THIRD EDITION

Managers and the Legal Environment: Strategies for the 21st Century

Constance E. Bagley

Graduate School of Business

Stanford University

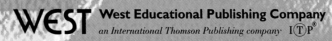

WEST **West Educational Publishing Company**
an International Thomson Publishing company I(T)P®

Cincinnati • Albany • Boston • Detroit • Johannesburg • London • Madrid • Melbourne • Mexico City
New York • Pacific Grove • San Francisco • Scottsdale • Singapore • Tokyo • Toronto

Publisher/Team Director: Jack W. Calhoun
Senior Acquisitions Editor: Rob Dewey
Acquisitions Editor: Scott D. Person
Senior Developmental Editor: Jan Lamar
Production Editor: Kara ZumBahlen
Media Technology Editor: Kurt Gerdenich
Media Production Editor: Mary Hufford
Marketing Manager: Michael Worls
Manufacturing Coordinator: Georgina Calderon
Production House: Pre-Press Company, Inc.
Composition: Pre-Press Company, Inc.
Interior Design: Cynthia Crampton Design
Cover Design: Joe Devine
Cover Image: ©1998, PhotoDisc, Inc. ©1998, Digital Stock

Bagley, Constance E.
    Managers and the legal environment : strategies for the 21st
century / Constance E. Bagley. — 3rd ed.
        p.   cm.
    Includes bibliographical references and index.
    ISBN 0-538-88485-1 (alk. paper)
    1. Business law—United States.   2. Trade regulation—United
States.   3. Business ethics—United States.   I. Title
KF889.B255   1999
346.7307—dc21   98-18789
                                                              CIP

123456789 WCBS 7654321098
Printed in the United States of America

I(T)P
International Thomson Publishing
West Educational Publishing is an ITP Company.
The ITP trademark is used under license.

Contents in Brief

Table of Contents

Table of Cases

The principal cases are in bold type. Cases cited or discussed are in light type.

Preface

While no business curriculum would be complete without an overview of the legal environment in which business takes place, the comprehensive and cutting-edge legal environment of business text must offer more. To achieve maximum effectiveness, such a text should provide an integrated treatment of law and management and serve as a practical reference that enables managers to spot legal issues before they become legal problems. It should also explain how a manager can use the law as a strategic asset to craft solutions that make it possible to attain the core business objectives. These goals have been foremost in the mind of the author of *Managers and the Legal Environment: Strategies for the 21st Century, Third Edition*. As its title implies, the text is designed as a "hands-on," transactional guide for future and current business managers, including entrepreneurs. It provides a broad and a detailed understanding of how law impacts daily management decisions and business strategies. No manager operating in the complex and everchanging global business environment of the late 1990s and the early 21st Century can compete successfully without such knowledge.

The topics covered in *Managers and the Legal Environment: Strategies for the 21st Century* demonstrate its focus on meeting the needs of business managers. The text covers not only such essential legal topics as agency, contracts, torts, criminal law, antitrust, and employment law, but also others of vital concern to business managers, such as intellectual property, lending transactions, and securities offerings, as well as international business transactions. The chapter on real property and land use illustrates the overall approach in the text: It includes not only the key legal concepts of property law and land use, but also a detailed discussion of the essentials of a commercial real estate lease.

In all instances, the form of presentation is dictated by a desire to convey the dynamic interplay between business decisions and the legal environment. When the most effective method of presenting the material is to demonstrate how actual business conflicts are resolved in the courts, an approach emphasizing judicial cases is used. This approach is employed in a majority of the chapters. When certain material, such as discussions of lending transactions and international trade, is best conveyed with text, this is the approach taken.

The legal topics discussed in the main body of the text are on the leading edge of business regulation. They include the World Trade Organization; copyright law in cyberspace; employer liability for sexual harassment; owner/operator liability under the Comprehensive Environmental Response, Compensation and Liability Act (CERCLA); the fiduciary duties of officers and directors in a corporate takeover; and HIV in the workplace.

This text is suitable for a class in the legal environment of business at the undergraduate, M.B.A., executive M.B.A., or executive education levels. The objective is a comprehensive and challenging, yet approachable and understandable, text that will work for those with substantial work experience and for those who are studying business at the undergraduate level for the first time.

Each chapter of *Managers and the Legal Environment: Strategies for the 21st Century* employs a wide array of effective teaching devices that reinforce the goals of the text.

Pedagogical Features

A Case in Point

Each chapter presents four to eight cases, set off from the body of the text, as examples of the law in action. These cases represent crucial court decisions that have shaped important business law concepts, or that present key legal conflicts that managers will address in their careers. Included are many modern cases that represent the most current statement of the law. These cases include, for example, the U.S. Supreme Court's June 1998 decisions *Clinton v. City of New York,* which struck down the line-item veto, and *Bragdon v. Abbott,* which extended the Americans with Disabilities Act to asymptomatic HIV-positive individuals. Other traditional cases, such as *Meinhard v. Salmon* and *MacPherson v. Buick Motor Co.,* are used to show early developments in the law that remain applicable today. The selection and approach to cases is guided by the author's above-stated goal of teaching students to identify legal issues before they become legal problems.

The format of the Case in Point section is designed to convey a detailed understanding of the cases, while simultaneously covering a large range of material. The case citation and facts are followed by a statement of the issue presented, which reinforces the legal principle being illustrated by the case. Each case discussion then proceeds with a presentation of the court's decision and then a description of the result.

The opinions in two cases in each chapter are presented in the language of the court, edited for clarity and brevity. Excerpts from dissenting opinions are used occasionally to demonstrate how reasonable people can come to different conclusions about the same facts. This is important for two reasons. First, today's dissent may be tomorrow's majority opinion. Second, comparing the arguments raised in the opinion with those of the dissent requires, and strengthens the student's ability to engage in, critical analysis. Each edited case is followed by two thought-provoking questions that challenge the student's understanding of the court's language and reasoning.

The opinions in the remaining cases in each chapter are summarized, thereby permitting the coverage of more cases and concepts than would be feasible if all cases were in the language of the court. The author believes that students benefit from reading a more rigorous treatment of cases than is provided by the short briefs found in many texts. Thus, students are provided

with a detailed recitation of the facts, the issues, the court's reasoning, and the result.

Many cases also include comments. The comments place the case in its proper legal perspective and offer commentary on why the case is important, why the court decided it a certain way, or what the ramifications of the decision are for business actors. Thus, cases are not presented in a vacuum. Instead, students are provided with an explanation of the key significance of the case. This helps students understand how an individual case impacts the legal environment as a whole. In addition, the comments encourage students to think critically about court decisions.

Ethical Considerations

This text places great emphasis on ethical concerns, stimulating students to understand how their actions as managers must incorporate considerations of ethics and social responsibility. Ethical considerations are emphasized in four ways. First, the opening chapter, "Ethics and the Law," includes topics such as exploitation of foreign workers, racial discrimination at Texaco and Avis, the Odwalla juice recall, and the Bhopal and Exxon Valdez disasters. Second, the text includes relevant excerpts from the *Dun & Bradstreet Code of Business Conduct* and the *American Express Company Code of Conduct.* Third, ethical considerations are highlighted throughout the text in separate boxed sections and raised in many of the end-of-chapter Questions and Case Problems. Finally, the Manager's Dilemma question in each chapter requires students to consider how ethics factor into a managerial decision.

These ethical considerations are commentaries on how standards of ethics and social responsibility do (and sometimes do not) inform the process of lawmaking. The text discusses the ethical implications of business decisions made in response to legal rules, as well as the moral boundaries of the legal regime. For example, cases discussing the legal rules regarding the payment of greenmail and hushmail by a target company are followed by a discussion of whether such payments, or anti-takeover measures generally, are ethical and socially responsible.

View from Cyberspace

New to this edition, most chapters include a boxed discussion of how the laws addressed in the chapter apply to electronic commerce, the Internet, and cyberspace generally. For example, the chapter on public and private offerings of securities discusses direct initial public offerings on the World Wide Web. The constitutional law chapter discusses the Communications Decency Act's ban on obscene or indecent material on the Internet. The consumer protection chapter addresses concerns about privacy on-line.

International Considerations

Two chapters cover international aspects of the legal environment. One chapter addresses international trade law, including the World Trade Organization and the European Monetary Union; the other is a transactional, integrated discussion of international business transactions. International considerations are also highlighted in most chapters. For example, both the product liability and the securities fraud and insider trading chapters describe the relevant European Union Directives. Taiwanese law is discussed in the environmental law and consumer protection chapters.

Economic, Historical, and Political Perspectives

Most chapters have a separate boxed section that puts the law in that chapter into economic, historical, or political perspective. For example, the labor-management relations chapter describes attempts by HMO physicians to unionize. The contracts chapter traces the doctrine of unconscionability from Roman law, and the environmental law chapter describes the economics of selling the right to pollute.

These Perspectives add a real-world dimension to the material. Too often law is presented in a vacuum, divorced from the larger political and economic context in which the law is created. The goal of these sections is to heighten students' awareness of these larger forces. In addition, business managers should be made aware of the complicated interplay between economics and the law. That interplay is crucial to the operation of a business, but it is often less than predictable.

In Brief

To provide a visual aid for the student, the text includes 22 boxed summaries, under the heading "In Brief," that break down into digestible pieces the key elements of material presented in that chapter. In some cases, this may be represented in the form of a flow chart; in others, it may appear in the form of a decision tree or matrix.

At the Top

Highlighted sections interspersed throughout the text reflect the importance of corporate governance, leadership, and vicarious liability in today's business and regulatory environment. These sections reflect matters that concern not only upper management and corporate officers, but also employees generally.

Inside Story

Each chapter contains case summaries that present fascinating and detailed descriptions of real-world business conflicts. A strong effort has been made to include up-to-the-minute, cutting-edge business disputes. The Inside Stories cover conflicts involving key-industry players, such as the antitrust suit *United States v. Microsoft Corp.,* Medicare fraud at HCA/Columbia Healthcare, the UPS–Teamsters strike, and executive compensation at Walt Disney Company. They bring the legal conflicts to life and reinforce the students' appreciation for how such conflicts are played out in the real world.

Defined Terms, Key Words and Phrases, and Glossary

Throughout the text, all crucial legal terms are placed in italics and defined immediately. A list of key terms used in a chapter appears immediately before the end-of-chapter Questions and Case Problems, with a page reference to the place where that term is defined.

In addition to the references to defined terms contained in Key Words and Phrases, there is also a comprehensive glossary at the end of the text. The Glossary defines each term that has been set in italics anywhere in the text. The definition of terms in the Glossary and the Key Words and Phrases helps convey the concepts and improves the students' legal and business vocabulary.

Internet Sources

New to this edition, each chapter contains a list of World Wide Web sites (including their electronic addresses, called URLs) relevant to the chapter. These sites give students a starting point for on-line legal research. The URLs are current as of July 1, 1998. Although every attempt was made to identify Internet sites that are maintained and updated regularly, the Internet is highly dynamic, and a hot site today may be gone in six months.

The Responsible Manager

Each chapter concludes with a section entitled "The Responsible Manager." This section is an in-depth discussion of the crucial legal considerations that the successful manager must take into account. The Responsible Manager sections summarize each chapter, but they are far more than a mere summary. In a concise yet sophisticated manner, they alert managers to the legal issues they must spot in order to avoid violating the law or plunging the company into expensive, time-consuming litigation. In addition, these sections highlight the ethical concerns managers need to confront to adequately serve their company and community.

These sections play a vital role in establishing this text as a "must-have" for upcoming and practicing business managers. In the Responsible Manager section for a particular area of the law, managers will find a wealth of practical information that will bring them up to speed on the key legal issues in that area. These sections are not merely check-lists—they contain a depth of analysis that is demanded by the complex, real-life nature of the problems at hand.

As examples, the Responsible Manager section for the chapter on alternative dispute-resolution provides a step-by-step guide to setting up an effective alternative dispute resolution procedure. The torts chapter provides a manager's guide to reducing risks of exposure for tort liability. The international business transactions chapter highlights the issues likely to arise in transactions involving more than one country and suggests strategies for managing successfully in a global setting.

End of Chapter Questions and Case Problems, Manager's Dilemma, and Answer Manual

Each chapter is followed by ten sophisticated and thought-provoking questions that require students to synthesize and review the material. The questions are diverse. Some are imaginative hypotheticals that raise the central legal issues in a creative and humorous fashion. Others are based directly on specific cases, presenting real-world legal conflicts as opportunities for students to apply the appropriate law. In most chapters, more than half the questions are based on actual cases, with the citation provided for enterprising students who want to look up the case in preparation for class. The questions that are based on actual cases often raise issues at the cutting edge of law and management.

New to this edition, the last question in each chapter, entitled "Manager's Dilemma," requires students to analyze the legal, business, and ethical aspects of a managerial decision.

A complete and separate Answer Manual, prepared by the author, identifies the issues presented in each of the questions and provides thorough, cogent model answers.

 ## Changes in the Third Edition

Roughly half of the cases presented as A Case in Point and many of the end-of-chapter Questions and Case Problems are new. The chapter on product liability includes a discussion of the Restatement (Third) of Torts: Product Liability. A majority of the Inside Stories and the Economic, Historical, and Political Perspectives are also new.

As noted above, this edition includes three new pedagogical features: View from Cyberspace, the Manager's Dilemma, and Internet Sources.

After teaching courses at Stanford where I used the first two editions and reviewing suggestions from other professors using the text, I concluded that it would be appropriate to add one new chapter and to reorder several others. The new chapter—Chapter 4, entitled "Alternative Dispute Resolution"—reflects the importance of using such alternatives as negotiation, arbitration, and mediation to resolve business disputes without litigation. It also identifies common barriers to settlement.

Several chapters have been shortened and combined with other chapters to reflect both the relative importance of the material and lessons learned in using the first two editions. In particular, the material on forms of business organizations previously presented in Chapter 5 entitled "Agency and Forms of Business Organizations" is combined with former Chapter 20 entitled "Corporations" to create a new Chapter 20 entitled "Forms of Business Organizations." New Chapter 20 includes an expanded discussion of limited liability companies. Agency is now a stand-alone chapter. The chapter on torts now follows the chapters on contracts and sales. The two international law chapters have been put into the same unit.

Ancillary Components

Instructor's Manual

The Instructor's Manual was developed by Ernest W. King (University of Southern Mississippi). This manual includes chapter outlines, case summaries, and teaching suggestions.

Test Bank

The Test Bank was developed by Arthur M. Levine (California State University–Long Beach) and Peter M. Lee (Pacific Coast University). It contains true/false test questions, multiple-choice test questions, and essay test questions. The Test Bank also includes multi-subject final exam essay questions prepared by the author.

Thompson World Class Testing Tools™ allows instructors to create edit, store, and print exams.

Study Guide

The Study Guide was prepared by Ernest W. King (University of Southern Mississippi). It includes chapter objectives, chapter outlines, study questions (fill-in-the-blank, true/false, multiple choice, and essay). Answers are provided in a separate answer key.

Other Teaching Aids

Cutting Edge Cases in the Legal Environment of Business (2nd ed.)   A collection of 17 recent legal environment of business edited cases from 1995 to 1998, using the court's own language in an expanded format, that may be purchased separately.

Business Law and Legal Environment Video Library   Includes a variety of professionally produced videos, including the complete Drama of the Law I and II series.

CD-ROM Resources for Business Law and the Legal Environment   Includes cases, key legislation and regulations, relevant articles of the UCC and more. This CD-ROM utilizes West's PREMISE © software which allows one to search for and retrieve specific items quickly.

Ten Free Hours of WESTLAW   West's computerized legal research and Dow Jones News/Retrieval service.

"You Be the Judge"   This software program provides case problems for ten topic areas. Students are given the facts and then asked how the case should be decided.

Contracts: An Interactive Guide and UCC Article 2 Sales: An Interactive Guide   These are interactive programs designed to aid in teaching contracts and sales.

West's Regional Reporters   Gives professors and students updated case decisions from their region throughout the year.

Please ask your West representative for the qualification details for the above listed supplements.

Pennzoil v. Texaco Case Study and Accompanying Video

The *Pennzoil v. Texaco* case study is the Inside Story for the contracts chapter. It includes excerpts from the court's opinion and the legal documents so students can have the experience of seeing such material first hand. This particular case study can serve as the basis for discussion or for the staging of a mock trial in which students can play the lawyers, executives, investment bankers, and jury. An edited videotape of the mock trial conducted by students in the author's class at the Graduate School of Business at Stanford University is also available.

 Acknowledgments

A number of professors reviewed portions of the manuscript and the first two editions, and provided guidance, correction and helpful commentary. I thank each of them.

Reviewers who provided insight for this edition include:

Royce de R. Barondes, Louisiana State University
Susan M. Denbo, Rider College
Joan T. A. Gabel, Georgia State University
Ernest W. King, University of Southern Mississippi
Eugene P. O'Connor, Canisius College
Lou Ann Simpson, Drake University

Reviewers for the second edition include:

Barbara Ahna, Pacific Lutheran University
Rodolfo Camacho, Oregon State University
Kenneth D. Crews, Indiana University
James G. Frierson, East Tennessee State University

John P. Geary, Appalachian State University

David G. Jaeger, Case Western Reserve University

Arthur Levine, California State University–Long Beach

Susan L. Martin, Hofstra University

William F. Miller, Stanford University

Alan R. Thiele, University of Houston

Reviewers for the first edition include:

Thomas M. Apke, California State University, Fullerton

Dawn Bennett-Alexander, University of Georgia

Robert L. Cherry, Appalachian State University

Frank B. Cross, University of Texas, Austin

Charles J. Cunningham, University of Tampa

Michael Engber, Ball State University

Andrea Giampetro-Meyer, Loyola College, Maryland

James P. Hill, Central Michigan University

Tom Jackson, University of Vermont

Roger J. Johns, Jr., Eastern New Mexico University

Jack E. Karns, East Carolina University

Mary C. Keifer, Ohio University

Nancy Kubasek, Bowling Green University

Paul Lansing, University of Iowa

Nancy R. Mansfield, Georgia State University

Arthur J. Marinelli, Ohio University

John McMahon, Stanford University

Gregory C. Mosier, Oklahoma State University

Patricia H. Nunley, Baylor University

Mark M. Phelps, University of Oregon

Michael W. Pustay, Texas A&M University

Roger Richman, University of Hartford

John C. Ruhnka, University of Colorado at Denver

Linda B. Samuels, George Mason University

Susan Samuelson, Boston University

Rudy Sandoval, University of Texas, San Antonio

John E. H. Sherry, Cornell University

S. Jay Sklar, Temple University

Larry D. Strate, University of Nevada, Las Vegas

Gary L. Tidwell, College of Charleston

William V. Vetter, Wayne State University

William H. Walker, Indiana-Purdue University, Ft. Wayne

Darryl Webb, University of Alabama

The following practitioners reviewed portions of the manuscript and provided leading-edge input from the trenches of business law practice:

Dale E. Barnes, Jr., McCutchen, Doyle, Brown & Enersen LLP

James C. Lu, General Counsel, Acer America

J. Thomas Rosch, Latham & Watkins

Diane Wilkins Savage, Cooley Godward LLP

Any mistakes or inadequacies are my own.

My Faculty Assistant, Marilyn Gildea, provided invaluable word processing, editing, and research support. Her keen eye for detail and consistency helped immeasurably to convert the manuscript into a clear, understandable text. She worked Herculean hours and yet always kept her sense of humor and perspective. Marilyn, thanks a million. I could not have done it without you. I mean that literally.

Kelly R. Young, a JD/MBA student at Stanford University, was the lead research assistant. The following students at the Stanford Law School also helped as research assistants: Kevin Jeffery, Steve Lee, and Matthew Robison. I thank each of them for their hard work and creativity. I also thank Pamela Givens, MBA student at the Stanford Graduate School of Business, and Rakesh Khanna, JD/MBA student at Stanford University, for their assistance.

Thanks to Rob Dewey and Scott Person of West Educational Publishing for their insightful and creative suggestions for this third edition and to Senior Developmental Editor Jan Lamar, who provided continuity and helped make it all come together. Thanks also to Production Editor Kara ZumBahlen for her even temper while meeting a seemingly impossible production schedule.

Finally, thanks to my colleague and friend Jeffrey Pfeffer, the Thomas D. Dee Professor of Organizational Behavior at Stanford University's Graduate School of Business, for his on-going advice, encouragement, and friendship.

Constance E. Bagley
Graduate School of Business
Stanford University

About the Author

Constance E. Bagley received her J.D., *magna cum laude*, from the Harvard Law School and her A.B., with distinction and departmental honors, from Stanford University, after being elected Phi Beta Kappa her junior year. Bagley received Honorable Mention for the Stanford Graduate School of Business Distinguished Teaching Award in 1993 and was GSB Trust Faculty Fellow for 1997–1998. Before joining the faculty at Stanford University's Graduate School of Business, she was a corporate partner at the San Francisco law firm of McCutchen, Doyle, Brown & Enersen. Bagley is the co-author of *The Entrepreneur's Guide to Business Law* (West Publishing 1998). She is a member of the Faculty Advisory Board of the *Stanford Journal of Law, Business & Finance,* the Editorial Board of the *Journal of Internet Law,* and the Advisory Board for the Bureau of National Affairs Corporate Practice Series.

Dedication

To my students at the Stanford Business School,
past, present and future.

C.E.B.

Foundations of the Legal and Regulatory Environment

CHAPTER 1

Ethics and the Law

INTRODUCTION

Importance of Ethics to the Manager

The corporate world has been rocked by a number of ethical scandals involving a variety of activities, including price-fixing, racial discrimination, insider trading, tax evasion, sale of unsafe products, overcharging on government contracts, disregard of safety or environmental regulations, shady corporate restructurings, use of child labor and sweatshops, and employee drug and alcohol abuse while on the job. In a Business Roundtable report on company conduct in the United States, a group of prominent business leaders called ethics in business "one of the most challenging issues facing the corporate community in this era." A survey by one of the Big Six accounting firms, Touche Ross, found that 94% of top corporate executives believed the business community was troubled by ethical problems.

Ethics can and do impact profits and even survival—as organizations such as Bre-X Minerals (bankrupt Canadian mining company that artificially inflated its gold reserves), Drexel Burnham (bankrupt junk-bond dealer engaged in securities fraud), Columbia/HCA Healthcare (hospital company under siege for Medicare fraud), and Hudson Foods (seller of tainted meat) can attest. An ethical manager considers not

just what is best for the bottom line in the short term but also the long-term effect a particular decision will have on customers, suppliers, employees, the environment, members of the surrounding community, and other stakeholders. A manager's ethics will affect not only his or her company and its reputation and long-term viability but also the manager's personal sense of worth and accomplishment.

Chapter Overview

The purpose of this chapter is to provide a framework for analyzing how ethics, business, and law interact. This chapter begins with a brief overview of several theories of ethics and systems of justice. Business ethics is defined and discussed in its relationship to economic performance. The chapter continues with a description of notable examples of social responsibility and irresponsibility on the part of corporations. It shows how certain conduct raises ethical as well as legal issues. The chapter concludes with a perspective on the role of the corporation and its managers in ensuring ethical conduct and the evolving role of the law in this area.

Different Theories of Ethics

It is sometimes difficult to define what constitutes good ethical behavior. This is due in part to the fact that there are several underlying ethical theories. People, consciously or not, employ ethical theories in their decision-making processes. The important thing for a manager to remember is that there are different "ethically correct" ways of looking at a decision. Because there are different ways of approaching a given situation, a manager's constituencies may not always reach a similar decision and hence may not be as willing to accept the implications and consequences of the manager's decision.

The two main schools of ethical thought are teleological and deontological. *Teleological theory* is concerned with consequences. The ethical good of an action is to be judged by the effect of the action on others. *Deontological theory* focuses more on the motivation and principle behind an action rather than on the consequences.

For example, suppose that a construction company donates materials to build shelters for the homeless. In judging this action within the teleological framework, the fact that some homeless people are given housing is the important issue. Within a deontological framework, one would want to know why the company was motivated to supply the materials for the shelters. On the other hand, suppose an employer makes a promise to throw a party if the firm reaches profitability and then breaks the promise. Under teleological theory, as long as the consequences of breaking the promise are insignificant, then the action of breaking the promise is not in and of itself bad. However, deontological theory would suggest that there is something intrinsically wrong with making a promise and breaking it, no matter what the consequences. Thus, a particular action can be evaluated differently, depending on the system under which it is examined.

For illustrative purposes, several theories within these two schools are briefly developed. *Utilitarianism* is a major teleological system of beliefs that operates under the proposition that the ideal is to maximize the total benefit for everyone involved. Under a utilitarian theory, no one person's particular interest is given more weight than another, but rather the utility of everyone as a group is maximized.

For example, suppose that a $10,000 bonus pool is to be divided among three executives and that their marginal benefits from receiving a portion of the money can be quantified. Imagine that the money must be allocated in one of two ways: Under Distribution 1, the three persons benefit 6, 12, and 24 units, respectively. Under Distribution 2, the three persons benefit 8, 12, and 16 units, respectively. A utilitarian would want Distribution 1 because the total benefit (6 + 12 + 24 = 42) is greater than under Distribution 2 (8 + 12 + 16 = 36). There is no concern that the other distribution seems more equal and fair; similarly, there is no concern that under the benefit-maximizing utility distribution, the worst-off person has considerably less than the worst-off person in Distribution 2.

On the other hand, *Rawlsian moral theory*, a deontological theory, aims to maximize the worst-off person in society. Rawlsian theory states that principles should be developed behind a "veil of ignorance." Each person in society is to imagine that he or she does not know what his or her allotment of society's resources will be and then decide what principles should govern society's interactions. Rawls believed that behind the veil of ignorance people would create a system that benefited the least-well-off people most. According to that theory, Distribution 2 is better. Under a Rawlsian scheme, the favored distribution is the one preferred by the person who faces the possibility of getting the worst share.

Kantian theory is another main deontological line of thought. Kant advocated maxims that epitomize a morality based on freedom and rationality. Kant's categorical imperative looks to the form of an action, rather than the intended result, in examining the ethical worth. The form of an action can be delineated into the universalizability and reversibility of an action. *Universalizability* asks whether one would want everyone to perform in this manner, and *reversibility* looks to whether one would want such a rule applied to one's self. For example, in deciding how long a break to give the workers on an assembly line, a manager might try to apply this theory. In choosing between a 10-minute break every three hours with bathroom breaks whenever necessary versus a longer lunch break, a manager might ask—under universalizability—whether he or she would like a world in which all companies applied a similar system. Under reversibility, the manager would decide whether he or she would want to be subjected to a particular break system as an employee.

The consequences of an action motivated by a certain ethical system can often be evaluated within a comparative justice framework. This allows a framework for comparing the rights-based moral theories of Kant or Rawls to, for example, a utilitarian framework. Three main categories within this framework are distributive, compensatory, and retributive theories of justice.

Distributive justice focuses on how the burden and benefits of a particular system are distributed. An ideal system maximizes the overall pie by dividing it such that incentives are enough to entice persons to produce more; the system also concerns itself with a fair distribution of these goods—compensating those who contributed while still upholding a certain minimum standard. For example, the use of progressively higher income tax rates for those with more income can be understood within a distributive justice framework.

Compensatory justice aims at compensating people for the harm done by others. For example, if someone is found responsible for making another person miss five days of work, a compensatory system of justice would ask that the victim be somehow compensated for the lost wages.

A *retributive justice system* framework also is appropriately employed when someone does harm to another, yet the focus is more on how to deter another harm from happening. Thus, suppose X steals an idea from Y and makes $10,000. If the idea had not been stolen, Y would have made $5,000. Under a compensatory framework, X would compensate Y for his thievery by paying Y $5,000. On the other hand, under a retributive framework, X should be taught that stealing an idea is wrong. X should be required to give up any benefit to Y and pay Y closer to $10,000.

"I KNOW THE DIFFERENCE BETWEEN RIGHT AND WRONG, BUT SO FAR I'VE NEVER HAD REASON TO ACT ON THAT INFORMATION."

HISTORICAL PERSPECTIVE

AQUINAS ON LAW AND ETHICS

Saint Thomas Aquinas (1225?–1274), theologian and philosopher, believed that an unjust law could not properly be considered a law at all. The only true laws were those that followed eternal law—as far as eternal law could be discovered by the use of human reason and revelation. Eternal law is the orderly governance of the acts and movements of all creatures by God as the divine governor of the universe.

Because not every individual follows a natural inclination to do good—that is, to act virtuously in order to achieve happiness and to avoid evil—human laws are framed to train, and sometimes compel, a person to do what is right, as well as to restrain the person from doing harm to others. According to Aquinas, in order for human law to be considered law, that is, binding on human conscience, it must be just. In order to be just, a human law must be (1) consonant with a reasoned determination of the universal good; (2) within the power of individuals to fulfill; (3) clearly expressed by legitimate authority; (4) approved by custom, that is, the declaration of right reason by a community; and (5) widely promulgated. To the extent that human law is just, it is in concert with eternal law, as discerned through human reason, and is binding on individuals. Human laws that promote private benefit over the common good are unjust, and individuals are bound not to obey them. Instead individuals should "disregard them, oppose them, and do what [they] can to revoke them."[a]

Most modern legal theorists separate the question of a law's status as law from the question of its inherent morality. They argue that a law may help to resolve moral issues, punish immoral action, and serve a moral purpose (as, for example, when laws permit participation in government); but a law need not be inherently moral to be a real law. In this so-called positive-law view, any law counts as a real law if it has been created according to recognized procedures by someone with the recognized authority to do so—a king, for instance, or, in the U.S. system, a legislature, a judge, or an administrative agency. A properly created law may, of course, be criticized as immoral. Persons may even wish to disobey it. But they do so in the full knowledge that they are disobeying a valid law.

In the United States, the split between legal and moral debate has always been less clear than positive-law theorists might wish. Americans have always given their moral debates a peculiarly legal flavor, mainly because certain important but ambiguous phrases in the U.S. and state constitutions invite a person to "constitutionalize" moral questions. Moral questions are readily translatable into questions about the meaning and scope of the constitutional doctrines of due process of law, liberty, equal protection under the laws, or cruel and unusual punishment. For example, in upholding a woman's right to have an abortion, the U.S. Supreme Court stated: "At the heart of liberty is the right to define one's own concept of existence, of meaning, of the universe, and of the mystery of human life."[b]

It has become a national trait of Americans to expect their constitutions to support their moral convictions. Just as Aquinas believed that unjust laws could not accord with eternal law, so many Americans believe that unjust laws cannot be constitutional. Perhaps it is for this reason that so many of the most controversial American moral debates, such as those on slavery, prohibition, civil rights, equal rights for women, gays in the military, the right to die, and abortion have focused on the interpretation of constitutions or have been framed in terms of possible constitutional amendments. In some ways, the tendency in the United States to look to constitutions for substantiation of the just quality of law is akin to the use by theologians of the Judeo–Christian scriptures as supernatural revelation or knowledge of the universal good that is eternal law.

As this comparison of present-day constitutional analysis to thirteenth-century theology indicates, the past is often a valuable pointer to the future. At the same time, one must be able to distinguish differences between doctrines that prevailed in the past and those that should prevail in the future. In this regard, it is important to recall the positivists' distinction between law and morals. If a person confuses what's "allowed" with what's "right," he or she risks cutting his or her ethical discussions short and missing opportunities both for the encouragement of morality by law and for the reform of law in the light of society's morals.

---

a. P. GLENN, A TOUR OF THE SUMMA 170 (1978).

b. Planned Parenthood v. Casey, 505 U.S. 833 (1992).

Business Ethics

Definition of Business Ethics

There is more to a successful company than meeting bottom-line financial objectives. A manager concerned with ethics must consider how these financial objectives are met and what the company contributes to the worth of society. Most, if not all, business executives would agree that upholding good business ethics is essential to the success of a company and a strong economy. John Akers, former chairman of IBM, has stated: "Ethics and competitiveness are inseparable . . . . The greater the measure of mutual trust and confidence in the ethics of a society, the greater its economic strength."[1]

AT THE TOP

Responsibility for ethical behavior and compliance with the law extends from the top of the management hierarchy down. It cannot be delegated away. Managers provide role models—be they good or bad—for their subordinates.

Despite the consensus on the importance of ethics, there is no precise definition of what constitutes good business ethics. Many decisions that at first glance may not appear to involve ethics have subsequent ethical implications.

Ethical conduct goes beyond merely complying with the law; conduct deemed legal can still be unethical. Many people associate ethics with such concepts as integrity, fairness, and honesty. For more than 75 years, the J. C. Penney Co. has considered ethical business behavior to be that which conforms to the Golden Rule: Do unto others as you would have them do unto you.

How does a manager decide what is ethical? The chief executive officer of a highly successful Scandinavian multinational tells his managers to conjure up the following scenario: Assume that the decision you are about to make in Timbuktu becomes public knowledge in our home country, the host country, and significant Third World countries where our company is operating. Assume further that you, as the decision maker, are called upon to defend the decision on television both at home and abroad. If you think you can defend it successfully in these public forums, the probability is high that your decision is ethical.[2]

International Focus: OECD Code of Business Conduct and Bribery Ban

In the past, business ethics differed somewhat from culture to culture. However, as the market shifts from a domestic to an international one and as advances in technology create a greater flow of information, business ethics are becoming more standardized. A generalized code of business conduct was drawn up by the Organization of Economic Cooperation and Development (OECD) in 1976. The OECD is comprised of 29 nations from North America, Europe, and Asia–Pacific whose members are committed to an open-market economy, pluralistic democracy, and respect for human rights. The OECD nations represent more than half of the goods and services produced worldwide and include some of the world's largest economies. The code, which discusses proper behavior and ethical conduct for multinationals, has had a significant impact on international business practice.

The code reflects the views of government, business, labor, and consumer groups. It requires multinational corporations to (1) act in accordance with the economic, commercial, and social goals and priorities of the host country; (2) abstain from bribery and other corrupt practices seeking favorable treatment from the host government; (3) abstain from political intervention in the host country; (4) make a positive contribution to the balance of payments of the host country; (5) abstain from borrowing from local financial institutions, so that they can reserve their capital for local enterprises; (6) monitor the multinational's impact on employment, wages, labor standards, working conditions, and industrial relations; (7) protect the environment of the host country; and (8) disclose information on the multinational's activities so that the home country and the host country can formulate government policy.

---

1. *Good Takes on Greed*, The Economist, Feb. 17, 1990, at 71.

2. Alden Lank, *The Ethical Criterion in Business Decision Making: Operational or Imperative?* in Touche Ross and Co., Ethics in American Business: A Special Report 48 (1988) (hereafter cited as Touche Ross Report).

In 1997, the OECD proposed that its members adopt a bribery ban and developed a treaty to go into effect in December of that year. The United States had been lobbying for such a ban since enacting the Foreign Corrupt Practices Act (FCPA) in response to the bribery scandals of the mid-1970s. The FCPA prohibits the payment by U.S. companies of bribes to government officials. Companies outside the United States, particularly those located in Europe, are in favor of the bribery ban, which they see as making it possible to operate ethically without losing business. One German legislator estimated that German companies paid 10 billion Deutsche marks (U.S. $5.7 billion) in bribes in 1997.[3] Unfortunately, the ban is unlikely to affect the business climate of the worst offenders; among the countries that ranked highest in the 1997, Corruption Perception Index were Russia, China, Argentina, Mexico, Colombia, Pakistan, Indonesia, Nigeria, and the Philippines.[4] However, the ban will hold the OECD countries to a higher standard of conduct with regard to use of bribes.

Relationship of the Law and Ethics

The following case illustrates how legal liability can depend a great deal on how one views the ethical nature of the situation.

---

3. Neil King, Jr., *Momentum Builds for Corporate-Bribery Ban*, WALL ST. J., Sept. 23, 1997, at A16.

4. *Id.*

| A CASE IN POINT | IN THE LANGUAGE OF THE COURT |

CASE 1.1
MEINHARD v. SALMON
Court of Appeals of New York
164 N.E. 545 (N.Y. 1928).

FACTS In 1902, Louisa Gerry leased the Bristol Hotel in New York City to the defendant, Walter Salmon. The lease was for a term of 20 years, beginning in 1902 and ending in 1922. The lessee, Salmon, was to renovate the hotel building for use as shops and offices at a cost of $200,000. Salmon needed funds in order to complete his proposed renovations to the building, and he persuaded Morton Meinhard to act as a financial backer. Salmon and Meinhard entered into a joint venture agreement with the following terms: Meinhard agreed to pay to Salmon half of the moneys necessary to reconstruct, alter, manage, and operate the property, and Salmon agreed to pay to Meinhard 40% of the net profits for the first five years of the lease and 50% for the years thereafter. If there were losses, each party was to bear them equally. Salmon, however, was to have sole power to "manage, lease, underlet and operate" the building.

In January 1922, with less than four months of the lease to run, Elbridge Gerry, who had become the owner of the property, approached the defendant, Salmon. Salmon and Gerry agreed to enter into a new 20-year lease for not only the Bristol Hotel but also an entire tract of property surrounding it. The new lessor (the entity leasing the property) was the Midpoint Realty Company, which was owned and controlled by Salmon. Under the new lease, the Bristol Hotel would eventually be torn down, and new buildings at a cost of $3 million would be built on the old Bristol site and adjacent lots.

The lease between Gerry and the Midpoint Realty Company was signed and delivered on January 25, 1922. Salmon had not told Meinhard anything about it. Meinhard was not informed even of the existence of a new project. The first that he knew of it was in February, when the new lease was a done deal.

Meinhard demanded to be included in the new lease. The defendants, Salmon and Gerry, refused to do so.

Meinhard sued. A referee found in favor of Meinhard but limited his interest in (and corresponding obligations under) the lease to 25%. Both the plaintiff and the

Case 1.1 continues

Case 1.1 continued

defendant cross-appealed to the Appellate Division of the New York court. On appeal, the plaintiff, Meinhard, was awarded one-half of the interest in (and corresponding obligations under) the lease. The defendant, Salmon, appealed to the New York Court of Appeals, the highest state court in New York.

ISSUE PRESENTED   Did Salmon, as Meinhard's joint venturer, have a relationship of trust (or fiduciary duty) to Meinhard that obligated him to give Meinhard the opportunity to be included in a new lease covering property that was originally leased by Salmon on behalf of the joint venture?

OPINION   CARDOZO, C. J. (later a justice of the U.S. Supreme Court), writing for the New York Court of Appeals:

Joint adventurers, like copartners, owe to one another, while the enterprise continues, the duty of the finest loyalty. Many forms of conduct permissible in a workaday world for those acting at arm's length are forbidden to those bound by fiduciary ties. A trustee is held to something stricter than the morals of the market place. Not honesty alone, but the punctilio of an honor the most sensitive, is then the standard of behavior. As to this there has developed a tradition that is unbending and inveterate. Uncompromising rigidity has been the attitude of courts of equity when petitioned to undermine the rule of undivided loyalty by the "disintegrating erosion" of particular exceptions. Only thus has the level of conduct for fiduciaries been kept at a level higher than that trodden by the crowd. It will not consciously be lowered by any judgment of this court.

The owner of the [property], Mr. Gerry, had vainly striven to find a tenant who would favor his ambitious scheme of demolition and construction. Baffled in the search, he turned to the defendant Salmon [who was] in possession of the Bristol, the keystone of the project. . . . To the eye of an observer, Salmon held the lease as owner in his own right, for himself and no one else. In fact he held it as a fiduciary, for himself and another, sharers in a common venture. If this fact had been proclaimed, if the lease by its terms had run in favor of a partnership, Mr. Gerry, we may fairly assume, would have laid before the partners, and not merely before one of them, his plan of reconstruction. . . . The trouble about [Salmon's] conduct is that he excluded his coadventurer from any chance to compete, from any chance to enjoy the opportunity for benefit that had come to him alone by virtue of his agency. This chance, if nothing more, he was under a duty to concede.

. . .

We have no thought to hold that Salmon was guilty of a conscious purpose to defraud. Very likely he assumed in all good faith that with the approaching end of the venture he might ignore his coadventurer and take the extension for himself. He had given to the enterprise time and labor as well as money. He had made it a success. Meinhard, who had given money, but neither time nor labor, had already been richly paid. There might seem to be something grasping in his insistence upon more. Such recriminations are not unusual when coadventurers fall out. They are not without their force if conduct is to be judged by the common standards of competitors. That is not to say that they have pertinency here. Salmon had put himself in a position in which thought of self was to be renounced, however hard the abnegation. He was

Case 1.1 continues

Case 1.1 continued

much more than a coadventurer. He was a managing coadventurer. For him and for those like him the rule of undivided loyalty is relentless and supreme. . . .

RESULT   The judgment for the plaintiff, Meinhard, was affirmed. He was granted one-half of the interest in (and corresponding obligations under) the new lease between Salmon and Gerry.

COMMENTS   In *Meinhard v. Salmon*, the court seemed to assume without explanation that joint venturers had a *fiduciary duty* to one another. Judges can disagree on what types of business relations give rise to a standard that is "higher than the morals of the market place," thereby giving rise to a fiduciary duty. Furthermore, there is even disagreement as to what constitutes proper morals of the marketplace. In one recent case, decided by the New York Court of Appeals, the same court that decided *Meinhard v. Salmon*, a majority of the judges concluded that a finder of a buyer for a business did not have a fiduciary duty to disclose to the seller the unsavory reputation of the potential buyer.[5] The dissenting judge disagreed. He argued that there was a fiduciary relationship between the parties, and, even if there were not, the morals of the marketplace would require disclosure. Fiduciary duty and this case are discussed more fully in Chapter 5.

Questions

1. Would the result in this case have been different if Gerry had offered Salmon a lease on property far removed from the Bristol property that was the subject of the Salmon–Meinhard joint venture?

2. Why is it appropriate to hold joint venturers to a legal and ethical standard that is higher than the norms of the marketplace?

---

5. Northeast Gen. Corp. v. Wellington Advertising, 624 N.E.2d 129 (N.Y. 1993).

Good Ethics Are Simply Good Business

Not only is ethical behavior good for business, it can even improve the bottom line. This conclusion has generally been accepted by corporate America, and a number of empirical studies support it. For example, the Touche Ross survey found that 63% of the respondents believed that high ethical standards strengthen a business's competitive position. In another study, the Ethics Resource Center in Washington, D.C., surveyed 21 companies that had a written commitment stating that the public was central to their existence. It found that $30,000 invested in these companies 30 years ago would have outperformed by nearly nine times the same investment in Dow Jones composite-index companies that had no written commitment.

Merck & Co., the number-one pharmaceutical company in the world, believes good ethics make good business. On the inside cover of Merck's 1996 Annual Report is a quote by George Merck II, who in 1950 stated the company philosophy as follows: "We try to remember that medicine is for the people. It is not for the profits. The profits follow, and if we have remembered that, they have never failed to appear. The better we have remembered it, the larger they have been."[6] After the end of World War II, Merck provided medicine to treat tuberculosis in Japan. The company did not make any money from that effort, but they are now the largest pharmaceutical company in the Japanese market.

But Sometimes Honesty Can Hurt

The publishing industry is driven by circulation numbers—the higher the circulation, the more publishers can charge advertisers. Given those incentives, it is not

---

6. MERCK & CO., INC. 1996 ANNUAL REPORT (1997).

surprising that overestimating circulation numbers is a common practice in the industry and often goes undetected. In September 1997, British publishing giant Reed Elsevier PLC revealed that for five years its managers had been padding their circulation figures, and the company was obligated to repay advertisers for the errors. This announcement was followed by several days of stock price declines on the London and Amsterdam stock exchanges.[7]

Social Responsibility and Profits

A company has an obligation to be both ethical and socially responsible, but what does it mean to be socially responsible? In his seminal article *The Social Responsibility of Business Is to Increase Its Profits*,[8] Nobel Prize winner in economics Milton Friedman asserts that the only guiding criterion for the corporation should be profitability. He argues that it is not the role of business to promote social ends in and of themselves. Friedman asserts that a corporation is an "artificial person" and therefore has no true responsibilities to any constituent other than its owners, or shareholders. When a company makes a decision to spend money for a social cause, it is in essence making the decision for someone else and spending someone else's money for a general social interest.

Friedman's main argument rests on his view that spending corporate funds on social issues is, in effect, usurping the role of government. Spending money in ways that are not consistent with shareholder wishes is tantamount to imposing a tax and unilaterally deciding where the money will be spent. Because taxation is a governmental function, and only the government has sufficient legislative and judicial provisions to ensure that taxation and expenditures fairly reflect the desires of the public, a corporation making taxation decisions on its own would render the executive "simultaneously legislator, executive and jurist."

Friedman concludes his landmark article by asserting that "social responsibility" is an inherently collectivist attitude and is a "fundamentally subversive doctrine." In a free society, "there is one and only one social responsibility of business—to use its resources and engage in activities designed to increase its profits so long as it stays within the rules of the game, which is to say, engages in open and free competition without deception or fraud."

Friedman's very polemic viewpoint has not gone uncriticized. For example, Richard Nunan argues that corporations are sometimes better equipped than the government to handle certain social issues. For example, soft drink companies have a much better and more credible forum to promote recycling of bottles than the public sector. Furthermore, sometimes corporations even "have moral obligations to pursue socially desirable goals. Specifically, they have a minimal moral obligation to avoid creating social injury and to correct any past social injuries for which they can be held directly responsible."[9]

Some companies have mandated ethical behavior and social commitment as an integral part of their business. Examples include Ben & Jerry's (ice cream and yogurt), The Body Shop (lotions, soaps and cosmetics), Odwalla (fresh juices), and Patagonia (outdoor apparel). Giant retailer Dayton Hudson (owner of Target and other retail stores) regularly gives a certain percentage of its profits to charitable causes.

The Tension: Stride Rite

Stride Rite shoe company found itself in the uncomfortable position of trying to balance "the demands of two masters—shareholders and society."[10] On the one hand, this nationwide company with $625 million in annual sales can be seen as a paradigm of a company able to help improve the quality of life in the community while maintaining a solid financial bottom line. A favorite on the New York Stock Exchange, having almost doubled its sales within the past seven years, Stride Rite was also recognized for its social commitments. It had received 14 public-service awards within the past three years from renowned institutions such as the National Women's Political Caucus and Harvard University. Among other things, the company has contributed 5% of pretax profits to a certain foundation, donated sneakers, set up

---

7. Patrick M. Reilly & Ernest Beck, *Publishers Often Pad Circulation Figures*, Wall St. J., Sept. 30, 1997, at B12.

8. Milton Friedman, An Economist's Protest 177–84 (1972).

9. Richard Nunan, *The Libertarian Conception of Corporate Property: A Critique of Milton Friedman's View on the Social Responsibility of Business*, 7 J. Bus. Ethics 891–906 (1988).

10. Joseph Pereira, *Social Responsibility and Need for Low Cost Clash at Stride Rite*, Wall St. J., May 28, 1993, at A1. This discussion of Stride Rite is derived from and based on this article. Reprinted by permission of *The Wall Street Journal* © 1993 Dow Jones & Company, Inc. All Rights Reserved Worldwide.

scholarships for inner city youths, and pioneered the effort in the corporate world to set up on-site facilities for day care and elder care.

Like other companies, Stride Rite has been forced to face the issue of social responsibility versus profitability. In 1984, Stride Rite laid off 2,500 people as a result of a decision to move certain factories abroad to take advantage of lower labor costs. In May 1993, the company announced the closing of its plant in New Bedford, Massachusetts. Facing an unemployment rate of about 14%, residents of New Bedford did not take the news of the announced closing well, and two suspicious fires caused damage estimated at $750,000. Chairman Ervin Shames spoke in defense of the company's seemingly split personality: "Putting jobs into places where it doesn't make economic sense is a dilution of corporate and community wealth. . . . It was a difficult decision. Our hearts said, 'Stay,' but our heads said 'Move.'"[11] A former chairman of the company, Arnold Hiatt, acknowledges the difficulty in the situation: "To the extent that you can stay in the city, I think you have to, [but] if it's at the expense of your business, I think you can't forget that your primary responsibility is to your stockholders."[12]

Others see the world of social responsibility as a variable-sum, win–win game. An act need not hurt to be socially responsible. It can help public relations or employee morale. Ewing Kauffman, owner of the Kansas City Royals baseball team and founder of Marion Laboratories, says:

> And the surprising thing, by doing these things, the company increases their image in the community and the region, but even more important is the fact that it creates a feeling of pride among the people who work at that company. They're proud to work at that company, they're proud that their company does those type of things.[13]

Trade-off between Good Ethics and Short-Term Economic Return

The proposition that good ethics is good business suggests that there may never be need for a trade-off between what is the best behavior from an ethical point of view and what might be best for short-term economic

results. As the Stride Rite example shows, however, this is not always the case. In today's rapidly changing business world, the success of a business is often measured by short-term earnings. Even though companies may preach ethics, the managers who are promoted are generally the ones who demonstrate profitability in their units. Other employees get the message that the bottom line is what really matters. Particularly when business turns sour or becomes more competitive, companies and individuals will often turn their backs on fairness and honesty.

The decay of cultural and social institutions and the complexities of conducting business in a multinational environment, have been cited as threats to the ethical conduct of business. Even organizations with institutional codes of ethics have encountered problems. For example, cadets at West Point were found guilty of cheating, despite the strong institutional requirements for honesty and integrity. In 1994, naval officials announced that the U.S. Naval Academy had implicated about 125 midshipmen, or about 15% of the class of 1994, for cheating. The Naval Academy, like West Point, has an honor code that prohibits lying, cheating, or stealing.

Balance between Economic Performance and Ethics

One possible solution to the tension between economic performance and ethics is to set minimum ethical standards that all employees must meet. Managers must try to demonstrate that high ethical standards lead to business success. For example, Johnson & Johnson CEO Ralph Larsen has said that Johnson & Johnson's high-level executives try hard to ensure that their employees live up to their corporate credo, which stresses honesty and integrity. In the words of Larsen: "The Credo shouldn't be viewed as some kind of social welfare program. It's just plain good business."[14]

On the other hand, in a survey done by *Industry Week*, there is evidence to suggest that the more highly compensated a manager, the more likely he or she is to compromise business ethics. Thirteen hundred managers were asked how they would handle the following situation: Their company is involved in bidding on a

11. *Id.* at A5.

12. *Id.*

13. Casey Gilmore, *Mr. K Looks Back, Looks Ahead: On Business and Civic Duty*, KAN. CITY BUS. J., Sept. 25, 1992.

14. Faye Rice et al., *Leaders of the Most Admired: Corporate Citizenship*, FORTUNE, Jan. 29, 1990, at 40.

contract for the U.S. Navy. Although their price is equivalent to that of their competitor's, their engineers tell them that it will take several more months than their competitor to develop and manufacture the same output. When questioned what the manager would tell the Navy when asked about their development schedule, the more highly compensated managers were more willing to be less than frank with the Navy to get the business (see Exhibit 1.1).

 Social Responsibility

The public's perception of socially responsible behavior influences the ethical decisions that businesses make. Many companies have faced severe financial setbacks caused by decisions that, in hindsight, were perceived by the public as unethical. Consumer products companies are particularly sensitive to public perception, given their reliance on individual retail sales. As William D. Smithburg, chairman and chief executive officer of the Quaker Oats Company, wrote: "[I] know ethical behavior is sound business practice because every day at the Quaker Oats Company I am reminded that we succeed or fail according to the trust consumers have in us."[15] Issues of social responsibility arise in the areas of product safety,

the environment, investment, advertising campaigns, underpaid foreign workers, and charitable contributions.

Customers and Product Safety

Socially responsible businesses place a heavy emphasis on the safety of their products. Huge costs have been associated with failure to meet the public's perception of what is safe.

Johnson & Johnson and Tylenol   Johnson & Johnson's Tylenol success story is a classic illustration of socially responsible behavior. In September 1982, some Tylenol capsules were tampered with and laced with cyanide poison. As soon as the first deaths were reported, the company recalled 31 million bottles of Tylenol. This recall cost Johnson & Johnson approximately $100 million. Although the short-term economic costs of such a move were enormous, within a matter of months Johnson & Johnson was able to regain the market share it had lost. By living up to its reputation for integrity and social responsibility, Johnson & Johnson enhanced both its public image and its long-term profitability. However, that image was recently tarnished by claims that Johnson & Johnson had failed to warn consumers that Tylenol, when taken with alcohol, can cause liver damage.

Hudson Foods and Tainted Hamburger   Hudson Foods experienced the biggest meat recall ever in the

---

15. Touche Ross Report at 45.

EXHIBIT 1.1   Relationship between Compensation and Ethics

You are a manager of a company bidding on a contract for the U.S. Navy. Although your price is the same as your competitor's, your engineers have told you that it will take your firm longer to develop and manufacture the product. What would you tell the Navy if asked about your development and manufacture schedule? Here's how the managers in *Industry Week*'s survey responded.

	SALARY UNDER $40K	SALARY $40K–$80	SALARY $80K–$120K	SALARY OVER $120K
Manager indicates company can match competitor's schedule and hopes to find a solution later.	5%	12%	18%	22%
Manager describes company's production schedule as engineers outlined it.	78%	59%	51%	41%

SOURCE   *Torn Between Halo & Horns*, INDUSTRY WK., Mar. 15, 1993. Used by permission.

United States in a hamburger-contamination scare that began with a recall of a few thousand pounds of meat and ended with the company eventually being bought out by Tyson Foods, Inc. In August 1997, several people in Colorado became ill from eating Hudson Foods hamburgers sold by Burger King. On August 12, Hudson issued a voluntary recall of 20,000 pounds of frozen hamburger patties. According to the U.S. Department of Agriculture (USDA), two days later Hudson shipped 40,000 pounds of potentially contaminated meat. The USDA called for an expansion of the recall in light of evidence that Burger King, Boston Market, and grocery stores had received the new shipments. On August 21, Hudson recalled all the ground beef produced since June at the plant where contamination was suspected—an estimated 25 million pounds. The scandal forced Hudson out of the beef-processing business. In September 1997, poultry producer Tyson Foods agreed to purchase all of the stock of Hudson Foods for $22.50 per share.

Odwalla Juice Contamination   In 1996, California-based fresh-juice producer Odwalla, Inc. experienced product contamination that led to illness and one fatality among its customers. Odwalla's vision statement read in part "living flavor, soil to soul, people to planet, nourishing the body whole."[16] That made the announcement by Washington state officials that there was epidemiological evidence that Odwalla apple juice had infected several people with *E. coli* bacteria a severe shock to the company and its customers. More than 60 people became ill, and one child died. Odwalla responded by carrying out a voluntary recall of all of its apple, carrot, and vegetable products, creating a hotline and Web site to handle customer inquiries, and offering to pay the medical expenses for all those stricken ill by Odwalla products. Odwalla also voluntarily began flash-pasteurizing its apple juice, a process it had eschewed before because of the potential adverse effect on the nutritional value of the juice. Although Odwalla temporarily lost customers and its stock took a beating, its responsible handling of the contamination was essential to restoring customer and shareholder confidence.

Communities and the Environment

Closely akin to product safety is environmental safety. Disregard for safety has resulted in some spectacular environmental disasters that have severely hurt the surrounding communities.

Union Carbide and Bhopal   The Union Carbide disaster at a pesticide factory outside of Bhopal, India, in 1984 provides a vivid example of the failure to make the right ethical decisions. Union Carbide, prior to the accident, had been warned by a team of experts that the plant had "serious potential for sizable releases of toxic materials."[17] In addition, there were six serious accidents at the Bhopal facility during the six years that preceded the disaster. Clearly, Union Carbide had reason to believe the facility was at risk. On December 3, 1984, in the most lethal industrial accident ever, some 40 tons of methyl isocyanate gas was emitted from the plant. As of 1991, more than 3,800 people had died as a result of the accident, and 20,000 were left seriously disabled. The Indian government has received more than 650,000 claims from individuals physically and psychologically affected; and, as of 1993, had accepted 300,000 claims.

If this disaster had occurred in the United States, Union Carbide would have been financially crippled, if not driven into bankruptcy, by the lawsuits that would have followed. In a settlement with the Indian government, however, Union Carbide—which had $5 billion in equity—agreed to pay $470 million to settle all present and future claims. Although this appears to be a great deal of money at first glance, the *Wall Street Journal* has estimated that the victims are likely to receive less than $1,000 apiece. Alok Pratap Singh, leader of one of the larger victim groups, estimates the needs of the Bhopal victims at $4.5 billion over the next 20 years.[18]

In October 1991, India's Supreme Court upheld the $470 million settlement. The attorney for one of the biggest groups of victims and other opponents of the settlement had unsuccessfully argued that Union Carbide should be required to pay "First World" not "Third World" rates for deaths and injuries.[19]

Exxon Valdez   Another environmental disaster with grave consequences was the Valdez, Alaska, oil spill. On March 24, 1989, 10.1 million gallons of crude oil spilled from the tanker *Exxon Valdez* into the waters of Prince William Sound. More than 36,000 migrating

16. ODWALLA, INC., 1996 ANNUAL REPORT 2 (1997).

17. Robert Sherrill, *Corporate Crime and Violence: Big Business Power and the Abuse of the Public Trust*, NATION, Nov. 28, 1988, at 568.

18. Anthony Spaeth, *Court Settlement Stuns Bhopal Survivors*, WALL ST. J., Feb. 22, 1989, at A12.

19. Scott McMurry, *India's High Court Upholds Settlement Paid by Carbide in Bhopal Gas Leak*, WALL ST. J., Oct. 4, 1991, at B8.

birds were killed, an estimated 1,000 miles of shoreline was affected, and one of the world's richest salmon fisheries was greatly impaired. Exxon estimated that the costs of cleaning up the most disastrous oil spill in North American history was upwards of $2 billion. The spill cut Exxon's earnings for 1989 to $3.81 billion compared with $5.26 billion in 1988.

Questionable ethical decisions by Exxon and unacceptable behavior by certain Exxon employees triggered severe worldwide criticism. The captain of the vessel was not at the helm of the tanker when it went aground. He had left the third mate, who was clearly unqualified under U.S. Coast Guard standards to navigate through Prince William Sound, to steer the tanker. The Coast Guard was also criticized for not keeping a closer watch on radar.

In February 1990, a U.S. federal grand jury indicted Exxon and its shipping subsidiary on five criminal charges (two of which were felonies) that carried possible penalties of more than $600 million. In 1991, Exxon reached a $1.025 billion settlement agreement with the federal government and the state of Alaska. The $900 million civil portion of the settlement is to be paid to the state over a 10-year period. Exxon also agreed to pay a $125 million criminal fine, including restitution of $100 million to be equally divided between the state and federal governments to pay for restoration in Alaska.

In March 1990, the captain of the tanker was convicted of negligently discharging oil. He was acquitted, however, of criminal mischief, operating the tanker while intoxicated, and reckless endangerment. The captain was sentenced to 1,000 hours of community service, mostly to help clean oil-soaked beaches, and ordered to pay $50,000 in partial restitution.

In August 1994, in a civil suit brought as a class action involving about 10,000 commercial fishermen, a federal court jury in Anchorage awarded compensatory damages against Exxon of $286.8 million. The jury awarded $5 billion in punitive damages in September 1994.

Public outrage at the Valdez oil spill and Exxon's cleanup efforts has not gone unnoticed by some corporations. Exxon appointed one of its top executives to monitor its environmental actions worldwide. It also placed a scientist on its board of directors, and the board formed a public-issues committee to respond to shareholder, consumer, and environmental concerns. Several oil companies, such as Chevron, advertise on television their sensitivity to environmental issues.

Individual and institutional investors are also taking steps toward more environmentally responsible behavior. The Social Investment Forum undertook a project called the Coalition for Environmentally Responsible Economies (CERES) to draft investor guidelines. The CERES principles, which were introduced in 1989, have been presented at numerous shareholder meetings. More than 75 companies (including General Motors and oil marketer Sun Company) had endorsed the principles by 1997. The guidelines focus on environmental awareness and corporate activities, such as using and preserving natural resources, safely disposing of pollutants, marketing safe products, and reducing environmental risks. Several pension funds and institutional investors have adopted the CERES principles and base their investment decisions in part on corporations' adherence to these principles.

MAXXAM, Pacific Lumber, and Old-Growth Redwoods　In 1985, MAXXAM Group, Inc., a Texas-based company headed by financier Charles Hurwitz, acquired Pacific Lumber in a hostile takeover. Pacific Lumber was a 100-year-old lumber-harvesting company whose assets included 200,000 acres of redwood trees in Humboldt County, California. These lands included 17,000 acres of old-growth redwood, including a 3,000-acre stand called the Headwaters Forest, which is the largest privately owned stand of old-growth redwoods in the world. Prior to the takeover, Pacific Lumber employed a conservative cutting program, which had as its goal sustained yield over a long period of time.

After the takeover, the new management doubled production, harvesting trees more than 1,000 years old in order to exploit the high profits such old wood commanded to pay down the debt MAXXAM incurred in the takeover. Pacific Lumber tried in 1991 and 1996 to log in the Headwaters Forest, but it was prevented from doing so by the government. In 1992, Californians rejected a $300 million bond issue to fund the purchase of the Headwaters from MAXXAM. In 1996, the California Department of Forestry denied permission to log based on potential impact on the marbled murrelet, a robin-sized seabird on the threatened-species list. MAXXAM continued to fight the restrictions in court, arguing that the restrictions constituted a taking of MAXXAM's property without just compensation. MAXXAM and the U.S. government reached a tentative agreement for the sale of 7,500 acres of virgin old-growth redwoods (including the Headwaters Forest) in exchange for $380 million in cash. Congress has approved the federal government's $250 million share.[20] Many environmentalists challenged the pact for failing to protect a much larger area, which they claim is necessary to preserve the animal, bird, and plant ecosystem.

Employees: Sweatshops, Child Labor, Restructurings, and Contingent Workers

Wal-Mart, Kmart, and Sweatshops In May 1996, labor activists alleged that top U.S. retailer Wal-Mart's Kathie Lee Gifford line of apparel was produced in overseas and U.S. sweatshops that held back workers' wages. Prior attempts at prompting Wal-Mart to investigate sweatshops had fallen on deaf ears. However, Kathy Lee Gifford, a popular TV talk show host, responded by joining then Labor Secretary Robert Reich in his call for retailers to take responsibility for the working conditions that exist at their contractors. Other retailers were also called on the carpet for selling apparel made in sweatshops. Kmart was the subject of reports that its Jaclyn Smith line of clothing was produced by children working for 31 cents per hour in sweatshops in Honduras. J.C. Penney Co. suspended purchases from two manufacturers that Secretary Reich claimed used sweatshops to produce their goods.[21] Critics have charged that the Nike athletic shoe company is using child labor and not paying its foreign workers a livable wage. These allegations and Nike's response are discussed in the "Inside Story" at the end of this chapter.

Child Labor at Wal-Mart In 1992, the press revealed that some of the products Wal-Mart labeled "Made in the U.S.A." were actually made in Bangladesh by child laborers working for pennies a day. The head of Wal-Mart's Bangladesh operation denied that they were children, saying, "The workers just look young because they are malnourished adults."[22] Wal-Mart chief executive officer David Glass denied that the retailer misled the public with its "Buy America" campaign and stated that Wal-Mart was unable to substantiate the fact that

children were working in factories in Bangladesh. Rosalene Costa, a human rights worker in Bangladesh interviewed by NBC "Dateline," said the children working at the factory were about 12 years old. The children told her their real ages when the supervisor was not around.[23]

Leveraged Buyouts and Restructurings During the 1980s, tax reforms and the *laissez-faire* ("let it be") approach of the Reagan administration toward mergers and acquisitions, plus a willingness by managers and financiers to take on huge amounts of debt to buy stock, triggered the popularity of leveraged buyouts funded by *junk bonds*—forms of high-yield, high-risk, unsecured corporate indebtedness that are not investment grade. A *leveraged buyout* (LBO) is a takeover financed with loans secured by the acquired company's assets. Groups of investors, including management, use borrowed money along with some of their own money to buy back the company's stock from its current shareholders. Like most other business trends, leveraged buyouts have both positive and negative implications, involving critical ethical considerations.

In some cases, leveraged buyouts proved favorable for the acquired company, because a more efficient and productive organization resulted. Corporate waste, such as lazy and unproductive management, excess layers of bureaucracy, and unprofitable divisions, triggered many of the early takeovers. By reducing such waste, these takeovers may have contributed to the resurgence in American productivity growth in the 1980s. Without junk-bond financing, for example, Ted Turner's cable empire might never have been built. The same holds true for the long-distance telephone carrier MCI Communications.

The junk-bond phenomenon has not been without its faults, however. A number of companies (including giant retailers Macy's and Federated) declared bankruptcy when they were unable to repay the debt incurred in their leveraged buyouts. Thousands of employees of acquired companies were laid off, had their wages cut, saw their employee pension funds diminish, and had their collective bargaining or labor union agreements circumvented.

Critics claim that LBOs financed by junk bonds evolved from an important financial innovation to an

20. Alex Barnum, *Breakthrough for Deal to Buy Headwaters*, SAN FRANCISCO CHRON., Jan. 24, 1998, at A13.

21. Susan Chandler, *Prime Time for Sweatshops*, BUS. WK., June 17, 1996, at 44.

22. *NBC Questions Wal-Mart's "Buy America" Campaign* (United Press International, Dec. 22, 1992).

23. *Id.*

extraordinarily abused one, which glorified greed, manifested as short-term wealth maximization at the expense of the long term. Those profiting had a rationale for their sudden surge in wealth. As corporate raider Gordon Gekko, in the 1987 movie *Wall Street*, put it: "Greed, for lack of a better word, is good. Greed is right. Greed works. Greed clarifies, cuts through, and captures the essence of the evolutionary spirit. Greed, in all of its forms—greed for life, for money, for love, knowledge—has marked the upward surge of mankind."[24]

Contingent Workers Many large companies not only substantially reduced their full-time work force in the early to mid-1990s, but also hired part-time, temporary, or contract workers for many of the jobs that remained. Such workers are often paid a lower hourly wage than full-time workers and usually are not eligible for employee benefits, such as medical insurance. This was a major issue in the UPS–Teamsters strike, which is discussed in Chapter 14.

Supporters of this trend argue that it is necessary to give U.S. companies the flexibility to adjust the work force to reflect changing and seasonal labor demand. Critics claim that the practice saps worker morale and ultimately adversely affects worker productivity.[25]

Edward Hennessy, Jr., former chairman and CEO of Allied-Signal, Inc., argues:

> If we choose to deny the larger human and social impact of the corporation, if we try to reduce the company to the bare essentials of a commercial transaction, we will end up with a work force that is less capable and less dedicated over the long run. We will also cause society to be indifferent—if not completely hostile—to the interests of corporations and their shareholders.[26]

Maquiladora Plants Maquiladora plants in Mexico, which give U.S. companies access to cheap Mexican labor, raise issues of what is fair pay. As with the Bhopal settlement, one must consider the ethics of having a "First World" and "Third World" rate of pay. Much of the opposition to the North American Free Trade Agreement (NAFTA), discussed in Chapter 25, related

to the feared "export" of U.S. jobs and the exploitation of workers in Mexico.

Customers and Price-fixing

In June 1995, the U.S. government served executives of Archer Daniels Midland (ADM), a leading agribusiness company, with subpoenas resulting from a three-year investigation of the company's participation in an international price-fixing scheme for lysine products. Company officials were charged with colluding with competitors to coordinate price increases and to allocate sales of lysine products among themselves. Ajinomoto Co. and Kyowa Hakko Kogyo Co., two Japanese companies,

INTERNATIONAL CONSIDERATION

Firms in Japan take a pluralistic approach to the responsibilities of a corporation, in contrast to American firms, which operate from the principle that the shareholders' interests are paramount. Indeed, the epistemological origins of *keiei*, the Japanese word for business, encompass the notion of improving society's well-being. A Japanese company concerns itself with the interests of a variety of stakeholders, including its main bank, suppliers, subcontractors, customers, and employees. When asked the question, "Under which of the following assumptions is a large company in your country managed?" 97% of Japanese firms surveyed selected "A firm exists for the interest of all stakeholders." Only 24% of U.S. companies, 30% of U.K. companies, 78% of French companies, and 82% of German companies selected this response.

In another survey of CEOs in Japan's 113 top corporations, 63.2% of the CEOs indicated that employees were the most important source of support for the CEO; only 11.5% identified shareholders as the most important source of support. Japanese companies have long had a no-layoff policy. As the 1990s brought about slower growth and other changes in the Japanese economy, Japanese CEOs have had to struggle with how to keep the promise of lifetime employment or, if the promise cannot be kept, how to minimize the adverse effect on employees' trust and loyalty.

---

24. Quoted in Joseph Nocera, *The Decade that Got Out of Hand*, Best of Bus. Q., Winter 1989–90, at 183.

25. *See* Jeffrey Pfeffer, The Human Equation: Building Profits by Putting People First 161–194 (1998).

26. Touche Ross Report at 44.

were also charged. Individual managers were targeted in the probe and were levied personal fines as a result of their involvement. ADM pled guilty to the price-fixing charges and paid $100 million in fines. The other companies also admitted guilt and paid fines of $10 million. Additionally, all of the companies remained subject to civil fines, as their customers filed lawsuits to recover damages from the inflated prices they paid as a result of the price-fixing.

Other Constituencies

Salomon Brothers and U.S. Treasury Bonds Scandal In 1991, Salomon Brothers was caught in a scandal involving the sale of government bonds. Government regulations prohibited any one company or individual from buying more than 35% of the bonds available for sale. In April of that year, Salomon's chief of government bond trading received a letter from a regulator requesting information about a discrepancy related to a bid. He brought this to the attention of his superiors and mentioned the illegal bidding his department had been engaged in. His superiors did not report this information to the authorities. One month later, Salomon bought at least 44% and controlled up to 85% of the issue of two-year notes; after the auction, prices rose sharply, and short sellers were "squeezed." Shortly thereafter, the Securities and Exchange Commission (SEC) and Justice Department initiated a secret investigation into Salomon's government bond trading activities. In response to subpoenas served against Salomon in June, Salomon initiated its own internal investigation. Resignations ensued, fines were levied, and the matter was finally resolved in May 1992 when the SEC settled with Salomon Brothers for $290 million.

Columbia/HCA Healthcare and Medicare Fraud The once high-flying hospital and medical services company, Columbia/HCA Healthcare, is under siege for alleged criminal fraud in connection with its Medicare billing practices. This is discussed in the "Inside Story" in Chapter 15.

Positive Action

Toyota Some companies make socially responsible choices without waiting for a problem to arise. In 1997, Toyota rushed to become the first seller of automobiles powered by a combination of an electric battery for slow speeds and an internal combustion engine for highway driving. Toyota touted the fuel efficiency and low emissions, especially in environmentally sensitive Europe where Toyota has traditionally had a modest market share.

Conoco In response to the *Exxon Valdez* debacle, Conoco, one of the United States' largest oil companies, announced in April 1990 that it was ordering two new oil tankers with double hulls. Experts believe that double-hull tankers can prevent or limit spills if the tanker runs aground. Conoco president and chief executive officer Constantine S. Nicandros stated, "We are in the business by the public's consent. We are sincere in our concern for the air, water and land of our planet as a matter of enlightened self-interest."[27]

Starbucks In 1995, Starbucks Coffee Co. adopted guidelines regarding treatment of employees by its foreign coffee suppliers. The guidelines cover many issues including child labor, housing, safe and clean facilities, and the right to associate freely. Starbucks admitted that the company began promoting the guidelines in response to consumer boycotts of its products. While activists applauded Starbucks's actions, some called for more to be done, as Starbucks will not punish suppliers who do not comply.

Wetherill Associates In 1978, using their own savings, E. Marie Bothe and Edith M. Gripton founded Wetherill Associates, Inc., which rebuilds and distributes replacement parts for automobiles. Their goal was to put into practice the business philosophy of Richard W. Wetherill, a management consultant and author in Philadelphia who exhorted businesspersons to "always do the right thing." Although the automotive-parts industry was rife with dishonest tactics such as bribery, kickbacks, and illegal sales practices, the two women instilled the company with a commitment to honesty, integrity, and quality, values that are shared and practiced by all who work there. Employees turned down cash payments offered under the table, refused to sell products they knew would be used improperly, and interacted honestly and openly with customers, suppliers, and each other. In 1994, Wetherill Associates, Inc. was

---

27. *Conoco Says It Will Order Oil Tankers with Double Hulls*, L. A. TIMES, Apr. 11, 1990, at D1.

the leading company in its industry, earning profits of $10 million on revenues of $98 million.

Merck Merck & Co. decided to develop and give away a drug that cured river blindness, a painful parasitic infection that eventually resulted in loss of vision. More than one million people in Third World countries had contracted the disease. Merck developed the drug expecting that governments or aid agencies would pay for and distribute the product when it was complete. When no organization did so, Merck continued development and distributed the medicine itself, at no cost to the recipients. The decision to do this was based on the company's vision and dedication to that vision, which is as follows: "We are in the business of preserving and improving human life. All of our actions must be measured by our success in achieving this goal."[28]

Royal Dutch/Shell Group Shell Oil is taking special care to avoid harming the vulnerable Amazon rain forest when it proceeds with its $3 billion, 40-year natural-gas project in Camisea, Peru.[29] The area is accessible only by air or river and is unusually rich in plant and animal life. Shell is also trying to ensure that local villagers directly affected by its operations actually benefit from them. Camisea is home to 5,000 Indians who have only recently settled in permanent villages.

This stands in sharp contrast to previous activities by Shell and other oil companies in South America. For example, oil companies dumped 19 billion gallons of toxic waste at Ecuador's Amazon oil fields between 1972 and 1989. The industry's old ways led to embarrassing boycotts, tarnished corporate images, and the enactment of stiff new laws. Thomas Lovejoy, a Smithsonian scientist and rain-forest expert, states that big companies are finally realizing "that if you do things right from the start, it will save you a lot of money and a lot of grief in the long run."[30]

Lessons

The examples in this section highlight three important needs. Companies and their managers must (1) think critically about the moral aspects of corporate activity; (2) be ethical and be perceived by the public as ethical; and (3) be socially responsible and be perceived as socially responsible and credible throughout the world, given the globalization of the marketplace and of information.

Other Manifestations of Ethical Dilemmas

What Shareholders Really Want

In a recent survey, 246 shareholders from across the United States were asked what they thought their corporations should spend money on. It turned out that money is not always the first thing on shareholders' minds. Sometimes the environment takes priority.[31] Two areas were targeted: (1) cleaning up plants and stopping environmental pollution, and (2) making safer products. In a list of 10 items, "higher dividends" ranked only third. Falling to the bottom of the list was "spending more money on charitable contributions and programs to benefit women or racial minorities." Concern for ethics *per se* fell to fifth place.

When seen in totality, the study seems to suggest that a corporation should do several things to manage expenditures and social concerns. There should be a corporate awareness of social, ethical, and environmental issues at all levels; methods should be developed to evaluate and report on the social and environmental impacts of corporate activities; and incentives to encourage employees to be responsible should be integrated into the performance evaluation system and corporate culture. The corporate structure should be modified to deal with social, environmental, and ethical crises.

Socially Responsible Investment

Besides being concerned about product and environmental safety, the public has put pressure on corporations and institutional investors to invest responsibly, that is, in such a way as to not lend support to unjust, oppressive regimes. For instance, many companies with direct or indirect economic ties to South Africa were the subject of consumer boycotts and shareholder

---

28. From Merck & Co., Inc., *Internal Management Guide 1989,* as quoted in James C. Collins & Jerry S. Porras, Built to Last: Successful Habits of Visionary Companies 46–47 (1994).

29. Jonathan Friedland, *Oil Companies Strive to Turn a New Leaf to Save Rain Forest,* Wall St. J., July 17, 1997, at A1.

30. *Id.*

---

31. Mark Epstein, *What Shareholders Really Want,* N. Y. Times, Apr. 28, 1991, sec. 3, p. 11.

resolutions prohibiting investment in South Africa. South Africa's policy of racial segregation (called *apartheid*) relegated its black citizens to a second-class status in employment, housing, and opportunity. The boycotts and shareholder resolutions were critical in helping end apartheid in South Africa, a result for which Nelson Mandela and F. W. de Klerk won the Nobel Peace Prize in 1993.

Advertising Campaigns

Targeted Marketing   In the summer of 1991, G. Heileman Brewing Co. planned to release a new malt liquor called Power Master. The name and label were designed to connote the product's high alcohol content of 5.9%, which would have made Power Master the strongest malt liquor on the market. Power Master was targeted through advertising and design specifically at the African-American community. African Americans and Hispanics are the largest consumers of malt liquors currently on the market. African-American activist groups threatened protests, including billboard whitewashing campaigns, in response to the new product. Michael L. Pfleger, pastor of St. Sabina Catholic Church in Chicago and one of the persons arrested for protesting outside Heileman headquarters in La Crosse, Wisconsin, stated: "We're not going to tolerate target marketing when the product is death or disease."[32] Heileman decided to withdraw the product before it was even released to the stores.

Marketing Tobacco and Beer to Children

Parents and public health officials sharply criticized RJR Nabisco (makers of Camel cigarettes) for its advertisements featuring a cartoon figure, Old Joe Camel. A number of studies showed that ads involving this sharply dressed camel who frequents pool halls and pickup bars were tremendously successful in targeting children. In a study involving 229 children ages three to six, more than half were familiar with the figure and associated him with cigarettes. Six-year-olds were nearly as familiar with Joe Camel as they were with the Mickey Mouse logo for the Disney Channel.[33]

After introducing Josephine Camel in 1994, RJR ran four-page, full-color ads in *People, Sports Illustrated,* and other magazines that depicted female and male camels drinking, smoking, shooting pool, and playing darts and cards at Joe's Place, a multilevel bar. Faced with the Food and Drug Administration's threat to regulate nicotine as a drug and increasingly hostile public opinion, RJR voluntarily agreed in 1997 to abandon the Joe Camel ad campaign in the United States. The proposed tobacco litigation settlement, discussed in the "Inside Story" in Chapter 10, would sharply curtail tobacco advertising.

However, Joe Camel continues to thrive outside the United States. In 1996, he started showing up in other countries. Argentinian antismoking activists became incensed when Joe Camel and friends began appearing in smoking advertisements and promotional gimmicks in that country. The antismoking groups protested that the promotions, which revolved around motorcycles and rock concerts, were primarily targeted at teenagers and young adults.[34]

In 1997, the Federal Trade Commission launched a probe of alcohol advertising to children. The *Wall Street Journal* reported that a survey by Competitive Media Reporting showed that during an arbitrarily chosen week, youths under the drinking age made up a majority of the audience for beer commercials on several occasions.[35] For example, Molson beer was advertised on MTV during a 10:00 P.M. episode of "Beavis and Butt-Head," 69% of whose viewers were under 21, the legal drinking age in all 50 states. Stroh advertised Schlitz Malt Liquor during MTV's prime-time music-video show when 56% of the audience was under 21. That same week, Adolph Coors ran two ads just after 8:00 P.M. on the Black Entertainment Network, when 65% of the audience was under age. These commercials violated the beer industry's own guidelines, which provide that beer advertising should not be aired on television programs when most of the audience is expected to be below the legal purchase age. The industry's own failure to police itself may well result in new federal restrictions on beer and liquor advertising.

---

32. Thomas Palmer, *A Target-Marketing Ploy Backfires—Malt Liquor Aimed at Blacks Dies Aborning, A Victim of Insensitivity,* BOSTON GLOBE, July 14, 1991, at 71.

33. Kathleen Deveny, *Joe Camel Is Also Pied Piper, Research Finds,* WALL ST. J., Dec. 11, 1991, at B1, B6.

34. Jonathan Friedland, *Under Siege in the U.S., Joe Camel Pops Up Alive, Well in Argentina,* WALL ST. J., Sept. 10, 1996, at B1.

35. Sally Goll Beatty, *Are Beer Ads on "Beavis and Butt-Head" Aimed at Kids?* WALL ST. J., Jan. 6, 1997, at B1.

Conflicts of Interest in Takeovers

Management-led buyouts present unique conflicts of interest. When management is doing the buying, it has a strong incentive to make a deal to purchase the company from the existing shareholders for the lowest possible price. This incentive conflicts with management's responsibility as a protector of the interests of the shareholders of the target company to obtain the highest price for the existing shareholders.

The large fees paid advisors in mergers and acquisitions can also present conflicts of interest. For example, Sterling Drug was a longtime client of Morgan Bank of New York, one of the most prestigious commercial banks in the United States. When Hoffmann–La Roche made its surprise move to take over Sterling, Morgan Bank was not surprised—because it was the financial advisor to Hoffmann–La Roche. John M. Pietruski, Sterling's chairman, stated in a public letter to the chairman of Morgan Bank, Lewis T. Preston: "I am shocked and dismayed by what I consider to be Morgan Bank's unethical conduct in aiding and abetting a surprise raid on one of its longtime clients."[36] Morgan Guaranty Trust Co. came under fire when it helped one client, Smith-Kline Beecham Corp., the Philadelphia pharmaceutical giant, buy a firm that another client, Corning Glass Works, had agreed to purchase. Corning officials were surprised by the rival bid and outraged by Morgan Guaranty's role. When asked for a reaction, Stephen Albertalli, director of investor relations of Corning Glass, said: "You can imagine what it might be. I just don't use four-letter words over the phone."[37]

Charitable Contributions

Although the law clearly permits companies to make charitable contributions, such contributions raise the issues cited by Milton Friedman earlier in this chapter concerning management's giving away of other people's money. Controversial charities include Planned Parenthood (which advocates a woman's right to an abortion) and the Boy Scouts (which refuses to admit homosexuals). One way out is to let shareholders decide, on a pretax basis, where they want the contributions to go.

Berkshire Hathaway, headed by lauded investor Warren Buffet, does just that. Each shareholder who holds Berkshire Hathaway stock in his or her own name (not through a broker) is permitted to designate where his or her pro rata share of contributions should go. Although Berkshire Hathaway's high share price ($78,500 per Class A share and $2,621 per Class B on June 23, 1998) and resultant low number of shareholders make this practice feasible, the concept could be applied elsewhere.

Even charity can be taken to extremes. The directors of oil giant Occidental Petroleum were sued by shareholders irate at the board's decision to build a $100 million art museum carrying chairman Armand Hammer's name to house his art collection (which had been purchased largely with Occidental corporate funds). Although the court held that the business judgment rule (discussed in Chapter 21) protected the directors from personal liability, it suggested that the shareholders would be fully justified in throwing out the board through a shareholder vote.

 Promoting Ethical Behavior

The CEO Sets the Ethical Tone of the Corporation

The chief executive officer plays the most significant role in instilling a sense of ethics throughout the organization. William F. May, chairman of the Trinity Center for Ethics and Corporate Policy, states: "The CEO has a unique responsibility; he's a role model. What he does, how he lives, and the principles under which he operates become pretty much those the rest of the corporation emulate."[38] John J. Mackowski, chairman and CEO of the Atlantic Mutual Companies, states:

> I think the CEO's responsibility is to view ethics within the corporate culture, understand how its values—good or bad—come to bear upon the company, its business, and its employees. In well-run corporations, for example, the great thing is the sense the staff has of fairness. And for most things, they know enough so that they really need not go to a supervisor to find out what is right or wrong. It's there in specific statements about how they are supposed to deal with customers or one another. And that direction has to come from the top.[39]

36. Quoted in Leslie Wayne, *How the Morgan Bank Struck Out*, N.Y. Times, Feb. 7, 1988, sec. 3, p. 1.

37. Quoted in Jed Horowitz, *Morgan's Role in Merger Pits It Against Client*, Am. Banker, Mar. 28, 1988, at 1.

38. Touche Ross Report at 28.

39. Touche Ross Report at 28.

This is not to downplay the role of middle management. It is often an employee's immediate supervisor who has the most direct effect on the employee. Direction from the top, however, makes middle management aware that the CEO is serious about his or her commitment to ethics. Ethics cannot be made a high priority of the corporation overnight, but it can be achieved through strong leadership and support from the CEO.

The chairman and chief executive officer of The Dun & Bradstreet Corporation (a global credit-rating agency) introduced his company's policy on business conduct with the letter shown in Exhibit 1.2.[40] Similarly, the chairman and chief executive officer of American Express Company (a global financial and travel services company) states, "American Express Company is committed to the highest standards of integrity" and "the Company's Code of Conduct is one of American Express Company's most important documents and is intended to be part of the foundation of our corporate culture."[41]

Treatment of Employees

Typically, corporations with high ethical standards emphasize employee self-esteem. If employees feel that they are being treated fairly, they take pride in both themselves and their company. If not, they may retaliate by stealing supplies or inventory, padding expense accounts, or calling in sick when they are not. They may simply not produce at their optimum level. John H. Stookey, president and chairman of Quantum Chemical Corporation, explains:

> If people work in an organization which demeans their sense of self-worth, they are humiliated by small amounts every day. But if they work for an organization that enhances their self-esteem, it is enormously valuable to them. So if by publishing a code of ethics or by setting an example you can reinforce a person's sense that he is part of an upstanding enterprise, you are reaffirming his faith in himself. He becomes prouder of who he is and of where he's working. If you understand that process, it is not difficult to raise the ethical standards of an institution, because you can play to those needs and a lot of people will work with you.[42]

---

40. All excerpts from the *Dun & Bradstreet Corporation Policy on Business Conduct* (1998) used by permission.

41. Used by permission of the American Express Company.

42. TOUCHE ROSS REPORT at 34.

EXHIBIT 1.2   A CEO's Message on Ethics

Dear Associate:

For more than 155 years, The Dun & Bradstreet Corporation has carefully nurtured a reputation for integrity. As associates of this great company, we are stewards of that reputation and must act in keeping with the highest standards of fairness, honesty and integrity in all our dealings with our fellow associates, customers, suppliers and investors around the world. . . .

Please familiarize yourself with this document and refer to it frequently when you are presented with a complex issue or predicament in your work at The Dun & Bradstreet Corporation. If you ever have a question about proper business conduct, please consult with your manager, a Human Resources representative or a member of your unit's Legal department before taking any action. The Dun & Bradstreet Corporation's Office of Business Practices is also available to assist you. . . .

. . .

Each and every day, it is imperative that all of our actions work to preserve and strengthen our commitment to integrity. That commitment has been a cornerstone of The Dun & Bradstreet Corporation's success for more than 155 years, and it will be a key to our success for the next 155 years and beyond.

Sincerely,

Terry Taylor
Chairman and Chief Executive Officer

Mission Statements

Corporations sometimes include ethical language in their corporate mission statements. This language may not mention ethics by name but stresses that the corporation has responsibilities in addition to profit maximization and that it has obligations to both employees and customers. For example, Toyo Glass Company, a Japanese supplier of glass products, has the following statement:

1. Our objective is to contribute our share of work towards the happiness of the public at large.
2. Profit is not our first aim to attain, it is a natural outgrowth of successful business activities.

3. Everybody is expected to do his duty as a service to the public, individually and collectively, and thus to benefit the property of his own as well as others.[43]

As mentioned earlier, Merck & Co., the most successful pharmaceutical company in the world, also has a vision that contains ethical values, which it lives by.

Codes of Ethics

Codes of ethics are the most widespread means by which companies communicate their ethical standards to their employees. A code of ethics is a written set of rules or standards that states the company's principles and clarifies its expectations of employee conduct in various situations. Although these codes vary from company to company, they govern such areas as selling and marketing practices, conflict of interest, political activities, and product safety and quality.

The Ethics Resource Center reported in 1987 that 74% of all large corporations in America had adopted a code of conduct. In 1986, the Center for Business Ethics found that of companies taking steps to institutionalize ethics, 93% had compiled codes of ethics.

Business leaders judge a code of ethics to be one of the most effective measures for encouraging ethical business behavior. James Burke, chairman of Johnson & Johnson, believes that Johnson & Johnson's code of ethics helped the company out of its Tylenol-tampering crisis. Johnson & Johnson's code begins: "We believe that our first responsibility is to the doctors, nurses, and patients, to mothers and all others who use our products and services. In meeting their needs, everything we do must be of high quality."[44] When it was discovered that Tylenol capsules had been tampered with, the company acted swiftly to remove the product from the shelves. "Dozens of people had to make hundreds of decisions on the fly," says Burke. "There was no doubt in their minds that the public was going to come first in this issue because we had spelled it out [in our credo] as their responsibility."[45]

It is important to note that a company code of ethics is ineffective without proper implementation. It is not enough simply to state the rules of the company; the code must give employees an understanding of prin-

ciples to guide them in making practical decisions. The code should be a living document, reviewed periodically to meet new circumstances. Managers should go over the code with personnel to ensure understanding of the company's values. The company should supplement the written code of ethics with ethics education programs conducted by professional trainers. The company should also pay increased attention to ethical standards in recruiting and hiring.

Exhibit 1.3 contains excerpts from the *American Express Company Code of Conduct* (1997).

Oversight

In an effort to enforce ethical standards, some companies have set up oversight committees. According to a 1992 survey by the Center for Business Ethics, nearly half of the respondents (all Fortune 1000 companies) had ethics officers. Nearly all of these officers had been appointed in the previous five years.[46]

In general, ethics committees are responsible for setting standards or policy and for handling employee complaints or infractions. The membership of these committees often includes executive officers or directors of the company. Ombudspersons investigate employee complaints. Judiciary boards usually decide cases of ethics code violations.

Another method of oversight is the social audit. Increasingly, companies have been performing social audits of their activities in sensitive or controversial areas. For example, a company might conduct an internal audit of its disposal of chemical waste, or a bank might audit the reporting practices of its securities trading division. The Body Shop retained an outsider—Kirk Hanson of the Stanford Business School—to audit the effect of its activities on the environment and the communities where it operates. An oversight committee may also be responsible for looking at ethical considerations in a company's benefits programs.

Ethics Training

Many companies hold workshops and courses in ethics for their employees or hire ethics consultants to run training sessions; 60% of the companies that provide ethics training do so during the orientation process for new employ-

---

43. Robert E. Allinson, GLOBAL DISASTERS: INQUIRIES INTO MANAGEMENT ETHICS (1997).

44. TOUCHE ROSS REPORT at 38.

45. Stanley J. Modic, *Corporate Ethics: From Commandments to Commitment*, INDUSTRY WK., Dec. 14, 1987, at 33.

46. Rosie Sherman, *Ethicists: Gurus of the '90s*, NAT'L L.J., Jan. 24, 1994, at 1.

EXHIBIT 1.3   Excerpts from the *American Express Company Code of Conduct*

PERSONAL RESPONSIBILITY

All employees are expected to protect and enhance the assets and reputation of American Express Company. Our business is based on a strong tradition of trust. It is the reason our customers come to us. Honesty and integrity are cornerstones of ethical behavior—and trustworthiness and dependability are essential to lasting relationships. Our continued success depends on doing what we promise—promptly, competently and fairly.

. . .

The Code of Conduct provides guidelines for a variety of business situations. It does not try to anticipate every ethical dilemma an employee may face. American Express therefore relies on the good judgment—the internal moral compass—of each of its employees. When faced with a difficult ethical decision, employees sometimes find it helpful to ask themselves certain basic questions. For example:

- Am I compromising my own personal ethics?
- Would I like to see my action become a general industry practice?
- How would I feel if my action were reported on the front page of my local newspaper?
- Would the Company lose customers—or shareholders—if they knew employees did this?
- Would I be comfortable explaining my action to my spouse? My parents? My children?

. . .

LEADERS' RESPONSIBILITY

Managers, by virtue of their positions of authority, must be ethical role models for all employees. An important part of a manager's leadership responsibility is to exhibit the highest standards of integrity in all dealings with fellow employees, customers, suppliers and the community at large.

Used by permission.

---

ees. Companies cite two primary goals of ethics training: (1) to develop a general awareness of ethics in business, and (2) to draw attention to practical ethical issues.

Some companies have developed innovative methods for educating their employees in ethics. Citicorp, one of the largest bank holding companies in the United States, created a board game to instruct its employees in Citicorp policies, laws governing the workplace, and ethical decision making. The game, called The Work Ethic—An Exercise in Integrity, has been played in company orientation sessions and training programs by more than 40,000 Citicorp employees at all levels of management.[47]

In the game, teams of employees are presented with ethical dilemmas and alternative courses of action. Each team, after discussion, selects one of four courses of action. The teams advance on the game board according to the ethical appropriateness of their responses. The questions cover a wide range of subjects, including bribery, customer confidentiality, sexual harassment, and discrimination. Two sample questions are shown in Exhibit 1.4.

---

47. Citicorp North America, *Business Ethics: What Is Business's Responsibility?*, ASSET-BASED FINANCE J., Fall/Winter 1987, at 8.

EXHIBIT 1.4   Sample Questions from the Citicorp Work Ethic Board Game

---

1. An important customer arranges a meeting for you and several of your staff at a private club. The meeting is about to begin when a waiter tells you that a member of your staff has been refused admittance because of his race. What do you do?
   (a) Ask the customer to move the meeting to a local restaurant so your colleague can attend.
   (b) Tell the customer that the meeting will have to be rescheduled at a Citicorp facility.
   (c) Ask your employee to leave and say you'll talk to him when you get back to the office.
   (d) Say an emergency has come up, you have to leave, but you'll reschedule the meeting.

2. You're responsible for purchasing office equipment and supplies for your department. After you've held the job for a year, your husband becomes a salesperson for a supplier and gets assigned to your unit as part of his sales territory. What do you do?
   (a) Do nothing.
   (b) Update your conflict of interest disclosure form and ask your supervisor to remove you from decisions concerning that supplier.
   (c) Replace equipment from your husband's company with equipment from another supplier.
   (d) Ask your husband to request another territory.

Citicorp feels that the game has been successful in communicating to employees the importance of ethics in business and in teaching them the standards and policies of Citicorp. The Work Ethic game is just one of several programs at Citicorp to increase awareness of the importance of ethics.

Making It Easier to Blow the Whistle

Many employees are reluctant to "blow the whistle"—to report illegal or unethical conduct that they observe at work—for fear of being considered a troublemaker or of being fired. A number of federal, state, and local laws prohibit reprisals against employees who report activities that they believe violate a law, rule, or regulation. These whistle-blowing laws are discussed in Chapter 12.

Even with legislative and judicial protections, however, whistle-blowers do suffer. For example, on the eve of the space shuttle *Challenger*'s takeoff in January 1986, two senior engineers from Morton Thiokol warned that the shuttle's O-ring gaskets (manufactured by Morton Thiokol) might be affected by the forecasted cold weather. The launch was not canceled, and seven astronauts died when the shuttle exploded in a ball of flame. According to the *Economist*, even though the two Morton Thiokol employees were praised for their actions, their careers suffered.[48]

Edna Ottney, a quality assurance engineer who has investigated employee concerns in the nuclear power industry since 1985, reported that 90% of the 1,700 whistle-blowers she interviewed had experienced negative reactions. A person who reported violations at the Comanche Peak nuclear plant in Glen Rose, Texas, warns: "Be prepared for old friends to suddenly become distant. Be prepared to change your type of job and lifestyle. Be prepared to wait years for blind justice to prevail."[49]

A study published in the September 1993 issue of the *British Medical Journal* shows that this is a problem that transcends national borders. Of 35 Australian whistle-blowers surveyed, 8 lost their jobs as a result of whistle-blowing, 10 were demoted, 10 resigned or re-

tired early because of ill health related to victimization, 15 were taking prescribed medication to deal with stress, and 17 had considered suicide.[50]

A manager can make it easier for employees to blow the whistle by protecting them from retaliation by their immediate supervisor and coworkers. A manager provides moral and psychological support by emphasizing to coworkers the courage shown by the whistle-blower and by providing free counseling to deal with any victimization by coworkers.

Having an Ethics Program Isn't Enough

General Electric (GE), a multibillion-dollar company employing 220,000 people, had one of the most elaborate ethics programs in corporate America in the early 1990s, including divisional ethics ombudspersons, toll-free ethics telephone lines, and a documented code of ethics. Yet with all of these things in place, GE had a very poor record of ethical conduct. From 1990 to 1994, GE paid at least $163 million in fines for 16 different cases of fraud, waste, and abuse in government contracts. Several of the cases were initiated by whistle-blowers from within GE's own ranks. If GE had an ethics hotline, why did whistleblowers go outside the system to report abuses? The organization Taxpayers Against Fraud maintained that it was because the whistle-blowers were fearful of what would happen to them if they reported the transgressions within the company.

GE's ethical mistakes were not confined to its government contracts. In 1992, its NBC division was caught using rockets to stage explosions of fuel tanks on GM trucks for a "Dateline" segment on the allegedly faulty tanks. The company immediately fired the persons involved, instituted ethics guidelines, and created an office of ombudsperson. GE's Kidder Peabody securities brokerage division suffered from an inflated trading profits scandal in 1994. One trader allegedly falsified profits of $350 million. The trader maintained that he was a scapegoat being used to explain poor profits that year.

GE has 72 Superfund environmental cleanup sites, which had cost GE $94 million through mid-1994. An-

48. "*Good Takes on Greed*, THE ECONOMIST, Feb. 17, 1990, at 72.

49. Quoted in Joel Chineson, *Bureaucrats with Conscience*, LEGAL TIMES, Apr. 17, 1989, at 50.

50. Marcy Mason, *The Curse of Whistle-Blowing*, WALL ST. J., Mar. 14, 1994, at A14.

other whistle-blowing suit in 1994 led to a government investigation of GE's misrepresentation of the ability of jet engines to withstand electromagnetic impulses. One of GE's contractors was providing parts that did not meet the specifications, which GE knew but failed to

correct. As one ethics professor put it, "Having an ethics program is no guarantee of propriety."[51]

---

51. Ed Petry quoted in Nanette Byrnes, *The Smoke at General Electric*, FIN. WORLD, Aug. 16, 1994, at 34.

INTERNATIONAL CONSIDERATION

There is increasing focus worldwide on ethics. In addition to the OECD activities mentioned earlier, individual countries are examining their business activities and assessing the need for instilling additional consideration for ethical issues in a business context. This examination is often in the wake of scandals or other events that highlight the lack of ethical thought in business dealings.

Japan As of 1991, only about 30% of Japanese businesses had adopted a code of ethics. A series of major scandals in the 1990s, including illegal contributions to political parties, payments to mob figures by Nomura Securities and Mitsubishi, collusion and rigging of bids for construction contracts, and sale and distribution of HIV-infected blood products, led to the formation of the Corporate Citizenship Committee.[a]

China The tension between *Li* (profits) and *Yi* (society's norms for distributing profits or benefits) is a long-standing one in China and is at the core of any debate about ethics. Despite recent problems U.S. companies have had with respect to their Chinese counterparts (such as massive software piracy and counterfeiting), the development of the Center for Applied Ethics in 1994 and the Beijing International Conference of Business Ethics in 1997 are signs that ethics is a topic of concern in China.[b]

Philippines The presence of 88 languages and dialects in the Philippines makes business ethics a difficult term to define. At the core of the concept of business ethics for Filipinos seems to be the ideas of *kasalanan* (sin) and *mabuting gawa* (virtuous action). The rapid growth of the Philippine economy created opportunities for corruption, and in 1996 the Philippines ranked high in surveys of national corruption. In addition, many workers labor in sweatshops for low wages, conditions fueled by the intense competition for international investment in the 1990s.

Although most Filipino businesses do not have an ethical code or provide ethical training for their employees, there are indications of interest in increasing ethical conduct. The Financial Executives Institute of the Philippines has offered seminars on ethics for its members and in 1997 created a publication titled *Ethics and Filipino Enterprise*.[c]

Russia Private business is a relatively new concept in Russia. Moving from the Communist economic structure to a capitalist one put strong pressures on an economy already in crisis. Given the transitional nature of business, from public to private enterprises, the opportunities for unethical business practices (including an underground market run by gangsters) were many. In reaction to the lack of stable relationships between government and private businesses, Ivan Kivelidi, an active supporter of honest and responsible business practices in Russia, created the Roundtable of Russian Business in 1993. Kivelidi was assassinated in 1995.[d]

Latin America Ethical behavior in Latin America seems to be viewed with a bit of disdain; materialism and selfishness guide many decisions and actions. There is a saying that captures the spirit governing many business interactions: "el que no tranza no avanza"—"one that does not act unethically does not succeed." In that environment, there is little respect for employees, who are usually poorly paid, and no attention is given to environmental issues.[e]

---

a. Iwao Taka, *Business Ethics in Japan*, 14 J. BUS. ETHICS 1499–1508 (1997).

b. Lu Xiaohe, *Business Ethics in China*, 14 J. BUS. ETHICS 1509–18 (1997).

c. Alejo José G. Sison & Antonette Palma-Angeles, *Business Ethics in The Philippines*, 14 J. BUS. ETHICS 1519–25 (1997).

d. Ruben G. Apressyan, *Business Ethics in Russia*, 14 J. BUS. ETHICS 1561–70 (1997).

e. M. Cecilia Arruda, *Business Ethics in Latin America*, 14 J. BUS. ETHICS 1597–1603 (1997).

The Law and the "Unethical"

Role of the Law

The law—civil as well as criminal—plays an important part in promoting ethical conduct. Ethical behavior often requires a higher standard than that prescribed by the law; an action that is unethical may nonetheless be legal. On the other hand, as shown in Exhibit 1.5, unethical behavior tends to result in illegal behavior over time.

When a manager breaks a law, he or she can expect to be punished. The same may not be true for those who demonstrate unethical conduct. However, courts and legislatures continually modify the law to take account of ethical standards. For example, scandals about American companies' payment of bribes to foreign officials led to passage of the Foreign Corrupt Practices Act, which generally makes such payments illegal. Similarly, over-billing by defense contractors led to the passage of the False Claims Act, which gives whistle-blowers a financial reward for revealing Pentagon fraud.

Employer's Liability for Acts of Employees

The ethical responsibility of a company is not limited to how it provides a service or manufactures a product. Companies have additional responsibilities to their employees and to society in general. The law enforces this responsibility by imposing liability on employers in

EXHIBIT 1.5   Relationship of Ethics to Law

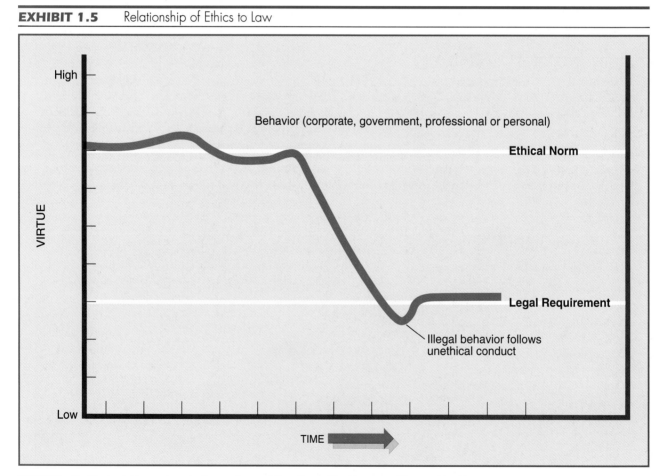

SOURCE Dr. Charles J. Cunningham, Jr., former director, Ethics Center, The University of Tampa. *Used by permission.*

certain instances. For example, companies are faced with the ethical decision of whether to serve alcohol at company gatherings. In some states, including New Jersey and Washington, an employer may be held liable for injuries caused by an employee's drunken driving after an office party.

In response to growing concern about drunken driving, there have been fewer office parties during the holidays and stricter controls on the amount of drinking at the parties that are held. Many companies still have parties but have banned the consumption of alcohol at them. Some smaller companies now throw their parties in hotels and pay for their employees to stay overnight. For example, Advanced Environment Technology Corporation of Flanders, New Jersey paid for hotel rooms for 68 employees and their guests, and for breakfast the next morning.

An employer may be held liable for sending home an intoxicated employee even if the employee did not become intoxicated at an office party but instead was found to be drinking on the job, as in the following case.

A CASE IN POINT | **IN THE LANGUAGE OF THE COURT**

CASE 1.2
**OTIS ENGINEERING
CORPORATION
v. CLARK**
Supreme Court of Texas
668 S.W.2d 307 (Tex. 1983).

FACTS   Robert Matheson worked the evening shift at the Otis Engineering plant. He had a history of drinking on the job and was intoxicated on the night of the automobile accident in which he killed himself and the wives of the plaintiffs Larry and Clifford Clark. Some of Matheson's coworkers told Matheson's supervisor, Donald Roy, that Matheson was acting strangely, including bobbing and weaving near his machine, and that he seemed intoxicated. Roy said that he observed Matheson's condition and was aware that other employees believed he should be removed from the machine. When Matheson returned from his dinner break, Roy suggested that he should go home. As he escorted Matheson to the company's parking lot, Roy asked Matheson if he was all right and if he could make it home. Matheson answered that he could. Thirty minutes later, some three miles away from the plant, the fatal accident occurred.

The medical examiner testified that Matheson had a blood alcohol content of 0.268%. This indicated he had ingested a substantial quantity of alcohol, an amount representing some 16 to 18 cocktails if consumed over a period of one hour, or 20 to 25 cocktails if consumed over a period of two hours. The doctor stated that persons working around Matheson would undoubtedly have known of his condition.

When some night-shift employees came to work around 10:30 P.M. and remarked there had been an accident on Belt Line Road, Roy immediately suspected Matheson was involved. Upon hearing of the accident, Roy, acting on a hunch and without any further corroborating information, voluntarily went to the police station to see if Matheson was involved.

The Clarks sued Matheson's employer, Otis Engineering Corporation, for the wrongful deaths of their wives in the car accident with Matheson. Otis moved for summary judgment, arguing that as a matter of law Otis was not liable for Matheson's conduct. The trial court granted Otis's motion for summary judgment and dismissed the Clarks' claims. The appeals court reversed and remanded (sent back) the case for trial, holding there were genuine issues of fact for a jury to decide. Otis appealed.

ISSUE PRESENTED   Can an employer who sent an intoxicated employee home be held liable for injuries to third parties caused by the employee's off-the-job drunken driving?

Case 1.2 continues

Case 1.2 continued

OPINION GARLIN, J., writing for the Texas Supreme Court:

Otis' motion for summary judgment was granted on the basis that as a matter of law Otis owed no duty to the Clarks. In order to establish tort liability, a plaintiff must initially prove the existence and breach of a duty owed to him by the defendant. As a general rule, one person is under no duty to control the conduct of another, even if he has the practical ability to exercise such control. . . .

What we must decide is if changing social standards and increasing complexities of human relationships in today's society justify imposing a duty upon an employer to act reasonably when he exercises control over his servants. . . .

• • •

As Dean Prosser [former Dean of the Law School at the University of California, Boalt Hall] has observed, "[C]hanging social conditions lead constantly to the recognition of new duties. No better general statement can be made, than the courts will find a duty where, in general, reasonable men would recognize it and agree that it exists." If . . . we change concepts of duty as changing social conditions occur, then this case presents the Court with the opportunity to conform our conception of duty to what society demands.

• • •

[T]he standard of duty that we now adopt for this and all other cases currently in the judicial process, is: when, because of an employee's incapacity, an employer exercises control over the employee, the employer has a duty to take such action as a reasonably prudent employer under the same or similar circumstances would take to prevent the employee from causing an unreasonable risk of harm to others. . . .

Therefore, the trier of fact in this case should be left free to decide whether Otis acted as a reasonable and prudent employer considering the following factors: the availability of the nurses' aid station, a possible phone call to Mrs. Matheson, having another employee drive Matheson home, dismissing Matheson early rather than terminating his employment, and the foreseeable consequences of Matheson's driving upon a public street in his stuporous condition. . . .

DISSENTING OPINION McGEE, J.:

In my opinion, Otis was under no legal duty to restrain Matheson or to refrain from sending him home before the end of his shift, as the majority holds. The inability of a majority of the court to state why Otis owed a duty to the Clarks' decedents convinces me that the imposition of liability on third parties for the torts of an intoxicated person is not the proper remedy.

To compound the problem, the majority reaches an incorrect result. No court in any jurisdiction has ever suggested that an employer may be held liable for the off-duty, off-premises torts of an intoxicated employee when the employer has not contributed to the employee's state of intoxication. Moreover, and because of the pervasiveness of alcohol-related accidents of all types, today's decision radically increases the potential liability of all Texans without even acknowledging those policies

Case 1.2 continues

Case 1.2 continues

that militate against the recognition of a duty in cases such as this. In my opinion, the bench, the bar, and the public are entitled to know the reasons for and the consequences of expanded liability, matters the majority opinion chooses not to address.

. . .

[W]hat is the action that a "reasonably prudent employer" must take to avoid liability under this rule? Concededly, the facts of this one case make this appear a simple question since Otis maintained a nurse's station for ill employees. The rule of this case, however, will apply to small and large employers alike, and most small employers have no such facility, nor do they have the practical ability to take the other steps suggested by the majority. . . . In an attempt to do justice in this one case, the majority has placed an impractical and unreasonable duty upon all employers.

. . .

[T]he majority erodes the concept that an individual is responsible for his or her own actions. I would adhere to the rule that an employee is not acting in the course and scope of his employment while traveling to and from work and that the employer will not be held liable to one injured by the employee's negligent operation of an automobile during these trips to and from work. It is well settled in Texas that a person is under no duty "to anticipate negligent or unlawful conduct on the part of another."

RESULT   The summary judgment for Otis was reversed, and the case was sent back to the trial court for a jury determination of whether Otis acted as a reasonable and prudent employer in light of the facts of the case. If the jury found that Otis did not act reasonably and prudently, then Otis would be liable to the plaintiffs for damages.

COMMENTS   The employer may also be responsible for an automobile accident caused by an employee on his way home who was not intoxicated but was exhausted from being forced to work 27 consecutive hours.[52]

Questions

1. Should a tavern owner who refused to serve an intoxicated person be liable for a fatal accident involving the intoxicated person if the tavern's employee jump-started the person's car?
2. What ethical or oversight policies could Otis have put into place that would have prevented this accident?

---

52. Robertson v. LeMaster, 301 S.E.2d 563 (W. Va. 1983). This case is discussed in Chapter 9.

Criminal Liability of Manager for Acts of Subordinates

The law increasingly holds managers responsible for both the misdeeds of their employees and for criminal violations by the employer corporation. This can result in not only civil but also criminal liability for a manager who fails to properly oversee compliance by the company. Application of this in the environmental law context is discussed in Chapter 16. The following case involves the Federal Food, Drug and Cosmetic Act, which makes it a criminal offense to mislabel or adulterate food, drugs, or cosmetics that are part of interstate commerce. A chief executive officer faced criminal charges under that act in this case.

A CASE IN POINT	SUMMARY

CASE 1.3
UNITED STATES
v. PARK
Supreme Court
of the United States
421 U.S. 658 (1975).

FACTS   John Park was the chief executive officer of Acme Markets, Inc., a national retail food chain headquartered in Philadelphia, Pennsylvania. Acme employed 36,000 people and had 874 retail outlets and 16 warehouses. In 1971, the Food and Drug Administration (FDA) informed Park of violations by his company of the Federal Food, Drug and Cosmetic Act, including the presence of rats in one of the warehouses in which food was stored.

Park was told by members of the company that the appropriate vice-president was looking into the matter and was taking corrective action. Park did not investigate further. Months later in 1972, the FDA found evidence of rodent infestation in the firm's Baltimore warehouse. A letter to Park, dated January 27, 1972, included the following: "We note with much concern that the old and new warehouse areas used for food storage were actively and extensively inhabited by live rodents. Of even more concern was the observation that such reprehensible conditions obviously existed for a prolonged period of time without any detection, or were completely ignored. . . . We trust this letter will serve to direct your attention to the seriousness of the problem and formally advise you of the urgent need to initiate whatever measures are necessary to prevent recurrence and ensure compliance with the law." A second inspection was done in March. On that occasion, the inspectors found that there had been improvement in the sanitary conditions, but that there was still evidence of rodent activity in the building and in the warehouses. The inspectors also found some rodent-contaminated lots of food items.

Acme and Park were charged with five criminal counts of violation of the Federal Food, Drug and Cosmetic Act by storing food shipped in interstate commerce in warehouses where it was exposed to rodent contamination. Acme, but not Park, pled guilty to the charges. At trial, Park was convicted on all five counts. He was found guilty under a theory of vicarious liability for the acts and omissions of other corporate employees. He was also found strictly liable under the statute's strict liability standard. Under strict liability, a defendant can be found guilty even without a showing of criminal intent by the defendant or any other member of the corporation.

ISSUE PRESENTED   Can the chief executive officer of a company be held vicariously and strictly criminally liable under the Federal Food, Drug and Cosmetic Act for the introduction of misbranded and adulterated articles into interstate commerce?

SUMMARY OF OPINION   The U.S. Supreme Court upheld Park's conviction under both the vicarious liability and the strict liability theories. The Court stated that strict liability was applicable because "the public interest in the purity of its food is so great as to warrant the imposition of the highest standard of care on distributors." The Court reasoned that Acme's employees were in a sense under Park's general direction. By virtue of Park's position, he had authority and responsibility to maintain the physical integrity of Acme's food products. The statute makes individuals, as well as corporations, liable for violations. An individual is liable if it is clear, beyond a reasonable doubt, that the individual had a responsible relation to the situation, even though he may not have participated personally. Thus, Park, as CEO, could be found criminally liable even if he did not consciously do wrong.

RESULT   The conviction of CEO Park for causing adulteration of food that had traveled in interstate commerce and that was held for sale was upheld.

Employer's Liability for Racial Discrimination by Employees

When the Civil Rights Act of 1964 was promulgated, the laws prohibiting discrimination in public accommodations, such as restaurants, were designed with Birmingham, Alabama, lunch counters in mind. Some 30 years later, in the largest settlement under the federal public-accommodation laws, Denny's Restaurants agreed to pay more than $54 million to settle lawsuits filed by African-American customers. Forty-six million dollars was paid to customers, and another $8.7 million was paid to their attorneys.

Since 1987, African-American customers of Denny's have filed more than 4,300 claims of discrimination. These claims converged into two class action suits based in California and Maryland. Among the claims were those of six African-American Secret Service agents assigned to President Bill Clinton's detail. In a Denny's in Annapolis, Maryland, 15 white Secret Service agents were seated and served, while the African-American agents were refused a table.

Another African-American customer, 15-year-old Rachel Thompson, was refused the free meal that Denny's advertises for a customer's birthday, despite having provided a baptismal certificate and school records containing her birthdate. She recalls the incident: "I felt embarrassed. It was humiliating because other families in there were looking at us, and I guess they thought we were some kind of bad criminals because . . . the staff members there were just gathered around our table, shaking their heads and screaming."[53]

Rachel Thomas, the 33-year-old vice-president of a skin-care company, recalled the incident in which she, her husband, and their three children waited for an hour and 20 minutes after a waitress took their order and never returned. About her children, she said, "Those babies don't have anything to do with this racism, and they were the ones put out by it. . . . You can't explain it to them; they don't understand."[54]

An African-American federal judge from Houston and his wife, who had been traveling for 18 hours, were forced to wait for almost an hour at a Denny's in California, while white teenagers taunted them, calling them "niggers."

In all, there were thousands of complaints of unequal treatment of African-American customers that included not being served, having to pay a cover charge, and having to prepay for meals. The company denied that it had a policy of discrimination. However, during pretrial fact-finding, a former manager testified about training sessions in which managers were told how to deal with "too many blacks in a restaurant at one time," which was referred to as a "blackout."[55] Jerome J. Richardson, the chairman and chief executive of Flagstar (the company that owns Denny's), said that the "settlements are not an admission that Denny's has had a policy or practice of discrimination against African Americans." Rather, he sought to portray the incidents as random: "We serve one million customers a day at Denny's and we have 40,000 employees. It would be naive on my part to say that customers are always satisfied."[56]

John Relman, a lawyer for the Washington Lawyers' Committee for Civil Rights, saw it differently: "We believe that there was, at the company, an attitude that went into the management level, but we don't know exactly how high. This attitude at the company, at the management level and working its way down, had the effect of causing discriminatory attitudes going down to the lowest levels of the company."[57]

As part of the settlement of the class action suits, Denny's agreed to hire Los Angeles civil rights lawyer Sharon Lybeck Hartmann to monitor any discrimination claims that may arise. In addition, African Americans posing as customers were used to help ensure that Denny's did not discriminate in the future.

In 1997, Texaco agreed to pay more than $100 million to settle claims by African–American employees of racial discrimination in hiring and promotion. This is discussed in the "Inside Story" in Chapter 13.

In October 1997, the Pennsylvania attorney general's office accused Avis Rent A Car, Inc. of discriminating against minority car renters after an undercover investigation revealed a "clear pattern of abuse."[58] This

53. Timothy Ziegler, *Denny's Victims Discuss Harassment*, SAN FRANCISCO CHRON., May 25, 1994, at A3.
54. *Id.*
55. Stephen Labaton, *Denny's Restaurants to Pay $54 Million in Race Bias Suit*, N. Y. TIMES, May 25, 1994, at A1.
56. *Id.*
57. *Id.*
58. Lisa Miller, *Avis Again Is Accused of Discriminating Against Minorities Seeking to Rent Cars*, WALL ST J., Oct. 15, 1997, at A4.

occurred within 12 months of the filing of two suits brought by Avis customers in North Carolina and Florida. In December 1997, Avis agreed to pay approximately $3.3 million to settle the North Carolina suit; the other suit is still pending.

Employee Drug Testing

Sometimes the law has to balance the conflicting interests of different groups in resolving a social issue. Such an issue is employee drug testing, which is expected to increase through the 1990s because of the prevalence of drug usage and its negative effects. The employer's interest in a drug-free workplace must be balanced against the employee's constitutional right to privacy. Employers are concerned about drug and alcohol abuse because it results in lower productivity, lower quality output, accidents, absenteeism, tardiness, and excessive use of medical facilities. Employees, on the other hand, argue that drug testing is an invasion of their privacy, particularly when there is no objective reason to think that the employee has been using drugs.

In January 1990, former U.S. Surgeon General C. Everett Koop stated that studies show that 14–25 percent of the nation's workers have illegal drugs in their systems on any given day. He believes that the American workplace is the proper arena in which to address the nation's drug problem.

Businesses can make and enforce rules against drug use or possession on work premises. They can prohibit employees from being under the influence of drugs while working. They can develop drug education programs and provide drug and alcohol rehabilitation programs and counseling. Regardless of how businesses deal with the problem of drug and alcohol abuse, they should not lose sight of their ethical responsibilities to their employees. Drug testing of employees is discussed further in Chapter 12.

White-Collar Crime

Liability for negligent conduct that results in harm to others may sometimes be debatable. Liability for criminal conduct is not. Unfortunately, the 1980s saw white-collar crime rise to the forefront of the business agenda. White-collar crime, such as fraud and embezzlement—crimes characterized by deceit and dishonesty on the

---

IN BRIEF

MAKING ETHICAL DECISIONS

Frequently, managers faced with ethical dilemmas do not have a clear process for evaluating and making a decision. Companies with ethical programs, such as American Express, typically provide employees with a checklist of questions for individuals to ask themselves when pondering a situation that requires an ethical response. The following steps can also help clarify the decision-making process:

- Identify the issue and get the facts.
  - *Is there a conflict at the personal, interpersonal, institutional, or societal level?*
  - *Does the issue have a moral or ethical component?*
  - *What are the relevant facts?*
  - *Whose interests are at stake?*
  - *What alternative actions are available?*

- Evaluate alternative actions from moral and personal points of view.
  - *Which alternative would do the following:*
    - *Lead to the best overall consequences?*
    - *Best respect and protect the moral rights of individuals?*
    - *Treat all parties in a fair or just manner?*
    - *Make a good general rule for people to follow in similar circumstances?*
  - *Do any alternatives conflict with my personal ethics?*
  - *How comfortable would I be if I had to explain my actions to shareholders, customers, family, and friends?*

- Make a decision.
  - *Does this action best address the ethical concerns?*
  - *Does this action have the potential to result in an outcome that I would be proud to have reported in the newspaper or on the news?*

- Evaluate the consequences.
  - *In retrospect, was this action and outcome the best one I could have made given the information I had available at the time?*
  - *What part of the decision-making process might I have approached differently?*

SOURCE Based on *An Approach to Ethical Decision-Making*, Markkula Center for Applied Ethics, Santa Clara University. *Used by permission.*

part of corporate executives and their employees—has proved quite costly. The short-term costs include lost profits. The long-term costs include erosion of the moral base of the organization, a loss of public confidence in business, and a threat to the free-enterprise system. To counteract white-collar crime, the corporate community needs to create an ethical business environment; individual businesses cannot do it alone.

The Federal Corporate Sentencing Guidelines provide a rating system, including aggravating and mitigating factors, to determine the appropriate sentence for companies convicted of federal crimes. A corporation's sentence will be reduced if it had in place an effective system designed to promote ethics and prevent violations of law. The sentencing guidelines and white-collar crime are discussed further in Chapter 15.

THE RESPONSIBLE MANAGER
Ensuring Ethical Conduct

Ethical behavior is reinforced when top management exemplifies the company's values and takes a leadership role in programs to promote ethics; when the company creates an atmosphere of openness and trust in which employees feel comfortable in reporting violations; and when activities to enhance and reward ethics are part of every operating level of the company.

At the outset, a business must accept the proposition that high ethical standards and business success go hand in hand. Although ethics alone may not ensure long-term success, unethical behavior leads to illegal activity and can result in business failure. Members of top management cannot just pay lip service to this notion. Rather, they should show a dedication and commitment to ethics. They should realize that ethical responsibility is not just a component of a successfully run business but in fact is a type of thinking that permeates an entire organization.

The manager should recognize the critical importance of self-esteem, both at the individual and the organizational levels. The company should create a proper balance between economic performance and ethics and demonstrate that a strong ethical culture is a prerequisite to long-term profitability. In doing so, the corporation must look at itself honestly and objectively. It should ask itself what factors, either because of its industry or its internal corporate structure, inhibit it from being ethical.

A corporation needs a clearly written policy, such as a code of ethics. This policy must be legitimized and reinforced through formal and informal interaction with the entire management, beginning with the CEO. It must include procedural steps for reporting violations of the code of ethics and enforcing the code. The company should include a reference to the code of ethics in its employment agreements.

A company should institute ethics training, including setting up a forum discuss ethical dilemmas. In deciding whether a decision is ethically right, a company should ask whether a decision is fair or unfair to its personnel, customers, suppliers, and the communities where it does business. Managers should consider the direct and indirect results of a particular decision, including the impact on public image. They should ask themselves how much short-term benefit they are willing to forego for long-term gain.

Ethics are related to laws, but they are not identical. The legal thing to do is usually the right thing to do—but managers often have to go beyond their legal obligations to act ethically.

The law acknowledges that in a business deal, misunderstandings may arise, unforeseen events may occur, expected gains may disappear, or dislikes may develop that tempt one party to act in bad faith. The law, by requiring each party to act in good faith, significantly reduces the risk of a party breaking faith.[59] When reading the chapters that follow, consider whether the courts, in applying the law, are doing anything more than requiring businesspersons to do what they knew or suspected they really should have been doing all along.

---

59. *See* Robert S. Summers, *"Good Faith" in General Contract Law and the Sales Provisions of the Uniform Commercial Code,* 54 VA. L. REV. 195 (1968).

NIKE AND EXPLOITATION OF FOREIGN WORKERS

Nike, Inc. is an $8-billion athletic footwear, apparel, and equipment company. The company has been extremely successful and in 1998 was the leading supplier of athletic footwear. Nike designs and markets its merchandise but subcontracts the manufacturing out to other companies. Production takes place mainly in Asia.

Nike pays high-profile athletes, such as basketball superstar Michael Jordan and golfer Tiger Woods, large sums of money to advertise its products. The company sponsors college sports teams and spends millions of dollars on creative print and television advertisements to establish the strong Nike brand image. In 1996, Nike earned a return on sales of 40%, which is not unusual in its industry, but are these huge profits made at the expense of Asian factory workers?

Nike CEO Phil Knight pioneered the manufacture of running shoes in Asia after conceiving of the idea while a Stanford Business School student in the early 1960s. Nike started having its shoes made in Japan in 1964, then moved production to other Asian countries as changes in the exchange rate and labor costs made Japan more costly. Labor troubles coupled with increased industrialization resulted in higher wages in South Korea and Taiwan in the mid-1980s. The search for cheaper labor led Nike and other shoe companies to China, Thailand, Indonesia, India, Vietnam, and the Philippines.

In June 1996, *Life* magazine featured a story about children in Pakistan who stitched leather panels together by hand for soccer balls with the Nike swoosh logo. Critics claimed that Nike was exploiting labor in Asia and Third World countries by working with subcontractors that used child labor, paid substandard wages, and provided hazardous working conditions. Indeed, several members of Congress sent a public letter to Knight in October 1997 stating:

As members of the United States Congress we are deeply disappointed and embarrassed that a company like Nike, headquartered in the United States, could be so directly involved in the ruthless exploitation of hundreds of thousands of desperate Third World workers, most of whom are women.[60]

At one factory producing Nike shoes, there were seven toilets available for 10,000 employees. Other factories were cited for having blocked fire exits and permitting only one bathroom break and two water breaks in an eight-hour day. Reports of abuse, both physical and verbal, were common, as was sexual harassment and corporal punishment. At one Vietnamese factory, 56 women were made to run laps around the building because they had not worn regulation shoes to work. They were forced to continue running even after women started to collapse; eventually 12 of the women had to be hospitalized.

Nike responded to the charges by sending its board members to investigate the factories, commissioning studies from independent researchers (though some questioned how independent the researchers were because they were funded by Nike and conducted all of their interviews through Nike interpreters), and hiring Ernst & Young to audit the employment practices at Nike's subcontractors.

In 1996, Indonesia raised its minimum wage, but the contractors producing Nike shoes received an exemption from having to pay the higher wage. Michael Jordan earned $20 million from wearing the Nike swoosh in 1996. Activist groups claim that this is $4 million more than all the women in the Indonesian factories earned in one year. Activists reported that Nike's contractors pay its workers a regular average wage of $2.33 per day, well below the $4.25 per day estimated to be the livable wage in Indonesia in 1996. In addition, allegations have been made that Nike forced its employees to work overtime. Nike says that its workers make on average $4.67 with that overtime, which Nike claims is voluntary.

Nike shoes are produced in 400 factories in 30 countries. Nike CEO Phil Knight maintains that Nike's presence in Indonesia and other Asian countries has provided more good than harm, both in improving the working conditions and increasing the standard of living. Knight asserts that good corporations are the ones that lead these countries out of poverty.[61] Other Nike executives have pointed out that the presence of companies such as Nike move people from farming jobs to factory jobs, a key step in industrializing farming-based economies. And Nike has some support in its point of view: Dramatic declines in the percentage of people living at the lowest levels of poverty and a tripling of per capita income in the last 20 years are clear signs of economic improvement.[62]

In response to the allegations of ill treatment, Nike has taken steps to clarify for its contractors what is acceptable treatment and to monitor for and correct abuses. Nike now requires every subcontractor that produces shoes for Nike to sign a Memorandum of Understanding. The subcontractor certifies that it will comply with certain broad criteria in the following areas: (1) government regulation of business; (2) safety and health; (3) worker insurance; (4) forced labor; (5) environment; (6) equal opportunity; and (7) documentation and inspection.

In early 1997, Nike and other companies agreed, at the urging of the Clinton administration and human rights groups, to eliminate overseas sweatshops, to pay minimum wage, and to allow workers to organize. Despite assurances by Nike of improved working conditions and pay meeting minimum wage, workers were reportedly still unhappy. In Indonesia, a factory that manufactured Nike shoes was shut down after workers protested that the company was paying less than the legal minimum wage. In South Vietnam, workers at another Nike subcontractor conducted two one-day walkouts in one month to protest their contract.

In June 1997, Nike commissioned civil rights leader Andrew Young and a group of Dartmouth College researchers to conduct a study of working conditions in its subcontractors' factories in Vietnam and Indonesia. The October 1997 report concluded that those workers earned enough money to cover their basic needs and discretionary spending or savings. The report stated that although there was no grievance committee, the workers seemed satisfied with the current working conditions. Earlier reports also showed workers satisfied with the working conditions. In September 1997, Nike ended contracts with four factories in Indonesia after discovering that they were not paying their workers minimum wage.

Although the criticism in the media has been intense, Nike itself noted that the bottom line has not been affected much. Sales were up 42% in 1996; the company realizes that its consumers—11- to 16-year-olds—don't really pay much attention to the reports in the newspapers and on television of abuses in faraway places.[63] Customer indifference, combined with the fact that Nike's shareholders rejected a proposal to require outside auditing of the subcontractor's factories, show that there may not be much incentive for Nike to alter its practices further.

The issues here are complex. Nike and others would say that Nike's presence in these countries is improving the lives of the workers, and there is some evidence of that. When the question of child labor, for example, is framed around Western standards, the answer seems obvious—children belong in the classroom, not in a sweatshop. But in some Asian cultures, being in a classroom is simply not an option, and the sweatshop may not look too bad when compared to the alternatives available in the reality in which those children live.

60. Bernie Sanders, *Nike Corporate Practices Come Under Attack*, CONGRESSIONAL PRESS RELEASES (Oct. 24, 1997).

61 Keith Richburg & Anne Swardson, *US Industry Overseas: Sweatshop or Job Source?; Indonesians Praise Work at Nike Factory*, WASH. POST, July 28, 1996, at A1.

62. Associated Press, *Nike's Foreign Workers Adequately Paid, Study Says*, BUFF. NEWS, Oct. 17, 1997.

63. Farhan Haq, *US Labor: Nike Not Worried at Criticism* (Int'l Press Service, Oct. 21, 1997).

KEY WORDS AND PHRASES

apartheid   **19**

compensatory justice   **4**

deontological theory of ethics   **3**

distributive justice   **4**

fiduciary duty   **9**

junk bonds   **15**

Kantian theory   **3**

leveraged buyout (LBO)   **15**

Rawlsian moral theory   **3**

retributive justice   **4**

reversibility   **3**

teleological theory of ethics   **3**

universalizability   **3**

utilitarianism   **3**

QUESTIONS AND CASE PROBLEMS

1. In 1993, shops began selling a line of clothes and other items depicting Charles Manson, the mass-murderer whose followers killed seven persons, including actress Sharon Tate, in two Los Angeles homes in August 1969. Manson has been denied parole repeatedly and remains in prison for the gruesome murders committed by him and members of his cult. In 1993, the rock band Guns 'N' Roses included in its new release a song written and sung by Manson.

Cecily Turner is in charge of ordering policies for Mammoth Records, a large national retail chain of stores selling compact discs, tapes, videos, and T-shirts. She has received a flood of letters and faxes from angry parent groups, church leaders, politicians, and others demanding that Mammoth pull the Guns 'N' Roses CD and tape and stop selling the Manson T-shirts. Turner knows that these are very popular items at the retail stores. If Mammoth stops selling them, its competitors will pick up the extra business, thereby reducing Mammoth's profits. What should Turner do?

2. Rose Stern is a manager/buyer in charge of purchasing blue jeans for a large retail store chain. She's also a die-hard football fan. This year, the Super Bowl will be played in New Orleans, Louisiana, her hometown. Stern's favorite team, the Miami Dolphins, is expected to reach the Super Bowl.

Currently, the store chain carries four brands of jeans. In an effort to streamline its product line, however, the CEO has decided to cut back to three brands of blue jeans, leaving to Stern the decision of which brand to cut. Assume that all four brands are equally profitable. What if the makers of Brand One send Stern a pair of Super Bowl tickets? Should she accept these tickets? What if the maker of Brand One is also a close friend of hers? Or a relative? Is this a bribe? Or is it simply a friendly business gesture?

3. Assume the same facts as in Question 2, except that Brand One underperforms the other three brands. How should that affect her decision? What if it is mid-January and the Dolphins are definitely in the Super Bowl? Stern has waited her entire life to watch the Dolphins play in the Super Bowl. Even if she would not accept the tickets before, should she accept them now? Can she get out of her dilemma by offering to pay the face value of the tick-ets? Should she accept the tickets if she has already decided to discontinue Brand One?

4. Juan Gonzales is one of two partners who own a family-style, 24-store restaurant chain in the Northeast. The restaurants have a reputation for serving quality food at bargain prices. Since the opening of the first restaurant 34 years ago, the restaurants have generated a loyal clientele. However, many of these customers are older. Because the restaurant business has recently taken a turn for the worse, Gonzales feels it is time to revamp his restaurant's image so that it appeals to the younger generation. Consequently, Gonzales and his partner have taken on a significant amount of debt in order to remodel and renovate.

Five of the 24 restaurants are in New York City. In the last few days, Gonzales has received 15 phone calls from people who claim that they have gotten sick after eating at his restaurant in the Bronx. After investigation, Gonzales discovers that a shipment of frozen sausage was contaminated with *Salmonella ohio*, a rare form of food poisoning. How should Gonzales respond to the 15 customers who have already called? How should he respond to any further complaints? If Gonzales denies that the contamination was caused by his restaurants, it is possible that no one will find out. After all, there are thousands of restaurants and grocery stores in New York City that could have poisoned the customers.

Should Gonzales pull all of the shipments of sausage from his freezers? What if he decides to compensate the victims but his partner disagrees? What if both Gonzales and his partner agree to compensate the poisoned victims, but because of the recent debt this is not financially feasible? How should he balance the ethical implications with the economic implications? Should his response vary depending on whether Gonzales's restaurants are insured?

5. Henry Sherman is the CEO of the nation's leading fur company. In years past, the fur trade has been incredibly lucrative. However, Sherman has recently become quite concerned about the future of the fur industry. A public outcry has erupted regarding the killing of the animals supplying the furs. Animal-rights activists are pressuring state legislatures to pass laws that would limit or prohibit the sale of furs in their jurisdictions. Rather than taking a wait-and-see approach, Sherman decides to monitor the most influential animal-rights group, Save the Animals.

Sherman hires a small public affairs firm to scrutinize the actions of Save the Animals. In addition to keeping a close eye on Save the Animals, the public affairs firm tracks other players in the industry, both groups and individuals.

Sherman is quite satisfied with the information that the public affairs firm provided. He was told that the information was gathered from newsletters, news reports, and other published material available to the public. The information allows Sherman to lobby effectively against antifur legislation, making his shareholders, employees, and customers all quite happy.

Six months later, Sherman learns that most of the crucial information he had received was not collected from public documents. Rather, it was gathered by an informant who had infiltrated Save the Animals. Should Sherman terminate his contract with the public affairs firm? Are the public affairs firm's actions ethical? Are they legal? Is this spying? Assuming that there is no legal protection against private surveillance and hence the monitoring is legal, is the legal thing to do the right thing to do?

An argument can be made that this is good business, because Sherman's stakeholders are happy. Is good business good ethics?

6. How would a responsible manager of a hostile-takeover target react to the following statement? How would a responsible partner of a leveraged buyout firm react?

> Amazing as it may seem, the battle between raiders and companies is sometimes said to be a Darwinian struggle that assists the evolution of business by creating organizations that are ever more efficient, more competitive, and more fit for survival.
>
> Actually, what we're seeing is the reverse of evolution. Our liberating of resources from managerial control has become so indiscriminate that we're undoing the very process of building for the future which business depends on. We're headed back down the Darwinian slope toward lower forms of organization as deal after deal leaves more and more of our operations either reduced to fragments or liquidated into money.
>
> So, business must work to build awareness that deal-making for fast bucks is wrongheaded and dangerous. We must stress the point that business people cannot con-

tribute to the good of society by concentrating on near-term profits alone. Even more important is the need to increase competitiveness and profitability over the long term. (TOUCHE ROSS REPORT at 40.)

7. After years of consulting in the beer business, three MBAs from Georgia State University decided to buy and operate a liquor retail store. When they located a target store, they sat outside to count cars and cases of beer moving out of the door, looked over the seller's purchase records, talked with his major suppliers, and analyzed his prices, inventory turns, and competitive position. After they had agreed on terms, signed a letter of intent, and obtained loans to buy the real estate and inventory, they signed a confidentiality agreement designed to prevent them from sharing the retailer's financial information with anyone if the deal fell through. When they went to see the retailer's accountant, she checked to see that they had signed the confidentiality statement, called her client to double-check that they were the buyers, and then gave them the ledger books and tax returns for the past four years, as well as the "real" books for the last four years.

The MBAs discovered that the seller was actually running his business illegally by selling part of his inventory wholesale to competing stores, rather than retail to customers. The retailer did not possess a wholesale liquor license; one cannot have both a wholesale and a retail license in the state in question. The seller was buying huge quantities of beer to gain the highest discounts from the distributors and then selling part at retail and part at wholesale. He reported his retail revenue as his gross revenue to the Internal Revenue Service, the state tax board, and the liquor board. His wholesale revenue went into the mattress.

The MBAs decided not to complete the transaction, as they had no intention of running the business that way. The store owner received an all-cash offer of $50,000 more than the MBAs had agreed on, but he liked the "young, enthusiastic guys." The MBAs told him to take the other offer, and they all parted on friendly terms.

What should the MBAs have done? Who was hurt by the retailer's illegalities?

8. What can a manager do to prevent retaliation for whistle-blowing?

9. Chrysler Corp. recently dropped its policy of requiring magazines in which it advertises to alert the company in advance of any editorial content that encompasses sexual, political, or social issues or any editorial that might be construed as provocative or offensive, as well as to provide Chrysler with written editorial summaries outlining major themes/articles appearing in upcoming issues. Other advertisers, including Ameritech Corp., continue to require prenotification. What ethical and business considerations should a magazine publisher take into account when deciding whether to provide prenotification?

MANAGER'S DILEMMA

10. Arnita Kim is the CEO of BioDef, a biotechnology company that depends heavily on a year-to-year contract with the Department of Defense to provide antidotes for use in the event of biological warfare. Antidotes are drugs that combat the diseases spread by release of deadly biological agents. The existing product has a shelf life of one year. This creates a current stream of income for BioDef as the government has to replace its supply of antidotes every year. However, the research director for BioDef has just told Kim of a major research breakthrough that makes it possible, at little extra cost, to extend the shelf life of the antidotes from one year to four years.

The current contract with the Department of Defense will expire in two months. Assume that BioDef is not legally required to tell the government about the breakthrough. Should Kim tell the government about the breakthrough? What factors should Kim consider in making this decision?

INTERNET SOURCES	
The Business Roundtable's page offers information about its efforts to affect public policy.	http://www.brtable.org
The International Business Ethics Institute's page provides information about implementing corporate ethics programs.	http://www.business-ethics.org
The Organization for Economic Cooperation and Development provides various information about ethics, both in and out of business, through its searchable home page.	http://www.oecd.org
The Novartis Foundation for Sustainable Development's page provides access to a large collection of ethics articles and links to other sites addressing ethics.	http://foundation.novartis.com/atoz/corporate _ethics/articles.html
The Centre for Applied Ethics in Hong Kong provides information about its research and other activities focusing on ethics.	http://158.182.44.53/cae
The Stanford University page contains its official Code of Conduct for Business Activities.	http://www.portfolio.stanford.edu/200006

The Better Business Bureau's searchable page offers information about ethics in business.	http://www.bbb.org
The American Legal Ethics Library at Cornell University Law School offers judicial opinions, legal codes of ethics, and related materials.	http://www.law.cornell.edu/ethics
The Institute for Business and Professional Ethics at DePaul University provides many resources regarding ethics.	http://www.depaul.edu/ethics

CHAPTER 2

Constitutional Bases for Business Regulation

INTRODUCTION

Effect of United States Constitution on Business

The United States Constitution, including the Bill of Rights, imposes limitations on the way business is conducted in the United States. It gives federal and state governments the power to regulate business activities, and it provides that certain rights cannot be taken away from private persons and businesses. It allocates responsibility for regulating business to the three branches of the federal government: the legislative, the executive (which includes the president), and the judicial.

The Constitution became effective in 1789, and the first ten amendments, called the Bill of Rights, were added in 1791. Seventeen other amendments have subsequently been added. The most recent, the Twenty-seventh Amendment, was adopted in 1992; it prohibits changes in congressional pay from taking effect until after an intervening election of representatives.

Chapter Overview

This chapter first discusses the structure of the government of the United States as established by the Constitution and the alloca-

tion of different responsibilities to the three branches of government. This allocation is referred to as the separation of powers. The scope of powers of the federal courts and the concept of judicial review are outlined, as is the Supremacy Clause. Next, the chapter details the scope of executive and legislative power. This is followed by an analysis of conflicts that arise among the three branches.

The chapter then discusses the doctrine of *federalism*, which serves to allocate power between the federal government and the various state governments. The central importance of the Commerce Clause of the Constitution to this doctrine is explored. Finally, the chapter outlines the individual rights established by the Constitution and the various methods of protecting those rights. Among the various constitutional issues discussed are the rights to free speech, freedom of religion, and due process guaranteed under the Bill of Rights, and the concepts of substantive due process, eminent domain, and equal protection.

Structure of Government

The Constitution divides governmental power between the state and federal governments, giving the federal government certain specified powers. Without a grant of power from the Constitution, the federal government cannot act. All powers not expressly given to the federal government in the Constitution rest with either the states or the people.

It should be noted that both the states and the federal government can regulate the same business activity. For example, there are both federal and state laws governing environmental protection, antitrust, and retail banking. If, however, a state law conflicts with federal law, the federal law takes precedence or *preempts* the state law.

 ## Separation of Powers

Within the federal government, power is separated among the judicial branch (the courts), the executive branch (the president and cabinet departments), and the legislative branch (the Congress). This division of power among the three branches is typically referred to as the *separation of powers*.

The Judicial Power

The power of the judiciary is established in various parts of the Constitution. Articles I and III give Congress the authority to establish federal courts. Article III provides the basis for the judicial power of federal courts.

Article III   Article III of the Constitution vests judicial power in the Supreme Court of the United States and such other lower courts as Congress may from time to time establish. Federal judicial power extends to all cases or controversies:

- Arising under the Constitution, laws, or treaties of the United States
- Of admiralty and maritime jurisdiction.
- In which the United States is a party
- Between two or more states
- Between a state and citizens of another state
- Between citizens of different states

- Between citizens of the same state claiming lands under grants of different states
- Between a state or citizens thereof and foreign states, citizens, or subjects.

This provision grants *subject matter jurisdiction* to the federal courts, meaning that federal courts have the power to decide these types of cases.

Article III gives the Supreme Court *appellate jurisdiction* in all such cases. Thus, a lower court tries the case, and the Supreme Court hears only appeals from the lower court's decision. The Supreme Court also has *original jurisdiction* over cases affecting ambassadors and cases in which a state is a party. This means that such cases are tried in the Supreme Court, not in a lower court. Today, the Supreme Court's original jurisdiction is mainly used to decide controversies between states.

Congress has used its authority under Article III to establish federal district courts and courts of appeal. The structure of the federal court system is discussed in Chapter 3. All cases that fall under one of the categories listed above, except those in which the Supreme Court has original jurisdiction, are tried in federal district courts, or in some instances in state courts with a right to remove them to federal court.

Article I   Article I allows Congress to establish special courts other than the federal district courts and courts of appeal established under Article III. These specialized courts are often granted administrative as well as judicial powers. Examples of such courts are the United States Tax Court, the United States Bankruptcy Court, and the courts of the District of Columbia.

Judicial Review   The federal courts also have the power to review acts of the other two branches of the federal government to determine whether they violate the Constitution. This power of *judicial review* makes the federal judiciary a watchdog over the government.

The Constitution does not explicitly state that the federal courts have this power of review. The power was established by a landmark decision of the Supreme Court in 1803. In *Marbury v. Madison*,[1] the Supreme Court stated that it is the duty of the Supreme Court to determine what the law is. The Supreme Court held that the written Constitution must be the fundamental and paramount law of the land. Any law enacted by Congress that conflicts with the Constitution is void.

---

1. 5 U.S. (1 Cranch) 137 (1803).

The Supremacy Clause Federal courts also have the power to review the executive, legislative, and judicial acts of the states. The Supremacy Clause of Article VI states that the Constitution, laws, and treaties of the United States take precedence over state laws and that the judges of the state courts must follow federal law.

The Executive Power

The executive power of the president is defined in Article II, Section I, of the Constitution. Various executive functions may be delegated within the executive branch by the president or by Congress.

Article II, Section 2, enables the president, with the advice and consent of the Senate, to appoint the justices of the U.S. Supreme Court. It also allows the president to appoint all ambassadors and consuls and all other officers of the United States whose appointments are not provided for elsewhere in the Constitution.

Article II, Section 2, also empowers the president to grant reprieves and pardons for offenses against the United States, except in cases of impeachment. President Gerald Ford invoked this section when he pardoned Richard Nixon after Nixon resigned from the presidency following the Watergate burglary scandal in the early 1970s.

Article I, Section 7, grants the president the power to either approve or disapprove acts of Congress before they take effect. The president thus has *veto power* over laws that do not meet his or her approval. Congress can *override* a president's veto by a two-thirds vote of both the House of Representatives and the Senate.

The president has extensive power over foreign affairs. Although only Congress can formally declare war, the president may take other military action through the president's power as commander-in-chief of the armed forces under Article II, Section 2. President George Bush used this power in 1989 to invade Panama and again in 1991 to drive Iraqi forces from Kuwait.

The president also has the power to make treaties with the advice and consent of the Senate—that is, with two-thirds of the senators voting to ratify the treaty. Ratified treaties, along with the Constitution, are the supreme law of the land. Any laws enacted in violation of either of these are void. The president may also make executive agreements that do not require the advice and consent of the Senate. These agreements are superior to state law but not to federal law. Treaties and executive agreements are discussed further in Chapter 25.

The Legislative Power

Article I, Section 8, of the Constitution enumerates the powers of the Congress, which consists of the House of Representatives and the Senate. Among other things, Congress has the power to (1) regulate commerce with foreign nations and among the states; (2) spend to provide for the common defense and general welfare; (3) coin money; (4) establish post offices; (5) lay and collect taxes; (6) issue patents and copyrights; (7) declare war; and (8) raise and support armies. The courts have given a broad interpretation to Congress's power to regulate commerce among the states and its power to spend for the common welfare. Congress also has the power to make laws that are "necessary and proper" to carry out any power vested in the government of the United States.

Conflicts Between the Branches

Inherent in the system of checks and balances is potential for conflict between the three branches of government. At times, the power of one branch of the government must be curbed in order to ensure the integrity of another branch.

Article I, Section 6, states that senators and representatives "shall not be questioned in any other Place" for "any Speech or Debate in either House." This immunity was clarified by the Supreme Court in a case in which a former senator was prosecuted for accepting a bribe relating to his actions on postal rate legislation.[2] The Supreme Court held that the immunity only "protects against inquiry into acts which occur in the regular course of the legislative process and the motivation for those acts." The immunity does not protect all acts "relating to the legislative process." The Supreme Court let the prosecution proceed. Because the issue was whether the senator accepted the bribe, it was not necessary for the prosecutor to inquire into whether the illegal promise was performed.

The Constitution does not expressly grant immunity to executive officials, but some immunities are implied. It has been inferred from the extensive impeachment proceedings outlined in the Constitution that the president is immune from criminal prosecution prior to impeachment. In addition, the president may not be sued for damages resulting from official acts. This immunity is based on the president's unique position in the constitutional scheme.

---

2. United States v. Brewster, 408 U.S. 501 (1972).

*"As a matter of fact, I **have** read the Constitution, and, frankly, I don't get it."*

Drawing by Weber; © 1988 The New Yorker Magazine, Inc. *Used by permission.*

The president also has a type of immunity known as *executive privilege*, which protects against the forced disclosure of presidential communications made in the exercise of executive power. Yet sometimes the executive privilege must give way to the judicial branch's need to obtain evidence in a criminal trial.

The leading case in this area involved President Richard Nixon and concerned his refusal to comply with a subpoena in a criminal trial.[3] After the burglary of the Democratic National Headquarters in the Watergate Hotel in 1972, seven of his associates were tried for conspiracy to obstruct justice and other offenses re-

lated to the burglary. In that trial, Nixon was ordered by the court to produce tape recordings and documents related to conversations between himself and his aides and advisors. The president released edited transcripts of some of the conversations and then filed to declare the subpoena invalid. Nixon claimed executive privilege as to the confidential conversations between himself and his advisors. The Supreme Court found that neither the separation-of-powers doctrine nor the need for confidentiality of high-level communications could justify a presidential privilege at all times, because this "unqualified" privilege would upset the constitutional balance of a workable government. In particular, the Court found that where the president's claim of privilege was based only on the generalized interest in confidentiality and

---

3. United States v. Nixon, 418 U.S. 683 (1974).

not on the need to protect military or diplomatic secrets, the president's interest could not prevail over the fundamental demands of due process of law in the fair administration of criminal justice.

Executive privilege also protects the president from being sued for his or her official acts. In 1982, in *Nixon v. Fitzgerald*,[4] the Court granted the president "absolute immunity from damages liability predicated on his official acts." Fifteen years later, in 1997, the Court made clear that such immunity does not extend to protect the president during his term of office from civil litigation over events that occurred before he took office. In *Clinton v. Jones*,[5] the Court held that President Clinton could be sued by Paula Jones, formerly an Arkansas state employee, for sexual harassment and tort claims arising from acts that allegedly took place in 1991, while Clinton was governor of Arkansas. Although such litigation would subject the president to the power of the judiciary, it would not violate the separation of powers.

The principle of separation of powers has also barred certain legislation. The Supreme Court invalidated a legislative-veto provision in *INS v. Chadha*.[6] A *legislative veto* allows Congress to veto the actions of the executive branch.

In this case, the Court held unconstitutional Section 244(c)(2) of the Immigration and Nationality Act, which authorized either house of Congress, by resolution, to invalidate the decision of the executive branch to allow a particular deportable alien to remain in the United States. The Court reasoned that action by a house of Congress pursuant to that section was essentially legislative. Thus, as detailed in Article I of the Constitution, it was subject to the constitutional requirements of passage by a majority of both houses and presentation of the action to the president for signature or veto. The one-house legislative veto violated the constitutional requirements of *bicameralism* (action by both houses of Congress) and presentment of legislation to the president.

Another allocation of power that raised separation-of-powers issues was the line-item veto given to the president by Congress effective January 1, 1997.[7] The *line item veto* allowed the president to sign a bill into law and then cancel any dollar amounts that he or she believed to be fiscally irresponsible. Essentially, the veto gave the president the power to strike specific provisions from tax and spending bills that usually include thousands of separate, discrete provisions. With such power, a president could shape budgetary policy without having to make the stark choice to accept or reject an entire package of provisions. Congress could effectively override any particular line item veto by adopting a disapproval bill by a two-thirds vote of both houses.

The U.S. Supreme Court, by a vote of six to three, declared the line item veto unconstitutional in the following case.

---

4. 457 U.S. 731 (1982).

5. 117 S. Ct. 1636 (1997).

6. 462 U.S. 919 (1983).

7. 2 U.S.C. § 691 *et seq.* (Supp. 1997).

A CASE IN POINT   SUMMARY

CASE 2.1
CLINTON v.
CITY OF NEW YORK
Supreme Court of the
United States
66 U.S.L.W. 4543
(June 25, 1998).

FACTS   In August 1997, President Bill Clinton signed the Balanced Budget Act into law. Six days later, pursuant to the Line Item Veto Act (the act), he canceled a provision benefiting the city of New York and certain hospitals, thereby reviving a $2.6 billion contingent liability that Congress had eliminated in the Balanced Budget Act. In that same month, President Clinton signed into law the Taxpayer Relief Act but canceled certain tax breaks favorable to farmers' cooperatives. The canceled provisions would have permitted persons selling their stock in a qualified agricultural refiner or processor corporation to a farmers' cooperative to defer paying $98 million in taxes over the next five years and $155 million over the next ten.

The city of New York sued to invalidate the line item veto, as did Snake River Potato Growers, Inc., which had been actively pursuing a transaction that was

Case 2.1 continues

Case 2.1 continued

dependent on the canceled tax breaks. The federal district court declared the line item veto unconstitutional, and President Clinton appealed.

ISSUE PRESENTED   Does the Line Item Veto Act violate the requirements of bicameral passage and presentment to the president or separation of powers?

SUMMARY OF OPINION   The U.S. Supreme Court began by considering whether the plaintiffs had standing to challenge the act. The Court held that they did have standing, because they suffered an immediate injury when President Clinton canceled legislation that provided them a benefit. The Court distinguished its decision in *Raines v. Byrd*,[8] in which it had ruled that six members of Congress had not alleged a sufficiently concrete injury to have standing to challenge the act before the president had actually used it. In contrast to the "institutional injury" in *Raines* that was "abstract and widely dispersed," the plaintiffs in this case had alleged a "personal stake" in having an actual injury redressed.

The Court then considered the plaintiffs' constitutional challenges. The Court held that the act impermissibly altered the "single, finely wrought and exhaustively considered, procedure" in Article I, Section 7, of the U.S. Constitution, which requires that laws be approved by both Houses of Congress then presented to the president. The president must approve all parts of a bill or reject it in toto. The amendment and repeal of statutes must meet these same requirements. If the act were valid, it would authorize the president to create a different law—one whose text was not voted on by either House of Congress or presented to the president for signature. The Court concluded that if there is to be a new procedure in which the president will play a different role in determining the final text of what may become a law, "such change must come not by legislation but through the amendment procedures set forth in Article V of the Constitution."

In an exercise of judicial restraint, the Court found it unnecessary to consider the district court's alternative holding that the act impermissibly disrupted the balance of powers among the three branches of government.

RESULT   The Line Item Veto Act was held unconstitutional.

COMMENTS   President Clinton called the decision "a defeat for all Americans" that "deprives the president of a valuable tool for eliminating waste in the federal budget and for enlivening the public debate over how to make the best use of public funds."

---

8. 117 S. Ct. 2312 (1997).

 Federalism

The federal government's powers are limited to those expressly granted in the Constitution. Its powers are also subject to specific restrictions, such as those in the Bill of Rights. State governments, on the other hand, have general powers not specified in the Constitution. These include the *police power* to protect the health, safety, welfare, or morals of the people of the state.

Some powers are exclusively federal because the Constitution expressly limits the states' exercise of those powers. Exclusive federal powers include the power to make treaties, to coin money, and to impose duties on imports. Other powers are inherently in the states' domain, such as the power to structure state and local governments.

To further protect this division of power between the federal and state governments, the Eleventh Amendment was added to the Constitution in 1798. It immunizes states from lawsuits in federal court brought by citizens of another state or of another nation. Although a state may waive this sovereign immunity, it must do so voluntarily and in accordance with its own law. Congress cannot abrogate that immunity even when it legislates pursuant to its own authority under Article I.[9] In *Schlossberg v. Maryland*,[10] for example, the U.S. Court of Appeals for the Fourth Circuit overturned a provision of the Bankruptcy Reform Act of 1994 that explicitly abrogated a state's sovereign immunity from suit in federal court.

The Supreme Court reaffirmed the system of dual sovereignty when it struck down provisions of the Brady Handgun Violence Prevention Act that required state law enforcement officers to receive reports from gun dealers regarding prospective handgun sales and to conduct background checks on prospective handgun purchasers.[11] As a result of the national debate over gun regulation, Congress passed the Brady Act, named after President Ronald Reagan's press secretary, James Brady, who was wounded by John Hinkley during his attempt to assassinate President Reagan. Among other things, the act established a five-day federal waiting period for handgun purchases and called for the attorney general to establish a computerized system for instantaneous background checks. Because such a system would take a few years to establish, the act also called for local law enforcement officials to conduct background checks until the national system was up and running.

The Court stated that "[t]he power of the Federal Government would be augmented immeasurably if it were able to impress into its service—and at no cost to itself—the police officers of the 50 States." Accordingly, it held that the federal government may not compel states to enact legislation or to administer by executive action a federal regulatory program.

Another boundary between federal and state powers is the Constitution's Commerce Clause.

The Commerce Clause

Article I, Section 8, gives Congress the power to regulate commerce with other nations, with Indian tribes, and between states. The Commerce Clause is both a restraint on state action and a source of federal authority. The commerce power has been interpreted to allow federal regulation of such areas as interstate travel, labor relations, and discrimination in accommodations.

The first Supreme Court discussion of the Commerce Clause was by Chief Justice John Marshall in the 1824 case *Gibbons v. Ogden*.[12] A steamboat monopoly affecting navigation between New York and New Jersey violated a federal statute regulating interstate commerce. The Court held that under the Supremacy Clause, the federal statute prevailed. In the decision, Justice Marshall discussed in detail his view that interstate commerce—which he defined as "commerce which concerns more states than one"—included every activity having any interstate impact. Therefore, Congress could regulate all such activities.

From 1887 to 1937, the Supreme Court developed a view of the Commerce Clause quite different from Marshall's view. The Court interpreted "commerce" narrowly, holding that activities such as mining and manufacturing were not commerce and therefore could not be regulated by Congress. The Supreme Court was not persuaded by the fact that the products of these activities would later enter interstate commerce. During this period, the Court struck down New Deal legislation, arguing that the Commerce Clause did not grant Congress the power to regulate such activities.

The turning point in the Supreme Court's attitude came in *NLRB v. Jones & Laughlin Steel Corp.*[13] The Court held that Congress could regulate labor relations in a manufacturing plant because a work stoppage at such a plant would have a serious effect on interstate commerce; the steel manufactured by the plant was shipped across state lines.

Today, most federal regulation of commerce is upheld under the Commerce Clause. The Supreme Court usually defers to the findings of Congress. If legislation has a "substantial economic effect" on interstate commerce, it is held to be a valid exercise of the commerce power. The Court will uphold such laws made by Congress as long as there is some rational ground for finding that the items regulated have an effect on interstate commerce.

For example, in *Heart of Atlanta Motel, Inc. v. United States*,[14] the Supreme Court upheld Title II of

---

9. Seminole Tribe of Florida v. Florida, 517 U.S. 609 (1996).

10. 119 F.3d 1140 (4th Cir. 1997).

11. Printz v. United States, 117 S. Ct. 2365 (1997).

12. 22 U.S. (1 Wheat) 1 (1824).

13. 301 U.S. 1 (1937).

14. 379 U.S. 241 (1964).

the Civil Rights Act of 1964, which prohibits discrimination or segregation on the ground of race, color, religion, or national origin in any inn, hotel, motel, or other establishment of more than five rooms that provides lodging to transient guests. Prior to passage of the act, the party challenging the act—the Heart of Atlanta Motel—had followed a practice of refusing to rent rooms to African Americans, and it alleged that it intended to continue to do so. The 216-room motel for transient guests was easily accessible by a major highway. The operator of the motel solicited patronage from outside the state of Georgia through various national advertising media, including magazines of national circulation. It maintained more than 50 billboards and highway signs within the state, soliciting patronage for the motel. It accepted convention trade from outside Georgia, and approximately 75% of its registered guests were from out of state.

The Court noted that the population had become increasingly mobile, with millions of people of all races traveling from state to state. African Americans in particular have been the subject of discrimination in transient accommodations, having to travel great distances to secure lodging. Often they have been unable to obtain accommodations and have had to call upon friends to put them up overnight. These conditions had become so acute as to require the listing of available lodging for African Americans in a special guidebook, which the Court called in itself "dramatic testimony to the difficulties Blacks encounter in travel."

The Court stated that the power of Congress to deal with these obstructions depended on the meaning of the Commerce Clause. The Court reasoned: "The determinative test of the exercise of power by the Congress under the Commerce Clause is simply whether the activity sought to be regulated is 'commerce which concerns more States than one' and has a real and substantial relation to the national interest." The Court concluded that the action of Congress in the adoption of the act as applied here to a motel that concededly served interstate travelers is within the power granted Congress by the Commerce Clause of the Constitution. Although it may be argued that Congress could have pursued other methods to eliminate the obstructions it found in interstate commerce caused by racial discrimination, this was a matter of policy that rested entirely with Congress and not with the courts.

In *Katzenbach v. McClung*,[15] a case argued concurrently with *Heart of Atlanta*, the Supreme Court upheld the application of the Civil Rights Act to a restaurant because a substantial portion of the food that it served had previously moved in interstate commerce. The Court reasoned that the restaurant's discrimination against African Americans, who were potential customers, resulted in its selling less food that had traveled in interstate commerce. Thus, the discrimination had a substantial effect on interstate commerce.

In 1995, in the following case, the Supreme Court surprised many when it struck down a federal law banning guns near schools as being beyond the power of Congress under the Commerce Clause. This was the first time since 1937 that the Court had invalidated a federal statute on that basis.

---

15. 301 U.S. 1 (1937).

A CASE IN POINT	IN THE LANGUAGE OF THE COURT

CASE 2.2
UNITED STATES v.
LOPEZ
Supreme Court of
the United States
115 S. Ct. 1624 (1995).

FACTS   After Alfonso Lopez, Jr. (Lopez), then a 12th-grade student, carried a concealed handgun into his high school, he was charged with violating the Federal Gun-Free School Zones Act of 1990. Section 922(q) of the act forbids "any individual knowingly to possess a firearm at a place that [he] knows . . . is a school zone." The federal district court denied Lopez's motion to dismiss the indictment, concluding that Section 922(q) was a constitutional exercise of Congress's power to regulate activities in and affecting interstate commerce. In reversing, the court of appeals held that, in light of what it characterized as insufficient congressional findings and legislative

Case 2.2 continues

Case 2.2 continued

history, Section 922(q) was invalid as beyond the power of Congress under the Commerce Clause. The United States appealed.

ISSUE PRESENTED   Does the Commerce Clause give Congress the power to regulate the possession of handguns near schools?

OPINION   REHNQUIST, C.J., writing for the U.S. Supreme Court:

We start with first principles. The Constitution creates a Federal Government of enumerated powers. As James Madison wrote, "[t]he powers delegated by the proposed Constitution to the federal government are few and defined. Those which are to remain in the State governments are numerous and indefinite.". . .

The Constitution delegates to Congress the power "[t]o regulate Commerce with foreign Nations, and among the several States, and with the Indian Tribes."

. . .The *Gibbons*[16] Court, however, acknowledged that limitations on the commerce power are inherent in the very language of the Commerce Clause.

> It is not intended to say that these words comprehend that commerce, which is completely internal, which is carried on between man and man in a State, or between different parts of the same State, and which does not extend to or affect other States. Such a power would be inconvenient, and is certainly unnecessary.
>
> Comprehensive as the word 'among' is, it may very properly be restricted to that commerce which concerns more States than one. . . .
>
> . . .

Jones & Laughlin Steel[17]. . . ushered in an era of Commerce Clause jurisprudence that greatly expanded the previously defined authority of Congress under that clause. In part, this was a recognition of the great changes that had occurred in the way business was carried on in this country. Enterprises that had once been local or at most regional in nature had become national in scope. But the doctrinal change also reflected a view that earlier Commerce Clause cases artificially had constrained the authority of Congress to regulate interstate commerce.

But even these modern-era precedents which have expanded congressional power under the Commerce Clause confirm that this power is subject to outer limits. In *Jones & Laughlin Steel*, the Court warned that the scope of the interstate commerce power "must be considered in the light of our dual system of government and may not be extended so as to embrace effects upon interstate commerce so indirect and remote that to embrace them, in view of our complex society, would effectually obliterate the distinction between what is national and what is local and create a completely centralized government." Since that time, the Court has heeded that warning and undertaken to decide whether a rational basis existed for concluding that a regulated activity sufficiently affected interstate commerce.

. . .

Case 2.2 continues

---

16. Gibbons v. Ogden, 22 U.S. (1 Wheat.) 1 (1824).
17. 301 U.S. 1 (1937).

Case 2.2 continued

. . . [W]e have identified three broad categories of activity that Congress may regulate under its commerce power. First, Congress may regulate the use of the channels of interstate commerce. Second, Congress is empowered to regulate and protect the instrumentalities of interstate commerce, or persons or things in interstate commerce, even though the threat may come only from intrastate activities. Finally, Congress' commerce authority includes the power to regulate those activities having a substantial relation to interstate commerce, i.e., those activities that substantially affect interstate commerce.

. . .

We now turn to consider the power of Congress, in the light of this framework, to enact § 922(q). The first two categories of authority may be quickly disposed of: § 922(q) is not a regulation of the use of the channels of interstate commerce, nor is it an attempt to prohibit the interstate transportation of a commodity through the channels of commerce; nor can § 922(q) be justified as a regulation by which Congress has sought to protect an instrumentality of interstate commerce or a thing in interstate commerce. Thus, if § 922(q) is to be sustained, it must be under the third category as a regulation of an activity that substantially affects interstate commerce.

. . .

Section 922(q) is a criminal statute that by its terms has nothing to do with "commerce" or any sort of economic enterprise, however broadly one might define those terms. Section 922(q) is not an essential part of a larger regulation of economic activity, in which the regulatory scheme could be undercut unless the intrastate activity were regulated. It cannot, therefore, be sustained under our cases upholding regulations of activities that arise out of or are connected with a commercial transaction, which viewed in the aggregate, substantially affects interstate commerce.

Second, § 922(q) contains no jurisdictional element which would ensure, through case-by-case inquiry, that the firearm possession in question affects interstate commerce. . . .

Although as part of our independent evaluation of constitutionality under the Commerce Clause we of course consider legislative findings, and indeed even congressional committee findings, regarding effect on interstate commerce, the Government concedes that "[n]either the statute nor its legislative history contain[s] express congressional findings, regarding the effects upon interstate commerce of gun possession in a school zone." We agree with the Government that Congress normally is not required to make formal findings as to the substantial burdens that an activity has on interstate commerce. But to the extent that congressional findings would enable us to evaluate the legislative judgment that the activity in question substantially affected interstate commerce, even though no such substantial effect was visible to the naked eye, they are lacking here.

. . .

The Government's essential contention, in fine, is that we may determine here that § 922(q) is valid because possession of a firearm in a local school zone does

Case 2.2 continues

Case 2.2 continued

indeed substantially affect interstate commerce. The Government argues that possession of a firearm in a school zone may result in violent crime and that violent crime can be expected to affect the functioning of the national economy in two ways. First, the costs of violent crime are substantial, and, through the mechanism of insurance, those costs are spread throughout the population. Second, violent crime reduces the willingness of individuals to travel to areas within the country that are perceived to be unsafe. The Government also argues that the presence of guns in schools poses a substantial threat to the educational process by threatening the learning environment. A handicapped educational process, in turn, will result in a less productive citizenry. That, in turn, would have an adverse effect on the Nation's economic well-being. As a result, the Government argues that Congress could rationally have concluded that § 922(q) substantially affects interstate commerce.

We pause to consider the implications of the Government's arguments. The Government admits, under its "costs of crime" reasoning, that Congress could regulate not only all violent crime, but all activities that might lead to violent crime, regardless of how tenuously they relate to interstate commerce. Similarly, under the Government's "national productivity" reasoning, Congress could regulate any activity that it found was related to the economic productivity of individual citizens: family law (including marriage, divorce, and child custody), for example. Under the theories that the Government presents in support of § 922(q), it is difficult to perceive any limitation on federal power, even in areas such as criminal law enforcement or education where States historically have been sovereign. Thus, if we were to accept the Government's arguments, we are hard-pressed to posit any activity by an individual that Congress is without power to regulate.

. . .

To uphold the Government's contentions here, we would have to pile inference upon inference in a manner that would bid fair to convert congressional authority under the Commerce Clause to a general police power of the sort retained by the States. Admittedly, some of our prior cases have taken long steps down that road, giving great deference to congressional action. The broad language in these opinions has suggested the possibility of additional expansion, but we decline here to proceed any further. To do so would require us to conclude that the Constitution's enumeration of powers does not presuppose something not enumerated and that there never will be a distinction between what is truly national and what is truly local. This we are unwilling to do.

RESULT   The Supreme Court affirmed the decision of the court of appeals, holding that Section 922(q) exceeds Congress's authority to regulate interstate commerce under the Commerce Clause and is therefore unconstitutional. Lopez's indictment under Section 922(q) was dismissed.

Questions

1. Would the result in this case have been different if Lopez had been charged with violating a federal law that made it a crime to possess cocaine within a school zone?
2. In a strongly worded dissent, Justice Breyer argued that having a well-educated workforce was essential to the ability of the United States to compete in global

Case 2.2 continues

Case 2.2 continued

markets and, therefore, items such as guns that hampered education directly impacted interstate commerce. If his view were accepted, could Congress legally enact legislation defining a national curriculum with national student testing and national standards for teacher accreditation? What are the policy arguments for and against giving Congress that power?

Limits on State Powers

Federal powers enumerated in the Constitution impose many limits on state action. This chapter discusses only the limits on state power resulting from the commerce power, but the principles apply to other federal powers as well.

Where Congress has indicated a policy by acting, Congress's action preempts state action because the Supremacy Clause makes federal laws supreme over state laws. Even when Congress has not taken action, the "dormant" Commerce Clause imposes restrictions on state action.

Preemption   State law is preempted when it directly conflicts with federal law or when Congress has manifested an intention to regulate the entire area without state participation.

In 1996, in *Medtronic, Inc. v. Lohr*,[18] the U.S. Supreme Court considered the issue of preemption with regard to claims of defective design, negligent manufacture, and failure to warn in the arena of medical devices. Twenty years earlier, Congress had passed the Medical Device Amendments (MDA) to the Food, Drug and Cosmetic Act, which created the federal Food and Drug Administration (FDA). Those amendments specifically forbid states from establishing "any requirement" that is different from or in addition to those of the MDA. In *Medtronic*, a pacemaker recipient sued the device's manufacturer under state product liability law. The manufacturer argued that the state law was preempted by the MDA. Reasoning that the MDA's requirements for pacemakers were too general to preempt state law, the Court rejected the manufacturer's challenge.

In contrast, in *Papike v. Tambrands, Inc.*,[19] the U.S. Court of Appeals for the Ninth Circuit ruled that the MDA's tampon-labeling requirements were sufficiently specific to preempt California common law liability for failure to warn. Unlike the general pacemaker regulations at issue in *Medtronic*, the FDA's treatment of tampon-labeling was quite specific: "Preemption results in this case because the FDA has established specific counterpart regulations with respect to labeling tampons."

The issue of preemption is especially important to a corporation that is trying to prevent a hostile takeover. In a *hostile takeover*, a third party, called a *raider*, seeks to obtain control of a corporation, called the *target*, over the objections of its management. (Hostile takeovers are discussed further in Chapter 21.) A number of state legislatures, in response to a wave of hostile takeovers that resulted in the loss of jobs and the relocation of corporate headquarters out of state, adopted antitakeover statutes. The constitutionality of these statutes was challenged by corporate raiders, who argued that federal law was exclusive in this area. One of the early forms of state antitakeover legislation was struck down in *Edgar v. MITE Corp.*[20]

MITE Corporation, an Illinois company, initiated a *tender offer* (an offer to shareholders to buy their shares) for all the outstanding shares of Chicago River and Machine Co. by filing with the Securities and Exchange Commission the schedule required by the Williams Act, which is the part of the federal Securities Exchange Act of 1934 governing tender offers. In following this procedure, MITE did not comply with legislation in effect at the time in Illinois.

---

18. 116 S. Ct. 2240 (1996).

19. 107 F.3d 737 (9th Cir. 1997), *cert. denied*, 118 S. Ct. 166 (1997) (mem.).
20. 457 U.S. 624 (1982).

The Illinois Business Take-Over Act required that any person or company intending to make a tender offer notify the secretary of state and the target company of the offer 20 days before it was to become effective. During that time the offeror could not communicate its offer to the shareholders, but the target company was free to disseminate information to its shareholders concerning the impending offer. Additionally, any takeover offer had to be registered with the Illinois secretary of state, who was authorized to hold a hearing on the fairness of the offer.

A plurality of the Supreme Court found that the act violated the Supremacy Clause. In particular, the Court found that three provisions of the act conflicted with congressional mandates: (1) the precommencement provisions insisting on 20-days' notice frustrated the no-notice objectives of the Williams Act, which intended to foil the target company's attempts to repel tender offers beneficial to shareholders; (2) the failure to provide a deadline by which a hearing on a contested takeover must be brought thwarted the Williams Act provision allowing the purchase of shares pursuant to the tender offer to proceed without unreasonable delay; and (3) the requirement that the Illinois secretary of state review the fairness of tender offers contravened the congressional intent to prevent investor protection from overriding investor authority.

In *CTS Corp. v. Dynamics Corp. of America*[21] the Supreme Court upheld Indiana's Control Share Acquisition Act. The Indiana act provided that a "control share acquisition" that would otherwise have given the acquirer the power to vote more than specified percentages of the stock of the target (that is, 20%, 33.3%, or 50%) would not in fact result in acquisition of the commensurate voting rights unless they were conferred by a majority of the disinterested shareholders at a meeting to be held within not more than 50 days. The Indiana act was one of many post-*MITE*, second-generation antitakeover statutes.

In finding that the Indiana act did not have the three traits of the Illinois statute struck down in *MITE*, the Supreme Court reasoned that the Indiana act did not give either the target company or the offeror an advantage in communicating with shareholders about an impending offer. The act did not impose an indefinite

delay, as did the statute in *MITE*, and it did not prevent an offeror from consummating an offer on the 20th business day, the earliest day permitted under applicable federal regulations, because the shareholders could agree to hold a special meeting within this period. Finally, the Court reasoned that, unlike the Illinois statute, which required the state government to interpose its views of fairness, the Indiana act allowed the shareholders collectively to evaluate the fairness of the offer.

The Court then focused on whether the Indiana act frustrated the purpose of the Williams Act. According to the Court, unlike the statute considered in *MITE*, the Indiana act did not operate in favor of management against offerors and to the detriment of shareholders. To the contrary, the Indiana act "protect[ed] the independent shareholder against both of the contending parties," thus furthering a basic purpose of the Williams Act, which is "placing investors on an equal footing with the takeover bidder." The Court further noted that the Indiana act "operated on the assumption, implicit in the Williams Act, that independent shareholders faced with tender offers are at a disadvantage." By providing shareholders with the opportunity to vote as a group to reject the offer, the Court stated, the Indiana act protected individual investors from the coerciveness of having to accept a tender offer for fear of having to sell later at a depressed price.

Ultimately, preemption depends on the specificity of federal regulation, any statutory language addressing preemption, and the nature of the conflict between the federal and state approaches. Federal preemption of state law claims related to tobacco is discussed in Chapter 10.

Dormant Commerce Clause   Since the mid-1930s, the Supreme Court has tried to clarify when state regulation is valid in the absence of preempting federal regulation. The principle the Court now follows is that state regulation affecting interstate commerce will be upheld if the regulation (1) is rationally related to a legitimate state end, and (2) does not create any undue burden on interstate commerce. A regulation creates an *undue burden* when the regulatory burden on interstate commerce outweighs the state's interest in the legislation.

The Supreme Court is hostile toward state protectionism and discrimination against out-of-state interests.

---

21. 481 U.S. 69 (1987).

However, not all state regulations found invalid under the Commerce Clause are protectionist or discriminatory. The problem lies in determining the purpose of the legislation. Protectionist regulations may be explicitly discriminatory; they may be enacted for a discriminatory purpose; or they may simply have the effect of favoring local interests at the expense of out-of-state concerns.

A Madison, Wisconsin, regulation that barred the sale of pasteurized milk unless it had been processed and bottled within a radius of five miles from Madison was struck down as discriminatory.[22] The city claimed that the ordinance was a health measure, but the Supreme Court found that it discriminated against milk originating in other states. On the other hand, a Minnesota statute banning plastic, nonreturnable milk containers was upheld in the face of claims that it discriminated against interstate commerce.[23] The statute, stated the Supreme Court, was not "simple protectionism"; it "regulated evenhandedly" by prohibiting all milk retailers from selling their products in the plastic containers. The regulation applied regardless of whether the milk, the containers, or the sellers were from inside or outside the state.

A North Carolina statute prohibited the sale of apples that bore a grade other than the applicable U.S. grade. Washington State apples bore their own state's grade on the container, a grade that was equal to or more stringent than the U.S. grade. The North Carolina statute was held invalid because, although neutral on its face, the effect of the statute was to discriminate against Washington apples.[24]

The Supreme Court struck down a Massachusetts law that required every milk dealer who sold milk in Massachusetts to contribute to a state fund based on the volume of the milk that the dealer had sold within the state, regardless of the price the dealer paid for the milk or its point of origin.[25] Massachusetts dairy farmers received a form of subsidy because they, but not the out-of-state producers, were entitled to disbursements from the fund, based on the volume of milk

they produced. The Court reasoned that the combination of the Massachusetts tax, which was levied on all producers, combined with the subsidy provided to only local Massachusetts dairy farmers, was akin to the kind of tariff that the Commerce Clause was meant to prohibit. In part because most of the milk sold in Massachusetts is produced by out-of-state entities, the Massachusetts law had the effect of enabling higher-cost Massachusetts dairy farmers to compete unfairly with lower-cost dairy farmers in other states. This "violates the principle of the unitary national market by handicapping out-of-state competitors, thus artificially encouraging in-state production even when the same goods could be produced at lower cost in other States."[26]

Federal Fiscal Powers

Two other federal powers, the taxing and spending powers, have been invoked to regulate traditionally local "police problems" as well as purely economic problems. The Constitution grants a broad taxing power to the federal government. The only specific limitations imposed are that (1) direct taxes on anything but income and capitation (per head) taxes must be allocated among the states in proportion to population; and (2) all custom duties and excise taxes must be uniform throughout the United States. The single prohibition is that no duty shall be levied upon exports from any state. The Fifth Amendment's due process clause is also a general limitation on the taxing power.

Taxes have an economic impact on business. The federal government has imposed taxes in order to affect the behavior of business as well as to raise revenues. The Supreme Court has, however, upheld taxes solely because of the power to tax granted to the government. The Court will not look into the purpose behind the tax in determining its validity.

Congress has the power to spend in order to provide for the common defense and general welfare. An exercise of the spending power will be upheld as long as it does not violate a specific check on the federal power.

22. Dean Milk Co. v. City of Madison, 340 U.S. 349 (1951).
23. Minnesota v. Clover Leaf Creamery Co., 449 U.S. 456 (1981).
24. Hunt v. Washington State Apple Advertising Comm'n., 432 U.S. 333 (1977).
25. West Lynn Creamery, Inc. v. Healy, 512 U.S. 186 (1994).
26. *Id.*

HISTORICAL PERSPECTIVE

THE INITIATIVE PROCESS

In 1898, South Dakota became the first state to establish a procedure whereby citizens could initiate change on their own without going through their elected representatives. During the next 20 years, 18 other states adopted initiative processes, and by the early 1990s the number had grown to 24. Unlike representative democracy, initiatives give direct legislative power to voters by allowing them to make new laws, either by amending the state constitution or enacting legislation. Some states, such as California, allow no executive veto of initiatives (unlike legislation passed by representatives) and forbid repeal except by subsequent voter initiative.

Since 1898, the initiative process has been used by citizens seeking to change governmental policy on a wide range of topics including child labor, women's suffrage, gambling, alcohol prohibition, prostitution, civil rights, the death penalty, environmental protection, and property taxes. Although 100 years old, the initiative has seen most of its use in recent years. For example, in

California in the 1950s, only 17 initiatives were circulated and only ten qualified for the ballot. In the 1980s, citizens proposed more than 200 initiatives and voted on more than 40.

In recent years, many major public policy battles have moved out of the state capitols and into the land of initiatives. In 1996, voters in California and Arizona legalized medical use of marijuana by ballot initiative. In that same year, Californians approved Proposition 209 to end racial preferences by state and local governments. One year later, voters in Houston turned down an initiative to end that city's affirmative action program. In 1994 and again in 1997, Oregon voters authorized physician-assisted suicide for competent, terminally ill adults.

SOURCE   This discussion is based on K. K. DuVivier, *By Going Wrong All Things Come Right*, 63 U. CIN. L. REV. 1185 (1995); P. K. Jameson & Marsha Hosack, *Citizen Initiatives in Florida*, 23 FLA. ST. U. L. REV. 417 (1995); and David L. Callies et al., *Ballot Box Zoning*, 39 WASH. U. J. URB. & CONTEMP. L. 53 (1991).

◆ Protection of Individual Liberties

The Constitution

Although most explicit guarantees of individual liberty are found in the amendments to the Constitution, the original Constitution contains three specific guarantees of individual rights.

The Contracts Clause   Article I, Section 10, of the Constitution specifically prohibits a state legislature

from impairing the obligation of existing contracts. The Fifth Amendment imposes a similar bar on federal legislation that would retroactively impair the obligations of a contract.

Insurance companies raised issues under the Contracts Clause in connection with insurance law changes mandated by California voter-approved Proposition 103 in the case that follows.

A CASE IN POINT	SUMMARY

CASE 2.3
CALFARM INSURANCE
COMPANY v.
DEUKMEJIAN
Supreme Court of California
771 P.2d 1247 (Cal. 1989).

FACTS   In 1988, the voters of California approved Proposition 103, an initiative that made fundamental changes to the regulation of automobile and other types of insurance. Seven insurers and the Association of California Insurance Companies filed suit against Governor George Deukmejian and others, contending that Proposition 103

Case 2.3 continues

Case 2.3 continued

was unconstitutional on its face, under both the U.S. and California constitutions. Among other challenges, the insurance companies challenged the part of the initiative that made it illegal for insurance companies to refuse to renew policies for automobile insurance except for (1) nonpayment of premiums; (2) fraud or material misrepresentations affecting the policy or the insured; or (3) a substantial increase in the hazard insured against. Before enactment of Proposition 103, insurers had an unfettered right to refuse to renew policies. Because the new restrictions on renewal applied to policies issued before enactment of Proposition 103, the insurers argued that it violated the constitutional prohibition against a "law impairing the obligation of Contracts."

ISSUE PRESENTED Do new restrictions on an insurance company's ability to refuse to renew an automobile insurance policy entered into prior to enactment of the new restrictions violate the Contracts Clause?

SUMMARY OF OPINION In analyzing the constitutionality of the nonrenewal provisions of Proposition 103, the California Supreme Court relied heavily on the law as set forth by the U.S. Supreme Court in *Exxon Corp. v. Eagerton*.[27] In that case, the U.S. Supreme Court upheld an Alabama law that imposed a severance tax on oil and gas while prohibiting price increases that would pass on the burden of the tax, even though some sellers had contracts that expressly authorized such price increases. The Court explained:

> Although the language of the Contracts Clause is facially absolute, its prohibition must be accommodated to the inherent police power of the State "to safeguard the vital interests of its people." This Court has long recognized that a statute does not violate the Contracts Clause simply because it has the effect of restricting, or even barring altogether, the performance of duties created by contracts entered into prior to its enactment. Thus, a state prohibition law may be applied to contracts for the sale of beer that were valid when entered into, a law barring lotteries may be applied to lottery tickets that were valid when issued, and workmen's compensation law may be applied to employers and employees operating under pre-existing contracts of employment that made no provision for work-related injuries.

Applying these standards and others from other jurisdictions, the California Supreme Court upheld the nonrenewal restrictions. The decision rested in part on the fact that insurance is a highly regulated industry in which further regulation can reasonably be anticipated. Proposition 103 does not prevent an insurer from discontinuing its California business; an insurer can still withdraw from doing business in California. Furthermore, Proposition 103, as interpreted by the California Supreme Court earlier in its opinion, guaranteed that insurers renewing policies would receive fair and reasonable rates. Because the nonrenewal impairment of contract was found by the court to be "relatively moderate and restrained," the constitutional hurdle that the law had to overcome was correspondingly low. The public interest in making insurance available to all Californians and the fear that insurance companies would refuse to renew in California, leaving drivers without the car insurance required by law, was sufficient, when measured

Case 2.3 continues

---

27. 462 U.S. 176 (1983).

Case 2.3 continued

against the relatively low degree of impairment of contract rights involved, to justify the nonrenewal provision under the U.S. and California constitutions, even as applied to existing policies.

RESULT California can legally change the nonrenewal provisions applicable to existing automobile insurance policies without violating the U.S. or state constitution.

COMMENTS The provision of Proposition 103 that rolled back insurance rates by 20% was upheld under a due process attack, because Proposition 103 provided an individualized mechanism whereby insurers could obtain rate increases that would give them a fair and reasonable return. However, the part of Proposition 103 that prohibited rate increases for one year following enactment of Proposition 103 unless the insurer was threatened with insolvency was struck down as unconstitutional on its face. Although price controls and rent controls are often upheld, they cannot be confiscatory. The property owner is entitled to a reasonable return on the owner's investment. Even if profits in the past were excessive, this would not justify an unreasonably low rate of return for the future.

Ex Post Facto Laws   Article I, Section 9, and Article I, Section 10, prohibit *ex post facto* laws. These are laws that punish actions that were not illegal when performed.

Bills of Attainder   Article I, Section 9, prohibits the federal government from enacting laws to punish specific individuals. Such laws are termed *bills of attainder*.

In 1997, eight regional Bell telephone operating companies (BOCs) successfully challenged portions of the 1996 Telecommunications Act as an unconstitutional bill of attainder. The BOCs argued and the federal district court agreed that the act singled out the companies by name for legislative punishment by restricting their ability to (1) enter the long-distance market; (2) provide telecommunications equipment; and (3) engage in electronic publishing.[28] However, the U.S. Court of Appeals for the District of Columbia Circuit apparently disagreed and held in a different case that restrictions on BellSouth's ability to offer electronic publishing was not punishment.[29]

The Bill of Rights

The first ten amendments of the Constitution constitute the Bill of Rights. The first eight amendments contain specific guarantees of individual liberties that limit the power of the federal government. Importantly, the last two make clear that the federal government's powers are limited and enumerated, whereas the rights of the people go beyond those listed in the Constitution.

The First Amendment guarantees freedom of religion, speech, press, and assembly. The Second Amendment grants persons the right to bear arms. The Third Amendment provides that no soldier shall be quartered in any house. The Fourth Amendment prohibits unreasonable searches and seizures and requires that warrants shall be issued only upon probable cause. The Fifth Amendment (1) contains the grand jury requirements; (2) forbids double jeopardy (that is, being tried twice for the same crime); (3) prohibits forcing a person to be a witness against himself or herself; (4) prohibits the deprivation of life, liberty, or property without due process of law; and (5) requires just compensation when private property is taken for public use. The Sixth Amendment guarantees a speedy and public jury trial in all criminal prosecutions. The Seventh Amendment gives the right to a jury trial in all civil (that is, noncriminal) cases when the value in dispute is greater than $20. The Eighth Amendment prohibits excessive bails or fines as well as cruel and unusual punishment. The Fourth, Fifth, and Sixth Amendments are discussed in Chapter 15.

Applicability to the States   The Fourteenth Amendment provides that no state shall "deprive any person of life, liberty, or property, without due process of law"

---

28. SBC Communications, Inc. v. FCC, 981 F. Supp. 996 (N.D.Tex. 1997).
29. BellSouth Corp. v. FCC, 144 F.3d 58 (D.C. Cir. 1998).

IN BRIEF

OUTLINE OF THE BILL OF RIGHTS

Amendment I

Establishment Clause
Free Exercise Clause
Freedom of Speech
Freedom of Press
Right to Assembly and Petition

Amendment II

Right to Keep and Bear Arms

Amendment III

Restrictions on Quartering Soldiers

Amendment IV

No Unreasonable Search and Seizure
Requirements for Warrants

Amendment V

Presentment or Indictment of a Grand Jury for Capital or
    Otherwise Infamous Crime
Prohibition on Double Jeopardy
Prohibition on Compulsory Self-Incrimination
Due Process Required Before Taking Life, Liberty, or Property
Just Compensation for Taking of Private Property

Amendment VI

In Criminal Prosecutions:
    Right to a Speedy and Public Trial
    Right to a Jury Trial
    Right to Confront Witnesses
    Right to Counsel

Amendment VII

Right to a Jury Trial in Civil Cases

Amendment VIII

No Excessive Bail
No Excessive Fines
No Cruel and Unusual Punishment

Amendment IX

Rights of the People Not Limited to Those Listed in the
    Constitution

Amendment X

Powers Not Delegated to the United States in the
    Constitution Are Reserved to the States or the People,
    Except for Those Powers Prohibited to the States by the
    Constitution, Which Are Reserved to the People

(the *Due Process Clause*) and "[n]o State shall make or enforce any law which shall abridge the privileges or immunities of citizens of the United States" (the *Privileges and Immunities Clause*). After the Fourteenth Amendment was passed, it was argued that the Due Process Clause and the Privileges and Immunities Clause made the Bill of Rights applicable to state governments.

The Supreme Court has rejected this theory. It has held that the provisions of the Bill of Rights are incorporated into the Fourteenth Amendment only if they are fundamental to the American system of law or are safeguards "essential to liberty in the American scheme of justice."[30]

Many provisions of the Bill of Rights have been held to limit the actions of state governments as well as the federal government. For example, if a state government were to abridge the freedom of speech, it would violate the First Amendment as applied to state governments through the Fourteenth Amendment.

---

30. Duncan v. Louisiana, 391 U.S. 145 (1968).

Other provisions have been held not to apply to the states: the Second Amendment right to bear arms, the Fifth Amendment requirement of a grand jury indictment before any criminal prosecution, and the Seventh Amendment guarantee of a jury trial in civil cases.

The Eighth Amendment prohibition against the imposition of excessive bail has not been explicitly applied to the states, but in a number of state cases the Supreme Court has assumed that it applied. The Fifth Amendment's prohibition against the taking of property without just compensation has not been incorporated into the Fourteenth Amendment, but the due process guarantee in the Fourteenth Amendment has been interpreted to provide the same protection.

The Supreme Court has not yet determined whether the Third Amendment, which prohibits the quartering of soldiers in private houses, and the excessive-fine provision of the Eighth Amendment are applicable to state governments.

Article IV, Section 2, of the Constitution and Section 1 of the Fourteenth Amendment both guarantee the privileges and immunities of citizens. Article IV provides that citizens of each state shall receive all the privileges and immunities of citizens of other states. This provision prohibits any unreasonable discrimination between the citizens of different states. Any such discrimination must reasonably relate to legitimate state or local purposes. The Fourteenth Amendment prohibits the states from making laws that would abridge the privileges or immunities of citizens of the United States—that is, the rights that go with being a citizen of the federal government, such as the right to vote in a federal election.

 ## Due Process

The due process clauses of the Fifth Amendment (which applies to the federal government) and the Fourteenth Amendment (which applies to the states) prohibit depriving any person of life, liberty, or property without due process of law. *Procedural due process* focuses on the fairness of the legal proceeding. *Substantive due process* focuses on the fundamental rights protected by the due process clauses.

Procedural Due Process

Whenever a governmental action affects a person's life, liberty, or property, the due process requirement applies,
and some form of notice and hearing is required. The type of hearing varies depending on the nature of the action, but some opportunity to be heard must be provided. In general, greater procedural protections are afforded to criminal defendants because the possibility of imprisonment and even death in capital cases is at stake.

The Due Process Clause of the Fourteenth Amendment has been interpreted to make virtually all of the procedural requirements in the Bill of Rights applicable to state criminal proceedings. These rights are discussed in Chapter 15.

Substantive Due Process

Disputes have raged over the years as to what fundamental rights people in our society possess, with which the government may not interfere. It has been argued that such rights and liberty interests, including the right to privacy, are guaranteed by the due process clauses of the Fifth and Fourteenth Amendments. This protection of fundamental rights is known as substantive due process. The notion of substantive due process was not wholeheartedly received by the Supreme Court until the end of the nineteenth century, mainly because substantive due process rights are not specifically listed in the Constitution.

Limit on Economic Regulation   The Supreme Court first invalidated a state law on substantive due process grounds in 1897.[31] A Louisiana law prohibited anyone from obtaining insurance on Louisiana property from any marine insurance company that had not complied in all respects with Louisiana law. The Court held that the statute violated the fundamental right to make contracts.

Early in the twentieth century, the concept was applied to more controversial areas, such as state statutes limiting working hours. In *Lochner v. New York*,[32] the Supreme Court struck down a New York statute that prohibited the employment of bakery employees for more than 10 hours a day or 60 hours a week. The Court held that the statute interfered with the employers' and employees' fundamental right to contract with each other.

In the period from 1905 to 1937, the Supreme Court invoked the doctrine of substantive due process

---

31. Allgeyer v. Louisiana, 165 U.S. 578 (1897).
32. 198 U.S. 45 (1905).

to invalidate a number of laws relating to regulation of prices, labor relations, and conditions for entry into business.

In 1937, the Supreme Court reversed direction. After President Franklin Delano Roosevelt threatened to "pack" the Court (discussed in the "Inside Story"), the Justices upheld a minimum wage law for women in Washington, overruling an earlier decision striking down a similar statute.[33] In 1938, the Court upheld a statute that prohibited the interstate shipment of "filled" milk (milk to which any fat or oil other than milk fat has been added).[34] The Court made clear that if any state of facts, either known or imaginable, pro-

33. West Coast Hotel Co. v. Parrish, 300 U.S. 379 (1937).
34. United States v. Carolene Products Co., 304 U.S. 144 (1938).

vides a rational basis for the legislation, the legislation will not be held to violate substantive due process. Under this test, economic regulation is rarely constrained by economic liberty.

Limit on Punitive Damages   In certain cases involving torts, or civil wrongs, the jury is entitled to award the plaintiff not only compensatory damages equal to the plaintiff's actual loss but also punitive or exemplary damages, designed to punish and make an example of the defendant. Usually, the size of the punitive damages bears some relationship to the size of the compensatory damages and the degree of reprehensibility. The following case addressed the issue of whether an award of punitive damages that was 500 times the amount of compensatory damages was so excessive as to violate substantive due process.

| A CASE IN POINT | IN THE LANGUAGE OF THE COURT |

CASE 2.4
BMW OF NORTH AMERICA, INC. v. GORE
Supreme Court of the United States
116 S. Ct. 1589 (1996).

FACTS   BMW of North America had a nationwide policy of not advising its dealers, and hence the ultimate customers, of predelivery damage to new cars when the cost of repair did not exceed 3% of the car's suggested retail price. As a result of this policy, Ira Gore, Jr. (Gore) unwittingly purchased a BMW car that had been damaged in transit and then repainted. When he learned that his BMW had been repainted, Gore brought an action against BMW, BMW's American distributor, and an authorized Alabama BMW dealer based on the distributor's failure to disclose that his BMW had been repainted after being damaged prior to delivery. An Alabama Circuit Court entered a judgment on a jury verdict awarding Gore compensatory damages of $4,000 and punitive damages of $4 million. The Alabama Supreme Court affirmed the judgment after reducing the punitive award to $2 million. BMW appealed.

ISSUE PRESENTED   Is a $2 million punitive award arising from actions justifying only $4,000 of compensatory damages so excessive as to violate the Due Process Clause of the Fourteenth Amendment?

OPINION   STEVENS, J., writing for the U.S. Supreme Court:
The Due Process Clause of the Fourteenth Amendment prohibits a State from imposing a "grossly excessive" punishment on a tortfeasor. . . .

. . .

III

Elementary notions of fairness enshrined in our constitutional jurisprudence dictate that a person receive fair notice not only of the conduct that will subject him to punishment but also of the severity of the penalty that a State may impose. Three

Case 2.4 continues

Case 2.4 continued

guideposts, each of which indicates that BMW did not receive adequate notice of the magnitude of the sanction that Alabama might impose for adhering to the nondisclosure policy adopted in 1983, lead us to the conclusion that the $2 million award against BMW is grossly excessive: the degree of reprehensibility of the nondisclosure; the disparity between the harm or potential harm suffered by Dr. Gore and his punitive damages award; and the difference between this remedy and the civil penalties authorized or imposed in comparable cases. We discuss these considerations in turn.

Degree of Reprehensibility

Perhaps the most important indicium of the reasonableness of a punitive damages award is the degree of reprehensibility of the defendant's conduct. As the Court stated nearly 150 years ago, exemplary damages imposed on a defendant should reflect "the enormity of his offense." . . .

In this case, none of the aggravating factors associated with particularly reprehensible conduct is present. The harm BMW inflicted on Dr. Gore was purely economic in nature. . . . To be sure, infliction of economic injury, especially when done intentionally through affirmative acts of misconduct or when the target is financially vulnerable, can warrant a substantial penalty. But this observation does not convert all acts that cause economic harm into torts that are sufficiently reprehensible to justify a significant sanction in addition to compensatory damages.

. . .

Ratio

The second and perhaps most commonly cited indicium of an unreasonable or excessive punitive damages award is its ratio to the actual harm inflicted on the plaintiff. The principle that exemplary damages must bear a "reasonable relationship" to compensatory damages has a long pedigree. . . .

In [*Pacific Mutual Life Ins. Co. v. Haslip*[35]] we concluded that even though a punitive damages award of "more than 4 times the amount of compensatory damages," might be "close to the line," it did not "cross the line into the area of constitutional impropriety." *TXO*,[36] following dicta in *Haslip*, refined this analysis by confirming that the proper inquiry is "whether there is a reasonable relationship between the punitive damages award and the harm likely to result from the defendant's conduct as well as the harm that actually has occurred [which was $19,000]." Thus, in upholding the $10 million award in *TXO*, we relied on the difference between that figure and the harm to the victim that would have ensued if the tortious plan had succeeded. That difference suggested that the relevant ratio was not more than 10 to 1.

The $2 million in punitive damages awarded to Dr. Gore by the Alabama Supreme Court is 500 times the amount of his actual harm as determined by the jury. Moreover, there is no suggestion that Dr. Gore or any other BMW purchaser was threatened with any additional potential harm by BMW's nondisclosure policy. The disparity in this case is thus dramatically greater than those considered in *Haslip* and *TXO*.

Case 2.4 continues

---

35. 499 U.S. 1 (1991).

36. TXO Production Corp. v. Alliance Resources Corp., 509 U.S. 443 (1993).

Case 2.4 continued

Of course, we have consistently rejected the notion that the constitutional line is marked by a simple mathematical formula, even one that compares actual and potential damages to the punitive award. . . . Once again, "we return to what we said . . . in *Haslip*: 'We need not, and indeed we cannot, draw a mathematical bright line between the constitutionally acceptable and the constitutionally unacceptable that would fit every case. We can say, however, that [a] general concer[n] of reasonableness . . . properly enter[s] into the constitutional calculus.'" In most cases, the ratio will be within a constitutionally acceptable range, and remittitur will not be justified on this basis. When the ratio is a breathtaking 500 to 1, however, the award must surely "raise a suspicious judicial eyebrow."

Sanctions for Comparable Misconduct

Comparing the punitive damages award and the civil or criminal penalties that could be imposed for comparable misconduct provides a third indicium of excessiveness. As Justice O'Connor has correctly observed, a reviewing court engaged in determining whether an award of punitive damages is excessive should "accord 'substantial deference' to legislative judgments concerning appropriate sanctions for the conduct at issue." In *Haslip*, the Court noted that although the exemplary award was "much in excess of the fine that could be imposed," imprisonment was also authorized in the criminal context. In this case the $2 million economic sanction imposed on BMW is substantially greater than the statutory fines available in Alabama and elsewhere for similar malfeasance.

The maximum civil penalty authorized by the Alabama Legislature for a violation of its Deceptive Trade Practices Act is $2,000; other States authorize more severe sanctions, with the maxima ranging from $5,000 to $10,000. . . . Moreover, at the time BMW's policy was first challenged, there does not appear to have been any judicial decision in Alabama or elsewhere indicating that application of that policy might give rise to such severe punishment.

RESULT   The Supreme Court reversed the judgment of the Alabama Supreme Court and ruled that the $2 million punitive damage award was so excessive as to violate the Due Process Clause of the Fourteenth Amendment of the U.S. Constitution. The Court remanded the case to Alabama for reconsideration of constitutional punitive damages.

COMMENTS   Justice Ginsburg, dissenting from the decision, claimed that the Court "unnecessarily and unwisely ventures into territory traditionally within the States' domain" by ruling for BMW. Similarly, Justice Scalia dissented and argued, "At the time of the adoption of the Fourteenth Amendment, it was well understood that punitive damages represent the assessment by the jury, as the voice of the community, of the measure of punishment the defendant deserved."

Another due process concern in awarding punitive damages is the availability of judicial review of the amount. Along with the substantive due process requirement illustrated in *BMW*, there is a procedural due process requirement that such awards be subject to appellate review. In *Honda Motor Co. v. Oberg*,[37] an Oregon jury had

Case 2.4 continues

---

37. 512 U.S. 415 (1994).

Case 2.4 continued

awarded $5 million in punitive damages to a plaintiff injured in a three-wheel all-terrain vehicle accident. Although Honda wished to appeal the penalty, Oregon's constitution barred review of punitive awards unless there was no evidence to support the jury's decision. The U.S. Supreme Court found the Oregon rule in violation of due process and insufficient to protect Honda's constitutional rights to due process.

Questions

1. What guidelines does the notion of "substantive due process" articulated by the Court give a manager contemplating a policy such as BMW's?
2. BMW deceived its customers by selling them cosmetically imperfect products. Would the result have been any different if BMW had cut costs by installing inexpensive and unreliable airbags?

Protection of Fundamental Rights   Substantive due process challenges are given more weight when fundamental rights other than the right to make contracts are at issue. Fundamental rights and liberty interests protected by the Due Process Clause include the guarantees of the Bill of Rights, the right to marry and to have children, the right to travel, the right to vote, and the right to associate with other people. The Supreme Court has made clear that the fundamental rights protected by substantive due process are not limited to those specifically enumerated in the Constitution or the Bill of Rights. Legislation that limits fundamental rights violates substantive due process unless it can be shown to promote a compelling or overriding government interest.

Substantive due process was extended to the right to privacy in *Griswold v. Connecticut*.[38] The executive director of the Planned Parenthood League of Connecticut and a physician who served as medical director for the league at its center in New Haven were arrested. They were charged with giving birth control advice in violation of a Connecticut statute that prohibited the use of any drug, medicinal article, or instrument for the purpose of preventing conception.

In finding that the Connecticut statute was an unconstitutional invasion of individuals' right to privacy, the Supreme Court discussed the penumbra of rights surrounding each guarantee in the Bill of Rights. The Court defined *penumbra* as the peripheral rights that are implied by the specifically enumerated rights. For example, the Court noted that the First Amendment's freedom of the press necessarily includes the right to distribute, the right to receive, the right to read, freedom of inquiry, freedom of thought, freedom to teach, and freedom of association. The Fourth Amendment, which prohibits unreasonable searches and seizures, similarly includes a "right to privacy, no less important than any other right carefully and particularly reserved to the people." The Supreme Court found that the Connecticut statute encroached on the right to privacy in marriage.

The right to privacy is an essential element in the debate between pro-choice and pro-life groups concerning a woman's right to an abortion. It is relevant in other areas as well. For example, in one case,[39] a schoolteacher sued a board of education alleging that the nonrenewal of her teaching contract was due to the fact that she was an unwed mother and her pregnancy had been by means of artificial insemination. The district court held that a woman has a constitutional privacy right to become pregnant by means of artificial insemination. The Supreme Court has upheld a person's right to refuse life-sustaining treatment (such as lifesaving hydration and nutrition)[40] but declined to recognize a right to physician-assisted suicide.[41]

---

38. 381 U.S. 479 (1965).

39. Cameron v. Board of Education, 795 F. Supp. 228 (S.D. Ohio 1991).
40. Cruzan v. Director, Missouri Dept. of Health, 497 U.S. 261 (1990).
41. Washington v. Glucksberg, 117 S. Ct. 2258 (1997).

Mandatory drug testing also presents privacy issues. The Supreme Court has upheld certain regulations concerning drug testing for public employees. This issue is discussed in Chapter 12.

 ## Compensation for Takings

One of the earliest provisions of the Bill of Rights incorporated into the Fourteenth Amendment was the Fifth Amendment provision that private property may not be taken for public use without just compensation. State and federal governments have the power of *eminent domain*, which is the power to take property for public uses such as building a school, park, or airport. If property is taken from a private owner for such a purpose, the owner is entitled to just compensation. A more complex situation arises when the government does not physically take the property but imposes regulations that restrict its use. If the regulation amounts to a taking of the property, the owner is entitled to just compensation. In a sense, all regulation takes some aspect of property away from the owner. The question is when does a regulation constitute a taking that requires compensation.

Takings Cases

In one instance, the Supreme Court held that there was a taking when a homeowner was required to grant a public right-of-way through his property in order to obtain a building permit to replace his oceanfront house with a larger one.[42] This case, and land use regulation generally, are discussed in Chapter 17.

Another case involved the Federal Communications Commission's regulation of the rates a utility company could charge for the attachment of television cables to the utility company's poles. The Supreme Court held that the regulation was not a taking, as long as the rates were not set so low as to be unjust and confiscatory.[43]

In another case, Penn Central Transportation Company, the owner of Grand Central Station in midtown Manhattan, was prohibited from constructing an office building above Grand Central Station. The pro-

hibition was ordered by the Landmarks Preservation Commission, which had designated the station a landmark. Under New York City law, the commission could prevent any alteration of the fundamental character of such buildings. A high-rise would arguably have altered the fundamental character of Grand Central Station. The Supreme Court found that the prohibition was not a taking.[44] This case is discussed in Chapter 17.

The disclosure of trade secrets by the government can constitute a taking requiring just compensation.[45] Trade secrets are discussed in Chapter 11.

 ## Equal Protection

The Equal Protection Clause of the Fourteenth Amendment places another limitation on the power of state governments to regulate; a comparable limitation is imposed on the federal government by the Due Process Clause of the Fifth Amendment. The Equal Protection Clause provides that no state shall "deny to any person within its jurisdiction the equal protection of the laws." The Supreme Court's interpretation of this clause is the subject of much debate.

Establishing Discrimination

In order to challenge a statute on equal protection grounds, it is first necessary to establish that the statute discriminates against a class of persons. Discrimination may be found on the face of the statute, in its application, or in its purpose. The statute may explicitly (on its face) treat different classes of persons differently; or the statute itself may contain no classification, but government officials may apply it differently to different classes of people. Finally, a statute may be neutral on its face and in its application but have the purpose of creating different burdens for different classes of persons.

In determining whether a facially neutral law is a device to discriminate against certain classes of people, the Supreme Court looks at three things: (1) the practical or statistical impact of the statute on different classes of persons; (2) the history of the problems that the

42. Nollan v. California Coastal Comm'n, 483 U.S. 825 (1987).
43. FCC v. Florida Power Corp., 480 U.S. 245 (1987).

44. Penn Central Transp. Co. v. New York City, 438 U.S. 104 (1978).
45. Ruckelshaus v. Monsanto Co., 467 U.S. 986 (1984).

statute seeks to solve; and (3) the legislative history of the statute. However, even if a government action has a disproportionate effect on a racial minority group, it will be upheld if there was no racially discriminatory purpose or intent.[46]

Validity of Discrimination

The Supreme Court has evolved three tests to determine the constitutionality of various types of discrimination, depending on how the statute classifies the persons concerned.

Rational Basis Test   The *rational basis test* applies to all classifications that relate to matters of economics or social welfare. Under this test, a classification will be held valid if there is any conceivable basis on which the classification might relate to a legitimate governmental interest. It is a rare regulation that cannot meet this minimal standard.

Strict Scrutiny Test   A classification that determines who may exercise a fundamental right or one that is based on a suspect trait such as race is subject to strict scrutiny. Under the *strict scrutiny* test, a classification will be held valid only if it is necessary to promote a compelling state interest. The right to privacy, the right to vote, the right to travel, and certain guarantees in the Bill of Rights are fundamental rights. Rights such as welfare payments, housing, education, and government employment are not fundamental rights.

Substantially Related Test   The Supreme Court occasionally applies a third test, which is stricter than the rational basis test but less strict than strict scrutiny. This intermediate test applies to classifications such as gender and legitimacy of birth. Under this test, a classification will be held valid if it is substantially related to an important governmental interest.

Racial Discrimination

Racial discrimination was the major target of the Fourteenth Amendment, so it is clear that racial classifications are suspect. However, some uncertainties arise over racial classifications that are intended to favor minorities.

From 1896 to 1954, the "separate but equal" doctrine allowed separate services to exist for minorities as long as they were equal to the services provided for whites. In *Plessy v. Ferguson*,[47] the Supreme Court upheld a law requiring that all railway companies provide separate but equal accommodations for African-American and white passengers. Fifty-eight years later, the Supreme Court held in *Brown v. Board of Education*[48] that the doctrine had no place in education. The justices unanimously decided that the "segregation of children in public schools solely on the basis of race, even though the physical facilities and other 'tangible' factors may be equal, deprives the children of the minority group of equal educational opportunities." Supreme Court rulings following *Brown* made it clear that no governmental entity may segregate people because of their race or national origin.

Complications concerning racial classifications have arisen more recently in the area of affirmative action intended to benefit racial or ethnic minorities. The debate has raged over whether strict scrutiny should be applied only to legislation that discriminates against a minority or to any legislation that generally discriminates based on race. The Supreme Court resolved that issue in *Adarand Constructors, Inc. v. Peña*,[49] when it held that all racial classifications—whether imposed by federal, state, or local government—are subject to strict scrutiny. In *Adarand*, the white owner of a construction company successfully challenged regulations adopted by the U.S. Department of Transportation that made use of race-based presumptions in awarding lucrative federal highway project contracts to economically disadvantaged businesses. The Court rejected the argument it had accepted in an earlier case[50] that because the Equal Protection Clause was adopted after the Civil War to protect African Americans, it permits "benign" racial classifications to protect minorities so long as there is a rational basis for the classification.

In the following case, the U.S. Court of Appeals for the Fifth Circuit considered an affirmative action program at the University of Texas that used reduced standards for African-American and Mexican-American applicants and employed a segregated evaluation process.

---

46. Arlington Heights v. Metropolitan Hous. Dev. Corp., 429 U.S. 252 (1977) (upholding a largely white suburb's refusal to rezone to permit multifamily dwellings for low- and moderate-income tenants, including members of racial minorities).

47. 163 U.S. 537 (1896).

48. 347 U.S. 483 (1954).

49. 515 U.S. 200 (1995).

50. Metro Broadcasting, Inc. v. FCC, 497 U.S. 547 (1990) (upholding two minority-preference policies mandated by Congress to achieve broadcast diversity).

A CASE IN POINT	SUMMARY

CASE 2.5
HOPWOOD v. TEXAS
United States Court of
Appeals for the Fifth Circuit
78 F.3d 932 (5th Cir. 1996),
cert. denied, 116 S. Ct.
2581 (1996).

FACTS   In 1991, Cheryl Hopwood and three other white residents of Texas applied to the law school at the University of Texas at Austin, a leading national law school. At that time, the law school administration based its offers of admission largely on a composite of the applicant's undergraduate grade point average and his or her law school admissions test score. In the admissions process, the school first separated applicants into three pools based on their composite scores: presumptive admit, discretionary, and presumptive deny. An applicant in the presumptive admit category was offered admission unless the dean of the school or the chair of the admissions committee downgraded his or her application based on a weak undergraduate education or other application deficiency. An applicant in the presumptive deny category was rejected unless upgraded by a reviewing professor, who might well be the only person to review that application. Applicants in the middle, discretionary category received extensive review: subcommittees of three members of the full admissions committee reviewed groups of thirty applications. Each reviewer was given a fixed number of votes to cast among the group of thirty applicants. Applicants who received two or three votes were offered admission. Applicants who received a single vote were placed on the waiting list, and those who received no votes were denied admission.

As part of its explicit affirmative action program, the school required lower composite scores for African-American and Mexican-American applicants than for all others. For example, the lowest presumptive admit score for whites and nonfavored minorities was 199, but favored minorities needed a score of only 189 to be placed in the highest category. Similarly, the presumptive deny hurdle for nonfavored applicants was 192, although for favored minorities it was only 179. The law school also segregated its evaluation process. While whites and nonfavored minorities in the discretionary zone were evaluated by a subcommittee of three, favored minorities in the discretionary zone were evaluated by a separate minority subcommittee that evaluated every favored minority candidate. Thus, each favored application could receive extensive review and discussion. Finally, the law school maintained segregated waiting lists to engineer further the racial composition of the entering class.

By their composite scores, Hopwood and the other plaintiffs placed at the top of the discretionary zone. As a result, none was offered admission, although favored minority applicants with scores under the discretionary hurdle for whites were offered admission. Alleging that the state law school's system violated their rights under the Equal Protection Clause of the Fourteenth Amendment, Hopwood and her fellow rejectees sued the law school. The law school argued that its system of racial classification and application segregation was constitutional because it was intended to remedy past discrimination by the state of Texas and was narrowly tailored to do so.

The trial court ruled unconstitutional the school's practice of separate review committees for favored minorities but refused to grant an injunction because the law school had already ended that particular procedure voluntarily. Furthermore, the court awarded only nominal damages of $1 and ordered the law school to allow the plaintiffs to reapply without paying the application fee. Importantly, the trial court refused to enjoin the use of racial preferences, to order the law school to admit the plaintiffs, or to award compensatory or punitive damages.

Case 2.5 continues

Case 2.5 continued

ISSUE PRESENTED   Does the Fourteenth Amendment's Equal Protection Clause permit a government school to discriminate in its admissions based on race?

SUMMARY OF OPINION   The U.S. Court of Appeals began by noting that "[t]he central purpose of the Equal Protection Clause 'is to prevent the States from purposefully discriminating between individuals on the basis of race.'" Ultimately, the Fourteenth Amendment seeks to render race irrelevant in government decision making. Relying on Supreme Court rulings, including *Adarand,* the court explained that all racial classifications by any governmental entity, regardless of "benign" or "remedial" intent, are subject to strict scrutiny under the Fourteenth Amendment. Hence, to withstand constitutional challenge such classifications must both (1) serve a compelling governmental interest and (2) be narrowly tailored to achieve that interest.

The law school had argued that its system of segregation was compelled by an interest in maintaining a diverse student body and remedying the present effects of past discrimination by both the University of Texas system and the state of Texas as a whole. The court rejected diversity as a compelling interest, holding that current Supreme Court jurisprudence establishes that only remedial interests, that is, reversing the current effects of past discrimination, justify racial classification. Such treatment of individuals based on their race in order to foster diversity frustrates, rather than facilitates, the goals of equal protection:

> Diversity fosters, rather than minimizes, the use of race. It treats minorities as a group, rather than as individuals. It may further remedial purposes but, just as likely, may promote improper racial stereotypes, thus fueling racial hostility.
> The use of race, in and of itself, to choose students simply achieves a student body that looks different. Such a criterion is no more rational on its own terms than would be choices based upon the physical size or blood type of applicants.
>
> . . .
>
> The assumption [of this program] is that a certain individual possesses characteristics by virtue of being a member of a certain racial group. This assumption, however, does not withstand scrutiny. . . .
> To believe that a person's race controls his point of view is to stereotype him. . . .
> Instead, individuals, with their own conceptions of life, further diversity of viewpoint.

The court then examined the law school's goal of remedying past discrimination. Unlike diversity, such remedial interests may justify racial classification. Relying on and quoting *City of Richmond v. J. A. Croson Co.,*[51] the court conceded that a state actor may racially classify when it has a "strong basis in the evidence for conclusion that remedial action was necessary." At issue, however, was the type of discrimination that one governmental entity can use as a basis for imposing a system of racial classification. The law school argued that the University of Texas's and the state of Texas's well-

Case 2.5 continues

---

51. 488 U.S. 469, 528 (1989).

Case 2.5 continued

documented history of discrimination against African Americans and Mexican Americans justified its admissions process. The court disagreed.

One state actor may act to remedy the current effects of its own past discrimination but not the current effects of another state actor's discrimination, discrimination in the general industry in question, or societal discrimination in general. Otherwise, without a limiting principle, racial classification—a highly suspect governmental practice—could go effectively unchecked. Hence, the relevant unit of analysis was the law school at the University of Texas at Austin, which could not establish that its past discrimination against African Americans and Mexican Americans had any current effects that a segregated admissions process attempted to remedy. Without such current effects of its own past discrimination, no remedial interest could justify its system of racial differentiation.

RESULT   The appeals court reversed the trial court's decision, ruling that the law school may not use race as factor in its admissions decisions. It also remanded the case for further consideration of damages in light of its analysis and conclusions.

COMMENTS   The U.S. Supreme Court denied the law school's petition for certiorari, thereby leaving as law in the states of Texas, Louisiana, and Mississippi (the states in the Fifth Circuit) the Fifth Circuit's rejection of diversity and broad remedial action as justification for racial classification by the government. In the same term, the Supreme Court refused to hear an appeal of a decision by the U.S. Court of Appeals for the Ninth Circuit refusing to preliminarily enjoin Proposition 209, a California state ballot initiative that amended the California constitution to prohibit the state and its subdivisions from granting racial preferences in college admissions, the awarding of contracts, and the hiring of employees.[52] The Ninth Circuit had concluded that Proposition 209 likely does not violate the Equal Protection Clause.

One year later, white applicants rejected by the University of Michigan filed lawsuits against that institution's undergraduate and law schools for violations of the Equal Protection Clause similar to those suffered by Cheryl Hopwood. Those cases are still under way, but court observers expect more suits to follow and the Supreme Court to speak eventually and definitively to the issue.

---

52. Coalition for Economic Equity v. Wilson, 122 F.3d 692 (9th Cir. 1997), *cert. denied*, 118 S. Ct. 397 (1997).

Quota systems setting aside a certain number of positions in schools or housing for minority members are usually struck down by the court. Under a strict quota system, individual circumstances are disregarded and members of minority races may have less of a chance of obtaining a position if a small number of positions are set aside for them.

Private employers are not limited by the Equal Protection Clause, which applies only to governmental actions. However, as explained in Chapter 13, private entities are subject to the Civil Rights Act and other regulations imposed by federal and state antidiscrimination statutes.

Other Forms of Discrimination

Three classifications are subject to the intermediate-level (substantially related) test of heightened scrutiny: gender, illegitimacy, and alienage.

Gender   Classifications based on gender will be upheld if substantially related to important governmental interests. In this area, the Supreme Court decides on a case-by-case basis. It invalidated statutory provisions that gave female workers fewer benefits for their families than male workers. It upheld differential treatment for women when it was compensatory for past discrimination, but not when it unreasonably denied benefits to men. It upheld a statutory rape law applying only to men, exemption from the draft for women, and the exclusion of insurance benefits for costs relating to pregnancy.

In 1996, in *United States v. Virginia*,[53] the Court ruled that the Virginia Military Academy, an all-male, state-supported military college, violated the Equal Protection Clause by excluding women. The Court held that classifications based on gender must (1) serve important governmental objectives, (2) be substantially related to achieving those objectives, and (3) rest on an "exceedingly persuasive justification." Justice Ginsburg's majority opinion can be read to require gender classifications to meet a standard somewhere between intermediate and strict scrutiny. Gender discrimination is discussed further in Chapter 13.

Illegitimacy   Classifications based on the legitimacy of children will be held invalid unless substantially related to a proper interest of the state. The Supreme Court will usually look at the purpose behind the classification and will not uphold any law intended to punish so-called illegitimate children.

Alienage   Aliens, that is, persons who are not citizens of the United States, do not receive the protection of all constitutional guarantees, many of which apply only to citizens. For example, in 1990, the Supreme Court held that the Fourth Amendment prohibition of search and seizure without a warrant did not apply to a drug raid of an alien's premises in Mexico.[54] Because of Congress's plenary power over aliens, classifications imposed by the federal government based on alienage are valid if they are not arbitrary and unreasonable. State and local laws that classify on the basis of alienage are, however, subject to the strict scrutiny test discussed earlier; however, a state law discriminating against alien participation in state government is evaluated under the rational basis test.

 Freedom of Speech

The First Amendment states that "Congress shall make no law . . . abridging the freedom of speech, or of the press." However, the Court does not apply the First Amendment to protect all speech to the same degree. The type of speech most clearly protected is political speech, including speech critical of governmental policies and officials. It has been argued that other types of speech, such as defamation, obscenity, advertising, and "fighting words," should be accorded a lesser degree of protection. Still other types of expression—bribery, perjury, and counseling to murder—are considered not to be protected by the First Amendment at all.

Determining whether a type of speech is protected by the First Amendment is only the first step of the analysis. If it is determined that a certain expression is protected, it must then be determined to what extent the expression may be regulated without violating the First Amendment.

"Clear and Present Danger" Test

Throughout most of the nineteenth and early twentieth centuries, Congress followed the mandate of the First Amendment literally and made "no law" restricting freedom of speech, assembly, or the press. In response to vocal resistance to World War I, Congress passed the Espionage Act of 1917 and the Sedition Act of 1918. In 1919, the Supreme Court, in a decision by Justice Oliver Wendell Holmes, first discussed the "clear and present danger" test in affirming a conviction under the Espionage Act.[55]

Schenck was convicted for circulating to men who had been called and accepted for military service a document that stated that the draft violated the Thirteenth Amendment, which prohibits slavery or involuntary servitude. The Supreme Court considered the defendant's actions in the context of a nation at war:

> [T]he character of every act depends upon the circumstances in which it is done. The most stringent protection of free speech would not protect a man in falsely

53. 116 S. Ct. 2264 (1996).

54. United States v. Verdugo-Urquidez, 494 U.S. 259 (1990).

55. Schenck v. United States, 249 U.S. 47 (1919).

shouting fire in a theatre and causing a panic. [The] question in every case is whether the words used are used in such circumstances and are of such a nature as to create a *clear and present danger* that they will bring about the substantive evils that Congress has a right to prevent. (Emphasis added.)

The Supreme Court held that many things that might be said in peacetime cannot be allowed in time of war. Schenck's conviction under the Espionage Act was upheld as constitutional.

Later, during the height of the Cold War, the clear and present danger doctrine was applied in a manner restricting First Amendment freedoms even more severely. In the 1960s, the test became stricter and more protective of free speech. In *Brandenburg v. Ohio*[56] the Supreme Court held that "the constitutional guarantees of free speech and free press do not permit a State to forbid or proscribe advocacy of the use of force or of law violation except where such advocacy is directed to inciting or producing imminent lawless action and is likely to incite or produce such action."

In 1997, the U.S. Court of Appeals for the Fourth Circuit held that the First Amendment did not bar a wrongful-death action against the publisher of *Hit Man: A Technical Manual for Independent Contractors*, a 130-page manual of detailed factual instructions describing how to become a professional killer.[57] A convicted murderer had used the book to commit a triple homicide. The publisher stipulated that it had targeted the market of murderers, would-be murderers, and other criminals for the sale of *Hit Man* and that it knew and intended that criminals would immediately use it to solicit, plan, and commit murder. The court rejected the publisher's claim that this was abstract advocacy protected under *Brandenburg v. Ohio*, stating:

[T]his book constitutes the archetypal example of speech which, because it methodically and comprehensively prepares and steels its audience to specific criminal conduct through exhaustively detailed instructions on the planning, commission, and concealment of criminal conduct, finds no preserve in the First Amendment.

A government act may violate the right to free speech not only by forbidding speech but by commanding it as well. In 1995, the U.S. Supreme Court ruled that Massachusetts had violated the First Amendment when it ordered organizers of South Boston's St. Patrick's Day Parade to include a group of gay and lesbian Bostonians of Irish ancestry.[58] Such compulsory inclusion of a group imparting a message the organizers did not wish to convey is forbidden by the Free Speech Clause.

Defamation

Defamatory words—words that harm a person's reputation—are protected by the First Amendment, even when they are false, if they are made by a media defendant (such as a newspaper or television network) about a public figure without knowledge they were false, that is, without actual malice. Defamation is discussed further in Chapter 9.

Obscenity

Obscene material does not enjoy any protection under the First Amendment. Obscene material is defined as material that (1) appeals to a prurient or sordid and perverted interest in sex; (2) has no serious literary, artistic, political, or scientific merit; and (3) is on the whole offensive to the average person in the community.

Commercial Speech

Commercial speech, especially advertising, has always been subject to substantial regulation. It was formerly thought that commercial speech was excluded from the coverage of the First Amendment; under the most recent case law, however, it has full protection. The government cannot suppress commercial speech, but it can make reasonable regulations regarding the time, place, and manner of such speech. For instance, in 1996, the U.S. Court of Appeals for the Ninth Circuit upheld a municipal ordinance banning the sale of merchandise or services on the sidewalks of Waikiki, a popular tourist area

56. 395 U.S. 444 (1969).

57. Rice v. Paladin Enter., Inc. 128 F.3d 233 (4th Cir. 1997), *cert. denied,* 118 S. Ct. 1515 (1998).

58. Hurley v. Irish-American Gay, Lesbian and Bisexual Group of Boston, 515 U.S. 557 (1995).

VIEW FROM CYBERSPACE

PORNOGRAPHY AND FREE SPEECH ON THE INTERNET

Concerned with the easy availability of pornography on the Internet, Congress in 1995 enacted the Communications Decency Act (CDA). Passed in part to protect children from sexually explicit materials in cyberspace, the law criminalized the interstate and international transmission of any obscene or patently offensive communications to any person under the age of 18 through the use of an interactive computer service, such as an on-line service provider giving access to the Internet. The CDA provided two affirmative defenses: one for those who took "good faith, reasonable, effective, and appropriate actions" to restrict access by minors to the prohibited communications, and a second for those who restricted access to covered material by requiring certain designated forms of age proof, such as a verified credit card or an adult identification number or code. The American Civil Liberties Union, joined by many businesses, libraries, and education societies, challenged the law as an unconstitutional violation of the First Amendment's protection of free speech. The case quickly found its way to the U.S. Supreme Court.

Demonstrating a fluency with cyberspace that surprised many commentators, the Court struck down much of the act but left in place its prohibition on on-line transmission of obscene speech, because obscenity is not protected speech.[a] Discussing e-mail, chatrooms, the World Wide Web, search engines, list servers, and Internet service providers, the Court dismissed the government's analogy to broadcast media, which have enjoyed only limited First Amendment protection. Unlike television and radio broadcasting, the Internet does not have an extensive history of government regulation, is not a scare resource in need of monitored allocation, and is not intrusive into individuals' homes.

Instead, the Court viewed the Internet as analogous to a public square, a place where speech is given heightened protection:

> This dynamic, multifaced category of communication includes not only traditional print and news services, but also audio, video, and still images, as well as interactive, real time dialogue. Through the use of chat rooms, any person with a phone line can become a town crier with a voice that resonates farther than it could from any soapbox. Through the use of Web pages, mail exploders, and newsgroups, the same individual can become a pamphleteer. As the [trial court] found, "the content on the Internet is as diverse as human thought."

Furthermore, given the nature of cyberspace, the law's affirmative defenses (restricting access by minors and verifying user ages) were unworkable. Credit cards are insufficient proxies, because many sites are noncommercial and many adults do not own credit cards. Ultimately, the Court agreed with the lower court: "[T]he CDA places an unacceptably heavy burden on protected speech, and the defenses do not constitute the sort of 'narrow tailoring' that will save an otherwise patently invalid unconstitutional provision. . . ."

Libertarians and other free speech advocates were overjoyed with Court's ringing endorsement of the First Amendment in cyberspace. Writing for the Court, Justice Stevens acknowledged the government's interest in protecting children from harmful material but reminded the government of the limits imposed by the Constitution:

> But that interest does not justify an unnecessarily broad suppression of speech addressed to adults. As we have explained, the Government may not "reduc[e] the adult population . . . to . . . only what is fit for children."

a. Reno v. ACLU, 117 S. Ct. 2329 (1997).

in Honolulu.[59] The plaintiffs, sellers of T-shirts imprinted with philosophical and inspirational messages, claimed that the ordinance violated their First Amendment rights. Relying on Supreme Court precedent,[60] the court reasoned that such restrictions are valid if they (1) are content-neutral, (2) are narrowly tailored to serve a significant governmental interest, and (3) leave open ample alternative channels of communication. Because Honolulu's restriction met the three-part test, it was upheld.

Misleading advertising, however, may be restricted or entirely prohibited. Truthful advertising relating to lawful activities is protected by the First Amendment. However, the government retains some authority to regulate. The government must have a substantial interest, and the interference with speech must be in proportion to the interest served.[61]

There is controversy over the extent of First Amendment protection of liquor and cigarette advertising. In 1971, the federal district court for the District of Columbia upheld federal legislation forbidding cigarette advertising on radio and television.[62] Similarly, in 1996, the U.S. Court of Appeals for the Fourth Circuit upheld a Baltimore ordinance banning cigarette advertising on outdoor billboards, building sides, and free-standing signboards.[63]

Such advertising is, of course, not wholly unprotected. In 1995, Coors Brewing Company successfully challenged a provision of the 1935 Federal Alcohol Administration Act that prohibited statements of alcohol content on malt beverage labels unless state law required disclosure.[64] Even though the government's asserted goal of preventing competition based on high alcoholic strength was legitimate, the Court found no evidence that the labeling restriction served the goal.

In 1996, the Court struck down a 40-year-old Rhode Island statute that prohibited the advertisement of liquor prices except at the point of sale.[65] Rhode Island asserted its interest in promoting temperance and argued that the law prevented retailers from competing on price and thereby encouraging alcohol consumption. The Court accepted that interest as legitimate but held the statute too restrictive to meet Free Speech Clause standards. Although commercial speech generally receives less protection than political speech under the First Amendment, the Court recognized a limit to that diminished standard:

> [W]hen a State entirely prohibits the dissemination of truthful, nonmisleading commercial messages for reasons unrelated to the preservation of a fair bargaining process, there is far less reason to depart from the rigorous review that the First Amendment generally demands.

---

65. 44 Liquormart, Inc. v. Rhode Island, 116 S. Ct. 1495 (1996).

INTERNATIONAL CONSIDERATION

In 1989, the Canadian parliament responded to the antismoking lobby by passing the Tobacco Products Control Act. The act aimed to decrease tobacco consumption by banning all tobacco advertising and promotion and requiring unattributed health warnings to be printed on all tobacco products. Cigarette manufacturers challenged the law as a violation of their right to free speech, which is protected by the Canadian Charter of Rights and Freedoms. Six years later, the Supreme Court of Canada overturned much of the act.[a]

The Court reasoned, "Smoking is a legal activity yet consumers are deprived of an important means of learning about product availability to suit their preferences and to compare brand content with an aim to reducing the risk to their health." Asserting its independence, the Court noted that Parliament does not have the right to determine unilaterally the limits of its intrusion on the rights and freedoms guaranteed by the Charter. In this case, the act's infringement on the right to free speech were neither reasonable nor "demonstrably justified in a free and democratic society."

---

a. RJR–MacDonald v. Attorney Gen. of Canada [1995] 127 D.L.R. 4th 1 (Can.).

---

59. One World One Family Now v. Honolulu, 76 F.3d 1009 (9th Cir. 1996), *cert. denied*, 117 S. Ct. 554 (1997) (mem.).

60. Ward v. Rock Against Racism, 491 U.S. 781 (1989). *See also* Clark v. Community for Creative Non-Violence, 468 U.S. 288 (1984) (defining "content neutral" as "justified without reference to the content of the regulated speech").

61. *In re* R.M.J., 455 U.S. 191 (1982).

62. Capital Broadcast Co. v. Mitchell, 333 F. Supp. 582 (D.D.C. 1971).

63. Penn Advertising of Baltimore, Inc. v. Schmoke, 63 F.3d 1318 (4th Cir. 1996).

64. Rubin v. Coors Brewing Co., 514 U.S. 476 (1995).

The First Amendment also protects seemingly non-speech business. The U.S. Court of Appeals for the Ninth Circuit in 1996 affirmed a lower court's decision enjoining California's Santa Clara County from enforcing its ban on gun sales at the county's fairgrounds.[66] The county argued that the ban did not regulate speech, but rather regulated the unprotected conduct of selling guns. The trial court had found that "some type of speech is necessarily involved in the sale of any gun,"[67] and the appeals court ruled that the offer to buy constituted commercial speech. Hence, the ban had to pass First Amendment scrutiny. Although the county asserted an interest in curtailing gun possession, the court ruled that the ban did not directly advance that interest and enjoined enforcement.

In 1996, a federal district judge in California ruled that encryption software is speech. In a lawsuit challenging the federal government's export restrictions on encryption software, a mathematics graduate student from the University of California at Berkeley sought to post on the Internet the underlying source code for his own encryption program. The U.S. State Department informed him that he would need an export license to do so, and he sued. In a preliminary ruling, the judge decided that the source code was speech and that the government's regulation would have to face First Amendment scrutiny, stating: "This court can find no meaningful difference between computer language . . . and German or French. . . ."[68]

Freedom of speech issues also arise in connection with "English only" laws, requiring that all government business be conducted in English. This is discussed in Chapter 13.

Prior Restraints

Prior restraints of speech, such as prohibiting in advance a demonstration in a public area, are considered a more drastic infringement on free speech than permitting the speech to occur but punishing it afterwards. Restrictions concerning the time, place, and manner of speech are usually acceptable under the First Amendment; but regulations that restrict speech in traditional public forums are scrutinized closely, as in the following case.

68. Bernstein v. United States Dep't of State, 922 F. Supp. 1426 (N.D. Cal. 1996). *See also* Jared Sandberg, *Judge Rules Encryption Software Is Speech in Case on Export Curbs*, WALL ST. J., Apr. 18, 1996, at B7. For ultimate disposition at the district court level, *see* Bernstein v. United States Dep't of State, 974 F. Supp. 1288 (N.D. Cal. 1997) (declaring regulations as unconstitutional prior restraints in violation of the First Amendment, inasmuch as encryption software was singled out and treated differently from other software regulated under the Export Administration Regulations).

66. Nordyke v. Santa Clara County, Calif., 110 F.3d 707 (9th Cir. 1997).
67. Nordyke v. Santa Clara County, Calif., 933 F. Supp. 903 (N.D. Cal. 1996).

A CASE IN POINT | **SUMMARY**

CASE 2.6
FW/PBS, INC. v.
CITY OF DALLAS
Supreme Court
of the United States
493 U.S. 215 (1990).

FACTS In 1986, the city of Dallas adopted an ordinance regulating sexually oriented businesses. A sexually oriented business was defined as "an adult arcade, adult bookstore or adult video store, adult cabaret, adult motel, adult motion picture theater, adult theater, escort agency, nude model studio, or sexual encounter center." The ordinance regulated such businesses through zoning, licensing, and inspections. The ordinance also banned motels that rented rooms for fewer than ten hours.

The court of appeals upheld the ordinance as a content-neutral regulation of time, place, and manner. The court found that the ordinance was "designed to serve a substantial government interest" and allowed for "reasonable alternative avenues of communication." FW/PBS appealed.

ISSUE PRESENTED Can a city ban adult bookstores and theatres and motels that rent rooms for less than ten hours?

Case 2.6 continues

Case 2.6 continued

SUMMARY OF OPINION The U.S. Supreme Court viewed the ordinance, except for the ban on ten-hour motels, as a prior restraint on speech. Any system of prior restraint comes to the Supreme Court bearing a strong presumption that it may be unconstitutional. The Court held that the ordinance did not comply with the procedural safeguards for that type of regulation. The safeguards necessary are: (1) any prior restraint must be for no longer than necessary to preserve the status quo until a court hearing; (2) the court hearing must be promptly available; and (3) the would-be censor must bear both the burden of going to court and the burden of proof once in court.

The Supreme Court upheld, however, the part of the ordinance that prohibited motels from renting rooms for less than ten hours. Such rooms are often used for prostitution. Dismissing the argument that the ordinance unconstitutionally interfered with the right of association, Justice O'Connor stated: "Any 'personal bonds' that are formed from the use of a motel room for less than 10 hours are not those that have 'played a critical role in the culture and traditions of the nation by cultivating and transmitting shared ideals and beliefs.'"

RESULT The city of Dallas could legally ban motels from renting rooms for less than ten hours but could not ban adult bookstores and theatres.

COMMENTS It should be noted that no question was presented or decided concerning whether the material regulated by the ordinance was obscene. The regulations were struck down as unconstitutional prior restraints on speech.

Prior restraint is particularly important to members of the media, who may need to publish immediately or not at all. In such a case, prior restraint might keep a magazine, for example, from publishing damaging, confidential information. In the financial-derivatives case between Bankers Trust and Procter & Gamble (P&G), such a situation arose. During P&G's suit against Bankers Trust for negligent sale of financial products, *Business Week* obtained confidential documents about both parties that emerged from their court-approved secret discovery process. The litigants asked the trial court for a temporary restraining order (TRO) to keep *Business Week* from publishing the information. The court granted the TRO and later enjoined the magazine from ever publishing the information. *Business Week* appealed the injunction, and the U.S. Court of Appeals for the Sixth Circuit struck it down as a violation of the

First Amendment.[69] Noting that "[a] prior restraint comes to a court 'with a heavy presumption against its constitutional validity,'" the appeals court found the trial court's grounds for granting the TRO insufficient to meet the high standard required for prior restraint.

 Freedom of Religion

Two clauses of the First Amendment deal with religion. The Establishment Clause prohibits the establishment of a religion by the federal government and through the Fourteenth Amendment by state governments. The Free Exercise Clause prohibits certain, but not all, restrictions on the practice of religion. For example, in

---

69. Procter & Gamble v. Bankers Trust, 78 F.3d 219 (6th Cir. 1996).

Employment Division, Oregon Department of Human Resources v. Smith,[70] the Supreme Court held that an Oregon statute that made criminal the use of peyote, an hallucinogenic drug, was constitutional even though used in Native American religious ceremonies. Accordingly, the Court held that it was constitutional to deny unemployment benefits to persons fired for their ingestion of peyote for sacramental purposes at a ceremony of the Native American Church. In deciding *Smith*, the Court announced a new, lower standard: Generally applicable laws that burden but do not target religion need not be justified by a compelling state interest to pass muster under the Free Exercise Clause of the First Amendment. Until then, laws burdening religion had to serve a compelling state interest, as articulated in the 1963 case *Sherbert v. Verner.*[71]

Outraged at the apparent ease with which the government could now intrude on the free exercise of religion, civil libertarians and religious leaders pressed Congress to enact remedial legislation to protect religious liberty. In response, Congress passed the Religious Freedom and Restoration Act (RFRA). The act attempted to strengthen religious freedom by codifying the earlier *Sherbert* standard, that is, courts hearing Free Exercise challenges would once again have to apply the stricter compelling interests test.

Soon after the passage of RFRA, the issue of government burdens on free exercise emerged again. When a Texas church sought a building permit, it was refused in accordance with a local historic-preservation law. The church, relying on RFRA and the First Amendment, challenged the ordinance. The city challenged RFRA itself as unconstitutional and argued that *Smith* and its lower standard applied. The Supreme Court struck down RFRA as an unconstitutional encroachment by Congress on the powers of the judiciary.[72] The power to interpret the Constitution belongs to the judicial, not legislative, branch. Because the First Amendment is a limitation and not an enumerated power of Congress, it "does not empower Congress to regulate all federal law in order to achieve religious liberty."

The government must remain neutral in matters of religion. However, in *Jimmy Swaggart Ministries v. Board of Equalization,*[73] the Supreme Court held that the imposition of general taxes on the sale of religious materials does not contravene the Free Exercise Clause of the First Amendment. The tax was only a small fraction of any sale, and it applied neutrally to all relevant sales regardless of the nature of the seller or purchaser. There was no danger that the seller's religious activity was being singled out for special and burdensome treatment. The Court also held that the tax did not violate the Establishment Clause. There was little evidence of administrative entanglement between religion and the government; the government was not involved in the organization's day-to-day activities. The imposition of the tax did not require the state to inquire into the religious content of the items sold or the religious motivation behind selling or purchasing them. The items were subject to the tax regardless of the content or motive for selling or purchasing them.

Religion in government offices is a difficult issue that may to bring the Establishment and Free Exercise Clauses into conflict. In 1996, the U.S. Court of Appeals for the Ninth Circuit ruled unconstitutional a near total ban on religious activity in the workplace imposed by the California Department of Education's Child Nutrition and Food Distribution Division.[74] Tensions arose in the division between computer analyst Monte Tucker and his supervisor after Tucker refused to stop signing office memos with his name and the acronym "SOTLJC," which stood for "Servant of the Lord Jesus Christ." After several warnings, the supervisor suspended Tucker and ordered all employees not to display religious materials outside their cubicles, not to engage in any religious advocacy, and not to put any acronym or other symbol on office communications. Although the state argued its interests in avoiding workplace disruption and the appearance of religious endorsement (which would constitute a violation of the Establishment Clause), the appeals court found such interests outweighed by Tucker's constitutional right to talk about religion. Such issues also come up in the private sector, which is regulated by various antidiscrimination statutes.

---

70. 494 U.S. 872 (1990).

71. 374 U.S. 398 (1963).

72. Flores v. Boerne, Texas, 117 S. Ct. 2157 (1997).

73. 493 U.S. 378 (1990).

74. Tucker v. State of Cal. Dep't of Ed., 97 F.3d 1204 (9th Cir. 1996).

THE RESPONSIBLE MANAGER
Preserving Constitutional Rights

Although the Constitution is directed at establishing and limiting the powers of federal and state governments, its provisions have a profound effect on private actors in society. Federal and state governments impose a myriad of regulations on businesses and on individuals. Regulation of activities such as commercial speech, employment practices, admissions policies, securities issuance, and production procedures must comply with the limitations established by the Constitution.

It is important for managers to know the limitations that may constitutionally be imposed on individuals and organizations. Although the costs are usually high, at times it may be worth it for a company to challenge a regulation on constitutional grounds. This was true for the insurance companies that successfully challenged Proposition 103's freeze on rate increases for one year.

Managers often have an interest in influencing legislation or other government action through political action committees or direct lobbying. When pursuing change, it is useful to know the constitutional limitations placed on different segments of the government.

A manager should be aware of the rights deemed valuable by the Constitution. Although the Constitution addresses only government actions, managers of private organizations should be aware of the societal values reflected in the Constitution.

It may seem at times that constitutional law is far removed from the world of business. This is a misconception. Constitutional law is as close as the nearest private club that does not admit African Americans, Jews, women, or homosexuals. Such clubs may be important places for conducting business and for networking in general. A manager invited to become a member of such a club or to accompany his or her boss or client as a guest faces a tough choice.

Cities such as New York and states such as California have enacted ordinances to ban such clubs if they are of a certain size and are used for the conduct of business. Such laws must pass constitutional muster. The courts will balance the First Amendment rights of association and free speech against the government's social policy against discrimination.

Such ordinances relate not to political speech (the most protected form of speech) but to commercial speech. Commercial speech is not wholly without protection, however. The Supreme Court has held, for example, that lawyers must be permitted to advertise. But the Court permits greater regulation of commercial speech than political speech. For this reason, ordinances banning discriminatory clubs usually extend just to clubs where business is conducted. For example, in *Warfield v. Peninsula Golf Country Club*,[75] the California Supreme Court held that a private country club that allowed nonmembers for a fee to use its golf course, tennis courts, or dining areas was a "business establishment" and therefore subject to the state law prohibiting discrimination against women and minorities. It will generally be assumed that business is conducted in a private club if the manager's employer pays for club dues, meals, or drinks or if it is a company-sponsored event.

In contrast, the California Supreme Court held that the Boy Scouts of America was not a business establishment but rather a charitable, expressive, and social organization, whose formation and activities were unrelated to the promotion or advancement of the economic or business interests of its members.[76] As a result, the Boy Scouts could deny a gay former Eagle Scout's application for scoutmaster on the basis of his homosexuality[77] and dismiss two Cub Scouts from their den for refusing to affirm a belief in God.[78]

---

75. 896 P.2d 776 (Cal. 1995).

76. Curran v. Mount Diablo Council of the Boy Scouts of America, 952 P.2d 218 (Cal. 1998). *Contra* Dale v. Boy Scouts of America, 706 A.2d 270 (N.J. Super. Ct. App. Div. 1998).

77. *Id.*

78. Randall v. Orange County Council, 952 P.2d 261 (Cal. 1998).

INSIDE STORY

EFFECT OF POLITICS ON SUPREME COURT APPOINTMENTS

The nomination process for the United States Supreme Court has grown increasingly politicized and controversial over time. Televised Supreme Court nomination hearings before the Senate Judiciary Committee have riveted the nation's attention as few other internal events in Congress have. Being nominated to the Supreme Court now brings along with it a process of public scrutiny akin to running for national political office. Politics, however, is not new to the process.

Franklin Delano Roosevelt was probably the first president in history to attempt explicitly and publicly to use the power of judicial appointment to change the Court's position on the key political issues of the day. Frustrated with the Supreme Court's overturning of much of his New Deal legislation on the basis of an historical commitment to limited government, President Roosevelt introduced his now-famous Court-packing bill that would have added one justice to the Court for every sitting Justice who had reached the age of 70. The bill would have increased the Court's membership to 15 and given Roosevelt a clear majority.

Although the bill was never passed by the Senate, the threat was clear. The Court quickly capitulated and abandoned its commitment to limited government, especially regarding economic liberty. One month after the plan was announced, Justice Roberts inexplicably changed his position and voted to overturn *Morehead v. Tipaldo*,[79] which had struck down New York's minimum wage law in 1936. The statute was subsequently upheld in *West Coast Hotel v. Parrish*.[80] This "switch in time that saved nine" allowed Roosevelt to implement his program of massive federal regulation. Over the next six years, Roosevelt made nine appointments to the Court. At the time of his death during his fourth term, Roosevelt had completely revamped the Court, secured passage of his New Deal legislation, and ushered in a new era of constitutional law.

Although Roosevelt's motivations were clearly political, other presidents have made considerations of diversity and representation key to their selection of nominees. Thurgood Marshall was clearly qualified for the nomination, having argued a number of monumental cases before the Court, including *Brown v. Board of Education*,[81] the landmark school-desegregation case. President Lyndon Johnson's appointment of Marshall also took into consideration the need for African Americans to be represented on the Court for the first time. Similarly, the appointments of Justices Sandra Day O'Connor (the first woman member of the Court) and Clarence Thomas by Presidents Reagan and Bush, respectively, served to expand and maintain the gender and racial diversity of the Court.

President Dwight Eisenhower's 1953 appointment of Earl Warren as the Chief Justice further demonstrates the influence of politics on the nomination process. At the time, Warren was the Republican governor of California and had been a critical factor in Eisenhower's 1952 bid for the presidency. Eisenhower repaid the political debt with the nomination, despite misgivings by powerful Republicans, such as Vice President Richard Nixon, about Warren's progressive stance on certain issues. Although Warren was believed to be a moderate Republican at the time of the nomination, the Warren Court became the most liberal, activist court in history, leading a constitutional revolution in the application of the Bill of Rights to the states.

The executive office holds the power to identify and nominate individuals to the judiciary. A cursory investigation reveals that some combination of personal friendship and political compatibility are often the overriding factors for appointment. The nomination of Abe Fortas in 1965 is one example. In 1965, Adlai Stevenson, then U.S. Representative to the United Nations, died of a heart attack while on a visit to London, England. As the nation mourned the death of a great public servant, President Lyndon Johnson recognized a tremendous opportunity. He was swift and deliberate in his action: Six days after Stevenson's death, Johnson nominated Arthur Goldberg, then an associate justice of the Supreme Court, to succeed Stevenson as

U.S. representative to the United Nations. This created a vacancy on the Court and sparked a battle over its composition.

Certainly, Johnson was not ignorant of the eminent power and prestige of the Court. Johnson had won a seat in the House of Representatives in 1937, about the time that President Roosevelt was threatening to "pack" the Supreme Court. Johnson had watched as the Court struck down his party's New Deal legislation.

He had also witnessed, firsthand, the power of the Court. After serving in Washington, Johnson ran for a Texas seat in the Senate. Following a narrow victory in the primary, Johnson's opponent made allegations of voting fraud and obtained a temporary restraining order prohibiting the secretary of state from printing Johnson's name on the ballot for the general elections. Despite an appeal by Johnson, the injunction remained in effect. Immediately thereafter a young lawyer by the name of Abe Fortas took over the case. Fortas argued Johnson's case to Justice Black in the U.S. Court of Appeals for the Fifth Circuit. Fortas won the case, as did Johnson the Senate election.

Two days after removing Goldberg from the Court, President Johnson made another announcement. On July 22, 1965, he appointed his longtime friend Abe Fortas as associate justice of the Supreme Court. The appointment of Fortas to the bench is a clear example of how friendship, both personal and political, influences the nomination process. President Johnson, in nominating Fortas,

not only placed a close friend on the Supreme Court but repaid an old political debt in the process.

Another pivotal nomination in the recent past was that of Robert Bork, a well-known constitutional scholar, by President Ronald Reagan in 1987. Bork was the last nominee to the Supreme Court to have a "paper trail" of opinions and writings on constitutional matters. The nightmare Senate hearings, in which Bork was forced to attempt to explain to the senators and the general public the reasoning behind some of his more radical statements over the years, of which there were many, were enough to convince any president of the impossibility today of nominating someone with that kind of record. The hearings surrounding Bork's nomination were controversial, as was Bork's constitutional scholarship. The Senate probed deeply and substantively for information central to Bork's constitutional views in an effort to determine whether Bork would overturn widely accepted, mainstream constitutional law. One newspaper even went so far as to gather the record of his movie rentals from his neighborhood video store and publish them. In the end, Bork's views and the resultant political uproar across the nation led to his being denied confirmation to the Court.

In response to this hostile and extensive probing by the Senate, more recent presidents have attempted to nominate individuals who have produced little or no legal opinions on critical issues. The nomination by President George Bush of David Souter, often re-

ferred to as a "stealth candidate" due to his anonymity prior to nomination, is illustrative.

The 1991 nomination of Clarence Thomas to the "black seat" on the Supreme Court, vacated by the resignation of Justice Thurgood Marshall, was supposed to be similarly quiet but resulted in another Bork-like public spectacle, the effects of which are still rippling throughout the country. The retirement of Justice Marshall, a staunch liberal activist, left the Court without an African-American member for the first time since the 1960s. President Bush nominated Thomas, a 43-year-old African-American conservative federal judge, to fill that void. Thomas seemed to be a safe bet: His writings and opinions were sparse and generally without controversy. Thomas even went so far as to deny ever having engaged in a debate on the issue of abortion:

> **Senator Leahy:** Have you [Judge Thomas] ever had discussion of *Roe v. Wade*[82] other than in this room, in the 17 or 18 years it's has been there?

> **Judge Thomas:** Only, I guess, Senator, in the fact in the most general sense that other individuals express concerns one way or the other, and you listen and you try to be thoughtful. If you are asking me whether or not I have ever debated the contents of it, the answer to that is no, Senator.[83]

Even this denial, preposterous as it seemed to some, could not derail Thomas's quest for a seat on this nation's highest court. Without extensive writings to defend, Thomas gained wide support in the Senate.

However, after completing an initial hearing, Thomas was called back before the Judiciary Committee to face allegations of sexual harassment put forward by African-American law professor and former colleague, Anita Hill. The ensuing melee, although shedding fascinating light on the intersection of race, gender, and ideology in the Senate and society in general, resulted in no substantial conclusions as to the truth of the allegations. Rather it became a circus in which actors on both sides paraded before the committee, asserting their versions of the truth.

In the end, only three senators, all Democrats, admitted to changing their votes. Thomas was approved by a vote of 52 to 48. Many members of the Senate sought to avoid the political fallout on both sides of the issue. Responding to allegations during the hearings about Anita Hill's mental stability, Senator Nancy Landon Kassebaum (R-Kansas), who voted to confirm Thomas, attempted to maintain the support of women, as well as that of her political party. In response to questions of committee members Arlen Spector and Howell Heflin that suggested that Professor Hill's accusations were the product of wild "fantasy and mental instability,"[84] Kassebaum condemned the tactics employed to discredit the allegations of misconduct, stating that she "found no evidence that Professor Hill was mentally unstable, is inclined to wild fantasy, or is part of a decade-long conspiracy to get Clarence Thomas." However, she also declined to change her vote in favor of Thomas's confirmation,

because she "saw no compelling reason to overturn that judgment."[85] Southern Democrats, responding to pressure from their large African-American and conservative constituencies, also refused to change their votes after Thomas, undaunted by the allegations, charged the committee with conducting a "high-tech lynching of uppity Blacks." This aggressive challenge to the Senators dulled the edge of their remaining questions.

Though public opinion polls following the hearings found that more Americans believed Judge Thomas than Professor Hill, the image of 12 white men grilling an African-American woman about her charges of sexual harassment set in motion a political movement that resulted in the election of historic numbers of women and African Americans to both the House of Representatives and the Senate. In 1992, Carol Mosely Braun became the first African-American woman to serve in the U.S. Senate, and California became the first state in history to send two women, Dianne Feinstein and Barbara Boxer, to the Senate. Partially in an effort to change the image of the Judiciary Committee, both Senators Braun and Feinstein were asked to join the committee.

Two years later, in 1993, President Bill Clinton nominated Ruth Bader Ginsburg to the Court. The politics of that nomination swirled around the question of whether the Senate should apply an abortion "litmus test" to her appointment, in light of the changing Supreme Court position on the

pivotal issue of whether a woman has a constitutional right to an abortion. President Clinton sought to nominate a person who would receive widespread support from the Senate Judiciary Committee. Any indication of a controversial hearing was immediately dispelled in Judge Ginsburg's opening remarks. In an effort to preempt potential litmus test-type questions, she hinted at the inappropriateness of deciding a case in advance, but promised to impartially hear each case before the Court "without reaching out to cover cases not yet seen." She stated:

> You are well aware that I come to this proceeding to be judged as a judge not an advocate. Because I am and hope to continue to be a judge it would be wrong for me to say or preview in this legislative chamber how I would cast my vote on questions the Supreme Court may be called upon to decide. Were I to rehearse here what I would say and how I would reason on such questions, I would act injudiciously. Judges in our civil system are bound to decide concrete cases not abstract issues. Each case comes to court based on particular facts and its decisions should turn on those facts and governing law stated and explained in light of the particular arguments the parties or their representatives present. A judge sworn to decide impartially can offer no forecasts, no hints, for that would show not only disregard for the specifics of a particular case; it would display disdain for the entire judicial process.[86]

Judge Ginsburg came to the hearing as a judge on the U.S. Court of Appeals for the District of Columbia, where she had served since being appointed to the bench by President Jimmy Carter in 1980. Her 13 years of judicial experience, coupled with impressive credentials, won her nearly unanimous support from the public as well as the Judiciary Committee. Justice Ginsburg was easily confirmed by a vote of 96 to 3, and her hearing served as an opportunity to reduce hostility in the nomination process.

One year later, President Clinton had another opportunity to nominate a justice to the Court. Having learned from his success with Justice Ginsburg and the difficulties of his predecessors, he avoided controversy and nominated "technocrat" Stephen Breyer, a judge on the U.S. Court of Appeals for the First Circuit known for his academic writings on regulatory economics. One reporter covering Breyer's nomination hearing characterized it this way:

> The most unlikely story of the moment is that the Senate Judiciary Committee's hearings on Stephen Breyer's appointment to the Supreme Court unexpectedly became a bore, albeit a pleasant bore. That is to Breyer's advantage, for it signals an overdue cooling of the passions superheated by earlier Supreme Court confirmation fights. . . .[87]

Like Ginsburg, Breyer successfully avoided controversy and received Senate confirmation with little public attention.

Whether these nominations demonstrate a return to the earlier practice of polite and deliberative advice and consent by the Senate or a temporary respite from raging political winds remains to be seen. Court watchers expect to know soon, however, as Chief Justice Rehnquist and Justices O'Connor and Stevens are all thought likely to leave the Court in the near future.

---

79. 298 U.S. 587 (1936).

80. *Id.*

81. 347 U.S. 483 (1954).

82. 410 U.S. 113 (1973).

83. Nomination of Judge Clarence Thomas to be Associate Justice of the Supreme Court of the United States: Hearings Before the Senate Comm. on the Judiciary, 102nd Cong., 1st. Sess. 222 (1991).

84. *Id.*

85. Adam Clymer, *The Thomas Confirmation: The Senate's Futile Search for Safe Ground*, N.Y. TIMES, Oct. 16, 1991.

86. Nomination of Judge Ruth Bader Ginsburg to be Associate Justice of the Supreme Court of the United States: Hearings Before the Senate Comm. on the Judiciary, 103rd Cong., 1st. Sess. 222 (1993).

87. Edwin M. Yoder, *Breyer's Hearings Lack Passion of Bork's*, DENVER POST, July 18, 1994, at B7.

KEY WORDS AND PHRASES

appellate jurisdiction **41**
bicameralism **44**
bill of attainder **56**
eminent domain **63**
executive privilege **43**
ex post facto **56**
federalism **40**
judicial review **41**

legislative veto **44**
line item veto **44**
penumbra **62**
original jurisdiction **41**
police power **45**
preempt **41**
prior restraints **72**
procedural due process **58**

rational basis test **64**
separation of powers **41**
strict scrutiny **64**
subject matter jurisdiction **41**
substantive due process **58**
undue burden **52**

QUESTIONS AND CASE PROBLEMS

1. What are the three branches of the U.S. government? What functions does each branch serve? How are they checked and balanced?

2. Chemical Waste Management owned and operated a hazardous waste treatment, storage, and disposal facility in Alabama. Alabama is one of only 16 states that have commercial hazardous waste landfills. In the late 1980s, the annual rate of hazardous waste received by the facility more than doubled. More alarming to some Alabamans, 90% of the tonnage buried each year was shipped in from other states. The Alabama government reacted to this situation by passing legislation that limited the amount of hazardous wastes or substances that could be disposed of in any one-year period. The new law also imposed an additional fee on waste generated outside of Alabama that was disposed of at a commercial hazardous waste site in Alabama. Chemical Waste Management challenged the new law as unconstitutional.

a. Is the new law constitutional? [*Chemical Waste Mgmt., Inc. v. Hunt*, 112 S. Ct. 2009 (1992)]

b. Instead of alarm over imports of waste from out of state, the municipal government of Clarkstown, New York, was concerned that too little waste was being received from anywhere to make the operation of its waste facility economical. Without the assurance of such a local facility, such waste might have to travel further and expose more of the state to danger from spills, leaks, and highway accidents. As a result, the town passed an ordinance requiring that all producers of nonhazardous solid waste in the town have it treated at the town's facility or pay a "tipping fee" to the town. Producers challenged the law as unconstitutional. What result? [*C&A Carbone v. Clarkstown, N.Y.*, 511 U.S. 383 (1994)]

3. In an exercise of its police power, Oregon enacted a bottle bill that required retailers of beer or carbonated beverages to accept empty containers in exchange for a statutory refund value. The bill also prohibited retail sale of beverages in metal containers with detachable pull-top openers. The purpose of the legislation was to reduce litter in Oregon and reduce injuries to people and animals caused by discarded pull-tops. Manufacturers of cans and out-of-state beverage bottlers challenged the legislation on the ground that it imposed an undue burden on interstate commerce and was thus invalid under the Commerce Clause of the Constitution.

a. What are the grounds on which state legislation may be struck down as violating the Commerce Clause?

b. Assuming that the manufacturers and canners showed that the bill would have a substantial impact on interstate commerce, how could the state of Oregon justify the legislation? [*American Can Co. v. Oregon Liquor Control Comm'n*, 517 P.2d 691 (Or. Ct. App. 1973)]

4. In 1994, Congress enacted the Violence Against Women Act, making crimes of violence motivated by gender a federal offense. The legislative history contained Congress's finding that such violence had an adverse effect on interstate commerce. Making use of the new law, a freshman at Virginia Tech in Blacksburg, Virginia, sued two football players in federal court for allegedly raping her in a university dorm within minutes of meeting her. The football players challenged the statute as unconstitutional.

a. Does Congress have the power, under the Commerce Clause, to make gender-based violence illegal? [*Brzonkala v. Virginia Polytechnic Inst. and State Univ.* 132 F.3d 949 (4th Cir. 1997)]

b. Congress enacted legislation making carjacking a federal crime. Its stated justification included transportation of carjacked vehicles across state lines, either in parts or intact, and the effect of car theft on insurance rates. Does Congress have the power, under the Commerce Clause, to make carjacking a federal crime? [*United States v. Oliver*, 60 F.3d 547 (9th Cir. 1995)]

5. The city of San Diego enacted an ordinance regulating billboards. The ordinance permitted billboards for on-site commercial advertising but not for other commercial advertising or for noncommercial communications. On-site commercial advertising was defined as a sign advertising goods or services available on the property where the sign was located. The city's stated purposes in enacting the ordinance were to reduce traffic hazards caused by distracting sign displays and to preserve and improve the appearance of the city.

a. Does the portion of the ordinance limiting commercial billboard advertising to on-site billboards violate the Constitution?

b. Does the portion of the ordinance banning the use of billboards for noncommercial communications violate the Constitution? [*Metromedia v. City of San Diego*, 453 U.S. 490 (1981)]

c. Can a municipality constitutionally prohibit all residential signs except For Sale and warning signs in order to prevent visual clutter? [*City of Ladue v. Gilleo*, 512 U.S. 43 (1994)]

6. The New York City Transit Authority had a rule excluding from employment any person who had participated in a methadone maintenance treatment program for heroin addiction. The rule was challenged under the Fourteenth Amendment's Equal Protection Clause and Due Process Clause.

a. What level of scrutiny should a court use to analyze the classification created by the transit authority's rule?

b. What arguments might the plaintiffs make for striking down the rule? What arguments might the transit authority make to justify the rule? [*New York City Transit Auth. v. Beazer*, 440 U.S. 568 (1979)]

7. Mr. Thomas, a Jehovah's Witness, was transferred to a department producing military tanks. He quit his job because his religious beliefs forbade participation in the production of armaments. The Indiana Employment Security Review Board denied Thomas's claim for unemployment benefits because a statute made benefits unavailable to those who voluntarily leave their employment without good cause. Did Indiana violate Thomas's constitutional rights? Frame the legal and ethical arguments for and against requiring Indiana to pay Thomas unemployment benefits. [*Thomas v. Review Bd.*, 450 U.S. 707 (1981)]

8. A Wisconsin law permitted creditors to freeze the wages of a debtor (in legal terms, to garnish the wages) until the completion of a trial to determine the debtor's liability. Under the law, creditors' lawyers could effect a garnishment by requesting a summons from a court and serving it on the debtor's employer. No notice to the debtor was required until ten days after the summons was served. Did the law authorizing garnishment without prior notice and opportunity for a hearing violate the constitutional rights of debtors? Explain why or why not. [*Sniadach v. Family Fin. Corp. of Bay View*, 395 U.S. 337 (1969)]

9. John Doe filed a complaint with New York City's Commission on Human Rights alleging that he was not hired because he was a single gay male suspected of having HIV. His case was settled and the city made public the terms of the conciliation agreement. Did New York City violate John Doe's right to privacy? [*Doe v. New York City*, 15 F.3d. 264 (2d Cir. 1994)]

MANAGER'S DILEMMA

10. Each chamber of Congress is responsible for setting and enforcing its own procedural rules to facilitate the conduct of its legislative business. The Senate's rules currently forbid the use of mechanical devices that, by their presence, "distract, interrupt or inconvenience the business or members of the Senate." Consequently, senators may not bring cellular phones or televisions onto the floor of the Senate. Recently, a Senator asked the chamber's Rules Committee to allow him to bring his laptop computer onto the Senate floor. The Senator argued that use of laptops would help senators track legislation and make more productive use of their time during those long and sometimes arcane floor debates. As well, several aides carrying briefcases are often needed to bring along material that could fit onto a single disk. Other senators worried about destroying the "mystique" of the Senate floor, distractions from the incessant click of keyboards, and the potential for on-line lobbying.

What other arguments are there, both for and against the request? What rule makes the most sense in light of the Senate's responsibilities under the Constitution? What position should a manager instruct his or her lobbyist to promote when lobbying members of the Rules Committee?

INTERNET SOURCES	
The Constitution page of the Louisiana State University's Department of Political Science contains annotated text of the U.S. Constitution, other founding documents, and related research.	http://www.lsu.edu/guests/poli/public_html/const.html

Internet Sources continue

Internet Sources continued

The Legal Information Institute page at Cornell University Law School offers a wide variety of resources related to the U.S. Constitution, including its various articles and amendments and related historical documents.	http://www.law.cornell.edu/topics/constitutional.html
The International Constitutional Law page at the University of Würzburg in Germany addresses constitutional law around the world and contains numerous national constitutions and related materials and links.	http://www.uni-wuerzburg.de/law
The Library of Congress's Broadside Collection offers a collection of materials concerning the formation of the U.S. Constitution.	http://lcweb2.loc.gov/ammem/bdsds/bdsdhome.html
This private, individual page contains the constitutions of the separate states and links to related newsgroups.	http://teaminfinity.com/~ralph/states/states.html
The Constitution Society's home page offers a variety of materials about the U.S. constitutional republic, including discussions of various constitutional principles, founding documents, and related resources.	http://www.constitution.org
Yahoo's own Constitutional Law page offers links to related sites and the opportunity to search for specific items.	http://www.yahoo.com/law/constitutional
White House	http://www.whitehouse.gov
U.S. House of Representatives	http://www.house.gov
U.S. Senate	http://www.senate.gov

CHAPTER 3

Courts, Sources of Law, and Litigation

INTRODUCTION

Equal Justice under the Law

"Equal justice under the law" is the inscription on the front of the United States Supreme Court building in Washington, D.C. It is a reminder that the judicial system is intended to protect the legal rights of those who come before a court. In a litigation-prone society, managers should understand the judicial system and be prepared to use it to protect their rights and the rights of their companies.

Chapter Overview

This chapter begins with a discussion of the federal and state court systems, including subject matter and personal jurisdiction and choice of law. It continues with a description of the sources of the law, including constitutions, statutes, regulations, and common law. The chapter outlines the litigation process, including discovery, the attorney–client privilege, class actions, various trial strategies for companies involved in a lawsuit, and document-retention programs. Alternatives to litigation, such as mediation and arbitration, are discussed in Chapter 4.

 ## How to Read a Case Citation

When an appellate court decides a case, the court writes an opinion, which is published in one or more *reporters*—collections of court opinions. Some trial courts also publish opinions. The citation of a case (the *cite*) includes the following information:

1. The plaintiff's name
2. The defendant's name
3. The volume number and title of the reporter in which the case is reported
4. The page number at which the case report begins

5. The court that decided the case (if the court is not indicated, it is understood to be the state or U.S. Supreme Court, depending on the reporter in which the case appears)
6. The year in which the case was decided

For example, *Chrysler Corporation v. Ford Motor Company*, 972 F. Supp. 1097 (E.D. Mich. 1997), indicates that in 1997 an opinion was issued in a case involving the Chrysler Corporation as the plaintiff with the Ford Motor Company as the defendant. The case was decided in the United States District Court for the Eastern District of Michigan. The case is reported in volume 972 of the Federal Supplement, beginning on page 1097. *In Re Barney's, Inc.*, 206 B.R. 328 (Bankr. S.D.N.Y 1997), refers to the bankruptcy proceedings of Barney's, Incorporated, the upscale clothing store. The case is reported in the Bankruptcy Reporter, volume 206, beginning on page 328. The parenthetical information indicates that this is a United States Bankruptcy Court sitting in the Southern District of New York.

Some cases are reported in more than one reporter. For example, the famous New York taxicab case discussed in Chapter 20, *Walkovszky v. Carlton*, is cited as 18 N.Y.2d 414, 276 N.Y.S.2d 585, 223 N.E.2d 6 (N.Y. 1966). One may locate this case in volume 18 of the second series of New York Reports, in volume 276 of the second series of the New York Supplement, or in volume 223 of the second series of the North Eastern Reports.

When quoting a particular passage from an opinion, one should include the page number on which the information is found after the page number at which the case report begins. A comma should separate the two numbers. For example, suppose one wanted to quote the specific page where the Court of Appeals of Virginia ruled that the plaintiff was entitled to worker's compensation benefits due to his exposure to asbestos while working for E. I. DuPont de Nemours & Company. The cite would read: *Jones v. E. I. DuPont De Nemours & Co.*, 480 S.E.2d 129, 130 (Va. Ct. App. 1997). Thus, the case report begins on page 129 of volume 480 of the second series of the South Eastern Reporter, and the cited material is on page 130. The parenthetical information identifies the adjudicating body as the Court of Appeals of Virginia and the year as 1997.

When the lawsuit is originally filed, the case name appears as *plaintiff v. defendant*. If the case is appealed, the case name usually appears as *appellant* or *petitioner* (the person who is appealing the case or seeking a writ of *certiorari*) *v. appellee* or *respondent* (the other party). So if the defendant lost at the trial level and appealed the decision to a higher court, the name of the defendant (now the appellant) would appear first in the case citation.

The Court System

The United States has two judicial systems: federal and state. Federal and state courts have different subject matter jurisdiction. In general, federal courts are courts of limited subject matter jurisdiction, meaning they can adjudicate only certain types of cases. The jurisdiction of the federal courts arises from the U.S. Constitution

and statutes enacted by Congress. By contrast, state courts have general subject matter jurisdiction and can therefore hear any type of dispute. The jurisdiction of a state's courts arises from that state's constitution and statutes. The two coexisting judicial systems are a result of the federalism created by the U.S. Constitution, which gives certain powers to the federal government while other powers remain with the states.

The basic structure of the federal and state court systems is diagrammed in Exhibit 3.1. In practice, the structure of the U.S. court system is more complex than the diagram indicates. For example, an applicant may appeal an adverse decision from the U.S. Patent and Trademark Office to the Board of Patent Appeals and Interferences. The person may then appeal an unfavorable ruling from this court to the Court of Appeals for the Federal Circuit. Alternatively, the applicant may appeal the unfavorable ruling of the Board of Patent Appeals and Interferences by filing a civil action, in the U.S. District Court for the District of Columbia, against the Commissioner of the U.S. Patent and Trademark Office.

Federal Jurisdiction

Federal courts derive their legal power to hear civil cases from three sources: diversity jurisdiction, federal question jurisdiction, and jurisdiction when the United States is a party.

Diversity Jurisdiction

Diversity jurisdiction exists when a lawsuit is between citizens of two different states and the amount in controversy, exclusive of interest and all costs, exceeds $50,000. The purpose of the monetary requirement is to prevent trivial cases from overwhelming the federal judicial system.

Diversity jurisdiction was traditionally justified by the fear that state courts might be biased against the out-of-state party. In federal district court, all litigants are in a neutral forum, and there should be no local prejudice for the home team.

Most diversity cases are decided under state laws and thus could also be resolved in state court. The following landmark case addressed the question of whether state or federal law should apply to a suit brought in a federal court exercising its diversity jurisdiction.

EXHIBIT 3.1   Hierarchy of the Federal and State Court Systems

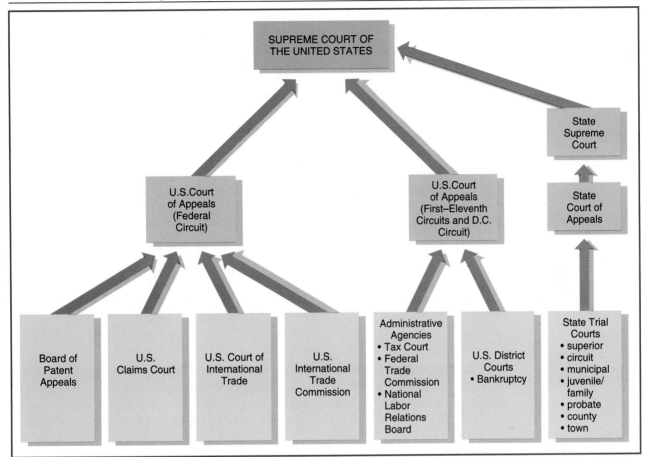

| A CASE IN POINT | SUMMARY |

CASE 3.1
ERIE RAILROAD CO.
v. TOMPKINS

Supreme Court of the
United States
304 U.S. 64 (1938).

FACTS   Tompkins, a citizen of Pennsylvania, was injured on a dark night by a passing freight train owned by the Erie Railroad Company. At the time of the accident, Tompkins was walking along the railroad's right of way near Hughestown, Pennsylvania. Tompkins alleged that the accident occurred through the negligent operation or maintenance of the train; that he was rightfully on the premises because he was walking along a commonly used footpath; and that he was struck by something that looked like a door protruding from one of the moving cars. Tompkins filed his lawsuit in federal district court in New York because Erie Railroad was a corporation of that state. Erie Railroad denied liability.

Case 3.1 continues

Case 3.1 continued

Pennsylvania had no statute applicable to this case. Cases of this type were decided under common law, that is, the body of law created by court decisions. Erie Railroad contended that the common law of Pennsylvania, and not what was known as federal common law, should apply to this cause of action. Under Pennsylvania common law, as declared by the Pennsylvania Supreme Court, persons who use the pathways alongside railroad tracks, rather than the proper crossways, are trespassers. According to Pennsylvania law, a railroad is not liable for injuries to trespassers resulting from its negligent actions.

The district court judge refused to instruct the jury about the Pennsylvania law; the case went to the jury under federal common law. The jury awarded Tompkins $30,000. Erie Railroad appealed. The court of appeals held that the jury did not need to consider whether the law of Pennsylvania applied in this situation because the issue at trial concerned "general law" rather than the specific law in Pennsylvania. The court stated that when there is an issue of general law, such as the responsibility of a railroad for injuries caused by its servants, then, in the absence of a state statute, a federal court is free to decide what the common law of the state is or should be. Thus, the court of appeals affirmed the jury verdict. Erie Railroad appealed.

ISSUE PRESENTED   Should state or federal law govern cases in federal court sitting in diversity actions that do not concern matters governed by the U.S. Constitution or acts of Congress?

SUMMARY OF OPINION   The U.S. Supreme Court ruled that in cases where a federal court exercises its diversity jurisdiction, it must apply the relevant state law as declared by either the state's legislature or its highest court. The Court further ruled that a federal court cannot ignore state law unless the lawsuit concerns the U.S. Constitution or a federal statute. In essence, the Supreme Court abolished the notion of federal common law in diversity cases.

RESULT   The Supreme Court reversed the decision of the court of appeals. Erie Railroad won the right to have the case tried using Pennsylvania law. Because under Pennsylvania law plaintiff Tompkins was considered a trespasser to whom Erie Railroad owed no duty of care, Erie Railroad was not liable to Tompkins.

COMMENTS   The *Erie doctrine*, as the holding of this case is known, serves an important purpose. It ensures that the outcome of a case in federal court will be similar to the outcome in a state court because the same law will govern either adjudication. This prevents litigants (the parties to a lawsuit) from *forum shopping* between federal and state courts in an attempt to have the more favorable law govern their dispute. Essentially, after *Erie*, a federal court sitting in diversity will apply the relevant law as if it were sitting as a state court.

When litigants are in federal court due to diversity jurisdiction, they cannot choose which state's law will govern the dispute. The court itself makes this decision, applying well-established conflict-of-law rules, which prescribe which state's law should apply to a particular kind of case.

Determining Citizenship   A natural person is a citizen of the state wherein the person has his or her legal residence or domicile. A person may have a house or residence in more than one state. A person is a citizen, however, only of the state that he or she considers home.

A corporation, on the other hand, may have dual citizenship. A corporation is deemed a citizen of the state in which it has been incorporated and of the state where the company has its principal place of business. Federal courts usually apply one of three tests in determining where a company engaged in multistate operations has its principal place of business.

The first is the nerve center test. To find the corporation's nerve center, courts consider (1) where the executive and administrative offices are located; (2) where the income tax return is filed; and (3) where the directors and shareholders meet. The second test focuses on the place of operations. This test requires locating the majority of the corporation's physical operations, such as manufacturing facilities or offices. The total activity test, a combination of the first two tests, considers all aspects of the corporate entity, including the nature and scope of the company's activities. The total activity test is gaining popularity among the courts.

Federal Question Jurisdiction

A *federal question* exists when the dispute concerns federal law, namely a legal right arising under the U.S. Constitution, a federal statute, an administrative regulation issued by a federal government agency, federal common law, or a treaty of the United States. There is no minimum monetary requirement for lawsuits involving a federal question.

United States Is a Party

Federal courts have jurisdiction over all lawsuits in which the U.S. government, or an officer or agency thereof, is the plaintiff or defendant. As with federal question jurisdiction, there is no minimum monetary requirement for lawsuits where the United States is a party.

Federal Courts

The main function of the federal courts is to interpret the Constitution and laws of the United States. George Washington told the Supreme Court in 1790, "I have al-

ways been persuaded that the stability and success of the National Government, and consequently the happiness of the American people, would depend in a considerable degree on the interpretation and execution of its laws."

President Washington signed into law the Senate's first piece of legislation, entitled "An Act to Establish the Judicial Courts of the United States." This act created federal trial courts. Two years later, Congress created the courts of appeal. The three-tiered system of district courts, courts of appeal, and the Supreme Court remains today. The president of the United States nominates each judge who serves on these federal courts. The United States Senate, pursuant to its "advice and consent" power, then votes to approve or reject the judicial nominees. The Constitution does not impose any age or citizenship requirements on judicial candidates. Once confirmed by the Senate, federal judges have a lifetime appointment to the bench. They may be removed from office only by legislative impeachment if they violate the law. As a result, the federal judiciary is more independent than either the executive or legislative branches; lifetime tenure protects federal judges from public reprisal for making unpopular or difficult decisions.

U.S. District Courts

The U.S. district courts are the trial courts of the federal system. Currently, the country is divided into 94 judicial districts. Each state has at least one district, and the more populous states have as many as four. Exhibit 3.2 shows various districts. Many districts have two or more divisions. For example, the main location for the U.S. District Court for the Western District of Texas is in San Antonio. However, the Western District of Texas also has courts in Austin, El Paso, Midland, and Waco. Thus, a plaintiff may file its lawsuit with the nearest federal district court, provided, of course, that the court has jurisdiction over the particular controversy.

U.S. Courts of Appeal

The primary functions of a court of appeals are (1) to review decisions of the trial courts within its territory; (2) to review decisions of certain administrative agencies and commissions; and (3) to issue *writs*, or orders, to lower courts or to litigants. Only final decisions of lower courts are appealable. A decision is final if it conclusively resolves an issue in a dispute or the entire controversy.

Cases before the courts of appeal are usually presented to a panel of three judges. Occasionally, all the judges of a court of appeals will sit together to hear and decide a particularly important or close case. This is called an *en banc* (or *in banc*) *hearing*. The court of appeals can either affirm or reverse the decision of the lower court. It may also *vacate*, or nullify, the previous court's ruling and *remand* the case—send it back to the lower court for reconsideration. Frequently, the panel of judges will decide an appeal based upon the legal briefs or written memoranda submitted to the court, rather than hearing oral arguments presented by the lawyers.

There are 13 courts of appeal, one for each of the 12 regional circuits in the United States and one for the federal circuit. The Ninth Circuit, encompassing 10 states and Guam, is the largest circuit, with 28 active judges. The Court of Appeals for the First Circuit has only 6 active judges. Exhibit 3.2 shows the geographical boundaries of the circuits.

The Court of Appeals for the Federal Circuit, created in 1982, does not have jurisdiction over a specific geographic region but rather hears appeals from various specialized federal courts, including the Claims Court, the Court of International Trade, and the Internal Trade Commission. Exhibit 3.3 lists the states and territories included within each circuit.

Specialized Federal Courts

The federal system has several specialized courts that resolve legal disputes within particular subject areas.

EXHIBIT 3.2 Geographical Boundaries of the U.S. District Courts and Circuit Courts of Appeal

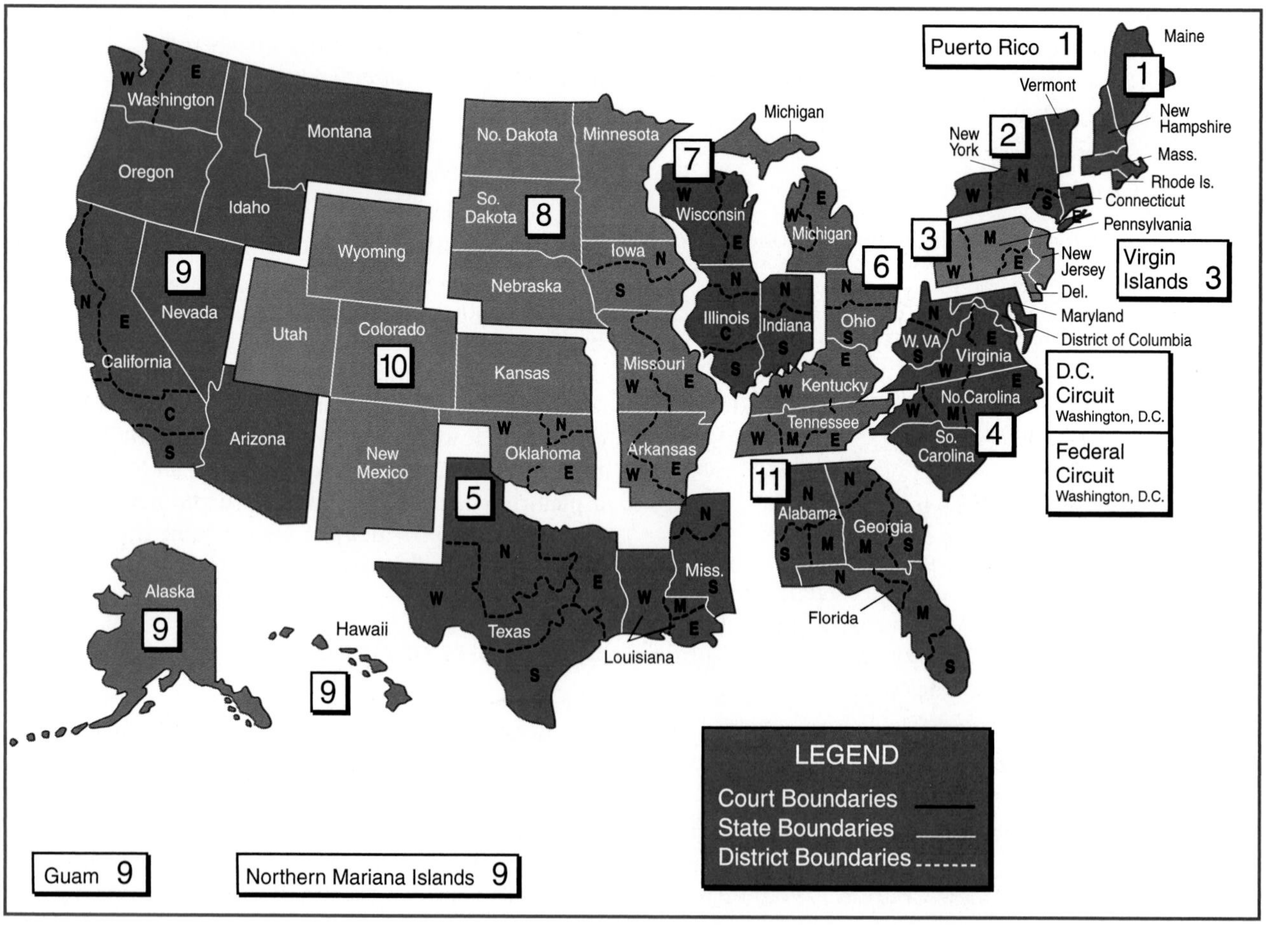

EXHIBIT 3.3   United States Courts of Appeal

CIRCUIT	REGION
District of Columbia	District of Columbia
First	Maine, Massachusetts, New Hampshire, Puerto Rico, Rhode Island
Second	Connecticut, New York, Vermont
Third	Delaware, New Jersey, Pennsylvania, Virgin Islands
Fourth	Maryland, North Carolina, South Carolina, Virginia, West Virginia
Fifth	Canal Zone, Louisiana, Mississippi, Texas
Sixth	Kentucky, Michigan, Ohio, Tennessee
Seventh	Illinois, Indiana, Wisconsin
Eighth	Arkansas, Iowa, Minnesota, Missouri, Nebraska, North Dakota, South Dakota
Ninth	Alaska, Arizona, California, Guam, Hawaii, Idaho, Montana, Nevada, Oregon, Washington
Tenth	Colorado, Kansas, New Mexico, Oklahoma, Utah, Wyoming
Eleventh	Alabama, Georgia, Florida
Federal	Based in Washington, D.C., but hears cases from all regions

POLITICAL PERSPECTIVE

SPLITTING THE NINTH CIRCUIT

Amid charges that the Ninth Circuit Court of Appeals is too large and overwhelmed, Congress has revisited the issue of whether and how the largest U.S. court of appeals should be divided. Although discussions of such a split began as early as 1973, advocates of reform have become more aggressive. In 1997, the Senate passed a bill that would split the Ninth Circuit in two. Other proposals include dividing the Ninth Circuit three ways and studying structural reform of the judiciary beyond the Ninth Circuit.

Advocates of breaking up the Ninth Circuit claim that it is too large, its unwieldy caseload is unbearable, and it is dominated by California. Republican Senator Ted Stevens recently lamented that only one of the 28 judges in the Ninth Circuit sits in Alaska. Opponents contend that the tremendous workload of the Ninth Circuit is due to partisan politics in Congress, not the size of the circuit. Presently, one third of the judicial seats on the Ninth Circuit are vacant. Opponents contend the delay is a tactic of Republicans seeking to block the nomination of judges they view as unduly liberal or activist. Opponents also argue that the driving force in splitting the Ninth Circuit is an attempt to liberate the Northwest states from the liberal leanings of the California-dominated federal appeals court.

Chief Justice Rehnquist recently decried the Senate's failure to vote on pending nominations.[a] Some argue that activist judges, not the Senate confirmation process, are the real problem. Senator Hatch, chairman of the Senate Judiciary Committee, stated that "The number one problem happens to be activist judges who continue to find laws that aren't there and expand the law beyond the intent of Congress."[b]

a. *Delay in Approving Judicial Nominees Angers Rehnquist*, WALL ST. J., Jan. 2, 1998, at 40.

b. *Chief Justice's Annual Report Criticizes Senate's Slowness in Confirming Judges*, 66 U.S.L.W. 2408 (Jan 13, 1998).

The bankruptcy courts are units of the federal district courts that hear proceedings involving the bankruptcy laws and regulations of the United States. When Drexel Burnham Lambert (Wall Street firm that pioneered junk bonds), Continental Airlines, and Barney's (high-end clothing store) filed for protection from their creditors under Chapter 11 of the bankruptcy laws, they did so in federal bankruptcy court. (The law of bankruptcy is discussed in Chapter 24.)

The tax courts hear taxpayer petitions or appeals regarding federal income, estate, and gift taxes. The Court of International Trade has jurisdiction over disputes involving tariffs or import taxes and trade laws. This court also hears cases on appeal from the U.S. International Trade Commission, which handles disputes involving unfair practices in import trade. The U.S. Court of Military Appeals hears cases from the lower courts and tribunals within the armed services.

U.S. Supreme Court

The Supreme Court was created by Article III of the Constitution. The Court consists of one chief justice and eight associate justices. At least six justices must be present to hear a case. The majority of the cases heard by the Supreme Court are on appeal from the U.S. courts of appeal. A decision by a state supreme court is also appealable to the U.S. Supreme Court, but only when the case concerns the U.S. Constitution or some other federal law. The Supreme Court may hear direct appeals from a federal district court decision if the court declared an act of the U.S. Congress unconstitutional. For example, the Supreme Court directly reviewed the District Court for the District of Columbia's invalidation of the Line Item Veto Act.[1]

The Supreme Court has discretionary review, meaning that it decides which cases within its jurisdiction it will adjudicate. When it decides to hear a case, the Supreme Court issues a *writ of certiorari* ordering the lower court to certify the record of proceedings below and send it up to the Supreme Court. Four justices must vote to hear a case before a writ can be issued. If a writ was sought but denied by the Supreme Court, the citation for the case will indicate *"cert. denied."*

The Court will not hear an appeal unless a real and substantial controversy is involved and resolving the lawsuit will provide actual relief to one party. Further, the party pursuing the appeal must have standing to sue. *Standing* means that the party seeking relief is the proper party to advance the litigation, has a personal interest in the outcome of the suit, and will benefit from a favorable ruling. The following case addressed the issue of whether persons who would be adversely affected economically by action taken under the Endangered Species Act had standing to challenge the action.

---

1. City of New York v. Clinton, 985 F. Supp. 168 (D.D.C. 1998).

A CASE IN POINT	SUMMARY

CASE 3.2
BENNETT v. SPEAR
Supreme Court of the
United States
117 S. Ct. 1154 (1997).

FACTS   The Endangered Species Act of 1973 (ESA) requires the identification of threatened animal species and their critical habitat to prevent federally induced environmental damage. If a proposed action may adversely affect an endangered species, the Fish and Wildlife Service authors a Biological Opinion exploring the consequences of the proposed action. If the action will harm the environment, the opinion must outline potential alternatives.

In light of these obligations under the ESA, the Bureau of Reclamation notified the Fish and Wildlife Service that the operation of the Klamath Project might harm two species of endangered fish, the Lost River and shortnose suckers. The Klamath Project is a federal reclamation scheme in northern California and southern Oregon spanning a

Case 3.2 continues

Case 3.2 continued

series of lakes, rivers, dams, and irrigation canals. The Fish and Wildlife Service issued a Biological Opinion that concluded the Klamath Project would harm the endangered fish, and it proposed maintaining minimum water levels in certain reservoirs as an alternative.

Irrigation districts and rancher owners that would be harmed if the proposed alternative were adopted challenged the Biological Opinion. They argued that the maintenance of reservoir levels in order to safeguard the fish would cause significant, irreparable economic hardship. The plaintiffs contended that the Biological Opinion was insufficiently supported by evidence and that it did not consider the economic impact of its proposed alternatives.

The trial court dismissed the complaint for lack of jurisdiction because the plaintiffs did not have standing to initiate the lawsuit. The appeals court affirmed, holding that the economic, recreational, and aesthetic interests of the plaintiffs did not fall within the "zone of interests" permitting a suit under the ESA. Rather, only plaintiffs seeking to preserve endangered species had standing to sue under the ESA. The plaintiffs appealed.

ISSUE PRESENTED   Are economic interests sufficient grounds for standing under the Endangered Species Act?

SUMMARY OF OPINION   The U.S. Supreme Court held that the petitioners did have standing to challenge the Biological Opinion. The statute specifically provided that "any person may commence a civil suit." Taking the statute at face value, the Court rejected the proposition that standing should be limited to environmentalists.

The Court also found that the traditional standing requirements were satisfied. The plaintiffs had articulated an injury in fact that could be traced to the Biological Opinion and such economic harm was redressable by the judiciary.

In terms of the reviewability of the ESA and the Biological Opinion, the Court found that both were within its proper jurisdiction. Plaintiffs would suffer an economic harm due to the misadministration of the ESA, and, to the extent that the Biological Opinion is the "consummation of the agency's decisionmaking," it is subject to legal challenge.

RESULT   The appeals court decision was reversed. The irrigation districts and ranch owners had standing to challenge the Biological Opinion.

In *National Credit Union Administration v. First National Bank & Trust Co.*,[2] the U.S. Supreme Court held that commercial banks had standing to challenge an interpretation of the National Credit Union Administra-tion (NCUA) permitting credit unions to be composed of multiple, unrelated employer groups, each having its own common bond of occupation. The banks argued that this was contrary to Section 109 of the Federal Credit Union Act (FCUA), which provides that "Federal credit union membership still be limited to groups having a common bond of occupation or association, or to

2. 118 S. Ct. 927 (1998).

groups within a well-defined neighborhood, community, or rural district."[3]

The Court held that the banks' interests were "arguably within the zone of interests" to be protected by the NCUA, even though there was no indication that Congress intended to benefit commercial banks. Section 109 limited membership in every federal credit union to members of definable groups, thereby limiting the markets that credit unions can serve. Therefore, one of the interests arguably to be protected by Section 109 was an interest in limiting the markets that federal credit unions could serve. As competitors of credit unions, the banks had the same interest, which was adversely affected by the NCUA's interpretation of Section 109.

The Court summarized the proper method of analyzing standing to challenge an agency interpretation of a statute as follows:

> [I]n applying the "zone of interests" test, we do not ask whether, in enacting the statutory provision at issue, Congress specifically intended to benefit the plaintiff. Instead, we first discern the interests "arguably . . . to be protected" by the statutory provision at issue; we then inquire whether the plaintiff's interests affected by the agency action in question are among them.

The Supreme Court will not decide cases in which a political question is involved. A *political question* is defined as a conflict that should be decided by either the executive or legislative branches of government. Under the political question doctrine, the Supreme Court identifies those disputes that are more appropriately decided by democratically elected officials.

 ## State Courts

State courts handle the bulk of legal disputes in the United States. Each state's constitution creates the judicial branch of government for that state. For example, the Constitution of Florida provides that "[t]he judicial power shall be vested in a supreme court, district courts of appeal, circuit courts, and county courts. No other courts may be established by the state. . . ."[4] The various sections then provide the details of the state judicial system. These include the number of justices sitting on the state's supreme court, the jurisdiction of the state courts, the geographic districts of the various courts of appeal, the way in which justices and judges are selected or appointed, and the tenure of the justices and judges.

For a state court to hear a civil case, the court must have personal jurisdiction. *Personal jurisdiction* means that the court has legal authority over the parties to the lawsuit. Personal jurisdiction may be based upon the residence or activities of the person being sued (called *in personam* jurisdiction) or upon the location of property at issue in the lawsuit (called *in rem* jurisdiction). For example, if an individual does any business in the state, then he or she is properly within the jurisdiction of the state courts. Owning property in a state, causing a personal injury or property damage within the state, or even paying alimony or child support to someone living within the state might justify the exercise of personal jurisdiction by that state's courts.

Most states have *long-arm statutes*, which subject an out-of-state defendant to jurisdiction where the defendant is doing business or commits a civil wrong in the state. Long-arm statutes must also comport with due process requirements. As long as the person has sufficient *minimum contacts* with a state such that it is fair to require him or her to appear in a court of that state, the state has personal jurisdiction over that person. The critical test is whether the entity has certain minimum contacts with the state "such that the maintenance of the suit does not offend 'traditional notions of fair play and substantial justice.'"[5]

The courts generally require the nonresident defendant to do some act or consummate some transaction in the forum in which it is being sued. Alternatively, the defendant may perform some act by which it purposefully availed itself of the privilege of conducting activities in the forum, thereby invoking the benefits and protections of the forum. Courts have held that negotiating business contracts by means of telephone calls, the mail, or even the telecopier is sufficient to provide a state court with personal jurisdiction over an individual or corporation.

3. 12 U.S.C. § 1759.
4. FLA.CONST. of 1968, art. V, § 1 (1968).

5. International Shoe Co. v. Washington, 326 U.S. 310, 316 (1945) (quoting Milliken v. Meyer, 311 U.S. 457, 463 (1940)).

VIEW FROM CYBERSPACE

PERSONAL JURISDICTION AND THE WEB

The ability to use the Internet to conduct business throughout the world from a desktop computer has raised new issues about the permissible scope of personal jurisdiction based on Internet use. Although this is an emerging area of law, thus far, "the likelihood that personal jurisdiction can be constitutionally exercised is directly proportionate to the nature and quality of commercial activity that an entity conducts over the Internet."[a] The Federal District Court for the Western District of Pennsylvania adopted a sliding scale, stating:

> At one end of the spectrum are situations where a defendant clearly does business over the Internet. If the defendant enters into contracts with residents of a foreign jurisdiction that involved the knowing and repeated transmission of computer files over the Internet, personal jurisdiction is proper. At the opposite end are situations where a defendant has simply posted information on an Internet Web site which is accessible to users in foreign jurisdictions. A passive Web site that does little more than make information available to those who are interested in it is not grounds for the exercise of personal jurisdiction. The middle ground is occupied by interactive Web sites where a user can exchange information with the host computer. In these cases, the exercise of jurisdiction is determined by examining the level of interactivity and commercial nature of the exchange of information that occurs on the Web site.[b]

Applying these principles, the Pennsylvania court held that it could assert jurisdiction over a California corporation with a Web site accessible in Pennsylvania that had 3,000 subscribers in Pennsylvania to whom it issued passwords and seven contracts with Internet access providers to furnish its services to their customers in Pennsylvania.

In contrast, the U.S. Court of Appeals for the Ninth Circuit ruled that an Arizona corporation (which owned the service mark "Cybersell") could not sue a Florida corporation (which used "Cyber Sell" on its Web page) for trademark infringement in Arizona.[c] The court held that "something more," beyond just placing an advertisement on the Web that could be viewed in Arizona, was required to confer jurisdiction over the defendant in Arizona. Absent evidence that the defendant deliberately targeted the Arizona audience or that its Web site actually generated business in Arizona, the defendant had insufficient contacts with Arizona to justify Arizona's assertion of personal jurisdiction.

---

a. Zippo Mfg. Co. v. Zippo Dot Com, 952 F. Supp. 1119, 1124 (W.D. Pa. 1997).

b. *Id.*

c. Cybersell v. Cybersell, 130 F.3d 414 (9th Cir. 1997).

State Trial Courts

At the lowest level of the state trial court system are several courts of limited jurisdiction. These courts decide minor criminal matters, small civil suits, and other specialized legal disputes. Examples include traffic courts, small claims courts, juvenile courts, and family courts. Within these courts, the procedures can be informal. Parties may appear without lawyers, the court may not keep a complete transcript or recording of the proceedings, and the technical rules of evidence and formal courtroom procedures may not apply. In small claims court, the jurisdiction of the court is usually limited to disputes involving less than, for example, $5,000. Any dispute involving more than this amount must be heard by a higher-level trial court.

The second level of state trial courts consists of courts of general or unlimited jurisdiction. These courts have formal courtroom procedures, apply the standard rules of evidence, and record all proceedings.

State court actions cover a broad spectrum of business activities. For example, in Fort Worth, Texas, the owner of a barbecue restaurant sued a former employee for absconding with a secret barbecue sauce recipe. In

Louisiana, a plant worker sued the chemical company Monsanto because she suffered an anxiety attack after a supervisor violently berated her for not working. Shell Oil Company's insurers were sued in state court—unsuccessfully—to provide coverage for the $2.5 billion cleanup of hazardous waste at the U.S. Army facility near Denver, Colorado.

State Appellate Courts

A state appellate court is similar to its counterpart in the federal system. It usually consists of a panel of three judges that reviews the lower court ruling for errors in application of the law or procedures. The court of appeals usually accepts the findings of fact of the trial judge or jury, unless a particular finding is clearly unsupported by the evidence presented at trial. The state appellate court is not required to accept the lower court's conclusions of law. The appellate court will consider legal issues *de novo*, or anew, as if the trial court had not made any conclusions of law. A state court of appeals may affirm, reverse, or vacate and remand any final decision of a lower court.

State Supreme Court

Each state has one court acting as the highest judicial authority in that state. Most states call that court the supreme court. (In New York, the highest state court is called the Court of Appeals; the intermediate appellate court is called the supreme court, appellate division; and the state trial courts are called supreme courts.) The number of justices on the court varies from three to nine. A state supreme court usually has discretionary jurisdiction over all decisions of a court of appeals. Further, a state supreme court may have jurisdiction over cases where a statute of the state or the United States has been ruled unconstitutional in whole or in part. A state supreme court also resolves appeals in criminal cases in which a sentence of death has been imposed.

◆ Choice of Law and Choice of Forum

The question of what law to apply comes up not only in the context of diversity cases heard in federal court but also in state court actions involving the citizens of

INTERNATIONAL CONSIDERATION

Although issues of choice of law and choice of forum often arise in cases involving parties from different jurisdictions within the United States, similar issues arise when parties are from different countries. In either context, the court adjudicating a dispute must balance the competing interests of different sovereignties and resolve the conflict according to one jurisdiction's conflict-of-laws rules. In order to avoid confusion, it is customary for a contract involving parties from different jurisdictions to specify which country's law will govern and where the dispute will be tried.

more than one state. This question is governed by a complicated set of conflict of law rules. In general, the state that has the greatest governmental interest in a case will provide the governing law. Put another way, selecting the governing law is guided by a grouping of contacts: the state with the strongest contacts with the litigants has the greatest interest in the application of its law.

Sometimes a state will use formalistic rules. Some states look only to where a contract was entered into in deciding which state's contract law should govern a dispute. For example, because Pennzoil and Getty Oil Company entered into their contract in New York, the lens of New York contracts law was used to evaluate whether there was a binding contract. (Texaco's intentional interference with this contract, and the related litigation, is discussed in the "Inside Story" in Chapter 7.)

The parties to a contract may agree in advance which law should govern their dispute in the event that one develops. This section is usually entitled Governing Law. Parties can also decide in advance where any disputes should be litigated. This is done by using a *choice of forum clause*. A contract can also provide that disputes will be decided by a method other than litigation in court. A common choice is arbitration, which is discussed in Chapter 4.

A court will usually uphold the contracting parties' choice of law and forum, as happened in the following case.

| **A CASE IN POINT** | **SUMMARY** |

CASE 3.3
RICHARDS v.
LLOYD'S OF LONDON
United States Court of
Appeals for the Ninth Circuit
135 F.3d 1289 (9th Cir.
1998) *(en banc)*.

FACTS Lloyd's of London is involved in the business of writing insurance and reinsurance. Although some individuals devote full time to Lloyd's business insurance and control it, others are wholly passive investors with unlimited liability.

Between 1970 and 1993, Lloyd's vigorously recruited investors (called names) in the United States in an attempt to increase its underwriting capacity. The information furnished by Lloyd's to potential investors did not meet the standards for prospectuses set forth by the Securities and Exchange Commission, nor were the investment contracts offered by Lloyd's registered under federal or state securities laws. As part of this campaign, Alan Richards and 573 other individuals (the plaintiffs) became passive investors in Lloyd's underwriting business.

In 1986, Lloyd's required the plaintiffs to execute a contract that included choice-of-law and forum-selection clauses. Paragraph 2.1 of the General Undertaking specified that "The rights and obligations of the parties . . . shall be governed by and construed in accordance with the laws of England." Paragraph 2.2 continued: "Each party irrevocably agrees that the courts of England shall have exclusive jurisdiction to settle any dispute and/or controversy of whatsoever nature arising out of or relating to the Member's membership of, and/or underwriting of insurance business of Lloyd's. . . ."

On October 9, 1994, the plaintiffs filed an amended complaint alleging securities fraud under the federal securities laws and violations of RICO (Racketeer Influenced and Corrupt Organizations Act). Lloyd's of London did not respond to this complaint, and the plaintiffs moved for a default judgment. Lloyd's then argued that the suit should be dismissed on the grounds of improper venue and *forum non conveniens* (a doctrine claiming that the present suit should be dismissed because an alternate, more convenient forum should adjudicate the dispute). The trial court dismissed the suit, then a panel of the court of appeals reversed. Lloyd's requested a rehearing by the full court of appeals.

ISSUE PRESENTED Are choice-of-forum and choice-of-law clauses requiring a U.S. citizen to litigate securities fraud claims under English law in English courts valid and enforceable?

SUMMARY OF OPINION The U.S. Court of Appeals began by acknowledging that the Securities Act of 1933 and the Securities Exchange Act of 1934 both provide that contracts in violation of the acts are void. Nonetheless, in 1972, the U.S. Supreme Court ruled in *The Bremen v. Zapata Off-Shore Co.*[6] that courts should enforce choice-of-law and choice-of-forum clauses in cases of "freely negotiated private international agreement[s]." Two years later, the Court relied on *Bremen* to uphold a choice-of-forum clause in a securities transaction, making clear that its policy favoring choice provisions did not yield to securities law. According to the Court, choice-of-forum provisions are "an almost indispensable precondition to achievement of the orderliness and predictability essential to any international business transaction." Otherwise, the scope of U.S. securities law would be boundless.

Case 3.3 continues

---

6. 407 U.S. 1 (1972).

Case 3.3 continued

Because the names signed a contract with English entities to participate in an English insurance market and flew to England to consummate the transaction, the contract was international and within *Bremen*'s reach. The fact that Lloyd's solicited the names in the United States does not change the contract's international nature.

The court identified three grounds for not enforcing a forum-selection clause: (1) if the clause was fraudulently included in the contact; (2) if enforcement would deprive a party "of his day in court"; and (3) if enforcement would contravene a strong public policy of the forum in which suit is brought. The names argued that the first and third grounds applied.

The first ground requires that the forum-selection clause itself was included in the contract by fraud, not that the contract as a whole was entered into fraudulently. The names never alleged that Lloyd's misled them as to the legal effect of the choice clauses, only that they did not appreciate the effect. Neither did they allege that Lloyd's fraudulently inserted the clauses without their knowledge. Hence, the first ground did not apply.

As for the third ground regarding public policy, six other circuits had already enforced such clauses. Moreover, U.S. Supreme Court precedent had held that in the context of an international agreement there is "no basis for a judgment that only United States laws and United States courts should determine this controversy in the face of a solemn agreement between the parties that such controversies be resolved elsewhere." The court concluded that to mandate that American standards govern such a controversy demeans the standards elsewhere and places U.S. law over that of other countries. Furthermore, it is simply not possible for the U.S. to trade in world markets and over international waters exclusively on its terms, governed by its laws, and resolved in its courts. As a result, the court held that the choice-of-forum and choice-of-laws clauses in the General Undertaking were valid and enforceable.

RESULT The full court of appeals reversed the panel's dismissal of the federal Securities Acts claims and required it to rule on the plaintiffs' motion for a default judgment.

COMMENTS The outcome of *Richards v. Lloyd's of London* conforms with the holdings of the U.S. Courts of Appeal for the Second, Fourth, Fifth, and Seventh Circuits.

 ## Sources of the Law

In applying the law, federal and state courts look to constitutions, statutes, regulations, and common (or case) law.

Constitutions

Courts may be called upon to interpret the U.S. or state constitutions. For example, the First Amendment provides that Congress shall make no law abridging the freedom of speech. Incidents of flag burning have required courts to interpret just what type of conduct constitutes speech protected by the First Amendment. Lawsuits concerning random drug testing of employees have centered on whether this testing violates the Fourth Amendment ban on unreasonable searches and/or the right to privacy.

The U.S. Constitution does not expressly set forth a right to privacy. As explained in Chapter 2, such a right is found in the penumbra of other articulated rights. Some state constitutions do specifically grant a right to privacy, however. The following case addresses the issue of whether a Montana law proscribing private, consensual, same-gender sexual conduct between adults violates the right to privacy specified in the Montana constitution.

| A CASE IN POINT | IN THE LANGUAGE OF THE COURT |

CASE 3.4
GRYCZAN v. MONTANA
Supreme Court of Montana
942 P.2d 112 (Mont. 1997).

FACTS   Three men and three women (respondents), who were homosexuals residing in Montana, filed a declaratory judgment action challenging Section 45-5-505 of the Montana criminal code. A *declaratory judgment action* seeks only a judicial order articulating the legal rights and responsibilities of the parties, rather than monetary damages. Section 45-5-505 provides for up to ten years imprisonment and/or a $50,000 fine for individuals who knowingly engage in "deviate sexual relations," defined as "sexual contact or sexual intercourse between two persons of the same sex or any form of sexual intercourse with an animal."

The state of Montana moved to dismiss the case, contending that the respondents lacked standing and that there was no justiciable controversy. The district court denied this motion and later concluded that Montana's deviate-sexual-relations statute violated respondents' right to privacy under the Montana constitution. The state appealed.

ISSUE PRESENTED   Do persons not yet prosecuted under Section 45-5-505 have standing to challenge it? If so, does Montana's deviate-sexual-conduct statute violate the right to privacy under the Montana Constitution?

OPINION   NELSON, J., writing for the Montana Supreme Court:

The State maintains that . . . Respondents are required to show an "injury in fact" and that no such injury exists here because there is no evidence of a credible threat of prosecution under the statute since no one has been prosecuted for engaging in consensual, adult, private, same-gender sexual conduct since the statute was enacted.

. . .

[However] [b]ecause the legislature does not regard the statute as moribund and because enforcement has not been foresworn by the Attorney General, we agree that Respondents suffer a legitimate and realistic fear of criminal prosecution along with other psychological harms. Respondents are precisely the individuals against whom the statute is intended to operate. This is sufficient to give Respondents standing to challenge the constitutionality of the statute.

. . .

The federal constitution does not explicitly grant citizens the right to privacy. That right has been inferred, however, from other provisions of the constitution and is used particularly in search and seizure contexts.

. . .

While the right of privacy enunciated in *Griswold*[7] [which held that laws forbidding the use of contraceptives by married couples in their own homes violate the right of marital privacy] has been recognized by the United States Supreme Court to protect certain personal decisions, other personal choices have been excluded. [The court

Case 3.4 continues

---

7. Griswold v. Connecticut, 381 U.S. 479 (1965).

Case 3.4 continued

cites *Bowers v. Hardwick*,[8] in which the majority held that the U.S.Constitution cannot support a fundamental right to engage in homosexual sodomy, while the dissent argued the issue was the "right to be left alone."] . . . Regardless of whether Bowers was correctly decided, we have long held that Montana's Constitution affords citizens broader protection of their right to privacy than does the federal constitution. . . . Unlike the federal constitution, Montana's Constitution explicitly grants to all Montana citizens the right to individual privacy [in Article II, Section 10].

. . .

. . . [I]t is hard to imagine any activity that adults would consider more fundamental, more private, and, thus, more deserving of protection from governmental interference than noncommercial, consensual adult sexual activity.

. . .

Quite simply, while legislative enactments may reflect the will of the majority, . . . there are certain rights so fundamental that they will not be denied to a minority no matter how despised by society. In Montana, the right of privacy is such a right. While nothing in this opinion should be construed to countenance nonconsensual sexual activity, sexual contact with a minor, or any form of sexual conduct for commercial purposes, Montana's constitutional right of privacy—this right of personal autonomy and right to be let alone—includes the right of consenting adults, regardless of gender, to engage in noncommercial, private, sexual relations free of governmental interference, intrusion and condemnation.

RESULT   The Montana Supreme Court held that Montana's deviate-sexual-conduct statute violated the state constitutional right to privacy and affirmed the district court's permanent injunction preventing enforcement of the statute.

Questions

1. Why were the respondents able to challenge the law when they had not been arrested or prosecuted for violating it?
2. Why did the U.S. Supreme Court precedent in *Bowers v. Hardwick* not bind the Montana Supreme Court?

---

8. 478 U.S. 186 (1986).

Statutes

Congress enacts statutes in such areas as public assistance, food and drugs, patents and copyrights, labor relations, and civil rights. For example, Title 42 of the United States Code, Section 2000(a), provides that "all persons shall be entitled to the full and equal enjoyment of the goods, services, facilities, privileges, advantages, and accommodations of any place of public accommodation . . . without discrimination or segregation on the grounds of race, color, religion or national origin."

Regulations

Courts sometimes hear cases arising under regulations issued by administrative agencies and executive departments. Federal regulations and rules are printed in the multivolume *Code of Federal Regulations* (*CFR*), which is revised and updated every year.

The CFR covers such varied topics as the regulations applying to federal highways, issued by the Department of Transportation; the Internal Revenue Service regulations, issued by the Department of the Treasury; the immigration and naturalization rules and procedures, issued by the Department of Justice; the regulations governing the sale of securities, issued by the Securities and Exchange Commission; and the regulations governing television, radio, and telecommunications, issued by the Federal Communications Commission. Administrative rules and regulations, and the various agencies, are discussed in Chapter 6.

INTERNATIONAL CONSIDERATION

Bulgaria's difficult struggle with both economic and political reform shows the effect of eliminating law as a means of regulation and dispute resolution. The regulations that were implemented after the breakup of the Soviet Union were "designed to protect the old order and did little to accomplish the legal reforms promised by the collapse of the former Eastern bloc."[a]

Any regulations that were passed were not enforced. Nonenforcement engendered a thriving underground economy, disregarding intellectual property rights, including trademark, copyright, and related restrictions. The pervasive, cash-based underground economy also enabled systematic tax avoidance in both personal and business transactions. Businesses routinely violated environmental regulations, knowing the probability of enforcement to be low and believing environmental protection to be bothersome.

Due to the government's tarnished public image, Bulgarians rarely litigate when faced with a breach of contract. Rather, "the local common wisdom holds that no matter how carefully a contract may be drawn, if it is breached, most of the time the parties will settle the dispute themselves. Such an approach usually means the more powerful or ruthless party wins. . . ."[b]

a. Katherine J. Wilkinson, *A Lawyer in a World without Law: An American's Odyssey in Bulgaria*, BUS. L. TODAY, Sept./Oct., 1997, at 41.
b. *Id.* at 44.

Common Law

Common law is case law—the legal rules made by judges when they decide a case in which no constitution, statute, or regulation exists to resolve the dispute. Common law originated in England and includes all of the case law of England and the American colonies before the American Revolution, as well as American case law since the colonial period.

Stare Decisis   Common law is developed through the doctrine of *stare decisis*, which translates as "to abide by decided cases." Once a court resolves a particular issue, other courts addressing a similar legal problem will generally follow that court's decision.

A legal rule established by a court's decision may be either persuasive or authoritative. A decision is *persuasive* if it reasonably and fairly resolved the dispute. Another court confronting a similar dispute will probably choose to apply the same reasoning.

An *authoritative decision*, by contrast, is one that must be followed, regardless of its persuasive power. The U.S. Court of Appeals for the Seventh Circuit explained:

> Whether a decision is authoritative depends on a variety of factors, of which the most important is the relationship between the court that decided it and the court to which it is cited later as a precedent. The simplest relationship is hierarchical: the decisions of a superior court in a unitary system bind the inferior courts. The most complex relationship is between a court and its own previous decisions.
>
> A court must give considerable weight to its own decisions unless and until they have been overruled or undermined by the decisions of a higher court, or other supervening developments, such as a statutory overruling. But [a court] is not absolutely bound by [its previous rulings], and must give fair consideration to any substantial argument that a litigant makes for overruling a previous decision.[9]

Federal courts interpreting state law must follow that state's courts—this was the principle established in *Erie Railroad Co. v. Tompkins*, discussed earlier in this chapter. Every court must follow a decision of the U.S. Supreme Court, unless powerfully convinced that the Supreme Court itself would change its decision at the first possible opportunity.

9. Colby v. J. C. Penney Co., 811 F.2d 1119, 1123 (7th Cir. 1987).

Although the Supreme Court rarely overrules its previous opinions, it does happen. For example, the Supreme Court rejected the "separate but equal" test adopted by *Plessy v. Ferguson*[10] in *Brown v. Board of Education*,[11] the 1954 school-desegregation case. More recently, many have called upon the Supreme Court to reverse its 1973 holding in *Roe v. Wade*[12] that a woman has a constitutionally protected right to an abortion. The importance of the doctrine of *stare decisis* was underscored in the following case.

10. 163 U.S. 537 (1896).
11. 347 U.S. 483 (1954).

12. 410 U.S. 113 (1973).

A CASE IN POINT   **IN THE LANGUAGE OF THE COURT**

CASE 3.5
PLANNED PARENTHOOD OF S.E. PENNSYLVANIA v. CASEY
Supreme Court of the United States
505 U.S. 833 (1992).

FACTS   The Pennsylvania Abortion Control Act of 1982 (as amended in 1988 and 1989) requires that a woman seeking an abortion give her informed consent prior to the abortion procedure and that she be provided with certain information at least 24 hours before the abortion is performed. For a minor to obtain an abortion, the act requires the informed consent of one of her parents, but provides for a judicial bypass option if the minor does not wish to or cannot obtain a parent's consent. Another provision of the act requires that, unless certain exceptions apply, a married woman seeking an abortion must sign a statement indicating that she has notified her husband of her intended abortion. The act exempts compliance with these three requirements in the event of a medical emergency and imposes reporting requirements on facilities that provide abortion services.

Five abortion clinics and one physician, representing himself as well as a class of physicians who provide abortion services, brought suit seeking declaratory and injunctive relief. Each provision was challenged as unconstitutional on its face. Relying on *Roe v. Wade*, the district court entered a preliminary injunction, held all the provisions at issue unconstitutional, and entered a permanent injunction against enforcing them. The appeals court upheld as constitutional all of the regulations except for the husband-notification requirement. The plaintiff appealed.

ISSUE PRESENTED   In light of *Roe v. Wade* and the doctrine of *stare decisis*, should the Pennsylvania abortion regulations be upheld as constitutional?

OPINION   O'CONNOR, KENNEDY, and SOUTER, J. J., writing for a plurality of the U.S. Supreme Court:

Liberty finds no refuge in a jurisprudence of doubt. Yet 19 years after our holding that the Constitution protects a woman's right to terminate her pregnancy in its early stages, *Roe v. Wade*, that definition of liberty is still questioned. Joining the respondents . . . the United States, as it has done in five other cases in the last decade, again asks us to overrule *Roe*.

. . .

After considering the fundamental constitutional questions resolved by *Roe*, principles of institutional integrity, and the rule of *stare decisis*, we are led to conclude this: the essential holding of *Roe v. Wade* should be retained and once again reaffirmed.

Case 3.5 continues

Case 3.5 continued

[The Court then gave a brief synopsis of the *Roe v. Wade* holding and its trimester approach to abortion regulation. Under *Roe*, a woman's right to an abortion is virtually absolute in the first trimester of pregnancy. Regulations designed to protect the woman's health, but not to further the state's interest in potential life, are permissible in the second trimester. In the third trimester, when the fetus is viable, the state may act to protect the potential life of the fetus, except when the life or health of the mother is at stake. The Court rejected the trimester framework, which it did not consider the "essential holding" of *Roe*. Instead, the Court concluded that a woman has a right to terminate her pregnancy prior to the time the fetus is viable, regardless of when that occurs.]

. . .

The obligation to follow precedent begins with necessity, and a contrary necessity marks its outer limit. . . . Indeed, the very concept of the rule of law underlying our own Constitution requires such continuity over time that a respect for precedent is, by definition, indispensable. At the other extreme, a different necessity would make itself felt if a prior judicial ruling should come to be seen so clearly as error that its enforcement was for that very reason doomed.

Even when the decision to overrule a prior case is not virtually foreordained, as in the rare, latter instance, it is common wisdom that the rule of *stare decisis* is not an "inexorable command," and certainly it is not such in every constitutional case. Rather, when this Court reexamines a prior holding, its judgment is customarily informed by a series of prudential and pragmatic considerations designed to test the consistency of overruling a prior decision with the ideal of the rule of law, and to gauge the respective costs of reaffirming and overruling a prior case. . . .

So, in this case, we may inquire whether *Roe*'s central rule has been found unworkable; whether the rule's limitation on state power could be removed without serious inequity to those who have relied upon it or significant damage to the stability of the society governed by the rule in question; whether the law's growth in the intervening years has left *Roe*'s central rule a doctrinal anachronism discounted by society; and whether *Roe*'s premises of fact have so far changed in the ensuing two decades as to render its central holding somehow irrelevant or unjustifiable in dealing with the issue it addressed.

[One] comparison that 20th century history invites is with the cases employing the separate-but-equal rule for applying the Fourteenth Amendment's equal protection guarantee. They began with *Plessy v. Ferguson* holding that legislatively mandated racial segregation in public transportation works no denial of equal protection, rejecting the argument that racial separation enforced by the legal machinery of American society treats the black race as inferior. The *Plessy* Court considered "the underlying fallacy of the plaintiff's argument to consist in the assumption that the enforced separation of the two races stamps the colored race with a badge of inferiority. If this be so, it is not by reason of anything found in the act, but solely because the colored race chooses to put that construction upon it." Whether, as a matter of historical fact, the Justices in the *Plessy* majority believed this or not, this understanding of the implication of segregation

Case 3.5 continues

Case 3.5 continued

was the stated justification for the Court's opinion. But this understanding of the facts and the rule it was stated to justify were repudiated in *Brown v. Board of Education*. . . .

The Court in *Brown* addressed these facts of life by observing that whatever may have been the understanding in *Plessy*'s time of the power of segregation to stigmatize those who were segregated with a "badge of inferiority," it was clear by 1954 that legally sanctioned segregation had just such an effect, to the point that racially separate public educational facilities were deemed inherently unequal. Society's understanding of the facts upon which a constitutional ruling was sought in 1954 was thus fundamentally different from the basis claimed for the decision in 1896. While we think *Plessy* was wrong the day it was decided, . . . we must also recognize that the *Plessy* Court's explanation for its decision was so clearly at odds with the facts apparent to the Court in 1954 that the decision to reexamine *Plessy* was on this ground alone not only justified but required.

. . .

. . . In constitutional adjudication as elsewhere in life, changed circumstances may impose new obligations, and the thoughtful part of the Nation could accept each decision to overrule a prior case as a response to the Court's constitutional duty.

Because the case before us presents no such occasion it could be seen as no such response. Because neither the factual underpinnings of *Roe*'s central holding nor our understanding of it has changed (and because no other indication of weakened precedent has been shown) the Court could not pretend to be reexamining the prior law with any justification beyond a present doctrinal disposition to come out differently from the Court of 1973. . . .

RESULT   The Court upheld what it considered to be the central holding of *Roe v. Wade* under the doctrine of *stare decisis*. At the same time, the Court upheld the Pennsylvania abortion regulations as constitutional, except for the spousal-notification requirement. The regulations imposed procedural requirements that the Court did not consider central to the holding of *Roe*.

COMMENTS   Chief Justice Rehnquist explicitly stated in his dissent that *Roe* was wrongly decided and could be overturned consistently with the traditional approach to *stare decisis* in constitutional cases. Justice Blackmun, author of the *Roe* opinion, strongly disagreed and argued that under the test of strict scrutiny, which he believed should be applied, all provisions of the Pennsylvania law should be struck down. He noted the slim margin behind the Court's decision to uphold *Roe*:

> In one sense, the Court's approach is worlds apart from that of the Chief Justice and Justice Scalia. And yet, in another sense, the distance between the two approaches is short—the distance is but a single vote.
> I am 83 years old. I cannot remain on this Court forever, and when I do step down, the confirmation process for my successor well may focus on the issue before us today. That, I regret, may be exactly where the choice between the two worlds will be made.

As discussed in the "Inside Story" for Chapter 2, Justice Ruth Bader Ginsburg refused to have an abortion litmus test applied to her nomination to the Court in 1993.

Case 3.5 continues

Case 3.5 continued

Questions

1. What factors did the Court consider in deciding whether to overturn *Roe v. Wade*?
2. Why did the Court conclude that overturning *Plessy* in *Brown v. Board of Education* was appropriate, but that overturning *Roe v. Wade* would not be?

One court of appeals does not have to follow another court of appeals. One trial court does not have to follow another trial court. It must follow the court of appeals above it but need not follow other appellate courts. Thus, if the U.S. Court of Appeals for the Tenth Circuit (based in Denver) interprets a federal air pollution regulation in a certain way, the U.S. Court of Appeals for the Sixth Circuit (based in Cincinnati) may follow that interpretation, but is not compelled to do so. The authority of the Tenth Circuit does not reach beyond its own geographical boundaries. However, a federal district court in Tulsa, which is within the Tenth Circuit, would be compelled to interpret the regulation in accordance with the decision of the Court of Appeals for the Tenth Circuit.

Restatements   Today, many rules that originated as common law have been collected into *restatements* compiled by legal scholars, practicing attorneys, and judges. There are restatements of various areas of the law, such as torts, contracts, property, and trusts. The restatements do not compel a judge to make a particular decision unless the rule has been adopted by the state's legislature. They are persuasive rather than authoritative.

 ## Civil Procedure

Civil procedure refers to the methods, procedures, and practices that govern the processing of a civil lawsuit from start to finish. The Federal Rules of Civil Procedure (FRCP) control the trial practices in all of the U.S. district courts. Each federal district court may also adopt its own local rules, applicable only within that district, to supplement the federal rules. Individual judges may even have particular rules as to how certain procedures operate in their own courts.

Each state has a set of rules governing the procedures in the state trial court system. Often, the state rules will be similar in many respects to the federal rules. There is also a separate set of rules for practicing before the various courts of appeal and supreme courts. These rules address every requirement, from the time deadline for filing an appeal, to the contents of the notice of appeal, to the paper size, line spacing, and type style for briefs filed with the court. Each court system has its own rules or guidelines to ensure the orderly processing of the lawsuit.

Filing a Claim

Complaint   The *complaint* briefly states a grievance and makes allegations of (1) the particular facts giving rise to the dispute; (2) the legal reason why the plaintiff is entitled to a remedy; and (3) the *prayer*, or request for relief. The complaint should also explain why this particular court has jurisdiction over the alleged dispute and whether the plaintiff requests a jury trial. If the plaintiff does not request a jury trial within the time limit, that right is deemed to be waived.

Summons   After the plaintiff files the complaint, the clerk of the court prepares a summons. The *summons* officially notifies the defendant that a lawsuit is pending against it in a particular court and that it must file a response to the complaint within a certain number of days. The clerk then stamps the official seal of the court on the summons. Next, the plaintiff or the clerk will serve the official summons and complaint on the defendant. Service is usually completed by sending the documents to the defendant by mail. After a defendant receives the summons and complaint, it will have from 20 to 30 days to file an answer.

Answer   The defendant's *answer* may admit or deny the various allegations in the complaint. If the defendant believes that it lacks sufficient information to assess the truth of an allegation, it should state this. Such a statement has the effect of a denial. The answer may also deny that the law provides relief for the plaintiff's claim regardless of whether the plaintiff's factual allegations are true.

The answer may put forth affirmative defenses to the allegations in the complaint. An *affirmative defense* admits that the defendant has acted in a certain way but claims that the defendant's conduct was not the real or legal cause of harm to the plaintiff. An example of an affirmative defense in a contract case is the requirement under the statute of frauds (discussed in Chapter 7) that certain agreements are not enforceable unless they are in writing.

An answer may also include a *counterclaim*, a legal claim by the defendant against the plaintiff. The counterclaim need not be related to the plaintiff's claim.

If the defendant does not file an answer within the time required, a *default judgment* may be entered in favor of the plaintiff. The defendant, however, may ask the court to set aside the default judgment if there were extenuating circumstances for not filing the answer to the complaint on time.

The complaint, the answer, and any reply to the answer filed by the plaintiff are referred to as the *pleadings*.

Discovery

Before a trial is held, the parties collect evidence to support their claims, through a process called *discovery*. In general, parties may obtain discovery regarding any matter relevant to the lawsuit. Discovery includes *depositions*, which are written or oral questioning of any person who may have helpful information about the facts of the case; *interrogatories*, which are written questions to the parties in the case and their attorneys; and *requests for production of documents*, such as medical records and personal files.

The basic purpose of discovery is to eliminate the "game" elements in a trial. If all the parties to the lawsuit have all the evidence before trial, everyone benefits. By revealing the strengths and weaknesses of the various claims, discovery frequently allows the lawsuit to be *settled*—resolved by agreement without a trial. At the least, discovery helps prevent any major surprises from occurring at trial because each side already has learned about the other's case.

Discovery serves other useful functions. First, it can preserve evidence. For example, depositions preserve the testimony of important witnesses who may otherwise be unavailable at trial. Second, discovery reduces the number of legal issues to be presented at trial, because the parties can see beforehand which claims they have evidence to support and which ones are not worth pursuing.

Discovery has its drawbacks, however. The process is very expensive, because discovery is labor intensive. Frequently, hours and days of depositions and hundreds of interrogatories will be undertaken. The strategy behind such a plan can be twofold: to wear down the opposing party by making the lawsuit more expensive than a victory would be worth; or to keep the papers flowing at such a rate that the other side cannot discern what all the documents really state. Such tactics often lead to discovery disputes that end up before the court. Taken too far, these strategies can lead to discovery abuse, which reduces the already slow pace of litigation, significantly increases costs, and can anger judges. Courts sometimes impose penalties upon companies and their counsel for discovery abuses. The sanctions leveled against the E. I. DuPont de Nemours and Company are described in the "Inside Story."

Not all relevant information is subject to discovery. For example, the *work-product doctrine* protects information that an attorney prepares in the course of his or her work. This information includes the private memoranda and personal thoughts of the attorney created while he or she is preparing a case for trial. The rationale behind the work-product rule is that lawyers, while performing their duties, must "work with a certain degree of privacy, free from unnecessary intrusion by opposing parties and their counsel."[13] Work-product materials may be obtained only with a showing of extreme necessity, such that the failure to obtain the materials would unduly prejudice an attorney's case or create hardship and injustice.

Attorney–Client Privilege

An even more important limitation on discovery and testimony at trial is the *attorney-client privilege*, which dates back to the sixteenth century and provides that a court cannot force the disclosure of confidential communications between a client and his or her attorney. The privilege survives the death of the client.

---

13. Hickman v. Taylor, 329 U.S. 495, 510 (1947).

ETHICAL CONSIDERATION

Suppose you are a top manager at a major corporation. You have recently been sued in federal district court by an individual who was injured by one of your widgets. Your in-house counsel tells you that the plaintiff's counsel is competent but a sole practitioner specializing in family law. You discuss litigation strategy with your attorney. One tactic is to overwhelm opposing counsel through the discovery process. Your counsel provides several options: (1) delivering 40 boxes of corporate documents a day for 4 days, of which perhaps 60 pages are relevant to the suit, then moving for dismissal on the fifth day; (2) actively mislabeling or hiding documents in the above "document dump"; (3) not providing any relevant information to opposing counsel but sending box after box of useless material; (4) stalling and delaying document requests because the corporation "is unable to locate them"; (5) accurately labeling the relevant material, but including it in a "document dump"; (6) declaring that only through extensive travel would opposing counsel be able to access the relevant information (sending individuals likely to be deposed all over the world on "important projects"); (7) continuously delaying and extending the number of depositions, interrogatories, and other materials needed in order to "effectively prepare for trial"; (8) promptly providing only the relevant information in a way the opposing counsel may easily access it; and (9) lying and destroying all relevant documents. Which option should you select and why?

The rationale of the attorney–client privilege is to promote the administration of justice. Clients are more likely to make a full and frank disclosure of the facts to an attorney if they know that the attorney cannot be compelled to pass the information on to adversary parties. An attorney is better able to advise and represent a client if the client discloses the complete facts. The privilege may also help to prevent unnecessary litigation, because an attorney who knows all the facts should be better able to assess whether litigation is justified.

The attorney–client privilege is an exception to the general rule of evidence that any person with knowl-

edge of a case may be called to testify in depositions or at trial. Thus, by protecting certain communications, the attorney–client privilege does limit the amount of evidence that can be produced at trial. As a result, courts will place certain limitations on the scope of the privilege.

To be protected by the privilege, a communication must occur between the attorney and the client. The communication must also be intended as confidential. If the client plans to relay the information to others or makes the communication in the presence of other individuals not involved in the lawsuit, there is no confidentiality.

The attorney–client privilege belongs to the client alone. The attorney, however, has an obligation to alert the client to the existence of the privilege and, if necessary, to invoke it on the client's behalf. The client can waive the privilege over the attorney's objection if the client so desires.

Limitations   The attorney to whom the communication is made must be a practicing attorney at the time of the communication, and the person making the communication must be a current or prospective client seeking legal advice. If the client were conversing with the attorney about nonlegal matters, the conversation would not be protected.

The attorney–client privilege does not protect client communications that are made to further a crime or other illegal act. If an executive were to ask his or her attorney about the best way to embezzle money, that conversation would not be privileged.

Tobacco Litigation and Attorney–Client Privilege
Although no one knows the extent of the tobacco industry's documentation, Stanton A. Glanz, a professor at the University of California at San Francisco and an experienced tobacco critic, believes that the attorney–client privilege has been used to conceal (1) market research and other information regarding plans to recruit teenage smokers; (2) studies documenting the dangers of tobacco and nicotine; and (3) political stratagems.

Tobacco companies may abandon the privilege at any time, as the Liggett Group did in its March 1997 settlement.[14] In this settlement, Liggett confessed that cigarette smoking causes lung cancer, heart disease, and

14. John Greenwald et al., *Smoking Gun: A Cigarette Maker Finally Admits that Its Product Is Dangerously Habit-Forming. Is This the End of Big Tobacco's Legal Invincibility?*, TIME, Mar. 31, 1997, at 32.

emphysema; that nicotine is an addictive substance; and that the tobacco companies had, for years, directed their advertising to youth. In July 1997, the Florida District Court of Appeal rejected the tobacco companies' claim of attorney–client privilege for eight confidential documents (which included attorney's notes from in-house meetings on legal strategy) turned over to the Liggett Group.[15] The court concluded that because the documents contained evidence that tobacco attorneys participated in an industrywide conspiracy to defraud the

public about the danger of smoking, they came within the exemption for communications to further commission of fraud or a crime.

Corporate Clients   With communications between a corporate client and an attorney, it is often difficult to define what element of the corporation can be considered the client. The corporation does not fit the common definition of a client, because the corporation itself is unable to communicate with the attorney except through its officers, directors, agents, or employees. The following case resulted in a key decision defining who is the client for purposes of applying the attorney–client privilege in a corporate setting.

---

15. 66 U.S.L.W. 1112 (Aug. 19, 1997).

A CASE IN POINT   SUMMARY

CASE 3.6
UPJOHN CO. v.
UNITED STATES
Supreme Court
of the United States
449 U.S. 383 (1981).

FACTS   In January 1976, independent accountants conducted an audit of one of the foreign subsidiaries of Upjohn, an international pharmaceuticals company. The accountants discovered that the subsidiary made payments to, or for the benefit of, foreign government officials in order to secure government business. The accountants informed Upjohn's vice-president and general counsel. In response to the accountants' information, the general counsel conducted an internal investigation of Upjohn's foreign subsidiaries. In conjunction with outside attorneys, Upjohn's general counsel distributed a questionnaire to foreign managers concerning these alleged practices. Upjohn's attorneys also interviewed 33 other company employees and officers. Upjohn voluntarily submitted a report to the Securities and Exchange Commission disclosing certain questionable payments. A copy of the report was submitted to the Internal Revenue Service (IRS), which immediately began an investigation to determine the tax consequences of the payments. The IRS issued a summons to Upjohn demanding to see the results of the questionnaires, files related to the questionnaires, and copies of the employee interviews. Upjohn refused to turn over these documents on the ground that the information was protected by the attorney–client and work-product privileges.

The IRS filed a lawsuit in federal district court, seeking to enforce the summons. The district court ruled that Upjohn must comply with the IRS summons. Upjohn appealed the decision to the court of appeals, which ruled that Upjohn did not waive its attorney–client privilege. This privilege, however, only covered communications made by officers and agents responsible for directing Upjohn's response to the lawsuit. Thus, only the communications of the company personnel who were within a control group—the senior level of officers and managers guiding the corporation—were considered confidential. According to the court of appeals, the communications of the regular employees to Upjohn's attorneys were not confidential, because these individuals were not identified with the corporation as a whole. Upjohn appealed.

ISSUE PRESENTED   Are the communications by a corporation's employees to corporate counsel protected by the attorney–client privilege when the employee

Case 3.6 continues

Case 3.6 continued

responses to counsel were confidential communications made while the corporation was seeking legal advice?

SUMMARY OF OPINION   The U.S. Supreme Court rejected the control group test on the ground that it would frustrate the very purpose of attorney–client privilege, which is to encourage communication of relevant information by all employees to the corporation's attorneys. The middle- and lower-level employees, rather than the senior officers, will normally be the ones whose actions embroil the corporation in serious legal difficulties. Accordingly, these same employees will be the ones possessing relevant information needed by corporate counsel to advise as to actual or potential legal problems.

The Supreme Court adopted a subject matter test to determine when the attorney–client privilege is available to a corporation. Under this test, the privilege protects the communications or discussions of any company employee with counsel so long as the subject matter of the communication relates to that employee's duties and the communication is made at the direction of a corporate superior. The Court also ruled that the attorney–client privilege extends to communications made to both in-house and outside counsel as long as the attorneys are acting in a legal capacity. Previously, courts addressing this issue had been reluctant to protect communications with in-house counsel.

RESULT   The Supreme Court reversed the ruling of the court of appeals. Communications between Upjohn's attorneys and all of its employees, not just a small, upper-level group, were deemed protected under the attorney–client privilege as long as those communications passed the subject matter test.

COMMENTS   The decision in *Upjohn* did not resolve all of the uncertainties regarding the application of attorney–client privilege to corporations. The Supreme Court did not decide whether the attorney–client privilege applies to communications with former employees. Nor did it resolve the issue of what exactly constitutes a voluntary waiver of the attorney–client privilege by a corporation. Finally, there is still uncertainty about the protection that the privilege gives corporations in suits brought against them by shareholders.

In *In Re Bieter Co.*,[16] the U.S. Court of Appeals for the Eighth Circuit held that the attorney–client privilege extends to communications between a partnership's attorney and a consultant to the partnership who was the functional equivalent of an employee. Even though the consultant was an independent contractor, not an employee, he was still a representative of the client partnership. Factors pointing to this included the fact that he had daily contact with the partnership's principals, he had acted as the partnership's sole representative in critical meetings, and he had worked with the partnership's attorneys on the lawsuit.

Guidelines   Following the Supreme Court's decision in *Upjohn*, there are a few guidelines for attorneys and corporations concerning the best method by which to keep communications within the scope of the attorney–client privilege.[17]

---

16. 6 F.3d 929 (8th Cir. 1994).

17. Based on Block & Remz, *After "Upjohn": The Uncertain Confidentiality of Corporate Internal Investigative Files*, in AMERICAN BAR ASSOCIATION SECTION ON LITIGATION, RECENT DEVELOPMENTS IN ATTORNEY–CLIENT PRIVILEGE, WORK-PRODUCT DOCTRINE AND CONFIDENTIALITY OF COMMUNICATIONS BETWEEN COUNSEL AND CLIENT (1983).

1. Communication between an attorney and a corporation is protected only when a client is seeking or receiving legal advice, not business advice. Thus, corporations should request legal advice in writing and assign communication with the attorney to a specific employee who has responsibility over the subject matter at issue.
2. Corporations should make sure that all communication between employees and corporate counsel is directed by senior management and that the employees know they must keep all communications confidential.
3. Corporations should demonstrate the confidentiality of attorney–client communications by dealing directly with counsel (not through intermediaries) and by maintaining confidential files and documentation.
4. When a corporation gives a governmental agency access to its communications or files, the corporation should negotiate a written agreement of confidentiality with the agency or an agreement that the agency will not take physical possession of the documents. The corporation should also investigate the possibility of statutory protection in this situation.

Pretrial Activity

Before the trial begins, the attorneys and the judge usually meet to discuss certain issues.

Motion to Dismiss The lawsuit may be resolved before trial by the judge granting a motion to dismiss. A motion formally requests the court to take some action. A *motion to dismiss* seeks to terminate the lawsuit on the ground that the plaintiff's claim is technically inadequate. A judge will grant a motion to dismiss if (1) the court lacks jurisdiction over the subject matter or the parties involved; (2) the plaintiff failed to properly serve the complaint on the defendant; or (3) the plaintiff has failed to state a claim on which relief can be granted.

A party may file a motion to dismiss immediately after the complaint and answer have been filed. This is known as a *motion for judgment on the pleadings*. One party, usually the defendant, argues that the complaint alone demonstrates that the action is futile.

The moving party may file *affidavits*, that is, sworn statements, or other written evidence in an attempt to show that the cause of action is without merit. When information or documents other than the pleadings are involved, the motion becomes a *motion for summary judgment*.

Summary Judgment A judge will grant *summary judgment* only if all of the written evidence before the court clearly establishes that there are no disputed issues of material fact and the party who requested the summary judgment is entitled to recover as a matter of law. If there is even a scintilla, that is, even the slightest bit, of evidence that casts doubt on an important fact in the lawsuit, the judge must not grant summary judgment. However, a judge may grant summary judgment on some issues of the case and let the other issues proceed to trial. This is called a *partial summary judgment*.

Pretrial Conference Pretrial or status conferences may be held either in open court or in the judge's chambers. During these conferences, the attorneys for the litigants meet with the judge to discuss the progress of their case. Topics discussed may include (1) the issues as stated in the pleadings; (2) any amendments to the pleadings; (3) the scheduling of future discovery and a plan for the timely completion of discovery; (4) the status of pending motions or prospective motions that a party may file; (5) a schedule of the disclosure of witnesses or exhibits; and most important, (6) the prospects for a settlement of the dispute. The main goal of a pretrial conference is to formulate an efficient plan for the trial.

Trial

A trial usually goes through the following stages.

1. Selection of the jury (if the trial is before a jury). The judge or attorneys may question the potential jurors.
2. Opening statements, first by the plaintiff's attorney and then by the defendant's attorney
3. Presentation of evidence and witnesses by the plaintiff's attorney. This consists of:
   a. Direct examination of witnesses by the plaintiff's attorney
   b. Cross-examination of witnesses by the defendant's attorney
   c. Redirect examination by the plaintiff's attorney
   d. Recross-examination by the defendant's attorney
   e. Redirect and recross-examination repeated until both sides have no further questions to ask
4. Presentation of evidence and witnesses by the defendant's attorney. This consists of:
   a. Direct examination of witnesses by the defendant's attorney

b. Cross-examination of witnesses by the plaintiff's attorney

c. Redirect and recross-examination until both sides have no further questions to ask

5. Motion for a directed verdict by either attorney

6. Closing arguments, first by the plaintiff's attorney, then by the defendant's attorney and then rebuttal by the plaintiff's attorney

7. The judge's instructions to the jury

8. Jury deliberations

9. Announcement of the jury verdict

Selection of Jury   Each side can challenge any number of jurors for cause during a process of questioning the potential jurors called *voir dire*. Cause includes any relationship between the juror and any of the parties or their counsel. Most jurisdictions also permit a limited number of preemptory challenges. These can be used by counsel to remove potential jurors who counsel thinks might be inclined to decide for the other side. The U.S. Supreme Court has held that it is unconstitutional to use a preemptory challenge to remove a potential juror due to race or gender.[18]

Motion for a Directed Verdict   At the close of the presentation of all the evidence, either attorney may ask the judge to grant a motion for a *directed verdict*. The moving party asserts that the other side has not produced enough evidence to support the legal claim or defense alleged. The motion requests that the judge take the case away from the jury and direct that a verdict be entered in favor of the party making the motion. Should the judge agree that there is not even an iota of evidence to support one party's claim or defense, the judge will issue a directed verdict. This does not happen very frequently.

Jury Verdict   After both sides have presented the closing arguments, the judge instructs the jury on applicable rules of law. After deliberating in private, the jury delivers its verdict, specifying both the prevailing party and the relief to which that party is entitled. In federal court, the six-person jury verdict must be unanimous. In state courts, a unanimous jury verdict is not always required. Frequently, 9 out of 12 votes is sufficient.

"Isn't it true that you did not love the victim, as you claim, but, in point of fact, feigned affection for the sole purpose of obtaining tuna fish?"

Posttrial Motions

The announcement of the jury verdict does not necessarily conclude the case. Either party may make a motion to set aside the verdict or to have the case retried.

Judgment Notwithstanding the Verdict   Immediately after the jury has rendered its verdict and the jury has been excused from the courtroom, the attorney for the losing party may make a motion for *judgment notwithstanding the verdict*. Such a judgment, also known as a *judgment n.o.v.*, from the Latin *non obstante veredicto*, reverses the jury verdict on the ground that the evidence of the prevailing party was so weak that no reasonable jury could have resolved the dispute in that party's favor. However, if there is any reasonable possibility that the evidence could support the jury verdict, the judge will deny a motion for a judgment n.o.v. or j.n.o.v.

New Trial   The judge may order a new trial if there were serious errors in the trial process—such as misconduct on the part of the attorneys or the jurors, or the improper admission of evidence that severely prejudiced one party's chances for a fair trial.

Appeal

If the trial judge does not grant the motion for a j.n.o.v. or a new trial, the losing party can appeal the decision. The appellate court will review the manner in which the

---

18. *See* Batson v. Kentucky, 476 U.S. 79 (1986) (race); J.E.B. v. Alabama, 511 U.S. 127 (1994) (gender).

trial judge applied the law to the case and conducted the trial. The court of appeals can review the presentation of evidence at trial, the denial of a motion for a directed verdict, the jury instructions, and even the jury award of damages.

If the appellant loses before the court of appeals, it may want to have the supreme court consider the decision. However, appeals are expensive. The losing party should seriously consider the likelihood of success at the higher court before pursuing an appeal.

 ## Class Actions

If the conduct of the defendant affected numerous persons in a common way, the case may be brought by a representative of the class of persons affected as a *class action*. This was done in the asbestos personal-injury cases brought against asbestos manufacturers such as GAF Corporation and Pfizer, Inc.; the silicone breast implant cases involving Dow Corning and others; and the smoking cases brought against the tobacco companies. Class actions are the norm in actions alleging securities fraud.

Written notice of the formation of the class must be mailed to all potential class members. Anyone who wants to litigate separately can opt out of the class. *Business Week* estimates that 260,000 out of millions of potential claimants for asbestos-related injury elected to opt out of a $1 billion settlement reached in 1993 involving 20 of the largest asbestos manufacturers.[19] If a

person does not opt out, he or she is a member of the class and will be bound by any decision or settlement reached in the class action.

Although historically corporate defendants have condemned class actions as an easy way for an eager plaintiff and his or her lawyer to get to court, this is changing. Some companies see class actions as a "strategic management tool" to end litigation nightmares and have found ways to use class actions to their advantage: avoiding potentially devastating jury awards, reducing litigation costs, and limiting long-term liability.[20]

A class action can have the following advantages in a major product liability case: (1) the settlement can bind not only present class members but also future claimants; (2) standardized payment schedules avoid the risk of widely divergent jury awards; (3) some claimants who suffered less harm than others can be excluded from the settlement; and (4) the filing of suits and the settlement can occur on the same day.[21]

Any settlement of a class action requires approval by the court hearing the case. Until recently, courts were hesitant to reject a mutually agreed upon settlement. However, as the following case indicates, the Supreme Court has tightened the requirements for class certification, making settlement more difficult.

19. Catherine Yang, *Look Who's Talking Settlement*, Bus. Wk., July 18, 1994, at 72.

20. Richard B. Schmitt, *The Deal Makers: Some Firms Embrace the Widely Dreaded Class-Action Lawsuit*, Wall St. J., July 18, 1996, at A1.

21. Yang, *supra* note 19.

A CASE IN POINT	SUMMARY

CASE 3.7
AMCHEM PRODUCTS,
INC. v. WINDSOR
Supreme Court
of the United States
117 S. Ct. 2231 (1997).

FACTS   Plaintiffs, nine individuals who were exposed to asbestos, filed a class action complaint, answer, and settlement proposal with the defendant Amchem Products, Inc. They never intended to litigate but merely sought judicial certification of the class, as required by Federal Rule of Civil Procedure 23. The petitioners claimed to represent the class of individuals who had not previously sued asbestos manufacturers and either (1) had been exposed to asbestos attributable to petitioner through their occupations or the occupations of a household member, or (2) had a spouse or family member who had been exposed to asbestos. The size of the class was indeterminate but estimated to include hundreds of thousands, perhaps millions, of individuals.

Case 3.7 continues

Case 3.7 continued

Of the nine named plaintiffs, half alleged presently manifested medical conditions as a result of asbestos exposure, while others had not yet developed any asbestos-related medical condition. The latter were considered "exposure-only" plaintiffs. The class was not divided into any subclasses.

The proposed settlement accomplished three things. First, the settlement prevented most class members from litigating any claims not previously filed against Amchem. Second, it outlined a procedure and schedule of payments for exposure-only and presently ill plaintiffs. It described categories of compensable cancers and specified the range of damages for each. Moreover, the number of claims paid per year was capped for each disease. Third, it denied recovery for any medical monitoring costs, emotional distress, loss of consortium, or any asbestos-related medical condition that did not result in a physical impairment.

The federal district court certified the class and enjoined class members from separately pursuing asbestos-related lawsuits in state or federal courts. The court of appeals, however, ordered decertification and vacated the district court's injunction. Amchem appealed.

ISSUE PRESENTED   Does the certification of a class to achieve a global settlement of current and future asbestos-related lawsuits comport with Federal Rule of Civil Procedure 23?

SUMMARY OF OPINION   The U.S. Supreme Court held that the proposed class did not satisfy the requirements of Rule 23. The Court ruled that although litigation was never contemplated, courts must evaluate the proposed certification as if it were.

The Court looked to Rule 23(b)(3)'s mandate that common questions "predominate over any question affecting only individual members," and it concluded that the humongous class size, with disparate individual interests, could not meet the requirement. The class members' shared experience of exposure to asbestos was not sufficient, because there were different categories of class members (different medical problems and the existence or absence of asbestos-related symptoms) and multiple individual differences (different medical histories, different levels and types of exposure, and varying degrees of severity of asbestos-related medical conditions). Characterizing the class as "sprawling," the Court concluded that the differences between the class members were greater than their commonalities. Therefore, the predominance requirement of Rule 23(b)(3) was not fulfilled.

The Court also found the class did not satisfy the Rule 23(a)(4) requirement for adequate representation. Essentially, Rule 23(a)(4) requires that the representatives of a class must be part of the class and have the same interests as the class members. However, in this case, the class members had different interests. Those currently injured would seek immediate payment while exposure-only plaintiffs would seek a generous, protected fund for future compensation. Thus, it was impossible to ensure that the class representatives could adequately represent their interests.

RESULT   The order of the court of appeals was affirmed. The class was decertified, and the injunction barring asbestos-related litigation was vacated.

Case 3.7 continues

Case 3.7 continued

COMMENTS   The *Amchem* decision was handed down as the Supreme Court's Advisory Committee on Civil Rules was considering a proposal to make settlements easier in class action lawsuits.[22] The decision was a signal to both the Advisory Committee and the lower courts to evaluate petitions for class certification and class action settlements more carefully. Indeed, lawyers working on the so-called fen-phen diet-pill related lawsuits (*ex post*, diet pills were linked to heart valve damage and a rare form of lung disease) indicate that class action lawsuits "are in a new era"[23] with courts less likely to accept class certifications and settlements.

22. Richard B. Schmitt, *High Court Upsets Class-Action Proposal*, WALL ST. J., July 10, 1997, at B10.

23. Richard B. Schmitt, *Thinning the Ranks: Diet-Pill Litigation Finds Courts Frowning on Mass Settlements*, WALL ST. J., Jan. 8, 1998, at A1.

ETHICAL CONSIDERATION

Is it ethical for a manufacturer of a product that caused harm to persons who will not discover it until a future date to enter into a class action settlement that provides limited funds for future claimants?

◆ Litigation Strategies for Plaintiffs

When planning to file a lawsuit, the plaintiff must decide which legal claim is most likely to succeed. The plaintiff must also decide in which court to pursue the lawsuit.

The Decision to Sue

Parties frequently file a lawsuit without giving sufficient thought to the various consequences. Before filing a lawsuit, one should consider (1) whether the likelihood of recovery and the amount of recovery are enough to justify the cost and disruption of litigation; (2) whether the defendant will be able to satisfy a judgment against it; (3) whether the defendant is likely to raise a counterclaim; (4) whether suing will cause any ill will among customers, suppliers, or other sources of corporate financing; (5) whether any publicity accompanying the suit will be harmful; and (6) the impact of the litigation on the company's relationship with the defendant. For example, a company may be advised not to sue the manufacturer of its multimillion-dollar computer over a $50,000 software problem if the company must rely on this manufacturer for support, service, and parts for the next few years.

If a lawsuit appears inevitable, there may be some advantage to filing a claim first. The plaintiff's claim determines in what court the case will be heard. The defendant, however, may be able to remove an action from state court to federal court if there is diversity of citizenship or a federal question. Alternatively, it may be able to remove the action to a more appropriate *venue*, or location.

Parties should always consider settling the suit. Recent figures show that more than 90% of cases settle out of court, saving all parties the time, cost, and ill will of a trial. Filing a lawsuit can be a tactic to encourage settlement of a dispute that neither party really wishes to bring to trial. Settlement discussions usually occur during the pretrial stages.

Parties should also consider alternatives to litigation, such as arbitration and mediation. Alternative dispute resolution techniques are discussed in Chapter 4.

Some attorneys recommend that companies construct a prelitigation "decision tree," which determines at each step of the proceeding the chances of prevailing or losing, the costs of going forward, and the potential amount of recovery. Developing a decision tree forces a company to conduct a substantial factual and legal analysis of its claim. This is in everyone's interest; courts are inclined to impose monetary penalties or "sanctions" on companies, individuals, and attorneys who file lawsuits without sufficient facts or the legal basis to support their claims.

The Decision to Settle

Some lawsuits are unlikely to settle, for example: (1) cases presenting legal questions—such as the meaning of an ambiguous term in a contract—that the court should clarify to avoid future disputes between the same parties; (2) cases that could bring a large recovery if the plaintiff wins and no great harm if it loses; and (3) cases where one side has acted so unreasonably that settlement is impossible.

Sometimes a lawsuit is worth pursuing simply to establish a company's credibility as one that will fight to support a legitimate business position. If applied too rigidly, such a philosophy can be expensive and may do more harm than good.

Settlement is likely in a case when pursuing the lawsuit all the way to trial is not cost efficient. For example, if a plaintiff alleges that a product is defective and caused him a loss of $4,500, the legal expenses will far exceed the original loss. Discovery alone is likely to cost more than $4,500. In such a case, it is in both parties' interest to settle the dispute if at all possible. However, if the plaintiff's claim is similar to many other identical claims that may be brought against the company, settling the first claim could appear to commit the defendant to paying all the other claims, too.

Pretrial Preparation

Having decided to file a lawsuit, the company should carefully select the personnel who will act as the contacts for the attorneys. These individuals should make sure that the necessary information and documents are gathered for the attorneys. The contact persons should have substantial authority in the company.

Executives or senior management who will be involved in the lawsuit or with the corporate attorneys should not handle public relations. This could lead to disputes regarding waiver of the attorney–client privilege.

The company should instruct all employees not to destroy any documents that may be relevant to the lawsuit. Destruction of these documents, particularly after the claim is filed, can be harmful and even illegal. Document-retention policies are discussed in greater detail later in this chapter.

The company should instruct employees not to discuss the lawsuit with anyone, including family or close friends. Casual comments about bankrupting the op-

---

AT THE TOP

It is important for members of higher management and, in some cases, the full board of directors to become involved in the decisions of when to sue, when to settle or dismiss, and how vigorously to defend. Sometimes the managers or employees intimately involved in the case lack the perspective and objectivity to determine the merits and the full impact a particular litigation decision will have on the company as a whole.

---

posing party or teaching an opponent a lesson may turn up as testimony at trial, with undesirable consequences.

The company and its attorney should develop a budget for the lawsuit. Then at each step of the case, strategic options can be discussed on the basis of cost-benefit analysis. The budget should include not only the lawyer's fees but also (1) the cost of employee time; (2) damage to company morale; (3) disruption of business; and (4) other hidden expenses. A budget will help the company manager and lawyer decide whether to pursue the lawsuit or attempt to settle.

The attorney and client should then select a court in which to file the lawsuit. Federal courts may be more accustomed to handling complex business litigation, such as that involving federal securities law or employment-discrimination laws. State courts are usually skilled in handling business disputes ranging from contract matters to personal-injury lawsuits. Other considerations about where to file include (1) the convenience and location of necessary witnesses and documents; (2) the location of trial counsel; (3) the reputation and size of the company and its opponent in a particular area; and (4) the possibility of favorable or unfavorable publicity.

All courts urge the parties to confer and settle the case if possible. The judge will act as a settlement mediator and objectively assist counsel in recognizing the strengths and weaknesses of their cases. Some state courts require a settlement conference before a specially designated settlement judge. The parties may also hire retired judges, professional mediators, law school professors, or mediators who are part of a bar association settlement program.

SHOULD THE UNITED STATES ADOPT THE BRITISH RULE THAT THE LOSER PAYS THE WINNER'S ATTORNEY'S FEES?

The costs of litigation are spiraling, and policymakers are scrambling to find the cause. With greater frequency, informed legal commentators have fingered plaintiffs who file lawsuits to extort a settlement, even when they know that the expected return from the trial will be negative. To deter such nuisance lawsuits and lessen the tide of excessive litigation in general, scholars, politicians, and ordinary citizens have called for an adoption of the British rule whereby the loser of a trial must provide for the legal expenses, including attorney's fees, of the victor. The American system, by contrast, requires each litigant to bear its own attorney's fees regardless of the trial's outcome, unless there is a contract providing that the loser must pay the attorney's fees for the winner.

In the early 1990s, these calls for legal reform entered mainstream politics. President George Bush's Council on Competitiveness established a working group on Federal Civil Justice Reform in January 1991, which recommended adoption of the British rule. The British rule—also known as the "loser pays" rule—simply states that the losing party at trial must pay the legal costs of the winner. Virtually every Western European country uses this system.

Under the council's recommendation, a modified "loser pays" rule would be adopted in cases involving state law brought under the federal court's diversity jurisdiction. The loser would pay the winner's costs of vindicating its prevailing position, but fee shifting would be limited to the amount in fees that the loser incurred, which could be further limited by judicial discretion.

> Adopting a "loser pays" rule for payment of attorney's fees will provide those bringing suit with a choice of methods to finance their litigation. The rule would help fund meritorious claims not currently initiated because the cost of pursuing the claim would have exceeded the expected recovery. . . . Because the losing party will be obligated to pay the winner's fees, this approach will encourage litigants to evaluate carefully the merits of their cases before initiating a frivolous claim or adopting a spurious defense.[a]

The report went on to state that the rule is also grounded in fairness—in the equitable principle that a party who suffers should be made whole.

Former American Bar Association President John Curtin stated that the proposal for a modified British rule was rejected by the ABA because of the "chilling effect" such a rule would have on the legal rights of certain individuals. He explained that execution of the "loser pays" rule would discourage potential litigants with bona fide claims from bringing suit due to trepidation over monetary ruin.[b]

Both consumer groups and civil libertarians also attacked the proposals. Public Citizen, a consumer advocate organization led by Ralph Nader, criticized the council's recommendations in an August 13, 1991, news release, calling the report an "anti-worker, anti-consumer, pro-corporate-wrongdoer blueprint for undermining America's system of common law."[c] Other critics contended that the fee-shifting rule would limit access to the judiciary for the indigent and would inhibit the bringing of novel or untested legal theories.

Efforts by the Republican majority in Congress in the mid-1990s to adopt the British rule as part of the "Contract With America" failed.

In practice, the British rule is not as detrimental to plaintiffs as might appear at first glance. As the *ABA Journal* reported,[d] only about 40% of British plaintiffs in court actions involving personal injury are subject to the "loser pays" risk of the British rule.[e] Most plaintiffs avoid the risk by one of three methods: (1) the government legal aid program; (2) trade unions who provide legal representation for their members and absorb litigation costs; and (3) legal expense insurance.

a. *Agenda for Civil Justice Reform in America* 24 (1991).

b. *Id.*

c. Herbert M. Kritzer, *The English Rule*, ABA J., Nov. 1992, at 55.

d. *Id.* at 55 (based on a 1986 study conducted for the Lord Chancellor's Department, which is the management arm of the English judiciary).

e. Judiciary, *ABA President Challenges Quayle Council Recommendations for Civil Justice Reforms*, DAILY REP. FOR EXECUTIVES (BNA), Aug. 14, 1991, at A-3.

Litigation Strategies for Defendants

A defendant receiving a complaint and summons should never let the lawsuit go unattended. An answer is required usually within 20 to 30 days. The defendant should also plan a defense strategy and follow it step by step. Factual and legal preparation should be done promptly, so that important evidence—such as the memory of key witnesses—is not lost.

When a company receives the complaint, efforts should be made to determine why the plaintiff felt it necessary to sue. Some of the factors may include (1) whether prior bargaining or negotiations with the plaintiff broke down, and why; (2) whether the company's negotiator was pursuing the wrong tactics or following an agenda inconsistent with the company's best interests; and (3) whether the lawsuit resulted from bad personnel practices that the company still needs to correct. Senior executives should also get together and decide whether it would be beneficial to discuss the lawsuit with the plaintiff.

A defendant should also promptly consider the possibility of a settlement and review the ways in which amicable negotiations could be commenced or resumed. The defendant may also want to consider mediation or arbitration as alternatives to an expensive trial. Sometimes, an apology can be more important than a vigorous defense in a case where the plaintiff feels unjustly wronged.

If the lawsuit cannot be settled, then the defendant should proceed with the same steps required of the plaintiff—plan a strategy, prepare a budget for the action, and so on. If the suit was filed in a state court, the defendant must decide whether it is possible, and desirable, to move the action to federal court.

If the plaintiff has sued in a place that is greatly inconvenient for the defendant and its witnesses, the defendant may file a motion for a change of venue. A federal district court may transfer the case to a federal district court in another state. A state court, however, can only transfer the case to another location within the state.

 ## Document Retention

When a company is a defendant in a lawsuit, company documents may be used to prove liability in court. According to the *Wall Street Journal*, some companies are

ETHICAL CONSIDERATION

You are a manager of Dow Chemical Company, overseeing the silicone breast implant litigation across the United States. Your market research tells you that most individuals distrust Big Business and that most consumers cannot identify many products of your company, except those involved in the litigation. With an upcoming trial in Louisiana, you are considering conducting a full-scale advertising campaign to boost the public image of Dow Chemical. The purpose is to influence public opinion in the jurisdiction of the suit, thereby creating a positive image in the minds of potential jurors. You have several options:

1. Emphasize in the campaign Dow Chemical's citizenship: employees volunteering, donating to charities, and the improvement of society as a result of Dow's products.
2. Describe the benefits of silicone products. Although not mentioning the breast implant issue, tell numerous heart-wrenching tales of silicone products saving the lives of children.
3. Begin the final campaign the week before jury selection. Highlight the greedy plaintiff's bar of attorneys and lament the growing litigiousness of our society. The final slogan: "You can stop the greedy lawyers!"
4. Same as 3, but also argue that silicone breast implants do no harm.[a]

What should you do? If you were the plaintiff, how would you respond to these tactics?

a. *See* Richard B. Schmitt, *Can Corporate Advertising Sway Juries?*, WALL ST. J., Mar. 3, 1997, at B1.

destroying three times as many documents as they did a decade ago. Companies have learned that nearly any corporate document can become a powerful weapon in court in the hands of opposing counsel. A well-designed and well-executed document management program can (1) reduce corporate liability; (2) protect trade secrets and other confidential information; and, most important, (3) save on litigation costs.[24] Time and money are wasted when corporate staff and lawyers are forced to search for documents during discovery. With an organized document management program, a company knows exactly what documents are in its possession and where these documents are located.

Most companies do not have established policies regarding document retention and destruction. They practice what some professionals call the "search and destroy" technique of file management: arbitrarily cleaning out file cabinets when storage space is running low.

However, federal and state regulations require companies to retain certain records. The Code of Federal Regulations contains more than 2,400 regulations requiring that certain types of business records be maintained for specific periods of time. Many regulatory agencies have increased their retention requirements, forcing some companies to increase their file capacities by more than 15% a year.

Designing a Policy

In general, documents that a company is not required to retain for any business or legal purpose should be eliminated from company files. Documents that are kept may be obtained by opposing counsel during discovery, and they may be harmful to the company in court. For example, an interoffice memorandum that described company strategy toward a competitor as "target and exploit their weak points to drive them out of the market" could be produced in court as evidence of intent to engage in an illegal and unfair business practice.

Documents containing elements of a company's decision-making process can sometimes be used out of context. A well-known example is the memorandum that was found in the files of Ford Motor Company during discovery for a 1972 trial arising out of a death caused by a Ford Pinto's allegedly defectively designed fuel tank. The memo, prepared in compliance with the regulations of a federal agency, compared the cost of design modifications to the Pinto fuel tank with the potential loss of life that might be caused by the existing design. During the trial,

the plaintiff's counsel convinced the jury that the memo was proof that Ford decided to defer redesign of the fuel tanks on the basis of this cost study. The jury awarded compensatory damages of $3.5 million and punitive damages of $125 million against Ford. (Compensatory damages compensate the injured party for the harm suffered; punitive damages are intended to punish the wrongdoer for conduct that is outrageous, willful, or malicious.)

Even if a company has been careful to destroy records, duplicates may exist in an employee's personal files, where they are still subject to discovery. For example, in the mid-1970s, the Weyerhauser Company paid $200 million in a case after company documents were found through discovery in personal files in the home of a retired company administrative assistant.

An employee's private diaries, calendars, and notebooks are also subject to discovery. Opposing counsel could glean from them a great deal about a company's operations. Companies should therefore include this type of record in its document management program.

Corporate Privacy

Besides protecting a company in the event of litigation, a document management program protects corporate privacy and trade secrets. A company should destroy confidential or proprietary materials as soon as possible. It should also preserve the confidentiality of employee records and destroy these records when they are no longer necessary. If an employee sues a company for wrongful termination, the employee's file is subject to discovery, and careless or unsubstantiated information in the file may be persuasive evidence at trial. Further, corporations can be liable for damages if confidential information in an employee's file, such as a medical record indicating past drug use, is made public.

Necessary Elements of a Document-Retention Program

Well-Planned and Systematic   To stand up in court, a document retention program must be well planned and systematic. Companies usually appoint a senior officer of the organization to be responsible for the supervision and auditing of the document management program. Policies should be established as to the types of documents to be destroyed, including documents stored on computer or word processing disks. The documents should then be

---

24. Much of the discussion of document retention that follows is based on the work of John Ruhnka, associate professor at the Graduate School of Business Administration, University of Colorado at Denver, and Robert B. Austin, CRM, CSP, of Austin Associates, Denver. *See* John Ruhnka & Robert Austin, *Design Considerations for Document Retention/Destruction Programs,* 1 Corp. Confidentiality & Disclosure Letter 2 (1988).

systematically destroyed according to an established time frame (for example, when they reach a certain age).

No Destruction in the Face of a Potential Lawsuit

It is illegal to destroy documents when the company has notice of a potential lawsuit. A company cannot wait until a suit is formally filed against it to stop destroying relevant documents. A company must halt destruction as soon as it has good reason to believe that a suit is likely to be filed or an investigation started. Companies that did not halt destruction of documents have been forced to pay damages even when they acted accidentally. For example, in *Carlucci v. Piper Aircraft*,[25] flight data information essential to the case was missing. The judge did not believe Piper Aircraft's claim that it had not deliberately destroyed the relevant document. The judge issued a directed verdict for the plaintiff and rendered a $10 million judgment against Piper.

No Selective Destruction

The importance of a systematic document-management program cannot be emphasized enough. The court will scrutinize whether document destruction was done in the ordinary course of business. Any hint of selective destruction jeopardizes the defensibility of a document-management program.

25. 102 F.R.D. 472 (S.D. Fla. 1984).

ETHICAL CONSIDERATION

You are a senior manager of a major manufacturer of in-line skates (rollerblades) that currently markets its products in North and South America. A recent memo from the vice-president for research and development explored how the skates would react to a new synthetic addition to concrete—ExtraLast. ExtraLast is still in the experimental phases in the United States but is currently being used in Europe. The memo found that under very specific conditions, the combined effects of heat, moisture, ExtraLast, and the plastic used on the wheels of the rollerblades creates a toxic carcinogenic substance. The top engineer expressed doubt, however, that anyone else would discover the toxic reaction for five to ten years; the toxic reaction was discovered by accident when a lab tech spilled a vial containing the reactive chemical in ExtraLast and failed to properly clean up the mess.

Given the potential for ExtraLast to be used in the United States in the next five years, what should you do? Is it ethical to shred the memo now?

THE RESPONSIBLE MANAGER
Reducing Litigation Expenses

Legal disputes often arise in the normal course of business operations. Some may be resolved amicably, but others may require a third party to adjudicate the dispute. Although the courts do provide one venue, a corporate manager should not rush to trial. The costs of effective counsel, the protracted nature of most commercial disputes, and the resultant opportunity costs can be significant. The allocation of corporate funds is one concern, but so is the distraction of corporate managers on litigation-related activities, such as depositions, interrogatories, trial, and document searches. And while most cases are settled, they are generally settled after hundreds of hours of pretrial activities.

In order to avoid these predictable pitfalls, a responsible manager seeks alternatives that maximize corporate value and interests. One solution is to engage in a continuing conversation with counsel in order to find

ways to reduce litigation costs.[26] In other words, find ways to settle cases cheaply and quickly. This requires identifying and overcoming litigious working assumptions of both the corporation and the lawyer. Emotions, a desire to pass the buck, and partisan bias can create a litigation trap that prevents some conflicts from being settled in a timely manner. Egos must be set aside—by both managers and lawyers—and optimal solutions to the *problem* of litigation must be pursued.

One option is for a manager to instruct counsel to develop a settlement strategy in addition to a litigation strategy. That is, while litigators are searching for ways to overcome a potential adversary, counsel should also seek ways to resolve the conflict as soon as possible. Such an organized approach enables the manager to keep the conflict in perspective by comparing the costs,

26. This discussion is based on Roger Fisher, *He Who Pays the Piper*, HARV. BUS. REV., Mar.–Apr., 1985, at 150.

advantages, and disadvantages of litigation and settlement. This approach also assists a manager in identifying those situations in which it is worthwhile to go to court, whether to establish a beneficial precedent or limit (or overturn) a disadvantageous one. Delineating specific settlement options and reviewing the results of settlement or litigation and the accuracy of cost predictions may also help reduce legal fees.

Frequent contact with counsel is also critical to reducing litigation expenses. Lack of good communication is often cited as a key problem by both managers and attorneys. Law firms often wrongly assume that they call the shots and spend more time and money on a case than the client may have intended.[27] A manager often needs legal advice to make an informed decision but should resist the temptation to just "leave it to the lawyers." Instead, the responsible manager treats litigation like any other business problem that requires a business solution.

27. Ann Davis, *Businesses' Poor Communications with Law Firms Is Found Costly*, WALL ST. J., July 17, 1997, at B5.

INSIDE STORY

DUPONT AND DISCOVERY ABUSE

The purpose of discovery is to facilitate the disclosure of all relevant information so that the ultimate resolution of a conflict may be based on a complete understanding of the facts, thereby facilitating a just result. Abuse of the discovery process is the use of the rules of discovery to avoid, hide, delay, and deceive the opposing party's understanding of one's facts and information. Often it involves strategic denials of information, hiding information, or making the information so costly to access that opposing counsel is severely burdened. Such discovery abuses infuriate judges and may result in the imposition of sanctions or penalties, including fines.

For example, in *In re E. I. DuPont de Nemours and Company*,[28] a federal district court held that the defendant, DuPont Company, had committed fraud, abused discovery, and violated court orders. As a result, it fined DuPont $6.8 million for discovery abuses and $100 million for civil contempt.

The latter sanction could be waived by compliance with the other court orders and taking out full-page ads in the *Wall Street Journal* and major papers in Georgia, Alabama, and Michigan admitting wrongdoing and describing the orders of the court. For every day that DuPont did not comply with the order, it would be fined $30,000.

DuPont had repeatedly failed to disclose test data that was critical to the plaintiff's claim that DuPont's Belnate DF fungicide was contaminated with herbicides that damaged the plaintiff's crops. After initial and supplemental requests, court orders to disclose, and promises of disclosure by DuPont's chief executive officer, legal department, and trial counsel, DuPont still did not reveal the test data. Moreover, DuPont had presented to the court a motion containing materially untrue statements, hoping to convince the court to vacate prior findings of discovery misconduct.

The judge stated:

Having heard and reviewed all of the relevant evidence, the Court concludes that DuPont, in light of the hundreds of claims and lawsuits which have arisen out of the use of its product Belnate 50DF, decided that it would not reveal the potentially damaging evidence generated by the Alta test.... DuPont consciously and deliberately withheld the Alta data and documents from the Plaintiffs and the Court.... DuPont urged falsely to the Court and elicited false testimony.... DuPont continued its concealment and deception to the extent of presenting to this Court knowingly untrue representations about DuPont's compliance with its discovery obligations and with this Court's orders with the accomplished purpose of fraudulently obtaining an untrue order from this Court to absolve DuPont of its misconduct, and to relieve DuPont of sanctions it richly deserved.

DuPont's conduct with regard to the Alta data and documents . . . was willful, deliberate, conscious, purposeful, deceitful, and in bad faith. . . . Put in layperson's terms, DuPont cheated. And it cheated consciously, deliberately and with purpose. DuPont has committed a fraud on this Court, and this Court concludes that DuPont should be, indeed must be, severely sanctioned if the integrity of the Court system is to be preserved.

. . .

By entering the monetary sanctions set forth herein it is the Court's purpose to deter DuPont and others who might likewise engage in such misconduct from engaging in such egregious discovery practices in the future and to deter it and others from committing similar frauds upon this or any other Court.

The fines imposed by the trial court were later overturned by the U.S. Court of Appeals for the Eleventh Circuit.[29] Although the appeals court was troubled by the conduct of DuPont and its lawyers, it held that the sanctions were overwhelmingly punitive and therefore criminal in nature. Because DuPont had not been provided the constitutional protections given to criminal defendants in this civil proceeding, the punitive fines against DuPont were vacated. However, the pattern of abuse by DuPont was so severe that the appeals court suggested a criminal investigation into the company and its counsel. As a result, the case was remanded to the district court for further hearings to determine the appropriate, nonpunitive discovery sanctions.

DuPont has been sanctioned for discovery abuses in other Belnate DF litigation. For example, a Hawaii state court judge found statements by an in-house counsel to be "fraudulent by clear and convincing evidence" and fined DuPont $1.5 million for discovery abuse.[30] DuPont was also fined $20,000 by a Florida state judge who, as a result of discovery abuses, ordered a victory for the plaintiff.[31] DuPont has appealed both judgments.

---

28. 918 F. Supp. 1524 (M.D. Ga. 1995).

29. *In re* E. I. DuPont de Nemours & Co.-Belnate Litigation, 99 F.3d 363 (11th Cir. 1996).

30. Milo Geyelin, *Fine Against DuPont in Belnate Case Is Overturned by Federal Appeals Court*, WALL ST. J., Oct. 21, 1996, at B10.

31. *Id.*

KEY WORDS AND PHRASES

QUESTIONS AND CASE PROBLEMS

1. Answer the following questions with regard to the case cite *Reno v. American Civil Liberties Union*, __ U.S. __, 117 S. Ct. 2329 (1997).

a. In what year was the case decided?

b. What court decided the case?

c. Can you tell from the cite which party originally brought the lawsuit?

d. Can you tell from the cite which party brought the appeal?

e. Suppose you wanted to cite the following passage that appeared on page 2351: "The interest in encouraging freedom of expression in a democratic society outweighs any theoretical but unproven benefit of censorship." Where would the page designation go?

2. One method of obtaining personal jurisdiction over an absent corporation is to attempt to gain jurisdiction over the parent through jurisdiction over the subsidiary. If a foreign corporation has no contact with a particular state except that it owns a subsidiary doing business in that state, should that be a sufficient contact to allow the state to claim jurisdiction over the parent? [*Newport Components v. NEC Home Elec (U.S.A.)* 671 F. Supp. 1525 (C.D. Cal. 1987)]

3. CompuServe, an Internet service provider located in Ohio, provided electronic access to more than 1,700 information services, in addition to serving as a conduit for individuals to acquire computer software. Patterson subscribed to CompuServe and placed his "shareware" on the electronic market of CompuServe access. As a result, CompuServe and Patterson entered into a Shareware Registration Agreement, which created an independent contractor relationship between Patterson and CompuServe and incorporated the CompuServe Service Agreement and Rules of Operation. These agreements specified that any conflict would be governed by Ohio law. Patterson sent an e-mail to CompuServe indicating that he agreed to the terms of the agreement. When CompuServe began marketing a product similar to Patterson's, Patterson complained and CompuServe changed the name of its product. However, Patterson continued to complain and demanded a $100,000 settlement. CompuServe sought a declaratory judgment in an Ohio court that CompuServe had not infringed upon Patterson's trademarks.

Patterson claimed that the Ohio courts lacked personal jurisdiction due to insufficient contacts with the state. [*CompuServe v. Patterson*, 89 F.3d 1257 (6th Cir. 1996)]

a. Do you agree with Patterson? Should he be subject to the Ohio courts?

b. Why would Patterson not want to submit to the Ohio judiciary?

4. Stig Slosh, a native of Albany, New York, was touring the United States with his band De Minimis Fringe. While playing a concert in the state of Nowhere, Slosh was struck in the head by the band's giant fiberglass armadillo, a prop suspended by ropes that glided across the stage during the opening song. The accident occurred because the stagehands assigned to manipulate the prop miscalculated its position in the air. Slosh and the band were forced to cancel the show, but they finished the remainder of the tour. The armadillo was damaged beyond repair and had to be discarded. However, the band was not too upset about this. They were already leaning toward dropping the prop from their act, as it didn't seem to add much. However, the band did not make this fact public. Instead, Slosh sued the local concert promoter, Graham Bell, a resident of Nowhere, in federal district court.

a. Bell tries to have Slosh's suit thrown out of federal court. Bell claims that a federal court has no subject matter jurisdiction over this lawsuit. What arguments can Slosh make to keep the suit in federal court? (If any additional facts are needed to make this argument, state what they are.) What is Bell's best argument for keeping this suit out of federal court? How might Bell get the information needed to make this argument?

b. Assume that Slosh succeeds in keeping the lawsuit in federal court. Slosh bases his suit against Bell on the general common law principle that employers are financially liable for the actions of their employees. The stagehands were in fact employed by Bell. Bell counters that the laws of the state of Nowhere should apply. Under Nowhere common law, performers assume full financial responsibility for any damage caused by props they use in their acts. Which law should govern? Why?

5. Whatawad, Inc. is a major producer of bubble gum. In the last year, Whatawad lost a significant portion of its market share to Humungo Bubble, Inc., its main competitor in the field. Humungo ads boasted that in a test conducted by independent researchers, Humungo gum blew larger bubbles than Whatawad. In fact, the test was conducted by Humungo's own research team. Before he quit the company, Ian Ventor, head of research at Humungo, told his supervisor that he wanted to inform Humungo's in-house counsel about the false statement in the ad. The supervisor told Ventor that it was his own choice whether to take such action. Ventor went ahead and told the in-house counsel. Lotta D. Kay, the vice-president of sales for Whatawad, was determined to prevent further erosion of her company's business. In a written memo, Kay instructed her sales representatives to offer kickbacks to the wholesalers who purchased bubble gum from Whatawad if they would increase orders by 10%. Although Kay instructed the sales representatives to destroy her memo, Kay's own secretary forgot to delete the memo from the company's computer system.

a. Suspecting the use of kickbacks, the district attorney's office brings charges against Whatawad. When these charges are brought, the CEO of Whatawad instructs both Kay and her sales representatives to reveal all the details of their activity to trial lawyers hired specifically to defend the firm in this suit. They do that. The district attorney demands to see the notes describing their discussions. Will he be successful in obtaining the notes covering either Kay's or the sales representatives' conversations? What policies shape the law in this area?

b. Immediately after the charges are brought, Kay finds out about the undeleted memo and deletes it herself from the system. Kay's secretary believes this is an unethical act and reports it to the district attorney. Does Kay have any liability for this action? What procedures should Whatawad have followed to ensure that this document did not remain in the system? Should a company use a document-retention system to destroy documents that clearly demonstrate wrongdoing on the part of the company?

c. The district attorney decides to prosecute Humungo for false advertising. He demands to see the notes of the conversation between Ian Ventor and the in-house counsel. What arguments can the district attorney make to obtain these notes? How should the company respond?

6. DuLac Corporation, a leading U.S. manufacturer of chemicals and synthetic fabrics, is incorporated in the state of Blue Waters. All of DuLac's business is conducted within Blue Waters, and all its offices are located within the state. Blue Waters, is under the federal jurisdiction of the U.S. Court of Appeals for the Fourth Circuit. The Environmental Protection Agency (EPA) commenced an investigation of DuLac's disposal procedures for DRT, a mixture of the toxic compound DNGR and the neutralizing agent HRMLS. Upon discovering that DuLac had disposed of DRT in dump sites not approved for toxic-waste disposal, the EPA filed suit against DuLac for cleanup costs and punitive damages under a federal statute forbidding the disposal of DNGR or any derivative thereof except in approved toxic-waste-dump sites. The action was brought in a federal district court sitting in Blue Waters. DuLac's only defense to the action is that, because the DNGR in DRT is fully neutralized, DRT should not be considered a derivative of DNGR for purposes of the statute. A month later, the lawyer for the EPA offers to settle the case for cleanup costs only.

a. Assume that the U.S. Court of Appeals for the Sixth Circuit recently interpreted the statute literally, upholding an award of punitive damages against a company that had disposed of fully neutralized DNGR. As DuLac's manager, would you recommend that the company accept the settlement offer?

b. Assume that another district court within the Fourth Circuit recently reached the same result as the Sixth Circuit. How would you advise DuLac regarding the settlement offer?

c. Assume that the U.S. Supreme Court recently reached the same result as the Sixth Circuit. Would your advice to DuLac remain the same?

7. A Massachusetts-based manufacturer of a cigarette filter containing asbestos placed its products into the stream of interstate commerce by delivering them to the cigarette manufacturer's plants in New Jersey and Kentucky. From there, the component part was shipped across the United States and was sold in Maryland. The filter manufacturer knew that the products would be sold in the state of Maryland. However, the filter manufacturer was not registered to do business in Maryland, did not have an office there, and did not employ any individuals within the state of Maryland. Can the Massachusetts company be sued in a wrongful-death suit in the courts of Maryland for producing a component part that potentially contributed to the deceased's lung cancer?

[*Lesnick v. Hollingsworth & Vose Co.*, 35 F.3d 939 (4th Cir. 1994), *cert. denied*, 513 U.S. 1151 (1995)]

8. The National Collegiate Athletic Association (NCAA) sponsors and regulates intercollegiate athletic competition throughout the United States. Under the NCAA's drug-testing program, randomly selected college student athletes competing in postseason championships and football bowl games are required to provide samples of their urine under closely monitored conditions. Urine samples are chemically analyzed for proscribed substances. Athletes testing positive are subject to disqualification.

Student athletes attending Stanford University sued the NCAA, contending its drug-testing program violated their right to privacy secured by Article I, Section I, of the California state constitution. That section provides: "All people are by nature free and independent and have inalienable rights. Among these are enjoying and defending life and liberty, acquiring, possessing, and protecting property, and pursuing and obtaining safety, happiness, and privacy." Stanford intervened in the suit and adopted plaintiffs' position.

a. Does the NCAA's drug-testing program violate athletes' right to privacy under the California state constitution?

b. Suppose the elements of the cause of action for violation of the state constitutional right to privacy are (1) a legally protected privacy interest; (2) a reasonable expectation of privacy; and (3) serious invasion of a privacy interest. How would you evaluate the constitutional claim?

c. Does it matter that the NCAA is a private organization and not a governmental agency? Should it be subject to a lesser standard in evaluating invasions of the right to privacy?

d. To monitor athletes as they provided urine samples, an NCAA official (of the same sex as the athlete) stood five to seven feet away as the athlete urinated. Should it matter that the NCAA could use less intrusive means to ensure a valid urine sample? [*Hill v. NCAA*, 865 P.2d 633 (Cal. 1994)]

9. Richard King operated a music club called the Blue Note in Columbia, Missouri. In an attempt to increase local exposure, King created a Web page with information regarding show dates, times, and ticket prices. In addition, King provided a hyperlink to a famous jazz club by the same name in New York City. Bensusan Restaurant Corporation, the operators of the Blue Note in New York, brought suit in New York, claiming that King was violating the Lanham Act, the federal Trademark Dilution Act (Bensusan had trademarked "The Blue Note"), and common law unfair competition principles. King's only contact with New York was the passive Web page. Does King have to respond to these allegations in a New York court? [*Bensusan Restaurant Corp. v. King*, 126 F.3d 25 (2d Cir. 1997)]

a. Would the answer be different if King had intentionally named his club the Blue Note in hopes of riding the coattails of the famous New York club? Why or why not?

b. What if King responded to New Yorkers' e-mail inquiries received through the Web site? What if he notified his regular customers in New York of new, upcoming shows either by phone or e-mail addressed to such persons?

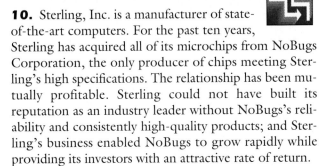

MANAGER'S DILEMMA

10. Sterling, Inc. is a manufacturer of state-of-the-art computers. For the past ten years, Sterling has acquired all of its microchips from NoBugs Corporation, the only producer of chips meeting Sterling's high specifications. The relationship has been mutually profitable. Sterling could not have built its reputation as an industry leader without NoBugs's reliability and consistently high-quality products; and Sterling's business enabled NoBugs to grow rapidly while providing its investors with an attractive rate of return.

Some months ago, several of Sterling's computers exploded shortly after installation. Upon investigation, Sterling discovered that tiny imperfections in NoBugs's microchips had aggravated a dormant design defect in the computers, causing the explosions. Analysis of the chips indicated that they were indeed below specification and that the imperfections were caused by a slight miscalibration of NoBugs's encoding equipment. NoBugs recalibrated the equipment and promptly resumed production of perfect chips. Sterling's losses from the explosions—lost profits, out-of-pocket costs associated with compensating customers for the explosions, and injury to business reputation—are estimated to exceed $20 million. Sterling and NoBugs disagree on the amount of the loss for which NoBugs should be responsible. Sterling's CEO is considering a lawsuit. She asks you to prepare a memo outlining the advantages and disadvantages of litigation and proposing a litigation strategy. Draft that memo.

INTERNET SOURCES	
This page offers new students of the law a variety of materials, including guides to case citations and research materials.	http://www.lawlib.uh.edu/guides
Courts.net provides directory listings for courts throughout the nation on a state-by-state basis.	http://www.courts.net
The state of California's judicial system has its own home page with information about its court system, including structure and recent decisions.	http://www.courtinfo.ca.gov
The National Center for State Courts' home page offers a variety of information pertaining to state courts.	http://www.ncsc.dni.us
The Cornell University Law School offers access to all U.S. Supreme Court decisions since 1990 as well as more than 500 of the most important historical decisions.	http://www.law.cornell.edu/supct
Under the direction of the U.S. Department of Commerce, this page offers access to more than 7,000 U.S. Supreme Court opinions from 1937 to 1975.	http://www.fedworld.gov/supcourt/index.html
FindLaw allows users to search for state and federal statutes, cases, and regulations.	http://www.findlaw.com/casecode
U.S. Code	http://law.house.gov/usc.htm
Congressional Record	http://www.access.gpo.gov/su_docs/aces/aces150.html
GPO Access Databases	http://www.access.gpo.gov/su_docs/aces/aces002.html
GPO Access Searching Tips	http://georgetown.edu/wtaylor/gposrch.html
Federal Web Locator	http://www.law.vill.edu/Fed-Agency/fedwebloc.html

CHAPTER 4

Alternative Dispute Resolution

INTRODUCTION

Why Not Just Sue?

Why would a manager consider alternative methods for resolving disputes when the manager has access to a judicial system provided by the government and financed through taxation?[1] For anyone who has used litigation and the courts to resolve a business dispute, the answer is obvious. Litigation is expensive and takes a toll on management and employees. In addition to generating legal fees, lawsuits distract management from the company's business, risk damaging the firm's public image, and jeopardize relationships with the opposing party.

To avoid the expense and disruption of legal battles, companies increasingly use out-of-court methods to resolve their disputes. Instead of automatically taking legal conflicts to the courthouse, more firms than ever are using alternatives to formal litigation to settle conflicts with customers, suppliers, and employees. For example, General Mills estimates that it has saved

hundreds of thousands of dollars through the use of alternative procedures.

Of all tort cases in the United States, only 5% are ever tried.[2] In California's state court system, only 7% of all civil cases ever go to trial.[3] Clearly, trials are not the only option when it comes to dispute resolution.

Chapter Overview

This chapter explains the manager's nonlitigation options for the resolution of business disputes. Alternative dispute resolution (ADR) methods include negotiation, mediation, and arbitration, as well as hybrids, such as minitrials, med-arb, and summary jury trials. The chapter also discusses barriers to successful dispute resolution and suggests strategies for resolving disputes out of court. It also explains how the law views these alternatives to litigation.

---

1. The author gratefully acknowledges the assistance of Kelly R. Young in the preparation of this chapter. Mr. Young received his M.B.A. and J.D. from Stanford University and is currently vice-president for research at the James Buchanan Center at George Mason University.

2. Robert Wilson, *Negotiation with Private Information: Litigation and Strikes,* Nancy L. Schwartz Memorial Lecture, Kellogg Graduate School of Management, Northwestern University, Chicago, Illinois, May 18, 1994.

3. *Infrequent Trials,* WALL ST. J., June 19, 1995, at B5. The remaining 93% of cases include both dismissed and settled cases.

Thinking about ADR

To select the best alternative to litigation, managers must be aware of their own needs and constraints. Like other business decisions, choosing a dispute resolution mechanism—including litigation—involves many trade-offs: Is the right decision more important than quick resolution, or is time of the essence? Is public attention helpful to the resolution of the conflict, or does the matter require confidentiality? Does the company need to preserve its relationship with the other party, or is this conflict the last interaction with that party? Will mutual resolution of the conflict make the company a desirable business partner, or will potential disputants seek conflict because the company appears weak and unwilling to defend itself vigorously?

Not all dispute resolution mechanisms are appropriate for all disputes. To choose the right mechanism, a manager should consider the nature of the alternatives, as well as his or her specific situation. To distinguish the alternatives from each other, a manager should consider the following questions about dispute settlement and the possible answers:[4]

1. How are the disputants represented?
    - by lawyers
    - by persons without formal legal training
    - by themselves without any outside representation
2. Who makes the final decision?
    - a judge or other government employee with formal legal training
    - an attorney or other legal professional
    - an expert in the industry
    - a representative of the community in which the company operates
    - the disputants with the help of a neutral third party
    - the disputants themselves
3. How are facts found and standards of judgment set?
    - the disputants or their representatives are responsible for the presentation of evidence of the facts and arguments to establish the standard for resolution
    - the dispute resolver, or final decision maker, could aid the disputants in performing any of these tasks
    - the dispute resolver alone could establish the standards and find the facts
4. What is the source of the standard for resolution?
    - rules already established by legislatures and courts
    - evolving rules and standards
    - prior practice of those whose disputes were resolved before this one
    - prevailing values and notions of fairness
    - the disputants themselves, determined either before or after the dispute arises
    - a delegated third party, such as the American Arbitration Association (AAA) or the American Mediation Council (AMC)
5. How will any decision be enforced?
    - by a court or threat of legal action
    - by the good faith of the disputants
    - by concern for reputation and future relationships
6. Who will pay for the dispute resolution procedure?
    - the losing party
    - all parties on an equal basis
    - the dispute resolver will allocate the costs
    - the employer (in the case of conflicts with employees) or the supplier (in the case of conflicts with customers)
    - the party bringing the dispute for resolution

Different alternatives answer these questions differently, and parties can often mix and match to suit their circumstances. Before attempting to resolve any dispute, good managers should think carefully about their own goals and the nature of dispute resolution alternatives.

"The first thing we do, let's kill all the lawyers."

—William Shakespeare, Henry VI, Part 2, Act IV, Scene ii, Line 75.

---

4. These questions and answers are based on JOHN J. COUND ET AL., CIVIL PROCEDURE: CASES AND MATERIALS 1311–13 (6th ed. 1993).

EARLY BINDING ARBITRATION

In one of the earliest examples of ADR, two women brought their dispute over the maternity of an infant boy to a leading official:[a]

> Then the king [Solomon] said, "The one says, 'This is my son, who is living, and your son is the dead one;' and the other says, 'No! For your son is the dead one, and my son is the living one.'"
>
> And the king said, "Get me a sword." So they brought a sword before the king. And the king said, "Divide the living child in two, and give half to the one and half to the other."
>
> Then the woman whose child was the living one spoke to the king for she was deeply stirred over her son and said, "Oh my lord, give her the living child and by no means kill him."
>
> But the other said, "He shall be neither mine nor yours; divide him!"
>
> Then the king answered and said, "Give the first woman the living child and by no means kill him. She is his mother."
>
> When all Israel heard of the judgment which the king had handed down, they feared the king; for they saw that the wisdom of God was in him to administer justice.

a. 1 *Kings* 3: 23–28.

Varieties of ADR

There are three basic varieties of ADR: negotiation, mediation, and arbitration. By mixing these with each other and the formal judicial system, a manger has three more options: minitrial, med-arb, and summary jury trials.

Negotiation

"Everyone negotiates," begins the popular book *Negotiating Rationally* by Professors Max Bazerman and Margaret Neale, and so they do. In a world of scarce resources, imperfect information, and miscommunication, conflict is inevitable. Suppose Matt puts a For Sale sign on his a car, and Kelly has $1,000 to spend on one. They both would like to have the car *and* the cash, but that is not possible. Therein lies the conflict. Almost naturally, they begin to discuss the situation. Kelly asks, "What year car are you selling? What condition is it in? What is the mileage?" Kelly also asks himself how much he can afford. What other cars has he seen for sale? How much does he value the high-end stereo and the low-quality paint job? Kelly offers $800; Matt balks and demands $2,000.

Somewhere in that story, Matt and Kelly began to negotiate. Like Supreme Court Justice Potter Stewart's quip about pornography, people may not be able to define negotiation precisely, but they know it when they see it. For the most part, though, *negotiation* is the give-and-take people engage in when coming to terms with each other.

The life of a manager is similar. Employees must be hired, supplies must be purchased, products must be sold, capital must be raised, and meetings must be scheduled. Conflict is inevitable. Job descriptions will be misinterpreted, suppliers will demand more favorable terms, customers will cancel orders, investment banks will demand larger fees, and busy project teams will have to find two-hour windows when sales representatives from Singapore and engineers from Silicon Valley are both available for conference calls to London-based advertisers.

Some of these examples are clearly beyond the pale of the law, but some are not. An employee may claim breach of contract when an expected promotion goes to someone else. A software developer might sue a customer who refused to pay for customized software.

Even when parties turn to the courts, a trial may not result. The judicial system, including many of the formal procedures of civil litigation, encourages parties to consider settling their disputes out of court. This is discussed in detail later in this chapter.

Approaches

One can view negotiation along several different dimensions. Negotiation can be either forward looking with concern for desired relationships—*transactional negotiation*—or backward looking to address past events that have caused disagreement—*dispute negotiation*. An example of a transactional negotiation is one between two firms involved in a joint venture. An example of a dispute negotiation is one between a steel manufacturer that failed to deliver I-beams and a construction company that has already paid for them. In the former, both parties are looking to the future with positive expectations; but in the latter, the parties are looking to the past and apportioning blame. Conflicts need not be simply one or the other. Labor negotiations often have elements of both transactions and disputes. The parties must work together in the future but may also feel the need to apportion blame for the event that precipitated the crisis.

Negotiation can be viewed as involving a fixed or a growing pie. In *distributive* or *zero-sum negotiations*, the only issue is the distribution of the fixed pie. For example, in the car sale example above, each dollar that Matt receives for the car is a dollar less that Kelly has left. The pie consists of the cash and the car; and more for one necessarily means less for the other. On the other hand, in *integrative* or *variable-sum negotiations*, mutual gains are possible as parties trade lower-valued resources for higher-valued ones.

In the car example, Matt might make the negotiation integrative by offering to include a new paint job or to remove the expensive stereo. If Matt owned an auto body shop, he might be able to repaint the car inexpensively. Kelly might highly value the fresh coat and pay considerably more for a freshly painted car. Similarly, if Kelly is tone-deaf and barely values the stereo system, Matt might remove the stereo and reduce the price substantially. The different values placed by Matt and Kelly on the stereo or the paint job allow them to gain from trading. For instance, Matt can enhance the original deal for both parties by taking off the table something he values more than Kelly does (the stereo) and replacing it with something Kelly very much wants (a reduced price). Or Matt could add something he values less than Kelly does (the paint job) and take away something Matt wants for himself (a higher price). In the employment context, parties often expand a distributive discussion about salary to integrate issues of medical benefits, vacation days, formal titles, and other perquisites, such as parking spaces, first-class air travel, and corporate credit cards.

Such integration of issues, or pie-growing, was popularized by Roger Fisher and Bill Ury in their book *Getting to Yes*. (After receiving criticism for paying undue attention to integrative negotiations and ignoring dull but common distributive situations, Ury published a follow-up book, *Getting Past No*.) Unsurprisingly, distributive negotiations can easily become adversarial and strain even the closest relationships. With nothing to do but fight over the pie, parties are left with nothing to do but fight. For that reason, managers should follow Fisher and Ury's advice and try to integrate other issues into the discussion. This creates the possibility of trade-offs that allow both parties to gain relative to their distributive starting point. For instance, in our car example, the addition of paint jobs and stereos into the discussion allows both parties to gain from trading and transforms a distributive negotiation into an integrative one.

Planning and Preparation

Professors Bazerman and Neale recommend asking and answering three questions before entering a negotiation (or at least before entering a negotiation one wishes to win): First, ask what is your *reservation price*, that is, that price at which you are indifferent between the success and failure of the negotiation. In their framework, a negotiator should first establish his or her *Best Alternative to a Negotiated Agreement (BATNA)*. This is the outcome a person will choose if the negotiation fails. By definition, it is the best outcome available outside the negotiation. Consequently, any settlement higher than one's BATNA is preferable to a failed negotiation. Although reservation price and BATNA are not the same, they are closely related. The transaction costs of executing the BATNA are the essential difference.

By understanding one's BATNA, a person can determine the highest price he or she should be willing to pay. If a manager makes an offer close to her reservation price and her opponent refuses, the manager knows that further concessions are not in her interest. As Bazerman and Neale remind us, "[T]he goal of negotiating is not to reach just any agreement, but to reach an agreement that is better for you than what you would get without one."[5] Well-intentioned managers can easily get caught up in the heat of an important negotiation and mistake agreement for success.

Second, ask what are your interests, as opposed to your positions. Positions are the stated requirements that one negotiator demands of his or her opponent. Interests are what he or she actually desires, whether revealed or withheld. Knowing one's interests allows a person to fashion integrative solutions.

Third, ask how important, comparatively, each negotiation issue is to you. Understanding one's priorities and distinguishing between positions and interests allows a manager to think systematically about trade-offs that create mutual gain. A prudent negotiator asks these three questions about his opponents as well as himself.

Exhibit 4.1 summarizes the steps to take in preparation for a negotiation. An unprepared negotiator is a manager's favorite opponent. Don't be someone else's favorite opponent.

Strategy

A basic lesson of game theory is to *look forward and reason back*. That is to say, one should think through the consequences of any potential decision and then work backwards step by step from the ultimate result to the choice at hand. In the classic *Prisoner's Dilemma*,[6] Alice and Bugsy conspire to commit a dastardly deed. The two criminal conspirators are arrested, separated, and interrogated by a cynical but clever detective with only enough evidence for a minor conviction. The detective offers each person the same deal: "Fink on your friend and go free right now; but if your friend finks on you too, you each get five years. Keep quiet and spend one year in jail if your buddy keeps quiet too, but spend eight years if you get finked out." The chart in Exhibit 4.2, called a *payoff table* in game theory, describes the possible outcomes.

Regardless of what the other chooses, each person can minimize his or her jail time if he or she rats out the

---

5. Max H. Bazerman & Margaret A. Neale, Negotiating Rationally 173 (1992).

6. Anatol Rappaport & Albert M. Chammah, Prisoner's Dilemma: A Study in Conflict and Cooperation (1965).

EXHIBIT 4.1   Negotiation Preparation

Before embarking on a negotiation, a manager should do the following:

1. Analyze the nature of the dispute
   - Ask why this particular constellation of actors is at the negotiating table now
2. Specify superordinate goals and objectives
   - Figure out what you want
3. Outline the scope of the negotiation
   - Identify the issues to be negotiated, both tangible and intangible
   - Determine your reservation price
   - Consider your alternatives to this negotiation
   - Analyze the priorities for each issue to be negotiated
   - Consider alternative proposals you could offer and you could accept
4. Understand your opponent by asking:
   - What issues will be of concern to her?
   - What are her priorities on those issues?
   - What is her reservation price?
   - What are her alternatives to this negotiation?
   - What is the history of negotiations between you and your opponent?
   - What is her reputation?
   - Is the opponent monolithic or a group with members having differing views?
5. Understand the particular negotiation situation and ask:
   - What are the deadlines or other time constraints?
   - Who has the authority to ratify any agreement and is that person at the negotiation?
   - Will this negotiation affect future negotiations and, if so, how?
   - How important is your relationship with the other party going forward?

SOURCE   Based on Professor Margaret Neale's course "Conflict and Negotiation" at the Stanford University Graduate School of Business. Used by permission.

---

other. Take Bugsy, for example. If Alice stays quiet, Bugsy goes free by finking or spends a year in prison for his silence. If Alice finks, Bugsy does five years instead of eight by finking. Not knowing Alice's decision before he

EXHIBIT 4.2 Prisoner's Dilemma Payoff Table

		Bugsy	
		Quiet	Fink
Alice	Quiet	A 1 yr B 1 yr	A 8 yrs B free
	Fink	A free B 8 yrs	A 5 yrs B 5 yrs

INTERNATIONAL CONSIDERATION

In negotiating across cultures or in international settings, cultural myopia is a serious barrier to success. For instance, eye contact implies dramatically different attitudes in Japan and the United States. In the United States, a negotiator who avoids eye contact will be perceived as being intimidated or shifty. In Japan, that same behavior is taken as a sign of respect. When signals are misinterpreted, complex negotiations get even more complicated. Consider the Tokyo conference room where respectful officials of Mitsubishi avoid eye contact as discussions begin with aggressive owners of a Texas car dealership who rarely avert their eyes. What of teetotaling in Moscow? Bare heads in Jerusalem? Shoed feet in Beijing?[a]

---

a. For discussions of issues in cross-cultural negotiation, *see* Frank E. A. Sader & Jeffrey Z. Rubin, *Culture, Negotiation, and Eye of the Beholder*, 7 NEGOTIATION J. 249 (1991); Stephen E. Weiss, *Negotiating with "Romans"—Part 1*, SLOAN MGMT. REV. 51 (Winter 1994); John L. Graham, *The Japanese Negotiation Style: Characteristics of a Distinct Approach*, 9 NEGOTIATION J. 123 (1993).

himself must decide, Bugsy should fink. (By introducing postgame information such as retribution for finking or pregame structures such as agreements to keep quiet, one can change the game and the conclusions.)

Game theorists would say that in this game, finking is the *dominant strategy*—it is always superior to the alternatives. Although the total time spent in jail is minimized by each person keeping quiet—two years total—this optimal outcome will not be achieved because neither person can be sure of the other. Thus, the dilemma. Perhaps a more appropriate term would be "Prisoner's Tragedy" because the same structure that allows a brief two years of jail time ensures a hefty 10 years.

To put this into a business context, imagine two litigating parties. Instead of prison terms, imagine millions of dollars in legal fees and judgments. Instead of finking and keeping quiet, imagine countersuing and capitulating. The bottom line is that under certain conditions, actors will not cooperate with each other even though cooperation would serve their combined interests.

If our prisoners or firms could get together and contract around the rules of the game, they might ensure the optimal outcome. That, rather than noncooperation, is the lesson of the often-misunderstood Prisoner's Dilemma.[7]

Barriers to Resolution

Negotiators often encounter barriers to the successful resolution of their disputes, although these barriers may be quite invisible to them or their opponents. In general, there are three types of barriers: strategic, structural, and psychological.[8]

Strategic barriers are those obstacles one party intentionally places before the other. For instance, a party may refuse to reveal what issues are important to him or her or may mislead opponents as to his or her sincere evaluation of various alternatives. This secrecy and deception may reflect a lack of trust, an unsophisticated negotiation strategy, or a motive ulterior to successful

---

7. For a thorough and entertaining discussion of game theory as applied to life, *see* AVINASH K. DIXIT & BARRY J. NALEBUFF, THINKING STRATEGICALLY : THE COMPETITIVE EDGE IN BUSINESS, POLITICS, AND EVERYDAY LIFE (1993).

8. For a discussion and analysis of barriers to successful dispute resolution, *see* Lee Ross & Andrew Ward, *Psychological Barriers to Dispute Resolution*, 27 ADVANCES IN EXPERIMENTAL PSYCHOLOGY 255 (1995).

negotiation. Playing hardball is another such barrier. By refusing to compromise and being difficult to deal with, a disputant may enhance his or her reputation for toughness with his or her colleagues. Even more strategically, a disputant may intentionally behave irrationally in order to discourage those who might seek conflict with him or her, reasoning that no one wants to pick a fight with Rambo.

Unlike strategic barriers, which are erected to interfere with the negotiation, *structural barriers* arise from the existing frameworks and institutions within which a manager operates. Common structural barriers include (1) unequal or *asymmetric information* between parties, (2) winner's curse in auction settings, (3) conflicts of interest between principals (such as equity owners) and the agents (such as corporate officers) employed to negotiate on their behalf, (4) restricted channels of communication between negotiators, and (5) political constraints on otherwise optimal solutions. The presence of these barriers makes negotiation progress and ultimate agreement quite difficult.

Take, for example, asymmetric information in the used car market. Assume that cars are either creampuffs (worth $5,000) or lemons (worth $3,000) and that only Matt, the seller, knows whether his car is a creampuff or a lemon. Thus, Kelly, the prospective buyer, is at an informational disadvantage. If Kelly offers $4,000, Matt's acceptance signals to Kelly that the car is worth only $3,000, but if the car is worth $5,000, Matt will refuse the offer. Knowing this ahead of time, Kelly will be reluctant to bid seriously.

The problem of *winner's curse* is related to asymmetric information. In an auction, the winner is the party with the highest bid. That reflects the winner's placing the highest value on the item. When the true value is uncertain, as with a locked safe or an unverified masterpiece, the winning bid reflects merely the highest expected value, which may well exceed the subsequently realized value. The winner's curse is the realization by the winner that he or she won because he or she most *overvalued* the item. Anticipating such a result, prospective bidders may be unwilling to bid even close to their expected value at all. These structural barriers may be remedied by changing the relevant structure, such as incorporating warranties in the face of asymmetric information.

Psychological barriers are perhaps the most difficult to understand and remedy because they arise from the very paradigms through which negotiators see the world. These barriers include (1) *reactive devaluation*, in which one party discounts proposals of the opposing party simply because the proposal came from an opponent; (2) *divergent construals*, that is, differing perceptions of the same events, such as pro-Israeli and pro-Palestinian television viewers believing that the same news broadcast about Jewish settlements on the West Bank was biased in favor of the other side; (3) *psychological dissonance* from past events or decisions as one tries to reconcile contradictory decisions or actions, such as the inability to reject one's previous but mistaken evaluation or announcement; (4) *optimistic overconfidence* in one's own argument, strategy, or position; and (5) *loss aversion*, that is, being risk seeking after suffering losses and risk averse after enjoying gains. Lacking consciousness of these barriers in one's self and one's opponents enhances conflict and makes successful negotiation exceedingly difficult. Awareness of them, however, is the first step towards overcoming them.

Exhibit 4.3 summarizes a number of common negotiation mistakes.

EXHIBIT 4.3   Common Negotiation Mistakes

Common negotiation mistakes include:

- Pursuing a negotiated course of action only to justify an earlier decision.
- Assuming that what is good for you is necessarily bad for your opponent and vice versa.
- Being irrationally affected by an initial anchor price, that is, a price that was suggested early in the negotiations and may now be an unnatural standard for evaluating other offers.
- Failing to look for another frame or characterization of the issues that would put a different perspective on the negotiation.
- Being affected by readily available information (such as personal experience or recent events) and ignoring other valid, but less accessible, data.
- Placing too much confidence in your own fallible judgment.

SOURCE Adapted with the permission of The Free Press, a Division of Simon & Schuster, from NEGOTIATING RATIONALLY by MAX H. BAZERMAN & MARGARET A. NEALE. Copyright © 1992 by Max H. Bazerman and Margaret A. Neale.

◆ Mediation

Litigation can turn business colleagues into bitter enemies. The win-lose nature of lawsuits usually makes it impossible for both parties to claim satisfaction, save face, or forgive-and-forget. After a lawsuit, one party feels vindicated and the other feels wronged. Even the ostensible winner often feels angry about the time and expense wasted on getting what he or she felt was his or her due to begin with. Mediation can be a less hostile alternative. Like negotiation, mediation can lead to joint gains. It can also help preserve relationships that might otherwise break under the strain of conflict.

In *mediation*, the parties agree to try to reach a solution themselves, but with the assistance of a neutral third party who helps them find a mutually satisfactory solution. This third party is the *mediator*.

In many ways, mediation is an extension of the negotiation process. One can view mediation as a facilitated negotiation. The mediator/facilitator guides the parties in a structured set of discussions about the issues and alternatives. He or she confers with both parties, together and in private, and points out the elements of their dispute and the areas of agreement. Sometimes the mediator helps the parties to identify their own goals.

As in negotiation, parties often confuse their positions with their interests, especially after publicly stating a commitment to a position. If seen as a neutral, a mediator is better positioned to ask questions and offer suggestions without creating the suspicion of ulterior motives. Parties to mediation are less likely to ask of a good mediator "What is she really trying to do?" Unlike the parties, a mediator can offer compromises without fear of appearing weak or too eager to settle.

A mediator's role is to suggest ways to resolve the dispute fairly and to guide the parties toward resolution. Unlike a judge, a mediator cannot enforce a solution; the parties must come to a resolution themselves and then agree to abide by it. Once agreement is reached, parties may formalize the arrangement with contracts, public statements, or letters of understanding.

History

The formal use of mediation is hardly a recent phenomenon. Early immigrant groups, including Quaker, Chinese, and Jewish communities, used mediation to resolve intragroup conflict and to avoid the American judicial system's foreign legal culture. Organized labor has used mediation since the nineteenth century. In 1926, Congress established the National Mediation Board, and in 1947 it created the Federal Mediation and Conciliation Service. These two entities remain active in dispute resolution.

When Congress created the Mediation and Conciliation Service, it unequivocally stated its support for labor mediation: "It is the policy of the United States that . . . the settlement of issues between employers and employees through collective bargaining may be advanced by making available full and adequate governmental facilities for conciliation, mediation, and voluntary arbitration to aid and encourage employers and representatives of their employees to reach and maintain agreements. . . ."[9]

In 1997, the Federal Mediation Board ordered a new union election for customer service agents at US Airways Group Inc. after it found the carrier "tainted" conditions required for a fair election.[10] That same year the Federal Mediation and Conciliation Service called for federally mediated meetings between Caterpillar, Inc. and the United Auto Workers. The two groups had been at odds since the early 1990s and had endured two large-scale strikes. Until the Conciliation Service's director intervened, the two sides had not met in two years to discuss the expired contract.[11]

Insurance companies have also used mediation to save money, time, and other resources. The Travelers Insurance Company found that more than 85% of the cases it submitted to mediation were settled. Even in the cases in which a settlement could not be reached, the mediation process helped the litigants focus on the most important issues, which allowed for a quicker resolution at trial. In the last few years, 37 insurance companies have entered pacts to mediate their claims against each other. Chubb & Son, Inc., a participating insurance company, has resolved nearly a dozen disputes under mediation pacts and saved between $150,000 and $200,000 per case.[12]

---

9. 29 U.S.C. § 171 (1978). This is the Labor-Management Relations Act of 1947, also known as the Taft-Hartley Act.

10. *New Union Election at US Air Is Ordered by Mediation Board*, WALL ST. J., June 23, 1997, at B12D.

11. *Caterpillar, UAW Agree to Mediation in Bid to End Strife*, WALL ST. J., May 5, 1997, at A6.

12. Margaret A. Jacobs, *Industry Giants Join Movement to Mediate*, WALL ST. J., July 21, 1997, at B1.

In the last three years, more than 100 large companies agreed to mediate any disputes arising out of their business dealings with each other. Participants include PepsiCo, Kellogg Company, Chase Manhattan, and DuPont.[13]

Because mediators can allow parties to vent their feelings and encourage parties to at least acknowledge each other's perspectives, mediation can diffuse difficult interpersonal tensions. Today, violence-plagued inner city schools are experimenting with mediation programs to help their students resolve conflicts with each other. Courts often mandate mediation before allowing disputes to go to trial. This is most common in family, housing, and small claims courts, which deal with the most personal of relationships.

Selecting a Mediator

Although not pronouncing final judgment, a mediator can powerfully affect the outcome of the mediation. By asking some questions but not others, the mediator can move the discussion to or from some issue. By suggesting solutions and reacting to proposals, the mediator can influence both parties' attitudes toward fairness, risk aversion, and trust. A skilled mediator knows how to bring disputing parties to genuine settlement; an unskilled mediator can push parties into agreements they later regret, or worse, he or she can inflame the situation.

In the 1980s the Society of Professionals in Dispute Resolution (SPDR) formed a commission to study the qualifications of mediators. After concluding that performance rather than credentials should be the central qualification criteria, it determined that qualified mediators should be able to (1) understand the negotiating process and the role of advocacy; (2) earn trust and maintain acceptability; (3) convert parties' positions into needs and interests; (4) screen out nonmediable issues; (5) help parties invent creative options; (6) help parties identify principles and criteria that will guide their decision making; (7) help parties assess their nonsettlement alternatives; (8) help parties make their own informed choices; and (9) help parties assess whether their agreement can be implemented.[14] Mediation agreements may or may not specify how a mediator will be selected.

The American Mediation Council (AMC), a for-profit dispute resolution firm, offers a standard mediation clause for parties to incorporate into their contracts: "Any controversy or claim arising out of or relating to this agreement shall be submitted to the American Mediation Council, LLC (AMC), under its Mediation Rules, before the parties resort to arbitration, litigation, or other dispute resolution procedure." These rules do not require parties to use an AMC mediator. Instead, they call for the mediator to be selected from the AMC panel of mediators unless the parties agree otherwise. This default provision serves even the most hostile parties who cannot even agree on a mediator. For those who can agree and choose to select their own mediator, the SPDR qualification list is a valuable guide.

Confidentiality

The issue of confidentiality is central to negotiation and mediation. If parties do not feel comfortable revealing important and sensitive information, they are less likely to identify opportunities for mutual gain. Unlike negotiation, mediation allows disputants to confide in a third party without fear of being exploited. Whether manifest

"Our mediator will meet with your mediator."

---

13. *Id.*

14. National Institute of Dispute Resolution, *Dispute Resolution Forum*, May 9, 1989.

ETHICAL CONSIDERATION

In many businesses, volume discounts are standard practice, and large customers reasonably expect to receive favorable treatment. How should a large, international corporation with a steady stream of disputes screen prospective mediators? Is it appropriate for a manager of the corporation to make clear to prospective mediators the potential for future lucrative business "if this one goes well"?

as caucusing or shuttle diplomacy, confiding in a mediator can allow the mediator to identify potential gains and point them out to the parties. If that confidentiality is doubted, however, parties will withhold useful but potentially damaging information. Even worse, if the

promise of confidentiality is not honored, parties will come to regret their mediation experience.

To protect such confidences, many states extend legal privileges to mediators, but these approaches are not uniform. New York, for example, provides a broad mediation privilege: "[A]ll memoranda, work products, and case files of a mediator are confidential and not subject to disclosure in any judicial or administrative proceeding."[15] Similar protection extends to communications made during the mediation between the mediator and the participants. This protects parties from later discovery and questioning at trial. In California, by contrast, confidentiality is protected only to the extent agreed upon in writing by the parties.[16] Although federal law does not directly address the question, federal courts have shown a willingness to recognize a mediation privilege, as was done in the following case.

15. N.Y. JUD. L. § 849-b(6).
16. CAL. EVID. CODE § 1152.5.

A CASE IN POINT   **IN THE LANGUAGE OF THE COURT**

CASE 4.1
NATIONAL LABOR RELATIONS BOARD v. JOSEPH MACALUSO, INC.
United States Court of Appeals for the Ninth Circuit 618 F.2d 51 (9th Cir. 1980).

FACTS   In 1976, the Retail Store Employees Union, Local 1001, successfully campaigned to organize the employees of Joseph Macaluso, Inc., a retailer of women's apparel, at its four stores in Washington state. After several months of bargaining, the company and the union failed to reach a collective bargaining agreement. The parties then decided to enlist the assistance of a mediator from the Federal Mediation and Conciliation Service (FMCS). Professional mediator Douglas Hammond attended three meetings between the parties at which the issues surrounding a collective bargaining agreement were negotiated with his assistance.

During the spring and summer of 1976, the company engaged in conduct that led the National Labor Relations Board (NLRB) to charge it with unfair labor practices toward pro-union employees. The NLRB also asserted that the company and the union had finalized a collective bargaining agreement at the three meetings with Hammond and that the company had violated the law by failing to execute the written contract incorporating this agreement. The company disputed that any collective bargaining agreement had ever been reached.

At trial before an NLRB administrative law judge (ALJ), the union representatives testified that at the third meeting there was an amicable explanatory discussion of the mutually accepted terms of the new collective bargaining agreement. The company negotiators, on the other hand, asserted that their refusal to give in to union demands caused the union negotiators to burst into anger, threaten lawsuits, and leave the room

Case 4.1 continues

Case 4.1 continued

at Hammond's suggestion. According to the company, Hammond was thereafter unable to bring the parties together, and the union negotiators ended the third meeting in anger.

In an effort to make its case, the company requested that the judge subpoena Hammond and obtain his description of the last two bargaining sessions. The subpoena was initially granted but later revoked upon motion of the FMCS. Without Hammond's tie-breaking testimony, the judge decided that the union witnesses were more credible and ruled that an agreement had been reached.

ISSUE PRESENTED   Does the goal of preserving mediator effectiveness by protecting mediator neutrality in labor disputes outweigh the public's interest in obtaining each person's evidence?

OPINION   WALLACE, J., writing for the U.S. Court of Appeals:

The NLRB's revocation of Hammond's subpoena conflicts with the fundamental principle of Anglo-American law that the public is entitled to every person's evidence. . . .

The facts before us present a classic illustration of the need for every person's evidence: the trier of fact is faced with directly conflicting testimony from two adverse sources, and a third objective source is capable of presenting evidence that would, in all probability, resolve the dispute by revealing the truth. . . . The public interest protected by revocation [of Hammond's subpoena] must be substantial if it is to cause us to "concede that the evidence in question has all the probative value that can be required, and yet exclude it because its admission would injure some other cause more than it would help the cause of truth, and because the avoidance of that injury is considered of more consequence than the possible harm to the cause of truth." We thus are required to balance two important interests, both critical in their own setting.

We conclude that the public interest in maintaining the perceived and actual impartiality of federal mediators does outweigh the benefits derivable from Hammond's testimony. . . .

[F]ederal mediation has become a substantial contributor to industrial peace in the United States. The FMCS, as amicus curiae, has informed us that it participated in mediation of 23,450 labor disputes in fiscal year 1977, with approximately 325 federal mediators stationed in 80 field offices around the country. Any activity that would significantly decrease the effectiveness of this mediation service could threaten the industrial stability of the nation. The importance of Hammond's testimony in this case is not so great as to justify such a threat. Moreover, the loss of that testimony did not cripple the fact-finding process. The ALJ resolved the dispute by making a credibility determination, a function routinely entrusted to triers of fact throughout our judicial system.

. . .

Public policy and the successful effectuation of the Federal Mediation and Conciliation Service's mission require that commissioners and employees maintain a reputation for impartiality and integrity. Labor and management or other interested

Case 4.1 continues

Case 4.1 continued

parties participating in mediation efforts must have the assurance and confidence that information disclosed to commissioners and other employees of the Service will not subsequently be divulged, voluntarily or because of compulsion, unless authorized by the Director of the Service.

. . .

We conclude, therefore, that the complete exclusion of mediator testimony is necessary to the preservation of an effective system of labor mediation, and that labor mediation is essential to continued industrial stability, a public interest sufficiently great to outweigh the interest in obtaining every person's evidence. . . .

RESULT The appeals court upheld the NLRB's revocation of a subpoena of the federal mediator and enforced the NLRB's order against the company.

Questions

1. Should the public policy to support mediator confidentiality and impartiality ever yield to the need for courts to make their decisions based on relevant evidence? How important are these two public policies? What are the consequences of favoring one over the other?
2. If mediators enjoyed no legal privileges of confidentiality, what could a disputant do before entering mediation to ensure that the mediator did not end up in court testifying for the other party?

When to Use Mediation

Mediation, like other forms of ADR, is better suited to some conflicts than to others. For mediation to be appropriate, the parties must sincerely desire to settle their dispute. If they are unwilling to compromise or seek to harm their opponents, mediation will be a frustrating waste of time. Conversely, parties who wish to preserve their relationship are best suited to mediation. Litigation is adversarial by nature and often leaves hard feelings in its wake. Arbitration too can pit one party against another such that future interactions are filled with animosity.

Legal uncertainty also makes mediation an attractive alternative. If the law is clear and one party's rights are clearly being violated by the other party, mediation will seem unnecessary. The less black-and-white the situation, the more risky legal action is. Mediation allows parties to resolve their differences more quickly and without appeal to undeveloped, ill-formed, or uncertain legal doctrine.

The need for privacy may also make some disputes more appropriate for mediation. Lawsuits require the filing of public documents and can alert the media to sensitive areas of business. Trade secrets, embryonic research, organizational structures, and internal training documents may need to be kept from the front pages of newspapers. Suppliers and customers may also become nervous if problems that could have been kept confidential are reported in the press. "Keeping it between ourselves" is much more realistic if few outsiders are involved.

Mediation Process

By definition, mediation is a flexible process that allows for many different structures, rules, and procedures. Because parties are less likely to agree to anything once a dispute has arisen, mediation organizations have evolved sets of default rules to which disputants can subscribe in advance of a specific conflict or to which they can defer once a conflict has arisen. Although many variations are possible, the Ground Rules of Proceeding from the AMC Rules and Procedures for Mediation of Business Disputes, excerpted in Exhibit 4.4, provide a good illustration.

These ground rules set a framework for mediation that anticipates many ambiguities and areas for disagreement, such as representation, caucusing, and confidentiality. The rules are, however, flexible. As the final rule makes clear, disputants may agree to alternative

---

EXHIBIT 4.4   American Mediation Council Ground Rules

The following ground rules will apply, subject to any changes on which the parties and the mediator agree.

a. The process is voluntary and nonbinding.

b. Each party may withdraw at any time after the mediation session has begun, and before execution of a written agreement, by written notice to AMC and the other party or parties.

c. The mediator shall be neutral and impartial.

d. The mediator shall control the procedural aspects of the mediation. The parties will cooperate fully with the mediator.

    i.   The mediator is free to meet and communicate separately or jointly with each party.

    ii. The mediator will decide when to hold joint meetings with the parties and when to hold separate meetings. The mediator will fix the time and place of each session and its agenda in consultation with the parties. There will be no stenographic record of any meeting. Formal rules of evidence or procedure will not apply.

e. Each party will be represented at the mediation by a person authorized to negotiate a resolution of the dispute, unless excused by the mediator as to a particular conference. Each party may be represented by more than one person, for example, a business executive and an attorney. The mediator may limit the number of persons representing each party.

f. The process will be conducted expeditiously. Each representative will make every effort to be available for meetings.

g. The mediator will not transmit information received in confidence from any party to any other party or any third party unless authorized to do so by the party transmitting the information, or unless ordered to do so by a court of competent jurisdiction.

h. Unless the parties agree otherwise, they will refrain from pursuing litigation or any administrative or judicial remedies during the mediation process or for a set period of time, insofar as they can without prejudicing their legal rights.

i. Unless all parties and AMC otherwise agree in writing, the mediator and any persons assisting the mediator will be disqualified as a witness, consultant or expert in any pleading or future investigation, action or proceeding relating to the subject matter of the mediation (including any investigation, action or proceeding which involves persons not party to this mediation).

j. The mediator may obtain assistance and independent expert advice, with the prior agreement of and at the expense of the parties. Any person proposed as an independent expert also will be required to disclose any circumstances known to him or her that would cause reasonable doubt regarding the candidate's impartiality.

k. Neither AMC nor the mediator shall be liable for any act or omission in connection with the mediation, except for its/his/her own willful misconduct.

l. The mediator may withdraw at any time by written notice to the parties (i) for serious personal reasons, (ii) if the mediator believes that a party is not acting in good faith, or (iii) if the mediator concludes that further mediation efforts would not be useful. If the mediator withdraws pursuant to (i) or (ii), he or she need not state the reason for withdrawal.

m. At the inception of the mediation process, each party and representative will agree in writing to all provisions of these Rules, as modified by agreement of the parties.

SOURCE   From AMERICAN MEDIATION COUNCIL LLC, RULES AND PROCEDURES FOR MEDIATION OF BUSINESS DISPUTES § 3. *Used by permission.*

---

rules if the AMC's default framework is ill suited to their particular conflict. The remainder of the AMC's rules and procedures, by which its clients agree to abide before entering mediation, addresses the entire mediation process: proposing mediation to one's disputant, selecting a mediator, exchanging information, preparing for the mediation, negotiating final settlement, and maintaining confidentiality.

Dangers

Mediation is often attractive because it offers resolutions that are speedy, inexpensive, and logistically simple when compared to litigation. Mediation can also be therapeutic for the parties involved if they can express their pent-up feelings of anger, frustration, or betrayal. On the other hand, critics of mediation have pointed to the lack of procedural protections in the process. Some parties may be surprised to find that their legal rights are not protected in mediation even though their rights would be protected in litigation. Parties with equal bargaining power may wisely agree to trade such rights for expediency, but unequal bargainers may unfairly take advantage of each other. For example, in a conflict between a landlord and rent-controlled tenants over rat infestation, a tenant might accept the placing of rat traps instead of the full-scale extermination that the housing code and a court would mandate.

Mediation may also deter or encourage change in the distribution of power in a relationship. For example, introducing mediation into a non-union plant may effectively diffuse current tensions and hinder efforts to unionize the plant.[17] Before agreeing to mediation, parties should consider the possibility of such unintended consequences, including possible effects on continued adjudication of the dispute, future dealings with the opponent, and one's reputation with internal and external constituencies.

ETHICAL CONSIDERATION

During a dispute with a competitor over copyrighted software that is similar to a competitor's products, you ask a mediator friend about his work in ADR. In the course of a few nameless anecdotes about his recent clients, you are shocked to learn how much sensitive information a skilled mediator can induce parties to share. At the same time, your attorneys tell you that without more evidence against your competitor, a lawsuit is not justified or economically prudent at this time. Should you propose mediation to the other company in the hope of learning enough information to justify legal action? If such a proposal is accepted, should you send as your representative a new employee who has no sensitive information to reveal? Should you hire a professional investigator as your representative to elicit as much damaging information as possible from your competitor?

◆ Arbitration

Arbitration is the resolution of a dispute by a neutral third party, called an *arbitrator*. For example, in July 1997, MovieFone, Inc. won a $22.7 million arbitration award against box-office equipment manufacturer Pacer/CATS Corp. for breach of contract. In 1992, the parties had entered into an agreement to sell movie tickets by telephone. Two years after the agreement, Pacer/CATS contributed its assets to a joint venture between its parent corporation, Wembley PLC, and Ticketmaster, Inc. MovieFone claimed the asset transfer violated its contract with Pacer/CATS. An American Arbitration Association (AAA) panel agreed and awarded MovieFone $22.7 million for the harm it suffered.[18] (The "Inside Story" for this chapter describes the big-ticket arbitration involving IBM and Fujitsu.)

Unlike mediation, arbitration usually results in a binding decision that is enforceable in court. In contrast, any resolution reached as a result of mediation is binding upon the parties only if they subsequently enter into a contract embodying the agreed-upon terms. In

arbitration, the parties typically agree beforehand to be bound by the results of the arbitration.

Although *nonbinding arbitration* is certainly an option, most parties enter into arbitration for its binding nature. For instance, in *final-offer arbitration*, used most notably in baseball salary disputes, each side submits its "best and final" offer to the arbitrator, who must choose one of the two proposals. Such a structure strongly encourages the parties to submit fair and reasonable offers. Otherwise, the less reasonable party is likely to lose with no chance for further concessions. Without its binding nature, such an exercise would be pointless. Still, some parties value the result of nonbinding arbitration as a guide to what is fair. If a neutral third party has heard the strongest evidence and best arguments of both sides in a dispute, his or her opinion can serve as a baseline for what a court might decide.

Arbitration Process

Arbitration is the most formalized of the ADR methods. It is unlike both negotiation, in which there is no structure unless the parties first negotiate one, and mediation, in which the mediator focuses more on creating dialog than on enforcing a technical format. In some

---

17. WILLIAM L. URY ET AL., GETTING DISPUTES RESOLVED 52 (1988).

18. *Arbitration Panel Awards Damages of $22.7 Million*, WALL ST. J., July 24, 1997, at B10.

ways, arbitration is like a trial. The first stage is usually a *prehearing*, in which parties may submit trial-like briefs, supporting documents, and other written statements making their case. Because neither federal nor state statutes grant arbitrators the authority to use discovery devices at this stage, prehearing discovery is usually limited to what the parties voluntarily disclose.

Because the hearing itself is adversarial, as with a formal judicial trial, it is more structured than the prehearing. The precise structure varies from arbitration to arbitration, but Rule 29 of the Commercial Arbitration Rules, promulgated by the AAA, provides an illustration:

> The Arbitrator may, at the beginning of the hearing, ask for statements clarifying the issues involved.
>
> The complaining party shall then present its claim and proofs and its witnesses, who shall submit to questions or other examination. The defending party shall then present its defense and proofs and its witnesses, who shall submit to questions or other examination. The Arbitrator has discretion to vary this procedure but shall afford full and equal opportunity to all parties for the presentation of any material or relevant proofs.
>
> Exhibits, when offered by either party, may be received in evidence by the Arbitrator.

Although no detailed rules of evidence or procedure need apply—unlike in state and federal court, where much statutory and case law addresses fine points in exacting detail—many arbitrators believe that compliance with some of these rules is useful and necessary. Arbitrators may also subpoena documents and witnesses for the hearing.

In the final, *posthearing* phase, the arbitrator makes his or her award after considering all the evidence presented in the prehearing and the hearing itself. Often, the award is unaccompanied by any discussion or explanation of the decision. "Written opinions can be dangerous because they identify targets for the losing party to attack," notes one arbitration scholar.[19] In a profession neither subject to appeal nor constrained by precedent, arbitrators may be reluctant to give extra grist to the loser's mill. On the other hand, the Supreme Court has noted that "a well reasoned opinion tends to engender confidence in the integrity of the process and aids in clarifying the underlying agreement."[20] In some set-

tings, such as federal labor arbitrations under the auspices of the NLRB, arbitrators are required to write an opinion. Also, parties can insist on such an opinion as part of their contract with the arbitrator.

This flexibility in the process of arbitration is one motivation to forgo formal litigation. Without the principle of *stare decisis* to bind the decision maker, arbitration allows for more flexibility in the outcome. That is not necessarily desirable because an arbitrator might surprise parties with his or her decision while a judge would be predictable. Still, issues of cost and time make arbitration an attractive option in many situations.

Choice of Arbitrator

The arbitrator is usually chosen by the parties to the dispute or by a third-party delegate, such as the American Arbitration Association, which represents 18,000 arbitrators. The choice of an arbitrator is crucial. Unlike a judge's decision, which can be set aside if erroneous, an arbitrator's ruling generally is binding. As New York's highest court stated nearly two decades ago, "An arbitrator's paramount responsibility is to reach an equitable result, and the courts will not assume the role of overseers to mold the award to conform to their sense of justice. Thus, an arbitrator's award will not be vacated for errors of law and fact committed by the arbitrator."[21]

---

21. Sprinzen v. Nomberg, 389 N.E. 2d 456, 458 (N.Y. 1979).

INTERNATIONAL CONSIDERATION

In 1997, two associations of Japanese attorneys announced the formation of a new ADR center to handle intellectual property disputes. Frustrated by the lack of expertise in the courts and other arbitration systems, the founders planned to employ experts from many fields who understand industrial property and the underlying science and technology. The center, scheduled to open in March 1998, is available to all disputants regardless of nationality.[a]

---

a. *Japanese IP Arbitration Center Planned*, 9 J. PROPRIETARY RTS. 6, 35 (1997).

---

19. R. COULSON, BUSINESS ARBITRATION—WHAT YOU NEED TO KNOW 29 (3d ed. 1986).

20. United Steelworkers of Am. v. Enterprise Wheel & Car Corp., 363 U.S. 593, 598 (1960).

An arbitration clause may list the names of potential arbitrators; if so, the parties should check the availability of these candidates before enlisting them. As with judges and their courts, particular arbitrators may be too busy to provide speedy resolution. Alternatively, the arbitration clause may refer the selection of an arbitrator to the AAA or another dispute resolution organization. American Arbitration Association arbitrators are skilled, and the association makes special efforts to identify arbitrators experienced in handling particular types of disputes. The AAA decides how many arbitrators to appoint (usually from one to three) and may include arbitrators from different professions—unless the arbitration clause specifies the number and kind of arbitrators desired. Arbitration clauses often provide that each party will choose its own arbitrator and that these two will pick a third. In some states, the government itself is willing to intervene. In New York, for instance, a court may name the arbitrator upon application by either party.[22] The Federal Arbitration Act (FAA) has a similar provision.[23]

The ability to select an arbitrator familiar with the industry or form of dispute further distinguishes arbitration from much of the judicial system. Judges tend to be experts in judicial procedure. Consequently, they hear cases touching on many substantive areas of the law. A federal district judge, for instance, could in a single day preside over cases ranging from felony narcotic sales to toxic tort class actions, and including price-fixing cases, contract disputes between financial institutions, and racially motivated employment discrimination. Arbitrators tend to focus on business sectors or conflict types, such as labor relations or landlord-tenant disputes. To the extent one is more concerned with substance than procedure, arbitration can be an attractive alternative to litigation.

Arbitration Clauses

A common device by which parties enter into arbitration is the inclusion of an arbitration clause in a contract. An *arbitration clause* specifies that in the event of a dispute arising out of the contract, the parties will arbitrate specific issues in a stated manner. Arbitration clauses are especially important in international contracts when each party wishes to avoid the labyrinth of a foreign legal system and the many pitfalls awaiting a novice litigant.

ETHICAL CONSIDERATION

A common premise underlying advocacy of ADR is that the parties to it have consented to the dispute resolution mechanism as opposed to the judicial system. Should the manager of a local appliance store whose sales contracts call for binding arbitration—in barely legible typeface buried in the middle of five pages of legalese—be able to enforce those arbitration clauses? Does it matter whether this is the only refrigerator distributor for miles in a poor urban area? If the store serves a predominately Chinese-only-speaking neighborhood, should the agreement be in Chinese?

When drafting a contract, managers should consider the scope of any arbitration clause. Usually, the parties to the contract are the parties to the arbitration. Sometimes, however, a dispute may arise between parties to several different contracts. For example, there may be a dispute between a construction subcontractor and an architect. The parties should ensure that there is an arbitration clause in each contract and that each party agrees to a consolidated arbitration with other parties on related issues. Foreseeing which disputes are better arbitrated than litigated is more difficult than foreseeing which parties might come into conflict. A broad arbitration clause, which may apply to tort as well as contract claims, is preferable. Parties should also agree upon a location close to their businesses and a reasonable timetable by which to settle their disputes. The arbitration clause may provide that the arbitration will commence with a prehearing conference.

Unfortunately, arbitration clauses often do not include details of how arbitration will proceed, when and where it will take place, and who will preside. Most arbitration clauses simply state that the parties will arbitrate all disputes relating to or arising out of their contract—leaving the parties to fight over the specifics of arbitration after a dispute arises. To minimize the conflict over such specifics, parties often designate that arbitrations will be done according to the rules of a third-party organization, such as the American Arbitration Association. As in mediation, such organizations have evolved rules and procedures that may serve as defaults for disputing parties.

22. N.Y. CIV. PRAC. L. & R. 7504 (1980).
23. 9 U.S.C. § 5 (1970).

INTERNATIONAL CONSIDERATION

When parties to a contract are from different nations, disputes between the parties can bring legal regimes into collision with one party's expectations. To avoid such difficulty, it is often helpful to include arbitration clauses in these contracts. After all, few managers would appreciate being hauled into a foreign-language court 5,000 miles from their home office and held to unfamiliar legal standards. Many European and Asian business leaders, for example, are uncomfortable with the U.S. legal system's discovery procedures for obtaining evidence prior to trial through depositions, written interrogatories, and document production. In addition, often the parties can draft an arbitration clause to mutual satisfaction; whereas parties cannot "negotiate around" many rules of a legal system once litigation has begun even if all parties are willing.

EXHIBIT 4.5   Sample Arbitration Clause in Employment Context

The Firm and I mutually consent to the resolution by final and binding arbitration of all claims or controversies, whether or not arising out of my employment (or its termination), that the Firm may have against me or that I may have against the Firm or its partners, employees or agents in their capacity as such, including, but not limited to, claims for compensation due; claims for breach of any contract or covenant (express or implied); tort claims; claims of discrimination (including, but not limited to, claims based on race, sex, sexual preference, religion, national origin, age, marital status, medical condition, handicap or disability); claims for benefits (except as set forth in paragraph 3, below [which excludes worker's compensation and unemployment benefits]); and claims alleging a violation of any federal, state or other governmental law, statute, regulation or ordinance (collectively, "Claims"), *provided however* that Claims shall not include claims excluded in [paragraph 3]. All Claims shall be arbitrated in accordance with the attached Arbitration Rules and Procedures, which are expressly incorporated herein and made part of this Agreement.

Arbitration of Employment Disputes   Employees are increasingly asked to sign employment agreements with arbitration clauses. Exhibit 4.5 contains an excerpt from an actual arbitration agreement used by a national professional services firm. All employees were required to sign it as a condition of their employment with the firm.

During the 1930s, only about 10% of collective bargaining agreements in the United States contained arbitration clauses. Ten years later, the rate had risen to 40%, and today nearly all major collective bargaining agreements include arbitration clauses.[24] The American Arbitration Association calls the growth of arbitration in employment contracts dramatic and reports that nearly 400 firms use such clauses in their dealings with employees.

In a contrary trend, some employment-discrimination claims are beginning to be excluded from mandatory arbitration agreements. In *mandatory arbitration*, one party will not do business with the other unless he or she agrees to arbitrate any future claims. In the labor context, that means that a firm will not hire an individual unless he or she agrees now to arbitrate future claims; that is, the agreement to arbitrate is a condition of employment.

The Equal Employment Opportunity Commission (EEOC) has long opposed the mandatory arbitration of claims of racial- and gender-based discrimination. In 1997, the EEOC won a major victory in its long-running battle with Wall Street over the issue. In August of that year, the National Association of Securities Dealers, Inc. (NASD), which regulates the securities sales profession, voted to rescind its requirement that all licensed brokerage employees arbitrate their discrimination claims.[25] In late 1997, Smith Barney, Inc. settled a class action sexual-discrimination case in part by agreeing to establish a new

---

24. ANTOINE, *Arbitration and the Law*, in ARBITRATION IN PRACTICE 9 (Zack ed. 1984).

25. *Elimination of Mandatory Arbitration of Discrimination Claims Proposed by NASD*, 66 U.S.L.W. 2105 (1997). For such NASD action to be effective, the Securities and Exchange Commission had to approve it, which the FCC did in 1998. Nonetheless, individual brokerage firms will remain free to make use of mandatory arbitration, subject to continued development of the law in this area.

ADR process to replace mandatory arbitration at the company,[26] and in early 1998 Merrill Lynch began drafting a new policy on dispute resolution as part of its attempt to settle a similar class action suit.[27]

---

26. *Smith Barney Settlement May Signal Shift in Mandatory Dispute Settlement Debate*, 66 U.S.L.W. 2355 (1997).

27. Patrick McGeehan, *Merrill Lynch Is Drafting a New Policy that Could Let Employees Sue in Court*, WALL ST. J., Jan. 22, 1998, at C1.

Some courts seem suspicious of mandatory arbitration in general (see Chapter 13), but especially if employees have not made it clear that they understand and appreciate their acceptance of mandatory arbitration. In the following case involving a man who claimed that his employer had violated the Americans with Disabilities Act (ADA), the court refused to enforce an arbitration clause buried in a personnel manual.

A CASE IN POINT   SUMMARY

CASE 4.2
NELSON v. CYPRUS
BAGDAD COPPER
CORP.
United States Court of
Appeals for the Ninth Circuit
119 F.3d 756 (9th Cir. 1997).

FACTS   In 1975, Melton Nelson began working for the Cyprus Bagdad Copper Corporation, a mining company with operations in Bagdad, Arizona. In 1993, Cyprus issued an employee handbook to all its employees, each of whom was required to sign an acknowledgment that he had received the handbook and would read and understand its contents. Among other policies and procedures, the handbook described the company's mandatory grievance procedures, which culminated in binding arbitration.

The next year, Cyprus initiated a corporate restructuring, and Nelson's department was reorganized. As a result, he was required to work rotating 12-hour shifts. Concerned that his health could not tolerate rotating shifts, Nelson so notified his supervisor. After the supervisor made some initial efforts to accommodate Nelson's medical situation, Cyprus fired Nelson.

Upon the advice of counsel, Nelson chose not to arbitrate his termination according to the procedures outlined in the employee handbook. Instead, he sued Cyprus for violations of the Americans with Disabilities Act and the Arizona Civil Rights Act (ACRA). In response, the company argued that Cyprus was bound to arbitrate his claims against the company arising from his termination.

The trial court held as matter of law that the arbitration clause was enforceable and that Nelson had waived his rights to bring his claims to court. Nelson appealed.

ISSUE PRESENTED   Do mandatory arbitration provisions contained in an employee handbook serve to waive an employee's rights to sue for unlawful discrimination?

SUMMARY OF OPINION   The U.S. Court of Appeals reversed the trial court's grant of summary judgment and returned the case to the lower court to hear Nelson's claims. The appeals court assumed for the sake of argument that claims under the ADA could indeed be waived. However, the court stated that waivers of statutory rights—such as the rights granted under the ADA and the ACRA—must be made knowingly and expressly. The employee must have been aware that he was agreeing to waive his rights to sue, and he must have agreed expressly to waive those rights.

When the court examined Nelson's waiver, it concluded that his signed acknowledgment of the employee handbook did not constitute a knowing agreement to waive his rights. Nothing in the acknowledgment mentioned that the handbook contained an

Case 4.2 continues

Case 4.2 continued

arbitration clause or that acceptance of the handbook constituted a waiver of rights to sue under the ADA. Instead, Nelson merely acknowledged receipt of the handbook and agreed to read it. By the court's reasoning, "Nelson agreed only to 'read and understand' the Handbook. He did not agree to be bound by its provisions." Hence, the waiver was invalid. As well, his continued employment at Cyprus could not be seen as a implied waiver because statutory rights must be waived expressly as well as knowingly.

RESULT   The decision of the trial court was reversed, and the case was remanded for judicial consideration of Nelson's claims. Nelson was not required to arbitrate his claims.

COMMENTS   The appeals court reached its conclusion without having to decide whether ADA claims can actually be waived. It simply assumed that they could because the court could decide the case on simpler grounds. Courts usually avoid setting precedent—for example, determining whether claims under the ADA can be waived—if they can frame the case as asking a different question and rely on an established precedent to resolve it. Instead of seeing the case as posing a question of first impression, courts often twist and turn to see the case as asking a question that has already been answered. While such judicial conservatism may or may not be jurisprudentially sound, it does reduce the likelihood of reversal by a higher court.

Arbitration can be a two-way street between businesses and their employees. In January 1997, BioSafe International, Inc. won an arbitration award of $800,000 against its former chairman and chief executive officer, Richard Rosen. The company claimed that Rosen made improper expenditures and breached his employment agreement.[28]

Judicial Enforcement

Arbitration was used by the medieval guilds and in early maritime transactions to help settle commercial disputes. Some scholars trace its history back to Roman law, whereas others discern the influence of ecclesiastical law. Judicial attitudes toward arbitration, however, did not develop in concert. Early English courts honored agreements to arbitrate controversies after an arbitrator had made an award, but would not enforce agreements to arbitrate. The judges received fees from each litigation, which may explain some of their hostility. Although the earliest U.S. courts tended to adopt the English attitude and undercut the effectiveness of arbitration, attitudes began to shift in the twentieth century.

28. *BioSafe Gets Arbitration Award*, WALL ST. J., Jan. 9, 1997, at B2.

INTERNATIONAL CONSIDERATION

Throughout the 1990s, India has undertaken significant reforms to liberalize its economy. As part of its effort to attract international business, India enacted its Arbitration and Conciliation Act of 1996. Although a signatory since 1958 to the United Nations' New York Convention on the Recognition and Enforcement of Foreign Arbitral Awards, arbitration in India had been viewed abroad with distrust. Indian courts had intervened during and after arbitrations, thus keeping parties from reliably avoiding local courts and enjoying closure to any specific dispute. The new law, based on the United Nations' Model Arbitration Law, brings international standards to both domestic and international arbitrations in India. Court interference during arbitration has been nearly eliminated, and the bases for judicial review of awards has been severely limited. India is one of the world's largest and most promising consumer markets; with a legal infrastructure better suited to resolution of commercial disputes, India is now poised to attract much commerce.

In 1920, New York enacted the first arbitration statute in the United States, giving parties the right to settle current disputes and control future ones through private arbitration. The New York act served as a model for the Uniform Arbitration Act enacted 35 years later. Today most states have amended their laws to conform to the Uniform Arbitration Act, making agreements to arbitrate and arbitration awards judicially enforceable. Five years after New York blazed the trail, Congress passed what is now known as the *Federal Arbitration Act*. When, many years later, the Supreme Court applied the act to a dispute between Southland Corporation and one of its 7–Eleven franchisees, the Justices proclaimed that in enacting the law "Congress declared a national policy favoring arbitration and withdrew the power of the states to require a judicial forum for the resolution of claims which the contracting parties agreed to resolve by arbitration."[29]

The U.S. Supreme Court has enforced arbitration clauses, even when the rights at issue were protected by federal law. For example, in *Rodriguez de Quijas v. Shearson/American Express, Inc.*,[30] the Supreme Court held that a predispute agreement to submit to compulsory arbitration any controversy relating to a securities investment was enforceable even though the plaintiff alleged claims under the Securities Act of 1933. The Court noted that in recent years it had upheld agreements to arbitrate claims under the Securities Exchange Act of 1934, the Racketeer Influenced and Corrupt Organizations Act (RICO), and the antitrust laws. By agreeing to arbitrate a statutory claim, the Court reasoned, a party does not forego the substantive rights afforded by the statute. The agreement means only that the resolution of the dispute will be in an arbitral, rather than judicial, forum. The Supreme Court strongly endorsed statutes, such as the Federal Arbitration Act, that favor this method of resolving disputes.

In *Shearson Lehman/American Express v. Bird*,[31] the Supreme Court vacated a decision in which the court of appeals had ruled unenforceable a predispute agreement to arbitrate statutory claims under the Employee Retirement Income Security Act (ERISA), which governs pensions and other employee benefit plans. The Supreme Court's action seems to indicate that predispute agreements to arbitrate claims under ERISA are enforceable. ERISA is discussed further in Chapter 12.

The Supreme Court has maintained its pro-ADR stance over the years, and it has upheld arbitration agreements that involve claims arising from the following: (1) collective bargaining provisions;[32] (2) Sherman Antitrust Act;[33] (3) Securities Exchange Act of 1934;[34] (4) Racketeer Influenced and Corrupt Organizations Act;[35] and (5) Age Discrimination in Employment Act.[36] In addition, the Court has routinely upheld agreements to arbitrate ordinary contract claims.[37]

State legislatures have enacted legislation designed to protect their citizens from unwittingly agreeing to mandatory arbitration. The following case considered whether such legislation was permissible given the Federal Arbitration Act.

31. 493 U.S. 884 (1989).

32. AT&T Technologies, Inc. v. Communication Workers of Am. 475 U.S. 643 (1986).

33. Mitsubishi Motors Corp. v. Soler Chrysler-Plymouth, Inc., 473 U.S. 614 (1985).

34. Shearson/American Express v. McMahon, 482 U.S. 220 (1987), *reh'g denied*, 483 U.S. 1056 (1987).

35. *Id.*

36. Gilmer v. Interstate/Johnson Lane Corp., 500 U.S. 20 (1991).

37. *See, e.g.*, Prima Paint Corp. v. Flood & Conklin Mfg. Co., 388 U.S. 395 (1967). More recently, *see* Doctor's Assoc. Inc. v. Casarotto, 116 S. Ct. 1652 (1996) (Case 4.3).

31. Southland Corp. v. Keating, 465 U.S. 1, 2 (1984).

30. 490 U.S. 477 (1989).

| A CASE IN POINT | IN THE LANGUAGE OF THE COURT |

CASE 4.3
DOCTOR'S ASSOCIATES, INC. v. CASAROTTO
Supreme Court
of the United States
116 S. Ct. 1652 (1996).

FACTS Subway sandwich-shop franchisees signed a standard franchise agreement, which included on page nine and in ordinary type a provision requiring all disputes arising under the agreement to be settled by arbitration. Nonetheless, these franchisees brought an action in state court against their Subway franchisor, Doctor's Associates,

Case 4.3 continues

Case 4.3 continued

Inc. (DAI), and its Montana development agent. Because of the mandatory arbitration provision in the franchise agreement, the trial court stayed the litigation, that is, did not allow it to go forward. The Subway franchisees appealed. The Montana Supreme Court reversed the trial court on the grounds that the standard franchise agreement's mandatory arbitration clause was unenforceable under a Montana statute that required that a mandatory arbitration clause be typed in underlined capital letters on the first page of the contract. The U.S. Supreme Court vacated the Montana Supreme Court's decision and remanded the case to the Montana Supreme Court for reconsideration in light of the Federal Arbitration Act. On remand, the Montana Supreme Court reaffirmed its prior opinion based on a finding that the FAA did not preempt the Montana statute. The franchisor appealed.

ISSUE PRESENTED   May a state legislature impose special requirements for an arbitration clause that are not applicable to contracts generally?

OPINION   GINSBURG, J., writing for the U.S. Supreme Court:

The Federal Arbitration Act . . . declares written provisions for arbitration "valid, irrevocable, and enforceable, save upon such grounds as exist at law or in equity for the revocation of any contract." Montana law, however, declares an arbitration clause unenforceable unless "[n]otice that [the] contract is subject to arbitration" is "typed in underlined capital letters on the first page of the contract." The question here presented is whether Montana's law is compatible with the federal Act. We hold that Montana's first-page notice requirement, which governs not "any contract," but specifically and solely contracts "subject to arbitration," conflicts with the FAA and is therefore displaced by the federal measure.

I

. . .

"States may regulate contracts, including arbitration clauses, under general contract law principles and they may invalidate an arbitration clause 'upon such grounds as exist at law or in equity for the revocation of any contract.' What States may not do is decide that a contract is fair enough to enforce all its basic terms (price, service, credit), but not fair enough to enforce its arbitration clause. The [Federal Arbitration] Act makes any such state policy unlawful, for that kind of policy would place arbitration clauses on an unequal 'footing,' directly contrary to the Act's language and Congress's intent."

. . .

II

Section 2 of the FAA provides that written arbitration agreements "shall be valid, irrevocable, and enforceable, save upon such grounds as exist at law or in equity for the revocation of any contract." . . . Thus, generally applicable contract defenses, such as fraud, duress or unconscionability, may be applied to invalidate arbitration agreements without contravening § 2.

Case 4.3 continues

Case 4.3 continued

Courts may not, however, invalidate arbitration agreements under state laws applicable only to arbitration provisions. By enacting § 2, we have several times said, Congress precluded States from singling out arbitration provisions for suspect status, requiring instead that such provisions be placed "upon the same footing as other contracts." Montana's § 27-5-114(4) directly conflicts with § 2 of the FAA because the State's law conditions the enforceability of arbitration agreements on compliance with a special notice requirement not applicable to contracts generally. The FAA thus displaces the Montana statute with respect to arbitration agreements covered by the Act.

RESULT The decision of the Montana Supreme Court was reversed, and the franchisees were required to arbitrate their dispute with the franchisor.

Questions

1. The clause in question called for arbitration of "[a]ny controversy or claim arising out of or relating to this contract" in accordance with the AAA's Commercial Arbitration Rules. The clause further called for any such arbitration to be carried out in Connecticut. Should one's evaluation of the decision depend on the franchisees' ability to get from Montana to Connecticut? Would it be different if the clause called for arbitration in Ulan Bator, Mongolia?
2. What bothered the Court about the Montana law was that it applied only to arbitration clauses. That, the Court held, was the province of the Federal Arbitration Act. Is it possible to craft a state law that would enable a court to invalidate an arbitration provision?

Judicial Review of Awards

The Federal Arbitration Act lists four circumstances in which an arbitration award may be set aside by a court: (1) the award was procured by corruption, fraud, or undue means; (2) the arbitrator was demonstrably impartial or corrupt; (3) the arbitrator engaged in misconduct by refusing to postpone the hearing when given sufficient reason or by refusing to hear pertinent evidence; and (4) the arbitrator exceeded his or her powers or executed them so badly that a final award on the issue put to arbitration was not made. Acknowledging the rights of parties to arbitration to agree to tailor-made procedural rules, one court held that the parties could agree to give a court the power to overturn an arbitration award if the court concluded that it was not supported by substantial evidence.[38] Overall, the courts look favorably on arbitration and favor its results.

Other case law suggests that awards may be reversed for reasons beyond those enumerated in the FAA or provided for in the arbitration agreement itself. For example, a court might set aside an arbitrator's decision if it would "violate some explicit public policy that is well defined and dominant"[39] or was "arbitrary and capricious."[40] The following case addressed the question of whether an award could be set aside because it was in "manifest disregard of the law."

---

38. LaPine Technology Corp. v. Kyocera Corp., 130 F.3d 884 (9th Cir. 1997).
39. United Paperworkers Int'l Union v. Misco, Inc., 484 U.S. 29 (1987).
40. Wilko v. Swan, 346 U.S. 427 (1953), *overturned by* Rodriquez de Quijas v. Shearson/American Express, Inc., 490 U.S. 477 (1989), on other grounds.

| **A CASE IN POINT** | **SUMMARY** |

CASE 4.4
MONTES v. SHEARSON LEHMAN BROTHERS, INC.
United States Court of Appeals for the Eleventh Circuit
128 F.3d 1456
(11th Cir. 1997).

FACTS   Delfina Montes went to work for Shearson Lehman Brothers and signed an agreement to arbitrate any disputes arising from her employment. After the termination of her employment, Montes filed suit for allegedly unpaid overtime under the Fair Labor Standards Act (FLSA), which mandates overtime pay for certain workers. Honoring the arbitration agreement, the trial court referred the dispute to arbitration. The arbitration panel ruled that Shearson did not owe Montes any overtime pay. Montes petitioned the trial court to vacate the arbitration panel's ruling as arbitrary and capricious because the panel heeded Shearson's urging that it disregard the FLSA. In support of her claim, Montes pointed out several statements made during the arbitration hearing by Shearson's attorney, including:

> I know, as I have served many times as an arbitrator, that you as an arbitrator are not guided strictly to follow case law precedent. That you can also do what's fair and just and equitable. . . .

> You have to decide whether you're going to follow the statutes . . . or do what is right and just and equitable in this case.

> . . . in this case this law is not right.

> . . . I now ask you in my closing, not to follow the FLSA if you determine that she's an exempt employee.

The court denied the petition, and Montes appealed.

ISSUE PRESENTED   Can a plea to deliberately disregard the relevant law provide a basis for overturning the result of an arbitration?

SUMMARY OF OPINION   Although the Eleventh Circuit had never expressly adopted the "manifest disregard of the law" rationale for overturning awards, the U.S. Court of Appeals noted that all other circuits—except the Fifth—had done so. Furthermore, the U.S. Supreme Court had carefully distinguished between a merely erroneous interpretation of the law—which is not grounds for overturning an award—and manifest disregard of the law—which is grounds for overturning.[41] Such "manifest disregard" requires an arbitrator to be conscious of the law and to deliberately ignore it. As well, the court noted that an agreement to arbitrate statutory claims is simply an agreement to submit such claims to an arbitral rather than judicial form; it is not an agreement to forfeit statutory rights. Hence, manifest disregard of the law can constitute grounds for vacating an arbitration award because it can amount to a forfeiture of statutory rights.

In this case, the arbitration record and formal decision lacked supporting facts to indicate the basis for the award. Similarly, the record and decision did not indicate that the panel had rejected Shearson's plea to disregard to law. The appeals court, therefore, could not be sure that Shearson's plea went unheeded by the panel and that the arbitrators' decision was not made in manifest disregard of the law.

RESULT   The appeals court reversed the district court's affirmation of the arbitration award and remanded the case for a new arbitration.

Case 4.4 continues

---

41. *Id. See also* First Options of Chicago, Inc. v. Kaplan, 514 U.S. 938, 942 (1995).

Case 4.4 continued

COMMENTS   The appeals court's inability to understand the full basis for the arbitration award underscores the importance of a thoroughly written arbitration decision outlining the rationale for the award. Had the court been confident that the arbitration panel had rejected Shearson's plea to disregard the Fair Labor Standards Act, it would likely have upheld the award and saved the parties further uncertainty, delay, and arbitration costs. The case also points out the folly of explicitly encouraging the arbitrators to disregard the law.

INTERNATIONAL CONSIDERATION

The United Nations Convention on the Recognition and Enforcement of Foreign Arbitral Awards, Article III, implemented in the United States by Chapter 2 of the Federal Arbitration Act,[a] provides: "Each Contracting State shall recognize arbitral awards as binding and enforce them in accordance with the rules of procedure of the territory where the award is relied upon, under the conditions laid down in the following articles." As of 1997, 106 countries were signatories to the convention.[b]

a. 9 U.S.C. § 201 (West Elec. Update 1997).

b. For the full text of the convention and the list of signatories, see the annotation to the section, 9 U.S.C.A. § 201 (West Elec. Update 1997).

with the situation from mediation. A danger of med-arb is that honesty in mediation could become damaging revelation in arbitration, especially if the mediator then acts as arbitrator. A decision-making arbitrator cannot forget what he or she has learned confidentially in mediation caucuses with a party. Looking ahead to such a possibility, parties in the "med" stage of med-arb may be reluctant to participate openly and in good faith, thus ensuring the final "arb" stage from the beginning. In such a scenario, time and money are wasted by the doomed mediation phase. For this reason, it is usually preferable to specify that a different person will act as arbitrator if mediation fails to resolve the conflict.

Minitrial

In a *minitrial*, lawyers conduct discovery for a limited period, usually a few weeks. They then exchange legal briefs or memoranda of law. At this point, the top management of the two businesses hears the lawyers from each side present their case in a trial format. The presentations are moderated by a neutral third party, often an attorney or a judge.

After the minitrial, the managers of the two businesses meet to settle the case. If they are unable to reach a settlement, the presiding third party can issue a nonbinding opinion. The managers can then meet again to try to settle on the basis of the third-party opinion. For this reason, minitrials are a cross between arbitration and negotiation.

Minitrials have several advantages. Like litigation, they allow a thorough investigation and presentation of the parties' claims; but they give the managers the opportunity to work out their differences directly rather than through their attorneys. By shortening the time

Hybrids

There are various hybrid forms of ADR available, including med-arb, minitrials, and summary jury trials.

Med-Arb

Med-arb is the most obvious hybrid form of ADR. In *med-arb* the parties to a dispute enter mediation with the commitment to submit to binding arbitration if mediation fails to resolve the conflict. Typically, the same person serves as mediator and arbitrator. Delay and expense are reduced if the arbitrator is already familiar

for discovery and presentation of the case, minitrials can reduce the possibility of the two sides becoming locked into opposing positions. The presence of a neutral third party gives the process an added element of discipline. Should the managers come to an impasse in their discussions, the third party can offer suggestions about a settlement. Finally, minitrials have the advantage of remaining relatively private. This is important to parties in disputes over confidential information or trade secrets.

An example of a successful minitrial is the 1986 settlement of the dispute between Telecredit and TRW. This minitrial took place in a hotel conference room. After brief presentations by both sides, Telecredit's cofounder conferred with a vice-president of TRW. Within half an hour, the two parties had agreed on the outlines of a settlement, which was negotiated over the following 11 weeks. The two companies estimated that the minitrial saved them at least $1 million in combined legal fees.

Because minitrials involve discovery, the production of briefs, oral argument, and the hiring of a third party, they can still be fairly expensive. Only when disputes are expected to involve large damage awards or protracted litigation do minitrials make economic sense.

Summary Jury Trial

In a *summary jury trial* (*SJT*), parties to a dispute put their cases before a real jury, which renders a nonbinding decision. Like nonbinding arbitration, this allows the parties to assess how a decision maker might decide the case in a real trial. The result is often the basis for a negotiated settlement. Like minitrials, summary jury trials offer disputants the opportunity to present their best case in a trial-like setting. Because the SJT makes use of abbreviated procedures, the result is achieved more quickly and with less expense.

A unique feature of SJTs is their focus-group opportunity. Disputants often debrief jurors after the trial to find out how and why they reached their decision. Like discovery, this helps align the parties' information and expectations so there is less reason to go through the expense of a formal trial. For example, a car accident victim suing for $5 million may balk at her insurance company's offer of $50,000 to settle the claim. If the jury in an SJT renders an award of only $75,000, the plaintiff will be more willing to consider settlement. On the other hand, if the jury awards $3 million, the defendant insurance company will wish to revise its settlement offer. Either way, the parties' expectations will be brought closer together, making settlement more likely.

Others

Because ADR is a dynamic area, these are not the only hybrid forms. *Early Neutral Evaluation* (*ENE*) was created by the U.S. District Court for the Northern District of California in 1985 to help litigants honestly appreciate their position. In ENE, a neutral attorney familiar with the law in the area reviews the case and offers each side his or her evaluation of the strengths and weaknesses. Such early feedback by a disinterested expert can assist parties before they become engrossed in the adversarial process.

Ombudspersons are also used to help parties in conflict. Such a person hears complaints, engages in fact-finding, and generally promotes dispute resolution through information methods such as counseling or mediation. An ombudsperson allows aggrieved parties to vent their concerns and alert *related* parties to problems before they become *opposing* parties.

As international trade grows and the resources of court systems are stretched thinner, scholars and organizations will seek new, more effective forms of ADR. What these will be, no one can say. Regardless, the need to solve disputes more efficiently will remain a strong motivation for managers to demand alternatives to litigation.

Legal Treatment of ADR

Although ADR is an alternative to the judicial system, the government is neither ignorant of nor indifferent to the alternatives. Federal ADR legislation has expanded significantly in recent years. One of the most comprehensive statutes, the Civil Justice Reform Act of 1990,[42] requires every federal district court to develop a civil justice expense and delay reduction plan (EDRP). The purpose of such plans is "to facilitate deliberate adjudication of civil cases on the merits,

---

42. 28 U.S.C. § 471 (1993).

monitor discovery, improve litigation management, and ensure just, speedy, and inexpensive resolution of civil disputes." The act recommends six methods for courts to use in developing EDRPs, one of which is referring appropriate cases "to alternative dispute resolution programs . . . including mediation, minitrial, and summary jury trial."

As discussed earlier, Congress declared a national policy in favor of arbitration in passing the Federal Arbitration Act; and case law protects the confidentiality of discussions with mediators. The government, including the judicial system, promotes alternatives to litigation in a variety of ways, including requiring pretrial settlement conferences, providing liberal discovery, penalizing plaintiffs who reject favorable settlement offers, limiting the ability of a party to introduce willingness to negotiate as evidence of fault, and generally enforcing agreements to arbitrate.

Pretrial Conferences

The procedural rules that govern civil litigation reveal a prosettlement bias. These rules, the *Federal Rules of Civil Procedure* (*FRCP*) in the federal system and with their counterparts in the state systems, allow judges to require disputants to meet and explore settlement before beginning a trial. Such meetings are not required, but the judge may order them at his or her discretion. For that reason, presettlement conferences may be thought of as compulsory mediation. As in mediation, the judge may be able to bridge differences and propose solutions that the parties could not negotiate on their own. In fact, the official advisory committee on the FRCP observed, "Empirical studies reveal that when a trial judge intervenes personally at an early stage to assume judicial control over a case and to schedule dates for completion by the parties of the principal pretrial steps, the case is disposed of by settlement or trial more efficiently and with less cost and delay than when the parties are left to their own devices."[43]

For example, the judge assigned to 10 of the suits brought by 27 utility companies against Westinghouse Corporation in 1975 forced the chief executives concerned to meet in his office to try to settle the case.

Westinghouse had breached its contracts to deliver about 70 million pounds of uranium because the price of uranium had more than doubled. The judge thought that a business solution to the lawsuits, rather than a legal one, might be more advantageous to all parties. If the court forced Westinghouse to pay damages, Westinghouse would be crippled financially. It might not be able to complete the construction of certain nuclear power plants that it was building for the same utility companies. Inventive and mutually beneficial settlements were reached in many of the cases. (The Westinghouse uranium cases are discussed in the "Inside Story" in Chapter 8.)

Liberal Discovery

As explained in Chapter 3, the entire discovery process is aimed at increasing both parties' access to information. If both plaintiff and defendant have similar information—through interrogatories, depositions, and production of documents—they are more likely to expect the same outcome at trial. With less uncertainty to resolve by a lengthy and expensive trial, parties are more likely to settle. In the terminology from the earlier discussion of barriers to resolution, the discovery process aims to reduce information asymmetry and to align parties' expectations about continued litigation. This makes settlement more likely.

Rejected-Offer Sanctions

In addition to the carrot of discovery, the rules of civil procedure provide a stick for plaintiffs unwilling to entertain settlement seriously. Rule 68 of the FRCP allows a defendant to offer to accept judgment against himself for a specific amount of money no less than 10 days before a trial begins. If the plaintiff accepts the offer, the case concludes and judgment is entered by the court per the agreement. If the plaintiff refuses and the case goes to trial, then the plaintiff must pay the defendant's legal expenses incurred subsequent to the offer if the final judgment is not more favorable than the rejected offer. Looking forward to such an unpleasant sanction, plaintiffs will think carefully before rejecting settlement proposals. This encourages defendants to make serious offers of settlement as early as possible, and in turn it encourages plaintiffs to consider those offers just as seriously.

---

43. FED. R. CIV. P. 16, Notes of Advisory Committee on Rules.

Negotiation as Evidence of Fault

While the FRCP govern procedure in litigation before federal courts, the *Federal Rules of Evidence* (*FRE*) govern the use of evidence in such litigation. Individual states have similar sets of rules, which, along with related case law, determine what evidence is admissible in court and, therefore, on what evidence a fact finder may rely. For a party exploring solutions or attempting to integrate issues, these rules are most important.

For example, a manager faced with a highly dubious claim of product defect may be willing to replace the item to preserve customer goodwill. At the same time, the manager may be unwilling to pay the customer for the profits it lost because of the alleged defect in the product. At a trial, the customer might want to introduce the manager's offer to replace the product as evidence of the defect and the validity of its case against the company: "After all, ladies and gentlemen of the jury, why would a company give my client a new product if there was nothing wrong with the old one?" Looking ahead to such a possibility, the manager will be reluctant to negotiate at all for fear that his

sincere efforts to preserve goodwill could appear later as admissions of fault. At a minimum, the manager will be exceedingly circumspect in his or her language. Both results make settlement more difficult and less likely.

To exclude that trial scenario and its chilling effect on negotiations beforehand, Rule 408 prohibits the use of settlement offers as evidence of liability. The protection extends to conduct and statements made in such negotiations, as well as formal offers of settlement. The goal is to insulate the entire negotiation process from the threat of exposure at trial. As Congress observed when enacting the restriction, "The purpose of [the] rule is to encourage settlements which would be discouraged if such evidence were admissible."[44]

Managers should not take too much comfort in Rule 408 because if damaging revelations made in negotiations are otherwise discoverable, they are admissible. Similarly, while offers to settle may not be used as evidence of liability, such offers may be used to show

---

44. SENATE COMMITTEE ON THE JUDICIARY, FEDERAL RULES OF EVIDENCE, 93d CONG., 2d SESS., 1974, S. REPT. NO. 1277, 10.

IN BRIEF

MODELS OF ALTERNATIVE DISPUTE RESOLUTION

	NEGOTIATION	**MEDIATION**	**ARBITRATION**
How are the disputants represented?	Disputants represent themselves or legal counsel negotiates on their behalf	By themselves	By legal counsel
Who makes the final decision?	Disputants mutually decide	Disputants mutually decide	If binding arbitration, arbitrator(s) decides
How are facts found and standards of judgment set?	Parties decide ad hoc	Parties decide ad hoc	Arbitrator(s) decides based on preset rules, e.g., those of the AAA
What is the source for the standard of resolution?	Mutual agreement	Mutual agreement	Arbitrator's sense of fairness
How will the resolution be enforced?	Agreement usually turned into a contract that is enforceable by the courts	Agreement usually turned into a contract that is enforceable by the courts	By courts, according to the agreement to arbitrate the dispute
Who will pay the dispute resolution fees?	Parties decide ad hoc	Parties decide ad hoc	Parties decide before entering arbitration, often in arbitration clause

Mediation Model

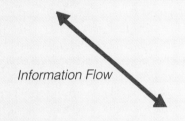

Lawyers   Participants   Participants   Lawyers

Mediator

1. Introduces, structures, gains rapport
2. Finds out facts, isolates issues
3. Helps identify alternatives
4. Guides negotiation and decision making
5. Clarifies/writes an agreement or plan
6. Provides for legal review and processing
7. Available for follow-up, review, revision

Negotiation Model

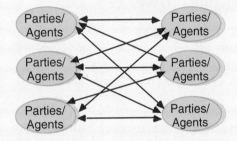

Information Flow

1. Parties or Party decide they want to settle a dispute.
2. Orientation and positioning are very important.
3. Discussion and arguing of Issues begins between a few designated participants or all the parties can participate.
4. Either an agreement or final impasse is reached

Adjudication Model
(Litigation & Arbitration)

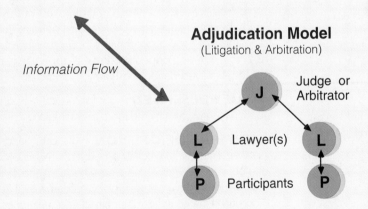

Information Flow

Judge or Arbitrator

Lawyer(s)

Participants

1. Listens to each side's presentation.
2. Decides outcome based on predetermined criteria (legislation, precedent, fairness, etc.).

witness bias or obstruction of criminal investigation or to disprove a suggestion of undue delay. In short, a clever lawyer can often find a way to introduce some evidence concerning negotiations.

Contract Law

After a successful negotiation or mediation, parties often contract with each other for the arrangement they have reached. Such contracts are governed by contract law, which is discussed in Chapter 7. Generally speaking, this body of law addresses the circumstances under which agreements between two parties will be enforced by courts and the form such enforcement may take.

Parties constrained by an arbitration clause may claim that the contract itself (including its arbitration clause) is void due to force, fraud, or the like. Thus, they would argue, neither the contract nor its arbitration clause should be enforced. The U.S. Supreme Court put that issue largely to rest in the following case.

| **A CASE IN POINT** | **SUMMARY** |

CASE 4.5
PRIMA PAINT CORP. v. FLOOD & CONKLIN MANUFACTURING CO.
Supreme Court of the United States
388 U.S. 395 (1967).

FACTS   In 1964, Prima Paint purchased Flood & Conklin's paint-selling business. As part of the overall transaction, Prima and Flood agreed that Flood would (1) provide Prima with consulting services for six years; (2) refrain for six years from selling paint and paint products in its existing sales territory and to its current customers; and (3) provide Prima with its customer list. In return for these three agreements, Prima agreed to pay Flood a percentage of its receipts during the six-year period. The agreement contained a broad arbitration clause by which the parties agreed to arbitrate all claims in New York City according to the rules of the American Arbitration Association.

Before the first payment was due, Prima concluded that Flood was insolvent and notified Flood of the discovery. Although late, Prima went ahead and made its first payment, but into escrow, not to Flood. Prima then filed a complaint against Flood in federal district court for rescission of the consulting agreement. Prima argued that it had been fraudulently induced to enter into the consulting contract, and therefore the contract was voidable. Flood responded by serving Prima with a notice to arbitrate in accordance with their contract. Prima moved to stay the arbitration pending the litigation, and Flood moved to stay the litigation pending the arbitration.

The trial court agreed with Flood and stayed the litigation pending the outcome of arbitration. Prima appealed, but the appeals court dismissed the appeal, leaving the litigation stayed pending arbitration. Prima appealed.

ISSUE PRESENTED   Is it for the court or an arbitrator to resolve a claim that a party was fraudulently induced to enter into a contract containing an arbitration clause?

SUMMARY OF OPINION   The U.S. Supreme Court identified the issue as one of *severability*, that is, whether an arbitration clause could be severed from the remainder of the contract or whether the clause had to stand or fall with the larger contract. If an arbitration clause were not severable, a court would be able to enforce it and require arbitration only if the court first determined in a judicial proceeding that the contract in which it appeared was valid. If the contract was voided, the arbitration clause would fall as well.

If the doctrine of severability applied, however, a court would uphold an agreement to arbitrate unless the agreement to arbitrate itself was challenged. For instance, Alpha might argue that Beta fraudulently included the arbitration clause in an otherwise valid contract by slipping it into the final draft. In that case, a court would have to

Case 4.5 continues

Case 4.5 continued

consider the validity of the agreement to arbitrate. But if Alpha argued that Beta fraudulently induced it to enter into the contract as a whole, the court would sever the arbitration clause, find the agreement to arbitrate controlling on the parties, and leave the issue of the contract's validity to arbitration.

Looking to the exact language of the Federal Arbitration Act and the underlying congressional intent to facilitate the arbitration process, the Court adopted the doctrine of severability. Consequently, once a court is satisfied that the validity of the agreement to arbitrate is not specifically challenged, the judge must order arbitration in accordance with the clause. Unless the arbitration clause itself is challenged by a party, questions of contract validity and interpretation are properly the subject of arbitration.

Because Prima did not claim that it had intended to exclude legal issues from arbitration or that it was fraudulently induced to agree to arbitrate claims, the lower court was correct to stay Prima's lawsuit pending the outcome of arbitration.

RESULT   The Supreme Court upheld the dismissal of Prima's appeal. Prima's lawsuit was stayed pending the arbitration initiated by Flood.

As shown in *Prima Paint,* arbitration clauses can significantly alter a company's judicial rights. Managers entering into a contract with an arbitration clause should understand that "any claims arising from this contract" may well include all claims related to the contract, including the validity of the contract itself.

Tortious Dispute Resolution

Although the law supports settlements through ADR, managers are not immune from the law simply because they pursue alternative mechanisms to resolve their disputes. The applicability of tort law is a good example.

The law of torts, which is discussed in Chapter 9, deals with civil wrongs causing injury to a person or his or her property. A claim of fraudulent misrepresentation requires proof that the defendant intentionally misled the plaintiff by making a material misrepresentation of fact upon which the plaintiff relied to his or her detriment. It is not difficult to imagine a negotiation in which one might be tempted to so mislead an opponent. Still, the law of fraud will apply, and a manager may be liable for the injury he or she causes. As well, an overly aggressive manager attempting to "resolve" a dispute by force or threats may be found liable for assault, intentional infliction of emotional distress, defamation, invasion of privacy, disparagement, injurious falsehood, interference with contractual obligations, or interference with prospective business advantage. Attempting to settle conflict outside of court does not exempt managers from the law.

THE RESPONSIBLE MANAGER
Staying Out of Court

Legal problems or disputes often arise in business, and an amicable solution to them is not always possible. Some form of dispute resolution then becomes the next step.

The courts exist to assist litigants in working out a fair solution to their dispute. But litigation is expensive, time consuming, and disruptive to everyone involved.

Consequently, all parties benefit when the courts are used as the last step in the legal process, rather than as the starting point.

Often communication, or the lack thereof, can make the difference between a minor disagreement and protracted litigation. Apologizing may be just as crucial as filing or defending a lawsuit.

A manager should decide when litigation, as opposed to a settlement or other method of resolving the dispute, is the company's best strategic move. If the problem is a recurring one, or if the opposing party is clearly making a frivolous claim or attempting to use the lawsuit as a way to extort money from the company, then the courtroom becomes the most practical alternative. Similarly, if the adverse publicity that attends a trial would be more damaging to one party than another, the party better positioned to endure the publicity may prefer to retain the right to threaten to take the dispute to court. In many cases, however, negotiation, mediation, a minitrial, or arbitration will enable the parties to conclude their dispute more quickly and with less expense and hardship.

The first step in implementing an alternative dispute resolution program is generating enthusiasm within the company for the program.[45] The general counsel or other appropriate person should explain to company officers and executives the benefits of an ADR program, including the savings of time and money, the decrease in disruption to employees and management, and the fact that solutions generally are more business-oriented in nature. High-level management should demonstrate its commitment to an ADR program and explain its benefits to other executives, who may be unfamiliar with such a program. The company needs to involve (1) in-house counsel; (2) the executives and corporate managers; (3) outside counsel; (4) the company's adversaries; and (5) certain field personnel, such as insurance industry claims personnel. Training of these various players is also essential.

Once a company establishes a formal program, the next step is for the general counsel and company manager to ensure that the alternative dispute resolution procedures are employed. Some companies negotiate ADR clauses into all of their standard business agreements or contracts. Other companies leave it to their attorneys to decide which disputes are best resolved by alternative dispute resolution rather than litigation.

After deciding that an alternative dispute resolution method will be the best way to achieve its goal, the company must persuade the opposing party to participate in the procedure. Certain forms of ADR, such as mediation, are usually accepted readily—the proceeding is informal and can be terminated at any time, and a mediator can also protect the confidentiality of sensitive data, which might be made public during litigation.

Once a company has developed an ADR program, continuous feedback from all participants is required in order to monitor, refine, and improve the program. Constructive criticism is vital. Frequently, corporate managers or executives are in a position to discover a weakness in a particular ADR procedure that could harm the company. The company may wish to designate one employee as the ADR "point person" who monitors the program to ensure that flaws are corrected and strengths are further refined.

Establishing an alternative dispute resolution program has cost-benefit advantages. Valuable management time is saved by avoiding litigation. Equally important, alternative dispute resolution procedures help pursue a relationship with the opposing party and allow flexibility in resolving legal disputes.

---

45. This discussion is based on CENTER FOR PUBLIC RESOURCES, MAINSTREAMING: CORPORATE STRATEGIES FOR SYSTEMATIC ADR USE (1989).

INSIDE STORY

THE $800 MILLION ARBITRATION: IBM AND FUJITSU

In the past, companies usually did not submit legal disputes to arbitration when there were significant sums of money or assets at stake. This has changed. International Business Machines Corporation (IBM) set a precedent in 1985

when it turned to arbitration to resolve its dispute with Fujitsu Ltd., a Japanese electronics firm that was trying to gain access to IBM programming materials.

The dispute began in 1982, when IBM accused Fujitsu of

copying IBM software to use as a base to develop its own operating system software. IBM claimed that Fujitsu was violating IBM's software copyrights. An agreement was reached in 1983, but the agreement fell through. IBM initiated arbitration with the American Arbitration Association in 1985. Two arbitrators were chosen to arbitrate the dispute: Robert Mnookin, then a professor at Stanford Law School and an authority in dispute settlement, and John Jones, a retired executive and expert in computer systems.

Two years later, the arbitrators issued the first of two decisions resolving the dispute. They held that Fujitsu had the right to obtain access to IBM programs in order to develop and market imitations of IBM mainframe software products. The arbitrators' order left unresolved the dollar amount that Fujitsu would pay IBM for access to the IBM programs. However, the order was perceived as a major breakthrough for companies trying to compete with IBM, the traditionally dominant force in the software market. Observers of this market thought that the arbitrators' decision could help to shape new trends in the mainframe industry worldwide.

A second order, issued in 1988, set dollar amounts for the payments that Fujitsu would make to IBM for access to the IBM software. The license for future use alone was valued at close to $400 million, bringing the total amount Fujitsu could conceivably pay to approximately $800 million.

In these two orders, the arbitrators set out a complex arrangement to govern the relationship between the two companies through the year 2002. The orders included provisions for mutual access to each company's programming material, a complex payout plan, and strict rules for governing the exchanges of information and software between the two companies.

In 1997, five years ahead of the schedule, IBM and Fujitsu agreed to terminate their arbitration arrangement. The decision, however, did not reflect failure on the part of the parties or the arbitrators. Instead, the companies preferred an even less confrontational relationship. In their joint statement announcing the end of arbitration, the companies said, "IBM and Fujitsu hope that the termination of the arbitration will enable them to explore mutually beneficial business opportunities to meet their customers' needs into the twenty-first century."[46]

The IBM and Fujitsu arbitration was unprecedented, not only for the magnitude of the assets involved but also for its potential impact on the level of competition in the international market for computer software. It signaled an increased willingness to use arbitration to resolve disputes in the international business environment.

---

46. As quoted in *IBM and Fujitsu Drop Pending Arbitration*, WALL ST. J., May 12, 1997, at B12A.

KEY WORDS AND PHRASES

QUESTIONS AND CASE PROBLEMS

1. As a manager, how would you design and implement a policy to limit litigation costs by taking advantage of alternative dispute resolution mechanisms? Be specific in your answer. How well does your design and implementation account for strategic, structural, and psychological barriers?

2. In the Prisoner's Dilemma discussed in this chapter, what types of agreements could increase the likelihood of conspirators cooperating and getting around the dilemma? What environmental factors would weaken such agreements and make cooperation less likely? More likely?

3. The Securities Act of 1933 was passed to require truthful disclosure in the sale of securities in order to promote efficient capital markets. The Age Discrimination in Employment Act was passed to protect the elderly from a culture biased toward youth and to make our culture more accepting of senior citizens. If those policies were important enough to codify into federal law, should they be left to private arbitration where only the interests of the individual parties, and not the public interest, will be represented? Does the public interest have a legitimate role in what are otherwise strictly private arbitrations? Should it have a role? If it does have a legitimate role, what procedures could be designed to ensure that that role is not neglected?

4. In *Nelson v. Cyprus Bagdad Copper Corp.*, 119 F.3d 756, 758 (1997) (Case 4.2), the employee signed the following acknowledgment:

> I have received a copy of the Cyprus Bagdad Copper Corporation Handbook that is effective July 1, 1993 and understand that the Handbook is a guideline to the Company's policies and procedures. I agree to read it and understand its contents. If I have any questions regarding its contents I will contact my supervisor or Human Resources Representative.

In light of the *Nelson* decision, how should this language be modified to ensure that new employees are bound by arbitration agreements?

5. Rich and Enza Hill picked up the phone, ordered a computer from Gateway 2000, and gave their credit card number. Thereafter, a box arrived containing the computer and a list of terms, said to govern unless the customer returns the computer within 30 days. One of the terms was an arbitration clause requiring the arbitration of all claims against Gateway 2000 arising from the purchase of the computer. The Hills kept their computer for more than 30 days, after which they complained about its components and performance. Gateway refused to refund their money. Outraged, the Hills filed a class action suit in federal court under the Racketeer Influenced and Corrupt Organizations Act (RICO). The Hills reasoned that Gateway had used the mail and telephone to sell the shoddy merchandise and hence committed mail and wire fraud. The Hills may also have been aware that a successful lawsuit would entitle them to treble damages under RICO.

The district court refused to enforce the arbitration agreement, holding that there was insufficient evidence to find that the arbitration agreement was a valid waiver of the Hills' right to sue or that the Hills were given adequate notice of the arbitration clause. On appeal, the U.S. Court of Appeals for the Seventh Circuit reversed the lower court and ordered the parties to submit their dispute to arbitration according to the arbitration clause. Rejecting the Hills' argument that the arbitration clause did not stand out, the court reasoned that "[a] contract need not be read to be effective; people who accept [the computer] take the risk that the unread terms may in retrospect prove unwelcome." [*Hill v. Gateway 2000, Inc.*, 105 F.3d 1147 (7th Cir. 1997)]

Is it possible to reconcile the *Gateway* decision with the Ninth Circuit's refusal in *Nelson v. Cyprus Bagdad Copper Corp.*, 119 F.3d 756 (1997) (Case 4.2) to enforce the arbitration clause in an employee handbook? In what ways are these cases similar? Dissimilar?

6. On November 6, 1991, orthopedic surgeon Lonnie Paulos performed a posterior cruciate ligament reconstruction on the left knee of patient Doncene Sosa. Less than one hour before the surgery and while Sosa was waiting in her surgical clothing, a representative of Dr. Paulos' office gave her three documents and asked her to sign them. The documents were (1) Patient Informed Consent and Release of Claims; (2) Consent for Use of Freeze Dried or Flesh Donor Tissue; and (3) Physician–Patient Arbitration Agreement.

The arbitration agreement stated that (1) all claims between the parties will be settled by arbitration; (2) both parties waive their constitutional rights to a jury trial for any claim between them; (3) arbitration will be by a panel of three board-certified orthopedic surgeons, one of which each party will choose and one of which the other two arbitrators will choose; (4) if the arbitrators award the patient less than one-half of the amount she seeks in arbitration, then the patient will be responsible for all expenses, costs, arbitrators' fees, and reasonable attorney's fees incurred by physician in connection with the arbitration, including payment to physician at the rate of $150.00 per hour for time spent by the physician defending himself in connection with the arbitration; (5) the agreement may be revoked by written notice delivered to the physician or mailed within 14 days after signature; and (6) the patient declares that she has read and understands the agreement, that the physician or his assistant has explained the above agreement to her and to her satisfaction, that she does not have any unanswered questions, and that she has executed the agreement of her own free will and not under any duress.

Upon awakening from the anesthesia, Sosa became aware of a surgical complication. Later she filed a complaint for medical malpractice against Dr. Paulos. He in turn asked the court to compel arbitration in accordance with the Physician–Patient Arbitration Agreement signed by Sosa. Sosa agreed that she signed all three documents before her surgery, although she alleges that she did so without reading them. Furthermore, she claims that neither Dr. Paulos nor any member of his staff ever discussed the arbitration agreement with her. Sosa argues that the facts surrounding her signing of the agreement, together with the substance of the agreement itself, demonstrate that it was procedurally and substantively unconscionable and therefore unenforceable. Dr. Paulos, on the other hand, argues that the agreement is fair and evenhanded and that Ms. Sosa had plenty of time to read the agreement and ask questions concerning its content. Because arbitration agreements are favored in this state, Dr. Paulos argues, the court should compel arbitration pursuant to the parties' agreement. What result? [*Sosa v. Paulos*, 924 P.2d 357 (Utah 1997)]

7. Two commercial fisherman, Gill and Brook, live on the edge of a lake teeming with 10,000 pounds of fish.

Each depends on the fish catch for his livelihood and has equipment to harvest immediately the lake's entire 10,000 pounds of fish, worth $10 per pound. For the population to sustain itself and offer both fishermen a lifetime of catch, no more than 4,000 pounds can be harvested in any one year. If less than 6,000 pounds are left behind to reproduce, the lake will be empty forever. But if at least 6,000 pounds are left to reproduce, a perpetual supply of 4,000 pounds, worth $40,000 now, will remain available.

If alone on the lake, Gill or Brook would happily harvest only 4,000 pounds per year and ensure a continual supply of fish. In competition with each other, however, both Gill and Brook are deeply suspicious of each other. Gill fears that Brook will harvest any fish Gill leaves behind, and Brook fears Gill will do the same if he limits his catch.

Without any additional information, what are the incentives for Gill and Brook to fish at various rates? What is the payoff table? What could Gill and Brook do to ensure the optimal outcome? What barriers would they face in such an attempt?

8. Describe a situation from your own experience, personal or business, where the resolution of a conflict was frustrated by a psychological barrier. Was the barrier yours, your opponent's, or both? What could you have done to overcome the barrier?

9. During her second year of business school at the University of Wisconsin, Ursula learned that Freedom Consulting wanted to hire an MBA with her experience, skills, and interests to come on board as a consultant in its Boston office. After discussing Freedom with some of her classmates, Ursula discovered that the firm offered few benefits: two weeks of vacation and basic health maintenance coverage by Kaiser Permanente. To her delight, she also learned that Freedom has an office in warm and sunny San Diego, although the firm was not recruiting for that office.

After interviewing with Freedom and feeling good about the position and the company overall, Ursula asked about compensation. Because she had a similar offer from Decisions Forever with a salary of $95,000, Ursula would not accept less than $95,000 in salary. Freedom had another candidate nearly as qualified as Ursula who was willing to work for $90,000. Freedom saw no reason to increase its offer to Ursula.

During their discussions, Freedom explained that it was considering switching medical insurance providers to a preferred provider plan with Blue Cross and had an immediate and pressing need for MBAs to join its Chicago office. After an unusually open and honest discussion, both parties learned the value the other placed on the following issues.

ISSUE	URSULA'S VALUE		FREEDOM'S VALUE	
Official title	Analyst	−$1000	Analyst	$0
	Consultant	0	Consultant	0
	Manager	2600	Manager	−500
Number of vacation days	10	0	10	0
	20	2000	20	−2500
Medical insurance provider	Blue Cross	500	Blue Cross	−3000
	Kaiser	0	Kaiser	0
Geographic location	Boston	0	Boston	0
	Chicago	−300	Chicago	2500
	San Diego	1000	San Diego	−5000
Matching 401(k) retirement plan	Yes	2000	Yes	−1600
	No	0	No	0
Start date	Immediately	−1000	Immediately	5000
	In 3 months	1000	In 3 months	−1000
Signing bonus of $5000	Yes	5000	Yes	−5000
	No	0	No	0

Why might Ursula and Freedom place differing values on these issues? How easy would it really be for Ursula to learn fully about Freedom's values and vice versa?

Given the information above, what should a manager of Freedom who wants to hire Ursula now offer her? What should Ursula be willing to accept? How much value has been created by integration? How much value remains to be distributed?

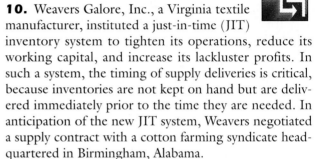

MANAGER'S DILEMMA

10. Weavers Galore, Inc., a Virginia textile manufacturer, instituted a just-in-time (JIT) inventory system to tighten its operations, reduce its working capital, and increase its lackluster profits. In such a system, the timing of supply deliveries is critical, because inventories are not kept on hand but are delivered immediately prior to the time they are needed. In anticipation of the new JIT system, Weavers negotiated a supply contract with a cotton farming syndicate headquartered in Birmingham, Alabama.

In the contract, the syndicate agreed to supply Weavers with 1¼ tons of top quality cotton on the Tuesday morning of each week for the next 18 months. In return, Weavers agreed to pay $.65 per pound, one month in advance of each shipment. For instance, on March 15, Weavers would pay $1625 for 1¼ tons of cotton to be delivered by the syndicate on the morning of Tuesday, April 15. Strict adherence to the delivery schedule was of paramount importance to Weavers, the first textile manufacturer in the region and the only customer of the syndicate to implement JIT.

On October 15, six months into the agreement, the syndicate announced that it would be unable to deliver the next few shipments to Weavers on time and complete. Poor harvests and equipment failures had disrupted the syndicate's operations, and its contracts with other customers were already straining its operations. Many of them would also have to receive late and/or incomplete shipments. For the time being, the syndicate announced, Weavers would have to make do with a single ton of cotton delivered on Wednesday evenings, at best.

Christina Snow, Weavers' CEO, was livid. Without the next few shipments of cotton on time, she might well lose customers, market share, and profits. Snow's first instinct was to have Weavers' general counsel fire off a terse letter to the syndicate reminding it of its contractual obligations and Weavers' willingness to enforce its rights in court. After that, she might file a lawsuit.

Should Snow turn this matter over to Weavers' general counsel? What else could Snow do to protect and further the interests of Weavers? What are the pros and cons of these courses of actions?

INTERNET SOURCES	
The American Arbitration Association's home page offers avenues into its many services.	http://www.adr.org
The Dispute Resolution Section of the American Bar Association offers information about the law of ADR.	http://www.abanet.org/dispute/home.html
The Mediation Information Research Center offers articles and other information about mediation as well as resources concerning professional mediators.	http://www.mediate.com
JAMS/Endispute's page offers information about its many dispute resolution services.	http://www.jams-endispute.com
The Securities Law Home Page offers information about arbitration of disputes involving securities and securities dealers and brokers.	http://www.seclaw.com/centers/arbcent.html
The U.S. House of Representatives Internet Law Library has a large collection of ADR-related statutes, court decisions, and articles.	http://law.house.gov/314.html

CHAPTER 5

Agency

INTRODUCTION

Agency and the Conduct of Business

In an *agency* relationship between two parties, one of the parties—the *agent*—agrees to act on behalf of another person—the *principal*. The agent has the authority to deal with third parties and to bind the principal to a contract. In the sphere of their agreement, the principal has the right to control the agent's conduct and is liable for the agent's torts. Agency is perhaps the most pervasive legal relationship in the business world. Businesses of all kinds require the assistance of agents in order to conduct multiple operations in various locations. Indeed, without the law of agency, corporations could not function at all. Only through its agents can the legal fiction of a corporation enter into any kind of binding agreement.

Chapter Overview

This chapter defines and discusses the central principles of agency law. First, it describes the different methods by which an agency relationship can be formed. The chapter identifies the different types of agency relationships and the consequences that flow from each. It examines the duties an agent owes to his or her principal, and an agent's authority to enter into agreements that are binding upon the principal. Finally, the chapter discusses the extent to which a principal may be liable for the tortious or illegal conduct of his or her agent.

 ## Formation of an Agency Relationship

The agency relationship is consensual in nature and is typically created by agreement of the parties. This agreement can be either written or oral. An agency agreement can also be implied from conduct. For instance, suppose computer maker C regularly ships inventory to distributor D with the understanding that D will sell the computers to retailers and end users. An agency relationship exists between C and D, even if they have not entered into a formal agreement.

Agency relationships can also be formed without agreement—by ratification or by estoppel. If a principal approves or accepts the benefits of the actions of an otherwise unauthorized agent, he or she has formed an *agency by ratification.* An *agency by estoppel* occurs in the following scenario. Jack causes Kendra to believe that Lori is his agent, and Kendra relies on this misrepresentation and proceeds to deal with Lori. Even if Lori is not in fact Jack's agent, Kendra's reliance creates an agency by estoppel; thus her dealings with Lori will be binding upon Jack. Jack is estopped (prevented) from denying that Lori is his agent.

Types of Agency Relationships

An agent may be either an employee of the principal or an independent contractor.

Employee

The most common form of agency relationship is the employer-employee relationship, sometimes still referred to as the master-servant relationship. The basic characteristic of this relationship is that the employer has the right to control the conduct of the employee. The employee may have the authority to bind the employer to a contract under theories of actual or apparent authority.

Independent Contractor

An *independent contractor*, such as a lawyer working for a client or a plumber working for a house builder, is not an employee of the person paying for his or her services, because his or her conduct is not fully subject to that person's control. The person hiring an independent contractor bargains only for results.

An independent contractor may or may not be an agent. Generally, an agency relationship exists when the hiring person gives the independent contractor authority to enter into contracts on his or her behalf. For example, suppose a builder contracts for $100,000 to build a house for Ken. Ken has no control over the builder's manner of doing the work because the house is one of a large group of houses that the builder is constructing in a housing subdivision. The builder is not Ken's agent. On the other hand, suppose Ken expressly authorized the builder to buy redwood siding from a lumber company on his behalf. Here, the independent contractor becomes Ken's agent.

Distinguishing between Employees and Independent Contractors

Determining whether a worker is an employee or independent contractor is a legal issue with several important consequences.

One significant difference between employees and independent contractors involves liability. Employers are liable for the torts of their employees, so long as the employee was acting within the scope of his or her employment. Persons hiring independent contractors, however, are generally not liable for torts committed by the independent contractor.

In addition, the distinction between employee and independent contractor status raises important tax and benefits issues. Employers are not required to deduct or pay income, Social Security, and unemployment taxes for independent contractors; independent contractors bear the responsibility to pay their own self-employment taxes. Moreover, independent contractors are generally not eligible for the same fringe benefits (such as medical insurance, stock options, and 401(k) retirement plans) received by employees. This was a crucial factor in the *Microsoft* case depicted in the "Inside Story" in this chapter. Because an employer does not pay taxes and may not provide fringe benefits for independent contractors, an employer may be able to hire an independent contractor for less money than it would cost to hire an employee to do the same work.

The distinction between employees and independent contractors is an important one, but there is no bright-line test to distinguish one from the other. Significantly, the label used in an employment contract does not determine the employment status of a worker. In other words, the outcome turns on "what you do" not "what you say." The law looks at a variety of factors, including the following:

1. How much control can the employer exercise over the details of the work?
2. Is the employed person engaged in an occupation distinct from that of the employer?
3. Is the kind of work being done usually performed under the direction of an employer or by a specialist without supervision?
4. What degree of skill does the work require?

5. Does the employer provide the worker with tools and a place of work?
6. For how long is the worker employed?
7. Is the worker paid on the basis of time or by the job?

Employee status is more likely to be found for workers who are lower paid and less skilled, lack bargaining power, and have a high degree of economic dependence on their employers.

Relationship of Agent to Principal

In an agency relationship, one person—the agent—acts for or represents another person—the principal. The principal delegates a portion of his or her power to the agent. The agent then manages the assigned task and exercises the discretion given to him or her by the principal. The agency relationship is created by an express or implied contract or by law.

Fiduciary Responsibility

In agreeing to act on behalf of the principal, the agent becomes a *fiduciary*. Loyalty and obedience are the hallmarks of the fiduciary relationship. An agent has a duty to act solely for the benefit of his or her principal in all matters directly connected with the agency undertaking. This is the *duty of loyalty*. For example, an agent entrusted with the power to buy a piece of land for her principal cannot buy the land for himself or herself instead.

An agent also has a duty to act with due care. This *duty of care* includes a duty to avoid mistakes, whether through negligence, recklessness, or intentional misconduct. Some states require an agent to use the same level of care a person would use in the conduct of his or her own affairs. Others use a comparative approach: An agent is to use the same level of care a reasonable person in a like situation would use. Application of these duties to officers, directors, and controlling shareholders is discussed in Chapter 21.

The following case examines the contours of the duty of loyalty. Specifically, it considers the propriety of a fiduciary, such as an accounting firm, establishing a business in direct competition with that of its client.

A CASE IN POINT   **SUMMARY**

CASE 5.1
STERN STEWART & CO.
v. KPMG PEAT
MARWICK LLP
Supreme Court of New York
N.Y.L.J., July 24, 1997, at 25
(N.Y. Sup. Ct. July 15, 1997).

FACTS   Stern Stewart is a leading New York boutique financial consulting firm specializing in corporate valuations and executive compensation. It uses a system called Economic Value Added; Stern Stewart has trademarked the acronym EVA.

KMPG Peat Marwick (KPMG) is a Big Six accounting firm that served as Stern Stewart's auditors and tax advisors. It had access to Stern Stewart's confidential financial records and executive compensation information. While still acting in this fiduciary capacity, and without notice to Stern Stewart, KPMG decided to establish an economic-consulting division that would compete with Stern Stewart. KPMG called this its Economic Value Management (EVM) unit.

Stern Stewart was not aware of KPMG's intentions until after a number of its employees had been hired by KPMG and the formation of KPMG's EVM practice was well underway. Stern Stewart sued KPMG under a variety of theories, including breach of fiduciary duty.

ISSUE PRESENTED   Did KPMG's undisclosed creation of an economic value management division constitute a breach of the fiduciary duty KPMG owed Stern Stewart as its accountant?

Case 5.1 continues

Case 5.1 continued

SUMMARY OF OPINION   The New York Supreme Court accepted the classic standard of fiduciary duty as pronounced by Justice Cardozo in *Meinhard v. Salmon*: A fiduciary must accord to a standard of behavior "not of honesty alone, but the punctilio of an honor the most sensitive." A fiduciary relationship, the court noted, is one in which the principal should be able to repose trust and not be on guard against the "unlimited ingenuity that overreaching entrepreneurs and trade pirates put to use."

The court found significance in the fact that KPMG had access to a large number of Stern Stewart's confidential documents, including financial statements and employee information. It noted that one initial step in the formation of KPMG's EVM division involved KPMG sending six staff members to a Stern Stewart seminar to secure information helpful to the implementation of their plan. A memorandum written by one of the attendees gloated over the value of the information derived. The court found that "[a]lthough many of the KPMG actions were innocent, it was clear that KPMG decided to 'buy, not build' an economic value consulting practice." The fact that KPMG lured away Stern Stewart employees by offering them bonuses and profit-sharing packages that were not offered to other KPMG hires contributed to this finding.

At bottom, the court reasoned, the claim was that a fiduciary, after learning of a profitable area of practice by way of its fiduciary relationship, breached its obligations by establishing a business to compete with its client. A fiduciary is "not entitled to engage in an actual secretive competitive venture when still in the embrace of an active relationship with a principal." The court concluded that KPMG's conduct violated these principles.

RESULT   The court found KPMG liable for breach of its fiduciary duty to Stern Stewart.

COMMENTS   The court held that KPMG had violated its fiduciary duty even though KPMG had not misappropriated trade secrets or engaged in unfair competition. This case highlights the problems accounting firms face as they expand into new areas of consulting.

The court said it was troubled by the difficulty it faced deciding on an appropriate remedy for this suit. It issued an injunction prohibiting KPMG's EVM unit from sending out teams that included two or more former Stern Stewart employees. It called this a small step designed to prohibit the use of "look-alike" teams formed of employees hired away while KPMG was a fiduciary. The court awarded Stern Stewart only nominal damages, however, because it could not prove that KPMG's actions had directly led to the loss of any business. The court deferred consideration of punitive damages, and as of early 1998 had still not resolved the issue.

The legal struggle between these two firms took another strange turn in December 1997, when KPMG sued Stern Stewart for trying to stifle competition. KPMG's suit, filed in federal court, contended that Stern Stewart tried to subvert KPMG's January 12, 1998, conference on economic value management by urging potential speakers to boycott the event.

Sometimes it is not clear whether a person acting on behalf of another does or does not have a fiduciary duty to the other person. This was the issue in the following case dealing with a person hired to find a buyer for a company.

A CASE IN POINT	IN THE LANGUAGE OF THE COURT

CASE 5.2
NORTHEAST GENERAL
CORPORATION v.
WELLINGTON
ADVERTISING, INC.
Court of Appeals of New York
624 N.E.2d 129 (N.Y. 1993).

FACTS In 1988, plaintiff Northeast General Corporation, through its agents Dunton and Margolis, entered into an agreement with defendant Wellington Advertising, Inc. relating to the sale of Wellington Advertising. Northeast was to act "as a non-exclusive independent investment banker and business consultant for the purposes of finding and presenting candidates for purchase, sale, merger or other business combination." The agreement further provided that Northeast General would be entitled to a finder's fee, based on the size of the transaction, if a transaction was completed within three years of when Wellington was introduced to the "found" buying party.

Margolis, one of Northeast General Corporation's agents, after consultation with Northeast's new president, Dunton, introduced Sternau to Wellington's president, Arpadi, as a potential purchaser of Wellington. Ultimately, Sternau and Wellington entered into a purchase agreement.

Before introducing Sternau to Wellington, Dunton was informed by an unidentified investment banker that Sternau had a reputation for buying companies, removing assets, rendering the companies borderline insolvent, and leaving minority investors unprotected. Dunton did not, prior to the closing of the Wellington-Sternau deal, disclose this information to Wellington.

After Northeast's introduction of Sternau to Wellington, but prior to signing the acquisition agreement, Dunton called Arpadi and offered further help with the transaction. Arpadi declined that help and discouraged Dunton from any further involvement. After the merger agreement was signed, companies controlled by Sternau purchased the controlling stock of Wellington, leaving Wellington's principals, including Arpadi, as minority investors. Ultimately, Wellington was rendered insolvent, and Arpadi and other minority investors suffered financial losses. Wellington delivered a check for Northeast's finder services; but, before the check could be negotiated, payment was stopped.

Northeast sued Wellington to recover its finder's fee. After a trial, the jury found in favor of Northeast and awarded it the agreed-on finder's fee. The trial court judge set aside the jury's verdict. The judge's decision, which rested on arguments of public policy, imposed a fiduciary-like duty on finders to disclose adverse information to their clients. The appellate division court upheld the trial court judge's action. Northeast appealed.

ISSUE PRESENTED Does a finder–seller agreement create a relationship of trust with a "fiduciary-like" obligation on the finder to share information with the seller regarding the potential buyer's bad reputation?

OPINION BELLACOSA, J., writing for the New York Court of Appeals:

Before courts can infer and superimpose a duty of the finest loyalty, the contract and relationship of the parties must be plumbed. We recognize that "[m]any forms of conduct permissible in a workaday world for those acting at arm's length, are forbidden to those bound by fiduciary ties" (*Meinhard v. Salmon*, 249 N.Y. 458, 464). Chief Judge Cardozo's oft-quoted maxim is a timeless reminder that "[a] trustee is held to something stricter than the morals of the market place. Not honesty alone, but the punctilio of an honor the most sensitive" (*id.*). If the parties find themselves or

Case 5.2 continues

Case 5.2 continued

place themselves in the milieu of the "workaday" mundane market place, and if they do not create their own relationship of higher trust, courts should not ordinarily transport them to the higher realm of relationship and fashion the stricter duty for them.

The Northeast-Wellington agreement contains no cognizable fiduciary terms or relationship. The dissent ascribes inordinate weight to the titles non-exclusive "independent investment banker and business consultant." These terms in the context of this agreement are not controlling, since Dunton did not perform the services of an investment banker or consultant. Instead, Dunton's sole function was "for purposes of finding and presenting candidates." That drives the analysis of this case because he was a traditional finder functioning under a finder's agreement, and his role ceased when he found and presented someone. The finder was not described or given the function of an agent, partner or co-venturer.

. . . Probing our precedents and equitable principles unearths no supportable justification for such a judicial interposition, however highly motivated and idealistic. Indeed, responding to this fine instinct would inappropriately propel the courts into reformation of service agreements between commercially knowledgeable parties in this and perhaps countless other situations and transactions as well.

This Court may sense a sympathetic impulse to balance what it may view as the equities of a situation such as this. The hard judicial obligation, however, is to be intellectually disciplined against that tug. Instead, courts must focus on the precise law function reposed in them in such circumstances, which is to construe and enforce the meaning and thrust of the contract of the parties, not to purify their efforts.

. . . The character of the Northeast-Wellington agreement was not one of trust importing duties beyond finding a prospect. The fact that Wellington did not employ its own independent, traditional methods to check out the reputation of the prospect and accepted what turned out to be a bad prospect does not warrant this Court rescuing it from its soured deal by any post-agreement fiduciary lifeline.

. . .

The commonplace mores of the market place suffice and are appropriate to govern relationships established by contract of the type involved here, which contemplates and asks nothing more of the parties than performance of a simple service. In sum, defendants' financial losses from their market mishap with Sternau is not reason enough to propel a sweeping new fiduciary-like doctrine into finders' agreements.

DISSENTING OPINION   HANCOCK, J.:

A fiduciary relationship is one founded on trust or confidence reposed by one person in the integrity and fidelity of another. The term is a very broad one. It is said that the relation exists, and that relief is granted, in all cases in which influence has been acquired and abused, in which confidence has been reposed and betrayed. The origin of the confidence and the source of the influence are immaterial. The rule embraces both technical fiduciary relations and those informal relations which exist whenever one man trusts in and relies upon another. Out of such a relation, the law raises the rules that neither party may exert influence or pressure upon the other.

. . .

Case 5.2 continues

Case 5.2 continued

The narrow question applying the above rules is whether Arpadi's and Dunton's relationship exhibits sufficient trust and de facto control upon which to ground Dunton's duty to disclose negative information regarding the very deal he was promoting. The record reveals more than enough evidence to demonstrate both elements. By imparting confidential business details as well as his personal plans and intentions [which included Arpadi's statement that he was "terrified" he "would lose everything" in a bad merger], Arpadi reposed trust in Dunton as a business counselor to find candidates likely to conform to Arpadi's investment goals. Arpadi expected Dunton to perform as a finder with Arpadi's interests at heart, i.e., not to remain silent as Wellington was being circled by a corporate predator. Dunton exerted de facto control and influence over Arpadi by fostering Arpadi's false belief that there was no reason not to accept Sternau as a suitable candidate. Dunton's review of the intimate details of Arpadi's business marked Dunton's acceptance of that trust. There is no doubt that as regards the proposed merger with [Sternau's company], Dunton and Arpadi stood in a fiduciary relation to each other.

. . .

There is a final point. Even if only the agreement between Northeast and Arpadi were to be considered, the law would, I submit, imply a duty on the part of Dunton to disclose critical adverse information in these circumstances. . . .

. . .

. . . Indeed, I believe that many would agree that even the "morals of the market place" would require it. Surely [Dunton] should not be rewarded for his failure.

RESULT   The judgment for Wellington was reversed by the New York Court of Appeals notwithstanding the dissent because a majority of the judges on the court voted for reversal. Accordingly, Wellington was ordered to pay the finder's fee to Northeast General.

Questions

1. Which arguments do you find more persuasive, those of the majority or the dissent?
2. The court stated that a broker, who helps negotiate a deal and thereby brings the parties to an agreement, has a fiduciary duty to act in the best interests of the person who hired him or her. Should a finder, who merely introduces the parties, be governed by a lesser ethical standard? If not, is it the role of the law to enforce that standard?

◆ Agent's Ability to Bind the Principal

An agent has the ability to bind the principal in legal relations with third parties if the agent has actual or apparent authority to do so. Even in the absence of such authority, the principal may be bound by the unauthorized acts of his or her agent if the principal subsequently ratifies those acts. A principal can be bound even if his or her identity is undisclosed to the third party.

Actual Authority

The principal may give the agent *actual authority* to enter into agreements on his or her behalf, that is, the principal may give consent for the agent to act for and bind the principal. This consent (or authority) may be express or implied.

Express Authority   *Express authority* may be given by the principal's actual words, for example, a request that the agent submit a budget for a proposed plan of action. Express authority may also be given by an action that indicates the principal's consent, for example, by sending the agent a check in partial payment for the purchase of materials necessary to execute the plan. An agent has express authority if the agent has a justifiable belief that the principal has authorized him or her to do what he or she is doing.

Although one purpose of minutes of meetings of the board of directors of a corporation is mere formality, another purpose is to answer agency questions that may arise from corporate transactions. Board minutes are one way a manager can determine whether an officer had actual authority to execute an agreement or to take other actions on behalf of the corporation.

Implied Authority   Once the agent is given express authority, he or she also has *implied authority* to do whatever is reasonable to complete the task he or she has been instructed to undertake. For example, if an agent is instructed to purchase a truck costing up to $20,000 for his or her principal, the agent has implied authority to select the appropriate make and model, negotiate the purchase price, and finalize the sale.

Persons in certain positions or offices have implied authority to do what is reasonable for someone in that position. For example, the vice-president of purchases for a trucking business, because of his or her position, has the implied authority to engage in the activities described in the preceding paragraph. There are limits to such implied authority, however. For example, the vice-president of purchases for a trucking division does not have the implied authority to buy an office building. Similarly, an officer of a corporation does not have the authority to bind the corporation to sell or grant rights to purchase shares of its stock; stock issuances must be approved by the board of directors of the corporation.

Apparent Authority

Apparent authority is created when a third party reasonably believes that the agent has authority to act for and bind the principal. This belief may be based on the words or acts of the principal or on knowledge that the principal has allowed its agent to engage in certain activities on its behalf over an extended period of time. As the following case illustrates, the existence of apparent authority may be shown by inference and circumstantial evidence.

A CASE IN POINT	SUMMARY

CASE 5.3
LUNDBERG v. CHURCH FARM, INC.
Appellate Court of Illinois,
Second District
502 N.E.2d 806
(Ill. App. Ct. 1986).

FACTS   Church Farm, Inc. was in the business of breeding thoroughbred racehorses. The company owned a "very well bred stallion" called Imperial Guard. Church Farm had purchased Imperial Guard for $700,000 and sought to syndicate breeding rights in the horse. It placed a full center-page advertisement in *Racing Form*, a publication directed to the horse-breeding and -racing community. The ad listed the cost of one syndication share as $50,000 and directed all inquiries to "Herb Bagley, Manager." (Ownership of the horse would be divided into 40 shares, so the owner of one share would essentially own a 1/40th interest in the horse. He or she would also be entitled to have three mares bred to the stallion each breeding season.)

Bagley lived on the Church Farm and was the farm manager. Church Farm provided Bagley with preprinted forms to serve as contracts for the syndication. Vern Lundberg met with Bagley several times at the farm to discuss Imperial Guard. In April

Case 5.3 continues

Case 5.3 continued

1982, Lundberg and Bagley executed a contract for one syndication share. Bagley verbally guaranteed to Lundberg that Imperial Guard would remain at Church Farm in Illinois until 1984. He told Lundberg that because the horse was to be registered in Illinois, he preferred Illinois purchasers. Therefore, he would guarantee six live foals to Lundberg in the first two breeding seasons under the contract, regardless of how many mares would have to be bred to Imperial Guard to accomplish that.

Bagley also added the following language in hand to the signature page of the preprinted form:

> I, Herbert F. Bagley, hereby agree to guarantee to Vern Lundberg 6 live foals in the first two years of this contract.
>
> H. Bagley

Finally, Bagley openly signed the contract on behalf of Church Farm's president. The contract contained signature lines for both Gilbert Church ("CHURCH FARM, INC., Gilbert G. Church, Pres.") and Bagley ("Herbert F. Bagley, Farm Mgr."). Bagley signed his own signature line and wrote "Gilbert G. Church by H. Bagley" on Church's line. Lundberg also signed the contract.

During the 1982 breeding season, Lundberg bred four mares to Imperial Guard, resulting in only one live foal. Later in 1982, Gil Church moved Imperial Guard to Oklahoma without giving notice to Lundberg. Lundberg sued Church Farm, claiming breach of contract. Church Farm defended by arguing that Bagley lacked authority to add any provisions to the preprinted form. The trial court awarded Lundberg $147,000 in damages. Church Farm appealed.

ISSUED PRESENTED   Does a manager have apparent authority to negotiate contract terms when he is held out as the contact person in a public advertisement?

SUMMARY OF OPINION   Lundberg did not dispute that Bagley lacked actual authority to negotiate a contract that differed from the preprinted form and to sign on behalf of Church Farm. Lundberg claimed, however, that Bagley had the apparent authority to do so.

The Appellate Court of Illinois acknowledged that the party asserting an agency relationship such as apparent authority has the burden of proving its existence, but noted that it may do so by inference and circumstantial evidence. The court defined an agent's apparent authority as that authority that the principal knowingly permits the agent to assume or which he holds his agent out as possessing. In other words, it is "the authority that a reasonably prudent [person] . . . would naturally suppose the agent to possess."

The agent's authority must be derived from some act or statement of the principal. The court noted that (1) Gil Church had approved the Imperial Guard ad listing Bagley as the farm's manager and directing all inquires to him, and (2) Church also permitted Bagley to live on the farm and to handle its daily operations. As a result, the court found "the conclusion is inescapable" that Gil Church affirmatively placed Bagley in a managerial position giving him complete control of Church Farm and its dealings with the public.

Case 5.3 continues

Case 5.3 continued

The court felt that this arrangement was "just the sort of 'holding out' of an agent by a principal that justifies a third person's reliance on the agent's authority." It held that Bagley did have apparent authority to deal with Lundberg; therefore, the contract with Lundberg was binding on Church Farm.

RESULT   The trial court's ruling that Bagley had apparent authority to bind Church Farm, Inc. was affirmed. Church Farm breached its contract with Lundberg when it failed to honor the terms to which Bagley and Lundberg had agreed.

Ratification

The principal can bind himself or herself to an agent's unauthorized acts through *ratification*, that is, affirmation, of the prior act. When an act has been ratified, it is then treated as if the principal had originally authorized it.

Ratification, like authorization, can be either express or implied. *Express ratification* occurs when the principal, through words or behavior, manifests an intent to be bound by the agent's act. For example, a principal could ratify his or her agent's unauthorized purchase of a truck either by saying "OK" or simply by paying the bill for the vehicle. *Implied ratification* occurs when the principal, by his or her silence or failure to repudiate the agent's act, acquiesces in it.

VIEW FROM CYBERSPACE

INTELLIGENT AGENTS AND CLICK-WRAP AGREEMENTS

Intelligent agents are semiautonomous computer programs that can be dispatched by the user to execute certain tasks. An important type of intelligent agent is one that can search the Internet and either retrieve relevant information or serve as a "personal shopping agent" that makes purchases on behalf of its user.[a]

A prominent feature of electronic commerce over the Internet or World Wide Web is the *click-wrap agreement*.[b] Under a click-wrap agreement, computer users assent to the terms of an on-line contract by clicking on an acceptance box. The convergence of these two forms of cyberspace technology raises an interesting legal question: What happens when an intelligent agent comes across a click-wrap agreement?

Intelligent agents may someday have the natural language abilities to parse through contract provisions and accept only those terms their users have preprogrammed. But at least for the near term, these agents will likely be able only to accept or reject on-line contracts in full. Because of the prevalence of click-wrap agreements, the value of an agent that completely avoids them will be significantly reduced. On the other hand, traditional agency law does not offer clear guidance as to whether an electronic device can bind an individual to a contract.

The drafters of the forthcoming Article 2B of the Uniform Commercial Code are addressing the issue. The tentative draft of the article seems to place the onus on the user of an intelligent agent, noting that the individual or company that adopted the agent is responsible for its conduct and bound by its performance. Critics of the draft, however, question whether it is appropriate to allow users to be bound by an agent that has been given such limited guidance.

---

a. This discussion is based on Stuart D. Levi & Robert Sporn, *Can Programs Bind Humans to Contracts?*, NAT'L L.J., Jan. 13, 1997, at B9.

b. The term *click-wrap agreement* is derived from shrink-wrap license. Under a *shrink-wrap license*, users are deemed to have assented to a licensing agreement with a software manufacturer by their act of tearing open the shrink wrap covering the software package. The U.S. Court of Appeals for the Seventh Circuit recently held that shrink-wrap licenses are generally enforceabale. *See* ProCD, Inc. v. Zeidenberg, 86 F.3d 1447 (7th Cir. 1996) (Case 8.1).

Undisclosed Principal

An agent may lawfully conceal his or her principal's identity, or even his or her existence. This may be desirable if, for instance, the principal is trying to buy up adjacent properties in one area before news of a business venture is made public, or if the principal's wealth would cause the seller to demand a higher price. If there is an *undisclosed principal,* that is, if the third party does not know the agent is acting for the principal, the principal will nonetheless be bound by any contract the agent enters into with actual authority. (If the agent acts without authority, the principal will not be bound; however, the agent himself or herself may be liable on such a contract.)

ETHICAL CONSIDERATION

Is it ethical to use an agent to enter into a contract with a third party who has made it clear that she is unwilling to enter into a deal with the undisclosed principal?

"We—your agents, successors, licensees, and assigns—would like to share a few thoughts with you."

Liability for Torts of Agents

A principal may be liable for not only the contracts but also the torts of his or her agents. According to the doctrine of *respondeat superior*, if an agent is acting within the scope of his or her employment, the agent's employer will be liable for any injuries or damage to the property of another that the agent causes. As stated in *Jones v. Hart*, decided in England in 1798:

> If the servants of A with his cart run against another cart, wherein is a pipe of wine, and overturn the cart and spoil the wine, an action lieth against A. For whoever employs another is answerable for him, and undertakes for his care to all that make use of him. The act of the servant is the act of his master, where he acts by authority of the master.

If the principal is required to pay damages to a third party because of an agent's negligence, the principal has the right to demand reimbursement from the agent.

Scope of Employment

Many cases in this area turn on whether the employee was acting within the scope of his or her employment. (Torts of independent contractors are discussed in the following section.) What constitutes scope of employment? Some of the relevant factors include (1) whether the employee's act was authorized by the employer; (2) the extent to which the employer's interests were advanced by the act; (3) whether the employer furnished the instrumentality (for example, truck, machine) that caused the injury; and (4) whether the employer had reason to know the employee would perform the act.

Given the play in these legal standards, it is not always clear whether the agent is acting within the scope of his or her employment. The following classic case is an illustration of this fact.

A CASE IN POINT   **SUMMARY**

CASE 5.4
RILEY v. STANDARD OIL CO. OF NEW YORK
Court of Appeals of New York
132 N.E. 97 (N.Y. 1921).

FACTS   Arthur Riley, a child, was hit and severely injured by a truck driver named Million. Million was an employee of the Standard Oil Company of New York, a large corporation even in the 1920s. Riley's mother, acting as a *guardian ad litem* (a person authorized to bring suit on behalf of a minor), sued Standard Oil. She sought to recover damages for personal injury from Standard Oil on the ground that the company was responsible for the tortious act of its agent, the truck driver.

Million had been instructed by his supervisor to drive a company truck from a Standard Oil mill to the freight yard of the Long Island Railroad, which was about two-and-a-half miles away. Million was supposed to pick up several barrels of paint at the freight yard and bring them back to the mill. Before leaving the mill, Million found some pieces of scrap wood and loaded them in the truck. As he pulled out of the mill, he did not turn in the direction of the freight yard. Instead, he drove to his sister's house, which was about four blocks in the opposite direction. After unloading the wood for his sister, he headed back toward the mill on his way to the freight yard. En route to the freight yard, but before he passed the mill, Million hit Arthur Riley. The only issue on appeal was whether Million was in fact acting as an agent for the company—that is, whether he was within the scope of his employment—when he hit Arthur Riley.

Standard Oil claimed that Million was not acting as an authorized agent of the company at the moment Million hit Riley. His supervisor had told him to go to the

Case 5.4 continues

Case 5.4 continued

freight yard, and he had no express actual authority to go in the opposite direction to deliver the wood to his sister. Nothing in his task indicated that Million had the implied actual authority to do so. Hence, the defendant argued that this personal errand was done without any authority and was outside the scope of employment. The defendant argued that, at least until Million returned to his initial point of departure (the entrance to the mill), he was not acting as an agent for Standard Oil and therefore the company could not be held liable for his actions.

ISSUE PRESENTED   For the purpose of determining a principal's liability for the conduct of its agent, does the scope of employment include returning to work after a diversion for a personal errand?

SUMMARY OF OPINION   The New York Court of Appeals rejected Standard Oil's argument. It held that if Million had hit Riley while on the way to his sister's house, it would have been up to the jury to decide whether this side trip was a separate journey on his own business, distinct from that of his master, or a mere deviation from the general route. If the jury found it to be a new journey, Million would not have been acting as Standard Oil's agent, and the company would not be liable for his negligence. However, the accident occurred when Million had already completed his personal errand and was headed back in the direction of his assigned destination. The court concluded, "At some point in the route Million again engaged in the defendant's business. That point, in view of all the circumstances, we think he had reached."

RESULT   Standard Oil was liable for employee Million's negligence. Million was deemed to be acting in the scope of employment when returning from his errand.

COMMENTS   Courts apply various standards in determining whether an agent is acting within the scope of his or her employment for purposes of tort liability. However, most courts consider such factors as when and where the tort occurred, what the employee was doing when the tort occurred, and why the employee was doing what he or she was doing.

Before the *Riley* case, there was much precedent for not holding an employer responsible for accidents caused by a driver-employee when he was using the employer's vehicle for his own purposes. The three-out-of-seven judges who dissented in *Riley* were able to cite a long list of such cases. The court could have held that Million, like the drivers in the previous cases, was still on his errand and not an agent when he hit Riley.

However, several of the judges were concerned with improving the tort system for victims of accidents. Standard Oil, as a large company, was in the best financial position to pay the damages for the serious injury caused by one of its drivers. To decide this close call the other way would have placed the financial burden on those least able to cover the loss.

Torts of Independent Contractors

The *respondeat superior* doctrine typically applies only to the action of employees. Principals may be held liable for the torts of independent contractors only in extraordinary circumstances, usually involving highly dangerous acts. For instance, if a principal hires an independent contractor to blast boulders off his land, the principal will be liable for any injuries damages resulting from the blast. In other words, a principal cannot avoid liability of damages resulting from ultrahazardous activities simply by contracting out the work. (Ultrahazardous activities are discussed further in Chapter 9.)

 ## Liability of the Principal for Violations of Law by the Agent

Under the theory of *vicarious liability*, a company can be held liable for violations of law by its employees even if a manager told the employee not to violate the law. This is demonstrated in the following case involving violations of federal housing and civil rights laws.

AT THE TOP

Although having a policy against illegal practices may not insulate the employer and its owner from civil liability for criminal acts of its lower-level employees, it reduces the chance the employees will break the law to begin with and it reduces the likelihood of the assessment of punitive damages against the employer and its owner.

A CASE IN POINT	IN THE LANGUAGE OF THE COURT

CASE 5.5
CHICAGO v. MATCHMAKER REAL ESTATE SALES CENTER, INC.
United States Court of Appeals for the Seventh Circuit
982 F.2d 1086
(7th Cir. 1992).

FACTS   In 1987, the Leadership Council, a nonprofit fair housing corporation in the city of Chicago, suspected that the agents of Matchmaker Real Estate Sales Center were engaging in the illegal practice of racial steering. *Racial steering* is a practice by which real estate brokers and agents preserve and encourage patterns of racial segregation in available housing. This is done by steering members of racial and ethnic groups to buildings and neighborhoods already predominantly inhabited by members of that same racial and ethnic group and away from buildings and neighborhoods inhabited primarily by members of other races or groups. Racial steering violates Section 1982 of the Civil Rights Act of 1866 and the Fair Housing Act of 1968.

Beginning in July 1987, the Leadership Council conducted a series of tests of Matchmaker's activities. Pairs of African-American and white "testers"—individuals who posed as home seekers—went to Matchmaker and inquired about buying homes in Chicago and its suburbs. The Leadership Council closely matched the African-American and white teams for financial qualifications (including income and possible down payments) and housing needs (such as family size and preferences).

In each test the Matchmaker agents engaged in blatant acts of racial steering. For example, the African-American testers and white testers were, in the same time period with very similar housing qualifications and requirements, given very different housing

Case 5.5 continues

Case 5.5 continued

listings that included only houses in neighborhoods already dominated by the testers' own racial groups. One Matchmaker agent, Carol Scarpiniti, even went so far as to tell one of the white tester couples behind closed doors that she knew she was "not supposed to steer," but because the white testers were unfamiliar with the area, she would give them "boundaries" to tell them "where not to live."

Matchmaker's sole shareholder and chief executive officer, Erwin Ernst, exercised day-to-day control over Matchmaker and its real estate agents. However, he did not engage in nor did he condone racial steering practices. He had created written office policies and procedures requiring that his agents comply with fair housing laws. He was also a signatory of an agreement by a national realtors organization ordering full compliance with fair housing laws and actively worked to get other Chicago brokers to sign the agreement. He required all his real estate agents to attend fair housing training courses sponsored by local real estate boards.

The city of Chicago, the Leadership Council, and the individual testers sued the realty corporation; its sole shareholder and chief executive officer, Ernst; and its sales agents. The agents were found liable for compensatory and punitive damages, as were Ernst and the realty company. The defendants appealed.

ISSUE PRESENTED   Should a realty firm and its sole owner and chief executive officer owner be held liable for the illegal acts of racial steering committed by the firm's real estate agents?

OPINION   BAUER, J., writing for the U.S. Court of Appeals:

The doctrine of *respondeat superior* "enables the imposition of liability on a principal for the tortious acts of his agent and, in the more common case, on the master for the wrongful acts of his servant."[1] "As a matter of well-settled agency law, a principal may be held liable for the discriminatory acts of his agent if such acts are within the scope of the agent's apparent authority, even if the principal neither authorized nor ratified the acts."[2] . . . A principal cannot free itself of liability by delegating to an agent the duty not to discriminate. [The court noted that the discriminatory acts of Matchmaker's agents were within the scope of their employment even though Matchmaker's policy prohibited discrimination.]

Federal courts have routinely applied these principles in fair housing cases and held principals liable for the discriminatory acts of their agents. For example, in *Walker v. Crigler*,[3] the plaintiff brought suit under the Fair Housing Act against the owner of rental property and his agent, a professional realtor. The plaintiff, a single mother, alleged that the realtor had discriminated against her because of her sex. A jury found the realtor liable, but ruled in favor of the owner. On appeal, the Fourth Circuit held that the evidence was sufficient "to support the conclusion that [the owner] specifically intended that [the realtor] not discriminate." Given this finding, the court noted that "[t]he central question to be decided . . . is which innocent

Case 5.5 continues

---

1. General Bldg. Contractors Ass'n v. Pennsylvania, 458 U.S. 375, 392 (1982).
2. Coates v. Bechtel, 811 F.2d 1045, 1051 (7th Cir. 1987).
3. 976 F.2d 900 (4th Cir. 1992).

Case 5.5 continued

party, the owner whose agent acted contrary to instruction, or the potential renter-who felt the direct harm of the agent's discriminatory failure to offer the residence for rent, will ultimately bear the burden of the harm caused." The court concluded that the Fair Housing Act's "overriding societal priority" requires that "the one innocent party with the power to control the acts of the agent, the owner of the property or other responsible superior, must act to compensate the injured party for the harm, and to insure that similar harm will not occur in the future." . . .

Here, Matchmaker (through Ernst), like the owner in Walker, specifically instructed its agents not to discriminate. As in Walker, the question we must decide is who among the innocent parties—the plaintiffs or Matchmaker and Ernst—should bear the responsibility for the discriminatory acts of Matchmaker's agents. We agree with the Fourth Circuit that "we must hold those who benefit from the sale and rental of property to the public to the specific mandates of anti-discrimination law if the goal of equal housing opportunity is to be reached."

RESULT The court affirmed the magistrate judge's decision holding Matchmaker and Ernst vicariously liable for compensatory damages due to the illegal acts of its agents, even though the principal had specifically instructed his agents not to act in such an illegal way. However, the court reversed the magistrate judge's order for punitive damages to be paid by Matchmaker and Ernst. A principal is liable for punitive damages for the discriminatory acts of his agent only if he knew of or ratified the acts.

Questions

1. Is it fair to hold Ernst liable for the illegal acts he did not condone?
2. Why were punitive damages against Matchmaker and Ernst inappropriate?

THE RESPONSIBLE MANAGER
Working with Agents

The relationship between a manager and his or her employer is one of trust. As an agent, a manager owes his or her employer fiduciary duties, which are most often summarized as the duty of care and the duty of loyalty. The duty of care typically requires a manager to avoid reckless or intentional behavior that would harm the company. Rarely will an act of simple negligence be treated as a breach of fiduciary duty. The duty of loyalty imposes more complex obligations. It requires a manager to avoid self-dealing or for-profit activity that competes with the business of the employer. In other words, a manager has a duty to act solely for the benefit of his or her employer in all matters related to its business. This duty includes an obligation to notify the employer of all relevant facts—all that the agent knows, the principal should know.

As a controlling officer of a company, a manager must be concerned with the scope of authority granted to the company's workers and the company's potential liability for the actions of those workers. Perhaps the most determinable aspect of this relationship is whether the worker is deemed an employee or an independent contractor. A manager may have several reasons to prefer labeling workers independent contractors rather than employees—for instance, lower tax and benefits costs or reduced exposure to liability. However, the manager must be aware that legally the status of workers will be determined by the manner in which they are used, not by the label written into the employment agreements.

Once a manager has hired an agent, he or she must be careful to leave little doubt about the scope of the agent's authority. If the manager does not do this, he or she may find, for example, that a purchasing agent has inadvertently been given the apparent authority to bind the business to a large purchase of supplies, above the actual needs of the business. A manager can help avoid scope-of-authority problems by making explicit, unambiguous statements to third parties that specify the limits on an employee's ability to enter into a binding contract. When dealing with third parties through an employee-agent, a manager must also monitor transactions to avoid conduct that might legally ratify an otherwise unauthorized agreement entered into by the employee.

The manager should ensure that the work environment and the machines and other equipment used in the business are safe. He or she should also stress to the employees the importance of not only complying with the law but also of being ethical and safety conscious. These concerns pertain mostly to the duties owed by employers to their employees. But employers may owe similar duties even to workers properly termed independent contractors, depending on where the independent contractor works and how much control the employer exerts over that work.

Finally, an employer must be concerned with liability for the wrongdoing of its workers. Because the employer will be liable for those torts of employees that are committed in the scope of employment, a manager should attempt to decrease the risk of such vicarious liability by defining the employees' scope of employment as narrowly as possible. A manager should also be aware that the employer is not able to avoid liability for injuries caused while it is engaged in an ultrahazardous activity, even if it is working through an independent contractor. Finally, as discussed in Chapter 15, employers may be responsible for the criminal acts of employees. For example, if an employee violates an industry-related regulation during the normal course of employment, the employer could be held vicariously liable. In some situations, the supervising manager may be liable as well.

INSIDE STORY

WHEN ARE "TEMPORARY" WORKERS EMPLOYEES?

In an economy that has seen many employers attempt to reduce labor costs and increase staffing flexibility by hiring temporary workers and independent contractors, the classification of workers has risen to new importance. The U.S. Court of Appeals for the Ninth Circuit recently caused a stir when it ordered Microsoft Corp., the world's largest computer software company, to provide fringe benefits to certain freelance workers even though they had signed agreements expressly stating that they were not eligible for such benefits.[4]

Microsoft employs a core staff of permanent employees, which it categorizes as "regular employees." Microsoft offers them a wide variety of benefits, including paid vacations, sick leave, holidays, short-term disability, group health and life insurance, and pensions, as well participation in its 401(k) retirement plan and its employee stock-purchase plan. Microsoft supplements its core staff of employees with a pool of individuals to whom it does not pay fringe benefits. It previously classified these individuals as "independent contractors" or "freelancers," but prior to the filing of this lawsuit began classifying them as "temporary agency employees." Freelancers were hired when Microsoft needed to expand its workforce to meet the demands of new product schedules. The company did not provide them with any of the employee benefits that its regular employees receive.

The named plaintiffs (who sued on their own behalf and as representatives of a class of workers) worked for Microsoft in the United States between 1987 and 1990 as freelancers in the company's international division. Although hired to work on specific projects, seven of the eight named plaintiffs had worked on successive projects for a minimum of two years prior to the time the action was filed, while the eighth had worked for more than a year. During that time, they performed services as software testers, production editors, proofreaders, formatters, and indexers. Microsoft fully integrated the plaintiffs into its workforce: They often worked on teams along with regular employees, sharing the same supervisors, performing identical functions, and working the same core hours. Because Microsoft required that they work on site, they received admittance card keys, office equipment, and supplies from the company.

Freelancers and regular employees, however, were not without their obvious distinctions. Freelancers wore badges of a diferent color, had different electronic-mail addresses, and attended a less formal orientation than that provided to regular employees. They were not permitted to assign their work to others, invited to official company functions, or paid overtime wages. In addition, they were not paid through Microsoft's payroll department. Instead, they submitted invoices for their services, documenting their hours and the projects on which they worked, and were paid through the accounts receivable department.

The plaintiffs were told when they were hired that, as freelancers, they would not be eligible for benefits. None contended that Microsoft ever promised them any benefits individually. All eight named plaintiffs signed Microsoft Corporation Independent Contractor Copyright Assignment and Non-Disclosure Agreements (nondisclosure agreements) as well as companion documents entitled In-dependent Contractor/Freelancer Information (information documents) when first hired by Microsoft or soon thereafter. The nondisclosure agreement, a three-page document primarily concerned with confidentiality, included a provision that stated that the undersigned "agrees to be responsible for all federal and state taxes, withholding, Social Security, insurance and other benefits." The information document likewise stated that "as an Independent Contractor to Microsoft, you are self-employed and are responsible to pay all your own insurance and benefits." Eventually, the plaintiffs learned of the various benefits being provided to regular employees from speaking with them or reading various Microsoft publications concerning employee benefits.

In 1989 and 1990, the Internal Revenue Service (IRS) examined Microsoft's employment records to determine whether the company was in compliance with the tax laws. Applying common law principles defining the employer-employee relationship, the IRS concluded that Microsoft's freelancers were not independent contractors but employees for withholding- and employment-tax purposes, and that Microsoft would thereafter be required to pay withholding taxes and the employer's portion of Social Security tax. Microsoft agreed to pay overdue employer withholding taxes and issue retroactive W-2 forms to allow the freelancers to recover Microsoft's share of Social Security taxes, which they had been required to pay. It apparently also agreed to pay freelancers retroac-tively for any overtime they may have worked.

After learning of the IRS rulings, the plaintiffs sought various employee benefits, including benefits under the Employee Stock Purchase Plan (ESPP) and Savings Plus Plan (SPP) benefits. The SPP is a cash or deferred-salary arrangement under Section 401k of the Internal Revenue Code that permits Microsoft's employees to save and invest up to 15% of their income through tax-deferred payroll deductions. Under the plan, Microsoft matches 50% of the employee's contribution in any year, with a maximum matching contribution of 3% of the employee's yearly compensation. The ESPP permits employees to purchase company stock at 85% of the lower of the fair market value on the first or on the last day of each six-month offering period through payroll deductions.

Microsoft rejected the plaintiffs' claims for benefits, maintaining that they were independent contractors who were personally responsible for all their own benefits. The named plaintiffs brought a lawsuit, challenging the denial of benefits.

A three-judge panel of the appeals court addressed the SPP and ESPP claims separately. The SPP document provided that "each employee who is 18 years of age or older and who has been employed for six months shall be eligible to participate in this Plan" and defined "employee" to mean "any common law employee who receives remuneration for personal services rendered to the employer and who is on the U.S. payroll of the employer." Microsoft conceded that the workers were common law employees (acknowledging the IRS's earlier finding) who rendered services to the company, and the workers were indisputably over the age of 18 and had been employed for longer than six months. Thus, the issue became one of specific plan interpretation: were these workers "on the U.S. payroll" of Microsoft?

The court held that the employment status of an individual is not determined by the label used in the contract between the parties and that evidence of an intent on the part of both parties to exclude the workers from plan eligibility was not controlling, because the parties mistakenly believed the workers were independent contractors, not common law employees. Finally, the court noted that Microsoft, as drafter of the plan, could easily have explicitly stated that these workers were not eligible to participate. Accordingly, the court construed the ambiguity in the plan against Microsoft and held that the workers were eligible to participate under the terms of the SPP.

The court's decision with respect to the ESPP claim turned on its view of Microsoft's objective intent as manifested in the language of the ESPP document. Specifically, the court held that, by stating within the plan that the plan was intended to comply with Section 423 of the Internal Revenue Code, Microsoft adopted the IRS's definition of common law employee. As a result, the court interpreted the ESPP as expressly extending eligibility to all of the workers in the plaintiffs' class.

Judge Stephen S. Trott filed a vigorous dissent. Judge Trott viewed the matter as a simple contract case and saw no reason why the IRS's one-time determination of the workers' status (motivated by an aggressive tax-collection policy) should control the question of their eligibility for specific fringe benefits. He pointed out that the rules regarding who is an employee and who is an independent contractor are unclear—at the time the workers signed on with Microsoft, both parties believed in good faith that the workers were independent contractors. On this understanding, the workers agreed they were not eligible for SPP and ESPP benefits, and Microsoft agreed to pay them a higher hourly wage than regular employees doing the same work. In Judge Trott's view, the majority obfuscated the existence of this basic, enforceable contract by wrongly suggesting that Microsoft intentionally misled the workers as to their status.

Microsoft was not content to give up its struggle after the decision of the three-judge panel. It petitioned for a rehearing by the U.S. Court of Appeals for the Ninth Circuit *en banc* (in other words, it asked the Ninth Circuit to assign 11 judges to hear the case anew). The appeals court agreed to the rehearing, but its decision—issued on July 24, 1997—was in substance not very different from that of the three-judge panel.[5]

The *en banc* appeals court began by noting that any insinuation by the panel court that Microsoft deliberately attempted to mislead the workers was inappropriate.

The court stated, "we could take either a negative or a positive view of Microsoft's intent and motives," and it chose to characterize the parties' initial choice of the independent contractor label as a simple, honest mistake.

Nevertheless, the *en banc* court generally left the analysis of the panel decision intact. It ruled that the language in the workers' employment contracts that denied their eligibility for the SPP and ESPP was not controlling. The court reasoned that such language was designed "merely [to] warn the workers about what [would happen] to them if they are independent contractors." Because the workers were in fact determined to be common law employees, the court deemed this explanatory language inapplicable. "[T]he independent contractor label was a mere error," the court stated, and "we see no reason to embrace and perpetuate that error."

By an eight-to-three margin, the *en banc* court sustained the ESPP holding of the panel court, ruling that the workers were eligible to participate. It departed from the panel's SPP decision, deciding by a six-to-five margin that the question of the workers' eligibility should go back to the plan administrator. The administrator had not addressed the specific question of whether the workers were "on the U.S. payroll" of Microsoft, and the court ruled that issues of plan interpretation should not be addressed by the courts until the plan administrator had made his determination.

Commentators were quick to note that the *en banc* decision did

"We're very sorry, Doyle, but you've been here for twelve years, and the other temps are starting to talk."

not alter the message of the panel court: If individuals are treated in every respect as employees, the mere fact that they are designated independent contractors will not establish that status. In order to establish independent contractor status, employers must show that the workers have the right to control the manner and means by which they perform their work. This can include setting their own hours, the right to refuse assignments, the right to subcontract work, or the right to work for other companies. Many administrative agencies also require some evidence that the individual has an investment in equipment and the ability to sustain both a profit and a loss.

Many companies have responded to this decision by leasing workers from temporary employment agencies instead of hiring them directly. Even this arrangement may not be fail-safe. The fact that leased workers are on the payroll of an employment agency does not preclude them from being considered the employees of the company—the agency and company could be considered joint employers. To determine whether a company is a joint employer of leased workers, a manager should consider such factors as whether the company (1) supervises the workers; (2) has the ability to hire and fire; (3) is involved in day-to-day labor relations; (4) establishes wage rates; or (5) has the power to promote or discipline the worker. As with questions surrounding the independent contractor label, the bottom line is this: If leased employees are treated the same as regular employees, they may be treated as common law employees of the company.

---

4. Vizcaino v. Microsoft Corp., 97 F.3d 1187 (9th Cir. 1996). The statement of facts that follows is excerpted from this opinion.

5. 120 F.3d 1006 (9th Cir. 1997).

KEY WORDS AND PHRASES

QUESTIONS AND CASE PROBLEMS

1. Singer was employed by General Automotive Manufacturing Company (GAMC) as its general manager from 1953 until 1959. He had worked in the machine-shop field for more than 30 years and enjoyed a fine reputation in machine-shop circles.

GAMC was a small concern with only five employees and a low credit rating. Singer attracted a large volume of business to GAMC and was invaluable in bolstering the company's credit rating. At times, when collections were slow, Singer paid the customer's bill to GAMC and waited for his own reimbursement until the customer remitted. Also, when work was slack, Singer would finance the manufacture of unordered parts and wait for recoupment until the stockpiled parts were sold. Some parts were never sold, and Singer personally absorbed the loss on them.

While working for GAMC, Singer set up his own sideline operation, in which he acted as a machinist-consultant. As orders came in to GAMC through him, Singer would decide that some of them required equipment GAMC lacked or that GAMC could not do the job at a competitive price. For such orders, Singer would give the customer a price, then deal with another machine shop to do the work at a lower price and pocket the difference. Singer conducted his operation without notifying GAMC of the offers that it (through Singer) did not accept. GAMC contended that this sideline business was in direct competition with its business.

GAMC sued Singer for breach of fiduciary duty. What result? What were Singer's duties to GAMC as its agent? Was Singer's operation of a sideline business ethical? Would it have been ethical had he disclosed it to his GAMC superiors? [*General Automotive Mfg. Co. v. Singer*, 120 N.W.2d 659 (Wis. 1963)]

2. Han Delbar was the sole proprietor of a bicycle shop called We Deal Wheels. He had two employees, Sandy Gear and Jebb Sprocket. Gear had the title of salesperson. She sold bikes and accessories to the public and also bought items from wholesalers. Sprocket had the title of repairperson; he did the repairs. Both employees sometimes did business-related errands outside the shop. At 10:00 A.M. one Monday, business was slow, so Delbar and Gear decided to test-ride a new mountain bike that the shop had just started selling. They left Sprocket to tend the store. At 10:30 A.M. a salesperson from R Tools R Jools, Inc., a wholesale tool supplier, walked into the shop. She found Sprocket there alone. She showed him a new line of high-priced bicycle repair tools. Sprocket was impressed and felt that the store should carry the tools. He said to the R Tools salesperson: "I'm in charge of repairs here, and so it makes sense for me to order these tools. You can bill us for $1,000 worth." The salesperson had done business with Gear in the past. Also, she had been told by Delbar that Sprocket was in charge of repairs and that We Deal Wheels would make good on any order purchased on credit. She was only too happy to make the sale by leaving the requested tools.

At 10:45 A.M. Delbar and Gear made it to a wooded area at the edge of town. Gear told Delbar that a true test of the bike's performance would require taking the long way back to the shop, across a rocky stretch of terrain. Delbar said that he himself wanted to go straight back, but that Gear could go the long way as long as she returned to the shop with all due haste. On her ride back, Gear stopped to buy a soda at the local grocery store. Rushing out of the store, Gear accidentally knocked over an elderly man, who broke his leg and arm in the fall.

At 11:30 A.M. Delbar returned to the store and saw the tools. He immediately called R Tools to cancel the order, believing they were too high priced. He told Sprocket that he should not order tools in the future.

a. R Tools refuses to take back the order, and Delbar refuses to pay for it. R Tools sues Delbar to collect the money. What arguments will each make in an attempt to win this suit? Who should win? How could Delbar have ensured his success on this issue?

b. The injured man sues Delbar, as Gear's employer, for his injuries. What arguments will Delbar make to avoid liability? Will he be successful? Assume that Delbar can succeed on his legal arguments. Does he have any ethical duty to pay?

3. Leonardo ran a small but prosperous rare-print shop. To keep the shop stocked with the finest prints, Leonardo needed to make purchases at trade shows throughout the world. When he was too busy to attend, Leonardo sometimes sent his employee, Rembrandt. On other occasions he paid for the services of an independent buyer named Rubens.

On March 14, Leonardo sent Rembrandt to Tokyo to buy 10 nineteenth-century Japanese prints. Leonardo told Rembrandt that he should use his own best judgment and buy the 10 prints that he considered to be of the finest quality. Price was no concern. While at the show, Rembrandt made a written list of the finest prints. The total came to 11. Rembrandt was unable to eliminate any from the list on the basis of quality. He closed his eyes and brought his finger down on the paper and it landed on print #4. Rembrandt purchased that print for himself and bought the other 10 for Leonardo.

On April 14, Rubens, who had his own business buying prints for himself and other dealers, called Leonardo. Rubens said he would be attending a show in Munich and asked if Leonardo wished him to purchase a few prints on Leonardo's behalf. Leonardo replied that he was interested, but only if Rubens agreed to fax him photocopies of all prints for sale, then let Leonardo select five before Rubens bought any. Rubens did not usually make such concessions, but he agreed to do it. Rubens and Leonardo signed Rubens's standard contract, with a typed-in clause for the faxing arrangement. Once at the show, Rubens faxed the copies. Leonardo selected five prints. One of the five was a forgery, but Leonardo could not detect it in a fax. Rubens had spotted the forgery and discreetly mentioned it to the show's organizer. Not wanting to create a scandal, the organizer offered Rubens $5,000 to remain silent. Rubens accepted the bribe.

a. Leonardo believes that the print Rembrandt purchased for himself is the best of the Tokyo lot. Rembrandt refuses to sell it to Leonardo. (After he returned, Rembrandt decided his print was the finest.) The dealer sues his employee to obtain possession. What arguments could Rembrandt's lawyers make? How would Leonardo's lawyers counter? Has Rembrandt violated a fiduciary duty to Leonardo?

b. Leonardo finds out about the Munich forgery. Leonardo's lawyer advises him that he cannot sue Rubens under contract law because Rubens's standard contract explicitly denies any liability for forged artwork. Does Leonardo have any other way to force Rubens to reimburse him for the loss? What can Leonardo recover in damages if he is successful?

4. Resop wanted to invest in jukeboxes. He engaged Tarnowski as his agent and gave him the job of researching and negotiating for the purchase of a number of jukeboxes found in restaurants and bars along a certain route in Wisconsin. Resop eventually purchased dozens of jukeboxes in a sale arranged by his agent Tarnowski.

Tarnowski was dishonest in reporting the extent and nature of his research. Tarnowski told Resop that he had made a thorough investigation of the route. He represented that it had 75 locations in operation, that each location had one or more machines, that these machines were not more than six months old, and that the gross income from all the locations amounted to more than $3,000 per month. In reality, Tarnowski made only a superficial investigation of five locations, and he knowingly gave Resop false information. The route actually had only 47 locations, not every location had a jukebox, some of the jukeboxes were seven years old, and the gross income on all the machines was far less than $3,000 per month. Moreover, Tarnowski collected a secret commission of $2,000 from the sellers for consummating the sale of the jukeboxes.

Did Tarnowski breach his fiduciary duty? If so, what damages will Resop be awarded? [*Tarnowski v. Resop*, 51 N.W.2d 801 (Minn. 1952)]

5. If a manager is in doubt whether a worker hired as an independent contractor is in fact a common law employee, what can he or she do to ensure that the worker retains his or her independent contractor status? What factors will be used to determine the worker's legal status?

6. The president of a corporation hired an assistant to be responsible for both his personal and business affairs, including review of vendor invoices and credit card statements for the corporate account. Without the knowledge of the president, the assistant obtained an additional credit card for the corporate account in her name. The corporation alleged that the assistant stole $412,000 via unauthorized credit card charges.

The corporation sued the credit card issuer, seeking to recover $276,000 in unauthorized charges and a declaration that it was not liable for the $51,000 outstanding balance on one of the cards. The applicable federal law limits the liability of cardholders from "unauthorized" charges.

The credit card issuer argued that the corporation, because of its negligence in failing to examine the credit card statements that would have revealed the assistant's fraudulent charges, had given the assistant apparent authority to make the charges. Therefore, the card issuer contended, the charges were not unauthorized under the meaning of the statute and the corporation was fully liable for those charges. What result? [*Minskoff v. American Express Travel Related Services Co.*, 98 F.3d 703 (2d Cir. 1996)]

7. Derek, a busy business school student at the University of Texas, hired Andrea to do landscaping and general maintenance work around his house. Todd and David worked for Andrea. Generally, Derek would tell Andrea what he wanted done, then Andrea would give Todd and David instructions, and they would complete the work.

One day Derek asked Andrea to make sure all the limbs of a large oak tree were cut away from the roof of his house. Because Andrea had no sophisticated tree-trimming equipment, she ordered Todd and David to climb the oak tree, shimmy out on the limbs that needed cutting, and saw them off. While Todd was on one of the uppermost limbs, it snapped, sending him tumbling onto David below him. David's limb then snapped, and the pair landed atop a pile of bricks, which Derek was storing in his backyard for a subsequent addition to his deck.

Todd and David claim they are employees of Derek and sue him for failing to provide and maintain safe working conditions. What result?

8. Johnson was the sole general partner of a large office building in Austin, Texas, along with several limited partners. The limited partners were also lessees of space in the office building. Each tenant of the building (including the limited partners/lessees) was responsible for the "finish-out" construction of that tenant's office space. Most of these tenants hired one of two contractors to finish out their office spaces. On most of these finish-out jobs, the contractors paid Johnson, the sole general partner, a 15% fee. Each contractor simply added this fee to the sum charged to the tenant. Some tenants knew about the fee and others did not. Did Johnson owe a fiduciary duty to his limited partners (who were also his tenants) to disclose the fee? [*Johnson v. J. Hiram Moore, Ltd.*, 763 S.W.2d 496 (Tex. Ct. App. 1989)]

9. The plaintiffs were models in a "fitness fashion show," featured as part of the Working Women's Survival Show exhibition at a convention center in St. Louis. B.P.S., doing business as Wells Fargo Guard Service, had contracted with the city to provide guards at the center.

Security arrangements at the convention center included a number of television-surveillance cameras scattered around the center, which were monitored on small screens in a central control room. The direction in which the cameras were pointing could be adjusted manually or automatically in the control room. The control room also had a large screen that the guards could use to view the image from the cameras or to monitor what was being taped on the VCR. The purpose of having the VCR was to enable the guards to videotape suspicious activities. The Wells Fargo guards were told to practice taping on the VCR.

Promoters for the Working Women's Survival Show had a makeshift curtained dressing area set up near the stage for the models in the fashion shows. Unbeknown to the models, the dressing area was in a location that could be monitored by one of the surveillance cameras. That fortuity was discovered by two Wells Fargo guards, Rook and Smith. Rook had the rank of captain within Wells Fargo, denoting supervisory capacity, though there was testimony that when he worked in the control room, he had no supervisory authority. Another supervisor with disputed supervisory authority, Ramey, walked by the control room and saw the guards using the large screen to view women in a state of undress.

Ramey said that he thought the guards were watching pornographic tapes that they had brought to work. (There was testimony that the guards watched their own pornographic tapes in the control room.)

Either Smith or Rook (each accuses the other) focused the camera on the plaintiffs and taped them as they were changing clothes for the fashion show. Another guard, Sonntag, took the tape home, leaving a decoy in its place. Sonntag decided to report the incident to Wells Fargo management. When he phoned Wells Fargo, he asked for a particular individual to accompany him in taking the tape to the police. Wells Fargo insisted that he turn the tape over to them. He decided to take it to the police station anyway, but stopped when he was frightened by a Wells Fargo car with men in it parked outside the station. He then noticed a television anchorman also outside the police station. He gave the tape to the anchorman, who aired a redacted (edited) version of it on the local television news.

Can Wells Fargo Guard Service be held liable for the unauthorized actions of its agents, even if those actions are done for reasons of personal pleasure rather than for work? [*Does v. B.P.S. Guard Serv., Inc., d/b/a Wells Fargo Guard Serv.*, 945 F.2d 1422 (8th Cir. 1991)]

MANAGER'S DILEMMA

10. Theis opened an account with the du-Pont, Glore Forgan brokerage firm in August 1967. Benjamin was Theis's account executive. Theis discovered that Benjamin had been making unauthorized transactions in his account from the beginning. Theis reprimanded Benjamin and threatened to close the account but did not complain to Benjamin's superiors. In March 1968, Theis wrote to Benjamin insisting that Benjamin make trades pursuant to Theis's requests only. Nevertheless, Benjamin's unauthorized trading continued. On May 24, 1968, Benjamin made a trade in direct contravention of Theis's orders. Later that day, Theis called duPont's cashier and cancelled his account.

Theis sought damages against duPont for the losses arising out of Benjamin's unauthorized trades. Will Theis recover for all the trades? What theory should duPont advance to prevent recovery on at least some of the unauthorized trades? How could Benjamin's immediate supervisor have prevented this problem? Does duPont have an ethical obligation to make good Theis's losses? [*Theis v. duPont, Glore Forgan, Inc.*, 510 P.2d 1212 (Kan. 1973)]

INTERNET SOURCES	
This page from *Windows 95* magazine provides a copy of its independent contractor agreement.	http://www.win95mag.com/archive/97_03/html/contractor.html
The University of Chicago offers an independent contractor user's guide for its employees that addresses many of the distinctions between independent contractors and employees.	http://www.uccomp.uchicago.edu/adminres/arunits/comptrollers/compt_ap/icug/icintro.htm
Northwestern Mutual Life Insurance Company's page offers detailed information about the different business forms.	http://www.northwesternmutual.com/business/owners/basics
The local government of Hendricks County, Indiana, offers a variety of important information for new small businesses, including the differences between forms of business.	http://www.hcedp.org/costbus/fstoc.htm

CHAPTER 6

Administrative Law

INTRODUCTION

Importance of Administrative Agencies

Administrative law concerns the powers and procedures of administrative agencies, such as the Internal Revenue Service (IRS), which collects taxes, and the Securities and Exchange Commission (SEC), which regulates securities markets. The activities of administrative agencies affect nearly everyone, frequently on a daily basis. Administrative agencies set limits on pollution and emissions and regulate disposal of hazardous waste. They regulate radio and television, food and drugs, and health and safety. Although the number of federal court trials in all cases is probably less than 10,000 annually, agencies such as the Social Security Administration act annually on millions of applications for benefits. Federal and state administrative agencies solve practical problems that cannot be handled effectively by the courts or legislatures.

Administrative agencies date back to the country's earliest days. The first Congress established three administrative agencies, including one for the payment of benefits to Revolutionary War veterans. The Patent Office was created in 1790, and ten other federal administrative agencies were created before the Civil War.

At three critical junctures in U.S. history, Congress made extensive use of administrative agencies. During the Progressive Era, from 1885 until 1914, Congress turned to agencies such as the Interstate Commerce Commission, the Federal Reserve Board, the Federal Trade Commission (FTC), and the Food and Drug Administration (FDA) to solve problems concerning railroads and shipping, banks, trade, and food and drugs. In response to

the stock market crash in 1929 and the subsequent Depression, Congress created many agencies to deal with the crisis and delegated broad authority to them. Finally, during the dawn of the environmental era in the 1970s, Congress turned extensively to federal administrative agencies to regulate health and restrict pollution. The Environmental Protection Agency (EPA), which did not even exist in 1960, today administers a budget of more than $6.5 billion and has more than 15,000 employees.

Chapter Overview

This chapter discusses the various ways in which administrative agencies operate. Agencies make rules to effectuate legislative enactments; they resolve conflicts by formal adjudication, a courtlike proceeding; they carry out informal discretionary actions; and they conduct investigations regarding compliance with specific laws and regulations.

This chapter also addresses the key principles of administrative law. Constitutional issues include the separation of powers, the delegation of authority, and the protections afforded by the Bill of Rights. Issues arising from the judicial review of agency actions include the doctrines of ripeness and exhaustion of administrative remedies. Doctrines that limit the decision-making power of agencies include the principles that agencies are bound by their own rules and that they must explain the basis for their decisions.

Finally, the chapter describes how to find the rules of a particular agency and how to obtain documents from the government.

How Administrative Agencies Act

The Fourth Branch of Government

Courts adjudicate legal disputes, the legislature adopts laws, and the executive branch administers the laws. Although usually part of the executive branch, administrative agencies can rightly be called a fourth branch of government. This fourth branch performs some of the functions of each of the other three branches, with quasi-legislative and quasi-judicial as well as executive roles. An administrative agency functions in four primary ways: making rules, conducting formal adjudications, taking informal discretionary actions, and conducting investigations.

Making Rules

A state legislature or Congress frequently lacks the time, human resources, and expertise to enact detailed regulations. Sometimes issues are so politically sensitive that elected officials lack the will to make the tough decisions. In such cases, the legislature will pass a law presenting general principles and guidelines and will delegate authority to an administrative agency to carry out this legislative intent. The agency will then adopt appropriate rules or regulations.

The process that administrative agencies use to adopt rules is similar, but not identical, to the legislative process. The basic procedure involves three steps.

Notice to the Public   First, the administrative agency gives notice to the public of its intent to propose a rule. Generally, the agency will publish the proposed rule and give the public an opportunity to submit written comments. Exhibit 6.1 shows a proposed rule published by an administrative agency. Exhibit 6.2 is a fictitious example of a written comment on the proposed rule. The letter (1) identifies the company that is concerned; (2) describes why it is concerned; (3) suggests a specific change in the language of the proposed rule; and (4) provides factual information to support its position. These kinds of comments are very helpful to an agency and can influence the final rule.

Agencies may, but are not always required to, hold a formal public hearing. They always allow people to comment on proposed rules by meeting informally or telephoning the agency personnel. If a company is particularly concerned about a proposed rule, it would be

wise to both call and meet with the proposing agency about its concerns.

Evaluation   Second, the administrative agency evaluates the comments, responds to them, and decides on the scope and extent of the final rule.

Adoption   Third, the agency will formally adopt the rule by publishing it in the *Federal Register* along with an explanation of changes. The final rule will also be *codified*, that is, added to the *Code of Federal Regulations (CFR)*. (These two publications are discussed later in the chapter.)

Federal agency officials who decide what rules are to be adopted are not elected. The president appoints some; others are hired through civil service procedures. In either instance, the rules they adopt are as binding as the laws passed by the legislative branch, and, like statutes, rules can be challenged in court. (Such challenges are discussed later in this chapter.)

The federal government has attempted to make the regulatory process less cumbersome and time-consuming, more informal, and less vulnerable to judicial review by applying the Japanese style of seeking consensus of the major affected groups on the substance of new regulations. This process is known as *regulatory negotiations* or "reg. neg." Representatives of major groups convene and work out a compromise through negotiation. Congress has facilitated this process by adopting amendments to the Administrative Procedures Act (APA) entitled Negotiated Rulemaking Procedure.[1]

Conducting Formal Adjudications

Courts do not have the time, money, and personnel to hear all the cases that might arise in the course of regulating individual and corporate behavior. Consequently, legislatures frequently give administrative agencies the responsibility for solving specific types of legal disputes, such as who is entitled to government benefits, or the imposition of civil penalties on regulated industries.

Formal agency adjudications are courtlike proceedings that can be presided over by one or more members of the agency or by an *administrative law judge*. The presiding official is entitled to administer oaths, issue subpoenas, rule on offers of proof and relevant

---

1. 5 U.S.C. §§ 561 *et seq.* (1993).

EXHIBIT 6.1   A Proposed Rule Published by an Administrative Agency

51622   Federal Register / Vol. 62, No. 191 / Thursday, October 2, 1997 / Proposed Rules

ENVIRONMENTAL PROTECTION AGENCY

40 CFR Part 745

[OPPTS-62128C; FRL-5749-1]

RIN 2070-AC64

Lead; Requirements for Lead-Based Paint Activities in Public Buildings, Commercial Buildings and Steel Structures; Extension of Comment Period

AGENCY: Environmental Protection Agency (EPA).

ACTION: Extension of comment period.

SUMMARY: EPA is extending the comment period on an August 22, 1997 document which announced a public meeting and requested written comments on the development of training and certification requirements and work practice standards for individuals and firms conducting lead-based paint activities in public buildings (except child-occupied facilities), commercial buildings, and steel structures.

DATES: Written comments should be submitted to EPA by November 3, 1997.

ADDRESSES: Comments must bear the docket control number "OPPT-62128B." All comments should be sent in triplicate to: OPPT Document Control Officer (7407), Office of Pollution Prevention and Toxics, Environmental Protection Agency, 401 M St., SW., Room G-099, East Tower, Washington, DC 20460.

Comments and data may also be submitted electronically to: oppt.ncic@epamail.epa.gov. Follow the instructions under Unit II. of this document. No Confidential Business Information (CBI) should be submitted through e-mail.

All comments which contain information claimed as CBI must be clearly marked as such. Three sanitized copies of any comments containing information claimed as CBI must also be submitted and will be placed in the public record for this rulemaking. Persons submitting information on any portion of which they believe is entitled to treatment as CBI by EPA must assert a business confidentiality claim in accordance with 40 CFR 2.203(b) for each such portion. This claim must be made at the time that the information is submitted to EPA. If a submitter does not assert a confidentiality claim at the time of submission, EPA will consider this as a waiver of any confidentiality claim and the information may be made available to the public by EPA without further notice to the submitter.

FOR FURTHER INFORMATION CONTACT: For more specific or technical information contact: Ellie Clark, National Program Chemicals Division (7404), Office of Pollution Prevention and Toxics, Environmental Protection Agency, 401 M St., SW., Washington, DC 20460, Telephone: 202-260-3402, Fax: 202-260-0770, e-mail: clark.ellie@epamail.epa.gov.

For general information or to obtain copies of the August 22, 1997 document contact: National Lead Information Clearinghouse (NLIC), 1025 Connecticut Avenue, NW., Suite 1200, Washington, DC 20036-5405 or toll free at 1-800-424-5323. Fax: 202-659-1192, e-mail: leadctr@nsc.org, Internet site: http://www.nsc.org/ehc/lead.htm.

SUPPLEMENTARY INFORMATION:

I. Background

In the **Federal Register** of August 22, 1997 (62 FR 44621) (FRL-5740-7), EPA announced a public meeting scheduled for September 3, 1997, in Washington, DC to take public comments and suggestions from a cross-section of stakeholders on the development of training and certification requirements and work practice standards for individuals and firms conducting lead-based paint activities in public buildings (except child-occupied facilities), commercial buildings, and steel structures. The notice stated that EPA specifically wanted additional public comment on the following subjects: (1) Coverage of lead-based paint activities, in particular clarification of the term "deleading"; (2) the interface between OSHA's lead standards and EPA's TSCA section 402 regulations; (3) distinguishing among various building and structure types; and (4) sources of information for EPA's regulations. EPA discussed each issue in detail and requested comments and additional information on specific items. In the document, EPA provided a 30-day comment period following the public meeting. In response to requests by interested parties, EPA is extending the comment period by 30 days. Comments must now be received by November 3, 1997.

II. Public Record and Electronic Submissions

The official record for this action, as well as the public version, has been established for this action under docket control number "OPPTS-62128B" (including comments and data submitted electronically as described below). A public version of this record, including printed, paper versions of electronic comments, which does not include any information claimed as CBI, is available for inspection from noon to 4 p.m., Monday through Friday, excluding legal holidays. The official record is located in the TSCA Nonconfidential Information Center, Rm. NE-B607, 401 M St., SW., Washington, DC.

Electronic comments can be sent directly to EPA at: oppt.ncic@epamail.epa.gov

Electronic comments must be submitted as an ASCII file avoiding the use of special characters and any form of encryption. Comments and data will also be accepted on disks in WordPerfect 5.1/6.1 or ASCII file format. All comments and data in electronic form must be identified by the docket control number "OPPTS-62128B." Electronic comments on this action may be filed online at many Federal Depository Libraries.

List of Subjects in 40 CFR Part 745

Environmental protection, Hazardous substances, Lead, Recordkeeping and notification requirements.

Dated: September 26, 1997.

Vanessa Vu,
Acting Director, Office of Pollution Prevention and Toxics.

[FR Doc. 97-26188 Filed 10-1-97; 8:45 am]
BILLING CODE 6560-50-F

EXHIBIT 6.2   Comment on a Proposed Administrative Rule

RIVERS ENVIRONMENTAL
One Windwood Circle
Portland, OR 99443
(503) 433-1234

October 3, 1997

OPPT-62128B
OPPT Document Control Officer (7407)
Office of Pollution Prevention and Toxins
Environmental Protection Agency
401 M Street, SW, Room G-099
Washington, DC 20460

Dear Sir or Madam:

On August 22, 1997, the EPA proposed an amendment to its requirements for lead-based paint activities in public buildings, commercial buildings, and steel buildings. 40 C.F.R. 745. The goal of the proposed amendment was to improve the development of training and certification requirements and work-practice standards for individuals and firms conducting lead-based paint activities in public buildings (except child-occupied facilities). We write to support the agency's proposed changes and to offer several additional actions that should be taken in order to improve the safety of the work crews and the public.

We are a small business specializing in removal of toxic materials. This includes the removal of lead-based paint with concentrations of over .05%. All of our workers are certified according to OSHA and EPA standards, yet we often face competition from uncertified commercial painting companies that ignore the training and environmental regulations in dealing with toxic substance removal. Any additional costs we spend on complying with safety standards will cause more violations of EPA and OSHA regulations by these companies, unless stricter enforcement and penalty measures are put into place.

Further, the agency has listed numerous procedures to protect workers involved in lead-based paint removal. We think that additional training should be required for workers in confined spaces and voids. In particular, we recommend the following procedures:

1.   A doctor specializing in industrial medicine should take blood samples to establish a baseline exposure level.
2.   A safety department worker should test the air quality before allowing the crew to enter. Voids are confined spaces and the potential for accidental death is ever present. The safety department has tested voids that have had a dangerously low oxygen level that could have resulted in death if entered without prior testing.
3.   It is essential that all men maintain a close shave to ensure a satisfactory seal between their respirators and their faces. Facial hair can collect enough dust to present a threat when eating.

Please call us if we can provide any additional information.

Sincerely,

Darren M. Stevens

President

evidence, authorize depositions, and decide the case at hand.

These formal adjudications typically include a pre-hearing discovery phase. The hearing itself is conducted like a trial. Each side presents its evidence under oath, and testimony is subject to cross-examination. The main difference between administrative adjudications and courtroom trials is that there is never a jury at the administrative level.

An administrative agency's decision in a formal adjudication can be appealed to a court. Agency actions that set rates for natural gas prices or that provide licenses for dams are examples of the types of cases that regularly go to court. In most instances, judicial review of an agency action is based on the *record*, that is, the oral and written evidence presented at the administrative hearing. The court's review is limited to determining whether the administrative agency acted properly based on the evidence reflected in the record. In some cases, the laws governing the administrative adjudication provide for a *de novo* (i.e., new) proceeding in court, where the entire matter is litigated from the beginning.

Taking Informal Discretionary Actions

The basic role of administrative agencies is to provide a practical decision-making process for repetitive, frequent actions that are inappropriate to litigate in courts. These *informal discretionary actions* have been called the lifeblood of administrative agencies. Common examples are the awarding of governmental grants and loans; workers' compensation cases; the administration of welfare benefits; the informal resolution of tax disputes; and the determination of Social Security claims. Informal discretionary action also governs most applications to government agencies for licenses, leases, and permits, such as driver's licenses, leases of federal lands, and the registration of securities offerings.

Informal discretionary actions also include matters such as contracting, planning, and negotiation. Thus, the process of negotiating a contract with a government agency to supply military parts or to build bridges or highways is within the realm of administrative law. In fact, most of what the governmental agencies do falls within the category of informal discretionary action.

The most noteworthy aspect of these informal actions is their lack of clear procedural rules. In court, there is a strict set of rules and procedures to be followed, and a specific person (the judge) is assigned to hear the case. In informal discretionary actions, the agency frequently has no formal procedures, such as notice to the public, opportunity to file briefs, or opportunity to submit oral testimony. Informal agency actions can lead to quick and practical problem resolution, but they can also lead to seemingly endless administrative paper shuffling.

Conducting Investigations

Many administrative agencies have the responsibility to determine whether a regulated company or person is complying with the laws and regulations. They can use their subpoena power to make mandatory requests for information, conduct interviews, and perform searches. Based on these investigations, the agencies may file administrative suits seeking civil penalty assessments, or they may go to court and seek civil and criminal penalties.

Since 1970, governmental agencies have increasingly relied on their investigatory and prosecutorial powers. The indictment and conviction of arbitrageur Ivan Boesky and numerous other financial figures for insider trading resulted from administrative investigations and the exercise of administrative prosecutorial powers.

The investigatory powers possessed by administrative agencies can lead to fines ranging from thousands of dollars to hundreds of millions of dollars. For example, the Securities and Exchange Commission settled its three-year securities fraud investigation of junk bond king Michael Milken in 1990 for $600 million. Note that administrative agencies, such as the Occupational Safety and Health Administration (OSHA), sometimes fail to collect the whole fine.

◆ Administrative Agencies and the Constitution

Constitutional issues raised by the creation of administrative agencies concern the separation of powers, the proper delegation of authority, and the limits imposed on agency actions by the Bill of Rights.

Separation of Powers

The Constitution of the United States provides for a legislature, an executive, and a judiciary. It does not specifically provide for administrative agencies, thus raising the question of whether the delegation of legislative and judicial powers to an administrative agency is constitutional.

The few cases addressing this issue have upheld the constitutionality of this "fourth branch" of government. In 1855, a court decision allowed the Department of the Treasury to audit accounts for money owed to the United States by customs collectors and to issue a warrant for the money owed. The Supreme Court rejected the position that such activity was a judicial action that only the courts of the United States were empowered to carry out.[2]

In 1935, in a case involving the Federal Trade Commission, the Supreme Court explained with approval that the FTC was an administrative body created by Congress to carry out legislative policies in accordance with a prescribed legislative standard and to act as a legislative or judicial aid by performing rule-making and adjudicatory functions. The Supreme Court said the FTC exercised power in the effectuation of quasi-legislative or quasi-judicial powers, or as an agency of the legislative or judicial departments of the government. It found no constitutional violation in allowing an administrative agency to perform judicial and legislative functions. It did not, however, provide much expla-

nation as to why this was permissible.[3] Justice Jackson subsequently said:

> [Administrative bodies] have become a veritable fourth branch of the Government which has deranged our three-branch legal theories as much as the concept of a fourth dimension unsettles our three dimensional thinking. . . . Administrative agencies have been called quasi-legislative, quasi-executive and quasi-judicial, as the occasion required. . . . The mere retreat to the qualifying "quasi". . . is a smooth cover which we draw over our confusion as we might use a counterpane to conceal a disordered bed.[4]

The separation-of-powers doctrine has not generally been an impediment to the exercise of authority by administrative agencies. The courts have held that the Constitution contemplates a practice that will integrate the separate powers of the three branches into a workable government. Administrative agencies are an essential part of such a government.

However, the following case, together with the legislative-veto case *INS v. Chadha*[5] (discussed in Chapter 2), shows that the concept of separation of powers retains some viability, especially when Congress attempts to retain control over the acts of an administrative agency.

---

2. *Den ex dem.* Murray v. Hoboken Land & Improvement Co., 59 U.S. 272 (1856).

3. Humphrey's Ex'r v. United States, 295 U.S. 602 (1935).
4. FTC v. Ruberoid Co., 343 U.S. 470, 487–88 (1952).
5. 462 U.S. 919 (1983).

A CASE IN POINT | **IN THE LANGUAGE OF THE COURT**

CASE 6.1
AIRPORTS AUTHORITY
v. CITIZENS FOR THE
ABATEMENT OF
AIRCRAFT NOISE, INC.
Supreme Court of
the United States
501 U.S. 252 (1991).

FACTS   In 1940, Congress authorized the executive branch to acquire a tract of land a few miles from the Capitol and to construct what is now Washington National Airport (National). From the time it opened until 1987, National was owned and operated by the federal government. National and Dulles International Airport (Dulles) in rural Virginia are the only two major commercial airports owned by the federal government.

Throughout its history, National has been the subject of controversy. Its location at the center of the metropolitan area is a great convenience for air travelers; but flight paths over densely populated areas have generated concern among local residents about safety, noise, and pollution. Those living closest to the airport have provided the strongest support for proposals to close National or to transfer some of its operations to Dulles.

An act of Congress (the Transfer Act) transferred operation and control of the airport from the federal Department of Transportation to the Metropolitan Washington Airports Authority (MWAA), an entity formed by the District of Columbia and the state of Virginia. The Transfer Act authorized MWAA's board of directors to create a board of review,

Case 6.1 continues

Case 6.1 continued

consisting of nine members of Congress, eight of whom serve on committees with jurisdiction over transportation issues. The board of review members were to serve in their individual capacities as representatives of the users of the airports. The board of review had a variety of powers, including the authority to veto decisions made by MWAA's directors.

The MWAA directors then adopted a new master plan providing for the construction of a new terminal at National, which would increase flight traffic. The congressional board of review allowed the plan to proceed. In November 1988, Citizens for the Abatement of Aircraft Noise, Inc. (CAAN), in order to prevent further expansion of airport traffic, brought an action seeking a declaration that the board of review's veto power was unconstitutional. CAAN argued that the review board was in essence a congressional agent with disapproval powers over key operational decisions that were quintessentially executive and therefore violated the separation of powers.

ISSUE PRESENTED   Does maintenance of congressional control over an administrative agency's operation of the airports by means of a review board violate the separation-of-powers principle?

OPINION   STEVENS, J., writing for the U.S. Supreme Court:

Because National and Dulles are the property of the Federal Government and their operations directly affect interstate commerce, there is no doubt concerning the ultimate power of Congress to enact legislation defining the policies that govern those operations. Congress itself can formulate the details, or it can enact general standards and assign to the Executive Branch the responsibility for making necessary managerial decisions in conformance with those standards. The question presented is only whether the Legislature has followed a constitutionally acceptable procedure in delegating decision-making authority to the Board of Review.

The structure of our Government as conceived by the Framers of our Constitution disperses the federal power among the three branches—the Legislative, the Executive, and the Judicial—placing both substantive and procedural limitations on each. . . .

To forestall the danger of encroachment "beyond the legislative sphere," the Constitution imposes basic and related constraints on the Congress. It may not "invest itself or its Members with either executive power or judicial power."

. . . If the power is executive, the Constitution does not permit an agent of Congress to exercise it. If the power is legislative, Congress must exercise it in conformity with the bicameralism and presentment requirements of Art. I, § 7. In short, when Congress "[takes] action that ha[s] the purpose and effect of altering the legal rights, duties, and relations of persons . . . outside the Legislative Branch," it must take that action by the procedures authorized in the Constitution.

. . . [T]he statutory scheme challenged today provides a blueprint for extensive expansion of the legislative power beyond its constitutionally confined role. . . .

RESULT   Congress's conditioning of transfer of District of Columbia area airports to a local airport authority upon creation of a board of review that was composed of

Case 6.1 continues

Case 6.1 continued

members of Congress with veto power over decisions of local authority's directors violated separation of powers.

Questions

1. Congress gave itself veto power over the decisions of the MWAA. *INS v. Chadha* also involved the power of Congress to veto the actions of an administrative agency. Do all legislative vetoes violate the Constitution's separation-of-powers principle? Would any legislative action short of exercise of a legislative veto violate the principle?

2. The Court noted that if a "power is executive, the Constitution does not permit an agent of Congress to exercise it." But how bright is the line between an "executive" and a "legislative" power? Would you characterize the rules and regulations enacted by administrative agencies as purely executive in nature? Purely legislative?

Delegation of Authority

The delegation of authority issue concerns the nature and degree of direction the legislature must give to administrative agencies. There are only two cases in which the Supreme Court has refused to uphold the delegation of power to administrative agencies. One case concerned delegation of power regarding shipments of oil between states in excess of government-set quotas.[6] The second case concerned the delegation of authority to the president to determine codes of fair competition for various trades and industries.[7] In both cases, the Supreme Court held that while Congress was free to allow agencies to make rules within prescribed limits, Congress itself must lay down the policies and establish the standards.

Both before and after these two cases, however, the Supreme Court upheld vague standards, such as those requiring rules to be set "in the public interest," "for the public convenience, interest or necessity," or "to prevent unfair methods of competition." As a practical matter, it is necessary to allow such broad delegations to administrative agencies. There is virtually no way Congress or the state legislative bodies can draft detailed legislation that anticipates all conceivable situations. The limitations imposed by these two Depression-era cases remain on the books, however, as a protection against overreaching legislative delegations that would place arbitrary and uncontrolled power in the hands of unelected officials.

Limits Imposed by the Bill of Rights

There is very little limit to the investigatory powers of administrative agencies. They must, of course, comply with constitutional principles protecting freedom from self-incrimination and from unreasonable search and seizure. Over the years, however, these principles have been severely eroded.

Self-Incrimination The Fifth Amendment's protection against self-incrimination does not apply to records that the government requires to be kept. Specifically, the Fifth Amendment protections do not apply to records that are regulatory in nature, are of a kind that the party has customarily kept, and have at least some public aspect to them. In addition, the Fifth Amendment's protection against self-incrimination does not apply to corporations.

Probable Cause Administrative agencies in carrying out their investigatory power are not required to have probable cause—that is, reason to suspect a violation—before beginning an investigation. The agencies may inquire into regulated behavior merely to satisfy themselves that the law is being upheld. For example, the Internal Revenue Service needs no specific cause to order an audit of a company's tax records.

---

6. Panama Ref. Co. v. Ryan, 293 U.S. 388 (1935).

7. Schechter Poultry Corp. v. United States, 295 U.S. 495 (1935).

Search and Seizure   In the administrative arena, the courts have largely obliterated the protection of the Fourth Amendment against unreasonable searches and seizures. Particularly for industries such as liquor and firearms, which are highly regulated, the government can conduct full inspections of property and records almost without restriction.

Right to Jury Trial

A formal adjudication before an administrative agency resembles a court trial before a judge. This resemblance raises the question whether the administrative adjudication violates the constitutional right to a trial by jury. In two cases, one decided in 1927 and one in 1937, the Supreme Court held there was no such constitutional right. One case upheld the system for collection of taxes without a jury trial;[8] the other upheld the right of the National Labor Relations Board (NLRB) to require reinstatement of discharged employees and payment of back wages based solely on an administrative hearing.[9] These cases held that the Seventh Amendment right to a jury trial extends only to cases for which a right to trial by jury existed in common law before the enactment of the Seventh Amendment. Because administrative agencies adjudicate statutory rights that were unknown at the time the Seventh Amendment was enacted, the Court held that the right to a jury trial did not apply.

 Principles of Administrative Law

Choice of Approach

Because, theoretically, an administrative agency can exercise legislative-type functions through its rule-making authority and judicial-type functions through its adjudicatory authority, the question of how administrative agencies were to choose between the two processes arose quickly. There are competing considerations.

On one hand, it is simple and efficient to set forth a general rule that applies to unknown parties in future activities. On the other hand, until the agency has had experience with the subject matter and has dealt with a number of individual cases, it may lack sufficient information to proceed with rule making.

In 1947, the Supreme Court held that administrative agencies have a fundamental right to decide whether to proceed on a case-by-case basis or by rule.[10] Such a right is necessary because an administrative agency cannot anticipate every problem it might encounter; problems could arise that were so specialized and varying in nature as to be impossible to capture within the boundaries of a general rule.

Over the years, the agency's choice on how to proceed has frequently been limited by Congress. Typically, legislation requires the agency to enact a regulatory program and provides a deadline for the issuance of final regulations. This congressional direction shows the interaction between Congress, the judiciary, and the administrative agencies. Although the courts will not interfere with the authority of administrative agencies to act, Congress, which is the source of the agencies' authority, may fill the gap left when the agency fails to adopt final regulations.

Authority to Act

Administrative agencies can be compared to large corporations in size, structure, and, to some extent, function. Agencies provide benefits, sign contracts, and produce products. In the private arena, a person acting on behalf of an organization may bind the organization in accordance with the person's actual authority and also in accordance with the person's apparent authority (concepts discussed in Chapter 5). Under the rules for government agencies, there is only actual authority.

The issue of apparent governmental authority is particularly important in the western states, where the United States owns up to 90% of the land. These lands are administered by the U.S. Forest Service and the Bureau of Land Management. Local citizens have a great deal of contact with these agencies. Not surprisingly, one of the first cases deciding the scope of a government official's authority was a case involving these public lands.

In 1917, the Supreme Court held that the United States was not bound by acts of its officials who, on behalf of the government, entered into an agreement that was not permitted by law.[11] The Court rejected the argument that the neglect of duty by officers of the

8. Wickwire v. Reinecke, 275 U.S. 101 (1927).

9. National Labor Relations Bd. v. Jones & Laughlin Steel Corp., 301 U.S. 1 (1937).

10. Securities & Exch. Comm'n v. Chenery Corp., 332 U.S. 194 (1947).

11. Utah Power Light Co. v. United States, 243 U.S. 389 (1917).

government was a defense to the suit by the United States to enforce a public right to protect a public interest. The Court has repeatedly upheld the fundamental principle that government employees acting beyond their authority cannot bind the government. The basic purpose of this rule is to prevent personal actions from circumventing Congress and the formal process of law. The negative effect of the rule, however, is to take away incentive for the government to make sure that its officials know the law and administer it properly.

The uninitiated naturally rely on the word of a government employee who explains the scope of his or her authority. This is a mistake. In fact, it is incumbent upon anyone dealing with government agencies to make sure that the person he or she is dealing with is authorized to act and that the proposed actions are permitted by law.

◆ Judicial Review of Agency Actions

If the courts control agency action with too heavy a hand, an agency can grind to a halt. If too little oversight is exercised, agencies can run roughshod over individual rights.

Congress or the appropriate state legislature sets the standards for judicial review of agency actions. Some agency actions are not reviewable because they are committed at the discretion of the agency. Most agency actions are, however, reviewable by the courts; but the basic standard of review is highly deferential to the agency.

Review of Rule Making and Informal Discretionary Actions

The basic standard for judicial review of agency rule making and informal discretionary actions is that the court will uphold the agency's action unless it is arbitrary and capricious. Under the *arbitrary and capricious standard*, if the agency has a choice between several courses of action, the court will presume that the chosen course is valid. It will uphold the action unless the person challenging it shows that it lacks any rational basis.

For example, under some laws, agencies must determine the reasonableness of rates set by regulated industries such as the electrical power and the radio and television industries. Under general accounting principles, depreciation could be calculated on a straight-line basis, by dividing the total cost of the asset by the years it will be in use, or on an accelerated basis that results in more depreciation in the earlier years. In those kinds of cases, the courts have deferred to the agency's choice of what method of accounting produced a reasonable cost, even when the company proposed an equally reasonable alternative. As long as the agency had a rational basis for its action, the courts defer to the agency's decision.

It is more difficult for an agency to persuade a court to uphold a rule when Congress has not expressly granted rule-making authority. In a case decided in early 1994, the U.S. Court of Appeals for the District of Columbia concluded that the Environmental Protection Agency had the power to adopt some rules but not others.[12] The statute at issue was the Comprehensive Environmental Response, Compensation and Liability Act (CERCLA). CERCLA, discussed further in Chapter 16, generally imposes *strict liability* (liability without fault) on all past and present owners of sites with hazardous waste. The EPA had adopted a rule designed to exempt secured creditors—persons who lend money secured by a security interest, mortgage, or deed of trust on the property—from liability under the act. The court concluded that there was no evidence that Congress intended the EPA to have the power to define who is liable under CERCLA, and it invalidated the EPA's rule. The EPA's lender-liability rule was not due judicial deference as an "interpretation" under *Chevron USA Inc. v. Natural Resources Defense Council Inc.*,[13] because there was no evidence that Congress expressly or implicitly gave the EPA authority to reconcile in a reasonable manner statutory ambiguities or to fill statutory interstices. As discussed in Chapter 16, Congress passed legislation in 1996 that codified the EPA's rule.[14]

An administrative agency cannot adopt rules that go beyond the grant of authority provided by Congress. The power of the Securities and Exchange Commission to adopt a rule relating to tender offers was at issue in the following case. In a *tender offer*, a company makes a public offer to buy securities at a price that is usually higher than the market price of the securities prior to the announcement of the tender offer.

---

12. Kelley v. Environmental Protection Agency, 15 F.3d 1100 (D.C. Cir. 1994).
13. 467 U.S. 837 (1984).
14. *See* 42 U.S.C. § 9601(20) (Supp. 1997).

CASE 6.2
UNITED STATES v.
O'HAGAN

Supreme Court of
the United States
117 S. Ct. 2199 (1997).

FACTS   James O'Hagan was a partner in the law firm of Dorsey & Whitney in Minneapolis, Minnesota. In July 1988, the London-based company Grand Metropolitan PLC (Grand Met) retained Dorsey & Whitney as local counsel for a potential tender offer for the common stock of the Pillsbury Company, headquartered in Minneapolis. Both Grand Met and Dorsey & Whitney took precautions to protect the confidentiality of Grand Met's tender offer plans. O'Hagan did not work on the Grand Met representation. Dorsey & Whitney withdrew from representing Grand Met on September 9, 1988. Less than a month later, Grand Met publicly announced its tender offer for Pillsbury stock.

While Dorsey & Whitney was still representing Grand Met, O'Hagan began purchasing Pillsbury stock and call options for Pillsbury stock. When Grand Met announced its tender offer in October, the price of Pillsbury stock rose to $60 per share. O'Hagan sold his Pillsbury call options and stock, making a profit of more than $4.3 million.

The Securities and Exchange Commission initiated an investigation into O'Hagan's transactions, culminating in a 57-count indictment, charging O'Hagan with, among other counts,[15] violation of Rule 14e-3(a). Rule 14e-3(a), adopted by the SEC pursuant to Section 14(e) of the Securities Exchange Act of 1934, makes it a crime to trade on nonpublic information about an upcoming tender offer if that information was obtained from the issuer, the offeror, or someone working on their behalf. O'Hagan was convicted by a jury of violating this rule. He appealed.

The appeals court reversed O'Hagan's conviction on all counts, holding, among other things, that Rule 14e-3(a) exceeded the SEC's Section 14(e) rule-making authority. The United States appealed.

ISSUE PRESENTED   Did the SEC exceed its rule-making authority by adopting Rule 14e-3(a), which made it a crime to trade on the basis of material nonpublic information concerning an upcoming tender offer, without requiring a showing that the trading at issue entailed a breach of fiduciary duty?

OPINION   GINSBURG, J., writing for the U.S. Supreme Court:

> The governing statutory provision, § 14(e) of the Exchange Act, reads in relevant part: "It shall be unlawful for any person . . . to engage in fraudulent, deceptive, or manipulative acts or practices, in connection with any tender offer . . . . The [SEC] shall, for the purposes of this subsection, by rules and regulations define, and prescribe means reasonably designed to prevent, such acts and practices as are fraudulent, deceptive, or manipulative."
> . . .
>
> Relying on § 14(e)'s rulemaking authorization, the Commission, in 1980, promulgated Rule 14e-3(a). . . . "One violates Rule 14e-3(a) if he trades on the basis of material nonpublic information concerning a pending tender offer that he knows or has reason to know has been acquired 'directly or indirectly' from an insider of the offeror or issuer, or someone working on their behalf. Rule 14e-3(a) is a disclosure provision. It creates a duty in those traders who fall within its ambit to abstain or

Case 6.2 continues

---

15. The other counts are discussed in Chapter 23.

Case 6.2 continued

disclose, without regard to whether the trader owes a pre-existing fiduciary duty to respect the confidentiality of the information."

. . .

. . . Rule 14e-3(a), as applied to cases of this genre, qualifies under § 14(e) as a "means reasonably designed to prevent" fraudulent trading on material, nonpublic information in the tender offer context. A prophylactic measure, because its mission is to prevent, typically encompasses more than the core activity prohibited. As we noted . . . § 14(e)'s rulemaking authority gives the Commission "latitude," even in the context of a term of art like "manipulative," "to regulate nondeceptive activities as a 'reasonably designed' means of preventing manipulative acts, without suggesting any change in the meaning of the term 'manipulative' itself." We hold, accordingly, that under § 14(e), the Commission may prohibit acts, not themselves fraudulent under the common law or § 10(b), if the prohibition is "reasonably designed to prevent . . . acts and practices [that] are fraudulent."

Because Congress has authorized the Commission, in § 14(e), to prescribe legislative rules, we owe the Commission's judgment "more than mere deference or weight." Therefore, in determining whether Rule 14e-3(a)'s "disclose or abstain from trading" requirement is reasonably designed to prevent fraudulent acts, we must accord the Commission's "controlling weight unless it is arbitrary, capricious, or manifestly contrary to the statute."

RESULT The Supreme Court reversed the lower court's ruling, holding that Rule 14e-3(a) did not exceed the SEC's authority. O'Hagan's Rule 14e-3(a) convictions were affirmed.

Questions

1. How much weight should a court give to the fact that Congress has not amended Section 14(e) since Rule 14e-3(a) was adopted?
2. Rule 10b-5 is an SEC antifraud rule that the U.S. Supreme Court has held requires a showing of *scienter*, that is, intent to defraud or breach of fiduciary duty (discussed further in Chapter 23). *Scienter* is not required under Rule 14e-3. Why should the SEC have greater authority to regulate fraud in connection with tender offers than it has in garden-variety cases of insider trading in violation of Rule 10b-5?

Review of Factual Findings

An agency's fact-findings are its determinations that can be made without knowledge of the relevant law or regulation. When an agency makes a formal adjudication in an administrative law court, the arbitrary and capricious standard of judicial review is not applied to the agency's factual findings. Instead, courts use a *substantial evidence standard* to review factual findings

that agencies make in formal adjudications. Under this standard, the courts ask whether the evidence could reasonably support the agency's conclusion.[16] In particular, courts will examine the process of the agency's fact-finding: how the agency collected the facts and

---

16. Consolidated Edison Co. v. National Labor Relations Bd., 305 U.S. 197 (1938).

evaluated the data. Courts will apply the substantial evidence standard to the whole record, meaning all the factual evidence collected, and not just the evidence that supports the agency's conclusion. However, under the substantial evidence standard, the courts defer to an agency's reasonable factual determinations, even if the record would support other factual conclusions. This standard of review is similar to an appellate court's review of jury verdicts in trial courts. Courts feel that the agency's fact finder is generally in a better position to judge the credibility of the witnesses and to evaluate the evidence, especially if the evidence is highly technical or scientific. This deference is strengthened by Congress's improvements in the qualifications and professionalism of administrative law judges since the 1950s.

Review of Statutory Interpretations

The earliest cases held that courts would decide the law but would defer to an agency's *construction* (i.e., interpretation) of a statute within its area of expertise. This allows those with the practical experience to have the greatest influence in deciding how to implement a particular law. Although the Supreme Court's position on this issue has varied somewhat, its most recent cases have reinforced the rule of deference to administrative interpretation of law. This is demonstrated in the following case.

A CASE IN POINT	SUMMARY

CASE 6.3
**SMILEY v. CITIBANK
(SOUTH DAKOTA), N.A.**
Supreme Court of
the United States
517 U.S. 735 (1996).

FACTS   Barbara Smiley, a resident of California, held two credit cards issued by Citibank (South Dakota), N.A., a national bank located in South Dakota. Her card agreements provided for the assessment of late fees ranging from $6 to $15 if she failed to make her monthly payment within 15 days of its due date. These late fees were permitted by South Dakota law. Smiley, however, argued that the fees were unconscionable penalties that violated California law. She brought a class action against Citibank on behalf of herself and other California residents who held Citibank credit cards.

The superior court dismissed Smiley's suit, reasoning that her claims were preempted by Section 30 of the National Bank Act of 1964, 12 U.S.C. § 85. This act gives national banks the right to charge such amounts of interest as are legal in the state in which the bank is located. The comptroller of the currency had interpreted of the term "interest" in Section 85 to include late fees. The California Court of Appeal and California Supreme Court affirmed. Smiley appealed.

ISSUE PRESENTED   Was the comptroller's interpretation of the term "interest" to include late fees a reasonable one?

SUMMARY OF OPINION   The U.S. Supreme Court first noted that "it is our practice to defer to the reasonable judgments of agencies with regard to the meaning of ambiguous terms in statutes they are charged with administering." The comptroller of the currency is charged with administering federal banking laws.

Smiley argued that the ordinary rules of deference should not apply because the regulation containing the comptroller's interpretation[17] was set forth more than 100 years after the enactment of Section 85. The Court rejected this argument. A court accords deference to agencies "not because of a presumption that they drafted the provisions in question, or were present at the hearings . . . ; but rather because of a

Case 6.3 continues

---

17. *See* 12 C.F.R. § 7.4001(a) (1998).

Case 6.3 continued

presumption that Congress, when it left ambiguity in a statute meant for implementation by an agency, understood that the ambiguity would be resolved, first and foremost, by the agency, and desired the agency (rather than the courts) to possess whatever degree of discretion the ambiguity allows."

Smiley also argued that there was no rational basis for distinguishing between the various charges the comptroller deemed interest (for example, numerical periodic rates, late fees, overlimit fees, annual fees, and cash advance fees) and those it deemed non-interest (for example, appraisal fees, finders' fees, fees for document preparation, and fees incurred to obtain credit reports). The Court, however, refused to find that the line drawn by the comptroller was arbitrary and capricious.

Finally, Smiley argued that the comptroller's regulation was not entitled to deference because it was inconsistent with a prior agency position. Upon review of the facts, the Court did not feel the agency had reversed its position. Even if it had, the Court held, a change in position is not invalidating because it was the intention of Congress to leave the discretion provided by the ambiguities of a statute with the implementing agency.

The Court concluded that the comptroller's regulation deserved deference. As a result, the Court sought to determine not whether the regulation represented the best interpretation of Section 85, but simply whether it represented a reasonable one. Its answer was "obviously yes."

RESULT   The Supreme Court affirmed the California courts' dismissal of Smiley's suit.

COMMENTS   In contrast, the Supreme Court struck down an interpretation of the Federal Credit Union Act by the Credit Union Administration that permitted credit unions to include members with unaffiliated employers.[18] The Court ruled that the interpretation was contrary to the clear wording of the statute.

---

18. National Credit Union Admin. v. First Nat'l Bank & Trust Co., 118 S. Ct. 927 (1998).

Review of Procedures   For a number of years, the courts have endeavored to bring greater fairness to the administrative process. Some courts began to require agencies to follow procedures not specified by statutes or required by the Due Process Clause of the Fifth Amendment to the Constitution. This occurred most frequently in the rule-making area, where rule-making proceedings were often challenged as being fundamentally unfair and in need of greater public participation. These challenges were most often made by public interest groups battling large corporations with entrenched positions of influence with the agency.

In 1978, in a case involving a challenge by an environmental advocacy group to the licensing of a nuclear power plant, the Supreme Court held that the courts may not impose additional procedural requirements on agencies.[19] Absent extremely compelling circumstances, administrative agencies are free to fashion their own rules of procedure and to pursue their own methods of inquiry to discharge their broad and varied duties. A court is not free to impose on an agency its view as to what procedures the agency must follow; the court may only require the agency to comply with its own procedural rules and to conform to the requirements of the Due Process Clause of the Fifth Amendment.

---

19. Vermont Yankee Nuclear Power Corp. v. Natural Resources Defense Council Inc., 435 U.S. 519 (1978).

The reason for these highly deferential review standards is evident: The role of administrative agencies is to relieve the burden on the courts by having the agencies make their own adjudications. If the courts were to engage in searching inquiry on all factual questions and exercise their own judgment on policy or procedural issues, the function of administrative agencies would be greatly diminished.

The scope of judicial review of a decision not to take an enforcement action is explored in the following case.

A CASE IN POINT   **SUMMARY**

CASE 6.4
HECKLER v. CHANEY
Supreme Court of
the United States
470 U.S. 821 (1985).

FACTS   Prison inmates were convicted of capital offenses and sentenced to death by lethal injection of drugs under the state laws of Oklahoma and Texas. The inmates claimed that the drugs used were approved by the Food and Drug Administration for the medical purposes stated on their labels, but were not approved for use in human executions. Furthermore, the drugs had not been tested for the purpose of execution; and, given that the drugs would likely be administered by untrained personnel, it was likely that the drugs would not induce the quick and painless death intended. The inmates argued that the use of these drugs for human execution was an " unapproved use of an approved drug."

The inmates petitioned the FDA, alleging that use of the drugs for such a purpose violated the Federal Food, Drug and Cosmetic Act (FDCA). Specifically, they requested the FDA to take various investigatory and enforcement actions to prevent these perceived violations. They asked the FDA to affix warnings to the labels stating that they were unapproved and unsafe for human execution, to send statements to the drug manufacturers and prison administrators stating that the drugs should not be so used, and to adopt procedures for seizing the drugs from state prisons and to recommend the prosecution of those involved in the chain of distribution who knowingly distributed or purchased the drugs with the intent to use them for human execution. The FDA refused the request.

The federal district court denied the inmates relief and the inmates appealed. The appeals court reversed and held that the FDA's refusal to take enforcement actions was both an abuse of discretion and reviewable; the court remanded the case with directions that the agency be required to "fulfill its statutory function."

ISSUE PRESENTED   Is the decision of the Food and Drug Administration not to take enforcement actions under the Federal Food, Drug and Cosmetic Act with respect to drugs used to carry out the death penalty subject to judicial review?

SUMMARY OF OPINION   The U.S. Supreme Court focused on the extent to which determinations by the FDA not to exercise its enforcement authority over the use of drugs in interstate commerce may be judicially reviewed.

The Court reviewed the Administrative Procedures Act's comprehensive provisions for judicial review of agency actions. The Court recognized that there are many factors that make judicial review of agency decisions to enforce something unsuitable. An agency decision not to enforce often involves a complicated balancing of a number of factors that are peculiarly within its expertise. The agency must not only assess whether a violation has occurred, but whether agency resources are best spent on this violation or another; whether the agency is likely to succeed if it acts; whether the particular enforcement action requested best fits the agency's overall policies; and whether the

Case 6.4 continues

Case 6.4 continued

agency has enough resources to undertake the action at all. An agency generally cannot act against each technical violation of the statute it is charged with enforcing. As well, the agency is far better equipped than the courts to deal with the many variables involved in the proper ordering of its priorities. In conclusion, the Court found that an agency's decision not to take enforcement action should be presumed immune from judicial review.

The Court concluded by noting that the fact that the drugs involved in this case are ultimately to be used in imposing the death penalty "must not lead this Court or other courts to import profound differences of opinion over the meaning of the Eighth Amendment to the United States Constitution into the domain of administrative law."

RESULT   The Supreme Court reversed the lower court's ruling and held that there is a presumption of unreviewability of decisions of an agency not to undertake enforcement action. The inmates could not force the FDA to act.

The Supreme Court has also significantly restricted standing to sue to obtain judicial review of federal agency action. In the following case, the Court held that members of an environmental organization could not challenge a federal action arguably violating the Endangered Species Act (ESA) unless they could show a certain personal connection with the species affected.

A CASE IN POINT	IN THE LANGUAGE OF THE COURT

CASE 6.5
LUJAN v. DEFENDERS
OF WILDLIFE
Supreme Court of
the United States
504 U.S. 555 (1992).

FACTS   Section 7 of the Endangered Species Act of 1973 is intended to protect species of animals against threats to their continuing existence caused by humans. The ESA instructs the secretary of the interior to promulgate by regulation a list of those species that are either endangered or threatened under enumerated criteria and to define the critical habitat of these species. Section 7(a)(2) of the act then provides, in pertinent part:

> Each Federal agency shall, in consultation with and with the assistance of the Secretary [of the Interior], insure that any action authorized, funded, or carried out by such agency . . . is not likely to jeopardize the continued existence of any endangered species or threatened species or result in the destruction or adverse modification of habitat of such species which is determined by the Secretary, after consultation as appropriate with affected States, to be critical.

In 1978, the Fish and Wildlife Service (FWS) and the National Marine Fisheries Service (NMFS), on behalf of the secretary of the interior and the secretary of commerce respectively, promulgated a joint regulation stating that the obligations imposed by Section 7(a)(2) extend to actions taken in foreign nations. The next year, however, the Interior Department began to reexamine its position. A revised joint regulation was proposed in 1983; it reinterpreted the section to require consultation only for actions taken in the United States or on the high seas.

Shortly thereafter, organizations dedicated to wildlife conservation and other environmental causes filed this action against Manuel Lujan, the secretary of the interior.

Case 6.5 continues

Case 6.5 continued

Plaintiffs sought a declaratory judgment that the new regulation, which required other agencies to confer with the secretary of the interior under Section 7 of the ESA only with respect to federally funded projects within the United States and on the high seas, was in error, and an injunction requiring the secretary to promulgate a new regulation restoring the initial interpretation of the geographic scope.

The federal district court dismissed the case for lack of standing and the court of appeals reversed. The secretary of the interior appealed.

OPINION SCALIA, J., writing for the U.S. Supreme Court:

The preliminary issue, and the only one we reach, is whether the respondents here, plaintiffs below, have standing to seek judicial review of the rule.

. . .

Over the years, our cases have established that the irreducible constitutional minimum of *standing* contains three elements: First, the plaintiff must have suffered an "injury in fact"—an invasion of a legally protected interest which is (a) concrete and particularized, and (b) "actual or imminent, not 'conjectural' or 'hypothetical.'" Second, there must be a causal connection between the injury and the conduct complained of—the injury has to be "fairly . . . trace[able] to the challenged action of the defendant, and not . . . th[e] result [of] the independent action of some third party not before the court." Third, it must be "likely," as opposed to merely "speculative," that the injury will be "redressed by a favorable decision."

The party invoking federal jurisdiction bears the burden of establishing these elements. . . .

. . .

[W]hen the plaintiff is not himself the object of the government action or inaction he challenges, standing is not precluded, but it is ordinarily "substantially more difficult" to establish.

. . .

. . . "But the 'injury in fact' test requires more than an injury to a cognizable interest. It requires that the party seeking review be himself among the injured." . . .

With respect to this aspect of the case, the Court of Appeals focused on the affidavits of two Defenders' members—Joyce Kelly and Amy Skilbred. Ms. Kelly stated that she traveled to Egypt in 1986 and "observed the traditional habitat of the endangered Nile crocodile there and intend[s] to do so again, and hope[s] to observe the crocodile directly," and that she "will suffer harm in fact as a result of [the] American . . . role . . . in overseeing the rehabilitation of the Aswan High Dam on the Nile . . . and [in] develop[ing] . . . Egypt's . . . Master Water Plan." Ms. Skilbred averred that she traveled to Sri Lanka in 1981 and "observed th[e] habitat" of "endangered species such as the Asian elephant and the leopard" at what is now the site of the Mahaweli Project funded by the Agency for International Development (AID), although she "was unable to see any of the endangered

Case 6.5 continues

Case 6.5 continued

species;" "this development project," she continued, "will seriously reduce endangered, threatened, and endemic species habitat including areas that I visited . . . [, which] may severely shorten the future of these species;" that threat, she concluded, harmed her because she "intend[s] to return to Sri Lanka in the future and hope[s] to be more fortunate in spotting at least the endangered elephant and leopard." When Ms. Skilbred was asked at a subsequent deposition if and when she had any plans to return to Sri Lanka, she reiterated that "I intend to go back to Sri Lanka," but confessed that she had no current plans: "I don't know [when]. There is a civil war going on right now. I don't know. Not next year, I will say. In the future."

We shall assume for the sake of argument that these affidavits contain facts showing that certain agency-funded projects threaten listed species—though that is questionable. They plainly contain no facts, however, showing how damage to the species will produce "imminent" injury to Mss. Kelly and Skilbred. That the women "had visited" the areas of the projects before the projects commenced proves nothing. As we have said in a related context, "'[p]ast exposure to illegal conduct does not in itself show a present case or controversy regarding injunctive relief . . . if unaccompanied by any continuing, present adverse effects.'" And the [women's] profession of an "inten[t]" to return to the places they had visited before—where they will presumably, this time, be deprived of the opportunity to observe animals of the endangered species—is simply not enough. Such "some day" intentions—without any description of concrete plans, or indeed even any specification of when the some day will be—do not support a finding of the "actual or imminent" injury that our cases require.

. . .

. . . To say that the Act protects ecosystems is not to say that the Act creates (if it were possible) rights of action in persons who have not been injured in fact, that is, persons who use portions of an ecosystem not perceptibly affected by the unlawful action in question.

Respondents' other theories are called, alas, the "animal nexus" approach, whereby anyone who has an interest in studying or seeing the endangered animals anywhere on the globe has standing; and the "vocational nexus" approach, under which anyone with a professional interest in such animals can sue. Under these theories, anyone who goes to see Asian elephants in the Bronx Zoo, and anyone who is a keeper of Asian elephants in the Bronx Zoo, has standing to sue because the Director of AID did not consult with the Secretary regarding the AID-funded project in Sri Lanka. This is beyond all reason. Standing is not "an ingenious academic exercise in the conceivable."

RESULT   The Supreme Court reversed the appeals court's ruling and held that the plaintiffs did not assert sufficiently imminent injury to have standing. Their claimed injury was not redressable.

COMMENTS   This case along with others is believed to have had a hampering effect on environmental organizations' access to court.

In contrast, in *Bennett v. Spear*[20] (Case 3.2), the Supreme Court held that ranchers and irrigation districts had standing to challenge a Fish and Wildlife finding that a waste-reclamation project might harm two endangered species of fish and its recommendation that minimum levels in certain reservoirs be maintained; they would be directly affected economically if the recommendation were implemented.

 ## Limits of Review

No Right to Probe the Mental Processes of the Agency

One of the most critical points of administrative law concerns the extent to which a court can inquire into the process by which an administrative agency makes its decision. This issue was one of the first decided in the administrative law arena. It was resolved in a case involving a decision of the secretary of agriculture that made news headlines at the end of the New Deal era.[21]

The Packers and Stockyards Act authorized the secretary of agriculture to determine reasonable rates for services rendered by cattle-marketing agencies. The marketing agencies of the Kansas Stockyards challenged the ultimate price set as too low. The federal district court had allowed the marketing agents to require the secretary to appear in person at the trial. He was questioned at length regarding the process by which he had reached his decision about the rates. The interrogation included questions as to what documents had been studied and the nature of consultations with his subordinates. The Supreme Court held that it was improper to permit this questioning relating to the mental processes of the secretary.

Today, formal federal review procedures limit judicial review of agency actions to the record compiled before the agency. Thus, once an administrative process is complete, there is generally no judicial opportunity to inquire into the whys and wherefores of the decision-making process. Without this shield from judicial review, agency actions would be tied up in court and would lose their efficacy.

Nevertheless, the system of checks and balances is maintained in this area. Although a court may not inquire into the decision-making process, the legislature may. Congress regularly holds oversight hearings on how agencies are administering the law. Criticism from a key member of Congress or a congressional committee can lead to newspaper headlines and changed agency policies. Congress can also use the appropriation process to withhold funds from disfavored programs and to fund favored ones.

Timing of Review

Two judicial doctrines are intended to prevent premature transfer of cases from the administrative arena to the courts: the doctrines of exhaustion of administrative remedies and of ripeness.

Exhaustion *Exhaustion of administrative remedies* concerns the timing and substance of the administrative review process. The general rule is that a court will not entertain an appeal to review the administrative process until the agency has had the chance to act and all possible avenues of relief before the agency have been fully pursued. The purpose is to conserve judicial resources. However, a party is not required to exhaust all administrative avenues when that would be futile.

The exhaustion doctrine can also be understood to require a party to present its arguments to the administrative agency and to give the agency the chance to rule on them in the first instance. In reviewing an administrative agency's action, the courts will not rule on issues that the party failed to present to the agency.

Ripeness The *ripeness* doctrine helps ensure that courts are not forced to decide hypothetical questions. Courts will not hear cases until they are "ripe" for decision. The issue of ripeness most frequently arises in pre-enforcement review of statutes and ordinances; that is, when review is sought after a rule is adopted but before the agency seeks to apply the rule in a particular case. The general rule is that agency action is ripe for judicial review when the impact of the action is sufficiently direct and immediate as to make review appropriate.[22]

---

20. 117 S. Ct. 1154 (1997).
21. United States v. Morgan, 313 U.S. 409 (1941).

22. Abbott Lab. v. Gardner, 387 U.S. 136 (1967) (pre-enforcement review of FDA generic drug-labeling rule was appropriate because the issue was purely legal, the regulations represented final agency action, and the impact of the rules was direct and immediate).

◆ Decision-Making Power of Agencies

There are a number of doctrines that limit administrative agencies' decision-making powers.

Only Delegated Powers

The general rule is that an administrative agency may do only what Congress or the state legislature has authorized it to do. Agency action contrary to or in excess of its delegated authority is void.

The Iran-Contra controversy, to some extent, involved the question of whether Colonel Oliver North, a government official, exceeded the authority delegated to the National Security Agency (NSA) or contravened a congressional enactment. Congress had placed limits on the ability of specified government agencies to raise funds to supply the efforts of rebels seeking to overthrow the government of Nicaragua. For many years, the NSA and the Central Intelligence Agency (CIA)—two administrative agencies in the national security area—had been authorized to aid the rebels. When Congress withdrew this authority, Oliver North's alleged transgression was to continue providing such aid without proper authority. The drama of the Oliver North case is repeated daily on a smaller scale as administrative agencies seek to determine the scope of their authority to act.

Obligation to Follow Own Rules

Not only are agencies required to act within the authority delegated to them, they are also required to follow their own rules and regulations. When an administrative agency adopts a regulation, it becomes binding on the public. It also binds the agency. For example, in *Service v. Dulles*,[23] the Supreme Court held that a State Department employee could not be discharged without being provided reasons, because that would be contrary to the agency's regulations regarding discharges under the State Department's Loyalty Security Program.

At the federal level, one of the most prominent procedural obligations is the requirement to prepare an environmental impact statement before approving major federal actions. The National Environmental Policy Act

---

23. 354 U.S. 363 (1957).

"I'm sorry, sir, but F.A.A. rules forbid the wearing of Hawaiian shirts in the Business Class section."

From the *Wall Street Journal.* Reprinted by permission of Cartoon Features Syndicate.

(NEPA), passed in 1969, changed dramatically how all federal agencies conduct their business.

Before 1969, an agency could focus exclusively on its substantive legal obligations (the legal rules that define the rights and duties of the agency and of persons dealing with it) and on its own duly adopted procedural obligations (the rules that define the manner in which these rights and duties are enforced). With NEPA's passage, each federal agency assumed a new procedural obligation to consider the environmental impacts of its proposed actions and the alternatives to those impacts. Each of the hundreds of thousands of federal actions must comply with NEPA. As a result, each agency attempts to document its compliance as a routine part of its procedures. The agencies have not found it easy to meet these procedural requirements. There are hundreds of cases invalidating agency action as a result of the failure to meet this obligation.

Explanation of Decisions

As discussed earlier in this chapter, courts will not inquire into the mental processes of the decision maker. The corollary to this principle is that the agencies must explain the basis for their decisions and must show that they have taken into account all relevant considerations as required by the statute. If an agency makes a decision and fails to provide an adequate explanation of why it acted, the courts will invalidate the agency's action.[24] In some instances, however, the court may permit the agency to explain deficiencies in the record and to add supplementary explanations of why it acted. The judiciary's insistence that an agency make a reasoned decision, supported by an explanation of why it acted, is a major restraint on improper agency action.

 ## Finding an Agency's Rules

The most important publication in dealing with federal agencies is the *Federal Register*, published daily by the U.S. Government Printing Office. Agencies are required by law to use the *Federal Register* to provide notice to the public of proposed and final rules. Rules that are not properly published in the *Federal Register* are void.

Once a rule is finally adopted by an agency, it is codified in the *Code of Federal Regulations*. The *CFR* contains more than 50 titles and includes the regulations of approximately 400 federal agencies and bureaus.

In addition to these officially published documents, federal agencies maintain internal guidance documents. For example, the U.S. Forest Service controls millions of acres of timber lands. Its formal rules are sparse, but it publishes a manual and a handbook that contain thousands of pages of guidance on such topics as how to conduct timber sales. The Forest Service's manual and handbook are not generally available and may be difficult to find, but they are an important source of law, agency practice, and policy. Reports of court cases provide equivalent information. Cases decided by agency adjudication are not usually reported.

 ## Obtaining Documents from an Agency

In court proceedings and in formal agency adjudications, documents may be obtained by discovery. In other situations, individuals are entitled to obtain copies of government records pursuant to federal and state statutes. The federal statute authorizing this procedure is the Freedom of Information Act (FOIA).[25] Under the FOIA any citizen may request records of the government on any subject that is of interest. Unlike discovery, an FOIA request need not show the relevance of the documents to any particular legal proceeding or that the requester has any specific interest in the documents. It is sufficient that the requester seeks the documents.

In theory, the Freedom of Information Act provides an easy way to obtain documents from a government agency. The agency is required to respond to a document request within ten days. In practice, months, weeks, or even years may pass before the government responds to an FOIA request. Moreover, requesters are required to pay the cost of locating and copying the records. However, these costs are waived for public interest groups, newspaper reporters, and certain other requesters.

Not all documents in the government's possession are available for public inspection. The FOIA exempts:

1. Records required by an executive order to be kept secret in the interest of national defense or foreign policy
2. Records related solely to the internal personnel rules and practice of an agency
3. Records exempted from disclosure by another statute
4. Trade secrets or confidential commercial and financial information
5. Interagency memorandums or decisions that reflect the deliberative process
6. Personnel files and other files that, if disclosed, would constitute a clearly unwarranted invasion of personal privacy
7. Information compiled for law enforcement purposes
8. Reports prepared on behalf of an agency responsible for the regulation of financial institutions
9. Geological information concerning wells

The government is not required to withhold information under any of these exemptions. It may do so or not in its discretion.

Frequently, regulated companies are required to submit confidential information to the government. From the perspective of a company submitting such information, the Freedom of Information Act presents a danger of disclosure to competitors. To protect information from disclosure, the company should mark each document as privileged and confidential, so that gov-

---

24. *See, e.g.*, Motor Vehicle Mfr. Ass'n v. State Farm Mut. Auto. Ins. Co., 463 U.S. 29 (1983).

25. 5 U.S.C. § 552 (1988).

ernment officials reviewing FOIA requests will not inadvertently disclose it.

From the perspective of those doing business with the government, the Freedom of Information Act provides an excellent opportunity to learn who is communicating with the agency and what the agency is thinking about a particular matter. The FOIA can also

be useful in obtaining government studies and learning generally about government activities.

Each federal agency has its own set of regulations relating to FOIA requests. These regulations must be complied with strictly or consideration of the request may be greatly delayed.

IN BRIEF

SEVEN BASIC STEPS FOR WORKING SUCCESSFULLY WITH AN ADMINISTRATIVE AGENCY

STEP 1
Investigate the applicable standards that will govern agency's actions.

STEP 2
Identify and evaluate the agency's formal structure.

STEP 3
Determine what facts are before the agency.

STEP 4
Identify the interests of others who may be involved in the decision-making process.

STEP 5
Adopt a strategy to achieve the desired goal.

STEP 6
Eliminate adverse impact on other interested parties.

STEP 7
Get involved in the administrative process early and stay involved.

THE RESPONSIBLE MANAGER
Working with Administrative Agencies

Administrative agencies are intended to be practical problem-solving entities. It is therefore easier for a nonlawyer to work with an administrative agency than to represent himself or herself in court. Most simple administrative matters do not require an attorney, but one may be necessary to handle more complicated matters.

Seven basic recommendations for working successfully with an administrative agency are offered in the "In Brief" above.

As recommended in Step 1, a manager working with an agency should first investigate the basic legal standards that will govern the agency's actions in the matter at hand. These include the agency's laws, its regulations, and its internal manuals and procedures. It is also important to investigate how the agency's administration of its laws and regulations is affected by its past history and by current political influences. Agencies, like any other bureaucracy, tend to have biases in how they carry out their laws and regulations.

These investigations are important for three reasons. First, a manager needs to know what facts must be presented in order to prevail in a claim. Second, it is possible that the agency personnel may not know the applicable legal standard. Many administrative agencies have little access to legal advice and find it helpful to have a clear presentation of the law under which a person is proceeding. Third, it is important to know the law at the outset of an administrative proceeding, because under the doctrine of exhaustion of administrative remedies, issues not raised before the agency are deemed to be waived if the matter is later brought before a court.

The second step is for the manager to identify and evaluate the agency's formal structure, to understand how the agency operates. Administrative agencies can have complicated structures. Because the power to make decisions may be vested in more than one official, it is important to know all of the decision maker's options before proceeding. A person can start at the top, the middle, or the bottom. The important point is to start at the right place. Finding out where that is takes some effort.

Next, the manager needs to determine what facts the agency already has (Step 3). In a judicial proceeding, the parties create the record by filing documents with the court. All parties have access to those documents and share the same factual record. The same is not true in an administrative agency proceeding. The factual record may be scattered about the agency in different files and offices. In order to function effectively before the agency, a manager must identify and locate this record.

Step 4 recommends the manager identify the interests of other agencies or parties who may be involved in the decision-making process. In a court proceeding, all the parties to a case are known; in an administrative matter, the parties may not be designated formally. It helps to identify the people concerned at the outset and to determine how the proposed action will affect those people.

Upon completing this background information, the manager should adopt a strategy to achieve the desired goal (Step 5). Investigation of an administrative matter could show that the agency lacks the authority to do what is proposed. In that case, the manager must persuade the agency to adopt new rules or go to the legislature to have new laws adopted. The most significant task, however, is to decide whether additional factual information should be gathered and presented to the agency. The record before the agency will normally be the record in court. The use of experts during the administrative process and the submission of key documents are important.

In reviewing a proposed action, the manager may find that the action would have undesirable impacts on other interested parties (Step 6). Elimination of those impacts is an effective way to avoid costly disputes.

Finally, as recommended in Step 7, the manager needs to participate in the administrative process at the earliest possible time and to continue participating throughout the proceedings. Once set in motion, agencies tend to stay in motion unless they are deflected by an outside force. The greater the momentum that has gathered, the harder it is to move the agency off the path it is pursuing. Therefore, it is important to participate early in the process in an effort to influence the agency before it makes up its mind rather than after.

INSIDE STORY

AUCTIONING THE AIRWAVES: STUCK IN C BLOCK

In the early 1990s, the U.S. government recognized the need to make use of market forces to allocate the electromagnetic spectrum if that resource were to be put to its highest and best use. Companies use the spectrum for radio and television broadcasts, portable radio communications, cellular telephones, and other wireless personal communication systems. In the past, licenses to use spectrum wavelengths were given away, based on either the public policy merits of applicants or a lottery.

In 1993, Congress amended the Communications Act of 1934, which created the Federal Communications Commission (FCC), to regulate recently pioneered uses of the spectrum.[26] Congress did not create a new system for allocating scarce wavelength, but rather empowered the FCC to enact regulations to create and administer a market-based system. Broad in its mandate, Congress authorized the

FCC to design and employ competitive bidding procedures for the licensing of certain uses of wavelength with the guidelines that (1) the spectrum be rapidly developed and efficiently used; (2) licenses be broadly distributed with economic opportunities for small businesses, minorities, and women; (3) the distribution of licenses among geographic areas be equitable; and (4) the public capture a portion of the value of the spectrum.

The FCC responded with a plan to auction Broadband Personal Communication Services (Broadband PCS), that is, 120 MHz of wavelength that encompasses a variety of emerging mobile and portable radio communications. Under its new authority, the FCC divided the 120 MHz into six blocks (A through F), which would be auctioned in the three stages for defined geographic regions. After consulting with experts in game theory (including Stanford Business School Professor Robert Wilson) to design the most effective procedures, the commission decided to conduct each auction through simultaneous multiple-round bidding with simultaneous stopping in between rounds. As one might expect, the system was quite complicated.

In the first auction (for Blocks A and B), two 20 MHz licenses for each of 51 state-sized Major Trading Areas throughout the nation were offered to all comers on a cash-only basis. The auction was conducted in early 1995, and after 112 rounds of bidding, a total of 18 successful bidders paid $7.7 billion for licenses. Three bidders, however, won licenses covering 95% of the U.S. population: AT&T; a consortium of regional Bell operating telephone companies; and a consortium of Sprint, TCI, Comcast, and Cox Cable.

The second auction (for Block C) was a license of 30 MHz in 493 city-sized Basic Trading Areas. The first auction had been open to all bidders; the second auction was restricted to entrepreneurs. The FCC defined *entrepreneurs* as companies with less than $125 million in gross revenues and less than $500 million in total assets. These entrepreneurs were given their own auction as part of the FCC's attempt to distribute at least some licenses to smaller, less established firms in accordance with Congress's mandate. In contrast to the cash-only terms for Blocks A and B, the C-Block auction required successful bidders to make only a 5% down payment at the conclusion of auction, a 5% down payment at the time of license issuance, and principal repayment of the remaining 90% over ten years at Treasury interest rates. Such generous financing terms—effectively subsidies—were intended to make bidding more attractive to new and small players in the telecommunications industry.

In addition to creating a system that disfavored large bidders, the FCC adopted special provisions, including a 10% bidding credit, for "small businesses," defined as companies with no more than $40 million in gross revenues. The FCC also attempted to give minority- and woman-owned bidders their own preferences: a 25% bidding credit and weaker affiliation restrictions, which permitted limited partnerships with otherwise unqualified bidders to bid.

Unfortunately for the FCC, three days before the initial C-Block bidder applications were due, the U.S. Supreme Court announced its opinion in *Adarand Constructors, Inc. v. Peña*,[27] which ruled that racial and gender classifications by the federal government are subject to strict judicial scrutiny. (This case is discussed in detail in Chapter 2.) Recognizing both the legal uncertainty of its bid preferences and the practical certainty of legal action if it granted such preferences, the FCC extended the preferential policies to all "small businesses," whether or not minority- or women-owned. Although the decision to eliminate the race and gender preferences was challenged by one hopeful beneficiary, the U.S. Court of Appeals for the District of Columbia rejected the challenge and allowed the auction to proceed.[28]

The C-Block auction finally began in late 1995. After 184 rounds of bidding, the auction concluded on May 6, 1996. Eighty-nine bidders won 493 licenses at a cost of $10.2 billion. Observers were astounded at the magnitude of the prices, which were effectively twice those paid per potential customer for Blocks A and B. NextWave placed the highest total bid: $4.2 billion for New York, Los Angeles, and Houston. The auction's generous financing terms, however, meant that much of that revenue was inflated and existed only on paper.

By June 1995, winners of 18 licenses had defaulted on their down payments, and in July the

FCC had to reauction those licenses. To forestall further defaults, the FCC amended its rules to allow licensees to partition and sell parts of their territories. Still, the owner of the Phoenix license, which had already been reauctioned in July, defaulted; and the FCC had to again reauction the license. By September 1995, nine licensees had defaulted on their full 10% down payments. Additionally, initial public offerings by the two of the highest bidders had to be called off when investors balked at the high prices paid for the licenses.

Further fueling the C-Block fire, Pocket Communications, the second highest bidder at $1.4 billion, filed for bankruptcy protection in April 1997. Concerned about the ability of licensees to make their scheduled payments,

the FCC suspended installment payments that same day. Six months later another licensee, General Wireless, followed Pocket into bankruptcy court. After considering the problem, the FCC reinstated the installment payments but offered licensees a limited menu of repayment options that revolved around the return of some or all licenses to the FCC.

Commenting on the new repayments options, FCC Chairman Reed Hundt said, "Our goal here is to make sure these companies are in business, not appearing before the commission or in bankruptcy court." Although outvoted by the other commissioners, Hundt had proposed even more generous repayment terms. Big Six accounting firm and consultancy Deloitte & Touche studied the new market in C-Block licenses

and concluded that given the high prices paid for the licenses, most licensees would do well to break even. Regarding the repayment options offered by the FCC, Deloitte's chief telecommunication's officer David Roddy remarked, "It seems like they're just rearranging deck chairs on the *Titanic*. It's not the right time for these companies to make money." It remains to be seen whether the bidding system set up by the FCC will result in the successful implementation of the congressional guidelines embodied in the 1993 amendments to the Communications Act of 1934.

26. 47 U.S.C. § 309 (j).
27. 515 U.S. 200 (1995).
28. Unpublished opinion, Sept. 28, 1995.

KEY WORDS AND PHRASES

administrative law judge   **185**
arbitrary and capricious standard   **193**
codified   **185**
construction   **196**
de novo   **188**
exhaustion of administrative

remedies   **202**
informal discretionary actions   **188**
record   **188**
regulatory negotiations   **185**
ripeness   **202**
scienter   **195**

standing   **200**
strict liability   **193**
substantial evidence standard   **195**
tender offer   **193**

QUESTIONS AND CASE PROBLEMS

1. Why are administrative agencies called the fourth branch of the U.S. government?

2. A statute gives the Department of the Interior the power to allow or to curtail mining within the national forests "as the best interests of all users of the national forest shall dictate." Is this a valid delegation of legisla-

tive power to the agency, or is it too broad a delegation of power?

3. Assume that on May 1, 1998, Congress enacted a statute to deal with the problem of toxic-waste-dump sites. These dump sites, in use for many years, leak toxic chemicals, and thereby poison groundwater and endanger people. The statute created a "superfund" to which all companies producing toxic waste must contribute. This superfund will pay for cleaning up the most dangerous toxic-waste-dump sites.

The statute also created the Toxic Waste Agency (TWA) to administer the superfund and cleanup operations. The TWA has adopted rules to determine how much each company must contribute to generate the $10 billion needed to clean up the waste sites. The contributions will depend on the toxicity of the chemical wastes that the company produces, the length of time the company has been in operation, and its ability to pay.

To help determine each company's required contribution, the TWA developed a list of all sources of toxic waste. Included on the list is the chemical XYZ, the manufacture of which produces toxic waste. However, the chemical ABC is not on the list. Nagel Corporation makes XYZ and concedes that it produces toxic wastes. Nagel also believes that the manufacture of ABC produces toxic wastes. ABC is manufactured exclusively by Seith Cooper Chemical Company.

Nagel appeals to the correct court concerning the absence of ABC from the list of toxic chemicals. The commissioner of the TWA asks the court to dismiss the appeal because Nagel lacks standing. What is the result?

4. The Occupational Health and Safety Act of 1970 created new statutory duties for employers. It permitted the federal government, in proceedings before an administrative agency without a jury, to impose civil penalties on employers violating the OSHA. Did the penalty provisions of the OSHA violate the Seventh Amendment rights of employers? Explain why or why not. [*Atlas Roofing Co., Inc. v. Occupational Safety and Health Review Comm'n*, 430 U.S. 442 (1977)]

5. Section 102(c) of the National Security Act of 1947 provides that "the Director of Central Intelligence may, in his discretion, terminate the employment of any officer or employee of the Agency whenever he shall deem such termination necessary or advisable in the interests of the United States" [50 U.S.C. § 5403(c)]. The director of the CIA terminated a homosexual CIA employee without stating any reason for the dismissal. The employee sought judicial review of his termination on the ground that it was arbitrary, capricious, or an abuse of discretion. Is judicial review of the director's actions proper? [*Webster v. Doe*, 486 U.S. 592 (1988), *aff'd in part, rev'd in part* by *Doe v. Gates*, 981 F.2d 1316 (D.C. Cir. 1993)]

6. The Food and Drug Administration, charged with implementation of the Federal Food, Drug and Cosmetic Act, refused to approve the cancer-treatment drug Laetrile on the ground that it failed to meet the statute's safety and effectiveness standards. Terminally ill cancer patients sued, claiming that the safety and effectiveness standards implemented by the FDA could have no reasonable application to drugs used by the terminally ill. The statute contained no explicit exemption for drugs used by the terminally ill. The case reached the court of appeals, which agreed with the plaintiffs and approved intravenous injections of Laetrile for terminally ill cancer patients. The United States appealed to the Supreme Court. Under what standard should the Supreme Court review the FDA's determination that an exemption from the Federal Food, Drug and Cosmetic Act should not be implied for drugs used by the terminally ill? [*United States v. Rutherford*, 442 U.S. 544 (1979)]

7. In 1985, President Reagan signed into law the Gramm-Rudman-Hollings Act. The purpose of the act was to reduce the federal deficit by setting a maximum deficit amount for fiscal years 1986 to 1991, progressively reducing the budget deficit to zero by 1991.

If the federal budget deficit were not reduced as the act required, an automatic budget process took effect. The comptroller would calculate, on a program-by-program basis, the amount of reductions needed to meet the target. He would then report that amount to the president, who was required to issue a sequestration order mandating these reductions. (A *sequestration order* directs spending levels to be reduced below the levels authorized in the original budget.) Unless Congress then acted to modify the budget to reduce the deficit to the required level, the sequestrations would go into effect.

The comptroller, unlike the employees of the executive branch and agency officials, does not serve at the pleasure of the president. He can be removed from office only by Congress.

Opponents of the Gramm-Rudman-Hollings Act felt the comptroller's role in the automatic budget process was an exercise of executive functions. Because the comptroller was controlled by Congress, they argued that this role violated the constitutional requirement of separation of powers. Were they right? [*Bowsher v. Synar*, 478 U.S. 714 (1986)]

8. It is not always clear whether an administrative agency is required to have a search warrant to pursue an investigation. Is a warrant required to conduct an investigation in the following cases?

a. An Occupational Safety and Health Administration inspector entered Joy and Barry's, an electrical and plumbing installation business, to conduct a search of the working areas of the business that were not open to the public. Joy and Barry's was selected for inspection at random by the agency. Ron, the general manager of the business, refused to allow the inspector to enter without a warrant. Must the inspector get a warrant to conduct the investigation, which is authorized under the Occupational Safety and Health Act? [*Marshall v. Barlow's, Inc.*, 436 U.S. 307 (1978)]

b. Jon is a liquor dealer holding a federal retail liquor dealer's occupational tax stamp. He refused to allow tax agents to inspect his locked storeroom. May they inspect the storeroom without a search warrant? [*Colonnade Catering Corp. v. United States*, 397 U.S. 72 (1970)]

c. Wendy, president of Tom and Barb's Silver Mines, refused to allow a government agent to conduct a warrantless search of the mine, even though the Federal Mine Safety and Health Act of 1977 authorized the secretary of labor to make warrantless inspections of mines. Additionally, the Mine Act specifies that underground mines must be inspected four times a year. Should the Supreme Court uphold Wendy's refusal to allow the inspector to enter? [*Donovan v. Dewey*, 452 U.S. 594 (1981)]

9. In 1977, Michael Pertschuk was appointed chairman of the Federal Trade Commission (FTC). On his accession to the chairmanship, Pertschuk sought to transform the agency into an efficient organization for advancing the interests of the consumer. The first major policy initiative undertaken by Pertschuk focused on the effects of television advertising on children.

Pertschuk began speaking frequently on the subject of children's television. On the October 31, 1977, broadcast of the "Today" show, he expressed his view that no advertising directed at preschoolers should be allowed to be broadcast. He also sent letters to the FCC chairman and the FDA commissioner describing his objections to advertising aimed at children.

On April 27, 1978, the FTC released a Notice of Proposed Rule Making that included three options. One of the options would have banned all television advertising for "any product which is directed to audiences composed of a significant proportion of children who are too young to understand the selling purpose of or otherwise comprehend or evaluate the advertising." In response to this notice, on May 8, 1978, the national trade associations of advertisers, advertising agencies, and toy manufacturers petitioned Pertschuk to remove himself from participation in the rule-making proceeding. They alleged that his public statements on the issue evidenced prejudgment and bias. Should Pertschuk remove himself from participating in the rule-making proceedings? [*Association of Nat'l Advertisers, Inc. v. Federal Trade Comm'n*, 627 F.2d 1151 (D.C. Cir. 1979), *cert. denied*, 447 U.S. 921 (1980)]

MANAGER'S DILEMMA

10. Dora Reilly is the executive vice-president of DNA in Combat, Inc., a genetic-engineering company based in Cambridge, Massachusetts. Eighteen months ago she filed an application for FDA approval of a promising anticancer drug, DBL. Two months ago she met Gene Splice at an après-ski party and invited him to her room at the ski lodge to listen to her CD collection. After that night, Splice returned to his job as a senior specialist in the division of the FDA responsible for approving new drugs based on recombinant DNA, and Reilly returned to Cambridge. Two weeks after her return, Splice wrote Reilly a letter on FDA letterhead, saying, "It was nice to see your name cross my desk on your company's petition for approval of DBL. I'd really like to see you again—why don't you fly down this weekend?"

Reilly considered requesting that the petition be referred to another specialist at the FDA. However, she is concerned that that would delay the approval process by at least 18 months. Her chief scientist has advised her that a key competitor is expected to have a similar drug on the market in four months. What should she do?

INTERNET SOURCES

The Federal Web Locator, a service of the Villanova Center for Information Law and Policy, offers users a chance to search for materials from and about the federal government, including its many agencies and their Web pages.	http://www.law.vill.edu/fed-agency/fedwebloc.html
The National Archives and Records Administration's page allows uses to search the entire *Code of Federal Regulations.*	http://www.access.gpo.gov/nara/cfr/cfr-table-search.html
This page of the National Archives and Records Administration allows uses to search the entire *Federal Register.*	http://www.access.gpo.gov/su_docs/aces/aces140.html
Cornell University's Legal Information Institute page provides the text of the entire U.S. Code, including the Administrative Procedures Act.	http://www.law.cornell.edu/uscode/5/ch5.html
Federal Communications Commission	http://www.fcc.gov

The Legal Environment

CHAPTER 7

Contracts

INTRODUCTION

Why Contract Law Is Important

Contract law defines which agreements will be enforced by the courts and which will not. Contracts are central to the conduct of business both in the United States and internationally. Without contract law, a seller could not ship goods to a buyer knowing that it has an enforceable right to be paid for the goods. Similarly, a buyer could not order goods knowing that the seller must deliver or pay damages for nondelivery. Leases of real property, loan agreements, employment agreements, settlement agreements, and joint venture agreements are all based on the parties' expectation that the promises made will be enforceable.

Contract law comes from statutes, case law, and tradition. It varies slightly from state to state. Many states follow the Restatement (Second) of the Law of Contracts, which is the basis for much of the discussion in this chapter. Common law contracts include contracts involving services and real property. Commercial transactions involving the sale of goods, that is, movable personal property, are governed by Article 2 of the Uniform Commercial Code (UCC), which has been adopted, with variations, in every state. Article 2 is discussed in more detail in Chapter 8.

Chapter Overview

This chapter discusses the elements necessary for a valid contract: agreement (formed by an offer and acceptance), consideration, contractual capacity, and legality. It explains the doctrine of promissory estoppel, which can, in certain circumstances, result in limited relief for a party who has relied on a noncontractual promise to his or her detriment. The need for genuine assent and the effects of fraud and duress are discussed, as are issues concerning misunderstanding or mistake about the meaning of a contract or the facts underlying the contract. The chapter explains the requirement that certain contracts be in writing and the rules for looking beyond the written terms of an agreement to discern the parties' intentions. It discusses damages for breach of contract and court orders for specific performance. The chapter then addresses precontractual liability, including the enforcement of an agreement to negotiate. It concludes with a look at the conflicts that may arise between a party's contractual obligations and its obligations to others, and liability for interference with a contract.

 ## Basic Requirements of a Contract

A *contract* is a legally enforceable promise or set of promises. If the promise is broken, the person to whom the promise was made—the *promisee*—has certain legal rights against the person who made the promise—the *promisor*. If the promisor fails to carry out its promise, the promisee may be able to recover money damages, or it may be able to get an injunction or a court order forcing the promisor to perform the promise.

Formation of a valid contract requires four basic elements. First, there must be an agreement between the parties formed by an offer and acceptance. Second, the parties' promises must be supported by something of value, known as consideration. Third, both parties must have the capacity to enter into a contract. Fourth, the contract must have a purpose that is legal.

In addition, courts may invalidate contracts that do not reflect a true "meeting of the minds." For instance, if one party is induced into a contract by fraud, duress, or misrepresentation, courts may refuse to enforce the contract because both parties did not genuinely assent to its terms.

 ## Agreement

A valid contract requires an offer and acceptance resulting in agreement between the two parties. Contract law has traditionally treated offer and acceptance as a rather sterile, step-by-step process. Despite its incongruity with the fluid nature of business deal-making today, this narrow view continues to give the rules governing contract formation a formalistic flavor.

 ## Offer

An *offer* is a manifestation of willingness to enter into a bargain that justifies another person in understanding that his or her assent to that bargain is invited and will conclude it. An offer is effective if the *offeror* (the person making the offer) has an intention to be bound by the offer, the terms of the offer are reasonably definite, and the offer is communicated to the *offeree* (the intended recipient).

Intention

Courts will evaluate the offeror's outward expression of intent, not his or her secret intentions. Thus, if a reasonable person would consider an offeror's statement to be a serious offer, an offer has been made. This means that offers made in obvious jest or in the heat of anger do not meet the intention requirement, because a reasonable person would know the offer was not serious. This objective standard of contract interpretation makes it possible to plan one's business based on reasonable expectations of what the other party's words mean.

Most advertisements are treated not as offers but as invitations to negotiate. Sellers do not have an unlimited ability to provide services or an unlimited supply of goods. If advertisements were offers, then everyone who "accepted" could sue the seller for breach of contract if the seller's supply ran out. An advertisement will be treated as an offer only in the rare case where a seller makes a promise so definite that it is clearly binding itself to the conditions stated. This can arise, for example, when the advertisement calls for some performance by the offeree, such as providing information that leads to the recovery of a lost or stolen article.

Definiteness

An offer will form the basis for a contract if it is definite, meaning that essential terms are not left open. If essential terms (such as price, subject matter, duration of the contract, and manner of payment) are left open, then there is no contract. (As discussed in Chapter 8, the UCC permits courts to supply a reasonable price term if the parties have clearly demonstrated an intention to contract but left the price term open.)

Communication

The offeror must communicate the offer to the offeree. For instance, a good Samaritan who returns a lost pet cannot claim a reward offered by the owner if he or she did not know about the reward beforehand.

Termination of Offer

An offer can be terminated either by operation of law or by action of the parties.

Termination by Operation of Law An offer terminates when the time of acceptance specified by the offeror has elapsed or at the end of a reasonable period if the offeror did not specify a time. Death or incapacitation of either party terminates an offer, as does destruction of the subject matter.

Termination by Action of the Parties The offeror can *revoke* its offer—that is, cancel it—at any time before the offeree accepts. An offer is also terminated if the offeree rejects it. Merely inquiring into the terms of an offer, however, is not a rejection. For example, suppose Cassandra offers Misha a managerial position at $105,000 per year, and Misha responds, "Does that include a five-week paid vacation?" This is an inquiry into terms, as distinguished from a counteroffer, and does not terminate the original offer.

A *counteroffer* is a new offer by the original offeree. A counteroffer constitutes a rejection of the original offer and has the effect of reversing the roles of the original offeror and offeree. Had Misha replied, "That salary is too low, but I'll take the job at $120,000 per year," he would have terminated the offer by making a counteroffer.

Irrevocable Offers

Sometimes an offer cannot be revoked by the offeror. *Irrevocable offers* arise in two circumstances: (1) when an option contract has been created, and (2) when an offeree has relied on an offer to his or her detriment.

Option Contracts One type of irrevocable offer occurs when an offeror agrees to hold an offer open for a certain amount of time in exchange for some consideration from the other party. Such an agreement is known as an *option contract*. Under such an agreement, the offeror cannot revoke the offer until the time for acceptance has expired. For example, a company might agree to keep the position of general manager open for ten days while the person offered the position decides whether to take the job in exchange for a $200 payment by the offeree.

Under the UCC, a merchant's firm offer, in writing, to buy or sell goods is equivalent to an option contract and is enforceable even if the other party gave no consideration for the firm offer. The merchant cannot revoke until the time has elapsed; if no time is stated, the offer must be held open for a reasonable amount of time, which cannot exceed three months.

Detrimental Reliance Another type of irrevocable offer can occur when an offeree has changed his or her position because of justifiable reliance on the offer. Sometimes courts will hold that such *detrimental reliance* makes the offer irrevocable.

Suppose Aunt Leila offers to give her niece Jaye the use of her Maui condo for Jaye's spring-break vacation in exchange for Jaye's promise to fix a hole in the condo roof during her stay. Under traditional contract law, Aunt Leila could revoke this offer at any time before Jaye accepts. But suppose Jaye relies on this offer, purchases a nonrefundable plane ticket to Maui, and passes up the opportunity to rent other condos for her stay. The modern view of this situation is quite different from traditional contract law. If Aunt Leila should reasonably

have known Jaye would act to her detriment in reliance on Aunt Leila's offer, then the doctrine of *promissory estoppel* would make Aunt Leila's offer irrevocable. In other words, Aunt Leila would be estopped—or barred—from revoking her offer. The doctrine of promissory estoppel is described in more detail in the discussion of consideration below.

 ## Acceptance

Acceptance is a response by the person receiving the offer that indicates willingness to enter into the agreement proposed in the offer. A typical example of an offer and acceptance is something like this: Nanci says to Jim, "I'll give you $100 for your new computer software package," and Jim says "Okay." A contract has been made. Nanci is now legally obliged to give Jim the money, and Jim is obliged to give Nanci the software.

Both offer and acceptance can be oral, written, or implied by conduct. For example, a manager offers a consultant $5,000 to develop a business plan for her company. The consultant begins interviewing key executives and drafting a business plan. By starting work on the business plan, he has accepted the offer. The acceptance is implied by his action, even though he did not actually say "I accept your offer."

Mode of Acceptance

The offeror is the "master of his offer" in that he or she can specify authorized and unauthorized means of acceptance. For example, the offeror could specify that his offer can be accepted only by a facsimile to a stated facsimile number and that the acceptance is not effective until actually received. In the absence of such a provision, acceptance is effective upon dispatch. Thus, if a person drops into the mailbox a properly addressed envelope with adequate postage containing a letter accepting an offer, a contract is formed when the letter is put in the mailbox; and the offeror cannot thereafter revoke the offer.

Mirror Image Rule The traditional concept of contract formation requires that acceptance be unequivocal. In other words, what the offeree accepts must be a mirror image of what the offeror has offered. If it is not, the *mirror image rule* dictates that no contract has been formed.

For example, suppose Alyssa offers to rent to Victor 6,000 square feet of office space in Houston for $60 per square foot. Victor accepts the offer of office space but says he wants ten free underground parking spaces included as well. The requirements of the mirror image rule have not been met because Victor's acceptance is not unequivocal. Victor's request for the parking spaces is considered a counteroffer rather than an acceptance. Accordingly, there is no contract.

Battle of the Forms   The narrow concept of contract formation reflected in the mirror image rule is difficult to apply to standardized or form contracts. Under traditional law, if parties struck a deal by exchanging preprinted forms, the second form constituted a counteroffer—not an acceptance—because it was not the mirror image of the first form. This problem often gives rise to a so-called *battle of the forms*, in which each party claims that its own form represents the actual terms of the contract.

The UCC, which applies only to sales of goods, offers two alternatives to the traditional rule. Depending on the circumstances, the terms agreed to will be either (1) the areas of agreement between the two forms, plus standard terms supplied by the UCC; or (2) the first form plus any nonessential changes in the second form. This is discussed more fully in Chapter 8.

Many contracts are a mixture of individually negotiated terms and standard, preprinted terms. When there is a conflict, the negotiated term will prevail. For example, in *Steiner v. Mobil Oil Corp.*,[1] Steiner, a gas station owner, told Mobil Oil Corporation that he wanted a Mobil franchise only if Mobil would guarantee a specific gas discount for the next ten years. Steiner's condition was stated verbally in the negotiations and again in a letter to Mobil. Mobil sent back a thick packet of docu-

_____
1. 569 P.2d 751 (Cal. 1977).

ments in which was buried a form limiting the discount to the first year of the franchise. The station owner stowed the packet in a drawer without reading all the forms. A year later, when Mobil discontinued the discount, the station owner sued. The California Supreme Court held that because Mobil had verbally agreed to the discount term, it was obligated to notify the station owner (with a cover letter, for example) of any change in the final printed documents. Although this case should not be read as an excuse for not reading documents before signing them, the court was probably influenced by the fact that the gas station owner was fighting Mobil, a major corporation, over a disputed form buried in the thick packet of documents Mobil had prepared.

Intent to Be Bound   Formalistic rules of contract formation often do not reflect the realities of how businesses enter into agreements. A joint venture agreement between contractors to build a hydroelectric dam, for example, can involve months of negotiations and a series of letters, memorandums, and draft contracts. As a result, it is sometimes difficult to determine exactly at what point the parties have entered into a valid legally binding contract.

At some point in negotiations, the parties will usually manifest an intention, either orally or in writing, to enter into a contract. Such *intent to be bound* can create an enforceable contract. The courts will look at the specific facts of each case when determining whether the parties regarded themselves as having completed a bargain.

A preliminary agreement that is subject to approval by a higher authority, such as the board of directors, may not be considered an expression of intent to be bound. This was a key issue in the following case.

A CASE IN POINT   SUMMARY

**CASE 7.1
APOTHEKERNES
LABORATORIUM FOR
SPECIALPRAEPARATER
v. IMC CHEMICAL
GROUP, INC.**
United States Court of
Appeals for the Seventh Circuit
873 F.2d 155 (7th Cir. 1989).

FACTS   Apothekernes negotiated to buy a biochemical division of IMC and had been assured by the person negotiating for IMC that the IMC board of directors would approve the purchase contract. All the substantial terms of the purchase agreement were agreed on, and a letter of intent was signed. The letter of intent stipulated that the terms were "subject to our concluding an Agreement of Sale which shall be acceptable to the Boards of Directors of our respective corporations, whose discretion shall in no way be limited by this letter." The IMC board rejected the deal, and Apothekernes sued on two grounds. First, Apothekernes argued that when the negotiators agreed to

Case 7.1 continues

Case 7.1 continued

all the terms, a binding contract was formed. Second, it asserted that the letter of intent imposed a duty to negotiate in good faith, which was violated when the IMC board rejected the deal.

ISSUE PRESENTED   Does rejection of a letter of intent by the board of directors constitute a breach of contract or a breach of the duty to negotiate in good faith when the negotiators had a meeting of the minds but the letter of intent explicitly provided that the board of directors had unlimited discretion to accept or reject the letter of intent?

SUMMARY OF OPINION   The U.S. Court of Appeals held that there was no contract. Even though there was a meeting of the minds of the negotiators, the fact that the letter of intent explicitly stated that the deal was subject to board approval should have put the buyer on notice that any promises of rubber-stamp board approval were not to be taken seriously. The court recognized IMC's duty to negotiate in good faith, but it held that good faith does not guarantee that such negotiations will result in a binding contract.

RESULT   The IMC board had the right to reject the letter of intent negotiated by a subordinate, so there was no contract.

COMMENTS   This is one of the first cases to recognize that there can be an enforceable agreement to negotiate in good faith, though here the court found IMC did not breach that agreement. The meaning of good faith is discussed later in this chapter.

 Consideration

A promise does not always constitute a valid contract. To form a valid contract, each side must provide something of value. The thing of value, known as *consideration*, can be money, an object, a promise, a service, or a giving up of the right to do something. For instance, an adult's promise to quit smoking for five years constitutes consideration because the promisor is giving up something he or she is legally entitled to do. A promise to take property off the market for 30 days constitutes consideration. So does a promise to do a midyear audit.

A promise to do something illegal, however, such as pay for sexual favors in a state where prostitution is prohibited, does not constitute valid consideration. Likewise, a promise to fulfill a preexisting legal obligation, that is, to do something the promisor is already obligated to do—either by law or by contract—is not consideration.

For example, suppose Brett's Builders Corporation (BBC) has a contract to build a production facility for Hardware, Inc. for $15 million. Halfway through the project, BBC demands an additional $3 million to finish the project. Because it wants the project done as quickly as possible, Hardware promises to pay the additional $3 million. Hardware's promise is not enforceable by BBC, because BBC's promise to "finish the project" did not constitute consideration. BBC was already contractually obligated to build the facility in its entirety. This type of situation is explored further in the discussion of contract modification below.

Adequacy of Consideration

Generally, courts will not scrutinize the value of the consideration or the fairness of a contract. This means that courts will deem consideration adequate—and thus hold parties to their bargain—unless they feel the purported consideration is nothing more than a sham. Thus the adage that even a peppercorn can be adequate consideration. The rare exception to this rule is the unconscionability doctrine discussed next.

Bilateral and Unilateral Contracts

Consideration can be either a promise to do a certain act or the performance of the act itself.

A *bilateral contract* is a promise given in exchange for another promise. One party agrees to do one thing, and the other party agrees to do something in return. For example, Ibrahim promises to give Mercedes $10 if Mercedes promises to drive Ibrahim to business school. The exchange of promises represents consideration and makes the promises binding.

A *unilateral contract* is a promise given in exchange for an act. A unilateral contract is accepted by performing the specified act. For example, Ibrahim promises to give Mercedes $10 if Mercedes drives him to business school. Mercedes can accept the contract only by driving Ibrahim to business school.

Mutuality of Obligation

The corollary of consideration is the concept of *mutuality of obligation*. Unless both parties are obligated to perform their side of the bargain, neither will be. Mutuality of obligation applies only to bilateral contracts. In the case of a unilateral contract, the promisor becomes bound only after the promisee has performed the required act. Thus, in the example above, Ibrahim has no obligation to pay Mercedes $10 until Mercedes drives him to school.

In other words, a bilateral contract must limit the behavior of both parties in some fashion for it to be enforceable. If one party has full freedom of action, there is no contract.

Illusory Promise

A promise that neither confers any benefit on the promisee nor subjects the promisor to any detriment is an *illusory promise*. Because there is no mutuality of obligation in such a case, the resulting agreement is unenforceable. For example, a classic case[2] involved a coal company, Wickham, that agreed to sell at a certain price all the coal that Farmers' Lumber, a lumber company, wanted to purchase from Wickham. The Iowa Supreme Court held that Farmers' Lumber's promise to purchase only what it wanted to purchase, which could be nothing at all, was illusory. Because there was no consideration flowing from Farmers' Lumber to Wickham, there was no contract. Farmers' Lumber could have avoided the finding of an illusory contract by agreeing to purchase all the coal it needed from Wickham. Such an agreement is called a requirements contract, which is further discussed next.

Sometimes a party may mischaracterize a unilateral contract as an illusory promise, as happened in the following case.

---

2. Wickham & Burton Coal Co. v. Farmers' Lumber Co., 179 N.W. 417 (Iowa 1920).

| A CASE IN POINT | IN THE LANGUAGE OF THE COURT |

CASE 7.2
DAHL v. HEM PHARMACEUTICALS CORP.
United States Court of Appeals for the Ninth Circuit
7 F.3d 1399 (9th Cir. 1993).

FACTS HEM Pharmaceuticals Corporation designed a new drug, Ampligen, to fight chronic fatigue syndrome. Typically, new medicines go through several phases of clinical evaluation before FDA approval and general release onto the market. As part of that process, HEM began a clinical trial with 92 patients to evaluate the effectiveness, side effects, and risks of Ampligen.

Dahl and the other patients signed consent forms warning of the experimental nature of Ampligen and its possible side effects. Although the patients were free to withdraw from the clinical trial at any time, if they remained in the study they were required to accept the risks of treatment, to forego other drugs, to not become pregnant, and to submit to intrusive and uncomfortable testing for one year. In return, after the testing ended they would be entitled to receive Ampligen for a full year at no charge.

Case 7.2 continues

Case 7.2 continued

At the end of the yearlong study, HEM refused to provide the year's supply of the drug to the patients free of charge. The patients sued HEM for breach of contract and asked for a preliminary injunction to compel the company to uphold its side of the contract and provide the drug without charge for one year.

The trial court granted the preliminary injunction, and HEM appealed.

ISSUE PRESENTED   Is voluntary participation in clinical trials sufficient consideration to form a contract when the participants could have dropped out of the trials at any time?

OPINION   KLEINFELD, J., writing for the U.S. Court of Appeals:

The arrangement with the experimental subjects was that they would participate in the double-blind study for a year. This was to facilitate evaluation of the safety and effectiveness of Ampligen. After the double-blind phase of testing ended, they would be entitled to receive Ampligen for a full year at no charge. The consent forms included a conditional promise of additional Ampligen after the double-blind study was completed:

> If statistical analysis of the endpoints show that Ampligen shows efficacy compared to placebo, then following completion of all termination procedures, you understand that if you received placebo on study, you will be offered Ampligen and will re-enter and follow the same protocol as if you had been randomized to receive Ampligen on study. If you received Ampligen on study, you understand that you will be offered continuation on Ampligen and will re-enter and follow the same protocol.
>
> …

HEM argues that as a matter of contract law, petitioners' probability of success on the merits was low, because its promise was not supported by consideration. This argument is without merit. The patients submitted themselves to months of periodic injections with an experimental drug or, unbeknownst to them, mere saline solution, combined with intrusive and necessarily uncomfortable testing to determine their condition as the tests proceeded. HEM sought to have them participate in its study so that it could obtain FDA approval for its new drug.

HEM argues that because petitioners participated voluntarily and were free to withdraw, they had no binding obligation and so gave no consideration. Somehow the category of unilateral contracts appears to have escaped HEM's notice. The deal was, "if you submit to our experiment, we will give you a year's supply of Ampligen at no charge." This form of agreement resembles that in the case taught in the first year of law school.[3] There, an uncle promised his nephew that if he would refrain from drinking, using tobacco, or playing cards and billiards until age 21, he would receive $5,000. The court held that consideration had been given because the nephew had refrained from the prohibited activities during the requisite period on the faith of his uncle's promise. He had accepted the offer by completing performance.

Case 7.2 continues

---

3. Hamer v. Sidway, 27 N.E. 256 (N.Y. 1891).

Case 7.2 continued

In this case, the petitioners performed by submitting to the double-blind tests. They incurred the detriment of being tested upon for HEM's studies in exchange for the promise of a year's treatment of Ampligen. Upon completion of the double-blind tests, there was a binding contract.

RESULT   The trial court's grant of a preliminary injunction was affirmed. HEM was required to provide Ampligen to the petitioners who wanted it.

COMMENTS   The court harshly notes HEM's failure to understand the validity of unilateral contracts, that is, contracts in which an act is traded for a promise. In a unilateral contract, the act—or refraining from the act—may constitute consideration. In the case of HEM's trial subjects, they both underwent experimentation and examination and refrained from taking other drugs that might have helped their chronic fatigue.

Perhaps HEM was hoping the court would confuse the contract in question with a bilateral contract, where one promise is exchanged for another. In that case, a promise that the promisor is free to fulfill or not is illusory. HEM's patients, however, did not make a promise; they acted and refrained from certain actions. There was nothing illusory about their intrusive and necessarily uncomfortable testing.

Questions

1.   Given that HEM promised sufferers of chronic fatigue syndrome a much-needed medicine if they helped HEM in its study, was it ethical to refuse to supply the drug, to require patients to litigate, and even to put forward a legal defense?

2.   What type of act or refraining from acting by the patients might have led the court to find for HEM and declare the contract void for lack of consideration?

Conditional Promises

Conditional promises often look illusory, but they are enforceable as long as the promisor is bound by conditions beyond his or her control. For example, Xerox promises to hire Diane as an inventor on condition that the Patent and Trademark Office issues a patent on her new photocopying process. Although the likelihood of obtaining a patent may be remote, the decision is out of the parties' hands. If the patent is issued, Xerox will be obligated to hire Diane. The contract is valid at the time it is agreed upon, but performance is not required until the condition is satisfied.

If the condition is not satisfied, either party can cancel the contract. For example, a partner might agree to sell his share of the partnership for ten times the partnership's earnings on condition that an audit of the partnership's books shows earnings of at least $5 million. The partner will not be obligated to sell his share if the earnings of the partnership are less than $5 million.

There are three types of conditions: (1) conditions precedent; (2) conditions concurrent; and (3) conditions subsequent. A *condition precedent* is a condition that must be satisfied before performance under a contract is due. For example, if Martin agrees to buy Josie's house, provided he can obtain financing at less than 8% for 30 years within 60 days of signing the contract, then Martin's obtaining the specified financing is a condition precedent to his duty to buy the house. If the condition is satisfied, he must buy the house; if it is not, the contract will fail and Martin will not be required to buy the house. When a condition is partially within the control of one party, that party will often have an implied-in-law duty to use best efforts to cause the condition to be satisfied.

Conditions concurrent occur when the mutual duties of performance are to take place simultaneously. For example, a buyer's obligation to pay for goods often does not become absolute until the seller tenders or delivers the goods. Similarly, the seller's obligation to deliver the goods does not become absolute until the buyer tenders or actually makes payment.

A *condition subsequent* is a contract term that operates to terminate an existing contractual obligation if that condition occurs. For example, Sarah promises to wash Kate's car on Tuesday unless it rains beforehand. If it rains Monday evening, the condition subsequent is fulfilled, and the parties' obligations under the contract are terminated.

Requirements and Output Contracts

In a *requirements contract*, the buyer agrees to buy all its requirements of a specified commodity, such as steel, from the seller, and the seller agrees to meet those requirements. The parties do not know how much steel the buyer will actually need, but whatever that amount is, the buyer will buy it all from that seller. The buyer is constrained from buying steel from another supplier.

In an *output contract*, the buyer promises to buy all the output that the seller produces. Again, the parties do not how know many units that will be, but the seller must sell all its output to that buyer. The seller cannot sell any of its product to another buyer.

These types of contracts are not enforceable if the requirement or output is unreasonable or out of proportion to prior requirements or outputs. For example, the buyer cannot take advantage of the seller by increasing its requirement to triple the usual amount. The seller will not be required to sell anything over the reasonable or usual amount required by the buyer.

Promissory Estoppel

The primary exception to the rule that only promises supported by consideration will be enforced is the doctrine of promissory estoppel. *Promissory estoppel* (sometimes referred to as *detrimental reliance*) provides an exception to this rule only if four requirements are met: (1) a promise, (2) justifiable reliance, (3) forseeability, and (4) injustice.

Promise   There must be a promise. A statement of future intent is not sufficient, nor is an estimate or a misstatement of fact. For example, Hank asks Bart the time, and Bart mistakenly tells Hank it is two o'clock when it is actually three o'clock. As a result Hank misses an important appointment. Hank relied on the information to his detriment, but there was no promise.

"The paper and ink content is within acceptable norms, but the contract itself appears to have too many clauses."

Copyright 1996 Ted Goff. *Used by permission.*

Justifiable Reliance   The promise must cause the promisee to take an action that he or she would not have otherwise taken. When the niece Jaye buys the plane ticket to Hawaii, she is relying on Aunt Leila's promise. If Jaye had not bought the ticket, there would be no reliance, and her aunt would be free to take back her promise.

Foreseeability   The action taken in reliance on the promise must be reasonably foreseeable by the promisor. It is foreseeable that the niece would buy a plane ticket as a result of her aunt's promise. It is not foreseeable that she would quit her job to take a six-month vacation in Hawaii. Therefore, the aunt would probably have to pay for the plane ticket but not for the niece's lost wages.

Injustice   A promise that has been reasonably relied on will give rise to relief only if the failure to do so would cause injustice. The exact meaning of "injustice" has been debated in a variety of legal tracts, but a good rule of thumb is to ask whether the promisee has been harmed by his or her reliance on the promise. If the niece had made a plane reservation that could be cancelled without penalty, there would be no injustice in letting the aunt take back her promise; thus promissory estoppel would not apply.

The original interpretation of promissory estoppel was that it applied only to gifts, not to bilateral exchanges. A series of cases in the mid-1960s, however, used promissory estoppel to enforce promises made in the course of contract negotiations. The leading case is set forth next.

| A CASE IN POINT | IN THE LANGUAGE OF THE COURT |

CASE 7.3
HOFFMAN v. RED OWL
STORES, INC.
Supreme Court of Wisconsin
133 N.W.2d 267 (Wis. 1965).

FACTS   Hoffman negotiated with Red Owl Stores, Inc. to open a Red Owl grocery store. The negotiations went through several stages and continued for more than two years before they broke down.

When Hoffman first approached Red Owl about buying a franchise, he said he had only $18,000 to invest. Red Owl assured him that this amount would be sufficient. Hoffman already owned a bakery and, with Red Owl's encouragement, he bought a small grocery store to get more experience. The store was profitable, but Red Owl advised Hoffman to sell it because he would have a larger Red Owl store within a few months. A site in the nearby city of Chilton was soon found for the new store, and Hoffman paid the $1,000 deposit. Meanwhile, Hoffman had also rented a residence for himself and his family near the new site.

Red Owl then told Hoffman that he had to sell his bakery before the franchise deal could go through. He sold it, and negotiations proceeded regarding the details of financing and leasing the new store. At this stage, Red Owl increased Hoffman's required investment from $18,000 to $24,100, and a few weeks later to $26,100. Hoffman requested money from his father-in-law, who agreed to put money into the business, provided he could come in as a partner. Negotiations broke down when Red Owl insisted that the father-in-law sign an agreement stating that the money he was advancing was an outright gift. Hoffman sued Red Owl for damages based on the defendant's failure to keep promises that had induced him to act to his detriment.

ISSUE PRESENTED   Can a party to failed negotiations successfully assert a claim for promissory estoppel based on precontractual negotiations and agreements and his acts taken in reliance thereon?

OPINION   CURRIE, C. J., writing for the Wisconsin Supreme Court:

Many courts of other jurisdictions have seen fit over the years to adopt the principle of promissory estoppel, and the tendency in that direction continues. As Mr. Justice McFaddin, speaking in behalf of the Arkansas court, well stated, the development of the law of promissory estoppel "is an attempt by the courts to keep remedies abreast of increased moral consciousness of honesty and fair representations in all business dealings."[4]

. . .

The record here discloses a number of promises and assurances given to Hoffman by Lukowitz on behalf of Red Owl upon which plaintiffs relied and acted upon to their detriment.

Foremost were the promises that for the sum of $18,000 Red Owl would establish Hoffman in a store. After Hoffman had sold his grocery store and paid the $1,000 on the Chilton lot, the $18,000 figure was changed to $24,100. Then in November 1961, Hoffman was assured that if the $24,100 figure were increased by $2,000 the deal would go through. Hoffman was induced to sell his grocery store fixtures and

Case 7.3 continues

4. Peoples Nat'l Bank of Little Rock v. Linebarger Constr. Co., 240 S.W.2d 12, 16 (Ark. 1951).

Case 7.3 continued

inventory in June 1961, on the promise that he would be in his new store by fall. In November, plaintiffs sold their bakery building on the urging of defendants and on the assurance that this was the last step necessary to have the deal with Red Owl go through.

. . .

There remains for consideration the question of law raised by defendants that agreement was never reached on essential factors necessary to establish a contract between Hoffman and Red Owl. Among these were the size, cost, design, and layout of the store building; and the terms of the lease with respect to rent, maintenance, renewal, and purchase options. This poses the question of whether the promise necessary to sustain a cause of action for promissory estoppel must embrace all essential details of a proposed transaction between promisor and promisee so as to be the equivalent of an offer that would result in a binding contract between the parties if the promisee were to accept the same.

Originally the doctrine of promissory estoppel was invoked as a substitute for consideration rendering a gratuitous promise enforceable as a contract. In other words, the acts of reliance by the promisee to his detriment provided a substitute for consideration. If promissory estoppel were to be limited to only those situations where the promise giving rise to the cause of action must be so definite with respect to all details that a contract would result were the promise supported by consideration, then the defendants' instant promises to Hoffman would not meet this test. However, . . . [it is not necessary that] the requirement that the promise giving rise to the cause of action must be so comprehensive in scope as to meet the requirements of an offer that would ripen into a contract if accepted by the promisee.

Rather the conditions imposed are:

(1) Was the promise one which the promisor should reasonably expect to induce action or forbearance of a definite and substantial character on the part of the promisee?
(2) Did the promise induce such action or forbearance?
(3) Can injustice be avoided only by enforcement of the promise?

We deem it would be a mistake to regard an action grounded on promissory estoppel as the equivalent of a breach of contract action. As Dean Boyer points out, it is desirable that fluidity in the application of the concept be maintained.[5]

. . .

We conclude that injustice would result here if plaintiffs were not granted some relief because of the failure of defendants to keep their promises that induced plaintiffs to act to their detriment.

. . .

"The wrong is not primarily in depriving the plaintiff of the promised reward but in causing the plaintiff to change position to his detriment. It would follow that the

Case 7.3 continues

---

[5]. Benjamin F. Boyer, *Promissory Estoppel: Requirements and Limitations of the Doctrine*, 98 U. PA. L. REV. 459, 497 (1950).

Case 7.3 continued

damages should not exceed the loss caused by the change of position, which would never be more in amount, but might be less, than the promised reward."[6]

RESULT   The Wisconsin Supreme Court awarded damages to the plaintiffs for all items except for one—damages for the loss, if any, on the sale of the grocery store, fixtures, and inventory—as to which a new trial was ordered to determine appropriate damages.

Questions

1. Assuming Hoffman relocated his family to be near the new store site, should the personal moving expenses of Hoffman's family be reimbursed?
2. Suppose Hoffman made less money at his new job at the grocery store than he had previously made at the bakery. Given that Hoffman had taken on this job at the grocery store only to gain experience before owning a Red Owl, should he be compensated for his lost profits?

---

6. Warren Seavey, *Reliance on Gratuitous Promises or Other Conduct*, 64 HARV. L. REV. 913, 926 (1951).

 Capacity

A valid contract requires that both parties possess the capacity to enter into an agreement. *Capacity* to contract is a legal term of art that refers to a person's ability to understand the nature and effect of an agreement. The widely accepted rule is that minors and mentally incompetent persons lack capacity.

The law's concern is that one party may take advantage of a person who is unable to protect his or her interests. As a result, the law generally gives minors or incompetent persons the power to repudiate their obligations under the contract. In other words, such contracts are *voidable* at the option of the person lacking capacity: He or she can enforce the contract if it is favorable to him or her, or avoid the contract if it is not. Moreover, in some states minors not only have the power to avoid their contractual obligations, they are even entitled to retain any property they may have acquired under the voidable contract.

These voidability rules are subject to certain limitations. Both minors and mentally incompetent persons will be held to contracts for necessaries, such as food, clothing, and shelter. Otherwise, no one would be willing to provide the necessaries a minor or mentally incompetent person needs to survive. Both minors and mentally incompetent persons can ratify (agree to be bound by) contracts after they reach majority or gain competency. In many states, minors cannot repudiate their contractual obligations if they misrepresented their age to the other party.

Finally, it should be noted that contracts entered into by incompetent persons have the potential to be either void, voidable (at the option of the incompetent person), or valid. If the party has been legally adjudged incompetent and appointed a guardian, the contract is void. If he or she simply lacked mental capacity to comprehend the subject matter, the contract is voidable. If the party was able to understand the nature and effect of the agreement, however, then even if he or she lacked capacity to engage in other activities, the contract is valid, with no voidability option.

 Legality

Contracts must have a purpose that is legal. Contracts that are either contrary to a statute or contrary to public policy are illegal and are generally considered void—that is, they are not valid contracts at all.

Licensing Statutes

Many states require licenses for the conduct of particular kinds of business, ranging from real estate and securities broker licenses to chauffeur licenses to contractor licenses. Many statutes provide that if a party fails to have a required license, the other party to the contract does not have to fulfill its side of the bargain, usually payment. This is true even if the unlicensed party performed the work perfectly and even if the other party knew that the person doing the work was unlicensed.

Other Contracts Contrary to Statute

Sometimes a statute will expressly make a contract illegal. For example, *usury statutes*, which limit the interest rate on loans, usually provide that any loan agreement in violation of the statute is unenforceable. In some jurisdictions, this means that no amount of interest can be collected; in some states, the principal amount of the loan is not collectible either. Loans that violate the usury statutes also violate criminal law.

Other examples of *illegal contracts* include price-fixing agreements in violation of the antitrust laws, bribes, wagering contracts, or bets in violation of applicable gambling laws, and unreasonable covenants not to compete. To be reasonable, a *covenant not to compete* entered into in connection with the sale of a business must be reasonable as to scope of activities, length of time, and geographic area and must be necessary to protect trade secrets or goodwill. The enforceability of covenants not to compete in the employment context is discussed in Chapter 12.

Unconscionability

A contract term is *unconscionable* if it is oppressive or fundamentally unfair. This concept is applied most often to consumer contracts when the consumer may have little or no bargaining power. The purchase terms are dictated by the seller, and the buyer can take it or leave it. For example, an exorbitantly high price, such as $900 for an item valued at $350, can be considered unconscionable if the item is a necessity and the consumer has no other option but to buy from that particular seller.

A recent case presents the issue vividly. In August 1997, the state of Florida settled a suit against the tobacco industry for more than $11 billion. Florida had hired a group of outside attorneys to represent it in the case. They entered into a contract that called for the attorneys to receive a 25% contingency fee. The settlement agreement with the tobacco industry called for attorney's fees to be determined by an independent

arbitrator. After the settlement agreement was signed, several of the state's outside attorneys went to court in an effort to enforce their 25% contingency-fee contract.

A Florida state judge denied their claim on unconscionability grounds. The court stated that a fee of tens of millions of dollars or perhaps even hundreds of millions could be reasonable, "but a fee of 2.8 *billion* dollars simply shocks the conscience of the court." The court calculated that if the 12 principal lawyers had worked around the clock beginning at the outset of negotiations in mid-1994 through the end of 1997, they would be paid the equivalent of $7,716 per hour if the contingent-fee agreement were upheld. The court found these figures to be "patently ridiculous" and "per se unreasonable."[7]

Courts usually refuse to enforce contract terms that they find unconscionable. When the term is central to the contract, the court can either rewrite the term (for example, by substituting a fair market price) or void the contract. As the Historical Perspective in this chapter describes further, the doctrine of unconscionability had its origins in Roman law.

Unconscionability has both a procedural and a substantive element.

Procedural Element   The procedural element focuses on two factors: oppression and surprise. *Oppression* arises from an inequality of bargaining power that results in no real negotiation and an absence of meaningful choice for one party to the contract. *Surprise* arises when the terms of the contract are hidden in a densely printed form drafted by the party seeking to enforce these terms. Form contracts are usually drafted by the party with the superior bargaining position.

Substantive Element   No precise definition of substantive unconscionability can be set forth. Courts have talked in terms of "overly harsh" or "one-sided" results. One commentator has pointed out that unconscionability turns not only on a "one-sided" result but also on an absence of justification for it. The most detailed and specific commentaries observe that a contract is largely an allocation of risk between the parties, and therefore a contractual term is substantively suspect if it reallocates the risk of the bargain in an objectively unreasonable or unexpected manner. But not all unreasonable risk allocations are

---

7. John McKinnon, *Florida Judge Blocks Lawyers' Bid to Collect Tobacco-Accord Fee*, WALL ST. J., Nov. 13, 1997, at B3.

HISTORICAL PERSPECTIVE

UNCONSCIONABILITY AND FREEDOM OF CONTRACT

The principle of freedom of contract embodies the idea that the judicial system should give effect to the expressed intention of parties to an agreement. This has always been a fundamental precept of Western legal systems. It is based on the belief that the terms of a contract express the free will of the contracting parties. Parties should be able to dispose of their property and services in any manner they see fit.

It is difficult for a court to evaluate the fairness of a contract and to figure out the relative values of a business deal to the parties. Accordingly, courts observe the general principle that they should not substitute their judgment about the fairness of a contract for that of the parties.

Freedom of contract ensures that the law does not unduly restrict the ability of the competitive market to bring about productive and allocative efficiency. *Productive efficiency* exists when competition among parties seeking to earn profits results in resources flowing to lowest-cost producers of a good. *Allocative efficiency* exists when goods and services are produced up to the point at which the cost of production of goods equals their price, which results in efficient allocation of scarce societal resources to the production of various goods.

Leaving the parties to define the contract terms as they see fit will result in greater maximization of profitability, provided three conditions are met: (1) the parties to the contract are better informed than the courts about the conditions under which the benefits of the deal can be maximized; (2) the parties are equally well informed and enjoy roughly equal bargaining power; and (3) the legislature is unable to provide rules detailed enough to govern the particular business situations in which the contract was agreed.

Naturally, these conditions are met more fully in some contexts than in others. Also, public policy concerns must be respected; contracts that produce results contrary to public policy should not be enforced, even if they enhance economic efficiency. Courts have therefore created exceptions to the principle of freedom of contract, voiding contracts in two types of cases: (1) when the three conditions mentioned above are not met; and (2) when the purpose or the result of the contract violates public policy.

The first type of case, in which the conditions necessary for freedom of contract to maximize economic efficiency are not met, may be characterized as involving procedural unconscionability. The second type of case, in which the contract leads to a result that is against public policy, may be characterized as involving substantive unconscionability.

These concepts date back to Aristotelian theory and Roman law.[a] Under Roman law, each party to an exchange had to give something equal in value to what he or she received. Unequal exchanges were considered fundamentally unjust. The law remedied the injustice in extreme cases through the doctrine of *laesio enormis*. This doctrine developed from language in the Code of Justinian that provided a remedy for those who sold land for less than half its "just price." *Laesio enormis* expanded this provision to cover contracts for goods whose contract price deviated by at least half from the just price. Under the Roman system, the just price was the market price for similar goods under similar circumstances. The German and French laws that relieve a party from its obligations under a contract that is not for the just price have their roots in the Roman doctrine of *laesio enormis*.

In the United States and England, the general principle of freedom of contract, embodied in the common law rule that the judiciary will not examine the fairness of an exchange, has always been limited by the doctrine of unconscionability. In the eighteenth century, unequal exchanges were considered evidence of fraud in the making of the contract. Courts would refuse to enforce unconscionable contracts, which were generally defined as those involving harsh or oppressive terms of exchange.

The coming of the Industrial Revolution and the emergence of large corporations in the mid-1800s brought about fundamental changes in the mode of analysis of contract law. As goods became more complex, the seller typically had greater knowledge of them

Historical Perspective continues

Historical Perspective continued

than the buyer, and the bargaining power of large corporations often greatly exceeded that of the individuals with whom they contracted. Thus, a greater number of contracts failed to satisfy the "equal footing" condition necessary to make freedom of contract efficiency-enhancing. Consequently, courts became less hesitant to intervene to protect the party to a contract who was perceived to be weaker. The doctrine of unconscionability was expanded to cover situations where the parties were not on an equal footing.

Modern courts have also been willing to void contracts on grounds of substantive unconscionability. For example, in *American Home Improvement, Inc. v. MacIver*,[b] the New Hampshire Supreme Court held that a contract for the payment of $1,750 plus

$800 in credit charges for the purchase and installation of 14 windows, a door, and a coating for the sidewalks of a house was unconscionable because the goods and services were worth far less than the price. The court focused not on the process by which the contract was formed but on the unjust result of the bargain struck. (Other cases applying the doctrine of unconscionability to the sale of goods under Article 2 of the Uniform Commercial Code are discussed in Chapter 8.)

---

a. The discussion of Roman, French, German, and English law and certain aspects of the discussion of U.S. law set forth above are based upon James Gordley, *Equality in Exchange*, 69 CAL. L. REV. 1587 (1981), and the authorities cited therein.

b. 201 A.2d 886 (N.H. 1964).

---

unconscionable. The greater the unfair surprise or the inequality of bargaining power, the less likely the courts will tolerate an unreasonable risk allocation.

Releases   Persons are sometimes asked to sign a general release, especially before embarking on a dangerous activity such as skydiving or race car driving. A *general release* purports to relieve the owner of the facility of

any liability for injuries suffered by the person using the facility, including liability for negligence. A number of earlier cases have held that the exculpatory language in a general release agreement was invalid because the agreement was unconscionable. There appears to be a trend toward honoring these releases, however, as demonstrated in the following case.

A CASE IN POINT	IN THE LANGUAGE OF THE COURT

CASE 7.4
KURASHIGE v. INDIAN DUNES, INC.
California Court of Appeal
246 Cal. Rptr. 310
(Cal. Ct. App. 1988).

FACTS   Indian Dunes Park, owned by Indian Dunes, Inc., was used by the general public for motorcycle dirt-bike riding. On December 21, 1982, Kurashige was injured while riding his motorcycle on the park's trails. Before using the park, Kurashige had signed a general release agreement, which was printed in red ink with ten-point bold type and capital letters saying: "SINCE ALL MOTORBIKE RIDING IS DANGEROUS WE REQUIRE ALL RIDERS AND VISITORS TO ASSUME ALL RISK BY SIGNING THIS GENERAL RELEASE." At the bottom of the agreement, the words "MOTORCYCLING IS DANGEROUS" were printed in red in 17-point bold type. Below the agreement were three columns of 28 lines each for the riders to sign. Printed on each of the 84 lines were the words "THIS IS A RELEASE" in capital letters.

The agreement provided in pertinent part that each of the undersigned "Hereby Releases, Waives, Discharges and Covenants not to sue [defendants], all for purposes herein referred to as Releasees, from all liability to the Undersigned . . . for all loss or damage and any claim or demands therefor, on account of injury to the person or

Case 7.4 continues

Case 7.4 continued

property or resulting in death of the Undersigned, whether caused by the negligence of Releasees or otherwise while the Undersigned is upon the Park premises. . . ."

Kurashige suffered injury and sued the owner of Indian Dunes. The trial court granted summary judgment in favor of Indian Dunes. By granting the motion for summary judgment, the court took the issue of liability away from the jury and decided as a matter of law that the defendant should prevail. Kurashige appealed.

ISSUE PRESENTED   Is the exculpatory language in a general release agreement enforceable as a general matter and, more specifically, as against a claim of unconscionability?

OPINION   SPENCER, J., writing for the California Court of Appeal:
[The court began by considering whether any general release, regardless of terms, was valid. Relying on *Tunkl v. Regents of the University of California*,[8] the court held that an exculpatory provision may stand only if it does not involve "the public interest."]

. . . [T]he "General Release" agreement used here was printed legibly, contained adequate, clear and explicit exculpatory language and indicated defendants were to be absolved from the consequences of their own negligence. Furthermore, it did not involve the public interest: defendants' business was not generally thought to be suitable for public regulation; defendants did not perform a service of great importance to the public, and the business was not a matter of practical necessity for members of the public; and defendants' customers did not place their persons under defendants' control.

. . .

[The court then addressed the plaintiff's contention that the general release was unconscionable.] Turning to the procedural element of unconscionability, the first question is whether the "General Release" agreement was oppressive, whether there was "an inequality in bargaining power which result[ed] in no real negotiation and 'an absence of meaningful choice.'"[9] The record shows there was no real negotiation; the "General Release" agreement was preprinted and all users of Indian Dunes Park were required to sign it before using the park. However, the record does not show plaintiff had no meaningful choice in deciding to sign the agreement. . . . There is no evidence plaintiff could not have ridden his motorcycle elsewhere without the constraints imposed upon him by defendants.

The next question is whether plaintiff was surprised by supposedly agreed-upon terms hidden within a printed form drafted by defendants. The entire release agreement was printed at the top of the form signed by plaintiff. Warnings as to the dangers of motorcycling, the rider's assumption of the risk and the release and waiver of all liability stood out and the exculpatory provisions of the agreement were clearly set forth. Thus, the agreement was not procedurally unconscionable.

Case 7.4 continues

---

8. 383 P.2d 441 (Cal. 1963).

9. A & M Produce Co. v. FMC Corp., 186 Cal. Rptr. 114 (Cal. Ct. App. 1982).

Case 7.4 continued

In examining the issue of substantive unconscionability, one question to be asked is whether the agreement was one-sided and, if so, whether the one-sidedness was justified. A further question is whether the agreement reallocated the risks of the bargain in an objectively unreasonable or unexpected manner. Risk reallocation which will be subjected to special scrutiny is that in which the risk shifted to a party is one that only the other party can avoid. Clearly, the agreement here was one-sided; all of the risk was reallocated to the Park's user, plaintiff. As previously discussed, the risk reallocation was not unexpected; the agreement clearly indicated the user assumed all risk of his use of the Park's facilities.

Was the risk reallocation objectively unreasonable? One signing the agreement warrants he knows "the present condition [of the Park and] that said condition may become more hazardous and dangerous during the time [he is] upon said premises." The agreement warned the user motorcycling is dangerous; implicit in the knowledge of the danger of motorcycling "is the knowledge that riding over rough, uneven terrain in an outdoor park poses a risk of injury from a fall" or other accident.[10] Moreover, to a certain extent, the risk of injury is conditioned upon the user's skill and experience as a motorcycle rider, factors over which the Park's owners and operators have no control. In view of the foregoing, the risk reallocation was not unreasonable and the "General Release" agreement was not substantively unconscionable.

RESULT   The appeals court upheld the general release and affirmed the trial court's grant of summary judgment for the defendant Indian Dunes.

COMMENTS   It would appear that the court would limit the use of general releases in a county hospital. Would it matter if the hospital were private?

Questions

1. Would the result in this case have been any different if the plaintiff had been thrown off his bike after riding into a barbed-wire fence not visible from the hill he had just crested? What about a big hole on the other side of the hill?
2. What would the court consider a practical necessity for members of the public? A bus? A cosmetic surgery clinic? A public park for camping that charges a small fee?

---

10. Coates v. Newhall Land & Farming, Inc., 236 Cal. Rptr. 181 (Cal. Ct. App. 1987).

 Genuineness of Assent

Even if a contract meets all the requirements of validity (agreement, consideration, capacity, and legality), it may not be enforceable if there was no true "meeting of the minds" between the two parties. In other words, a court will refuse to enforce a contract if it feels one or both of the parties did not genuinely assent to the terms of the contract. The discussion below examines a variety of problems that could prevent a true meeting of the minds.

Fraud

A contract is voidable if it is tainted with fraud. There are two types of fraud: fraud in the factum and fraud in the inducement. *Fraud in the factum* occurs when a party is persuaded to sign one document thinking that it is another. For example, if a person were given a deed

ETHICAL CONSIDERATION

Envelopes for the processing of photographic film typically contain printed language on the outside of the envelope stating that in the event of loss, defect, or negligence in the processing, the purchaser's damages are limited to the replacement of the film and processing. Shortly before Mr. Sam Smoke died of a heart attack, his wife, Sara Smoke, took pictures of him playing with his new granddaughter. After his death, Mrs. Smoke took the film to Photo-Finish for processing. She gave the company her name but did not sign anything. Photo-Finish lost the film. Mrs. Smoke sued for negligence and claimed damages to compensate her for the emotional distress caused by the loss of the invaluable pictures. What is Photo-Finish legally required to do? What should it do?

to sign for the transfer of real property, after being told he was signing an employment agreement, the deed could be voided by the defrauded party.

The second type of fraud, *fraud in the inducement*, occurs when a party makes a false statement to persuade the other party to enter into an agreement. For example, if a jeweler told a customer that the stone in a ring was a diamond, when the jeweler knew it was zirconium, an agreement to purchase the ring would be fraudulent, and the purchaser would have the right to rescind, that is, cancel, the contract. A contract is not voidable due to fraudulent misrepresentation unless the misrepresentation was material to the bargain and relied on by the party seeking to void the contract.

A variation of the second kind of fraud—called *promissory fraud*—occurs when one party induces another to enter into a contract by promising to do something without having the intention to carry out the promise. Because a promise to do something necessarily implies the intention to perform, when a promise is made without such an intention, there is an implied misrepresentation of fact that can give the other party the right to rescind the contract.

Another variation of fraud in the inducement occurs when a party has a duty to disclose information to

the other party but fails to do so. For example, a partner who knows the true value of a piece of property cannot sell it to a fellow partner without disclosing the true value. Often a duty to disclose arises out of a special relationship between the parties (that is, a fiduciary relationship), such as between partners or between a trustee and beneficiary.

Duress

A contract is also voidable if one party was forced to enter into it through fear created by threats. Thus, inducing someone to sign a contract by blackmail or extortion is duress. There can be more subtle forms of pressure, such as an implied threat that at-will employees will lose their jobs unless they sign agreements waiving certain rights to employee benefits. Because duress is present only if the threatened act is wrongful or illegal, this type of pressure would not constitute duress.

Economic duress is usually not enough to invalidate a contract. Thus, many courts would uphold an agreement to sell a farm even if the owner had to sell it at a bargain price to avoid bankruptcy. Similarly, threats to withhold future business from a supplier unless more favorable terms are negotiated are not grounds to void a subsequent contract.

Under the related doctrine of *undue influence*, a court may invalidate an agreement if one party had sufficient influence and power over the other as to make genuine assent impossible. For example, if an invalid living alone, with few contacts with the outside world and dependent on a caregiver, agreed to sell her house to the caregiver at a bargain price, that agreement might be set aside based on undue influence.

Ambiguity

Misunderstandings may arise from ambiguous language in a contract or from a mistake as to the facts. If the

ETHICAL CONSIDERATION

Is it unethical to take advantage of someone's financial hardship to drive a hard bargain?

terms of a contract are subject to differing interpretations, some courts will construe the ambiguity against the party who drafted the agreement. More often, courts will apply the following rule: The party that would be adversely affected by a particular interpretation can void, or undo, a contract when (1) both interpretations are reasonable, and (2) the parties either both knew or both did not know of the different interpretations. If only one party knew or had reason to know of the other's interpretation, the court will find for the party who did not know or did not have reason to know of the difference.

For example, in a case involving Mark Suwyn, an executive vice-president of International Paper Company (the world's largest paper company), a federal court refused to enjoin Suwyn from joining Louisiana-Pacific, a producer of wood products.[11] Suwyn had signed a broad covenant not to compete with International Paper after allegedly being assured by International Paper's chairman and chief executive officer John Georges that the covenant was aimed at preventing Suwyn from going to one of the big paper companies. Suwyn had attached to the signed agreement a note indicating that it was meant to prevent him from joining a major paper company such as Georgia-Pacific, Champion, or Weyerhauser. Because Louisiana-Pacific did not make paper and was not on the list, Suwyn argued that he was free to join the company. Georges responded that the noncompete agreement was broad and included wood products, such as plywood and lumber, that both companies produced. The judge ruled that Suwyn and Georges had such different meanings in mind that there had been no real agreement on the noncompete pact. As a result, there was no contract.

Mistake of Fact

Like misunderstanding due to ambiguity, a *mistake of fact* can make a contract voidable, that is, subject to being undone by one or more parties. A court's willingness to undo a contract based on a mistaken assumption of fact depends heavily on the particular circumstances. The court will look at three factors to determine if a mistake has been made: (1) the substantiality of the mistake; (2) whether the risks were allocated; and (3) timing.

Substantiality of the Mistake   A court is more likely to void the contract when the mistake has a material effect on one of the parties. For example, in the classic case *Raffles v. Wichelhaus*,[12] two parties had signed a contract in which Wichelhaus agreed to buy 125 bales of cotton to be brought by Raffles from India on a ship named *Peerless*. There were, however, two ships named *Peerless*, both sailing out of Bombay during the same year. Raffles meant the *Peerless* that was sailing in December, and Wichelhaus meant the *Peerless* that was sailing in October. When the cotton arrived in the later ship, Wichelhaus refused to complete the purchase, and Raffles sued for breach of contract. The English court held that the contract was voidable due to the mutual mistake of fact. The court described the situation as one of "latent ambiguity" and declared that there was no meeting of the minds and therefore no contract.

Note that the three-month delay made the cotton worthless to the buyer and thus the mistake was substantial. What if the delay had been only a few days? In that case, the court would probably have enforced the contract. On the other hand, even if the delay had only been a few days, if the buyer had planned to resell the cotton on the open market and the price of cotton had dropped sharply between the arrival of the first and the arrival of the second ship, then the mistake would probably have been substantial enough to make the contract voidable.

Allocation of the Risks   If one party accepts a risk, then this allocation of risk becomes part of the bargain even if it is doubtful the risk will materialize, and that party must bear the consequences. For example, suppose Gerald wants to sell Cameron a house. He says he is uncertain whether the house needs a retaining wall to bolster the foundation. Cameron does not want to pay for a report by a structural engineer. She says she doesn't think the house needs a retaining wall and that she is willing to take the risk of being wrong about that if Gerald will lower the selling price. They sign a contract to this effect. Structural damage is subsequently discovered. The parties have allocated the risk of a mistake about the need for a retaining wall, and the contract is valid.

If the parties have not expressly allocated a risk, sometimes a court will place the risk on the party that

---

11. William M. Carley, *CEO Gets Hard Lesson in How Not to Keep His Top Lieutenants*, WALL. ST. J., Feb. 11, 1998, at A1.

12. 159 Eng. Rep. 375 (Exch. 1864).

had access to the most information. In other cases, it might impose the risk on the party better able to bear it.

Timing The party alleging a mistake of fact must give prompt notice when the mistake is discovered. If too much time passes before the other party is notified, undoing the contract might create more problems than letting it stand.

Mistake of Judgment

A *mistake of judgment* occurs when the parties make an erroneous assessment about some aspect of what is bargained for. For example, in a futures contract a seller agrees to sell a buyer a crop of sugar in three months at a price of 50 cents per pound. The seller is betting that the market price in three months will be less than 50 cents. The buyer is betting that the market price will be higher. One of them will be mistaken, but the futures contract will still be valid. This is a mistake of judgment. Such a mistake is not a valid defense to enforcement of the contract. (The UCC doctrine of commercial impracticability does allow a contract to be voided if there is too great a price shift. This doctrine was at issue in the Westinghouse uranium-supply cases, discussed in Chapter 8.)

The line between judgment and fact is unclear, and cases with similar circumstances can have different outcomes. In one case, the Wisconsin Supreme Court held that a contract to sell a stone for $1 was enforceable when neither party knew at the time that the stone was in fact a diamond.[13]

Under seemingly similar facts, the Michigan Supreme Court held that a contract for the sale of a cow thought to be barren, but later found to be with calf, was a mistake of fact that made the contract unenforceable.[14] The court reasoned:

> If there is a difference or misapprehension as to the substance of the thing bargained for; if the thing actually delivered or received is different in substance from the thing bargained for, and intended to be sold, then there is no contract. . . . A barren cow is substantially a different creature than a breeding one.

A dissenting judge pointed out that the buyer had believed the cow could be made to breed, in spite of the

seller's statements to the contrary, and had decided to take a chance on the purchase. He reasoned:

> There was no mistake of any material fact by either of the parties in the case as would license the vendors to rescind. . . . As to the quality of the animal, subsequently developed, both parties were equally ignorant, and as to this each party took his chances. If this were not the law, there would be no safety in purchasing this kind of stock.

It is unclear whether the assumption that a stone is worth only a dollar or a cow is barren is an assumption of fact or of judgment. As the majority and dissenting opinions in the Michigan case demonstrate, different judges reach different conclusions. One judge might consider the distinction to be merely semantic, whereas another might consider it significant.

Much of contract law comes down to the expectations of the parties involved. In the diamond case, both parties agreed that the value of the stone was unknown. The transaction was thus a conscious allocation of the risks involved. In the cow case, however, the seller did not consider the possibility that the cow was fertile. The buyer did not make known his secret belief that the cow could be made to breed. From the seller's point of view, the transaction was for a barren cow with no chance of breeding. However, the buyer did not see the transaction that way. The case might have come out differently if the buyer had explicitly said to the seller, "I know you believe the cow is barren, but I believe she can be made to breed, and I'm willing to take the chance in buying her."

Disclosing all expectations may make for firm contracts, but it is not the most effective negotiating technique. If the seller believes a cow is fertile, he or she will demand a higher price. Why pay the higher price when the vast majority of business transactions are completed without any need to do battle in the courtroom? One of the challenges of business is balancing the slim (but expensive) chances of litigation against the desire to make an advantageous deal.

 ## Statute of Frauds

Although most oral contracts are enforceable, many states have statutes requiring certain types of contracts to be evidenced by some form of written communication. Such a statute is called a *statute of frauds*. If a contract covered by the statute is oral, it is still a valid contract, but the courts will not enforce it if the statute of

---

13. Wood v. Boynton, 25 N.W. 42 (Wis. 1885).
14. Sherwood v. Walker, 33 N.W. 919 (Mich. 1887).

ETHICAL CONSIDERATION

The possibility that only one party may know the true value of an item being sold raises ethical issues. For example, an antique dealer at a garage sale might see a desk for sale for $50 that he recognizes as a Louis XV desk worth $15,000. Does he have an obligation to disclose the true value to the person holding the garage sale?

Under current law, he probably is not required to disclose the desk's true value unless he has some special relationship to the seller, such as family ties or a business connection in which the other party is relying on him to protect her interest. (See Chapter 1 for a discussion of such a fiduciary duty.) From an ethical point of view, is it fair for the dealer to take advantage of the ignorance of the homeowner, particularly if financial circumstances made it necessary for the homeowner to sell the desk? Should the antique dealer get some reward for the effort he has spent in becoming an expert in antiques and for the time he may have spent pawing through junk at countless garage sales?

Both the stone/diamond case and the barren cow case were decided in the nineteenth century. Similar mistakes about value occur today. A person recently sold a map for $3 that later turned out to be worth more than $19 million. This case appears to be similar to the stone/diamond case in that the parties knew what they were dealing with, namely a map. If a court decided that it should be governed by the stone/diamond case, then the purchaser of the map would have no legal duty to pay the seller any part of the $19 million. Is there a moral duty to share the windfall with the seller? Would the seller have a moral duty to share the loss if the buyer paid $19 million for a map worth only $3?

What if a framed picture sold for $25 turned out to have an original copy of the U.S. Constitution behind the picture? Is this a mistake of judgment or of fact? What, if anything, is the buyer's ethical responsibility to the seller in such a case?

frauds is raised as a defense. Therefore, if neither party raises the issue, the contract will be enforced. Similarly, even if the party seeking to enforce the contract has not

signed anything, it can still enforce the contract against a party that has signed a writing embodying the essential terms of the deal.

There are four traditional justifications for requiring certain contracts to be evidenced by writing. First, requiring a written document avoids fraudulent claims that an oral contract was made. Second, the existence of a written document avoids fraudulent claims as to the terms of the contract. Third, the statute encourages persons to put their agreements in writing, thereby reducing the risk of future misunderstandings. Fourth, the writing required by the statute has the psychological effect of reinforcing the importance of the parties' decision to enter into a contract.

Transactions Subject to the Statute of Frauds

Contracts that must be evidenced by some writing include (1) a contract for the transfer of any interest in real property (such as a deed, lease, or option to buy); (2) a promise to pay the debt of another person; (3) an agreement that by its terms cannot be performed within a year; and (4) a *prenuptial agreement* (that is, an agreement entered into before marriage that sets forth the manner in which the parties' assets will be distributed and the support to which each party will be entitled in the event of divorce).

The statute-of-frauds issue most litigated is whether a contract can by its terms be performed in one year. If it cannot—that is, if the contract is longer than one year in duration—then it must be put in writing to be enforceable.

A typical "performed within one year" case is one involving an oral promise of "lifetime employment." For example, *McInerney v. Charter Golf, Inc.*[15] involved a golf-apparel sales representative who received an offer to join a rival company, which promised to pay him an 8% commission. When notified of this offer, his employer orally promised to guarantee the sales rep a 10% commission "for the remainder of his life," subject to discharge only for dishonesty or disability. The sales rep accepted this offer and passed up the rival's offer. When he was fired three years later, he sued for breach of contract.

_____

15. 680 N.E. 2d 1347 (Ill. 1997).

The Illinois Supreme Court ruled that a lifetime employment contract is intended to be permanent. It inherently anticipates a relationship of long duration—certainly longer than one year. Thus, the court found the contract subject to the statute of frauds and unenforceable because it was not put in writing.

Other courts, however, have taken a contrasting approach. Those courts construe the words "not to be performed" to mean "not capable of being performed within one year." Because, theoretically, an employee can die at any time, these courts reason that lifetime employment contracts are *capable* of being performed within one year. As a result, they deem them outside the scope of the statute of frauds and valid even if not put in writing.

The statute of frauds does not require the agreement to be embodied in a formal, legal-looking document. An agreement can be represented by an exchange of letters that refer to each other, even if no single letter is sufficient to reflect all essential terms. Details or particulars can be omitted; only the essential terms must be stated. What is essential depends on the agreement, its context, and the subsequent conduct of the parties. The UCC has its own statute of frauds, discussed in Chapter 8.

Under the *equal dignities rule*, if an agent acts on behalf of another (the principal) in signing an agreement of the type that must under the statute of frauds be in writing, the authority of the agent to act on behalf of the principal must also be in writing. Thus, an individual signs a written *power of attorney* to authorize a person, called an attorney-in-fact (who need not be a lawyer), to sign documents on the individual's behalf. Corporations authorize officers to sign through a combination of written authority specified in the bylaws of the corporation and the minutes of the governing body, the board of directors.

If there is clear evidence that a person made an oral promise, a court will strain to recharacterize the nature of the agreement so that it does not come within the statute of frauds.[16] One cannot count on such leniency, however; so the prudent manager will put any and all agreements that might fall within the statute of frauds in writing.

---

16. *See, e.g.,* Wilson Floors Co. v. Sciota Park, Ltd., 377 N.E.2d 514 (Ohio 1978) (oral promise by construction lender to pay subcontractor if he returned to work served lender's own pecuniary interest so the agreement did not have to be in writing to be enforceable).

 ## The Parol Evidence Rule

If a contract is in writing, when will a court go beyond the words of the contract and look to other evidence to ascertain the intent of the parties? Under the *parol evidence rule*, when there is a written contract that the parties intended would encompass their entire agreement, parol (that is, oral) evidence of prior or contemporaneous statements will not be permitted to alter the terms of the contract. Such extrinsic evidence is inadmissible in court and cannot be used to interpret, vary, or add to the terms of an unambiguous written contract that purports to be the entire agreement of the parties. A court will usually not look beyond the "four corners" of the document to discern the intentions of the parties.

Clarifying Ambiguous Language

The parol evidence rule does not prohibit showing what the contract means. Thus, courts are willing to look beyond the written agreement if its language is ambiguous. For example, if the contract stated that a party was to purchase a carload of tomatoes, it would not violate the parol evidence rule to present evidence showing that "carload" in the relevant commercial setting means a train carload, not a Chevy truckload. This evidence merely explains the ambiguous term "carload"; it does not vary the term. Parol evidence is also admissible to show mistake, fraud, or duress.

Modern courts make a particular effort to discern the parties' intentions, notwithstanding the words that are written in the contract. In the landmark case of *Pennzoil v. Texaco*, which the "Inside Story" in this chapter discusses, the court held that the jury had reasonable evidence before it to conclude that the parties had intended to enter into a binding agreement—even though the document that was signed by two of the three parties was entitled a "memorandum of agreement" and the transaction was expressly made subject to the signing of other documents.

 ## Changed Circumstances

Contracts often contain provisions for a variety of future events so that the parties involved can allocate the risks of different outcomes. It is not always possible, however, to anticipate every occurrence. There are

VIEW FROM CYBERSPACE

UNIFORM ELECTRONIC TRANSACTIONS ACT

As managers conduct more and more of their business over the Internet, traditional contract law is being strained. Is an "electronic signature" sufficient to execute a contract? Does it satisfy the statute of frauds? Should the click of a mouse on an "Accept" box on a computer screen irrevocably bind parties to the contract terms set forth on the screen? Has a party communicated its offer to contract when the e-mail message arrives in the "Inbox" of the recipient, or when it has been opened, or when it has been read by the recipient? These questions posed by cyber-commerce are challenging contract law and the judges and legislators who make it.

To answer these questions, the National Conference of Commissioners on Uniform State Laws has taken up the issue. The conference's uniform acts serve as models for state legislatures, who take the conference's recommendations seriously and often enact the uniform laws exactly as recommended. In the summer of 1997, the conference began to review the first draft of its Uniform Electronic Transactions Act. By early 1998, it was clear from the early tentative drafts that the conference is seeking to break down barriers to the conduct of electronic commerce by validating electronic records and electronic signatures in the face of legal requirements for paper writings.

---

three theories used to address this situation: impossibility, impracticability, and frustration of purpose.

Impossibility

If Antonio signs a contract to sell Trevor computer chips of a special type manufactured only in Antonio's factory, which later burns down through no fault of Antonio's before he can manufacture the computer chips, it becomes impossible to perform the contract. The destruction of Antonio's factory is a changed circumstance that neither party contemplated when they made the contract.

Is Trevor entitled to money damages for Antonio's nonperformance? No, because Antonio's performance has become impossible, he is discharged from his obligations under the contract due to *impossibility*, and Trevor is not entitled to damages. If, however, the computer chips could be manufactured in another factory, Antonio would have an obligation to have them manufactured there when his factory burned down. This is the case even if it costs Antonio more money to manufacture them at another facility.

Impracticability

Closely related to impossibility is the concept of *impracticability*, where performance is possible but is commercially impractical. As a rule, impracticability is difficult to prove.

Impracticability was invoked by several shipping companies in 1967 when political turmoil in the Middle East gave rise to Egypt's nationalization of the Suez Canal and temporary closing of the key waterway. A number of merchant ships had to detour around the Cape of Good Hope at the southern tip of Africa. The detour increased shipping costs so much that the shipping companies suffered substantial losses. Several of these companies sued to nullify the contracts they had entered into before the Suez Canal was closed. They claimed performance was impractical and sought to recover the full costs of sailing the longer route around the Cape of Good Hope. In only one case did the court grant relief. The other courts found that the added costs were not so great as to make performance impracticable. (Chapter 8 addresses impracticability in contracts for the sale of goods.)

Frustration of Purpose

Frustration of purpose occurs when performance is possible, but changed circumstances have made the contract useless to one or both of the parties. A famous example is the King Edward VII coronation case.[17] Henry contracted to rent a room in London from Krell

---

17. Krell v. Henry, 2 K.B. 740 (C.A. 1903).

for the acknowledged purpose of viewing King Edward VII's coronation procession. Krell had advertised the room as one that would be good for viewing the coronation. When the King became ill with appendicitis and the coronation was postponed, Henry refused to pay for the apartment. Krell sued. The English court ruled that Henry did not have to pay because the entire reason for the contract had been "frustrated."

Note that performance of the contract was not impossible: Henry still could have rented the room. The outcome of the case would have been different if the room had been rented for the express purpose of viewing the coronation. In that case, Krell would have won because the purpose of the contract would have just been for the rental of the room, not for the viewing of the coronation.

The contract defense of frustration requires that (1) the parties' principal purpose in making the contract is frustrated, (2) without that party's fault, (3) by the occurrence of an event, the nonoccurrence of which was a basic assumption on which the contract was made. For performance to be excused, this frustration of purpose must have occurred without the defendant's fault. The defense of frustration is unavailable if the defendant helped cause the frustrating event or if the parties were aware of the possibility of the frustrating event when they entered into the contract.

Sovereign Acts Doctrine

Changes in the law also can affect contracts. When a party's performance is made illegal or impossible because of a new law, performance of the contract is usually discharged and damages are not awarded. But what happens when a party contracts with the government, and the government then promulgates a new law making its own performance impossible? Can the government simply change the law for contracts it no longer wishes to follow to make performance illegal, thereby discharging its obligations? According to the *sovereign acts doctrine*, the government cannot be held liable for breach of contract due to legislative or executive acts. Because one Congress cannot bind a later Congress, the general rule is that subsequent acts of the government can discharge the government's preexisting contractual obligations.

This doctrine has limitations, however. If Congress passes legislation deliberately targeting its extant contractual obligations, the defense otherwise provided by

the sovereign acts doctrine is unavailable. On the other hand, if a new law of general application indirectly affects a government contract and makes the government's performance impossible, the sovereign acts doctrine will protect the government in a subsequent suit for breach of the contract.

United States v. Winstar Corporation[18] involved a controversy arising out of the federal bail out of the savings and loan (S&L) industry in the 1980s. Because the government lacked the funds to prop up the many failing S&Ls, it gave healthy thrifts an incentive to acquire their ailing competitors by providing certain contractual assurances. In particular, the government agreed that the acquiring S&Ls could count the excess of the purchase price over the fair market value of the failing thrifts (the supervisory goodwill) toward their capital-reserve requirements, making acquisition more attractive. After the S&L crisis subsided, Congress enacted the Financial Institutions Reform Recovery and Enforcement Act of 1989 (FIRREA), which provided that supervisory goodwill could no longer be counted in calculating capital reserves. The thrifts then sued the government for breach of contract. The government, relying on the sovereign acts doctrine, argued that its obligations to the S&Ls had been extinguished because FIRREA prevented the government from fulfilling its side of the bargain. The Supreme Court rejected the sovereign acts defense because the government had deliberately enacted FIRREA in order to repudiate its contractual obligations. The Court held that when the government entered into the contract, it assumed the risk that future regulatory changes might make it impossible for the government to honor the contract. Thus, the government could not successfully assert the impossibility defense and was liable for its breach.

The sovereign acts doctrine remains important as general laws of broad application that make performance by the government impossible still provide a defense to the government's breach. *Winstar* only establishes limits to the doctrine; namely, the government cannot use its power to enact laws and regulations for the purpose of extinguishing specific contractual obligations. Furthermore, even in a *Winstar* situation, the government is not prevented from changing the law. It simply must pay damages for its legislatively chosen breach.

---

18. 116 S. Ct. 2432 (1996).

Contract Modification

Traditional contract law does not allow a contract to be modified if the modification would change the obligations of only one party. Under this view, no consideration has been given for the change. Over time, lawyers developed a variety of techniques to meet the formal requirements of consideration. One technique was *novation*, by which a new party is substituted for one of the old parties, and a new contract is written (with the consent of all old and new parties) effecting the desired change. Another technique was formal change, where the consideration for the desired modification is a formal but meaningless change, such as making the payment in cash rather than with a bank check. Similarly, if both parties agree to terminate the contract and enter into a new one, the new one will be valid.

In the modern business environment, modifications to contracts are often necessary. The UCC allows modification of contracts for the sale of goods without consideration as long as the change meets the test of good faith.

 Discharge of Contract

Once a manager has entered into a legally enforceable contract, his or her next concern is determining when the contractual obligations have been terminated, or *discharged*. The most common discharge of contracts occurs when both parties have fully performed their obligations toward one another. But what happens when one party performs and the other does not? Or when one party performs only half of its obligations under the contract? These questions are answered under the rules on discharging contracts.

If one party fails to perform a contract according to its essential terms, such as by not delivering the product after receiving payment, that party has *materially breached* the contract. Any material breach of a contract discharges the nonbreaching party from its obligations and provides grounds to sue for damages. Unlike a material breach, a minor breach occurs when the essential terms and purpose of the contract have been fulfilled. In the case of minor breach, the nonbreaching party still retains its contractual obligations but may suspend performance or sue for damages.

If a manager knows ahead of time (before performance is due) that the other party will breach the contract, there is an *anticipatory repudiation* of the contract. Such a repudiation is treated as a material breach of the contract. By treating an anticipatory repudiation as a breach, the nonbreaching party can avoid having to wait until an actual breach before taking action.

Contracts may also be discharged by the failure or occurrence of certain conditions stipulated in the contract, such as a condition precedent or a condition subsequent, as discussed above. If both parties agree, they may terminate the contract by *mutual rescission*. A mutual rescission is itself a type of contract and, as such, requires a valid offer, acceptance, and consideration. Often the consideration is simply the agreement by both parties not to enforce their legal obligations.

If one party prefers to retain the original contract but wants to contract with someone else, a third party may be substituted for one of the original parties. The third party will assume the original party's rights and responsibilities. All parties must agree to the substitution. Formally a new contract is formed, with the same terms but with different parties.

An *accord and satisfaction* is any agreement to accept performance that is different from what is called for in the contract. For example, a contract involving a debt under good faith dispute can be discharged by accord and satisfaction. Assume a creditor believes he is owed $100,000, but the debtor feels she owes only $75,000. An *accord* is formed when the creditor accepts the debtor's offer to settle the dispute for an amount less than the creditor claims is due (say, by cashing the debtor's check for $80,000 with "Full Payment" written on it). *Satisfaction* is the discharge of the debt.

Parties may sometimes have a valid contract that is discharged by operation of law. Certain types of changed circumstances, such as impossibility, impracticability, or frustration of purpose (described above), may discharge the contractual obligations of both parties. A bankruptcy proceeding by one party can also discharge its contractual obligations. Similarly, failing to file suit for breach of contract before the time specified in the statute of limitations has passed effectively discharges a contract, because the courts will no longer enforce it. In many states, an action for breach of a written contract must be filed within four years after the breach occurs.

◆ Duty of Good Faith and Fair Dealing

Every contract contains an implied covenant of good faith and fair dealing in its performance. This implied covenant imposes on each party a duty not to do anything that will deprive the other party of the benefits of the agreement. One court defined a lack of good faith as "some type of affirmative action consisting of at least . . . a design to mislead or to deceive another."[19] The covenant has been implied and enforced in a variety of contexts, including insurance contracts, agreements to make mutual wills, agreements to sell real property, employment agreements, and leases. (Its application in the employment context is discussed in Chapter 12.)

For example, suppose Reese is looking for an apartment. He comes upon Tara's apartment building and proceeds up the stairs to speak with the manager. Reese trips on a broken step, falls, and breaks his arm and leg. It is clear that the steps had not been maintained very well. Tara has insurance of $125,000 to cover this type of liability claim. Reese's lawyer originally demands $120,000, which includes a claim for punitive damages. Tara's insurance company refuses to pay the claim. Tara's insurance company still does not believe that Tara was negligent and takes the case to trial. The jury awards Reese $180,000. Tara is liable for the full amount, although she was insured for only $125,000. Tara then brings an action against her insurance company for not settling the claim within the policy limits. Under the implied covenant of good faith and fair dealing, the insurance company will have the obligation to pay the full $180,000 judgment. An insurance company can refuse to settle within the policy limits. But once an insurance company refuses an offer to settle within the policy limits and instead goes to trial, the insurance company becomes contractually responsible under the implied covenant of good faith and fair dealing for paying whatever amount is awarded at trial.

Courts have long deemed the relationship between insurance companies and their insured a special relationship that calls for a careful examination of the faithfulness of contractual dealings. In 1984, the California Supreme Court extended this special relationship rationale and created a tort action for bad faith denial of the

ETHICAL CONSIDERATION

Alejandro purchased a 40-foot-wide strip of land from a homeowner for a small sum of money. He then sold most of the land to the county, which laid down a road on the land. Alejandro kept a two-foot-wide strip of the land between the homeowner's property and the new road. When the homeowner crossed over this two-foot strip to get to the road, Alejandro threatened to sue for trespass. He then offered to sell back the two-foot strip for an extravagant sum. Should a court rescind the contract? On what theory? Was Alejandro's conduct ethical?

existence of a contract.[20] This decision generated intense criticism, however. In 1995, the court overruled the 1984 decision and held that a party could not receive tort damages for the bad faith denial of a contract.[21]

The precise meanings of "good faith" and "fair dealing" are the subject of extended debate among legal scholars. The terms themselves are ambiguous, and the practical meanings may vary over time. What was considered fair dealing 20 years ago may be considered unfair today, and vice versa.

Two commonly used rules of thumb, while not precise, do offer guidance. The manager in doubt can ask himself if his actions would embarrass him or his company if they should become public. He can also ask himself if he would follow the same course of action if he were dealing with a friend or relative.

Although these questions address moral rather than legal issues, they can be useful in evaluating whether a contemplated action would meet the legal test of good faith. (Good faith in the context of negotiations is discussed more fully later in this chapter.)

◆ Third-Party Beneficiaries

A person who is not a party to a contract can sometimes enforce the contract between the contracting parties. For example, suppose Sheila agrees to sell to Fernando a

19. Bunge Corp. v. Recker, 519 F.2d 449, 452 (8th Cir. 1975).

20. Seaman's Direct Buying Serv., Inc. v. Standard Oil Co. of Cal., 686 P.2d 1158 (Cal. 1984).

21. Freeman & Mills, Inc. v. Belcher Oil Co., 900 P.2d 669 (Cal. 1995).

piece of real property in exchange for a $100,000 payment by Fernando to Jack. Fernando is the promisor, Sheila is the promisee, and Jack is the *third-party beneficiary* or intended beneficiary. A person is not a third-party beneficiary with legal rights to enforce the contract unless the contracting parties intended to benefit that party.

Creditor Beneficiary

If the promisee entered into the contract in order to discharge a duty he or she owed the third party, then the third party is a *creditor beneficiary* and has the right to enforce the contract between the promisor and promisee. The third party must prove, however, that the promisee intended the contract to satisfy her obligation to him. For example, if Sheila owed Jack $100,000 and she and Fernando agree that she would sell land to Fernando in order to pay off that debt, Jack has enforceable rights under the contract as a creditor beneficiary. Jack can sue Fernando directly to compel performance. If the contract is not carried out, Jack also has the option of suing Sheila for the $100,000 she owes him.

Donee Beneficiary

A *donee beneficiary* is created when the promisee does not owe an obligation to the third party but rather wishes to confer a gift. For example, if Sheila agreed to sell her property to Fernando for $100,000 in order to make a $100,000 gift to Jack, Jack would be a donee beneficiary and could enforce the contract in most jurisdictions, but only against Fernando. Some jurisdictions, such as New York, require a family relationship between the donee beneficiary and the promisee before allowing the beneficiary to sue under the contract.

 Damages

If one party breaches a contract, the other party is entitled to monetary damages or to a court order requiring performance. The purpose of damages is to give the plaintiff the benefit of the bargain it contracted for, that is, to put the plaintiff in the position it would have been in had the contract been performed. A secondary purpose of damages is to discourage breaches of contract.

Over the years, a variety of methods have developed to measure appropriate monetary damages. The three standard measures are (1) expectation, (2) reliance, and (3) restitution. These measures may seem similar, but the resulting damage awards can be very different, as discussed below. However, recognizing that it is sometimes economically efficient to breach a contract, the legal system generally does not punish a party for breach of contract alone. Punitive damages, traditionally a tort remedy, may be awarded if the court finds oppressive, malicious, or fraudulent conduct. For example, if one party enters into a contract knowing that it will not perform its obligations under the contract, that party may be liable for promissory fraud.

Types of Damages

Expectation Damages   *Expectation damages* give the plaintiff the benefit of its bargain, putting the plaintiff in the cash position it would have been in if the contract had been fulfilled. For example, suppose a seller contracts to sell a buyer ten bales of cotton at $20 per bale. When the time comes to deliver the cotton, the seller reneges. The buyer can buy cotton elsewhere, but the market price is now $25 per bale. This extra cost will cut into the profit margin on the cloth the buyer had planned to weave from the cotton. Instead of spending $200 for ten bales of cotton, the buyer must now pay $250. The buyer's expectation damages are the difference between the two expenditures, that is, $50.

In the world of electronic banking, Mellon Bank Corporation recently sued Deluxe Corporation, a provider of electronic funds transfers and check authorization services, for breach of contract. In 1994, the two firms had teamed up to bid on a contract with the federal government to provide Social Security payments and food stamps via electronic transfers instead of paper checks. Their agreement called for exchange of confidential information and exclusive dealings with each other. In 1995, Deluxe, citing concerns over cashflow, ended its agreement with Mellon but six weeks later submitted a bid for the government contract with Citibank. After the U.S. Treasury awarded the contract to Deluxe and Citibank, Mellon sued Deluxe, claiming Deluxe's breach had cost Mellon $30 million in foregone profits. In 1997, a federal jury in Philadelphia agreed and awarded Mellon $30 million for its lost profits.[22]

22. Matt Murray, *Mellon Is Awarded $30 Million in Suit Against Deluxe*, WALL ST. J., Oct. 31, 1997, at A12.

Consequential Damages In addition to damages that compensate for the breach itself, the plaintiff is entitled to *consequential damages*, that is, compensation for losses that occur as a foreseeable result of the breach. For example, suppose the buyer in the example above buys the cotton elsewhere, but the transportation costs from this other location are $10 higher. This $10 is added to the $50 in damages. If the delay in finding a new vendor causes the buyer to be late in delivering cloth to one of its customers, any late fees the buyer pays will also be added to the damages.

Consequential damages must be reasonably foreseeable. They will be awarded only if the breaching party knew, or should have known, that the loss would result from a breach of the contract.

For example, in *Hadley v. Baxendale*,[23] the plaintiff owned a mill in which the crankshaft broke. The crankshaft was sent by carrier to be repaired. Because this was the only crankshaft the mill owned, the mill was completely shut down until the carrier returned with the repaired crankshaft. The carrier did not deliver the shaft as quickly as promised. The mill owner sued the carrier for profits lost during the time the mill was closed. The English appellate court did not award damages for lost profits because the carrier had no way of knowing that the nondelivery of the crankshaft would mean the closure of the mill, because most mills had more than one crankshaft. In order for lost profits to have been awarded, the lost profits would have to have been reasonably foreseeable or a natural consequence of the breach. Neither was the case here.

In another case, a stove manufacturer paid a carrier $50 to ship a new model of stove to a major exhibition.[24] The stove did not arrive until the exhibition was over. The manufacturer sued for the value of all the lost business he had expected to get at the exhibition. The court found that the $50 was too small an amount to serve as insurance for the entire business. Moreover, the value of the lost business was too speculative to calculate with any certainty. Damages were limited to the shipping expenses of $50.

Uncertainty of Damages In the stove case just described, it was impossible to measure the consequential damages (the stove manufacturer's lost business). Sometimes it is not possible to know even what the benefit of the bargain would have been. For example, Publisher & Sons signs a contract to publish a book Rachel Author has written. It is her first book. Publisher later decides not to publish the book. To what damages is Rachel entitled? The benefit of her bargain would be the royalties from a published book, but the parties have no way to measure how much those royalties would have been. Because Rachel has the burden of proving the amount of her loss, she may collect very little in damages.

Similarly, new businesses have no record of past profits by which to estimate the loss caused by a breach. Traditionally, this prevented start-ups from collecting anything for lost profits. New businesses are having more success recovering damages as more sophisticated methods are developed for projecting future profits.

Reliance Damages *Reliance damages* compensate the plaintiff for any expenditures it made in reliance on the contract that was subsequently breached. Instead of giving the plaintiff the benefit of the bargain, reliance damages return it to the position it was in before the contract was formed. For example, a seller agrees to sell a buyer a heavy drill press. The buyer invests in renovation work to strengthen the floor where the drill press will be placed. The buyer tells the seller of this work. The seller then sells the drill press to someone else. Reliance damages will require the seller to reimburse the buyer for the renovation expenses.

Restitution and Quantum Meruit Restitution is similar to reliance damages, but while reliance damages look at what the plaintiff has lost, *restitution* looks at what the other party has gained from the transaction. The usual measure of restitution is the amount it would cost the receiver of the benefit to buy that benefit elsewhere.

A court will order restitution under the doctrine of *quantum meruit* if one party has received a benefit for which it has not paid when there was no contract between the parties. The obligation to give restitution is implied as a matter of law. For example, suppose a doctor provides medical service to an unconscious accident victim. The doctor normally charges $200 for the care rendered. The patient could have gotten the same care from another doctor for $100. The value of the care to the patient is therefore $100. Because the patient was

23. 156 Eng. Rep. 145 (1854).

24. Security Stove & Mfg. Co. v. American Ry. Express Co., 51 S.W.2d 572 (Mo. App. Ct. 1932).

unconscious, he was unable to bargain for the services and enter into a contract. In a situation like this, a court will act as if there were a contract in order to prevent the patient from benefiting unfairly. The court will order the patient to make restitution by paying the doctor $100 for her services.

Mitigation of Damages

When one party breaches a contract, the other party has a duty to use reasonable efforts to *mitigate*, or lessen, the amount of damages that flow from the breach. As a general rule, the nonbreaching party cannot recover damages that it could have reasonably avoided. This gives the nonbreaching party an incentive to make the best of a bad situation.

For example, suppose a dairy farmer and butter manufacturer enter into a contract whereby the farmer agrees to provide raw milk to the manufacturer at 50 cents per gallon. If the farmer fails to deliver the milk, the manufacturer should *cover*—buy substitute milk at the current market price, say 65 cents per gallon at the time of breach. The manufacturer would still be entitled to expectation damages, measured by the difference between the market price at the time it learned of the breach (65 cent per gallon) and the contract price (50 cents per gallon), plus any consequential damages, such as extra shipping fees, late fees, and expenses incurred in finding substitute goods.

The buyer could also elect not to cover. If it does not cover, however, the buyer is limited to expectation damages (as measured above) and cannot recover any consequential damages that could have been prevented by covering, such as late fees. If no cover is available, then the buyer is entitled to foreseeable consequential damages resulting from the breach.

Additionally, the buyer must avoid compounding damages from the breach. Suppose in the dairy farmer example that milk were available on the open market at both 62 cents and 65 cents per gallon. If the quality is the same at both prices, the butter manufacturer is required to purchase at the lower price, thus reducing its expectation damages to 12 cents per gallon, instead of 15 cents. Any expenses incurred by the buyer in reasonably attempting to mitigate damages, such as the costs of finding another seller, are also recoverable under consequential damages, regardless of whether the efforts were successful.

From the seller's perspective, the duty to mitigate damages works similarly. For example, suppose a software company contracts to develop a customized program for a small architecture firm. The developer learns midway through the software-development stage that the firm plans to breach the contract. The developer should cover by finding another buyer for the software and charging the breaching firm for the difference between the contract price and the resale price (expectation damages), plus any consequential damages. If no other buyer is available, perhaps because the program is too customized, the developer should immediately stop its work and charge the breaching firm for expenses incurred plus the expected net profit.

Mitigation of damages is also important in the context of employment. If, for instance, an accountant were wrongfully terminated and filed suit against her employer for lost wages, she could not go away on vacation until the case concluded and still collect all her lost wages. Her duty to mitigate her damages requires that she use reasonable efforts to obtain similar employment elsewhere, such as an accounting position in the same city. Any recovery of lost wages under a wrongfully terminated employment contract will be reduced by what the employee earned or reasonably could have earned at a comparable job. Conversely, if the accountant had quit while under an employment contract, the employer would be required to use reasonable efforts to find a replacement for her. Courts will limit the employer's recovery to the difference between the cost of the replacement and the compensation specified in the original employment contract.

Liquidated Damages

The parties to a contract may include a clause that specifies the amount of money to be paid if one of them should later breach the agreement. Such *liquidated damages* clauses are frequently used in real estate and construction contracts. The amount of the liquidated damages should be the parties' best estimate of what the expectation damages would be. Courts will not enforce penalties. Thus, clauses that provide for damages that are substantially higher than the losses will not be enforced. The purpose of contract damages is to restore the aggrieved party to the position it would have been in had the contract been performed, not to punish the party who has committed the breach.

Specific Performance

Instead of awarding monetary damages, a court may order the breaching party to complete the contract as promised. *Specific performance* is ordered only when (1) the goods are unique (for example, an antique car or a painting); (2) the subject of the contract is real property; or (3) the amount of the loss is so uncertain that there is no fair way to calculate damages.

Courts never force an employee to provide services under an employment contract because it would constitute involuntary servitude in violation of the Thirteenth Amendment of the U.S. Constitution. For example, suppose a chief executive officer agrees to work for a corporation for five years. If he walks out after three years, the court will not force him to continue his employment. The court may, however, issue an injunction barring him from working for someone else. Similarly, if a professional baseball player with a seven-year contract with the Chicago Cubs breaches his contract and starts playing for the Houston Astros, an injunction can be granted to prevent him from playing for the Astros.

 ## Precontractual Liability

Cases have extended promissory estoppel to provide compensation for losses incurred when business negotiations fail. Liability for such losses, when negotiations fail to ripen into a contract, is now known as *precontractual liability*. This doctrine deserves considerable attention because of its importance to complex business negotiations and its evolving nature. In addition, although the law may not always require fair dealing in negotiations, ethical considerations may. E. Allan Farnsworth, professor of law at Columbia University, has written an insightful summary of the current state of the law concerning precontractual liability and the likely direction of future developments. His article, *Precontractual Liability and Preliminary Agreements: Fair Dealing and Failed Negotiations*, is excerpted and summarized in this section.[25]

Introduction

Business contracts today are often formed through complex negotiations, often involving many parties. These negotiations are a far cry from the simple bargaining envisioned by the traditional rules of offer and acceptance. During negotiations, there is often no actual offer or counteroffer but rather a series of agreements reached through a gradual process.

If negotiations fail before a contract has been signed, a number of questions of law can arise that the classic rules of offer and acceptance do not address: Does the disappointed party have a claim against the other for expenses or opportunity costs? Do parties in negotiation have to conform to a standard of fair dealing?

The principles of existing contract law can be applied to all three stages of the process of contract formation. These are (1) negotiation, (2) preliminary agreements, and (3) the ultimate agreement.

Negotiation

Under traditional contract law, the offeror is free to back out and revoke the offer at any time before a contract is made. Under this doctrine a party entering negotiations does so at the risk of the negotiations breaking off.

In recent decades, however, courts have shown increasing willingness to impose precontractual liability on grounds of unjust enrichment, misrepresentation, or specific promise.

Unjust Enrichment   *Unjust enrichment* occurs when a negotiating party unfairly appropriates the benefits of negotiation for its own use. For example, if one party discloses a trade secret in the interest of the negotiation, it would be unfair for the other party to use that secret for its own benefit if negotiations fail.

The normal time and effort put into a negotiation is considered part of the risk of negotiating. However, if an architect, for example, renders a service to a developer, such as drawing plans, the developer cannot then use the plans to award the contract to another party.

If a court finds that there was unjust enrichment, it may order the unjustly enriched party to pay for the benefits it has received. In practice, restitution has been ordered in only a few cases, where ideas were misappropriated during negotiations.

Misrepresentation   *Misrepresentation* occurs when a party (1) enters into a negotiation without serious intent to reach agreement; (2) fails to give prompt notice of a change in mind or intent; (3) alleges more authority to negotiate than it actually has; or (4) fails to disclose something it has a duty to disclose. For example, the Supreme Court of Washington found misrepresentation when the owner of a warehouse told the lessee that he intended to renew the lease for three years, when he was actually negotiating the sale of the facility. The owner was entering into negotiations without serious intent to reach agreement. The court held that the owner must carry out his promise to renew the lease. In practice, courts have rarely applied the law of misrepresentation to failed negotiations.

Specific Promise   Parties to a business negotiation will say many things in order to move discussions along and get the best bargain possible. A negotiating party who breaks a promise made during negotiations may be liable if the other party acted in reliance on that promise. This application of promissory estoppel was used in *Hoffman v. Red Owl Stores* [Case 7.3].

Preliminary Agreements

Preliminary agreements are made during negotiations in anticipation of some later, final agreement. Examples from business include letters of intent between a buyer and a seller of a business, commitment letters by a bank to lend money, and memoranda of understanding between two companies that plan to merge.

Two common types of preliminary agreements are agreements with open terms and agreements to negotiate.

Agreements with Open Terms   In a preliminary agreement with open terms, the parties leave some terms to be negotiated later. If those terms remain unresolved because one party did not fulfill its obligation to negotiate, a court will hold that party liable.

If the parties fail to agree on the open terms despite continued negotiation, they are bound by the terms of their original agreement, and the courts are left to supply the missing terms as they see fit. For example, some agreements for the sale of goods leave the price open for later determination. Should later negotiations on the price fail, a court will supply the missing price.

The important point here is that preliminary agreements with open terms are binding even if the parties cannot later agree on the missing terms.

An agreement with open terms imposes on the parties a duty of fair dealing. A breach of this duty entitles the injured party to out-of-pocket damages, and it also entitles the injured party to refuse to perform under the agreement. In some cases, it may be regarded as a breach of the contract, entitling the injured party to benefit-of-the bargain damages.

To determine the enforceability of preliminary agreements, courts examine (1) the intent of the parties to be bound, and (2) the definiteness of the terms of the agreement. The great bulk of litigation concerning the enforceability of preliminary agreements with open terms has involved the problem of intent, as in the case of *Pennzoil v. Texaco* [discussed in the "Inside Story" for this chapter].

The parties can make a preliminary agreement nonbinding by stating their intention not to be bound. However, courts will honor such an intent only if it is expressed in the clearest language. For example, titling an agreement a "letter of intent," or using the phrase "formal agreement to follow" might not be enough to prove to a court that the parties did not intend to be bound.

In deciding whether the parties to a preliminary agreement intended to be bound, courts look to a variety of factors, including (1) the degree to which the terms of the agreement are spelled out; (2) the circumstances of the parties (e.g., the importance of the deal to them); (3) the parties' prior course of dealing with each other, if any; and (4) the parties' behavior subsequent to the execution of the agreement (for example, issuing a press release may demonstrate intent).

Agreements to Negotiate   In a preliminary agreement to negotiate, the parties do not agree to be bound by the terms of the agreement. They are simply agreeing to continue the process of negotiations with the aim of reaching an ultimate agreement. For example, in mergers and acquisitions, a letter of intent between the acquiring company and the target does not bind the two parties if, after continued negotiations, the parties are unable to agree on the formal or definitive documents.

The parties to an agreement to negotiate should deal fairly. Courts, however, have refused to enforce agreements to negotiate even when there has been a breach of the duty of fair dealing. The courts have argued that (1) a court cannot fashion an appropriate remedy for breach of the duty because there is no way to know what the ultimate agreement would have been; and (2) a court cannot properly determine the scope of the duty of fair dealing under such agreements.

[Eds.: However, in two cases decided after Professor Farnsworth's article was written, the courts indicated greater willingness to give relief for violation of an agreement to negotiate. The U.S. Court of Appeals for the Seventh Circuit recognized that a letter of intent can create a duty to negotiate in good faith in *Apothekernes Laboratorium for Specialpraeparater v. IMC Chemical Group, Inc.*[26] The U.S. Court of Appeals for the Second Circuit applied the doctrine of promissory estoppel in *Arcadian Phosphates, Inc. v. Arcadian Corp.*[27] In that case, the parties had begun negotiating the sale of Arcadian's phosphate fertilizer facility to Arcadian Phosphates, Inc. (API). A four-page memorandum of understanding, which made the deal subject to the approval of Arcadian's board, was signed. The memo outlined the assets to be purchased, the purchase price, and an option for Arcadian to purchase up to 20% of API. It further provided that both parties would "cooperate fully and work judiciously in order to expedite the closing date and consummate the sale of the business."

[While final negotiations were continuing, the market for phosphates changed dramatically. Market prices for diammonium phosphate, the bellwether of the industry, went up 25% in five weeks. The consensus at the next board meeting of Arcadian was that the joint venture could not proceed as originally contemplated. When Arcadian informed API of its change in position, API sued Arcadian, claiming breach of contract or, in the alternative, promissory estoppel.

[The U.S. Court of Appeals for the Second Circuit upheld dismissal of API's breach of contract claim but reversed the lower court's dismissal of the promissory estoppel claim. The court stated that it was unclear whether Arcadian made an unambiguous promise to negotiate in good faith. If it did, and if API sustained an injury when it relied on the promise, a finding of promissory estoppel would be appropriate. In that event, the appropriate measurement of damages would be API's out-of-pocket expenses, not the profits API could expect to make through the joint venture.]

26. 873 F.2d 155 (7th Cir. 1989) (Case 7.1).
27. 884 F.2d 69 (2d Cir. 1989).

The Ultimate Agreement

Even when parties agree to and sign an ultimate agreement, it may not become final until certain conditions are met. If the conditions are not met, the contract terminates automatically. For example, a contract can be drafted as binding subject to obtaining financing or government approval. A buyer of real estate may condition its purchase on a pending government ruling on zoning. Courts have even allowed the parties to leave open the precise nature of a financing.

Conditional clauses must not be illusory promises. For example, courts usually disallow clauses that condition an agreement on the approval of a party's own lawyer.

The Meaning of Fair Dealing

Parties to a negotiation should describe as specifically as possible the duty of fair dealing to which they have agreed. Instead of simply pledging to use "best efforts" to negotiate fairly, the parties should specify whether the negotiations are to be exclusive, how long they must continue, what must be disclosed, and what must be held in confidence. Given the uncertain state of the law on these matters, no drafter should leave these items to a court to fill in.

Courts will go beyond the language of a preliminary agreement and look at the circumstances surrounding the negotiation to determine whether the dealings were fair. For example, courts will examine trade practices and the previous relationship of the parties.

Unfair Dealing Unfair dealing can be broadly grouped under seven headings: (1) refusal to negotiate, (2) improper tactics, (3) unreasonable proposals, (4) nondisclosure, (5) negotiation with others, (6) reneging, and (7) breaking off negotiations.

A refusal to negotiate can take several forms, besides an outright refusal to talk about terms. Delay tactics can be tantamount to outright refusal. Refusal to negotiate except on certain terms can also be considered a breach. For example, a party cannot condition its willingness to bargain on a change in the composition of the other party's bargaining team.

Stubborn and unyielding bargaining alone does not constitute unfair dealing, but it can be evidence of it. For example, an employer who consistently rejects out of hand all of a union's proposals would likely be found to be bargaining in bad faith, that is, dealing unfairly.

Although it is difficult for courts to judge the reasonableness of a proposal made in a negotiation, some cases are clear. For example, a proposal to renew a franchise on terms significantly less favorable to the franchisee, when there has been no change in circumstances, would most likely be considered unreasonable.

Successful negotiation often requires skillful judgment about what to communicate to the other party. In some instances, failure to disclose facts amounts to a misrepresentation. In general, parties are under an obligation not to misstate facts or intentions. There is a heavier burden of disclosure when the parties are not on equal footing, for example, when a fiduciary (such as a trustee) negotiates with a beneficiary.

Fairness does not generally require a party to negotiate with one party to the exclusion of all others. It seems reasonable, however, for each party to keep the other apprised of relevant proposals from third parties and to give opportunities to respond to counteroffers. The agreement to negotiate may contain an exclusive-negotiation clause that obligates one party to refrain from negotiating with others. Courts have not always upheld these clauses, but they are more inclined to do so if the clause specifies a time limit on the exclusivity.

Reneging on an agreement to negotiate can be considered a breach of the duty of fair dealing, particularly if the negotiations are well advanced. Reneging can amount to a refusal to negotiate.

There are some situations in which a party is justified in breaking off negotiations, such as changed circumstances, mistake, unfair dealing by the other party, or an impasse in the negotiations that makes it clear that the negotiations have no chance of success. However, a party cannot arbitrarily break off negotiations without making a reasonable effort to reach an agreement.

Fair Dealing   The standard of fair dealing ordinarily requires at least three things. First, each party must actually negotiate and refrain from imposing improper conditions on the negotiation. Second, each party must disclose enough about parallel negotiations to allow the other party to make a counterproposal. Third, each party must continue to negotiate until an impasse or an agreement has been reached. The standard does not require a party to bargain exclusively, to bargain for a specific length of time, or to disclose the basis of its proposals.

INTERNATIONAL CONSIDERATION

When doing business with companies in other nations, it is important to remember that although the law in the United States stems from a common law tradition, most non-English-speaking countries follow the civil law tradition. This system of jurisprudence was originally used in the Roman Empire, where it included institutes, codes, digests, and novels. Civil law countries rely primarily on codes (such as the Napoleonic Code in France) rather than case-by-case common law to develop rules for behavior. Therefore, it is prudent to include in multinational contracts a provision stating which country's law will apply (a choice-of-law provision) and in which jurisdiction a dispute must be brought (a choice-of-forum provision).

 Conflicting Duties

Sometimes there is a conflict between the duties owed under a contract and a duty owed to other parties. This arises frequently in the context of mergers and acquisitions.

Merger Agreements

A *merger agreement* is an agreement between two companies to combine into a single entity. A merger generally cannot be completed until it is approved by the shareholders of both companies.

A merger agreement will frequently require the board of directors of the target company—that is, the company being acquired—to recommend the deal to the shareholders and to use its best efforts to consummate the transaction. Such a provision is called a *best-efforts clause*. What happens if a third party comes along and offers a higher price to the target company? May the board of directors of the target company negotiate with the third party? May it recommend the new deal to the shareholders? Has the third party incurred any liability by interfering with the previously signed merger agreement, or is the third party just being competitive by offering a better price?

The third party will be liable for *tortious interference with a contract* if the following requirements are

IN BRIEF

DECISION TREE FOR CONTRACT ANALYSIS

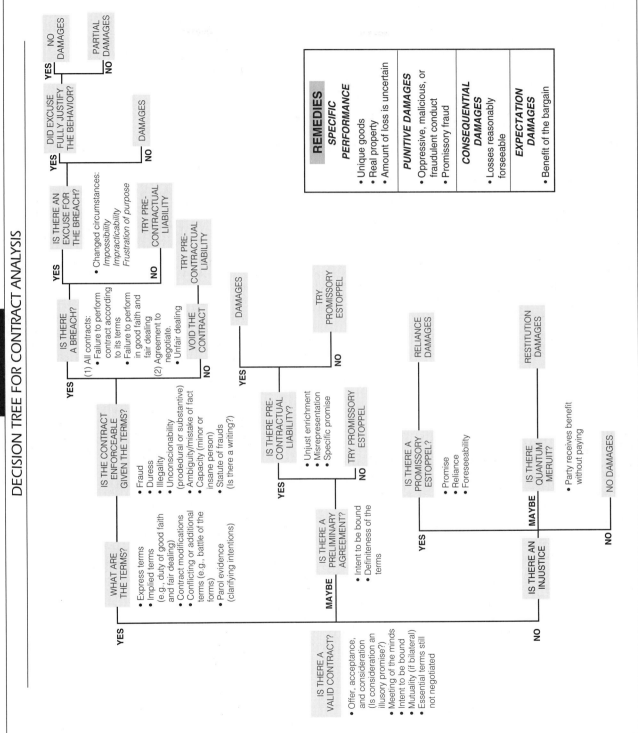

REMEDIES

SPECIFIC PERFORMANCE
- Unique goods
- Real property
- Amount of loss is uncertain

PUNITIVE DAMAGES
- Oppressive, malicious, or fraudulent conduct
- Promissory fraud

CONSEQUENTIAL DAMAGES
- Losses reasonably forseeable

EXPECTATION DAMAGES
- Benefit of the bargain

IS THERE A VALID CONTRACT?
- Offer, acceptance, and consideration (Is consideration an illusory promise?)
- Meeting of the minds
- Intent to be bound
- Mutuality (if bilateral)
- Essential terms still not negotiated

WHAT ARE THE TERMS?
- Express terms
- Implied terms (e.g., duty of good faith and fair dealing)
- Contract modifications
- Conflicting or additional terms (e.g., battle of the forms)
- Parol evidence (clarifying intentions)

IS THE CONTRACT ENFORCEABLE GIVEN THE TERMS?
- Fraud
- Duress
- Illegality
- Unconscionability (procedural or substantive)
- Ambiguity/mistake of fact
- Capacity (minor or insane person)
- Statute of frauds (Is there a writing?)

IS THERE A BREACH?
(1) All contracts:
- Failure to perform contract according to its terms
- Failure to perform in good faith and fair dealing
(2) Agreement to negotiate:
- Unfair dealing

IS THERE AN EXCUSE FOR THE BREACH?
- Changed circumstances: *Impossibility Impracticability Frustration of purpose*

DID EXCUSE FULLY JUSTIFY THE BEHAVIOR?

YES — **NO DAMAGES**

NO — **PARTIAL DAMAGES**

YES — **DAMAGES** (Is there an excuse — NO)

TRY PRE-CONTRACTUAL LIABILITY

VOID THE CONTRACT

IS THERE PRE-CONTRACTUAL LIABILITY?
- Unjust enrichment
- Misrepresentation
- Specific promise

TRY PROMISSORY ESTOPPEL

DAMAGES

TRY PROMISSORY ESTOPPEL

IS THERE A PRELIMINARY AGREEMENT?
- Intent to be bound
- Definiteness of the terms

IS THERE A PROMISSORY ESTOPPEL?
- Promise
- Reliance
- Foreseeability

RELIANCE DAMAGES

IS THERE QUANTUM MERUIT?
- Party receives benefit without paying

RESTITUTION DAMAGES

IS THERE AN INJUSTICE

NO DAMAGES

met: (1) a contract must exist between the plaintiff and another; (2) the defendant must have knowledge of the contract between the plaintiff and the other party; (3) the defendant's actions must cause the other party to breach the contract with the plaintiff; (4) the plaintiff must be damaged in some way; and (5) the defendant must intentionally and wrongfully induce the other party to breach the contract with the plaintiff.

Different courts have disagreed on what actions the target company's board of directors may or must take with regard to best-efforts clauses and what liability a competing bidder has if it succeeds in persuading the board of directors of the target company to breach the agreement with the first suitor and recommend the second deal to the shareholders.

In *Jewel Companies, Inc. v. Pay Less Drug Stores Northwest, Inc.*,[28] the U.S. Court of Appeals for the Ninth Circuit held that the board of directors of a target company that had signed a merger agreement with one suitor could bind itself to refrain from negotiating or accepting a second merger proposal prior to the shareholder vote on the first proposal. The court stated:

> It is nowhere written in stone that the law of the jungle must be the exclusive doctrine governing parties within the world of corporate mergers. The legitimate exercise of the right to contract by responsible boards of directors can help bring some degree of much needed order to these transactions.

The court held that the third party, which offered a higher price, could be liable for tortious interference with contract if the target company and the first suitor intended an agreement not to deal with any other party until the first deal was put to the target company's shareholders for a vote.

In *ConAgra, Inc. v. Cargill, Inc.*,[29] the merger agreement between the target company and the first suitor stated that "nothing herein contained shall relieve either Board of Directors of their continuing duties to their respective shareholders." The Nebraska Supreme Court interpreted this clause to mean that the parties agreed that the target company was not contracting out of its duty to recommend the deal that would be best for its shareholders. The court held that the third party, which offered a higher price, could

disrupt the merger with the first suitor without facing liability for tortious interference with contract.

The Delaware Supreme Court cited *ConAgra* with approval in *Paramount Communications Inc. v. QVC Network Inc.*[30] Paramount had entered into a friendly merger agreement with Viacom. As part of the deal, Paramount granted Viacom an option to buy Paramount shares at a favorable price (a *lock-up option*) together with a termination fee payable if the merger did not go through. QVC made a hostile bid for Paramount and sought to invalidate the lock-up option, which was worth about $500 million. The Delaware Supreme Court held that because the directors of Paramount had violated their fiduciary duties by granting the option, Viacom had no enforceable contractual right to the option. This case is discussed further in Chapter 21.

Fiduciary Outs

A merger agreement can be drafted to prevent the target company from soliciting other offers yet allow it to consider unsolicited offers. For example, supermarket chain Lucky Stores, Inc. and a management buyout group led by Gibbons, Green, van Amerongen entered into a merger agreement while Lucky was facing a hostile takeover bid by American Stores. The American bid was for $45 a share; the Gibbons bid was for $61 a share. The agreement between Lucky and Gibbons gave the Lucky directors a *fiduciary out*, which allows the target company's directors to remain faithful to their fiduciary duties to their shareholders even after signing an agreement with a suitor. In this case, the fiduciary out allowed the directors of Lucky to recommend to their shareholders unsolicited offers other than the Gibbons offer. In return for this privilege, Lucky agreed to pay Gibbons a $20 million break-up fee if Lucky's directors recommended a deal other than the one with Gibbons. A *break-up fee* is an agreed-on payment to a suitor if, through no fault of the suitor's, the merger is not consummated.

After hearing of the Gibbons bid and receiving access to certain confidential information concerning Lucky, American raised its bid to $65 a share. Lucky's board of directors recommended the higher American bid. American eventually acquired Lucky, and Gibbons was paid the $20 million break-up fee.

28. 741 F.2d 1555 (9th Cir. 1984).

29. 382 N.W.2d 576 (Neb. 1986).

30. 637 A.2d 34 (Del. 1994).

THE RESPONSIBLE MANAGER

*Acting in Good Faith
and Dealing Fairly*

It is virtually always preferable to put the terms of an agreement or deal in writing. Memories of even the most well-intentioned parties fade over time. A manager should review any contract before signing it. If the terms are unfamiliar or unclear to the manager, he or she should consult with an attorney. A manager should never sign a contract he or she does not understand.

It is rarely to a manager's advantage to try to slip a provision by the other party that the manager knows would be unacceptable if it were pointed out. It is far preferable to hash out any ambiguities at the negotiation stage while the parties are on good terms and in the mood to make a deal. Positions tend to polarize once the agreement is signed and a dispute arises.

Similarly, it is inappropriate and often unethical to bury offensive terms in a preprinted form contract in the hope that the other party will not spot them. Courts will sometimes refuse to enforce such terms, especially when they conflict with the position taken in the negotiations or are contrary to the spirit of the deal. It makes both legal and ethical sense to abide by the covenant of good faith and fair dealing in negotiating a contract. It is also good business. Contract litigation is expensive and time consuming.

Managers should avoid signing a letter of intent unless they intend to be bound by its proposed terms. Many courts will let a jury decide whether there was intent to be bound, even when the letter of intent states that it is not meant to be binding. If a letter of intent is necessary to obtain financing or to begin due diligence, then the manager not intending to be bound if negotia-tions of the definitive agreement break down should consider doing the following: First, insert clear language into the letter stating that it is not binding, that there is no contract unless and until the parties execute a definitive written contract, and that the letter creates no obligation to negotiate in good faith and cannot be reasonably relied upon. Second, label the document "tentative proposal" or "status letter." Third, do not sign the document.[31]

A manager should carefully consider whether there will be a conflict between the acts required by a contract and his or her fiduciary duties to the corporation and its shareholders. In general, a manager should not bind the directors to recommend a particular deal to the shareholders, because it is always possible that a better offer will come along. The manager should reserve the right to recommend the best deal, even if to do so requires paying a break-up fee to the first bidder.

A manager should ensure that he or she is not tortiously interfering with the contract of another. As *Pennzoil v. Texaco*, discussed in the Inside Story below, demonstrates, even a very large company can be driven into bankruptcy if its executives guess wrong on either the question of whether there is a contract or the question of whether their deal tortiously interferes with it.

It is sometimes tempting to view the drafting and review of contracts as a necessary evil. However, astute managers realize that contract drafting and negotiation can provide opportunities to strengthen business relationships and to protect key assets such as trade secrets, which give a firm a competitive edge.

---

31. *See* William G. Schopf et al., *When a Letter of Intent Goes Wrong*, 5 BUS. L. TODAY 31 (Jan./Feb. 1996).

INSIDE STORY

PENNZOIL v. TEXACO

In 1983, Pennzoil Company and Getty Oil Company negotiated a memorandum of agreement for a merger. Their cadres of lawyers were in the process of drafting the final documents when Texaco, Inc. came along and offered a better price for Getty. Getty accepted Texaco's offer, and Pennzoil subsequently sued Texaco for tortious interference with contract. To win, Getty had to prove (1) the existence of a contract, (2) Texaco's knowledge of the existence of the contract, (3) Texaco's intentional inducement of a breach of the contract, and (4) damages.[32] Texaco asserted that Pennzoil never had a contract, because the parties had not yet agreed on every essential term of the deal. A Texas jury disagreed and awarded Pennzoil $10.5 billion in compensatory and punitive damages.

It took the two parties four and a half months to present all the facts and arguments to the jury. The published opinion of the Texas Court of Appeals summarizes the events in question.[33]

Excerpts from the Opinion of the Court of Appeals: Facts

For several months in late 1983, Pennzoil had followed with interest the well-publicized dissension between the board of directors of Getty Oil Company and Gordon Getty, who was a director of Getty Oil and also the owner, as trustee, of approximately 40.2% of the outstanding shares of Getty Oil. On December 28, 1983, Pennzoil announced an unsolicited, public tender offer for 16 million shares of Getty Oil at $100 each.

Soon afterwards, Pennzoil contacted both Gordon Getty and a representative of the J. Paul Getty Museum, which held approximately 11.8% of the shares of Getty Oil, to discuss the tender offer and the possible purchase of Getty Oil. In the first two days of January 1984, a "Memorandum of Agreement" was drafted to reflect the terms that had been reached in conversations between representatives of Pennzoil, Gordon Getty, and the Museum.

Under the plan set out in the Memorandum of Agreement, Pennzoil and the Trust (with Gordon Getty as trustee) were to become partners on a 3/7ths to 4/7ths basis, respectively, in owning and operating Getty Oil. Gordon Getty was to become chairman of the board, and Hugh Liedtke, the chief executive officer of Pennzoil, was to become chief executive officer of the new company. The plan also provided that Pennzoil and the Trust were to try in good faith to agree upon a plan to restructure Getty Oil within a year, but if they could not reach an agreement, the assets of Getty Oil were to be divided between them, 3/7ths to Pennzoil and 4/7ths to the Trust.

The Memorandum of Agreement stated that it was subject to approval of the board of Getty Oil, and it was to expire by its own terms if not approved at the board meeting that was to begin on January 2. Pennzoil's CEO, Liedtke, and Gordon Getty, for the Trust, signed the Memorandum of Agreement before the Getty Oil board meeting on January 2, and Harold Williams, the president of the Museum, signed it shortly after the board meeting began. Thus, before it was submitted to the Getty Oil board, the Memorandum of Agreement had been executed by parties who together controlled a majority of the outstanding shares of Getty Oil.

The Memorandum of Agreement was then presented to the Getty Oil board, which had previously held discussions on how the company should respond to Pennzoil's public tender offer.

The board voted to reject recommending Pennzoil's tender offer to Getty's shareholders, then later also rejected the Memorandum of Agreement price of $110 per share as too low. On the morning of January 3, Getty Oil's investment banker, Geoffrey Boisi, began calling other companies, seeking a higher bid than Pennzoil's for the Getty Oil shares.

When the board reconvened at 3 P.M. on January 3, a revised Pennzoil proposal was presented, offering $110 per share plus a $3 "stub" that was to be paid after the sale of a Getty Oil subsidiary ("ERC"), from the excess proceeds over $1 billion. Each shareholder was to receive a pro rata share of these excess proceeds, but in any case, a minimum of $3 per share at the end of five years. During the meeting, Boisi briefly informed the board of the status of his inquiries of other companies that might be interested in bidding for the company. He reported some preliminary indications of interest, but no definite bid yet.

The Museum's lawyer told the board that, based on his discussions with Pennzoil, he believed that if the board went back "firm" with an offer of $110 plus a $5 stub, Pennzoil would accept it. After a recess, the Museum's president (also a director of Getty Oil) moved that the Getty board should accept Pennzoil's proposal provided that the stub be raised to $5, and the board voted 15 to 1 to approve this counterproposal to Pennzoil. The board then voted themselves and Getty's officers and advisors indemnity for any liability arising from the events of the past few months. There was evidence that during another brief recess of the board meeting, the counteroffer of $110 plus a $5 stub was presented to and accepted by Pennzoil. After Pennzoil's acceptance was conveyed to the Getty board, the meeting was adjourned, and most board members left town for their respective homes.

That evening, the lawyers and public relations staff of Getty Oil and the Museum drafted a press release describing the transaction between Pennzoil and the Getty entities. The press release, announcing an agreement in principle on the terms of the Memorandum of Agreement but with a price of $110 plus a $5 stub, was issued on Getty Oil letterhead the next morning, January 4, and later that day, Pennzoil issued an identical press release.

On January 4, Boisi continued to contact other companies, looking for a higher price than Pennzoil had offered. After talking briefly with Boisi, Texaco management called several meetings with its in-house financial planning group. . . .

On January 5, the *Wall Street Journal* reported on an agreement reached between Pennzoil and the Getty entities, describing essentially the terms contained in the Memorandum of Agreement. The Pennzoil board met to ratify the actions of its officers in negotiating an agreement with the Getty entities, and Pennzoil's attorneys periodically attempted to contact the other parties' advisors and attorneys to continue work on the transaction agreement.

The board of Texaco also met on January 5, authorizing its officers to make an offer for 100% of Getty Oil and to take any necessary action in connection therewith. Texaco first contacted the Museum's lawyer, Marty Lipton, and arranged a meeting to discuss the sale of the Museum's shares of Getty Oil to Texaco. Lipton instructed his associate, on her way to the meeting in progress of the lawyers drafting merger documents for the Pennzoil/Getty transaction, not to attend that meeting, because he needed her at his meeting with Texaco. At the meeting with Texaco, the Museum outlined various issues it wanted resolved in any transaction with Texaco, and then agreed to sell its 11.8% ownership in Getty Oil [for $125 per share].

At noon on January 6, Getty Oil held a telephone board meeting to discuss the Texaco offer. The board voted to withdraw its previous counterproposal to Pennzoil and unanimously voted to accept Texaco's offer. Texaco immediately issued a press release announcing that Getty Oil and Texaco would merge.

Soon after the Texaco press release appeared, Pennzoil telexed the Getty entities, demanding that they honor their agreement with Pennzoil. Later that day, prompted by the telex, Getty Oil filed a suit in Delaware for declaratory judgment that it was not bound to any contract with Pennzoil. The merger agreement between Texaco and Getty Oil was signed on January 6; the stock purchase agreement with the Museum was signed on January 6; and the stock exchange agreement with the Trust was signed on January 8, 1984.

In addition to the facts described in the excerpts from the opinion of the court of appeals, the Pennzoil lawyers emphasized several other events as evidence that both Pennzoil and Getty intended to be bound by the five-page memorandum of agreement.

At the conclusion of the January 3 Getty board meeting approving the Pennzoil merger, congratulations were exchanged, and many of the individuals present, including several Pennzoil representatives, shook hands. At trial, Texaco pointed out that, handshakes notwithstanding, the Getty board of directors left the meeting without signing the memorandum of agreement.

At trial, Pennzoil made this an issue of honor and the value of a man's word, asserting that a handshake could and often did seal a bargain. For its part, Texaco pointed to the fact that it had not made an offer until it was invited to do so by Getty. John McKinley, chairman of Texaco, repeatedly asked if Getty Oil were free to deal and was assured by Gordon Getty and by the Getty Museum that there was no contract with Pennzoil. In addition, under the law of New York, where all the deals were made, a contract does not exist until the parties have agreed on all the essential terms of the deal. Texaco argued that in a $5 billion deal involving four parties (Pennzoil, Getty Oil Company, the Sarah Getty Trust, and the Getty Museum), a five-page memorandum cannot possibly cover all the essential terms. Why else were upwards of 30 lawyers working around the clock to draw up the merger documents?

Before going further into the many legal arguments involved, it is useful to look more closely at the memorandum of agreement reproduced in Exhibit 7.1.

Getty and Pennzoil had an agreement in principle, but did they have a contract? As soon as the board meeting adjourned on the evening of January 3, work began on the legal documents and on the press release to announce the deal. Both were supposed to be completed by the next morning, but only the press release was ready. Typed on Getty Oil letterhead and dated January 4, 1984, it announced that Getty Oil and Pennzoil had "agreed in principle" to a merger. It further stated: "The transaction is subject to execution of a definitive merger agreement, approval by the stockholders of Getty Oil and completion of various governmental filing and waiting period requirements."

The Texaco deal was much simpler than the Pennzoil deal. Texaco simply bought out everyone at $125 a share. By 8 A.M. on January 6, a news release on Texaco letterhead had gone out. At 9 A.M., the Getty board of directors held another board meeting and approved the deal with Texaco. Texaco acquired Getty Oil, and Pennzoil was left out in the cold.

No one on Wall Street saw anything wrong with the deal, but the attitude in the Texas oil business was different. At the 1984 Pennzoil stockholder meeting, Hugh Liedtke described the decision to sue Texaco:

> It's one thing to play hardball. It's quite another thing to play foul ball. Conduct such as Texaco's is not made legal simply by protestations that the acts involved were, in fact, legal. All too often such assertions go unchallenged, and so slip into some sort of legal limbo, and become accepted as the norm by default. In this way, actions previously considered amoral somehow become clothed in respectability. [34]

EXHIBIT 7.1   The Pennzoil-Getty Memorandum of Agreement

Memorandum of Agreement
January 2, 1984

The following plan (the "Plan") has been developed and approved by (i) Gordon P. Getty, as Trustee (the "Trustee") of the Sarah C. Getty Trust dated December 31, 1934 (the "Trust"), which Trustee owns 31,805,800 shares (40.2% of the total outstanding shares) of Common Stock, without par value, of Getty Oil Company (the "Company"), which shares as well as all other outstanding shares of such Common Stock are hereinafter referred to as the "Shares", (ii) The J. Paul Getty Museum (the "Museum"), which Museum owns 9,320,340 Shares (11.8% of the total outstanding Shares) and (iii) Pennzoil Company ("Pennzoil"), which owns 593,900 Shares through a subsidiary, Holdings Incorporated, a Delaware corporation (the "Purchaser"). The Plan is intended to assure that the public shareholders of the Company and the Museum will receive $110 per Share for all their Shares, a price which is approximately 40% above the price at which the Company's Shares were trading before Pennzoil's subsidiary announced its Offer (hereinafter described) and 10% more than the price which Pennzoil's subsidiary offered in its Offer for 20% of the Shares. The Trustee recommends that the Board of Directors of the Company approve the Plan. The Museum desires that the Plan be considered by the Board of Directors and has executed the Plan for that purpose.

1. Pennzoil agreement. Subject to the approval of the Plan by the Board of Directors of the Company as provided in paragraph 6 hereof, Pennzoil agrees to cause the Purchaser promptly to amend its Offer to Purchase dated December 28, 1983 (the "Offer") for up to 16,000,000 Shares so as:

(a) to increase the Offer price to $110 per Share, net to the Seller in cash and

(b) to increase the number of Shares subject to the Offer to 23,406,100 (being 24,000,000 Shares less 593,900 now owned by the Purchaser).

Exhibit 7.1 continues

Exhibit 7.1 continued

2. Company agreement. Subject to approval of the Plan by the Board of Directors of the Company as provided in paragraph 6 hereof, the Company agrees:
   (a) to purchase forthwith all 9,320,340 Shares owned by the Museum at a purchase price of $110 per Share (subject to adjustment before or after closing in the event of any increase in the Offer price or in the event any higher price is paid by any person who hereafter acquires 10 percent or more of the outstanding Shares) payable either (at the election of the Company) in cash or by means of a promissory note of the Company, dated as of the closing date, payable to the order of the Museum, due on or before thirty days from the date of issuance, bearing interest at a rate equivalent to the prime rate as in effect at Citibank, N.A. and backed by an irrevocable letter of credit (the "Company Note")
   (b) to proceed promptly upon completion of the Offer by the Purchaser with a cash merger transaction whereby all remaining holders of Shares (other than the Trustee and Pennzoil and its subsidiaries) will receive $110 per Share in cash, and
   (c) in consideration of Pennzoil's agreement provided for in paragraph 1 hereof and in order to provide additional assurance that the Plan will be consummated in accordance with its terms, to grant to Pennzoil hereby the option, exercisable at Pennzoil's election at any time on or before the later of consummation of the Offer referred to in paragraph 1 and the purchase referred to in (a) of this paragraph 2, to purchase from the Company up to 8,000,000 Shares of Common Stock of the Company held in the treasury of the Company at a purchase price of $110 per share in cash.
3. Museum agreement. Subject to approval of the Plan by the Board of Directors of the Company as provided in paragraph 6 hereof, the Museum agrees to sell to the Company forthwith all 9,320,340 Shares owned by the Museum at a purchase price of $110 per Share (subject to adjustment before or after closing as provided in paragraph 2(a)) payable either (at the election of the Company) in cash or by means of the Company Note referred to in paragraph 2(c).
4. Trustee and Pennzoil agreement. The Trustee and Pennzoil hereby agree with each other as follows:
   (a) Ratio of Ownership of Shares. The Trustee may increase its holdings to up to 32,000,000 Shares and Pennzoil may increase its holdings to up to 24,000,000 Shares of the approximately 79,132,000 outstanding Shares. Neither the Trustee nor Pennzoil will acquire in excess of such respective amounts without the prior written agreement of the other, it being the agreement between the Trustee and Pennzoil to maintain a relative Share ratio of 4 (for the Trustee) to 3 (for Pennzoil). In connection with the Offer in the event that more than 23,406,100 Shares are duly tendered to the Purchaser, the Purchaser may (if it chooses) purchase any excess over 23,406,000; provided, however, (i) the Purchaser agrees to sell any such excess Shares to the Company (and the company shall agree to purchase) forthwith at $110 per Share and (ii) pending consummation of such sale to the Company the Purchaser shall grant to the Trustee the irrevocable proxy to vote such excess Shares.
   (b) Restructuring plan. Upon completion of the transactions provided for in paragraphs 1, 2 and 3 hereof, the Trustee and Pennzoil shall endeavor in good faith to agree upon a plan for the restructuring of the Company. In the event that for any reason the Trustee and Pennzoil are unable to agree upon a mutually acceptable plan on or before December 31, 1984, then the Trustee and Pennzoil hereby agree to cause the Company to adopt a plan of complete liquidation of the Company pursuant to which (i) any assets which are mutually agreed to be sold shall be sold and the net proceeds therefrom shall be used to reduce liabilities of the Company and (ii) individual interests in all remaining assets and liabilities shall be distributed to the shareholders pro rata in accordance with their actual ownership interest in the Company. In connection with the plan of distribution, Pennzoil agrees (if requested by the

Exhibit 7.1 continues

Exhibit 7.1 continued

Trustee) that it will enter into customary joint operating agreements to operate any properties so distributed and otherwise to agree to provide operating management for any business and operations requested by the Trustee on customary terms and conditions.

(c) Board of Directors and Management. Upon completion of the transactions provided for in paragraphs 1, 2 and 3 hereof, the Trustee and Pennzoil agree that the Board of Directors of the Company shall be composed of approximately fourteen Directors who shall be mutually agreeable to the Trustee and Pennzoil (which Directors may include certain present Directors) and who shall be nominated by the Trustee and Pennzoil, respectively, in the ratio of 4 to 3. The Trustee and Pennzoil agree that the senior management of the Company shall include Gordon P. Getty as Chairman of the Board, J. Hugh Liedtke as President and Chief Executive Officer and Blaine P. Kerr as Chairman of the Executive Committee.

(d) Access to Information. Pennzoil, the Trustee and their representatives will have access to all information concerning the Company necessary or pertinent to accomplish the transactions contemplated by the Plan.

(e) Press releases. The Trustee and Pennzoil (and the Company upon approval of the Plan) will coordinate any press releases or public announcements concerning the Plan and any transactions contemplated hereby.

5. Compliance with regulatory requirements. The Plan shall be implemented in compliance with applicable regulatory requirements.

6. Approval by the Board of Directors. This Plan is subject to approval by the Board of Directors of the Company at the meeting of the Board being held on January 2, 1984, and will expire if not approved by the Board. Upon such approval the Company shall execute three or more counterparts of the "Joinder by the Company" attached to the Plan and deliver one such counterpart to each of the Trustee, the Museum and Pennzoil.

IN WITNESS WHEREOF, this Plan, or a counterpart hereof, has been signed by the following officials thereunto duly authorized this January 2, 1984.

/s/ GORDON P. GETTY
Gordon P. Getty as Trustee of the Sarah C. Getty Trust

The J. Paul Getty Museum

By /s/ HAROLD WILLIAMS
    Harold Williams, President

Pennzoil Company
By _____
    J. Hugh Liedtke, Chairman of the Board and
    Chief Executive Officer

Joinder by the Company

The foregoing Plan has been approved by the Board of Directors.

Getty Oil Company
By_____

January 2, 1984

On January 10, 1984, Pennzoil filed suit in Delaware against Getty Oil, Gordon Getty, the Getty Museum, and Texaco. Pennzoil wanted specific performance—that is, a court order that would give them back their deal with Getty. A few days later, Pennzoil discovered the indemnity clauses and added tortious interference with contract to its claims against Texaco.

The Delaware case was to be tried before a judge, not a jury. Through some legal maneuvering on Pennzoil's part and Texaco's failure to file an answer in the Delaware case right away, the case against Texaco ended up in a Texas court before a jury. (The suits against Getty, the Trust, and the Museum continued in Delaware.) For four and a half months, the two sides presented their evidence. Before the jury retired to the jury room, the judge instructed them how to apply the law to the facts they had heard. The word "contract" never appeared in the jury instructions. Instead the judge used the word "agreement."

The jury deliberated and then returned a verdict in favor of Pennzoil. For Texaco's interference with contract, the jury awarded Pennzoil $7.53 billion compensatory damages and $3 billion punitive damages. (The punitive damages were eventually reduced to $1 billion. The compensatory damages were not changed.)

What did the judges for the Court of Appeals for the First Supreme Judicial District of Texas think of all this? In a lengthy opinion, excerpted below, they upheld the jury's verdict.

Excerpts from the Opinion of the Court of Appeals: Legal Analysis

Under New York law, if parties do not intend to be bound to an agreement until it is reduced to writing and signed by both parties, then there is no contract until that event occurs. If there is no understanding that a signed writing is necessary before the parties will be bound, and the parties have agreed upon all substantial terms, then an informal agreement can be binding, even though the parties contemplate evidencing their agreement in a formal document later.

Thus, under New York law, the parties are given the power to obligate themselves informally or only by a formal signed writing, as they wish. The emphasis in deciding when a binding contract exists is on intent rather than on form.

To determine intent, a court must examine the words and deeds of the parties, because these constitute the objective signs of such intent. Only the outward expressions of intent are considered—secret or subjective intent is immaterial to the question of whether the parties were bound.

Several factors have been articulated to help determine whether the parties intended to be bound only by a formal, signed writing: (1) whether a party expressly reserved the right to be bound only when a written agreement is signed; (2) whether there was any partial performance by one party that the party disclaim-ing the contract accepted; (3) whether all essential terms of the alleged contract had been agreed upon; and (4) whether the complexity or magnitude of the transaction was such that a formal, executed writing would normally be expected.

Although the magnitude of the transaction here was such that normally a signed writing would be expected, there was sufficient evidence to support an inference by the jury that the expectation was satisfied here initially by the Memorandum of Agreement, signed by a majority of shareholders of Getty Oil and approved by the board with a higher price, and by the transaction agreement in progress that had been intended to memorialize the agreement previously reached.

. . .

Texaco claims that even if the parties intended to bind themselves before a definitive document was signed, no binding contract could result because the terms that they intended to include in their agreement were too vague and incomplete to be enforceable as a matter of law. For a contract to be enforceable, the terms of the agreement must be ascertainable to a reasonable degree of certainty. The question of whether the agreement is sufficiently definite to be enforceable is a difficult one. The facts of the individual case are decisively important. The agreement need not be so definite that all the possibilities that might occur to a party in bad faith are explicitly provided for, but it must be sufficiently complete so that parties in good faith can find in the agreement words that will fairly define their respective duties and liabilities. . . .

EXHIBIT 7.2   Pennzoil Comment on Texaco Bankruptcy

© 1987 Margulies, *The Houston Post*. Reprinted by permission.

Texaco's attempts to create additional "essential" terms from the mechanics of implementing the agreement's existing provisions are unpersuasive. The terms of the agreement found by the jury are supported by the evidence, and the promises of the parties are clear enough for a court to recognize a breach and to determine the damages resulting from that breach.

Burdened by the largest damages award in U.S. history, Texaco filed for bankruptcy in 1987 after its appeals in the Texas courts failed. As part of its reorganization plan, Texaco agreed to settle the case with Pennzoil for $3 billion.

This case had a tremendous impact on Wall Street, which the *Wall Street Journal* dubbed "the Texaco chill." Investment banker Alan Rothenberg summarized the new attitude: "No longer can we say, 'We stole a deal fair and square.'"[35] *Pennzoil v. Texaco* is still on the books and can be cited as precedent in similar cases. In legal circles, the arguments still continue as to whether the Texas judges properly understood New York contract law and the jury reached the correct verdict.

32. *See, e.g.*, Kronos, Inc. v. AVX Corp., 612 N.E.2d 289 (N.Y. 1993).

33. Texaco, Inc. v. Pennzoil Co., 729 S.W.2d 768 (Tex. Ct. App. 1987).

34. THOMAS PETZINGER, JR., OIL AND HONOR: THE TEXACO–PENNZOIL WARS 275–76 (1987).

35. *Id.* at 459–60.

KEY WORDS AND PHRASES

QUESTIONS AND CASE PROBLEMS

1. Leslie Landlord agreed to rent Ted Tenant an office for $3,000 per month for three years. Tenant encountered financial difficulties. Landlord agreed to reduce the rent to $2,200 per month, and Tenant agreed not to file for bankruptcy. Tenant had no plans to file for bankruptcy. Unbeknownst to both Landlord and Tenant, a promise not to file for bankruptcy is unenforceable under the Bankruptcy Code. Was the agreement to reduce the rent binding? Would it make a difference if Tenant had planned to file for bankruptcy if he couldn't get the rent reduction? Was Tenant's conduct ethical?

2. Jane Murcello, contract administrator for Tommy's Restaurants, contacted the Fresh Bread Company and made an agreement with the bread company that it would supply Tommy's with all the hamburger buns that it needed. The Fresh Bread Company began supplying Tommy's with the hamburger buns. Murcello then contacted the Fresh Bread Company, stating that Tommy's was going to produce a fish sandwich and would need a special type of bun. She gave the dimensions of the new fish bun and the projected quantities. She stated, "I look forward to increasing our business with you." The Fresh Bread Company made several changes to its kitchen in preparation for baking the buns. Murcello called back two months later saying that she had decided to give the contract to Bake'm Company. The Fresh Bread Company sues Tommy's for breach of contract. Who should prevail?

3. Andy Barstow, owner of a store, entered into a detailed letter of intent to negotiate in good faith the lease of a store with Zandra Ingalls, a prospective tenant. The letter included an outline of what terms needed to be negotiated, including rent. Barstow promised to withdraw the store from the marketplace during the negotiations. Ingalls, during the time of the negotiations, spent money developing a marketing plan for her business.

She also brought in a carpenter, who started building some furniture and cabinets specially designed for the new store. Barstow called Ingalls the following week, saying that he had decided to lease the store to his friend, Bob Burke. What damages, if any, can Ingalls recover?

4. Lanci was involved in an automobile accident with an uninsured motorist. Lanci and Metropolitan Insurance Co. entered settlement negotiations and ultimately agreed to settle all claims for $15,000. Lanci's correspondence accepting the settlement offer clearly indicated his belief that his policy limit was $15,000. However, Lanci did not have a copy of his policy and, in fact, Lanci's policy limit was $250,000. When Lanci learned the correct policy limit, he refused to accept the settlement proceeds of $15,000. Should Lanci be able to void the contract? On what basis? [*Lanci v. Metropolitan Insurance Co.*, 564 A.2d 97 (Pa. Super. Ct. 1989)]

5. Brooks filled out, signed, and submitted a job application at one of Circuit City's stores. The application stated:

> This agreement requires you to arbitrate any legal dispute related to your application for employment with Circuit City. Circuit City will not consider your application unless this agreement is signed. . . . I recognize that if I signed the Agreement and do not withdraw within three days of signing I will be required to arbitrate any and all employment-related claims I may have against Circuit City, whether or not I become employed by Circuit City.

Circuit City offered Brooks only seasonal part-time employment at the store where she wished to work. She rejected this offer and filed an employment-discrimination suit against Circuit City. Circuit City sought to remove the employment-discrimination suit from court and bring it to arbitration, pursuant to the "agreement" in Brooks's job application. What result? [*Brooks v. Circuit City Stores, Inc.*, 73 Fair Empl. Prac. Cas. (BNA) 1838 (D. Md. 1997)]

6. Sutton and Epperson were the largest stockholders in Old Southern Life Insurance Co. Sutton had become dissatisfied with Epperson's management of the closely held corporation. He called a special meeting of the board of directors at which Epperson was removed from further management of the company.

Sutton subsequently agreed to purchase the Epperson family's stock in Old Southern for $1.75 million. Both parties were represented by counsel in the transaction, and no objection was made to a liquidated dam-

ages clause. The clause provided that if Sutton failed or refused to consummate the sale within the period allowed, a $50,000 binder would be retained by the Eppersons as liquidated damages for breach of the contract.

Sutton delivered a $50,000 binder check to Epperson on March 9, 1990. On April 25, 1990, the date set for consummation of the sales agreement, the parties met to close the transaction. However, Epperson's son, who was part owner of some of the shares, was not present. As a result, the transaction was not consummated because the son failed to sign the necessary closing documents. The next day, April 26, Sutton learned that the financial condition of Old Southern had deteriorated. He immediately informed the Eppersons that he was withdrawing his offer and would not complete the purchase.

The Eppersons cashed Sutton's check for $50,000. Should they be able to keep the money? [*Sutton v. Epperson*, 631 So. 2d 832 (Ala. 1993)]

7. Hydrotech, Inc., a New York corporation, agreed to sell wave-pool equipment to Oasis Waterpark, an amusement park in Palm Springs, California. Although Hydrotech was not licensed to install such equipment in California, it agreed to install the wave-pool equipment after Oasis promised to arrange for a California-licensed contractor to "work with" Hydrotech on any construction.

The contract between Hydrotech and Oasis called for Oasis to withhold a specific portion of the contract price pending satisfactory operation of the wave pool. Although the pool functioned properly after installation, Oasis continued to withhold payment for both the equipment and the installation services.

Section 7031 of the California Business and Professions Code states that one may not sue in a California court to recover compensation for any act or contract that requires a California contractor's license unless one alleges and proves that he or she was duly licensed at all times during the performance.

Can Hydrotech recover its compensation due under the contract? Does Hydrotech have a valid action against Oasis for fraud? Is it ethical for Oasis to use the California law to defend itself? [*Hydrotech Systems, Ltd. v. Oasis Waterpark*, 803 P.2d 370 (Cal. 1991)]

8. Prometheus Takeles, a relatively unknown Hollywood screenwriter, contracted with Star Motion Pictures Corporation (Star) to write a tragic comedy for a low-budget film. Star offered Prometheus 25% of the film's net profits for the first year the film was played.

Prometheus noticed that the document contained a very complicated formula defining "net profit." When he asked about the formula, which was six pages long, Star told him that its net profit formula for screenwriters was standard for the film industry. Prometheus signed the contract. Later, the film became a huge Hollywood success, earning more than $500 million in gross profits in the first year.

When Prometheus demanded his payment, the studio told him that the film had earned no net profit. Outraged, Prometheus sued Star for damages, claiming that the contract terms defining net profit were unconscionable. Star produced detailed financial documents demonstrating how the film had failed to earn any net profit. From the $500 million in gross revenues, Star deducted distribution fees totaling nearly 35% of the gross receipts, additional distribution costs, advertising fees (adding a flat 10% overhead fee), production costs (adding a flat 15% overhead charge), taxes (whether paid or not), political lobbying and guild expenses, and interest charges of 125% on expenses until the film broke even on all costs. Thus calculated, there remained no net profit on the seemingly successful film. Star argued that this formula reflects its huge risk in producing films, and that if it did not so compute net profit, it could not remain in business. Who should prevail? Was Star's conduct ethical?

9. Emmett Employer called Sally Denoco and offered her a two-year employment contract. Denoco said, "Great, I accept," and quit her present job, forfeiting unvested stock options. After Denoco had worked for Employer for six months, Employer fired Denoco. She then sued. Who should win? Does it matter if Employer made a note to himself after the phone call: "Sally Denoco—two-year contract. Salary to be negotiated"? If Denoco were to win, what would be her damages? Would she be entitled to anything if she quit her old job but never started work for Employer? What should Employer and Denoco each have done to protect their rights?

MANAGER'S DILEMMA

10. As lawyers assembled closing documents for a refinancing of some of the outstanding debt of United States Lines (USL), a secretary working on "Amendment No. 1 to the First Preferred Ship Mortgage" omitted three zeros from the number representing USL's outstanding indebtedness to Prudential Insurance. As a result, the document showed the amount of Prudential's first mortgage as "$92,885.00" instead of "$92,885,000.00." No one noticed the error until eight months later when USL defaulted on the notes secured by the amended mortgage and went bankrupt.

When Prudential tried to foreclose its $92,885,000 first mortgage, USL's bankruptcy trustee objected, arguing that the mortgage should be limited to $92,885. In addition, General Electric Capital Corporation (GECC), which had lent money to USL secured by a second mortgage, brought suit for a declaration that Prudential's first mortgage was valid only to the extent of $92,885. Since GECC had lent money to USL secured by a mortgage junior to that of Prudential, GECC stood to gain by reducing the value of Prudential's first mortgage.

GECC had been intimately involved in USL's financing for some years and knew that Prudential had a $92,885,000 first mortgage. Neither GECC nor any other creditor of USL asserted that it had relied on erroneous information about the amount of USL's outstanding debt.

Is Prudential legally entitled to a $92,885,000 first mortgage?

If you had been the manager at GECC in charge of the USL account, what would you have done once the typo was discovered? What would be the ethical thing to do? [*See* Andrew Kull, *Zero-Based Morality: The Case of the $31 Million Typo*, 1 BUS. L. TODAY 11 (July/Aug. 1992).]

INTERNET SOURCES

The law firm of Fenwick and West supports a page offering information about contract issues regarding electronic commerce.	http://www.fenwick.com/pub/351684.html
The Law Journal Extra provides news and other information about commercial law.	http://www.ljx.com/practice/commercial/index.html
The Contract Law Information network page provides a variety of information about Australian contract law and related issues.	http://law.anu.edu.au
The Buyer's Resource home page provides an extensive glossary of contract and other business terminology.	http://homes.inresco.com/Bglossary.html
The 'Lectric Law Library page offers a variety of business contract forms.	http://www.lectlaw.com/formb.html
This site contains the discussion draft of the Uniform Electronic Transactions Act.	http://www.law.upenn.edu/library/ulc/ulc.htm

CHAPTER 8

Sales

INTRODUCTION

When Does Article 2 of the UCC Apply?

Virtually all commercial enterprises engage in the purchase or sale of goods. Sales of goods within the United States are governed by Article 2 of the Uniform Commercial Code (UCC); most international sales are governed by the Convention on Contracts for the International Sale of Goods. Section 2-105 of the UCC defines *goods* as "all things (including specially manufactured goods) which are movable at the time of identification to the contract for sale." *Identification to the contract* means the designation—by marking, setting aside, or other means—of the particular goods that are to be supplied under the contract. The UCC has attempted to eliminate some of the legal formalities of traditional contract law to be in greater accord with the needs and realities of the business world. Many provisions of the UCC can be changed by the express agreement of the parties. To the extent that the UCC is silent on a subject, the common law contract provisions described in Chapter 7 apply.

The UCC does not govern the rendering of services or the sale of land. Contracts for selling services or land are governed by common law contract principles.

Sometimes the characterization of an activity as a sale of goods or of services is not clear. For example, when a hospital performs a blood transfusion, is it selling blood or rendering medical services?[1] This distinction can be critical for purposes of both the UCC warranties and product liability in tort (discussed in Chapter 10).

Similarly, there can be an issue as to whether something attached to land is considered goods or land. This gray area includes *fixtures*, which are items of personal property that are attached to real property and cannot be removed without substantial damage. Fixtures are not considered goods under Article 2. They are generally subject to the rules governing real property.

The UCC regulates sales of goods by both merchants and nonmerchants, to whom different rules may apply. Thus, for example, if Sam were to sell a car to Jay, the UCC would dictate both parties' rights and obligations under the sales contract, whether Sam was employed as a car dealer or was simply selling his personal possessions on his own behalf. Section 2-104 of the UCC defines a *merchant* as "a person who deals in goods of the kind or otherwise by his occupation holds himself out as having knowledge or skill peculiar to the practices or goods involved in the transaction."

Chapter Overview

This chapter addresses contract formation under the UCC and the UCC approach to the "battle of the forms," which occurs when the form accepting an offer contains terms different from those on the form that constitutes the offer. The special warranty provisions of the UCC are discussed, including express warranties and implied warranties of merchantability and fitness for a particular purpose. The chapter explains how the risk of loss is allocated and a buyer's right to reject nonconforming goods. The chapter then reviews excuses for nonperformance, including unconscionability and commercial impracticability, and remedies for unexcused nonperformance. It concludes with a discussion of the international sale of goods.

Contract Formation

Under common law, a contract is enforceable only if all necessary terms were expressed at the time of contracting. The UCC departs from this approach and permits a contract to be enforced if the parties intended a binding contract, even though important terms may have been left open for later agreement. If a dispute later arises over a missing term, the court may simply use a "gap-filler" as provided by the UCC. The court will fill in missing terms, however, only if the party attempting to enforce the contract can prove that there was a genuine agreement, not a mere proposal or intention to continue negotiations. It must be apparent that there has been an offer, acceptance, and consideration.

---

1. To precisely address the issue, many states have passed special amendments to their versions of the UCC. These so-called blood shield statutes define blood transfusions as the provision of services, rather than the sale of goods, in order to limit hospital and blood bank liability for reasons of public policy. *See, e.g.,* Zichichi v. Middlesex Memorial Hosp., 528 A.2d 805 (Conn. 1987), and Garcia v. Edgewater Hosp., 613 N.E.2d 1243 (Ill. App. Ct. 1993). In other states, the common law has led to the conclusion that such sales are incidental to the provision of medical services and, therefore, outside the scope of the UCC. *See, e.g.,* Lovett v. Emory Univ., Inc., 156 S.E.2d 923 (Ga. Ct. App. 1967).

Offer

Offer is not defined by the UCC, although it is used in several important sections. Therefore, traditional common law principles (discussed in Chapter 7) determine whether an offer has been made. Under the UCC, as in common law, neither an invitation for bids nor a price quotation is an offer. Similarly, a proposal by a sales representative that is subject to approval by the home office is not an offer.

Acceptance

The UCC does not define *acceptance* either, except to state that an acceptance may contain terms additional to or different from those in the offer. This is different from the common law mirror-image rule, which requires the acceptance to contain the exact same terms as the offer.

Unless the offeror indicates unambiguously that his or her offer can only be accepted in a particular way, an offer may be accepted in any manner and by any medium that is reasonable in the circumstances.

In our heavily technological age, the issue of what constitutes acceptance can be murky, as the following case illustrates.

A CASE IN POINT	**IN THE LANGUAGE OF THE COURT**

CASE 8.1
ProCD, Inc. v.
ZEIDENBERG
United States Court of
Appeals for the Seventh Circuit
86 F.3d 1447 (7th Cir. 1996).

FACTS   ProCD compiled information from more than 3,000 telephone directories into a single database. The database cost more than $10 million to compile and was expensive to keep current. ProCD sold a version of this database, called SelectPhone, on CD-ROM. Each SelectPhone CD-ROM package contained within it a *shrink-wrap license,* that is, a license that customers could not read when they made their decision to purchase SelectPhone but were deemed to have accepted when they opened the wrapping around the envelope containing the disks or clicked on the "I Accept" box on the computer screen. Among other things, the shrink-wrap license prohibited the unauthorized resale of the SelectPhone database.

Zeidenberg purchased a SelectPhone in Wisconsin and opened the packaging, including the shrink wrap. He also clicked on the "I Accept" box on the computer screen but decided to ignore the terms of the license. Instead, he formed Silken Mountain Web Services, Inc. (Silken Mountain)-to resell the information in the SelectPhone database. Silken Mountain made the SelectPhone database available on the Internet to anyone willing to pay Silken Mountain's price, which was less than that charged by

Case 8.1 continues

Case 8.1 continued

ProCD. Zeidenberg later purchased two updated versions of the database to make the latest SelectPhone information available via the Internet.

ProCD sued Zeidenberg and Silken Mountain for violating the license contained within the SelectPhone packages. The trial court found in favor of Zeidenberg and Silken Mountain on the grounds that the shrink-wrap license was not enforceable as a matter of Wisconsin contract law. ProCD appealed.

ISSUE PRESENTED   Is a shrink-wrap license whose terms are unknown at the time of purchase binding on the buyer?

OPINION   EASTERBROOK, J., writing for the U.S. Court of Appeals:

. . . [C]onsider the purchase of an airline ticket. The traveler calls the carrier or an agent, is quoted a price, reserves a seat, pays, and gets a ticket, in that order. The ticket contains elaborate terms, which the traveler can reject by canceling the reservation. To use the ticket is to accept the terms, even terms that in retrospect are disadvantageous. Just so with a ticket to a concert. The back of the ticket states that the patron promises not to record the concert; to attend is to agree. A theater that detects a violation will confiscate the tape and escort the violator to the exit. One could arrange things so that every concertgoer signs this promise before forking over the money, but that cumbersome way of doing things not only would lengthen queues and raise prices but also would scotch the sale of tickets by phone or electronic data service.

Consumer goods work the same way. Someone who wants to buy a radio set visits a store, pays, and walks out with a box. Inside the box is a leaflet containing some terms, the most important of which usually is the warranty, read for the first time in the comfort of home. By Zeidenberg's lights, the warranty in the box is irrelevant; every consumer gets the standard warranty implied by the UCC in the event the contract is silent; yet so far as we are aware no state disregards warranties furnished with consumer products. Drugs come with a list of ingredients on the outside and an elaborate package insert on the inside. The package insert describes drug interactions, contraindications, and other vital information—but, if Zeidenberg is right, the purchaser need not read the package insert, because it is not part of the contract.

Next consider the software industry itself. Only a minority of sales take place over the counter, where there are boxes to peruse. A customer may place an order by phone in response to a line item in a catalog or a review in a magazine. Much software is ordered over the Internet by purchasers who have never seen a box. Increasingly software arrives by wire. There is no box; there is only a stream of electrons, a collection of information that includes data, an application program, instructions, many limitations . . . and the terms of sale. The user purchases a serial number, which activates the software's features. On Zeidenberg's arguments, these unboxed sales are unfettered by terms—so the seller has made a broad warranty and must pay consequential damages for any shortfalls in performance, two "promises" that if taken seriously would drive prices through the ceiling or return transactions to the horse-and-buggy age.

Case 8.1 continues

Case 8.1 continued

According to the [trial] court, the UCC does not countenance the sequence of money now, terms later. . . .

What then does the current version of the UCC have to say? We think that the place to start is § 2-204(1): "A contract for sale of goods may be made in any manner sufficient to show agreement, including conduct by both parties which recognizes the existence of such a contract." A vendor, as master of the offer, may invite acceptance by conduct, and may propose limitations on the kind of conduct that constitutes acceptance. A buyer may accept by performing the acts the vendor proposes to treat as acceptance. And that is what happened. ProCD proposed a contract that a buyer would accept by using the software after having an opportunity to read the license at leisure. This Zeidenberg did. He had no choice, because the software splashed the license on the screen and would not let him proceed without indicating acceptance. So although the district judge was right to say that a contract can be, and often is, formed simply by paying the price and walking out of the store, the UCC permits contracts to be formed in other ways. ProCD proposed such a different way, and without protest Zeidenberg agreed. Ours is not a case in which a consumer opens a package to find an insert saying "you owe us an extra $10,000" and the seller files suit to collect. Any buyer finding such a demand can prevent formation of the contract by returning the package, as can any consumer who concludes that the terms of the license make the software worth less than the purchase price. . . .

. . .

Some portions of the UCC impose additional requirements on the way parties agree on terms. . . . Zeidenberg has not located any Wisconsin case—for that matter, any case in any state—holding that under the UCC the ordinary terms found in shrinkwrap licenses require any special prominence, or otherwise are to be undercut rather than enforced. In the end, the terms of the license are conceptually identical to the contents of the package. Just as no court would dream of saying that Select-Phone must contain 3,100 phone books rather than 3,000, or must have data no more than 30 days old, or must sell for $100 rather than $150—although any of these changes would be welcomed by the customer, if all other things were held constant—so, we believe, Wisconsin would not let the buyer pick and choose among terms. Terms of use are no less a part of "the product" than are the size of the database and the speed with which the software compiles listings. Competition among vendors, not judicial revision of a package's contents, is how consumers are protected in a market economy. ProCD has rivals, which may elect to compete by offering superior software, monthly updates, improved terms of use, lower price, or a better compromise among these elements. As we stressed above, adjusting terms in buyers' favor might help Matthew Zeidenberg today (he already has the software) but would lead to a response, such as a higher price, that might make consumers as a whole worse off.

RESULT   The appeals court reversed the decision of the trial court and ruled that the terms of a shrink-wrap license are binding on the buyer unless the terms are objectionable on grounds applicable to contracts in general.

Case 8.1 continues

Case 8.1 continued

Questions

1. Would the result have been different if the terms had included restrictions on the number of hours per day the buyer could use the software? Restrictions on the number of different users allowed to use the software? Restrictions on the use of the information, for example, no fundraising for abortion rights?

2. Even though shrink-wrap licenses are most common in the software industry, are there limits to the types of products to which such licensing terms may be applied?

VIEW FROM CYBERSPACE

SOFTWARE AND UCC ARTICLE 2B

Reacting to the rapid growth in information transactions and the rise of electronic commerce, the National Conference of Commissioners of Uniform State Laws is planning a major revision to the Uniform Commercial Code. A new Article 2B would cover many transactions otherwise not within the scope of the UCC. Such "transactions in information" would include licenses and agreements to support, maintain, develop, and modify information (including software). For purposes of the new article, "information" includes data, text, images, sounds, software, and databases. This will effectively eliminate the distinction between "goods" and "services" in software transactions. The licensing of trademarks and patents, however, will remain outside the scope of the UCC.

Other provisions of the new article address (1) issues arising from electronic data interchange, which enables parties to place orders electronically without human intervention; (2) enforceability of shrink-wrap and click-wrap licenses; (3) conduct constituting acceptance of offers; and (4) express and implied warranties for software and related services.

Perhaps the most controversial provisions in Article 2B, as currently drafted, are those that generally validate nonnegotiable shrink-wrap licenses for mass-marketed software. Some consumer rights advocates fear that such validation would give software vendors the ability to force consumers to forfeit important rights protected by the Copyright Act. In particular, consumers could be required to agree contractually to give up their right to "fair use" of copyrighted material and their right to copy and use uncopyrightable material. In November 1997, Representative Rick Bowcher (D-Va.) introduced a bill to the House of Representatives—The Digital Era Copyright Enhancement Act (H.R. 3048)—that would preempt state laws that give owners of information greater rights than they would have under the federal copyright law.

Once the commissions agree on the final wording of Article 2B, each state legislature must adopt it before it will become effective in that state.

Consideration

As with other contracts, contracts for the sale of goods ordinarily must have consideration to be enforceable. However, a *firm offer*, that is, a signed offer by a merchant that indicates that the offer will be kept open, is not revocable for lack of consideration. The offer must be kept open during the time stated, or for a reasonable period of time if none is stated, up to a maximum of three months. This rule is just one example of how the UCC provides more stringent standards for merchants than for nonmerchants.

Under common law, an agreement to modify a contract is binding only if there is consideration for the modification. Under the UCC, however, an agreement to modify a contract is binding even if there is no consideration for the modification as long as the modification was made in good faith. However, if the original contract was required to be in writing to satisfy the statute of frauds (discussed later in this chapter), then the agreement to modify the contract must be in writing also.

 ## Battle of the Forms

In a battle of the forms, the parties negotiate on the essential terms of the contract (for example, quantity, quality, and delivery date) but neglect to bargain over items that are less immediately important (for example, whether disputes will be subject to arbitration, for how long a period after delivery the buyer may assert complaints of defects, or on whom the risk of loss during shipment falls). The parties then exchange standard printed forms, each of which is filled with fine print listing all kinds of terms advantageous to the party that drew up the form. Often goods are shipped, received, and paid for before both parties have expressly accepted the same document as their contract. As a result of these exchanges, two questions arise: (1) Is there a contract? and (2) If so, what are its terms?

The UCC calls a truce in the battle of the forms by effectively abolishing the mirror-image rule. It is not necessary for an offer and acceptance to match exactly in order for a contract for the sale of goods to exist. Adding to or modifying terms in the offer does not make the acceptance a counteroffer, as is true under common law.

Section 2-207 of the UCC provides that a contract exists whenever the parties act as if there is a contract between them. It is not necessary to determine which document constitutes the offer and which the acceptance. The only issue to be decided is what the terms of the contract will be.

Definite Response

A definite and timely assent to an offer constitutes an acceptance. The presence of additional or different terms is not a bar to contract formation. The crucial inquiry is whether the parties intended to close a deal. If the offeree's response manifests the intent to enter into a deal, the offer has been accepted. For example, if additional or different terms merely appear in the standard printed language of a form contract, it is likely that the offeree intended to close a deal.

If, however, the response indicates only a willingness to continue negotiations, it is not an acceptance but a counteroffer. For example, an additional or different term that directly pertains to one of the negotiated terms, such as price or quantity, is evidence that the parties are still negotiating and have not reached an agreement.

Conditional Response

If the offeree wants to make a counteroffer rather than an acceptance, he or she should state clearly that acceptance is conditioned on the offeror's agreement to the additional or different terms. The safest course is to use language of the UCC; for example: "This acceptance is expressly made conditional on offeror's assent to all additional or different terms contained herein. Should offeror not give assent to said terms, there is no contract between the parties." Less direct language (such as "The acceptance of your order is subject to the conditions set forth herein," and "Acceptance of this order is expressly limited to the condition of purchase printed on the reverse side") has been held an acceptance rather than a counteroffer.

Acceptance with Missing Terms

What happens when the parties ship, receive, and pay for goods without first agreeing on all material terms? In that case, Section 2-207(3) provides that the terms of the contract will be those on which the writings exchanged by the parties agree, supplemented by the UCC's gap-fillers where needed.

Acceptance with Additional Terms

What is the effect of additional terms in an acceptance when the contract is not expressly made subject to the offeror's agreeing to those terms? The answer depends on whether the parties are merchants. Under Section 2-207(2), if even one of the parties is not a merchant, additional terms are construed as proposals for additions to the contract that the acceptance has created. Unless the offeror expressly agrees to the added provisions, they do not become part of the contract. If both parties are merchants, on the other hand, the additional provisions in the acceptance automatically become part of the contract, unless (1) the offer expressly limits acceptance to the terms of the offer; (2) the new terms materially alter the original offer; or (3) the party making the original offer notifies the other party within a reasonable time that it objects to the new terms. If one of these exceptions applies, the additional terms serve as proposals requiring the express consent of the offeror to become part of the contract.

Acceptance with Different Terms

What is the effect of different—as opposed to additional—terms in an acceptance when the acceptance is not expressly made subject to the offeror's agreeing to those terms? As in the case of additional terms in a response to an offer, different terms neither defeat the acceptance nor impede the formation of the contract. But what is the effect of those different terms? Mysteriously, the language of Section 2-207 does not address this situation. There are generally three possible answers: (1) as with additional terms governed by Section 2-207(2), the different terms could become part of a contract between merchants unless one of the three conditions discussed previously is met; (2) the additional terms could be ignored or treated as separate offers to modify the accepted contract; and (3) the opposing terms could "knock out" each other and UCC gap-fillers could be put in their place.

The following case illustrates how most courts deal with the situation in which the parties have sent conflicting forms, transacted their business, and then realized that they disagree about the terms of their contract.

A CASE IN POINT	SUMMARY

CASE 8.2
IONICS, INC. v.
ELMWOOD SENSORS,
INC.
United States Court of
Appeals for the First Circuit
110 F.3d 184 (1st Cir. 1997).

FACTS   Elmwood Sensors manufactures and sells thermostats, and Ionics makes hot- and cold-water dispensers, which it leases to its customers. On three separate occasions in 1990, Ionics purchased thermostats from Elmwood for use in its water dispensers. On each occasion, Ionics sent Elmwood a purchase order form that contained, in small type, various conditions.

Condition 18, entitled "Remedies," provided:

The remedies provided Buyer herein shall be cumulative, and in addition to any other remedies provided by law or equity. A waiver of a breach of any provision hereof shall not constitute a waiver of any other breach.

Condition 19, entitled "Acceptance," provided:

Acceptance by the Seller of this order shall be upon the terms and conditions set forth in items 1 to 17 inclusive, and elsewhere in this order. Said order can be so accepted only on the exact terms herein and set forth. No terms which are in any manner additional to or different from those herein set forth shall become a part of, alter or in any way control the terms and conditions herein set forth.

Before placing its first order, Ionics sent Elmwood a letter stating:

The information preprinted, written and/or typed on our purchase order is especially important to us. Should you take exception to this information, please clearly express any reservations to us in writing. If you do not, we will assume that you have agreed to the specified terms and that you will fulfill your obligations according to our purchase order. If necessary, we will change your invoice and pay your invoice according to our purchase order.

Case 8.2 continues

Case 8.2 continued

Following receipt of each order, Elmwood prepared and sent an "Acknowledgment" form containing the following language in small type:

This will acknowledge receipt of buyer's order and state seller's willingness to sell the goods ordered but only upon the terms and conditions set forth herein and on the reverse side hereof as a counteroffer. Buyer shall be deemed to have accepted such counteroffer unless it is rejected in writing within ten (10) days of the receipt hereof, and all subsequent action shall be pursuant to the terms and conditions of this counteroffer only; any additional or different terms are hereby objected to and shall not be binding upon the parties unless specifically agreed to in writing by seller.

For each of its three orders, Ionics received Elmwood's Acknowledgment prior to receiving the thermostats. Among the terms and conditions listed on the back of Elmwood's form was the following warranty term:

All goods manufactured by Elmwood Sensors, Inc. are guaranteed to be free of defects in material and workmanship for a period of ninety (90) days after receipt of such goods by Buyer or eighteen months from the date of manufacturer [*sic*] (as evidenced by the manufacturer's date code), whichever shall be longer. There is no implied warranty of merchantability and no other warranty, expressed or implied, except such as is expressly set forth herein. Seller will not be liable for any general, consequential or incidental damages, including without limitation any damages from loss of profits, from any breach of warranty or for negligence, seller's liability and buyer's exclusive remedy being expressly limited to the repair of defective goods f.o.b. the shipping point indicated on the face hereof or the repayment of the purchase price upon the return of the goods or the granting of a reasonable allowance on account of any defects, as seller may elect.

Several of the Ionics dispensers subsequently caused fires that allegedly resulted from defects in the Elmwood sensors. Ionics filed suit against Elmwood for breach of the implied warranty of fitness in an effort to recover costs incurred in the wake of the fires. Elmwood moved for partial summary judgment limiting its exposure to the warranty in its Acknowledgment. The trial court held that the conflicting terms would be stricken and that UCC warranty terms would apply in their place. As a result, warranties of fitness attached to the thermostats. Elmwood appealed.

ISSUE PRESENTED   If there has been an acceptance of an offer, but the offer and acceptance are on printed forms that contain contradictory terms, is there a contract? If so, what are its terms?

SUMMARY OF OPINION   The U.S. Court of Appeals began with a literal reading of Section 2-207, which addresses additional terms made in acceptance or confirmation of an order between merchants. Under Section 2-207, the additional terms become part of the contract unless (1) the offer expressly limits acceptance to the terms of the offer; (2) the terms materially change the contract; or (3) notification of objection is given within a reasonable time after the terms are received. The section goes on to state that conduct by both parties recognizing a contract will establish the contract, the terms of which will consist of the terms on which the writings of the parties agree and any supplementary terms provided by the UCC.

A case decided 25 years earlier by the same court, however, held that an acceptance with conflicting terms was outside the scope of Section 2-207. In *Roto-Lith, Ltd.*

Case 8.2 continues

Case 8.2 continued

v. *F.P. Bartlett & Co.*,[2] the court applied the first part of Section 2-207 and ruled that a response to an offer that includes a term "materially altering the obligation solely to the disadvantage of the offeror" is an acceptance conditional on agreement to the new term. The *Roto-Lith* court then reverted to common law and concluded that the buyer had accepted the seller's terms by accepting the goods. Hence, the new terms were part of the contract.

The *Ionics* court then turned to the final part of Section 2-207, allowing conduct between merchants to establish a contract whose disputed terms are filled in by the UCC. Comment 6 to that section squarely addressed the issue:

> If no answer is received within a reasonable time after additional terms are proposed, it is both fair and commercially sound to assume that their inclusion has been assented to. Where clauses on confirming forms sent by both parties conflict, each party must be assumed to object to a clause of the other. . . . As a result, the requirement that there be notice of objection . . . is satisfied and the conflicting terms do not become part of the contract. The contract then consists of the terms originally expressly agreed to, terms on which the confirmations agree, and terms supplied by [the UCC].

(Note that the official comments to the UCC help courts to understand the drafters' intentions, but they are not binding. If a judge believes there is a conflict between the statute and the comment, the judge will follow the statute.)

Facing the stark contradiction between *Roto-Lith*'s clear precedent and "the clear dictates of the [UCC]," the court had to make a choice. Noting the majority view in favor of the UCC comment, extensive criticism of the *Roto-Lith* approach, and the intent of Section 2-207 to modify the mirror image rule, the court overturned *Roto-Lith*. In conclusion, the court noted, "The reality of modern commercial dealings, as this case demonstrates, is that not all participants read their forms. To uphold Elmwood's view would . . . fly in the face of good sense."

RESULT The appeals court affirmed the trial court's decision to strike the contradictory terms and to use the UCC implied warranty of fitness as a gap-filler. Hence, Elmwood's thermostats were sold subject to the implied warranty of fitness.

COMMENTS By formally adopting the knockout rule instead of the old approach under *Roto-Lith*, the appeals court made it much harder to game the system by exchanging preprinted forms with boilerplate rejection of the other party's terms. With conflicting terms simply thrown out and replaced by UCC gap-fillers, managers using such forms should be aware of what UCC provisions might replace their standard terms.

---

2. 297 F.2d 497 (1st Cir. 1962).

 Statute of Frauds

Section 2-201 of the UCC is a *statute of frauds*. It provides that a contract for the sale of goods for $500 or more is unenforceable unless it is at least partly in writing. It states:

1. There must be some writing evidencing the sale of goods.
2. The writing must be signed by the party against whom enforcement is sought.
3. The writing must specify the quantity of the goods sold.

"Some Writing"

Statutes of frauds generally require all the essential terms of the contract to be in writing; the UCC's requirement for "some writing" is relatively lenient. The official comments to Section 2-201 state: "All that is required is that the writing afford a basis for believing that the offered oral evidence rests on a real transaction. It may be written in lead pencil on a scratch pad." The comments go on to state: "The price, time and place of payment or delivery, the general quality of the goods, or any particular warranties may all be omitted."

Signature

The writing must be signed by the party against whom enforcement is sought, unless the sale is between merchants and (1) a confirmation of the contract has been received, (2) the party receiving it has reason to know its contents, and (3) that party has not made a written objection within ten days after the confirmation was received. For example, an invoice that a seller sent to a buyer would be a contract enforceable against the buyer if there was no response from the buyer within ten days after receiving the invoice.

Quantity of Goods

The only term that must appear in the writing is that which designates the quantity of goods. This term is necessary to provide a basis for awarding monetary damages in the case of a breach. The contract is not enforceable beyond the quantity of goods shown in the writing. If no quantity is specified, the contract is unenforceable unless (1) the goods were specially manufactured for the buyer and are not suitable for resale to others in the ordinary course of the seller's business; (2) the defendant admits in a judicial proceeding that there was an agreement; or (3) payment for the goods was made and accepted or the goods were received and accepted.

◆ Warranties

Goods delivered pursuant to a contract may not live up to the buyer's expectations. In many such cases, the buyer can sue the seller for breaching an express or implied warranty that the goods sold would have certain qualities or would perform in a certain way.

The UCC's warranty provisions attempt to determine what attributes of the goods the parties have agreed upon. The UCC allows a great deal of flexibility in this regard, permitting consideration of the description of the goods, the seller's words, common uses in the trade, the price paid, and the extent to which the buyer has communicated particular needs to the seller to determine which warranties apply. As a result, the seller of goods may find itself bound, perhaps unintentionally, by one of the three warranties provided by the UCC: express warranty, implied warranty of merchantability, and implied warranty of fitness for a particular purpose.

Express Warranty

An *express warranty* is an explicit guarantee by the seller that the goods will have certain qualities. Section 2-313 of the UCC has two requirements for the creation of an express warranty. First, the seller must either make a statement or promise relating to the goods, provide a description of the goods, or furnish a sample or model of the goods. Second, this statement, promise, description, sample, or model must become a "part of the basis of the bargain" between the seller and the buyer. This second requirement is intended to ensure that the buyer actually relied on the seller's statement when making a purchasing decision. For example, if a car dealer asserts that a car will reach 130 mph, and the buyer's response is "I'm never going to take it above 55," it is unlikely that the buyer could claim breach of warranty if the car failed to go over 70 mph.

Puffing   Section 2-313(2) provides that a warranty may be found even though the seller never uses the word "warranty" or "guarantee" and has no intention of making a warranty. The seller has the burden of proving that the buyer did not rely on his or her representations. However, if a seller is merely *puffing*—that is, expressing an opinion about the quality of the goods—he or she has not made a warranty. For example, a car salesperson's statement that "this is a top-notch car" is puffing, whereas a factual statement such as "it will get 25 miles to the gallon" is an express warranty.

Unfortunately, the line between opinion and fact is not always easy to draw. Much turns on the circumstances surrounding the representation, including the identities and relative knowledge of the parties involved.

A number of courts employ a two-prong test to distinguish warranty language from opinion. The first prong is whether the seller asserted a fact of which the buyer was ignorant. If so, the assertion may be a warranty. The second prong is whether the seller merely stated a view on something about which the buyer could be expected to have formed his or her own opinion and whether the buyer could judge the validity of the seller's statement. In this second instance, the seller's statement is an opinion, not a warranty. The following case illustrates the difficulty of making these distinctions.

A CASE IN POINT   **IN THE LANGUAGE OF THE COURT**

CASE 8.3
WENG v. ALLISON
Appellate Court of Illinois
678 N.E.2d 1254
(Ill. App. Ct.1997).

FACTS   Michael and Karla Weng bought from Thomas Allison a 10-year-old car that had been driven 96,000 miles. In his prepurchase discussions with the Wengs, Allison told them that the car was "mechanically sound," "in good condition," "a good, reliable car," "a good car," and had "no problems." Without test-driving it, the Wengs purchased the car for $800.

As they drove the car home, the Wengs noticed that it did not seem to operate properly. They took their new car to an automobile dealership for an inspection and learned that it needed extensive repairs costing $1,500 and that it was not even safe to drive. Greatly dissatisfied, the Wengs sued Allison for breach of express and implied warranties.

The trial judge found that Allison's statements indicated to the buyers that he had never had any problems with the car. But Allison's statements were not express warranties unless they constituted the "basis of the bargain" with the Wengs. Allison's statements could not become the basis of the bargain unless the Wengs reasonably relied upon them. Reasoning that no one could have reasonably relied upon statements that a 10-year-old car, driven 96,000 miles, and selling for $800 had "no problems" and was "mechanically sound," the trial court ruled that because the statements did not constitute the basis of the bargain, they were not express warranties. The trial court entered judgment in favor of Allison, and the Wengs appealed.

ISSUE PRESENTED   When do statements made by a seller about a used car constitute an express warranty?

OPINION   HOLDRIDGE, J., writing for the Appellate Court of Illinois:

Express warranties are enforceable if the statements at issue are (1) affirmations of fact or promise which relate to the goods and become part of the basis of the bargain; or (2) descriptions of the goods which are made part of the basis of the bargain. If the goods fail to conform to the affirmations or promises, the seller may be held accountable for breach of warranty.

In this matter, the seller's statements to the buyers that the car was "mechanically sound," "in good condition," and had "no problems" were affirmations of fact and descriptions of the car that created an express warranty.

We find the trial court's ruling that the statements of the seller could not have been part of the basis of the bargain simply because no reasonable persons could have

Case 8.3 continues

Case 8.3 continued

relied upon those statements was erroneous. The trial court misconstrued the role of reliance in determining whether an affirmation of fact or description is part of the basis of the bargain. Affirmations of fact made during the bargain are presumed to be part of the basis of the bargain unless clear, affirmative proof otherwise is shown. It is not necessary, therefore, for the buyer to show reasonable reliance upon the seller's affirmations in order to make the affirmations part of the basis of the bargain. The burden is upon the seller to establish by clear, affirmative proof that the affirmations did not become part of the basis of the bargain.

In this matter, the record shows no clear, affirmative proof that the seller's affirmations of fact were not part of the basis of the bargain. Instead, the trial court simply assumed that no one could have reasonably relied upon the seller's statements that the car was mechanically sound, in light of the age, price and mileage of the car. We disagree. Any car of the age and mileage of the car sold to the plaintiffs can be "mechanically sound" and yet worth only $800; many other factors enter into the price of a car, i.e., the condition of the body, the condition of the paint, the presence or absence of rust, the condition of the tires, the condition of the interior of the car, the presence or absence of broken glass, etc. A "mechanically sound" car, in otherwise poor condition, can reasonably be worth $800.

To say, as the trial court did, that because of the age, mileage and price of the car no reasonable person could expect it to be mechanically sound is insufficient to overcome the presumption that the seller's affirmations concerning the condition of the car created an express warranty. The trial court's judgment was, therefore, against the manifest weight of the evidence.

RESULT   The appeals court reversed the trial court and ordered judgment for the buyers. The seller had made an express warranty, which it breached.

COMMENTS   Whether a statement about a product is an express warranty or merely an opinion depends on the context in which it is made, the degree to which the buyer is ignorant of the subject matter of the statement, the extent to which the seller was merely puffing, the time when the statement was made, and other factors concerning the relationship between the two parties.

Questions

1. Would the result have been different if the buyer had been an automobile dealer taking the car as a trade-in? A professional auto mechanic buying a car for his son?
2. Would the court have analyzed the issue differently if the seller had prefaced each description with "as far as I know" or "in my opinion"? What if the car's published *Blue Book* value had been $3,000?

Implied Warranty of Merchantability

The *implied warranty of merchantability* guarantees that the goods are reasonably fit for the general purpose for which they are sold and that they are properly packaged and labeled. The warranty applies to all goods sold by merchants in the normal course of business. It does not depend on the seller's statements or use of a sample or model. Rather, it depends on the identity of the seller as a merchant who deals in goods of a certain kind.

To be merchantable under Section 2-314(2) of the UCC, goods must (1) pass without objection in the trade under the contract description; (2) be fit for the ordinary purposes for which such goods are used; (3) be within the variations permitted by the agreement and be of even kind, quality, and quantity within each unit and among all units involved; (4) be adequately contained, packaged, and labeled as the agreement may require; and (5) conform to the promises or affirmations of fact made on the container or label, if any. Fungible goods, such as grain, must be of average quality within the contract description.

Reasonable Expectations The key issue in determining merchantability is whether the goods do what a reasonable person would expect of them. The contract description is crucial. Goods considered merchantable under one contract may be considered not to be merchantable in another. A bicycle with a cracked frame and bent wheels is not fit for the ordinary purpose for which bicycles are used, but it will pass under a contract for the sale of scrap metal.

When no contract description exists, the most frequent claim on which breach is based is that the goods are not fit "for the ordinary purposes for which such goods are used." Proof that the goods are imperfect or flawed is often insufficient to succeed on this claim. Even imperfect goods can be fit for their ordinary purposes.

The courts will not uphold all claims by dissatisfied buyers against sellers. In *Cardozo v. True*,[3] Ingrid Cardozo purchased a cookbook from True's bookstore. Several days later, Cardozo followed a recipe in the book for the preparation of the dasheen plant commonly known as elephant ears. While preparing the roots for cooking, she ate a small slice and immediately experienced a burning of the mouth area, coughing, gasping, and intense stomach cramps. She sued the bookstore for breach of implied warranty of merchantability. The Florida District Court of Appeals held that a bookstore is not liable under the implied warranty of merchantability for the content of the books the store sells but only for the physical characteristics of the books, such as printing and binding. The implied warranty of merchantability does not include the thought processes or suggestions conveyed by the authors of the book.

---

3. 342 So. 2d 1053 (Fla. App. 1977), *cert. denied*, 353 So. 2d 674 (Fla. 1977).

ETHICAL CONSIDERATION

What investigations should a seller make before putting goods on the market? Should a bookstore test every recipe in every cookbook it sells? If not, should a bookstore buy cookbooks only from well-regarded publishers that have test kitchens?

Implied Warranty of Fitness for a Particular Purpose

The *implied warranty of fitness for a particular purpose* is set forth in Section 2-315 of the UCC. It guarantees that the goods are fit for the particular purpose for which the seller recommended them. Broad in its scope, it may apply to merchants and nonmerchants alike. A "particular purpose" differs from the ordinary purpose for which a good is used in that "particular purpose" contemplates a specific use by the buyer that is peculiar to him or his business. By contrast, the ordinary purpose is that contemplated by the concept of merchantability and used in analyses of warranties of merchantability. For example, dress shoes are generally used for the purpose of walking on ordinary ground and not warranted for mountain climbing, but a seller may know that a particular pair was selected for mountain climbing.

Unlike the implied warranty of merchantability, this warranty does not arise in every sale of goods. It will be implied only if four elements are present: (1) the buyer had a particular purpose for the goods; (2) the seller knew or had reason to know of that purpose; (3) the buyer relied on the seller's expertise; and (4) the seller knew or had reason to know of the buyer's reliance. Although the warranty usually arises when the seller is a merchant with some level of skill or judgment, it is not restricted to such circumstances.

Reliance In order to prove that the buyer did not in fact rely on the seller's expertise, the seller may try to show that (1) the buyer's expertise was equal to or superior to the seller's; (2) the buyer relied on the skill and judgment of persons hired by the buyer; or (3) the buyer supplied the seller with detailed specifications or designs that the seller was to follow.

Identifiable patents and trademarks play an interesting role in this area of the law. If the buyer is insisting on a particular brand and style, he or she cannot be relying on the seller's skill or judgment. Hence, no warranty results. The mere fact that a good has an identifiable patent or trade name, however, does not prove nonreliance, especially if the seller recommended the product to the buyer.

Managers must provide adequate instruction and training to salespersons and agents about express and implied warranties. An aggressive salesperson willing to say what it takes to close a deal may unwittingly cause his or her company to be held liable under an implied warranty of fitness for a particular purpose when it never intended to make any such warranty at all.

Limiting Liability

The seller can avoid responsibility for the quality of the goods under any of these warranties. First, the seller need not make any express warranties. This may be difficult to do, however, because even a simple description of the goods may constitute a warranty. Second, a seller may disclaim any warranties of quality if it follows specifically delineated rules in the UCC designed to ensure that the buyer is aware of, and assents to, the disclaimers. For example, Section 2-316 allows a seller to exclude all implied warranties by using "expressions like 'AS IS,' 'WITH ALL FAULTS' or other language which in common understanding calls the buyer's attention to the exclusion of warranties and makes plain that there is no implied warranty." This language means that the buyer takes the entire risk as to the quality of the goods involved. Third, the seller can refrain from professing expertise with respect to the goods and can leave the selection to the buyer.

More commonly, the seller limits its responsibility for the quality of the goods by limiting the remedies available to the buyer in the event of breach. A typical method is the inclusion of a provision limiting the seller's responsibility for defective goods to repair or replacement. Some states limit a seller's right to limit liability especially for personal injury.

Under the UCC, a seller is not an absolute insurer of the quality of goods sold. In order to recover for breach of warranty, a buyer must prove that (1) the seller made an express or implied warranty under the UCC; (2) the goods were defective at the time of the sale; (3) the loss or injury was caused by the defect rather than the buyer's negligent or inappropriate use of the goods; and (4) the seller has no affirmative defenses, such as a disclaimer of warranty.

As an alternative to suing for breach of warranty, the plaintiff may sue in tort for strict product liability. A product liability claim may succeed where a breach-of-warranty claim would not. This may happen when there is no contractual relationship between the buyer and the seller. Chapter 10 discusses this issue.

 ## Magnuson-Moss Warranty Act

The Magnuson-Moss Warranty Act[4] is a federal law that protects consumers against deception in warranties. It requires that express warranties be made easy to understand.

No seller is required to make a written warranty under this act. If the seller does make a written promise or affirmation of fact, however, then it must also state whether, for example, the warranty is a full or a limited warranty. A *full warranty* gives the consumer the right to free repair or replacement of a defective product. A *limited warranty* might restrict the availability of free repair or replacement. This act is discussed further in Chapter 19.

 ## Right to Reject Nonconforming Goods

Generally, a buyer that has contracted to purchase goods from a seller must fulfill its obligation and pay for those goods. A buyer, however, has the right to reject nonconforming goods. Under Section 2-601 of the UCC, if the goods or the tender of delivery fails to conform to the contract in any respect, the buyer may reject any or all of the goods. Section 2-602 requires that any rejection be made within a reasonable time after the goods are delivered. After such a rejection, the buyer may not treat the goods as if it owned them. To the contrary, if the buyer has taken possession of the goods before rejecting them, then it must hold the goods with reasonable care for a time sufficient to permit the seller to remove them. As the following case illustrates, the right to reject is important but limited.

---

4. 15 U.S.C. §§ 2301–12 (1997).

A CASE IN POINT	SUMMARY

**CASE 8.4
MOORE &
MOORE GENERAL
CONTRACTORS, INC. v.
BASEPOINT, INC.**
Supreme Court of Virginia
485 S.E.2d 131 (Va. 1997).

FACTS   In late 1990, General Mills Restaurants, Inc. made plans to build a Red Lobster restaurant in Spotsylvania, Virginia. After requesting bids from various subcontractors for the elements of the project, general contractor Moore & Moore awarded a millwork subcontract to Basepoint. The subcontract called for Basepoint to provide custom-made cabinets of "melamine" for use throughout the restaurant. Even in the industry, the meaning of that term was unclear. Some evidence suggested that "melamine" referred to a composite product with a particular type of hard finish; other evidence suggested that it referred only to a finish and did not imply use of composite material.

In March and April of 1991, Basepoint delivered its cabinets to the job site, where they were received by Moore & Moore. Allen Lyle, Moore & Moore's field superintendent, and Donnie Hall, Lyle's subordinate, inspected the cabinets and noticed they were made of particle board instead of sturdier plywood, as called for in the master plans prepared by the project's architects. Believing that General Mills Restaurants would not know the difference and that he would be saving money by accepting delivery of the particle-board cabinets, Lyle directed the installation of all the cabinets.

On May 1, an inspector from General Mills Restaurants examined the installed millwork and rejected the cabinets as not conforming to the plans and specifications. The next day, Moore & Moore sent Basepoint a letter stating, "On Wednesday, May 1, 1991, it was discovered that most of your casework is constructed of particle board. Since the plans . . . we provided you for the above referenced job . . . call for plywood, all of the casework that has particle board does not conform and must be replaced." In the letter, Moore & Moore set the following Tuesday as the deadline for delivery of the replacement material, noting that Basepoint already had notified Lyle it could not meet the deadline. Upon removal of the cabinets made of particle board, Moore & Moore immediately procured plywood replacements from another subcontractor. The new cabinets were installed promptly, and the project was completed nearly on time.

Subsequently, Moore & Moore refused to pay Basepoint for the cabinets it had delivered. Basepoint then sued Moore & Moore for the $28,080 price of the cabinets. Moore & Moore denied any indebtedness to Basepoint, claiming the materials supplied were defective. In addition, Moore & Moore filed a cross-complaint against Basepoint for the $47,000 cost of removing the particle-board casework, rebuilding the casework with plywood, and finishing the remaining work under the contract.

The trial court found for Basepoint and rejected Moore & Moore's cross-claim. Moore & Moore appealed.

ISSUE PRESENTED   Can a buyer's acceptance of goods be revoked because of their nonconformity? If not, is the buyer entitled to recover from the seller the cost of substitute goods?

SUMMARY OF OPINION   The Virginia Supreme Court first noted that as a sale of goods between merchants, the dispute was controlled by the UCC. Section 2-601 provides that if goods fail to conform to the contract, the buyer may (1) reject the whole; (2) accept the whole; or (3) accept any commercial unit or units and reject the rest. Section 2-606(1)(c) provides that acceptance of goods occurs when the buyer

Case 8.4 continues

Case 8.4 continued

performs any act that is inconsistent with the seller's ownership of the goods. Because Moore & Moore's installation of the cabinets was an act inconsistent with Basepoint's ownership, the court found that Moore & Moore had accepted the goods. Even though Moore & Moore could have rejected any or all of the cabinets at delivery, its installation of them served as its acceptance.

Moore & Moore did not dispute this conclusion but instead contended that it had revoked its acceptance of the cabinets because of their nonconformity. The court, however, turned to Section 2-607(2), which provides that a buyer's acceptance of goods precludes their rejection and that acceptance cannot be revoked if it was given with knowledge of the nonconformity. Lyle and Hall's awareness that the cabinets were made of particle board amounted to such knowledge. Therefore, the court found, Moore & Moore could not revoke its acceptance.

Regardless of its liability to Basepoint for the cost of the cabinets, Moore & Moore pointed to Section 2-607(2), which provides that acceptance by a buyer "does not of itself impair any other remedy provided by this title for nonconformity." By its argument, Moore & Moore was entitled to an award based on the cover remedy of Sections 2-711 and 2-712, which allow a buyer to recover for procurement of substitute goods. The court, however, noted that under Section 2-711, the cover remedy is available in only four situations: (1) when the seller fails to make delivery; (2) when the seller repudiates the contract; (3) when the buyer rightfully rejects the goods; and (4) when the buyer justifiably revokes its acceptance of the goods. Here, Basepoint did make delivery and did not repudiate the contract. Moreover, Moore & Moore accepted the goods, thereby precluding rejection, and accepted with knowledge of nonconformity, making any revocation unjustified. With none of the four situations applicable, the court rejected Moore & Moore's cross-claim.

RESULT   The trial court's decision was affirmed. Moore & Moore was required to pay for the cabinets.

 ## Allocation of Risk of Loss

Goods can be lost in transit due to such events as fire, earthquake, flood, and theft. In the absence of an agreement to the contrary, Section 2-509 of the UCC places the risk of loss on the party controlling the goods at the time loss occurs, because that party is better able to insure against loss and to take precautions to protect the goods. Section 2-319 expressly authorizes the buyer and seller to allocate risk of loss between them as they see fit and provides shorthand symbols, such as "FOB" (free on board), with defined meanings to facilitate the expression of such an agreement between the parties.

Goods Shipped by Carrier

If a sales contract requires or authorizes the seller to ship the goods by carrier, the risk of loss passes to the buyer (1) at the time the goods are properly delivered to the carrier, if the contract does not require delivery at a particular destination; or (2) at the time the carrier tenders the goods to the buyer at the specified destination, if the contract specifies one. If nothing is said about delivery, the contract is not a delivery contract and does not require delivery to the destination.

If the parties indicate that shipment is to be made "FOB seller's place of business," delivery at a particular place is not required, so the risk of loss shifts to the buyer once the goods are properly placed in the possession of the carrier. An indication in the contract that shipment is to be made "FOB buyer's place of business" means that delivery at a particular place is required, so the risk of loss will not shift to the buyer until the goods are tendered to the buyer at its place of business. The parties' selection of an FOB term in a sales contract controls the allocation of the risk of loss even if contrary language exists elsewhere in the contract.

Goods Held by Independent Warehouse

When the goods are in the possession of an independent warehouse and the seller provides the buyer with a document enabling it to pick up the goods at the warehouse, the risk of loss passes to the buyer when the buyer receives the document entitling it to pick up the goods.

All Other Cases

When the goods are neither to be shipped by carrier nor held by an independent warehouse, the allocation of the risk of loss in transit depends on whether the seller is a merchant. (A seller is a merchant if he or she possesses experience and special knowledge relating to the goods in question.) If the seller is a merchant, the risk of loss passes to the buyer only when the buyer receives physical possession of the goods. If the seller is not a merchant, the risk passes to the buyer when tender of delivery is made. Tender of delivery is made when the seller notifies the buyer that it has the goods ready for delivery.

The following case deals with the question of when a buyer has physical possession of the goods and thus bears the risk of loss.

A CASE IN POINT	**SUMMARY**

CASE 8.5
LYNCH IMPORTS,
LTD. v. FREY
Appellate Court of Illinois
558 N.E.2d 484
(Ill. App. Ct. 1990).

FACTS On October 22, 1987, the buyers agreed to purchase a 1987 Volkswagen automobile from the seller for the price of $8,706. The agreement was set forth in a purchase order in which the following phrases were handwritten on the purchase contract: "Car to be in totally acceptable condition or money will be refunded to the customer" and "Acceptance subject to inspection."

On October 24, the buyers took possession of the vehicle and paid the seller $4,706 as partial payment of the purchase price. The balance of the purchase price was to be financed. It was understood that the car was to come with air-conditioning, but at the time of delivery it was not yet installed. One of two riders attached to the purchase contract provided that the buyer was responsible to have the vehicle fully covered under liability and collision automobile insurance from the instant that the buyer took possession. The rider also stated that the buyer was not authorized to return the vehicle without the seller's authorization and that no vehicle was to be sold with the condition that the buyer may later return it.

Two to three days thereafter, the buyers brought the vehicle to the seller so that the air conditioner could be installed. When they returned in the evening to pick up the vehicle, they were informed that the air conditioner had been installed but that the vehicle had sustained body damage in an accident. The buyers refused to take delivery of the automobile because of the damage and demanded that a new and undamaged car be substituted. When the seller refused, the buyers stopped payment on the check and cancelled their application for financing the balance of the purchase price.

The car dealership sued the automobile purchasers for damages of $8,706 for breaching the sales contract and $4,706 for wrongfully stopping the check. The buyers filed a counterclaim for the seller's breach of contract in failing to deliver an acceptable

Case 8.5 continues

Case 8.5 continued

car and sought damages of $1,330.35, representing the difference between the price paid by the buyers when they subsequently purchased a similar automobile and the contract price of the Volkswagen. The trial court granted summary judgment to the seller. The buyers appealed.

ISSUE PRESENTED   When a buyer takes possession of a car, but it is understood that the buyer will return with the car to have air-conditioning installed per the purchase order, has the buyer fully accepted the car and assumed complete responsibility for it?

SUMMARY OF OPINION   The Illinois Appellate Court stated that there existed an issue of material fact as to whether the buyers "accepted" the vehicle on October 24. The buyers argued that they did not accept the vehicle and therefore had the right to reject it, which they properly did, when it was damaged upon its return to the seller to install the air conditioner.

Under the provisions of Section 2-606 of the UCC, acceptance is deemed to have occurred when the buyer either signifies that the vehicle was conforming or "takes or retains" the vehicle in spite of its nonconformity. It was unclear to the court what the agreement was on October 24, 1987 just prior to the buyers' taking the vehicle. This uncertainty as to what transpired between the parties when the buyers took possession of the vehicle was of particular significance because the original purchase order contained the handwritten phrases: "Car to be in totally acceptable condition or money will be refunded to customer" and "Acceptance subject to inspection."

Section 1-202 of the UCC provides that the effect of the provisions of the UCC may be varied by agreement. The court concluded that the handwritten notations in the purchase agreement were sufficient to raise an inference that the buyers did not intend to waive their right to defer acceptance until the vehicle was brought to full conformity, even though they took interim possession of the vehicle.

Under Section 2-509 of the UCC, the risk of loss does not pass to the buyer until the buyer accepts the goods, even though the buyer obtains an insurable interest under Section 2-501 after the goods are identified to the purchase contract. Thus Rider 2, which required the buyer to obtain insurance, was not conclusive on its face to pass the risk of loss of the buyer.

RESULT   The Appellate Court reversed the lower court's grant of summary judgment for the seller. There were material issues of disputed fact, precluding summary judgment. The case was remanded to determine whether the buyers had accepted the vehicle on October 24 and whether they had the right to reject it when it was later discovered to be damaged upon its return from the seller to install air-conditioning.

 Unconscionability

A party is normally bound by the terms of a contract he or she signs. However, if the contract is so unfair as to shock the conscience of the court, the judge may decline to enforce the offending terms or the entire contract.

Section 2-302(1) of the UCC provides procedural guidelines for judicial review of unconscionable clauses in contracts for the sale of goods, but it does not define "unconscionable." The official comments, however, provide some guidance. For example, Comment 1 to Section 2-302 states:

> The basic test is whether, in the light of the general background and the commercial needs of the particular trade or case, the clauses involved are so one sided as to be unconscionable under the circumstances existing at the time of the making of the contract. . . . The principle is one of the prevention of oppression and unfair surprise . . . and not of disturbance of allocation of risks because of superior bargaining power.

In deciding whether a contract is unconscionable, the court considers evidence in addition to the contractual language, particularly (1) whether the contractual obligation was bargained for, and (2) whether the parties understood and accepted the obligation. As under common law (discussed in Chapter 7), unconscionability can be either procedural—relating to the bargaining process—or substantive—relating to the provisions of the contract.

Procedural Unconscionability

A contract is procedurally unconscionable when one party is induced to enter a contract without having any meaningful choice. For example, in highly concentrated industries with few competitors, all the sellers may offer the same unfair contracts on a "take it or leave it" basis. Such contracts are known as *adhesion contracts*. They are most prevalent in consumer transactions where bargaining power is unequal.

It is also procedurally unconscionable for a seller to tuck oppressive clauses into the fine print or for high-pressure salespersons to mislead illiterate consumers. In commercial transactions, however, it is presumed that the parties have the sophistication to bargain knowledgeably. Procedural unconscionability in the commercial setting is, therefore, more difficult to prove.

Substantive Unconscionability

A contract is substantively unconscionable if its terms are unduly harsh or oppressive or unreasonably favorable to one side, such as in the case of an excessive price or a limitation of one party's rights and remedies.

The courts have not agreed on any well-defined test for determining when a price is so excessive as to be unconscionable. However, prices that were two to three times the price of similar goods sold in the same area have been held unconscionable.

In another example, parties to a contract are allowed to limit the remedies available for breach but only to a certain extent. If, for example, consumer goods are involved, a provision that limits the purchaser's ability to recover monetary damages for personal injury is *prima facie* (or on its face) evidence of unconscionability.

The following case was among the first to raise the issue of unconscionability under the UCC.

| A CASE IN POINT | IN THE LANGUAGE OF THE COURT |

CASE 8.6
WILLIAMS v.
WALKER-THOMAS
FURNITURE CO.
United States Court of
Appeals for the District
of Columbia
350 F.2d 445
(D.C. Cir. 1965).

FACTS   Ova Lee Williams, a welfare mother of limited education, purchased household items from Walker-Thomas Furniture Company on credit over the course of several years. An obscurely worded provision in the purchase agreement form provided that all installment payments would be credited pro rata to all then outstanding purchases. The effect of this *cross-collateralization clause* was to keep a balance due on all items purchased until all the buyer's accounts were reduced to zero. Each new item purchased increased the balance due, giving the seller a continued security interest in all previously purchased items. When Williams's balance was down to $164, she bought a stereo costing $514. This brought her balance up to $678. When she defaulted on a payment, the furniture store tried to repossess all the goods she had previously purchased on credit over the years. She claimed that repossession of all the goods under the contract was unconscionable.

The trial court decided in favor of Walker-Thomas Furniture. Williams appealed.

ISSUE PRESENTED   Is a cross-collaterization clause in a sales contract between a store and a buyer unconscionable if one party has limited bargaining power and lacks specific knowledge to understand the terms if all the terms are clearly spelled out and the buyer has the option to not buy or to go elsewhere?

OPINION   WRIGHT, J., writing for the U.S. Court of Appeals:

We cannot condemn too strongly appellee's [Walker-Thomas Furniture's] conduct. It raises serious questions of sharp practice and irresponsible business dealings. A review of the legislation in the District of Columbia affecting retail sales and the pertinent decisions of the highest court in this jurisdiction disclose, however, no ground upon which this court can declare the contracts in question contrary to public policy. . . .

. . .

Congress has recently enacted the Uniform Commercial Code, which specifically provides that the court may refuse to enforce a contract which it finds to be unconscionable at the time it was made. . . . Accordingly, we hold that where the element of unconscionability is present at the time a contract is made, the contract should not be enforced.

Unconscionability has generally been recognized to include an absence of meaningful choice on the part of one of the parties together with contract terms which are unreasonably favorable to the other party. Whether a meaningful choice is present in a particular case can only be determined by consideration of all the circumstances surrounding the transaction. In many cases the meaningfulness of the choice is negated by a gross inequality of bargaining power. The manner in which the contract was entered is also relevant to this consideration. Did each party to the contract, considering his obvious education or lack of it, have a reasonable opportunity to understand the terms of the contract, or were the important terms hidden in a maze of fine print and

Case 8.6 continues

Case 8.6 continued

minimized by deceptive sales practices? Ordinarily, one who signs an agreement without full knowledge of its terms might be held to assume the risk that he has entered a one-sided bargain. But when a party of little bargaining power, and hence little real choice, signs a commercially unreasonable contract with little or no knowledge of its terms, it is hardly likely that his consent, or even an objective manifestation of his consent, was ever given to all the terms. In such a case the usual rule that the terms of the agreement are not to be questioned should be abandoned, and the court should consider whether the terms of the contract are so unfair that enforcement should be withheld.

In determining reasonableness or fairness, the primary concern must be with the terms of the contract considered in light of the circumstances existing when the contract was made. The test is not simple, nor can it be mechanically applied. The terms are to be considered "in the light of the general commercial background and the commercial needs of the particular trade or case." Corbin suggests the test as being whether the terms are "so extreme as to appear unconscionable according to the mores and business practices of the time and place."

RESULT The appeals court held that where the element of unconscionability is present at time the contract is made, the contract should not be enforced. Because the trial court that had granted judgment to the furniture company had not recognized that contracts could be unenforceable on that basis and the record was not sufficient for the appeals court to decide the issue as a matter of law, the case was remanded to the trial court for further proceedings.

COMMENTS The New York Supreme Court (the state trial court in New York) applied the same logic in *Jones v. Star Credit Corp.*[5] The plaintiff was a welfare recipient who purchased a freezer on credit for $900. With the addition of time credit charges, credit life insurance, credit property insurance, and sales tax, the purchase price totaled $1,234.80. At trial it was established that the freezer's value was only $300. In holding the freezer contract unconscionable, the New York court noted the fundamental tension underlying cases like *Williams*: "On the one hand it is necessary to recognize the importance of preserving the integrity of agreements and the fundamental right of parties to deal, trade, bargain and contract. On the other hand there is the concern for the uneducated and often illiterate individual who is the victim of gross inequality of bargaining power."

Questions

1. Would the result have been any different if the items in question were not furniture and other things of "necessity" but rather luxury items such as fur coats and diamond watches?
2. Was the court focusing more on the buyer's lack of money or the possibility that she was unable to comprehend fully the terms? What if she had a Ph.D. in economics but was on welfare? What if she were of moderate wealth but had a learning disability that limited her capacity to understand the implications of the terms of the contract?

---

5. 298 N.Y.S.2d 264 (N.Y. Sup. 1969).

Commercial Impracticability

Under the common law doctrine of impossibility, discussed in Chapter 7, a person may be excused from performing his or her contractual obligation if performance is rendered impossible by the occurrence of unforeseen events. In applying the doctrine of impossibility in a business context, the common law developed the doctrine of *commercial impossibility*. This doctrine allows the risk of nonperformance, under certain circumstances, to shift from the promisor to the promisee.

Application under the UCC

The UCC has adopted the doctrine of *commercial impracticability* rather than that of strict impossibility. Section 2-615 states that unless the contract provides otherwise, a failure to perform is not a breach if performance is made impractical by an event unforeseen by the contract. Section 2-615, the associated official comments, and the cases that have arisen under Section 2-615 establish certain criteria that a party seeking discharge from performance must show.

Underlying Condition   There must be a failure of an underlying condition of the contract, that is, a condition that was not included in the parties' bargain. Certain occurrences are provided for fully in contracts, and the seller is assumed to have figured an appropriate "insurance premium" into the contract price. Other risks are deemed too remote and uncertain to be included in the contract price. The function of the court in applying the doctrine of commercial impracticability is to determine which risks were, or properly should have been, allocated to the buyer and which to the seller.

Unforeseen Contingency   In addition to showing that a condition was not reflected in the contract price, a seller seeking discharge must prove that the contingency that prevents performance was both unforeseen and unforeseeable. To some extent every occurrence is foreseeable—there is always some probability that a fire will destroy the anticipated source of supply, that a key person will die, or that various acts of God will occur. Legally, however, a foreseeable contingency is one that the parties should have contemplated in the circumstances surrounding the contracting. If there is a standard trade custom for allocating the risk, it is assumed that a particular contract follows that custom, unless it specifies differently.

Official comment 4 provides an illustrative, but not exhaustive, list of contingencies that are considered unforeseeable. Wars and embargoes are considered unforeseeable; market fluctuations are not.

Impracticable Performance   Even if a party is able to show that there was a failure of an underlying condition of the contract and that it did not implicitly assume the risk of this occurrence, the party still must prove that the performance was impracticable. Increased cost alone is not sufficient reason to excuse performance, unless it is a marked increase. In one case, a 10- to 12-fold increase was considered sufficient. In another case, the court observed: "We are not aware of any cases where something less than a 100% cost increase has been held to make a seller's performance impracticable."[6] Transactions that have merely become unprofitable will not be excused. Sellers cannot rely on Section 2-615 to get them out of a bad bargain.

The Westinghouse Uranium Cases

The article excerpted in the "Inside Story" at the end of this chapter discusses the Westinghouse Electric Corporation uranium cases, in which Westinghouse unsuccessfully argued that the doctrines of impracticability and impossibility should relieve it of its obligation to supply uranium at a fixed price to utilities with nuclear power plants after a sharp increase in uranium prices.

Damages

The UCC, like the common law of contracts, generally tries to put the nonbreaching party in the same position it would have been in if the contract had been performed. This is usually done through the award of monetary damages.

Seller's Remedies

If a buyer wrongfully cancels a contract or refuses to accept delivery of the goods covered by the contract, the

---

6. Publicker Indus., Inc. v. Union Carbide Corp., 17 UCC Rep. Serv. 989 (E.D. Pa. 1975).

seller is entitled to damages under Section 2-708 of the UCC. The measure of damages is the difference between the market price at the time and place for delivery and the unpaid contract price, less expenses saved because of the buyer's breach. If this measure of damages is inadequate to put the seller in as good a position as performance would have, then the seller is entitled to recover the profit (including reasonable overhead) that it would have made from full performance by the buyer. Such a seller is called a *lost volume seller.*

Buyer's Remedies

If a seller wrongfully fails to deliver the goods or repudiates the contract, or if the buyer justifiably rejects the tendered goods, then under Section 2-711 of the UCC the buyer has several choices. The buyer may cancel the contract and recover as much of the price as has been paid and then either (1) *cover*, that is, buy the goods elsewhere and be reimbursed for the extra cost of the substitute goods; or (2) recover damages for nondelivery.

If the buyer elects to cover under Section 2-712, it must make, in good faith and without reasonable delay, a reasonable purchase of substitute goods. The buyer may then recover from the seller the difference between the cost of cover and the contract price.

If the buyer elects not to cover, under Section 2-713 the buyer is entitled to damages. The measure of damages is the difference between the market price at the time the buyer learned of the breach and the contract price. The buyer may also recover consequential damages. Section 2-715 of the UCC permits the buyer to recover consequential damages for (1) any loss resulting from general or particular requirements and needs of the buyer that the seller at the time of contracting had reason to know and that could not reasonably be prevented by cover or otherwise; and (2) injury to person or property proximately resulting from any breach of warranty.

 ## Specific Performance

If the promised goods are unique, then under Section 2-716 of the UCC a court may order the seller to deliver them. For example, if there is only one antique Mercedes-Benz of a certain vintage, then damages alone will not be adequate to remedy the loss suffered by the disappointed buyer. Only delivery of the promised car will suffice. On the other hand, if the car is one of thousands, monetary damages will suffice, because an equivalent car can be purchased elsewhere.

 ## International Sale of Goods and CISG

The UCC's Article 2 largely unified the laws of the separate states in the United States governing the domestic sale of goods. International sales of goods, however, remain outside its scope. As international trade and the global economy grew throughout the twentieth century, the need for more uniform laws throughout the world became apparent. Under the auspices of the United Nations, representatives of 66 countries adopted the Convention on Contracts for the International Sale of Goods (CISG) in 1980. With ratification by 12 signatories, including the United States, CISG became efffective in 1988. More than 50 countries have ratified the convention, including many of the world's largest economies: Canada, China, France, Germany, Russia, and Singapore.[7] Today, the signatories to CISG account for nearly two-thirds of the world's imports and exports.

Scope of Convention

CISG sets out substantive provisions of law to govern the formation of international sales contracts between merchants and the rights and obligations of buyers and sellers.[8] It applies to sales contracts between parties with places of business in different countries if those countries are bound by the convention, unless the parties have expressly opted out of CISG. Thus, CISG is the default provision that applies if a sales contract involving merchants from different countries is silent as to applicable law. As with the UCC, parties are free to specify applicable law and vary the effect of CISG provisions.

CISG applies to oral as well as written contracts of sale. CISG contains no statute of frauds requiring certain contracts to be in writing, unless one party has its

---

7. For the most up-to-date information about the convention, including its signatories, *see* the U.N. Web site at <http://www.un.or.at/uncitral>.

8. For extensive materials relating to CISG, including international cases and commentary, *see* the Pace University School of Law's Web site on the convention at <http://www.cisgw3.law.pace.edu>.

place of business in a country that has made a reservation to the convention in this regard. The United States did not make this reservation.

Although broad in its ambition, CISG does not apply to sales (1) of goods bought for personal, family, or household use, unless the seller neither knew nor should have known that the goods were bought for such use; (2) by auction; (3) on execution of a judgment or otherwise by authority of law; (4) of stocks, shares, investment securities, negotiable instruments, or money; (5) of ships, vessels, hovercraft, or aircraft; and (6) of electricity. As for the distinction between goods and services, CISG does not apply to contracts in which goods are sold in conjunction with services unless the preponderance of the obligations of the seller consists of the supply of goods. Neither does it apply to liability of the seller for death or personal injury to any person caused by its goods.

Offer and Acceptance

Under CISG, an offer becomes effective when it reaches the offeree, and it may be withdrawn if the withdrawal reaches the offeree before or at the same time as the offer. Until a contract is concluded, an offeror may revoke its offer if the revocation reaches the offeree before the offeree has dispatched its acceptance. An offer cannot be revoked, however, if the offer indicates that it is irrevocable or if the offeree reasonably relied on its irrevocability. Even if irrevocable, an offer is terminated when the offeree's rejection reaches the offeror.

A statement made by the offeree indicating its assent is an acceptance. Conduct indicating assent is also acceptance, but silence or inactivity does not in itself amount to acceptance. Acceptance becomes effective when it reaches the offeror, although acceptance is not effective if it fails to reach the offeror within the time the offeror has specified. If the offeror has specified no time, then the acceptance must reach the offeror within a reasonable time. If the offer is oral, however, it must be accepted immediately unless circumstances indicate otherwise.

Recognizing the importance of custom and practice, CISG also provides that if the parties have established practices between themselves, the offeror may accept the offer by performing an appropriate act, such as sending the goods or paying the price, without noti-

fying the offeror. In such a case, acceptance is effective as soon as the act is performed. Such acceptance by performance without notification differs from the UCC, which allows for acceptance by performance but requires notification. Ultimately, a contract is concluded at the moment acceptance of an offer becomes effective.

Battle of the Forms

An important difference between the UCC and CISG is the approach to battles of the forms. Under the convention, a reply to an offer that purports to be an acceptance but contains additional terms or other modifications that materially alter the terms of the offer is a rejection of the offer and constitutes a counteroffer. Thus, there is no contract. If the modifications do not materially alter the terms of the offer and the offeror fails to object in a timely fashion, then there is a contract that will include the terms of the offer with the modifications stated in the acceptance. CISG lists those categories of differences that are presumed to alter the terms of the offer materially: price, payment, quality and quantity of the goods, place and time of delivery, extent of one party's liability to the other, and settlement of disputes. The list leaves little for the sphere of "immateriality" and largely effects the old mirror image rule.

Good Faith

CISG provides that in interpreting the convention there shall be regard for promoting "the observance of good faith in international trade." Similarly, Section 1-203 of the UCC states a good faith requirement: "Every contract or duty within this Act impose a duty of good faith in its performance or enforcement." At the most superficial level, the UCC provision is broader than the CISG principle, which literally applies only to the interpretation of the convention rather than the conduct of merchants under it. Throughout CISG, however, are numerous requirements of "reasonableness," such as those for giving notice, making substitutions, relying, measuring inconvenience and expense, delaying performance, examining goods, incurring expenses, and making excuses.

Some commentators have suggested that the combination of CISG's requirements of good faith in interpretation and of reasonableness in so many areas of merchant behavior makes for a broad, albeit uncertain, duty for merchants to conduct themselves with good faith.[9] If that interpretation is correct, then, for example, if a seller requests additional time to deliver goods, a buyer would be required to act in good faith in deciding whether to grant that request. The buyer could not whimsically decide to enforce the letter of the contract to the seller's detriment. Managers are always well advised to act in good faith rather than arbitrarily, both for their own long-term interests and reputation and to enhance their ability to attain a sympathetic hearing by possible legal decision makers.

Implied Warranties

Under CISG, the seller must deliver goods that are of the quantity, quality, and description required by the contract, and such goods must be packaged as specified by the contract. As with the UCC, the convention also holds sellers liable for implied warranties of merchantability and fitness for particular use and for any express warranties they make. In the language of CISG:

> Unless the parties agree otherwise, goods do not conform unless they (a) are fit for the purposes for which goods of the same description would ordinarily be used; (b) are fit for any particular purpose expressly or impliedly made known to the seller at the time of the conclusion of the contract, except where the circumstances show that the buyer did not rely, or that it was unreasonable for him to rely, on the seller's skill and judgment; (c) possess the qualities of goods which the seller has held out to the buyer as a sample or model. . . .[10]

CISG makes clear, however, that the implied warranty of merchantability does not attach if the buyer knew that the goods were not fit for ordinary use.

---

9. *See, e.g.,* Phanesh Koneru, *The International Interpretation of the UN Convention on Contracts for the International Sale of Goods: An Approach Based on General Principles,* 6 MINN. J. GLOBAL TRADE 105 (1997).

10. 15 U.S.C. app. (1997), Convention on Contracts for the Sale of International Goods, art. 35.

THE RESPONSIBLE MANAGER
Operating under UCC Contract Law

Any manager who enters into contracts in his or her own name or in the name of his or her business should know which body of contract law will govern the transaction. In particular, the manager should determine whether the transaction is governed by Article 2 of the UCC, the common law rules concerning contracts, or CISG. Article 2 applies only to the sale of goods, not services or land. Although some things are clearly designated as goods, others may be more difficult to categorize. CISG will apply to most international sales of goods, unless the parties affirmatively opt out of its provisions. A manager should obtain legal advice if there is any doubt as to which body of law controls in a particular situation.

Once a manager has determined that Article 2 of the UCC controls, he or she should be aware of the requirements that must be met for the valid formation of a contract. This knowledge is crucial to ensuring that the company can enforce the contracts it has entered into and wishes to uphold. In addition, a manager may have a valid reason to attempt to avoid an agreement that was not formed in the correct manner. Only if the manager knows the rules of contract formation can he or she assess whether a contract was validly created.

Managers should also focus on one of the key elements in creating a valid contract: the process of offer and acceptance. The manner of making an appropriate offer is the same under the UCC as it is under common law. However, a manager should note that Article 2 allows an offeree to accept an offer even if the offeree's acceptance contains terms additional to or different from those in the offer. The UCC rules in this area and the corresponding case law are both complex and fact specific. Nonetheless, it is crucial that managers understand these rules before they engage in negotiations. Failure to develop this understanding can lead to adverse results. A manager or company may be legally bound to a contract even when there was no intention to be bound.

Article 2 of the UCC also establishes three types of warranties that buyers may rely upon when purchasing goods. Managers of companies that produce goods should be aware of how each warranty is created, how they are applied, and how liability for products can be limited under the UCC framework. It is essential that managers obtain legal advice in this area, because lawsuits under the UCC warranties can lead to large awards of damages. These warranties also provide guidelines for managers regarding what is expected from a product in terms of quality and suitability for its intended use.

Managers should also be familiar with the legal doctrines that allow parties legally to back out of contracts. The doctrine of impracticability can protect a party when unexpected changes in circumstances make performance not literally impossible but commercially ruinous. The doctrine of unconscionability provides managers with guidelines on the legal limits to one-sided contracts.

Both the UCC and CISG require the parties to act in good faith and in a commercially reasonable manner. Managers should avoid acting in an arbitrary manner and try to accommodate the reasonable requests of the other side (e.g., a seller's request to delay delivery when the delay would not have an adverse effect on the buyer's business).

INSIDE STORY

THE WESTINGHOUSE URANIUM CONTRACTS

Westinghouse Electric Corporation surprised and shocked the business and legal communities when, on September 8, 1975, it announced that it would not deliver about 70 million pounds of uranium under fixed-price contracts to 27 utility companies.

Westinghouse supported its position by relying on a relatively obscure and little-used provision of the Uniform Commercial Code, Section 2-615, which provides that a party may be excused from performing contractual obligations on the basis of commercial impracticability. It claimed that the potential loss of $2 billion made it commercially impractical to meet its obligations.

The utilities responded predictably enough by filing civil suits in 13 different federal jurisdictions. All 13 cases were combined and sent to the U.S. District Court for the Eastern District of Virginia on the basis that the commonality was

greater than the differences, particularly Westinghouse's defense of commercial impracticability and the problem of how to distribute the uranium that Westinghouse had on hand. Three utilities brought suit in a Pennsylvania state court, and three Swedish utilities took action in Stockholm.

This is only part of the picture as ripples from this bombshell spread out. In an effort to protect its interests, in 1976 Westinghouse brought suit against its suppliers of uranium claiming that an international cartel had caused an unforeseen and precipitous increase in the price of uranium. Preliminary maneuvers resulted in a decision from the Supreme Court of Ontario and one from the British House of Lords that prevented Westinghouse from getting documents and testimony relating to its case from foreign corporations. Similar action was taken in South Africa and Australia.

The suits against Westinghouse were delayed until September 1981 by Federal District Judge Prentice Marshall because "he was afraid people just weren't going to be ready in time." As of August 1979, more than seven million pages of documents had been submitted during the discovery proceedings. This may be one of the factors that led the judge to observe that this was "the lawyers' full employment case." The direct and indirect costs to the various participants in the uranium dispute are considerable. Westinghouse alone spent $25 million for out-of-house legal expenses in 1976.

On June 18, 1978, Westinghouse named Douglas D. Danforth to the new number two post of vice-chairman and chief operating officer so that the chairman, Robert E. Kirby, would have more time to spend trying to solve the company's uranium problem.

Westinghouse Position

Westinghouse claimed that dramatic, unprecedented, and unforeseeable events occurred that raised the price of uranium from about $6.50 to $9.00 per pound to $26 per pound in September 1975. This could lead to a potential loss to Westinghouse of about $2 billion. By July 1978, the price had risen to about $44 per pound, and the potential loss escalated to approximately $3 billion.

Westinghouse contended that the unexpected Arab oil embargo of 1973–1974 was one of the factors that resulted in a major increase in the price of all energy resources including uranium. Later, it argued that an international cartel was establishing prices for uranium and thus artificially increasing the price. For these reasons, Westinghouse sought refuge under Section 2-615 of the Uniform Commercial Code, arguing that it would be commercially impracticable to complete a contract that could result in bankruptcy.

On October 27, 1978, after having arrived at several out-of-court settlements, Westinghouse contended that Section 2-712 of the Uniform Commercial Code requires that if the injured party is to cover [that is, to buy substitute goods] they must do it "without unreasonable delay." Although the plaintiffs could have covered for $26 to $30 per pound for the first four months after the announcement of default, many still had not covered and were seeking damages of $43 per pound. Thus, Westinghouse argued that if they were to be assessed damages, or if out-of-court settlements should be arrived at, it should be on the basis of the cost of uranium at the date of rescission and not the current $43 per pound.

International Ramifications

Westinghouse's apparently weak case was unexpectedly bolstered when, in the summer of 1976, Friends of the Earth, an environmentally oriented group based in San Francisco and interested primarily in energy, discovered evidence in Australia of the possibility of the existence of an international cartel that was established to control the price of uranium. They immediately took action to take advantage of this windfall on October 15, 1976, by filing suits against 29 foreign and domestic suppliers of uranium including Gulf Oil Corporation and Rio Algom Corporation.

Westinghouse's efforts were somewhat frustrated by the fact that some of the potential suppliers of uranium were foreign corporations, or U.S. subsidiaries of a foreign corporation, or foreign subsidiaries of American corporations. So, when they attempted to acquire pertinent documents from Rio Algom Corporation, for example, they were not successful. Rio Algom is a Delaware corporation operating a uranium mine in Utah but is a wholly owned subsidiary of Rio Algom Limited, a Canadian corporation with Toronto as its principal place of business. The two corporations have common officers, directors, and marketing vice-presidents, and all records are kept in Toronto. Rio Tinto Zinc Corporation Limited, a British Corporation based in London, owns the majority of the stock in Rio Algom, Ltd.

Out-of-Court Settlements

Where does this leave Westinghouse in its attempt to chart new applications to the concept of impossibility and specifically to commercial impracticability as contained in Uniform Commercial Code Section 2-615? It seems very doubtful that all of this activity will result in a decision that could be used as a precedent in further defining the application of Uniform Commercial Code Section 2-615. After all, who would relish the idea of rendering a decision involving a potential award of $2.6 billion against the 36th largest corporation in the United States with a net worth of $2.29 billion at the end of 1977? Rarely have judges worked so diligently to avoid handing down decisions. For instance, Judge I. Martin Wickselman of the Court of Common Pleas for Allegheny County, Pennsylvania, Civil Division, was quoted as saying on February 10, 1977:

> I am tired of pussyfooting and, more than that, I am tired of talking to lawyers when other, more powerful men, who have the ultimate power of decision, have not been here. The fiscal well-being, possibly the survival of one of the world's corporate giants is in jeopardy. Any decision I hand down will hurt someone and, because of the potential damage, I want to make it clear that it will happen only because certain captains of industry could not

together work out their problems so that the hurt might have been held to a minimum.

Judge Wickselman then ordered the chief executives concerned to meet in his office on February 15. On February 16, the Judge stated "Solomon-like as I want to be, I can't cut this baby in half." He also indicated that, in any event, he would hand down a decision in the first week of April. Then on March 31, 1977, after several months of trial, Westinghouse and the three utilities, Duquesne Light Co., Ohio Edison Co., and the Pennsylvania Power Co., announced a settlement in which the utilities claimed they were to receive cash, equipment, and services worth up to $11.5 million and Westinghouse contended that the package would cost them about $6 million before taxes because the value of the settlement to the utilities exceeded the actual cost to Westinghouse. (This type of discrepancy occurred in every settlement and still remains unexplained.) Westinghouse also agreed to share with the utilities any proceeds it might receive from its conspiracy suits against its suppliers of uranium.

On another front, Judge Robert Merhige, Jr. of the U.S. District Court for the Eastern District of Virginia was doing what he could to have the 17 suits before him settled out of court. On the day the trial opened, October 17, 1977, Judge Merhige stated, "I don't ever expect to finish these cases. I expect [them] to get settled." At least partially as a result of the urging of the judge, cases in-

volving four utilities were settled within two months. Westinghouse settled with Alabama Power Co. for about $5 million and with Texas Utilities Services, Inc. for $70 million. These settlements included a supply of uranium, future services, and equipment, as well as cash. Westinghouse claimed that its cost to settle the Texas Utilities claim was $27 million.

During the final arguments of the case in early June 1978, Judge Merhige ordered, as he had on November 10, 1977, all of the utilities to outline proposals they would accept and present them to a special master appointed to oversee the negotiations. He also warned that he would summon all of the companies' boards of directors to a meeting before he ruled. This action apparently did not have the desired result because no additional agreements were forthcoming as the adversaries continued to maneuver to improve their position until Judge Merhige ruled on October 27, 1978:

> Westinghouse did not meet its burden of establishing that it is entitled to excuse from the contractual obligations which the court finds exists with Plaintiffs, either by reason of section 2-615 of the Uniform Commercial Code, or the force majeure clauses in its contracts with Plaintiffs.

The court's reluctance to issue a final and binding decision is indicated by the following:

> Having thus announced the Court's decisions on these basic points, the Court believes that there are sound reasons for not is-

suing its supporting findings of facts and conclusions of law at this time. I know that, if they are filed, they may well result in standing in the way of these cases ending, as I think they ought to end, in settlement. The Plaintiffs should not be misled by today's holding to the effect that Westinghouse is not excused from its contractual obligations. If anything, the Court is disposed to believe that, just as Westinghouse is not entitled to excuse from its contractual obligations, the Plaintiffs are not entitled to anything near the full measure of their prayer for relief.

> [T]hese are cases which I think everybody admits should be settled if at all possible, in the public interest, and they are really business problems, and should be settled as business problems by businessmen, as I have been urging from the very first.

It appears that these admonitions had some effect because as of 1980, 14 out of the original 17 lawsuits representing about 85% of the claims against Westinghouse have been settled in out-of-court agreements. It would seem that Westinghouse has been successful in its endeavor to minimize its losses and shift much of the economic costs of its managerial decisions from its shareholders, employees, and distributors to a broader base consisting of the utility companies and their customers and then on to the ultimate consumer.

SOURCE This "Inside Story" is excerpted from William Eagan, *The Westinghouse Uranium Contracts: Commercial Impracticability and Related Matters*, 18 AM. BUS. L.J. 281 (1980). Reprinted and excerpted by permission of the *American Business Law Journal*.

KEY WORDS AND PHRASES

adhesion contracts 279
commercial impossibility 282
commercial impracticability 282
cover 283
cross-collateralization clause 280
express warranty 270
firm offer 265
fixtures 261

full warranty 274
goods 261
identification to the contract 261
implied warranty of fitness for a
   particular purpose 273
implied warranty of merchantability
   272
limited warranty 274

lost volume seller 283
merchant 261
prima facie 280
puffing 270
shrink-wrap license 262
statute of frauds 269

QUESTIONS AND CASE PROBLEMS

1. Paul Lewis, a sawmill operator, acquired a new hydraulic pump for his facility. In need of hydraulic fluid to operate the pump, Lewis contacted Mobil Oil Corporation. Mobil's local representative, Frank Rowe, handled the inquiry. Lewis confessed his ignorance about the hydraulic pump, the type of fluid it required, and his necessary reliance on Mobil to supply the proper product. Without inquiring further, Rowe sold Lewis plain mineral oil without any chemical additives. Within a few days of using the oil, Lewis began to experience problems with the pump and asked Rowe several times if he was sure that the oil was appropriate for the pump. After several months, Lewis discovered that the oil he had bought from Mobil was improper for his pump. On what grounds could Lewis sue Mobil? What result? [*Lewis v. Mobil Oil Corp.*, 438 F.2d 500 (8th Cir. 1971)]

2. In planning the construction of a chemical plant in the fall of 1976, Daitom, Inc. solicited bids for two rotary vacuum dryers to dry the chemicals. In September, Pennwalt Corporation submitted a typewritten proposal to supply the dryers, specifying the equipment, the price, and the terms of delivery and payment and attached to it a preprinted form that specified the conditions of the sale. A reference in the sheet made the preprinted form an integral part of the proposal. In response, Daitom issued a purchase order to Pennwalt on a preprinted form that included lengthy standard terms and conditions. On the purchase order, Daitom typed a description of the dryers and referenced the Pennwalt proposal.

Pennwalt delivered the dryers to Daitom in May 1977, but Daitom did not install them until construction of the building was completed 13 months later in June 1978. Upon installation, the dryers did not function properly, so Daitom notified Pennwalt of the problems. Although representatives from Pennwalt visited the plant, they failed to repair the dryers. Daitom then filed suit, alleging that Pennwalt had breached a contractual warranty.

In response, Pennwalt claimed that under the contract, no warranty claims could be asserted more than one year after delivery of the dryers. Pennwalt pointed to language in its September proposal that conditioned Pennwalt's offer on Daitom's agreeing to a one-year limit on warranty claims. Pennwalt argued that the September proposal was an offer that was accepted by Daitom's purchase order. Daitom contended that its purchase order was not an acceptance of the one-year warranty limitation, because the purchase order contained standard language preserving all of Daitom's rights and remedies available at law. Among these legal rights was the right to make warranty claims up to four years after delivery—the standard limitation period specified by the UCC. Daitom's acceptance of the deal was expressly conditioned upon Pennwalt's assenting to the different terms contained in the purchase order. Did Daitom and Pennwalt enter into a contract? If so, what were its terms? [*Daitom, Inc. v. Pennwalt Corp.*, 741 F.2d 1569 (10th Cir. 1984)]

3. The Essex Group manufactured aluminum wire products. In 1967, Essex entered into a contract with Aluminum Co. of America (Alcoa) whereby Alcoa agreed, for a 16-year period (with a five-year renewable option at Essex's pleasure) to smelt Essex's alumina into the molten aluminum Essex needed in its production process.

The contract contained an escalation clause that tied the price Alcoa charged Essex to the Wholesale Price Index-Industrial Commodities (WPI-IC). WPI-IC is one of several indices available to measure inflation. Both parties agreed to the use of this index after concluding that its past record showed stability. Alcoa's objective was to achieve stable income of approximately four cents per pound of converted aluminum. Essex's objective was to ensure a long-term supply of aluminum.

Until 1972, the contract satisfied both parties' needs. However, because of the energy crisis that began in 1973, and increased pollution control costs that were unanticipated in 1967, Alcoa's electricity costs increased at a rate far more rapid than the WPI-IC index. Alcoa estimated that if it were to fulfill the terms of the contract it would lose in excess of $60 million. Alcoa brought suit seeking reformation or equitable adjustment of the agreement. Essex counterclaimed seeking damages for breach of contract. Result? [*Aluminum Co. of America v. Essex Group, Inc.,* 499 F. Supp. 53 (W.D.Pa. 1980)]

4. Before deciding what remedies are available under Article 2 of the UCC, one must first determine whether the transaction involved the sale of goods.

a. Wabash County REMC, a local electric utility, transmitted at least 135 volts of electricity to Thomas Helvey's home one day. As is standard, Helvey's household appliances could safely handle no more than 110 volts. As a result of the overload, Helvey's hair dryer exploded in his hand, causing him personal injury. In a suit against the utility, Helvey alleged breach of implied and express warranties and claimed damages for his personal injuries as well as the destruction of his hair dryer. What rights does Helvey have under Article 2 of the UCC? [*Helvey v. Wabash County REMC,* 278 N.E.2d 608 (Ind. App. Ct. 1972); *contra, Sterling Power Partners, L.P. v. Niagra Mohawk Power Corporation,* 657 N.Y.S.2d 407 (N.Y. App. Div. 1997)]

b. After suffering an interruption in his cable television, Kenneth Kaplan filed a class action lawsuit against his cable television provider, Cablevision of PA, Inc. Alleging that Cablevision had failed to provide continuous, uninterrupted cable service to himself and other contractual subscribers to Cablevision, Kaplan demanded damages for breach of Cablevision's implied warranty of merchantability under the UCC. What result? [*Kaplan v. Cablevision of PA, Inc.,* 671 A.2d 716 (Pa. Super. Ct. 1996)]

5. Fanny and Fred Farmer constructed a grain storage shed on some property they owned. Before the Farmers constructed this shed, they took out a first and second mortgage on the land. A few years after they constructed the shed, the Farmers decided to sell their farming business. According to the purchase agreement between the Farmers and the buyer, the shed was not to become a part of the land on which it sat until the realty was paid for in full. Is the shed a fixture, as defined by the UCC? If so, is it covered by the UCC? [*Metropolitan Life Insurance Co. v. Reeves,* 389 N.W.2d 295 (Neb. 1986)]

6. Dalton Department Store sold Mary Walsh a television made by Dalton. With the television, Walsh received a warranty that covers all electric and electronic parts for two years and all other metal parts for one year. Walsh had the television for six weeks and then took it out of the box. She noticed that one legs was shorter than the others; the screen had several scratches on it; and the remote control did not work. Walsh brought the television set back and demanded that Dalton repair all the problems at no charge. Dalton refused to do so. What rights does Walsh have? What if Mary had had the television for six months and then the glass screen suddenly shattered and the picture tube burned out?

7. Larry Lumberjack had a profitable lumber business. He sold his lumber to most of the major construction companies and contractors around the state. Lumberjack usually shipped his lumber by either freight car or truck, depending upon the location of the customer. Cameron Contractor, one of Lumberjack's best customers, recently ordered three trainloads of lumber from him. Lumberjack was to deliver the lumber to the rail yard and inform Contractor when it arrived. Lumberjack delivered Contractor's lumber, but before he had informed him of the delivery, a fire devastated the rail yard and destroyed Contractor's lumber. However, a number of Contractor's employees had observed the lumber being delivered. Lumberjack is now trying to secure payment from Contractor for the lumber, but Contractor is refusing to pay. Who should prevail? [*Lumber Sales, Inc. v. Brown,* 469 S.W.2d 888 (Tenn. Ct. App. 1971)]

8. A Ferrari originally commissioned by King Leopold III of Belgium was bought in 1969 by an American, Wayne. Another Ferrari fan, Lee, made Wayne a series of offers for the car, culminating in an offer of $275,000. This was a price previously set by Wayne to discourage offers. Lee, at Wayne's request, produced four checks, one of which was endorsed by Wayne's girlfriend. Wayne then wrote Lee, as he had told him before, that the sale required Wayne's parents' consent. The letter from Wayne to Lee recited that, after talking with his parents, Wayne decided the car would not be sold. Lee sued for breach of contract. Who should prevail? [*Lee v. Voyles*, 898 F.2d 76 (7th Cir. 1990)]

9. In July 1993, Werner Siebenmann sold a painting to David Rogath for $570,000. The piece, entitled *Self-Portrait*, was supposedly painted by Francis Bacon in 1792. In the bill of sale, Siebenmann warranted that he was the sole owner of the painting, that the piece was authentic, and that he was unaware of any challenges to its authenticity. Three months later, Rogath sold the piece to a New York art gallery for $950,000. The gallery soon learned of an existing challenge to *Self-Portrait*'s authenticity, first asserted in June by a London art dealer. The gallery requested Rogath to refund its money and take back the piece, which he did.

Rogath then sued Siebenmann for breach of contract and warranty. Siebenmann admitted that he knew of the challenge to *Self-Portrait* but claimed that he told Rogath about it, notwithstanding the language in the bill of sale. What result if (a) Siebenmann had said nothing about any challenge to Rogath? (b) Siebenmann had described the London art dealer's challenge to Rogath before concluding the sale? (c) Siebenmann said nothing of any challenge but Rogath learned independently of the London art dealer's doubts the day before purchasing the piece? [*Rogath v. Siebenmann*, 127 F.3d 261 (2d Cir. 1997)]

MANAGER'S DILEMMA

10. Sandy Singlefather has two children and lives in a subsidized housing development in New City. He receives federal assistance to help raise his two children. Singlefather recently read an advertisement for household appliances. The advertisement stated that he could "rent to own" his appliances with no credit. Singlefather was in need of a washing machine, and he had a poor credit history, so he answered the advertisement. The appliance store was more than delighted to accommodate him. Singlefather now pays $30 a week for his washing machine and will own it after he makes 78 payments. A washing machine usually sells for $350.

Has Singlefather entered into an unconscionable bargain? Should the manager of the rent-to-own business repossess the washing machine if Singlefather fails to pay the $30 weekly rent after possessing the machine and paying rent for 50 weeks?

Suppose that a rent-to-own business rents a large-screen television that retails for $3,000 for $100 a week with the right to own it after 80 weeks. The renter defaults after possessing the television and paying the $100 weekly rent for 50 weeks. Should the manager treat that transaction any differently from rental of the washing machine? How could the manager structure pricing to permit the transactions to withstand legal challenge yet still be profitable for the rent-to-own company? [*Murphy v. McNamara*, 416 A.2d 170 (Conn. Supp. 1979)]

INTERNET SOURCES	
Pace University's Institute for International Commercial Law sponsors a page about the U.N. Convention on Contracts for the International Sale of Goods.	http://www.cisg.law.pace.edu
The Uniform Law Commissioners, who draft the UCC, have a Web site at the University of Pennsylvania Law School that contains the entire UCC, including Article 2, and its history and proposed changes, as well as other uniform laws.	http://www.law.upenn.edu/library/ulc/ulc.htm
The Communications Media Center at New York Law School sponsors a page addressing the use of disclaimers on the Web.	http://www.cmcnyls.edu/public/mlp/udsciwww.htm
The United Nations Web site provides updated information about CISG, including its signatories.	http://www.un.or.at/uncitral

CHAPTER 9

Torts

INTRODUCTION

What Is a Tort?

A *tort* is a civil wrong resulting in injury to a person or property. A tort case is brought by the injured party to seek compensation for the wrong done. A crime, by contrast, is a wrong to society that is prosecuted by the state. (Criminal law is discussed in Chapter 15.) Even though a crime may be perpetrated against an individual, the victim is not a party to a criminal action. Criminal law generally is not concerned with compensating the victim, but with protecting society and punishing the criminal.

However, the distinctions between tort and criminal law are not always as clear as they first appear. A criminal statute might call for the criminal to compensate the victim. The victim might sue the perpetrator of the crime in tort, using the violation of a criminal statute as a basis for the tort claim. In some cases, tort law purports, like criminal law, to protect society through the award of punitive damages.

Chapter Overview

This chapter first discusses intentional torts, which fall into three general categories: (1) torts to protect individuals from physical and mental harm; (2) torts to protect interests in property; and (3) torts that protect certain economic interests and business relationships. The chapter then addresses negligence and strict liability. Tortious activity by more than one individual or entity raises the issues of vicarious liability and apportioned responsibility. The chapter applies these various theories to the evolving law of toxic torts.

Elements of an Intentional Tort

In order for a party to prevail in a tort action, the plaintiff must prove all elements of a claim. Intentional torts require the plaintiff to prove (1) actual or implied intent; (2) a voluntary act by the defendant; (3) causation; and (4) injury or harm. The act must be the actual and legal cause of the injury. The act required depends on the specific intentional tort.

Intent

Intent is the subjective desire to cause the consequences of an act. *Actual intent* can be shown by evidence that the defendant intended a specific consequence to a particular individual. Intent is implied if the defendant knew that the consequences of the act were certain or substantially certain even if he or she did not actually intend any consequence at all.

As the degree of certainty of the result decreases, the defendant's conduct loses the character of intent and becomes recklessness. As the result becomes even less certain, the act becomes negligence, which is treated later in this chapter. For example, if Metro Corporation's custodian, Hal, dumped garbage out of Metro's third-floor office window onto a busy sidewalk and hit Alexis, the law would likely imply intent to hit Alexis. Even though Hal may have had no subjective intention of hitting Alexis with the garbage, throwing it onto a busy sidewalk was substantially certain to result in at least one pedestrian being hit. However, if late one night Hal put garbage in the middle of the sidewalk in front of the office building for morning pickup and Alexis tripped over it, the intent to cause harm is not so clear. If intent is not established, Hal will not be liable for the intentional tort of battery, which requires intent to bring about a harmful contact. However, Alexis might be able to establish negligence if she can show that a reasonable person would not have left the garbage on the sidewalk.

Intent may be transferred. If the defendant intended to hit one person but instead hit the plaintiff, the intent requirement is met as to the plaintiff.

Defenses

Even if a plaintiff has proved all elements of a tort, the defendant may raise a legal defense to absolve himself or herself of liability. The most frequently raised defense is consent. If the plaintiff consented to the act of the defendant, there is no tort. Even if the plaintiff did not explicitly consent, the law may imply consent. For example, a professional athlete injured during practice is deemed to have consented to the physical contact attendant to practice.

The defendant may also be absolved of liability by a claim of self-defense or defense of others.

Types of Intentional Torts

The intentional torts of battery, assault, false imprisonment, intentional infliction of emotional distress, defamation, and invasion of privacy are designed to protect individuals from physical and mental harm. The torts of trespass to land, nuisance, conversion, and trespass to personal property protect interests in property. Certain economic interests and business relationships are protected by the torts of disparagement, injurious falsehood, fraudulent misrepresentation, malicious prosecution, interference with contractual relations, and interference with prospective business advantage. A single set of facts may give rise to claims under more than one theory.

Intentional Torts to Protect Persons

Battery

Tort law recognizes a basic right to have one's body free from harmful or offensive contact. Battery is the violation of that right.

Battery is the intentional, nonconsensual, harmful, or offensive contact with the plaintiff's body or with something in contact with it. Offensive contact, such as dousing a person with water or spitting in his or her face, may be a battery, even though the plaintiff has suffered no physical harm. The contact may be by the defendant directly or by something the defendant has set in motion. For example, putting poison in someone's food is a battery.

Another example of battery occurred after a New York Mets–Los Angeles Dodgers baseball game in July 1993. Amanda Santos, a two-year-old girl, was injured by an explosive device tossed in the parking lot by Vince Coleman, then a Mets outfielder. The young girl's family filed suit against Coleman and a number of other parties, alleging battery, infliction of emotional distress (discussed later in this chapter), conspiracy to commit battery and inflict emotional distress, negligence, and negligent infliction of emotional distress.[1] The suit requested unspecified general, special, and punitive damages.

An example of a controversial case of battery occurred when a San Francisco cab driver used his taxicab to apprehend an escaping mugger by pinning him to a wall. The escaping mugger sued the cabbie for use of excessive force, and the jury rendered a verdict of more than $24,000. The judge ordered a new trial, stating: "It is not now, nor was it ever the law, that before submitting to a lawful arrest, a fleeing felon is entitled to a fair fistfight."[2]

---

1. *Family Files Suit Against Coleman,* SAN JOSE MERCURY NEWS, Oct. 18, 1993, at 2D.
2. McClure v. Luxor Cab Co. (1992).

Assault

Assault also protects the right to have one's body left alone. Unlike battery, however, it does not require contact. *Assault* is an intentional, nonconsensual act that gives rise to the apprehension (though not necessarily fear) that a harmful or offensive contact is imminent.

Generally, assault requires some act, such as a threatening gesture, and the ability to follow through immediately with a battery. A punch thrown from close range that misses its target may be an assault, but a threat to punch someone is not. If a defendant makes a threatening gesture and says, "I would hit you if I weren't behind this desk," and the defendant is in fact behind the desk, there is no assault. The immediacy requirement has not been met. Similarly, the threat "I'll beat you up if you come to class next week" is not immediate enough to be an assault.

False Imprisonment

False imprisonment protects the right to be free from restraint of movement. It is intentional, nonconsensual confinement by physical barriers or by physical force or threats of force. It requires that the plaintiff either knew he or she was confined or suffered harm as a result of the confinement.

False imprisonment has been found when the plaintiff's freedom of movement was restricted because of force applied to the plaintiff's valuable property. For example, if a store clerk grabs a package from a customer walking out the door, this is false imprisonment because the customer cannot be expected to abandon the package to leave the store.

Shopkeepers who detain and later release a person mistakenly suspected of shoplifting are sometimes sued for false imprisonment. Most states have legislation exempting shopkeepers from such claims if the shopkeeper has acted in good faith and the detention is made in a reasonable manner, for a reasonable time, and is based on reasonable cause.

Intentional Infliction of Emotional Distress

The tort of *intentional infliction of emotional distress* protects the right to peace of mind. The law has been slow to redress purely mental injuries and is still evolving in this area. Jurisdictions differ sharply in their acceptance of this tort. In most jurisdictions, in order to prove intentional infliction of emotional distress, a plaintiff must show (1) outrageous conduct by the defendant; (2) intent to cause, or reckless disregard of the probability of causing, emotional distress; (3) severe emotional suffering; and (4) actual and proximate (or legal) causation of the emotional distress. The reluctance of the courts to accept intentional infliction of emotional distress as an independent tort most likely stems from the fear that plaintiffs will file false claims. Therefore, some jurisdictions also require a physical manifestation of the emotional distress.

The mental distress must be foreseeable. The defendant is liable only to the extent that the plaintiff's response is reasonably within the range of normal human emotions.

The acts of the defendant must be outrageous or intolerable. Insulting, abusive, threatening, profane, or annoying conduct is not in itself a tort. Everyone is expected to be hardened to a certain amount of abuse. In determining outrageousness, courts will consider the context of the tort, as well as the relationship of the parties. For example, in the workplace, the plaintiff can expect to be subjected to evaluation and criticism, and neither criticism nor discharge is in itself outrageous. On the other hand, sexual harassment by a supervisor in the workplace is less tolerated than it might be, for example, if done by a patron in a nightclub. The following case concerns an employer's liability for sexual harassment in the workplace.

A CASE IN POINT   **IN THE LANGUAGE OF THE COURT**

CASE 9.1
FORD v. REVLON, INC.
Supreme Court of Arizona
734 P.2d 580 (Ariz. 1987).

FACTS   Plaintiff Leta Fay Ford was an employee of Revlon in the Phoenix office's purchasing department. In 1979, Revlon hired Karl Braun as the new manager for the purchasing department, which made him Ford's supervisor.

Case 9.1 continues

Case 9.1 continued

In April 1980, Braun invited Ford to dinner, supposedly to discuss business. However, at the end of the evening when Ford tried to leave, Braun told her to stay because he planned to spend the night with her. When she rejected his advances, he told her, "You will regret this." This was only the first of several incidents in which Braun harassed Ford, including one a month later at a company picnic at which Braun held Ford in a chokehold, fondled her, and made lewd comments to her. Ford testified at trial that after the initial incident of harassment, her working relationship with Braun was strained and uncomfortable.

Ford had not reported the first incident to Revlon management. After the picnic incident, however, she began a series of meetings with several members of Revlon management in order to report her complaints. She contacted managers at both her Phoenix office and at Revlon headquarters in New Jersey. She told them that she was afraid of Braun and wanted help, and that the strain was making her sick.

The harassment continued throughout 1980. Braun threatened that he would destroy Ford and said that so long as she worked for him she was never going to go anywhere. When no action had been taken by December 1980, Ford called the manager at the New Jersey office to which she had complained earlier. That person, Marie Kane, told Ford that the situation was too hot for her to handle and that she did not want to be involved. Kane suggested that Ford put the matter in the back of her mind and try to forget the situation.

During the time of the harassment, Ford developed high blood pressure, a nervous tic in her left eye, chest pains, rapid breathing, and other symptoms of emotional stress. Ford felt weak, dizzy, and generally fatigued. She consulted a physician about her condition.

In February 1981, Ford submitted a written request for transfer out of the purchasing department. Finally, in late February, a meeting was held in personnel at Ford's demand so she could have something done about her situation with Braun. She again gave the details of her complaint and submitted a handwritten complaint that read in part:

> I am asking for protection from Karl Braun. I have a right to be protected.
> I am collapsing emotionally and physically and I can't go on.

Not until three months later did the representative from personnel submit a report on Ford's complaint to a Revlon vice-president. The report confirmed Ford's charge of sexual assault and recommended that Braun be censured. In May 1981, a full year and one month after Braun's initial act of harassment, Braun was issued a letter of censure from Revlon.

In October 1981, Ford attempted suicide. Later that month Revlon, fired Braun.

In April 1982, Ford sued both Braun and Revlon for assault and battery and for intentional infliction of emotional distress. At trial, two written personnel policies were admitted as evidence. The policies stated in part that "any employee who has a complaint about any aspect of his or her employment is entitled to have the complaint heard, investigated and, if possible, resolved" and that "legitimate complaints are to be satisfied as promptly and as fully as possible."

Case 9.1 continues

Case 9.1 continued

The trial court jury found both Braun and Revlon liable for assault and battery and found intentional infliction of emotional distress by Revlon. The court of appeals reversed. Ford appealed.

ISSUE PRESENTED   Can an employer's failure to take appropriate action in response to an employee's complaint of sexual harassment constitute the tort of intentional infliction of emotional distress?

OPINION   CAMERON, J., writing for the Arizona Supreme Court:

Elements of the tort of intentional infliction of emotional distress have been set out by this court. . . . The three required elements are: first, the conduct by the defendant must be "extreme" and "outrageous"; second, the defendant must either intend to cause emotional distress or recklessly disregard the near certainty that such distress will result from his conduct; and third, severe emotional distress must indeed occur as a result of defendant's conduct.

We believe that the conduct of Revlon met these requirements. First, Revlon's conduct can be classified as extreme or outrageous. Ford made numerous Revlon managers aware of Braun's activities at company functions. Ford did everything that could be done, both within the announced policies of Revlon and without, to bring this matter to Revlon's attention. Revlon ignored her and the situation she faced, dragging the matter out for months and leaving Ford without redress. Here is sufficient evidence that Revlon acted outrageously.

Second, even if Revlon did not intend to cause emotional distress, Revlon's reckless disregard of Braun's conduct made it nearly certain that such emotional distress would in fact occur. Revlon knew that Braun had subjected Ford to physical assaults and vulgar remarks, that Ford continued to feel threatened by Braun, and that Ford was emotionally distraught, all of which led to a manifestation of physical problems. Despite Ford's complaints, Braun was not confronted for nine months, and then only upon Ford's demand for a group meeting. Another three months elapsed before Braun was censured. Revlon not only had actual knowledge of the situation but it also failed to conduct promptly any investigation of Ford's complaint.

Third, it is obvious that emotional distress did occur. Ample evidence, both medical and otherwise, was presented describing Ford's emotional distress. Ford testified about her emotional distress and her development of physical complications caused by her stressful work environment. The evidence convinced the jury, which found that emotional distress had occurred.

We also note that Revlon had set forth a specific policy and several guidelines for the handling of sexual harassment claims and other employee complaints, yet Revlon recklessly disregarded these policies and guidelines. Ford was entitled to rely on the policy statements made by Revlon. . . . We hold that Revlon's failure to take appropriate action in response to Ford's complaint of sexual harassment by Braun constituted the tort of intentional infliction of emotional distress.

Case 9.1 continues

Case 9.1 continued

RESULT The Arizona Supreme Court vacated the decision of the court of appeals and reinstated the judgment of the trial court. Ford received the monetary award for damages that she had been granted by the jury.

Questions

1. Would Revlon still have been held liable in this case if it did not have a specific policy, which it failed to follow, for handling sexual-harassment claims? How important a factor should that policy be in the court's decision? Is it possible that this court's decision will discourage other companies from instituting their own sexual-harassment policies and guidelines?
2. What qualifies as the "severe emotional distress" necessary to prove that the defendant is liable for the intentional infliction of emotional distress? What if Ford had only felt very uncomfortable and inhibited in her work environment as opposed to attempting suicide and suffering from other physical ailments?

Defamation

Defamation is the communication (often termed *publication*) to a third party of an untrue statement of fact that injures the plaintiff's reputation by exposing him or her to "hatred, ridicule or contempt."

Libel is written defamation, and *slander* is spoken defamation. The distinction between libel and slander is sometimes blurred with respect to modern communications.

Special rules apply to the requirement of injury to reputation. In an action for slander (spoken defamation), the plaintiff must prove he or she has suffered actual harm, such as the loss of credit, a job, or customers, unless the statement is so obviously damaging that it falls into the category of slander per se. *Slander per se* means that the words are slanderous in and of themselves, for example, a statement that a person has committed a serious crime, is guilty of sexual misconduct, or is not fit to conduct business. In an action for libel (written defamation), the law presumes injury; that is, no actual harm need be shown unless the statement on its face is not damaging.

As the following case illustrates, an opinion is defamation only if it implies a statement of objective fact.

A CASE IN POINT	SUMMARY

**CASE 9.2
SAGAN v. APPLE
COMPUTER, INC.**
United States District
Court for the Central
District of California
874 F. Supp. 1072
(C.D. Cal. 1994)

FACTS Apple Computer began using the name of famed astronomer Carl Sagan in connection with a personal computer in 1993. After Apple Computer's use of "Carl Sagan" was publicized in computer periodicals and other publications, Sagan's attorneys demanded that Apple Computer cease use of the name. Apple Computer informed Sagan that it was using Sagan's name as a "code name" for a new personal computer and indicated that it would cease use of the name. In January 1994, Apple Computer changed the code name to "Butt-Head Astronomer." This name was published by Apple Computer and appeared in numerous newspapers and in other media. In April 1994, Sagan sued Apple Computer alleging libel.

Case 9.2 continues

Case 9.2 continued

ISSUE PRESENTED   Would a reasonable person conclude that Apple Computer, by changing a product code name from "Carl Sagan" to "Butt-Head Astronomer," made statements that imply a libelous assertion of fact?

SUMMARY OF OPINION   The Federal District Court ruled that the dispositive question in determining whether a statement of opinion can form the basis of a state libel action is whether a reasonable factfinder could conclude that the statements imply an assertion of fact. Factors to consider include (1) whether the defendant used figurative or hyperbolic language that would negate the impression that he was seriously maintaining an assertion of fact; (2) whether the general tenor of the communication negated the assertion of fact; and (3) whether the assertion is susceptible of being proved true or false.

There can be no question that the use of the figurative term "Butt-Head" negates the impression that Apple Computer was seriously implying an assertion of fact. It strains reason to conclude that Apple Computer was attempting to criticize Sagan's reputation or competency as an astronomer. One does not seriously attack the expertise of a scientist using the undefined phrase "butt-head." Thus, the figurative language militates against implying an assertion of fact.

Furthermore, the tenor of any communication of the information, especially the phrase "Butt-Head Astronomer," would negate the impression that Apple Computer was implying an assertion of fact. Any reader would likely understand that Apple Computer was clearly attempting to retaliate in a humorous and satirical way against Sagan's reaction to Apple Computer's use of his name. A reasonable reader would further conclude that the use of the term "astronomer" did not imply that Sagan was a less than able astronomer but that the word was merely a means of identifying Sagan.

Finally, the bare statement that Sagan is a "Butt-Head Astronomer" cannot rest on a core of objective evidence, so it cannot be proved true or false. Sagan did not suggest any other assertions of objective fact that could be reasonably implied from the phrase.

Therefore, the statement made by Apple Computer was protected under California law and could not form the basis of a claim for libel.

RESULT   The court dismissed Sagan's lawsuit.

The requirement of publication generally means that the statement must be made in the presence of a third person. Thus, the statement "You are a thief" made in a one-on-one conversation is not defamation. However, some courts have adopted the doctrine of *self publication* to give an employee a claim for defamation when the employer makes a false assertion in firing an employee, which the employer could reasonably expect the employee to repeat to a prospective employer.

Defenses   Defenses to defamation actions are framed in terms of privilege and may be asserted in a number of circumstances. An *absolute privilege* cannot be lost. A *qualified privilege* can be lost under certain conditions. If the defendant has an absolute privilege, he or she can publish with impunity a statement he or she knows to be false. The defendant can even do it with the most evil intention. Absolute privilege is limited to situations in which (1) the defendant has consented to the publica-

ETHICAL CONSIDERATION

The damage done to a person's reputation by defamation can be instantaneous, because the false statements frequently receive attention in the electronic and print media. The public, quick to latch on to the initial defamatory statements, is less likely to notice a court decision some years later that holds that the statements were in fact false.

Because of this phenomenon, someone determined to cast doubt on another person's reputation has a good chance of success. Once the damage is done, it is largely irreversible. Therefore, ethical restraint must sometimes take the place of legal restraint.

tion; (2) the statement is a political broadcast made under the federal "equal time" statute; (3) the statement is made by a government official in the performance of governmental duties; (4) the statement is made by participants in judicial proceedings; or (5) the statement is made between spouses.

In most jurisdictions, truth is an absolute defense to a defamation claim. The law will not protect a reputation the plaintiff does not deserve. However, the burden is on the defendant to prove that the derogatory statements are true. The law in most jurisdictions presumes that the plaintiff has a pristine reputation unless the defendant proves otherwise.

There is a qualified privilege to make statements to protect one's own personal interests, including statements to a peer review committee. There is a qualified privilege to make statements to protect legitimate business interests, such as statements to a prospective employer, or to provide information for the public interest, such as credit reports. Qualified privileges can be lost if the person making the statement abuses the privilege.

In addition to privileges, statutory devices may protect "speakers." For instance, the 1996 Communications Decency Act specifically states that a provider of Internet services will not be treated as the publisher of information provided by another information content provider. Hence, the U.S. Court of Appeals for the Fourth Circuit refused to hold America Online (AOL) liable for one AOL user's false characterization of an

other user as sympathizing with the Oklahoma City terrorists.[3] Because the federal statute preempts state law, Virginia's tort of defamation did not apply to AOL.

Media Defendants The media, such as newspapers, television, or radio, when they are commenting on a public official or public figure, have a qualified privilege that is almost absolute. Public officials include legislators, judges, and police officers. The definition of a public figure is addressed below.

The U.S. Supreme Court, in applying the First Amendment right of freedom of the press, has held that in order for a public official or public figure to recover damages for defamation by a media defendant, there must be a showing of *actual malice*. That means the statement must have been made with the knowledge that it was false or with a reckless disregard as to whether it was false. (Other aspects of the First Amendment are discussed in Chapter 2.)

Public figures are those who, by reason of the notoriety of their achievements or the vigor and success with which they seek the public's attention, are injected into the public eye. In *Time, Inc. v. Firestone*[4] the U.S. Supreme Court made it clear that social prominence does not automatically indicate public-figure status sufficient to trigger the actual malice requirement. Mary Alice Firestone had married into the famous and wealthy industrial family of Russell Firestone. When she and her husband divorced, Time, Inc. falsely reported the basis of her divorce. Mrs. Firestone sued Time, Inc. for defamation. The Supreme Court rejected the argument that Mrs. Firestone was a public figure. The Court stated that although Mrs. Firestone was prominent in the social circle of Palm Beach, Florida, this did not make her a public figure. It further stated that not all controversies of interest to the public are "public controversies" of the type that triggers the actual malice requirement. The Court concluded that Mrs. Firestone did not have to prove actual malice to prevail.

If the plaintiff is not a public figure, he or she need not prove malice. A private plaintiff may raise a defamation claim if the defendant acted with knowledge, acted in reckless disregard of the facts, or was negligent in

3. Zeran v. America Online, Inc., 129 F.3d 327 (4th Cir. 1997).
4. 424 U.S. 448 (1976).

failing to ascertain the facts. If the plaintiff proceeds on a negligence theory, he or she must prove actual damages, such as loss of business or out-of-pocket costs. If the plaintiff proves malice, damages are presumed, meaning no proof of damages is required.

Invasion of Privacy

Invasion of privacy is a violation of the right to keep personal matters to oneself. It can take several forms.

Intrusion is objectionable prying, such as eavesdropping or unauthorized rifling through files. Injunctions or court orders are usually available to prevent further intrusion. There must be a reasonable expectation of privacy in the thing into which there is intrusion. For example, courts have held there is no legitimate expectation of privacy in conversations in a public restaurant. The tort of intrusion does not require publication of the information obtained.

Public disclosure of private facts does require publication, for example, stating in a newspaper that the plaintiff does not pay debts or posting such a notice in a public place. The matter made public must not be newsworthy. The matter must be private, such that a reasonable person would find publication objectionable. Unlike in a defamation case, truth is not a defense.

Appropriation of a person's name or likeness may be an invasion of privacy. Often this tort is committed for financial gain. For example, using a fictitious testimonial in an advertisement, or using a person's picture in an advertisement or article with which he or she has no connection, would be a tort.

◆ Intentional Torts to Protect Property

Trespass to Land

The previously described torts have involved interference with personal rights. *Trespass to land* is an interference with a property right. It is an invasion of property without consent of the owner. The land need not be injured by the trespass. The intent required is the intent to enter the property, not the intent to trespass. Thus, a mistake as to ownership is irrelevant.

Trespass may occur both below the surface and in the airspace above the land. Throwing something, such as trash, on the land, or shooting bullets over it, may be

trespasses, even though the perpetrator was not standing on the plaintiff's land.

Refusing to move something that at one time the plaintiff permitted the defendant to place on the land may be a trespass. For example, if the plaintiff gave the defendant permission to leave a forklift on the plaintiff's land for one month, and it was left for two, the defendant may be liable for trespass.

Nuisance

Nuisance is a nontrespassory interference with the use and enjoyment of property, for example, by an annoying odor or noise.

Public nuisance is unreasonable and substantial interference with the public health, safety, peace, comfort, convenience, or utilization of land. A public nuisance action is usually brought by the government. It may also be brought by a private citizen who experiences special harm different from that of the general public.

Private nuisance is interference with an individual's use and enjoyment of his or her land. Destruction of crops by flooding, the pollution of a stream, or playing loud music late at night in a residential neighborhood can constitute a private nuisance.

The Wisconsin Supreme Court recently held that stray voltage that reduced a dairy herd's milk production is actionable on a private nuisance theory.[5] The court noted that the common law doctrine of private nuisance was broad enough to meet a wide variety of possible invasions and flexible enough to adapt to changing social values and conditions.

The focus of both public and private nuisance claims is on the plaintiff's harm, not on the degree of the defendant's fault. Therefore, even innocent behavior on the part of the defendant is actionable—that is, it may be the basis for a claim—if that behavior resulted in unreasonable and substantial interference with the use and enjoyment of the plaintiff's property. To determine whether the defendant's conduct is unreasonable, the court will balance the utility of the activity creating the harm and the burden of preventing it against the nature and the gravity of the harm. For example, hammering noise during the remodeling of a house may be easier to justify than playing loud music purely for recreation.

---

5. Vogel v. Grant-LaFayette Elec. Coop., 548 N.W.2d 829 (Wis. 1996).

Conversion

Conversion is the exercise of dominion and control over the personal property, rather than the real property (that is, land), of another. This tort protects the right to have personal property left alone. It prevents the defendant from treating the plaintiff's property as if it were his or her own. It is the tort claim a plaintiff would assert to recover the value of property stolen, destroyed, or substantially altered by the defendant.

The intent element for conversion does not include a wrongful motive. It merely requires the intent to exercise dominion or control over goods, inconsistent with the plaintiff's rights. The defendant need not know that the goods belonged to the plaintiff.

Trespass to Personal Property

When personal property is interfered with but not converted—that is, taken, destroyed, or substantially altered—there is a *trespass to personal property* (sometimes referred to as *trespass to chattels*). No wrongful motive need be shown. The intent required is the intent to ex-

ercise control over the plaintiff's personal property. For example, an employer who took an employee's car on a short errand without the employee's permission would be liable for trespass to personal property. However, if the employer damaged the car or drove it for several thousand miles, thereby lowering its value, he or she would be liable for conversion.

The tort of trespass to chattels can include demonstrations that involve private property on private land. For example, in an Oregon case a logging company sued six members of an environmental group who climbed on and chained themselves to the company's logging equipment.[6] The members of the environmental group had to pay punitive damages for demonstrating against government policies while on private property. The court ruled that the enforcement of these tort punitive damages did not violate the protesters' First Amendment rights.

---

6. Huffman and Wright Logging Co. v. Wade, 857 P.2d 101 (Or. 1993).

VIEW FROM CYBERSPACE

STAMPING OUT SPAM

Recently, the trespass to chattels action has found novel application in the on-line world. Frustrated by the proliferation of unsolicited e-mail advertisements clogging its servers, known as "spam," on-line service provider CompuServe sued a prominent Internet junk mailer, Cyber Promotions.[a] The court found that the volume of Cyber Promotions' mass mailings placed a tremendous burden on CompuServe's equipment. Moreover, the messages were largely unwanted by CompuServe customers, many of whom terminated their accounts specifically because of the unabated receipt of bulk e-mail messages. Thus, insofar as Cyber Promotions' mailings diminished the capacity of CompuServe's equipment and harmed CompuServe's business reputation and goodwill with its customers, those mailings were actionable as a common law trespass to chattels.

Similarly, America Online sued Over the Air Equipment for sending unsolicited e-mail messages promoting adult entertainment sites to AOL members. Perhaps fearing a repeat of Cyber Promotions' defeat, Over the Air settled the suit for an undisclosed sum and agreed to cease sending messages to AOL members. On the same day it proclaimed the settlement with Over the Air, AOL announced new lawsuits against Squeaky Clean Marketing and Cyber Services. Still, one AOL member laments, "The junk mail keeps coming and coming."[b]

---

a. CompuServe, Inc. v. Cyber Promotions, Inc., 962 F. Supp. 1015 (S.D. Ohio 1997).

b. Jared Sandberg, *AOL Declares Win Over Junk E-Mailer and Will Receive Unspecified Damages*, WALL ST. J., Dec. 19, 1997, at B6

Intentional Torts that Protect Certain Economic Interests and Business Relationships

Disparagement

Disparagement is the publication of statements derogatory to the quality of the plaintiff's business, to the business in general, or even to the plaintiff's personal affairs, in order to discourage others from dealing with him or her.

To prove disparagement, the plaintiff must show that the defendant made false statements about the quality or ownership of the plaintiff's goods or services, knowing that they were false, or with conscious indifference as to their truth. The plaintiff must also prove that the statements caused him or her actual harm; damages will not be presumed.

Injurious Falsehood

False statements that are knowingly made, although they may not be disparaging of the plaintiff's business, may nevertheless give rise to an *injurious falsehood* claim. For example, a false statement that the plaintiff has gone out of business or does not carry certain goods, if it results in economic loss to the plaintiff, is a tort.

The range of damages for injurious falsehood is more restricted than for defamation. Injurious falsehood permits recovery of only pecuniary (that is, monetary) losses related to business operations, whereas defamation permits recovery for loss of reputation, including emotional damages, as well as pecuniary losses.

Defenses   The defenses available to the defendant in a defamation action apply to injurious falsehood. In the case of comparison of goods, the privilege is even broader than the privilege available in defamation. For example, a defendant who favorably compares his or her own goods to those of a competitor is privileged, even though the defendant may not honestly believe in the superiority of his or her own goods.

Fraudulent Misrepresentation

The tort of *fraudulent misrepresentation*, also called fraud or deceit, protects economic interests and the right to be treated fairly and honestly. Fraud requires proof that the defendant intentionally misled the plaintiff by making a material misrepresentation of fact upon which the plaintiff relied. It also requires that the plaintiff suffer injury as a result of the reliance. For example, a shareholder who has relied to his or her detriment upon an intentionally misleading accountant's opinion regarding the company's financial statements might sue the accountant for fraud.

The fraud in a fraudulent misrepresentation action can be constructive—in other words, a court will sometimes impute a fraudulent intent to the defendant if the defendant showed reckless disregard for the truth.[7] (Negligent misrepresentation is discussed later in this chapter.)

An action for fraudulent misrepresentation can also be based upon the defendant's omission of a material fact when the defendant has a duty to speak because of a special relationship with the plaintiff. For example, in one case,[8] Williams, the plaintiff owner of a Buick dealership, had relied on a bank for several years for financial advice. The plaintiff was 25 years old and had worked his way up from lot boy. When Williams wanted to purchase a new dealership, Security Pacific, the bank, suggested he purchase Viking. Viking was losing money and owed Security Pacific money. In the meantime, Security Pacific was seeking a bailout from its financial obligations. The bank withheld all of this information from Williams. Williams then suffered great financial hardship and eventually lost both dealerships after the bank refused to extend financing.

---

7. *See, e.g.*, Citizens Nat'l Bank of Wisner v. Kennedy & Co., 441 N.W.2d 180 (Neb. 1989), and Software Design and Application, Ltd. v. Price Waterhouse, LLP, 57 Cal. Rptr. 2d 36 (Cal. Ct. App. 1996).

8. Security Pacific Nat'l Bank v. Williams, 262 Cal. Rptr. 260 (Cal. Ct. App. 1989).

ETHICAL CONSIDERATION

If a person knows that his or her goods are inferior, is it ethical to claim that they are better than a competitor's?

The California Court of Appeal upheld a jury verdict of $4.5 million, including $2.5 million in punitive damages. The court held that the bank owed Williams a *fiduciary duty*, that is, a duty to act with integrity.

Although statements as to future actions are generally deemed opinions and therefore not actionable, the court also held that an exception is found when (1) the defendant held itself out to be specially qualified and the plaintiff acted reasonably in relying upon the defendant's superior knowledge; (2) the opinion is that of a fiduciary or other trusted person; and (3) the defendant stated its opinion as an existing fact or as implying facts that justify a belief in its truth.

Malicious Prosecution and Defense

A plaintiff can successfully sue for *malicious prosecution* if he or she shows that a prior proceeding was instituted against him or her maliciously and without probable cause or factual basis. In addition, the earlier case must have been resolved in the plaintiff's favor. This tort originated in the misuse of the criminal process but has been adapted to redress malicious civil prosecution as well. A victorious plaintiff can recover damages for attorney's fees paid in connection with the prior action, injury to reputation, and psychological distress.

Courts frequently state that the malicious prosecution action is disfavored under the law. Because the action has the potential to produce a chilling effect that discourages legitimate claims, courts have been reluctant to expand its reach.

Nevertheless, one state expanded the doctrine to recognize an action for *malicious defense*. In *Aronson v. Schroeder*,[9] the defendant allegedly created false material evidence while serving as defense counsel in a prior case and then gave false testimony advancing the evidence. In a ruling for the plaintiff, the New Hampshire Supreme Court said it "merely recognize[d] that when a defense is based upon false evidence and perjury or is raised for an improper purpose, the litigant is not made whole if the only remedy is reimbursement of counsel fees. It follows that upon proving malicious defense, the aggrieved party is entitled to the same damages as are recoverable in a malicious prosecution claim."

---

9. 671 A.2d 1023 (N.H. 1995).

Interference with Contractual Relations

The tort of *interference with contractual relations* protects the right to enjoy the benefits of legally binding agreements. It provides a remedy when the defendant intentionally induces another person to breach a contract with the plaintiff. The basis of interference with contractual relations is intent to interfere. Thus, courts usually require that the defendant induce the contracting party to breach, rather than merely create the opportunity for the breach. The defendant must know of the existence of the contract between the plaintiff and the other person, or there must be sufficient facts that would lead a reasonable person to believe there was such a contract.

Interference with contractual relations also requires an unacceptable purpose in some jurisdictions. If good grounds exist for the interference, the defendant is not liable. For example, if a manager of a corporation is incompetent, a stockholder of a corporation may be able to induce breach of the employment agreement between the manager and the corporation. The stockholder's motive would be to protect his or her investment. On the other hand, a defendant may not interfere with another person's contract in order to attract customers or employees away from that person. Similarly, a defendant that knowingly participates in or induces a breach of fiduciary duty by another commits the tort of *participation in a breach of fiduciary duty*.

Perhaps the most famous case involving tortious interference with contract was *Pennzoil v. Texaco*, discussed in the "Inside Story" in Chapter 7. A jury decided against Texaco for interfering with Pennzoil's contract to buy Getty Oil, awarding $10.5 billion to Pennzoil. The case was ultimately settled for $3 billion.

Defenses   As in defamation, truth is a defense to a claim for interference with contractual relations. There is no liability if a true statement was made to induce another to break relations with the plaintiff.

Interference with Prospective Business Advantage

Courts are less willing to award damages for interference with prospective contracts than they are to

protect existing contracts. A party still engaged in negotiating a contract has fewer rights not to have its
deal disturbed than a party that has already entered
into a contract.

To prove *interference with prospective business advantage*, the plaintiff must prove that the defendant interfered with a relationship the plaintiff sought to
develop and that the interference caused the plaintiff's
loss. The interference must be intentional. However, in
rare cases courts have permitted recovery when the defendant was merely negligent.

Defense   Most jurisdictions recognize a privilege
to act for one's own financial gain. In some jurisdictions, the plaintiff has the burden of showing that the
defendant acted from a motive other than his or her
own financial gain, such as revenge. In others, the defendant has the burden of proving that he or she acted
only for financial gain. Any purpose sufficient to create
a privilege to disturb existing contractual relations will
also justify interference with prospective business
advantage.

As in defamation and interference with contractual
relations, truth is a defense. Some jurisdictions have applied the First Amendment defenses available in defamation cases.

Interference with prospective business advantage is
usually done by a competitor, or at least by one who
stands to benefit from the interference. However, it is
not a tort to compete fairly. For the purposes of competition, a defendant may attempt to increase its business
by cutting prices, allowing rebates, refusing to deal with
the plaintiff, secretly negotiating with the defendant's
customers, or refusing to deal with third parties unless
they agree not to deal with the plaintiff.

ETHICAL CONSIDERATION

Is it ethical to refuse to deal with the plaintiff, to secretly
negotiate with the plaintiff's customers, or to refuse to
deal with third parties unless they agree to refuse to
deal with the plaintiff?

 ## Elements of Negligence

An essential element of every intentional tort is the mental element of intent. Negligence does not include a mental element. Rather, the focus is on the conduct of the
defendant. The law of negligence requires that all people
must act as reasonable persons, taking appropriate care in
any given situation. It does not require that the defendant
intended, or even knew, that his or her actions would
harm the plaintiff. In fact, even if the defendant was full
of concern for the safety of the plaintiff, the defendant's
conduct may still be negligent. It is enough that the defendant acted carelessly or, in other words, that his or her
conduct created an unreasonable risk of harm.

Negligence is defined as conduct that involves an unreasonably great risk of causing injury to another person
or damage to property. In order to establish liability under a negligence theory, the plaintiff must show that (1)
the defendant owed a duty to the plaintiff to act in conformity with a certain standard of conduct, that is, to act
reasonably under the circumstances; (2) the defendant
breached that duty by failing to conform to the standard; (3) a reasonably close causal connection exists between the plaintiff's injury and the defendant's breach;
and (4) the plaintiff suffered an actual loss or injury.

Duty

A person with a *legal duty* to another is required to act
reasonably under the circumstances to avoid harming
the other person. The required standard of care is what
a reasonable person of ordinary prudence would do in
the circumstances. It is not graduated to include the
reasonably slow person, the reasonably forgetful person,
or the reasonable person of low intelligence.

**Duty of Accountants and Other Professionals to
Third Parties**   The issue of duty takes on special significance when the plaintiff asserts a claim of professional negligence, or malpractice, against a lawyer, an
architect, or an accountant. Although a professional
clearly owes a duty to his or her client, a professional
may not have a duty to a third party, with whom he or
she does not have a contractual relationship.

The following case outlines the three different approaches courts have taken to the question of professionals' duty to third parties.

| A CASE IN POINT | IN THE LANGUAGE OF THE COURT |

**CASE 9.3
ML-LEE ACQUISITION
FUND, L.P. v.
DELOITTE & TOUCHE**
Court of Appeals
of South Carolina
463 S.E.2d 618
(S.C. Ct. App. 1995).

FACTS   Big Six accounting firm Deloitte & Touche was retained by Emb-Tex (a textiles company) to audit its financial statements from 1982 to 1988. ML-Lee was a partnership formed in 1987 that invested in high-risk securities.

At the time that the reports for 1982 through 1986 were prepared, Deloitte & Touche was not aware of ML-Lee or of any intention by Emb-Tex to deal with ML-Lee. By early 1988, Emb-Tex and ML-Lee had begun to negotiate a deal that would result in ML-Lee investing $16 million in Emb-Tex. Deloitte & Touche was aware of these negotiations as it prepared Emb-Tex's 1987 financial statements, and the 1987 reports were included in an offering memorandum Emb-Tex issued to ML-Lee.

ML-Lee's investment went sour. It retained another auditor to review the financial statements Deloitte & Touche had prepared and found that the reports were based on several questionable assumptions and accounting practices. ML-Lee then sued Deloitte & Touche for negligent misrepresentation.

The trial court granted summary judgment to Deloitte & Touche, concluding as a matter of law that Deloitte & Touche did not owe a duty to ML-Lee. ML-Lee appealed.

ISSUE PRESENTED   Under what circumstances can an accountant be liable to third parties for negligent misrepresentation in the preparation of an audit report?

OPINION   HOWELL, C.J., writing for the South Carolina Court of Appeals:

III. Negligent Misrepresentation

To state a claim for negligent misrepresentation, the plaintiff must allege that . . . the defendant made a false representation to the plaintiff [and that] . . . the defendant owed a duty of care to see that he communicated truthful information to the plaintiff. . . .

The scope of a public accountant's duty to third persons who use and rely on their reports is an issue of first impression in South Carolina. However, in the states considering the issue, three main approaches have developed. The most restrictive approach, requiring strict contractual privity before liability could be imposed, was first enunciated by Chief Judge Cardozo of the New York Court of Appeals in *Ultramares Corp. v. Touche, Niven & Co.*[10] The Ultramares strict privity standard was relaxed somewhat by the court in *Credit Alliance Corp. v. Arthur Andersen & Co.*[11] to extend recovery to third parties enjoying a relationship to the accountant that "sufficiently approaches privity." Thus, under New York's "near privity" approach, accountants may be liable to third parties only if (1) the accountants actually know their reports will be used for a particular purpose; (2) the accountants know that a nonclient is expected to rely on the reports in furtherance of a particular purpose; and (3) there has been some conduct on the part of the accountants linking them to

Case 9.3 continues

---

10. 174 N.E. 441 (N.Y. 1931).
11. 483 N.E.2d 110 (N.Y. 1985).

Case 9.3 continued

that party or parties, which evinces the accountant's understanding of that party's or parties' reliance. Several states follow New York's "near privity" approach. . . .

The second approach, which ML-Lee wishes this Court to adopt, is the foreseeability approach, which extends an accountant's liability to all persons who the accountant should reasonably foresee might obtain and rely on the accountant's work. This approach, which subjects accountants to liability on the same basis as other tortfeasors, has been adopted in few jurisdictions.

The majority view, adopted recently in Georgia and North Carolina, is set forth in the Restatement (Second) of Torts § 552 (1977). . . .

[U]nder the Restatement, an accountant's duty is limited to the client and third parties whom the accountant or client intends the information to benefit. The Restatement approach recognizes that an accountant's duty should extend beyond those in privity or near-privity with the accountant, but is not so expansive as to impose liability where the accountant knows only of the possibility of distribution to anyone, and their subsequent reliance.

Determining the scope of a public accountant's duty to third parties requires a consideration and balancing of competing public policy concerns. A primary function of public accountants is to perform audits for their clients. When performing an audit, the accountant reviews the client-prepared statements and issues an opinion regarding whether the statements fairly represent the financial condition of the client company. For practical reasons, an audit rarely examines every transaction of a business. Instead, the accountant evaluates the internal controls of a business, and tests their efficacy with sample transactions. The end product of an audit is an audit report generally written to the client. The audit report may be used by the company to satisfy federal securities requirements (if the company's stock is publicly traded), or to satisfy the requirements of potential lenders. An audit, therefore, may be relied upon by the company, commercial lenders, and members of the investing public. Thus, accountants to some extent perform a public watchdog function, and therefore should provide the public with accurate information. An expansive view of the scope of an accountant's duty is consistent with the expansive uses to which the accountant's work product is put, and would encourage accountants to take extreme care before issuing an audit. In fact, some states adopting the foreseeability approach compare defective audits with defective products, refusing to insulate accountants with a privity requirement when no such requirement is imposed on manufacturers of defective products. . . . However, accountants typically have little control over the ultimate dissemination of their work. To hold them liable to any person who eventually relies on their work could "expose accountants to a liability in an indeterminate amount for an indeterminate time to an indeterminate class. . . ."

In explicitly rejecting the foreseeability approach, the North Carolina Supreme Court recognized the competing public policy concerns, but concluded that the foreseeability approach would result in liability more expansive than an accountant should be required to bear.

A more fundamental difference between product designers and manufacturers and accountants lies in their differing expectations concerning their work product.

Case 9.3 continues

Case 9.3 continued

Manufacturers and designers fully expect that their products will be used by a wide variety of unknown members of the public. Indeed, this is their hope. . . . This is not the case when an accountant prepares an audit. An accountant performs an audit pursuant to a contract with an individual client. The client may or may not intend to use the report for other than internal purposes. It does not benefit the accountant if his client distributes the audit opinion to others. Instead, it merely exposes his work to many whom he may have had no idea would scrutinize his efforts. We believe that in fairness accountants should not be liable in circumstances where they are unaware of the use to which their opinions will be put. Instead, their liability should be commensurate with those persons or classes of persons whom they know will rely on their work. With such knowledge the auditor can, through purchase of liability insurance, setting fees, and adopting other protective measures appropriate to the risk, prepare accordingly. . . .

   . . . As did the North Carolina Supreme Court, we conclude that the Restatement approach balances "the need to hold accountants to a standard that accounts for their contemporary role in the financial world with the need to protect them from liability that unreasonably exceeds the bounds of their real undertaking."

RESULT   The Court of Appeals affirmed the decision of the trial court in part, and reversed in part. Deloitte & Touche owed a duty to ML-Lee with respect to its 1987 audit report and thus could be liable for negligent misrepresentation. Because, at the time it prepared the reports, Deloitte & Touche could not have intended that ML-Lee would rely on its 1985 and 1986 reports, no such duty existed with respect to those reports.
   The South Carolina Supreme Court subsequently affirmed these rulings.

COMMENTS   The California Supreme Court adopted the Restatement's "intended beneficiary" rule in *Bily v. Arthur Young & Co.*[12] and suggested the following jury instruction on negligent misrepresentation in auditor liability cases:

> The representation must have been made with the intent to induce plaintiff, or a particular class of persons to which plaintiff belongs, to act in reliance upon the representation in a specific transaction, or a specific type of transaction, that defendant intended to influence. Defendant is deemed to have intended to influence [its client's] transaction with plaintiff whenever defendant knows with substantial certainty that plaintiff, or the particular class of person to which plaintiff belongs, will rely on the representation in the course of the transaction. If others become aware of the representation and act upon it, there is no liability even though defendant should reasonably have foreseen such a possibility.

Questions

1. Why should accountants be held to a lesser standard of liability than manufacturers?
2. Would Deloitte & Touche have been liable for negligent misrepresentation if it was not aware of the negotiations with ML-Lee but knew that Emb-Tex would be doing a securities offering in the near future?

---

12. 834 P.2d 745 (Cal. 1992).

In a case of intentional misrepresentation or fraud, if an accountant intends that a person or class of persons will rely on his or her opinion, then the accountant is liable to any such person. Suit can also be brought by any person whom the accountant reasonably should have foreseen would rely upon the intentional misrepresentation. Thus, the greater the defendant's degree of fault, the wider the scope of potential plaintiffs.

The issues surrounding auditor liability to third parties closely parallel those surrounding the liability of investment bankers who issue fairness opinions in leveraged buyouts. Should shareholders be able to sue the investment bankers directly for negligent misrepresentation? Do investment bankers owe shareholders a duty? The actual client of the investment banker is the board of directors of the target company. However, some courts have upheld negligent misrepresentation actions by shareholders against investment bankers on either a foreseeability basis or using a Restatement Section 552 analysis similar to the one adopted by the *ML-Lee* court.[13]

Attorneys may also be liable to third parties for their negligence. In 1995, the New Jersey Supreme Court held a property seller's attorney liable for providing incomplete inspection reports in the course of a sale of land.[14] When the complete—and unfavorable—information was later discovered by the purchaser, he sued the seller and the seller's attorney. Although the attorney claimed he had no duty to the purchaser and therefore could not be liable, the court disagreed.

To the contrary, the court held, when an attorney knows or should know that a nonclient buyer will rely on his or her professional capacity, the attorney owes a duty to the third party and may be liable for breaching that duty.

Duty of Employers to Third Parties Based on Letters of Recommendation   In recent years, employers have backed away from providing letters of recommendation, primarily because of the fear of lawsuits. A 1996 survey by the Society for Human Resource Management found that 63% of personnel managers refused to provide reference information about former employees to prospective employers.[15]

Employers have chosen this route—to issue "no comment" or "name, rank and serial number" reference letters—largely because writing a substantive reference puts in them in a "damned if you do, damned if you don't" legal conundrum. On the one hand, employers who disclose "too much" information that might be deemed negative may be subject to a defamation suit by the former employee. On the other hand, employers who disclose "too little" negative information may be held liable to injured third parties for negligent misrepresentation.

The following negligent misrepresentation case was widely publicized among human resources professionals and gave further resolve to their "no comment" approach.

---

13. For an excellent discussion of the potential liability of investment bankers to shareholders, *see* Bill Shaw & Edward J. Gac, *Fairness Opinions in Leveraged Buy Outs: Should Investment Bankers Be Directly Liable to Shareholders?*, 23 Sec. Reg. L.J. 293 (1995).

14. Petrillo v. Bachenberg, 139 N.J. 472 (1995).

---

15. *Note: Addressing the Cloud over Employee References: A Survey of Recently Enacted State Legislation*, 39 Wm. & Mary L. Rev. 177 (1997).

A CASE IN POINT	SUMMARY

CASE 9.4
RANDI W. v. MUROC
JOINT UNIFIED
SCHOOL DISTRICT
Supreme Court of California
929 P.2d 582 (Cal. 1997).

FACTS   Robert Gadams was a school administrator at Livingston Middle School. Randi W. was a 13-year-old student at Livingston. On February 1, 1992, Gadams allegedly molested and "engaged in sexual touching of" Randi.

The administrators at Livingston based their decision to hire Gadams in part on recommendation letters written by officials from three other school districts that had employed Gadams between 1985 and 1991. Gadams had been accused of sexual misconduct with female students at each of these districts and at two of them was

Case 9.4 continues

Case 9.4 continued

forced to resign on account of such accusations. The officials who wrote Gadams's recommendation letters were aware of these incidents. Nevertheless, each district provided a "detailed recommendation" that glowingly reviewed Gadams's work. One letter writer concluded: "I wouldn't hesitate to recommend Mr. Gadams for any position!" Another stated he "would recommend [Gadams] for almost any administrative position." A third recommended Gadams "for an assistant principalship or equivalent position without reservation." None of the letters made any reference to the allegations of Gadams's sexual misconduct.

Randi alleged that the letters constituted negligent misrepresentations and that the letter writers should have foreseen that these misrepresentations would cause injury to children at public schools. As a result, Randi argued that the letter writers owed a duty not only to the recipients of their letters but also to the children at public schools who were injured as a result of the misrepresentations.

The trial court dismissed Randi's claim on the basis that the defendants owed no duty to Randi. The court of appeal reversed. It relied on Sections 310 and 311 of the Restatement (Second) of Torts in imposing liability on one who intentionally or negligently gives false information to another person that results in physical injury to the recipient or another person. The school district appealed.

ISSUE PRESENTED   Can an employer who writes a favorable recommendation letter that omits known, material negative information be held liable to a third party who suffered physical injury as a result of the employer's omission?

SUMMARY OF OPINION   The California Supreme Court first addressed the question of whether the defendants owed Randi a duty, which hinged on the foreseeability of the actual harm. The court found that while "the chain of causation leading from defendants' statements and omissions to Gadams's alleged assault on [Randi] is somewhat attenuated," the assault was reasonably foreseeable. Specifically, the defendants could foresee that (1) Livingston's officers would read and rely on the defendants' letters in hiring Gadams; (2) had they not unqualifiedly recommended Gadams, Livingston would not have hired him; and (3) Gadams, after being hired by Livingston, might molest or injure a Livingston student such as Randi.

Two other important factors in the court's holding that the defendants owed Randi a duty were the availability of an alternative course of action and the balance of public policies. The defendants could just have easily written "full disclosure" letters that revealed all relevant facts about Gadams's background or "no comment" letters that offered no affirmative representations about his background but simply verified basic employment dates and details. In addition, the court recognized that its ruling might discourage employers from writing full recommendation letters for fear of tort liability but felt that this effect was outweighed by the high priority society placed on protecting children from physical and sexual abuse.

Having established the existence of a duty, the court went on to reject the defendants' alternative argument that their letters represented "mere nondisclosure," not "misleading misrepresentation." The court ruled that the defendants, having undertaken to provide some information about Gadams's ability and character, were obliged to

Case 9.4 continues

Case 9.4 continued

disclose all other facts that would "materially qualify" the limited facts disclosed. Instead, the defendants completely omitted the materially qualifying facts surrounding Gadams's alleged sexual misconduct. Thus, their letters were "misleading half-truths," upon which liability for negligent misrepresentation could be founded.

RESULT   The California Supreme Court affirmed the court of appeal's decision. The defendants were liable to Randi for negligent misrepresentation.

COMMENTS   State legislatures recognized that the beneficial free exchange of employment references is significantly stifled by the "damned if you do, damned if you don't" conundrum. In an effort to respond to this problem, at least 26 states had by 1997 enacted some type of statutory immunity for employers when they provide a reference.[16]

---

16. *Id.*

Duty in Other Contexts

Duty of Landowner or Tenant   A possessor of land (such as a tenant) or its owner has a legal duty to keep the property reasonably safe. Such a person can be liable for injury that occurs outside, as well as on, the premises. For example, a landowner may be liable for harm caused when water from a cooling tower covers the highway; or when sparks from a railroad engine, which is not properly maintained, start a fire on adjacent property; or when a roof sheds snow onto the highway.

A landowner must exercise care in the demolition or construction of buildings on his or her property and in the excavation of his or her land. Landowners have been held liable when a pole on a landowner's property collapsed after it was hit by a car and injured a pedestrian and when a landowner erected a sign that obstructed the view and caused an accident.

Generally, landowners are not liable for harm caused by natural conditions on their property, such as uncut weeds that obstruct a driver's view, the natural flow of surface water, or falling rocks. However, the landowner may be liable if he or she has altered the natural state of the land, for example, by erecting a dam that flooded a highway, by erecting a canopy so that water dripped from it to freeze on the sidewalk, or by planting a row of trees that obstructed the view of motorists.

In a few jurisdictions, landowners have a duty to maintain sidewalks that abut, that is, are right next to, their property. In all jurisdictions, a landowner has a general duty to inspect his or her land and keep it in repair, and he or she may be liable if a showroom window, a downspout, a screen, or a loose sign falls and injures someone.

Duty to Trespassers   In general, a landowner owes no duty to an undiscovered trespasser. Occasionally, a landowner may be liable even to a trespasser who is on his or her property without permission. One such case was brought by a burglar who was hurt when he fell through a skylight while trying to break into a house.

If a substantial number of trespassers are in the habit of entering at a particular place, the possessor has a duty to take reasonable care to discover and to protect the trespassers from activities he or she carries on. Some courts have also established a duty to protect such trespassers from dangerous conditions, such as concealed high-tension wires, that do not result from the possessor's activities. Some jurisdictions require the possessor to exercise reasonable care once he or she knows of the trespasser's presence.

Trespassing children are owed a higher level of duty. The *attractive nuisance* doctrine imposes liability for physical injury to child trespassers caused by artificial conditions on the land if (1) the landowner knew or

"To answer your question. Yes, if you shoot an arrow into the air and it falls to earth you know not where, you could be liable for any damage it may cause."

should have known that children were likely to trespass; (2) the condition is one the landowner would reasonably know involved an unreasonable risk of injury to such children; (3) the children because of their youth did not discover the condition or realize the risk involved; (4) the utility to the possessor of maintaining the condition is not great; (5) the burden of eliminating the risk is slight compared with the magnitude of the risk to the children; and (6) the possessor fails to exercise reasonable care to protect the children.

Duty to Licensees   A *licensee* is anyone who is on the land of another person with the possessor's express or implied consent. The licensee enters for his or her own purposes, not for those of the possessor. Social guests and uninvited sales representatives are licensees.

The possessor must exercise reasonable care for the protection of the licensee. This duty differs from that to a trespasser because the possessor is required to look out for licensees before they enter the land. However, he or she is not required to inspect for unknown dangers. The duty arises only when the possessor has actual knowledge of a risk.

Duty to Invitees   An *invitee*, or business visitor, is someone who enters the premises for the purposes of the possessor's business. The possessor owes a higher duty to an invitee than to a licensee. The possessor must protect invitees against known dangers and also against those dangers that he or she might discover with reasonable care.

The invitee is of particular importance to a manager. There are thousands of "slip and fall" cases each year due to wet floors, icy sidewalks, or broken steps. A customer is clearly an invitee and is accordingly owed a higher duty of care than a licensee such as a social guest.

A business's duty to invitees may even include an obligation to protect invitees from criminal conduct by third parties. States have been mixed in their application of this standard. The New Jersey Supreme Court recently held a supermarket liable when a 79-year-old woman was abducted from its parking lot and later killed.[17] Despite the fact that there had never been an abduction or similar incident on its property, the court ruled that Food Circus was negligent in failing to provide any security or warning signs in its parking lot. Employing an analysis that considered the "totality of the circumstances," the court concluded that it was foreseeable that over the course of time an individual would enter the supermarket's parking lot and assault a customer.

The Washington Supreme Court has also held that businesses have a duty to take reasonable steps to protect invitees from criminal conduct by third parties. However, in Washington this general duty does not necessarily include a duty to provide security personnel. In *Nivens v. 7-11 Hoagy's Corner*,[18] the court denied a claim by an assaulted convenience store patron. Its rationale was that imposing a requirement that businesses provide guards in all cases would unfairly shift responsibility for policing from the government to the private sector. In *dicta*, the court said that a duty to provide security guards may arise if "the construction or maintenance of the premises brings about a . . . peculiar temptation . . . for criminal misconduct" by third parties, but such facts were not present in *Nivens*.

Emergencies   In determining duty, the law allows reasonable mistakes of judgment in some circumstances. In emergency situations, the duty is to act as a reasonable person would act in the circumstances.

---

17. Clohesy v. Food Circus Supermarkets, Inc., 694 A.2d 1017 (N.J. 1997).
18. 943 P.2d 286 (Wash. 1997).

The defendant is expected to anticipate emergencies. Drivers must drive defensively. Innkeepers must anticipate fires and install smoke alarms and, in some cases, sprinkler systems and must provide fire escapes and other fire-safety features. Owners of swimming pools in subdivisions with children must fence their property.

Duty to Rescue   The law does not impose a general duty to rescue. However, once one undertakes a rescue, the law imposes a duty to act as a reasonable person and not to abandon the rescue effort unreasonably. Thus, if Ciril Wyatt sat on a river shore and watched Edward Donnelly drown, she would not be liable in negligence for Donnelly's death. However, if Wyatt saw Donnelly drowning, jumped in her boat, sped to him, tried to pull him into the boat and then changed her mind and let him drown, she would be liable.

A special relationship between two people may create a duty to rescue. If Donnelly were Wyatt's husband or child or parent, Wyatt would have a duty to rescue him. Other relationships that create a duty to rescue are employer and employee; innkeeper and guest; teacher and student; employee of bus, train, or other common carrier and passenger; and possibly team members, hunting partners, or hiking partners.

There is a duty to rescue those whom one has placed in peril. For example, if Wyatt had been driving her boat in a negligent manner, thereby causing Donnelly to fall overboard, she would have a duty to rescue him.

Breach of Duty

Once it is determined that the defendant owed the plaintiff a duty, the next issue is whether the defendant breached the duty.

Standard of Conduct   In many cases, the required standard of conduct will be that of the reasonable person. However, a person who is specially trained to participate in a profession or trade will be held to the higher standard of care of a reasonably skilled member of that profession or trade. For example, the professional conduct of a doctor, architect, pilot, attorney, or accountant will be measured against the standard of the profession. A specialist within a profession will be held to the standard of specialists.

The court will also look to statutes and regulations to determine whether the defendant's conduct amounted to a breach of duty. Some jurisdictions merely allow the statute to be introduced into evidence

INTERNATIONAL CONSIDERATION

Some jurisdictions do impose a general duty to rescue. France, for example, requires that bystanders try to help those in danger if the bystanders' effort will not put them at risk. This "good Samaritan" law grabbed the spotlight when Diana, Princess of Wales, her companion Emad Mohamed (Dodi) al-Fayed, and their French driver were killed in a 1997 automobile accident.[a] At the time of the crash, Princess Diana's car was being pursued by the paparazzi—a band of professional celebrity photographers. French authorities detained seven of these photographers, who faced possible charges under the good Samaritan law (as well as other possible charges). Initial eyewitness reports alleged not only that the paparazzi failed to assist the injured passengers of Princess Diana's car but also that they took rolls of photos of the accident scene and even may have told rescuers to get out of their field of vision.

a. *How Would Paparazzi Who Stalked Diana Fare in French Court?* WALL ST. J., Sept. 2, 1997, at A1.

to establish the standard of care. Others shift the burden to the defendant to prove he or she was not negligent once the plaintiff shows the defendant violated a statute and the violation caused the injury. This is often an impossible burden to satisfy. This rule, sometimes referred to as *negligence per se*, applies only if the statute or regulation was designed to protect a class of persons from the type of harm suffered by the plaintiff and if the plaintiff is a member of the class to be protected.

Courts will also look to the custom or the practice of others under similar circumstances to determine the standard of care. Although the custom in the industry may be given great weight, it is not ordinarily dispositive or conclusive.

Res Ipsa Loquitur   The doctrine of *res ipsa loquitur* ("the thing speaks for itself") allows the plaintiff to prove breach of duty and causation (discussed below) indirectly. *Res ipsa loquitur* applies when an accident has occurred, and it is obvious, although there is no direct proof, that the accident would not have happened absent someone's negligence. For example, if a postoperative X-ray showed a surgical clamp in the plaintiff's abdomen, even if no one testifies as to how the clamp got there, it can reasonably be inferred that the surgeon negligently left it there.

Res ipsa loquitur has three requirements. First, the plaintiff's injury must have been caused by a condition or instrumentality that was within the exclusive control of the defendant. This requirement eliminates the possibility that other persons, not named as defendants, were responsible for the condition that gave rise to the injury. Second, the accident must be of such a nature that it ordinarily would not occur in the absence of negligence by the defendant. Third, the accident must not be due to the plaintiff's own negligence.

Once *res ipsa loquitur* is established, jurisdictions vary as to its effect. In some jurisdictions, it creates a presumption of negligence and the plaintiff is entitled to a directed verdict (whereby the judge directs the jury to find in favor of the plaintiff), unless the defendant can prove he or she was not responsible. This rule has the effect of shifting the burden of proof, normally with the plaintiff, to the defendant. Other jurisdictions leave the burden of proof with the plaintiff, requiring the jury to weigh the inference of negligence and to find the defendant negligent only if the preponderance of the evidence (including the *res ipsa* inference) favors such a finding.

Causal Connection

In addition to establishing duty and breach, the plaintiff must prove that the defendant's breach of duty caused the injury. The causation requirement has two parts: actual cause and proximate (or legal) cause.

Actual Cause   The plaintiff establishes *actual cause* if he or she proves that but for the defendant's negligent conduct, the plaintiff would not have been harmed. The defendant is not liable if the plaintiff's injury would have occurred in the absence of the defendant's conduct. For example, if George Broussard put a garbage can out on the sidewalk for morning pickup and Anna Chang came along and broke her ankle, Broussard's conduct would not be the actual cause of Chang's injury if it were established that Chang had caught her heel in the sidewalk, turned her ankle, and then bumped into Broussard's garbage can.

When the plaintiff names more than one defendant, the actual-cause test may become a substantial-factor test: Was the defendant's conduct a substantial factor in bringing about the plaintiff's injury?

A further problem may arise if more than one individual could possibly have been the negligent party. A classic case involved two hunters shooting quail on an open range.[19] Both shot at exactly the same time, using identical shotguns. A shot from one of the guns accidentally hit another hunter. Clearly only one of the two defendants caused the injury, but there was no way to determine which one it was. The court imposed the burden on each defendant to prove that he had not caused the injury. Because neither could do so, both were held liable for the whole injury.

Proximate Cause   Once the plaintiff has proved that the defendant's conduct is an actual cause of the plaintiff's injury, he or she must also prove that it is the *proximate cause*, that is, that the defendant had a duty to protect the particular plaintiff against the particular conduct that injured him or her. Through the requirement of proximate cause, the law places limits on the defendant's liability. A defendant may not be liable for all of the injuries for which actual cause is established, as is demonstrated in the following leading case.

---

19. Summers v. Tice, 199 P.2d 1 (Cal. 1948).

A CASE IN POINT	SUMMARY

CASE 9.5
PALSGRAF v. LONG ISLAND RAILROAD CO.
Court of Appeals of New York
162 N.E. 99 (N.Y. 1928).

FACTS   Mrs. Palsgraf, the plaintiff, was standing on a platform of the defendant's railroad. A train stopped at the station. Two men ran forward to catch it. The train began moving. Although it was moving, one of the men was able to reach the train without a problem. The other man, who was carrying a package, jumped aboard the train

Case 9.5 continues

Case 9.5 continued

but seemed unsteady and about to fall. A guard on the train, who had held the door open, reached forward to help him in. Another guard who was on the platform pushed the man from behind. Because of the guard's pushing, the package that the man was carrying was dislodged and fell on the railroad tracks.

The package was small and covered by a newspaper. It contained fireworks, but there was no way to tell what the contents were just from observing the outside of the package. The fireworks exploded when they fell. The shock of the explosion made some scales many feet away at the end of the platform fall. The scales struck Mrs. Palsgraf, causing her injury.

Mrs. Palsgraf sued the railroad. The trial court jury entered a verdict in favor of Mrs. Palsgraf. This judgment was affirmed by the appellate court. The railroad appealed again.

ISSUE PRESENTED   Can the act of one person that results in harm to another person be considered negligence even though the harm was unintentional and unforeseeable to the person acting?

SUMMARY OF OPINION   The New York Court of Appeals reversed the trial and appellate courts' decisions and dismissed Mrs. Palsgraf's complaint. The court based its decision on its finding that the railroad's guard had not acted negligently in relation to Mrs. Palsgraf. The court explained that negligence must be considered in relation to the surrounding circumstances and factors of a given situation. In this case, the railroad guard could not have possibly known that the falling package would pose a danger to persons standing far away from it.

In order to sustain a claim of negligence, Mrs. Palsgraf needed to show that the defendant's guard had acted negligently and had exposed her to an unreasonable hazard. This claim could be sustained even if it were shown that he had done so unintentionally. However, Mrs. Palsgraf would need to show that the hazard would have been apparent to the reasonable person. Thus, she would have to argue that the guard had acted unreasonably, without the level of care that the typical reasonable person would have used in a similar situation.

Because the hazard of the exploding package was impossible for anyone, even the most reasonable and careful person, to detect, the court held that the defendant could not be held liable. Even if the defendant's guard had deliberately thrown the package down to the ground, the defendant would not have been held liable because there was nothing to indicate that this activity could pose a danger to anyone, especially someone standing as far away as Mrs. Palsgraf.

RESULT   The decisions of the trial and appellate courts were reversed. Mrs. Palsgraf's complaint was dismissed.

COMMENTS   Note that if the railroad guard had, for instance, stumbled over a package that appeared to be a bundle of newspapers on the platform, when the package was actually a bundle of dynamite, the railroad still would not be liable for

Case 9.5 continues

Case 9.5 continued

negligence to a person standing at the other end of the platform because the harm would have been similarly unforeseeable as in the above case. However, a person who was, for example, driving at a reckless speed through a crowded street would be liable for negligence regardless of the consequences because the act involves a foreseeable risk of harm to others.

The defendant is not required to compensate the plaintiff for injuries that were unforeseeable, even if the defendant's conduct was careless. Courts apply the foreseeability requirement in two different ways. Some courts limit the defendant's liability to those consequences that were foreseeable. Others look to whether the plaintiff was a foreseeable plaintiff, that is, whether the plaintiff was within the *zone of danger* caused by the defendant's careless conduct.

Injury

Finally, the plaintiff must prove injury to the plaintiff or the plaintiff's property. Even if a defendant is negligent, the plaintiff cannot recover if he or she can show no harm suffered as a result of the defendant's conduct.

This requirement is often the controlling factor in actions for *negligent infliction of emotional distress.* The traditional rule is that a plaintiff cannot recover for negligent infliction of emotional distress unless he or she can show some form of physical injury. However, recent cases involving exposure to HIV have prompted a reexamination of this "physical manifestation" requirement. In other words, courts have permitted plaintiffs to recover for emotional distress (over the fear of contracting HIV) without imposing a requirement that they actually contracted the virus.

Nevertheless, in dealing with this issue, courts have been careful to recognize a public policy interest in not fostering hysteria about the virus. Thus, they have set forth objective standards that prevent someone basing an action on an irrational fear that he or she contracted HIV. Tennessee's standards are among the most stringent. In *Bain v. Wells,* the Tennessee Supreme Court ruled that a plaintiff must have been actually exposed to HIV in order to recover for emotional distress.[20] Presumably, this means the plaintiff must demonstrate some medically sound channel of transmission. The plaintiff in *Bain* was paired with an HIV-positive roommate in a drug rehabilitation center. He had an open cut on his buttocks and shared a toilet with the roommate for eight days. The plaintiff's roommate also inadvertently used his disposable razor. The court denied the plaintiff's claim because medical evidence unequivocally states that HIV can only be transmitted through fluid-to-fluid contact.

The standards set forth by the New Jersey Supreme Court are more relaxed. In *Williamson v. Waldman,*[21] the court said that a plaintiff can recover if a reasonable person would have experienced emotional distress over the prospect of contracting HIV under the circumstances. However, this hypothetical reasonable person would be presumed to have "then-current, accurate, and generally available" knowledge concerning the transmission of HIV. Again, an irrational fear of catching the virus would not be a valid basis for an emotional distress suit.

 ## Defenses to Negligence

In some jurisdictions, the defendant may absolve itself of part or all of the liability for negligence by proving that the plaintiff was also negligent.

Contributory Negligence

Under the doctrine of *contributory negligence,* if the plaintiff was also negligent in any manner, he or she cannot recover any damages from the defendant. Thus,

---

20. 936 S.W.2d 618 (Tenn. 1997).
21. 696 A.2d 14 (N.J. 1997).

if a plaintiff was 5% negligent and the defendant was 95% negligent, the plaintiff's injury would go unredressed. To address this inequity, most courts have replaced the doctrine of contributory negligence with that of comparative negligence.

Comparative Negligence

Under the doctrine of *comparative negligence*, the plaintiff may recover the proportion of his or her loss attributable to the defendant's negligence. For example, if the plaintiff was 5% negligent and the defendant 95%, the plaintiff can recover 95% of the loss. Comparative negligence may take two forms: ordinary and pure. In an *ordinary comparative negligence* jurisdiction, the plaintiff may recover only if he or she is less culpable than the defendant. Thus, if the plaintiff is found 51% negligent and the defendant 49% negligent, the plaintiff cannot recover. In a *pure comparative negligence* state, the plaintiff may recover for any amount of the defendant's negligence, even if the plaintiff was the more negligent party. For example, if the plaintiff was 80% negligent and the defendant was 20% negligent, the plaintiff may recover 20% of his or her loss.

Assumption of Risk

The *assumption of risk* defense requires that the plaintiff (1) knew the risk was present and understood its nature and (2) voluntarily chose to incur the risk. It applies when the plaintiff, in advance of the defendant's wrongdoing, expressly or impliedly consented to take his or her chances of injury from the defendant's actions. Such consent, like consent to an intentional tort, relieves the defendant of any liability. For example, the plaintiff assumes the risk if he consents to take the chance of injury by riding in a car he knows had faulty brakes, or if he voluntarily chooses to walk where the defendant has negligently scattered broken glass.

In those jurisdictions that have adopted the comparative negligence doctrine, there is a strong trend to abolish assumption of risk as a defense. Sometimes courts use duty to determine the viability of the defense of assumption of risk, as in the following case.

| **A CASE IN POINT** | **SUMMARY** |

CASE 9.6
MOSCA v.
LICHTENWALTER
California Court of Appeal
68 Cal. Rptr. 2d 58
(Cal. Ct. App. 1997).

FACTS   Joseph Mosca and 23 others boarded a sportfishing boat for a day of ocean fishing off San Clemente Island. Another fisherman, David William Lichtenwalter, was fishing near Mosca off the stern. Lichtenwalter's line became entangled in kelp, and he tried to release it to no avail. A deckhand approached Lichtenwalter to assist in freeing his line. At about the time Lichtenwalter backed up and handed his pole to the deckhand, the line "sling-shotted" back over the rail towards Mosca, who was struck in the eye with the sinker, causing a partial vision loss.

Mosca sued Lichtenwalter for negligence. The trial court granted summary judgment in favor of Lichtenwalter. Mosca appealed.

ISSUE PRESENTED   Is getting hit in the eye by a sinker an inherent danger in sportfishing and one for which Mosca assumed the risk when he boarded the sportfishing boat?

SUMMARY OF OPINION   The California Court of Appeal first looked to "primary" assumption of risk, which is a policy-driven legal concept in which the courts declare there is no duty at all. Primary assumption of risk is often imposed when the parties are engaged in a sport. To decide whether to impose a duty, the courts must determine whether the injury arises from a risk inherent in the activity and whether

Case 9.6 continues

Case 9.6 continued

imposing a duty might chill participation in the activity and alter its fundamental nature. Determination of what constitutes an inherent risk is a legal question for the court.

The appellate court held that the trial court's determination that the danger of injury from a hook or sinker flying toward a participant is an inherent risk in sportfishing and that imposing the specter of liability regarding the danger would chill or alter the sport was reasonable.

RESULT   The appellate court affirmed the trial court's ruling of summary judgment in favor of the defendant Lichtenwalter.

COMMENTS   The fact that any safety precautions suggested by Mosca would, in the court's view, have fundamentally altered the nature of sportfishing seemed to weigh heavily in the court's decision.

The California Supreme Court extended the doctrine of assumption of risk to skiing in *Cheong v. Antablin* when it held that a fellow skier is not liable for injury to another skier unless the defendant intentionally caused the injury or engaged in conduct that was so reckless as to be totally outside the range of ordinary activity involved in the sport.[22]

◆ Vicarious Liability and Respondeat Superior

It is possible for one person to be held vicariously liable for the negligent, or in some cases the intentional, conduct of another.

Under the doctrine of *respondeat superior*—"let the master answer"—a "master" or employer is vicariously liable for the torts of the "servant" or employee if the employee was acting within the scope of his or her employment. The doctrine of *respondeat superior* may also apply when the person is not paid but acts on behalf of another person out of friendship or loyalty.

Underlying the doctrine of *respondeat superior* is the policy of allocating the risk of doing business to those who stand to profit from the undertaking. Because the employer benefits from the business, it is deemed more appropriate for the employer to bear the risk of loss than for the innocent customer. The employer is in a better position to absorb such losses or to shift them, through liability insurance or price increases, to customers and insurers and, thus, to the community in general.

An employer is liable for his or her own negligence in supervising or hiring an employee. The employer may also be vicariously liable for his or her employee's wrongful acts, even if the employer had no knowledge of them and in no way directed them, provided the acts were committed while the employee was acting within the scope of employment.

Activities within the scope of employment are activities closely connected to what the employee is employed to do or reasonably incidental to it. Courts will consider numerous factors in determining the scope of employment, such as the time, place, and manner of the act; the degree of deviation from normal methods of carrying out the employment; whether the act is generally done by such employees; and whether the employer could reasonably expect that the employee would do the act. Generally, an employee's conduct is considered within the scope of his or her employment if it (1) is of the nature that he or she was employed to perform; (2) is within the time and space limitations normally authorized by the employer; and (3) furthers, at least in part, the purpose of the employer.

In determining scope of employment, courts will consider evidence that the employer has forbidden the

---

22. 946 P.2d 817 (Cal. 1997).

act or forbidden doing it in a certain manner. However, giving such orders does not in itself absolve the employer; an employer cannot avoid vicarious liability simply by instructing the employee to act carefully.

If the wrongful act occurs while the employee has interrupted his or her employment to engage in an activity for the employee's own benefit, the employer is not vicariously liable. However, it is often unclear whether the employee's act was entirely outside the employer's purpose (called a *frolic*) or only a *detour*. Jurisdictions differ in their treatment of such cases.

Some courts look solely to the employee's purpose. So long as the employee is fulfilling his or her own objectives, the employee is outside the scope of employment. However, when any part of the employee's purpose is to accomplish the employer's objectives, then the employee is acting within the scope of employment.

The majority of jurisdictions focus on foreseeability. The employer is liable if the employee's deviation might reasonably be expected, even if the deviation was for the employee's own ends.

If intentional conduct caused the plaintiff's injury, courts will look to the nexus, or connection, between the conduct and the employment. They will first examine whether the employee was acting within the scope of employment. Usually, intentional torts exceed the scope of employment. For example, a security company was found not liable when one of its security guards raped a worker in a client's building, even though the guard used his position to create the circumstances for the rape.[23] Some courts may look beyond the scope of employment to determine whether the employee exercised authority conferred by his or her employer. Thus, one court held a county vicariously liable for battery, among other things, when one of its law enforcement officers stopped a woman, placed her in his patrol car, drove to an isolated place, and threatened to rape and murder her.[24]

In general, an employer is liable for his or her employee's intentional torts if the wrongful act in any way furthered the employer's purpose, however misguided the manner of furthering that purpose. Whether an act was in the scope of employment is an issue for the jury to decide.

Some courts, such as the Supreme Court of Texas in *Otis*,[25] have held that under certain circumstances employers have a legal duty to protect strangers from injuries caused by their off-duty employees. *Otis* concerned an automobile accident involving an intoxicated employee sent home by his employer. The Court of Appeals of Arizona declined to follow *Otis* in a case involving an employee with a history of drug abuse known to the employer.[26] She came to work high on cocaine and consumed additional cocaine while at work. Recognizing her intoxicated condition and severely impaired motor function, her supervisor ordered her to leave the premises before the end of her work shift. Shortly after leaving the premises, the employee drove her vehicle across the centerline, colliding head-on with the plaintiff's vehicle and seriously injuring him. The court dismissed the plaintiff's suit against the employer, holding that an employer's duty to exercise reasonable care to control its employee while he or she is acting outside the scope of employment is limited to torts committed by employees on the employer's premises or with the employer's personal property. Because the employer had no duty to use some care to avoid injury to the plaintiff, the defendant was not liable even though the defendant could foresee the risk that an impaired driver might cause an accident.

The employer may also be responsible for the safe passage home of an employee who was not intoxicated but was tired from working too many consecutive hours. In *Robertson v. LeMaster*,[27] LeMaster was an employee of the Norfolk and Western Railway Company. He was doing heavy manual labor, including lifting railroad ties and shoveling coal. After 13 hours at work he told his supervisor that he was tired and wanted to go home. The supervisor told him to continue working. This happened several times, until finally LeMaster said that he could no longer work because he was too tired. His supervisor told him that if he would not work, he should get his bucket and go home. He had been at work a total of 27 consecutive hours. On his way home, he fell asleep at the wheel and was involved in an accident, causing injuries to Robertson. Robertson sued the railroad.

23. Rabon v. Guardsmark, Inc., 571 F.2d 1277 (4th Cir. 1978), *cert. denied*, 439 U.S. 866 (1978).

24. White v. County of Orange, 212 Cal. Rptr. 493 (Cal. Ct. App. 1985).

25. Otis Engineering Corp. v. Clark, 668 S.W.2d 307 (Tex. 1983) (Case 1.2).

26. Riddle v. Arizona Oncology Services, Inc., 924 P.2d 468 (Ariz. Ct. App. 1996).

27. 301 S.E.2d 563 (W. Va. 1983).

The Supreme Court of Appeals of West Virginia concluded that requiring LeMaster to work such long hours and then setting him loose on the highway in an obviously exhausted condition was sufficient to sustain a claim against the railroad. The court regarded the issue in this case as not the railway's failure to control LeMaster while he was driving on the highway but rather whether the railroad's conduct prior to the accident created a foreseeable risk of harm. The court concluded that the railway's actions created such a foreseeable risk.

As in *Otis*, the accident occurred off-site and outside of regular working hours. But in this case, the accident was caused by fatigue and not intoxication. Because it was the employer's fault that LeMaster was so tired, this decision seems even more compelling than that in *Otis* from both an ethical and legal standpoint.

 ## Successor Liability

Under the doctrine of *successor liability*, individuals or entities who purchase a business or real property may be held liable for the tortious acts of the previous owner. For example, if a company buys the assets of a ladder manufacturer and continues in the same line of business, the acquiring company can be held liable for defective ladders manufactured and sold before the acquisition. Successor liability may also apply in the area of toxic torts, discussed later in this chapter.

 ## Liability of Multiple Defendants

The plaintiff may name numerous defendants. In some cases, the defendants may ask the court to join, or add, other defendants. As a result, when a court determines what liability exists, it must grapple with the problem of allocating the losses among multiple defendants.

Joint and Several Liability

Under the doctrine of *joint and several liability*, multiple defendants are jointly (that is, collectively) liable and also severally (that is, individually) liable. This means that once the court determines that multiple defendants are at fault, the plaintiff may collect the entire judgment from any one of them, regardless of the degree of that defendant's fault. Thus, it is possible that a defendant

who played a minor role in causing the plaintiff's injury must pay for all the damages. This is particularly likely when only one defendant is solvent, that is, when only one has money to pay the damages.

Thirty-four states have adopted statutes to limit the doctrine of joint and several liability for tort defendants. Most states that have abolished joint and several liability have moved to a "contributory" regime. Under a joint and several liability regime, a defendant can be liable for all of a plaintiff's damages, even if the defendant was only 1% responsible for causing the plaintiff's injuries. This would be the result if the other defendants (those 99% responsible for causing the injuries) lacked funds to pay the judgment. The same defendant under contributory rules would in no circumstance be liable for more than 1% of the total damage award.

Contribution and Indemnification

The doctrines of contribution and indemnification can mitigate the harsh effects of joint and several liability. *Contribution* distributes the loss among several defendants by requiring each to pay its proportionate share to one defendant, which discharges their joint liability. *Indemnification* allows a defendant to shift its individual loss to other defendants whose relative blame is greater. These other defendants can be ordered to reimburse the one that has discharged a joint liability.

However, the right to contribution and the right to indemnification are worthless to a defendant if all the other defendants are insolvent or lack sufficient assets to contribute their share.

 ## Strict Liability

Strict liability is liability without fault, that is, without either intent or negligence. Strict liability is imposed in two circumstances: (1) in product liability cases (the subject of Chapter 10), and (2) in cases revolving around abnormally dangerous activities.

Ultrahazardous Activities

If the defendant's activity is *ultrahazardous*, that is, so dangerous that no amount of care could protect others from the risk of harm, the defendant is strictly liable for any injuries that result from his or her act. An activity is

THE CHANGING TIDE OF TORT REFORM

The Traditional Arguments

For years, supporters and critics of the U.S. tort system have rehearsed largely unchanged arguments about the perceived need for tort reform. Critics claim that the present tort system—especially its product liability and medical malpractice suits—is unfairly expensive for defendants. Large and unpredictable jury awards have resulted in sharply higher liability insurance prices, which in turn (1) increase the cost of vital products and services; (2) stifle innovation in valuable but potentially dangerous products; and (3) render U.S. firms less equipped to compete with rivals abroad. Moreover, claim the critics, the tort system is inefficient: Attorney's fees and administrative costs are so extensive that less than half of the amount awarded by verdict or settlement is paid to injured plaintiffs.[a]

Supporters of the present tort system respond that it is the one place where the average citizen can battle the powerful on nearly equal terms. They claim that without the threat of lawsuits and their accompanying discovery process, large corporations would have every incentive to conceal harmful information about the effects of their products. Tort reform legislation would weight the system in favor of these deep-pocket defendants and insurance companies without giving them adequate incentive to reduce activities that cause injury. The supporters believe that if any reform of the system is necessary, judicial review and self-policing would be more effective tools than legislation at either the state or federal level.

Punitive Damages: Horror Stories and Calmer Studies

In recent years, the critics have asserted that the tort system has a random, Russian roulette flavor to it. To buttress this claim, they point to several recent cases in which juries have granted multimillion-dollar punitive damage awards to injured plaintiffs. These well-publicized horror stories include a $2.7 million award to a woman who spilled scalding-hot McDonald's coffee on her lap, a $4 million award against BMW for selling as new a car that had been damaged by acid rain and repainted,[b] and a $100 million award against General Mo-

tors in a case where the injured plaintiff was involved in a single-car accident, had admittedly consumed at least one beer, and was not wearing a seatbelt.

Separate studies, however, have found that punitive damage awards are both extremely rare and closely related to the size of compensatory damages. In a 1995 survey of the country's 75 most populous counties, the Department of Justice found that only 2% of the 762,000 cases disposed of—whether by settlement, trial, or other means—even reached a jury. Plaintiffs won just over half of those cases, received punitive damages in just 6% of the cases they won, and won more than $50,000 in only half of all punitive awards.[c]

A similar study of 45 populous counties, conducted by two Cornell University professors, found that punitive damages are not only less prevalent, but also less random than often alleged.[d] The study found that when compensatory damages were $10,000, punitives averaged $10,860; when compensatory damages were $100,000, punitives averaged $65,720; and when compensatory damages were $1 million, punitives averaged $397,810.

Those in favor of overhauling the present system say that these findings do not alleviate the concern that excessive punitive damages pose a threat to America's corporations. First, they note that these studies were conducted in highly populated counties, while many huge punitive damage awards have come from carefully selected rural counties. Moreover, while the actual number of punitive damage awards may be small, the recognized threat or potential for large awards has a ripple effect that distorts the entire system, especially settlement negotiations.

Congressional Proposals Stalled

The movement to reform the tort system from the federal level gained momentum when the Republicans won control of both houses of Congress in 1994. House Republicans listed tort reform as Tenet Nine in their Contract with America. They fulfilled their promise under the contract by introducing four bills designed to revamp the civil justice system in early 1995. These bills—collectively referred to as the "Common Sense" reform bills—called for a variety of tort reforms, including punitive damage caps and "loser pays" rules, which require the loser in a lawsuit to pay the attorney's fees of the winner.

A large number of the Common Sense reforms were quickly passed by the House in the form of H.R. 956. The Senate was far more deliberate, however, and was determined to pursue reform in a focused, rather than broad, sweeping manner. As a result, the Senate eventually passed H.R. 956, but not until early 1996 and not before the bill had been significantly watered down. As passed by the Senate, the Common Sense Product Liability Legal Reform Act of 1996 (as H.R. 956 came to be known) was narrowly targeted to reforming product liability law. Among the act's more prominent features were the prohibition of joint liability for noneconomic loss and a set of substantive restrictions on the availability of punitive damages. The "loser pays" rules and an outright cap on punitive damages were notably absent.

Even in this diluted version, the consensus behind H.R. 956 was not broad enough. Despite the Senate's efforts to make the bill more palatable to President Clinton, he vetoed H.R. 956 in May 1996. Neither house was able to muster a two-thirds vote to override.

Not surprisingly, the veto proved an effective damper on the movement to reform tort law from Washington, especially after President Clinton won re-election in 1996. The president was widely perceived to be a staunch supporter of trial lawyers, whose opposition to tort reform was unwavering. Senator Hatch introduced another reform effort in early 1997. Like H.R. 956, the Civil Justice Fairness Act of 1997 (S. 79) would have rewritten both punitive damages and joint and several liability rules. The bill, however, never made it out of the Senate Judiciary Committee.

Reform at the State Level Proceeds

Interestingly, at the same time tort reform was stumbling in Washington, the states were actively passing legislation to curb perceived abuses. By August 1997, nearly all 50 states had some type of tort reform statute in place.

Thirty-four states had taken steps to eliminate joint and several liability for tort defendants.[e] Thirty-one states have either placed a cap on punitive damages or evidentiary standards restricting their availability. In addition, several states have placed caps on non-economic damages

(such as pain and suffering) and/or passed collateral source rules (which provide that plaintiff's damage awards are to be reduced by any amount they receive from an insurance company or other "collateral source").[f]

State reforms, however, are not beyond challenge because they must comport with both state and federal constitutional requirements. At the end of 1997, the Illinois Supreme Court struck down much of that state's Civil Justice Reform Amendments of 1995 as a violation of the Illinois state constitution.[g] The amendments limited compensatory awards for noneconomic injury, restricted pretrial fact-finding of medical records, and abolished joint liability. At least 70 other state courts have struck down similar attempts at reform.[h]

Thus, much of what Congressional reformers tried to accomplish is already being done at the state level. Reformers argue that federal legislation is still needed because state reforms offer only patchwork protection. Because more than 70% of products made in one state are sold in another, businesses claim they need uniform federal rules to give them full protection. Nevertheless, there is no question that the prevalence of state legislation is changing the face of the U.S. tort system, even if gradually. With a tepid supporter of tort reform sitting in the White House until the next millennium, advocates of a tort system overhaul may have to content themselves with patchwork, state-by-state progress.

---

a. Philip Shuchman, *It Isn't That the Tort Lawyers Are So Right, It's Just That the Tort Reformers Are So Wrong*, 49 RUTGERS L. REV. 485 (1995).

b. The Alabama Supreme Court subsequently reduced this award to $2 million. BMW of North America, Inc. v. Gore, 646 So.2d 619 (Ala. 1994). The U.S. Supreme Court then declared the $2 million award void as "grossly excessive" and unconstitutional. BMW of North America, Inc. v. Gore, 517 U.S. 559 (1996). On remand, the Alabama Supreme Court further reduced the award to $50,000. BMW of North America, Inc. v. Gore, 701 So.2d 507 (Ala. 1997).

c. Richard C. Reuben, *Plaintiffs Rarely Win Punitives, Study Says*, 81 A.B.A. J. 26 (1995).

d. Edward Felsenthal, *Punitive Awards Are Called Modest, Rare*, WALL ST. J., June 17, 1996, at B2.

e. The data in this paragraph are derived from information published by the American Tort Reform Association, <http://atra.org/atra/atri2c.htm>.

f. Catherine Yang, *Tort Reform Needs Reforming*, BUS. WK., Apr. 15, 1996, at 67.

g. Best v. Taylor Machine Works, PROD. LIAB. REP. (CCH) ¶ 15,123 (Ill. 1997).

h. For an interesting debate about the normative question of whether tort reform should be addressed at the federal level, *see* Spencer Abraham, *Litigation Tariff: The Federal Case for National Tort Reform*, <http://www.heritage.org/heritage/p_review/summer95/thabra.html>, and William Niskanen, *Do Not Federalize Tort Law: A Friendly Response to Senator Abraham*, <http://www.cato.org/pubs/regulation/reg18v4a.html>.

ultrahazardous if it (1) necessarily involves a risk of serious harm to persons or property that cannot be eliminated by the exercise of utmost care, and (2) is not a matter of common usage.

Courts have found the following activities ultrahazardous: (1) storing flammable liquids in quantity in an urban area; (2) pile driving; (3) blasting; (4) crop dusting; (5) fumigating with cyanide gas; (6) constructing a roof so as to shed snow onto the highway; (7) emission of noxious fumes by a manufacturing plant located in a settled area; (8) locating oil wells or refineries in populated communities; and (9) test-firing solid-fuel rocket motors. However, courts have considered parachuting, drunk driving, maintaining power lines, and letting water escape from an irrigation ditch not to be ultrahazardous. Discharging fireworks is not ultrahazardous because the risk of serious harm could be eliminated by proper manufacture. In most jurisdictions, liability does not attach until the court determines that the dangerous activity is inappropriate to the particular location.

Under strict liability, once the court determines that the activity is abnormally dangerous, it is irrelevant that the defendant observed a high standard of care. For example, if the defendant's blasting injured the plaintiff, it is irrelevant that the defendant took every precaution available. Although evidence of such precautions might prevent the plaintiff from recovering under a theory of negligence, it does not affect strict liability. If a business involves an ultrahazardous activity, the managers should realize that in the event of injury they may have no defense to a claim of strict liability. The role of insurance for ultrahazardous activities is therefore particularly important.

 ## Damages

Tort damages generally attempt to restore the plaintiff to the same position he or she was in before the tort occurred. (In contrast, contract damages try to place the plaintiff in the position he or she would have been in had the contract been performed, as explained in Chapter 7.) Tort damages may include punitive as well as compensatory damages.

Actual Damages

Actual damages, also known as *compensatory damages*, measure the cost to repair or replace an item, or the de-

crease in market value caused by the tortious conduct. Actual damages may also include compensation for medical expenses, lost wages, and pain and suffering.

Punitive Damages

Punitive damages, also known as *exemplary damages*, may be awarded to punish the defendant and deter others from engaging in similar conduct. Punitive damages are awarded only in cases of outrageous misconduct. The amount of punitive damages may properly be based on the defendant's wealth and, in most jurisdictions, must be proportional to the actual damages. Several states have limited punitive damage awards to situations in which the plaintiff can prove by clear and convincing evidence that the defendant was guilty of oppression, fraud, or malice.

As discussed in the "Political Perspective," controversy has surrounded the size and nature of some punitive damage awards and led to calls for legal reform. Businesses have tended to be the strongest supporters of efforts to cap or eliminate punitive damages. Such enthusiasm, however, is largely limited to product liability cases, where businesses are defendants but rarely the plaintiffs. In other areas, where businesses tend to be the plaintiffs as well as the defendants (such as contracts, unfair competition, and misleading advertising), reform of punitive damages appears to be less of a priority.[28]

 ## Equitable Relief

If a monetary award cannot adequately compensate for the plaintiff's loss, courts may apply *equitable relief*. For example, the court may issue an *injunction*, that is, a court order, to prohibit the defendant from continuing a certain course of activity. This remedy is particularly appropriate for torts such as trespass or nuisance, when the plaintiff does not want the defendant's conduct to continue. The court may issue an injunction ordering the defendant to perform a certain activity. For example, a newspaper could be ordered to publish a retraction. In determining whether to grant injunctive relief, the courts will balance the hardship to the plaintiff against the benefit to the defendant.

28. Richard B. Schmitt, *Why Businesses Sometimes Like Punitive Awards*, WALL ST. J., Dec. 11, 1995, at B1.

BUSINESS TORTS

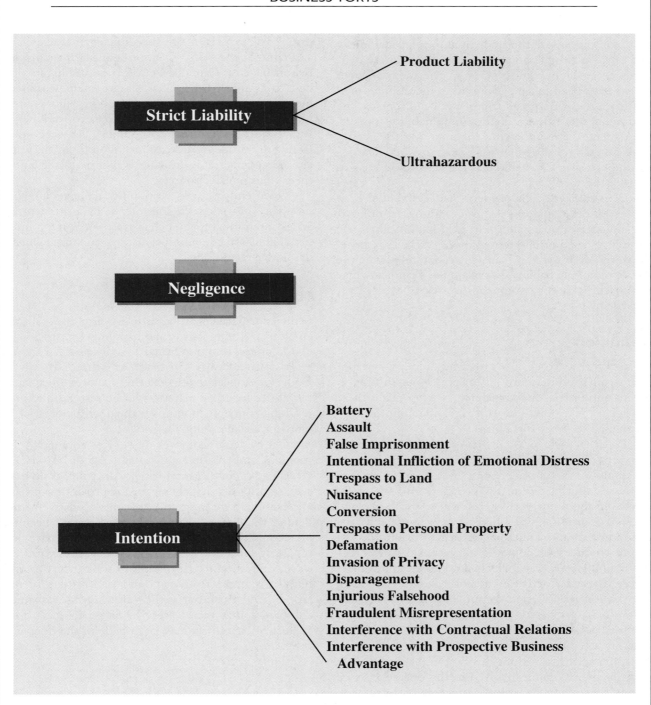

Strict Liability
- Product Liability
- Ultrahazardous

Negligence

Intention
- Battery
- Assault
- False Imprisonment
- Intentional Infliction of Emotional Distress
- Trespass to Land
- Nuisance
- Conversion
- Trespass to Personal Property
- Defamation
- Invasion of Privacy
- Disparagement
- Injurious Falsehood
- Fraudulent Misrepresentation
- Interference with Contractual Relations
- Interference with Prospective Business Advantage

◆ Toxic Torts

Since the 1970s, tort law has been evolving in response to sustained social and political concern over toxic substances and their potential for personal injury and environmental and property damage. These concerns are evident almost daily in the media. When courts have been asked to adjudicate the disputes arising from the widespread use of toxic substances, the traditional tort rules for determining liability, measuring damages, and allocating them among the parties have not always provided for ready answers. The resulting pressure for change has caused some courts to modify these rules and even to recognize new categories of damages. The prudent manager should keep abreast of developments in this emerging area of tort law and strive to reduce the risk of liability for toxic substances used or distributed in his or her enterprise. However, even the best managers cannot eliminate the risk of toxic tort liability. For example, a company may find itself liable for toxic exposures that have not yet caused any injury.

Definition

A *toxic tort* is a wrongful act that causes injury by exposure to a harmful, hazardous, or poisonous substance. Modern industrial and consumer society utilizes these substances in a variety of ways, creating countless opportunities for toxic tort claims.

Potential toxic tort defendants include those manufacturers (1) that utilize substances that may injure an employee, a consumer, or a bystander; (2) whose processes emit hazardous by-products into the air or discharge them into a river; (3) whose waste material goes to a disposal site where it may migrate to the groundwater and contaminate nearby wells; or (4) whose product itself contains or creates substances that can injure. However, liability is not limited to manufacturers. Everyday activities of governmental agencies, distribution services, and consumers may provide a basis for toxic tort claims. Some substances once thought safe, such as asbestos, have resulted in ruinous litigation when it was later established that they were harmful. Even financial institutions can be caught in the toxic tort net by becoming involved in the operations of a business handling hazardous materials or by buying contaminated land at a foreclosure sale.

Expensive to Defend

Toxic tort claims are among the most difficult and expensive of lawsuits to defend or prosecute. Expert witness costs alone can run into the millions for a single case. Toxic tort claims are also difficult to evaluate and, as a consequence, often cannot be insured against at a reasonable cost. Cause-and-effect relationships are difficult to establish because of disagreement within the medical and scientific community. When illness or injury does occur, it is often years after exposure began. Because exposures causing the injury can accumulate from a multitude of sources, including food, air, water, and skin contact, it is difficult to allocate blame among the various possible sources.

Open-ended claims for punitive damages are commonplace in toxic tort cases. Thus, plaintiffs typically allege intentional torts such as trespass, battery, intentional infliction of emotional distress, and outrageous or despicable conduct.

Strict Liability

Some courts have held hazardous-waste disposal to be an ultrahazardous activity and have imposed strict liability for injuries resulting from it. For instance, in *Sterling v. Velsicol Chemical Corporation*,[29] the Sixth Circuit Court of Appeals held that the operator of a waste-burial site for toxic material will be responsible for all resulting contamination under the doctrine of strict liability for ultrahazardous activities.

The federal Comprehensive Environmental Response, Compensation and Liability Act of 1980 (CERCLA) embodies this strict liability doctrine, as do many state statutes that largely mirror the provisions of CERCLA. Some have suggested that the legislative history behind these statutes indicates they should be interpreted and applied broadly. However, courts have been reluctant to extend strict liability to parties without a close connection to the hazardous substance. Strict liability may apply to owners and transporters of hazardous substances; but as the following case illustrates, companies that merely service or repair hazardous-substance containers may be outside of the doctrine's reach.

---

29. 855 F.2d 1188 (6th Cir. 1988).

| A CASE IN POINT | SUMMARY |

CASE 9.7
FARM BUREAU
MUTUAL INSURANCE
COMPANY v. PORTER &
HECKMAN, INC.
Court of Appeals of Michigan
560 N.W.2d 367
(Mich. Ct. App. 1996).

FACTS   The Carricos owned a home in Michigan with an outdoor, above-ground heating-oil tank. In 1991, the tank leaked, causing groundwater and soil contamination. The Carricos were sued by their neighbors in a separate action.

In this suit, Farm Bureau Mutual Insurance Company (the Carricos' insurance company) sued the company that serviced the Carricos' heating-oil tank (Porter & Heckman) for contribution. In other words, if Farm Bureau was forced to pay a claim to the Carricos' neighbors, Farm Bureau wanted Porter & Heckman to pay part of it.

Farm Bureau filed its claim against Porter & Heckman under Michigan's Environmental Response Act (MERA). It argued that, because Porter & Heckman was in the business of servicing equipment containing a hazardous substance (the heating oil), it should be strictly liable for any damage attributable to the oil. The trial court rejected this argument and dismissed Farm Bureau's claim. Farm Bureau appealed.

ISSUE PRESENTED   Can a company that merely services a system that contains a hazardous substance be held strictly liable for any damage caused by the substance?

SUMMARY OF OPINION   The Michigan Court of Appeals analyzed Farm Bureau's claim under MERA, which states that a defendant will be held strictly liable for contamination damage if (1) it is an operator of a facility that deals in hazardous substances, or (2) it otherwise arranges for the disposal of a hazardous substance.

As for the "operator" claim, the court ruled that a defendant is an operator only if it has authority to control the area where the hazardous substances were located. One who services a system does not automatically control the operation of the system. Thus, Porter & Heckman was not liable as an "operator" merely because it serviced the Carricos' heating oil tank.

Nor was it liable as an "arranger for disposal." The court ruled that this portion of the statute required an intent to dispose of the hazardous substance, as well as some ownership of or authority to control the actual substance. Here, Porter & Heckman had the intent and authority only to repair the heating-oil tank, not to dispose of or control the oil itself.

RESULT   The trial court's dismissal of Farm Bureau's claim was affirmed. Farm Bureau was neither an owner nor an operator under MERA.

New Theories of Damages

Under traditional tort principles, toxic tort plaintiffs who prove exposure to a toxic substance and a defendant's liability for that exposure may still not receive a damage award because the rules require proof of an actual injury. The plaintiffs may be at risk of developing cancer or some other disease in the future, but tort law generally has not allowed recovery for risk of future disease unless some precursor symptom is present, or unless the plaintiff proves he or she is more likely than not to get the disease. In the face of these limitations on damages, courts are being asked to allow awards for emotional distress in the absence of either physical symptoms or an intentional tort.

In *Sterling*, the trial judge who found Velsicol Chemical strictly liable also awarded compensatory damages to individuals who had consumed contaminated well water. The trial court awarded damages for physical symptoms caused by drinking the well water and also gave awards for increased risk of cancer, fear of increased risk of cancer, impairment of the immune system, and for a psychological ailment known as posttraumatic stress disorder. The trial judge also awarded damages for impairment of the residents' quality of life, under the traditional tort of nuisance, and punitive damages.

Applying Tennessee law, the U.S. Court of Appeals for the Sixth Circuit disallowed the award for increased risk of cancer, because no expert had testified that there was more than a 50% chance the plaintiffs would develop cancer. The awards for impairment of the immune system and for posttraumatic stress disorder were also thrown out, on the ground that the medical evidence was insufficient. The award for fear of increased risk of cancer was allowed, but was reduced to a fixed annual sum multiplied by the number of years of exposure. This limited measure of damages for fear of future cancer is unusual and may not be applied in other states.

Another novel remedy that is being urged is the award of damages to cover the future cost of medical monitoring in order to detect the disease at the onset, when treatment may be more effective.

THE RESPONSIBLE MANAGER
Reducing Tort Risks

Managers should implement ongoing programs of education and monitoring to reduce the risks of tort liability. Because torts can be committed in numerous ways, the programs should cover all possible sources of liability. For example, the management of a company that does not respond satisfactorily to an allegation of sexual harassment may be liable for intentional infliction of emotional distress. Statements made by representatives of a company about some individual or product can constitute defamation.

In addition to preventing intentional torts, managers should work to prevent their employees from committing acts of negligence, which can lead to large damage awards against the company. Any tort-prevention program must recognize that under the principle of *respondeat superior*, employers will be held liable for any torts their employees commit in the scope of their employment. It is crucial, therefore, to define the scope of employment clearly.

Managers should use care to avoid committing torts that are related to contractual relations and competition with other firms. For example, a company may be held liable for interference with contractual relations if a court finds that the company intentionally tried to induce a party to breach a contract. Also, although competition itself is permissible, intentionally seeking to sabotage the efforts of another firm is not. Managers may need to consult counsel when they are unsure whether their activity has crossed the line from permissible competition to tortious interference with a prospective business advantage.

In the toxic torts area, managers should adopt a long-term policy to protect employees, customers, and the environment from excess toxic exposure. They should identify any hazardous toxic substances used in their business activities or products or released into the environment. Where appropriate, managers should test and monitor to determine levels of exposure. Often, it is necessary to obtain an expert assessment of the hazards of toxicity of these substances. Managers should develop a plan to control and reduce toxic exposure. This can be done by reducing the quantity of toxic substances used, by recycling, by seeking less toxic alternatives, and by educating and training employees. Managers should implement a plan by assigning responsibilities, allocating resources, and auditing compliance. The waste-management plan should include criteria for choosing third-party contractors. Insurance should be obtained, if available, and coverage should be reviewed periodically. Management should adopt a contingency plan for responding to toxic accidents and develop a public relations plan both for routine (that is, safe) use of toxic substances and for possible toxic accidents.

A program of overall risk management and reduction is essential to limit the potential of tort liability. It is often desirable to designate one person to be in charge of risk management. That person should keep track of all claims and determine what areas of the business merit special attention. The head of risk management should be free to report incidents and problems to the chief executive officer and the board of directors, in much the same way as an internal auditor reports directly to the independent directors on the audit committee. This enhances independence and reduces the fear of reprisals if the risk manager blows the whistle on high-ranking managers.

INSIDE STORY

EMF LITIGATION

A new area of tort litigation is emerging that may prove to be more widespread and costly than the asbestos litigation that consumed millions of dollars in the 1980s—electromagnetic fields, commonly known as EMFs.

EMFs are found virtually everywhere in modern life, from microwave ovens to TVs, electric blankets, cellular phones, computers, and the power lines that run above houses. Although scientists are certain that EMFs exist and can measure their levels to a high degree of accuracy, no one really knows about the effects of EMF exposure. Some studies link it to leukemia and brain cancer. Other studies find that there is no link at all. Although there has been a large number of studies, the results have been contradictory and inconclusive.

The lack of conclusive evidence has not stopped an emergence of EMF litigation. In *Zuidema v. San Diego Gas & Electric,* a family sued its local utilities company alleging that their daughter's rare kidney cancer was caused by her exposure to EMFs from the power lines. The family lost its claim, but the case is still a landmark one because it is the first EMF personal injury lawsuit to be decided by a jury.[30]

The loss in the *Zuidema* case has not deterred other plaintiffs. Similar to asbestos litigation, cases are being brought while the scientific debate continues. And "[p]resently, more studies exist that appear to link EMF exposure to an increased risk of cancer than existed linking asbestos exposure to an increased risk of cancer at a similar embryonic stage of asbestos litigation."[31] Because EMFs are virtually everywhere, almost anyone of any class or age could be a plaintiff. In contrast, the asbestos cases were generally brought by the shipyard workers, insulation installers, and others who were typically exposed to asbestos in World War II.

Litigants sue under a number of theories, including negligence and failure to warn. The greatest bar to recovery thus far has been the inability to prove a strong enough linkage between EMFs and cancer in order to show causation. This may come in the future with further studies.

EMF litigation was featured in ABC's prime-time attorney drama "The Practice" in 1998. Although the jury awarded millions in damages to the cancer-ridden plaintiffs in this fictitious case, the judge granted a defense motion to set aside the verdict. As in real cases, the judge found that the plaintiffs had not proven that power lines cause cancer.

Another basis of litigation has been the loss of property value. Using this ground, it is unnecessary to prove actual EMF danger; one only has to prove that public fear of EMFs led to a loss of one's property value. This area of EMF litigation is probably the one utilities companies have to fear the most in the immediate future. For example, in *San Diego Gas & Elec. v. Daley,*[32] the California Court of Appeal held that fear of EMFs could lead to recovery of damages for diminution of property value. In that case, the plaintiff was awarded more than $2 million in damages and fees.

However the scientific debate comes out, the battle in the courtroom is sure to be interesting . . . and costly.[33]

---

30. *Power Struggles,* 13 CAL. LAW. 20 (June 1993).

31. Roy W. Kreiger, *On the Line,* 80 A.B.A. J. 40, 44 (1994).

32. 205 Cal. App. 3d 1334 (1988).

33. *See* Stanley Pierce & Charlotte A. Bilbow, *Electromagnetic Fields Attract Lawsuits,* NAT'L. L.J., Feb. 8, 1993, at 20.

KEY WORDS AND PHRASES

absolute privilege **298**
actual cause **313**
actual damages **322**
actual intent **292**
actual malice **299**
appropriation of a person's name
  or likeness **360**
assault **294**
assumption of risk **316**
attractive nuisance **310**
battery **293**
comparative negligence **316**
compensatory damages **322**
contribution **319**
contributory negligence **315**
conversion **301**
defamation **297**
detour **318**
disparagement **302**
equitable relief **322**
exemplary damages **322**
false imprisonment **294**
fiduciary duty **303**
fraudulent misrepresentation **302**
frolic **318**
indemnification **319**

injunction **322**
injurious falsehood **302**
intent **292**
intentional infliction of emotional
  distress **299**
interference with contractual relations
  303
interference with prospective business
  advantage **304**
intrusion **300**
invasion of privacy **300**
invitee **311**
joint and several liability **319**
legal duty **304**
libel **297**
licensee **311**
malicious defense **303**
malicious prosecution **303**
negligence **304**
negligence *per se* **312**
negligent infliction of emotional
  distress **315**
nuisance **300**
ordinary comparative negligence **316**
participation in a breach of fiduciary
  duty **303**

private nuisance **300**
proximate cause **313**
publication **297**
public disclosure of private
  facts **300**
public figure **299**
public nuisance **300**
punitive damages **322**
pure comparative negligence **316**
qualified privilege **298**
res ipsa loquitur **313**
respondeat superior **317**
self publication **298**
slander **297**
slander *per se* **297**
strict liability **319**
successor liability **319**
tort **292**
toxic tort **324**
trespass to chattels **301**
trespass to land **300**
trespass to personal property **301**
ultrahazardous **319**
zone of danger **315**

QUESTIONS AND CASE PROBLEMS

1. Francoise is at the beach swimming. Someone is drowning. She sees a rope next to her. She decides not to help the person, and the person drowns. Can the person's family successfully sue her? What if someone else wanted to save the person, but Francoise hid the rope and the swimmer drowned? What if Francoise is the swimmer's mother? Lawyer? Business competitor? What if, instead, Pierre saw a baby fall into a bathtub while the baby's parents were away. If Pierre does not help the baby, and the baby drowns, is Pierre liable? Do your answers depend on where the accidents occur?

2. Linda owned Clowntown USA, a successful amusement park. The main attraction of the amusement park was a very steep and fast rollercoaster. Although Linda maintained the rollercoaster meticulously, she knew that it was unsafe for riders under four feet tall. Accordingly, she instructed her employee, Oliver, not to permit any-

one less than four feet tall to ride on the rollercoaster. On a particularly busy day in June, Oliver forgot his instructions and allowed several children below four feet tall to ride on the rollercoaster. The children were thrown from the ride and suffered serious bodily injury.

a. Under what doctrine could the children's parents sue Linda for damages? What would Linda's lawyer assert as a defense? Who would be likely to prevail?

b. Would your answer change if Linda had merely told Oliver to be careful in operating the rollercoaster, without specifically telling him not to permit anyone under four feet tall to ride it?

c. What additional defense could Linda assert if she could prove that the children's parents had read and understood a conspicuous sign posted at the rollercoaster ticket booth stating that the ride was dangerous for those under four feet tall and that anyone under that height rode at their own risk?

3. Joe, Alice, and their baby, Pearl, live in a house next to a closed city dump. Since they moved in five years ago, the only source of water for drinking, cooking, and bathing has been a well under the house. Last month, Joe discovered that the well was contaminated by small amounts of waste solvents leaking from the dump. Joe and Alice show no symptoms but worry that the contamination will eventually make them sick. Baby Pearl has a condition that may become leukemia, and Joe and Alice are concerned that future children may be harmed as well. As a result of stress caused by worrying about the effects of the contamination on themselves and their family, Joe and Alice begin to smoke, and do so even while Alice is nursing Pearl. Joe and Alice learn that Big Corporation sent 5% of the solvents to the dump. Big has $10 million in insurance. Last year, Big shut down the local plant, laying off 2,000 employees. Ten percent of the solvents came to the dump from Small Company. Small dissolved last year. Its former owner, Bill Small, is worth $3 million. The other 85% of the solvents came from thousands of separate households and small businesses throughout the city, all of which paid the city trash-collection fees.

a. What torts can Joe and Alice claim against the city? Big Corporation? Small Company? Bill Small? The local dry cleaner?

b. If the city condemns the home, paying full market value, what types of damages can Joe and Alice still claim?

c. What torts can Pearl claim if she develops leukemia and lung cancer 30 years later? Against whom?

4. Assume the facts in Question 3. Joe and Alice's lawyer discovers that ten years ago Big Corporation and Small Company received copies of federal regulations classifying the solvent wastes as hazardous. No one at Small Company bothered to read the regulations, and the solvents continued to be disposed of at the city dump. However, Big Corporation's environmental engineer issued orders that the solvents be sent to a hazardous-waste site instead of the city dump. However, no one was assigned to police the order, and about once a month some solvent went to the city dump by mistake. The environmental engineer reissued the orders twice after hearing of the mistakes, but occasional violations continued until the plant closed.

a. Can Joe and his family recover punitive damages against Big Corporation? Small Company? Bill Small?

b. What additional facts would improve the chances of securing a large punitive damages award?

5. Traditionally, the liability associated with injury on the premises of another has hinged on the distinctions between trespassers, licensees, and invitees. In 1993, the New Jersey Supreme Court questioned the validity of these distinctions and articulated a more general framework: "Whether a person owes a duty of reasonable care toward another turns on whether the imposition of such a duty satisfies an abiding sense of basic fairness under all of the circumstances in light of considerations of public policy." *Hopkins v. Fox & Lazo Realtors*, 625 A.2d 1110 (N.J. 1993). For that court, the analysis involves balancing many factors, including the relationship between the parties, the nature of the attendant risk, the opportunity and ability to exercise care, and the public interest in the proposed solution.

Four years later in New Jersey, a golfer was struck by lightning during a golf game and suffered serious injuries. He sued the golf course for negligence, alleging that it had breached a duty of care to him by not protecting him from lightning strikes. In light of the framework articulated by the New Jersey Supreme Court in 1993, what result? [*Maussner v. Atlantic City Country Club, Inc.*, 691 A.2d 826 (N.J. Super. 1997)]

6. During one of his typical end-of-the-show presentations on "60 Minutes," Andy Rooney discussed the many products that manufacturers send to him in the mail. While Mr. Rooney was lamenting the vast amount of junk mail he receives, he mentioned Rain-X, a product that was sent to Rooney by its inventor and manufacturer. The product was sent after Rooney had complained in another episode that he thought cars needed larger windshield wipers. Rooney then, on the air, said that he had tried the sample of Rain-X on his windshield and that it didn't work. Should the inventor/manufacturer be able to sue Andy Rooney for business disparagement? How about defamation? [*Unelko Corp. v. Rooney*, 912 F.2d 1049 (9th Cir. 1990), *cert. denied*, 499 U.S. 961 (1991)]

7. A Kmart shopper, Burrow, wanted to purchase two lamps. A salesperson placed the two lamps into two cardboard boxes that were not the original cartons. The salesperson then carried the boxes to the cashier and told the cashier the price of the lamps. The cashier rang up the purchase and gave Burrow a receipt. Burrow placed the receipt in her purse and waited for her daughters to pay for their purchases before leaving the store. When she was leaving the store, an employee approached her and insisted on searching her boxes. According to Burrow, the employee then snatched the boxes from her hands and, after searching the boxes, told her she could go. A jury awarded Burrow $2,000 based on her false imprisonment claim. Should the jury award stand? [*Burrow v. Kmart Corp.*, 304 S.E.2d 460 (Ga. App. Ct. 1983)]

8. *Mindis Metals* sold acid-filled batteries to a battery-recycling facility. During the recycling process, lead from the batteries escaped from the facility. The resulting lead contamination caused both personal injuries and property damage to the facility's immediate neighbors. One neighbor sued Mindis under a theory of strict liability, arguing that because battery recycling is an ultrahazardous activity, Mindis is liable for all injuries and damages resulting therefrom. What result? [*Thompson v. Mindis Metals, Inc.*, 692 So. 2d 805 (Ala. 1997)]

9. Chris Beck, an employee of Henrietta Marlow, attended a Christmas party that Marlow sponsored for her employees. The party was held on Marlow's business premises. No one was required to attend the party, which started late in the afternoon and continued into the early evening. Beck was served many drinks by Marlow's secretary and became intoxicated. One hour later, Beck left the party, ran a red traffic light, and struck another car. Carl Timmons, the driver of the other car, had been speeding, and he was killed in the accident. Timmons's car had a broken headlight before the collision.

Whom can Carl's widow sue? Under what theory? What should the attorney for Beck try to show the jury? What should the attorney for Marlow try to prove to the jury?

MANAGER'S DILEMMA

10. *The New Yorker* published an article detailing a falling out among professors working on the Sigmund Freud archives. Masson, one of the professors, sued *The New Yorker* and the article's author for defamation, after the article quoted him referring to himself as an "intellectual gigolo." The author attributed the following quote to Masson:

> Then I met a rather attractive older graduate student, and I had an affair with her. One day, she took me to some art event, and she was sorry afterward. She said, "Well, it is very nice sleeping with you in your room, but you're the kind of person who should never leave the room—you're just a social embarrassment anywhere else, though you do fine in your own room." And you know, in their way, if not in so many words, Eissler and Anna Freud told me the same thing. They like me well enough "in my own room." They loved to hear from me what creeps and dolts analysts are. I was like an intellectual gigolo—you get your pleasure from him, but you don't take him out in public. . . .

Tape recordings contained the substance of Masson's reference to the graduate student but no suggestion that Eissler or Anna Freud considered him, or that he considered himself, an "intellectual gigolo." Instead, Masson said, on the tapes:

> They felt, in a sense, I was a private asset but a public liability. . . . They liked me when I was alone in their living room, and I could talk and chat and tell them the truth about things, and they would tell me. But that I was, in a sense, much too junior within the hierarchy of analysts, for these important training analysts to be caught dead with me.

The author of the article argued that not all of the conversations were recorded. She explained that at times her tape recorder was broken. In addition, she claimed to have taken notes (which she later typed up) during conversations between the two of them while walking or traveling by car.

Assume that the author faithfully captured the substance of Masson's comments but that he never said the exact words in quotation marks attributed to him. Does the author's alteration or reconstruction of the actual language used rise to the level of "actual malice"? If so, do all such alterations, except technical corrections of grammar or syntax, demonstrate actual malice? How much "proof" should a manager/editor demand from his or her authors or reporters to substantiate direct quotations? [*Masson v. The New Yorker Magazine, Inc.*, 501 U.S. 496 (1991)]

INTERNET SOURCES	
The Northern Illinois University page provides access to its 1995 study of the costs of the U.S. tort system.	http://www.icjl.org/data2/niu.htm
The Law Journal Extra page provides the text of recent judicial decisions dealing with tort law.	http://www.ljextra.com/practice/intentionaltorts/trde.html
The Worldwide Legal Information Association page provides information about tort law around the world.	http://www.wwlia.org/tort2.htm
The British law firm of Sweet & Maxwell provides a collection of reports on professional negligence and liability.	http://www.smlawpub.co.uk/journal/pnlr/index.html
The New York law firm of Queller & Fisher maintains a page dedicated to issues of negligence.	http://www.quellerfisher.com/negli.html
The Alexander Law Firm of San Jose, California, maintains the Consumer Law Page to disseminate information about torts, especially personal injury.	http://consumerlawpage.com
The U.S. House of Representatives Internet Law Library has a large collection of tort-related statutes, court decisions, and articles.	http://law.house.gov/110.htm
The American Tort Reform Association hosts a page addressing various issues about tort reform.	http://www.aaabiz.com/ATRA

CHAPTER 10

Product Liability

INTRODUCTION

Definition of Product Liability

Product liability is the legal liability of the manufacturer or seller of a product that, because of a defect, causes injury to the purchaser, user, or bystander. Liability extends to anyone in the business of selling the goods or in the chain of distribution.

Today, most states in the United States have adopted strict product liability, whereby an injured person may recover damages without showing that the manufacturer was negligent or otherwise at fault. No contractual relationship is necessary between the manufacturer and the injured person. The injured person merely needs to show that the product was sold in a defective or dangerous condition and that the defect caused his or her injury.

Chapter Overview

This chapter discusses the evolution of the strict liability doctrine, beginning with its origin in warranty and negligence theories. It then focuses on the bases for strict liability, including manufacturing defect, design defect, and failure to warn. The chapter examines who may be held liable for defective products and the allocation of liability among multiple defendants. Defenses to a product liability claim are discussed, along with legislative reforms designed to correct perceived abuses in the system. Finally, the law of product liability in the European Union is described.

 Theories of Recovery

The primary theories on which a product liability claim can be brought are breach of warranty, negligence, and strict liability.

Breach of Warranty

In a warranty action, the reasonableness of the manufacturer's actions is not at issue. Rather, the question is whether the quality, characteristics, and safety of the product were consistent with the implied or express representations made by the seller. A buyer may bring a warranty action whenever the product fails to meet the standards that the seller represents to the buyer at the time of purchase.

UCC Warranties As explained in Chapter 8, a warranty may be either express or implied. An express warranty is an affirmation made by the seller relating to the quality of the goods sold. An implied warranty is created by law and guarantees the merchantability and, in some circumstances, the fitness for a particular purpose of the goods sold.

Privity of Contract   A breach-of-warranty action is based on principles of contract law. In order for an injured person to recover, he or she must be in a contractual relationship with the seller. This requirement is known as *privity of contract*. It necessarily precludes recovery by those persons, such as bystanders, who are not in privity with the seller. In the *MacPherson* case discussed below, MacPherson was not in privity of contract with Buick and could not sue for breach of warranty.

Negligence

To prove negligence in a products case, the injured party must show that the defendant did not use reasonable care in designing or manufacturing its product or in providing adequate warnings (see Chapter 9). This can be quite difficult to prove. Moreover, injured persons are often negligent themselves in their use or misuse of the product. This precludes recovery in a contributory-negligence state and reduces recovery in a comparative-negligence state.

Significantly, a product liability claim based on negligence does not require privity of contract between the plaintiff and the defendant. Thus, one of the obstacles posed in breach-of-warranty actions is avoided.

MacPherson, which follows, is the landmark negligence case in which the defendant was found liable without privity of contract. Although still based on the negligence principles of reasonableness and due care, *MacPherson*'s abandonment of the privity requirement makes it an important forerunner to the doctrine of strict product liability.

⊙ A CASE IN POINT   SUMMARY

CASE 10.1
MacPHERSON v. BUICK MOTOR CO.
Court of Appeals of New York
111 N.E. 1050 (N.Y. 1916).

FACTS   MacPherson purchased a new Buick car with wooden wheels from a Buick Motor Company dealer who had previously purchased the car from Buick Motor Company, the manufacturer of the car. MacPherson was injured when the car ran into a ditch. The accident was caused by the collapse of one of the car's wheels because the spokes were made from defective wood. The wheel had been made by a manufacturer other than Buick.

MacPherson sued Buick Motor Company directly. He proved that Buick could have discovered the defects by reasonable inspection and that such an inspection had not been conducted. No claim was made that the manufacturer knew of the defect and willfully concealed it. After the trial court found in favor of MacPherson, Buick appealed. Buick argued that MacPherson could not sue Buick because there was no contract between Buick and MacPherson; the sale contract was between the dealer and MacPherson.

ISSUE PRESENTED   Can a consumer who purchases a product from a retailer sue the manufacturer directly for negligent manufacture of the product even though there is no contract per se between the consumer and the manufacturer?

SUMMARY OF OPINION   The New York Court of Appeals held that Buick could be held liable for negligence. As a manufacturer, it owed a duty to any person who could foreseeably be injured as a result of a defect in an automobile it manufactured. A manufacturer's duty to inspect was held to vary with the nature of the thing to be inspected. The more probable the danger, the greater the need for caution. Because the action was one in tort for negligence, no contract between the plaintiff and the defendant was required.

Case 10.1 continues

Case 10.1 continued

RESULT   The Court of Appeals affirmed the lower court's finding that the manufacturer, Buick Motor Company, was liable for the injuries sustained by the plaintiff. The manufacturer was found to be negligent in not inspecting the wheels and was responsible for the finished product.

COMMENTS   This case established the rule, still applicable today, that a manufacturer can be liable for failure to exercise reasonable care in the manufacture of a product when such failure involves an unreasonable risk of bodily harm to users of the product. This rule is embodied in Sections 1 and 2(a) of the recently approved Restatement (Third) of Torts: Product Liability (1997).[1] The foundations of the law discussed in this case were laid down in *Thomas v. Winchester*,[2] in which the manufacturer of a drug who accidentally mislabeled a poison was held responsible to the customer that ultimately bought the drug from the pharmacist.

---

1. The Restatement (Second) of Torts (1977) reflected this rule in Section 395.
2. 6 N.Y. 397 (1852).

Strict Liability in Tort

Strict liability in tort allows a person injured by an unreasonably dangerous product to recover damages from the manufacturer or seller of the product. Negligent conduct on the part of the manufacturer or seller is not required. Because the defect in the product is the basis for liability, the injured person may recover damages even if the seller has exercised all possible care in the manufacture and sale of the product.

For a defendant to be held strictly liable, the plaintiff must prove that (1) the plaintiff, or his or her property, was harmed by the product; (2) the injury was caused by a defect in the product; and (3) the defect existed at the time it left the defendant and did not substantially change along the way. Most states follow the formulation of Section 402A of the Restatement (Second) of Torts, which states:

1. One who sells any product in a defective condition unreasonably dangerous to the user or consumer or to his property is subject to liability for physical harm thereby caused to the ultimate user or consumer, or to his property, if
    a. the seller is engaged in the business of selling such a product, and
    b. it is expected to and does reach the user or consumer without substantial change in the condition in which it is sold.

2. The rule stated in Subsection (1) applies although
    a. the seller has exercised all possible care in the preparation and sale of his product, and the user or consumer has not bought the product from or entered into any contractual relation with the seller.[3]

As discussed later in this chapter, however, the Restatement (Second) of Torts (including Section 402A) was superseded by the Restatement (Third) of Torts: Product Liability in May 1997. The Restatement (Third) proposes to do away with the notion of "strict" liability, opting instead for a standard that asks: (1) was there a defect in the product? and (2) if so, could it reasonably have been avoided by use of an alternative design?

Note that, although judges often regard the Restatement as persuasive authority and an accurate depiction of present case law, courts are free to either follow or ignore the Restatement's formulation. As we will discuss later, it remains to be seen whether courts will broadly adopt the Restatement (Third) view of product liability.

In light of this dynamic, the doctrine of strict product liability outlined in Section 402A of the Restatement (Second) is by no means obsolete. The first state supreme court to adopt strict product liability was California in 1963, in the following case.

---

3. Restatement (Second) of Torts § 402A (1977).

| A CASE IN POINT | IN THE LANGUAGE OF THE COURT |

**CASE 10.2
GREENMAN v.
YUBA POWER
PRODUCTS, INC.**
Supreme Court of California
377 P.2d 897 (Cal. 1963).

FACTS   William Greenman's wife purchased a Shopsmith combination power tool that could be used as a saw, drill, and wood lathe for her husband's Christmas present. The power tool was manufactured by Yuba Power Products. Mr. Greenman had seen a Shopsmith demonstrated by the retailer and had studied a brochure prepared by the manufacturer. After Mr. Greenman secured an attachment to the tool to make it more useful as a lathe for turning a large piece of wood, he was injured when the wood flew from the machine and hit him in the forehead, causing serious injuries.

Mr. Greenman claimed that the tool was defective and not suitable to perform the work for which it was intended. He sued the manufacturer and retailer for breach of express and implied warranties and for negligent construction of the tool. At trial, evidence was introduced showing that "inadequate set screws" held together the part of the tool that injured Mr. Greenman. The jury returned a verdict for Mr. Greenman and against the manufacturer, based upon negligence and the express warranties.

ISSUE PRESENTED   Can a manufacturer be held strictly liable in tort when, knowing that its product would be used without inspection for defects, it places on the market a defective product that causes injury to a person?

OPINION   TRAYNOR, J., writing for the California Supreme Court:
. . . The jury could therefore reasonably have concluded that the manufacturer negligently constructed the Shopsmith. The jury could also reasonably have concluded that statements in the manufacturer's brochure were untrue, that they constituted express warranties, and that plaintiff's injuries were caused by their breach.

. . .

. . . A manufacturer is strictly liable in tort when an article he places on the market, knowing that it is to be used without inspection for defects, proves to have a defect that causes injury to a human being. Recognized first in the case of unwholesome food products, such liability has now been extended to a variety of other products that create as great or greater hazards if defective.

Although . . . strict liability has usually been based on the theory of an express or implied warranty running from the manufacturer to the plaintiff, the abandonment of the requirement of a contract between them, the recognition that the liability is not assumed by agreement but imposed by law, and the refusal to permit the manufacturer to define the scope of its own responsibility for defective products make clear that the liability is not one governed by the law of contract warranties but by the law of strict liability in tort. . . .

We need not recanvass the reasons for imposing strict liability on the manufacturer. . . . The purpose of such liability is to insure that the costs of injuries resulting from defective products are borne by the manufacturers that put such products on the market rather than by the injured persons who are powerless to protect themselves. Sales warranties serve this purpose fitfully at best. In the present case, for example, plaintiff was able to plead and prove an express warranty only because he read and relied on the representations of the Shopsmith's ruggedness contained in the manufacturer's brochure. Implicit in the machine's presence on the market, however,

Case 10.2 continues

Case 10.2 continued

was a representation that it would safely do the jobs for which it was built. Under these circumstances, it should not be controlling whether plaintiff selected the machine because of the statements in the brochure, or because of the machine's own appearance of excellence that belied the defect lurking beneath the surface, or because he merely assumed that it would safely do the jobs it was built to do. It should not be controlling whether the details of the sales from manufacturer to retailer and from retailer to plaintiff's wife were such that one or more of the implied warranties of the sales act arose. . . . To establish the manufacturer's liability it was sufficient that plaintiff proved that he was injured while using the Shopsmith in a way it was intended to be used as a result of a defect in design and manufacture of which plaintiff was not aware that made the Shopsmith unsafe for its intended use.

RESULT   The California Supreme Court affirmed the trial court's finding that the manufacturer was liable to the plaintiff and the monetary award of $65,000. It held that a manufacturer is strictly liable in tort when an article he places on the market, knowing that it is to be used without inspection for defects, proves to have a defect that causes injury to a human being.

Questions

1. What are the policy reasons in favor of imposing strict liability?
2. Suppose Mrs. Greenman had never read the brochure, yet had seen her husband use the tool successfully several times as a lathe. How would the court have decided the claim for breach of express warranties if she had been the one who had been injured and asserted the claim?

Rationale   The legal principle of strict product liability is grounded in considerations of public policy. The rationale has three basic parts: (1) the law should protect consumers against unsafe products; (2) manufacturers should not escape liability simply because they typically do not sign a formal contract with the end-user of their product (or with non-users who might be injured by their product); and (3) manufacturers and sellers of products are in the best position to bear the costs of injuries caused by their products, because they can pass these costs on to all consumers in the form of higher prices. In short, the goal of strict product liability is to force companies to internalize the costs of product-caused injuries. The crafters of the doctrine recognized this would give manufacturers an incentive to improve the safety of their products.

Strategy   Although negligence and breach of warranty are alleged in most product liability cases, they play a secondary role compared to strict liability. Under strict liability, the injured person does not have the burden of proving negligence and does not have to be in privity with the seller. Thus, strict liability is easier to prove than either negligence or breach of warranty.

Nonetheless, plaintiffs' attorneys usually try to prove negligence as well as strict liability. Proof of negligence will often stir the jury's emotions, leading to higher damages awards and, in some cases, punitive damages. On the other hand, once the plaintiff has raised the issue of negligence, the defense can introduce evidence that its products were "state-of-the-art" and manufactured with due care. Such evidence would be irrelevant to the issue of strict liability and hence inadmissible.

Testimony by Former Employees   A recent U.S. Supreme Court decision allowing a former General Motors Corporation (GM) engineer to testify in a product liability lawsuit against GM made it more difficult for manufacturers to keep former employee whistle-blowers off the witness stand.[4] The family of a Missouri woman who had burned to death when the engine in her GM car caught fire after a highway accident wanted Robert Elwell, a former GM engineer, to testify against the auto manufacturer in their Missouri suit. Elwell had previously agreed as part of an employment settlement with GM not to testify in product liability suits against GM without the company's consent. To enforce this settlement, a Michigan judge issued an injunction prohibiting Elwell from testifying against GM in any case.

Nonetheless, the trial court in Missouri allowed Elwell to testify. The plaintiffs won a jury verdict; but that judgment was reversed by the U.S. Court of Appeals for the Eighth Circuit, which ruled that Missouri was required to give full faith and credit to the Michigan injunction, and therefore Elwell was not permitted to testify.

The U.S. Supreme Court reversed, holding that Michigan had no authority to control other states' courts "by precluding them, in actions brought by strangers to the Michigan litigation, from determining for themselves what witnesses are competent to testify and what evidence is relevant and admissible in their search for the truth." It therefore allowed Elwell's testimony to stand and reinstated the Missouri trial court's judgment.

 ## Defective Product

An essential element for recovery in strict liability is proof of a defect in the product. The injured party must show (1) that the product was defective when it left the hands of the manufacturer or seller and (2) that the defect made the product unreasonably dangerous. Typically, it is dangerous if it does not meet the consumer's expectations as to its characteristics. For example, a consumer expects a stepladder not to break when someone stands on the bottom step. A product may be dangerous because of a manufacturing defect; a design defect; or inadequate warnings, labeling, or instructions. It may also be an unavoidably unsafe product.

Manufacturing Defect

A *manufacturing defect* is a flaw in the product that occurs during production, such as a failure to meet the de-

sign specifications. A product with a manufacturing defect is not like the others rolling off the production line. For example, suppose the driver's seat in an automobile was designed to be bolted to the frame. If the worker forgot to tighten the bolts, the loose seat would be a manufacturing defect.

Design Defect

A *design defect* occurs when, even though the product is manufactured according to specifications, its inadequate design or poor choice of materials makes it dangerous to users. Typically, there is a finding of defective design if the product is not safe for its intended or reasonably foreseeable use. A highly publicized example was the Ford Pinto, which a jury found to be defectively designed because the car's fuel tank was too close to the rear axle, causing the tank to rupture when the car was struck from behind.

Inadequate Warnings, Labeling, or Instructions

To avoid charges of *failure to warn*, a product must carry adequate warnings of the risks involved in the normal use of the product. For example, the manufacturer of a ladder must warn the user not to stand on the top step. A product must also be accompanied by instructions on the safe use of the product. For example, sellers have been found liable for failing to provide adequate instructions about the proper use and capacity of a hook and the assembly and use of a telescope and sun filter.

Although a warning can shield a manufacturer from liability for a properly manufactured and designed product, it cannot shield the manufacturer from liability for a *defectively* manufactured or designed product. For example, an automobile manufacturer cannot escape liability for defectively designed brakes merely by warning that "under certain conditions this car's brakes may

ETHICAL CONSIDERATION

Does a company have an ethical obligation to issue a warning about a defect that is discovered after a product is sold?

---

4. Baker v. General Motors Corp., 118 S. Ct. 657 (1998).

VIEW FROM CYBERSPACE

COMPUTERS AND REPETITIVE-STRESS INJURIES

In recent years, computer manufacturers have been sued by thousands of users who claim that a defectively designed computer keyboard has caused them repetitive-stress injuries. As of December 1997, however, not a single plaintiff had won a jury verdict.

In December 1996, a former secretary named Patricia Geressy found success employing a different strategy. She won a $5.3 million jury verdict against Digital Equipment Corporation, not for design defect, but for failure to warn against the potential hazards of using a computer keyboard. At the time of the verdict, several computer makers (such as Compaq and NEC) had begun to place warning labels on their keyboards, while others such as Digital and IBM had not.[a]

Repetitive-stress plaintiffs and their lawyers thought the Geressy verdict would set a favorable precedent and specifically precipitate further success on the failure-to-warn theory. Their expectations were never fulfilled, however. By the end of 1997, not a single jury had followed the Geressy lead. In fact, even Geressy's verdict did not hold up. In September 1997, a retrial was ordered because of new evidence tending to show that Geressy actually sustained her injuries prior to using a Digital keyboard. After a six-week trial in 1998, the jury found in favor of Digital.[b]

---

a. Jon Auerbach & Laura Johannes, *Companies Split on Warnings for Keyboards*, WALL ST. J., Dec. 11, 1996, at B1.

b. *N.Y. Jury Clears Digital Equipment Corp.*, CTDNEWS ONLINE EDITION, <http://ctdnews.com/news.html>.

ETHICAL CONSIDERATION

You are a manager of a major manufacturing corporation. An interview with a low-level engineer leads you to believe that the design specifications for your model PaZazz-4 are in fact the cause of numerous deaths. You are facing a wrongful death and products liability suit for defective design. The plaintiffs have not deposed this engineer, though his name was provided as one of the hundreds who worked on this project. Thus, while you believe the design for PaZazz-4 was defective, it will be extremely difficult—if not impossible—for the plaintiffs to prove this. What should you do?

fail." However, as will be explained later, some products, such as certain prescription drugs, are unavoidably unsafe. In cases involving such products, the adequacy of the warning determines whether the product, known to be dangerous, is also "defective."

Causation Requirement   In order to prevail on a failure-to-warn claim, a plaintiff must show both that the defendant breached a duty to warn and that the defendant's failure to warn was the proximate cause (or legal cause) of the plaintiff's injuries. The question of proximate cause is one for the jury to determine. As a result, the vast majority of courts will not disturb jury findings that a failure to warn was the proximate cause of an injury. However, in an extreme case—one in which the court believes no reasonable person could have deemed the failure to warn a proximate cause of the plaintiff's injury—the court may set aside a verdict on causation grounds.

Bilingual Warnings   The United States is a heterogeneous country. Diversity is one of its great strengths. With diversity can come challenges, however. Misunderstandings may arise due to differences in culture or language. Legislatures in states with a substantial non-English-speaking population have recognized the need for bilingual or multilingual documents in such areas as voting and public services. The following case addresses the need for bilingual warnings on nonprescription drugs.

| A CASE IN POINT | SUMMARY |

CASE 10.3
RAMIREZ v.
PLOUGH, INC.
Supreme Court of California
863 P.2d 167 (Cal. 1993).

FACTS In March 1986, when he was less than four months old, plaintiff Jorge Ramirez exhibited symptoms of a cold or similar upper respiratory infection. To relieve these symptoms, the plaintiff's mother gave him St. Joseph's Aspirin for Children (SJAC). Although the product label stated that the dosage for a child under two years old was "as directed by doctor," the plaintiff's mother did not consult a doctor before using SJAC to treat the plaintiff's condition. Over a two-day period, the plaintiff's mother gave him three SJAC tablets. On March 15, the plaintiff's mother took him to a hospital. There, the doctor advised her to administer Dimetapp or Pedialyte (nonprescription medications that do not contain aspirin), but she disregarded the advice and continued to treat the plaintiff with SJAC. Jorge thereafter developed the potentially fatal Reye's syndrome, resulting in severe neurological damage, including cortical blindness, spastic quadriplegia, and mental retardation.

Reye's syndrome occurs in children and teenagers during or while recovering from a mild respiratory tract infection, flu, chicken pox, or other viral illness. The disease is fatal in 20% to 30% of cases, with many of the survivors sustaining permanent brain damage. Several studies showing an association between the ingestion of aspirin during a viral illness, such as chicken pox or influenza, and the subsequent development of Reye's syndrome prompted the U.S. Food and Drug Administration (FDA) to impose a labeling requirement for aspirin products warning of the dangers of Reye's syndrome. Yet, even before the federal regulation became mandatory, packages of SJAC displayed this warning: "Warning: Reye Syndrome is a rare but serious disease which can follow flu or chicken pox in children and teenagers. While the cause of Reye Syndrome is unknown, some reports claim aspirin may increase the risk of developing this disease. Consult doctor before use in children or teenagers with flu or chicken pox." The package insert contained a similar warning.

The medication purchased by the plaintiff's mother had such warnings only in English, despite the fact that the defendant was aware that Hispanics were purchasing the medication. Because the plaintiff's mother could not read English, she was unable to read the warnings on the SJAC label and package insert. Yet she did not ask anyone to translate the label or package insert into Spanish, even though other members of her household could have done so.

The plaintiff sued defendant Plough, Inc., alleging that he contracted Reye's syndrome as a result of ingesting a nonprescription drug, St. Joseph's Aspirin for Children, that was manufactured and distributed by the defendant. The plaintiff sought compensatory and punitive damages on, among other things, a theory of product liability. The complaint alleged that the SJAC plaintiff ingested was defective when it left the defendant's control and that the product's reasonably foreseeable use involved a substantial and not readily apparent danger of which the defendant failed to adequately warn.

In finding no duty to warn and no causal relation between the defendant's actions and the plaintiff's illness, the trial court granted summary judgment for the defendant. On appeal, the court of appeal reversed because it found a duty to warn and felt that a jury question existed as to the adequacy of the necessary warning. The defendant appealed.

Case 10.3 continues

Case 10.3 continued

ISSUE PRESENTED May a manufacturer of nonprescription drugs that can lead to a deadly illness when taken as "normally expected" incur tort liability for distributing its products with warnings only in English despite the fact that the manufacturer knows that there are non-English-reading users?

SUMMARY OF OPINION The California Supreme Court began by noting that the defendant conceded that a manufacturer of nonprescription drugs has a duty to warn purchasers about dangers in its products. The issue was whether the defendant's duty to warn required it to provide label or package warnings in Spanish.

Courts have generally not looked with favor upon the use of statutory compliance as a defense to tort liability. But there is some room in tort law for a defense of statutory compliance. Where the evidence shows no unusual circumstances, but only the ordinary situation contemplated by the statute or administrative rule, then the minimum standard prescribed by the legislation or regulation may be accepted by the triers of fact, or by the court as a matter of law, as sufficient for the occasion.

The defendant manufacturer argued that the standard of care for packaging and labeling nonprescription drugs, and in particular the necessity or propriety of foreign-language label and package warnings, has been appropriately fixed by the dense layer of state and federal statutes and regulations that control virtually all aspects of the marketing of its products. The federal government regulates the labeling of nonprescription drugs through Section 502 of the Food, Drug and Cosmetic Act.[5]

The Food and Drug Administration regulations specify both the subject matter of required warnings and the actual words to be used. For example, the labeling for aspirin, and for most other over-the-counter drugs, must contain a general warning on use by pregnant or nursing women . . . and a warning about Reye's syndrome.

The FDA has stated that it "encourages the preparation of labeling to meet the needs of non-English-speaking or special user populations so long as such labeling fully complies with agency regulations." But the controlling regulation requires only that manufacturers provide full English labeling for all nonprescription drugs except those "distributed solely in the Commonwealth of Puerto Rico or in a Territory where the predominant language is one other than English. . . ." The regulation further states that if the label or packaging of any drug distributed in the 50 states contains "any representation in a foreign language," then all required "words, statements, and other information" must appear in the foreign language as well as in English.

The court reasoned that defining the circumstances under which warnings or other information should be provided in a language other than English is a task for which legislative and administrative bodies are particularly well suited. The California legislature has already performed this task in a variety of different contexts, enacting laws to ensure that California residents are not denied important services or exploited because they lack proficiency in English.

These statutes demonstrate that the legislature is able and willing to define the circumstances in which foreign-language communications should be mandated. Given

Case 10.3 continues

---

5. 21 U.S.C. § 352 *et seq.* (1997).

Case 10.3 continued

the existence of a statute expressly requiring that package warnings on nonprescription drugs be in English, the court stated that it was reasonable to infer that the legislature has deliberately chosen not to require that manufacturers also include warnings in foreign languages. The same inference was considered warranted on the federal level. The court concluded that the prudent course was to adopt for tort purposes the existing legislative and administrative standard of care on this issue.

RESULT   Plaintiff Ramirez's case was dismissed as a matter of law. Because both state and federal law require warnings in English but not in any other language, a manufacturer is not liable in tort for failing to label a nonprescription drug with warnings in a language other than English.

COMMENTS   The California Supreme Court was influenced by the experience of FDA-mandated Spanish inserts for prescription drugs. Recognizing that "the United States is too heterogeneous to enable manufacturers, at reasonable cost and with reasonable simplicity, to determine exactly where to provide alternative language inserts," the FDA for a time required manufacturers, as an alternative to multilingual or bilingual inserts, to provide Spanish-language translations of their patient package inserts on request to doctors and pharmacists. But the FDA later noted that manufacturers were having difficulty obtaining accurate translations and eventually it abandoned altogether the patient package insert requirement for prescription drugs.

Should the result be different if the nonprescription medicine is for an illness particular to a certain non-English-speaking group residing in the United States? What if there are advertisements for a particular medicine in a language other than English?

Unavoidably Unsafe Product

If the societal value of using an inherently dangerous product outweighs the risk of harm from its use, the manufacturer may be exonerated from liability for sale of such an *unavoidably unsafe product*. For example, certain drugs are generally beneficial but are known to have harmful side effects in some cases. The authors of the Restatement (Third) of Torts recognized that there should be a separate concept of product liability for manufacturers of prescription drugs.

Comment b to Section 6 of the Restatement (Third) reads in part:

The traditional refusal by courts to impose tort liability for defective designs of prescription drugs and medical devices is based on the fact that a prescription drug or medical device entails a unique set of risks and benefits. What may be harmful to one patient may be beneficial to another. Under Subsection (c) [of Section 6] a drug is

defectively designed only when it provides no net benefit to any class of patients. . . . [M]anufacturers must have ample discretion to develop useful drugs and devices without subjecting their design decisions to the ordinary test applied to products generally. . . .[6]

The Restatement (Second) of Torts reflected a similar view of product liability for manufacturers of prescription drugs.[7] Nearly every jurisdiction in the United States has followed the reasoning of the Restatement (Second) in some form or another. For example, in a 1986 case, the plaintiff had contracted polio from the Sabin oral polio vaccine. The odds of contracting polio from the vaccine are one in a million. The Kansas Supreme Court held that harm resulting from the use of a drug would not give rise to

---

6. Restatement (Third) of Torts: Product Liability § 6 cmt. b (1997).

7. *See* Restatement (Second) of Torts § 402A cmt. k (1977).

strict liability if it was "unavoidably unsafe," if its benefits outweighed its dangers, and if proper warnings were given.[8]

The California legislature has gone beyond the prescription drug area to bar failure to warn claims against manufacturers and sellers of alcohol and other products intended for personal consumption. (The statute does not bar suits alleging a manufacturing defect or a breach of warranty.) In 1997, the law was amended to specifically deny its protections to manufacturers of tobacco products.[9]

Definition of Product

Strict liability in tort applies only to products, not services. What qualifies as a *product* is sometimes not clear. Courts that have addressed the definition-of-product question have required that the product giving rise to liability be a tangible item. In *Winter v. G.P. Putnam's Sons*,[10] the plaintiffs were mushroom enthusiasts who purchased a book entitled *The Encyclopedia of Mushrooms*, which was published by the defendant. The plaintiffs relied on descriptions in the book to determine which wild mushrooms were safe to eat, then became critically ill after eating a poisonous variety. The court rejected the plaintiffs' strict product liability claim because the "product" involved was a collection of ideas and expressions, not a tangible item. The court reasoned that a high value should be placed on the unfettered exchange of ideas and that the threat of strict liability on the contents of books could seriously inhibit that exchange.

Massachusetts extended this "tangible item" requirement to the promotion of a sport or game. The plaintiff in *Garcia v. Kusan, Inc.*,[11] was an elementary school student who was hit in the eye by a wayward stick in a physical education class floor hockey game. His claim was that Kusan marketed the sport of floor hockey to elementary schools and then sold them the equipment necessary to play. Garcia did not argue that the stick was defective; instead he argued that the game of floor hockey itself (as marketed by Kusan) was defective. Garcia referred the court to an old Kusan floor

hockey instruction manual, which stated that the game required no protective equipment. The court, citing the rationale of *Winter,* entered summary judgment for Kusan. It reasoned that a game—the concept and instructions—could not constitute a "product" that would give rise to product liability; the necessary "tangible item" was lacking.

Who May Be Liable

In theory, each party in the chain of distribution may be liable: manufacturers, distributors, wholesalers, and retailers. Manufacturers of component parts are frequently sued as well.

A manufacturer will be held strictly liable for its defective products regardless of how remote the manufacturer is from the final user of the product; the only requirement for strict liability in this instance is that the manufacturer be in the business of selling the injury-causing product. Thus, occasional sellers, such as people who host garage sales, are not strictly liable. The manufacturer may be held liable even when the distributor makes final inspections, corrections, and adjustments of the product. Wholesalers are usually held strictly liable for defects in the products they sell. However, in some jurisdictions a wholesaler is not liable for latent or hidden defects if the wholesaler sells the products in exactly the same condition that he or she received them.

A retailer may also be held strictly liable. For example, in the automobile industry, retailers have a duty to inspect and care for the products. There are several jurisdictions, however, where a retailer will not be liable if it did not contribute to the defect and played no part in the manufacturing process.

Sellers of used goods are usually not held strictly liable because they are not within the original chain of distribution of the product. In addition, the custom in

---

8. Johnson v. American Cyanamid Co., 718 P.2d 1318 (Kan. 1986).

9. CAL. CIV. CODE § 1714.45 (Deering 1997).

10. 938 F.2d 1033 (9th Cir. 1991).

11. 655 N.E.2d 1290 (Mass. App. Ct. 1995).

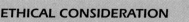
ETHICAL CONSIDERATION

Do publishers have an ethical obligation to warn readers that information in a book is not complete and should not be relied upon?

the used-goods market is that there are no warranties or expectations relating to the quality of the products (although some jurisdictions have adopted rules requiring warranties for used cars). A seller of used goods is, however, strictly liable for any defective repairs or replacements he or she makes.

A maker of component parts to manufacturer's specifications is not liable if the specifications for the entire product are questioned, because such a shortcoming is considered a design defect. For example, the maker of a car's fuel-injection system would not be liable if the automaker's specifications for the fuel-injection system turn out to be defective because the engine provides insufficient power to change lanes safely on a freeway. Makers of component parts are liable for manufacturing defects, however.

There is no strict liability in the service industries, only liability for negligence. In some cases it is unclear whether an injury was caused by a defective product or a negligently performed service. For example, a person may be injured by a needle used by a dentist or the hair solution used by a beautician. Some courts apply strict liability in these situations. Other courts will not go so far down the chain of distribution.

Successor Liability

A corporation purchasing or acquiring the assets of another is liable for its debts if there is (1) a consolidation or merger of the two corporations, or (2) an express or implied agreement to assume such obligations. There is also successor liability in situations where (1) the purchasing corporation is merely a continuation of the selling corporation, or (2) the transaction was entered into to escape liability.[12]

Thus, the acquiring corporation can be liable to a party injured by a defect in the transferor corporation's product. For example, a corporation that acquired all of a truck manufacturing company's assets was held liable for an injury caused by a defect in one of that company's trucks. The court reasoned that the new company was essentially a continuation of the predecessor corporation and that the acquiring corporation was in a better position to bear and allocate the risk than the consumer.[13]

Market-Share Liability

When there are multiple defendants, the injured party may not be able to prove which of the defendant manufacturers caused the injury. In certain cases, particularly those involving prescription drugs, the court may allocate liability on the basis of each defendant's share of the market. This doctrine of *market-share liability* was developed by the California Supreme Court in *Sindell v. Abbott Laboratories*[14] to address the specific problem of DES litigation.

Persons whose mothers took the drug diethylstilbestrol (DES) during pregnancy alleged that they were injured by the DES, which, among other things, increased their likelihood of developing cancer. They sought damages from a number of DES manufacturers. Many of the plaintiffs could not pinpoint which manufacturer was directly responsible for their injuries.

A number of factors made it difficult to identify particular DES manufacturers. All manufacturers made DES from an identical chemical formula. Druggists typically filled prescriptions from whatever stock they had on hand. During the 24 years that DES was sold for use during pregnancy, more than 300 companies had entered and left the market. The harmful effects of DES were not discovered until many years after the plaintiffs' mothers had used the drug. By the time the lawsuit was filed, memories had faded, records had been lost, and witnesses had died.

Given the difficulty of pinpointing the defendant responsible for each plaintiff, the court held that fairest way was to apportion liability based upon each manufacturer's national market share. The New York Court of Appeals followed California's lead in *Hymowitz v. Eli Lilly & Co*[15] The *Hymowitz* court stressed that "the DES situation is a singular case, with manufacturers acting in a parallel manner to produce an identical, generally marketed product, which causes injury many years later." Given this unusual scenario, the court reasoned, it was more appropriate that the loss be borne by those who produced the drug rather than those injured by it.

Market-share liability has been rejected in many jurisdictions. It has been criticized for being a simplistic response to a complex problem and for implying that manufacturers must be the insurers of all their industry's products.

---

12. Conway *ex rel.* Roadway Express, Inc. v. White Trucks, 639 F. Supp. 160 (M.D. Pa. 1986).

13. *Id.*

14. 607 P.2d 924 (Cal. 1980), *cert. denied*, 449 U.S. 912 (1980).

15. 539 N.E. 2d 1069 (N.Y. 1989).

Market-share liability has also been challenged on the constitutional ground that it violates the defendants' right to due process of law because it denies them the opportunity to prove that their individual products did not cause the plaintiff's injury.

 ## Defenses

The defendant in a product liability case may raise the traditional tort defenses of assumption of risk and, in some jurisdictions, a variation of comparative negligence known as comparative fault. In addition, other defenses, such as obvious risk, unforeseeable misuse of the product, the statute of limitations, the government-contractor defense, and the state-of-the-art defense, apply only to product liability cases. Finally, in certain circumstances state product liability law is preempted by federal law. Acceptance of the following defenses varies from state to state.

Comparative Fault

Contributory negligence by the plaintiff is not a defense in a strict liability action. However, the plaintiff's damages may be reduced by the degree to which his or her own negligence contributed to the injury. This doctrine is known as *comparative fault*.

Assumption of Risk

Under the doctrine of *assumption of risk*, when a person voluntarily and unreasonably assumes the risk of a known danger, the manufacturer is not liable for any resulting injury. For example, if a ladder bears a conspicuous warning not to stand on the top step, yet a person steps on it anyway and falls, the ladder manufacturer will not be liable for any injuries caused by the fall.

In a leading case in this area, a Washington appellate court found no assumption of risk when a grinding disc exploded and hit a person in the eye.[16] The court reasoned that although the injured person should have been wearing goggles, he could not have anticipated that a hidden defect in the disc would cause it to explode. By not wearing goggles, the injured person assumed only the risk of dust or small particles of wood or metal lodging in his eyes.

The following case addressed the issue of when an employee will be deemed to have assumed the risk of injury while working on the job.

---

16. Haugen v. Minnesota Mining & Mfg. Co., 550 P.2d 71 (Wash. Ct. App. 1976).

A CASE IN POINT	SUMMARY

CASE 10.4
VANCOPPENOLLE v. KAMCO INDUSTRIES, INC.
Court of Appeals of Ohio
1997 WL 679631 (Ohio Ct. App. Oct. 31, 1997).

FACTS   VanCoppenolle worked for a company that manufactured carpet-covered, molded plastic automobile trunk inserts. Her work included recycling old trunk inserts. A machine manufactured by Kice Metal Products Company, Inc. was used in the recycling process. It separated the plastic from the carpet. VanCoppenolle was injured while cleaning carpet fuzz from the Kice machine; she sued Kice on a product liability theory.

The trial court dismissed VanCoppenolle's claim on the ground that she had assumed the risk of her injury.

ISSUE PRESENTED   Is assumption of risk a viable defense against an employee injured by a defective product in the employment setting?

SUMMARY OF OPINION   The Ohio Court of Appeals first noted that assumption of risk is not a valid defense against an employee injured by a defective product in the employment setting if (1) the job duties require the employee to encounter the risk, and (2) the employee is injured while engaging in normal job-related tasks.

In this case, however, the court found VanCoppenolle to have acted in contravention of clear safety procedures outlined by her employer. The court noted that

Case 10.4 continues

Case 10.4 continued

VanCoppenolle had been provided with a machine manual, which specified that carpet fuzz was to be pushed out of the machine with a metal rod. VanCoppenolle also testified that she knew the correct procedure was to use a rod. At the time she was injured, VanCoppenolle was cleaning fuzz from the machine with her bare hands.

In light of this, the court ruled that VanCoppenolle's job duties did not require her to encounter the risk of injury. Rather, her testimony "supported the proposition that [she] voluntarily exposed herself to known risk." As a result, Kice could raise a valid assumption-of-risk defense.

RESULT   The appeals court affirmed the trial court's summary judgment for Kice.

© 1998 Ted Goff. *Used by permission.*

Obvious Risk

If the use of a product carries an *obvious risk*, the manufacturer will not be held liable for injuries that result from ignoring the risk. Often a plaintiff will argue that the manufacturer had a duty to warn of the dangers of a foreseeable use of the product. Courts often apply the standard that a manufacturer need not warn of a certain danger if that danger is generally known and recognized.

For example, *Maneely v. General Motors Corporation*[17] involved two men who were riding in the cargo bed of a pickup truck and were seriously injured in a collision. The men sued General Motors (GM), the manufacturer of the truck, for failure to warn of the dangers of riding in a cargo bed. The court rejected their claims, noting that, at some point, manufacturers must be relieved of the paternalistic responsibility of warning users of every possible risk that could arise from the use of their product. The court felt the public recognized the dangers of riding unrestrained in the cargo bed of a moving pickup truck; therefore, GM had no duty to warn of those dangers.

Unforeseeable Misuse of the Product

A manufacturer or seller is entitled to assume that its product will be used in a normal manner. The manufacturer or seller will not be held liable for injuries resulting from abnormal use of its product. However, an unusual use that is reasonably foreseeable may be considered a normal use.

For example, operating a lawn mower with the grass bag removed was held to be a foreseeable use, and the manufacturer was liable to a bystander injured by an object that shot out of the unguarded mower.[18] However, the alteration and misuse of fertilizer to create the bomb used in the 1993 terrorist bombing of the World Trade Center in New York were held not to be "objectively foreseeable" by fertilizer manufacturers. As a result, the owner of the World Trade Center could not hold fertilizer manufacturers liable for failing to use additives to make it more difficult to turn their products into explosives.[19]

Statute of Limitations

A *statute of limitations* is a time limit, defined by the statute, within which a lawsuit must be brought. Ordinarily, the statute of limitations starts to run at the time

---

17. 108 F.3d 1176 (9th Cir. 1997).

18. LaPaglia v. Sears Roebuck & Co., 531 N.Y.S.2d 623 (N.Y. App. Div. 1988).
19. Port Authority of New York & New Jersey v. Arcadian Corp., 991 F. Supp. 390 (D.N.J. 1998).

a person is injured. There are, however, exceptions. In many cases of injuries caused by exposure to asbestos, for example, the plaintiff did not become aware of the injury until after the statute of limitations had run out. This led to the adoption of *discovery-of-injury* statutes, which generally provide that the statute of limitations for asbestos cases does not begin to run until the person discovers the injury from exposure to asbestos.

For prenatal injuries caused by the drug DES, *revival statutes* have been enacted that allow plaintiffs to file lawsuits that had been barred previously by the running of the statute of limitations. DES manufacturers have argued that the revival statutes violate their right to due process of law. The manufacturers have also argued that their right to equal protection of the laws has been violated because the revival statutes typically designate only a few substances, such as DES or asbestos, but not other dangerous chemical substances. They claimed that this categorization was without sufficient basis and that it was the result of political compromise. Nevertheless, most courts hold that state revival statutes have a rational basis and that legislatures enacting such statutes are acting within their broad discretion.[20]

Many statutes of limitations have been amended to define more precisely when a cause of action arises. For example, the Ohio statute provides:

- An asbestos cause of action arises when the claimant learns or should have realized that he was injured by exposure to asbestos, whichever is earlier.
- An Agent Orange type cause of action involving exposure of a veteran to chemical defoliants or herbicides arises when the claimant learns that he was injured by the exposure.
- A DES cause of action arises when the claimant learns from a physician that her injury might be related to DES exposures or when she should have realized she had such an injury, whichever is earlier.[21]

Government-Contractor Defense

Under the *government-contractor defense*, a manufacturer of products under contract to the government can avoid product liability if (1) the product was produced according to government specifications; (2) the manufacturer possessed less knowledge about the specifications than did the government agency; (3) the manufacturer exercised proper skill and care in production; and (4) the manufacturer did not deviate from the specifications. The rationale for this immunity is that the manufacturer is acting merely as an agent of the government and to hold the manufacturer liable would unfairly shift the insurance burden from the government to the manufacturer.

Preemption Defense

Perhaps the most significant and controversial of the defenses to product liability is the *preemption defense*. Certain federal laws and regulations set minimum safety standards for products. For example, the National Traffic and Motor Vehicle Safety Act sets standards for auto manufacturers, and the Safe Medical Devices Act sets standards for the manufacture of medical devices. Manufacturers that meet those standards will sometimes be granted immunity from product liability claims, which are based on state law. The rationale is that the federal regulatory scheme preempts state product liability law; allowing states to impose 50 different sets of requirements would frustrate the purpose of a uniform federal scheme.

Manufacturing groups want preemption to serve as a "silver bullet" defense, effectively eliminating the possibility of state law product liability claims in any sphere governed by federal safety law and regulation. Commenting on a recent medical-device case before the Supreme Court, one of the manufacturers' most vocal representatives put the argument this way: "What it boils down to is whether we want to have the experts at the FDA tells us what is a safe pacemaker, or do we want each jury designing its own pacemaker—one doing it one way in Brooklyn and one doing it another way in Missouri?"[22]

In practice the preemption defense is not the sweeping tool manufacturing groups want it to be. Instead, its availability depends closely on the language and context of the federal statute at issue. In recent years, courts have struggled to determine whether federal safety statutes preempt state product liability claims involving tobacco, faulty medical devices, and automobiles without air bags.

20. *See, e.g.*, Hymowitz v. Eli Lilly & Co., 539 N.E.2d 1069 (N.Y. 1989), *cert. denied*, 493 U.S. 944 (1989).

21. OHIO REV. CODE ANN. § 2305.10 (Anderson 1997).

22. Paul M. Barrett, *Lora Lohr's Pacemaker May Alter Liability Law*, WALL ST. J., Apr. 9, 1996, at B1 (quoting Victor Schwartz).

The following case resolved the question of whether "no air bag" claims were preempted in Pennsylvania, at least until the U.S. Supreme Court specifically addresses the issue. A discussion of recent U.S. Supreme Court decisions examining preemption in tobacco and medical-device cases follows.

| **A CASE IN POINT** | **IN THE LANGUAGE OF THE COURT** |

CASE 10.5
CELLUCCI v. GENERAL MOTORS CORP.
Supreme Court
of Pennsylvania
706 A.2d 806
(Pa. 1998).

FACTS Daniel Cellucci suffered serious brain injuries when the 1986 Chevrolet Cavalier in which he was a passenger went off the road and collided with a tree. The Cavalier was equipped with three-point lap and shoulder harness safety belts and a dashboard warning light and buzzer, which were designed to promote occupant use of manufacturer-installed seat belts.

Cellucci brought an action against the manufacturer of the vehicle, General Motors (GM), claiming that he was wearing his seat belt at the time of the accident but that the Cavalier was defectively designed because air bags were not installed in it. In response, GM filed a motion for partial summary judgment contending that federal law preempts Cellucci's claim that the vehicle was defective because it did not have air bags. The trial court denied GM's motion. GM appealed to the superior court. The *en banc* superior court reversed the trial court and held that the National Traffic and Motor Vehicle Safety Act of 1996 (the Safety Act) impliedly preempted Cellucci's air bag claim. Cellucci appealed.

The court consolidated the Cellucci suit with a similar suit filed against Volvo by Susan Muntz, who was injured in a vehicle without an air bag, and her husband. The intermediate appellate court had held that the Muntzes' claim was not preempted by the Safety Act.

ISSUE PRESENTED Does the Safety Act preempt state tort claims based upon a manufacturer's failure to equip a vehicle with air bags?

OPINION CASTILLE, J., writing for the Pennsylvania Supreme Court:

The United States Congress enacted the Safety Act in order "to reduce traffic accidents and deaths and injuries to persons resulting from traffic accidents." The preemption clause of the Safety Act provides:

> Preemption.—
> (1) When a motor vehicle safety standard is in effect under this chapter, a State or a political subdivision of a State may prescribe or continue in effect a standard applicable to the same aspect of performance of a motor vehicle or motor vehicle equipment only if the standard is identical to the standard prescribed under this chapter. . . .
> (2) A State may enforce a standard that is identical to a standard prescribed under this chapter.

However, the Safety Act also provides that "compliance with a motor vehicle safety standard prescribed under this chapter does not exempt a person from liability at common law."

Case 10.5 continues

Case 10.5 continued

Pursuant to the powers which are authorized under the Safety Act, the Secretary of Transportation promulgated three safety options for occupant crash protection of passenger vehicles at Federal Motor Vehicle Safety Standard 208. For cars manufactured in 1985 and 1986, such as the vehicles at issue, Standard 208 provided that a manufacturer had the option for occupant restraint systems to equip the vehicle with (1) a complete passive restraint system for front and lateral crashes, (2) passive restraints for frontal crashes plus lap belts, shoulder harnesses and a warning system, or (3) a three-point manual seat belt with a warning system. Both of the vehicles at issue in this appeal had three-point manual seat belts and a warning system installed.

GM and Volvo argue that since they complied with one of the three safety options promulgated pursuant to the Safety Act, the common law tort claims raised by Cellucci and the Muntzes related to the failure of their cars to have air bags or other type of passive restraint systems (collectively, "no air bag" claims) are preempted by the Safety Act. Conversely, Cellucci and the Muntzes argue that Congress never intended for the Safety Act to preempt such claims. This Court's resolution of this dispute depends on an analysis of federal preemption law. . . .

The United States Supreme Court has held that federal preemption of state law can occur (1) where Congress explicitly preempts a state law, (2) where a state law actually conflicts with federal law, and (3) where Congress has implicitly indicated an intent to occupy a given field to the exclusion of state law.

The first line of analysis this Court will undertake is whether the Safety Act explicitly preempts the "no air bag" claims at issue. Here, Congress did not make explicit reference to state common law tort actions in the express preemption provision of Section 30103(b) of the Safety Act. However, Congress, in Section 30103(e), enacted a separate provision in the Safety Act authorizing common law liability. Therefore, when sections 30103(b) and (e) are read together, this Court finds that the intent of Congress is too ambiguous to conclude that common law actions such as the ones raised in these two matters were intended to be explicitly preempted. Accordingly, this Court holds that the Safety Act does not explicitly preempt common law actions concerning GM and Volvo's failure to install air bags or other passive restraint systems.

Since we concluded that the Safety Act does not explicitly preempt the state common law tort claims at issue, this Court must determine if Congress intended to impliedly preempt such claims. As noted above, Congress may have impliedly intended to preempt state common law actions where the state law conflicts with federal law. [As the United States Supreme Court has stated,] "a conflict will be found 'when it is impossible to comply with both state and federal law, or where the state law stands as an obstacle to the accomplishment of the full purposes and objectives of Congress.'" The United States Supreme Court has interpreted "stands as an obstacle" to mean that: "[a] state law also is preempted if it interferes with the methods by which the federal statute was designed to reach this goal." Thus, the seminal question is whether the state common law tort claims raised here conflict with the meth-

Case 10.5 continues

Case 10.5 continued

ods formulated under the Safety Act to achieve the goal of reducing deaths and injuries to people arising from traffic accidents.

Here, Cellucci and the Muntzes first assert that no conflict exists between the
Safety Act and their state common law tort claims because such claims do not inter-
fere with the three passive restraint options promulgated by the Secretary of Trans-
portation pursuant to the Safety Act in order to achieve the stated purpose of the
Safety Act: to reduce deaths and injuries arising from traffic accidents. As the United
States Court of Appeals for the Ninth Circuit has stated:

> the Safety Act does not mandate safety standards at any cost, but only those safety stan-
> dards determined by the Secretary of Transportation to be "reasonable, practicable and
> appropriate." Pursuant to Congress' direction, the Secretary considered and rejected a
> safety standard requiring airbags. In doing so, the Secretary considered, inter alia, the in-
> creased safety achieved by airbags as well as their cost. As members of the judiciary, we
> are not in a position to second-guess the Secretary's decision.

Moreover, the United States Senate published a report on the National Traffic
and Motor Vehicle Safety Act in which it stated that "the centralized, mass production, high-volume character of the motor vehicle manufacturing industry in the
United States requires that motor vehicle safety standards be not only strong and
adequately enforced, but that they be uniform throughout the country." Thus, since
Congress gave manufacturers three passive restraint options to choose from and indicated that such options must be uniform throughout the country, any state liability claim that deviates from allowing a manufacturer to use any of the three options
that Congress allowed conflicts with the Safety Act and the regulations promulgated
under it.

Cellucci and the Muntzes argue that the state common law tort claims at issue
do not impose any burden on the manufacturers which are additional to that of the
Safety Act. However, to argue that no conflict exists between allowing common law
liability for "no air bag" claims and the Safety Act fails. To assert that the common
law does not compel manufacturers to install certain types of passive restraints disregards the reality of the situation since "an automobile manufacturer faced with the
prospect of choosing the [passive restraint options], or facing potential exposure
to compensatory and punitive damages for failing to do so, has but one realistic
choice."

Thus, this Court finds that to allow common law liability where, as here, the underlying claims are that either an air bag or a different passive restraint system should
have been installed "frustrates the goals of the federal regulatory framework and undermines the flexibility that Congress and the Department of Transportation intended to give to automobile manufacturers in this area."

RESULT   The Pennsylvania Supreme Court held that the state product liability claims
asserted by Cellucci and the Muntzes were preempted by the Safety Act and dismissed them.

The *Cellucci* court noted that its decision was in line with most courts that have addressed the preemptive effect of the Safety Act. Courts in seven states, however, have ruled that "no air bag" claims are *not* preempted by the Safety Act (Arizona, California, Florida, Indiana, Missouri, New Hampshire, and Ohio). Despite this conflict, as of early 1998 the U.S. Supreme Court had yet to grant *certiorari* on this issue.

In light of the U.S. Supreme Court's recent preemption decisions in the context of other products, the fact that state courts are split on the "no air bag" cases should not be surprising. In *Cipollone v. Liggett Group, Inc.* (a 1992 decision), the Court found that Congress intended the Public Health Cigarette Smoking Act of 1969 to have a broad preemptive effect.[23] In particular, the Court held that the act preempted claims based on a failure to warn and the neutralization of federally mandated warnings to the extent that those claims relied on omissions or inclusions in a tobacco company's advertising or promotions. However, the Court ruled that the act did not preempt claims based on express warranty, intentional fraud and misrepresentation, or conspiracy. Four years later, in *Medtronic, Inc. v. Lohr,* the Court examined similar statutory language in the Medical Device Amendments of 1976 and found no preemption.[24]

Medtronic involved a pacemaker that the Food and Drug Administration (FDA) had cleared for distribution under a statutory provision requiring premarket notification for some types of medical devices. In the wake of the Court's decision, the FDA in December 1997 proposed regulations to clarify its position on preemption. The thrust of these regulations is that neither (a) an FDA grant of premarket approval nor (b) an investigational device exemption from approval constitutes the establishment of device-specific federal requirements. Therefore, neither of these actions should trigger preemption of state common law suits.

Medtronic makes it clear that compliance with a regulatory scheme is not always a valid defense. However, the more rigorous the regulatory process, the more likely that product liability claims will be preempted. In *Medtronic,* Medtronic's pacemaker was not closely scrutinized by the FDA: it had received an exemption from thorough review because it was deemed "substantially equivalent" to pacemakers already on the market. The fact that the pacemaker had not undergone rigorous regulatory examination was an important factor in the Court's decision not to preempt product liability claims against Medtronic.[25]

State-of-the-Art Defense

The *state-of-the-art defense* shields a manufacturer from liability if no safer product design is generally recognized as being possible. State courts have split over how to analyze this defense, on two grounds. First, states have differed in their definition of "state of the art." Some states have defined state-of-the-art evidence either in terms of industry custom (e.g., Alaska and New Jersey) or in terms of compliance with existing governmental regulations (e.g., Illinois).[26] The majority of states, however, deem state-of-the-art to refer to what is technologically feasible at the time of design. Accordingly, a manufacturer may have a duty to make products pursuant to a safer design even if the custom of the industry is not to use that alternative.[27]

States have also split on whether the state-of-the-art defense is available in design defect cases. Some courts have ruled that state-of-the-art evidence is irrelevant in strict product liability cases because it improperly focused the jury's attention on the reasonableness of the manufacturer's conduct. Other courts have made state-of-the-art evidence a complete defense to a design-defect claim. The overwhelming majority of states, though, hold that state-of-art evidence is simply relevant to determining the adequacy of the product's design. As the Connecticut Supreme Court concluded, "state of the art is a relevant factor in considering the adequacy of the design of a product and whether it is in a defective condition unreasonably dangerous to the ordinary consumer."[28]

The contours of the state-of-the-art defense are often first laid down by judges, then codified by state legislatures. This is especially true with respect to failure-to-warn claims. For example, an Indiana statute provides: "It is a defense that the design, manufacture,

23. 505 U.S. 504 (1992).
24. 518 U.S. 470 (1996).

25. This interpretation is supported by the FDA's recent proposal of regulations that serve to clarify its position.
26. *See* Potter v. Chicago Pneumatic Tool Co., 694 A.2d 1319, 1345–46 (Conn. 1997) (Case 10.6).
27. *Id.* at 1347.
28. *Id.*

IN BRIEF

BASES FOR PRODUCT LIABILITY AND DEFENSES

THEORY OF LIABILITY	DEFENSES
Breach of Warranty	No privity of contract
Negligence	Defendant used reasonable care
	Contributory or comparative negligence
Strict Liability in Tort	Unavoidably unsafe product
	Comparative fault (only reduces damages)
	Assumption of risk
	Obvious risk
	Abnormal misuse
	Government contractor
	Preemption
	State of the art

inspection, packaging, warning, or labeling of the product was in conformity with the generally recognized state of the art at the time the product was designed, manufactured, packaged, and labeled."[29] A Missouri statute provides that if the defendant can prove that the dangerous nature of the product was not known and could not reasonably be discovered at the time the product was placed in the stream of commerce, then the defendant will not be held liable for failure to warn.[30]

 ## Legislative Developments

Legislative reforms are developing in response to larger jury awards, perceived inconsistent treatment of litigants, and the insurance crisis of the 1980s, which made it prohibitively expensive or impossible to obtain product liability insurance in some industries.

Statutes of Repose

A *statute of repose* cuts off the right to assert a cause of action after a specified period of time from the delivery of the product or the completion of the work. The statute of repose is different from a statute of limitations, in which the time period is measured from the time when the injury occurred. Thus, under a statute of repose, if the repose period is 10 years, a person injured 11 years after the product was delivered would be time-barred from suing by the statute of repose, though not by the statute of limitations.

Statutes of repose have usually been upheld on the ground that they serve some legitimate state purpose, such as encouraging manufacturers to upgrade their products. Absent a statute of repose, a manufacturer might not upgrade, out of fear that upgrading might be seen as an admission that the earlier version was inadequate.

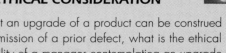
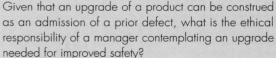

ETHICAL CONSIDERATION

Given that an upgrade of a product can be construed as an admission of a prior defect, what is the ethical responsibility of a manager contemplating an upgrade needed for improved safety?

---

29. IND. CODE ANN. § 33-1-1.5-4.5 (Michie 1997).

30. MO. REV. STAT. § 537.764 (1996).

Limitations on Punitive Damages

Large awards of punitive damages have been criticized for providing windfalls to injured parties far in excess of their actual losses and for motivating plaintiffs and their lawyers to engage in expensive and wasteful litigation rather than settling the case.

In response to these criticisms, 25 states enacted legislation limiting punitive damages awards between 1986 and 1989. By August 1997, the number of states with such legislation had increased to 31. These reforms have typically taken three basic forms. Some states have placed limits on when punitive damages are available or have required a higher standard of evidence (such as clear and convincing evidence rather than a mere preponderance of evidence) before punitives will be awarded. For example, in 1997 North Dakota passed a law requiring plaintiffs to prove oppression, fraud, or actual malice before claiming punitive damages. Other states have placed outright caps on punitive damages (Georgia, for instance, caps punitives at $250,000) or have tied punitive damages to compensatory damages (such as Florida's limitation that punitives cannot exceed three times compensatory damages). Finally, a few states, such as New Hampshire, have banned punitive awards altogether.

Codification of Defenses

As discussed in the previous section, an injured person's conduct can be the basis for a defense to a strict liability action. Several states have enacted statutes to codify such defenses, that is, to add them to the code of laws, that courts must follow.

Plaintiff's Negligence   Michigan law provides that the negligence of the plaintiff does not bar recovery, but damages are reduced by his or her degree of fault—that is, the negligence attributed to the plaintiff.[31] Under Illinois law, if the jury finds that the degree of the plaintiff's fault exceeds 50%, then the plaintiff cannot recover damages. If the jury finds that the degree of the plaintiff's fault is less than 50%, the plaintiff can recover damages, but the damages will be reduced in proportion to the plaintiff's fault.[32]

Assumption of Risk   Under Ohio law, if the claimant's express or implied assumption of risk is the direct and proximate cause of harm, recovery is completely barred.[33]

Misuse of Product   Unforeseeable misuse or modification is a defense under Indiana law if it is the proximate cause of the harm and the misuse or modification is not reasonably expected by the seller at the time the seller conveyed the product to another party.[34]

Limitations on Nonmanufacturer's Liability

Rather than holding all companies in the chain of distribution liable, many states limit the liability of nonmanufacturers. For example, a Minnesota statute provides that once an injured person files a claim against the manufacturer of the product, the court must dismiss the strict liability claim against any other defendants. A nonmanufacturer can be held strictly liable, however, if it was involved in the design or manufacture of the product or provided instructions or warnings about the defect, or if it knew of or created the defect. The nonmanufacturer may also be held strictly liable if the manufacturer is no longer in business or if it cannot satisfy a judgment against it.[35]

An Illinois statute provides that an action against a defendant other than the manufacturer will be dismissed unless the plaintiff can show that (1) the defendant had some control over the design or manufacture of the product, or instructed or warned the manufacturer about the alleged defect; (2) the defendant actually knew of the defect; or (3) the defendant created the defect.[36]

Limitations on Joint Liability

Traditionally, all defendants in a strict liability action were held jointly and severally liable. Each defendant was held liable not only for the injuries it severally—that is, individually—caused, but also for all of the injuries caused by all of the defendants jointly.

Many states have placed limits on joint and several liability. In fact, as of August 1997, three states had

---

31. Mich. Comp. Laws § 600.2959 (1997).

32. 735 Ill. Comp. Stat. Ann. 5/2-1116 (Michie 1997).

33. Ohio Rev. Code Ann. § 2315.20 (Anderson 1997).

34. Ind. Code Ann. § 33-1-1.5-4 (Michie 1997).

35. Minn. Stat. § 544.41 (1997).

36. 735 Ill. Comp. Stat. Ann. 5/2-621 (Michie 1997).

passed legislation either abolishing joint liability altogether or restricting its application. (Also, Tennessee abolished joint liability in 1992 by a court decision.) An Oregon statute, for example, provides:

> Liability of each defendant for non-economic damages is several, not joint. Liability of a defendant who is less than 15% at fault for economic damages is several only. Liability of a defendant who is 15% or more at fault for the economic damages is joint and several, except that a defendant whose fault is less than the plaintiff's is liable only for that percentage of the recoverable economic damages.[37]

Penalties for Frivolous Suits

Some states have enacted penalties to deter frivolous lawsuits. For example, a Wisconsin statute provides that if a claim or defense is found to be frivolous, the prevailing party can be awarded its legal costs and attorney's fees.[38] Minnesota and South Dakota passed similar legislation in 1997.

Attempts to Pass Federal Legislation

As described in the "Political Perspective" in Chapter 9, at the same time the states have been actively reforming their tort and product liability systems, Congress has had no success passing uniform federal legislation. President Clinton's veto of the Common Sense Product Liability Legal Reform Act of 1996 was a major blow to those seeking a congressional overhaul of product liability law.

In 1997, the 105th Congress set out to accomplish what the 104th could not. Representative Slade Gorton (R-Wash.) introduced new legislation—which became known as the Product Liability Reform Act of 1997 (S. 648)—that was based largely on the 1996 act vetoed by the President. After introducing the new bill, however, Gorton handed the reins to Senator J. D. Rockefeller (D-W.Va.), a leading party advocate of product liability reform, to broker a compromise that both the president and Republican leaders could accept. But this change in strategy brought about no immediate change in result.

Despite President Clinton's 1996 campaign promise to sign meaningful product liability legislation, his negotiating stance with Rockefeller and Gorton was rigid throughout 1997. By early 1998, it had become clear that the president would accede only to small, piecemeal measures (such as a cap on punitive damages that applied only to small-business defendants). He would not approve two measures valued highly by Republicans: a uniform ban on joint liability and an 18-year statute of repose that would cover virtually all manufactured products. In turn, Republican congressional leaders voiced determination to pass a sweeping reform of the product liability system or nothing at all. As of early 1998, they seemed content to highlight their differences with the president and thereby make product liability reform a congressional election-year campaign issue.

 ## Tobacco and Guns

One of the most dramatic applications of product liability law has been the lawsuits against tobacco companies for illness, death, and medical expenses resulting from the use of tobacco or from secondhand smoke. The "Inside Story" discusses this in detail.

Gun-control advocates have begun using a similar strategy in an effort to hold gun manufacturers liable for violence involving guns.[39] Results to date have been mixed.

For example, in a two-to-one split decision, the U.S. Court of Appeals for the Second Circuit dismissed a negligence case against Olin Corporation by victims of the December 7, 1993, shooting on a Long Island Railroad commuter train.[40] The shooter had used a 9mm handgun loaded with Olin's Black Talon ammunition, which has razor-sharp edges designed to rip and tear through a victim's body, to kill 6 people and wound 19 others. The court rejected the plaintiffs' arguments that Olin was negligent in marketing the Black Talon bullets to the general public. Dissenting judge Guido Calabresi stated that there was no question that Olin's marketing of Black Talons created an unreasonable risk that the public would be harmed and that their sale was the legal cause of the victims' severe injuries. Judge Calabresi

---

37. OR. REV. STAT. § 18.485 (1995).

38. WIS. LAWS § 814.025 (1996).

39. Many of the arguments for holding gun manufacturers liable are set forth in the Web page for the Center to Prevent Handgun Violence's Legal Action Project, <http://www.handguncontrol.org>.

40. McCarthy v. Olin Corp., 119 F.3d 148 (2d Cir. 1997).

argued that the case should have been referred to the New York Court of Appeals for its determination of whether Olin owed these victims a duty not to market the Black Talons even though the bullets had not been banned in the state of New York.

In contrast, a federal district court in Illinois permitted a suit by the families of two Chicago police officers gunned down with a TEC-DC9 assault pistol to proceed against the manufacturer Navegar, Inc., on the theory that Navegar created a public nuisance when it made a weapon with no legitimate sporting or self-defense use that had the sole purpose of killing and injuring human beings. Based in part on this case, the city of Philadelphia is reportedly considering suing the gun industry for creating a public nuisance to recoup the public costs associated with gun violence incurred by the city. Such a suit would be patterned after the suits brought against tobacco companies by state attorneys general seeking to recoup medical expenses associated with smoking.

 ## Problems with the System

The product liability scheme that has evolved has increasingly been criticized because of the financial burden it imposes on industry. The cornerstone of the scheme is the assumption that manufacturers are in the best position to insure against loss or to spread the risk of loss among their customers. Nevertheless, the costs to manufacturers—huge jury awards and high insurance premiums—have been enormous. Moreover, manufacturers often find it difficult to obtain an insurance policy that does not include a substantial deductible, which the manufacturer must pay. Sometimes insurance is not available at all, and companies have to pay all claims themselves. This leads to higher manufacturing costs.

The product liability scheme also takes its toll on industry efficiency and competitiveness. Companies have become unwilling to invest in product creation or modification because this is seen as an admission of guilt. In most jurisdictions, a modification of a product is admissible as evidence of the product's prior defective condition. Companies find themselves in Catch-22 situations: Failure to remedy a defect may expose the company to punitive damages, but remedying the defect may expose the company to compensatory damages in subsequent suits.

Restatement (Third) of Torts: Product Liability

Informed by these concerns, the American Law Institute (ALI) recently completed its effort to synthesize current case law of product liability. The ALI is a body of lawyers and law professionals that periodically undertakes efforts to produce a restatement of various subject areas of the law (such as agency, contracts, property). These restatements provide judges and lawyers with a comprehensive view of the status of American case law (drawn from a survey of courts throughout the country) and the rationale behind it. The restatements are, of course, infused with their drafters' vision of the way that particular area of the law should evolve.

Such is the case with the Restatement (Third) of Torts: Product Liability, which the ALI approved in May 1997 after five years of discussion and debate. The new Restatement proposes bold changes in the doctrine of product liability. Most importantly, it requires that any claim of design defect be supported by a showing of a reasonable alternative design. The effect of this change is to move away from strict liability for defectively designed products. (The new Restatement avoids using the term *strict liability* altogether.) Instead, the reasonable-alternative-design requirement forces plaintiffs to prove that defendants acted wrongly or negligently in choosing an improper design.

In many respects, those who failed in their ardent attempts to push tort and product liability reform through Congress saw their ideas embodied in the new Restatement. Indeed, the most vocal critics of the Restatement (Third) charged that the effort had been captured by defense attorneys seeking to accomplish through the ALI what they could not on Capitol Hill.

As noted earlier, no court is bound by the Restatement's formulation of product liability law. As of early 1998, few courts had even cited the "reasonable alternative design" requirement—the cornerstone of the Restatement (Third) approach. Two intermediate appellate courts in New Jersey did follow the Restatement's reasoning in 1997 decisions.[41] However, the only state supreme court to grapple with the "reasonable alternative design" proposal explicitly rejected it. That case follows.

---

41. *See* Congiusti v. Ingersoll-Rand Co., 702 A.2d 340 (N.J. Super. Ct. App. Div. 1997); Grzanka v. Pfeifer, 694 A.2d 295 (N.J. Super. Ct. App. Div. 1997).

CASE 10.6
POTTER v. CHICAGO
PNEUMATIC TOOL CO.
Supreme Court
of Connecticut
694 A.2d 1319
(Conn. 1997).

FACTS   John Potter and his fellow plaintiffs were shipyard workers injured in the course of their employment at a General Dynamics Corporation electric-boat facility as a result of using pneumatic tools manufactured by the defendants. The plaintiffs used the tools to chip, grind, and smooth metal surfaces at General Dynamics for approximately 25 years. They developed permanent vascular and neurological impairment of their hands, which caused blanching of their fingers, pain, numbness, reduction of grip strength, and intolerance of cold. Consequently, the plaintiffs were unable to continue their employment as grinders and their ability to perform other activities was restricted.

The plaintiffs claimed that (1) the tools were defectively designed because they exposed the plaintiffs to excessive vibration, and (2) the defendants failed to provide adequate warnings about the potential danger of excessive vibration.

The jury found for the plaintiffs. The defendants appealed and the case went directly to the Connecticut Supreme Court.

ISSUE PRESENTED   Are plaintiffs in a defective-design suit required to support their claim by demonstrating the existence of a reasonable alternative design?

OPINION   KATZ, J., writing for the Connecticut Supreme Court:

We first address the defendants' argument that the trial court improperly failed to render judgment for the defendants notwithstanding the verdicts because there was insufficient evidence for the jury to have found that the tools had been defectively designed. Specifically, the defendants claim that, in order to establish a prima facie design defect case, the plaintiffs were required to prove that there was a feasible alternative design available at the time that the defendants put their tools into the stream of commerce. We disagree.

. . .

Although courts have widely accepted the concept of strict tort liability, some of the specifics of strict tort liability remain in question. In particular, courts have sharply disagreed over the appropriate definition of defectiveness in design cases. As the Alaska Supreme Court has stated: "Design defects present the most perplexing problems in the field of strict products liability because there is no readily ascertainable external measure of defectiveness. While manufacturing flaws can be evaluated against the intended design of the product, no such objective standard exists in the design defect context."[42]

Section 402A [of the Restatement (Second) of Torts] imposes liability only for those defective products that are "unreasonably dangerous" to "the ordinary consumer who purchases it, with the ordinary knowledge common to the community as to its characteristics." Under this formulation, known as the "consumer expectation" test, a manufacturer is strictly liable for any condition not contemplated by the ultimate consumer that will be unreasonably dangerous to the consumer.

Case 10.6 continues

---

42. Caterpillar Tractor Co. v. Beck, 593 P.2d 871, 880 (Alaska 1979).

Case 10.6 continued

[Some jurisdictions apply a competing approach:] a balancing test that inquires whether a product's risks outweigh its benefits. Under [this test], otherwise known as the "risk-utility" test, the manufacturer bears the burden of proving that the product's utility is not outweighed by its risks in light of various factors. . . .

With this history in mind, we turn to the development of strict products liability law in Connecticut. . . .

This court has long held that in order to prevail in a design defect claim, "the plaintiff must prove that the product is unreasonably dangerous." We have derived our definition of "unreasonably dangerous" from comment (i) to § 402A, which provides that "the article sold must be dangerous to an extent beyond that which would be contemplated by the ordinary consumer who purchases it, with the ordinary knowledge common to the community as to its characteristics." This "consumer expectation" standard is now well established in Connecticut strict products liability decisions.

The defendants propose that it is time for this court to abandon the consumer expectation standard and adopt the requirement that the plaintiff must prove the existence of a reasonable alternative design in order to prevail on a design defect claim. We decline to accept the defendants' invitation.

In support of their position, the defendants point to the second tentative draft of the Restatement (Third) of Torts: Products Liability (1995) (Draft Restatement [Third]), which provides that, as part of a plaintiff's prima facie case, the plaintiff must establish the availability of a reasonable alternative design. Specifically, § 2 (b) of the Draft Restatement (Third) provides: "[A] product is defective in design when the foreseeable risks of harm posed by the product could have been reduced or avoided by the adoption of a reasonable alternative design by the seller or other distributor, or a predecessor in the commercial chain of distribution, and the omission of the alternative design renders the product not reasonably safe." The reporters to the Draft Restatement (Third) state that "very substantial authority supports the proposition that [the] plaintiff must establish a reasonable alternative design in order for a product to be adjudged defective in design."

We point out that this provision of the Draft Restatement (Third) has been a source of substantial controversy among commentators. . . . Contrary to the rule promulgated in the Draft Restatement (Third), our independent review of the prevailing common law reveals that the majority of jurisdictions do not impose upon plaintiffs an absolute requirement to prove a feasible alternative design.

. . . Our research reveals that, of the jurisdictions that have considered the role of feasible alternative designs in design defect cases: (1) six jurisdictions affirmatively state that a plaintiff need not show a feasible alternative design in order to establish a manufacturer's liability for design defect; (2) sixteen jurisdictions hold that a feasible alternative design is merely one of several factors that the jury may consider in determining whether a product design is defective; (3) three jurisdictions require the defendant, not the plaintiff, to prove that the product was not defective; and (4) eight jurisdictions require that the plaintiff prove a feasible alternative design in order to establish a prima facie case of design defect.

Case 10.6 continues

Case 10.6 continued

In our view, the feasible alternative design requirement imposes an undue burden on plaintiffs that might preclude otherwise valid claims from jury consideration. Such a rule would require plaintiffs to retain an expert witness even in cases in which lay jurors can infer a design defect from circumstantial evidence. Connecticut courts, however, have consistently stated that a jury may, under appropriate circumstances, infer a defect from the evidence without the necessity of expert testimony.

Moreover, in some instances, a product may be in a defective condition unreasonably dangerous to the user even though no feasible alternative design is available. In such instances, the manufacturer may be strictly liable for a design defect notwithstanding the fact that there are no safer alternative designs in existence. . . . Accordingly, we decline to adopt the requirement that a plaintiff must prove a feasible alternative design as a sine qua non to establishing a prima facie case of design defect.

RESULT   Though the Connecticut Supreme Court did not require the plaintiffs to support their claim by demonstrating the existence of a reasonable alternative design, it vacated the jury verdict and ordered a new trial on separate grounds. Specifically, it found that General Dynamics, the plaintiffs' employer, had substantially modified the pneumatic tools prior to their use by the plaintiffs.

Questions

1. Would the adoption of the reasonable-alternative-design standard eviscerate strict liability for defective products and replace it with a negligence standard?
2. Should a plaintiff injured by a defective product be prevented from reaching a jury until he or she can provide an expert who outlines an alternative way to design that product?

 ## Product Liability in the European Union

Differences between the product liability laws of states within the European Union (EU) created two major problems. First, there was uncertainty as to what the applicable law was. This uncertainty was harmful to both the consumer and the manufacturer of the product. Second, competition was distorted within the EU because liability and the severity of financial repercussions varied from one nation to another. The need for a uniform product liability directive was recognized.

The Council of Ministers of the EU adopted a product liability directive in July 1985, after nearly a decade of debate. The directive was intended to provide increased consumer protection and to harmonize competitive conditions within the EU.[43] In 1995, the European Commission decided to leave the directive unchanged, rejecting the urging of consumer groups to strengthen the liability provisions.[44]

The directive's basic purpose is to hold manufacturers or producers strictly liable for injuries caused by defects in their products. This purpose represents a fundamental change for manufacturers of products marketed in Europe. Traditionally, in most of the 12 member states, an injured consumer had to prove both negligence and privity of contract in order to recover damages from the producer of a defective product. Only France had previously imposed strict product liability.

---

43. 1985 O.J. (L 210) 29.

44. Robert Rice, *Business and the Law: A Question of Safety—The European Union's Product Liability Legislation,* FINANCIAL TIMES, Jan. 16, 1996, at 13.

Comparison with U.S. Strict Liability

The EU product liability directive is quite similar to the strict liability doctrine prevalent in the United States. In order to recover damages, an injured party has to prove that there was a defect, an injury, and a causal relationship between the defect and the injury. (Plaintiffs may also sue under the traditional negligence and contract laws of the EU member states.) In determining whether a product is defective, the courts in the EU countries, like those in the United States, consider such factors as the product's foreseeable uses and the instructions and warnings provided by the manufacturer. The directive does not apply to services, which remain governed solely by national law.

The available defenses are similar to those available in the United States. For example, a manufacturer will not be liable if (1) the manufacturer did not put the product into circulation; (2) the defect did not exist when the product went into circulation; (3) the product was a component that was neither manufactured nor distributed by the manufacturer of the overall product; or (4) the defect was due to compliance of the product with mandatory regulations. The manufacturer of a component part will not be liable if the defect was attributable to the design of the product into which the component was fitted.

The directive includes a statute of limitations and a statute of repose. An injured person must sue within three years of when he or she knew, or should have known, of the injury, the defect, and the manufacturer's identity. A manufacturer's liability will be extinguished 10 years after the product was put into circulation, unless the injured party has commenced proceedings in the meantime. Thus, as in some states in the United States, a defect that does not become apparent until 11 years after the product went into circulation may leave the injured person without a remedy. Most EU member states previously had statutes of repose with a 30-year period.

Unlike in the United States, a supplier or wholesaler is not strictly liable unless the injured party is unable to identify the manufacturer. In such an instance, the supplier can escape liability by informing the injured person of the manufacturer's identity.

The directive provides for a "development risks" or state-of-the-art defense. A producer can escape liability by proving that the state of scientific knowledge when the product went into circulation was insufficient to allow it to discover the defect. This provision is controversial because it introduces an element of fault, which is precisely what the strict liability doctrine attempts to exclude. The initial directive required the Council of Ministers to consider whether to repeal the state-of-the-art defense in 1995; as stated above, the council chose to leave this defense, as well as the remainder of the directive, unchanged.

It should be noted that importers of products into the EU are strictly liable under the directive. Thus, U.S. exporters may be required to indemnify overseas importers. U.S. exporters should carry product liability insurance and adhere to EU safety standards.

Implementation by Member States

Member states were required to implement the provisions of the directive by July 1988, but more than a decade after the initial adoption of the directive, implementation struggles continued. The directive contains three provisions that are optional. States can choose whether to (1) allow the development-risks defense described above, (2) impose a cap on damages of not less than 55 million British pounds (approximately $90 million), and (3) exclude all agricultural products from liability under the law.

As of early 1996, all member countries except Finland, Luxembourg, and Norway had elected to allow the development-risks defense. Only Germany, Greece, Portugal, and Spain have imposed any cap on damages. Agricultural products were excluded from product liability in all countries except Luxembourg and Sweden.

France has not enacted any portion of the directive. It claims that its preexisting product liability law is more strict than that required by the directive, and French courts appear to be interpreting French national law in accordance with the directive.[45]

Despite suffering a setback in the European Commission's 1995 decision not to modify or strengthen the directive, consumer organizations continued to argue that the laws of member states needed to be harmonized and that liability standards needed to be raised. In October 1997, in light of separate outbreaks of mad cow disease, *E. coli*, and salmonella, the commission adopted an amendment to the 1985 directive that would extend product liability to cover agricultural products. The commission took the action to help restore consumer confidence in the safety of agricultural products; it set a target date of January 1, 1999, for adoption by member states. Commentators, however, expect opposition from agricultural lobbies to be vigorous and predict that few states will enact new legislation before the target deadline.[46]

---

45. Christopher Hodges, *The EC's 1995 Review of the Product Liability Directive*, LLOYD'S PRODUCT LIABILITY INT'L, Feb. 29, 1996, at 19.

46. Celia Hampton, *Product Liability: EU Farm Produce; Market Access*, BUS. L. EUROPE, Oct. 14, 1997, at 8.

THE RESPONSIBLE MANAGER
Reducing Product Liability Risk

Managers have the responsibility to minimize their company's exposure to liability in the design, manufacture, assembly, and sale of its products. They should implement a product-safety program in order to ensure that products are sold in a legally safe condition. They also have an obligation to discover and correct any defects in the product. The goal should be to prevent accidents. If an accident does occur, evidence of a product-safety program is crucial for limiting the manufacturer's liability for punitive damages.

To protect against potential liabilities, managers should implement internal loss-control procedures, obtain insurance protection, and seek the advice of product liability counsel from the earliest stages of product development.

Managers should check the safety of their products both in their intended use and in reasonably foreseeable misuse. Managers should develop adequate instructions and comprehensive warnings. They should consider the reasonably foreseeable risks of using the product, ways to avoid those risks, and the consequences of ignoring the risks. Managers may find it helpful to follow industry standards; but sometimes a company must break new ground and go beyond what the industry has done in the past.

Managers should have a thorough understanding of all statutes, regulations, and administrative rulings to which a product must conform. Failure of the product to comply with any of these rules will typically be deemed a product defect. Mere conformance with these rules is considered a minimum requirement, however, and does not automatically release a manufacturer from liability.

Managers should keep internal records of their product engineering and manufacturing decisions. These records should include design specifications, design-failure tests, and safety reviews. Managers should monitor the product at every stage of production. The records must indicate that the design process was carefully considered; the records must include more than the mere suggestions or ruminations of employees.

Companies should be careful how they advertise and warrant their products. In product liability litigation, the overall impression of such representations may be criticized by opposing counsel. Careless advertising may even lead to product misuse, resulting in an injury for which the manufacturer will be liable.

Managers should continuously monitor field reports of injuries caused by both use and misuse of their company's products. Appropriate reaction to such information may bear on the issue of punitive damages.

Managers have a postsale duty to warn of any hazards of which they have become aware, even if the product was initially thought to be safe. This duty may simply require sending a letter to purchasers of the product. Or it may require providing the purchaser with a corrective device. In addition to updating consumers on product safety concerns, some jurisdictions require management to inform its consumers of technological advances or safety improvements. Section 15 of the Consumer Product Safety Act[47] imposes substantial product-safety reporting requirements. It requires management to notify an administrative agency if a product does not comply with applicable product-safety rules or if it contains a defect that could create a "substantial risk of injury to the public."

Managers should ensure that their products are performing as intended over the lives of the products and that the products have as little adverse effect on the environment as possible under current technology. It is helpful to establish a product-safety committee and to conduct regular safety audits in order to identify and correct problems. The advice of experienced counsel can be helpful in this area.

---

47. 15 U.S.C. § 2064 (1997).

INSIDE STORY

TOBACCO LITIGATION STILL SMOKING

The American tobacco industry generates annual revenue of nearly $50 billion. Health experts estimate that each year the industry's products claim the lives of 425,000 smokers.

Nevertheless, prior to 1995, the tobacco industry enjoyed virtual immunity from legal liability for its products. Before 1995, the industry had never paid a penny to settle a smoking-related lawsuit. Only one jury had awarded a plaintiff damages for injuries caused by tobacco products. The family of Rose Cipollone (a victim of lung cancer) won $400,000 in a 1988 jury trial. But even that victory was short-lived. The U.S. Court of Appeals for the Third Circuit quickly reversed the jury's decision. And by the time the U.S. Supreme Court ordered a new trial in 1992, the Cipollones had decided to bow out.

ABC's Exposé, Then Apology

This air of legal invincibility still surrounded the tobacco industry when it launched a highly publicized counterattack on the ABC television network and its news magazine *Day One*.

In February 1994, *Day One* aired a series alleging that tobacco companies regularly "spike" their cigarettes with nicotine. The broadcasts opened a national debate over the broad question of whether the cigarette industry artificially controlled nicotine levels to keep smokers hooked. Philip Morris immediately filed a mammoth $10 billion libel lawsuit against ABC. Philip Morris seized on the *Day One* assertion that a powerful tobacco extract containing nicotine and flavor was provided by outside suppliers and added as a filler. Instead, Philip Morris insisted, it merely added back nicotine that gets taken out of the filler in the course of the manufacturing process.[48]

ABC responded to the suit by announcing publicly that it stood by its story. After sifting through two million pages of tobacco industry documents in pretrial discovery, however, ABC's lawyers felt they could not sufficiently support the *Day One* account of nicotine extract coming from outside suppliers. As a result, the network made a stark turnabout: It agreed to issue a public apology to Philip Morris (broadcast on *ABC World News Tonight* and *Monday Night Football*) and to pay the tobacco maker $15 million to cover its legal fees.

The tobacco industry and its lawyers congratulated themselves heartily. Accounts had Philip Morris attorneys stopping a victory party to crank up the volume as the announcers on *Monday Night Football* read the apology. As it turned out, this was to be their high-water mark. Ironically, although ABC backed down in the face of a legal battle with the tobacco industry, it was precisely the allegations that *Day One* pursued—that tobacco makers altered the level of nicotine in their cigarettes—that would torment the industry in the courtroom and legislative arenas for years to come.

The Liggett Settlement

A watershed event occurred in March 1996, when the Liggett Group, the smallest of the five U.S. tobacco companies, settled what was at the time the largest lawsuit hanging over the industry. The settlement's significance lay in the fact that it marked the first time a cigarette maker assumed financial responsibility for tobacco-related diseases and deaths. Liggett's move was a stunning break from the rest of its industry.

As Liggett's controlling shareholder, Bennett LeBow, commented at the time, "For the past 10 years, on this litigation front, Liggett has pretty much been following everybody. If Philip Morris said jump, we jumped."[49] Anticipating the rationale that the industry's heavy-hitters would adopt in years to come, Liggett saw no reason to keep spending $10 million a year on legal fees if there was a way to settle and thereby control its liability.

The Liggett deal consisted of three primary features. First, the company settled lawsuits with the attorneys general of four states seeking recoupment of their smoking-related health-care costs. Second, Liggett agreed to phase in compliance with proposed FDA regulations designed to curb underage smoking, without conceding the FDA's authority to regulate tobacco. Finally, Liggett settled its portion of the *Castano* case, a class action suit against cigarette makers on behalf of smokers nationwide. (The outcome and impact of *Castano* is discussed following.)

Under the settlement, Liggett agreed to pay an annual maximum of 12% of its pretax income, which at that time was approximately $11 million. Thus the amount of money Liggett would contribute was not exorbitant (no more than $1.3 million annually), and none of it went to individual smokers (the *Castano* funds were to pay for smoking-cessation programs). Nevertheless, cracks in the tobacco industry's once impenetrable line of defense had been revealed. In addition, the internal documents furnished by Liggett in the years since the settlement added greatly to the efforts of

tobacco foes. The documents have helped establish that cigarette makers long knew of nicotine's addictive effect and deliberately increased the level of nicotine in their cigarettes to keep smokers hooked.

Castano and Subsequent Private Litigation

The legal opponents of the tobacco industry began their current assault in March 1994 with the filing of a huge class action suit in a Louisiana federal district court. The suit was revolutionary, both for its potential size and for the

"More nicotine."

widespread collaboration of plaintiff's attorneys it represented. It reflected the efforts of almost 60 law firms. Named *Castano* after the lead plaintiff, the suit was filed on behalf of every allegedly addicted smoker in the United States.

In March 1995, the class was certified by the district court. As previously discussed, Liggett deemed the potential liability from this suit to be so great that it was driven to settle its portion. Just months after that settlement, however, the U.S. Court of Appeals for the Fifth Circuit rejected the class action approach, reasoning that the issues raised by different state laws and the difficulty of assessing the addictions of individual class members made it impractical to collapse tobacco litigation into one federal class action.[50] This May 1996 ruling changed the landscape of the legal struggle significantly. The prospect of one centralized battle in federal court gave way to a fragmented series of suits in the state courts.

After *Castano*, the legal assault on the tobacco industry took three distinct forms. The first was an attempt to certify class action lawsuits in state courts, where the class would consist of every allegedly addicted smoker in that state. This effort is still ongoing. As of early 1998, plaintiff's lawyers had gained certification for a Louisiana class action and had failed in a similar effort in Pennsylvania.

The second form was the continued filing of traditional suits on behalf of individual plaintiffs or smaller classes of plaintiffs. In individual cases, the industry's record had remained remarkably good, reflecting the fact that its traditional defense—that smokers bear responsibility for their decision to light up—continues to resonate with juries. In August 1996, the industry suffered just its third-ever setback when a Jacksonville, Florida, jury ordered Brown & Williamson to pay $750,000 to Grady Carter, a 66-year-old Florida man who began smoking in 1947 at the age of 17. Plaintiff's attorney Woody Wilner gained national attention for successfully presenting to the jury evidence from Brown & Wil-liamson internal documents that suggested tobacco executives had long understood the addictiveness of nicotine and manipulated its content in cigarettes.

Wilner won again in June 1998, when another Jacksonville jury awarded the family of a deceased smoker, Roland E. Maddox, $500,000 in compensatory damages plus $450,000 in punitive damages. But later that month, the Florida appeals court reversed the verdict in the Carter case, using language that called into question the Maddox verdict.[51]

But at the same time tobacco companies were successfully defending suits on behalf of individual smokers, they were forced to acknowledge a new legal threat— the claims of victims of secondhand smoke. In October 1997, the major cigarette companies settled a class action suit brought by flight attendants who alleged they were harmed by secondhand smoke on airline flights. Many criticized the deal on the grounds that the plaintiffs' lawyers received a $49 million fee but obtained little of value for their clients. The tobacco companies agreed to establish a $300 million fund for research on smoking illnesses, but not a cent went directly to individual plaintiffs. They were relegated to proving their claims against the industry case-by-case, and the settlement gave the industry immunity from punitive damages in those cases. The terms of the deal aside, many experts predicted that the industry's decision to settle would serve as an invitation to narrow, well-defined class action suits brought on behalf of individuals claiming illness from regular exposure to cigarette smoke in a confined workplace.

In the first lawsuit blaming secondhand smoke for a person's death to reach trial, a six-person jury in Indiana ruled in March 1998 that cigarette manufacturers were not liable for the death of a nonsmoking nurse. The jurors concluded that cigarettes were not a defective product and that the tobacco companies were not negligent for failing to tell people that secondhand smoke was dangerous.[52]

State Lawsuits and the Universal Settlement

Certainly, the potential liability the industry could face as a result of statewide class actions (the progeny of *Castano*) and suits brought by individuals or narrow, well-defined classes is significant. However, the dollar amounts involved in such cases to date have been dwarfed by the staggering, multibillion-dollar sums being negotiated between cigarette makers and the individual states.

As the Liggett deal indicated, certain states had undertaken as early as 1995 to recover smoking-related health-care costs in lawsuits filed against the industry. Attorneys general in 40 states had filed such cases. The threat of virtually unlimited liability from the state suits, plus the specter of ongoing liability from the individual and class action suits, finally drove the cigarette makers into an effort to negotiate an all-encompassing settlement. Throughout the first half of 1997, tobacco lawyers met with representatives of the attorneys general and the group of lawyers who initiated the *Castano* litigation. They addressed four primary issues: (1) the amount of money the industry would pay to the states; (2) ways to control the industry's potential liability in future lawsuits; (3) the scope of the FDA's authority to regulate tobacco; and (4) what to do about teen smoking.

In June 1997, the negotiators emerged to announce a "universal" settlement. The tobacco makers would pay $368.5 billion to help cover health-care costs and issue warning labels declaring cigarettes addictive; in return, the state attorneys general would drop their current suits, and the industry would get protection from future claims. Also, curbs would be placed on the FDA's ability to regulate nicotine, and tobacco companies would agree to pay penalties if teen-smoking rates did not drop below specified levels.

Because federal legislation was required to curtail the FDA's authority and to impose the teen-smoking fees, congressional approval was required. In March 1998, Senate Commerce Committee Chairman John McCain (R-Ariz.) unveiled a bill that would increase tobacco-industry payments to $506 billion over 25 years, permit the FDA to regulate nicotine, and limit the industry's protection from private suits. The industry rejected the proposed amendments to the settlement previously reached with the states.

Nevertheless, the promise of a comprehensive settlement seemed to spur the tobacco industry to prevent any of its ongoing cases from reaching a courtroom verdict. In July and August 1997, the industry settled suits with Mississippi and Florida for an aggregate $15.3 billion before either case went to trial. The tobacco makers also settled the flight attendants' secondhand-smoke case and a case brought by California residents challenging the use of Joe Camel advertisements, both in late 1997. In January 1998, the industry gave the state of Texas $15 billion—the richest legal settlement in American history—to drop a health-care-cost-recovery suit just weeks into trial. Finally, the case brought by the state of Minnesota was settled in May 1998 for $6.1 billion.

Throughout early 1998, the industry continued to suffer embarrassment from the release of internal memoranda clearly demonstrating tobacco executives' knowledge of nicotine addictiveness and, worse yet, their determination to target advertisements at children as young as age five to ensure a future market for their cigarettes. The stream of damning documents put the tobacco industry in a bad light.

The Senate rejected an ambitious antitobacco bill in June 1998. As of July 1998, the major cigarette makers were negotiating with several state attorneys general a proposed settlement of the remaining state suits for $200 billion.[53] No congressional approval would be required, but the proposed settlement would not affect the FDA's ability to regulate tobacco or ban class-action lawsuits.

---

48. Alix Freedman et al., *Why ABC Settled with the Tobacco Industry*, WALL ST. J., Aug. 24, 1995, at B1.

49. Alix Freedman et al., *Breaking Away: Liggett Group Offers First-Ever Settlement of Cigarette Lawsuits*, WALL ST. J., Mar. 13, 1996, at A1.

50. Castano v. American Tobacco Co., 84 F.3d 734 (5th Cir. 1996).

51. Milo Geyelin & Ann Davis, *Verdict Against Tobacco Firm Is Reversed*, WALL ST. J., June 23, 1998, at A3.

52. Suein L. Hwang, *Jury Finds Tobacco Firms Not Liable in a Pivotal Secondhand Smoke Case*, WALL ST. J., Mar. 20, 1998, at A3.

53. Suein L. Hwang, *Tobacco Takes New Stab at a Settlement*, WALL ST. J., July. 10, 1998, at B1.

KEY WORDS AND PHRASES

assumption of risk   **344**

comparative fault   **344**

design defect   **337**

discovery-of-injury statute   **346**

failure to warn   **337**

government-contractor defense   **346**

manufacturing defect   **337**

market-share liability   **343**

obvious risk   **345**

preemption defense   **346**

privity of contract   **333**

product liability   **322**

revival statute   **346**

state-of-the-art defense   **350**

statute of limitations   **345**

statute of repose   **351**

unavoidably unsafe product   **341**

QUESTIONS AND CASE PROBLEMS

1. A product may be deemed unreasonably dangerous as a result of a manufacturing defect, a design defect, or a failure to warn. Explain the differences between the three types of defects.

2. How many times does it take for a misuse of a product to become a hazard about which a warning must be given? When does the obligation to warn actually stop?

3. SemiCorp manufactures electronic components, including a pressure sensor. SemiCorp publishes a catalog that gives the specifications of the sensor and suggests uses ranging from automobile emission systems to medical instruments. SemiCorp sells the sensors through an independent distributor.

SureBeat Company buys sensors from the distributor and uses them in pacemaker devices. Dr. Art Cardi implanted a SureBeat pacemaker in one of his patients, Ed Goodheart. The pacemaker sensor failed while Goodheart was water-skiing, and he drowned.

a. Who is subject to liability for Goodheart's death?

b. Does the plaintiff's attorney need an expert to prove that the pacemaker is defective?

c. What arguments can the defense raise to avoid liability? To reduce damages?

d. As risk manager of SemiCorp, do you recommend the issuance of a warning to customers? A product recall? Both?

4. Assume the facts of Question 3. Breath Company, a medical start-up company, tested a few of the sensors manufactured by SemiCorp as a component to control an alarm in a new product: a life-support respirator for use on patients in intensive-care and cardiac-care units of hospitals. Breath Company's business plan projected profits of $10 million from sales of the respirator over the next three years. Breath Company bought 500 sensors at $20 each from the distributor and built 100 respirators.

Just before Breath Company began selling respirators, SemiCorp was sued by Ed Goodheart's widow. SemiCorp also learned that an automobile manufacturer had tested the sensors for use in emission-control systems and rejected them as too unreliable. An internal audit of SemiCorp reported that the sensor production facility did not follow all of the company's internal quality control standards.

While SemiCorp's management evaluated the economics of the medical market for sensors, Breath Company delivered the 100 respirators to hospitals at $20,000 each. These were soon hooked up to patients as life-support systems. It had orders for 100 more. Two months later, SemiCorp issued a warning that its sensors were not suitable for medical life-support systems. After it had delivered 50 of the additional respirators, Breath Company actually received the warning from the distributor.

Breath Company recalled all 150 respirators, tested and selected a reliable $100 sensor from another source, and began to reintroduce the respirator six months later. Meanwhile, Life Company, a competitor, introduced a similar respirator. Breath Company's efforts to reintroduce the respirator fell short of its business plan and, after a loss of $5 million, the company shut its doors.

a. As attorney for Breath Company, what warranty and tort theories of liability would you plead against SemiCorp?

b. What torts would allow Breath Company recovery of damages for the following?

1. The $10,000 cost of the SemiCorp sensors

2. The loss of the $5 million investment

3. The current value of the $10 million profit projected by the business plan
4. Punitive damages

c. As counsel for SemiCorp, what arguments would you advance to avoid liability altogether? To limit damages?

5. Terrell Redman, senior vice-president of Alligator Corporation, is evaluating a potential acquisition for the company. The entity he wishes to acquire has several divisions, two of which manufacture chemicals and industrial tools.

a. What risks does the acquisition present to Alligator Corporation under product liability law?
b. Are there ways to limit the company's exposure?
c. To the extent that product liability law will expose the company to liability for the acquired company's prior conduct, what steps must be taken at the time of the acquisition to ensure the ability to defend potential claims? [*Tolo v. Wexco*, 993 F.2d 884 (9th Cir. 1993)]

6. What factors should a court consider in deciding whether a common law tort action for failure to install anti-lock brakes in a tractor-trailer truck is preempted by the National Traffic and Motor Vehicle Safety Act? [*Taylor v. General Motors Corp.*, 875 F.2d 816 (11th Cir. 1989), *as modified by Myrick v. Freuhauf Corp.*, 13 F.3d 1516 (11th Cir. 1994)]

7. Many states have laws regulating sales that impose an implied warranty of merchantability to the effect that the merchandise is fit for consumer use. Should the same durational limit that is provided buyers by express warranties by the manufacturer be applied to implied warranties? [*Carlson v. General Motors Corp.*, 883 F.2d 287 (4th Cir. 1989), *cert. denied*, 495 U.S. 910 (1990)]

8. Richard Welge loves to sprinkle peanuts on his ice cream sundaes. One day Karen Godfrey, with whom Welge boards, bought a 24-ounce vacuum-sealed plastic-capped glass jar of peanuts at a convenience store in Chicago. In order to obtain a $2 rebate that the manufacturer was offering to anyone who bought a "party" item, such as peanuts, Godfrey needed proof of her purchase from the jar of peanuts. Using an Exacto knife, she removed the part of the label that contained the bar code. She then placed the jar on top of the refrigerator. About a week later, Welge removed the plastic seal from the jar, uncapped it, took some peanuts,

replaced the cap, and returned the jar to the top of the refrigerator, all without incident.

A week later, Welge took down the jar, removed the plastic cap, spilled some peanuts into his left hand to put on his sundae, and replaced the cap with his right hand. But as he pushed the cap down on the open jar, the jar shattered. His hand was severely cut and is now, he claims, permanently impaired.

Welge has brought suit and has named three defendants: the convenience store, the manufacturer of the peanuts, and the manufacturer of the jar itself.

a. From whom will Welge be able to recover?
b. What defenses, if any, are available to the defendants? [*Welge v. Planters Lifesavers Co.*, 17 F.3d 209 (7th Cir. 1994)]

9. Darleen Johnson was driving her Ford car under rainy conditions on a two-lane highway through Missouri. The car's front tires had a reasonable amount of tread remaining on them, but the back tires were nearly bald. For an undetermined reason, Johnson lost control of the car, spun into the other lane, and collided with a pickup truck driven by Kathyleen Sammons. Johnson was killed instantly.

Johnson's father claimed that the inboard C.V. joint boot on the front axle was torn, which allowed debris to contaminate the joint. (The boot is a covering that contains the grease that lubricates the joint.) This contamination allegedly made the joint act like a brake on the left front wheel and caused Johnson's car to pivot around that wheel and into the path of the oncoming pickup truck.

Ford admits that the joint boot can become torn, which will allow contamination of the joint. In its manuals, Ford recommends periodic inspection of the boots. However, Ford contends that the joint on Johnson's car was contaminated during or after the accident. Ford also contends that contamination of the joint could not result in the joint seizing and creating a loss of steering control, and that the worst that could result from contamination would be some vibration and noise. According to Ford, Johnson's accident was caused by road conditions and driving error.

The case is submitted to the jury on theories of strict liability and negligent design and manufacture.

a. Is Ford liable for Johnson's death?
b. Are there any additional arguments that Ford can raise in its defense?
c. Who will prevail in this case? [*Johnson v. Ford Motor Co.*, 988 F.2d 573 (9th Cir. 1993)]

MANAGER'S DILEMMA

10. You are a product manager at Beak, Inc., a company that manufactures construction equipment. The head of your department, Kimura Kim, recently received a visit from the company's CEO, who described for Kim a problem with the performance of Beak's Titan cranes. Apparently, the hook portion of the crane has broken off on several occasions, resulting in the release of the object being moved. As yet, no serious injuries have resulted from the accidents. Research by the company's engineering department indicates that the problem occurs only when the cranes are used at full capacity on windy days and could be eliminated by reinforcing certain joints on the crane. The CEO is considering various alternatives, including doing nothing; sending a letter to all owners of the crane warning them not to use the crane at full capacity on windy days; recalling the cranes to make the adjustment; and changing the design of the cranes to incorporate the reinforcements. Recalling the cranes would involve a cost to Beak of approximately $100 million. Changing the design of the cranes would require retooling a significant portion of the company's equipment at a cost of $50 million.

Kim asks you to draft a memo outlining Beak's possible liability for injuries resulting from operation of the cranes and recommending a course of action designed to minimize that liability. Draft that memo, paying particular attention to the liability implications of each alternative course of action and the company's ethical responsibilities to its customers.

INTERNET SOURCES

The U.S. Consumer Product Safety Commission's page provides information about recent recalls and other agency activity.	http://www.cpsc.gov
The Federal Trade Commission's page provides information about its enforcement actions, consumer protection, and its regional offices.	http://www.ftc.gov
The Better Business Bureau's page provides consumers with information about its private regulation of business, including recent warnings and local offices.	http://www.bbb.org
The International Organization for Standardization's page provides information about its attempt to create various technical and product standards for business and government.	http://www.iso.ch
This site includes almost 39,000 documents subpoenaed by the House Commerce Committee from the tobacco industry.	http://www.house.gov/commerce/TobaccoDocs/documents.html
This site, maintained by the tobacco industry, promotes a universal settlement.	http://www.tobaccoresolution.com

CHAPTER 11

Intellectual Property

INTRODUCTION

Strategic Importance of Intellectual Property

Intellectual property is any product or result of a mental process that is given legal protection against unauthorized use. Different types of intellectual property are protected in different ways. Properly protected, intellectual property can give a firm a strategic competitive advantage.

A *patent* is a government-granted right to exclude others from making, using, or selling an invention. The patent holder need not personally make use of the invention. After a period of time (20 years from the application date for utility patents and 14 years for design patents in the United States), the patent expires and the invention is dedicated to the public.

A *copyright* is the legal right to prevent others from copying the original expression embodied in a literary work, musical work, sound recording, audiovisual work, sculptural work, pictorial work, computer program, or any other work of authorship fixed in a tangible medium. The protection also extends to derivative works, that is, works based upon the protected work. It is the expression that is protected, not the ideas underlying the expression. The owner also has exclusive rights to distribute, display, and perform the work. Protection is provided for at least 50 years.

Trademarks—that is, words or symbols (such as brand names) that identify the source of goods or services—are also given legal protection. Because trademarks tend to embody or represent the goodwill of the business, they are not legally transferable without that goodwill. Trademarks are protected for an indefinite time. They can be valuable marketing and business assets.

Trade secrets are another valuable form of intellectual property in today's world economy. A *trade secret* is information that gives a business an advantage over its competitors who do not know the information. The classic example of a trade secret is the formula for Coca-Cola. Trade secrets are protected for an indefinite time.

Know-how—that is, detailed information on how to make or do something—can be a trade secret or it can be show-how. *Show-how* is nonsecret information used to teach someone how to make or do something. It is generally not legally protectable.

Chapter Overview

This chapter describes the law of patents, copyrights, trademarks, and trade secrets in detail. It also discusses technology licensing, that is, the selling of permission to use a patented invention, a copyrighted work, a trade secret, or a trademark.

 Patents

Patents are one of the oldest recognized forms of intellectual property. Their importance has increased as our

society has become more technologically advanced. Texas Instruments, for example, received $391 million from patent royalties in 1992 on net revenues of $7.4 billion. Patents have formed the basis for whole businesses, such as the production of instant cameras, and industries, such as high-engineering plastics and biotechnology. Patent disputes have become one of the battlegrounds on which high-technology battles are fought.

Patent protection is specifically authorized by Article I of the U.S. Constitution. The Constitution grants Congress the power "to promote the Progress of Science and useful Arts, by securing for limited times to . . . Inventors the exclusive Right to their . . . Discoveries." U.S. patent law provides for three types of patents: utility patents, design patents, and plant patents.

Utility Patents

Utility patents are the most frequently issued type of patent. A *utility patent* protects any novel, useful, and nonobvious process, machine, manufacture, or composition of matter, or any novel, useful, and nonobvious improvement thereof. If the U.S. Patent and Trademark Office (PTO) issues a patent, the patent owner has the exclusive right to make, use, sell, and import for use the invention for a nonrenewable period of 20 years from the date on which the patent application was filed.

An invention is *novel* if it was not anticipated, that is, if it was not previously known or used by others in the United States and was not previously patented or described in a printed publication in any country. For instance, the PTO awarded patent 5,471,373 to four individuals who invented a lollipop holder that offers a light-and-music show with each lick. The lollipop holder has a switch in its handle that activates an integrated circuit that plays songs and flashes lights at the face of the person eating the candy.

Even if the invention is novel, it will be denied patent protection if its novelty merely represents an obvious development over *prior art*, that is, existing technology. That was the concern of two New Yorkers who applied for a patent for their device to remove garbage bags blown into tree branches. Although similar to the fruit picker, invented in 1869, the "bag-snagger" was found sufficiently different to warrant a separate patent.

The inventor must be diligent in his or her effort to file for patent protection. A *statutory bar* precludes protection in the United States if, prior to one year before the inventor's filing, the invention was described in a printed publication in the United States or a foreign country or if it was publicly used or sold in the United States. In most other countries, a patent application must be filed *before* the invention is described in a publication, publicly used, or sold.

Even when the inventor files promptly for protection of a novel, useful, and nonobvious invention, he or she may still be denied a patent. There is no protection for nonstatutory subject matter, such as abstract ideas (rather than specific applications of ideas), methods for doing business, mental processes, naturally occurring substances, arrangements of printed matter, scientific principles, or laws of nature.

Some commentators have suggested that some sports moves are potentially patentable. Under such thinking, patent contenders might include Pete Gogolak's soccer-style placekicking in American football, former Giant manager Roger Craig's split-fingered fastball in baseball, and Dick Fosbury's backward high-jumping first introduced at the 1968 Olympics (a.k.a. the Fosbury flop).[1]

Biotechnology   One of the most controversial applications of the patent law has been championed by the biotechnology industry. As the following Supreme Court case demonstrates, living organisms, if they are humanmade, can be patented.

---

1. *Can't Touch This?* SAN JOSE MERCURY NEWS, June 25, 1996, at 1E.

| **A CASE IN POINT** | **SUMMARY** |

CASE 11.1
DIAMOND v. CHAKRABARTY
Supreme Court of the United States
447 U.S. 303 (1980).

FACTS   In 1972, Ananda Chakrabarty, a microbiologist, filed a patent application related to his invention of a humanmade, genetically engineered bacterium that is capable of breaking down crude oil. Because no naturally occurring bacteria possess this property, Chakrabarty's invention was believed to have significant value for the treatment of oil spills.

Case 11.1 continues

Case 11.1 continued

The patent examiner rejected the patent application for the bacterium. The Patent Office Board of Appeals affirmed the examiner's decision on the ground that living things are not patentable. After various appeals, the U.S. Supreme Court agreed to hear the case.

ISSUE PRESENTED   Is a live, humanmade microorganism patentable subject matter under the U.S. patent laws?

SUMMARY OF OPINION   The issue before the U.S. Supreme Court was whether Chakrabarty's bacterium constituted a "manufacture" or "composition of matter" within the meaning of Section 101 of Title 35 of the United States Code. That section provides that the types of inventions that are patentable include "any new and useful process, machine, manufacture, or composition of matter, or any new and useful improvement thereof." In its decision, the Supreme Court did not attempt to determine into which of the categories the new bacterium fell.

The Court concluded that, though a previously unknown natural organism that is merely discovered cannot be patented, an organism that is created by a person can be. Chakrabarty's bacterium is markedly different from any organism found in nature. It does not fall into the nonpatentable categories of a law of nature, a physical phenomenon, or an abstract idea. It is the result of human ingenuity and research into a wholly new technology. Stating that the patent statutes should include "anything under the sun that is made by man," the Supreme Court extended patent protection to Chakrabarty's new organism.

RESULT   The Supreme Court held that a live, humanmade microorganism is patentable subject matter.

COMMENTS   This case demonstrates the dramatic economic effects that can occur because of developments in the law. The Supreme Court prophetically noted that its decision to allow the patent of Chakrabarty's bacterium could determine whether research efforts would be accelerated by the hope of reward or slowed by the want of incentives. In fact, the Chakrabarty decision spawned a whole new industry. It allowed small biotechnology firms to attract venture capitalists and other investors. It spurred investment in commercial genetic-engineering research. The very existence of some biotechnology firms can be traced to the *Chakrabarty* decision.

In 1987, PTO Commissioner Donald Quigg issued a notice that non-naturally occurring, non-human multicellular living organisms (including animals) are patentable subject matter. The PTO issued a patent in 1988 on a transgenic mouse that was engineered to be susceptible to cancer. It issued three more mouse patents in 1993.

In April 1998, a cellular biologist filed a patent application on a technique for combining human and animal embryo cells to produce a single animal-human embryo. The embryo could then be transplanted into a human or animal surrogate mother to develop into a two-species mixture or chimera. In response, the PTO issued a media advisory entitled "Facts on Patenting Life Forms Having a Relationship to Humans." The advisory stated that inventions directed at a human/non-human chimera could, under certain circumstances, not be patentable because they would fail to meet the public policy and morality aspects of the utility requirement. PTO Commissioner Bruce Lehman stated that the advisory was necessary to make clear that "there will be no patents on monsters, at least not while I'm commissioner."

ETHICAL CONSIDERATION

What ethical issues are raised by efforts to patent the process for creating a chimera? Should an inventor be allowed to patent the process for making human clones?

Computer Software   The law's embrace of software patenting began in 1981, when the Supreme Court held that:

> [if a] claim containing a mathematical formula implements or applies that formula in a structure or process, which when considered as a whole, is performing a function which the patent laws were designed to protect (e.g., transforming or reducing an article to a different state or thing), then the claim [may be patentable].[2]

Since then, software patents have been sought by developers and granted by the PTO at a quickening pace. The PTO issued 4,569 software patents in 1994 and 6,142 in 1995.

Many experts believe the PTO is issuing software patents too readily. Most software code is not published, so much of the relevant prior art is not accessible to the PTO examiners. In addition, U.S. patent applications are not published until and unless a patent is issued. As a result, the PTO has been issuing patents for computer programs that many believe are not novel or are merely obvious improvements of existing programs. This has created a great deal of concern in the software industry and spawned a movement to publish patent applications immediately upon filing so that industry experts have the opportunity to introduce evidence of prior art to limit or prevent the issuance of an overbroad or invalid patent.

In March 1994, in part in response to charges from intellectual property lawyers that the patent was overly broad, the PTO took the unusual step of reversing a patent granted to Compton's New Media and Encyclopedia Britannica. The patent, which covered virtually all ways of storing and retrieving text, sound, and images stored on compact disks, appeared to give Compton's a

dominant position in the fast-growing multimedia market. The fact that the patent was issued in the first place was cited by the Interactive Multimedia Association as evidence of the need to improve the training of the PTO's software examiners.

Design Patents

A *design patent* protects any novel, original (rather than nonobvious), and ornamental (rather than useful) design for an article of manufacture. Design patents protect against the copying of the appearance or shape of an article such as a computer terminal cabinet, a perfume bottle, typeface, or the icons and screen displays used in computer programs. A design dictated by function rather than aesthetic concerns cannot be protected by a design patent, but it may be protectable by a utility patent. A design patent has a duration of 14 years from the date on which the patent application was filed, compared to 20 years for utility and plant patents.

Design patents traditionally have been rarely used in the United States; other forms of protection, such as unfair competition law, have been relied upon instead. However, the use of design patents has been increasing recently.

Plant Patents

Plant patents protect any distinct and new variety of plant that is asexually reproduced (that is, not reproduced by means of seeds). The variety must not exist naturally. Thus, a plant patent will not be issued to someone who merely discovers a wild plant not previously known to exist. Once a plant patent is granted, the patent owner will have the exclusive right to exclude others from asexually reproducing, using, or selling the plant. Currently, the Senate is reviewing the Omnibus Patent Act, which would widen the scope of patents related to proprietary, specially bred plants to include fruit and flowers.

Filing for Patent Protection

In order to obtain patent protection in the United States, the inventor must file a patent application with the U.S. Patent and Trademark Office (PTO). Each

---

2. Diamond v. Diehr, 450 U.S. 175, 176 (1981).

patent application contains four parts: the specifications, the claims, the drawings (except in chemical cases), and a declaration by the inventor. After filing the patent application with the PTO, the applicant is required to make a full disclosure of relevant prior art about which he or she is aware.

The *specifications* must describe the invention (as defined by the claims) in its best mode and the manner and process of making and using the invention so that a person skilled in the relevant field could make and use it. The description of the *best mode* must be the best way the inventor knows of making the invention at the time of filing the application. All descriptions must be clear, concise, and exact.

The *claims* (the numbered paragraphs at the end of the patent) describe those elements of the invention that will be protected by the patent. Any element not specifically set forth in the claims is unprotected by the patent. Thus, the drafting of the claims is crucial in obtaining adequate protection.

The *drawings* must show the claimed invention. The *declaration by the inventor* must state that the inventor has reviewed the application and that he or she believes that he or she is the first inventor of the invention. The inventor is also required to make a full disclosure of any known relevant prior art, that is, of developments that relate to the claimed invention. Knowing the prior developments assists the patent attorney in drafting the claims to avoid the prior art; it also permits the patent examiner to determine whether the patent is novel or whether it would have been obvious to those familiar with the relevant field.

The patent examiner may initially reject the application as being precluded by prior inventions or otherwise lacking the statutory requirements. (Ninety-nine percent of all patent applications are initially rejected by the PTO.) The inventor may then present arguments (and in extreme cases, evidence) to contest the examiner's rejection or may seek to amend the application to overcome the examiner's rejection. If the application is finally rejected, the inventor can either refile the application as a continuation application, or appeal to the Patent Office's Board of Appeals and subsequently to either the United States District Court for the District of Columbia or the United States Court of Appeals for the Federal Circuit. Once the examiner agrees that a patent should be issued, and the examiner and applicant agree on the precise language of the claims, a patent may be issued.

Drawing by Chas. Addams © 1986, The New Yorker Magazine, Inc.

◆ Patent Infringement

There are three ways in which a patent may be infringed: directly, indirectly, or contributorily. The patent law defines *direct infringement* as the making, use, or sale of any patented invention within the United States during the term of the patent. When an accused device or process does not have precisely each element of a particular claim of a patent (that is, the patent is not literally infringed), but the patented invention is replicated in a product or process that works in substantially the same way and accomplishes substantially the same result, a direct infringement can be found under the *doctrine of equivalents. Indirect infringement* is defined as the active inducement of another party to infringe a patent. *Contributory infringement* occurs when one party knowingly sells an item that has one specific use that will result in the infringement of another's patent. For example, if a company sells a computer add-on card for a specific use that will infringe another's patent, the sale is a contributory infringement even though the add-on card itself does not violate any patent. Direct infringement can be committed innocently and unintentionally; indirect and contributory infringement require some knowledge or intent that a patent will be infringed.

◆ Defenses

A defendant to a patent-infringement action may claim a variety of defenses to a patent infringement claim, including (1) noninfringement of the patent, (2) invalidity of the patent, or (3) misuse of the patent.

Noninfringement

The defense of *noninfringement* asserts that the allegedly infringing matter does not fall within the claims of the issued patent. This defense compares the specific language of the patent claims with the allegedly infringing matter. If the allegedly infringing matter is not described by the patent claims, then the defense of noninfringement is successful. The patent owner may not assert any claim interpretation at odds with the application on file with the PTO. This doctrine is known as *file-wrapper estoppel*. Because the patent holder has previously negotiated the scope of his or her invention with the PTO, the patent holder may not renegotiate that scope in a subsequent court proceeding.

Invalidity

A patent is presumed to be valid, but a court may find it invalid if (1) the invention was not novel, useful, or nonobvious when the patent was issued; (2) the patent covers nonstatutory subject matter such as an abstract idea, a scientific principle, a mental process, or a method of doing business; (3) there was a statutory bar created by a publication or sale of the invention more than one year prior to the filing of the patent application; or (4) any other requirement of the patent law was not met.

Patent Misuse

A defense based on *patent misuse* asserts that although the defendant has infringed a valid patent, the patent holder has abused his or her patent rights and therefore has lost, at least temporarily, his or her right to enforce them. Patent misuse is not statutorily defined, but courts have found misuse when a patent holder has conditioned the granting of a patent license upon the purchase of other, unrelated goods or technologies. The patent holder will be barred from recovering for any infringement of his or her patent during the period of misuse. If the patent holder later "purges" himself or herself of the misuse, however, the patent holder may recover for any subsequent infringement.

◆ Remedies

If a valid patent has been infringed, the patent holder has a variety of remedies: (1) preliminary and permanent injunctive relief, (2) damages, (3) court costs, and (4) attorney's fees.

A preliminary injunction may be used to prevent any further infringement of the patent pending the court's ultimate decision. Most courts, however, are reluctant to grant injunctive relief before they have determined that a valid patent has actually been infringed. Once such a determination has been made, the patent holder is entitled to permanent injunctive relief.

Damages may also be awarded, based on a reasonable royalty for the infringer's use of the invention. Court costs, as fixed by the court, may be added. The court also has discretion to increase the award of damages by up to three times for intentional or willful infringement and to award attorney's fees in exceptional cases.

The instant-camera litigation between Polaroid Corporation and Eastman Kodak Company illustrates the potential for large damages awards for patent infringement. In the late 1960s, Polaroid asked Kodak to produce a new type of film to be used for a new one-step

ETHICAL CONSIDERATION

Some inventors have made their fortunes by turning out a steady stream of blueprints and drawings for new or improved devices without bothering to develop them into commercial products or even to create prototypes. Instead, they design their claims on top of existing products in order to create infringements by current manufacturers, and they delay filing their applications as long as possible to maximize their patents' value and longevity.[a] Is it ethical to use the patent system simply to collect revenue rather than spurring innovation?

----

a. For an example of such a controversy, *see* Bernard Wysocki, Jr., *How Patent Lawsuits Make a Quiet Engineer Rich and Controversial,* Wall St. J., Apr. 9, 1997, at A1.

camera that Polaroid was developing. In return for its agreement to develop and manufacture the new film, Kodak wanted Polaroid to license it to produce its own instant cameras and film. The parties were unable to reach an agreement. Polaroid began to manufacture its own film, and Kodak began a project to develop an instant camera and film. This development effort resulted in the introduction of Kodak's instant camera and film in 1976, which caused Polaroid to file suit against Kodak.

Seven years and 300,000 pages of discovery documents later, a federal district court held that Kodak had infringed 20 claims of seven Polaroid patents and enjoined Kodak from any further infringements. The injunction terminated Kodak's instant-camera business and left it with $200 million worth of useless manufacturing equipment and losses of $600 million. Kodak had to pay more than $150 million to 28 million customers who had purchased a Kodak camera that was now unusable because the injunction also prohibited Kodak from manufacturing or selling film for the cameras. Although Kodak appealed, the trial court's decision was affirmed.[3]

The parties litigated the issue of damages separately. Kodak claimed that Polaroid was entitled to damages of $177 million, representing a reasonable royalty of 5% for all instant cameras and film sold by Kodak from 1976 until 1985. Polaroid, however, claimed that it was entitled to $12 billion, comprising $4 billion in profits that Polaroid claimed it would have made if Kodak had not entered the instant-photography business in 1976, to be tripled because Kodak willfully infringed Polaroid's parents. In 1990, Kodak was ordered to pay $910 million to Polaroid for infringing its patents, including $454.2 million in lost profits and royalties and $455.3 million in interest. This is the largest award ever granted in a patent-infringement suit. Still, the award "disappointed Polaroid and heartened Kodak."[4]

◆ Role of Juries in Patent Infringement Cases

The role of juries in patent disputes has proven to be an important and controversial issue. Plaintiffs alleging infringement of their patents usually prefer a jury trial to

a bench trial based on the belief that lay people are more sympathetic to their cause than are professional and expert judges. For that reason, plaintiffs rarely waive their Seventh Amendment right to a jury trial. Juries, however, are only fact finders. Even in a jury trial, it is the judge who decides matters of law. But where is the line between fact and law?

In 1996, the U.S. Supreme Court held that construction of the words in the claims is a matter of law for

INTERNATIONAL CONSIDERATION

Given the international scope of manufacturing and distribution, many inventors file for patent protection in a number of countries. There are almost 200 countries in the world that grant patents; and, in each country, an issued patent provides the patent holder with the exclusive right to make, use, and sell the patented invention in that country. International patent protection for U.S nationals is governed by the patent laws of the foreign country and any treaty that the United States may have with that country. The laws regarding statutory bars in foreign jurisdictions are radically different from U.S. patent law. A rule of thumb is that any public disclosure of an invention prior to filing the patent application will bar an inventor's ability to obtain foreign patent protection.

The patent practice of other countries is often different from that of the United States. Some jurisdictions are more receptive to certain types of patents than others. In 1989, 30 years after its application was filed, Texas Instruments was granted a patent in Japan on an invention related to integrated circuits. The delay helped Japan's then fledgling computer-chip companies by allowing them to make, use, and sell the U.S.–patented integrated circuits in Japan without infringing Japanese patent laws. A patent had been granted on the same invention in the United States in 1964. Securities analysts estimate that the Japanese patent could bring Texas Instruments $100 million to $700 million annually until it expires in 2004.

A number of countries do not permit invention patents for pharmaceuticals, although they may be entitled to some protection under process patents. Given the differences in patent practice, it is important to discuss the rules that apply in the foreign country with an attorney, prior to disclosure or sale of any patentable subject matter.

3. Polaroid Corp. v. Eastman Kodak Co., 789 F.2d 1556 (Fed. Cir. 1986), *cert. denied*, 479 U.S. 850 (1986).

4. Lawrence Ingrassia & James S. Hirsch, *Polaroid's Patent-Case Award, Smaller than Anticipated, Is a Relief for Kodak*, WALL ST. J., Oct. 15, 1990, at A3.

the court, not the jury, to decide.[5] The Court reasoned that "[t]he construction of written instruments is one of those things that judges often do and are likely to do better than jurors unburdened by training in exegesis."

 Copyrights

Best-selling novels, award-winning films, off-the-shelf software packages, and compact disks are all copyrightable works. So are restaurant menus, laser disks, designer linens, plush toy animals, and cereal boxes. The United States Copyright Act of 1976 requires that the material for which copyright protection is sought be original (not copied) and fall within one of the following categories: (1) literary works; (2) musical works; (3) dramatic works; (4) pantomimes and choreographic works; (5) pictorial, graphic, and sculptural works; (6) motion pictures and other audiovisual works; and (7) sound recordings.

The act further requires that the works be fixed in a tangible medium from which they can be perceived, reproduced, or communicated. For example, stories may be fixed in written manuscripts, computer software on floppy disks, recordings of songs on compact discs, and staging of a play recorded on videotape. Protection is automatic. Neither registration nor the use of a copyright notice is required. However, it is usually helpful for a growing company to register so that statutory damages and attorney's fees are available. Other-

---

5. Markman v. Westview Instruments, Inc., 116 S. Ct. 1384 (1996).

INTERNATIONAL CONSIDERATION

The United States is a party to a number of international copyright treaties, including the Berne Convention for the Protection of Literary and Artistic Works and the Universal Copyright Convention. American works receive the same protection that is afforded to the works of a national in foreign countries that are signatories of the same treaties. Before distributing a copyrightable work outside the United States, it is important to discuss with an attorney what, if any, copyright protection is available for the work in the relevant foreign jurisdictions and what steps are necessary to obtain such protection.

wise, the company can recover only its actual damages, which a company with a limited track record or a new product with uncertain prospects often will have difficulty proving.

Originality and Compilations

Copyright protection extends only to original works of authorship evidencing some degree of creativity. Facts are not copyrightable. The following case addresses the question of when a compilation of facts is sufficiently original to warrant protection.

| A CASE IN POINT | IN THE LANGUAGE OF THE COURT |

CASE 11.2
WARREN PUBLISHING INC. v. MICRODOS DATA CORP.
United States Court of Appeals for the Eleventh Circuit
115 F.3d 1509
(11th Cir. 1997), *cert. denied,* 118 S. Ct. 397 (1997) (mem.).

FACTS   Warren Publishing (Warren) annually compiles and publishes a printed directory of cable-television systems throughout the United States (the *Factbook*). The "Directory of Cable Systems" section of the *Factbook* contains extensive information on cable systems, including the name, address, and telephone number of the cable-system operator; the number of subscribers; the channels offered; the price of service; and the types of equipment used. The entries in this section are arranged alphabetically by state and within each state alphabetically by community. The "Group Ownership" section contains listings of selected information on "all persons or companies which have an interest in 2 or more systems or franchises." To save space, a determination is made

Case 11.2 continues

Case 11.2 continued

as to which community is the "principal" community served by a particular cable system. Warren then prints the data only under the name of the principal community. Under the entries for the nonprincipal communities of a multiple-community cable system, there is a cross-reference to the principal community listing.

Microdos Data Corp. (Microdos) also markets a compilation of facts about cable systems in the form of a computer software package called "Cable Access." The Cable Access program, like Warren's *Factbook*, provides detailed information on cable operators. The software package is broken into three databases. The first database provides information on the individual cable systems, the second provides information on multiple-system operators, and the third is a historical database that provides selected information on the cable industry from 1965 to the present. Although the software package comes pre-sorted by state and city, a customer may rearrange the data in a format of its choosing. The customer may construct searches of the database's information on cable systems as required to fit its particular needs, as well as output the data to a hard copy in various formats, again to fit the specific needs of the customer.

Warren began publishing cable-television information in 1948, and Microdos began marketing Cable Access in 1989. In July 1990, Warren filed suit against Microdos, alleging copyright infringement and unfair competition. Warren alleged that Cable Access infringed upon its *Factbook* copyright in three areas: (1) the communities covered/principal community system, (2) the data fields, and (3) the data-field entries.

The district court found that Microdos had not infringed Warren's data-field format and that the data-field entries were uncopyrightable facts. Regarding the communities-covered issue, the district court found that Warren's principal community system was sufficiently creative and original to be copyrightable and that Microdos's system was substantially similar to Warren's. Therefore, the district court granted Warren's motion for a preliminary injunction. Microdos appealed.

ISSUE PRESENTED   Can the system for selecting information in a compilation be protected by copyright? If so, what are the requirements for protection of a selection system?

OPINION   BIRCH, J., writing for the U.S. Court of Appeals:

The Supreme Court, in its most recent decision focusing on compilation copyrights, noted that "[t]he sine qua non of copyright is originality."[6] The Court emphasized that originality is a constitutional requirement, noting that the Constitution "authorizes Congress to 'secur[e] for limited times to Authors . . . the exclusive Right to their respective Writings.'" The Court also admonished that:

> Facts, whether alone or as part of a compilation, are not original and therefore may not be copyrighted. A factual compilation is eligible for copyright if it features an original selection or arrangement of facts, but the copyright is limited to the particular selection or arrangement. In no event may copyright extend to the facts themselves.

Case 11.2 continues

6. Feist Publications, Inc. v. Rural Tel. Serv. Co., 499 U.S. 340, 345 (1991).

Case 11.2 continued

Thus, the compiler's choices as to selection, coordination, or arrangement are the only portions of the compilation that arguably are even entitled to copyright protection. As the *Feist* Court noted, these choices must be made "independently by the compiler and entail a minimal degree of creativity" in order to be entitled to compilation copyright protection. [In *Fiest*, the Supreme Court held that an alphabetical listing of names, addresses, and telephone numbers in a directory did not entail the minimal degree of creativity required for copyright protection. The Court rejected the so-called sweat of the brow theory, which would give protection to a compilation of facts that required effort to compile.] The *Feist* Court further explained:

> This protection is subject to an important limitation. The mere fact that a work is copyrighted does not mean that every element of the work may be protected. Originality remains the sine qua non of copyright; accordingly, copyright protection may extend only to those components of a work that are original to the author.

Given these limitations on the scope of copyright protection in a factual compilation, it is abundantly clear that "copyright in a factual compilation is thin." Only when one copies the protected selection, coordination, or arrangement in a factual compilation has one infringed the compilation copyright; copying of the factual material contained in the compilation is not infringement.

. . .

To establish its claim of copyright infringement, Warren must prove "(1) ownership of a valid copyright, and (2) copying of constituent elements of the work that are original." The first element is not at issue here, because Microdos does not contest that the Factbook, considered as a whole, is entitled to copyright protection. To prove the second element, Warren must demonstrate that Microdos, by taking the material it copied from the Factbook, appropriated Warren's original selection, coordination, or arrangement.

. . .

Section 102(b) of the Copyright Act specifically excludes "any idea, procedure, process, system, method of operation, concept, principle, or discovery" from copyright protection "regardless of the form in which it is described, explained, illustrated, or embodied in such work." Nonetheless, the district court concluded that Warren's "system" of selecting communities was original and entitled to copyright protection. This conclusion is contrary to the plain language of [the statute] and is clearly incorrect. If Warren actually does employ a system to select the communities to be represented in the book, then section 102(b) of the Act bars the protection of such a system.

. . .

At oral argument, Warren asserted, and the dissent agrees, that the district court was correct in finding that Warren is entitled to copyright protection in its "selection" of communities, which is based on its putatively unique definition of a cable system.

Case 11.2 continues

Case 11.2 continued

The problem with this is that Warren does not undertake any "selection" in determining what communities to include in the Factbook. Warren claims that its system of listing communities does not include the entire universe of cable systems, and thus there is "selection" involved as to which communities they include in their Factbook. This assertion, however, is plainly wrong.

. . .

The Second Circuit has noted that "[s]election implies the exercise of judgment in choosing which facts from a given body of data to include in a compilation."[7] [Warren] did not exercise any creativity or judgment in "selecting" cable systems to include in its Factbook, but rather included the entire relevant universe known to it. The only decision that it made was that it would not list separately information for each community that was part of a multiple-community cable system; in other words, it decided to make the Factbook commercially useful. Therefore, it cannot prevail in its claim that it "selected" which communities to include in its Factbook. The district court erred in determining that Warren's system of selecting communities was copyrightable.

. . .

Even were we to assume that the presentation of the selection of principal communities made by Warren was creative and original and therefore copyrightable, its claim that it is entitled to protection would nonetheless fail, because the selection is not its own, but rather that of the cable operators. The district court found that the principal community was "selected by contacting the cable operator to determine which community is considered the lead community within the cable system." As we observed in *BellSouth*,[8] "these acts are not acts of authorship, but techniques for the discovery of facts."

. . .

. . . Simply because Warren may have been the first to discover and report a certain fact on cable systems does not translate these acts of discovery into acts of creation entitled to copyright protection. "Just as the Copyright Act does not protect 'industrious collection,' it affords no shelter to the resourceful, efficient, or creative collector."

The record indicates that it is the cable operators, not Warren, that determine, in the case of a multiple-community system, the community name under which to list the factual data for the entire cable system. Therefore, Warren cannot prevail in its claim that it undertakes original selection in employing the principal community concept. Rather, it has created an effective system for determining where the cable operators prefer to have the data listed. While Warren may have found an efficient method of gathering this information, it lacks originality, which is the sine qua non of copyright.

Case 11.2 continues

---

7. Key Publications, Inc. v. Chinatown Today Publishing Enters., Inc., 945 F.2d 509, 513 (2d Cir. 1991).

8. BellSouth Advertising & Publishing Corp. v. Donnelley Info. Publishing, Inc., 999 F.2d 1436, 1441 (11th Cir. 1993) (*en banc*).

Case 11.2 continued

RESULT   The appeals court vacated the lower court's granting of an injunction and remanded the case for further consideration in light of its decision. Warren's principal community system was not copyrightable.

COMMENTS   Attorney Rebecca Edelson has distilled the following principles from *Warren*:

1. A selection of data is not copyrightable when the entire universe is "selected," even if the compiler is the first to think of compiling the information and even if the compilation is commercially useful.
2. A selection is not copyrightable when it is not the result of the compiler's own judgment, even if the compiler is the first to think of making the selection in the particular manner.
3. A "system" of selecting is not subject to copyright protection even if it is creative and original.
4. Organizing principles and discovery techniques are not subject to copyright protection no matter how commercially useful, novel, or industrious they are.[9]

The European Union provides greater protection for compilations of data than does the United States under current law. As of mid-1998, Congress was considering whether to pass legislation to strengthen database protection in the United States.

9. Rebecca "Bec" Edelson, *Another Factual Compilation Bites the Dust under the Copyright Laws: Warren Publishing, Inc. v. Microdos Data*, 22 New Matter 9–11 (Fall/Winter 1997).

Protected Expression

The act prohibits unauthorized copying of the *protected expression* of a work, but the underlying ideas embodied in the work remain freely usable by others. Section 102 of the act excludes from copyright protection any "idea, procedure, process, system, method of operation, concept, principle or discovery, regardless of the form in which it is described, explained, illustrated, or embodied."

When an idea and its expression are inseparable, the *merger doctrine* dictates that the expression is not copyrightable. If it were, this would confer a monopoly over the idea. Thus, a manufacturer of a karate video game cannot keep a competitor from producing another video game based on standard karate moves and rules. The idea of a karate game (including game procedures, karate moves, background scenes, a referee, and the use of computer graphics) is not protected expression. The manufacturer can, however, keep a competitor from copying any original graphics it has used in the game so long as they are not inseparable from the idea of karate or of a karate video game.

Useful Articles Doctrine

Under the *useful articles doctrine*, copyright protection does not extend to a useful article, that is, the useful application of an idea. The application of ideas is considered to be within the province of patent law. The act defines pictorial, graphic, and sculptural works to include "works of artistic craftsmanship insofar as their form but not their mechanical or utilitarian aspects are concerned." For example, blank forms, which are used to record information rather than convey information, are considered articles of use and are not copyrightable.

If the expression of a pictorial, graphic, or sculptural work cannot be identified separately from and exist independently of such utilitarian aspects, copyright protection will be denied to the whole work. An example of an article whose expression is separable from its utilitarian aspects would be a lamp that incorporates a statue of a woman in its base. An example of an article whose expression is not separable from its utilitarian aspects is the layout of an integrated circuit. Although a drawing of the circuit is copyrightable, the actual circuitry is not copyrightable because it is impossible to separate the utilitarian aspect of the circuit from its expression or layout. It is the layout of the circuit that enables the circuit to operate correctly. The circuit may be patentable, however. In addition, the layout or topography of the circuit is protected by the Semiconductor Chip Protection Act of 1984.

Exclusive Rights

To encourage the production of new works, copyright owners are given exclusive economic rights in the work. These rights can be conveyed to others. The copyright owner has the exclusive right to make copies of his or her work and to create derivative new works based upon it. He or she also has the exclusive right to distribute, publicly perform, and publicly display the work and to

INTERNATIONAL CONSIDERATION

In December 1997, the European Commission released a draft directive to update and harmonize member state copyright laws and bring those laws into conformity with two recent digital copyright treaties, the World Intellectual Property Organization (WIPO) Copyright Treaty and the WIPO Performances and Phonograms Treaty. The directive identifies four areas that require legislative action if the European Union is to achieve harmony in its copyright laws: (1) a reproduction right, (2) a communication to the public right, (3) a distribution right, and (4) protection against circumvention of abuse and protection systems.

If approved, the directive would outlaw the manufacture of devices that facilitate circumvention of copyright-protection technology. The draft would also provide authors with the exclusive right to authorize or prohibit communication of their work to the public, by wire or wireless means, including interactive Internet sites that offer such works without the author's permission. Debate on the draft will take place throughout 1998.

import into the United States copies of the work made overseas.

First Sale Doctrine   However, under the *first sale doctrine,* codified in Section 109(a) of the Copyright Act, once the copyright owner places a copyrighted item in the stream of commerce by selling it, the owner has exhausted his or her exclusive statutory right to control its distribution. In 1998, the U.S. Supreme Court applied that rule to the unauthorized importation of copies in a case involving L'anza Research International, Inc., a U.S. manufacturer and distributor of shampoos, conditioner, and other hair-care products.[10] L'anza had sold discounted products bearing a copyrighted label to a foreign company, expecting it to sell the products in Malta. Instead, the products were sold to an importer, Quality King Distributors, which brought them back into the United States for resale by unauthorized retailers at a discounted price. L'anza claimed that it was illegal for Quality King to import the goods into the United States and resell them because the goods bore a copyrighted label. The Supreme Court rejected that argument, holding that L'anza lost the right to control the import of the copyrighted item when it sold the products to the foreign company.

This decision was a blow to U.S. manufacturers and distributors that have been trying to combat the gray market, whereby another company buys their products then resells them outside the normal channel of distribution, often at a discounted price.[11] L'anza, for example, sold exclusively to domestic distributors who agreed to resell only to authorized retailers, such as barber shops, beauty salons, and professional hair-care colleges. L'anza argued that the American public is generally unwilling to pay the price charged for high-quality products when they are sold along with the less-expensive, lower-quality products, which are generally carried by supermarkets and drugstores. Big retailers, including Costco and Wal-Mart, favored application of the first sale doctrine to imports, because it made it possible for consumers to buy brand name products at discounted prices.

---

10. Quality King Distrib., Inc. v. L'anza Research Int'l, Inc., 188 S. Ct. 1125 (1998).

11. *See* Edward Felsenthal, *Copyright Scope Limited for Some Firms,* WALL ST. J., Mar. 10, 1998, at B5.

Copyright Ownership

The author of a work is the original owner of the copyright. The author is either the creator of the work or, in the case of a work made for hire, the party for whom the work was prepared. A *work made for hire* is either (1) a work created by an employee within the scope of his or her employment, or (2) a work in one of nine listed categories that is specially commissioned through a signed writing that states that the work is a "work made for hire."

The author can transfer ownership by an assignment of copyright. Assignments are often sought by parties that commission independent contractors to produce works—such as computer programs—that fall outside the nine categories of the act. Thus, if commissioning a work or preparing a work as an independent contractor, one should consult with an experienced copyright attorney to ensure that the desired party obtains copyright ownership.

The advent of non-print media, such as CD-ROMs and electronic databases, has given rise to disputes between freelance writers and photographers and the newspapers and magazines to which they sold their work about who owns electronic rights to the material. For example, in 1997, a group of freelance writers sued the newspapers to which they sold their stories, alleging that the newspapers' publishing of their work in non-print media was beyond the newspapers' copyrights and violated the writers' copyrights. A federal district court in New York rejected that challenge and declared that the Copyright Act gives the holder of the copyright in a compilation—in this case, the publisher of the newspaper or magazine—the rights to revise and republish.[12] Republication in electronic form was within those rights to the compilation. This case underscores the importance to a company acquiring rights to a work of drafting a broad assignment of the author's rights to revise and republish the work in any media.

Term

The duration of copyright ownership depends upon the identity of the author. If the author is a known individual, the term is the life of the author plus 50 years. For a work made for hire or for an anonymous or pseudonymous work, the term is the lesser of 75 years after first publication or 100 years after creation of the work.

Preemption of State Law and "Hot News"

Because the Copyright Act is a federal statute, it preempts state law that conflicts with it. The following case concerning electronic transmission of sporting-event scores illustrates the continued viability of state laws on misappropriation.

---

12. Tasini v. New York Times Co., 972 F. Supp. 804 (S.D.N.Y. 1997).

A CASE IN POINT   **SUMMARY**

CASE 11.3
NATIONAL
BASKETBALL
ASSOCIATION v.
MOTOROLA, INC.
United States Court
of Appeals for the
Second Circuit
105 F.3d 841 (2d Cir. 1997).

FACTS   Motorola manufactures and markets the SportsTrax paging device, and STATS, another defendant, supplies sporting-event information that is transmitted to the pagers. The pager, which became available to the public in 1996, can display the following information on National Basketball Association (NBA) games in progress: (1) the teams playing; (2) score changes; (3) the team in possession of the ball; (4) whether the team is in the free-throw bonus; (5) the quarter of the game; and (6) time remaining in the quarter. The information is updated every few minutes throughout the game with a two- to three-minute lag.

SportsTrax's operation relies on a data feed supplied by STATS reporters who watch the games on television or listen to them on the radio. The reporters key into a personal

Case 11.3 continues

Case 11.3 continued

computer changes in the score and other information, such as successful and missed shots, fouls, and clock updates. The information is relayed by modem to STATS's host computer, which compiles, analyzes, and formats the data for retransmission. The information is then sent to a common carrier, which sends it via satellite to various local FM radio networks that in turn emit the signal received by the individual SportsTrax pagers.

When the pager was introduced, the NBA sued Motorola and STATS in federal district court for federal copyright infringement, state law unfair competition by misappropriation, and false advertising. The trial court dismissed the copyright-infringement and false-advertising claims, but it found Motorola and STATS liable for misappropriation under New York state law. The court issued a permanent injunction against Motorola and STATS, who then appealed.

ISSUE PRESENTED   Does the real-time transmission of information regarding a sporting-event infringe on the copyright of the event's organizers or broadcasters? If not, does such transmission violate New York State law on misappropriation?

SUMMARY OF OPINION   Although the NBA did not appeal the lower court's dismissal of its copyright-infringement claims, the U.S. Court of Appeals began with that issue because of federal preemption. As amended in 1976, the Copyright Act provides protection to simultaneously recorded broadcasts of live performances, including sports events.[13] Although the event itself is not an "original [work] of authorship" and is therefore not copyrightable, broadcast of the event is entitled to copyright protection. In spite of that protection, reproduction of facts from such broadcasts does not violate the copyright, because no author may copyright facts or an idea. Hence, the lower court was correct to dismiss the NBA's copyright claims.

The 1976 amendments to the act also provide for preemption of state law claims that enforce rights "equivalent" to the exclusive copyright protection provided to works within the scope of the Copyright Act. Hence, the protection provided by federal copyright law could not also be offered by state law. The court, however, ruled that this preemption was subject to a "hot-news" exception, whereby such information, although potentially protected by copyright law, could also be protected by state law. Relying on an 80-year-old U.S. Supreme Court precedent and the legislative history of the 1976 amendments, the court ruled that such a hot-news exception applied only to cases in which (1) plaintiff generates or gathers the information at a cost; (2) the information is time sensitive; (3) the defendant's use of the information amounts to free riding on the plaintiff's efforts; (4) the defendant is in direct competition with the plaintiff; and (5) the availability of other parties to free ride on the plaintiff's efforts would so reduce the plaintiff's incentive to provide the product or service that its existence or quality would be threatened.

The court found that the hot-news exception did not apply, because the NBA failed to show any competitive effect by SportsTrax based on free-riding as required by the

Case 11.3 continues

---

13. 17 U.S.C. § 101 (1997).

Case 11.3 continued

fifth element. Without all five elements, the hot-news exception did not apply. Without that exception, the state misappropriation claim was preempted by federal copyright law, which provided no protection.

RESULT   The appeals court reversed the trial court's injunction, allowing Motorola and STATS to continue offering their product to sports fans.

◆ Copyright Formalities

Using proper copyright notices and registering works for which copyright protection is desired affords the copyright owner substantial benefits.

Copyright Notice

Although copyright notices are not mandatory for works first published after March 1, 1989, the use of a notice is advisable because it prevents an infringer from claiming innocent infringement. For works first published prior to March 1, 1989, most copyright authorities agree that notices should still be used to avoid the risk of releasing the work into the public domain. A proper U.S. copyright notice for works distributed within the United States includes these elements:

"Copyright" or "Copr." or "©"; the year of first publication; and the name of the copyright owner.

Registration

Registration with the U.S. Copyright Office is a prerequisite for filing an infringement suit for a work of U.S. origin. Statutory damages and attorney's fees are available only if the work was registered within 90 days after the first publication or was registered prior to the infringement at issue. In addition, registration creates a legal presumption of ownership and copyright validity, which can be extremely helpful to a plaintiff in a copyright-infringement suit. Because the timing of registration is critical to obtaining some of the related benefits, it is important to consult with a copyright attorney before beginning to publicly distribute a work.

ECONOMIC PERSPECTIVE

INTELLECTUAL PROPERTY RIGHTS AND INCENTIVES TO INNOVATE

A basic tenet of neoclassical economic theory is that productive efficiency and allocative efficiency will be achieved through free competition by private parties interested in maximizing their own welfare. Productive efficiency exists when competition among individual producers drives all but the lowest-cost producers of goods or services out of the market. Allocative efficiency exists when scarce societal resources are allocated to the production of various goods and services up to the point at which the cost of producing each good or service equals the benefit society reaps from its use.

In general, the economic policy of the United States is to foster the functioning of free markets in which individuals may compete. For example, the antitrust laws, discussed in Chapter 18, are designed to protect competition by prohibiting any individual entity or group of entities from monopolizing an industry.

The area of intellectual property is an exception to the general free-market orientation of the U.S. economy. Patent laws provide inventors with the opportunity to gain a legally enforceable monopoly to prevent the manufacture, use, and sale of their inventions for a limited time.

The economic rationale for granting monopolies to inventors is based on the high value of innovation to society and the need to give inventors an incentive. Free competition cannot lead to productive and allocative efficiency in an economy as a whole unless an efficient market exists for each product. Innovation may be regarded as a product. Allocative efficiency for innovation will exist only if it is produced up to the point at which the benefit to society from innovation equals the cost of its production.

Technological advances are crucial to a growing economy. Development of new techniques increases productive efficiency, thereby expanding the quantity of goods and services that can be produced with a given level of societal resources. Development of new products meeting previously unfulfilled needs increases the welfare of society as a whole. In the past decade, such innovation has taken on increasing importance for the United States in the international context. Although countries with lower-cost labor have a competitive advantage in the manufacture of goods with established production techniques, the United States's competitive advantage lies in its ability to develop new technologies.

The immense benefits society gains through innovation are difficult for individual innovators to capture. Absent legal rules protecting the ownership of inventions, once a valuable new product or cost-saving technique is introduced, others will immediately copy it and profit from it.

Individuals will only produce innovation up to the point at which the rewards they reap equal their costs. To ensure that innovation is produced fully up to the point at which its social cost equals its social benefit, the law must guarantee to innovators a significant part of the benefit from their innovations. The U.S. solution to this problem is to provide inventors, if their inventions meet the requirements for a patent, with a limited monopoly to exclude others from the manufacture, use, and sale of their inventions. This system ensures that inventors will be able to capture the full benefit of their inventions during the period of their monopoly, and that the innovation will be freely available to others after that period. The stringent requirements for patents prevent unnecessary restrictions on free competition.

An important secondary objective of providing inventors with patent protection is allowing the scientific community access to knowledge about state-of-the-art technology. Absent a legal monopoly, innovators would keep their advances secret to prevent others from copying them. Such secrecy would result in waste of scarce societal resources, as other researchers would struggle to discover what is already known.

In practice, the granting of a legal monopoly does not often interfere with the condition necessary for productive efficiency, namely, production of goods and services only by the lowest-cost producers. Although a patent holder has the legal right to exclude others from the manufacture, use, and sale of the invention, if another can use the invention more efficiently, it will be more profitable for the patent holder to sell or license his or her rights than to retain them for his or her exclusive use.

For example, assume that a patent holder can reap profits of $10 million per year by producing and selling her patented product. Suppose another company with better production facilities can produce the product at a lower cost, resulting in profits of $12 million per year. The other company would (theoretically) be willing to pay up to $11,999,999 per year in license fees for the right to produce the product. The patent holder would be willing (at least in theory) to license her rights for any amount in excess of $10 million per year. Thus, the legal monopoly in practice provides the inventor with a means of ensuring that others who profit from her creativity pay her for her contribution.

For example, Jack Kilby of Texas Instruments and Robert Noyce of Fairchild Semiconductor, inventors of the microchip, engaged in a lengthy legal battle to determine which of them would obtain a patent for the chip. Although the patent issue dragged on from 1959 to 1970, the two companies agreed in 1966 to cross-license each other and to jointly license other companies to produce the microchip.

The World Bank has identified property rights, including intellectual property rights, as one of the keys to energizing countries in transition to market-based economies. Noting that many developing and transitioning economies have adopted intellectual property laws similar to the developed nations, the World Bank acknowledges that these laws are difficult to enforce. But enforcement of these laws will encourage development of intellectual property and the foreign investment needed to spur growth in these countries.

Copyright Infringement

Copyright infringement is the copying, modification, display, performance, or distribution of a work without the permission of the copyright owner. A plaintiff in a copyright infringement suit must show substantial similarity of the protected expression, not merely substantial similarity of the ideas contained in the work. In addition, the plaintiff must prove that the alleged infringer had access to the plaintiff's work.

Piracy

Private companies in industries ranging from software to designer clothing, cosmetics, toys, liquor, and audiocassettes are increasingly forming alliances to work with government officials in a variety of countries to combat piracy. For example, 60 companies doing business in Mexico, including Levi Strauss, Reebok, Hard Rock Café, Walt Disney, and Tequila Herradura, banded together in 1998 to fight piracy. The International Intellectual Property Alliance estimated that U.S. companies lost $414 million to piracy in Mexico in 1996. In 1997, Mexican officials carried out 1,525 inspections at street markets and small stores and confiscated six million pirated products.[14]

Software companies estimate that they lose more than $15 billion a year due to the illegal copying or pirating of software. Exhibit 11.1 identifies various countries in which software publishers and distributors lost more than $100 million in 1994 due to software piracy and the percentage of the business software that was pirated in each country in 1994.

The rapid growth of the Internet has facilitated such piracy and created new problems for copyright holders. In addition to software publishers, music publishers are being challenged by the new technology. According to Frank Creighton, vice-president of the Recording Industry Association of America (RIAA), "Technology has created this animal, and technology will need to fix it."[15] One such "fix" is the use of Web robots, programs that search and index the Internet for specific content by visiting Web sites, requesting documents based on certain criteria, and following up with

---

14. Rogelio Varelo, *Mexican Officials, Companies Working To Fight Piracy, Heighten Awareness*, WALL ST. J., Feb. 20, 1998, at B9A.

15. *Copyright Owners Learning to Police Online Sales, Performance of Musical Works*, 66 U.S.L.W. 2483 (1998).

EXHIBIT 11.1   Software Piracy's Global Reach

COUNTRY	PIRACY RATE	$ US LOSSES (MILLIONS)	COUNTRY	PIRACY RATE	$ US LOSSES (MILLIONS)
Argentina	74%	$ 208	Netherlands	78%	$ 216
Australia	37	128	New Zealand	55	105
Brazil	77	551	Poland	91	201
Canada	58	255	Russia	94	541
China	98	527	Saudi Arabia	90	101
Czech Republic	83	108	South Korea	78	546
France	57	771	Spain	73	240
Germany	50	1875	Sweden	52	151
Hong Kong	62	133	Taiwan	72	232
Hungary	85	102	Thailand	98	174
India	82	128	Turkey	97	159
Indonesia	99	118	United Kingdom	43	544
Japan	67	2076	United States	35	2877
Mexico	78	200	Venezuela	71	104

SOURCE   From SAN FRANCISCO CHRONICLE, Sept. 19, 1996, at B4.

requests for documents referenced in those documents already retrieved. Music publisher BMI, for instance, uses the Web robot MusicBot to gather information from the Internet. Encryption and watermarking can also be used to provide protection for copyrighted works. Creighton estimates that his association focuses at least three-fourths of its anti-piracy resources on the Internet and new technology. Those resources include lawsuits against on-line music archives that serve as distribution points for hundreds of unauthorized copies of digital sound recordings.

Remedies

A plaintiff is entitled to recover his or her actual damages and the defendant's profits attributable to the infringement as well as attorney's fees under certain circumstances, to the extent that these are not duplicative of each other. Alternatively, if the copyright is registered within three months of first publication or prior to the alleged infringement, a plaintiff may elect to recover statutory damages, which can be up to $100,000 for willful infringement, and attorney's fees under certain circumstances. Injunctive relief, seizure of the infringing copies, and exclusion of infringing copies from import into the United States are also available under certain circumstances.

Infringers may also face criminal penalties. Until 1997, such criminal penalties applied only to willful copyright violations for commercial gain; those who stole copyrighted works and gave them away were immune to criminal prosecution. In December 1997, President Clinton signed into law the No Electronic Theft Act,[16] which closed a loophole in the federal wire-fraud statute that required proof that a defendant commercially gained from an infringing act. The new law punishes with fines and prison those who copy compact discs, videocassettes, or software worth more than $1,000 without permission of the copyright holder.

Fair Use Doctrine

Under the *fair use doctrine*, a person may infringe the copyright owner's exclusive rights without liability in the course of such activities as literary criticism, social comment, news reporting, education, scholarship, or research. In deciding what constitutes fair use, the courts balance the public benefit of the defendant's use against the effect on the copyright owner's interests. The factors they consider are the purpose of the use (including whether it was for profit); the economic effect of the use on the copyright owner; the nature of the work used; and the amount of the work that is used. In the following case, the limits of fair use were explored in the context of satire and parody.

---

16. The law (Pub. L. No. 105–145) amends the copyright-infringement sections of Titles 17 and 18 of the U.S. Code.

A CASE IN POINT	SUMMARY

CASE 11.4
DR. SEUSS ENTERPRISES, L.P. v. PENGUIN BOOKS USA, INC.
United States Court of Appeals for the Ninth Circuit
105 F.3d 1394
(9th Cir. 1997).

FACTS In 1995, Alan Katz and Chris Wrinn wrote and illustrated *The Cat NOT in the Hat! A Parody by Dr. Juice* satirizing the O. J. Simpson double-murder trial. The book was to be published and distributed by Penguin Books USA, Inc. (Penguin) and Dove Audio, Inc. (Dove). A prepublication advertisement for the book proclaimed:

> Wickedly clever author "Dr. Juice" gives the O. J. Simpson trial a very fresh new look. From Brentwood to the Los Angeles County Courthouse to Marcia Clark and the Dream Team, *The Cat Not in the Hat* tells the whole story in rhyming verse and sketches as witty as Theodore [sic] Geisel's best. This is one parody that really packs a punch!

The book traces the story of the Simpson trial with rhymes about Simpson's trip to Chicago, the noise outside Kato Kaelin's room, the bloody glove found by Detective

Case 11.4 continues

Case 11.4 continued

Mark Fuhrman, the Bronco chase, the arrest and booking, the hiring of attorneys, the assignment of Judge Lance Ito, the talk show interest, the comment on DNA, and the selection of the jury. On the hiring of attorneys, Katz wrote:

> A plea went out to Rob Shapiro / Can you save the fallen hero? / And Marcia Clark, hooray, hooray / Was called in with a justice play. / A man this famous / Never hires / Lawyers like / Jacoby-Meyers. / When you're accused of a killing scheme / You need to build a real Dream Team. / Cochran! Cochran! / Doodle-do / Johnnie, won't you join the crew? / Cochran! Cochran! / Deedle-dee / The Dream Team needs a victory.

With such flair, the book broadly mimics Dr. Seuss's characteristic style.

Dr. Seuss Enterprises, L.P. (Seuss) owns most of the copyrights and trademarks to the works of the late Theodor S. Geisel, the author and illustrator of the famous children's educational books written between 1931 and 1991 under the pseudonym Dr. Seuss. In *The Cat in the Hat*, first published in 1957, Geisel created a mischievous but well-meaning character, the Cat, that is almost always depicted with his distinctive scrunched and somewhat shabby red and white stovepipe hat.

Neither the authors, publisher, nor distributor of *The Cat Not in the Hat!* was licensed or authorized to use any of the works, characters, or illustrations owned by Seuss. They also did not seek permission from Seuss to use these properties. After seeing the advertisement, Seuss filed a complaint for copyright and trademark infringement, and an application for a temporary restraining order and a preliminary injunction.

In its complaint, Seuss alleged that *The Cat NOT in the Hat!* misappropriated substantial protected elements of its copyrighted works, used six unregistered and one registered Seuss trademark, and diluted the distinctive quality of its famous marks. Katz subsequently filed a declaration stating that *The Cat in the Hat* was the "object for [his] parody" and portions of his book derive from *The Cat in the Hat* only as "necessary to conjure up the original."

The district court granted Seuss's request for a preliminary injunction. About 12,000 books (at an expense of approximately $35,500) had been printed to date but were enjoined from distribution. Penguin and Dove appealed.

ISSUE PRESENTED   Under what conditions does a parody or satire qualify as fair use of a copyrighted work?

SUMMARY OF THE OPINION   The U.S. Court of Appeals began by noting that Seuss, as the owner of Dr. Seuss's copyrights, owns the exclusive rights (1) to reproduce the copyrighted work, (2) to prepare derivative works based on the copyrighted work, (3) to distribute copies or phonorecords of the copyrighted work to the public, (4) to perform the work publicly, and (5) to display the copyrighted work publicly. Proving copyright infringement requires proving both ownership of a valid copyright and infringement of that copyright by invasion of one of these exclusive rights.

Seuss's ownership of the copyrights to the works of Dr. Seuss in question easily satisfied the first prong. Because the allegedly infringing work was not a literal copy, however, the second prong required proof that it be "substantially similar" to the copyrighted work. Penguin and Dove argued that the test should be applied element

Case 11.4 continues

Case 11.4 continued

by element to those elements allegedly similar: title; lettering design; poetic meter; whimsical style involving neologisms and onomatopoeia; and the visual style of line drawing, coloring, and shading. None of these individual elements could be given copyright protection, Penguin and Dove noted, so the "substantial similarity" test could not be met. The appeals court rejected this argument, because the trial court based its decision on the back-cover illustration and the use of the Cat's hat.

The court then addressed Penguin and Dove's affirmative defense of fair use. The Copyright Act provides four factors for a court to weigh when considering the defense: (1) the purpose and character of the accused use, (2) the nature of the copyrighted work, (3) the importance of the portion used in relation to the copyrighted work as a whole, and (4) the effect of the accused use on the market for or value of the copyrighted work.

Although Penguin and Dove argued that *The Cat NOT in the Hat!* was a parody and therefore within the traditional understanding of fair use, the court disagreed. Relying on a recent U.S. Supreme Court case, the court noted that if '"the commentary has no critical bearing on the substance or style of the original composition, which the alleged infringer merely uses to get attention or to avoid the drudgery in working up something fresh, the claim to fairness in borrowing from another's work diminishes. . . .'" Here the work simply imitated Dr. Seuss's style without targeting his work. Instead, the target was the O. J. Simpson trial and its many characters and events.

The court then looked at the second factor, the nature of the copyrighted work. Although recognizing the limited role of this factor, the court found that the creativity, imagination, and originality embodied in *The Cat in the Hat* went against fair use as compared to other works. Similarly, the central nature of the Cat in Dr. Seuss's original work, made the third factor—the amount and substantiality of the portion of copyrighted work used for supposedly fair use—weigh against the defense. Regarding the fourth factor's concern for market effects, the court thought that the new work would at best displace the copyrighted work; more likely, it would cause harm. More importantly, because Penguin and Dove offered no evidence on this last factor, the court weighed it against them.

With all four factors weighing against fair use, the court rejected it as a defense.

RESULT The appeals court affirmed the trial court's granting of a preliminary injunction to prohibit the publication and distribution of the work.

COMMENTS In an earlier case, the U.S. Supreme Court found that the commercial use of a copyrighted Roy Orbison song "Pretty Woman" in a parody by rap group 2 Live Crew did not presumptively constitute unfair use with respect to either the character and purpose of use of the copyrighted work or the harm caused by that use to the potential market for the copyrighted work.[17] The Court held that a parody that uses no more than necessary of the lyrics and music of the original work to make it recognizable does not de facto copy an unreasonable part of the copyrighted work, even if the copied part is the heart of the original work.

---

17. Campbell v. Acuff-Rose Music, Inc., 510 U.S. 569 (1994).

In a 1992 case,[18] the U.S. Court of Appeals for the Second Circuit held that internal copying of scientific articles from periodicals purchased by a profit-seeking firm was not fair use under the Copyright Act. In this case, publishers of copyrighted scientific and technical journals brought an infringement action against Texaco for making unauthorized copies of copyrighted articles for use by the company's scientific research employees. Texaco scientists were in the practice of making copies of helpful articles from the circulating library copy of the scientific and technical journals to keep in their personal files or in the laboratory. The court was not persuaded by the task Texaco confronted in subscribing to a large number of journals in an effort to keep 400 to 500 employees in six U.S. research centers abreast of new scientific findings.

In a more recent case, the U.S. Court of Appeals for the Sixth Circuit considered fair use in the academic environment.[19] In this case, a Michigan photocopy shop was in the business of preparing course readers for university professors. The professors selected excerpts from a variety of copyrighted works belonging to authors and publishers. The copy shop then compiled and numbered the excerpts, created a table of contents, photocopied the compilation, and sold copies of the assembled reader to students for use in the course. Neither the professor nor the copy shop sought permission to use the excerpts. One publisher challenged the copy shop, suing it in federal district court for copyright infringement.

The copy shop argued that its photocopying was fair use because of the ultimately educational use of the course readers by university students, the transformative value of the compilation over the separate copyrighted works, the insubstantial portion of each excerpt compared to the larger copyrighted work, and the lack of displacement for demand of the copyrighted works. The appeals court rejected these arguments for fair use as unpersuasive: the copy shop's motivation was commercial profit, not education; the "transformative" value was slight at best; the excerpts were substantial; and the market value of the larger, copyrighted works was harmed. Without its defense of fair use, the copy shop was liable for copyright infringement and enjoined from further infringement.

In reversing the trial court's finding of fair use, the appeals court reached the same result a federal district court in New York had reached in a case with nearly identical facts involving the copy shop Kinko's.[20] In the New York case, a publisher sued Kinko's for copyright infringement for its preparation and sale of similar course readers. Like the copy shop in the Sixth Circuit case, Kinko's was found liable for copyright infringement.

Types of Infringement

Direct Infringement   In the Michigan and New York copy-shop cases discussed above, publishers had accused the shops of *direct infringement;* that is, one party was alleged to have violated at least one of the five exclusive rights of the copyright holder by its own actions. Its alleged infringement was directly against one of the exclusive rights.

Contributory Infringement   A party may also be liable for *contributory infringement*—inducing, causing, or materially contributing to the infringing conduct of another with knowledge of the infringing activity. In 1995, the Church of Scientology sued Internet service provider Netcom On-Line Communications Services, Inc. for contributory infringement. The church based its claim on an ex-member's posting of copyrighted works by the church's founder to a Usenet news group. To post the works, the ex-member allegedly uploaded them to an electronic bulletin board service (BBS) that used Netcom to access the Internet. The federal district court in California concluded that Netcom could be liable for contributory infringement if it knew or should have known of the infringement but did nothing to remove the posting.[21] Similarly, in 1997, a federal district court in Ohio found a BBS liable for contributory infringement of *Playboy* magazine's copyright in its adult photographs by encouraging BBS subscribers to upload electronic versions of the pictures so that other subscribers could then download them.[22]

---

18. American Geophysical Union v. Texaco Inc., 802 F. Supp. 1 (S.D.N.Y. 1992), *aff'd*, 60 F.3d 913 (2d Cir. 1994).

19. Princeton Univ. Press v. Michigan Document Services, 99 F.3d 1381 (6th Cir. 1996), *cert. denied*, 117 S. Ct. 1336 (1997) (mem.).

20. Basic Books, Inc. v. Kinko's Graphics, Inc., 758 F. Supp. 1522 (S.D.N.Y. 1991).

21. Religious Technology Ctr. v. Netcom On-Line Comm. Servs., Inc., 907 F. Supp. 1361 (N.D. Cal. 1995). In 1996, the parties settled the case. The settlement included agreement by Netcom to establish a protocol on its home page for handling future intellectual property disputes. The protocol can be found at <http://www.netcom.com/about/protectcopy.html>.

22. Playboy Enters., Inc. v. Russ Hardenburgh, Inc., 982 F. Supp. 503 (N.D. Ohio 1997).

In an earlier case, the U.S. Supreme Court considered whether Sony Corporation of America had contributed to the infringement of copyrights held by Universal City Studios, Inc.[23] Universal alleged that Sony, by manufacturing and selling the Betamax videocassette recorder (VCR), had contributed to the infringement of Universal copyrights on programs that were broadcast over the public airwaves that some viewers would presumably copy by means of Sony's device. The Court held that the sale of copying equipment does not constitute contributory infringement if the product has substantial non-infringing uses. In Sony's case, the trial court had found that time-shifting of television programs by private, non-commercial viewers was harmless and that many other copyright holders would not object to viewers so shifting their viewing times. Hence, the Court rejected Universal's claim and found that Sony's manufacture and sale of VCRs did not contributorily infringe on Universal's copyrights. The concept of contributory infringement has also been applied to trademark law.[24]

Vicarious Infringement   Liability also extends to vicarious infringement of copyrights. A defendant may face *vicarious liability* for the actions of a primary infringer if the defendant (1) has the right and ability to control the infringer's acts, and (2) receives a direct financial benefit from the infringement. Unlike contributory infringement, vicarious infringement does not require that the defendant know of the primary infringement. Although "direct financial benefit" certainly includes a percentage of the value of each illegal sale, it is not limited to such per unit arrangements.

In 1996, the U.S. Court of Appeals for the Ninth Circuit held that a swap-meet organizer could be held vicariously liable for creating and administering a market in which bootleg music was bought and sold.[25] Although the swap-meet organizer did not receive a percentage of sales, it did receive daily rental fees from the infringing vendors, admission fees from customers purchasing the illegally copied music, and incidental payments for parking, food, and other services. Furthermore, the availability of such bootleg music was a significant attraction of the swap meet. The court held that such a financial benefit could satisfy the second prong of the test for vicarious liability.

23. Sony Corp. of America v. Universal City Studios, 464 U.S. 417 (1984).

24. Hard Rock Café Licensing Corp. v. Concession Serv., Inc., 955 F.2d 1143 (7th Cir. 1992).

25. Fonovisa, Inc. v. Cherry Auction, Inc., 76 F.3d 259 (9th Cir. 1996).

 ## The Look and Feel Debate

The courts have come out strongly in favor of copyright protection for computer code, regardless of the medium. Source code, object code, and microcode can all be copyrighted. A more controversial issue is whether copyright protection should extend to the nonliteral aspects of a computer program that comprise its user interface. These nonliteral aspects have frequently been referred to in the media as the software's "look and feel."

User Interface

User interfaces are those commands, menu screens, instructions, icons, video images, and other screen displays that function as a communication link between a computer program and the computer user. Because users like to minimize the time needed to learn a computer program, those programs whose interfaces are easy to use are often more successful than competing programs. A successful program may also become the standard in the market because users resist having to learn to use a new interface. The economic value of user interfaces has led software developers to claim copyright protection for them. Competitors of successful programs argue that user interfaces should not be copyrightable.

Arguments against Protection   Opponents of copyright protection for user interfaces argue that industry standards should be allowed to develop so that users will not have to learn different interfaces for different programs. They further argue that because interface developments are incremental and are made by merely refining already existing interfaces, no company should have the right to claim exclusive ownership.

Many of the elements of a user interface can be analyzed as uncopyrightable ideas, useful articles, or as blank forms for recording information. Opponents of copyright protection argue that interfaces such as the desktop metaphor (at issue in the *Apple v. Microsoft* case discussed below) or a spreadsheet are simply ideas for communicating computer commands. They also argue that a user interface is a useful article, analogous to the instruments in an automobile such as a standard "H" pattern gearshift knob. Finally, they argue that when interfaces are used to input data or commands, they are simply uncopyrightable blank forms.

Arguments for Protection. The proponents of copyright protection for user interfaces argue that many elements of an interface can be analyzed under traditional copyright law, which protects nonliteral elements of literary works. The proponents also argue that nonliteral imitation of user interfaces should be considered copyright infringement under the "total concept and feel" test, initially applied to works unrelated to computer software. Under total concept and feel, a copyright is infringed if an ordinary observer would regard the subsequent work as a copy of the original work's total concept and feel, even if the subsequent work does not copy any individual element of the original work.

Total Concept and Feel

In 1988, Apple Computer, Inc. sued Microsoft Corporation and Hewlett-Packard Company, claiming that the graphic user interfaces (GUI) of Microsoft's Windows program and Hewlett-Packard's New Wave program imitated the look and feel of the user interface of the Macintosh computer.[26] This computer features a visual desktop metaphor with pull-down menus and easy-to-understand icons representing computer commands.

The trial court rejected Apple's argument that copyright law protected the gestalt of the elements in its user interface. Instead, the court required Apple to identify each element and prove that it was copyrightable subject matter. Infringement could not be based on the use of items not protected by copyright law. Applying this doctrine of analytical dissection, the trial court ruled that all of the claimed infringements but one—the use of a trash can as an icon for the delete-file function—related to items that Microsoft had a license to use based on a 1985 agreement with Apple Computer or to unprotected elements.[27]

The U.S. Court of Appeals for the Second Circuit took a different approach in a case decided in 1997.[28] In that case, a software engineer fired by his client claimed that the client had written new software based on the engineer's work and in violation of his copyright. The engineer claimed that his combination of four elements had been improperly copied: (1) an external file structure; (2) English-language commands; (3) functional modules, including those to operate hardware; and (4) a hierarchical series of menus with a touchscreen. The lower court ruled against the engineer after conducting an element-by-element analysis. The appeals court, relying on *Feist* and other decisions, instructed the trial court to reconsider the issue based on the specific use of the four elements in relation to each other.

The following case addressed the issue of whether the menu-command structure of a computer program, taken as a whole—including the choice of command terms, the structure, sequence and organization of these terms, their presentation on the screen, and the long prompts—is entitled to copyright protection.

---

26. Apple Computer, Inc. v. Microsoft Corp., 799 F. Supp. 1006 (N.D. Cal. 1992).

27. Apple Computer, Inc. v. Microsoft Corp., 821 F. Supp. 616 (N.D. Cal. 1993), *aff'd,* 35 F.3d 1435 (9th Cir. 1994), *cert. denied,* 513 U.S. 1184 (1995).

28. Softel, Inc. v. Dragon Medical and Scientific Communications, Inc., 118 F.3d 995 (2d Cir. 1997).

A CASE IN POINT	**SUMMARY**

CASE 11.5
LOTUS DEVELOPMENT CORP. v. BORLAND INTERNATIONAL, INC.
United States Court of Appeals for the First Circuit
49 F.3d 807 (1st Cir. 1995),
aff'd, 516 U.S. 233 (1996).

FACTS Lotus Development Corp. sued Borland International, Inc. for allegedly infringing its copyright on the software spreadsheet program Lotus 1-2-3. Lotus contended that Borland's Quattro and Quattro Pro programs copied Lotus's user interface, including menu commands, hierarchical menu structures, long prompts, and keystroke sequences. The trial ruled that the Lotus menu-command hierarchy was copyrightable expression subject to protection. Borland appealed.

ISSUE PRESENTED Are the functional relationships found in the menu-command hierarchy of a computer software program copyrightable?

Case 11.5 continues

Case 11.5 continued

SUMMARY OF OPINION   The U.S. Court of Appeals began by noting that the Copyright Act forbids copyright protection for any idea, procedure, process, system, method of operation, concept, principle, or discovery. For that reason, a copyrightable text describing how to operate something would not extend copyright protection to the method of operation itself. Here, the issue was whether the Lotus 1-2-3 command hierarchy was a "method of operation" and therefore not copyrightable.

In the case of Lotus 1-2-3, the court noted, the menu command hierarchy "does not merely explain and present Lotus 1-2-3's functional capabilities to the user; it also serves as the method by which the program is operated and controlled." Analogizing to videocassette recorders, the court found that Lotus 1-2-3's use of commands labeled "Print" and "Copy" was no different from VCR buttons labeled "Play" and "Fast Forward." That such VCR buttons are arranged and labeled does not make them an expression of the abstract method of operating a VCR. Rather, the buttons *are* the method of operating the VCR.

To the extent there is expression in Lotus 1-2-3's choice of terms such as "Exit" or "Save," it is part of the method of operation and cannot be copyrighted either. Quoting the U.S. Supreme Court's *Feist* decision, the court noted that "copyright assures authors the right to their original expression, but encourages others to build freely upon the ideas and information conveyed by that work."

RESULT   Ruling that the Lotus 1-2-3 hierarchy was not copyrightable, the appeals court reversed the trial court and found Borland not liable for copyright infringement.

COMMENTS   Although the decision by the Court of Appeals was affirmed by the U.S. Supreme Court, the Supreme Court split four-to-four and did not issue an opinion.

Registered Mask Work

The Semiconductor Chip Protection Act of 1984 created a highly specialized form of intellectual property, the *registered mask work*. This was the first significant new intellectual property right in the United States in nearly 100 years. Semiconductor masks are detailed transparencies that represent the topological layout of semiconductor chips. The act gives the owner exclusive rights in the mask for a period of 10 years and proscribes copying or use by others. However, the act specifically allows reverse engineering. Because this law is relatively new, the legal protections afforded to mask owners are still developing. The law was aimed primarily at counterfeiters who would replicate the semiconductor masks for a chip already on the market and produce the chips without having to expend their own resources on development. The remedies for infringement are an injunction, damages, and the impoundment of the infringing mask and chips.

In the first case litigated under the Semiconductor Chip Protection Act, Brooktree Corporation, a manufacturer of semiconductor chips, sued competitor Advanced Micro Devices, Inc. (AMD) for patent infringement and infringement-of-mask-work registration in connection with semiconductor chips used in color video displays. The AMD chips involved a design in which 80% of the circuitry was "similar" to Brooktree's design, and two of the three patents that were allegedly infringed related to portions of the registered mask works. Brooktree won at trial in federal district court, but AMD appealed. AMD did not challenge the validity of the mask-work registrations or the fact that the chips are protected property. Instead, it simply asserted that its chips were not infringements. To make its case, AMD produced voluminous amounts of paper attempting to show that it had conducted extensive research to reverse engineer the chip. By its argument, even though AMD's end product looked like Brooktree's chip, the path in arriving there was not by copying. Therefore, there could be no infringement.

The U.S. Court of Appeals for the Federal Circuit rejected AMD's attempted defense of reverse engineering.[29] After a rather technical analysis involving a close look at the circuitry involved in the individual patents, the court affirmed the validity and infringement of the patents. The court concluded that Brooktree was entitled to actual damages suffered as a result of the infringement, plus any profits made by AMD that were attributable to the infringement.

 ## Trademarks

Most people associate a particular trademark with the product to which it is applied without considering how this association has been generated. For example, when consumers purchase Apple computers, they usually do not think about how the word for a type of fruit has become representative of that particular brand of personal computer. Trademark law concerns itself with just such questions: how trademarks are created, how trademark rights arise, how such rights can be preserved, and why certain marks are given greater protection than others.

Statutory Definition

The federal trademark act, otherwise known as the Lanham Act, and the 1988 Trademark Law Revision Act[30] define a trademark as "any word, name, symbol, or device or any combination thereof adopted and used by a manufacturer or merchant to identify and distinguish his goods, including a unique product, from those manufactured or sold by others, and to indicate the source of the goods, even if that source is unknown."

This definition has been interpreted as recognizing four different purposes of a trademark: (1) to provide an identification symbol for a particular merchant's goods; (2) to indicate that the goods to which the trademark has been applied are from a single source; (3) to guarantee that all goods to which the trademark has been applied are of a constant quality; and (4) to advertise the goods.

Basically, a trademark tells a consumer where a product comes from and who is responsible for its creation. A trademark also implies that all goods sold under the mark are of a consistent level of quality. A consumer purchasing French-fried potatoes at a McDonald's restaurant, for instance, can reasonably expect them to taste as good as those sold at any other McDonald's. The trademark does not necessarily reveal the product's manufacturer. For example, the trademark Sanka identifies a brand of decaffeinated coffee. We may not know whether the manufacturer is a company called Sanka, but we know that all coffee products bearing the Sanka mark are sponsored by a single company (or its licensees).

Although most trademarks are verbal or graphic, trademark law also protects distinctive shapes, odors, packaging, and sounds. For instance, there is trademark protection for the unique shape of the Coca-Cola bottle and NBC's three chimes. An extension of trademark law, protection for trade dress, is discussed in the "Inside Story." The following case addresses the use of color as a trademark.

---

29. Brooktree Corp. v. Advanced Micro Devices, Inc., 977 F.2d 1555 (Fed. Cir. 1992).

30. 15 U.S.C. §§ 1051–1072 (1994).

A CASE IN POINT	**IN THE LANGUAGE OF THE COURT**

CASE 11.6
QUALITEX CO. v. JACOBSON PRODUCTS CO.
Supreme Court of the United States
514 U.S. 159 (1995).

FACTS Qualitex manufactures pads for use on dry-cleaning presses and, since the 1950s, has used a special shade of green-gold color on them. In 1989, rival Jacobson Products began to sell its own press pads to dry-cleaning firms and colored them a similar green-gold. In 1991, Qualitex registered the special green-gold color on its

Case 11.6 continues

Case 11.6 continued

press pads with the Patent and Trademark Office as a trademark. Qualitex subsequently sued Jacobson for trademark infringement.

Although Qualitex won at trial, the court of appeals set aside the judgment on the grounds that the Trademark Act does not permit registration of "color alone" as a trademark. Qualitex appealed.

ISSUE PRESENTED   Does the Trademark Act permit the registration of a trademark that consists solely of a color?

OPINION   SOUTER, J., writing for the U.S. Supreme Court:

The [Trademark] Act gives a seller or producer the exclusive right to "register" a trademark and to prevent his or her competitors from using that trademark. Both the language of the Act and the basic underlying principles of trademark law would seem to include color within the universe of things that can qualify as a trademark. The language of the Act describes that universe in the broadest of terms. It says that trademarks "includ[e] any word, name, symbol, or device, or any combination thereof." Since human beings might use as a "symbol" or "device" almost anything at all that is capable of carrying meaning, this language, read literally, is not restrictive. . . .

A color is also capable of satisfying the more important part of the statutory definition of a trademark, which requires that a person "us[e]" or "inten[d] to use" the mark "to identify and distinguish his or her goods, including a unique product, from those manufactured or sold by others and to indicate the source of the goods, even if that source is unknown."

True, a product's color is unlike "fanciful," "arbitrary," or "suggestive" words or designs, which almost automatically tell a customer that they refer to a brand. The imaginary word "Suntost," or the words "Suntost Marmalade," on a jar of orange jam immediately would signal a brand or a product "source"; the jam's orange color does not do so. But, over time, customers may come to treat a particular color on a product or its packaging (say, a color that in context seems unusual, such as pink on a firm's insulating material or red on the head of a large industrial bolt) as signifying a brand. And, if so, that color would have come to identify and distinguish the goods—i.e., to "indicate" their "source"—much in the way that descriptive words on a product (say, "Trim" on nail clippers or "Car-Freshner" on deodorizer) can come to indicate a product's origin. In this circumstance, trademark law says that the word (e.g., "Trim"), although not inherently distinctive, has developed "secondary meaning." Again, one might ask, if trademark law permits a descriptive word with secondary meaning to act as a mark, why would it not permit a color, under similar circumstances, to do the same?

We cannot find in the basic objectives of trademark law any obvious theoretical objection to the use of color alone as a trademark, where that color has attained "secondary meaning" and therefore identifies and distinguishes a particular brand (and thus indicates its "source"). In principle, trademark law, by preventing others from copying a source-identifying mark, "reduce[s] the customer's costs of shopping and making purchasing decisions," for it quickly and easily assures a potential customer that this item—the item with this mark—is made by the same producer as other similarly marked

Case 11.6 continues

Case 11.6 continued

items that he or she liked (or disliked) in the past. At the same time, the law helps assure a producer that it (and not an imitating competitor) will reap the financial, reputation-related rewards associated with a desirable product. The law thereby "encourage[s] the production of quality products," . . . and simultaneously discourages those who hope to sell inferior products by capitalizing on a consumer's inability quickly to evaluate the quality of an item offered for sale. It is the source-distinguishing ability of a mark—not its ontological status as color, shape, fragrance, word, or sign—that permits it to serve these basic purposes. And, for that reason, it is difficult to find, in basic trademark objectives, a reason to disqualify absolutely the use of a color as a mark.

Neither can we find a principled objection to the use of color as a mark in the important "functionality" doctrine of trademark law. The functionality doctrine prevents trademark law, which seeks to promote competition by protecting a firm's reputation, from instead inhibiting legitimate competition by allowing a producer to control a useful product feature. It is the province of patent law, not trademark law, to encourage invention by granting inventors a monopoly over new product designs or functions for a limited time after which competitors are free to use the innovation. If a product's functional features could be used as trademarks, however, a monopoly over such features could be obtained without regard to whether they qualify as patents and could be extended forever (because trademarks may be renewed in perpetuity). Functionality doctrine therefore would require, to take an imaginary example, that even if customers have come to identify the special illumination-enhancing shape of a new patented light bulb with a particular manufacturer, the manufacturer may not use that shape as a trademark, for doing so, after the patent had expired, would impede competition—not by protecting the reputation of the original bulb maker, but by frustrating competitors' legitimate efforts to produce an equivalent illumination-enhancing bulb. This Court consequently has explained that, "[i]n general terms, a product feature is functional," and cannot serve as a trademark, "if it is essential to the use or purpose of the article or if it affects the cost or quality of the article," that is, if exclusive use of the feature would put competitors at a significant non-reputation-related disadvantage. Although sometimes color plays an important role (unrelated to source identification) in making a product more desirable, sometimes it does not. And, this latter fact—the fact that sometimes color is not essential to a product's use or purpose and does not affect cost or quality—indicates that the doctrine of "functionality" does not create an absolute bar to the use of color alone as a mark.

It would seem, then, that color alone, at least sometimes, can meet the basic legal requirements for use as a trademark. It can act as a symbol that distinguishes a firm's goods and identifies their source, without serving any other significant function. Indeed, the District Court, in this case, entered findings (accepted by the Ninth Circuit) that show Qualitex's green-gold press pad color has met these requirements. The green-gold color acts as a symbol. Having developed secondary meaning (for customers identified the green-gold color as Qualitex's), it identifies the press pads' source. And, the green-gold color serves no other function. (Although it is important to use some color on press pads to avoid noticeable stains, the court found "no competitive need in the press pad industry for the green-gold color, since other

Case 11.6 continues

Case 11.6 continued

colors are equally usable.") Accordingly, unless there is some special reason that convincingly militates against the use of color alone as a trademark, trademark law would protect Qualitex's use of the green–gold color on its press pads.

RESULT   The Supreme Court reversed the court of appeals and reinstated Qualitex's judgment against Jacobson for trademark infringement.

Questions

1. How would the court have analyzed the case if dry-cleaning chemicals formed toxic gases when mixed with most dyes?
2. One argument against allowing trademarks of purely color is that such a system would create much uncertainty and unresolvable legal disputes as parties bickered over subtle hues and glosses, in contrast to the relative certainty of verbal and graphical marks. What is the strongest response to such an argument?

Benefits

Trademarks benefit both consumers and producers. For consumers, trademarks reduce the cost of finding information about products by dividing the many available products into a few brand types. Without such reference points, a buyer would have to gather information about each individual item he or she purchased. Trademarks also encourage the production of quality goods, because consumers can trace goods, especially low-quality goods, to their source through their mark.

For producers, a trademark represents the goodwill of a business, that is, an accumulation of satisfied customers who will continue buying from that business. Trademark rights are determined predominantly by the perceptions and associations in the minds of the buying public, so maintaining a strong trademark is essential to preserving the success of a business.

Exhibit 11.2 sets forth the 15 most valuable brand names in the world in 1995, according to a survey by *Financial World* magazine, and the percentage change in value from 1994.

Other Marks

Trademarks should not be confused with other forms of legally protected identifying marks, such as service marks, trade names, and certification marks.

Service Marks   A trademark is used in connection with a tangible product; a *service mark* is used in connection with services. The law concerning service marks is almost identical to that of trademarks.

Trade Names   While a trademark is used to identify and distinguish products, a *trade name* or a corporate name identifies a company, partnership, or business. Trade names cannot be registered under federal law, unless they are also used as trademarks or service marks. However, trade names are protectable under some of the same common law principles that apply to trademarks. The use of a trade name—evidenced by the filing of articles of incorporation or a fictitious business name statement—gives the company using the name certain common law rights.

Certification Marks   A *certification mark* placed on a product indicates that the product has met the certifier's standards of safety or quality. An example is the "Good Housekeeping" seal of approval placed on certain consumer goods.

Choosing a Trademark

To get a sense of how one chooses a trademark, consider a hypothetical entrepreneur who has developed a new form of computer software. This entrepreneur's program takes personal information—such as place and date of birth and daily biorhythms—and processes it to give the user predictions as to what may happen in the future (on the basis of "the past," that is, on the basis of the inserted

EXHIBIT 11.2   Most Valuable Brand Names

RANK	BRAND	COMPANY	VALUE (BILLIONS)	PERCENTAGE CHANGE (FROM PRIOR YEAR)
1.	Coca-Cola	Coca-Cola Co.	$39.05	14
2.	Marlboro	Philip Morris Cos.	38.71	13
3.	IBM	International Business Machines Corp.	17.15	*
4.	Motorola	Motorola Inc.	15.28	73
5.	Hewlett-Packard	Hewlett-Packard Co.	13.17	74
6.	Microsoft	Microsoft Corp.	11.74	31
7.	Kodak	Eastman Kodak Co.	11.59	(6)
8.	Budweiser	Anheuser-Busch Cos.	11.35	6
9.	Kellogg's	Kellogg Co.	11.00	2
10.	Nescafe	Nestle, SA	10.34	(2)
11.	Intel	Intel Corp.	9.71	55
12.	Gillette	Gillette Co.	9.67	12
13.	Pepsi	PepsiCo Inc.	7.81	3
14.	GE	General Electric Co.	7.42	25
15.	Levi's	Levi Strauss & Co.	6.92	10

*change not meaningful

information). He has chosen three possible names for his software: Viron, Gypsy in a Disc, and Venus.

The entrepreneur wants to be certain that the trademark he chooses for his software is protectable. Under trademark law, the degree of protection is determined by where a trademark can be classified on a scale of distinctiveness. The more distinctive a mark is, the less likelihood of confusion with other marks. Hence, marks that are the most distinctive are given, at least initially, the greatest legal protection. The policy is to reward originality in the creation of a mark.

Inherently Distinctive

Inherently distinctive marks are marks that need no proof of distinctiveness. They are often called strong marks, because they are immediately protectable. Fanciful, arbitrary, or suggestive marks are all inherently distinctive.

Fanciful Marks   A fanciful mark is a coined term having no prior meaning until used as a trademark in connection with a particular product. Fanciful marks are usually made-up words, such as Kodak for camera products and Exxon for gasoline. In the preceding hypothetical, "Viron" is an example of a fanciful, made-up mark.

Arbitrary Marks   Arbitrary marks are real words whose ordinary meaning has nothing to do with the trademarked product, for example, Apple for computers, Camel for cigarettes, and Shell for gasoline. In the preceding hypothetical, "Venus" is an example of an arbitrary mark.

Suggestive Marks   A suggestive mark suggests something about the product without directly describing it. After seeing the mark, a consumer must use his or her imagination to determine the nature of the goods. For instance, Chicken of the Sea does not immediately create an association with tuna fish; it merely suggests some type of seafood. In the hypothetical, "Gypsy in a Disc" would be an example of a suggestive mark. It merely suggests a future-predicting software program.

Not Inherently Distinctive

Marks that are not inherently distinctive are not immediately protectable. Granting trademark rights for a description of a product that may apply equally to different products would frustrate the fundamental distinguishing purpose of a trademark.

INTERNATIONAL CONSIDERATION

In 1997, Japan enacted a new trademark law to harmonize its trademark procedures with the international community and bring itself into compliance with the Trademark Law Treaty. The new law also addresses the accumulation of unused registered trademarks by allowing anyone to petition for the cancellation of a mark that has gone unused and by making it more difficult to defend against such petitions. The new law also shortens the time required to approve trademark applications. Observers expect that the trademark regime will make it easier for non-Japanese to register and protect their marks in Japan. Among its many provisions, the new law allows for the registration of three-dimensional marks for the first time.

Secondary Meaning   However, marks that are initially unprotectable can become protectable by acquiring *secondary meaning*, that is, a mental association by the buyer that links the mark with a single source of the product. Through secondary meaning, a mark obtains distinctiveness. Once this occurs, the mark is granted trademark protection. Thus, Microsoft was able to register "Windows" as a trademark once it had acquired secondary meaning.

Establishment of secondary meaning depends on a number of factors, such as the amount of advertising, the type of the market, the number of sales, and consumer recognition and response. The testimony of random buyers or of product dealers may be required in order to prove that a mark has acquired secondary meaning.

Secondary meaning is necessary to establish trademark protection for descriptive marks, geographic terms, and personal names.

Descriptive Marks   *Descriptive marks* specify certain characteristics of the goods, such as size or color; proposed uses; the intended consumers for the goods; or the effect of using the goods. Laudatory terms, such as First Rate or Gold Medal, are also considered descriptive marks.

Geographic Terms   Geographic descriptive terms are usually considered nondistinctive unless secondary meaning has been established. However, geographic terms used in an arbitrary manner are inherently distinctive, for example, Salem for cigarettes and North Pole for bananas.

Personal Names   Personal first names and surnames are not inherently distinctive. However, an arbitrary use of a historical name, such as Lincoln for a savings bank, does not require secondary meaning.

Nondistinctive and Generic

No protection is given to generic terms, such as "spoon" or "software," because doing so would permit a producer to monopolize a term that all producers should be able to use equally. It would be ridiculous to permit one manufacturer to obtain the exclusive right to use the word "computer," for example, and force all competitors to come up with a new word, rather than a brand name, for the same type of product. Generic terms are not protected even when they acquire secondary meaning.

Many terms that were once enforceable trademarks have become generic. For example, "escalator" was once the brand name of a moving staircase, and "cellophane" was a plastic wrap developed by DuPont. Due to misuse or negligence by the owners, these marks lost their connection with particular brands and became ordinary words (see Exhibit 11.3). That is the reason Xerox Corp. spends more than $100,000 a year explaining that you don't "Xerox" a document, you "copy" it on a Xerox copier.[31]

For terms that describe products made by only one company, the problem of genericism—the use of the product name as a generic name—is acute. Without competitive products, buyers may begin to think of the trademark as indicative of what the product is rather than where the product comes from. Manufacturers can try to avoid this problem by always using the trademark as an adjective in conjunction with a generic noun. It is all right to say "Sanka decaffeinated coffee" or "an Apple computer," but not "a cup of Sanka" or "an Apple." Once the buying public starts using the mark as a synonym for the product, rather than as a means of distinguishing its source, loss of the trademark is imminent.

---

31. Weigel, *Whatever You Do with This Article, Don't "Xerox" It,* Chicago Sun-Times, Oct. 7, 1990, at 57.

EXHIBIT 11.3   Attempts to Preserve a Trademark

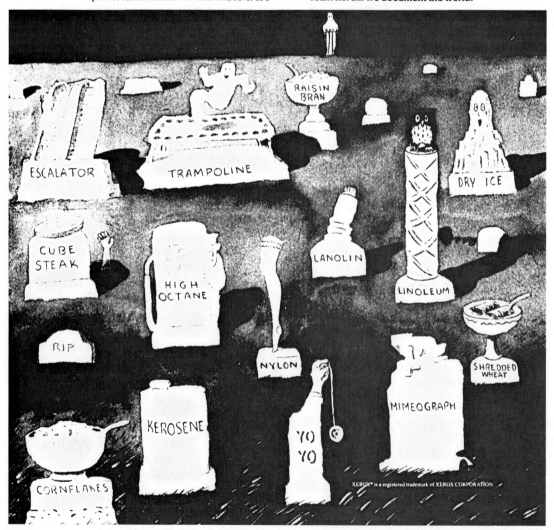

INTERNATIONAL CONSIDERATION

India, the world's most populous democracy, is paying increasing attention to intellectual property rights as it attempts to attract foreign investment and take its place in international trade. Although the Indian legal system is notoriously slow, its courts are acting with relative speed to issue injunctions and search-and-seize orders to halt the sale of fake goods. Still, trademark applications, which rose four-fold between 1992 and 1997, take five to seven years to process. Violations of software copyrights have also fallen. Such pirating accounted for 89% of the software market in 1991 but accounted for only 60% in 1996. The fall is the result of stronger copyright laws, elimination of duties on software imports, and aggressive litigation by copyright holders and support from international business associations. Despite these positive trends, India remains on the U.S. trade representative's priority watch list, mainly because of its failure to meet World Trade Organization obligations on agricultural and pharmaceutical patent protections. Still, observers say the situation is improving.[a]

a. Jonathan Karp, *India's Laws a Mixed Blessing for Investors*, WALL ST. J., July 11, 1997, at A10.

◆ Creating Rights in a Trademark

Trademark rights initially are obtained in the U.S. through use of the mark in commerce. Following use in interstate commerce, additional rights may be obtained by federal registration. State registration requires only intrastate use.

Use

A trademark is used in commerce if it is physically attached to the goods which are then sold or distributed. Each subsequent use of a trademark creates greater rights, because increased sales and advertising generate greater customer awareness of the mark as representing the product. Advertising and promotional activities in the United States by a foreign restaurant bearing a foreign trademark, but providing no restaurant services in the United States, was held not to constitute sufficient "use" of that trademark in commerce to merit protection.[32]

For marks that are not inherently distinctive, use is also necessary to establish secondary meaning. Although its application was denied initially, Microsoft Corporation succeeded in registering the mark "Windows" five years later after it presented studies demonstrating that users associated the mark with Microsoft's operating system for personal computers.

For inherently distinctive marks in the United States, ownership is governed by priority of use. The first seller to sell the goods under a mark becomes the owner and senior user of the mark. The mark is protected immediately, provided the adoption and use of the mark are done in good faith and without knowledge, actual or constructive, of any superior rights in the mark. Thus, when an entrepreneur first attempts to acquire trademark rights, he or she should check whether the entrepreneur is the first user of the proposed mark or any confusingly similar mark for similar products. If this is not done, the entrepreneur's use of the mark may be seen as infringing the trademark of a senior user, and he or she will not obtain any rights in the mark.

There is an exception to the rule of first use. If a subsequent, or junior, user establishes a strong consumer identification with its mark in a separate geographic area, the junior user may be granted superior rights for that area. The senior user, by failing to expand its business to other parts of the country, takes the risk that a junior user may be permitted to use the same or confusingly similar mark in a distant area. The junior user's use must be in good faith, that is, the junior user must take reasonable steps to determine whether any preexisting mark is confusingly similar to the one it plans to use.

This geographic rule is inapplicable, however, if the senior user has applied for or obtained federal registration. Once the senior user has filed an application or has obtained federal registration, it is permitted to claim nationwide constructive notice of the mark. This precludes any use—even a good faith use—of the mark by a junior user. However, the senior user may not take any action against the junior user in a geographically removed area until the senior user is likely to expand into that area.

32. Buti v. Impressa S.R.L., 139 F.3d 98 (2d Cir. 1998).

Federal Registration

Although not a requirement for obtaining U.S. rights in a mark, registration on the federal Principal Register provides many legal advantages. Such registration provides constructive notice of a claim of ownership in all 50 states. This makes it easier to enjoin subsequent users, because unauthorized use of a federally registered mark cannot be in good faith. Other benefits of registration on the Principal Register include (1) prima facie evidence of ownership; (2) the "incontestable" right (subject to certain defenses) to use the mark, obtainable after five years of continuous use following registration; and (3) the right to prevent importation into the United States of articles bearing an infringing mark.

Registration on the Principal Register makes strategic sense. It deters others from using the mark, as they are on constructive notice of the mark's ownership. It also gives the owner the right to preempt junior users if the owner expands into their territories.

Certain marks that do not qualify for registration on the Principal Register may be registered on the Supplemental Register. However, such registration does not afford the owner any of the above benefits. This type of registration should be pursued only upon the advice of counsel.

Federal registration of trademarks is conducted by the United States Patent and Trademark Office (PTO). The 1988 Trademark Law Revision Act dramatically changed the character of federal trademark law and the registration process. Whereas the prior system required use of the mark before an application could be filed, under the 1988 act an applicant may file either an "actual use" application or an "intent to use" application. For the latter, the applicant must state a bona fide intent to use the mark, must then commence use, and must provide the PTO with a statement of use within six months of receiving notice that its application is entitled to registration. The six-month period can be extended for up to 30 months, giving applicants a total of three years from the date of the notice of allowance in which to file the statement of use. Registration is postponed until the applicant actually uses the mark. However, the applicant has priority rights against any party who, before the application filing date, neither used the same mark nor filed an application for it.

The "intent to use" provision of the 1988 act is aimed at preventing the loss of time, money, and effort that previously occurred when a company developed and marketed a new product under a proposed trademark, only to find that the PTO did not agree that the trademark was registrable.

The registration process can be complex and confusing, and consultation with legal counsel is strongly advised before proceeding. It is also time consuming. It can take up to 18 months after an application is filed for a federal registration to be issued. Most state registrations take less time. Consequently, a company waiting on federal registration may simultaneously register the mark on the state level to ensure more immediate protection.

State Registration

State registration does not provide as much protection as federal registration. However, it does offer certain benefits. In most states, registration can be obtained within a few weeks of filing and is proof of ownership of the mark. For marks that are not eligible for federal registration, state registration usually provides at the least a modicum of protection, as long as there has been sufficient use of the mark. The degree of protection is determined by the relevant state statute.

State registration cannot preempt or narrow the rights granted by federal registration. For example, a junior user with a state registration predating a senior user's federal registration gains exclusive rights in the mark only in the geographic area of continuous usage preceding the federal registration, and not the entire state. A state trademark law that purported to reserve the entire state for the junior user would be preempted by the Lanham Act.

Trademark Searches

A company about to use a new trademark needs first to conduct a trademark search. Without conducting a search, the company has no way of knowing whether use of the proposed mark will constitute an infringement. The time, money, and effort spent on promotion and advertising will be wasted if use of the mark is ultimately prohibited.

There are various ways of searching a mark. The records of the PTO provide information on federally registered marks; the office of the secretary of state usually can provide relevant data for state marks. Both state and federal registrations describe the mark and the

INTERNATIONAL CONSIDERATION

As part of the normalization of trade relations with the United States in 1996, Cambodia signed a bilateral treaty with the United States. In exchange for formally receiving Most Favored Nation status in the United States and the lower tariffs that accompany such status, Cambodia agreed to allow U.S. trademark holders to take legal action against companies using their already established and popular names. For instance, one company in Phnom Penh had been selling pizza under the name "Pizza Hot" and using the familiar red triangle roof of PepsiCo's Pizza Hut. The new law will allow PepsiCo to petition to have the imitator's mark cancelled.

goods it identifies, the owners of the mark, the date of registration, and the date on which the mark was first used. Most of this registration material has been computerized, and can be accessed by an attorney.

Searching for unregistered marks is more difficult. Trade and telephone directories are often a good source of common law uses of marks. There are also several professional trademark search firms that search databases for customers. Although there is always the risk that a new mark or a common law user may be untraceable, any search is better than no search. Searching is evidence of a good faith effort to determine whether any other entity has preexisting rights in a mark.

 ## Loss of Trademark Rights

Failure to use one's mark—known as *abandonment*—may result in the loss of rights. A federally registered mark that has been abandoned can be used by a junior user. A trademark search can reveal whether a previously registered trademark has lost its enforceability. There are two types of abandonment: actual and constructive.

Actual Abandonment

Actual abandonment occurs when an owner discontinues use of the mark with the intent not to resume use.

Mere nonuse for a limited period does not result in loss of protection. However, there is a presumption of abandonment after two years of nonuse. Because protection for federally registered marks is nationwide, the abandonment must be nationwide for loss of rights to result.

Constructive Abandonment

Constructive abandonment results when the owner does something, or fails to do something, that causes the mark to lose its distinctiveness. Constructive abandonment can result from a mark lapsing into genericism through improper use, such as using "thermos" as a noun rather than a brand name. It can also result from the failure of an owner to adequately control companies licensed to use its mark. Thus, a licensor should carefully exercise quality controls and approval procedures for its licensees' products in order to ensure a consistent quality level.

 ## Trademark Infringement

Every trademark owner runs the risk either of having a mark infringed or of being the infringer of someone else's mark. A trademark can be infringed whether or not it is registered; the test for determining infringement in both cases is similar. To establish infringement, a trademark owner must prove (1) the validity of the mark (note that a federally registered mark is *prima facie* valid); (2) priority of usage of the mark; and (3) a likelihood of confusion in the minds of the purchasers of the products in question.

Proving validity and priority of usage is fairly straightforward if the mark is registered; even if the mark is not registered, proof is a factual matter. The likelihood-of-confusion standard, on the other hand, although a factual test, involves subjectively weighing a variety of factors. These include (1) the similarity of the two marks with respect to appearance, sound, connotation, and commercial impression; (2) the similarity of the goods; (3) the similarity of the channels of trade in which the goods are sold; (4) the strength of the marks, as evidenced by the amount of sales and advertising and the length of use; (5) the use of similar marks by third parties with respect to related goods and services; (6) the length of time of concurrent use without actual confusion; and (7) the extent and nature of any actual confusion of the two marks in the marketplace.

Taking advantage of trademark confusion, however, does not necessarily amount to infringement. In 1996, the U.S. Court of Appeals for the Sixth Circuit ruled that a travel agency had not infringed Holiday Inns' trademark in its vanity toll-free telephone number by using a similar number.[33] To promote itself, Holiday Inns had widely publicized its toll-free reservation line as 1-800-HOLIDAY, which translates to 1-800-465-4329 on a numeric keypad. Perhaps anticipating that dialers would mistake Holiday Inns' letter "O" for the number zero, the travel agency had reserved the toll-free number 1-800-405-4329. Acknowledging the potential for confusion, the court rejected Holiday Inns' claim of trademark infringement because the travel agency did not create the confusion; it merely took advantage of it.

In 1996, Congress amended the federal Trademark Act by enacting the Federal Trademark Dilution Act of 1995.[34] Under the new law, owners of famous trademarks are entitled to damages from and can enjoin parties whose commercial use of a mark "begins after the mark has become famous and causes dilution of the distinctive quality of the mark." In one of the first cases under the new law, Ringling Brothers and Barnum & Bailey sued to protect its registered mark "THE GREATEST SHOW ON EARTH." The circus promoter sought to enjoin the state of Utah from using the slogan "THE GREATEST SNOW ON EARTH" on its license plates, advertisements, and tourism promotions. Although the marks were not identical—"SNOW" instead of "SHOW"—the court ruled that the new statute protects marks from dilution by the use of identical as well as similar marks.[35] Ultimately, however, the court found in favor of Utah on the grounds that Ringling Brothers had not proven any dilution of their mark.[36]

In another case that year, Hormel Foods Corporation sued Jim Henson Productions, Inc. to enjoin it from using a new character "Spa'am" in the then-upcoming film *Muppet Treasure Island*. Hormel argued that such use by Henson would dilute its trademark "Spam" luncheon meat. Although conceding the similarity and likely lampooning intention of Henson, the court rejected Hormel's claim.[37] Instead of harming Hormel, the court concluded, Henson's use of "Spa'am" would likely increase public identification of Hormel's mark with Hormel.

First Sale Doctrine

As with copyrighted items, under the first sale doctrine, the right of a producer to control the distribution of a trademarked product extends only to the first sale of the product. Resale by the first purchaser of the original product is neither trademark infringement nor unfair competition. The first sale doctrine attempts to strike a balance among (1) trademark law's goal of allowing producers to reap the benefits of their reputation, (2) consumer's desire to receive genuinely what they bargain for, and (3) maintenance of competitive markets by limiting producer control of resale.

In 1995, Sebastian International, a consumer-products manufacturer, attempted to get around the first sale doctrine by affixing a special mark on its products. The mark read "Sebastian Collective Salon Member" and referred to an organization of professional hair salons and distributors that Sebastian created and controlled. When Longs Drug Stores, which was not a member of the group, attempted to sell Sebastian products with the mark, Sebastian sued for trademark infringement and unfair competition. Although a trial court preliminarily enjoined Longs from selling Sebastian products, the U.S. Court of Appeals for the Ninth Circuit relied on the first sale doctrine's letter and spirit to reverse that decision and allow Longs to continue selling the products.[38]

Remedies

The remedies for trademark infringement include injunctive relief, an accounting for lost profits due to customer confusion, and damages. The type of relief granted is determined on a case-by-case basis.

33. Holiday Inns, Inc. v. 800 Reservation, Inc., 86 F.3d 619 (6th Cir. 1996), *cert. denied*, 117 S. Ct. 770 (1997).

34. 15 U.S.C. § 1125(c)(1) (1997).

35. Ringling Bros.–Barnum & Bailey, Combined Shows, Inc. v. Utah Div. Travel Dev., 935 F. Supp. 763 (E.D.Va. 1996).

36. 955 F. Supp. 605 (E.D.Va. 1997).

37. Hormel Foods Corp. v. Jim Henson Prod., Inc., 73 F.3d 497 (2d Cir. 1996).

38. Sebastian Int'l Inc. v. Longs Drug Stores Corp., 53 F.3d 1073 (9th Cir. 1995), *cert. denied*, 116 S. Ct. 302 (1995) (mem.).

INTERNATIONAL CONSIDERATION

Every country has its own methods for determining what is a protectable trademark, how to obtain and maintain trademarks, and the scope of protection available for trademarks. In most countries, unlike the United States, use of a mark confers no rights, and registration is essential. In addition, registration of a trademark in the United States confers no rights in foreign countries, although a U.S. registration can provide an easy basis for registration of corresponding trademarks in countries that participate in multilateral trademark conventions with the United States.

◆ Trade Secrets

In our free-market system, the value of many types of information decreases with availability. With a highly mobile work force, the demand for modern technologies and innovation may lead to unauthorized disclosure of sensitive information. Trade-secret law is necessary to protect the owners of such information. As social theorist Alvin Toffler noted in his 1990 analysis *Powershift*:

> No one buys a share of [Apple Computer, Inc.] or IBM stock because of the firm's material assets. What counts are not the company's buildings or machines, but the contacts and power of its marketing and sales force, the organizational capacity of its management and the ideas crackling in the heads of its employees.[39]

39. ALVIN TOFFLER, POWERSHIFT (1990).

VIEW FROM CYBERSPACE

DOMAIN NAMES VS. TRADEMARKS

Telecommunications and the Internet have given birth to a new form of intellectual property: domain names. Through these electronic addresses, entities such as Ford Motor Company (ford.com), Stanford University (stanford.edu), and the Federal Communications Commission (fcc.gov) can communicate with each other. More important for managers, these addresses also allow potential customers, investors, and employees to find and transact with companies. Originally doled out by the National Science Foundation (NSF), these addresses are currently administered by Network Solutions, Inc., a small Herndon, Virginia, firm under contract with NSF. The role of trademark law in this area is still developing and is important for the estimated 500,000 businesses and 50 million people who use the Internet.

The courts have held that the commercial use of a domain name will infringe on a third party's trademark rights when the name is used by a company offering the same products as the trademark owner or when use of the name dilutes a famous trademark. For example, a court granted Panavision International's motion for a summary judgment against a domain-name "pirate" or

"cybersquatter" who registered the trademarked name "Panavision" in an attempt to force the trademark owner Panavision International to pay $13,000 to buy the domain name.[a] The court concluded that the cybersquatter had diluted Panavision's famous trademark. Similarly, registration of a domain name that was confusingly similar to a registered trademark constituted trademark infringement when the Internet site included a reference to a similar company name and offered the same services.[b]

In late 1997, a federal court ruled that although the use of a domain name falls under the Trademark Act, registration of a mark by a domain-name registrar does not constitute a commercial use of a mark under trademark laws.[c] Similarly, domain-name registrars do not have a duty to review domain-name applications to determine whether the requested domain names might infringe a third party's trademark rights.[d] Nonetheless, Network Solutions has a policy of putting domain names on hold when challenged by the owner of a federally registered trademark.

View from Cyberspace continues

View from Cyberspace continued

If this decision is followed, trademark holders would need to pursue individual domain-name registrants to protect their marks. Such pursuit may become more difficult in 1999, when NSF's contract with Network Solutions expires and NSF ends its own involvement with the entire issue of domain-name registration. At that point, the Internet community will have to police itself.

Some Internet groups have proposed overhauling the domain-name system to allow for seven generic top-level domains with specific suffixes, such as ".firm" and ".store," to ease a growing shortage of available names. This would create many more addresses for trademark holders to worry about. The proposal would also create 28 different domain-name registries.

Several prominent trademark attorneys recommend that trademark owners register with as many domains as possible.[c] Although identical trademarks can coexist under national laws when they relate to different product areas, only one party can register a particular name in each domain. Thus, "ford.com" can be owned by Ford Motor Company or Ford Models Inc. but not by both, even though the trademark "Ford" may be owned by Ford Motor Company, as applied to automobiles, and by Ford Models, as applied to modeling agencies.[f]

The federal government has proposed its own plan for privatizing the Internet by creating a not-for-profit corporation to oversee domain names. That plan calls for five new top-level domain names. Six for-profit companies would act as name registries.[g] The Internet Council of Registrars (CORE), a nonprofit group of 87 domain-name registrars from around the world, has challenged the U.S. proposal. The chairman of CORE's executive committee argues that the U.S. government does not have the authority to act in this matter and encourages "the U.S. government to quietly step aside."[h]

a. Panavision Int'l L.P. v. Toeppen, 141 F.3d.1316 (9th Cir. 1998).

b. Cardservice Int'l, Inc. v. McGee, 950 F. Supp. 737 (E.D.Va. 1997).

c. Lockheed Martin Corp. v. Network Solutions, Inc., 985 F. Supp. 949 (C.D. Cal. 1997).

d. Panavision Int'l v. Toeppen, 945 F. Supp. 1296 (C.D. Cal. 1996), *aff'd*, 141 F.3d 1316 (9th Cir. 1998).

e. *Attorneys Advise Trademark Owners To Register in Any Newly Created gTLDs*, 66 U.S.L.W. 2563 (Mar. 24, 1998).

f. *Id.*

g. *U.S. Plan to Revise Domain Name System Advocates Competition between Registries*, 66 U.S.L.W. 2476 (1998).

h. Rebecca Quick, *Group Contests Plan to Dispense Domain Names*, WALL ST. J., Mar. 24, 1998, at B4.

This increased emphasis on the value of trade-secret information has fueled a growing trend of litigation in this area. For example, during 1993, Procter & Gamble Co. filed suit to prevent one of its top executives, Neil P. DeFeo, from joining Clorox Company, claiming that the executive's knowledge of laundry and cleaning products would harm Procter & Gamble if shared with bleach maker Clorox.[40]

Volkswagen AG of Germany paid General Motors Corporation (GM) $100 million in 1997 as part of its settlement of GM's allegations that its purchasing chief stole trade secrets, including plans for future GM models and car-building techniques, when he left GM to join Volkswagen. The settlement also called for Volkswagen to purchase $1 billion of auto parts from GM over seven years, sever all business ties to the ex-employee in question, and return documents belonging to GM.

In 1997 alone, at least ten major companies battled over an executive's proprietary knowledge. As explained more fully later in this chapter, under the emerging doctrine of *inevitable disclosure* an employer can challenge a former employee's decision to work for a competitor, even in the absence of a covenant not to compete, if the new position would result in the inevitable disclosure or use of the former employer's trade secrets. After initiating a lawsuit, Campbell Soup Co. agreed to let the former head of its U.S. soup business join Heinz's tuna and pet-food businesses on the condition he stay out of Heinz's soup business for one year. After the plastics unit of General Electric

---

40. The settlement of this dispute in October 1993 illustrates possible ways to resolve such disputes in the future. The Procter & Gamble executive, DeFeo, agreed not to assume responsibilities for Clorox's hard-surface cleaners, such as Pinesol and Formula 409, until March 1, 1994. These two products compete with Procter & Gamble's Spic & Span, Top Job, and Mr. Clean. DeFeo agreed not to assume oversight for Clorox's powdered bleach until September 1, 1994, and for liquid bleach products until January 1, 1995. The parties agreed that DeFeo could manage the rest of Clorox's U.S. operations immediately. Ann Wozencraft, *Procter & Gamble Co. Settles with Former Exec Hired by Clorox*, CONTRA COSTA TIMES, Oct. 27, 1993, at C1.

Company (GE) hired away 14 employees from Dow Chemical Co., Dow sued GE for attempting to steal trade secrets. The two companies settled their dispute out of court and confidentially. Supposedly the settlement included no financial payment but called for the return of Dow documents taken by some of the departing employees. A subsidiary of Eastman Kodak Co. sued its former executive vice-president when he left to work for Fuji Photo Film Co. of Japan. Eastman Kodak alleged that the executive was breaching a noncompete clause in his employment contract. Fuji and Kodak settled their dispute by agreeing that the executive would not work for Fuji for one year. When an executive of Bayer AG of Germany left to join General Electric, Bayer sued, alleging that the marketing vice-president for electronic imaging systems had gone out of his way to learn trade secrets in anticipation of joining GE. The companies settled their dispute confidentially.

The term "trade secret" is difficult to define due to the fact-specific nature of the case law. Trade secrets can take almost any form. Plans, formulas, customer lists, research and development results, sales data, pricing information, computer programs, marketing techniques, and production techniques all can qualify as trade secrets. This list is by no means exhaustive. Anything that makes a company unique, or that a competitor would like to know because the information gives a competitive advantage, may be a trade secret.

The Supreme Court has held that trade-secret law is the province of the states. Until recently, the law of trade secrets was developed by the courts on a case-by-case basis, applying the laws of the relevant state. The decisions were based on tort theories in cases involving theft or misappropriation of trade secrets and on contract theories when a special relationship or duty was present. Many trade-secret cases involved a combination of the two theories.

Common Law

Under the common law, the definition most widely accepted by the courts is contained in the Restatement (Second) of Torts. Section 757(b) provides:

> A trade secret may consist of any formula, pattern, device, or compilation of information which is used in one's business, and which gives him an opportunity to obtain an advantage over competitors who do not know or use it. It may be a formula for a chemical compound, a process of manufacturing, treating or preserving materials, a pattern for a machine or other device, or a list of customers.

The courts have developed a number of factors to determine whether specific information qualifies as a trade secret. These factors include (1) the extent to which the information is known outside the business, (2) the extent to which measures are taken to protect the information, (3) the value of the information, (4) the amount of money or time spent to develop the information, and (5) the ease of duplicating the information.

Unfortunately, even with this formal definition and set of factors, a certain amount of guesswork still is required to determine whether a particular type of information qualifies as a trade secret under the common law. The courts have classified identical types of information differently when the factual settings were only slightly different.

The Uniform Trade Secrets Act

In 1979, the Uniform Trade Secrets Act (UTSA) was promulgated in an attempt to provide a coherent framework for trade-secret protection. The drafters of the UTSA hoped to eliminate the unpredictability of the common law by providing a more comprehensive definition of trade secrets. In particular, the drafters expanded the common law definition by adding the terms "method," "program," and "technique" to the Restatement's list of types of information that are protected. The intention was to specifically include know-how, that is, technical knowledge, methods, and experience. In addition, the common law definition was broadened by deleting the requirement that the secret be continuously used in a business. Accordingly, the UTSA defines a trade secret as:

> Information, including a formula, pattern, compilation, program, device, method, technique, or process, that (1) derives independent economic value, actual or potential, from not being generally known to, and not being readily ascertainable by proper means by, other persons who can obtain economic value from its disclosure or use, and (2) is the subject of efforts that are reasonable under the circumstances to maintain its secrecy.

Although the common law does not protect information unless it is in use, the UTSA definition is broad enough to include (1) information that has potential value from being secret; (2) information regarding one-time events; and (3) negative information, such as test results showing what will not work for a particular process or product.

The most significant difference, however, between the UTSA and the common law definitions is in the overall approach to determining whether information is protectable as a trade secret. As discussed above, at common law a fairly objective five- or six-part test was developed. Although many courts adopted a reasonableness standard when interpreting the individual factors of the test, the focus was on objectivity, as delineated in this test. The UTSA, on the other hand, uses a more flexible test indicating that the steps taken to preserve the information as a trade secret must be reasonable and the owner must derive independent economic value from secrecy. The latter is a somewhat subjective determination; there are not yet enough cases interpreting the "independent economic value" factor to indicate whether it will become significant over time.

Adopted, at least in part, in 40 states, the UTSA has only partially fulfilled its goal of standardizing trade-secret law. States have tended to incorporate only those parts of the UTSA that embody the existing common law of the particular state. Consequently, in states that have adopted the UTSA, the courts rely on a combination of common law and the UTSA.

While the UTSA seems to have fallen short of its goal of establishing consistent protection for trade secrets, it may provide broader protection to owners of trade secrets in the states where it has been adopted. Its definition of the term trade secret is broader than the common law definition, so that the burden of proof on the owner is reduced. In addition, the UTSA provides more effective remedies.

However, the UTSA did not improve on the common law definition in all areas. For example, the UTSA adopted separate definitions of the terms "trade secret" and "misappropriation"; but, because the definitions overlap, it is almost impossible to apply them separately. In addition, the protection of unique trade secrets, such as customer lists, may have been undermined because the UTSA does not directly address this controversial type of trade secret. In a recent California case under the UTSA, however, the court ruled that departing employees of a roofing company had misappropriated trade secrets by taking with them their collection of business cards representing 75% of the company's customers.[41] In its decision, the court noted that customer lists need not take any specific form and that the standard for protection is flexible: The more difficult and expensive information is to obtain, the more worthy it is of protection by the court as a trade secret.

Economic Espionage Act

The federal Economic Espionage Act,[42] enacted in 1996, imposes criminal liability (including fines and prison sentences) on any person who intentionally or knowingly steals a trade secret or knowingly receives or purchases a wrongfully obtained trade secret. The act's definition of trade secret is substantially similar to the definition in the Uniform Trade Secrets Act.

Although the act was prompted by a desire to remedy perceived problems facing U.S. businesses from foreign theft of trade secrets, it applies to any products placed in interstate commerce. Organizations (other than foreign instrumentalities) can be fined up to $5 million (or two times either the defendant's gain or the trade secret owner's loss, if greater). Foreign instrumentalities, defined as entities substantially owned or controlled by a foreign government, can be fined up to $10 million; individuals knowingly benefiting a foreign instrumentality can be fined up to $500,000 and imprisoned up to 15 years.

The act has extraterritorial application: It applies to any violation outside of the United States by a U.S. citizen or resident alien or by an organization organized in the United States. It also applies to violations outside of the United States if any act in furtherance of the offense was committed in the United States.

Comparison with Other Forms of Protection

Unlike the more formal procedures for patent and copyright protection, there are no lengthy application and filing procedures for trade-secret protection. No review or approval by a governmental agency is required. To create and protect a trade secret, one need only develop and maintain a trade-secret protection program. When the information being protected has a short shelf life, trade-secret protection may be a more practical solution than copyright or patent protection.

---

41. Morlife, Inc. v. Perry, 66 Cal. 2d 731 (Cal. Ct. App. 1997).
42. Pub. L. No. 104–294, 110 Stat. 3488 (1996).

Trade secrets are immediately protectable; and, unlike patents or copyrights, there is no fixed length of time for ownership. As long as the protected information remains confidential and is not developed independently by someone else, a trade secret will continue to be protectable under the law.

Another advantage of trade-secret protection is that material that would not qualify for patent or copyright protection is often protectable as a trade secret. A trade secret need not be as unique as a patentable invention or as original as a copyrightable work. It need only provide a competitive advantage. It may be merely an idea that has been kept secret, such as a way to organize common machines in an efficient manner, a marketing plan, or a formula for mixing the ingredients of a product.

Finally, patent and copyright protection usually require disclosure of trade-secret information. Patent law requires the disclosure of the best method of making the invention; and copyright law requires a deposit of the copyrightable work, with certain exceptions. There is always a risk that the protection will not be granted by the reviewing agency after the sensitive information has been revealed. To avoid this risk, trade-secret protection may be the safest course of action.

There are two disadvantages to utilizing trade-secret protection. First, the confidentiality procedures must be continuously and rigidly followed in order to preserve trade-secret status. The cost of a full-fledged program to protect trade secrets can be substantial. Second, trade-secret protection provides no protection against reverse engineering or independent discovery. The uncertainty of protection may limit the productive uses of the trade secret.

Protecting a Trade Secret

To properly protect trade-secret information, the owner must develop a program to preserve its confidentiality. In almost every jurisdiction, the test of a trade-secret program's adequacy may be reduced to the question of whether the owner has taken reasonable precautions to preserve the confidentiality of his or her trade secrets.

The most common forms of misappropriation of trade secrets are inadvertent disclosure and disclosure by employees. A program to protect against such disclosures should contain the elements discussed below. This outline, however, should not be relied upon to develop

an actual policy. An attorney knowledgeable in the area should always be consulted.

A trade-secret program should be in writing, with a statement explaining its purpose. It should cover four areas in detail: (1) notification, (2) identification, (3) security, and (4) exit interviews. The program must then be properly implemented and maintained.

Notification

A written indication that all employees are aware of the trade-secret program is critical; at a minimum, a written notice should be posted. Ideally, the company's trade-secret policy should be explained to each new employee during orientation, and each new employee should sign a confidentiality agreement. The agreement should specify how long confidentiality will be required. The duration of the agreement should not be so long, however, that a court would view it as overly restrictive and thus unreasonable.

Labeling is another means of notification. A rubber stamp denoting confidential material and the posting of signs in areas containing sensitive materials will in most cases satisfy the reasonableness requirement. However, because in practice it is difficult to ensure consistent and continuous labeling procedures, some authorities believe labeling may actually hurt the trade-secret status of the information. These authorities claim that failure to label some of the documents may be seen as evidence that the information in those documents should not be afforded trade-secret status. More advanced kinds of labeling, such as passwords, lend additional support for a finding of reasonableness.

The company should also provide written notice to any consultant, vendor, joint venturer, or other party to whom a trade secret must be revealed. The notice should take the form of a confidentiality agreement that describes the protected information and limits the receiving party's rights to use it. Without such notice, the receiving party may be unaware of the nature of the information and unwittingly release it into the public domain.

Identification

There is some controversy concerning the appropriate method of identifying trade secrets. One view is that everything within the workplace, or pertaining to the business, is a trade secret. The problem with this umbrella approach is that a court may find it overly restrictive of commerce and therefore against public policy. Such a finding could undermine the company's trade-secret program, exposing all of its trade secrets to unrecoverable misappropriation.

At the other extreme is a program that attempts to specify each trade secret of the company. This approach may be too narrow, because any legitimate trade secrets that are not specified will not be protected. Also, it is often difficult to pinpoint all of a company's potential trade secrets. For example, although it may be easy to designate all research and development projects as trade secrets, gray areas such as sales data, customer lists, or marketing surveys may cause problems.

The best solution may be a program that specifies as much information as possible while also including a limited number of catchall categories.

Security

Measures must be taken to ensure that trade-secret information remains secret, at least from the public. The disclosure of a trade secret, whether intentional (for example, as part of a sale) or by mistake, destroys any legal protection.

A common cause of this disastrous result is the unintentional disclosure of a trade secret during a public tour of the facility. An offhand remark in the hall overheard by a visitor, or a formula left written on a chalkboard in plain view of a tour group, is all that is needed. The best way to avoid this situation is to keep all trade secrets in areas restricted from public access. If such physical barriers are not possible, visitors' access should be controlled through a system that logs in all visitors, identifies them with badges, and keeps track of them while they are on the premises.

Trade secrets may also be inadvertently disclosed by employees participating in trade groups, conferences, and conventions, and through publication of articles in trade journals and other periodicals. To avoid this problem, an employer should consistently and continuously, as part of its trade-secret program, remind its employees and contractors of when and how to talk about the company's business activities.

Exit Interviews

When an employee who has had access to trade secrets leaves the company, he or she should be given an exit interview. The exit interview provides an opportunity to reinforce the confidentiality agreement that the employee signed on joining the company. If no confidentiality agreement exists, the exit interview is even more important. It will provide the notice and possibly the identification necessary to legally protect a trade secret. The exit interview also lets the departing employee know that the company is serious about protecting its trade secrets and that any breach of confidentiality could result in legal proceedings against him or her. After such a warning, any misappropriation would be deliberate and could therefore result in punitive damages.

In some states, posttermination obligations imposed on a departing employee may be unenforceable. In California, for example, a provision in an employment contract that prohibits an employee from later working for a competitor is void as an unlawful business restraint, except to the extent necessary to prevent the misappropriation of trade secrets. It is therefore important to consult with legal counsel concerning the scope of posttermination restrictions.

 ## Misappropriation of Trade Secrets

The UTSA defines *misappropriation* by listing the various permutations of when an individual uses the trade secret of another or learns of a trade secret through improper means. The UTSA defines "improper means" by a list of deceitful actions. The list, however, is not exclusive, and anything that strikes a court as improper would probably qualify as an improper means.

Remedies

Once a trade secret has been misappropriated, the law provides a choice of remedies. These are not mutually exclusive, and the typical trade-secret case involves more than one form of relief.

Injunction   A court may issue an injunction ordering the misappropriator to refrain from disclosing or using the stolen trade secret. An injunction is desirable because it preserves the confidentiality of the trade secret.

However, an injunction is available only to prevent irreparable harm. If the secret has already been disclosed, an injunction is usually no longer proper, unless there was only limited disclosure or all of those to whom the secret was disclosed knew of the misappropriation.

INTERNATIONAL CONSIDERATION

Most foreign countries will enforce reasonable nondisclosure restrictions in contracts, at least against parties to the contract. Although such contract restrictions against nondisclosure are generally enforceable, most countries do not recognize the tort law aspect of trade secrets that is recognized in the United States. In some countries, the judicial process itself may destroy the confidential character of the misappropriated information. For example, the Japanese judicial system does not have a procedure equivalent to the America *in camera* (confidentiality) procedure for review of trade-secret information.

Even if the trade secret has been disclosed, however, an injunction may still be appropriate. The court may enjoin the misappropriator from using the information, even though his or her disclosure has made it no longer a trade secret. The purpose of such an injunction is to deny the misappropriator the benefits of his or her misappropriation. In this situation, the injunction is often combined with an award of damages.

The owner may also be able to seek an injunction or damages from anyone receiving the misappropriated trade secret or anyone hiring the individual who misappropriated it.

Finally, an injunction is appropriate when an individual threatens to use or disclose a trade secret. In that situation, the real damage has yet to occur. In reality, however, very few cases involve threatened disclosure. The owner of a trade secret usually discovers the misappropriation only after the secret has been disclosed.

In a 1993 case in Massachusetts, GE Superabrasives sued a competitor that had hired a geochemistry expert previously employed by GE.[43] Upon leaving GE, the employee took an abundance of documents, including drawings and process instructions, related to the production of saw-grade industrial synthetic diamonds. The expert later entered into several agreements obliging him to transfer technology related to the production of the diamonds. GE then sued its ex-employee and rival, alleging that the technology transferred constituted a GE trade secret. The court ruled that GE had the fact-intensive burden of proving that (1) the information transferred was in fact a GE trade secret, and (2) the rival company that hired the expert knew or should have known that the information was a GE trade secret. After a jury trial, the court found in favor of GE on its claim of misappropriation of trade secrets and enjoined the competitor from manufacturing saw-grade diamonds for seven years, the amount of time it would have taken the competitor to develop or reverse engineer a technology for commercial production of high-grade saw diamonds.

The following case addressed the issue of whether a corporate manager's knowledge of trade secrets can cause inevitable disclosure of the trade secrets if the manager goes to work for a competitor.

---

43. General Elec. Co. v. Iljin Corp., 27 U.S.P.Q.2d (BNA) 1372 (D. Mass. 1993).

A CASE IN POINT	SUMMARY

CASE 11.7
PEPSICO, INC. v. REDMOND
United States Court of Appeals for the Seventh Circuit
54 F.3d 1262 (7th Cir. 1995).

FACTS In the mid-1990s, PepsiCo, Quaker Oats Company, and Coca-Cola Company were engaged in fierce competition for the growing sports-drink market with their products AllSport, Gatorade, and PowerAde, respectively. From 1984 to 1994, William Redmond, Jr. worked for PepsiCo in its Pepsi-Cola North America division. In his last year at PepsiCo, Redmond served as general manager of the California business unit, which enjoyed annual revenues of $500 million, generating 20% of the

Case 11.7 continues

Case 11.7 continued

division's profits. Redmond's high-level position gave him access to inside information and trade secrets, including the division's complete strategic and operating plans. As was customary for all PepsiCo employees, Redmond had signed a confidentiality agreement promising never to use or disclose to anyone outside the company confidential information about PepsiCo that he had obtained while in its employ.

In November 1994, Quaker offered to hire Redmond as the vice-president of field operations in its combined Gatorade and Snapple drinks subsidiary. Redmond accepted the offer two days later. Upon receipt of his resignation notice, PepsiCo brought suit to enjoin him from working at Quaker and to prevent him from disclosing PepsiCo trade secrets.

In December 1994, the trial court ruled in favor of PepsiCo and issued a preliminary injunction enjoining Redmond from assuming his position at Quaker for six months and enjoining him permanently from using or disclosing PepsiCo trade secrets. Redmond appealed.

ISSUE PRESENTED   What constitutes "threatened misappropriation" of trade secrets? Given that definition, did PepsiCo have a "reasonable likelihood of success" on its claims, as is the standard for issuing a preliminary injunction?

SUMMARY OF OPINION   The Illinois Trade Secrets Act provides that a court may enjoin the "actual or threatened misappropriation" of a trade secret, which is defined similarly to that in the Uniform Trade Secrets Act. The U.S. Court of Appeals reasoned that a company may prove a claim of trade-secret misappropriation by demonstrating that the employee's new position will inevitably lead him to rely on his ex-employer's trade secrets. Because of the competition between AllSport and Gatorade, the court concluded that Redmond could not help but rely on PepsiCo trade secrets as he plotted Gatorade's course. Specifically, Quaker would have a substantial advantage by knowing how PepsiCo will price, distribute, and market its sports drinks. Therefore, Quaker will be able to plan more strategically as it competes with PepsiCo.

Although Quaker may not intend to use such trade secrets from Redmond in order to duplicate PepsiCo's systems or co-opt its ideas, Quaker will be able to anticipate PepsiCo's distribution, packaging, pricing, and marketing moves. Taking a cue from the product market at stake, the court analogized, "In other words, PepsiCo finds itself in the position of a coach, one of whose players has left, playbook in hand, to join the opposing team before the big game."

RESULT   The Court of Appeals affirmed the trial court's preliminary injunction. Redmond could not join Quaker for six months and was prohibited from ever disclosing PepsiCo's trade secrets.

COMMENTS   Some legal commentators believe this decision will have widespread ramifications because it was based on Illinois's version of the Uniform Trade

Case 11.7 continues

Case 11.7 continued

Secrets Act, which has been adopted in 40 states. By recognizing the notion of inevitable disclosure as within the act's provision of "threatened disclosure," the case gives employers greater leverage over departing employees and a powerful weapon against competitors who would lure away valuable employees. According to Silicon Valley attorney James DiBoise, "In essence, the doctrine is a powerful noncompete clause. You are going to see it used more and more at the highest end of the workforce against employees who hold information that is valuable to the competition." If correct, the new doctrine will be particularly important in states that give little weight to, or that will not enforce, noncompete clauses in employment contracts.

Damages   Monetary damages are often awarded when the owner of the trade secret has suffered financial harm. The situations in which monetary damages are received are fact-specific. Damages may be awarded based upon either a contract theory or a tort theory. The technical differences between the two measures of damages make little practical difference. Most courts will attempt to fairly compensate the owner of a misappropriated trade secret regardless of how the case is characterized.

Under the tort theory of trade secrets, the purpose of the damages is not only to make the owner whole, but to disgorge any profits the misappropriator may have made due to his or her wrongful act. The key to the tort measure of damages is that there was either a harm or an unjust gain, or both.

The contract theory of trade secrets, on the other hand, measures damages by the loss of value of the trade secret to the owner as a result of a breach of contract. The loss of value is determined by adding the general loss to any special losses resulting from the breach and subtracting any costs avoided by the owner as a result of the breach.

Punitive Damages   Punitive damages are available when the misappropriation was willful and wanton. A misappropriation that can be characterized only as a breach of contract does not warrant punitive damages. In some states, attorney's fees are also recoverable by the prevailing party if the misappropriation was willful and malicious.

 Technology Licensing

Technology licensing is big business worldwide. The volume of commercial technology transfers has increased dramatically since World War II and is accelerating. For many modern business enterprises, intellectual property makes up some of their most significant productive assets.

One way for a technology owner to benefit from its technology is to use it itself. Another way is to license others to use it. Conversely, a potential acquirer of technology may choose either to develop the technology itself or to obtain it under license from another. Depending upon the circumstances of the parties and the market, a commonality of interest may develop that leads to a license transaction.

Advantages to the Licensor

From a licensor's perspective, there are a variety of reasons to license technology. One obvious reason is to generate revenue. License transactions constitute a substantial source of income for many technology-based companies. Licensing may be a way for a licensor to exploit its older technology. Often a somewhat dated technology is what a licensee can best use.

Licensing is often an inexpensive way to gain a presence in a target market. In essence, through the mechanism of a license, a licensor may be able to push many of the costs of market development onto the licensee in exchange for a share of the profits from the venture. A

IN BRIEF

INTELLECTUAL PROPERTY PROTECTION: COMPARATIVE ADVANTAGES

	TRADE SECRET	COPYRIGHT	PATENT	TRADEMARK
Benefits	Very broad protection for sensitive, competitive information; very inexpensive	Prevents copying of a wide array of artistic and literary expressions, including software; very inexpensive	Very strong protection; provides exclusive right to exclude others from making, using, and selling an invention; protects the idea itself	Protects marks that customers use to identify a business; prevents others from using confusingly similar identifying marks
Duration	As long as the information remains valuable and is kept confidential	Life of author plus 50 years; for corporations, 75 years from date of first publication or 100 years from date of creation, whichever is shorter	20 years from date of filing utility or plant patent application; 14 years from date of filing design patent application	As long as the mark is not abandoned and steps are taken to police its use
Weaknesses	No protection from accidental disclosure, independent creation by a competitor, or disclosure by someone without a duty to maintain confidentiality	Protects only particular way an idea is expressed, not the idea itself; apparent lessening of protection for software; hard to detect copying in digital age	Must meet high standards of novelty, utility, and non-obviousness; often expensive and time consuming to pursue (especially when overseas patents are needed); must disclose invention to public	Limited scope; protects corporate image and identity but little else; can be costly if multiple overseas registrations are needed
Required Steps	Take reasonable steps to protect—generally a trade-secret protection program	None required; however, notice and filing can strengthen rights and registration is required before an action for infringement can be filed	Detailed filing with U.S. Patent and Trademark Office that requires search for prior art and hefty fees	Only need to use mark in commerce; however, filing with U.S. Patent and Trademark Office is usually desirable to gain stronger protections
International Validity of U.S. Rights?	No. Trade-secret laws vary significantly by country, and some countries have no trade-secret laws	Generally, yes	No. Separate patent examinations and filings are required in each country; however, a single filing in the European Patent Office can cover a number of European countries	No. Separate filings are required in foreign jurisdictions, and a mark available in the U.S. may not be available overseas

SOURCE Excerpted from Constance E. Bagley & Craig E. Dauchy, The Entrepreneur's Guide to Business Law, 471–72 (1998). *Used by permission.*

licensor seeking new technology may condition its license upon a cross-license of the licensee's existing technology or may require a grant-back of any future technology developed by the licensee.

A license transaction may also give the licensor an inexpensive source of supply of the licensed product. When the licensee is operating in a low-cost labor market, such product-purchase rights may be highly valued by the licensor.

Advantages to the Licensee

There are also several reasons why a licensee might wish to license technology. By taking a license, a licensee can obtain immediate access to new technology, and can avoid the research and development costs that would be necessary to duplicate the technology. A license may enable the licensee to penetrate its target market sooner. Without having to independently develop the necessary technology, the licensee may be able to get a head start on its competitors.

A licensee may be seeking a long-term relationship with its licensor, which will enable it to graduate to higher and higher levels of the licensor's technology (including future developments). A licensee may seek to share in the goodwill of its licensor through the license transaction. If the licensor has strong trademarks or is otherwise the beneficiary of substantial goodwill, the licensee may be able to benefit in its local market.

Disadvantages to the Licensor

There are a variety of reasons why a licensor may choose not to license its technology. By far the greatest risk for a licensor is that its licensee may become its future competitor. Numerous examples abound of this phenomenon.

A licensor that relies exclusively upon its licensee for the manufacture of the licensed product may find that it loses the ability to manufacture the product efficiently itself. Licensors may be reluctant to undertake the service obligations that often arise in license transactions. A licensee may require a lot of training and assistance for the license transaction to be successful. The licensor may not be able ultimately to recoup such costs.

The managements of the licensor and licensee may differ on fundamental aspects of the license transaction, such as commitment, strategy, and marketing, thereby making success improbable. If language and cultural differences are added, the licensor may well decide that a proposed transaction is not worthwhile.

Disadvantages to the Licensee

A licensee, too, may decide that its differences with the licensor make the transaction not worthwhile. There are several other reasons why a potential licensee may choose not to carry through a license transaction.

A licensee may have concerns about technology transfer problems. Just because a licensor can operate its technology at a certain level does not necessarily mean it can effectively teach the licensee to use it at the same level. Licensees are often bitterly disappointed by the technology they have paid so dearly to acquire. In addition, continuing royalty payments can become burdensome to a licensee, particularly if competitors enter the market who are not paying a comparable royalty.

Intellectual Property Dispute Settlement

A license may be utilized as a means of settling an intellectual property dispute. Patent litigation, for example, is risky both for the defendant, who may face a treble damages award, and for the plaintiff, who may find his or her patent invalidated. To minimize such risks, the parties may enter into a license agreement. Two biotechnology companies, Cetus Corporation and Amgen, Inc., took such an approach. Amgen had brought an action against Cetus claiming that certain of Cetus's patents relating to Interleukin-2 were invalid; Cetus had counterclaimed that Amgen was infringing Cetus's patents. Rather than letting a court determine their fate, the parties settled the suit through an agreement whereby certain of Amgen's patent rights were assigned to Cetus and Cetus granted Amgen a license to use Cetus's patents.

INTERNATIONAL CONSIDERATION

If either the licensee or the licensor is located outside the United States, the export control laws of the United States must be carefully complied with to avoid potential liability. Unfortunately, such compliance may result in undue expense or delay. Also, it should be borne in mind that other countries may not offer the same intellectual property protection as the United States.

THE RESPONSIBLE MANAGER
Protecting Intellectual Property Rights

Some of a company's most important assets may be intangible forms of intellectual property. Consider the formula for Coke, never registered as a patent but kept as a trade secret by generations of executives at the Coca-Cola Company. An effective trade-secret policy is essential to almost all forms of business today. This chapter has provided suggestions regarding the implementation of such a policy. Exhibit 11.4 shows one company's code of conduct on this subject.

Problems can arise when a manager leaves the employment of one company to assume a position at another. It is critical that the manager and the new employer ensure that no confidential information, including trade secrets, is conveyed to the new employer, either in the form of documents or information in the manager's head. A company should provide written notice to all employees that it has a policy against receiving, using, or purchasing any trade secrets belonging to third parties. Misappropriation of trade secrets is a civil and criminal offense.

If the manager cannot fulfill all the duties of his or her new job without using trade secrets, it is necessary to scale back the manager's activities and responsibilities. This can be accomplished by having the former employer and the new employer agree that the manager will not assume responsibility for certain product lines that compete with his or her former employer's until a date when the strategic and other confidential information known by the manager is stale. If at all possible, the departing manager should address this issue up front, and negotiate this as part of his or her severance arrangements, rather than wait for a costly lawsuit to be brought by the former employer.

In addition to trade secrets, intellectual property is given legal protection through patents, copyrights, and trademarks. Patents are extremely important to high-technology companies. In fact, patents have formed the basis for whole businesses, such as biotechnology. A manager should strive to protect his or her company's patents from infringement by others. Royalties from patents can add tens or even hundreds of millions of dollars to a company's revenues.

Patents also have an important strategic use as a defensive measure in the event that another company claims patent infringement. In such a case, it is very helpful for a manager to have patents that can be used as bargaining chips to negotiate a settlement, which often takes the form of cross-licenses.

A manager should develop a global patent strategy because 179 different jurisdictions grant patents, each of which gives the holder exclusive rights only in the granting jurisdiction. Moreover, few countries share the U.S. system. For instance, only one other country, the Philippines, uses a "first-to-invent" instead of "first-to-file" approach in issuing patents. As well, many countries do not share the U.S. practice of keeping patent applications confidential until the patent is issued, thereby risking revelation of trade secrets if the patent is denied.

Copyrights prevent others from copying literary work, musical work, sound recordings, computer software, and other forms of expression fixed in a tangible medium. A manager should be aware that copyright registration with the U.S. Copyright Office is a prerequisite for filing an infringement suit for a work of U.S. origin. Statutory damages and attorney's fees are available only to owners who have registered the work within 90 days of first publication or prior to the infringement that forms the basis of the infringement suit.

Trademarks that identify brands of goods or services are protected for an indefinite time. However, managers must work to preserve trademarks. Once the buying public starts using the trademark as a synonym for the product, rather than as a means of distinguishing its source, loss of the trademark is imminent.

A company may benefit from technology licensing. Such arrangements offer advantages and disadvantages for both the licensor and licensee.

A manager should not only protect his or her company's own intellectual property, he or she should also ensure that the company does not infringe the intellectual property rights of others, whether they be patents, copyrights, trademarks, or trade secrets.

EXHIBIT 11.4   Confidential Information and Trade Secrets

All persons who work for the Company may learn, to a greater or lesser degree, facts about the Company's business, plans, operations or "secrets of success" that are not known to the general public or to competitors. Sensitive information such as customer lists, the terms or fees offered to particular customers, marketing or strategic plans, or proprietary or product systems developments are examples of the Company's confidential information or trade secrets. Similarly, during the course of performing their responsibilities, employees may obtain information concerning possible transactions with other companies or receive confidential information about other companies.

You may not disclose any confidential information or trade secret of the Company to others or use any such information for your own or someone else's benefit. Each of us who possesses or has access to confidential information or trade secrets has an important responsibility to keep that information confidential and to prevent it from being improperly disclosed to others inside or outside the Company. This obligation applies both during and subsequent to employment with the Company. We must be careful not to discuss such matters with family members or business or social acquaintances or in places where we can be overheard, such as taxis, elevators or restaurants. Within the Company, confidential information or trade secrets should be divulged only to other employees who need the information to carry out their business responsibilities. It is also the responsibility of each employee to maintain the confidentiality of sensitive employee information, such as salary, bonus, or performance appraisal data.

Finally, no employee should disclose to the Company or be asked by the Company to reveal confidential, proprietary or trade secret information of others. More specifically, employees are not permitted to possess or circulate improperly obtained confidential, proprietary or trade secret information belonging to a competitor.

SOURCE   From AMERICAN EXPRESS COMPANY'S CODE OF CONDUCT (1997). Used by permission of American Express Company.

INSIDE STORY

INTELLECTUAL PROPERTY IN A BOTTLE

In 1995, the best-selling chardonnay in the United States was Vintner's Reserve, a product of Kendall–Jackson Winery Ltd. (K–J), located in Santa Rosa, California. In sharp contrast, the world's largest winery, E. & J. Gallo Winery (Gallo) of Modesto, California, sold the 649th best-selling chardonnay, Turning Leaf. The sharp difference between the two products' successes underscored the dramatic differences between the two wineries in general.

Founded in 1933, Gallo had 5,000 employees and served the low end of the wine market. Selling 61 million cases of wine each year for more than $1 billion in sales, its average case sold for less than $17. A short drive up the California coast, fifteen-year-old K–J operated a smaller, more upscale business. With only 800 employees, it sold 2.5 million of cases of wine each year. Those cases, however, sold for $230 million, an average of $92 per case. As one wine expert noted, "Kendall–Jackson is a very distinctive wine with intense tropical fruit flavors. Turning Leaf is lighter and simpler. It's a good, solid commercial-grade wine."

By the following year, Gallo's Turning Leaf had improved its relative position in the U.S. chardonnay market, leaping from 649th to second place. Threatening K–J's top-selling Vintner's Reserve, the upscale Turning Leaf was a remarkable departure from Gallo's jug-wine image. In fact, the Gallo name did not appear on the label. More worrisome to K–J, Turning Leaf's packaging shared many traits with that of its own Vintner's Reserve: (1) a colored-leaf logo;

(2) a gradually tapering bottleneck; (3) a ¾-inch bottleneck label design; and (4) an uncovered leaf-stamped cork. So similar were the two that Paul Dolan, president of third-place chardonnay maker Fetzer Vineyards Co., called Gallo's packaging "a knockoff, no question about it."

Apparently, K–J shared Dolan's perspective; it filed suit against Gallo in April 1996. Claiming infringement of its trademark, K–J asked the federal district court to award it $30 million against Gallo, plus punitive damages.

At the heart of K–J's case against Gallo was a fast-growing area of intellectual property law called trade dress. A manifestation of trademark law, the concept of *trade dress* is to protect the overall look of a product as opposed to just a particular design. For example, a company might stake legal claim to a combination of common elements, such as the design, decor, and product offerings of a restaurant chain.[44]

In this case, K–J sought to protect its unique use of a combination of five elements: (1) a lip around the mouth of the bottle; (2) a visible cork; (3) a label around the bottle neck; and (4) a label with (a) a white background and (b) a foreground picture of a grape leaf. It accused Gallo of using focus groups to determine what packaging traits consumers most remembered about Vintner's Reserve. According to K–J, Gallo then ordered its designers to add orange color to the leaf on Turning Leaf's label to make it look more like the K–J brand. "They were copying so much they even forgot to put their name on the bottle," quipped K–J attorney Frederick Furth.

In contradiction, Gallo accused K–J of redesigning its label after initiating the litigation in order to make Vintner's Reserve's leaf look more like Gallo's. It also alleged that a K–J salesman arranged for a customer to move Gallo bottles for a posed photograph of a supermarket wine display, possibly in violation of state law prohibiting alcohol vendors from touching each other's products in display. The acrimony was in contrast to wine's image of cultivated civility. However, K–J's suit against Gallo was at least the third against Gallo for trademark infringement or deceptive advertising. K–J owner Jess Jackson had spent most of his career as a litigator, including representation of Joseph Gallo against his brothers Earnest and Julio in a failed attempt to win a one-third stake in Gallo.

Along with the parties themselves, competing vintners could not help but join the fray. As mentioned above, Fetzer publicly agreed with K–J's claim that Gallo stole the design of Vintner's Reserve. On Gallo's side, representatives of both Mondavi and Sebastiani Vineyards testified that they also use lipped bottles, weakening K–J's claim that Gallo stole that element from it. To support its case, K–J offered into evidence a "confusion" study purporting to show that its customers were easily confused people who purchased wine based primarily on appearance. In rebuttal, Gallo offered two of its own studies purporting to show no such confusion between Turning Leaf and Vintner's Reserve.

On April 3, 1997, one year after it began, K–J lost its lawsuit against Gallo.[45] After a two-week trial and two days of deliberation, a seven-person jury unanimously rejected K–J's claims that Gallo infringed K–J's trade dress. Commenting on the verdict after the trial, jury foreman Michael Willis said, "There was never any solid proof of intent. I think it's business; everybody does it. Gallo was very aware of K–J . . . but I'm not sure they stole [the packaging]."

Looking to the future of similar trade-dress lawsuits against competitors, Gallo attorney Joe Cotchett predicted, "People will think twice before they bring these suits."

---

44. Two Pesos, Inc. v. Taco Cabana, Inc., 505 U.S. 763 (1992).

45. The verdict was upheld on appeal. Kendall–Jackson Winery v. E. & J. Gallo Winery,—F.3d— (9th Cir. 1998).

KEY WORDS AND PHRASES

abandonment **401**
best mode **371**
certification mark **395**
claims **371**
contributory infringement **388**
copyright **367**
declaration by the inventor **371**
descriptive marks **397**
design patent **370**
direct infringement **388**
doctrine of equivalents **371**
drawings **371**
fair use doctrine **385**
file-wrapper estoppel **372**

first sale doctrine **379**
indirect infringement **371**
inevitable disclosure doctrine **404**
inherently distinctive marks **396**
intellectual property **367**
know-how **367**
merger doctrine **378**
misappropriation **408**
noninfringement **372**
novel **368**
patent **367**
patent misuse **372**
prior art **368**
protected expression **378**

registered mask work **391**
secondary meaning **397**
service mark **395**
specifications **371**
statutory bar **368**
trade dress **416**
trademark **367**
trade name **395**
trade secret **405**
useful articles doctrine **378**
utility patent **368**
vicarious liability **389**
work made for hire **370**

QUESTIONS AND CASE PROBLEMS

1. Meredith Corporation and Publications International Limited (PIL) publish magazines and books containing cooking recipes. In 1988, Meredith published *Discover Dannon: 50 Fabulous Recipes With Yogurt*, for which it received a copyright. The cookbook offers a cornucopia of culinary delights featuring Dannon yogurt, from "Simple Snacks" to "Exciting Entres" to "Dazzling Desserts." As inspiration, the book contains pictorial representations of the final products. In its copyright certificate, Meredith claimed protection for the book as a collective work and described the book's subject matter as a "compilation of recipes tested with Dannon yogurt."

In 1993 and 1995, PIL published two books containing 22 similarly yogurt-based recipes: *Dannon Healthy Habit Cookbook: Great-Tasting Recipes Lower in Fat And Calories* and *Taste Why It's Dannon: Collection of Great-Tasting Recipes*, respectively. The 22 recipes are functionally identical to their counterparts in *Discover Dannon*. As well, the PIL recipes have the same titles but display some differences in the listing of ingredients, directions for preparation, and nutritional information. PIL's cookbooks echo Meredith's celebration of Dannon yogurt as a nutritional bonanza for anyone immersed in today's health-conscious culture; and, like

Discover Dannon, both PIL cookbooks prominently display the Dannon trademark on the cover.

What claims can Meredith make against PIL? If Meredith sues to vindicate those claims, how should the court rule? [*Publications Int'l, Ltd. v. Meredith Corp.*, 88 F.3d 473 (7th Cir. 1996)]

2. Both State Street Bank and Trust Company and Signature Financial Group serve as administrators and accounting agents for mutual funds. In 1993, Signature received a patent entitled "Data Processing System for Hub and Spoke Financial Services Configuration." The invention provides a data-processing system and a method for monitoring and recording the information flow and data and for making all calculations necessary for maintaining a partnership portfolio and partner fund (hub-and-spoke) financial services configuration. Essentially, a hub-and-spoke arrangement is an investment structure whereby mutual funds ("spokes") pool their assets in an investment portfolio ("hub") organized as a partnership. This configuration involves (1) an entity that is treated as a partnership for federal income tax purposes and that holds the investment portfolio, and (2) funds that invest as partners in the partnership portfolio. Enabling mutual funds to pool their assets in this manner reduces fund administration costs and generates beneficial tax consequences. This complex financial structure, however, creates its own set of administrative challenges.

Signature's invention is for a system operated by means of a personal computer, with software capable of performing the required functions, data storage, and a means of display. State Street wants to challenge Signature's patent so that it can safely implement a similar system. On what grounds can it challenge the patent? What result? [*State Street Bank & Trust Co. v. Signature Fin. Group, Inc.,*—F. 3d— (Fed. Cir. 1998)]

3. Cecil Hudson worked for Cataphote Corp. Hudson did not know anything about making glass when he joined the company. However, during his employment and with the help of Cataphote, Hudson developed a way to produce glass beads by the vertical-updraft-furnace method. This process is not patent protected; it employs principles that are in the public domain. Nevertheless, the combination of public-domain techniques employed is novel and has been kept secret by Cataphote.

Hudson left Cataphote and started his own glass company. After six months of construction, he was ready to begin manufacturing. Cataphote management then called Hudson and stated that they would sue Hudson if he did not stop using the Cataphote updraft-furnace method.

Hudson comes to you, his attorney, for help. He asks you, "How can Cataphote sue me if the method is not patentable, and will Cataphote win?"

What do you tell Hudson, and what questions should you ask him to determine whether Cataphote's claim is actionable? [*Cataphote Corp. v. Hudson*, 422 F.2d 1290 (5th Cir. 1970)]

4. E.I. duPont de Nemours & Co. developed a new and very efficient process for manufacturing automobiles. You work for McKivex Company and are writing a consultant's report for a competitor about the manufacturing processes of its competitors. DuPont has a new plant, but the roof has not yet been built over it. You want to learn about the process without getting sued.

Can you take aerial photographs of the plant? Can you go through the garbage cans on the company's grounds looking for information that would describe the process? Can you go through the garbage that is at the city dump?

Can you interview the manufacturing manager on the telephone and write in your report whatever she says?

What if you did consulting for DuPont and knew the process—could you then include it in your report for its competitor?

What is ethical? [*E. I. duPont de Nemours & Co. v. Christopher*, 431 F.2d 1012 (5th Cir. 1970), *cert. denied*, 400 U.S. 1024 (1971)]

5. Virgil Richards conceived a way to regulate the translation of heterologous DNA in bacteria. He worked on this invention with three other people. Richards conceived of the idea in May 1996, reduced it to practice on May 14, 1997, and filed a patent application on June 1, 1998. Richards is being sued by the co-inventors for not including their names on the application.

On May 3, 1997, Richards published an article that explained his idea in detail. Clyde Taylor reduced this idea to practice on May 14, 1997, making only minor changes to the procedure disclosed in the article. He applied for a patent on June 1, 1997.

Can Richards or Taylor obtain a patent for the technology? The process includes some basic scientific principles. Does that mean that both patent applications will be rejected? [*In re O'Farrell*, 853 F.2d 894 (Fed. Cir. 1988)]

6. You are the intellectual property manager for Immuno, Inc., a pharmaceutical company that develops, markets, and licenses drugs. Your research scientists have developed a drug that appears to be effective in slowing the effects of the AIDS virus. The drug is based on a genetically engineered bacterium that was developed in part using simulation software capable of predicting the efficacy of the bacterium based on numerous design options. The software was written by one of your in-house scientists.

Immuno would like to begin clinical trials of the drug and, depending on the preliminary results of the trials, begin marketing the still-unnamed drug. Draft a plan for protecting the company's proprietary rights and state any assumptions you need to make about any procedures that are already in place.

7. A hypothetical new software product is described below. After reading the product description, think up three trademarks for this product: one that is inherently distinctive; one that is potentially, but not inherently, distinctive; and one that is nondistinctive.

New Product Description

This new software programming language is suited for Internet programming, as well as general telecommunications management. Whether you are currently programming in HTML or Java, you will find this new language appropriate for your project. Not only does the system offer total platform transparency, it also provides tremendous flexibility in designing Web-based products.

Importantly, the system is easy to learn. If you already know any simple programming language, then you already know enough of our software to get started. No professional programing expertise is required. The system is also fast, using little overhead and incorporating the most up-to-date Internet technology. In addition, many different libraries (collections of predesigned elements and procedures) have already been created and will soon be available for purchase.

8. Plato Systems designs, manufactures, and sells computer software. In February 1998, Plato received a letter from Titan Computers, a major computer hardware and software manufacturer. In the letter, Titan notified Plato that Titan had begun licensing certain patents relating to computer graphics, including ten patents on an attached list, and stated that Titan believed one or more of these patents might be of interest to Plato. Titan's letter offered a patent license at a royalty rate of 1% of Plato's revenues for covered products per patent used, up to a maximum of 3%, plus payment at the same rates for any past infringements of the patents.

Upon review of the ten listed patents, Plato discovered that its Platonic Frames 1.01 program, which uses a method for manipulating multiple, overlapping windows on a computer display, is substantially the same as a method claimed in one of the patents (the Slick patent). The remaining patents listed in Titan's letter do not appear to cover Plato's current products. The Slick patent was issued on May 1, 1994, based upon an application filed on July 1, 1991. Plato began commercial shipment of Platonic Frames 1.01 in March 1997. However, the same windowing method used in Platonic Frames 1.01 had been used in Plato's earliest product, which was first shipped in September 1993. One of Plato's engineers recalls that the windowing method claimed in the Slick patent was used in an experimental system developed in the late 1980s by Digilog Corporation and was described in a technical article by one of Digilog's engineers published in December 1990.

How should Plato respond to Titan's letter?

9. Sega manufactures video game consoles and cartridges for home entertainment use. Accolade is a competitor in the video cartridge market but does not manufacture its own consoles. Sega developed a system to protect its trademark rights—the Licensed Trademark Security System (TMSS)—by which the Sega console "reads" a video cartridge for specific computer code. If the video cartridge includes the computer code, it prompts a visual display on the television screen before the game commences, which states "PRODUCED BY OR UNDER LICENSE FROM Sega." Accolade analyzed Sega's game cartridges using a process known as reverse engineering to figure out which pieces of code were required for compatibility with the Sega console, and developed several video cartridges that include the Sega code necessary for the video game cartridges to be compatible with the Sega console. Because Accolade also copied the TMSS code, however, Accolade's video cartridges prompt the message that the Accolade games are "PRODUCED BY OR UNDER LICENSE FROM Sega," even though Accolade has no license from Sega to produce compatible video cartridges.

Does Sega have actionable claims against Accolade for the Accolade video game cartridges? What are the claims? Does Accolade have any defense to Sega's claims? If so, what are the defenses? [*Sega Enterprises Ltd. v. Accolade, Inc.*, 977 F.2d 1510 (9th Cir. 1992)]

MANAGER'S DILEMMA

10. You are the vice-president for sales at QuickGifts, Inc., a small start-up headquartered in Chicago, Illinois. QuickGifts specializes in supplying on short notice a variety of inexpensive gifts for all occasions, including cards, flowers, perfume, gift baskets, wine, books, and compact discs. Since QuickGifts' launch six months ago, the bulk of its revenue has come from catalog-driven telephone sales, often from frantic spouses and children the day before a wife or father's birthday. For a premium fee, QuickGifts arranges immediate delivery of a tasteful gift, usually overnight, but often within hours.

Recently, QuickGifts hired a Web designer to create an Internet outlet for its products. The designer has nearly completed his work on the site but has asked you about meta-tagging the site. Meta-tagging, he explains, is the labeling of your site with terms and phrases so that search engines, such as Yahoo, can identify it to users as they surf the Web. He recommends numerous conventional tags, including "gifts," "cards," and "flowers," but warns that many companies have already established a name in this business. Without quite recommending it, the designer notes that using the names of your rivals will at least give prospective customers the chance to see your Web site when they search for a specific rival. For instance, you could use meta-tags like "Hallmark," "FTD," "Amazon," and "CDnow." Is it legal to use these names as mega-tags? Would it be ethical? [*Playboy Enterprises, Inc. v. Calvin Designer Label*, 985 F. Supp. 1220 (N.D. Cal. 1997)]

INTERNET SOURCES	
The Law Engine site provides lots of useful links for federal and state statutes, rules, and court opinions.	http://www.fastsearch.com/law
This site includes free sources of the law of any state.	http://www.azstarnet.com/~frey/fed.htm
Japanese Patent Office	http://www.jpo-miti.go.jp
Foreign and International Law Resources on the Internet: Annotated from Cornell Law Library (International)	http://www.law.cornell.edu/library/guides/forin
PTO Guidelines on Domain Names as Trademarks	http://www.uspto.gov/web/offices/tac/domain/tmdomain.htm
The U.S. House of Representatives Internet Law Library site contains a variety of links to useful intellectual property articles and resources on the Web.	law.house.gov/105.htm
"Thomas": The U.S. Congress's Official Legislative Information Page is an extremely well-organized page describing pending bills, committee information, and Internet sources.	http://thomas.loc.gov
The President's Information Infrastructure Task Force	http://www.iitf.nist.gov

Human Resources in the Legal and Regulatory Environment

CHAPTER 12

The Employment Agreement

INTRODUCTION

Employee Rights, Powers, and Protection

Over the past 60 years, there has been an explosion in the laws regulating the employment relationship. As a result of the union movement, employees acquired economic and political power in their dealings with employers. With the emergence of the civil rights movement and the antidiscrimination legislation of the 1960s, employers began to examine their hiring and other employment practices more closely with respect to the treatment of women, minorities, and other protected groups.

The courts have developed new doctrines that limit the employer's traditional right to discharge an employee. These judicial decisions have recognized implied contractual obligations to show just cause for a discharge. Indeed, under the current law, an employer may be bound by contracts with its employees without even knowing it.

At the same time, both Congress and state legislatures have enacted legislation protecting all employees in the workplace and regulating the right to discharge employees. With the increasing concern over toxic wastes, for example, many environmental statutes contain provisions prohibiting retaliation against employees who raise concerns about the use of dangerous substances in the workplace. Many states now have *whistle-blower statutes*, which prohibit discharging an employee who has complained to a government agency about working conditions that he or she believes violate the law. Employers must devote an ever-increasing amount of attention and resources to complying with the sometimes bewildering array of statutes, regulations, and common law principles that bear upon their relations with their employees.

Chapter Overview

This chapter discusses the traditional rule that employees can be terminated at will and the exceptions that have developed in recent years, including wrongful termination based on a violation of public policy, breach of an implied contract, and breach of the implied covenant of good faith and fair dealing. It also examines the tort of fraudulent inducement and the enforceability of covenants not to compete. The laws relating to drug testing, genetic testing, lie detector tests, and certain hiring practices are also addressed. The chapter describes the employer's responsibility for worker safety and the system of workers' compensation. The requirements for paying minimum wage and overtime are also explained.

The chapter concludes with a discussion of three other statutes regulating the employer-employee relationship: the Employee Retirement Income Security Act of 1974 (ERISA), the Consolidated Omnibus Budget Reconciliation Act of 1985 (COBRA), and the Worker Adjustment and Retraining Notification Act of 1988 (WARN Act). Chapter 13 describes the major pieces of civil rights legislation that prohibit discrimination. Chapter 14 outlines the labor-relation laws applicable to unionized workers and their employers.

At-Will Employment

Most nonunionized American workers have no written employment contract. They are hired for a job without any express agreement about how long the job will last. For at least the last 100 years, the American rule has been that an employment agreement of indefinite duration is an *at-will contract*; that is, the employee can quit at any time, and the employer can discharge the employee at any time, for any reason, with or without notice. Whether by statute or judicial decision, all states originally followed this rule. The courts reasoned that denying the employer the right to discharge its employee, while the employee was at liberty to quit at any time for any reason, would deprive the employer of property without due process of law. Today, however, the at-will rule has been largely buried under its exceptions.

Employees Not Subject to the Rule

Public employees and employees who negotiated express contracts with their employers have generally not been subject to the at-will rule.

Public Employees Most employees of federal, state, and local government agencies have long worked under civil service or merit systems that provide for tenure, require just cause for discharge, and guarantee administrative procedures to determine whether there is just cause for discharge.

Employees with Contracts A private-sector employee can avoid at-will status by negotiating a contract that provides for a specific term of employment and defines how the contract can be terminated. Persons in professional or managerial positions are more likely to be able to negotiate individual contracts. Other employees rely on union contracts, which almost universally require just cause for termination and establish arbitration procedures whereby an employee can challenge his or her discharge.

 ## Wrongful Discharge

Beginning in the early 1970s, courts in a number of states began to recognize new causes of action for *wrongful discharge*, that is, termination of employment without good cause. Wrongful discharge is a common law-based claim supported by three theories: public policy, implied contract, and implied covenant of good faith.

These causes of action are based on both contract and tort law. Although the line between wrongful discharge and fraud is not always clear, each claim receives different damages. The former gives rise only to contract damages, but the latter gives rise to personal injury and punitive damages. However, even this distinction is hazy. Thus, some wrongful-discharge plaintiffs may be able to collect damages for emotional distress and punitive damages, not simply lost wages. Although some state courts have declined to recognize these exceptions to the at-will doctrine, the trend is toward some level of protection against discharge in certain circumstances. Employers are well advised to consider whether the reasons for any termination will pass muster as "good cause."

The Public Policy Exception

One of the earliest exceptions to the at-will rule was the *public policy exception*. Even if an individual is an at-will employee, the employer is prohibited from discharging the employee for a reason that violates public policy. The greatest protection is given to an employee discharged due to a refusal to commit an unlawful act, such as perjury or price-fixing, at the employer's request. Indeed, an employer's request that an employee violate a criminal statute—or even statutes that are not criminal—is almost always deemed against public policy and thus not a valid ground for discharge.

The following case addressed the issue of whether termination for refusal to violate a professional code of ethics constituted wrongful termination contrary to public policy.

A CASE IN POINT	SUMMARY

CASE 12.1
ROCKY MOUNTAIN
HOSPITAL AND
MEDICAL SERVICE
v. MARIANI

Supreme Court of Colorado
916 P.2d 519 (Colo. 1996).

FACTS   Diana Mariani was a certified public accountant employed for three years by the defendant, Rocky Mountain Hospital and Medical Service. She began as the general manager of the human resources department and later became the manager of special projects. In these capacities, Mariani objected to questionable accounting practices by Rocky Mountain. In particular, she discovered expense-allocation practices that enabled otherwise unprofitable enterprises to appear profitable and, as a result, benefit from artificially high solvency ratings. In response to Mariani's observations, her supervisor told Mariani that the allocation of expenses was a business decision.

Later, Mariani was assigned to draft materials regarding a proposed merger of regional insurance companies. Properly adjusting for the improper accounting, Mariani could not discern any benefits of the proposed merger. After she reported this to her supervisor, her supervisor told her that if she did not find any benefits, she would be fired. Questionable practices continued, including inappropriate tax breaks, misstated liabilities, and making what Mariani considered material omissions in various reports.

Mariani was fired. She considered this to be the direct result of her objections to Rocky Mountain's irregular accounting practices. Rocky Mountain claimed that Mariani was an at-will employee whose position was eliminated due to financial restructuring. Mariani sued for wrongful discharge. She argued that dismissal of an accountant for refusing to violate the Colorado State Board of Accountancy Rules of Professional Conduct prohibiting an accountant from knowingly misrepresenting facts or subordinating her judgment to others constituted wrongful termination contrary to public policy. The district court judge found for the employer. The state appellate court reversed and remanded part of the case. Mariani appealed.

ISSUE PRESENTED   Can an at-will employee state a claim for wrongful discharge under the public policy exception based on a professional code of ethics?

SUMMARY OF OPINION   In a bold move, the Colorado Supreme Court held that the rules of professional conduct for accountants do embody principles of public policy and, as a result, can be the source of a wrongful termination claim. The court began by outlining the public policy exception to the at-will rule, noting that the sources of public policy in previous cases had been specific statutory mandates. Nevertheless, the court held that to the extent the ethical codes of a profession serve a public purpose greater than mere professional advancement and are sufficiently specific so as to create a clear mandate, courts may look to ethical codes of conduct for sources of public policy.

The court found that the accountants' code of professional ethics serves the public by creating a standard ensuring the accurate computation and reporting of financial information. The requirements of the ethical code were also sufficiently specific to specify the rights and responsibilities of an accountant. As a result, Rocky Mountain violated Colorado public policy when it dismissed Mariani for refusing to violate the Colorado State Board of Accountancy Rules of Professional Conduct.

RESULT   The Colorado Supreme Court ruled that Mariani had been wrongfully discharged in violation of the state of Colorado's public policy.

The Colorado Supreme Court acknowledged that jurisdictions are split as to whether to recognize nonlegislative sources of public policy. Some jurisdictions, including California,[1] limit the sources of public policy to statutory or constitutional provisions. Others have recognized that nonlegislative sources, including professional ethical codes, may provide the basis for a public policy claim.[2]

In *Tameny v. Atlantic Richfield*,[3] the California Supreme Court held that an employee may maintain both tort and contract actions if the employee's discharge violated fundamental principles of public policy. As a result, damages for pain and suffering and possibly punitive damages were available.

A body of law related to the law governing retaliation for refusing to commit an illegal act recognizes a tort cause of action for discharge in retaliation for exercising a statutory right or privilege. For example, an employee claimed he was discharged by the Central Indiana Gas Company for filing a workers' compensation claim. Although there was no state statute that prohibited such a discharge, the Indiana Supreme Court recognized a tort cause of action for retaliatory discharge.[4] In another case, an employee of Firestone Tire and Rubber Company was discharged for refusing to take a lie detector test; a Pennsylvania statute prohibited employers from requiring such tests. The U.S. Court of Appeals for the Third Circuit found that the termination gave rise to a tort claim—not just a claim under the statute—because the statute represented a public policy.[5]

Employees who are discharged for carrying out important civic duties are also usually protected by the courts under the public policy doctrine. For example, the Oregon Supreme Court held that an employee could not be fired for participation in jury duty activities.[6] The court reasoned that jury duty was an important civic duty and that the will of the community and the effectiveness of the jury system would be thwarted if employers were allowed to discharge employees for fulfilling such an obligation.

Statutory Protections   The judicially created cause of action for discharge contrary to public policy exists alongside specific statutory provisions that prohibit retaliatory discharge. For example, the National Labor Relations Act prohibits discharge for union activities or for filing charges under the act.[7] The Fair Labor Standards Act prohibits discharge for exercising rights guaranteed by the minimum-wage and overtime provisions of that act.[8] The Occupational Health and Safety Act prohibits discharge of employees in retaliation for exercising rights under the act, such as complaining about work procedures or about health and safety violations in the workplace.[9] Many state acts contain similar provisions.

A more recent development has been the adoption of whistle-blower statutes. For example, the New York state statute[10] protecting private-sector whistle-blowers provides:

> An employer shall not take any retaliatory personnel action against an employee because such employee does any of the following:
> (a) discloses, or threatens to disclose to a supervisor or to a public body an activity, policy or practice of the employer that is in violation of law, rule or regulation which violation creates and presents a substantial and specific danger to the public health or safety;
> (b) provides information to, or testifies before, any public body conducting an investigation, hearing or inquiry into any such violation of a law, rule or regulation by such employer; or
> (c) objects to, or refuses to participate in any such activity, policy or practice in violation of a law, rule or regulation.

The rationale behind the protection of whistle-blowing is that it is in the public interest to promote compliance with law. It would be irresponsible to blindly protect all employee disclosures, however, because some disclosures may be intended merely to harass the employer. Consequently, the courts have established standards of review by which to judge the actions of both employers and employees. For example,

---

1. Gantt v. Sentry Ins. Co., 824 P.2d 680 (Cal. 1992).
2. *See, e.g.*, Winkelman v. Beloit Memorial Hosp., 483 N.W.2d 211 (Wis. 1992) (administrative rules).
3. 610 P.2d 1330 (Cal. 1980).
4. Frampton v. Central Indiana Gas Co., 297 N.E.2d 425 (Ind. 1973).
5. Perks v. Firestone Tire & Rubber Co., 611 F.2d 1363 (3d Cir. 1979).
6. Nees v. Hocks, 536 P.2d 512 (Or. 1975).

7. 29 U.S.C. § 158(a) (1), (3), and (4) (1994).
8. 29 U.S.C. §§ 215(a) (3), 216(b) (1994).
9. 29 U.S.C. § 660(c) (1988).
10. N.Y. LABOR LAW § 740 (McKinney 1989).

when a dismissed employee seeks reinstatement, the U.S. Court of Appeals for the Federal Circuit requires a showing of a "genuine nexus" (or connection) between the whistle-blowing and the employee's dismissal.[11] Proving this connection is often difficult.

Other cases have established a fair process by which to review claims in whistle-blower cases. Courts must balance the public interest in the enforcement of laws, the whistle-blower's interest in being protected from reprisal, and the employer's interest in managing its work force.

Implied Contracts

The second judicial exception to the at-will rule arises from the willingness of courts to interpret the parties' conduct as implying a contract limiting the employer's right to discharge, even though no written or express oral contract exists. Such a contract is known as an *implied contract*. Some factors that can give rise to an implied obligation to discharge the employee only for good cause are (1) she had been a long-term employee; (2) she had received raises, bonuses, and promotions throughout her career; (3) she was assured that her employment would continue if she did a good job; (4) she had been assured before by the company's management that she was doing a good job; (5) the company had stated that it did not terminate employees at her level except for good cause; and (6) she had never been formally criticized or warned about her conduct. Other relevant factors include the personnel policies or practices of the employer and the practices of the industry in which the employee is engaged.

A personnel manual stating that it was the employer's policy to release employees for just cause only, together with oral assurances that the employee would be with the company as long as he did his job properly, can give rise to a reasonable expectation that an employee will not be terminated except for good cause. In so holding, the Michigan Supreme Court stated in *Toussaint*[12] that there could be a contractual obligation binding on the employer without negotiations or any meeting of the minds, or even any communication of the policies to the employee:

No pre-employment negotiations need take place and the parties' minds need not meet on the subject; nor does it matter that the employee knows nothing of the particulars of the employer's policies and practices or that the employer may change them unilaterally. It is enough that the employer chooses, presumably in its own interest, to create an environment in which the employee believes that, whatever the personnel policies and practices, they are established and official at any given time, purport to be fair, and are applied consistently and uniformly to each employee. The employer has then created a situation "instinct with an obligation."

Although few courts have been willing to go as far as the Supreme Court of Michigan went in *Toussaint*, some courts have agreed that a personnel manual given to employees may give rise to contract obligations. The Oklahoma Court of Appeals held that the manual constitutes an offer of terms and conditions, and the employee's continuing to work is deemed an acceptance of the offer.[13]

Other courts have been unwilling to treat written personnel policies as contracts. For example, an employee of Citibank claimed the right not to be discharged except for cause, basing this claim on provisions of a personnel manual. A New York appellate court rejected this claim and held that the manual did not create any legal obligation upon the employer because the employee was still free to terminate the relationship at will.[14] Similarly, in a case involving Westinghouse Electrical Corporation, the North Carolina Court of Appeals held that unilaterally implemented employment policies are not part of the employment contract unless expressly included in it.[15]

The California Supreme Court, which had previously held that an implied contract not to terminate without good cause could be based on the employee's reasonable reliance on the company's personnel manual or policies,[16] applied the same principles to a claim of wrongful demotion.[17] Two engineers employed by Pacific Gas and Electric Company (PG&E) for 24 and 20 years, respectively, who were senior managers in the technical and ecological service unit, were demoted,

11. Warren v. Department of Army, 804 F.2d 654, 656 (Fed. Cir. 1986).

12. Toussaint v. Blue Cross & Blue Shield of Mich., 292 N.W.2d 880 (Mich. 1980).

13. Langdon v. Saga Corp., 569 P.2d 524 (Okla. Ct. App. 1976).

14. Edwards v. Citibank, N.A., 74 A.D.2d 553, *appeal dismissed*, 414 N.E.2d 400 (N.Y. 1980).

15. Walker v. Westinghouse Elec. Corp., 335 S.E.2d 79 (N.C. Ct. App. 1985).

16. Foley v. Interactive Data Corp., 765 P.2d 373 (Cal. 1988).

17. Scott v. Pacific Gas & Elec. Co., 904 P.2d 834 (Cal. 1995).

stripped of all supervisory authority, and had their pay cut by 25%. PG&E had a progressive discipline policy embodied in a document entitled "Pacific Gas and Electric Company: Positive Discipline Guidelines," which provided for progressively more serious, but constructively oriented, responses to employee misconduct. Demotion was discussed as an intermediate disciplinary step short of discharge, particularly appropriate when the employee showed an "ability deficiency." A PG&E personnel manager testified that PG&E expected employees to rely on company discipline policies so that employees knew what the company expected and what employees could expect from the company. The California Supreme Court held that the progressive discipline policy gave rise to an implied contractual agreement prohibiting demotion without good cause, which PG&E had breached. The court upheld a jury award for both engineers of $1,325,000 in damages for past and anticipated future lost earnings from the decreased salary and benefits as a result of the demotion and noneconomic damages of $150,000 for emotional distress.

Even when there is an implied contract not to terminate except for good cause, an employer may legally terminate an employee suspected of misconduct if, acting in good faith and following an investigation that was appropriate under the circumstances, the employer had reasonable grounds for believing that the employee had engaged in misconduct. For example, in one case,[18] a male manager was terminated following charges by two female employees of sexual harassment. The employer conducted a thorough investigation, which included interviews with the male manager, the two accusers, and 21 other people who had worked with the manager. The investigation was inconclusive, however; it was not possible to know with certainty whether the acts of harassment had actually taken place. The company felt that the accusers were credible, and the company's investigator concluded it was more likely than not that the harassment had occurred. Fearing a suit by the two women, the company terminated the male manager. He sued for wrongful termination; and the jury awarded him $1.78 million, after apparently finding that the charges against him were false. The California Supreme Court reversed and sent the case back for retrial so that the jury could determine whether the

company had a good faith belief, following a reasonable investigation, that the manager had engaged in sexual harassment. If so, the company would not be liable for wrongful termination.

Implied Covenant of Good Faith and Fair Dealing

The third prong in the developing law of wrongful discharge is the recognition of an *implied covenant of good faith and fair dealing* in the employment relationship. For example, the Supreme Judicial Court of Massachusetts held that a 25-year employee of National Cash Register Company, with a written contract providing for at-will employment, could sue for wrongful termination when the employer discharged him to deprive him of $46,000 in commissions.[19]

Courts in Texas, New Mexico, Florida, and Wisconsin have expressly declined to recognize an implied covenant of good faith and fair dealing in employment cases. California, like Massachusetts, recognizes such an implied covenant but provides only contract remedies for breach of the implied covenant; tort remedies, such as damages for pain and suffering and punitive damages, are not available.[20]

---

19. Fortune v. Nat'l Cash Register Co., 364 N.E.2d 1251 (Mass. 1977).
20. Foley v. Interactive Data Corp., 765 P.2d 373 (Cal. 1988).

IN BRIEF
LIMITS ON AT-WILL EMPLOYMENT

The employer's right to terminate an employee without cause may be subject to and restricted by:

- civil service systems
- union contracts
- express employment contracts (must be in writing if for more than one year)
- the public policy exception
- whistle-blower statutes
- implied contracts
- the implied covenant of good faith and fair dealing

---

18. Cotran v. Rollins Hudig Hall Int'l, 948 P.2d. 412 (Cal. 1998).

Right to Fair Procedure and Managed Care

The California courts have acknowledged a common law right to fair procedure protecting individuals from arbitrary exclusion or expulsion from private organizations that control important economic interests. Individuals having this right must be given notice of the charges brought against them and an opportunity to respond to those charges. They cannot be expelled from membership for reasons that are arbitrary, capricious, or contrary to public policy, notwithstanding provisions to the contrary in the organization's bylaws. This right has become increasingly important for health-care providers belonging to managed-care networks.

For example, in 1997, the California Court of Appeal applied this doctrine to a physician terminated by a health-care-provider network without the opportunity for a hearing.[21] The physician was an at-will independent contractor. The court reasoned that the right to fair procedure should extend to health-care providers' membership in provider networks, because managed-care providers control substantial economic interests. Prior cases had applied the doctrine to dentists and podiatrists.

 ## Fraudulent Inducement

During difficult economic times, a business may engage in puffery and exaggeration to keep and attract highly qualified personnel. The following case serves as a warning that a company may be held liable for overzealous sales pitches under a theory of fraudulent inducement.

---

21. Potvin v. Metropolitan Life Ins. Co., 63 Cal. Rptr. 2d 202 (Cal. Ct. App. 1997), *cert. granted*, 941 P.2d 1121 (Cal. 1997).

A CASE IN POINT	**IN THE LANGUAGE OF THE COURT**

CASE 12.2
STEWART v.
JACKSON & NASH
United States Court of
Appeals for the Second Circuit
976 F.2d 86 (2d Cir. 1992).

FACTS Victoria A. Stewart was an attorney who was employed in the environmental law department of a New York law firm. In October 1988, Ronald Herzog, a partner of the law firm Jackson & Nash, contacted Stewart regarding employment at his firm. Herzog allegedly represented to Stewart that Jackson had recently secured a large environmental law client, that Jackson was in the process of establishing an environmental law department, and that Stewart would head the environmental law department and be expected to service the firm's substantial existing environmental law client.

Stewart accepted employment at Jackson and, upon her arrival, was primarily assigned general litigation matters. Herzog repeatedly assured her that the promised environmental work would be forthcoming and consistently advised her that she would be promoted to a position as head of Jackson's environmental law department. Finally, in May 1990, a Jackson & Nash partner allegedly informed Stewart that Jackson never had environmental work, nor had it secured an environmental law client. Jackson & Nash dismissed Stewart on December 31, 1990.

Stewart filed suit, alleging that Jackson & Nash fraudulently induced her to enter into and remain in its employment. The district court dismissed Stewart's claim for failure to state a claim upon which relief could be granted. Stewart appealed.

Case 12.2 continues

Case 12.2 continued

OPINION   WALKER, J., writing for the U.S. Court of Appeals:

The district court found that Stewart's fraud claim arose from her termination from the firm and dismissed [the fraudulent-inducement claim] on the authority of *Murphy v. American Home Prod. Corp.*[22] *Murphy* held that because at-will employees "may be freely terminated . . . at any time for any reason or even for no reason," they can neither challenge their termination in a contract action nor "bootstrap" themselves around this bar by alleging that the firing was in some way tortious. Following *Murphy*, the court concluded that Stewart, an at-will employee, could not state a fraud claim based on facts arising out of her termination.

We find *Murphy* distinguishable. In *Murphy*, the plaintiff, an at-will employee of the defendant, claimed that he had been fired in a tortious manner. He alleged his firing was deliberately and viciously insulting, was designed to and did embarrass and humiliate the plaintiff and was intended to and did cause plaintiff severe mental and emotional distress thereby damaging plaintiff. These tort allegations, springing as they do directly from the termination itself, are a transparent attempt to restate the forbidden contractual challenge in the guise of tort.

Stewart's alleged injuries, on the other hand, commenced well before her termination and were, in several important respects, unrelated to it. According to the complaint, Jackson & Nash's misrepresentations caused Stewart, a budding environmental lawyer, to leave a firm with an environmental practice and spend two years in one in which she was largely unable to work in her chosen specialty. The resulting damage to her career development was independent of her later termination from Jackson & Nash and began while she was still at the firm. As she stated in her complaint, Stewart's "career objective—continuing to specialize in environmental law—was thwarted and grossly undermined during her employment with Jackson." Although *Murphy* precludes an award of damages for injuries caused by her termination, it does not prevent her from recovering for injuries that resulted from her reliance on false statements.

. . .

In this case Jackson & Nash's declarations that it "had recently secured a large environmental law client" and "was in the process of establishing an environmental law department" were not future promises but representations of present fact. . . . [T]hese representations support a claim for fraudulent inducement which is distinct and separable from any contract action.

. . . [Stewart] asserts that Jackson & Nash informed her that she "would be promoted to a position as head of Jackson's environmental law department . . . [although], upon information and belief, at the time Jackson made the aforesaid representations to Stewart, it knew that it did not intend to make her the head of the environmental law department." While [this] representation . . . appears, initially, to be a future promise (Stewart would be made head of the department), the New York

Case 12.2 continues

22. 448 N.E.2d 86 (N.Y. 1983).

Case 12.2 continued

Court of Appeals has explained that while mere promissory statements as to what will be done in the future are not actionable, . . . it is settled that, if a promise was actually made with a preconceived and undisclosed intention of not performing it, it constitutes a misrepresentation of material existing fact upon which an action for recission [based on fraudulent inducement] may be predicated. Stewart's assertion that Jackson & Nash, at the time it made the promise, "knew that it did not intend" to fulfill it, makes [the] representation . . . an allegation of present fact which gives rise to a claim of fraudulent inducement.

RESULT   Jackson & Nash's motion to dismiss was denied. Stewart could sue for fraudulent inducement.

COMMENTS   *Stewart* is notable in that it allows certain plaintiffs to proceed with their case even though fired at-will employees in most states are permitted to sue their employers for wrongful termination only under limited circumstances, such as breach of a public policy or discrimination. Although *Stewart* involved the hiring practices of a New York law firm, its legal principle is not easily limited to the specific facts of the case. Neal Brickman, Stewart's lawyer, suggested that the holding might prompt suits by fired employees, from several different professions, who claim hiring companies deceived them about working conditions. Because many similar claims have been dismissed by courts viewing them as wrongful termination suits in disguise, Brickman saw newfound potential for claims based not on promises about the future but about the circumstances at the firm when the employee was hired.

Questions

1. What is the difference between breach of contract and fraud in the inducement?
2. Why was it necessary for the plaintiff to couch her claim in terms of the tort of fraudulent inducement?

In 1996, the California Supreme Court unanimously held in *Lazar v. Rykoff-Sexton, Inc.* that a former New York executive could sue for fraud when a Los Angeles firm lured him to the West Coast with false promises of job security and regular bonuses.[23] The firm failed to tell the executive that it had just come off its worst economic year, had a dismal outlook, and was planning a merger that would eliminate the executive's position. Although the executive did an exemplary job, he was not paid the promised bonus and his job was terminated. The court held that the executive could re-

cover not only back pay and future lost wages, but also damages for emotional distress and punitive damages, which usually far exceed the amount of lost wages. The court distinguished *Hunter v. Up-Right, Inc.*,[24] an earlier case in which the California Supreme Court had held that an at-will employee who was induced to resign because he had been falsely told that his job was being eliminated could not state a valid tort claim for fraud. The *Lazar* court reasoned that the employer in *Hunter* had used deception when it could have directly fired the employee. In contrast, the employer in *Lazar* did not

---

23. 909 P.2d 981 (Cal. 1996).

24. 864 P.2d 88 (Cal. 1993).

have the power to force the executive to leave his company in New York. As a result, the executive's reliance on the employer's representations was truly detrimental.

 ## Noncompete Agreements

A *covenant not to compete* is a device, ancillary to another agreement (such as an employment contract), designed to protect a company's interests by limiting a former employee's ability to use trade secrets in working for a competitor or setting up a competing business. Enforcing a noncompete agreement can be difficult because rules vary by jurisdiction. For example, California, Texas, and Florida severely limit the enforceability of noncompetes.

Even if an employment agreement does not contain an express noncompetition clause, any provisions having a similar effect will be unenforceable in a jurisdiction banning noncompetes. For example, Dean Witter's employment agreement forced brokers in Los Angeles, California, to repay training costs if they left the company within two years. In a settlement of a class action suit in October 1997, Dean Witter agreed to return $540,000 collected from 34 former brokers and to pay another $1.2 million in legal fees for "involuntary servitude" in violation of California's ban on noncompetes unrelated to the sale of a business.[25]

In many cases, a noncompete agreement can be overturned due to "unreasonableness." Unreasonableness can be found on many grounds, including duration of limitation, geographic scope, and the employer's relation to the interests being protected. For example, the Nevada Supreme Court invalidated a noncompete agreement restricting a lighting-retrofitting employee from competing with his former employer within a 100-mile radius of the former employer's site for five years.[26] The duration placed a great hardship on the employee and was not necessary to protect the former employer's interests.

Thus, care must be taken when drafting noncompete agreements so that they will hold up in court. Corporate managers should keep the following guidelines in mind:[27]

- Know the relevant state laws. Given that different states apply different standards for reviewing noncompetes, be sure to structure each agreement in a way that courts will recognize and uphold.

- Be specific. Clarify the specific roles and responsibilities of a given employee, so the noncompete does not overly restrict the employee, thereby reducing the risk of judicial invalidation.

- Provide consideration for the noncompete. The noncompete may be a condition of employment; but for existing employees, be sure to provide something in exchange, such as a bonus or a promotion.

One court imposed noncompete obligations in the absence of a written agreement to protect trade secrets. A New York state judge enjoined former employees of DoubleClick Inc., who had not signed noncompete agreements, from working in the same industry for six months.[28] The court reasoned that the similarity in the two businesses and positions made it inevitable that the employees would use the former employer's trade secrets in their work for the new company. Trade-secret protection is discussed further in Chapter 11.

 ## At-Will Employment and Preemployment Practices

Employers seeking to preserve at-will employment need to consider not only their practices once an employee is hired, but also their preemployment practices.

---

25. Patrick McGeehan, *Attempt to Dun a Former Broker Costs Dean Witter $1.8 Million*, WALL ST. J., Oct. 23, 1997, at B12.

ETHICAL CONSIDERATION

What role should the law play in penalizing an employer that lies to its employee about the reason for termination in order to persuade the employee to resign? What role do ethics play in this situation?

---

26. Jones v. Deeter, 913 P.2d 1272 (Nev. 1996). *See also* Rollins Burdick Hunter of Wisconsin, Inc. v. Hamilton, 304 N.W.2d 752 (Wis. 1981).

27. *See* Christopher Caggiano, *Think All Noncompetes Stink? Think Again*, INC., Oct. 1997, at 114.

28. Frances A. McMorris, *Judge Restricts Two Executives Despite Lack of Noncompete Pacts*, WALL ST. J., Nov. 25, 1997, at B10.

In some states, it may be difficult to maintain an at-will relationship except by an express contract or by a disclaimer in the employment application or the personnel manual stating that nothing in the employment relationship and no personnel policy or benefit shall create a right to continued employment. If such a disclaimer is plainly contrary to the company's stated policy, however, it may be rejected by a court. For example, a statement on an application form that employment is at will probably will not be upheld if the company's written personnel policy expressly provides that employees will be given progressive discipline and will not be fired without just cause.

Second, if an employer chooses to have a written personnel policy, care should be taken to see that the language expressly reserves those rights that the employer wishes to maintain, especially with respect to discharge. Also, if employees are given handbooks that purport to summarize the official personnel manuals, the handbook and the manuals must be consistent. Otherwise, courts and juries are likely to uphold the policy that is most favorable to the employee.

Third, if an employer chooses to have a policy of progressive discipline, it is essential that supervisors and managers, as well as the human resources staff, are trained to administer the policy. In particular, they should be trained to document performance problems and to counsel employees about the need to improve.

Fourth, an employer can enter into an agreement with the employee that any dispute shall be subject to arbitration. An arbitration clause in a fairly negotiated written contract will withstand judicial scrutiny; however, a *boilerplate clause*—that is, standardized, non-negotiable language—in an employment application form may be found invalid.

Fifth, an employer should decide whether to establish an internal grievance procedure. Such a procedure can result in fewer lawsuits. If the employer establishes a grievance procedure, however, the employer must follow it. Otherwise, the employer may face claims for failure to follow its own procedure, especially when the procedure is elaborate.

The bottom line is that the employer should have in place a system of checks and balances to ensure that the company's policies are properly communicated and followed. Discharges should be well documented and handled in accordance with these policies. Employees should be treated in a fair and consistent manner.

In deciding whether there is an express or implied contractual right not to be fired except for cause, a court may consider statements made during preemployment interviews and on application forms. Consequently, if an employer wants to preserve the traditional legal right to discharge employees at will, it should see that limitations on this right are not inadvertently created.

To illustrate, an application form might include the following language above the employee signature line: "I understand that, if hired, my employment can be terminated with or without cause, at either my employer's or my option." Inclusion of such language reminds the employee that his or her employment is at will—and verifies that he or she was so informed—and lessens the likelihood that the employee will be able to establish an implied contractual right to be discharged only for cause. Additionally, no statements should be made during interviews that could create an impression that the applicant would not be fired without good cause. "Employees are never fired from here without good reason," "Your job will be secure, as long as you do your work," and "We treat our employees like family" are examples of such statements. In short, the employer should not mislead an applicant about the security of the job offered.

◆ Recommendations for Former Employees

Employers are often asked to give references regarding former employees to prospective employers. An employee always hopes that such a reference will be favorable, but such is not always the case. At any rate, the employee hopes that the reference will at least be fair. If the reference is not fair and an employer defames the reputation of a former employee, the former employee can sue the employer for defamation.

INTERNATIONAL CONSIDERATION

Before making a decision to move abroad, a manager should check to see whether the company will have flexibility in its hiring. A business should also make sure that its workers can get necessary visas to work abroad. Many countries have quotas requiring that a certain percentage of a foreign company's labor force be nationals of the host country.

Traditionally, defamation law requires publication, meaning that the communicator of the defamatory information tells the information to a third party, such as a prospective employer. However, some jurisdictions have an interesting exception to this rule in the employment context. Under the *doctrine of self-publication*, a defamatory communication by an employer to an employee may constitute publication when the employer could foresee that the employee would be required to repeat the communication, for instance, to a prospective employer. The doctrine is designed to provide a cause of action to the job-seeking employee who is forced to "self-publicize" the former employer's defamatory statement. So that disgruntled former employees will not overuse the doctrine, most jurisdictions require a showing of abuse on the part of the former employer and some reasonable degree of foreseeability of a compelled future self-publication.

Fear of a defamation claim may make it tempting for an employer to give an overly positive recommendation. This is not prudent. As explained in Chapter 9, an employer giving an untrue assessment of a former employee may be liable not only to the new employer who relies on the recommendation, but also to third persons physically harmed as a foreseeable result of the recommendation.

For example, in *Randi W. v. Muroc Joint Unified School District*,[29] a school district wrote letters of recommendation for a former administrative employee, inducing a school to hire the individual. However, the letters of recommendation did not include charges and complaints against the former employee for sexual misconduct. When the former employee sexually assaulted a student, the student sued the school district for fraud and negligent misrepresentation. The California Supreme Court ruled that once a recommender provides some information about a former employee, it is "obliged to disclose all other facts that 'materially qualify' the limited facts disclosed." Having provided "misleading half-truths," the former employer was liable to third parties who were injured as a foreseeable consequence of its representations.

Employee Drug and Genetic Testing

In recent years, there has been increasing public discussion about the abuse of drugs and alcohol in our society and, in particular, in the workplace. There is a widespread belief that drug and alcohol abuse lead to decreased productivity, quality control problems, absenteeism on the job, accidents, and employee theft. Many employers are adopting drug-screening programs for their employees and applicants. Indeed, according to the American Management Association, 77% of large companies in the United States test their employees for drugs.[30] Some employers are using drug testing in conjunction with a comprehensive drug program that includes employee education and assistance to the employee with a drug or alcohol problem.

Even apart from the legal implications, the practical usefulness of drug testing is limited. First, even the most sophisticated tests (which usually involve a urine or blood sample) cannot establish whether the employee was using drugs at any particular time. The tests can detect certain substances in the employee's body, but they do not tell how long the substance has been present. Second, depending on the level of sophistication of the test and the quality of the testing program, the test may produce erroneous results.

The issue of drug testing generally comes before the courts in the context of discipline or discharge of an employee for refusing to take a test. Although there seems to be great public support for drug testing, there is wide divergence in judicial opinions on the subject. Nonetheless, certain trends emerge. Whether testing will be deemed permissible in a particular situation depends on four factors: (1) the scope of the testing program; (2) whether the employer is a public or private employer; (3) any state constitutional guarantees of right to privacy; and (4) any state statutes regulating drug testing.

The first major factor, scope, concerns who is being tested: all employees (random testing); only employees in a specific job where it is felt there is a legitimate job-related need (for example, nuclear power plant employees); groups of employees (for example, all employees in one facility because there is a general suspicion of drug use within that group); or specific individuals who are believed to be using drugs. The smaller the group to be tested and the more specific the reason for testing, the more likely a court will uphold the test. Random testing is the most difficult to defend. The final three factors are discussed in more detail below.

---

29. 929 P.2d 582 (Cal. 1997) (Case 9.4).

30. *Who's Watching?* UFCW ACTION, Jan.–Feb. 1998, at 16.

Public Employees

Because public employees are protected by the U.S. Constitution's Fourth Amendment prohibition against unreasonable searches and seizures, there are greater limitations on testing than those imposed on private employers. It has long been recognized that urine tests and blood tests are a substantial intrusion upon bodily privacy and are therefore searches subject to regulation. With some exceptions, there is no federal constitutional limitation on drug testing in the private sector.

In 1989, the Supreme Court decided two cases that provided some guidance regarding the appropriate balance between the need for safety and a public employee's right to be free from an unreasonable search. Both decisions upheld employee drug-testing programs against Fourth Amendment challenges.

Skinner v. Railway Labor Executives' Association[31] addressed the constitutionality of drug testing of railroad employees. The Supreme Court held that railroads can be required to test public employees involved in a major train accident and have the authority to test employees who violate certain safety rules. The Court reasoned that any intrusion upon individual privacy rights in the railroad context was outweighed by the government's compelling interest in public and employee safety. In rejecting an individualized assessment of drug use, the Court noted that a substance-impaired railroad employee in a safety-sensitive job can cause great human loss before any signs of the impairment become noticeable. Thus, the regulations provided an effective means of deterring employees from using drugs or alco-

hol by putting them on notice that they are likely to be discovered if an accident occurs.

The Supreme Court also held mandatory drug testing of U.S. Customs Service employees in line for transfer or promotion to certain sensitive positions involving drug interdiction or the handling of firearms did not violate their constitutional rights.[32] Although there was no perceived drug problem among Customs employees, the Court held that the program was justified by the need for national security and by the extraordinary safety hazards attendant to the positions involved.

In 1997, the U.S. Court of Appeals for the District of Columbia upheld suspicionless drug testing of all Office of Management and Budget employees with passholder access to an office building within the White House security perimeter, regardless of the nature of their jobs, as a reasonable way to protect the president and vice-president from harm.[33] In contrast, in *Rutherford v. City of Albuquerque*,[34] the U.S. Court of Appeals for the Tenth Circuit concluded that drug testing without warning on a municipal truck driver returning from a one-year leave of absence was an unreasonable search in violation of the Fourth Amendment.

Health screening has recently become an important issue and involves many of the same issues that arise in the context of drug testing. The following case addresses the privacy interest implicated when a public employer uses fluid samples of employees to test for contagious and congenital diseases.

---

31. 489 U.S. 602 (1989).

32. National Treasury Employees Union v. Von Raab, 489 U.S. 656 (1989).

33. Stigile v. Clinton, 110 F.3d 801 (D.C. Cir 1997).

34. 77 F.3d 1258 (10th Cir. 1996).

A CASE IN POINT	SUMMARY

CASE 12.3
NORMAN–BLOODSAW v. LAWRENCE BERKELEY LABORATORY
United States Court of Appeals for the Ninth Circuit
135 F.3d 1260 (9th Cir. 1998).

FACTS   The Lawrence Berkeley Laboratory (Laboratory) is a research facility operated by the state of California pursuant to a contract with the Department of Energy (DOE). The DOE requires its contractors to create an occupational medical program that implements mandatory health screening after an offer of employment is made, but before commencement of work obligations, and periodic health examinations thereafter. The mandatory health examinations included a detailed survey regarding the individual's medical history as well as blood and urine samples. The questionnaires

Case 12.3 continues

Case 12.3 continued

asked the employees about any infection with venereal diseases, plus medical conditions such as sickle cell anemia and menstrual disorders.

Without the consent or knowledge of the employees, the Laboratory tested blood and urine samples for syphilis, sickle cell anemia, and pregnancy. Seven current and former administrative and clerical employees learned of this practice and sued, claiming violations of their privacy rights under the California and federal constitutions, the Americans with Disabilities Act, and Title VII of the Civil Rights Act of 1964. The district court dismissed each of their claims. The plaintiffs appealed.

ISSUE PRESENTED   May an employee who undergoes a general medical examination be tested, without his or her knowledge, for highly private and sensitive information, such as syphilis, sickle cell anemia, and pregnancy?

SUMMARY OF OPINION   The U.S. Court of Appeals held that testing for highly sensitive information without an employee's knowledge is actionable under the federal and California constitutions and Title VII. Because the disclosure of medical information has been recognized as an essential component of privacy, the performance of unauthorized tests struck at the heart of this constitutional interest. Indeed, the tests revealed information unknown even to the individual. Thus, such unauthorized tests implicated the Fourth Amendment bar on unreasonable searches and seizures, in addition to the privacy considerations of the Due Process Clause of the Fourteenth Amendment.

The court then analyzed the medical tests through the lens of the Fourth Amendment and balanced the government's interest in general medical examinations with the plaintiffs' expectation of privacy. The plaintiffs' privacy interest was deemed more significant for "[o]ne can think of few subject areas more personal and more likely to implicate privacy interests than that of one's health or genetic makeup." Insofar as each exam implicated information regarding one's sexual history or reproductive decision making, the court held that "the conditions tested for were aspects of one's health in which one enjoys the highest expectations of privacy."

Moreover, the court rejected the government's claim that the medical history questionnaire, which included questions on syphilis, sickle cell anemia and pregnancy, put the plaintiffs on notice that their fluid samples would be tested for these conditions. It found that the questions and actual testing were qualitatively different and that "revealing one's personal knowledge as to whether one has a particular medical condition has nothing to do with one's expectations about actually being tested for that condition."

The court reinstated the plaintiffs' cause of action under the California constitution with the same reasoning applied to the federal privacy interest. In terms of the Title VII claims, the court found that the plaintiffs had articulated a claim of race and sex discrimination. Black employees were screened for sickle cell anemia and women were screened for pregnancy; both tests were conditions of employment that were not applied to similarly situated white men. The court upheld the dismissal of the claims under the Americans with Disabilities Act.

RESULT   The appeals court reversed the district court's dismissal of the federal and state constitutional and Title VII claims and remanded the case for further proceedings.

Case 12.3 continues

Case 12.3 continued

COMMENTS   This is the first case decided by a federal appeals court ruling on genetic privacy in the workplace.[35]

35. *See* Carol Smith, *Other Perspectives: Some Cases of Genetic Discrimination*, SAN FRANCISCO SUNDAY EXAMINER & CHRON., Feb. 22, 1998, at CL 15.

Private Employers

Constitutional Limitations   The private employer must also respect employees' right to privacy. In some states, there is a right to privacy under tort law or the state constitution. For example, in California, Article 1, Section 1 of the state constitution specifically guarantees a right to privacy. That right extends to employees of private as well as public entities. Thus, the ban on genetic and pregnancy tests at issue in *Norman–Bloodsaw* (Case 12.3) applies to private as well as public employers.

The right to privacy is the right to be left alone. The courts balance this individual right with the competing public interest in public safety and welfare. Because of the nature of drug testing, which usually involves a blood or urine sample and therefore deals with private functions or requires a bodily intrusion, there is little doubt that drug testing raises privacy issues under state law, as it does under federal constitutional law. Therefore, to justify the test, an employer will have to establish a compelling interest, such as a reasonable belief that the individual was using drugs on the job. Even if the employer has good grounds to believe that the employee is using drugs, a court might require the employer to use impairment tests (such as walking a straight line) to determine whether the employee is actually impaired on the job, rather than blood or urine tests, which determine only whether a substance has been ingested at some recent time. In general, testing by private employers is more likely to be upheld when the persons being tested do not have a reasonable expectation of privacy.

A state constitution's guarantee of privacy was applied to the drug testing of a private employee in *Luddtke v. Nabors Alaska Drilling, Inc.*[36] In that case, the Supreme Court of Alaska held that the right to privacy in the state constitution did not apply to private entities,

only to the government; thus, the state constitution did not shield its citizens from drug tests by a private employer. Moreover, even if there was a right, the company's interest in maintaining the health, safety, and welfare of its workers would outweigh any privacy interest.

In 1990, the California Court of Appeal held that a nonintrusive pupillary-reaction test given to all employees of Kerr–McGee Corporation at its chemical plant in Trono, California, might violate the California constitution's right to privacy, depending on the intrusiveness of the test and the employer's safety needs.[37] The test consisted of shining a light in the person's eye and observing how much the pupil contracts. Although the court acknowledged that the pupillary test was less intrusive than urine, blood, or breath tests, it held that the trial court needed more facts to determine just how intrusive the test was.

Statutory Limitations   A number of states have adopted legislation regarding drug testing by private employers. Such legislation often sets forth the notice procedures an employer must follow before asking an employee to submit to a drug test. For example, in Vermont, the employer must, before administering the test, give the employee a copy of a written policy setting forth the circumstances under which persons may be tested, the drugs that will be screened, the procedures involved, and the consequences of a positive result. A Vermont employer must also tell the employee that a false positive result can be caused by medications and other substances.

A number of states have comprehensive drug- and alcohol-testing laws that require reasonable suspicion or probable cause before an employer may test. The requirements for establishing reasonable suspicion or probable cause vary from state to state. For instance, Connecticut's law permits testing when "the employer

36. 768 P.2d 1123 (Alaska 1989).

37. Semore v. Pool, 217 Cal. App. 3d 1087 (Cal. Ct. App. 1990).

has reasonable suspicion that the employee is under the influence of drugs or alcohol which adversely affects or could adversely affect such employee's job performance."[38] In addition, Connecticut's law prohibits determination of employment status or promotion based on drug testing.[39] Minnesota permits testing when there exists reasonable suspicion that the employee is under the influence, possesses drugs or alcohol on the employer's premises, or has sustained a personal injury or caused a workplace accident.[40]

Although it appears that there may be some limit on implementing a drug-testing program for private as well as public employees, it should be noted that employers have the right to make and enforce rules prohibiting drug use or possession of drugs on work premises, as well as rules prohibiting employees from being under the influence of drugs while at work. When there are visible signs of intoxication or impairment, or inadequate performance, the employer may take disciplinary action. Because of the inadequacy of drug tests and the uncertainty about the scope of employees' rights, the employer may wish instead to develop drug-assistance and drug-education programs, and identify and counsel employees about the performance problems that drug abuse can cause.

Employee Challenges An employee may challenge a drug test in many ways. The employee may claim the test breached his or her employment contract; that there was no justification for the test; that it violated the public policy that protects privacy; that he or she was defamed by false accusations of drug use based on an erroneous test; that he or she suffered emotional distress, especially if the test result was in error; or that the testing disproportionately affects employees of one race or sex and therefore is discriminatory.

 ## Polygraph Testing of Employees

Polygraph testing is another area in which employees' right to privacy may limit an employers' investigative rights. The Employee Polygraph Protection Act of 1988[41] (EPPA) generally makes it unlawful for employ-

ers to (1) request an applicant or employee to take a polygraph exam or other lie detector test; (2) rely on or inquire about the results of a lie detector test that an applicant or employee has taken; (3) take or threaten to take any adverse action against an applicant or employee because of a refusal to take, or on the basis of the results of, any lie detector test; or (4) take or threaten to take any adverse action against an employee or applicant who has filed a complaint or participated in a proceeding relating to the polygraph law.

The EPPA does not completely ban the use of polygraph exams. Employers may test employees who are reasonably suspected of conduct injurious to the business, as well as applicants or employees in certain businesses involving security services or the handling of drugs.

These rights cannot be waived by the employee in advance. For example, a federal district court held that although a bartender signed a release form stating that her employer had reasonable suspicion of theft before requesting that she take a polygraph test, the bartender could still sue for violation of the EPPA.[42] The court held that an employee can waive rights or procedures under the EPPA only pursuant to a written settlement of a pending lawsuit.

The EPPA does not restrict federal, state, or local government employers from administering polygraph exams. However, several states have laws restricting or prohibiting the use of polygraph examinations. For example, in Massachusetts, an employer cannot request that an applicant or employee take a lie detector test as a condition of employment.[43] Rhode Island,[44] Delaware,[45] and Pennsylvania[46] have similar statutes. Even when lie detector tests are permitted, no question should be asked during the test that could not lawfully be asked on an application form or during an interview.

 ## Employee Surveillance

Employers have a legitimate interest in observing their employees to ensure quality control and productivity. However, one developing area of law explores under what circumstances an employer may observe an

38. CONN. GEN. STAT. ANN. § 31–51x (West Supp. 1993).

39. CONN. GEN. STAT. ANN. § 31–51u(a) (West Supp. 1993).

40. MINN. STAT. ANN. § 181.951 (West 1993).

41. 29 U.S.C. §§ 2001–2009 (1988).

42. Long v. Mango's Tropical Café, Inc., 958 F. Supp. 612 (S.D. Fla. 1997).

43. MASS. GEN. LAWS ANN. ch. 149, § 19B (West 1996).

44. R.I. GEN. LAWS § 28–6.1–1 (1996).

45. DEL. CODE ANN. tit. 19, § 704 (1997).

46. 18 PA. CONS. STAT. ANN. § 7321 (West 1998).

employee without transgressing the employee's privacy rights. The watershed case in this area was *O'Connor v. Ortega*.[47] In that case, the U.S. Supreme Court ruled that a public employee may, in certain circumstances, enjoy a reasonable expectation of privacy in his or her workplace in relation to his or her employer. However,

the employer's privacy interest was to be balanced by the "operational realities" of the workplace.

After *Ortega*, lower courts have looked to (1) whether the employee was provided exclusive working space; (2) the nature of the employment; and (3) whether the employee was on notice that parts of the workplace were subject to employer intrusions. The following case analyses the issue of electronic surveillance of employees in light of these factors.

47. 480 U.S. 7009 (1987).

A CASE IN POINT	**IN THE LANGUAGE OF THE COURT**

CASE 12.4
VEGA-RODRIGUEZ v. PUERTO RICO TELEPHONE COMPANY
United States Court of Appeals for the First Circuit
110 F.3d 174 (1st Cir. 1997).

FACTS   Plaintiffs were security operators who monitored computer banks to detect alarm-system signals emanating from facilities owned by the Puerto Rico Telephone Company (PRTC) throughout Puerto Rico. PRTC installed three video-surveillance cameras to monitor the open area in which the security operators work. The cameras did not record any sound nor was the rest area within its field of vision. The office of PRTC's general manager contained a video monitor, a switcher unit, and a video recorder. The cameras operated all day, every day, and the tapes were stored in the general manager's office. Plaintiffs sued the PRTC, alleging violations of their constitutional rights to privacy after management ignored their complaints about the video surveillance. The district court granted PRTC's motion for summary judgment. Plaintiffs appealed.

ISSUE PRESENTED   Does a public employer's soundless video surveillance of the workplace violate an employee's right to privacy?

OPINION   SELYA, J., writing for the U.S. Court of Appeals:

To be actionable under the Fourth Amendment, a privacy expectation must meet both subjective and objective criteria: The complainant must have an actual expectation of privacy, and that expectation must be one that society recognizes as reasonable.

. . .

Generally speaking, business premises invite lesser privacy expectations than do residences. Still, deeply rooted societal expectations foster some cognizable privacy interests in business premises.

. . .

Here it is simply implausible to suggest that society would recognize as reasonable an employee's expectation of privacy against being viewed while toiling in an open and undifferentiated work area. The employer did not provide the work station for the employees' exclusive use, and its physical layout belies any expectation of privacy.

. . .

Employers possess a legitimate interest in the efficient operation of the workplace, and one attribute of this interest is that supervisors may monitor at will that which is in plain view within an open work area. Here, moreover, this attribute has a greater claim on our allegiance because the employer acted overtly in establishing the

Case 12.4 continues

Case 12.4 continued

video surveillance: It notified its work force in advance that video cameras would be installed and disclosed the cameras' field of vision.

. . .

The employees also contend that the Constitution spawns a general right, in nature of a privacy right, to be free from video surveillance in the workplace. We disagree.

. . .

The courts have identified two clusters of personal privacy rights recognized by the Fourteenth Amendment. One bundle of rights relates to ensuring autonomy in making certain kinds of significant personal decisions; the other relates to ensuring the confidentiality of personal matters. PRTC's monitoring does not implicate any of these rights.

. . .

Because the appellants do not have an objectively reasonable expectation of privacy in the open areas of their workplace, the video surveillance conducted by their employer does not infract their federal constitutional rights. PRTC's employees may register their objections to the surveillance system with management, but they may not lean upon the Constitution for support.

RESULT The security operators' case was dismissed, and PRTC was permitted to continue electronic surveillance of its employees.

COMMENTS According to a 1997 survey by the American Management Association, 35% of businesses in the United States said that they use various strategies to check up on employees, including listening in on employee's voicemail and phone calls, inspecting their computer files, and using video surveillance.[48] Moreover, 25% of businesses surveyed indicated that they conducted these activities without the consent or awareness of employees.

Questions

1. Why did the court find the employee's expectation of privacy "implausible"?
2. If the defendant had been a private employer, rather than a public entity, would this have altered the outcome?

48. *Who's Watching?* UFCW ACTION, Jan.–Feb. 1998, at 16.

 Responsibility for Worker Safety

Occupational Safety and Health Act

The Occupational Safety and Health Act of 1970 (OSHA)[49] was enacted to require employers to establish safe and healthy working environments. The federal

49. Pub. L. No. 91-596, 84 Stat. 1590 (1970) (codified as amended at 29 U.S.C. §§ 651–678 (1988 & Supp 1992)).

agency responsible for enforcing the provisions of OSHA is the Occupational Safety and Health Administration (also called OSHA). This agency is authorized by Congress to govern additional workplace issues, including exposure to hazardous chemicals, protective gear, fire protection, and workplace temperatures and ventilation.

An employer governed by OSHA must provide a place of employment that is free from *recognized hazards* that are causing or are likely to cause death or serious physical harm to employees. What constitutes a recognized hazard is not entirely clear. However, its reach is broad and includes anything from sharp objects to radiation. Conditions that are obviously dangerous or are considered by the employer or other employers in the industry to be dangerous are considered recognized hazards.

In April 1997, the Occupational Safety and Health Review Commission for the first time decided that OSHA has the power to prosecute employers that expose workers to ergonomic hazards, because the act imposes on employers a "general duty" to abate workplace hazards.[50] In December 1997, OSHA proposed $840,000 in penalties against Hudson Foods, Inc., based on 12 alleged ergonomics violations at its Noel, Missouri, poultry-processing plant.

OSHA has proposed a rule on how to monitor and prevent injuries stemming largely from repetitive motions on the job.[51] However, due to the contentious nature of ergonomic hazards, OSHA is carefully developing a recommended ergonomics-compliance program and studying corporate responses to the problem.[52]

Although state and federal health and safety laws specify that employers must have a certain number of toilets in the workplace depending on the size of the workforce, until April 1998 they did not specify that employees must be allowed to use the facilities. Some workers, especially those on assembly lines, were denied regular access to restrooms and were forced to wear adult diapers or suffer urinary tract infections from being forced to wait hours for permission to use a restroom. In response, OSHA issued an interpretation of its restroom standard to make it clear that providing restrooms is not enough; employees must be allowed to use them. "Restrictions on access must be reasonable and may not cause extended delay."[53]

OSHA also requires employers to maintain certain records, including the OSHA Form 200, which lists and summarizes all work-related injuries and illnesses. (Certain industries, such as retail, finance, and insurance, are exempt from this record-keeping requirement.) A summary of these records must be posted annually at the job site. In addition, employers must post in a conspicuous place (1) OSHA's official Job Safety Poster; (2) any OSHA citations for violations; and (3) notices of imminent danger to employees, including exposure to toxic substances.

OSHA inspectors are allowed to conduct surprise inspections at work sites when (1) OSHA believes an imminent danger is present, (2) an employee has filed a complaint, or (3) a fatality or catastrophe has occurred. During the inspection, the OSHA investigator may review company records, check for compliance with the relevant OSHA standards, inspect fire-protection and other safety equipment, examine the company's safety and health-management programs, interview employees, and walk through the facility.

When the inspection has been completed, the inspector meets with the employer and the employee representative, if any. The inspector discusses the results of the inspection and, if appropriate, issues a written citation for violations. There are five types of violations: (1) de minimis (that is, unimportant) violations, for which no notice is posted and no penalty is imposed; (2) nonserious violations, which present hazards that are not likely to cause death or serious bodily harm, for which a fine of up to $7,000 for each violation may be imposed; (3) serious violations, which have a substantial likelihood of resulting in death or serious bodily harm, for which a fine of up to $7,000 for each violation may be imposed; (4) willful violations, which are deliberate or intentional, for which a fine of at least $5,000 and up to $70,000 may be imposed for each violation; and (5) repeated violations, which occur within three years of a previously cited violation, for which a fine of up to $70,000 for each violation may be imposed. Courts may also impose criminal sanctions for health and safety infractions (see Chapter 15).

For purposes of sanctioning violations, the U.S. Court of Appeals for the Fifth Circuit recently held that the hazardous condition is the proper unit of prosecution, rather than the number of employees exposed to the hazardous condition.[54] Thus, if 87 employees are threatened by a chemical explosion, then one violation (the explosion), rather than 87 (the number of individuals exposed to the risk of heat, burns, and flying debris as a result of the explosion), may be cited.

50. Reich v. Pepperidge Farm, 66 U.S.L.W. 2095 (OSHRC 1997).

51. Laura M. Litvan, *Repetitive Regulation Syndrome,* INVESTOR'S BUS. DAILY, July 18, 1997, at A1.

52. *OSHA Acting on Only Some Ergonomics Recommendations, Work Group Reports,* 66 U.S.L.W. 2395 (Jan. 6, 1998).

53. *OSHA Issues Interpretation Letter for Standard on Bathroom Facilities,* 66 U.S.L.W. 2636 (Apr. 21, 1998).

54. Reich v. Arcadian Corp., 110 F.3d 1192 (5th Cir. 1997).

If OSHA finds a violation, the employer is required to remedy the problem immediately. If remedial action is not taken, OSHA will seek a court order to ensure compliance. The employer may either settle the violation or seek review of the OSHA decision by the Occupational Safety and Health Review Commission. OSHA may penalize egregious violations by imposing a separate fine for each violation rather than an overall fine for a group of violations. Additionally, punitive damages are available and the courts have upheld their application in extreme cases. For example, a federal district court recently permitted punitive damages in a suit against a nursing home that "blatantly" retaliated against a nurse for filing a complaint with OSHA regarding the lack of latex gloves at the site.[55]

In an attempt to increase corporate compliance with national safety standards and recognizing the limitations of traditional inspection procedures, OSHA has adopted cooperative compliance programs. *Cooperative compliance programs* are a national alternative enforcement mechanism that (1) offers employers a choice between a partnership with OSHA or traditional enforcement; (2) targets workplaces with high injury and illness rates using site-specific data; (3) requires participating businesses to establish or improve existing safety programs; and (4) allocates resources to the most dangerous workplaces in an attempt to prevent injury and illness.[56] Through cooperative compliance programs, OSHA hopes to develop a nationwide database on work-related illness and injury to target the most hazardous work environments and make them more safe. Yet, some employer groups claim that OSHA is unfairly targeting employers and coercing compliance with standards.

The Chamber of Commerce of the United States and several other industry groups sued to enjoin OSHA from implementing its cooperative compliance program on the grounds that it constituted a standard that had not been properly promulgated. In February 1998, the U.S. Court of Appeals for the District of Columbia Circuit temporarily enjoined OSHA from implementing its program.[57]

There is a trend toward increasing the number of criminal prosecutions of employers for OSHA violations. Although the word "employer" has not been defined, it appears to include those corporate officers who are responsible for ensuring compliance with OSHA standards.

State Criminal Prosecutions

Recognizing OSHA's financial and staff limitations, prosecutors in at least 14 states have charged employers with crimes ranging from assault and battery to reckless homicide for ignoring warnings to correct workplace safety hazards.[58]

A number of managers and officers of corporations have been criminally prosecuted for serious violations that led to the death of employees. These prosecutions have had mixed results. For example, in 1990, the Michigan Court of Appeals found that a supervisor was not guilty of involuntary manslaughter because he did not own the equipment that caused the accident.[59] In 1992, after 25 workers died in a fire at a chicken plant in North Carolina because fire-exit doors were locked, allegedly to prevent employees from stealing chickens, the plant owner pled guilty to involuntary manslaughter and was sentenced to nearly 20 years, the stiffest prison term to date.[60]

California and Maine recently enacted laws specifically providing for criminal penalties for employers who endanger their employees. In 1996, Massachusetts charged two metal-processing companies and their owners with assault and battery with a dangerous weapon: lead dust that workers inhaled while standing over giant kettles, stirring molten metals. The vacuum device that was supposed to suck up the vapors was broken. The Massachusetts attorney general claimed that this was not an accident: "They knew that they had created illegal conditions which were dangerous."[61]

Violence in the Workplace

Employers also face potential liability for violence in the workplace perpetrated by employees or their former boyfriends or spouses. Homicide was the second most

---

55. Reich v. Skyline Terrace Inc., 977 F. Supp. 1141 (N.D. Okla. 1997).

56. *OSHA's Cooperative Compliance Programs Expanded Nationwide, Herman Announces*, 66 U.S.L.W. 2349 (Dec. 9, 1997).

57. 66 U.S.L.W. 2522 (1998).

58. Ann Davis, *Treating On-the-Job Injuries as True Crimes*, WALL ST. J., Feb. 26, 1997, at B1.

59. Michigan v. Hegedus, 451 N.W.2d 861 (Mich. Ct. App. 1990).

60. Davis, *supra* note 58.

61. *Id.*

AT THE TOP

A manager can be held criminally responsible for serious workplace-safety violations. Diligent oversight of health and safety aspects of the workplace serves to reduce both the chance of employee serious injury and death in the first place and the likelihood that an individual manager will be found criminally liable if, despite his or her diligence, a fatal accident does occur.

---

common cause of death in the workplace in 1992.[62] In the year ended July 1993, more than two million people were attacked at work.[63]

To help prevent domestic violence in the workplace, some companies hold seminars on domestic-violence issues on company time, provide a 24-hour telephone counseling service for employees and their partners, and tap the phones of women who fear an attack and provide them with escorts to and from parking lots. Sometimes, the employer seeks restraining orders in its name to keep alleged abusers from potential victims' worksites.[64]

Once an employer is informed about the risk of violence or takes an interest in the case, it exposes itself to liability for negligence if it fails to take reasonable steps to prevent injury. For example, in 1995, both the employer of a woman killed in her Houston office by a former boyfriend and the office-building manager agreed to pay more than $350,000 to settle a case brought by the woman's family. The woman had told them that the former boyfriend was subject to a restraining order and that she feared that he would kill her, but according to her mother, "They didn't believe her story."[65]

Increasingly, employers are banning guns from the workplace. For example, Luby's Cafeterias Inc., site of the worst mass-shooting incident in the United States when a gunman in Killeen, Texas, shot 23 people and then killed himself in 1991, prohibits employees from bringing weapons to work.[66] Companies hope that hav-

ing a written policy banning guns will help reduce liability for workplace violence.

Some employers fear that new state laws permitting the carrying of concealed weapons might restrict their ability to ban guns, but legislation in most states permits employers to ban guns on business premises.[67] Other steps to reduce violence include beefing up security and developing violence-prevention programs to teach managers and employees how to defuse hostility, handle threatening situations, and respond to crises.[68]

 Workers' Compensation

State workers' compensation statutes provide for coverage of income and medical expenses for employees who suffer work-related accidents or illnesses.[69] The statutes are based on the principle that the risks of injury in the workplace should be borne by industry. The system is no-fault, and an employee is entitled to benefits regardless of the level of safety in the work environment and the degree to which the employee's carelessness contributed to the incident. However, the monetary awards are generally lower than those that might be obtained in lawsuits for negligence or other torts. Independent contractors are generally excluded from workers' compensation.

Workers' compensation can be provided through (1) self-insurance, (2) insurance purchased through a state fund, or (3) insurance purchased through a private company. A properly implemented workers' compensation insurance program for all employees enables employers to argue against other, more expensive remedies an injured employee may seek, such as tort damages. For example, the California Supreme Court ruled that a firefighter's claim of intentional infliction of emotional distress was barred by the workers' compensation statutes.[70]

Some courts have recognized exceptions to the general rule that workers' compensation is the sole remedy available for workplace injuries. For example, the Washington Supreme Court permitted a suit involving employee expsure to toxic chemicals in a fiber-

62. Joseph Pereira, *Employers Confront Domestic Abuse*, Wall St. J., Mar. 2, 1995, at B1.

63. *Id.*

64. *Id.*

65. *Id.*

66. Andrea Gerlin, *Concealed-Gun Laws Give Businesses the Jitters*, Wall St. J., Mar. 5, 1996, at B1.

67. *See* Center to Prevent Handgun Violence Legal Action Project, Guns & Business Don't Mix: A Guide to Keeping Your Business Gun-Free (1997).

68. Gerlin, *supra note 66*, at B1, B7.

69. *See* Constance E. Bagley & Craig E. Dauchy, The Entrepreneur's Guide to Business Law 378–89 (1998).

70. Cole v. Fair Oaks Fire Protection Dist., 729 P.2d 743 (Cal. 1987).

glass cloth used in airplane construction to continue.[71] The court held that the employer's conduct amounted to deliberate intent to injure. As a result, the suit was not barred by the workers' compensation remedy.

 ## Minimum Wage, Overtime, and Child Labor

The federal Fair Labor Standards Act (FLSA),[72] enacted in 1938 and amended many times thereafter, was established primarily to regulate the minimum wage, overtime pay, and the use of child labor. Many, if not all, states have established wage and hour regulations as well. In general, when the federal and state laws vary, employers must abide by the stricter law. Because of the wide variance in state laws, this discussion focuses on the federal law.

Who Is Covered

The FLSA applies to employees who individually are engaged in interstate commerce or in the production of goods for interstate commerce, or who are employed by employers who engage in interstate commerce. As a practical matter, employers of any size who participate in interstate commerce or in the production of goods for interstate commerce are covered by the FLSA.

The FLSA does not apply to independent contractors. Proper characterization of workers can be hotly contested. Chapter 5 outlines the factors courts use in deciding whether a worker is an employee or an independent contractor.

Hours Worked

The FLSA does not limit the number of hours that an employee may work in a workweek or workday, so long as the employee is paid appropriate overtime. (But, as noted in Chapter 9, if an employer forces an employee to work too many hours, the employer may be liable under common law for injury to a third party resulting from the employee's fatigue.)

Compensation

The FLSA requires that employees be compensated for all hours worked. In the case of professional or off-site employees, the number of hours worked may be hotly contested. In general, the hours that an employer knows or has reason to know that an employee has worked, even though the employee has not been requested to work, are deemed hours worked. If an employee is asked to be on standby—that is, available to return to work while off duty—the hours spent on standby will not be counted as hours worked if the employee is free to use the time for his or her own purposes.

Minimum Wage and Overtime

In 1938, the FLSA first established the minimum wage at 25 cents per hour; the federal minimum wage in July 1998 was $5.15 per hour. The FLSA also requires that, with some exceptions, every nonexempt employee be paid one and one-half times the regular rate of pay for hours worked in excess of 40 in a workweek.

Exempt Employees   Certain types of employees are exempt from the minimum-wage and overtime requirements of the FLSA, for example, salespersons and executive, administrative, and professional employees.[73] The regulations of the Wage and Hour Division of the Department of Labor define the characteristics of executive, administrative, and professional employees in terms of salary and work duties.

For a person to qualify as an executive, his or her primary duty must consist of the management of the enterprise by which he or she is employed or of a customarily recognized department or subdivision of the enterprise. The person must also (1) customarily and regularly direct the work of two or more other full-time employees, (2) have the authority to hire or fire other employees, (3) customarily or regularly exercise discretion, and (4) not devote more than 20% of his or her time to other types of duties.

To qualify as an administrative employee, a person's primary duty must consist of nonmanual work directly related either to management policies or to the general business operations of the employer or the employer's customers. The person's primary duty must require the exercise of discretion and independent judgment. For

71. Birklid v. Boeing Co., 904 P.2d 278 (Wash. 1995).

72. 29 U.S.C. §§ 201–219 (1988 & Supp. 1992).

73. 29 U.S.C. § 213(a) (1).

example, the U.S. Court of Appeals for the First Circuit held that insurance company marketing representatives qualify as administrative employees and are therefore exempt from the FLSA's overtime provisions.[74] The court rejected the Department of Labor's argument that the representatives were not given discretion in "matters of consequence." Instead, the court looked to the nature of the work and held that the discretion and independent judgment, in addition to its substantial economic consequences, satisfied the requirements of an administrative employee.

For a person to qualify as a professional employee, he or she must have a position requiring advanced knowledge in a field of science or learning customarily acquired by a prolonged course of specialized intellectual instruction and study. In *Freeman v. National Broadcasting Co.*,[75] the U.S. Court of Appeals for the Second Circuit held that writers and producers for a national television news program were exempted from the overtime provisions under the FLSA. The court reasoned that the workers were artistic professionals and could not be considered nonexempt employees.

The distinction between exempt and nonexempt is not always clear. For example, a group of engineers recently sued their employers for unpaid overtime after the company changed their classification from nonexempt to exempt.[76]

The U.S. Supreme Court reformulated the legal standards for determining the exempt status of workers under the FLSA in 1997 in *Auer v. Robbins*.[77] In *Auer*, St. Louis police officers sued the municipal police commissioners for overtime pay under the FLSA. The police officers claimed that because their compensation could theoretically be reduced due to variations in the quality or quantity of work, they did not meet the Department of Labor's salary test. An *exempt employee* is paid a minimum salary per week or month, while nonexempt employees are often paid an hourly wage. The Court upheld the prohibition on disciplinary deductions and found the salary test had been met if an employee's compensation may not as a practical matter be reduced

due to work-product variations. If, however, there is either an actual practice of making deductions or a significant likelihood of such deductions, then the employees are covered by the overtime provisions of the FLSA.

The U.S. Court of Appeals for the Ninth Circuit held that subjecting an employee's pay to deductions for absences of less than a day was antithetical to the concept of a salaried employee.[78] However, the Ninth Circuit has accepted the Department of Labor's position that additional compensation in the form of hourly overtime payment does not defeat exempt status under the salary-basis test.[79]

As a result, managers should reevaluate disciplinary policies and employee handbooks for exempt personnel to avoid reclassification of their employees.[80] If employees have been subject to pay deductions, employers may preserve the exempt status by reimbursing those employees and promising to comply with the test in the future.

Child Labor

The FLSA child-labor provisions were enacted to cure the early twentieth-century abuses of many employers who employed child labor at minimal wages. Under federal law, it is illegal to employ anyone under the age of 14, except in specified agricultural occupations. Children aged 14 or 15 may work in some occupations, but only if the employment occurs outside of school hours and does not exceed daily and weekly hour limits. Individuals aged 16 to 18 may work in manufacturing occupations, but they may not work in jobs that the secretary of labor has declared to be particularly hazardous, such as operating a power-driven woodworking machine, a hoisting apparatus, a metal-forming machine, or a circular or band saw. Jobs entailing exposure to radioactive materials are also deemed to be hazardous.

Modern-Day Slavery

Responding to several recent cases, including one involving a farm labor contractor who pled guilty to coercing

74. Reich v. John Alden Life Ins. Co., 126 F.3d 1 (1st Cir. 1997).

75. 80 F.3d 78 (2d Cir. 1996).

76. Dennis O'Brien, *Workers Suing Virginia's Newport News Shipbuilding for Overtime Pay*, KNIGHT–RIDDER TRIBUNE BUS. NEWS, Dec. 4, 1997.

77. 117 S. Ct. 905 (1997).

78. Abshire v. County of Kern, 908 F.2d 483 (9th Cir. 1990).

79. Boykin v. Boeing Co., 128 F.3d 1279 (9th Cir. 1997).

80. John D. Canoni, *Supreme Court Revises the Salary Basis Test for Exempt Employees*, 23 EMPLOYEE REL. L. J. 105–113 (1997).

migrant workers in South Carolina to harvest cucumbers against their will, U.S. Attorney General Janet Reno established the Worker Exploitation Task Force in April 1998 to investigate and prosecute cases of "modern-day slavery" in the United States. She cited one case involving Thai garment workers in California who were forced by armed guards to work 20-hour shifts in sweatshop conditions and another involving 60 deaf Mexicans forced to peddle key chains in the streets and subways of New York City. The task force will bring civil cases for back wages and criminal cases under the FLSA, as well as cases under the civil rights laws and the Thirteenth Amendment to the U.S. Constitution, which prohibits slavery and involuntary servitude.

 ## Other Laws Affecting the Employment Relationship

Federal legislation concerning employee benefits and layoffs indirectly affects employee relations. These laws, which apply regardless of whether employees belong to a union, are discussed below.

Employee Retirement Income Security Act

For several decades before 1974, the number of pension plans, the number of employees covered by those plans, and the annual benefits paid to retirees from these plans grew tremendously. Despite these increases, however, many employees who expected to receive pension plan payments upon retirement received either no benefits or far fewer benefits than they had anticipated. Plan officials made ill-advised investments; employees quit or were discharged with few or no vested benefits; or the employer terminated an underfunded plan with insufficient assets to cover its obligations.

To help avoid these problems, Congress enacted the Employee Retirement Income Security Act of 1974 (ERISA).[81] With few exceptions, ERISA applies to all pension plans, and many other types of employee benefit plans, established by employers engaged in interstate commerce. With regard to pension plans, ERISA,

among other things, (1) establishes minimum funding requirements and participation and vesting standards; (2) imposes fiduciary obligations on pension plan administrators; (3) requires detailed disclosure and reporting of certain pension plan information; (4) restricts substantially the investment of pension plan assets; and (5) calls for pension plan administrators to provide annual, audited financial statements to the government and participants.

ERISA requires plan fiduciaries to act solely in the interest of the plan's participants and beneficiaries in providing benefits and the plan itself in defraying expenses. These duties must be discharged with the care, skill, prudence, and diligence that a prudent person acting in a like capacity would exercise.[82]

Other employee benefit plans are covered by ERISA if a reasonable person could determine from the surrounding circumstances the existence of intended benefits, beneficiaries, financing for the benefits, and procedures for receiving the benefits. For example, many types of group severance pay plans are deemed to be either pension plans or welfare plans and thus regulated by ERISA. However, individually negotiated severance agreements are not.

Nonpension benefit plans are subject to ERISA's reporting, disclosure, and fiduciary-responsibility rules. For example, employees must be provided with documents such as a summary plan description, a summary annual report, and a summary of any material modifications to the plan.

The U.S. Court of Appeals for the Third Circuit held that if an employer is considering a specific proposal to alter employee benefits presented by managers empowered to implement the changes, then the employer has a fiduciary duty to disclose to the potentially affected employees that it is considering modifying employee benefits.[83] The U.S. Court of Appeals for the First Circuit adopted the same rule in *Vartanian v. Monsanto Co.*[84]

The Eighth Circuit considered the fiduciary duties imposed by ERISA in the context of health maintenance organizations in the following case.

---

81. 29 U.S.C. §§ 1001–1461 (1988 & Supp. 1992).

82. 29 U.S.C. §§ 1104 *et seq.* (1988 & Supp. 1992).

83. Fischer v. Philadelphia Elec. Co., 49 F.3d 982 (3d Cir. 1996).

84. 131 F.3d 264 (1st Cir. 1997).

| A CASE IN POINT | SUMMARY |

CASE 12.5
SHEA v. ESENSTEN
United States Court of
Appeals for the Eighth Circuit
107 F.3d 625 (8th Cir. 1997).

FACTS   Patrick Shea was an employee of Seagate Technologies, Inc., which provided employee health-care benefits through Medica, a health maintenance organization (HMO). While Shea was overseas on a business trip, he was hospitalized for chest pains; when he returned home, he visited his family doctor, an authorized primary care doctor affiliated with Medica. Shea discussed the history of heart disease in his family and his symptoms, which included chest pains, shortness of breath, muscle tingling, and dizziness. Shea's doctor said a referral to a cardiologist was unnecessary. Shea's symptoms continued, and he offered to pay for the cardiologist himself. Again, Shea's doctor convinced him that, as a forty-year-old, he was too young for heart problems and did not suffer from symptoms serious enough to justify visiting a cardiologist. Shea died of heart disease a few months later.

After Mr. Shea's death, Mrs. Shea discovered that Medica's contracts with its primary care physicians created financial incentives to minimize referrals. Indeed, Medica rewarded doctors for not making referrals and reduced a portion of their fees if they provided too many. Mrs. Shea initiated a wrongful death suit alleging that Medica violated its fiduciary duties under ERISA. The district court dismissed, and Mrs. Shea appealed.

ISSUE PRESENTED   Does an HMO have a fiduciary duty under ERISA to disclose its approach to discouraging referrals to specialists?

SUMMARY OF OPINION   After finding that Mrs. Shea had standing to bring the wrongful-death action, the U.S. Court of Appeals held that Medica had violated its fiduciary duty to the members of its HMO by not disclosing the financial incentives deterring physician referral to specialists. Noting that the fiduciary duties require acting only in pursuit of the interests of the plan's participants and beneficiaries, the court cited U.S. Supreme Court precedent requiring a fiduciary to deal with fairness and honesty with plan members. This duty includes disclosing any material fact that could negatively impact a beneficiary's interests.

Specifically, the financial incentive structure created by Medica should have been disclosed, because then patients would know that a physician's judgment could be influenced by self-serving economic considerations. Without this disclosure, Mr. Shea was unable to make a fully informed decision, which may have caused his death.

RESULT   The district court's dismissal of Mrs. Shea's wrongful-death suit was reversed. Mrs. Shea was permitted to proceed with her breach-of-fiduciary-duty suit against Medica.

COMMENTS   The scope of an HMO's fiduciary duties under ERISA is ill-defined. The relatively recent emergence of HMOs has left many courts to decide the issues without the guidance of fully developed common law, and conflicts between courts are still emerging. For example, in *Weiss v. CIGNA Healthcare, Inc.,*[85] a federal district court held that an HMO's restriction of treatment options that a member physician may discuss with a patient states a cause of action under ERISA. The court declined to follow *Shea,*

Case 12.5 continues

---

85. 972 F. Supp. 748 (S.D.N.Y. 1997).

Case 12.5 continued

however, and it rejected the notion that an HMO has a fiduciary duty to disclose to plan participants its financial-incentive structures with doctors.

In mid-1998, Congress was considering legislation that would amend ERISA to provide enrollees in health plans governed by ERISA the right to sue plan administrators for injury or death caused by administrative decisions that denied or restricted health care.

Under ERISA, an employer must maintain records of each employee's years of service and vesting percentage. Further, the employer or plan administrator must maintain sufficient records, usually including age, hours worked, salary, and employee contributions, to calculate each employee's benefits.

ERISA imposes various penalties for failure to conform to requirements. Plan participants or beneficiaries may sue for lost benefits and for loss of the plan's tax benefits. Any fiduciary of a plan who breaches a duty is personally liable for the losses resulting from the breach. ERISA also provides for civil penalties for breach of its prohibited transaction rules (which bar many transactions between an ERISA plan and a fiduciary of that plan) of up to 100% of the amount of the prohibited transaction.[86]

To minimize costs and maximize benefit levels, many employers belong to multiemployer pension plans. Under the Multiemployer Pension Plan Amendments Act of 1980, withdrawal from such a plan may result in stiff penalties.

Consolidated Omnibus Budget Reconciliation Act

The Consolidated Omnibus Budget Reconciliation Act (COBRA)[87] was established in 1986 to allow group health, dental, and visual benefits to continue for employees who are terminated voluntarily or involuntarily (unless the discharge was for gross misconduct) and for employees whose hours are reduced to the point that coverage would normally cease. COBRA applies to employers of 20 or more workers that sponsor a group health plan. Churches and federal government agencies are exempt from the requirements of COBRA. Employers must notify employees of their rights when they begin participation in a group health plan or when coverage has been threatened by an event such as termination or reduced hours.

Under COBRA, eligible employees must be given at least 60 days from the date their coverage ceases to elect to have their coverage continued. If coverage continuation is elected, the employer is required to extend, for up to 18 months, coverage identical to that provided under the plan for similarly situated employees or spouses. The eligible employee may be required to pay all or part of the premium. Disabled employees are eligible for continued coverage for up to 29 months. If the employee declines to continue coverage, the employer has no further coverage obligations.

An employer may discontinue coverage for one of five reasons: (1) the employer ceases to provide group health coverage to any of its employees; (2) the premium for the coverage is not paid; (3) the employee, or former employee, becomes insured under another group plan; (4) the employee, or former employee, becomes eligible for Medicare; or (5) a spouse of the employee, or former employee, becomes divorced, remarries, and becomes covered under the new spouse's plan.

Under the Technical and Miscellaneous Revenue Act of 1988,[88] employers who fail to comply with COBRA's requirements are subject to adverse tax consequences.

---

86. 29 U.S.C. §§ 1106, 1132 (1988 & Supp. 1992).

87. Pub. L. No. 99-272, 100 Stat. 82 (1986) (codified as amended in scattered sections of 29 U.S.C.).

88. Pub. L. No. 100-647, 102 Stat. 3342 (1989) (codified as amended in scattered sections of 26 U.S.C.).

Health Insurance Portability and Accountability Act

The Health Insurance Portability and Accountability Act of 1996 (HIPAA)[89] is an employee health-care reform law that provides special protection to individuals with lifelong illnesses. The law requires that new employees and their dependents be eligible for insurance coverage if they have had health insurance for at least 18 months and joined the company within 63 days of leaving a previous employer. The previous employer must provide a certificate to a leaving employee documenting the previous health-insurance coverage.

HIPAA also provides that the duration of an employee's previous coverage may be applied to fulfilling a new employer's waiting period and extends COBRA for individuals who leave work as a result of illness or disability for up to 29 months, provided they apply within 60 days of leaving. Companies are prohibited from charging higher health-insurance premiums to individuals with preexisting health problems. HIPAA also requires companies to offer the same health coverage whether the illness is physical or mental; it also provides greater health-related tax deductions for self-employed individuals.

The principal provisions of HIPAA cover all companies with 50 or more employees and went into effect on January 1, 1998. Despite its multiple provisions, HIPAA has not resolved all health-insurance-reform issues. For example, HIPAA did not include insurance pools for small businesses nor did it raise the lifetime caps on insurance benefits.

The General Accounting Office reported in March 1998 that some insurance carriers were using a variety of pricing and marketing tactics to discourage people from applying for health coverage under HIPAA. Some carriers were charging 140% to 600% of the standard premium for eligible individuals and had eliminated or reduced agent commissions for sales to HIPAA-eligible individuals.[90]

ETHICAL CONSIDERATION

Although the withholding of commissions is a circumvention of HIPAA, it may not rise to the level of a failure to offer coverage under federal law. Is it ethical for a manager to adopt a policy of withholding commissions when it is not clearly illegal to do so?

Worker Adjustment and Retraining Notification Act

The Worker Adjustment and Retraining Notification Act of 1988 (WARN Act)[91] requires an employer to provide timely notice to its employees of a proposal to close a plant or to reduce its work force permanently. The WARN Act attempts to strike a balance between the employer's interest in maintaining employee productivity and efficiency and the employee's interest in being forewarned of a mass layoff or plant closing.

The essential features of the WARN Act are as follows. The act applies to employers with 100 or more employees, either all working fulltime or working an aggregate of at least 4,000 hours per week. It requires employers to give employees 60 days' advance notice of any plant closing that will result in a loss of employment during any 30-day period for 50 or more employees. A shutdown of a product line or operation within a plant is included within the act's definition of a plant closing. The act also requires 60 days' notice for layoffs during any 30-day period that affect at least 500 employees, or at least 50 employees if they comprise one-third of the work force. Employers are required to give written notice of the plant closing or layoff to each representative of the affected employees or, if there is no representative, to each affected employee. Employers are also required to give written notice to the state and local governments in which the layoff or plant closing will occur.

The WARN Act permits an employer to order the shutdown of a plant before the conclusion of the 60-day

---

89. Pub. L. No. 104-191, 110 Stat. 1936 (1996) (codified in scattered sections of 18, 26, 29, 42 U.S.C.).

90. *HCFA Threatens Action Against Insurers That Violate HIPAA Guarantees of Coverage*, 66 U.S.L.W. 2619 (Apr. 14, 1998).

91. Pub. L. No. 100-379, 102 Stat. 890 (1988) (codified at 29 U.S.C. §§ 2101–2109 (1988)).

notice period if (1) at the time notice would have been required, the employer was actively seeking capital or business that would enable it to avoid or postpone the shutdown, and the employer reasonably and in good faith believed that giving the required notice would preclude it from obtaining the needed business or capital; or (2) the plant closing or mass layoff was caused by a natural disaster or by business circumstances that were not reasonably foreseeable at the time notice would have been required. The terms "actively seeking capital" and "business circumstances that were not reasonably foreseeable" remain largely undefined.

The WARN Act does not apply to the closing of a temporary facility. It also does not apply to a closing or mass layoff that results from the completion of a particular project if the affected employees were hired with the understanding that their employment would not continue beyond the duration of the project. Finally, it does not apply to a closing or layoff that results from a strike or lockout that is not intended to evade the requirements of the act.

The WARN Act includes several enforcement provisions. Aggrieved employees are entitled to receive back wages and benefits for each day that the employer is in violation. The court has discretion to award the prevailing party reasonable attorney's fees. In addition, an employer who violates the act may be subject to a civil penalty of up to $30,000, to be paid to affected communities.

THE RESPONSIBLE MANAGER
Avoiding Wrongful Discharge Suits

Many courts appear to be moving toward providing all employees the protection against discharge without good cause that traditionally was offered only by union contracts or by individually negotiated contracts. As a result, employers often find themselves in costly litigation, attempting to convince a jury that a discharge was justified. In light of these developments, an employer needs to develop a human resource approach that takes into account the statutory rights of employees, its own business needs, and the evolving common law of the state.[92]

An employer can do many things to limit its exposure to unwanted contractual obligations.[93] First, the employer should articulate the kind of contractual relationship it wishes to have with its employees. That relationship may not be the same for every employee or job classification. In some instances, it may be appropriate to maintain an at-will relationship. In other cases, the employer may prefer to have a written contract that specifies the terms and conditions of employment, including the circumstances under which the employment relationship may be terminated by either party. If the company has a code of conduct (as discussed in Chapter 1), violations of the code may be good cause for termination, particularly if the employee has signed an agreement to comply with it. For example, American Express Company requires each of its approximately 15,000 managers to sign an agreement to abide by the policies set forth in the company's code of conduct.

Recently, companies have been exploring the viability of peer review of employment conflicts, rather than judicial review. For example, Darden Restaurants, the company that owns the Red Lobster and Olive Garden chains of restaurants, has been using peer review of employee complaints since 1994.[94] The company has found that peer review (1) reduces the quantity, and therefore the costs, of litigation; (2) reduces tensions in the workplace; and (3) often avoids the costs of hiring and training a new person because the process facilitates reconciliation rather than conflict.

Red Lobster takes peer review seriously. Employees who have been fired or disciplined may seek a peer review; the decision of the peer review panel is binding and can overturn management's decision. The panels can even award damages. The program has reduced annual legal fees by $1 million.

---

92. *See* Jeffrey Pfeffer, Competitive Advantage through People 137–48 (1994).

93. *See* Constance E. Bagley & Craig E. Dauchy, The Entrepreneur's Guide to Business Law, 389–97 (1998).

94. Margaret A. Jacobs, *Red Lobster Tale: Peers Decide Fired Waitress's Fate*, Wall St. J., Jan. 20, 1998, at B1.

INSIDE STORY

WORKING "OFF THE CLOCK"

The Fair Labor Standards Act (FLSA) requires all nonexempt employees working more than forty hours per week to receive overtime, that is, pay for one and one-half times the hours worked. However, many businesses are finding ways to avoid this requirement. Called "off the clock," it is the phenomenon of workers not being compensated for the time they put in. Ways used to avoid paying overtime include (1) not marking the hours employees work on their time cards; (2) having employees come to work at different hours; (3) rolling one week's overtime to another week; (4) encouraging a work atmosphere where everyone puts in extra time; and (5) even qualifying promotions and social acceptance upon working the extra hours without pay.

The practice is surprisingly pervasive. The Department of Labor estimates that 142,468 workers were owed more than $82 million in overtime pay last year. Analysts attribute the rise of off-the-clock work to employers seeking to cut costs and workers' ignorance and fear that they would lose their jobs if they complained. But as workers learn their rights and news about the practice spreads, more cases are appearing.

For example, the U.S. Court of Appeals for the Second Circuit recently held that workers required to remain at outdoor worksites over their lunch break were providing a valuable service and are entitled to compensation for that time.[95] The court upheld the lower court's award of $5 million in overtime pay and almost $10 million in damages for the treatment of 1,500 telecommunications employees.

Many other cases are settled. For instance, a Taco Bell in Seattle recently settled a class action lawsuit alleging that workers were systematically denied proper compensation. Perhaps as many as 16,000 people will receive compensation for work done before and after the official work shift. Nordstrom's department stores also settled a suit in which it was charged with requiring employees to deliver packages to customers' homes off the clock. Albertson's, a grocery chain based in Idaho, is being sued in federal court for allegedly not recording the time employees worked on their time cards.

Captain D's, a division of Shoney's, Inc., provides a good example of reclassification of workers as exempt employees to avoid having to pay overtime. Managers of 370 stores who spend

more than 80% of their time preparing food are challenging their classification as salaried managerial employees in court. This is the third suit against the parent company in a relatively short period of time.

Not all claims of off-the-clock work have been successful however. The U.S. Court of Appeals for the Eleventh Circuit rejected a claim by police officers that physical training necessary to pass mandatory physical fitness tests constitutes work under the FLSA.[96] The court reasoned that the officers' exercise time is not compensable because it is undertaken outside of regular working hours, is neither compulsory nor productive work, and is not related to the police officer's jobs. Moreover, the court found that the benefits of the exercise transcended their employment requirements and, as a result, was not directly related to their jobs. Thus, although off-the-clock-work claims are increasingly brought by disgruntled employees, courts do not blindly accept the plaintiffs' charges.

---

95. Reich v. Southern New Eng. Telecommunications Corp., 121 F.3d 58 (2d Cir. 1997).

96. Dade County v. Alvarez, 124 F.3d 1380 (11th Cir. 1997).

KEY WORDS AND PHRASES

QUESTIONS AND CASE PROBLEMS

1. Frank Jacob was a supervisor with Kerr–McGee Corporation, a coal company, for more than 15 years. Jacob liked his job and was under the impression that he would be terminated only for cause. When the company had some bad times, Jacob was one of the people who was laid off. Although he had greater seniority than some of the other supervisors who were not laid off, he was at the bottom of the supervisors' rankings. Jacob brought a lawsuit claiming an implied contract to terminate only for just cause. In support, he produced one of the first employee handbooks he received from the company. The 1976 handbook indicated that employees of the coal company were permanent. The company produced the 1980, 1985, and 1988 revisions, which were given to each employee. Jacob received these versions of the personnel manual. The revisions contained specific disclaimers asserting that the employment relationship was at-will and stating that any person could be terminated without cause. Can Jacob successfully assert an implied contract claim? [*McIlravy v. Kerr–McGee Corp.*, 119 F.3d 876 (10th Cir. 1997)]

2. In March 1987, 43-year-old Peter Barnes read an ad in the *Chicago Tribune* that Pentrix was seeking experienced word processors to work in its Chicago office. Pentrix is a national corporation specializing in the design and manufacture of hand-held computers. The ad stated that Pentrix was looking for "experienced word processors seeking a career in a stable and growing company." On March 8, 1987, Barnes interviewed with Renee Thompson, the head of Pentrix's word processing department in Chicago. Thompson was impressed with Barnes's prior experience and reassured him that although Pentrix is a national corporation, the employees in Pentrix are like a family and look after one another. Thompson offered Barnes a job at the end of the interview, and Barnes began work on March 15, 1987.

Barnes received an updated policy manual from the personnel department every year that he worked for Pentrix. In addition to discussing such things as vacation, salary, and benefits, the policy manual described Pentrix's progressive discipline system.

Pentrix's progressive discipline system consisted of three basic steps. First, an employee's supervisor must discuss the employee's deficiencies with the employee and suggest ways for the employee to improve his or her work performance. Second, the employee must receive written notice of his or her poor performance with suggestions of how the employee's performance can improve. Third, the employee must receive a written warning that if the employee's performance does not improve, he or she will be terminated.

The manual provides that in cases of "material misconduct" a supervisor has the discretion to decide whether to follow the progressive discipline procedures. The policy manual also provided that Pentrix has complete discretion to decide who will be discharged in the event of a company layoff. In 1989, the following language was added to the policy manual:

> These policies are simply guidelines to management. Pentrix reserves the right to terminate or change them at any time or to elect not to follow them in any case. Nothing in these policies is intended or should be understood as creating a contract of employment or a guarantee of continued employment with Pentrix. Employment at Pentrix remains terminable at the will of either the employee or Pentrix at any time for any reason or for no reason.

Barnes signed an acknowledgment of receipt of the 1989 policy manual.

Barnes received several good performance reviews during the time he worked at Pentrix. On a few occasions, Thompson discussed with Barnes the importance of arriving at work on time, but no record was kept of the times that Barnes was late. Thompson noted in Barnes's 1995 and 1996 performance evaluations that Barnes should proofread his work more carefully.

In 1996, Barnes received an offer to work as a word processor for Lintog, another computer manufacturing corporation in Chicago. Barnes discussed this offer with Thompson. Thompson persuaded Barnes to remain at Pentrix by suggesting that Barnes might be promoted to day-shift word processing supervisor when the current day-shift supervisor resigned. The day-shift supervisor has yet to resign from Pentrix.

Barnes was discharged from Pentrix on September 1, 1998. Thompson told Barnes that he was being fired because Pentrix was experiencing a slowdown and that two word processors were being let go in each of Pentrix's 20 offices across the country. Thompson wrote on the separation notice placed in Barnes's personnel file that Barnes was being discharged as a result of a work force reduction. Before leaving on September 1, Barnes saw David George, Pentrix's vice-president of computer design, getting into his car. George said to Barnes, "Too bad about your job, but maybe this will teach you to stop leaking our computer designs to other companies."

Barnes had trouble sleeping and felt depressed after being fired from Pentrix. He waited three weeks before he began looking for another job. He then submitted an application to Lintog, the company that had offered him a job in 1996. Rob Grey, the head of the word processing department at Lintog, called Renee Thompson at Pentrix to find out why Barnes had left. Thompson responded that Barnes worked in Pentrix's word processing department for more than ten years and was discharged as a result of a slowdown. Barnes interviewed with Grey on September 28, 1998. During the interview, Grey asked Barnes why he had left his job at Pentrix. Barnes responded that although he was officially told that he was being discharged because of a reduction in force, he was fired because he was wrongly suspected of leaking the corporation's computer designs. Barnes was not hired by Lintog.

a. What claims might Barnes bring against Pentrix, Inc.?

b. If you were investigating whether Barnes could sue Pentrix, what information would you want to know?

c. What damages might Barnes be entitled to recover?

3. Frank Deus was an agent for Allstate Insurance Company in its Jackson, Mississippi, region from 1968 until August 1987, when he suffered a nervous breakdown that rendered him unable to work. He now suffers from severe tinnitus (ringing in the ears) and depression. He claims that Allstate intentionally inflicted emotional distress upon him, causing his breakdown.

Throughout his 19 years with Allstate, Deus was a company office agent (COA). His status as a COA was established through an employment agreement with Allstate. The agreement stated that Allstate could not terminate Deus for unsatisfactory work unless it first gave him notice, pursuant to a multiphase procedure to determine that his work was unsatisfactory and that his job was in jeopardy.

In 1984, Allstate fired 20% of the managers in Deus's office and brought in a number of new people. There was evidence that these changes increased tension for everyone in that office. But there was no indication that Deus was the only agent affected or that the changes were made with the intent of causing anyone emotional distress. Three years later, after his work performance declined due to his tinnitus, and after being

placed on probation, Deus was fired. Deus claims that he was wrongfully terminated. Does he have a valid claim? What will be Allstate's defense? [*Deus v. Allstate Insurance Co.*, 15 F.3d 506 (5th Cir. 1994)]

4. On October 15, 1984, George Anderson was hired by Electronic Data Systems Corporation (EDS) for a managerial position in its domestic treasury department. From October 1984 to October 1985, Anderson served as the cash manager in the domestic treasury department, where his responsibilities included managing all cash operations, short-term investments, cash forecasting, and related information systems, plus consulting with various groups within the EDS system.

In October 1985, Anderson was promoted to the position of manager of investments and debt in the domestic treasury department. In that position, Anderson had responsibilities for all domestic short- and long-term investments and all pension portfolios, corporate portfolios, and Title IX portfolios. In this position, Anderson was charged with the responsibility of administering investment assets totaling approximately $1.3 billion. The petition alleges that he was demoted and discharged for his refusal to commit illegal acts at the behest of another employee, Douglas Crow, and for reporting Crow's activities.

Anderson refused to commit these acts and reported these incidents and other improper conduct by Crow to management. Anderson asserts a cause of action for wrongful discharge, on the theory that under Texas law at-will employment contracts cannot be terminated because of an employee's refusal to commit illegal acts. Will Anderson prevail? [*Anderson v. Electronic Data Systems Corp.*, 11 F.3d 1311 (5th Cir. 1994)]

5. Robinson was the branch manager of one of Smith Barney's brokerage offices. One of his most important duties was to recruit experienced brokers. He contracted annually with Smith Barney in 1991, 1992, and 1993 under three separate but identical agreements. The 1993 agreement provided that:

> [I]n consideration of payment of the 1993 Incentive Compensation to me, I agree that should my employment with Smith Barney terminate for any reason and I become employed at a competitor organization, I will not for a one-year period directly or indirectly solicit or induce any Smith Barney employee to resign from either (a) the Smith Barney branch office at which I worked; or (b) any other Smith Barney office within a 50-mile radius of the competitor organization's office at which I work in

order for that employee to accept employment at the competitor organization at which I work.

Robinson made this promise in return for a promise from Smith Barney to allow him to participate in the firm's 1993 incentive compensation program. The exact amount of Robinson's incentive compensation was to be calculated after Smith Barney's 1993 profits were determined. He was to receive quarterly advances toward the compensation that he would ultimately be paid. In the event that Robinson were to resign or were to be terminated for cause during 1993, he would be required to return any advances received in that year. In April 1993, Robinson received a $7,000 advance, which he did not repay after he voluntarily left Smith Barney's employ on June 17, 1993.

Robinson conceded that during 1993 he left Smith Barney's employ, began to work for a competitor organization, and, having been advised that the agreement was unenforceable, knowingly breached the agreement not to solicit Smith Barney's employees by actively recruiting them. Did Robinson breach the noncompetition agreement? Will Robinson succeed in challenging the validity of the noncompetition agreement? [*Smith, Barney, Harris Upham & Co., Inc. v. Robinson*, 12 F.3d 515 (5th Cir. 1994)]

6. Susan Weissman sued her former employer, Crawford Rehabilitation, for breach of implied contract based on Crawford's failure to abide by the termination procedures set forth in the employee manual. Thereafter, Crawford discovered that Weissman had made fraudulent representations on her application for employment. Does this after-acquired evidence provide a complete defense? [*Crawford Rehabilitation Services, Inc. v. Weissman*, 938 P.2d 540 (Colo. 1997)]

7. IBP, Inc., which operates a meat processing plant, hired DCS Sanitation Management, Inc. as an independent contractor to clean the plant's machinery after the close of production each day. The DCS contract gave IBP the right to terminate the agreement if DCS violated IBP's contractor safety policy. IBP's employees pointed out numerous safety violations by DCS's employees to DCS supervisors and management, but IBP did not terminate the contract. Is IBP liable under the Occupational Safety and Health Act (OSHA) for the failure of DCS's employees to comply with OSHA safety procedures? Was IBP's conduct ethical? [*IBP, Inc. v. Herman*, 144 F.3d 861 (D.C. Cir. 1998)]

8. In 1976, Leonard Linton was a 17-year-old high school student in Dearborn Heights, Michigan. Linton and a companion were arrested by Dearborn police in a field near the high school. Police searched them and found marijuana on Linton's companion. Linton claims that he was not aware that his companion had the marijuana. Linton pled guilty to loitering in a field. He was released upon his parents' payment of a $50 fine. Linton claims that he was not told that he was charged with a crime; he was not offered the assistance of counsel; and he did not know that pleading guilty to loitering would give him a criminal record.

After finishing high school, Linton filled out an application for employment with United Parcel Service (UPS). On that application, Linton was asked, "Have you ever been convicted of a crime?" to which he answered, "No." Linton was hired as a part-time loader–unloader and he continued to work there from 1979 to 1988. UPS admits that during these nine years Linton was a hard-working employee.

In September 1988, Linton applied for a full-time position as a next-day specialist air driver. UPS required a second employment application for this position. This application also asked whether he had ever been convicted of a crime, and Linton again answered, "No." Both employment applications unequivocally stated that misrepresentation or omission of facts constituted grounds for termination.

UPS conducted a criminal-history check in connection with Linton's 1988 application. On October 7, 1988, Linton was discharged on the basis of a report from the state police stating that he had committed a "violation of controlled substance laws." The discharge letter claimed that "employment applications submitted to UPS on August 7, 1979, and September 20, 1988 were falsified." The discharge was pursuant to Article 17 of the UPS–union collective bargaining agreement, which sets forth the grounds for discharge or suspension.

Pursuant to the collective bargaining agreement, Linton filed a grievance with the union. On the advice of his union steward, Linton refused to take a "voluntary quit" deal and expressed his desire to take his grievance to the state committee. This claim was denied.

Did UPS have just cause for terminating Linton? Should the fact that Linton had no intent to deceive UPS affect the outcome of the case? [*Linton v. UPS*, 15 F.3d 1365 (6th Cir. 1994)]

9. The plaintiffs worked as floor hands on Rig 191, one of several rigs owned by Parker Drilling. As floor hands, their job was to connect 90-foot segments of steel pipe, each weighing 1,500 pounds, and place them in the drilling hole in the floor of the rig. This is demanding work. In addition, the drilling hole is often overflowing with mud, making the rig floor slick and treacherous. The work is performed at temperatures as low as –30°F, and requires use of heavy tools. Injuries are frequent, ranging from severed fingers to death.

Parker, in the interest of safety, enforced strict discipline aboard the rigs. This included a ban on the use or possession of drugs on the rigs. The drug ban extended to the company-provided sleeping areas, but it did not address employees' drug use during their off time, as long as they were off the drilling site. The plaintiffs testified that they were aware of Parker's drug policy.

During a routine safety inspection of the North Slope rigs, Parker's safety director, John Haynes, was told by two employees, Bill Reynolds and Joe Watkins, that the plaintiffs were routinely smoking marijuana on the rig and during their breaks.

Based on the written allegations of Reynolds and Watkins, Parker suspended the plaintiffs pending an investigation. At the time of the suspension, the plaintiffs were off the rig on their normal two-week rotation.

After confronting the plaintiffs, who denied using drugs, and based on the information above, Parker fired the plaintiffs. They then brought a wrongful-termination action.

Did Parker have adequate cause for terminating the plaintiffs' employment? [*Sanders v. Parker Drilling Co.,* 911 F.2d 191 (9th Cir. 1990)]

MANAGER'S DILEMMA

10. Chelsea Laman joined a high-tech start-up in 1996, immediately after graduating from the Sloan School at the Massachusetts Institute of Technology. She forewent better-paying consulting and investment banking opportunities to get in at the ground floor of a young, fast-growing company. As compensation, Laman receives a nominal salary and stock options. Because the company's product will require three years to bring to market, the options do not vest for three years. This means that Laman forfeits all of the stock options if she leaves the company before 1999.

In 1998, the company began having serious problems. Even though the project is on schedule and is anticipated to be a huge success, costs are skyrocketing and your investors demand a significant reduction in operating expenses.

You are considering firing Laman. Although she has performed well, Laman was the most recent person hired. She is an at-will employee, but, with less than one year until she can exercise her stock options and given the close-knit character of the company, you fear a lawsuit. At this critical stage, a wrongful termination lawsuit could bankrupt the company just in legal fees.

a. Should you fire Laman to reduce operating expenses?

b. If Laman is terminated, on what basis could she sue the company? Would she prevail?

c. How could you have structured the relationship to avoid this potential lawsuit?

INTERNET SOURCES

Department of Labor	http://www.dol.gov
Index of laws and articles on employment law	http://www.findlaw.com/01topics/27labor
United Food and Commercial Workers International Union	http://www.ufcw.org
AFL-CIO	http://www.aflcio.org
OSHA	http://www.osha.gov

CHAPTER 13

Civil Rights and Employment Discrimination

INTRODUCTION

Laws Designed to Eliminate Employment Discrimination

The abolition of slavery and the civil rights movement of the 1960s were two great forces behind modern civil rights legislation. From the Civil Rights Act of 1866 to that of 1991, the law has been moving in a direction to eliminate discrimination based on race, sex, color, religion, national origin, age, or disability. Civil rights laws help ensure that every person has the opportunity to reach his or her full potential.

Chapter Overview

This chapter provides an overview of federal legislation barring employment discrimination, with special attention to Title VII, the Americans with Disabilities Act, and the Age Discrimination in Employment Act. It also illustrates the various legal theories pursued under each piece of legislation, and how those theories relate to legal and appropriate behavior by managers in a business environment.

 ## Overview of Civil Rights Legislation

The federal statutes that forbid various kinds of discrimination in employment are summarized in this section. Many states have passed their own fair employment acts which, in some instances, provide greater protection than their federal counterparts.

The federal statutes discussed below apply only to employees, not independent contractors. As explained in Chapter 5, there is no bright-line distinction between the two categories. The courts tend to use two primary criteria to distinguish independent contractors from

employees. First, independent contractors control the outcome of a piece of work and the means and manner of achieving the outcome. Second, independent contractors offer services to the public at large, not just to one business.

Section 1981

The earliest piece of legislation in the area of employment and civil rights is the Civil Rights Act of 1866.[1] This statute (referred to as *Section 1981*) forbids racial

---

1. 42 U.S.C. § 1981 (1994).

discrimination by employers of any size in the making and enforcement of contracts, including employment contracts. Under Section 1981, as amended by the Civil Rights Act of 1991, the bar against racial discrimination applies not only to hiring, promotion, and termination but also to working conditions, such as racial harassment, and to breaches of contract occurring during the term of the contract.

Section 1981 applies to cases involving state or private conduct. Employees suing under Section 1981 are entitled to a jury trial of their claims and may be awarded greater monetary sanctions than are available under Title VII, discussed below.

The civil rights movement in the 1960s led to the next wave of legislation limiting the right of employers to establish the terms and conditions of employment.

Equal Pay Act

In 1963, Congress passed the Equal Pay Act,[2] which mandates equal pay for equal work without regard to gender. The act covers all public and private employers with 20 or more employees, including federal, state, and local governments. It is enforced by the Equal Employment Opportunity Commission (EEOC).

Title VII

The most significant piece of employment legislation is Title VII of the Civil Rights Act of 1964.[3] This statute, which is enforced by the EEOC, prohibits discrimination in employment on the basis of race, color, religion, national origin, or sex. Congress later amended Title VII to provide that discrimination on the basis of sex includes discrimination on the basis of pregnancy, childbirth, or related medical conditions.

Age Discrimination in Employment Act

In 1967, Congress passed the Age Discrimination in Employment Act (ADEA),[4] which protects persons 40 years and older from discrimination on the basis of age. The ADEA was amended in 1990 by the Older Workers' Benefit Protection Act, which prohibits age dis-

crimination in providing employee benefits and establishes minimum standards for waiver of one's rights under the ADEA. The ADEA is discussed later in this chapter.

Vietnam Era Veterans' Readjustment Assistance Acts

The Vietnam Era Veterans' Readjustment Assistance Acts of 1972 and 1974,[5] enforced by the Department of Labor, require affirmative action to employ disabled Vietnam-era veterans. They apply only to employers holding federal contracts of $10,000 or more.

Vocational Rehabilitation Act

The Vocational Rehabilitation Act of 1973,[6] enforced by the U.S. Department of Labor, prohibits discrimination against the physically and mentally disabled. Section 503 of the act imposes affirmative-action obligations on employers having contracts with the federal government in excess of $2,500 and makes the act applicable to employers receiving federal financial assistance of any amount. This legislation was the precursor to and guided the development of the Americans with Disabilities Act.

Veterans Re-Employment Act

The Veterans Re-Employment Act of 1974[7] gives employees who served in the military at any time the right to be reinstated in employment without loss of benefits and the right not to be discharged without cause for one year following such reinstatement.

Americans with Disabilities Act

The Americans with Disabilities Act (ADA),[8] which became law in 1990, provides millions of disabled Americans with access to employment, transportation, public accommodations, and telecommunications services. The ADA is the most sweeping civil rights measure since the Civil Rights Act of 1964.

2. 29 U.S.C. § 206(d) (1994).

3. 42 U.S.C. §§ 2000e–2000e-17 (1994).

4. 29 U.S.C. §§ 621–634 (1994).

5. 38 U.S.C. §§ 4100 *et seq.* (1994).

6. 29 U.S.C. §§ 701–797 (1994).

7. 38 U.S.C. §§ 4301–4307 (1994).

8. 42 U.S.C. §§ 12101–12213 (1994).

The ADA's definition of a disability includes any physical or mental impairment that substantially limits one or more major life activities, such as walking, talking, or working. Under this definition, persons who have recovered from cancer, alcoholism, or drug abuse, persons with HIV disease, and persons who are considered disabled are protected from discrimination.

The act requires all businesses to provide "reasonable accommodations" to the disabled, unless such an accommodation would result in "undue hardship" on business operations. It also prohibits discrimination in employment on the basis of a person's disability.

The employment provisions of the ADA apply to all private employers with 15 or more employees and are discussed later in this chapter.

Civil Rights Act of 1991

After two years of debate, the Civil Rights Act of 1991[9] was adopted in November 1991. The act amended Section 1981 of the Civil Rights Act of 1866, the Civil Rights Act of 1964, the Age Discrimination in Employment Act of 1967, the Attorney's Fees Awards Act of 1976, and the Americans with Disabilities Act of 1990. Most importantly, the act legislatively overruled several parts of recent Supreme Court rulings that were unfavorable to the rights of plaintiffs in employment-discrimination cases. The act also extended coverage of the major civil rights statutes to the staffs of the president and the Senate. In addition, the act provided for the establishment of a "glass ceiling" commission to study barriers to the promotion of women and minorities, and required the EEOC to engage in educational/outreach activities and to create a Technical Assistance Training Institute.

Provisions of the Civil Rights Act of 1991 are discussed both in the context of the statutes to which they relate throughout the chapter and as a distinct nondiscrimination statute.

Family and Medical Leave Act of 1993

President Clinton signed the Family and Medical Leave Act of 1993[10] into law on February 5, 1993. The act is designed to allow employees to take time off from work to handle domestic responsibilities, such as the birth or adoption of a child or the care of an elderly parent. Employees are guaranteed job security despite familial responsibilities. Though applicable to both men and women, the act seems to have special significance for women, who often are forced to choose between job security and caregiving.

The act seeks to promote the stability and economic security of American families. The specific provisions of the act are discussed in detail later in this chapter.

 ## Enforcement

The Equal Employment Opportunity Commission (EEOC) is the primary enforcer of civil rights legislation in the United States. A part of the Department of Justice, the EEOC processes hundreds of complaints, investigating and evaluating their merit. If the claim is unfounded, then it is dismissed. If the claim withstands initial inquiry and the EEOC is unable to pursue the case due to staff and resource constraints, the agency will provide a right-to-sue letter to the private party. Without this administrative permission, private litigants cannot initiate suits under various statutes, including the ADA and Title VII.

The EEOC has recently become more proactive in its approach to enforcing antidiscrimination laws. In early 1998, the EEOC began contracting with private organizations in Washington, D.C., and Chicago to explore the use of "testers" to identify employers that discriminate.[11] Employment-discrimination testing is the practice of sending pairs of individuals that are equally qualified to apply for entry-level positions in an effort to determine if impermissible factors such as race, gender, national origin, or disability influence employment decisions. The results of each $100,000 pilot program will determine whether the EEOC further pursues employment-discrimination testing.

 ## Title VII

Scope

Title VII prohibits all public and private employers with 15 or more employees, including federal, state, and local

---

9. Pub. L. No. 102–106, 105 Stat. 1071 (1991) (codified in scattered sections of the U.S.C.)

10. 29 U.S.C. §§ 2601–2654 (1994).

---

11. *EEOC Contracts with Private Testers To Uncover Employers' Discriminatory Hiring*, 66 U.S.L.W. 2391–92 (Jan. 8, 1998).

governments, from making decisions based upon an individual's race, color, religion, national origin, or sex. The racial discrimination suit against Texaco, discussed in the "Inside Story," was initiated under Title VII.

One of the largest sex-discrimination cases was settled by Lucky Stores, a large grocery-store chain, which agreed to pay almost $75 million in damages to women who were denied promotions, and to invest an additional $20 million in affirmative-action programs for its female employees. The protracted litigation was initiated by a group of female employees who were denied desirable assignments, management training, and movement into full-time positions that would have improved their chances for promotions. A federal district court found that from 1984 to 1989, women accounted for 46.6% of the new employees at Lucky Stores, but made up 84% of the new employees assigned to low-paying jobs; and that these women were offered few chances to move into management positions.

The proper role of religion in the workplace is a source of growing litigation under Title VII. The EEOC documented a 31% increase in claims of discrimination on the basis of religion from 1990 to 1995.[12] With some employees demanding the opportunity to express their religious beliefs in the workplace and others wanting to be free from any religious exposure, employers are often caught in the middle.

Title VII also prohibits retaliation against employees for filing complaints with the EEOC. In 1997, the U.S. Supreme Court unanimously ruled that this antiretaliation provision protected both current and former employees.[13] The case involved an employer who allegedly gave a former employee a negative reference because he had filed a claim of racial discrimination against the company. The Court reasoned that although the statute's definition of "employee" was ambiguous, certain statutory provisions contemplated former employees and such protection was necessary to provide comprehensive protection against racial discrimination.

One final noteworthy aspect of Title VII suits is that the otherwise rigorous standing requirements may be relaxed. In *Trafficante v. Metropolitan Life Insurance Company*,[14] the Supreme Court held that white tenants of an apartment complex had standing to sue their landlord under Title II of the Civil Rights Act of 1964 (which bars housing discrimination) for not renting to African Americans due to a "loss of important benefits from interracial associations." The U.S. Courts of Appeal for the Fifth, Sixth, and Ninth Circuits have extended this logic and held that white male employees have standing to sue for race and sex discrimination under Title VII as a result of a supervisor's disparaging remarks about black and female coworkers. The U.S. Courts of Appeal for the Fourth and Seventh Circuits refused to extend the *Trafficante* rationale to Title VII cases.[15]

Remedies

Remedies available under Title VII include compensation for lost salary and benefits, reinstatement or "front pay" equal to what the employee would have received had the individual not been discharged, and injunctive relief to stop prohibited discriminatory actions. Front pay is awarded when reinstatement is inappropriate because the position is unavailable or hostility raises a practical barrier.

The plaintiff may also recover compensatory damages for future pecuniary losses, emotional pain and suffering, inconvenience, mental anguish, loss of enjoyment of life, and other nonpecuniary losses. While front pay is limited in duration because it compensates for the immediate effects of discrimination, lost future earnings compensate an employee for a lifetime of diminished earnings resulting from the reputational harms suffered as a result of discrimination. Therefore, an employee may be awarded both front pay and damages for lost future earnings.[16] In addition, punitive damages are available and can be awarded even if the jury awarded no compensatory damages.[17]

The compensatory and punitive damages available for discrimination based on sex or religion are capped at $50,000 for employers of 100 or fewer employees; $100,000 for employers with 101 to 200 employees;

---

12. Margaret A. Jacobs, *Courts Wrestle with Religion in Workplace*, WALL ST. J., Oct. 10, 1995, at B1.

13. Robinson v. Shell Oil Co., 117 S. Ct. 843 (1997).

14. 409 U.S. 205 (1972).

15. Childress v. Richmond, 134 F.3d 1205 (4th Cir. 1998) (*en banc*); Bermudez v. TRC Holdings, 138 F.3d 1176 (7th Cir. 1998).

16. Williams v. Pharmacia Inc., 137 F.3d 944 (7th Cir. 1998).

17. Timm v. Progressive Steel Treating Inc., 137 F.3d 1008 (7th Cir. 1998).

$200,000 for employers with 201 to 500 employees; and $500,000 for employers with more than 500 employees. However, the compensatory caps do not apply to intentional racial or ethnic discrimination. Punitive damages are available only when the employer acted with "malice or with reckless indifference to" an employee's rights. Any party to a case for damages can demand a jury trial, but the court may not inform the jury of the caps on damage awards.

Legal Theories under Title VII

Litigation under Title VII has produced two distinct legal theories of discrimination: (1) disparate treatment, and (2) disparate impact.

Disparate Treatment   A plaintiff claiming *disparate treatment* must prove that the employer intentionally discriminated against him or her by denying a benefit or privilege of employment because of his or her race, religion, sex, or national origin. The Supreme Court has established a systematic approach toward proof of these claims. First, the employee must prove a *prima facie* case. This means he or she must prove that (1) he or she is a member of a class of persons protected by Title VII; and (2) he or she was denied a position or benefit he or she sought, for which he or she was qualified, and which was available. If the employee proves the *prima facie* case, the employer then must present evidence, but need not prove, that it had legitimate, nondiscriminatory grounds for its decision. If the employer meets this burden of producing evidence, the employee then must prove that the grounds offered by the employer were only a pretext for unlawful discrimination.

The Supreme Court held in *St. Mary's Honor Center v. Hicks*[18] that a showing of pretext is insufficient, in and of itself, to compel judgment for the employee. Therefore, even if an employer gives a false justification or reason for how it treated an employee, the employee will not prevail unless he or she can show that the given reason was false and that the employer's real reason for its action was discrimination. Such a showing may be very difficult for employees to make.

In a disparate-treatment case, for example, an African-American employee may claim that he was fired because of his race. He would show in the first instance that he is an African-American, he was fired, and he possessed at least the minimum qualifications for the job. Some courts may require that he also show that his job was not eliminated but was filled by someone else after his termination. Once he proves this, his employer might present evidence that the employee was terminated for excessive absenteeism. The employer might produce the employee's attendance records and a supervisor's testimony that his attendance was unacceptable. The employee may attempt to prove pretext in a number of ways. He may show that his supervisor uttered racial slurs from time to time. He may show that his employer's attendance policy requires a written warning about poor attendance before the employee can be terminated on that ground, and that he received no such warning. He may show that white employees with similar attendance records were not fired. In any event, the employee has the burden of proving that his employer fired him because of his race.

When an employee proves that the employer's decision was motivated in part by impermissible discrimination, the employer has engaged in an illegal employment practice. However, no damages can be awarded and reinstatement, hiring, or promotion cannot be ordered if the employer demonstrates that it would have taken the same action in the absence of the impermissible motivating factor. In such a case,

INTERNATIONAL CONSIDERATION

Managers should be aware of civil rights laws of foreign countries when exploring globalization strategies and managing the workforce of foreign subsidiaries. A foreign jurisdiction's interpretations of acceptable behavior, in addition to the country's regional or international commitments, should be researched. For example, the British government has had trouble comporting its employment policies with European sexual-equality laws, despite opting out of the social chapter of the Maastricht Treaty.[a]

a. Robert Rice & James Blitz, *Sex Equality Ruling May Spark Compensation Moves*, FIN. TIMES, Aug. 1, 1995, at 6.

18. 509 U.S. 502 (1993).

declaratory relief is still available, as is an award of attorney's fees and costs.

The courts have long recognized that creation of a hostile working environment for an employee because of his or her race violates Title VII. An example of such *hostile-environment harassment* would be continually subjecting an African-American employee to ridicule and racial slurs.

To be actionable, the alleged racial harassment must be so severe or pervasive that it altered the working environment. Hostile-environment sexual harassment is discussed later in this chapter.

Although some courts have held that a one-time incident is not enough to create a hostile environment, the trend appears to be to find hostile environment if the incident is severe enough. For example, one case[19] involved an African-American female county employee who alleged that, while she was training at a police academy firing range, her direct supervisor turned to a deputy and said: "There's the jungle bunny." The New Jersey Supreme Court identified several factors that made the incident severe enough to create actionable hostile-environment discrimination under the New Jersey Law Against Discrimination (patterned after Title VII): (1) the derogatory term used by the sheriff was "patently a racial slur, and [was] ugly, stark and raw in its opprobrious connotation"; (2) the sheriff was the plaintiff's ranking supervisor, effectively closing her avenue for redress; (3) the sheriff was a chief law enforcement officer; and (4) the remark was made not only in the plaintiff's presence but in front of the deputy.

Disparate Impact   The *disparate-impact* theory arose out of Title VII class actions brought in the 1970s against large employers. These suits challenged testing and other selection procedures, claiming that they systematically excluded women or particular ethnic groups from certain types of jobs. It is not necessary to prove intentional discrimination to prevail in a disparate-impact case. Discrimination can be established by proving that an employment practice, although neutral on its face, had a disparate impact on a protected group.

For example, suppose an employer has a policy that it will hire for security guard positions only persons who are at least 5 feet 8 inches tall, weigh at least 150 pounds, and can pass certain agility tests. This would seem like a neutral policy, in that it does not expressly exclude women or some Asian males. However, if the number of women or Asian males who are refused employment is proportionately greater than the number of white males refused employment, then that policy has a disparate impact.

To prove disparate impact, the plaintiff must demonstrate that the specific employment practice, policy, or rule being challenged has caused a statistically significant disproportion between the effects on different groups. The employer then has the burden to demonstrate that the challenged practice is job-related for the position in question and consistent with business necessity.

The business justification must relate to job performance. Inconvenience, annoyance, or expense to the employer will not suffice. For example, a Latina applicant who is denied employment because she failed an English-language test may challenge the language requirement. If she has applied for a sales job, the employer may justify the requirement on the ground that ability to communicate with customers is an indispensable qualification. On the other hand, if she has applied for a job on the production line, that justification may not suffice. As under disparate-treatment analysis, the ultimate burden of persuasion rests with the plaintiff.

In *Wards Cove Packing Company v. Atonio*,[20] the U.S. Supreme Court held that the proper statistical analysis compares the racial or other composition of the persons holding the jobs at issue to the racial or other composition of the *qualified* persons in the relevant labor market. *Ward's Cove* involved a racially stratified workforce in which unskilled, lower-paying jobs were filled predominantly by nonwhites and skilled, higher-paying jobs were filled predominantly by whites. The Court held that it was not enough to show that the percentage of nonwhite individuals in skilled, higher-paying jobs was less than the percentage of nonwhite individuals in the labor market. The Court also held that a plaintiff must identify with specificity the discriminatory employment practice, such as a method of testing.

The following case illustrates that if a job requires no special skills, then all members of the labor pool are considered when doing the statistical analysis necessary to determine whether a facially neutral policy has a disparate impact.

---

19. Taylor v. Metzger, 706 A.2d 685 (N.J. 1998).

20. 490 U.S. 64 (1989).

| **A CASE IN POINT** | **IN THE LANGUAGE OF THE COURT** |

CASE 13.1
EQUAL EMPLOYMENT
OPPORTUNITY
COMMISSION v.
STEAMSHIP CLERKS
UNION, LOCAL 1066
United States Court of
Appeals for the First Circuit
48 F.3d 594 (1st Cir. 1995),
cert. denied, 516 U.S. 814
(1995).

FACTS   The Steamship Clerks Union, Local 1066 (the Union) is a 124-member labor organization representing the individuals who check cargo against inventory lists as products and materials are loaded and unloaded in the port of Boston. The work is neither difficult nor requires specialized training. In October 1980, the Union adopted a membership sponsorship policy (MSP) that required Union applicants to be sponsored by an existing member. When the Union adopted the MSP, there were no African-American or Hispanic members of the Union. Over the next six years, the Union accepted 30 new members, who all were Caucasian. After 1986, the Union closed its membership rolls.

In 1991, the EEOC initiated a suit against the Union for disparate-impact discrimination. The EEOC noted that while African Americans and Hispanics constituted between 8% and 27% of the relevant labor pool in the Boston area, none were hired by the Union. The Union responded that its MSP was merely a form of nepotism, not racial discrimination, because every member admitted between 1980 and 1986 was closely related to an existing member of the Union. The district court ruled in favor of the EEOC, and the Union appealed.

ISSUE PRESENTED   Did the Union MSP unlawfully discriminate against potential union members based on its disparate impact upon African-American and Hispanic laborers?

OPINION   SELYA, J., writing for the U.S. Court of Appeals:

It has long been understood that discrimination, whether measured quantitatively or qualitatively, is not always a function of a pernicious motive or malign intent. Discrimination may also result from otherwise neutral policies and practices that, when actuated in real-life settings, operate to the distinct disadvantage of certain classes of individuals. . . . [T]he disparate impact approach roots out "employment policies that are facially neutral in their treatment of different groups but that in fact fall more harshly on one group than another and cannot be justified by business necessity."

. . .

Population statistics for the Boston area, proffered by the EEOC and unchallenged by the Union, show that in the relevant time frame African Americans comprised 21%, and Hispanics 6%, of the available labor force. Although there are no known statistics on the racial composition of the steamship clerk industry—if such an "industry" exists—Census Bureau statistics that merge the transportation industry's employment statistics with similar statistics for public utilities . . . show that blacks and Hispanics participate in the labor force as clerical/clerks at a rate of 7% and 1% of the total, respectively. Despite the fact that the combined pool of potential black and Hispanic applicants for union membership ranged between 8% and 27% of the overall pool of potential applicants, no African-American or Hispanic was granted Union membership. Finally, during the MSP's heyday—the six-year period from 1980 through 1986—the Union admitted 30 new members. Based on a comparison of these figures with the profile of the newly minted Union members—0 of 30, or

Case 13.1 continues

Case 13.1 continued

zero percent—the district court found that the EEOC adequately demonstrated a race-based disparate impact.

. . .

The utility of statistical evidence "depends on all of the surrounding facts and circumstances." In this instance, the sample, though small, is telling. Given the unique factual mosaic from which the statistical scaffolding hangs, and the logical force of the conclusion that the numbers suggest, it would blink reality to conclude that a serious "sample size" problem lurks here. In our judgment, the lower court did not err in considering the available statistical evidence, and drawing founded inferences from it, en route to a disparate impact determination.

. . .

As for the absence of identifiable minority applicants, the Union would have us rule that causation may be proven only by demonstrating that a flesh-and-blood African-American or Hispanic, who applied and was turned away, would have been admitted as a member but for the MSP. This isthmian view is a product of tunnel vision. The concept of causation under Title VII, like the larger concept of discrimination itself, is sometimes only discernible and inferable when viewed in context. Here, the unvarnished reality of the situation—a sponsorship-based membership policy, enacted by an all-white union, and a six-year track record of zero minority members despite 30 new white members, all of whom had family ties to existing members— renders the district court's conclusion irresistible notwithstanding the lack of a specific unsuccessful minority applicant.

. . .

The Union suggests that the MSP is job-related and consistent with business necessity because it represents an important vehicle for continuing family traditions.

. . .

Here, the Union has not shown even the glimmerings of a business necessity defense. Instead, it asks us to undertake a leap of faith. It makes absolutely no effort to explain, logically, why family tradition, and, thus, the MSP, are necessary adjuncts to carrying on the business of steamship clerks; and we, like the district court, can discern no essential connection. If courts were to accept an employer's arbitrary *ipse dixit* as a satisfactory justification for retaining a policy that produces an invidiously discriminatory impact, Title VII would be reduced to no more than a toothless tiger. A policy that is neutral on its face, but that discriminates in fact, cannot elude the proscriptions of the law merely because its sponsor prefers to retain it.

. . .

We affirm the district court's grant of partial summary judgment in favor of the EEOC on its claim of disparate impact discrimination. The Union adopted a membership policy which, by its very nature, created a strong likelihood that no nonwhite face would ever appear in the Union's ranks. Based on the evidence we have recounted, the EEOC established a *prima facie* case of discrimination. Because the Union failed either to rebut that case or to offer a legitimate, nondiscriminatory

Case 13.1 continues

Case 13.1 continued

justification for maintaining the membership policy, the district court did not err in finding for the EEOC in respect to liability.

RESULT   The case was remanded to the district court to determine the appropriate remedy for the EEOC in light of the Union's illegal, race-based discrimination.

Questions

1. How did the EEOC demonstrate that the Union was unlawfully discriminating against nonwhites in the Boston area?
2. Why does the court not consider the maintenance of family traditions a legitimate business necessity?

Historically, disparate-impact analysis has been limited to objective selection criteria, such as tests and degree requirements. However, the Supreme Court has held that this analysis may also apply to subjective bases for decisions, such as interviews and supervisor evaluations. Thus, if an employer makes hiring decisions on the basis of interviews alone and if the percentage of women or African Americans hired differs significantly from the percentage of qualified women or African Americans in the relevant labor pool, a claim may be made that this process is unlawful under Title VII. The issue then will be whether the process is justified by business necessity.

For example, the EEOC sued Joe's Stone Crab Restaurant in Miami and other expensive restaurants nationwide for having all-male servers.[21] The EEOC claimed that the restaurants' policy of not posting job openings but rather relying on word of mouth for applicants had a disparate impact on women who were not made aware of the openings.

Defenses under Title VII

Title VII sets forth several statutory defenses to claims of discriminatory treatment. Of these defenses, the one most frequently cited is the defense of bona fide occupational qualification.

Bona Fide Occupational Qualification   Title VII provides that an employer may lawfully hire an individual on the basis of religion, sex, or national origin if re-

ligion, sex, or national origin is a bona fide occupational qualification (BFOQ) reasonably necessary to the normal operation of that particular business. This is known as the *BFOQ defense.* Because BFOQ is an affirmative defense, the employer has the burden of showing a reasonable basis for believing that the category of persons (for example, women) excluded from a particular job was unable to perform that job.

The BFOQ defense has been narrowly construed. For example, regulations promulgated by the Equal Employment Opportunity Commission provide that gender will not qualify as a BFOQ where a gender-based restriction is based on (1) assumptions of the comparative employment characteristics of women in general (such as the assumption that women have a higher turnover rate than men); (2) stereotyped characterizations of the sexes (for example, that men are less capable of assembling intricate equipment than women); or (3) the preferences of coworkers, employers, or customers for one sex or the other.[22] Gender will be considered a BFOQ, for example, when physical attributes are important for authenticity (as with actors) or when a gender-based restriction is necessary to protect the rights of others to privacy (as with restroom attendants).

Men seeking to be servers at Hooters restaurant argued that the restaurant would not hire them solely on the basis of their sex. Hooters argued that being female was a BFOQ, because the restaurant was providing entertainment, not just food. The case was recently settled out of court for $3.75 million. Under the agreement,

---

21. Christopher Simon, *Restaurant Seeks Waitresses after Suit,* WALL ST. J., Oct. 7, 1997, at B8.

22. 29 C.F.R. § 1604.2(a)(1)(i)–(iii) (1997).

the serving staff will continue to be all female, but the company will create more nonserving jobs for men.[23]

The BFOQ defense is not available when discriminatory treatment is based on a person's race or color.

Seniority and Merit Systems Bona fide seniority and merit systems are not covered by Title VII, as long as such systems do not result from intentional discrimination. This is considered an exemption rather than an affirmative defense. Consequently, the plaintiff has the burden of proving a discriminatory intent or illegal purpose. Moreover, although a disproportionate impact may be some evidence of a discriminatory intent, such an impact is not, in itself, sufficient to establish discriminatory intent.

After-Acquired Evidence When an employee initiates a suit under Title VII, sometimes over the course of discovery, an employer will learn that the individual violated company rules. Under these circumstances, employers have argued that the plaintiff's discrimination claim should fail because, had the employer known of the employee misconduct, the employee would have been discharged anyway.

In *McKennon v. Nashville Banner Publishing Company*,[24] the U.S. Supreme Court held that after-acquired evidence of misconduct does not bar a discrimination claim. *McKennon* involved an age-discrimination claim under the ADEA by an employee who, fearing a discrim-

inatory discharge, photocopied numerous confidential company documents. When the company discovered her misconduct, it moved to dismiss her claim because it would have fired her immediately had it known of her actions. The Court held that after-acquired evidence cannot bar a discrimination claim under the ADEA, or similar statutes such as Title VII, because that would frustrate the broader goal of nondiscrimination. However, the employee misconduct is not ignored. Thus, remedies available to plaintiffs in cases involving misconduct should be limited to back pay; remedies should not include reinstatement or front pay.

Lower courts have further refined the *McKennon* standard, which did not specify the burden of proof upon employers to demonstrate that they would have disciplined the employee for his or her misconduct. For example, the Ninth Circuit held that in discrimination suits in which employers rely upon after-acquired evidence, the employer must prove by a preponderance of the evidence that it would have made the disputed employment decision once it had the after-acquired evidence.[25]

 Special Applications of the Laws

The civil rights legislation was founded on the fundamental premise that people ought not be denied a job or opportunity on the job because of their race, religion, or sex. The law has expanded beyond that basic premise to reach more subtle forms of discrimination.

Pregnancy Discrimination

Traditionally, female employees have been disadvantaged due to their role as childbearers. In the past, many employers did not provide pregnancy leave; an employee who decided to have a child would either have to work throughout her pregnancy or quit.

In 1976, the Supreme Court held that denying a woman disability insurance benefits for a temporary disability caused by pregnancy was not sex discrimination.[26] The Supreme Court reasoned that the denial of benefits was based not on being female but on being pregnant, and that a distinction between pregnant persons (albeit all female) and nonpregnant persons was not sex discrimination.

23. *Hooters Chain Settles Sex Discrimination Suit*, SAN FRANCISCO CHRON., Oct. 1, 1997, at A3.

24. 513 U.S. 352 (1995).

ETHICAL CONSIDERATION

Civil rights legislation has done more than simply prohibit intentional discrimination against minority groups and women. It has fostered a major shift in public attitudes about the capabilities of individuals and contributed to the breakdown of stereotypes regarding ethnic and gender groups. As a result, many longstanding stereotypes held by employers and society in general have been challenged. What obligations do managers have to identify and redress group-based animus within their organization? What can a manager do to change racist or sexist attitudes?

25. O'Day v. McDonnell–Douglas Helicopter Co., 79 F.3d 756 (9th Cir. 1996).

26. General Elec. Co. v. Gilbert, 429 U.S. 129 (1976).

Congress, recognizing the increasing number of women in the work force and the widespread need for medical insurance and medical leave for pregnancies, responded by passing the Pregnancy Discrimination Act. The act provided that Title VII's prohibition on the basis of sex extends to pregnancy; discrimination on the basis of pregnancy is, on its face, a form of sex discrimination.[27] Employers must provide the same compensation for disabilities related to pregnancy and childbirth as they provide for any other disability. Many states have followed suit and, as in other areas of discrimination law, some provide greater protection than required under federal law.

These protections, however, are not absolute. The U.S. Court of Appeals for the First Circuit, for example, ruled that an employer could discharge a manager who was on maternity leave, because it realized the company could function effectively without her.[28] The court reasoned that discharge is an ordinary risk of employment, whether or not one is pregnant, and ruled that the employer had demonstrated that it would have eliminated her position regardless of her pregnancy.

Pregnancy-related complaints of employment discrimination increased 6% from 1997 to 1998.[29] Thus, while the legal climate for pregnant workers has become more favorable, bias on the basis of pregnancy continues and will likely become more salient as women make up a greater percentage of the work force.[30]

Fetal-Protection Policies

Certain substances used in manufacturing are harmful to the fetus being carried by a pregnant woman. In an effort to avoid such harm, and related lawsuits for unsafe working environments, some companies adopted what are called "fetal-protection policies." A *fetal-protection policy* bars a woman from certain jobs unless her inability to bear children is medically documented. Such a plan was challenged under Title VII in the case that follows.

---

27. 42 U.S.C. § 2000e(k) (1994).

28. Smith v. F.W. Morse & Co., 76 F.3d 413 (1st Cir. 1996). *Accord* Rhett v. Carnegie Ctr. Assoc., 129 F.3d 290 (3d Cir. 1997).

29. Sue Shellenbarger, *Work & Family: Recent Suits Make Pregnancy Issues Workplace Priorities*, WALL ST. J., Jan. 14, 1998, at B1.

30. *Id.*

A CASE IN POINT	IN THE LANGUAGE OF THE COURT

**CASE 13.2
AUTOMOBILE
WORKERS
v. JOHNSON
CONTROLS, INC.**
Supreme Court
of the United States
499 U.S. 187 (1991).

FACTS Since 1982, Johnson Controls, Inc., a manufacturer of batteries, has maintained a fetal-protection policy designed to prevent unborn children and their mothers from suffering the adverse effects of lead exposure. Lead attacks the fetus's central nervous system and retards cognitive development. Under the policy, women with childbearing capacity will neither be hired for nor be allowed to transfer into those jobs in which lead levels are defined as excessive. The United Automobile, Aerospace and Agricultural Implement Workers of America, several UAW local unions, and a group of individual employees brought suit alleging that this policy violated Title VII. The plaintiffs included a woman who had chosen to be sterilized in order to keep her job as well as women who had suffered losses in compensation when transferred out of jobs that exposed them to lead. The federal district court and the court of appeals found in favor of Johnson Controls.

The U.S. Supreme Court granted certiorari "to address the important and difficult issue of whether an employer, seeking to protect potential fetuses, may discriminate against women just because of their ability to become pregnant."

OPINION BLACKMUN, J., writing for the U.S. Supreme Court:

The bias in Johnson Controls' policy is obvious. Fertile men, but not fertile women, are given a choice as to whether they wish to risk their reproductive health for a particular job. . . .

. . . Johnson Controls' policy classifies on the basis of gender and childbearing capacity, rather than fertility alone. Respondent does not seek to protect the unconceived

Case 13.2 continues

Case 13.2 continued

children of all its employees. Despite evidence in the record about the debilitating effect of lead exposure on the male reproductive system, Johnson Controls is concerned only with the harms that may befall the unborn offspring of its female employees. . . . Johnson Controls' policy is facially discriminatory because it requires only a female employee to produce proof that she is not capable of reproducing.

. . .

. . . [T]he absence of a malevolent motive does not convert a facially discriminatory policy into a neutral policy with a discriminatory effect. Whether an employment practice involves disparate treatment through explicit facial discrimination does not depend on why the employer discriminates but rather on the explicit terms of the discrimination. . . .

. . . We hold that Johnson Controls' fetal-protection policy is sex-discrimination forbidden under Title VII unless respondent can establish that sex is a "bona fide occupational qualification."

. . .

The BFOQ defense is written narrowly and this Court has read it narrowly. . . . Johnson Controls argues that its fetal-protection policy falls within the so-called safety exception to the BFOQ. Our cases have stressed that discrimination on the basis of sex because of safety concerns is allowed only in narrow circumstances. . . .

. . .

Our case law, therefore, makes it clear that the safety exception is limited to instances in which sex or pregnancy actually interferes with the employee's ability to perform the job. This approach is consistent with the language of the BFOQ provision itself, for it suggests that permissible distinctions based on sex must relate to ability to perform the duties of the job. Johnson Controls suggests, however, that we expand the exception to allow fetal-protection policies that mandate particular standards for pregnant or fertile women. We decline to do so. Such an expansion contradicts not only the language of the BFOQ and the narrowness of its exception but the plain language and history of the Pregnancy Discrimination Act [PDA].

. . . [W]omen as capable of doing their job as their male counterparts may not be forced to choose between having a child and having a job.

. . .

We have no difficulty concluding that Johnson Controls cannot establish a BFOQ. Fertile women, as far as appears in the record, participate in the manufacture of batteries as efficiently as anyone else. Johnson Controls' professed moral and ethical concerns about the welfare of the next generation do not suffice to establish a BFOQ of female sterility. Decisions about the welfare of future children must be left to the parents who conceive, bear, support, and raise them rather than to the employers who hire those parents. Congress has mandated this choice through Title VII, as amended by the Pregnancy Discrimination Act. Johnson Controls has attempted to exclude women because of their reproductive capacity. Title VII and the PDA simply do not allow a woman's dismissal because of her failure to submit to sterilization.

Nor can concerns about the welfare of the next generation be considered part of the "essence" of Johnson Controls' business. Judge Easterbrook in this case perti-

Case 13.2 continues

Case 13.2 continued

nently observed: "It is word play to say that 'the job' at Johnson [Controls] is to make batteries without risk to fetuses in the same way 'the job' at Western Airlines is to fly planes without crashing."

. . . Johnson Controls' fear of prenatal injury, no matter how sincere, does not begin to show that substantially all of its fertile women employees are incapable of doing their jobs.

A word about tort liability and the increased cost of fertile women in the workplace is perhaps necessary. . . . More than 40 states currently recognize a right to recover for a prenatal injury based either on negligence or on wrongful death. . . . It is worth noting that OSHA gave the problem of lead lengthy consideration and concluded that "there is no basis whatsoever for the claim that women of childbearing age should be excluded from the workplace in order to protect the fetus or the course of pregnancy." Instead, OSHA established a series of mandatory protections which, taken together, "should effectively minimize any risk to the fetus and newborn child." Without negligence, it would be difficult for a court to find liability on the part of the employer. If, under general tort principles, Title VII bans sex-specific fetal-protection policies, the employer fully informs the woman of the risk, and the employer has not acted negligently, the basis for holding an employer liable seems remote at best.

. . .

The tort-liability argument reduces to two equally unpersuasive propositions. First, Johnson Controls attempts to solve the problem of reproductive health hazards by resorting to an exclusionary policy. Title VII plainly forbids illegal sex discrimination as a method of diverting attention from an employer's obligation to police the workplace. Second, the specter of an award of damages reflects a fear that hiring fertile women will cost more. The extra cost of employing members of one sex, however, does not provide an affirmative Title VII defense for a discriminatory refusal to hire members of that gender.

Our holding today that Title VII, as so amended, forbids sex-specific fetal-protection policies is neither remarkable nor unprecedented. Concern for a woman's existing or potential offspring historically has been the excuse for denying women equal employment opportunities. Congress in the PDA prohibited discrimination on the basis of a woman's ability to become pregnant. We do no more than hold that the Pregnancy Discrimination Act means what it says. It is no more appropriate for the courts than it is for individual employers to decide whether a woman's reproductive role is more important to herself and her family than her economic role. Congress has left that choice to the woman as hers to make.

RESULT   The judgment of the court of appeals was reversed and the case was remanded for further proceedings consistent with the Supreme Court's opinion. Women cannot be excluded from certain jobs because of their childbearing capacity.

Questions

1. Would the Court have decided the case differently if all fertile employees, male and female alike, were banned from jobs involving lead?
2. What must Johnson Controls do to avoid suits for prenatal injury based on negligence or wrongful death?

In the wake of *Johnson Controls*, employers have been forced to walk a fine line between not limiting the positions available for a female employee and limiting or reducing potential workplace hazards. Indeed, in eight states employers may be liable for not providing a safe work environment for a pregnant employee's fetus.[31] Employers have been held liable for falling machines, triggering premature birth and brain damage to the child, and requiring pregnant employees to work beyond their doctor's orders, resulting in premature birth and later death of the fetus.[32]

English-Only Laws

The national origin provisions of Title VII have been used to challenge English-only workplace rules and laws. Such rules have increased dramatically in recent years and the EEOC is challenging them, arguing that language is closely linked with national origin.[33] Moreover, some state governments, including New Hampshire, South Carolina, South Dakota, Nebraska, and Arizona, have adopted strongly worded laws enforcing English as the only recognized language.[34] The Arizona Supreme Court struck down the Arizona initiative that required state government employees to speak only English, but the case was rendered moot when the plaintiff resigned from her job.[35]

Sexual Harassment

As more women have entered the work force and risen to positions previously dominated by men, courts have recognized sexual harassment as a form of sexual discrimination. Sexual harassment, which can be asserted by male or female employees, is one of the more complex and emotional issues in antidiscrimination law.

Early on, the courts recognized that a specific, job-related adverse action, such as denial of promotion, in retaliation for a person's refusal to respond to his or her supervisor's sexual advances was a violation of Title VII. Such retaliation is referred to as *quid pro quo harassment*. One court has held that a person will be treated as a supervisor, even if he or she does not have ultimate authority to hire or fire an employee, if he or she has significant input into the employee's hiring, firing, or conditions of employment.[36]

A threat of adverse job action does not constitute *quid pro quo* harassment if the threat is not carried out. Instead, it is a form of hostile environment.[37]

In *Meritor Savings Bank v. Vinson*,[38] the Supreme Court ruled that creation of a hostile environment by sexual harassment is a form of sex discrimination barred by Title VII. The case was brought by a female branch manager who claimed that for four years she had been constantly subjected to sexual harassment. After her probationary period, a male manager requested that she engage in a sexual relationship with him. Out of fear of losing her job, she eventually agreed and later testified to his explicit sexual conduct in front of other employees. She also claimed that her manager had assaulted her on several occasions. She never reported this harassment to any of his supervisors and never used the bank's complaint procedure, because it required an employee to report any grievances first to one's superior—who in this case was the cause of the grievance.

The Court held that there can be sexual harassment solely by the creation of a hostile work environment, even if there is no retaliatory employment action against the employee. Thus, it is not necessary for the employee to show a concrete economic effect on employment, such as discharge or denial of a raise or promotion, to establish a violation. The Supreme Court noted that not every sexually offensive comment or act constitutes actionable sexual harassment; there must be sufficiently offensive conduct to give rise to a pervasively hostile atmosphere. This determination should be based upon the totality of the circumstances.

The Supreme Court in *Meritor* placed heavy reliance on the EEOC's regulations defining sexual harassment. They are a useful guide to the employer in developing an anti-sexual-harassment policy or in educating its supervisors. They state:

> Harassment on the basis of sex is a violation of section 703 of title VII. Unwelcome sexual advances, requests for sexual favors, and other verbal or physical conduct of a sexual nature constitute sexual harassment when (1) submission to such conduct is made either explicitly or implicitly a term or condition of an individual's employment, (2) submission to or rejection of such conduct by

31. *Id.*

32. *Id.*

33. *At Panel Discussion on National Origin Bias EEOC Says English-Only Challenges Are Rising,* 66 U.S.L.W. 2375 (Dec. 23, 1997).

34. Paul M. Barrett, *Justices to Decide Case Involving Official Use of English Language,* WALL ST. J., Mar. 26, 1996, at B6.

35. Ruiz v. Hull, 957 P.2d 984 (Ariz. 1998).

36. Reinhold v. Virginia, 135 F.3d 920 (4th Cir. 1998).

37. Burlington Indus., Inc. v. Ellerth, 118 S. Ct. 2257 (1998).

38. 477 U.S. 51 (1986).

'GREAT NEWS, LURLINE MAE... SUPREME COURT SAYS YOU GOTTA RIGHT TO WORK HERE, PREGNANT OR NOT!'

an individual is used as the basis of employment decisions affecting such individual, or (3) such conduct has the purpose or effect of unreasonably interfering with an individual's work performance or creating an intimidating, hostile, or offensive working environment.[39]

In *Harris v. Forklift Systems, Inc.*,[40] the Supreme Court clarified its ruling in *Meritor*. The Court ruled that no showing of a serious effect on an employee's psychological well-being, or other injury, is necessary for a hostile work environment claim under Title VII. The case involved a female manager of an equipment-rental company who was harassed for two years by its president. In the presence of other employees, the president said such things as "You're a woman, what do you know?" and "We need a man as the rental manager" and telling her she was a "a dumb-ass woman." The president also made sexual innuendoes suggesting that they "go to the Holiday Inn to negotiate her raise" and occasionally asked female employees to get coins from his front pants pocket. Despite complaints, the sexual comments continued. The female manager quit, then filed suit alleging that the president's conduct had created an abusive work environment for her because of her gender.

The Court ruled in favor of the female manager. It held that no showing of a serious effect on an employee's psychological well-being or other injury was

necessary for an action for abusive or hostile work environment under Title VII, reasoning that "Title VII comes into play before the harassing conduct leads to a nervous breakdown." The Court reaffirmed its holding in *Meritor* that Title VII is not limited to economic or tangible discrimination, but covers the entire spectrum of disparate treatment of men and women at work.

The Court stated that although a discriminatory work environment often has numerous negative repercussions, the abusive environment itself violates Title VII. Thus, if a work environment would reasonably be perceived, and is perceived, as hostile or abusive, Title VII does not require psychological injury. In order to determine a hostile or abusive environment, courts must look at all the circumstances, including (1) the frequency and severity of the discriminatory conduct; (2) whether it is physically threatening or humiliating, or a mere offensive utterance; and (3) whether it unreasonably interferes with an employee's work performance.

The Supreme Court provided additional guidance in *Faragher v. City of Boca Raton*.[41] To be actionable under Title VII, sexual harassment must be so severe or pervasive as to alter the conditions of the victim's employment and create an abusive working environment. "'[S]imple teasing,' offhand comments, and isolated incidents (unless extremely serious) will not amount to discriminatory changes in the terms and conditions of

39. 29 C.F.R. § 1604.11(a) (1997).

40. 510 U.S. 17 (1993).

41. 118 S. Ct. 2275 (1998) (Case 13.3).

employment.'" The conduct must be "extreme." The standards for judging hostility are sufficiently demanding to prevent plaintiffs from converting Title VII into a "general civility code"; they are intended to filter out "complaints attacking 'the ordinary tribulations of the workplace, such as the sporadic use of abusive language, gender-related jokes, and occasional teasing.'"

Defining a Hostile Work Environment Lower courts have struggled with defining when workplace incidents are sufficiently offensive to create a hostile work environment. They have construed *Meritor* broadly in finding that sexual conduct in the workplace, even when not directed at the plaintiff, may violate Title VII. For example, in a case involving a female attorney for the Securities and Exchange Commission, the court held that open sexual activity in exchange for tangible employment benefits creates a hostile working environment.[42] The plaintiff had testified that she had rebuffed sexual overtures and that the sexually permissive atmosphere made it impossible for her to work as a professional or to have a good working relationship with those managers. The court found that these facts established sexual harassment, as defined by the Supreme Court in *Meritor*.

Some courts have held that even one instance of sexual harassment may be sufficient to create a hostile work environment. For example, the Supreme Judicial Court of Maine ruled that a supervisor's request for sexual favors in exchange for money over the course of a business lunch was sufficiently severe to state a hostile work environment under *Meritor* and *Harris*.[43] By contrast, the Federal District Court for the Western District of Pennsylvania ruled that a waitress who had been harassed by a customer had not established that the behavior was severe, pervasive, or regular.[44] The waitress had identified three instances of sexual comments that were offensive. The U.S. Supreme Court seemed to acknowledge in *Faragher* that an "extremely serious" isolated incident might give rise to a finding of hostile environment. The Court reserved the issue of whether a single unfulfilled threat by a supervisor of adverse job action is sufficient in *Burlington Industries, Inc. v. Ellerth*.[45]

In a highly publicized lawsuit, former Arkansas state employee Paula Jones sued President Bill Clinton

---

INTERNATIONAL CONSIDERATION

Although sexual harassment is often litigated in the United States, many other countries have just begun to recognize claims for sexual harassment. For example, many behaviors that would be considered sexual harassment in the United States are considered appropriate by some in Japan.[a] Although 26.5% of female workers in Japan have reported having some unpleasant job-related sexual experiences, most do not sue for a number of reasons.

First, women often have a secondary status to men in Japan. Entertaining clients may explicitly involve women, ranging from idle chatter at "hostess bars" to naked women bathing men, even prostitution. Women in large corporations often are considered "office ladies" who serve tea or perform clerical duties, but are not promoted and are expected to retire after getting married. Second, sexual harassment is not an important issue to Japanese women. Before the first sexual-harassment lawsuit in 1989, there was no word to describe the behavior and, as an editor of a Japanese magazine for working women commented, the magazine focuses upon "issues and problems that are more closely related to [women's] daily lives."[b]

Finally, when women do complain about treatment by male supervisors and coworkers, they generally go to the local labor commission, which is more receptive to their claims. Courts are more skeptical of sexual-harassment suits, focusing on the behavior of the woman, rather than the man.

---

a. Andrew Pollack, *In Japan, It's See No Evil; Have No Harassment,* N.Y. TIMES, May 7, 1996, at C1.

b. *Id.*

---

for acts she alleged occurred in his hotel suite while he was Governor of Arkansas. Jones alleged that Clinton had said "I love the way your hair flows down your back" and "I love your curves" while sliding his hand up her leg toward her pelvic area and attempting to kiss her neck. She allegedly rebuffed his advances and sat down on a sofa near the door. Clinton allegedly then sat down, lowered his trousers and underwear, exposed his erect penis, and told her to kiss it. Jones sued under

42. Broderick v. Ruder, 715 F. Supp. 1 (D.D.C. 1989)

43. Nadeau v. Rainbow Rugs Inc., 675 A.2d 973 (Me. 1996).

44. Hallberg v. Eat'n Park, No. 94-1888, 1996 U.S. Dist. WL 182212 (W.D. Pa. Feb 28, 1996).

45. 118 S. Ct. 2257 (1998)

Section 1983, claiming that Clinton had violated her right to equal protection by engaging in *quid pro quo* and hostile-work-environment sexual harassment. She also sued under Arkansas law for sexual assault and intentional infliction of emotional distress (or outrage).

The Federal District Court for the Eastern District of Arkansas granted Clinton's motion for summary judgment in April 1998.[46] The court held that Clinton's conduct, if true, was "boorish and offensive" but was not sexual assault. In considering Jones's claims for sexual harassment under Section 1983, the court ruled that they were governed by the case law interpreting Title VII. The court then ruled that Jones had failed to show that her refusal to submit to the alleged unwelcome sexual advances had resulted in a tangible job detriment: There was no diminution in her salary or change in her job classification, and she continued to receive positive reviews. Therefore, her claim of *quid pro quo* harassment failed. The court similarly rejected her claim of a hostile work environment, ruling that the alleged single episode was not sufficiently severe to alter the conditions of employment and create an abusive working environment. Finally, the court held that the alleged conduct was not extreme and outrageous enough to constitute intentional infliction of emotional distress or outrage. Jones indicated that she would appeal the decision.

Recently, several large multinational corporations with offices in the United States were charged with sexual harassment. Astra USA, a unit of the pharmaceutical giant Astra AB of Sweden, was investigated by the EEOC regarding hundreds of claims of sexual harassment. An investigative report by *Business Week* uncovered a corporate culture in which women employees were regularly groped, expected to go to executives' hotel rooms and have drinks, sexualized at work, and regularly subjected to sexual advances by the president and other members of top management.[47] Those who complained suffered retaliation by being discredited, passed up for promotion, and even discharged. After an internal probe, the president was fired.[48] In 1998, Astra agreed to pay $9.85 million to at least 79 women and to one man who was punished for speaking out.[49]

ETHICAL CONSIDERATION

A rule that no employee should be subjected to requests for sexual favors is not sufficient. Sexual harassment may include overt or subtle sexual advances, even if there is no retaliation when such advances are rebuffed; sexual joking; leering; or any unwelcome touching. The difficult situation is the workplace where physical familiarity has come to be accepted, or where sexual comments are laughed at or tolerated. If management appears to condone such conduct, the employee may feel compelled to go along with it, even if he or she finds it intimidating or if it interferes with his or her ability to work.

Mitsubishi Motor Manufacturing of America, Inc. faced the largest sexual-harassment case ever. The EEOC alleged that more than 400 men sexually harassed more than 300 female employees by groping them, calling them "bitches" and "whores," and placing drawings of female body parts on car fenders.[50] The EEOC's class action suit alleged that sexual harassment was persistent and pervasive, and that the plant manager retaliated against those who complained. Initially, Mitsubishi denied all allegations of sexual harassment[51] and took the offensive. It organized employee protests of the lawsuit and encouraged employees to rally behind the company, sought access to the plaintiffs' gynecological and psychological records, and argued that some plaintiffs were merely promiscuous. In 1997, Mitsubishi paid $10 million to settle a separate private sexual-harassment lawsuit brought by 29 female employees. The EEOC class action suit was settled in June 1998. Mitsubishi agreed to pay $34 million, the largest sexual-harassment settlement ever obtained by the EEOC. The executive vice-president at Mitsubishi Motor Manufacturing of America apologized, saying "We again extend our sincere regret to any woman who has been harmed."[52]

46. Jones v. Clinton, 990 F. Supp. 657 (E.D. Ark. 1998).

47. Mark Maremont, *Abuse of Power: The Astonishing Tale of Sexual Harassment at Astra USA*, Bus. Wk., May 13, 1996, at 86.

48. Laura Johannes, *Astra USA Fires Bildman from Top Post*, Wall St. J., June 27, 1996, at A3.

49. Associated Press, *Drug Firm to Pay Record $9.85 Million*, San Francisco Chron., Feb. 6, 1998, at A3.

50. Rochelle Sharpe, *EEOC Sues Mitsubishi Unit for Harassment*, Wall St. J., Apr. 10, 1996, at B1.

51. Rochelle Sharpe, *Fighting Back: A Mitsubishi U.S. Unit Is Taking a Hard Line In Harassment Battle*, Wall St. J., Apr. 22, 1996, at A1.

52. Washington Post, *Mitsubishi Settles Suit for $34 Million*, San Francisco Chron., June 12 1998, at A3.

Vicarious Liability In *Burlington Industries,* the Supreme Court relied on general common law agency principles to determine an employer's liability for sexual harassment by a supervisor, noting that generally sexual harassment by a supervisor is not conduct within the scope of employment. The Court cited Section 219(2) of the Restatement (Second) of Agency for the proposition that an employer is liable for the torts of employees not acting in the scope of employment if (1) the employer intended the conduct; (2) the employee's high rank makes him or her the employer's alter ego; (3) the employer was negligent; or (4) the employee was aided in accomplishing the tort by the existence of the agency relation.

The employer is negligent with respect to sexual harassment if it knew or should have known of the harassment but failed to stop it. This negligence standard would govern hostile environment by coworkers (and probably customers with whom the employee must deal as part of his or her job).

In addition, the employer is always vicariously liable under the aided-in-the-agency-relation standard when a supervisor takes a tangible employment action against a subordinate (such as firing, failing to promote, reassign-

ment with significantly different responsibilities, or reducing benefits). Thus, in a case resulting in adverse job action, the employer is vicariously liable for the hostile environment created by a supervisor with immediate (or successively higher) authority over the victimized employee regardless of whether the employer knew or should have known about the supervisor's conduct.

However, if there was no tangible employment action, then the defending employer can raise an affirmative defense to liability by proving, by a preponderance of the evidence, that (1) the employer exercised reasonable care to prevent and correct promptly any sexually harassing behavior; and (2) the plaintiff employee unreasonably failed to take advantage of any preventive or corrective opportunities provided by the employer (such as a complaint procedure) or to avoid harm otherwise. Thus, this affirmative defense would potentially be available in a case in which there was an unfulfilled threat of adverse job action but not in a case in which the threat was carried out.

The Supreme Court further explained the affirmative defense available in cases not involving a tangible employment action in the following case.

A CASE IN POINT   **SUMMARY**

CASE 13.3
FARAGHER v. CITY OF
BOCA RATON
Supreme Court
of the United States
118 S. Ct. 2275 (1998).

FACTS   Beth Ann Faragher worked for the City of Boca Raton, Florida (the City) as an ocean lifeguard intermittently from September 1985 to June 1990. Faragher alleged that over the course of these five years, two supervisors had subjected her to unwanted sexual advances, including touching her shoulders and waist on a number of occasions, patting her thigh, and slapping her on the buttocks. Another female lifeguard, Nancy Ewanchew, was treated similarly. Neither Faragher nor Ewanchew complained to the recreation department of the City, but they did speak to a supervisor in a personal capacity. The supervisor did not pass on the information to other supervisors. In 1990, Ewanchew wrote a letter to the City complaining of the sexual advances of her supervisors. In response, the City investigated and reprimanded them.

In 1992, Faragher initiated a lawsuit against the City of Boca Raton under Title VII alleging sexual harassment. She argued that her supervisors were quintessential agents of the City, which made the City liable for their conduct. Faragher also argued that the harassment was sufficiently pervasive to conclude that the City had constructive knowledge of the illicit conduct. Thus, she asserted that the City should be held both indirectly and directly liable for the hostile work environment.

The City responded that there was no showing that the supervisors were acting within the scope of their authority nor were they assisted by virtue of their relationship with the City. The City argued that it should not be held liable for the conduct of its employees acting within their personal capacities. The City also argued that there was insufficient evidence to impose constructive knowledge upon the City; as soon as it knew of the harassment, it took action.

Case 13.3 continues

Case 13.3 continued

The district court ruled in favor of Faragher, holding the City vicariously liable and directly liable because the City had constructive knowledge of the harassment due to its pervasiveness. The appeals court reversed, and Faragher appealed.

ISSUE PRESENTED   Is an employer liable for a supervisor's hostile-environment sexual harassment, regardless of the employer's actual or constructive knowledge of the harassment?

SUMMARY OF OPINION   As it had in *Burlington Industries*, the U.S. Supreme Court considered the aided-by-agency-relation principle embodied in Section 219(2)(d) of the Restatement (Second) of Agency an appropriate starting point for determining an employer's vicarious liability for a hostile environment created by a supervisor. The Court acknowledged that there is a sense in which a harassing supervisor is always assisted in his or her conduct by the supervisory relationship. "When a fellow employee harasses, the victim can walk away or tell the offender where to go, but it may be difficult to offer such responses to a supervisor" with the power to hire, fire, and set work schedules and pay raises.

Even so, the Court felt constrained by its holding in *Meritor* that the employer is not automatically liable for harassment by a supervisor. It also noted that the primary objective of Title VII is to avoid harm. To implement that statutory policy, the Court considered it appropriate "to recognize the employer's affirmative obligation to prevent violations and give credit here to employers who make reasonable efforts to discharge their duty." At the same time, the Court acknowledged an employee's duty to avoid or mitigate harm. If the employee unreasonably failed to avail himself or herself of the employer's preventive or remedial apparatus, the employee should not recover damages that could have been avoided if he or she had done so.

Accordingly, the Court held that if the supervisor's harassment does not culminate in a tangible employment action (such as discharge, demotion, or undesirable assignment), then the employer may raise an affirmative defense to liability or damages. To establish the defense, the employer must prove two things: (1) it exercised reasonable care to prevent and correct promptly any sexually harassing behavior; and (2) the employee unreasonably failed to take advantage of any preventive or corrective opportunities provided by the employer or to avoid harm otherwise. For example, if an employer has provided a proven, effective mechanism for reporting and resolving complaints of sexual harassment available to the employee without undue risk or expense, then the employee's unreasonable failure to use that complaint procedure will normally suffice to satisfy the employer's burden under the second element of the defense.

Applying these principles to the facts of the case at hand, the Court ruled as a matter of law that the City did not exercise reasonable care to prevent the supervisors' harassing conduct. The City failed to disseminate its policy against sexual harassment among the beach employees. The City's policy did not include a sensible complaint procedure because it did not provide any assurance that the harassing supervisors could be bypassed in registering complaints. Its officials made no attempt to keep track of the conduct of supervisors, even though the supervisors were given virtually unchecked authority over subordinates who were completely isolated from the City's higher management.

Case 13.3 continues

Case 13.3 continued

RESULT   The Supreme Court reversed the appeals court and remanded the case for entry of judgment in Faragher's favor. The City was vicariously liable for the hostile environment created by the supervisors.

COMMENT   The Court stated that the promulgation of an antiharassment policy with a complaint procedure was not necessary as a matter of law, but the need for a stated policy suitable to the employment circumstances would be relevant to determining whether the employer acted reasonably. Although the Court raised the possibility that the employer of a small workforce might be able to prevent harassing behavior by acting informally, it is clear that every employer, regardless of the size of the workforce, is well advised to adopt, disseminate, and enforce a written policy prohibiting harassment and providing a reasonable complaint procedure.

Same-Sex Sexual Harassment   The U.S. Supreme Court resolved the split in the circuits over whether same-sex harassment may be actionable under Title VII in the following case.

A CASE IN POINT	SUMMARY

CASE 13.4
ONCALE v.
SUNDOWNER
OFFSHORE
SERVICES, INC.
Supreme Court
of the United States
118 S. Ct. 998 (1998).

FACTS   Joseph Oncale was employed by Sundowner Offshore Services as one of eight men on an oil platform in the Gulf of Mexico. On numerous occasions, Oncale was subjected to sex-related humiliation in the presence of the rest of the crew. Two of his supervisors worked in tandem to restrain Oncale as one of them placed his penis on Oncale's neck on one occasion and on his arm on another. While on the company premises, one supervisor restrained Oncale as he showered, as the other forced a bar of soap into Oncale's anus, and both threatened anal rape. Both Oncale and his supervisors claimed to be heterosexual.

Oncale's complaints were unheeded by the company's safety compliance clerk, who participated in the mistreatment. Oncale eventually resigned as a result of the continuing abuse, then filed a complaint for same-sex harassment under Title VII. The district court dismissed the claim. The district court was affirmed on appeal, and Oncale appealed.

ISSUE   Is harassment between individuals of the same sex prohibited under Title VII's ban on discrimination on the basis of sex?

SUMMARY OF OPINION   A unanimous U.S. Supreme Court held that Title VII's ban on discrimination on the basis of sex includes sexual harassment between individuals of the same gender. Noting the split between the courts of appeal, the Court found nothing in the Court's precedents that restricted sexual harassment to individuals of different genders. Although same-sex harassment was not the evil Congress sought to remedy when it passed Title VII, the Court saw "no justification in the statutory language or our precedents for a categorical rule excluding same-sex harassment claims from the coverage of Title VII." Insofar as the essence of the sexual harassment claim was present—that the disputed conduct constituted discrimination because of sex—then fears "that recognizing liability for same-sex harassment will transform Title VII into a general civility code for the American workplace" were unfounded.

Case 13.4 continues

Case 13.4 continued

But the Court made it clear that harassing conduct need not be motivated by sexual desire to support an inference of discrimination on the basis of sex. Thus, the plaintiff in a same-sex case is not required to allege that the harasser was homosexual.

At the same time, the Court stated that "the statute does not reach genuine but innocuous differences in the ways men and women routinely interact with members of the same sex and of the opposite sex." It requires "neither asexuality nor androgyny in the workplace." Workplace harassment is not automatically discrimination because of sex merely because the words used have sexual content or connotations. Title VII prohibits only "behavior so objectively offensive as to alter the 'conditions' of the victim's employment." The conduct must be severe or pervasive enough to create an objectively hostile or abusive work environment.

The Court concluded by emphasizing that the perspective of a reasonable person in the plaintiff's position is the relevant reference point. Thus, although a pat on the bottom by a football coach to a player running onto the field may not constitute sex discrimination, a similar touching of a secretary might. The Court concluded that the "real social impact of workplace behavior often depends on a constellation of surrounding circumstances, expectations, and relationships," and it called on juries and judges to use "common sense" in differentiating sex discrimination from horseplay.

RESULT   The Supreme Court reversed the appeals court.

Appropriate Corrective Measures   Supervisors and nonsupervising employees should be taught that all forms of sexual conduct and sexual talk in the workplace are inappropriate. This should be stated in a written policy. The management of a company, whether through its human resource staff or otherwise, must be familiar with the atmosphere of its workplace and be vigilant in maintaining an appropriate environment in which employees can work comfortably.

It is also important to develop an atmosphere in which the employee feels free to bring a complaint. This has two components. First, victims of sexual harassment should be given information and support to identify and report sexual harassment.[53] Second, because the harasser is often the employee's supervisor, an effective procedure provides more than one resource person to whom the employee can complain. There should be persons of both genders so that the employee has a choice; sexual harassment is not a problem for only female employees.

The company should also ensure that all complaints are thoroughly investigated. The employer should meet with the complaining employee at the employee's earliest convenience and immediately interview the accused person, coworkers, and other witnesses. If the investigation reveals a problem, then the employer should consider whether termination or reassignment of the harasser or a reprimand is in order. Any reprimand should be in writing and be put in the harasser's personnel file. The reprimand should make it clear to the harasser that his or her conduct is unacceptable and warn that any recurrence will be grounds for severe discipline (including termination). The harasser should also be instructed to avoid having contact with the victim or talking about him or her. The employer should follow up with the victim to ensure that there are no continuing problems and to assure him or her that it will do whatever it can to support the victim's career goals.[54] Even if the investigation is inconclusive, it may be appropriate for the employer to offer the alleged victim a reassignment.

Although such protective measures may reduce liabilities, a company may still be sued for sexual harassment.

---

53. *See* Bernice R. Sandler, *Handling Sexual Harassment*, WOMEN IN MEDICINE AND THE MEDICAL SCIENCES, Fall 1997, at 1 (discussing strategies that victims may use to address workplace sexual harassment).

54. *See* Casenas v. Fujisawa USA, Inc., 58 Cal. App. 4th 101 (1997) (describing the employer's timely investigation of, and response to, the sexual-harassment allegations as "a textbook example of how to respond appropriately to an employee's harassment complaint.").

For example, Adolph Coors was sued in federal court even though it took extraordinary measures to respond to a claim of sexual harassment.[55] The company has a written policy against sexual harassment and conducts training sessions for management and employees. In responding to the reported sexual harassment, Coors fired eight people after a year-long investigation, hired a lawyer for the female employee to obtain restraining orders against two of the fired coworkers, installed a security system in the victim's home, paid for security guards to protect the woman twenty-four hours a day and seven days a week, provided her with a cellular phone and an escort, and granted her full paid medical leave and long-term disability benefits when she was too fearful to return to work. Commentators note that, while such efforts significantly reduce the likelihood of punitive damages, they cannot immunize a company from liability.

If an employer does not take appropriate action, then a company is exposing itself to potentially astronomical jury awards. For example, Baker & McKenzie, the world's largest law firm with 1,670 lawyers in 30 countries, learned the hard way in September 1994 about an employer's liability for sexual harassment by a manager. A California jury awarded legal secretary Rena Weeks $50,000 compensatory damages and $6.9 million punitive damages from Baker & McKenzie for its failure to provide a harassment-free workplace. Martin Greenstein, a former Baker & McKenzie partner who allegedly grabbed her breasts and buttocks and dropped M&M candies in her blouse pocket, was ordered to pay $225,000 in punitive damages. At trial, Weeks presented evidence that for several years before Baker & McKenzie hired her, Greenstein had engaged in similar conduct with other women employees. The incidents were reported to the firm's management, and the firm did little in response other than to speak to Greenstein and document the reports in the women's personnel files. Each time the firm spoke to him, Greenstein denied the accusation and the firm warned him not to engage in such conduct, but it never took further action.

In assessing punitive damages equal to 10% of Baker & McKenzie's net worth, jurors were, according to juror Frank Lewis, "highly cognizant of the fact that we were sending a message not only to Baker & McKenzie but to corporate America."[56] The trial court reduced the punitive damage award to $3.5 million.

The California Court of Appeal upheld the award under Section 3294 of the California Civil Code, which permits a punitive damage award against an employer for its employee's acts of oppression, fraud, or malice if the employer, through its managing agents, had advance knowledge of the employee's unfitness and employed him or her with a conscious disregard of the rights and safety of others.[57] The court held that an employer may not employ or continue to employ a harasser without taking action reasonably designed to protect others. The court rejected Baker & McKenzie's argument that an employer is left in the impossible situation of either terminating every accused harasser or facing punitive damage liability for the employee's later acts. Although an employer is not required to terminate a harassing employee, it is required to take reasonable measures to prevent a known harasser from committing future acts of harassment.

---

56. Rachel Gordon, *Amount of Award Split Harassment Jury*, SAN FRANCISCO EXAMINER, Sept. 3, 1994, at A1.
57. Weeks v. Baker & McKenzie, ___ Cal. Rptr. 2d ___ (Cal. Ct. App. 1998).

IN BRIEF

ELEMENTS OF A SEXUAL HARASSMENT CLAIM

Unwelcome sexual advances, requests for sexual favors, and other verbal or physical conduct of a sexual nature constitute sexual harassment when

1. an individual's employment depends on the submission to such conduct;
2. submission to or rejection of such conduct is used as the basis of employment decisions; or
3. such conduct unreasonably interferes with the individual's work performance or creates an intimidating, hostile, or offensive working environment.

In order to establish a claim of hostile-environment sexual harassment under Title VII, it must be shown that

1. the harassment created an abusive working environment;
2. the harassment was based on sex; and
3. the harassment was so severe or pervasive as to alter the conditions of the victim's employment.

---

55. Bob Ortega, *Sex-Harassment Lawsuit Names Coors Despite Its Protective Moves*, WALL ST. J., Nov. 14, 1997, at B9.

In light of such liabilities, some companies have acted quickly to fire individuals accused of sexual harassment. However, as discussed in Chapter 12, without a full investigation and a good faith belief that harassment occurred, the employer may find itself sued by a discharged employee for wrongful termination.[58]

Although employers are clearly liable if they know of a hostile work environment and do nothing, there are limited circumstances in which an employer that does not immediately act on a claim of sexual harassment may not be liable. In *Torres v. Pisano*,[59] the U.S. Court of Appeals for the Second Circuit ruled that a supervisor who did not act on an employee's sexual-harassment claim in order to honor the victim's request for confidentiality did not expose the employer to liability. The court reasoned that the supervisor's failure to act was not in violation of his duty to take reasonable steps to eliminate the sexual harassment because of the specific instructions of the victim not to share the information with anyone else.

Sexual Stereotyping

In *Price Waterhouse v. Hopkins*,[60] Ann Hopkins had been denied partnership in the Big Six accounting firm Price Waterhouse. She claimed that the firm had discriminated against her on the basis of sex. She produced evidence that the policy board had advised her that, in order to improve her chances for partnership, she should "walk more femininely, talk more femininely, dress more femininely, wear make-up, have her hair styled, and wear jewelry."

The Supreme Court concluded that the evidence produced by Hopkins was sufficient to establish that sexual stereotyping played a part in the firm's decision not to promote her. With respect to sexual stereotyping, the Supreme Court stated: "An employer who objects to aggressiveness in women but whose positions require this trait places women in an intolerable and impermissible Catch-22: out of a job if they behave aggressively and out of a job if they don't. Title VII lifts women out of this bind."[61] In addition, although the case dealt with gender discrimination, the Supreme Court expressly stated that all references to gender and all principles announced in the opinion "apply with equal force to discrimination based on race, religion, or national origin."

 ## Age Discrimination

The principal federal law prohibiting discrimination in employment on the basis of age is the Age Discrimination in Employment Act (ADEA). The ADEA prohibits age discrimination in employment with respect to individuals aged 40 years or older. Because the ADEA protects only persons aged 40 or above, individuals under age 40 have no protection from discrimination based on age. The U.S. Court of Appeals for the Second Circuit ruled that members of a company's board of directors who were retired officers are considered employees and protected from mandatory board retirement if they continued to perform their previous duties and reported to a senior board member.[62]

The substantive provisions of the ADEA are similar to those of Title VII. The ADEA generally prohibits age discrimination with respect to employee hiring, firing, compensation, and the terms, conditions, and privileges of employment.

The ADEA applies to all employers that affect interstate commerce and have at least 20 employees. Courts have held that the employer, not the individual making the alleged discriminatory decision, is liable for age discrimination.[63]

Plaintiffs under the ADEA may also employ the hostile-work-environment rationale often used in the context of sex- and race-based harassment. The U.S. Court of Appeals for the Sixth Circuit extended the hostile-work-environment claim to the context of age discrimination, finding the hostile-work-environment claim a "relatively uncontroversial proposition."[64] The ADEA also prohibits retaliation against an individual aged 40 or older because of the individual's opposition to unlawful age discrimination or because he or she has made a charge or testified or assisted in an investigation, proceeding, or litigation under the ADEA. Standing issues have also been contested under the ADEA. One federal district court held that former insurance company employees were ineligible to sue under the ADEA

---

58. Howard Mintz, *Proving Sex Harassment: Firms Struggle Over Employee Rights vs. Workplace Protection*, SAN JOSE MERCURY NEWS, Oct. 20, 1997, at A1.

59. 116 F.3d 625 (2d Cir. 1997).

60. 490 U.S. 228 (1989).

61. *Id.*

---

62. EEOC v. Johnson & Higgins, Inc., 91 F.3d 1529 (2d Cir. 1996).

63. Stults v. Conoco Inc., 76 F.3d 651 (5th Cir. 1996).

64. Crawford. v. Medina Gen. Hosp., 96 F.3d 830 (6th Cir. 1996).

because they were independent contractors, not employees.[65] However, courts have held that former employees do have standing to sue under the ADEA.[66]

The ADEA also prohibits unlawful age discrimination among persons within the protected age group. Thus, for example, if two individuals aged 41 and 53 apply for the same position, the employer may not lawfully reject either applicant on the basis of age. In other words, an employer may still have engaged in age discrimination even if it hires a person who is over 40.

In *O'Connor v. Consolidated Coin Caterers Corporation*,[67] a unanimous Supreme Court explained that age discrimination cannot be inferred simply because the replacement is outside of the protected class. That is, a 40-year-old employee who is replaced by a 39-year-old employee does not give rise to a stronger inference of discrimination than a 52-year-old employee who is replaced by a 40-year-old employee. Rather, "the fact that a replacement is substantially younger than the plaintiff is a far more reliable indicator of age discrimination." Thus, the Court suggested that there is no age discrimination unless the person hired is substantially younger than the person fired.

Older Workers' Benefit Protection Act

The Older Workers' Benefit Protection Act[68] (OWBPA) was a 1990 amendment to the Age Discrimination in Employment Act. It prohibits age discrimination in providing employee benefits. The OWBPA also establishes minimum standards for employees who waive their rights under the ADEA.

In order to meet minimum standards, the waiver must be "knowing and voluntary." The employee must be given at least 21 days to consider whether to enter into an agreement waiving rights under the ADEA. This period is extended to 45 days when the waiver is in connection with an early retirement or exit-incentive plan offered to a group or class of employees. The agreement must also give the employee a period of at least seven days following execution of the agreement, during which the employee may revoke it. An employee who has accepted a severance payment in exchange for

waiving his or her rights under the ADEA can sue the employer for violation of the ADEA without having to return the payment if the waiver was not made in accordance with the OWBPA.[69]

Many states also have enacted laws designed to protect the employment rights of older individuals. There appears to be increasing support for expanding protection against discrimination on the basis of age.

Defenses

An employer faced with an age-discrimination claim may assert in its defense that (1) age is a BFOQ reasonably necessary to the normal operation of the business (extremely difficult to prove); (2) the differential treatment is based on reasonable factors other than age; (3) the employer's action is based on a bona fide seniority system or employee benefit plan—such as a retirement, pension, or insurance plan—that is not invoked as a subterfuge to evade the purposes of the ADEA; or (4) the discharge of or discipline of a protected individual was for good cause.[70] Although these defenses are set forth in the ADEA itself, employers should proceed with caution because the courts construe them strictly.

 ## Disability Discrimination

Title I of the Americans with Disabilities Act (ADA) prohibits employers from discriminating against a qualified individual because of a disability in regard to job-application procedures, hiring, advancement, discharge, compensation, job training, and other terms, conditions, and privileges of employment. Such discrimination includes the use of selection criteria to screen out individuals with disabilities unless the criteria are job-related and consistent with business necessity. Even in that event, the employer may not exclude a disabled individual if that individual with some "reasonable accommodation" could perform the essential functions of the position, unless the accommodation would impose an "undue hardship" upon the employer.

The broad scope of the ADA includes preemployment questions and application procedures. The EEOC has indicated that employers may ask questions about reasonable accommodations, though employers are still barred from asking about disabilities or requiring med-

65. Strange v. Nationwide Mut. Ins. Co., 867 F. Supp. 1209 (E.D. Pa. 1994).

66. McKeever v. Ironworker's Dist. Council, No. 96-5858, 1997 U.S. Dist. WL 109569 (E.D. Pa. Mar. 7, 1997).

67. 517 U.S. 308 (1996).68.

68. 29 U.S.C. § 623(f) (1994).

69. Oubre v. Entergy Operations, Inc., 118 S. Ct. 838 (1998).

70. 29 U.S.C. § 623(f) (1994).

ECONOMIC PERSPECTIVE

EFFECT OF DOWNSIZING ON OLDER WORKERS

Companies that have attempted to decrease operating costs by restructuring and downsizing their work forces have primarily used two approaches: voluntary retirement programs and involuntary layoffs. Other companies have encouraged the retirement of older employees to make way for younger, less-expensive workers.

Older workers have borne the brunt of corporate downsizing. Although the companies allege that severance and retirement packages are more humane than layoffs, there is a monetary motive behind them as well. Older workers generally receive higher paychecks; and, even if only a few opt for early retirement, the company payroll may be greatly decreased.

Many workers between the ages of 45 and 65 accept severance packages even though the pension offered is smaller than that they would receive if they were employed until retirement. They do so because they would otherwise have to pay for health insurance, and the prospects of finding another job at their age are poor. It is of little consequence that the severance packages typically require that the recipient forfeit any right to legal remedies for age or other types of discrimination because the benefits they provide are often greater than those obtained from filing a lawsuit; age-discrimination cases are difficult to prove and jury awards are typically small.

One Wall Street firm has been attacked for implementing "Operation Fresh Meat," a campaign that allegedly is designed to replace older workers with younger workers who can be paid much less.[a] Former middle-aged employees of the company claim that the firm was laying off older workers while simultaneously hiring college graduates. None of the employees filed a complaint against the company, however; they waived their right to sue for age discrimination in return for severance packages.

Many companies dispute the fact that older employees are bearing the brunt of corporate downsizings. The Commonwealth Fund, a New York nonprofit organization, conducted a survey among 400 companies in 1991 in which managers stated that older workers were not disproportionately affected by downsizing. They did acknowledge, however, that workers over 55 were often encouraged to accept early retirement.

The American work force is getting older. More than one in eight Americans is over 65, and experts predict that by 2030 one in five will be in that age bracket. In anticipation of this trend, Congress eliminated mandatory retirement to allow employees to work as long as they desire.

However, managers must take steps to eliminate age stereotypes. Some of the myths about older workers are that they are set in their ways, cannot adapt to new situations, and rely on outdated information to make business decisions. Companies are often reluctant to train and promote people over 45, because they feel it is a waste to train and promote someone with perhaps only seven to ten years of employment left.

A number of high-technology firms, including many in Silicon Valley, are lobbying Congress to increase the number of visas available for skilled foreign workers to remedy a claimed critical shortage of engineers and programmers. Yet, a number of older skilled American workers claim that they have been unable to get high-technology jobs, because of companies' erroneous assumptions about older workers and their abilities. In a world that emphasizes the possession of critical knowledge and information, many companies appear to be throwing away valuable resources in discarding or refusing to hire workers with experience, knowledge, and skill.

a. Bruce Caldwell, *Old Before Your Time,* INFO. WK., Sept. 20, 1993, at 30.

---

ical tests that are not a business necessity.[71] The ADA also extends to employee benefit packages.

For example, the EEOC sued Chase Manhattan Corporation in 1997, alleging that the disparity between physical and mental disability benefit packages violated the ADA.[72] Chase Manhattan offered physical-disability benefits until age 65, but terminated mental-disability benefits after 18 months. To date, the U.S. Courts of

71. Asra Q. Nomani, *EEOC Eases Question Limits for Disabled,* WALL ST. J., Oct. 11, 1995, at A5.

72. Glenn Burkins, *Chase Faces Suit over Benefits to Mentally Ill,* WALL ST. J., Sept. 9, 1997, at B6.

Appeal for the Sixth and Seventh Circuits have rejected the EEOC's assertion that distinctions between mental and physical disabilities violate the ADA. Nonetheless, Israel Discount Bank of New York settled a similar case in 1998 by agreeing to provide the same benefits to employees with mental conditions as those provided to employees with physical conditions.[73]

Enforcement and Remedies

Title I of the ADA is enforced in the same manner as Title VII of the Civil Rights Act of 1964. Thus, the Equal Employment Opportunity Commission initially investigates claims of discrimination and may sue to enforce Title I's provisions. If the individual receives a right-to-sue letter, the complaining applicant or employee may sue and obtain the same remedies available under Title VII, including back pay, reinstatement or hiring, and attorney's fees and costs. Compensatory and punitive damages are subject to the same caps as those applicable to discrimination based on sex or religion. Disability-related claims now account for about 20% of all discrimination charges filed by the EEOC, which has significantly increased the agency's caseload.[74] Despite such difficulties, the EEOC has successfully litigated many cases, including a $5.5 million jury award, the largest award under the ADA to date.[75]

Impermissible Discrimination

The ADA codifies existing judicial analysis of what constitutes impermissible discrimination. Under the ADA, employers are prohibited from intentionally discriminating against disabled persons and from engaging in employment practices that are not intentionally discriminatory, but have the effect of discriminating against disabled persons or perpetuating the past effects of such discrimination. The term "discriminate" as construed by the ADA includes the following prohibited practices:

1. Limiting, segregating, or classifying an applicant or employee because of his or her disability so as to adversely affect his or her opportunities or status;

2. Entering into a contractual relationship with an employment or referral agency, union, or other organization that has the effect of subjecting employees or applicants with a disability to prohibited discrimination;

3. Utilizing standards, criteria, or methods of administration that have the effect of discriminating or perpetuating the effects of discrimination because of disability;

4. Denying equal job benefits to a qualified individual because of the known disability of a person with whom the qualified individual is known to have a relationship or association;

5. Not making reasonable accommodations to the known physical or mental limitations of an otherwise qualified employee or applicant with a disability unless to do so would impose undue hardship on the employer;

6. Denying job opportunities to an otherwise qualified employee or applicant with a disability in order to avoid having to make reasonable accommodations for that disability;

7. Using qualification standards or employment tests that tend to screen out individuals with disabilities, unless the qualification standards or employment tests are shown to be job-related and are consistent with business necessity; and

8. Failing to select and conduct job testing in such a way as to ensure that when the test is administered to an applicant or employee with a disability that impairs his or her sensory, manual, or speaking skills, the results of the test accurately reflect the skills or aptitude that test is designed to measure, rather than reflecting the sensory, manual, or speaking impairment.

Definition of Disability

The ADA codifies existing law developed under the Vocational Rehabilitation Act of 1973 by defining a "person with a disability" as (1) a person with a physical or mental impairment that substantially limits one or more of that person's major life activities, (2) a person with a record of a physical or mental impairment that substantially limits one or more of that person's major life activities, or (3) a person who is regarded as having such an impairment. Because "working" is included among the "major life activities," any impairment that limits the individual's ability to work, or that

---

73. *Bank's Accord with EEOC Eliminates Distinctions in Long-Term Disability Plans*, 66 U.S.L.W. 2519 (Mar. 3, 1998).

74. Lisa J. Stansky, *Opening Doors*, ABA J., Mar. 1996, at 66.

75. *Federal Jury Hands Victory to the EEOC in Disabilities Case*, WALL ST. J., Jan. 7, 1997, at B10.

the employer perceives as limiting those abilities, is considered a disability.

The first prong of the ADA's definition of a disability is functional; that is, it focuses upon how and to what extent the individual is impaired. This has lead to considerable confusion and conflicting outcomes. One example is the status of cancer as a disability. The U.S. Court of Appeals for the Fifth Circuit has ruled that a woman with breast cancer who was discharged from her job after undergoing radiation treatments for breast cancer was not disabled.[76] The court held that she had a physical impairment, but that none of her major life activities were limited. The serious side effects of her treatment were not sufficient to trigger protection under the ADA. The U.S. Court of Appeals for the Eleventh Circuit came to a similar conclusion.[77] By contrast, the Federal District Court for the Southern District of New York held that an individual discharged while diagnosed with cancer and undergoing chemotherapy was disabled under the ADA due to his cancer-related hospitalizations.[78]

Another example of judicial conflict is in determining what constitutes a major life activity. The U.S. Supreme Court resolved a split in the circuits when it ruled in *Bragdon v. Abbott*[79] that reproduction is a major life activity, rejecting the Eighth Circuit's holding to the contrary.[80]

In terms of work performance, courts have given employers greater leeway. For example, the U.S. Court of Appeals for the Seventh Circuit ruled that an employee who was discharged due to low performance immediately following a heart attack was not protected under the ADA, because the employment decision was based only upon reasons related to the disability, not the disability itself.[81]

Although the definition of a disability under the ADA is relatively vague, the statute does clearly exclude many things. For example, the ADA specifically excludes homosexuality, bisexuality, sexual-behavior disorders, compulsive gambling, kleptomania, and pyromania from the definition of a disability. Psychoactive-substance-use disorders resulting from current illegal use of drugs, including the use of alcohol in the workplace against the employer's policies, are also excluded from the ADA's definition of a disability. The ADA also amends the Vocational Rehabilitation Act of 1973 to be consistent with these provisions. Although "current use" is not specifically defined in the statute, it has been interpreted to include drug use weeks or months before discharge.[82] However, an employee or applicant who is no longer engaged in the illegal use of drugs or alcohol on the work site, but who is involved in or has completed a supervised rehabilitation program, may be regarded as a disabled person. Also, although an individual may not be fired on the basis of his or her alcoholism, an employer may discharge the person based upon behavior related to the alcoholism.[83]

The third prong of the definition of a disability is based on the notion that societal stereotypes and prejudice may constrain individuals with disabilities more than their actual limitation. *School Board of Nassau County v. Arline*[84] is a landmark decision because it is the first time the Supreme Court explained the significance of the "regarded as" prong of the definition of a handicap. The Court held that a teacher was handicapped due to her infection with tuberculosis and as a result of the Board's action regarding her as disabled. The Court reasoned that "the contagious effects of a disease cannot be meaningfully distinguished from the physical effects on a claimant." As a result, an employer may not discriminate against an individual based on the effects of a disease on others because their reactions may be based upon stereotypes, misinformation, and long-held misconceptions of handicapped individuals. The Court noted that "Congress acknowledged that society's accumulated myths and fears about disability and disease are as handicapping as are the physical limitations that flow from actual impairment." Thus, the reactions of others may be as limiting, if not more so, than the individual's handicap.

Although *Arline* was initiated under the Vocational Rehabilitation Act of 1973, the precursor to the ADA, it is considered a seminal case articulating how individuals may be "regarded as" disabled, whether or not they actually have a disability. In the context of the

---

76. Ellison v. Software Spectrum Inc., 85 F.3d 187 (5th Cir. 1996).

77. Gordon. v. E.L. Hamm & Assocs. Inc., 100 F.3d 907 (11th Cir. 1996), *cert. denied*, 118 S. Ct. 630 (1997).

78. Mark v. Burke Rehabilitation Hosp., No. 94-3596, 1997 U.S. Dist. WL 189124 (S.D.N.Y. Apr. 17, 1997).

79. Bragdon v. Abbott, 118 S Ct. 2196 (1998) (Case 13.5).

80. Krauel v. Iowa Methodist Med. Ctr., 95 F.3d 674 (8th Cir. 1996).

81. Matthews. v. Commonwealth Edison Co., 128 F.3d 1194 (7th Cir. 1997).

82. Shafer v. Preston Mem'l Hosp. Corp., 107 F.3d 274 (4th Cir. 1997).

83. James Podgers, *Disability and DUIs: ADA Claims by Fired or Demoted Alcoholic Employees Fail*, ABA J., Feb. 1996, at 46.

84. 480 U.S. 273 (1987).

ADA, *Arline* stands for the proposition that an employer's prejudice, stereotypes, or misconceptions of a disability may be the source of nondiscrimination protection.

Obesity as a Disability   State and federal courts are grappling with the issue of whether obesity should be considered a disability and thus protected from discrimination by employers. Plaintiffs have advocated two types of claims: (1) obesity is a physical disorder that severely limits their major life activities, and (2) the individual is regarded as disabled due to his or her obesity. In 1993, the U.S. Court of Appeals for the First Circuit ruled that the Rehabilitation Act protected obese people from employment discrimination as a result of a perceived disability.[85] By contrast, other courts have rejected claims that individuals may be regarded as disabled as a result of their weight. The U.S. Court of Appeals for the Fourth Circuit ruled that the EEOC regulations indicate that obesity should be recognized as a disability only in rare circumstances and denied the plaintiff's claim.[86] A district court in Virginia came to a similar conclusion in denying a claim by a former state trooper that she was wrongly perceived as disabled when she was forced to work as a dispatcher after she exceeded the applicable weight requirements.[87]

Reasonable Accommodation

The ADA requires that employers make reasonable accommodations to an employee's disability, as long as doing so does not cause the employer "undue hardship." Thus, even if a disability precluded an individual from performing the essential functions of the position, or presented a safety risk, the employer is required to assess whether there is a reasonable accommodation that will permit the individual to be employed despite his or her disability. Title I sets forth a nonexhaustive list of what might constitute "reasonable accommodation," including the following: (1) making work facilities accessible; (2) restructuring jobs or modifying work schedules; (3) acquiring or modifying equipment or devices; (4) modifying examinations, training materials, or policies; and (5) providing quali-

fied readers or interpreters or other similar accommodations for individuals with disabilities.

The extent to which an employer is required to accommodate an individual with a disability is an evolving area of the law. Courts have not been receptive to claims that a reasonable accommodation includes transferring the individual to a new supervisor.[88] The courts are split on the question of whether an employer is required to reassign a disabled employee to a new job if the employee is not qualified, even with reasonable accommodation, for the job he or she currently holds or from which he or she was terminated.[89] However, reassignment can be used as a means of accommodating a disabled employee when accommodating the employee in the current position is possible but difficult for the employer.

A minimum requirement seems to be that employers are required to discuss with a disabled employee potential accommodations and should not make unilateral decisions regarding the adequacy of potential accommodations.[90] However, a plaintiff in a disability-discrimination lawsuit bears the burden of producing evidence that accommodations exist and that such accommodations would be reasonable.[91]

Studies indicate that most accommodations required under the ADA are generally inexpensive. One study analyzed the reasonable accommodations provided to employees of Sears, Roebuck & Company and found that nearly three-quarters were made at no cost.[92] In terms of the accommodations that were formally requested, the average cost was $45.20 for 71 individuals,[93] much less than the $1,800–$2,400 per employee the company spends in terminating and rehiring employees.[94] Although other studies have found more expensive estimates, most accommodations still cost less than $500.[95] The fear that the ADA

85. Cook v. Rhode Island Dept. of Mental Health, 10 F.3d 17 (1st Cir. 1993).

86. Torcasio v. Murray, 57 F.3d 1340 (4th Cir. 1995).

87. Smaw v. Virginia, 862 F. Supp. 1469 (E.D. Va. 1994).

88. Frances A. McMorris, *Employee's Transfer Plea Rejected in Another Disabilities-Act Ruling*, WALL ST. J., Jan. 21, 1997, at B5.

89. *Compare* Smith v. Midland Brake, Inc., 138 F.3d 1304 (10th Cir. 1998) *with* Bultemeyer v. Fort Wayne Community Schls., 100 F.3d 1281 (7th Cir. 1996).

90. Bultemeyer v. Fort Wayne Community Schls., 100 F.3d 1281 (7th Cir. 1996).

91. Willis v. Conopco Inc., 108 F.3d 282 (11th Cir. 1997).

92. Francine Schwadel, *Sears Sets Model for Compliance with Disabilities Act, Study Says*, WALL ST. J., Mar. 4, 1996, at B5.

93. Terry Carter, *Unhappy to Oblige*, ABA J., July 1997, at 36.

94. Schwadel, *supra* note 92.

95. Lisa J. Stansky, *Opening Doors*, ABA J., Mar. 1996, at 67.

would be inordinately expensive to businesses has not materialized.

Undue Hardship   A reasonable accommodation is not required if it would impose an undue hardship on the employer. The ADA defines "undue hardship" to mean an activity requiring significant difficulty or expense when considered in light of (1) the nature and cost of the accommodation needed; (2) the overall financial resources of the facility, the number of persons employed at the facility, the effect on expenses and resources, or any other impact of the accommodation on the facility; (3) the overall financial resources of the employer and the overall size of the business with respect to the number of employees and the type, number, and location of its facilities; and (4) the type of operation of the employer including the composition, structure, and functions of the workforce, the geographic separateness, and administrative or fiscal relationship of the facility in question to the employer.

One example of an accommodation that was deemed unreasonable involved an employee with various mental impairments that made it impossible for him to work in an unduly stressful environment. The employee asked for a transfer out of the stressful work environment and later sued when the employer did not honor his request. The U.S. Court of Appeals for the Third Circuit ruled that transferring the employee away from the stressful work environment was not a reasonable accommodation because it would impose extraordinary administrative costs on the employer.[96]

Permissible Exclusion

If an applicant or employee is disabled, he or she may be excluded from the employment opportunity only if, by reason of the disability, he or she (with or without reasonable accommodation) cannot perform the essential functions of the job or if the employment of the individual poses a significant risk to the health or safety to others. In determining whether a job function is essential, the ADA requires that consideration be given to the employer's judgment as to what functions are essential, but also looks to any written job description prepared *before* advertising or interviewing for the job

commenced. The applicant or employee does not have to prove his or her ability to perform all the functions of the job, only the essential functions.[97]

EEOC regulations issued in 1991 state that the risk of injury applies if there is risk to others or the disabled employee. However, the risk of injury must be a probability of substantial harm under the person's current condition for it to be used to deny a job due to risk of future injury. Also, employers cannot rely on their own physician's opinion; risk of injury must be based upon generally accepted medical opinion. For example, the U.S. Court of Appeals for the Sixth Circuit ruled that a hospital acted lawfully when it laid off an HIV-positive surgical technician after concluding that he posed a direct threat to the health and safety of others. His job included, on an infrequent basis, engaging in invasive, exposure-prone activities, such as inserting his fingers into a patient's incision during surgery.[98] The presence of sharp instruments on which the technician could prick his hand increased the risk of HIV transmission.

HIV Discrimination

A major issue today is the employer's relationship with an employee who has HIV disease, that is, an individual who has been infected with the human immunodeficiency virus (HIV). Due to recent advances in drug treatments, more individuals are living healthy, productive lives while infected with HIV. This is called asymptomatic HIV disease. When an individual's immune system is compromised and the person becomes ill due to HIV-related complications, the individual is considered symptomatic. Acquired Immune Deficiency Syndrome (AIDS) refers to the most serious stage of symptomatic HIV disease.

Although the ADA does not specifically list HIV disease as a disability, legislative history, EEOC regulations, and many courts have considered HIV disease to be a disability. Under the Vocational Rehabilitation Act of 1973, AIDS was deemed a protected handicap. The following case addressed the issue of whether asymptomatic HIV-positive individuals are disabled within the meaning of the ADA.[99]

---

96. Gaul v. Lucent Techs., Inc., 134 F.3d 576 (3d Cir. 1998).

97. Deane v. Pocono Medical Ctr., 142 F.3d 138 (3d Cir. 1998) (*en banc*).

98. Estate of Mauro v. Borgess Medical Ctr., 137 F.3d 398 (6th Cir. 1998).

99. John Gibeaut, *Filling a Need*, ABA J., July 1997, at 48.

A CASE IN POINT	**SUMMARY**

CASE 13.5
BRAGDON v. ABBOTT
Supreme Court of
the United States
118 S. Ct. 2196 (1998).

FACTS   In September 1994, Sidney Abbott scheduled an appointment with her dentist, Dr. Randon Bragdon. Abbott noted on her patient registration form that she was HIV-positive. She was asymptomatic at the time. When Bragdon discovered a cavity, he told Abbott that he would fill her cavity only in a hospital, rather than in his office. Bragdon would charge no extra fee, though Abbott would have to bear the costs of the hospital facilities. Abbott refused and filed suit under the ADA alleging discrimination on the basis of a disability, HIV infection, in a place of public accommodation, a dentist's office. The district court granted summary judgment for Abbott, concluding that the procedure could safely be performed in Bragdon's office. The appeals court affirmed, and Bragdon appealed.

ISSUE PRESENTED   Is an asymptomatic HIV-positive woman disabled for purposes of the ADA?

SUMMARY OF OPINION   The U.S. Supreme Court ruled that Abbott was disabled under the first prong of the definition of a disability. The Court found that infection with HIV constituted a physiological disorder with a constant and detrimental effect on the infected person's hemic and lymphatic systems from the moment of infection.

This physical impairment substantially limited the major life activity of reproduction. The Court reasoned that "Reproduction and the sexual dynamics surrounding it are central to the life process itself." The Court rejected Bragdon's attempt to limit the phrase "major life activity" to those aspects of a person's life that have a public, economic, or daily character.

Although the HIV infection did not make it impossible for Abbott to reproduce, it substantially limited her ability to reproduce by (1) imposing on the man a significant risk of becoming infected, and (2) creating a risk that the child would be infected during gestation and childbirth. The Court noted testimony that Abbott had foregone a family and children due to the risk of HIV transmission. These statements provided the necessary nexus between the physical impairment of HIV disease and the major life activity of reproduction.

The Court acknowledged that Bragdon could have refused to treat Abbott if her infectious condition posed a direct threat to the health or safety of others. A direct threat is a significant risk that cannot be eliminated by a modification of policies, practices, or procedures. The risk assessment must be based on medical or other objective evidence. Even if a health care professional believes in good faith that a significant risk exists, he or she will still be liable for refusing to provide treatment if the court objectively determines that the belief is not reasonable.

RESULT   The appeals court's determination that asymptomatic HIV infection is a disability was affirmed, but the case was remanded to determine whether there was an objective, scientific basis for Bragdon's belief that filling the cavity in his office posed a significant risk of transmission.

COMMENTS   The Court's analysis in *Bragdon* would appear to be relevant to cases involving a far more prevalent issue, namely, whether individuals who have medical conditions that are either in remission or alleviated with medication, such as cancer, diabetes, and high blood pressure, are disabled for purposes of the ADA. Given the court's approach in *Bragdon*, is it more or less likely than before that the Court would treat diseases in remission or controlled by medication as disabilities?

In the context of HIV disease, courts have narrowly construed the direct-threat exception in accordance with medical evidence that HIV cannot be transmitted through casual contact. Thus, only those professions that could lead to the transmission of bodily fluids, such as health-care workers, are given closer analysis under the direct-threat exception.

The ADA includes a special provision that employers may discriminate against individuals with contagious diseases in food-handling positions. The secretary of health and human services was directed to publish a list of infectious and communicable diseases; HIV was not included. Nonetheless, the U.S. Court of Appeals for the Sixth Circuit held that a grocery store could require a produce clerk who said that he was HIV-positive to undergo a physical examination to verify his condition.[100]

Dealing with HIV Disease in the Workplace An employer cannot justify discrimination against a person with AIDS on the basis of coworker or customer preference. Similarly, the fact that the employment of someone with AIDS will increase group health insurance costs or cause absenteeism does not make discrimination permissible. In 1993, the EEOC issued guidelines suggesting that disability-based distinctions in employer-provided health insurance programs violate the ADA except under extremely narrow circumstances.

Additionally, many states recognize either a common law or constitutional right to privacy. This protects individuals from improper communication of their HIV status, even though the information is true and was properly obtained for a specific purpose. Communication of such personal information might be protected by the qualified-privilege defense as long as it is confined only to those people who have a legitimate need to know. General communication of someone's HIV status among coworkers is probably not protected by the privilege. Statutes prohibiting disclosure of medical information, specifically HIV-related information, may also be a source of employer liability. Thus, HIV-related information should be kept in confidence among individuals who need to know.

The employer also runs the risk of being sued for libel or slander if careless statements are made about employees. For example, falsely accusing an employee of being gay or of having AIDS could be grounds for a slander action (if the accusation is oral) or a libel action (if the accusation is in writing). Truth, however, is a complete defense to a libel or slander action.

An increasingly popular means of protecting against such a dilemma is to have an HIV-education program for all employees. Several employers, especially larger corporations, have aggressively developed and utilized such programs. They show videotapes, circulate pamphlets and articles in employee newsletters, and invite medical professionals to give presentations. They strive to give employees accurate medical information about how HIV is transmitted, to assure employees that the employer is not going to discriminate against an employee infected with HIV, and to assure all employees that attention will be given to their health needs.

Genetic Discrimination

The Council for Responsible Genetics, a bioethics group based in Cambridge, Massachusetts, estimates that at least 200 people have suffered employment discrimination based on genetic information. For example, a job applicant who mentioned to the interviewer that her father had Huntington's disease, a fatal genetic disorder, was told that the company would not hire her because it could not afford the 50–50 chance that she, too, might develop Huntington's.[101] University of Washington professor Phil Bereano argues that using genetic tests to predict who will get sick creates a class of people who are considered "damaged goods," making them especially vulnerable to discrimination by employers and insurers.[102]

Approximately 18 states have enacted privacy laws to eliminate genetic discrimination by insurers and employers. In 1996, Congress passed legislation prohibiting group health plans from using information obtained from genetic tests as a basis for denying or limiting coverage or for charging more for coverage. Although having an asymptomatic genetic defect would not appear to limit a major life activity under the ADA, President Clinton has proposed to Congress legislation to ban genetic discrimination.[103]

---

100. EEOC v. Prevo's Family Market Inc., 135 F. 3d 1089 (6th Cir. 1998).

101. Carol Smith, *Other Perspectives: Some Cases of Genetic Discrimination*, SAN FRANCISCO SUNDAY EXAMINER & CHRON., Feb. 22, 1998, at CL 15.

102. *Id.*

103. *White House Warns of Misuses of Genetic Tests: Call to Congress to Protect Workers from Potential Bias*, SAN FRANCISCO CHRON., Jan. 20, 1998, at A3.

Sexual-Orientation Discrimination

Discrimination in employment based on sexual orientation is not barred by Title VII or other federal laws, but is prohibited by many local and several state statutes. Legislation to amend Title VII to include sexual orientation has been introduced in every term of Congress since 1975, but was not passed. In 1997, the Employment Nondiscrimination Act (ENDA), which would have prohibited employment-related discrimination on the basis of sexual orientation, fell one vote short of passing the Senate. Congressional studies of such nondiscrimination laws indicate that they would not significantly increase bias complaints.[104]

Seven states presently prohibit discrimination on the basis of sexual orientation. In these states, gay and lesbian employees who are fired because of their sexual orientation may bring wrongful-termination suits under state law. In a 1991 California case, Shell Oil Company and its subsidiary Triton Biosciences were ordered to pay $5.3 million in back pay and damages to a gay executive who was fired solely because he was gay.[105] The executive had been with Shell for 19 years and had received consistently high work performance evaluations. When Shell accidentally discovered he was gay, it fired him, refused to pay earned bonuses and other benefits, and later shared the executive's sexual orientation with prospective employers and agencies. A California court found Shell and Triton guilty of outrageous conduct and intentional infliction of emotional distress.

Some states have attempted to prevent such statewide nondiscrimination protections. In Colorado, an initiative narrowly passed that would have repealed existing gay-rights ordinances in three cities and prevented future legislation protecting individuals from discrimination on the basis of sexual orientation. However, in 1996, the U.S. Supreme Court struck down the Colorado voter initiative, arguing that it violated the Equal Protection Clause of the Fourteenth Amendment on its face because it singled out and imposed special disadvantages upon one population, nonheterosexuals.[106]

---

104. *Gay Rights Legislation Would Not Cause Surge of Bias Complaints, GAO Reports,* 66 U.S.L.W. 2280 (Nov. 11, 1997).

105. Collins v. Shell Oil Co., 56 Fair Empl. Prac. Cas. (BNA) 440 (Cal. App. Dep't Super. Ct. 1991).

106. Romer v. Evans, 517 U.S. 620 (1996).

> ### AT THE TOP
>
> An employee tends to take her cue from the conduct of her employer. For example, if the employer discriminates in its hiring, retention, and promotion policies, the employee may be more likely to believe that like conduct is acceptable. The employee may take this as an indication of not only how she can but how she should act in the workplace.

In order to attract the most talented employees, many corporations have adopted domestic-partnership policies. Domestic partners are same-sex partners of an employee to whom benefits, such as health insurance, are extended. Municipalities and universities have also adopted such policies. Although this may enable a company to stay competitive in hiring, it may present unique issues. For example, in 1993, the Williamson County (Texas) commissioners voted three-to-two to deny tax breaks worth $750,000 to Apple Computer because of Apple's domestic-partners policy, citing the high moral and family values of their community. The debate prior to the vote included much anti-gay sentiment and suggestions that a yes vote would bring homosexuals and AIDS to Williamson County. However, one week later the commission reversed its decision in another three-to-two vote. Political, economic, and public pressure, rather than a change of heart, seemed to have motivated the change in decision.

 ## Affirmative Action

Affirmative-action programs are generally viewed as a means to remedy past acts of discrimination. Such programs are usually established pursuant to court orders, court-approved consent decrees, or federal and state laws that impose affirmative-action obligations on government contractors.

Executive Order 11246 requires federal government contractors to include in every government contract not exempted by the order a provision that states that the contractor will not discriminate in employment on the basis of race, color, religion, sex, or national origin, and that the contractor agrees to take affirmative steps to prevent discrimination.[107] In some cases, a contractor's affirmative-action plan must be put in writing. Although individuals have no private right of action based on an alleged violation of the order, the Department of Labor, through its Office of Federal Contract Compliance Programs, has a wide range of sanctions available to it. These sanctions include, for example, suspending or terminating a government contract and disqualifying the contractor from entering any future government contracts.

Government contractors are subject to affirmative-action obligations under other federal laws as well. For example, Section 503 of the Vocational Rehabilitation Act of 1973 requires employers with government contracts or subcontracts of more than $2,500 to employ qualified disabled persons and to take affirmative action with respect to such individuals. Similarly, the Vietnam Era Veterans' Readjustment Assistance Act of 1972 requires employers with federal contracts or subcontracts of $10,000 or more to take affirmative action to employ and to advance in employment disabled Vietnam-era veterans.

As explained in Chapter 2, the U.S. Supreme Court, in *Adarand Constructors, Inc. v. Pena*,[108] applied its most rigorous judicial scrutiny to affirmative-action programs by requiring the government to provide a compelling interest that is accomplished through narrowly tailored means. The Court, in reinstating a reverse-discrimination claim by a white-owned construction company that lost a contract to a minority-owned business, held that benign and invidious racial classifications should be subject to the same standards. This was a significant ruling because it required the government to show a specific history of discrimination in order to justify preferential treatment of minority-owned businesses in government contracts.

In response to *Adarand*, the Department of Justice embarked on an ambitious program reassessing minority set-aside programs.[109] Beneficiaries of the program will be more closely scrutinized, but the centerpiece of the initiative is to construct an evidentiary basis for affirmative action by documenting any history of discrimination faced by racial minorities in specific industries. The analysis will determine the percentage of minority-owned firms that are awarded government contracts in 80 industries and compare this to the total number of minority-owned firms in that industry.[110] If the difference between the two figures is large enough, this will be presented as evidence of discrimination and will justify the implementation of flexible benchmarks that identify targets, rather than rigid quotas, for contract dispersal. When the disparity between the total number of firms and the number of government contracts they win decreases, the Department of Commerce will eliminate the benchmarks.

The U.S. Court of Appeals for the District of Columbia Circuit struck down in 1998 the Federal Communications Commission's affirmative action requirements for radio and television broadcast licenses.[111] The court held that *Adarand*'s requirement of strict scrutiny applied not just to racial preferences in hiring but to any race-conscious decision making that affects employment opportunities even if it does not establish preferences, quotas, or set asides. The court explained:

> [W]e do not think it matters whether a government hiring program imposes hard quotas, soft quotas, or goals. Any one of these techniques induces an employer to hire with an eye toward meeting the numerical target. As such, they can and surely will result in individuals being granted a preference because of their race.

The court also held that the FCC's interest in fostering diverse programming was not compelling. Even if the diversity goal could be deemed a compelling state interest, the court concluded that the FCC's equal employment opportunity rules were not narrowly tailored to foster diverse programming.

Although government programs have been struck down by the courts, some affirmative-action programs by private employers have been accepted. For example, the Court upheld a collective-bargaining agreement between a union and a company that contained an affirmative-action plan giving preference to African-American

---

107. Executive Order No. 11246, 3 C.F.R. § 339 (1964–1965), *reprinted in* 42 U.S.C. § 2000e (1994).

108. 515 U.S. 200 (1995).

109. *Affirmative Action Changes Unveiled by Justice Department*, 64 U.S.L.W. 2737 (May 28, 1996).

110. Rochelle Sharpe, *Who Benefits?: Asian-Americans Gain Sharply in Big Program of Affirmative Action*, WALL ST. J., Sept. 9, 1997, at A1.

111. Lutheran Church–Missouri Synod v. Federal Communications Commission, 141 F.3d 344 (D.C. Cir 1998).

employees entering into skilled-craft training positions.[112] Concluding that Title VII did not preclude all private, voluntary, race-conscious affirmative-action programs, the Court noted that the plan (1) like Title VII, was designed to break down patterns of racial segregation and hierarchy; (2) "did not unnecessarily trammel the interests of white employees"; and (3) was a temporary measure intended to attain rather than maintain racial balance. The EEOC has promulgated regulations regarding voluntary affirmative-action plans.[113]

In *Taxman v. Board of Education*,[114] the U.S. Court of Appeals for the Third Circuit struck down, as a violation of Title VII, a school board's affirmative-action plan. The plan gave preference to minority teachers over nonminority teachers in lay-off decisions when teachers were equally qualified. The court read *United Steelworkers v. Weber* to permit race-based employment decisions only when it is necessary to remedy past discrimination. A mere desire to promote diversity in education was not sufficient to warrant a discriminatory policy. The U.S. Supreme Court granted the petition for *certiorari* and heard oral arguments; but, before it ruled, the parties settled the case. Several civil rights groups feared that the Supreme Court would use this case as an occasion to ban all affirmative-action programs, so they contributed the bulk of the money paid in settlement.

The Civil Rights Act of 1991 limited the ability of persons to challenge affirmative-action litigated judgments and consent decrees. A person cannot challenge a judgment or consent decree if any of the following three conditions is applicable: (1) the person had actual notice of the proposed judgment or order sufficient to let that person know that the judgment or decree might adversely affect the interests and legal rights of that person, and had an opportunity to present objections; (2) the person had a reasonable opportunity to present objections to the judgment or order; or (3) the person's interests were adequately represented by another person who had previously challenged the judgment or order on the same legal grounds and with a similar factual situation.

 ## Civil Rights Act of 1991

This chapter describes, in context, many of the provisions and effects of the Civil Rights Act of 1991. Other provisions not yet covered are discussed below.

The act overturns *Lorance v. AT&T Technologies*[115] by providing that a seniority system adopted for an intentionally discriminatory purpose can be challenged under Title VII when the seniority system is adopted, when an individual becomes subject to the system, or when a person aggrieved is injured by the application of the seniority system.

The act provides that Title VII and the Americans with Disabilities Act, like the Age Discrimination in Employment Act, apply to U.S. citizens employed in foreign countries by American-owned or controlled companies unless compliance with Title VII or the ADA would cause the employer to violate the law of the foreign country in which it is located.

The act expanded the categories for which compensatory and punitive damages could be recovered to include intentional religious, disability, and sex discrimination. Under prior law, recovery of damages was limited to victims of intentional racial or ethnic bias.

The act banned so-called *race norming of employment tests*, which is a device designed to ensure that a minimum number of minorities and women are in the application pool. The act prohibits an employer, in connection with the selection or referral of applicants or candidates for employment or promotion, from adjusting the scores of, using different cutoff scores for, or otherwise altering the results of, employment-related tests on the basis of race, color, religion, sex, or national origin.

The act includes, as Title II, the Glass Ceiling Act of 1991. In its findings and purposes section, this act states that "(1) despite a dramatically growing presence in the workplace, women and minorities remain underrepresented in management and decision-making positions in business; (2) artificial barriers exist to the advancement of women and minorities in the workplace." The act established a Glass Ceiling Commission to study and make recommendations concerning elimination of artificial barriers to advancement and increas-

112. United Steelworkers of America v. Weber, 443 U.S. 193 (1979).

113. *See* 29 C.F.R. § 1608.1–12 (1997).

114. 91 F.3d 1547 (1996) (*en banc*); Eva M. Rodriguez, *Rights Group's Settlement Settles Little*, WALL ST. J., Nov. 24, 1997, at A3.

115. 490 U.S. 900 (1989) (holding that the period for filing a challenge began with the date the system was adopted).

ing opportunities and development experiences of women and minorities to foster advancement to management and decision-making positions in business.

Family and Medical Leave Act of 1993

The Family and Medical Leave Act of 1993[116] has a number of specific and rather straightforward guidelines regarding employee eligibility and employer obligations. The employee must have worked at the place of employment for at least 12 months and have completed at least 1,250 hours of service to the employer during that 12-month period to be eligible for a family leave.

The act applies only to employers with 50 or more employees at work sites within 75 miles of each other. Part-time employees are excluded from the act's coverage and are not be counted in calculating the 50 employees necessary for an employer to be covered by the act.

Eligible employees are entitled to 12 weeks of unpaid leave per year. There are four situations in which an employee may use leave under the act: (1) the birth of a child; (2) the placement of an adopted or foster-care child with the employee; (3) care of a child, a parent, or a spouse; or (4) a serious health condition that renders the employee unable to do his or her job.

An employee cannot contract out of his or her right to leave time under this act. However, the employer may require, or an employee may choose, to substitute any or all accrued paid leave for the leave time that is now provided for under this act. The act should be considered a floor, not a ceiling, to what employers can provide their employees in terms of a leave option. Even if employers provide for more generous leave provisions, however, they must provide employees with notice regarding the consequences of taking the extra leave.[117]

Finally, an important aspect of the act is that it requires the employer to restore the employee to the same position, or one with equivalent benefits, pay, and other terms and conditions of employment, following the expiration of the leave. Unfortunately, studies indicate that many companies are not complying with the law.[118] A significant minority of businesses either are not guaranteeing the jobs of people who take leaves or are not providing health benefits during the leave. Many more companies provide for no appeals process and do not have formal written policies regarding the FLMA.

To vindicate one's rights under the FMLA, a plaintiff may sue both the employer and his or her supervisor individually.[119] This interpretation is distinctive because a supervisor cannot be sued in his or her individual capacity under Title VII, the ADEA, or the ADA.

Mandatory Arbitration of Employment Disputes

A key issue in employment law today is the enforceability of agreements to arbitrate future discrimination claims. Employees often prefer to go to court where they are entitled to extensive discovery, witnesses of their own choosing, and possible punitive damages.

In *Alexander v. Gardner-Denver Co.*[120] the U.S. Supreme Court struck down an arbitration clause in a collective bargaining agreement, holding that arbitration cannot provide an adequate substitute for a judicial proceeding in protecting federal statutory rights under Title VII. Yet in 1991, the Supreme Court held in *Gilmer v. Interstate/Johnson Lane Corp.*[121] that brokerage employees who had signed individual agreements to arbitrate could be required to arbitrate age discrimination claims under the Age Discrimination in Employment Act. It is not yet clear what effect, if any, passage of the Older Workers Benefit Protection Act will have on this matter. The act requires all waivers, including potentially a waiver of the right to a jury trial, to be made knowingly and voluntarily.

116. Pub. L. No. 103-3, 107 Stat. 6 (1993) (codified at 5 U.S.C. § 6381 *et seq.* and 29 U.S.C. § 2601 *et seq.*).

117. Fry v. First Fidelity Bancoporation, No. 95-6019, 1996 U.S. Dist., WL 36910 (E.D. Pa. Jan. 30, 1996).

118. *Family-Leave Compliance Is Falling Short*, WALL ST. J., Mar. 16, 1994, at B1.

119. Freeman v. Foley, 911 F. Supp. 326 (N.D. Ill. 1995).

120. 415 U.S. 36 (1974). Notwithstanding this precedent and contrary to seven other circuits, the U.S. Court of Appeals for the Fourth Circuit concluded in 1997 that *Gardner-Denver* was no longer the law and held that employees could be compelled to submit claims under the Americans with Disabilities Act and Title VII to binding arbitration pursuant to a collective bargaining agreement. The Supreme Court has granted *certiorari* in this case. Wright v. Universal Maritime Serv. Corp., 121 F.3d 702 (4th Cir. 1997) (table), *cert. granted*, 118 S. Ct. 1162 (1998).

121. 500 U.S. 20 (1991).

The U.S. Court of Appeals for the First Circuit enforced a voluntary, prospective agreement with the employer to arbitrate all claims under the Americans with Disabilities Act (ADA).[122] Similarly, the Fifth Circuit enforced an arbitration clause applicable to ADA claims to which the employee had agreed at a performance review.[123]

The U.S. Court of Appeals for the Ninth Circuit held in 1994 that employees who do not "knowingly" agree to arbitrate Title VII claims cannot be required to submit those claims to arbitration.[124] The Ninth Circuit went a step further in 1998 and held in *Duffield v. Robertson Stephens & Co.*[125] that employers may not require employees to waive their right to a jury trial for future Title VII claims as a condition of employment. The court ruled that a securities trader at investment banking firm Robertson Stephens & Company could litigate her claims of sex discrimination and sexual harassment in court even though she, like all broker-dealer employees, had signed an agreement to submit all employment-related disputes to binding arbitration.

The court based its decision on the Civil Rights Act of 1991, which gave employees the right to a jury trail and encouraged the parties, "where appropriate and to the extent authorized by law," to pursue alternative dispute resolution, including arbitration, to resolve their Title VII disputes.[126] The court analyzed the legislative history and concluded that "Congress intended to adopt *Gardner-Denver*'s firm rule precluding enforcement of compulsory agreements to arbitrate future Title VII claims, not *Gilmer*'s possible validation of such agreements." The court did appear willing to enforce knowing and voluntary agreements to arbitrate Title VII claims that employers and employees enter into after a dispute has arisen.

The Third Circuit expressly rejected the Ninth Circuit's *Duffield* analysis, after finding nothing in the Civil Rights Act of 1991 to suggest that Congress intended, by implication, to repeal the Federal Arbitration Act as applied to Title VII claims.[127] The Third Circuit also concluded that nothing in the Older Workers Benefit Protection Act of 1990 precludes mandatory arbitration of ADEA claims.

There is now a split in the circuits on the enforceability of compulsory arbitration clauses as applied to Title VII claims.[128] The Supreme Court has espoused in other contexts (including claims under the federal securities laws) a "liberal federal policy favoring arbitration,"[129] so it remains to be seen whether the Court will construe the language and legislative history of the Civil Rights Act of 1991 as evidencing congressional intent not to permit compulsory arbitration of Title VII claims.

 Preemployment Practices

From both a legal and a practical standpoint, the employer–employee relationship begins at the start of the application process. Recent years have seen an increase in litigation concerning preemployment practices, such as job advertising, employment applications, job interviewing, and testing. Employers must take care to avoid unlawful discrimination in these activities.

Obviously, a policy or a particular decision not to hire an applicant because she is a woman or an African American would be subject to challenge under disparate-treatment analysis. A policy or decision must not treat some applicants differently from others simply because of their gender or race.

A more common problem in today's business environment concerns hiring practices and policies that appear to be race- or gender-neutral but that have a disparate impact on one race or gender. Where a hiring practice or policy is found to have a disparate impact on a protected class of persons, the employer must show that the policy is a business necessity. The business necessity must be related to job performance and not to inconvenience, annoyance, or expense.

Job Advertisements

Many employers begin the recruitment process by posting or publishing a Help Wanted notice. Title VII and

122. Bercovitch v. Baldwin School, Inc., 133 F.3d 141 (1st Cir. 1998).

123. Miller v. Public Storage Mgmt., Inc., 121 F.3d 215 (5th Cir. 1997).

124. Prudential Ins. Co. v. Lai, 42 F.3d 1299 (9th Cir. 1994), *cert. denied*, 516 U.S. 812 (1995).

125. 144 F.3d 1182 (9th Cir. 1998).

126. Pub. L. 102-166 § 118 (1991), reprinted in notes to 42 U.S.C. 1981.

127. Seus v. John Nuveen & Co., ___ F.3d ___ (3d Cir. 1998).

128. The following cases upheld such clauses but did not consider the effect of the Civil Rights Act of 1991: Paladino v. Avnet Computer Techs., Inc., 134 F.3d 1054 (11th Cir. 1998); Cole v. Burns Int'l Security Servs., 105 F.3d 1465 (D.C. Cir. 1997); Rojas v. TK Communications, Inc., 87 F.3d 745 (5th Cir. 1996); Austin v. Owens-Brockway Glass Container Inc., 78 F.3d 875 (4th Cir. 1996).

129. Moses H. Cone Mem'l Hosp. v. Mercury Constr. Corp. 460 U.S. 1 (1983). *See also* the cases discussed in Chapter 4 of this book.

the ADEA prohibit employers from publishing or printing job notices that express a preference or limitation based on race, color, religion, sex, national origin, or age, unless such specifications are based on good faith occupational qualifications. For example, an advertisement for a "waitress" implies that the employer is seeking a woman for the job. If there is no bona fide reason why the job should be filled by a woman rather than a man, the advertisement might be considered discriminatory. Similarly, terms such as "young woman" or "girl" should never be used because they discourage job candidates from applying for positions because of their sex or age.

Many state laws also prohibit discriminatory advertisements. For example, Massachusetts and Ohio prohibit notices that express, directly or indirectly, any limitations or specifications concerning race, color, religion, national origin, sex, age, ancestry, or disability. Word-of-mouth recruitment practices, which normally involve current employees informing their family and friends of job openings, also can be discriminatory. When information is disseminated in this way, it may tend to reach a disproportionate number of persons of the same race or ethnicity as the employer's current employees. Thus, reliance on word-of-mouth recruiting practices may perpetuate past discrimination. Where word-of-mouth is used, it should be supplemented with other recruiting activities that are designed to reach a broader spectrum of people.

Employers advertising for jobs should avoid placing advertisements in publications with sex-segregated help-wanted columns. They should indicate that the employer is an equal opportunity employer, and should use media designed to reach people in both minority and nonminority communities.

Applications and Interviews

Employers use the application and interview process to gain information about an individual's personal, educational, and employment background. Unless it has a valid defense, an employer should avoid making inquiries on an application form, during a preemployment interview, or in some other manner, that identify the protected characteristics of a job candidate. Although federal laws do not expressly prohibit preemployment inquiries concerning an applicant's race, color, national origin, sex, marital status, religion, or age, such inquiries are disfavored because they create an inference that these factors will be used as selection criteria. These inquiries may be expressly prohibited under state law.

INTERNATIONAL CONSIDERATION

A study of help-wanted advertisements in the English-language *Bangkok Post* from 1985 to 1996 revealed that approximately 25% of all ads by American, French, and British companies specified the gender of the applicants they were seeking.[a] Companies typically specified men for senior positions such as product managers and engineers while women were specified for jobs such as secretaries, administrative assistants, and receptionists. However, several companies, including Pizza Hut and Lucent Technologies, specifically stated in their ads that the advertised positions were available to men or women.

a. Jonathan Marshall, *Sex Bias Found in Job Ads for Asia*, SAN FRANCISCO CHRON., May 12, 1998, at C1.

Often the line between permissible and impermissible areas of inquiry is not clear. Because the actions of recruiters, interviewers, and supervisors can expose an employer to legal liability, it is crucial that they understand which questions should and should not be asked. As a general rule, recruitment personnel should ask themselves "What information do I really need to decide whether an applicant is qualified to perform this job?"

Sex and Marital/Family Status Any preemployment inquiry that explicitly or implicitly indicates a preference or limitation based on an applicant's sex is unlawful unless the inquiry is justified by a bona fide occupational qualification. In rare cases a candidate's sex may be a valid criterion for a job, as in the case of actors or actresses or fashion models. However, questions concerning an applicant's sex, as well as marital/family status, should be avoided. For example, application forms and interviewers should not ask:

1. whether an applicant is male or female
2. the number or ages of an applicant's children
3. how an applicant will arrange for child care
4. an applicant's views on birth control
5. whether an applicant is pregnant or plans to become pregnant

6. whether a female applicant prefers to be addressed as Mrs., Miss, or Ms.
7. the applicant's maiden name.

In addition, an interviewer should not direct a particular question, such as whether the applicant can type, only to female or only to male applicants.

Some of the above information eventually will be needed for benefits, tax, and EEOC profile purposes; but it can be collected after the applicant is employed.

There are exceptions to this general rule. For example, state law may require employers to collect data regarding the race, sex, and national origin of each applicant, and the job for which he or she has applied. Certain government contractors are also obligated to collect applicant-flow data. Such data are collected for statistical and record-keeping purposes only and cannot be considered by the employer in its hiring decision. In general, if an employer is required to collect such data, the employer should ask applicants to provide self-identification information on a form that is separate or detachable from the application form.

Age Application forms and interviewers should not try to identify applicants aged 40 and older. Accordingly, job candidates generally should not be asked their age, their birth date, or the date that they completed elementary or secondary school. An employer can inquire about age only if (1) age is a bona fide job requirement, as for a child actor; or (2) the employer is trying to comply with special laws, such as those applying to the employment of minors. The claim that it may cost more to employ older workers as a group does not justify differentiation among applicants based on age.

Race Employers should not ask about an applicant's race. Questions concerning complexion or skin, eye, or hair color should be avoided; and applicants should not be asked to submit photographs.

National Origin An applicant should not be asked about his or her nationality or ancestry, because Title VII prohibits discrimination on the basis of national origin. The Immigration Reform and Control Act of 1986 (IRCA)[130] makes it unlawful for an employer with four or more employees to discriminate against applicants or employees on the basis of either their national origin or their citizenship status. If the employer has 15 or more employees and therefore is covered by Title VII,

charges of national-origin discrimination must be filed under Title VII, not IRCA.

IRCA also makes it unlawful for an employer of any size to knowingly hire an individual who is not authorized to work in the United States. Violators can be subject to civil and criminal penalties. However, employers must not discriminate against persons solely because they appear to be foreign or speak a foreign language. The act specifies the correct procedure for determining whether an applicant is authorized to work.

Under the act, any newly hired employee is required to complete a Form I-9 certifying that he or she is authorized to work in the United States and has presented documentation of work authorization and identification to the employer. After examining the documents presented, the employer must complete the remainder of the form, certifying that the documents appear genuine, relate to the employee, and establish work authorization. The Form I-9 must be completed within a prescribed period of time.

Religion An employer generally should not ask questions about an applicant's religion. An employer can tell an applicant what the normal work schedule is, but should not ask which religious holidays the applicant observes or whether the applicant's religion will interfere with his or her job performance. Title VII's ban on religious discrimination encompasses more than Sabbath observance. It applies to all conduct motivated by religion, such as dress or maintenance of a particular physical appearance. Title VII imposes a duty upon employers to make reasonable accommodation to their employees' religious practices as long as such accommodation will not cause undue hardship to the employer's business.

An employer can ask about a candidate's religious beliefs if they are a bona fide occupational qualification. For example, a school that is owned, supported, or controlled by persons of a particular religion can require that its employees have a specific religious belief. In an extreme case, a federal district court ruled that a helicopter pilot could be required to convert to the Moslem religion in order to fly over certain areas of Saudi Arabia that are closed to non-Moslems.[131] The court ruled that the requirement was a bona fide occupational qualification justified by safety considerations, because Saudi Arabian law prohibits non-Moslems from entry into Mecca; non-Moslems risk being beheaded if caught entering this area.

130. Pub. L. No. 99-603, 100 Stat. 3359 (1986) (codified as amended in scattered sections of the U.S.C.).

131. Kern v. Dynalectron Corp., 577 F. Supp. 1196 (N.D. Tex. 1983), *aff'd*, 746 F.2d 810 (5th Cir. 1984).

Disabilities and Physical Traits Applicants should not be questioned about their general medical condition. Although Title VII does not prohibit discrimination on the basis of disability, the Americans with Disabilities Act prohibits all discrimination on the basis of disability. In addition, several states prohibit such discrimination, and the federal Vocational Rehabilitation Act of 1973 forbids discrimination against disabled persons by certain government contractors and by employers receiving federal financial assistance. After an employer has described a job's requirements, the employer can ask the applicant if he or she can perform the job. If the applicant answers no, the employer should ask if there is any way to accommodate the applicant's limitation. An applicant also can be told that the job offer is contingent on passing a job-related medical exam (discussed further below).

Applicants generally should not be asked questions about their height or weight. Height and weight requirements have been deemed unlawful when such standards disqualify physically disabled persons, women, and members of certain ethnic or national-origin groups, and the employer could not establish that such requirements were directly related to job performance.

Conviction Record Although an employer can ask applicants if they have ever had a criminal conviction, this question should be followed by a statement that the existence of a criminal record will not automatically bar employment. Because in many geographical areas a disproportionate number of minorities are convicted of crimes, the use of conviction records as an automatic exclusion may have a disparate effect on minorities and therefore may be unlawful.

Consideration of a criminal record generally will be lawful only if the conviction relates to the requirements of the particular job. For example, an employer may be justified in rejecting an applicant convicted of theft for a hotel-security position. When a job applicant has been convicted of a crime involving physical violence, the employer may be faced with a delicate problem. Some courts have held the employer liable when an applicant with a record of violent behavior was hired and later assaulted another employee or a third party. Liability is based on the theory that the employer was negligent in its duties to protect the health and safety of the injured person by hiring such an employee. If the employee is operating in a jurisdiction that recognizes this *negligent-hiring theory*, a policy against hiring any person with a criminal conviction for a violent act is justified. This is an increasingly difficult area for employers, given recent instances of violence in the workplace.

Employers should not ask applicants if they have ever been arrested. Some states, such as Washington and Illinois, prohibit or restrict employers from asking applicants about arrests or detentions that did not result in conviction.

Education Employers can ask applicants questions regarding their education and work experience, but all requirements, such as possession of a high school diploma, must be job-related. Inflated standards of academic achievement, language proficiency, or employment experience may be viewed as a pretext for unlawful discrimination against women and members of minority groups.

Credit References Rejection of an applicant because of a poor credit rating may be unlawful unless the employer can show that the decision not to hire the applicant was due to business necessity. Because the percentage of minority-group members with poor credit ratings generally is higher than that of nonminority-group members, rejection of applicants on this basis can have a disparate impact upon minority groups.

Use of Resume Scanning Software

A majority of the Fortune 1000 companies use resume-scanning technologies, which often electronically search resumes for certain key words. In 1998, four African Americans sued Walt Disney Company, claiming that its method of screening unlawfully discriminated against African-American applicants who, due to cultural differences, were likely to use "key words" on their resumes that were different from those used by white applicants.[132] One attorney warns that resume-scanning software could result in "digital redlining," because of its ability to easily winnow out particular factors, such as age, gaps in employment, and zip codes.[133]

Preemployment Tests

Many employers use preemployment tests as a screening mechanism. Title VII prohibits employers from using any test that is designed, intended, or used to disqualify applicants in one of the protected groups. In addition, there are restrictions on the use of tests that have the effect of

132. *Employers' Use of Resume Scanning Software Raises New Issues of Discrimination in Hiring*, 66 U.S.L.W. 2611 (Apr. 14, 1998).

133. *Id.*

screening out protected-group members. An employer considering a test as a means to select employees must (1) determine if the test will have an adverse effect on a protected group of applicants; and (2) have the test validated in accordance with procedures specified by the EEOC.

A test has an adverse effect on members of a protected group if the pass rate of any sex, race, or ethnic group is less than 80% of the pass rate for the highest group passing the test. For example, if 100% of whites and only 79% of African Americans pass a particular test, the test is presumed to be unlawful because it has an adverse effect on African Americans.

A test that has an adverse impact on a protected group must be validated under the Uniform Guidelines on Employee Selection Procedures, published by the EEOC. Validation is expensive and complicated. Even if a test is job-related, it may still be challenged if alternative, less-discriminatory selection procedures would equally aid the employer in making hiring decisions.

Physical Examinations

The Americans with Disabilities Act prohibits preemployment medical examinations or inquiries concerning the existence, nature, or extent of the disability of an applicant unless the inquiries relate directly to that individual's general ability to perform job-related functions and a tentative offer of employment has been made. Medical examinations may be required only after a definite employment offer has been made and before the employee begins his or her employment duties. The offer of employment may be conditioned on the job-related results of the medical examination only if all entering employees are subject to such an examination. Moreover, the results of such an examination must be treated as confidential medical records and kept separate from other personnel information.

 ## Applicability of Civil Rights Laws to Temporary Workers

The EEOC has responded to the growth in the number of temporary or contingent workers (2.3 million in 1997) by extending potential liability for discrimination against such workers to both the employment agencies or temporary staffing firms and their client-employers.[134] If both the staffing firm and its client have the right to control the worker, then they are treated as joint employers and subject to liability for both back and front pay as well as compensatory and punitive damages. If the staffing firm learns that one of its clients has discriminated against a temporary employee, the firm should not assign other workers to that work site unless the client has taken the necessary corrective and preventive measures to ensure that the discrimination will not recur. Otherwise, the staffing firm will be liable along with the client if a worker later assigned to that client is subjected to similar misconduct.

---

134. Text of the EEOC's guidance on application of the employment discrimination laws to contingent workers is available at <http://www.eeoc.gov/press/12-8-97.html>.

THE RESPONSIBLE MANAGER
Honoring Employees' Civil Rights

Managers must be aware that there are federal, state, and local statutes forbidding certain types of discrimination, such as discrimination on the basis of race, color, religion, national origin, sex, sexual orientation, age, or disability. They should therefore familiarize themselves with these laws and notify their employees of their existence. Managers must prevent unlawful discrimination in both the preemployment and employment process.

In order to prevent unlawful discrimination, management should develop a written policy, clearly outlining discriminatory acts prohibited by federal, state, and local statutes. Employees should be advised that any form of discrimination is inappropriate. The policy should have an enforcement mechanism and should clearly state that violations of the policy will result in poor performance reviews or termination. Such a policy would not only curb discriminatory acts but would demonstrate that management diligently attempted to prevent such behavior in the event that litigation should arise.

The firm should also create a working environment in which employees feel comfortable in bringing complaints against fellow workers and supervisors. Each complaint should be thoroughly investigated and, if necessary, the violator should be punished. In addition, there should be at least two individuals in the company, a male and a female, to whom such complaints may be brought. Because supervisors are often the discriminators, this system would have an advantage over one in which an employee must first complain to his or her supervisor before an investigation could take place.

Although the establishment of such a policy is one way to prevent unlawful discriminatory practices, it is not sufficient in itself. Managers must also abide by the policy and comply with all federal, state, and local statutes prohibiting unlawful discrimination. If management participates in discriminatory acts, its employees will have little incentive to abide by the firm's policy against discrimination, and employees will hesitate to bring a claim for discriminatory treatment.

At the same time, managers should avoid being so afraid of sexual-harassment claims that they fail to have the informal contacts, such as a beer after work or a game of golf, necessary for mentoring. Otherwise, the very persons that Title VII was meant to benefit can find themselves unable to establish rewarding working relationships.

Yet, managers are rightly concerned that if mentoring leads to romance, then morale can suffer as coworkers feel that the object of the manager's attention is receiving favorable treatment. Also, if the relationship turns sour, the company may lose a valued employee.

Extramarital office romance is particularly troubling when there is a significant power and age gap between partners. Such relationships are very perilous. If the parties have a falling out, the subordinate may claim that the relationship was not consensual, because he or she feared adverse employment consequences for rebuffing the manager's advances.

Nonetheless, employers have been forced to acknowledge that "trying to outlaw romance [in the workplace] is like trying to outlaw the weather."[135] Adults spend the bulk of their time at work and, for many, offices have replaced churches, gyms, parties, and bars as the primary dating meeting ground.

Only 3% of the companies surveyed by the American Management Association have strict fraternization policies banning managers from having a romantic relationship with a subordinate. In the mid-1990s, International Business Machines abandoned the following policy:

> A manager may not date or have a romantic relationship with an employee who reports through his or her management chain, even when the relationship is voluntary and welcome.[136]

Today, IBM managers may become romantically involved with subordinates as long as the manager steps forward and transfers to another job within or outside the company so he or she is not supervising or evaluating the performance of the subordinate he or she is dating. Because the manager usually has more flexibility, the onus is on the manager to transfer.

---

135. IBM manager quoted in Carol Hymowitz & Ellen Joan Pollock, *The Once Clear Line in Interoffice Romance Has Become Blurred*, WALL ST. J., Feb. 4, 1998, at A1, A8.

136. *Id.*

INSIDE STORY

TEXACO PAYS $176 MILLION TO SETTLE RACE-DISCRIMINATION LAWSUIT

In March 1994, six African-American employees of oil giant Texaco, Inc. filed a class action lawsuit on behalf of 1,500 current and former employees, charging Texaco with racial discrimination. The suit alleged that African-American employees lost out in promotions and were subject to racial slurs at work. The company responded by saying it expected to prevail and characterized the lawsuit as "riddled with falsehoods."[137] The lawsuit received little attention for the next two-and-a-half years.

However, a series of events forced Texaco to admit that it had a serious problem with the way it treated its African-American employees. In June 1996, the EEOC determined that from 1992 to 1994 Texaco had given African Americans significantly fewer promotions than other employees.

Then in August 1996, a dismissed Texaco executive provided plaintiff's attorneys with clandestine tape recordings he had made of high-ranking Texaco officials disparaging African-American workers during the meetings held to improve the position of minorities at Texaco. Part of the transcript of the conversations that were made public included the following statement by one executive regarding the lack of promotions for African-American employees: "All the black jelly beans seem to be glued to the bottom of the bag."[138] The jelly bean reference came from a diversity training exercise during which an analogy was made between the different backgrounds of Texaco's employees and different flavors of jelly beans in a candy jar. The initial transcription of a hotly disputed section of the tape quoted the executive as saying, "I'm still having trouble with Hanukkah. Now, we have Kwanzaa. (Expletive) niggers, they (expletive) all over us with this."[139] A later investigation stated that the phrase "St. Nicholas" was mistaken for the word "nigger"; that report quotes the disputed phrase as: "I'm still

struggling with Hanukkah . . . and now we have Kwanzaa. . . . Poor Saint Nicholas, they s---tted all over his beard."[140]

Public reaction ranged from the threat of boycotts to divestiture of Texaco stock by public pension plans. The Philadelphia city pension plan divested its Texaco stock, and others considered following suit.[141]

Texaco's newly installed chief executive officer and chairman, Peter Bijur, quickly responded to these developments and expressed sincere sorrow and disappointment that such events had happened. He denounced all racially motivated behavior, met with Jesse Jackson and other African-American leaders to prevent a boycott, and launched an internal investigation into Texaco's diversity and equal opportunity policies. The internal investigation later faulted three executives for interfering with the lawsuit by not providing requested documents and in other ways.[142]

One week after the disclosure of the tapes, Texaco settled the lawsuit at a total cost of $176 million, including cash payments, salary raises, and the design and implementation of new diversity programs.[143] Most of the executives involved were suspended with pay and eventually fired.

The unprecedented settlement includes several components. First, Texaco agreed to pay $115 million in cash to the plaintiff class. Of this sum, $26.1 million provided a one-time 11% pay raise for every salaried black employee. Thirty-five million dollars was allocated

for company diversity-related programming, and the remaining $53.9 million was dispersed among the class members as cash payments.

Second, Texaco agreed to create an Equality and Tolerance Task Force composed of three Texaco appointees, three appointees of the plaintiffs' attorneys, and a mutually agreed on chair. The Task Force is considered extraordinary by the business community because of its expansive authority to monitor and review Texaco's progress in achieving diversity of its 27,000-person employee base.[144] Moreover, half of the sitting board is composed of individuals not otherwise affiliated with Texaco. The task force includes the vice chairman of the board of Texaco in addition to Deval Patrick, former chief of the Civil Rights Division of the Department of Justice, and Mari Matsuda, a Georgetown University Law Center professor known for her work in critical race theory.[145] The task force has its own budget and support staff to generate recommendations, but final decision-making authority will still rest with the Texaco's board of directors.

According to company reports,[146] Texaco has taken other steps to increase diversity. It has articulated work force composition goals, such as increasing the percentage of its work-force composed of racial minorities from 22% to 29% by the year 2000. In order to accomplish this, Texaco has implemented various strategies to enhance the representation of minorities among job applicants from within the organization and is working to increase the percentage of minorities hired outside the firm. Outside recruitment efforts have included expanding internship and scholarship programs for qualified minority students, recruiting from more predominantly minority colleges, and training managers and supervisors to make more effective decisions. The compensation packages of supervisors and managers are affected by their efforts to increase diversity of the company. Texaco is also increasing the amount of business it does with minority-owned businesses in the areas of contracting and services, including finance, insurance, and diversification of its wholesalers and retailers.

Although some commentators expressed doubts as to whether Texaco was genuinely pursuing these efforts, the evidence indicates that progress has been made. Initial reviews indicated that 38% of all new hires and 24% of promotions were minorities, although minorities constituted only 22% of the Texaco workforce.[147] Ten percent of the performance-based bonuses of top executives is based on the success of the company's diversity programs.

Nevertheless, some of Texaco's African-American employees feel that things have not changed

and that the promotions and cash payments have even engendered resentment from their coworkers. One source of the problem is that white and black employees seem to have interpreted the same events in different way: white employees tended to be surprised by the allegations of racial discrimination whereas black employees tended to consider the Texaco tapes as external validation of the bias with which they were all too familiar.[148] Some employees question how much can really change. "How do you legislate how someone feels?" remarked one Texaco employee. "There haven't been a lot of changes. The old feelings have just gone underground; there is a real effort to just say nothing."[149]

The Texaco settlement has forced U.S. companies to assess the status of racial and ethnic diversity within their organizations.[150] Previously relegated to human resource divisions, diversity has become an issue at the board of directors level. Board members have begun to demand information and assessments of liability and to recommend action plans. For example, in 1996, Chase Manhattan Corporation's board of directors grilled top executives for more than three hours on the status of women and minorities in the company.[151] This was the first time

the full board had ever addressed the issue.

137. *Texaco, Inc.: Suit Alleges Discrimination against Black Professionals*, WALL ST. J., Mar. 31, 1994, at A6.

138. *Black Hole: Race in the Workplace/Racism and Texaco*, THE ECONOMIST, Nov. 16, 1996.

139. Tribune Wires, *Texaco Exec Didn't Use Racial Slur, Lawyer Says Analysis Suggests Word on Tape Was "Nicholas,"* CHICAGO TRIB., Nov. 12, 1996.

140. Jolie Solomon, *Texaco's Troubles: A Scandal over Racial Slurs Forces the Oil Giant to Rethink—and Remake—its Corporate Identity*, NEWSWEEK, Nov. 25, 1996, at 48.

141. Del Jones, *City Pension Fund to Sell Texaco Stock*, USA TODAY, Nov. 22, 1996, at 1A.

142. Allanna Sullivan, *Texaco's Race-Bias Inquiry Faults Three Executives*, WALL ST. J., July 15, 1997, at B5.

143. Allanna Sullivan & Peter Fritsch, *Texaco Is Trying to Reach a Settlement in 1994 Racial-Discrimination Lawsuit*, WALL ST. J., Nov. 11, 1996, at A3; Anne Reifenberg, *Texaco Settlement in Race-Bias Case Endorsed by Judge*, WALL ST. J., Mar. 26, 1997, at B9.

144. *Texaco to Pay 176.1 Million in Bias Suit: Record Settlement Includes Task Force Possessing Broad Oversight Power*, WALL ST. J., Nov. 18, 1996, at A3.

145. Press Release from Texaco Public Relations (June 23, 1997).

146. TEXACO, INC., EQUAL OPPORTUNITY AND DIVERSITY AT TEXACO: 1997 REPORT (1997).

147. Leon Wynter & Allanna Sullivan, *Business and Race*, WALL ST. J., Nov. 5, 1997, at B1.

148. Jonathan Kaufman & Alex Markels, *Blacks, Whites Differ on Lesson of Texaco Tape*, WALL ST. J., Nov. 18, 1996, at B1.

149. Leon Wynter & Allanna Sullivan, *Business and Race*, WALL ST. J., Nov. 5, 1997, at B1.

150. Joann S. Lublin, *Texaco Case Causes a Stir in Boardrooms*, WALL ST. J., Nov. 22, 1996, at B1.

151. *Id.*

KEY WORDS AND PHRASES

BFOQ defense   **463**
disparate impact   **460**
disparate treatment   **459**

fetal-protection policy   **465**
hostile-environment harassment   **460**
negligent-hiring theory   **493**

quid pro quo harassment   **469**
race norming of employment
   tests   **488**

QUESTIONS AND CASE PROBLEMS

1. Sheila Prescott is an employee at Ladet, Inc. in Miami, Florida. Ladet manufactures tennis clothes for men and women and has more than 600 employees. Prescott has worked for Ladet since 1993. She is employed in the personnel department and reports directly to the director of personnel, Frank Allen. In May 1997, Prescott and Allen traveled together to the University of Wisconsin on a recruiting trip. While in Wisconsin, Prescott and Allen had sexual intercourse.

In June 1998, Prescott was passed over for a position as head of the personnel department in Ladet's newly opened Denver branch office. This job would have provided Prescott with higher pay. Another woman at Ladet was offered the job.

Prescott has brought a sexual-harassment claim against Allen and Ladet. Although Allen and Prescott had sexual intercourse only on that one occasion in Wisconsin, Prescott contends that Allen refused to recommend her for the Denver position because he wanted to keep her in the Miami office. Prescott has not been demoted and has not received a cut in pay.

If you were investigating Prescott's sexual-harassment claim, what information would you want to know? What relief might Prescott be granted?

2. Tony Sadler is a production supervisor for Zydos, Inc., a Nevada manufacturer of printed circuit boards. Several years ago, Sadler worked in Ohio for Axion, Inc. When Zydos was just starting up, it recruited Sadler by offering him better money and a ground-floor role in Zydos's development. Sadler was persuaded to quit his job at Axion and move to Nevada. He has been a successful supervisor at Zydos ever since, receiving several raises, good performance reviews, and a recent promotion.

In his new position, Sadler supervises the Zydos Quality Assurance and Test Department, which comprises 12 employees who test A and B units before sealing and shipping them. The department is made up of one Caucasian, six Hispanics, and five Vietnamese. Most of the employees know how to test both A and B units, but a few have been trained on only one unit. Because Zydos is experiencing significant financial difficulties, the human resources manager has instructed Sadler to prepare a list of potential layoff candidates from his department. He is to examine his employees' flexibility and the importance of their skills to the work at hand. Sadler's layoff candidate list reads:

NAME	REASON
Tran Trinh	Elimination of lead position
Yin Chia	Not trained to test A units
Quyen Lam	Not trained to test A units
Dzung Tien	Not trained to test A units

The human resources manager of Zydos has contacted you for advice. In addition to providing you with the above information, he tells you that he was contacted this morning by Raul Lopez, a quality assurance tester who had recently received a poor performance review. He complained that he was "getting a raw deal" because Sadler "spends all his time with those geeks." When pressed for details, Lopez complained that Tony favored the Vietnamese, often went to lunch with them, and spent long periods of time talking to them (and especially to a young Vietnamese woman named Hye Nguyen) to the exclusion of others in his department. He confided that everyone thinks Hye and Tony are having an affair.

The human resources manager also tells you that the Vietnamese people are a tightly knit group; that Hye is a very good tester; that she is very shy and submissive; and that, when she came to work at Zydos several months before, destitute and helpless after leaving an abusive Vietnamese boyfriend, Sadler befriended her and helped her get on her feet. He also tells you that the lead tester, Tran Trinh, is a 54-year-old "Vietnamese godfather type" who "rules the roost for the Vietnamese" in Sadler's department and has wide connections within the Vietnamese community. Tran disapproves of Hye's association with Sadler and is a family friend of Hye's ex-boyfriend. Sadler has received a couple of threatening phone calls from Hye's ex-boyfriend regarding things that have occurred at work.

The human resources manager has asked both Hye and Sadler whether they are having a romantic relationship. Both have denied anything but a warm friendship.

What legal liabilities could result from the situation in Sadler's department and what advice would you give Sadler to help avoid each potential liability?

3. Assume the facts in Question 2. Further assume that a week has passed and Hye has told the human relations manager that she and Sadler have been having a romantic relationship, that initially it was what she wanted, but that now she wants it to stop. She says that she has told Sadler that it is over, and he is angry. She is afraid that he will fire her or keep "talking like a lover" to her. The human relations manager tells you he fired Sadler immediately.

What legal liability might Zydos have toward Sadler? If either of Hye's worries had come to fruition before Sadler was fired, what legal liabilities might have resulted to Zydos?

4. Ralph, a male carpenter, suffered a mental breakdown after being repeatedly taunted by his coworkers, who accused him of being a homosexual and a child molester. He asked his employer, Lucent Technologies, to allow him to go back to work for four weeks on a part-time basis while he tried to adjust to normal life. Ralph's therapist asserted that this opportunity was essential to Ralph's recovery. Lucent Technologies had paid Ralph previously for disability leave, but refused to permit him to return to work on a part-time basis. Ralph sued under the Americans with Disabilities Act. Will he prevail? [*Ralph v. Lucent Technologies, Inc.*, 135 F.3d 166 (1st Cir. 1998)]

5. Plaintiff Candelaria Cuello-Suarez, a U.S. citizen who was born in the Dominican Republic and was a 17-year veteran employee of the Puerto Rico Electric Power Authority (PREPA), held various positions as clerk and typist. She possessed a bachelor's degree in business administration with a major in accounting and a minor in management and, shortly after commencement of her lawsuit, obtained her license as a certified public accountant. Over the years, she successfully passed at least 10 different tests required for promotion and always received above-average evaluations in her performance reviews. She never received a reprimand. Prior to filing her lawsuit, the plaintiff filed applications for promotions to supervisory positions, with no success. Subsequent to the filing of her suit in 1988, she applied for the position of supervisor of consumer services. The position was filled by a native Puerto Rican who had been employed by PREPA for seven months and had a bachelor's degree in marine biology.

The plaintiff claims that she was denied a promotion on many occasions because of her national origin. What must she prove in order to make a *prima facie* case of discrimination? What type of nondiscrimina-

tory justification for its actions will the Puerto Rico Electric Power Authority present? [*Cuello-Suarez v. Puerto Rico Elec. Power Authority*, 988 F.2d 275 (1st Cir. 1993)]

6. Seven white, male police officers complained to their precinct captain that their immediate supervisor repeatedly made disparaging remarks to and about female and African-American police officers. They claimed that the supervisor's remarks created a sexually and racially hostile environment that interfered with the sense of teamwork among officers of different sexes and races needed to ensure that officers of one group would assist officers of another group in the performance of their duties. The department investigated the complaint but took no remedial action. Instead, the complaining officers received involuntary shift changes and transfers and unfavorable performance evaluations. They then sued, arguing that the department had violated Title VII. Result? [*Childress v. Richmond*, 134 F.3d 1205 (4th Cir. 1998)]

7. In March 1988, Ellie Grizzle was hired at age 42 as a general ledger accountant by Travelers, a health maintenance organization (HMO) "umbrella" company in Las Colinas, Texas. Although she did not have a bachelor's degree in accounting, Grizzle had 10 years of experience working as an accountant. For the initial period of her employment, March 1988 through March 1989, Grizzle achieved an above-average rating of 2, only because the highest rating of 1 was reserved for a perfect performance. Grizzle also won an award for outstanding achievement during this period.

In September 1988, Grizzle applied for but did not receive a supervisory position. According to Grizzle, during an interview with finance director Glen Marconcini she was informed by him that, although she was qualified for the promotion, she would not receive it because she rubbed him the wrong way, she smoked, and also, he was not wild about her age. Thereafter, Grizzle complained to her immediate supervisor, Leon Nary, who interceded on her behalf. As a result of her complaint to Nary, Grizzle received a $2,000 a year raise and was given supervisory authority within her department. No formal complaint was made with respect to Marconcini's alleged comment; in fact, favorable employment action followed her informal complaint to Nary.

In March 1989, the Travelers Las Colinas and Atlanta offices merged. The following month, Kent Latiolais, a transferee from the Travelers Atlanta office, was made Grizzle's supervisor. The appointment of Latiolais was in effect a demotion for Grizzle. Grizzle testified that she met with Traveler's regional vice-president and comptroller Dave Goltz and expressed concern that she had been passed over for Latiolais's job because of her age and that Goltz "kind of lost his composure for a second," then assured her that he would never discriminate against anyone, including Grizzle, on the basis of age.

From approximately April 1989, Grizzle, Latiolais, and Loretta Scott, a younger co-worker who performed the same function at Travelers as Grizzle, all shared the same small office. In July 1989, Travelers switched to a new computer system on which the plaintiff lacked proficiency, with the result that she made many ledger errors. In the summer of 1989, Grizzle complained to Traveler's director of Internal Accounting, Beverly Snyder, that she was being subjected to increased surveillance and scrutiny of her work by Latiolais, while Scott was not, and that she was being given insufficient computer training. According to Grizzle, Snyder responded that there was nothing that Grizzle could do about it because she was not over the age of 55. Snyder later denied making that statement and also testified that she did not know that the ADEA prohibits age discrimination against people aged 40 and above. In July and December 1989, Grizzle received two warnings by Latiolais regarding her lack of productivity and her ledger entry mistakes. In January 1990, she was placed on "final warning." Documentation of her errors continued during this period. On February 16, 1990, Latiolais told Grizzle that her performance had not improved and that she was being discharged. Grizzle was only 44 years old on the date of her discharge and only two years older than she was at the time Travelers made the decision to hire her.

Latiolais, Goltz, and Snyder, each of whom was approximately ten years younger than Grizzle, participated in making the decision to fire her. She was replaced by a 23-year-old recent college graduate. On March 16, 1990, Grizzle filed a complaint with the Equal Employment Opportunity Commission (EEOC).

Does Grizzle have a valid claim against Travelers? Should the age of the supervisors who chose to discharge her factor into the court's decision? [*Grizzle v. Travelers Health Network*, 14 F.3d 261 (5th Cir. 1994)]

8. Pam Armstrong was employed by Flowers Hospital as a nurse in the Home Care Services division. Her employment in this position required her to visit and treat patients in their homes. Armstrong was assigned patients in the Headland, Midland, and Dothan areas, and worked during the day, Monday through Friday. When Armstrong was initially hired, she was required to attend a one-day orientation. Following that orientation, she spent the first two weeks riding with another nurse. Upon completion of that two-week period, Armstrong was assigned a number of patients with varying conditions.

On December 12, 1990, Armstrong was informed that she had been assigned a patient who was diagnosed as HIV-positive. He was further diagnosed as having cryptococcal meningitis, an infectious disease common among AIDS patients.

On the same day, Armstrong informed Cheryl Wynn, her supervisor at Home Care Services, that she did not believe that she should treat this patient because she was in the first trimester of her pregnancy. She expressed concern that if she were required to treat this patient, she might jeopardize her baby. Armstrong stated that it was not the presence of AIDS that concerned her as much as the opportunistic infections commonly present with AIDS patients. She further stated that it was not her own health that she was concerned about, because she, as a healthy adult, would be capable of recovering from most of these infections. Her primary concern was the health of her unborn baby.

Wynn informed Armstrong that the policy of Home Care Services was to not make exceptions and not allow reassignment of patients to other nurses. Home Care's policy on the treatment of AIDS patients stated that the "Universal Precautions" provided by the Centers for Disease Control (CDC) were to be followed by all nurses in treating patients with infectious diseases. Any nurse who refused to treat a patient was subject to termination. After discussing the situation with her supervisor, Wynn informed Armstrong that she would be given two days in which to reconsider her decision. If Armstrong still refused to treat the AIDS patient, she would be given the option of resigning or facing termination. On December 14, 1990, Armstrong had not changed her mind about treating the patient, and she refused to resign. She was terminated.

After her termination, Armstrong filed a Title VII claim with the Equal Employment Opportunity Commission. The EEOC investigated the matter and returned a finding that there was no reasonable determination of a Title VII violation. Do you agree? [*Armstrong v. Flowers Hosp.*, 812 F. Supp. 1183 (M.D. Ala. 1993)]

9. Oak Rubber Company was a manufacturer of industrial vinyl gloves. The company operated six production machines around the clock with three shifts of workers. Each machine was required to be staffed with six glove-strippers and one packer. The machines operated continuously through the employees' breaks and lunch periods. Oak scheduled extra workers to substitute for the employees on break, and also to cover for employees who were absent or on vacation. The list of excused absences included a number of reasons an employee might occasionally miss work, but did not include observance of the Sabbath. If Oak did not have enough workers for each machine, it was forced to shut down the affected machine, suffering a loss of production.

The Saturday work schedule was either full or partial production. For those Saturdays scheduled for full production, Oak gave all of its employees 48-hours notice and made it mandatory for all employees on all shifts to report to work. If, after the employees reported to work, Oak determined that extra workers were available, employees could exercise "work options" to go home without pay.

Cooper was hired by Oak in 1975 as a glove-stripper/packer, and worked the night shift from 11:00 P.M. to 7:00 A.M. In January 1984, Cooper attended her first Seventh Day Adventist service and attended regularly thereafter. Cooper knew that the church prohibited all work from sundown on Friday until sundown on Saturday. Cooper nonetheless worked numerous Saturdays in 1984, but was able to attend church services after ending her shift at 7 A.M. She worked a total of nine Saturday shifts in 1985, and reported for work on seven other occasions, but exercised work options to leave early on those occasions. Oak did not schedule any full production Saturdays between July 1985 and November 1986.

In November 1986, Cooper exercised her seniority right to transfer to the day shift. Coincidentally, one day later, Oak announced that the following Saturday was scheduled for full production. Cooper informed her su-

pervisor that she could not work because of her religious beliefs.

Cooper did not work that Saturday or the remaining full-production Saturdays in 1986. She received a verbal warning. In January 1987, Cooper talked to her new supervisor about her religion's prohibition against working on Saturdays. The supervisor suggested that Cooper use her 17 accrued vacation days to avoid working Saturdays, but Cooper was unwilling to use them in this manner. Cooper's supervisor also suggested that she trade back to the night shift so that she could attend services on Saturday mornings. This alternative was also unacceptable to Cooper because it would still require her to work on the Sabbath. Cooper testified that although she had been willing to work the Friday night shift prior to July 1985, her commitment to the church had grown since that time and prevented her from continuing to do so. Cooper resigned to avoid disciplinary suspension and what she claimed would be her inevitable termination from employment. One month after Cooper's resignation, Oak hired an additional 18 glove-strippers/packers, enhancing its ability to maintain production despite work absences.

Cooper filed suit under Title VII, claiming that she was disciplined and constructively discharged because she adhered to her sincere religious beliefs against working on the Sabbath. Was Cooper constructively discharged from her employment, even though she could have used her accrued vacation days rather than resign? Did Oak reasonably accommodate Cooper's religious beliefs when it offered her the option of trading shifts? What type of relief should be granted to Cooper if she wins her suit? [*Cooper v. Oak Rubber Co.*, 15 F.3d 1375 (6th Cir. 1994)]

MANAGER'S DILEMMA

10. It is important that an employer protect itself against claims of sexual harassment, not only to meet legal obligations, but also to maintain a workplace conducive to the physical and mental well-being of all employees. Many commentators recommend that a company have a written policy that clearly prohibits sexual harassment and provides a procedure for employees to bring a claim of sexual harassment without intimidation. Such a policy is essential to limit the company's vicarious liability. Moreover, a company should provide for nondiscriminatory behavior in its corporate code of ethics.

On the other hand, excessive fear of sexual-harassment claims can result in a dehumanized work environment in which supervisors and employees are afraid to make compliments or engage in mentoring for fear their conduct will be misconstrued. How should a manager balance these considerations?

INTERNET SOURCES	
Equal Employment Opportunity Commission	http://www.eeoc.gov
Texaco, Inc.	http://www.texaco.com
American Civil Liberties Union	http://www.aclu.org

CHAPTER 14

Labor–Management Relations

INTRODUCTION

Resurgence of Unions

Although union membership has declined since its all-time high of 35.5% of all U.S. nonagricultural workers in 1945 (see Exhibit 14.1), the power of unions appears to be on the upswing. In 1997, the Teamsters' union organized a successful strike by 185,000 workers at the United Parcel Service of America (UPS), which resulted in substantial concessions by UPS. (The UPS strike is described in the "Inside Story" at the end of this chapter.) *Business Week* dubbed the strike a "wake-up call for business" and argued that businesses can no longer take workers for granted.

At the same time, heretofore non-unionized classes of workers are beginning to try to organize. Health-care workers, includ-

ing physicians and nurses who feel squeezed by managed care and health maintenance organizations (HMOs), are hoping that a union will give them more negotiating leverage with HMOs.

Chapter Overview

This chapter discusses the coverage and operation of the National Labor Relations Act (NLRA), which governs labor relations in the United States. It outlines the procedure for employees to vote on whether they wish to be represented by a union; the types of employer conduct that are unlawful under the NLRA; strikes and the rights of strikers; and unlawful union conduct. Labor–management relations in selected countries are reviewed briefly.

 History

Congress has comprehensively regulated labor–management relations in an attempt to balance equitably the economic power of employers, individual employees, and unions. Before the mid-1930s, attempts by employees to band together and demand better wages and working conditions were largely ineffective. Organized economic action, such as strikes and picketing, were enjoined as unlawful conspiracies. Employers squelched attempts to organize by lawfully discharging union organizers.

In 1932, Congress enacted the Norris–La Guardia Act,[1] which regulated and largely prohibited the is-

suance of injunctions or court orders in labor disputes. Through the Wagner Act[2] in 1935 and the Taft–Hartley Act[3] in 1947, Congress sought to provide employees with greater economic bargaining power by allowing them to organize, but also sought to curb perceived union excesses. The Landrum–Griffin Act was enacted in 1959 primarily to address problems created by corruption within union leadership. These laws are known collectively as the National Labor Relations Act.

---

1. 29 U.S.C. §§ 101–115 (1988).
2. 29 U.S.C. §§ 151–169 (1994).
3. 29 U.S.C. §§ 141–144 (1994).

EXHIBIT 14.1   U.S. Union Membership, 1921–97

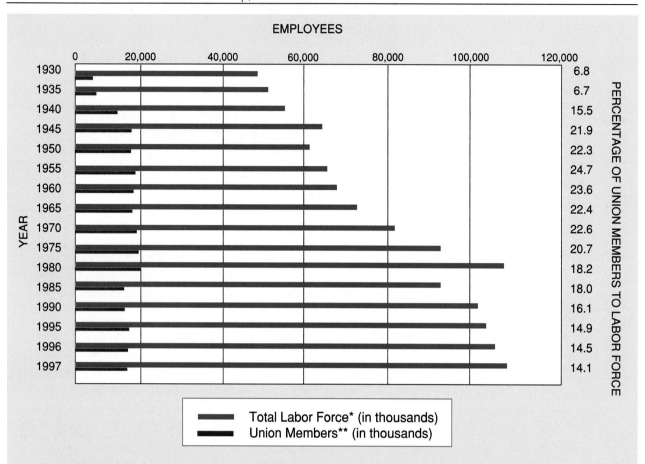

*Labor force statistics from the Current Population Survey of the Bureau of Labor Statistics. Includes agricultural workers.

**Union members are the annual average number of dues paying members reported by labor unions. Data exclude members of professional and public employee associations. These data are not available after 1980.

SOURCE   U.S. Department of Labor, Bureau of Labor Statistics.

 ## Coverage of the National Labor Relations Act

The National Labor Relations Act covers all enterprises whose operations affect interstate or foreign commerce. However, the National Labor Relations Board (NLRB), which administers the act, has, with court approval, limited its jurisdiction to enterprises having a substantial effect on commerce. The dollar volume of an employer's revenues or purchases determines whether that employer's impact on commerce is sufficiently substantial to bring it within the NLRB's jurisdiction.

In general, the NLRA covers only employees located within the territorial United States, not U.S. employees located elsewhere. However, the NLRB has ruled that its jurisdiction extends to foreign employers doing business within the United States that would otherwise be under the NLRB's jurisdiction.

Employees of Nonprofit Institutions

In 1974, Congress extended the NLRB's jurisdiction to employees of all health-care institutions, including non-profit hospitals. Before 1974, the NLRB had taken the position that it would not assert jurisdiction over non-profit organizations except in exceptional circumstances. In recent years, however, the NLRB has shown increasing willingness to take jurisdiction over such organizations.

Supervisors

Section 7 of the NLRA grants rights only to employees, not to supervisors. The statute defines a *supervisor* as anyone with authority to hire, suspend, lay off, pro-mote, discharge, discipline, or direct employees, or to effectively recommend such action, provided the exercise of that authority is not of a merely routine or clerical nature but requires the use of independent judgment. (The characterization of nurses as supervisors is a key issue in their attempt to join unions, which is discussed in the "Economic Perspective.")

The NLRB will not allow supervisors to vote in union elections; and, in most cases, the NLRB does not have the authority to find that supervisors have been treated unlawfully under the NLRA.

Independent Contractors

Independent contractors are not covered by the NLRA because they are not employees. In determining whether an individual is an independent contractor, the NLRB invokes the common law right-to-control test (which is discussed in Chapter 5). A person is deemed to be an *independent contractor* if the employer exercises no control over either the means of performing the work or the end result of the work. (The characterization of physicians working with a health maintenance organization as inde-pendent contractors is a key issue in their attempt to join unions, also discussed in the "Economic Perspective.")

Agricultural Laborers

The NLRA specifically excludes from its coverage any individual employed as an agricultural laborer. An agri-cultural laborer is one who performs work primarily in connection with (1) an agricultural operation, or (2) an operation that is both an integral part of ordinary agri-cultural production and an essential step before the products can be marketed in normal outlets.

Representation Election Procedure

The five-member NLRB has established a number of re-gional offices throughout the country to handle the day-to-day tasks of overseeing *representation elections*, that is, elections among employees to decide whether they want a union to represent them for collective bargaining.

Filing a Petition

The procedure for conducting a representation election is initiated by the filing of a petition with a regional of-fice of the NLRB. The vast majority of those petitions are filed by labor organizations.

In order to obtain an election, a union must make a *showing of interest;* that is, it must prove to the NLRB that a sufficient number of employees have an interest in an election. This is nearly always done by submitting to the NLRB *union authorization cards* from at least 30% of the employees in an appropriate collective-bargaining unit. Generally, these cards contain a state-ment that the individual signing it wishes to be represented for purposes of collective bargaining by a certain union. If the union cannot provide a showing of interest, the NLRB will dismiss the petition.

An individual employee may file a petition to decer-tify an incumbent union if at least 30% of the employees in the bargaining unit sign a statement that they no longer wish to be represented for collective bargaining by their union.

Petitions may also be filed by employers at certain intervals to test the union's continuing support. To do so, an employer must show objectively that the majority of employees in the collective-bargaining unit no longer wish to be represented by the union.

Appropriate Unit

Regardless of whether the union, the employer, or an employee files the petition for election, the election procedures are essentially the same, except that in the case of an initial organizing campaign, the parties or the NLRB may have to determine which employees should be allowed to vote in an election. The NLRB will hold elections only in appropriate collective-bargaining units. An appropriate unit is one in which the employees share a community of interest; that is, they have similar compensation, working conditions, and supervision, and they work under the same general employer policies. In determining whether a unit is an appropriate collective-bargaining unit, the NLRB also looks at (1) the kind of work performed, (2) similarity in the qualifications and skills of employees, (3) frequency of contact among employees, (4) geographic proximity of employees, and (5) the wishes of affected employees.

Scope of Unit

With certain limitations, the union and the employer are free to agree on the scope of the unit in which an election should be conducted. However, if the proposed unit will include both professional and nonprofessional employees, the consent of the professional employees must be obtained. In addition, Section 9(b)(3) of the NLRA prohibits a labor organization from representing security guards if that organization admits nonguards to membership or is affiliated with a labor organization that admits nonguards to membership. As a result, the NLRB will refuse to hold an election among a unit of guards if the petitioning labor organization represents nonguards or is affiliated with a union that represents nonguards. These special rules for security guards are necessary to prevent guards from having conflicts during strikes between their responsibility as employees and their loyalty as union members.

If the employer and the union cannot agree on the scope of the unit, the NLRB will conduct a hearing to resolve the issue. A common issue at a representation hearing is whether a certain position is supervisory as defined by the NLRA. If it is, that position will be excluded from the unit. If it is not, the individual in that position will be included in the unit and allowed to vote. The director of the regional office in which the petition is filed makes such determinations, which are appealable to the NLRB.

Conduct of Election

Following an agreement between the parties for an election or a decision from the regional director over disputed unit issues, the regional office will conduct an election. The NLRB agent travels to the employer's location, erects a portable voting booth, and oversees the election process. The specific place and time for the election are agreed on between the employer and union.

The NLRB agent ensures that no irregularities occur during the election and hands out ballots to the employees. Each employee enters the place of voting and indicates by placing a mark in an appropriate square on the ballot whether he or she wishes to be represented for collective bargaining by the specified union. The employee then deposits the marked ballot into a ballot box, which is opened at the close of the election by the NLRB agent. The NLRB agent then tallies the election results and signs a ballot count. With a unit of previously unrepresented employees, the union needs 50% plus one of the valid votes cast in the election to win.

Objections

The party losing the election may file objections to it. Objections typically allege misconduct either by the other party before or during the election or by the NLRB agent at the election. For example, a union that has lost an election may allege that, just before the election, the employer unlawfully threatened employees with reprisals if they voted for the union. If the objections are deemed without merit, the election will be certified by the NLRB. If they are deemed meritorious, the NLRB will conduct a new election. If an employer's misconduct was so serious that a free and fair election is impossible, the NLRB will order the employer to bargain with the union, even without an election.

◆ Unfair Labor Practices by Employers

Section 8(a) of the NLRA prohibits employers from engaging in specified activities against employees or their unions. Such activities, known as *unfair labor practices*, are investigated and prosecuted by the general counsel of the NLRB and his or her representatives.

Unfair labor practice charges may be filed in the NLRB's regional offices. Ordinarily, the time limit for filing a charge is six months. A charge is usually investigated by a field examiner or a field attorney of the local office. The regional director then decides whether, based on evidence disclosed by the investigation, the charge has merit.

If the charge is meritorious, the local office will attempt to arrange a settlement. If the matter cannot be settled at the local level, it will be tried before an administrative law judge (ALJ). The decision of the ALJ is reviewable by the NLRB, which may adopt, modify, or reverse the decision. The NLRB's decision is in turn appealable to a federal appellate court and, ultimately, to the Supreme Court of the United States.

Interference with Protected Activities

Section 8(a)(1) of the NLRA makes it illegal for an employer to interfere with, restrain, or coerce employees in the exercise of their Section 7 rights to organize and bargain collectively and to engage in other protected, concerted activities. This prohibition covers a wide range of employer conduct, including (1) threatening employees with any adverse action for organizing or supporting a union; (2) promising employees any benefits if they abandon support for a union; (3) interrogating employees about union sentiment or activity; and (4) engaging in surveillance of employees' union activities. Such conduct is generally thought to chill employees' exercise of their Section 7 rights. For example, an employer may not threaten to shut down its business or to take away benefits if the union wins a representation election. Similarly, an employer may not interrogate employees about whether they have signed a union representation card or about the union activities of other employees.

Section 8(a)(1) also prohibits an employer from enforcing an overly broad rule against soliciting other employees (perhaps for union support) or distributing literature on company premises. In general, an employer may only prohibit solicitation or distribution of literature by employees on company property during work time. It is not yet clear whether an employer must give employees access to the employer's electronic mail system for solicitation and distribution of information.

However, nonemployee union organizers do not have the same rights as employees for solicitation and the distribution of literature. The U.S. Supreme Court held in *Lechmere, Inc. v. National Labor Relations Board*[4] that nonemployee union organizers do not have a right to trespass on an employer's private property for the purpose of communicating with and organizing employees, except in very limited circumstances. *Lechmere* involved the efforts of a union to gain access to a parking lot partially owned by a retail store. The court reasoned that although employees have an unrestricted right to organize themselves, nonemployees are not afforded such protection unless the employees are inaccessible because they live on the employer's property. Thus, the retail store could ban nonemployee labor organizers from its property.

Sometimes a union will pay individuals to seek work with non-union employers with the intent of having them organize the other workers once hired. This practice is often referred to as "salting." The U.S. Supreme Court considered whether such a job applicant is an employee protected by the NLRA in the following case.

---

4. 502 U.S. 527 (1992).

A CASE IN POINT	SUMMARY

CASE 14.1
NATIONAL LABOR RELATIONS BOARD v. TOWN & COUNTRY ELECTRIC INC.
Supreme Court of the United States
516 U.S. 85 (1995).

FACTS Town & Country Electric, Inc. (T&C), a non-union electrical contractor, sought several licensed Minnesota electricians for construction work. T&C advertised the openings, but refused to interview ten of the eleven union applicants and dismissed the eleventh after only a few days of work. The union applicants sought to work at T&C while being paid by the union to organize T&C's workers. Members of the International Brotherhood of Electrical Workers, Locals 292 and 343, filed a complaint with the NLRB alleging unfair labor practices by T&C.

An administrative law judge found that T&C had refused to interview and hire the union applicants on the basis of their union activities. The NLRB affirmed, interpreting "employee" to include job applicants and finding the applicants' union affiliations and intentions to organize of no importance. The U.S. Court of Appeals reversed, and the NLRB appealed.

Case 14.1 continues

Case 14.1 continued

ISSUE PRESENTED   Can a worker be an employee of a business if he or she is simultaneously paid by a union to organize the company's workers?

SUMMARY OF OPINION   The U.S. Supreme Court deferred to the NLRB's interpretation of the term "employee," finding its interpretation consistent with the purpose of the National Labor Relations Act, in addition to being within the scope of ordinary dictionary definitions. The Court looked to precedent and legislative history, finding additional support for the proposition that the term "employee" should be interpreted broadly and should not be restricted. Moreover, one provision of the NLRA seemed to contemplate an employee of a company being paid by an union. Section 186 of the 1947 Labor Management Relations Act prohibits an employer from paying a person employed by a union, except for monies paid to "any . . . employee of a labor organization who is also an employee."

In response to T&C's claim that under agency law a servant cannot have two masters, the Court reasoned that as long as service to one does not lead to the abandonment of obligations owed to another, there is no conflict. Moreover, the Court rejected the employer's assertion that a worker being paid by a union is disloyal, because there was no indication that salted employees were any more likely to undermine the interests of the company than other employees.

RESULT   The Supreme Court reversed the court of appeals' decision and upheld the NLRB's decision. T&C had violated the NLRA by firing and refusing to interview individuals paid by a union solely on the basis of their union activities.

COMMENTS   *Town & Country* was a blow to non-union contractors, who have since then been lobbying Congress to pass anti-salting legislation.[5] The House of Representatives passed a bill to end salting (Fairness for Small Business and Employees Act (H.R. 3246)) on March 26, 1998, which President Clinton promised to veto.[6] Even if a salted worker is considered an employee for purposes of the NLRA, however, an employer may still refuse to hire a full-time union organizer on the basis of a general company rule against hiring individuals with full-time jobs. The U.S. Court of Appeals for the Sixth Circuit held in *Architectural Glass & Metal Company v. National Labor Relations Board*[7] that refusing to hire individuals with full-time jobs constitutes a legitimate, nondiscriminatory reason for refusing to hire an applicant, provided the rule was applied and promulgated in a nondiscriminatory manner.

---

5. *Supreme Court Speaks*, 66 U.S.L.W. 2292 (Nov. 18, 1997).

6. *House Narrowly Passes GOP 'Fairness' Bill to Amend Federal Labor Law, End 'Salting,'* 66 U.S.L.W. 2602 (Apr. 7, 1998).

7. 107 F.3d 426 (6th Cir. 1997).

Section 8(a)(1) also protects employees who engage in concerted activities for mutual aid and protection. For example, an employer may not retaliate against a group of employees who approach it and complain about some aspect of their working conditions, such as poor lighting or uncomfortable temperatures in the workplace. For an activity to be *concerted*, it must be "engaged in with or on the authority of other employees, and not solely by and on behalf of the employee himself."[8] The NLRB will find a violation of the National Labor Relations Act only when (1) the employer knows of the concerted nature of the employee's activity; (2) the concerted activity is protected by the NLRA; and (3) the discipline at issue is in retaliation for the employee's protected, concerted activity. The following case explores one aspect of the right to engage in concerted activities for the purpose of mutual aid and protection.

8. Meyers Indus., Inc., 268 N.L.R.B. 493, 497 (1984), *remanded sub nom.* Prill v. NLRB, 755 F.2d 941 (D.C. Cir. 1985), *cert. denied*, 474 U.S. 971 (1985).

A CASE IN POINT	SUMMARY

CASE 14.2
NATIONAL LABOR RELATIONS BOARD v. J. WEINGARTEN, INC.
Supreme Court of the United States
420 U.S. 251 (1975).

FACTS   The employer, J. Weingarten, Inc., operated a chain of retail stores that contained food operations. Leura Collins, a salesperson, was represented by the Retail Clerks Union. The employer suspected that she had taken some merchandise without properly purchasing it. Collins was summoned to an interview with an investigator and the store manager. During the questioning, she asked the store manager several times to call the union shop steward or some other union representative, but those requests were denied. The employer also questioned Collins about her disclosure that she had not been paying for her lunches. During this part of the questioning, Collins repeated her request for a shop steward, which was again denied. The employer then terminated the questioning and asked Collins not to discuss the matter with anyone else because it was a private matter.

ISSUE PRESENTED   May an employer deny an employee's request that a union representative be present at an investigatory interview that the employee reasonably believes might result in disciplinary action?

SUMMARY OF OPINION   The U.S. Supreme Court observed that an employee's seeking the assistance of a union representative at a confrontation with the employer clearly falls within the literal wording of Section 7 that employees have the right to engage in concerted activities for the purpose of mutual aid and protection. The employee sought "aid or protection" against a perceived threat to her employment security. The union representative, whose participation was sought, safeguards not only the particular employee's interest, but also the interests of the entire bargaining unit by ensuring that the employer does not initiate or continue a practice of imposing punishment unjustly. Further, the Court said, requiring a lone employee to attend an investigatory interview that she reasonably believes may result in the imposition of discipline perpetuates the inequality in bargaining power between employees and employers that the National Labor Relations Act was designed to eliminate.

RESULT   An employer may not deny a union employee's request that a union representative be present at an investigatory interview.

COMMENTS   It is important to keep in mind the limitations of the *Weingarten* decision. It applies only to situations where an employee who is a union member asks for the assistance of a union representative at an investigatory interview that the employee reasonably believes might result in discipline.

ETHICAL CONSIDERATION

Should a manager honor a request by a non-union employee to have another individual present at an investigatory interview?

Domination of a Labor Organization

Under Section 8(a)(2) of the NLRA, an employer may not dominate or assist a labor organization. This provision was enacted to cure the abuse of employers assisting compliant organizations to represent their employees and then imposing "sweetheart" collective-bargaining contracts—that is, contracts unduly favorable to the employer. Under this provision, a company may not give financial support to a labor organization. It may not instigate, encourage, or directly participate in the formation of a labor organization.

The U.S. Court of Appeals for the Seventh Circuit held that an employer that created and maintained employee "action committees" violated the NLRA, because they constituted representational labor organizations dominated by management.[9] At issue were committees created by management to develop solutions to employee dissatisfaction with attendance and pay policies. The court reasoned that unlike independent employee participation organizations, the committees at issue had their structures, duration, and subject matter defined by management. Additionally, the employer was represented on every committee. Similarly, the U.S. Court of Appeals for the Sixth Circuit upheld a determination of the NLRB that an employer-created "plant counsel" with three of eight members representing management, which met on company property during working hours, was a company-dominated labor organization.[10]

An employer may not attempt to influence the making of union policy. For example, supervisors may not serve as union officials or on a union bargaining team. An employer may not recognize a union as the bargaining representative of a unit of employees when a majority of its employees do not support the union.

Discrimination Against Union Supporters

Section 8(a)(3) prohibits employers from discriminating against any employee to encourage or discourage membership in any labor organization. If an employee has been unlawfully discharged, the NLRB may order that the employee be reinstated and given full back pay. A common Section 8(a)(3) allegation is a worker being discharged for attempting to organize fellow employees. To prove a violation of Section 8(a)(3), it must be shown that the employee's conduct, protected by Section 7, was a substantial or motivating factor in the discharge. In such a case, the employer may allege a legitimate business reason for the termination, but the alleged business reason may be a pretext, intended to cover up an unlawful discharge.

In some cases, there may be mixed motives, that is, evidence of both a proper and an improper reason for termination. When there is some evidence of both lawful and unlawful reasons for discharge, the NLRB must prove that the employee's protected conduct was a substantial motivating factor in the discharge. To escape liability, the employer must then show by a preponderance of the evidence that the employee would have been discharged for legitimate reasons regardless of the protected activity.[11]

Section 8(a)(3) permits a union and employer to incorporate a *union security clause* into a collective-bargaining contract. Such a clause requires, as a condition of employment, that employees in the collective-bargaining unit either become members of the union after a certain period of time or pay fees to the union equivalent to the periodic union dues. The laws of a number of states forbid union security clauses.

In *Communications Workers of America v. Beck*,[12] the Supreme Court held that employees in a represented unit who are not union members need pay only those fees necessary for the union to perform activities related to collective bargaining, contract administration, and grievance adjustment. Thus, a union cannot use a

---

9. Electromation Inc. v. NLRB, 35 F.3d 1148 (7th Cir. 1997).
10. Webcor Packaging Inc. v. NLRB, 118 F.3d 1115 (6th Cir. 1997).

11. NLRB v. Transportation Mgt. Corp., 462 U.S. 393 (1983).
12. 487 U.S. 735 (1988).

union security clause to require non-union employees to pay fees expended on organizing employees of other employers, lobbying for labor legislation, and participating in social, charitable, and political events. However, union members may be required to pay the entire dues amount.[13] Moreover, the NLRB has approved a notice remedy whereby a union pledges to inform employees of their rights under *Beck*. Indeed, if the union does not provide an employee notice of his or her rights, it commits an unfair labor practice.[14]

Discrimination Against Employees Who File Charges

Under Section 8(a)(4) of the NLRA, it is an unfair labor practice for an employer to discharge or otherwise discriminate against an employee because he or she has filed charges or given testimony to the NLRB, either in a representation proceeding or pursuant to an unfair labor practice charge.

Failure to Bargain in Good Faith

Section 8(a)(5) of the NLRA imposes upon unionized employers a duty to bargain collectively. For example, the employer must be willing to meet union representatives at reasonable times to bargain over the conditions of employment. A related provision, Section 8(d), requires employers to bargain in good faith, that is, to approach negotiations with an honest and serious intent to engage in give-and-take bargaining in an attempt to reach an agreement. However, the obligation to bargain in good faith does not compel either party to agree to a proposal or to make concessions. The examination of whether an employer has bargained in good faith is difficult because it involves determining the employer's subjective frame of mind. The NLRB will look at all of the surrounding circumstances, including the employer's willingness to negotiate and its conduct at the bargaining table.

In *National Labor Relations Board v. General Electric Company*,[15] the court found that an employer did not bargain in good faith when it adopted a take-it-or-leave-it posture and then publicized that position to establish the idea that the union was powerless. In 1960, many of the employees of General Electric (GE), one of the best-known manufacturers of electrical equipment and appliances in the United States, were represented by the International Union of Electrical, Radio and Machine Workers. Having suffered a crippling strike and having agreed to a contract settlement that it viewed as excessive, GE adopted a new approach in its 1960 collective-bargaining negotiations. It announced to the union that it would hold nothing back when it made its offer to the union. GE stated that, though it was willing to accept any suggestions based on facts that the company might have overlooked, it would not engage in give-and-take bargaining but would hold firmly to its offer. GE then advertised that position extensively to employees. Through a "veritable avalanche of publicity," GE described its proposal as both fair and firm.

The appeals court, affirming a decision of the NLRB, held that the company's collective-bargaining posture violated Section 8(a)(5). Its well-publicized policy of firmness tended to back the company into an inflexible position and to establish in the minds of employees the idea that the union was unnecessary.

The duty to bargain collectively in good faith prohibits an employer from unilaterally changing some term or condition of employment unless, after bargaining with the union to an impasse, the employer's unilateral changes are consistent with the union's pre-impasse proposal. This is the *implementation after impasse doctrine*. However, in *McClatchy Newspapers v. National Labor Relations Board*,[16] the appeals court deferred to the NRLB's wage exception to the implementation after impasse doctrine, which prohibits an employer from unilaterally altering wages after a bargaining impasse. Accordingly, the court held that a publisher who unilaterally granted merit pay increases after a collective-bargaining impasse over wages acted unlawfully.

The duty to bargain in good faith also requires employers to bargain over certain subjects. The NLRB and courts have held that there are three categories of bargaining subjects: mandatory, permissible, and illegal.

13. Monson Trucking Inc., 324 N.L.R.B. 149 (1997).

14. *NLRB Renews Support for* Beck *Notice, But Gould Favors Broad Nationwide Remedy*, 66 U.S.L.W. 2329 (Dec. 2, 1997).

15. 418 F.2d 736 (2d Cir. 1969), *cert. denied*, 397 U.S. 965 (1970).

16. 131 F.3d 1026 (D.C. Cir. 1997).

Employers must bargain over mandatory subjects—those that vitally affect the terms and conditions of employment, such as wages and work hours. Employers may, but are not obligated to, bargain over permissible subjects. Employers must not bargain over illegal subjects.

There has been much litigation over what subjects are mandatory. In the following case, the Supreme Court considered whether an employer must bargain over a decision to close part of its operation.

| A CASE IN POINT | SUMMARY |

CASE 14.3
FIRST NATIONAL MAINTENANCE CORP. v. NATIONAL LABOR RELATIONS BOARD
Supreme Court of the United States
452 U.S. 666 (1981).

FACTS   First National Maintenance Corporation was engaged in the business of providing housekeeping, cleaning, maintenance, and related services for commercial customers. Following a dispute with a nursing home over fees, First National terminated its contract with that customer and discharged its employees who worked there. The union representing those employees requested bargaining over the decision to terminate the contract. First National refused. The union alleged that the employer's refusal breached its duty to bargain in good faith.

ISSUE PRESENTED   Does an employer need to bargain over a decision to shut down part of its business for purely economic reasons?

SUMMARY OF OPINION   Congress did not intend that the union would become an equal partner with the employer in the running of the business enterprise. An employer must bargain over a decision, the U.S. Supreme Court ruled, only if bargaining would "promote the fundamental purpose of the Act by bringing a problem of vital concern to labor and management within the framework established by Congress as most conducive to industrial peace." The Court also noted that an employer needs to make certain decisions fundamental to its operation without the encumbrance of the collective-bargaining obligation. The Court concluded that bargaining over management decisions that have a substantial impact on the continued availability of employment should be required only if the benefit, for labor–management relations and the collective-bargaining process, outweighs the burden placed on the conduct of the business.

RESULT   The Supreme Court ruled that an employer is not required to bargain over every decision that it makes.

COMMENTS   Even though an employer may not be required to bargain over a decision to close part of its operations for economic reasons, the employer will be required to bargain with the union over the effects of such a decision on employees represented by the union. Moreover, the Supreme Court in *First National Maintenance* explicitly limited its holding to "partial closings" accomplished for economic reasons and stated that it was not expressing a view as to other management decisions, including plant relocations, sales, or other kinds of subcontracting or automation. Finally, bargaining over a management decision to close or modify its operations may be required when the decision hinges on labor costs over which the union has some control.

ETHICAL CONSIDERATION

The law prevents an employer from attempting to escape its collective-bargaining obligation by shutting down a unionized operation and moving the functions of that former operation to a nearby site. This violation, known as a *runaway shop,* is to be distinguished from an employer's decision to close permanently a unionized facility and not transfer its functions elsewhere. Is this a fair distinction?

In 1989, the NLRB ruled that drug testing is a mandatory subject of bargaining.[17] Johnson–Bateman Company, a manufacturer of concrete pipe, announced a new policy that any employee suffering a work-related injury would be required to take a drug and alcohol test. The union, which had not been given advance notice of this policy or an opportunity to bargain over it, demanded that the company rescind the policy. Johnson–Bateman refused, and proceeded as it had announced.

The NLRB held that the company's proposed drug and alcohol testing was a mandatory subject of bargaining. The testing of employees who require medical treatment for work injuries is germane to the working environment. By requiring testing, the employer had changed the method by which it would investigate possible employee responsibility for accidents and the character of proof on which an employee's job security might depend.

In a companion case, *Star Tribune,*[18] the NLRB ruled that the employer, a daily newspaper, did not violate the NLRA by failing to bargain over the implementation of a mandatory drug- and alcohol-testing policy for job applicants. The NLRB noted that such testing would not vitally affect either workplace safety or the terms and conditions of employment for current employees represented by the union. Thus, preemployment testing of applicants was not a mandatory subject of bargaining.

The NLRB ruled that the use of video surveillance cameras in the workplace was a mandatory subject of bargaining in the following case.

---

17. Johnson–Bateman Company, 295 N.L.R.B. 26 (1989).

18. 295 N.L.R.B. 63 (1989).

A CASE IN POINT	SUMMARY

CASE 14.4
COLGATE–PALMOLIVE COMPANY
National Labor Relations Board
323 N.L.R.B. 82 (1997).

FACTS Colgate–Palmolive Company installed hidden cameras throughout the work environment, including the restrooms and fitness area, in order to reduce workplace theft and employee misconduct. The International Chemical Workers Union, Local 15, issued a bargaining demand letter to Colgate–Palmolive. It argued that the video surveillance was a mandatory subject of bargaining because employees could be discharged on the basis of misconduct documented by the camera. Colgate–Palmolive refused, and the union filed a complaint with the NLRB. An administrative law judge held that the union had a statutory right to bargain over the use of the hidden surveillance cameras and agreed with the union that the cameras were a mandatory subject of bargaining. Colgate–Palmolive appealed to the NLRB.

ISSUE PRESENTED Does an employer's installation of hidden surveillance cameras constitute a mandatory subject of bargaining?

SUMMARY OF OPINION The NLRB upheld the administrative law judge's ruling that video surveillance was a mandatory subject of collective bargaining between the employer and the union. The NLRB looked to *Ford Motor Company v. NLRB,*[19] in which the U.S. Supreme Court outlined two factors for determining which decisions are

---

19. 441 U.S. 488 (1979).

Case 14.4 continues

Case 14.4 continued

mandatory subjects of bargaining. A decision is a mandatory subject of bargaining if the decision is both (1) "plainly germane to the work environment"; and (2) "not among those managerial decisions, which lie at the core of managerial control." The NLRB considered video surveillance analogous to physical examinations, drug testing, and polygraph testing in that all were investigatory tools an employer may use to discharge an employee. As a result, the subject of video surveillance was "unquestionably germane" to the working environment.

In terms of the second factor, the NLRB reasoned that the cameras were not fundamental to the direction of the enterprise and did not directly impinge on the employer's security. As a result, the decision to implement video surveillance was not at the core of managerial control. Therefore, Colgate–Palmolive had a duty to bargain with the union regarding the use of video surveillance of employees.

RESULT   The NLRB held that Colgate–Palmolive's refusal to bargain regarding the video surveillance violated Sections 8(a)(1) and (5) of the NLRA because the use of video surveillance was a subject of mandatory bargaining.

If an employer does not bargain in good faith, a union may seek an injunction for unfair labor practices from the NLRB. During the Reagan and Bush administrations, injunctions were rarely issued. However, the board under the Clinton administration has been much more active and much more willing to issue injunctions to jump-start collective-bargaining efforts.[20] Indeed, under the Clinton administration the number of injunctions has jumped from 35 to approximately 140 per year.

Presumption of Majority Support

A union that is certified by the NLRB as the bargaining agent for a unit of employees enjoys an *irrebuttable presumption* of majority support for one year. Its

support may not be questioned during that time, and the employer may not refuse to bargain with the union. Such a refusal is a *per se violation* of the National Labor Relations Act, that is, a violation in itself, without the need for proof of any further misconduct. After the first year, the employer may rebut the presumption of majority support by showing either that (1) the union does not in fact have majority support, or (2) the employer has a good faith doubt of the union's majority support.

When an employer replaces striking employees, the question arises whether the replacements support or oppose the incumbent union. The NLRB has followed a no-presumption approach and ruled that the replacements' union sentiments should be decided on a case-by-case basis. The Supreme Court approved that approach in the following case.

---

20. Richard C. Reuben, *Baseball Strike Teaches Legal Lessons: Lawyers Should Reassess Strategies, Avoid Animosities in Negotiations*, ABA J., June 1995, at 42.

A CASE IN POINT	**SUMMARY**

CASE 14.5
NATIONAL LABOR RELATIONS BOARD v. CURTIN MATHESON SCIENTIFIC, INC.
Supreme Court of the United States
494 U.S. 775 (1990).

FACTS   On May 21, 1979, the collective-bargaining agreement between Teamsters Local 960 and Curtin Matheson Scientific expired. Curtin Matheson is a company engaged in the purchase and sale of laboratory equipment and supplies. The collective-bargaining agreement covered production and maintenance employees.

After the union rejected the company's final offer for a new agreement, Curtin locked out the 27 union employees. The union called for an *economic strike*, that is, a strike based not on unfair labor practices but on the economics of the offer made by the employer. Curtin hired 29 workers to replace the 22 striking employees. Two

Case 14.5 continues

Case 14.5 continued

months later, the union ended the strike and offered to accept Curtin's final offer. Curtin revoked this offer and withdrew recognition of the union, stating that it doubted that the union had majority support. The union filed an unfair labor practice charge, alleging that the employer lacked good faith doubt of majority status.

The NLRB held that, although replacements often will not favor the incumbent union, the likelihood of such opposition is insufficient to justify an anti-union presumption.

ISSUE PRESENTED   Should the NLRB assume that workers who replace striking employees are anti-union in determining whether an employer is justified in doubting the union's majority support?

SUMMARY OF OPINION   The U.S. Supreme Court agreed with the NLRB, finding that the circumstances of each strike and the replacements' reasons for crossing the picket line may vary. For example, a replacement who otherwise supports the union may be forced to work for a struck employer for financial reasons. A replacement also may desire union representation even though he or she refuses to support a particular strike. The Court noted that an anti-union presumption could allow an employer to eliminate the union entirely merely by hiring a sufficient number of replacement employees. The Court concluded that the NLRB's adoption of a case-by-case approach was rational, was consistent with the NLRA's policy of maintaining industrial peace, protected the bargaining process, and preserved employees' rights to engage in protected activity.

RESULT   The NLRB need not assume that workers who replace striking workers are anti-union. The NLRB may determine the union sentiments of striker replacements on a case-by-case basis.

 Strikes

Lawful strikes are of two kinds: economic strikes and unfair labor practice strikes. Other types of strikes violate the NLRA.

Economic Strikes

Unions often strike employers when they are unable to extract acceptable terms and conditions of employment through collective bargaining. An employer that suffers such an economic strike is permitted to hire permanent replacements for the striking employees. If it does so, the employer need not rehire striking employees who offer to return to work, unless the departure of the replacements creates vacancies. However, a company is required to reinstate striking workers who make unconditional offers to return to work if vacancies are later created by the departure of strike replacements.[21]

The right to replace striking employees set forth by the NLRA has been upheld, even against an executive order by President Clinton. The U.S. Court of Appeals for the District of Columbia Circuit held that an executive order barring federal agencies from contracting with employers that permanently replace protected striking workers illegitimately impinged upon the NLRB's specific policy provision to the contrary.[22]

An employer may not be required to reinstate a striking employee, even when a vacancy occurs, if (1) the former striker has secured regular and equivalent employment elsewhere; or (2) the employer has legitimate and substantial business reasons, such as a striker's lack of necessary skills; or (3) the striker has committed sufficiently serious misconduct during the strike.

The following case addressed the issue of whether an employer may reinstate a striking worker to a lower-paid position due to the employer's fear that keeping the employee as a supervisor posed a potential threat to the business enterprise.

---

21. Laidlaw Corp. v. NLRB, 414 F.2d 99 (7th Cir. 1969), *cert. denied*, 397 U.S. 920 (1970).

22. Chamber of Commerce v. Reich, 74 F.3d 1322 (D.C. Cir. 1996).

A CASE IN POINT	IN THE LANGUAGE OF THE COURT

CASE 14.6
DIAMOND WALNUT GROWERS INC. v. NATIONAL LABOR RELATIONS BOARD
United States Court of Appeals for the District of Columbia Circuit
113 F.3d 1259
(D.C. Cir. 1997) (en banc).

FACTS   Diamond Walnut Growers Inc. (Diamond) processes and packages walnuts. In September 1991, approximately 500 of Diamond's workers went on strike after collective bargaining between management and the Cannery Workers, Processors, Warehousemen and Helpers Local 601 of the International Brotherhood of Teamsters, AFL–CIO (the union) failed. A bitter strike ensured. Diamond hired replacement workers to carry on business; and the union engaged in acts of violence, an international economic boycott, and a public relations campaign to discredit Diamond. This campaign included a national bus tour distributing information describing Diamond as employing "scabs" and packaging walnuts contaminated with "mud, dirt, oil, worms and debris."

Before a union election, six striking workers unconditionally offered to return to work. Three returning strikers were unable to resume their previous positions. However, one individual, Miller, had been a quality control supervisor before the strike, but was given a seasonal packing position upon returning. The NRLB filed a complaint alleging violation of Section 8(a)(1) and (3) of the NLRA for unlawfully discriminating against Miller for her protected union activities. Diamond appealed.

ISSUE PRESENTED   Does risk of sabotage by an employee who engaged in product disparagement constitute a substantial business justification enabling the employer to place the worker in a nonsupervisory position?

OPINION   SILBERMAN, J., writing for the U.S. Court of Appeals:

The employer admits that it took into account Miller's . . . protected activity in choosing to place . . . [her] in jobs that were objectively less desirable than those for which . . . [she] was qualified, and does not dispute that its action discriminated against . . . Miller within the meaning of the NLRA.

. . .

After discrimination is shown, the burden shifts to the employer to establish that its treatment of the employees has a legitimate and substantial business justification.

. . .

When a union claims that a food product produced by a struck company is actually tainted, it can be thought to be using the strike equivalent of a nuclear bomb; the unpleasant effects will long survive the battle. . . . The employer does not challenge the board's conclusion that the "tainted walnuts" campaign was protected. But to conclude the campaign was protected obviously does not determine whether the company's justification was substantial.

. . .

The issue, then, is . . . whether the employer had a legitimate concern, based on the undisputed evidence and the employer's claimed factual inferences—presented to and unchallenged by the board—that her employment as a quality control assistant would have posed an unusual and serious risk that she would engage in future misconduct of a particular kind. The board seems to have ignored those concerns without discussion. . . .

Miller, as a quality control assistant, could simply avert her eye and cause the feared damage with apparently little risk of discovery. There is no remedy that might lie against her that could compensate the employer for the type for damage even a

Case 14.6 continues

Case 14.6 continued

moment's lapse on her part could cause. In short, she would have had special motive, a unique opportunity, and little risk of detection to cause severe harm.

Our colleagues accuse us of forcing the board in the future to "draw fine lines" between those cases in which an employer's discriminatory placement of returning strikers has a substantial justification and those that do not. Exactly so. That is the board's job. . . .

RESULT The NLRB decision against Diamond regarding Miller's work assignment was reversed. Diamond did not violate the NLRA.

Questions

1. What legitimate business justification did Diamond Walnuts provide for reinstating Miller to a lower-paying position?
2. How did the court evaluate the legitimacy of Diamond Walnuts' business justification?

Unfair Labor Practice Strikes

Workers sometimes strike an employer wholly or partly to protest an unfair labor practice. For example, a union may strike because it believes that the employer is not bargaining in good faith. Workers who engage in such an *unfair labor practice strike* have a right to be reinstated to their former positions if they make an unconditional offer to return to work. If the employer refuses to rehire them, the NLRB may award them reinstatement plus back pay. This difference between the rights of economic strikers and those of unfair labor practice strikers may cause debate as to whether the employer committed an unfair labor practice and whether the strike was called to protest that practice.

Unlawful Strikes

The NLRA prohibits certain kinds of *organizational strikes* or picketing, whose purpose is to organize employees, and certain kinds of *recognitional strikes*, whose purpose is to force the employer to recognize the union as a collective-bargaining agent for its employees. It also outlaws certain *secondary boycotts*, which are strikes called against an outside company to induce it to put pressure (usually by withholding business) on the employer with whom the union has a dispute.

Organizational Strikes Section 8(b)(7) of the NLRA prohibits organizational or recognitional strikes or picketing when (1) the employer has already lawfully

recognized another labor organization as the representative of its employees and the union may not properly raise a question concerning that representation; (2) the

INTERNATIONAL CONSIDERATION

Managers with operations outside the United States need to consider the labor-relations laws of the foreign countries in which they have employees. Trade unions, often more active than in the United States, commonly work more closely with management. For example, at Germany's Volkswagen plants, trade unions sit on special "work councils" that approve or reject company changes in production. Work councils typically represent all workers in an establishment, whether or not they are unionized.

By contrast, Chile provides very little protection for labor organizing. Workers must organize within individual companies, rather than across industries, and many blatant anti-union tactics outlawed in the United States are perfectly legal. These practices have led some to oppose granting President Clinton fast-track authority in an attempt to block Chile's entrance into the North American Free Trade Agreement (NAFTA).[a] Fast-track authority and NAFTA are discussed in Chapter 25.

a. Matt Moffett, *Pinochet's Legacy: Chile's Labor Law Hobbles Its Workers and Troubles the U.S.*, WALL ST. J., Oct. 15, 1997, at A1.

"Actually, Tommy, we're just about full-blooded management, except for your grandfather on your mom's side, who was one-quarter labor."

NLRB has conducted a representation election under the NLRA within the preceding 12 months; or (3) the union has not filed a petition for a representation election within a reasonable period of time, not to exceed 30 days, from the date picketing commenced.

Recognitional Strikes   Section 8(b)(4)(i)(C) of the NLRA makes it unlawful for a labor organization to induce employees (for example, through picketing) to engage in a work stoppage to force the employer to recognize a labor organization if another labor organization has been certified as the employees' representative.

Secondary Boycotts   Section 8(b)(4) of the NLRA was enacted primarily to address the problem of a union unfairly involving neutral employers, with whom the union has no quarrel, in a labor dispute. Section 8(b)(4)(B) makes it illegal for a union to engage in or encourage a strike with the object of forcing any person to cease handling the products of an employer or to cease doing business with that employer.

Section 8(b)(4)(B) allegations arise quite commonly in the construction industry, where, typically, a number of employers work on a single construction site. A union that has a dispute with one of those employers may picket the entire job site, thereby hoping to shut down the work completely and put maximum pressure on that employer. Employers have countered this tactic by directing the employees and vendors of the *primary employer*, that is, the employer with whom the union has a dispute, to use a gate that is physically separated from the gate to be used by all other persons. Under this arrangement, known as the *neutral-gate system*, the union may picket only at the gate reserved for the employees and vendors of the primary employer.

ECONOMIC PERSPECTIVE

THE UNIONIZATION OF HEALTH-CARE PROVIDERS

As health-care costs have spiraled over the last decade, both businesses and individuals have sought to reduce expenditures while continuing to receive high-quality care. After proposed federal reforms were abandoned, managed care operations, or health maintenance organizations (HMOs), swept the country. Since 1990, the number of individuals enrolled in HMOs has doubled to 64 million, and the pace of reform continues unabated. HMOs have been successful at reining in the costs of health care because they approach medicine as a business, with efficiency and profit margins governing most decisions. HMOs have changed the way medical care is provided in the United States, by introducing economics into the calculus for health-care decisions.

Health-care providers are increasingly dissatisfied with these changes. Doctors and nurses are losing decision-making authority to HMO executives. HMOs now restrict what doctors can tell patients about treatments, limiting the number of days a patient may stay in a hospital after surgery (pejoratively called "drive-by" surgery), and limiting referrals to specialists. In addition, patient loads are being increased, support staff cut, and autonomous decision-making authority replaced with bureaucratic processes.

In response, doctors and nurses are organizing themselves and seeking collective-bargaining status to change the policies of the HMOs. In 1997, doctors at the prestigious Thomas–Davis Medical Center in Tucson, Arizona, voted of 93 to 32 to join the Federation of Physicians and Dentists, an affiliate of the American Federation of State, County and Municipal Employees (AFSCME).[a] According to AFSCME's director of organizing, a majority of physicians favor the opportunity to bargain collectively and would have already done so if legal and political climates were different.[b]

Some health-care providers have expressed alarm with practices they assert sacrifice quality health care in order to serve economic interests. One doctor in New Jersey commented, "We need to find a way to put the patients first and corporate profits for the insurance companies second. It should be our job as doctors to worry about the actual health of our patients and not just the financial health of our employers, the insurance companies and HMOs."[c] And the public seems to concur. Polls indicate that nine out of every ten respondents agree with the statement "Doctors need to take the important health-care decisions about families out of the hands of insurance companies."[d]

Despite the interest in organizing, health-care providers must first overcome several legal obstacles. In the past, doctors have been held to be independent contractors, rather than rank-and-file employees, and therefore not capable of forming a bargaining unit. Alternatively, HMOs may argue that health-care providers are supervisors. Supporters of unionizing retort that managed care companies have transformed autonomous health-care providers into employees with little decision-making authority. They cite HMO-mandated working conditions and influence over medical and office procedures.

On January 8, 1998, the regional director for the NLRB in Philadelphia rejected the United Food and Commercial Workers' bid to represent 500 New Jersey physicians. The regional director rejected the union's claim that AmeriHealth HMO's provider contracts included such strict controls over all aspects of physicians' activities that they were effectively employees of the company. She ruled that the physicians were independent contractors, in part because they themselves made the fundamental decisions that determined the profitability of their practices.[e] The union appealed the issue to the full board.

To date, the courts have come out differently on related subjects. For example, the U.S. Court of Appeals for the Sixth Circuit held that licensed practical nurses (LPNs) were "supervisors" under the NLRA, because they directed the work of nurse's aides and exercised independent judgment.[f] By contrast, the U.S. Court of Appeals for the District of Columbia Circuit, in an unpublished decision, ruled that licensed practical nurses were not "supervisors" under the NLRA.[g] In that case, the nurses directed some certified nursing assistants, but were not responsible for various administrative tasks regarding the assistants, such as scheduling

Economic Perspective continues

Economic Perspective continued

and disciplining. Similarly, the U.S. Court of Appeals for the Fourth Circuit held that licensed practical nurses at a nursing home were employees, not supervisors, even though they were the senior professionals on site at the nursing home at night and on weekends.[h] The LPNs directed the work of certified nurse assistants, but they were not empowered to affect anyone's terms of employment. Also, most of the decisions they were called on to make while nominally "in charge" were made in accordance with pre-selected choices and routine procedures. As health-care providers seek collective-bargaining status to command greater attention from HMOs, this area of the law is bound to expand.

a. Andrea Adelson, *Physician, Unionize Thyself: Doctors Adapt to Life as HMO Employees*, N.Y. TIMES, Apr. 5, 1997, at 35. A physician bargaining unit consisting of employee physicians was recognized by the NLRB. Thomas–Davis Medical Centers, 324 N.L.R.B. 15 (1997).

b. *Physician Organizing Continuing Despite Legal, Political Obstacles*, 66 U.S.L.W. 2608 (Apr. 7, 1998).

c. *Doctors Turn to UFCW for Managed Care Cure*, UFCW ACTION, Jan.–Feb. 1998, at 12.

d. *Id.*

e. *New Jersey Doctors Are Not Employees, May Not Organize, Labor Board Says*, 66 U.S.L.W. 2443 (Jan. 27, 1998).

f. Caremore, Inc. v. NLRB, 129 F.3d 365 (6th Cir. 1997).

g. Beverly Enterprises–Pa Inc. v. NLRB, 129 F.3d 1269 (D.C. Cir. 1997).

h. Beverly Enterprises, West Virginia Inc. v. NLRB, 136 F.3d 353 (4th Cir. 1998).

Unfair Labor Practices by Unions

Section 8(b) of the NLRA specifies several activities, besides unlawful strikes, in which unions may not engage.

Coercion of Employees

Section 8(b)(1)(A) of the NLRA prohibits unions from coercing employees to join the union or to support its activities. For example, a union may not attempt to intimidate employees into voting for it in a representation election. A union is also prohibited from coercing employees to join, or refrain from abandoning, a strike.

Unions—and employers—are also prohibited from influencing election results by offering monetary or nonmonetary benefits to employees. For example, the U.S. Court of Appeals for the Fifth Circuit ruled that a union's promise to throw "the biggest party in the history of Texas" if the union won the election was a conditional inducement that invalidated the election results.[23] The court reasoned that the only motivation for the promise was to encourage employees to vote for the union, as opposed to attempts to cultivate good employee–management relations. Thus, like employer promises of a Christmas party[24] or union promises of a

raffle made before election,[25] the union's promise interfered with and therefore invalidated the election.

Section 8(b)(1) has also been held to obligate a union to represent fairly and honestly all of the employees in the collective-bargaining unit, without regard to their union affiliation. The Supreme Court held in *Vaca v. Sipes*[26] that, as the exclusive bargaining representative of the employees, the union has a statutory duty to represent fairly all of the employees in collective bargaining and in enforcement of the collective-bargaining agreement. Under this doctrine, the union has an obligation to represent all members of a designated unit without hostility or discrimination toward any employees. It must exercise its discretion with complete good faith and honesty and avoid arbitrary conduct.

Inducing Employer Discrimination against Non-Union Workers

Under Section 8(b)(2) of the NLRA, a union may not cause or attempt to cause an employer to discriminate against an employee on the basis of union affiliation or activities. For example, a union may not encourage an employer to discharge someone because he or she does not belong to the union. In addition, a union may not cause or attempt to cause an employer to discriminate against

23. Trencor v. NLRB, 110 F.3d 268 (5th Cir. 1997).
24. NLRB v. Lou Taylor, Inc., 564 F.2d 1173 (5th Cir. 1977).

25. Crestwood Manor, 234 N.L.R.B. 1097 (1978).
26. 386 U.S. 171 (1967).

an employee who has been denied union membership for any reason other than failure to pay union dues.

Failure to Bargain in Good Faith

Section 8(b)(3) requires the union to bargain in good faith with the employer. This section requires the union to meet with the employer at reasonable times; and Section 8(d) requires it to approach bargaining with a serious and honest intent to conclude a collective-bargaining contract. It is rarely alleged that a union has failed to bargain in good faith.

 ## Labor Relations in Selected Countries

A discussion of the labor-relations laws of certain European countries and Japan follows.

United Kingdom

Workers in the United Kingdom are free to organize and join labor unions. A trade union that has been recognized by the employer for collective-bargaining purposes enjoys certain rights, including (1) the right of time off for union officials and members, (2) the right to appoint a representative to handle safety matters, (3) the right to be consulted prior to the transferring of the place of business, and (4) the right to receive certain information related to collective-bargaining issues.

Although collective-bargaining agreements are commonplace, they are not generally enforceable as contracts unless incorporated into an individual employment contract.

Germany

German workers are allowed to form unions, known under German law as "associations." There are three main national unions: (1) the DGB, representing tradespersons; (2) the DAG, representing salaried employees; and (3) the DBB, representing civil service workers. Approximately one-third of the German work force is represented by unions.

A single collective-bargaining agreement applies to

IN BRIEF

UNFAIR LABOR PRACTICES

By Employers

1. Interfering with employees' rights to organize and bargain collectively:
   - Threatening employees with any adverse action for organizing or supporting a union
   - Promising employees any benefits if they fail to support a union
   - Questioning employees regarding union activity
   - Engaging in surveillance of employees' union activities
2. Enforcing an overly broad rule against soliciting other employees for union support or distributing union literature
3. Punishing employees for engaging in concerted activities for mutual aid and protection
4. Dominating or assisting a labor organization
5. Discriminating against any employee to encourage or discourage membership in any labor organization
6. Discharging or otherwise discriminating against an employee because he or she has filed charges with the NLRB
7. Failing to bargain collectively and in good faith:
   - Changing some term or condition of employment, unless bargaining with the union has come to an impasse and the changes are consistent with the union's pre-impasse proposal
   - Failing to bargain over mandatory subjects
8. Refusing to reinstate workers who engage in an unfair labor practice strike

By Unions

1. Unlawful strikes
2. Coercing employees to join the union or support its activities
3. Failing to fairly and honestly represent all of the employees in a collective bargaining unit, without regard to their union affiliation
4. Inducing employer discrimination against non-union workers
5. Failing to bargain in good faith

all unionized workers within a particular trade or industry. In some cases, upon approval by the federal minister of labor, a collective-bargaining agreement may bind all workers in an industry, whether unionized or not. A German statute establishes the right to strike.

France

French labor relations are governed primarily by laws and regulations rather than by collective-bargaining agreements.[27] These laws and regulations establish wages, the work week, health and safety conditions, legal holidays, and paid vacations. They also prohibit certain types of discrimination.

French workers are free to organize and join unions if they so choose. Workers may elect employee representatives or, in larger companies, a personnel committee to express their concerns to management. The *Code du travail* (Employment Code) provides for the negotiation of collective agreements between workers and employers, and the right to strike is fundamental.[28]

Italy

The Italian Constitution grants workers the right to unionize and strike. Organized labor in Italy is dominated by a number of national labor unions. The *Statuto dei lavoratori*, the Workers' Bill of Rights, regulates most aspects of working conditions and union activities. Collective-bargaining agreements negotiated between representatives of management and labor unions legally bind only those who belong to the organizations who signed the agreements and those who have elected to adopt them.

Spain

Spanish workers are represented by works councils, which voice their concerns to and bargain with management. Collective-bargaining agreements are negotiated by a maximum of 24 representatives, half from management and half from labor. An agreement is reached when 60% of each side votes in favor of adopt-

ing an agreement.

Belgium

Article 20 of the Belgian Constitution and Section 1 of the Law of May 24, 1921 give workers in Belgium the right to unionize or refrain from doing so. Belgian unions not only participate in collective bargaining but also influence the enactment of government regulations and participate in the management of public organizations in the labor field.

Bargaining is conducted by approximately 20 employer federations. Most collective-bargaining agreements concluded at the national level bind all employers, even if they are not members of the employers' organization that signed the agreement. Similarly, the majority of collective-bargaining agreements concluded at the industry level bind all employers in the industry at issue, even if they do not belong to the employers' organization that signed the agreement.

Switzerland

The Swiss Constitution does not give workers the right to unionize and strike. However, federal legislation has established the right of workers to join or refrain from joining a union. There are six major labor unions in Switzerland, organized along trade or industry lines. Collective-bargaining agreements are common, and nonunion workers may enjoy the benefits of such agreements with the consent of the parties to the agreement.

Japan

Three major statutes govern labor conditions and relations in Japan. The Labor Standards Law regulates matters such as labor contracts, wages, and discrimination; the Labor Union Law and the Labor Relations Adjustment Law regulate unionization, strikes, and related matters. Collective bargaining occurs only during April and May of each year. Labor–management councils assist in collective bargaining. Of Japan's approximately 72,700 unions, Rengo (Private-Sector Trade Union Confederation) is the largest.[29]

---

27. C. TRAV., arts. L 131-1–136-4, R 132-1–136-11.

28. Declaration of Rights of the Constitution of October 27, 1946, Preamble ¶ 6, confirmed by the Preamble of the Constitution of October 4, 1958; C. TRAV., art. L 521-1.

29. INVESTING, LICENSING AND TRADING CONDITIONS ABROAD 2:21 (Business Intl. Corp., 1989); *Hosokawa to Canvass Coalition Heads on Cabinet Reshuffle*, JAPAN ECON. NEWSWIRE, Feb. 25, 1994.

THE RESPONSIBLE MANAGER
Building Good Labor Relations

A manager should, at a minimum, observe the restrictions that the National Labor Relations Act places upon employer activity. He or she should not threaten adverse treatment if employees support a union, interrogate employees about their union activities, promise employees benefits if they abandon the union, or spy on union activities.

However, a manager is permitted by law to discuss certain matters with employees. He or she may tell employees that the company opposes a union. A manager may review with employees the disadvantages of unionism, such as the possibility of strikes and the payment of union dues and initiation fees. Managers may also discuss with employees their current benefits and the company's history of favorable treatment of employees, which has occurred without a union. He or she may tell employees that it is unlawful for the union to attempt to harass or intimidate them into supporting it.

Most managers in the United States have a visceral negative reaction to attempts to unionize their workers, believing that unions interfere with management control in the workplace and hinder efforts to achieve competitive levels of costs, quality, and productivity.[30] Yet, some academics argue that there is systemic empirical evidence indicating that unions were positively associated with training expenditures, successful employee involvement, and successful quality-improvement programs and organizational innovation.[31] Indeed, many of the best-known examples of high-performance production systems occur at unionized plants, such as those at Saturn, Xerox, Corning, Levi Strauss, NUMMI, and AT&T.[32] Thus, it behooves managers to consider carefully the potential benefits as well as disadvantages of unionization when deciding whether to oppose efforts to unionize.

When a union lawfully represents a unit of employees, management is required by the NLRA to meet at reasonable times with the union and confer in good faith with respect to wages, hours, and other terms and conditions of employment. The law does not specify how many times or for how long the employer must meet with the union. At a minimum, the employer cannot refuse to meet with the union at all or meet on so few occasions that it is almost impossible to attain an agreement. If a union accuses an employer of unlawfully attempting to delay bargaining, the NLRB will look at all of the surrounding circumstances, including the number and length of meetings, the reasons given by the employer for any delays, and any conditions placed upon bargaining by the employer. Some courts have held that an employer must approach collective bargaining with the same seriousness with which it would approach the negotiation of a commercial contract. In this regard, it may be useful for the manager to review the suggestions for good faith negotiations provided in Chapter 7.

The NLRA also requires management to give the union the information it needs to discharge its collective-bargaining duties adequately. The general rule is that management must disclose relevant information, such as employees' wages, overtime hours, surveys leading to changes in working conditions, layoffs resulting from subcontracting, and seniority lists. However, some courts hold that the employer need disclose only information that is both relevant and necessary. Thus, management may not be required to disclose particularly sensitive employee data, such as the results of employee aptitude or intelligence tests.

Management must be careful about withdrawing any proposals it has made during bargaining. An employer's reneging upon such proposals may be evidence of bad faith, though it is not normally a *per se* violation of the law. In determining whether the withdrawal of collective bargaining offers amounts to bad faith, the NLRB considers such factors as the subjects on which the offer was withdrawn, the number of times the employer reneged, and the reasons offered by the employer for reneging.

If management questions the validity of union activities relating to an election, then it may challenge the election in court. Although this may be an effective tool to address unfair labor practices by a union, management should not abuse the process by needlessly delaying the implementation of election results.[33] Moreover, management should abide by the directives of the NRLB and court orders. For example, one poultry producer in Texas delayed implementation of a successful organizing effort through litigation for ten years, then refused to respond to court and administrative orders to comply. The NLRB sought a contempt order against the poultry producer. Such intransigence engenders distrust and resentment by workers and is fundamentally disrespectful to the judiciary and the NLRB.

31. *Id.* at 248.

32. *Id.*

33. *See* G. Pascal Zachary, *Long Litigation Often Holds Up Union Victories,* Wall St. J., Nov. 17, 1995, at B1.

30. *See* Jeffery Pfeffer, The Human Equation: Building Profits by Putting People First 226 (1998).

INSIDE STORY

UPS STRIKERS DELIVER A WAKE-UP PACKAGE TO BUSINESS

On August 19, 1997, the Teamsters Union reached an agreement with the United Parcel Service of America (UPS) ending a 185,000-worker strike that had crippled the package-delivery giant. The Teamsters won concessions from UPS on its core demands, including higher wages, better pay for part-time workers, and more full-time positions. Specifically, UPS agreed to convert 10,000 part-time jobs to full-time positions, thereby doubling the hourly pay. UPS abandoned a plan to opt out of the Teamsters' pension plan, and agreed to average pay raises of 15% over five years for part-time workers. Full-time workers would benefit from a 35% pay raise over five years.

The UPS strike was significant for a number of reasons. First, it was the first strike in years that the general public supported. Although many people were inconvenienced, polls indicated that the public supported the strikers by a 2-to-1 ratio over management.[34] Essentially, the UPS strikers became the symbol for all part-time workers in America. As wages and other compensation as a percentage of national income have de-

clined from 1993 through 1996, corporate profits have increased.[35] As a result, more people are feeling excluded from the benefits of economic prosperity. As John W. Alden, UPS vice-chairman, remarked after the settlement, "If I had known that it was going to go from negotiating for UPS to negotiating for part-time America, we would've approached it differently."[36]

Second, the UPS strike contravened the common wisdom that the labor movement in the United States is dead. Although the percentage of American workers who are union members has consistently declined over time, the UPS strike indicates that labor is still strong. Indeed, UPS had difficulty recovering from the strike and may have permanently lost a substantial portion of its most profitable customers.[37]

Hoping to ride a wave of optimism and success, union organizers have intensified their efforts to organize low-wage and part-time workers. This coincides with other ways labor has been renewing itself, from updating its songs of solidarity[38] to strategic union mergers to

reduce in-fighting and consolidate political power.[39] Thus, many opine that the UPS strike will give more confidence to other collective-bargaining units.

For example, after the successful Teamsters strike, the Independent Pilots Association, UPS's in-house pilot union, authorized a strike amidst continuing contract negotiations. UPS and the pilots reached an agreement shortly thereafter. Additionally, shortly after the UPS–Teamsters strike, labor won the largest organizing victory in the private sector since 1987 when non-union ground workers of US Airways Group, Inc. decided to be represented by the Communications Workers of America.[40]

The third way in which the UPS strike was significant was that the parties resolved the dispute themselves. After the strike by the American Airlines flight attendants in 1993, in which President Clinton took the unusual step of brokering an agreement, commentators were unclear whether the White House would intervene.

In the American Airlines strike, President Clinton had personally called the chairman of

American Airlines and the president of the flight attendants' union. These were the most direct steps taken by a president to influence the outcome of a work stoppage since President Reagan dismissed striking air traffic controllers in 1981. President Bush had refused to intervene in an Eastern Airlines strike in 1989 and had given his approval to federal intervention in a freight-rail strike in 1992 only after Congress passed a law calling for such action.

Although presidential pressure can be effective, after the American Airlines strike, experts cautioned that such efforts could induce managers and unions to rely upon government officials to broker settlements, rather than using existing dispute resolution mechanisms. Indeed, President Clinton indicated that the White House would mediate labor conflicts only in "extreme situations" that "pose a threat" to the public. Thus, the resolution of the UPS strike without intervention by politicians signaled the reluctance of the President to resolve such private problems and forced UPS and the Teamsters to come to a mutually beneficial settlement.

Finally, the UPS sparked many objections to organized labor. For example, the *Wall Street Journal* ran two editorials denouncing union coercion by featuring the misfortune of Rod Carter. Carter was a nonstriking UPS employee who was assaulted and stabbed with an ice pick by strike supporters.[41] And even though union officials denounced such violence, hundreds of individuals complained to organizations and on Web sites of harassment, heckling, threats of violence, and actual violence related to the UPS strike. Thus, although the UPS labor conflagration symbolized the strength and vitality of unions in America, opponents denounced such organizing as coercive and prone to violence.

34. Paul Magnusson et al., *Wake-up Call for Business: The Teamsters' Win Means Workers Can No Longer Be Taken for Granted*, BUS. WK., Sept. 1, 1997, at 28.

35. Aaron Bernstein, *Sharing Prosperity*, BUS. WK., Sept. 1, 1997, at 64.

36. Paul Magnusson et al., *supra* note 34, at 29.

37. Douglas A. Blackmon, *UPS Still Fails to Wrap Up Its Recovery from Strike: Some Customers Have Never Returned, and Pilots Threaten New Disruption*, WALL ST. J., Dec. 8, 1997, at B4.

38. Asra Q. Nomani, *Unions Sing, But Not the Same Old Songs*, WALL ST. J., Sept. 19, 1995, at B1.

39. *Unions of Auto Workers, Steelworkers and Machinist Agree to Merge by 2001*, WALL ST. J., July 27, 1995, at A3.

40. Susan Carey, *US Air Workers Choose CWA in Rerun Ballot*, WALL ST. J., Sept. 30, 1997, at C20.

41. *Union Casualties*, WALL ST. J., Sept. 2, 1997, at A18; *Brother Acuna*, WALL ST. J., Sept. 15, 1997, at A22.

KEY WORDS AND PHRASES

concerted activity **508**
economic strike **514**
implementation after impasse doctrine **511**
independent contractor **505**
irrebuttable presumption **514**
neutral-gate system **518**

organizational strikes **517**
per se violation **514**
primary employer **518**
recognitional strike **517**
representation elections **505**
runaway shop **513**
secondary boycott **517**

showing of interest **505**
supervisor **505**
unfair labor practices **506**
unfair labor practice strike **517**
union authorization cards **505**
union security clause **510**

QUESTIONS AND CASE PROBLEMS

1. Terry Spence, a computer trainer at Compuware Corp., was discharged after he threatened to tell Compuware's client about work-related problems. Although Spence was the only employee who threatened to complain, he had consulted with other employees before threatening to speak out. Was Spence engaged in concerted activity? Did his discharge violate the NLRA? Does it matter whether Compuware knew that Spence had consulted with other employees? [*Compuware Corp. v. NLRB*, 134 F.3d 1285 (6th Cir. 1998)]

2. For some time, the Acme Dye Company suspected that a union was attempting to organize its production and maintenance workers. The employer's suspicions were confirmed when Local 123 of the Teamsters Union filed a petition with the National Labor Relations Board asking it to hold a union representation election. Because Acme believed that its employees were unhappy with their relatively low wage levels, Acme sent out a memorandum to all employees immediately after the filing of the petition, thanking them for their hard work and announcing an immediate 5% pay increase for all employees.

Does the announcement of the pay increase, which came as a complete surprise to the employees, violate the National Labor Relations Act? Would it make any difference if the employer could demonstrate that it had planned for several weeks before the filing of the petition to grant a wage increase and that it was merely coincidence that the announcement came on the heels of the union petition? Would the answer be the same if the employer made the announcement just before the filing of the petition? [*NLRB v. Exchange Parts Co.*, 375 U.S. 405 (1964)]

3. Beverly Health and Rehabilitation Services (Beverly) owns and operates over 750 health-care facilities for elderly or infirm individuals nationwide. The service and maintenance employees at 20 of these health-care facilities in Pennsylvania are unionized. In November, the most recent collective-bargaining agreements expired but the staff worked as negotiations proceeded. The unionized employees complained of numerous unfair labor practices under the NLRA to the NLRB, including removal of union bulletin boards, denial of established access of union representatives to union members, changes in health-care insurance, reduction in work hours, unilateral changes in employee policies, denial of information relevant to contract negotiations, prohibitions against wearing union insignia, prohibitions against bringing union literature onto the premises, and Beverly's direct contact with unionized employees to influence continued union membership. As a result, the union commenced an unfair labor practice strike at 15 facilities. After the strike, Beverly refused to reinstate many of the striking employees, despite their unconditional offer to return to work. Nine months after the strike, Beverly had not reinstated

66 employees; and 115 employees had either quit or been fired. The NLRB sought a temporary injunction seeking cessation of the alleged unfair labor practices in addition to reinstatement of striking employees.

a. Should the NLRB be granted a temporary injunction to facilitate a peaceful resolution to labor–management friction? Why? Are there any themes in the alleged unfair labor practices of Beverly? [*Kobell v. Beverly Health and Rehabilitation Services, Inc.*, 987 F. Supp. 409 (W.D. Pa. 1997)]

b. What if Beverly had only prevented union members from posting union material on company bulletin boards on which any employee was permitted to post non-union material, such as For Sale signs? Would this practice, during a union organizing campaign, violate the NLRA by making organizational efforts more expensive; or is the company simply not subsidizing unions by distributing their literature free of charge? [*Guardian Indus. Corp. v. NLRB*, 49 F.3d 317 (7th Cir. 1995)]

4. After a successful union organizing attempt at one of its facilities, the Hastings Rug Company decided that it would not be able to afford the substantial increases in labor costs that it believed would result from unionization. It decided to shut down that plant and go out of business altogether. This closure of its entire business resulted in the layoff of all of its employees, many of whom had voted for the union.

Would the closure of the business, with the resultant layoff of union supporters, violate the National Labor Relations Act? Would it make any difference if the company had simply shut down that facility and transferred its work to its other, non-union, plants rather than closing the entire business? What would the result be if the company simply closed the non-unionized facility and opened an entirely new facility in a nearby town? [*Local 57, ILGWU v. NLRB*, 374 F.2d 295 (D.C. Cir. 1967), *cert. denied*, 387 U.S. 942 (1967)]

5. Teamsters Local Union 122 was engaged in a labor dispute with August A. Busch & Company, a beer distributor. On three occasions numerous union members descended on the employer's stores and bought small items, such as packs of bubble gum or bags of potato chips, and paid for them with bills of large denominations. These shopping expeditions, involving between 50 and 125 participants, crowded the employer's store and created long checkout lines, full parking lots, and delays for regular customers on days that were usually particularly lucrative for the employer. The activity was not presented to the general public as an official union activity. The employer filed a complaint with the NLRB that the associational shopping constituted a secondary boycott insofar as it aimed to deter retailers from purchasing the employer's beverages. Are the "shop-ins" a secondary boycott that should be enjoined as an unfair union practice? [*Pye v. Teamsters Local Union No. 122,* 61 F.3d 1013 (1st Cir. 1995)]

6. The International Brotherhood of Electrical Workers petitioned the NLRB to hold an election among clerical employees of the Phoenix Tire Company. Forty-two of the 100 employees in the appropriate collective-bargaining unit signed cards stating that they wished the union to represent them for collective bargaining. During the course of the election campaign, the company committed many unfair labor practices, such as interrogating employees about their union activities, threatening employees with loss of benefits if they voted for the union, and promising them increased wages and free vacations to Hawaii if the union were voted down. In addition, the three employees who were believed to be the principal union supporters were discharged, ostensibly for legitimate business reasons, but actually because of their union activity. In the union representation election, of the 96 employees who cast ballots, only 10 voted for the union.

Following the election, the union filed objections based upon the employer's conduct. Is the NLRB likely to set aside the results of the first election and order a second one?

The union then filed charges alleging that the employer's actions were illegal. It requested the NLRB to order the company to bargain with the union even without a second election because the employer's illegal acts were so pervasive that there was no reasonable chance for a free and fair election. Should the NLRB order the employer to bargain with the union, even without a second election? Should it make any difference in the analysis if more than half of the employees in the collective-bargaining unit had signed cards requesting the union to represent them? [*NLRB v. Gissel Packing Co.,* 395 U.S. 575 (1969)]

7. In May 1990, the United Food and Commercial Workers Local 400 started organizing the workers of approximately 30 Be-Lo grocery stores in southern Virginia. Less than one year later, the union informed management that a majority of its workers had signed authorization cards indicating that they supported collective representation by the union. As a result, an election was scheduled for late March 1991. Between February and March, the company initiated a campaign to dissuade its workers from voting for the union. Its tactics included videos, memoranda, meetings, and the dissemination of information about stores that had been forced to close after unionization, through flyers in the form of a mock "pink slip." The company focused on the potential harms that would result from a union win. In March, the union lost the election by a vote of 377 to 220. Did Be-Lo engage in any unfair labor practices before the election? If so, what is the appropriate remedy? If not, does the union have the right to picket at a number of Be-Lo grocery stores? Why? [*Be-Lo Stores v. NLRB,* 126 F.3d 268 (4th Cir. 1997)]

8. The Armstrong Rubber Company provides rubber to a nearby tire manufacturer, Steelbelt Tire. The Rubber Workers of America (RWA), which represents the production and maintenance workers of Steelbelt, recently struck Steelbelt after the breakdown of collective-bargaining negotiations. Ordinarily, Armstrong drivers deliver the rubber to Steelbelt, but they now refuse to cross the picket line established by the RWA. Steelbelt sent one of its replacement workers over to Armstrong to pick up a load of rubber. A group of strikers followed that driver and picketed Armstrong's facility while the driver from Steelbelt was on Armstrong's premises collecting the rubber. When that driver left, the picketers left as well.

Is the RWA's picketing of Armstrong unlawful under these circumstances? Would it make any difference if the pickets remained at Armstrong long after they knew that the driver from Steelbelt had left? Would it be a violation of the National Labor Relations Act for the RWA to picket Armstrong at all times, simply because Armstrong did business with the tire manufacturer? [*IBEW, Local 861 (Plauche Elec., Inc.),* 135 N.L.R.B. 250 (1962)]

9. In the course of collective-bargaining negotiations, the union and the employer are far apart on the question of proposed wage increases. The union has demanded a wage increase of $1.00 per hour; the employer has offered three increases of 25 cents per hour over the next three years. The employer tells the union that it simply cannot afford the union's wage demands and that, if it grants them, it will no longer be competitive. The union believes that the employer can easily afford its requested wage increases. The union asks to inspect the company's financial records so it can determine for itself whether the employer is in a position to afford its wage demands. The employer refuses, telling the union that those records are highly confidential and that their disclosure to competitors would be extremely damaging.

May the company lawfully refuse to disclose the requested records? Would it make any difference if the union agreed to keep the records confidential? Should it make a difference if the company refused to accede to the union's wage demands, not on the ground that it cannot afford them, but on the ground that those demands are out of line with the collective-bargaining agreements that have been reached recently with its competitors? [*NLRB v. Truitt Mfg. Co.*, 351 U.S. 149 (1956)]

MANAGER'S DILEMMA

10. The Jonestown Metal Company manufactures metal rods for construction. The 200 members of the production and maintenance unit are represented by the Teamsters Union. The collective-bargaining contract contains a provision that there will be no strikes or work stoppages of any kind during the term of the contract. With the employer's agreement, the union designated four employees to act as shop stewards to represent it in day-to-day matters with the employer. On a hot summer day, the employer's air-conditioning system broke down, but the employer refused to allow employees to go home because of the critical need to fill an order immediately. Nearly all the represented workers then walked out of the plant, without obtaining the union's approval. The shop stewards walked out too; but they neither encouraged nor discouraged other employees to do the same. When the workers returned the next day, the employer informed them that all regular employees would be suspended for one day for their walkout. The shop stewards were discharged because they failed to take any action to halt the strike, which violated the collective-bargaining agreement.

Is the employer entitled to impose more severe discipline on the union shop stewards than on the other employees? Would it make a difference if the collective-bargaining contract stated that shop stewards would use their best efforts to prevent employees from engaging in strikes that violate the collective-bargaining contract? [*Metropolitan Edison Co. v. NLRB*, 460 U.S. 693 (1983)]

INTERNET SOURCES	
Department of Labor	http://www.dol.gov
Teamsters Union	http://www.teamster.org
Index of laws and articles on labor law	http://www.findlaw.com/01topics/27labor
This National Right to Work Legal Defense Foundation site provides links to articles, cases, and laws applicable to compulsory unionism, union violence, and use of union dues for political lobbying.	http://www.nrtw.org
United Food and Commercial Workers International Union	http://www.ufcw.org
AFL-CIO	http://www.aflcio.org

CHAPTER 15

Criminal Law

INTRODUCTION

Impact on Corporate Behavior

Criminal law is a powerful tool for controlling corporate behavior and ensuring ethical conduct. In the corporate setting, significant resources are devoted to preventing and defending criminal law violations. For instance, Motorola, Inc., a Fortune 100 electronics company that specializes in such products as semiconductors, pagers, and cellular telephones, has an 80-attorney in-house legal staff. Rich Weise, the general counsel, recalls that in 1984 no one on his legal staff worked full-time on criminal law issues. In 1994, Weise estimated that six attorneys at Motorola, including a former federal prosecutor, work full-time on criminal law issues. These attorneys counsel managers on how to avoid criminal liability in such areas as defense procurement contracts, antitrust law compliance, securities trading by officers and directors, and toxic substances restrictions as spelled out in the Occupational Safety and Health Act and in the environmental laws. Motorola has also assembled a multidisciplinary investigation team, com-

posed of attorneys, accountants, and other personnel, that is deployed if a crisis arises.

Criminal liability may be imposed in several ways. Individuals are always responsible for their criminal acts, even if working under orders from top management. Individuals may also be responsible for the acts of their subordinates. A corporation itself may also be found guilty of a criminal act, even though the corporation's employees committed the criminal act.

Chapter Overview

This chapter defines the elements necessary to create criminal liability. It discusses the statutory sources of criminal law and describes criminal procedure—the mechanics of a criminal action, the plea options, and the trial. Constitutional issues include search warrant requirements and restrictions on police interrogation. The chapter concludes with a discussion of white-collar and computer crime as well as the Racketeer Influenced and Corrupt Organizations Act (RICO) and other federal criminal statutes.

 ### Definition of a Crime

A *crime* is an offense against the public at large. It may be defined as any act that violates the duties owed to

the community, for which the offender must make satisfaction to the public. An act is criminal only if it is defined as criminal in a federal or state statute or in a local ordinance enacted by a city or county.

Two elements are necessary to create criminal liability: (1) an act that violates an existing criminal statute, and (2) the requisite state of mind.

The Criminal Act

The term *actus reus* (guilty act or wrongful deed) is often used to describe the act in question. A crime is not committed unless some overt act has occurred. Merely thinking about a criminal activity is not criminal.

The State of Mind

Generally, a crime is not committed unless the criminal act named in the statute is performed with the requisite state of mind, known as *mens rea* (guilty mind). However, under some statutes, a person can be guilty regardless of his or her state of mind. This is known as *strict liability.*

Strict Liability   Strict liability statutes are generally disfavored. Most courts will require clear legislative intent before they will construe a statute as imposing strict liability. The Supreme Court has stated that the requirement of "a relation between some mental element and punishment for a harmful act is almost as instinctive as the child's familiar exculpatory 'But I didn't mean to.'"[1] Typically, strict liability statutes address issues of public health and safety. (Strict liability statutes that provide for vicarious criminal liability are discussed later in the chapter.)

Mens Rea   The three forms of *mens rea* are negligence, recklessness, and intention to do wrong. Negligence is the least culpable state of mind, while intention to do wrong is the most culpable. The statute that defines the criminal act also defines the requisite state of mind. Generally speaking, crimes associated with a higher degree of culpability are punished more severely. Convictions for intentional homicide, for instance, bring penalties far more harsh than those for negligent homicide.

Negligence is the failure to see the possible negative consequences that a reasonable person would have seen. An individual may be negligent even if he or she did not know of the possible harm of his or her act. All that is necessary is that a reasonable person would have known of the possible harm. A reasonable person is often thought of as a rational person using ordinary care under the circumstances. *Recklessness* in the criminal context is conscious disregard of a substantial risk that the individual's actions would result in the harm prohibited by the statute. Recklessness is found when the individual knew of the possible harm of his or her act, but ignored the risk. A person has an *intention to do wrong* when he or she consciously intends to cause the harm prohibited by the statute, or when he or she knows such harm is substantially certain to result from his or her conduct.

Merely being able to define these terms, however, often does not provide an answer to more complex questions of real-world guilt. Consider the intention-to-do-wrong requirement in the context of the federal false-statement statute.[2] The statute makes it a crime to "knowingly and willfully" make any false statement or representation "in any manner within the jurisdiction of any department or agency of the United States." Suppose a defendant makes a statement to a federal agent that she knew was false. However, she did not know that the person to whom she directed the statement was a federal agent. Would this defendant be convicted?

In *United States v. Yermian*,[3] the U.S. Supreme Court ruled that she would be. The Court applied the "intention to do wrong" requirement only to the "false statement" portion of the statute. In other words, it required only that a defendant knowingly lie to a person who is in fact a federal agent, rather than requiring that she knowingly lie to person that she knows is a federal agent.

A commonly invoked platitude is "ignorance of the law is no excuse." While true as a general principle, this is an imprecise rule that, taken alone, does not tell courts how to apply the *mens rea* requirements of particular criminal statutes. The following case illustrates the substantial room for interpretation and debate that often exists.

---

1. Morissette v. United States, 342 U.S. 246, 250–51 (1952).

2. 18 U.S.C. § 1001 (1994).

3. 468 U.S. 63 (1984).

| A CASE IN POINT | SUMMARY |

CASE 15.1

LIPAROTA v.
UNITED STATES

Supreme Court
of the United States
471 U.S. 419 (1985).

FACTS   Frank Liparota owned a sandwich shop in Chicago. He was indicted for acquiring and possessing food stamps in violation of the federal statute governing food stamp fraud. The statute provides that "whoever knowingly uses, transfers, acquires, alters or possesses coupons or authorization cards in any manner not authorized by [the statute] or the regulations" is subject to a fine and imprisonment. Neither the statute nor the regulations authorize the sale of food stamps for cash.

On three occasions, Liparota purchased food stamps from an undercover Department of Agriculture agent for substantially less than their face value. Liparota was convicted by a jury at trial. The court of appeals affirmed the conviction. Liparota appealed.

ISSUE PRESENTED   In order to obtain a conviction under the federal food-stamp-fraud statute, must the government prove (1) that the defendant acquired food stamps in a manner that *he knew* was unauthorized, or (2) merely that the defendant acquired food stamps in a manner that was in fact unauthorized?

SUMMARY OF OPINION   The U.S. Supreme Court acknowledged that it was unclear how far down the sentence "knowingly" travelled and that there were two ways to interpret the mental state (or *mens rea*) required by the federal food-stamp-fraud statute. The government argued that Liparota violated the statute if he knew that he was acquiring food stamps and if in fact that acquisition was not authorized by statute or regulations. Liparota argued that an individual violates the statute only if he knows he has acquired food stamps and if he also knows he has done so in an unauthorized manner. The Court's task was to determine which meaning Congress intended.

The question was made more difficult by the fact that either interpretation would accord with ordinary usage. Moreover, the legislative history of the statute contained nothing that clarified the congressional purpose on this point.

Accordingly, the Court looked for guidance in the "background assumption[s] of our criminal law." The Court noted that when statutory language is ambiguous, it traditionally assumes some *mens rea* is required.

The Court felt this construction was particularly appropriate because to interpret the statute otherwise would criminalize a broad range of apparently innocent conduct. For instance, the broad reading of the statute advanced by the government would render criminal someone who possessed food stamps because they were mistakenly sent to him through the mail due to clerical error. The Court determined that such a result was not what Congress intended.

In order to convict Liparota, the government needed to prove that he knew that his acquisition of the food stamps was in a manner unauthorized by statute or regulations. However, the government was not required to introduce any extraordinary evidence that would conclusively demonstrate the defendant's state of mind. "Rather, as in any other criminal prosecution requiring *mens rea*, the Government may prove by reference to facts and circumstances surrounding the case that petitioner knew that his conduct was unauthorized or illegal."

Case 15.1 continues

Case 15.1 continued

RESULT The decision of the court of appeals was reversed and Liparota's conviction was overturned.

COMMENTS The Supreme Court held in *Bryan v. United States*[4] that as a general matter, when used in the criminal context, a "willful" act is "one undertaken with a 'bad purpose.' In other words, in order to establish a 'willful' violation of a statute, 'the Government must prove that the defendant acted with knowledge that his conduct was unlawful.'" In contrast, the term "knowingly" merely requires proof of knowledge of the facts that constitute the offense, not knowledge of unlawfulness, unless (as in *Liparota*) the text of the statute dictates a different result.

4. 118 S. Ct. 1939 (1998).

 ## Sources of Criminal Law

Conviction of a crime can lead to a substantial fine, a jail sentence, or even the death penalty. Because the results of a criminal conviction can be so serious, all criminal liability is specifically defined in statutes, which are binding on a court. In contrast, much of civil law was developed by the courts without applicable statutes.

A criminal charge and prosecution are brought by either the state or federal government. Under most federal and state laws, crimes are divided into two categories. A *felony* is a crime punishable by death or by imprisonment for more than one year. A *misdemeanor* is a less serious crime, punishable by a fine or a jail sentence of one year or less.

The Model Penal Code

The criminal statutes of the individual states and the federal government are similar, but not exactly the same. This is because most states have adopted the Model Penal Code but have modified it to meet their own needs. The Model Penal Code is a set of criminal law statutes that were proposed by the National Conference of Commissioners of Uniform State Laws for adoption by the states.

 ## The Federal Sentencing Guidelines

State and federal criminal statutes normally specify penalties that include both jail time and monetary fines. The length of a jail sentence is usually within a specified range. In a state court, if the defendant is found guilty, the judge generally has sentencing discretion within that range. In a federal court, the judge has considerably less discretion and must follow the Federal Sentencing Guidelines.

Federal Sentencing Guidelines for Individuals

The United States Sentencing Commission is an independent agency in the judicial branch charged with monitoring criminal-sentencing practices in the federal courts. In creating the commission, Congress sought to create an honest, fair, and effective federal-sentencing system, with reasonable uniformity in the sentences imposed for similar criminal offenses committed by similar offenders. The commission established sentencing guidelines, which create categories of "offense behavior" and "offender characteristics." A sentencing court must select a sentence (up to the maximum authorized by statute for each federal crime) from within the guide-line ranges specified by the combined categories. In unusual cases, a court may depart from the guidelines but must specify reasons for the departure.

Congress abolished federal parole in 1984. Rather than permit a parole commission to decide how much of a sentence an offender actually serves, an offender serves the full sentence imposed by the court under the sentencing guidelines, less approximately 15% for good behavior.

The average length of prison sentences imposed for offenders in federal district courts in 1994 was 133.5 months for murder, 68.5 months for rape, 15.6 months for tax law violations, 22 months for bribery, 21 months for fraud, 3.2 months for antitrust offenses, and 12.6 months for embezzlement.[5]

Federal Sentencing Guidelines for Organizations

The Federal Sentencing Guidelines for Organizations, enacted in 1991, specify stiff fines for companies convicted of fraud, antitrust violations, and most types of corporate wrongdoing. According to the Sentencing Commission, the guidelines for organizations were "designed so that the sanctions imposed upon organizations and their agents . . . will provide just punishment, adequate deterrence, and incentives for organizations to maintain internal mechanisms for preventing, detecting and reporting criminal conduct."[6]

The guidelines take a carrot-and-stick approach. The "stick" is that organizations are held liable for the criminal actions of all their employees and agents. The "carrot" is that a company's maintenance of a meaningful voluntary-compliance program is deemed a mitigating factor that will reduce otherwise applicable fines. A company can also achieve significant mitigation of fines by cooperating with or self-reporting misconduct to authorities.

Experts claim the guidelines "have been a watershed, especially as a policy initiative in terms of how government should affect corporate misconduct."[7] Indeed, the guidelines are consistently cited as one of the

---

5. BUREAU OF JUSTICE STATISTICS, SOURCEBOOK OF CRIMINAL JUSTICE STATISTICS 1996, 442 (1997).

6. Itamar Sittenfeld, *Federal Sentencing Guidelines*, INTERNAL AUDITOR, Apr. 1996, at 58.

7. *Criminal Sentencing Guidelines Are Working, Conference Speakers Say*, 66 U.S.L.W. 2287 (1997).

AT THE TOP

To take advantage of the Federal Sentencing Guidelines provisions that reduce culpability for a company with an effective compliance program, a company must have in place the following due diligence strategies:

1. **Standards and procedures to reduce criminal conduct**   A viable code of conduct is a good starting point.
2. **High-level personnel in charge of program**   The audit committee of the board could accept oversight of the program.
3. **Due care in delegating authority**   The fox can't guard the hen house.
4. **Effective communication and training**   A well-designed video can help ensure ongoing training about the standards.
5. **Mechanisms for monitoring and reporting criminal misconduct**   An anonymous toll-free hotline might help encourage reporting of misconduct.
6. **Consistent enforcement of standards, including investigation and discipline**
7. **Procedures for feedback and correction**

SOURCE   This summary of the seven-step program is drawn from Itamar Sittenfeld, *Federal Sentencing Guidelines*, INTERNAL AUDITOR, Apr. 1996, at 58.

---

most important motivators behind corporate America's rush to embrace compliance programs.

Punishment under the Guidelines   To fully understand the incentive structure created by the guidelines, it is helpful to walk through its calculation of fines for criminal offenses. The first step is to determine the base fine, which is determined according to the severity of the crime. For instance, the base fine for price fixing or making market-allocation agreements among competitors is $20,000 (offense level 10), and the base fine for laundering of money instruments (such as checks) is $1,600,000 (offense level 23). However, if this base fine is exceeded by either the organization's gain or the plaintiff's loss from the crime, then that amount will supplant the base fine.

The second step is to determine the culpability of the organization. A variety of factors come into play, including whether the organization itself was convicted of a crime, whether management condoned or willfully ignored the criminal misconduct, whether management assisted authorities in their investigation, and whether the organization had an effective compliance program in place at the time of misconduct.

As the following example illustrates, the beneficial effects of self-reporting misconduct and maintaining an effective compliance program can be profound. Consider a company being fined for a criminal trademark infringement, where the value of the goods exceeds $500,000. Its base fine would be $175,000, based on an offense level of 16. If the company were convicted of a criminal violation and had a prior history of such violations, it would have a culpability score of 7 (see Table 2 in Exhibit 15.1). This would mean that its fine range would be between $245,000 and $490,000 without any "good news." However, if that company reported its own violation to authorities and had an effective compliance program in place, its net culpability score would be minus 1 (see Table 3 in Exhibit 15.1), resulting in a multiplier of 0.05 to 0.20 (see Table 4 in Exhibit 15.1). In this case, its final fine range would be between $8,750 and $35,000.

Misgivings about the Guidelines The Federal Sentencing Guidelines for Organizations have been credited with encouraging corporations to self-police their own misconduct and to assist authorities in their criminal investigations. The guidelines may tend to foster a "checklist mentality" in many corporations, however, without necessarily bringing about a more law-compliant and ethical work force. One possible shortcoming of the guidelines is that they can encourage companies to adopt all the compliance "bells and whistles," but still send out conflicting—"wink and nod"—signals to employees.

Experts note that criminal misconduct within a corporation is often a function of performance measures and goal-setting that induces people to do what they should not do. Managers should be careful to avoid sending mixed signals that reward performance at all costs regardless of compliance with the law.

Letting Employees Take the Rap When facing a criminal probe, corporations have increasingly responded to the guidelines' encouragement to cooperate with authorities by increasingly turning on their employees to win leniency for themselves. One of the cor-

porate actions viewed favorably by the guidelines is the application of "adequate discipline" to employees deemed responsible for criminal violations. Obviously, a company has an incentive to isolate a small group of "fall guys," fire them, and cooperate with the federal government in their prosecution. This is true despite the fact that it can often be difficult to separate who is really responsible for corporate crimes from who is not.

Consider the case of Darling International, Inc., an animal-feed manufacturer accused of polluting the Blue Earth River in Minnesota.[8] Under financial pressure in 1990–91, the company boosted production, thereby overloading its manufacturing plant's wastewater system. Beginning in the autumn of 1991, the company began illegally dumping millions of gallons of contaminated water, which killed aquatic life in the river. By the spring of 1992, the wastewater system manager, on orders from the plant manager, began diluting wastewater test samples with tap water to try to fool pollution-control authorities. When those authorities found illegal pollution levels in the river, Darling blamed it on a one-time spill.

The federal government began a grand jury investigation in 1993. But that investigation languished until Darling began its own internal investigation in 1996. Under pressure from company counsel conducting this investigation, the wastewater-system manager confessed to the entire dumping and cover-up scheme. Unbeknownst to him, Darling passed this information directly to the government prosecutor. Darling also submitted the manager's name along with the names of three other employees whom the company intended to fire and hold responsible for the scheme. The four Darling employees maintain that they were not the only ones aware of the company's illegal dumping.

The U.S. attorney prosecuting the case said that Darling's disclosure provided the first corroboration of serious crimes and pushed his investigation "light years ahead." He thought the outcome was fair because Darling paid a significant fine and four individuals were held responsible for their actions. Not surprisingly, the four employees, who lost their jobs and faced criminal charges, had a different perspective. In their view, because of the sentencing guidelines, Darling got "to pay

---

8. Details of the *Darling* case are drawn from Dean Starkman, *More Firms Let Employees Take the Rap*, WALL ST. J., Oct. 9, 1997, at B3.

EXHIBIT 15.1   Calculating Corporate Fines under the Federal Sentencing Guidelines

---

Step 1: Determine the base fine (Table 1).
Step 2: Calculate the preliminary culpability score (Table 2).
Step 3: Calculate the mitigating factors score (Table 3).
Step 4: Subtract the mitigating factors score from the preliminary culpability score to find the net culpability score.
Step 5: Determine the appropriate multipliers (Table 4).
Step 6: Multiply the base fine by the multipliers to find the final fine range.

Note that the judge has discretion to determine the actual fine from the final range.

TABLE 1: BASE FINE

The greatest of:

a. Offense level amount:

OFFENSE LEVEL	FINE ($)
6 or less	5,000
. . .	. . .
10	20,000
. . .	. . .
20	650,000
. . .	. . .
30	10,500,000
. . .	. . .
37	57,500,000

b. Gain to the organization
c. Loss incurred by the plaintiff

TABLE 2: PRELIMINARY CULPABILITY SCORE

Score from 5 to 16:

ACTIVITY	SCORE
Conviction	+5
Tolerating, condoning, willfully ignoring	+4
Prior history	+1 or +2
Violating judicial orders	+1 or +2
Obstructing justice	+3

TABLE 3: MITIGATING FACTORS

First, the most beneficial of:

ACTIVITY	SCORE
Self-reporting to authorities	−5
Cooperating with authorities	−2
Accepting responsibility	−1

Then, subtract 3 more for an effective compliance program.

TABLE 4: MULTIPLIERS

CULPABILITY SCORE	MINIMUM MULTIPLIER	MAXIMUM MULTIPLIER
10 or more	2.00	4.00
9	1.80	3.60
8	1.60	3.20
7	1.40	2.80
6	1.20	2.40
5	1.00	2.00
4	0.80	1.60
3	0.60	1.20
2	0.40	0.80
1	0.20	0.40
0 or less	0.05	0.20

their measly fine and wash their hands of the rest of us." Indeed, the employees who cooperated with the investigation bore the brunt of the punishment. As their lawyer asked, is it fair that federal prosecutors set out to destroy individual lives when they could have gone after just the company?

Criminal versus Civil Liability

Many regulatory statutes provide for both criminal and civil sanctions if they are violated. An individual or a corporation may therefore be sued under both criminal and civil law for a single act.

Civil law, and in particular tort law (discussed in Chapter 9), compensates the victim for legal wrongs committed against the person or his or her property. Criminal law protects society by punishing the criminal. It does not compensate the victim. However, the victim of a crime may bring a civil suit for damages against the perpetrator. Violation of a criminal statute is *negligence per se*; this means that in a subsequent civil suit, the court will accept the criminal conviction as sufficient proof that the accused was negligent, that is, that the defendant did not act with the care a reasonable person would have used under the same circumstances. Consequently, defendants must carefully review their criminal defense strategy in light of possible future civil litigation.

Burden of Proof

Criminal trials differ from civil trials in imposing a much heavier *burden of proof*. Generally, to prevail in a civil trial, the plaintiff need only establish the facts by a *preponderance of the evidence*. If the evidence tips the scales only slightly in favor of the plaintiff, he or she wins. In a criminal case, the accused is presumed innocent until proven guilty beyond a reasonable doubt.

ETHICAL CONSIDERATION

Is it ethical for a corporation to "turn in" some but not all of the managers who participated in criminal wrongdoing?

This difference in the degree of proof required is typical of the procedural and constitutional safeguards protecting defendants' rights throughout criminal proceedings. In a criminal case, the formidable resources of the state are focused on an individual. In this contest of unequal strength, it seems only fair to require the state to meet a higher standard of proof. Moreover, the deprivation of personal liberty and the lifelong stigma of criminal conviction are at stake in a criminal prosecution, whereas in a civil lawsuit only monetary damages are at stake.

Criminal Procedure

A criminal action begins with the arrest of the person suspected of a crime and proceeds through a preliminary hearing to plea bargaining and trial.

Arrest

After a person is arrested, he or she is taken to a police station and booked; that is, the charges against him or her are written in a register. The arresting police officer must then file a report with the prosecutor. Based on this report, the prosecutor must decide whether to press charges against the arrested person. If charges are to be pressed, many states require that the accused be taken before a public judicial official, usually a justice of the peace or magistrate, to be informed of the charges against him or her. Bail is often determined during this initial appearance before the public official.

Plea

If the accused is charged with only a misdemeanor, the accused will be asked at this initial appearance whether he or she pleads guilty or not guilty. In the case of a felony, the next step in many states is a preliminary hearing, at which the prosecutor must present evidence demonstrating probable cause that the defendant committed the felony. Following this hearing, formal charges are usually filed either by the prosecutor through an *information*, a document filed with the court, or by a grand jury through an *indictment*. The accused will then be arraigned before a trial court judge. At the arraignment, the accused will be informed of the charges against him or her and be asked to enter a *plea* of guilty or not guilty.

The accused can also plead *nolo contendere*, which means that he or she does not contest the charges. For the purpose of the criminal proceedings, this plea is equivalent to a guilty plea. However, a plea of *nolo contendere*, unlike a guilty plea, cannot be introduced at a subsequent civil trial. Therefore, a *nolo contendere* plea may be used by corporate defendants who anticipate civil suits based on the same activity for which they face criminal charges.

If the defendant enters a plea of not guilty, the case is set for trial.

Plea Bargaining

Very few cases ever reach trial. Most cases are resolved through plea bargaining between the accused and the prosecutor. *Plea bargaining* is the process whereby the prosecutor agrees to reduce the charges in exchange for a guilty plea from the accused.

Frequently, a lower-ranking member of a criminal conspiracy will "cop a plea," that is, provide the prosecutor with testimony incriminating his or her criminal superiors, in exchange for a reduced sentence or immunity from prosecution. The immunity granted may be either use immunity or transactional immunity. *Use immunity* prohibits the testimony of the witness from being used against him or her in any way. *Transactional immunity*, which is broader, prohibits any criminal prosecution of the witness that relates to any matter discussed in his or her testimony.

Consent decrees are common in the corporate context. A *consent decree* is a court order based on an agreement by the defendant corporation to take measures to remedy the problem that led to criminal charges. Like a plea of *nolo contendere*, a consent decree cannot be introduced as evidence of guilt in a subsequent civil trial, and it raises the same ethical considerations for corporations.

Trial

A criminal trial proceeds in much the same way as civil trials, which were discussed in Chapter 3. There are opening statements, direct examination and cross examination of witnesses, and closing arguments. The jury then deliberates to reach a verdict of guilty or not guilty.

◆ Fourth Amendment Protections

The Fourth Amendment to the United States Constitution provides:

> The right of the people to be secure in their persons, houses, papers, and effects, against unreasonable searches and seizures, shall not be violated, and no Warrants shall issue, but upon probable cause, supported by Oath or affirmation, and particularly describing the place to be searched, and the persons or things to be seized.

This provision was intended to prevent the arbitrary and intrusive searches that had characterized British rule during the colonial period. Courts have struggled, however, to strike the appropriate balance between the individual's expectation of privacy and the government's legitimate need to secure evidence of wrongdoing to prevent criminal acts and apprehend criminals. The Fourth Amendment applies only to actions by government officials, unless a private person is acting on behalf of the government.

The Arrest Warrant Requirement

An *arrest* is a Fourth Amendment seizure in which police take a person into custody against his or her will for purposes of criminal prosecution or interrogation. No arrest is valid unless there is probable cause. *Probable cause* for arrest is defined as a reasonable belief that the suspect has committed a crime or is about to commit a crime. The Fourth Amendment does not require that a warrant be obtained prior to an arrest in a public place

ETHICAL CONSIDERATION

A plea of *nolo contendere* is appropriate if the cost of defending a long, drawn out criminal trial is significantly higher than any fines for which the corporation is liable. A *nolo contendere* plea is also appropriate to avoid the emotional costs of defending at a criminal trial. But is it ethical for a corporation to plead *nolo contendere* when its management knows the corporation is guilty of the wrong? Does a corporation have an ethical duty to confess guilt even if it will result in stiffer economic penalties and civil damages?

as long as there is probable cause. Thus, an officer may make a warrantless arrest when the officer has reasonable grounds to believe a felony has been committed by the suspect or when a misdemeanor has been committed in the officer's presence. In general, an arrest warrant is required only for arrests in the suspect's own home or in another person's home.

Some limited stops and detentions may be justified without a showing of probable cause (e.g., brief questioning when police observe unusual conduct that leads to a reasonable suspicion of criminal activity).

Unreasonable Searches

Before conducting any search that would be deemed unreasonable under the Fourth Amendment, a law enforcement agent must obtain a warrant. The touchstone of the Supreme Court's analysis in Fourth Amendment search warrant cases has been whether the individual has a reasonable expectation of privacy under the circumstances. In the Court's landmark Fourth Amendment case, *United States v. Katz*,[9] Justice Harlan's concurring opinion framed the issue as follows: Has government action intruded upon an individual's subjective expectation of privacy; if so, is that expectation one that society deems reasonable? If an individual did not have a subjective privacy expectation, or if he or she had an expectation that society would not deem reasonable, then the police were entitled to conduct a search without a warrant.

In applying this framework, courts have held that a citizen's interest in freedom from governmental intrusions is very strong in his or her private home—an expectation of privacy there is quite reasonable. However, in places open to the public, such as a business office, law enforcement has been given broader scope. For instance, the Supreme Court has permitted warrantless searches of business offices in which the government agent enters during business hours and observes whatever is visible to customers or the public from the public areas of the business establishment. Similarly, the Court permitted a warrantless search of garbage cans placed at curbside for collection where it was readily accessible to animals and other persons, including the trash haulers who could have sorted through it before commingling it with garbage collected from other dwellings.

Other examples of circumstances where the *Katz* test requires no search warrant include border searches (such as by customs agents at an international airport) in order to enforce national boundaries. Similarly, no search warrant is required for government officials to search an individual's bank deposit records. This is because an individual's expectation of privacy is lessened when the individual reveals his or her affairs to the bank. The individual assumes the risk that the information will be revealed to the government.

Warrantless Searches   Most police searches are not pursuant to a warrant. These searches either (i) are deemed not "unreasonable searches" under the *Katz* test, or (ii) fall within one of six established exceptions to the search warrant requirement. The six exceptions are: (1) search incident to a lawful arrest; (2) search of an automobile if there is probable cause to believe evidence of a crime will be found; (3) anything discovered by police in plain view if the officers are legitimately on the premises; (4) stop and frisk of a suspect if the officer reasonably believes the suspect is dangerous; (5) search when the owner or a person who appears to have authority voluntarily and intelligently consents to the search; and (6) instances when the police are in "hot pursuit" or when the evidence may disappear before a warrant can be obtained (e.g., blood samples containing alcohol). If a person is validly arrested (pursuant to an arrest warrant or following a criminal act observed by a police officer), the officer has the authority to search the arrestee and the area immediately within the arrestee's control to protect the safety of the officer.

In three recent decisions, the Supreme Court has given police a broader scope to conduct traffic stop searches. In *Whren v. United States*,[10] the Court ruled that if a traffic law was violated by the vehicle being stopped, it is irrelevant that the police officer might have used the violation only as a pretext to stop the car. (After stopping the *Whren* defendant, the police observed that he was holding plastic bags of crack cocaine in his hands.) The Court ruled in *Ohio v. Robinette*[11] that police officers need not inform detained drivers that they are "legally free to go" before asking for consent to search their vehicles. Finally, in *Maryland v.*

---

9. 389 U.S. 347 (1967).

10. 116 S. Ct. 1769 (1996).
11. 117 S. Ct. 417 (1996).

Wilson,[12] the Court held that a police officer may order passengers out of a vehicle during the course of a traffic stop. (When the defendant in *Wilson* exited the car, "a quantity of cocaine fell to the ground.")

Administrative Searches

When the purpose of government action is regulatory and not prosecutorial, a search warrant may not be required for entry onto private property, usually a business. The probable cause standard is relaxed and is satisfied by the showing of a general and neutral enforcement plan.

Thus, a government agency (for example, the Occupational Safety and Health Administration) may conduct administrative searches if it demonstrates that its inspections can be effective only if they are a complete surprise and the agency statute prescribes some schedule of inspections. Similarly, no warrant is required to search airline passengers before boarding, to seize contaminated food, or for school officials to conduct searches in the school (school officials need only a reasonable suspicion). A warrant is also often not required when the government performs or requires drug testing of employees. Drug testing of employees is discussed in Chapter 13.

The following case examines the contours of the exception for regulatory searches of commercial property used in "closely regulated" industries.

---

12. 117 S. Ct. 882 (1997).

A CASE IN POINT	IN THE LANGUAGE OF THE COURT

CASE 15.2
UNITED STATES v.
ARGENT CHEMICAL
LABORATORIES, INC.
United States Court of
Appeals for the Ninth Circuit
93 F.3d 572 (9th Cir. 1996).

FACTS   Argent Chemical Laboratories manufactures and repackages veterinary drugs. Food and Drug Administration (FDA) agents inspected Argent several times between the summer of 1993 and May 1994 to ensure compliance with the Food, Drug and Cosmetic Act. The FDA cited Argent for certain deficiencies. Several months after the last inspection, FDA agents and U.S. marshals seized over $100,000 worth of veterinary drugs from Argent's premises.

The United States filed an action to condemn the property seized. Argent contested the constitutionality of the seizure. The district court held that the seizure violated the Fourth Amendment; it accordingly ordered the government to return the property. The government appealed.

ISSUE PRESENTED   Was the seizure of Argent's veterinary drugs without a warrant an unreasonable seizure that violated the Fourth Amendment?

OPINION   CANBY, J., writing for the U.S. Court of Appeals:

. . .

III. The Fourth Amendment and the *Colonnade–Biswell* Exception

Argent argues that . . . the seizure violated the Fourth Amendment's prohibition of unreasonable searches and seizures and its requirement that warrants issue upon probable cause. We conclude, however, that Argent's argument is defeated by the nature of its business and the regulation to which it is subject.

The Fourth Amendment applies to commercial premises as well as to private homes.[13] But under the so-called *Colonnade–Biswell* exception, warrantless searches and seizures on commercial property used in "closely regulated" industries are constitutionally permissible.[14] Persons engaging in pervasively regulated industries have a diminished expectation of privacy.[15] With regard to such industries, "Congress has

Case 15.2 continues

---

13. *See* See v. City of Seattle, 387 U.S. 541 (1967).

14. *See* Colonnade Catering Corp. v. United States, 397 U.S. 72 (1970); United States v. Biswell, 406 U.S. 311 (1972).

15. *See* New York v. Burger, 482 U.S. 691 (1987).

Case 15.2 continued

broad authority to fashion standards of reasonableness for searches and seizures." Thus in *Colonnade* and *Biswell*, the Court held that there was no constitutional violation when the businesses of dispensing liquor and selling firearms, respectively, were subjected to inspections and seizures without a warrant issued by a judicial officer upon probable cause.

Argent asserts that . . . its veterinary drug business is not the kind of industry that is subject to the *Colonnade–Biswell* exception. We reject [this contention].

IV. Manufacture of Veterinary Drugs as a Closely Regulated Industry

In *New York v. Burger,* the Supreme Court set forth the standards for determining when the *Colonnade–Biswell* exception applies. A warrantless inspection will be deemed reasonable only if the business is closely regulated and if three criteria are met:

First, there must be a "substantial" government interest that informs the regulatory scheme pursuant to which the inspection is made.

Second, the warrantless inspections must be "necessary to further [the] regulatory scheme." . . .

Finally, "the statute's inspection program, in terms of the certainty and regularity of its application, [must] provide a constitutionally adequate substitute for a warrant."

We conclude that all of these standards are met in this case.

As a threshold matter, the veterinary drug industry is "closely regulated." The Food, Drug and Cosmetic Act prohibits the adulteration or misbranding of any drug, whether that drug is intended for use by either humans or animals. "Virtually every phase of the drug industry is heavily regulated, from packaging, labeling, and certification of expiration dates, to prior FDA approval before new drugs can be marketed." Regulations implementing the Act are quite extensive. For example, good manufacturing practices for the preparation of human and animal drugs are set forth in detail. The veterinary drug industry is certainly regulated as extensively as the vehicle dismantling industry, which the Supreme Court has held to be "closely regulated."

. . .

FDA regulation of Argent's industry also meets the three enumerated criteria of *Burger*. First, there is "a 'substantial' government interest that informs the regulatory scheme pursuant to which the inspection is made." . . . Congress has seen fit, either for human safety or for economic reasons, to regulate animal drugs to ensure their safety and effectiveness. Whether the interest is human health, economic health, or both, we conclude that it is substantial.

Second, "the warrantless inspections [are] 'necessary to further [the] regulatory scheme.'" Unannounced inspections have a deterrent effect; forcing inspectors to obtain a warrant before inspection might frustrate the purpose of the Act by alerting owners to inspections. Moreover, this court has recognized the "need for swift governmental action to remove misbranded products from the stream of commerce." Thus, warrantless searches and seizures are necessary to further the regulatory scheme that ensures the integrity of veterinary drugs.

Finally, the regulatory scheme, "in terms of the certainty and regularity of its application, [provides] a constitutionally adequate substitute for a warrant," thereby

Case 15.2 continues

Case 15.2 continued

satisfying the third *Burger* requirement. . . . Inspections are conducted with notice furnished at the time, and their scope is limited by statute. Seizures are limited to drugs that are adulterated or misbranded, the articles to be seized must be described "with reasonable particularity," and the government's complaint must be "verified on oath or solemn affirmation." Moreover, in most cases, the seizure is subject to the approval of one of the Food and Drug Administration's district offices, the appropriate office (or "center") in the Food and Drug Administration headquarters, the Food and Drug Administration's Office of Enforcement, the Office of the Chief Counsel, and the Department of Justice.

We conclude, therefore, that Argent's operation, as regulated by the FDA, falls within the *Colonnade–Biswell* exception to the Fourth Amendment's warrant requirement.

. . .

VI. Conclusion

Under the *Colonnade–Biswell* exception to the Fourth Amendment, Argent had a "reduced expectation of privacy." As a consequence, the seizure of Argent's drugs from its premises . . . did not violate the Fourth Amendment.

RESULT   The decision of the district court was reversed. The government was permitted to condemn the veterinary drugs seized from Argent.

Searches Employing New Technology

The framers of the Fourth Amendment protections could not have conceived of the technological tools at the disposal of today's law enforcement agencies. As a result, it has been the duty of the courts to apply those protections in a modern, technologically sophisticated context. The seminal *Katz* decision involved the government's use of an electronic bug on the outside of a pay-phone booth. The Court ruled this mode of surveillance unconstitutional without a warrant.

Technological innovation has simply made the issues more complex. Consider the deployment of surveillance cameras on the public lampposts and telephone poles of city streets. Police in Tacoma, Washington, and Baltimore, Maryland, currently use such surveillance systems to monitor criminal activity (such as drug dealing and prostitution) in public places. Officials in at least 75 other cities, including Cincinnati, Honolulu, Miami, New Orleans, New York, and Portland, Oregon, have inquired about Baltimore's program.[16] The use of this type of surveillance is almost certainly constitutionally permitted because it intrudes only upon public space, revealing what any member of the public could see.

However, a host of new devices designed to detect weapons and contraband have far more invasive capabilities. One device now being tested in a Los Angeles courtroom and a North Carolina prison uses back-scattered X-ray technology to develop a computer-enhanced outline of a person's body and everything that person is carrying. Another device being tested by the Justice Department employs passive millimeter wave-imaging technology to "see" through clothes, as

---

16. Mark Hansen, *No Place to Hide*, ABA J., Aug. 1997, at 44.

well as most building materials. It has the added advantages of being both portable and capable of operating at a distance.[17]

A less complex technology now in widespread use by law enforcement agencies is an infrared thermal-image scanner. A common use of the scanner involves pointing it at the homes of suspected marijuana cultivators. "Hot spots" that show up on the scanner can indicate the heat being released from grow lights for the otherwise hidden marijuana crop.

Police generally use thermal-image scanners without a warrant, as part of their effort to compile enough information to obtain a warrant for a physical search of the premises. This use has given rise to a heated legal debate about its constitutionality under the Fourth Amendment. Four of the six federal circuit courts of appeal that have considered the issue have determined that this use of thermal-image scanners is constitution-

ally permitted without a warrant.[18] Appellate courts in seven states have addressed this question: three have found the scanner use permissible,[19] four have found it unconstitutional.[20] The Washington Supreme Court held scanner use unconstitutional in the following case.

---

18. *See* United States v. Ishmael, 48 F.3d 850 (5th Cir. 1995); United States v. Myers, 46 F.3d 668 (7th Cir. 1995); United States v. Robinson, 62 F.3d 1325 (11th Cir. 1995); United States v. Pinson, 24 F.3d 1056 (8th Cir. 1994). A three-judge panel of the U.S. Court of Appeals for the 10th Circuit held this use of the scanner unconstitutional. United States v. Cusumano, 67 F.3d 1497 (10th Cir. 1995). However, the court reheard the issue *en banc* and vacated the panel decision. The *en banc* opinion resolved the case on other grounds and declined to address the constitutional question. United States v. Cusumano, 83 F. 3d 1247 (10th Cir. 1996). The Ninth Circuit held that the use of a thermal scanning device was a "search" requiring a warrant because of people's expectation of privacy in the heat signatures of the activities, intimate or otherwise, that they pursue within their homes. United States v. Kyllo, 140 F.3d 1249 (9th Cir. 1998).

19. State v. Cramer, 851 P.2d 147 (Ariz. Ct. App. 1992); LaFollette v. Commonwealth, 915 S.W.2d 747 (Ky. 1996); State v. McKee, 510 N.W.2d 807 (Wis. Ct. App. 1993).

20. People v. Deutsch, 52 Cal. Rptr. 2d 366 (Cal. Ct. App. 1996); State v. Siegal, 934 P.2d 176 (Mont. 1996); Commonwealth v. Gindlesperger, 706 A.2d 1216 (Pa. Super. Ct. 1997); State v. Young, 867 P.2d 593 (Wash. 1994).

---

17. *Id.*

| A CASE IN POINT | IN THE LANGUAGE OF THE COURT |

CASE 15.3
STATE v. YOUNG
Supreme Court
of Washington
867 P.2d 593 (Wash. 1994).

FACTS On August 14, 1990, the Edmonds police department received an anonymous note in the mail. It stated that Robert Young operated "a big marijuana grow" and provided Young's address and telephone number.

The police investigated, and found that Young had no criminal record. A detective went to Young's home numerous times and observed that the basement windows were always covered. However, he never observed any bright lights in the home nor did he detect any odor of marijuana. The detective obtained power consumption records for Young's home, and found the abnormally high usage levels at Young's home to be consistent with a marijuana-growing operation.

A few days later, the detective obtained assistance from a special agent from the U.S. Drug Enforcement Agency (DEA) who had been trained in the use of infrared thermal-detection devices. Used at night, the device highlights manmade heat sources as a white color and cooler temperatures as a shade of gray.

On the night of August 21, 1990, the detective and DEA special agent went to Young's address and conducted a thermal surveillance of the home. The scanner revealed abnormal heating patterns, indicating that the basement was warmer than the upstairs. The detective and special agent then conducted thermal surveillance on

Case 15.3 continues

Case 15.3 continued

the homes of Young's neighbors. They noted that the heating pattern in Young's home differed from that of his neighbors, and concluded there was a marijuana-growing operation in his home.

Based on an affidavit containing the facts described, the detective obtained a search warrant for Young's home on August 28, 1990. The search warrant was executed and a quantity of marijuana was seized. Young was charged with possession of marijuana and intent to manufacture and deliver.

Prior to trial, Young moved to suppress the evidence, arguing that the use of infrared surveillance to obtain evidence was unconstitutional. His motion was denied, and Young was convicted at trial. Young appealed.

ISSUE PRESENTED   Does the use of an infrared thermal-image scanner to detect heat sources within a private home constitute an unreasonable search that violates the Fourth Amendment?

OPINION   JOHNSON, J., writing for the Washington Supreme Court:

We hold the infrared surveillance violated the Fourth Amendment.

A search occurs for Fourth Amendment purposes when "an expectation of privacy that society is prepared to consider reasonable is infringed." People have a reasonable expectation of privacy in their own homes.

. . . Homes enjoy a special status in federal constitutional jurisprudence. "[T]he right of a man to retreat into his own home and there be free from unreasonable governmental intrusion" stands at the "very core" of the Fourth Amendment. Therefore, searches and seizures in public places are treated differently than searches and seizures occurring in the home. Accordingly, the Supreme Court has differentiated between the use of sensory enhancement devices in homes from their use on other objects. Compare *United States v. Karo*[21] with *United States v. Knotts.*[22]

In *Knotts*, the defendant purchased a drum of chloroform containing an electronic beeper, or tracking device. He placed the drum in his vehicle, and drove to a cabin in the woods. Federal agents tracked the movement of the vehicle to the cabin, but did not continue to monitor the beeper once it had moved indoors. The Court held this use of the beeper did not constitute a search. Rather, the Court characterized the activity as "amount[ing] principally to the following of an automobile on public streets and highways," and noted the information discovered by tracing the beeper could have been discovered by unenhanced, visual surveillance. Moreover, the beeper trace did not constitute a search because a person has a lesser expectation of privacy in a car because "it seldom serves as one's residence."

In contrast, *Karo* involved an electronic beeper which was taken inside a home. *Karo* contains the Supreme Court's most recent statement on the use of a sensory

Case 15.3 continues

---

21. 468 U.S. 705 (1984).
22. 460 U.S. 276 (1983).

Case 15.3 continued

enhancement surveillance device on a private residence. The Court found the warrantless monitoring of the electronic beeper inside a private residence, a location not observable by the naked eye, violated the Fourth Amendment.

. . .

In this case, the infrared device used was at least as intrusive as the beeper in *Karo*. In *Karo*, the beeper was not sensitive enough to reveal the can's precise location within an enclosed structure. In contrast, the infrared device at issue here reveals the specific location of heat within the home. An infrared device need not produce the equivalent of a photographic image before it is declared intrusive under the Fourth Amendment.

. . .

Here, like *Karo*, the information conveyed by the infrared device was critical to the government. The police relied heavily on the infrared surveillance results, and the inferences that could be drawn from them, in obtaining the search warrant.

. . .

When the police use sense-enhancing devices to obtain information from someone's home that could not be obtained by unaided observation of the exterior, they should have a search warrant. Because the police did not obtain a warrant prior to using the device in this case, we hold the search also violated the Fourth Amendment.

RESULT   Young's conviction was reversed. The marijuana seized after the illegal thermal scan was not admissible.

COMMENTS   The federal courts of appeal that have allowed police use of thermal-image scanners have relied on two different rationales. One theory is that the scanner is simply measuring "waste heat," and the individual defendants had no subjective expectation of privacy in that waste heat. These opinions analogize garbage searches, which have been ruled constitutional, and dog-sniff searches, which have been held constitutional because individuals have no subjective expectation of privacy in the odors they give off.

The second theory is that even if an individual demonstrates a subjective expectation of privacy, the use of the scanner is so minimally intrusive that society would not deem that privacy expectation reasonable. This rationale compares thermal imaging to the use of a mapping camera on a high-altitude surveillance flight, and the use of a pen register, which discloses only the telephone numbers that have been dialed and not the content of communications. The crucial factor, under this analysis, is that the government's use of surveillance was too imprecise to reveal "intimate details" about the defendant or his or her property.

Cordless and Cellular Phones and E-mail   No search warrant is required for a search of the phone numbers a person has called. A search warrant is required to listen to or record conversations conducted on traditional telephones (wiretapping), but not on cordless telephones.

In one case,[23] a man named Tyler was convicted of stealing $35,000 in merchandise from his employer. His conviction was in part based on intercepted telephone conversations Tyler had made from his cordless telephone. The U.S. Court of Appeals for the Eighth Circuit rejected Tyler's argument that the recording, which would have required judicial approval if the conversation had taken place on a regular phone, violated his Fourth Amendment rights. The court held that Tyler had no reasonable expectation of privacy when he used the cordless phone. The owner's manual stated that the cordless phone operates by broadcasting radio signals between a base unit and a mobile handset, and that communications on the unit can be overheard by other cordless units. The *Tyler* opinion also stated that persons using a standard telephone to speak to a cordless telephone user are generally thought to be protected, because such a person has no reason to know his or her words are being broadcast from the cordless phone user's base unit to a handset. Cellular phones have been treated by courts as similar to cordless phones in that the person initiating the cellular conversation has no justifiable expectation of privacy.[24]

Likewise, a commercial on-line service user was deemed to have lacked a reasonable expectation of privacy in e-mail messages and chat room "conversations."[25] Accordingly, the Fourth Amendment was not violated when a federal agent lurking in a chat room collected e-mail and chat messages containing child pornography from the defendant.

Obtaining a Search Warrant

When a law enforcement agent needs to obtain a search warrant, the agent must persuade a "neutral and detached" magistrate that a search is justified. The rights of private citizens are protected by the requirement that a magistrate, rather than a law enforcement agent, determine whether probable cause exists for a search.

A valid search warrant must (1) be based on probable cause; (2) be supported by an oath or affirmation; and (3) describe in specific detail (with particularity) what is to be searched or seized. The Supreme Court

has indicated that probable cause is to be determined by the totality of the circumstances, balancing the privacy rights of the individual against the government's law enforcement needs.

When government authorities obtain a warrant to conduct a physical search of a business, the scope of the search typically must have some limits. A recent decision by the U.S. Court of Appeals for the Ninth Circuit made clear that the government may obtain a broad warrant to conduct a sweeping raid of a company only when the government has made a showing that a company is "pervaded by fraud."[26] Federal officials had been investigating Solid State Devices, Inc. on charges that the company sold dozens of inexpensive, commercial-grade semiconductors as "high-reliability" devices suitable for premier weapons and space applications.[27] The court found that the companies to which the "pervaded by fraud" exception applied were little more than "boiler-shop" sales operations engaged only negligibly in legitimate business activities. Even if a company, such as Solid State, has allegedly routinely engaged in fraudulent practices, it will be very difficult for the government to obtain a sweeping warrant so long as that company is "engaged in some legitimate activity."

The Exclusionary Rule

The *exclusionary rule* is virtually unique to the U.S. legal system. It prohibits, in many circumstances, the introduction in a criminal trial of evidence offered as proof of guilt that was obtained by an illegal search or seizure in violation of the Fourth Amendment. Illegal evidence includes evidence found when the search went beyond the scope of the warrant, evidence gathered without a warrant when a warrant was required, and evidence acquired directly or indirectly as a result of an illegal search or arrest (called *fruit of the poisonous tree*).

The exclusionary rule is often criticized in the media as simply a device to set guilty criminals free on a technicality. Supporters of the rule argue that it is necessary to protect personal freedom.

---

23. Tyler v. Berodt, 877 F.2d 705 (8th Cir. 1989).

24. *See, e.g.*, Edwards v. State Farm Ins. Co., 833 F.2d 535 (5th Cir. 1987).

25. *See* United States v. Charbonneau, 979 F. Supp. 1177 (S.D. Ohio 1997).

26. *In re* Grand Jury Investigation Concerning Solid State Devices, Inc., 130 F.3d 853 (9th Cir. 1997).

27. *See* Andy Pasztor, *U.S. Appeals Panel Ruling Clouds Probe of Faulty Electronic Parts*, WALL ST. J., Jan. 5, 1998, at B10.

Exceptions to the Exclusionary Rule After a shift in its composition during the 1980s, the Supreme Court began to sharply limit the application of the exclusionary rule. The two most important limitations the Court has elaborated are the "good faith" exception and the "inevitable discovery" exception.

The "good faith" exception maintains that evidence obtained by police in good faith will not be excluded from trial, even if it was obtained in violation of the Fourth Amendment. In *United States v. Leon*,[28] the Court's seminal "good faith" case, the Court recognized that the exclusionary rule was designed to deter police misconduct. Thus, if police were acting in good faith when they unconstitutionally obtained evidence, the Court reasoned that no deterrent purpose would be served by excluding such evidence.

Recently, the Court extended the "good faith" exception to cover errors made by court personnel. As a result, if police conduct an unconstitutional search relying on erroneous information from a court employee, the exclusionary rule will not apply.

The "inevitable discovery" exception provides that illegally obtained evidence can lawfully be introduced at trial if it can be shown that the evidence would have inevitably been found by other legal means.[29] For example, *United States v. Pimentel*[30] concerned Duroyd Manufacturing Company, a corporation that submitted a successful bid to the Defense Department for the manufacture

of parts of artillery shells. Under the contract, Duroyd falsified documents and charges to the Defense Department. Evidence of this fraud was contained in a letter to Duroyd from one of its subcontractors. The government obtained this letter in an illegal search, and Duroyd sought to apply the exclusionary rule. The court, however, noted that under the contract, the Defense Department's auditors had the right to examine all "books, records, documents and other evidence . . . sufficient to reflect properly all direct and indirect costs . . . incurred for the performance of this contract." Therefore, the court held that this letter would inevitably have been discovered, and refused to apply the exclusionary rule on that ground.

 Fifth Amendment Protections

The Fifth Amendment prohibits forced self-incrimination, double jeopardy, and criminal conviction without due process of law.

Self-Incrimination

The Fifth Amendment provides that no person "shall be compelled in any criminal case to be a witness against himself." This protection against self-incrimination extends to the preliminary stages in the criminal process as well as the trial itself. In the landmark self-incrimination case that follows, the Supreme Court laid down what has become known as the *Miranda* rule: a statement made by a defendant in custody is admissible only if the defendant was informed prior to police interrogation of his or her constitutional rights to remain silent and to have counsel present.

---

28. 468 U.S. 897 (1984).

29. *See* Nix v. Williams, 467 U.S. 431 (1984).

30. 810 F.2d 366 (2d Cir. 1987).

A CASE IN POINT	SUMMARY

CASE 15.4
MIRANDA v. ARIZONA
Supreme Court
of the United States
384 U.S. 436 (1966).

FACTS Ernesto Miranda was arrested at his home for the kidnapping and rape of an 18-year-old woman. He was brought to a police station and questioned by two officers. Two hours later, the officers emerged from the interrogation room with a written confession signed by Miranda. At the top of the statement was a typed paragraph stating that the confession was made voluntarily, without threats or promises of immunity, and "with full knowledge of my legal rights, understanding any statement I make may be used against me." Miranda was not advised that he had a right to remain silent and a right to have counsel present.

Case 15.4 continues

Case 15.4 continued

At trial, the confession was admitted into evidence, and Miranda was convicted. The Arizona Supreme Court affirmed the conviction, and Miranda appealed.

ISSUE PRESENTED   If a defendant has not been informed of his constitutional right to remain silent and consult with counsel, can statements obtained from him during police interrogation be admitted into evidence at trial?

SUMMARY OF OPINION   The U.S. Supreme Court observed that the case before it raised questions that "go to the roots of our concepts of American criminal jurisprudence: the restraints society must observe consistent with the Federal Constitution in prosecuting individuals for crime." It then succinctly stated its holding: "the prosecution may not use statements . . . stemming from custodial interrogation of the defendant unless it demonstrates the use of procedural safeguards effective to secure the privilege against self-incrimination."

By "procedural safeguards," the Court meant that law enforcement authorities must inform accused persons of their right to silence and assure a continuous opportunity to exercise it. Prior to any questioning, the person must be warned that he has a right to remain silent, that any statement he does make may be used as evidence against him, and that he has a right to the presence of an attorney (either retained or appointed by the court if the defendant cannot afford to retain one himself).

RESULT   Miranda's conviction was reversed. His confession was inadmissible as evidence.

A witness in a U.S. proceeding who is not facing prosecution in the United States may not invoke the privilege to avoid having to give testimony that might incriminate the witness in another country, unless the sovereign that the witness fears will prosecute him or her is itself bound by the privilege. However, the Supreme Court has left open the question of whether the privilege against self-incrimination may be asserted if the cooperation between the United States and another country reached a point at which prosecution in the other country could not fairly be characterized as "foreign."[31]

The Fifth Amendment privilege against self-incrimination applies only to compelled testimonial evidence. The Supreme Court has determined that forcing defendants to provide tangible evidence such as fingerprints, body fluids (urine and blood), or voice or handwriting samples does not violate the Fifth Amendment prohibition against self-incrimination. Requiring appearance in a lineup also does not violate the privilege.

The Fifth Amendment protection for business records and papers is very limited. Corporations enjoy no protection. Under the *collective entity doctrine,* the Supreme Court has held that the custodian of records for a collective entity (such as a corporation) may not resist a subpoena for such records on the ground that the act of production will incriminate him or her. Recognizing a Fifth Amendment privilege on behalf of record custodians for collective entities, the Court has said, would have

---

31. United States v. Balsys, 66 U.S.L.W. 4613 (1998).

ETHICAL CONSIDERATION

The possibility that a company might have to produce incriminating documents in a criminal investigation provides added impetus for systematically destroying documents pursuant to a document retention policy (which can also protect the company from having to produce damaging documents in civil cases, as discussed in Chapter 3). Is it ethical for a company to destroy specific documents because it knows them to be incriminating?

a detrimental impact on the government's efforts to prosecute white-collar crime. Nonetheless, the custodian cannot be compelled to testify as to the contents of the documents if that testimony would incriminate him or her personally. However, the custodian would still have to turn the documents over to the prosecution.

The business records compiled by a sole proprietor might have some protection. The Supreme Court has held that courts must at least assess the Fifth Amendment rights at issue when the business records of a sole proprietor are subpoenaed.[32] However, this analysis is not concerned with the content of the documents. Rather, a privilege may be invoked only if the government cannot authenticate the documents without the proprietor; in that case, the act of furnishing documents may have the qualities of self-incriminating testimony.

The Fifth Amendment privilege may not be invoked to resist compliance with a regulatory regime, as long as that regime is designed with a public purpose unrelated to the enforcement of criminal laws.[33] Thus records that government regulations require a business to keep can be used against the reporting individual in a criminal prosecution.

Double Jeopardy

The Double Jeopardy Clause of the Fifth Amendment protects criminal defendants from multiple prosecutions

for the same offense. If the defendant is found not guilty, the defendant is cleared of all charges, and the prosecutor may not appeal the verdict. If the defendant is found guilty, however, the defendant can appeal. Double jeopardy does not bar a second prosecution if there was a hung jury in the first proceeding.

There are important limitations on the double jeopardy protection. A single criminal act may result in several statutory violations for which the defendant may be prosecuted even if each prosecution is based on the same set of facts. For example, a prosecutor could bring criminal charges for securities law violations, wire and mail fraud, false statements, and tax evasion against a defendant for his actions in operating a securities scam. In addition, the Double Jeopardy Clause does not protect against prosecutions by different governments (such as state and federal) based on the same underlying facts. Thus, two police officers who beat Rodney King in 1991, whose acquittal of California state criminal charges spawned the 1992 Los Angeles riots, could still be tried and convicted one year later of federal charges of violating his civil rights.

Finally, the prohibition against double jeopardy does not preclude a civil suit being brought against a criminal defendant by the alleged crime victim. Thus, although O. J. Simpson was acquitted on criminal murder charges in 1996, the families of his alleged victims were still able to secure multimillion-dollar monetary judgments against Simpson in a 1997 civil trial.

Civil and Criminal Prosecutions by the Government   In recent years, a vital issue for the prosecutors and perpetrators of business crimes has been whether the government could seek both civil sanctions and criminal punishment for the same illegal conduct. A 1989 Supreme Court decision indicated that some civil sanctions might rise to the level of "punishment" that triggered the Double Jeopardy Clause, thereby prohibiting criminal prosecution.[34] In light of that decision, some government agencies shied away from seeking civil penalties in cases that were also the subject of criminal prosecution.

In 1997, however, the Supreme Court, in the following case, clarified the law in this area, making it far more difficult for defendants to argue that a civil sanction implicates the Double Jeopardy Clause.

---

32. *See* Fisher v. United States, 425 U.S. 391 (1976). *See also* Braswell v. United States, 487 U.S. 99 (1988).

33. *See* Shapiro v. United States, 335 U.S. 1 (1948).

34. *See* United States v. Halper, 490 U.S. 435 (1989).

A CASE IN POINT	**SUMMARY**

CASE 15.5
HUDSON v.
UNITED STATES
Supreme Court
of the United States
118 S. Ct. 488 (1997).

FACTS   During the early and mid-1980s, John Hudson was the chairman and controlling shareholder of the First National Bank of Tipton and the First National Bank of Hammon. Tipton and Hammon are two very small towns in western Oklahoma.

The Office of the Comptroller of the Currency (OCC) investigated the Tipton and Hammon banks. The OCC found that Hudson had used his bank positions to arrange a series of loans that, while nominally made to third parties, were in reality made to Hudson in order to enable him to redeem bank stock that he had pledged as collateral on defaulted loans.

The OCC alleged that by causing the banks to make these loans, Hudson violated various federal banking statutes and regulations. The OCC also alleged that the illegal loans resulted in losses to the Tipton and Hammon banks of almost $900,000 and contributed to the failure of those banks. In February 1989, the OCC assessed a "Civil Money Penalty" of $100,000 against Hudson. Later that year, the OCC issued Hudson notice that it intended to bar him from further participation in the conduct of "any insured depository institution."

Hudson resolved the OCC proceedings against him in October 1989 by agreeing (1) to pay $16,500, and (2) not to participate in any manner in the affairs of any banking institution without the written authorization of the OCC and all other relevant regulatory agencies.

In August 1992, Hudson was indicted in the Western District of Oklahoma in a 22-count indictment on charges of criminal conspiracy and misapplication of bank funds. The violations charged in the indictment rested on the same lending transactions that formed the basis for the prior administrative actions brought by the OCC.

Hudson moved to dismiss the indictment on double jeopardy grounds, but the federal district court denied the motions. The court of appeals affirmed. That court held, following *Halper*, that the actual fines imposed by the Government were not so grossly disproportional to the proven damages to the Government as to render the sanctions "punishment" for double jeopardy purposes. Hudson appealed.

ISSUE PRESENTED   Under what circumstances does a civil sanction constitute a "punishment" that implicates the Double Jeopardy Clause, thereby prohibiting criminal prosecution?

SUMMARY OF OPINION   The U.S. Supreme Court noted that the Double Jeopardy Clause protects only against the imposition of multiple criminal punishments for the same offense. Legislative intent is the guiding factor in determining whether a particular penalty is "civil" or "criminal." When the legislature has indicated an intention to establish a civil sanction, courts can under certain circumstances transform it into a criminal penalty for double jeopardy purposes. However, "it is important to note that . . . the statute [must be considered] on its face, and only the clearest proof will suffice to override legislative intent."

The Court proceeded to reject the double jeopardy test laid out in *Halper*, stating that its opinion in *Halper* had deviated from "longstanding double jeopardy principles." The *Halper* opinion wrongly tried to assess the "character" of the sanctions

Case 15.5 continues

Case 15.5 continued

imposed. It focused on whether the sanctions, regardless of whether they were civil or criminal, were so grossly disproportionate to the harm caused as to constitute "punishment." Instead, the Court held that double jeopardy analysis should focus on the "statute on its face"—that is, the label attached to a penalty by the legislature should figure heavily in the court's evaluation of the penalty.

Moreover, the Court noted that other constitutional provisions already address some of the ills at which *Halper* was directed. The Due Process and Equal Protection Clauses protect individuals from sanctions that are downright irrational. The Eighth Amendment protects against excessive civil fines.

Applying "traditional double jeopardy principles" to the facts of this case, the Court found it evident that Congress intended the OCC monetary penalties and disbarment sanctions imposed upon Hudson to be civil in nature. Therefore, the criminal prosecution of Hudson would not violate the Double Jeopardy Clause.

RESULT   The Supreme Court affirmed the decision of the court of appeals, thereby permitting the criminal case against Hudson to proceed.

COMMENTS   Within one month after the *Hudson* decision, the Securities and Exchange Commission decided to seek civil fines routinely in cases where there is also a parallel criminal prosecution. In the past, when litigating cases that were also being criminally prosecuted, the SEC typically sought non-punitive relief, such as disgorgement of illegal profits and court injunctions that ban future violations of the law. SEC officials read *Hudson* to mean "that the issue of double jeopardy has largely been removed." The general counsel of the SEC remarked that "now, we are more free to pursue the full range of statutory remedies that Congress provided us."[35]

---

35. Paul Beckett, *SEC May Seek Civil Fines in Some Cases Involving Parallel Criminal Prosecution*, WALL ST. J., Jan. 8, 1998, at B6.

Due Process and Voluntary Confessions

When the conduct of law enforcement officials in obtaining a confession is outrageous or shocking, the Due Process Clauses of the Fifth and Fourteenth Amendments bar the government from using the involuntary confession, even if the *Miranda* warnings were given. For example, physical coercion or brutality invalidates a confession. However, the courts have usually held that misleading or false verbal statements that induce the suspect to confess are not grounds for invalidating the confession, unless the statements rise to the level of unduly coercive threats.

A Florida appeals court invalidated a confession elicited through the use of false scientific documents in *Florida v. Cayward*.[36] The police in that case intentionally fabricated laboratory reports linking the defendant to the crime and exhibited the reports to the defendant during an interrogation, hoping to induce a confession. The false reports were presented as genuine, and the defendant confessed during the interrogation. The court held that the police tactics violated the defendant's constitutional right to due process of law. Other

---

36. 552 So. 2d 971 (Fla. Dist. Ct. App. 1989).

courts, however, have said that there is no "bright line" which dictates that all uses of false documents are unconstitutional. These courts have held that confessions similarly obtained were in fact "voluntary," after considering the "totality of the circumstances."[37]

Before a confession of guilt will be admitted into evidence, the trial judge must determine whether the confession was voluntarily made, as required by the Due Process Clauses. The Supreme Court has held, however, that the erroneous admission at trial of a coerced confession will not always require that the conviction be overturned.[38]

 ## Sixth Amendment Protections

The Sixth Amendment grants the criminal defendant a number of procedural protections.

Assistance of Counsel

The defendant in most criminal prosecutions has the right "to have the Assistance of Counsel." This means, first, that the accused has the right to his or her own attorney. If the defendant cannot afford an attorney, he or she will be entitled to a court-appointed attorney. Second, once the accused is taken into custody, the accused must be informed of his or her right to counsel as part of the *Miranda* warnings. Third, the assistance of counsel must be effective, that is, within the range of competence required of attorneys in criminal cases. In practice, counsel is presumed effective and only in outrageous cases is counsel considered ineffective. Fourth, an attorney must be appointed for an appeal of a verdict. The right to a court-appointed attorney for a second appeal, however, has not been granted.

Jury Trial

Most defendants in criminal cases have the right to a jury trial. Jury trials are not required in cases in which authorized punishment for the charged offense is six months or less and also is not required in juvenile proceedings. State court juries consist of 6 to 12 individuals, with a mini-

mum of 6 jurors. Federal courts have 12 jurors. To render a verdict in a criminal trial, a federal court jury must be unanimous in its decision. The Supreme Court has ruled that juries of six in state courts must also be unanimous in order to reach a verdict in a criminal case, but it has not ruled on juries of seven or more.

Other Procedural Rights

The Sixth Amendment also guarantees the right to a speedy trial and the right to confront and cross-examine witnesses.

 ## Nonconstitutional Protections

In a criminal prosecution, the prosecutor is obligated to show the defendant all evidence that the defendant specifically requests. In addition, certain items must be turned over regardless of whether the defendant requests them. The accused may also be required to reveal certain information to the prosecutor, such as statements made by witnesses who have testified in a sworn statement.

More requirements to reveal evidence are imposed on the prosecutor than on the defendant. The rationale for this protection is the need to neutralize the natural advantage of the state against the individual defendant.

Attorney–Client Privilege

When criminal charges are brought against a corporate employee, one might ask to whom the attorney–client privilege is applied. It may be unclear whether the client is the employee charged with the offense, the corporation that is paying the lawyer, or both. In general, a client must establish a relationship with the attorney for the attorney–client privilege to apply. Thus, if the employee is the client, the employee should obtain an engagement letter from the attorney that expressly states that the employee is the client even if the employer is paying the attorney's fees. (The attorney–client privilege is discussed in Chapter 3.)

 ## Liability for Criminal Actions

Liability may be imposed on the person who committed the crime, on that person's supervisors as individuals, and on the corporation that employs the person.

---

37. *See, e.g.,* Sheriff, Washoe County v. Bessey, 914 P.2d 681 (Nev. 1996); Arthur v. Virginia, 480 S.E.2d 749 (Va. Ct. App. 1997).

38. *See* Arizona v. Fulminante, 499 U.S. 279 (1991) (harmless error test applies to determine whether conviction must be overturned).

Individual Liability

Individuals may commit a criminal act either against a corporation for their own gain, or on behalf of the corporation.

If an officer, director, or employee commits a crime against the corporation, such as theft, embezzlement, or forgery, that person will be prosecuted as an individual.

Officers, directors, or employees who commit crimes while acting in their corporate capacities will also be prosecuted as individuals. Even if the employee was acting in the best interest of the corporation, the employee is still individually liable for his or her criminal acts. As discussed below, that person's supervisor may also be held responsible.

If a supervisor asks an employee to commit an act that the employee suspects is criminal, the employee should bear two things in mind. First, if there is a criminal prosecution, it is not a valid defense for the employee to state that he or she was just following the orders of upper-level officers or directors of the corporation. Second, as discussed in Chapter 12, an employee cannot be terminated for refusing to commit a criminal act.

Vicarious Liability

Vicarious liability (also called *imputed liability*) is the imposition of liability on one party for the wrongs of another. Under the theory of vicarious liability, officers, directors, and managers may be found guilty of a crime committed by employees under their supervision. Criminal statutes that provide for the vicarious liability of corporate officers require that the officer commit some wrongful act. However, this requirement can typically be fulfilled simply by the officer's failure to provide adequate supervision, or by the officer's failure to satisfy a duty imposed by the statute. In other words, the "wrongful act" need not always be an affirmative act.

The more delicate issue is what kind of *mens rea*, or mental state, is required to find a corporate officer vicariously liable for a crime. In cases involving criminal vicarious liability, the crucial questions are most often "How much did the manager know?" and "How much does the statute require that the manager know before he or she can be held criminally liable?"

Responsible Corporate Officer Doctrine   The *responsible corporate officer doctrine* addresses these questions. It is important to note at the outset that two different but interwoven issues are involved. The first is a vicarious liability issue: whether an officer bears responsibility for the actions of his or her subordinates. The second is a *mens rea* issue: whether the officer must have known about or intended the violation before he or she can be held criminally liable.

The Supreme Court laid the groundwork for the responsible corporate officer doctrine in *United States v. Park*.[39] The Court held that a chief executive officer (CEO) could be found criminally liable for his company's distribution of "adulterated" food in violation of the Food, Drug and Cosmetics Act (FDCA). At trial, the government had shown that Park's company stored food in rodent-infested warehouses.

John Park was the CEO of Acme Markets, a national retail food chain that employed 36,000 people and operated 874 retail outlets. Despite this enormous size and the multiple layers of authority between Park and the employees whose acts ultimately "caused" the FDCA violations, Park was found guilty of a crime as an individual. The Court noted that "Congress has seen fit to enforce the accountability of responsible corporate agents dealing with products which may affect the health of customers" by enacting "rigorous" penal sanctions. As a result, the Court felt it was obligated to broadly apply the statute in question. It held that corporate officers had a "duty to implement measures that will insure that violations will not occur"; in other words, the FDCA imposed "requirements of foresight and vigilance."

Thus, at first glance, the Supreme Court established a sweeping precedent for the criminal prosecution of corporate officers. Seemingly, under *Park*, any corporate officer could be found guilty of a crime if he or she bore a "responsible relationship" to a violation of a statute dealing with "products which may affect the health of customers."

This is not, however, how the responsible corporate officer doctrine has been applied. Courts of appeal have recognized an important limitation on the doctrine: it should be applied only when the statute at issue is a misdemeanor statute that contains no *mens rea* requirement (in other words, a strict liability statute). The FDCA, the statute involved in *Park*, was a strict liability misdemeanor statute. After being found guilty, Park was subject only to a fine and not incarceration.

---

39. 421 U.S. 658 (1975).

Courts generally have not applied the responsible corporate officer doctrine in cases involving felony statutes, though the government has often attempted to prosecute felonies under the doctrine. When a statute requires that a defendant "knowingly" commit a wrongful act, courts have ruled that the responsible corporate officer doctrine will not apply. For example, the Federal Meat Inspection Act and environmental statutes such as CERCLA and RCRA (discussed in Chapter 16) all require that defendants knowingly commit wrongful acts before being found guilty. Despite the fact these statutes clearly concern public health and safety, appellate courts have refused to affirm convictions under the responsible corporate officer doctrine.[40] On the other hand, appellate courts have used the responsible corporate officer doctrine to impose monetary penalties (but not imprisonment) under OSHA[41] and the Radiation Control for Health and Safety Act.[42]

In sum, the responsible corporate officer doctrine is an important tool in the government's effort to enforce compliance with statutes that regulate health and safety issues. By invoking the doctrine, the government can prosecute corporate officers for failing to exercise adequate supervision. Courts, however, have been careful to apply the responsible corporate officer doctrine only in cases involving misdemeanor violations, not to felony prosecutions.

Impossibility Defense to Strict Liability   A corporate officer might not be held strictly (and vicariously) liable if he or she had done everything possible, yet the company was still unable to comply with the applicable standards. In these circumstances, the officer can argue the defense of impossibility. "To establish the impossibility defense, the corporate officer must introduce evidence that he exercised extraordinary care and still could not prevent violations of the Act."[43]

Corporate Liability

A corporation can be held liable for criminal offenses committed by its employees if the acts were committed within the scope of their employment (whether actual or apparent). Many jurisdictions also require that the employee or agent was acting, at least in part, in furtherance of the corporation's business interests. This form of vicarious liability is known as *respondeat superior*, which means "let the superior give answer." (The doctrine of *respondeat superior* in civil cases is discussed in Chapters 5 and 9.)

In cases involving misdemeanor offenses or regulatory crimes, the well-established rule is that corporations are criminally liable for all violations committed by any of its agents or employees.[44]

A small minority of courts holds that corporations cannot be guilty of a non-strict liability crime—that is, a crime requiring a guilty mental state such as "knowledge" or "intent." However, it is now the generally accepted rule that a corporation may be indicted for a crime (such as negligent homicide) for which a specific guilty mental state is essential. In such cases, the knowledge or intent of employees and agents is imputed to the corporation.[45] In many cases, the legislature has clearly indicated (either in the language of the statute or in legislative history) a desire to impose criminal liability on corporations, and courts consistently enforce such legislative intent.[46]

Most courts hold that the fact an agent may have acted contrary to a corporate policy or express instructions will not absolve the corporation from criminal liability.[47] As long as the agent was acting within his or her apparent authority (and, some states require, at least in part for the benefit of the corporation), the fact that a corporation's board or upper management did not expressly ratify the action does not absolve the corporation from liability. The defense argument that a corporation should not be judged guilty of a crime unless the

---

40. *See, e.g.,* United States v. Agnew, 931 F.2d 1397 (10th Cir. 1991); United States v. MacDonald & Watson Waste Oil Co., 933 F.2d 35 (1st Cir. 1991).

41. *See, e.g.,* United States v. Doig, 950 F.2d 411 (7th Cir. 1991).

42. *See, e.g.,* United States v. Hodges X-Ray, Inc., 759 F.2d 557 (6th Cir. 1985).

43. United States v. Gel Spice Co. 773 F.2d 427 (2d Cir. 1985) (quoting United States v. New England Grocers Co., 488 F. Supp. 230 (D. Mass. 1980)).

44. *See* 18 Am. Jur. 2d *Corporations* § 2136 (1985).

45. *See, e.g.,* Boise Dodge v. United States, 51 F.3d 1390 (9th Cir. 1969); Vaughn and Sons, Inc. v. State, 737 S.W.2d 805 (Tex. Crim. App. 1987); 18 Am. Jur. 2d *Corporations* § 2137 (1985).

46. *See, e.g.,* Hanlester Network v. Shalala, 51 F.3d 1390 (9th Cir. 1995); People v. Mattiace, 568 N.E.2d 1189 (N.Y. 1990).

47. *See, e.g.,* United States v. Beusch, 596 F.2d 871 (9th Cir. 1979); State v. Hy Vee Food Stores, Inc., 533 N.W.2d 147 (S.D. 1995).

INTERNATIONAL CONSIDERATION

Many European nations do not recognize corporate criminal liability because (1) the corporation does not possess a guilty mind; (2) the corporation is not viewed as the real offender in a crime that is committed; and (3) the corporation is not considered well suited for either punishment or rehabilitation. For example, the German constitution prohibits imposition of criminal liability on corporations. These countries focus instead on identifying and punishing the individuals responsible for the criminal acts.

wrongful act was consistent with a wrongful corporate policy typically has been rejected.[48] As a practical matter, courts have been willing to impose liability upon the corporation if the agent's actions were at least "tolerated" by management.[49] Typically, these courts have made this determination based on the totality of the circumstances surrounding the agent's actions.

The following two cases are examples of circumstances under which corporations can be judged guilty of non-strict liability crimes based on the actions of employees. One case involved only a low-level employee, the driver of a school bus (owned by a corporation) who ran over and killed a six-year-old who was crossing in front of the bus. The bus driver, who had just let the child off the bus, could not see the child because mirrors that were required by state statute were missing. The court held that the corporation was criminally liable for homicide by vehicle.[50]

In another case exhibiting employee activity not expressly ratified by the corporation,[51] the president of defendant Penn Valley Resorts, Edwin Clancy, agreed to provide dinner and an open bar for 60 undergraduate

students from the State University of New York at Alfred, New York. Despite the fact that most of the students were not of legal drinking age, many of them were served alcohol.

A 20-year-old minor, William Edward Frazer, Jr., became noticeably intoxicated such that he was staggering, slurred his speech, and had quickly altering moods. Despite protests from his friends, Frazer attempted to drive himself back to the university. In the course of the 45-minute trip back, he caused an automobile accident in which he was killed. Frazer had driven his car into the opposite lane and struck a bridge abutment, causing his vehicle to overturn and become airborne for 75 feet. At the time of death his blood alcohol content was .23; a level of .10 is normally considered sufficient to make a person intoxicated.

The Pennsylvania court held that a corporation could be found liable for a criminal action even if the corporation's board of directors did not condone the action. Furthermore, if the illegal conduct is performed or tolerated by a high managerial agent acting on behalf of the corporation within the scope of his or her office or employment, the corporation can be held criminally, as well as civilly, liable. The appellate court found that the defendant corporation was properly convicted of criminal involuntary manslaughter, reckless endangerment, and furnishing liquor to minors and visibly intoxicated persons: "[T]he serving of intoxicating beverages to a minor or visibly intoxicated person alone does not constitute involuntary manslaughter or reckless endangerment. Here, it was the serving of alcohol, coupled with several crucial elements known to Clancy, which established causation, and therefore the offenses."

◆ White-Collar Crime

White-collar crime is violation of the law by a corporation or one of its managers. White-collar employees—that is, managers or professionals—may be either the victims or the perpetrators of crime. Most white-collar crime is nonviolent, either committed against a business or the government or committed by a business against a large group of individuals. Although there is no precise definition of white-collar crime, government estimates put the cost of nonviolent fraud and commercial crime at more than $100 billion a year.

---

48. *See, e.g.,* State v. Pinarfville Athletic Club, 594 A.2d 1284 (N.H. 1991).

49. *See* Minnesota v. Christy Pontiac–GMC, Inc., 354 N.W.2d 17 (Minn. 1984).

50. Commonwealth v. McIlwain School Bus Lines, 423 A.2d 413 (Pa. Super. 1980).

51. Commonwealth v. Penn Valley Resorts, Inc., 494 A.2d 1139 (Pa. Super. 1985).

IN BRIEF

LIABILITY FOR CRIMINAL ACTIONS

Type of Defendant	Standard for Liability
Individual	Must have performed *actus reus* (criminal act) with *mens rea* (guilty mind).
Corporate Officers	Vicarious liability. Under responsible corporate officer doctrine, officers can be liable for criminal actions of their subordinates if the officer bore a "responsible relationship" to the violation of a law dealing with products that affect public health and safety. Typically, the doctrine is used to apply criminal liability only in misdemeanor situations.
Corporations	*Respondeat superior* liability. A corporation can be held liable for criminal offenses committed by employees if the acts were committed (1) within the scope of their employment (whether actual or apparent), and (2) in furtherance of the corporation's business interests.

Many white-collar criminal statutes do not have a *mens rea* requirement. It is, therefore, possible to commit crime in the corporate setting without having the intention of committing the crime.

White-collar criminals are often treated less harshly than perpetrators of violent crimes. Juries and judges are often more sympathetic to white-collar criminals than to other criminals. White-collar criminals do receive jail sentences and large fines, however, especially for violations of environmental statutes and in cases involving what is perceived as extreme greed.

Crime against the Corporation

Examples of crimes committed by an employee against his or her employer include theft, embezzlement, fraud, and acceptance of a bribe.

Theft, technically known as *larceny*, is simply the taking of property without the owner's consent. White-collar theft ranges from taking home pens and pencils from the office to stealing money through the company's computer system.

Embezzlement is the taking of money or property that is lawfully in the employee's possession by reason of his or her employment. For example, a company's treasurer who takes money that belongs to the company by writing checks to dummy accounts is guilty of embezzlement.

Fraud is any deception intended to induce someone to part with property or money. Fraud may involve a false representation of fact, whether by words or by conduct, or concealment of something that should have been disclosed. Examples of fraud are the padding of an expense account and the submission of falsely inflated Medicare reimbursement bills of the sort alleged against Columbia/HCA Healthcare Corp. (discussed in the "Inside Story").

Acceptance of a bribe may also be a crime against the employer. For example, a sales representative cannot legally accept a kickback from a purchaser of his or her employer's products. Similarly, a purchasing agent for a corporation must not accept a bribe from an outside salesperson.

ETHICAL CONSIDERATION

It is not always clear where the line is drawn between accepting gifts and taking bribes. For instance, if a data-processing manager will make the decision on the purchase of a mainframe computer, it is unethical and illegal for him or her to accept a percentage of the sales price of the computer from the seller. Some data-processing managers accept expensive meals, sports tickets, and other "perks" from computer salespersons. Is acceptance of such gifts ethical?

"I'M AFRAID, WILKINS, THAT WHEN YOU EMBEZZLE SIX MILLION DOLLARS, IT'S HARD TO CLAIM YOU DID IT IN SELF-DEFENSE."

© 1998 by Sidney Harris

Crime by the Corporation

Examples of crimes perpetrated by corporations and their employees include consumer fraud, securities fraud, tax evasion, and environmental pollution.

Corporations can also commit crimes against other corporations. Examples include price-fixing (discussed in Chapter 18) and misappropriation of trade secrets or violations of copyright or patent laws (discussed in Chapter 11).

Racketeer Influenced and Corrupt Organizations Act

The Racketeer Influenced and Corrupt Organizations Act (RICO)[52] was originally designed to combat organized crime and provide a mechanism of enforcement

---

52. 18 U.S.C.A. §§ 1961–68 (West 1984 and Supp. 1998).

period, and (4) conspiring to engage in any of these activities.

RICO Requirements

Section 1961(4) of the RICO statute broadly defines an *enterprise* as "any individual, partnership, corporation, association, or other legal entity, and any union or group of individuals associated in fact although not a legal entity." Racketeering activity is defined to include various state and federal offenses, specifically including mail and wire fraud and fraud in the sale of securities. Consequently, almost any business fraud can serve as the basis for a criminal RICO violation.

In order to demonstrate a pattern of racketeering activity, a plaintiff must show that at least two related predicate acts have occurred within a 10-year period. Two isolated acts are not considered sufficient.

Use of RICO

Use of the RICO statute is particularly effective against groups of traders, brokers, and others who have developed a continuous relationship of passing and trading on inside information. In July 1988, for example, Alfred Elliot was charged with making $680,000 in illegal profits from trading on confidential information he had acquired while a partner at a Chicago law firm. Also charged with wire fraud and securities fraud, Elliot was alleged to have engaged in nine incidents between 1984 and 1986 in which he learned of large pending stock acquisitions by clients and invested heavily in the target company.

Although RICO is generally given a liberal construction to ensure that Congress's intent is not frustrated by an overly narrow reading of the statute, the reach of the statute is not unlimited, as seen in *Reves v. Ernst & Young*.[53] Purchasers of demand notes from a farmer's cooperative brought a securities fraud and RICO action against the accountants of the cooperative. The Supreme Court held that the accountants hired to perform an audit of the cooperative's records did not exert control over the company and did not "participate in the operation or management" of the

against syndicate bosses and masterminds who might otherwise escape liability. Recently, however, the criminal provisions of RICO have been used against classic white-collar crimes.

The RICO statute prohibits (1) the investment in any enterprise of income derived from racketeering, (2) the acquisition of an interest in an enterprise through a pattern of racketeering activity, (3) participation in an enterprise through a pattern of racketeering activity involving at least two related predicate acts in a 10-year

53. 507 U.S. 170 (1993).

cooperative's affairs. Such a finding of participation would have been necessary to find the accountants liable under RICO for failing to inform the cooperative's board of directors that the cooperative was insolvent.

Reves is an important case for accountants, underwriters, attorneys, and others who work with a company issuing securities. Such persons can no longer be found liable under RICO just because they were involved in the offering process. Instead, some involvement in the management of the issuer of the securities is required.

Penalties under RICO

Prosecutors have indicated that criminal RICO charges will be used widely in future prosecutions. Persons convicted of criminal RICO violations are subject to a fine and imprisonment for up to 20 years (or life if the violation is based on a racketeering activity for which the maximum penalty includes life imprisonment).

In addition to criminal penalties, the statute grants a private right of action that permits individuals to recover treble damages (that is, three times their actual damages) and also their costs and attorney's fees. The private right of action apparently was intended as a tool against businesses fueled by funds generated through organized crime. The statute contains no explicit requirement that organized crime be involved, however, and RICO has been used in numerous civil suits against legitimate businesses.

In 1995, Congress foreclosed the use of the RICO civil private right of action against alleged perpetrators of securities fraud. Denying the potential for RICO-based shareholder lawsuits was one of the many measures in the Private Securities Litigation Reform Act designed to curb abusive shareholder litigation.[54] However, criminal RICO charges can still be based on securities fraud.

 Computer Crime

White-collar crime increasingly involves computers. Most computer-related crimes are likely to go undetected, how-

ever, because computer offenses generally involve little or no visible physical activity. The computer may be used not only to commit the offense, but also to hide or destroy the evidence. Because most computer crime is perpetrated by insiders, the individuals who are in the best position to discover the crime are often the ones who committed it.

Even if computer crime is detected, it often goes unreported and unpenalized. Most businesses, especially financial institutions, do not want it publicly known that an employee or an outsider used the company's computer system to steal from the company. In some cases, the affected company, instead of prosecuting the computer criminal, has hired him or her as a computer security consultant.

Even when computer crimes are reported, they are not always prosecuted. Many prosecutors are overworked, and their offices understaffed; as a result, they give low priority to nonviolent crimes.

Computer Fraud

Computer fraud is the use of a computer to steal company or government funds. This type of theft generally involves improper or unauthorized access to the computer system and the creation of false data or computer instructions. The computer system then generates fraudulent transfers of funds or bogus checks that are cashed by the wrongdoer.

More than 40 different sections of the federal criminal code may apply to thefts by computer, ranging from embezzlement from an Indian tribal organization to wire fraud. The Computer Fraud and Abuse Act broadly addresses the general problem of theft by computer. Most computer-aided thefts can also be prosecuted under traditional state larceny laws.

The Computer Fraud and Abuse Act   The Computer Fraud and Abuse Act[55] prohibits gaining access to a computer without authorization, if by such access the user (1) obtains financial records from a financial institution, card issuer, or credit reporting agency; (2) obtains information from any department or agency of the United States, or (3) obtains information from any protected computer if the conduct involved an interstate or

---

54. Private Securities Litigation Reform Act of 1995, Pub. L. No. 104-67, § 107, 109 Stat. 737, 758 (codified at 18 U.S.C.A. § 1964(c) (West Supp. 1998)).

55. 18 U.S.C.A. § 1030 (West Supp. 1998).

foreign communication. The act also makes the knowing transmission of computer viruses (discussed below) illegal.

If the computer fraud perpetrated by a defendant was committed for commercial advantage or private gain, or if the value of information obtained by the fraud exceeds $5,000, the defendant is subject to up to five years imprisonment and a fine up to $250,000, or up to twice the amount of the gross gain or loss for the offense.

Computer Piracy

Computer piracy is the theft or misuse of computer software. (With the increasing value and decreasing size of computer equipment, the theft of computer hardware is increasing. This is larceny, however, not computer piracy.)

Concerned with the increasing amount of computer software theft, Congress amended the Copyright Act in 1980 to cover computer software. (Copyright law is discussed further below and in Chapter 11.)

Most states have made the theft of computer software a crime. For example, New York enacted a computer crime statute in 1986. Sections 156.30 and 156.35 of the New York Penal Law now define six crimes related to computer misuse. The act makes it a felony to duplicate a computer software program without authorization if either the software has a value in excess of $2,500 or the duplication is done in connection with another felony. The legislation also prohibits the possession of unlawfully duplicated materials with a value in excess of $2,500.

Computer Viruses

A computer virus is a computer program that can replicate itself into other programs without any subsequent instruction, human or mechanical. A computer virus may destroy data, programs, or files, or it may prevent user access to a computer. A computer virus need not be destructive. It may be benign and temporary. The virus may act immediately or when a trigger condition is met, such as a certain date of the year.

The proliferation of personal computers has created millions of entry points for viruses. A virus can be concealed in any software and then passed on to other computers through time-sharing services, information services, disks, or other means. The increasing linkage of computers through networking also increases vulnerability to a virus.

Although computer viruses were first publicized in 1983, it was in 1988 that government, businesses, and the public generally began to grasp the threat posed by viruses. In a widely publicized incident in 1988, a Cornell graduate student released a virus into the nationwide Internet computer network. In 1990, he became the first person convicted under the Computer Fraud and Abuse Act and faced penalties of up to five years in prison and a $250,000 fine.[56] He was sentenced in May 1990 to three years probation, a $10,000 fine, payment of probation costs, and 400 hours of community service. Experts generally agree that the virus, which clogged computer memory and communications lines, effectively shut down approximately 6,000 computer systems of various sizes. The program caused no actual damage to any files, although with minor modifications it apparently could have been transformed into a malignant virus that would have destroyed large amounts of data. However, the virus cost many thousands of employee hours to locate and undo.

 Other Federal Criminal Laws

A large number of federal regulatory laws provide for criminal as well as civil penalties for their violation. Some of the more important are discussed in this section.

Wire and Mail Fraud Acts

Next to RICO, the Wire and Mail Fraud Acts[57] may be the prosecutor's most powerful weapon against the white-collar criminal defendant. Chief Justice Warren Burger characterized the Mail Fraud Act as a "stopgap" provision that criminalizes conduct that a court finds morally reprehensible but that is not mentioned in any other criminal statute.

To establish *mail fraud* or *wire fraud* under the acts, the prosecutor must demonstrate (1) a scheme intended to defraud or to obtain money or property by fraudulent means; and (2) the use of the mails or of interstate tele-

---

56. *See* United States v. Morris, 928 F.2d 504 (2d Cir. 1991).
57. 18 U.S.C. § 1343, 1341 (1994).

VIEW FROM CYBERSPACE

ON-LINE VANDALISM AND PORNOGRAPHY

The ability of computer hackers to access protected financial and governmental records is one of the primary concerns spawned by increased use of the Internet. The threat posed by hackers is not an idle one for the federal government. A 1996 study by the General Accounting Office estimated that in 1995 alone, the two million computers on the 10,000 networks of the Defense Department were broken into as many as 250,000 times.[a] The private sector has been equally afflicted. Recent examples include a gang that hacked into Equifax, a credit-reporting agency, and gained access to 176 credit card numbers. Those numbers could be used or sold on the black market. Another hacker broke into a Seattle hotel's reservation system and stole the credit card numbers of the hotel's guests.[b]

A recent method of disruption devised by Internet hackers, called "smurfing," does not involve the access of any protected information, but it temporarily cripples the victim's network connection by flooding it with data. The threat of the nuisance is magnified by the fact that smurfing programs are widely available on the World Wide Web; so virtually any computer user can simply "choose a victim and launch an attack."[c]

This latest phase of on-line vandalism raises further questions about the capabilities of the Internet, which was not initially designed as a global marketplace. Some security experts have compared smurfing to the prank of sending dozens of pizzas to someone who never ordered them, but others note that the effects of the temporary lack of access can be extremely costly for companies doing extensive business on-line.

A separate cyberspace-spawned concern has been the enhanced ability of pedophiles to prey on children. Often this issue has been linked to the proliferation of on-line pornography. In 1996, Congress reacted to this problem by passing the Communication Decency Act. The act sought to protect children from harmful material on the Internet by criminalizing the "knowing" transmission of "obscene or indecent" messages to any recipient under 18 years of age. In 1997, the Supreme Court upheld the ban on obscenity but ruled that the ban on indecent material was an unconstitutional infringement of the freedom of speech.[d]

Although no federal legislation may emerge, individual states have shown a willingness to prosecute the distribution of on-line pornography. In 1994, a Memphis, Tennessee, jury found a California couple that operated an Internet bulletin board service guilty on 11 counts of transmitting obscenity through interstate telephone lines.[e]

Legal experts caution, though, that reaching across geographic jurisdictional lines as Tennessee did is a troubling exercise. The Internet is a worldwide phenomenon. For instance, what if the defendants in the Tennessee case had been foreign nationals, not California residents? One commentator has wryly noted that if U.S. prosecutors want to try foreign nationals for the content they put on the Internet, then Americans should be prepared for some prosecutor from Afghanistan to yank college sophomores out of Iowa because the words on their Web pages are crimes in that society.[f]

---

a. *See* Jon Jefferson, *Deleting Cybercrooks*, ABA J., Oct. 1997, at 68.

b. *Id.*

c. Jared Sandberg, *Internet Vandals Pose Threat by Using New Mode of Attack Called "Smurfing,"* WALL ST. J., Jan. 8, 1998, at B17.

d. *See* Reno v. ACLU, 117 S. Ct. 1239 (1997).

e. *See* Jefferson, *supra* note a.

f. *Id.*

---

phone lines in furtherance of the fraudulent scheme. Exactly what constitutes a fraudulent scheme has never been established. It remains a factual question determined on a case-by-case basis. The Supreme Court has broadly construed "fraud" to encompass "everything designed to defraud by representations as to the past or present, or suggestions and promises as to the future."[58] Violations

---

58. Durland v. United States, 161 U.S. 306, 313 (1896).

of the acts are punishable by a fine not to exceed $1,000 and a jail sentence not to exceed five years. If the violation affects a financial institution, the violator may be fined up to $1 million or imprisoned up to 30 years, or both.

Federal prosecutions under these acts have involved such diverse activities as defense procurement fraud, insurance fraud, false financial statements fraud, medical advertising fraud, tax fraud, divorce mill fraud, and securities fraud. Indeed, it is rare for a white-collar criminal prosecution to be brought without alleging a violation of the Wire and Mail Fraud Acts. Also, violation of these acts can trigger RICO liability; as a result, Wire and Mail Fraud and RICO prosecutions often proceed in tandem.

As the following case demonstrates, the Wire and Mail Fraud Acts can be used to prosecute a broad array of fraudulent activity.

A CASE IN POINT	SUMMARY

CASE 15.6
SCHMUCK v.
UNITED STATES
*Supreme Court
of the United States
489 U.S. 705 (1989).*

FACTS   Wayne T. Schmuck, a used-car distributor, purchased used cars, rolled back their odometers, and sold them to Wisconsin retail dealers at prices artificially inflated by the low-mileage readings. The unwitting dealers, relying on the altered readings, resold the cars to customers at inflated prices. The dealers consummated these transactions by mailing title-application forms to the state authorities on behalf of the buyers.

Schmuck was indicted for mail fraud. He filed a pretrial motion to dismiss on the ground that the mailings by the dealers were not in furtherance of his fraudulent scheme and, thus, did not satisfy the mailing element of the crime of mail fraud. The district court denied his motion, and, after trial, the jury returned a guilty verdict. Schmuck appealed.

ISSUE PRESENTED   Can a mailing that is routine and innocent in and of itself, and that is merely tangentially related to a fraudulent scheme, constitute a "mailing" that triggers liability under the Mail and Wire Fraud Acts?

SUMMARY OF OPINION   The U.S. Supreme Court held that the mailings at issue satisfied the mailing element of the crime of mail fraud. Contrary to Schmuck's contention, such mailings need not be an essential element of the scheme to defraud. Rather, they are sufficient as long as they are incidental to an essential part of the scheme.

Here, although the mailings may not have contributed directly to the duping of either the retail dealers or the customers, they were necessary to the successful passage of title to the cars. This passage of title was, in turn, essential to the perpetuation of the scheme to defraud, because a failure in the passage of title would have jeopardized petitioner's relationship of trust and goodwill with the dealers upon whose unwitting cooperation the scheme depended.

RESULT   The Supreme Court affirmed Schmuck's conviction.

A prosecution for wire and mail fraud can be brought in addition to other prosecutions based on the same events. Thus, the defendant may be charged with violation of the securities laws, the bankruptcy laws, the tax laws, or the Truth in Lending Act, as well as for wire or mail fraud.

A prosecutor can choose under which statutes to charge the defendant. This prosecutorial discretion increases the plea-bargaining power of the government. Additionally, by presenting multiple statutory violations to the jury, the prosecutor increases the chances of conviction and the likelihood of a stiffer sentence.

False Statements Act

The False Statements Act provides that:

> Whoever, in any manner within the jurisdiction of any department or agency of the United States knowingly and willfully
>
> (1) falsifies, conceals or covers up by any trick, scheme, or device a material fact;
>
> (2) makes any false, fictitious or fraudulent statements or representations, or
>
> (3) makes or uses any false writing or document knowing the same to contain any false, fictitious or fraudulent statement or entry, shall be fined [not more than $5,000] or imprisoned not more than five years, or both.[59]

Although not used as frequently as the Wire and Mail Fraud Acts, the False Statements Act has become an effective tool for criminal prosecutions of businesses and employees who deal dishonestly with governmental administrative agencies. For example, in *United States v. Yermian*,[60] an employee of Gulton Industries, a defense contractor, was convicted of making false statements to the Department of Defense in connection with his application for a security clearance.

The Tax Laws

Certain violations of the Internal Revenue Code are subject to criminal penalties. The strictest penalties are found in Section 7201, which prohibits willful attempts to evade any tax imposed under the code, including employee withholding requirements. Anyone convicted under this provision is subject to a fine not to exceed $100,000 ($500,000 for a corporation) plus all costs of the prosecution and/or a prison term not to exceed five years. Section 7206 forbids any false statements in a tax return, punishable with the same fine structure but with a maximum prison sentence of three years. Under Section 7207,

willful delivery of a fraudulent return to the secretary of the treasury is punishable with up to one year in jail and a fine of $10,000 ($50,000 in the case of a corporation).

A tax fraud prosecution must allege willful misconduct on the part of the accused. Consequently, prosecutors in tax fraud cases often add a mail fraud charge, which can result in a conviction even if willful misconduct is not proved. Moreover, mail fraud, unlike tax fraud, can be the basis for a RICO claim.

The Sherman Act

The antitrust laws are designed to encourage active business competition. (These laws are discussed in detail in Chapter 18.)

Criminal prosecutions under the antitrust laws occur most frequently in actions brought under Sections 1 and 2 of the Sherman Act.[61] Section 1 of the Sherman Act prohibits, among other things, all agreements in restraint of trade, including price-fixing. Section 2 prohibits monopolization, that is, the willful acquisition or maintenance of monopoly power coupled with the intent to monopolize.

Penalties under the Sherman Act Criminal prosecutions under the Sherman Act are initiated under the direction of the attorney general through the Antitrust Division of the Department of Justice or the appropriate U.S. attorney. Individuals who violate the act are subject to a statutory maximum of three years in prison and/or a $350,000 fine per violation. Corporations that violate the Sherman Act are subject to a fine of up to $10 million per violation, and the fine can be increased under other statutes to twice the gain to the violators or twice the loss to the victims, whichever is greater.

Because the Sherman Act contains both criminal and civil sanctions, the government must always determine whether to bring a criminal action, a civil action, or both. In making this determination, the government continues to rely on a report of the U.S. attorney general issued in 1955, under which the criminal sanction has generally been limited to particularly egregious conduct, such as price-fixing or group boycotts, or has been applied to individuals previously convicted of an antitrust offense.

59. 18 U.S.C. § 1001 (1994).

60. 581 F.2d 595 (7th Cir. 1978).

61. 15 U.S.C §§ 1–2 (1998).

Prosecutions   A dramatic rise in the number of criminal convictions under the antitrust laws occurred in the 1980s, with more than 100 criminal convictions requiring imprisonment handed down between 1980 and 1983 alone. Many of the convictions were for bid rigging in highway contracting. The U.S. Sentencing Commission has promulgated only one federal sentencing guideline for antitrust offenses. It deals with horizontal agreements in restraint of trade (for example, horizontal price-fixing, bid rigging, and market allocation), and guides federal courts in setting penalties up to the statutory maximum. In most cases, first-time offenders sentenced under the federal guideline serve a minimum six- to twelve-month jail sentence. Many defendants in Sherman Act prosecutions plead *nolo contendere* (no contest) to forestall the use of a guilty verdict in a subsequent civil action.

The Federal Securities Laws

The two main federal securities laws are the Securities Act of 1933[62] (1933 Act) and the Securities Exchange Act of 1934[63] (1934 Act). Both of these statutes were drafted in the wake of the stock market crash of 1929 as a way to restore investor confidence in the nation's securities markets. The Securities and Exchange Commission (SEC) administers both the 1933 Act and the 1934 Act. These acts are discussed more fully in Chapters 22 and 23 but are briefly described here.

1933 Act   The 1933 Act covers the initial distribution of a security from the issuer to the public. Unless an exemption applies, the issuer must file a registration statement (including a detailed prospectus) with the SEC. To encourage proper disclosure of all information demanded by the statute, Section 24 of the act provides for criminal penalties in addition to civil sanctions. Any person or entity that willfully violates the 1933 Act or any regulation promulgated by the SEC is subject to a maximum fine of $10,000 and/or a five-year jail sentence. The U.S. attorney, not the SEC, decides whether to bring criminal charges.

1934 Act   The 1934 Act focuses on the need for public companies (that is, those with securities trading in

the public market) to periodically update disclosures initially made under the 1933 Act. The 1934 Act requires public companies to file annual reports, quarterly reports, and additional reports to reflect any material change in the company, such as a merger or sale of substantially all of its assets. The 1934 Act regulates, among other things, insider transactions, proxy solicitations, tender offers, brokers and dealers, and the securities exchanges. The 1934 Act also contains a general prohibition on securities fraud and on *insider trading*, that is, trading while in possession of material nonpublic information.

The 1934 Act provides for criminal penalties for willful violations of the act or the related SEC rules. Violators can be punished with a fine not to exceed $1 million and/or a 10-year prison sentence, except that if the violator is a person other than a natural person (such as a corporation), a fine up to $2.5 million may be imposed. Violators who prove they had no knowledge of the rule or regulation will not be subject to imprisonment, however. The penalties for insider trading are set forth in Chapter 23.

Fall of the Junk-Bond King   One of Wall Street's most notorious criminal scandals involved Michael Milken, the erstwhile "junk-bond king" of Drexel Burnham Lambert Inc. The charges levied against Milken were broad in scope. They included unlawful concealment of security positions, cheating clients out of trading profit by falsely reporting sales prices to them, and evasion of income taxes by illegally manufactured trading losses.

Milken eventually settled the criminal and civil cases against him by agreeing to $600 million in fines and pleading guilty to charges resulting in a 10-year prison sentence. He ended up serving only 22 months in prison.

At the time of the settlement, U.S. Attorney General Richard Thornburgh characterized Milken's crimes as "some of the most serious efforts undertaken to manipulate and subvert Wall Street's securities markets." He added that the case sent a strong message about "crime in the suites: Those white-collar criminals are never so powerful or clever that they cannot be caught by diligent and persistent law enforcement efforts."

The SEC chairman also said he was "extremely pleased" by the $600-million Milken settlement, which was the largest in the SEC's history. Of the $600-million payment paid by Milken, $200 million was a fine that went directly to the U.S. Treasury. The $400-

---

62. 15 U.S.C.A. §§ 77a *et seq.* (West 1997).
63. 15 U.S.C.A. §§ 78a *et seq.* (West 1997).

million portion was administered by the SEC and made available to satisfy claims by investors and others who asserted that Milken had defrauded them.

The Savings and Loan Crisis   Milken's exploits have been tightly linked to the crisis that resulted in the failure of hundreds of U.S. banks and thrifts in the 1980s and early 1990s. Many of the savings and loans (S&Ls) that failed had invested in junk bonds (high-yield non-investment-grade debt) issued by Milken's firm Drexel Burnham Lambert. When the junk-bond market collapsed, so did the S&Ls that had invested so heavily in it. Financial experts have argued that blame for the crisis should be laid at the feet of Congress—first for deregulation that made it possible for S&Ls to buy junk bonds, then for passing a knee-jerk law forcing S&Ls to sell off their portfolios en masse, which virtually guaranteed that the junk-bond market would collapse. Nevertheless, the Justice Department assigned a special counsel to investigate the S&L crisis and pursued criminal prosecutions against alleged culprits with vigor.

From 1988 to 1995, the federal government's effort to "find and prosecute those who looted our financial institutions during the savings and loan crisis" resulted in a total of 6,405 persons being charged with bank-related crimes. In cases that had been resolved as of the expiration of the special counsel's term, the government had achieved a conviction rate of 96.5%. Of those convicted in major financial institution fraud prosecutions, 75.5% received jail sentences. Fines totaling $45 million were imposed upon those convicted of fraud in the operation of banks, S&Ls, and credit unions; and a total of $2.9 billion in restitution was ordered.[64]

The Foreign Corrupt Practices Act

The Foreign Corrupt Practices Act,[65] discussed in Chapter 26, makes it a crime for any U.S. firm to make payments to an official of a foreign government in an attempt to influence the actions of the official. The act also requires detailed record-keeping and internal control measures by all public companies, whether international or purely domestic. The penalties for vio-

lations of the Foreign Corrupt Practices Act are set forth in Chapter 26.

The Environmental Laws

During the past several decades, Congress has passed or significantly modified existing laws to protect the environment (see Chapter 16). These laws provide for criminal sanctions against both the corporation and its employees. The Wire and Mail Fraud Acts and the False Statements Act supplement the criminal sanctions included in the environmental statutes. As explained in Chapter 16, the Environmental Protection Agency has proposed more lenient treatment for those who self-report violations.

Two examples of environmental laws that impose criminal sanctions are the Clean Water Act and the Resource Conservation and Recovery Act.

The Clean Water Act   The Clean Water Act[66] requires all industrial and municipal entities to obtain a permit from the Environmental Protection Agency (EPA) prior to discharging specified pollutants into a water source. Detailed records of all discharges and periodic testing of sample discharges are required. Criminal penalties under the act vary, depending on whether the violation was negligent, knowing, or knowing and endangered others. First-time violators are subject to prison terms ranging from 1 to 15 years and fines ranging from $2,500 to $100,000 per day. Organizations that knowingly endanger others can be fined up to $1 million. For second and subsequent violations, prison terms and fines are doubled.

Any person who knowingly falsifies any records required to be maintained under the act may be fined $10,000 and imprisoned for up to two years. Prison terms and fines are also doubled for subsequent violations.

The Resource Conservation and Recovery Act
The Resource Conservation and Recovery Act (RCRA) of 1976, as amended in 1984,[67] provides for cradle-to-grave monitoring of hazardous-waste material. This statute and the accompanying regulations set out procedures and record-keeping requirements for the transportation, storage, and treatment of hazardous waste.

64. *See* Michelle Singletary, *Justice Dept. Hails Prosecutions at Banks, S&Ls*, WASH. POST, Nov. 14, 1995, at A10 (citing Justice Dept. report).
65. 15 U.S.C. § 78dd-2 (1994).
66. 33 U.S.C. §§ 1351 *et seq.* (1994).
67. 42 U.S.C. §§ 6901 *et seq.* (1994).

Criminal penalties can be levied both against the corporation and against individual employees who dispose of hazardous waste without the appropriate RCRA permit.

The Occupational Safety and Health Act

The Occupational Safety and Health Act (OSHA)[68] applies to all employers engaged in a business affecting interstate commerce. OSHA is discussed in Chapter 12.

OSHA Requirements   OSHA requires employers to provide a place of employment free from recognized hazards that are likely to cause death or serious physical harm. Employers are also required to comply with many detailed safety regulations.

Penalties under OSHA   Most violations of OSHA are punished by civil penalties. The penalties are mandatory when the employer receives a citation for a serious violation, discretionary when the violation is nonserious. More severe civil penalties (that is, fines up to $70,000) are imposed for willful or repeated violations. The terms "serious," "nonserious," "willful," and "repeated" are all defined in the act.

Section 666(e) of the act provides for even harsher penalties if the employer commits a willful violation that results in the death of an employee. In this case, the employer may suffer a fine, imprisonment, or both. If the employer had not previously been convicted of a violation, he or she may be punished by a fine of not more than $10,000 or by imprisonment of up to six months, or both. For a second conviction, the punishment can be a fine of up to $20,000 or imprisonment of up to one year, or both.

State Law Prosecutions of Workplace Safety Hazards   As noted in Chapter 12, state prosecutors have recently taken an aggressive approach toward workplace safety hazards that result in injuries. Recognizing OSHA's financial and legal limitations, prosecutors in at least 14 states have charged employers with crimes ranging from assault and battery to reckless homicide for ignoring safety warnings.[69] For example, a vice-president and manager of a Massachusetts pewter manufacturer was charged with assault and battery by means of a dangerous weapon for allegedly exposing an employee to hazardous chemical solvents and oils that had been dumped into a pit inside the manufacturing facility.[70] California and Maine recently enacted laws specifically providing for criminal penalties for employers who endanger their employees.

Employers have defended against such charges by claiming that OSHA preempts state prosecutions based on failure to maintain workplace safety. However, the U.S. Court of Appeals for the First Circuit has rejected this argument,[71] and several other courts have adopted the First Circuit's reasoning.[72]

The Copyright Act

The Copyright Act criminalizes willful infringement of copyrights. Section 506(a) of the act provides that any person who infringes a copyright willfully and for purposes of commercial advantage or private financial gain shall be subject to a maximum prison term of five years and a maximum fine of $250,000.[73] In addition to copyright infringement, Section 506 of the act also criminalizes fraudulent use of a copyright notice, fraudulent removal of a notice, and false representation in connection with a copyright application.

Before 1998, a necessary element of criminal infringement under Section 506(a) was that the perpetrator acted for private or commercial gain. In *United States v. La Macchia*,[74] a 1994 case before the Massachusetts federal district court, a computer bulletin board operator who provided users with free unauthorized copies of copyrighted software escaped prosecution because his activities lacked the element of commercial gain. On December 16, 1997, however, President Clinton signed a bill that closed this "*La Macchia* loophole." The No Electronic Theft Act (NET) amended Section 506(a) to criminalize willful acts of infringement without requiring proof of financial gain.[75]

---

68. 29 U.S.C. §§ 651 *et. seq.* and 29 U.S.C.A. §§ 651 *et. seq.* (West Supp. 1997).

69. *See* Ann Davis, *Treating On-the-Job Injuries as True Crimes,* WALL ST. J., Feb. 26, 1997, at B1.

70. *See* Martin E. Levin, *Avoiding Workplace Crime Is "Common Sense,"* MASS. LAW. WKLY., Apr. 7, 1997, at 11.

71. *See* Pedraza v. Shell Oil Co., 942 F.2d 48 (1st Cir. 1991).

72. *See, e.g.,* Wickham v. American Tokyo Kasei, Inc., 927 F. Supp. 293 (N.D. Ill. 1996); Donovan v. Beloit Co., 655 N.E.2d 313 (Ill. App. Ct. 1995).

73. 17 U.S.C.A. § 506(a) (West Supp. 1998); 18 U.S.C.A. § 2319 (West Supp. 1997).

74. 871 F. Supp. 535 (D. Mass. 1994).

75. Pub. L. No. 105–147, 111 Stat. 1678 (1997).

Economic Espionage Act

In 1996, Congress passed the Economic Espionage Act, which for the first time made theft of trade secrets a federal crime. The act was passed in response to a dramatic rise in the incidence of industrial espionage. In 1996, the FBI reported 800 pending probes of economic espionage (involving nationals of 23 different countries), twice as many as in 1994.[76] A survey released by the American Society for Industrial Security showed a 323% increase in incidents from 1992 to 1995, resulting in an estimated annual loss to U.S. companies of $25 billion.[77]

The act targets theft of trade secrets both by foreigners and domestic spies. For foreign defendants, it defines economic espionage as knowingly stealing, or by fraud or deception obtaining, a trade secret with the intention that it will benefit a foreign government or agent. On the domestic side, the test is whether the defendant (1) intends to convert a trade secret to the economic benefit of anyone other than the trade-secret owner, and (2) intends or knows that this act will injure the owner. In order for information to be considered a trade secret, the owner must have taken "reasonable measures to keep such information secret," and the value of the information must stem from its proprietary nature.[78]

Within a year of the Economic Espionage Act's enactment, the FBI had conducted a number of high-profile sting operations under its authority. One sting nabbed two Taiwanese businesspersons attempting to buy stolen data about Bristol-Myers Squibb's blockbuster cancer drug, Taxol.[79] Another involved a contract worker for PPG Industries Inc., who attempted to sell secret fiberglass formulas to Owens–Corning.[80]

Perhaps the most elaborate system of espionage uncovered under the auspices of the act was perpetrated by a senior chemical engineer at Avery Dennison Corp. Before being caught on videotape rifling through confidential files in a darkened room, Victor Lee had for years routinely passed on "highly confidential" formulas and reports to a Taiwanese adhesive-tape maker, Four Pillars Enterprise Co. On annual trips to Taiwan, Lee had given regular lectures to Four Pillars engineers detailing sensitive Avery production methods. In 1997, Lee agreed to a plea bargain that temporarily made him an undercover agent aiding the FBI's case against Four Pillars. Later that year, two Four Pillars executives were indicted under the Economic Espionage Act. A federal judge in Cleveland, Ohio, ordered the executives to remain in Ohio until a trial date had been set.[81]

Penalties under the act can reach 15 years imprisonment and fines of up to $10 million, depending on the value of the trade secrets stolen.[82] However, critics have already complained that sentencing is not severe enough to adequately deter the immensely profitable industry of industrial espionage. They note that because many white-collar corporate spies are first-time offenders, the Federal Sentencing Guidelines are lenient. For instance, the defendant in the Owens–Corning case was sentenced to only 15 months in jail, despite the fact that PPG estimated the value of the information stolen at up to $20 million.[83]

76. See Dan Gottlieb, *Justice Enforces "Spy Act" of 1996*, Purchasing, Apr. 1997, at 18.

77. See Stan Crock & Jonathan Moore, *Corporate Spies Feel a Sting*, Bus. Wk., July 14, 1997, at 76.

78. See 18 U.S.C.A. §§ 1831, 1832 (West Supp.1998).

79. See Crock & Moore, *supra* note 77.

80. See Gottlieb, *supra* note 76.

81. See Dean Starkman, *Secrets and Lies: The Dual Career of a Corporate Spy*, Wall. St. J., Oct. 23, 1997, at B1.

82. See 18 U.S.C.A. § 1831 (West Supp.1998).

83. See Crock & Moore, *supra* note 77.

THE RESPONSIBLE MANAGER
Ensuring Criminal Law Compliance

Senior management can implement various actions and procedures to encourage criminal law compliance.

The corporation should develop a code of ethics, as discussed in Chapter 1. All criminal acts should be outlawed by the code. The code of ethics should have an enforcement mechanism and should clearly state that violations of the code will result in sanctions such as salary reductions, poor performance ratings, and, in extreme cases, termination of employment.

As suggested in the discussion of the Federal Sentencing Guidelines, the corporation should develop a comprehensive program to ensure compliance with laws and regulations. Senior management should oversee the program. The corporation should have educational procedures to remind all employees about the provisions of the compliance program. Some corporations require that employees sign a yearly statement saying that they have read the code of ethics.

It should be clear throughout the company that ethical behavior is expected. A policy of honesty should be stressed. What top management does when it sees criminal law–related problems will influence all employees. It is much harder for an employee to justify committing a criminal act against the corporation when he or she cannot claim that the top management is also guilty of criminal acts.

As in the *Park* case, top management may be found vicariously liable for crimes committed by employees under their supervision. Organizations themselves can also be assessed large fines as a result of criminal acts committed by their managers and employees if the acts were committed within the scope of employment and for the benefit of the corporation.

Corporate in-house counsel should be independent and report directly to the chief executive officer. They should not succumb to pressure from division managers to give the go-ahead to an action that counsel believes may violate a criminal statute.

Some courts will excuse a corporation from criminal liability if the corporation shows that it diligently tried to prevent the criminal behavior. The Federal Sentencing Guidelines specifically provide for reduced sentences if a company has an effective compliance program in place. A good reporting structure is a crucial feature of such a compliance program. Prosecutors and courts are very inclined to mitigate the punishment of a corporation if it consistently reports the criminal misconduct of its employees.

Outside firms can be hired to audit the corporation's methods of ensuring criminal law compliance. These firms can also make suggestions to improve the corporation's methods.

The corporation should also focus on the continuing education of its employees. All employees need to know the criminal law that affects them. In-house training can keep corporate employees abreast of changes in the criminal law and can help ensure that employees do not forget their obligations under criminal law.

INSIDE STORY
COLUMBIA/HCA IN NEED OF A GOOD DOCTOR

More than any other company, Columbia/HCA Healthcare Corp. embodied the dramatic consolidation of power that shaped the health-care industry in the mid-1990s. Columbia took over one rival after another and diversified to provide virtually the full spectrum of hospital services, from hospital care to home care.

By early 1997, Columbia was the nation's largest health-care company, owning 343 hospitals and 143 free-standing surgery centers.[84] Its chief executive and founder, Richard L. Scott, was a former mergers-and-acquisitions lawyer whose initial investment of $125,000 had mushroomed into an equity stake worth over $300 million. Scott's vision for Columbia was to expand annual revenue from its 1997 range of $20 billion to a total over $100 billion. He also drove the company's obsession with the bottom line—one that produced a consistent earnings growth rate in the double digits.[85]

Wall Street loved the story. Columbia's stock price rose from about $8 per share in January 1991 to a high of $44.875 per share in February 1997.

The rest of the health-care industry watched in awe, wondering how Columbia managed to sustain this pace. By early 1997, details about Columbia's management and operation began to surface. And the details were anything but flattering. Former employees declared that patient care was not a Columbia priority: "Columbia hospitals exist to make money—period." One ex-employee said that while at Columbia he "committed felonies every day."[86]

The questionable practices at Columbia were many, but at least three types stood out. The first was the way Columbia structured its dealings with doctors. Despite federal laws prohibiting self-referral, Columbia allowed doctors to buy syndication shares in its hospitals and clinics. These shares would rise in value if hospital earnings did, thereby giving doctors a strong incentive to refer patients only to Columbia facilities. Some Columbia hospitals also used directorships to give thousands of dollars in extra monthly fees to specialists who were in a position to boost patient traffic. Medical directors who did not bring in additional patients—such as radiologists and pathologists, who typically see patients that have already been admitted—received no directorship pay.[87]

Federal agencies also questioned whether Columbia hospitals were guilty of "patient dumping." In August 1994, a disoriented, elderly homeless man entered the emergency room of a Columbia hospital. Doctors discharged him without performing a CAT scan. Hours later, the man made it to a Catholic hospital that performed a CAT scan and found a brain hemorrhage that required surgery. The Columbia hospital refused to take the patient back. Federal regulators investigating this incident found that on the same day, another patient with similar symptoms—but with insurance coverage—received a battery of tests and was admitted to the Columbia hospital.[88]

Several months later, another homeless man was denied treatment at the emergency room of a Columbia hospital. The doctor gave the man a glass of juice and noted on his chart that he was "filthy" and suffering from "acute homelessness." The man was discharged. An hour later, he died of pneumonia on the hospital lawn.[89]

Perhaps most revealing of the "profit-at-any-cost" culture that drove Columbia were the categories tracked by its quarterly score cards of hospital performance. The score cards sent out by Columbia headquarters rated and ranked each hospital each month on nearly a dozen measures, from costs of supplies to number of surgeries—but not on the quality of care.[90]

The most questionable category on the score card was something called the "Case Mix Index." This index measured the severity of the procedures each hospital billed to Medicare and, thus, the reimbursement level. The score-cards set a lofty "budgeted" index. If a hospital coded its procedures to indicate additional problems, enough to meet the index, it would generate far higher collections from Medicare.

Former Columbia managers have said that Columbia managers faced pressure to illegally "upcode" their Medicare cases. Indeed, some have claimed that Columbia headquarters set "impossible, insane" goals for what portion of Medicare cases should carry medical "complications," which result in higher reimbursement.[91] Health-care industry analysts estimate that community hospitals typically have complications in about 40% to 60% of cases, while large teaching hospitals with more patients requiring specialized treatment might hit complication rates of 80%. At Columbia, however, some former executives were told to try to ensure that 97% or 98% (in one case even 100%) of their Medicare patients were coded as having complications.[92]

Health-care consultants called this practice "unbelievable." One commented: "My first question to Columbia is: Are you asking for trouble? This is a red flag. It is saying, 'Here I am, come look at my records.'"[93]

Columbia seemed undaunted. It proclaimed that the case mix index didn't really set a goal, it was just a parameter.[94] With respect to its dealings with doctors, which pushed the boundaries of self-referral restrictions, a Columbia spokeswoman said, "We think that we are within the law. And if the law is incorrect, change the law."[95]

Still, on the inside, Columbia officers were worried about having the details of their reimbursement practices revealed. Two witnesses cited in a federal affidavit claimed that the company established a policy whereby almost all internal documents related to cost reports and reimbursements were to be stamped "Attorney/Client Privileged." Generally, law enforcement officials aren't entitled to view such documents during criminal investigations. The witnesses claimed that the attorney–client designation was placed on papers that were the result of internal financial audits, having nothing to do with the legal department.[96]

As it turned out, federal regulators had noticed the red flags. By July 1997, Columbia had become fully embroiled in one of the largest health-care fraud investigations ever. The Justice Department's criminal division coordinated the probe, which involved several federal agencies, including the FBI and the criminal inspection arms of the Department of Health and Human

Services, the Defense Department, and the Postal Service. After federal authorities seized business records in a series of raids on Columbia hospitals and clinics, Scott resigned as CEO and left the company on July 25, 1997.

In an affidavit filed as part of a grand jury investigation, the federal government stated that the FBI and other investigative agencies had uncovered a "systemic corporate scheme perpetrated by corporate officers and managers" of Columbia facilities to improperly inflate the amount of reimbursement it received each year from federal programs such as Medicare, Medicaid, and the military health-care program.[97] The government outlined several examples of this "systemic corporate scheme" to defraud federal health programs. One involved a Columbia policy to improperly shift costs from its hospitals to its home-health agencies to take advantage of reimbursement rules that treated these facilities differently, thereby inflating the total funds Columbia received from Medicare. Another alleged Columbia practice was to secure low prices for its mergers and acquisitions by excluding the value of "goodwill" for such things as patient rolls and make up the difference by offering lucrative management contracts to principals on the other side of the deal.[98] Confidential witnesses cited in the affidavit testified that Columbia officers made an effort to hide from federal regulators internal documents that could have disclosed fraud. Also, they claimed that Columbia's top executive in charge of internal audits told his

employees to "soften" the language used in internal financial audits and to delete the word "fraud" from any reports.[99]

One important episode described by the witnesses involved a $14-million error in Columbia's favor that Columbia officials decided not to report to Medicare. This case led to the first criminal indictments against Columbia managers, on charges of Medicare fraud. According to the witnesses, Columbia discovered that a fiscal intermediary responsible for reviewing a hospital cost report had erroneously accounted for interest on a $14-million loan. The mistake meant extra reimbursement to Columbia. Instead of reporting the error, Columbia executives sought out and obtained a legal opinion saying they weren't obligated to bring the matter to the government's attention. They also established a "reserve" of $500,000 per year to repay any money the government might later decide that Columbia owed.[100]

Columbia soon realized that the federal government's wide-ranging investigation was not going away. The new management team decided that Columbia's corporate culture had to be reformulated from the ground up. In October 1997, they took a substantial step in that direction by hiring attorney Alan Yuspeh to take charge of Columbia's ethics overhaul.[101] Yuspeh had played a key role in the defense industry's efforts to rebound from scandal in the 1980s. At a time when the defense industry was under fire for billing the government $9,000 for wrenches and $1,500 for toilet

seats, Yuspeh set up a framework for defense contractors and government compliance officers to discuss how to do business properly. In this process, leading defense contractors pledged to strictly enforce their individual codes of ethics and to alert government authorities if they found evidence of impropriety.

Yuspeh quickly announced a plan for Columbia that tracked his experience in defense. He claimed there were many similarities between the defense and health-care industries in that both involve complex regulatory and accounting schemes and both depend heavily on government reimbursement. Yuspeh and Columbia's new management team agreed that their immediate priority was to create at Columbia "the finest compliance program in the country."[102] As part of the overhaul, Columbia created audit teams that would be dispatched to hospitals to review the coding of patients' illnesses and generally ensure that the company did not take advantage of the "ambiguities" in Medicare rules.[103] Ultimately, under the new compliance program, Columbia's goal is to disclose overbilling to the government on its own.

Key federal health regulators saw promise in the early stages of Columbia's voluntary compliance model. The inspector general at the Department of Health and Human Services voiced approval of Yuspeh's efforts at Columbia. She said that in spite of the temptations for hospitals to find loopholes in the complex federal reimbursement rules, she was a big believer in the efficacy of corporate voluntary compliance programs.[104] Still, even if Columbia successfully transitions to a company fully committed to self-reporting its improper billing practices, such a program would not wipe clean the systemic pattern of past fraud alleged by the government.

Moreover, the perpetrators of health-care fraud today face far more severe penalties than defense contractors faced in the 1980s. In 1996, Congress passed a law that orders a five-year suspension from the Medicare program for any company convicted of a medical fraud felony. According to industry experts, exclusion from Medicare is the "death sentence" for any health-care entity. Indeed, one analyst commented, "companies are willing to do anything, even see their executive go to jail, to avoid conviction."[105]

Perhaps it should not be surprising, then, that jail time is precisely what may loom for the first group of Columbia officials to be indicted in the federal investigation. Three company officers were set to go to trial in early 1998 on Medicare fraud charges related to Columbia's decision not to disclose the significant accounting error described above. Lawyers close to the case, however, said the government hoped to gain cooperation from these three defendants and other witnesses to piece together a trail of evidence that could lead to criminal indictments of key executives in Columbia's Nashville headquarters.[106] The government seems to have adopted the strategy endorsed by its top FBI special agent, who had come to believe that the best way to deter health-care companies

from ripping off taxpayers was not to settle for money. It was to throw "bodies"—executives of miscreant companies—behind bars.[107]

Needless to say, a dark cloud will hang over Columbia's operations for some time. Some predict a fine of at least one billion dollars. Because such a wide array of fraudulent practices had been alleged at Columbia hospitals and health-care centers around the country, the Justice Department was, as of early 1998, still reluctant to even begin negotiations toward a comprehensive settlement. To add to Columbia's worries, several state medical insurance bodies also had lawsuits pending. Finally, the ripple effects of Columbia's alleged Medicare fraud were being felt in Columbia's dealing with the private sector. In the months after the investigation became public, emboldened managed-care companies and other insurers began balking at paying some of Columbia's larger bills and were scrutinizing all other patient bills before paying up.[108]

In light of the Columbia/HCA revelations, the Justice Department has aggressively pursued fraudulent practices in the health-care industry. Attorney General Janet Reno has said that fighting and preventing health-care fraud remain top priorities, stressing that "we cannot allow financial incentives to corrupt" the provision of medical services. "Health care must be based on what is best for patients' health, not the bottom line of providers," Reno said.[109]

The Justice Department has used the False Claims Act for civil actions against health-care providers. Hospital executives expressed concern that the government was prosecuting honest billing mistakes or mere negligence. However, the attorney general defended the use of the False Claims Act, stating that the Justice Department would take action only against providers that knew that a claim was false or acted with "reckless disregard" or "deliberate ignorance" of the fact that false and fraudulent bills were submitted for payment.[110]

The government's ultimate goal is for the health-care industry to become self-regulating through widespread use of corporate compliance programs. In February 1998, the Department of Health and Human Services's Office of Inspector General released compliance program guidelines to help hospitals promote adherence to Medicare and Medicaid regulations.[111]

According to the guidelines, if a hospital official discovers credible evidence of misconduct from any source and, "after a reasonable inquiry," has reason to believe that the misconduct may violate criminal, civil, or administrative law, the hospital should promptly report the existence of the misconduct to the appropriate governmental authority.

Although adherence to the guidance is strictly voluntary, implementation of an effective compliance program could earn a company leniency in any future governmental investigation. The inspector general would not guarantee that a health-care provider would be completely protected against prosecution. But the existence of an effective compliance program will be taken into account in determining the nature and level of any administrative sanctions that the inspector general might seek to impose.[112]

84. *See* Lucette Lagnado, *Ex-Manager Describes the Profit-Driven Life inside Columbia/HCA*, WALL ST. J., May 30, 1997, at A1; David S. Hilzenreth, *Massive Fraud Investigation Centers on Columbia/HCA*, WASH. POST, July 18, 1997, at G1.

85. *See* Lucette Lagnado, *Columbia/HCA Warns of Profit Decline*, WALL ST. J., Sept. 10, 1997, at A3.

86. Lagnado, *Ex-Manager, supra* note 84.

87. *See id.*

88. *Id.*

89. *Id.*

90. *See* Lucette Lagnado, *Columbia/HCA Graded Its Hospitals on Severity of Their Medicare Cases*, WALL ST. J., May 30, 1997, at A6.

91. *Id.*

92. *Id.*

93. *Id.*

94. *Id.*

95. Lagnado, *Ex-Manager, supra* note 84.

96. *See* Eva M. Rodriguez & Lucette Lagnado, *U.S. Claims Deep Fraud at Columbia*, WALL ST. J., Oct. 7, 1997, at A3.

97. *See id.*

98. *See* Eva M. Rodriguez, *Florida Fraud Case Gives Feds, Columbia a Focus in Their Fight*, WALL ST. J., Dec. 24, 1997, at A1.

99. *See* Rodriguez & Lagnado, *supra* note 96.

100. *Id.*

101. *See* Lucette Lagnado, *Columbia Taps Lawyer for Ethics Post; Yuspeh Led Defense Initiative of 1980s*, WALL ST. J., Oct. 14, 1997, at B6.

102. *Id.*

103. *See* Andy Pasztor & Lucette Lagnado, *Ethics Czar Aims to Heal Columbia*, WALL ST. J., Nov. 26, 1997, at B6.

104. *Id.*

105. *Id.*

106. *See* Rodriguez, *supra* note 98.

107. *See id.*

108. *See* Lucette Lagnado & Joseph B. White, *Columbia/HCA May Need More Time to Map Strategy*, WALL ST. J., Oct. 30, 1997, at B4.

109. *Reno Assures Hospitals False Claims Act Won't Be Used to Punish Mere Billing Errors*, 66 U.S.L.W. 2489 (1998).

110. *Id.*

111. *HHS IG Releases Guidance for Hospitals to Self-Regulate, Prevent Health Care Fraud*, 66 U.S.L.W. 2506 (1998).

112. *Id.*

KEY WORDS AND PHRASES

actus reus   **531**

arrest   **538**

burden of proof   **537**

collective entity doctrine   **548**

computer fraud   **559**

computer piracy   **560**

consent decree   **538**

crime   **530**

embezzlement   **556**

enterprise   **558**

exclusionary rule   **546**

felony   **533**

fraud   **556**

fruit of the poisonous tree   **546**

imputed liability   **553**

indictment   **537**

information   **537**

insider trading   **564**

intention to do wrong   **531**

larceny   **556**

mail fraud   **560**

mens rea   **531**

Miranda warnings   **548**

misdemeanor   **533**

negligence   **531**

negligence *per se*   **537**

nolo contendere   **538**

plea   **538**

plea bargaining   **538**

preponderance of the evidence   **537**

probable cause   **538**

recklessness   **531**

respondeat superior   **554**

responsible corporate officer doctrine   **553**

strict liability   **531**

transactional immunity   **538**

use immunity   **538**

vicarious liability   **553**

white-collar crime   **555**

wire fraud   **560**

QUESTIONS AND CASE PROBLEMS

1. The United States Gypsum Company (Gypsum) was charged with price-fixing in violation of the Sherman Act. Gypsum produces gypsum board, a laminated type of wallboard that is the primary component of interior walls and ceilings in residential and commercial construction.

Beginning in 1966, the Justice Department and Federal Trade Commission became involved in investigations into possible antitrust violations in the gypsum board industry. In late 1973, an indictment was filed in federal district court charging Gypsum, five other major gypsum-board manufacturers, and various of their corporate officials with sustaining "a continuing agreement . . . to (a) raise, fix, maintain and stabilize the prices of gypsum board; (b) fix, maintain and stabilize the terms and conditions of sale thereof; and (c) adopt and maintain uniform methods of packaging and handling such gypsum board." It was further alleged that the defendants "telephoned or otherwise contacted one another to exchange and discuss current and future published or market prices and published or standard terms and conditions of sale and to ascertain alleged deviations therefrom."

If the government can show that prices in the industry were in fact "fixed," but cannot show that Gypsum had an intent to fix prices, can Gypsum be found guilty of criminal price-fixing under the Sherman Act? [*United States v. United States Gypsum Co.*, 438 U.S. 422 (1978)]

2. All manufacturers of prescription drugs must receive approval from the government for their operations. The police received a tip that Scott Chan was manufacturing prescription drugs without the appropriate governmental clearance in a warehouse located at 4292 Wilkie Way. Without obtaining a search warrant, the police raided the warehouse and found the illegal drug-making apparatus. They then seized all the drugs and relevant business records concerning the manufacturing operation for use as evidence.

At trial, Chan claimed that both the drugs and the business records should be suppressed and not admitted into evidence. Is he correct? On what grounds should he base his argument? Suppose instead that it was agents for the Food and Drug Administration who seized the evidence instead of the police. Does the analysis change? What if Chan lived in the warehouse?

[For legal analysis of these questions, *see United States v. Katz*, 389 U.S. 347 (1967); *United States v. Argent Chemical Laboratories, Inc.*, 93 F.3d 572 (9th Cir. 1996); *In re Grand Jury Investigation Concerning Solid State Devices, Inc.*, 130 F.3d 853 (9th Cir. 1997).]

3. Dow Chemical Company operated a 2,000-acre chemical-manufacturing facility with numerous covered buildings in Midland, Michigan. Dow maintained extensive security around the facility. Security measures around the perimeter of the facility prevent ground-level public viewing, and Dow also investigates any low-level aircraft flights over the facility.

The Environmental Protection Agency (EPA) sought to inspect two of Dow's power plants in the facility for violations of federal air-quality standards. Without obtaining a search warrant to enter the property and despite Dow's refusal to voluntarily agree to a search, the EPA employed a commercial airplane with precision aerial-camera mapping equipment to photograph Dow's large manufacturing and research facilities from the air. The powerful equipment allowed power lines as small as 0.5 inches in diameter to be observed. Yet, at all times, the aircraft stayed within navigable airspace.

Dow somehow became aware of the EPA's actions and claimed that its Fourth Amendment rights had been violated. In making this contention, however, Dow conceded that a simple flyover with naked-eye observation, or the taking of a photograph from a nearby hillside overlooking such a facility, would give rise to no Fourth Amendment problem. Did the EPA's photographs constitute an unreasonable search in violation of the Fourth Amendment? [*Dow Chemical Co. v. United States*, 476 U.S. 227 (1986)]

4. Cronic and two associates were indicted on mail fraud charges involving the transfer of more than $9 million in checks between banks in Tampa, Florida, and Norman, Oklahoma, over a four-month period. Right before the trial was to begin, the attorney for the defendants withdrew. The court-appointed substitute counsel turned out to be an attorney who specialized in real estate and had never argued before a jury.

Once counsel was appointed, the court allowed the attorney only 25 days of pretrial preparation, even though it had taken the government more than four years to investigate the case and review all the documents. Cronic's two codefendants ended up testifying for the government. Cronic was convicted and received a 25-year sentence.

On appeal, Cronic claimed that the conviction cannot stand because he did not have effective assistance of counsel. Is he correct? [*United States v. Cronic*, 466 U.S. 648 (1984)]

5. Bert's Sporting Goods, Inc., with stores located throughout the state of Lys, sells a wide variety of sporting goods, including guns. Lys Penal Code § 123.45 requires sellers of guns to verify that the purchaser has not committed a felony within the last five years. If the purchaser has committed a felony within the last five years, the seller is not allowed to make the sale. "Willfully" selling a gun to a recent felon is considered a misdemeanor and is punishable by up to one year in jail and/or a maximum $10,000 fine.

Jim Dandy, who was convicted of a felony under Lys's penal code four years ago, went to purchase a gun at one of the Bert's Sporting Goods stores. Joe Mountain, a salesman at Bert's, sold Dandy the gun without asking for identification or checking to see whether Dandy was a convicted felon.

As a matter of fact, Mountain never checked whether any of the customers to whom he sold guns were felons. Mountain did not know of the Lys law requiring that he check on the customer's prior criminal history. However, Jay Lake, Mountain's supervisor, knew of the law and also knew that Mountain never checked whether a customer was a felon. Bert, the sole shareholder and director of Bert's Sporting Goods, Inc., knew about the law but did not know that Mountain did not check on his customers' prior criminal history.

Dandy used the gun in a robbery and shot two police officers during his getaway. He was never captured. Can Mountain be punished under Lys Penal Code § 123.45? What about Lake? Bert? Bert's Sporting Goods, Inc.? What penalties should be assessed? [For legal analysis of these questions, see *United States v. Park*, 421 U.S. 658 (1975); *United States v. Bi–Co Pavers, Inc.*, 741 F.2d 730 (5th Cir. 1984); *Bryan v. United States*, 118 S. Ct. 1939 (1998).]

6. Barry Engel was president of Gel Spice Company, which imported, processed, and packaged spices. As president he was responsible for the purchasing and storing of spices in the company's Brooklyn, New York, warehouse. In June 1972, the FDA inspected the Gel Spice warehouse and found widespread rodent infestation. Upon reinspection in August 1972, the FDA found evidence of continuing infestation. Following the two 1972 inspections, the FDA considered a criminal prosecution against Gel Spice. Before referring the case to the Department of Justice, however, an additional inspection was performed. At that July 1973 inspection, no evidence of rodent infestation was found, and the criminal prosecution was dropped. Three years later, in July 1976, the FDA inspected Gel Spice and again found active rodent infestation. Four additional inspections were performed from 1977 to 1979, each of which revealed continuing infestation. Thereafter, the government instituted criminal proceedings against Gel Spice and its president, Barry Engel. Under what theory of criminal liability could Engel be held liable for violating the Food, Drug and Cosmetic Act? Could Engel successfully assert the de-

fense of impossibility? [*United States v. Gel Spice Co.*, 773 F.2d 427 (2d Cir. 1985)]

7. An employee of Ladish Malting Co. was killed when he fell from a dilapidated fire-escape platform when it collapsed. Ladish was charged and indicted under a provision of the Occupation Safety and Health Act (OSHA) that imposes criminal penalties on any employer who "willfully violates" any occupational safety or health standard and thereby causes the death of an employee.

At trial, the government did not prove that Ladish had actual knowledge that the fire-escape platform was hazardous. The trial judge's instruction to the jury permitted the conclusion that Ladish "willfully" violated the applicable regulation if it "should have known" that the fire escape was in disrepair. The jury found Ladish guilty of "willfully violating" a safety standard and thereby causing the death of an employee, and the judge imposed a $450,000 fine. On appeal, should the verdict be upheld? [*United States v. Ladish Malting Co.*, 135 F.3d 484 (7th Cir. 1998)]

8. Bermel Enterprises, Inc. is a supplier of computer programming consulting services to the federal government. Alex and Margot Frankel, two Bermel systems analysts, have consistently overstated the time they spend working on the government projects on their time reports. It is these time reports that determine how much money the government pays the company. Additionally, Michelle Laff, a manager at Bermel, has falsified the results of systems tests conducted on the computer systems installed for the government. As a result, it appears that the systems are bug-free when in fact they have many errors.

What criminal charges may the government bring against the employees? Against Larry Bermel, owner of Bermel Enterprises, Inc.? Against Bermel Enterprises, Inc. itself?

9. Anthony Viola was the proprietor of Blue Chip Coffee, a wholesale coffee company in Brooklyn, New York. Michael Formisano performed odd jobs for Viola, mostly consisting of light cleanup and maintenance work. Viola, Formisano, and other defendants were convicted under the Racketeer Influenced and Corrupt Organizations Act (RICO) and for other substantive and conspiracy violations arising from their involvement in a drug-and-stolen-property importation and distribution ring.

The government alleged that the defendants assisted narcotics dealers in their efforts to import drugs into the United States through the Brooklyn waterfront. The drug owners would contact Viola who, in turn, would use his influence and access to information to locate the drugs and remove them from the pier in circumvention of U.S. Customs agents inspecting imported goods. The government also alleged that the defendants purloined cargo from the waterfront and sold the goods on the black market.

The government established at trial that Formisano was employed by Viola to perform menial tasks and that, on two occasions, Formisano agreed to sell goods for Viola knowing they were stolen. Also, the government showed that Formisano once was present when Viola ordered another employee to load stolen goods on a delivery truck. However, in the wealth of evidence presented at trial to show the existence and scope of the Viola enterprise, Formisano was hardly ever mentioned. Formisano argued that he could not be convicted under RICO because he had no part in the operation or management of the Viola enterprise. Should Formisano's RICO conviction be upheld on appeal? [*United States v. Viola*, 35 F.3d 37 (2d Cir. 1994)]

MANAGER'S DILEMMA

10. Many consulting firms try to finish fixed-price projects under the budgeted hours, thus earning more profit. As a result, consultants are often in a hurry.

Speeding tickets can result from the haste to make deadlines, meetings, or planes. Although many consulting firms bill clients for expenses relating to specific projects, it is not legitimate to bill a client for speeding tickets, because the client did not ask the consultant to break the law. Because fines for illegal activities are not tax-deductible, the consulting firm cannot write off this expense, either. A common way of passing on the expense is by padding dinner receipts or adding several small amounts to the client's bill, without supplying specific receipts.

If the consultant gets a speeding ticket while on company business, should the consultant absorb the cost personally? Lie to the client? Have the partner on the project reimburse him or her? What if the consultant is self-employed?

INTERNET SOURCES

This site for Corporate Compliance, Ltd. provides information on establishing and testing criminal compliance systems.	http://www.corporatecompliance.com
This FindLaw site, when searched using the word "criminal," provides links to a variety of cases and sites dealing with federal and state criminal law.	http://www.findlaw.com
The Columbia/HCA Healthcare Corporation Code of Conduct (dated May 13, 1998) is available at the corporation's site.	http://www.columbia-hca.com

CHAPTER 16

Environmental Law

INTRODUCTION

Role in Business Management

Environmental law consists of numerous federal, state, and local laws with the common objective of protecting human health and the environment. These laws are of great concern to businesses, many of which might not have considered environmental liability when they first undertook an activity.

For example, General Electric Co. (GE) built electric transformers in Pittsfield, Massachusetts. For decades, GE used polychlorinated biphenyls (PCBs) to insulate the transformers against fires. By 1976, the federal government had banned PCBs as carcinogenic. Since then, GE has been working to remove the chemicals from its 250-acre plant. In 1996, however, regulators discovered that in the 1940s and 1950s GE had donated PCB-soaked debris to local landfills for the creation of residential housing lots. Some lots had at least 10,000 times the concentration of the cancer-causing chemical allowed by state regulation. GE has been forced to pay for tests on the lots, to purchase contaminated lots, and to defend lawsuits for diminished property values.[1]

Some industries (such as petroleum, mining, and chemical manufacturing) are well accustomed to intense government regulation of the environmental effects of their operations. In recent years, however, the scope and impact of environmental laws

have grown steadily. Today, real estate owners and investors, developers, insurance companies, and financial institutions find that their operations, too, are often affected by laws and regulations intended to protect the environment.

Chapter Overview

This chapter introduces four federal environmental laws that illustrate the importance of environmental regulation for an expanding scope of business activities. The Clean Air Act, the Clean Water Act, and the Resource Conservation and Recovery Act are discussed as examples of environmental statutes that control the release of pollutants into the air, water, and land. The Comprehensive Environmental Response, Compensation, and Liability Act is discussed as an example of a remedial statute with broad application to all kinds of businesses and individuals. The chapter also addresses the potential liability under the environmental laws of shareholders, directors, officers, and managers, as well as affiliated companies. It outlines the key elements of effective compliance programs and audits, and it concludes with a discussion of international considerations.

---

1. William M. Carley, *Pollution from PCBs Keeps GE in Trouble with Pittsfield, Mass.*, WALL ST. J., Dec. 4, 1997, at A1.

Environmental Laws

Common Law Nuisance

Historically, public officials relied primarily on the common law theory of nuisance (discussed in Chapter 9) to control industrial and agricultural activities that interfered with the health or comfort of the community. Thus, industrial odors, noise, smoke, and pollutants of all kinds were the subjects of numerous lawsuits that attempted to balance the legitimate business interests of the polluter with the private interests of the surrounding community. However, the need to file a lawsuit in each case and the complexity of the common law made nuisance a cumbersome way to control environmental pollution in an industrial society. Moreover, a lawsuit could not prevent pollution; it could only provide a remedy after the fact. Today, state and federal regulatory programs have largely replaced common law nuisance as a means of pollution control.

Statutes

Environmental statutes establish policy, set goals, and authorize the executive branch or one of its administrative agencies to adopt regulations specifying how the law will be implemented. The statutes and regulations are interpreted and applied in administrative and judicial proceedings. Thus, environmental laws consist of the statutes, the regulations, and the administrative and judicial interpretations of their meaning. In addition, the administrative agency often issues policy statements and technical guidance that, while not having the force of law, guide enforcement efforts or provide assistance to the regulated community.

Three Categories   Environmental laws can be divided into three broad categories. The largest category consists of environmental laws that regulate the release of pollutants into the air, water, or ground. These laws usually authorize the government to issue and enforce permits for releases of pollutants. They may also authorize emergency responses and remedial action if, for example, improper waste disposal or accidental chemical spills threaten human health or the environment. Statutes in this category include the Clean Air Act; the Federal Water Pollution Control Act, as amended by the Clean Water Act; the Solid Waste Disposal Act, as amended by the

Resource Conservation and Recovery Act (RCRA); the Comprehensive Environmental Response, Compensation, and Liability Act (CERCLA or Superfund), as amended by the Superfund Amendments and Reauthorization Act of 1986; and similar state laws. These four pollution-control laws are discussed in this chapter.

A second category includes laws that govern the manufacture, sale, distribution, and use of chemical substances as commercial products. This category includes the Federal Insecticide, Fungicide and Rodenticide Act, which applies to pesticide products, and the Toxic Substances Control Act, which applies to all chemical substances both manufactured in and imported into the United States, excluding certain substances that are regulated under other federal laws. The Safe Drinking Water Act, which governs the quality of drinking water served by public drinking-water systems, can also be included in this category.

A third category includes laws that require government decision makers to take into account the effect of their decisions on the quality of the environment. This category includes the National Environmental Policy Act (NEPA) and the similar laws adopted by most states. NEPA, discussed in Chapters 6 and 17, is the cornerstone of environmental protection in the United States. Together with its state law counterparts, it affects all business activities that require governmental authorizations, permits, or licenses.

Popular Initiatives

Sometimes the public grows impatient with the legislative process and takes matters into its own hands through the initiative process. An *initiative* is a law submitted directly to the electorate for approval. If a majority of the voters vote in favor of the initiative, it becomes law without the need for approval by the legislature.

For example, in California, citizens were concerned that many commercial products contain substances known to cause cancer. In 1986, they voted for Proposition 65, which requires the state to identify all substances known to the state to cause cancer. As of mid-1998, more than 500 toxic chemicals were on the California list. Any business that knowingly causes exposure to such substances must provide a warning to the persons exposed unless the exposure presents no significant risk. Also exempted are exposures for which federal warning law preempts state authority. Many companies, including Gillette Co., the maker of Liquid Paper correction fluid, have reformulated their products rather than label them with cancer warnings. Because California represents 15% of the U.S. market, the law has affected the formulation of products nationwide.

Industry Participation

Companies affected by environmental laws should pay close attention to legislative, regulatory, and popular initiatives. Frequently, companies can take an active role in shaping such initiatives to protect their interests. Congressional or administrative agency staff may be unaware of how a proposed law or regulation may affect a particular industry. Usually, congressional and administrative agency staff welcome constructive industry participation in the law- and rule-making process, particularly when a company can propose alternative ways to accomplish the same legislative goals. Environmental laws and regulations are constantly changing as new threats to human health and the environment become apparent and as new ways are discovered to manage such threats safely and economically. The prudent company anticipates these changes and participates constructively in the legislative- and rule-making process.

Natural Resources Laws

Although environmental law contributes to the protection of natural resources, it generally does not include wilderness preservation, wildlife protection, coastal

ETHICAL CONSIDERATION

Environmental laws establish minimum standards to which companies must adhere. Companies also have fiduciary duties to their shareholders, and many labor activists argue that companies have similar duties to their employees. Is it ethical for a manager to adhere to stricter standards than mandated by law when such adherence will raise costs, reduce shareholder returns, and possibly jeopardize existing jobs? Is it more ethical, or less, when the standards are to be implemented in a Third World jurisdiction with no environmental laws whatsoever?

zone management, energy conservation, national park designation, and the like. Those laws are commonly referred to as *natural resources laws.* Nor does environmental law cover land-use regulation and zoning. Such laws, generally administered by local governments, are commonly referred to as land-use laws. They are discussed in Chapter 17.

◆ Administration of Environmental Laws

All the federal laws that set national goals and policies for environmental protection are administered by the Environmental Protection Agency (EPA), except for the National Environmental Policy Act, which is administered by the Council on Environmental Quality. State programs administer state laws and also federal laws, with the authorization of the EPA.

The Environmental Protection Agency

The *Environmental Protection Agency (EPA)* was created in 1970 by an executive order and operates under the supervision of the president. The EPA administrator and assistant administrators are appointed by the president with the advice and consent of the Senate. However, the EPA is neither an independent agency nor a cabinet-level department.

Several of the assistant administrators are responsible for administering the agency's regulatory programs; others have internal administrative functions. These national program managers share responsibility with the 10 regional administrators who head each of the 10 EPA regional offices. The national managers at headquarters develop policy and set goals for the regional offices. The regional administrators take responsibility for day-to-day program operation.

State Programs

State environmental laws and programs often predate the comparable federal programs. Moreover, many states have laws that are more stringent and more comprehensive than the federal laws. For example, California's hazardous-waste-management laws, water-quality-control laws, underground-tank regulations, and ban on land disposal of certain hazardous wastes all predate and in some cases provided the model for subsequent federal legislation.

Because of the prior existence of state environmental programs, and in order to reduce the burden of administration for the EPA, the EPA may authorize or approve a state program in lieu of the federal program in that state. The EPA does not delegate its federal authority; it merely approves a state program as "equivalent to or more stringent than" the federal program and then refrains from implementing the federal program in that state. However, the EPA generally provides oversight. It retains its enforcement authority and may revoke its authorization if the state program fails to meet federal requirements.

 ## The Clean Air Act

The Clean Air Act, as amended by the Clean Air Act of 1990,[2] sets four kinds of air quality goals. First, it requires the EPA to establish *national ambient air quality standards*, that is, to establish the maximum levels of pollutants in the outdoor air that, with adequate margins of safety, are compatible with public health. Standards have been set for six pollutants: (1) particulate matter, (2) sulfur dioxide, (3) ozone, (4) nitrogen dioxide, (5) carbon monoxide, and (6) lead. Every state and locality must seek to achieve and maintain these national air quality standards, which are revised periodically.

Second, the Clean Air Act requires that air quality not be allowed to deteriorate in those areas that already meet the national ambient air quality standards. Third, the act requires the preservation of natural visibility within the major national parks and wilderness areas. Fourth, it requires the EPA to establish emission standards that protect public health, with an ample margin of safety, from hazardous air pollutants.

The national ambient air quality standards are to be achieved through (1) state implementation plans approved by the EPA; (2) technological controls, including new source performance standards, set by the EPA; and (3) mobile-source controls set by the EPA. The *state implementation plans (SIPs)* prescribe emission-control measures for motor vehicles and for stationary sources existing prior to 1970. The SIPs also establish programs for state regulation of the "modification, construction, and operation of any stationary source." The SIPs include special programs for areas in each state that have

not yet attained the national ambient air quality standards. For those areas that have attained ambient air quality standards, the SIPs contain a program for prevention of significant deterioration. The SIPs vary considerably in their content and procedures from state to state. In large states, such as California, the SIPs may be developed and administered by local or regional districts. These districts often promulgate their own rules, which are often, but not always, incorporated into the SIP.

The EPA establishes performance standards for new sources, based on the best control technology available for a category of similar sources. The idea is that by requiring new sources to utilize the best control technology available, the sources of pollution will gradually be eliminated. Also, it is hoped that adherence to the performance standards will ensure roughly equal treatment of similar sources throughout the nation.

Before construction of major sources of emissions in areas that have achieved national ambient air quality goals is allowed to begin, a case-by-case determination of the *best available control technology (BACT)* is required. BACT is defined as an emission limitation that the permitting authority determines achieves the maximum reduction of pollutants, taking into account energy, environmental, and economic considerations. The permitting authority may consider the cost of the technology only in relation to the reduction of pollutants it achieves. Before construction of major sources of emissions in nonattainment areas, case-by-case determinations of the *lowest achievable emission rate (LAER)* for the sources are required. New sources include not only new plants but also modifications of existing plants if these cause a significant increase in emissions.[3] By affecting land-use decisions and transportation changes, as well as imposing emission controls, the law helps determine what areas of the country and what industrial sectors will be able to grow over the next 20 years or more.

The law also provides deadlines for attaining ambient air quality standards and puts pressure on those areas of the country that do not yet meet national ambient air quality standards. If a nonattainment area fails to develop an adequate plan to attain the national standard, the federal government is required to impose penalties, such as bans on construction of new sources of pollution, limits on the use of federal highway funds,

2. 42 U.S.C. §§ 7401 *et seq.* (1995).

3. Pub. L. No. 101-549, 104 Stat. 2399 (1990) (codified in 42 U.S.C. §§ 7408, 7479, and 7511 (1995)).

limits on drinking-water hookups, and the withholding of federal air-pollution funds.

The law also requires reductions in vehicle tail-pipe emissions of certain pollutants and the use of reformulated gasoline; it also mandates that fleets use clean, low-emission fuels in some nonattainment areas. Major sources of some 200 hazardous air pollutants are required to meet new emission limits based on maximum achievable control technology. Electric power plants must reduce emissions that lead to the formation of acid rain. Finally, the law phases out methylchloroform and chlorofluorocarbons and places limitations on the production of certain substitute chemicals.[4]

 ## The Clean Water Act

The Federal Water Pollution Control Act[5] was adopted in 1972 and was substantially amended by the Clean Water Act of 1977 and by the Water Quality Act of 1987. The act, as amended, is commonly referred to as the Clean Water Act. The principal goal of the Clean Water Act is to eliminate the discharge of pollutants into the navigable waters of the United States. *Navigable waters* are all "waters of the United States which are used in interstate commerce," including "all freshwater wetlands that are adjacent to all other covered waterways."

The principal regulatory program established by the Clean Water Act is the *National Pollutant Discharge Elimination System (NPDES)*, which requires permits for the discharge of pollutants from any point source to navigable waters. EPA regulations establish national *effluent limitations*, which impose increasingly stringent restrictions on pollutant discharges, based on the availability of economic treatment and recycling technologies. More stringent restrictions are imposed on new sources through the setting of national standards of performance. General and specific industry pretreatment standards are set for discharges to *publicly owned sewage treatment works (POTWs)*. The pretreatment standards are designed to ensure the effective operation of the POTW and to avoid the pass-through of pollutants. The POTW in turn must comply with its own NPDES

INTERNATIONAL CONSIDERATION

In the summer of 1997, Indonesia suffered two months of fires that enshrouded nearly 50 million people across Southeast Asia in smoke. Exacerbated by drought, the fires caused the region's worst-ever smog crisis. According to some, the real culprit was not fire but politics. "There is no good ethic of land management in Indonesia," remarked a senior environmental official at the World Bank. "The underlying view is that this is a developing country; they feel they need to develop with nothing getting in their way."[a]

Centrally run from the capital in Jakarta, the powerful Indonesian government aggressively sets industrial policy instead of leaving private individuals free to operate in a market. All permits for big projects are issued in Jakarta, as are production quotas for most major commodities. In recent years, the government demanded significant increases in output for timber products, palm oil, and rubber. To increase these plantation products, the government allocated vast tracts of public lands, which workers set ablaze in order to clear for planting. Although ostensibly outlawed in 1995, land-clearing fires are largely uncontrolled. When one environmental ministry official fingered three companies for setting fires, the agriculture ministry challenged him. "They have a conflict of interest," the former official observed softly. Upon seeing two men apprehended for setting fires, one plantation official praised their work: "We need the land to plant more rubber trees. Otherwise, we won't meet our expansion plans."[b]

a. Peter Waldman, *Southeast Asian Smog Is Tied to Politics*, WALL ST. J., Sept. 30, 1997, at A17.
b. *Id.*

---

4. For a discussion of the impact of the act on an industrial company, *see* Barbara Rosewicz, *Sweeping Change: How Clean-Air Bill Will Force DuPont into Costly Moves*, WALL ST. J., May 25, 1990, at A1.

5. 33 U.S.C. §§ 1251 *et seq.* (1998).

permit for the discharge of treated waters. The NPDES program is administered largely through approved state programs. However, the EPA maintains NPDES authority in areas not within the jurisdictions of states housing EPA-approved programs.

The following case, which addresses the EPA's regulations of effluent discharges by the offshore oil and gas industry, suggests the complexity of this area.

| A CASE IN POINT | SUMMARY |

CASE 16.1
BP EXPLORATION
& OIL, INC. v.
ENVIRONMENTAL
PROTECTION AGENCY

United States Court of
Appeals for the Sixth Circuit
66 F.3d 784 (6th Cir. 1995).

FACTS On April 3, 1993, after 18 years of rule making, the EPA issued final regulations under the Clean Water Act limiting effluent discharge for the offshore oil and gas industry. Specifically, the regulations articulated the BPT, BAT, BCT, and NSPS standards for drilling fluids, drill cutting waste, produced water, and produced sand in effluent discharge for offshore oil and gas drilling.

BPT (best practicable control technology currently available) is the average of the best existing performances by industrial plants of various sizes and ages within a point source category. For toxic pollutants, *BAT (best available technology economically achievable)* represents the best economically achievable performance in the category. For conventional pollutants, *BCT (best conventional pollutant control technology)* is intended to prevent unnecessarily stringent treatment that might be required under BAT. *New source performance standards (NSPS)* require use of technology chosen as BAT for new sources of pollutants.

BP Exploration and other oil companies challenged the regulations as too stringent. They alleged that the EPA violated the act by (1) setting an unreasonable standard for the discharge of oil and grease; (2) prohibiting discharge of certain drilling wastes within three miles of shore; and (3) banning discharge of contaminated sand. At the same time, the Natural Resources Defense Council, Inc. (NRDC), an environmental activist group, alleged that the EPA violated the act by promulgating standards that were too lenient. The NRDC argued that the EPA (1) illegally rejected zero discharge of drilling wastes; (2) violated the act by failing to regulate radioactive pollutants; and (3) should have required reinjection of polluted water.

ISSUE PRESENTED Were the Clean Water Act regulations issued by the EPA for the offshore oil and gas industry legal?

SUMMARY OF OPINION The U.S. Court of Appeals first rejected BP's challenge to the EPA's selection of improved gas flotation in its best available technology economically achievable standards and new source performance standards for limiting oil and grease in produced water. BP had failed to prove its claim that improved gas flotation does not remove dissolved oil. The EPA's decision to use the method was reasonable and based on reliable data. The court next held that the EPA reasonably decided that insufficient evidence existed to regulate radioactive pollutants in produced water, as the NRDC had urged. Also, the EPA acted within its statutory authority in not requiring zero discharge of produced waters through reinjection.

The court then turned to challenges to the EPA's BAT, NSPS, and BCT standards for drilling fluids and drill cuttings. These standards require dischargers within three nautical miles from shore in the Gulf of Mexico and in California waters to transport drilling fluids and drill cuttings to shore by barge and to dispose of the discharge in landfills. The court rejected BP's challenge to the EPA's calculation of the BCT cost-effectiveness test.

The court rejected BP's challenge to the BAT and NSPS levels for drilling fluids and cuttings, because it failed to show that zero discharge does not achieve any additional environmental benefit. The court upheld the EPA's determination on waste volume and landfill capacity for drilling fluids and cuttings in the Gulf of Mexico. The EPA had made its decision after considering all the options the NRDC raised and after weighing the benefits and drawbacks of those options.

Case 16.1 continues

Case 16.1 continued

The court also upheld the EPA's rejection of the zero-discharge option for drilling wastes in California beyond the three-mile limit. Weighing all the factors, the EPA determined that the increased air emissions from transporting the drilling wastes to the California coast by barge vastly outweighed the benefit of a zero-discharge limitation beyond three miles from shore.

In addition, the court upheld the EPA's decision to reject zero discharge of drilling wastes in Alaska, because the EPA carefully examined the possibility of requiring reinjection of drilling wastes in Alaska and rejected this option due to geologic concerns and the large amount of space required for reinjection technologies.

Turning to challenges to the EPA's zero-discharge limitation for produced sand, the court noted that the amount of produced sand is so minimal and irregular that existing barges that transport barrels of product or that service the offshore platforms are capable of carrying the produced sand to shore.

RESULT   The appeals court upheld the EPA regulations, rejecting the challenges from both industry and environmental activists.

 ## The Resource Conservation and Recovery Act

The Solid Waste Disposal Act, as amended by the Resource Conservation and Recovery Act (RCRA) of 1976 and the Hazardous and Solid Waste Amendments of 1984,[6] governs the management of hazardous wastes. The act authorizes the EPA to identify and list hazardous wastes, to develop standards for the management of hazardous wastes by generators and transporters of wastes, and to set standards for the construction and operation of hazardous-waste treatment, storage, and disposal facilities.

Cradle-to-Grave Responsibility

RCRA imposes "cradle-to-grave" responsibility on generators of hazardous waste. Each generator must obtain an EPA identification number and use a transportation manifest when transporting wastes for treatment or disposal. This allows the EPA to track the transportation, treatment, and disposal of hazardous wastes from the generator's facility to the final disposal site. A manifest is also required to transport hazardous wastes to an authorized storage facility.

Owners and operators of hazardous-waste facilities must obtain permits and comply with stringent standards for the construction and operation of their facilities. These standards include maintaining certain liability insurance coverage and providing financial assurances that show the owner/operator has the financial wherewithal to close the facility at the appropriate time and to maintain it properly after closure.

Even though hazardous-waste facilities are closely regulated, companies that generate hazardous wastes must carefully select treatment, transportation, and disposal facilities. Liability may be imposed on persons who "own or operate" the facility or who have used the facility for the storage, treatment, or disposal of wastes. Under RCRA, as under most environmental laws, *person* includes both corporations and individuals and does not exclude officers and shareholders. Moreover, persons who "contributed" to the improper waste disposal can include persons who had no direct involvement but

---

6. 42 U.S.C. §§ 6901 *et seq.* (1995).

ECONOMIC PERSPECTIVE

SELLING THE RIGHT TO POLLUTE

In the 1980s, Congress passed a number of laws to reduce sulfur dioxide pollution. Sulfur dioxide, a by-product of burning coal, causes acid rain. Each law was hotly debated: Environmentalists expressed concern with ever increasing amounts of pollution, while businesses were afraid that excessive controls would increase costs substantially. Congress tried to appease both sides by imposing regional restrictions on companies but allowing the amount of pollution to grow with the economy.

Economists proposed another solution: tradable pollution rights. A pollution right gives the holder permission to generate a specific amount of sulfur dioxide emissions. Economists argued that such rights would give rise to a market through which companies could find the least expensive way to reduce their emissions. Those firms that could cheaply reduce emissions could sell their pollution rights to firms facing more expensive pollution-reduction needs. Because different industries, companies, and facilities can reduce their emissions at different costs, those firms with a comparative advantage could do the bulk of emissions reduction and preserve scarce social resources. With a fixed number of pollution rights, total emissions would still be reduced to the desired level but in the most efficient way possible.

In 1990, Congress amended the Clean Air Act to allow companies that exceed air-quality requirements to sell their pollution rights to other companies, such as public utilities that burn high-sulfur coal to generate power. The first public auction of emission allowances took place in March 1993, when the Chicago Board of Trade offered sulfur dioxide–emission allowances issued by the EPA. Utility companies purchased 95% of the 50,010 emission allowances. Each allowance enabled the buyer to discharge one ton of sulfur dioxide. The utilities claimed that the allowances would enable them to delay the need to install scrubbers.

In the 1998 auction, the winning bidder paid $115 per allowance, up from $107 in 1997.[a] By requiring polluters to buy a limited number of permits, the EPA hopes to cut annual sulfur dioxide emissions in half by the year 2000.

The Chicago Board of Trade began trading futures contracts on the pollution permits in 1994. The concept of trading pollution rights has been hailed by utilities and environmentalists as a crucial element in the plan to control acid rain by creating a cost-efficient mechanism to reduce sulfur dioxide emissions by power plants.

Several brokerage firms have formed their own market for selling air-pollution-credit commodities, challenging the Chicago Board of Trade. A brokered trade in 1994 involving a New Jersey utility and a Connecticut utility was the first interstate trade involving nitrogen oxide credits under the free-market system. Nitrogen oxide contributes to smog. Trading in pollution credits, which is favored by economists and some environmentalists, seeks to achieve emissions reductions at minimum cost by allowing the cleanup to be made wherever it is cheapest.

Pollution reduction arrived on the global stage as concerns over global warming grew in the 1990s. At an international conference in Kyoto, Japan, in December 1997, the nations of the world considered the need to reduce greenhouse gases—primarily carbon dioxide emissions. Although tradable rights to pollute were discussed, no specific proposal was accepted. The Kyoto Conference is discussed in the "Inside Story."

---

a. Christopher Harder & Mark Golden, *Pollution Rights Fetch Premium at EPA Sale*, WALL ST. J., Mar. 27, 1998, at B7C.

---

had the authority to control the corporation's actions and failed to do so.

Many wholesalers and distributors are concerned about the extent of their liability for actions taken by their customers. The following case addresses whether liability attaches to a company with the power to control a hazardous site if it does not exercise that power.

"It's great! You just tell him how much pollution your company is responsible for and he tells you how many trees you have to plant to atone for it."

Ed Fisher © 1989 from The New Yorker Collection. All Rights Reserved.

A CASE IN POINT   **IN THE LANGUAGE OF THE COURT**

CASE 16.2
SHELL OIL CO. v.
LOVOLD CO.
Indiana Court of Appeals
687 N.E.2d 383
(Ind. Ct. App. 1997), *reh'g*
granted by 691 N.E.2d 521
(Ind. Ct. App. 1998).

FACTS   Lovold Co. is the owner of a gasoline service station in Brownsburg, Indiana. Lovold purchased the gasoline for its underground storage tanks from an intermediate wholesaler that, in turn, purchased the gasoline from its wholesaler, Shell Oil. Lovold later discovered that its underground storage tanks had leaked petroleum and contaminated the soil in the surrounding area. Lovold spent $150,000 to clean the contaminated soil and replace the tanks.

Case 16.2 continues

Case 16.2 continued

On December 20, 1995, Lovold filed suit against Shell, alleging that Shell violated Indiana's Underground Storage Tanks Act (USTA). Specifically, Lovold alleged that Shell was liable for Lovold's corrective costs under the act, because Shell operated the tanks at the time the leaks had occurred. In response, Shell filed a motion for summary judgment, arguing that it was not an operator under the statute because it was not responsible for the daily operation of the underground storage tanks. The trial court denied Shell's motion, and Shell appealed.

ISSUE PRESENTED   Is a company with the authority to control an underground storage tank liable under state environmental law for leaks even if it did not in fact operate the tank itself?

OPINION   BAKER, J., writing for the Indiana Court of Appeals:

Shell argues that the trial court erred in denying its motion for summary judgment. Specifically, Shell argues that it could not be liable under the Act because it did not "operate" the underground storage tanks.

In order for a party to be held liable for costs under the USTA, it must be shown that the party either "owned or operated the underground storage tank at the time" when the petroleum leak occurred. According to the statute, an operator is defined as a person "in control of, or having responsibility for, the daily operation of an underground storage tank."

Recently, another panel of this court concluded that the term "operator" was ambiguous because the legislature failed to define the words control and responsible. As a result, [that] court applied rules of statutory construction, and determined that an operator was someone who had the authority to control the underground storage tanks. Unlike [that] court, we do not conclude that the terms "control" and "responsible" are ambiguous and, therefore, subject to statutory construction.

Our rules of statutory construction forbid this court from interpreting a statute that is facially clear and unambiguous. Further, when the legislature defines a word, we are bound by that definition. As stated above, an operator is defined as a person "in control of, or having responsibility for, the daily operation of an underground storage tank." Responsible is defined as "answerable" or "accountable." MERRIAM WEBSTER'S COLLEGIATE DICTIONARY, 998 (10th ed. 1993). Further, "control" is defined as "to exercise restraining or directing influence over." In order to be considered an operator under the Act, therefore, Shell must have had more than the "authority to control." Rather, Shell must have exercised immediate control over or have been directly answerable for the daily operations of the storage tanks.

In the present case, nothing in the record indicates that Shell exercised such influence or was otherwise accountable for the daily operations of the storage tanks. The record reveals that the relationship between Shell and the operators of the Brownsburg station was tenuous. Shell, as a wholesaler, merely supplied gasoline to an intermediate wholesaler who, in turn, supplied gasoline to the Brownsburg station. However, there is no evidence that Shell had a contract with the station to supply the gasoline. Additionally, there is no evidence that Shell leased the facility; rather, the intermediate wholesaler, who leased the facility from a third party, sublet the station to the Brownsburg station operators. Finally, although Shell may have

Case 16.2 continues

Case 16.2 continued

taken certain remedial actions over the past several years to ensure that the underground storage tanks would not pose a health risk to the local residents, these isolated acts were insufficient to make Shell responsible for the daily operations of the Brownsburg station's underground tanks. Under these circumstances, we cannot conclude that Shell was an operator under the Act. To hold otherwise, would impose a definition that the legislature could not have intended.

RESULT   The appeals court reversed the trial court's denial of Shell's motion for summary judgment. Shell was not liable under the Indiana act.

COMMENTS   The recent contrary case referred to by the court was *Shell Oil Co. v. Meyer.*[7] Decided by another panel of the same Indiana Court of Appeals only three months before *Shell Oil Co. v. Lovold, Meyer* held that to be an "operator," an entity need not have exercised actual control over a facility if it had authority to control the facility. Because the Indiana statute was modeled on the federal Resource Conservation and Recovery Act and resembles the statutes of many other states, *Meyer* was thought to signal the beginning of a major increase in the liability of oil companies for the cleanup of groundwater pollution at sites across the nation. The potential for national impact was implied by the many *amici curiae* (friend of the court) briefs filed, including those by the Natural Resources Defense Council, Inc. and the National Coalition of Petroleum Retailers.

On February 5, 1998, the Indiana Court of Appeals granted Lovold a rehearing, leaving the law uncertain.

Questions

1. What type of relationship would Shell have to have with the gas station owner before Shell could be considered an operator? Would a long-term, exclusive contract to supply petroleum products suffice? Would a revolving line of credit with Shell suffice?
2. Given the uncertain and evolving nature of the law on this issue, what protections could Shell take in its future dealings to avoid, limit, or mitigate its liability for damages arising from underground leaks at gas stations?

---

7. 684 N.E.2d 504 (Ind. Ct. App. 1997).

Criminal Liability

Although RCRA imposes strict civil liability, a civil violation requires some sort of knowledge. In particular, RCRA provides criminal sanctions for any person who "knowingly transports any hazardous waste identified or listed under this subchapter to a facility which does not have a permit."[8] As explained in Chapter 15, it is not always clear how far down the sentence the word "knowingly" travels.

The U.S. Court of Appeals for the Eleventh Circuit held in *United States v. Hayes International Corp.*[9] that knowledge of the regulation banning transport of hazardous waste to an unlicensed facility was not an element of the offense. Furthermore, the defendants could be found guilty even if they did not know that the substance

---

8. 42 U.S.C. §§ 6928 (d)(1).

9. 786 F.2d 1499 (11th Cir. 1986).

being disposed of (a mixture of paint and solvents) was a hazardous waste within the meaning of the regulations. It was enough that they knew that what was being disposed of was a mixture of paint and solvents. The court distinguished *Liparota v. United States*,[10] which required knowledge that the purchase of food stamps was illegal, on the grounds that (1) the food stamp law required "knowing violation of a regulation"; and (2) RCRA, unlike the food stamp law, was a public welfare statute involving a heavily regulated area with great ramifications for the public health and safety. The court concluded that it was fair to charge those who chose to operate in such an area with knowledge of the regulatory provisions.

However, the court held that the government did have to prove that the defendants knew that the facility to which the waste was sent did not have a permit. Thus, even if the transporter does not know a permit is required, so long as he knows the facility does not have one or knows he has not inquired, that is sufficient knowledge for a conviction. Such knowledge can be shown circumstantially. For example, given that it is common knowledge that properly disposing of wastes is an expensive task, if someone is willing to take away wastes at an unusual price or under unusual circumstances, then a juror could infer that the transporter knows the wastes are not being taken to a permit facility.

The court did acknowledge that mistake of fact would be a defense if the defendants had had a good faith belief that the materials were being recycled. The regulations applicable at the time provided an exemption from the permit requirement for waste that was recycled. The court distinguished a case in which the Supreme Court had held that a person who believed in good faith that he was shipping distilled water when in fact he was shipping dangerous acid did not "knowingly" ship dangerous chemicals in violation of applicable regulations.[11] Unlike the defendant in that case, the defendants in *Hayes* knew what was being shipped—a combination of waste and solvents—and did not have a good faith belief that they were being recycled. Therefore, the convictions were upheld.

New Concepts for Waste Management

RCRA bans the disposal of hazardous wastes onto land without treatment to render them less hazardous. To comply with the EPA's land-disposal requirements, companies that generate hazardous waste may have to make substantial capital investments in treatment systems or may have to incur increased costs for having wastes treated elsewhere prior to disposal.

Generators of hazardous waste must certify that they have a program in place to reduce the quantity and toxicity of their wastes. They must also certify that they are disposing of their wastes in a manner that, to the extent practicable, minimizes future threats to human health and the environment. Many companies are changing their raw materials and production processes and are developing ways to recycle or otherwise use wastes. For some companies, these changes may result in reduced costs of operation over the long term.

Environmental regulatory programs can both increase costs and create opportunities for cost savings. Because the costs of hazardous-waste management can be substantial, the company that develops cost-efficient and forward-looking waste-management practices may have a considerable advantage over its less-efficient competitors.

The Federal Superfund Law

More than any other environmental law, the Comprehensive Environmental Response, Compensation, and Liability Act (CERCLA) of 1980, as amended by the Superfund Amendments and Reauthorization Act of 1986,[12] has affected businesses and individuals that do not themselves produce environmental pollutants. CERCLA authorizes the federal government to investigate and take remedial action in response to a release or threatened release of hazardous substances to the environment. CERCLA established what is now called the *Hazardous Substance Superfund* to finance federal response activity. Since its creation, the Superfund has been replenished with tax revenue numerous times, for a total replenishment of more than $15 billion.

How federal Superfund money will be spent is determined in part by the EPA's National Priorities List, which identifies sites that may require remedial action. The sites are listed by the EPA in a rule-making proceeding based on a *hazard ranking score*, which represents the degree of risk that the site presents to the environment and public health.

10. 471 U.S. 419 (1985) (Case 15.1 in this book.)

11. United States v. International Minerals, 402 U.S. 558 (1971).

12. 42 U.S.C. §§ 9601 *et seq.* (1998).

The EPA may undertake remedial action itself or require responsible persons to do so. If the EPA performs the remedial work, it can recover its costs from the responsible persons. The *responsible persons* include (1) the present owner or operator of the facility, (2) the owner or operator at the time of disposal of the hazardous substance, (3) any person who arranged for treatment or disposal of hazardous substances at the facility, and (4) any person who transported hazardous substances to and selected the facility.[13]

The average cost of response by the EPA at a Superfund site is estimated at $25 million. Response costs for some sites may be much higher. The magnitude of this liability has caused dramatic changes in the way companies, their lenders, and their investors investigate business transactions involving interests in real property. Many companies engage expert environmental counsel and consultants to assist in what is called a due-diligence investigation. Allocation of the risk of liability under CERCLA and other environmental laws has become a significant issue in the negotiation of agreements and documents relating to business transactions.

The U.S. Court of Appeals for the Ninth Circuit has ruled that long-term medical-monitoring costs for persons exposed to toxic substances during hazardous-waste cleanup are not recoverable as part of these "response" costs.[14] While CERCLA allows for the recovery of costs to monitor a site for release or threat of release of hazardous substances, it does not allow for recovery of costs to monitor an exposed individual's long-term health. Rather, the CERCLA provision is aimed at the public health and general welfare.

Strict Liability

The courts interpret the liability provisions of CERCLA broadly in order to effectuate the remedial policies of the statute. It is now well established that the present owner of the land is liable for the cleanup of hazardous substances disposed of on the land by another person, usually a previous owner or tenant, unless it can establish the third-party defense (also called the innocent landowner defense) discussed following.

CERCLA imposes strict liability, meaning that the responsible parties are liable regardless of fault. The law also allows the imposition of joint and several liability, which means that any one responsible party can be held liable for the total amount of response costs and natural resource damages even though others also may be responsible for the release. A responsible party held jointly and severally liable can seek cost recovery or contribution from other responsible parties, provided the other parties are still in existence and able to pay. Many times they are not. Thus, joint and several liability allows the government to select financially sound parties from whom to collect response costs and puts the burden of collecting these costs on the selected defendants.

In the following case, a present owner that was sued by the government sought contribution from a prior owner whose disposal of hazardous substances consisted solely of a soil investigation involving nine drill borings.

---

13. 42 U.S.C. § 9607 (1998).
14. Price v. U.S. Navy, 39 F.3d 1011 (9th Cir. 1994).

A CASE IN POINT	SUMMARY

CASE 16.3
UNITED STATES v. CDMG REALTY CO.
United States Court of Appeals for the Third Circuit
96 F.3d 706 (3d Cir. 1996).

FACTS   From 1945 until 1972, Sharkey's Farm Landfill operated as a municipal landfill for Morris County, New Jersey. During its operation, the landfill received waste from several New Jersey counties. In addition, the landfill received 750,000 pounds of hazardous chemical waste from a pharmaceutical company; three million gallons of wastewater of unknown composition from a chemical company; and chemical waste from various other sources. During the late 1960s and early 1970s, neighbors continually complained about odors, smoke from fires, lack of proper cover, and the presence of dead animals at the landfill. In 1972, the landfill was closed; and, in the mid-1970s, the EPA began investigating the site under CERCLA.

Case 16.3 continues

Case 16.3 continued

In 1981, Dowel purchased the vacant property. Three months before finalizing its purchase, Dowel conducted a soil investigation to determine the land's suitability for construction. The investigation, Dowel's only activity on the land, involved nine drill borings, each twelve to eighteen feet deep. The engineer's records showed that the drill bored through various waste materials and groundwater and that several of the boreholes caved in during the testing. During its period of ownership, Dowel kept the property vacant and deposited no waste at the site.

In 1983, the New Jersey Department of Environmental Protection and Energy (NJDEPE) advised Dowel that it was investigating the property and that Dowel should cease any planned activities at the site. The next year, the EPA informed Dowel that it was potentially liable for cleanup costs under CERCLA. In 1987, Dowel sold the property to HMAT Associates, Inc., after full disclose of the site's history, investigation by environmental regulators, and possible Superfund designation and liability.

In 1989, the EPA and the NJDEPE commenced legal action under CERCLA against parties potentially responsible for the costs of cleaning up the site. The parties sued included HMAT as the current owner but not Dowel. HMAT then sued Dowel seeking contribution from it as a former owner of the property "at the time of disposal." The trial court granted summary judgment for Dowel, and HMAT appealed.

ISSUE PRESENTED   Does CERCLA liability attach to a former owner "at the time of disposal" if that "disposal" consists only of passive seepage or leaching? Does liability attach if "disposal" consists only of soil testing?

SUMMARY OF OPINION   Under CERCLA, the term "disposal" means "the discharge, deposit, injection, dumping, spilling, leaking, or placing of any solid waste or hazardous waste into or on any land or water so that such solid waste or hazardous waste or any constituent thereof may enter the environment or be emitted into the air or discharged into any waters, including ground waters." Although the terms "leaking" and "spilling" do not generally denote active conduct, the U.S. Court of Appeals held that in this context, they should be read to require affirmative human action, because the surrounding words all envision human action. The law also makes a prior owner liable only in the event of a "release" or "threatened release." Because "release" is defined broadly in the statute to include leaching, Congress was clearly aware of the concept of passive migration in landfills and knew how to refer to it. That it did not refer to it when defining "dispose" suggests it meant to exclude it.

Similarly, CERCLA provides an "innocent owner" defense to liability if the defendant can prove the release was caused soled by an act or omission of a third party. Because this defense is conditioned on the defendant's having purchased the property "after the disposal," the "disposal" cannot constitute a constant, passive spreading of contaminants. Otherwise, the defense would almost never apply because there would be no point "after disposal."

As for liability arising out of Dowel's soil testing, CERCLA does not immunize a party from liability because its dispersal of contaminants was insubstantial. To the contrary, the dispersal need not reach any particular level in order to constitute disposal and trigger liability. In the case of soil testing, however, automatic liability would undermine CERCLA's innocent owner defense because a party merely investigating a

Case 16.3 continues

Case 16.3 continued

property could be held responsible for disposal. Such testing must not be negligent, though. If a party is negligent in testing, it may be held liable for any disposal caused by the tests.

RESULT   The appeals court vacated the decision of the trial court and remanded the case for further consideration of Dowel's liability for the disposal caused by its testing under a standard of negligence.

Retroactive Application As the following case demonstrates, owners can be held liable for hazardous waste disposed of before CERCLA became law.

| A CASE IN POINT | IN THE LANGUAGE OF THE COURT |

CASE 16.4
UNITED STATES v.
OLIN CORP.

United States Court
of Appeals for the
Eleventh Circuit
107 F.3d 1506
(11th Cir. 1997).

FACTS   For nearly 50 years, Olin Corp. operated a chemical-manufacturing facility in McIntosh, Alabama. During its first 30 years, the plant produced mercury- and chlorine-based commercial chemicals that contaminated significant segments of the company's property. As a result, groundwater and soil pollution on one part of the property made it unfit for future residential use. In response, the government sued Olin under CERCLA, seeking a cleanup order against it and reimbursement for response costs. After negotiations with the government, Olin agreed to a consent decree calling for it to pay all costs associated with remediation of the site. The decree also resolved Olin's liability for contamination caused by disposal activities before and after CERCLA's effective date of December 11, 1980.

Olin contended that CERCLA was not intended to impose liability for conduct predating the statute's enactment. Agreeing with Olin, the district court rejected the consent decree and dismissed the government's complaint against Olin. The government appealed.

ISSUE PRESENTED   Does CERCLA liability apply retroactively to disposals occurring prior to its enactment?

OPINION   KRAVITCH, J., writing for the U.S. Court of Appeals:

The district court also based its dismissal order on its conclusion that CERCLA's response cost liability scheme applies only to disposals after the statute's enactment. This ruling not only conflicts with this court's recent description of CERCLA, but also runs contrary to all other decisions on point. . . .

. . .

Because CERCLA contains no explicit statutory command regarding retroactive application of its cleanup liability regime, this court must decide what, if any, further

Case 16.4 continues

Case 16.4 continued

inquiry should occur. Although the [U.S. Supreme Court] reaffirmed the presumption against retroactive application of statutes, it emphasized that courts must effectuate congressional intent regarding retroactivity. The Court ruled that its approach simply was designed to "assure [ ] that Congress itself has affirmatively considered the potential unfairness of retroactive application and determined that it is an acceptable price to pay for the countervailing benefits." As a result, we conclude that even absent explicit statutory language mandating retroactivity, laws may be applied retroactively if courts are able to discern "clear congressional intent favoring such a result." . . .

We examine first CERCLA's language. As noted above, the statute contains no explicit statement regarding retroactive application of its cleanup liability provisions. Olin mistakenly contends that CERCLA's text therefore offers no insight into Congress's intent on this subject. CERCLA imposes liability for response costs upon "owners and operators" of "any site or area where a hazardous substance has been deposited. . . ." Its reach also extends to "any person who at the time of disposal of any hazardous substance owned or operated" such a facility. Congress thus targeted both current and former owners and operators of contaminated sites. By imposing liability upon former owners and operators, Congress manifested a clear intent to reach conduct preceding CERCLA's enactment.

. . .

An analysis of CERCLA's purpose, as evinced by the statute's structure and legislative history, also supports the view that Congress intended the statute to impose retroactive liability for cleanup. . . . Congress's twin goals of cleaning up pollution that occurred prior to December 11, 1980, and of assigning responsibility to culpable parties can be achieved only through retroactive application of CERCLA's response cost liability provisions; this fact provides additional evidence of clear congressional intent favoring retroactivity.

Further review of CERCLA's legislative history confirms that Congress intended to impose retroactive liability for cleanup.

RESULT The appeals court reversed the district court's dismissal of the government's complaint and remanded the case for further proceedings. Olin was liable for waste disposed of before CERCLA became law.

COMMENTS The lower court's decision stood noticeably alone in holding that CERCLA did not apply to acts predating its enactment. By reversing the district court, the Eleventh Circuit reaffirmed the general understanding that retroactivity is no defense to CERCLA liability.

Questions

1. Given that Congress can pass environmental laws that penalize actions previously thought innocuous, or at least quite legal, what should a manager do when making decisions that may affect the environment?

2. How would the court have analyzed the issue if the law's legislative history had contained no references to retroactive liability?

ETHICAL CONSIDERATION

What may be cost effective in the short term may not be in the long term, particularly when the environment and human health are concerned. Given the possibility of retroactive liability, managers should consider not just what the law requires of them at the time but also what effects their actions now might have on the environment in the future. But, if there is no possibility of retroactive liability, is it ethical for managers to ignore those possible but uncertain future effects?

Affiliated Companies and Piercing the Corporate Veil Corporate relatives must also worry about CERCLA liability. In every state, corporations have limited liability so that shareholders risk only their invested capital. Hence, a plaintiff suing a corporation may go after that company's assets but not the assets of its shareholders, including a parent corporation. To protect plaintiffs against corporate schemes to use this protection merely to inappropriately evade responsibility, courts may "pierce the corporate veil" that separates a firm from its subsidiary. Such a collapsing of the legal distinction between parent and subsidiary is only appropriate if the distinction is a fiction meant simply to protect shareholders from illegal activity. In the following case, the court considered the responsibility of two parent corporations for the hazardous-disposal activities of their subsidiaries.

A CASE IN POINT   SUMMARY

CASE 16.5
UNITED STATES v.
BESTFOODS
Supreme Court
of the United States
118 S. Ct. 1876 (1998).

FACTS Beginning in 1957, a series of owners manufactured chemicals at a site in Dalton Township, Michigan. During the initial owner's tenure, groundwater underneath the site became contaminated. In 1965, a subsidiary of CPC International, Inc. purchased the property, becoming its second owner. The subsidiary's disposal of chemical waste in unlined lagoons caused further pollution of soil, surface water, and groundwater. Overflows of chemicals contained in a cement-lined equalization basin and chemical spills from train cars and storage drums caused further contamination. In 1972, a third owner acquired the property but went bankrupt five years later. At that time, the bankruptcy trustee took title to the property and attempted to sell it with the assistance of the Michigan Department of Natural Resources (MDNR), which had become concerned about the property because of its extensive pollution.

In October 1977, the MDNR concluded its efforts to find a purchaser that would help clean up the property. The state agency signed an agreement with Cordova Chemical Company of California (Cordova/California), a wholly owned subsidiary of Aerojet–General Corporation (Aerojet). In the agreement, Cordova/California accepted responsibility to clean up specific types of contamination, and the MDNR agreed to clean up other specific types of contamination. The company also agreed to pay the MDNR $600,000 to help offset the agency's cleanup costs. The agreement stated: "Cordova Chemical Company shall not have any responsibility or liability in connection with any other corrective actions which the [MDNR] or any other governmental agency may hereafter deem necessary. . . ." Immediately after signing the agreement, Cordova/California purchased the site from the bankruptcy trustee. The next year, Cordova Chemical Company of Michigan (Cordova/Michigan), a wholly owned subsidiary of Cordova/California, acquired ownership of the site. In time, both Cordova/California and the MDNR fulfilled their cleanup responsibilities. Although the agreement did not address all forms of pollution on the property, neither Cordova/California nor Cordova/Michigan exacerbated the remaining problems.

Case 16.5 continues

Case 16.5 continued

In 1981, the EPA became involved in cleaning up the site. Eventually, it formulated a long-term response to the environmental damage, which was expected to cost millions of dollars. To recover those costs, the United States later sued all related parties: (1) the current owner, Cordova/Michigan; (2) its parent and previous site owner, Cordova/California; (3) its parent, Aerojet; (4) CPC, the parent corporation of the second owner; and (5) the MDNR for having arranged the transfer of the property to Cordova/California.

The trial court ruled that the first four parties—the owner-connected parties—were all liable, but it found the MDNR not liable. Cordova/Michigan accepted its liability, but Cordova/California, Aerojet, and CPC appealed the decision. The appeals court reversed, holding that Aerojet and CPC were not liable because there was no basis for piercing the corporate veil under state corporate law. The United States appealed.

ISSUE PRESENTED What is the standard under CERCLA for holding a parent corporation financially liable for pollution that occurred on a site owned by its subsidiary?

SUMMARY OF OPINION Under CERCLA, liability for cleanup costs of a polluted site attaches to (1) the present "owner or operator" of a facility from which there is a release of hazardous substances, and (2) any prior "owner or operator" of a facility whose involvement coincided with disposal of hazardous substances. The U.S. Supreme Court held that there are two bases for imposing liability on parent corporations under CERCLA for operating facilities ostensibly under the control of their subsidiaries. First, a parent corporation will have derivative CERCLA liability for its subsidiary's actions when (but only when) the corporate veil may be pierced. Piercing is appropriate when the corporate form would otherwise be misused to accomplish certain wrongful purposes such as fraud. Second, a parent corporation may have direct liability as an operator for its own actions in operating a facility owned by its subsidiary. The Court held that "an operator must manage, direct, or conduct operations specifically related to pollution, that is, operations having to do with the leakage or disposal of hazardous waste, or decisions about compliance with environmental regulations." Thus, the question is not whether the parent operates the subsidiary, but rather whether it operates the facility.

The Court acknowledged that it is common for directors of the parent to serve as directors of its subsidiary. Directors and officers holding positions with a parent and its subsidiary can and do "change hats" to represent the two corporations separately. Courts generally presume that the directors are wearing their "subsidiary hats" and not their "parent hats" when acting for the subsidiary. As a result, the parent is not liable just because dual officers and directors made policy decisions and supervised activities at the facility. However, the parent may be held directly liable if (1) the parent operates the facility in the stead of its subsidiary or alongside the subsidiary in some sort of joint venture; (2) a dual officer or director departs so far from the norms of parental influence exercised through dual officeholding as to serve the parent, even when ostensibly acting on behalf of the subsidiary, in operating the facilty; or (3) an agent of the parent with no hat to wear but the parent's hat manages or directs activities at the facility. However, activities that involve the facility that are consistent with the parent's investor status (such as monitoring of the subsidiary's performance, supervision of the subsidiary's finance and capital budget decisions, and articulation of general policies and procedures) should not give rise to direct operator liability for the parent.

Case 16.5 continues

Case 16.5 continued

RESULT   The Supreme Court vacated the appeals court decision and remanded for determination of the role played by CPC's agents in operating the facility. If CPC's agents went beyond the actions necessary to protect CPC's investor status and took actions directed to the facility that "are eccentric under accepted means of parental oversight of a subsidiary's facility," then CPC would have direct liability as an operator.

COMMENTS   The Supreme Court expressly left open the question of whether, in enforcing CERCLA's indirect liability, courts should borrow state law or instead apply a federal common law of veil piercing.[15]

---

15. *Compare* United States v. Cordova/Michigan, 113 F.3d 572 (6th Cir. 1997) (*en banc*) (applied Michigan veil-piercing law) *with* Lansford-Coaldale Joint Water Auth. v. Tonolli Corp., 4 F.3d 1209 (3d Cir. 1993) (applied federal common law).

In *Bestfoods*, the Sixth Circuit turned to Michigan corporate law in deciding whether to pierce the Michigan firm's corporate veil. Other courts have turned to federal common law, that is, the principles found in cases that the courts have developed for interpreting federal statutes like CERCLA. Under federal common law, courts may give less respect to the corporate form than under the common law of many states.

In *United States v. Kayser-Roth Corp.*,[16] for example, the court relied on federal common law in applying CERCLA to hold a parent corporation directly liable for response costs as the owner and operator of a facility that was actually owned and operated by its subsidiary. The court determined that the parent Kayser-Roth could not be held liable under CERCLA as an operator merely because of its stock ownership in the subsidiary Stamina Mills. However, the court held that Kayser-Roth was liable as an operator because of the pervasive control it exercised over Stamina Mills's operations. The court relied on these facts: (1) Kayser-Roth had total monetary control, including control over budgeting and collection of accounts receivable; (2) all contracts with governmental agencies regarding environmental matters had to be funneled through the parent; (3) all real estate transactions, including leases, had to be approved by the par-

ent; (4) all capital expenditures exceeding $5,000 had to be approved by the parent; and (5) Kayser-Roth personnel were placed in nearly all of Stamina Mills's officer and director positions. The court further determined that the corporate veil of Stamina Mills should be pierced to impose liability on Kayser-Roth as an owner under CERCLA. The court reasoned that to allow the parent company to escape liability would frustrate the purpose of the federal statute, which did not place any particular importance on the corporate form. Because of its pervasive control of Stamina Mills, Kayser-Roth was therefore liable as an owner under CERCLA.

Successor Liability   An important issue related to parent–subsidiary liability is *successor liability*, that is, the responsibility of an acquirer of corporate assets for the liabilities of the corporation that sold its assets. Ordinarily, a purchaser of corporate assets—as opposed to a purchaser of all the stock of corporation—does not assume any liabilities from the seller. The doctrine of successor liability arose out of attempts by companies to evade liability by selling the bulk of their business or assets. In such a scheme, a corporation expecting liability might sell off everything but its corporate name and distribute the proceeds to shareholders, thereby leaving claimants against it with no assets to collect against. Although this aspect of corporate law is a province of state common law, CERCLA has raised the specter of a federal common law of successor liability regarding environmental cleanup under that statute.

---

16. 724 F. Supp. 15 (D.R.I. 1989), *aff'd*, 910 F.2d 24 (1st Cir. 1990), *cert. denied*, 498 U.S. 1084 (1991).

In 1997, the U.S. Court of Appeals for the Ninth Circuit ruled that a federal common law of successor liability was unnecessary under CERCLA,[17] thereby agreeing with the First, Sixth, and Eleventh Circuit decisions relying on state common law to determine successor liability. The Second, Third, Fourth and Eighth Circuits have adopted the contrary position, which relies on federal common law to determine successor liability. Instead of resolving the debate, the Court of Appeals for the Ninth Circuit simply evened up the score: federal common law 4, state common law 4. Such a situation is commonly resolved by the U.S. Supreme Court, which may happen here.

Punitive Damages

CERCLA allows recovery for cleanup costs, but under Section 107(a) does not allow punitive damages unless recklessness is found. The case of *United States v. Hooker Chemicals & Plastics Corp.*[18] examined the extent to which one company was liable for the adverse effects of chemical dumping. Hooker Chemicals had used a 16-acre plot of land, the Love Canal site, in the city of Niagara Falls, New York, as a landfill for toxic chemical wastes from Hooker's Niagara Falls plant between 1942 and 1954. There was evidence that some of the containers were not properly sealed. Due to poor drainage and Hooker's dumping practices, the landfill presented serious problems to the surrounding area. The presence of flammable chemicals with flashpoints of less than 100°F led to frequent fires, some with flames as high as 20 feet. After rainstorms, noxious fumes would permeate the neighborhood. Frequent explosions from the site would propel debris for distances as great as two blocks. Children swimming in unfilled parts of the nearby canal reported cases of skin rash.

In 1953, Hooker transferred the site to the city school board to build a school and playground. A year later, an elementary school was built in the central section of the parcel. Even after Hooker learned of the potential hazards of the substances it had dumped, the company did not offer the school board additional information that might have protected the site's users. In 1978, a health emergency was announced when noticeable quantities of chemical residue began seeping into the basements of nearby homes. In 1985, Hooker settled a lawsuit with 1,300 current and former residents of the area for $20 million for personal-injury and property-damage claims.

The state of New York alleged reckless or wanton disregard for the health and safety of the local residents surrounding the Love Canal site. The district court found that Hooker Chemical Company's behavior was negligent, but did not rise to the level of recklessness. Therefore, punitive damages were not appropriate.

Defenses

CERCLA provides only three defenses to liability. The defendant must show that the release of hazardous substances was caused solely by (1) an act of God (that is, an unavoidable natural disaster, such as an earthquake); (2) an act of war; or (3) the act or omission of a third party, provided that certain other requirements are met. To assert the *third-party defense* (also referred to as the *innocent landowner defense*), a responsible party must show that the third party was not an employee and had no contractual relationship with the person asserting the defense. If the facility was acquired from the third party, the written instrument of transfer is deemed to create a contractual relationship, unless the purchaser acquired the facility after the hazardous substances were disposed of and without any knowledge or reason to know that hazardous substances had previously been disposed of at the facility. To establish that the purchaser had no reason to know that hazardous substances were disposed of at the facility, the purchaser must show that, prior to the sale, it undertook "all appropriate inquiry into the previous ownership and uses of the property consistent with good commercial or customary practice in an effort to minimize liability."[19]

Lender Liability

Lenders also face liability under CERCLA because foreclosure of a contaminated property potentially makes a lender the owner and, therefore, liable. In 1996, Congress passed the Asset Conservation, Lender Liability,

17. Atchison, Topeka & Santa Fe Rwy. Co. v. Brown & Bryant Inc., 132 F.3d. 1295 (9th Cir. 1997). *Contra* Zollo Drum Co. v. B. F. Goodrich Co., 99 F.3d 505 (2d Cir. 1997).

18. 850 F. Supp. 993 (W.D.N.Y. 1994).

19. 42 U.S.C. § 9601(35)(B) (Supp. 1997).

and Deposit Insurance Protection Act of 1996, which modified CERCLA's definition of "owner or operator" to limit the potential exposure of lenders that foreclose on real property.[20]

The new definition excludes from "owner or operator" a lender that did not participate in the management of a facility prior to foreclosure. Participation in management means "actually participating in the management or operational affairs" of the facility; mere capacity to influence management is not a sufficient basis for imposing operator liability on a lender. Although a lender may take steps to sell the property or buy it at the foreclosure sale, the lender must attempt to sell or re-lease the property as soon as practicable for a commercially reasonable price. The new definition also allows a lender to hold "indicia of ownership," such as a deed of trust, to protect its security interest without facing liability.

Under the amended law, a fiduciary's liability is limited to the assets held in trust. There is also a safe harbor for fiduciaries that undertake lawful response actions, but the safe harbor does not protect against negligence that causes or contributes to the release or threatened release of hazardous substances.[21]

Legislation has been introduced in some states to overcome the effect of antideficiency statutes when financial institutions find they have loaned monies for the purchase or improvement of what turns out to be polluted property. (*Antideficiency statutes* prevent the holder of a mortgage or deed of trust secured by real property from suing the borrower to recover whatever is still owing after a foreclosure sale.)

◆ Enforcement of Environmental Laws

Enforcement includes the monitoring of regulated companies' compliance with the environmental laws and the correction or punishment of violations.

Self-Reporting

Many statutes and regulations require regulated companies to report certain facts to the EPA, such as the con-

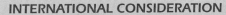

INTERNATIONAL CONSIDERATION

The environmental laws of other nations are generally not as pervasive and do not establish regulatory requirements as strict as those of the United States. However, U.S. and some European environmental laws may serve as models for other nations as they develop regulatory programs to protect their environments. Therefore, forward-looking companies recognize that the global environmental regulation of the future may look very much like current environmental regulation in the United States and Western Europe.

centrations and/or the amounts of pollutants discharged from a facility. These reports may indicate a violation and may therefore be the subject of an enforcement action by the agency. There are severe penalties for filing false reports, including criminal sanctions for knowingly providing false information to a government agency. The EPA may reduce or eliminate fines for civil or administrative violations by companies that discover such violations through their own systematic compliance reviews, report them to the EPA, and remedy them. It also may recommend against criminal prosecution by the Department of Justice if the company cooperates with the EPA.[22]

Agency Inspections

The environmental laws provide broad authority to the administering agencies to conduct on-site inspections of plant facilities and their records. Many laws authorize the agency to collect samples for analysis. Inspections may be conducted routinely or in response to reports or complaints from neighbors or employees. If criminal violations are suspected, the agency may choose to conduct an inspection under the authority of a search warrant. Violations observed during the inspection may be the subject of civil or criminal enforcement actions.

---

20. 42 U.S.C. § 9601(20) (Supp. 1997).
21. 42 U.S.C. § 9607(n) (Supp. 1997).

22. *EPA May Recommend Not Prosecuting Companies that Uncover, Report Crimes,* 66 U.S.L.W. 2520 (1998). *See* <http://es.epa.gov/oeca/oceft/audpol2.html> for the official EPA memo on the policy.

Enforcement Actions

Because the environmental laws are intended to accomplish such important societal goals and violations of the laws may cause serious harm or injury, environmental regulatory agencies generally are given strong enforcement powers. For a first violation, the agency might issue a warning and impose a schedule for compliance. If the schedule is not met or the violations are repeated, more aggressive enforcement action will likely follow. Such action may take the form of an administrative order to take specified steps to achieve compliance or a formal administrative complaint containing an assessment of administrative penalties. The penalties vary; but because they can be assessed for each day of each violation, they can be substantial for repeated, multiple, or long-standing violations.

In more egregious cases, the enforcing agency may initiate a civil lawsuit and/or a criminal prosecution. Courts are authorized in most instances to impose penalties of $25,000 to $100,000 per day of violation and to sentence individuals to jail terms of one year or more.[23] (See also the discussion of penalties in Chapter 15.) In some cases, the agency may have authority to close down the violator's operations.

Environmental Justice

A new area of enforcement addresses so-called environmental justice. *Environmental justice* is the notion that decisions with environmental consequences (such as where to locate incinerators, dumps, factories, and other sources of pollution) should not discriminate against poor and minority communities. Because such decisions usually require state or municipal permitting, enforcement is often by the federal government and against states, cities, and counties.

Between 1993 and 1998, the EPA received 51 environmental justice complaints, most of which addressed the granting of state and local permits. As of mid-1998, fifteen cases were still under active consideration, including a challenge to a $700 million chemical plant to be built in the heavily industrialized corridor between Baton Rouge, Louisiana, and New Orleans.

The EPA adopted an interim policy that provides that even when a pollution permit passes the ordinary

tests under the environmental laws, it might still be illegal under Title VI of the Civil Rights Act of 1964 if it contributes to a pattern of disproportionate pollution in a minority neighborhood (a practice that civil rights activists call "environmental racism").[24] While certain state governments and major industrial groups oppose the new policy as unworkable, some civil rights groups fault it for not going far enough. As of spring 1998, the EPA was still formulating its final policy on investigating such claims and enforcing the bans on discriminatory permitting.[25]

◆ Management of Environmental Compliance

Knowledgeable corporate officials today recognize the need to adopt corporate policies and create management systems to ensure that company operations are protective of human health and the environment. These programs generally include several key elements.

Corporate Policy

A strong corporate policy of environmental protection, adopted and supported at the highest levels of management, is usually the keystone of an effective program. Mere compliance with environmental laws may not be enough. A practice that is lawful today could nevertheless lead to environmental harm and future liability. For example, underground storage of flammable materials was once considered a sound practice and was actually required by many local fire codes. Little thought was given to the possibility of leaks or spillage around the tanks, with resulting harm to underground water supplies. If the risks had been perceived properly, double containment could have been provided when the tanks were first installed. This lack of foresight caused many companies to incur substantial costs for groundwater restoration.

The corporate policy should require every employee to comply with environmental laws. It should encourage management to consider more stringent measures than those required by law if such measures

---

23. *See, e.g.,* 33 U.S.C. § 1319 (1995) and 42 U.S.C. § 6928 (1995).

24. John H. Cushman, Jr., *Industry Bridles at Pollution Policy,* SAN FRANCISCO EXAMINER, May 10, 1998, at A4.

25. *EPA Issues Guidance for Investigating Claims that State, Local Permits Are Discriminatory,* 66 U.S.L.W. 2504 (1998).

are necessary to protect human health and the environment. Finally, the policy should encourage a cooperative and constructive relationship with government agency personnel and should support active participation in legislative and administrative rule-making proceedings.

Well-Defined Organization

Management of environmental compliance requires a well-defined organization with clear responsibilities and reporting relationships. The complex and technical nature of environmental laws and regulations requires a highly trained professional staff with legal and technical expertise.

Periodic Assessment

A program of periodic internal assessments of environmental compliance should be developed to test the effectiveness of the management system, to identify instances of noncompliance, and to ensure that such instances are corrected. It is important in planning the assessment to determine whether the company wishes to maintain the confidentiality of any assessment reports.

Long-Term Strategies

The company should develop strategies for reducing the costs of compliance and the risk of liability over the long term. Corporate strategies might include minimizing the amounts and kinds of pollutants produced, developing ways to recycle waste products, and investing in new technologies to render wastes nonhazardous. If hazardous wastes are produced that must be disposed of, the company should have procedures for evaluating and selecting well-managed and well-constructed disposal facilities.

AT THE TOP

A corporation can be held liable for the malfeasance of its employees. In addition, an employee participating in this conduct can be held personally criminally liable. Therefore, it is necessary for a corporation to conduct an education program designed to make its employees aware of their environmental responsibilities.

Record-Keeping and Accounting

Good record-keeping and cost-accounting systems are also essential. Many environmental laws require certain records to be developed and maintained for specified periods of time. These laws need to be consulted when a company develops a record-retention policy. Because the costs of environmental compliance may be significant and in some circumstances must be separately reported to the Securities and Exchange Commission, cost-accounting procedures need to be developed that allow the company to forecast and report the costs of environmental compliance.

Reporting Policies and Procedures

The company should have policies and procedures for reporting environmental law violations to corporate management and for managing the company's reporting obligations to government agencies. Top management needs to ensure that whistle-blowers are not subject to retaliation.

Agency Inspection Policies and Procedures

Government agencies may undertake inspections with little or no advance notice. The company should be prepared in advance for such an event by having a protocol for handling the inspection. Individuals trained in company protocol should accompany the inspector to ensure that the inspection is conducted properly and within the inspector's authority. The person who accompanies the inspector should prepare a report to management and make sure that any instances of noncompliance identified during the inspection are corrected.

Education and Training

The most essential component of good environmental management is comprehensive education and training. Every employee must know about and understand the company's environmental policy and recognize his or her responsibilities in carrying it out.

Public Relations

As popular sentiment increasingly favors environmental sensitivity and protection, companies must pay attention to the public relations consequences of their environment-affecting actions. Dissatisfaction with a company's environmental record can lead to adverse publicity, activist protests, consumer boycotts, and more stringent regulation.

In 1998, two U.S. companies in the Mitsubishi Group of Japan reached an agreement to end years of protests by the Rainforest Action Network, an aggressive environmental activist group. The group had opposed the company's environmental practices, especially its logging in rain forests. Mitsubishi Motor Sales America and Mitsubishi Electric America agreed to stop using products from old growth or otherwise rare forests beginning in April 1998. Praising the agreement, one Mitsubishi Electric executive declared, "Global companies increasingly are realizing that we have a responsibility to the ecosystems in which we do business."[26]

Of course, environmental activists are not above the law. In June 1997, an English court awarded McDonald's nearly $100,000 after the fast-food franchiser sued London Greenpeace for libel. Eleven years earlier, London Greenpeace had published a pamphlet criticizing McDonald's and accusing it of Third World starvation, rainforest destruction, and various other injustices. After the longest trial in English history, a judge found that the activists had not proved the truth of their accusations, as required by English libel law. Vindicated in the courts, McDonald's suffered in the press. One publication noted the differing conclusions about whether the verdict was "McLibel or McCensorship."[27]

Environmental Audit

An important first step in comprehensively managing environmental liability is to conduct an environmental audit. Such a candid, internal self-assessment documents and measures (1) compliance with occupational health and safety requirements; (2) compliance with federal, state, and local emissions limits and other requirements of a company's licensing, if any; (3) current practices for the generation, storage, and disposal of hazardous wastes; and (4) potential liability for past disposal of hazardous substances. According to a mid-1990s study by Price Waterhouse, 75% of firms have environmental auditing programs.

Although such programs can generate valuable information for management, they may also be self-incriminating and the basis for liability. A thorough audit that reveals contaminated properties, shoddy disposal practices, and lax compliance with regulations will certainly aid a company seeking to improve its environmental compliance. However, if the results of such an audit were available, plaintiffs in the discovery stage of litigation might find their case fully supported. For that reason, several states have enacted laws making such information privileged in order to motivate companies to produce and use it. At least one court has established a qualified privilege for certain self-critical analyses,[28] and the EPA has announced that it will take such audits favorably into account when pursuing civil liability. Still, managers must carefully weigh the costs and benefits of investigating and documenting environmental compliance.

 ## International Aspects

The National Environmental Policy Act, enacted in 1970, was the first element of the new environmental regulatory regime in the United States. Other countries, too, have initiated environmental regulatory schemes with environmental policy acts. Central to each of these acts is the requirement that the government expressly consider environmental values in its decision making and that it document this consideration in written environmental impact reports that can be reviewed by the public. These requirements are especially important when the government itself is responsible for major development projects.

A fundamental element of the U.S. scheme is the policy that the polluter pays. The European Union has also adopted this policy: "The cost of preventing and eliminating nuisances must, as a matter of principle, be borne by the polluter."[29] In 1987, the Single European Act added environmental provisions to the EC Treaty, and additional provisions were added in the 1992 Treaty on European Union. The European Union policy on the environment includes the following objectives:

26. Charles McCoy, *Mitsubishi Units Reach Accord with Activists*, WALL ST. J., Feb. 11, 1998, at A11.

27. Colleen Graffy, *Big Mac Bites Back*, ABA J., Aug. 1997, at 22.

28. Reichhold Chemicals, Inc. v. Textron, Inc., 157 F.R.D. 522 (N.D. Fla. 1994).

29. Objective 17, Restatement of the Objectives and Principles of a Community Environment Policy, 1977 O.J. (C 139).

IN BRIEF

DEVELOPING AN ENVIRONMENTAL COMPLIANCE PROGRAM

In evaluating or developing an environmental program, a manager should consider the following areas and ask the following questions:

1. Achieving and maintaining compliance
   - What laws and regulations affect the company's facilities?
   - What procedures effectively balance compliance costs with liability?
   - How can those procedures be communicated to those responsible for their implementation?
   - How can employees be persuaded they have a stake in the program's success?
2. Obtaining timely notice of new requirements
   - What is being done to keep abreast of new requirements?
   - Will management receive notice early enough to make necessary changes cost effectively?
3. Influencing future requirements
   - What environmental laws and regulations are on the horizon?
   - How are they being tracked?
   - What is being done to influence their wording and enactment?
4. Monitoring compliance accurately
   - What kind of monitoring is required?
   - Who will perform that monitoring?
   - How will the results be assessed?

5. Timely and accurate reporting
   - When must a manager report information to regulators?
   - What procedures ensure that reportable incidents are brought to management's attention?
   - Does the company have databases for tracking chemical use and other technical information?
6. Responding to emergencies
   - What systems are in place to respond to emergencies?
   - Are responsible employees trained to respond appropriately?
7. Maintaining community relations
   - How strong is the company's relationship with the surrounding community?
   - What kind of programs maintain and grow that relationship?
   - How would management expect the community to respond to emergencies?

SOURCE Based on Steven J. Koorse, *When Less is More—Trouble*, BUS. L. TODAY, Sept./Oct. 1997, at 24.

---

preserving, protecting, and improving the quality of the environment; protecting human health; prudent and rational utilization of natural resources; and promoting measures at the international level to deal with regional or worldwide environmental problems.

This concept is also being introduced in Asia. Taiwan, for example, has begun the process of enacting an environmental law modeled, in part, on the U.S. Superfund statute (CERCLA), with modifications to address the local culture, issues, and concerns.

When the laws of other nations are closely patterned on U.S. laws, compliance may be easier for U.S. companies operating in those countries. However, U.S. companies must be careful to note the differences between the U.S. laws and the laws of their host countries.

Public understanding of the importance of protecting the environment in order to preserve the planet is

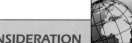

INTERNATIONAL CONSIDERATION

Environmental concerns are becoming increasingly intertwined with trade regulations. Many environmental activists have argued that the ability of U.S. pesticide manufacturers to ship their products to Third World nations subverts U.S. environmental regulations, because the products often return to the United States.

increasing. There is a growing international recognition of environmental problems such as global warming, ozone depletion, acid rain, and habitat destruction. (The Kyoto international summit on global warming is described in the "Inside Story.") As nations act individually and together to address these environmental problems, they will develop environmental regulatory schemes that will affect where development can occur and where factories can be constructed; what products can be produced; how these products must be produced, distributed, used, and discarded; and how wastes must be managed and discarded.

Sustainable Development

An environmental issue of increasing importance is the concept of sustainable development. *Sustainable development* "holds that future prosperity depends on preserving 'natural capital'—air, water, and other ecological treasures—and that doing so will require balancing human activity with nature's ability to renew itself. It also recognizes that growth is necessary to eliminate

poverty, which leads to the plunder of resources."[30] Such a concept is politically controversial because it entails significant changes in national regulatory and economic policies. Increased cooperation among industrialized and developing nations, the possibility of industrialized nations scaling back their transformation of the world's resources into wealth, and the use of new technology to preserve the earth's environment and prevent pollution would also be important.

Sustainable development is also controversial among business leaders because two concerns central to the concept—slowing world population growth and fighting poverty in developing nations—are issues that most managers do not see as their concern or problem. Nonetheless, a number of U.S. companies, such as 3M, have set goals to reduce air, water, and solid-waste emissions. In the case of 3M, its environmental policies will enable 3M to make and distribute products more efficiently, cutting its costs per unit on most products by 10%.[31]

---

30. Emily T. Smith, *Growth vs. Environment*, Bus. Wk., May 11, 1992, at 66.
31. *Id.* at 74.

 THE RESPONSIBLE MANAGER

Managing Risks of Environmental Liability

Several sources of potential environmental liability present risks to the parties in business transactions. In evaluating a company for purposes of acquisition, investment, or financing, a manager must consider that the company's earnings may be affected by the costs of compliance with environmental laws. The value of its equipment assets may be affected by regulatory limitations that make the equipment obsolete. Its ability to expand in existing locations may be impaired as a result of limitations on new sources of air emissions or the availability of nearby waste treatment or disposal facilities. A company's cash flow may be affected by needed capital investments or by increased operating costs necessitated by environmental regulations. Failure to comply with existing regulations may lead to the imposition of substantial penalties, also affecting cash flow. Small companies or companies that are highly leveraged may not be able to meet these additional demands for cash.

Similarly, a small company may not be able to survive the imposition of liability for response costs under CERCLA or similar state laws. A large company with a long history of operations in a number of locations may also have potential liabilities under CERCLA that are not reflected on its balance sheets. Finally, a company's operations or the condition of its properties may present risks of injury to other persons and their property, giving rise to possible tort claims.

The most important element in managing the risk of these potential liabilities is *due diligence*, that is, a systematic process for determining whether property contains or emits hazardous substances and whether the company is in compliance with environmental laws. The object of environmental due-diligence investigations is to identify and characterize the risks associated with the properties and operations involved in the business transaction. In recent years, such investigations have become highly sophisticated undertakings, often requiring the use of technical consultants and legal counsel with special expertise. Although much of the effort is focused on the review of company documents and available public records, it may also involve physical inspections of the properties, including soil and groundwater sampling and analysis. Care should be taken to avoid negligent soil investigations, which can create liability for disposal of hazardous waste. Environmental due-diligence efforts may represent a significant cost of the transaction and may take a much longer time to complete than traditional due-diligence efforts.

The scope of the due-diligence effort will depend on the nature of the assets and the structure of the transaction. For example, if the transaction is a simple purchase and sale of real estate, then the due diligence can be limited to the property to be acquired and its surroundings. If the transaction involves the acquisition of a business with a long history of operations in many locations, however, then the due-diligence investigation must cover not only the current operating locations, but also prior operating locations and the sites used for off-site disposal of wastes. This is particularly true in the case of an acquisition by merger, because the surviving company takes over all of the liabilities of the disappearing company.

The parties to the transaction can allocate the identified risks of environmental liability by undertakings of specified obligations, assumptions and retentions of contingent liabilities, adjustments to the purchase price, representations and warranties, indemnifications, and the like. It is important to remember that contractual arrangements to shift environmental liability are not binding on the federal or state government. Thus, even if the seller of property agrees to indemnify the purchaser for any environmental claims arising out of the seller's activities, the EPA can still recover response costs from the present owner. The present owner could sue the seller for indemnification and contribution, but will bear the entire cleanup cost if the previous owner is insolvent or has insufficient assets.

Care must be exercised when risks are identified that are not yet quantifiable. For example, if liability for response costs is accepted in return for a reduction in the purchase price, it should be borne in mind that response costs often exceed by a wide margin the initial estimate provided by a consultant or a government agency.

Regardless of comprehensive due diligence, crises will arise from time to time. To prepare for them, a manager should have a crisis-management plan. Such a plan should include the designation of someone other than the CEO to coordinate the response. That response, in turn, should include immediate stabilization of the crisis, objective inquiry into it, and some immediate action to assure the company's constituencies that things are being put under control. For that reason, constituencies must receive information as the response continues. To the extent crises are at least foreseeable, more detailed plans should be developed ahead of time.[32]

Under CERCLA, secured lenders, and in some cases equity investors, may be deemed liable for response costs as present operators if they participate in the day-to-day management of the borrower. If a lender takes title at foreclosure, it may also be deemed liable for response costs as a present owner unless it attempts to dispose of the property reasonably quickly. Thus, the risk of hazardous-substance releases on the subject property should be carefully evaluated in connection with the loan application. The operations of the borrower should also be carefully reviewed in order to evaluate the risks they present during the life of the loan. If a release of hazardous substances occurs on the property, its value as collateral is impaired. Upon default, the lender may not be able to recover the outstanding amount of the debt.

In addition, some states have adopted *superlien* provisions, which secure recovery of response costs incurred by state agencies. Where a superlien exists, it may take priority over existing security interests.

In trying to protect against diminishment of the value of collateral, a lender must be careful not to participate in management, however. Overly strict loan covenants that involve the lender in making decisions (such as approval of major capital expenditures) may create operator liability for the lender.

When an owner leases property, it must take care to evaluate the environmental risks of the tenant operations. Use of the property should be carefully limited to prevent any unauthorized activities. If the tenant's activities present significant risks, financial assurances in the form of parent corporation guarantees, letters of credit, or performance bonds might be obtained to make sure that any damage caused by the tenant will be remedied. Tenants also should be cautious in taking possession of property formerly occupied by others. Many tenants perform *baseline assessments* to establish the environmental condition of the property at the commencement of the lease and at the termination of the lease. These assessments may provide some protection from liability for conditions caused by prior or succeeding tenants.

The costs of environmental law compliance and the potential environmental liabilities must be carefully evaluated for purposes of Securities and Exchange Commission (SEC) disclosure and reporting requirements. The SEC requires special disclosure of environmental enforcement proceedings and litigation and requires the disclosure of estimated costs of environmental compliance, including capital expenditures and

any effects of compliance on earnings and competitive position that may be material. The EPA provides information to the SEC in order to assist the SEC in enforcing these reporting requirements.

32. Stanley Sporkin, *A Plan for Crisis Management and Avoidance* (Address at Nonprofit Risk Management Institutes (Nov. 12, 1997).

INSIDE STORY

DEBATE OVER GLOBAL-WARMING TREATY HEATS UP

I am I plus my surroundings and if I do not preserve the latter, I do not preserve myself.
—José Ortega y Gasset, Spanish essayist and philosopher

Green politics at its worst amounts to a sort of Zen fascism; less extreme, it denounces growth and seeks to stop the world so that we can all get off.
—Chris Patten, British Conservative politician and secretary of state for the environment

Numerous studies of the atmosphere and the Earth's environment have turned up two indisputable facts: the levels of greenhouse gases in the atmosphere (there are six of them, the most prevalent being carbon dioxide (CO_2)) are rising and the temperature of the Earth's surface is increasing. Some scientists believe there is a link between these two facts; namely, that the greenhouse gases trap more of the sun's heat than normal inside the atmosphere, elevating temperatures on the Earth's surface to unnatural levels. A number of scientists and environmentalists claim that if something is not done soon about this problem, temperatures all over the world will rise 1 to 3.5 degrees Centigrade and the oceans will rise

anywhere from 15 to 95 centimeters.[33] For other scientists, the evidence linking greenhouse gases and the global rise in temperatures is unclear. Some businesses resist government mandates to clean up their acts (and the air) in response to what businesses feel are alarmist warnings of an impending environmental Armageddon.

In 1990, the United States tackled one piece of this issue by instituting the issuance and trading of sulfur dioxide pollution permits in an effort to curb the acid rain problem. In the face of the growing evidence of global warming, in December 1997, representatives from 129 nations met in Kyoto, Japan, to consider signing the United Nations Global Climate Change Treaty, which set

restrictions on industrialized nations' production of greenhouse gases. The aim of the treaty is to set a worldwide limit on the amount of hydroflurocarbons, perflurocarbons, sulfur hexafluoride, and carbon dioxide released into the atmosphere from industrial processes. The restrictions are imposed only on the industrialized nations; the developing nations are not required to reduce emissions. The treaty also seeks to protect large forested areas, particularly the rain forests of Central and South America, because of the ability of the trees to absorb some of the carbon dioxide gas.

Carbon dioxide is introduced into the atmosphere through the burning of fossil fuels, such as petroleum products and coal, and natural gas. Annual CO_2 emissions in 1995 were 5.475 billion tons (20.52 tons per capita) for the United States, 3.196 billion tons (2.68 tons per capita) for China, 1.82 billion tons (12.26 tons per capita) for Russia, 833 million tons (10.24 tons per capita) for Germany, and 433 million tons (14.83 tons per capita) for Canada.[34]

U.S. critics of the treaty maintained that adherence to the treaty's restrictions would damage the U.S. economy by increasing costs, lowering output, and lessening investment. Some estimate the negative effect on the gross national product (GNP) to be as much as $200 billion a year in lost jobs, higher fuel prices, lower exports, and lower productivity. For example, the American Corn Growers Association (ACGA) quantified the yearly effect of compliance with the pact and predicted dire consequences: an 8.5% increase in the cost of production, 130% increase in natural gas costs, 500% increase in coal costs, 33% increase in gasoline costs, and a $17.4 billion increase in the cost of food to consumers.[35]

The success of pollution permit trading led President Clinton to attempt to extend the model to the global arena. Instead of companies being allocated pollution permits, under the Clinton proposed plan, each industrial nation would be budgeted a portion of the total allowable emissions cap, which the United States proposed to set to 1990 levels of emissions. The United States wanted to include the developing nations in the cuts; but developing nations resisted,

stating that it unfairly imposed restrictions that would hinder their ability to develop industrially and compete globally. There were concerns that a global pollution permit trading solution may lead to "eco-colonialism," whereby rich nations invest in cleaning up environmental problems in poorer nations, at the expense of the poorer nations' economic growth. However, in the absence of controls in developing nations, the opposite could also occur, whereby pollution-heavy industries move to lesser developed countries with fewer restrictions on spewing gases, to the detriment of the local and global environments.

The Kyoto treaty was opened for signature by the United Nations on March 16, 1998. The European Union countries were expected to be among the first to sign. The treaty would reduce the average industrialized nation's emissions of greenhouse gases by 5% from the base year 1990. Enforcement of limits of developed nations was scheduled to begin in 2008.

The trading of emissions rights sought by the United States may phase out after eight years.[36] Trading and compliance details were to be included in negotiations set for November 1998 in Buenos Aires. The president of the United States was expected to wait until the treaty details were hammered out before submitting the treaty to the U.S. Senate for ratification.

Notwithstanding the uncertainty about the effects of greenhouse gases, not all businesses are denying that the problem exists or fighting to preserve the status quo. A group of more than 50 CEOs

ran a full-page advertisement in the *Wall Street Journal* (shown following) that said, in part: "We are confident that if the government develops a reasonable climate policy, industry can step up to the challenge without threatening American jobs or living standards. It will take hard work, leadership, and ingenuity, three of our nation's most abundant—and renewable—natural resources."

British Petroleum Group (BP) chief executive John Browne expressed his company's philosophy in this way: "We must now focus on what can and what should be done, not because we can be certain climate change is happening, but because the possibility can't be ignored. If we are all to take responsibility for the future of our planet, then it falls to us to begin to take precautionary action now."[37] Toward that end, BP instituted measurable objectives in 1997 to ensure that it was doing what it could to create a sustainable planet; these objectives included participating in the policy debate searching for global solutions to the problem, developing alternative fuels for the long term, funding continuing scientific research, and controlling the company's own CO_2 emissions.

Other businesses are also coming forward to take responsibility for sustaining the planet. Niagara Mohawk Power, a New York state power-generation company, lowered its carbon dioxide emissions by 2.5 million tons. Then, under the U.S. emission trading program, it swapped those CO_2 emission rights for sulfur dioxide allowances, which it gave to local

A BUSINESS CLIMATE CHALLENGE

America Needs to Get Serious About Global Warming

As business executives, we recognize that the vast majority of scientists believe that the "balance of evidence suggests a discernible human influence on global climate."* Left uncontrolled, a changing climate could threaten the future prosperity of our nation and the world.

To reduce this threat, we call upon the United States government to exert strong leadership by promoting climate change policies that provide incentives to act quickly. The government must set clear and reasonable goals, allow maximum flexibility and promote cooperation among nations.

Business leaders, who constantly manage risks in the face of uncertainty, are particularly well-suited to help the nation address the challenge of climate change. Many of us are already taking action to reduce our own greenhouse gas emissions. We are confident that if the government develops a reasonable climate policy, industry can step up to the challenge without threatening American jobs or living standards. It will take hard work, leadership and ingenuity, three of our nation's most abundant – and renewable – natural resources.

 Richard Recchia
Executive VP and CEO
Mitsubishi Motor Sales
of America, Inc.

 Aaron Feuerstein
President and CEO
Malden Mills Industries, Inc.

 David Olsen
Chief Executive Officer
Patagonia, Inc.

 Howard Schultz
chairman and ceo
Starbucks Coffee Company

 Larry Papay
Senior Vice President
Bechtel Group, Inc.

 Harry V. Quadracci
President and Founder
Quad/Graphics, Inc.

 George P. Mitchell
Chairman and CEO
Mitchell Energy
    Development Corp.

 Ray Anderson
Chairman and CEO
Interface, Inc.

 Philip H. Knight
Founder and CEO
Nike, Inc.

 Gary Hirshberg
President and CEO
Stonyfield Farm Yogurt

 Mark Farber
President
Evergreen Solar, Inc.

 Mason Willrich
Principal
Nth Power Technologies, Inc.

Ted Turner

World Climate Change Threatens Our Prosperity

For more information: 1-888-363-9197

A message from Business Challenge, 1636 Connecticut Ave. NW, Suite 300, Washington, DC 20009. Phone 1-888-363-9197.
* "Climate Change 1995: The Science of Climate Change." Intergovernmental Panel on Climate Change (IPCC). The IPCC is a scientific panel of 2,500 climate experts from around the world.

SOURCE Original ad from the *Wall Street Journal* and *USA Today*, October 1997. Provided by Ozone Action, Washington, D.C. *Used by permission.*

environmental groups, who retired them. Additionally, the company used $125,000 of its tax rebate from the emissions donation to install solar power at a Mexican fishing village. Niagara Mohawk Power's chief environmental scientist, Martin A. Smith, asks the question, "Do we just stand by and let these gases accumulate?"[38]

Lee R. Raymond, chairman of Exxon, would say yes. Raymond, who in 1997 was head of the American Petroleum Institute, a U.S. oil industry lobbying group, has been urging developing nations to resist emissions limitations until the cause and effect of climate change are better understood. His stance is that Nature is the cause of the Earth's current temperature change, and that such changes occur often. Raymond reportedly stated, "The ice ages are a good example."[39] He argues that imposing environmental controls will restrict foreign investment, which would derail growth in these developing countries.

Executives from other U.S. industries also expressed their criticism of the global-warming treaty. Aluminum manufacturers felt it would reduce their ability to compete with manufacturers in countries with fewer restrictions. The Big Three automakers were critical of the pact, because it will likely result in higher gasoline prices, which will fuel demand for smaller, more fuel-efficient (and less profitable) automobiles. The American Iron and Steel Institute expressed concern about the U.S. steel industry's ability to be competitive against firms producing steel in developing nations such as China, Vietnam, and Korea, which will not face restrictions as a result of the treaty. A spokesperson for the U.S. Steel Group of USX Corp. stated, "We would oppose any agreement that doesn't include developing nations, as that would put us in a competitive disadvantage."[40]

But some economists believe that the limits imposed can create competitive advantage. Harvard Business School Professor Michael E. Porter maintains that firms can remain competitive and in fact gain competitive advantage through innovation offsets. Porter and colleague Claas van der Linde use the term *innovation offsets* to describe technological advantages gained by companies that met the challenge of environmental regulations and discovered lower costs and better quality products as a result. He points to several examples of U.S. industries that have made such gains and believes that the new tighter rules could spur additional innovation. Critics of this approach point out that innovation offsets amount to only $2 of every $100 spent on environmental compliance.[41] To decrease the costs to industry of reducing greenhouse gases, some businesses have recommended drastically increasing the price of gasoline—that would reduce consumption rather than forcing industries to find a way to innovate to find cleaner ways to burn the gas consumed.

Even after the signing of the global-warming treaty in 1997, questions continue to arise about what is really at stake and how much it will cost the global economy to deal with it. Two months after the treaty was signed, scientists commented that the limitations imposed by the treaty would make very little real difference. Top climate experts predict that near the end of the twenty-first century, greenhouse gases will be twice preindustrial levels, global temperatures will be higher, and serious disruption to agricultural and other ecosystems could develop. An assessment of the potential impact of the treaty indicated that at best the restrictions will reduce the rate at which levels increase, but not actually decrease the levels.

Some critics fault the failure of agreement from the developing nations for the lack of meaningful standards. Others see the Kyoto treaty as the first in a series of agreements that will tackle the problem in bigger and more ambitious actions.

33. John Browne, *Breaking Ranks,* STANFORD BUS., Sept. 1997, at 18.

34. From Oak Ridge National Laboratory data, as reported by John J. Fialka, *Breathing Easy: Clear Skies are Goal as Pollution Is Turned into a Commodity,* WALL ST. J., Oct. 3, 1997, at A1.

35. Shaun Schafer, *Lobbyists Claim UN Emissions Treaty Would Devastate US Farmers,* TULSA (OKLA.) WORLD, Nov. 8, 1997.

36. John J. Fialka, *Emissions Trading in Warming Pact May Be Phased Out,* WALL ST. J., Mar. 17, 1998, at A12.

37. Browne, *supra* note 33, at 18.

38. John J. Fialka, *Breathing Easy: Clear Skies Are Goal as Pollution is Turned into a Commodity,* WALL ST. J., Oct. 3, 1997, at A1.

39. Ian Johnson, *Exxon Urges Developing Nations to Shun Environmental Curbs Hindering Growth,* WALL ST. J., Oct. 14, 1997, at A17.

40. Wall Street Journal News Roundup, *Big US Industries Launch an Attack on Warming Treaty,* WALL ST. J., Dec. 12, 1997, at A3.

41. *Is Cleanup of Greenhouse Gases Really Worth the Big Price Tag?* INVESTOR'S BUS. DAILY, Nov. 11, 1997, at A8.

KEY WORDS AND PHRASES

antideficiency statutes **596**
baseline assessments **602**
best available control technology
   (BACT) **579**
best available technology economically
   achievable (BAT) **581**
best conventional pollutant control
   technology (BCT) **581**
best practicable control technology
   currently available (BPT) **581**
due diligence **601**
effluent limitations **580**
environmental justice **597**
environmental law **576**

Environmental Protection Agency
   (EPA) **578**
hazard ranking score **587**
Hazardous Substance Superfund **587**
initiative **597**
innocent landowner defense **595**
innovation offsets **606**
lowest achievable emission rate
   (LAER) **579**
national ambient air quality
   standards **579**
National Pollutant Discharge
   Elimination System (NPDES) **580**
natural resources laws **578**

navigable waters **586**
new source performance standards
   (NSPS) **581**
person **582**
publicly owned sewage treatment
   works (POTWs) **580**
responsible persons **588**
state implementation plans
   (SIPs) **579**
successor liability **602**
superlien **602**
sustainable development **601**
third-party defense **595**

QUESTIONS AND CASE PROBLEMS

1. Northeastern Pharmaceutical and Chemical Company (NEPACCO) had a manufacturing plant in Verona, Missouri, that produced various hazardous and toxic by-products. The company pumped the by-products into a holding tank, which a waste hauler periodically emptied. Michaels founded the company, was a major shareholder, and served as its president. In 1971, a waste hauler named Mills approached Ray, a chemical-plant manager employed by NEPACCO, and proposed disposing of some of the firm's wastes at a nearby farm. Ray visited the farm and, with the approval of Lee, the vice-president and a shareholder of NEPACCO, arranged for disposal of wastes at the farm.

Approximately eighty-five 55-gallon drums were dumped into a large trench on the farm. In 1976, NEPACCO was liquidated, and the assets remaining after payment to creditors were distributed to its shareholders. Three years later the EPA investigated the area and discovered dozens of badly deteriorated drums containing hazardous waste buried at the farm. The EPA took remedial action and then sought to recover its costs under RCRA and other statutes. From whom and on what basis can the government recover its costs? [*United States v. Northeastern Pharm. and Chem. Co.*, 810 F.2d 726 (8th Cir. 1986), *cert. denied*, 484 U.S. 848 (1987)]

2. George Lu has been named the executive director of the Cornell University Foundation, a nonprofit association organized to support the university. As part of its efforts, the foundation has begun a program to preserve open-space land and ecologically sensitive environments near the university's campus in upstate New York. The foundation plans to buy or receive gifts of land, especially from alumni, and then sell the land to public entities for permanent preservation. The difference between the purchase price and the sale price will be used to finance the association's efforts and to support Cornell generally. One of Lu's first tasks is to develop a protocol and prepare model agreements for making acquisitions.

a. As a nonprofit, educational organization, does the association have potential liability under the environmental laws?

b. What procedures should Lu establish to protect the association from potential environmental law liabilities in connection with its acquisitions?

c. What kinds of contractual arrangements should be considered to protect the association from environmental law liabilities? [*United States v. Alcan Aluminum Corp.*, 34 E.R.C. 1744 (N.D.N.Y. 1991)]

3. ABC Investment Company is considering the leveraged buyout of a small, privately held manufacturing company that has been in operation since the 1930s. ABC is analyzing the cash flow expected from the company's operations over the next five years in order to evaluate the economics of the buyout. To do this, the managers of ABC estimate the future capital and operating expenses of the company. What information should they have to properly estimate future capital and operating costs related to environmental law compliance?

4. Martin Sanchez is a loan officer for a financial institution and is considering whether to finance the leveraged buyout described in Question 3. The loan would be secured by the real property on which the plant is located, the equipment assets, and all personal property located on the plant premises.

a. What financial risks do the environmental laws present to the lender?

b. What steps can the financial institution take to protect the lender against these risks?

c. If the debtor begins defaulting on its payment obligations, should the lender provide management consultation and advice to the borrower?

d. If the debtor defaults, what steps should the lender take before commencing foreclosure proceedings? [*Kelley v. Tiscornia*, 104 F.3d 361 (6th Cir. 1996) (table)]

5. Johanna Landing has been hired by Newco Corporation to identify possible sites for construction of a major new manufacturing facility. Newco's operations will involve the production of substantial quantities of hazardous waste and constitute a major new source of air emissions.

a. How will these facts affect Landing's consideration of possible construction sites?

b. How will these facts and the location affect Newco's analysis of its costs of construction and operation?

6. Gregg Entrepreneur is organizing a small company to manufacture a new biotechnology product. Entrepreneur will be a principal shareholder and president of the company. What measures should Entrepreneur take to ensure that his company operates in compliance with environmental laws?

Despite all the measures Entrepreneur has taken to ensure environmental law compliance, his vice-president of operations reports that the production manager has been disposing of wastes into the sewer in violation of national pretreatment standards and that she has been submitting false reports to the publicly owned sewage treatment works (POTW) to cover up the violations. All of the reports have been signed by the vice-president of operations, who had no knowledge that they contained false statements. What steps should Entrepreneur take? Should he report the violations to the POTW even if it could result in personal civil or criminal liability? What about the vice-president? The production manager? What is Entrepreneur's ethical responsibility? [*United States v. Alley*, 775 F. Supp. 771 (N.D. Ill. 1990)]

7. American Widgets is a manufacturing company that has gained a large share of the international widget market, largely because of high quality and competitive pricing. However, the disposal of the company's wastes has become increasingly expensive. A new ban on land disposal will require that one of the company's largest waste streams be incinerated. Plants of competitors located in Southeast Asia and in South America are subject to increasing environmental regulation modeled after the laws in the United States, but they are not subject to a land-disposal ban and will have a significant competitive advantage over plants located in the United States. Jimmy Tsai, an American Widgets manager, is considering the possibility of locating a new plant in Southeast Asia. What factors should he take into account? What alternatives are there besides relocation?

8. An enterprising young Texas A&M M.B.A. graduate, Nancy Schmidt, purchased land near Houston from Winetka Development, Inc. for $12 million. Schmidt was speculating that the demands, and consequently the inflated prices, of Houston suburbia would soon reach her property. Within two years, Schmidt formed a joint venture with a developer and broke ground on her subdivision plan, expending $1.4 million on streets, plumbing, and irrigation for the planned championship golf course designed by Arnold Palmer. Much to her chagrin, an Environmental Protection Agency (EPA) investigation identified this parcel of land as a former municipal waste landfill and a source of groundwater pollution. The EPA notified Schmidt and her partner that, as the present owners and operators of the property, pursuant to Section 107 of CERCLA they were "potentially responsible parties," jointly and severally liable for all of the costs of cleanup, with cleanup costs estimated to be upwards of $29 million.

Who will be liable for the cleanup costs? Is the developer liable? Is it relevant that Schmidt knew or did not know about the landfill prior to the purchase? Does it matter that this was a municipal waste landfill? If a vice-president of Winetka Development lied to Schmidt about the prior uses of the land, is Winetka liable for the cleanup costs? For the purchase price and development costs? If a lower-level manager of Winetka is the person who lied to Schmidt, does the analysis change? Does the analysis change if Winetka and all of its employees had not known about the waste? Can Schmidt just give the property back to Winetka in order to free herself from any legal entanglements? [*Tanglewood East Homeowners v. Charles–Thomas, Inc.*, 849 F.2d 1568 (5th Cir. 1988)]

9. Lansford–Coaldale Joint Water Authority (the Authority) provides public water in Carbon County, Pennsylvania. The Authority's groundwater production and supply wells are adjacent to a site formerly used for lead smelting that is now owned by Tonolli Pennsylvania (Tonolli PA). Because there had been release of hazardous substances on the ex-smelting site, the Authority is concerned that there might be contamination in its wells. After conducting an environmental study, the Authority sued three parties for private cost recovery under CERCLA: (1) Tonolli PA; (2) Tonolli Canada, a Canadian corporation and Tonolli PA's sister corporation; and (3) the parent corporation IFIM, a Dutch corporation. The Authority alleged that, among other things, the defendants were owners or operators of a company that posed a threat of future contamination to their water supply.

Tonolli PA subsequently became insolvent, but the proceedings remained against Tonolli Canada and IFIM. On what basis, if any, can the surviving entities be held liable? [*Lansford–Coaldale Joint Water Authority v. Tonolli Corp.*, 4 F.3d 1209 (3d Cir. 1993)]

MANAGER'S DILEMMA

10. You are the CEO of a Brazilian real estate company that owns several hundred thousand acres of rain forest. A representative of a large American hamburger chain approaches you with an offer to buy a portion of the land at a very attractive price. The revenue from the sale of the land would permit your company to undertake a large development project in Rio de Janeiro, which would both provide new jobs and increase the amount of low-cost housing in the city. However, you are aware that the hamburger chain intends to convert the rainforest acreage into grazing lands for cattle. What should you do? Discuss the trade-offs between environmental preservation and economic development. Describe sustainable development. How do environmental laws affect national policy with regard to industrial growth and economic development in the United States? Competition in international markets? How do state environmental laws affect competition between states for industrial development?

INTERNET SOURCES	
American Petroleum Institute	http://www.api.org
British Petroleum	http://www.bp.com
Environmental Protection Agency	http://www.epa.gov
Greenpeace	http://www.greenpeace.org
National Environmental Defense Council	http://www.nedc.org
The Chemical Scorecard Web site, developed by the Environmental Defense Fund, combines more that 150 government and university databases to allow users to locate polluters in their community, research the dangers of common household products, and compile sophisticated pollution rankings.	http://www.scorecard.org
Sierra Club	http://www.sierraclub.org

CHAPTER 17

Real Property and Land Use

INTRODUCTION

Importance

It is difficult to imagine any business enterprise that does not involve real property in some manner. From the global company with factories or retail outlets on several continents to a mail-order business operated out of an apartment, real estate is important to the successful functioning of most businesses.

Real estate is one of the largest industries in the United States and has a powerful impact on the general economy. Real estate also has the power to evoke strong national sentiment. Many Americans who would not think twice about the large purchase of treasury bills by Japanese banks reacted with emotion when Japanese investors bought a 51% share of the Rockefeller Center in New York City, home of Radio City Music Hall and the Rockettes.

Real estate law finds its roots in both English common law and Spanish civil law. Many of the laws are determined by municipalities, others by the state. In recent years, the federal government has played an increasingly active role, through tax policy and environmental regulations that affect the density of real estate development. The federal government is also interested in the safety of real estate (through the Occupational Safety and Health Administration), physical accessibility to commercial facilities (under the Americans with Disabilities Act), foreign investment in U.S. real estate, and the preservation of parklands.

Chapter Overview

This chapter discusses the forms of real estate ownership and the transfer of ownership, including the different types of deeds and the effect of recording statutes. It explains the role of brokers and the effect of express and implied warranties concerning the condition of the property. The chapter outlines the alternatives to acquiring real property for cash, including tax-deferred exchanges, sale and leasebacks, and real estate investment trusts. Certain types of preliminary agreements, including option contracts, rights of first refusal, and letters of intent, are then described. Methods of financing are also addressed, as are leasing and lease terms. Finally, the chapter outlines governmental regulation of the use of real property by the exercise of police and condemnation powers and the circumstances in which government restrictions on land use are deemed "takings," requiring compensation of the owner under the U.S. Constitution.

Forms of Ownership

Real property can be held in a variety of ways. It can be owned by a single individual; it can be owned by two or more individuals or entities as tenants in common; and it can be owned by two or more individuals as joint tenants or by a husband and wife as tenants by the entirety or as community property. Real property can also be held in a trust or owned by a general partnership, limited partnership, or corporation.

Individual Ownership

The simplest type of ownership is a property owned by a single individual. From a business perspective, individual ownership is often undesirable because the individual owner may be liable in tort for any accidents occurring on the property. The risk of unlimited personal liability, however, can be covered by insurance.

Tenancy in Common

Tenants in common each own an undivided fractional interest in a parcel of real property. For example, one tenant in common may have a two-thirds interest and another a one-third interest. Two or more persons can hold property as tenants in common. Regardless of the percentage ownership interest, however, each tenant in common has an equal right to possession of the property, and no co-tenant has the right of exclusive possession of the property against any other co-tenant. However, a co-tenant has the right to exclusive possession of the entire property against any third party. Co-tenants share the income and burdens of ownership. An action for contribution from the other co-tenants is available to a co-tenant who has paid more than his or her share. The interest of a tenant in common is assignable and inheritable without the consent of any other co-tenant.

Joint Tenancy

A *joint tenancy* is the ownership of property in equal shares by two or more persons. The key characteristic of a joint tenancy is the right of survivorship. If a joint tenant dies, his or her interest passes automatically to the remaining joint tenant or tenants. However, an attempt by a single joint tenant to convey separately his or her interest in the property will destroy the joint tenancy and convert it to a tenancy in common. Moreover, use of joint tenancy property in a business may also terminate the joint tenancy.[1]

Tenancy by the Entirety

Historically, English common law recognized a special type of co-ownership of real property between husband and wife called *tenancy by the entirety*. Like joint tenancy, tenancy by the entirety includes a right of survivorship. However, unlike in a joint tenancy, the right of survivorship was historically held to be indestructible by the separate acts of the parties. Consequently, neither spouse could convey an individual interest to a third party and thereby terminate the right of survivorship. Additionally, unlike joint tenancy, where joint tenants have equal rights to possession of the property, tenancy by the entirety entitled only the husband to possession, use, and enjoyment of the property. In effect, he acted as a guardian over the wife's interest.

Although many people find the concept incompatible with the status of married women in modern society, approximately 22 states recognize some form of tenancy by the entirety. Most states have retained the indestructible right of survivorship, but they give the husband and wife equal rights to the possession, use, and revenues of the property. Additionally, the modern view is that divorce converts a tenancy by the entirety to a tenancy in common.[2]

However, tenancy by the entirety represents an historical anomaly that may not serve a justifiable purpose today. The indestructible right of survivorship can act to the disadvantage of one or both of the spouses. Because neither spouse can compel a severance of the property, a deadlock between the spouses may result while both spouses are alive.

Community Property

In Arizona, California, Idaho, Louisiana, Nevada, New Mexico, Texas, and Washington, property acquired by

---

1. Williams v. Dovell, 96 A.2d 484 (Md. 1953).

2. Markland v. Markland, 21 So. 2d 145 (Fla. 1945).

either spouse during marriage is considered to be *community property;* that is, each spouse owns an undivided one-half interest in the property. Property acquired prior to the marriage or by gift or inheritance during the marriage is separate property, unless the spouse owning it has converted it to community property. Separate property is converted into community property when (1) one spouse gifts separate property to the other spouse, (2) the parties treat the separate property in such a manner that a presumption of a gift arises, or (3) the separate and common property have been commingled, or mixed together. *Separate property* belongs solely to the spouse who acquired it before marriage or received it by gift or inheritance.

Conveyance   Community property cannot be conveyed unless both spouses execute the instrument by which the conveyance is effected. It should be noted, however, that when the instrument is not signed by one of the spouses, but both spouses were present during negotiations and were fully aware of the terms and conditions, the nonsigning spouse may not claim that the transaction is void due to the absence of a signature.[3]

The community-property interest of a spouse may be separately willed upon death. In the absence of a will, community property passes to the other spouse.

Divorce   Most of the cases interpreting what is or is not community property arise in the divorce context. Community-property laws vary from state to state. Complicated issues can arise, for example, when one spouse inherits land from his or her family (which is separate property at the date of inheritance), but subsequently one or both spouses improve or develop the property. In this case, some or all of the inherited property may turn into community property. Similarly, if one spouse uses separate property as seed capital for a business that is operated by the spouse during the marriage, then part of the value of the business will be separate property and part will be community property.

Among the factors to be considered in determining whether all or part of the property has been transformed from separate to community property are (1) whether the value of the separate property has increased due to factors other than the inherent investment qual-

ity of the property; or (2) whether the party responsible for increasing the value of the property has been compensated, by salary or some other special allocation. Any increase in value resulting from factors other than the inherent investment quality of the property or compensation received by one spouse from development activities undertaken on the property during marriage is community property.

Joint tenancy between spouses and community property are theoretically different; but in the divorce context, courts frequently ignore the differences. In the context of income or estate tax on substantial investments, community property is generally a more desirable form of ownership than joint tenancy.

Trust

Property may be also held in a *trust,* whereby the property is owned and controlled by one person, the *trustee,* for the benefit of another, the *beneficiary.* The duration of the trust, the powers of the trustee and the trustor (the person creating the trust), and the express rights of the beneficiary are set forth in a trust agreement.

General Partnership

When property is held in a general partnership, the partners have rights similar to those of co-tenants, and each partner is liable for all the debts of the partnership. A general partner has no right to possess partnership property for other than partnership purposes. In addition, a general partner may not assign his or her individual interest in specific partnership property. On the other hand, a general partner can effectively convey the entire partnership property to a bona fide purchaser who has no knowledge of any restriction that might exist on the general partner's authority to convey partnership property.

Limited Partnership

Real property may be held in a limited partnership, consisting of one or more general partners, who manage the property, and one or more limited partners. The liability of a limited partner is usually restricted to the amount of capital he or she has contributed to the partnership. The authority of the general partner to convey the property

---

3. Calvin v. Salmon River Sheep Ranch, 658 P.2d 972 (Idaho 1983).

is determined by the limited partnership agreement and the jurisdiction's limited partnership law.

Corporate Ownership

A corporation may own real property. Corporate authority to convey the property is governed by the corporation's articles of incorporation and by-laws, as well as the jurisdiction's corporate law. The board of directors must authorize most transfers of real property.

A business will normally own real estate in the name of the business. Whether that business is organized as a partnership (general or limited) or a corporation will depend on tax, financial, securities, and liability factors. The choice of the proper entity for owning real estate is particularly important at the beginning of an investment or development. It may be difficult to make a change at a later date without adverse tax consequences. The issue of choice of entity is discussed further in Chapter 20.

 Transfer of Ownership

Ownership of land is transferred by a document known as a *deed*, which is recorded at a public office, typically the office of the county recorder in the county where the real property is located. Any document transferring an interest in real estate, such as a deed or a lease, is called a *conveyance.* The person conveying the property is the *grantor,* and the person to whom the property is conveyed is the *grantee.* Occasionally, but seldom in business, ownership is obtained through an installment sales contract, with the deed to follow when payment for the real estate has been completed. Ownership of property subject to probate is transferred by a court order from the probate court.

In most purchases of real estate, the type of interest conveyed is a *fee simple* interest, that is, absolute ownership of the property. However, many other transactions, such as a lease, convey less than an absolute ownership interest in the property.

Title

A seller of real estate is generally required to convey *marketable title,* that is, a fee simple interest free from defects. Defects of title that make it unmarketable include any cloud on the title that would cause the buyer to receive less than a fee simple interest. For example, the existence of a lien on the property would constitute a defect of title sufficient to make the title unmarketable.

The type of interest (usually fee simple) and the quality of title (that is, whether it is marketable) are set forth in a deed executed by the party conveying the property. The type of deed determines the scope of warranties granted.

Types of Deeds

An interest in real property can be conveyed only by a signed deed that specifically describes that interest and is delivered to and accepted by a named grantee. There are three basic types of deeds: grant deeds, quitclaim deeds, and warranty deeds. These differ in the specific warranties they contain.

Grant Deed   A *grant deed* contains implied warranties that (1) the grantor has not previously conveyed the same property or any interest in it to another person, and (2) the title is marketable. A grant deed also conveys *after-acquired title.* This means that if at the date the deed is executed the grantor does not have title to the real property referred to in the grant deed, but subsequently acquires it, the title will be automatically transferred to the grantee.

Quitclaim Deed   A *quitclaim deed* contains no warranties, and the grantor only conveys whatever right, title, and interest it holds, if any, at the time of execution. A quitclaim deed does not convey after-acquired title.

Warranty Deed   A *warranty deed* contains the implied warranties of a grant deed; in addition, the grantor expressly warrants the title to and the quiet possession of the property. Warranty deeds may also contain other express warranties.

 Recording Statutes

Deeds and other instruments of conveyance must be recorded with a government official in a public office, where copies will be available to anyone. The documents must be in *recordable form.* The requirements vary from state to state, but typically include legibility and some type of notarization by a notary public. The record in the public office is the principal basis for determining the state of title of real estate, and there is an extensive body of law concerning what and how recording controls that title.

Recording statutes establish an orderly process by which claims to interests in real property can be resolved. There are three types of recording statutes: (1) race statutes, (2) pure notice statutes, and (3) race–notice statutes.[4]

Under *race statutes,* recording is a race—the rule is "first in time is first in right." The first to record a deed has superior rights, regardless of whether he or she knew that someone else had already bought the property but had failed to record the deed.

Under *pure notice statutes,* a person who has notice that someone else has already bought the property cannot validate his or her deed by recording it first. Notice may be *actual* or constructive. Courts may find *constructive notice* if a reasonable inquiry (for instance, inspection of the property) would have disclosed the prior interest. A pure notice statute protects good faith subsequent purchasers. A *good faith subsequent purchaser* is one who purchases for value, in good faith, without knowledge of a prior outstanding interest. Thus, if, at the time a subsequent purchaser acquires a deed, he or she had no notice (actual or constructive) of a prior deed, then the subsequent purchaser will have superior rights.

Race–notice statutes protect only those good faith subsequent purchasers who record their deed before the prior purchaser records its deed.

 Title Insurance

Despite the existence of recording statutes, the condition of title to a specific property and the priority of any claims against the property are often difficult to ascertain. In some states, title is searched by attorneys, in others by title abstract companies on which attorneys rely, and in still others by title insurance companies, which may also insure the condition of title or the pri-

ority of one's interest. In some states, lawyers' opinions are still used rather than title insurance.

Extent of Coverage

A title insurance policy insures against loss as a result of (1) undisclosed liens or defects in title to the property; or (2) errors in the abstraction of the title, that is, in the summary of the relevant recorded deeds and liens. Generally, the policy limit is the purchase price of the property, or the amount of the *encumbrance,* that is, the claim against the property.

It is important to review a title report or insurance policy carefully before acquiring title to property. The exceptions listed in the report may be defects in title.

A title company may have a claim against the seller of real property if the seller conveys the property pursuant to a grant deed and it turns out that there is an encumbrance that the title company did not discover.

Escrow

In addition to issuing title insurance policies, title companies often hold the purchase money in *escrow,* that is, in a special account, until the conditions for the sale have all been met. The money is then paid to the seller. If the sale does not go through, the money is returned to the would-be purchaser. Banks also perform this service, and in some jurisdictions there are separate escrow companies.

The *escrow agent* acts as a neutral stakeholder, allowing the parties to close the transaction without the physical difficulties of passing instruments and funds between the parties. Additionally, it is the duty of the escrow agent to coordinate the closing with the recording of documents, the issuance of title insurance, and other activities that take place concurrently with the closing.

Neutral Party As a neutral party, the escrow agent is an agent of all parties to the transaction and must follow their specific instructions. Because an escrow agent has a fiduciary duty to all of the parties, it cannot act when the parties have submitted conflicting instructions. Generally, if conflicts between instructions are not resolved by the parties, the escrow agent will go to court for a resolution of the conflict.

The following case addressed the scope of an escrow agent's fiduciary duty to one of its principals.

---

4. Only two states (Delaware and North Carolina) use race statutes. Usage in other states is split about evenly between pure notice statutes and race–notice statutes.

A CASE IN POINT	SUMMARY

CASE 17.1

SCHOEPE v. ZIONS FIRST NATIONAL BANK

United States District Court
for the District of Utah
750 F. Supp. 1084
(D. Utah 1990).

FACTS   In October 1980, Lion Hill, a Nevada partnership, contracted to sell Nevada mining property to Pacific Silver Corporation. In February 1981, pursuant to the terms of the 1980 contract, Lion Hill and Pacific Silver signed an escrow agreement with Zions First National Bank. Under the escrow agreement, Pacific Silver agreed to pay the purchase price in installments to Zions, which, as escrow agent, would deliver the payments to Lion Hill. (Schoepe was the sole surviving Lion Hill partner.)

In March 1984, Zions made a $1.6 million loan to Pacific Silver. Zions made the loan without the knowledge or consent of Lion Hill. In January 1985, again without the knowledge or consent of Lion Hill, Zions made a $700,000 loan to Pacific Silver.

Later in 1985, Lion Hill agreed to an extension of Pacific Silver's payment schedule. The payment schedule of the original October 1980 contract was modified to decrease current payments and increase later payments. This 1985 extension was also made part of the escrow agreement.

After making the 1986 payment on the loan, Pacific Silver defaulted. Lion Hill claimed that it would not have agreed to the 1985 extension had it known of the $2.3 million in loans that Zions had made to Pacific Silver. Lion Hill claimed that Zions, acting as escrow agent, owed it a duty to disclose these loans, and that such nondisclosure was the proximate cause of Lion Hill's damages. Lion Hill claimed these damages included the payments it would have received from Pacific Silver had the 1985 extension not been made.

ISSUE PRESENTED   Does an escrow agent have a fiduciary duty to disclose dealings with principals that fall outside the scope of the controlling escrow agreement?

SUMMARY OF OPINION   The Federal District Court first noted that the duties of an escrow agent do not reach the level of common law agency duties. The escrow agent is a limited agent whose authority derives from the escrow agreement. The scope of an escrow agent's fiduciary duty is limited by the terms of the escrow agreement. An escrow agent's primary obligation is to exercise reasonable skill and ordinary diligence in following the escrow instructions.

The court then addressed the scope of the escrow agent's duty to disclose information to its principals. Previous cases found an obligation to disclose a known fraud being committed on a party to the escrow agreement. Others held that an escrow agent has a duty to disclose knowledge of material facts that might affect the principal's decision as to a pending transaction, if such knowledge was acquired in the course of his or her agency. This duty to disclose is most likely to attach when the escrow agent "knows the principal is looking to him for protection as to those very facts of which the [escrow agent] has knowledge."

It was uncontested that Zions exercised reasonable skill and ordinary diligence in following the escrow instructions. It also was uncontested that the escrow agreement contained no language imposing a duty on Zions to disclose any information to its principals. Finally, Lion Hill did not allege that Zions was engaged in fraud or that it had knowledge of a third party committing a fraud upon Lion Hill.

Case 17.1 continues

Case 17.1 continued

Lion Hill argued that Zions' knowledge of the loans it made to Pacific Silver constituted "knowledge of material facts" that gave rise to a duty to disclose. The court disagreed. It concluded that, whether or not the existence of the loans was "material" to Lion Hill, Zions had no duty to disclose it because it did not acquire the knowledge "in the course of its agency." Instead, Zions was acting outside of the scope of the escrow agreement when it made the loans to Pacific Silver.

The court justified its decision on policy grounds, maintaining that the burden of obtaining information about other indebtedness is better placed with the principals. Lion Hill, for instance, could have required Pacific Silver to submit a financial statement before it agreed to the payment extensions. Alternatively, Lion Hill could have contracted for such disclosure from Zions in the escrow agreement.

RESULT   The court awarded Zions summary judgment and dismissed Lion Hill's claim.

Brokers

The market for real estate is imperfect, and brokers serve to maintain that market by putting together buyers and sellers. The levels of competence and the areas of expertise of commercial brokers vary greatly. Most brokers specialize in a particular market segment, such as raw land, industrial leasing, or office buildings.

Compensation

Brokers are customarily retained by the seller through a listing agreement that, to be enforceable, must be in writing. Generally, brokers are compensated by a payment based on a percentage of the gross selling price (or aggregate rental income). The percentage can vary from 1% to 3% for large commercial properties to 10% for raw land. To the extent that the buyer's or lessee's broker is compensated, it is usually by sharing the commission paid by the seller.

Listing Agreements

There are several types of listing agreements: open, exclusive, and net.

Open Listing   In an open listing, the listing broker will receive a commission only if he or she procures a

ready, willing, and able buyer. Because it is understood that the seller will be contracting with more than one broker, the first broker to procure a buyer is the one who will receive a commission. Because of the uncertainty of earning a commission even if a buyer is found, it is hard to get a broker to work diligently to sell a commercial property with an open listing.

Exclusive Listing   An exclusive listing grants the broker the right to sell the property; any sale of the property during the term of the listing will entitle the broker to a commission. If a seller is going to give an exclusive listing, he or she may wish to restrict from the listing agreement particular buyers with whom the seller has dealt before signing the listing agreement.

Net Listing   A net listing involves a completely different compensation scheme. The broker will receive any sales price in excess of the net listing amount specified by the seller. Net listings are uncommon.

Effect of Seller Financing   In commercial transactions, the seller may provide the financing for the buyer. Thus, the sale may net very little cash to the seller. In that event, the seller often will be unwilling to pay most of it to a broker in the form of a commission. Therefore, the listing agreement may provide that if the seller accepts payment of the purchase price on terms, such as installments, the broker will accept payment of his or her commission on the same terms.

Regulation of Brokers

In most states, real estate brokers are heavily regulated. They are generally required to have a license to perform brokerage activities. Brokerage activities are broadly defined as any sale or offer to sell, any purchase or offer to purchase, any solicitation related to the sale of real property or of a business opportunity, and any leases, loans secured by real property, or real property sales contracts. A mere finder, who does nothing more than introduce two parties for a fee, does not need a broker's license. If the person has engaged in brokerage activities without a license, he or she will not be able to sue successfully to recover his or her fee.

In many states, real estate brokers must report and keep records of the transactions in which they deal. Brokers may also be required to meet continuing education requirements and requirements regarding the particulars of real estate loans.

Agency Relationship

Brokers may also be subject to regulations concerning disclosure of the agency relationship between the broker and the parties to the transaction. As a general rule, a broker may not act for more than one person in a transaction without the knowledge or consent of all parties to the transaction. When a broker acts for both the buyer and the seller, the relationship is characterized as a *dual agency*. In most instances, a dual agent is prohibited from disclosing to the buyer that the seller is willing to sell the property for less than the listing price without the consent of the seller. Similarly, a dual agent may not disclose to the seller that the buyer is willing to pay a price greater than the listing price. Agency issues are discussed further in Chapter 5.

 Acquisitions and Dispositions

Acquisitions and dispositions of real estate interests are contracted for in the same manner as most commercial transactions. To be enforceable, however, a contract for the sale of a real property interest must be in writing. Although standardized contracts are often used in relatively simple transactions, such as the conveyance of a single-family residence or a small commercial property, most large transactions require custom-drafted contracts.

Generally, contracts for the sale of an interest in real property are the result of protracted negotiations between the parties. In addition to essential terms such as price, time, and method of payment, common areas of negotiation include types of acceptable financing, the condition of title, closing costs, taxes, and compliance with zoning laws, building codes, and environmental regulations. In many purchase and sale agreements, the most heavily negotiated provisions are the seller's representations and warranties concerning the condition of the property.

Representations and Warranties

In the past, real estate transactions were governed by the traditional rule of *caveat emptor* ("let the buyer beware"). Under this rule, the seller of a home or other property made no warranties to the buyer other than those expressly included in the deed or contract of sale. Current law is more protective of the buyer, especially when a person is buying a home.

Implied Warranty of Habitability   Current law imposes on builders of houses an implied warranty of habitability. Under this modern approach, which has been adopted by the majority of states, the seller of a home is in effect a guarantor of the home's fitness. As with the UCC's implied warranty of merchantability for sales of goods (discussed in Chapter 8), sellers under the implied warranty of habitability warrant that the house is in reasonable working order and is of reasonably sound construction.

Seller's Duty to Disclose   The traditional rule of *caveat emptor* is also giving way to a duty on sellers to disclose defects in real property transactions. In most states, sellers have an obligation to disclose any known defect that (1) materially affects the value of the property, and (2) the buyer could not reasonably discover. As the following case illustrates, sellers (and their brokers) can be liable for nondisclosure of certain off-site conditions that materially affect the value of the property.

A CASE IN POINT | **IN THE LANGUAGE OF THE COURT**

CASE 17.2
STRAWN v. CANUSO
Supreme Court
of New Jersey
657 A.2d 420 (N.J. 1995).

FACTS   The plaintiffs are more than 150 families who purchased new homes in Voorhees Township. The homes were developed and marketed by companies controlled by the Canuso family. The homebuyers sought damages against the Canusos and their companies because—unbeknownst to them—the new homes they purchased had been constructed near the Buzby Landfill, a hazardous-waste dumpsite.

Between 1966 and 1978, large amounts of hazardous materials and chemicals were dumped at the Buzby Landfill. Toxic materials escaped, contaminating the groundwater and air. The federal Environmental Protection Agency recommended that the site be considered for a Superfund cleanup.

The homebuyers alleged that the developers and brokers (1) knew of the Buzby Landfill before they considered the site for residential development, and (2) that, although specifically aware of the existence and environmental hazards of the landfill, they failed to disclose those facts to the families when they purchased their homes. In particular, an officer of the brokerage firm urged the Canusos to disclose the existence of the Buzby Landfill to homebuyers. The Canusos refused that request and instead followed a policy of nondisclosure. That policy continued even after early purchasers complained about odors. The representatives of the Canuso brokerage and development companies were instructed never to disclose the existence of the Buzby Landfill, even when asked about such conditions.

The trial court granted the defendants' motion for summary judgment, ruling that the developers and brokers did not owe a duty to prospective purchasers to disclose conditions of the property. The appellate division reversed the decision of the trial court, ruling that the Canuso brokerage and development companies had a duty to disclose to potential buyers the existence of the nearby, abandoned hazardous-waste dump. Canuso appealed.

ISSUE PRESENTED   Do the developers of new homes and the real estate brokers marketing those homes have a duty to disclose to prospective buyers that the homes have been constructed near an abandoned hazardous-waste dump?

OPINION   O'HERN, J., writing for the New Jersey Supreme Court:

Weintraub establishes that a seller of real estate or a broker representing the seller would be liable for nondisclosure of on-site defective conditions if those conditions were known to them and unknown and not readily observable by the buyer. Such conditions, for example, would include radon contamination and a polluted water supply. Whether and to what extent we should extend this duty to off-site conditions depends on an assessment of the various policies that have shaped the development of our law in this area.

As noted, the principal factors shaping the duty to disclose have been the difference in bargaining power between the professional seller of residential real estate and the purchaser of such housing, and the difference in access to information between the seller and the buyer. Those principles guide our decision in this case.

The first factor causes us to limit our holding to professional sellers of residential housing (persons engaged in the business of building or developing residential housing) and the brokers representing them. Neither the reseller of residential real estate

Case 17.2 continues

Case 17.2 continued

nor the seller of commercial property has that same advantage in the bargaining process. Regarding the second factor, professional sellers of residential housing and their brokers enjoy markedly superior access to information. Hence, we believe that it is reasonable to extend to such professionals a similar duty to disclose off-site conditions that materially affect the value or desirability of the property.

The silence of the [brokerage firm's] representatives and the Canuso Management Corporation's principals and employees "created a mistaken impression on the part of the purchaser." Defendants used sales-promotion brochures, newspaper advertisements, and a fact sheet to sell the homes in the development. That material portrayed the development as located in a peaceful, bucolic setting with an abundance of fresh air and clean lake waters. Although the literature mentioned how far the property was from malls, country clubs, and train stations, "neither the brochures, the newspaper advertisements nor any sales personnel mentioned that a landfill [was] located within half a mile of some of the homes." . . .

. . . In the case of on-site conditions, courts have imposed affirmative obligations on sellers to disclose information materially affecting the value of property. There is no logical reason why a certain class of sellers and brokers should not disclose off-site matters that materially affect the value of property.

The duty that we recognize is not unlimited. We do not hold that sellers and brokers have a duty to investigate or disclose transient social conditions in the community that arguably affect the value of property. In the absence of a purchaser communicating specific needs, builders and brokers should not be held to decide whether the changing nature of a neighborhood, the presence of a group home, or the existence of a school in decline are facts material to the transaction. Rather, we root in the land the duty to disclose off-site conditions that are material to the transaction. That duty is consistent with the development of our law and supported by statutory policy.

We hold that a builder-developer of residential real estate or a broker representing it is not only liable to a purchaser for affirmative and intentional misrepresentation, but is also liable for nondisclosure of off-site physical conditions known to it and unknown and not readily observable by the buyer if the existence of those conditions is of sufficient materiality to affect the habitability, use, or enjoyment of the property and, therefore, render the property substantially less desirable or valuable to the objectively reasonable buyer. Whether a matter not disclosed by such a builder or broker is of such materiality, and unknown and unobservable by the buyer, will depend on the facts of each case.

RESULT   The verdict in favor of the homebuyers was affirmed. The defendants had violated their duty to disclose the existence of the landfill.

Questions

1. Would the court have reached a different result if the sellers had not touted the development's bucolic setting, fresh air, and clean lake waters?
2. Why should a seller of commercial property have a lesser obligation to disclose adverse off-site conditions?

Contractual Protections and Due Diligence A skillful buyer will request express contractual representations and warranties from the seller as to the condition of the property. This is particularly important in commercial transactions, because courts are less willing to impose implied warranties and a duty to disclose when the buyer is not an individual but rather a commercial entity. From the seller's perspective, the representations and warranties are a potential source of liability. From the buyer's perspective, the representations and warranties provide some assurance that the buyer is getting what it expected. If nothing else, the negotiation of representations and warranties frequently leads to additional disclosures regarding the physical condition of the property

However, the buyer should not rely upon the representations and warranties as an alternative to its own careful investigation of the condition of the property. Although the seller is generally required to indemnify the buyer against liability arising from the inaccuracy of any of its representations and warranties, the right to indemnification is not worth much if the seller does not have the resources to back it up. Perhaps more important, defects in the property can seriously disrupt the buyer's operations and business.

Environmental Considerations

Due diligence is particularly necessary with respect to environmental issues (discussed in Chapter 16). Because liability under federal and state environmental laws and regulations can be so large as to overshadow any other economic aspect of the property, the buyer should diligently investigate whether there are toxic or hazardous substances on or under the property. The buyer should determine the prior uses of the property and look for any indications of underground tanks or other physical evidence that would indicate possible environmental problems.

Under the Comprehensive Environmental Response, Compensation, and Liability Act (CERCLA), the current owner or operator of a contaminated facility is jointly and severally liable for the costs associated with cleaning up the facility. This liability attaches even if the current owner purchased the property with no knowledge of the prior contamination, unless it can show that it made all due inquiry and still had no reason to know about the contamination.

To establish the *innocent landowner defense,* the purchaser must do extensive due diligence in the form of environmental tests of the water and soil and research into prior uses of the property and any adjacent property from which waste might have spread. As a result, one commentator has stated that "the innocent landowner defense provides effectively no reliable defense to a purchaser of real estate today."[5] In the absence of the innocent landowner defense, CERCLA holds present owners or operators and the owners or operators at the time of waste disposal jointly and severally liable for cleanup costs. As a result, if the prior owner is insolvent or nonexistent, the current owner can be responsible for the entire cleanup.

As the following case illustrates, courts tend to apply the innocent landowner defense strictly, particularly in commercial transactions.[6]

---

[5] *See* L. Jager Smith, *CERCLA's Innocent Landowner Defense: Oasis or Mirage?*, 18 COLUM. J. ENVTL. L. 155, 157 (1993).

[6] *See* Eva M. Fromm et al., *Allocating Environmental Liabilities in Acquisitions,* 22 IOWA J. CORP. L. 429 (1997).

| **A CASE IN POINT** | **SUMMARY** |

CASE 17.3
BCW ASSOCIATES, LTD.
v. OCCIDENTAL
CHEMICAL CORP.
United States District Court for the Eastern District of Pennsylvania
1988 WL 102641 (E.D. Pa. Sept. 29, 1988).

FACTS In 1984, Occidental Chemical Corporation (Occidental) sold a warehouse to BCW Associates, Ltd. (BCW). The sales contract provided that BCW would purchase the warehouse "as is." The contract also provided that BCW would have 45 days to inspect the warehouse and could terminate the sale during this period. BCW formally waived this termination right and acquired the property. BCW subsequently leased the warehouse to Knoll International, Inc. Knoll used the warehouse to store and distribute inventory from its office-furniture business.

Case 17.3 continues

Case 17.3 continued

Both BCW and Knoll had noticed a significant amount of dust present in the warehouse, but viewed the dust as merely a nuisance. Three different consulting firms evaluated the warehouse and reported to BCW and Knoll that there were no environmental hazards at the facility. In addition, Occidental gave comfort letters to BCW in which Occidental represented that no hazardous materials were stored in the warehouse.

In the fall of 1985, Knoll's activity in the warehouse caused dust to "rain down" from the rafters. When the dust was analyzed, Knoll learned that the dust showed dangerous levels of lead.

Firestone Tire and Rubber Company had owned and operated the warehouse prior to Occidental, from 1952 to 1980. The dust in the warehouse was created by the white sidewall grinding phase of Firestone's production of white sidewall tires. Firestone conducted these operations throughout its occupation of the warehouse.

Knoll and BCW jointly undertook a thorough cleaning of the warehouse. BCW paid for the cleanup of the warehouse structure, in part because Knoll's lease required BCW to indemnify Knoll for costs associated with cleaning the dust. Knoll paid for the cost of cleaning its inventory and equipment, and it incurred costs to provide its employees with personal protective equipment.

BCW and Knoll sued Occidental and Firestone for the costs associated with cleaning the dust from the warehouse. BCW and Knoll asserted the innocent landowner defense under the Comprehensive Environmental Response, Compensation, and Liability Act.

ISSUE PRESENTED   To what extent must a purchaser or lessor of property investigate possible environmental hazards in order to qualify for CERCLA's innocent landowner defense?

SUMMARY OF OPINION   The Federal District Court concluded that neither BCW nor Knoll could take advantage of innocent landowner defense. Both were liable for an appropriate share of the cleanup costs.

The court noted that BCW could have negotiated an indemnification clause from Occidental, but chose not to. As a result, BCW accepted the risk that there might be an environmental problem with the warehouse, and this was reflected in its purchase price. In light of BCW's knowledge of the dust prior to purchasing the warehouse and its knowledge of Knoll's planned activities, the court determined that "it cannot be said [BCW] exercised due care or took adequate precautions."

The court found that Knoll knew it was leasing a dusty, old warehouse and that this fact was reflected in its lease price. The court also emphasized that Knoll's officers were suspicious about the environmental condition of the warehouse, but they declined to investigate the matter further because of the expense of additional testing and the urgent need for warehouse space.

RESULT   The court ruled that Firestone, BCW, and Knoll were each one-third responsible for the costs associated with cleaning up the lead dust.

COMMENTS   Because it is so difficult for a buyer to prove that it had no reason to know of the hazardous waste at the time the property was acquired, buyers should

Case 17.3 continues

Case 17.3 continued

always demand representations and warranties about environmental compliance and the condition of the property with a right to indemnification if an environmental problem comes to light.

Tax-Deferred Exchanges

An alternative to acquiring real property for cash is a *tax-deferred exchange,* whereby the seller exchanges its property for another piece of property. This can have favorable tax consequences. In particular, the capital gains tax owed by the seller may be deferred if the seller (1) is disposing of a property held for investment or for productive use in a trade or business, and (2) is acquiring a property that qualifies under the Internal Revenue Code. Tax-deferred exchanges take many forms. The most common is the three-party exchange, in which the buyer purchases a piece of property designated by the seller and exchanges it for the seller's property.

There are a number of pitfalls in utilizing a tax-deferred exchange. For example, in a three-party exchange, under the environmental laws the buyer may be liable for the cleanup of any toxic or hazardous materials on the property acquired for the purpose of exchange. Changes in tax rates may affect the desirability of a tax-deferred exchange. For example, if the tax rate is likely to increase, it may be better to pay the tax at the time of the transfer of the property rather than at a later date, when the rate may be higher. Because of the complex nature of these exchanges, it is prudent to consult an attorney specializing in tax and real estate issues when acquiring real property through a tax-deferred exchange.

Sale and Leaseback

A *sale and leaseback* arrangement involves a simultaneous two-step transaction. In the first step, an institutional lender with funds to invest, such as a life insurance company or a pension fund, purchases real property from a corporation. In the second step, or often simultaneously, the property is leased back to the corporation for its use. The term of the lease is long, often ranging from 20 to 40 years. The tenant may have the option of repurchasing the property at or before the termination date of the lease.

The amount of rent payable is structured so that during the term of the lease, the lessor will recoup the purchase price of the property and realize an acceptable return on its investment. The lessee pays all taxes and maintenance and operating costs.

The advantage to a company of selling and leasing back its real property is that capital funds are obtained at a lower cost and for a longer period than would be available with other sources of financing. A sale and leaseback transaction may also be used to reduce the company's debt structure by freeing up cash that would otherwise be tied up in the property. Also, rent is fully tax deductible, whereas only the interest portion of loan payments is deductible.

On the other hand, from the purchaser's point of view, the investment quality of a sale and leaseback transaction depends upon the financial stability of the seller/lessee. Such transactions are usually available only to corporations with strong track records.

Real Estate Investment Trusts (REITs)

Real estate investment trusts, commonly referred to as *REITs,* are a 1960s creation of the Internal Revenue Code and can provide a good tax vehicle for investors seeking to invest in a portfolio of real property. As long as at least 95% of a REIT's net income is distributed to shareholder–beneficiaries, the REIT itself pays no income tax; taxes are paid at the shareholder–beneficiary level only. REITs are limited in the types of operations they may conduct. Ownership concentration is also limited: No five persons can own more than 50% of the REIT's beneficial interests. REITs sell beneficial shares that are traded in the stock markets and permit small investors to invest in a diversified portfolio of real estate, similar to an investment in common stocks through a mutual fund. Although REITs had financial difficulties in the 1970s and 1980s, due to plummeting real estate values and risky development projects, returns on REITs in the mid-1990s were generally very attractive.

Transactions with Foreigners

Sales of real property interests to foreign persons are regulated by the federal government. Under the Foreign Investment in Real Property Tax Act, the purchaser of a U.S. real property interest from a foreign person is required to withhold 10% of the purchase price to ensure that U.S. capital gains tax is collected on the sale. Additionally, the Agricultural Foreign Investment Disclosure Act requires foreign acquirers of U.S. agricultural land to file an informational report with the U.S. secretary of agriculture.

Water Rights

In drought-prone and largely arid parts of the western United States, the water rights associated with parcels of real property—especially agricultural property—can substantially impact the property's value. The federal government has long given farming interests enhanced water rights, allowing them to purchase water at a sharp discount.

This century-old policy has drawn the ire of environmentalists, who view it as an economically perverse system that discourages conservation. For example, the scheme has left a relatively small number of farmers in control of approximately 80% of the water consumed in California. Environmentalists argue that if farmers paid the true market value of water, then far less of it would be poured over desert acres to grow crops, and more would be used for drinking water and producing high-tech goods, and for conservation projects such as restoring salmon runs.[7]

In 1996, the Westlands Water District, located in California's Central Valley, launched an electronic market for the trading of water rights. Experts called this the first true market for the buying and selling of nature's most essential commodity. It was immediately hailed as a role model by both agricultural interests and conservationists.[8] Many saw the broad support for the plan as a sign of the growing role that economic thinking plays in debates over natural resources. According to the president of the World Resources Institute, the

---

INTERNATIONAL CONSIDERATION

Many countries will not allow foreigners to own land. In these countries, a foreigner must therefore obtain a long-term lease on the property.

Mexico's laws restricting foreign ownership offer a complex example. Foreigners cannot buy title to any property within 31 miles of the ocean, or within 62 miles of the U.S. or Guatemalan borders. All a foreigner can legally acquire near the beach or border is the right to use the land for up to 50 years through a Mexican bank trust called a *fideicomiso translativo de dominio*.[a]

Even these trusts can be invalidated if the title to the land is not clear. Mexican title records are not thorough, and title insurance is rare. Public notaries in Mexico can search for liens against property title; typically, however, they search back no more than a decade.[b]

The legal regime governing Russia's real property completely shuts out foreigners. The Communist legislators who, as of early 1998, still dominated the parliament, steadfastly refused to privatize the market for rural land. The parliament speaker has said it would it be like "selling the motherland."[c] Even if the barrier to foreign ownership were lifted, there are no legal mechanisms for transferring ownership of Russian land. Thus, rural land can neither be freely bought and sold nor used as collateral for loans.

In any country where foreign ownership is permitted, an investor should be cautious when purchasing property. Many countries do not have adequate means for searching the title of property. In addition, many countries allow for *squatter's rights*, whereby ownership of property that is not occupied by its owner for a certain period of time will be transferred to those who have been unlawfully occupying it. Such a transfer is usually not reflected in the official land records.

---

a. *See* Bob Ortega, *Quirky Laws for Americans Buying Mexican Property*, WALL ST. J., Oct. 17, 1997, at B1.

b. *See id.*

c. *See* Matthew Brzezinski & Scott Kilman, *Collectively, Farms Are a Worsening Mess in Post-Soviet Russia*, WALL ST. J., Jan. 12, 1998, at A1.

---

7. *See* G. Pascal Zachary, *Water Rights May Become More Liquid*, WALL ST. J., Feb. 15, 1996, at A2.

8. *Id.*

keener appreciation for economic ideas among conservationists has been "part of a recognition that the important decisions are being made by people who listen to economists."[9] Indeed, environmentalists asserted that "as we move into an era without new supplies, trading will more and more play a role in moving water to its highest-value uses."[10]

Farmers saw this as a way to make more informed business decisions. Water rights have historically been sold through informal coffee-shop meetings or telephone deals between farmers. The advent of widely available pricing information was eagerly anticipated. One California farmer lamented that before the opening of the market, "You may [have been] paying too much or too little for water; you [didn't] know." Now, as the use of the electronic market expands, farmers will be able to compare the cost of conservation methods with the real value of water that might be used instead.[11]

One issue that could stand in the way of the market's expansion is the potential for farmers to reap windfall profits. Some experts point out that there are many taxpayers who would be outraged at the idea of building a publicly subsidized project for farmers, only to have them sell off that same water to municipalities at a premium and pocket the difference. However, even many environmental groups accept the fact that water will never be freed up for transfer unless there is some profit for the seller. Moreover, a 1992 change in federal law sanctioned profits earned by farmers on the sale of federally granted water rights.

 ◆ Preliminary Agreements

Often, the parties to a real estate transaction are able to reach a general agreement on terms and conditions, but need more time either to negotiate specific representations and warranties or to further investigate the sale. A number of alternatives to the traditional contract for the sale of real property have been developed. Examples of alternative methods of acquiring rights in real estate include option contracts, rights of first refusal, and letters of intent.

---

9. *Id.*
10. *Id.*
11. *Id.*

Option Contract

In an *option contract,* the potential buyer pays the seller for the right, but not the obligation, to purchase the property during a given time period. The option gives the buyer time to conduct investigations, determine whether the purchase of the property is economically feasible, and obtain financing. The seller receives payment for taking the property off the market for a specified period of time.

For an option contract to be enforceable, it must be in writing and consideration must be paid to the seller. Additionally, the option contract must state the major terms of the proposed purchase agreement and must specify the manner in which the option may be exercised. It is also advisable to record the option to provide constructive notice to third parties and thereby prevent the sale of the property to a third party before the option has expired.

Right of First Refusal

A *right of first refusal* is the right, conferred by a contract, to purchase the property on the same terms offered by or to a third party. Perhaps its most frequent use is with a tenant of a leasehold interest. The holder of the right of first refusal should require that it be recorded.

A right of first refusal often provides great leverage to the holder. Its very existence can chill the owner's ability to sell the property. Few buyers will want to start investigations and negotiations knowing that they could lose the deal if the party with the right of first refusal exercises its right.

Consequently, it may be advisable to modify the right of first refusal, giving the holder only the right to negotiate the purchase of the property before the seller enters negotiations with another party. This is sometimes called a *right of first negotiation.* Another method of accommodating the needs of the seller is to provide for a very short time, such as 72 hours, for the holder to exercise its right of first refusal.

Letter of Intent

A letter of intent may create the right to acquire an interest in a specific property. A *letter of intent* sets forth the general terms and conditions of a proposed purchase until a formal acquisition agreement can be signed. Letters of intent are often viewed as unenforceable by the parties, but courts have increasingly treated them as enforceable contracts. In one case, the court focused on the conduct of the parties to determine whether an enforceable agreement was intended despite express written statements to the contrary.[12] Consequently, if the parties do not wish to be bound by their letters of intent, they must ensure that the terms and conditions are not set forth so specifically that a binding legal obligation is created; and they must conduct themselves consistently with the absence of a binding contract.

When properly utilized, letters of intent allow the parties to investigate the proposed transaction to determine whether it is worth pursuing. Although letters of intent are generally not as effective as options or rights of first refusal in removing property from the market, they can create an ethical commitment to consummate the transaction. In some states, the execution of a letter of intent creates an implied covenant of good faith and fair dealing between the parties, requiring good faith negotiation of a formal acquisition agreement.

 Financing

Financing the purchase of real estate may involve borrowing funds for a long or short term. The loan is usually secured by a lien on the property, known as a *mortgage* or *deed of trust*. The availability of financing depends on the intrinsic value of the property or on both its value and its potential for the production of income. There are an almost unlimited number of types of financing. Some of the more common forms are discussed in this section.

Permanent Loans

The most common type of real estate loan is the permanent loan. This is usually a long-term loan, repaid over 25 or 30 years.

Fixed-Interest Loans   Traditionally, permanent loans have a fixed interest rate; that is, the rate of interest does not change over the term of the loan. The lender assumes the risk of losing the benefit of any rise in inter-

est rates, and the borrower assumes the risk of losing the benefit of any fall.

In order to benefit from any increases in market interest rates, many lenders reserve the right to call (that is, demand repayment of) fixed-interest loans after a specified period, often after five, ten, or fifteen years. Conversely, to prevent borrowers from refinancing their obligation when market interest rates fall below the fixed interest rate of the loan, some lenders may insert a lock-in clause to prohibit prepayments of principal, or they may impose a penalty, called a *prepayment penalty,* if the loan is paid off early.

Variable-Interest Loans   Variable-interest loans allow lenders to avoid the risk of fluctuating interest rates. In a variable-interest loan, the rate of interest is set in relation to a specified standard or base rate. It is often set at a fixed number of percentage points over the *prime rate,* that is, the interest rate offered by major lending institutions to their most creditworthy customers. Over the term of the loan, the interest rate fluctuates with changes in the base rate or index. The interest rate is usually adjusted annually or semiannually. The total amount of the change over the term of the loan is generally subject to some cap or maximum top rate. A floor may also be established to ensure that the interest rate does not fall below a specified percentage.

Points   In addition to interest, real estate lenders charge a loan fee, called *points.* The fee is the amount funded, multiplied by a fixed percentage. Each 1% is a point. For example, a $2\frac{1}{2}$-point fee on a $100,000 loan would be $2,500. Points are usually paid at the time the loan is made. The deductibility of points as a payment of interest is determined under the Internal Revenue Code.

Loan-to-Value Ratio   The availability of financing for the acquisition of commercial property through the use of a permanent loan is frequently determined by the property's income-producing potential. Permanent loans often have loan-to-value ratios of 60% to 80%; that is, the principal amount of the loan is as much as 60% to 80% of the lender's appraised value of the property.

Construction Loans

Construction loans generally have a term slightly longer than the estimated construction period. Upon completion of construction, a construction lender may

---

12. Computer Systems of America v. International Business Machs. Corp., 795 F.2d 1086 (1st Cir. 1986).

be repaid from either permanent (take-out) financing or interim (gap) financing obtained by the developer. *Interim* or *gap financing* is financing that a developer obtains to pay off the construction loan when it becomes due before the permanent financing is available. This financing is provided by someone other than the construction lender and is more long term. A *take-out commitment* is an agreement by a lender to replace the construction loan with a permanent loan, usually after certain conditions, such as the timely completion of the project, have been met. Prior to negotiating a construction loan, the developer should establish a relationship with a lender willing to make a permanent loan or provide gap financing.

Development Loans

Although developers use construction loans for the acquisition and improvement of commercial properties, they use *development loans* for the acquisition, subdivision, improvement, and sale of residential properties. Funds are advanced by the lender as development progresses. The lender normally requires that the developer obtain performance bonds and personal guarantees by principals of the developer. Development lenders usually do not require take-out commitments by other lenders because the development loan is repaid upon the sale of building sites. From the lender's perspective, development loans are more risky than construction loans. The ability to pay off the development loan depends on the developer's ability to sell parcels of the development.

Equity Participation by Lender

Many lenders attempt to increase their yield from real estate projects by participating in the *equity*, or ownership, of the property. Such participation can be beneficial to both the lender and the developer. The lender can improve its yield from the project by sharing in the profits as well as receiving interest on its loan. The developers can benefit from the higher loan-to-value ratio, lower interest rates, and slower repayment terms that a participating lender will accept.

Equity participation by lenders is a relatively recent phenomenon. Historically, federal and state statutes prohibited banks and other lenders from owning real estate. In recent years, however, these statutory restraints have been substantially liberalized.

Structure of Participation   The most common form of equity participation by lenders is a *kicker*, that is, the receipt of a percentage of gross or net income in excess of a stipulated base. The lender may, for example, receive a kicker in the amount of a stipulated percentage of income over a break-even point determined by a set formula. Alternatively, the lender may actually purchase an interest in the property or in the entity owning the property.

 ## Wraparound Financing

Occasionally, an owner will require financing in addition to an existing loan secured by a deed of trust or mortgage on the property. Unless the second lender is willing to take a position subordinate to the holder of the first loan with respect to rights to the property, the owner will need to obtain a second loan sufficient to satisfy (pay off) the first loan and still provide sufficient funds to meet its financing requirements.

It may not be economically attractive to pay off the first loan, however, because of prepayment penalties or because the interest rate on the first loan may be lower than on a new loan. In such instances, wraparound financing can provide additional funds without requiring the owner to first pay off the original loan.

In a *wraparound financing* transaction, the second lender lends the owner the additional funds and agrees to take over the servicing of the first loan. In exchange, the owner executes a deed of trust or mortgage and an all-inclusive note, covering the combined amount of the first and second loans. The new lender benefits because the rate charged on the all-inclusive note is higher than the weighted-average interest rates of the first and second loans. The owner benefits because the interest rate on the all-inclusive note is lower than the rate it would have to pay if it paid off the first loan and took out a new loan to cover the entire amount.

 ## Appraisal Methods

The value of an income-producing property may be appraised by (1) the cost approach, whereby the construction cost of building a given improvement on the property is added to the value of the unimproved land; (2) the market approach, which looks at the selling prices in recent sales of properties with similar income-producing characteristics; or (3) the income approach, which establishes the present value of the estimated annual cash flow over the anticipated holding period.

The appraisal of property is an inexact science, and it is relatively unregulated by state governments. Because the funds available to a developer, and the financial institution's loan fees, are based upon the property's appraised value, the appraiser may be pressured to inflate its appraisal. Although increased loan fees and increased funds for development may provide short-term benefits, inflated appraisals can have disastrous long-term effects.

The savings and loan crisis in the 1980s was in part caused by inflated appraisals that induced savings and loan associations to make reckless loans. The resulting failure of many savings and loans cost taxpayers in excess of $300 billion. Upon disposal of a failed savings and loan's assets, the government was often able to recoup only a small portion of a property's inflated appraisal value. An article in the *Wall Street Journal* in the spring of 1990 lamented that some of the appraisers responsible for the crisis will have to be relied on in its resolution.

Protective Laws

There are laws in every jurisdiction to regulate the conduct of lenders and borrowers, especially in the area of what interest rate can be charged (the *usury laws*) and the remedies if a borrower fails to pay or is otherwise in default. Both sets of laws are designed primarily to protect individuals more than businesses. Many of the default laws were originated to protect farmers during the Great Depression.

It is worth noting that many of the protective laws apply to all loans, not just to noncommercial loans. However, lenders frequently ask commercial borrowers to waive these protections. Most large lenders use standard documents for loan agreements, although changes are sometimes made. In substantial transactions, it is essential that all documents be reviewed and negotiated by all parties to a transaction and their counsel.

In recent years, usury laws have tended to disappear, because an out-of-date usury law (e.g., limiting the interest rate to 8% when the prevailing rate is 12%) will simply cause loan money to go to a more liberal jurisdiction. There are still states, however, in which the usury laws apply unless the title to the property is held by a corporation. In other states, equity participation by a lender may result in an illegally high interest rate. The penalties for violating the usury laws can be severe, and treble damages are sometimes available. A borrower cannot effectively agree to waive the benefits of a usury law; such a waiver is considered contrary to public policy.

Foreclosure

The legal process by which a mortgagee may have a piece of property put up for sale in the public arena to raise cash in order to pay off a debt due the mortgagee is known as *foreclosure*. The property is sold to the highest bidder; the proceeds are then first used to satisfy the debt obligation (plus interest) of the unpaid mortgage and court costs. Any remainder is given to any other secured creditors holding a mortgage or deed of trust on the property. The mortgagor receives nothing until all creditors with a security interest in the property are paid in full.

In some states, the lender can bid the amount of the outstanding indebtedness in the foreclosure sale. If the lender is the highest bidder, it acquires the property, and the debt is extinguished.

The exact details of the foreclosure process differ from state to state. Some states allow *rights of redemption*, which give the mortgagor and certain other categories of interested persons the right to redeem the property within a statutory limited period varying from two months to two years after sale. If payment of the foreclosure amount plus interest is not made by the expiration of the redemption period, the purchaser at the foreclosure sale receives the deed and clear ownership of the land.

 ## Commercial Leasing

A *commercial lease* involves not only a conveyance of an interest in real property from the landlord to the tenant, but also a contract that governs the respective rights and obligations of the parties during the lease term. Because most businesses do not own the premises in which their business operations are conducted, the availability and the terms and conditions of commercial leasing can be crucial factors in determining the success or failure of a business. There are four types of commercial leases: office leases, retail leases, industrial leases, and ground leases.

Office Leases

Most office premises constitute a portion of an office building. Unless the tenant is to occupy a substantial portion of the building, the landlord will ordinarily present a standard lease form used for all of the tenants of the building. The landlord has a significant economic interest in using a standardized form. Because the landlord is more interested in obtaining occupants than in obtaining any particular tenant as an occupant, it is often unwilling to negotiate each lease provision separately or to permit the tenant to prepare the lease. In a tight market for tenants, however, more negotiation is possible.

Specific provisions of a form office lease, however, may be negotiable. A tenant should try to negotiate modifications to those lease provisions that need to be tailored to that tenant's occupancy. In addition, the money terms of the lease—such as basic and additional rent; responsibility for taxes, operating expenses, and maintenance; and escalation provisions—should be specifically negotiated by the tenant.

Rental Charge   Most office leases set forth the basic rent for the premises, usually in dollars per square foot or per rentable square foot. It is important for the tenant to inquire how the landlord established the rentable square feet in the premises. In some cases, the owner measures from the outside walls, even though the usable space is within the interior walls. The difference may be substantial. In other cases, the landlord includes public areas, such as parts of corridors shared with other tenants.

The landlord should be asked to provide detailed plans that clearly indicate the gross rentable space and how much of that space is actually usable. In larger lease transactions, it may be beneficial for the tenant to hire an architect to determine the proportion of rentable square feet to usable space.

Alterations   After the rent has been established, a tenant should determine other costs. If the premises have to be adapted to meet the tenant's needs, the tenant should negotiate what alterations will be acceptable to the landlord and how much of the cost the landlord will credit against the rent.

Such issues are often addressed in a separate agreement, called a *work letter agreement,* attached to the lease. The work letter agreement should describe the alterations, specify the time period for making them, and specify who is to bear the costs. As an incentive to lease the premises, most landlords will provide tenants with either an improvement allowance or an allowance for free rent for a specified period. The amount of such allowances is dictated by the marketplace.

Additional Space   The tenant may be given either an option or a right of first refusal for leasing additional adjoining space.

Assignments and Subleases   An *assignment* of the lease is a permanent transfer of the lease to a third party. The third party acquires the tenant's rights under the lease; however, the tenant remains liable for the rent if the third party defaults unless the lessor has agreed to look only to the third party. A *sublease* is a temporary transfer of the lease to a third party.

If the premises fail to meet the tenant's needs, or if the tenant can no longer afford the lease, it may wish to assign or sublease. Landlords, on the other hand, may be hesitant to grant the right to assign or sublease. In an escalating market, a lease may develop a substantial bonus value if market rents exceed the rent due under the lease. Therefore, the landlord may condition the assignment or subleasing of space on the tenant's paying over any bonus value or splitting it with the landlord. Moreover, landlords are often concerned about the financial wherewithal of any assignees or sublessees. Therefore, most leases require the landlord's written consent for an assignment or a sublease.

Most landlords are willing to provide in the lease that they will not withhold consent unreasonably. However, a landlord may attempt to require a provision stating that it has absolute discretion to grant or withhold consent. In some states, such a provision is considered an unreasonable restraint on the conveyance of a tenant's interest in a commercial lease and is therefore unenforceable.

Retail Leases

In the negotiation of retail leases, the focus is on the operation of the tenant's business. Retail leases frequently contain a percentage rent clause that requires the tenant to pay, in addition to a base monthly rent, a percentage of its gross sales to the landlord. A percentage rent provision provides a hedge against inflation for the landlord, as well as a means for the landlord to participate in a successful tenant's business. In addition, the provision may compensate for a low base rent received from the *anchor tenant,* that is, a department store or supermarket that determines the economic success of a shopping center.

The definition of gross sales usually covers all sales of merchandise and services for cash or credit. Tenants should try to exclude from the percentage rate provision sources of revenue that do not produce a profit, such as customer services, sales to employees, and carrying charges. The tenant should also require an adjustment to gross sales to allow for bad debts. Although landlords will generally demand the right to audit the tenant's books, the tenant should attempt to limit the frequency of such audits. Some commercial leases have a *kick-out clause,* which gives the tenant the right to leave if certain gross revenue goals are not met.

Anchor Tenants A primary concern of most tenants in shopping centers is the identity and longevity of anchor tenants. To protect its economic position, a tenant should strive to build concessions in the lease whereby the lease is terminated or rent is decreased if an anchor tenant leaves and a replacement anchor tenant is not readily found.

Business Hours For the convenience of customers in all stores in a shopping center, it is generally necessary for stores to maintain similar business hours. Retail leases therefore often require the tenant to maintain the same hours as most stores in the center. However, because not all businesses require the same hours, and the hours of operation of a business may fluctuate due to seasonal variations, a tenant should closely scrutinize any lease provisions concerning hours of operation.

Parking Tenants should seek commitments from the landlord regarding the availability and configuration of parking. The landlord may consider parking lots as spaces into which to expand. As protection against the loss of parking areas to expansion of the center, the tenant should attempt to negotiate a provision precluding the landlord from reducing the ratio of parking areas to leased space in the center below an agreed minimum. Alternatively, a tenant may be able to negotiate a nonrevocable, nonexclusive easement that provides that the ratio will remain constant if the landlord expands the center.

Landlords often seek to regulate the areas in which employees of tenants are allowed to park. The tenant will want some assurance that any designated employee parking areas will be within a specified distance of its premises and in a safe location.

Exclusivity Clauses An *exclusivity clause* limits or prevents the operation of a competing store in the shopping center. It can be both a positive and negative part of the retail lease. Such a clause may provide the tenant with protection against competition. However, competition among tenants is usually important to the viability of a shopping center—many shoppers are attracted to shopping centers because they are able to compare goods and services.

Other Considerations As with office leases, the ability of a tenant to assign and sublet the premises is important. The tenant will want to preserve flexibility, particularly in the event of a sale of its business. The landlord will want to control the use of the space to monitor the retail mix of the center.

Often the tenant will be required either to join a merchant's association, which charges tenants to establish and maintain an advertising fund, or to make payments to a general promotional fund.

Environmental concerns are also significant in retail leases. The existence of a paint store or a dry cleaner as a tenant can impose liability upon the landlord under federal and state environmental laws and regulations.

Industrial Leases

Industrial leases tend to have a three-year term with renewal options. They usually contemplate substantial capital improvements by the tenant in the form of plant and equipment. Industrial leases are almost always *triple net,* which means the tenants pay all taxes, insurance, and maintenance expenses. Additionally, because the industrial use tends to be very site-specific, assignments of industrial leases are usually allowed only upon the sale of a tenant's business, and subleasing is usually strictly prohibited.

One of the major considerations in industrial leasing is the financeability of the lease. Some industrial leases contain provisions that allow the tenant to obtain a leasehold mortgage or other security device to secure a lender's interest in the capital improvements that the tenant constructs on the leased premises.

Ground Leases

A *ground lease* is a very long-term lease, sometimes as long as 99 years. Ground leases are used when a landowner desires to obtain a steady return of income from undeveloped commercial property without the expense of improving or managing the property. Alternatively, a ground lease may be proposed by a tenant that does not wish to invest its own funds in the land but is willing to erect improvements for its own use and at its own risk.

The Internal Revenue Code has helped to increase the use of ground leases as an alternative to sales of real property. If the landowner has a low tax basis in the real property, it would incur a heavy capital gains tax if it were to sell, but not if it leased, the property. The lessee has tax advantages, too: both the rent paid to the lessor and the depreciation of the building erected by the lessee are deductible expenses.

 ## Government Regulation of Land Use

Land use is most heavily regulated at the local level. However, several states regulate at least some aspects of land use on a regional or statewide level. In Florida, the state has preempted the authority of local jurisdictions to regulate land use. The state determines what is permissible in part by deciding what is a sufficient infrastructure. Federal and state laws concerning environmental matters, such as air and water quality and the protection of wetlands and endangered species, can also affect the permitted uses of property.

The discussion that follows first outlines federal and state regulations, then explains general principles of local land-use regulation. Each state has its own scheme for land-use regulation at the local level. Local regulatory systems operating under a state's scheme may vary from city to city, although some states require more uniformity than others ("city" is used here to refer to both cities and counties, unless otherwise noted). The specific laws and regulations applicable in each state and local jurisdiction must be consulted in order to understand how land use in that local jurisdiction is regulated.

The National Environmental Policy Act

The National Environmental Policy Act (NEPA)[13] requires all federal agencies to preserve and enhance the environment so that "man and nature can exist in productive harmony, and fulfill the social, economic, and other requirements of present and future generations of Americans." To implement this goal, NEPA requires all

agencies of the federal government to consider the environmental consequences of their actions. In any proposal for legislation or other major federal action that may significantly affect the quality of the environment, the government must include an *environmental impact statement (EIS)*. The EIS considers (1) the environmental impact of the proposed action, (2) any adverse environmental effects that the proposed action would unavoidably have, (3) alternatives to the proposed action, (4) the relationship between the short-term uses of the environment and the maintenance and enhancement of long-term productivity, and (5) any irretrievable commitments of resources that the proposed action would involve.

EIS Requirement   Some federal actions are categorically exempt from the EIS requirement because they do not have any environmental impact. If the action is not categorically exempt, an *environmental assessment (EA)* is prepared, which identifies any significant impact on the environment. If the EA indicates that the action will not have significant impact on the environment, no EIS is prepared. If there may be significant impact, an EIS is required. In some cases, courts have determined that an EIS may not be required when the agency proposing the action performs an environmental review substantially equivalent to an EIS. Some environmental statutes expressly state that decisions made in accordance with the statute are not subject to the EIS requirement.

State Law Counterparts   Most states have adopted environmental quality laws similar to NEPA, which require state and local agencies to consider the environmental impact of their decisions. The procedures followed are similar to federal procedures but vary from state to state. NEPA and its state law counterparts are enforced mainly through litigation by persons who wish to challenge a government agency decision. NEPA and state law complaints have been used extensively by groups opposing real estate developments and federal leases of public lands for private use. Such litigation can delay projects for many years.

Planning   Planning for compliance with NEPA or its state law counterparts is an important part of planning for any business project that requires state or federal decisions, approvals, or permits. This means not only the preparation of an EIS, if required, but also planning the project to minimize adverse effects on the environment.

---

13. 42 U.S.C. §§ 4321 *et seq.* (1994).

The Police Power

The legal basis for land-use planning and regulation is the *police power,* that is, the inherent authority of a city or county to protect the health, safety, and welfare of its residents. The scope of the police power has been given wider and wider interpretation. Its exercise is no longer limited to addressing immediate threats to the public health and safety, such as fires or unsanitary conditions. The Supreme Court has stated:

> The concept of the public welfare is broad and inclusive. . . . The values it represents are spiritual as well as physical, aesthetic as well as monetary. It is within the power of the Legislature to determine that the community should be beautiful as well as healthy, spacious as well as clean, well-balanced as well as carefully patrolled.[14]

Under this broad reading of public welfare, regulations as varied as architectural review, rent control, limitations on condominium conversions, and restrictions on off-site advertising signs have all been upheld as being appropriate uses of a city's police power.

Limits   Although the range of activities a city can engage in is broad, there are limitations to the police power. A land-use regulation will be upheld if it is reasonably related to the public welfare, but the city may not act arbitrarily or capriciously in enacting or applying land-use regulations. In addition, regulations are sometimes challenged on the ground that they amount to a taking of the

INTERNATIONAL CONSIDERATION

Nation states have the right to expropriate or nationalize foreign property under the power of eminent domain. Western countries tend to consider expropriation or nationalization proper as long as (1) it is for a legitimate public purpose; (2) it does not discriminate against a particular class of foreigners; and (3) the state promptly pays fair compensation. Many Third World countries object to having to pay fair market value for expropriated property, citing, among other things, the history of European imperialism and colonialism.

property without just compensation, in violation of the Fifth Amendment to the U.S. Constitution (made applicable to the states by the Fourteenth Amendment). The U.S. Supreme Court has stated that a *regulatory taking* (sometimes referred to as *inverse condemnation*) has occurred if the regulation either (1) does not substantially advance legitimate state interests, or (2) denies the owner all economically viable use of its land.[15]

In the case that follows, the Supreme Court explored the question of what constitutes a taking requiring just compensation.

---

14. Berman v. Parker, 348 U.S. 26, 33 (1954).

15. Agins v. Tiburon, 447 U.S. 255, 260 (1980).

| **A CASE IN POINT** | **IN THE LANGUAGE OF THE COURT** |

CASE 17.4
PENN CENTRAL
TRANSPORTATION CO.
v. CITY OF NEW YORK
Supreme Court
of the United States
438 U.S. 104 (1978).

FACTS   New York City's Landmarks Preservation Law was enacted to protect historic landmarks and neighborhoods from alterations. Under the law, an 11-member landmark commission may designate a building or district a landmark. Once the designation is approved, the owner of the landmark is responsible for keeping it in good repair, and any exterior alterations require commission approval. The Grand Central Terminal in midtown Manhattan, New York City, was designated such a landmark site.

Penn Central (owners of the terminal) and UGP Properties entered into an agreement whereby UGP was to construct and lease out a 50-story office building over Grand Central Terminal. UGP would pay Penn Central $1 million per year during construction and then at least $3 million per year for an estimated period of at least 25

Case 17.4 continues

Case 17.4 continued

years. Penn Central submitted an application for the construction of the 50-story office building over the terminal that met all local zoning requirements, but was subsequently denied permission by the landmark commission. However, Penn Central was granted permission to transfer the right to build a tall building to other parcels in the vicinity.

Penn Central sued the City of New York, claiming that the application of the Landmarks Law had deprived it of its property without just compensation. The trial court granted an injunction, and the New York Court of Appeals reversed, concluding that no taking was involved. Penn Central appealed.

ISSUE PRESENTED   May a city, as part of a comprehensive program to preserve historic landmarks and districts, place restrictions on the development of individual landmarks without effecting a "taking" requiring "just compensation"?

OPINION   BRENNAN, J., writing for the U.S. Supreme Court:

Over the past 50 years, all 50 states and over 500 municipalities have enacted laws to encourage or require the preservation of buildings and areas with historic or aesthetic importance. These nationwide legislative efforts have been precipitated by two concerns. The first is recognition that, in recent years, large numbers of historic structures, landmarks, and areas have been destroyed without adequate consideration of either the values represented therein or the possibility of preserving the destroyed properties for use in economically productive ways.

The second is a widely shared belief that structures with special historic, cultural, or architectural significance enhance the quality of life for all. Not only do these buildings and their workmanship represent the lessons of the past and embody precious features of our heritage, they serve as examples of quality for today. . . . New York City, responding to similar concerns and acting pursuant to a New York State Enabling Act, adopted its Landmarks Preservation Law in 1965. The city acted from the conviction that "the standing of [New York City] as a world-wide tourist center and world capital of business, culture and government" would be threatened if legislation were not enacted to protect historic landmarks. . . .

. . . While the law does place special restrictions on landmark properties as a necessary feature to the attainment of its larger objectives, the major theme of the law is to ensure the owners of any such properties both a "reasonable return" on their investments and maximum latitude to use their parcels for purposes not inconsistent with the preservation goals.

. . .

. . . The Terminal . . . is one of New York City's most famous buildings. Opened in 1913, it is regarded not only as providing an ingenious engineering solution to the problems presented by urban railroad stations, but also as a magnificent example of the French beaux-arts style. . . .

. . .

. . . Stated baldly, appellants' position appears to be that the only means of ensuring that selected owners are not singled out to endure financial hardship for no reason is to hold that any restriction imposed on individual landmarks pursuant to the New

Case 17.4 continues

Case 17.4 continued

York City scheme is a "taking" requiring the payment of "just compensation." Agreement with this argument would, of course, invalidate not just New York City's law, but all comparable landmark legislation in the Nation. We find no merit in it.

. . .

In any event, appellants' repeated suggestions that they are solely burdened and unbenefited is [sic] factually inaccurate. This contention overlooks the fact that the New York City law applies to vast numbers of structures in the city in addition to the Terminal—all the structures contained in the 31 historic districts and over 400 individual landmarks, many of which are close to the Terminal. . . . [W]e cannot conclude that the owners of the Terminal have in no sense been benefited by the Landmarks Law. . . .

. . .

. . . We now must consider whether the interference with appellants' property is of such a magnitude that "there must be an exercise of eminent domain and compensation to sustain [it]." That inquiry may be narrowed to the question of the severity of the impact of the law on appellants' parcel, and its resolution in turn requires a careful assessment of the impact of the regulation on the Terminal site.

. . .

. . . Its designation as a landmark not only permits but contemplates that appellants may continue to use the property precisely as it has been used for the past 65 years: as a railroad terminal containing office space and concessions. So the law does not interfere with what must be regarded as Penn Central's primary expectation concerning the use of the parcel. More importantly, on this record, we must regard the New York City law as permitting Penn Central not only to profit from the Terminal but also to obtain a "reasonable return" on its investment. . . .

DISSENTING OPINION   REHNQUIST, J.:

Of the over one million buildings and structures in the city of New York, appellees have singled out 400 for designation as official landmarks. The owner of a building might initially be pleased that his property has been chosen by a distinguished committee of architects, historians, and city planners for such a singular distinction. But he may well discover, as appellant Penn Central Transportation Co. did here, that the landmark designation imposes upon him a substantial cost, with little or no offsetting benefit except for the honor of the designation. The question in this case is whether the cost associated with the city of New York's desire to preserve a limited number of "landmarks" within its borders must be borne by all of its taxpayers or whether it can instead be imposed entirely on the owners of the individual properties.

. . .

. . . If the cost of preserving Grand Central Terminal were spread evenly across the entire population of the city of New York, the burden per person would be in cents per year—a minor cost appellees would surely concede for the benefit accrued. Instead, however, appellees would impose the entire cost of several million dollars per year on Penn Central. But it is precisely this sort of discrimination that the Fifth Amendment prohibits.

Case 17.4 continues

Case 17.4 continued

RESULT   The Court affirmed the decision of the lower court. New York City could prevent Penn Central from building an office building above Grand Central Terminal without having to pay Penn Central anything for the restriction on development.

COMMENTS   The Court's decision in this case seemed particularly influenced by the fact the terminal owners were still making a substantial return from their property and that their principal use of the terminal was unaffected.

Questions

1. The landmark law requires the owner to pay for the costs of maintaining the landmark. What happens if the company cannot afford the necessary costs to maintain the property to the extent the law would require?

2. Suppose that a fire caused major damages to an historical landmark and substantial amounts of money would be required to restore the property to its original state. Could the owner be required to expend such funds? Could an owner be required to maintain an expensive insurance policy against the property to protect against such occurrences?

In a 1992 case,[16] the U.S. Supreme Court reviewed a lower court ruling in which a regulation had been found to deny a landowner all economically viable use of his land. In 1986, Lucas paid $975,000 for two residential lots on which he intended to build single-family homes. In 1988, the South Carolina legislature enacted the Beachfront Management Act, which effectively barred him from erecting any permanent structure on his parcels. Lucas sued, claiming that he was a victim of a taking without just compensation. The state trial court held that his land had been rendered economically useless. The South Carolina Supreme Court reversed the trial court's granting of $1.2 million in compensation, holding that if a regulation is designed to prevent harmful or noxious uses, no compensation is required. The U.S. Supreme Court ruled that the South Carolina Supreme Court erred in applying this test and remanded the case. The proper test, according to the U.S. Supreme Court in *Lucas,* is whether the land-use regulation permits results that could not have been achieved under state common law nuisance doctrine. If the regulation does no more than duplicate the result under nuisance law, no compensation is required. If, however, the regulation prohibits activity not prohibited by common law nuisance and denies an owner economically viable use of his

land, compensation may be required. The U.S. Supreme Court in *Lucas* said that in such cases the burden of proof is on the state to show that its regulation is not a taking.

Takings questions also arise when a regulatory agency imposes a condition that must be satisfied before a building permit or other land-use approval is granted. This is addressed later in this chapter as part of the discussion of regulatory schemes.

 Regulatory Schemes

The fundamental components of most land-use regulatory schemes are a general plan, a zoning ordinance, and a subdivision ordinance. Some jurisdictions also employ more specialized planning documents, often called specific plans or community plans, that function somewhere between the general plan and the zoning ordinances.

The General Plan

Many cities have a general development plan, known variously as the general plan, city plan, master plan, or comprehensive plan. (All such plans are referred to as the general plan in this chapter.) A *general plan* is a long-range planning document that addresses the physical development and redevelopment of a city. It is comprehensive in that it addresses the entire city and a wide range

---

16. Lucas v. South Carolina Coastal Council, 505 U.S. 1003 (1992).

ARIZONA VOTERS REJECT TAKINGS INITIATIVE

In November 1994, Arizona voters decided the fate of a controversial land-use initiative. Proposition 300 was a "takings" law, which would have required state and local governments to compensate landowners for any value their private property lost as a result of government land-use regulation. Proposition 300 marked the first time a state's voters had voted on a property-rights referendum. As a result, property rights groups viewed the measure as a pivotal battle, saying that its passage would encourage private property laws in other states and restrictions on federal environmental laws.

Environmental activists were outspent by Proposition 300 proponents two-to-one, but they were not without support. An *Arizona Republic* editorial opined that the proposition's "hard-to-define requirements sound more like ways to hamstring government agencies than to promote the general welfare." The state

Department of Transportation estimated that its cost to implement Proposition 300 would reach into the hundreds of millions of dollars. The Fish and Game Department predicted that the law would cost it $10 million a year—one quarter of its annual budget.

After an intense campaign, Proposition 300 was rejected by a three-to-two margin. Conservationists said the vote should send a message to lawmakers. "People still clearly support environmental health and safety, even in places like Arizona," said the Sierra Club's Southwest Coordinator. "If Arizona can figure it out, other places—including Washington, D.C.—can figure it out."

SOURCE   This discussion is drawn from *The Big November Win: Arizona's "Takings" Bill Went Down Hard*, 6 AMICUS J. 25 (1995).

---

of concerns, such as housing, natural resources, public facilities, transportation, and the permitted locations for various land uses. It includes goals, objectives, policies, and programs related to these concerns.

The practical effect of the general plan varies from state to state. In some states, a general plan is not required at all. In certain states, the general plan is strictly an advisory document that need not be adhered to when planning decisions are made. In other states, the plan functions as the "constitution" for development and, by law, planning decisions (such as zoning, subdivision approval, and road and sewer construction) must be consistent with it. When the general plan has this significance, anyone contemplating development of a specific piece of property should determine what the general plan says about the allowed uses for that property. If development of the type contemplated is not authorized by the general plan, a general plan amendment will be required. The general plan may also be amended to preclude a contemplated development.

The general plan may provide important information about the city's policies regarding growth, where

and when public services and facilities will be provided, and whether developers will be expected to provide or pay for needed infrastructure.

Authorization of a type of development in the general plan is not a guarantee that a specific development will be permitted. The development must also be authorized by the zoning ordinance, and other land-use approvals could be required.

Other Planning Documents

Some jurisdictions employ other planning documents in addition to the general plan. Called specific plans, special plans, community plans, area plans, and a number of other names, these plans usually encompass just a portion of the city's geographic area. They may focus on areas in particular need of planning, such as a downtown area slated for redevelopment, an environmentally sensitive area, a transportation corridor, or an area facing unusual development pressure. Typically, these plans are more detailed than the general plan.

Zoning

Zoning is the division of a city into districts and the application of specific land-use regulations in each district. Zoning regulations are divided into two classes: (1) regulations regarding the structural and architectural design of buildings (such as height or bulk limitations), and (2) regulations regarding the uses, such as commercial or residential, to which buildings within a particular district may be put. These types of regulations are employed both in traditional zoning systems and in more recently developed approaches to zoning.

Traditional Zoning   Traditional zoning separates different land uses. For example, residential areas are separate from commercial and industrial areas, and residential areas of varying densities are separate. This approach to zoning finds its roots in the earliest land-use regulations, which promoted health and safety by separating residences from certain types of manufacturing and service industries. Early zoning also protected property values by preventing apartments from being built near more desirable single-family dwellings.

Planned Unit Development   Although many cities still employ some form of traditional zoning, others have adopted different approaches. For example, under *planned unit development (PUD)* zoning, the land-use regulations for a given piece of property reflect the proposed development plans for that property. These plans may include a mixture of uses, such as residential, office, and retail commercial, which could not be accommodated under the separation of uses required by traditional zoning. Residential development may be clustered on a portion of the property, at densities that exceed what would be permitted under traditional zoning, but in such a manner that larger areas of open space are provided. Many feel that this more flexible approach to zoning allows greater creativity and shows greater sensitivity to environmental and aesthetic concerns.

Zoning Relief   Variances and conditional-use permits may create exceptions to a zoning ordinance. A *variance* allows a landowner to construct a structure or carry on an activity not otherwise permitted under the zoning regulations. It allows the property owner to use the property in a manner basically consistent with the established regulations, with such minor variations as are necessary to avoid inflicting a unique hardship on that property owner. In some states, variances may be granted to allow uses not authorized by the zoning regulations. In other states, variances are limited to sanctioning deviations from regulations governing physical standards, such as minimum lot size, the maximum number of square feet that may be developed, and off-street parking requirements.

A *conditional-use permit* allows uses that are not permitted as a matter of right under the zoning ordinance. The permit imposes conditions to ensure that the use will be appropriate for the particular situation.

Nonconforming Uses   A *nonconforming use* is an existing use that was originally lawful, but that does not comply with a later-enacted zoning ordinance. A zoning ordinance may not compel immediate discontinuance of a nonconforming use (unless it constitutes a public nuisance). A city can require that nonconforming uses be eliminated within a reasonable time or upon application for a building permit to modify the premises.

Subdivision

Frequently, development requires the division of land into separate parcels. This process is known as *subdivision*. It is a necessary step in residential development and often in industrial or commercial development.

The subdivision process allows the city to regulate new development and to limit harm, deterioration of water quality, soil erosion, and building in areas subject to earth movement. The subdivider may also be required to address, for example, the impact of the subdivision on views and other aesthetic concerns or on traffic circulation.

Subdivision approval frequently requires that the subdivider provide streets, utilities, sewers, drainage facilities, and other infrastructure to serve the subdivision. It may be required to dedicate land for parks, schools, libraries, and fire stations, and to pay impact fees to offset the increased burden on public facilities and services resulting from the subdivision. The conditions may include constructing on-site or off-site facilities, or paying fees for purposes as varied as acquiring parkland or providing day-care centers, public art, or low-income housing.

Conditions

Conditions to a land-use approval will be upheld if they are reasonably related to the burdens on the community created by the development being approved. Thus, if the development will result in an influx of residents or employees, a fee to fund traffic improvements made necessary by that influx will be upheld. The courts have described the legally required relationship between a condition to an approval and the impacts of the development being approved as a *nexus*. In the absence of the required nexus, the condition may be struck down, as in the case of *Nollan v. California Coastal Commission.*[17]

In 1982, James and Marilyn Nollan sought a permit from the California Coastal Commission to demolish their existing single-story beachfront house and replace it with a two-story, three-bedroom house approximately three times larger than the existing structure. Public beaches were located within one-half mile to the north and south of the Nollans' property. Finding that the new house would further obstruct the ocean view, increase private use of the beach, and establish a "psychological barrier" to access to the nearby public beaches, the commission approved the construction subject to the condition that the Nollans dedicate an easement for public access across the portion of their property lying between the high-water mark and a sea wall approximately 10 feet inland. The Nollans challenged this condition.

The U.S. Supreme Court, in a five-to-four decision, held that the dedication condition amounted to an unconstitutional taking. Citing its holdings in earlier takings cases, the Court stated that a land-use regulation, including a dedication condition, amounts to a taking if it can be shown that the regulation either (1) does not substantially advance a legitimate governmental interest, or (2) denies an owner economically viable use of his land. The Court found that the regulation failed on the first prong of this test: The condition

did not in fact further the governmental interest advanced as its justification.

The Supreme Court elaborated on the lack of connection, or nexus, between the identified impacts of the project and the easement condition. The Court concluded it was quite impossible to understand how a requirement that people already on the public beaches be able to walk across the Nollans' property reduced any obstacles to viewing the beach created by the new house. It was also impossible for the Court to understand how it lowered any "psychological barrier" to using the public beaches, or how it helped to remedy any additional congestion on them caused by construction of the Nollans' new house. The Court therefore found that the commission's imposition of the permit condition could not be treated as an exercise of its land-use power for any of these purposes.

The Supreme Court concluded that the condition was not a valid land-use regulation, but an "out-and-out plan of extortion." Although the Court recognized California's right to advance its programs and use its power of eminent domain for a "public purpose," the Court concluded by saying that if the government wanted an easement across the Nollans' property, "it must pay for it." The Supreme Court did indicate that a condition that protected the public's ability to see the beach and ocean despite the construction of the Nollans' new house—such as a height limitation, a ban on fences, or even a requirement that the Nollans provide a viewing area for the public—would probably be constitutional.

The following case addressed a question left open by the Supreme Court in *Nollan;* namely, what is the required degree of connection between the conditions imposed by a city and the projected impact of the proposed development.

17. 483 U.S. 825 (1987).

A CASE IN POINT | **SUMMARY**

CASE 17.5
DOLAN v.
CITY OF TIGARD
Supreme Court
of the United States
512 U.S. 374 (1994).

FACTS Florence Dolan, owner of a plumbing and electrical supplies store located on Main Street in the central business district in the city of Tigard, Oregon, applied to the city for a permit to redevelop the site. Her proposed plans called for nearly doubling the size of the store to 17,600 square feet and paving a 39-space parking lot. She also proposed building an additional structure on the site for complementary businesses and to provide more parking. The proposed expansion and intensified use were consistent with the city's zoning scheme in the central business district.

Case 17.5 continues

Case 17.5 continued

The City Planning Commission granted Dolan's permit application subject to certain conditions imposed by the city's Community Development Code (CDC). The CDC required that new developments facilitate a reduction of congestion in the central business district by dedication of land for pedestrian/bicycle pathways intended to encourage alternatives to automobile transportation for short trips. In addition, as part of a drainage plan designed to alleviate flooding that occurs along Fanno Creek, including areas near Dolan's property, the CDC required dedication of sufficient open land area for greenway adjoining and within the floodplain.

Applying the CDC, the City Planning Commission required that Dolan dedicate the portion of her property lying within the 100-year floodplain for improvement of a storm drainage system along Fanno Creek and that she dedicate an additional 15-foot strip of land adjacent to the floodplain as a pedestrian/bicycle pathway. The dedication required by the conditions encompassed approximately 7,000 square feet, or roughly 10% of the property.

Dolan challenged the city's dedication requirements, arguing that they constituted an uncompensated taking of her property under the Fifth Amendment, as applied to the states through the Fourteenth Amendment.

ISSUE PRESENTED   What relationship must exist between conditions to a land-use approval and the projected impact of a proposed development for the conditions not to constitute an unconstitutional taking of property?

SUMMARY OF OPINION   The U.S. Supreme Court, in a five-to-four decision, held that the city had failed to show that there was "rough proportionality" between the conditions imposed on Dolan's permit and the nature and extent of the proposed development's impact. Citing *Nollan*,[18] the Court stated that had the city simply required Dolan to dedicate a strip of land along Fanno Creek for public use, rather than conditioning the grant of a permit to redevelop her property on such a dedication, a taking would have occurred. The Court noted that the purpose of the Takings Clause is to prohibit the government from forcing some people alone to bear public burdens that, in all fairness and justice, should be borne by the public as a whole.

In evaluating Dolan's claims, the Court first determined whether the required "essential nexus" existed between the legitimate state interest and the permit condition exacted by the city. The Court found that the essential nexus was present. The prevention of flooding along Fanno Creek and the reduction of traffic congestion in the central business district qualify as legitimate public purposes. A nexus existed between preventing flooding along Fanno Creek and limiting development within the creek's 100-year floodplain. Dolan proposed to double the size of her retail store and to pave her now-gravel parking lot, thereby expanding the impervious surface on the property and thus increasing the amount of stormwater runoff into Fanno Creek. Similarly, the Court upheld the city's attempt to reduce traffic congestion by providing for alternate means of transportation for workers and shoppers by requiring a pedestrian/bicycle pathway.

Case 17.5 continues

---

18. Nollan v. California Coastal Comm'n., 483 U.S. 825 (1987).

Case 17.5 continued

The Court then considered whether the degree of exactions demanded by the city's permit conditions bore the required relationship to the projected impact of Dolan's proposed development. The Court created a test of "rough proportionality" to decide what constitutes a taking. Under this test, while no precise mathematical calculation is required, the city must make some sort of individualized determination that the required dedication is related both in nature and extent to the impact of the proposed development.

Applying this test to Dolan, the Court held that requiring her to create a public greenway, as compared with a private greenway, was not justified by the city's interest in flood control. Such an interest could be satisfied equally well by a private greenway, which would give Dolan control over the time at which the public entered the greenway.

With respect to the pedestrian/bicycle pathway, the Court acknowledged that the larger retail sales facility would increase traffic on the streets of the central business district by roughly 435 additional trips per day. The Court noted that dedications for streets, sidewalks, and other public ways are generally reasonable exactions to avoid excessive congestion for a proposed property use. But in this case, the Court found that the city had not met its burden of demonstrating that the additional number of vehicle and bicycle trips generated by Dolan's development reasonably relate to the city's requirement for dedication of the pedestrian/bicycle easement. The city had simply found that the creation of the pathway could offset some of the traffic demand and lessen the increase in traffic congestion, but the city failed to make an effort to quantify its findings in support of the dedication for the pedestrian/bicycle pathway beyond the conclusory statement that it could offset some of the traffic demand generated.

RESULT   The proposed exactions required by Dolan's permit constituted an unconstitutional condition in violation of the Fifth Amendment. The city failed to show rough proportionality, that is, that there had been an individualized determination that the required dedication was related both in nature and extent to the impact of Dolan's proposed development.

COMMENTS   In a joint dissent, Justices Stevens, Blackmun, and Ginsburg noted that this was "unquestionably an important case." They attacked the decision of the majority, both because it reversed a long-standing presumption that land-use regulation of commercial space is constitutional, and because it changed the burden in takings cases. These justices argued:

> If the government can demonstrate that the conditions it has imposed in a land-use permit are rational, impartial and conducive to filling the aims of a valid land-use plan, a strong presumption of validity should attach to these conditions. The burden of demonstrating that those conditions have unreasonably impaired the economic value of the proposed improvement belongs squarely on the shoulders of the party challenging the state action's constitutionality. That allocation of burdens has served us well in the past. The Court has stumbled badly today by reversing it.

Vested Development Rights

Until a developer obtains a *vested right*—that is, a fully guaranteed right—to develop a property, the regulations governing that property may be changed. In other words, a developer has no claim to the land-use regulations in effect when the property was acquired, when preliminary steps to development were taken, or at any other time prior to the vesting of the right to develop. A change in the land-use regulations prior to vesting may thus preclude a proposed development.

In some states, the right to develop vests when substantial work is done and substantial liabilities are incurred in reliance on a building permit. In other states, vesting is tied to obtaining the "last discretionary approval" required for development. States differ on what constitutes the last discretionary approval.

Early Vesting   Late vesting of the right to develop leaves a developer vulnerable to loss of time and money should the land-use regulations be changed prior to vesting. For this reason, mechanisms to allow early vesting are available in several states. One such mechanism is a development agreement, which is authorized in Arizona, California, Colorado, Florida, Hawaii, and Nevada. The development project is governed by the regulations in effect when the agreement is entered into and is immune from subsequent changes in the land-use regulations.

Environmental Assessment

Some states, before approving a development project, require a detailed evaluation of the effects of the project on the environment. The state may also require a discussion of alternatives to the proposed project and an identification of measures to mitigate adverse environmental effects.

 ## Physical Accessibility to Commercial Facilities

Under the Americans with Disabilities Act (ADA),[19] any new renovations or alterations to commercial facilities must be accessible to disabled persons, including those in wheelchairs. Commercial facilities are defined

---

19. 42 U.S.C. § 12101 *et seq.* (1994).

LIMITS ON LAND-USE REGULATION

1. Regulation must be reasonably related to the public welfare.
2. Regulation cannot deny the owner all economically viable use of its land.
3. Regulation must substantially advance legitimate state interests.
4. Conditions to a land-use approval must be reasonably related to the burdens on the community created by the development being approved (nexus).
5. There must be rough proportionality between the conditions imposed and the nature and extent of the proposed development's impact.

---

under the act as all structures except those intended for residential use. However, this accessibility rule applies only to the areas being renovated and requires compliance only to the extent feasible. New construction, on the other hand, is subject to more complex accessibility rules. In building new structures, architects and builders must comply with regulations established by the U.S. attorney general regarding accessibility. In general, new structures must be designed and constructed so that they are "readily accessible to and usable by individuals with disabilities," unless it is structurally impossible to do so. Violation of the physical-accessibility rules for renovations and new construction can result in a private lawsuit or action by the U.S. attorney general. Violators may be required to pay damages as well as civil penalties of up to $50,000 for a first violation and $100,000 for subsequent violations.

The ADA also requires minor physical changes to existing workplaces to accommodate disabled workers. For example, the ADA mandates removal of architectural barriers in existing stores, offices, and firms where the removal is "readily achievable." Modifications are readily achievable if they are easy to accomplish and can be done without significant expense. Readily achievable changes might include ramping of a few steps or lowering of a public telephone for wheelchair users, installation of grab bars in rest rooms, raised letters and numerals on elevator controls, and rearrangement of office furniture to provide increased accessibility.

Property Taxes and Proposition 13

In 1978, California voters staged what has been described as a "property tax revolt" when they approved Proposition 13. This statewide ballot initiative amended the California state constitution and limited the rate at which real property was taxed within the state and the rate at which real property assessments were increased. Proposition 13 raised questions of equity and fairness because two very similar pieces of property could have drastically different tax consequences depending on when the property was last transferred. Property was reassessed when it was sold, so the new buyer often paid substantially more property tax than the neighbor with a comparable house who had owned the property for a number of years. Nevertheless, in a 1992 case,[20] the U.S. Supreme Court upheld the constitutionality of the acquisition-value property-tax assessment scheme Proposition 13 created, rejecting arguments that it violated the Equal Protection Clause of the Fourteenth Amendment.

---

20. Nordlinger v. Hahn, 505 U.S. 1 (1992).

In *Nordlinger,* the Court had "no difficulty in ascertaining at least two rational or reasonable considerations . . . that justif[ied]" California's system, which often taxed neighbors (owning similar properties) at dramatically different rates. First, the Court felt California could have a legitimate interest in local neighborhood preservation, continuity, and stability. The state therefore legitimately could decide to structure its tax system to discourage rapid turnover in ownership of homes and businesses. Second, the Court determined that California legitimately could conclude that a new owner does not have the same reliance interest warranting protection against higher taxes as does an existing owner. As a result, the state could deny a new owner at the point of purchase the right to "lock in" to the same assessed value as is enjoyed by an existing owner of comparable property.

In a scathing dissent, Justice Stevens decried the fact that as a result of Proposition 13, California property owners who bought before enactment of Proposition 13 in 1978 (referred to by Justice Stevens as "the Squires") owned 44% of the owner-occupied residences, yet paid only 25% of the total taxes collected in 1989. He argued that the severe inequalities created by Proposition 13 were arbitrary and unreasonable and did not further a legitimate state interest.

THE RESPONSIBLE MANAGER
Buying and Using Real Estate

The typical manager who does not manage real estate full-time will probably find that there are more laws, administrative regulations, and governmental practices associated with real estate than with many other management activities. The manager will not always be able to rely on common sense in managing real estate, because the laws and administrative practices can impact real estate in surprising ways.

When acquiring real estate, the manager should (1) determine that the property is properly located for the company's operations; (2) determine whether the improvements, if already built, comply with applicable building codes and are suitable for the company; (3) determine whether the facility complies with physical accessibility regulations under the Americans with Disabilities Act; (4) determine that previous owners have fully complied with federal, state, and local environmental and hazardous-waste laws and that the company will not be liable under any of those laws; (5) decide whether the company should lease or buy the property; (6) decide, if the property is rental property, for how long and under what terms it should be leased; (7) decide, if the property is for sale, how best to negotiate the purchase contract and finance the purchase; and (8) keep senior executives and/or the board of directors informed about the manager's actions and decisions throughout the process.

The magnitude of the investment and the permanence of the acquisition render these decisions some of the most important that a manager will make. Although large corporations generally have a department for facilities management, smaller organizations do not. The manager will need to have access to responsible professionals, including knowledgeable commercial/industrial real estate brokers, attorneys who specialize in real estate, environmental consultants, and attorneys specializing in environmental law. If the company is acquiring bare land and building its own improvements, the manager will also need to have available expertise in planning and land use. With the heavy use of outside consultants comes the responsibility of managing the consultants and controlling the costs of the real estate operations.

Similar responsibilities accompany the occupancy of real estate. If a company occupies premises under a full-service lease, which requires the lessor to maintain the property, the tenant's responsibilities may be limited to seeing that the services provided are adequate. Most manufacturing companies, however, do not occupy leased premises on a full-service basis. This may mean that the management is responsible for continuing maintenance, repairs, and compliance with laws, including environmental laws. In any type of occupancy, management must always plan ahead so that the facilities

will continue to be adequate for present and future operations. It is often difficult to anticipate needs, and it is easy to overspend or, conversely, to fail to anticipate a new demand.

Finally, the manager is likely to find that he or she has less control than desired over real estate decisions. For example, building or other occupancy permits may need to be obtained from several agencies, such as building departments and fire departments. Those agencies may not be responsive to the urgent demands of a company, and the official involved may be given a great deal of discretion in both the timing and interpretation of the applicable laws. Delays beyond the company's control frequently try managers' patience and cause inconvenience and downtime. In either the acquisition or disposition phase, a manager would be well advised to allow considerable extra time for delay.

INSIDE STORY
ANOTHER PEBBLE ACROSS AN OCEAN OF RETREAT

As the saying goes, the whole is greater than the sum of its parts. This time-worn expression certainly applies to real estate, where local communities often attach sentimental value to land or a building. This sentimentality is frequently difficult to pinpoint, and its value can be distinctly separate from the property's fair market value. The foray by Japanese investors to acquire the famous Pebble Beach Golf Course in northern California is an excellent case in point.

Nestled along the breathtaking views of the famed 17-Mile Drive lies the exclusive town of Pebble Beach. In addition to its legendary seaside golf course, which has hosted the U.S. Open, this resort on the tip of the Monterey peninsula is known for picturesque

serenity. The rare stands of Monterey pines in the Del Monte Forest create a natural playground for the enormous population of deer, which often wander aimlessly across fairways to the chagrin of golfers. Along the coast, not far from the famed Lone Cypress, hundreds of sea lions have made a home of the rocks jutting from the Pacific Ocean. As they lazily soak up the sun and bark at each other, these docile creatures seem oblivious to the sea kayaks that drift slowly by. It is no wonder that residents of Pebble Beach have come to view their peaceful environment as nothing short of sacred.

Minoru Isutani, the owner of the real estate firm Cosmo World, failed to account for this community's ongoing romance with its

surroundings when he paid $841 million to buy the Pebble Beach resort from a partnership headed by oilman Marvin Davis in August 1990. To raise the funds necessary to buy Pebble Beach, Isutani sold a large block of membership certificates for his four Japanese golf courses to Itoman, the Osaka trading house made infamous in 1991 for its scandalous activities.[21] Soon after, reports trickled out in the Japanese and U.S. press that Isutani paid such a high price for the Pebble Beach resort because he hoped to sell private Pebble Beach club memberships and use the proceeds to pare down his hefty debt. The price to become a member at the famous course, which had always been open to the public, would not be cheap. Initial reports were that he expected to persuade golf-loving Japanese to pay as much as $740,000 per membership.[22]

However, the gamble proved to be disastrous. If Isutani had done his research, he might have realized that his plan to convert a relatively democratic establishment into a Japanese millionaire's club would prompt an outcry from the concerned citizens of Pebble Beach. Instead, Isutani went forward with the acquisition only to later abandon the membership scheme in the face of implacable local opposition. When this occurred, the Japanese investor was financially ruined, forced to abruptly sell the resort at nearly a $350-million loss.

The new owners—Japanese investors calling themselves the Lone Cypress Co. after the landmark tree along 17-Mile Drive—learned much from Isutani's failed attempt to sell expensive memberships. In addition to lavishing attention and millions of dollars on the Pebble Beach course and The Lodge at Pebble Beach, the owners did their best to display good citizenship by making generous donations to local charities and keeping officials and homeowners apprised of any developmental plans. The open communication contrasted sharply with the business style of golf course developer Isutani, whose bulldozer approach to land-use issues did not sit well with local government officials, residents, or the California Coastal Commission.[23] Despite ongoing rumors of its intention to sell the landmark property, the Lone Cypress Co. had, as of early 1998, held on to Pebble Beach for a successful six-year tenure.

Isutani's experience was merely symptomatic of what had become a trend of retreating Japanese investments.[24] Japanese investors became seriously interested in American real estate after the Western industrial powers reached an agreement in 1985 to lower the value of the dollar against the yen and European currencies. Although this accord was designed to reduce the U.S. trade deficit, it also made the purchase of U.S. property a much better bargain for those with foreign currency. Japan had accumulated huge supplies of capital through its large trade surpluses and needed to invest it somewhere. The U.S. property market was booming in the mid-1980s and even when investors paid a premium, as many did, the market value often quickly caught up.

Every week, it seemed, newspapers reported high-profile sales of famous American resorts, movie studios, sports teams, and landmarks. In Hawaii, Japanese agents negotiated purchases of hotels on Waikiki Beach and made offers on private homes in high-value residential neighborhoods. In 1989, Mitsubishi Estate Company attracted nationwide publicity in the United States by paying $846 million for a controlling interest in the firm that owned Rockefeller Center, the coveted Manhattan address that includes the famed Radio City Music Hall. Even cattle ranches were being sold to Japanese investors, who seemed to have endless supplies of money and optimism about the U.S. market.

To some Americans, the buying spree was a troubling sign that

Japan was "buying up" their country. The purchases brought home dramatically Japan's emergence as a potent force in the world economy. Real estate purchases became fodder for jokes on TV talk shows and commentary for Congress. In Tokyo, Japanese officials became concerned that the investments would put new strain on trans-Pacific trade relations and discouraged further purchases of so-called trophy buildings. When Chicago's Sears Tower, the world's tallest building, went on the market in 1989, the Japanese government was widely reported to have urged Japanese businesses to keep their distance.

Annual Japanese real estate investment in the United States peaked in 1988 at $16.7 billion. Then the American economy stumbled into recession, prodding a collapse in real estate prices. Investors who made their original real estate–backed purchases with cash faced a double-whammy. Besides declining property values, they were hit with severe currency exchange losses as they converted their dollar proceeds into yen. These factors, combined with an economic downturn in Japan and its weak stock market, caused Japanese investment to drop precipitously throughout the 1990s. By 1993, the Japanese were investing only $705 million in U.S. real property.

Indeed, this chain of events caused not just a reduction in buying, but a mass sell-off. Many Japanese investors put their U.S. properties back on the market for a substantial loss. For example, Mitsubishi lost more than $600 million on its investment in

Rockefeller Center. During 1994 and 1995 alone, the Japanese divested themselves of approximately $20 billion worth (or close to one quarter) of their total U.S. real estate holdings. Experts expect the rate of divestitures to accelerate further, with Japanese investors forecast to sell as much as $50 billion of U.S. real estate assets from 1996 to 2000. The spread of the economic "Asian flu" from Thailand and Korea to Japan in 1998 will force Japan to focus even more on internal affairs and strengthening countries in the region, leaving little cash available for buyouts of American firms, overseas facilities, and the high-profile real estate purchases that dominated the 1980s.

21. *Prosecutors to Probe Isutani's 55 Billion Golf Handicap: Aftermath of Pebble Beach Fiasco Leaves a Question of Fraud*, COMLINE DAILY NEWS TOKYO FIN. WIRE, Apr. 8, 1992.

22. Martha Groves, *New Pebble Beach Owners Are Playing Finesse Game*, LOS ANGELES TIMES, May 19, 1992, at D1.

23. *Id.*

24. This discussion draws upon the following sources: John Burgess, *Rush to Buy U.S. Property Slows to a Cautious Walk*, INT'L HERALD TRIB., June 22, 1992; Jerry Dubrowski, *Rapid Pullout: In an Accelerating Withdrawal, Japanese Triple U.S. Land Sales*, CHICAGO TRIB., Apr. 21, 1996, at K7; Loretta Kalb, *Japanese Fleeing U.S. Real Estate*, SACRAMENTO BEE, June 9, 1995, at F1; Arthur M. Louis, *Japanese Dump U.S. Properties*, SAN FRANCISCO CHRON., April 19, 1994, at D1; Ronald E. Yates, *Foreigners' Investment in U.S. Plunges*, CHICAGO TRIB., June 10, 1992, at C1; and *Japanese Cut Losses in U.S. Real Estate: Once-High-Priced Trophy Properties Are Being Sold as Market Rebounds*, CHICAGO TRIB., June 3, 1996, at A5.

KEY WORDS AND PHRASES

after-acquired title 613
anchor tenant 628
assignment 628
beneficiary 612
caveat emptor 617
commercial lease 627
community property 612
conditional use permit 636
constructive notice 614
conveyance 613
deed 613
deed of trust 625
development loans 626
dual agency 617
encumbrance 614
environmental assessment (EA) 630
environmental impact statement (EIS) 630
equity 626
escrow 614
escrow agent 614
exclusivity clause 629
fee simple 613
foreclosure 627
gap financing 626
general plan 634
good faith subsequent purchaser 614

grant deed 613
grantee 613
grantor 613
ground lease 629
innocent landowner defense 620
interim financing 626
inverse condemnation 631
joint tenancy 611
kicker 626
kick-out clause 629
letter of intent 624
marketable title 630
mortgage 625
nexus 637
nonconforming use 636
option contract 624
planned unit development (PUD) 636
points 625
police power 631
prepayment penalty 625
prime rate 625
pure notice statutes 614
quitclaim deed 613
race-notice statutes 614
race statutes 614
real estate investment trust (REIT) 622

recordable form 613
recording statutes 614
regulatory taking 631
right of first negotiation 624
right of first refusal 624
rights of redemption 627
sale and leaseback 622
separate property 612
squatter's rights 623
subdivision 636
sublease 628
take-out commitment 626
tax-deferred exchange 622
tenancy by the entirety 611
tenants in common 611
triple net lease 629
trust 612
trustee 612
usury laws 627
variance 636
vested right 640
view easement 645
warranty deed 613
work letter agreement 628
wraparound financing 626
zoning 636

QUESTIONS AND CASE PROBLEMS

1. Miller granted his neighbor a *view easement,* that is, an interest in Miller's property that entitled the neighbor to an unobstructed view. The easement was recorded. Miller later contracted to sell the property and disclosed the existence of the view easement to the buyer, Gazzo. A preliminary title report issued by Fidelity National Title Insurance Company failed to disclose the existence of the easement. Gazzo then requested that Fidelity investigate the possible existence of the easement. Fidelity assured Gazzo that the easement did not exist and maintained that, except for those items set forth in Fidelity's title report, Miller had free title. Miller executed a grant deed conveying the property to Gazzo.

Gazzo later found out that the easement had in fact been recorded, and he recovered $125,000 from Fidelity for the diminution of the property's value as a result of the easement. Gazzo assigned any claim that he had against Miller to Fidelity, and Fidelity sued Miller for breach of warranty. Fidelity claimed that by executing the grant deed Miller had implicitly warranted that title to the property was being conveyed free of any encumbrances. Does Miller's prior disclosure of a recorded encumbrance to Gazzo prevent Fidelity from relying on the warranty against encumbrances that is typically implied in a seller's grant deed? [*Fidelity National Title Ins. Co. v. Miller,* 264 Cal. Rptr. 17 (Cal. Ct. App. 1989)]

2. Ace owns Whiteacre, a 40-acre parcel of unimproved real estate on the outskirts of a burgeoning city in the state of Calvada. In June 1988, the legislature of Calvada approved the construction of a freeway adjacent to Whiteacre. Shortly after the completion of the freeway in 1995, Ace was approached by Greenhorn, who desired to construct an apartment building on Whiteacre. Greenhorn is a licensed general contractor previously employed by several large apartment building developers. Although Greenhorn could not arrange financing to purchase Whiteacre outright, he was able to negotiate a 60-year ground lease from Ace on the express condition that Greenhorn complete construction of the apartment building before July 1, 1997. The lease was duly executed by both Ace and Greenhorn, and a memorandum of the lease was legally recorded.

Greenhorn obtained a $10-million loan at 10% interest that was due and payable on or before July 1, 1997, from Construction Lender. To secure repayment of the construction loan, Greenhorn executed a leasehold mortgage in favor of Construction Lender and legally recorded it.

Concurrently with the funding of the construction loan, Greenhorn obtained a standby commitment from Permanent Lender to advance $10 million at 8% interest contingent on (1) the issuance of certificates of occupancy for 80% of the apartment building, and (2) the leasing of 60% of the total rentable space of the apartment building to tenants acceptable to Permanent Lender. Greenhorn contracted with various subcontractors for the construction of the apartment building. Certificates of occupancy for 80% of the apartment building were issued on or before May 31, 1997. Certificates of occupancy for the remaining units were not obtained until July 3, 1997. The leasing of units was hampered by the availability of apartments at a lower cost in competing complexes. As of May 31, 1997, Permanent Lender had approved leases for only 45% of the rentable space.

Fearful of defaulting on the construction loan, Greenhorn approached both Construction Lender and Permanent Lender and was successful in negotiating a letter of intent between Greenhorn, Construction Lender, and Permanent Lender, whereby it was agreed in principle that the term of the construction note would be extended to December 31, 1997, subject to approval by counsel for both Construction Lender and Permanent Lender. Upon the execution of the letter of intent, the officer of Construction Lender negotiating it exclaimed that he was glad that an agreement had been reached to extend the construction loan. The officer representing Permanent Lender replied that he should receive a memento to mark the importance of the occasion.

Subsequently, the prime interest rate rose from 8% to 13% in a two-month period, the lending policies of Permanent Lender were scrutinized by the federal regulatory authorities, and its reserve requirements were substantially increased. Permanent Lender, unbeknownst to Greenhorn and Construction Lender, was not in a position to fund the permanent loan because of its increased reserve requirements.

Prior to December 31, 1997, Greenhorn submitted executed leases to Permanent Lender sufficient to meet the 60% lease contingency. The financial condition of the tenants who signed these leases was equal to or greater than that of the tenants previously approved by Permanent Lender. Recognizing the tight position that it was in, Permanent Lender's attorneys uncovered an ancient deed restriction that precluded the sale or lease of Whiteacre or any portion thereof to any person of Chinese descent and refused to approve several leases to individuals with Chinese surnames. Thus, Greenhorn was unable to fulfill the 60% lease contingency prior to December 31, 1997, and Permanent Lender refused to fund the permanent loan.

On January 5, 1998, Construction Lender sent a notice of default to Greenhorn and announced its intent to foreclose the leasehold mortgage.

What are the legal rights and obligations of Ace, Greenhorn, Construction Lender, and Permanent Lender?

3. The Rocking K Ranch is located in state X, which utilizes a race–notice recording system. Although the ranch had been operated for many years by Abel, record title was actually held by Abel's reclusive uncle, Meier. After a number of years of unexpectedly low cattle prices, Abel encountered severe cash flow difficulties. In an attempt to solve his financial problems, Abel entered into the following transactions:

a. On January 1, 1998, Abel sold the ranch to Baker for $250,000. Abel delivered a duly executed and acknowledged grant deed to Baker, but the grant deed was not recorded by Baker until September 2, 1998.

b. On February 1, 1998, Abel leased the ranch to his neighbor, Carter, for a period of five years. Carter immediately removed the fences surrounding the Rocking K and operated both his ranch and the Rocking K as a single outfit.

c. On February 26, 1998, Abel sold the ranch to Dalton for $250,000, delivering a duly executed and acknowledged quitclaim deed to Dalton. The quitclaim deed was duly recorded by Dalton on March 5, 1998.

d. Meier died on March 10, 1998. Under the terms of Meier's will, Abel inherited the ranch. A grant deed (the Meier deed) was delivered to Abel by the executor of Meier's estate on August 10, 1998.

e. On August 25, 1998, with the Meier deed in his back pocket, Abel approached his other neighbor, Everready, offering to sell the ranch to Everready for $240,000. Everready was reluctant to purchase it because he knew that Carter had recently been operating the Rocking K. After talking with Carter and determining that Carter's only interest in the ranch was a leasehold interest, Everready agreed to purchase the ranch from Abel for $220,000. At the consummation of the sale Everready received the Meier deed and a grant deed executed by Abel in favor of Everready. On September 3, 1998, Everready first recorded the Meier deed and then recorded the grant deed executed by Abel.

As of September 4, 1998, who is the lawful owner of the Rocking K Ranch?

4. Patricia and Bobby Star were married in New Mexico in July 1992. They had been living together since 1989. In July 1998, they separated. They had purchased a residence as joint tenants in April 1991. Bobby made the down payment from his separate funds. The mortgage payments were made out of commingled funds before and after marriage.

In August 1993, Patricia founded BioGene Corporation, a biotechnology firm, with $20,000 that she received as an inheritance from her grandmother. All of the stock of BioGene was issued in Patricia's name, and Patricia worked full time for BioGene. Bobby retained his job with another employer and was not involved in the operations of BioGene. Due to limited financial resources, Patricia did not draw a salary from BioGene until August 1998. In September 1998, BioGene's first product was approved by the FDA. Shortly thereafter, Patricia sold all of her BioGene stock to a large pharmaceutical concern for $30 million. Two days after the sale of the stock, Patricia filed for dissolution of the marriage.

You are the judge in the Family Law Court. Is the residence that Patricia and Bobby acquired community property or property held in joint tenancy? Would it matter if after marriage they had written a document stating that they wanted to hold the property as community property? In joint tenancy? Does Bobby have any interest in the proceeds from the sale of the BioGene stock?

5. David Ross and Chuck McCabe entered into a purchase contract whereby Ross agreed to purchase a 10-acre parcel from McCabe for $3 million. Under the terms of the purchase contract, Ross deposited the purchase contract and $100,000 into an escrow account with Title Company. The purchase contract also provided that the closing was to occur on or before December 31, 1997, and that if McCabe desired to enter into a tax-free exchange, Ross would cooperate in facilitating the exchange at no cost to Ross.

After discussing the transaction with a real estate attorney, McCabe determined that it would be to his advantage to structure the transaction as a three-party exchange. On June 12, 1997, McCabe and Ross entered into a letter of intent outlining the proposed terms of the exchange as follows:

a. McCabe would attempt to locate an exchange property with a purchase price greater than $2,900,000 on or before September 30, 1997.

b. Ross would purchase the exchange property through a separate escrow and would exchange that property with McCabe. McCabe further agreed to reimburse Ross to the extent that the purchase price of the exchange property was greater than $2,900,000.

c. If McCabe did not locate an exchange property on or before September 30, 1997, the purchase price of the 10-acre parcel would be paid by Ross's deposit of the following into escrow: (1) a certified check in the amount of $500,000; (2) a duly executed promissory note in the amount of $2,400,000; and (3) a deed of trust on the 10-acre parcel in favor of McCabe, securing the payment of the $2,400,000 promissory note.

A formal addendum to the purchase contract, incorporating the terms of the letter of intent, was drafted by McCabe's attorney but never executed by either party.

On September 15, 1997, Ross delivered escrow instructions to Title Company, incorporating the purchase contract by reference but making no mention of the letter of intent or the addendum. The escrow instructions stated that the purchase price was to be paid by Ross's $100,000 deposit, his delivery of a certified check in the amount of $500,000 and his execution of a $2,400,000 promissory note secured by a deed of trust on the 10-acre parcel. The escrow instructions also fixed the closing date as December 14, 1997.

On September 29, 1997, McCabe called Ross and told him that he had not been able to select a suitable property for the exchange. He requested that David extend McCabe's period for locating an exchange property

by 10 days. Ross agreed to extend it, but the parties never executed a written agreement to that effect. On October 5, 1997, McCabe located an exchange property. In a letter delivered to Ross on October 6, 1997, McCabe demanded that Ross purchase the exchange property and consummate the three-party exchange in accordance with the terms of the letter of intent.

On December 14, 1997, Ross deposited the certified check, the promissory note, and the deed of trust into escrow and demanded that Title Company close the transaction in accordance with the terms set forth in the purchase contract. Later on the same day, McCabe delivered a letter signed by him demanding that Title Company cancel the escrow.

What are the respective rights and obligations of Ross, McCabe, and Title Company?

6. Developer purchased a 400-acre, unimproved parcel of real property located in Altair City. Developer proposes to construct 450 single-family residences on the parcel. Altair City is concerned that construction of 450 single-family residences will overburden Altair City's streets. Which of the following conditions imposed by Altair City for the issuance of a building permit to Developer would be likely to constitute a taking under the Fifth Amendment to the U.S. Constitution?

a. Altair City requires Developer to dedicate 50 of the 400 acres for use as city parks.

b. Altair City imposes a $2.00 per square foot assessment on each single-family unit constructed by Developer. The fees collected from the assessment accrue to the city's general fund and may or may not be used to finance public transportation projects.

c. Altair City requires Developer to dedicate 10 acres of the parcel that abut a major thoroughfare for the construction of a park-and-ride lot.

Would a two-year delay in the grant of a construction permit, occasioned by the coastal commission's erroneous belief that a lot-line adjustment procured by the prior owner was illegal, constitute a regulatory taking? [*First Lutheran Church v. Los Angeles County*, 482 U.S. 304 (1987); *Landgate Inc. v. California Coastal Comm'n*, 953 P.2d 1188 (Cal. 1998)]

7. William and Jean Hall own and operate a mobile home park in Santa Barbara, California. They provide plots of land on which to install mobile homes. The tenants pay rent for the use of the land and the facilities.

The Halls bought the park in 1984. In 1998, the city enacted a rent control ordinance applicable to mobile home parks. The ordinance required park operators to offer their tenants leases of unlimited duration. The leases must also let the tenant terminate at will, whereas the operator can only terminate for cause as narrowly defined by the ordinance. Rent increases are strictly limited by the ordinance.

The Halls consult you, their attorney, about the ordinance. They want to know what they can do about it. What will you tell them? Does it matter that shortly after the ordinance was enacted the resale price of these homes shot up dramatically? [*Hall v. City of Santa Barbara*, 833 F.2d 1270 (9th Cir. 1986)]

8. Lucy Dunworth, developer of a shopping mall, entered into an easement and operating agreement with three major department stores. One of the covenants in the agreement was that each occupant promised to operate its store area as a first-class department store under its trade name for a 20-year period. The occupants each purchased their commercial space in fee (that is, they actually purchased the land) from the developer. Kaufman–Straus Co., one of the tenants, sold its place to a discount store two years later. The other two first-class department stores bring an action against the discount store because it is not a first-class operation. What is the result? [*Net Realty Holding Trust v. Franconia Properties, Inc.*, 544 F. Supp. 759 (E.D. Va. 1982)]

9. In December 1992, Innovative Health Systems, Inc. (IHS), an outpatient drug- and alcohol-rehabilitation treatment center, decided that its program should move from its current facility to a building located in downtown White Plains, New York. The new site was more than five times as large as the current site and was closer to a bus line and to other service providers that IHS clients frequently visited. IHS planned to expand the services it offered at the new site to include a program for children of chemically dependent persons. Therefore, IHS predicted an increase in the number of clients it would serve.

In December 1992, the deputy commissioner of building for the city of White Plains informed IHS that its proposed use of the downtown site—counseling offices with no physicians on staff for physical examinations or dispensing of medication—qualified as a business or professional office under White Plains' zoning ordinance and thus would be permissible in the zoning district. In January 1994, IHS signed a lease for the new space.

In April 1994, IHS filed an application with the White Plains Department of Building for a building permit. Because the application requested a change of use from "retail" to "office," the building commissioner referred it to the planning board for approval as required by the local zoning ordinance, with a recommendation that the application be approved.

The application provoked tremendous opposition from the surrounding community, including residents who lived in the remainder of the downtown building in which IHS sought to relocate and the owner of a shopping mall located near the proposed IHS site. The opponents expressed their concern about the condition and appearance of people who attend alcohol- and drug-dependence treatment programs and the effect such a program would have on property values. At regulatory hearings, opponents repeatedly referred to IHS clientele as "undesirable elements" who pose a real security risk. In a follow-up letter to the zoning board, a local resident stated his belief that even if IHS clients were middle-class—which he questioned—they still could "exhibit the erratic, antisocial and sometimes illegal behavior we associate with an impecunious backslider."

On July 5, 1995, the White Plains zoning board of appeals voted four-to-one to reject IHS's application for a building permit. The board did not issue a written resolution, as required by the zoning ordinance, but rather stated on the record that, based on its understanding of the services IHS provides, it was better classified as a clinic than an office. Absent in their discussion, however, was any reference to the zoning ordinance or the building commissioner's prior interpretation—which classified IHS's operations as an office and recommended granting the permit.

IHS sued the city of White Plains and its zoning board, claiming disability-discrimination prohibited by the Americans with Disabilities Act. Does it have a valid claim? [*Innovative Health Systems, Inc. v. White Plains*, 117 F.3d 37 (2d Cir. 1997)]

MANAGER'S DILEMMA

10. Prior to acquisition by the United States, landowners in the Hawaiian Islands developed an extensive feudal land-ownership system that has proved remarkably resistant to change. Although Hawaiian leaders and American settlers have repeatedly attempted to divide the large Hawaiian land estates, the results have generally been unsuccessful. As of the late 1980s, the 18 largest landowners in the state owned 40% of the available land. The 72 largest landowners owned 47%. With the federal and state governments owning 49% of the land in the state, little was left for the rest of the population. As might be expected in an area of desirable real estate with little land for sale, the price of owning land in Hawaii has grown exponentially over the past several decades.

The large private landowners have adopted a pattern of leasing their land for long terms rather than selling it. Often the land is leased to a developer who builds condominiums on the property. The condominiums are then sold subject to the ground lease. Sometimes the landowners themselves build and sell the condominiums, subject to a ground lease. The leases, commonly for 55 years or longer, require a substantial initial payment and lease payments for 25 to 30 years at a fixed rate. At the end of the initial term, the rent is renegotiated pursuant to the terms of the lease. In almost all cases, the renegotiated rent substantially exceeds the initial fixed rate.

To break up this pattern of land ownership and control the escalating prices of housing, the city of Honolulu passed Ordinances 91-95 and 91-96 on December 18, 1991. Ordinance 91-95 provides a mechanism for converting leasehold interests in condominium units to fee interests, through the use of the city's condemnation power. Ordinance 91-96 is a rent-control measure that limits increases in ground rent due the owner of the land under the condominium units.

You have been retained by several Hawaiian landowners to review the ordinances and make a recommendation on how to proceed. What do you recommend? [*Richardson v. City and County of Honolulu*, 124 F.3d 1150 (9th Cir. 1997)]

INTERNET SOURCES

National Association of Realtors	http://nar.realtor.com
This site includes home listings and information.	http://www.realtor.com
The American Real Estate and Urban Economics Association site includes a biannual newsletter for professionals and academics interested in real estate and urban policy.	http://www.areuea.org
The National Association of Real Estate Investment Trusts site includes information regarding legal issues affecting real estate investment trusts.	http://www.nareit.com

CHAPTER 18

Antitrust

INTRODUCTION

Firms Pay Record Fines

In 1998, Ucar International was fined a record $110 million for rigging prices and squelching competition in the international market for graphite electrodes, an essential component in furnaces used to produce steel.[1] Two years earlier, the Justice Department fined Archer–Daniels–Midland (self-described "Supermarket to the World") $100 million for fixing prices in the markets for citric acid and lysine, a livestock-feed additive.[2] Both firms violated the *antitrust laws*, which prohibit monopolistic combinations of companies (*trusts*), and other unreasonable restraints on competition, such as price-fixing among competitors.

The basic principle of antitrust law is that the economy functions best when firms are free to compete vigorously with one another. A competitive economy allows the consumer to enjoy better goods at lower prices, or, as economists say, it maximizes consumer wealth. If, however, competition is decreased or eliminated by firms seeking jointly or independently to wield monopoly power, consumers suffer and the performance of the economy declines.

The antitrust statutes contain certain very general prohibitions on business conduct. These general prohibitions often have little content until courts apply them to the particular facts of a case. Thus, bright lines that clearly separate lawful from unlawful conduct are rare in this field. A business practice that harms competition in one market setting might not harm competition in another. The courts and agencies that enforce the antitrust laws must distinguish between the pernicious and the benign.

Chapter Overview

This chapter offers a general overview of the federal antitrust laws, pointing out which aspects are settled and which are not. It begins with a discussion of Sections 1 and 2 of the Sherman Act, then addresses the Clayton Act provisions relating to mergers and combinations. The chapter outlines the Robinson–Patman Act's prohibitions on price discrimination, and it concludes with a discussion of international application of the U.S. antitrust laws.

---

1. Gordon Fairclough, *Ucar to Pay Record Fine in Antitrust Case*, WALL ST. J., Apr. 8, 1998, at B15.

2. Bryan Gruley, *ADM's $100 Million Price-Fixing Fine Blows Lid off Usual Maximum Penalty*, WALL ST. J., Oct. 16, 1996, at A4.

Politics, History, and Economics

The first antitrust law, the Sherman Act, was passed by Congress in 1890 as fear of corporate power grew during the Progressive Era. It was part of a populist movement to combat the rise of powerful trusts in such basic industries as oil and steel. "You must heed [the voters'] appeal or be ready for the socialist, the communist, and the nihilist," Senator Sherman declared during the debate over his bill. The Sherman Act's general prohibitions have evolved over the past hundred years through judicial decisions. This rather ad hoc development of the law has led to some seemingly confused results. For example, business practices forbidden by the Sherman Act in the early twentieth century are often permissible in today's changed economic environment.

A century after the Sherman Act was passed, the United States finds itself in the midst of a world economy in which competition in many industries takes place on an international scale. Often the United States is no longer the dominant economic power. A new generation of academics, lawyers, and judges has challenged their predecessors' conclusions that certain business practices or market conditions are inherently anticompetitive. This school of thought, known as Law and Economics, concludes that market forces defeat most anticompetitive practices. It questions the efficacy of the government's regulation of commerce and markets, arguing that instead of promoting competition, attempts at regulation often increase the anticompetitive structure of the markets. Law and Economics scholars would ask skeptics to identify a single monopoly that harmed consumers and was sustained without the aid of government.

Even the antitrust enforcers have lost much of their zeal for interfering with the market out of principle or an antipathy for corporate power. Twenty years ago, Robert Pitofsky, now chairman of the Federal Trade Commission, wrote an appeal to the antitrust regulators that they not allow concerns for business efficiency to cloud their pursuit of antitrust's overriding political goal: no entity in a democracy should become too powerful. In 1997, Mr. Pitofsky noted that such political content remains a part of his calculus, but said that it would not dictate the decision of an individual case. "The economy really is dynamic," he observed. "Over time, if prices go up, there is a tendency for others to

enter." That same year, Joel Klein, head of the Antitrust Division of the Department of Justice, noted, "The single biggest mistake is to view this process from 30,000 feet. What we do depends on intense market analysis."[3]

As economics increasingly informs legal decisions and market-based arguments are made and refined, the evolution of antitrust law continues. To many, this evolutionary process is antitrust's greatest strength and the reason it has entered its second century.

Restraint of Trade: Section 1 of the Sherman Act

Section 1 of the Sherman Act provides that "[e]very contract, combination in the form of trust or otherwise, or conspiracy, in restraint of trade or commerce among the several States, or with foreign nations, is declared to be illegal."[4] On its face, Section 1 appears to prohibit all concerted activity that restrains trade. However, almost every business transaction, even a contract for the purchase of goods or services, restrains trade to a certain extent. A contract, for example, restrains the parties from doing things that would constitute a breach. Read literally, Section 1 would outlaw every type of business transaction.

In order to avoid an unworkable construction of the Sherman Act, the courts have concluded that Section 1 prohibits only those restraints of trade that unreasonably restrict competition. This chapter explores in some detail the circumstances under which conduct unreasonably restrains trade.

Enforcement

The Sherman Act is enforced in a number of ways. First, violations of Section 1 may be prosecuted as felonies. Corporations can be fined under the Sherman Act up to $10 million for each violation, and the fine can be increased under other statutes to twice the gain to the violators or twice the loss to the victims, whichever is greater. Individuals can be fined up to $350,000 for each violation, and imprisoned for up to three years.

---

3. Roger Lowenstein, *Antitrust Enforcers Drop the Ideology, Focus on Economics,* WALL ST. J., Feb. 27, 1997, at A1.

4. 15 U.S.C. § 1 (1997).

Second, the Justice Department may bring civil actions to enforce the Sherman Act. Third, private plaintiffs, sometimes called private attorneys general, are entitled to recover three times the damages they have sustained as a consequence of the Sherman Act violation. Finally, state attorneys general may bring civil actions for injuries sustained by residents of their respective states. In these *parens patriae actions*, treble damages may also be recovered. (In addition to the federal antitrust laws, there are state antitrust laws giving causes of action both to private persons and to state attorneys general.) Exhibit 18.1 shows the 18 largest criminal price-fixing fines levied.

 Violation of Section 1

In order for liability to attach under Section 1, a plaintiff must demonstrate (1) there is a contract, combination, or conspiracy among separate entities; (2) it unreasonably restrains trade; (3) it affects interstate or foreign commerce (this requirement is of little practical import, because the Supreme Court has interpreted interstate commerce as including virtually all commerce); and (4) it causes an antitrust injury.

A Contract, Combination, or Conspiracy

Section 1 does not prohibit unilateral activity in restraint of trade. Acting by itself, an individual or firm may take any action, no matter how anticompetitive, and not violate Section 1. (However, Section 2 of the Sherman Act, discussed later in this chapter, does prohibit some forms of unilateral conduct.)

This threshold requirement of concerted action is one of the most frequently litigated issues in antitrust cases. In 1984, the Supreme Court ruled that a parent corporation and its wholly owned subsidiary cannot "agree" within the concerted-action requirement of

EXHIBIT 18.1   The Top Criminal Price-Fixing Fines

COMPANY	PRODUCT	FINE($000,000)	YEAR
Ucar International	Graphite electrodes	110	1998
Archer–Daniels–Midland	Lysine	70	1996
Bayer AG	Citric acid	50	1997
Archer–Daniels–Midland	Citric acid	30	1996
Showa Denko KK	Graphite electrodes	29	1998
Dyno Nobel	Commercial explosives	15	1995
F. Hoffman LaRoche Ltd.	Citric acid	14	1997
Jungbunzlauer Int'l AG	Citric acid	11	1997
ICI Explosives USA	Commercial explosives	10	1995
Mrs. Baird's Bakeries	Bread and bread products	10	1995
Ajinomoto	Lysine	10	1996
Kyowa Hakko Kogyo	Lysine	10	1996
American Home Products	Agricultural chemicals	7.3	1997
Premdor	Residential doors	6	1994
Stanley Works	Architectural hinges	5	1993
Miles	Scouring pads	4.5	1993
Kanzaki Specialty Paper	Fax paper	4.5	1994
Comet Products	Plastic dinnerware	4.2	1994

SOURCE   Compiled from Bryan Gruley, *ADM's $100 Million Price-Fixing Fine Blows Lid Off Usual Maximum Penalty*, Wall St. J., Oct. 16, 1996, at A4; Gordon Fairclough, *Ucar to Pay Record Fine in Antitrust Case*, Wall St. J., Apr. 8, 1998, at B15; Scott Kilman, *Two Swiss Chemical Firms Will Plead Guilty, Pay Fines in Price-Fixing Case*, Wall St. J., Mar. 27, 1997, at B5; and *American Home Products Corp.: Unit Will Pay $7.3 Million in Price-Fixing Settlement*, Wall St. J., Jan. 31, 1997, at A12.

Section 1.[5] Whether sister corporations or corporations that are less than wholly owned can impermissibly agree remains an open issue.

Conspiracies, especially illegal conspiracies, are inherently secretive. Most price-fixers do not keep minutes of their meetings or send confirming letters. Consequently, requiring direct proof of a conspiracy would likely permit many undesirable activities to escape Section 1 liability. On the other hand, because unilateral behavior is not a violation, courts must be careful in relaxing the requirement that conspiracy be proven. Courts have struggled to develop mechanisms that allow lawsuits under Section 1 to go forward without direct proof of a conspiracy or agreement while ensuring that only the truly guilty are convicted.

One such mechanism is the distinction between horizontal and vertical agreements. *Horizontal agreements* are those between firms that directly compete with each other, such as retailers selling the same range of products. *Vertical agreements* are those between firms at different levels of production or distribution, such as a retailer and its supplier.

The judicial characterization of an agreement as horizontal or vertical has dramatic consequences. A horizontal agreement may be proved by *circumstantial evidence,* that is, evidence of the parties' actions from which an agreement may be inferred. A vertical agreement, on the other hand, can be proved only by direct evidence that there was an agreement or by circumstantial evidence that tends to exclude the possibility of independent action.

Proving a Horizontal Conspiracy Because an agreement among horizontal competitors, such as two automakers, almost invariably reduces interbrand competition, such agreements are generally disfavored under the antitrust laws. *Interbrand competition* is competition between companies producing the same type of product. For example, Ford Motor Co. and General Motors engage in interbrand competition for trucks and automobiles.

The classic definition of conspiracy, whether horizontal or vertical, focuses on whether the alleged conspirators had a meeting of the minds in a scheme that violates the law. The courts will not require evidence of an explicit agreement to violate the law. As the U.S. Court of Appeals for the Ninth Circuit has stated with respect to a horizontal conspiracy, a "knowing wink can mean more than words."[6]

Plaintiffs often attempt to infer a horizontal conspiracy from evidence of parallel behavior by ostensibly independent firms, for example, that they consistently set prices at the same levels and change prices at the same times. The problem with this type of evidence (particularly where a homogenous product or service is included) is that it is ambiguous as an indicator of anticompetitive behavior. Parallel pricing of similar products or services can result either from illegal price-fixing or from vigorous competition.

The Supreme Court addressed parallel behavior as an indicator of an illegal conspiracy in *Theatre Enterprises, Inc. v. Paramount Film Distributing Corp.,*[7] a horizontal-restraints case. The case involved a suburban Baltimore movie theater that sought to exhibit first-run films from major film distributors. All of the distributors refused the request and instead continued to distribute first-run films exclusively to downtown theaters. The issue was whether proof of conscious parallel business behavior, without more, supported an inference of conspiracy sufficient to prove a violation of Section 1 of the Sherman Act. The Supreme Court found no conspiracy in restraint of trade, because there was no agreement among the distributors to act in concert. Instead, the refusals were made by the distributors, individually, based on sound economic reasons and in response to the same market conditions.

To infer an agreement or conspiracy from parallel behavior, the courts have required that the plaintiff show additional facts or "plus factors." Under the *Theatre Enterprises* standard, parallel behavior that would appear to be contrary to the economic interest of the defendants, were they acting independently, would support an inference of conspiracy. On the other hand, if the defendants can produce reasonable business explanations for the behavior, as the movie distributors did in *Theatre Enterprises,* a court will not infer a conspiracy. Other circumstantial evidence of an agreement, such as a meeting between two defendants, may be a plus factor. Increasing prices and persistent profits despite a decline in demand for the good or service may also be plus factors.

5. Copperweld Corp. v. Independence Tube Corp., 467 U.S. 752 (1984).

6. Esco Corp. v. United States, 340 F.2d 1000, 1007 (9th Cir. 1965).

7. 346 U.S. 537 (1954).

Proving a Vertical Conspiracy   Vertical agreements, such as those between an automaker and its local dealers, may reduce *intrabrand competition,* that is, price competition between local dealers selling the same manufacturer's products. But they often enhance interbrand competition, that is, competition between dealers selling different manufacturers' products. It is in the best interests of both the automaker and its dealers to provide the most marketable product so as to receive the greatest possible share of available consumer dollars. Courts look more favorably on reductions in intrabrand than interbrand competition when there is vigorous interbrand competition that can prevent the reduction in intrabrand competition from harming consumers.

Since the mid-1980s, the courts have generally been unwilling to allow proof of vertical conspiracies by circumstantial evidence alone. The Supreme Court has held that firms in a vertical arrangement, unlike competitors, have many legitimate reasons to communicate with each other. Therefore, a plaintiff seeking to prove an unlawful conspiracy must introduce evidence that tends to exclude the possibility that the firms acted independently.[8] Evidence of action that could be either concerted or independent is insufficient to prove a Section 1 violation under this test. Since this case, few plaintiffs lacking direct evidence of a conspiracy have been successful in asserting a Section 1 claim based on a vertical restraint.

Unreasonable Restraint of Trade

There are two approaches to analyzing the reasonableness of a restraint: the *per se* rule and the rule of reason.

Per se Violations   *Per se analysis* condemns practices that are completely void of redeeming competitive rationales. This is appropriate when the practice always or almost always tends to restrict competition and decrease output. Once identified as *illegal per se,* a practice need not be examined further for its impact on the market or its procompetitive justifications. Indeed, the defendant will not be permitted to offer excuses or explanations to avoid liability.

Scholarship, which originated in the Law and Economics movement at the University of Chicago, has argued that very few practices are inherently anticompetitive. Because this scholarship has been accepted by

many courts, the number of truly *per se* violations of the antitrust laws has declined.

The Rule of Reason   If the plaintiff has not proven a *per se* violation, the activity will be evaluated under the *rule of reason.* The objective of this rule is to determine whether, on balance, the activity promotes or restrains competition. In making this determination, the court will consider the structure of the market as well as the defendant's action. The court will analyze the anticompetitive and procompetitive effects of the challenged practice. Activity that has a substantial net anticompetitive effect is deemed an unreasonable restraint of trade and hence is unlawful.

 ## Types of Horizontal Restraints

Unlawful horizontal restraints, that is, restraints between direct competitors, include price-fixing, market division, and some kinds of group boycotts. These have traditionally been treated as *per se* violations of Section 1 of the Sherman Act. Trade associations may also be found to be acting unlawfully under the rule of reason in some circumstances.

INTERNATIONAL CONSIDERATION

In October 1996, Archer–Daniels–Midland (ADM) was fined $100 million by the U.S. government for criminally fixing the price of lysine, a livestock-feed additive. The conspiracy involved agreements between ADM and at least three Asian firms: Kyowa Hakko Kogyo Co. Ltd. and Ajinomoto Co. of Japan, and Sewon Co. of South Korea. The government's case against ADM was helped by the cooperation of the Asian firms, who pled guilty earlier that year and accepted fines of $20 million. In turn, the corporate convictions gave the government leverage against three executives at the Asian firms who pled guilty for their individual roles in the scheme. In exchange for relatively light sentences—fines of no more than $75,000—they then assisted the Justice Department in its prosecution of executives at ADM.[a]

_____

a. *Asian Businessmen Enter Pleas in ADM Price-Fixing,* WALL ST. J, Jan. 15, 1997, at B2.

_____

8. Monsanto Co. v. Spray-Rite Serv. Corp., 465 U.S. 752 (1984).

Horizontal Price-Fixing

Horizontal price-fixing, such as an agreement between retailers to set a common price for a product, is the classic example of a *per se* violation of Section 1. *Horizontal price-fixing* agreements include (1) setting prices (including maximum prices); (2) setting the terms of sale, such as customer credit terms; (3) setting the quantity or quality of goods to be manufactured or made available for sale; or (4) rigging bids (agreements between or among competitors to rig contract bids).

The Justice Department views price-fixing as "hard crime," to be punished by jail sentences whenever possible, and many executives have been imprisoned for price-fixing. Indeed, under the Federal Sentencing Guidelines, some term of confinement is mandatory for individuals convicted of horizontal price-fixing, bid rigging, or market-allocation agreements; in most cases, first-time offenders serve a minimum six- to twelve-month jail sentence.

Multimillion-dollar fines against corporations convicted of price-fixing are the rule rather than the exception. But civil actions, in particular class actions (which inevitably follow criminal prosecutions), can have even more drastic financial consequences. Liability for antitrust damages is joint and several among all of the conspirators, so that each conspirator is potentially liable for treble damages for the losses caused by all of the defendants. In one series of cases involving price-fixing in the corrugated paper industry, the trial judge estimated the potential treble damages at more than $3.5 billion. Seven defendants settled for more than $24 million each, and ten more settled for between $5 and $20 million. One nonsettling defendant was tried and found liable for $800 million in treble damages but later settled for nearly $50 million while the case was on appeal.

Some products, such as sporting events, may require horizontal restraints in order to exist at all. Economists suggest that the sporting league comprising the different teams should be viewed as a single firm in the business of providing competition. Hence, constraints on teams are simply attempts to put "departments" within the firm on an equal footing so that customers can enjoy balanced contests among them. Courts, however, take a more formalistic view but make allowances for the needed horizontal constraints. As the following case concerning limits on college coaching salaries shows, the courts use a "quick look" rule of reason to examine such constraints.

A CASE IN POINT   **SUMMARY**

CASE 18.1
LAW v. NATIONAL COLLEGIATE ATHLETIC ASSOCIATION
United States Court of Appeals for the Tenth Circuit
134 F.3d 1010
(10th Cir. 1998).

FACTS The National Collegiate Athletic Association (NCAA) is an association of approximately 1,100 educational institutions that coordinates the intercollegiate athletic programs of its members. As part of that coordination, the NCAA adopts and promulgates playing rules, standards of amateurism, standards for academic eligibility, student-recruitment regulations, and rules governing the sizes of athletic squads and coaching staffs. The rules vary based on division status, which reflects differences in program size and scope.

Concerned with rapidly rising program costs at Division I schools in the 1980s, the NCAA promulgated new rules in 1991 to limit the number of basketball coaches at those schools to four—one head coach, two assistant coaches, and one entry-level coach. The new rules also restricted the annual salary of an entry-level coach to $16,000 but allowed these so-named restricted-earnings coaches (RECs) to receive additional compensation for performing duties in other departments of the institution.

A group of RECs from Division I schools for the 1992–93 academic year challenged the compensation limit as an illegal attempt to restrain trade under Section 1 of the Sherman Act. The NCAA argued that some horizontal restraints were necessary to provide its product, namely competition. Furthermore, it argued that these limits were reasonable and procompetitive. On a motion for summary judgment, the trial court ruled in favor of the RECs. Having found that the NCAA had violated the Sherman

Case 18.1 continues

Case 18.1 continued

Act, the court permanently enjoined it from enforcing any salary limitations against the plaintiffs and from reenacting the limits in another form. The NCAA appealed.

ISSUE PRESENTED   When horizontal restraints are necessary for the provision of a good or service, under what antitrust standard should such restraints be evaluated?

SUMMARY OF OPINION   The U.S. Court of Appeals began by noting that normally horizontal price-fixing is illegal *per se*. Some products, however, require horizontal restraints in order to exist at all. In 1984, the U.S. Supreme Court applied the rule of reason to review a NCAA plan for televising college football that involved both output limits and price-fixing.[9] As in that case, the product here is competition itself, which relies on horizontal constraints for its very existence. In such a case where horizontal agreements are so necessary, all such horizontal agreements must be evaluated under a rule of reason.

While under the rule of reason plaintiffs usually must show that a defendant has market power in order to prove substantial adverse effects on trade, no such proof is necessary when the very purpose and effect of the agreement is to fix prices. This "quick look" rule of reason is appropriate whenever the practice has obvious anticompetitive effects and allows for immediate inquiry into procompetitive justifications.

The NCAA offered three justifications. First, retention of entry-level coaches would allow younger, less experienced coaches entry into Division I schools. The court ruled that although perhaps socially laudable, such entry was not necessary to preserve competition in intercollegiate sports. Second, the NCAA argued that salary limits would allow schools to reduce costs, which would in turn allow them to maintain money-losing programs in low-profile sports. The NCAA did not, however, present any evidence that money saved on the salaries of basketball coaches would not simply be spent on other aspects of the basketball program. Third, the NCAA argued that the rules would keep wealthier schools from placing more experienced coaches in the restricted-earnings coaching slot, thereby skewing the needed balance of competition. The NCAA's evidence, however, simply showed that the cost reductions would be achieved without harming the existing competitive balance rather than achieving competitive balance. After this "quick look" rule of reason, the court concluded that there were no justifications for the restraints.

RESULT   The appeals court affirmed the trial court's grant of summary judgment and permanent injunction. The NCAA's salary restraints were unreasonable restraints on trade in violation of Section 1.

COMMENTS   By applying a "quick look" rule of reason standard, the court pointed out the multi-level nature of antitrust analysis. Under the *per se* rule, an act is illegal without regard to actual effects. Under the *"quick look" rule of reason*, adverse effects are taken for granted, and the court considers only the possible justifications. Under the rule of reason, the court studies both positive and negative effects on competition and weighs them against each other. Although a *per se* rule gives a manager more predictability, the rule of reason contemplates a complex and dynamic marketplace where reasonableness varies with the circumstance.

---

9. NCAA v. Board of Regents, 468 U.S. 85 (1984).

Horizontal Market Division

The Supreme Court considers market divisions so inherently anticompetitive as to constitute *per se* violations of Section 1. *Horizontal market division* can take various forms. For instance, competitors might divide up a market according to class of customer or geographic territory or restrict product output. In 1972, the U.S. Supreme Court considered the legality of an agreement to divide the grocery market by an association of supermarket chains.[10] The association's members, 25 small- and medium-sized independent supermarket chains, each agreed to sell a particular trademarked brand only in an assigned area. They also agreed not to sell the brand's products to other retailers. Although the association argued that exclusive territories were necessary to encourage local advertising of the fledgling brand, the Court ruled that market division is prohibited even if it is intended to enable small competitors to compete with larger companies and foster interbrand competition. More recently, the Supreme Court has emphasized that horizontal market division by potential as well as actual competitors is *per se* illegal.[11]

Group Boycotts

It is a fundamental principle of liberty and freedom of contract that an individual may choose to do business with whomever he or she wants. Nevertheless, an agreement among competitors to refuse to deal with another competitor—a *group boycott*—has traditionally been treated as a *per se* violation of Section 1. An agreement between or among competitors that deprives another competitor of something it needs to compete effectively is considered so inherently anticompetitive that no economic motivation for the action may be offered as a defense.

For example, the Supreme Court held that manufacturers of appliances could not agree with a distributor's competitors to refrain from selling to the distributor or to do so only at higher prices. Such an agreement was treated as a *per se* violation of Section 1 even if there was no agreement on the exact price, quantity, or quality of the appliances to be sold.[12]

More recently, the Supreme Court has begun to distinguish some forms of group boycotts that it believes are not so inherently anticompetitive as to merit *per se* treatment. For instance, in 1985, the Court found no Sherman Act violation when a purchasing cooperative of office-supply retailers expelled a member for violating a cooperative bylaw requiring notification of changes in ownership.[13] As a result, the remaining members would not transact business with the expellee, but it had alternative suppliers available to it. Although boycotts cutting off a competitor from necessary supplies justify *per se* treatment, some boycotts involving restraints and exclusions encourage competition and call for analysis under the rule of reason. Using such a rule of reason, the Court held that the cooperative had not violated the Sherman Act.

Trade Associations

Courts do not look favorably upon attempts at self-regulation by trade and professional associations, particularly when such attempts result in group boycotts. For example, an American Medical Association rule of ethics, which forbade salaried practice and prepaid medical care, was held to violate the Sherman Act.[14] In 1996, an association of 450 retailers of scuba and diving equipment was found liable for antitrust violations after it sought to prevent a discounting snorkel manufacturer from selling its products via mail order by threatening to publish a negative article about the manufacturer in the association's magazine and threatening a leading scuba magazine with boycott if it carried the mail order company's advertising.[15]

In 1997, the U.S. Court of Appeals for the Ninth Circuit struck down rules by the California Dental Association forbidding all advertising that referred to "low" or "reasonable" prices, offered volume discounts, or made any claims about quality of service.[16] Although the nonprofit trade association of dentists called its rules a code of ethics, the court characterized the rules as a "naked restraint" on price competition and the supply of information. Such restrictions are not illegal *per se*, as the FTC had argued, but instead are reviewed under the "quick look" rule of reason.

---

10. U.S. v. Topco Assocs., Inc., 405 U.S. 596 (1972).

11. Palmer v. BRG of Georgia, Inc. 498 U.S. 46 (1990).

12. Klor's, Inc. v. Broadway–Hale Stores, Inc., 359 U.S. 207 (1959).

13. Northwest Wholesale Stationers, Inc. v. Pacific Stationery & Printing Co., 472 U.S. 284 (1985).

14. American Medical Ass'n v. United States, 317 U.S. 519 (1943).

15. United States v. Scuba Retailers Ass'n, Inc., 1996 WL 335423 (S.D. Fla. 1996).

16. California Dental Ass'n v. FTC, 128 F.3d 720 (9th Cir. 1997).

Trade and professional associations often disseminate information among their members. The Sherman Act requires that the exchange of information be monitored to ensure that it does not facilitate anticompetitive behavior, such as price-fixing or market division. Association agreements rarely state goals that violate the Sherman Act, so courts must draw inferences about the probable effects of the information exchanged. The courts will look at the market structure and the type of information exchanged.

A large *cartel,* or group of competitors that agrees to do something, is inherently unstable. Conversely, the fewer the companies that must agree, the more likely they will agree and be able to enforce the agreement. Therefore, the more concentrated the industry, the more closely courts will scrutinize trade-association activity.

The type of information exchanged plays an even more critical role in the analysis. For example, a weekly report disseminated by a hardwood manufacturers' trade association listed the names of companies that sold lumber and the prices at which they sold it. Additionally, monthly reports discussed future price trends and provided future estimates of production. The Supreme Court held that this information violated Section 1 of the Sherman Act, as members could utilize the information to police secret agreements setting uniform prices or terms.[17] Another manufacturers' association disseminated information on average costs and the terms of past transactions. It did not identify individual sellers or buyers and did not discuss future pricing. The Supreme Court found no violation of Section 1.[18]

Information that does not involve prices or terms of sale receives less scrutiny by the courts. Activities such as cooperative industrial research, market surveys, and joint advertising concerning the industry have been upheld. The exchange of information concerning contractors whose payments were two months in arrears was upheld as a reasonable way to help members avoid contractor fraud.[19]

 Types of Vertical Restraints

Unlawful *vertical restraints,* that is, restraints between firms at different levels in the chain of distribution, include price-fixing, market division, tying arrangements, and some franchise agreements.

Vertical Price-Fixing

The Supreme Court has determined that agreements on price between firms at different levels of production or distribution can be as anticompetitive as agreements between direct competitors at the same level of production or distribution. Thus, for many years, vertical price-fixing (also known as *resale price maintenance (RPM)* when the agreement fixes minimum prices) had been held a *per se* violation of the Sherman Act. RPM agreements have been challenged by consumers claiming overcharges, by competitors claiming loss of sales, and by dealers or retailers terminated by the manufacturer for offering discounts from list or suggested prices. As discussed later in this chapter, a competitor cannot successfully bring an action challenging RPM unless it can show antitrust injury.

Resale price maintenance has been unlawful *per se* since 1911, when the Supreme Court held that an agreement between a drug manufacturer and its distributors setting both wholesale and retail prices violated Section 1 of the Sherman Act. Such restrictions impermissibly limited the freedom of choice of other drug distributors and retailers. As a result, society was deprived of the benefits that it would have received from unrestricted distribution of the drugs.[20]

Some academics and jurists have challenged the treatment of resale price maintenance as a *per se* violation. For example, Robert Bork, a noted legal scholar and Reagan Supreme Court nominee whose appointment was blocked by the Senate, argued that most vertical price restrictions do not limit competition among competitors or give them power to restrict output or to raise prices. Bork contended that vertical price restrictions ensure economic efficiencies and maximize consumer welfare by preventing price competition that forces retailers to cut back on nonprice items such as consumer service. In fact, Bork argued, the blanket prohibition of vertical price restrictions lessens consumer welfare by allowing discount retailers to free-ride on the services provided by other retailers.

Consumer electronics stores provide a classic example of the problem Bork describes. For example, suppose

---

17. American Column & Lumber Co. v. United States, 257 U.S. 377 (1921).

18. Maple Flooring Mfrs. Ass'n v. United States, 268 U.S. 563 (1925).

19. Cement Mfrs. Protective Ass'n v. United States, 268 U.S. 588 (1925).

20. Dr. Miles Medical Co. v. John D. Park & Sons Co., 220 U.S. 373 (1911).

Highbrow Home Theatre Centre provides its patrons with very sophisticated viewing and listening rooms and highly trained salespersons to assist in their selection of video players, receivers, and speakers. Three blocks away is Lou's Discount Appliances, which sells the same equipment at discount prices but does not provide viewing and listening rooms or knowledgeable salespersons. A consumer might spend hours at the Highbrow Home Theatre Centre listening and learning, then walk three blocks and buy the products from Lou's Discount Appliances. If this becomes a pattern, Highbrow will be forced to cut back its service in order to compete with Lou's prices. High-quality service will be eliminated as a consumer option.

The Supreme Court has so far rejected these arguments with regard to maintenance of minimum prices and retained the *per se* rule against vertical minimum price-fixing. It has, however, greatly increased the plaintiff's burden of proof by requiring evidence of an agreement on specific price levels. Many antitrust lawyers believe this change in the analysis has dealt a fatal blow to attempts by terminated discounters to invoke the *per se* rule in cases alleging resale price maintenance. Very few manufacturers are clumsy enough to insist that their dealers agree on specific minimum prices.

In the following case, the Supreme Court reconsidered the *per se* rule against the vertical fixing of maximum prices.

A CASE IN POINT | **IN THE LANGUAGE OF THE COURT**

CASE 18.2
STATE OIL CO. v. KHAN
Supreme Court
of the United States
118 S. Ct. 275 (1997).

FACTS Barkat U. Khan (Khan) entered into an agreement with State Oil Company (State Oil) to lease and operate a gas station and convenience store owned by State Oil. The agreement provided that Khan would purchase the station's gasoline from State Oil at a price equal to a suggested retail price set by State Oil, less a margin of 3.25 cents per gallon. Under the agreement, Khan could charge any price to his customers, but if the price charged was higher than State Oil's suggested retail price, the excess was to be rebated to State Oil. Similarly, if Khan sold gasoline for less than the suggested retail price, it would reduce his 3.25 cent margin.

A year after Khan began operating the station, he fell behind in his lease payments to State Oil, which then notified Khan of its intent to terminate the agreement due to his breach and to evict him from the station. Khan then sued State Oil, alleging that it had engaged in price-fixing in violation of the Sherman Act. The trial court held that Khan did not allege a *per se* violation of the antitrust law and did not demonstrate antitrust injury or harm to competition. The appeals court reversed, holding that the claim did allege a *per se* violation and that Khan could have suffered antitrust harm. State Oil appealed.

ISSUE PRESENTED Is vertical maximum price-fixing a *per se* violation of the Sherman Act?

OPINION O'CONNOR, J., writing for the U.S. Supreme Court:
Although the Sherman Act, by its terms, prohibits every agreement "in restraint of trade," this Court has long recognized that Congress intended to outlaw only unreasonable restraints. As a consequence, most antitrust claims are analyzed under a "rule of reason," according to which the finder of fact must decide whether the questioned practice imposes an unreasonable restraint on competition, taking into account a variety of factors, including specific information about the relevant business, its condition before and after the restraint was imposed, and the restraint's history, nature, and effect.

Case 18.2 continues

Case 18.2 continued

Some types of restraints, however, have such predictable and pernicious anticompetitive effect, and such limited potential for procompetitive benefit, that they are deemed unlawful *per se*. *Per se* treatment is appropriate "[o]nce experience with a particular kind of restraint enables the Court to predict with confidence that the rule of reason will condemn it." Thus, we have expressed reluctance to adopt *per se* rules with regard to "restraints imposed in the context of business relationships where the economic impact of certain practices is not immediately obvious."

[The Court then discussed in detail its previous decisions on the subject, including *Albrecht v. Herald Co.*,[21] in which the Court ruled that maximum vertical price-fixing was *per se* illegal.]

Thus, our reconsideration of *Albrecht*'s continuing validity is informed by several of our decisions, as well as a considerable body of scholarship discussing the effects of vertical restraints. Our analysis is also guided by our general view that the primary purpose of the antitrust laws is to protect interbrand competition. "Low prices," we have explained, "benefit consumers regardless of how those prices are set, and so long as they are above predatory levels, they do not threaten competition." Our interpretation of the Sherman Act also incorporates the notion that condemnation of practices resulting in lower prices to consumers is "especially costly" because "cutting prices in order to increase business often is the very essence of competition."

So informed, we find it difficult to maintain that vertically-imposed maximum prices could harm consumers or competition to the extent necessary to justify their *per se* invalidation.

. . .

We recognize that the *Albrecht* decision presented a number of theoretical justifications for a *per se* rule against vertical maximum price fixing. But criticism of those premises abounds. The *Albrecht* decision was grounded in the fear that maximum price fixing by suppliers could interfere with dealer freedom. In response, as one commentator has pointed out, "the ban on maximum resale price limitations declared in *Albrecht* in the name of 'dealer freedom' has actually prompted many suppliers to integrate forward into distribution, thus eliminating the very independent trader for whom *Albrecht* professed solicitude." For example, integration in the newspaper industry since *Albrecht* has given rise to litigation between independent distributors and publishers.

The *Albrecht* Court also expressed the concern that maximum prices may be set too low for dealers to offer consumers essential or desired services. But such conduct, by driving away customers, would seem likely to harm manufacturers as well as dealers and consumers, making it unlikely that a supplier would set such a price as a matter of business judgment. In addition, *Albrecht* noted that vertical maximum price-fixing could effectively channel distribution through large or specially-advantaged dealers. It is unclear, however, that a supplier would profit from limiting its market by excluding potential dealers. Further, although vertical maximum price-fixing

Case 18.2 continues

---

21. 390 U.S. 145 (1968).

Case 18.2 continued

might limit the viability of inefficient dealers, that consequence is not necessarily harmful to competition and consumers.

. . .

Not only are the potential injuries cited in *Albrecht* less serious than the Court imagined, the *per se* rule established therein could in fact exacerbate problems related to the unrestrained exercise of market power by monopolist-dealers. Indeed, both courts and antitrust scholars have noted that *Albrecht*'s rule may actually harm consumers and manufacturers. Other commentators have also explained that *Albrecht*'s *per se* rule has even more potential for deleterious effect on competition after [another decision of this Court] because, now that vertical nonprice restrictions are not unlawful *per se*, the likelihood of dealer monopoly power is increased. . . .

After reconsidering *Albrecht*'s rationale and the substantial criticism the decision has received, however, we conclude that there is insufficient economic justification for *per se* invalidation of vertical maximum price fixing. That is so not only because it is difficult to accept the assumptions underlying *Albrecht*, but also because *Albrecht* has little or no relevance to ongoing enforcement of the Sherman Act. Moreover, neither the parties nor any of the *amici curiae* have called our attention to any cases in which enforcement efforts have been directed solely against the conduct encompassed by *Albrecht*'s *per se* rule.

Respondents argue that reconsideration of *Albrecht* should require "persuasive, expert testimony establishing that the *per se* rule has distorted the market." Their reasoning ignores the fact that *Albrecht* itself relied solely upon hypothetical effects of vertical maximum price fixing. Further, *Albrecht*'s dire predictions have not been borne out, even though manufacturers and suppliers appear to have fashioned schemes to get around the *per se* rule against vertical maximum price fixing. In these circumstances, it is the retention of the rule of *Albrecht*, and not, as respondents would have it, the rule's elimination, that lacks adequate justification.

. . . For the reasons we have noted, however, the remedy for respondents' dispute with State Oil should not come in the form of a *per se* rule affecting the conduct of the entire marketplace.

. . .

Although we do not "lightly assume that the economic realities underlying earlier decisions have changed, or that earlier judicial perceptions of those realities were in error," we have noted that "different sorts of agreements" may amount to restraints of trade "in varying times and circumstances," and "[i]t would make no sense to create out of the single term 'restraint of trade' a chronologically schizoid statute, in which a 'rule of reason' evolves with new circumstances and new wisdom, but a line of *per se* illegality remains forever fixed where it was." . . .

Although the rule of *Albrecht* has been in effect for some time, the inquiry we must undertake requires considering "the effect of the antitrust laws upon vertical distributional restraints in the American economy today." As the Court noted [in an earlier case] there has not been another case since *Albrecht* in which this Court has

Case 18.2 continues

Case 18.2 continued

"confronted an unadulterated vertical, maximum-price-fixing arrangement." Now that we confront *Albrecht* directly, we find its conceptual foundations gravely weakened.

In overruling *Albrecht,* we of course do not hold that all vertical maximum price fixing is *per se* lawful. Instead, vertical maximum price fixing, like the majority of commercial arrangements subject to the antitrust laws, should be evaluated under the rule of reason. In our view, rule-of-reason analysis will effectively identify those situations in which vertical maximum price fixing amounts to anticompetitive conduct.

RESULT   The Supreme Court vacated the decision of the appeals court and ordered it to reconsider State Oil's pricing policies under the rule of reason.

COMMENTS   The Court did not deem vertical maximum price-fixing legal *per se*, but only ruled that it should be analyzed under a rule of reason "to identify those situations in which [it] amounts to anticompetitive conduct." But the Court was careful to point out that vertical *minimum* price-fixing remains illegal *per se*, although it did not offer a new rationale for that prohibition.

Questions

1. Under what "situations" would vertical maximum price-fixing "amount to anticompetitive conduct"?
2. What arguments, if any, would persuade the Court to reconsider its *per se* rule against minimum vertical price-fixing?

As noted earlier, Section 1 of the Sherman Act addresses only concerted action. Because unilateral action is not prohibited, a manufacturer or distributor can announce list prices to dealers, and the dealers may decide independently to follow those suggestions. Similarly, manufacturers and distributors may advertise suggested retail prices. Indeed, a manufacturer or distributor may (absent any intent to create or maintain a monopoly) announce that it will terminate any dealer who does not charge its suggested list prices and then terminate those who do not do so (because the conduct is entirely unilateral).[22] However, most manufacturers and distributors do not want to terminate dealers who violate the policy. They, therefore, frequently use termination as a threat to coerce agreement. Once there is agreement, there is a violation of Section 1. Similarly, if the manufacturer or distributor becomes a clearinghouse for complaints by dealers about another dealers' failure to charge the suggested list price and agrees to police the prices charged by the other dealers, then there would be concerted action.

If a manufacturer or distributor coerces retailers to adhere to its suggested price levels, it will violate the Sherman Act. Any threats of sanctions that interfere with the retailer's freedom to set its own minimum price for the goods or services that it sells will constitute an unreasonable restraint of trade in violation of the Sherman Act. However, the line separating persuasion from coercion is not always clear.

Nonprice Vertical Restraints and Vertical Market Division

Vertical market division is an arrangement imposed by a manufacturer on its distributors or dealers that limits the freedom of the dealer to market the manufacturer's product. Such an agreement may establish exclusive distributorships, territorial or customer restrictions, location clauses, areas of primary responsibility, and the like.

---

22. United States v. Colgate & Co., 250 U.S. 300 (1919).

These nonprice vertical restrictions are not illegal *per se.* Rather, they are judged under the rule of reason.

The central inquiry is whether the reduction in intrabrand competition is justified by interbrand competition. The higher the market share of a particular manufacturer's product, the greater the likelihood that a decline in intrabrand competition will violate the rule of reason. For example, suppose Pixel Unlimited controls 80% of the market for high-definition television (HDTV) screens in Atlanta, Georgia, and sells its products through five independent retail outlets. Pixel agrees with three of its dealers to terminate the other two. Although a reduction in competition among Pixel dealers might arguably increase interbrand HDTV competition, given Pixel's high market share that would not offset the anticompetitive effect of the decrease in Pixel intrabrand competition. Accordingly, the reduction in the number of Pixel dealers might violate Section 1.

Exclusive Distributorships In an *exclusive distributorship,* a manufacturer limits itself to a single distributor in a given territory or, perhaps, line of business. So long as a manufacturer does not have dominant market power, it may allocate different geographic areas to its distributors and refuse to sell to other potential distributors in those areas. Exclusive distributorships have been upheld under the rule of reason when there is some competitive pressure that limits the market power of the retailers holding them. Exclusive automobile dealerships for particular geographic regions are the classic example. This restriction on intrabrand competition is permissible because of the intense interbrand competition among U.S. and foreign automobile manufacturers.

In the following case, the court considered the legality of exclusive distributorships in the provision of supplemental news to Chicago's newspapers.

A CASE IN POINT	IN THE LANGUAGE OF THE COURT

CASE 18.3
PADDOCK PUBLISHING INC. v. CHICAGO TRIBUNE CO.
United States
Court of Appeals for
the Seventh Circuit
103 F.3d 42 (7th Cir. 1996).

FACTS The two largest newspapers in Chicago are the *Chicago Tribune* and the *Sun–Times.* In addition to printing the work of its own staff, the *Tribune* prints stories from the New York Times News Service, a supplemental news service to which it subscribes and which provides news and other material of interest to newspapers around the world. The New York Times News Service is one of many supplemental news providers that offer exclusive contracts to newspapers in each metropolitan area. The *Sun–Times* subscribes to the Los Angeles Times/Washington Post News Service. As a result, stories provided by the Los Angeles Times/Washington Post News Service to the *Sun–Times* are not available to the *Tribune* or any other Chicago newspaper, and stories provided by the New York Times News Service to the *Tribune* are not available to the *Sun–Times* or any other newspapers in Chicago.

Because the news providers charge their subscribers according to circulation, they strive to sign up the largest paper in each market. Similarly, newspapers prefer exclusive licensing, because printing the same stories as their competitors would make them less distinctive and valuable to readers. As a result, the larger newspapers subscribe to the more popular services, and the smaller newspapers are left to subscribe to the less popular services for their supplemental news. Chicago's third-largest newspaper, the *Daily Herald,* was further disadvantaged because the third most popular provider was owned by the *Tribune,* which refused to license its stories to a competitor in its home market.

The *Daily Herald* challenged the pattern of exclusive distributorships as a violation of Section 1 of the Sherman Act, because it effectively denied the *Herald* the opportunity to subscribe to the best supplemental news services. The trial court dismissed the *Daily Herald's* complaint for failure to state a claim. The paper appealed.

Case 18.3 continues

Case 18.3 continued

ISSUE PRESENTED   Does a pattern of exclusive distributorships in a market violate the Sherman Act?

OPINION   EASTERBROOK, J., writing for the U.S. Court of Appeals:

The *Herald* does not contend that the *Tribune* has conspired with the *Sun-Times* to bring about this state of affairs. Nor does it contend that the supplemental news services and features syndicators (or their contributing papers and authors) have agreed among themselves. It concedes that each has adopted its method of doing business independently; they take the same approach to distribution because each has discovered that it is the most profitable way to do business. All of the contracts between services and newspapers are terminable at will or on short notice (usually 30 days, although some features require a year's notice). . . .

This is fundamentally an "essential facilities" claim—but without any essential facility. There are three supplemental news services that the *Herald* is willing to acknowledge as major competitors (and others besides, though the *Herald* denigrates them). There are hundreds, if not thousands, of opinion and entertainment features; a newspaper deprived of access to the *New York Times* crosswords puzzles can find others, even if the Times has the best known one. . . . [T]his case does not involve a single facility that monopolizes one level of production and creates a potential to extend the monopoly to others. We have, instead, competition at each level of production; no one can "take over" another level of production by withholding access from disfavored rivals. . . . [T]he existence of three competing facilities not only means that none is an "essential facility" but also means that each of the three is entitled to sign an exclusive contract with a favored user. Other firms that want to enter the market can do so by competing at intervals for these contracts.

Competition-for-the-contract is a form of competition that antitrust laws protect rather than proscribe, and it is common. Every year or two, General Motors, Ford, and Chrysler invite tire manufacturers to bid for exclusive rights to have their tires used in the manufacturers' cars. Exclusive contracts make the market hard to enter in mid-year but cannot stifle competition over the longer run, and competition of this kind drives down the price of tires, to the ultimate benefit of consumers. Just so in the news business—if smaller newspapers are willing to bid with cash rather than legal talent. In the meantime, exclusive stories and features help the newspapers differentiate themselves, the better to compete with one another. A market in which every newspaper carried the same stories, columns, and cartoons would be a less vigorous market than the existing one. And a market in which the creators of intellectual property (such as the *New York Times*) could not decide how best to market it for maximum profit would be a market with less (or less interesting) intellectual property created in the first place. No one can take the supply of well researched and written news as a given; legal rulings that diminish the incentive to find and explicate the news (by reducing the return from that business) have little to commend them.

In what way could the news services' practices harm consumers? Tacit collusion (economists' term for "shared monopoly") could be a source of monopoly profits and injury to consumers even if none of the stages of production is monopolized. Some distribution arrangements might be objectionable because they facilitate tacit

Case 18.3 continues

Case 18.3 continued

collusion. But collusion, tacit or express, requires some horizontal cooperation, or at least forbearance from vigorous competition among rivals. Although the newspaper market is concentrated on the readers' side, the inputs to newspaper production are unconcentrated and therefore do not facilitate tacit collusion in the more concentrated market. The New York Times News Service competes for column inches of ink not only with other supplemental news services but also with the Associated Press, Reuters, and the reporters of the subscribing papers. . . .

What the *Herald* does argue is that a mixture of fewness of firms, exclusive contracts, and relations between suppliers and users of news that endure despite short contract terms, hampers the growth of small rivals even though each market is competitive. Such an argument does not come within any of the economic approaches to tacit collusion—but it does, the *Herald* insists, come within the holding of [previous cases].

    . . .

[The case relied on by the *Daily Herald*] involved exclusive dealing, while this case involves exclusive distributorships. Despite the similarity in nomenclature, there is a difference. . . . An exclusive dealing contract obliges a firm to obtain its inputs from a single source. . . . None of the newspapers in Chicago (or anywhere else) has promised by contract to obtain all of its news from a single source—and the sources have not locked all of their output together. . . . A new entrant to the supplemental news service business could sell to every newspaper in the United States, if it chose to do so. . . .

[In *Theatre Enterprises, Inc. v. Paramount Film Distributing Corp.*, the] FTC and the Supreme Court concluded that even exclusive dealing contracts are lawful if limited to a year's duration. The Commission saw that exclusivity can promote competition by making it feasible for firms to invest in promoting their products—for these costs would not be recoverable if the contracts were of very short terms, or if rivals could exhibit the same films and obtain the benefit of this promotional activity. Moreover, with year-long contracts, the entire market is up for grabs. A new entrant can sell to a twelfth of the theaters in the first month, a sixth of all theaters by the end of the second month, and so on; competition for the contract makes it possible to have the benefits of exclusivity and rivalry simultaneously. Things work similarly in the newspaper business. Contract terms are short, so competition for the contract can flourish. Meanwhile, exclusive distribution of news or features through a single paper in a city helps the paper distinguish itself from, and compete with, its rivals. The *Sun–Times* will not promote a readership for a particular columnist if the *Tribune* and the *Herald* carry the same column; free-riding would spoil the investment and thwart this aspect of competition.

RESULT   The trial court's dismissal of the case was affirmed. The exclusive distribution agreements were not unreasonable restraints on trade.

COMMENTS   In addition to rejecting the *Daily Herald's* claim, the court showed its contempt for the paper's attempt to use antitrust law against its successful competitors by noting that the *Herald* had never even tried to outbid the *Tribune* or *Sun–Times* for their supplemental news service subscriptions. In its conclusion, the court sharply

Case 18.3 continues

Case 18.3 continued

offered the paper some advice: "The *Herald* has never tried to make a better offer, and we conclude that it has come to the wrong forum. It should try to outbid the *Tribune* and *Sun–Times* in the marketplace, rather than to outmaneuver them in court."

Questions

1. If the publishers of the *Tribune* and the *Sun–Times* had agreed with each other to subscribe to supplemental news services only on an exclusive basis, how would the court have viewed the *Daily Herald*'s claim?
2. How would the market for news have been affected if the *Daily Herald* had succeeded in eliminating exclusive distribution agreements?

Territorial and Customer Restrictions   *Territorial* and *customer restrictions* prevent a dealer or distributor from selling outside a certain territory or to a certain class of customers. For example, a Dow representative selling industrial chemicals might be permitted to sell only to hardware stores, and only in a specified area. The Supreme Court has held that vertical territorial or customer restrictions are not *per se* violations of Section 1. Such restrictions often increase interbrand competition; thus an accompanying reduction of intrabrand competition may be permissible.

However, a manufacturer cannot disguise an agreement to maintain resale prices as a territorial restriction. A court will look beyond the form of the transaction to the substance and will use the *per se* rule to strike down what is in reality a vertical minimum price restraint. Similarly, where a number of retailers combine to force a manufacturer to impose an ostensibly vertical agreement on its retailers, the agreement is in reality horizontal and will be deemed a *per se* violation of Section 1.

Dual Distributors   A manufacturer that sells its goods both wholesale and at retail is called a *dual distributor*. Early decisions held that such an arrangement was unlikely to create the efficiencies and increased competition created by permissible forms of vertical nonprice agreements. Accordingly, restraints imposed by dual distributors were considered illegal *per se*. The trend in recent decisions, however, is to analyze such restraints under the rule of reason (as long as they originate with the manufacturer, not the retailers), because they can have beneficial economic effects.

Tying Arrangements

Tying arrangements can be challenged under Section 1 of the Sherman Act or Section 3 of the Clayton Act. The Clayton Act specifically prohibits tying arrangements in commodities, while the Sherman Act prohibits tying arrangements generally. The legal analysis applied under the two statutes has converged; thus, the following analysis applies to both Clayton Act and Sherman Act claims.

In a *tying arrangement,* the seller will sell product A (the *tying,* or desired, product) to the customer only if the customer agrees to purchase product B (the *tied* product) from the seller. A tying arrangement is a way of forcing a buyer to purchase a product or service it would not buy on the product's or service's own merits.

For example, suppose Metro Cable expands its cable-television service into a new town. The public utilities commission grants Metro the exclusive right to provide cable service in the new town. Metro is a subsidiary of Moviemax, a company that provides a cable-television movie channel for subscribers. To improve Moviemax's profit margin, the marketing vice-president decides to require all of Metro's customers to subscribe to Moviemax. In this example, the tying product is the basic cable service. The tied product is the Moviemax television channel.

Tying arrangements unreasonably restrain trade by preventing competitors from selling their goods to customers obliged to buy the tied product. In the Moviemax example, the tying arrangement would make it more difficult for other movie channels, such as

HBO, to sell their product to cable customers in the new town. Tying arrangements also restrict the freedom of choice of purchasers who are forced to buy the tied product.

Tying arrangements have traditionally been held to be *per se* violations, provided that (1) the tying and tied products are separate products, (2) the availability of the tied product is conditioned upon the purchase of the tying product, (3) the party imposing the tie has enough market power in the tying product market to force the purchase of the tied product, and (4) a "not insubstantial" amount of commerce in the tied product is affected.

Separate Products Whether there are separate products may be difficult to determine. Firms often label or market a combination of goods and services as a single product. The courts attempt to determine whether there are two economically distinct products by determining whether there is a separate demand for them. For example, in one case the Supreme Court found that below-market financing that was provided to buyers of prefabricated metal homes was a separate product from the homes themselves. A key issue in the Justice Department's case against Microsoft Corporation, discussed in the "Inside Story," is whether Microsoft's Internet Explorer Web browser is a separate product from Microsoft's Windows operating system.

Condition of Sale If the tying product can be purchased on nondiscriminatory terms, without the tied product, there is no tie. It has been suggested that a manufacturer should not make a second product technologically interdependent with the purchased product such that technology, rather than contract terms, forces customers to buy both. To date, however, these technological ties have been found lawful as long as there is not separate demand for the products involved.

Market Power The nature and extent of the market power required is frequently litigated. As the Supreme Court defines it, market power is "the power to force a purchaser to do something that he would not do in a competitive market."[23] It is ordinarily inferred from a firm's predominate share of the market, but in tying

claims the issue is how power in one market translates into power in another. The extent to which power in one market allows a producer or seller to exploit another market depends on the *cross-elasticity of demand*, that is, the sensitivity of consumer demand for one good to the price of another good. The lower the cross-elasticity of demand between, say, gasoline and cars, the less sensitive is consumers' demand for cars to the price of gasoline. Hence, a car dealership with dominant market power in cars would be better able to leverage that power to dominate the gasoline market. The higher the cross-elasticity, the more sensitive the demand for cars is to the price of gasoline and the less able the dealership is to translate its market power in cars to market power in gasoline. Hence, the first dealership would be better able to dominate the gasoline market by requiring its car customers to purchase its gasoline even as it raises the cost of that gasoline.

A firm's ability to translate power in one market to power in another is often a function of product complementarity. If one needs product B to make product A work, then the firm controlling the market for product A will have a good shot at forcing consumers to buy the complementary product (B) from it.

Courts have not fashioned any precise formula using market share and cross-elasticity of demand by which firms can know ahead of time the line between antitrust violation and shrewd business.

Effect on Commerce A "not insubstantial" amount of commerce is affected if more than a trifling dollar amount is involved.

Business Justification Unlike other *per se* violations, a tying arrangement may be upheld if there is a business justification for it. In a Ninth Circuit decision,[24] Mercedes–Benz's policy of requiring its dealers to sell only factory-made parts was upheld. The court ruled that this tying arrangement was justified by the assurance it provided to Mercedes that service on its automobiles, important in preserving their high-quality image, would not be performed with substandard parts.

Some lower courts have allowed tying arrangements in fledgling industries. For example, one court

---

23. Eastman Kodak Co. v. Image Technical Servs., Inc., 112 S. Ct. 2072 (1992).

24. The Mozart Co. v. Mercedes–Benz of North Am., Inc., 833 F.2d 1342 (9th Cir. 1987), *cert. denied*, 488 U.S. 870 (1988).

upheld a tying arrangement whereby purchasers of cable-television satellite antennas were required to purchase service contracts to ensure proper functioning of the antennas.[25]

Thus, although the courts continue to say that tying arrangements are *per se* illegal, they apply a flexible *per se* rule that considers market power and business justifications. Tying arrangements are in effect judged under a type of rule of reason.

Franchise Agreements

A *franchise* is a business relationship in which one party (the franchisor) grants to another party (the franchisee) the right to use the franchiser's name and logo and to distribute the franchiser's products from a specified locale. The franchise agreement may provide that the franchisor will not grant another franchise within a specified distance of the franchisee's business location. To ensure uniformity and quality, the franchisor may impose conditions on the operation of the franchise. For example, a McDonald's hamburger franchisee might be required to have all employees wear an approved uniform and to decorate the restaurant in an approved fashion.

Antitrust issues are raised when a franchisor, in an effort to promote uniformity and name recognition, imposes certain types of limitations on the franchisee. For example, ice cream manufacturer Baskin Robbins was accused of imposing an illegal tying arrangement when it required all franchisees to buy their ice cream from Baskin Robbins. However, the seller (Baskin Robbins) was held to have no market power over the tying product. Ice cream franchises, like automobile franchises, face intense interbrand competition. No one franchisor has the ability to dominate the market even if it does require all of its franchises to buy its products.

However, several recent cases suggest that a franchisor might have market power if the franchisor keeps the purchase requirement secret from the would-be franchisee and the franchisee cannot easily recoup its investment in the franchise. In such a case, the franchisee could be "locked in" and not free to acquire a different franchise on more favorable terms.

The Supreme Court has held that under the rule of reason, vertical market division between a franchisor and a franchisee may be lawful when interbrand competition is enhanced by the limitation on intrabrand competition.[26] Such division may take the form of limits on the number of franchisees in a geographic region and restrictions on sale of franchisor products to specifically franchised locations.

Antitrust Injury

To recover damages, a plaintiff must establish that it sustained an *antitrust injury,* that is, a loss due to a competition-reducing aspect or effect of the defendant's violation of the Sherman Act. A plaintiff may not recover under the antitrust laws for losses that resulted from competition as such.

In 1990, the Supreme Court considered whether resale price maintenance gives rise to an antitrust injury in the absence of predatory pricing. USA Petroleum, an independent gasoline retailer, claimed that Atlantic Richfield Company (ARCO), an integrated oil company, conspired with retail service stations selling ARCO-brand gasoline to fix prices at below-market levels. USA Petroleum argued that this was an illegal resale price maintenance scheme whereby the competition that would otherwise exist among ARCO-brand dealers was eliminated by agreement. As a result, the retail price of ARCO-brand gasoline was maintained at artificially low and uncompetitive levels. This allegedly drove many independents in California out of business.

The U.S. Supreme Court held that USA Petroleum could not recover damages for ARCO's resale price maintenance because there was no showing of predatory pricing, that is, pricing below cost designed to drive competitors out of the market.[27] The Court reasoned that when the prices are set under a resale price maintenance program at nonpredatory levels, there is generally no anticompetitive effect. Such pricing may reduce the market share of competitors or the price that competitors may charge consumers. Without doubt, those competitors are injured as a result of the practice, but there is nothing anticompetitive about that in and of itself. Indeed, such a result benefits the consumer. In such a case, the Court held, the competitor may not recover damages under the antitrust laws.

25. United States v. Jerrold Elecs. Corp., 187 F. Supp. 545 (E.D. Pa. 1960), *aff'd,* 365 U.S. 567 (1961).

26. Continental T.V., Inc. v. GTE Sylvania Inc., 433 U.S. 36 (1977).
27. Atlantic Richfield Co. v. USA Petroleum Co., 495 U.S. 328 (1990).

This decision was viewed by some scholars as another victory for Law and Economics.[28] Charles Rule, a Washington lawyer and former Justice Department antitrust chief, said that the decision is consistent with the Supreme Court's approach of viewing the antitrust laws as protecting competition rather than individual competitors.[29] The Supreme Court also expressly stated in its *Atlantic Richfield* opinion that consumers and the manufacturers' own dealers may bring suit to enforce the rule against a vertical maximum price-fixing scheme if anticompetitive consequences result.

Limitations on Antitrust Enforcement

The courts have limited the private enforcement rights of individual citizens and states by invoking the doctrine of standing. They have also limited the liability of state governments by applying state-action exemptions.

Standing

To prevent private parties from jumping on the treble-damages bandwagon, the Supreme Court requires that a private plaintiff have *standing* to sue, that is, that the plaintiff has suffered an injury from the defendant's vio-

lation of the antitrust law. For example, a consumer buying goods from an innocent middleman does not have standing to recover from the manufacturer who was a member of a price-fixing cartel.

More complicated standing issues arise where a company alleges that its competitors are violating the antitrust laws. For example, suppose that Connaught Gin complains that its competitor, Profumo Gin, has imposed an illegal exclusive dealing agreement on Connaught's former dealer, Liquor World. At first, Connaught's injury appears indirect compared with that of Liquor World. However, the central reason that the antitrust law is concerned with exclusive dealing agreements is their impact on the market opportunities of competitors. Accordingly, Connaught is granted standing, because it has suffered injury of the kind that the antitrust laws are designed to prevent (and is a more likely plaintiff than Liquor World). The courts thus hold substance over form to promote the primary goal of the antitrust laws—fostering competition.

State-Action Exemption

More than 50 years ago, the Supreme Court declared that the antitrust laws apply to anticompetitive actions by private parties, not to anticompetitive actions by state legislatures or administrative bodies. Thus, state action is exempt as long as (1) there is a clear state purpose to displace competition, and (2) the state provides adequate public supervision. For example, the California legislature passed a law designed to limit the production, and consequently raise the price, of raisins. Given that California produced nearly one-half of the world's raisins, the effect of this statute on interstate commerce was substantial. Nevertheless, the Supreme Court enunciated and applied the state-action exemption in this case.[30]

The courts have refused to extend the exemption to local municipalities, except in certain limited circumstances. However, Congress did pass the Local Government Antitrust Act of 1984 in response to municipalities' fears of treble damages. This act eliminated all liability for antitrust damages by local governments but preserved equitable remedies, such as injunctions. The act extended immunity from damages to all officials or employees acting in an official capacity.

---

28. Reuben, *High Court Narrows Test for Antitrust,* San Francisco Banner Daily J., May 15, 1990, at 1.

29. Stephen Wermiel, *Supreme Court Hardens Stance on Pricing Suits,* Wall St. J., May 15, 1990, at A3.

ETHICAL CONSIDERATION

False disparaging statements about a rival may rise to the level of antitrust violation only when they have significant and enduring anticompetitive effects.[a] Is it ethical to make such statements before they rise to the level of an antitrust violation? Is it ethical to threaten antitrust litigation to quiet a competitor's accurate but disparaging remarks about one's products?

a. American Prof. Testing Service, Inc. v. Harcourt Brace Jovanovich Legal & Prof. Pub., Inc., 108 F.3d 1147 (9th Cir. 1997).

---

30. Parker v. Brown, 317 U.S. 341 (1943).

AT THE TOP

Any communications by a company's employees regarding price-fixing, or any director involvement in such activity, may subject the company to potential liability in the form of civil damages and criminal penalties. It is therefore very important that the company maintain an adequate supervisory mechanism.

 ## Monopolies: Section 2 of the Sherman Act

Section 2 of the Sherman Act provides:

> Every person who shall monopolize, or attempt to monopolize, or combine or conspire with any other person or persons, to monopolize any part of the trade or commerce among the several States, or with foreign nations, shall be deemed guilty of a felony.[31]

As under Section 1 of the Sherman Act, corporations can be fined up to $10 million (or double the gain to the violator or double the loss to the victim if that is more than $10 million) for each violation, and individuals can be fined up to $350,000 for each violation and imprisoned for up to three years. As a practical matter, however, violators of Section 2 are not prosecuted criminally.

A firm that possesses monopoly power is able to set prices at noncompetitive levels, harming both consumers and competitors. Consequently, Section 2 condemns actual or attempted monopolization of any market. Unlike Section 1, Section 2 does not require proof of an agreement or any other collective action.

Section 2 does not, however, prohibit the mere possession of monopoly power. The offense of monopolization has two elements. The plaintiff must first show that the defendant has monopoly power in a relevant market and then that the defendant willfully acquired or maintained that power through anticompetitive acts. A firm that has monopoly power thrust upon it by circumstances or attains it by superior performance does not violate Section 2. There is thus a status element (the defendant must be an entity with monopoly power) and a conduct element (the defendant must commit anticompetitive acts).

---

31. 15 U.S.C. § 2 (1997).

INTERNATIONAL CONSIDERATION

Article 85(1) of the Treaty of Rome, which created the European Union, prohibits agreements whose object or effect is to restrict competition in the European Union. Agreements that violate Article 85(1) are automatically void under Article 85(2) and unenforceable before the national courts in the member states of the European Union.

Article 85(2) prohibits abuse of an entity's dominant position. The question of what constitutes a dominant position is complex and depends on a number of factors, such as the firm's market share in the relevant market, the competitive pressures it faces, its ability to control price, and barriers to entry to its market.

For example, in 1980 the European Commission opened a proceeding against IBM, the world's largest computer manufacturer. The commission claimed that IBM had abused its dominant position in the supply of two key products (the central processing unit and the operating system) for its most powerful range of computers, System/370, in an effort to control the markets for the supply of all products compatible with System/370. The alleged abuses included (1) failing to supply other manufacturers in sufficient time with the technical interface information needed to permit competitive products to be used with System/370, (2) not offering System/370 central processing units (CPUs) without main memory included in the price, (3) not offering System/370 CPUs without the basic software included in the price, and (4) refusing to supply certain software installation services to users of non-IBM CPUs.

In 1984, IBM entered into an undertaking in which it agreed to offer its System/370 CPUs either without main memory or with only such capacity as was strictly required for testing and to disclose, in a timely manner, sufficient interface information to enable competitors to attach both their hardware and software products to System/370. IBM had previously advised the commission that it had taken steps to make installation services available to all users of its software and was in the course of unbundling all software.[a]

---

a. Commission of the European Communities, *Fourteenth Report on Competition Policy* (1984).

Trade and Commerce

The Sherman Act applies only to "trade or commerce" among states or with foreign nations. The Supreme Court has held that the phrase "commerce among the several States" extends the reach of the Sherman Act to as far as constitutionally allowed under the Commerce Clause.[32] The resulting scope of antitrust jurisdiction is therefore broad and encompasses more than restraints on trade that are motivated by a desire to limit interstate commerce or that have their sole impact on interstate commerce. The commerce requirement of the act may be satisfied when (1) the defendant's conduct directly interferes with the flow of goods in the stream of commerce, or (2) the defendant's conduct has a substantial effect on interstate commerce.

In 1997, a fraternity at Hamilton College in New York argued that the school's new policy of requiring all students to live in college-owned facilities and to purchase college-sponsored meal plans was an attempt to monopolize the housing and dining markets in that area. The fraternity alleged substantial effects on interstate commerce, including Hamilton's out-of-state student population (56%) and its annual revenue for room and board from those students ($4 million). The district court dismissed the complaint on the grounds that the provision of residential services under the new policy did not involve "trade or commerce." The appeals court reversed the dismissal, however, and ruled that such a question was suitable for trial.[33]

Monopoly Power

Courts define *monopoly power* (also called *market power*) as the power to control prices or exclude competition in a relevant market. Monopoly power is marked by supracompetitive prices (that is, prices that are higher than they would be in a competitive market) over an extended period of time and the unavailability of substitute goods or services. The determination of whether a particular corporation has monopoly power usually requires complex economic analysis. Presumptions based on market share and other structural characteristics of markets are used to simplify the analysis;

but in practice, each case turns on its unique (and usually disputed) facts.

Competition takes place in discrete markets. Therefore, the existence of monopoly power can be determined only after the relevant market for the product is determined. Markets have two components: a product component and a geographic component.

Multiple-Brand Product Market   The *multiple-brand product market* is made up of product or service offerings by different manufacturers or sellers that are economically interchangeable and may therefore be said to compete. Sometimes it is easy to identify substitutes. No one would deny that Coca-Cola competes against Pepsi. Frequently, the question is more complex. Does Coca-Cola compete against Dr. Pepper? Almost certainly. Against Koala Springs orange and mango juice and mineral water? Maybe. Against powdered iced tea? That is hard to say.

These questions are important because the power of a seller to set prices above competitive levels is limited by the ability of purchasers to substitute other types of products. If purchasers are unable to substitute other goods in the face of a price increase, the seller can set prices at monopoly levels. The product market is that collection of goods or services that customers deem to be practically substitutable.

Single-Brand Product Market   The Supreme Court in *Eastman Kodak Co. v. Image Technical Services, Inc.* held that "[b]ecause service and parts for Kodak equipment are not interchangeable with other manufacturers' service and parts, the relevant market from the Kodak-equipment owner's perspective is composed of only those companies

INTERNATIONAL CONSIDERATION

In a case brought in France by Orangina against Coca-Cola of France for abuse of dominant position, the French court ruled in 1997 that the relevant product market was all colas, not all soft drinks as Coca-Cola had asserted.[a]

a. David Buchan, *Orangina Takes Some Fizz Out of Coke*, FIN. TIMES, Jan. 30, 1997, at 2.

32. Summit Health, Ltd. v. Pinhas, 500 U.S. 322, 329 n.10 (1991).

33. Hamilton Chapter of Alpha Delta Phi Inc. v. Hamilton College, 128 F.3d 59 (2d Cir. 1997).

that service Kodak machines."[34] The Court rejected Kodak's argument that the relevant market was all copy machines and that Kodak could not have market power as to Kodak parts and service for copy machines because it did not have market power in copy machines. Evidence in the case showed that Kodak controlled nearly 100% of the Kodak parts market and 80% to 95% of the Kodak service market, with no readily available substitutes for Kodak-equipment owners. Because of the high costs of switching to another brand, consumers could not readily change copy-machine manufacturers if Kodak unilaterally raised its service fees. Thus, in some cases, a single brand of a product or service may constitute a separate market in a Section 2 analysis.

Geographic Market   Competition is also affected by geographical restraints on product movement. If a firm in Michigan is the only maker of widgets in the Midwest, it has the potential to exercise monopoly power unless widget makers from other parts of the country can profitably ship their products to that area. Some markets are national or even international in scope, for example, the markets for long-distance telephone service, supercomputer sales, and nuclear power plant–design services. Other markets are localized, for example, markets for products that are expensive to transport, such as wet cement. The contours of geographic markets may also be affected by government regulations that confine firms to certain regions.

By defining the geographic market, antitrust courts try to separate firms that affect competition in a given region from those that do not. The geographic market encompasses all firms that compete for sales in a given area at current prices or would compete in that area if prices rose by a modest amount.

Market Share   Once the relevant market is determined, the plaintiff must show that, within this market, the defendant possessed monopoly power. The Supreme Court has held that monopoly power may be inferred from a firm's predominant share of the market, because a dominant share of the market often carries with it the power to control output across the market and thereby control prices. In determining market share, the initial definition of the relevant market is crucial. For example,

---

34. 504 U.S. 451 (1992).

INTERNATIONAL CONSIDERATION

The European Commission has taken a similar approach in deciding whether a nondominant manufacturer of a primary product can be dominant with respect to a secondary market consisting solely of replacement parts, consumables, and maintenance services that must be technically compatible with the primary product. Relevant factors include the price and time-life of the primary product, transparency of prices of secondary products, prices of secondary products as a proportion of the primary product value, and information costs.

Applying these factors, the commission rejected in 1995 the complaint of Pelikan, a German manufacturer of toner cartridges for printers, against Kyocera, a Japanese manufacturer of computer printers, including toner cartridges for those printers. The commission did not find that Kyocera had a dominant position in the market of consumables. Purchasers were well informed about the price charged for consumables and appeared to take it into account in making their decision to buy a printer. Life-cycle costs of consumables (mainly toner cartridges) represented a very high proportion of the value of a printer. Therefore, if the prices for consumables of a particular brand were raised, consumers would have a strong incentive to buy another brand of printer.[a]

---

a. European Comm'n, *XXVth Report on Competition Policy 1995* (1996), at 41–42.

Perrier mineral water could be considered part of the market for imported mineral water. Perrier's competitors would include other imported mineral-water sellers like Pellegrino. Perrier has a major share of that market. On the other hand, if the market is defined as all mineral water, then Perrier's market share would be considerably smaller. Consequently, how a relevant market is defined often determines whether a particular firm has a dominant share of the market.

In one case, the Supreme Court found that 87% of the market was a predominant share sufficient to create a presumption of monopoly power. As a general proposition, firms with market shares in excess of 60% are especially vulnerable to Section 2 litigation. When a single brand of a product or service constitutes the relevant market, market share may be 100%.

Barriers to Entry   Market shares do not, however, conclusively establish monopoly power. Market share must be analyzed in the context of other characteristics of the market in question. The plaintiff must show that new competitors face high market barriers to entry and that current competitors lack the ability to expand their output to challenge a monopolist's high prices. Common entry barriers include patents, governmental licenses or approvals, control of essential or superior resources, entrenched buyer preferences, economies of scale, and, according to some authorities, high initial capital requirements. Courts will also look at profit levels, market trends, pricing patterns, product differentiation, and government regulation. Essentially, the court is trying to determine the likelihood that another company will become a viable competitor in the relevant market if there is a small but significant nontransitory increase in price levels. The discussion of the breakup of the Bell Telephone System in the "Economic Perspective" of this chapter highlights these issues.

Monopolistic Intent

Once the presence of monopoly power is established, the defendant's intent may be relevant. Some cases hold that the plaintiff must prove that the defendant's conduct lacks a legitimate business purpose; other cases hold that the burden is on the defendant to prove such a purpose. The plaintiff must then prove a monopolistic intent. It is possible to prove intent through evidence of statements by the monopolist's executive expressing a desire to eliminate competition. Hostility between competitors is commonplace, however, and may even be beneficial to vigorous competition. Therefore, the courts often require that *monopolistic intent* be proved by evidence of conduct (not merely statements) that is inherently anticompetitive.

A defendant may rebut allegations of monopolistic intent by showing that its success in the marketplace is the result of "superior skill, foresight, and industry." A monopoly earned by superior performance is not unlawful. Indeed, the law recognizes that the possibility of attaining such a monopoly may be a powerful incentive to vigorous competition, which benefits consumers.

Therefore, a key issue in Section 2 litigation is whether the defendant acquired or maintained its monopoly by procompetitive acts or by anticompetitive acts. Anticompetitive acts include predatory pricing and, under certain circumstances, refusal to deal.

Predatory Pricing   The courts have not settled on a single definition of *predatory pricing,* that is, the attempt to eliminate rivals by undercutting their prices to the point where they lose money and go out of business, so that the monopolist can then raise its prices because it is no longer restrained by competition. The courts have struggled to develop principles that distinguish between such anticompetitive pricing and the procompetitive pricing that occurs when a more efficient firm competes vigorously yet fairly against its rivals. In the latter case, the more efficient firm could undercut its rivals, forcing them out of business, and a lawful monopoly would result.

When prices are above average variable cost but below average total cost and the company has excess capacity, courts will usually find the pricing legal. (*Variable cost* is the cost of producing the next incremental unit; *total cost* includes variable cost and fixed costs, such as rent and overhead.) If a company does not have excess capacity, the legality of the pricing depends on the company's intent; the cases are very fact-specific. Prices below average variable cost are presumptively illegal unless the business can demonstrate that the pricing is an introductory offer or that costs will fall dramatically as the company progresses along the learning curve. At some point, pricing below cost becomes economically irrational unless the predator is anticipating the long-term gains that would result from destroying its rivals.

Some academics have argued that predatory pricing is self-defeating in all but a few market scenarios. Having eliminated its rivals, the predator needs to keep them, and new entrants, out of the market when it raises its prices to recoup its losses. That will be difficult as the high prices—and high profits—can be expected to attract new entrants. Thus, predatory pricing is an irrational strategy unless the market, because of barriers to entry or other factors, is structurally conducive to monopolization.

The Supreme Court has accepted this argument. In 1986, the Court rejected a claim brought by U.S. television manufacturers against their Japanese counterparts. It held that some allegations of predation are inherently implausible, because the marketplace cannot be successfully monopolized. In such cases, there is no Sherman Act violation, whatever monopolistic intent the defendant may have had. This has been referred to as the *rule of impossibility*.[35]

Refusal to Deal   As a general proposition, the antitrust laws do not prevent a firm from deciding with whom it will or will not deal. Yet the courts have long recognized that there are circumstances in which a unilateral refusal to deal may allow a firm to acquire or maintain monopoly power.

A monopolist has a duty to deal with its rivals when it controls an *essential facility,* that is, some resource necessary to its rivals' survival that they cannot feasibly duplicate. There are four elements a court considers in an essential-facility case. First, the court must determine

---

35. *See, e.g.,* Matsushita Elec. Indus. Co. v. Zenith Radio Corp., 475 U.S. 574 (1986), and Brooke Group Ltd. v. Brown & Williamson Tobacco Corp., 509 U.S. 209 (1993).

whether the defendant prevents would-be competitors from using the facility. Second, the court must determine whether it is feasible for the defendant to permit access to the facility by its would-be competitors. Third, the court must determine whether the defendant has monopoly power and control of the facility. Fourth, and most critical, the court must determine whether the competitors are able to duplicate the essential facility. This approach was followed in the *AT&T* case, which led to the breakup of the Bell Telephone System.

The essential-facility doctrine does not require a firm to share with its competitors resources that are merely useful. It has been held that a company need not share technology that would allow them to compete more effectively and need not share resources that the competitors could duplicate on their own. As demonstrated in the following case, even if a monopolist does not control an essential facility, Section 2 prohibits a monopolist from refusing to deal in order to create or maintain a monopoly absent a legitimate business justification.

A CASE IN POINT	SUMMARY

CASE 18.4
IMAGE TECHNICAL SERVICES, INC. v. EASTMAN KODAK CO.
United States Court of Appeals for the Ninth Circuit
125 F.3d 1195 (9th Cir. 1997), *cert. denied,* 118 S. Ct. 1560 (1998).

FACTS   After independent service organizations (ISOs) began servicing copying and micrographic (microfilm) equipment manufactured by Eastman Kodak Co. (Kodak), Kodak adopted policies to limit the availability to ISOs of replacement parts for its equipment and to make it more difficult for ISOs to compete with it in servicing such equipment.

The ISOs sued, alleging that Kodak had unlawfully monopolized and attempted to monopolize the sale of service and parts for Kodak machines, in violation of Section 2 of the Sherman Act, by leveraging its monopoly power in the equipment market. After the Supreme Court affirmed the denial of Kodak's motion for summary judgment because of genuine issues of material fact regarding Kodak's market power, a federal district court found that Kodak had violated Section 2. It awarded the ISOs $71.8 million in damages and issued a 10-year injunction requiring Kodak to sell the ISOs all parts, manuals, and tools needed to service Kodak equipment. Kodak appealed, in part on the grounds that its patents and copyrights on equipment parts provided justification for its refusal to sell those parts to ISOs.

ISSUE PRESENTED   Do patent and copyright protections provide a legitimate business justification for refusing to license products?

SUMMARY OF OPINION   Section 2 of the Sherman Act prohibits monopolies and attempts to form monopolies. A claim of monopolization requires proof that the

Case 18.4 continues

Case 18.4 continued

entity possessed monopoly power in the relevant market and willfully acquired or maintained that power. A claim of attempted monopolization requires proof of (1) intent to control prices or destroy competition, (2) anticompetitive conduct aimed at that purpose, and (3) a dangerous probability of achieving monopoly power. Both claims require proof of antitrust injury.

The U.S. Court of Appeals concluded that the ISOs had proved by substantial circumstantial evidence that Kodak had monopoly power in the separate markets for Kodak copiers and Kodak copier parts. Kodak manufactured 30% of the parts itself, controlled another 20% to 25% through contracts with original-equipment manufacturers, and discouraged self-servicing and resale of parts by end users. Furthermore, barriers to entry made this market power monopolist: Kodak holds 220 copier patents, controls its designs and tools, and enjoys brand name power and economies of scale. Hence, a jury could reasonably believe that Kodak had monopoly power. Kodak's refusal to sell parts to ISOs intentionally and effectively leveraged its equipment monopoly to achieve a similar monopoly in parts.

Although Kodak argued that its parts were not an essential facility and that therefore it could refuse to deal with the ISOs, the court ruled that essential facility is not the only circumstance in which a firm cannot refuse to deal. Instead, the Sherman Act prohibits refusal to deal in order to create or maintain a monopoly unless there is a legitimate business justification. Intellectual property rights may create such a justification.

There is, however, tension between antitrust law and patent and copyright law. On the one hand, antitrust law challenges monopoly as a threat to competition; but, on the other hand, patent and copyright law grant monopoly power as an incentive to innovate. The court acknowledged that patent and copyright holders may refuse to sell or license protected work, but stated that a monopolist who acquires a dominant position in one market through patents and copyrights may violate Section 2 if the monopolist exploits that dominant position to extend the lawful monopoly into a separate market. Thus, while exclusionary conduct can include a monopolist's unilateral refusal to license a patent or copyright or to sell its patented or copyrighted work, a monopolist's desire to exclude others from its protected work is a presumptively valid business justification for any immediate harm to consumers. That presumption may be rebutted by, for example, evidence that the intellectual property protection was acquired unlawfully or that its use as a business justification was merely pretext.

The trial judge's failure to instruct the jury on this point was error. However, the error was harmless, because there was sufficient evidence of pretext that a jury would probably have found Kodak's presumption of valid business justification rebutted. Kodak's parts manager had testified that patents "did not cross [his] mind" at the time Kodak began the parts policy. Kodak's contracts did not distinguish between so-called proprietary parts and patented or copyrighted products. Although Kodak's equipment required thousands of parts, only 65 were patented. Yet, Kodak refused to sell both protected and unprotected products.

RESULT   The appeals court affirmed the trial court's finding of liability against Kodak. On other grounds, it amended the terms of the injunction and remanded the case for a new trial on the issue of damages regarding sales of used equipment.

Case 18.4 continues

Case 18.4 continued

COMMENTS   This case underscores the importance for managers to be clear about the reasons why they are refusing to sell or license a product and to ensure that the refusal to deal does not extend to unrelated products for which there is no business justification. If Kodak's refusal to sell or license parts was motivated by a desire to reap the monopoly profits it was entitled to exact under the patent and copyright laws and if Kodak had agreed to sell or license unprotected products, then the court would most likely have found no violation of Section 2.

Derivative Markets

Ordinarily, Section 2 liability is restricted to monopolistic behavior within the specific market in which the firm has monopoly power. Through leveraging, however, a firm with monopoly power in one market can use that power to gain an advantage in a separate market. It is clear that when such an advantage amounts to monopoly power in the second market, the firm has violated Section 2. It is less clear whether a firm can use its monopoly power in one market to gain a competitive advantage, short of actual monopolization, in another market. A federal appeals court explored this issue in another *Kodak* case, this time involving Kodak's film market.

Kodak had introduced a pocket-sized camera with a new type of film, which was capable of producing photographs that could previously be taken only by much larger cameras. For 18 months after the introduction of the camera system, only Kodak produced the new type of film, which required special photo-processing equipment to develop. Kodak possessed a monopoly in the film and camera markets.

In *Berkey Photo, Inc. v. Eastman Kodak Co.,*[36] Berkey Photo, a seller and processor of film, challenged the introduction of the new camera system. It accused Kodak of attempting to use its monopoly power in the film market to gain leverage in the photo-finishing equipment and services markets in violation of Section 2 of the Sherman Act. In rejecting Berkey's claim, the court concluded that Kodak's invention resulted from its superior business skill, product, and foresight. Thus, the failure to disclose the product innovation prior to intro-

duction of the new product did not constitute willful maintenance of monopoly power in violation of the Sherman Act.

However, the *Berkey Photo* court did suggest that the use of monopoly power in one market to obtain a competitive advantage in another market might violate Section 2. Recent Supreme Court decisions tend to undercut this suggestion, but they do not do so decisively. More specifically, in another case,[37] the Supreme Court held that the plaintiff in every Section 2 case involving unilateral conduct must prove a dangerous probability that the defendant's conduct will create or maintain monopoly power in a market. That holding seems to suggest that "leveraging" that only confers a "competitive advantage" in a market cannot violate Section 2.

The U.S. Court of Appeals for the Ninth Circuit adopted this approach when it held that two airlines that had developed the two largest proprietary computerized airline reservation systems did not violate Section 2 merely because the systems gave them a competitive advantage in the air-transportation market.[38] The court held that unless the monopolist uses its power in the first market to acquire and maintain a monopoly in the second market, or to attempt to do so, there is no Section 2 violation. The plaintiffs had conceded that the two airlines did not have a monopoly in the leveraged, downstream air-transportation market and that there was no dangerous probability that either defendant would acquire such a monopoly. Therefore, their Section 2 claims were rejected.

On the other hand, there is some language in *Eastman Kodak Co. v. Image Technical Services, Inc.*

36. 603 F.2d 263 (2d Cir. 1979), *cert. denied,* 444 U.S. 1093 (1980).

37. Spectrum Sports, Inc. v. McQuillan, 506 U.S. 447 (1993).

38. Alaska Airlines, Inc. v. United Airlines, Inc., 948 F.2d 536 (9th Cir. 1991).

that indicates that leveraging monopoly power in one market to create a competitive advantage in another market can be a Section 2 violation. Therefore, the Supreme Court's position on monopoly leveraging that only confers a competitive advantage is not yet totally clear.

Underlying the decisions under Section 2 is the conflict between the goal of preventing anticompetitive behavior and the goal of promoting consumer welfare by encouraging innovation. In certain cases, firms are permitted to adopt practices that, though they might exclude competition, also foster innovation.

For example, a firm is entitled to introduce technological innovations that adversely affect competitors, even if, in order to do so, it erects barriers to other firms' entry into the market. Consumers pay for such exclusion in the form of higher prices. Nevertheless, the courts and legislators have decided that, as a matter of policy, these higher prices are acceptable as the cost of technological change. If firms were denied the right to act as Kodak did, there would be no incentive to innovate. Technological innovation, in the long run, increases social welfare.

Other Anticompetitive Acts Other practices that have been held to indicate the presence of monopolistic intent include the allocation of markets and territories, price-fixing, fraudulently obtaining a patent, or engaging in sham litigation against a competitor. Firms can also incur Section 2 liability by acquiring or maintaining monopoly power through corporate mergers or acquisitions.

 ## Mergers: Section 7 of the Clayton Act

If a merger or acquisition unreasonably restrains trade, it violates Section 1 of the Sherman Act. If it results in monopolization, it violates Section 2. These statutes, however, are rarely invoked to challenge mergers. Dissatisfied with the ability of the government to attack mergers under the Sherman Act, Congress amended the Clayton Act in 1950 to prohibit mergers that threatened to harm competition. Section 7 of the Clayton Act provides:

> No person engaged in commerce or in any activity affecting commerce shall acquire, directly or indirectly, the whole or any part of the stock or other share capital and no person subject to the jurisdiction of the Federal Trade

Commission shall acquire the whole or any part of the assets of another person engaged also in commerce or in any activity affecting commerce, where in any line of commerce or in any activity affecting commerce in any section of the country, the effect of such acquisition may be substantially to lessen competition, or to tend to create a monopoly.[39]

Two types of mergers are covered by Section 7: *horizontal mergers* between actual or prospective competitors at the same level of distribution, which are likely to reduce competition; and *vertical mergers* between firms at different points along the chain of production and distribution. In recent years, challenges to vertical mergers have been rare.

Unlike the Sherman Act, the Clayton Act does not provide criminal sanctions for violations of its terms. The Justice Department, through the courts, and the Federal Trade Commission (FTC), through its own administrative proceedings, may seek (1) divestiture of acquired stock or assets; (2) sale of particular subsidiaries, divisions, or lines of business; (3) compulsory sale of needed materials to a divested firm; (4) compulsory sharing of technology; or (5) temporary restrictions upon the defendant's own output.

Private parties, such as competitors of the merging firms, may also bring actions for injunctive relief. Recently, however, some courts have come to look with disfavor upon such actions, fearing that they might halt mergers that would actually intensify competition. Firms that are targets of hostile takeovers frequently attempt to use Section 7 litigation to prevent the takeover, although recent limitations on antitrust standing—that is, the right to bring such actions—have greatly limited the availability of this tactic.

State attorneys general may also enforce Section 7, and they have begun to do so with increasing frequency. For example, the California attorney general challenged the American Stores–Lucky Stores merger after the FTC approved the transaction. If the proposed merger had been completed as planned, the resulting entity would have been the top-volume food retailer in the United States with 600 supermarkets and estimated annual sales exceeding $21 billion. The Supreme Court's decision in the case makes it clear that state law enforcement officials have the power to enforce the federal antitrust laws, if they desire. American Stores was ordered

---

39. 15 U.S.C. § 18 (1997).

to divest itself of 161 stores.[40] States also may utilize state antitrust laws to challenge proposed mergers.

In contrast to the Sherman Act, which is often enforced by private plaintiffs, the Clayton Act is enforced mainly by the federal agencies. Justice Department or FTC action can delay, if not abort, a corporate merger or acquisition.

---

40. California v. American Stores Co., 495 U.S. 271 (1990).

Hart–Scott–Rodino Antitrust Improvements Act

The Hart–Scott–Rodino Antitrust Improvements Act amended Section 7 in 1976 to provide a premerger notification procedure whereby the FTC and Justice Department can review the anticompetitive effects of proposed mergers meeting certain size-of-party and size-of-transaction tests. A premerger notification must be filed if one party to the transaction has assets or annual sales of at least $10 million and the other has assets

---

ECONOMIC PERSPECTIVE

THE REGULATION OF NATURAL MONOPOLIES

In the imagined world of perfect competition, *productive efficiency* (an equilibrium in which only the lowest-cost producers of goods and services survive) and *allocative efficiency* (an equilibrium in which scarce societal resources are allocated to the production of various goods and services up to the point where the cost of the resources equals the benefit society reaps from their use) would go hand in hand. In the real world, however, this is not always so. For example, the most cost-efficient way to provide telephone connections to homes is to link all of the homes to one central station, using one set of lines. Competition would require duplication of this expensive infrastructure; productive efficiency is best served by a monopoly. But the pricing policy of a monopolist is not controlled by competition. Consequently, the unregulated price of local telephone service would rise above the socially efficient level, and allocative efficiency would be impaired (see Exhibit 18.2). This can be remedied only by regulation of such industries, which are known as natural monopolies.

For many years, the American Telephone and Telegraph Company (AT&T) enjoyed a regulated monopoly in both local and long-distance telecommunications. The provision of long-distance service is not a natural monopoly, because more than one network of intercity telephone lines can be profitably operated. Nonetheless, there was no competition in long-distance service because AT&T controlled access to the lines to individual homes.

In 1974, the U.S. government brought an antitrust suit against AT&T, charging monopolization of the telecommunications industry in violation of Section 2

of the Sherman Act. The case was decided in 1983.[a] In 1984, AT&T signed a consent decree to enable competition to flourish in the long-distance market. The decree provided for (1) the breakup of AT&T's monopoly over local service by creating seven regional telecommunications companies, known as the Baby Bells, and (2) a complex set of rules to ensure that both AT&T and other companies providing long-distance service, such as MCI and Sprint, would have equal access to the local networks. The Baby Bells would, of course, be subject to regulation because each of them would still enjoy a monopoly in the provision of local telephone service.

In the years since the signing of the consent decree, long-distance rates have fallen by 40% in nominal dollars as MCI, Sprint, and other entrants have proven effective competitors to AT&T. These long-distance competitors are now applying their skills to local phone service. In 1994, MCI announced plans to build a local telephone network, and it has spent nearly $2 billion building the necessary facilities. Using old telegraph right-of-ways it bought from Western Union in 1990, MCI provided local service in more than 30 cities at the end of 1997. If it succeeds in merging with WorldCom, Inc., that number will climb to 100.[b] In the meantime, the Baby Bells are making plans to offer long-distance service in their home territories.

---

a. United States v. American Tel. & Tel. Co., 552 F. Supp. 131 (D.D.C. 1982), *aff'd sub nom.*, Maryland v. United States, 460 U.S. 1001 (1983).

b. *MCI Communications Corp.: Local Calling for Business Is Rolled out in Six Cities*, WALL ST. J., Dec. 19, 1997, at B4.

EXHIBIT 18.2 Welfare Loss from Monopoly

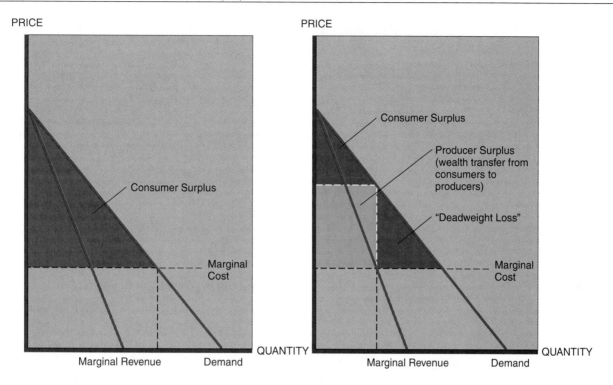

COMPETITIVE MARKET   MONOPOLY

DEFINITION OF TERMS

Consumer surplus The difference between the value of a good to consumers (measured by the price they would be willing to pay for the good) and the price they actually must pay to obtain the good.

Producer surplus The difference between the cost to producers of producing a good (measured by the minimum price at which they would sell a given quantity of the good) and the price they actually receive in the market.

Total surplus The sum of producer and consumer surplus. Total surplus represents the difference between the cost to society of the inputs used to make a good, including raw materials and labor, and the value of the finished good to society. Total surplus measures the overall increase in societal wealth attributable to production of a good.

Deadweight loss The difference between total surplus in a competitive market and total surplus in a monopolized market.

or annual sales of at least $100 million. The transaction must involve a purchase of at least $15 million or 15% of the voting securities of the acquired company. Failure to notify can result in fines and reversals of transactions.

In 1997, the FTC fined German auto-parts maker Mahle GmbH $5.1 million for failing to alert authorities to its $40-million purchase of 50.1% of a Brazilian rival's

voting stock. Because both companies have U.S. subsidiaries, the FTC had authority to intervene.[41] In 1996, Sara Lee Corporation paid a fine of $3.1 million after

41. John R. Wilke & Bryan Gruley, *Fines Grow for Evading Antitrust Review*, WALL ST. J., Feb. 28, 1997, at A2.

INTERNATIONAL CONSIDERATION

As the members of the European Union (EU) continue to plan for monetary convergence, antitrust regulation remains a point of contention for some key member states. Most notably, Germany, Britain, and France have strenuously resisted European merger law as insufficient to police colluding and monopolizing companies.

In Germany, for instance, regulators have called for the EU law to be strengthened, while industry has pressed the government to drop German law in favor of the current European law. Industry representatives argue that the German law is too complex and that its rulings are frequently overturned by European rulings anyway. More importantly, they say, German law absurdly requires that regulators make their judgments based on effects only in Germany when international mergers are increasingly common. German regulators, on the other hand, believe the EU law insufficiently distinguishes between vertical mergers and more dangerous horizontal mergers. As well, the EU law has no clear trigger for investigating proposed mergers, whereas German law automatically confers regulatory jurisdiction if one company takes control of more than 25% of another.[a]

In 1996, the European Commission's competition directorate published a new green book to stimulate discussion about reforming EU merger law. The paper specifically recommended that the EU law's threshold requirements for merger applications be lowered and that internationally merging firms be allowed to register just once with the commission instead of having to register multiple times with the relevant member states. Signaling its willingness to compromise, Germany announced in 1997 its plan to double its threshold for referring mergers to regulators, effective 1999.[b] Harmonization, however, remains more aspiration than plan.

a. Matt Marshall, *German Competition Law Is Criticized by Companies, Praised by Politicians*, WALL ST. J., Feb. 9, 1996, at B7B.

b. Peter Norman, *Bonn Plans Cartel Law Change*, FIN. TIMES, Apr. 28, 1997, at 2.

the FTC challenged its failure to notify authorities in 1991 of its purchase of $26 million of assets from a company in the United Kingdom. Sara Lee had counted the deal as two transactions: $13.1 million for the company's U.S. assets and $12.7 million for its U.K. assets. In addition to the fine, the FTC forced Sara Lee to sell one of the brands it had acquired from the U.K. company and another brand it had acquired previously.[42]

In general, parties to a merger must give the FTC and Justice Department 30 days to review their filings, or 15 days in the case of a tender offer. Either period can be extended in the event of a request for additional information by the government. Requests for additional information should be avoided, if possible, because they cause further delays before the merging parties know whether the Justice Department will challenge the proposed merger.

Merger Guidelines

In connection with their enforcement obligations, the Federal Trade Commission and the Justice Department have together developed a series of guidelines as to the kinds of transactions that are likely to be challenged as violations of the Clayton Act.

Under the 1992 merger guidelines, the FTC and Justice Department (the reviewing agencies) seek to determine whether a proposed corporate combination will more likely than not reduce competition, using basically the same analysis as the courts use in applying Section 2 of the Sherman Act (discussed earlier in this chapter). The reviewing agency will first determine the relevant geographic and product markets. Then, it will calculate the market shares of the companies proposing to merge. Finally, it will determine the effect of the merger on the relevant market.

If the merger appears to increase concentration in the relevant market by a certain amount, the reviewing agency will ordinarily challenge the transaction. However, the question of whether to challenge a combination is left to the discretion of the agency.

As an aid to the interpretation of market data, the Justice Department uses the *Herfindahl–Hirschman Index* (*HHI*) of market concentration. The HHI is

42. *Id.*

calculated by summing the squares of the individual market shares of all the firms in the market. For example, in a market with four competitors having market shares of 35%, 25%, 25%, and 15%, the HHI is 2,700 ($35^2 + 25^2 + 25^2 + 15^2 = 1,225 + 625 + 625 + 225 = 2,700$).

When the postmerger HHI is less than 1,000, the Justice Department characterizes the market as unconcentrated. In such cases, the department will not challenge the merger or other combination.

When the postmerger HHI is between 1,000 and 1,800 and the merger will produce an HHI increase of 100 points or more, the 1992 merger guidelines state that the merger will possibly raise significant competitive concerns.

When the postmerger HHI is above 1,800, the department considers the market to be highly concentrated. In such cases, an increase in the HHI of 100 points or more creates a rebuttable presumption of anticompetitive effects. For example, a merger between firms with market shares of 5% and 10% will result in a 100-point increase in the HHI ($15^2 = 225, 5^2 + 10^2 = 125$), whereas a merger between firms with market shares of 7% and 8% will result in a 112-point increase ($15^2 = 225, 7^2 + 8^2 = 113$).

When the increase in the HHI is less than 50 points, Justice Department action is unlikely. When the increase is between 50 and 100 points, the department will challenge the transaction if it determines, based on a broad-ranging analysis of the market, that the effect of the merger is "substantially to lessen competition." The department will consider such factors as changing market conditions, the relative strength or weakness of the firms in the market, and barriers to entry into the relevant market. It should be noted that even if the Justice Department or the FTC approve the merger, it may still be challenged in court by another party.

 ## Litigation under Section 7

Although the Department of Justice's merger guidelines are of considerable persuasive value, the standards applied by courts differ in several significant respects. Moreover, a court's analysis may vary depending on the type of merger or corporate combination that has been challenged.

Horizontal Mergers

A horizontal merger is the combining of two or more competing companies at the same level in the chain of production and distribution. The first step in determining the lawfulness of such a merger is to identify the relevant product and geographic markets. The same standards discussed in connection with Section 2 of the Sherman Act are used.

Once the market is defined, the court will look primarily at three factors: (1) the market shares of the firms involved in the transaction, (2) the level of concentration in the market, and (3) whether the market is structurally conducive to anticompetitive behavior.

The case of *United States v. Philadelphia National Bank*[43] illustrates this method of analysis. In the early 1960s, Philadelphia National Bank (PNB) was the second largest bank in the Philadelphia market, which consisted of 42 commercial banks in the metropolitan area of Philadelphia, Pennsylvania, and its three contiguous counties. After PNB had signed a merger agreement with Girard Bank, the third largest bank in the same market, the United States sued to enjoin the merger on the grounds that it would violate Section 7 of the Clayton Act. Referring to the Clayton Act, the Court noted "that a merger which produces a firm controlling an undue percentage share of the relevant market, and results in a significant increase in the concentration of firms in that market is so inherently likely to lessen competition substantially that it must be enjoined in the absence of evidence clearly showing the merger is not likely to have such anticompetitive effects."

In this case, first, the merger would have resulted in PNB's controlling at least 30% of the commercial banking business in the four-county Philadelphia metropolitan area, which the Court viewed as a threat to competition. Second, after the merger, the two largest banks would control 59% of the market, whereas the two largest banks before the merger controlled only 44%. This increase in concentration also worried the Court. Third, neither the high level of government regulation of the banking business nor the banks' provision of services and intangible credit rather than tangible products made the banking industry immune from the

---

43. 374 U.S. 321 (1963).

anticompetitive effects of undue concentration. Because of these three elements, the Court directed the district court to enter judgment enjoining the merger.

The figure of 30% market share which the Court held to be excessive has been taken by many lower courts to create a presumption of illegality. However, the Supreme Court has insisted that no single numerical standard can be applied to all markets. In one case the Supreme Court enjoined a merger between competing grocery stores when the acquiring grocery store had a 4.7% market share and the acquired grocery store had a 4.2% market share. The top four firms in the relevant market controlled only 24.4% of the market.[44] (This decision, however, has been relentlessly criticized.) Most courts today require that, in the absence of a highly concentrated market, the merging firms have a combined market share of at least 30% before a Section 7 violation will be found.

In a more recent case, the Federal Trade Commission challenged the merger of office-supply retailers Office Depot, Inc. and Staples, Inc., the first and second largest operators of office-supply superstores, respectively. In 1996, the two firms agreed to merge their operations (with more than $8 billion of revenue), joining their more than 1,000 stores. As required by Hart–Scott–Rodino, the companies notified the FTC of their plan. For seven months, the FTC investigated the proposed merger. Although Staples and Office Depot did not compete with each other in many geographic markets, the FTC contended that the merger would hurt consumers on balance by reducing competition in the markets in which the two companies did compete. Consequently, the commissioners voted four-to-one to challenge the merger.

To satisfy the regulators, the companies negotiated a consent decree with the FTC staff to permit the merger on the condition that the companies sell off 63 stores to OfficeMax, the third-largest office-supply superstore retailer, in those markets in which the FTC most feared a reduction in competition. Nonetheless, the FTC commissioners again ruled against the merger by a vote of three-to-two and asked the district court to enjoin the companies from joining.

Defining the relevant product market as consumable office supplies sold through office-supply super-stores, the court rejected the argument that Wal-Mart and other retailers compete in the same market with Staples, Office Depot, and OfficeMax. The court relied heavily on pricing data that indicated, among other things, that prices were on average 13% higher in geographic markets in which Staples was the only office superstore than in markets in which all three superstores competed, even though retail and discount chains selling consumable office supplies were present in both markets. Turning then to market concentration, the court noted that before the merger, the least concentrated market had an HHI of 3,597 and the most concentrated had an HHI of 6,944. After the proposed merger, those figures would rise to 5,003 and 10,000, respectively. Thus, these markets were already "highly concentrated" and would see an average increase of 2,715 HHI points. Furthermore, the industry's large economies of scale meant that new entrants would have to open many large stores nationally in order to compete. The large amount of capital necessary to do this would be a barrier to entry. Ultimately, the district court sided with the FTC and, in 1997, issued an injunction, killing the $3.4 billion deal.[45]

Even if a merger or combination is determined to be presumptively illegal on the basis of market shares, the defendants may still show that the transaction is not likely to decrease competition. First, if there are no barriers to entry in the relevant market, any transitory increase in concentration will be quickly eroded by the entry of new competitors into the market. Second, if one of the combined firms is failing, the proposed transaction may be the only alternative to that failure. In either of these cases, Section 7 liability can be avoided.

Vertical Mergers

A vertical merger is the acquisition by one company of another company at a higher or lower level in the chain of production and distribution. For example, the merger of an airplane manufacturer and an airplane-engine manufacturer would be a vertical merger. In vertical merger cases, courts tend to focus on whether the merger has excluded competitors from a significant sector of the market. For example, when competing suppliers were denied access to approximately 25% of the

---

44. United States v. Von's Grocery Co., 384 U.S. 270 (1966).

45. Federal Trade Comm'n v. Staples, Inc., 970 F. Supp. 1066 (D.D.C. 1997).

highly concentrated automobile market, Section 7 was held to be violated. When the market is less concentrated, however, the courts will analyze the market more thoroughly to determine whether the transaction has any anticompetitive effects.

For example, the U.S. Supreme Court in *Brown Shoe Co. v. United States*[46] pointed to a number of factors that demonstrated the anticompetitive effect of Brown Shoe Company's purchase of retail shoe chain G. R. Kinney Company: (1) an industry trend toward vertical integration, (2) the strength of the parties involved relative to their competitors, (3) the absolute number of shoe sales involved (eight million), and (4) the express purpose of Brown Shoe to restrict competing shoe suppliers from access to the Kinney distribution outlets it sought to control. That decision, however, has been severely criticized; and it is unlikely that the Justice Department would now challenge a proposed merger with market-share effects similar to those in *Brown Shoe,* where only 2% of the nationwide retail shoe market was foreclosed by the merger.

Conglomerate Mergers

In the 1960s and 1970s, many academics and government prosecutors favored expanding Section 7 prohibitions to cover mergers that were neither horizontal nor vertical in the traditional sense. The effort to prohibit *conglomerate mergers*—that is, the acquisition of a company by another company in a different line of business—has largely been abandoned. Because the merging companies are in different markets, there is no threat to competition.

One theory advanced during this period has endured, although it has been rarely applied. A merger between firms that are not competitors at the time of the acquisition but that might, absent the merger, have become competitors may be held to violate Section 7. This is because potential competition is useful in keeping prices at competitive levels. When prices rise above competitive levels, potential competitors will have an incentive to enter the market and charge competitive prices. When there is no such potential entrant into the market, there is no pressure to keep prices at competitive levels. Monopoly pricing may result.

Consequently, it can be argued that a merger violates Section 7 if a plaintiff proves that (1) the market is highly concentrated; (2) one of the merging firms is an actual, substantial competitor in the market and the other is one of a small number of firms that might have entered the market; (3) entry of that firm *de novo* or anew or by a "toehold" acquisition into the market would be reasonably likely to have procompetitive effects; and (4) entry by that firm absent the merger was likely. Some attorneys argue that a merger does not have to eliminate an actual potential entrant in order to violate Section 7. Under this theory it is sufficient if the merger eliminates a perceived potential entrant.

◆ Price Discrimination: The Robinson–Patman Act

Section 2 of the Clayton Act, as amended by the Robinson-Patman Act, prohibits *price discrimination,* that is, selling the same product to different purchasers at the same level of distribution at different prices. By outlawing price discrimination, the legislators believed that they could protect independent business by preventing the formation of monopolies. It was assumed that price discrimination was the means by which trusts were built and that discriminatory price concessions were the means by which large retail chains expanded at the expense of smaller independent retailers.

Today, enforcement of the Robinson–Patman Act is a low priority of the Federal Trade Commission; the Justice Department does not enforce the act at all. However, private enforcement through civil litigation continues.[47]

Elements of a Robinson–Patman Case

In order to establish a price-discrimination case under the Robinson–Patman Act, six elements must be established. First, there must be discrimination in price, that is, a difference in the price at which goods are sold, or in the terms and conditions of sale, or in such items as freight allowances or rebates.

---

46. 370 U.S. 294 (1962).

47. *See* Meyerowitz, *Beware of Price-Discrimination Pitfalls,* BUS. MARKETING, June 1986, at 136.

Second, some part of the discrimination must involve sales in interstate commerce, that is, at least one sale must be across state lines or involve the instrumentations of interstate commerce. A seller may discriminate in price as long as no sale across state lines occurs.

Third, the discrimination must involve sales for use, consumption, or resale within the United States. Fourth, there must be discrimination between different purchasers. In other words, there must be at least two sales. Fifth, the discrimination must involve sales of tangible commodities of like grade and quality.

Finally, there must be a probable injury to competition. The probable injury to competition is assessed at three levels: (1) the seller level, (2) the buyer level, and (3) the customer level.

Defenses

Even if a plaintiff has shown the elements of a Robinson–Patman violation, there are a number of defenses available.

Meeting Competition   Discriminatory prices are not prohibited if the seller acted in "good faith to meet an equally low price of a competitor."[48] As defined by the Federal Trade Commission, good faith is "a flexible and pragmatic, not a technical or doctrinaire, concept. The standard of good faith is simply the standard of the prudent businessman responding fairly to what he reasonably believes is a situation of competitive necessity."[49]

Cost Justification   Price differentials that would be otherwise prohibited by the Robinson–Patman Act are not prohibited if the differentials "make only due allowance for differences in the cost of manufacture, sale or delivery resulting from the differing methods or quantities" in which the goods are sold and delivered.[50] In order to establish this defense, the defendant must show actual cost savings, not merely generalized assertions of cost savings, to justify the

price reduction. Defendants may show savings not only in manufacturing costs but also in selling and delivery costs (such as costs of billing; credit losses; costs of advertising, promotion, and selling; and freight and delivery charges). The FTC interprets this defense restrictively, and it is expensive to compile the necessary paper trail.

Changing Conditions   Section 2(a) does not prohibit price changes

> from time to time where in response to changing conditions affecting the market for or the marketability of the goods concerned such as but not limited to actual or imminent deterioration of perishable goods, obsolescence of seasonal goods, distress sales under court process, or sales in good faith in discontinuance of business in the goods concerned.[51]

In the few cases where this defense has been raised, the issue was whether the price discrimination was a response to one of the conditions listed in the statute. The changing-conditions defense has generally been confined to situations caused by the physical characteristics of the product, such as the perishable nature of fruit. For example, a court permitted price differentials on bananas from a single shipload because they reflected the perishable nature of bananas.

 ## International Application of the Antitrust Laws

Sovereign Immunity

To avoid antitrust disputes with foreign governments, the U.S. courts apply a *sovereign immunity* doctrine. This doctrine protects foreign governments from applications of U.S. laws. (The sovereign immunity doctrine is discussed further in Chapter 26.) Much litigation turns on whether a foreign firm's anticompetitive activity was directed by its government or if it was merely tolerated. If the foreign government tolerates but does not require the anticompetitive acts, the U.S. antitrust laws apply.

48. 15 U.S.C. § 13(b) (1997).

49. Continental Baking Co., 63 F.T.C. 2071, 2163 (1963).

50. 15 U.S.C. § 13(a) (1997).

51. *Id.*

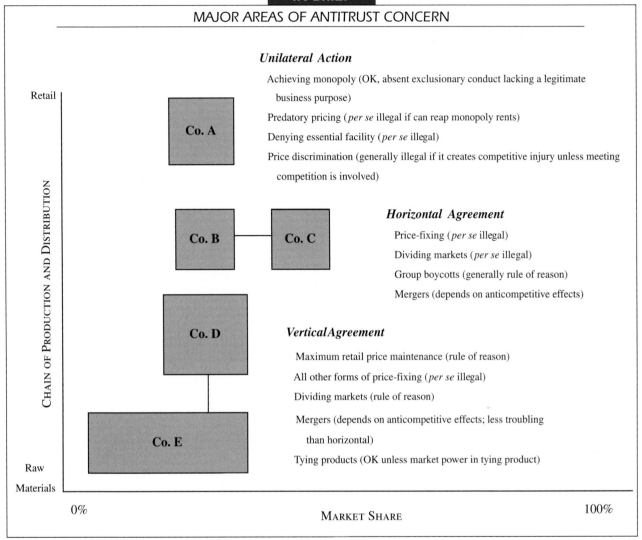

IN BRIEF

MAJOR AREAS OF ANTITRUST CONCERN

Unilateral Action

Achieving monopoly (OK, absent exclusionary conduct lacking a legitimate business purpose)

Predatory pricing (*per se* illegal if can reap monopoly rents)

Denying essential facility (*per se* illegal)

Price discrimination (generally illegal if it creates competitive injury unless meeting competition is involved)

Horizontal Agreement

Price-fixing (*per se* illegal)

Dividing markets (*per se* illegal)

Group boycotts (generally rule of reason)

Mergers (depends on anticompetitive effects)

Vertical Agreement

Maximum retail price maintenance (rule of reason)

All other forms of price-fixing (*per se* illegal)

Dividing markets (rule of reason)

Mergers (depends on anticompetitive effects; less troubling than horizontal)

Tying products (OK unless market power in tying product)

Co. A

Co. B — Co. C

Co. D

Co. E

Retail

Raw Materials

CHAIN OF PRODUCTION AND DISTRIBUTION

0%   MARKET SHARE   100%

Extraterritorial Application of U.S. Law

The Supreme Court has interpreted the Sherman Act to apply extraterritorially when (1) the intent of parties is to affect commerce within the United States, and (2) their conduct actually affects commerce in the United States. However, this relatively straightforward statement of the law obscures the complex issues in-volved in applying U.S. antitrust laws to activities occurring outside its borders.

The following case dealt with the question of whether conduct by a non-U.S. company outside of the United States but having an effect on commerce in the United States could form the basis for a criminal antitrust case.

A CASE IN POINT	**SUMMARY**

CASE 18.5
UNITED STATES v.
NIPPON PAPER
INDUSTRIES CO.
United States Court of
Appeals for the First Circuit
109 F.3d 1 (1st Cir. 1997),
cert. denied, 118 S. Ct. 685
(1998) (mem.).

FACTS   In 1995, a federal grand jury indicted Nippon Paper Industries Company, Ltd. (NPI), a Japanese manufacturer of facsimile (fax) paper, for criminally violating Section 1 of the Sherman Act. The indictment alleged that in 1990 NPI and certain unnamed co-conspirators held meetings in Japan during which they agreed to fix the price of thermal fax paper throughout North America. To achieve this goal, NPI and other manufacturers purportedly sold the paper in Japan to unaffiliated trading houses on the condition that the houses charge inflated prices for the paper when they resold it in North America. The trading houses then shipped and sold the paper to their subsidiaries in the United States, which in turn sold it to American consumers at artificially high prices.

NPI moved to dismiss the indictment, in part because the alleged conduct took place entirely in Japan and was, therefore, beyond the reach of the Sherman Act in a criminal case. Accepting this argument, the district court dismissed the case. The government appealed.

ISSUE PRESENTED   May a criminal antitrust prosecution be based on conduct that took place entirely outside the United States?

SUMMARY OF OPINION   The U.S. Court of Appeals began by noting that the courts presume that congressional legislation applies only within the territorial jurisdiction of the United States unless contrary intent appears. The first Supreme Court case to address extraterritorial application of the Sherman Act found that it did not apply to a civil action concerning conduct wholly outside the United States that had no discernible effect on imports to the United States.[52] Since then, however, the Court has upheld civil liability under the Sherman Act for conduct outside the United States that had substantial anticompetitive effects in the United States.[53] The issue of criminal liability for extraterritorial conduct has never been addressed.

In this case, however, the same language of the same section of the same statute (Section 1 of the Sherman Act) governs both civil and criminal liability: "Every contract, combination in the form of trust or otherwise, or conspiracy, in restraint of trade or commerce among the several States, or with foreign nations, is declared to be illegal." Common sense suggests that courts should interpret the same language uniformly, whether the impetus for interpretation is civil or criminal. Such understanding flows from the basic canons of statutory interpretation and Supreme Court interpretation of other statutes.

Although there is no direct precedent for antitrust criminal liability for wholly extraterritorial conduct, the court reasoned that "[t]here is a first time for everything." The absence of earlier criminal actions reflects more the increasingly global economy and less Section 1's limited reach. As well, there is precedent for application of state criminal laws to conduct occurring wholly outside the state.

Case 18.5 continues

---

52. American Banana Co. v. United Fruit Co., 213 U.S. 347 (1909).

53. Hartsford Fire Ins. Co. v. California, 509 U.S. 764 (1993).

Case 18.5 continued

The principle of lenity provides that when interpreting statutes in criminal cases, ambiguity should favor the accused. Here, however, there is no such ambiguity. Lenity applies when inquiry yields ambiguity, not simply because the meaning of a statute is not readily apparent without inquiry. Similarly, the principle of comity counsels forbearance when two sovereigns both have legitimate claims to jurisdiction in a dispute. More aspiration than fixed rule, comity in antitrust applies only when another sovereign's law mandates conduct that violates U.S. antitrust law. That was not the case here.

RESULT The decision of the trial court was reversed, and the indictment reinstated. NPI could be criminally prosecuted in the United States for fixing prices of products sold in the United States even though the meetings to fix prices took place in Japan.

COMMENTS As one commentator critically noted, "Inch by inch, for half a century the courts have given the Justice Department a longer and longer leash in allowing it to pursue antitrust cases abroad. A First Circuit Court of Appeals panel may have cut that leash entirely."[54] On the other hand, former Deputy Assistant Attorney General Diane P. Wood has pointed out the difficulties of effectively implementing international antitrust enforcement without taking into account events, transactions, and parties beyond the enforcing country's borders.

---

54. John Gibeaut, *Sherman Goes Abroad*, ABA J., July 1997, at 42.

Foreign nations do not always accept the applicability of U.S. antitrust laws. For example, Canada, Australia, and South Africa all enacted laws forbidding their citizens to make available to U.S. courts any documents bearing on the nature and existence of an alleged uranium cartel. This action prevented U.S. courts from gathering the information necessary to ascertain whether an antitrust violation had occurred. (The alleged uranium cartel was one of the defenses Westinghouse Electric Corporation raised in the lawsuit discussed in the "Inside Story" in Chapter 8.)

Many countries do not accept treble damages as a remedy. For example, the United Kingdom does not allow any recovery in excess of single damages. Suppose a U.S. court awards a U.S. corporation, USCO, $15 million in damages, after trebling, in a suit against UKCO, a U.K. corporation. When USCO attempts to collect $15 million of UKCO's assets, the U.K. court will treat two thirds of the $15 million award, or $10 million, as an illegal treble damages award. Thus, USCO will be able to recover only $5 million in the U.K. court. Even when a U.S. court finds a foreign corporation in violation of the antitrust laws, any award of damages is meaningless without foreign enforcement of the award.

As the global economy becomes more of an economic reality, the antitrust analysis of the relevant market will have to take account of foreign goods produced but not sold in the United States. Another issue that must be resolved in the future is how the antitrust laws will apply to U.S. companies purchasing foreign entities that have potentially valuable national security or technology applications in highly concentrated markets.

INTERNATIONAL CONSIDERATION

Invocation of another nation's antitrust laws can be an important strategy for international expansion. During the past 10 years, Procter & Gamble (P&G) has successfully wielded antitrust laws against competitors to support its move into Latin America. After losing to Colgate–Palmolive in a bidding war to acquire a Brazilian toothpaste manufacturer with 52% market share, P&G contacted the Brazilian trade commission. P&G pointed out that Colgate already controlled 27% of the market, whereas P&G was simply trying to get its foot in the door. In 1996, after a two-year review, the agency ordered Colgate to pull the acquired Brazilian brand from the shelves for four years. Earlier that year, P&G complained to Mexican regulators about the likely effects of the merger between Kimberly–Clark and Scott Paper. Because the merger would give the new entity control over 90% of the Mexican tissue market, P&G supplied the Mexican officials with reams of data about the Mexican tissue business and pointed out that the earlier rulings on the merger by United States and European officials required Kimberly to sell off its worldwide baby-wipes operation. As a result, Mexican regulators required Kimberly to divest itself of a popular brand of tissue with 20% market share. P&G has used similar tactics against Unilever Group in Argentina, where Argentine officials are still investigating charges that Unilever used unfair trade practices in the market for laundry detergent.[a]

a. Tara Parker-Pope, *P&G Calls the Cops as It Strives to Expand Sales in Latin America*, WALL ST. J., Mar. 20, 1998, at A1.

THE RESPONSIBLE MANAGER
Avoiding Antitrust Violations

Although it is impossible for a manager to eliminate all possible antitrust violations, there are a number of steps that should be implemented. The underlying purpose of the antitrust statutes is to promote competition. The economy functions best when firms compete vigorously, but fairly, with one another. In antitrust, however, the line between legal and illegal conduct is often blurry. Consequently, there are few rules that a manager can give his or her employees. Rather, the manager must identify the activities or conditions that most often trigger antitrust liability, such as discussions with competitors, discussions with buyers about their future prices, and activities that may increase concentration in any market that is already highly concentrated.

The code of conduct from Dun & Bradstreet excerpted in Exhibit 18.3 is an excellent example of the type of information that companies should provide all their employees. A code of conduct is not sufficient in itself, however. It simply provides a solid foundation from which compliance values are imparted to employees on an ongoing basis.

Discussions among competitors receive the highest degree of antitrust scrutiny. Trade and professional associations are particularly vulnerable. If they disseminate information that identifies parties to individual transactions and the price of even past or current individual transactions, the antitrust laws may be violated. Equally hazardous is the dissemination of information that may result in market division or output restriction. As a general rule, any trade association information concerning prices should be immediately forwarded to in-house or outside counsel to address potential antitrust concerns.

Antitrust scrutiny is also heightened whenever price is discussed, even between manufacturers and retailers. A corporation must make clear to its salespersons that they cannot coerce the retailer regarding the minimum price it charges the end consumer. Such conduct will raise the specter of treble-damages liability.

Finally, antitrust scrutiny is heightened where markets are highly concentrated. The fewer the entities that compete in a particular market, the more likely that agreements among them can be effectuated and that mergers can lead to unlawful monopolies. Consequently, corporations operating in concentrated markets should be particularly cautious. A manager can obtain rough approximations of market concentration from company counsel.

Employees should be encouraged, through an appropriate award system, to inform the manager whenever any of the above "red flags" appear. A manager should not hesitate to seek assistance from counsel in analyzing any activity that might violate the antitrust laws.

Common sense and education are the keys. Actions that don't seem fair usually are not. Continuing education programs will keep corporate employees aware of potential antitrust problems. A manager should always stress that short-term gains through unethical or illegal behavior are always outweighed by longer-term losses, particularly in the area of antitrust with its treble-damages awards.

EXHIBIT 18.3   Excerpts on Antitrust and Competition from the *Dun & Bradstreet Policy of Business Conduct*

Dun & Bradstreet will not tolerate any business transaction or activity that violates the letter or spirit of the antitrust and competition laws of any country that apply to the Company's business.

The antitrust and competition laws define acceptable behavior for competing in the marketplace. The general aim of these laws is to promote competition and let businesses compete on the basis of quality, price and service.

U.S. and European Community (EC) law prohibits agreements or actions that might eliminate or discourage competition, bring about a monopoly (in the U.S.) or abuse a dominant market position (in the EC), artificially maintain prices, or otherwise illegally hamper or distort normal commerce.

Individual European countries, Canada, Japan, Australia and a number of other countries have similar laws.

In addition to criminal fines and jail terms, U.S. antitrust violations often allow a private party to recover "treble damages" from the Company. Treble damages are three times the actual money damages. Antitrust lawsuits have frequently resulted in judgments against companies amounting to tens of millions—and on occasion, hundreds of millions—of dollars. Violations of EC competition law are punishable by substantial fines.

The antitrust laws are deliberately broad and general in their language. They contain sweeping provisions against restraints that threaten a competitive business economy, but they provide no definitive list of those activities. This means D&B associates must pay careful attention to possible antitrust implications of the Company's business activities. The Legal Department should be contacted in all cases of doubt.

. . .

SOCIAL DISCUSSIONS AND COMPANY COMMUNICATIONS

. . . Any kind of casual understanding between two companies that a business practice adopted by one would be followed by the other may be used in court to prove an illegal agreement.

Even social conversations can be used as evidence that an agreement existed. Memos and other written communications that use casual or inappropriate language might some day be examined by a government agency or opposing lawyers. Using loose language may raise questions about conduct that is entirely legal and may undermine all our efforts to comply with the antitrust and competition laws.

Example: Sales managers of two competing information companies met socially after work. After a few drinks, they agreed that it would be great if they reduced their workload by not chasing after the same customers. The bartender overheard the conversation.

In actuality, neither sales manager stopped selling to particular customers. Later, one company won most of the information business from law firms in the region, while the other company won most of the business from newspapers. This led to an investigation into market allocation of both companies, and the bartender's testimony was used against them.

But aren't my files and memos confidential?

No! Except for certain "privileged" communications with lawyers, all Company documents and computer files, including the most casual note or electronic-mail message, may be disclosed to government enforcement organizations or private parties in lawsuits against the Company. You should also know that stamping documents "restricted" or "confidential" does not protect them from being disclosed in court.

Exhibit 18.3 continues

Exhibit 18.3 continued

How can I avoid being tripped up by my own memos?

Follow these general guidelines:

- Report facts, be concise and objective, and indicate where information came from to establish that there is no cooperation with competitors.
- Do not draw legal conclusions.
- Avoid expressions that may imply guilt, such as "Please destroy after reading" or, "We stole this customer from Acme Widget Corp."
- Do not refer to "industry policies," "industry price" or similar expressions that imply a common course of action exists even though it does not.
- Do not use language that would suggest a false intent to harm competitors, such as, "This new program will 'destroy' the competition" or "establish a dominant position."
- Do not overstate your share of the market or refer to a market that is unreasonably narrow in order to make your market share appear larger.
- Consult with the Legal Department about when communications with a lawyer can be "privileged."

QUESTIONS AND ANSWERS

I work in sales and am friendly with a sales representative from one of our competitors. Our kids are on the same soccer team, so we see each other every week. Last weekend, we talked about a new sales promotion my company is offering. This promotion is no secret; we ran a big advertisement in the trade magazines. Did I do anything wrong?

Yes. You should never discuss price or other terms of sale with competitors under any circumstances. It is too easy for others to misinterpret any conversations you have, however innocent you believe them to be.

My boss asked me how a sales call to a prospective customer went. I mentioned that the customer seemed very interested, but was locked into a three-year contract with one of our competitors that still had two years to go. My boss told me to follow up immediately. I was supposed to convince the customer that no contract was "written in stone" and he shouldn't be so timid about walking away from the other contract. I do not feel comfortable telling the customer what to do about his contract.

You are correct to feel uncomfortable. It is against Company policy to interfere with the contracts of competitors. You might suggest that the customer review his contract to see if he has a right to terminate early, but never advise a customer to violate a contract or offer advice on how to interpret a competitor's contract.

Our main service is so popular that it almost sells itself. We are definitely the industry leaders in this field, and our sales show it. However, some of our other services are a bit stagnant and haven't moved much lately. So, I started to offer the main service only as a partner service to a couple of the slow movers. The customers want the main service so badly they don't seem to care. Isn't this a great idea?

No. If a product with a dominant market share is sold only to customers if they also agree to buy another product, this could be an illegal tying arrangement. While there are exceptions, any such plan should be cleared by your Legal Department.

At a trade association meeting, a few of us from competing companies met for drinks and the talk turned to what we each charge our customers. This seemed wrong but I didn't know how to deal with the situation.

You should say forcefully that you can't participate in price or similar discussions. If the talk continues, walk out and make a show of it (such as spilling your drink) so your protest will be remembered. Discussions like these are frequently used as evidence of illegal agreements, even against people who participated unwillingly but silently.

SOURCE From *The Dun & Bradstreet Corporation's Policy of Business Conduct* (1998). Used by permission.

INSIDE STORY

AN OPERATING SYSTEM BY ANY OTHER NAME WOULD BROWSE AS SWEETLY

In 1994, the U.S. Department of Justice's Antitrust Division charged Microsoft Corporation, the largest software company in the world, with unlawful monopoly and restraint of trade under Sections 1 and 2 of the Sherman Act. Among other things, the regulators alleged that Microsoft had engaged in anticompetitive marketing practices directed at personal computer (PC) manufacturers that preinstall operating system software on the PCs they produce for retail sale. These included charging per-processor royalties, whereby PC manufacturers were offered a discount if they agreed to pay a royalty to Microsoft for each computer processor sold, regardless of whether the unit was shipped with the Microsoft operating system or a competitor's operating system.

After a year of legal wrangling, Microsoft signed a consent decree on August 21, 1995. Microsoft agreed not to charge per-processor royalties. The decree also prohibited Microsoft from conditioning the licensing of its operating system software to original equipment manufacturers (OEMs) on their agreement to license other Microsoft products. However, Microsoft retained the right to develop integrated products. In particular, the Section IV(E)(I) of the consent decree provided:

> Microsoft shall not enter into any License Agreement in which the terms of that agreement are expressly or impliedly conditioned upon:

> (1) the licensing of any other Covered Product, Operating System Software product or other product (provided however that this provision in and of itself shall not be construed to prohibit Microsoft from developing integrated products).

The government based its demand on the notion of "network economies," a condition in which the value of owning a product rises as other consumers own the same product. Facsimile machines are an obvious example. Having the only fax machine in the world is worthless, but having one of a million fax machines is quite valuable because it allows one to communicate with 999,999 other fax-machine owners. Much of the value of the product arises from being part of the network.

Such networks can be physical or virtual. The former includes telephones and railroads; the latter includes most shared technologies and standards. For instance, there are networks of VHS video recorders and Macintosh computers whereby members of the network can interact with each other in valuable ways, such as by exchanging videotapes or computer files. The interaction is possible because users share a common technology or standard. Computer operating system software is another example; software developers generally prefer to invest their resources in designing applications for platforms in widespread rather than limited use. Once there are many applications for an operating system, that system becomes more attractive to consumers as well.

For this reason, Microsoft's stunning success in the market for PC operating system software worried the regulators. Because most PC owners used Microsoft's operating system, the regulators argued, Microsoft could coerce them into buying other products simply by tying the two together. For instance, Microsoft might condition the sale of Windows on the purchase of its word-processing software Word. By so tying the products together, Microsoft would force PC users to combine rather than separate their choices for operating systems and word processors. As a result, consumers of PCs would end up buying Microsoft's operating system and its word processor even if they would prefer Microsoft's operating system and a non-Microsoft word processor. Of course, consumers could still purchase the non-Microsoft word processor, but the additional purchase price and switching costs would probably deter some.

Microsoft argued, however, that operating systems are dynamic and must respond to consumer demand and technological advancement. Microsoft reasoned that initially operating systems did not include modules for data compression, memory management, file backup, or device driving. Such "extras" were provided separately. Over time, these functions were integrated into the operating system as consumers began to expect them as standards rather than options. In fact, Microsoft's DOS operating system and its Windows graphical user interface (GUI) were originally separate products, with the latter running on top of the former like any other separate application. As the GUI became standard, it was integrated into the operating system. To protect this long-term strategy of continually enhancing its operating system by integrating new and better functions, Microsoft demanded and received permission in the consent decree to continue developing "integrated" products.

While the antitrust guardians were battling Microsoft and hammering out the consent decree, the World Wide Web came into being and promised to give everyone access to everything. In April 1994, Microsoft founder, chairperson, and CEO Bill Gates publicly announced Microsoft's intention to include Internet-browsing software in Windows 95. Soon after, Microsoft unveiled Internet Explorer to compete with Netscape Communications Corporation's wildly popular Navigator browser. By the time Microsoft signed the consent decree in 1995, Microsoft had already supplied to manufacturers a version of Windows 95 bundled with Explorer at no additional cost. In addition to receiving Internet Explorer bundled with Windows, OEMs were prohibited from disassembling the package.

Historically, PC operating systems have always served to coordinate a user's access to various sources of information, including internal hard drives, floppy disk drives, random access memory, and CD-ROM drives. With the birth of the Internet, Microsoft reasoned, it was time for operating systems to provide access to this next, great source of information. By its logic, integration of Web browsers was the natural next step in operating system evolution. Within two years, Internet Explorer had garnered more than 40% of the Web browser market, largely at Netscape's expense. No doubt, Internet Explorer's rapid success arose in part from Microsoft's provision of the browser with Windows for the same price. Its functionality, however, made it a worthy rival to Navigator. Many critics concluded that Internet Explorer 4.0, released in 1997, was a better product than Netscape Navigator.[55] Dell Computer Corporation chairperson Michael Dell claimed that his customers would demand Windows with Internet Explorer even if the products were not bundled.[56]

On October 20, 1997, the Department of Justice petitioned the U.S. District Court for the District of Columbia to find Microsoft in contempt of court for violating the 1995 consent decree and to fine the company $1 million per day until it complied. The regulators argued that the company had violated the decree by conditioning its licensing of Windows 95 on the licensing of Internet Explorer. "Microsoft is not entitled to require computer manufactures and consumers to take Internet Explorer when they license Windows 95," claimed Assistant Attorney General Joel Klein. In addition to the fine, the government asked the court (1) to stop Microsoft from requiring PC manufacturers to accept Internet Explorer as a condition of receiving Windows 95; and (2) to require Microsoft to notify Windows 95 consumers that they are not required to use Internet Explorer and to give consumers simple instructions for removing the Internet Explorer icon from their computer desktop.

In its defense, Microsoft claimed that Internet Explorer was integrated with Windows and, therefore, within the consent decree's bounds. "This is capitalism," exclaimed Gates after the government filed its petition. "We create a product called Windows. Who decides what's in Windows? It's the customers who buy Windows." Not, it would seem, government bureaucrats, at least as far as Gates was concerned. To the contrary, argued Klein, "[E]veryone knows you have an operating system, you have a browser."[57]

Judge Thomas Penfield Jackson framed the issue as follows:

> A critical element of the present dispute, therefore, is whether Internet Explorer is to be deemed an "integrated" component of Windows 95, or, to the contrary, an "other product," distinct and severable from the operating system without otherwise impairing the system's operational integrity.[58]

The government asserted a violation of the court-approved consent decree, not the antitrust laws. Hence, contempt of court was the government's charge against Microsoft. That turned out to be a doubled-edged sword for the antitrust warriors. Because judicial orders must provide "explicit notice of precisely what conduct is outlawed," the court had to resolve any ambiguities in the terms of the consent decree in Microsoft's favor. Judge Jackson found Microsoft's interpretation of "integrated" versus "other product" plausible and, therefore, rejected the government's request to find the company in contempt and fine it $1 million per day.

However, that did not end the case. Judge Jackson had found only that the terms of the consent decree were ambiguous, not that Microsoft actually was in compliance with those terms. Without further evidence, he could not issue a final ruling, because the record was incomplete and there were many disputed issues of technological fact and contract interpretation. Judge Jackson then issued a preliminary injunction prohibiting Microsoft from further conditioning its licensing of PC operating system software (including Windows 95 or any successor version) on the licensing of any Microsoft browser pending development of the record. The injunction did not affect PCs on which Internet Explorer had already been installed.

Many commentators questioned the Antitrust Division's pursuit of Microsoft on this point. "There may well be a tremendous amount of market power exercised by a company like Microsoft, but there is a question of what you can do about it," observed economist Robert Tollison, director of the Center for the Study of Public Choice at George Mason University. "By the time you do something about it, the world has innovated 10 times over again. A lot of what you can do is either harmful or irrelevant."[59] Robert Crandall, a senior fellow at the Brookings Institution in Washington, D.C., noted that *first-mover advantages* (e.g., the advantages accruing to the firm that is first to enter a market) can be real but are often ephemeral. When asked if anything could or should be done about a significant first-mover advantage in order to help the U.S. economy, Crandall answered, "Probably very little."[60]

Netscape retained antitrust scholar and former judge Robert H. Bork, a fellow of the American Enterprise Institute, to represent the company in its efforts to persuade the Justice Department to bring a broader case against Microsoft under Section 2. Bork asserted that Microsoft had engaged in predatory business practices "intended to preserve the company's monopoly of personal computer operating systems through practices that exclude or severely hinder rivals but do not benefit consumers."[61] Bork alleged that (1) Microsoft's operating system licenses have forbidden makers of personal computers to alter the first display screen from that required by Microsoft, thereby controlling what the consumer sees; (2) Microsoft has forbidden Inter- net service providers to advertise or promote any non-Microsoft Web browser; and (3) Internet content providers (such as Disney that provide news, entertainment, and other information from sites on the Web) have been forced to agree not to promote content developed for competing platforms as a condition to gaining access to Microsoft's screen display.[62]

On May 12, 1998, the U.S. Court of Appeals for the District of Columbia stayed the injunction insofar as it applied to Windows 98 (which further integrated Internet Explorer into the operating system).[63] The court held that "The United States presented no evidence suggesting Windows 98 was not an 'Integrated Product' and thus exempt from the prohibitions of Section IV (E)(I)."

Faced with the imminent launch of Windows 98 and perhaps believing that it was now or never, the Department of Justice (DOJ) filed a wide-ranging complaint against Microsoft on May 18, 1998. The attorneys general of 20 states filed similar suits the same day. The DOJ suit alleged that Microsoft's restrictive agreements with Internet and on-line service providers (such as America Online) and Internet content providers, whereby those companies agreed not to license, distribute, or promote non-Microsoft products (or to do so only on terms that materially disadvantaged such products), and Microsoft's agreements with OEMs restricting modification or customization of the PC boot-up sequence and screen, unreasonably restrict competition in violation of

Section 1. The complaint also alleged that Microsoft engaged in a series of anticompetitive practices (including tying and unreasonably exclusionary agreements) with the purpose and effect of maintaining its PC operating system monopoly and extending that monopoly to the Internet browser market in violation of Section 2.

As relief, the Government requested an injunction enjoining Microsoft from (1) requiring any person to license Microsoft's Internet browser or any other software product or service as a condition of licensing or distributing any Microsoft operating system product; (2) requiring any person to agree not to license, distribute, or promote any non-Microsoft Internet browser software or other software product or to do so on disadvantageous, restrictive or exclusionary terms; (3) restricting the right of any person to modify the screens, boot-up sequence or functions of any Microsoft operating system product to add or substitute a non-Microsoft Internet browser or other software products, as long as such addition or substitution does not materially impair the performance of the Microsoft operating system product; (4) for a period of three years, distributing a single version of its operating system that includes Microsoft's browser software unless Microsoft also includes the most current version of the Netscape Internet browser (a condition Microsoft analogized to requiring Coca Cola Company to include two Pepsi colas in every six-pack of Coke); and (5) distributing at a single price a version of

Windows 98 bundled with software providing the Internet Explorer icon unless Microsoft gives OEMs a practical and commercially reasonable option of deleting or not installing the software that provides the Internet Explorer icon and Microsoft deducts from the Windows 98 royalty an amount equal to the OEM's reasonable cost of deleting or not installing the software.

The case was assigned to Judge Jackson, who scheduled the trial for September 1998. Regardless of the suit's outcome, there is a consensus building in the high-tech industry that this case will alter how the computer industry and the Internet develop in the future.[64] *Business Week* reports that sources close to the DOJ and state attorneys general say that the government hopes the suits will establish general principles on practices, such as exclusionary contracts and product bundling, that will apply to markets beyond browsers.[65] This could affect Microsoft's ability to integrate into Windows new features, such as voice recognition and visual recognition, and to extend the Windows platform to consumer appliances (such as interactive television) and to computer servers for electronic commerce by using its opening screen for Windows as the portal to the Internet. Roberta R. Katz, general counsel for Netscape, claimed: "Anyone who cares about the Internet and the digital marketplace has got to care that there be competitive, alternative routes to get there."[66]

For his part, Bill Gates predicted that Microsoft would win

the case, saying that "this is a lawsuit where the government had its best day when it filed the suit."[67] He characterized Microsoft's conduct as pro-consumer and stated that the law on Microsoft's ability to innovate on behalf of consumers was "crystal clear."[68] He noted that Internet Explorer had been in Windows from the beginning, yet did not gain significant market share until Microsoft listened to its customers and made a better product. Gates characterized the software industry as being highly competitive and warned against undue government interference in an industry that has been a major engine for growth in the United States and a significant generator of export revenues.

55. For a list of product reviews, *see* <http://www.microsoft.com/ie/press/>.

56. David Bank, *Why Software and Antitrust Law Make an Uneasy Mix*, WALL ST. J., Oct. 22, 1997, at B1.

57. *Id.*

58. United States v. Microsoft Corp., 980 F. Supp. 537 (D.D.C. 1997).

59. Anna Bray Duff, *Are Successful High-Tech Firms Next Target of Antitrust Action?* INVESTOR'S BUS. DAILY, Oct. 11, 1997, at A6.

60. *Id. See also* John R. Wilke & Bryan Gruley, *Is Antitrust Relevant in This Digital Age? Watch Microsoft's Case*, WALL ST. J., Oct. 22, 1997, at A1.

61. Robert H. Bork, *What Antitrust Is All About*, N. Y. TIMES, May 4, 1998, at A23.

62. *Id.*

63. Microsoft Corp. v. United States, ___ F.3d ___ (D.C. Cir. 1998).

64. Amy Cortese et al., *The Battle for the Cyber Future*, BUS. WK., June 1, 1998, at 38.

65. *Id.* at 39.

66. *Id.* at 40–41.

67. *Id.* at 40.

68. *Id.*

KEY WORDS AND PHRASES

QUESTIONS AND CASE PROBLEMS

1. SpeeDee Oil Change Systems is a nationwide franchisor of car-care centers offering oil changes, tune ups, and other basic automotive services. Its franchises are sold throughout the United States and abroad. SpeeDee entered into a contract with Mobil Oil under which Mobil would provide promotional assistance to SpeeDee franchisees and make contributions to an advertising fund. In return, SpeeDee made the Mobil brand of motor oil the recommended primary lubricant at all SpeeDee franchised outlets. In effect, this made the Mobil brand the only approved brand for purchase in bulk by SpeeDee franchisees.

Jim Elliot is a SpeeDee franchisee. He wants to offer oil and other products by Castrol but is constrained by his franchise agreement, or so say SpeeDee attorneys who have threatened to terminate his franchise. He thinks the franchise agreement is unfair. What legal action can he take? What would he have to prove? [*Wilson v. Mobil Oil Corp.*, 984 F. Supp. 450 (E.D. La. 1997)]

2. A manufacturer of electronics in New Orleans, Louisiana, authorized Hayman Electronics and Radio World to sell its products in the New Orleans area. Hayman had been a retailer of these products for several years; Radio World's relationship with the manufacturer was more recent. Hayman complained to the manufacturer that Radio World was price cutting and requested that the manufacturer terminate Radio World as a retailer. The manufacturer did so. Radio World comes to you, the company attorney, asking you what Radio World can do about the termination. What additional information would you like to know, and how will you respond?

3. Queen City Pizza is a franchisee of Domino's Pizza, Inc. By Domino's standard franchise agreement, all pizza ingredients, beverages, and packaging materials used by Queen City must conform to standards set by Domino's. The agreement also gives Domino's sole discretion to require franchisees to purchase these items only from Domino's or approved suppliers. As a result, Domino's supplies 90% of the $500 million in ingredients used by its 3,500 franchisees each year. Except for fresh dough, Domino's purchases the ingredients from approved suppliers and then resells them to franchisees at a markup.

Queen City claims that Domino's has monopolized the market in pizza supplies and ingredients for use in Domino's stores in violation of Section 2 of the Sherman Act. Analyze the merits of this claim. [*Queen City Pizza, Inc. v. Domino's Pizza, Inc.*, 124 F.3d 430 (3d Cir. 1997)]

4. After their collective-bargaining agreement expired, the National Football League (NFL) and the NFL Players Association began to negotiate a new contract. The NFL presented a plan that would permit each of its teams to establish a "developmental squad" of substitute players, each of whom would be paid the same $1,000 weekly salary. The union disagreed, insisting that individual squad members should be free to negotiate their own salaries. When negotiations reached an impasse, the NFL unilaterally implemented the plan. The squad players brought suit against the league, claiming that the agreement among the NFL team owners to pay the players $1,000 per week restrained trade in violation of the Sherman Act. Can the NFL owners all agree to pay only $1,000 per week? [*Brown v. Pro Football, Inc.,* 518 U.S. 231 (1996)]

5. United States manufacturers want to bring a suit against Japanese manufacturers, alleging a conspiracy to take over the U.S. automobile industry by exporting low-priced products to the United States while keeping the prices artificially high in Japan. The U.S. manufacturers tell you, their attorney, that the Japanese manufacturers have formed an association in which they discuss market conditions in the United States, potential or actual import restrictions, surcharges, and simplification of export procedures, as well as other topics.

a. In light of these facts, what are the chances of successfully bringing an antitrust suit against these manufacturers? Assume that there are no conflict-of-law or other procedural problems due to the manufacturers' being in another country.

b. What if, instead of discussing the topics listed above, they discussed the details of individual sales, production, inventories, current price lists, and future price trends?

c. What if they discussed average costs, freight rates, and terms of past transactions, without identifying buyers or sellers? [*Matsushita Elec. Indus. Co. v. Zenith Radio Corp.,* 475 U.S. 574 (1986)]

6. Lillian Alexander worked for Western Propane Company in Colorado. After becoming disgruntled with the company, she left and opened her own propane company, which competed directly with Western Propane. The two companies fought for the same customers. Within two years, Alexander's company went from 0% to 25% of the market, and Western Propane's share dropped from 75% to 50%. Alexander comes to you, her attorney, wanting to bring suit against Western

Propane for predatory pricing. She tells you that during a recent price war Western Propane priced its product below average total cost. What must you prove to show predatory pricing, and what are your chances of success? [*McGahee v. Northern Propane Gas Co.,* 858 F.2d 1487 (11th Cir. 1988), *cert. denied,* 490 U.S. 1084 (1989)]

7. The National Society of Professional Engineers (NSPE), with a membership of 69,000 engineers, adopted a code of ethics that prohibited its members from engaging in competitive bidding. As interpreted by the NSPE's board of ethical review, the rule against competitive bidding barred engineers from submitting any price information to prospective customers and from entering into any discussion of fees until after an engineer is selected for a particular job. When the NSPE's code of ethics was challenged as violating Section 1 of the Sherman Act, the NSPE argued that its rule against competitive bidding was reasonable. The NSPE argued that price competition among engineers might adversely affect the quality of engineering and was accordingly contrary to the public interest.

a. Should the NSPE's code of ethics be analyzed under the rule of reason or under the *per se* rule?

b. Assuming analysis under the rule of reason, should the code of ethics be held to violate Section 1 of the Sherman Act? Make the arguments for and against holding the code of ethics to be illegal price-fixing. [*National Soc'y of Professional Engrs. v. United States,* 435 U.S. 679 (1978)]

8. The Aspen Skiing Company (Aspen Ski) owned three of the four mountain skiing facilities in Aspen, Colorado. The fourth facility was owned by the Aspen Highlands Skiing Corporation (Highlands). Between 1962 and 1977, Aspen Ski and Highlands jointly offered a six-day ticket providing skiers with unlimited access to all four facilities. Revenues from the "all-Aspen" ticket, which was very popular with skiers, were divided on the basis of usage. In 1976–77, Aspen Ski's share of the market for downhill skiing services in Aspen was approximately 80%.

In the late 1970s, Aspen Ski's management came to believe that Aspen Ski could expand its market share if it discontinued the all-Aspen ticket. For the 1977–78 season, Aspen Ski refused to market the all-Aspen ticket unless Highlands accepted a fixed share of the revenue, rather than a share based on usage. In 1978–79, Aspen Ski refused to market the all-Aspen ticket unless Highlands accepted an extremely low fixed share of the revenue, which Highlands declined to do. An Aspen Ski official admitted that Aspen Ski intended to make Highlands an offer that it could not accept. In addition, Aspen Ski took affirmative steps to make it difficult for Highlands to market its own all-Aspen ticket. This included refusing to sell lift tickets for Aspen Ski's facilities to Highlands and refusing to accept guaranteed Highlands vouchers in exchange for lift tickets to Aspen Ski's facilities.

As a result of these actions, Highlands's share of the market for downhill-skiing facilities in Aspen steadily declined, reaching 11% in 1980–81. In 1979, Highlands sued Aspen Ski for monopolization of the downhill-skiing market in Aspen.

a. What elements are required to prove a charge of monopolization?

b. Did Aspen Ski enjoy monopoly power in the relevant market?

c. Could the all-Aspen ticket be fairly characterized as an essential facility? If so, did Aspen Ski's refusal to provide Highlands with access to the all-Aspen ticket constitute evidence of intent to monopolize? [*Aspen Skiing Co. v. Aspen Highlands Skiing Corp.*, 472 U.S. 585 (1985)]

9. Honeywell Incorporated manufactures and sells industrial control equipment that controls the manufacturing processes at various refineries and factories. The equipment depends heavily on printed circuit boards, which contain many components. These components periodically fail, which in turn often causes the circuit board and the industrial control equipment also to fail. When a circuit board fails, Honeywell will replace it with a new or refurbished board, charging its customer 50% of the list price, as long as the customer returns the defective board.

Roughly 95% of the components on the circuit boards can be purchased either from the component manufacturer or from a component distributor. The other 5% are designed specifically for Honeywell by third-party manufacturers. Honeywell has restrictive agreements with these manufacturers whereby the manufacturers agree not to sell these components to either Honeywell equipment owners or service organizations. Honeywell also has a stated policy of not selling its components to anyone. When a circuit board fails, equipment owners cannot usually identify which component caused the failure. As a result, equipment owners essentially must return to Honeywell to obtain an entire replacement board.

PSI Repair Services offers circuit-board repair services to owners of industrial control equipment. PSI provides board services for customers who own systems manufactured by Honeywell's competitors by purchasing the necessary components from either the equipment or component manufacturer. It is also able to obtain any firmware and documentation necessary for the non-generic components either from the manufacturer's marketing information or by purchasing this information from the manufacturer. Because PSI is unable to obtain any of the components manufactured exclusively for Honeywell, it is, for all practical purposes, unable to compete in the market for repair of Honeywell boards. What legal claims does PSI have against Honeywell? [*PSI Repair Servs., Inc. v. Honeywell, Inc.*, 104 F.3d 811 (6th Cir. 1997), *cert. denied*, 117 S. Ct. 2434 (1997)]

MANAGER'S DILEMMA

10. You are the vice-president for marketing at Lucky Liquor, a manufacturer of liquor. During a meeting with your staff, several pricing proposals are made with strong arguments to support each proposal.

a. The manufacturer sets a minimum price per ounce that the wholesalers can charge.

b. The manufacturer sets a maximum price per ounce that the wholesalers can charge.

c. The wholesalers can charge any price they want within a certain range; if they charge a higher price, they must give the customer a rebate coupon for the differential.

d. The wholesalers can charge any price they want, but if they advertise a price that is less than Lucky Liquor's specified minimum advertised price, the wholesalers are not entitled to receive the marketing funds that Lucky Liquor provides wholesalers that do not advertise prices that are less than the specified minimum advertised price.

After the meeting, you are considering the pros and cons of each plan so you can make a recommendation to the president. Although each plan has different marketing advantages, your staff estimates approximately the same level of sales for each. What other factors should you consider before making your recommendation? What are the legal pros and cons of each proposal? What else do you need to know before calculating the legal tradeoffs among the proposals?

INTERNET SOURCES

The Competition Online site, maintained by the editors of *Competition Journal* in Dublin, Ireland, is a gateway to numerous U.S., European, and other antitrust sites.	http://www.clubi.ie/competition/ WorldsBiggestAntiTrustSitesList.html
Department of Justice	http://www.usdoj.gov
Federal Trade Commission	http://www.ftc.gov
Microsoft Corporation	http://www.microsoft.com
Netscape Communications	http://www.netscape.com

CHAPTER 19

Consumer Protection

INTRODUCTION

Role of Consumer Protection Law in Business

Historically, consumers had little recourse in the event of a dispute with a creditor, vendor, manufacturer, producer, or service provider. The words commonly associated with consumer transactions were *caveat emptor* ("let the buyer beware"). Now many federal and state laws protect consumers from discriminatory credit requirements, unfair and deceptive trade practices and fraud, and unsafe or harmful consumer products. Managers must, of course, comply with the laws. In addition, by being proactive and promoting industry self-regulation, managers may be able to forestall new regulatory restrictions.

Chapter Overview

This chapter examines four primary areas of consumer protection law and the agencies, departments, and commissions that administer and enforce it: (1) consumer credit and consumer bankruptcy under Chapter 13 of the Bankruptcy Code; (2) unfairness, deception, and fraud (including the regulation of advertising, packaging and labeling, pricing, warranties, and certain sales practices); (3) consumer privacy; and (4) consumer health and safety (including the regulation of alcohol, tobacco, smoking, gambling, firearms, drugs, medical devices, food, automobiles, broadcasting, and the Internet). The chapter focuses primarily on federal legislation, although numerous state law topics are discussed. In general, consumer protection law at the state level is more stringent than federal law.

 Commissions and Agencies

Federal regulatory agencies involved in consumer protection are either independent commissions or executive branch agencies. Independent commissions include the Federal Trade Commission (FTC), the Federal Communications Commission (FCC), the Securities and Exchange Commission (SEC), the Federal Reserve System, and the Consumer Product Safety Commission (CPSC). The Federal Trade Commission, for example, has five commissioners appointed by the president and confirmed by the Senate for seven-year terms. No more than three of them can be from the same political party. The commissioners vote on decisions by majority vote and issue rules.

Executive branch regulatory agencies, on the other hand, are located in cabinet departments. Examples of executive branch regulatory agencies are the Food and Drug Administration (located within the U.S. Department of Health and Human Services), the Office of Interstate Land Sales Registration (U.S. Department of Housing and Urban Development), and the National Highway Traffic Safety Administration (U.S. Department of Transportation).

The "In Brief" identifies the key commissions and agencies charged with administering major consumer protection laws.

 ## Consumer Credit

At the turn of the century there were general *usury statutes* in most states that applied to lending transactions. These statutes set legal caps on what interest rates lenders could charge. In general, the maximum interest allowed under these laws was 6% to 12%. As a result, many consumers were unable to procure small loans and an illegal lending market that often involved organized crime developed. In response, Congress made it a federal crime to engage in the *extortionate extension of credit*, defined in the law as the making of a loan for which violence was understood by the parties as likely to occur in the event of nonpayment.

Because credit continues to play an important role in many consumer transactions, a range of consumer protection laws address this area. This chapter discusses federal and state regulation of consumer credit, as well as consumer bankruptcy issues. Business bankruptcy is covered in Chapter 24.

 ## Consumer Credit Protection Act

Federal consumer credit law can be confusing because of the many acts with similar names. However, these complex acts and regulations are all part of the lengthy Consumer Credit Protection Act (CCPA),[1] which was initially passed by Congress in 1968. Since 1968, several additional acts (or titles) have been added to the original legislation. An overview of the CCPA is provided in Exhibit 19.1. Not all titles or provisions of the act are discussed in this chapter; those that are omitted are so noted.

---

1. 15 U.S.C. §§ 1601 *et seq.* (1998).

EXHIBIT 19.1   Consumer Credit Protection Act (CCPA)

TITLE	CONSUMER CREDIT PROTECTION ACT
I.	Truth-in-Lending Act (TILA)
	Chapter 1: General Provisions [omitted]
	Chapter 2: Credit Transactions
	Chapter 3: Credit Advertising
	Chapter 4: Fair Credit Billing Act
	Chapter 5: Consumer Leasing Act
II.	Extortionate Credit Transactions [discussed above]
III.	Restrictions on Garnishment
IV.	National Commission on Consumer Finance [omitted]
V.	General Provisions [omitted]
VI.	Fair Credit Reporting Act
VII.	Equal Credit Opportunity Act
VIII.	Fair Debt Collection Practices Act
IX.	Electronic Fund Transfer Act

Truth-in-Lending Act

Title I, the Truth-in-Lending Act (TILA), is intended "to assure a meaningful disclosure of credit terms so that the consumer will be able to compare more readily the various credit terms available and avoid the uninformed use of credit."[2] In particular, the act makes uniform the actuarial method for determining the rate of charge for consumer credit. But the act is not a usury statute, and nowhere in the act are interest rates set. The TILA applies only to credit transactions (for example, sales, loans, and leases[3]) between creditors and consumers, not to credit transactions between two consumers. Debtors must be natural persons, so corporations and other entities are not protected by the act.

The TILA also draws a distinction between open-end credit and closed-end credit. The former occurs when the parties intend the creditor to make repeated

---

2. 15 U.S.C. § 1601 (1998).

3. Under federal law, consumer lessees are also protected by the 1976 Consumer Leasing Act, which is Chapter 5 of the TILA. The Federal Reserve Board has issued regulations (known collectively as Regulation M) to implement the act. Under these regulations, consumer leases are defined to include leases that last more than four months and do not exceed $25,000. The act and accompanying regulations control both advertising and disclosure in connection with these consumer leases.

IN BRIEF

CONSUMER PROTECTION LAWS AND THEIR ADMINISTRATION

Agency, Department, or Commission	Consumer Credit	Unfairness, Deception, and Fraud	Consumer Health and Safety
Federal Trade Commission Established: 1914 Commissioners: 5 1996 Budget: $100 million	Credit Advertising; Fair Credit Reporting Act; Fair Debt Collection Practices Act	Advertising; Sales Practices	
Food and Drug Administration (U.S. Department of Health and Human Services) Established: 1930 Commissioners: 1 1996 Budget: $877 million		Labeling of Food (except meat, poultry, and eggs), Drugs, and Cosmetics	Adulterated Food and Cosmetics; Approval of Drugs and Medical Devices
U.S. Department of Agriculture Established: 1862 1996 Budget: $58.7 billion		Labeling of Meat, Poultry and Eggs	Inspection of Meat, Poultry and Egg Processing Facilities
Federal Communications Commission Established: 1934 Commissioners: 5 1996 Budget: $1 billion		Telemarketing	Broadcast Standards
U.S. Postal Service Established: 1775 Reorganized 1970 1996 Budget: $60.3 billion			
Office of Interstate Land Sales Registration (U.S. Department of Housing and Urban Development) Established: 1969		Interstate Land Sales	
Securities and Exchange Commission Established: 1934 Commissioners: 5 1996 Budget: $376 million		Securities Fraud	
Federal Reserve Board Established: 1913 Governors: 7	Truth in Lending Act (Regulation Z); Consumer Leasing Act (Regulation M); Equal Credit Opportunity Act (Regulation B); Electronic Fund Transfer Act (Regulation E)		
National Highway Transportation Safety Administration (NHTSA) (U.S. Department of Transportation) Established: 1970 Administrators: 1 1996 Budget: $242 million			Automobile Safety Standards; Driver Safety
Consumer Product Safety Commission (CPSC) Established: 1972 Commissioners: 3 1996 Budget: $41 million			Consumer Product Safety Act (CPSA); Consumer Product Safety
U.S. Department of Labor, Est.: 1913 1996 Budget:$33.4 billion	Garnishment of Wages		
State Law, Departments and Commissions	Installment Sales; Loans to Consumers; Uniform Consumer Credit Code (UCCC)	State Labeling Laws; State Deceptive Practices Statutes; Insurance Regulation; Lemon Laws; Uniform Commercial Code (UCC)	State Departments of Consumer Affairs
Other Federal Law	Chapter 13 Consumer Bankruptcy		

SOURCE Budget of the United States Government Fiscal Year 1998, Appendix.

EXHIBIT 19.2   Loan Model Form

ANNUAL PERCENTAGE RATE The cost of your credit as a yearly rate. %	FINANCE CHARGE The dollar amount the credit will cost you. $	Amount Financed The amount of credit provided to you or on your behalf. $	Total of Payments The amount you will have paid after you have made all payments as scheduled. $

You have the right to receive at this time an itemization of the Amount Financed.

☐ I want an itemization.   ☐ I do not want an itemization.

Your payment schedule will be:

Number of Payments	Amount of Payments	When Payments Are Due

Insurance

Credit life insurance and credit disability insurance are not required to obtain credit, and will not be provided unless you sign and agree to pay the additional cost.

Type	Premium	Signature
Credit Life		I want credit life insurance. _____(signature)
Credit Disability		I want credit disability insurance. _____(signature)
Credit Life and Disability		I want credit life and disability insurance. _____(signature)

You may obtain property insurance from anyone you want that is acceptable to _____(creditor). If you get the insurance from _____ (creditor), you will pay $_____.

Security: You are giving a security interest in:
_____   the goods or property being purchased.
_____   (brief description of other property).
Filing fees $_____   Non-filing insurance $_____
Late Charge: If a payment is late, you will be charged $_____/_____% of the payment.

Prepayment: If you pay off early, you
_____may   _____will not   have to pay a penalty.
_____may   _____will not   be entitled to a refund of part of the finance charge.
See your contract documents for any additional information about nonpayment, default, any required repayment in full before the scheduled date, and prepayment refunds and penalties.

_____
e means an estimate

extensions of credit (for example, Visa or MasterCard), whereas the latter involves only one transaction (for example, a car or house loan). Open-end consumer credit plans must make certain disclosures at three separate times: (1) in an initial disclosure statement when the account is opened; (2) in subsequent periodic billing statements; and (3) annually when a consumer must be notified of his or her rights under the Fair Credit Billing Act. In general, the required information includes finance and other charges, security interests (collateral), previous balance and credits, identification of transactions, closing date and new balance, and annual percentage rates and period rates.

Closed-end credit plans require disclosure for each transaction of at least the following: identity of creditor, amount financed, finance charge, annual percentage rate, variable rate, payment schedule, total of payments, total sale price, prepayment provisions, late payment fee, security interest, credit insurance, loan assumption policy, and required deposit. Special rules apply for certain residential mortgages and adjustable rate transactions.

Regulation Z Congress directed the Federal Reserve Board (FRB) to interpret and enforce the TILA. To that end, the FRB issued regulations, known collectively as *Regulation Z*.[4] The FRB has also produced model disclosure forms for use with credit sales and loans. An example of the model form for loans appears as Exhibit 19.2.[5]

Regulation Z applies to any transaction (in which both parties are subject to the TILA) that involves an installment contract in which payment is to be made in more than four installments and the credit is primarily for personal, family, or household purposes. The two most important terms in a TILA disclosure statement are the finance charge (interest over the life of the loan expressed as a dollar amount) and the annual percentage rate (APR) (interest expressed as a percentage), both as defined in Regulation Z. Typical transactions include car loans, student loans, home improvement loans, and certain real estate loans in which the amount financed is less than $25,000. Regulation Z also contains provisions dealing with disclosure of the terms of any credit or mortgage insurance offered in connection with a loan. In the following case, the court considered the TILA responsibility of an automobile retailer who retains part of the price of third-party warranties.

---

4. 12 C.F.R. § 226 (1998).

5. 12 C.F.R. § 226.18 app. H-2 (1998).

A CASE IN POINT   SUMMARY

CASE 19.1
GIBSON v.
BOB WATSON
CHEVROLET–GEO, INC.
United States
Court of Appeals
for the Seventh Circuit
112 F.3d 283 (7th Cir. 1997).

FACTS Ruthie Gibson purchased a used car from Chicago car dealer Bob Watson Chevrolet–Geo, Inc. To facilitate her purchase, Gibson took advantage of the dealership's offer to finance her acquisition. As a part of the transaction, Bob Watson gave Gibson a statement entitled "Itemization of Amount Financed." The statement contained a category labeled "Amounts Paid to Others on Your Behalf," under which was the entry "To North American for Extended Warranty $800.00." Gibson discovered that a substantial amount of that $800 was retained by Bob Watson rather than paid to North American, the company that provided the extended warranty. Gibson sued Bob Watson, alleging that its undisclosed retention of a portion of the $800 made its statement false, thereby violating the Truth-in-Lending Act. Similarly, Gibson alleged that because Bob Watson marked up the price of warranties more for credit customers than for cash customers, it retained more of the warranty price and effectively levied an additional and undisclosed finance charge in violation of the TILA. The district court dismissed the complaint, and Gibson appealed.

Case 19.1 continues

Case 19.1 continued

ISSUE PRESENTED   Does the TILA require the seller of a car on credit to disclose that a portion of the price of third-party–provided services is retained by the dealer? Does the TILA require disclosure as "finance charges" of the difference between the retention portions for cash and credit customers?

SUMMARY OF OPINION   The U.S. Court of Appeals began by noting that Gibson alleged two different violations of the TILA. First, she alleged that when Bob Watson sold cars for cash rather than credit, it marked up the cost of the warranty by a lesser amount, thereby retaining a smaller amount of the warranty charge for cash customers. Hence, credit customers paid more for the same car and warranty than cash customers. This difference, she argued, is a "finance charge," which the TILA requires the dealer to disclose. Second, the act requires the lender to provide "a written itemization of the amount financed," including "each amount that is or will be paid to third persons by the creditor on the consumer's behalf, together with an identification of or reference to the third person."[6] Gibson alleged that although Bob Watson disclosed that $800 would be paid to North American for the extended warranty, it paid only a portion of that $800 to North American and retained the difference. Hence, its disclosure to her contained a false representation regarding payments to third persons on her behalf.

If Bob Watson did systematically charge credit customers more for the extended warranty than it charged cash customers, the cost of credit is implicated and, therefore, so is the TILA. "This is a type of fraud that goes to the heart of the concerns that actuate the [act]," the court explained.

Even if Bob Watson did not systematically charge credit customers more than cash customers for the extended warranty, the requirement to itemize for credit customers the amounts paid to third parties is free standing. Gibson alleged that Bob Watson's statement disclosed that it paid $800 to North American for the extended warranty when, in fact, it paid less. If proven, that would clearly violate the act's provision.

In its defense, Bob Watson argues that commentary by the Federal Reserve Board (FRB), whose Regulation Z implements the TILA, allows it to act as it did. The FRB commentary states that when a creditor retains a portion of the fee charged to a consumer for a service provided by a third party, such as an extended warranty, "the creditor . . . may reflect that the creditor has retained a portion of the amount paid to others." The commentary goes on to provide an example: "For example, the creditor could add to the category 'amount paid to others' language such as '(we may be retaining a portion of this amount).'" The use of the term "may" does not mean that creditors may or may not disclose their retention, as Bob Watson argued. That interpretation would be preposterous and contradict the statute. Instead, the commentary use of the term "may" suggests that creditors need not disclose how much of the amount they are retaining but only the fact that they may be retaining a portion of it.

RESULT   The appeals court reversed the trial court's dismissal of the case and ordered that the case continue.

---

6. 15 U.S.C. § 1638(a)(2)(B)(iii) (1998).

Credit Cards   One provision of the TILA limits the liability of credit card holders to $50 per card for unauthorized charges made before a card issuer is notified that the card has been lost or stolen. Once a card issuer has been notified, a card holder incurs no liability from unauthorized use. A credit card company also cannot bill a consumer for unauthorized charges if the card was improperly issued by the card company.

Although Regulation Z is usually triggered by credit arrangements in which a finance charge is imposed, the TILA and Regulation Z were amended in 1970 to include regulation of both credit cards (such as Visa or MasterCard, which permit deferred payment over a period of time) and charge cards (such as American Express, which require payment of the full balance upon receipt of the bill).

Regulation Z also has specific provisions that cover disclosure of information in credit card applications. Information, which must be presented in the form of a table, includes annual fee, annual percentage rates, variable rate information, grace period, minimum finance charge, method of computing balance, cash advance fee, late fee and over-limit fee, as well as any fees that vary by state. Every credit card offer or application must contain such a table. The FRB model form for applications and solicitations for credit cards appears as Exhibit 19.3.[7]

Home Equity Lending Plans   The TILA employs specific protections for consumers who use their home

---

7. 12 C.F.R. § 226.5a(b) app. G-10A (1998).

EXHIBIT 19.3   Applications and Solicitations Model Form (Credit Cards)

Annual percentage rate for purchases	_____ %
Variable rate information	Your annual percentage rate may vary. The rate is determined by [*explanation*].
Grace period for repayment of balances for purchases	You have [____ days] [until _____] [not less than _____ days] [between _____ and _____ days] [days on average] to repay your balance [for purchases] before a finance charge on purchases will be imposed. [You have no grace period in which to repay your balance for purchases before a finance charge will be imposed.]
Method of computing the balance for purchases	
Annual fees	[(Annual) [Membership] fee: $_____ per year] [(*type of fee*): $_____ per year] [(*type of fee*): $_____.]
Minimum finance charge	$_____
Transaction fee for purchases	[$____] [____% of ____]
Transaction fee for cash advances, and fees for paying late or exceeding credit limit	Transaction fee for cash advances: [$____] [____% of ____] Late payment fee: [$____] [____% of ____] Over-the-credit-limit fee: $_____

as collateral for a second mortgage or open-end line of credit. Because losing one's home has such significant consequences, Congress felt special disclosure requirements were in order for home equity loans. The TILA provides consumers a *right of recission* (that is, a right to cancel the contract) whenever their home is used as collateral except for original construction or acquisition. These cancellation rights are generally available for three days if all procedures are properly followed by the lender, three years if they are not. The TILA also mandates disclosure requirements including up-front costs, repayment schedules, and the annual percentage rate and its method of calculation.

Credit Advertising　　Chapter 3 of the TILA includes specific provisions that regulate credit advertising. The idea behind these provisions is that consumers equipped with complete and accurate credit information will be able to find the best terms. Regulation Z requires that any advertised specific credit terms must be actually available and that any credit terms (for example, finance charge or annual percentage rate) mentioned in the advertisement must be explained fully. The FTC enforces the advertising provisions of Regulation Z. Unlike the other sections of the TILA, there is no private cause of action for a consumer to sue credit advertisers directly.

Credit Billing: The Fair Credit Billing Act　　Chapter 4 of the TILA is known as the Fair Credit Billing Act. By 1974, Congress had become concerned about the problems consumers were having in getting creditors to respond to their complaints. In response, Congress enacted the Fair Credit Billing Act, which requires creditors, such as credit card companies, to respond to consumer complaints with an acknowledgment of the complaint, followed by a reasonable investigation to determine whether the complaint is justified. Companies cannot evade this requirement by canceling a cardholder's account.

For example, in 1982, American Express Company canceled a cardholder's account during a dispute about incorrect billings. Although it argued that its contract with the cardholder allowed it to revoke a credit card at any time for any reason, the U.S. Court of Appeals for the District of Columbia ruled that the Fair Credit Billing Act's protections were not waivable.[8] As the court explained:

The rationale of consumer protection legislation is to even out the inequalities that consumers normally bring to the bargain. To allow such protection to be waived by boiler plate language of the contract puts the legislative process to a foolish and unproductive task. A court ought not impute such nonsense to a Congress intent on correcting abuses in the market place.

Hence, the Fair Credit Billing Act protected the cardmember despite the provisions of the Cardmember Agreement that purported to waive the protections of the act.

Restrictions on Garnishment

Garnishment is the legal procedure by which a creditor may collect a debt by attaching a portion of a debtor's weekly wages. Title III of the CCPA puts limits on the ability of creditors to garnish wages. In particular, the act restricts the amount of a debtor's wages that is available for garnishment to the lesser of either (1) 25% of the "disposable earnings" for that week (defined by the act as the amount remaining after deductions required by law), or (2) the amount by which "disposable earnings" for that week exceed 30 times the current federal minimum hourly wage. The secretary of labor enforces the provisions of this title. Some states prohibit garnishment of wages altogether.

Fair Credit Reporting Act

Qualifying for credit is important because of the widespread use of credit in consumer transactions. Almost everyone over the age of 18 has a credit report on file somewhere. Lenders look to these various reporting agencies for information on an individual's creditworthiness. Because negative information in a credit report can make obtaining credit considerably more difficult, it is helpful for consumers to be able to access these credit reports and correct any false information before it is reported to lenders or shared with any other reporting agency's computer.

A tort law cause of action for defamation may provide a remedy when a reporting agency circulates false information. However, such a claim can be defeated if the person transmitting the information did not know it was false. (Defamation and tort defenses are discussed in Chapter 9.)

Congress became concerned about potential injury to consumers through errors in credit reports and in

---

8. Gray v. American Express Co., 743 F.2d 10 (D.C. Cir. 1984).

1970 passed the Fair Credit Reporting Act (FCRA), which became Title VI of the Consumer Credit Protection Act (CCPA). Under the act, consumers can request all information (except medical information) on themselves, the source of the information, and any recent recipients of a report. The FCRA also gives consumers a right to have corrected copies of their credit reports sent to creditors. The FTC has primary responsibility for the enforcement of the FCRA.

Credit bureaus must investigate disputed information in credit reports and resolve consumer complaints within 30 days. The credit-reporting agency must go beyond the original source of information to determine whether it is accurate. Thus, when a consumer notified the agency that she had never held the credit cards her report showed as being delinquent, the agency could not just rely on the credit card companies' statements that the applications for the cards had the correct information; instead, the agency should have checked the handwriting on the credit applications and determined whether the applications were obtained by fraud.[9] Credit bureaus must give consumers written notice of the results of the investigation within five days after it is completed.

When a consumer disputes information in a file with a credit bureau, creditors must conduct an investigation, review all relevant information, and report inaccurate or incomplete information to all national credit bureaus. The act also contains restrictions on *investigative consumer reporting* (reports that contain information on character and reputation, not just credit history), including the requirement that in most cases a consumer be notified in writing that such a report may be made.

Amendments to the FCRA that became effective in September 1997 impose new restrictions on the use of credit reports by employers. These are designed to ensure that individuals (1) are aware that their credit reports may be used for employment purposes; (2) agree to such use; and (3) are notified promptly if information in their credit reports results in a negative employment decision. The employer must notify the individual in writing that a report may be used and obtain the individual's consent before asking a credit bureau for the report. Before an employer may rely on a credit report to take adverse action (defined as denying a job applicant a position, reassigning or terminating an employee, or denying a promotion), it must first provide the individual with a "pre–adverse action disclosure" that includes a copy of the credit report and the FTC's "A Summary of Your Rights Under the Fair Credit Reporting Act."

After an employer has taken adverse action, it must give the individual notice—orally, in writing, or electronically—that the action has been taken. The notice must include (1) the name, address, and phone number of the credit bureau that supplied the credit report; (2) a statement that the credit bureau did not make the decision to take adverse action and cannot give specific reasons for it; and (3) a notice of the individual's right to dispute the accuracy or completeness of any information the bureau furnished and the individual's right upon request to an additional free credit report from the credit bureau within 60 days.

Employers that fail to get permission before requesting a credit report or to provide the pre–adverse action disclosures are subject to suits for damages (including punitive damages for deliberate violations) by individuals and civil penalties by the FTC.

Equal Credit Opportunity Act

Passed by Congress in 1974, the Equal Credit Opportunity Act (Title VII of the CCPA) was originally intended to address the difficulty many women had in obtaining credit; it prohibited discrimination in the granting of credit on the basis of sex or marital status. The current list of protected categories includes race, color, religion, national origin, sex or marital status, age (except that older applicants may be given favorable treatment), applicants whose income derives from public assistance, and applicants who have exercised in good faith any right under the CCPA.

The Federal Reserve Board has issued regulations (known collectively as Regulation B) to implement the act. Unlike most of the other acts covered so far, the Equal Credit Opportunity Act applies to business credit as well as consumer credit. In general, the rejection of an application for credit triggers the act and various compliance steps, which include written notification of the reasons for denial. The regulations also establish methods for evaluating the creditworthiness of an applicant.

---

9. Cushman v. Trans Union Corp., 115 F.3d 220 (3d Cir. 1997).

ETHICAL CONSIDERATION

Is it ethical for a lender to call a friend in the police department to see whether a loan applicant has a criminal record? Should the applicant be notified of that investigation?

Fair Debt Collection Practices Act

Prior to enactment of the Fair Debt Collection Practices Act in 1978 (Title VIII of the CCPA), the common law was used to protect debtors from outrageous collection practices. For example, if a loan shark broke a debtor's kneecaps, the debtor would have an action for battery. Defamation and invasion of privacy actions were also common.

Since 1978, the Fair Debt Collection Practices Act, which is enforced by the FTC, has regulated debt collectors and debt-collection practices and provided a civil remedy for anyone injured by a violation of the statute. The act covers only third-party debt collectors (for example, collection agencies) or someone pretending to be a third-party collector. First-party debt collectors (for example, retail store collection departments) are not covered under the act, although the FTC can reach these individuals under its duty to address "unfair and deceptive trade practices" under Section 5 of the Federal Trade Commission Act. In general, FTC guidelines require collectors to tell the truth and not use any deceptive means to collect a debt or locate a debtor. For example, a collector may not give the impression that it is a government agency or credit bureau. As the following case illustrates, debt collectors have serious obligations toward those from whom they attempt to collect.

A CASE IN POINT   **IN THE LANGUAGE OF THE COURT**

CASE 19.2
BARTLETT v. HEIBL
United States
Court of Appeals
for the Seventh Circuit
128 F.3d 497 (7th Cir. 1997).

FACTS   Micard Services, a credit card company, hired attorney John Heibl to collect a consumer credit card debt of approximately $1,700 from Curtis Bartlett. Heibl sent Bartlett a letter, which Bartlett received but did not read, in which Heibl told him that "if you wish to resolve this matter before legal action is commenced, you must do one of two things within one week of the date of this letter": (1) pay $316 toward the satisfaction of the debt, or get in touch with Micard (the creditor), or (2) "make suitable arrangements for payment. If you do neither, it will be assumed that legal action will be necessary." Under Heibl's signature appeared a near-verbatim description of Section 1692g(a) of the Fair Debt Collection Practices Act (FDCPA). The section advised Bartlett that he had 30 days within which to dispute the debt, in which case Heibl would mail him a verification of it. At the end of the paraphrase, Heibl added that "suit may be commenced at any time before the expiration of this thirty (30) days."

Alleging that Heibl's letter violated the act by stating the required information in a confusing manner, Barlett filed suit against the debt collector. The trial court found for Hiebl, and Bartlett appealed.

ISSUE PRESENTED   Does a dunning letter violate the FDCPA by describing the debtor's and collector's respective rights in a way that confuses the debtor about his rights?

OPINION   POSNER, C.J., writing for the U.S. Court of Appeals:
The Fair Debt Collection Practices Act provides that within five days after a debt collector first duns a consumer debtor, the collector must send the debtor a written

Case 19.2 continues

Case 19.2 continued

notice containing specified information. The required information includes the amount of the debt, the name of the creditor, and, of particular relevance here, a statement that unless the debtor "disputes the validity of the debt" within thirty days the debt collector will assume that the debt is valid but that if the debtor notifies the collector in writing within thirty days that he is disputing the debt, "the debt collector will obtain verification of the debt [from the creditor] . . . and a copy of [the] verification . . . will be mailed to the consumer." A similar provision requires that the debtor be informed that upon his request the debt collector will give him the name and address of his original creditor, if the original creditor is different from the current one. If the debtor accepts the invitation tendered in the required notice, and requests from the debt collector either verification of the debt or the name and address of the original creditor, the debt collector must "cease collection of the debt . . . until the [requested information] is mailed to the consumer." These provisions are intended for the case in which the debt collector, being a hireling of the creditor rather than the creditor itself, may lack first-hand knowledge of the debt.

If the statute is violated, the debtor is entitled to obtain from the debt collector, in addition to any actual damages that the debtor can prove, statutory damages not to exceed $1,000 per violation, plus a reasonable attorney's fee.

. . .

The letter is said to violate the statute by stating the required information about the debtor's rights in a confusing fashion. Finding nothing confusing about the letter, the district court rendered judgment for the defendant after a bench trial. The plaintiff contends that this finding is clearly erroneous. The defendant disagrees, of course, but also contends that even if the letter is confusing this is of no moment because Bartlett didn't read it. That would be a telling point if Bartlett were seeking actual damages, for example as a consequence of being misled by the letter into surrendering a legal defense against the credit-card company. He can't have suffered such damages as a result of the statutory violation, because he didn't read the letter. But he is not seeking actual damages. He is seeking only statutory damages, a penalty that does not depend on proof that the recipient of the letter was misled. . . .

. . .

The main issue presented by the appeal is whether the district judge committed a clear error in finding that the letter was not confusing. The statute does not say in so many words that the disclosures required by it must be made in a nonconfusing manner. But the courts, our own included, have held, plausibly enough, that it is implicit that the debt collector may not defeat the statute's purpose by making the required disclosures in a form or within a context in which they are unlikely to be understood by the unsophisticated debtors who are the particular objects of the statute's solicitude.

Most of the cases put it this way: the implied duty to avoid confusing the unsophisticated consumer can be violated by contradicting or "overshadowing" the required notice. . . .

As with many legal formulas that get repeated from case to case without an effort at elaboration, "contradicting or overshadowing" is rather unilluminating—even, though we hesitate to use the word in this context, confusing. . . .

Case 19.2 continues

Case 19.2 continued

It would be better if the courts just said that the unsophisticated consumer is to be protected against confusion whatever form it takes. A contradiction is just one means of inducing confusion; "overshadowing" is just another; and the most common is a third, the failure to explain an apparent though not actual contradiction—as in this case. . . . On the one hand, Heibl's letter tells the debtor that if he doesn't pay within a week he's going to be sued. On the other hand, it tells him that he can contest the debt within thirty days. This leaves up in the air what happens if he is sued on the eighth day, say, and disputes the debt on the tenth day. He might well wonder what good it would do him to dispute the debt if he can't stave off a lawsuit. The net effect of the juxtaposition of the one-week and thirty-day crucial periods is to turn the required disclosure into legal gibberish. That's as bad as an outright contradiction.

. . . The cases . . . leave no room to doubt that the letter to Bartlett was confusing; nor as an original matter could we doubt that it was confusing—we found it so, and do not like to think of ourselves as your average unsophisticated consumer. So the judgment must be reversed. But we should not stop here. Judges too often tell defendants what the defendants cannot do without indicating what they can do, thus engendering legal uncertainty that foments further litigation. . . .

. . . We here set forth a redaction of Heibl's letter that complies with the statute without forcing the debt collector to conceal his intention of exploiting his right to resort to legal action before the thirty days are up. We are not rewriting the statute; that is not our business. We are simply trying to provide some guidance to how to comply with it. We commend this redaction as a safe harbor for debt collectors who want to avoid liability for the kind of suit that Bartlett has brought and now won. . . .

Dear Mr. Bartlett:

I have been retained by Micard Services to collect from you the entire balance, which as of September 25, 1995, was $1,656.90, that you owe Micard Services on your Master-Card Account No. 5414701617068749.

If you want to resolve this matter without a lawsuit, you must, within one week of the date of this letter, either pay Micard $316 against the balance that you owe (unless you've paid it since your last statement) or call Micard at 1-800-221-5920 ext. 6130 and work out arrangements for payment with it. If you do neither of these things, I will be entitled to file a lawsuit against you, for the collection of this debt, when the week is over.

Federal law gives you thirty days after you receive this letter to dispute the validity of the debt or any part of it. If you don't dispute it within that period, I'll assume that it's valid. If you do dispute it—by notifying me in writing to that effect—I will, as required by the law, obtain and mail to you proof of the debt. And if, within the same period, you request in writing the name and address of your original creditor, if the original creditor is different from the current creditor (Micard Services), I will furnish you with that information too.

The law does not require me to wait until the end of the thirty-day period before suing you to collect this debt. If, however, you request proof of the debt or the name and address of the original creditor within the thirty-day period that begins with your receipt of this letter, the law requires me to suspend my efforts (through litigation or otherwise) to collect the debt until I mail the requested information to you.

Sincerely,

John A. Heibl

Case 19.2 continues

Case 19.2 continued

We cannot require debt collectors to use "our" form. But of course if they depart from it, they do so at their risk. . . .

RESULT The appeals court reversed the trial court's decision and ordered judgment for the plaintiff and computation of statutory damages, costs, and attorney's fees.

Questions

1. How would the court have analyzed the case if Bartlett had been a consumer rights attorney himself and, in spite of Hiebl's letter, well aware of his FDCPA rights and Hiebl's corresponding obligations?
2. What are the arguments for and against statutory damages that allow a debtor who did not read a dunning letter to challenge it based on the letter's confusing, but never read, text?

ETHICAL CONSIDERATION

In communicating with a debtor, certain practices are specifically forbidden by the act, including having a debt collector contact a debtor at any time if that debtor is represented by an attorney. What self-imposed limits, if any, might a debt collector adopt and what role should a debtor's personal circumstances (for example, unemployment or terminal illness) play in how aggressive a debt collector might choose to be?

People who write bad checks for goods and services are protected from abusive debt collection practices by the FDCPA. The courts of appeal for the Seventh,[10] Eighth,[11] and Ninth circuits[12] have each held that the payment obligation that arises from a bounced check is "debt" within the meaning of the act even though the transaction involved no offer of credit or extension of credit.

Electronic Fund Transfer Act and Debit Cards

On-Line Debit Cards and Preauthorized Fund Transfers   The Electronic Fund Transfer Act (Title IX of the CCPA), passed by Congress in 1978, covers on-line debit cards issued by banks for use with automatic teller machines (ATMs) and point-of-sale transactions, as well as preauthorized electronic fund transfers or automatic payments from a consumer's account. As with credit cards, banks are prohibited from sending out debit cards except in response to a consumer's request.

In accordance with the act, the Federal Reserve Board (FRB) has issued regulations (called collectively Regulation E) and model forms for banks to use to satisfy disclosure requirements under the act. In general, the FRB forms ensure disclosure regarding contract terms, potential customer liability for unauthorized use (as with credit cards customer liability is usually limited to no more than $50), and consumer complaint procedures. Banks are also required to issue receipts with every ATM transaction and to mail periodic statements showing electronic fund transfer activity on a consumer's account during the period. For preauthorized transfers or automatic payments, banks are required to provide either (1) written or oral notice within two days of the scheduled transaction date that the transaction did or did not occur, or (2) provide a telephone line for consumers to call and ascertain whether the transfer occurred. Most financial institutions have adopted the latter approach.

---

10. Bass v. Stolper, Koritzinsky, Brewer & Neider, 111 F.3d 1322 (7th Cir. 1997).

11. Duffy v. Landberg, 133 F.3d 1120 (8th Cir. 1998).

12. Charles v. Lundgren & Assocs., P.C., 119 F.3d 739 (9th Cir. 1997).

Off-Line Debit Cards On-line debit cards are PIN-protected; that is, cash cannot be withdrawn from an ATM and a deduction cannot be made at a point-of-sale terminal unless the holder uses a personal identification number (PIN). In contrast, off-line debit cards (which may bear the Visa or MasterCard logo) have the characteristics of both an ATM card and a credit card, and they can be used without a personal identification number. For example, the holder of an off-line debit card could authorize a deduction from the consumer's bank account by signing a charge slip at a restaurant.

Federal law does not currently limit consumer liability for lost or stolen off-line debit cards. Thus, a thief could steal someone's debit card and empty that person's checking account by using the card for purchases before the card is even missed. Senator Jack Reed (D-RI) introduced legislation in September 1997 that would require financial institutions to limit consumer liability for lost or stolen debit cards to $50.[13] Visa and MasterCard voluntarily agreed in August 1997 to impose a $50 cap on liability for their debit cards.

 State Law

U–Triple C

All states have statutes regulating consumer credit. Two types of consumer credit transactions are addressed primarily at the state level: installment sales and loans to consumers. These state statutes vary widely, and an attempt to create uniform state laws on consumer credit through adoption of the Uniform Consumer Credit Code (UCCC, called the U–Triple C), has been largely unsuccessful. The UCCC has been adopted by only a handful of states, and in each of those it has been so significantly altered that little uniformity remains. The UCCC is intended to replace a state's consumer credit laws, including those that regulate usury, installment sales, consumer loans, truth in lending, and garnishment.

Installment Sales

State installment sales laws set caps on the legal interest rate and permissible charges such as late charges and de-ferral charges. In addition, the state statutes discuss remedies and attorney's fees, as well as any party's right to assign the sales contract.

Consumer Loans

Most states also have a statute (or several statutes) pertaining to consumer loans. In general, these statutes require compliance with the state's usury statute, although often a lender may be granted an exemption from the usury statute by obtaining a specified license in the state. If a lender is exempted from coverage of the usury laws, it can charge whatever rate of interest the market will bear.

State Credit Card Regulation

State usury statutes are also of concern to the credit card industry. In the early 1980s, in response to New York state's particularly stringent usury statute and credit card fee limits, Citibank moved its entire credit card operations from New York to South Dakota, a state with virtually no credit card regulations. The Supreme Court had previously ruled that the usury statutes and credit card fee limits in effect in the state in which the credit card operation is located apply to all customers, regardless of where they live.[14] Thus, a bank with credit card operations in a state such as South Dakota or Delaware can charge a resident of Massachusetts the high rates of interest and fees permitted in that state even though they are in excess of the Massachusetts limits.

 Consumer Bankruptcy: Chapter 13

Chapter 13 (consumer bankruptcy) of the Bankruptcy Code deals with adjustments to the debt of an individual or married couple with regular income. Chapters 7 (liquidation) and 11 (reorganization) of the act are discussed in detail in Chapter 24. Although an individual may also be the subject of a Chapter 7 liquidation or Chapter 11 reorganization, only individuals or small proprietorships are eligible under Chapter 13.

13. Dual-use Debit Cardholder Protection Act of 1997, S. 1154 (1997).

14. Marquette Nat'l Bank of Minneapolis v. First of Omaha Serv. Corp., 439 U.S. 299 (1978).

Chapter 13 Requirements

Individuals with regular income, including wage earners and individuals engaged in business, may qualify for Chapter 13 status if their unsecured debts do not exceed $100,000 and their secured debts do not exceed $350,000. Chapter 13 is similar to a reorganization in that it provides for a plan for repaying creditors.

Chapter 13 plans can be proposed only by debtors and usually are quite simple. The plan ordinarily allows the debtor to retain all of his or her assets, not just those that would be exempt (exempt property is defined below); but his or her future disposable income (which would be the debtor's to keep in a Chapter 7 or 11 bankruptcy) must be paid to a disbursing trustee for the next three to five years. Creditors holding claims secured by a mortgage, deed of trust, or security interest are entitled to the equivalent of the present value of their lien rights, except that Chapter 13 plans cannot modify home mortgage loans unless they provide for payments to cure default. Unlike under Chapter 11, creditors do not vote on Chapter 13 plans. However, they can object to confirmation if the plan is proposed in bad faith, is not feasible, or offers them less than what they would get in Chapter 7 liquidation.

A Chapter 13 plan may be either a composition plan or an extension plan. In a *composition plan*, creditors receive a percentage of the indebtedness and the debtor is *discharged* of the remaining obligation, meaning that the debtor is no longer legally liable for that amount. In an *extension plan*, creditors receive the entire indebtedness, but the period for payment is extended beyond the original due date.

After completing all plan payments, the debtor obtains a Chapter 13 discharge. An earlier discharge may be granted in hardship cases if the creditors have at least as much as they would have under Chapter 7. Apart from the hardship situation, this fresh start (sometimes called *super discharge*) will extinguish otherwise nondischargeable debts such as claims for fraud, theft, willful and malicious injury, or drunk driving, but not spousal or child support.

Advantages of Chapter 13

Chapter 13 has many advantages for overextended consumers. For example, the filing of a bankruptcy petition stops all creditor collection activity other than the filing of a claim in the bankruptcy proceeding. In addition, unlike in a Chapter 7 liquidation, a Chapter 13 debtor does not surrender any assets. A good faith effort to pay creditors can preserve goodwill and future credit prospects. Unfortunately, Chapter 13 debtors are often unable to make the payments outlined in their plan and eventually convert from Chapter 13 to Chapter 7. After conversion, the debtor's nonexempt property is liquidated, and the debtor receives a Chapter 7 discharge.

Individual Debtors under Chapter 7

A Chapter 7 liquidation results in the discharge of certain debts. (Chapters 11 and 13 may discharge a portion of a debt through a composition plan, but often plans only modify a repayment schedule.) Certain obligations are nondischargeable, including taxes, student loans (unless repayment would constitute an undue hardship), spousal or child support, fines or penalties, drunk-driving liabilities, or claims arising from fraud, theft, or willful or malicious conduct. The most widely used criteria in assessing undue hardship in the student loan context are (1) whether the debtor, for most of the loan repayment period, can maintain on current income and expenses a minimal standard of living; and (2) whether the debtor has made good faith repayment efforts. Other relevant considerations include the amount of the debt, the accumulation of interest, and the debtor's claimed expenses and current standard of living. A bankruptcy court may partially discharge student loans when full repayment would impose undue hardship on a debtor who could nonetheless manage partial payment.

A Chapter 7 discharge is not available to debtors who have received a discharge in a bankruptcy filed in the preceding six years. It will also be denied if the debtor has mistreated his or her creditors or abused the system, such as by fraudulently transferring or concealing property, by destroying or falsifying financial information, or by disobeying lawful court orders. (Unlike in Chapter 7, a debtor's prior misconduct or discharge within the past six years will not bar Chapter 13 discharge.)

Under Chapter 7, individuals are permitted to retain exempt property. *Exempt property*, excluded from the bankruptcy estate, is intended to provide for the individual's future needs and generally includes such things as a homestead, one or more motor vehicles, household or personal items, tools of the debtor's trade, health aids, personal injury awards, alimony or support payments, disability or retirement benefits (including IRAs), life insurance or annuities, and some special deposits or cash. Available exemptions vary from state to state and are usually limited to a maximum dollar amount or by a necessity standard.

The Bankruptcy Code permits debtors to nullify involuntary liens that impair their allowable exemptions. They can even invalidate consensual liens on most household items, tools of the trade, or health aids, unless the secured creditor financed the debtor's purchase of the property or was given possession of it. To take full advantage of the exemptions, debtors often convert assets from nonexempt to exempt forms before filing their bankruptcy cases. However, they must be careful not to take steps that could be considered fraudulent, because fraudulent conduct could jeopardize the right to discharge existing debts.

On June 10, 1998, the House of Representatives passed the Bankruptcy Reform Act of 1998 (H.R. 3150), which would severely curtail the ability of individuals earning a regular income equal to or greater than the national median income from filing under Chapter 7. Such individuals would be required to file under Chapter 13 if they could pay at least 20% of their unsecured, nonpriority debts over a five-year period and could pay at least $50 per month. If enacted, the act would also make credit card debt nondischargeable. The Senate was expected to pass its version of consumer bankruptcy reform (S. 1301) by the end of 1998.

◆ Unfairness, Deception, and Fraud

Many regulatory agencies, both federal and state, are involved in the area of unfair and deceptive trade practices and consumer fraud. Among the federal agencies that respond to unfair and deceptive trade practices and consumer fraud are the Federal Trade Commission, the Food and Drug Administration, the Federal Communications Commission, the U.S. Post Office, the U.S. Department of Housing and Urban Development, and the Securities and Exchange Commission. (Securities fraud is discussed in Chapter 23.)

Each of these agencies protects consumers from unfair and deceptive trade practices and fraud in consumer transactions. The areas that these agencies regulate in-

ETHICAL CONSIDERATION

A manager contemplating personal bankruptcy faces ethical issues when deciding whether to convert non-exempt property to exempt property. For example, buying a large house in Florida may be a legal way to make private funds unavailable, but is it fair to the creditors who relied on the debtor's general net worth in making an unsecured loan?

clude advertising, packaging and labeling, pricing, warranties, and numerous sales practices. Through government regulation, consumers are shielded from trade practices that are considered unfair, deceptive, or fraudulent.

For example, the FTC sued Toys "R" Us, the largest toy retailer in the United States, for unfair methods of competition under Section 5 of the Federal Trade Commission Act. In 1997, the administrative law judge held that Toys "R" Us had violated Section 5 by keeping prices for popular toys (such as Barbie, Mr.

ETHICAL CONSIDERATION

Publication of a newspaper article entitled "A Car Buyer's Guide to Sanity," which taught consumers how to negotiate lower prices, so angered car dealers that they pulled at least $1 million worth of advertising from the newspaper. The FTC challenged the dealers' actions under the antitrust laws, claiming that they had deprived consumers of essential price information in the form of newspaper advertising and had chilled the newspaper from publishing similar stories in the future.[a] Should the government become embroiled in an advertiser's decision to pull advertising from a news publication? Was the advertisers' conduct ethical?

---

a. Anthony Ramirez, *Car Dealers to Stop Ad Threat*, SAN FRANCISCO CHRON., Aug. 2, 1995, at B3.

Potato Head, and Hall of Fame G.I. Joe dolls) artificially high by forcing major suppliers (including Mattel and Hasbro) to agree not to sell best-selling toys to club retailers and warehouses such as Sam's and Price Club.[15]

State attorneys general and state departments of consumer affairs are also involved on the state level in protecting consumers through their administration of various state labeling laws, state warranty provisions (such as "lemon laws"), state deceptive sales practices statutes, and state privacy laws.

 ## Advertising

Consumers are bombarded daily by the competing claims of various advertisers trying to generate new sales. From billboards to television to publications and even the back of grocery receipts, advertisers vie for the consumer's attention. In this competitive environment, companies sometimes make claims that are deceptive or false. Legal solutions to this problem have historically involved three separate approaches: the common law, statutory law, and regulatory law. Regulatory law, enacted and enforced through the Federal Trade Commission (FTC), has proven to be the most effective approach in combating false advertisements.

Common Law

A traditional common law approach provides two remedies for a consumer who has been misled by false advertising. First, a consumer can sue for breach of contract. In this instance, however, it may be difficult to prove the existence of a contract because advertisements are usually considered by the courts to be only an offer to deal. A consumer might also sue for the tort of deceit. Deceit requires the proof of several elements, including knowledge by the seller that the misrepresentation is false. In addition, the misrepresentation must be one of fact and not opinion, a difficult distinction to make in the context of advertising. (Chapter 7 provides additional coverage of breach of contract. Deceit, also called fraudulent misrepresentation, is discussed in Chapter 9.)

Statutory Law

The Uniform Commercial Code (UCC) and the Lanham Trademark Act are two statutes that may protect consumers from false advertising. Under Section 2-313 of the UCC, any statement, sample, or model may constitute an *express warranty* if it is part of the basis of the bargain. Thus, an advertising term may be construed as an express warranty for a product. If the product does not conform to the representation made, the warranty is breached. Express warranties can be disclaimed in a sales contract, however, so the UCC does not generally provide a strong response to false advertising claims. (UCC warranties are discussed in Chapter 8.)

The Lanham Trademark Act forbids the use of any false "description or representation" in connection with any goods or services and provides a claim for any competitor (rather than consumer) who might be injured by any other competitor's false claims. The purpose of the act is to ensure truthfulness in advertising and eliminate misrepresentations of quality regarding one's own product or the product of a competitor.

For example, the Coca-Cola Company, maker of Minute Maid orange juice, sued Tropicana Products, Inc. in the early 1980s under the Lanham Trademark Act. At issue was a television commercial in which athlete Bruce Jenner squeezed an orange while saying, "It's pure, pasteurized juice as it comes from the orange," and then pouring the juice into a Tropicana carton. Coca-Cola claimed that commercial was false because it represented that Tropicana contains unprocessed, fresh-squeezed juice when in fact the juice is heated (pasteurized) and sometimes frozen before packaging. The court agreed that the representation was false because it suggested that pasteurized juice comes directly from oranges. The court granted an injunction to prevent Tropicana from continuing to use the advertisement.[16]

FTC Regulatory Law

The Federal Trade Commission is charged with preventing unfair and deceptive trade practices, which includes false advertising. Its jurisdiction over advertising was not explicitly established until 1938, however, when Congress amended the Federal Trade Commission Act and

---

15. *Judge: Toys R Us Plays Unfair,* SAN JOSE MERCURY NEWS, Oct. 1, 1997, at 1C. *See also* FTC Press Release, *FTC Judge Upholds Charges against Toys "R" Us,* Sept. 30, 1997, <http://www.ftc.gov/opa/9709/toys-id.htm>.

---

16. Coca-Cola Co. v. Tropicana Prods., Inc., 690 F.2d 312 (2d Cir. 1982).

declared "unfair or deceptive acts or [trade] practices" to be unlawful. Among the areas that the FTC has addressed under Section 5 are deceptive price and quality claims and false testimonials and mock-ups.

If the FTC believes a violation of Section 5 exists, it will attempt to negotiate a consent order with the alleged violator. A *consent order* is an agreement to stop the activity that the FTC has found illegal. If an agreement cannot be reached, the matter will be heard by an administrative law judge. The judge's decision can be appealed to the full commission, and from the full commission the decision can be appealed to the U.S. Court of Appeals.

Deceptive Price   One example of deceptive pricing practices involves the sale of advertised items at higher prices to customers unaware of the advertised price. In one case, a man purchased a blue 1986 Chevrolet Celebrity with 29,000 miles from an automobile dealer for $8,524.[17] Unbeknownst to him, the dealership was currently advertising a blue 1986 Celebrity with 29,000 miles for $6,995 in a local newspaper. When he returned home, the man saw the ad and telephoned the dealership to demand that the deal be renegotiated. The salesman refused, claiming that the advertised car had been sent to auction. The customer sued under the Illinois Consumer Fraud Act, which forbids false misrepresentations as well as omission of material facts. The trial court held that the dealership had a duty to inform the customer of the advertised price and awarded him the difference in prices, plus costs.

Deceptive pricing practices also include offers of free merchandise with a purchase or two-for-one deals in which the advertiser recovers the cost of the free merchandise by charging more than the advertiser's regular price for the merchandise bought. Another example of deceptive pricing, *bait and switch advertising*, is regulated by the FTC. An advertiser violates FTC rules if it refuses to show an advertised item, fails to have a reasonable quantity of the item in stock, fails to promise to deliver the item within a reasonable time, or discourages employees from selling the advertised item.

Quality Claims   Advertisements often include quality claims. These quality claims imply that the advertiser has some reasonable basis for making the claim. For example, television and print ads from an October 1990

ad campaign show a Volvo automobile withstanding the impact of a giant-tired "monster truck" named Bear Foot that flattens the rest of a long line of cars. What is not readily apparent from the advertisements is the fact that the Volvo's roof had been reinforced, and some of the other vehicles' supports had been weakened. In response, the Federal Trade Commission required, for the first time, the ad agency—and not just the advertiser—to pay a fine for the deceptive ad. Thus, the automaker and its New York ad firm each agreed to pay a $150,000 penalty, though neither admitted violating laws against false advertising.[18]

Under the FTC's general view, quality claims made without any substantiation are deceptive. On the other hand, obvious exaggerations and vague generalities are considered *puffing* and are not considered deceptive because they are unlikely to mislead consumers. (Puffing is also discussed in Chapter 8.) To determine whether an advertiser has made a deceptive quality claim, the FTC must first identify the claim and then determine whether the claim is substantiated.

For example, the marketers of Doan's pills were held to have disseminated false and deceptive statements in advertisements claiming greater effectiveness to relieve back pain than other over-the-counter pain relievers.[19] The marketers lacked any reasonable basis for substantiating the representations.

ETHICAL CONSIDERATION

Is the Volvo ad just an example of puffing? Was Volvo and the ad agency's behavior unethical?

Testimonials and Mock-ups   Testimonials and endorsements in which the person endorsing a product does not, in fact, use or prefer it have also been determined to be deceptive and therefore in violation of the FTC Act. Additionally, it is deceptive for the endorser to imply falsely that he or she has superior knowledge or experience. The use of comparative advertising is illustrated by the case that follows.

---

17. Affrunti v. Village Ford Sales, Inc. 597 N.E.2d 1242 (Ill. App. Ct. 1992).

18. *F.T.C. Accord on Volvo Ads,* N.Y. TIMES, Aug. 22, 1991, at D19.

19. *In re* Novartis Corp., FTC Docket No. 9279 (Mar. 9, 1998), 66 U.S.L.W. 2582 (Mar. 31, 1998).

| A CASE IN POINT | SUMMARY |

CASE 19.3
L&F PRODUCTS
v. PROCTER &
GAMBLE CO.
United States Court
of Appeals for the
Second Circuit
45 F.3d 709
(2d Cir. 1995).

FACTS   L&F Products, a division of Sterling Winthrop, Inc., manufactures and markets Lysol cleaning products, including Lysol Basin Tub & Tile Cleaner, a bathroom cleanser, and Lysol Deodorizing Cleaner, an all-purpose product often employed for bathroom cleaning. Procter & Gamble Company (P&G) manufactures and sells several Spic and Span household cleaning products, including Spic and Span Basin–Tub–Tile Cleaner, Spic and Span Bathroom Cleaner, and Ultra Spic and Span, a general cleanser.

In July 1993, P&G began a television advertising campaign in which its products were compared to those of an unnamed competitor obviously intended to be Lysol Deodorizing Cleaner. In three different commercials, a Spic and Span product and Lysol Deodorizing Cleaner were used by two custodians on identical soiled shower stalls, tubs, or tile floors set in a large, white room. The surfaces are visibly dirty when the custodians begin their tasks, and each custodian is shown making one swipe across the dirty surface. The screen then "dissolves," and the custodians leave, looking pleased with their work. Two new characters enter, and each contrives to casually pass a white cloth over the just-cleaned stalls, tubs, or floors. The surface cleaned with Lysol is ultimately revealed to have left a residue that is seen to sully the cloth. The white cloths passed over the tub, shower, and floor cleaned with Spic and Span are not similarly dirtied.

Two of the commercials employed templates made of the same materials that formed the tubs and showers themselves. Like other manufacturers, P&G developed its own soap scum for use in testing its products. Its formula includes carbon black, a dark pigment used as a laboratory marker. In order to mimic the tenacity of household soap scum, the laboratory-developed product is baked onto a test surface at high temperatures. Because of the impossibility of baking an entire shower stall or tub, templates are used. The third commercial addressed floor grime, for which P&G did not need to bake the laboratory version into the test surface.

The soiled templates were wiped with the competing products off-screen an equal number of times with a comparable degree of force. They were later inserted into the shower and steambath sets and, on-screen, white cloths were rubbed against them. However, the initial swipe across the shower and tub tiles by the custodians was performed on tiles dirtied with ordinary soil, rather than the laboratory-developed scum.

L&F sued P&G, alleging that the commercials were false or misleading. The district court dismissed the lawsuit, and L&F appealed.

ISSUE PRESENTED   Is it a deceptive trade practice (1) to make cleaning residue more easily filmed by adding substances, or (2) to simulate without disclosure the wiping of ordinary soil with the actual wiping of laboratory-developed soil?

SUMMARY OF OPINION   The U.S. Court of Appeals began by noting that the Lanham Act forbids the use of a "false designation or origin, or any false description or misrepresentation, including words or other symbols tending falsely to describe or represent the same. . . ." To successfully sue under this act, a plaintiff must demonstrate that either the challenged advertisement is literally false or, although literally true, is still likely to mislead or confuse consumers. . . .

L&F claimed that the use of carbon black and tile templates constituted false advertising *per se.* Carbon black, however, exists in many household items and is

Case 19.3 continues

Case 19.3 continued

thus a natural component of organic soap scum. The court stated, "The inescapable fact is that Lysol products sometimes leave a residue," and held that P&G was entitled to make the residue camera-registerable by using carbon black. As for the use of tile templates, the court found nothing inherently misleading about simulating cleaning on-screen while conducting the actual cleaning off-screen, nor did the court find anything deceptive in showing the custodians wiping ordinary soil rather than the laboratory-developed scum that was used for the actual test results.

RESULT   The appeals court affirmed the dismissal of the complaint.

COMMENTS   Not all advertisements withstand challenge so easily. In the mid-1960s, the Federal Trade Commission successfully challenged a series of three television commercials by Colgate–Palmolive Company of its Rapid Shave shaving cream.[20] Each of the commercials featured a sandpaper test, in which the announcer informed the audience that "To prove Rapid Shave's super-moisturizing power, we put it right from the can onto this tough, dry sandpaper. It was apply . . . soak . . . and off in a stroke." While the announcer was speaking, Rapid Shave was applied to a substance that appeared to be sandpaper, and immediately thereafter a razor was shown shaving the substance clean. The Federal Trade Commission issued a complaint charging that the commercials were false and deceptive. Evidence disclosed that sandpaper of the type depicted in the commercials could not be shaved immediately following the application of Rapid Shave, but required a soaking period of approximately 80 minutes. The evidence also showed that the substance resembling sandpaper was in fact a simulated prop, or "mock-up," made of plexiglass to which sand had been applied. Ultimately, the U.S. Supreme Court agreed with the FTC and ruled the commercials unlawfully deceptive.

20. FTC v. Colgate–Palmolive Co., 380 U.S. 374 (1965).

The FTC has the authority to issue cease and desist orders to advertisers who violate Section 5 of the Federal Trade Commission Act, such as those advertisers who employ deceptive price or quality claims or false testimonials. A *cease and desist order* instructs advertisers to stop using the methods deemed unfair or deceptive. In one case, the FTC required the maker of Listerine to cease and desist from making the claim that Listerine prevented colds and sore throats or lessened their severity. Testing performed by the FTC revealed that this claim, which the company had made for more than 50 years, was false. To counteract years of false claims, the FTC required the company to disclose in any future advertisements for Listerine that, contrary to prior advertising, Listerine did not help prevent colds or sore throats or lessen their severity.

The order applied to the next $10 million of Listerine advertising only.[21]

FTC remedies include civil damages, affirmative advertising (advertiser required to include specific information), counter or corrective advertising (as with Listerine), and multiple product orders (advertiser required to cease false claims regarding all of its products).

Drug Advertising

In 1997, the FDA, which regulates drug advertising, eased the restrictions on the advertising of prescription

21. Warner–Lambert Co. v. FTC, 562 F.2d 749 (D.C. Cir. 1977), *cert. denied*, 435 U.S. 950 (1978).

drugs on television and radio. Drug companies can now tout the drug's benefits without listing all the side effects and explaining how to properly use the drug. Television ads must, however, warn of major risks and provide a quick way (such as a toll-free telephone number, Web address, or magazine advertisement) for consumers to obtain full information about the drug.

Infomercials

Infomercials, also known as long-form marketing programs or direct response television, are advertisements generally presented in the format of half-hour television talk shows or news programs. Their very format, however, may present problems by blurring the line between advertising and regular television programming.[22] The next trend in infomercials appears to be the "sitcommercial," a full-length show resembling a family sitcom. For example, Bell Atlantic filmed "The Ringers," a sitcom intended to show off and sell telephone equipment.

Infomercials first became popular in 1984 after the Federal Communications Commission (FCC) deregulated the amount of time that broadcast stations could dedicate to advertisements. As a result, infomercials be-

came a forum for advertising questionable products such as cures for baldness and impotence.

Since 1984, consumer advocate groups have lodged numerous complaints alleging deceptive advertising. As a result, the infomercial industry established an internal watchdog agency, the National Infomercial Merchandising Association, in 1990. The association offers guidelines to combat deceptive practices, endorses legitimate infomercial producers, and reports violations to the FTC.

◆ Packaging and Labeling

Both the Federal Trade Commission and the Food and Drug Administration (FDA) regulate the packaging and labeling of products. For example, the FTC has adopted guidelines specifying when manufacturers and marketers can label their products "Made in U.S.A." Under the Federal Food, Drug and Cosmetic Act,[23] the FDA regulates the misbranding of food, drugs, medical devices, and cosmetics. Numerous state laws cover such items as food, drugs, medical devices, cosmetics, clothing, tobacco, and alcohol.

Food, Drugs, Medical Devices, and Cosmetics

The FDA has primary responsibility for regulating the packaging and labeling of food (except meat, poultry, and eggs, which are under the jurisdiction of the U.S. Department of Agriculture), drugs, medical devices, and cosmetics. In 1966, Congress passed the Fair Packaging and Labeling Act[24] in response to the surge in pre-packaged items available at supermarkets, and the perceived subtle deceptions some manufacturers employed.

---

22. Karen Zagor & Gary Mead, *Illumination from the Stars: A Look at the New-Found Respectability of So-Called "Infomercials*," FIN. TIMES, Nov. 5, 1992, at 18.

23. 21 U.S.C. §§ 301 *et seq.* (1998).
24. 15 U.S.C. §§ 1451 *et seq.* (1998).

Under the act, a food label must contain the name and address of the manufacturer, packer, or distributor; the net quantity on the front panel, placed in a uniform location; and the quantity given in servings with the net quantity of each serving stated and the quantity listed in certain ways, depending on how the product is classified. This last provision requires dual declarations of sizes (for example, one quart and 32 ounces) and forbids the use of terms such as "jumbo quart" and "super ounce."

Another area of concern for Congress was the proliferation of various package sizes, making price comparison extremely difficult for consumers. For example, a "jumbo" size of one product might contain the same amount as the "large" size of another. Similarly, the terms "small, medium, and large" have often been embellished with terms like "ketchup-lover size," "family size," and "fun size." The 1966 act provides authority to add requirements concerning the use of such terms, as well as terms associated with value claims such as "economy size." Many supermarkets now provide unit pricing information so that consumers can more easily compare the prices of competing products.

Nutrition Facts   The Nutrition Labeling and Education Act, passed by Congress in 1990, requires mandatory nutrition labeling of almost all foods, a nutrition panel entitled Nutrition Facts, expanded ingredient labeling requirements, and restrictions on nutrient content claims and health claims.

Under the act, approximately 90% of processed food must carry nutrition information. Some exceptions include plain coffee and tea, delicatessen items, and bulk food. The Nutrition Facts panel, mandated by the act, includes the amount per serving of saturated fat, cholesterol, dietary fiber, sodium, and other nutrients. In addition, these panels provide information on how the food fits into an overall daily diet. Point-of-purchase nutrition information is voluntary under the act for many raw foods including meat, poultry, raw fish, and fresh produce. Such information may be shown, for example, in a poster or chart at a butcher's counter or a produce stand.

The FDA regulation also governs the use of nutrient claims such as "light," "fat free," and "low calorie," and provides uniform definitions so that these terms mean the same for any product on which they appear. Because of an exemption the dairy industry won from Congress, however, 2% milk may continue to be labeled "low fat" even though it does not meet the standard FDA definition.

Health Claims   Health claims are also regulated under the act. In particular, claims linking a nutrient or food to the risk of a disease or health-related condition are allowed only under certain circumstances. For example, statements regarding the relationship between calcium and osteoporosis, saturated fat and heart disease, and sodium and hypertension are permitted. Health claims made about dietary supplements are also regulated under the act. Dietary supplements include products such as vitamins, minerals, amino acids, and fatty acids. In general, the act requires that health claims about dietary supplements cannot be misleading, and that claims must be supported by available scientific evidence.

Organic Foods   Congress created the National Organic Standards Board in 1990 to establish a federal definition of the term "organic." Organic generally means free of synthetic chemicals and pesticides but also is generally understood to include use of environmentally sound growing techniques. As of May 1998, Secretary of Agriculture Dan Glickman was expected to exclude genetically engineered and irradiated food and crops fertilized with sewage sludge from the definition of organic, but to allow the use of antibiotics, nonorganic feed, and long-term confinement of animals in the production of organic meat.[25]

---

25. Rick Weiss, *'Organic' Label Ruled Out for Biotech, Irradiated Foods*, WASH. POST, May 1, 1998, at A2.

ETHICAL CONSIDERATION

The FDA permits milk producers to stimulate increased milk production in diary cows with the growth hormone BST (bovine somatotropin). BST (also known as BGH or bovine growth hormone) is a protein hormone created naturally by the pituitary gland of cows. Traces of the hormone occur naturally in milk. Milk producers are not required to disclose hormone use on the labels for products containing milk from cows injected with BST. Should hormone use be disclosed to milk consumers? What marketing advantage might be gained from labeling milk produced by cows not injected with BST? Could the milk be labeled "hormone free" when, in fact, trace amounts of the hormone occur naturally in milk?

Medical Devices   Labeling of medical devices is also under the jurisdiction of the FDA. The application of

those labeling requirements is demonstrated in the following case.

A CASE IN POINT	SUMMARY

CASE 19.4
O'GILVIE v.
INTERNATIONAL
PLAYTEX, INC.
United States
Court of Appeals
for the Tenth Circuit
821 F.2d 1438 (10th Cir.
1987), *cert. denied,*
486 U.S. 1032 (1988).

FACTS   Kelly O'Gilvie brought this action, individually and on behalf of the estate of his deceased wife, Betty, against International Playtex, Inc. O'Gilvie alleged that Mrs. O'Gilvie's use of Playtex super-absorbent tampons caused her death from toxic shock syndrome, and he sought damages from Playtex under the Kansas law of strict liability in tort. In answers to special interrogatories, the jury found that Playtex tampons had caused Mrs. O'Gilvie to develop toxic shock syndrome, and that Playtex had failed to adequately warn of the fatal risk of toxic shock from the use of its product. The jury awarded actual damages of $1,525,000, and punitive damages of $10 million.

After the entry of judgment and apparently in response to the trial court's suggestion, Playtex represented that it was discontinuing the sale of some of its products, instituting a program of alerting the public to the dangers of toxic shock syndrome, and modifying its product warning. The trial court thereupon ordered the punitive damage award reduced to $1,350,000. Both parties appealed.

ISSUE PRESENTED   Was Playtex's warning to tampon consumers of the danger of toxic shock syndrome adequate as a matter of law because it complied with Food and Drug Administration regulations?

SUMMARY OF OPINION   Playtex contended that it was entitled to a directed verdict because O'Gilvie presented no evidence that the warning accompanying its super-absorbent tampons was inadequate or that the warning was the cause of Mrs. O'Gilvie's injury. The U.S. Court of Appeals disagreed.

O'Gilvie argued at trial that the warning was inadequate because it did not properly apprise users of the causal connection between toxic shock and the use of tampons, or of the increased risk from the use of super-absorbent tampons. Experts testified that the warning did not alert buyers to the increased risk from use of high-absorbency tampons, and that simply mentioning an association between toxic shock and tampon use did not adequately alert users to the cause and effect relationship.

The court's review of the record revealed abundant evidence that Playtex deliberately disregarded studies and medical reports linking high-absorbency tampon fibers with increased risk of toxic shock at a time when other tampon manufacturers were responding to this information by modifying or withdrawing their high-absorbency products. Moreover, there was evidence that Playtex deliberately sought to profit from the situation by advertising the effectiveness of its high-absorbency tampons when it knew other manufacturers were reducing the absorbency of their products due to the evidence of a causal connection between high absorbency and toxic shock. This occurred in the face of Playtex' awareness that its product was far more absorbent than necessary for its intended effectiveness.

The appeals court concluded that the trial court had, in reducing the punitive damages award, rewarded Playtex for continuing its tortious conduct long enough to use it as a bargaining chip. The possibility that other potential defendants would be

Case 19.4 continues

Case 19.4 continued

able to reduce their liability for punitive damages in the same way might encourage the very behavior that the punitive award was intended to deter.

Playtex argued that the presence of a warning that complied with FDA requirements precluded, as a matter of law, any finding that Playtex exhibited the reckless indifference necessary to support an award of punitive damages. The court disagreed. It found that compliance with FDA standards was not dispositive under Kansas law if a reasonable manufacturer would have done more. Under the circumstances in this case, compliance with the FDA regulations did not preclude punitive damages, because there was evidence sufficient to support a finding of reckless indifference to consumer safety.

RESULT   The $10 million punitive damage award was reinstated.

COMMENTS   The FDA issued tampon labeling rules in 1989 that standardized absorbency terms like "junior," "regular," "super," and "super plus." This change was important because there is medical evidence of a direct relationship between tampon absorbency and the risk of TSS, with the least absorbent tampons being the safest.

Clothing

The FTC has primary responsibility for regulating the packaging and labeling of commodities other than food, drugs, medical devices, and cosmetics. For example, numerous federal laws regulate the labeling of clothing. Among these are the Wool Products Labeling Act,[26] the Fur Products Labeling Act,[27] the Flammable Fabrics Act,[28] and the Textile Fiber Products Identification Act.[29] Each of these acts is intended to protect distributors and consumers against misbranding and false advertising. Critics of these acts have suggested that the false advertising aspects of each act could have been covered by Section 5 of the Federal Trade Commission Act, and that the principal value of these acts has been to protect one producer from another producer's false claims.

Tobacco

Tobacco product packages are required to contain one of several health warnings about the hazards associated with smoking. Such warnings were first required after passage of the Federal Cigarette Labeling and Advertising Act of 1966. In 1986, Congress passed the Smokeless Tobacco Health Education Act, which requires similar warnings on packages of smokeless chewing tobacco products.

As discussed more fully in Chapter 10, a number of states have sued the tobacco companies to recover the costs of government-provided health care for tobacco-related illnesses. Although the tobacco industry reached a tentative $368.5 billion global settlement with the states in June 1997, Congress refused to assent and provide the immunity from further liability that was a critical aspect of the deal. Furthermore, some members of Congress called for even higher taxes and more draconian regulation, including the prohibition of human and cartoon images on tobacco advertising and packaging. As of June 1998, there was no consensus in Congress as to how to respond to the settlement and what changes to make in the regulation of the industry.[30]

Alcohol

In 1989, a congressionally mandated warning label began to appear on bottles, cans, and packages of wine, beer, and spirits. It states that alcohol consumption

26. 15 U.S.C. §§ 68 *et seq.* (1998).

27. 15 U.S.C. §§ 69 *et seq.* (1998).

28. 15 U.S.C. §§ 1191 *et seq.* (1998).

29. 15 U.S.C. §§ 70 *et seq.* (1998)

30. *GOP Mulls Narrower Tobacco Measure that May Withhold Liability Protection,* WALL ST. J., Apr. 20, 1998, at A3.

increases the risks of birth defects, says that consuming alcoholic beverages can impair one's ability to drive a car, and cautions against its use with machinery.[31]

The warning label was implemented by the Bureau of Alcohol, Tobacco and Firearms (BATF), a branch of the Treasury Department that also regulates the wine industry. Beyond warning labels, BATF regulates everything that appears on packages of alcoholic beverages. All such products must have certain mandatory information on their labels. Wine, which changes with every vintage, has labeling regulations that differ from spirits and beer. BATF receives approximately 4,500 wine label applications per month, many of them identical to the previous year's label. Each wine label must be approved by BATF before it can be used.

BATF regulations attach legal meanings to various statements made on wine labels, including the vintage year, grape variety, producer, and alcohol content. Warnings are also required to alert those who are allergic to sulfites that trace amounts of the substances, which may be used in production as a preservative and which are also produced naturally during fermentation, are contained in the wine.

State Labeling Laws

Many states, through their use of labeling laws, have taken steps to protect consumers from dangerous products. Historically, these laws have sought to protect consumers from risks that involve the danger of imminent bodily harm. Recently, however, some states have enacted more extensive state labeling laws. Most notable among these statutes is California's Safe Drinking Water and Toxic Enforcement Act of 1986, better known as Proposition 65. Proposition 65 provides that "no person . . . shall knowingly and intentionally expose any individual to a chemical known to the state to cause cancer or reproductive toxicity without first giving clear and reasonable warning to such individual."[32]

The law requires the governor to compile a list of the chemicals requiring warnings, and to update the list annually. The current list includes ingredients such as alcohol and saccharin, as well as potential contaminants such as lead and mercury. The labeling requirements apply to manufacturers, producers, packagers, and retail sellers, and may be in the form of product labels, signs at retail outlets, or public advertising. An example of a Proposition 65 warning is "Warning: This product contains a chemical known to the State of California to cause birth defects or other reproductive harm." The FDA has the authority to issue regulations that would preempt state labeling requirements such as Proposition 65, but the FDA has so far chosen not to do so.

 ## Pricing

Utilities

Price regulation is another form of consumer protection. Various entities, primarily at the state level, are involved in setting rates and price levels for certain commodities. For example, state public utilities commissions often regulate natural monopolies, including local telephone service and other public utilities. (Chapter 18 contains additional information on natural monopolies and antitrust regulation.)

In 1998, California became the first state to fully end utility monopolies, making it possible for businesses and consumers to buy electric power from the cheapest supplier. Although competition was expected to bring big cost savings, experts now predict that the real benefits of competition won't be felt until 2002.[33]

The attorneys general of Arkansas, Iowa, Maine, New Hampshire, and Wisconsin warned consumers in 1997 to be wary of scam artists, pyramid schemes, and *slamming*, the illegal practice of switching the electrical supplier of an individual without first getting permission (a practice that has been prevalent in the deregulated long-distance telephone market). A key issue in deregulation is how to allocate *stranded costs*, the outstanding liabilities for plants and programs that were incurred while the utilities were a regulated monopoly.

Drugs

Azidothymide (AZT) is a medicine used for treating complications of AIDS. The Burroughs Wellcome

31. Dan Berger, *Modern Wine Industry Still Fears the "Feds" But For Labeling Reasons*, L.A. TIMES, Nov. 24, 1989, at H2.

32. CAL. HEALTH & SAFETY CODE § 25,249.6 (West 1997).

33. Benjamin A. Holden, *Electricity Savings to Be Short-Circuited*, WALL ST. J., Sept. 24, 1997, at A2.

Company has been at the center of a controversy over the price charged for this drug. AZT treatment often costs as much as $6,500 per year, which is prohibitively expensive for many AIDS patients, particularly those with inadequate insurance coverage. The new cocktail of protease inhibitors recommended for people with HIV or AIDS costs even more.

Consumer Warranties

Uniform Commercial Code Warranties

State warranty law provides an important basis for many consumer protection claims. In consumer product transactions in which the Uniform Commercial Code applies, Article 2 provides a buyer of goods a remedy for a seller's breach of an express or implied warranty. UCC warranties are discussed in Chapter 8.

Magnuson–Moss Warranty Act

In addition to the statutory protections provided by the UCC, the federal government has passed an act that is designed to inform consumers about the products they buy. This law, which applies only when a seller offers a written warranty, is the Magnuson–Moss Warranty Act.[34] The act does not require any seller to provide a written warranty, but if a seller does offer one, the act requires certain disclosure in connection with that written warranty. In addition, the act restricts disclaimers

---

34. 15 U.S.C. §§ 2301 *et seq.* (1998).

ETHICAL CONSIDERATION

Should free market, competitive forces determine the price of "essential" goods such as pharmaceuticals, or should their prices be regulated? What constitutes "reasonable" profits on a product such as AZT?[a]

---

a. For a complete discussion of the AZT controversy, *see Ethics, Pricing and the Pharmaceutical Industry,* J. Bus. Ethics, Aug. 1992, at 617. *See also* Brian O'Reilly, *The Inside Story of the AIDS Drug,* Fortune, Nov. 5, 1990, at 112.

for implied warranties and permits consumers to sue violators of the Magnuson-Moss Warranty Act and to recover damages plus costs, including reasonable attorney's fees.

Disclosure under the act requires a manufacturer or seller, when offering a written warranty on goods costing more than $15, to "fully and conspicuously disclose in simple and understandable language the terms and conditions of the warranty." The FTC has issued various rules relating to this provision, including one that requires consumer notification that some states do not allow certain manufacturer exclusions or limitations.

A manufacturer or seller who offers a written warranty on goods costing more than $10 must also state whether the warranty is full or limited. The act requires that in order for a warranty to be "full" it must meet the following minimum federal standards. First, a full warranty must give the consumer the right to free repair of the product within a reasonable time or, after a reasonable number of failed attempts to fix the product, permit the customer to elect a full refund or replacement. Second, the warrantor may not impose any time limit on the warranty's duration. Lastly, the warrantor may not exclude or limit damages for breach of warranty unless such exclusions are conspicuous on the face of the warranty. Any warranty that does not meet these minimum federal standards must be designated as "limited."

Also under the act, a seller who offers a written warranty may not disclaim *implied warranties,* such as the implied warranty of merchantability. These implied warranties may be limited to the duration of the written warranty, but then the written warranty must be designated as "limited." Still, a seller may disclaim all implied warranties by not offering any written warranty or service contract at all and selling a product "as is."

FTC rules allow a seller to establish an informal dispute resolution procedure, and require consumers to use this procedure before filing a lawsuit under the act. Magnuson-Moss also requires that the warrantor be given an opportunity to remedy its noncompliance before a lawsuit is filed.

Multiple Causes of Action

Often, a plaintiff will allege several causes of action arising out of the same alleged defect. For example, a consumer who bought Norton AntiVirus Version 2.0 anti-virus software in April 1997 from the manufacturer Symantec filed suit in February 1998 because the product was not Year 2000–compliant, that is, it could not process dates for year 2000 and beyond.[35] The software uses date information to run scheduled diagnostic testing of the user's computer. In August 1997, Symantec released a new version Norton AntiVirus Version 4.0, which was Year 2000–compliant, but refused to provide the plaintiff a free fix for Year 2000 problems inherent in its Version 2.0 software.

The plaintiff, who sought class action status for the suit, alleges four causes of action: (1) breach of the implied warranties of merchantability and fitness for ordinary use; (2) violation of the Magnuson–Moss Warranty Act due to Symantec's failure to certify Version 2.0 as Year 2000–compliant and remedy the defect; (3) fraudulent and unfair business practices in violation of the state statute banning "unlawful, unfair or fraudulent business practices"; and (4) violation of the California Consumer Legal Remedies Act. This is the third lawsuit nationwide to specifically focus on Year 2000 issues.[36]

State Lemon Laws

A majority of states have laws dealing with warranties on new cars and new mobile homes. These *lemon laws* are designed to protect consumers from defective products that cannot be adequately fixed. The statutes vary considerably from state to state, but there are several common features. In general, a new car must conform to the warranty given by the manufacturer. This means that if, after a reasonable number of attempts (usually four), the manufacturer or dealer is unable to remedy a defect that substantially impairs the value of the car, the car must be replaced or the purchase price refunded. Lemon laws also typically require replacement or refund if a new car has been out of service ("in the shop") for 30 days during the statutory warranty period.

In addition to permitting the revocation of a new car sales contract, state lemon laws are designed (like the Magnuson–Moss Warranty Act) to encourage informal resolution of disputes concerning defective new cars. Lemon laws achieve this objective by requiring that a consumer use a manufacturer's arbitration pro-

gram before litigating, as long as the manufacturer has established an informal dispute resolution program that complies with FTC regulations. Some states, including New York, have adopted their own standards for these dispute resolution programs.

In 1997, five car buyers sued General Motors (GM) and more than 400 California dealerships, alleging that hundreds, and possibly thousands, of GM customers had unknowingly bought problem-plagued vehicles previously repurchased by dealers under the California lemon law. That law requires dealers reselling cars previously repurchased under the lemon law to stamp "lemon law buyback" on the title and put a sticker on the car itself. The plaintiffs, who brought the suit as a class action, claimed that GM and the dealers failed to brand the cars as lemons, but instead represented them as being fit. The plaintiff's counsel claimed that if the cars had been properly labeled, they would have been worth one-third to one-half of what the plaintiffs paid.[37]

Sales Practices

Many laws that are designed to protect consumers from unfair and deceptive trade practices involve disclosure requirements in various sales transactions and regulation of some specific forms of sales practices. Regulations related to sales practices may cover all industries or they may be industry specific, such as the FTC's rules for used cars sellers or state insurance regulations. A number of state and federal agencies currently regulate sales practices, including the FTC, the FCC, the Postal Service, and the Department of Housing and Urban Development.

Sometimes a party can use laws of general application to protect consumers. For example, a lawyer in Washington, D.C., won two state court judgments totaling $11.6 million against affiliates of Tele-Communications, Inc. for charging excess late fees on monthly cable-TV bills.[38] He successfully argued that the fees violated the general principle of contract law that damages assessed for breach of contract cannot be disproportionate to the actual harm caused by the breach.

35. Cappelan v. Symantec, Cal. Super. Ct., Santa Clara County, No. 772147 (complaint filed Feb. 19, 1998).

36. *Maker of Software Sued for Failing To Make Product Year 2000 Compliant,* 66 U.S.L.W. 2534 (Mar. 10, 1998).

37. Kathryn Kranhold, *Lawsuit Accuses General Motors of Violating State 'Lemon Law,'* WALL ST. J., Oct. 1, 1997, at CA2.

38. Eben Shapiro, *Attorney Finds a Way to Battle Bills' Late Fees,* WALL ST. J., Oct. 6, 1997, at B1.

State Deceptive Practices Statutes

Most state consumer protection laws are directed at deceptive trade practices. Under these laws, sellers are prohibited from providing false or misleading information to consumers. Although there is considerable variation among state laws, they often provide more stringent protections than do federal laws.

UCC Unconscionability Principle

Also on the state level, the Uniform Commercial Code protects consumers from unfair sales practices through the unconscionability principle contained in Section 2-302 of the UCC. This section prohibits the enforcement of any contracts for the sale of goods that are so unfair and one-sided that they shock the conscience of the court. This provision is discussed in Chapter 8.

Door-to-Door Sales

Door-to-door sales are those transactions initiated and concluded at a buyer's home. For a number of reasons, they have invited regulation at both the state and federal level. Door-to-door sales are unique in that individuals may feel more pressured to buy something from someone standing at their door, or they may make a purchase just to get rid of a persistent salesperson. As a result, the FTC has mandated a three-day cooling-off period during which a consumer may rescind a door-to-door purchase. Under FTC rules, the seller must also notify a buyer of the right to cancel. Laws in some states provide longer periods during which consumers can cancel a sale.

Referral Sales and Pyramid Sales

A number of states have enacted legislation restricting referral and pyramid sales. In a *referral sale*, the seller offers the buyer a commission, rebate, or discount for furnishing the seller with a list of additional prospective customers. The discount, however, is usually contingent on the seller actually making later sales to those buyers referred by the original customer.

Pyramid selling involves a scheme whereby a consumer is recruited as a product "distributor" and receives commissions based on the products he or she sells and on the recruitment of additional sellers (or even receives commissions on the sales of the recruits).

The problem with both referral and pyramid sales is that unless the buyer or "distributor" becomes involved early in the chain, the supply of prospective recruits is quickly exhausted.

Telemarketing

Aggressive telemarketing sales practices, particularly the use of autodialers and "900" telephone numbers, have resulted in congressional intervention. For example, Congress passed the Telephone Consumer Protection Act (TCPA) of 1991,[39] which directed the FCC to adopt rules and regulations to curb telemarketing abuses. In general, the TCPA prohibits the use of either autodialers or simulated or prerecorded voice messages to deliver calls to emergency telephone lines, healthcare facilities, radio telephone services, and other services where the called party will incur some charge for the call. The only exception is if the called party has given prior consent to such calls. A second provision prohibits the use of prerecorded messages when calling residential telephone numbers, except with the prior consent of the called party or in the case of an emergency. Although enforcement of this second provision was initially enjoined by a federal court in Oregon on free speech grounds, the provision was later upheld by the U.S. Court of Appeals for the Ninth Circuit.[40]

In July 1993, the FCC and the FTC adopted final rules regulating the advertising, operation, and billing of 900 numbers. The rules were enacted pursuant to the Telephone Disclosure and Dispute Resolution Act of 1992,[41] which directed the FTC and the FCC to

---

39. 47 U.S.C. § 227 (1998).

40. Moser v. FCC, 46 F.3d 970 (9th Cir. 1995), *cert. denied*, 515 U.S. 1161 (1995).

41. 15 U.S.C. § 5701 (1998).

issue regulations governing pay-per-call services. Various provisions of the rules require that (1) calls to 900 numbers in excess of two minutes include a preamble disclosing the name of the information provider and a brief description of the service; (2) any advertisements include the cost of the call adjacent to and in a type size no less than one-half the size of the 900 number; and (3) the cost per minute and any minimum charges be disclosed to consumers.

In 1997, the North American Securities Administrators Association and the FTC announced that their six-month "Field of Schemes" fraud crackdown on investment-related telemarketing fraud had resulted in 61 enforcement actions. The schemes ranged from Ostrich ranching in Idaho, to digital fingerprint identification in Indiana, to worthless oil and gas programs in Kentucky.

Mail Order Sales

Unscrupulous mail order sales practices have led to a high incidence of consumer complaints and resulting state and federal regulation in this area. In general, two practices that have been regulated are processing procedures for mail orders and the receipt of unsolicited goods. Order-processing procedures basically require sellers to respond to consumer orders by shipping merchandise or offering refunds within a reasonable time.

Unsolicited or unordered merchandise sent by U.S. mail, as provided by the Postal Reorganization Act of 1970, may be kept or disposed of by the recipient without the recipient incurring any obligation to the sender. The U.S. Postal Service has authority to assess criminal and civil penalties for fraudulent mail schemes that injure consumers. Book and record clubs are generally legal as long as they comply with state law provisions requiring sellers to provide consumers with forms or announcement cards that the consumer may use to instruct the seller not to send the offered merchandise.

Industry-Specific Sales Practices

Since the early 1980s, the FTC has become more involved in regulating the sales practices of specific industries. For example, the FTC in 1985 began to require used car sellers to affix a Buyer's Guide label to the cars that they sell.[42] The Buyer's Guide is intended to disclose to potential buyers information about the car's warranty and any service contract provided by the dealer. If the car is sold without a warranty, the label must state that the car is being sold "as is."

A related and well-developed area of state and federal consumer law concerns restrictions on tampering with car odometers. The Motor Vehicle Information and Cost Savings Act[43] makes it a crime to change car odometers. In its findings, Congress concluded that consumers purchasing a motor vehicle rely heavily on odometer readings as an indication of a car's safety and reliability. Federal odometer regulations issued by the National Highway Traffic Safety Administration require that mileage be disclosed in writing each time a car's title is transferred. The transferor must also certify that, to the best of his or her knowledge, the odometer reading reflects the actual mileage.

On the state level, industry-specific regulation covers the insurance industry. State insurance commissioners not only establish regulations regarding the disclosure of information to perspective policyholders, they also set maximum rates within a state.

Real Estate Sales

A number of state and federal laws protect consumers in real estate transactions. In general, these laws, including the Real Estate Settlement Procedures Act and the Interstate Land Sales Full Disclosure Act, are designed to prevent fraud and require disclosure of certain relevant information. Certain disclosure requirements of the Truth-in-Lending Act apply to real estate credit transactions as well. In some transactions, real estate buyers have the right to cancel the purchase contract if certain

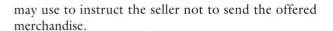

ETHICAL CONSIDERATION

Should caller ID be used by telemarketers to identify those individuals who call their 800 or 900 telephone numbers?

---

42. 16 C.F.R. § 455 (1998) (Used Motor Vehicle Trade Regulation Rule).
43. 15 U.S.C. § 1901 *et seq.* (1998).

information is not disclosed to them or if other procedures are not properly followed.

The Real Estate Settlement Procedures Act and revisions made to it in 1976 are designed to assist home buyers by requiring disclosure of any requirements for settlement proceedings, which may include title insurance, taxes, and fees for attorneys, appraisers, and brokers. In general, lenders must give an estimate of settlement costs, identify service providers the applicant is required to use, and provide a statement showing the annual percentage rate for the mortgage.

In the early 1960s, Congress became concerned with fraudulent practices used in the sale of subdivided land for investment purposes or for second or retirement homes. Hearings held at that time indicated that many older Americans had invested their savings in new subdivisions, particularly in Florida and the Southwest, in which the lots were unbuildable. Because the lots were often marketed through newspaper advertisements or other interstate means, sales were often finalized before the purchaser had the opportunity to see the property.

To remedy this situation, Congress in 1968 passed the Interstate Land Sales Full Disclosure Act,[44] which is administered by the secretary of the Department of Housing and Urban Development (HUD). Under the act, the secretary created the Office of Interstate Land Sales Registration, and federal disclosure requirements were imposed on the sale of undeveloped subdivided land. The act gives the secretary of HUD the power to bring suit in federal district court to enjoin sales by developers who have not registered in accordance with the act.

The act was modeled after the Securities Act of 1933 and requires developers to file an initial statement of record with HUD's Office of Interstate Land Sales Registration for approval before the lots can be leased or sold. Only developments of 100 or more lots of unimproved land promoted through a common plan and deemed part of interstate commerce are covered under the act. As discussed in Chapter 2, interstate commerce is a very broad concept and can include almost any otherwise intrastate activity that makes use of the U.S. mail or the telephone.

---

44. 15 U.S.C. § 1701 *et seq.* (1998).

ETHICAL CONSIDERATION

When, if ever, does an advertiser possess too much information about a consumer's preferences and buying habits? What implications might interactive television have for consumer privacy?

The act provides both criminal and civil penalties for a land promoter's fraud, misrepresentation, or noncompliance. Purchasers affected by a promoter's wrongdoing have a private cause of action and may cancel the purchase contract.

◆ Privacy Protections

A number of states have passed laws that are intended to protect consumer privacy. Privacy bills were introduced in 35 states in 1993 alone. Among the bills that passed in 1993 was one in Maine that prohibited the sale or rental of lists containing the names, addresses, and account numbers of credit card holders without their express written permission. A New York law regulates use of information about videocassette rentals and sales.[45]

---

45. John H. Awerdick, *Marketing Regulation Will Get Tougher*, DIRECT, Nov. 1993, at 110.

INTERNATIONAL CONSIDERATION

Germany has been an international pioneer in protecting individuals' right to privacy since the late 1960s. The German constitutional court ruled in 1983 that all citizens have a constitutional right to know what data is being kept about them and by whom. They are also guaranteed access to that data to ensure its accuracy. Thus, personal information that is given freely and used for marketing purposes by credit card companies in the United States is off-limits in Germany.

© Signe Wilkinson, from *Philadelphia Daily News*. Reprinted by permission of the Cartoonists and Writers Syndicate.

VIEW FROM CYBERSPACE

PRIVACY IN THE ELECTRONIC AGE

Federal and state governments, credit-tracking bureaus, and purveyors of direct mail lists have all been collecting information about consumers for years. All of that information can wind up on the Internet and almost anyone can gain access to it.

Internet ad-tracking companies put "cookies" on Web-surfers' computer hard drives that contain information about which Web sites the users visit, what companies they work for, what city they're in, and what kind of computers they're using—and it collects this information without any notification or consent of the user. Web sites request personal information when a user reg-

isters to gain access to the services and information provided at that site. Companies use this information to tailor their marketing pitches to the tastes of the individual consumer.

The increasing use of the Internet to conduct personal and commercial transactions, as well as to provide access to information, raises a number of privacy issues. Privacy concerns, including fear that credit card numbers will be used without the consumer's consent, have hampered electronic commerce.

State common law and federal statutes provide limited recourse in the event of invasion of privacy in

View from Cyberspace continues

electronic communication. The Restatement (Second) of Torts prohibits (1) intentional intrusion into one's solitude, seclusion, or private affairs; (2) misappropriation of a name or likeness for personal benefit; (3) public disclosure of private facts; and (4) placing another in a false light in the public eye.[a]

These protections would cover such acts as intercepting private e-mail, selling information for personal benefit, and misappropriating names or likenesses.

The Electronic Communications Privacy Act (EPCA)[b] provides for criminal and civil penalties for intrusion and invasion of privacy involving electronic communications. Part 1 prohibits intentional or attempted interception or disclosure of electronic communications; Part 2 disallows unauthorized intentional access to stored electronic communications.

Under current law, the FTC cannot force firms to disclose their privacy policies. If a Web site posts a privacy policy, however, the FTC considers failure to abide by it a deceptive trade practice under Section 5(a) of the FTC Act. The FTC also takes the position that failure to obtain parental consent before collecting information from children is an unfair trade practice, because it presents special risks to children.[c]

Members of Congress have proposed several pieces of legislation to deal with various issues surrounding collection and availability of personal information over the Internet.[d] For example, the Consumer Internet Privacy Protection Act would require Internet providers to get consent in writing from subscribers before giving information to third parties. The Identity Theft and Assumption Deterrence Act would increase punishment for taking an individual's information (such as Social Security number and mother's maiden name) and using that information to fraudulently obtain credit or commit other financial crimes (so-called *identity theft*). The Personal Information Privacy Act would limit the government's ability to use personal information to stop computerized abuses and would provide for civil damages if Social Security numbers are used without authorization.

In an effort to prevent government from imposing costly restrictions, the computer industry has made some attempts to police itself. The Information Technology Industry Council (ITI) issued voluntary guidelines to its member organizations in November 1997. The guidelines, *The Protection of Personal Data in Electronic Commerce*, define eight principles intended to apply both to

data-collection practices and electronic database use over the Internet.[e] The eight principles are as follows:

1. *Providing Information on Data-Protection Policies* Collectors and users of personal data should give individuals easily understood information about their policies regarding the collection, use, and disclosure of personal data.
2. *Notifying and Empowering the Consumer* Individuals have the right to be informed about, and exercise reasonable control over, the collection and use of their personal data. ITI member companies are developing market-driven technological solutions enabling individual data providers to exercise choice and control over their personal data. In many cases, electronic technologies offer greater personal data protection.
3. *Limiting Data Collection* Collectors and users of personal data should limit the collection of personal data to that which is needed for valid business reasons, and any such data should be obtained by lawful and fair means.
4. *Ensuring Data Accuracy* Collectors and users should strive to maintain the accuracy of the personal data held, including establishing, where appropriate, mechanisms allowing individuals to have the opportunity to review and correct their personal data in defined and secure circumstances.
5. *Enabling Informed Choice* At the time of collection of personal data, collectors and users should furnish individuals with information on the intended use of such data and with mechanisms permitting the exercise of choice on its disclosure.
6. *Safeguarding Security* Collectors and users of personal data should take appropriate steps to ensure that personal data is protected from unauthorized access and disclosure, including limiting access to such data to only those employees with a business need to know.
7. *Educating the Marketplace* Collectors and users of personal data, and particularly ITI companies with expertise to share, should support and participate in consumer-education efforts about the importance of fair information practices and privacy protection. Individuals should use their powers of choice in the marketplace to safeguard their personal data and that of their children.

View from Cyberspace continues

View from Cyberspace continued

8. *Adapting Privacy Practices to Electronic and On-line Technologies*   To the maximum extent possible, privacy principles and practices should be the same regardless of the specific technologies employed for data collection and use. Individuals should have a reasonably consistent expectation of privacy in both electronic and paper-based environments.

The Direct Marketing Association (DMA) has taken a stronger stance. In December 1997, the association announced mandatory standards for its members and threatened expulsion for those organizations that did not comply with the new standards. These standards include notifying consumers of information practices, allowing consumers to chose to opt out of providing information, and honoring the posted policy.

European countries favor a more legislative approach to privacy protection, with governments defining the standards to which industry should comply. The European Union (EU) Data Protection Directive,[f] scheduled to go into effect in late 1998, will generally require firms to obtain permission before collecting personal data. The directive also will prevent companies operating in the EU from transmitting data electronically to third countries, including the United States, unless those countries provide "adequate" protection for personal information. The directive does not define what is adequate protection; the EU will make the adequacy determination on a case-by-case basis. Although the directive will accommodate voluntary codes of conduct and industry guidelines, they must protect individuals as a whole and be effective, enforceable, and provide for redress.

TRUSTe, a California company that rates Web sites according to their level of privacy, has surveyed Web users and found that 41% would leave a Web page rather than reveal personal information. The survey results also revealed that at least 25% supply false data when they do comply with requests for information.

---

a. Phillip J. Crihfield & Alan J. Goldman, *Privacy? What Privacy? Don't Assume Your Journey into the Net Is Secure,* Bus. L. Today, Mar./Apr. 1996, at 48.

b. 18 U.S.C. § 2510 (1998).

c. *Firms Not Abiding by Their Privacy Policies May Face Section 5 Action,* FTC *Official Says,* 66 Legal News 24 (1997).

d. Rebecca Quick, *Don't Expect Your Secrets to Get Kept on the Internet,* Wall St. J., Feb 6, 1998, at B5.

e. *The Protection of Personal Data in Electronic Commerce,* (Nov. 20, 1997), Information Technology Industry Council Web site <http://www.itic.org>.

f. Council Directive 95/46/EC.

Consumer Health and Safety

As with unfairness, deception, and fraud, many federal, state, and local regulatory agencies protect consumers' health and safety. Among the federal agencies that work to prevent consumer injury are the Food and Drug Administration, the Department of Agriculture, the Department of Transportation's National Highway Traffic Safety Administration, and the Federal Communications Commission.

The areas that these agencies regulate include alcohol, tobacco, smoking, gambling, firearms, drugs, medical devices, food, pesticides, automobiles, and broadcasting. Through government regulation, consumers are shielded from products or practices that are considered detrimental to health and safety. However, consumer protection law should not be confused with product liability law, discussed in Chapter 10. Product liability law provides a common law remedy enforced by private action, whereas consumer protection law provides a statutory remedy enforced by the government (or, in some cases, also by private parties).

At the state level, consumer health and safety laws cover a wide variety of areas, such as the availability of alcohol, tobacco, and gambling. State and local provisions also address no-smoking regulations, restaurant inspections, and the competency of professional workers through the granting of various occupational licenses.

Alcohol and Tobacco

Regulation of the "vices" alcohol and tobacco (as they relate to consumer health and safety) is achieved, since repeal of the Eighteenth Amendment and the end of Prohibition, primarily at the state and local government levels. States no longer prohibit the use of alcohol and tobacco, but they do regulate access to both by establishing minimum ages for purchase and enacting laws that limit the hours during which alcohol may be sold at liquor stores, bars, and clubs. In addition, an Indiana law prohibits the sale of alcohol on credit.[46]

Increasing evidence of the addictive qualities of nicotine has led to support for regulation of cigarettes as a drug. In 1997, a federal district court in North Carolina ruled that the FDA could regulate tobacco as a drug,[47] but that decision was appealed. After a panel of three judges of the Fourth Circuit heard the appeal in late 1997, reargument of the case was ordered because one judge had died and another began suffering serious medical problems. The reargument was scheduled for June 1998.[48]

Smoking

The regulation of smoking and the recent proliferation of nonsmoking laws, especially in California, has been mostly at the local government level, primarily because of the significant influence of the tobacco industry at the state and federal levels. The passage of many tough local ordinances, banning all smoking in restaurants and offices, was also helped by a 1993 Environmental Protection Agency report that found that secondhand cigarette smoke causes cancer.

Philip Morris, maker of Marlboro cigarettes, sued the city of San Francisco to overturn that city's anti-smoking ordinance. Philip Morris claimed that state workplace safety rules are responsible for regulating the safety of workers and therefore preempt enforcement of the local smoking regulation.[49] In a 1992 case based on a similar claim, a California judge overturned a San Francisco ordinance regulating the use of video display terminals (VDTs) in private business. Concern over secondhand smoke prompted statewide efforts as well. In 1994, California outlawed smoking in restaurants and most other workplaces to protect employees and customers; and, in 1998, it extended the prohibition to bars and casinos, making it the first state to outlaw smoking so broadly.[50] Although attempts to repeal the ban on smoking in bars have been made, thus far none has succeeded.[51]

Gambling

Gambling is also a consumer protection issue. Once limited to Nevada, gambling has seen enormous growth in other states, on waterways, and on Native American reservations or reservation-owned property. There are dozens of on-line gambling sites on the World Wide Web, most of which are based off-shore. Several states, including Minnesota,[52] have tried to ban these virtual casinos. As of mid-1998, Congress was considering a federal ban.

Highly promoted lotteries in 33 states and the District of Columbia fund public projects from education to environmental preservation. With this expansion, however, has come increased concern that consumers might be deceived by lottery advertisements or become compulsive gamblers, spending beyond their means.

Firearms

At least 34 U.S. Postal Service employees have been murdered by coworkers in the past decade and an additional 26 have been wounded. As explained in Chapter 12, advocates of gun control measures have cited rising workplace violence as one reason to restrict access to firearms. Gun control laws vary from state to state. In 1994, major federal crime legislation included a ban on the manufacture, future sale, and possession of 19 brands of combat-style assault weapons and their look-alikes.

---

51. *Assembly Moves to Lift Smoking Ban*, L.A. TIMES, Jan. 1, 1998, at A1.

52. Minnesota v. Granite Gate Resorts, Inc., 568 N.W. 2d 715 (Minn. 1997).

ETHICAL CONSIDERATION

What can managers do to decrease workplace violence? Would gun-control laws help prevent the type of violence that has plagued the U.S. Postal Service in recent years?

---

46. IND. CODE ANN. § 7.1-5-10-12 (West 1997).

47. Coyne Beahm, Inc. v. FDA., 966 F. Supp. 1374 (M.D.N.C. 1997).

48. Suein L. Hwang & Ann Davis, *Tobacco Firms' Hopes in Lawsuit Are Dashed by Reargument Order*, WALL ST. J., Apr. 20, 1998, at B9.

49. Eben Shapiro, *Philip Morris Sues City over No-Smoking Rules*, WALL ST. J., Feb. 2, 1994, at B1.

50. CAL. LABOR CODE § 6404.5 (West 1998).

Drugs, Medical Devices, and Cosmetics

The Food and Drug Administration (FDA) plays a broad role in consumer protection law. It monitors the production and sale of $1 trillion of food and medical products each year. In addition to its involvement in food, drug, medical device, and cosmetic labeling (*misbranding*), the FDA regulates the new-drug approval process.

FDA Standards for Drug Approval

The FDA has authority to require that certain drugs be available only by prescription. Thus, if a drug authorized only for prescription use is sold over-the-counter, it is misbranded and the FDA will halt its sale. In general, the FDA will require prescription use only when a drug is, for example, toxic, requires a physician's supervision for safe use, or is addictive.

The first step in the approval process for new drugs is their classification by the Drug Enforcement Agency (DEA) into one of five schedules based on potential for abuse and currently accepted medical use. Only Schedule I drugs, those with the highest potential for abuse and no currently accepted medical use, cannot be approved by the FDA.

The drug-approval process for non–Schedule I drugs begins with preclinical research (which includes animal testing) aimed at discovery and identification of drugs that are sufficiently promising to study in humans. The drugmaker then submits this preclinical research, along with a document called "Claimed Exemption for Investigational New Drug," to the FDA. The FDA can then permit or deny continued research. If approved for investigational purposes, a drug will be tested in humans in three separate phases, with FDA review at the end of each phase. This framework is designed to protect the safety of the human subjects used in the study, to develop necessary data on the drug, and to ensure that all studies are done properly. Once all of the testing data are assembled, they are submitted to the FDA, which may approve or deny. Approval is based on a drug's safety and effectiveness; it may require marketing restrictions, and can be contested by anyone. The FDA must also approve the description of a drug (for example, labels and package inserts).

Drugs with a high potential for therapeutic gain and no satisfactory alternative may be given priority (ex-

pedited) review by the FDA. In addition, such drugs may be available during the investigational stage, to people not within the clinical test group, through open protocols. For example, people with AIDS may have access to new drugs under investigation if preliminary evidence of effectiveness exists.

Congress passed legislation in 1997 to speed up the approval of new drugs, medical devices, and food products by permitting the FDA to use outside reviewers to evaluate medical devices and make it easier for seriously ill patients to obtain experimental drugs.[53]

53. Food and Drug Administration Modernization Act of 1997, Pub. L. No. 105-115 (1997).

ETHICAL CONSIDERATION

Drug companies provide financial support to academic researchers in the form of employment or consulting fees, research funds, money to attend symposiums, and speaking honorariums. Should scientists disclose their ties to drug companies when publishing articles about their research? Should drug companies disclose these financial ties?

ETHICAL CONSIDERATION

Invitro International in 1993 secured U.S. approval for its product Corrositex, the first legal substitute for live rabbits in testing the corrosiveness of chemicals. Invitro's customers are mainly cosmetics and household products companies, such as Helene Curtis and S.C. Johnson, that have stopped using tests on live rabbits.[a] Animal rights activists have praised the company. What ethical concerns are present in product testing? Does the type of product being tested (for example, food, drugs, or cosmetics) affect these ethical concerns?

a. Nina Munk, *Bunny Money*, FORBES, Dec. 20, 1993, at 212.

HISTORICAL PERSPECTIVE

FOOD AND DRUG REGULATION

Thalidomide Tragedy Spurs New Laws, 1962

[T]he thalidomide tragedy of the 1960s, though Americans were spared its worst effects, produced the still-stronger drug-testing laws of 1962.

Thalidomide, developed in Germany, had been hailed as the greatest sleeping pill in history. After it became a bestseller in Germany, Britain and Canada, the century-old William Merrell Company asked the U.S. Food and Drug Administration in September 1960 for approval to sell it in the United States. The application, backed by four telephone-book-sized volumes of data, was assigned to Frances Kelsey, a Canadian-born physician and pharmacologist who had just joined the FDA.

Dr. Kelsey thought thalidomide looked "peculiar." For one thing, the sleeping pill didn't make test animals sleepy. Despite constant—and angry—pressure from Merrell, she blocked approval, asking Merrell for more and more data.

Meanwhile, German and other European doctors were puzzling over an epidemic of phocomelia, children born with flipper-like appendages instead of proper arms and legs. In November 1961, Widiking Lenz, a Hamburg pediatrician, discovered the link: Mothers of the deformed babies had been using thalidomide. The drug was withdrawn that month and Merrell dropped its application for FDA approval.

When the thalidomide story hit the United States, it caused shudders that had seismic effects in Congress. Sen. Estes Kefauver, whose tough drug-regulating bill had been gutted on Capitol Hill, now saw it revived, strengthened and sped on its way to President Kennedy's desk. He signed it into law in October 1962, two months after he had awarded Dr. Kelsey the Distinguished Federal Civilian Service Award.

SOURCE   WALL ST. J., Sept. 6, 1989, at B1. Reprinted by permission of the *Wall Street Journal*, © 1989, Dow Jones & Company, Inc. All Rights Reserved Worldwide.

Update

In a strange historical twist, this birth-defect causing drug came back in vogue in the 1990s as a hopeful response to AIDS. In 1995, the FDA gave Celgene Corporation permission to conduct clinical trials of thalidomide to counteract the severe weight loss and deterioration that often accompanies AIDS.[a] In the following year, Celgene applied for federal permission to use thalidomide to treat an especially painful form of leprosy.[b] In 1997, the FDA Advisory Committee recommended approval of thalidomide for this treatment, signaling a new found respect for this scourge of the 1960s.[c]

a. *Once-Feared Thalidomide to Be Offered AIDS Patients*, SEATTLE POST-INTELLIGENCER, Aug. 29, 1995, at A3.

b. *Company Applies to Use Thalidomide for Leprosy*, ORLANDO SENTINEL, Dec. 24, 1996, at A8.

c. *FDA Approves Thalidomide's Use against ENL*, ECN—EUROPEAN CHEM. NEWS, Sept. 15, 1997, at 51.

Food Safety

Product Definition: Food or Drug?

Drugs, as defined by the act, include (1) articles intended for use in the diagnosis, cure, mitigation, treatment, or prevention of disease; and (2) articles (other than food) intended to affect the structure or any function of the body. Thus, many things that are, in fact, food may fit this definition. For example, orange juice may be said to be used to prevent disease. Under the act, *food* is defined as (1) articles used for food or drink; (2) chewing gum; and (3) articles used for components of either.

Because the distinction between drugs and food is important in the application of both the mislabeling and adulteration provisions of the act, as well as the drug-approval process, the FDA must categorize each product. In general, the FDA looks at the intent to use a product as a drug in determining how to categorize it. Intent may be apparent from the manufacturer's intent or reasons for consumers' use, or it may be inferred from labels, promotional material, or advertisements. The following case provides an example of this analysis.

| **A CASE IN POINT** | **IN THE LANGUAGE OF THE COURT** |

CASE 19.5
UNITED STATES v. KASZ ENTERPRISES, INC.
United States District Court for Rhode Island
855 F. Supp. 534 (D.R.I. 1994), *amended*, 862 F. Supp. 717 (D.R.I. 1994).

FACTS James Kaszyk was the owner and president of Kasz Enterprises, Inc. (Kasz). Kasz sold and distributed two hair care products under the trade names Solution 109 Herbal Shampoo and Solution 109 Herbal Cosmetic Scalp Cleanser (Solutions 109, collectively). The two products were sold together for a combined retail price of $100. The FDA had never approved the products as a drug. Beginning in 1991, the FDA inspected Kasz three times. Each time the FDA found that Kasz was distributing the products in interstate commerce and promoting them as a hair-growth and hair-loss-prevention system in violation of the Food, Drug and Cosmetic Act.

Kasz conceded that it sold the Solutions 109 in interstate commerce, but it argued that the only claim it made regarding Solutions 109 was that they make hair fuller and thicker. The FDA, however, argued that Kasz touted the products as hair-growth stimulants and hair-loss preventors by incorporating opinions and testimonials from third-party users of Solutions 109.

Despite numerous FDA warnings, Kasz continued to distribute and promote Solutions 109. The FDA then sought to permanently enjoin Kasz from manufacturing, selling, and distributing Solutions 109 and any other unapproved new drugs in interstate commerce.

ISSUE PRESENTED When does a product become a drug for purposes of the Food, Drug and Cosmetic Act (FDCA)?

OPINION PETTINE, J., writing for Federal District Court, and quoting the Report and Recommendation of U.S. Magistrate Judge Lovegreen:

The threshold question in this analysis is whether Solutions 109 are drugs which would thus subject them to regulation by FDA under the FDCA. If a product is intended for use in the treatment of disease or is intended to affect the structure or function of the human body, it is a drug under the FDCA.

The intended use of a product is determined by the vendor's objective intent in promoting, distributing, and selling the product. Objective intent can be demonstrated by, among other things, "labeling" claims, advertising material, oral and written statements, and evidence that the vendor is aware that his product is being offered or used by others for a purpose for which it is neither labeled nor advertised. For example, claims in circulars and newspaper advertisements that explain the curative properties of products may establish that such products are drugs. Similarly, testimonials regarding a product's curative properties or ability to affect the structure or function of the human body may be used to establish the intended use of the article as a drug.

Case 19.5 continues

Case 19.5 continued

Solutions 109 are drugs within the meaning of [the act's second definition]. Products intended for use in the treatment, prevention, or cure of baldness or thinning hair, are drugs within the meaning of [the act] because hair loss can be a manifestation of disease. . . . It is clear that Kasz has marketed Solutions 109 as hair growth stimulation and hair loss prevention products notwithstanding Kasz' disclaimer that Solutions 109 only make hair look fuller and thicker. The promotional materials accompanying Solutions 109 are replete with claims (testimonials) that hair growth has occurred and hair loss prevented with use of these products. Therefore, Solutions 109 are intended by Kasz for use in the mitigation, treatment or prevention of hair loss and are thus drugs within the meaning of [the act].

Solutions 109 are also drugs within the meaning of [the act's third definition] because they are represented to have a physiological effect on the body of man, namely, to cause hair growth and to prevent hair loss. The hair growth process is a function of the human body. . . . Products that claim to be effective for growing hair or preventing hair loss, thus claim to alter the functioning of the hair growth and hair loss process. Likewise, such products are intended to alter the structure of the hair itself, to make it grow longer or thicker, or to prevent the hair from becoming thinner.

. . .

The statutory definition does not require that a product be intended both to treat disease and to affect the structure or function of the body; these are two different ways in which a product may be considered a drug under the FDCA.

. . .

Kasz also points out that certain disclaimer language is contained in some of their promotional material. There is no dispute as to this fact. . . .

Disclaimers relating to intended drug uses are ineffective where the overall circumstances demonstrate the seller's true intent to communicate to the consumer that a product has drug uses. . . .

. . . The intent and effect of the FDCA in protecting consumers from drug claims that have not been supported by competent scientific proof cannot be circumvented by linguistic game-playing. If Kasz really did not intend for consumers to purchase their products in the belief that the products would grow hair, Kasz would simply have removed all references to hair growth in their labeling and promotional literature. They have not done so, doubtless because they know that consumers will not purchase normal shampoo for the $100 price now being charged for Solutions 109 unless they believe that it will grow hair.

RESULT   The court permanently enjoined Kasz from manufacturing, selling, and distributing Solutions 109 and any other unapproved new drugs in interstate commerce.

Questions

1. Why didn't the disclaimer language keep Solutions 109 from being characterized as a drug?
2. Why was the price charged for Solutions 109 relevant?

CHAPTER 19   CONSUMER PROTECTION   **737**

FDA Standards for Food Condemnation

The FDA also protects consumer health and safety through the confiscation of contaminated or adulterated foods. The standards for condemnation are different depending on whether the product is a natural food or contains additives. An *additive* is anything not inherent in the food product, including pesticide residue, unintended environmental contaminants, and unavoidably added substances from packaging. If an additive (in the quantity present in the food product) is injurious to any group in the general population, then the product will be deemed adulterated.

Natural foods are adulterated if they "consist in whole or in part of any filthy, putrid or decomposed substance, or if it is otherwise unfit for food." All foods contain some level of unavoidable natural defects, so the FDA sets minimum tolerance standards for defects that will be tolerated. Articles that exceed those minimum levels are deemed adulterated and seized by the FDA. In some cases a seized product may be rehabilitated by a manufacturer and released by the FDA for sale.

In the largest recall of its kind, Hudson Foods recalled 25 million pounds of hamburger meat contaminated with a virulent strain of *E. coli* bacteria in 1997. Tainted food causes an estimated 6.5 million to 33 million illnesses and 9,000 deaths annually in the United States.

INTERNATIONAL CONSIDERATION

Recent trade treaties have made the U.S. food market one of the most open in the world. Food imports have doubled in the last five years and have risen to 30 billion tons. The importation of fresh fruits and vegetables, gourmet cheeses, meats, and shellfish present new challenges for regulators. For example, raspberries imported from Guatemala carried a food-borne parasite that struck hundreds of people in 1996.

To allay concerns in the United States, authorities in Mexico (which ships 90% of its $4.5 billion in annual food exports to the United States) are encouraging produce exporters to have their operations certified by private U.S. laboratories that inspect the fields, irrigation water and packing conditions, and the bathrooms workers use. Mexican growers of mangoes destined for the United States employ 60 USDA inspectors. Still experts argue that the ultimate burden of ensuring safe food may fall on the globalized food industry.[a]

a. Paul Magnusson et al., *News: Analysis & Commentary*, Bus. Wk. Sept. 8, 1997, at 30–32.

"It's only the Ericksons, so why don't you just use the recalled hamburger meat."

Jack Ziegler © 1997 from The New Yorker Collection. All Rights Reserved.

The U.S. Department of Agriculture also plays a major role in food safety. The Department's primary consumer protection activities all involve food and include inspecting facilities engaged in the slaughtering or processing of meat, poultry, and egg products; preventing the sale of mislabeled meat or poultry products; and offering producers a voluntary grading program for various agricultural products.

Pesticides

Under the Food, Drug and Cosmetic Act, the FDA shares with the Environmental Protection Agency (EPA) the responsibility for regulating pesticide residues on food. The EPA registers pesticides and establishes tolerances under the act. The FDA enforces the tolerance levels and deems a food to be adulterated if it does not conform to the pesticide tolerance levels set under the act.

Genetically Engineered Food

Calgene, Inc., a California-based biotech company, began marketing its genetically engineered Flavr Savr tomato in mid-1994, after waiting several years for FDA approval. With antisense technology, genetic engineers used the plant's own genetic design to overcome unwanted traits. In the case of the Flavr Savr tomato, a copy of the gene responsible for rotting is cloned and reinserted in reverse order. The two opposites bind to one another, effectively blocking the rot-producing function. As a result, the Flavr Savr tomato is expected to last longer and taste better than conventional tomatoes.

Marvin Cetron, president of Forecasting International, predicted in April 1998 that in the next two years the food biotechnology industry will create potatoes made disease-resistant with the addition of a chicken gene; rice fortified with a pea gene to improve protein balance; and pork made leaner with the addition of a cow or chicken gene.[54]

Although there is still considerable consumer resistance to genetically engineered foods, consumers' growing concerns about the environment may lead to greater acceptance. Genetically engineered pest-resistant plants may reduce the need for chemical pesticides, thereby helping to protect the environment.

Irradiated Foods

In December 1997, the FDA authorized the irradiation of fresh and frozen red meat as a means to kill foodborne bacteria (including *E. coli*) and to lengthen shelf life. Irradiation is a process by which food is passed through a sealed chamber where it is exposed to gamma ray radiation from cobalt 60 or cesium 137 or to an electron beam.

Wheat was the first food approved for radiation in the United States. Since approving wheat in 1963, the FDA has approved the irradiation of potatoes (1964), dried spices and vegetable seasonings (1983), pork (1986), fruits and vegetables (1986), poultry (1992), and red meat (1997). FDA regulations require irradiated foods to be prominently and conspicuously labeled with the radura symbol (a stylized green flower) and the words "Treated with Radiation" or "Treated by Irradiation."

For many consumers, irradiation conjures up images of mushroom clouds and Chernobyl.[55] Some activists have threatened to organize consumer boycotts of companies selling irradiated foods and to launch media campaigns against irradiation. Yet, experts predict that consumers will be won over by irradiation's safety and effectiveness in protecting consumers from bacteria and other microbes. Former FDA commissioner Dr. David Kessler agrees and draws parallels to the public's shunning of pasteurized milk in the early twentieth century and the initial distrust of microwave ovens in the 1970s.[56]

AT THE TOP

A chief executive officer of a food company may be held vicariously and strictly liable for introducing adulterated articles into interstate commerce.[a]

---

a. United States v. Park, 421 U.S. 658 (1975).

---

54. *Irradiation Education Effort Needed from Industry and Government, Futurist Tells Food Update,* FOOD CHEMICAL NEWS (May 4, 1998).

55. Martha Groves, *Less-Than Glowing Image Hampers Food Irradiation,* L.A. TIMES, Mar. 15, 1998, at A1.

56. Joanna Ramey, *Food Industry Groups Near Start of Irradiation Campaign,* SUPERMARKET NEWS, Apr. 17, 1998, at 23.

Health Insurance and Managed Care

As explained in Chapter 12, the Health Insurance Portability and Accountability Act, adopted by Congress in 1996, made health insurance coverage portable, renewable, and available for workers as they moved from job to job. The National Association of Insurance Commissioners has drafted a model state law designed to protect the confidentiality of personally identifiable health insurance information by restricting health insurers use and disclosure of such information. President Clinton conveyed his administration's proposal for privacy legislation to Congress in September 1997.

The growth of health maintenance organizations (HMOs) and managed care has led to pressure for a patient's bill of rights that would give patients the right to choose health-care providers and a way to hold health plans accountable for their health-care treatment decisions. Texas became the first state to give injured patients the right to sue health plans for malpractice over decisions to deny coverage for treatment.

Employer-sponsored health plans are governed by the federal Employee Retirement Income Security Act (ERISA). As explained in Chapter 12, ERISA prohibits patients injured as a result of coverage denials from suing employer-sponsored plans for lost wages, pain and suffering, or punitive damages. Several bills pending in Congress in mid-1998 would allow patients to sue health plans and their administrators for damages arising out of managed care decisions. Proponents argue: "Health plans can't have it both ways. They can't take the position that they save money through effective utilization review, and then, when something goes wrong, say, 'It has nothing to do with us.'"[57] Opponents fear runaway health costs and argue that consumers can "vote with their feet" to solve quality problems.

One employee is taking a different tack. She sued Cigna HealthCare of California, alleging that it engaged in false and misleading advertising by promising more than it delivered in violation of the state ban on "unfair and deceptive business practices."[58]

Most managed care plans provide for mandatory arbitration of all controversies with the plan. Some patient-rights advocates seek to ban mandatory arbitration and give patients the right to seek an immediate court ruling when a managed care plan denies treatment. Notwithstanding a mandatory arbitration clause in the plan, the California Supreme Court refused to require arbitration when it found that the plan's method of arbitration was unfair and not implemented in compliance with its own stated policies.[59]

Automobiles

Automobile safety has seen enormous gains since Ralph Nader first brought the issue to the nation's attention in the 1960s.[60] Air bags (for the driver and front passenger) and anti-lock brakes have become popular safety features and are standard equipment on many new cars. Before consumers began to request air bags, many car manufacturers met the legal requirement for passive restraints through the use of automatic seat belts.

In response to consumer-group pressure, the National Highway Traffic Safety Administration (NHTSA) may require automakers to list safety data on new-car window stickers, along with fuel economy data and national origin of parts. Surveys have shown that many consumers want the government to provide more information about crashworthiness by adding data on side impact, offset frontal, and rollover crashes to frontal collision data currently being gathered. For more than 15 years, the New Car Assessment Program has assessed frontal collision safety by crashing cars at 35 mph, which is one-third more destructive than the 30-mph crashes that vehicles must pass to meet federal safety standards.

The NHTSA, created in 1970, is an agency of the U.S. Department of Transportation. By law, the NHTSA has the power to establish motor vehicle safety standards,[61] establish a National Motor Vehicle Safety Advisory Council, engage in testing and development

---

57. Laurie McGinley, *Broad Battle to End HMOs' Limited Liability for Treatment-Coverage Denials Gains Steam*, WALL ST. J., Jan. 12, 1998, at A22.

58. K. Oanh Ha, *Lawsuit Seeks to Bypass HMO Arbitration Process*, WALL ST. J., Sept. 10, 1997, at CA2.

59. Engalla v. Permanente Medical Group, Inc., 938 P.2d 903 (Cal. 1997).

60. RALPH NADER, UNSAFE AT ANY SPEED (1965) (criticizing in particular General Motors Corporation's Corvair model). For a critique of Ralph Nader's consumer activist activities, *see* DAN BURT, ABUSE OF TRUST (1982).

61. Boats are subject to safety regulation under the Federal Boat Safety Act of 1971 (46 U.S.C. §§ 4301 *et seq.* (1998)), and aircraft safety is regulated by the Federal Aviation Act of 1958 (49 U.S.C. §§ 1421 *et seq.* (1998)).

of motor vehicle safety, prohibit manufacture or importation of substandard vehicles, and develop tire safety.[62] In addition, the NHTSA is charged with developing national standards for driver safety performance, accident reporting, and vehicle registration and inspection. States refusing to comply with established federal standards are denied federal highway funds.[63]

It is often prudent for a manufacturer to recall a product with defects even before required legally to do so. For example, in 1998, Volkswagen of America recalled its New Beetles to correct a problem that could cause engine fires. It also gave its dealers money that could be used to give customers some compensation for having to bring in the car for the one-hour repair needed to correct the problem.

 ## Broadcasting and the Internet

Broadcasting

The U.S. attorney general and the chairman of the FCC warned broadcasters in 1994 to voluntarily reduce television violence or risk having the government step in to regulate it for them. Dissatisfied with industry's failure to reduce television violence (on average, an American child sees about 8,000 murders on television before reaching high school), the Telecommunications Act of 1996[64] requires television makers to include the V-chip in television sets sold in the United States. The *V-chip* is a set of internal controls that can read the TV-show

ratings transmitted by television networks and block all shows with a certain rating.

FCC regulations adopted in 1998 require television manufacturers to include the V-chip in at least half of all sets bigger than 13 inches by July 1999 and in all such sets by January 2000.[65] The FCC also approved the rating system that television networks will use to work with televisions with the V-chip. The system includes age limits and identifies programs with violence, sex, suggestive dialogue, or profanity and children's programs containing fantasy violence. News programs are not rated.

Use of the ratings is voluntary, however. To date, NBC and the BET cable network have declined to use the content-rating system that the rest of the industry began using in the fall of 1997. NBC gives age limits but does not include content descriptions (such as S for sexual situation and L for adult language); BET does not rate shows at all.

---

65. Laurie J. Flynn, *V-Chip and Ratings Are Close to Giving Parents New Power*, N.Y. TIMES, Apr. 2, 1998, at G6.

---

62. Motor Vehicle Safety Act of 1966, 15 U.S.C. §§ 1381 *et seq.* (1998).

63. Highway Safety Act of 1966, 23 U.S.C. §§ 401 *et seq.* (1998).

64. Pub. L. No. 104-104, 110 Stat. 56 (1996).

ETHICAL CONSIDERATION

Adding new safety requirements for automobiles can increase product cost and shut some consumers out of the market. Should governments coerce individuals into paying for unwanted safety features or should individual consumers be allowed to choose which features they pay for?

INTERNATIONAL CONSIDERATION

The Central Council for Education subcommittee in Japan was expected in March 1998 to recommend the introduction of the V-chip in Japan or the establishment of a system requiring warnings to appear in advance of programs not suitable for children.[a] Some experts attribute the rising juvenile crime rate to violent images on television.

The president of Japan Broadcasting Corporation (NHK) indicated that the public network will not introduce the V-chip censoring system. He said that the V-chip would be superfluous because NHK does not broadcast any sexually explicit or violent scenes.[b] However, private networks (such as TBS and TV Asahi) do carry violent crime shows.

---

a. Norma Reveler, HOLLYWOOD REPORTER, Mar. 13, 1998.

b. *Id.*

Regulation of broadcasting by the FCC seeks to ensure that broadcast media are competitive and operate for the public's benefit and use. Enforcement of FCC policies is achieved primarily through its ability to withhold license renewals. Licenses cannot be transferred or assigned without permission of the FCC and a finding that such a transfer will serve the public interest. FCC regulation of the content of broadcast programming raises First Amendment issues.

First Amendment Concerns

George Carlin recorded a 12-minute monologue entitled "Filthy Words" before a live audience in a theater. He began by referring to his thoughts about "the seven words you can't say on the public airwaves." He then proceeded to list those words and repeat them over and over in a variety of colloquial phrases. A radio station broadcasted a recording of the "Filthy Words" monologue on a weekday afternoon as part of a program about contemporary society's attitude toward language. The station advised listeners before the broadcast that the piece included language that might be offensive to some listeners.

A few weeks after the broadcast, a man who stated that he heard the broadcast while driving with his young son wrote a letter of complaint to the FCC. In response to the letter, the FCC issued an order condemning the broadcast as indecent and threatened to revoke the station's broadcast license if additional complaints were received.

In upholding the FCC's order, the U.S. Supreme Court concluded that of all forms of communication, broadcasting has the most limited First Amendment protection.[66] Among the reasons for the special treatment of indecent broadcasting was the uniquely pervasive presence that the medium of expression occupies in people's lives. Broadcasts, the Court said, extend into the privacy of the home, and it is impossible to avoid completely those that are patently offensive. Broadcasting, moreover, is uniquely accessible to children.

Internet

As explained in Chapter 2, the Supreme Court extended greater First Amendment protection to the Internet

ETHICAL CONSIDERATION

Does television violence create a violent society? Can content-based regulation of broadcasting protect consumer health and safety? What additional precautions (such as time, place, and manner restrictions), if any, should be taken to protect children?

when it struck down the Communications Decency Act (CDA) in 1997.[67] Nonetheless, the World Wide Web Consortium (W3C), a high-tech, international industry organization created in 1994 to develop protocols to aid in the evolution of the Web, created a labeling system to help parents control their children's surfing on the Internet. The Platform for Internet Content Selection (PICS) provides a standard format for labels so that any PICS-complaint software can read the ratings. Web publishers self-rate their content through a labeling service such as SafeSurf.

SafeSurf has one of the most prevalent and detailed ratings systems in the world. It includes ratings on profanity; heterosexual and homosexual themes; nudity; violence; intolerance of another's race, religion, gender, or sexual orientation; glorifying drug use; and gambling. For example, a site's rating on sexual themes could range from a 1 for subtle innuendo implying sexual acts through use of metaphor to a 9 for explicit and crude graphic descriptions of intimate details of sexual acts designed to arouse.

Parents can install PICS-filtering technology to block sites with ratings considered inappropriate for children. A W3C policy analyst stated that the adoption of the self-rating system was designed to "help show the industry is productive and responsible" and to reduce the likelihood that Congress will attempt to regulate the Internet by adopting "a CDC Part 2 of some sort down the road."[68]

The FTC began searching the Internet in mid-1998 to determine whether industry's efforts to self-regulate

---

66. FCC v. Pacifica Found., 438 U.S. 726 (1978).

67. Reno v. ACLU, 117 S. Ct. 2329 (1997).

68. Gillian Flynn, *The Web Cops*, San Francisco Examiner, Oct. 26, 1997, at B5.

to prevent Internet fraud were effective. Types of Internet fraud include (1) Web auctions with nonexistent or overvalued goods; (2) charges for free or never-supplied Internet services; (3) sales of computer products that were not delivered or that were misrepresented; (4) pyramid schemes; (5) false promises of credit cards; and (6) prizes or sweepstakes that request up-front fees.[69]

Other Consumer Products: The Consumer Product Safety Commission

Congress created the Consumer Product Safety Commission (CPSC), an independent regulatory agency, in 1972. Its purposes include protection of the public against unreasonable risks of injury associated with consumer products and assistance to consumers in evaluating the comparative safety of such products. Under the Consumer Product Safety Act[70] (which created the CPSC), the CPSC is authorized to set consumer product safety standards, such as performance or product-labeling specifications.

The statute provides a detailed scheme governing the adoption of such a standard. Any interested person may petition the CPSC to adopt a standard and may resort to judicial remedies if the CPSC denies the petition. The CPSC itself can begin a proceeding to develop such a standard by publishing in the Federal Register a notice inviting any person to submit an offer to do the development. Within a specified time limit, the CPSC can then accept such an offer, evaluate the suggestions submitted, and publish a proposed rule. The actual issuance of the final standard is subject to notice and comment by interested persons.

The penalty provisions of the act make it unlawful to manufacture for sale, offer for sale, distribute in commerce, or import into the United States a consumer product that does not conform to an applicable standard. Violators are subject to civil penalties, criminal penalties, injunctive enforcement and seizure, private suits for damages, and private suits for injunctive relief.

This means that if a product cannot be made free of unreasonable risk of personal injury, the CPSC may ban its manufacture, sale, or importation altogether. The supplier of any already-distributed products that pose a substantial risk of injury may be compelled by the CPSC to repair, modify, or replace the product, or refund the purchase price.

Before implementing a mandatory safety standard, the CPSC must find that voluntary standards are inadequate. One obvious concern for the commission is that a producer motivated by profits may not be willing or able to self-regulate. Any standards that the CPSC issues must also be reasonably necessary to eliminate an unreasonable risk of injury that the regulated product presents. To determine whether a standard is reasonably necessary, the commission weighs the standard's effectiveness in preventing injury against its effect on the cost of the product.

The CPSC administers several consumer protection acts, including the Flammable Fabrics Act, Federal Hazardous Substances Act,[71] Poison Prevention Packaging Act (child-resistant bottle caps), and the Refrigerator Safety Act. The CPSC currently has no jurisdiction over tobacco products, firearms, pesticides, motor vehicles, food, drugs, medical devices, or cosmetics.[72] These matters are regulated by other entities, such as the FDA, or are unregulated. In addition to its other duties, the CPSC maintains an Injury Information Clearinghouse to collect and analyze information relating to the causes and prevention of death, injury, and illness associated with consumer products.

State Occupational Licensing

State departments of consumer affairs protect the public by examining and licensing firms and individuals who possess the necessary education and demonstrated skills to perform their services competently. Among the occupations generally regulated are accountants, architects, barbers, contractors, cosmetologists, dentists, dry cleaners, marriage counselors, nurses, pharmacists,

69. *Internet Fraud Legislation Premature; Self-Regulatory Efforts Could Work, FTC Says*, 66 U.S.L.W. 2502 (Feb. 24, 1998).

70. 15 U.S.C. §§ 2051 *et seq.* (1998).

71. This act is a composite of three significant acts: the Hazardous Substances Labeling Act, the Child Protection Act, and the Child Protection and Toy Safety Act. 15 U.S.C. § 2052 (1988).

72. 15 U.S.C. § 2052 (1998).

INTERNATIONAL CONSIDERATION

Under Section 2067 of the Consumer Product Safety Act, goods produced in the United States that are manufactured for export only are exempt from compliance with U.S. product safety standards. Goods declared "banned hazardous substances" by the CPSC are also exempt from regulation as long as they are intended for export. Exporters of such goods must, however, file a notifying statement with the CPSC 30 days before shipping the product so that the CPSC can notify the government of the foreign country of the shipment and the basis for the applicable U.S. safety standard.

ETHICAL CONSIDERATION

Exporting unsafe products to foreign markets raises serious ethical concerns. Should U.S. managers approve the sale of products determined to be hazardous by the CPSC to countries where government regulations are less stringent? Consider the related example of breast implants (regulated by the FDA, not the CPSC). As recently as 1992, three of the four silicone-filled breast-implant manufacturers were continuing to export the devices, which were subject to a sales moratorium in the United States earlier that year.[a]

a. Robert L. Rose, *Breast Implants Still Being Sold Outside U.S.*, WALL ST. J., Mar. 4, 1992, at B1.

physical therapists, physicians, and social workers.[73] State departments of consumer affairs also investigate and resolve consumer complaints and hold public hearings involving consumer matters.

Attorneys are regulated by state bar associations and the courts. In 1998, the Texas Supreme Court appointed a committee to investigate Nolo Press, the largest publisher of self-help legal books, to determine whether it was engaged in the unauthorized practice of law.[74]

73. As noted in Chapter 7, any person required to be licensed who is in fact not licensed cannot enforce a promise to pay for unlicensed work.

74. Richard B. Schmitt, *Texas Probes Self-Help Legal Books Firm*, WALL ST. J., Mar. 26, 1998, at B9.

THE RESPONSIBLE MANAGER

Complying with Consumer Protection Laws

Managers have a responsibility to make sure that current and potential customers are treated fairly and in a manner that will not subject them to injury, economic or physical. In that regard, managers must take steps to ensure that their company is aware of and in compliance with various federal and state consumer protection regulations.

A manager should maintain open lines of communication with his or her employees. Employees should be aware of the steps necessary to comply with consumer protection laws. Because both managers and employees can be held legally accountable for their actions (and criminally liable in some cases), specific procedures should be in place to educate others in the company on important consumer law topics.

Managers whose companies extend credit to customers need to be aware that many discriminatory practices in the extension of credit are illegal. In particular, the Equal Credit Opportunity Act covers the following protected categories: race, color, religion, national origin, sex, marital status, age (except that older applicants may be given favorable treatment), and applicants whose income derives from public assistance. Some states also prohibit discrimination in credit based on sexual orientation.

In a competitive marketplace, managers often need to be aggressive in their advertising of products or services. Nonetheless, managers must refrain from making claims that may be deceptive or false. The FTC aggressively pursues companies that make false advertising claims. FTC remedies can include civil damages and corrective advertising campaigns, which can cost millions of dollars.

Managers in a manufacturing setting must recognize that product recalls may be necessary to correct a defective product. These recalls may be voluntary; or the government may, under consumer protection laws, order a company to remedy a potentially hazardous situation. Companies have an ethical obligation to issue a warning about a product defect it discovers after its product is sold.

Managers should consider establishing an internal product safety committee to conduct regular product safety inspections. Production-line employees and others should be empowered to make suggestions on how to improve product safety and thereby protect consumers. Critical also is some form of whistle-blower protection for an employee who brings possible con-

sumer protection law violations to the attention of a manager. Concealment or inaction on the part of a manager may subject him or her to criminal prosecution and a possible jail sentence.

Managers should not be satisfied merely to meet minimum government standards with regard to consumer protection laws. Mere compliance may not be sufficient to release a manager or his or her company from liability when the manager has superior product information and should have taken additional precautions.

Managers should embrace the opportunity to self-regulate or, at least, work closely with a regulatory agency to establish industry standards that meet the concerns of both the agency and the company. A good example of a self-regulating industry is the infomercial industry. Faced with possible government regulation, the industry established its own watchdog agency. In doing so, it was able to avert government involvement and the possibility of more restrictive regulation.

INSIDE STORY
PRUDENTIAL INSURANCE'S DECEPTIVE SALES PRACTICES

In 1994, Prudential Insurance Company of America (Prudential) admitted to its customers, shareholders, and the public that its sales agents had engaged in deceptive sales practices in violation of federal and state consumer protection laws and federal racketeering laws. Prudential claimed that it was taking steps to remedy the problems. Yet, the ensuing three years brought a series of missteps and attempted cover-ups that could wind up costing the company much more than the estimated $1 billion settlement Prudential was able to negotiate originally with regulators and the courts.

Insurance companies make money by issuing policies in ex-

change for premiums. Insurance agents make commissions and bonuses by selling policies; the more policies they sell, the more money they make. Sometime in the 1980s, Prudential's agents began engaging in deceptive sales practices: churning customers' policies to create new business, misrepresenting policies to customers as private pension plans, and identifying themselves as financial planners instead of insurance agents. *Churning* is a practice whereby agents were writing new policies for customers and paying for the new policies with the cash value of existing policies. This usually hurt the policyholder because the built-up cash value of the old policy was often wiped out.

An article in the *Wall Street Journal (WSJ)* reported that Prudential executives had received information about the abuses long before they were made public.[75] Internal audit records from 1986 examined by *WSJ* reporters indicated that agents were engaging in churning practices. A report from the following year recommended a company-wide audit to determine the scope of the problem. Other irregularities included agents having customer statements mailed to Prudential branch offices or to the agents' homes rather than to the customer. This action was taken to hide the churning. Customers never received statements so they were unaware of the decrease in the cash value of their policies.

Audits conducted in the early 1990s indicated that churning was continuing and that Prudential had not instituted effective procedures to detect these abuses. In 1994, Prudential commissioned a study by Coopers and Lybrand to review its sales practices and internal policies. The Coopers and Lybrand study stated that Prudential had not devoted sufficient attention at senior levels of management to the annual warnings contained in the audit reports. In fact, it was only the scrutiny of state regulators that caused Prudential to conduct an internal investigation of promotional materials to prevent agents from using misleading and unacceptable materials.

Compliance problems continued into 1996. An internal audit report generated in the third quarter of 1996 mentioned ongoing problems such as incorrect addresses for at least 10% of policyholders, opening up the potential for activity on those accounts going undetected by the customer. A separate memo regarding compliance systems suggested that the systems were not effective in being able to detect abuses of the sort they were designed to prevent. Additional reports showed that customer complaints were coming into Prudential at a rate of 2,500 per month.[76] Members of the board of directors for Prudential stated that the problems had been accorded an appropriate amount of attention.

Prudential repeatedly lost or destroyed documents related to the case. After a series of incidents in Massachusetts, a fire in a Pennsylvania warehouse that contained thousands of pages of company files destroyed records pertaining to the case. The court cited the company without imposing any penalties, despite requests for severe sanctions from the plaintiffs' lawyers. Many of those documents had yet to be examined, and experts following the case expect the plaintiffs to use that fact to have the original settlement overturned.

In 1997, Prudential took a write-off related to the lawsuits of $1.6 billion, increasing to $2.1 billion the amount the company had set aside to deal with this problem.

---

75. Leslie Scism, *Prudential Sales Problems Lasted into '96*, WALL ST. J., Dec. 22, 1997, at B12.

76. *Id.*

KEY WORDS AND PHRASES

additive   737
bait and switch advertising   716
caveat emptor   699
cease and desist orders   718
churning   744
composition plan   713
consent order   716
discharged   713
drug   734
exempt property   713
express warranty   715

extension plan   713
extortionate extension of credit   700
food   734
garnishment   706
identity theft   730
implied warranties   724
infomercial   719
investigative consumer reporting   707
lemon laws   725
misbranding   733
puffing   716

pyramid selling   726
referral sale   726
Regulation Z   703
right of recission   706
slamming   723
stranded costs   723
super discharge   713
usury statutes   700
V-chip   740

QUESTIONS AND CASE PROBLEMS

1. On March 19, 1997, Gulender Ozkaya wrote a check for $1041.55 to pay an automobile dealership for repairs to her car. When she realized that her car had not been properly repaired, Ozkaya stopped payment on the check. The canceled check was then purchased by Telecheck Services, Inc., which sent Ozkaya a form dunning letter attempting to collect payment. In the letter, Telecheck said, "Until this is resolved, we may not approve your checks or the opening of a checking account at over 90,000 merchants and banks who use Telecheck nationally." It also warned, "We have assigned your file to our Recovery Department where it will be given to a professional collection agent. Please be aware that we may take reasonable steps to contact you and secure payment of the balance in full." To resolve the issue and update her record quickly, Ozkaya was instructed to send a cashier's check or money order for the amount due in a return envelope that was provided. Telecheck added a $25 service charge, listed as a "fee" at the top of the letter, to the amount of the original check. Finally, it cautioned that "[a]ny delay, or attempt to avoid this debt, may affect your ability to use checks."

At the bottom of the page, the reader was referred to the back "for important legal notice and corporate address." The reverse side of the letter contained a standard debt validation notice, which indicated that if the consumer disputed the debt, she should contact Telecheck in writing within 30 days.

Ozkaya filed suit against Telecheck. What claims under the Fair Debt Collection Practices Act could she make against the company, and what are Telecheck's strongest defenses? [*Ozkaya v. Telecheck Servs., Inc.*, 982 F. Supp 578 (N.D. Ill. 1997)]

2. Americans consume an estimated 80 billion aspirin tablets a year and more than 50 over-the-counter drugs contain aspirin as the principal active ingredient. Yet aspirin labeling intended for the general public does not discuss its use in arthritis or cardiovascular disease because treatment of these conditions—even with a common over-the-counter drug—has to be medically supervised. The consumer labeling contains only a general warning about excessive or inappropriate use of aspirin and specifically warns against using aspirin to treat children and teenagers who have chicken pox or the flu because of the risk of Reye's syndrome, a rare but sometimes fatal condition. The FDA in 1993 proposed a new label for aspirin products which would read, "IMPORTANT: See your doctor before taking this product for your heart or for other new uses of aspirin because serious side effects could occur with self treatment." As new uses for old drugs are discovered, how should the FDA respond to protect consumers from possible injury?

3. In 1989, John M. Stevenson began receiving phone calls from bill collectors regarding overdue accounts that were not his. After Stevenson obtained a copy of his credit report from TRW Inc., a credit-reporting agency, he discovered many errors in the report. The report included information on accounts that belonged to another John Stevenson; it also included accounts belonging to his estranged son, John Stevenson, Jr., who had fraudulently obtained some of the disputed accounts by using the senior Stevenson's Social Security number. In all, Stevenson disputed sixteen accounts, seven inquiries, and much of the identifying information.

TRW investigated the complaint; and on February 9, 1990, it told Stevenson that all disputed accounts containing negative credit information had been removed. Inaccurate information, however, either continued to appear on Stevenson's reports or was reentered after TRW had deleted it. Stevenson then filed suit, alleging both common law libel and violations of the Fair Credit Reporting Act. Did TRW violate the Fair Credit Reporting Act in its handling of Stevenson's dispute? [*Stevenson v. TRW, Inc.*, 987 F.2d 288 (5th Cir. 1993)]

4. Rehavem and Eleanor Adiel entered into a contract with Lakeridge Associated, Ltd. to purchase a townhouse to be built by Lakeridge. Thereafter, Lakeridge executed and delivered a mortgage application to Chase Federal Savings & Loan Association. The loan was approved and Lakeridge executed a promissory note payable to Chase. The funds were used by Lakeridge to construct the townhouse. Under the terms of the Adiels' purchase agreement, the Adiels were required to submit a mortgage loan application to Chase for the same amount as the Lakeridge loan. The Adiels' application to Chase was for a residential consumer loan. Once approved, the Adiels were to assume the Lakeridge loan.

Chase did not provide a truth-in-lending statement in connection with the original loan to Lakeridge or when the Adiels assumed the Lakeridge mortgage. Was the original loan a commercial loan or a consumer loan? Does the Truth-in-Lending Act apply to both? Can an argument successfully be made that if Chase was aware of the prearrangement it should have provided truth-in-lending documents with the original loan? [*Adiel v. Chase Fed. Sav. & Loan Ass'n*, 810 F.2d 1051 (11th Cir. 1987)]

5. You lose your purse or wallet, which contains all of your credit cards, checkbook, automatic teller machine (ATM) card, Visa debit card, and numerous personal items. You later learn that someone found it and charged several thousand dollars on your credit cards before you had the opportunity to notify your credit card companies. He or she also forged a $500 check. This person used the Visa debit card to purchase a $10,000 home theater system, resulting in a $10,000 deduction from your checking account. In addition, he or she found your personal identification number (PIN) and was able to withdraw $400 from your checking account at an ATM. What are your liabilities to the credit card companies and your bank under the Truth-in-Lending Act and the Electronic Fund Transfer Act? Can you force your bank to return the $10,400 deducted from your checking account? Assume the finder uses your Social Security number to obtain new credit accounts in your name and then never pays the bills. What are your remedies under the Fair Credit Reporting Act?

6. In 1974, a flood caused by storm-driven waves from the Bering Sea swept through the city of Nome, Alaska. The floodwaters caused extensive damage to the commercial district of Nome, including the Bering Sea Saloon. The floodwaters burst through the back door of the saloon, resulting in merchandise being thrown to the ground and being exposed to various amounts of seawater and possibly to raw sewage. As a result, the FDA ordered the destruction of 1,638 cases of alcoholic beverages. On what basis can the FDA seize contaminated food or beverages? What criteria does it employ? Might it be possible for the Bering Sea Saloon to recondition the seized articles? [*United States v. 1,638 Cases of Adulterated Alcoholic Beverages and Other Articles of Food*, 624 F.2d 900 (9th Cir. 1980)]

7. From 1934 to 1939, Charles of the Ritz Distributors sold more than $1 million worth of its "Rejuvenescence Cream." Advertisements for the cosmetic product typically referred to "a vital organic ingredient" and certain "essences and compounds" that the cream allegedly contained. Users were promised that the cream would restore their youthful appearance, regardless of the condition of their skin. How might the FTC analyze the representations made by Charles of the Ritz? What evidence might the FTC consider to determine whether the advertisements are deceptive? Is it important that consumers actually believe that the product will make them look younger? How might the product's name affect the FTC's analysis? [*Charles of the Ritz Distribs. Corp. v. FTC*, 143 F.2d 676 (2d Cir. 1944)]

8. You have just graduated from college, but the economy has taken a turn for the worse and you are unable to find a job. While looking for work, you decide to move back in with your parents. Although your parents are willing to feed and shelter you temporarily, they tell you that your student loans are your own responsibility. After several months of missed loan payments, a friend of yours who went to law school suggests that you file for bankruptcy under Chapter 13 and attempt to get your loans discharged under the "hardship" exception, because you are unemployed and have no income. What is the likely result in the bankruptcy court? Is the result different under Chapter 7? Is it ethical to file for bankruptcy if you expect to get a good job once the economy improves? [*In re Claxton*, 140 B.R. 565 (N.D. Okla. 1992); *In re Coveney*, 192 B.R. 140 (W.D. Tex. 1996)]

9. In a 1991 attempt to persuade soft drink bottlers to switch from 7UP to Sprite, Coca-Cola Company, the distributor of Sprite, developed a promotional campaign entitled "The Future Belongs to Sprite." In its presentation, Coca-Cola used charts and graphs to compare the two drinks' relative sales and market share during the previous decade. The campaign was especially targeted at 74 "cross-franchise" bottlers, who distribute 7UP along with Coca-Cola products other than Sprite. After Coca-Cola made the presentation to eleven of these cross-franchise bottlers, five decided to switch from 7UP to Sprite. In response, Seven-Up Company filed suit against Coca-Cola, alleging that the presentation violated the Lanham Act's prohibition on misrepresentations "in commercial advertising or promotion." Coca-Cola argued that its presentation was not sufficiently disseminated to the public to constitute advertising under the statute. Was Coca-Cola's presentation "advertising" and therefore subject to the Lanham Act? [*Seven-Up Co. v. Coca-Cola Co.*, 86 F.3d 1379 (5th Cir. 1996)]

MANAGER'S DILEMMA

10. Your company manufactures recreational all-terrain vehicles (ATVs). The Consumer Product Safety Commission (CPSC) has expressed concern that ATVs may be unnecessarily dangerous. As a result, the CPSC is contemplating regulations regarding the sale and use of ATVs. How might your company respond to the CPSC? In what way might your company work with other ATV manufacturers to avert governmental involvement? What powers does the CPSC have over your business? [*Consumer Fed'n of Am. v. CPSC*, 990 F.2d 1298 (D.C. Cir 1993)]

INTERNET SOURCES

Federal Trade Commission	http://www.ftc.gov
Food and Drug Administration	http://www.fda.gov
Federal Communications Commission	http://www.fcc.gov
U.S. Postal Service	http://www.usps.gov
Securities and Exchange Commission	http://www.sec.gov
National Highway Traffic Safety Administration	http://www.nhtsa.dot.gov
Consumer Product Safety Commission	http://www.cpsc.gov
This site, maintained by the FTC's Bureau of Consumer Protection, provides consumer news on product recalls, tips for avoiding scams, smart shopping suggestions, and contacts for lodging consumer complaints as well as links to other Web sites containing consumer information.	http://www.consumer.gov
The *Georgia Institute of Technology Survey on Internet Privacy* is available at this site.	http://www.epic.org/privacy/survey
Position of the American Dietetic Association on Food Irradiation is available at this site.	http://www.eatright.org/airradi.htm
Full text of Bankruptcy Reform Act of 1998 (H.R. 3150) can be viewed at this site.	http://thomas.loc.gov
The Privacy Information page on the FTC's Web site contains information on how to protect personal information from public access, including sample "opt-out" letters for consumers to send to credit bureaus and the Direct Marketing Association requesting that their personal information not be sold, shared with third parties, or used for marketing purposes.	http://www.ftc.gov/privacy

UNIT

V

Ownership and Control

CHAPTER 20

Forms of Business Organizations

INTRODUCTION

Choosing the Proper Form

One of the first questions facing any entrepreneur wishing to start a business is which form of business organization will best suit the enterprise. In weighing the advantages and disadvantages associated with the various forms, four considerations take on primary importance. First, to what extent will the personal assets of the founders and investors be exposed to the liabilities of the business? Second, how can taxes be minimized? Third, which format will make the business most attractive to potential investors, lenders, and employees? Finally, what costs are associated with creating and maintaining the organization?

Entrepreneurs selecting a form of entity enjoy a broad range of options. And while this decision comes in the earliest stages in the life of a business, it is nonetheless a crucial one. Changing the form of organization can be very costly—not just in terms of administrative and legal fees, but a change may also give rise to tax

liability or cause a business opportunity to be lost. Thus, at the outset of their venture, entrepreneurs should consider carefully its expected evolution and choose the form of organization accordingly. In addition, once the form of entity is chosen, its managers must be diligent in complying with all statutory requirements.

Chapter Overview

This chapter begins with a description of the most frequently used forms of business organizations: sole proprietorships, partnerships (both general and limited), corporations (including S corporations), limited liability companies, and limited liability partnerships. It examines their advantages and disadvantages. Next, the chapter summarizes the basic tax treatment of these different entities. The remainder of the chapter offers a more detailed discussion of how partnerships and corporations are structured and operated.

 Sole Proprietorship

The sole proprietorship is the simplest and most prevalent form of business enterprise in the United States. In a *sole proprietorship,* one person owns all of the assets of the business and is solely liable for all of its debts. In other words, the sole proprietor is the business; therefore, any

individual who does business without creating a separate organization is operating as a sole proprietorship.

There are no formal requirements for forming a sole proprietorship. However, if the business operates under a *fictitious business name*—that is, a name other than the name of the owner—that name must be registered with the state. A sole proprietorship ends upon either the discontinuation of the business or the death of the proprietor.

Advantages of a sole proprietorship include the flexibility afforded by having one person in complete control of the business. Also, because a sole proprietorship can be created without formal agreements or state filings, it is the easiest and least costly form of business organization to set up. Sole proprietorships pay only one level of income tax—the proprietor reports income from the business on his or her personal tax returns. Finally, an important advantage of a sole proprietorship is that the proprietor receives all of the profits generated by the business.

If the business loses money, however, the proprietor alone bears liability for the losses. This element of risk is the major disadvantage of the sole proprietorship. In addition, it is more difficult for sole proprietorships to raise capital. A sole proprietor can tap only personal funds and the funds of those willing to lend money.

 ## General Partnership

A *general partnership* is created when two or more persons agree to place their money, efforts, labor, or skills in a business and to share the profits and losses.[1] Their agreement can be express or implied, and they must share in real profits, not just receive wages or compensation. In some respects, a partnership is like a marriage or a family. Its members share not only the benefits of the relationship but the burdens as well. Absent an express agreement to the contrary, each partner has some control over the business, and each may have the authority to bind the other partner with respect to third parties. The partners are co-owners of the partnership's property; they hold it as tenants in partnership. Thus, a partnership is, in effect, a mutual agency relationship. (See Chapter 5 for a discussion of agency principles.)

One of the key advantages of a partnership is that it allows for a wide variety of operational and profit-sharing arrangements. In essence, partners may agree to any terms in forming a partnership as long as they are not illegal or contrary to public policy. An example of this flexibility is the fact that partners may make contributions to the business in the form of either capital or services. Suppose Pro and Ron decide to form a partnership, called Rad Waves, to manufacture windsurfing equipment. Ron contributes the start-up and operating capital, and Pro contributes only his management services. Even though Pro has not contributed capital to the partnership, he is (unless agreed otherwise) an equal partner with Ron in Rad Waves.

Like a sole proprietorship, a partnership has the advantage of being subject to only one level of tax. Though they must file an informational return with the Internal Revenue Service (IRS), partnerships do not pay income taxes as a separate entity. Instead, the profit earned by the partnership (whether or not distributed) "passes through" to the individual partners, who report it as income on their individual returns. Thus, a partnership is a *pass-through entity*.

General partnerships face a disadvantage similar to sole proprietorships in that individual partners are subject to personal liability for the obligations of the partnership. Thus, if the partnership is unable to pay its debts, creditors of the partnership have claims against the assets of individual partners.

Joint Venture

A *joint venture* is a one-time partnership of two or more persons for a specific purpose, such as the construction of a hydroelectric dam or a cogeneration plant. Like a general partnership, a joint venture requires that the parties (1) share a community of interest; (2) have the mutual right to direct and govern; (3) share the partnership's profits and losses; and (4) combine their property, money, efforts, skill, or knowledge in the undertaking. Unlike a general partnership, a joint venture is not a continuing relationship; it terminates when the project is completed.

In a joint venture, there is no mutual agency relationship, unless the partners specifically provide for it. Thus, the authority of one member to bind the others is more limited than in a general partnership. To avoid inadvertently conferring apparent authority to bind the other members, a joint venture should make it clear in its dealings with third parties that it is a joint venture and not a partnership. This distinction should be reflected in the entity's name and in the recitation of its legal status in its contracts.

---

1. The Uniform Partnership Act, which has been adopted by 49 states, defines a partnership as "an association of two or more persons to carry on as co-owners of a business for profit."

Revised Uniform Partnership Act

The preceding discussion of general partnerships is based on the Uniform Partnership Act (UPA). The UPA has been adopted in some form in every state except Louisiana. The Revised Uniform Partnership Act (RUPA) has been adopted by several states (including California), and others are considering its adoption. Exhibit 20.1 outlines several significant changes the RUPA makes to the UPA.

 ## Limited Partnership

The basic form of partnership described above is called a general partnership. A *limited partnership* is a special type of partnership consisting of general partners and limited partners. General partners of a limited partnership remain jointly and severally liable for partnership obligations (just like partners in a general partnership), and they are responsible for the management of the partnership. *Limited partners*, however, assume no liability for partnership debts beyond the amount of capital they have contributed, and they have no right to participate in the management of the partnership.

Limited partnerships are often used to raise capital—the limited liability for limited partners makes them attractive to investors. In the Rad Waves example, the general partners might desire to raise capital to finance a sportswear line to promote their other products. To

do so, they could restructure their partnership as a limited partnership with Ron and Pro remaining as general partners. They could then offer an investor a limited partnership interest in the business, renamed Rad Waves, L.P. If Olivia contributed $1,000 to the partnership, she would then be a limited partner in Rad Waves (assuming the relevant state statute was complied with), and her personal liability for Rad Waves' obligations would be limited to her $1,000 original investment.

This ability to attract investors with the assurance of limited liability is the main advantage of a limited partnership. A limited partnership is more difficult to create. Unlike a general partnership, a limited partnership does not come into existence until a certificate of limited partnership has been filed with the appropriate state agency. Moreover, courts are generally strict about enforcing the formal requirements of limited partnership status. If a partnership runs afoul of those requirements, courts will treat it as a general partnership instead.

 ## Corporations

A *corporation* is an organization authorized by state law to act as a legal entity distinct from its owners. As a separate legal entity, the corporation has its own name and operates with limited powers to achieve specific purposes. Corporations are owned by shareholders, who

---

EXHIBIT 20.1   Significant Changes in the Revised Uniform Partnership Act

- Generally, the Revised Uniform Partnership Act (RUPA) shifts emphasis from protecting partners against the unauthorized acts of their fellow partners toward protecting the rights of third parties that deal with the partnership in good faith.
- A partnership is treated as an entity distinct from its partners.
- A partner is not a co-owner of partnership property; the concept of "tenancy in partnership" is eliminated.
- Property that is not acquired in the name of the partnership is nonetheless partnership property if the instrument transferring title refers to either (1) the person taking title as a partner, or (2) the existence of the partnership.
- RUPA codifies specific fiduciary duties owed by a partner to the partnership and the other partners.
- A partnership is not automatically dissolved upon a partner's bankruptcy, death, or withdrawal; instead, the partners holding a majority of the partnership interests may elect to continue the general partnership within 90 days after the occurrence of such events.

SOURCE This information is drawn from Jack S. Johal et al., *Practicing Under California's Revised Uniform Partnership Act*, Bus. L. News, Winter 1997, at 3.

have purchased an ownership stake in the business. The board of directors, which is elected by the shareholders, has central decision-making authority. The board of directors typically employs officers to manage the day-to-day operations of the business.

One of the most attractive features of the corporation is that the liability of its shareholders is limited to their investments. Only the corporation itself is responsible for its liabilities. (An important exception to this general rule, the piercing the corporate veil theory, is discussed later in this chapter.) This cap on liability permits entrepreneurs and investors to undertake risky ventures without the worry of losing personal assets if things go badly.

Another benefit of the corporation is that it has the ability to raise significant capital by selling ownership shares of corporate stock (also known as equity) to investors. Finally, corporations have the advantage of perpetual life. Thus, if a key investor dies, or decides to sell his or her interest in the business, the corporation as an entity continues to exist and to conduct business.

The main disadvantage of the corporate form of organization is that it is subject to two levels of taxation: both corporate and shareholder. The corporation pays tax on the income generated by the business, and shareholders pay tax on that same income when it is distributed as dividends.

S Corporations

Some small corporations can avoid this double taxation by electing to be treated as an S corporation under Subchapter S of the Internal Revenue Code. *S corporations* are taxed as a pass-through entity. In other words, the corporation itself is not taxed on its income; rather, shareholders pay tax on their pro rata share of the corporation's income. An election to be taxed under Subchapter S does not affect the status of the organization as a corporation for state corporate law purposes. Any corporation that has not elected to be an S corporation is called a *C corporation* because it is governed by the tax rules in Subchapter C of the Internal Revenue Code.

To qualify for S corporation status, a corporation must satisfy the following requirements:

1. The corporation must have no more than 75 shareholders, all of whom must be individuals who are citizens of the United States or U.S. resident aliens, or certain types of tax-exempt organizations, trusts, or estates.

2. The corporation must have only one class of stock.
3. The corporation generally may not own 80% or more of any other corporation.
4. The corporation must file a timely election to be treated as an S corporation.

Close Corporations

Some states have enacted laws that give close corporations extra operating flexibility. A *close corporation* is one whose shares are held by a small number of persons, often members of a family. The statutory limit on the number of shareholders a close corporation may have is typically 30. A corporation must elect to become a close corporation by stating in its certificate of incorporation that it is a close corporation; otherwise, the corporation will, regardless of the number of shareholders, not be treated as a close corporation. State close corporation laws can permit significant departure from formalities imposed by traditional corporation laws, such as the requirements that the corporation conduct annual shareholder and board meetings, adopt bylaws, and maintain formal records of board and shareholder decisions.

Limited Liability Companies

The limited liability company is a relatively new form of business organization, rapidly gaining popularity in the United States. A *limited liability company (LLC)* combines the tax advantages of a pass-through entity with the limited liability advantages of a corporation. Like corporations and limited partnerships, the LLC is a creature of state law. To form an LLC, a charter document must be filed with the appropriate state agency (usually the office of the secretary of state). This LLC charter document is typically called the *articles of organization* (as in California) or the *certificate of formation* (as in Delaware). Also, the name of the business must include the initials L.L.C. or the words Limited Liability Company.

The rights, obligations, and powers of the owners of the company (the *members*), the managers, and the officers are set forth in an *operating agreement*. The members elect the *managers* who, like a board of directors, are responsible for managing the business, property, and affairs of the company. The managers appoint the officers of the company.

In 1997, the IRS issued regulations that clarified the status of LLCs as entities that are not taxed at the firm level (unless they elect to be taxed as corporations). In effect, these new "check the box" regulations permit the founders to decide whether an entity—other than a corporation under state law or a publicly held entity—is to be taxed as a corporation or a pass-through entity. State-law corporations and publicly traded entities are taxed as corporations.

The LLC form of business organization offers the advantages of both the limited partnership and the S corporation, without their respective drawbacks. Properly formed LLCs will be taxed as partnerships, but unlike the general partners in limited partnerships, even the controlling persons in LLCs can limit their liability to the amount invested. Moreover, all owners of an LLC can participate fully in the management of the business. An LLC (like a partnership) also can have flexible allocations of profits and losses. The main advantage of the LLC form over the S corporation is the lack of restrictions on shareholders. Specifically, there is no limit on the number of members an LLC can have; and, in contrast with an S corporation, its investors can be corporations, partnerships, and foreigners.

One disadvantage of the LLC form of business organization is the cost of preparing a customized operating agreement. However, as LLCs become more common, standardized forms have started to emerge.[2] They provide a good starting point for drafting but must be tailored to the individual company and the needs of its members.

Limited Liability Partnerships

The *limited liability partnership* (*LLP*) is an even more recently developed form of business organization. The first LLP statute was enacted in Texas in 1991, and by 1997 nearly all states had enacted some form of LLP statute. The LLP has features similar to the LLC and is designed primarily for professionals who typically do business as a partnership. The main function of an LLP is to insulate its partners from *vicarious liability* for certain partnership obligations, such as liability arising from the malpractice of another partner. Partners in an

LLP usually have unlimited liability for their own malpractice.

LLPs are created by filing appropriate forms with a central state agency. A major advantage of the LLP form for existing partnerships such as law firms or accounting firms is that attaining LLP status requires no significant modification of the business's partnership agreement. Difficulties relating to negotiating and drafting the agreements required to convert an existing partnership to a limited liability entity such as a corporation or LLC were often cited as major obstacles to such a conversion.[3] In addition, like other forms of partnerships, LLPs retain pass-through taxation treatment.

LLP statutes are not uniform. Most statutes provide that liability will be limited at least for debts and obligations arising from the malpractice, or negligent or wrongful conduct, of other partners. However, a few states, such as Minnesota and New York, protect partners from commercial liabilities (such as trade debt) as well.[4] This type of expanded protection further narrows the distinction between an LLP and an LLC. In fact, the trend in LLP statutes enacted after 1995 has been to provide the broader type of liability protection exemplified by Minnesota and New York.[5]

Income Tax Considerations

The analysis that follows is concerned solely with federal income tax consequences under the Internal Revenue Code of 1986, as amended and in force as of January 1, 1998. Many state income tax provisions follow the federal rules. Because provisions in the tax laws change often, it is more important to understand the general issues than to strive for a detailed knowledge of the tax laws for any given year.

Comparing Separate Taxable Entities with Pass-Through Entities

The tax treatment of a C corporation is different from that of pass-through entities (such as partnerships, S corporations, and LLCs) in several respects. Each may

2. *See, e.g.,* Allan B. Duboff (ed.), Guide to Organizing and Operating a Limited Liability Company in California (1995), published by the Partnerships and Unincorporated Business Organizations Committee of the Business Law Section of the State Bar of California. This guide includes annotated sample short-form and long-form operating agreements and other useful exemplars.

3. *See* Elizabeth G. Hester, *Keeping Liability at Bay*, Bus. L. Today, Jan.–Feb. 1996, at 59.

4. *See id.* at 60.

5. *Id.*

have favorable or unfavorable tax consequences, depending upon the circumstances.

Property Transfers   Because a C corporation is a separate taxable entity, a transfer of cash or any other kind of property between the corporation and its owners is a taxable transaction unless it comes within one of the statutory exceptions in Subchapter C.

It is easier to transfer property to and from a partnership on a tax-free basis than it is with either a C corporation or an S corporation. For example, a transfer of property to either type of corporation in exchange for stock is tax-free only if the persons transferring the property own 80% or more of the stock of the corporation immediately after the transaction. In contrast, an exchange of property for a share in a partnership is tax-free, without regard to the percentage share in the partnership.

Similarly, property that has appreciated in value may be more easily distributed on a tax-free basis from a partnership than from a corporation. The partnership is not subject to tax on the appreciated property. The partner receiving the property is not taxed until he or she subsequently sells the property. In contrast, a corporation will be taxed on the appreciation in value just as if it had sold the property for cash, and the shareholders will be taxed on the fair market value of the property they have received. Thus, in the case of a C corporation there will be both a corporate-level tax and a shareholder-level tax on the distribution. For an S corporation, the taxable income is passed through and will be taxed only at the shareholder level.

Cash Distribution   The income of a C corporation is taxed at the corporate level, and it is taxed again at the individual level when it is distributed. This double taxation does not occur with the other forms of business organizations. This difference alone may make a pass-through entity preferable to a C corporation as the chosen form of business organization.

Double taxation can be reduced in two ways. First, the tax liability of the corporation can be reduced to the extent that corporate income can be offset by tax-deductible payments to shareholders. For example, if personal services are a major source of the corporation's income, payment of compensation to shareholders active in the business will reduce the corporation's taxable income. If capital investment is a major source of income, payment of interest or rent to shareholders may provide similar relief. Second, the tax liability of the shareholders can be reduced to the extent that the business income is

retained by the corporation and not distributed to shareholders. However, the accumulated earnings of a corporation may be taxed if they are not being retained for a legitimate business purpose of the corporation.

Cash distributions from partnerships and S corporations are tax-free to the recipients, up to the amount of their previous capital contributions less any income previously passed through to them. Distributions from C corporations, on the other hand, generally result in taxable dividend income to the shareholders.

Operating Losses   If the business operations of a C corporation produce a loss, as is frequently the case with start-up companies and real estate investments in their early years, the operating loss will be recognized at the corporate level. This means that the shareholders receive no tax benefits from the operating loss, and the corporation receives no benefit until it has operating income against which its prior losses can be deducted.

On the other hand, if the same business is operated by a partnership or S corporation, the operating loss each year will be passed through to the individual partners or shareholders. They may, if certain tax law requirements are satisfied, deduct the operating loss from their other income. However, passive-loss limitations allow only owners who materially participate in the business to deduct its losses from other ordinary income (such as wages or interest). Passive investors may not deduct such losses from ordinary income, but can use passive losses to offset passive gains (such as capital gains on the sale of stock).

Capitalization   A C corporation has no tax-law restrictions as to its capitalization. As business needs require, the corporation may issue common stock, preferred stock, bonds, notes, warrants, options, and other instruments. These instruments may confer the right to varying degrees of control and varying shares of earnings and may be convertible, redeemable, or callable. However, the tax treatment of each type of capital instrument is not always the same as its classification by the corporation. For example, shareholder debt may be treated as stock if the corporation has too little *equity capital*, that is, capital received in exchange for shares in the ownership of the corporation. As a consequence, tax-deductible "interest" payments may be recast as nondeductible "dividends."

Allocation of Losses   Items of partnership income or loss generally can be allocated to specific partners at specific times as long as these allocations have a substantial economic effect apart from tax considerations. Thus, a partnership can allocate a disproportionate amount of losses or depreciation to a particular partner in the early years and allocate a disproportionate amount of later income to the same partner until the loss is recovered. This form of allocation may generate a valuable tax deferral for that partner.

No comparable allocation can be made by a C corporation, except to a limited extent by capitalizing the corporation with different classes of stock and debt. An S corporation is even more limited in this respect. It may have only one class of stock, and all income and losses must be allocated strictly in proportion to stock ownership.

 ## Partnership Mechanics

The following section describes in more detail how partnerships are formed, operated, and terminated.

Formation of a General Partnership

A general partnership can be created with nothing more than a handshake and a general understanding between the partners. For example, students agree to work together on a business plan; a baker and a chef agree to open a restaurant together; an engineer and a mechanic agree to design bicycles together—in each case, a partnership is formed. However, the intention of one party alone cannot create a partnership. There must be a meeting of the minds. Hence, in the Rad Waves example, if Ron viewed his agreement with Pro as forming a partnership, while Pro contemplated a mere employee–employer relationship, a partnership would not be formed.

A partnership does not require a minimum of capital in order to be formed. However, partners usually contribute cash or property, or agree to provide personal services to the partnership. In some instances, a partnership interest may be received as a gift. The partnership need not be given a name. There may or may not be a written partnership agreement.

Without a Written Agreement   If there is no written partnership agreement, the state laws will determine whether the relationship is to be treated as a partnership or some other relationship, such as an agency. If the relationship is recognized as a partnership, state partnership laws will govern the partnership if there is no

written agreement. Some provisions of those laws could lead to undesirable business results.

In the Rad Waves example, Pro and Ron could form a partnership with a simple oral agreement. However, under state partnership law, Pro and Ron will be required to share the profits and losses equally. Furthermore, until the partnership is terminated, neither partner may withdraw capital without the consent of the other. If there were a third partner, his or her death would terminate the partnership even if Pro and Ron preferred to continue it. These are just a few examples of the dangers of forming a partnership without a written partnership agreement.

With a Written Agreement   A written partnership agreement can prevent future misunderstandings. It can also provide for a dispute resolution mechanism, such as arbitration. A written partnership agreement can override many of the provisions of partnership statutes that could turn out to be undesirable to the partners.

A partnership agreement usually includes the term of the partnership's existence, the capital characteristics of the partnership, the division of profits and losses between the partners, partnership salaries or withdrawals, the duties of the partners, and the consequences to the partnership if a partner decides to sell his or her interest in the partnership or becomes incapacitated or dies. Also included are the name of the partnership, the names and addresses of the partners, the type of business to be conducted, and the location of the business.

Drafting a partnership agreement focuses the partners' attention on matters that might not be considered if less formal partnership arrangements were made. For example, will all partners have an equal voice in management? What limits will be placed on the managing partners? How will disputes be settled? May a partner be expelled? May new partners be admitted? If so, by what process?

Operation of a General Partnership

The operation of a general partnership may be informal. Decisions may be made by consensus rather than by formal votes. However, lack of formality should not be equated with lack of responsibility for the fortunes, or misfortunes, of the partnership. For example, if Pro and Ron form Rad Waves as a general partnership, they will each be responsible for the full amount of any liabilities incurred by the partnership or by either partner acting

IN BRIEF

CHOICE OF BUSINESS ENTITY: PROS AND CONS

The following chart lists the principal considerations in selecting the form of business entity and applies them to the C corporation, S corporation, general partnership, limited partnership, limited liability company, and limited liability partnership. The considerations are listed in no particular order, in part because their importance will vary with each business formation depending on the nature of the business, sources of financing, and the plan for providing financial returns to the owners (for example, distributions of operating income, a public offering, or a sale of the business). Other factors that are not listed will also influence choice of entity. In addition, the "yes or no" format oversimplifies the applicability of certain attributes.

	C Corporation	S Corporation	General Partnership	Limited Partnership	Limited Liability Company	Limited Liability Partnership
Limited Liability	Yes	Yes	No	Yes[A]	Yes	Yes[B]
Flow-through Taxation	No	Yes	Yes	Yes	Yes	Yes
Simplicity/Low Cost	Yes	Yes	No	No	No	No
Limitations on Eligibility	No	Yes	No	No	No	No
Limitations on Capital Structure	No	Yes	No	No	No	No
Ability to Take Public	Yes	Yes[C]	No[D]	No[D]	No[D]	No[D]
Flexible Charter Documents	No	No	Yes	Yes	Yes	Yes
Ability to Change Structure without Tax	No	No	Yes	Yes	Yes	Yes
Favorable Employee Incentives (including incentive stock options)	Yes	Yes/No[E]	No[F]	No [F]	No[F]	No[F]
Qualified Small Business Stock Exclusion for Gains	Yes[G]	No	No	No	No	No
Special Allocations	No	No	Yes	Yes	Yes	Yes
Tax-Free In-Kind Distributions	No	No	Yes	Yes	Yes	Yes

(A) Limited liability for limited partners only; a limited partnership must have at least one general partner with unlimited liability.

(B) Partners in LLPs generally are protected from liability for malpractice and other wrongful conduct of fellow partners; states are split on whether LLP partners can be held individually liable for other partnership liabilities, such as commercial debt.

(C) S corporation would convert to C corporation upon a public offering because of the number of shareholders.

(D) Although the public markets are generally not available for partnership offerings, partnerships (including LLPs) and LLCs can be incorporated without tax and then taken public.

(E) Although an S corporation can issue incentive stock options (ISOs), the inability to have two classes of stock limits favorable pricing of the common stock offered to employees.

(F) Although partnership and LLC interests can be provided to employees, they are poorly understood by most employees. Moreover, ISOs are not available.

(G) Special low capital gains rate for stock of U.S. C corporations with not more than $50 million in gross assets at the time stock is issued if the corporation is engaged in an active business and the taxpayer holds the stock for at least five years.

within the scope of his authority as a partner. Hence, Ron's personal assets could be seized if Rad Waves's partnership assets were insufficient to satisfy a judgment against Rad Waves. Ron's personal assets might also be seized if Rad Waves breached a contract entered into by Pro on behalf of the partnership.

A partnership is a form of mutual agency. Each partner has authority to act on behalf of the other in the conduct of the partnership's business. Each partner in a general partnership is liable for the debts incurred by another partner acting in the name of the partnership if that partner had express authority to assume the debt or was carrying on the business of the partnership in the usual way. Partners also owe one another certain fiduciary duties. The following case explores the scope of such duties.

| **A CASE IN POINT** | **SUMMARY** |

CASE 20.1
BOHATCH v. BUTLER
Supreme Court of Texas
41 Tex. Sup. Ct. J. 308
(1998).

FACTS In February 1990, Collette Bohatch was named a partner in the Washington, D.C. office of Butler & Binion, a Houston-based law firm. John McDonald was then the managing partner of the firm's D.C. office, which did work almost exclusively for Pennzoil. Bohatch soon became privy to internal firm reports showing the number of hours each attorney worked, billed, and collected. After reviewing such reports, she became concerned that McDonald was overbilling Pennzoil.

On July 15, 1990, Bohatch met with Louis Paine, Butler & Binion's managing partner, to report her concerns about McDonald's billing practices. Paine told Bohatch he would investigate. The following day, McDonald met with Bohatch and informed her that Pennzoil was not satisfied with her work and wanted her work to be supervised. Bohatch later testified that this was the first time she had ever heard criticism of her work for Pennzoil.

After looking into Bohatch's complaint and discussing the allegations with Pennzoil's in-house counsel, who said that Pennzoil believed the firm's bills were reasonable, Paine informed Bohatch in August that he found no basis for her contentions. Paine also told her she should begin to look for other employment. In June 1991, she was informed that that month's partnership distribution would be her last. She was asked to leave by November.

Bohatch filed suit for breach of fiduciary duty and other claims in October 1991. The firm voted to expel her three days later. At trial, a jury found that the firm had breached its fiduciary duty to Bohatch. The court of appeals reversed, holding that the firm's only duty to Bohatch was not to expel her in bad faith. Bohatch appealed.

ISSUE PRESENTED Can a partnership expel a whistle-blowing partner merely for reporting in good faith the alleged misconduct of another partner?

SUMMARY OF OPINION The Texas Supreme Court first recognized that the relationship between partners "is fiduciary in character, and imposes upon all the participants the obligation of loyalty . . . and the utmost good faith, fairness, and honesty in their dealings with each other." Nevertheless, partners have no obligation to remain partners—"at the heart of the partnership concept is the principle that partners may choose with whom they wish to be associated."

Case 20.1 continues

Case 20.1 continued

Thus, the question the court addressed was whether, in this case, the fiduciary relationship between and among partners gave rise to a duty not to expel a partner who in good faith reported suspicions of overbilling by another partner. The court concluded that there should be no such whistle-blower exception to the basic at-will nature of partnerships. Although the public policy arguments in favor of the exception were "not without force," courts had consistently held that a partnership may expel a partner for "purely business reasons."

An allegation such as Bohatch's can create a fundamental schism in a partnership, severely damaging the personal confidence and trust essential to the partner relationship. Once such charges are made, partners may find it impossible to continue to work together. In these circumstances, expulsion of the accusing partner may be the only way to preserve the partnership. As a result, the court concluded that the fiduciary duty that partners owe one another "does not encompass a duty to remain partners or else answer in tort damages."

RESULT The Texas Supreme Court affirmed the appellate court decision that Butler & Binion did not breach any fiduciary duty it owed to Bohatch.

COMMENTS Members of a professional corporation also have fiduciary duties to fellow members. The Illinois Supreme Court held that two lawyers who resigned from the law firm of Dowd & Dowd, a professional corporation, violated their fiduciary duties if they surreptitiously solicited firm clients before resigning.[6] The New York Court of Appeals characterized the loyalty owed partners as what "distinguishes partnerships (including law partnerships) from bazaars."[7]

---

6. Dowd & Dowd, Ltd. v. Gleason, 693 N.E.2d 358 (Ill. 1998).

7. Graubard Mollen Dannett & Horowitz v. Moskovitz, 653 N.E.2d 1179, 1183 (N.Y. 1995).

Decision Making in a General Partnership

Unlike a corporation, which has a centralized board of directors and a staff of hired executives for decision making, a general partnership is characterized by direct owner management and control of the business. Each partner's assets are vulnerable to the poor business decisions of the fellow partners. It is therefore important that each partner have a voice in the business decisions of the partnership.

A partnership may choose to cede managerial control of the business to one or more of its partners. Unless partners expressly agree otherwise, partnership law requires unanimous agreement of all partners on all but the most ordinary matters. If the partners in an informal partnership cannot agree on a decision, they may disband the partnership, distribute its assets, and terminate it.

Dissolution of a General Partnership

Dissolution of a general partnership occurs when the partners no longer carry on the business together. There are many reasons for dissolving a partnership. The agreed term for the partnership may expire, or the partners may decide to dissolve the partnership prior to the expiration of the agreed term. A particular undertaking specified in the partnership agreement may be completed. One or more partners may desire to dissolve the partnership.

(Absent an agreement to the contrary, withdrawal of a general partner results in the dissolution of the partnership.) A partner may be expelled, and the remaining partners may thereafter agree to terminate the partnership. A partner may die or go bankrupt, and the agreement may not provide for the partnership's continuation.

A partnership will also be dissolved if the business for which the partnership was formed becomes unlawful—for example, if there is a war between the countries of two or more of the partners. In such a case, the partnership will be dissolved regardless of the wishes of the partners. In other situations, a court may issue a decree of dissolution if a partner becomes disabled, insane, or otherwise unable to perform as a partner. Courts also have the power to dissolve a partnership when a partner willfully breaches the agreement or performs in such a manner as to make it impractical to carry on the partnership. Because the purpose of partnerships is to make a profit, a partnership may be dissolved by court decree if it becomes apparent that it is unprofitable and lacks any real prospect of success. If the partnership has reasonable prospects of earning money in the future, however, it may not be dissolved by court decree despite recent losses.

Winding Up the General Partnership

Upon dissolution, all of the partners' authority ceases except their authority to complete transactions begun but not yet finished, and to wind up the partnership. *Winding up* involves settling the accounts and liquidating the assets of the partnership for the purpose of making distributions and terminating the concern. The liabilities and obligations of the partners do not end at dissolution; the partnership continues throughout the winding-up period.

During the winding-up process, the partners' fiduciary duties to one another continue. The winding-up partners may not run the business for their own benefit, but must account as trustees to the withdrawing partners or to the estate of a deceased partner.

Termination of the General Partnership

Termination occurs when all the partnership affairs are wound up and the partners' authority to act for the partnership is completely extinguished. A dissolved partnership may terminate or may be continued by a new partnership formed by the remaining partners (including perhaps the estate or heirs of a deceased partner).

 ## Limited Partnership Requirements

The basic rules that govern formation, operation, and termination of general partnerships apply as well to limited partnerships. Some additional requirements placed on limited partnerships are discussed below.

Limited Participation

A limited partner's liability is limited unless he or she takes part in the control of the business. Thus, if a limited partner had a voice in the business decisions of the partnership, she would be opening herself up to the possibility of liability beyond her original capital investment. Furthermore, a limited partner may contribute money or property to the partnership, but generally not services. Hence, in the Rad Waves example, if Olivia assisted with the design of the sportswear line, in most states her liability could exceed her original $1,000 capital contribution. Therefore, limited partners should not take part in any partnership activity beyond monitoring the progress of their investment and exercising such statutory rights as the right to vote on the removal of a general partner. Moreover, the limited partner's name cannot appear in the name of the partnership without incurring unlimited liability.

Formal Requirements

In addition to the requirement that a certificate of limited partnership be filed with the appropriate state authority, most states' statutes require the partnership agreement to clearly designate the limited partners as such. Any partnership that does not substantially meet this and other statutory requirements will be treated as a general partnership, with mutual liability and apparent authority attaching to each partner. As the following case demonstrates, a person who intended to be only a limited partner may face liability if there has not been substantial compliance in good faith with the formal requirements.

A CASE IN POINT	IN THE LANGUAGE OF THE COURT

CASE 20.2
REIMAN v.
INTERNATIONAL
HOSPITALITY
GROUP, INC.
Court of Appeals for the
District of Columbia
614 A.2d 925 (D.C. 1992).

FACTS Richard Reiman was a real estate broker with a contract to broker the sale of a Washington, D.C.–area motel on behalf of his client, the Connecticut Inn Partnership (CIP). In September 1982, as a result of Reiman's work, CIP and Connecticut Avenue Associates (CAA), a putative limited partnership, executed a letter of intent for the sale and purchase of the motel. CAA had not filed a certificate of limited partnership before executing the letter of intent. Reiman and CIP claimed that on January 17, 1983, CAA anticipatorily breached the letter of intent agreement. As a result, CIP put the motel back on the market and eventually sold it to another buyer.

In September 1983, Reiman brought suit to recover his commission against CAA and certain individual defendants that Reiman alleged were partners of CAA. Henry Lieberman was one of these individual defendants. At trial, the court ruled that the CAA partnership and some individual defendants were liable to Reiman. The court, however, ruled that Lieberman was not liable because he intended to be only a limited partner of CAA.

Reiman appealed the Lieberman ruling. Reiman argued that, because CAA had failed to comply with statutory limited partnership filing requirements, CAA was in fact a general partnership and that Lieberman must be held liable as a general partner.

ISSUE PRESENTED Can an individual who intended to become only a limited partner in a limited partnership be held liable as a general partner if the partnership fails to comply with the statutory filing requirements?

OPINION STEADMAN, J., writing for the District of Columbia Court of Appeals:
. . . Section 11 [of the Uniform Limited Partnership Act (ULPA)], which appears as D.C. Code § 41-211, reads:

> A person who has contributed to the capital of a business conducted by a person or partnership erroneously believing that he has become a limited partner in a limited partnership is not, by reason of this exercise of the rights of a limited partner, a general partner with the person or in the partnership carrying on the business, or bound by the obligations of such person or partnership; provided, that on ascertaining the mistake he promptly renounces his interest in the profits of the business, or other compensation by way of income.

Thus, it is no longer correct to say that any individual associated with a purported limited partnership where the proper formalities have not been complied with is necessarily as a matter of law liable as a general partner. As cases have recognized, compliance with Section 11 "promptly" after the discovery of a mistake will prevent any general partner liability from being imposed upon the putative limited partner. . . . The converse of Section 11, however, . . . is that if such a renunciation is not effectuated and no other section of the UPLA provides protection, the putative limited partner faces liability in an individual capacity for debts of the partnership. . . .

. . .

Lieberman invokes the section of the ULPA . . . providing that a limited partnership is formed if there has been "substantial compliance in good faith" with the formal requirements. He invokes a line of cases which hold that the filing of the

Case 20.2 continues

Case 20.2 continued

certificate within a "reasonable time" constitutes "substantial compliance" and has retroactive effect to activities undertaken by the partnership prior to the filing.

The filing of the certificate is, however, a crucial statutory step. We think analogous law in this jurisdiction impels us to follow a competing line of contrary cases, which hold that protection under the ULPA begins only from the time of the filing of the certificate.

. . .

This history and the wording of Section 11 itself make it plain that one is not absolved from any potential liability simply because one intended only to be a limited partner. . . . Thus, the trial court stopped too soon when it absolved Lieberman from liability simply because no certificate of partnership had been prepared and Lieberman had no intent to enter anything other than a limited partnership.

RESULT   The appeals court vacated the trial court's judgment in favor of Lieberman and remanded the case back to the trial court to determine whether Lieberman "substantially complied in good faith" with the requirements of the District of Columbia version of the ULPA.

COMMENTS   Some states have adopted provisions that more clearly deal with the liability of a purported limited partner. For example, Section 15633 of the California Revised Limited Partnership Act provides that a person who makes a capital contribution to a purported limited partnership, believing in good faith that he or she has become a limited partner, is liable only to third parties that both transacted business with the purported limited partnership before the certificate of limited partnership was filed and reasonably believed that the person was a general partner at the time of the transaction.

Questions

1. Why wasn't Lieberman's intent to be only a limited partner enough to make him a limited partner?
2. Should it matter whether Reiman had any dealings with Lieberman before the CAA certificate of limited partnership was filed?

Although it is prudent and usually necessary to follow the formal requirements for formation of a limited partnership, the would-be limited partners cannot escape liability for the partnership's obligations by claiming that a formality was not followed. Courts typically hold that the technical filing requirements for limited partnership status (like those for corporate status) are designed to protect third parties.

 Incorporation

Incorporation is the process by which a corporation is formed. The corporate statutes of each state set forth the steps that must be taken to establish a corporation in that state. Many states' statutes are based in whole or in part on the Model Business Corporation Act, an annotated uniform statute prepared by academics and practitioners. The state under whose laws a corporation is formed is called the corporation's *corporate domicile*. A corporation is not limited to doing business in its corporate domicile. It can conduct business as a foreign corporation in other states. Typically, in order to do so, it must file a statement of *foreign corporation* with the appropriate secretary of state and state taxing authority.

Where to Incorporate

Corporations can choose to incorporate in any state; it need not be the state in which most of their business is located. Two important factors affect the decision of where to incorporate: (1) the costs of incorporation in a given state; and (2) the relative advantages and disadvantages of that state's corporation laws. If the corporation is privately held and its business will be conducted largely within one state, incorporation in that state is probably the best choice. If the corporation will be large from the outset or will be engaged in substantial interstate business, however, then incorporation in a jurisdiction with the most advantageous corporate statutes and case law should be considered.

Corporation laws may be favorable either to management or to the shareholders. Some states, such as Delaware, are known to be pro-management because their statutes and court decisions tend to give control on a wide range of issues to the officers and directors. Other states, such as California, make it difficult for corporate managers to do certain things without the approval and participation of the shareholders. These states are thought of as pro-shareholder.

A discussion of the Delaware statutes helps highlight some of the key corporate governance choices. The power to elect the board of directors is the primary way in which shareholders exercise control and it is provided for in all jurisdictions. Delaware permits, but does not require, cumulative voting (discussed further below), which allows a minority shareholder greater opportunity to elect someone to the board. Delaware also permits a *staggered* (or *classified*) *board*, whereby directors serve for specified terms, usually three years, with only a fraction of them up for reelection at any one time. A classified board makes it more difficult to replace the entire board at once. In Delaware, classified boards are the norm. Delaware prohibits the removal of directors on a classified board without cause, unless the certificate of incorporation provides otherwise. In addi-

tion, as explained further in Chapter 21, Delaware permits broad limitations on directors' monetary liability.

More than half of the large businesses incorporated in the United States are Delaware corporations. When deciding whether to incorporate in the local state or Delaware, incorporators must weigh the advantages Delaware law provides for managers against the expense of paying Delaware corporate taxes, the expense of hiring lawyers familiar with Delaware law, and the possibility of having to defend a lawsuit in Delaware. Businesses incorporated in their local state often reincorporate in Delaware once they have grown large enough to justify the effort and expense of reincorporation.

It should be noted that the balance between shareholder and management powers in each state does not remain static. California, a traditionally pro-shareholder state, amended its Corporations Code as of January 1, 1990, to permit publicly held companies to have a staggered board and to make cumulative voting optional. (However, *privately held corporations* incorporated in California must still have cumulative voting and cannot have a staggered board.) On the other hand, the traditionally pro-management Delaware courts have held that certain decisions affecting the corporation must be made by shareholders, not directors.

How to Incorporate

To create a corporation, one or more incorporators must prepare a document called the *certificate* or *articles of incorporation* (or the *corporate charter*). This document must be filed with the appropriate state governmental agency, usually the secretary of state for the jurisdiction that will become the corporate domicile.

The articles of incorporation are generally quite short. For example, the Pennsylvania Business Corporation Law specifies that the articles need only set forth the name of the corporation, the location and mailing address of the corporation's registered office in Pennsylvania, a brief statement of the purpose of the corporation, the term for which the corporation is to exist (which may be perpetual), the total number of shares that the corporation is authorized to issue, the name and mailing address of each of the incorporators, and a statement of the number of shares to be purchased by each.

Section 204 of the Pennsylvania Business Corporation Law, like most modern corporation statutes, goes on to provide that the purpose clause "may consist of or include a statement that the corporation shall have unlimited power to engage in and to do any lawful act concerning any or all lawful business for which corporations may be incorporated under this act." Pennsylvania's corporate law goes on to specify corporate powers, so there is no need to have a long purpose clause in the articles of incorporation. Indeed, to do so invites trouble, because one might inadvertently exclude an activity in which the corporation may later want to engage.

After the articles of incorporation are filed, the incorporators adopt the *bylaws*, that is, the rules governing the corporation (including the number of authorized directors), and elect the initial board of directors. This can be done either at an organizational meeting or by unanimous written consent. The incorporators are exclusively empowered to place the directors in office. After electing the board of directors, the incorporator signs a written resignation. The directors then have an organizational meeting at which they (1) ratify the adoption of the bylaws by the incorporators or adopt new bylaws, (2) appoint officers, (3) designate a bank as depository for corporate funds, (4) authorize the sale of stock to the initial shareholders, and (5) determine the consideration to be received in exchange for such shares—cash, other property, or past (but not future) services rendered to the corporation.

Exhibit 20.2 outlines the steps required to form a corporation.

Defective Incorporation

Because a corporation does not have a common law existence, but only a statutory one, any defect in the incorporation process can have the effect of denying corporate status. A business organization that was intended to function as a corporation but has failed to comply with the statutory requirements is in fact a partnership or, if there is only one shareholder, a sole proprietorship. The owners will not enjoy the protection of limited liability and can be held personally responsible for all debts of the enterprise. However, the courts have developed several doctrines to avoid this result if it would be unfair.

De Jure Corporation   When incorporation has been done correctly, a *de jure corporation* is formed. This means that the entity is a corporation by right and cannot be challenged. Most jurisdictions will find de jure corporate status so long as the incorporators have sub-

---

EXHIBIT 20.2   Steps Required to Form a Corporation

- Select a corporate name and agent for service of process.
- File certificate of incorporation (also known as articles of incorporation or charter in some jurisdictions) signed by incorporator(s).
- Sign action by incorporator(s) that:
  - adopts bylaws,
  - specifies initial directors.
- Obtain written resignation of incorporator(s).
- Hold first directors' meeting or take action by unanimous written consent of the directors. Among other items of business,
  - ratify the adoption of the bylaws by the incorporator(s) or adopt new bylaws,
  - elect officers,
  - issue stock,
  - authorize corporate bank account.

---

stantially complied with the incorporation requirements. For example, substantial compliance will be found even if the incorporators failed to obtain a required signature or submitted an improper notarization.

De Facto Corporation   If the incorporators cannot show substantial compliance, a court may treat the entity as a *de facto corporation,* that is, as a corporation in fact even though it is not technically a corporation by law. For the court to find a de facto corporation, the incorporators must demonstrate that they were unaware of the defect and that they made a good faith effort to incorporate correctly. For example, if a clerk for the secretary of state delayed filing the articles, the business would not be a corporation de jure, but would probably be a corporation de facto.

Corporation by Estoppel   An entity that is neither a de jure nor a de facto corporation may be a *corporation by estoppel.* If a third party, in all of its transactions with the enterprise, acts as if it were doing business with a corporation, the third party is prevented or *estopped* from claiming that the enterprise is not a corporation. It is considered unfair to permit the third party to reach shareholders' personal assets when all along it had believed it was dealing with a corporation whose shareholders had limited liability. The court found such a corporation by estoppel in the following case.

A CASE IN POINT	SUMMARY

CASE 20.3
CRANSON v.
INTERNATIONAL
BUSINESS MACHINE
CORP.
Supreme Court of Maryland
200 A.2d 33 (Md. 1964).

FACTS   In April 1961, Albion C. Cranson was asked to invest in the Real Estate Service Bureau (the Bureau), a new business about to be incorporated. He met with other interested individuals and an attorney and agreed to purchase stock and become an officer and director of the enterprise. Upon being advised by the attorney that the Bureau had been formed under the laws of Maryland, he paid for and received a stock certificate evidencing ownership of shares in the corporation. He was elected president of the corporation and was shown the corporate seal and minute book.

The new venture was conducted as a corporation. It had corporate bank accounts; auditors maintained corporate books and records; it leased the office where it did business. All of the transactions that Cranson conducted for the corporation, including the dealings with International Business Machines (IBM), were made as an officer of the corporation. At no time did he assume any personal obligation or pledge his individual credit to IBM.

Due to an oversight on the part of the attorney, of which Cranson was not aware, the certificate of incorporation, although signed and acknowledged prior to May 1, 1961, was not filed until November 24, 1961. Between May 17 and November 8, the Bureau purchased eight typewriters from IBM. Partial payments were made, leaving a balance due of $4,333.40. IBM sued Cranson for the balance due, on the theory that he was a partner in the business conducted by the Bureau and as such was personally liable for its debts.

ISSUE PRESENTED   Is a person who is an officer, director, and shareholder of a corporation personally liable for debts incurred before the articles of incorporation were filed, if he believed in good faith that the articles had been filed and the creditor relied on the existence of the corporation when it extended credit?

SUMMARY OF OPINION   IBM contended that the failure of the Bureau to file its certificate of incorporation barred any claim to corporate existence. However, the Maryland Supreme Court found that IBM, having dealt with the Bureau as if it were a corporation and having relied on its credit rather than that of Cranson, was estopped from asserting that the Bureau was not incorporated at the time the typewriters were purchased.

RESULT   IBM was estopped from denying the corporate existence of the Bureau. Cranson was not liable for the balance due on the typewriters.

 Piercing the Corporate Veil

The corporation is built around the central premise of limited liability. Under certain circumstances, courts will deny this central premise and hold the shareholders liable for claims against the corporation. A court will *pierce the corporate veil* in this way if necessary to prevent the evasion of statutes, the perpetration of fraud, or other activities against public policy. The need to pierce arises only if the corporation is unable to pay its own debts.

INTERNATIONAL CONSIDERATION

Before a business decides to incorporate abroad, its management should consult a lawyer in the country in which the incorporation is to take place, in order to be advised of the country's laws governing tax, labor, and corporate issues. Parties contemplating a partnership or joint venture should note that civil law jurisdictions do not usually recognize common law–style partnerships. They instead look through the partnership to the partners and view the partners as the legal owners.

There are two legal approaches to piercing the corporate veil. The *alter ego theory* applies when the owners of a corporation have so mingled their own affairs with those of the corporation that the corporation does not exist as a distinct entity—instead, it is an alter ego of its owners. The *undercapitalization theory* applies when the corporation is a separate entity, but its deliberate lack of adequate capital allows it to skirt potential liabilities. Such undercapitalization constitutes a fraud upon the public.

Courts usually apply some combination of these theories. If a court suspects wrongdoing or bad faith on the part of shareholders, it will be more inclined to pierce the corporate veil. Because a publicly traded corporation generally does not have one controlling shareholder, attempts to pierce the veil of such corporations are rare. Usually the cases involve small, closely held corporations, including subsidiaries of larger corporations.

Alter Ego Theory

There are several factors that a court will consider when deciding whether a corporation is merely the alter ego of a shareholder.

Domination by Shareholder   If an individual or another corporation owning most of the stock of the corporation exerts a great deal of control, such that the standard corporate decision-making mechanisms are not in operation, the courts may find that the corporation has no will of its own.

Commingling of Assets   The courts will also examine whether the books and funds of the corporation and of the controlling shareholder have been commingled; for example, whether the shareholder uses company checks to make personal purchases or payments.

Bypassing Formalities   If an action that requires approval by the board proceeds without a board meeting being held, or if other procedural rules (such as the requirement of an annual shareholders meeting) are consistently broken, the courts will be inclined to view the corporation as the instrument of the controlling shareholder.

However, recognizing that small businesses are run in a more informal manner than large ones, legislators have created the statutory category of the close corporation, that is, a corporation with a limited number of shareholders that is explicitly designated as a close corporation in its charter. Under some close corporation statutes, if a close corporation's shareholders agree not to observe corporate formalities relating to meetings of directors or shareholders in connection with the management of its affairs, the bypassing of these formalities may not be considered a factor tending to establish that the shareholders have personal liability for corporate obligations. In addition, many statutes permit the management of a close corporation to reside in the shareholders as long as a certain percentage of the shareholders agree to this in writing.

Undercapitalization Theory

In deciding whether a corporation is undercapitalized, a court will consider whether the founders should have reasonably anticipated that the corporation would be unable to pay the debts or liabilities it would incur. (Of course, the amount of capital invested does not have to guarantee business success—if it did, all failed businesses would be deemed undercapitalized.)

For example, assume a new corporation is formed to build airplanes, an activity that requires large expenditures and entails substantial risks of liability for third-party injury. The corporation has raised only $1,000 in capital. It is obvious that the corporation will run out of funds quickly and be unable to pay its bills. It will not have money to buy adequate product liability insurance or to self-insure against claims for injuries caused by defective airplanes. A court may, because of the undercapitalization, ignore the corporate form and hold the owners of the corporation personally liable for its debts and liabilities.

The above example is an exaggerated case. In reality, it is often difficult for a court to decide how much capital is enough. Two judges examining the same facts may come to different conclusions as to whether the owner should have reasonably anticipated that the corporation would need more capital. Judges may also disagree as to whether undercapitalization alone is sufficient grounds to pierce the corporate veil. In the following case, the majority opinion and the minority dissent reflect two sides of this issue.

A CASE IN POINT	IN THE LANGUAGE OF THE COURT

CASE 20.4
WALKOVSZKY v.
CARLTON
Court of Appeals of New York
223 N.E.2d 6 (N.Y. 1966).

FACTS   The plaintiff was severely injured in New York City when he was run down by a taxicab owned by the defendant, Seon Cab Corporation (Seon). The individual defendant, Carlton, was a shareholder of ten corporations, including Seon, each of which had two cabs registered in its name. Each cab was covered by only the minimum $10,000 per cab automobile liability insurance required by New York law.

Although seemingly independent of one another, these corporations were, according to the plaintiff, "operated . . . as a single entity, unit and enterprise" with regard to financing, supplies, repairs, employees, and garaging, and all were named as defendants. The plaintiff also asserted that the multiple corporate structure constituted an unlawful attempt "to defraud members of the general public" who might be injured by the cabs. He therefore sought to hold their sole shareholder personally liable for his injury.

ISSUE PRESENTED   May the corporate veil be pierced solely because the corporation is undercapitalized?

OPINION   FULD, J., writing for the New York Court of Appeals:

The law permits the incorporation of a business for the very purpose of enabling its proprietors to escape personal liability but, manifestly, the privilege is not without its limits. Broadly speaking, the courts will disregard the corporate form, or, to use accepted terminology, "pierce the corporate veil," whenever necessary "to prevent fraud or to achieve equity."

. . .

The individual defendant is charged with having "organized, managed, dominated and controlled" a fragmented corporate entity but there are no allegations that he was conducting business in his individual capacity. . . . The corporate form may not be disregarded merely because the assets of the corporation, together with the mandatory insurance coverage of the vehicle which struck the plaintiff, are insufficient to assure him the recovery sought. If Carlton were to be held individually liable on those facts alone, the decision would apply equally to the thousands of cabs which are owned by their individual drivers who conduct their businesses through corporations organized pursuant to [the New York Business Corporation Law] and carry the

Case 20.4 continues

Case 20.4 continued

minimum insurance required. . . . These taxi owner-operators are entitled to form such corporations, and we agree . . . that, if the insurance coverage required by statute "is inadequate for the protection of the public, the remedy lies not with the courts but with the Legislature." It may very well be sound policy to require that certain corporations must take out liability insurance which will afford adequate compensation to their potential tort victims. However, the responsibility for imposing conditions on the privilege of incorporation has been committed by the Constitution to the Legislature and it may not be fairly implied, from any statute, that the Legislature intended, without the slightest discussion or debate, to require of taxi corporations that they carry automobile liability insurance over and above that mandated by the Vehicle and Traffic Law.

DISSENTING OPINION   KEATING, J.:

From their inception these corporations were intentionally undercapitalized for the purpose of avoiding responsibility for acts which were bound to arise as a result of the operation of a large taxi fleet having cars out on the street 24 hours a day and engaged in public transportation. And during the course of the corporations' existence all income was continually drained out of the corporations for the same purpose.

The issue presented by this action is whether the policy of this State, which affords those desiring to engage in a business enterprise the privilege of limited liability through the use of the corporate device, is so strong that it will permit that privilege to continue no matter how much it is abused, no matter how irresponsibly the corporation is operated, no matter what the cost to the public. I do not believe that it is.

[Judge Keating then cited with approval a California Supreme Court case[8] holding that the corporate veil could be pierced based on undercapitalization alone.]

. . .

What I would merely hold is that a participating shareholder of a corporation vested with a public interest, organized with capital insufficient to meet liabilities which are certain to arise in the ordinary course of the corporation's business, may be held personally responsible for such liabilities. Where corporate income is not sufficient to cover the cost of insurance premiums above the statutory minimum or where initially adequate finances dwindle under the pressure of competition, bad times or extraordinary and unexpected liability, obviously the shareholder will not be held liable.

The only types of corporate enterprises that will be discouraged as a result of a decision allowing the individual shareholder to be sued will be those such as the one in question, designed solely to abuse the corporate privilege at the expense of the public interest.

RESULT   In New York, the corporate veil may not be pierced solely because the corporation is undercapitalized. Accordingly, plaintiff Walkovszky cannot sue Carlton in his individual capacity.

Case 20.4 continues

---

8. Minton v. Cavaney, 364 P.2d 473 (Cal. 1961).

Case 20.4 continued

COMMENTS In *Walkovszky,* the court rejected the argument that undercapitalization alone constituted fraud. However, the court suggested that the plaintiff amend the complaint to allege that the individual defendants were "shuttling . . . personal funds in and out of the corporation 'without regard to formality and to suit their immediate convenience,'" thus stating a valid cause of action under the alter ego theory.

Questions

1. From a public policy standpoint, with which opinion do you agree, the majority or the dissent?
2. Would the result have been different if defendant Carlton's name had been conspicuously displayed on the sides of all of the taxis owned by the various corporations of which Carlton was the sole shareholder and if Carlton actually serviced, inspected, repaired, and dispatched the taxis?

ETHICAL CONSIDERATION

Should a person be allowed to use the corporate form without ensuring that the corporation has sufficient funds to act in a socially responsible manner?

Tort versus Contract

A tort plaintiff's contact with the corporation (for example, being hit by a taxi) may be completely involuntary. Many courts are therefore more sympathetic to the tort victim who faces an undercapitalized corporate defendant than to a plaintiff seeking to pierce the corporate veil in a breach-of-contract case. Why should someone who voluntarily contracted to provide credit to a weakly capitalized corporation, perhaps charging a premium interest rate in so doing, later be entitled to reach the owner's personal assets? After all, the creditor had, or could have negotiated, access to the corporation's financial statements. The voluntary decision to do business with the undercapitalized company contrasts quite sharply with the plight of a party who is a victim of a tort committed by an officer or employee of the corporation.

Management of the Corporation

Corporate control is apportioned among the directors, officers, and shareholders. The directors are the overall managers and guardians of the shareholders' interests in the corporation. The officers are the day-to-day managers. The shareholders, as the owners of the corporation, do not participate directly in management, but they elect the directors. The shareholders also must approve certain major transactions.

Directors

Most state statutes provide that the business and the affairs of the corporation shall be managed, and all corporate powers shall be exercised, by or under the direction of the board of directors. The board may delegate the management of the day-to-day operations of the business of the corporation to a management company or to other persons, such as officers. A member of the board may also serve as an officer. Such a person is called an *inside director.* A director who is not also an officer is called an *outside director.* An understanding of the dynamics between the board and the officers is essential to comprehend the workings of a corporation.

"Now that you've all put in your two cents' worth, I should like to interject my fifty-one per cent controlling interest."

Officers

The officers appointed by the board of directors are agents of the corporation and have the power to act on its behalf. A corporation will normally have a president, a secretary, a chief financial officer, and other officers as designated in the bylaws or determined by the board.

Any number of offices may be held by the same person, unless the articles or bylaws provide otherwise. Officers are chosen by the board and serve at the pleasure of the board. If an officer is terminated in violation of a contract of employment, he cannot sue to get his job back, but he can sue for damages. An officer may resign at any time upon written notice to the corporation. The corporation can sue for damages if an officer's resignation breaches his or her employment contract.

Shareholders

The shareholders elect the directors. The courts have held that directors have no inherent right to remain in office. In some states, directors can be removed by the shareholders with or without cause at any time. In other states, such as Delaware, a director who is elected to a staggered board (whereby directors serve for designated terms) may not be removed without cause, unless the certificate of incorporation provides otherwise. However, the shareholders might be able to accomplish the same result by first eliminating the charter or bylaw provision requiring the staggered board, then by voting to remove the directors. There are also certain transactions, such as a merger or the sale of substantially all of the corporation's assets, that can be approved only by a vote of the shareholders.

ETHICAL CONSIDERATION

Directors and officers are allowed to be shareholders in the corporation they manage. In fact, giving the managers an ownership stake is a standard strategy for increasing their motivation. A manager's duty is to act in the best interest of all of the shareholders. However, if there are conflicting interests among the shareholders, how should a director or officer who is also a shareholder resolve conflicts between his or her own interests and those of other shareholders?

Shareholder Voting Rules

Shareholders can act by vote at a meeting or by written consent. A shareholder who cannot be present at a meeting can vote by *proxy*, that is, by a written authorization for another person to vote on his or her behalf. Only *shareholders of record*, that is, persons whose names appear on the corporation's shareholder list on a specified date, are entitled to vote.

No action can be taken at a shareholder meeting unless there is a *quorum*; the quorum requirements are set forth in each state's corporate statute. In most jurisdictions, there is no quorum unless the holders of at least 50% of the outstanding shares are present in person or by proxy.

Cumulative Voting

In the election of directors, shareholders can cast one vote per share for each director. A shareholder's total number of votes is thus equal to the number of directors to be elected multiplied by the number of shares owned by the shareholder. Some states permit, and some require, cumulative voting, whereby each shareholder may cast all of his votes for one nominee, or allocate them among nominees as he sees fit.

In an election permitting *cumulative voting*, the number of shares, *x*, required to elect a given number of directors, *y*, may be calculated by the following formula:

$$x = \frac{y \times z}{1 + d} + 1$$

where *z* is the total number of shares voting, and *d* is the total number of directors to be elected.

To illustrate, assume a shareholder wants to elect three directors (*y* = 3) to a board with five members up for election (*d* = 5). There are 100 shares of the corporation outstanding and they are all voted (*z* = 100). Then

$$x = \frac{3 \times 100}{1 + 5} + 1$$

$$x = 51$$

With cumulative voting, a shareholder would need 51 shares to elect three directors.

Shareholders' Right of Inspection

Shareholders have a common law right to inspect the corporate books and records, including the stock register and/or shareholder list, the minutes of board meetings and shareholder meetings, the bylaws, and books of account. In making the examination, shareholders are permitted the assistance of an accountant, lawyer, or other expert.

The right of inspection is limited, however, by the requirement that the inspection be conducted for a proper purpose. States vary in their interpretation of this limit. Some jurisdictions construe "proper purpose" liberally, leaving shareholder inspection rights virtually unfettered. These states reason that inspection rights should be broad because everything that affects a corporation eventually has an effect on its shareholders. Other states, more concerned with the potential for the inspection right to be an abusive tool, protect against "fishing expeditions" by requiring more than a vague allegation of mismanagement to establish a proper purpose.

Many of the most intense shareholder inspection battles involve access to the list of shareholders. Shareholders seeking to change a corporate policy or gain control of the corporation want to identify and target their message to the holders of large blocks of stock. In order to do this, the insurgents need a copy of the shareholder list. Precisely because the list is so valuable to its shareholder critics, incumbent managers are likely resist efforts to obtain it.

Acknowledging that access to the shareholder list can be vital to a successful corporate power struggle, some jurisdictions allow such access without requiring a proper purpose, provided the shareholder owns a substantial block of shares. For example, Section 1600(a) of the California Corporations Code provides that any 5% shareholder can inspect and copy the record of shareholders' names and addresses and shareholdings during usual business hours upon five business days' written notice.

Most states still require a proper purpose to obtain a shareholder list, however. The following case considers which motivations will qualify as a proper purpose.

| A CASE IN POINT | SUMMARY |

CASE 20.5
STATE EX REL.
PILLSBURY v.
HONEYWELL, INC.
Supreme Court of Minnesota
191 N.W.2d 406
(Minn. 1971).

FACTS   Charles Pillsbury opposed the Vietnam war. On July 3, 1969, he attended a protest meeting at which he learned that Honeywell, Inc. had a large government contract to produce anti-personnel fragmentation bombs for use in the war. Upset that such bombs were being produced in his own community by a company that he had known and respected, Pillsbury resolved to stop Honeywell's munitions production.

On July 14, 1969, Pillsbury purchased 100 shares of Honeywell. He admitted that the sole purpose of the purchase was to give himself a voice in Honeywell's affairs so he could persuade Honeywell to cease producing munitions. Pillsbury submitted two formal demands to Honeywell requesting that it produce its current shareholder list and all corporate records dealing with weapons and munitions manufacture. Honeywell refused.

Pillsbury filed suit to force Honeywell to comply with his inspection request. The trial court dismissed his suit, holding that Pillsbury's purpose was not proper. Pillsbury appealed.

ISSUE PRESENTED   Does a shareholder whose desire to change a corporate policy is motivated by social or political concerns have a proper purpose required to gain access to a shareholder list?

SUMMARY OF OPINION   The Minnesota Supreme Court said that the act of inspecting a corporation's shareholder list must be viewed in its proper perspective. In the context of the large firm, inspection can be more akin to a weapon in corporate warfare. "Considering the huge size of many modern corporations and the necessarily complicated nature of their bookkeeping, it is plain that to permit thousands of stockholders to roam at will through their records would render impossible . . . the proper carrying on of their business." Because the power to inspect may be the power to destroy, the court reasoned, it is important that only those with a bona fide interest in the corporation enjoy that power.

The court determined that a proper purpose under Delaware law (which governed the case because Honeywell was incorporated in Delaware) contemplated a concern with investment return. Pillsbury had "utterly no interest" in Honeywell's affairs before he learned of their production of fragmentation bombs. His avowed purpose in buying Honeywell was to place himself in a position to try to impress his social and political opinions upon Honeywell management and its other shareholders. Such an interest, the court concluded, could hardly be deemed a proper purpose germane to his economic interest as a shareholder.

RESULT   The Minnesota Supreme Court affirmed the trial court's denial of Pillsbury's petition to compel Honeywell to provide corporate records for inspection.

Structural Changes

State laws establish mechanisms by which the fundamental structure of the corporation can be changed. These changes can range from a reorganization of the enterprise to the end of the corporation as a separate entity. Because structural changes have far-reaching consequences, they cannot be made easily.

State corporation law prohibits certain changes, such as a merger or the sale of substantially all of the corporation's assets, unless they are approved by both the board of directors and the shareholders. Approval by the shareholders usually means approval by a simple majority of the outstanding shares, but the articles of incorporation may require approval by a larger majority, such as two-thirds of the shareholders. Such a requirement for supermajority approval reflects the importance of structural changes.

Merger

A *merger* is the combination of two or more corporations into one. The *disappearing corporation* no longer maintains its separate corporate existence, but becomes part of the *surviving corporation*. The surviving corporation assumes, that is, becomes responsible for, all of the liabilities and debts of the disappearing corporation, and automatically acquires all of its assets, by operation of law. The new corporation may take on the name of one of the parties to the merger, or a new corporate name may be chosen. For example, when Burroughs merged with Sperry Univac, the new corporation was named Unisys.

An agreement of merger, negotiated between the two companies, will specify such crucial matters as who will comprise the management team of the new enterprise. A merger generally cannot occur unless the boards and the shareholders of both companies approve the transaction. Once the requisite approval is given, the agreement of merger is filed with the secretary of state.

In a noncash merger, the shares in the disappearing corporation are automatically converted into shares in the surviving corporation. Shareholders are required to surrender their old stock certificates for new certificates representing the stock of the surviving corporation. If a shareholder does not surrender his or her old certificate, it is deemed by operation of law to represent shares of the surviving corporation.

In a cash merger, some shareholders (usually the public shareholders) are required to surrender their shares in the disappearing corporation for cash. They retain no interest in the surviving corporation. Hence, such a merger is also called a *freeze-out merger*.

If a proposed merger meets certain size-of-party and size-of-transaction tests, a premerger notification must be filed with the Federal Trade Commission and the Department of Justice. This notification enables the federal agencies to review the anticompetitive effects of the proposed merger before the combination occurs. (Such Hart–Scott–Rodino filings and antitrust in general are covered in Chapter 18.)

Sale of Assets

A company may want to acquire the assets of another company but not its liabilities. To achieve this goal, it can purchase all or most of the other company's assets without merging with the other company. The proceeds of the sale of assets can be distributed to the selling company's shareholders as part of a dissolution of the corporation. Alternatively, the selling company may choose to continue its corporate existence and invest the proceeds of the sale of assets in a new business.

A sale of all or substantially all of the assets of a corporation must be approved by both the board and the shareholders of the selling company. Most states consider a sale of 50% or more of the assets of a company to be a sale of substantially all of the assets.

Some states do not require that the transaction be approved by the shareholders of the acquiring company, on the theory that the acquisition of assets is a routine management decision, in which the shareholders should not be involved.

Appraisal Rights

In a merger or a sale of assets, dissenting shareholders—those who voted against the transaction—are frequently granted *appraisal rights*, that is, the right to receive the fair cash value of the shares they were forced to give up as a result of the transaction. This right is available only if the transaction was subject to shareholder approval and if the dissenting shareholder complies with certain statutory procedures.

For example, minority shareholders of Alabama By-Products Corporation were cashed out at $75.60

pursuant to a merger in 1985. They sought appraisal of their shares pursuant to Section 262 of the Delaware Corporations Code. On August 1, 1990, the Delaware Court of Chancery (the trial court in Delaware that hears corporate law cases) issued an opinion that valued the minority's shares in excess of $180 per share, using the discounted future cash flow methodology. The court also awarded the minority shareholders interest on the award of 12½%, or 5% above the 7½% federal discount rate in August 1985. The court rejected the defendants' argument that a lower short-term rate should be used, stating:

> Appraisal cases are akin to wars of attrition, with the dissenting shareholder forced to wait years for a return on his litigation investment. Short-term interest rates would be unfair for such shareholders, and a windfall to the surviving corporation.[9]

◆ Ownership Changes

One company may gain control of another by buying a majority of its voting shares, rather than by merging with it or purchasing its assets.

Tender Offers

A *tender offer* is a public offer to all the shareholders of a corporation to buy their shares at a stated price, usually higher than the market price. The party making the offer is called a *bidder*, or sometimes a raider, because of the hostile nature of the bid. The bidder may offer either cash or other securities in exchange for the stock it seeks to acquire. The bidder is often a new corporation formed for the purpose of making the offer.

The shareholders are free to reject or accept the tender offer without the approval of the board of the

---

9. Neal v. Alabama By-Products Corp., Del. Ch., C.A. No. 8282 (Aug. 1, 1990).

target. If shareholders sell sufficient stock to the bidder, it will acquire control of the *target corporation*. Hence, the term *takeover* is commonly used to describe this transaction. Because a takeover is almost sure to change substantially the corporate structure of the target, tender offers are the subject of much regulation by federal statutes, as well as by the laws of the individual states. (Takeovers and the defensive tactics that boards can use to thwart them are discussed more fully in Chapter 21.)

An example of a takeover that results in a major change in corporate structure is the *second-step back-end merger*, whereby the bidder acquires more than 50% of the shares of a company through a tender offer and then eliminates the remaining shareholders in a subsequent merger. The bidder first replaces the target company's board of directors with its own people. These new board members then approve the merger of the target company into a company owned by the bidder, with the shareholders of the target company receiving cash or securities for their stock. As the majority shareholder of the target company, the bidder can outvote any dissenters and provide the required shareholder approval. The remaining shareholders are thus frozen out of the new company, and the bidder ends up with all the equity interest.

Leveraged Buyouts

Any tender offer can be structured as a *leveraged buyout* (*LBO*), that is, a stock purchase financed by debt. Many LBOs involve members of corporate management in the group of investors seeking to gain control of a corporation. The debt financing an LBO is typically secured by the assets of the target company (such as real estate or plant and equipment), and it may take the form of the issuance of bonds, a commercial bank loan, or a loan from an investment bank. An LBO often results in a high debt load, which requires the company to make a series of substantial interest payments.

THE RESPONSIBLE MANAGER

Choosing the Appropriate Business Organization

The individuals who participate in the creation of a business organization will often go on to become its

managers. These managers have a strong incentive to maximize the new enterprise's potential for success. To do this, several concerns must be addressed during the entity-selection process.

First, a founder should define and clarify the business goals of the enterprise in a business plan. For example, if the enterprise will need capital from a large number of individuals, it will be necessary to ensure limited liability for some or all of these investors. A general partnership would not be suitable, as there would be no limited liability for passive investors. A related concern is clarifying the goals of the individual participants in the enterprise. For example, experienced managers who have developed a new product that requires little capital outlay would probably want exclusive control of the new business. A general partnership might be best suited to their needs.

If a general partnership is chosen, there are additional concerns. For example, it is important to put the partnership agreement in writing. A written partnership agreement forces people to think through their business objectives and relationships before they begin working together. It also avoids the imposition of certain statutory partnership rules that apply when there is no written agreement.

If several persons work together on an informal basis with a common business objective, and then one leaves, the *forgotten founder* problem can arise. The person who left may have ownership rights in the enterprise. Such rights can be based on the laws of intellectual property if the person leaving created a protectable piece of property, such as a patentable invention or computer software that is protected by copyright law. (Intellectual property is discussed in Chapter 11.) Even if a founder created no protectable intellectual property before leaving, he or she may have been a partner in an informal oral general partnership if the parties had been sharing profits and losses. As such, that founder would be entitled to a share of the partnership assets.

One way to mitigate the forgotten founder problem is to incorporate early and issue shares that are subject to vesting over time. A common vesting schedule provides that if a person leaves in the first year, he or she forfeits all rights to any stock. Under this approach, called *cliff vesting*, one-quarter of the stock is often vested at the end of the first year. The remainder is vested monthly over the next three to four years.

If early incorporation is either infeasible or otherwise undesirable, it is important to spell out in writing at the beginning of a joint project what will happen if someone leaves. Otherwise, those who remain could find themselves sued years down the road for a share of the company that finally is formed or for a partnership interest or for royalties for use of intellectual property.

Tax considerations play a major role in the choice of a business entity. Because tax law is constantly changing, its impact on a particular business form cannot be predicted with certainty. Nonetheless, the larger issues, such as whether taxation will be at both the entity and owner level or only at the owner level, must be considered. In addition, optimal tax planning does not necessarily mean tax minimization. When deciding how to organize a business, the company must weigh the tax advantages against the agency costs.

If a founder decides that incorporation is the best course, he or she should obtain competent legal advice. State statutes vary in their requirements for incorporation. As a practical matter, founders should always request that their lawyer send them a certified copy of the articles of incorporation to confirm that the articles were in fact filed with the secretary of state on the specified date.

Even if a corporation is formed in accordance with the appropriate legal requirements, a court may still disregard the corporate form. In some jurisdictions, the corporate veil may be pierced solely because the corporation is undercapitalized. The founders should consult with counsel as to the capital requirements in the jurisdiction of incorporation. Courts may also pierce the corporate veil if the shareholders fail to respect the corporate form in their execution of daily activities or if they commingle personal and corporate funds. Managers should make it clear in all of their dealings with third parties that they are acting on behalf of a corporation. All firm stationery and agreements should indicate corporate status.

Once the corporation has been established, the managers will oversee the process of capitalization. To decide what percentages of debt and equity are to be used in financing the operation, managers should have a realistic idea of the existing demand and the distinct markets for both types of financing. In addition, managers must be aware of the rates at which the corporation can borrow money and the terms that debt and equity holders will require. Tax considerations are crucial to this process.

The final capital structure can take a variety of forms, and much creativity can be employed in this area. Managers will often seek assistance from attorneys specializing in finance and tax law, as well as from investment bankers. The more a manager understands about capitalization, however, the better the manager can utilize the information provided by lawyers and bankers to achieve a suitable capital structure.

The officers of a corporation are empowered by the board to manage the day-to-day operations of the business. They are also agents for the corporation and must be concerned with the impact of agency law on their actions. First, a manager must be certain that he or she is acting with actual authority (such as a resolution from the board of directors, passed in a procedurally correct manner, that approves a proposed action). Second, a manager has the power to delegate authority to subordinates to bind the corporation. Accordingly, the manager should clearly define the scope of employment for all employees of the corporation and clearly indicate to third parties the extent of each employee's authority.

Managers are often directors, as well as officers. As board members, they should ensure that the board acts in accordance with the articles of incorporation and the applicable corporate law. Board actions are valid only if the directors act in their collective role and not in their individual capacity. The duties of board members to act in an informed manner and to make decisions based on the best interests of the corporation are discussed in Chapter 21.

INSIDE STORY

THE 3DO COMPANY: A "VIRTUAL" CORPORATION

The 3DO Company was founded by William M. (Trip) Hawkins in 1991. 3DO was formed to create a new interactive multimedia platform and to develop technology that could achieve a breakthrough in home audiovisual realism at an affordable price. In addition, the company planned to broadly license the technology to hardware system manufacturers, software title developers, and software publishers. The company targeted its initial product design, the 3DO Interactive Multiplayer, to be the first interactive multimedia product that would appeal to the entire family, bridging the gap between children's video games and adults' home computers. The Multiplayer was designed to run new entertainment, education, and information compact disk (CD) applications developed specifically for the 3DO format and to also play conventional audio CDs and display photo CDs. The 3DO Multiplayer was not compatible with any other software formats that were currently commercially available. New

applications developed for the 3DO format included realistic adventure games, lifelike sports and flight simulations, interactive movies, children's storybooks, education programs, and a variety of information services.

Hawkins saw a trend in the confluence of computer, communication, and consumer electronics products. As communication lines carried more information, including video images, and as computers became more powerful even as their prices fell, he developed the concept of a technology standard that would allow powerful multimedia players connected to a communication network to download game software titles and other interactive entertainment for the family. A number of large industry players stood to capitalize on these trends, including (1) computer companies such as Apple Computer, IBM, and Silicon Graphics; (2) telecommunications companies such as AT&T, MCI, and US West; (3) cable companies such as Tele-Communications Inc. (TCI) and Time Warner Cable;

(4) consumer electronics companies such as Sony and Matsushita; and (5) game software companies such as Electronic Arts, Nintendo, and Sega.

Hawkins decided that the focus of 3DO should be the development of a technology standard used for multimedia players and game software. The company developed quickly for a new start-up. From the beginning, Hawkins realized the importance of bringing in other partners, such as product suppliers and technology promoters, to share the technological and financial risks. He signed agreements with AT&T to develop the computer graphics integrated circuits (chipset), Matsushita to manufacture the interactive game players, and Time Warner to contribute portions of its media archives and develop interactive software titles. In addition, he signed agreements with a host of software companies to produce the game software titles that would run using 3DO's technology standard, including Electronic Arts.

He also brought in venture capital investors Kleiner Perkins Caufield & Byers, which had invested in many successful start-ups and would provide funding to other companies developing software titles for the 3DO platform.

In May 1993, 3DO went public in an initial public offering (IPO) at $15 per share, raising more than $40 million for the development of the technology, working capital needs, and the acquisition of complementary businesses, products, and technologies. For a company with no revenues, and losses totaling more than $13 million in the year and a half since it was founded, the IPO looked a lot like those for biotechnology companies, which often go public with little revenue and no profits. The total market valuation of 3DO was almost $300 million, and investor interest in the multimedia company was overwhelming—the stock rose quickly to $20 on the first day of trading, and by the next month had risen to more than $25 per share, putting the company's total valuation at more than $450 million.

By October, the stock had reached $48 a share. But seven months later, in May 1994 (one year after the company went public), the stock price fell to below $10 per share. Hurt by slow sales of the Interactive Multiplayer—due in part to its relatively high price and the dearth of software titles to play on the Multiplayer—and increased competition from rivals Sony Corporation, Sega, and Nintendo, 3DO had run into tough times. In June 1994, 3DO sold $36.8 million of stock at $12.375 a share to new Asian investors and its initial equity partners. This capital infusion was necessary to keep 3DO afloat. In August 1994, the stock traded at $13.50 a share.

What had investors seen in this company that made it unique from other game software companies? To begin with, most of the company's revenues were expected to come from the technology licenses it granted to others, not from the sale of the game players and software titles that it manufactured. This allowed the company to focus on its core capability, the development of a technology standard around which other multimedia hardware and software companies could coalesce. The 3DO technology license was provided at no cost to the hardware game manufacturers; and by April 1994, Matsushita, AT&T, Sanyo, Toshiba, Samsung, and Goldstar had signed hardware license agreements with 3DO. Software title producers were required to pay a royalty of $3 per copy of a software title to use the 3DO license. By May 1994, the company had shipped more than 550 software development systems to more than 200 licensee companies worldwide. 3DO provided the training and technical support for its standard, but it was not involved in the sales or distribution of any products.

In a sense, Hawkins had developed the company into a "virtual" corporation. This organizational form was characterized by a web of close relationships among its customers, suppliers, and potential competitors that enabled the company to take advantage of a market opportunity by combining the core capabilities of different companies to bring a new product to market faster than if the company itself had developed all of the capabilities internally.[10] 3DO did not plan to manufacture or market any of the game players or software titles. Rather, it sought to maintain technological leadership and support its licensees.

The 3DO Company went beyond a normal joint venture or strategic alliance. Joint ventures are typically a collection of two or more companies that partner up for a specific project, each holding an ownership stake in the joint venture firm. A strategic alliance is usually a collection of companies that agree on the technical direction of their respective business, without sharing equity ownership in a distinct joint venture. What Hawkins had done was to combine unique features of the joint venture and the strategic alliance. He brought a host of companies from different industries together to agree upon a technical standard, and signed them to contracts as suppliers of computer chips, hardware game players, and game software titles, all of which would run on the 3DO technology standard. Furthermore, he aligned the companies' interests with 3DO's by selling them equity stakes in 3DO. Thus, 3DO shared the financial risk of development with the investors, while at the same time giving them a significant opportunity of upside return if the technology became a multimedia standard and gained mass market popularity. To gain credibility in the financial world and ease the transition from a start-up to a public company, Hawkins brought in venture investors such as Kleiner Perkins Caufield & Byers, which had contributed to the development of other successful start-up companies such as Apple Computer and Silicon Graphics.

3DO's strategy and form of business organization brought it and its corporate partners much initial publicity and success. In fact, soon after the IPO, the four corporate partners and the venture capital firm all had large "paper" returns on their initial investments of capital and technology in the company. The large initial investment returns for these companies predicted success for 3DO's unique form of business organization and the potential of the inter-active multimedia market. Yet 3DO's own interests and the fortunes and future of its alliance partners were intricately intertwined, which brought some problems for the company.

In particular, 3DO was threatened by conflicts of interest with its corporate partners who had joined a number of alliances that compete with the 3DO technology standard. AT&T formed an alliance with and invested money in the EO Corporation and General Magic to develop personal intelligent communicators that might be applicable to interactive information or video services. Matsushita was also a member of the General Magic alliance. In addition, Time Warner entered into a number of alliances with cable, computer, and communication companies to exploit the growing multimedia market. Furthermore, Electronic Arts's position as a major supplier to Nintendo and Sega, both of which would be affected by 3DO's entry into the interactive multimedia market, put it in a conflicted situation with 3DO. The 3DO organizational structure brought benefits in product development and the establishment of a technology standard. However, it also carried the burden of conflict and coordination problems.[11]

---

10. *See* WILLIAM H. DAVIDOW & MICHAEL S. MALONE, THE VIRTUAL CORPORATION (1992); John A. Byrne, *The Virtual Corporation*, BUS. WK., Feb. 8, 1993, at 98–103.

11. *Home Entertainment: Tripping*, ECONOMIST, June 12, 1993, at 80.

KEY WORDS AND PHRASES

QUESTIONS AND CASE PROBLEMS

1. Amy Rockwell was a brilliant but penniless electrical engineer. She had designed a new type of cogeneration plant that she believed had great commercial potential. On January 15, she approached Benjamin Furst, a successful and experienced manager in the energy field, with the idea of starting Cogen, Inc., a corporation devoted to building a plant based on this new design. Furst was enthusiastic. On January 28, he enlisted the support of Clyde Pfeffer, a well-known venture capitalist who had retired from venture capital work but was looking to invest the proceeds of his past endeavors. Pfeffer gave the green light on February 16 to establish the new enterprise.

Furst retained the law firm of Fumble & Botchem to handle the details of incorporation. Fumble, one of the partners, drafted the articles of incorporation, signed them as the incorporator, and filed them with the secretary of state on February 28. He then advised his clients that the articles had been filed. Because of a typographical error, the articles of incorporation filed with the secretary of state referred to the company as Cogene, not Cogen.

Rockwell, Furst, and Pfeffer decided that they would save further expense by completing the incorporation process without any more assistance from Fumble & Botchem. On March 3, they held what they called the meeting of incorporators to elect the directors, and proceeded to elect themselves to the board. As board members, they appointed themselves as the company's officers. They typed up the minutes of this meeting.

On March 4, the daily operations of Cogen, Inc. commenced. In all of their transactions with third parties, the officers represented themselves as doing business for the corporation. One of these transactions was with Firstloan Bank, which lent the company $5 million. The representations in the loan agreement stated that the corporation had been duly formed, that it existed as a valid corporation under Texas law, and that the shares of stock owned by the various shareholders had been duly authorized and were fully paid.

On May 5, the corporation began building its cogeneration plant. Three months later, energy prices dropped drastically, and there was no longer a need for a cogeneration facility in that location. The corporation was forced to default on the bank loan. The lawyers for the bank, upon being informed that it would not receive any more loan payments, reviewed the original loan documents, the articles of incorporation, and the minutes of the first meeting of the incorporators. Upon reviewing these documents, they initiated an action directly against the three founders in their individual capacity for liability on the bank loan.

a. What arguments can the lawyers for the bank make in their effort to hold the founders personally liable for the debt of the corporation? Should their arguments prevail?

b. What counterarguments can the founders make to avoid such liability?

2. Robert Dexter was the sole force behind In Over Our Heads, Inc., a corporation designed to run a year-round community swimming pool. The enterprise was incorporated in the correct manner in January, with Dexter as the sole director and shareholder. Dexter contributed $100,000 of starting capital, which was just enough to purchase the pool, finance initial advertising, and leave a reserve of $10,000. The corporation had no liability insurance.

On March 10, the pool opened for business. The corporation operated with a profit over the next few months. In June, Dexter took a two-week vacation to Europe and used a check from the company bank account to purchase his airline ticket. In November, he decided to have the pool repainted. Because business had slowed and the corporation's bank account did not have sufficient funds, Dexter wrote a personal check for this job.

Dexter feared he would not make enough money through the winter to turn a profit, so he decided to take a part-time job as a telephone salesperson for a real estate company. He used the swimming pool's office phone to make his calls and made a substantial profit.

On February 11, a child drowned in the pool. The parents brought suit for wrongful death against the corporation and against Dexter in his individual capacity as owner. At the time of suit, the corporation had the $10,000 reserve and less than $1,000 in its bank account. Because of these limited funds, the child's parents hoped to recover most of their damages directly from Dexter.

What arguments can be made to hold Dexter liable for any debt of the corporation arising from this death? Should they prevail? How could Dexter have protected himself against such potential liability? Can an owner-manager of a small corporation guarantee that he will not be held liable for the corporation's debts?

3. Sullivan purchased an American Football League (AFL) franchise for a professional football team for $25,000. Several months later, he organized a corporation, the American League Professional Football Team of Boston. Sullivan contributed his AFL franchise, and nine other people contributed $25,000. In return, each of the ten investors received 10,000 shares of voting common stock in the corporation. Approximately four months later, the corporation sold 120,000 shares of nonvoting common stock to the public at $5 per share.

In 1975, Sullivan obtained control of all 100,000 voting shares of the corporation. He immediately used his control to vote out the other directors and elect a friendly board. In order to finance the purchase of the voting shares, Sullivan borrowed approximately $5,000,000. As a condition of the loan, Sullivan was to use his best efforts to organize the corporation so that its income could be devoted to the payment of the personal loan and its assets pledged to secure the loan. In order to accomplish this goal, Sullivan had to eliminate the interests in the nonvoting shares.

In 1976, Sullivan organized a new corporation. The boards of directors of the new and old company executed a merger agreement for the two corporations, providing that after the merger the voting stock of the old corporation would be extinguished and the nonvoting stock would be exchanged for cash at $15 per share.

David Coggins owned 10 shares of nonvoting stock in the old corporation. He voted against the merger and brought suit against what he alleged was an unfair and illegal transaction. Was the transaction unfair to the nonvoting shareholders? Should Coggins be able to obtain an injunction to stop the merger? [*Coggins v. New England Patriots Football Club*, 492 N.E.2d 1112 (Mass. 1986)]

4. While attending Georgia Tech, Alan, Brian, Cathy, and Diane conceived of an innovative design for a hospital management software system, but they did not actually write the code. At the time, there was some talk among them of starting a business after graduation, but there was no formal agreement. Four months after graduation, Alan, Brian, and Cathy formed a company to develop the system. They initially took the position that Diane was not entitled to share in the new enterprise because of the enormous amount of work that would be required to develop the code and make it commercially viable. Their lawyer suggested reaching an agreement with Diane, whereby she would receive a 5% equity interest in the new company in exchange for any rights she might have in the technology.

Should Alan, Brian, and Cathy accept their lawyer's advice? What risks do they face if they do not?

5. Francis McQuade was the manager of the New York Giants baseball team. Charles Stoneham (father of Horace Stoneham, who acquired the baseball franchise in 1936 and moved it from New York to San Francisco in 1958) owned a majority of the stock of the company that owned the Giants and sold shares in that company to McQuade and John McGraw. As part of this transaction, these three shareholders each agreed to use his best efforts to continue to keep each of the others as directors and officers of the company at their present salaries. Stoneham and McGraw subsequently failed to use their best efforts to continue to keep McQuade as a director and treasurer of the company. McQuade sued for specific performance of the agreement. What result? [*McQuade v. Stoneham*, 189 N.E. 234 (N.Y. 1934)]

6. Smith Construction contracted with Wolman, Duberstein & Thompson (WBT), a general partnership, to build two homes. The partnership then failed to pay the balance due on the homes (approximately $107,000), thereby breaching the contract. Smith Construction obtained a judgment against WBT for the balance due, but received only about $2,000 of that judgment, which was garnished from WBT's bank account. WBT had no other assets.

Can Smith Construction execute the remainder of its judgment against the assets of the individual partners of WBT? If so, are the individual partners jointly and severally liable, or are they only jointly liable for this business debt? (Joint and several liability means each partner is potentially liable for the entire debt of the partnership; joint liability means each is liable only for a portion of the debt.) Will the terms of the WBT partnership agreement affect the outcome? [*Wayne Smith*

Constr. Co., Inc. v. Wolman, Duberstein & Thompson, 604 N.E.2d 157 (Ohio 1992)]

7. In 1987, William Myers injured his hand while operating a cement pump. The pump had been manufactured in 1981 by Thomson Equipment. In 1982, Putzmeister, Inc., purchased the assets of Thomson Equipment but did not expressly assume the liabilities. Is Putzmeister liable to Myers for product liability? What factors would the court consider in determining whether Putzmeister must assume Thomson Equipment's liability for wrongfully manufactured products? [*Myers v. Putzmeister, Inc.,* 596 N.E.2d 754 (Ill. App. Ct. 1992)]

8. Theodore Bentley was acting as managing partner of Eaglewood Associates, Ltd. (Eaglewood). Eaglewood included James Shindler, Ralph Reamer, and Bentley. In July 1977, Bentley signed as managing partner a letter confirming a brokerage commission agreement with Marr & Associates (Marr). Subsequently, Marr successfully negotiated certain financing for the construction of an apartment project. At the closing of the financing, Eaglewood refused to pay Marr the $60,000 finder's fee, claiming (1) that Eaglewood was not operating as a limited partnership in July 1977 when Bentley signed the agreement, and (2) that Bentley was not authorized to act on its behalf.

The jury found that the parties were operating as a limited partnership in July 1977 even though the certificate of limited partnership was not filed with the secretary of state until December 1977. Eaglewood appealed. What result? [*Shindler v. Marr & Assoc.,* 695 S.W.2d 699 (Tex. Ct. App. 1986)]

9. Mary Doting was a partner in the Frank J. Trunk and Son Partnership. In 1988, Doting successfully petitioned the court to order a dissolution of the partnership. The court concluded that the partnership could not be wound up until the affairs of the partnership were completed. At the time, the partnership still had receivables under contract that would not be payable until 1997 at the earliest and 2001 at the latest.

Frank and Mary Trunk wanted the partnership to continue and succeeded in preventing its termination through October 1992. At that time, Doting filed a second petition to terminate the partnership. The Trunks argued the partnership could not be terminated until the last receivable had been received. Must all partnership receivables be received by a partnership before a court can order its termination? [*Doting v. Trunk,* 856 P.2d 536 (Mont. 1993)]

MANAGER'S DILEMMA

10. Ernie Jameson is a design engineer with a proven track record in the field of electronic musical instruments. He recently designed a new VLSI (very large scale integrated) chip. This chip is meant to be the heart and soul of a digital sampling keyboard to be called Echo. Jameson believes the Echo will set a new industry standard. He wishes to organize a business enterprise to build and market it. He has a meeting with his lawyer, at which he conveys to her the following bits of information:

a. It will take approximately two years to turn the VLSI chip into a marketable product.

b. Jameson has more than $200,000 in savings from previous ventures. He does not want any of that money at risk in this new venture. However, he wants a part of the ownership; he is unsure what percentage he wants.

c. There are five private investors currently willing to put up money in this venture. Only two out of the five want to play an active role in the enterprise. Jameson is willing to give these two some limited control.

d. Jameson knows that he is not qualified to manage the new endeavor. Nonetheless, he wants a significant say in how it proceeds.

e. Five more investors could be attracted to this project, but only if they could be guaranteed some fixed return on their money or could realize immediate tax benefits from investing.

f. Jameson would like Bernie Lord, a manager much in demand in the electronics field, to be his CEO. It would take significant incentives to attract him to the enterprise.

Jameson is not committed to using any particular type of business organization; he is interested in weighing the alternatives. What possible types of business organizations could accommodate the needs of the various players? What are the advantages and disadvantages of each alternative? Which one should Jameson choose?

INTERNET SOURCES	
Small Business Administration	http://www.sbaonline.sba.gov/
First Draft (July 1997) of Proposed Revisions to the Revised Uniform Limited Partnership Act	http://www.law.upenn.edu/library/ulc/llp/rulpa.txt
Uniform Partnership Act of 1994	http://www.lamission.cc.ca.us/law/partners.htm
Implications of California's Newly Adopted Revised Uniform Partnership Act	http://www.taxlawsb.com/resources/BusTax/ptshp.htm
Uniform Partnership Acts	http://lawlibrary.ucdavis.edu/LAWLIB/Nov97/0451.html
This site for Richards, Layton & Finger, the largest law firm in Delaware, contains excellent articles on Delaware corporate and partnership law and provides links to other legal-related sites.	http://www.rlf.com/
LLC-USA.com operates a Web site dedicated to issues surrounding limited liability companies.	http://www.llc-usa.com

CHAPTER 21

Directors, Officers, and Controlling Shareholders

INTRODUCTION

Fiduciary Duties

Directors and officers are agents of the corporation and owe a fiduciary duty to the corporation and its shareholders. They are legally obliged to act primarily for the benefit of the shareholders. Under certain circumstances, a majority or controlling shareholder owes a fiduciary duty to other shareholders as well.

These duties take two basic forms: a duty of care and a duty of loyalty. Generally, the *duty of care* requires fiduciaries to make informed and reasonable decisions and to exercise reasonable supervision of the business. The *duty of loyalty* mandates that fiduciaries act in good faith and in what they believe to be the best interest of the corporation, subordinating their personal interests to the welfare of the corporation. As then-Judge Benjamin Cardozo stated, many forms of conduct permissible in the business world for those acting at arm's length are forbidden to those bound by fiduciary ties. A trustee, he said, is held to

something stricter than the morals of the marketplace. Not mere honesty, but a "punctilio of honor the most sensitive," is the standard of behavior with which fiduciaries must comply.[1]

Chapter Overview

This chapter outlines the duties of directors, officers, and, in certain situations, controlling shareholders. First, it analyzes the duty of care in terms of the most applicable judicial doctrine, the business judgment rule. Next, it addresses issues arising under the duty of loyalty, including corporate opportunities. The chapter discusses the fiduciary duties of directors that arise when the directors must decide whether to sell the company or resist a corporate takeover bid. Legislative responses to these issues are also described. Finally, the chapter looks at the duties of controlling share-holders in connection with sales of corporate control and squeeze-out mergers.

 ## The Business Judgment Rule and the Duty of Care

In cases challenging board decisions for breach of the duty of care, the courts generally defer to the business judgment of the directors, acknowledging that courts

are ill equipped to second-guess directors' decisions at a later date. Thus, under the *business judgment rule*, as long as certain standards are met, a court will presume that the directors have acted in good faith and in the

---

1. Meinhard v. Salmon, 164 N.E. 545, 546 (N.Y. 1928). *See* Case 1.1.

honest belief that the action taken was in the best interest of the company. The court will not question whether the action was wise or whether the directors made an error of judgment or a business mistake.

In order to take advantage of the rule, directors must have made an informed decision with no conflict between personal interests and the interests of the corporation and its shareholders. If the business judgment rule does not apply to a transaction, courts generally shift to directors the burden of proving that their acts were not grossly negligent (or in cases involving trans-

actions in which the directors are interested, that the transaction was fair and reasonable).

Informed Decision

The business judgment rule is applicable only if the directors make an informed decision. The general corporation law of most jurisdictions authorizes directors to rely on the reports of officers and certain outside experts. However, passive reliance on such reports may result in an insufficiently informed decision, as in the following case.

A CASE IN POINT	SUMMARY

CASE 21.1
SMITH v.
VAN GORKOM
Supreme Court of Delaware
488 A.2d 858 (Del. 1985).

FACTS Trans Union Corporation was a publicly traded, diversified holding company engaged in the railcar-leasing business. Its stock was undervalued, largely due to accumulated investment tax credits. Jerome W. Van Gorkom, the chairman of the board of Trans Union, was reaching retirement age. He asked the chief financial officer, Donald Romans, to work out the per-share price at which a leveraged buyout could be done, given current cash flow. Romans came up with $55, based on debt-servicing requirements. He did not attempt to determine the intrinsic value of the company. Van Gorkom later met with Jay Pritzker and worked out a merger at $55 per share. Trans Union stock was then trading at about $37 per share.

Van Gorkom called a board meeting for September 20, 1980, on one day's notice, to approve the merger. All of the directors were familiar with the company's operations as a going concern, but they were not apprised of the merger negotiations before the board meeting on September 20. They were also familiar with the current financial status of the company; a month earlier they had discussed a Boston Consulting Group strategy study. The ten-member board included five outside directors who were CEOs or board members of publicly held companies, and a former dean of the University of Chicago Business School.

Copies of the merger agreement were delivered to the directors, but too late for study before or during the meeting. The meeting began with a 20-minute oral presentation by chairman Van Gorkom. The chief financial officer then described how he had arrived at the $55 figure. He stated that it was not an indication of a fair price, only a workable number. Trans Union's president stated that he thought the proposed merger was a good deal.

The board approved the merger after a two-hour meeting. Board members later testified that they had insisted that the merger agreement be amended to ensure that the company was free to consider other bids before the closing; however, neither the board minutes nor merger documents reflected this clearly.

Plaintiff Smith sued to challenge the board's action, arguing that the merger price was too low. The Delaware Court of Chancery held that, given the premium over the

Case 21.1 continues

Case 21.1 continued

market value of Trans Union stock, the business acumen of the board members, and the effect on the merger price of the prospect of other bids, the board was adequately informed and did not act recklessly in approving the Pritzker deal. In making its findings, the court relied in part upon actions taken by the board after the board meeting on September 20, 1980, that were intended to cure defects in the directors' initial level of knowledge.

ISSUE PRESENTED   Were directors who accepted and submitted to the shareholders a proposed cash merger without determining the intrinsic value of the company grossly negligent in failing to inform themselves adequately before making their decision?

SUMMARY OF OPINION   The Delaware Supreme Court reversed the lower court and held that the directors were grossly negligent in failing to reach a properly informed decision. They were not protected by the business judgment rule even though there were no allegations of bad faith, fraud, or conflict of interest. The court found that the directors could not reasonably base their decision on the inadequate information presented to the board. They should have independently valued the company.

The court found that the directors had inadequate information as to (1) the role of Van Gorkom, Trans Union's chairman and chief executive officer, in initiating the transaction; (2) the basis for the proposed stock purchase price of $55 per share; and, most importantly, (3) the intrinsic value of Trans Union, as opposed to its current and historical stock price. The court held that in the absence of any apparent crisis or emergency, it was grossly negligent for the directors to approve the merger after a two-hour meeting, with eight of the ten directors having received no prior notice of the proposed merger.

The court stated:

> None of the directors, management or outside, were investment bankers or financial analysts. Yet the board did not consider recessing the meeting until a later hour that day (or requesting an extension of Pritzker's Sunday evening deadline) to give it time to elicit more information as to the sufficiency of the offer, either from inside management (in particular Romans) or from Trans Union's own investment banker, Salomon Brothers, whose Chicago specialist in mergers and acquisitions was known to the Board and familiar with Trans Union's affairs.
>
> Thus, the record compels the conclusion that on September 20 the Board lacked valuation information adequate to reach an informed business judgment as to the fairness of $55 per share for sale of the Company.

The court additionally held that the directors' subsequent efforts to find a bidder willing to pay more than Pritzker were inadequate to cure the infirmities of their uninformed exercise of judgment.

The court rejected the directors' argument that they properly relied on the officers' reports presented at the board meeting. The court stated that a pertinent report may be relied on in good faith, but not blindly. In the circumstances, the directors were duty bound to make reasonable inquiry of Van Gorkom, the chief executive officer, and Romans, the chief financial officer. If they had done so, the inadequacy of those officers' reports would have been apparent. Van Gorkom's summary of the terms of the deal was inadequate because he had not reviewed the merger documents and was

Case 21.1 continues

Case 21.1 continued

basically uninformed as to essential terms. (Indeed, he had signed the merger agreement at the opening of the Chicago Lyric Opera without first reading it.) Romans's report on price was inadequate because it was not a valuation study, just a cash flow–cash feasibility study.

The court also held that the mere fact that a substantial premium over the market price was being offered did not justify board approval of the merger. According to the court, a premium may be one reason to approve a merger, but sound information as to the company's intrinsic value is required to assess the fairness of an offer. In this case, there was no attempt to determine the company's intrinsic value.

RESULT   The Delaware Supreme Court found that the Trans Union directors were grossly negligent in making an uninformed decision regarding the proposed merger agreement. The case was remanded to the Delaware Court of Chancery for an evidentiary hearing to determine the fair value of the shares based on Trans Union's intrinsic value on September 20, 1980, the day of the board's meeting in which the Pritzker offer was considered. If that value was found by the chancellor to be higher than $55 per share, the directors would be liable for the difference.

COMMENTS   The case was settled for $23.5 million—$13.5 million in excess of the directors' liability insurance coverage. Although the purchasers, the Pritzker family, ultimately paid the amount by which the settlement exceeded the directors' coverage, they were not legally obligated to do so.

Smith v. Van Gorkom was one of the most highly debated corporate law cases ever decided. Three years after the decision, one of the key defendants—Trans Union's chief executive officer, Jerome W. Van Gorkom—wrote an article giving the defendants' side of the story. The article makes it clear that the defendants and the Delaware Supreme Court had very different views about what the directors actually did and what their options really were.

In his article, Van Gorkom stated that at the September 20 meeting:

> The directors, all broadly experienced executives, realized that an all-cash offer with a premium of almost 50 percent represented an unusual opportunity for the shareholders. They also knew, however, that $55 might not be the highest price obtainable. At the meeting, therefore, there was considerable discussion about seeking an outside "fairness opinion" that might shed further light on the ultimate value of the company.[2]

2. J. W. Van Gorkom, *Van Gorkom's Response: The Defendant's Side of the Trans Union Case*, reprinted in MERGERS & ACQUISITIONS, Jan./Feb. 1988. Excerpts reprinted by permission.

Furthermore, Van Gorkom explained that:

> Acceptance of the offer was not a decision by the directors that the company should be sold for $55 a share. The acceptance was the only mechanism by which the offer could be preserved for the shareholders. *They* would make the ultimate decision as to the fairness of the price and they would do so only after the free market had had ample time in which to determine if $55 was the top value obtainable. The market's opinion would be definitive and worth infinitely more to the shareholders than any theoretical evaluation opinion that the directors could obtain in 39 hours or even longer. On this reasoning the offer was accepted.

Following the meeting, the Trans Union directors hired Salomon Brothers to conduct an intensive search for a higher bidder. In addition, Van Gorkom stated that once the $55 offer became a matter of public knowledge, an auction occurred in the market with Trans Union's stock sometimes selling above $56 on the New York Stock Exchange. After three months of the intensive search and the public auction, no higher bid was ever received. "[T]he market had proven beyond a shadow of a doubt that $55 was the highest price obtainable."

Because of the above factors, Van Gorkom believes that he and the other Trans Union directors wholeheartedly fulfilled their fiduciary obligations. He concludes that their actions clearly should have been protected under the business judgment rule.

Although the holding in *Van Gorkom* seems clear, sometimes boards of directors still do not follow the rules regarding their duties to make informed decisions about the sale of the corporation. For example, in *Cede & Co. v. Technicolor, Inc.*,[3] the Delaware Supreme Court found at least five problems with the Technicolor board's exercise of due care in approving a merger agreement whereby Technicolor was acquired by MacAndrews & Forbes Group (a company controlled by Ronald O. Perelman). The five problems identified by the court were (1) the agreement was not preceded by a prudent search for alternatives; (2) given the terms of the merger and the circumstances, the directors had no reasonable basis to assume that a better offer from a third party could be expected to be made following the agreement's signing; (3) although the buyer's approach had been discussed with several of the directors before the meeting, most of the directors had little or no knowledge of an impending sale of the company until they arrived at the meeting, and only a few of them had any knowledge of the terms of the sale and of the required side agreements; (4) the intended buyer did, probably, effectively lock up the transaction before the meeting when he acquired rights to buy certain shares from two of the largest shareholders of Technicolor; and (5) the board did not satisfy its obligation to take reasonable steps to be adequately informed before it authorized the execution of the merger agreement.

Reliability of Officers' Reports

As underscored by *Van Gorkom*, not every statement of an officer can be relied on in good faith, and no statement is entitled to blind reliance. The passivity of the Trans Union directors in *Van Gorkom* unquestionably influenced the court's finding of gross negligence. When the chief financial officer, Romans, told the board that the $55 figure was within a "fair price range" for a leveraged buyout,

> no director sought any further information from Romans. No director asked him why he put $55 at the bottom of his range. No director asked Romans for any details as to his study, the reason why it had been undertaken or its depth. No director asked to see the study;

and no director asked Romans whether Trans Union's finance department could do a fairness study within the remaining 36-hour period available under the Pritzker offer.... [If he had been asked,] Romans would have presumably ... informed the Board of his view, and the widespread view of Senior Management, that the timing of the offer was wrong and the offer inadequate.[4]

When the CEO, Van Gorkom, told the board that $55 per share was fair, no questions were asked.

> The Board thereby failed to discover that Van Gorkom had suggested the $55 price to [the bidder] Pritzker and, most crucially, that Van Gorkom had arrived at the $55 figure based on calculations designed solely to determine the feasibility of a leveraged buy-out. No questions were raised either as to the tax implications of a cash-out merger or how the price for the one million share option granted Pritzker was calculated.[5]

Reliability of Experts' Reports

Two principles regarding the use of experts' reports emerge from the cases. First, a board should engage a reputable investment banking firm, aided if necessary by an outside appraiser, (1) to prepare a valuation study, and (2) to give a written opinion as to the financial fairness of the transaction and of any related purchase of assets or options.

Second, directors have a duty to pursue reasonable inquiry and to exercise reasonable oversight in connection with their engagement of investment bankers and other advisors. A conclusory fairness opinion (that is, an opinion that merely states a conclusion without giving the factual grounds for that conclusion) of an investment banker, however expert, is not a sufficient basis for a board decision, particularly if the investment banker's conclusion is questionable in light of other information known to the directors. As the directors of SCM Corporation learned in *Hanson Trust PLC v. ML SCM Acquisition, Inc.*,[6] an expert's opinion must be in writing and be reasoned.

SCM was the subject of a hostile tender offer by a British conglomerate, Hanson Trust PLC. SCM's board negotiated a friendly management leveraged buyout led by "white knight" Merrill Lynch. As part of this agreement, SCM granted Merrill Lynch an *asset lock-up option* to purchase two divisions of SCM, considered SCM's key assets or *crown jewels*. The option was exercisable if

---

3. 634 A.2d 345 (Del. 1993).

4. Smith v. Van Gorkom, 488 A.2d 858, 876 (Del. 1985).

5. *Id.*

6. 781 F.2d 264 (2d Cir. 1986).

Merrill Lynch were not successful in acquiring control of SCM. A lock-up option is a kind of consolation prize for the loser in a bidding war; depending on how it is priced, a lock-up option can have the effect of deterring other bids.

SCM's investment banker, Goldman Sachs, issued a written fairness opinion on the overall deal, stating that the sale of SCM to Merrill Lynch was fair to the shareholders of SCM from a financial point of view. A partner at Goldman Sachs also orally advised SCM's directors that the option prices were "within the range of fair value." However, the directors did not inquire what the range of fair value was or how it was calculated. The directors had been advised by preeminent outside counsel that the decision whether to approve the lock-up was within the discretion of the board in exercising its business judgment. Further, white knight Merrill Lynch had represented in negotiations that it would not proceed with its leveraged buyout offer without the lock-up. Notwithstanding these factors and the directors' own working knowledge of the company, the U.S. Court of Appeals for the Second Circuit held that the SCM directors' "paucity of information" and "their swiftness of decision-making" strongly suggested a breach of the duty of care.

Note that the SCM board did receive a written fairness opinion on the sale of SCM to Merrill Lynch. However, it received only an off-the-cuff oral opinion on the fairness of the prices at which two divisions were to be sold to Merrill Lynch under the lock-up option. Unfortunately for the directors, the banker had not in fact calculated the fair value of the two divisions. In relying on his opinion, therefore, the board was not adequately informed.

The Second Circuit contrasted the actions of the SCM directors with what the Delaware Supreme Court referred to as the grossly negligent actions of the directors in *Van Gorkom* and with the commendable actions of the directors in another case, *Treadway Companies, Inc. v. Care Corp.*[7] (Treadway, a New Jersey corporation that operated bowling alleys and motor inns, faced a hostile takeover attempt by Care Corporation, which operated health care and recreational facilities, including bowling alleys.) The court stated:

> [T]he SCM directors failed to take many of the affirmative directorial steps that underlie the finding of due care

in *Treadway* on which the district court herein relied. In *Treadway*, the directors "armed" their bankers with financial questions to evaluate; they requested balance sheets; they adjourned deliberations for one week to consider the requisitioned advice; and they conditioned approval of the deal on the securing of a fairness opinion from their bankers.

As in the case of officers' reports, blind reliance on the reports of experts creates a risk that the directors will not receive the protection of the business judgment rule.

Investment Banker's Fee Structure   Another principle, noted in the commentaries but yet to emerge from the case law, is that directors should exercise care to ensure that the terms of the investment banker's compensation do not impair its independence. Certain compensation schemes are difficult to reconcile with the best interests of the corporation and its shareholders, and should therefore be avoided.

For example, the investment banker may be promised a flat fee if the raider is successful at its initial price or, if a higher price is obtained, a percentage of that price (the percentage fee being larger than the flat fee). In some cases, the investment banker is to receive a flat fee plus a percentage of the difference between the bidder's initial price and the price ultimately received by the shareholders. In still others, the investment banker is to receive expenses plus a straight percentage of the sale price. Directors need to recognize that some of these arrangements create a financial incentive for the investment banker to close a transaction at any price, or at a price that is any amount higher (even if by only one cent) than the original offer. The fee structure that is most favorable for the target company is one that aligns the incentives of the investment banker with those of the company's shareholders.

Reasonable Supervision

As fiduciaries, directors have a responsibility to exercise reasonable supervision over corporate operations. Because the prescribed role of the corporate director is to establish broad policies and then rely on managers to implement them, the question of what constitutes reasonable supervision is necessarily one of degree. The outcome in reasonable supervision cases depends heavily on particular facts. The Delaware Court of Chancery refined and clarified the reasonable supervision doctrine in the following case.

---

7. 638 F.2d 357 (2d Cir. 1980).

A CASE IN POINT	SUMMARY

CASE 21.2
IN RE CAREMARK INT'L
DERIVATIVE LITIGATION
Court of Chancery
of Delaware
698 A.2d 959
(Del. Ch. 1996).

FACTS   The parties in this shareholder derivative action petitioned the court to approve as fair and reasonable a proposed settlement of their case. The suit involved claims that the members of Caremark's board of directors breached their fiduciary duty of care to Caremark in connection with alleged violations by Caremark employees of federal and state laws and regulations applicable to health-care providers.

As a result of the alleged violations, Caremark was subject to an extensive four-year investigation by the Department of Health and Human Services and the Department of Justice. In 1994, Caremark was charged in an indictment with multiple felonies. It thereafter entered into a number of plea agreements in which it agreed to pay civil and criminal fines and make payments reimbursements to various private and public parties. In all, Caremark was required to make payments totaling approximately $250 million.

When the shareholder derivative suit was filed in 1994, the plaintiff initially sought to recover these losses from the individual members of the Caremark board of directors. The complaint charged that the directors allowed a situation to develop and continue that exposed the corporation to enormous legal liability and, in so doing, they violated a duty to be active monitors of corporate performance. The complaint did not charge either director self-dealing or the breach of the duty of loyalty. The proposed settlement included no payment by individual board members, but rather outlined a series of procedures the company would implement to promote future compliance with applicable laws and regulations.

ISSUE PRESENTED   What is the scope of a director's duty to exercise reasonable supervision over corporate operations?

SUMMARY OF OPINION   The Delaware Chancery Court began by noting that director liability for a breach of the duty to exercise appropriate attention may, in theory, arise in two distinct contexts. First, such liability may follow from a board decision that results in a loss because that decision was ill advised or negligent. Second, liability to the corporation for a loss may arise from an unconsidered failure of the board to act in circumstances in which due attention would, arguably, have prevented the loss.

The court explained that compliance with a director's duty of care can never appropriately be judicially determined by reference solely to the content of the board decision that led to a corporate loss; the court must always also consider the good faith or rationality of the process employed. Even if a judge or jury considering the matter after the fact believes a decision is substantively wrong (or degrees of wrong extending from "stupid" to "egregious" or "irrational"), this provides no ground for director liability, as long as the court determines that the process employed was either rational or employed in a good faith effort to advance corporate interests. The court reasoned that to employ a different rule—one that permitted an objective evaluation of the decision—would expose directors to substantive second guessing by ill-equipped judges or juries, which would, in the long-run, be injurious to investor interests. Thus, the business judgment rule is process oriented and informed by a deep respect for all good faith board decisions.

Case 21.2 continues

Case 21.2 continued

The second class of cases involving potential director liability for inattention arises when a loss eventuates not from a decision but from unconsidered inaction. Most of the decisions that a corporation, acting through its human agents, makes are, of course, not the subject of director attention. Legally, the board itself will be required only to authorize the most significant corporate acts or transactions: mergers, changes in capital structure, fundamental changes in business, appointment and compensation of the CEO, and the like. However, ordinary business decisions that are made by officers and employees deeper in the interior of the organization can vitally affect the welfare of the corporation and its ability to achieve its various strategic and financial goals. This raises the question: What is the board's responsibility with respect to the organization and monitoring of the enterprise to ensure that the corporation functions within the law to achieve its purposes?

The court noted an increasing tendency, especially under federal law, to employ the criminal law to ensure corporate compliance with external legal requirements, including environmental, financial, employee, and product safety, as well as assorted other health and safety regulations. The federal Organizational Sentencing Guidelines offer powerful incentives for corporations to have in place compliance programs to detect violations of law; to promptly report violations to appropriate public officials when discovered; and to take prompt, voluntary remedial efforts.

In light of these developments, the court held that directors cannot satisfy their obligation to be reasonably informed concerning the corporation unless they assure themselves that appropriate information and reporting systems exist in the organization. These systems must be reasonably designed to provide to senior management and to the board itself timely and accurate information sufficient to allow management and the board to reach informed judgments concerning both the corporation's compliance with law and its business performance.

The level of detail that is appropriate for such an information system is a question of business judgment. The court acknowledged that no rationally designed information and reporting system will remove the possibility that the corporation will violate laws or regulations. But the board is required to exercise a good faith judgment that the corporation's information and reporting system is in concept and design adequate to assure the board that appropriate information will come to its attention in a timely manner as a matter of ordinary operations, so that it may satisfy its responsibility.

Thus, the court ruled that a director's obligation includes a duty to attempt in good faith to ensure that there is a corporate information and reporting system that the board concludes is adequate. Failure to do so under certain circumstances may, in theory at least, render a director liable for losses cause by noncompliance with applicable legal standards.

RESULT   The court concluded that the settlement was fair and reasonable and, therefore, approved it.

COMMENTS   The court noted that if the shareholders are not satisfied with the informed good faith judgment of the directors, their recourse is to elect different directors.

The Securities and Exchange Commission issued a release in 1997 emphasizing the affirmative responsibility of officers and directors under the federal securities laws to ensure the accuracy and completeness of public company filings with the SEC, such as annual and quarterly reports and proxy statements.[8] They are required to conduct a full and informed review of the information contained in the final draft of the filings. If an officer or director knows or should have known about an inaccuracy in a proposed filing, he or she has an obligation to correct it. An officer or director may rely on the company's procedures for determining what disclosure

is required only if he or she has a reasonable basis for believing that those procedures are effective and have resulted in full consideration of those issues.

If a director or officer is aware of facts that might have to be disclosed, he or she must go beyond the established procedures to inquire into the reasons for nondisclosure of that information. Officers and directors cannot blindly rely on legal counsel's conclusions about the need for disclosure if they are aware of facts that seem to suggest that disclosure is required. They must then discuss the issue specifically with disclosure counsel, telling counsel exactly what they know and asking specifically whether disclosure is required. If they are not satisfied with the answers provided, they should insist that the documents be revised before they are filed with the SEC.

---

8. Report of Investigation Pursuant to Section 21(a) of the Securities Exchange Act of 1934 concerning the Conduct of Certain Former Officers and Directors of W. R. Grace & Co., Exchange Act Release No. 39157 (Sept. 30, 1997).

VIEW FROM CYBERSPACE

DIRECTORS FACE Y2K

The millenium bug—the software crisis that promises to ring in the new millenium when computers programmed with just a two-digit date field (e.g., 00 for 1900) will think the year is 1900 not 2000 and therefore not recognize any dates in the 21st century— could pose significant liability problems for corporate directors. Plaintiff's lawyers are already exploring the possibility of suing directors for breach of fiduciary duty in the event that a crisis does occur.[a] Such actions would be based on the theory that directors failed to adequately monitor the operations of the company and, thus, breached their duty of care. The claim would be that the Year 2000 (Y2K) problem should have been anticipated and corrected before 2000.

If directors completely ignore the potential for a Year 2000 problem and a costly crisis within their company in fact occurs, a breach of duty of care suit would have a fair chance of success.[b] However, directors can take steps to significantly reduce their exposure to liability in the face of a millenium bug. Directors should examine how well the corporate computer system is

equipped to deal with Year 2000 issues, ideally hearing presentations from the appropriate officers and employees and, perhaps, outside consultants. If the board makes a reasonable decision based on such presentations—either to take additional remedial action or that the problem has been adequately addressed—then future actions based on directors' failure to monitor will be unlikely to succeed.[c]

In addition, the Securities and Exchange Commission requires publicly held companies to disclose to shareholders the costs of addressing the Y2K problem if those costs constitute a material event or uncertainty that is reasonably likely to affect future financial results.[d]

---

a. Dennis J. Block & Stephen A. Radin, *Year 2000 Director Liability Issues, Part I*, N.Y.L.J., Jan. 13, 1998, at 1.

b. *Id.*

c. *Id. See also* Juli Wilson Marshall, *Cyber Esq: Turning Points*, L.A. DAILY J., Feb. 26, 1998.

d. *Companies Take Variety of Approaches to Disclosing Y2K Problems to Investors*, 66 U.S.L.W. 2339 (Dec. 9, 1997).

Disinterested Decision

Even when the board makes an informed decision, the business judgment rule is not applicable if the directors have a financial or other personal interest in the transaction at issue. For example, if a board of inside directors (that is, directors who are also officers of the corporation) were setting executive compensation, they could be required to prove to a court that the transaction was fair and reasonable. To be disinterested in the transaction normally means that the directors can neither have an interest on either side of the transaction nor expect to derive any personal financial benefit from the transaction (other than benefits that accrue to all shareholders of the corporation, which are not considered self-dealing).

One or more individual directors may have an interest in the transaction, provided it is approved by a majority of the disinterested directors. However, if the board delegates too much of its authority or is too much influenced by an interested party, then the entire board may be tainted with that individual's personal motivations and lose the protection of the business judgment rule.

In some jurisdictions, a relevant factor in determining whether a board is disinterested is whether the majority of the board consists of outside directors. The fact that outside directors receive directors' fees but not salaries is viewed as heightening the likelihood that the directors were not motivated by personal interest.

Application of these rules in the context of takeovers, mergers, and acquisitions is discussed later in this chapter.

Statutory Limitations on Directors' Liability for Breach of Duty of Care

Cases such as *Van Gorkom* had a devastating impact on the market for directors' and officers' liability insurance and on the availability of qualified outside directors. In response, Delaware adopted legislation in 1986 to allow shareholders to limit the monetary liability of directors for breaches of the duty of care in any suit brought by the corporation or in a *shareholder derivative suit*, that is, a suit by a shareholder on behalf of the corporation. Most other states followed suit. Most statutes require that the limitation be contained in the original articles of incorporation or in an amendment approved by a majority of the shareholders.

The statutes do not affect directors' liability for suits brought by third parties; they merely allow the shareholders to agree that, under certain circumstances, they will not seek monetary recovery against the directors. The directors' liability for breach of the duty of loyalty may not be limited. Also, most states do not allow officers to be exonerated from liability for breach of the duty of care or the duty of loyalty.

Delaware's Statute

Section 102(b)(7) of the Delaware Corporation Code permits the certificate of incorporation to include a provision limiting or eliminating the personal liability of directors to the corporation or to its shareholders for monetary damages for breach of fiduciary duty. (Delaware law is especially relevant because many large public companies are incorporated there.) Such a provision, however, cannot eliminate or limit the liability of a director (1) for any breach of the directors' duty of loyalty to the corporation or its shareholders; (2) for acts or omissions not in good faith or that involve intentional misconduct or knowing violation of law; (3) for unlawful payments of dividends or stock purchases; or (4) for any transaction for which the director derived an improper personal benefit.

California's Statute

Section 204(a)(10) of the California Corporation Code, which applies to corporations organized under California law, is more restrictive. In addition to the four exceptions contained in the Delaware statute, California prohibits elimination or limitation of director liability for (1) acts or omissions that show a reckless disregard for the director's duty to the corporation or its shareholders in circumstances in which the director was aware, or should have been aware, of a risk of serious injury to the corporation or its shareholders; and (2) an unexcused pattern of inattention that amounts to an abdication of the director's duties to the corporation or its shareholders.

 Duty of Loyalty

To comply with their duty of loyalty, directors and managers must subordinate their own interests to those of

"All in favor of a cap on our liability?"

the corporation and its shareholders. As a result, when a shareholder attacks a transaction in which managers or directors are engaged in self-dealing or have a self-interest other than that of corporate fiduciary, courts will closely review the merits of the deal. Traditionally, such a transaction has been voidable unless its proponents could show it was fair and reasonable to the corporation.

The Delaware Supreme Court in *Mills Acquisition Co. v. Macmillan, Inc.*[9] reiterated the duty that corporate directors have to demonstrate their utmost good faith and fairness in transactions in which they possess a financial, business, or other personal interest that is not shared by the corporation or all shareholders generally. In *Mills*, the court struck down the asset lock-up option granted to a white knight by the target corporation as part of a merger agreement was deemed invalid. The other participant in the auction had indicated its intent to top any offer made by the white knight. Under the agreement between the target and the white knight, target management would receive different consideration from that given the public.

Therefore, the lock-up option, which had the effect of terminating any further bidding, did not enhance general shareholder interests. Furthermore, the court held that independent members of the corporation's board of directors should have attempted to negotiate alternative bids for the corporate assets before they granted any bidder a lock-up option intended to end the active auction.

Corporate Opportunities

One central corollary of the fiduciary duty of loyalty is that officers and directors may not take personal advantage of a business opportunity that rightfully belongs to the corporation. This is known as the *corporate opportunity doctrine*. For example, suppose a copper-mining corporation is actively looking for mining sites; if an officer of the corporation learns of an attractive site in the course of his business for the corporation, he may not buy it for himself. If he attempted to do so, a shareholder could block the sale or impose a *constructive trust* on any profits he makes from the acquisition, that is, force him to hold such profits for the benefit of the corporation and pay them over to the corporation on request.

---

9. 559 A.2d 1261 (Del. 1989).

The courts have devised several tests for determining whether an opportunity belongs to a corporation. Perhaps the most widely used is the *line-of-business test.* Under this test, if an officer, director, or controlling shareholder learns of an opportunity in the course of his or her business for the corporation and the opportunity is in the corporation's line of business, a court will not permit the officer, director, or controlling shareholder to keep the opportunity for himself or herself.

For example, the Delaware Supreme Court ruled that the president and director of Loft, Inc., a company engaged in the manufacturing of candies, syrups, beverages, and foodstuffs, could not set up a new corporation to acquire the secret formula and trademarks of Pepsi Cola.[10] He had unsuccessfully sought a volume discount for Loft's purchases of syrup from Coca-Cola Company and was contemplating substituting Pepsi for Coke.

If the officer or director develops an idea on company time using company resources, then a court will be more likely to find a breach of fiduciary duty if the officer or director then leaves to pursue the idea. If the officer or director has signed an assignment of inventions, then the idea usually will belong to the company under the terms of that agreement. Even absent such an agreement, use of company time or resources may restrict the ability of the officer or director to define the line of business narrowly.

For example, the Georgia Court of Appeals estopped three ex-officers of the Atlanta-based commuter airline Metro Express who had left to form a company offering commuter services in Memphis from claiming that Metro Express was incorporated solely to provide services from the Atlanta hub and was therefore not interested in the Memphis route.[11] They had developed the idea on company time and using company resources.

Other courts have considered (1) whether it would be fair for the fiduciary to keep the opportunity, (2) whether the corporation has an expectancy or interest growing out of an existing right in the opportunity, or (3) whether the interference by the fiduciary will hinder the corporation's purposes. Because different states apply different tests, it is important for a corporate fiduciary to consult local counsel if there is any question of the fiduciary's actions interfering with a corporate opportunity.

The following case dealt with the issue of whether failure to disclose a corporate opportunity to the directors automatically results in liability.

10. Guth v. Loft, Inc., 5 A.2d 503 (Del. 1939).

11. Phoenix Airline Servs., Inc. v. Metro Airlines, Inc., 403 S.E.2d 832 (Ga. Ct. App. 1991).

A CASE IN POINT   SUMMARY

CASE 21.3
OSTROWSKI v. AVERY
Supreme Court
of Connecticut
703 A.2d 117 (Conn. 1997).

FACTS Avery Abrasives, Inc. was a manufacturer of large abrasive cutting wheels, particularly wheels 20 inches or more in diameter. Craig Avery was the company's vice-president of manufacturing and a director. Michael Passaro was the finishing supervisor.

Avery and Passaro became convinced that there was a market for small cutting wheels of less than four inches in diameter. Avery asked his father (who was the president, CEO, and controlling shareholder of Avery Abrasives) whether he and Passaro could pursue this opportunity and retain their jobs at Avery Abrasives. Avery's father consented. Then, without notifying the board or minority shareholders of Avery Abrasives, Avery and Passaro set up their own company, ISW, to manufacture small cutting wheels.

The minority shareholders of Avery Abrasives sued Avery and Passaro, claiming that their creation of ISW usurped a corporate opportunity to which Avery Abrasives was rightly entitled.

Case 21.3 continues

Case 21.3 continued

ISSUE PRESENTED If an officer or director of a corporation personally takes advantage of a corporate opportunity, will prior disclosure of that opportunity serve as a defense to liability? Will lack of disclosure automatically result in liability?

SUMMARY OF OPINION The Connecticut Supreme Court first determined that (1) Avery and Passaro owed fiduciary duties to Avery Abrasives and its shareholders, and (2) the chance to develop small cutting wheels constituted a "corporate opportunity" for Avery Abrasives. The court then turned to the central question in its opinion: "What role does disclosure to other directors and shareholders play in determining whether a corporate opportunity was in fact usurped?"

The court noted that the law of corporate opportunity contemplates that disclosure will be made to disinterested directors, who then are given an opportunity to accept or reject the opportunity. Adequate disclosure of a corporate opportunity will provide defendants with a safe harbor from liability for breach of fiduciary duty. But Avery and Passaro had apparently failed to give adequate notice. Their disclosure was to Avery's father, who could not be considered disinterested. Moreover, the board as a whole (including its disinterested directors) was not informed of the opportunity until after Avery and Passaro had established ISW.

However, the court held that, under Connecticut law, failure to disclose would not give rise to automatic liability. In the absence of adequate disclosure, a corporate fiduciary could avoid liability only if he or she could prove by clear and convincing evidence that exploitation of a corporate opportunity did not damage the corporation. The court declined to apply this rule to the facts of Avery and Passaro's case, instead leaving the issue to be addressed by the trial court on remand.

RESULT The case was remanded to trial court, which was ordered to determine whether Avery and Passaro either (1) made a disclosure sufficient to avail themselves of the safe harbor from liability for breach of fiduciary duty, or (2) could establish by clear and convincing evidence that their conduct did not harm Avery Abrasives. If they could satisfy either of these affirmative defenses, the shareholders' claims would be dismissed.

The Delaware Supreme Court recently held that corporate officers and directors who usurp a corporate opportunity must disgorge to the corporation any gains obtained through their breach of loyalty, even though they, acting in their capacity as controlling shareholders, could have prevented the corporation from taking advantage of the opportunity. In *Thorpe v. CERBCO Inc.*,[12] two brothers were officers, directors, and controlling shareholders of CERBCO. When a potential acquiror brought up the possibility of buying one of CERBCO's subsidiaries, the brothers instead proposed to sell their own shares to the acquiror. The court found that, because the brothers (in their capacity as shareholders) could have blocked every viable sale of the subsidiary, CERBCO was not in fact able to take advantage of the opportunity. Thus, CERBCO suffered no damages as a result of this lost opportunity because there was zero probability of the acquisition occurring (due to the brothers' lawful right to vote against it). Nevertheless, the brothers were fiduciaries of CERBCO and, as such, had the duty to present the acquisition opportunity to CERBCO. The court held that the brothers were not entitled to the profit gained by their breach of this duty. As a result, they were not entitled to keep the profit they had made on the sale of their stock to the potential acquiror of CERBCO's subsidiary.

---

12. 703 A.2d 645 (Del. 1997).

Executive Compensation

One of the most controversial issues in corporate governance today is the high level of executive compensation, which can add up to tens or hundreds of millions of dollars for chief executive officers with a substantial number of stock options. Institutional investors stress the need for pay for performance. This is often done with stock options, which are usually exercisable at the market price at the time of grant for up to ten years.

Options are designed to align the incentives of the management and the shareholders—if the stock price goes up, the executive can exercise the option and sell his or her stock at a premium over the exercise price. However, in a rising stock market, such as the bull market in the mid-to-late-1990s, an executive could be rewarded not for company-specific performance but simply because the broader market had gone up—the rising-tide-lifts-all-boats phenomenon.

Worse yet, sometimes the company's stock price goes down and drops below the exercise price; so the board agrees to re-price the options, that is, make them exercisable at the lower price. With re-pricing, the executive can earn additional compensation even though all the shareholders have lost money.

To date, the SEC and institutional investors have sought to address the issue of executive compensation through (1) disclosure of executive compensation and company performance compared to its peer group to shareholders in the proxy statement for the election of directors, (2) the establishment of compensation committees consisting solely of independent directors, and (3) the adoption of other measures designed to improve corporate governance.[13] Popular ideas include separating the role of CEO and chair (or appointing an independent director as lead director)[14] and having a majority of the board independent of management.

As the "Inside Story" dealing with Walt Disney Company explains, however, sometimes a company may do very well and reward its shareholders with a high stock price even though executive compensation is very high and the board is not very independent. This raises the proverbial "If it ain't broke, don't fix it." To which institutional investors respond, it may not be broken yet but it will break in the future, with often disastrous results, unless a proper governance structure is in place before there is a crisis (such as the death of the CEO with no clear succession plan for training and selecting his or her successor).

 ## Duties in the Context of Takeovers, Mergers, and Acquisitions

In deciding whether to sell a company, the courts have held that directors should consider seven key factors: (1) the company's intrinsic value, (2) nonprice considerations, (3) the reliability of officers' reports to the board, (4) the appropriateness of delegating negotiating authority to management, (5) the reliability of experts' reports, (6) the investment banker's fee structure, and (7) the reasonableness of any defensive tactics. As explained earlier, the directors must act in good faith and be adequately informed.

The Company's Intrinsic Value

The ability to make an informed decision as to the acceptability of a proposed buyout price requires knowledge of the company's intrinsic value. Determining intrinsic value entails more than an assessment of the premium of the offering price over the market price per share of the company's stock. When, as in *Van Gorkom*, it is believed that the market has consistently undervalued the company's stock, evaluating the offered price by comparing it with the market price is "faulty, indeed fallacious."

Thus, the directors must not only assess the adequacy of the premium and how the premium compares with that paid in other takeovers in the same or similar industries; they must also assess the intrinsic or fair value of the company (or division) as a going concern and on a liquidation basis.

---

13. *See, e.g., The California Public Employees Retirement System Principles of Corporate Governance for U.S. Companies*, available at <http://www.calpers.ca.gov/site/invest.htm#CORPORATE>.

14. *See, e.g.*, Constance E. Bagley & Richard H. Koppes, *Leader of the Pack: A Proposal for Disclosure of Board Leadership Structure*, 34 SAN DIEGO L. REV. 149 (1997).

Practitioners have read *Van Gorkom* as virtually mandating participation by an investment banker if directors are to avoid personal liability. However, the *Van Gorkom* court expressly disclaimed such an intention:

> We do not imply that an outside valuation study is essential to support an informed business judgment; nor do we state that fairness opinions by independent investment bankers are required as a matter of law. Often insiders familiar with the business of a going concern are in a better position than are outsiders to gather relevant information; and under appropriate circumstances, such directors may be fully protected in relying in good faith upon the valuation reports of their management.[15]

Hence one commentator's quip that it would be "an overstatement to consider the *Van Gorkom* case as the Investment Bankers' Relief Act of 1985."

For all practical purposes, however, directors should look to both internal and external sources for guidance. The most reliable valuation information will consist of financial data supplied by management and evaluated by investment bankers.

The *Hanson Trust* decision makes it clear, however, that the mere presence of investment bankers in the target's boardroom will not shield its directors from personal liability. In that case, the Goldman Sachs partner's oral opinion that the option prices were "within the range of fair value" did not withstand the scrutiny of the Second Circuit on appeal.

Delegation of Negotiating Authority

If members of management are financial participants in the proposed transaction, the delegation of negotiation responsibilities to management or inside directors will expose the board to greater risks of liability. The Second Circuit observed in *Hanson Trust*:

> SCM's board delegated to management broad authority to work directly with Merrill to structure an LBO proposal, and then appears to have swiftly approved management's proposals. Such broad delegations of authority are not uncommon and generally are quite proper as conforming to the way that a Board acts in generating proposals for its own consideration. However, when management has a self-interest in consummating an LBO, standard post hoc review procedures may be insufficient. SCM's management and the Board's advisers presented the various agreements to the SCM directors more or less as faits accompli, which the Board quite hastily approved. In short, the Board appears to have failed to ensure that negotiations for alternative bids were conducted by those whose only loyalty was to the shareholders.[16]

Nonprice Considerations

In evaluating a buyout proposal, directors have a fiduciary duty to familiarize themselves with any material nonprice provisions of the proposed agreement. Directors are duty bound to consider separately whether such provisions are in the best interest of the company and its shareholders or, if not, whether the proposal as a whole, notwithstanding such provisions, is in the best interest of their constituencies.

In *Van Gorkom*, for example, several outside directors maintained that Pritzker's merger proposal was approved with the understanding that "if we got a better deal, we had a right to take it." The directors also asserted that they had "insisted" upon an amendment reserving to Trans Union the right to disclose proprietary information to competing bidders. However, the court found that the merger agreement reserved neither of these rights to Trans Union. In the court's view, the directors had "no rational basis" for asserting that their acceptance of Pritzker's offer was conditioned upon a market test of the offer or that Trans Union had a right to withdraw from the agreement in order to accept a higher bid.

Directors should therefore ensure not only that they correctly understand the nonprice provisions of a proposed merger agreement, but also that the provisions find their way into the definitive agreement. They should verify this by reading the documents prior to execution.

As indicated in *Unocal Corp. v. Mesa Petroleum Co.*[17] (discussed further following), when analyzing a takeover bid and its effect on the corporate enterprise,

---

15. Smith v. Van Gorkom, 488 A.2d 858, 876 (Del. 1985).

16. Hanson Trust PLC v. ML SCM Acquisition, Inc., 781 F.2d 264, 277 (2d Cir. 1986).
17. 493 A.2d 946 (Del. 1985) (Case 21.4).

the board may consider (1) the adequacy of the price offered; (2) the nature and timing of the offer; (3) questions of legality; (4) the impact on constituencies other than the shareholders, for example, creditors, customers, employees, and perhaps the community generally; (5) the risk of nonconsummation; (6) the quality of the securities being offered in exchange; and (7) the basic shareholder interests at stake.

Takeover Defenses

The business judgment rule creates a powerful presumption in favor of actions taken by the directors of a corporation. As noted earlier, however, the business judgment rule does not apply if the directors have an interest in the transaction being acted upon. If a hostile raider is successful, it is probably going to replace the company's management and board of directors as its first step after assuming control. A successful defense against the takeover has the effect of preserving the positions of current management and directors. Thus, the directors arguably have a personal interest whenever a board opposes a hostile takeover.

The following case established the principle that the business judgment rule applies to takeover defenses, provided the directors can show that there was a perceived threat to the corporation to which the defense was a reasonable response.

A CASE IN POINT	IN THE LANGUAGE OF THE COURT

CASE 21.4
UNOCAL CORP. v. MESA PETROLEUM CO.
Supreme Court of Delaware
493 A.2d 946 (Del. 1985).

FACTS   On April 8, 1985, Mesa Petroleum Co., the owner of approximately 13% of oil company Unocal's stock, commenced a two-tier "front-loaded" cash tender offer for 64 million shares, or approximately 37%, of Unocal's outstanding stock at a price of $54 per share. Mesa was controlled by T. Boone Pickens. The "back-end" was designed to eliminate the remaining publicly held shares by an exchange of securities purportedly worth $54 per share. Pursuant to a court order, however, Mesa issued a supplemental proxy statement to Unocal's shareholders disclosing that the securities offered in the second-step merger would be highly subordinated and that Unocal's capitalization would differ significantly from its present structure. Unocal rather aptly termed such securities "junk bonds."

Various defensive strategies were available to the board if it concluded that Mesa's two-step tender offer was inadequate and should be opposed. One of the devices was a discriminatory *self-tender* by Unocal for its own stock. Unocal's vice-president of finance and its assistant general counsel made a detailed presentation to

Case 21.4 continues

Case 21.4 continued

the Unocal board of the proposed terms of the exchange offer. A price range between $70 and $80 per share was considered; and, ultimately, the directors agreed upon $72. The board was also advised about the debt securities that would be issued (the cost of the proposal was estimated to be $6.1 to $6.6 billion) and about the necessity of placing restrictive covenants upon certain corporate activities until the obligations were paid.

Based on the advice of its investment bankers and the board's own deliberations, the directors unanimously approved the exchange offer. Their resolution provided that if Mesa acquired 64 million shares of Unocal stock through its own offer, Unocal would buy the remaining 49% of Unocal's outstanding shares for an exchange of debt securities having an aggregate par value of $72 per share. The board resolution also stated that the offer would be subject to conditions described to the board at the meeting or deemed necessary by Unocal's officers, including the exclusion of Mesa from the proposal.

Legal counsel advised that under Delaware law Mesa could be excluded only if the directors reasonably believed that exclusion served a valid corporate purpose. The directors' discussion centered on the objective of adequately compensating shareholders at the "back-end" of Mesa's proposal, which Mesa would finance with junk bonds. To include Mesa would defeat that goal, because under the proration aspect of the exchange offer, every Mesa share accepted by Unocal would displace one held by another shareholder. Further, if Mesa were permitted to tender to Unocal, the latter would in effect be financing Mesa's own inadequate proposal.

The Delaware Court of Chancery temporarily restrained Unocal from proceeding with the exchange offer unless it included Mesa. The trial court recognized that directors could oppose, and attempt to defeat, a hostile takeover that they considered adverse to the best interests of the corporation. However, the Delaware Court of Chancery decided that in a selective purchase of the company's stock, the corporation bears the burden of showing (1) a valid corporate purpose, and (2) that the transaction was fair to all of the shareholders, including those excluded. Unocal appealed.

ISSUE PRESENTED   Can a board of directors make a discriminatory stock exchange offer in order to protect a corporation and its shareholders from one of the corporation's own shareholders that is attempting to make a hostile takeover? What standard of judicial review applies to defensive tactics designed to thwart a hostile takeover?

OPINION   MOORE, J., writing for the Delaware Supreme Court:

. . . [I]t is now well established that in the acquisition of its shares a Delaware corporation may deal selectively with its stockholders, provided the directors have not acted out of a sole or primary purpose to entrench themselves in office.

. . .

When a board addresses a pending takeover bid it has an obligation to determine whether the offer is in the best interests of the corporation and its shareholders. In that respect a board's duty is no different from any other responsibility it shoulders, and its decisions should be no less entitled to the respect they otherwise would be

Case 21.4 continues

Case 21.4 continued

accorded in the realm of business judgment. There are, however, certain caveats to a proper exercise of this function. Because of the omnipresent specter that a board may be acting primarily in its own interests, rather than those of the corporation and its shareholders, there is an enhanced duty which calls for judicial examination at the threshold before the protections of the business judgment rule may be conferred.

. . .

. . . [D]irectors must show that they had reasonable grounds for believing that a danger to corporate policy and effectiveness existed because of another person's stock ownership. However, they satisfy that burden "by showing good faith and reasonable investigation. . . ."[18] Furthermore, such proof is materially enhanced, as here, by the approval of a board comprised of a majority of outside independent directors who have acted in accordance with the foregoing standards.

IV.

A.

In the board's exercise of corporate power to forestall a takeover bid our analysis begins with the basic principle that corporate directors have a fiduciary duty to act in the best interests of the corporation's stockholders. As we have noted, their duty of care extends to protecting the corporation and its owners from perceived harm whether a threat originates from third parties or other shareholders. But such powers are not absolute. A corporation does not have unbridled discretion to defeat any perceived threat by any Draconian means available.

The restriction placed upon a selective stock repurchase is that the directors may not have acted solely or primarily out of a desire to perpetuate themselves in office. . . . [This] is designed to ensure that a defensive measure to thwart or impede a takeover is indeed motivated by a good faith concern for the welfare of the corporation and its stockholders, which in all circumstances must be free of any fraud or other misconduct. . . .

B.

A further aspect is the element of balance. If a defensive measure is to come within the ambit of the business judgment rule, it must be reasonable in relation to the threat posed. This entails an analysis by the directors of the nature of the takeover bid and its effect on the corporate enterprise. Examples of such concerns may include: inadequacy of the price offered, nature and timing of the offer, questions of illegality, the impact on "constituencies" other than shareholders (that is, creditors, customers, employees, and perhaps even the community generally), the risk of nonconsummation, and the quality of securities being offered in the exchange. While not a controlling factor, it also seems to us that a board may reasonably consider the basic stockholder interests at stake, including those of short term speculators, whose actions may have fueled the coercive aspect of the offer at the expense of the long term investor. Here, the threat posed was viewed by the Unocal board as a grossly inadequate two-tier coercive tender offer coupled with the threat of greenmail.

Case 21.4 continues

---

18. Cheff v. Mathes, 199 A.2d 548, 554–55 (Del. 1964).

Case 21.4 continued

[*Greenmail* occurs when a raider acquires stock in a target company then threatens to commence a hostile takeover unless its stock is repurchased by the target at a premium over the market price.]

. . .

V.

Mesa contends that it is unlawful, and the trial court agreed, for a corporation to discriminate in this fashion against one shareholder. . . .

. . .

[W]hile the exchange offer is a form of selective treatment, given the nature of the threat posed here the response is neither unlawful nor unreasonable. If the board of directors is disinterested, has acted in good faith and with due care, its decision in the absence of an abuse of discretion will be upheld as a proper exercise of business judgment.

. . .

VI.

In conclusion, there was directorial power to oppose the Mesa tender offer, and to undertake a selective stock exchange made in good faith and upon a reasonable investigation pursuant to a clear duty to protect the corporate enterprise. Further, the selective stock repurchase plan chosen by Unocal is reasonable in relation to the threat that the board rationally and reasonably believed was posed by Mesa's inadequate and coercive two-tier tender offer. Under those circumstances the board's action is entitled to be measured by the standards of the business judgment rule. Thus, unless it is shown by a preponderance of the evidence that the directors' decisions were primarily based on perpetuating themselves in office, or some other breach of fiduciary duty such as fraud, overreaching, lack of good faith, or being uninformed, a Court will not substitute its judgment for that of the board.

RESULT   The board of directors of Unocal could legally make a discriminatory stock repurchase plan available to some of its shareholders in order to protect them and the corporation from a coercive hostile takeover attempt by Mesa Petroleum, one of the other shareholders.

COMMENTS   The strategy used in this case is no longer available because of the SEC's "all holders rule." According to the rule, a selective stock repurchase plan is deemed a tender offer in which all holders of securities of the same class must be allowed to participate. Nonetheless, this case remains a key Delaware precedent for the analysis of defensive tactics, including shareholder rights plans (also called poison pills) which can have much the same effect as a discriminatory self-tender.

Questions

1. Should the fact that some members of the board of directors were large shareholders in the corporation disqualify them from making a decision regarding a selective stock repurchase plan such as the one found in this case?
2. In the 1990s, there have been fewer hostile takeover attempts than there were in the 1980s. Should the laws regarding defensive maneuvers available to boards of directors be tightened to reflect this trend?

Once the judgment is made that a sale or breakup of the corporation is in the best interests of the shareholders or is inevitable, directors have a fiduciary duty to obtain the best available price for the shareholders. This rule was first articulated in a case involving a hostile takeover bid for Revlon, Inc. by Pantry Pride.[19]

After initially resisting the takeover attempt, the Revlon board elected to go forward with a friendly buyout from another company at a lower price than that offered by the hostile bidder. The Revlon board sought to justify the lower price by pointing out the benefits of the friendly buyout for other corporate constituencies, such as the Revlon noteholders. The hostile bidder sued to enjoin the friendly buyout.

The Delaware Supreme Court required the Revlon board to seek the highest price for the shareholders. The court defined the duty of the directors as follows:

> The Revlon board's authorization permitting management to negotiate a merger or buyout with a third party was a recognition that the company was for sale. The duty of the board had thus changed from the preservation of Revlon as a corporate entity to the maximization of the company's value at a sale for the stockholders' benefit. . . . The directors' role changed from defenders of the corporate bastion to auctioneers charged with getting the best price for the stockholders at a sale of the company.

In *Barkan v. Amsted Industries, Inc.,*[20] the Supreme Court of Delaware held that the basic teaching of cases such as *Revlon* is simply that directors of corporations must act in accordance with their fundamental duties of care and loyalty. However, the court ruled that acting in accordance with these duties does not mean that every change of corporate control necessitates an auction. If fairness to shareholders and the minimizing of conflicts of interest can be demonstrated, the added burden of having an auction may not be necessary.

The court in *Barkan* declined making a specific rule for determining when a market test (or "market check") is required. The court simply stated: "[I]t must be clear that the board had sufficient knowledge of relevant markets to form the basis for its belief that it acted in the best interests of the shareholders."[21]

It is doubtful that a failure of directors to consider every conceivable alternative would in itself amount to a breach of fiduciary duty. Such a rule would be unduly harsh. In hindsight, a complaining shareholder could almost always conjure up at least one alternative that the directors failed to consider. On the other hand, the failure of a board to consider any alternatives at all, or the unwillingness of a board to negotiate with anyone other than its chosen white knight (or with the initial offeror), would be a breach of fiduciary duty unless there were special circumstances.

When Is a Company in Revlon Mode?

The case of *Paramount Communications, Inc. v. Time Inc.*[22] examined the question of what constitutes an event triggering the *Revlon* duty to maximize shareholder value. (A company with such an obligation is deemed to be in *Revlon mode*.) Time had entered into a friendly stock-for-stock merger agreement with Warner Communications. Under that agreement, roughly 60% of the stock of the new combined entity Time–Warner would be held by former public shareholders of Warner. The merger agreement was subject to the approval of Time's shareholders.

Shortly before the Time shareholder vote was to take place, Paramount Communications made a hostile, unsolicited cash tender offer for all Time shares. In response, Time proceeded with its own highly leveraged cash tender offer to acquire 51% of Warner, to be followed by a back-end, second-step merger of the two companies. This tender offer, which would preclude acceptance of the Paramount tender offer, did not require approval by the Time shareholders. Paramount challenged the actions of Time's directors in opposing its offer, arguing that the Time board had put Time in the *Revlon* mode when it agreed to the stock merger with Warner.

The Delaware Supreme Court held that this transaction did not trigger *Revlon* duties because there was no change in control. Majority control shifted from one "fluid aggregation of unaffiliated shareholders" to another and remained in the hands of the public. As a result, the Time board could properly take into account such intangibles as the desire to preserve the Time culture and journalistic integrity in deciding to

---

19. Revlon, Inc. v. MacAndrews & Forbes Holdings, Inc., 506 A.2d 173 (Del. 1986).
20. 567 A.2d 1279 (Del. 1989).
21. *Id.* at 1288.

---

22. 571 A.2d 1140 (Del. 1990).

reject Paramount's hostile tender offer, which was arguably worth more to shareholders than the Time–Warner combination. The court considered this to be a strategic alliance, not a sale of Time to Warner, which would have triggered the *Revlon* duty to maximize shareholder value.

Relying heavily on the precedent established by the *Time–Warner* case, Paramount entered into a friendly merger agreement with Viacom Inc. in September 1993. When QVC Network, Inc. made a hostile unsolicited offer for Paramount at a price worth $1.3 billion more than what Viacom was offering, the Paramount board refused to negotiate with QVC and instead stood by its merger agreement with Viacom. In the following case, the Delaware Supreme Court examined the propriety of the Paramount board's action, especially in light of the fact that Viacom was controlled by a single individual, Sumner Redstone.

ETHICAL CONSIDERATION

The fight between the management of Revlon and Pantry Pride for control of Revlon was one of the most acrimonious takeover battles on record. After the Delaware Supreme Court's decision, Pantry Pride won control of the company. The exiting CEO of Revlon received more than $15 million in a severance bonus that Revlon was required to pay in the event he was fired or resigned after a change of control in the corporation. Such a severance arrangement, called a *golden parachute*, is a form of takeover defense that increases the bidder's expense to purchase the target. Under what circumstances might it be ethical for the board to adopt golden parachutes?

A CASE IN POINT	**IN THE LANGUAGE OF THE COURT**

CASE 21.5
*PARAMOUNT
COMMUNICATIONS
INC. v. QVC NETWORK
INC.*
Supreme Court of Delaware
637 A.2d 34 (Del. 1994).

FACTS   Beginning in the late 1980s, Paramount Communications Inc., which owned and operated a diverse group of entertainment businesses, investigated the possibility of acquiring or merging with other companies in the entertainment, media, or communications industry. Paramount considered such transactions to be desirable, and perhaps necessary, in order to keep pace with competitors in the rapidly evolving field of entertainment and communications.

In April 1993, Martin Davis, chairman and CEO of Paramount, met with Sumner Redstone, CEO, chairman, and majority owner of Viacom, a communications company that included MTV and Showtime Networks. After five months of discussions, they entered into a friendly merger agreement between Paramount and Viacom, along with other related agreements. Under these merger agreements, the Paramount shareholders would receive a combination of stock and cash that was then valued at $69.14 per share. In addition, Paramount amended its poison pill so that it would not be triggered by the Viacom deal.

Viacom and Paramount both made public statements to the effect that outside bids were unwelcome. However, in September 1993, QVC Network Inc., owner of a television shopping channel, proposed to Davis an acquisition of Paramount by QVC for cash and stock worth approximately $80 per share. In response to the hostile QVC offer, Viacom increased its bid to $80 per share cash at the front end, to be followed by a second-step stock-for-stock merger of equivalent value. In the next two months, QVC and Viacom each continued to enter competing bids. Paramount repeatedly rebuffed QVC, although QVC often submitted offers of higher value than those of Viacom.

Case 21.5 continues

Case 21.5 continued

QVC then sued the Paramount directors, arguing that the Paramount board had put Paramount in the *Revlon* mode when it committed to a transaction that would shift control of Paramount from the public shareholders to Redstone. The Delaware Court of Chancery agreed, and Paramount appealed the decision.

ISSUE PRESENTED   Does a board of directors have an obligation to consider an unsolicited tender offer from one corporation when the board has expressed a desire not to receive competing bids because it is engaging in a friendly merger agreement with another corporation?

OPINION   VEASEY, J., writing for the Delaware Supreme Court:

II. APPLICABLE PRINCIPLES OF ESTABLISHED DELAWARE LAW

. . .

A. The Significance of a Sale or Change of Control

. . .

In the case before us, the public stockholders (in the aggregate) currently own a majority of Paramount's voting stock. Control of the corporation is not vested in a single person, entity, or group, but vested in the fluid aggregation of unaffiliated stockholders. In the event the Paramount–Viacom transaction is consummated, the public stockholders will receive cash and a minority equity voting position in the surviving corporation. Following such consummation, there will be a controlling stockholder. . . . Irrespective of the present Paramount Board's vision of a long-term strategic alliance with Viacom, the proposed sale of control would provide the new controlling stockholder with the power to alter that vision.

Because of the intended sale of control, the Paramount–Viacom transaction has economic consequences of considerable significance to the Paramount stockholders. Once control has shifted, the current Paramount stockholders will have no leverage in the future to demand another control premium.

. . .

C. Enhanced Judicial Scrutiny of a Sale or Change of Control Transaction

. . .

The key features of an enhanced scrutiny test are: (a) a judicial determination regarding the adequacy of the decisionmaking process employed by the directors, including the information on which the directors based their decision; and (b) a judicial examination of the reasonableness of the directors' action in light of the circumstances then existing. The directors have the burden of proving that they were adequately informed and acted reasonably.

. . .

. . . Accordingly, a court applying enhanced judicial scrutiny should be deciding whether the directors made a reasonable decision, not a perfect decision. If a board selected one of several reasonable alternatives, a court should not second-guess that choice even though it might have decided otherwise or subsequent events may have cast doubt on the board's determination. Thus, courts will not substitute

Case 21.5 continues

Case 21.5 continued

their business judgment for that of the directors, but will determine if the directors' decision was, on balance, within a range of reasonableness.

D. *Revlon* and *Time–Warner* Distinguished

. . .

Under Delaware law there are, generally speaking and without excluding other possibilities, two circumstances which may implicate *Revlon* duties. The first, and clearer one, is when a corporation initiates an active bidding process seeking to sell itself or to effect a business reorganization involving a clear break-up of the company. However, *Revlon* duties may also be triggered where, in response to a bidder's offer, a target abandons its long-term strategy and seeks an alternative transaction involving the break-up of the company.

The Paramount defendants have misread the holding of *Time–Warner*. Contrary to their argument, our decision in *Time–Warner* expressly states that the two general scenarios discussed in the above-quoted paragraph are not the only instances where "*Revlon* duties" may be implicated. The Paramount defendants' argument totally ignores the phrase "without excluding other possibilities. . . ."

. . .

Accordingly, when a corporation undertakes a transaction which will cause: (a) a change in corporate control; or (b) a break-up of the corporate entity, the directors' obligation is to seek the best value reasonably available to the stockholders. This obligation arises because the effect of the Viacom–Paramount transaction, if consummated, is to shift control of Paramount from the public stockholders to a controlling stockholder, Viacom. Neither *Time–Warner* nor any other decision of this Court holds that a "break-up" of the company is essential to give rise to this obligation where there is a sale of control.

III. BREACH OF FIDUCIARY DUTIES BY PARAMOUNT BOARD

. . .

A. The Specific Obligations of the Paramount Board

. . .

Since the Paramount directors had already decided to sell control, they had an obligation to continue their search for the best value reasonably available to the stockholders. This continuing obligation included the responsibility, at the October 24 board meeting and thereafter, to evaluate critically both the QVC tender offers and the Paramount–Viacom transaction to determine if: (a) the QVC tender offer was, or would continue to be, conditional; (b) the QVC tender offer could be improved; (c) the Viacom tender offer or other aspects of the Paramount–Viacom transaction could be improved; (d) each of the respective offers would be reasonably likely to come to closure, and under what circumstances; (e) other material information was reasonably available for consideration by the Paramount directors; (f) there were viable and realistic alternative courses of action; and (g) the timing constraints could be managed so the directors could consider these matters carefully and deliberately.

Case 21.5 continues

Case 21.5 continued

B. The Breaches of Fiduciary Duty by the Paramount Board

. . .

Throughout the applicable time period, and especially from the first QVC merger proposal on September 20 through the Paramount Board meeting on November 15, QVC's interest in Paramount provided the opportunity for the Paramount Board to seek significantly higher value for the Paramount stockholders than that being offered by Viacom. QVC persistently demonstrated its intention to meet and exceed the Viacom offers, and frequently expressed its willingness to negotiate possible further increases.

. . .

V. CONCLUSION

The realization of the best value reasonably available to the stockholders became the Paramount directors' primary obligation under these facts in light of the change of control. That obligation was not satisfied, and the Paramount Board's process was deficient. The directors' initial hope and expectation for a strategic alliance with Viacom was allowed to dominate their decisionmaking process to the point where the arsenal of defensive measures established at the outset was perpetuated (not modified or eliminated) when the situation was dramatically altered. QVC's unsolicited bid presented the opportunity for significantly greater value for the stockholders and enhanced negotiating leverage for the directors. Rather than seizing those opportunities, the Paramount directors chose to wall themselves off from material information which was reasonably available and to hide behind the defensive measures as a rationalization for refusing to negotiate with QVC or seeking other alternatives. Their view of the strategic alliance likewise became an empty rationalization as the opportunities for higher value for the stockholders continued to develop.

RESULT   The Paramount board of directors, in order to fulfill its fiduciary duties to its shareholders, must entertain competing merger bids because the board had already agreed to a change in control in the attempted friendly merger deal with Viacom.

COMMENTS   The arguably new standards set forth by the Delaware court for the triggering of the *Revlon* duty to maximize shareholder value is troubling for several reasons. First (although the court denies this fact), the decision cannot help but have a chilling effect on strategic acquisitions by Delaware corporations. The court's opinion invites a competing bidder to enter the fray as soon as a target company enters into a strategic merger involving a change of control.

Although a bidder might otherwise be concerned under those facts about tortious interference with contract, the Delaware Supreme Court opinion made it clear that, under Delaware law at least, any contractual limitations on selling a company to someone else must yield to the directors' fiduciary duties. In this respect, it is ironic that one of the Paramount directors is Hugh Liedtke, CEO of Pennzoil, who successfully sued Texaco for $3 billion in a case involving Texaco's interference with Pennzoil's contract to acquire Getty Oil. (This case is discussed in the "Inside Story" in Chapter 7.)

Second, the Delaware court's decision leaves open the question of what constitutes a change in control. In the 1989 case in which Paramount sought to establish

Case 21.5 continues

Case 21.5 continued

that Time's merger with Warner constituted a change of control and thus effectively put Time up for sale, the Delaware Supreme Court concluded that there was no change in control even though after the merger approximately 60% of the shares of the combined entity would be owned by former Warner shareholders. The court accepted the argument that, for this purpose at least, public shareholders are fungible.

Questions

1. Why was it relevant that the acquiring company, Viacom, had such a large shareholder in Redstone?
2. Could Paramount and Viacom have structured their deal in a different way to avoid putting Paramount in *Revlon* mode?

Allocation of Power Between the Directors and the Shareholders

A key issue that emerges from cases involving hostile takeovers and defensive tactics is who gets to decide whether the corporation should be sold—the board of directors or the shareholders. Theoretically, the board of directors is the guardian of the shareholders' interests, but the interests and obligations of the two groups sometimes conflict.

For example, a hostile takeover attempt frequently presents such a conflict. Sometimes the proposed terms are attractive to the shareholders because the acquiring corporation offers to pay a substantial premium for their stock. However, the board of directors may believe that the acquiring company's plans for the corporation are ultimately destructive, as in the case of a bust-up takeover, in which the acquired corporation is taken apart and its assets sold piecemeal. The directors may have legitimate concerns about the effect of such a takeover on the company's employees or on the community where the corporation is located. Or the directors might believe that the long-term value of the company is greater than the price being offered. Of course, a director might oppose a transaction just to maintain his or her own place on the corporation's board in violation of the director's legal obligation to put the corporation's interests before his or her own.

One of the first cases addressing the allocation of power between the directors and the shareholders in deciding whether the corporation should be sold in-

volved the adoption by a board of directors, without shareholder approval, of a *poison pill*, that is, a plan that would make any takeover not approved by the directors prohibitively expensive.[23] In 1984, the directors of Household International, fearing that Household might be taken over and busted up, adopted a poison pill in the form of a Preferred Share Purchase Rights Plan. This plan provided that, under certain triggering circumstances, common shareholders would receive a "right" per every common share of Household. In the event of a merger in which Household was not the surviving corporation, the holder of each common share of Household would have the right to purchase $200 of the common stock of the acquiring company for only $100. If this right were triggered and exercised, it would dilute the value of the stock of the acquiring company, making a takeover prohibitively expensive for the acquiring company.

The Delaware Supreme Court upheld the board's power to adopt the plan. It found that the plan did not usurp the shareholders' ability to receive tender offers and to sell their shares to a bidder without board approval of the sale. Household's poison pill left "numerous methods to successfully launch a takeover." For example, a bidder could make a tender offer on the condition that the board redeem the rights, that is, buy them back for a nominal sum before they were triggered. A bidder could set a high minimum of shares and

---

23. Moran v. Household Int'l, Inc., 500 A.2d 1346 (Del. 1985).

IN BRIEF

DECISION TREE ANALYSIS OF BUSINESS JUDGMENT RULE

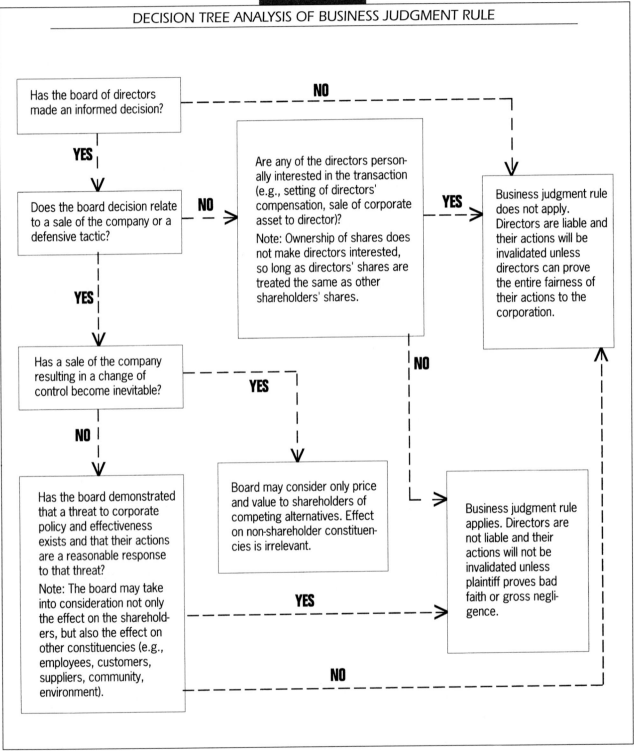

rights to be tendered; it could solicit consents to remove the board and replace it with one that would redeem the rights; or it could acquire 50% of the shares and cause Household to self-tender for the rights. In a self-tender, the company would agree to buy back the shareholders' rights for a fair price.

The court also found that the plan did not fundamentally restrict the shareholders' right to conduct a proxy contest. In a *proxy contest*, someone wishing to replace the board with his or her own candidates must acquire a sufficient number of shareholder votes to do so. Such votes are usually represented by *proxies*, or limited written powers of attorney entitling the proxy holder to vote the shares owned by the person giving the proxy. The court found that a proxy contest could be won with an insurgent ownership of less than 20% (the threshold for triggering distribution of the rights), and that the key to success in a proxy contest is the merit of the insurgent's arguments, not the size of his or her holdings.

The court concluded that the decision to adopt the poison pill plan was within the board's authority. Moreover, because the directors "reasonably believed Household was vulnerable to coercive acquisition techniques and adopted a reasonable defensive mechanism to protect itself," the court held that the board had discharged its fiduciary duty appropriately under the business judgment rule.

As of 1998, more than half of Fortune 500 companies had poison pill plans in effect. A number of institutional investors have urged companies to put their poison pill plans up for a shareholder vote. Texaco did so in 1998, and it was successful in getting approval from more than 50% of its shares.

Although the Delaware Supreme Court upheld the adoption of a poison-pill plan in *Moran*, it reserved judgment on how such a plan would operate in practice. In particular, it left open the question of when directors must redeem the poison pill rights to permit shareholders to tender their shares to a bidder.

The question of whether a board must redeem a pill is fact specific—a court will look at all of the circumstances in making its decision. Certain factors will favor keeping the pill in place. These include (1) a tender offer that is only slightly above the market price of the stock; (2) a tender offer for less than all of the shares; (3) an active attempt by the board to solicit other offers; (4) a conscious effort by the board to

allow its outside directors, deemed more disinterested, to make the decisions in this area; and (5) the fact that the tender offer is only in its early stages. The *Time–Warner* case made it clear that, under certain circumstances, a board faced with a hostile takeover bid can "Just Say No."

A number of takeover cases have drawn a distinction between the exercise of two types of corporate power: (1) the power over the assets of the corporation; and (2) the power relationship between the board and the shareholders.[24] As explained earlier, directors have broad power over the assets of the corporation. Such decisions are generally protected by the business judgment rule or subjected to *Unocal*'s proportionality analysis if they relate to defensive tactics. As the Delaware Chancellor William Allen explained in *Paramount Communications Inc. v. Time Inc.*:

> The corporation law does not operate on the theory that directors, in exercising their powers to manage the firm, are obligated to follow the wishes of a majority of shares.[25]

Thus, the Time directors had the power to acquire Warner Communications even though the holders of a majority of Time's stock probably would have preferred to take Paramount's offer.

However, if a board's unilateral decision to adopt a defensive measure touches on issues of control, then further judicial scrutiny is required to protect the shareholder franchise essential for corporate democracy. In particular, the court must decide whether the board purposefully disenfranchised its shareholders (that is, interfered with their right to elect the directors). If so, the action is strongly suspect under *Unocal* and cannot be sustained without a compelling justification.[26]

Based on these principles, the U.S. District Court for Nevada, applying Delaware law to a Nevada corporation in the absence of a Nevada precedent, struck down a reorganization plan adopted by the board of directors of ITT Corp. to thwart a hostile tender offer bid and proxy contest by Hilton Hotels Corp.[27] The

---

24. *See* Hilton Hotels Corp. v. ITT Corp., 978 F. Supp. 1342 (D. Nev. 1997).

25. Fed. Sec. L. Rep. (CCH) ¶ 94,514 (Del. Ch. July 14, 1989), *aff'd*, 571 A.2d 1140 (Del. 1990).

26. *See* Stroud v. Grace, 606 A.2d 75 (Del. 1992); Unitrin, Inc. v. American Gen. Corp., 651 A.2d 1361 (Del. 1995).

27. Hilton Hotels Corp. v. ITT Corp., 978 F. Supp. 1342 (D. Nev. 1997).

plan called for the break-up of ITT into three new entities, the largest of which (ITT Destinations) would hold more than 90% of ITT's current assets. The board of directors of ITT Destinations would consist of the current directors of ITT; but the ITT Destinations board would, unlike the current ITT board, be classified or staggered. The board would be divided into three classes with each class of directors serving for a term of three years and with one class to be elected each year. A shareholder vote of 80% would be required to remove the directors without cause or to repeal the classified board.

The ITT board proposed to implement this plan prior to ITT's annual meeting and without obtaining shareholder approval. The net effect of the plan was to make it impossible for the ITT shareholders to elect at the 1997 annual meeting a majority of the directors nominated under Hilton's proxy contest.

The court ruled that ITT had failed to show a threat to corporate policy and effectiveness, in part because ITT was now doing exactly what Hilton said it would do if its slate were elected. Even if Hilton's offer constituted a cognizable threat under *Unocal*, ITT's board was not allowed to adopt measures that were preclusive or coercive; that is, the board could not "cram down" on shareholders the management-sponsored alternative. ITT's plan was preclusive and coercive because it forced the ITT shareholders to accept the plan and a majority of ITT's incumbent board members for another year.

The court looked at a variety of factors (including the timing, entrenchment of current directors, ITT's stated purpose, and the effect of the classified board) and concluded that the primary purpose of the plan was to disenfranchise the ITT shareholders. As such, it was not a reasonable response unless a compelling justification existed. The ITT directors had provided no such justification. Thus, even if an action (such as amending the bylaws to adopt a classified board or to expand the size of the board) is normally permissible if the board adopts it in good faith and with proper care, a board cannot undertake such an action if the primary purpose is to disenfranchise the shareholders and entrench the current board in the face of a proxy contest.[28]

AT THE TOP

Protecting the shareholder franchise is critical because the business judgment rule provides the directors and officers great latitude in managing the day-to-day affairs of the corporation. As a result, shareholders who are displeased with the business performance generally have only two options: sell their shares or vote to replace the incumbent board members. The corporate governance system loses a key control if unhappy shareholders cannot vote the directors out of office.

Duty of Directors to Disclose Preliminary Merger Negotiations

Directors can face a difficult decision when deciding when they must disclose an offer to buy the company or the company's participation in merger negotiations. As is discussed more fully in Chapter 23, disclosure can be required even if the parties have not reached an agreement in principle on the price and structure of the transaction. The Supreme Court held in *Basic Inc. v. Levinson*[29] that such "soft information" can be material. Yet directors may fear that disclosure of negotiations will put the company in *Revlon* mode.

Managers planning a management buyout (MBO) of a company have a real conflict of interest in deciding whether to disclose their offer to the public, because disclosure will often bring forth competing bidders. Prudent directors, like the independent directors of RJR Nabisco when faced with CEO Ross Johnson's bid, will often require public announcement of the bid even if it puts the company "in play."

Duties of Controlling Shareholders

A shareholder who owns sufficient shares to outvote the other shareholders, and thus to control the corporation, is known as a *controlling shareholder*. In certain situations, controlling shareholders owe a fiduciary duty to

---

28. *See* Blasius Indus. Inc. v. Atlas Corp., 564 A.2d 651 (Del. Ch. 1988).

29. 485 U.S. 224 (1988).

THE PENNSYLVANIA ANTITAKEOVER STATUTE

The interest of state legislators—or at least of those persons with enough power to successfully promote legislation—in regulating takeovers and corporate changes of control has resulted in a variety of state statutes designed to challenge the rules of the takeover game. Most of this legislation is the result of anti-takeover sentiment. A prime example is Pennsylvania Senate bill 1310, also known as Act 36, which was signed into law by Governor Bob Casey (D) on April 27, 1990.[a] This statute employs a number of state-of-the-art strategies to impede the progress of a corporate raider. An examination of the events surrounding the enactment of this controversial statute highlights the current phase in the ever-changing battle over defining, shaping, and reshaping the law in this area.

Background

The impetus for drafting the statute came from an actual takeover attempt. Armstrong World Industries, Inc., a Fortune 500 company specializing in flooring and furnishings, is headquartered in Lancaster, Pennsylvania. Armstrong was the target of a hostile bid by the Belzberg family, based in Canada. The Belzbergs made an offer to the Armstrong's board to buy the company, but the offer was rejected. Next, the Belzbergs' holding company, First City Financial Corporation, initiated a proxy fight for control of four directors' seats on the board. The shareholders' meeting at which the results of the proxy fight were to be announced was scheduled for April 30.

Noah W. Wenger (R), the state senator from the Lancaster district, introduced a comprehensive anti-takeover bill while the Belzbergs and Armstrong were in the midst of their conflict. The bill, drafted in part by the Pennsylvania Chamber of Business and Industry, was designed not only to throw a wrench in the plans of corporate raiders in general but perhaps also to impede the Belzberg bid in particular. Armstrong down-played the notion that the company was the force behind the bill, but a company spokesperson acknowledged that the bill would be "highly beneficial" to the company.

The Statute

The Pennsylvania's antitakeover statute attacks bids for corporate control on three major fronts. First, it requires controlling persons (defined as those who own, or control proxies for, 20% of a company's stock) to disgorge—that is, give back to the company—any profits they make by selling stock of the company within 18 months after becoming a controlling person. Such disgorgement is required if stock acquired within 24 months before or within 18 months after becoming a controlling person is sold by the controlling person within 18 months after becoming a controlling person.

This provision is aimed at those who, after failed takeover attempts, attempt to reap short-term profits by selling acquired stock at a premium. Institutional investors and other shareholders who launch proxy fights for purposes other than gaining control of a majority of the board are exempted from the disgorgement provision. This exemption was a last-minute modification to the bill designed to placate the large institutional investors. These investors did not want to lose a major source of profit simply because they had a large stake in a company and wanted to exert a certain degree of control over its operation.

Second, the statute expands the directors' ability to consider other constituencies when making change-of-control decisions. Subsection (d) of Section 511 provides an expansive list of constituencies that a director may consider when exercising his or her duty to the corporation:

> In discharging the duties of their respective positions . . . directors may, in considering the best interests of the corporation, consider to the extent they deem appropriate:
> (1) The effects of any action upon *any or all groups affected by such action*, including shareholders, employees, suppliers, customers and creditors of the corporation, and upon communities in which offices or other establishments of the corporation are located.
> (2) The short-term and long-term interests of the corporation, including benefits which may accrue to the corporation from its long-term plans and the *possibility that these interests may be best served by the continued independence of the corporation.*

Political Perspective continues

Political Perspective continued

(3) The resources, intent and conduct (past, stated and potential) of person seeking to acquire control of the corporation.

(4) *All other pertinent factors.* [Emphasis added.]

The implication is clear. A director's duty when considering a proposal for a change of control is not simply to maximize shareholder value. Under the statute, a director's duty is to consider a broad range of interests, including "all other pertinent factors."

Numerous court decisions have indicated that directors may in some instances consider other constituencies. However, directors could only guess how the interests of other constituencies ranked against the interests of shareholders. The Pennsylvania statute clarified this issue by stating that directors shall not be required to regard any particular corporate interest or the interest of any group as "a dominant or controlling interest or factor."

The drafters' concern for minimizing director liability is evident in Subsection (f), which states that there is no heightened duty of directors in a takeover situation. This is in direct contrast with the *Unocal* line of cases from the Delaware courts. (*See* Case 21.4.) In those cases, before the directors could invoke the business judgment rule, they had the burden of proving that there was a threat to corporate policy and effectiveness and that their response was reasonable in relation to that threat. (It is usually the plaintiff who has the burden of proving that the directors breached their duties.)

Third, like some other states' antitakeover statutes, the Pennsylvania law deprives a shareholder of its voting rights when it crosses certain ownership lines, placed at 20%, 33%, and 50% of the company's stock. The voting rights can be regained only if the majority of shareholders—excluding holders of shares acquired in the previous 12 months—give their approval at a special shareholders' meeting.

The statute also protects the employees of a company that is taken over. Existing labor contracts must be honored, and a successful bidder must pay severance benefits to employees who lose their jobs within two years of the takeover.

Corporations are allowed to opt out of various provisions of the antitakeover statute. The corporation's bylaws could be amended to state that the provisions in question do not apply, provided this was done within 90 days after the statute's enactment. Alternatively, the articles of incorporation can be amended at any time.

Responses

Directly after the statute's enactment, most commentators agreed that the Pennsylvania antitakeover statute was the most stringent passed by any state legislature. It met with some sharp criticism. In a speech to the Council of Institutional Investors, former SEC Chairman Richard Breeden stated that the statute would "tilt the balance of corporate power in favor of corporate management and against shareholders by protecting decisions of the board of directors from effective challenge by shareholders."

Economists attacked the statute for reducing the value of Pennsylvania corporations. One study by professors from the University of Washington showed that Pennsylvania stocks underperformed the Standard & Poor's 500 by 6.9% in the period from October 1989, when Act 36 was announced, to January 1990, when it passed the Pennsylvania Senate.[b] Another study found a $4 billion drop in the combined market capitalization or value of Pennsylvania companies between the date the act was announced and the date it was signed. The market drop for companies in 25 other states was $6 billion *combined.*[c]

Several leading Pennsylvania corporations chose to opt out of the statute. One such company was Hunt Manufacturing, a leading manufacturer and distributor of office and arts and crafts products. The CEO, Ronald J. Naples, stated on June 26, 1990:

> The Board of Directors concluded that, both as a matter of principle and as a practical matter, the scope and uncertain effect of the new Pennsylvania anti-takeover amendments make them undesirable. We believe the company's legitimate interest in controlling its own destiny can be protected in ways more consistent with shareholder rights.

One of Pennsylvania's largest companies, Westinghouse Electric, which had actively promoted the opt-out provisions before the bill was passed, announced on May 31, 1990, that its board of directors had decided to opt out of the statute. As of 1992, more than 66 of the estimated 200 corporations affected by the statute had opted out of at least one of its subchapters.[d]

Two Armstrong shareholders brought suit in federal court on April 27, 1990, against the board of directors of Armstrong and the Pennsylvania secretary of state. The suit raised broad claims of violation of the U.S. Constitution, but it was dismissed by the district court. The U.S. Court of Appeals for the Third Circuit

Political Perspective continues

affirmed the district court's decision, concluding that the plaintiffs' claims were not ripe for judicial review.[c]

The Belzberg family also filed suit in U.S. district court in Philadelphia, alleging that the law was unconstitutional. The Belzbergs had reason to fight. At the Armstrong annual shareholders' meeting, held just a few days after the legislation was approved, the Belzbergs gained only one seat on the board. The *Wall Street Journal* reported that they subsequently were forced to sell their 11.7% share of Armstrong at a loss.

Recent Use

The Pennsylvania statute proved important in the successful attempt by Mellon Bank (a Pennsylvania corporation) in 1998 to thwart a hostile bid by the Bank of New York.[f] In rejecting Bank of New York's $23.6 billion offer (which represented a premium of 28% over Mellon's clos-

ing stock price the day before the offer was announced and a premium of 34% over Mellon's average closing stock price over the last 30 trading days), the chairman of Mellon's board seemed to be invoking the Pennsylvania statute when he criticized the proposed merger as not benefiting "our shareholders, employees, customer and —in particular—the communities we serve."[g]

a. The independent sections are codified as 15 PA. CONS. STAT. ANN. §§ 511, 512, 1721, 2502 (1990); 15 PA. CONS. STAT. ANN. §§ 2561–2567, 2571–2574, 2581–2583, 2585–2588 (1990).

b. Vineeta Anand, *Pennsylvania Anti-Takeover Law Slams Stock Prices, Study Finds*, INVESTORS DAILY, Oct. 1, 1990, 31.

c. Jeffrey L. Silberman, *How Do Pennsylvania Directors Spell Relief? Act 36*, 17 DEL. J. CORP. L. 115 (1992).

d. *Id.*

e. Armstrong World Industries, Inc. v. Adams, 961 F.2d 405 (3d Cir. 1992).

f. *See* Bloomberg News, *In Pennsylvania, Watch Out What You Try to Take Over: Thanks to Tough Rules, Mellon Bank Is Able to Flatly Reject an Offer from Bank of New York*, L.A. TIMES, Apr. 23, 1998, at D7.

g. Associated Press, *Mellon Bank Sues Bank of New York to Avoid Takeover; $23 Billion Bid Was Rejected*, STAR TRIBUNE (Minneapolis), Apr. 24, 1998, at 1D.

---

the corporation and to its other shareholders. Generally, controlling shareholders have a responsibility to minority shareholders to control the corporation in a fair, just, and equitable manner. They may not engage in a bad faith scheme to drain off the corporation's earnings, ensuring that minority shareholders are frozen out of all financial benefits.[30]

Sale of Control

The obligation not to exercise control in a manner that intentionally harms the corporation and minority shareholders spills over into a sale of control. For instance, if a controlling shareholder knows or has reason to believe that the purchaser of its shares intend to use controlling power to the detriment of the corporation, the controlling shareholder has a duty not to transfer the power of management to such a purchaser.

A controlling interest in a corporation usually commands a higher price per share than a minority interest. Does this control premium belong to the corporation or to the majority shareholder? The widely accepted rule is that controlling shareholders normally have a right to derive a premium from the sale of a controlling block of

stock.[31] For instance, in *Zetlin v. Hanson Holdings, Inc.*,[32] the New York Court of Appeals commented:

> In this action plaintiff Zetlin contends that minority stockholders are entitled to an opportunity to share equally in any premium paid for a controlling interest in the corporation. This rule would profoundly affect the manner in which controlling stock interests are now transferred. It would require, essentially, that a controlling interest be transferred only by means of an offer to all stockholders, that is, a tender offer. This would be contrary to existing law and if so radical a change is to be effected it would be best done by the Legislature.

In extreme circumstances, however, courts may be willing to characterize the control premium as a corporate asset, thus entitling minority shareholders to a portion. The U.S. Court of Appeals for the Second Circuit took such an approach in *Perlman v. Feldmann*.[33] *Perlman* involved Newport Steel Corp., whose mills produced steel sheets for sale to manufacturers of steel products. C. Russell Feldmann was the chairman of the board of directors and president of the corporation; he was also the controlling shareholder. In August 1950,

---

30. Sugarman v. Sugarman, 797 F.2d 3 (1st Cir. 1986).

31. *See, e.g.,* Essex Universal Corp. v. Yates, 305 F.2d 572 (2d Cir. 1962).

32. 397 N.E.2d 387 (N.Y. 1979).

33. 219 F.2d 173 (2d Cir. 1955), *cert. denied*, 349 U.S. 952 (1955).

Because European banks are not subject to the regulatory strictures applicable to U.S. banks, they are much more important institutional investors and exert a more powerful force on how a company is run than comparable U.S. banks. For example, German banks exercise extraordinary control over company access to capital. By law, the banks can represent shareholders who deposit their shares with the banks. Because only the banks are allowed to trade on the floor of the German stock exchanges, and therefore have the best knowledge of stock performance, most shareholders take advantage of this service.

In 1986, German banks held on average proxies for 65% of the shares present at the shareholder meetings at 100 of the largest German companies. For example, at the 1986 shareholder meeting of Siemens, approximately 61% of the outstanding shares were present at the meeting. Of the shares voted, Deutsche Bank voted 18%, Dresdner Bank 11%, and Commerzbank 4%. All banks taken as a group voted approximately 80% of the shares voted at the meeting.[a] Banks are also permitted to purchase directly up to 100% of the shares of a company, although it is considered imprudent for them to invest substantial portions of their capital in any single company.

---

a. Theodor Baums, *Corporate Governance in Germany: The Role of Banks*, 40 AM. J. COMP. L. 503, 524 (1992).

when the supply of steel was tight due to the Korean War, Feldmann and some other shareholders sold their stock to a syndicate of end users of steel who were interested in securing a source of supply.

Minority shareholders brought a shareholder derivative suit to compel the controlling shareholders to account for, and make restitution of, their gains from the sale. The court held that the consideration received by the defendants included compensation for the sale of a corporate asset, namely the ability of the board to control the allocation of the corporation's product in a time of short supply.

Note that the court did not seek to prohibit majority shareholders from ever selling their shares at a premium; it was careful to circumscribe its holding with an emphasis on the extreme market conditions:

> We do not mean to suggest that a majority stockholder cannot dispose of his controlling block of stock to outsiders without having to account to his corporation for profits or even never do this with impunity when the buyer is an interested customer, actual or potential, for the corporation's product. But when the sale necessarily results in a sacrifice of this element of corporate good will and consequent unusual profit to the fiduciary who has caused the sacrifice, he should account for his gains. So when a time of market shortage, where a call on a corporation's product commands an unusually large premium, in one form or another, we think it sound law that a fiduciary may not appropriate to himself the value of this premium.

The following case involved elements of abuse of control and sale of control. The dominant shareholders took a series of steps to ensure that they participated in the financial benefits of the company, without letting the minority shareholders also participate.

| A CASE IN POINT | SUMMARY |

CASE 21.6

JONES v. H. F. AHMANSON & CO.

Supreme Court of California
460 P.2d 464 (Cal. 1969).

FACTS   The shares of the United Savings and Loan Association were not actively traded due to their high book value, the closely held nature of the association, and the failure of its management to provide information to shareholders, brokers, or the public.

In 1958, investor interest in shares of savings and loan associations and holding companies increased. Savings and loan stocks that were publicly marketed enjoyed a steady increase in market price. The controlling shareholders of the United Savings and Loan Association decided to create a mechanism by which the association, too, could

Case 21.6 continues

Case 21.6 continued

attract investor interest. They did not, however, attempt to render the association's shares more readily marketable.

Instead, a holding company, the United Financial Corporation of California, was incorporated in Delaware on May 8, 1959. On May 14, pursuant to a prior agreement, certain association shareholders owning a majority of the association's stock exchanged their shares for those of United Financial.

After the exchange, United Financial held 85% of the association's outstanding stock. The former majority shareholders of the association had become the majority shareholders of United Financial and continued to control the association through the holding company. They did not offer the minority shareholders of the association an opportunity to exchange their shares.

The first public offering of United Financial stock was made in June 1960. An additional public offering in February 1961 included a secondary offering (that is, an offering by selling shareholders) of 600,000 shares. There was active trading in the United Financial shares. Sales of the association shares, however, decreased from 170 shares per year before the formation of United Financial to half that number by 1961. United Financial acquired 90% of the association's shares that were sold.

A shareholder of the association brought suit, on behalf of herself and all other similarly situated minority shareholders, against United Financial and the individuals and corporations that had set up the holding company. The plaintiff contended that the defendants' course of conduct constituted a breach of fiduciary duty owed by the majority shareholders to the minority. She alleged that they used their control of the association for their own advantage and to the detriment of the minority when they created United Financial, made a public market for its shares that rendered the association's stock unmarketable except to United Financial, and then refused either to purchase the minority's association stock at a fair price or to exchange the stock on the same terms afforded to the majority. She further alleged that they created a conflict of interest that might have been avoided had they offered all association shareholders the opportunity to participate in the initial exchange of shares.

ISSUE PRESENTED   Did majority shareholders who transferred their shares to a holding corporation, then took it public without allowing the minority to exchange their shares, breach their fiduciary duty to the minority shareholders?

SUMMARY OF OPINION   The California Supreme Court began its analysis by stating that the majority shareholders, acting either singly or in concert, have a fiduciary responsibility to the minority and to the corporation. They must use fairly their ability to control the corporation. They may not use it to benefit themselves alone, or in a manner detrimental to the minority. Any use to which they put their power to control the corporation must benefit all shareholders proportionately and must not conflict with the proper conduct of the corporation's business. The court summarized the rule as one of "inherent fairness from the viewpoint of the corporation or those interested therein."

The court noted that there were two other ways the controlling shareholders of the association could have taken advantage of the bull market in savings and loan stock. They could have caused the association to effect a stock split, thereby increasing the

Case 21.6 continues

Case 21.6 continued

number of outstanding shares, or they could have created a holding company and permitted all shareholders to exchange their shares before offering the holding company's shares to the public. Either course would have benefited all of the shareholders alike, although the majority shareholders would have had to relinquish some of their control shares. However, the defendants chose to set up a holding company which they controlled, but did not allow minority shareholders to exchange association shares for shares of the holding company. Moreover, the market created by the defendants for United Financial shares would have been available for association shares had the defendants chosen a stock split of the association's shares.

The court stated that when a controlling shareholder sells or exchanges his or her shares, the transaction is subject to close scrutiny, particularly if the majority receives a premium over market value for its shares. If the premium constitutes payment for what is properly a corporate asset, all shareholders are entitled to a proportionate share of the premium (citing *Perlman v. Feldmann*). The defendants' exchange of association stock for United Financial stock was an integral part of a scheme that the defendants could have reasonably foreseen would destroy the potential public market for association stock. The remaining association shareholders would thus be deprived of the opportunity to realize a profit from those intangible characteristics that attach to publicly marketed stock.

RESULT   The majority shareholders who transferred their shares to a holding corporation, then took it public without allowing the minority to exchange their shares, breached their fiduciary duty to the minority shareholders. The minority shareholders were awarded damages that would place them in a position at least as favorable as the majority shareholders created for themselves.

Freeze-outs

The Delaware Supreme Court has held that a majority shareholder may *freeze out* the minority, that is, force the minority to convert their shares into cash, as long as the transaction is fair.[34]

Sometimes a freeze-out is effected by merging a subsidiary into its parent, as in *Rosenblatt v. Getty Oil Co.*[35] In this case, Skelly Oil Company and Mission Corporation merged into Getty Oil Company, which was indirectly the majority shareholder of both Skelly and Mission. All three corporations were in the oil business. At issue was the fairness of the exchange ratio in the merger, that is, the ratio that would be used to convert the minority shareholders' stock into cash.

The Delaware Supreme Court stated that the concept of fairness in parent–subsidiary mergers has two aspects: fair dealing and fair price. Both must be examined together in resolving the ultimate question of entire fairness.

As to fair dealing, a court will look at the timing of the transaction; how it was initiated, structured, negotiated, and disclosed to the board; and how director and shareholder approval was obtained. The court cited a number of factors leading to a conclusion of fair dealing by Getty, including the adversarial nature of the negotiations between the parties to the merger.

Regarding fair price, a court will look at such economic factors as asset value, market value, earnings, and future prospects, and at any other elements that affect the intrinsic value of a company's stock. Both Getty and Skelly believed that the real worth of an oil company is centered in its reserves. Therefore, the court was especially impressed with the fact that they had employed D & M, a petroleum consulting engineering firm with a

---

34. Weinberger v. UOP, Inc. 457 A.2d 701 (Del. 1983).
35. 493 A.2d 929 (Del. 1985).

worldwide reputation and with nearly 37 years of experience, to estimate Getty's and Skelly's respective oil and natural gas reserves.

The court concluded that Getty had dealt fairly with the Skelly minority shareholders in the merger.

 ## Greenmail

While still a senior in college, Saul Steinberg acquired a 3% interest in the O'Sullivan Rubber Company. He demanded that the company diversify into automotive parts. The company refused. Steinberg threatened a proxy fight to replace the existing directors. The company then bought out Steinberg for three times what he had paid for his stock and thereby "helped Saul Steinberg invent greenmail."[36]

---

36. Eric Allison, The Raiders of Wall Street (1987).

Decades later, in 1984, Steinberg, through a syndicate called MM Acquisition Corporation (MM for Mickey Mouse), took a run at Walt Disney Productions. Within 12 hours of his threatening a cash tender offer for Disney, Steinberg was bought out for $325.4 million, giving him a profit of about $60 million. Some Disney shareholders sued the Disney directors for paying greenmail. Before the trial, the plaintiffs sought to impose a constructive trust on the greenmail proceeds received by Steinberg. (A constructive trust is used to make available to their rightful owners any assets misappropriated by a fiduciary.) The trial court imposed constructive trust, and an appellate court affirmed. (In 1989, after three weeks of trial, the case was settled for $89.5 million.) The case presented here addresses the extent to which a shareholder who receives greenmail from a company's board of directors is an aider and abettor of that board's breach of duty to the company.

A CASE IN POINT	SUMMARY

CASE 21.7
HECKMANN v.
AHMANSON
Court of Appeal of California
214 Cal. Rptr. 177
(Cal. Ct. App. 1985).

FACTS In March 1984, a group headed by Saul Steinberg purchased more than two million shares of stock of Walt Disney Productions, the owner of Disneyland. Disney responded by announcing that it would acquire the Arvida Corporation for $200 million in newly issued Disney stock and it would assume Arvida's $190 million debt. The Steinberg group countered with a shareholder derivative suit in federal court, seeking to block the Arvida transaction. A shareholder derivative suit is a suit brought on behalf of the corporation by one or more of its shareholders. All of the proceeds of such a suit (less expenses) go to the corporation for the benefit of all of its shareholders.

While the shareholder derivative suit was pending, the Steinberg group proceeded to acquire two million additional shares of Disney stock, increasing its ownership position to approximately 12% of the outstanding Disney shares. On June 8, 1984, the Steinberg group advised Disney's directors of its intention to make a tender offer for 49% of the outstanding shares at $67.50 a share, and its intention to later tender for the balance at $72.50 a share.

The Disney directors responded by offering to repurchase all the Disney stock held by the Steinberg group. Disney repurchased that stock for $297.4 million and reimbursed the estimated cost incurred in preparing the tender offer, $28 million, for a total of $325.4 million, or about $77 per share. The Steinberg group garnered a profit of about $60 million. In return, the Steinberg group agreed not to purchase any more Disney stock and to drop the Arvida litigation. It did not actually dismiss the derivative claims, but it agreed not to oppose a motion to dismiss made by Disney.

After the repurchase of the Steinberg group's shares was announced, several Disney shareholders brought an action seeking to rescind Disney's purchase agreement

Case 21.7 continues

Case 21.7 continued

with the Steinberg group. They also sought an accounting and the imposition of a constructive trust upon all funds the Steinberg group received from Disney. At a preliminary hearing, the trial court granted a constructive trust. The Steinberg group appealed.

ISSUES PRESENTED   Was a shareholder who induced the board of directors to pay greenmail liable as an aider and abettor of the board's breach of its duty to the company? Was the shareholder, who (as part of the greenmail transaction) abandoned a derivative suit against the company, also liable to the other shareholders for breaching his fiduciary duty to them?

SUMMARY OF OPINION   The California Court of Appeal found that the plaintiffs had demonstrated a reasonable probability of success at trial and upheld the trial court's imposition of a constructive trust.

First, the court found that the plaintiffs had made a sufficient showing of personal interest on the part of the directors to shift the burden onto the board to show that the transaction was fair. The court held that the directors had not sustained that burden merely by making a vague assertion that their objective in repurchasing the stock was to avoid the damage to Disney and its shareholders that would have resulted from the Steinberg tender offer. Thus, the directors were not given the protection of the business judgment rule.

The court further found that the Steinberg group could be held liable as an aider and abettor of the board in its alleged breach of fiduciary duty. The court noted that the Steinberg group knew it was reselling its stock at a price considerably above market value to enable the Disney directors to retain control of the corporation. It also knew or should have known that Disney was borrowing the $325 million purchase price. From its previous dealings with Disney, including the Arvida transaction, it knew that the increased debt load would adversely affect Disney's credit rating and the price of its stock.

Second, the court found that the plaintiff shareholders had adequately demonstrated a breach of the fiduciary duty owed directly by the Steinberg group to the Disney shareholders. When the Steinberg group filed the derivative suit against Disney to block Disney's purchase of Arvida, it assumed a fiduciary duty to the other shareholders. It could not abandon the suit for its own financial advantage. The plaintiff's duty in a derivative action is analogous to the duty of care owed by a volunteer rescuer to the rescuee. The court stated that the members of the Steinberg group "are like the citizens of a town whose volunteer fire department quits fighting the fire and sells its equipment to the arsonist who set it (who obtains the purchase price by setting fire to the building next door)." Thus, the plaintiffs had demonstrated a reasonable probability that the Steinberg group breached its fiduciary duty to the other Disney shareholders by abandoning the Arvida litigation two weeks after it was filed.

RESULT   The shareholder who induced the board to pay greenmail was liable as an aider and abettor of the board's breach of its duty to the company. He was also liable for his breach of fiduciary duty to his fellow shareholders when he abandoned the shareholder derivative suit.

In another case involving the repurchase of shares at a premium to forestall a takeover attempt, the U.S. District Court for the Southern District of New York found the basis for claiming a similar breach of the directors' fiduciary duty.[37] The plaintiffs had sued to recover $41 million paid to Carl Icahn by tire manufacturer B.F. Goodrich Company when it repurchased one million shares of its stock from Icahn at an above-market price. This transaction resulted in an $8 million loss to Goodrich, with no corresponding benefit to Goodrich shareholders. According to the court, "[t]he only beneficiaries under the repurchase, other than Icahn, were the Goodrich directors, who insured their continued control of the company." Chairman of the board Ong admitted that the transaction could be characterized as greenmail and that the directors agreed to purchase the shares because they did not wish to have Goodrich put into play for a possible takeover bid. The court held that under New York law the allegation that the board of directors repurchased stock at a premium over market in an attempt to prevent a hostile takeover stated a claim for breach of fiduciary duty and waste of corporate assets if the repurchase conferred no benefit on the other shareholders.

Delaware courts analyze the payment of greenmail in the same way they analyze other defensive tactics under *Unocal.* If the board demonstrates that the shareholder to be bought out poses a threat to corporate policy and effectiveness and the repurchase of shares at a premium is a reasonable response to that threat, then the payment will be protected by the business judgment rule.

The payment of greenmail by boards of directors has led to a number of shareholder proposals designed to prohibit the practice. For example, the holders of more than 50% of the outstanding shares of Gillette Company approved the following shareholder resolution in 1988:

RESOLVED, That the stockholders of Gillette Company recommend our Board of Directors take the necessary steps to amend the by-laws as follows:
(a) The Company shall not acquire any of its voting equity securities at a price above the average market price of such securities from any person who is the beneficial owner of more than three percent of the Company's voting equity securities and has been such for less than two years, unless such acquisition is pursuant to the same offer and terms as made to all holders of securities of such class and to all holders of any other class from or into which such securities may be converted.
(b) This provision shall not apply to any acquisition that has been approved by a vote of two-thirds of the shares entitled to vote.
(c) This provision shall not restrict the Company from:
(1) reacquiring shares in the open market in transactions in which all shareholders have an equal chance to sell their shares, and in number of shares that do not exceed in any one day the daily average trading volume for the preceding three months; (2) offering to acquire at market price all shares, but no less than all shares, of any shareholder owning less than 100 shares of common stock; or (3) reacquiring shares pursuant to the terms of a stock option plan that has been approved by a vote of a majority of the common shareholders.

Professor Rita Kosnick of Texas A&M University compared 53 companies that paid greenmail with 57 that resisted. She found that the boards that resisted had more outside directors and more directors with executive experience than the boards that paid up.[38]

Hushmail

The Delaware Supreme Court has characterized as *hushmail*—that is, a combination of greenmail and hush money—a repurchase of shares at a premium over market to ensure silence. The term was first used in *Grobow v. Perot.*[39]

General Motors Corporation (GM), one of the Big Three U.S. automobile manufacturers, repurchased certain GM stock and contingent notes owned by H. Ross Perot and his close associates for nearly $745 million. Perot, a U.S. presidential candidate in 1992, himself characterized the price at which his securities were repurchased as being at a "giant premium."

Perot resigned immediately from GM's board. He also resigned as chairman of GM's subsidiary Electronic Data Systems (EDS), which he had founded and of which he was the largest shareholder. Perot further

---

37. Feinberg Testamentary Trust v. Carter, 652 F. Supp. 1066 (S.D.N.Y. 1987).

38. Rita Kosnick, *Greenmail: A Study of Board Performance in Corporate Governance,* ADMIN. SCI. Q. 32, 163 (1987).

39. 539 A.2d 180 (Del. 1988).

agreed (1) to stop criticizing GM management, in default of which he agreed to pay GM damages of up to $7.5 million; (2) not to purchase GM stock or engage in a proxy contest against the board for five years; and (3) not to compete with EDS for three years or recruit EDS executives for 18 months. The commitment by Perot not to criticize the GM board was later characterized as the hushmail feature of the agreement.

The GM repurchase came at a time when GM was experiencing financial difficulty and was engaged in cost cutting. Public reaction to the announcement ranged from mixed to adverse. The repurchase was sharply criticized by industry, including members of GM's management ranks. The criticism focused on the size of the premium over the market price of the repurchased stock and on the hushmail provision. A shareholder suit ensued.

The Delaware Supreme Court found that the plaintiffs' complaints regarding the hushmail provision failed to plead with particularity any facts that would support a conclusion that the primary purpose of the board's payment of the giant premium was to buy Perot's silence. To the contrary, the plaintiffs themselves stated in their complaints two legitimate business purposes for the GM board's decision to sever its relationship with Perot: (1) the board's determination that

it would be in GM's best interest to retain control over its wholly owned subsidiary EDS; and (2) the decision to rid itself of the principal cause of the growing internal policy dispute over EDS's management direction. In addition, GM secured significant covenants from Perot besides the hushmail provision: (1) not to compete or hire EDS employees; (2) not to purchase GM stock or engage in proxy contests; and (3) to stay out of GM's and EDS's affairs. Moreover, Perot agreed to pay liquidated damages should he breach his no-criticism covenant. The court found that the plaintiffs' effort to measure the fairness of the premium paid by GM was flawed by their inability to place a dollar value on these promises made by Perot, particularly his covenant not to compete with EDS or attempt to hire away EDS employees.

The court concluded that, although the board of directors might be subject to criticism for the premium paid Perot and his associates for the repurchase of their interest in GM, on the present record the repurchase could only be seen legally as an exercise of business judgment by the General Motors board with which a court may not interfere.

In the spring of 1990, in response to continuing shareholder pressure, General Motors adopted a bylaw prohibiting the payment of greenmail.

THE RESPONSIBLE MANAGER
Carrying Out Fiduciary Duties

Officers, directors, and controlling shareholders are fiduciaries. They owe their principal (the corporation and its shareholders) undivided loyalty. They must act in good faith. They may not put their own interests before those of the corporation and its shareholders. They cannot, for example, fight off a hostile takeover just to keep their jobs. They cannot use the company's confidential information for their personal gain.

Officers and directors also owe the corporation and its shareholders a duty of care. They should act with the care reasonable persons would use in the management of their own property. They have a duty to make only

informed decisions. They cannot rely blindly on the advice of other people, even experts.

The duty to make informed decisions, which is a part of the duty of care, takes various forms. In the context of takeovers, board members cannot reject an offer without taking sufficient time to analyze its merit. Managers must be able to demonstrate that they made their decisions only after sufficient deliberation and after review of all relevant information. They should consider the possible effects of both the monetary and the nonmonetary aspects of the transaction.

A manager should never sign a document without first reading it. Ideally, each director should read the document the board is asked to approve. If that is not practical, the directors should demand and read a written summary prepared by counsel. They should also make sure that the officers who are authorized to sign the agreement have read it before signing it.

A manager should be informed as to the rules in the company's state of incorporation regarding the duty of care. Some jurisdictions permit the shareholders to amend the articles of incorporation to relieve directors of any financial liability for violations of the duty of care. But even with such provisions in place, directors must still act in good faith and in what they honestly believe is the best interest of the corporation. Otherwise, they will breach their duty of loyalty. Such a breach not only can result in monetary liability, but can also demoralize the shareholders and employees of the corporation, and make it difficult to maintain a high level of ethical behavior among them.

In a situation involving a potential conflict of interest, a manager should excuse himself or herself and leave the decision to others who do not have a conflict. It is common, for example, to establish special independent committees of the board of directors, either to examine the fairness of a management offer to acquire the company or to review the merits of shareholder litigation against the directors or officers.

A repurchase of stock at a premium from a dissident (or unhappy) shareholder may violate both the directors' duty to the corporation and the shareholder's duty to the other shareholders. Different courts view such repurchases differently, and local counsel should always be consulted. It is often appropriate for the board not only to obtain a written opinion of counsel that such a repurchase is permissible, but also to convene a special independent committee of directors to decide whether the consideration that will be paid for the stock is fair.

Any controlling shareholder engaging in a transaction such as a merger with the company it controls must be able to prove that the transaction is fair both procedurally and substantively. The use of independent committees, advised by independent financial consultants and counsel, helps show procedural fairness, as does a willingness to negotiate the proposed transaction with such a committee on an arm's length basis. Paying a fair price for corporate assets or for shares of a corporation shows substantive fairness. The fairness of a price can be demonstrated by evidence of competing offers or independent appraisals or evaluations. The form of compensation of the appraiser or investment banker should not give that person an interest in the outcome of the appraisal or of the transaction. It is often preferable to pay the appraiser or investment banker a flat fee regardless of whether the deal goes through, rather than an incentive fee based on the value of the deal struck.

Certain acts of directors, officers, and controlling shareholders are both illegal and unethical, such as the seizing of a corporate opportunity by an officer. Other conduct may be legal yet ethically questionable, such as the payment of hushmail or, in some circumstances, greenmail.

Some situations present conflicting ethical concerns. The Delaware Supreme Court has held that the directors must maximize shareholder value, that is, get the best price available, if they decide to sell control of the corporation. Yet a sale to a bust-up artist who will sell the company's assets, or to a union buster, might adversely affect the corporation's other constituencies, such as employees, suppliers, and the community in which the corporation does business. A manager should try to select a course of action that protects the corporation's constituencies without sacrificing the shareholders' right to the best price. If the management team itself bids for the company, the board may find itself forced to become an auctioneer whose sole goal is to get the best price for the shareholders.

A board of directors can use various defensive measures to prevent a hostile takeover, provided the measures are reasonable in relation to the threat posed, and provided the board considers it in the best interests of the company and its constituencies for the company to remain independent. Any measures designed to interfere with the shareholder franchise require proof by the directors of a compelling justification.

Similarly, if the board adopts a strategy resulting in a change of control of a corporation, it cannot use defensive tactics such as no-shop provisions (whereby the board agrees not to consider other offers) or large asset or stock lock-ups to deter competing bidders. In short, if the board agrees to a change of control, it breaches its fiduciary duties if it makes competing offers impossible by adopting a scorched-earth policy that leaves the successful bidder with a depleted target. Although legal counsel will advise managers and directors in this area, a knowledge of the rules of the game is essential to good management.

INSIDE STORY

NO MICKEY MOUSE PAY AT DISNEY

BURBANK, Calif.—[. . . Michael] Eisner's intuition has consistently won big returns for shareholders during his 12½ years at the helm [of Walt Disney Co.]. But his way of doing things is getting him something much less appealing: shareholder pressure to reform a hand-picked board that some corporate-governance experts say isn't independent enough. Disney counts 12 of its 16 directors as independent, but most of them have some close personal or professional ties to Mr. Eisner or the company. They include his personal lawyer, his children's former elementary-school principal, an architect who has done work for Disney and three former Disney executives.

Some shareholders are also upset about two cases of executive pay: the contract the board recently gave Mr. Eisner to stay another 10 years that included eight million stock options, and a multimillion-dollar payout the board made to terminate Michael Ovitz's failed 14-month stint as company president. "Executive Compensation Reports," a newsletter, estimates that Mr. Eisner's package is the largest options grant ever to a sitting chief executive.

. . .

While a number of major corporations have felt heat from shareholder activists in recent years, Disney has until now been protected from such critics by its strong returns. As Mr. Eisner likes to point out, Disney's market capitalization has soared to $53 bil-

lion from $2 billion under his leadership. Critics acknowledge Disney's impressive track record, but counter that the company's snowballing success has left it dangerously dependent on just one man who, despite a talented team of division heads, has a propensity to micromanage, a history of heart trouble and no heir apparent. The current flare-up raises a key question: Is success a substitute for strong corporate-governance standards that check a company's management in good times as well as bad?

"I would say that [the Disney board] is living in the Dark Ages of good corporate-governance practices," says John Nash, president of the National Association of Corporate Directors, an independent organization with no connection to Disney or its shareholders. "It would not meet the standard that's being demanded by institutional shareholders and corporate-governance authorities. It's too beholden to Eisner. There are too many conflicts of interest. There are too many business relationships that cloud independence."

. . .

Mr. Eisner defends the board's independence and promises: "When this CEO stops performing, they should get rid of me—and they will.". . .

. . .

Besides directors' links to Mr. Eisner, critics say there are other signs that the board's practices haven't kept up with evolving

standards. Ownership of the company's stock is low; four directors own no shares at all. (As a Jesuit priest, Father O'Donovan [President of Georgetown University to which Mr. Eisner has donated more than $1 million since 1989] isn't allowed to own any.) Though Mr. Eisner floods members with memoranda, the board doesn't hold a regular strategic-planning retreat. Outside directors don't meet regularly in the absence of company executives such as Mr. Eisner. The board doesn't give Mr. Eisner an annual written assessment of his performance, even though 89% of the nation's biggest industrial corporations do, according to a 1996 survey by executive recruiters Korn/Ferry International.

Disney has recently shown signs of responding to investor concerns, without admitting to any shortcomings. A new sheaf of corporate-governance guidelines, just passed by the board, says ownership of $15,000 worth of Disney stock by board members is "highly desirable." The guidelines also offer a broad definition of director independence and call for an annual review of each board member's status. Mr. Litvack [Disney senior executive vice president and a board member] says all 12 Disney directors who aren't currently company employees pass the new test of independence.

But the company's definition falls far short of the standards recommended by groups like the

Council of Institutional Investors, which says directors can't be labeled independent if they are former employees or have any professional or consulting relationship with the company.

The recent complaints might never have surfaced had it not been for back-to-back blockbusters in December and January: Mr. Ovitz's firing and Mr. Eisner's new contract. In the latter case, Mr. Eisner, not the board, selected executive-pay-expert Graef Crystal to consult for the board "as a favor," Mr. Crystal says. Like Mr. Eisner's previous contracts, the new one gives him a relatively low annual salary of $750,000, with the prospect of greater rewards if the company performs well. The contract includes a plan tying his bonus to the growth of Disney's earnings per share. It would allow Mr. Eisner to receive a bonus in some years even if earnings per share remain unchanged.

The contract negotiations were marked by a bizarre circumstance involving Irwin Russell, who is both chairman of the board's compensation committee and Mr. Eisner's personal lawyer. Mr. Russell relinquished his committee role during the discussion because he needed to represent Mr. Eisner's interests. Other directors concede it is an unusual arrangement, but say it worked because of Mr. Russell's integrity. "I agree that that's not a profile you would normally want to see," says director Raymond L. Watson, a compensation-committee member who stepped in as chairman for Mr. Russell. "But you've got to go to the individuals."

Mr. Watson says Mr. Russell's overarching fairness made it "very difficult to tell during the discussion whom he did represent. At times, I said there were certain things I was willing to concede that Irwin said, 'No, he shouldn't get that.'" Mr. Crystal concurs that Mr. Russell's "straddled role might have cost Michael money." Mr. Russell says: "I would never do anything that I thought wasn't appropriate. I have a very, very high standard of behavior, both for myself and others."

. . .

Under fire recently over the Ovitz exit package, which included a $38.8 million payment and three million stock options, Mr. Eisner and other directors point to the company's action as proof that the board identifies problems quickly and acts. "Michael was sharing with board members his concerns," Mr. Watson recalls.

. . .

Mr. Eisner now believes his eventual successor will come from inside the company. "There's a list of 40, and it could be any one of those 40 depending on when I get hit by the truck." In the meantime, the board is nudging Mr. Eisner to show them his current management team in action. "He's on a real campaign to expose the board to the various executives at that company," Mr. Watson said.

But Mr. Eisner doesn't plan on going anywhere. He feels no need to apologize for doing little community service, not serving on other corporate boards and "all the other things CEOs do. It's very worthy and I wish I had time to do it and someday I will do that. But it's not the job of the CEO in one of these kinds of companies."

SOURCE Bruce Orwall & Joann S. Lublin, *The Plutocracy: If a Company Prospers, Should Its Directors Behave by the Book? Disney's Eisner Shoots Back at Critics Who Say Board Isn't Truly Independent*, WALL ST. J., Feb. 24, 1997, at A1. Reprinted with permission of the *Wall Street Journal,* © 1997 Dow Jones & Company, Inc. All Rights Reserved Worldwide.

KEY WORDS AND PHRASES

asset lock-up option **787**
business judgment rule **784**
constructive trust **793**
controlling shareholder **810**
corporate opportunity doctrine **793**
crown jewels **787**
duty of care **783**

duty of loyalty **783**
freeze out **816**
golden parachute **803**
greenmail **801**
hushmail **819**
line-of-business test **794**
poison pill **807**

proxy **809**
proxy contest **809**
Revlon mode **802**
self-tender **798**
shareholder derivative suit **792**

QUESTIONS AND CASE PROBLEMS

1. Zapp Corporation is a large, publicly held corporation. The board of directors consists of nine individuals. Three are members of management: Mary Kay Yellow, the CEO; Gordon Green, the CFO; and Collette Gray, the VP of Marketing.

On January 15, these three inside directors announce their intention to attempt a management buyout (MBO) of Zapp. After several discussions between Green and Oliver Oldhouse, Zapp's longtime investment banker, the management team proposes to buy all of Zapp's shares for $72 per share, which is a $12 premium over the current market price of $60. The board is scheduled to meet on February 24 and must approve this transaction if it is to proceed. Yellow establishes a special committee of three outside directors to review the proposal before it reaches the board. Norm Newhouse, an investment banker not affiliated with Zapp, is hired to advise the special committee.

On February 24, at 9 A.M., the special committee meets with Newhouse to assess the MBO proposal. One of the documents they review is a letter from Oldhouse that states that the price offered is fair, but that he has not negotiated the best price, nor has he been given authority to seek other bidders for the company. The entire board meets at 11 A.M. At this meeting, the special committee reports that it endorses the MBO. The board approves the transaction 9–0. The MBO proceeds and is successfully completed.

Paul Pink, a shareholder in Zapp, is not satisfied with the amount of money he received for his shares and sues Zapp's board of directors. What arguments will Pink make to win his case? What counterarguments, legal or otherwise, can be made by the directors?

2. Missouri Fidelity Union Trust Life Insurance Co. stock was trading at $2.63 per share. Eight directors sold their shares for $7.00 per share, conditioned on the resignation of eleven of the fifteen directors of the corporation and the provision that five nominees of the buyer be elected as a majority of the executive and investment committees.

Did the directors violate a fiduciary duty by selling corporate control through their directorships? Would the answer be different if the directors had controlled a majority of the voting stock? [*Snyder v. Epstein*, 290 F. Supp. 652 (E.D. Wis. 1968)]

3. The After-School Care Corporation owned more than 40 day-care centers specializing in providing care to elementary-aged children in the afternoons. The president of the company, Clark Holmes, received a phone call at work one day from Marney Stein, the owner and sole proprietor of Pro Providers, a firm that owned six nursery schools for children aged two to four. Stein indicated that she wanted to sell Pro Providers for $1 million and asked if After-School was interested. Holmes proposed the sale to the After-School board of directors. The directors were divided on the issue because they were not certain whether branching out into nursery care would be a smart move. However, as funds were not available, there was no need at the time to vote on the issue.

Holmes decided that he would try to purchase Pro Providers on his own. After securing a loan, Holmes entered into negotiations with Stein. They agreed on a price of $900,000, and the sale went through. Holmes did not inform the board of his activity until after the sale was completed.

A shareholder sues Holmes, alleging that he is taking for himself a corporate opportunity that belongs to the corporation. What kinds of arguments will the shareholder make? Will she be successful? Would the result be different if Holmes expands one of the Pro Provider nursery schools into a nursery/after-school center?

4. Ann O. Yance owned 15% of Kalas Airlines. Yance was an extremely visible and critical shareholder who attended all of the annual meetings of the company and often made public statements that openly criticized its management. Because Yance was a celebrated stunt pilot, these statements garnered much attention in the press. The board of directors of Kalas repeatedly asked Yance not to make these criticisms publicly, but rather to make them directly to the board. Yance did not comply. At a meeting of the board of directors, she proposed that the board, acting on behalf of the company, buy back her shares. The price at which Yance was willing to sell was $45 per share, $16 over the market price. The board agreed to the sale on condition that Yance agree not to speak out against the company or buy any more stock in the company for ten years.

What precautions should the board take to protect this transaction against attack from a shareholder of the company? What grounds would a shareholder have to make such an attack? What are the defenses available to the board? Can the behavior of the board or Yance be criticized on ethical grounds?

5. The Engulf Corporation is a large media and entertainment conglomerate with its stock trading on the

New York Stock Exchange. Engulf is a major producer of films and videos and also publishes several magazines. The company has a shareholders' rights plan (that is, a poison pill), which would make any hostile takeover financially prohibitive unless the pill is redeemed by Engulf's board of directors. On January 10, the Megaclout Corporation, in a move designed to gain control of Engulf, announced a tender offer for 51% of Engulf's shares at $140, an $11 premium over the market price.

On January 14, in a board meeting that lasted more than 13 hours, the Engulf board of directors met to consider Megaclout's offer. Engulf's lawyers and investment bankers attended, and they made detailed presentations on the adequacy of the offer. The next day, the board officially announced that they believed the Megaclout offer was unacceptable for two reasons. First, the board believed that the long-term value of the Engulf stock ranged from $160 to $170, and thus $140 was financially inadequate. Second, the board claimed that Engulf had a distinct corporate culture that included special ways of doing business, an outstanding record of management–employee relations, and strong support of community projects in the towns in which Engulf businesses were located. Acceptance of Megaclout's tender offer would pose a direct threat to this corporate culture. For these reasons, the board refused to redeem the poison pill.

Megaclout brought suit as a shareholder of Engulf against the Engulf board of directors, demanding that the board redeem the poison pill, which would allow all the shareholders to decide whether they wanted to accept the offer by tendering their shares.

a. Must the board of directors of Engulf redeem the poison pill at this time?

b. The board argues that the offer, which is $11 over the market price of the stock, is financially inadequate. Is their argument convincing or not? Why?

c. Should managers be concerned about corporate constituencies other than shareholders, such as employees or communities in which businesses are located? What if these different concerns conflict?

6. Shlensky was a minority stockholder of Chicago National League Ball Club, Inc., which owned and operated the Chicago Cubs baseball team. The defendants were directors of the club. Shlensky alleged that since night baseball was first played in 1935, every major-league team except the Cubs had scheduled most of its home games at night. This had allegedly been done for the specific purpose of maximizing attendance, thereby maximizing revenue and income.

The Cubs have sustained losses from its direct baseball operations. Shlensky attributes the losses to inadequate attendance at the Cubs' home games, which are played at Wrigley Field. He feels that if the directors continue to refuse to install lights at Wrigley Field and schedule night baseball games, the Cubs will continue to sustain similar losses.

Shlensky further alleges that Philip Wrigley, the president of the corporation, has refused to install lights not, as Wrigley claims, for the welfare of the corporation, but because of his personal opinion that "baseball is a daytime sport." Additionally, Shlensky alleges that the other directors have acquiesced in Wrigley's policy.

In his complaint, Shlensky charges that the directors are acting for reasons contrary to the business interests of the corporation and that such acts constitute mismanagement and waste of corporate assets. Does the directors' decision fall within the scope of their business judgment? Have the directors failed to exercise reasonable care in the management of the corporation's affairs? [*Shlensky v. Wrigley*, 237 N.E.2d 776 (Ill. App. Ct. 1968)]

7. McDonald, a potential buyer of financial institutions, visited Halbert at the Tulane Savings and Loan Association. Halbert was president, manager, and chairman of the board, and, along with his wife, the owner of 53% of the stock of the association. McDonald asked if the association were for sale. Halbert replied that it was not for sale but that he and his wife would sell their controlling stock for $1,548 per share. Halbert did not tell the association's board of directors or its shareholders about McDonald's interest in acquiring the association.

In addition to agreeing to sell his stock, Halbert also agreed to cause the association to withhold the payment of dividends. After Halbert's shares were purchased, Halbert, who had not yet relinquished his corporate offices, helped McDonald solicit the minority shareholders' shares and even advised them that, because McDonald was going to withhold dividends for 10 to 20 years, they ought to take his offer of $300 per share. McDonald bought some of the minority shares at $300 and others for between $611 and $650.

Did Halbert owe the minority shareholders a fiduciary duty? If so, what was his duty in selling his minority stock position? Was his conduct ethical? [*Brown v. Halbert*, 76 Cal. Rptr. 781 (Cal. App. Ct. 1969)]

8. Axton–Fisher Tobacco Corp. had a large inventory of tobacco that had greatly appreciated in value, although investors were unaware of its worth. The company had issued two classes of common stock: Class A and Class B. The controlling shareholder, Transamerica, held mostly Class B stock.

Using its power as controlling shareholder, Transamerica caused Axton–Fisher to redeem the Class A stock and then caused the distribution of the valuable tobacco inventory to the remaining shareholders as a liquidating distribution. This was obviously a bad outcome for the Class A shareholders.

Management had two other options. First, it could have disclosed the company's true value and the liquidation plan and could then have given notice of intent to redeem the Class A stock. Second, the managers could have declined to issue a notice of redemption and proceeded with the liquidation.

Did the managers breach their fiduciary duties to the shareholders in the course of action they chose? Which, if any, course of action would not have resulted in a breach of their duties? [*Zahn v. Transamerica*, 162 F.2d 36 (3d Cir. 1947)]

9. Holland had 883,585 shares outstanding, approximately 18.5% of which were owed by Hazelbank, a family holding company. Three of the directors had significant interests in the company: Cheff, the chief executive officer; Mrs. Cheff; and Landwehr. Of the four other directors, only Trenkamp (the general counsel) and one other had interests in the company. All received $300 per diem for monthly board meetings. Cheff received an annual salary of $77,400, and Trenkamp received significant fees as general counsel.

In June 1957, Maremont, an active corporate financier, inquired about merging Holland into one of its companies. When he was rebuffed, he indicated no further interest in Holland. The Holland board investigated and discovered that Maremont had bought 55,000 Holland shares and that he had the reputation of acquiring and liquidating companies.

In August 1957, Maremont informed Cheff that he owned 100,000 shares and demanded a place on the board. He then indicated that Holland's distribution technique was obsolete and that its products could be sold wholesale through half a dozen salespeople. Con-

sequently, Holland's sales force became fearful of a Maremont acquisition.

Maremont later suggested that Hazelbank either sell its Holland shares or purchase his. In October, Holland's directors considered purchasing Maremont's shares. The board was informed that Mrs. Cheff and Hazelbank were ready to buy the shares if Holland did not and that Holland would have to borrow substantial sums to finance the purchase. Nevertheless, the board decided to buy the shares at $14.40 a share, somewhat higher than current market price.

Did the board violate any duty when it decided to purchase Maremont's shares? [*Cheff v. Mathes*, 199 A.2d 548 (Del. 1964)]

MANAGER'S DILEMMA

10. Bell Atlantic Corp. entered into merger negotiations with NYNEX Corp. to create one of the nation's largest telecommunications companies. NYNEX stated that it would execute a binding merger agreement only if the agreement included a termination fee provision under which either company would be forced to pay the other $550 million if its shareholders did not approve the deal. The termination fee arguably reflected each company's costs for negotiating and structuring the merger; however, it also clearly gave shareholders a disincentive to reject the merger. As a Bell Atlantic director who otherwise favored the NYNEX merger, would you approve the agreement with the fee provision?

Assume the merger was approved by the shareholders of both companies. A dissenting Bell Atlantic shareholder sues the company's directors for breach of fiduciary duty, claiming that the termination fee impaired shareholder voting rights by inequitably coercing shareholders into voting for the merger. Was the Bell Atlantic board's adoption of the merger agreement (including the $550 million termination fee) a valid exercise of its business judgment? [*Brazen v. Bell Atlantic Corp.*, 695 A.2d 43 (Del. 1997)]

INTERNET SOURCES	
This site for Richards, Layton & Finger, the largest law firm in Delaware, contains excellent articles on Delaware corporate and partnership law and provides links to other legal-related sites.	http://www.rlf.com

Securities and
Financial Transactions

CHAPTER 22

Public and Private Offerings of Securities

INTRODUCTION

Raising Capital through Securities Offerings

Most businesses reach a certain point at which the founders' initial capital investment and ongoing bank loans are insufficient for continued growth. At this juncture, the directors and managers of the company must decide whether to rein in the company's growth consistent with its existing capital asset base or to sell an interest in the company to raise capital for continued expansion. Although companies often turn first to venture capital or private investment firms, eventually many will seek to raise capital through an initial public offering of the company's shares. Even those companies that can internally generate the cash flow for growth may decide to sell securities to spread the concentration of risk in the business venture and to give the founders and early investors liquidity.

Because registered public offerings are very expensive (often costing more than $900,000), sales of securities to private investors or venture capitalists are almost always structured to be exempt from the federal registration requirements. Whether the directors and managers of a company seek an exemption or go through the public offering process, they must understand and comply with securities laws. Penalties for noncompliance include damages, fines, and imprisonment.

Chapter Overview

This chapter first provides an overview of the federal statutory scheme that regulates the offer and sale of securities. It then defines the key terms "security," "offer," and "sale" under the Securities Act of 1933 (the 1933 Act).

Next, the chapter describes the public offering process, including the registration of securities, the role of an underwriter, the importance of due diligence, preparation of the registration statement, and a managerial timeline for a public offering.

Some of the most relied on exemptions from registration for offerings by the issuer, including the private offering and small business exemptions, are then outlined. A table that lists the key elements of certain exemptions is also provided.

The chapter goes on to discuss exemptions for secondary offerings by shareholders, the restrictions on the resale of registered and unregistered securities, foreign offerings under Regulation S, and sales to qualified institutional buyers under Rule 144A. The periodic reporting and certain other requirements under the Securities Exchange Act of 1934 (the 1934 Act) are listed.

The chapter then highlights liability for failure to meet the registration and prospectus-delivery requirements under Section 12(1) of the 1933 Act and for misstatements or omissions in the registration statement. The discussion focuses on Section 11, under which issuers are strictly liable for misstatements or omissions in a registration statement and certain officers, all directors, accountants, and underwriters are liable if they fail to act with due diligence. The chapter explains who may sue, who may be sued, the elements of liability, the available defenses, the calculation of damages, and the guidelines for due diligence.

Section 12(2) of the 1933 Act, which provides a remedy for any person who purchases a registered or unregistered security in a public offering by means of a misleading prospectus or oral communication, is then discussed. The broader antifraud provisions contained in Section 10(b) of the 1934 Act and Rule 10b-5 (which apply to both registered and exempt offerings of securities) are discussed in Chapter 23. The chapter concludes with a discussion of criminal penalties for violations of the 1933 Act.

 ## Federal Statutory Scheme

Regulations governing securities offerings in the United States stem from the public and governmental outrage and distrust of the nation's financial markets that followed the stock market crash of 1929. According to Representative (later Speaker of the House) Sam Rayburn:

> Millions of citizens have been swindled into exchanging their savings for worthless stocks. The fraudulent promoter has taken an incredible toll from confiding people. . . .
>
> These hired officials of our great corporations who permitted, who promoted, who achieved the extravagant expansion of the financial structure of their respective companies today present a pitiable spectacle. Five years ago they arrogated to themselves the greatest privileges. They scorned the interference of the Government. They dealt with their stockholders in the most arbitrary fashion. They called upon the people to bow down to them as the real rulers of the country. Safe from the pitiless publicity of Government supervision, unrestrained by Federal statute, free from any formal control, these few men, proud, arrogant, and blind, drove the country to financial ruin. Some of them are fugitives from justice in foreign lands; some of them have committed suicide; some of them are under indictment; some of them are in prison; all of them are in terror of the consequences of their own deeds.[1]

The two principal federal acts that regulate securities transactions and issuers, the Securities Act of 1933 and the Securities Exchange Act of 1934, were adopted during the depths of the Great Depression. These and subsequent acts embodied the belief that (1) investors should be provided with all essential information prior to investing in speculative ventures, (2) corporate insiders should not be allowed to abuse their position and use nonpublic information concerning their companies to their own financial advantage, and (3) injured investors should receive adequate relief even in the absence of common law fraud.

The 1933 Act

In adopting the 1933 Act, the U.S. Congress sought to ensure adequate disclosure to investors of material information about the issuer and the offering. The act requires that promoters of securities offerings register them with the Securities and Exchange Commission (SEC), an agency of the U.S. federal government, and provide to prospective purchasers a prospectus containing material information about the issuer and the offering, unless the security or the type of transaction is exempt from registration.

Congress rejected suggestions that it also regulate the content or quality of securities offerings. As a result, investors are not protected from making highly speculative or foolish investments. The 1933 Act requires only that they be advised of all material facts before they invest their money.

---

1. House Consideration, Amendment and Passage of H.R. 5480, May 5, 1932, 77 Cong. Rec. 2910, 2918 (1933), as reprinted in 1 Fed. Sec. L. Legis. Hist. 1933–1982, at 2948 (1983).

In addition to requiring registration, the 1933 Act expressly creates private rights of action for certain violations of its provisions. This means that in addition to public enforcement by the SEC or criminal proceedings by the U.S. Attorney's Office, any investor can bring a private suit for damages.

The 1934 Act

The 1934 Act sought to build upon the 1933 Act by implementing a policy of continuous disclosure. Companies of a certain size and with a certain number of shareholders or whose stock is traded on a national securities exchange are required to file periodic reports with the SEC. The 1934 Act also contains stringent antifraud provisions and implements filing requirements for insiders dealing in their own company's stock. In addition, the 1934 Act established a framework for the self-regulation of the securities industry under the ultimate supervision of the SEC.

The Private Securities Litigation Reform Act of 1995

The Private Securities Litigation Reform Act of 1995[2] (the Reform Act) was the most sweeping reform of the U.S. securities laws in the last 20 years. The Reform Act was designed to correct perceived abuses in private securities litigation, particularly class actions that coerced settlements and thereby increased the cost of raising capital and chilled corporate disclosure to investors.

The Reform Act included a variety of procedural provisions designed to prevent the filing of frivolous suits by so-called professional plaintiffs who often owned a limited number of shares in many companies and stood ready to lend their names to class action complaints they often had not even read. The act introduced the idea that the "most adequate plaintiff" should be the lead plaintiff and select counsel to represent the class. There is a rebuttable presumption that the plaintiff with the largest financial interest in the relief being sought by the class is the most adequate.

The act limited discovery to prevent "fishing expedition" lawsuits designed to force the defendants to settle frivolous claims to avoid the cost of discovery. Except in extraordinary circumstances, courts must stay discovery pending a ruling on a motion to dismiss. Stricter and uniform pleading requirements require the investor to specify each statement alleged to be misleading and the reason or reasons the statement is misleading. The plaintiffs also must plead and then prove that the misstatement or omission alleged in the complaint actually caused their loss. The investor must also specifically allege facts giving rise to a "strong inference" that the defendant acted with the required state of mind. Thus, in securities fraud cases under Section 10(b), which require *scienter,* the plaintiffs must allege facts giving rise to a strong inference of fraudulent intent on the part of the defendant.

The combination of the stricter pleading requirements and the staying of discovery pending a decision on a motion to dismiss makes it more likely that defendants will be able to resolve frivolous claims more quickly and cheaply by winning motions to dismiss before incurring the time and expense of extensive discovery.

The act generally eliminates joint and several liability in cases under Section 10(b) of the 1934 Act for defendants who did not commit knowing violations and requires such defendants to pay only their "fair share" of the damages, that is, the portion attributable to their percentage of responsibility. Outside directors are given the same protection for suits under Section 11 as a way to encourage capable outsiders to serve on corporate boards.

The act imposes new requirements for independent public accountants auditing the financial statements of publicly traded companies. These requirements, which are designed to result in early detection of fraud and disclosure, are discussed more fully in Chapter 23.

Finally, the act created a new statutory safe harbor for written and oral forward-looking statements by issuers and certain persons retained or acting on behalf of the issuer. This is discussed further in the sections dealing with liability under Sections 11 and 12(2) of the 1933 Act. Its application to fraud cases under Section 10(b) of the 1934 Act and Rule 10b-5 is discussed in Chapter 23.

---

2. Pub. L. No. 104-67, 109 Stat. 737 (1995) (codified in scattered sections of 15 U.S.C.). The complete text of the act is available at <http://thomas.loc.gov/c104/h1058.enr.txt>.

As of mid–1998, Congress was considering legislation that would limit a plaintiff's ability to bring a securities fraud case involving a publicly traded company in state court. State court proceedings have become more prevalent since the passage of the Reform Act, because most state laws do not provide the protections afforded companies and their officers and directors by the Reform Act.

SEC Rules and Regulations

Since Congress adopted the 1933 Act and the 1934 Act, the SEC has used its power as an administrative agency to adopt a number of rules and regulations. The SEC uses these rules and regulations to address some of the ambiguity of the securities acts, make case-specific exemptions, carry out informal discretionary actions, and conduct investigations regarding compliance with the securities acts.

For instance in 1972, the SEC adopted Rule 144 to clarify definition of the term "underwriter." In 1982, the SEC adopted Regulation D with rules that outlined the requirements and limitations for exempt private offerings and offerings by small businesses. Subsequently, it adopted Rule 701 to exempt offers and sales of securities pursuant to employee benefit plans. Recently, the SEC revised Regulation A to make it easier for small businesses to raise capital without going through a public offering.

All of the securities acts have been amended numerous times since their adoption. Exhibit 22.1 briefly describes the main sections of the two acts. More detailed excerpts from both acts can be found in Appendices J and K of this book.

EXHIBIT 22.1   Important Sections of the 1933 and 1934 Acts

1933 ACT

- *Section 2*—defines terms, including security, offer, sale, and underwriter.
- *Sections 3 and 4*—list exempt securities and describe exempt transactions.
- *Section 5*—requires the registration of all securities offered and sold in the United States (unless an exemption from registration is available) and the delivery of a prospectus.
- *Sections 6–8 and 10*—outline the general procedures of the registration process and detail the guidelines for the registration statement and the accompanying prospectus.
- *Sections 11 and 12*—describe the penalties, elements of liability, damages, and parties held liable for violation of the 1933 Act.

1934 ACT

- *Section 10*—regulates the use of manipulative and deceptive devices in the purchase or sale of securities.
- *Section 12*—lists the reporting requirements for registered public companies.
- *Section 16*—provides the reporting requirements for insiders including directors, officers, and principal shareholders and the limitations on insider transactions.

Blue Sky Laws

In addition to the federal securities laws, there are state statutes called *blue sky laws*. An issuer selling securities must comply not only with the federal securities laws, but also with the securities laws of all of the states in which the securities are offered or sold. Fortunately, many states, the District of Columbia, and Puerto Rico have adopted the Uniform Securities Act, and thus there is some consistency among state laws. Other states, including New York and California, have retained their own version of securities regulatory schemes.

Like the federal statutes, the Uniform Securities Act emphasizes disclosure as the primary means of protecting investors. However, some states authorize the securities administrator to deny a securities selling permit unless he or she finds that the issuer's plan of business and the proposed issuance of securities are fair, just, and equitable. Even if the state statute does not state this provision specifically, a state securities commissioner can usually deny registration until he or she is satisfied that the offering is fair. This process is referred to as *merit review*.

In late 1996, Congress passed the Capital Markets Efficiency Act of 1996,[3] a law designed in part to provide more uniformity between federal and state securities regulation. Under the new law, states are no longer permitted, in connection with transactions involving only accredited investors that are exempt pursuant to Rule 506 under Regulation D, to require more than the type of filing required by the SEC (including any amendments), a consent to service of process, and a filing fee. Accordingly, pre-offer and pre-sale notice filings and merit review requirements of the states have been preempted in connection with Rule 506 offerings. The law similarly preempts state registration requirements and merit review in connection with most initial public offerings registered with the SEC. The new law also provides federal preemption for the issuance of securities to "qualified purchasers," a category of investors to be defined by the SEC at a later time.

 ## Definition of Terms

It is necessary to define three basic terms used in the 1933 Act—security, offer, and sale. Their meanings in a securities law context may be different from their everyday meanings.

Security

The term *security* for purposes of the 1933 Act—and most other securities statutes—is much broader than the common conception of the term. Section 2(1) of the 1933 Act defines a security as:

> any note, stock, treasury stock, bond, debenture, evidence of indebtedness, certificate of interest or participation in any profit-sharing agreement, collateral-trust certificate, pre-organization certificate or subscription, transferable share, investment contract, voting-trust certificate, certificate of deposit for a security, fractional undivided interest in oil, gas, or other mineral rights, any put, call, straddle, option, or privilege on any security, certificate of deposit, or group or index of securities (including any interest therein or based on the value thereof), or any put, call, straddle, option, or privilege entered into on a national securities ex-

INTERNATIONAL CONSIDERATION

On most American stock exchanges, foreign securities are traded in the form of American Depository Receipts (ADRs). The securities themselves are held by a financial institution called a depository, which issues the ADRs traded by foreign investors and handles any foreign-exchange transactions. This structure allows the foreign securities to trade at a per-share price level customary in the U.S. market. In addition, it allows investors to trade interests in foreign securities in compliance with U.S. clearance and settlement requirements.

change relating to foreign currency, or, in general, any interest or instrument commonly known as a "security," or any certificate of interest or participation in, temporary or interim certificate for, receipt for, guarantee of, or warrant or right to subscribe to or purchase, any of the foregoing.

Because the term security is defined so broadly, the circumstances of a particular transaction must be analyzed to determine whether in fact it involves a security and is subject to regulation.

Certain investments that are commonly agreed to be securities include the stock and bonds of public and private companies. However, some investments, which by their name fall into the definition of securities, are not necessarily considered securities. An example is the stock in a cooperative association owning an apartment building, whereby an occupant of the building owns shares of stock that are inextricably linked to the lease of a particular unit of the building. In *United Housing Foundation v. Forman*,[4] the U.S. Supreme Court held that because the dwelling was used as a place of habitation, the inducement to purchase was solely to acquire living space and not to invest for profit. Consequently, the Court ruled that the shares of stock were not securities under the 1933 Act.

The scope of the law goes further than just the category of commonly agreed-on securities. Under federal law, one type of security—an *investment contract*—is

3. Pub. L. 104-290, 110 Stat. 3416 (1996).

4. 421 U.S. 837 (1975).

present if the transaction involves an investment of money in a common enterprise with profits to come solely from the efforts of others. This test was first enunciated in the following case.

A CASE IN POINT	SUMMARY

CASE 22.1
SEC v. W. J.
HOWEY CO.
Supreme Court
of the United States
328 U.S. 293 (1946).

FACTS   The W. J. Howey Company (Howey) owned large tracts of citrus acreage in Lake County, Florida. Expansion of the citrus acreage was financed, in part, by the sale of strips of land bearing citrus trees to persons living in various parts of the United States. Each prospective investor was offered both a land-sale contract and an optional service contract (with a ten-year term) after being told that it was not feasible to invest in a grove unless service arrangements were made. Although investors were free to use any service company, approximately 85% of the acreage sold was serviced by a company affiliated with Howey.

Most of the investors were unskilled in agriculture. The primary motivation for investing was the expectation of substantial profits, projected to be 10% annually over a ten-year period.

ISSUE PRESENTED   Does the offer and sale of parcels of land bearing citrus trees, coupled with optional management contracts pursuant to which the promoter cares for the trees, constitute an investment contract and hence a security under Section 2(1) of the 1933 Act?

SUMMARY OF OPINION   The U.S. Supreme Court held that the transactions in this case clearly involved investment contracts as listed in Section 2(1). The plan involved a scheme "whereby a person invests his money in a common enterprise and is led to expect profits solely from the efforts of the promoter or a third party." The persons buying the land were not skilled in the cultivation, harvesting, or marketing of citrus fruits, had no intent to occupy the land and develop it for themselves, and were attracted solely by the prospect of a return on their investment.

The Court held that the critical element in the transaction was the large-scale cooperative nature of the enterprise and the managerial efforts of the promoters. The transfer of real property rights was purely incidental. Accordingly, there was no question that an investment contract was involved. The fact that some investors chose not to accept the optional service contract was immaterial, the Court concluded, because the 1933 Act prohibits the offer, as well as the sale, of unregistered, nonexempt securities.

RESULT   Howey had offered and sold securities.

COMMENTS   This case makes it clear that a security can be present even in schemes that are not purely speculative or promotional in nature and that involve investments in tangible assets having intrinsic value. The Supreme Court shifted the focus in determining whether or not a security was involved from the surface appearance of a transaction to the expectations of the parties. Subsequent cases have expanded the *Howey* test and have held that Section 2(1) is not to be read literally, because Congress intended the application of the federal securities laws to turn on the economic realities underlying a transaction and not on the name attached to it.

Although the *Howey* test required that the investor rely solely on the efforts of others for the expectation of profits, subsequent decisions have established that there can be an investment contract, and thus a security, even if the investor participates in the generation of profits.[5]

An interest in a general partnership is generally held not to be a security, because each partner by law has the right to exercise control in the operation of the partnership. However, the courts have found a general partnership interest to be a security if it meets any of the following three tests:

1. The partnership agreement leaves so little power to the partners that the arrangement is tantamount to a limited partnership.
2. The investor is so inexperienced in business affairs that he or she is incapable of intelligently exercising his or her partnership powers.
3. The investor is so dependent on the unique management ability of the promoter or manager that he or she cannot replace the manager or exercise meaningful partnership powers.[6]

A limited partnership interest is almost always held to constitute a security because limited partners, in order to protect their limited liability, are prohibited by law from taking part in the control of the partnership business. An interest in real estate is not in itself considered a security, though it may be a security if combined with a management contract, as in *Howey*.

The SEC and at least 35 state securities regulators have taken the position that interests in a limited liability company (LLC) are securities. Regulators base their conclusion on either the theory that LLC interests constitute an investment contract under *Howey* or that they have all the characteristics of stock. The U.S. Supreme Court has not yet ruled on this issue.

In recent years, there was a controversy as to whether the sale of an entire business through the sale of its corporate stock involved the sale of a security. Under the *sale-of-business doctrine*, certain courts held that compliance with federal securities laws was not necessary because the economic reality of the transaction was that a business was being sold, rather than securities. The U.S. Supreme Court rejected this doctrine in *Landreth Timber Co. v. Landreth*, holding that the sale of a business through a stock transaction is a securities transaction if the stock sold possesses all of the characteristics traditionally associated with common stock.[7]

Promissory notes and other evidences of indebtedness may or may not constitute a security, depending on the factual context. In the following case, the Supreme Court set forth the *family resemblance test* for determining which types of notes are securities.

---

5. SEC v. Glenn W. Turner Enters., Inc., 474 F.2d 476 (9th Cir. 1973), *cert. denied*, 414 U.S. 821 (1973).

6. The test to determine whether a general partnership constitutes a security was set forth in *Williamson v. Tucker*, 645 F.2d 404 (5th Cir. 1981), *cert. denied*, 454 U.S. 897 (1981), and later applied in *Holden v. Hagopian*, 978 F.2d 1115 (9th Cir. 1992).

7. 471 U.S. 681 (1985).

| **A CASE IN POINT** | **SUMMARY** |

CASE 22.2
REVES v. ERNST & YOUNG
Supreme Court of the United States
494 U.S. 56 (1990).

FACTS Farmers' Cooperative of Arkansas and Oklahoma, Inc. (the Co-op) was an agricultural cooperative of approximately 23,000 members. In order to raise money to support its general business operations, the Co-op sold demand notes, that is, promissory notes payable at any time that the holder of the note requested payment. The notes were not collateralized and were uninsured; they paid a variable rate of interest that was adjusted monthly to keep it higher than the rate paid by local financial institutions. The Co-op offered the notes to both members and nonmembers, marketing the scheme as a safe and secure "investment program."

Despite such assurances, the Co-op filed for bankruptcy, leaving approximately $10 million in demand notes unpaid. A group of holders of the notes sued the Co-op's

Case 22.2 continues

Case 22.2 continued

auditors under Section 10(b) of the 1934 Act, claiming that the auditors intentionally failed to follow generally accepted accounting principles in evaluating the financial condition of the Co-op.

The note holders prevailed at the trial level, receiving a $6.1 million judgment. The auditors appealed, claiming that the demand notes were not securities under the 1934 Act. (The definition of "security" under Section 3(a)(10) of the 1934 Act is virtually identical to the definition under Section 2(1) of the 1933 Act.) The appeals court reversed, and the note holders appealed.

ISSUE PRESENTED   Are demand notes issued by a farmers' cooperative to its members securities?

SUMMARY OF OPINION   The U.S. Supreme Court adopted a family resemblance test to use in determining whether a promissory note is a security. Under this test, a promissory note is initially presumed to be a security based upon the literal language of the Securities Acts ("The term 'security' means any note . . ."). This presumption may be rebutted, however, by a showing that the note bears a "strong resemblance" (in terms of four specific factors) to an enumerated category of instruments commonly held not to constitute securities. The four specific factors used in evaluating an instrument are

1. the motivations that would prompt a reasonable seller and buyer to enter into the transaction;
2. the plan of distribution of the instrument;
3. the reasonable expectations of the investing public; and
4. whether some factor, such as the existence of another regulatory scheme, significantly reduces the risk of the instrument, thereby rendering application of the federal securities laws unnecessary.

The category of instruments commonly held not to constitute securities includes notes delivered in connection with consumer financing, notes secured by a home mortgage, and short-term notes secured by accounts receivable.

Applying these four factors to the case at hand, the Court observed the following: (1) the Co-op sold the notes in an effort to raise capital for its general business operations, and the purchasers bought them in order to earn a profit in the form of interest; (2) the notes were distributed to a wide group of people over an extended period; (3) the notes were characterized to the public as investments, and it is likely that the public perceived them as such; and (4) there was no risk-reducing factor making application of the federal securities law unnecessary (for example, the notes were not federally insured certificates of deposit). Because the notes bore no family resemblance to the types of notes commonly held not to constitute securities and, in fact, resembled the types of instruments the federal securities laws were designed to regulate, the Court held the notes were securities.

In reaching its decision, the Court expressly rejected the use of the *Howey* test in determining whether or not a note constitutes a security. It stated that the *Howey* test is useful in determining whether an instrument constitutes an investment contract, but is not helpful in determining whether an instrument is a note within the statutory definition of security.

Case 22.2 continues

Case 22.2 continued

The Court also expressly rejected the use of an investment-versus-commercial test, which previously had been used by the majority of circuits in determining whether a note constituted a security. Under this test, notes issued in a commercial or consumer context were held not to be securities, but those issued in an investment context were held to be securities.

The Court lastly rejected the auditor's argument that because the notes were demand notes, they fell within the literal terms of Section 3(a)(10) of the 1934 Act ("the term 'security' . . . shall not include . . . any note . . . which has a maturity at the time of issuance of not exceeding nine months"). The Court held that a demand note does not necessarily mature in nine months. In light of this patent ambiguity and in light of Congress's broad purposes in enacting the federal securities law, the Court chose not to interpret the exclusion in Section 3(a)(10) to cover the Co-op's demand notes.

RESULT   The demand notes issued by the farmers' cooperative to its members were securities.

COMMENTS   The holding in *Reves v. Ernst & Young* removed much of the uncertainty regarding the status of promissory notes for securities law purposes. Prior to this decision, the courts were widely split as to the proper test to use in evaluating promissory notes.

Offer

Section 2(3) of the 1933 Act defines an *offer* as "every attempt or offer to dispose of, or solicitation of an offer to buy, a security or interest in a security, for value." This definition is much broader than that in contract law. An offer that is unacceptably vague for contract law purposes may well constitute an offer for federal securities laws purposes. However, Section 2(3) expressly provides that preliminary negotiations or agreements between an issuer and an underwriter or among underwriters do not constitute an offer to sell.

Sale

A *sale* is defined by Section 2(3) to include "every contract of sale or disposition of a security or interest in a security, for *value.*" The crucial term in this definition is value. It has been defined by the courts very broadly; more broadly, for example, than in state corporations statutes, which require that stock can only be issued for "value" in the form of cash, property, or compensation for past services.

The "In Brief" provides a decision tree for determining whether an instrument is a security and for analyzing the securities registration requirements discussed below.

 The Public Offering

Once it is determined that an investment offering does in fact involve a security, the issue of registration must be addressed.

Registration of Securities

Section 5 of the 1933 Act requires the registration of all securities offered and sold in the United States, unless an exemption from registration is available. Section 5 can be summarized as follows.

1. Section 5(a) prohibits the sale of a security before a registration statement has been filed with the SEC. The *registration statement* consists of filing forms and the *prospectus*, the disclosure document

that an issuer of securities provides to prospective purchasers. Section 5(c) prohibits the use of any means of interstate commerce to offer to sell or buy any security during this time.

2. During the waiting period between the filing of the registration statement and the date the registration statement becomes effective with the SEC, written and oral offers to sell the security may be made,

but all written offers must meet the standards required of a prospectus.

3. Once the registration becomes effective with the SEC (referred to as *going effective*), offers and sales of securities may be made. However, Section 5(b) continues to require that any written offer or sale of a security be preceded or accompanied by a prospectus meeting the requirements of the 1933 Act.

IN BRIEF

DECISION TREE ANALYSIS OF SECURITIES REGISTRATION REQUIREMENTS

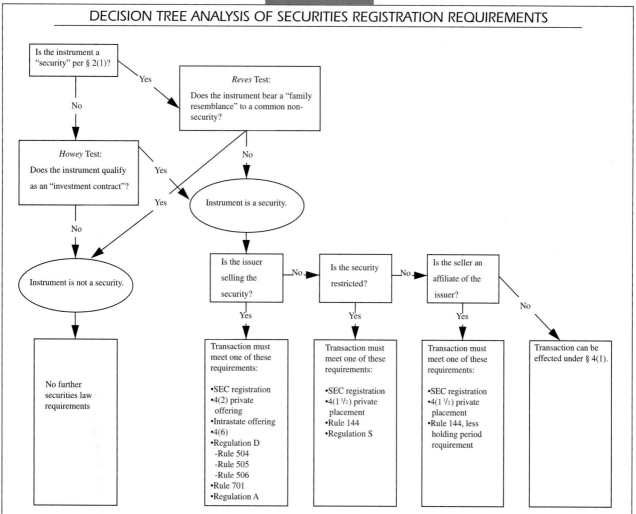

SOURCE This decision tree was created by John Lee based on information provided by Constance E. Bagley. Copyright © 1998 by Constance E. Bagley. Used by permission.

In general, every public offering of securities must be registered with the SEC. The registration requirement is designed to ensure that certain information is filed with the SEC and distributed to potential investors by means of a prospectus. Unlike certain state securities authorities, the SEC does not have statutory authority to approve or disapprove an offering on its merits. Instead, the registration process is designed to ensure that the information provided to investors is accurate and complete. The general procedures to be followed in the registration process are found in Sections 6 and 8 of the 1933 Act.

The registration of a public offering is an expensive and time-consuming affair. The process includes the preparation of the registration statement—that is, the document filed with the SEC—and of the prospectus, which must be included in the registration statement and provided to prospective investors. Securities lawyers, independent accountants, investment bankers, a printer, and an engraver all become involved in the process. The out-of-pocket fees and expenses for an initial public offering, excluding compensation for the investment bankers who underwrite the offering, can easily exceed

$900,000. All such fees must be paid by the issuer of the securities (or in the case of offerings by persons other than the issuer, by the seller of the securities).[8]

The Role of the Underwriter

A public offering of securities is typically, though not necessarily, underwritten by one or more broker-dealers or investment banking firms.

Firm Commitment Underwriting   In a *firm commitment underwriting*, the underwriters agree to purchase the entire offering, thus effectively shifting the risk of the offering from the issuer to the underwriters. The lead underwriter is responsible for negotiating with the issuer the terms of the underwriter. The lead underwriter is responsible for negotiating with the issuer the terms of the offering and compensation and for putting

---

8. The process of doing an initial public offering is discussed in detail in CONSTANCE E. BAGLEY & CRAIG E. DAUCHY, *The Entrepreneur's Guide to Business Law* 494–540 (1998).

"Would everyone check to see they have an attorney? I seem to have ended up with two."

together an underwriting group (the *syndicate)*. Each member of the underwriting group agrees to purchase a certain number of the securities of the issuer once the offering is declared effective by the SEC.

Such a commitment places the underwriters in a risky position. Therefore, the underwriting agreement between the issuer and the lead underwriter as representative of the underwriting group, and the agreements among the members of the underwriting group, are typically not signed until immediately before the offering is declared effective by the SEC. The price at which the securities will be offered and the underwriters' commission are usually not formally determined until the evening before the offering goes effective.

Once the offering becomes effective, the underwriters attempt to sell the securities that they are obligated to purchase. Most firm underwriting agreements are of short duration. Usually, the sale closes within one week of the day the agreement is signed. As of the closing date, the underwriters are obligated to purchase any securities that remain unsold.

The "Inside Story" highlights a situation in which a stock offering of British Petroleum by the British government coincided with the October 1987 stock market crash. Weeks in advance of the proposed offering, the U.S. investment banks involved in the deal provided a firm commitment underwriting to the government. After stock prices plummeted in the market crash, the U.S. underwriters lost up to $500 million from the post-crash offering.

Because a firm commitment underwriting will provide the issuer with a predetermined amount of money within a specified period, it is attractive to issuers. A firm commitment underwriting is also attractive to investors because it implies that the underwriters themselves are willing to take a risk on the offering. Because it places the members of the underwriting group at risk for the amount of the offering, broker-dealers and investment bankers will usually only agree to a firm underwriting if they are certain that they will be able to sell the offered securities quickly. Such certainty will depend upon a variety of factors, including the amount of money being sought, the performance and prospects of the company, whether the company is seasoned or relatively new, and the condition of the public securities market.

Best-Efforts Underwriting   In a *best-efforts underwriting*, the underwriters do not agree to purchase the securities being offered. Instead, they agree to use their best efforts to find buyers at an agreed-on price. Best-efforts underwritings are often used for initial public offerings or for companies that are unseasoned.

A best-efforts offering leaves the risks of the offering entirely with the issuer. However, some established, successful companies may prefer a best-efforts offering because the cost of distribution is lower than for a firm commitment underwriting.

The Registration Statement

Sections 7 and 10 of the 1933 Act, and the rules promulgated by the SEC under the act, contain detailed guidelines as to what must be included in the registration statement and the accompanying prospectus. Regulations C and S–K, adopted by the SEC pursuant to the 1933 Act, list the general information required in connection with most public registrations.[9] In addition, the SEC has issued a variety of forms that list the information required in connection with particular types of transactions.

Forms   Securities offered in an initial public offering are registered in a registration statement meeting the requirements of *Form S–1* (or if the issuer is a small business, *Form SB–1)*. The registration statement must include a complete description of the securities being offered, the business of the issuer, the risk factors, the management, and the major shareholders. It must also include audited financial statements.

Companies that have been filing periodic reports under the 1934 Act, but that are not followed so widely that the SEC could be confident that information previously filed would be disseminated in the marketplace, file on Form S–2. *Form S–2* allows these companies to present certain information in a streamlined form and to incorporate previous filings by reference, so that investors can obtain more information if desired. This is part of the SEC's integrated disclosure system, which is designed to integrate the reporting requirements under the 1934 Act with the prospectus delivery requirement under the 1933 Act.

Form S–3 applies to a category of companies that have filed periodic reports under the 1934 Act for at least three years and have a widespread following in the marketplace. For an offering by an issuer of common

---

9. 17 CFR § 230.400 *et seq.* (1997); 17 CFR § 229 (1997).

stock, for example, the issuer can use Form S–3 only if the aggregate market value of the voting stock held by nonaffiliates is $150 million or more; or alternatively, if the aggregate market value of the voting stock held by nonaffiliates is $100 million or more and the issuer has an annual trading volume of three million shares or more. (*Affiliates* include officers, directors, and controlling shareholders. The SEC has a rebuttable presumption that any shareholder with 10% of the issuer's stock is an affiliate.)

For companies filing on Form S–3, information about the registrant that has been reported in annual and quarterly reports filed under the 1934 Act need not be provided to investors in the prospectus, unless there has been a material change in the registrant's affairs or financial statements. However, such reports are incorporated by reference and are deemed a part of the prospectus for liability purposes.

As part of the SEC's Small Business Initiatives (SBI) designed to ease the cost of raising capital for small businesses, the SEC simplified offering methods for small companies by the adoption of new registration forms, Form SB–1 and Form SB–2, for small business issuers. *Small business issuers* are defined as companies with revenues less than $25 million whose market value of publicly held securities (other than those held by affiliates) is less than $25 million. Other aspects of the SBI changes that affect exemptions from registration and reporting requirements are discussed later in this chapter.

The SEC adopted Form SB–1, under which nonreporting and transitional small business issuers can offer up to $10 million annually. *Form SB–2* has no limit on the amount of offerings by small business issuers. Both forms can be used for initial and repeat offerings as well as for primary and secondary offerings. In addition, the SB forms reduce the need for audited financial statements compared to what is required under Form S–1. Only the last fiscal year's audited balance sheet and the previous two years' audited income statements are required under Forms SB–1 and SB–2. Exhibit 22.2 compares some of the requirements of registered offerings on Forms S–1, SB–1 and SB–2.

Prospectus The prospectus is the document provided to prospective purchasers of an issuer's securities. It is contained within the registration statement.

The tone of a prospectus frequently strikes nonlawyers as dry, bleak, and confusing. Such a perception arises out of the conflicting purposes of the prospectus. On the one hand, it is a selling document, designed to present the best possible view of the investment and the issuing company. On the other hand, it is a disclosure document, an insurance policy against claims of securities fraud. It is this second function that usually predominates. The prospectus usually contains only provable statements of fact, with numerous disclaimers regarding the future success of the issuer. Businesspeople, accustomed to presenting their

EXHIBIT 22.2	Comparison of Public Offering Requirements		
	FORM S–1 OFFERING	**FORM SB–1 OFFERING**	**FORM SB–2 OFFERING**
Amount of offering	No limit	Up to $10 million in any fiscal year	No limit
Type of issuer	Any issuer	Must be a nonreporting or a transitional small business issuer	Must be a small business issuer
Type of offering	No limitations	No limitations	No limitations
Type of disclosure required	S–1 basic registration form for most offerings. S–1 items referenced in Regulation S–K.	Offering statement with three models: 1) Q&A, Form U–7 2) Form 1–A, old form 3) Form SB–2, part I.	Simplified Form SB–2. SB–2 items referenced in Regulation S–B, a simplified version of Regulation S–K.

company in the best possible light, frequently have difficulty adjusting to the somber tone of the prospectus.

As of October 1, 1998, companies selling securities to the public in the United States must use plain English in the design and language of the cover page, summary, and risk factors sections of the prospectus. In these sections, companies must (1) use short sentences with everyday words, (2) avoid legal jargon and highly technical business terms, (3) use the active voice, (4) not use multiple negatives, and (5) use bullet lists for complex information, if possible. Companies are encouraged, but not required, to use plain English throughout the prospectus.

A sample cover page of a prospectus appears as Exhibit 22.3.

Due Diligence

A key step in preparing the registration statement is the process of *due diligence,* whereby the company, the underwriters, and their respective counsel assemble and review the information about the company in the registration statement. The company must be prepared to back up every claim it makes in the prospectus. Even if the claim is stated as an opinion (such as "The company believes that it is the industry leader"), the company must be able to demonstrate the reasonableness of the belief.

Underwriters cannot simply rely on the representations of issuers or the officials of issuers, but must perform their own independent due diligence investigation. They should go beyond the corporate documents provided by the issuer and examine information in press releases and news reports concerning key competitors and others important to the issuer's business. Underwriters should also monitor relevant Web sites and public agency filings.

Exhibit 22.4 provides a long but useful list of tasks that should be undertaken by officers, directors, underwriters, and counsel engaged in the offering of securities.

Registration Procedure

The registration statement must be filed with the SEC. Section 8 of the 1933 Act provides that the registration automatically becomes effective on the twentieth day after filing, unless the SEC fixes an earlier date. Most registrants file their registration statement with language stating that it shall not become effective until declared effective by the SEC, so that the staff of the SEC has the necessary time (which usually exceeds the statutory 20-day period) to review the filing.

Each amendment to the registration statement filed prior to the effective date starts the 20-day period running again; however, if the SEC has consented to the amendment, the waiting period may be accelerated. If, on the other hand, the SEC finds that the registration statement is materially defective in some respect, it may, after notice and a hearing, issue a stop order suspending the effectiveness of the offering.

Review   Registration statements received by the SEC are subject to review by the SEC staff. The extent of review is usually affected by the nature of the offering and the number of filings that the SEC is faced with reviewing. In general, all first-time registrants will receive a complete review. Most repeat registrants will receive a more limited review, and some will receive no review.

Comments of the SEC staff are conveyed through a letter of comment, which is either read over the telephone to the issuer's counsel or, less often, mailed to counsel directly. The members of the SEC staff are usually available to discuss these letters of comment either by telephone or in person. Although the comment letters contain only suggestions without force of law, they generally result in the filing of an amendment to the registration statement. Acceding to the staff's reasonable suggestions is less expensive and less time-consuming than fighting an issue in an administrative hearing and in court. The amended registration statement is usually filed with a letter from counsel answering, item by item, the issues raised by the staff.

Waiting Period   The time between the filing of the registration statement and its becoming effective is called the *waiting period* or the *quiet period* because the law severely limits what the issuer and underwriters can say or publish during this time. No sale of securities can occur prior to the effectiveness of the registration statement; however, the underwriters may assemble selling groups, distribute copies of the preliminary prospectus, and even solicit offers to buy the securities. The preliminary prospectus—sometimes referred to as a *red-herring prospectus* because a notice on the cover states in red ink that it is not final and is subject to completion—is an incomplete version of the final prospectus. It sets forth the proposed range for the selling price and omits underwriters except for the lead underwriters, whose

EXHIBIT 22.3   Prospectus Cover Page

I n k t o m i

2,254,000 Shares

Inktomi Corporation

Common Stock
(par value $0.001 per share)

Of the 2,254,000 shares of Common Stock offered hereby, 2,000,000 are being sold by Inktomi Corporation ("Inktomi" or the "Company") and 254,000 are being sold by the Selling Stockholders. See "Principal and Selling Stockholders". The Company will not receive any of the proceeds from the sale of the shares being sold by the Selling Stockholders.

Prior to this offering, there has been no public market for the Common Stock of the Company. For factors considered in determining the initial public offering price, see "Underwriting".

See "Risk Factors" beginning on page 5 for certain considerations relevant to an investment in the Common Stock.

The Common Stock has been approved for quotation on the Nasdaq National Market under the symbol "INKT".

THESE SECURITIES HAVE NOT BEEN APPROVED OR DISAPPROVED BY THE SECURITIES AND EXCHANGE COMMISSION OR ANY STATE SECURITIES COMMISSION NOR HAS THE SECURITIES AND EXCHANGE COMMISSION OR ANY STATE SECURITIES COMMISSION PASSED UPON THE ACCURACY OR ADEQUACY OF THIS PROSPECTUS. ANY REPRESENTATION TO THE CONTRARY IS A CRIMINAL OFFENSE.

	Initial Public Offering Price	Underwriting Discount(1)	Proceeds to Company(2)	Proceeds to Selling Stockholders
Per Share	$18.00	$1.26	$16.74	$16.74
Total (3)...........................	$40,572,000	$2,840,040	$33,480,000	$4,251,960

(1) The Company and the Selling Stockholders have agreed to indemnify the Underwriters against certain liabilities, including liabilities under the Securities Act of 1933, as amended. See "Underwriting".
(2) Before deducting estimated expenses of $700,000 payable by the Company.
(3) The Company has granted the Underwriters an option for 30 days to purchase up to an additional 338,100 shares of Common Stock at the initial public offering price per share, less the underwriting discount, solely to cover over-allotments. If such option is exercised in full, the total initial public offering price, underwriting discount, proceeds to Company and proceeds to Selling Stockholders will be $46,657,800, $3,266,046, $39,139,794 and $4,251,960, respectively. See "Underwriting".

The shares offered hereby are offered severally by the Underwriters, as specified herein, subject to receipt and acceptance by them and subject to their right to reject any order in whole or in part. It is expected that certificates for the shares will be ready for delivery in New York, New York, on or about June 15, 1998, against payment therefor in immediately available funds.

Goldman, Sachs & Co.

BT Alex. Brown

Hambrecht & Quist

The date of this Prospectus is June 9, 1998.

EXHIBIT 22.4   Due Diligence Checklist

THE PRODUCT

1. Examine and operate each product, particularly new products, to assess appearance, function, design, and so on.
2. Assess the threat of obsolescence for each significant product line.
3. Review new product and service plans and development progress.
4. Compare the product with those of competitors and assess the threat from new competitors.
5. Perform an analysis of unproven technology, using experts if necessary.

THE INDUSTRY

1. Estimate the size of the industry, present and projected, in each significant product line and compare company growth projections with anticipated market size for consistency.
2. Review government and trade reports and trade literature regarding the company's market segments to check for consistency with the representations and unstated premises in the prospectus.
3. Analyze competitors' SEC filings for unanticipated trends or developments.
4. Evaluate the importance of proprietary products, copyrights, and trademarks within the industry.
5. Interview trade association personnel concerning trends of relevance to the prospectus.
6. Assess the effect of macroeconomic trends (for example, interest rate fluctuations, inflation rates, and economic growth rates) on the issuer's prospects for success.
7. Assess the comparative strengths and weaknesses of competitors in terms of the dominant competitive factors in the industry (price, service, performance, and so on).
8. Compare the company's financial performance with that of its competitors.
9. Determine whether research and development (R&D) expenditures are consistent with industry practice.

MARKETING AND DISTRIBUTION

1. Evaluate the importance of original equipment manufacturers (OEMs), present and future.
2. Interview principal customers regarding the company's products and services, complaints, anticipated future needs, and so on.
3. Analyze each significant contract regarding contingencies, extent of warranties and other service obligations, rights of cancellation, and so on. Check contracts with customers for completeness and to determine the existence of side written or oral commitments or other terms that materially vary company contracts. Evaluate the quality of the backlog.
4. Evaluate the adequacy of the distribution network, the degree of control over distribution, and the like.
5. Evaluate the effectiveness of marketing personnel.
6. For new products, estimate the cost of introduction, and determine whether the cost is adequately reflected in cash-flow projections.
7. Assess the likelihood of discontinuation of products or services and whether the prospectus should disclose this information.

TECHNOLOGY

1. Review the company's R&D plans to determine whether any radical changes in product direction are anticipated and what cost burden will be imposed on the company in coming years.
2. Evaluate the effectiveness of R&D personnel and organization to assess the company's capacity for technological innovation.
3. Evaluate the company's patent position and the enforceability of its technology licenses.
4. Analyze any litigation regarding technology rights.
5. Review royalty contracts for contingencies, etc., and contact the licensees to determine the existence of any agreement or understanding that varies the terms of the contract.

Exhibit 22.4 continues

Exhibit 22.4 continued

6. With regard to government contracts, determine what if any interest the government asserts or may assert in company technology.
7. Evaluate other professional affiliations of management or R&D personnel (such as academic affiliations) to assess the likelihood of competing claims on company technology.
8. Evaluate the effectiveness of the company's efforts to police its patents, preserve its trade secrets, maintain its copyrights and marks, and other intellectual property; assess the company's resources to perform these tasks.
9. Determine whether the company's exports are consistent with export-control laws.

MANAGEMENT

1. Investigate the prior experience of management and directors in the same industry and the same size company, their experience with large firms, and so on. Also, investigate backgrounds of officers and directors, standing in the community, reputation in the industry, and so on.
2. Evaluate the responsiveness of management to previous auditors' management letters.
3. Assess the effectiveness of management through interviews with outside customers and suppliers, bankers, auditors, and so on.
4. Review prior transactions between the company and insiders for fairness, propriety, full disclosure, and so on.
5. Determine whether any significant defections from management or the board are imminent, and assess the effect on company competitiveness.

EMPLOYEES

1. Compare the company's stock option plans, pension plans, salaries, and other executive compensation with those of competitors to assess the company's ability to attract and retain skilled employees.
2. Consider whether the public offering is likely to result in loss of key employees to retirement.
3. Review employee contracts for term, unrecorded benefit obligations, contingencies, and the like. Interview key employees to determine whether unrecorded written or oral commitments have been made to them.
4. Determine whether compensation obligations have been properly accounted for in the company's books.
5. Assess the adequacy of the labor supply for each operating division.
6. Evaluate the company's labor–relations history, union contracts, prospects of union activity, and so on.

PRODUCTION

1. Assess the ability of production facilities to handle anticipated volumes and whether the cost of new plant and equipment is consistent with anticipated cash flow.
2. Evaluate product and process obsolescence, and compare production facilities to those of industry competitors to determine future competitiveness, both technical and economic.
3. Inquire into anticipated plant closings as well as plans for new facilities, and consider whether disclosure in the prospectus would be advisable.
4. Evaluate adequacy of management information systems and inventory-control programs.
5. Assess the exposure from single-source suppliers, and evaluate the company's contingency plan for responding to an interruption to supplies.
6. Contact major suppliers to determine their satisfaction with the company and their plans to retire, reduce, or raise the price of key supplies and components.

ACCOUNTING

1. Determine whether intangible expenses, such as R&D expenditures, are being or should be expensed.
2. Analyze company finances, including supporting work papers where necessary, for prior years.
3. Review budgets and projections in order to determine material changes in the company's financial position, and compare past budgets and projections with actual experience in order to assess the accuracy of management's estimates.

Exhibit 22.4 continues

Exhibit 22.4 continued

4. Compare the company's revenue-recognition policy and other accounting conventions with those of the industry.
5. Evaluate the effect of customer financing practices on present and future revenues.
6. Evaluate the effect of changes in tax laws and the company's position with respect to open tax years.
7. Verify that the use of proceeds matches financial needs quantitatively and qualitatively.
8. Determine whether inventory turns are consistent with industry ratios.
9. Assess the accuracy of the inventory reported and the adequacy of the inventory obsolescence reserve, and determine the suitability of the mix of materials inventory.
10. Review aging receivables for consideration of reserve or write-off, and assess the adequacy of the bad-debt reserve and other reserves against income.
11. Obtain a report as to the adequacy of the company's accounting controls.
12. Ascertain that the preeffective auditor's "cold comfort" letter is complete.

LEGAL

1. Identify and assess the effect of new and proposed governmental regulations on operations, expenses, and the like.
2. Check title, title insurance, encumbrances, liens, and so on, on company property and equipment.
3. Review incorporation documents, bylaws, and minutes of all shareholder, board, and board committee meetings for several years, both to confirm regularity and to identify events that might require further investigation.
4. Review stock transfer records for regularity, and check for agreements affecting ownership or control of shares.
5. Evaluate pending litigation, review the terms of significant concluded litigation, and investigate the existence of threatened claims or future exposure for statutory or regulatory violations.
6. Determine whether any acquisitions, mergers, reorganizations, and so on, are impending or likely and what effect they will have on the company.
7. Review all press releases, promotional literature, company reports, news accounts, etc., for consistency with the prospectus.
8. Review company banking, leasing, factoring arrangements, and the like, and assess the likelihood and effect of disruption or termination.
9. Determine that all insurable risks have been adequately insured against and that policies do not have material adverse exclusions or omissions.

SOURCE   Derived from Robert Alan Spanner, *Limiting Exposure in the Offering Process*, REV. SEC. & COMMODITIES REG. 64–66 (Apr. 8, 1987). Copyright © 1987, Standard & Poor's Corporation. Reprinted by permission.

names appear on the cover page of the preliminary prospectus.

Selling efforts during the waiting period must be done in strict compliance with the securities laws. They usually include oral presentations to large institutional investors in key cities in the United States, Europe, and Asia called *roadshows*. Any offers to buy can only be accepted after the registration statement is declared effective by the SEC and only after each prospective investor is provided with a copy of the final prospectus. Notice of a proposed offer can be circulated by means of a *tombstone ad*, so named because of its appearance and somewhat somber tone. Exhibit 22.5 depicts a tombstone ad.

Tombstone ads are governed by Rule 134 of the 1933 Act. Such ads are not intended to be selling devices, but merely a means of identifying the existence of a public offering and indicating where a prospectus may be obtained. Rule 134 restricts the notice to 14 limited categories of information. If the notice has more, it will be deemed a prospectus and will be required to meet more rigorous information standards.

The information that may be contained in such a notice includes the name of the issuer, the title of the securities, the amount offered, the price of the securities, and similar factual information. This type of advertisement may not solicit offers to buy the securities

EXHIBIT 22.5   Tombstone Ad

$1,371,562,500

STMicroelectronics

19,000,000 Common Shares

Price US$72.1875 Per Share
FRF428.58
ITL125,900

Copies of the Prospectus may be obtained in any State in which this
announcement is circulated only from such of the undersigned
as may legally offer these securities in such State.

Joint Global Coordinators and Joint Global Bookrunners

Deutsche Bank   **Lehman Brothers**   **Morgan Stanley Dean Witter**

Banca D'Intermediazione Mobiliare IMI   Salomon Smith Barney
SG   SBC Warburg Dillon Read

Banca Commerciale Italiana   Banque Nationale de Paris
Goldman, Sachs & Co.   NationsBanc Montgomery Securities LLC   Paribas

---

Bear, Stearns & Co. Inc.   BT Alex. Brown International
Union Européenne de CIC   Cofiri S.p.A.
Crédit Lyonnais   Credit Suisse First Boston
Credito Italiano   Istituto Bancario San Paolo di Torino S.p.A.
J.P. Morgan & Co.   Dresdner Kleinwort Benson

June 5, 1998

unless it is preceded or accompanied by a prospectus and unless it contains a statement that no offer to buy the securities can be accepted, and no part of the purchase price can be received, until the registration statement becomes effective.

The issuing company and its underwriter must be careful about the information they release to the public during the waiting period. If an issuer or underwriter conditions the market with a news article or press release about the company and its upcoming offering, the act is referred to as *gun-jumping*. In such circumstances, the company may be in violation of the 1933 Act, and the SEC may require the issuer to postpone the offering.

Going Effective   Once a registration statement has been informally cleared by the SEC staff or the registrant has received notice that the registration statement will not be reviewed, a preeffective amendment will be filed with the SEC. This is typically accompanied by a request that the waiting period be accelerated so that the registration statement will become effective at a particular date and time. Without the request for acceleration, the registration statement would not become effective until the expiration of an additional 20-day period.

Once an offering is declared effective, sales of the securities may be consummated, provided that each purchaser is given a copy of the final prospectus. Information concerning the price of the securities and under-

ETHICAL CONSIDERATION

Large institutional investors are frequently shown earnings projections, the assumptions underlying the company's business model, and industry comparisons during the roadshow. This information should not be provided in writing unless the underwriters gather it up after the meeting. Nonetheless, it sometimes finds its way into "cheat sheets" that are meant for the underwriters' internal use but are sometimes given to favored clients. Is it fair to give additional information—beyond that contained in the prospectus—to big institutional investors but not to individual investors?

writing arrangements is filed with the SEC as part of the final prospectus. Supplemental sale literature, which in most cases need not be reviewed by the SEC, may be provided to prospective purchasers. Such sales literature must be preceded or accompanied by the final prospectus. Often, the underwriters will run a tombstone ad to publicize their involvement in the offering.

Exhibit 22.6 suggests a timeline for managers who are considering a public securities offering.

EXHIBIT 22.6   Managerial Timeline for a Public Securities Offering

Day 1 – 30	• Decide upon a public offering of securities to raise capital, and choose a securities underwriting firm.
Day 30 – 60	• With the aid of the underwriter, prepare the forms and prospectus for the registration statement.
Day 60 – 90	• File the registration statement with the SEC for review, and submit any amendments to the filing.
Day 90 – 120	• During the quiet period, the underwriter can assemble selling groups, distribute copies of the preliminary prospectus, and solicit offers to sell the securities. The company must not disclose information to the public, except that required in the ordinary course of business.
Day 120 +	• Once the offering is declared effective and the pricing amendment is filed, sales of the company's securities may begin.

Shelf Registration

Rule 415 under the 1933 Act provides for the *shelf registration* of securities, that is, the registration of a number of securities at one time for issuance later. The securities can then be issued over a period of time, for example, in connection with continuous acquisition programs or employee stock-benefit plans, or at a later date, for example, when interest rates or market conditions are more favorable to the issuance of securities. Shelf registration can result in reduced legal, accounting, and printing expenses, and increased competition among underwriters. Moreover, the issuer can respond more flexibly to rapidly changing market conditions, by varying the structure and terms of the securities on short notice.

Registration is intended to ensure that current information is available to prospective underwriters and purchasers of securities. Accordingly, shelf registration is restricted to offerings in which the information contained in the registration statement will not become stale or inaccurate after some months or years.

Rule 415 limits the availability of shelf registration to ten types of offerings, which can be broken down into two basic categories: (1) traditional shelf offerings, and (2) offerings of securities of certain large, publicly traded companies that are eligible to use short-form registration procedures such as Form S-3.

Traditional shelf offerings include (1) securities offered pursuant to employee benefit plans; (2) securities offered or sold pursuant to dividend or interest reinvestment plans; (3) warrants, rights, or securities to be issued upon conversion of other outstanding securities; (4) mortgage-related securities; and (5) securities issued in connection with business combination transactions.

With respect to offerings by certain large, publicly traded companies, the SEC has decided that because the market receives a steady stream of high-quality information concerning these issuers, the risks of stale information are minimal.

Reorganizations and Combinations

When securities holders are asked to approve a corporate reorganization or combination—such as a reclassification of securities, a merger involving an exchange of securities, or a transfer of assets of one corporation in exchange for the securities of another—they are in effect faced with an investment decision. In recognition of this fact, the SEC adopted Rule 145, which expressly provides that the protections provided by the 1933 Act's registration requirements are applicable to certain types of business reorganizations and combinations. An offer, offer to sell, or sale occurs when a plan of reorganization is submitted to shareholders for approval. Transactions that fall within the guidelines specified in Rule 145 should be registered with the SEC in a combined registration statement and proxy statement on *Form S-4*, unless an exemption from registration is available.

Because shareholder approval of mergers and other combinations necessarily involves communications between a corporation and its shareholders, Rule 145 also contains specific rules as to whether such communications will not be deemed to be a prospectus or an offer to sell for purposes of the 1933 Act.

Rule 145 also provides that under certain circumstances affiliates of the acquired company, such as officers, directors, or controlling shareholders, are deemed *underwriters*, that is, persons selling securities on behalf of the issuer or a person who controls or is under common control with the issuer. Such affiliates cannot resell their securities without compliance with certain resale restrictions that include limitations on the amount of securities sold in a three-month period.

Secondary Offerings

A principal advantage of registering a securities offering with the SEC and the appropriate state securities authorities is that the securities may be traded relatively freely following the initial public offering. A *secondary offering*, that is, a subsequent offering by a person other than the issuer, must either be registered with the SEC or be exempt from registration. If the secondary offering is of nonrestricted securities and is made by a nonaffiliate, there are no limitations on the size of the offering or the number of offerees.

◆ Exemptions for Offerings by the Issuer

In adopting the 1933 Act registration provisions, Congress provided exemptions from registration when there is no practical need for it or the public benefits from it would be too remote. Exemptions from registration fall into two categories: exempt securities and exempt transactions.

Exempt securities, listed in Section 3 of the 1933 Act, include the following:

1. Any security issued or guaranteed by the United States or any state of the United States
2. Any security issued or guaranteed by any national bank
3. Any security issued by a charitable organization
4. Any security that is part of an issue offered and sold only to persons residing within a single state or territory, if the issuer is a resident of the same state or territory. (*Note*: Even though the intrastate offering exemption is listed under Section 3, the SEC treats it like the transactional exemptions under Section 4.)

Exempt transactions are described in Section 4 of the 1933 Act. They include the following:

1. "Transactions by any person other than an issuer, underwriter or dealer" (Section 4(1))
2. "Transactions by an issuer not involving any public offering" (Section 4(2), the private-offering exemption)

Most state blue sky laws have exemptions from registration that roughly correspond to the federal exemptions.

Private Offerings

Because of the expense and burdens of public offerings, companies trying to raise money usually attempt to qualify for an exemption from registration. The one most frequently relied upon is the exemption for private offerings. A *private offering* is a transaction not involving an offer to the public, but rather to selected qualified investors. Private offerings are often referred to as private placements. A private offering can be consummated more quickly and with far less expense than a public offering.

Because securities offered under the private offering exemption are unregistered, their subsequent transfer is restricted and their price will be discounted accordingly. In addition, purchasers of privately offered securities may demand a greater voice in the operation of the business or sweeteners such as dividend preferences or mandatory redemption privileges, which force the company to repurchase the stock upon the occurrence of certain events.

Under Section 4(2), an offering is exempt from registration if it does not involve a "public offering." This term is not defined in the 1933 Act and thus has been the subject of much judicial interpretation. The SEC originally took the position that "under ordinary circumstances an offering to not more than 25 persons is not an offering to a substantial number and presumably does not involve a public offering."[10] This guideline was rejected by the Supreme Court in the following landmark case.

10. Securities Act Release No. 285 (1935).

A CASE IN POINT   SUMMARY

CASE 22.3
SEC v. RALSTON PURINA CO.
Supreme Court of the United States
346 U.S. 119 (1953).

FACTS   Ralston Purina, a feed and cereal company, offered common stock at market prices to the employees of the company. Among those employees responding to the offer were artists, bake-shop foremen, chow-loading foremen, clerical assistants, clerks, stenographers, and at least one veterinarian. Between 1947 and 1951, the company sold to 2,000 of its employees a total of $2 million worth of stock. The employees lived in various locations throughout the United States. Ralston Purina took the position that because the stock was offered only to "key employees" of the company, it was a private offering exempt from registration under the 1933 Act.

ISSUE PRESENTED   Does the determination of whether a transaction is a public or private offering depend primarily on the sophistication of the offerees or the number of offerees?

Case 22.3 continues

Case 22.3 continued

SUMMARY OF OPINION The U.S. Supreme Court held that the offering was not exempt from registration. The Court stated that absent a showing of special circumstances, employees are indistinguishable from other members of the investing public as far as the securities laws are concerned.

The Supreme Court also rejected a strict numerical test. Instead, the Court held, the critical consideration is whether the class of persons offered the securities needs the protection of the 1933 Act: "An offering to those who are shown to be able to fend for themselves is a transaction not involving any public offering." If, as in the present case, an offering is made to those who are not able to fend for themselves, the transaction is a public offering. The Court noted that an important factor affecting this determination is whether the offerees have access to the same kind of information that the 1933 Act would make available through a registration statement.

RESULT Ralston Purina's offer of stock to its employees was not exempt from registration.

COMMENTS The Supreme Court ruling in *Ralston Purina* refocused attention under Section 4(2) from a strict numerical test to the sophistication of the offerees. The ruling did little to clarify the private-offering exemption, and reliance on Section 4(2) therefore remained an uncertain and somewhat risky proposition.

Regulation D: Safe-Harbor Exemptions

Responding to the need for greater certainty in connection with the private-offering exemption, the SEC adopted Regulation D in 1982. Regulation D offers a safe harbor for those seeking exemption from registration: An issuer that fails to comply with all of the requirements of the applicable rule will not necessarily have no exemption because the transaction may still meet the more general conditions of Section 4(2).

Regulation D contains three separate exemptions from registration, defined by Rules 504, 505, and 506. Rules 501–503 define terms and concepts applicable to one or more of the exemptions.

Accredited Investors The concept of an accredited investor, derived from earlier federal regulations and state securities laws, is based upon the idea that certain investors are so financially sophisticated that they do not need all the protections afforded by the securities laws. Rule 501 defines an *accredited investor* as any one of the following:

1. Any national bank
2. Any corporation, business trust, or charitable organization with total assets in excess of $5 million
3. Any director, executive officer, or general partner of the issuer
4. Any natural person who had individual income in excess of $200,000 in each of the two most recent years, or joint income with that person's spouse in excess of $300,000 in each of those years, and who has a reasonable expectation of reaching the same income level in the current year
5. Any natural person whose individual net worth, or joint net worth with that person's spouse, at the time of the purchase exceeds $1 million.

Integration of Sales If an issuer makes successive sales within a limited period of time, the SEC may *integrate* the successive sales; that is, it may deem them to be part of a single sale. Integrating two or more offerings may increase the number of unaccredited investors beyond acceptable limits, resulting in the loss of a private-offering exemption. The SEC and the courts look at a variety of factors to determine whether offerings should be integrated. If the offerings (1) are part of a single plan of financing, (2) are made at or about the same time, (3) involve the same type of consideration, and (4) are made for the same purpose, then the SEC may recommend integration of the offerings.

Rule 502(a) provides an integration safe harbor for Regulation D offerings. Under Rule 502(a), offers and sales made more than six months before the start of a Regulation D offering or more than six months after its completion will not be considered part of the Regulation D offering, provided that the same issuer makes no offers or sales of a similar class of securities during those six-month periods.

Rule 504   Rule 504 exempts offerings of up to $1 million within a 12-month period. There may be an unlimited number of purchasers under Rule 504. Rule 504 is not available to issuers registered under the 1934 Act—known as public companies—or to investment companies like mutual funds. It is also not available to *blank check companies,* which are development-stage companies that have no specific business plan or have a business plan to acquire a presently unknown business. The issuer must file with the SEC a notice on Form D within 15 days after the first sale of securities.

Rule 505   Rule 505 exempts offerings of up to $5 million within a 12-month period. General solicitations and advertising are not permitted in connection with a Rule 505 offering, and the issuer must reasonably believe that there are not more than 35 unaccredited investors. Rule 505 is not available to investment companies. Rule 505 requires that certain specified information be provided to purchasers (unless all are accredited investors). This information is generally compiled in a private-placement memorandum or offering circular. Rule 505 also requires that purchasers have the opportunity to ask questions and receive answers concerning the terms of the offering. A notice on Form D must be filed with the SEC within 15 days of the first sale of securities.

Rule 506   Rule 506 exempts offerings that in the issuer's reasonable belief are limited to no more than 35 unaccredited investors, provided that the issuer reasonably believes immediately prior to making any sale that each unaccredited investor either alone or with his or her purchaser representative has enough business experience to evaluate the merits and risks of the prospective investment. There can be an unlimited number of accredited investors. However, general solicitations and advertising are not permitted in connection with a Rule 506 offering.

Like Rule 505, Rule 506 requires that certain specified information be provided to purchasers (unless all purchasers are accredited investors), and that purchasers have the opportunity to ask questions and receive answers concerning the terms of the offering. A notice on Form D must be filed with the SEC within 15 days of the first sale of securities.

Section 4(6) Exemption

Section 4(6) of the 1933 Act exempts offers and sales by any issuer to an unlimited number of accredited investors, provided that the aggregate offering price does not exceed $5 million and there is no public solicitation or advertising in connection with the offering. The Section 4(6) definition of "accredited investor" is almost identical to that of Regulation D. The availability of this exemption does not depend upon the use of any type of disclosure document.

Regulation A

The 1992 SEC Small Business Initiatives expanded the previously largely unused Regulation A exemption and included the adoption of a "testing the waters" provision, which permits issuers to solicit indications of interest before filing any required disclosure documents.

Size of Offering and Eligible Companies   Under Regulation A, $5 million of securities can be offered and sold in a 12-month period, of which up to $1.5 million may be sold by the selling security holders. Only U.S. and Canadian companies that are not required to report under the 1934 Act can qualify to use Regulation A.

In addition, the regulation cannot be used by an investment company, a company issuing oil and gas rights, or a blank check company.

Under Rule 262, the "bad boy" provision, Regulation A is unavailable if the issuer or its officers, directors, principal shareholders, or affiliates have been subject to specified proceedings, convictions, injunctions, or disciplinary orders from the SEC or other regulatory agencies arising from the securities business or postal fraud. To disqualify the company from using Regulation A, the misconduct must have occurred within five years preceding the filing, or within ten years for officers, directors, and principal shareholders.

Testing the Waters   Regulation A issuers can determine interest in a proposed offering prior to filing an offering statement. The issuer need only to file a solicitation of interest document with the SEC, along with copies of any written or broadcast media ads. There is no prohibition on general solicitation or advertising. Radio and television broadcasts and newspaper ads are permitted to determine investor interest in the offering.

No sales may be made or payment received during the test-the-waters period. To move forward, the company must file Form 1–A with the SEC, and the Regulation A offering statement must be qualified by the SEC. Once the offering statement is filed, testing-the-waters activity ceases. Sales can be made only after the passage of a required 20-day waiting period from the time of the last solicitation of interest.

By late 1993, more than 30 issuers had used the testing-the-waters provision for a variety of businesses. Of the 30, only five companies actually proceeded with the Regulation A offering. According to an official of the SEC and a number of attorneys, the real success stories were the companies that, after testing the waters and finding them unfavorable, did not spend the considerable amount of money required to do a public offering.[11]

Offerings to Employees

Nonpublic companies that are not registered pursuant to the 1934 Act often face a problem when instituting employee stock plans. If the company relies on Rule 504, it can issue only $1 million in one 12-month period. Because employee offerings are usually continuous, the issuer may face serious integration problems. It is seldom practical to shut a stock plan down for six months to take advantage of Regulation D's integration safe harbor.

In response to these problems, the SEC adopted Rule 701 and temporary Rules 702T and 703T. Rule 701 exempts offers and sales of securities made (1) pursuant to a written compensatory benefit plan for employees, directors, general partners, trustees (if the issuer is a business trust), officers, consultants, or advisors; or (2) pursuant to a written contract relating to the compensation of such persons. If the benefit plan is for consultants or advisors, they must render bona fide services not connected with the offer and sale of securities in a capital-raising transaction. Exempt compensatory

benefit plans include purchase, savings, option, bonus, stock-appreciation, profit-sharing, thrift-incentive, and pension plans. The issuer must provide each plan participant with a copy of the plan and each contractor with a copy of his or her contract, but no other disclosure document is required by Rule 701.

Rule 701 applies only to securities offered and sold in an amount not more than the greatest of (1) $500,000; (2) 15% of the total assets of the issuer; or (3) 15% of the outstanding securities of the class being offered and sold. Moreover, the aggregate offering price of securities subject to outstanding offers made in reliance on Rule 701 plus securities sold in the preceding 12 months in reliance on Rule 701 may not exceed $5 million.

Rule 701 provides additional integration relief for issuers who sell both under Rule 701 and under Rules 504 or 505 of Regulation D. Offerings under Rule 701 are not integrated with those under Rules 504 and 505, and vice versa.

Rule 702T requires that a Form 701 be filed not later than 30 days after the first sale that brings the aggregate sales under Rule 701 above $100,000, and thereafter annually within 30 days following the end of the issuer's fiscal year. Rule 703T makes Rule 701 unavailable to issuers subject to injunctions for failure to file Form 701.

Exhibit 22.7 summarizes the key elements of certain exemptions from registration discussed in this section.

The Private Placement Memorandum

The *private-placement memorandum* is the private offering counterpart to the prospectus. Like the prospectus, the private-placement memorandum is both a selling document and a disclosure document. The disclosure function is usually primary, so the memorandum may not be as upbeat as the issuer might like.

The content of the private-placement memorandum is determined by the exemption upon which the issuer relies. For example, Rule 502(b) under Regulation D provides that if an issuer is selling securities under Rule 505 or 506 to any purchaser that is not an accredited investor, certain specified information must be provided to the purchaser. On the other hand, if the issuer is offering securities under Rule 504 or only to accredited investors, or in reliance upon the general Section 4(2) exemption, the issuer is not required to provide any specific information. State blue sky laws

11. *SEC Pleased with SBI, Agency Official Declares*, Sec. Reg. & L. Rep. (BNA), Oct. 8, 1993, at 1341.

EXHIBIT 22.7   Key Elements of Certain Exemptions from Registration

TYPE OF EXEMPTION	DOLLAR LIMIT OF THE OFFERING	LIMITS ON THE PURCHASERS	PURCHASER QUALIFICATIONS	ISSUER QUALIFICATIONS
Section 4(2)	No limit	Generally limited to small number of sophisticated offerees able to understand and bear risk	Offerees and purchasers must have access to information and be sophisticated investors	No limitations
Regulation D[a] Rule 504[b]	Up to $1 million in 12 months	No limit	No requirements	Not a 1934 Act public-reporting company nor an investment or blank check company
Regulation D[a] Rule 505	Up to $5 million in 12 months	No limit on the number of accredited investors, but limited to 35 unaccredited investors	No requirements for unaccredited investors	Not an investment company
Regulation D[a] Rule 506	No limit	No limit on the number of accredited investors, but limited to 35 unaccredited investors	Unaccredited investors must have sufficient experience to evaluate the investment	No limitations
Section 4(6)[a,b]	Up to $5 million	No limit on the number of accredited investors	All purchasers must be accredited—no unaccredited investors allowed	No limitations
Regulation A	$5 million in 12 months, with a maximum of $1.5 million sold by the selling security holders	No limit	No requirements	A U.S. or Canadian company, but not a 1934 Act public-reporting company, nor an investment company, nor a blank check company, nor a company issuing oil/gas/mineral rights, nor disqualified under "bad boy" Rule 262
Rule 701[c,d]	The greatest of $500,000 or 15% of the total assets of the issuer or 15% of the outstanding securities of the same class, up to a limit of $5 million over 12 months	No limit on the number of employees, directors, officers, advisors, or consultants	Advisory and consulting services must not be connected with the offer and sale of securities in a capital-raising transaction	Not a 1934 Act public-reporting company nor an investment company

a. All issuers relying on these exemptions are required to file a notice on Form D with the SEC within 15 days after the first sale of securities. In addition, solicitations, advertising, and the provision of information during such offerings are limited.

b. This exemption does not depend on the use of any type of disclosure document.

c. All issuers relying on this exemption must file Form 701 with the SEC within 30 days after the sale of more than $100,000 worth of securities and annually thereafter.

d. Must be pursuant to written compensatory benefit plans or written contracts relating to compensation.

ETHICAL CONSIDERATION

Because federal law only requires disclosure of all material information, who bears the responsibility for ensuring the quality and fairness of an offering? The managers and directors of the issuing company? The investment bankers? The securities lawyers?

may also influence the content and format of a private-placement memorandum.

In many circumstances, no private-placement memorandum is technically required. However, an issuer is well advised to create such a document in order to clearly demonstrate the disclosure made to prospective investors. Such disclosure is important to rebut claims of securities fraud, a topic discussed in Chapter 23.

Exhibit 22.8 summarizes the definitions of certain key terms from the 1933 Act and the SEC regulations promulgated thereunder.

◆ Exemptions for Secondary Offerings

A principal advantage of registering a securities offering with the SEC and the appropriate state securities authorities is that the securities may be traded relatively freely following the initial public offering. However, securities issued in a private placement cannot be the subject of a secondary offering, that is, a subsequent offering by a person other than the issuer, unless they are either registered or exempt from registration. Securities issued in a private placement are thus called *restricted securities.*

Section 4(1) Exemption

Section 4(1) of the 1933 Act provides that "transactions by any person other than an issuer, underwriter, or dealer" are exempt from registration.

Section 2 of the 1933 Act defines an *issuer* as any person "who issues or proposes to issue any security." A *dealer* is defined as "any person who engages either for all or part of his time, directly or indirectly, as agent,

broker, or principal, in the business of offering, buying, selling, or otherwise dealing or trading in securities issued by another person."

An *underwriter* is defined as "any person who has purchased from an issuer with a view to, or offers or sells for an issuer in connection with, the distribution of any security." As used in the definition of an underwriter, the term "issuer" includes "any person directly or indirectly controlling or controlled by the issuer, or any person under direct or indirect common control with the issuer." For example, the sale of securities to the public by a controlling shareholder is a transaction involving an underwriter. In this case, the Section 4(1) exemption is therefore unavailable.

If the person desiring to sell unrestricted securities is not an issuer, underwriter or dealer, he or she may sell the securities without registration under Section 4(1). There is no limit to the size of the offering or the number of offerees. Section 4(1) is the exemption most often relied upon by persons who sell securities in the secondary market in an ordinary transaction involving a broker.

Rule 144

Because of the uncertainty in the definition of the term underwriter, the SEC adopted Rule 144 in 1972. Rule 144 is not meant to be the exclusive means through which restricted securities may be sold, but merely to provide objective criteria for deciding whether a person is an underwriter. Under Rule 144, a person is *not an underwriter* if the following conditions are met.

1. Adequate current public information must be available concerning the issuer. This requirement effectively means that the issuer is a publicly traded company that has complied with the periodic reporting requirements imposed by the 1934 Act (discussed later in this chapter).
2. The securities must have been beneficially owned—with all economic rights belonging to the owner—and fully paid for at least one year prior to the date of sale.
3. In any three-month period, the seller must not sell more than the greater of (i) 1% of the outstanding securities of the class, or (ii) the average weekly trading volume in the securities during the four calendar weeks preceding the filing of the notice of sale on Form 144.

EXHIBIT 22.8   Key Terms of the Securities Act of 1933 and SEC Regulations

Security	Most commonly used criteria under federal law: 1. Investment of money 2. Common enterprise 3. Profits derived "solely" from efforts of others [Section 2(1)]
Offer	"Every attempt or offer to dispose of, or solicitation of an offer to buy, a security or interest in a security, for value." [Section 2(3)]
Sale	"Every contract of sale or disposition of a security or interest in a security, for value." [Section 2(3)]
Accredited Investor	As defined by Rule 501 under Regulation D: 1. National bank, savings and loan, registered broker-dealer, insurance company, investment company, SBIC (small business investment company), employee benefit plan if the investment decision is made by a "plan fiduciary" 2. Charitable organization, corporation, or business trust with total assets greater than $5 million 3. Any director, executive officer, or general partner of the issuer 4. Any natural person with individual income greater than $200,000 in each of the two most recent years or joint income with spouse greater than $300,000 in each of those years with a reasonable expectation of the same income level in the current year 5. Natural person with individual net worth or joint net worth with spouse greater than $1 million at time of purchase 6. Entity owned by any of the above 7. Trust with assets greater than $5 million with purchases directed by a sophisticated investor 8. Private development company (as defined)
Restricted Securities	"Securities issued in a transaction not involving a public offering." [Rule 144]
Issuer	"Every person who issues or proposes to issue any security," including, for purposes of definition of underwriter, "any person directly or indirectly controlling or controlled by the issuer, or any person under direct or indirect common control with the issuer." [Section 2(4)]
Affiliate	Any officer, director, or major shareholder (generally presumed to include one holding at least 10% of issuer's stock). Someone who controls, or is controlled by, or co-controls with the issuer. [Rule 144]
Underwriter	"Any person who has purchased from an issuer with a view to, or offers or sells for an issuer in connection with, the distribution of any security." [Section 2(11)]
"Not an Underwriter"	"Not an underwriter" safe-harbor requirements of Rule 144: 1. Adequate public information available 2. One-year holding period (unless affiliate sells unrestricted securities) 3. Sales limitations for any three-month period: the greater of 1% of the outstanding securities of the class, or the average weekly trading volume for the preceding four weeks 4. Must sell through a broker or directly to a market maker 5. Form 144 filing if more than 500 shares or greater than $10,000 aggregate price in three months 6. Must have bona fide intention to sell within a reasonable amount of time after filing Form 144
Rule 144(k)	A nonaffiliate who has held the security for more than two years may resell without restriction.
Rule 144A	A nonaffiliate may resell without restriction to a "qualified institutional buyer."

4. The securities must be sold in "broker's transactions" as defined in the 1933 Act, or directly to a "market maker," as defined in the 1934 Act. Solicitation of offers to buy is not permitted, and no commissions for the sale may be paid to any person other than the broker who executes the order of sale.

5. If the amount of the securities sold during any three-month period will exceed 500 shares or have an aggregate sale price in excess of $10,000, a notice on Form 144 must be filed with the SEC and with the principal stock exchange (if any) on which the securities are traded.

6. The person filing the Form 144 must have a bona fide intention to sell the securities within a reasonable time after the filing of the notice.

Rule 144(k) provides that a person who is not an affiliate of the issuer, and has not been an affiliate for three months preceding the sale, may sell restricted securities without regard to items 1, 3, 4, and 5 above if such person has owned the securities for at least two years prior to their sale. This is of particular importance for privately held companies that do not file 1934 Act reports. Affiliates include officers, directors, and major shareholders. The SEC has a rebuttable presumption that anyone owning at least 10% of the issuer's stock is an affiliate.

If the requirements of Rule 144 are met, restricted securities may be sold publicly without registration. Usually, restricted securities are identified as such by legends appearing on the face or back of their stock certificates. Accordingly, an opinion from the issuer's attorney may be required before a transfer agent is willing to consummate a transaction involving restricted securities. Certificates issued following a sale pursuant to Rule 144 may be issued without restrictive legends.

If an affiliate of the issuer wants to sell stock, he or she must sell in accordance with Rule 144 (except for the one-year holding period requirement which is inapplicable if the securities being sold were acquired in a registered offering) or use another available exemption. The most common is the *Section 4(1½) exemption* for private offerings by an affiliate. These offerings could qualify as private placements under Section 4(2) if made by the issuer. Thus, the securities can be offered only to persons capable of bearing and understanding the risk of the investment who acquire the securities for investment purposes only and not with a view to distribution.

 Rule 144A and Regulation S

In 1990, the SEC adopted two new regulations governing the resale of unregistered securities and the offering of securities outside the United States. The rules were designed to liberalize primary and secondary trading of private-placement securities.

Rule 144A

Rule 144A permits the resale of unregistered securities to *qualified institutional buyers*—that is, institutional investors holding and managing $100 million or more of securities—if the securities are not of the same class as any securities of the issuer listed on a U.S. securities exchange or quoted on an automated interdealer quotation system (such as Nasdaq Stock Market). The rule creates a safe harbor for trading unregistered securities that are often issued to institutional investors in private placements and generally subject to Rule 144's holding periods. The creation of a secondary market for eligible unregistered securities has increased the liquidity and value of these securities and reduced the private offering discount for them.

If a transaction meets the terms of Rule 144A, it is deemed not to be a distribution. Therefore, the seller is not an underwriter as defined in the 1933 Act. If the seller is also not an issuer or dealer, it may rely on the Section 4(1) exemption for transactions by persons who are not issuers, underwriters, or dealers.

Dealers may also take advantage of Rule 144A. Under Section 4(3) of the 1933 Act, dealers are entitled to an exemption from registration, unless they are participants in a distribution or in a transaction taking place within a specified period after securities have been offered to the public. If a transaction complies with Rule 144A, the dealer will be deemed not to be a participant in a distribution and the securities will be deemed not to have been offered to the public. Accordingly, the transaction will be exempt from registration.

Rule 144A is a nonexclusive exemption. If the requirements of Rule 144A cannot be met, the parties to the transaction may still rely on the facts-and-circumstances analysis commonly associated with nonpublic transfers of unregistered stock. For example, the Section 4(1½) exemption for private resales of restricted securities may apply.

VIEW FROM CYBERSPACE

OFFERINGS ON THE INTERNET

In 1995, Spring Street Brewing Co. Inc. became the first company to conduct an initial public offering over the Internet.[a] Spring Street raised $1.6 million in an offering exempt under Regulation A. The securities were qualified under the blue sky laws of 18 states, on the assumption that the majority of potential purchasers resided in those states.

Other small companies have done offerings of up to $1 million under Rule 504 of Regulation D, which does not prohibit general solicitation for offerings of up to $1 million. Rule 505 (with its $5 million limit) and Rule 506 (with no dollar limit) do prohibit general solicitation. The SEC has taken the position that offerings on the Internet violate that ban unless access to offering materials is restricted to prequalified, accredited investors. This is normally done by making the sites offering the securities accessible only by pass-word and only to investors shown by questionnaire to be accredited.[b]

Companies doing registered offerings can post the registration statement on their Web site. In addition, NETRoadshow and other firms have begun to make audiovisual transmissions of live investor roadshows to authorized investors via the Internet. The transmission is not edited for content and contains the oral presentations by management, questions and answers, and charts and graphics presented at the roadshow.[c]

_____

a. *See* Constance E. Bagley & John Arledge, *SEC Could Ease Offerings of Securities via the Web*, NAT'L L.J., Jan. 13, 1997, at B9.

b. *See* Constance E. Bagley & Robert J. Tomkinson, *Internet Is Seeing Its Share of Securities Offerings*, NAT'L L.J., Feb. 2, 1998, at C3.

c. *Id.* at C4

Regulation S

Regulation S clarifies the general rule that any offer or sale outside the United States is not subject to the federal registration requirements. The SEC has long held the view that the Section 5 registration requirements do not apply to offers and sales effected in a manner that would result in the securities coming to rest abroad. Transactions meeting the requirements of certain safe harbors for the issuance and resale of securities set forth in Regulation S will be deemed to occur outside the United States.

All offers and sales of any security under Regulation S must be made in *offshore transactions*, defined as those in which no offer is made to a person in the United States and either (1) at the time the buy order is originated, the buyer is outside the United States; or (2) the transaction is one executed in, on, or through the facilities of a designated offshore securities market. No directed selling efforts may be made in the United States.

Exhibit 22.9 provides a flow chart of the registration and exemption requirements applicable to primary and secondary offerings of securities.

INTERNATIONAL CONSIDERATION

The combination of Rule 144A and Regulation S has expanded the private-placement market by increasing the liquidity of privately placed securities. The clear exemptions from registration and its related expenses have made the U.S. market more attractive to both U.S. and foreign companies. Regulation S additionally has enabled U.S. companies to offer securities abroad with greater certainty that such securities are exempt from registration.

◆ Reporting Requirements of Public Companies

The completion of a public offering does not terminate the issuer's relationship with the SEC. Under Section

EXHIBIT 22.9   An Outline of Registration and Exemption Requirements

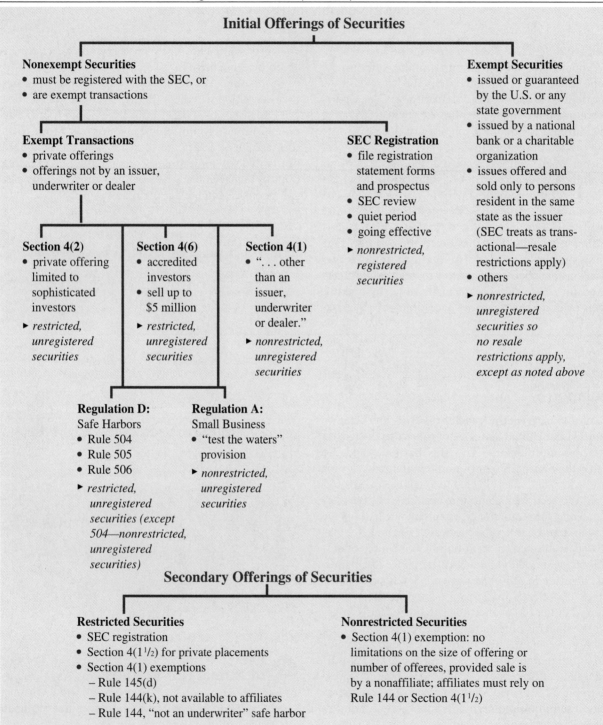

Initial Offerings of Securities

Nonexempt Securities
- must be registered with the SEC, or
- are exempt transactions

Exempt Securities
- issued or guaranteed by the U.S. or any state government
- issued by a national bank or a charitable organization
- issues offered and sold only to persons resident in the same state as the issuer (SEC treats as transactional—resale restrictions apply)
- others
- ▸ *nonrestricted, unregistered securities so no resale restrictions apply, except as noted above*

Exempt Transactions
- private offerings
- offerings not by an issuer, underwriter or dealer

SEC Registration
- file registration statement forms and prospectus
- SEC review
- quiet period
- going effective
- ▸ *nonrestricted, registered securities*

Section 4(2)
- private offering limited to sophisticated investors
- ▸ *restricted, unregistered securities*

Section 4(6)
- accredited investors
- sell up to $5 million
- ▸ *restricted, unregistered securities*

Section 4(1)
- ". . . other than an issuer, underwriter or dealer."
- ▸ *nonrestricted, unregistered securities*

Regulation D:
Safe Harbors
- Rule 504
- Rule 505
- Rule 506
- ▸ *restricted, unregistered securities (except 504—nonrestricted, unregistered securities)*

Regulation A:
Small Business
- "test the waters" provision
- ▸ *nonrestricted, unregistered securities*

Secondary Offerings of Securities

Restricted Securities
- SEC registration
- Section 4(1½) for private placements
- Section 4(1) exemptions
  - Rule 145(d)
  - Rule 144(k), not available to affiliates
  - Rule 144, "not an underwriter" safe harbor

Nonrestricted Securities
- Section 4(1) exemption: no limitations on the size of offering or number of offerees, provided sale is by a nonaffiliate; affiliates must rely on Rule 144 or Section 4(1½)

15(d) of the 1934 Act, a company with registered securities in a public offering must file periodic reports. Usually, under Section 12 of the 1934 Act, the company must also register the class of equity securities offered to the public.

Section 12

Under Section 12 of the 1934 Act, an issuer engaged in interstate commerce and having total assets exceeding $5 million must register with the SEC each nonexempt class of security that (1) is listed on a national stock exchange, or (2) is an equity security held of record by at least 500 persons. Registration subjects the issuer to various reporting requirements and to certain rules and regulations concerning proxies, tender offers, insider trading, and so on. A company registered with the SEC under Section 12 is commonly referred to as a public or *reporting company.*

Registration under the 1934 Act is intended to supplement the 1933 Act registration and to keep current information concerning the issuer available to the public, enabling investors to make informed decisions about securities purchases. Although registration under the 1934 Act imposes additional burdens on an issuer, some issuers voluntarily register with the SEC in order to receive the protections afforded by the 1934 Act in proxy contests, which are attempts to oust the existing management of a company by appealing directly to its shareholders.

The following are some of the significant requirements associated with becoming a registered company under Section 12 of the 1934 Act.

10–Q   An unaudited quarterly statement of operations and financial condition must be filed on Form 10–Q with the SEC within 45 days after the end of each fiscal quarter.

10–K   An annual audited report must be filed on Form 10–K with the SEC within 90 days of the end of an issuer's fiscal year.

8–K   Certain events, including changes in control, acquisitions or dispositions of key assets, and resignation of directors, require a report to be filed on Form 8–K with the SEC within 15 days of the event.

Small business issuers that are required to file periodic reports under the 1934 Act can do so with simplified forms under Regulation S–B. These abbreviated forms include *Form 10–KSB* for annual reports and *Form 10–QSB* for quarterly reports.

Other Sections of the 1934 Act

Other sections of the 1934 Act regulate such activities as proxy solicitations, insider trading, and tender offers.

Proxy Solicitations   The proxy regulation provisions of Section 14 of the 1934 Act apply to all public companies. They govern the solicitation of written powers of attorney, or *proxies,* that give the proxy holder the right to vote the shares owned by the person who signs the proxy card. Proxy solicitations relate not just to the board of directors, but to shareholder proposals as well. In recent years, proxy proposals have dealt with corporate governance issues (such as executive compensation, cumulative voting, repeal of the classified board, recission of poison pill provisions, and confidential voting) and social issues (such as doing business in South Africa and China and getting out of the tobacco business).

Insider Trading   Section 16 of the 1934 Act requires that reports be filed with the SEC listing securities holdings of officers, directors, and persons holding more than 10% of the issuer's equity securities, and any changes in such holdings. Form 5 states that these reports must be filed "both initially and on an annual basis." (These reports are described more fully in Chapter 23.) Insiders of companies not registered under the 1934 Act need not file regular reports with the SEC.

Tender Offers   Any person making a *tender offer* to shareholders, whereby shareholders are asked to sell their shares to that person for a stated price, must comply with the tender offer rules found in Section 14 of the 1934 Act. Some rules, such as the requirement that a tender offer be left open for at least 20 business days, apply even if the company is not registered under the 1934 Act if it has a significant number of shareholders. Other rules, such as the rule giving shareholders the right to withdraw their shares once they are tendered, and the rule requiring proration if the offer is oversubscribed, apply only if the company is registered under the 1934 Act.

Schedule 13D   Under Section 13, any person acquiring at least 5% of the shares of a reporting company must file a Schedule 13D within 10 days of that acquisition. The Schedule 13D must disclose the number of shares acquired and the intentions of the person acquiring them. Often, the person acquiring the shares will state that he or she is buying the shares for investment purposes only. Sometimes, however, the company suspects an ulterior motive, such as preparation for a hostile takeover attempt.

◆ Violation of the Registration and Prospectus–Delivery Requirements of the 1933 Act: Section 12(1)

As explained above, Section 5 of the 1933 Act provides that, absent an exemption, all securities must be registered and may be sold only after delivery of a prospectus meeting the requirements of the 1933 Act. The penalty for violation of Section 5 is simple and severe. Section 12(1) provides that, absent an exemption, anyone who offers or sells a security without an effective registration statement is liable to the purchaser for recission or damages.

Elements of Liability

To establish a Section 12(1) claim, the plaintiff must show that the defendant sold or offered securities without an effective registration statement or by means of a noncomplying prospectus, through the use of interstate transportation or communication. A plaintiff typically satisfies the interstate transportation or communication requirement by proving that the mails, telephone, or other interstate means were used in the offer or sale to that particular plaintiff. The plaintiff must file suit within one year from the date the securities were offered or sold.

Section 12(1) imposes a standard of strict liability; that is, the plaintiff need not show that the defendant acted willfully or negligently, only that the defendant committed the act of selling unregistered securities.

Damages

If the plaintiff still owns the securities, he or she is entitled to rescind the purchase. To rescind, the plaintiff returns the securities, together with any income (such as dividends) he or she received from them, in exchange for what the plaintiff paid for the securities, plus interest. If the plaintiff has sold the securities, the plaintiff is entitled to recover damages—usually the difference between what the plaintiff paid and what the plaintiff received for the securities.

Who May Be Sued

The severity of the remedy under Section 12(1) has naturally led to a great deal of interest as to just who may be considered to have offered or sold securities within the meaning of the statute. It clearly includes the issuer. But what about others involved in an unregistered securities transaction, such as attorneys, accountants, underwriters, and investment bankers?

Before the U.S. Supreme Court decided the following case, many courts had held that a defendant had seller status under Section 12(1) if it engaged in actions that were a substantial factor in bringing about the plaintiff's securities purchase. The Supreme Court rejected the substantial-factor test in this case.

A CASE IN POINT	IN THE LANGUAGE OF THE COURT

CASE 22.4
PINTER v. DAHL
Supreme Court
of the United States
486 U.S. 622 (1988).

FACTS   Maurice Dahl was a California real estate broker and investor. Dahl purchased unregistered securities in the form of oil and gas interests from B. J. Pinter, an oil and gas producer and registered securities dealer in Texas. Enthusiastic about his investment, Dahl successfully encouraged his friends and family to purchase additional securities from the defendant. When the investment failed, the purchasers sued Pinter for violation of Section 12(1) of the Securities Act of 1933.

Pinter claimed that Dahl, who encouraged his friends and family to invest, was a substantial factor in those sales. Pinter therefore contended that Dahl was a seller and should be held liable under Section 12(1).

Case 22.4 continues

Case 22.4 continued

ISSUE PRESENTED   Is a person with no financial interest in an offering of unregistered securities a seller under Section 12(1) of the 1933 Act?

OPINION   BLACKMUN, J., writing for the U.S. Supreme Court:

In determining whether Dahl may be deemed a "seller" for purposes of 12(1), such that he may be held liable for the sale of unregistered securities to the other investor-respondents, we look first at the language of 12(1). That statute provides, in pertinent part: "Any person who . . . offers or sells a security in violation of the registration requirement of the Securities Act shall be liable to the person purchasing such security from him." This provision defines the class of defendants who may be subject to liability as those who offer or sell unregistered securities. But the Securities Act nowhere delineates who may be regarded as a statutory seller, and the sparse legislative history sheds no light on the issue. The courts, on their part, have not defined the term uniformly.

At the very least, however, the language of 12(1) contemplates a buyer–seller relationship not unlike the traditional contractual privity. Thus, it is settled that 12(1) imposes liability on the owner who passes title, or other interest in the security, to the buyer for value. Dahl, of course, was not a seller in this conventional sense, and therefore may be held liable only if 12(1) liability extends to persons other than the person who passes title.

    . . .

Although we conclude that Congress intended 12(1) liability to extend to those who solicit securities purchases, we share the Court of Appeals' conclusion that Congress did not intend to impose rescission based on strict liability on a person who urges the purchase but whose motivation is solely to benefit the buyer. When a person who urges another to make a securities purchase acts merely to assist the buyer, not only is it uncommon to say that the buyer "purchased" from him, but it is also strained to describe the giving of gratuitous advice, even strongly or enthusiastically, as "soliciting." Section 2(3) defines an offer as a "solicitation of an offer to buy . . . for value." The person who gratuitously urges another to make a particular investment decision is not, in any meaningful sense, requesting value in exchange for his suggestion or seeking the value the titleholders will obtain in exchange for the ultimate sale. The language and purpose of 12(1) suggest that liability extends only to the person who successfully solicits the purchase motivated at least in part by a desire to serve his own financial interests or those of the securities owner. If he had such a motivation, it is fair to say that the buyer "purchased" the security from him and to align him with the owner in a rescission action.

    . . .

We are unable to determine whether Dahl may be held liable as a statutory seller under 12(1). The District Court explicitly found that "Dahl solicited each of the other plaintiffs in connection with the offer, purchase and receipt of their oil and gas interests." We cannot conclude that this finding was clearly erroneous. It is not clear, however, that Dahl had the kind of interest in the sales that make him liable as a statutory seller. We do know that he received no commission from Pinter in connection with the

Case 22.4 continues

Case 22.4 continued

other sales, but this is not conclusive. Typically, a person who solicits the purchase will have sought or received a personal financial benefit from the sale, such as where he "anticipat[es] a share of the profits," or receives a brokerage commission. But a person who solicits the buyer's purchase in order to serve the financial interests of the owner may properly be liable under 12(1) without showing that he expects to participate in the benefits the owner enjoys.

The Court of Appeals apparently concluded that Dahl was motivated entirely by gratuitous desire to share an attractive investment opportunity with his friends and associates. This conclusion, in our view, was premature. The District Court made no findings that focused on whether Dahl urged the other purchases in order to further some financial interest of his own or of Pinter. Accordingly, further findings are necessary to assess Dahl's liability.

RESULT   The Supreme Court vacated the judgment of the appeals court and remanded the case for further proceedings consistent with its opinion.

Questions

1. Was Dahl partially responsible for the failure to register the securities? If so, should he have been liable for violating Section 5?
2. What facts do you need to know to determine whether Dahl was a seller within the meaning of Section 5?

Who May Sue

Anyone who purchases shares issued in violation of the registration requirements can bring suit. If the securities were sold to a number of persons, then a plaintiff could bring a class action suit, which is filed on behalf of all persons who have allegedly been harmed by the acquisition of the illegally issued securities.

 ## Section 11 of the 1933 Act

Section 11 provides a remedy for a person who purchases a security pursuant to a misleading registration statement. Note that Section 11 applies only to registered securities. The section is the most lengthy and detailed civil liability provision in the 1933 Act, spelling out who may sue, who may be sued, the elements of the offenses, the permitted defenses, and the damages that may be awarded. Under Section 11, an issuer of securities is liable for its false statements even if they were not made with intent to defraud.

Who May Sue

Tracing Requirement   Any person who has acquired a registered security may sue under Section 11. However, the purchaser must prove that the security at issue was actually one of those sold with the misleading registration statement. Although this requirement does not present a problem for direct purchasers of an initial public offering, open-market purchasers may find it difficult to trace their securities back to a sale made under the defective registration statement.

Class Actions   Plaintiffs in a Section 11 case will typically bring a class action, in which the named plaintiffs act on behalf of themselves and "all others similarly situated." The advantage to the plaintiffs (and their attorneys) of proceeding in this manner is that the individual plaintiffs' claims, worth only a few hundred or a few thousand dollars, together amount to millions of dollars. Indeed, these suits are potentially so lucrative that some investors send their monthly brokerage statements to their attorneys as a routine practice, and thus a private enforcement mechanism of sorts is created.

Who May Be Sued

Section 11 lists, and thereby limits, the entities and persons who may be sued: (1) the issuer offering the security; (2) the underwriters; (3) any member of the board of directors at the time of the offering; (4) persons who give their consent to be named in the registration statement as future directors; (5) every person who signed the registration statement (under Section 6(a) of the 1933 Act, it must be signed by the issuer, its principal executive officer, its principal financing officer, and its principal accounting officer); and (6) experts who consent to give authority to the "expertized" portion of the registration statement, such as accountants who audit the financial statements contained in it. No person can be named in the registration statement as an expert unless that person has consented in writing to being named.

All defendants in a Section 11 case have joint and several liability for violations, meaning that one defendant can be held responsible for all the damages awarded the plaintiff even if that defendant was only partially responsible for the violation, with one exception. Outside directors who did not commit knowing violations are generally liable only for the portion of the damages attributable to their percentage of responsibility.

Plaintiffs often allege that persons or entities other than those specified in Section 11 are liable under a theory of secondary liability, such as aiding and abetting or conspiracy. Most (but not all) courts reject such attempts to expand liability under Section 11. In 1994, the U.S. Supreme Court held that a private plaintiff may not maintain an aiding and abetting suit under Section 10(b).[12]

Controlling Persons   Section 15 imposes liability on anyone who "controls any person liable under Section 11 or 12." The term "control" is not defined in the 1933 Act. Congress left this issue for the courts to decide:

> It was thought undesirable to attempt to define the term. It would be difficult if not impossible to enumerate or to

anticipate the many ways in which actual control may be exerted. A few examples of these methods used are stock ownership, lease, contract, and agency. It is well known that actual control sometimes may be exerted through ownership of much less than a majority of the stock of a corporation either by the ownership of such stock alone or through such ownership in combination with other factors.[13]

Unsurprisingly, the courts do not agree as to when there is *controlling-person liability*. Some courts will find control if the defendant had the power to directly or indirectly control or influence corporate policy or the power to control the general affairs of an entity.[14] Other courts require that the person must have actually participated in the securities violation.[15] Most courts will find liability if a person merely possesses the power to control the specific activity that is the basis for the securities violation, regardless of whether that power was exercised, provided that the person did actually exercise some degree of general control or influence over the Section 11 defendant.

A controlling person is usually an officer or director of the company. In *Metge v. Baehler*,[16] the plaintiff claimed that the company's bank was a controlling person and therefore liable under the securities laws. The U.S. Court of Appeals for the Eighth Circuit applied the following two-prong test to determine whether Banker's Trust was a controlling person. A plaintiff must establish both (1) that the defendant actually participated in (that is, exercised control over) the company's operations in general; and (2) that the defendant possessed the power to control the specific transaction or activity upon which the primary violation was predicated. Because the court found no actual exercise of control by Banker's Trust, the court concluded that the bank had no controlling-person liability.

The case illustrates the flexibility of the securities laws and the creativity of plaintiffs. Had the bank obtained more restrictive covenants in its lending agreements, the court might have found that it was liable as a controlling person even though it did not participate in

---

12. Central Bank of Denver, N.A. v. First Interstate Bank of Denver, N.A., 511 U.S. 164 (1994).

13. H.R. REP. No. 1383, 73rd Cong., 2d Sess. § 19 at 26 (1934).

14. *See, e.g.,* Abbott v. Equity Group, Inc., 2 F.3d 613 (5th Cir. 1993).

15. *See, e.g.,* Sharp v. Coopers & Lybrand, 649 F.2d 175 (3d Cir. 1981) (interpreting identical language in Section 20(a) of the 1934 Act to require culpable participation in the securities violation).

16. 762 F.2d 621 (8th Cir. 1985), *cert. denied*, 474 U.S. 1057 (1986).

the specific violations of the securities laws. A lender that overprotects itself via restrictive covenants and control of its borrower may thus create a problem for itself.

Section 15 does not impose strict liability on controlling persons. Controlling persons are not liable if they had no knowledge of the facts giving rise to the controlled person's alleged liability and had no reasonable ground to believe in the existence of such facts. The majority view is that the defendant bears the burden of establishing the defenses of "no knowledge" and no "reasonable ground to believe." This is normally done by proving that the defendant acted in good faith and took reasonable measures, in light of the situation, to prevent the securities violation.[17]

Elements of Liability

The elements of a Section 11 offense are straightforward. The plaintiff must show that at the time the registration statement became effective either (1) it contained a false or misleading statement of a material fact, or (2) it omitted to state a material fact required to be stated in the registration statement or necessary to make the statements contained in the registration statement not misleading.

The Supreme Court has defined a *material fact* as one that a reasonable investor would most likely have considered important in deciding whether to buy or sell—that is, what a reasonable hypothetical investor would have considered important, not necessarily what the actual investor considered important. The Supreme Court has held that an omitted fact is material if there is "a substantial likelihood that the disclosure of the omitted fact would have been viewed by the reasonable investor as having significantly altered the 'total mix' of information made available."[18]

The plaintiff does not have to establish that he or she relied upon the misstatement or omission except in the following instance: A plaintiff who purchases a security on the open market after the issuing company has released its income statements for the year following the registration statement must show that the misrepresentation influenced his or her decision to buy.

ETHICAL CONSIDERATION

There is an incentive for plaintiffs to urge the courts to construe broadly the guidelines as to who may be a defendant—particularly when the plaintiff is looking for a "deep pocket" defendant, that is, someone who can pay large damages. A plaintiff has every right to use the securities laws to their fullest extent to redress a wrong covered by one of the statutes. However, some commentators believe that there are plaintiffs who attempt to recover losses beyond the scope of the statutes. Although some claim that plaintiffs cannot be faulted for trying, the better view is that plaintiffs should proceed only if they believe in good faith that the suit is justified, given the legal guidelines.

Indeed, Rule 11 of the Federal Rules of Civil Procedure, which is designed to deter bad faith claims, provides for sanctions against an attorney who signs a complaint that the attorney does not reasonably believe has merit. The Reform Act gave Rule 11 new teeth by requiring courts to include in the record, at the conclusion of the action, specific findings as to whether all parties and all attorneys complied with each requirement of Rule 11(b). If the action was brought for an improper purpose, was unwarranted by existing law, legally frivolous, or not supported by facts, then the act creates a presumption that the appropriate sanction is an award to the prevailing party of all attorney's fees and costs incurred in the case.

Defenses

Section 11 sets forth several defenses to a claim under its provisions. The defenses of no reliance and no causation focus on the effects of the misstatements on the behavior of investors and the market, while the defense of due diligence looks to the culpability of the defendants.

No Reliance   The defense of no reliance relates to the investor's knowledge. An investor who knows that there was a misstatement or omission cannot claim to have relied on it; he or she is presumed to have acted despite the misstatement or omission. Thus, if the defendant can establish that the plaintiff knew that a statement was false or that there was an omission, there is no liability under Section 11.

17. *See* Lewis D. Lowenfels & Alan R. Bromberg, *Controlling Person Liability under Section 20(a) of the Securities Exchange Act and Section 15 of the Securities Act,* 53 Bus. Law. 1, 26–27 (1997).

18. TSC Indus., Inc. v. Northway, Inc., 426 U.S. 438, 449 (1976).

No Causation The defense of no causation concerns itself with the link between the misstatement and the investor's loss. Even if there was a misstatement or omission of material fact, a defendant will not be liable if it can show that the misstatement or omission did not actually cause the plaintiff to suffer any loss. In other words, the plaintiff may have lost money on a trade, but that loss may not have been due to the defendant's conduct. This showing typically consists of an expert analysis of the various factors that influenced the price movements of the securities in question.

Due Diligence The defense of due diligence focuses on the behavior of the defendants. It is available to all defendants except the issuing company. A defendant is not liable for a misrepresentation or omission if it acted with due diligence, that is, if (1) it conducted a reasonable investigation; and (2) it reasonably believed (a) that the statements made were true, and (b) that there were no omissions that made those statements misleading. A reasonable investigation is what a prudent person managing his or her own property would conduct.

The primary wrinkle in the due diligence defense arises in connection with the expertized portions of the registration statement, such as audit reports on the company's financial statements, appraisal reports, or engineering reports. Nonexpert defendants are entitled to rely on the experts. They can establish due diligence by showing that they had no reasonable basis to believe that the experts' reports were misleading and in fact did not believe them to be misleading. Significantly, they need not show that they undertook any investigation of those reports.

The experts are, of course, responsible for their own reports, provided that the reports are identified as having been prepared by them and provided that the experts have given their consent to the use of their reports in the registration statement. The experts are generally not responsible under Section 11 for portions of the registration statement other than their reports.

The case that follows was the first to articulate the due diligence standards applicable to the various participants in the offering process.

A CASE IN POINT	IN THE LANGUAGE OF THE COURT

CASE 22.5
ESCOTT v. BARCHRIS CONSTRUCTION CORP.
United States District Court for the Southern District of New York
283 F. Supp. 643
(S.D.N.Y. 1968).

FACTS BarChris was in the business of building bowling alleys. It obtained capital through a public offering in May 1961. Due to financial problems, the company filed for protection under the Bankruptcy Act in October 1962. A class action followed, alleging Section 11 claims against the company, its officers and directors, and its underwriters.

ISSUE PRESENTED When is the due diligence defense available to the principal officers or the inside directors of the issuer? May a chief financial officer rely on the audited financial statements if he had reason to believe those statements were incorrect? Have outside directors and underwriters, who relied on the management's statements and made no independent investigation, acted with due diligence?

OPINION McLEAN, J., writing on behalf of the Federal District Court:
[The court first found that both the expertized and nonexpertized portions of the registration statement were misleading. Every defendant raised the defense of due diligence except the issuer, to whom the defense was not available.]
[The court applied the most stringent standards to the company's principal officers and inside directors. It first noted that principal officers and inside directors (directors who are also officers of the corporation) who sign a registration statement have a significant burden. Because of their extensive knowledge of the company's affairs, it is rare that they can successfully establish a due diligence defense. The court held that the chief financial officer was not entitled to rely on the outside auditors as

Case 22.5 continues

Case 22.5 continued

to the accuracy of the financial statements, because he had reason to believe that those statements were incorrect. The court concluded that the liability of principal officers and inside directors approaches that of the company itself. They cannot escape liability for the nonexpertized portions of the statement even if they did not read the statement, did not understand it, and relied on assistants and lawyers to make adequate disclosures.]

[The court then considered the liability of two outside directors who had become directors a month before the offering. Neither had read the registration statement in final form, and both relied on assurances from the officers that everything was in order.]

Section 11 imposes liability in the first instance upon a director, no matter how new he is. He is presumed to know his responsibility when he becomes a director. He can escape liability only by using that reasonable care to investigate the facts which a prudent man would employ in the management of his own property. In my opinion, a prudent man would not act in an important matter without any knowledge of the relevant facts, in sole reliance upon representations of persons who are comparative strangers and upon general information which does not purport to cover the particular case. . . .

[The court then considered whether the underwriters had established the due diligence defense.] [I]t is clear that no effectual attempt at verification was made. The question is whether due diligence required that it be made. Stated another way, is it sufficient to ask questions, to obtain answers which, if true, would be thought satisfactory, and to let it go at that, without seeking to ascertain from the records whether the answers in fact are true and complete?

. . .

The underwriters say that the prospectus is the company's prospectus, not theirs. Doubtless this is the way they customarily regard it. But the Securities Act makes no such distinction. The underwriters are just as responsible as the company if the prospectus if false. And prospective investors rely upon the reputation of the underwriters in deciding whether to purchase the securities.

. . .

In a sense, the positions of the underwriter and the company's officers are adverse. It is not unlikely that statements made by company officers to an underwriter to induce him to underwrite may be self-serving. They may be unduly enthusiastic. As in this case, they may, on occasion, be deliberately false.

The purpose of Section 11 is to protect investors. To that end the underwriters are made responsible for the truth of the prospectus. If they may escape that responsibility by taking at face value representations made to them by the company's management, then the inclusion of underwriters among those liable under Section 11 affords the investors no additional protection. To effectuate the statute's purpose, the phrase "reasonable investigation" must be construed to require more effort on the part of the underwriters than the mere accurate reporting in the prospectus of

Case 22.5 continues

Case 22.5 continued

"data presented" to them by the company. It should make no difference that this data is elicited by questions addressed to the company officers by the underwriters, or that the underwriters at the time believe that the company's officers are truthful and reliable. In order to make the underwriters' participation in this enterprise of any value to the investors, the underwriters must make some reasonable attempt to verify the data submitted to them. They may not rely solely on the company's officers or on the company's counsel. A prudent man in the management of his own property would not rely on them.

RESULT None of the defendants could rely on the due diligence defense, except for the outside directors, who were permitted to rely on the opinion of the auditors as to the audited financial statements.

COMMENTS The degree of reliance a participating underwriter may place on a principal underwriter remains unclear. The court in *BarChris* summarily noted that the participating underwriters who relied solely on the primary underwriters did not establish due diligence. An SEC release has since suggested that a participating underwriter has met its due diligence requirements if it satisfies itself that the managing underwriter has made the kind of investigation the participant would have performed were it the manager.

Questions

1. Why were the underwriters not permitted to take management's representations at face value?
2. To what standard should accountants be held: to the standard of their profession or that of a reasonable person?

Bespeaks Caution Doctrine

According to the *bespeaks caution doctrine*, a court may determine that the inclusion of sufficient cautionary statements in a prospectus renders immaterial any misrepresentations and omissions contained therein. The doctrine stands for the proposition that a statement or omission must be considered in context, so that accompanying statements may render it immaterial as a matter of law.

In 1993, Trump Castle Funding issued a prospectus conveying to potential investors the risks inherent in the proposed venture, the financing of the Taj Mahal casino. The prospectus alerted potential investors that there was a chance that the partnership would be unable to repay the bondholders. The court held that the extensive cautionary statements, tailored to the specific risks involved, negated any potentially misleading effect of the optimistic projections in the prospectus on a reasonable investor. Trump was therefore not liable for violating Rule 10b-5.[19]

Not all courts have adopted the bespeaks caution doctrine. In addition, cautionary language may render an alleged omission or misrepresentation immaterial, but only if the cautionary statements are substantive and tailored to specific future projections, estimates, or opinions in the prospectus.

---

19. *In re* Donald J. Trump Casino Securit. Litig., 7 F.3d 357 (3d Cir. 1993), *cert. denied*, 510 U.S. 1178 (1994). *See also* Grossman v. Novell, Inc., 120 F.3d 1112 (10th Cir. 1997); Moorhead v. Merrill Lynch, 949 F.2d 243 (8th Cir. 1997); *In re* Worlds of Wonder Securit. Litig., 35 F.3d. 1407 (9th Cir. 1994), *cert. denied sub nom*, Deloitte & Touche v. Miller, 516 U.S. 909 (1995).

In 1994, the Fifth Circuit stated:

> . . . cautionary language is not necessarily sufficient, in and of itself, to render predictive statements immaterial as a matter of law. . . . The appropriate inquiry is whether, under all the circumstances, the omitted fact or the prediction without a reasonable basis "is one [that] a reasonable investor would consider significant in [making] the decision to invest, such that it alters the total mix of information available about the proposed investment." Inclusion of cautionary language . . . is, of course, relevant to the materiality inquiry. . . . Nevertheless, cautionary language as such is not dispositive of this inquiry.[20]

Reform Act Safe Harbor for Forward-Looking Statements

The Reform Act provides a statutory safe harbor for certain forward-looking statements by issuers subject to the 1934 Act's reporting requirements and persons acting on their behalf. However, it is not available for initial public offerings or offerings by a blank check company, a partnership, a limited liability company, or a direct participation investment program. The safe harbor also does not apply to any forward-looking statement included in a financial statement prepared in accordance with generally accepted accounting principles.

The safe harbor provides two independent and alternative grounds for precluding liability. Under the first prong, liability for a written or oral forward-looking statement is precluded if it was identified by the speaker as a forward-looking statement and accompanied by meaningful cautionary statements that identify important factors that could cause actual results to differ materially from those in the statement. Even if the statement does not satisfy the criteria of this prong, there is a second prong that precludes liability for a forward-looking statement unless the person who made the statement did so with actual knowledge that the statement was false or misleading. A company is not liable for a forward-looking statement it issues unless the plaintiff proves that the statement was made by, or with the approval of, an executive officer who had actual knowledge that the statement was false or misleading.

This safe harbor is discussed further in Chapter 23.

---

20. Rubinstein v. Collins, 20 F.3d 160 (5th Cir. 1994).

Damages

Section 11 sets forth the damages recoverable for violation of its provisions. If the plaintiff has not sold the securities in question, the recoverable damages are the amount paid for each security minus its value at the time the plaintiff brings the claim. The value at the time the plaintiff brings the claim is usually the market price, unless the market price has been affected by the misrepresentation or omission. If the securities have been sold before the plaintiff brings the claim, the recoverable damages are the amount paid for the security minus the amount received at sale.

 ## Section 12(2) of the 1933 Act

Section 12(2) provides a remedy for any person who purchases a security, by means of a misleading prospectus or oral communication. To establish a Section 12(2) claim, the plaintiff must prove that (1) through the mails or other means of interstate commerce, (2) the defendant offered or sold a security, (3) by means of a prospectus or oral communication, (4) which included a material misrepresentation or omission. Materiality under Section 12(2) is the same as materiality under Section 11. The purchaser may rescind the purchase unless the defendant proves that the depreciation in the value of the security resulted from factors unrelated to the alleged misstatement or omission. If the purchaser has sold the security, he or she generally may recover damages equal to the difference between what the purchaser paid and what he or she received for the security. However, if the defendant demonstrates that part or all of the decline in the value of the security was caused by factors other than the misstatement or omission alleged in the complaint, then the plaintiff may not recover damages based on that portion of the decline.

Section 12(2) does not require the plaintiff to prove that he or she relied on the misrepresentation or that the defendant acted with *scienter*, that is, an intent to deceive. On the other hand, Section 12(2) applies only to those who offer or sell a security. Under Section 12(2), the plaintiff must bring the action within one year from when the plaintiff discovered or should have discovered the fraud, or three years after the sale, whichever is the shorter.

The Supreme Court interpreted Section 12(2) to apply only to public offerings in the following case.

A CASE IN POINT	SUMMARY

CASE 22.6
GUSTAFSON v.
ALLOYD CO.
Supreme Court
of the United States
513 U.S. 561 (1995).

FACTS   Three individuals (Sellers) who owned all the stock of Alloyd Co., Inc. (Alloyd), a corporation engaged in the manufacture of clear plastic blister-packaging and automatic heat-seal packaging equipment, entered into a stock-purchase agreement, whereby they agreed to sell their stock to Wind Point Partners II, L.P. (Wind Point), an experienced and sophisticated venture-capital investment partnership. Sellers represented that they had estimated Alloyd's inventory and that the interim financial statements presented fairly Alloyd's financial condition. The stock-purchase agreement expressly stated that there would be an adjustment in the purchase price to take account of any variance between the inventory estimates in the interim financials and the year-end audit. Wind Point also expressly waived any right it had to seek rescission.

When the year-end audit revealed a substantial inventory shortfall, Wind Point sought to rescind the transaction under Section 12(2). Wind Point claimed that the stock-purchase agreement was a prospectus in which Sellers had materially misrepresented Alloyd's financial condition as of the date of the interim financials. Because Section 14 of the 1933 Act renders invalid waivers of the act's protections, the contractual agreement to waive rescission would not apply to a Section 12(2) claim.

The district court granted Sellers' motion for summary judgment, but the appeals court reversed. Sellers appealed.

ISSUE PRESENTED   Does Section 12(2) apply to misrepresentations in a stock-purchase agreement in connection with a private offering of stock?

SUMMARY OF OPINION   The U.S. Supreme Court first focused on Section 10, which provides that a "prospectus" is a document, related to a public offering by an issuer or its controlling shareholders, that must contain the information contained in a registration statement. Although Section 10 does not define what a prospectus is, the Court reasoned that it does indicate what a prospectus cannot be if the 1933 Act is to be interpreted as a symmetrical and coherent regulatory scheme.

There was no dispute that the stock-purchase agreement was not required to contain the information contained in a registration statement. The sale was a private placement exempt under Section 4(2). Therefore, the Court held that the stock-purchase agreement was not a prospectus under Section 10 and thus not a prospectus for purposes of Section 12(2) either.

The Court limited Section 12(2) to transactions involving a Section 10 statutory prospectus (and transactions involving exempt securities that are exempt from that requirement by reason of Section 3). A document can still be a prospectus if it omits a required piece of information, but it is not a prospectus if it need not comply with Section 10's requirements in the first place.

RESULT   Wind Point's claim under Section 12(2) was dismissed.

COMMENTS   *Gustafson* makes it clear that Section 12(2) liability extends to fraudulent statements or omissions in statutory prospectuses (those contained in the registration statement) used in a registered public offering, but does not extend to fraudulent documents used in connection with secondary market transactions, at least

Case 22.6 continues

Case 22.6 continued

those not involving resales by affiliates. Resales by affiliates under Rule 144 or Rule 144A should not fall within the scope of Section 12(2). However, resales by affiliates that would constitute a distribution under traditional Section 2(11) analysis are probably public offerings subject to Section 12(2).[21]

---

21. *See* Stephen M. Bainbridge, *Securities Act Section 12(2) after the Gustafson Debacle,* 50 Bus. Law. 1231, 1258 (1995).

Section 12(2) liability would appear to extend to selling documents, such as a brochure sent to investors along with the statutory prospectus, used in connection with registered offerings. Section 12(2) clearly applies to oral communications made in connection with a registered public offering. Although the *Gustafson* opinion is not clear on this point, Section 12(2) probably would not apply to oral communications made in connection with a private placement.[22]

The Supreme Court did not define what it meant by public offerings. Private placements under Section 4(2) are clearly not public offerings. But what about sales under Regulation D? The SEC adopted Rules 504 and 505 of Regulation D not under Section 4(2) but under its authority in Section 3(b) to exempt offerings of less than $5 million. The SEC relied on Section 4(2) for its statutory authority to adopt Rule 506, but the rule's safe harbor is far more liberal than the case law under Section 4(2). It is not yet clear whether the term "public offering" applies to (1) all offerings not exempted under Section 4(2), or (2) all offerings that must be registered under Section 5 and all offerings of securities exempted under Section 3. The later reading would exclude offerings under Regulation D from Section 12(2)'s reach.

Who May Be Sued

Section 12(2)'s language relating to who may be liable is identical to that of Section 12(1): anyone who "offers or sells" a security by means of a misleading prospectus

or oral communication. Accordingly, most courts treat Sections 12(1) and 12(2) as the same for the purposes of identifying potential defendants. In *Pinter v. Dahl,*[23] the Supreme Court considered only Section 12(1) and declined to extend its holding to Section 12(2). Some subsequent cases in the lower courts have, however, applied *Pinter* to Section 12(2), holding that only those in privity with the plaintiff or those who solicit the securities sale for financial gain face liability under Section 12(2). Those in privity would include underwriters, brokers, and dealers having a direct contractual relationship with the plaintiff.

Reasonable Care Defense

Section 12(2) provides a defense of reasonable care. A defendant will not be liable for a Section 12(2) violation if it can prove that it did not know, and in the exercise of reasonable care could not have known, about the misrepresentations or omissions. In contrast to the due diligence defense of Section 11, the defense of reasonable care is not spelled out in detail. Commentators have suggested that reasonable care may require a defendant to undertake an investigation. In *Sanders v. John Nuveen & Co.,*[24] the U.S. Court of Appeals for the Seventh Circuit held that there is no difference between the duties imposed on an underwriter by Section 11, which requires a reasonable investigation, and Section 12(2). An underwriter, the Seventh Circuit held, must look beyond published data and undertake some inves-

---

22. *See* Ballay v. Legg Mason Wood Walker, Inc., 925 F.2d 682 (3d Cir. 1991), *cert. denied,* 502 U.S. 820 (1991).

23. 486 U.S. 622 (Case 22.4).

24. 619 F.2d 1222 (7th Cir. 1980), *cert. denied,* 450 U.S. 1005 (1981).

tigation of that part of the data that is verifiable. Because the underwriter in *Sanders* did not examine the issuing company's records, contracts, or tax returns, the underwriter did not act with reasonable care.

 ## Criminal Penalties

In addition to buying back the securities or paying damages, defendants also face criminal penalties for violations of state or federal securities laws that include fines and imprisonment. Under Section 24 of the 1933 Act, any person who willfully violates the provisions of the

act shall upon conviction be fined not more than $10,000 or imprisoned for up to five years, or both. A violation can be willful even if the defendant did not know that the transaction at issue involved securities or that the law was being violated. In cases claiming false statements or omissions of material facts, the government need show only that the defendant knew what investors were and were not being told, accompanied by proof that the statement or omissions were objectively material.[25]

25. United States v. English, 92 F.3d 909 (6th Cir. 1996).

 ## THE RESPONSIBLE MANAGER
Complying with Registration Requirements

Any person offering securities must comply with the registration requirements of the 1933 Act. This includes start-up companies, as well as large, publicly traded companies. Failure to comply gives the purchaser of the security the right to keep the proceeds if the investment is successful or to return the security to the seller if the investment does not turn out as hoped. Moreover, as was explained in Chapter 15, a willful failure to comply is a criminal offense. Even if a security is exempt from registration, it is not exempt from the antifraud provisions of the 1934 Act, discussed in Chapter 23.

Managers, particularly those of small firms, should be familiar with the four-part *Howey* test. They should be aware that certain contracts that are not normally thought of as securities may run afoul of the 1933 and 1934 acts.

Furthermore, securities held by officers, directors, and other affiliates cannot be freely resold. They must be sold under Rule 144, subject to its volume and public information requirements, or in a private offering to sophisticated, eligible buyers. Companies must put legends on affiliates' share certificates, issue stop-transfer orders to the transfer agent, or take such other steps as may be reasonable to ensure compliance with these rules.

The preparation of a private-placement offering memorandum is an involved process that requires an intimate knowledge of the statutory requirements. Managers face considerable liability for incorrect or misleading statements in these documents.

Any person involved in a public offering of securities has a legal and ethical duty to ensure that the prospectus contains no misleading statements or omissions. Experts, such as accountants, have a particularly heavy responsibility. The underwriters and outside directors cannot rely passively on the representations of management. Violations of these rules give rise to both civil and criminal liability.

Managers should work closely with counsel during the waiting period to ensure that there are no gun-jumping problems due to any eagerness on behalf of the underwriter or the company's public relations department. It is very important that the company not issue an abnormal number of press releases or increase the amount of its advertising prior to the registration going effective. In other words, the manager should make sure that the company does not depart from its ordinary routine and that the company remains quiet.

In addition, a manager should ensure that there are no material misstatements or omissions in any public disclosures (for example, Form 10–K or Form 10–Q). Once a disclosure is made, even if there was no legal obligation to disclose, the statements contained within it must be truthful and are subject to securities law.

INSIDE STORY

THE BRITISH PETROLEUM STOCK OFFERING

To participate in the British government's share offering of British Petroleum Company plc, a multinational group of investment bankers agreed to a firm commitment underwriting in which the stock price was set weeks before the bankers actually could sell the stock. In addition, to gain a piece of the multibillion dollar offering, the underwriting banks agreed to an unusual out-clause that gave the British Parliament total control over the transaction.

Before the government's offering came to market, worldwide share prices plummeted in the October 1987 stock market crash. The value of British Petroleum's shares dropped more than 20% from the fixed-offer price. The British, European, Canadian, and Japanese underwriters pre-sold portions of their shares of the offering before the market crash and mitigated their losses. However,

the U.S. underwriters, which included Goldman Sachs, Morgan Stanley, Salomon Brothers, and Shearson Lehman, were prohibited from pre-selling due to SEC regulations and faced combined losses of up to $500 million if the offering went to market. Consequently, they argued vociferously for the government to pull or delay the offering.

Despite the underwriters' pleas, the British government did not want to let the underwriters off the hook; such a step would have cost the British taxpayers more than $2 billion in lost proceeds.[26] Many Britons had charged that the banks merely took profits from government privatizations without ever really being at risk, according to attorney Simon MacLachlan of London's Clifford Schance, who observed the events. "Underwriters had to be seen to be taking a loss from time to time."[27]

The U.S. underwriters understood what their firm commitment underwriting meant. According to Charles S. Whitman III of Davis Polk & Wardell, the New York law firm that represented all four U.S. underwriters involved in the deal, "We made it clear what the contract was. But no one knew what could happen to the market. No one I know is saying it can't happen again."[28] Although the underwriters could not persuade the British Parliament to let them out of the firm commitment-underwriting agreement, they were successful in persuading the government to cap their losses.

26. Anatole Kaletsky & Richard Tomkins, *Financial Markets in Turmoil; Arguments Are Strong for Lawson to Proceed with Offering*, FIN. TIMES, Oct. 28, 1987, at 2.

27. Sherry R. Sontag, *Can a Market Crash Be an 'Act of God'?; Out-Clauses Revisited*, NAT'L L.J., Dec. 14, 1987, at 1.

28. *Id.*

KEY WORDS AND PHRASES

accredited investor **850**

affiliate **840**

bespeaks caution doctrine **867**

best-efforts underwriting **839**

blank check companies **851**

blue sky laws **831**

controlling-person liability **863**

dealer **845**

due diligence **841**

family resemblance test **834**

firm commitment underwriting **838**

Form S–1 **839**

Form S–2 **839**

Form S–3 **839**

Form S–4 **848**

Form SB–1 **839**

Form SB–2 **840**

going effective **837**

gun-jumping **847**

integrate **850**

investment contract **832**

issuer **854**

material fact **864**

merit review **831**

not an underwriter **854**

offer **836**

offshore transactions **857**

private offering **849**

private-placement memorandum **852**

prospectus **836**

proxy **859**

qualified institutional buyer **856**

quiet period **841**

red-herring prospectus **841**

registration statement **836**

reporting company **859**

restricted securities **854**

roadshow **845**

sale **836**

QUESTIONS AND CASE PROBLEMS

1. Life Partners Inc. is the leading promoter of interests in viatical settlements, whereby investors purchase at a discount interests in a pool consisting of terminal AIDS patients' life insurance benefits. Is Life Partners engaged in the sale of securities? [*SEC v. Life Partners Inc.*, 87 F.3d 536 (D.C. Cir. 1996)]

2. Devour Corporation proposes to issue common stock in exchange for the assets of Quarry Inc. Quarry will first obtain the approval of its shareholders and then distribute the Devour common stock to its shareholders. Does Devour have to register the stock that it will give Quarry in exchange for Quarry's assets?

3. Tommy Long owns 5,000 shares of Super Corporation. There are 100,000 shares outstanding, and the stock is actively traded on the New York Stock Exchange. Long is not an issuer, underwriter, or dealer as defined in the Securities Act of 1933. Long publicly purchased the shares on the advice of Mark Fynch. When Long goes to sell these shares, must he register them under the 1933 Act?

4. Ventura Corporation of Denver, Colorado, made a private offering of its common stock on January 1 and additional offerings on March 1, August 1, and November 1. All of the private placements are with the same group of 50 individuals and pension funds. Do these separate private offerings constitute one continuous public offering by Ventura?

5. Susan Newton, 38, founded her own software firm at age 15 and acquired her stock in an offering under Rule 505 of Regulation D. She now has a position on the board of directors of EBM Corporation and owns 15% of its outstanding common stock. Newton grew her firm to $20 million in revenue before it was purchased by EBM for EBM common stock in a private placement under Section 4(2). She no longer is an officer or active in the day-to-day management of her business. She proposes to sell her interest in EBM to the public. The stock

is actively traded on the American Stock Exchange. Must she register her stock under the 1933 Act?

6. Security Pacific National Bank had extended a line of credit to Integrated Resources under which it obtained short-term loans from the bank. Participations in these loans were sold to various institutional investors under a master agreement containing a disclaimer stating that each investor participated in the loans without relying on Security Pacific. Integrated later defaulted on the loans and declared bankruptcy. Several investors sued Security Pacific, arguing that the loan participations were securities under the 1933 Act, and sought to rescind their purchase agreement. Did Security Pacific sell securities? [*Banco Español de Crédito v. Security Pac. Nat'l Bank*, 973 F.2d 51 (2d Cir. 1992), *cert. denied*, 509 U.S. 903 (1993)]

7. In January, Arbor Corporation, a paper company with annual sales of more than $2 billion and assets of more than $5 billion, issued four million registered common shares at an average price of $50 per share. In preparing the registration statement, Charles Controller relied on a report by Acme Appraisers, which stated that the company's woodlands were worth $900 million. Acme's report was not included in the registration statement, and Acme was not mentioned. Ollie Olson, the company's newly elected outside director (and Controller's brother-in-law) questioned whether the woodland estimate might be too high. Controller reassured him that "if the numbers are good enough for our CPAs, they're good enough for me."

In February, the company discovered that the woodland appraisal was overstated by $150 million. Management and the directors are livid about the error. To add to Arbor's problems, a major competitor shocked the industry by announcing that it will double its paper production capacity. Arbor's stock price is now $20 per share.

Do the shareholders have a basis for a suit? Who can they sue? What problems or defenses will they likely encounter? Assuming that the suit is otherwise successful, how will damages be determined?

8. Duke Distribution, Inc. recently had a public offering of its shares. The company's attorneys, its CPAs, and the underwriter's attorneys worked diligently to meet a tight deadline that management had imposed. Unfortunately, in its haste to meet the deadline, Duke's team failed to include some important information in the registration statement. The prospectus failed to mention that while Duke's inventory-to-sales ratio was constant over the past few years, most competitors' ratios had declined significantly over the same period. It also failed to mention that the company leases warehouses from a partnership consisting of three of its directors. The leases require rent that is about 8% higher than the market rate for equivalent facilities. After the initial public offering, the company engaged in additional transactions with insiders.

Now the economy has softened and competition has increased. The price of Duke stock has fallen from $15 to $10. Is there a cause of action? Against whom? What are the defenses?

9. Gateway 2000, Inc. (Gateway), the leading direct marketer of personal computers in the United States, issued 11.7 million shares of common stock at a price of $15 per share in an initial public offering in December 1993. The prospectus included the following language: "Although the company anticipates significant growth in the future, it does not expect its growth to continue at the rates previously experienced." The prospectus also identified 16 risk factors, including (1) "Short Product Life Cycles," which warned that there could be no assurance that the new products and features introduced in 1993 will be successful or that the introduction of new products will not materially and adversely affect the sale of the company's existing products; (2) "Management of Growth," stating that the company has experienced and may continue to experience problems with its management information systems and inventory controls; (3) "Potential for Fluctuating Operating Results," noting that the personal computer industry generally has been subject to seasonality and to significant quarterly and annual fluctuations in operating results; (4) "Potential Liability for Sales, Use or Income Taxes," stating that the company does not collect or remit sales or use taxes with respect to its sales in any state other than South Dakota, where its physical plant

and employees are located, and warning that in the future the company may be required to collect sales and use taxes in states other than South Dakota; and (5) "Absence of Public Market and Possible Volatility of Stock Price," warning that the market price for the company's common stock may be highly volatile.

The per share earnings for the first quarter of 1994 declined, triggering a drop in Gateway's stock price from $20.44 to $15.50 per share. Earnings dropped again during the second quarter of 1994, and the stock price plummeted to $9.25 per share on June 23, 1994. Gateway attributed the reduced earnings to product transitions, unanticipated sales mix, and technical problems with a new line of portable computers.

The plaintiffs, who had purchased Gateway stock soon after the stock was publicly offered, sued under Sections 11 and 12(2) of the 1933 Act and Section 10(b) and Rule 10b-5 of the 1934 Act. They alleged that the prospectus (1) overstated earnings in 1993 and 1994 by failing to adequately reserve for uncollectable accounts receivable and product returns; (2) misrepresented Gateway's prospect for growth; (3) misrepresented the existence and extent of obsolete and defective inventories; (4) misrepresented that Gateway's reserves for doubtful accounts were adequate, thereby overstating Gateway's assets by $6.8 million; (5) misrepresented the quality of Gateway's new portable computers; (6) misrepresented serious deficiencies in Gateway's purchasing and inventory control systems, management information and order systems, and management and forecasting procedures; and (7) misrepresented Gateway's obligations to pay sales taxes to states other than South Dakota.

Should any of the plaintiffs' claims be dismissed? On what theory? [*Parnes v. Gateway 2000, Inc.,* 122 F.3d 539 (8th Cir. 1997)]

MANAGER'S DILEMMA

10. Shares in "hot" initial public offerings (IPOs) are by definition in high demand. Most shares are allocated to large institutional investors. However, in a practice dubbed "spinning," the investment banks may allocate shares to the personal accounts of executives of the bank's corporate clients or would-be corporate clients. Because hot deals usually trade at a premium over the IPO price, the executives can sell the shares on the day of the IPO for quick profits.

Cristina Morgan, Hambrecht & Quist's managing director of investment banking, defended the practice of allocating IPOs to the personal brokerage accounts of clients who also direct corporate-finance business to the firm, saying, "Is it appropriate? Well, yeah." She reasoned: "If you sell doughnuts, you do everything you can to enhance the image and service of your doughnut shop to customers. You're just doing your job. That's what we all are doing." Morgan points out that the amounts involved, often 500 to 1,000 shares, are small compared to the net worth of her clients, and she asserts that there is no way that the IPO allocations could influence the corporate decisions made by the executives who receive the allocations.[29]

_____

29. Ms. Morgan is quoted in Michael Siconolfi, *Hambrecht & Quist Goes on Offensive on 'Spinning,'* WALL ST. J., Nov. 26, 1997, at C1, C20. *See also* Michael Siconolfi, *SEC, NASD Begin Probes of IPO 'Spin' Accounts,* WALL ST. J., Nov. 13, 1997, at A3.

Regina Taoka is the newly appointed head of investment banking at an old-line Wall Street investment banking firm that is eager to shake off its stodgy image and to increase its share of high-technology initial public offerings. Taoka knows that the firm's personal clients include venture capitalists owning substantial shares in privately owned companies that are contemplating going public and officers and directors of public companies that may engage in secondary offerings or mergers and acquisitions.

The manager in charge of business development has proposed that the firm give these individuals "a taste" of future hot IPOs, in hopes that "they will remember who their friends are" when selecting a lead underwriter or financial advisor for their companies. He tells Taoka that "everyone is doing it."

What restrictions, if any, should Taoka put on spinning? Is allocation to the personal account of a private company executive more or less defensible than allocation to the account of an executive of a publicly traded company?

INTERNET SOURCES	
This site maintained by Houlihan Smith & Company, a specialized investment banking firm, includes a helpful article on due diligence entitled *The Investment Banker's Perspective on Due Diligence for Mergers, Acquisitions and Securities Offerings.*	http://www.houlihansmith.com
Securities and Exchange Commission	http://www.sec.gov
The SEC's guidance on how to comply with the plain English requirements—*A Plain English Handbook: How to Create Clear SEC Disclosure Documents*—is posted on this site.	http://www.sec.gov/consumer/plaine.htm
Nasdaq Stock Market	http://www.nasdaq.com
New York Stock Exchange	http://www.nyse.com
This site provides free access to electronic filings with the SEC.	http://www.freeedgar.com

CHAPTER 23

Securities Fraud and Insider Trading

INTRODUCTION

Maintaining the Integrity of the Securities Markets

The principal antifraud provisions of the federal securities laws are Sections 11 and 12(2) of the Securities Act of 1933 (the 1933 Act), discussed in Chapter 22, and Section 10(b) of the Securities Exchange Act of 1934 (the 1934 Act). As explained in Chapter 22, Section 11 applies only to registered offerings, and Section 12(2) applies only to public offerings not exempt from the 1933 Act's registration requirements. In contrast, Section 10(b) applies to all purchases and sales of securities, regardless of whether they are registered or exempt from registration.

Under Section 10(b) and Rule 10b–5, promulgated by the Securities and Exchange Commission (SEC) pursuant to the 1934 Act, it is unlawful for any person to use a fraudulent, manipulative, or deceptive device in connection with the purchase or sale of any security. Rule 10b–5 also prohibits *insider trading*, that is, trading securities while in possession of material nonpublic information in violation of a duty to the corporation or its shareholders or the source of the information. Section 16(b) of the 1934 Act also regulates trading by insiders. In particular, it allows a public corporation to sue for damages if any officer or director of the corporation or any person who owns more than 10% of the corporation's securities engages in short-swing trading, that is, the purchase and sale, or sale and purchase, of securities of the corporation within a six-month period.

Chapter Overview

This chapter focuses on Section 10(b) and Rule 10b–5. It sets forth the seven elements necessary in a Rule 10b–5 case and the fraud-on-the-market theory of liability. The safe-harbor for certain forward-looking statements is discussed. Section 17(a) of the 1933 Act, under which the U.S. government can bring fraud claims, is briefly discussed. The chapter defines insider trading and discusses in detail the legal elements of an insider-trading case. Short-swing trading is then defined, and the rules for calculating the recoverable profits are discussed, as well as the requirements for reporting by insiders.

Section 10(b) of the 1934 Act

Section 10(b) gives the SEC power to prohibit individuals or companies from engaging in securities fraud by authorizing the SEC to prescribe specific rules for the protection of investors.

Rule 10b–5

The SEC promulgated Rule 10b–5 as a means to achieve the goals of Section 10(b): to encourage disclosure of information relevant to the investing public, to protect investors, and to deter fraud in the securities industry. Rule 10b–5 states:

> It shall be unlawful for any person, directly or indirectly, by the use of any means or instrumentality of interstate commerce, or of the mails, or of any facility of any national securities exchange,
>
> (1) to employ any device, scheme, or artifice to defraud,
>
> (2) to make any untrue statement of a material fact or to omit to state a material fact necessary in order to make the statements made, in the light of the circumstances under which they were made, not misleading, or
>
> (3) to engage in any act, practice, or course of business which operates or would operate as a fraud or deceit upon any person, in connection with the purchase or sale of any security.

The SEC has broad power to investigate apparent violations of Rule 10b–5 and to order that the violator stop its wrongful conduct or to recommend criminal prosecution for willful violations.

More suits are brought under Rule 10b–5 than under any other provision of securities law, including those, such as Sections 11 and 12(2) of the 1933 Act, that explicitly create private rights of action. Although there is some overlap, Rule 10b–5 extends to misconduct not covered by other securities laws. Under Rule 10b–5, managers could be liable for misleading statements contained in any document—such as a press release or a letter to shareholders—or even a speech to a trade association as long as the statements were made in a manner reasonably calculated to influence the investing public.

Since 1946, courts have held that Rule 10b–5 also creates an implicit private right of action giving individual investors the right to sue a violator for damages. Although the Supreme Court has lately shown increasing hostility toward implied rights of action under other provisions of the securities laws, most commentators do not expect it to abrogate the right of action under Rule 10b–5.

Controlling Persons   Section 20(a) imposes joint and several liability on every person who, directly or indirectly, controls any person liable under the 1934 Act, unless the controlling person acted in good faith and did not directly or indirectly induce the acts constituting the violation. This provision is generally interpreted in the same way as Section 15 of the 1933 Act, which is discussed in Chapter 22.

Aiding and Abetting   In *Central Bank of Denver, N. A. v. First Interstate Bank of Denver, N.A.*,[1] the Supreme Court ruled that a private plaintiff may not maintain an aiding and abetting suit under Section 10(b). In that case, the plaintiff attempted to hold the bank that was the indenture trustee for a municipal bond issue secondarily liable as an aider and abettor of the fraud perpetrated by the issuers of the bonds. The Court began by noting that it had interpreted Section 10(b) to impose private civil liability on those who commit a manipulative or deceptive act in connection with the purchase or sale of securities. However, the Court held that a private plaintiff may not bring a Rule 10b–5 suit against a defendant for acts not prohibited by the text of Section 10(b). Because the text of Section 10(b) does not prohibit aiding and abetting, the Court concluded that a private plaintiff may not maintain an aiding and abetting suit under Section 10(b).

The Court noted that the absence of Section 10(b) aiding and abetting liability did not mean that secondary actors in the securities markets were always free from liability under the securities laws. Any person or entity, including a lawyer, accountant, or bank, who employs a manipulative device or makes a material misstatement (or omission) on which a purchaser or seller of securities relies may be liable as a primary violator under Rule 10b–5, assuming all of the requirements for primary liability under Rule 10b–5 are met.

In reaching its decision, the Supreme Court noted the vexatious nature of Rule 10b–5 suits and the fact that it requires secondary actors to expend large sums

---

1. 511 U.S. 167 (1994).

for pretrial defense and the negotiation of settlements. The Court went on to state:

> This uncertainty and excessive litigation can have ripple effects. For example, newer and smaller companies may find it difficult to obtain advice from professionals. A professional may fear that a newer or smaller company may not survive and that business failure would generate securities litigation against the professional, among others. In addition, the increased costs incurred by professionals because of the litigation and settlement costs under 10b-5 may be passed on to their client companies, and in turn incurred by the company's investors, the intended beneficiaries of the statute.

The SEC can still bring aider-and-abettor cases seeking injunctive relief or damages under Section 10(b). To prove that a person is an *aider and abettor*, it is necessary to show (1) the existence of a primary violation of Section 10(b) or Rule 10b–5, (2) the defen-

dant's knowledge of (or recklessness as to) that primary violation, and (3) substantial assistance of the violation by the defendant.

Conspiracy   In *Dinsmore*,[2] the U.S. Court of Appeals for the Second Circuit applied *Central Bank*'s reasoning to a claim of conspiracy to fraudulently buy or sell securities and held that there was no private implied cause of action for conspiracy under Section 10(b).

Primary Liability for Secondary Actors   Both the Supreme Court in *Central Bank* and the Second Circuit in *Dinsmore* took pains to make it clear that secondary actors can be liable in private suits if their conduct satisfied the requirements for primary liability, as happened in the following case.

---

2. Dinsmore v. Squadron, Ellenoff, Plesent, Sheinfeld & Sorkin, 135 F.3d 837 (2d Cir. 1998).

A CASE IN POINT	**SUMMARY**

CASE 23.1
McGANN v.
ERNST & YOUNG
United States Court of
Appeals for the Ninth Circuit
102 F. 3d 390
(9th Cir. 1996), *cert. denied,*
117 S. Ct. 1460 (1997).

FACTS   Ernst & Young was the outside auditor for Community Psychiatric Centers (CPC), a publicly traded corporation. The plaintiffs alleged that Ernst & Young failed to disclose the fact that CPC had a major accounts receivable problem and thereby issued a false and misleading audit opinion regarding CPC's financial statements for the fiscal year ending in November 1990.

Moreover, the plaintiffs alleged that Ernst & Young knew that CPC would include this audit opinion in its annual report on Form 10–K filed with the SEC. The plaintiffs claimed that the suppression of this information caused CPC's stock price to be artificially inflated. In September and November 1991, when CPC announced a major drop in earnings due to $37 million in uncollectible debts, the value of CPC's stock declined precipitously.

The plaintiffs were the class of people who purchased CPC between the time Ernst & Young published its audit opinion for CPC's 1990 fiscal year and the time CPC announced its bad debts. They alleged that Ernst & Young, by producing a fraudulent audit report with the knowledge that its client would disseminate the report to the securities market, committed fraudulent acts "in connection with" the trading of securities and thus violated Section 10(b) of the 1934 Act. The district court dismissed the claim, and the plaintiffs appealed.

ISSUE PRESENTED   Is an accounting firm subject to primary liability under Section 10(b) of the 1934 Act when it prepares a fraudulent audit report that it knows its client will include in a Form 10–K?

Case 23.1 continues

Case 23.1 continued

SUMMARY OF OPINION The U.S. Court of Appeals began by noting that accountants have no aider-and-abettor liability under Section 10(b) per *Central Bank of Denver*.[3] However, the court held that *Central Bank* did not undercut *SEC v. Texas Gulf Sulphur Co.*,[4] which stands for the proposition that any false and misleading assertions made "in a manner reasonably calculated to influence the investing public" are made "in connection with" the purchase or sale of securities within the meaning of Section 10(b). The language of Section 10(b) does not limit liability to those who actually trade securities. One who "introduces fraudulent information into the securities market does no less damage to the public because that party did not trade stocks." Therefore, Ernst & Young could be liable for a primary violation of Section 10(b) if the plaintiff could prove that Ernst & Young made a misleading statement in the audit opinion knowing that the opinion would be included in CPC's Form 10–K.

RESULT The appeals court reversed the district court's judgment in favor of Ernst & Young and remanded the case back to district court. The allegations survived the motion to dismiss on the pleadings.

---

3. 511 U.S. 164 (1994).

4. 401 F.2d 833 (2d Cir. 1968) (Case 23.2).

Note that *McGann* involved an alleged failure to disclose that caused the audit opinion to be false and misleading. Accountants are generally not responsible for misrepresentations or omissions in other parts of a document that they did not certify.[5] Thus, the U.S. District Court for the Southern District of New York dismissed a case in which the plaintiffs claimed that the accountant that certified the financial statements for fiscal years 1993 and 1994, which were included in a prospectus dated February 22, 1996, had a duty to disclose the disastrous results for the last quarter of 1995.[6] The plaintiffs had argued that the financial figures in the audit report and elsewhere in the prospectus gave the impression that the company had "turned the corner" and become profitable when in fact the company had experienced a record loss in the final quarter of 1995. The court rejected the notion that an accurate report becomes misleading because an issuer suffers a material loss subsequent to the period covered by the report. However, the court acknowledged that accountants do have a duty to take reasonable steps to correct misstatements they have discovered in financial statements they audited previously.[7]

Accountants must sign a written consent before their audited report can be included in a registration statement. Before doing so, they should do an *S–1 review*, which is a review of events subsequent to the date of the certified balance sheet in the registration statement to ascertain whether any material change has occurred in the company's financial position that should be disclosed to prevent the balance sheet figures from being misleading. This review includes comparing recent financial statements to earlier ones, reading minutes of the shareholders' and directors' meetings, and investigating changes in material contracts, bad debts and newly discovered liabilities.

The U.S. Court of Appeals for the Sixth Circuit held that an attorney for a securities issuer who had direct contacts with potential investors may be liable under Section 10(b) and Rule 10b–5 for talking with the

---

5. *See* Shapiro v. Cantor, 23 F.3d 717 (2d Cir. 1997).

6. Adair v. Kaye Kotts Assocs., Inc., Fed. Sec. L. Rep. (CCH) ¶90,192 (S.D.N.Y. 1998).

7. *See* IIT v. Cornfeld, 619 F.2d 909 (2d Cir. 1980).

ETHICAL CONSIDERATION

If, in the course of the S–1 review, the accountants learn that the company's earnings have dropped dramatically from earnings for the comparable periods included in the registration statement, should the accountants refuse to sign the consent for inclusion of their opinion on the financial statements for the previous period unless the adverse results are disclosed?

potential investors concerning material details of the proposed investment, without revealing certain additional facts he knew that had to be disclosed to prevent the statements he made from being misleading.[8] "In sum, while an attorney representing the seller in a securities transaction may not always be under an independent duty to volunteer information about the financial condition of his client, he assumes a duty to provide complete and non-misleading information with respect to subjects on which he undertakes to speak."

The Third Circuit had held that investors may sue a law firm that had a significant role in preparing the client's offering documents for primary liability under Section 10(b), even though the investors were not aware of the firm's role.[9] To hold the lawyer liable, the plaintiff had to prove that (1) the lawyer knew or was reckless in not knowing that the statement would be relied on by investors, (2) the lawyer was aware or was reckless in not being aware of the material misstatement or omission, (3) the lawyer played such a substantial role in the creation of the statement that the lawyer could fairly be said to be the author or co-author of the statement, and (4) the other requirements of primary liability are satisfied. However, the Third Circuit decided to rehear the case, leaving the value of the earlier decision as precedent in doubt.

Statute of Limitations   Suits under Section 10(b) must be brought within one year of the date the plaintiff discovered or should have discovered the fraud

or within three years of the date of the violation, whichever is shorter.[10]

◆ Elements of a Rule 10b–5 Cause of Action

In order to recover damages from a defendant under Rule 10b–5, a plaintiff must show each of the following elements:

1. The defendant used either an instrumentality of interstate commerce or the mails or a facility of a national securities exchange.
2. The defendant made a statement that either misrepresented or omitted a fact.
3. The fact was of material importance.
4. The misrepresentation or omission was made with *scienter* (culpable state of mind).
5. There was a purchase or sale of securities.
6. The plaintiff acted in reliance either on the defendant's misrepresentation or on the assumption that the market price of the stock accurately reflected its value.
7. The defendant's misrepresentation or omission caused the plaintiff to suffer losses.

Each of these seven elements is described in more detail below.

Interstate Commerce

The requirement that the defendant used interstate commerce, the mails, or a national securities exchange gives Congress the power to regulate the defendant's conduct under the U.S. Constitution. The requirement is usually easy to satisfy. Use of interstate commerce includes use of a radio broadcast heard in more than one state; use of a newspaper advertisement in a newspaper delivered to more than one state; or use of a telephone wired for interstate calls, even if no interstate calls were actually made. Use of the mails includes sending a letter within a state, because the mail is an instrumentality of interstate commerce. Use of a national securities exchange includes use of any facility of such an exchange.

8. Rubin v. Schottenstein, Zox & Dunn, 143 F.3d 263 (6th Cir. 1998) *(en banc)*.

9. Klein v. Boyd, Fed. Sec. L. Rep. (CCH) ¶90,136 (3d Cir. 1998), *vacated and reh'g granted,* Fed. Sec. L. Rep. (CCH) ¶90,165 (3d Cir. 1998).

10. Lampf, Pleva, Lipkind, Prupis & Petigrow v. Gilbertson, 501 U.S. 350 (1991).

Misstatement or Omission

A *misstatement* is a misrepresentation of a fact; in other words, a lie. An *omission* is a fact left out of a statement, such that the statement becomes misleading.

Misstatement   In the following case, a company's attempts to dispel rumors were found to misrepresent the facts.

A CASE IN POINT   **SUMMARY**

CASE 23.2
SECURITIES AND
EXCHANGE
COMMISSION v. TEXAS
GULF SULPHUR CO.
United States District
Court for the Southern
District of New York
312 F. Supp. 77 (S.D.N.Y.
1970), *aff'd,* 446 F.2d 1301
(2d Cir. 1971), *cert. denied,*
404 U.S. 1005 (1971).

FACTS   Texas Gulf Sulphur Company (TGS) drilled a test hole on November 12, 1963, which indicated the possible discovery of copper. TGS did not immediately disclose the results of its drill hole or undertake further drilling because it wanted to acquire property in the surrounding area and did not want to drive up the price of the property.

On April 12, 1964, in response to rumors about the copper discovery, TGS issued a press release. By this time, the company had confirmed the discovery of copper. Preliminary tests indicated that the discovery was significant. The press release, however, minimized the importance of the discovery. It said (in part):

For Immediate Release
TEXAS GULF SULPHUR COMMENT ON TIMMINS, ONTARIO, EXPLORATION
NEW YORK, April 12—The following statement was made today by Dr. Charles F. Fogarty, executive vice president of Texas Gulf Sulphur Company, in regard to the company's drilling operations near Timmins, Ontario, Canada. Dr. Fogarty said:
During the past few days, the exploration activities of Texas Gulf Sulphur in the area of Timmins, Ontario, have been widely reported in the press, coupled with rumors of a substantial copper discovery there. These reports exaggerate the scale of operations, and mention plans and statistics of size and grade of ore that are without factual basis and have evidently originated by speculation of people not connected with TGS.

The facts are as follows. TGS has been exploring in the Timmins area for six years as part of its overall search in Canada and elsewhere for various minerals—lead, copper, zinc, etc. During the course of this work, in Timmins as well as in Eastern Canada, TGS has conducted exploration entirely on its own, without the participation by others. Numerous prospects have been investigated by geophysical means and a large number of selected ones have been core-drilled. These cores are sent to the United States for assay and detailed examination as a matter of routine and on advice of expert Canadian legal counsel. No inferences as to grade can be drawn from this procedure.

Most of the areas drilled in Eastern Canada have revealed either barren pyrite or graphite without value; a few have resulted in discoveries of small or marginal sulphide ore bodies.

Recent drilling on one property near Timmins has led to preliminary indications that more drilling would be required for proper evaluation of this prospect. The drilling done to date has not been conclusive, but the statements made by many outside quarters are unreliable and include information and figures that are not available to TGS.

The work done to date has not been sufficient to reach definite conclusions and any statement as to size and grade of ore would be premature and possibly misleading. When we have progressed to the point where reasonable and logical conclusions can be made, TGS will issue a definite statement to its stockholders and to the public in order to clarify the Timmins project.

Case 23.2 continues

Case 23.2 continued

The SEC contended that TGS's April 12 release was a misstatement because the impression it left with investors was contrary to the known facts at the time.

ISSUE PRESENTED   Does a press release giving a misleading impression about the results of a drilling operation violate Rule 10b–5?

SUMMARY OF OPINION   The Federal District Court acknowledged that the timing of disclosure is a matter for the business judgment of the corporate officers. However, when a company chooses to issue a press release to respond to spreading rumors regarding its activities, it must describe the true picture at the time of the press release. This should include the basic facts known, or which reasonably should be known, to the drafters of the press release. Such facts are necessary to enable the investing public to make a reasonable appraisal of the existing situation.

Because the press release misled reasonable investors to believe either that there was no ore discovery, or that any discovery was not a significant one, TGS violated Section 10(b) and Rule 10b–5.

RESULT   TGS violated Section 10(b) and Rule 10b–5.

COMMENTS   A company may have excellent reasons to attempt to dispel rumors. TGS, for example, had an interest in keeping the find quiet in order to keep down the acquisition costs of land. Or consider a company involved in merger negotiations asked by the press whether there is any reason for unusual trading in its stock. The company may well want to keep the negotiations under wraps for a variety of legitimate reasons. Yet, if it says that it is unaware of any corporate developments, it runs the risk of Rule 10b-5 liability. The SEC has indicated that it considers such a statement in these circumstances to be a violation of Rule 10b–5. The Supreme Court addressed this issue in *Basic, Inc. v. Levinson* (Case 23.4).

A prediction about the future can be a misstatement, but only if the person making the prediction does not believe it at the time. A prediction is not a guarantee, and it does not become a misstatement simply because the facts do not develop as predicted. If there is no reasonable basis for a prediction, however, then it is a misstatement, because the person who made it could not honestly have believed it.[11]

The Private Securities Litigation Reform Act of 1995 (the Reform Act) contains a safe-harbor for certain forward-looking statements. It is discussed later in this chapter.

Omission   It is clear that a company must be careful if it chooses to speak. What if it chooses not to speak?

The general rule is that a company has no duty under Rule 10b–5 to reveal corporate developments unless it or its insiders trade in its securities, recommend trading to someone else, or disclose the information as a *tip*—that is, a disclosure made to an individual and withheld from the general public. The fact that information is material does not, in itself, give rise to a duty to disclose.[12]

However, stock exchange rules require that issuers promptly reveal material developments unless there is a business reason not to do so, and the securities laws require that certain information be disclosed in registration statements, annual and quarterly reports, and

---

11. *See* Virginia Bankshares v. Sandberg, 501 U.S. 1083 (1991) (holding that a statement as to beliefs or opinions may be actionable if the opinion is known by the speaker at the time it is expressed to be untrue or to have no reasonable basis in fact).

12. Backman v. Polaroid Corp., 893 F.2d 1405 (1st Cir. 1990).

proxy solicitations. In particular, Management's Discussion and Analysis must disclose any known material event or uncertainty that would cause reported financial information not to be necessarily indicative of future operating results or financial condition.[13]

Once the company has said something about a particular topic, it then has a duty to disclose enough relevant facts so that the statement is not inaccurate, incomplete, or misleading. The statement may be an obligatory one. Or the statement may be voluntary; for example, a company may choose to publicize information about favorable new developments or to respond to unfavorable rumors. Whether the statement is obligatory or voluntary, the company's officials must tell the whole truth with respect to that topic or risk being sued later for a misleading omission.

An omission can occur when a company makes a statement that is true at the time but that becomes misleading in light of later events. If investors are reasonably relying on the previous statements, the company can be held liable for failing to disclose the new information. For example, a company incurs a duty to update its financial projections when a projection changes or the company discovers that the projection was incorrect from the outset.

INTERNATIONAL CONSIDERATION

Under the London Stock Exchange rules, if a listed company's share price moves significantly on the basis of rumor and the rumor is true, then the company must disclose the existence of the rumored event. For example, in January 1998, drug powerhouse SmithKline Beecham PLC was required to disclose that it was engaged in merger negotiations with American Home Products after rumors of a deal sent shares of both companies rising.[a] Although there is no numerical threshold for disclosure, a rule-of-thumb is that a 10% move in the stock triggers the duty to disclose the accuracy of truthful rumors. Thus, if a British company's stock moves by 10% in response to truthful rumors, the company cannot continue to say "no comment." On the other hand, if the rumors are not true, then the company can continue to say "no comment."

a. Steven Lipin & Sara Calian, *Did U.K.'s Strict Rules Spur Deal?* WALL ST. J., Feb. 2, 1998, at C1.

---

13. *See* Item 303 of SEC Regulation S-K, Management's Discussion and Analysis of Financial Condition and Results of Operations, 17 C.F.R. § 229.303(a)(3)(ii) (1996).

The following case addressed the issue of whether a company has a duty to updates or correct statements that have become misleading in light of subsequent events.

<table>
<tr><td>**A CASE IN POINT**</td><td>**IN THE LANGUAGE OF THE COURT**</td></tr>
</table>

CASE 23.3
WEINER v. QUAKER OATS CO.
United States Court of Appeals for the Third Circuit
129 F.3d 310 (3d Cir. 1997).

FACTS On November 2, 1994, the Quaker Oats Company (Quaker) and Snapple Beverage Corp. (Snapple) announced that Quaker would acquire Snapple in a tender offer and merger transaction for $1.7 billion in cash. The market disapproved of the deal. Subsequent to the announcement, Quaker's stock price fell $7.375 per share—approximately 10% of the stock's value.

To finance the acquisition, Quaker had obtained $2.4 billion of credit from a banking group led by NationsBank Corp. The Snapple acquisition nearly tripled Quaker's debt, from approximately $1 billion to approximately $2.7 billion. The acquisition also increased Quaker's total debt-to-total capitalization ratio to approximately 80%.

Over the course of the year prior to its acquisition of Snapple, Quaker had announced in several public documents the company's guideline for debt-to-equity

Case 23.3 continues

Case 23.3 continued

ratio and its expectations for earnings growth. The announcements formed the basis for the plaintiff's action.

In its 1993 Annual Report (dated October 4, 1993), Quaker stated that "our debt-to-total capitalization ratio at June 30, 1993 was 59 percent, up from 49 percent in fiscal 1992. For the future, our guideline will be in the upper-60 percent range." Quaker's president reiterated this "guideline" in a letter contained in the same Annual Report. Quaker's Form 10–Q for the quarter ended September 30, 1993 (filed with the SEC in November 1993) repeated the total debt-to-total capitalization ratio guideline.

In its 1994 Annual Report (dated September 23, 1994), Quaker stated that "we are committed to achieving real earnings growth of at least 7 percent over time." In addition, the report noted that Quaker's total debt-to-total capitalization ratio was 68.8 percent, "in line with our guideline in the upper-60 percent range."

Negotiations between Quaker and Snapple apparently began in the spring of 1994. By early August 1994, Quaker had advised Snapple that it was interested in pursuing a merger of the two companies and had commenced a due diligence investigation. As noted, the merger was completed in November of that year.

The gist of the plaintiffs' complaint was that, even if Quaker's announcements about its total debt-to-total capitalization ratio and projected earnings growth were true at the time made, Quaker still had a duty to update or correct those statements if it knew they had become materially misleading in light of subsequent events. The plaintiffs alleged that (1) Quaker knew those statements were materially misleading as soon as it was reasonably certain the Snapple merger would be finalized, and (2) Quaker had such certainty at least sometime prior to its formal announcement of the merger on November 2, 1994.

The district court dismissed both portions of the plaintiffs' claim, on the basis that neither Quaker's statements relating to its total debt-to-total capitalization ratio nor its statements relating to its projected earnings growth were material. The plaintiffs appealed.

ISSUE PRESENTED   In what circumstances do a corporation and its officers have a duty to update, or at least not to repeat, particular projections regarding the corporation's financial condition (for example, total debt-to-total capitalization ratio or earnings growth projections)?

OPINION   POLLAK, J., writing for the U.S. Court of Appeals:

Rule 10b–5, promulgated pursuant to § 10(b) of the [1934] Act, provides the framework for a private cause of action for violations involving false statements or omissions of material fact. To establish a valid claim of securities fraud under Rule 10b–5, plaintiffs must prove that the defendant: (1) made misstatements or omissions of material fact, (2) with *scienter*, (3) in connection with the purchase or sale of securities, (4) upon which plaintiffs relied, and (5) that plaintiffs' reliance was the proximate cause of their injury.

In the present litigation, the plaintiffs allege that . . . they purchased shares in reliance on statements made by Quaker . . . about (1) Quaker's guideline for the ratio of total debt-to-total capitalization (in the upper 60 percent range) governing the company's financial planning and (2) Quaker's expected earnings growth in fiscal 1995.

Case 23.3 continues

Case 23.3 continued

The statements about expected earnings growth were made in August and September of 1994 . . . and it is plaintiffs' contention that, at a point when Quaker was in active pursuit of Snapple, Quaker and Smithburg must have known that the projections were illusory.

Plaintiffs' central complaint with respect to [the statements regarding the guideline for the ratio of total debt-to-total capitalization] is that, when the Snapple negotiations went into high gear, Quaker . . . had to have known that a . . . ratio in the high 60 percent range was no longer a realistic possibility. At that point, plaintiffs contend, defendants had a duty publicly to set the guidelines record straight.

. . .

A. The Total Debt-to-Total Capitalization Ratio Guideline

Plaintiffs' claims under this heading are claims of nondisclosure. "When an allegation of fraud under Section 10(b) is based upon a nondisclosure, there can be no fraud absent a duty to speak." In general, Section 10(b) and Rule 10b–5 do not impose a duty on defendants to correct prior statements—particularly statements of intent—so long as those statements were true when made. However, "[t]here can be no doubt that a duty exists to correct prior statements, if the prior statements were true when made but misleading if left unrevised." To avoid liability in such circumstances, "notice of a change of intent [must] be disseminated in a timely fashion." Whether an amendment is sufficiently prompt is a question that "must be determined in each case based upon the particular facts and circumstances."

. . .

1. Materiality

. . .

In *Basic*, the Court adopted in the context of § 10(b) and Rule 10b–5 the standard of materiality set forth in *TSC Industries*. The *Basic* Court approved . . . the principle that "[a]n omitted fact is material if there is a substantial likelihood that a reasonable shareholder would consider it important in deciding how to [proceed]."

. . .

Therefore, "[o]nly if the alleged misrepresentations or omissions are so obviously unimportant to an investor that reasonable minds cannot differ on the question of materiality is it appropriate for the district court to rule that the allegations are inactionable as a matter of law."

. . .

In sum, in the present case, we find that a trier of fact could conclude that a reasonable investor reading the 1993 Annual Report published on October 4, 1993, and then the 1994 Annual Report published on September 23, 1994, would have no ground for anticipating that the total debt-to-total capitalization ratio would rise as significantly as it did in fiscal 1995. There was after all no abjuration of the "upper 60-percent range" guideline. The company had predicted the rise from 59 percent to the "upper 60-percent range" in the 1993 report and that rise had occurred by and was confirmed in the 1994 report. Therefore, it was reasonable for an investor

Case 23.3 continues

Case 23.3 continued

to expect that the company would make another such prediction if it expected the ratio to change markedly in the ensuing year.

. . .

B. Earnings Growth Projections

For the reasons discussed above, we have concluded that plaintiffs' claim based on defendants' statements about the total debt-to-total capitalization guideline ratio should not have been dismissed. We do not, however, think that plaintiffs' claim based on defendants' projections of earnings growth merits resuscitation.

Quaker's 1994 Annual Report—issued on September 23, 1994, more than five weeks prior to the November 2 merger announcement—contained the statement that "we are committed to achieving a real earnings growth of at least 7 percent over time." We conclude that the phrase "over time" in this second statement inoculates Quaker from any claims of fraud that point to a decline in earnings growth in the immediate aftermath of the Snapple acquisition. No reasonably careful investor would find material a prediction of seven-percent growth followed by the qualifier "over time." Therefore, we hold that no reasonable finder of fact could conclude that the projection influenced prudent investors.

RESULT   The claim relating to Quaker's total debt-to-total capitalization ratio guideline was reinstated and remanded to the district court; the dismissal of the claim relating to Quaker's earnings growth projections was affirmed.

Questions

1. Given that a wealth of data compiled by market analysts demonstrates that, over the long run, stock prices follow corporate earnings, which piece of information would you find more important to your investment decision to buy or sell Quaker stock: (a) forecasts relating to the company's total debt-to-total capitalization ratio, or (b) forecasts relating to the company's real earnings growth?
2. Would an announcement by Quaker that it was contemplating increasing its total debt-to-total capitalization ratio have "tipped the market" to a pending acquisition? What result might that have brought?

There is a duty to disclose the results of product safety tests, if they make previously disclosed test results false. For example, A. H. Robins Company, a pharmaceutical manufacturer, reported in 1970 that its Dalkon Shield intrauterine contraceptive device was safe and effective. In 1972, internal studies indicated that the Dalkon Shield was not as safe or effective as originally reported.[14] The U. S. Court of Appeals for the Second Circuit held that Robins's omission of the new information rendered its earlier statements misleading. Because investors were still relying on the statement that the Dalkon Shield was safe, the company had a duty to correct that statement once it learned that it was inaccurate.

Statements by Third Parties   Even if the company itself did not publish the misleading projection, or make the statement, or start the rumor, it may nevertheless have a duty to reveal all of the facts regarding the issue. This is the case when the company is so entangled with the third party's statement that the statement can be attributed to the company; the company is then responsible for making sure that the statement is accurate. For example, if a company makes it a practice to review and correct drafts of analysts' forecasts, then the company impliedly represents that the corrected forecast is in accord with the company's

---

14. Ross v. A. H. Robins Co., 607 F.2d 545 (2d Cir. 1979), *cert. denied*, 446 U.S. 946 (1980).

ETHICAL CONSIDERATION

If there is no legal obligation to disclose bad news, is there an ethical duty to disclose it?

view, and it has a duty to reveal all facts necessary to ensure that the analyst's report is not misleading. Similarly, a company's distribution of copies of an analyst report to investors or other members of the public may be construed as an implied representation that the information in the report is accurate or reflects the company's views.

Material Fact

A buyer or seller of stock cannot win damages just because an executive misrepresented or omitted a fact about the company. The fact must be material. Materiality is judged at the time of the misstatement or omission.

Vague statements of corporate optimism that are not capable of objective verification and mere puffing are immaterial as a matter of law because reasonable investors do not rely on them in making investment decisions.[15] However, a prediction that the company "expects . . . a net income of approximately $1.00 a share" for the fiscal year to close in two months was held to be a material statement.[16]

---

15. *See, e.g.,* Raab v. General Physics Corp., 4 F.3d 286 (4th Cir. 1993) (statements in annual report that company expected 10% to 30% growth rate over the next several years and was "poised to carry the growth and success of 1991 well into the future" held to be immaterial puffing); San Leandro Emergency Medical Group Profit Sharing Plan v. Philip Morris Cos., 75 F.3d 801 (2d Cir. 1996) (statement that company was "optimistic" about its earnings in 1993 and that it should deliver income growth consistent with its historically superior performance was mere puffery and lacked the sort of definite positive projections that might require later correction).

16. Marx v. Computer Sciences Corp., 507 F.2d 485 (9th Cir. 1974).

The Supreme Court has recognized that for contingent or speculative events, such as negotiations regarding a potential merger, it is difficult to tell whether a reasonable investor would consider the omitted fact material at the time. The Supreme Court has declined to adopt a bright-line rule; materiality is a fact-specific determination. If a misstatement or omission concerns a future event, its materiality will depend upon a balancing of the probability that the event will occur and the anticipated magnitude of the event in light of the totality of the company activity.

It is not always possible to predict which facts a court will consider material. However, some issues are nearly always considered material. For example, any statements about the earnings, distributions, or assets of a company (unless the misrepresentation concerns a minor amount—if a press release misstates a major corporation's yearly earnings by $100, that is not material).

Materiality is not affected by the intent of the party making the statement. There can be liability even if the manager did not know the omitted or misrepresented fact came within the legal definition of a material fact.

Significant facts about a parent or a subsidiary of a company are usually material. These include the discovery of embezzlement or falsification of financial statements, an impending tender offer, or the loss of a manufacturer's major customer. Other facts that are probably material include inability to obtain supplies, increased costs of supplies, a decision to close a plant, information regarding the outlook in the industry, an intention to market a new product or cease marketing an old one, potential liability for damages in a lawsuit, a major discovery or product development, cost overruns, a change in management or compensation of corporate officers, and an increase in real estate taxes. As this list illustrates, a material fact is any fact that is likely to affect the market value of the company's stock.

As the following case demonstrates, even "soft"— that is, speculative—information can be deemed material under Rule 10b–5.

A CASE IN POINT   **SUMMARY**

CASE 23.4
BASIC INC. v. LEVINSON
Supreme Court
of the United States
485 U.S. 224 (1988).

FACTS   In September 1976, officers and directors of Basic Inc. began discussions with representatives of Combustion Engineering, Inc. concerning the possibility of a merger. Basic was a publicly traded company primarily engaged in the business of

Case 23.4 continues

Case 23.4 continued

manufacturing chemical refractories for the steel industry. Combustion produced mostly alumina-based refractories.

Basic made three public statements in 1977 and 1978 denying the existence of ongoing merger negotiations. On December 18, 1978, Basic announced the possibility of a merger.

The plaintiffs had sold their Basic shares after Basic's first public denial of negotiations and before the public announcement of the possibility of a merger. They sued Basic, alleging that its denials violated Rule 10b–5.

ISSUE PRESENTED Can even the existence of very preliminary merger negotiations short of an agreement in principle on price and structure be a material fact?

SUMMARY OF OPINION The U.S. Supreme Court began by noting that the materiality of statements concerning contingent or speculative events will depend at any time upon a balancing of both the indicated probability that the event will occur and the anticipated magnitude of the event in light of the totality of the company activity. The Court quoted with approval the late Judge Friendly, who applied the *Texas Gulf Sulphur* probability/magnitude approach in the specific context of preliminary merger negotiations:

> Since a merger in which it is bought out is the most important event that can occur in a small corporation's life, to wit, its death, we think that inside information, as regards a merger of this sort, can become material at an earlier stage than would be the case as regards lesser transactions—and this even though the mortality rate of merger in such formative stages is doubtless high.

Thus, whether merger discussions in any particular case are material depends on the facts. Generally, in order to assess the probability that the event will occur, a fact finder will need to look to indicia of interest in the transaction at the highest corporate levels. Without attempting to catalog all such possible factors, the Court noted by way of example that board resolutions, instructions to investment bankers, and actual negotiations between principals or other intermediaries may serve as indicia of interest. To assess the magnitude of the transaction to the issuer of the securities allegedly manipulated, a fact finder will need to consider such facts as the size of the two corporate entities and of the potential premiums over market value.

No particular event or factor short of closing the transaction need be either necessary or sufficient by itself to render merger discussions material.

RESULT The case was remanded (sent back) for further proceedings consistent with the opinion. The Supreme Court rejected the lower court's holding that merger discussions short of an agreement in principle as to price and structure are immaterial as a matter of law.

COMMENTS The Supreme Court's advice does not much help executives to predict with certainty whether a fact concerning a future event will be considered material. Most commentators advise that if a company is involved in a speculative matter, aspects of which it wishes to remain private, the only safe way to avoid liability under Rule 10b–5 is not to say anything during the early stages of negotiation.

Silence or a "no comment" statement in response to rumors will not lead to liability if the company has not previously spoken on the subject and insiders are not trading or tipping. However, there is a caveat: A policy of not commenting on rumors must be adhered to in the face of both true and untrue rumors. If the company always says "no comment" when the rumor is true, but provides facts to dispel untrue rumors, then the "no comment" acts as an admission that the rumor is true.

Although keeping silent may be safer under Rule 10b–5, in many cases it will be hard to do. If a corporation's stock is traded on rumors of some major development, silence may contribute to disorderly market activity, distrust of company management, and possible abuse by those with access to inside information. Moreover, a blanket "no comment" policy makes it impossible to dispel false but damaging rumors. Once the silence is broken, of course, the company must be exceedingly careful in its statements even as to speculative events.[17]

Bespeaks Caution Doctrine   As explained in Chapter 22, under the judicially developed *bespeaks caution doctrine*, a court may determine that the inclusion of sufficient cautionary statements in a document renders immaterial any misrepresentation and omission contained therein. The doctrine applies only to projections, estimates, and other forward-looking statements that are accompanied by precise cautionary language that adequately discloses the risks involved. The cautionary language must relate to the specific information that the plaintiffs allege is misleading.[18] Unlike the safe harbor provided in the Reform Act, the bespeaks caution doctrine applies to forward-looking statements in any context, including initial public offerings. The legislative history of the Reform Act makes it clear that Congress did not intend its statutory safe-harbor provisions to replace the judicial bespeaks caution doctrine or to foreclose further development of that doctrine by the courts.

Scienter

Rule 10b–5 does not impose liability for innocent misstatements or omissions. The misstatements or omissions must be made with *scienter*, that is, a mental state embracing the intent to deceive, manipulate, or defraud. Intent to deceive means that the defendant says something she believes is untrue that she expects others to rely on, or that she omits a fact that she hopes will cause others to misunderstand what she does say. The Supreme Court has made clear that *scienter* is more than mere negligence or lack of care.

Recklessness   A majority of jurisdictions have held that recklessness qualifies as *scienter*. Different jurisdictions define recklessness slightly differently. In some circuits, such as the Seventh (which includes Illinois), a defendant is held to have acted recklessly if he or she either knew that his or her statements would probably be misleading or should have known it because the misleading quality of the statements was so obvious. In the Second Circuit (which includes New York), recklessness requires a showing that the defendant either knew his or her statement was misleading or untrue or was put on notice that it might be, but made the statement anyway without investigating the facts. In the Ninth Circuit (which includes the West Coast), the definition of recklessness is that the defendant's conduct was an extreme departure from the standards of ordinary care that presented a danger of misleading buyers or sellers that was either known to the defendant or was so obvious that the defendant must have been aware of it.

The officers of a national corporation (which could be sued in any of these jurisdictions) would want to avoid recklessness under all of these definitions. Thus, before making any statement, the officers should investigate what the facts are, and they should make no statement unless they in good faith believe it to be true. The investigation must be fairly thorough. An officer may be liable for misrepresenting facts that he or she should have been aware of, even if the officer was not in fact aware of them. For example, directors may be deemed to have knowledge of facts in the corporate books regardless of whether they have actually examined the books.

The Reform Act requires the plaintiff to plead with particularity specific facts giving rise to a strong inference that the defendant acted with *scienter*. Several district courts have interpreted this heightened pleading standard to preclude liability under Section 10(b) for

---

17. *See* Dale E. Barnes, Jr. & Constance E. Bagley, *Great Expectations: Risk Management through Risk Disclosure,* 1 STAN. J.L., BUS. & FIN. 155 (1994).

18. *See, e.g.,* Kaplan v. Rose, 49 F.3d 1363 (9th Cir. 1994).

recklessness.[19] Others have held that the *scienter* standard for non-forward-looking statements may still be satisfied by a showing of recklessness using the Second Circuit's definition of recklessness.[20] As of early 1998, the issue was pending in the U.S. Courts of Appeal for the Sixth and Ninth Circuits.

The tough new pleading requirements make it more important than ever for insiders to avoid trading while in possession of material nonpublic information. As one court noted, "[I]nsider trading in suspicious amounts or at suspicious times is probative of bad faith and *scienter*."[21] Plaintiffs can be expected to claim that insiders who sold before the announcement of bad news knew of the impending negative developments so they sold their stock while the market price was artificially high, thereby "cashing in" on their alleged misrepresentations and omissions.[22] This arguably creates an inference of fraud.[23]

The U.S. District Court for the Northern District of California rejected this argument in a case involving Silicon Graphics, Inc. and held that the Reform Act eliminated the motive-and-opportunity test, by which the inference of fraud can be made by showing that the defendant had a motive for committing fraud (usually profits from personal trades) and the opportunity to do so.[24] The SEC filed an *amicus* brief in the *Silicon Graphics* appeal, arguing that Congress meant to adopt the pleading standard applied in the Second Circuit. It is not yet clear how other courts will rule on this issue; but until there is a definitive ruling, managers and companies would be well advised to assume that insider trading shortly before the announcement of bad news will create an inference of fraud sufficient to satisfy the Reform Act's pleading requirements.

Purchase or Sale

Rule 10b–5 requires that the conduct occur "in connection with the purchase or sale of any security." This requirement defines both those who can sue and those who can be sued under Rule 10b–5.

The Supreme Court has made it clear that only persons who actually purchase or sell securities can sue under Rule 10b–5. Persons who have not purchased (or sold) cannot sue on the theory that they would have purchased (or sold) had they known the true facts. Thus, liability under Rule 10b–5 does not extend to the whole world of potential investors, but only to those who actually buy or sell stock after a misstatement or omission.

Parties that can be sued under Rule 10b–5 are those that make or are responsible for misstatements and omissions in connection with the purchase or sale of securities.

In Connection With Statements are made "in connection with" the purchase or sale of securities if they were made in a manner reasonably calculated to influence the investing public or if they were of the sort upon which the investing public might reasonably rely.

A company must be careful to monitor its public statements, such as those made in periodic reports, press releases, proxy solicitations, and annual reports. Even when addressing noninvestors such as creditors or labor union representatives, a manager should exercise caution if the statements can reasonably be expected to reach investors.

Reliance

To establish liability under Rule 10b–5, an investor must show that he or she relied either directly or indirectly on the misrepresentation or omission. If the investor did not rely on the misstatement or omission in deciding to buy or sell stock, then any loss he or she incurred could not be blamed on the company that made the misrepresentation or omission.

Direct Reliance A plaintiff may show reliance by showing that he or she actually read the document, such as a press release or prospectus, that contained the misstatement. In the case of an omission, the Supreme Court has ruled that the plaintiff will be presumed to have relied on the omission, if it was material. That presumption of reliance can be rebutted—that is, shown to be not true—by a showing that the plaintiff would have bought (or sold) the stock even if the omitted fact had been included.

19. *See, e.g., In re* Silicon Graphics, Inc. Sec. Litig., 970 F. Supp. 746 (N.D. Cal. 1997).

20. Marksman Partners, L.P. v. Chantal Pharm. Corp., 927 F. Supp. 1297 (C.D. Cal. 1996).

21. *In re* Apple Computer Sec. Litig. 886 F. 2d 1109 (9th Cir. 1989), *cert. denied*, 496 U.S. 943 (1990).

22. *See* Dale E. Barnes, Jr. & Karen Kennard, *Greater Expectations: Risk Disclosure under the Private Securities Litigation Reform Act of 1995—An Update*, 2 STAN. J.L., BUS. & FIN. 331, 347–48 (1996).

23. *See, e.g.,* the class action complaint dated Dec. 2, 1997, filed by Ronald L. Reiser, Trustee, and Richard Buck against Silicon Graphics, Inc. and its chief executive officer Edward R. McCracken and others, *Reiser v. Silicon Graphics, Inc.,* No. C-97-4362-TEH, available at <http://securities.milberg.com>.

24. *In re* Silicon Graphics, Inc. Sec. Litig., 970 F. Supp. 746 (N.D. Cal. 1997).

Fraud on the Market   In the securities market, however, direct reliance is rare because transactions are not conducted on a face-to-face basis. The market is interposed between the parties, providing important information to the parties in the form of the market price. As the federal court for the Northern District of Texas said in the LTV Securities Litigation: "The market is acting as the unpaid agent of the investor, informing him that, given all the information available to it, the value of the stock is worth the market price."

The theory underlying this view is known to economists as the *efficient-market theory.* It holds that in an open and developed securities market, the price of a company's stock equals its true value. The market is said to evaluate information efficiently and to incorporate it into the price of a company's securities.

Against this background, the courts have approved the *fraud-on-the-market theory.* If the information available to the market is incorrect, then the market price will not reflect the true value of the stock. Under this theory, an investor who purchases or sells a security is presumed to have relied on the market, which has in turn relied on the misstatement or omission when it set the price of the security. In *Basic Inc. v. Levinson* (Case 23.4), the Supreme Court affirmed this theory. Quoting one of the earlier lower court decisions, the Supreme Court noted that: "It is hard to imagine that there ever is a buyer or seller who does not rely on market integrity. Who would knowingly roll the dice in a crooked crap game?"

Thus, plaintiffs do not have to show that they read or heard a defendant's misstatement in order to recover damages from that defendant. Instead, reliance is presumed if the investor shows that the defendant made a public material misrepresentation that would have caused reasonable investors to misjudge the value of the defendant's stock and that the investor traded shares of the defendant's stock in an open securities market after the misrepresentations were made and before the truth was revealed.

A defendant can rebut the fraud-on-the-market presumption by showing that the plaintiff traded or would have traded despite knowing the statement was false. For example, an insider who is aware of nonpublic information that results in the stock being undervalued, but who sells for other reasons, cannot be said to have relied on the integrity of market price.

Lower courts have declined to apply the fraud-on-the-market presumption in cases in which there is not an efficient, open, and developed market. The courts have identified at least five factors to consider in identifying an efficient market: (1) sufficient weekly trading volume, (2) sufficient reports and analyses by investment professionals, (3) the presence of market makers and arbitrageurs, (4) the existence of issuers eligible to file Form S–3 short-form registration statements, and (5) an historical showing of immediate price response to unexpected events or financial releases. In short, for a market to be open and developed, it must have a large number of buyers and sellers, and a relatively high level of trading activity and frequency. It also must be a market that rapidly reflects new information in price.

Truth on the Market   Defendants have also used the efficient-market theory to their advantage. For example, even if the defendant makes the misrepresentation that it is not involved in merger negotiations, if the market makers were privy to the truth, there is no fraud on the market. In the following case, an appellate court found that the market was aware of one set of facts undisclosed by the defendants, but was not aware of another set of undisclosed facts.

A CASE IN POINT	**SUMMARY**

CASE 23.5
IN RE APPLE
COMPUTER SECURITIES
LITIGATION
United States Court of
Appeals for the Ninth Circuit
886 F.2d 1109
(9th Cir. 1989), *cert. denied,*
496 U.S. 943 (1990).

FACTS   In late 1982 and early 1983, Apple Computer, Inc. made several optimistic public statements concerning its newly developed office computer, the Lisa. For example, in a January 31, 1983, *Business Week* article, Apple's chairman of the board, Steven Jobs, was quoted as saying: "I don't think we will have any problem selling all the Lisa's we can build." In an April 14, 1983, *Wall Street Journal* article, he was quoted as stating: "Lisa is going to be phenomenally successful in the first year out of the chute."

Case 23.5 continues

Case 23.5 continued

Many of the risks and problems associated with Lisa, however, were widely publicized. The same *Business Week* article quoting Mr. Jobs as saying that Apple would have little trouble selling Lisa also stated: "One indication of how uncertain Apple's prospects are is that expert estimates of how many Lisa's the company will sell are all over the lot—from 2,000 to 30,000." The article also questioned whether vendors would write software to support Lisa and whether the price tag for Lisa was too high. Similarly, the *Wall Street Journal* article in which Mr. Jobs predicted Lisa's great success was captioned: "Some Warm Up to Apple's 'Lisa,' but Eventual Success is Uncertain." The article discussed Lisa's incompatibility with IBM products, the difficulties in attracting software suppliers, and the high price tag.

The Lisa was a commercial failure and was discontinued shortly after its introduction. As a result of this disappointing news, Apple's stock price fell by almost 75%.

The plaintiffs, purchasers of Apple stock, brought a Section 10(b) fraud-on-the-market suit against Apple and its officers and directors, alleging that they failed to disclose problems with the Lisa that would have contradicted their earlier, optimistic public statements.

ISSUE PRESENTED   Was there fraud on the market when a manufacturer made optimistic predictions about a new product, even though analysts and others following the company discounted the predictions and publicized the true state of affairs?

SUMMARY OF OPINION   The U.S. Court of Appeals held that in a fraud-on-the-market case a defendant's failure to disclose material information may be excused if that information has been made credibly available to the market by other sources. As the court explained, "individuals who hear [only good news or only bad news] may receive a distorted impression . . ., and thus may have an actionable claim. But the market, and any individual who relies only on the price established by the market, will not be misled."

The press portrayed the Lisa as a risky gamble. At least 20 articles explored the risks Apple was taking. Moreover, many of the optimistic statements challenged by the plaintiffs appeared in those same articles. In the words of the court, "The market could not have been made more aware of Lisa's risks." Therefore, the defendants were not liable, as a matter of law, for failing to disclose those risks. Accordingly, the defendants' motion for summary judgment on the claims related to the Lisa was granted.

The court reached a different conclusion with respect to two optimistic statements Apple made concerning Twiggy, the new disk drive to accompany the Lisa computer. In a November 29, 1982, press release, Apple had claimed that Twiggy "represents three years of research and development and has undergone extensive testing and design verification during the past year." The release went on to state that Twiggy "ensures greater integrity of data than the other high density drives by way of a unique, double-sided mechanism designed and manufactured by Apple."

The court concluded that certain technical problems relating to Twiggy had not been revealed to the market. Neither the press nor anyone else disclosed (1) that the internal tests conducted by Apple indicated that Twiggy was slow and unreliable, (2) that the Apple division responsible for the production of Lisa warned top executives that Twiggy's unreliability could delay the introduction of Lisa by several months, and (3) that Mr. Jobs expressed "virtually zero confidence" in the division that was

Case 23.5 continues

Case 23.5 continued

responsible for the design and development of Twiggy. Accordingly, the court concluded that if Twiggy's technical problems were material facts tending to undermine the optimism of the two statements, the defendants could be liable for failing to reveal those facts. Materiality was thus left as a triable issue of fact, and the defendants' motion for summary judgment on the claims related to Twiggy was denied.

RESULT   The plaintiffs' claims relating to the Lisa computer were dismissed as a matter of law. The claims related to the Twiggy disk drive were not dismissed because they raised questions of fact for a jury to decide. In 1991, after two former executives were found guilty of making "materially misleading statements," Apple agreed to set up a $16 million fund to settle the suit.

COMMENTS   The Ninth Circuit pointed out that a defendant is not relieved of its duty to disclose material information unless that information has been transmitted to the public with a degree of intensity and credibility sufficient to counterbalance any misleading impression created by the defendant. A brief mention of the omitted fact in a few poorly circulated or lightly regarded publications would be insufficient.

Integrated Disclosure   The SEC has adopted at least some of the premises of the efficient-market theory in its disclosure rules. In 1982, the SEC adopted the *integrated disclosure system*. As explained in Chapter 22, there are two separate disclosure systems: one under the 1933 Act and one under the 1934 Act. The integrated disclosure system seeks to eliminate duplicative or unnecessary disclosure requirements under the two acts.

Issuers that have been filing periodic reports under the 1934 Act can incorporate certain information from those reports into a registration statement filed under the 1933 Act. The market is deemed to have already absorbed such information in its evaluation of the issuer, so that information can be omitted from the prospectus.

Causation

A plaintiff must prove that the defendant's misstatement or omission caused him or her to suffer losses. Increasingly, this is an economic question—what factors influence the price of a stock in the securities market?

In a securities case involving Nucorp Energy, for example, investors claimed that a misrepresentation by the company of the value of its oil reserves caused them to suffer losses. The claim was based on the contention that the stock price was maintained at an artificially high level as a result of the misrepresentation. The investors attributed the later drop in the stock price to the revela-

tion of the true facts. At trial, the defendants presented the testimony of an economist that the drop in the price of the stock was not attributable to any misrepresentation of the value of the oil reserves, but rather was caused by a drop in the price of oil. The jury found that the plaintiffs had failed to prove their claim.

As a result of these developments in the area of causation, proponents of the efficient-market theory may be right when they predict that in the future the entire Rule 10b–5 case may boil down to one question: Did the misleading statement artificially affect market price?

Fraud-Created-the-Market Theory

In some cases in which the alleged fraud is so pervasive that without it the issuer would not have been able to

ETHICAL CONSIDERATION

Managers of companies frequently act as promoters, describing the company's products to the press and the public in an aggressive, upbeat manner. It is reasonable to expect them to engage in a certain amount of puffing and exaggeration. Are these exaggerations ethically justifiable if they do not violate the securities laws?

sell the securities because the information to the market would have shown them to be worthless, the court will dispense with the reliance requirement and apply a variation of the fraud-on-the-market theory, called the *fraud-created-the-market theory.* Under this theory, the causal connection between the defendant's fraud and the plaintiff's injury is not established by alleging and proving that the fraud affected the market price. Rather, the causal connection is established by alleging and proving that the securities could not have been marketed at any price absent fraud.

The courts are split on when plaintiffs can rely on the fraud-created-the-market-theory. The Seventh Circuit, for example, has rejected the fraud-created-the-market theory[25] on the grounds that the existence of a security does not depend on the adequacy of disclosure. It reasoned that many securities are on the market even though the issuer or a third party has made inaccurate or incomplete disclosures. Therefore, full disclosure of adverse information may lower the price of a security, but it will not exclude the security from being sold on the market.

◆ Reform Act Safe Harbor for Forward-Looking Statements

The Reform Act provides issuers subject to the 1934 Act's reporting requirements and persons acting on their behalf a two-prong safe harbor for certain forward-looking statements. *Forward-looking statements* include (1) a statement containing a projection of revenues, income, earnings per share, capital expenditures, dividends, capital structure, or other financial items; (2) a statement of the plans and objectives of management for future operations, including plans relating to the issuer's products and services; (3) a statement of future economic performance, including any such statement in the management's discussion and analysis of financial condition or in the results of operations (MD & A) required to be included by the SEC; and (4) any statement of the assumptions underlying or relating to such a statement.

However, the safe harbor does not apply to forward-looking statements in connection with (1) an initial public offering, (2) an offering of securities by a blank check company, (3) a rollup or going-private transaction, (4) a

tender offer, or (5) an offering by a partnership, limited liability company, or direct participation investment program. The safe harbor also does not apply to any forward-looking statement included (1) in a financial statement prepared in accordance with generally accepted accounting principles, or (2) a report of beneficial ownership on Schedule 13D.

As explained in Chapter 22, the statutory safe harbor for forward-looking statements was designed to promote market efficiency by encouraging companies to disclose projections and other information about the company's future prospects. Anecdotal evidence indicated that corporate counsel were advising their clients to say as little as possible due to fear that if the company failed to satisfy its announced earning projections—perhaps due to an industry downturn or the timing of a large order or release of a new product—the company would automatically be sued.

Under the first prong of the safe harbor, a person is protected from liability for a misrepresentation or omission based on a written forward-looking statement as long as (1) the statement is identified as forward-looking, and (2) the statement is accompanied by meaningful cautionary statements identifying important factors that could cause actual results to differ materially from those projected in the statement. The safe harbor also protects forward-looking oral statements if the person making the statement (1) identifies the statement as a forward-looking statement, (2) states that results may differ materially from those projected in the statement, and (3) identifies a readily available written document (such as a document filed with the SEC) that contains factors that could cause results to differ materially.

The stated factors must be relevant to the projection and of a nature that could actually affect whether the forward-looking statement is realized. Boilerplate warnings will not suffice. Failure to include the particular factor that ultimately causes the forward-looking statement not to come true will not mean that the statement automatically is not protected by the safe harbor. The company must disclose all important factors, not all factors. In this respect, the safe harbor provides greater protection than the bespeaks caution doctrine.

In ruling on a motion to dismiss based on this prong of the safe harbor, the state of mind of the person making the statement is not relevant. The court looks only at the cautionary language accompanying the forward-looking statement.

---

25. Eckstein v. Balcor Film Investors, 8 F.3d 1121 (7th Cir. 1993), *cert. denied,* 510 U.S. 1073 (1994).

Even if a person cannot rely on this prong, there is an independent prong based on the state of mind of the person making the statement. A person or business entity will not be liable in a private lawsuit involving a forward-looking statement unless the plaintiff proves that the person or business entity made a false or misleading forward-looking statement with actual knowledge that it was false or misleading. A statement by a business entity will come within the safe harbor unless it was made by or with the approval of an executive officer of the entity with actual knowledge by that officer that the statement was false or misleading.

Auditor Disclosure of Corporate Fraud

The Reform Act added a new Section 10A to the 1934 Act to promote disclosure by independent public accountants of illegal acts committed by their publicly traded audit clients. Each audit must include, in accordance with generally accepted auditing standards, (1) procedures designed to provide reasonable assurance of detecting illegal acts that would have a direct and material effect on the determination of financial statement amounts, (2) procedures designed to identify material related-party transactions (such as those involving officers, directors, and controlling shareholders of the company being audited), and (3) an evaluation of whether there is substantial doubt about the ability of the company to continue as a going concern during the ensuing fiscal year.

If in the course of the audit, the independent public accountant detects or otherwise becomes aware of information indicating that an illegal act has or may have occurred (regardless of whether it is perceived to have a material effect on the financial statements), then the accountant must (1) determine whether it is likely that an illegal act has occurred and, if so, determine and consider the possible effect on the financial statements; and (2) inform the appropriate level of the management of the company. The accountant must ensure that the audit committee, or the board of directors in the absence of such a committee, is adequately informed with respect to the illegal acts, unless the illegal act is clearly inconsequential. If after informing the audit committee or board, the accountant concludes that (1) the illegal act has a material effect on the financial statements of

the company, (2) the senior management has not taken timely and appropriate remedial actions with respect to the illegal act, and (3) the failure to take remedial action is reasonably expected to warrant departure from a standard audit report or resignation, then the accountant must, as soon as practicable, directly report its conclusions to the board of directors. The board is then required to notify the SEC within one business day after its receipt of the report. If the board fails to do so, the accountant must furnish the SEC a copy of its report (or the documentation of any oral report given).

Damages for Violation of Rule 10b–5

The measure of damages in a Rule 10b–5 case is typically the out-of-pocket loss, that is, the difference between what the investor paid (or received) and the fair value of the stock on the date of the transaction. Alternately, an investor can elect to rescind the transaction, returning what he or she received and getting back what he or she gave. In the court's discretion, *prejudgment interest*—that is, interest on the amount of the award between the date the securities were purchased and the date of the judgment—may also be awarded. Punitive damages are not available.

In theory, damages must be proven with reasonable certainty. In practice, however, damages are awarded on the basis of expert testimony, which can be highly conjectural. For example, a claim that a company's failure to reveal negative information about its new product artificially inflated the price of its stock is quite difficult to evaluate with any scientific certainty because even the experts do not agree to what extent any particular piece of information affects the price of a company's securities.

In addition, there can be only estimates for the number of traders who can claim damage. For example, in-and-out traders' trades are included in the total volume of trading; but such traders who buy, then quickly sell, suffer no damage if they sell the securities before the price drop.

Evidence of damages is therefore often presented on the basis of a comparison with industry or market performance, on the assumption that the industry or the market was not subject to the same artificial inflation. This clearly remains a fertile field for argument and future litigation.

Section 17(a) of the 1933 Act

Section 17(a) of the 1933 Act prohibits fraud in connection with the sale of securities. It is similar in scope to Section 10(b) of the 1934 Act, which prohibits fraud in both the sale and the purchase of securities. Unlike Section 10(b), Section 17(a) does not require proof of *scienter* (or bad intent). Several courts formerly extended a right of action under Section 17(a) to private parties; however, most recent decisions reject this extension as inconsistent with the language and purpose of the statute.

 ## What Is Insider Trading?

Insider trading refers in general terms to trading by persons (often insiders such as officers and directors) while in possession of material nonpublic information. However, not every instance of trading on inside information constitutes a securities violation. Rather, the term insider trading refers to activities that the courts have held to be proscribed by the broad language of Rule 10b–5. Because there is no statutory definition of insider trading, the law in this area has developed on a piecemeal basis. This lack of a clear definition has caused enforcement problems for the SEC and federal prosecutors. It can also make it difficult for investors to know whether their actions constitute prohibited insider trading.

The safest course is never to trade while in possession of material nonpublic information; however, such a premise is unduly restrictive. The nature of insider trading can best be understood by examining the purposes underlying the laws that prohibit it.

A fundamental goal of the securities laws in general is the protection of the investing public and the maintenance of fairness in the securities markets. Allowing a party who knows that the market is incorrectly pricing a security to exploit another party's ignorance of that fact is fundamentally unfair. However, the Supreme Court has held that not every trade while in possession of material nonpublic information violates Section 10(b). For such a trade to be illegal there must be some breach of a duty by the person trading; or if the person trading is the recipient of a *tip*—a piece of inside information— there must be a breach of duty by the person who gave the tip. The person giving the tip is known as the *tipper*; the person receiving it is known as the *tippee*.

Corporate officers and directors, for example, have specific legal duties to the corporation and shareholders they serve that prohibit them from engaging in insider trading. As corporate fiduciaries, these individuals are required to subordinate their self-interests to the interests of the shareholders, as discussed in Chapter 21.

The following case was the first decided by a U.S. court of appeals to rule on whether an insider who trades while in possession of material nonpublic information can escape liability by proving that he or she did not actually use the information in deciding to buy or sell.

A CASE IN POINT	SUMMARY

CASE 23.6
SECURITIES AND
EXCHANGE
COMMISSION v. ADLER
United States Court
of Appeals for
the Eleventh Circuit
137 F. 3d 1325
(11th Cir. 1998).

FACTS   Robert Adler, Harvey Pegram, Philip Choy, and Domer Ishler were all business associates and social acquaintances. Adler was an outside director of Comptronix, Inc. At a board meeting on November 15, 1992, Comptronix directors were informed of a potential fraud in which the company's chief executive officer, president, and treasurer had made millions of dollars of false accounting entries and had misstated Comptronix's sales and earnings records.

On November 16, Pegram placed a call to Adler's home. Two minutes later, Pegram called his wife at home. Approximately 12 minutes later, Pegram's wife called the Pegrams' stockbroker and placed an order to sell 50,000 shares of Comptronix stock. Between November 16 and November 24, the Pegrams sold 150,000 shares of Comptronix common stock. The SEC contended that Adler tipped Pegram and that the Pegrams avoided losses of $2,315,375. The Pegrams claimed that Adler had

Case 23.6 continues

Case 23.6 continued

given them no information about Comptronix and maintained that they had planned to sell their Comptronix stock anyway.

Pegram also placed a call to Choy on November 16. Later that evening, Choy faxed his broker an order to sell 5,000 shares of Comptronix stock. The SEC contended that Pegram tipped Choy and that Choy avoided losses of approximately $75,000. Choy and Pegram denied that their conversation was related to Comptronix.

Phone records showed that both Adler and Pegram spoke to Ishler on November 23. On November 24, Ishler purchased 300 put options for Comptronix stock. He later realized gains on this transaction approximating $368,750. The SEC claimed that Ishler was tipped by either Adler or Pegram. All three men denied talking to one another about Comptronix.

On November 24, Comptronix's common stock closed at a price of $22 per share. On November 25, Comptronix publicly announced that its CEO, president, and treasurer were suspended from all decision-making responsibilities and that the board of directors had formed a special committee to investigate "certain matters relating to the company's financial statements." That day, Comptronix stock lost 72% of its value, closing at a price of $6.125 per share.

The SEC brought civil actions for insider trading against Adler, Pegram, Choy, and Ishler. At trial, the jury deadlocked and a mistrial was declared. The judge granted each of the defendants' motions for judgment as a matter of law. The SEC appealed.

ISSUE PRESENTED   Does the mere fact that an insider traded while in possession of material nonpublic information give rise to liability, or must some causal connection be shown between the possession of that information and the insider's trading?

SUMMARY OF OPINION   The U.S. Court of Appeals first set out to determine the applicable rule in this relatively uncharted area of the law. The court acknowledged the familiar maxim that under Section 10(b) of the 1934 Act a corporate insider has a duty to disclose material nonpublic information or to abstain from trading on the information.[26] The SEC argued that this disclose-or-abstain rule supported its position that knowing possession of material nonpublic information while trading is sufficient to establish liability under Section 10(b)—whether or not the insider actually used that undisclosed information for his or her own benefit.

The court disagreed, primarily because it was convinced by a review of Supreme Court precedent that Section 10(b) liability must be based on some showing of fraud. Thus, mere "knowing possession"—that is, proof that an insider traded while in possession of material nonpublic information—is not a *per se* violation of the insider trading laws. However, when an insider trades while in possession of material nonpublic information, a "strong inference arises" that such information was used by the insider in trading. The insider can attempt to rebut this inference of *scienter* by introducing evidence of preexisting plans or other "innocuous" reasons for making the trade. To avoid liability, the insider would have to show that there was no causal connection between the information and the trade—that is, that the information was

Case 23.6 continues

---

26. *See In re* Cady, Roberts & Co., 40 S.E.C. 907 (1961); Chiarella v. United States, 445 U.S. 222 (1980).

Case 23.6 continued

not used. The fact finder would then weigh all the evidence and make a finding as to whether the information was in fact used.

Having determined the test it deemed appropriate, the court applied it to the present facts. In short, the court found that the suspicious sequence of phone calls involving Adler, Pegram, Choy, and Ishler was more than enough evidence to allow a reasonable jury to find that (1) Adler possessed material nonpublic information, (2) he shared it with Ishler and Pegram (who shared it with Choy), and (3) Ishler, Pegram, and Choy profitably traded Comptronix stock based on that material nonpublic information. As a result, the court struck down the district court's judgments in favor of the defendants.

RESULT   The judgments in favor of the defendants were reversed, and their cases were remanded to the district court for trial.

COMMENTS   It is not yet clear whether other courts of appeal or the U.S. Supreme Court will agree with the Eleventh Circuit's decision in *Adler*. Until the issue is resolved definitively, insiders would be well advised to refrain from trading while in possession of material nonpublic information.

If the *Adler* test is adopted by other courts, defendants who traded while in possession of material nonpublic information will have the opportunity to rebut the strong inference of wrongdoing with evidence of innocuous reasons for their seemingly illegal trade. The most persuasive evidence is usually a preexisting plan to sell securities, either to diversify an investment portfolio or to generate cash. Note that someone who *purchases* securities while in possession of material nonpublic information cannot avail himself or herself of these rationales and thus will have a much more difficult time rebutting the strong inference that his or her trade was an illegal use of the undisclosed information.

Insider-trading cases focus specifically on the duty to disclose, before trading, material information that is not publicly known (that is, not commonly available to the investing public). An insider must either disclose material nonpublic information in his or her possession or refrain from trading. The fundamental question in an insider-trading case is whether this obligation should be imposed on a particular trader. Besides officers and directors (who have a clear duty of disclosure), there are other traders who, though not having an independent fiduciary duty to shareholders, should nevertheless be prohibited from trading on inside information. The persons prohibited from such trading—insiders, tippees, and others—are the subject of the following sections.

 Insiders

An *insider* is a person with access to confidential information and an obligation of disclosure to other traders in the marketplace. Insiders include not only traditional insiders—such as officers and directors—but also temporary insiders, such as outside counsel and financial consultants.

Traditional Insiders

Traditionally, only persons closely allied with the corporation itself were considered insiders. They are true insiders because they acquire information by performing duties within or on behalf of the issuer corporation. Persons or entities traditionally considered insiders include (1) officers and directors, (2) controlling shareholders, (3) employees, and (4) the corporation itself.

Officers and Directors   Officers and directors have a fiduciary obligation of loyalty and care to the corporate shareholders. They also have the greatest access to sensitive information regarding corporate events.

Controlling Shareholders   Because of their majority stock ownership, controlling shareholders are generally in a position to control the activities of the corporation. They are therefore likely to be aware of impending corporate events.

Employees   As agents or servants of a corporation, employees have a duty of loyalty. They may not personally profit from confidential information that they receive in the course of their employment.

The Corporation   Often, a corporation (or other issuer) will engage in the purchase or sale of its own securities. Under these circumstances, the corporation and those acting on its behalf are insiders and must not trade while in possession of material nonpublic information. This was made clear by the Second Circuit in *Texas Gulf Sulphur* (Case 23.2), in which a corporation with nonpublic information about its discovery of copper deposits was prohibited from purchasing its own shares on the open market until the true nature of the find was disclosed.

Temporary Insiders

Outside attorneys, accountants, consultants, and investment bankers who are not directly employed by the corporation, but who acquire confidential information through the performance of professional services, are also considered insiders. The Supreme Court extended liability under Section 10(b) to such *temporary insiders* in footnote 14 to the *Dirks* case, which is presented as Case 23.7.

 Tippees

Tippees—that is, persons who receive information from a traditional or temporary insider—may also be subject to liability under Rule 10b–5, but only if they can be considered derivative insiders. In most cases, a tippee has no independent duty to the shareholders of a corporation, with which he or she may have little or no connection. A tippee will not be held liable as a *derivative insider* unless the insider's duty of disclosure can somehow be imposed upon the tippee. This rule was established in the following landmark case.

A CASE IN POINT   **SUMMARY**

CASE 23.7
DIRKS v. SECURITIES AND EXCHANGE COMMISSION
Supreme Court of the United States
463 U.S. 646 (1983).

FACTS   Raymond Dirks, an officer of a New York broker-dealer firm, specialized in providing investment analysis of insurance company securities to institutional investors. Dirks was contacted by Ronald Secrist, a former employee of Equity Funding of America. Secrist was seeking aid in exposing the fraudulent activities of that corporation. These fraudulent activities had resulted in an overvaluation of Equity Funding's assets. Dirks was thus the potential tippee, with Secrist the tipper. After corroborating Secrist's story, Dirks advised certain clients that they should sell their shares in the company. When the corporate fraud was later revealed, the price of the company's stock went down.

The SEC brought proceedings against Dirks on the theory that he had constructively breached a fiduciary duty. In effect, the SEC maintained that anyone receiving information from an insider stands in the insider's shoes and should be held to the same standards and be subject to the same duties as that insider.

Case 23.7 continues

Case 23.7 continued

ISSUE PRESENTED   Is a tippee liable absent a violation of fiduciary duty by the tipper?

SUMMARY OF OPINION   The U.S. Supreme Court rejected the argument that anyone receiving information from an insider should be held to the same standards as the insider. The Court held instead that a tippee is not liable unless the tippee and the tipper join in a coventure to exploit the information. Only in such a case will the fiduciary duty of the tipper be derivatively imposed on the tippee. For the tippee to the liable, therefore, the tipper must have a duty to the corporation not to disclose the information and must breach this duty by seeking to benefit personally from the disclosure of the information. The benefit sought by the tipper can be either tangible or intangible. Intangible benefits might include an enhanced reputation or the intangible benefit received through the giving of gifts.

In this case, the insider was motivated solely by a desire to expose fraudulent conduct. He did not breach any fiduciary duties because it was in the interests of the corporation that this information be disclosed.

RESULT   Absent a breach of duty on the part of the insider/tipper, no derivative duty could be imposed on Dirks, the tippee. Dirks was not guilty of illegal insider trading.

The requirement that the tipper must be seeking some benefit implies that the tipper must desire that the tippee trade on the information; but it is unclear whether such a showing is necessary. For example, the tipper could derive a benefit merely from impressing the tippee with his or her access to confidential information. Such a desire could stem from social or career aspirations of the tipper and could have nothing to do with the stock-trading ramifications of the information.

Breach of Fiduciary Duty

In addition to the desire to benefit himself or herself, the tipper must also be acting in breach of a fiduciary duty to the corporation (or to another under the misappropriation theory, discussed later in this chapter) by disclosing the information to the tippee. The information must be nonpublic at the time it is divulged, and it must be in the interests of the corporation (or the other party in a misappropriation case) to keep the information confidential.

The tippee is liable only if he or she knew or should have known that the tipper's disclosure of the confidential information constituted a fiduciary breach. If the tippee has reason to know that the insider's disclosure was wrong or against the interest of the corporation, the tippee's actual knowledge will be irrelevant.

Remote Tippees

Remote tippees—that is, the tippees of tippees—may be found to have violated Section 10(b) and Rule 10b–5 even if they are completely unacquainted with and removed from the original insider tipper. However, remote tippees are not liable unless they knew or should have known that the first-tier tipper was breaching a fiduciary duty in passing on the nonpublic information.[27] The phrase "should have known" is key to this formulation. It means that a tippee cannot insulate himself or herself from liability merely by failing to inquire as to the source of the information. If the tippee has reason to suspect that the information was wrongfully acquired, such conscious avoidance of knowledge will not prevent a finding of *scienter*.

---

27. SEC v. Musella, 678 F. Supp. 1060 (S.D.N.Y. 1988).

Misappropriation Theory

From time to time, the SEC has unsuccessfully attempted to impose liability on anyone who trades while in possession of material nonpublic information. In *Chiarella v. United States*,[28] the Supreme Court rejected the argument that every trade based on nonpublic material information should be held to violate the securities laws.

Under the *misappropriation theory*, there is a Rule 10b–5 violation if a person breaches a fiduciary duty to the owner of nonpublic information by trading on that information after misappropriating it for his or her own use. No independent duty of disclosure to the person from whom the securities were bought or sold or the issuer is required. Liability is imposed because the trader converted the confidential information to his or her own use. The U. S. Supreme Court embraced this theory in the following case.

---

28. 445 U.S. 222 (1980).

A CASE IN POINT   **IN THE LANGUAGE OF THE COURT**

CASE 23.8
UNITED STATES
v. O'HAGAN
Supreme Court
of the United States
117 S. Ct. 2199 (1997).

FACTS   Attorney James Herman O'Hagan purchased stock and options for stock in Pillsbury Company (Pillsbury) prior to the public announcement of a tender offer for Pillsbury's stock by Grand Met PLC (Grand Met). O'Hagan possessed material nonpublic information about Grand Met's intentions, which he had obtained as a partner of the law firm representing Grand Met in connection with its acquisition of Pillsbury. O'Hagan realized a profit in excess of $4,000,000 on his Pillsbury-related transactions.

O'Hagan was convicted of 57 counts of securities fraud, mail fraud, and money laundering. [The counts under Rule 14e–3(a) (which prohibits a person with nonpublic information about a tender offer from buying stock in the target company) are discussed in Chapter 6 (Case 6.2).]. The appeals court reversed, and the United States appealed.

ISSUE PRESENTED   Is a person who trades in securities for personal profit, using confidential information misappropriated in breach of fiduciary duty to the source of the information, guilty of violating Section 10(b) and Rule 10b–5? [The Rule 14e–3 counts are discussed in Chapter 6 (Case 6.2).]

Case 23.8 continues

Case 23.8 continued

OPINION   GINSBURG, J., writing for the U. S. Supreme Court:
In pertinent part, § 10(b) of the Exchange Act provides:

> It shall be unlawful for any person, directly or indirectly, by the use of any means or instrumentality of interstate commerce or of the mails, or of any facility of any national securities exchange—
>
> . . .
>
> b.   To use or employ, in connection with the purchase or sale of any security registered on a national securities exchange or any security not so registered, any manipulative or deceptive device or contrivance in contravention of such rules and regulations as the [Securities and Exchange] Commission may prescribe as necessary or appropriate in the public interest or for the protection of investors.

The statute thus proscribes (1) using any deceptive device (2) in connection with the purchase or sale of securities, in contravention of rules prescribed by the Commission. The provision, as written, does not confine its coverage to deception of a purchaser or seller of securities; rather, the statute reaches any deceptive device used "in connection with the purchase or sale of any security."

Pursuant to its § 10(b) rulemaking authority, the Commission has adopted Rule 10b–5, which, as relevant here, provides:

> It shall be unlawful for any person, directly or indirectly, by the use of any means or instrumentality of interstate commerce, or of the mails or of any facility of any national securities exchange,
>
> (a) To employ any device, scheme, or artifice to defraud, [or]
>
> . . .
>
> (c) To engage in any act, practice, or course of business which operates or would operate as a fraud or deceit upon any person, in connection with the purchase or sale of any security.

Liability under Rule 10b–5, our precedent indicates, does not extend beyond conduct encompassed by Section 10(b)'s prohibition.

Under the "traditional" or "classical theory" of insider trading liability, § 10(b) and Rule 10b–5 are violated when a corporate insider trades in the securities of his corporation on the basis of material, nonpublic information. . . .

The "misappropriation theory" holds that a person commits fraud "in connection with" a securities transaction, and thereby violates § 10(b) and Rule 10–5, when he misappropriates confidential information for securities trading purposes, in breach of a duty owed to the source of the information. Under this theory, a fiduciary's undisclosed, self-serving use of a principal's information to purchase or sell securities, in breach of a duty of loyalty and confidentiality, defrauds the principal of the exclusive use of that information. In lieu of premising liability on a fiduciary relationship between company insider and purchaser or seller of the company's stock, the misappropriation theory premises liability on a fiduciary turned trader's deception of those who entrusted him with access to confidential information.

Case 23.8 continues

Case 23.8 continued

. . .

B

We agree with the Government that misappropriation, as just defined, satisfies § 10(b)'s requirement that chargeable conduct involve a "deceptive device or contrivance" used "in connection with" the purchase or sale of securities. We observe, first, that misappropriators, as the Government describes them, deal in deception. A fiduciary who "[pretends] loyalty to the principal while secretly converting the principal's information for personal gain" . . . defrauds the principal.

. . .

We turn next to the § 10(b) requirement that the misappropriator's deceptive use of information be "in connection with the purchase or sale of [a] security." This element is satisfied because the fiduciary's fraud is consummated, not when the fiduciary gains the confidential information, but when, without disclosure to his principal, he uses the information to purchase or sell securities. The securities transaction and the breach of duty thus coincide. This is so even though the person or entity defrauded is not the other party to the trade, but is, instead, the source of the nonpublic information. A misappropriator who trades on the basis of material, nonpublic information, in short, gains his advantageous market position through deception; he deceives the source of the information and simultaneously harms members of the investing public.

. . .

In sum, considering the inhibiting impact on market participation of trading on misappropriated information, and the congressional purposes underlying § 10(b), it makes scant sense to hold a lawyer like O'Hagan a § 10(b) violator if he works for a law firm representing the target of a tender offer, but not if he works for a law firm representing the bidder. The text of the statute requires no such result.

RESULT   O'Hagan's conviction was upheld. He violated § 10(b) and Rule 10b–5 by trading on material nonpublic information in violation of his duty to his partners and the firm's client.

Questions

1. Would the misappropriation theory apply to a case in which a person defrauded a bank into giving him a loan or embezzled cash from another and then used the proceeds of the misdeed to purchase securities?
2. If the fiduciary disclosed to the source of the nonpublic information that he or she planned to trade on that information, would trading on that information constitute a Section 10(b) violation? Would it violate any other laws? Would it be ethical?

Liability under the misappropriation theory requires that the defendant's trading threaten some injury to the defrauded party or the source of information. Actual injury need not be demonstrated. The threatened injury need not be pecuniary; it may be reputational or intangible.

The trader must know that the information utilized was meant to be confidential and that it was not intended to be used for anyone's personal benefit.

The misappropriation theory widens the class of persons who can be found liable for insider trading, but the requirement that there be a fiduciary duty remains a limiting factor. For instance, one who merely overhears a conversation relating to confidential information has no fiduciary duty and therefore no liability. Similarly, one who infers from the movements of corporate executives that an event will likely take place owes no duty to the corporation or its employees.

In *U.S. v. Chestman*,[29] the U.S. Court of Appeals for the Second Circuit held that the nephew-in-law of a controlling shareholder and family patriarch did not violate Rule 10b–5 when he passed on inside information to his broker, who traded on the information. The nephew-in-law was not in the inner circle of the family. Although he was married to the sister of one of the patriarch's daughters, the fact of marriage, taken alone, did not create a fiduciary relationship. Although spouses may by their conduct become fiduciaries, the marriage relationship alone does not impose fiduciary status. The court identified certain relationships that are inherently fiduciary: attorney and client, executor and heir, guardian and ward, principal and agent, trustee and trust beneficiary, and senior corporate official and shareholder.

The Supreme Court upheld the conviction of R. Foster Winans, author of the *Wall Street Journal* column entitled "Heard on the Street," under the Mail and Wire Fraud Acts, thereby providing an additional way to prosecute insider trading. Winans had misappropriated the content of his soon-to-be-published columns and tipped the information to two stockbrokers, who used the information to make trades based on the anticipated positive market response to the column's publication. The Court held that if confidential information is generated by a business, and if the business has the right to control the use of such information prior to public disclosure, then use of that information to trade can be prohibited under the wire and mail fraud statutes.

---

29. 947 F.2d 551 (2d Cir. 1991) *(en banc), cert. denied,* 503 U.S. 1004 (1992).

INTERNATIONAL CONSIDERATION

Germany's insider-trading laws prohibit directors from selectively divulging nonpublic information without issuing a broad public announcement. For example, in June 1997, the Federal Securities Regulatory Office began investigating whether Daimler–Benz AG board member Eckhard Cordes had illegally given a profit forecast to a handful of reporters at a dinner during the Geneva Motor Show when he told them that Daimler's 1996 net profits would likely "have a 2 before the decimal point," thereby signaling that profits would be more than two billion marks.[a]

---

a. Brandon Mitchener, *Daimler Official Is the Subject of Investigation,* WALL ST. J., June 6, 1997, at A9A.

 RICO

A securities fraud claim cannot be used as a predicate act in a civil case under the Racketeer Influenced and Corrupt Organizations Act (RICO) (discussed in Chapter 15) unless the defendant has been criminally convicted in connection with the fraud. Similarly, a criminal conviction under the Wire and Mail Fraud Acts for misappropriation of an employer's confidential information could, assuming other requirements are met, be the basis for a civil RICO case.

 Enforcement of Insider-Trading Prohibitions

Persons who violate the insider-trading provisions of the federal securities laws are subject to civil enforcement actions by the SEC, private suits for damages, and criminal prosecution. In both government and private actions, the complaining party must demonstrate these five elements: (1) a misstatement or omission of a material fact, (2) *scienter*, (3) reliance by the injured party, (4) causation, and (5) loss.

Private Actions

In private actions, the plaintiff must have standing to sue; that is, the plaintiff must be an actual purchaser or seller of securities, and the plaintiff's loss must have been proximately caused by the acts of the defendant. A private plaintiff may recover only his or her actual out-of-pocket damages.

Civil Enforcement

In an SEC civil enforcement action, the defendant may be liable for treble damages and disgorgement of profits and may be subject to an injunction prohibiting future trading.

Criminal Prosecutions

The SEC itself has no criminal enforcement power. Criminal prosecutions are brought by the Department of Justice through the U.S. Attorney's Office, often on referral from the SEC. If criminally convicted, a defendant faces a fine of up to $1 million and/or imprisonment for up to ten years for willful violations. Willfulness has been interpreted as awareness by the defendant that he or she was committing a wrongful act; the defendant need not specifically know that he or she was violating a statute.

INTERNATIONAL CONSIDERATION

The EC Insider-Trading Directive requires each member state to enact its own penalties. Many nations with less active trading markets impose civil rather than criminal sanctions. However, since 1993, Britain, France, and Germany have all instituted criminal sanctions against persons engaging in insider trading.

"I think I can get you off with a lighter sentence, but it might screw up your movie deal."

Arnie Levin © 1992 from The New Yorker Collection. All Rights Reserved.

◆ The Securities Fraud Enforcement Act

Immediately following the massive insider-trading charges against Michael Milken and Drexel Burnham Lambert in the late 1980s (discussed more fully in this chapter's "Inside Story"), Congress passed and President Reagan signed the Insider Trading and Securities Fraud Enforcement Act of 1988. The act raised the maximum penalty for insider trading from five to ten years in prison and increased the likelihood that persons found guilty would actually be incarcerated for some period of time. (Previously, the average sentence for insider trading was less than one year, and community service was often ordered in lieu of prison.) In addition, the maximum fine was raised from $100,000 to $1 million. Violators and their firms could also be liable for civil penalties of triple the profit gained or loss avoided as a result of the wrongful trading.

The legislation also provided strong encouragement to the brokerage industry to police itself. A brokerage house can be fined if it "knew or recklessly disregarded" information that would indicate insider-trading activities on the part of its employees. Intended to force firms to police their employees, to institute compliance systems, and to monitor suspicious activities, the act specifically requires registered brokers and dealers to maintain and enforce reasonably designed written policies and procedures to prevent the misuse of material nonpublic information. The maximum criminal penalty that could be imposed on brokerage firms was raised from $500,000 to $2.5 million.

Although this legislation does not explicitly require it, many commentators have suggested that it is prudent for other companies not in the brokerage business to implement such policies and procedures in light of their potential liability.

Bounty Payments

The act provides for bounty payments to individuals whose tips result in insider-trading prosecutions, in a manner similar to that utilized by the Internal Revenue Service in tax cases. These bounties could be as high as 10% of any revenues recovered from a defendant through penalties or settlement.

Private Right of Action

The act provides a private right of action for contemporaneous traders, that is, persons who purchased or sold securities of the same class at the same time the insider was trading. The total amount of damages that may be recovered is limited to the amount of the profit gained or loss avoided in the unlawful transaction. Any amounts disgorged pursuant to court order or at the instance of the SEC will offset the amount of recoverable damages by contemporaneous traders. Of significance to potential tippers and tippees is the provision that makes tippers and all direct and remote tippees jointly and severally liable. That means that any individual in the chain can be found liable for all of the profits gained or losses avoided in every transaction within the chain of information.

◆ Short-Swing Trading

Section 16(b) of the 1934 Act governs *short-swing trading*—the purchase and sale, or the sale and purchase, by officers, directors, and greater-than-10% shareholders of equity securities of a public company within a six-month period. Unlike Section 10(b), which requires *scienter* (that is, a showing of bad intent), liability is imposed under Section 16(b) regardless of the insider's state of mind.

ETHICAL CONSIDERATION

A number of brokerage houses have investigated whether any of their employees were involved in insider trading. Most of these firms turned over their trading records to the New York Stock Exchange for computer analysis. Persons suspected of illicit activities could be subject to SEC enforcement actions and criminal prosecutions. Such investigations send a stern message to employees and encourage ethical behavior and compliance with the insider-trading laws. They also improve the public's perception of the brokerage industry. How stringently should managers of brokerage houses follow these procedures?

Although the purpose of Section 16(b) is to prevent insiders of publicly held companies from exploiting information not generally available to the public in order to secure quick profits, it need not be proven that the insider actually possessed any material nonpublic information at the time the insider traded in the securities. To establish liability under Section 16(b) it is sufficient to prove that an insider purchased and then sold, or sold and then purchased, equity securities within a period of six months.

Section 16(a) of the 1934 Act imposes certain reporting obligations on officers and directors and shareholders owning more than 10% of a public company's equity securities. Section 16(c) prohibits such persons from *selling securities short*, that is, from selling securities they do not yet own.

Definitions

Section 16(b) of the 1934 Act provides that each officer, director, and greater-than-10% shareholder of an issuer that has registered any class of its equity securities under the 1934 Act must surrender to the issuer "any profit realized by him from any purchase and sale, or any sale and purchase, of any equity security of such issuer (other than an exempted security) within any period of less than six months."

Equity Security   An *equity security* includes (1) any stock or similar security; (2) any security that is convertible, with or without consideration, into such a security; (3) any security carrying any warrant or right to subscribe to or purchase such a security; (4) any such warrant or right; and (5) any other security that the SEC deems to be of a similar nature and that, for the protection of investors or in the public interest, the SEC considers appropriate to treat as an equity security. Thus, equity securities may include hybrids that are not ordinarily considered equity securities, such as convertible debt securities that have not been registered under the 1934 Act.

Special problems can arise in connection with the grant and exercise of stock options and other derivative securities. A set of complicated rules embodied largely in Rule 16b–3 (adopted by the SEC under Section 16(b) of the 1934 Act) governs this area. Before becoming an officer or director, a person should consult counsel to avoid inadvertent Section 16(b) liability.

Matching   The shares that are sold need not be the same shares that were purchased. Any purchase and any sale will incur liability if they occur less than six months apart, regardless of whether the transactions involve the same shares. For example, if on January 1, an officer of XYZ Corporation sold 100 shares of XYZ Corporation common stock that he had held for ten years, then on February 1 purchased 200 shares of XYZ Corporation common stock at a lower price, he would be liable for the short-swing profits on 100 of the shares. The January 1 sale would be matched with the February 1 purchase, even though the officer had held the securities for ten years before he sold them.

Profit Calculation   To calculate the profits recoverable under Section 16(b), the sale price is compared with the purchase price. If several purchases and sales occur within a six-month period, the lowest purchase price will be matched with the highest sale price; then the next lowest purchase price with the next highest sale price; and so on, regardless of the order in which the purchases and sales actually occurred. By matching purchases and sales in this manner, the recoverable profit is maximized.

Short-swing profits cannot be offset by trading losses that were incurred in the same period. Thus, there may be recoverable profits under Section 16(b) even though the officer or director suffered a net loss on the trading transactions.

The following example illustrates the "lowest-in, highest-out" matching principle just described. Assume that an officer made purchases and sales, each of 100 shares, as follows:

Date	Transaction	Price
Jan. 1	Purchase	$ 9
Jan. 30	Sale	10
Feb. 15	Sale	15
Feb. 28	Purchase	12
March 15	Purchase	6
March 30	Sale	4

These transactions would result in a recoverable short-swing profit of $1,000, calculated as follows. The February 15 sale is matched with the March 15 purchase, for a profit of $15 – $6 = $9 per share, or $900. Then the January 30 sale is matched with the January 1 purchase, for a profit of $10 – $9 = $1 per share, or $100. Even though the March 15 purchase at $6 per share and the subsequent sale at $4 per share resulted in a loss of $2 per share, or $200, that loss will not be taken into account. The officer would have to surrender $900 + $100 = $1,000, even though the officer in fact realized only $200 of net profit in the trading transactions (total sales of $2,900 less purchases of $2,700).

Six Months   To result in recoverable short-swing profits, the purchase and sale, or sale and purchase, must have occurred "within any period of less than six months." That period commences on the day on which the first purchase or sale occurred and ends at midnight two days before the corresponding date in the sixth succeeding month. For example, for a transaction on January 1, the six-month period ends at midnight on June 29, two days before July 1.

Officer or Director   A person may be liable under Section 16(b) if he or she was an officer or director at the time of either the purchase or the sale; it is not necessary that both transactions occur during the person's tenure.

For example, if an officer purchased 100 shares of XYZ Corporation common stock at $10 per share on January 1, resigned as an officer on February 1, then sold 100 shares of XYZ Corporation common stock at $20 per share on March 1, she would be liable for $1,000 of short-swing profits because she was an officer when she made the January 1 purchase. Similarly, if a person purchased 100 shares of XYZ Corporation at $10 per share on January 1, became an officer of XYZ Corporation on February 1, and sold the shares at $20 on March 1, that person would be liable for $1,000 of short-swing profits because he was an officer at the time of sale. On the other hand, if an officer who had not traded for more than six months before March 1 resigned on March 1, bought 100 shares of XYZ Corporation at $10 on April 1, then sold them at $20 on April 2, she would not have recoverable profits because she was not an officer or director at the time of either the purchase or the sale.

Greater-than-10% Shareholder   The rule is different for persons who are not officers or directors but are owners of more than 10% of the issuer's equity securities. Such persons are liable under Section 16(b) only if they hold more than 10% of the securities both at the time of the purchase and at the time of the sale. The transaction whereby the person becomes a 10% shareholder does not count.

For example, if a person purchased 10.5% of XYZ Corporation's common stock at $10 on January 1, then sold those shares at $20 on March 1, that person would have no recoverable short-swing profits. However, if the same person had purchased another 2% of XYZ common stock in February, then the February purchase could be matched against the March sale because the shareholder owned more than 10% of the stock at the time of the February purchase and also at the time of the March sale.

Beneficial Ownership of Shares   Officers, directors, and greater-than-10% shareholders can be liable for purchases and sales of shares they do not own of record but are deemed to beneficially own. Under Section 16(b), a person will be considered the *beneficial owner* of any securities held by his or her immediate family—his or her spouse, any minor children, or any other relative living in his or her household. There is a rebuttable presumption that a person is the beneficial owner of any securities over which he or she has the practical power to vest title in himself or herself, or from which he or she receives economic benefits (such as sales proceeds) substantially equal to those of ownership.

Purchases and sales of securities held beneficially by an officer, director, or greater-than-10% shareholder will be attributed to him or her in determining the person's liability for short-swing trading. For example, the purchase of securities by an officer's wife could be matched under Section 16(b) with the sale of other securities by the officer himself within six months of his wife's purchase, thereby resulting in liability for short-swing profits. Thus, any officer, director, or greater-than-10% shareholder planning a purchase or sale must consider not only his or her own trading record but also the record of those persons whose securities he or she is deemed to beneficially own.

Unorthodox Transactions

If a purchase or sale by an officer, director, or greater-than-10% shareholder that would otherwise result in recoverable short-swing profits was involuntary and did not involve the payment of cash, and if there was no possibility of speculative abuse of inside information, then a court may hold that there was an *unorthodox transaction* to which no liability will attach. These situations generally arise in the context of exchanges in mergers and other corporate reorganizations, stock conversions, stock reclassifications, and tender offers in which securities are sold or exchanged for consideration other than cash. On the other hand, in a tender offer or acquisition, an exchange of securities for cash by an officer, director, or greater-than-10% shareholder would almost certainly be deemed a sale for which the person receiving the cash could be liable under Section 16(b).

Beneficial-Ownership Reports

Section 16(a) of the 1934 Act requires that officers, directors, and greater-than-10% shareholders of companies that have registered any class of equity securities under the 1934 Act file beneficial-ownership reports with the SEC and with any national securities exchange on which their company's equity securities are listed. Within ten days of becoming an officer or director, a person must file an initial ownership report on Form 3, even if the person does not beneficially own any securities of the company at that time. In the case of greater-than-10% shareholders, a Form 3 must be filed within ten days of the date they acquire a greater-than-10% interest. (In addition, as noted in Chapter 22, any person who acquires more than 5% of the voting securities of a public company must file a Schedule 13D within ten days of the date he or she acquires that interest. An amendment to the Schedule 13D must be filed promptly after any material change in beneficial ownership or investment purpose.)

Subsequently, an officer, director, or greater-than-10% shareholder must file a Form 4 within ten days after the end of each month in which any change in beneficial ownership occurs. In the initial Form 4, an officer or director must report all purchases or sales that occurred within the previous six months, even if those transactions were effected before the person became an officer or director. A Form 5 showing changes in beneficial ownership during the preceding year must be filed

annually. However, if there were no changes in beneficial ownership during the year, an officer or director may instead present to the company a certificate stating that there were no reportable events. The company must keep this certificate on file.

A person who ceases to be an officer or director must continue to report any changes in beneficial ownership that occur within six months of the last reportable transaction while the person was an officer or director.

Acquisitions of shares through reinvestment of cash dividends under a qualifying dividend reinvestment plan do not require the filing of a Form 4. However, participation in the plan and the ownership of shares under the plan must be disclosed in Form 4 reports that are otherwise required to be filed.

The SEC has brought enforcement actions to force executives to file these ownership reports within the required time frame. The SEC also adopted rules that require a corporation to disclose in its proxy statement and in its annual report on Form 10–K whether its officers and directors have complied with their Section 16(a) reporting obligations.

Prohibition on Selling Short

Section 16(c) of the 1934 Act prohibits officers or directors from selling any of their company's equity securities short, that is, from selling a security that the seller does not own. If the officer or director owns the security being sold, he or she must deliver it within 20 days after the sale, or deposit it in the mails or other usual channels of delivery within five days. If the officer or director fails to do this, he or she will be liable under Section 16(c) unless (1) he or she acted in good faith and was unable to make the delivery or deposit within the specified time, or (2) he or she acted in good faith and satisfying the time requirements would have caused undue inconvenience or expense.

THE RESPONSIBLE MANAGER
Preventing Securities Fraud and Insider Trading

Managers have an obligation not to mislead investors in company public announcements, periodic reports,

or speeches. Although a company can remain silent about material developments if neither the company nor insiders are trading, early disclosure is often the better course. This gives all investors equal access to current information about the company. There is a trade-off here, however. Sometimes the company's business or transactions may be in a state of flux. For example, the company might have received an offer to buy the company's assets from an unreliable party who may not have any visible source of financing. It may be worse to get the market's hopes up by disclosing the offer than to wait to see whether in fact the offer is real. Managers, together with their lawyers, must make these judgment calls.

Another reason for early disclosure is to avoid illegal insider trading. A company must make disclosure if it knows its insiders, such as officers or directors, are trading in the company's securities while they are in possession of material nonpublic information.

Each company that takes advantage of the capital markets has a legal and ethical duty to ensure the integrity of those markets. Securities fraud, in any form, erodes investor confidence and makes it more difficult and expensive for honest businesses to raise capital.

Any forward-looking statements should be identified as such and be accompanied by meaningful cautionary language identifying important factors that could cause actual results to differ materially from those in the forward-looking statement. It is often helpful (1) to prioritize the order of risk factors, (2) to state the risk in the first sentence, (3) to be specific, (4) to convey the magnitude of the risk, and (5) to focus risk factors on the negatives, without softening them by including positives.

Trading by a manager while in possession of material nonpublic information is illegal. It violates the manager's fiduciary duty to subordinate his or her personal interests to the interests of the corporation and shareholders he or she serves. A manager is given access to nonpublic information not for the manager's own personal gain but to better enable the manager to serve his or her principal—the corporation and its shareholders. Violation of those rules erodes shareholder confidence and erodes the confidence of investors generally in the capital markets. It is also unethical.

A manager cannot give tips to others in exchange for money or even just to enhance his or her reputation as "someone in the know." A manager should carefully guard the information given in confidence by his or her employer or client. Managers must also instill these values in their subordinates. Everyone, from the person who empties the trash or runs the copy machine to the person who occupies the largest office in the executive suite, must be told to follow these rules or risk dismissal. This edict should be made clear in the corporation's code of ethics and in its personnel manual. All corporations, and especially brokerage firms, without adequate procedures in place to prevent illegal insider trading face potential liability for their insiders' illegal trades.

A company cannot disclose material information only to certain favored analysts. This is unfair to the public investors and can result in liability for the company and for the manager who tips an analyst whose clients then trade based on the tip.

An officer or director of a public company who buys and sells securities within a six-month period has a legal and ethical responsibility to come forward and pay all profits over to the corporation. This is true even if the short-swing trade was inadvertent, as might happen if an officer sold securities not realizing that his or her spouse had bought securities less than six months before. A corporation that discovers a short-swing trade must try to persuade the insider to voluntarily turn the profits over to the corporation. If the insider refuses to do so, the corporation has an obligation to bring suit to recover the profits from the short-swing trading. If a corporation fails to bring suit, any shareholder has the right to sue on behalf of the corporation.

Officers and directors of public companies must report their security holdings and their trades in a timely manner. Disregard of these filing requirements breeds contempt for the law and encourages illegal or unethical behavior by others in the organization.

Each manager has a role to play in preventing securities fraud and insider trading. As with preventing the other types of criminal behavior described in Chapter 15, a manager leads by example. If the manager permits his or her company to engage in unlawful or unethical conduct, the manager exposes himself or herself and the company to considerable risk of civil and criminal liability. Such a manager also is likely to encourage illegal behavior by subordinates.

1980s INSIDER-TRADING SCANDALS

Inquiries into insider trading tend to focus on high-volume trading that occurs before major corporate announcements. Enforcement agencies generally watch organized trading rings and well-known public figures because of their high profiles. However, ordinary investors and isolated violations are also detected and prosecuted. Surveillance groups monitor daily trading and investigate any suspicious activity. One such group, the American Exchange Stock Watch Group, was instrumental in breaking the "Heard on the Street" case discussed earlier.

Dennis Levine and Ivan Boesky

Prosecutors and enforcement agencies also rely heavily on information gathered from informers and persons already under indictment. For example, the arrest and prosecution of Dennis Levine and Ivan Boesky in 1986 set off the most comprehensive investigation of securities-trading practices in the history of federal regulation. Levine, a former managing director of Drexel Burnham Lambert, was initially charged with illegal trading in approximately 54 stocks. An investment banker, Ira B. Sokolow, then pleaded guilty to passing stolen information to Levine. As a result of cooperation by Levine, the SEC was able to bring insider-trading

charges against one of Wall Street's richest and most active speculators, Ivan Boesky.

Boesky, the son of an immigrant restaurateur, made his career and fortune as a risk arbitrageur who concentrated on the purchase and sale of stock in target corporations that were the subject of tender offers. Generally, the stock of a target corporation will be bought by the acquiring corporation at a premium; thus, people who invest prior to the announcement of the acquisition are in a position to make swift and substantial profits. The SEC alleged that Levine, who worked on mergers and acquisitions, would pass on information to Boesky, who was able to purchase shares in the target prior to public announcement of the impending takeover. It is further believed that Boesky offered Levine a 5% commission for any information leading to an initial stock purchase and a 1% commission for information pertaining to stocks already owned by Boesky.

In 1985, Levine was alleged to have passed to Boesky information received from Sokolow regarding the merger of Nabisco and R. J. Reynolds. Use of this information resulted in approximately $4 million in profits for Boesky. In all, Boesky was alleged to have made approximately $50 million through these insider-trading activities. Both Levine and

Boesky pleaded guilty to criminal charges, and Boesky settled the SEC's civil charges by agreeing to pay $100 million and to cooperate with the government in future prosecutions of others. Both men were sentenced to prison for their actions.

Drexel Burnham Lambert

Approximately two years later, with the cooperation of Ivan Boesky, the SEC brought dramatic charges against Drexel Burnham Lambert and four of its prominent employees, including the head of its junk-bond department, Michael Milken. According to the SEC, Drexel had entered into a secret agreement with Boesky to defraud its clients and drive up the price of target-company stocks. The complaint, filed in September 1988, alleged that Drexel utilized Boesky to engage in *stock parking*—the temporary sale of shares to another entity or individual, intended to hide the true ownership of the shares in order to avoid tax-reporting requirements or the net-margin requirements of the securities laws applicable to brokerage firms. Drexel, which assisted companies interested in acquisitions, was also accused of advising Boesky to purchase massive amounts of shares in certain companies in order to give the appearance of active trading in them and to drive up the takeover price.

In December 1988, Drexel agreed to plead guilty to six felony counts, pay a $680 million fine, and submit to SEC oversight, contingent upon its settlement of civil charges (which occurred in April 1989). As a part of both settlements, Drexel was required to terminate the employment of Michael Milken. (The Milken case is discussed in Chapter 15.)

Other Boesky-Related Prosecutions

Another prosecution evolving out of the Boesky affair involved Martin A. Siegel, a former managing director of Drexel. Siegel was fingered by Boesky and pleaded guilty in February 1987 to stock parking and tax evasion to the tune of $9 million. In June 1990, he was sentenced to two months in prison; he had faced a possible maximum sentence of ten years. Reuters quoted U.S. District Judge Robert Ward as saying there were three mitigating factors that affected the sentencing decision: Siegel's "cooperation, contrition and candor in a difficult situation."[30]

---

30. Reuters, *Key Scandal Figure Gets Light Sentence*, SAN FRANCISCO CHRON., June 16, 1990, at B1.

KEY WORDS AND PHRASES

QUESTIONS AND CASE PROBLEMS

1. E. Jacques Courtois, Jr. and Franklin Courtois worked for various New York investment banking firms in the 1970s, including Morgan Stanley and Kuhn Loeb. These individuals misappropriated information entrusted to their employers regarding clients' imminent merger transactions and tipped James Newman, a broker, who traded on the information. The SEC brought charges against the two investment bankers under Section 10(b) and Rule 10b–5, alleging that they had breached the trust and confidence placed in them by their employers and indirectly by the employers' corporate clients and the clients' shareholders. Result? [*United States v. Newman*, 664 F.2d 12 (2d Cir. 1981)]

2. During a session with her psychiatrist, Dr. Robert Willis, Joan Weill mentioned in confidence the imminent merger of the company headed by her husband, Sanford Weill, with another company. Willis, upon hearing of the merger, communicated the information to Martin Sloate, who traded in the company's securities for his own account and for his customers' accounts.

Did Willis or Sloate engage in illegal insider trading? Was the conduct of the parties ethical? [*SEC v. Willis*, 777 F. Supp. 1165 (S.D.N.Y. 1991)]

3. Gallop, Inc. is a toy manufacturer specializing in games for boys and girls aged 8 to 12. Gallop had predicted first-quarter earnings of $.20 per share on March 30. On April 15, Gallop received a fax from its key distributor reporting a $10 million claim for personal injury of a nine-year-old child who was allegedly injured by a design defect in Gallop's most popular product line, the Spartan Warriors. Gallop's outside counsel was instructed to prepare a press release describing the claim. Before the press release was sent to the copy center at Gallop's executive office, the vice-president of marketing, one director, and the outside counsel sold all of their Gallop shares at the prevailing market price of $25.25 per share.

Collin Copier, who ran the photocopying machine at Gallop's executive office, saw the draft press release; called his broker, Barbara Broker; told her about the press release; and ordered her to sell the 500 shares of Gallop that Copier had acquired in Gallop's initial public offering. Broker then called her best client, Charleen Client, and suggested that she sell her 100,000 shares of Gallop stock, but did not tell her why. Client agreed, and Broker sold Copier's and Client's stock at $25.25 a share right before the market closed on April 17.

The press release was publicly announced and was reported on the Business Wire after the market closed on April 17. The next day, Gallop's stock dropped to $20.75 per share. A class action suit has been brought, and the SEC has commenced enforcement proceedings. Criminal prosecution is threatened by the U.S. Attorney's Office.

What are the bases on which each proceeding could be brought? Who is potentially liable? For how much?

4. Ann Boland, a freelance writer, called her mother to boast about a press release that she was writing for Empire Corporation. The assignment called for the strictest confidence because it involved the announcement of a takeover.

Later in the day, Ann's mother casually tells her son Tim, a business student, about his sister's press release. She does not mention the name of the takeover target, but she naively provides Tim with enough details that he is almost certain who it is.

Tim calls his rich buddy, Carl Consultant, and tells him the story. They decide to buy options on the target company's stock and to split any profits 50–50. In a week, the two have made a small fortune. Are there any Rule 10b–5 violations? If so, who may be required to disgorge profits?

5. Santa Fe Industries, Inc. acquired control of 60% of the stock of Kirby Lumber Corporation, a Delaware corporation. Through additional purchases, Santa Fe increased its control of Kirby stock to 95%. Santa Fe then decided that it wanted to acquire 100% ownership of Kirby.

After obtaining an independent appraisal of Kirby's physical assets, Santa Fe submitted the appraisals, along with additional financial information, to Morgan Stanley to appraise the fair market value of Kirby's stock. Morgan Stanley appraised Kirby's physical assets at $320 million and valued its stock at $125 per share.

Based on Morgan Stanley's findings, Santa Fe decided to enter into a short-form merger with Kirby. In accordance with the short-form merger statute, the minority shareholders were notified the day after the merger became effective and advised of their right to obtain an appraisal in Delaware court if they were dissatisfied with the offer of $150 per share. They were also supplied copies of Morgan Stanley's appraisal concluding that the fair market value of the stock was $125 per share.

The minority shareholders of Kirby objected to the merger, but did not pursue their appraisal remedy. Instead, they filed suit in federal court seeking to enjoin the merger or recover what they viewed was the fair market value of their shares, $772 per share. Their complaint alleged that Santa Fe fraudulently obtained the appraisal report from Morgan Stanley and offered $25 above the appraisal in order to deceive the minority shareholders into believing that their offer was generous. It was further alleged that these acts violated Rule 10b–5 because Santa Fe employed a "device, scheme or artifice to defraud."

Did Santa Fe, as a majority shareholder, breach a duty to deal fairly with the minority shareholders? Was Santa Fe's conduct "manipulative or deceptive"? Was it ethical? [*Santa Fe Indus., Inc. v. Green*, 430 U.S. 462 (1977)]

6. Verifone manufactures and designs products used by retail merchants to automate a variety of transactions, such as authorizing credit card purchases. In 1990, Verifone filed a registration statement and prospectus describing the company's past growth trends in revenues and earnings, including a list of its well-known customers, markets for potential growth, and companies that were considering using its products.

The prospectus also contained a section on the risks associated with its stock.

The plaintiffs contended that the discussion of the risks was merely boilerplate and did not disclose with sufficient detail the risks faced by Verifone shareholders. The plaintiffs further alleged that the company's historic growth trends had ceased, and that the company was "facing a brick wall" in existing markets. Therefore, the plaintiffs alleged, the prospectus was materially misleading.

If the plaintiffs assert the fraud-on-the-market theory, what will they need to show in order to prevail? Will the plaintiffs also have a claim against the underwriters? [*In re Verifone Sec. Litig.*, 784 F. Supp. 1471 (N.D. Cal. 1992), *aff'd*, 11 F.3d 865 (9th Cir. 1993)]

7. National Industries acquired 34% of TSC Industries' voting stock from TSC's founder and principal shareholder and his family. After the sale, the TSC founder resigned from the TSC's board of directors. Subsequently, five National nominees, including National's president and chief executive officer, were placed on TSC's board. Several months later, TSC's board, with the National nominees abstaining, approved a proposal to liquidate and sell all of TSC's assets to National. One month later, the two companies issued a joint proxy statement to their shareholders, recommending approval of the proposal. The proxy solicitation was successful, TSC was liquidated, and the exchange of shares was effected.

A TSC shareholder brought an action against the two companies claiming that their joint proxy statement was materially misleading. The basis of the claim was that the proxy statement omitted material facts relating to the degree of National's control over TSC. Were the omitted facts material? [*TSC Indus., Inc. v. Northway, Inc.*, 426 U.S. 438 (1976)]

8. On November 8, 1990, the *Wall Street Journal* reported rumors of a possible merger of AT&T and NCR. AT&T declined to comment on the rumors. That same day, Charles Brumfield, vice-president of labor relations for AT&T, called his friend Joseph Cusimano and told him that he believed the contents of the newspaper article were true and that "AT&T was going to be attempting to acquire NCR." Cusimano made a series of trades in NCR securities on November 9, 12, and 15 through 20. The AT&T board authorized the acquisition of NCR on November 14 and publicly announced its interest on December 2.

Did either Brumfield or Cusimano violate Section 10(b) and Rule 10b–5? On what theory? Was Brumfield's information nonpublic and material? [*United States v. Mylett*, 97 F.3d 663 (2d Cir. 1996); *United States v. Cusimano*, 123 F.3d 83 (2d Cir. 1997), *cert. denied*, 118 S. Ct. 1090 (1998)]

9. Texas International Speedway, Inc. (TIS) filed a registration statement for $4,398,900 in securities with the proceeds to be used to construct an automobile racetrack called the Texas International Speedway. The entire issue was sold on the offering date, October 30, 1969. On November 30, 1970, TIS filed for bankruptcy.

The prospectus stated that the speedway was under construction. It also included a pro forma balance sheet showing that, upon completion of the public offering and application of the proceeds to the construction costs of the speedway, TIS would have $93,870 in cash on hand on the speedway's opening date.

The TIS prospectus warned that "THESE SECURITIES INVOLVE A HIGH DEGREE OF RISK" and that the construction costs might be underestimated. If the plaintiff investors present evidence from which a jury could infer that, on the effective date of the registration statement, the two officers and directors of TIS and its accountant knew that the cost of construction was understated and that consequently TIS's working capital position would not be as favorable as the prospectus reflected, will the plaintiff win a suit under Section 10(b) and Rule 10b–5? What would be the result if the Reform Act applied? [*Huddleston v. Herman & MacLean*, 640 F.2d 534 (5th Cir. 1981), *rev'd in part and aff'd in part*, 456 U.S. 914 (1982)]

MANAGER'S DILEMMA

10. On June 24, 1994, Novell, Inc., the world's leading provider of network operating software, merged with WordPerfect in a stock-for-stock exchange registered under the 1933 Act pursuant to a registration statement initially filed April 22, 1994, and last amended on June 23, 1994.

The registration statement included a warning that the integration of Novell and WordPerfect could be difficult due to intense competition in WordPerfect's market sector and the company's declining financial performance. It further cautioned that the acquisitions of

WordPerfect and the Quattro Pro spreadsheet software program from Borland Inc. in the first part of 1994 could be difficult because they were large acquisitions in new markets where Novell did not have management or marketing experience. The registration statement warned that no assurance could be given that the various businesses could be successfully integrated. Also, the dominant competition expected from Microsoft was stressed. In addition, Novell warned that the merger and acquisition would lead to higher expenditures in sales, marketing and support and higher other costs. Novell predicted that its future earnings and stock prices could be subject to "significant volatility, particularly on a quarterly basis" and warned that WordPerfect's market was "characterized by severe competitive pressure" that could "materially adversely affect Novell." The June 10 amendment to the registration statement advised that "disruptions associated with the merger and the acquisition of Quattro Pro have resulted in declines in sales of Quattro Pro in recent periods." Also, significant deteriorations in the sales and profitability of WordPerfect were disclosed.

The merger was completed five weeks before the end of the third quarter. On August 19, 1994, Novell announced that its consolidated third-quarter earnings would fall between 15% and 20% below analysts' projections and that the company would recognize a $120 million charge against earnings for the quarter related to its acquisition of Quattro Pro. The next business day, August 22, Novell's stock price fell from $15.12 per share to $14 per share, a 7% drop.

The plaintiff class members purchased shares of Novell stock during the period between April 27, 1994, and August 19, 1994. They alleged that beginning on April 27, 1994, Novell issued a series of false and misleading statements and omissions of material fact to the press and to financial analysts regarding the effect of the WordPerfect merger on Novell's operations and near-term earnings potential. They did not claim that the registration statement itself was misleading.

In particular, the plaintiffs alleged that the following statements had inflated the price of Novell stock during the class period: (1) a statement by defendant Wise (Novell's senior vice-president for finance) on April 27, 1994, that there were "indications" that WordPerfect was "gaining market share . . . from less than 20% in 1992 to more than 40% today" and that "the combination wouldn't dilute future earnings"; (2) a statement by defendant Frankenberg (Novell's CEO, president, and chairperson) on June 27, 1994, that Novell had experienced substantial success in the integration of the sales forces and operations of WordPerfect and that the merger process had been moving "faster than we thought it would"; (3) Frankenberg stated in the same June 27, 1994, publication that "we have not slowed down the effort to create new products, we've accelerated it" and that he believed there was "a compelling set of opportunities" available to the new Novell; (4) a statement by Rietveld (CEO of WordPerfect and later the president of Novell's WordPerfect/Novell applications group) on June 28, 1994, that the merger had been "perhaps the smoothest of mergers in recent history"; (5) Frankenberg's statement on June 28, 1994, that "he was pleased with the accelerating pace of product development since the acquisition was completed in March"; and (6) Novell's statement on July 20, 1994, that "[b]y moving rapidly to a fully integrated sales force, we are leveraging our combined knowledge of the expanding scope of network solutions," and "Novell expects that network applications will quickly reshape customer expectations and expand the role of our channel partners in supporting end-user network solutions."

Novell and the other defendants made a motion to dismiss the complaint. Result? Is there anything that Novell's officers should have done differently? Was their conduct ethical? [*Grossman v. Novell, Inc.*, 120 F.3d 1112 (10th Cir. 1997)]

INTERNET SOURCES	
Securities and Exchange Commission	http://www.sec.gov
Investors can register complaints by e-mail with the Securities and Exchange Commission by following the instructions at this site.	http://www.sec.gov/consumer/reachus.htm
Milberg Weiss is perhaps the largest (and in Silicon Valley the most feared and hated) law firm specializing in representing plaintiffs in securities fraud suits and class actions.	http://securities.milberg.com http://www.milberg.com
The brainchild of Stanford Law School professor (and former SEC commissioner) Joseph Grundfest, this Securities Class Action Clearinghouse site has been called the "mecca for the securities lawyer." This is the first Designated Internet Site for required electronic posting of court documents in the United States.	http://securities.stanford.edu
The Securities Law Home Page provides access to many important securities law cases and useful links to other law-related sites.	http://www.seclaw.com

CHAPTER 24

Debtor–Creditor Relations and Bankruptcy

INTRODUCTION

Salvaging a Business in Financial Trouble

The reasons for borrowing money, and the uses to which the loan proceeds are applied, are many and varied. A business will generally decide to borrow when it needs funds and believes it is in a position to pay interest for the use of such funds. Although lenders sometimes take equity positions in a borrower, whereby they receive returns based on the profits or losses of the borrower, lenders in a loan transaction are entitled only to interest at a stated rate on the amount borrowed (generally called the *principal*) and the return of the principal at the end of the term.

When a business is in trouble, because of external events or internal miscalculations or misdeeds, it will inevitably run short of cash and fall behind in its payments. Creditors may be temporarily appeased; but those with collateral will ultimately pursue foreclosure, and others will file lawsuits in a race for the remaining assets. Defending against these actions can absorb resources and hamper management's ability to cure the company's underlying ills. Successful collection can cripple or kill the business.

Predatory dismemberment may destroy a company's real economic value. This loss in value will ultimately hurt creditors if there are not enough assets to go around. Even if all debts can be paid, the equity holders in the company will suffer. The collapse of a large enterprise could leave many unemployed and send disruptive waves through related industries.

The legal tools used to stem this potentially destructive tide are found mainly in the Bankruptcy Code.[1] Under the U.S. Constitution, Congress is given the power to enact bankruptcy laws. A successful reorganization under Chapter 11 of the Bankruptcy Code results in the restructuring of financial relationships among the owners and creditors of a business and, ideally, the preservation of a viable going concern. Even when reorganization is not possible, the bankruptcy system is designed to realize the maximum value from the available assets, to provide equitable distribution among claimants, and to foster fair and efficient administration through a collective or multiparty process.

Chapter Overview

This chapter categorizes commercial loans according to the type of lender, the purposes to which the loan proceeds will be applied, and whether the loan is secured or unsecured. This discussion is followed by a summary of the typical terms of a loan

---

1. Codified in scattered sections of 11 U.S.C.

agreement. Methods for securing a loan under Article 9 of the Uniform Commercial Code are discussed, together with a description of the terms of a typical security agreement. Equipment leasing, guaranties, and subordination are addressed. This is followed by a discussion of business bankruptcies under Chapter 7 and Chapter 11 of the Bankruptcy Code, workouts, and lender liability. (Consumer credit and consumer bankruptcy are covered in Chapter 19.)

 ## Loans Categorized by Lender

Commercial loans are most commonly made by banks, insurance companies, and purchasers of *commercial paper*, that is, short-term corporate indebtedness. Both banks and insurance companies are highly regulated. Extensive federal and state legislation prescribes the types of entities that may call themselves banks, who may own them, and, once they become banks, what they may or may not do. Similarly, insurance companies are restricted by state legislation in connection with their business of insuring against risk. The regulatory framework within which banks, insurance companies, and other types of lenders operate will affect their sources and availability of funds; these factors in turn will affect the terms on which they will offer to lend money. Banks generally are more flexible in the length of the terms of their loans, the interest-rate formulas, and the mechanics of loan administration. Among insurance companies, medium- to long-term loans at fixed interest rates are more common. Whether it is a bank or an insurance company, a lender may have particular expertise in the industry in which the borrower does business or in making loans for particular purposes.

 ## Loans Categorized by Purpose

A borrower may require funds to meet everyday working capital needs, to finance an acquisition of assets or a business, or to finance a real estate construction project or an engineering project. Under regulations promulgated by the board of governors of the Federal Reserve System, lenders and borrowers may not enter into transactions whereby secured credit will be used to acquire stock, unless certain requirements are met. Apart from these basic restrictions and additional restrictions that apply to borrowers in regulated industries, borrowers may borrow money for a wide variety of reasons. These reasons will dictate whether the loan will be a term loan or a revolving loan.

Term Loans

Funds required for a specific purpose, such as an acquisition or a construction project, are generally borrowed in the form of a *term loan*. A specified amount is borrowed, either in a lump sum or in installments. It is to be repaid on a specified date (known as the *maturity date*) or *amortized* (paid off over a period of time). For example, in an acquisition the buyer may be required to pay the purchase price up front and thus will require a lump-sum loan. By contrast, the owner of a construction project will require a loan to be disbursed in installments as scheduled progress payments become due. Amounts repaid under a term loan cannot be reborrowed.

Revolving Loans

A borrower may project its working capital needs for a given period but desire flexibility as to the exact amount of money borrowed at any given time. A *revolving loan* or *revolving line of credit* allows the borrower to borrow whatever sums required, up to a specified maximum amount. The borrower may also reborrow amounts it has repaid (hence the term "revolving"). The lender will require a *commitment fee* as consideration for its promise to keep the commitment available, as it receives no interest on amounts not borrowed.

 ## Secured Loans

In making a loan, the lender relies on the borrower's cash flow, the borrower's assets, or the proceeds of another loan as sources of repayment. If the lender relies solely on the borrower's promise to repay the loan, the lender's recourse for nonpayment is limited to suing the borrower. Moreover, even if the lender does sue the borrower, it stands in no better position than other general creditors of the borrower with no special claim to any specific assets of the borrower as a source of repayment. Because of this risk, lenders are often unwilling to make loans without something more than the borrower's promise of repayment. Lenders usually require *collateral,* that is, property belonging to the borrower that will become the lender's if the loan is not repaid. A loan backed up by collateral is known as a *secured loan.* Unsecured loans, if they are available at all, are priced at a higher rate to reflect the greater credit risk to the lender.

If the borrower fails to repay a secured loan, the lender, in addition to suing for return of the monies lent, may *foreclose* on—that is, take possession of—the collateral and either sell it to pay off the debt or keep it in satisfaction of the debt. It should be noted that under some *antideficiency* and *one-form-of-action laws* lenders seeking remedies against real property security may be restricted from suing the borrower personally. In cases in which a lender has recourse to the borrower or to other property of the borrower and exercises such rights, the lender may be precluded from foreclosing on real estate mortgaged by the borrower. These laws, which date back to the Great Depression, are designed to protect borrowers from forfeiting their properties to overzealous lenders.

Loan Agreements

Given the variety of loans described above, the basic structure of loan agreements is surprisingly standard. Lenders are concerned about the administration of the loan, their ongoing relationship with the borrowers, and the rights they have if the borrowers breach their promises. At times, these concerns must be addressed in specially tailored documentation; however, banks generally use a collection of standard forms, which are distributed to loan officers along with instructions for their use. This section discusses the basic features common to all loan agreements.

Parties to the Agreement

The parties to a loan agreement are the lender and the borrower. There may be more than one lender and more than one borrower. If the lender is an insurance company, the loan agreement will be called a *note purchase agreement.*

Lenders When two or more lenders, usually banks, together make one loan to a borrower, it is called a *syndicated loan.* In a syndicated loan, the lenders enter into concurrent direct obligations with the borrower to make a loan, typically on a pro rata basis. The loan is coordinated by a lead lender who serves as agent for all of the lenders in disbursing the funds, collecting payments of interest and principal, and administering and enforcing the loan.

A *participation loan* is a loan in which the original lender sells shares to other parties, called participants. Each participant acquires an undivided interest in the loan. The sale may be made without the borrower's involvement.

Borrowers Multiple borrowers are usually related entities, such as a parent corporation and its subsidiaries. It is important to remember that corporate law recognizes each corporation as a separate entity. From the lender's point of view, the parent and its subsidiaries are one economic entity; but from the subsidiaries' point of view, if each subsidiary is jointly and severally liable for the entire debt, its obligation may outweigh the economic benefit it receives from the loan. (To the extent that the loan is used by the parent rather than the subsidiary, the transaction may be invalidated as a fraudulent transfer under state law and the federal Bankruptcy Code, as discussed below.)

Additional Parties In more complicated transactions, additional parties may become involved in the negotiations for a loan, even though they are not parties to the loan agreement. For example, in a leveraged buyout, the acquisition of a company is financed largely by debt secured by its assets. The lender will want assurances from the seller that the assets being sold to the borrower are free and clear of all liens, and this concern may affect the structure of the buyout; or, if the seller is taking a note from the buyer for part of the purchase price, the lender will want to negotiate with the seller an agreement setting forth their relative rights to repayment. In a construction loan, the construction lender will advance sufficient funds to complete the construction project with the expectation of being repaid when a permanent, long-term lender steps in. In such a situation, the construction lender will negotiate with the permanent lender as well as the borrower.

In certain types of project financings, a limited partnership may be formed for the sole purpose of constructing, say, a power plant. The general partner's liability is normally unlimited; however, for tax and other reasons, a lender may agree that it will look only to the partnership's assets for repayment of a loan. In such a case, the lender would need to assure itself that the limited partnership has sufficient resources to repay the loan. Such resources include, for example, fees from the sale of goods or services provided by the enterprise. The nature of the partnership's contracts for the sale of goods or services will therefore be of concern to the lender.

In all of these examples, the lender has a legitimate interest in seeing that the borrower's relationships with third parties will not adversely affect the loan.

Commitment to Make a Loan

A loan agreement may be preceded by a *term sheet*, which is a letter outlining the terms and conditions on which the lender will lend. A commitment to make a loan need not be in writing to be enforceable; but an oral promise may be difficult to enforce, because reasonable people may have honest differences in their recollections of what was said. However, a jury may award damages for breach of an oral loan commitment, as in the following case.

A CASE IN POINT	SUMMARY

**CASE 24.1
LANDES
CONSTRUCTION CO.,
INC. v. ROYAL BANK
OF CANADA**
United States Court of
Appeals for the Ninth Circuit
833 F.2d 1365
(9th Cir. 1987).

FACTS   An officer of the Royal Bank of Canada made an oral promise to lend the Landes Construction Company funds to purchase real property for development. He allegedly said, over dinner, "We are going to lend you $10 million for this project." The bank subsequently maintained that no such commitment had been made and refused to provide the loan. Landes Construction was unable to obtain alternative financing and forfeited a $3 million deposit. It sued the bank for breach of contract. Landes Construction presented evidence at trial that it had lost between $29 million and $79.6 million in profits. The jury awarded Landes Construction $18.5 million.

ISSUE PRESENTED   Is an oral agreement to lend money enforceable?

SUMMARY OF OPINION   The U.S. Court of Appeals upheld the jury verdict, even though it characterized the trial as "little more than a swearing contest." The jury verdict, it said, was supported by substantial evidence. Neither party disputed that various meetings occurred, that the bank had advanced $3 million, that these funds went to the seller, or that Landes Construction was the buyer named in the purchase agreement. The bank's arguments against the verdict centered on what inferences should be drawn from this evidence. One reasonable inference, the court concluded, was that the bank promised to lend Landes Construction the $10 million for the project. The only possible error of law that the court found was admission of evidence of lost profits. This alleged error, however, was harmless, according to the court.

RESULT   The jury award of $18.5 million for breach of a promise to lend was valid.

In response to cases like *Landes Construction,* state legislatures have proposed, and at least one has adopted, legislation specifically requiring loan commitments that exceed a threshold dollar amount to be in writing in order to be enforceable. Even in the absence of such legislation, a prudent lender will use a written term sheet or commitment letter to specify the terms of a proposed loan (including the amount, the interest

ETHICAL CONSIDERATION

Managers should be careful not to make oral promises that they cannot, or will not, perform. The business environment is always changing, and it is better to qualify one's statements than to make a strong commitment today that may be regretted tomorrow.

Managers should recognize that many types of oral contracts are binding. When there is no independent witness to an oral contract, a contracting party may be tempted to alter his or her version of the facts, leading to a contest of "your word against mine." This type of behavior is clearly unethical.

rate, fees, and repayment provisions) and to disclaim any obligation to lend until additional investigation is completed, additional terms and conditions are negotiated, and formal documentation is signed.

Description of the Loan

A loan agreement contains the lender's promise to lend a specified amount of money. Frequently, this will be the only promise that the lender will make in the loan agreement. The loan agreement also describes the mechanics by which funds will be disbursed, the rate of interest to be charged, the manner of computing such interest, and the repayment terms.

Mechanics of Funding   The funds are usually sent by wire transfer to an account specified by the borrower. If the timing is important, the borrower will want to discuss with the lender the logistical details of the loan agreement, such as the lender's deadline for sending wire transfers. The logistics may become critical if the lender and the borrower are in different time zones or if there are multiple lenders, as in a syndicated loan.

Interest Rates   Interest rates may be fixed or *floating*, that is, fluctuating throughout the life of the loan according to the interest rate that the lender would pay if it borrowed the funds in order to relend them. Fixed-rate term loans from insurance companies are common; banks generally prefer a floating rate. The floating rate may be pegged to the bank's *prime rate*, that is, the

lowest published rate of interest at which the bank lends to its best and most creditworthy commercial customers. Because a bank may lend money at a rate that is less than its so-called prime rate, banks often use the terms *base rate* or *reference rate*. Some banks include in their definition an explicit statement that the prime (or base or reference) rate is not the bank's best or lowest rate. The floating rate may be expressed either as a percentage of the prime rate (such as 110% of the prime rate) or, more commonly, as the sum of the prime rate and a specified number of percentage points (such as the prime rate plus 10%).

Alternatively, the floating rate may be pegged to the London Interbank Offered Rate (LIBOR) or to the certificate of deposit (CD) rate. These rates are based on the theoretical cost that a bank incurs to obtain, for a given period of time, the funds it will lend. To this cost is added a spread (or margin) to arrive at the actual interest rate. Frequently, a loan agreement will offer prime-rate, LIBOR, and CD-rate options for the borrower to select during the life of the loan.

The *London Interbank Offered Rate (LIBOR)* interest rate is based on the cost of borrowing offshore U.S. dollars in the global interbank market, which nowadays is centered in several locations in addition to London. Deposits made through the interbank offering market are generally for periods of 1, 2, 3, 6, 9, or 12 months; LIBOR loans are made for corresponding periods. At the end of an interest period, the borrower may elect to (1) roll over the LIBOR loan, that is, to continue it for another interest period; (2) repay the loan; or (3) convert it to a loan based on a different interest rate.

The *certificate of deposit (CD) rate* is based on the average of the bid rates quoted to the bank by dealers in the secondary market for the purchase at face value of certificates of deposit of the bank in a given amount and for a given term. CD-rate loans are commonly available for interest periods of 30, 60, 90, or 180 days.

Computation of Interest   Interest is generally computed on a daily basis according to one of several methods. Under the *365/360 method*, the nominal annual interest rate is divided by 360, and the resulting daily rate is then multiplied by the outstanding principal amount and the actual number of days in the payment period. Thus, for a year of 365 or 366 days, the actual rate of interest will be greater than the nominal annual rate.

Under the *365/365 method*, the daily rate is determined by dividing the nominal annual interest rate by

365 (or 366, in leap years), then this daily rate is multiplied by the outstanding principal amount and the actual number of days in the payment period.

Under the *360/360 method,* it is assumed that all months have 30 days; thus the monthly interest amounts are always the same.

The method used to compute interest is significant when large principal amounts are involved. It may also be significant if the lender or the loan is subject to state *usury* laws, which limit the maximum rate of interest that may be charged. National banks and other specified classes of lenders are subject to federal legislation that preempts state usury laws; and many states permit higher interest rates for exempt commercial transactions over a given dollar amount. Unless a state or federal exemption applies, lenders and borrowers should analyze whether a loan is usurious by virtue of its terms and conditions. For example, compensation paid for a loan, such as commitment fees, expenses, and prepayment penalties, may be deemed to constitute interest.

Repayment Terms A revolving loan may be repaid from time to time at the borrower's discretion, subject to a final maturity date when all sums outstanding become due and payable. In a term loan, the lender may require the entire principal to be repaid in one lump sum upon maturity or in equal or unequal installments.

Term-loan agreements and revolving-loan agreements may also require mandatory prepayment when certain events occur. For example, in a receivables and inventory line of credit, a prepayment will be required if the level of receivables and/or inventory supporting the outstanding borrowings drops. Other events that may mandate a prepayment are a sale of assets outside the ordinary course of business or financial earnings above a specified level.

Asset-based Loans In structuring a loan agreement, the fact that a loan is secured or unsecured is not particularly significant, except in certain types of asset-based financing in which the amount lent is determined according to the levels of assets available from time to time. One example of an asset-based loan is a revolving line of credit based on receivables, inventory, or both. Subject to certain criteria as to what inventory or receivables are eligible—that is, acceptable to the lender—the borrower borrows against such assets, and repays such loans on a revolving basis out of collections of the receivables generated from the sale of inventory. Sometimes, payments may be made directly to the lender

through such mechanisms as a locked-box or blocked account, which allow the lender to take the outstanding loan repayments out of the proceeds collected, before they are distributed to the borrower.

Representations and Warranties

Before committing to make a loan, a lender will investigate the potential borrower's financial condition and creditworthiness. It will also require the borrower to confirm:

- The legal status of the borrower, including, in the case of a corporation, its proper incorporation and good standing
- That corporate and other actions have authorized the proposed borrowing
- That regulatory and other approvals that might be required for the borrowing have been obtained
- That there are no court orders or contracts that would be in conflict with the loan agreement
- Whether the borrower is involved in any litigation
- That the borrower has good and marketable title to all of its assets, including any assets that constitute collateral for the loan
- That the loan agreement is legal, valid, and binding
- That no default has occurred or would result from entering into the loan agreement.

The purpose of these representations and warranties is to specify the assumptions on which the lender is willing to lend. In the negotiation process, the representations and warranties serve as a checklist of major areas of investigation by the lender. They also provide a framework for the borrower to examine its legal and financial position.

Qualifications Often, a borrower will state that a representation is true to the best of its knowledge. The borrower will want to be held accountable only for what it knows, not for what it does not know. The lender will want the borrower to take steps to ascertain the accuracy of its representations. The risk of a representation proving to be untrue is usually placed on the borrower rather than the lender. Any qualification based on the borrower's knowledge is therefore likely to be phrased in terms of what the borrower either knows or should know after diligent inquiry. It may include a definition of the appropriate standard of diligence.

In the loan agreement, the borrower states that the representations and warranties are true and complete as of the date of the loan agreement. They do not apply prospectively. However, the loan agreement may provide that if advances are to be made, the representations and warranties will be updated as of the time of the advances.

Truthfulness of Representations   Before a disbursement is made under the loan agreement, the lender will require an opinion of counsel and a certification by an independent public accountant, confirming the representations made by the borrower. The lender's obligation to continue to lend will likewise be conditioned upon the continuing truthfulness of the representations in the loan agreement.

Conditions to Closing

Authority to Approve the Loan   The lender will require evidence that the borrower's internal requirements for approving the loan have been met. It may require copies of the relevant corporate resolutions, with a certification by the corporate secretary. It may also require certification of the incumbency of the officers authorized to execute the loan agreement.

Completion of Documents   The loan agreement is typically only one of several documents that must be signed in connection with a loan. The lender will also require a promissory note and, if the loan is secured, a security agreement and financing statements.

Payment of Fees   Some fees, such as commitment fees, must be paid before any funds are disbursed.

Other Conditions   Other conditions may apply in certain circumstances. For example, in the case of a term loan to finance a merger or acquisition, the lender will condition any disbursement on the consummation of the merger or acquisition.

Regulatory approval may be required because of the nature of the borrower's business. In such cases, the particular permits and approvals that must be obtained or issued before the lender is willing to disburse funds will be enumerated.

Lenders are becoming increasingly concerned about the liability they may face when real property held by them, either as security or outright after a foreclosure, is required to comply with environmental cleanup laws. The lender may, therefore, require an opinion of environmental counsel, an environmental audit by qualified consultants and engineers, and indemnity agreements with the borrower and with any third parties that may be responsible for the environmental condition of the property.

Conditions Precedent

If the basic assumptions and facts upon which the lender has relied change materially after a commitment to lend has been made, the lender will need to reevaluate the loan. It may (1) refuse to advance the funds committed; (2) refuse to advance additional funds if some disbursements have already been made; or (3) accelerate the maturity of the loan. The loan agreement will specify the conditions that must be met before the lender's obligations arise under the agreement. These are known as *conditions precedent.*

Covenants

Covenants are the borrower's promises to the lender that it will or will not take specific actions as long as either a commitment or a loan is outstanding. If a covenant is breached, the lender is free to terminate the loan.

Whereas the lender's obligation is simply to make the loan once the stated conditions are met, the list of obligations imposed upon the borrower can be quite lengthy. The borrower's obligations may also affect nonparties to the loan agreement. For example, the lender may require that the borrower and its subsidiaries maintain a specified net worth, computed on a consolidated basis. Because the subsidiaries are not parties to the loan agreement, that agreement cannot directly impose such an obligation on them. However, the borrower may be required to cause its subsidiaries to comply with the covenant. Such a covenant assumes that the borrower is in a position to influence the nonparties' actions.

Affirmative Covenants   *Affirmative covenants* state what the borrower undertakes to do, for example, maintain its corporate existence, pay taxes, maintain insurance, and comply with applicable laws.

The borrower is usually required to keep the lender informed of its financial condition and to submit unaudited financial reports monthly or quarterly and audited financial reports annually. Financial tests relating to income statement and balance sheet items may be imposed. A catchall covenant will require the borrower to inform the lender of any material adverse change in its operations or financial condition.

Negative Covenants   *Negative covenants* state what the borrower undertakes not to do, for example, not to incur additional debt beyond a specified amount, and not to grant liens other than those specifically enumerated or those arising in the ordinary course of business. (A *lien* is a claim on property that secures a debt owed by the owner of the property.)

Scope   Covenants are generally heavily negotiated. Financial covenants, because they are based on projections of future financial results, require flexibility in long-term loans. A covenant will be resisted by the borrower if it is perceived to interfere with the borrower's control and operation of its businesses. A lender sensitive to borrowers' fears of lender control will draft its covenants carefully to impose no more control than is needed to protect the lender's right to be repaid. For example, a provision that effectively gives the lender the right to select the borrower's management may be difficult to justify. Lawsuits, some resulting in multimillion-dollar punitive judgments against unduly interfering lenders, have alerted lenders to the need for caution in drafting and enforcing such provisions.

Events of Default

A loan agreement lists the events that will trigger the lender's right to terminate (or *call*) the loan, accelerate the repayment obligations, and, if the loan is secured, take possession of the property securing the loan. These events, known as the *events of default*, may be defined by the parties to the loan agreement. They usually include (1) failure to pay on time any amounts due under the loan agreement; (2) making false or misleading representations or warranties in connection with the loan; and (3) failing to live up to any covenant in the loan agreement. In addition, if the borrower, any subsidiary, or a guarantor enters into bankruptcy, the lender will want to put its obligations on hold while it considers the next course of action.

Some events of default are outside the control of the borrower. For example, if a loan is made to a corporation on the strength of the lender's confidence in a particular individual's management ability, the death of that individual may be included as an event of default. Similarly, involuntary liens or legal judgments against the borrower, although more or less outside of the bor-

rower's control, change the fundamental bases on which a loan was originally made. A loan agreement cannot require the borrower to take or not take actions that are outside of its control. Nevertheless, because the consequences of certain events, regardless of how they are caused, are of concern to the lender, the lender will want to include these events in the default section.

Cross-Default   A *cross-default* provision provides that any breach by the borrower under any other loan agreement constitutes an event of default under this loan agreement. A borrower will want to limit the provision to apply only to a serious breach of a loan agreement covering the loan of an amount greater than a specified minimum. The borrower may also want the lender to agree that the borrower's breach of another agreement will not constitute an event of default under this agreement unless the other lender terminates its loan on account of the breach.

The lender, on the other hand, will want a broad definition of the events of default. It will want the right to join with other creditors to negotiate some form of protection for its position as soon as the borrower's financial condition deteriorates.

Provided the borrower does not seek bankruptcy, the lender and borrower are free to renegotiate the terms and conditions on which the loan will remain outstanding. For example, the lender may agree to continue the loan in exchange for new or additional collateral, new guaranties, or a higher rate of interest. Such negotiations are a practical alternative to the more drastic measure of calling, that is, terminating, the loan. (If the borrower seeks bankruptcy, the lender's efforts to restructure the loan will be subject to the jurisdiction of the bankruptcy court.)

Remedies for Default

The default section sets forth the remedies for default. These remedies are optional for the lender. If the lender *waives* a default—that is, decides not to exercise any of its remedies—it may exact additional consideration from the borrower, in the form of an increase in the interest rate or additional security.

It is prudent to set forth a waiver in writing to avoid any misunderstanding as to the scope of the waiver and the terms and conditions upon which it is being granted, including any additional obligations that the borrower will now be expected to satisfy. In lender liability lawsuits, express terms in a loan agreement have been found to be superseded by oral or written communications between the lender and the borrower, or by the actions of the borrower or lender. Reducing understandings to writing and avoiding actions that may be inconsistent with the written documents will avoid surprises and failed expectations on both sides.

Secured Transactions under the UCC

The mechanics of taking a security interest in personal property and fixtures, and the consequences of taking such a security interest, are governed by Article 9 of the Uniform Commercial Code (UCC), which has been adopted with certain variations in all states. Before Article 9 was adopted, such common law security devices as the pledge, the chattel mortgage, the conditional sale, the trust receipt, and the factor's lien were all governed by different rules. Article 9 of the UCC was intended to provide a unified, comprehensive scheme for all types of *secured transactions,* that is, loans or other transactions secured by collateral put up by the borrower. Article 9 applies "to any transaction (regardless of its form) which is intended to create a security interest in personal property or fixtures including goods, documents, instruments, general intangibles, chattel paper or accounts."

Terminology

Part 1 of Article 9 defines terms. In place of the various common law security devices, the UCC uses the single term *security interest* to signify any interest in personal property or fixtures that are used as collateral to secure payment or the performance of an obligation. The parties to a secured transaction are (1) the *debtor,* that is, the person who owes payment or other performance of the obligation secured, whether or not that person owns or has rights in the collateral; and (2) the *secured party,* that is, the lender, seller, or other person in whose favor there is a security interest. A *security agreement* is an agreement that creates or provides for a security interest.

Formal Requisites

Part 2 of Article 9 prescribes the formal requisites for creating an enforceable security interest and describes the rights of the parties to a security agreement. If the se-

cured party takes possession of the collateral, an oral agreement is sufficient to create a security interest; otherwise, a signed security agreement containing a description of the collateral is required. For a security interest to be enforceable, the UCC requires that value has been given in exchange for it, and that the debtor has rights in the collateral. These requirements do not have to be fulfilled in any particular order. When all of the requirements have been met, a security interest is said to have *attached.*

Rights and Remedies

The remainder of Article 9 sets forth the rights of the secured party as against other creditors of the debtor; the rules for *perfecting* a security interest, that is, making it valid as against other creditors of the debtor; and the remedies available to a secured party when a debtor defaults.

Scope of Article 9

Article 9 provides a single source of reference for most consensual security interests; but some security interests are outside of its scope. Article 9 does not apply to liens on real property. Various state and federal laws preempt the UCC in the areas of ship mortgages, mechanic's liens, and aircraft liens. Notices of security interests in trademarks are commonly filed in the Patent and Trademark Office, in addition to being perfected as general intangibles under the UCC. Article 9 does not apply to security interests subject to a landlord's lien, to a lien given by statute or other rule of law for services or materials, or to a right of setoff. (A *right of setoff* permits one party to deduct automatically from payments due the other party amounts due the first party.) Security interests in securities are governed by Article 8 of the UCC.

Security Agreements

A security agreement identifies the parties and the property to be used as collateral. It may also specify the debtor's obligations and the lender's remedies in case of default.

Parties to the Agreement

Security agreements typically use the UCC terminology to identify the parties. In a loan transaction, the secured party is the lender. The debtor is the borrower, if it owns the collateral or if the owner has authorized it to use the property for collateral. If the third-party owner acts as a guarantor of the borrower's obligation, it may also be referred to as the debtor. (Guaranties are discussed later in this chapter.)

Granting Clause

Unless the security interest is a possessory interest (traditionally called a *pledge*), the security agreement must be signed by the debtor and must expressly grant a security interest in some specified property. The standard operative words are: "The debtor hereby grants to the secured party a security interest in . . . ." No precise form is required by the UCC; however, the collateral must be described.

Description of the Collateral

The description of the collateral need not be specific, as long as it reasonably identifies what is described. Loans to finance the purchase of specific property, such as an equipment loan, will typically be secured by the property purchased; the security agreement will contain a specific description of such property.

For example, a working capital loan may be secured by receivables and inventory, with the inventory described as "any and all goods, merchandise, and other personal property, wherever located or in transit, that are held for sale or lease, furnished under any contract of service, or held as raw materials, work in process, supplies, or materials used or consumed in the debtor's business." Frequently, a secured party will take a security interest in all of the assets of the debtor—not only fixed assets, inventory, and receivables, but also trademarks, trade names, goodwill, licenses, books, and records. In such cases, the collateral may be described as all tangible and intangible property that, taken together, is intended to preserve the value of the debtor as a going concern.

After-Acquired Property   *After-acquired property* is property that the debtor acquires after the execution of the security agreement. After-acquired assets may be included in the security agreement either in addition to, or as replacements of, currently owned assets. A security interest in after-acquired collateral will attach when the debtor acquires rights in the collateral, assuming that

the other prerequisites for attachment have previously been met.

Proceeds   The UCC provides that, unless otherwise agreed, a security agreement gives the secured party a security interest in the proceeds if the collateral is sold, exchanged, collected, or otherwise disposed of. The security interest is equally effective against cash, accounts, or whatever else is received from the transaction. This feature makes a security interest created under Article 9 a *floating lien.*

Debtor's Obligations

The debtor is obligated to repay the debt and to pay interest and related fees, charges, and expenses. In addition, the debtor will have nonmonetary obligations, such as obligations to maintain prescribed standards of financial well-being, measured by net worth, cash flow, and debt coverage (the ratio of debt to equity). These obligations are typically set forth in detail in a loan agreement or a promissory note, although occasionally they may be found in a security agreement.

Cross-Collateralization

The collateral for one loan may be used to secure obligations under another loan. This is done by means of a *cross-collateralization* provision—sometimes called a *dragnet clause*—in the security agreement. For example, a lender extending an inventory and receivables line of credit to a borrower may insist that the line be secured not only by inventory and receivables, but also by equipment owned by the borrower and already held by the lender as collateral for an equipment loan. Thus, if the lender forecloses on the equipment, any proceeds in excess of the amounts owed under the equipment loan will be available to pay down the inventory and receivables line of credit. Similarly, if the equipment loan is cross-collateralized with collateral for the inventory and receivables line of credit, any proceeds realized from foreclosure of the inventory and receivables will be available to pay down the equipment loan.

Remedies for Default

The remedies described in a security agreement track the rights and procedures set forth in Article 9. After default, the secured party has the right to take possession of the collateral, without judicial process if this can be done without breach of the peace. The secured party must then dispose of the collateral at a public or private sale. If there is a surplus from the sale of the collateral, the secured party is required to return it to the debtor. If there is a deficiency, the debtor remains liable for that amount. The proceeds from the sale must be applied in this order: (1) to the reasonable expenses of foreclosure and, if provided for in the agreement, reasonable attorney's fees and legal expenses; (2) to the satisfaction of the obligations secured; and (3) to the satisfaction of indebtedness secured by a subordinate security interest, if a written demand for such satisfaction is timely received.

Although the UCC establishes a framework within which the lender may exercise its remedies, some details must be provided for by contract. For example, the parties may agree to apply the proceeds of a foreclosure sale to attorney's fees and legal expenses, or they may agree that the debtor will assemble the collateral and make it available to the secured party at a designated place. All such provisions are subject to the requirement that the secured party's disposition of the collateral must be commercially reasonable. This term is not defined in the UCC, but it is generally interpreted to require conformity with prevailing standards and to prevent one party from taking undue advantage of another. However, the secured party and the debtor are free to fashion a mutually acceptable standard of commercial reasonableness; and security agreements typically contain a description of such standards.

Perfecting a Security Interest

In order to protect its rights in the collateral, a lender must ensure that its security interest is perfected, that is, valid against other creditors of the debtor and against a trustee in bankruptcy of the debtor. The UCC does not define perfection; instead, it describes the situations in which an unperfected security interest will be subordinated to the rights of third parties. For example, a security interest is subordinate to the rights of "a person who becomes a lien creditor before the security interest is perfected." Subordination to lien creditors means in effect that the security interest is not valid against the debtor's trustee in bankruptcy.

Methods of Perfection

Security interests can be perfected by possession of the collateral, by filing a financing statement, or automatically.

By Possession A security interest in letters of credit and advices of credit, goods, instruments (other than certificated securities, which are covered by Article 8 of the UCC—see below), money, negotiable documents, or chattel paper is perfected by the secured party's taking possession of the collateral.

By Filing For other types of collateral, perfection is accomplished by filing a financing statement. Standard printed forms, known as *UCC-1 forms*, are widely available for this purpose.

Automatic Perfection Some security interests require neither possession nor filing for perfection. For example, a *purchase-money security interest* in consumer goods (created when the seller of consumer goods lends the buyer the money with which to buy them) is automatically perfected. Under certain circumstances, a security interest in instruments or negotiable instruments is temporarily perfected without filing or possession. Automatic perfection is of limited duration, however, and it must be followed by possession or filing if perfection is to survive for a longer period.

Uncertificated Securities The once fundamental distinction between possessory and nonpossessory security interests has become blurred by the introduction of uncertificated, or book-entry, securities. In 1967, the U.S. Treasury Department promulgated procedures for the issuance and maintenance of book-entry Treasury securities; other agencies, including the Federal National Mortgage Association and the Federal Home Loan Mortgage Corporation, followed suit. These agencies no longer issue securities in certificate form. Even when the securities are in the form of bearer instruments (meaning that they are payable to the holder thereof) or registered instruments (meaning that they are payable to the registered owner), the owners of the securities seldom have possession of the instruments; the securities are frequently held in brokerage accounts or mutual funds. Article 8 of the UCC, which governs investment securities, was revised in 1977 to provide for the creation and perfection of security interests in certificated and uncertificated securities; and these topics were removed from Article 9.

Filing Procedure

The fundamental concept behind perfection by filing is to provide notice "to the world" that assets of one person are subject to the security interest of another. If a security interest is not perfected by possession, the collateral remains in the debtor's possession and control. This occurs, for example, when the collateral is intangible (such as accounts), or when possession by the secured party is impractical (as in the case of inventory). A centralized system gives effective public notice that property in the possession and under the apparent control of the debtor is actually subject to the rights of another. The filing system enables a prospective creditor to determine whether in claiming its rights to such assets it will be competing with other creditors or with a trustee in bankruptcy. It also enables a purchaser of goods to determine whether the seller's creditors have any claims against the goods. (It should be noted that, under certain circumstances, a purchaser of goods is protected from liens on such goods created by the seller; for example, consumers are protected from inventory liens on a seller's goods by UCC Section 9-307(1).)

Where to File   The proper place to file in order to perfect a security interest is in the office of the secretary of state in the state in which the property is located or, in the case of intangible property, in which the debtor is located. A security interest in collateral closely associated with real property, such as fixtures, growing crops, timber, or minerals, must be filed in the office in which a mortgage on the real estate would be recorded, usually the county recorder's office in the county where the real property is located.

What to File   To perfect a nonpossessory security interest in personal property, a financing statement must be filed. The financing statement merely gives notice that a financing transaction is being or is about to be entered into, without describing the transaction. It need only contain the signatures of the parties to the transaction, their addresses, and a description of the kinds of collateral in which a security interest has been or may be granted. If a financing statement covers crops grown or to be grown or goods that are or are to become fixtures, the UCC also requires a legal description of the land concerned.

When to File   A financing statement may be filed in advance of the transaction or the security agreement. This is important because, under the UCC, a security interest is perfected when the statement is filed. Thus, the first secured party to file has priority over other parties with security interests in the same debtor's property, unless special priority rules apply, as in the case of purchase-money security interests.

◆ Equipment Leasing

In order to conserve its working capital, a company may desire to lease the equipment it needs, rather than purchase it. Leasing sometimes offers an attractive alternative to borrowing funds to purchase the equipment because a leasing company may be willing to provide more lenient terms than a bank or other lender. A leasing company may also be willing to accept a greater credit risk than banks, but it will probably charge higher interest rates than a bank to accommodate the greater

---

VIEW FROM CYBERSPACE

ELECTRONIC FILING UNDER ARTICLE 9

The American Law Institute (ALI) has proposed amendments to Article 9 to make its filing provisions medium neutral. Because the record will not be limited to paper or other tangible media, states will be free to implement electronic searching. To facilitate electronic filing, revised Article 9 would eliminate the requirement that the debtor sign the financing statement. However, the secured party would have to be identified, and the debtor would be required to authorize the statement indicating the collateral covered by the financing statement. The ALI anticipated presenting the final draft to state legislatures in 1999.

credit risk involved. A newer enterprise may sometimes be asked for a security deposit or personal guaranty in connection with an equipment lease.

When equipment is leased, three parties are involved: the seller of the equipment, the leasing company, and the user of the equipment. The user determines its needs and negotiates a purchase price for the equipment, then engages a leasing company to purchase the equipment and lease it to the user. The manufacturer or seller of the equipment may lease it to the user, either directly or through a leasing subsidiary, but third-party leasing companies are more frequently used.

Differences from True Lease

An equipment lease that serves the purpose of financing is known as a *finance lease.* A finance-lease agreement is a lengthy document that differs from a true lease in several ways. It gives the lessor some degree of control over the use, alteration, and location of the equipment. It prohibits major changes in the user's business operations without the consent of the lessor, unless the lessee first repays the lessor in full. The lessee is required to keep the equipment in good repair and to insure it against loss or damage. The lessor is given a security interest in the equipment, and it may foreclose and sell the equipment in the event of default by the user. In addition to the terms of the lease agreement, the rights and remedies of the lessor and lessee are governed by Article 9 of the Uniform Commercial Code.

For accounting purposes, a finance lease is treated as a long-term debt of the lessee, who is deemed to own the leased equipment; the lessee may therefore enjoy tax benefits such as depreciation deductions. The lessee may have the right to purchase the equipment at the end of the lease term. In this case, the lease will often provide that the purchase price shall be the fair market value of the equipment at that time.

 ## Guaranties

A *guaranty* is an undertaking by one person, the *guarantor,* to become liable for the obligation of another person, the *primary debtor.* A guaranty allows the party that is to receive payment to look to the guarantor in the event the primary debtor fails to pay. The guarantor can be an individual, a corporation, a partnership, or any other type of entity willing to lend its credit support to another's obligation. The most common form of guaranty is a guaranty that indebtedness or other payment obligations of another will be paid when due. A less common form is a guaranty that specified nonpayment obligations will be performed; this is sometimes referred to as a *guaranty of performance.* The type of guaranty and the duties of the guarantor will be determined by the language of the guaranty instrument. The Statute of Frauds requires that a guaranty be in writing to be enforceable.

In lending transactions, a guaranty is often required when, after completing its credit analysis, the lender determines that the credit of the borrower is not sufficient to support the requested loan. The lender will evaluate the credit of each guarantor and decide whether to make the loan based on the combined credit of the borrower and the guarantors. Also, a lender may require guaranties from officers, directors, or shareholders of a borrower, especially when the borrower is a closely held corporation. A lender may seek to protect its position under a guaranty by requiring that the guarantor refrain from incurring additional debt or granting liens on its assets.

Payment versus Collection

Under a *guaranty of payment,* the guarantor's obligation to pay the lender is triggered, immediately and automatically, when the primary debtor fails to make a payment when due. In contrast, under a *guaranty of collection,* the guarantor becomes obliged to pay only after the lender has attempted unsuccessfully to collect the amount due from the primary debtor. With a collection guaranty, the lender will generally have to commence a lawsuit and take other steps to collect a debt before calling on the guarantor to pay (unless the primary debtor is insolvent or is otherwise clearly unable to pay). This condition makes the enforcement of collection guaranties so cumbersome and expensive that lenders almost always require payment guaranties.

Limited versus Unlimited

The amount of a guarantor's liability under a guaranty may be either limited or unlimited. In the case of a *limited guaranty,* the maximum amount of the guarantor's liability is expressly stated in the guaranty instrument. This maximum liability is usually a specific dollar amount, although it can be based on other criteria, such as a percentage of the primary debtor's total indebtedness to the lender.

Continuing versus Restricted

A *restricted guaranty* is enforceable only with respect to a specified transaction or series of transactions. A guaranty that covers all future obligations of the primary debtor to the lender is referred to as a *continuing guaranty*. The objective of the continuing guaranty is to make the guarantor liable for any debt incurred at any time by the primary debtor, regardless of whether the debt was contemplated at the time the guaranty was entered into. Lenders naturally favor continuing guaranties over restricted guaranties.

Revocation In many jurisdictions, a continuing guaranty may be revoked by the guarantor during his or her lifetime. The effect of such a revocation is to prevent the guarantor from becoming liable for debts incurred by the primary debtor in connection with transactions not yet entered into. Revocation also results from the death of the guarantor; however, the guarantor's estate will remain liable for debts incurred by the primary debtor prior to the guarantor's death.

Discharging the Guarantor A lender who makes a guaranteed loan must avoid any actions that would have the effect of discharging the guarantor, such as altering the terms of the agreement between the lender and the primary debtor (for example, increasing the interest rate on the loan or increasing the amount of the scheduled payments); extending the time for payment of the loan or renewing the indebtedness; or releasing or impairing the lender's rights with respect to collateral pledged by the primary debtor. A well-drafted guaranty can alleviate some of these potential pitfalls. However, the best approach is for the lender to obtain the consent of the guarantor before making any material change to the arrangement between the lender and the primary debtor.

Fraudulent Conveyances

A guaranty may be attacked as a fraudulent conveyance under the federal Bankruptcy Code or state fraudulent transfer statutes. A *fraudulent conveyance* is the direct or indirect transfer of assets to a third party with the actual intent to, or the effect of, hindering, delaying, or defrauding creditors by putting the assets out of the creditors' reach. A guaranty may be a fraudulent conveyance if it confers no benefit on the guarantor but makes the guarantor's assets unavailable to creditors other than the party receiving the guaranty. For example, if the guarantor did not receive fair value in exchange for giving its guaranty and the guarantor was insolvent at the time it gave its guaranty, or if the guarantor was rendered insolvent or left with unreasonably small capital as a result of giving its guaranty, the party receiving the guarantee may have an unfair advantage over other creditors of the guarantor. In such a case, the other creditors would be able to invalidate the guaranty. These issues must be carefully examined by the lender before accepting a guaranty.

Upstream Guaranty An *upstream guaranty* occurs when subsidiaries guarantee the parent company's debt or pledge their assets as security for the parent's debt. An upstream guaranty may be found fraudulent if the guarantor received none of the loan proceeds or received an inadequate amount compared to the liability it incurred. Other creditors of the subsidiary (and the creditor's minority shareholders, if the subsidiary is less than wholly owned by the parent) may claim that the lender, as the beneficiary of the guaranty, received an unfair advantage at the other creditors' expense.

Leveraged Buyouts Leveraged buyouts, in which acquisition of a company is financed largely through debt, may be subject to attack as fraudulent conveyances. For example, if a leveraged buyout is structured so that a newly formed corporation will acquire the stock of the target company using proceeds from a loan, the lender's source of repayment will be dividends paid from the target company to the borrower. In order to ensure that such a source of repayment will be available, the lender may require the target company to give a guaranty, which may or may not be secured by assets of the target company. Alternatively, the lender may require a merger between the target company and the borrower. Such guaranties or mergers will be invalidated if both (1) the target company did not receive a reasonably equivalent value; and (2) the target company was left insolvent, with assets that were unreasonably small in relation to its business, or with insufficient working capital.

Preferences

A transfer from a debtor to an outsider creditor that results in a reduction in the guaranty liability of an insolvent insider may be a voidable preference if it occurs within one year of the date the insider files bankruptcy.[2] For example, suppose that on February 1, 1997, ABC Corp. borrows $1 million from Friendly Bank and that Henri-Claude, a major shareholder of ABC Corp., guarantees the loan. ABC Corp. makes a $100,000 payment to Friendly Bank on March 1, 1998. On October 1, 1998, Henri-Claude files bankruptcy. Henri-Claude's creditors will be able to set aside the $100,000 payment because it reduced Henri-Claude's guarantor liability dollar for dollar and thereby preferred Friendly Bank by paying off part of Henri-Claude's debt to Friendly Bank with funds not available to other creditors of Henri-Claude.

 ## Subordination

A *debt subordination* is an agreement whereby one or more creditors of a common debtor agree to defer payment of their claims until another creditor of the same debtor is fully paid. The indebtedness that is subordinated under the agreement is referred to as the subordinated or *junior debt.* The indebtedness that benefits from the subordination is called the *senior debt.*

The primary purpose of a debt subordination is to protect the senior creditor in the event of the debtor's insolvency. As long as the debtor is solvent, both the junior debt holder and the senior debt holder can expect to be paid. If the debtor becomes insolvent, there will be insufficient assets to satisfy all of its creditors. In such circumstances, creditors can expect to receive only a partial payment on their claims. In subordinating its claim, the holder of the junior debt agrees to yield its right of payment to the senior creditor until the senior creditor has been paid in full.

Corporations frequently use subordinated debt as a means of raising capital. The use of subordinated notes or subordinated debentures (long-term secured bonds) may have certain advantages over equity financing. For example, the interest payable on subordinated debt will be tax-deductible. In addition, the interest rate payable on subordinated debt is often less than the dividend rate that would have to be offered on comparable preferred stock.

Indebtedness to Insiders

When a borrower seeks short-term borrowings from a bank or other commercial lender, the lender will often require that the indebtedness of the borrower to insiders, such as officers, directors, and shareholders, be subordinated. This is especially the case when the borrower is a closely held corporation and the insider debt is significant in relation to the amount of the lender's loans.

Lien Subordination

A *lien subordination* is an agreement between two secured creditors whose respective security interests, liens, or mortgages attach to the same property. The subordinating party agrees that the lien of the other creditor shall have priority notwithstanding the relative priorities that the parties' liens would otherwise have under applicable law. Unlike debt subordination, a lien subordination does not limit the right of the subordinating party to accept payment from the debtor. Instead, the lien subordination has the effect of limiting the subordinating party's recourse to the collateral until the prior secured party's claim has been satisfied.

Equitable Subordination

A creditor's claim may be involuntarily postponed through application of the doctrine of *equitable subordination.* This doctrine was developed in bankruptcy law to prevent one creditor, through fraud or other wrongful conduct, from increasing its recovery at the expense of other creditors of the same debtor. The court will order that the creditor that acted wrongfully shall receive no payment from the debtor until the claims of all other creditors have been fully paid.

 ## Business Bankruptcies

There are two major types of business bankruptcies: liquidation under Chapter 7 and reorganization under

---

2. *See, e.g.,* Levit v. Ingersoll Rand Fin. Corp. (*In re* V. N. Deprizio Constr. Co.), 874 F.2d 1186 (7th Cir. 1989).

Chapter 11. (Adjustments of debts for individuals under Chapter 13 are covered in Chapter 19.) The pros and cons of filing bankruptcy, under Chapters 7 and 11, from the points of view of the debtor and the creditors, and out-of-court resolutions, called *workouts,* are discussed in the following sections.

 ## Chapter 7 Liquidations

A bankruptcy case is initiated by filing a petition. The filing of a bankruptcy petition automatically creates a *bankruptcy estate,* which consists of virtually all the debtor's existing assets. A trustee is appointed to administer the estate. In a Chapter 7 bankruptcy, sometimes called a *straight bankruptcy,* the trustee liquidates the estate and distributes the proceeds, first to secured creditors (to the extent of their collateral) and then in a prescribed order and pro rata within each level. The unencumbered funds are applied, first, to pay priority claims, such as bankruptcy administrative expenses, wages or benefits up to $2,000 per employee, consumer deposits up to $900, and most unsecured taxes; next, to pay general unsecured creditors (with timely filed claims coming before tardy ones); then, to pay noncompensatory fines or penalties; and, last, to pay legal interest on unsecured claims. In practice, the estate is rarely adequate to pay unsecured creditors even 50 cents on the dollar; and no-asset cases are quite common.

Individual Debtors

Individual debtors normally are *discharged*—that is, relieved—from bankruptcy (also called prepetition) obligations, except for nondischargeable debts such as (1) taxes; (2) educational loans; (3) spousal or child support; (4) fines or penalties; (5) drunk-driving liabilities; and (6) claims arising from fraud, theft, or willful and malicious injury. Punitive damages awarded on account of the debtor's fraudulent acquisition of money, property, services, or credit are also nondischargeable.[3] An individual who has filed under Chapter 7 can enter into a contract with a creditor (a *reaffirmation agreement*) whereby the debtor agrees to repay a debt even though the debt would otherwise be discharged in the

debtor's bankruptcy case. The creditor must file the reaffirmation agreement with the bankruptcy court, which has the power to disapprove it if the court finds that the agreement is not in the debtor's best interests.

From 1985 to 1997, Sears, Roebuck & Co. unlawfully dunned more than 200,000 consumers who had outstanding debt on Sears credit cards and had filed for bankruptcy protection. Sears persuaded them to sign reaffirmation agreements, but Sears failed to file the agreements with the bankruptcy courts. Sears entered into a settlement with the Federal Trade Commission in June 1997, whereby it agreed to refund $100 million to consumers for its improper credit card collection practices.[4] Sears also agreed to write off the unpaid portion of the balances on the invalid reaffirmation agreements.

There is a split in the circuit courts of appeals as to whether an individual debtor who has filed for protection under Chapter 7 may retain property that secures a loan if the debtor remains current on the loan payments without having to reaffirm the debt. The U.S. Court of Appeals for the Ninth Circuit held that a Chapter 7 debtor who was current on his car payments could retain a car financed by a credit union by making the loan payments specified in the loan agreement without having to reaffirm the debt.[5] The Second, Fourth, and Tenth Circuits reached the same result. In contrast, the Fifth, Seventh, and Eleventh Circuits have held that once a debtor decides to retain rather than surrender the property, the debtor must claim an exemption, redeem the property by paying off the debt, or reaffirm the debt.

Individual debtors under Chapters 7 and 13 are discussed further in Chapter 19.

Nonindividual Debtors

Chapter 7 does not provide a discharge for corporations, partnerships, or similar business entities. Once their assets are sold, these debtors essentially become defunct shells whose unpaid obligations have no significance. Thus, from the vantage point of the debtor firm's management, the only virtue of a liquidation may be that the task of selling property and paying creditors

---

3. Cohen v. de la Cruz, 118 S. Ct. 1212 (1998).

4. Robert Berner & Bruce Ingersoll, *Sears to Repay Card Holders $100 Million,* WALL ST. J., June 5, 1997, at A3.

5. McClellan Fed. Credit Union v. Parker (*In re* Parker), 139 F.3d 668 (9th Cir. 1998).

falls to a trustee. The principals of closely held companies are often better advised to avoid bankruptcy and to handle these chores themselves. Rather than adhering to the *pro rata* distribution model, they may wish to prefer some creditors by channeling funds first to those who are most likely to pursue them personally (such as holders of guaranties). Also, they may not want to expose earlier transactions (such as preferential payments) to scrutiny by a trustee, who can become a more troublesome foe than any of the company's creditors by invoking the avoiding powers discussed below.

 ## Chapter 11 Reorganizations

Chapter 11 is designed for reorganizing troubled businesses, from single-asset limited partnerships and joint ventures (such as Dow Corning, manufacturer of silicon breast implants) to huge publicly held corporations, such as the oil giant Texaco, the pharmaceutical manufacturer A. H. Robins, the retailer Federated Department Stores, or the building materials supplier Johns-Manville. The treatment of the debtor's creditors and holders of ownership interests and the future of its business are set forth in a plan developed by one or more of the parties. If the plan meets the statutory requirements and is confirmed by the court, it becomes a master contract that redefines the legal relationships among all who have claims against (or interests in) the debtor; it binds even those who do not consent to its terms.

The Plan

All plans divide claims and equity interests into separate classes according to their legal attributes. For example, lienholders' claims are classified by collateral and rank (often resulting in one claim per class, because each lien confers distinct rights and usually secures only one claim). Relevant priority claims (such as wages or consumer deposits) are put into discrete classes, separate from general unsecured claims. Holders of preferred shares are grouped separately from common shareholders.

A plan also must prescribe treatment for the claims and interests in each class. Some plans simply extend the time for repaying debts; others reduce the amounts payable. A reduction in the amount payable is known as a *composition*. In many cases, creditors exchange all or part of their claims for preferred or common stock or other ownership interests in the business, thereby diluting or extinguishing the rights of the prebankruptcy shareholders. Sometimes, the entire business will be sold free of claims, with creditors dividing the sale proceeds. A plan can even call for liquidation and distribution comparable to the Chapter 7 process. Unless they agree otherwise, priority claimants usually are entitled to full payment when the plan becomes effective, except that prepetition unsecured taxes may be paid in installments over six years from the assessment date, with interest at the market rate.

In addition, the plan must explain the intended means for its execution. Plans often provide for payments from cash on hand, future earnings, asset sales, new capital contributions, or some combination of sources.

Confirmation

To be confirmed, a plan must meet numerous statutory requirements. Some of the less technical requirements are discussed below.

Feasibility   The plan must be feasible. There is no point in replacing the debtor's existing obligations with a new set of obligations that the debtor cannot meet.

Best Interests of Creditors   Unless accepted unanimously, the plan must pass the *best interests of creditors test*. Dissenters must be given a bundle of rights with a current value at least as great as the distribution they would receive through a Chapter 7 liquidation.

Reorganization Bonus   It should be relatively easy to satisfy the fixed minimum standards for confirmation if the business has significant value as a going concern. In that case, the viability of a plan often turns upon how it proposes to split what might be labeled the reorganization bonus. This bonus or premium is the difference between the aggregate liquidation value of the assets and the worth of the business as an operating whole. Ordinarily, it must be distributed according to existing priorities. Unless it accepts less favorable treatment, each class of creditor is paid fully before any distribution is made to any junior class. Similarly, creditors are paid in full (with postconfirmation interest) before equity holders receive anything.

Disclosure Statement   Before deciding whether to accept the plan, creditors and shareholders are entitled to receive a disclosure statement that the court has found contains adequate information to enable them to make an informed judgment. This disclosure process largely displaces otherwise applicable laws and regulations governing the issuance and sale of securities, including the requirements of the Securities Act of 1933, described in Chapter 22.

Acceptance   A creditor class accepts the plan if the affirmative ballots represent a simple majority and represent two-thirds of the total claim amounts of those voting. An equity class accepts if the favorable ballots represent two-thirds of the voted interests.

Impaired Claims   If a plan impairs any class of claims, then it cannot be confirmed unless at least one impaired class accepts it (excluding favorable votes cast by insiders). Claims are considered *impaired* if the plan does not provide for full cash payment on its effective date and if it alters the creditors' legal, equitable, or contractual rights in any way (except by curing defaults and reinstating the maturity of the claim).

If the basic requirements discussed above are met and all impaired classes accept the plan, the plan should be confirmed.

Cram-Down Confirmation

Though rejected by a class, the plan can still be confirmed by a *cram down*, that is, confirmed over the objections of creditors. However, a cram down can occur only if the court finds that the plan does not discriminate unfairly and that it is fair and equitable. Although both phrases have technical meanings that are open to interpretation, it is the phrase "fair and equitable" that is more frequently the subject of debate. If the rejecting class consists of secured claims, the plan ordinarily can be found fair and equitable only if creditors will retain their liens until they receive full payment in cash of the secured claims. The cash payments must have a present value at least as great as the present value of the collateral. If the debtor elects to retain and use the creditor's collateral, the value of the collateral (and thus the secured claim) is the replacement value, that is, what the debtor would have to pay for comparable property.[6] For other creditors and equity holders, the plan will be con-

sidered fair and equitable only if no class junior to the naysayers will receive anything under the plan or if the rejecting class is to receive value equivalent to immediate payment in full.

Thus, to cram down a plan that would distribute stock in satisfaction of claims, the proponent must show that the stock will neither overpay nor underpay those who receive it. The value of the stock turns on the going-concern value of the business, which is often a controversial issue. When classes have not accepted a debt-for-stock plan, the confirmation hearing can easily become a battle among expert witnesses arguing over whether higher or lower multiples or multipliers should be used to capitalize the reorganized debtor's expected earnings, which are themselves subject to competing projections.

Plan Negotiations

Because confirmation by cram down is both difficult and uncertain, plan proponents frequently try to draft terms that will encourage broad acceptance. For the first 120 days (or for a longer or shorter time that the court may fix), only the debtor can propose a plan. After this exclusivity period expires, any party may propose a plan. Thus, a debtor who does not bargain reasonably may be faced with a competing plan that might be threatened or proposed by a major secured creditor or by the official committee that is appointed in Chapter 11 cases to represent the interests of unsecured creditors. Even if the debtor is the only party proposing a plan, an endorsement from the creditors' committee can be essential to obtain the creditor support necessary to achieve confirmation without a cram down. Taken together, these dynamics promote negotiation and accommodation among the interested parties. Most successful plans in large Chapter 11 cases reflect such compromises.

Discharge

Just as a discharge under Chapter 7 can give individual debtors a fresh start, confirmation under Chapter 11 can give reorganized debtors a new financial beginning under the plan. For individual debtors, however, the same debts that would be nondischargeable under Chapter 7 are excluded from the Chapter 11 discharge. Also, a plan that calls for liquidation and cessation of business will only af-

---

6. Associates Commercial Corp. v. Rash, 117 S. Ct. 1879 (1997).

ford a discharge to individuals who would have been eligible for one in Chapter 7. Because entities such as corporations or partnerships are not eligible for a discharge under Chapter 7, they will similarly not be discharged under Chapter 11 in the event of a liquidation. If the business is rehabilitated, the debtor entity is liable for pre-confirmation claims only insofar as they are expressly preserved by the plan. No bankruptcy discharge, whether under Chapter 11 or otherwise, protects the debtor's co-obligors, such as guarantors or joint tortfeasors.

INTERNATIONAL CONSIDERATION

Winding-up proceedings in Australia are essentially *ex parte:* only the creditors appear before the court. As a result, they do not provide debtors the same recourse as U.S. bankruptcy rules. Other countries, such as Germany, do not provide for the complete discharge of debts in bankruptcy, only arrangement for their payment over time.

Other Chapters

In addition to Chapter 7 (which includes special subchapters for commodity and stockbroker liquidations), Chapter 11 (which includes a subchapter for railroad reorganizations), and Chapter 13 (consumer bankruptcy), the Bankruptcy Code contains two chapters that are more limited, and three others of broader significance. Chapter 12, a hybrid of chapters 11 and 13, provides debt adjustment, but not a superdischarge, for family farmers (a technically defined term) whose aggregate debts do not exceed $1.5 million. Chapter 9, largely patterned after Chapter 11, provides debt adjustment for municipalities. Chapters 1, 3, and 5 apply to all bankruptcies. These chapters contain important provisions—discussed in the sections that follow—such as the automatic stay, rules for claim allowance and priority, the

"For Heaven's sake, Haskell, we're only bankrupt - you act like we're broke."

From *The Wall Street Journal*–Permission, Cartoon Features Syndicate definition of the bankruptcy estate and framework for its administration, and the trustee's avoiding powers.

 Bankruptcy Procedures

Individuals can wipe the slate clean immediately through a Chapter 7 liquidation or obtain a superdischarge by devoting their future earnings to creditors through a Chapter 13 plan. Troubled business debtors who file under Chapter 11 may be able to preserve value for the benefit of shareholders or other equity interests. Bankruptcy also offers several other advantages for debtors.

Automatic Stay

The most immediate and dramatic advantage of any bankruptcy filing is the *automatic stay*, which instantly suspends most litigation and collection activities against the debtor, its property, or that of the bankruptcy estate. Many debtors file for bankruptcy on the eve of foreclosure to forestall the loss of crucial assets; others file primarily to stave off litigation or collection activities. The latter group includes such notable bankruptcy refugees as Dow Corning (facing 19,000 lawsuits involving 400,000 women claiming immune-system illness caused by silicon breast implants), Johns-Manville (sued for thousands of asbestos-related injuries), and Texaco (unable to post a bond while appealing the multibillion-dollar judgment against it for interfering with Pennzoil's efforts to acquire Getty Oil).

Though they may feel frustrated, creditors must honor the automatic stay. As the following case demonstrates, failure to do so can be costly.

A CASE IN POINT	SUMMARY

CASE 24.2
IN RE COMPUTER COMMUNICATIONS, INC.
United States Court of Appeals for the Ninth Circuit 824 F.2d 725 (9th Cir. 1987).

FACTS   Codex Corporation, a designer and manufacturer of communications equipment and networks used for transmitting information between complex computer systems, entered into a joint marketing and development agreement in April 1979 with Computer Communications, Inc. (CCI), a manufacturer of computer equipment and software. Under the agreement, Codex agreed to make minimum quarterly purchases of equipment and software from CCI for incorporation in Codex's products. The agreement was amended on November 4, 1980, and its term was extended to four years commencing in April 1979. The amended agreement required CCI to continue to provide technical support and spare parts. On November 6, 1980, two days after the parties executed the amended agreement, CCI filed a petition under Chapter 11.

On December 30, 1980, Codex notified CCI that it was terminating the agreement pursuant to a clause in the amended agreement that expressly permitted termination in the event of a filing in bankruptcy. Codex failed to make its minimum purchases for the quarter ending December 31, 1980, and failed to make any of its quarterly minimum purchases after that.

CCI filed suit in bankruptcy court on January 30, 1981, alleging that Codex's termination of the agreement violated the automatic-stay provision of the Bankruptcy Code. On February 23, 1981, Codex notified CCI that it was terminating purchases of equipment from CCI pursuant to a clause in the amended agreement that permitted unilateral notice of termination by Codex upon payment of not more than $400,000.

The bankruptcy court held that Codex had willfully violated the automatic stay. The court awarded general damages of $4,750,000 (apparently based on loss of projected profits), plus $250,000 in punitive damages. Codex appealed.

Case 24.2 continues

Case 24.2 continued

ISSUE PRESENTED   Does unilateral termination of an agreement with a debtor who has filed for bankruptcy violate the automatic-stay provision?

SUMMARY OF OPINION   The U.S. Court of Appeals upheld the award, holding that Codex violated the automatic-stay statute by terminating its contract unilaterally, rather than applying for relief from the bankruptcy court. According to the legislative history, the purpose of the automatic stay is to give the debtor a "breathing spell" from creditors, stop all collection efforts, and permit the debtor to attempt repayment or reorganization.

   Codex argued that the contract was not property of the bankrupt estate and was therefore not automatically stayed. The court rejected this argument, finding that the contract did fall within the definition of "property of the estate."

RESULT   Codex violated the automatic stay and was liable for the debtor's loss of projected profits and for punitive damages.

COMMENTS   This case makes it clear that even if a party to a contract has a unilateral right to terminate it, once the other party is in bankruptcy, the contract cannot be terminated unless the bankruptcy court orders relief from the automatic stay. Willful violations of the automatic stay may also constitute contempt of court and warrant punitive damages.

ETHICAL CONSIDERATION

In Case 24.2, CCI extended its agreement with Codex only two days before filing for bankruptcy. It seems clear that Codex would not have renewed the agreement if it had known that CCI was going to declare bankruptcy. The managers of CCI locked in a favorable contract by concealing their intentions from Codex. Was the CCI managers' conduct unethical or just good business?

The U.S. Supreme Court ruled that a bank could, without violating the automatic stay, put a temporary administrative hold on the portion of the bankrupt debtor's checking account that the bank claimed was subject to setoff.[7] The bank refused to pay withdrawals from the bankrupt's account that would reduce the balance below the sum the bank claimed was due on its loan to the bankrupt party. The bank then filed in the bankruptcy court a motion for relief from the automatic stay. The Court acknowledged that the bankruptcy filing gives rise to an automatic stay of various types of activities by creditors, including "the setoff of any debt owing to the debtor that arose before the commencement of the [bankruptcy case] against any claim against the debtor." However, the Court held that a setoff has not occurred until three steps have been taken: (1) a decision to effectuate a setoff, (2) some action accomplishing the setoff, and (3) a recording of the setoff. Thus, there is no setoff unless the creditor intends to permanently settle accounts.

   The Court reasoned that a bank account is not money belonging to the depositor but rather represents a promise by a bank to pay the depositor an amount equal to the money in the account. Therefore, by imposing an administrative hold, the bank does not exercise dominion over the bankrupt's property. Rather, it is a temporary refusal of a creditor to pay a debt that is subject to setoff against a debt owed by the bankrupt.

---

7. Citizens Banks of Maryland v. Strumpf, 516 U.S. 16 (1995).

ETHICAL CONSIDERATION

Would it be ethical for the manager of company about to file bankruptcy to withdraw all company funds from accounts at banks to which the company owes money to avoid having an administrative hold imposed on the accounts?

By stopping creditors in their tracks, the stay provides a breathing spell that can enable a Chapter 11 debtor to focus on the operation of the business and the reorganization of its financial affairs. The stay is not a permanent shield, however. The court may authorize creditors to resume collection efforts, most often foreclosure on collateral, for cause—that is, if there is inadequate protection of the creditors' property interests, such as when the value of collateral declines with use and no replacement security is provided. Relief from the stay will also be granted if the debtor has no equity in property and a stay is not necessary for effective reorganization. Such relief from the automatic stay becomes more likely as time passes without progress toward reorganization. However, the automatic stay is rarely lifted to permit garden-variety litigation against the debtor.

Administration of Claims

Instead of lawsuits, creditors file a relatively simple *proof of claim*. This serves to centralize the administration of most claims in the bankruptcy court, where the process is streamlined. The proof-of-claim requirement in a Chapter 11 bankruptcy is deemed satisfied for claims listed in the debtor's schedules as uncontingent and undisputed (unless the creditor wishes to claim more than the debtor acknowledges is due).

HISTORICAL PERSPECTIVE

FROM MOSAIC LAW TO VULTURE CAPITALISTS

The principle that debtors should be permitted to discharge certain debts has ancient roots. As early as 1400 B.C., Mosaic law required unconditional forgiveness of debts every seven years to encourage a proper focus on social relationships. The word "bankruptcy" is believed to have evolved from the Latin words "banca" and "rupta," referring to the broken bench or moneychangers' table left behind by failed merchants fleeing from their creditors. In 1542 A.D., lawmakers under King Henry VIII passed a Bankruptcy Act to regulate failing English merchants. Over the centuries, strong sanctions for insolvency, including imprisonment, generally made bankruptcy a remedy for creditors rather than a relief for debtors.

The roots of the American bankruptcy system can be traced to the experiences of colonists who were refugees from debtors' prisons in Europe. The drafters of the Constitution, recognizing the importance of debtor relief, gave Congress the exclusive right to establish national bankruptcy laws and thereby override the states' treatment of debtors and creditors. The first bankruptcy enactments, early in the nineteenth century, contained no provisions for voluntary bankruptcy. It was not until 1898, when a severe depression forced many railroads into receivership, that Congress used its bankruptcy power to allow troubled enterprises to reorganize. The Bankruptcy Act of 1898 enabled failing railroads and other businesses to continue operating while reorganizing, generally stripping shareholders of their interests.

Financier J. P. Morgan reorganized so many busted railroads that his work in this area became known as "Morganization." Fifty years after Morgan, the trustee for the estate of Alfred I. du Pont obtained control of the Florida East Coast Railway by holding 56% of its defaulted mortgage bonds. Astute purchases of defaulted rail bonds in the 1940s provided the start for a number of Wall Street fortunes.[a]

In 1978, Congress enacted the Bankruptcy Reform Act, which created the Bankruptcy Code. That legislation, the result of nearly a decade of intensive study and debate about problems in the bankruptcy system and proposed reforms, made sweeping changes in the law, most of them favorable to debtors.

In light of the massive defaults on junk bonds in 1989 and the early 1990s, some questioned whether

Congress gave debtors too much relief under the Bankruptcy Code. The lead-in to a *Forbes* article on the subject summarizes the state of affairs as of 1990: "In the old days, a debt was an obligation and bankruptcy was a disgrace. Nowadays bond issuers concoct ever more ways to stiff investors."[b]

In the *Forbes* article, commentator Matthew Schifrin compares the debtor-lenient U.S. system with other Western countries, in which a debtor's property is auctioned off if it can't pay its debts:

> That's why Australian conglomerator Alan Bond is scrambling to save his highly leveraged empire. The bankruptcy laws in Australia have scant provision for reorganization. If you owe and you can't pay, your creditors can liquidate your company.[c]

In the United States, the debtor usually retains control of the enterprise while it is being reorganized.

Even in the United States, however, bondholders are fighting back. A new breed, called vulture capitalists, is beginning to develop. They buy up bonds at depressed prices and then seek to throw out existing management. Or as happened to Chapter 11 debtor R. H. Macy & Co. in 1994, a competitor—in this case, Federated Department Stores—can buy up senior debt and promise bond holders more than they might otherwise receive if the debtor stays independent, then force a merger of the two companies as part of the plan of reorganization needed for the debtor to emerge from bankruptcy.[d]

Personal bankruptcies increased more than 25% in 1997 from the prior year. In 1997, credit card companies wrote off $24 billion, or about 6% of their credit card loans.[e] Of the 1.3 million Americans who filed for bankruptcy protection in 1997, 70% filed under Chapter 7. A survey by Ernst & Young indicated that 10% of those who successfully filed for Chapter 7 bankruptcy in four surveyed cities in the early 1990s could have repaid all their debts within five years. Another 25% could have repaid 45% of their debts over the same period.[f] Believing that the 1978 reforms had been overly protective of debtors, Congress considered amending the Bankruptcy Code in 1998 to make it more difficult for individuals to discharge debts under Chapter 7 that they could pay pursuant to a repayment plan under Chapter 13.

a. Matthew Schifrin, *Enough Already!,* Forbes, May 28, 1990, at 126.

b. *Id.*

c. *Id.* at 128.

d. Patrick M. Reilly & Laura Jereski, *Macy, Federated Reach Accord in Merger Talks,* Wall St. J., July 15, 1994, at A3.

e. Peter Sinton, *Many Bankruptcy Filers Can Pay Off Their Debts,* San Francisco Chron., Feb. 23, 1998, at B2.

f. *Id.*

Filed claims are deemed valid or allowed unless and until someone objects. Except for personal-injury or wrongful-death claims, which are triable to a jury in the district court, disputed claims normally are resolved through a quick hearing before the bankruptcy judge. If resolution would unduly delay administration of the bankruptcy case (such as when a claim is contingent upon a future event), the bankruptcy court will estimate the allowable amount of certain claims.

Some claims are limited in bankruptcy. For example, a landlord's damages claim for termination of a lease cannot exceed rent for the greater of one year or 15% (but not to exceed three years) of the remaining term. Similarly, a terminated employee's damages claim may not exceed one year's compensation. Unless the estate can pay all claims in a liquidation, postpetition interest is allowed only to secured creditors that can recover it from their collateral.

Control

Though handling claims effectively is important, preserving value to pay them is more important. The debtor's track record for good management may be uneven. Nevertheless, based upon the debtor's presumed knowledge of the business and incentive to save it for the benefit of all concerned, Chapter 11 leaves the debtor in possession of the bankruptcy estate. A *debtor in possession (DIP)* has basically the same powers and duties as a trustee. (Because of this general congruity, and unless the context clearly indicates otherwise, references to the DIP below should be understood to apply equally to a duly appointed trustee.)

Under Chapter 11, an independent trustee normally will not be appointed to displace the DIP without proof that current management is either dishonest or clearly incompetent. Thus, subject to the constraints discussed below, Chapter 11 usually permits the debtor to operate in the ordinary course of business. This, together with the automatic stay and the initial exclusive right to propose a plan, may represent the distressed debtor's best opportunity to exercise control over its fate.

The following case dealt with the question of whether acrimony between the debtor and the creditors is sufficient cause to justify appointment of a bankruptcy trustee in the Chapter 11 case.

A CASE IN POINT | **SUMMARY**

CASE 24.3
IN RE Marvel
Entertainment
Group Inc.
United States Court of
Appeals for the Third Circuit
140 F.3d 463 (3d Cir. 1998).

FACTS   After Marvel Entertainment Group filed for bankruptcy protection under Chapter 11, tensions arose between several of the creditors. Eventually, one creditor acquired control of Marvel, thereby assuming the roles of DIP and creditor. The new DIP and the other creditors attempted to settle their claims against the estate, but negotiations broke down. The new DIP then commenced adverse litigation against the other creditors. The other creditors petitioned for the appointment of a trustee, arguing that the new DIP was incapable of neutrality. The district court appointed a trustee, and the new DIP appealed.

ISSUE PRESENTED   Is acrimony between the DIP and certain creditors sufficient cause to justify appointment of a trustee?

SUMMARY OF OPINION   The U.S. Court of Appeals began by noting that appointment of a trustee should be the exception rather than the rule. Nonetheless, a court does have the power to appoint a trustee "for cause, including fraud, dishonesty, incompetence, or gross mismanagement of the affairs of the debtor by current management" or "if such an appointment is in the interests of the creditors, any equity security holders, and other interests of the estate." Because the new DIP's dual role had caused extreme acrimony, the court concluded that the appointment of a trustee was not an abuse of discretion by the district court.

The court explained that the determination of what kind of acrimony would rise to the level of cause was within the district court's discretion and should be made on a case-by-case basis "when the inherent conflicts extend beyond the healthy conflicts that always exist between debtor and creditor, or . . . when the parties 'begin working at cross purposes.'"

RESULT   The appointment of a trustee was affirmed.

Obtaining Credit

The DIP's first priority often is to stay in business and continue (or resume) providing goods and services to customers at a profit. Yet, as observed at the outset, poor cash flow often paves the way to Chapter 11. Although the bankruptcy system does not manufacture money, it may enhance or create some funding possibilities.

Customer's Payments   The debtor's liquidity crisis sometimes stems from a secured lender's insistence that all encumbered customer payments be applied to the loan, leaving little or no cash to operate. If a bankruptcy petition is filed, customer payments on prebankruptcy accounts will remain the lender's cash collateral, but the court may authorize the DIP to use the funds if the lender's position is adequately protected. Such protection might be found in surplus collateral that gives the lender an ample equity cushion, or it might be provided by granting the lender a substitute lien on postpetition inventory and receivables. Of course, the court may underestimate the need for protection, and this risk often prods an otherwise recalcitrant lender to negotiate terms for use of its cash collateral.

Extension of Unsecured Credit   Filing for reorganization may encourage suppliers (and perhaps other lenders) to extend unsecured credit. During the debtor's prebankruptcy decline, conventional trade terms (such as payment due 30 days after invoice) often become unavailable as the debtor falls behind on accounts payable and word of its shaky condition spreads. Fearful that they may recover only pennies on the dollar from credit sales if the debtor collapses, vendors typically begin requiring cash on delivery or even in advance. This only aggravates the debtor's problems. Ironically, the same suppliers, particularly those who are sophisticated and who value the debtor's patronage most, may be willing to resume regular credit transactions with the DIP.

Flexibility returns because postpetition debts incurred in the ordinary course of doing business are allowable as administrative expenses, which are accorded priority over virtually all other unsecured claims. Thus, vendors that extend postpetition credit expect full payment on those transactions. In so doing, they may strengthen the debtor's business and promote a greater recovery on their prepetition claims.

Secured Borrowings   The debtor's ability to borrow on a secured basis can be similarly enhanced in a Chapter 11 reorganization, mainly because collateral may be more available. For example, assets acquired after the bankruptcy petition is filed (other than those derived directly from prebankruptcy collateral) will not be subject to prepetition security agreements designed to cover such after-acquired property. Therefore, a debtor who can produce inventory or generate accounts receivable after the bankruptcy filing may have enough unencumbered property to support new secured loans. Moreover, if credit is not otherwise available, the court can authorize borrowing that is secured by a priming lien, provided that the preexisting lienholder is adequately protected. A *priming lien* is a lien that is senior to a previously granted security interest. Thus, for example, a first mortgage on raw land might be involuntarily subordinated to a new lien that will secure a DIP–developer's construction financing.

Court Oversight   On occasion, the bankruptcy court's oversight alone may help the debtor arrange new secured loans. By obtaining court approval after giving appropriate notice to other creditors, lenders can virtually immunize their repayment rights and security interests from the attacks by other creditors that sometimes undermine prebankruptcy loans.

Turnover of Debtor's Property   Though usually less expeditious than borrowing, other bankruptcy tools also can help the DIP obtain funds for operations and enhance the value of the estate. Almost anyone can be compelled to turn over property of the estate that could be used by the DIP. Thus, if adequate protection is provided, a lender who has frozen the debtor's deposit accounts at the banking institution or a taxing authority that has seized them may be required to relinquish these funds.

Avoiding Powers

Still more striking is the DIP's ability to invoke the potent *avoiding powers* that trustees can use to invalidate or reverse certain prebankruptcy transactions.

Strong-Arm Clause   Under the *strong-arm clause*, the DIP is granted the rights of a hypothetical creditor who extended credit to the debtor at the time of bankruptcy and who, as a result, either obtained a judicial lien on all property in which the debtor has an interest or obtained an execution against the debtor that was returned unsatisfied. The DIP also has the rights that a bona fide purchaser of real property from the debtor would have if the transfer was perfected. The DIP has these powers and rights regardless of whether a judgment-lien creditor or a bona fide purchaser actually exists.

Thus, if a deed of trust or mortgage was not properly recorded before bankruptcy or a security interest in personal property was not duly perfected against third-party claims under applicable law (typically, the Uniform Commercial Code), the DIP can establish superior rights to the affected property for the benefit of the estate. This is the case even if the debtor could not have recovered such assets outside of bankruptcy. In addition, the DIP can avoid—that is, invalidate—any transaction that an existing unsecured creditor could invalidate. This might include unauthorized dividends to shareholders, procedurally defective bulk sales, or transfers considered fraudulent as to creditors under nonbankruptcy laws such as a state fraudulent transfer statute.

The scope of the DIP's strong-arm powers usually depends on state property law, so it may differ from case to case. For example, in many states, the rights of a creditor holding a judicial lien against real property are superior to those of a party with an unrecorded mortgage against the same property. Using the strong-arm powers, a DIP can avoid the unrecorded lien. Similarly, where a judicial creditor's lien would have priority over an unperfected security interest, the DIP may use his hypothetical status to invalidate a security interest that was not perfected by filing or possession, but would otherwise be valid between a debtor and its creditor. If state law permits, the DIP may reverse other transfers of the debtor's property and void otherwise valid obligations of the debtor. Any value the DIP recovers pursuant to the strong-arm clause inures to the benefit of the creditors of the bankruptcy estate.

Fraudulent Transfers   The DIP may invoke the Bankruptcy Code to avoid fraudulent transfers or obligations. In general, these arise from transactions that occurred within a year before bankruptcy that (1) are actually intended to hinder, delay, or defraud creditors, or (2) provide less than reasonably equivalent value in exchange and leave the debtor insolvent or without sufficient capital to engage in business or to pay expected debts. Thus, a leveraged buyout that leaves a company with insufficient capital and high debt leverage after the payouts to equity holders may be voidable as a fraudulent conveyance.[8] Most states have roughly parallel fraudulent-transfer laws, but the Bankruptcy Code's version may be broader. For example, the state laws may be inapplicable to distressed foreclosure sales that are noncollusive and procedurally proper; bankruptcy law has been applied to invalidate such sales if the proceeds are less than 70% of the collateral's fair market value. Thus, although a good faith buyer should have a lien for the value given (which is usually the amount of the secured debt), the DIP may be able to reverse the foreclosure and recapture equity.

Preferences   The avoiding power used most extensively is the ability to recover preferences. *Preferences* are transfers to (or for the benefit of) creditors on account of antecedent debts that are made from an insolvent debtor's property within 90 days before bankruptcy and that enable the creditors to receive more than they would through a Chapter 7 liquidation. (The preference window is enlarged to a year before bankruptcy if the benefited creditor is an insider—that is, someone in a position to control the debtor's conduct, such as a relative, partner, director, officer, or substantial shareholder.) Preferences are made avoidable in bankruptcy both to discourage creditors from dismembering a troubled business in their race for its assets and to foster equal distribution among similarly situated claimants. Subject to limited exceptions, the DIP can recover voluntary or involuntary preferential payments and strip away preferential security interests or collection liens, all for the benefit of the bankruptcy estate.

A payment is only a preference if it is for an antecedent (or preexisting) debt. However, to avoid penalizing creditors that continue to deal in a customary fashion with the debtor during its slide into bankruptcy, current payments in the ordinary course of business cannot be recovered as preferences. As the following case demonstrates, it is not always clear whether a payment is for an antecedent debt or is a current payment in the ordinary course of business.

---

8. *See, e.g.,* United States v. Tabor Court Realty Corp., 803 F.2d 1288 (3d Cir. 1987), *cert. denied,* 483 U.S. 1005 (1987).

A CASE IN POINT	**IN THE LANGUAGE OF THE COURT**

CASE 24.4
UNION BANK
v. WOLAS
Supreme Court of
the United States
502 U.S. 151 (1991).

FACTS   ZZZZ Best Company, Inc. made two interest payments and paid a loan commitment fee on a long-term debt to Union Bank. Within 90 days, ZZZZ Best filed a petition under Chapter 7 of the United States Bankruptcy Code. Herbert Wolas was appointed Chapter 7 trustee of the company's estate and filed a complaint against the bank to recover the payments, claiming that they were voidable preferences under 11 U.S.C. § 547(b). The bankruptcy court held that the payments on this long-term debt were made "in the ordinary course of business" under 11 U.S.C. § 547(c)(2) and therefore excepted from the scope of § 547(b). The federal district court agreed with the bankruptcy court, but the appeals court reversed.

Case 24.4 continues

Case 24.4 continued

ISSUE PRESENTED   Can payments on long-term debt qualify for the ordinary-course-of-business exception to the trustee's power to avoid preferential transfers?

OPINION   STEVENS, J., writing for the U.S. Supreme Court:

III

The Bank and the trustee agree that § 547 is intended to serve two basic policies that are fairly described in the House Committee Report. The Committee explained:

> . . . The purpose of the preference section is two-fold. First, by permitting the trustee to avoid prebankruptcy transfers that occur within a short period before bankruptcy, creditors are discouraged from racing to the courthouse to dismember the debtor during his slide into bankruptcy. The protection thus afforded the debtor often enables him to work his way out of a difficult financial situation through cooperation with all of his creditors. Second, and more important, the preference provisions facilitate the prime bankruptcy policy of equality of distribution among creditors of the debtor. Any creditor that received a greater payment than others of his class is required to disgorge so that all may share equally. . . .

As this comment demonstrates, the two policies are not entirely independent. On the one hand, any exception for a payment on account of an antecedent debt tends to favor the payee over other creditors and therefore may conflict with the policy of equal treatment. On the other hand, the ordinary course of business exception may benefit all creditors by deterring the "race to the courthouse" and enabling the struggling debtor to continue operating its business.

Respondent places primary emphasis, as did the Court of Appeals, on the interest in equal distribution. When a debtor is insolvent, a transfer to one creditor necessarily impairs the claims of the debtor's other unsecured and undersecured creditors. By authorizing the avoidance of such preferential transfers, § 547(b) empowers the trustee to restore equal status to all creditors. Respondent thus contends that the ordinary course of business exception should be limited to short-term debt so the trustee may order that preferential long-term debt payments be returned to the estate to be distributed among all of the creditors.

But the statutory text—which makes no distinction between short-term debt and long-term debt—precludes an analysis that divorces the policy of favoring equal distribution from the policy of discouraging creditors from racing to the courthouse to dismember the debtor. Long-term creditors, as well as trade creditors, may seek a head start in that race. . . .

IV

In sum, we hold that payments on long-term debt, as well as payments on short-term debt, may qualify for the ordinary course of business exception to the trustee's power to avoid preferential transfers. We express no opinion, however, on the question whether the Bankruptcy Court correctly concluded that the Debtor's payments of interest and the loan commitment fee qualify for the ordinary course of business exception, § 547(c)(2).

RESULT   The judgment of the appeals court was reversed and the case was remanded for determination of whether the loan was incurred in the ordinary course of the

Case 24.4 continues

Case 24.4 continued

debtor's business and of the bank's business, whether the payments were made in the ordinary course of business, and whether the payments were made according to ordinary business terms. Payments on long-term debt may qualify for the ordinary-course-of- business exception to the trustee's power to avoid preferential transfers.

Questions

1. Would a policy of encouraging short-term credit transactions enable troubled debtors to regain their financial footing without resorting to bankruptcy?
2. Might the *Wolas* decision increase the availability to debtors of unsecured funds?

Setoff Rights   A creditor exercising a setoff right automatically deducts what the debtor owes the creditor from what the creditor owes the debtor. By analogy to the preference provision, creditors who exercise setoff rights within 90 days before bankruptcy can be required to disgorge such offsets to the extent that they decreased their obligations to the debtor within the 90-day period.

Statutory Liens   The DIP can avoid certain statutory liens, including those that first arise upon insolvency or that would not have been enforceable against a bona fide purchaser of the encumbered property when the bankruptcy was filed. This prevents state law from creating hidden priorities that would distort the federal bankruptcy distribution scheme.

Collective Bargaining Agreements   The rules for avoiding collective-bargaining agreements changed after Frank Lorenzo used Chapter 11 to avoid Continental Airlines' collective-bargaining agreements. In the early 1980s, when labor rejected his demands for sizable wage concessions, Frank Lorenzo took Continental into a Chapter 11 proceeding and repudiated its collective-bargaining agreements. Continental Airlines emerged from bankruptcy a nonunion carrier with a reduced wage structure.

Organized labor protested the use of the Bankruptcy Code by Lorenzo (and, increasingly, others) to break unions. In 1984, Congress responded, amending the Bankruptcy Code so that a debtor no longer has broad discretion to abrogate unilaterally its labor contracts. Instead, a debtor may reject collective-bargaining agreements over the objection of its unions only if (1) it has presented labor with a proposal showing that rejection is economically necessary and fair to the affected parties; (2) it has bargained to impasse; and (3) the bankruptcy court finds that, on balance, fairness clearly favors rejection.

In 1989, with Lorenzo at its helm, Eastern Airlines demanded that its unions agree to reductions in wages and other benefits. Labor refused, and a strike ensued. Within days, Eastern filed a bankruptcy petition for reorganization.

History appeared to be about to repeat itself, but the similarities with the Continental bankruptcy ended there. The consummation of Lorenzo's agreement to sell Eastern Airlines' assets to former baseball commissioner Peter Ueberroth was killed by the demands of Eastern's unions.

Executory Contracts and Leases

The DIP has the option of assuming or rejecting prebankruptcy *executory contracts*—that is, contracts that have not yet been performed—or unexpired leases. Assumption preserves the debtor's rights and duties under the existing relationship, whereas rejection terminates them.

If an executory contract or unexpired lease is a valuable asset, the DIP will want to assume it so that it can be preserved for the reorganizing business or sold at a profit. For example, assumption is advantageous when it allows the debtor to sell or buy goods at a favorable price or to lease space or equipment at better-than-market rents. Even a contract or lease in default can be assumed provided the DIP cures and compensates for the breach and gives adequate assurance of future performance. Once assumed, the contract or lease obligations are allowable as administrative expenses, like those arising from other authorized postpetition transactions.

Despite contrary contractual restrictions, any assumed contract or lease can be sold and assigned intact if the prospective assignee's future performance is adequately assured.

On the other hand, by rejecting a disadvantageous contract or lease, the DIP can escape burdensome performance obligations. The nondebtor party to the contract or lease will be deemed to have a prepetition damages claim for breach and thus will be treated like others whose claims arise from prebankruptcy transactions.

The following case addressed the issue of whether an option to buy property is an executory contract.

| A CASE IN POINT | IN THE LANGUAGE OF THE COURT |

CASE 24.5
UNSECURED CREDITORS COMMITTEE OF ROBERT L. HELMS CONSTRUCTION & DEV. CO. v. SOUTHMARK CORP.
(In re Robert L. Helms Construction and Development Co. Inc.),
United States Court of Appeals for the Ninth Circuit
139 F.3d 702
(9th Cir. 1998) (en banc).

FACTS   Southmark, a Texas corporation, sold the Double Diamond Ranch in Nevada to the Double Diamond Ranch Limited Partnership (Double Diamond), retaining an option to buy back part of the ranch. Southmark later filed for bankruptcy in Texas. As part of its Chapter 11 reorganization plan, it assumed various executory contracts by filing a notice of assumption. The plan provided that all executory contracts not listed were deemed rejected. The notice didn't list the option to buy back the ranch; therefore, it would have been deemed rejected if it was an executory contract.

Double Diamond then itself filed for bankruptcy in Nevada. The committee administering the Double Diamond bankruptcy decided to sell the ranch to South Meadows Properties Limited Partnership. The committee asked the bankruptcy court to allow sale of the ranch free and clear of Southmark's option. A free-and-clear sale was appropriate only if the option was no longer valid because it had been stripped away in the Texas bankruptcy proceeding. The Nevada bankruptcy court held that the option was an executory contract that had been rejected in Southmark's bankruptcy. Therefore, it allowed Double Diamond to sell the ranch to South Meadows free and clear of Southmark's option. Southmark appealed.

ISSUE PRESENTED   Is an option to buy property an executory contract?

OPINION   KOZINSKI, J., writing for the U.S. Court of Appeals:

An executory contract is one "on which performance remains due to some extent on both sides." More precisely, a contact is executory if "the obligations of both parties are so unperformed that the failure of either party to complete performance would constitute a material breach and thus excuse the performance of the other."

A paid-for but unexercised option presents a puzzle. Is it executory or isn't it? Each side may have unperformed obligations, but they are contingent on the optionee's decision to exercise the option. If it does, the optionor has a duty to deliver the property, and the optionee may have a duty to tender payment, depending on the mechanics of the option. But if the option is not exercised, nothing happens and neither party commits a breach. The contingent nature of the obligations has troubled courts. Some have said that these are contingent obligations, but obligations nonetheless, hence options are executory. Other courts have held that the optionee has fulfilled its only true obligation under the option by paying for it; the creation of further obligations lies within the optionee's sole discretion, so the contract isn't executory.

. . .

A better approach . . . is to ask whether the option requires further performance from each party at the time the petition is filed. Typically the answer is no, and the

Case 24.5 continues

Case 24.5 continued

option is therefore not executory. The optionee need not exercise the option—if he does nothing, the option lapses without breach. The contingency which triggers potential obligations—exercising the option—is completely within the optionee's control. While some options may be executory, *Easebe*[9] is overboard in holding that they all are.

. . .

We therefore reject *Easebe*'s broad rule that all options are executory contracts. Instead, we look to outstanding obligations at the time the petition for relief is filed and ask whether both sides must still perform. Performance due only if the optionee chooses at his discretion to exercise the option doesn't count unless he has chosen to exercise it. An option may on occasion be an executory contract, for instance, where the optionee has announced that he is exercising the option, but not yet followed through with the purchase at the option price.

The question thus becomes: At the time of filing, does each party have something it must do to avoid materially breaching the contract? Typically, the answer is no; the optionee commits no breach by doing nothing.

It appears likely that the option here wasn't executory when Southmark filed its petition, but the record is not entirely clear.

RESULT   The case was remanded to the bankruptcy court with instructions to determine the effect of the confirmed Southmark reorganization plan. If the plan did not resolve the question, the bankruptcy court was instructed to apply the legal test described above to determine whether the option contract was executory at the time of filing and to fashion a remedy if it found that the option was not an executory contract and remained an asset of the Southmark estate.

Questions

1. If Southmark had given written notice of its intent to exercise the option, but had not yet paid the purchase price, before filing for bankruptcy, would the option have been an executory contract?

2. The option agreement expressly provided that the option was for a period of 15 years "provided, however, that the option granted herein shall terminate in the event Southmark files for protection under Chapter 11 for the Bankruptcy Code." Why wasn't the option automatically terminated when Southmark filed under Chapter 11?

---

9. Gill v. Easebe Enters. (*In re* Easebe Enters.), 900 F.2d 1417 (9th Cir. 1990).

Sale of Property

Bankruptcy can facilitate favorable sales of assets other than contracts or leases. For example, if partition or division of property jointly owned by the debtor and another is impractical and if separate sale of the debtor's undivided interest would yield significantly less for the estate, the DIP can sell both interests and disburse the net proceeds proportionately, as long as the resulting benefit would outweigh the detriment to the other owner. Similarly, the DIP may sell property free and clear of liens or other interests (which normally will be shifted to the proceeds) if the price will exceed all encumbrances or if the nondebtor's interest is in bona fide dispute. Thus, although the debtor's sale before bankruptcy might be stymied, the DIP can sometimes break the logjam and pass clear title under Chapter 11.

This cleansing power of bankruptcy extends beyond specific property. It can be the key to successful reorganization through the sale of the entire business or through new capital infusions. When a business is troubled and its future is in doubt, potential investors may shy away despite the venture's intrinsic worth. Similarly, the price a prospective going-concern purchaser will pay may be seriously depressed by the fear that acquiring all of the assets will also subject the buyer to the debtor's obligations under doctrines of successor liability (discussed in Chapter 9). The same investors or buyers are often less jittery, and hence more willing to recognize the true value of the debtor's business, if the transaction proceeds under a confirmed plan or other court order that quantifies or cuts off preexisting claims. Subject to possible constitutional due process protections for unknown future claimants, Chapter 11 can thus dispel uncertainties that would otherwise prevent the debtor from realizing the equity in its business.

 ## Workouts

Because the high transaction costs and the adverse publicity of a Chapter 11 bankruptcy can be disadvantageous for debtors and creditors alike, the parties often try to negotiate an out-of-court settlement. Such an agreement, called a *workout*, restructures the debtor's financial affairs in much the same way that a confirmed plan would, but it can bind only those who expressly consent.

The foundation of any successful workout is trust. Creditors will not sign an agreement that leaves the business in the hands of management they consider to be dishonest or incompetent. If the debtor has lost credibility by misleading creditors or evading their reasonable inquiries (a common problem), its management may need to recruit and defer to a turnaround specialist in order to restore confidence. Full disclosure and candor are especially important when creditors are agreeing to accept partial payment in full satisfaction of undisputed debts. The debtor's misrepresentation or concealment of material facts probably would invalidate an otherwise binding release.

Workouts are forged in the shadow of bankruptcy, and the parties measure their concessions against the obvious alternative. The debtor and major creditors may be willing to accept something less than unanimity (for example, to preclude dissenters from extorting preferred treatment), but the deal will unravel if there are too many holdouts. When this risk is apparent from the outset, the workout agreement can be drafted in the form of a Chapter 11 plan. If necessary, and provided the information disclosed in soliciting assent to the agreement was adequate, the debtor can then file for reorganization and use the prepetition votes to transform the workout into a confirmed plan that binds dissenters. This is called a *prepackaged bankruptcy.*

Regardless of its terms, a workout agreement cannot stop the debtor from taking refuge in Chapter 11 if the restructured obligations prove too great. The right to file bankruptcy cannot be waived. Sometimes, however, creditors have strategic reasons to defer the debtor's filing, perhaps to buttress their positions with new guaranties, or to season transfers against the avoiding powers. In any event, if the debtor has broken faith with the workout pact, the court may consider previous creditor concessions in deciding whether to lift the stay, to allow creditors to propose a plan at the outset, to appoint a trustee, or to convert the case to a Chapter 7 liquidation.

 ## Lender Liability

A series of court decisions has expanded the recoveries available to borrowers against lenders and, as a consequence, lenders have become more aware of the risks of lender liability. The most notable development is not so much the legal theories on which lender liability claims are based, but rather the frequency with which such claims are being asserted. Some theories on which lender liability claims may be based are described in this section.

Breach of Contract

A breach of contract results from a lender's failure to act or to refrain from acting as required by the terms of a loan document or other agreement. Compensatory damages will be awarded to place the borrower in the same position it would have been in if the lender had properly performed the agreement.

IN BRIEF

ADVANTAGES AND DISADVANTAGES OF BANKRUPTCY

Category	Advantages	Disadvantages
Debtors	*Automatic Stay* • Instantly suspends most litigation and collection activities against the debtor, its property, or the bankruptcy estate *Control* • Debtor retains possession of the bankruptcy estate (unless a trustee is appointed) • Chapter 11 permits the debtor to operate in the ordinary course of business *Contracts, Leases, and Property* • Debtor in possession (DIP) has option of assuming or rejecting prebankruptcy executory contracts or unexpired leases • DIP may (in certain circumstances) sell property free and clear of liens or other interests	*Administrative Costs* • Legal and accounting expenses • Official creditors' committee fees *Reduction in Autonomy* • Creditor oversight • Management's ability to make and implement decisions rapidly and autonomously is curtailed *Stigma of Bankruptcy* • Morale or confidence problems among staff, vendors, or customers • Customer anxiety regarding future warranty claims or product support
Creditors	*Enhanced Value and Participation* • Preserves going-concern value of an insolvent business • DIP more accountable due to bankruptcy reporting and notice requirements *Equitable Distribution* • When inequitable conduct by any creditor (typically an insider) has prejudiced others, bankruptcy court has authority to subordinate all or part of transgressor's claim to payment of other creditors *Involuntary Petitions* • Creditors may file an involuntary petition for relief under Chapter 7 or (more rarely) Chapter 11 and force the debtor into bankruptcy	*Suspension of Individual Remedies* • Automatic stay stalls foreclosure • Nondebtor parties to executory contracts and unexpired leases left in limbo *Unequal Effects* • Some bankruptcy procedures affect various creditors unequally (e.g., avoiding actions, claim caps, equitable subordination) *Reduced Distribution* • Only a small fraction of Chapter 11 cases filed result in a successful reorganization. Continued operation results in less funds to distribute at liquidation

Breach of Duty of Good Faith

Some cases have imposed an implied obligation of good faith and fair dealing on lenders. This duty requires the lender to act reasonably and fairly in dealing with the borrower and in exercising its rights and remedies under the loan documents and under applicable law.

Where there is a fiduciary relationship between the lender and borrower or where the parties are of unequal bargaining strength, punitive damages may be recoverable for breach of the implied duty of good faith and fair dealing. For example, the U.S. Court of Appeals for the Sixth Circuit affirmed a judgment of $1.5 million compensatory damages and punitive damages against the Irving Trust Company. The company was found to have breached an implied covenant of good faith and fair dealing when it failed to give notice to the borrower before refusing to make further advances under a discretionary line of credit.[10]

Fraudulent Misrepresentation

A lender may be liable for making false statements to a borrower if, for example, it represents that it will make a

---

10. K.M.C. Co. v. Irving Trust Co., 757 F.2d 752 (6th Cir. 1985).

> ### AT THE TOP
>
> Some large banks have begun to place mandatory arbitration clauses in their loan agreements. These clauses affect the claims a debtor may assert regarding the lender's breach of an implied duty of good faith and fair dealing and avoid the costs involved with a jury trial.

loan facility available to the borrower when, in fact, it has decided not to extend any credit to the borrower. If a fiduciary relationship exists between the lender and the borrower, the lender may have an additional duty to disclose information if nondisclosure would result in injury to the borrower. Both compensatory and punitive damages may be recovered for fraudulent misrepresentation.

Economic Duress

Economic duress is the coercion of the borrower by threatening to do an unlawful act that might injure the borrower's business or property. If the lender pressures the borrower into doing something that the borrower is not required to do under the loan documents, a court may find the lender's action constitutes economic duress. For example, a threat by the lender to accelerate the loan unless the borrower provides additional collateral may constitute economic duress if there is no default under the loan documents. Compensatory and punitive damages may be recovered for economic duress.

Tortious Interference

The lender was found liable for wrongful or tortious interference with the borrower's corporate governance in the following case, which set a precedent for claims of this kind.

A CASE IN POINT | **SUMMARY**

CASE 24.6
STATE NATIONAL BANK OF EL PASO v. FARAH MANUFACTURING CO.
Court of Appeals of Texas
678 S.W.2d 661
(Tex. App. 1984).

FACTS   The loan agreement between the bank lenders and the borrower, Farah Manufacturing Co. (FMC), contained a clause prohibiting any change in the borrower's management "which any two Banks shall consider, for any reason whatsoever, to be adverse to the interests of the Banks." The lenders threatened to accelerate the loan if a certain individual, of whom the lenders disapproved, was reappointed as chief executive officer of the borrower. In response to this threat, the borrower appointed a series of chief executive officers proposed by the lenders. The financial position of the borrower seriously deteriorated during the tenure of these chief executives.

The borrower sued the lenders for fraud, duress, and tortious interference. In particular, the lenders' threats to accelerate the loan under the management-change clause, in order to influence the choice of managers, was found to be an excessive interference with the borrower's internal affairs. The lenders were found liable for the

Case 24.6 continues

Case 24.6 continued

losses suffered by the borrower while under the bank-imposed management, resulting in a judgment against the banks in excess of $18 million. The banks appealed.

ISSUE PRESENTED   Is a bank that requires the borrower to hire chief executive officers recommended by the bank liable to the borrower for excessive interference with the borrower's internal affairs?

SUMMARY OF OPINION   The Texas Court of Appeals began by noting that interference with another's business relations with a third party is actionable only if the interference is motivated by malice and no useful purpose of the inducing party is subserved. Malice, in this connection, is not to be understood in its proper sense of ill will against a person, but in its legal sense, as characterizing an unlawful act, done intentionally without just cause or excuse. Actual malice (ill will, spite, evil motive, or purposing the injury of another) need not exist.

To establish a *prima facie* case of interference with contract, the plaintiff must prove that (1) there was a contract subject to interference, (2) the act of interference was willful and intentional, (3) the intentional act was a proximate cause of plaintiff's damage, and (4) actual damage or loss occurred. The plaintiff is not required to show that the defendant's acts were undertaken with an intent to harm.

The burden then shifts to the defendant to show that its acts were either justified or privileged. In all cases, the act of interference must be without legal right or justifiable cause on the part of the defendant.

The court held that interference embraces within its scope all intentional invasions of contractual relations, including any act injuring or destroying property and so interfering with the performance of the contract itself, regardless of whether breach of contract is induced.

FMC claimed that the lenders interfered with FMC's own business relations and protected rights. Although the lenders may have been acting to exercise legitimate legal rights or to protect justifiable business interests, the court ruled that their conduct failed to comport with the standards of fair play. The social benefits derived from permitting the lenders' interference were clearly outweighed by the harm to be expected therefrom.

The court found the evidence legally sufficient to establish that the lenders interfered with FMC's business relations, its election of directors and officers, and its protected rights. FMC was entitled to have its affairs managed by competent directors and officers who would maintain a high degree of undivided loyalty to the company. The interference compelled the election of directors and officers whose particular business judgment and inexperience and whose divided loyalty proximately resulted in injury to FMC. The interference by the lenders was done willfully, intentionally, and without just cause or excuse. As a matter of law, the court held that FMC had established a cause of action for interference.

RESULT   The Texas Court of Appeals affirmed the judgment. State National Bank of El Paso was liable to the borrower, Farah Manufacturing, for excessive interference with the borrower's internal affairs.

Intentional Infliction of Emotional Distress

A lender was found liable for intentional infliction of emotional distress when, after deciding not to make any additional advances to the borrower, bank officials publicly ridiculed him, pointing at him, using profanities, and laughing about his financial difficulties. To recover for intentional infliction of emotional distress, the lender's conduct must be extreme and outrageous and must intentionally or recklessly cause emotional distress to the borrower. Compensatory and punitive damages may be recovered.

Negligence and General Tort Liability

Claims that do not fall into one of the other established categories may be characterized as negligence or general tort liability. Negligence is the failure to exercise reasonable care, resulting in injury to the borrower. General tort liability arises from conduct that intentionally causes injury to a borrower.

Statutory Bases of Liability

A lender may be liable to the borrower if it violates a statutory standard of conduct. For example, the federal Racketeering Influenced and Corrupt Organizations Act (RICO) has been used by private litigants in lender liability cases. Although RICO was adopted by Congress as a tool for fighting organized crime, the definition of a "pattern of racketeering activity" is arguably broad enough to encompass fraud or misrepresentation by banks or other lenders. The treble damages available under RICO provide an incentive for borrowers to claim RICO violations in their lender liability suits.

The federal antitying statutes prohibit banks and thrifts from conditioning a loan or other financial service on the borrower's purchase of an unrelated property or service from the lender or on the borrower's providing to the lender a product or service unrelated to the original loan. A lender may be subject to penalties in cases brought by the Securities and Exchange Commission for aiding or abetting a borrower in violating federal securities laws if it knew, or should have known, that a violation was taking place or if it is found to be a controlling person with respect to the borrower.

Under the federal Comprehensive Environmental Response, Compensation and Liability Act (CERCLA, discussed in Chapter 16) and state law counterparts, if the lender falls within the statutory definition of an owner or operator of a site contaminated by hazardous wastes and does not come within the statutory safe harbor for lenders, it may find itself liable for all the costs of cleanup even if they exceed the amount of the loan.

Special Defenses Available to Failed Banks and Savings and Loans

When a bank or savings and loan has failed and federal banking agencies have taken control, a doctrine called *D'Oench, Duhme*[11] has been used by the Federal Depository Insurance Corporation (FDIC) and Resolution Trust Corporation (RTC) to increase the value of the failed institution by easing the federal agencies' ability to collect on loans. In effect, *D'Oench, Duhme* bars many claims and defenses against conservators and receivers that might have been valid against the failed bank itself. The doctrine bars enforcement of any agreements (including secret agreements) unless those agreements are in writing and have been approved contemporaneously by the bank's board or loan committee and recorded in the bank's written records. This permits federal and state bank examiners to rely exclusively on the bank's written records in evaluating the worth of the bank's assets.[12] The result of this doctrine is that the federal agencies are often victorious over borrowers in cases in which a borrower asserts certain common law defenses to escape a loan obligation assumed by the FDIC or RTC. *D'Oench, Duhme* applies only to banking transactions engaged in by federally insured institutions. It does not apply to nonbanking transactions or to transactions engaged in by a bank's nonbank subsidiaries.

---

11. From the Supreme Court case of the same name, *D'Oench, Duhme & Co. v. FDIC*, 315 U.S. 447 (1942).

12. Alexandria Assocs. v. Mitchell Co., 2 F.3d 598 (5th Cir. 1993).

However, support for the doctrine may be eroding. The U.S. Court of Appeals for the Ninth Circuit ruled in 1997 that the *D'Oench, Duhme* doctrine does not protect the FDIC as receiver of a failed bank.[13] It relied on two recent U.S. Supreme Court cases[14] in which the Supreme Court declined to apply federal common law in suits brought by the FDIC as receiver for federally chartered and insured banks. In contrast, the Eleventh Circuit held that the FDIC, acting as receiver of a federal bank, was still protected by the common law doctrine.[15] The Eleventh Circuit discerned "no indications that *D'Oench* is ripe for overruling." The U.S. Supreme Court will most likely be called upon to resolve this split in authority in the circuit courts of appeal.

13. Ledo Fin. Corp. v. Summers, 122 F.3d 825 (9th Cir. 1997). *Accord* Murphy v. FDIC, 61 F.3d 34 (D.C. Cir. 1995); DiVall Insured Income Fund Ltd. Partnership v. Boatmen's First Nat' Bank, 69 F.3d 1398 (8th Cir. 1995).

14. Atherton v. FDIC, 117 S. Ct. 666 (1997); O'Melveny & Myers v. FDIC, 512 U.S. 79 (1994).

15. Motorcity of Jacksonville Ltd. v. Southeast Bank, N.A., 120 F.3d 1140 (11th Cir. 1997) (*en banc*). *Accord* Young v. FDIC, 103 F.3d 1180 (4th Cir. 1997).

THE RESPONSIBLE MANAGER
Managing Debtor–Creditor Relations

A responsible manager must understand lender liability risks. The following steps will help lenders minimize those risks.

In negotiating loan terms, the lender should indicate clearly that any commitment must be in writing and approved by the loan committee or other appropriate officials of the lender. The lender's written communications to the borrower should disclaim any commitment if none is intended.

The lender should avoid provisions in loan documents giving it a broad right to control the borrower's management decisions or day-to-day business activities. The lender should refrain from using its financial leverage to influence such activities as the selection of management, the hiring or firing of employees, or the payment of other creditors.

The loan documents should contain a merger clause stating that the written loan documents supersede any prior oral understandings and that the borrower is not relying on any prior oral promise or representation by the lender. The loan documents should provide that any amendment, modification, or waiver of the terms of the documents or of the rights of the parties must be in writing and signed by both the lender and the borrower.

The lender may ask the borrower to insert in the loan documents a waiver of its right to a jury trial. Juries are often perceived as sympathetic to borrowers; a judge may be less likely to award large compensatory or punitive damages to the borrower. The lender may want to specify in the loan documents that any legal action by the borrower must be brought in a court in a specific state or city to avoid the possible disadvantage the lender may have as a defendant in a court in the borrower's home territory. The lender may want to add an arbitration clause to the loan documents, stating that any disputes arising under the loan documents will be resolved through binding arbitration instead of litigation in a court.

The lender should maintain accurate and complete credit files supporting all the actions it takes. Virtually all of the documents in the lender's files may be subject to legal discovery; it is wise to assume that any entry in the credit files may someday be read to a judge or jury in a lender liability case.

The lender should not threaten to take actions that are not yet authorized or which the lender does not actually intend to take. The lender should give reasonable warning and, if possible, written notice to the borrower before terminating a line of credit, changing an established course of conduct, accelerating a loan, or exercising any remedies.

Except when acting as a trustee or other fiduciary, the lender should refrain from giving any legal, financial, or investment advice to the borrower that might create a fiduciary relationship between the lender and borrower. The lender should be cautious about giving other creditors the financial history of the borrower or opinions as to the borrower's creditworthiness.

In a workout situation, when the borrower is trying to renegotiate a loan it cannot pay or if it becomes apparent that the borrower may be preparing a lender liability suit, the lender should consult with legal counsel.

At all times the lender's loan officers should behave professionally, regardless of their level of frustration with the borrower. Any personality conflicts with the borrower should be avoided. If a personality conflict does develop, the matter should be transferred to other loan officers.

It has become fashionable in some circles to view Chapter 11 as a strategic option for creative business planning. Apart from the fresh start granted to individual debtors, however, the bankruptcy system generally respects a debtor's obligations existing under state or other federal law; it merely provides a forum for dealing fairly, efficiently, and flexibly with the rights of all the creditors and equity holders. Thus, although insolvency is not a prerequisite for relief, a bankruptcy filing is generally not appropriate unless the business is in serious financial difficulties.

If those difficulties are present, the bankruptcy system can be an effective mechanism for overcoming them while preserving a productive enterprise. Yet for each celebrated success, there are countless failed Chapter 11 cases, in which no plan is confirmed and creditors are left with less than they would have received through prompt liquidation. This is partly the price of giving depressed businesses the chance to rebound, but it also reflects fundamental problems.

Many debtors, most of them single-asset or other small businesses, file Chapter 11 cases without any realistic prospect for reorganization. In some instances, the principals refuse to recognize and deal with financial ills until the business is too weak to survive. Continuing their ostrichlike pattern, they then file a Chapter 11 petition, awash in a sort of terminal euphoria, not recognizing that liquidation is inevitable. Other debtors see the writing on the wall but file to buy time, hoping for a miracle cure. Still others file merely to postpone the management's impending unemployment.

Congress gave creditors the means to protect their interests, however. If management acts improperly, a trustee can be appointed; if reorganization is improbable, the case can be dismissed or converted to a Chapter 7 liquidation. Unfortunately, these remedies are rarely invoked before the creditors' interests are seriously prejudiced. Not surprisingly, individual unsecured creditors tend to be reluctant to throw good money after bad by policing the debtor's conduct. For the same reason (though with less justification), they frequently decline to serve or participate actively on the official creditors' committee, so this watchdog may be somnolent or nonexistent in smaller cases. Thus, unless a secured creditor is motivated to overcome this inertia, a Chapter 11 case may have a bleak outcome.

Absent prompting from an interested party, the bankruptcy judge ordinarily will not intervene until the situation becomes egregious, as when the DIP does not comply with the rules, such as those requiring regular financial and tax reporting. Because the court is not well equipped to investigate the progress of each Chapter 11 debtor, an abusive case can languish for considerable time before the court itself initiates corrective action.

The effectiveness of the bankruptcy system depends largely upon knowledgeable and responsible conduct by the interested parties. In general, both debtors and creditors benefit by addressing financial problems early and pursuing a constructive workout. Because the charged emotional climate often makes this difficult, it is important to obtain objective and practical advice from counsel. If a workout is not possible, the debtor's management should consider whether a reorganization is plausible before filing for relief under Chapter 11. If the case is filed, creditors must recognize that meaningful participation, ideally through the official creditors' committee, is usually necessary to protect their interests.

Directors of a corporation in financial trouble assume new responsibilities to protect not only shareholders but the entire community of interests represented by creditors, employees, and other parties with a stake in the continued viability of the corporation. Once a corporation becomes insolvent or files for bankruptcy, the directors owe a fiduciary duty to creditors as well as shareholders.

INSIDE STORY

RJR NABISCO LEVERAGED BUYOUT

From time to time, a company may incur long-term indebtedness in the form of bonds. The proceeds of such debt will generally be used for long-term purposes, such as the acquisition of machinery or the construction of a new plant. Bonds are usually negotiable and are available for purchase and sale by investors in the public market. The company that sells the bonds, called the issuer, will normally sell them to an underwriter who, in turn, markets them to the public.

The agreement governing a bond issue is contained in a written document called an *indenture*. Like a loan agreement or a note purchase agreement, an indenture contains a description of the terms, or characteristics, of the bonds. Such terms include the interest rate; the security, if any, for the bonds; and the terms for repayment of the principal and retirement of the bonds. In addition, the issuer will make certain representations and warranties about itself, the bonds, and certain promises (or covenants) with respect to what it will or will not do while the bonds are outstanding. Because of the public market that exists for bonds, many of the terms found in indentures have become standardized.

In the past, the standard indenture did not contain protections against changes in corporate structure, such as leveraged buyouts, mergers, or hostile takeovers. Such

events, called *event risks,* cause the prices of high-grade investments to plummet. For example, in a leveraged buyout (LBO), in which the buyer acquires the stock or assets of a company by borrowing large sums of debt and using little equity, the company's assets must be pledged as security for the debt. Frequently, after the LBO is consummated, the acquired company's assets are sold off to reduce the debt burden.

The case of *Metropolitan Life Insurance Company v. RJR Nabisco, Inc.*[16] arose when two institutional bondholders found themselves holding bonds whose values had declined after the issuer's LBO. They sued the issuer in the Federal District Court for the Southern District of New York. Even though the indentures did not expressly prohibit an LBO, the bond holders argued that the issuer was required to repurchase the bonds because it had breached an implied covenant of good faith and fair dealing when it entered into the LBO. The court held that, because the written agreement did not contain an express LBO prohibition, to imply a covenant of good faith and fair dealing that prohibited the LBO would add to the indenture a term that was neither bargained for nor contemplated by the parties.

Background

On October 20, 1988, F. Ross Johnson, then the chief executive

officer of RJR Nabisco, Inc., proposed a $17 billion leveraged buyout of the company. A bidding war began, and Kohlberg Kravis Roberts and Company (KKR) submitted the successful bid. KKR's proposal called for a $24 billion buyout valued at approximately $109 per share.

Even before the company had accepted KKR's proposal, the bond holders, Metropolitan Life Insurance Company (MetLife) and Jefferson Life Insurance Company, filed suit. They alleged that the company's actions drastically impaired the value of the bonds they held by "misappropriating" the value of those bonds to help finance the acquisition, thereby creating a windfall to the company's shareholders. The plaintiffs argued that the acquisition contradicted the understandings of the market on which the plaintiffs had relied. They also said that RJR had actively solicited, and had received, investment-grade ratings for their bonds; and, because the ratings would be adversely affected by the LBO, the LBO contradicted a basic premise for their investment.

MetLife and Jefferson were sophisticated investors in the bond market, having held approximately $350 million in bonds issued by RJR between July 1975 and July 1988. MetLife had assets exceeding $88 billion and debt holdings exceeding $49 billion. Jefferson had more than $3 billion in total assets and $1.5 billion in debt securities.

The court acknowledged that the plaintiffs, like other holders of public bond issues, had acquired the bonds after the indentures had been negotiated and memorialized. Nevertheless, the court noted, the underwriters who ordinarily negotiate the terms of the indentures with the issuers must then sell the bonds; and, thus, they must negotiate with the interests of the buyers in mind. Moreover, the plaintiffs presumably reviewed the indentures carefully before lending large sums to any company.

The indentures all contained the same basic provisions. None restricted the creation of unsecured debt or the payment of dividends by RJR. All permitted mergers as long as the surviving corporation assumed existing debt. Two of the indentures had previously included restrictions on incurring the type of debt contemplated by the LBO, but these restrictions had been deleted in subsequent negotiations unrelated to the LBO. In one case, MetLife bargained for a guarantee from the parent of RJR's predecessor, R. J. Reynolds, in exchange for its agreement to delete the restrictive covenants. In the other case, MetLife had bargained for a new rate and different maturity in exchange for such deletion.

The Court's Decision

The plaintiffs had argued that the company, explicitly or implicitly, had agreed with the bond holders' premise that the bonds would maintain their investment ratings. However, the court determined that the indentures contained no explicit prohibition against the LBO with KKR and that they unambiguously permitted the LBO. Because the indentures were unambiguous, the court said, the plaintiffs could not introduce extrinsic evidence—that is, evidence outside of the indenture language—to show that the intention of the parties was to prohibit the LBO. Thus, documents indicating that MetLife had recognized the risk of an LBO to public debt (but had not taken any steps to protect against such risk) were inadmissible as evidence.

The court said that under certain circumstances, courts will consider extrinsic evidence to evaluate the scope of an implied covenant of good faith. However, the court noted that under applicable precedents, a different rule applied in interpreting boilerplate provisions of indentures used in the securities market. The court explained that boilerplate provisions do not result from the relationship of particular borrowers and lenders and thus do not depend upon the particularized intentions of the parties. Because the efficiency of capital markets relied upon uniform interpretation of indentures, the meaning of boilerplate provisions in such indentures was not subject to case-by-case determination.

The court noted that, even though the plaintiffs had not alleged that an express covenant had been breached, a covenant of good faith and fair dealing could be implied if the "fruits of the agreement" between the parties had

been "spoiled." In this analysis, the court determined that the "fruits" guaranteed by the indentures included the periodic and regular payment of interest and the eventual repayment of principal. Yet interest payments had been continuing, and there was no indication that principal would not be paid when due. The court said that a restriction against incurring new debt would be an additional "fruit" or benefit that the parties had not bargained for. The court added that it had no reason to believe that the market, in evaluating bonds, did not discount for the possibility that the issuer might engage in a debt-financed buyout. Thus, the loss in bond value was a market risk that public bond holders accepted.

The court noted that the indentures contained provisions for adding new covenants on the mutual agreement of RJR and the bond holders, and it suggested that these provisions could be used to add restrictions against LBO debt. The court acknowledged that huge, sophisticated companies like RJR might not accept such new covenants, but said that multibillion-dollar investors like MetLife and Jefferson presumably had some say in the terms of the investments they make and continue to hold. If the issuers were to need new infusions of capital, for example, the bond holders would have an opportunity to impose new covenants. Because of the plaintiffs' and RJR's relatively equal bargaining positions, the court concluded that the contract between them was not inequitable.

Protecting against Event Risk

In response to bond purchasers' concern about event risk, underwriters have begun to include new, express covenants. In one recent bond issue, the indenture included a provision granting bond holders the right to sell their bonds back to the issuer in the event of a change of control or leveraged buyout. Some lenders have devised debts in which the interest rate is adjusted if the issuer's debt rating is downgraded.

Standard and Poor Corporation responded by introducing a rating system called "event risk covenant rankings." Bonds are ranked on a scale of "E–1, strong protection" to "E–5, insignificant or no protection," based on the degree of covenant protection provided in a bond indenture.

---

16. 716 F. Supp. 1504 (S.D.N.Y. 1989).

KEY WORDS AND PHRASES

QUESTIONS AND CASE PROBLEMS

1. What is necessary for a perfected security interest in goods?

2. ABC Food Corporation, a food company with annual sales of more than $1 billion, operated a paper division which supplied ABC with packaging for its food products. The management of ABC determined that ABC should concentrate on its core business of manufacturing food products, and recommended to the ABC board of directors that the assets of the paper division be sold.

Newcorp, Inc. is a newly formed corporation with two shareholders who have experience in the timber industry. Those two shareholders also jointly own Lumber Corporation, which operates two lumber mills in the state of Washington. Newcorp was formed specifically to acquire the assets of ABC's paper division.

On February 1, 1997, ABC and Newcorp signed a letter of intent specifying a closing no later than July 1, 1997, subject to Newcorp obtaining satisfactory financing. The letter of intent provided that ABC and Newcorp would enter into a long-term contract whereby Newcorp would supply specified quantities of paper packaging to ABC.

On February 15, 1997, Newcorp approached the Bank of Hope to request a term loan to acquire the assets of ABC's paper division and a revolving line of credit to meet its day-to-day working capital requirements. On March 31, 1997, the Bank of Hope delivered to Newcorp a letter stating that it would agree to extend a credit facility to Newcorp on the terms and conditions described in a term sheet attached to the letter.

Bank of Hope required, as a condition to its credit facility, that the credit be secured by all fixed and current assets of Newcorp. Carlos Banker, the account officer for the Bank, took all steps necessary to give Bank of Hope a valid first-priority lien on all collateral.

A major source of revenue for Newcorp will be the long-term supply contract with ABC. The Bank of Hope is requiring an assignment of the supply contract. The assignment would prohibit ABC and Newcorp from making any amendments to the contract without the bank's consent.

a. You are a manager of Newcorp. What objections would you have to such an assignment?

b. You are a manager of ABC. Any objections?

3. Assume the facts in Question 2. One of the terms of the Bank of Hope's loan is a guaranty from each shareholder and from Lumber Corporation.

a. You are Sylvia Daily, president of Newcorp. As president, you will be involved in the day-to-day operations of Newcorp. What arguments might you make against giving such a guaranty?

b. You are Joe Lucre. You own 51% of the stock of Newcorp, and you made loans to Newcorp during the initial stages of its existence. You have since left the running of Newcorp to Sylvia Daily and the other managers of Newcorp. What arguments could you make against giving such a guaranty?

c. You are the Bank of Hope's attorney. What advice would you give the bank about taking a guaranty from Lumber Corporation?

4. Assume the facts in Questions 2 and 3. On June 1, 1997, Revolving Credit Bank takes over the revolving line of credit from Bank of Hope and acquires Bank of Hope's security interest in Newcorp's accounts receivable and inventory. Beginning in early 1998, due to a combination of internal and external conditions, Newcorp's business failed to generate sufficient revenue to meet its debt obligations. The loan agreement between Newcorp and Revolving Credit Bank contains an advance clause, which states that Revolving Credit Bank may, at its discretion, advance up to $2 million based on eligible accounts receivable and inventory. Revolving Credit Bank informed Newcorp that Newcorp has failed to maintain certain financial covenants contained in their credit agreement. Without declaring a default, Revolving Credit Bank required from then on that Newcorp establish a locked-box arrangement with the bank, so that all payments made to Newcorp can be used first to repay any advances outstanding. On March 1, 1998, Newcorp's treasurer called Valerie Lender, Revolving Credit Bank's account officer, and asked for a $350,000 advance to cover checks that would be presented to the bank that day. Revolving Credit Bank refused to lend the full amount requested, but did advance $200,000 to pay certain suppliers.

You are the manager of one of the trade creditors of Newcorp that has not been paid. Do you have any rights against Revolving Credit Bank?

5. Assume the facts in Questions 2 through 4. In April 1998, Newcorp began to have difficulty meeting its monthly repayment obligations on the term loan from the Bank of Hope. Although Newcorp never missed a payment, the payments were all a few days late. In May 1998, Carlos Banker called the treasurer at Newcorp, assuring him that the Bank of Hope "would stand by the company" and that Newcorp should do whatever it could to keep the payments current. In September 1998, Revolving Credit Bank, concerned about continuing deteriorating conditions, decided to initiate foreclosure proceedings. The Bank of Hope followed suit only when Revolving Credit Bank began foreclosure proceedings. When the Bank of Hope began foreclosure proceedings against the paper plant, it discovered that the nearby Temecula River was polluted due to wastewater discharged from the plant.

a. You are a manager of Newcorp. What defenses would you raise against Revolving Credit Bank's foreclosure? Against the Bank of Hope's foreclosure?

b. You are a manager of Revolving Credit Bank. How would you respond to Newcorp's arguments?

c. You are a manager of the Bank of Hope. How would you respond to Newcorp's arguments? Should the Bank of Hope proceed to foreclose against the plant? Should it require Newcorp to clean up the river? What recourse does the Bank of Hope have against Newcorp if it does not foreclose? Does it have any recourse against any other party?

d. You are a manager of ABC and hold a junior deed of trust on the property. How would you react to the Bank of Hope's latest action?

e. Was the Bank of Hope's foreclosure ethical?

6. On September 22, Robert Herriford borrowed $6,500 from Avemco Investment Corp. and executed a promissory note for $9,607.92. The promissory note was secured by an agreement granting Avemco a security interest (or mortgage) in an airplane.

On July 4, Herriford entered into a lease option agreement with the three plaintiffs (Don Brown, Josef Miller, and Allen McAlear) whereby the plaintiffs would pay hourly rentals for the plane and contribute equally toward Herriford's debt retirement with Avemco. Upon full payment of the mortgage on the airplane, the plaintiffs would have an option to purchase one-fourth ownership (each) of the plane for the sum of $1. The plaintiffs became co-insureds with Herriford on the airplane, and copies of the policy were sent to Avemco.

On July 9, the plaintiffs advised Avemco that they had exercised the option with Herriford and tendered to Avemco the $4,859.93 still owed by Herriford. On July 18, Avemco refused the offer and wrote to Herriford announcing that, because of his failure to comply with the note and security agreement, Avemco was accelerating the payments and the entire balance of $5,078.97 was due and payable on or before July 28. The additional amount was to reimburse Avemco for its purchase of "Vender's Single Interest Insurance."

On July 25, plaintiff McAlear advised Avemco that the plaintiffs did not accept Avemco's rejection of the tender and that the money to retire the debt was available to Avemco at the First Security Bank of Bozeman, upon representation of a satisfaction of the mortgage.

On July 29 or 30, a representative of Avemco used a passkey to start the plane and flew it to Seattle. Avemco then notified Herriford of the repossession. Avemco demanded payment of $5,578.97 by August 10 or the aircraft would be sold, with the proceeds to be applied first to sale expenses and second to Herriford's account. On September 22, Avemco sold the plane for $7,000.

Assume that Herriford agreed that if he were to lease any of the property covered by the security interest without Avemco's consent, Avemco had the right to accelerate the loan. Avemco could accelerate if Herriford violated a specific provision of the agreement and if it deemed itself insecure. Should Herriford be held to the agreement? Should Avemco be entitled to call the loan because Herriford violated a specific provision of the agreement, or should it also have to show that it was insecure? [*Brown v. Avemco Inv. Corp.*, 603 F.2d 1367 (9th Cir. 1979)]

7. On June 29, 1982, Timbers, Ltd. executed a note in the amount of $4,100,000. United Savings Association was the holder of the note, as well as of the security interest created the same day in an apartment project owned by Timbers in Houston, Texas. On March 4, 1985, Timbers filed a voluntary petition under Chapter 11 of the Bankruptcy Code.

On March 18, 1985, United Savings Association moved for relief from the automatic stay of enforcement of liens triggered by the petition on the ground that there was lack of "adequate protection" of its interest. At a hearing before the bankruptcy court, it was established that Timbers owed them $4,366,388.77 and the value of the collateral was between $3,650,000 and $4,250,000. United Savings was therefore an undersecured creditor. Timbers had agreed to pay United Savings the postpetition rents from the apartment project, minus operating expenses. United Savings wanted additional compensation. The bankruptcy court agreed; on April 19, it conditioned continuance of the stay on monthly payments by Timbers on the estimated amount realizable on foreclosure ($4,250,000). The court held that postpetition rents could be applied to these payments.

Should an undersecured creditor be entitled to interest on its collateral during the stay to secure adequate protection? [*United Savings Ass'n of Texas v. Timbers of Inwood Forest Assocs., Ltd.*, 484 U.S. 365 (1988)]

8. Brodie Hotel Supply, Inc. sold some restaurant equipment to Standard Management Company, Inc. for use in a restaurant in Anchorage, Alaska. Standard Management went bankrupt. Brodie repossessed the equipment but left it in the restaurant. With the consent of Brodie, James Lyon took possession of the restaurant and began operating it in June. Throughout the summer, Brodie and Lyon negotiated over the price and terms under which Lyon was to purchase the equipment.

In November, Lyon borrowed $17,000 from the National Bank of Alaska and, as security for the loan (which was evidenced by a promissory note), executed a security agreement (or chattel mortgage) covering the restaurant equipment. This equipment consisted of 159 separate types of items, including a refrigerator, a dishwasher, an ice cream cabinet, spoons, and chinaware. The bank assigned its security interest to the Small Business Administration (SBA), represented in this action by the United States. In late November, the bank filed a financing statement, showing the SBA as assignee.

Brodie then delivered to Lyon a bill of sale covering the equipment, and Lyon executed a security agreement (or chattel mortgage) on the equipment, naming Brodie as secured party (or mortgagee). This security interest was given to secure the unpaid purchase price of the equipment.

Which of the parties had priority, under the respective security agreements, to the proceeds of the sale of the restaurant equipment? [*Brodie Hotel Supply v. United States*, 431 F.2d 1316 (9th Cir. 1970)]

9. Rembert ran up gambling losses of between $18,000 and $24,000. She obtained a second mortgage on her house and repaid some of her credit card debt, but she continued gambling and incurred further losses. When she filed bankruptcy under Chapter 7, the two credit card companies from whom she had received cash advances claimed that her debts (totaling $11,000) were procured by fraud and therefore nondischargeable. They argued that by using the credit cards, she represented that she had the ability to repay the debt when in fact her financial condition made repayment impossible. Rembert countered that there was fraud only if at the time she used the cards she had no intent to repay the debt incurred. Who is correct? Is it ethical to incur debt without knowing how one will be able to repay it? [*Rembert v. AT&T Universal Card Service*, 141 F.3d 277 (6th Cir. 1998); *Citibank (South Dakota) N.A. v. Eashai (In re Eashai)*, 87 F.3d 1082 (9th Cir. 1996)]

MANAGER'S DILEMMA

10. Bill and Bob Green were principal owners of Greenbrook Carpet Company. They attempted to obtain a loan from the bank in order to purchase a controlling block of stock in Lewis Carpet Mills, Inc. The bank refused to make the loan because it considered the Greens's collateral to be inadequate. The bank subsequently agreed to lend $350,000 to Greenbrook in return for a security interest in Greenbrook's inventory. Greenbrook then transferred the loan proceeds to the Greens in return for a note. The Greens used the funds to purchase the Lewis stock and granted Greenbrook a security interest in that stock. The Greens were not personally liable on the note.

Did the transaction between Greenbrook and the Greens constitute a fraudulent transfer? Was it ethical? [*In re Greenbrook Carpet Co.*, 722 F.2d 659 (11th Cir. 1984)]

INTERNET SOURCES

This site provides links to bankruptcy journals and publications and to law firm Web sites providing bankruptcy information.	http://findlaw.com/01topics/03bankruptcy
This site, maintained by the American Bankruptcy Institute, includes legislative updates.	http://www.abiworld.org/legis
The Bankruptcy Lawfinder site, maintained by the law offices of Warren E. Agin in Massachusetts, provides answers to frequently asked bankruptcy questions.	http://www.agin.com/bkfaq
This site, maintained by Cornell Law School, contains a full-text version of UCC Article 9.	http://www.law.cornell.edu/ucc/9

International Business

CHAPTER 25

International Trade

INTRODUCTION

High-Priority Concern

The financial crisis in Thailand, Indonesia, and Korea in 1997 and 1998 (dubbed the Asian flu) and its impact on U.S. exports and stock markets underscored the existence of a global economy and the importance of international trade.[1] Trade contributed almost $1 trillion to the U.S. economy in 1997 and accounted for a third of its growth since 1992.[2] Because a far greater number of countries are exporting their goods to the United States than ever before, domestic products are faced with increased competition. Indeed, the United States amassed a $181.9 billion trade deficit in 1997.

Dealing with import competition and opening foreign markets for U.S. exports are the targets of U.S. international trade policy and trade law. For corporate managers, a basic knowledge of these laws and issues is more important than ever.

Chapter Overview

This chapter begins with a discussion of trade law and policy, followed by a summary of how the U.S. government is organized to regulate international trade. The bulk of the chapter addresses the major U.S. laws and international agreements in this field, including the North American Free Trade Agreement and the agreement that established the World Trade Organization. The final section discusses the European Union and its plan for economic, monetary, and political integration.

 Developments in Trade Policy

The U.S. government has given trade policy increasingly higher priority over the last few decades. The office of U.S. Trade Representative, created less than 45 years ago, now has cabinet-level rank. Policymakers have come under increasing pressure to protect U.S. industries from import competition and to press foreign governments to open their markets to U.S. exports.

The Past as a Warning for the Future

As the following article demonstrates, U.S. trade policy can have a dramatic effect on business.

---

1. *See* Bob Davis, *Asia's Troubles Swell U.S. Trade Deficit*, WALL ST. J., June 19, 1998, at A2.
2. Paul Magnusson et al., *Clinton's Trade Crusade*, BUS. WK., June 8, 1998, at 34, 35.

Economists Are Right for a Change, 1930

PRESIDENT HERBERT HOOVER, ignoring the pleas of 1,028 economists to veto it, signed with six gold pens the Smoot–Hawley Tariff Act on June 17, 1930. It was a hollow celebration.

The day before, anticipating the signing, the stock market suffered its worst collapse since November 1929, and the law quickly helped push the Great Depression deeper.

Its tariffs, which by 1932 rose to an all-time high of 59% of the average value of imports (today it's 5%), were designed to protect U.S. farm and textile products from foreign competition. Economists warned that angry nations would retaliate, adding that foreigners would also have fewer dollars to buy U.S. goods as well as to settle their World War I debts.

Within two years, Great Britain and more than 20 other nations raised their tariffs and reduced buying of U.S. imports. Within the U.S., prices and output continued their fast fall.

From 1930 to 1931, U.S. imports dropped 29%, but U.S. exports fell even more, 33%, and continued their collapse to a modern-day low of $2.4 billion in 1933.

One long-lasting effect of the act: The definition of "ornamental apparel," which has braid or lace, has stuck over the years and still adds to the duty paid. But in 1930, it was 90%; now it's 30%. In the 1930s it was another reason for women to use plainer lingerie.

In 1934, Congress passed the Reciprocal Trade Agreements Act to empower the president to reduce tariffs by half the 1930 rates in return for like cuts in foreign duties on U.S. goods. The "beggar thy neighbor" policy was dead.

SOURCE WALL ST. J., Apr. 28, 1989, at B1. Reprinted with permission of the *Wall Street Journal*, © 1989 Dow Jones & Company, Inc. All Rights Reserved Worldwide.

 ## U.S. Trade Law

U.S. trade laws are enacted by Congress and administered by the federal government and administrative agencies.

The Role of Congress

Under the U.S. Constitution, Congress has exclusive power to regulate foreign commerce, which includes imports and exports, foreign investment, licensing of technology, and other commercial activities. This chapter deals primarily with trade laws; that is, those laws directed at imports and exports, although some of these laws affect other activities as well.

Trade laws are generally designed either to restrict or to facilitate imports and exports. Imports are restricted primarily by means of tariffs and quantitative limitations; certain imports are facilitated by being exempted from U.S. tariffs. Exports are controlled by means of export licenses; certain exports are facilitated by special federal government financing, certain tax breaks, and Section 301 of the Trade Act of 1974, which is discussed later in this chapter.

The Role of the President

The president administers U.S. trade laws pursuant to the authority delegated to him or her by Congress. In addition, as chief executive, the president has broad power to negotiate trade agreements. However, the president has no power to regulate trade without congressional delegation or approval. Nevertheless, as the case below shows, the president can negotiate nonbinding, voluntary undertakings.

A CASE IN POINT | **IN THE LANGUAGE OF THE COURT**

CASE 25.1
CONSUMERS UNION, INC. v. KISSINGER
United States Court of Appeals for the District of Columbia
506 F.2d 136 (D.C. Cir. 1974), *cert. denied*, 421 U.S. 1004 (1975).

FACTS In order to assist the U.S. steel industry, President Nixon (through his secretary of state, Henry Kissinger) sought to reduce steel imports from Japan and Europe by convincing foreign producers to limit their exports to the United States. The undertakings to do so were voluntary, and no attempt was made by the United States to legally enforce them.

Consumers Union, believing that U.S. consumers were hurt by this restriction on supplies of foreign steel, sued the secretary of state. It argued that the president had,

Case 25.1 continues

Case 25.1 continued

in effect, regulated foreign commerce without any specific statutory delegation of authority from Congress and, thus, exceeded his authority.

ISSUE PRESENTED   Did President Nixon act within his powers in negotiating nonbinding, voluntary undertakings by foreign producers to reduce their exports to the United States?

OPINION   McGOWAN, J., writing for the U.S. Court of Appeals:

The steel import restraints do not purport to be enforceable, either as contracts or as governmental actions with the force of law; and the executive has no sanctions to invoke in order to compel observance by the foreign producers of their self-denying representations. They are a statement of intent on the part of the foreign producer associations. The signatories' expectations, not unreasonable in light of the reception given their undertakings by the executive, are that the executive will consult with them over mutual concerns about the steel import situation, and that it will not have sudden recourse to the unilateral steps available to it under the Trade Expansion Act to impose legal restrictions on importation. The President is not bound in any way to refrain from taking such steps if he later deems them to be in the national interest, or if consultation proves unavailing to meet unforeseen difficulties: and certainly the Congress is not inhibited from enacting any legislation it desires to regulate by law the importation of steel.

The formality and specificity with which the undertakings are expressed does not alter their essentially precatory nature insofar as the executive branch is concerned. In effect the President has said that he will not initiate steps to limit steel imports by law if the volume of such imports remains within tolerable bounds. Communicating, through the Secretary of State, what levels he considers tolerable merely enables foreign producers to conform their actions accordingly, and to avoid the risk of guessing at what is acceptable. Regardless of whether the producers run afoul of the antitrust laws in the manner of their response, nothing in the process leading up to the voluntary undertakings or the process of consultation under them differentiates what the executive has done here from what all presidents, and to a lesser extent all high executive officers, do when they admonish an industry with the express or implicit warning that action, within either their existing powers or enlarged powers to be sought, will be taken if a desired course is not followed voluntarily.

RESULT   The export restraints by the foreign producers were upheld. The president did not exceed his constitutional authority, because the export restraints were accomplished through an informal, voluntary agreement. The restraints were not legally binding on the foreign exporters, and they were not enforced by U.S. authorities.

COMMENTS   In order for the U.S. Customs Service to enforce this agreement by excluding imports in excess of the agreed limits, congressional approval would have been required. The effect of the voluntary restraints was perhaps the same as if quotas had been imposed by Congress; but the court did not feel it could interfere with the president's power to conduct foreign relations. Congress later approved the steel restraints. President Reagan negotiated new steel-export restraints with foreign governments in 1984, and President Bush extended them in 1988; Congress approved both actions.

Case 25.1 continues

Case 25.1 continued

Questions

1. What incentives do foreign exporters have to voluntarily refrain from exporting their goods to the United States?
2. Could the U.S. Customs Service have enforced this agreement by excluding imports in excess of the agreed limits?

Administrative Agencies

The agencies primarily responsible for administration of the trade laws are the U.S. Trade Representative (USTR), the Department of Commerce, the Department of State, the Department of the Treasury, the U.S. International Trade Commission, and the U.S. Customs Service (which is part of the Treasury Department).

The USTR is responsible for the development of U.S. trade policy and the negotiation of trade agreements with other countries, with the assistance of the other agencies. The USTR makes all policy decisions concerning the operation of these agreements. The Department of Commerce is generally responsible for implementing U.S. trade policy, enforcing certain import-relief laws and export controls, and promoting U.S. exports. The Department of State administers controls on munitions exports and defends U.S. economic interests through U.S. embassies abroad.

The Department of the Treasury administers embargoes imposed on U.S. trade with countries such as Iraq, Cuba, and Libya. The International Trade Commission is an independent agency with a variety of responsibilities, including investigations concerning the effect of imports on U.S. industries. The Customs Service enforces all U.S. customs laws and import restrictions and collects U.S. tariffs. Other agencies, such as the U.S. Department of Agriculture, administer restrictions on U.S. trade falling in their particular areas of responsibility, with the assistance of the Customs Service.

The Interagency Committee

The president makes trade-policy decisions based on the recommendations of an interagency committee, headed by the USTR. Included on the committee are the agencies listed above, in addition to the Department of Labor, the Council of Economic Advisors, and other agencies interested in trade policy. Private interests are typically given the opportunity to express their views to any of these agencies, or to the interagency committee directly. For example, tariffs on a particular product are rarely changed without first consulting the affected industry. Government officials at all the agencies are generally receptive to requests and comments from U.S. companies. In many cases, public hearings are held before decisions are made.

 ## Tariffs

Tariffs are the basic tool for limiting imports to protect domestic industries. Today, most tariffs are *ad valorem tariffs*, meaning that the importer must pay a percentage of the value of the imported merchandise. For instance, a 10% tariff on a shipment of imports valued at $10,000 would result in a *duty*, that is, a required payment, of $1,000.

U.S. tariffs are established by federal law. They can be changed only by law or by administrative action authorized by law. Congress frequently changes U.S. tariffs. However, under the auspices of the Trade Agreement Program begun in 1934, Congress has also periodically delegated to the president the authority to reduce U.S. tariffs in exchange for tariff concessions by other nations. In addition, Congress has for many years delegated to the president the power to increase tariffs temporarily in order to protect domestic industries in certain specified situations. These import-relief laws are discussed later in this chapter.

The Harmonized Tariff Schedule

The United States has accepted an internationally harmonized tariff system. Current tariffs are found in a document entitled the *Harmonized Tariff Schedule of the United States (HTS)*.[3] The HTS lists the tariffs imposed by Congress and the president on goods, based on their country of origin. Exhibit 25.1 reproduces the first two pages from the General Notes (that is, the general instructions) to the HTS. Exhibit 25.2 reproduces a page from the schedule covering beverages.

For each product category, there are two basic rates of duty. There is one column for most countries (column 1) and a second one for Afghanistan, Cuba, Laos, North Korea, and Vietnam (column 2). These columns reflect tariffs imposed by Congress or negotiated by the president under the Trade Agreements Program. Column 1 is subdivided into general and special tariffs. Special tariffs reflect preferential rates for certain countries on certain products; these are described later in this chapter. Temporary increases in U.S. tariffs are listed in Chapter 99 of the HTS.

Country of Origin

U.S. tariffs vary depending on the country of origin. A good is considered the product of the country from which it was first exported, unless it has been substantially transformed into a new article of commerce. If

---

3. Published by the U.S. International Trade Commission.

EXHIBIT 25.1 Harmonized Tariff Schedule of the United States: General Notes

HARMONIZED TARIFF SCHEDULE of the United States (1997)
Annotated for Statistical Reporting Purposes

GNs 1--3(a)(iv)(B)

GENERAL NOTES

1. Tariff Treatment of Imported Goods and of Vessel Equipments, Parts and Repairs. All goods provided for in this schedule and imported into the customs territory of the United States from outside thereof, and all vessel equipments, parts, materials and repairs covered by the provisions of subchapter XVIII to chapter 98 of this schedule, are subject to duty or exempt therefrom as prescribed in general notes 3 through 14, inclusive, and general note 16.

2. Customs Territory of the United States. The term "customs territory of the United States", as used in the tariff schedule, includes only the States, the District of Columbia and Puerto Rico.

3. Rates of Duty. The rates of duty in the "Rates of Duty" columns designated 1 ("General" and "Special") and 2 of the tariff schedule apply to goods imported into the customs territory of the United States as hereinafter provided in this note:

   (a) Rate of Duty Column 1.

      (i) Except as provided in subparagraphs (iv) and (v) of this paragraph, the rates of duty in column 1 are rates which are applicable to all products other than those of countries enumerated in paragraph (b) of this note. Column 1 is divided into two subcolumns, "General" and "Special", which are applicable as provided below.

      (ii) The "General" subcolumn sets forth the general most-favored-nation (MFN) rates which are applicable to products of those countries described in subparagraph (i) above which are not entitled to special tariff treatment as set forth below.

      (iii) The "Special" subcolumn reflects rates of duty under one or more special tariff treatment programs described in paragraph (c) of this note and identified in parentheses immediately following the duty rate specified in such subcolumn. These rates apply to those products which are properly classified under a provision for which a special rate is indicated and for which all of the legal requirements for eligibility for such program or programs have been met. Where a product is eligible for special treatment under more than one program, the lowest rate of duty provided for any applicable program shall be imposed. Where no special rate of duty is provided for a provision, or where the country from which a product otherwise eligible for special treatment was imported is not designated as a beneficiary country under a program appearing with the appropriate provision, the rates of duty in the "General" subcolumn of column 1 shall apply.

      . . .

HARMONIZED TARIFF SCHEDULE of the United States (1997) -- Supplement 1
Annotated for Statistical Reporting Purposes

GN 3(b)--3(c)(iv)

(b) <u>Rate of Duty Column 2</u>. Notwithstanding any of the foregoing provisions of this note, the rates of duty shown in column 2 shall apply to products, whether imported directly or indirectly, of the following countries and areas pursuant to section 401 of the Tariff Classification Act of 1962, to section 231 or 257(e)(2) of the Trade Expansion Act of 1962, to section 404(a) of the Trade Act of 1974 or to any other applicable section of law, or to action taken by the President thereunder:

Afghanistan	Laos	Vietnam
Cuba	North Korea	

(c) <u>Products Eligible for Special Tariff Treatment.</u>

(i) Programs under which special tariff treatment may be provided, and the corresponding symbols for such programs as they are indicated in the "Special" subcolumn, are as follows:

Generalized System of Preferences	A, A* or A+
Automotive Products Trade Act	B
Agreement on Trade in Civil Aircraft	C
North American Free Trade Agreement:	
Goods of Canada, under the terms of general note 12 to this schedule.	CA
Goods of Mexico, under the terms of general note 12 to this schedule	MX
Caribbean Basin Economic Recovery Act	E or E*
United States-Israel Free Trade Area	IL
Andean Trade Preference Act	J or J*
Agreement on Trade in Pharmaceutical Products	K
Uruguay Round Concessions on Intermediate Chemicals for Dyes	L

(ii) Articles which are eligible for the special tariff treatment provided for in general notes 4 through 14 and which are subject to temporary modification under any provision of subchapters I, II and VII of chapter 99 shall be subject, for the period indicated in the "Effective Period" column in chapter 99, to rates of duty as follows:

(A) if a rate of duty for which the article may be eligible is set forth in the "Special" subcolumn in chapter 99 followed by one or more symbols described above, such rate shall apply in lieu of the rate followed by the corresponding symbol(s) set forth for such article in the "Special" subcolumn in chapters 1 to 98; or

(B) if "No change" appears in the "Special" subcolumn in chapter 99 and subdivision (c)(ii)(A) above does not apply, the rate of duty in the "General" subcolumn in chapter 99 or the applicable rate(s) of duty set forth in the "Special" subcolumn in chapters 1 to 98, whichever is lower, shall apply.

(iii) Unless the context requires otherwise, articles which are eligible for the special tariff treatment provided for in general notes 4 through 14 and which are subject to temporary modification under any provision of subchapters III or IV of chapter 99 shall be subject, for the period indicated in chapter 99, to the rates of duty in the "General" subcolumn in such chapter.

(iv) Whenever any rate of duty set forth in the "Special" subcolumn in chapters 1 to 98 is equal to or higher than, the corresponding rate of duty provided in the "General" subcolumn in such chapters, such rate of duty in the "Special" subcolumn shall be deleted; except that, if the rate of duty in the "Special" subcolumn is an intermediate stage in a series of staged rate reductions for that provision, such rate shall be treated as a suspended rate and shall be set forth in the "Special" subcolumn, followed by one or more symbols described above, and followed by an "s" in parentheses. If no rate of duty for which the article may be eligible is provided in the "Special" subcolumn for a particular provision in chapters 1 to 98, the rate of duty provided in the "General" subcolumn shall apply.

1/ Pursuant to Pub.L. 102-420, Oct. 16, 1992 (106 Stat. 2149), nondiscriminatory treatment was withdrawn from goods that are products of Serbia or Montenegro effective Oct. 31, 1992.

EXHIBIT 25.2   Sample Page from the Harmonized Tariff Schedule

HARMONIZED TARIFF SCHEDULE of the United States (1997)

IV

Annotated for Statistical Reporting Purposes

Heading/ Subheading	Stat. Suf- fix	Article Description	Units of Quantity	Rates of Duty		
				1		2
				General	Special	
2201		Waters, including natural or artificial mineral waters and aerated waters, not containing added sugar or other sweetening matter nor flavored; ice and snow:				
2201.10.00	00	Mineral waters and aerated waters.............	liters..	0.33¢/liter	Free (A,CA,E,IL,J, MX)	2.6¢/liter
2201.90.00	00	Other..	t.......	Free		Free
2202		Waters, including mineral waters and aerated waters, containing added sugar or other sweetening matter or flavored, and other nonalcoholic beverages, not including fruit or vegetable juices of heading 2009:				
2202.10.00		Waters, including mineral waters and aerated waters, containing added sugar or other sweetening matter or flavored................	....	0.3¢/liter	Free (A,CA,E,IL,J) 0.1¢/liter (MX)	4¢/liter
	20	Carbonated soft drinks: Containing high-intensity sweeteners (e.g., aspartame and/or saccharin)..................	liters			
	40	Other..............................	liters			
	60	Other.............................	liters			
2202.90		Other:				
2202.90.10		Milk-based drinks:				
2202.90.10	00	Chocolate milk drink...............	liters..	18.5%	Free (A+,E,IL,J) 2% (CA) 4% (MX)	20%
2202.90.22	00	Other: Described in general note 15 of the tariff schedule and entered pursuant to its provisions.....	liters.v kg	17.5%	Free (A+,E,IL,J, MX) 1.7% (CA)	35%
2202.90.24	00	Described in additional U.S. note 10 to chapter 4 and entered pursuant to its provisions...................	liters v kg	17.5%	Free (A+,E,IL,J) 1.7% (CA)	35%
2202.90.28	00	Other 1/......................	liters v kg	25.6¢/liter + 16.2%	See 9906.22.01- 9906.22.03 (MX)	27.6¢/liter + 17.5%
2202.90.30	00	Fruit or vegetable juices, fortified with vitamins or minerals: Orange juice: Not made from a juice having a degree of concentration of 1.5 or more (as determined before correction to the nearest 0.5 degree)...........	liters..	4.9¢/liter	Free (A+,E,IL,J) 0.5¢/liter (CA) See 9906.22.04- 9906.22.05 (MX)	18¢/liter
2202.90.35	00	Other........................	liters..	8.55¢/liter	Free (A+,E,IL,J) 0.9¢/liter (CA) 6.7¢/liter (MX)	18¢/liter
2202.90.36	00	Other: Juice of any single fruit or vegetable............	liters..	The rate applicable to the natural juice in heading 2009	Free (E,IL,J) The rate applicable to the natural juice in heading 2009 (A*,CA,MX)	The rate applicable to the natural juice in heading 2009
2202.90.37	00	Mixtures of juices............	liters..	The rate applicable to the natural juice in heading 2009	Free (E,IL,J) The rate applicable to the natural juice in heading 2009 (A,CA,MX)	The rate applicable to the natural juice in heading 2009
2202.90.90		Other...........................	....	0.3¢/liter	Free (A,CA,E,IL,J, MX)	4¢/liter
	10	Nonalcoholic beer.................	liters			
	90	Other.............................	liters			

such a *substantial transformation* occurs, the country of origin is considered to be the country in which the transformation took place.

Tariff Classification

Tariffs also vary depending on the article's *tariff classification*, that is, where it is best described in the HTS. Determining an article's classification is often a simple matter because many articles are described exactly in the schedules. For example, on the sample page shown in Exhibit 25.2, mineral waters are classified under item 2201.10. However, articles are not always as clearly described, and disagreements may occur. This is especially true of newly developed products. For example, under an earlier tariff schedule, optical fibers were not specifically described. Consequently, there was a question whether optical fibers should be classified as an article of glass, or an optical element, or part of a communications system.

Customs Valuation

The duty paid on an imported article depends on the value assigned to it by the Customs Service, that is, on the *customs valuation* of the article. The lower the valuation, the lower the duty.

The basic rule of customs valuation in the United States is that the value of an article for customs purposes is the *transaction value*, which is the price indicated on the sales invoice. Following this rule makes customs valuation for most imports a simple matter. However, there are exceptions to this rule. For example, if the importer and the foreign seller are related, the Customs Service is authorized to determine whether the invoice reflects a price negotiated by two parties at arm's length.

There are further rules to keep in mind. For example, the cost of foreign inland freight is not *dutiable* (subject to duty) if charged separately from the invoice price. If, however, the cost of foreign inland freight is included in the invoice price, then it is included in the valuation and becomes dutiable. Careful customs planning can avoid such needless costs.

Customs Laws

Proper customs planning can not only minimize the import duties paid but also help to avoid violations of the customs laws. Penalties can be severe and can involve forfeiture of the imported articles, along with heavy fines.

The U.S. customs laws are administered by the Customs Service. Its headquarters are in Washington, D.C., but the service has a district office at every U.S. port. Tariff rulings by the district offices can be appealed to headquarters and then to the U.S. Court of International Trade. Appeals from this court are to the U.S. Court of Appeals for the Federal Circuit and then to the U.S. Supreme Court. The customs laws are found in Title 19 of the U.S. Code. The regulations of the Customs Service are in Title 19 of the Code of Federal Regulations.

 ## Tariff Preferences

Pursuant to authority delegated by Congress, the president has established preferential tariffs for imports from certain developing countries. The most important of these tariffs is based on the Generalized System of Preferences.

The Generalized System of Preferences

The Generalized System of Preferences (GSP), which was agreed to multilaterally, is a program developed by the industrialized countries to assist developing nations by improving their ability to export. Under the GSP, which was adopted in Title V of the Trade Act of 1974,[4] the president has designated certain products as eligible for duty-free treatment if they are produced in developing countries designated as eligible beneficiaries of the program. The eligible countries and products are listed in General Note 3(c)(i) of the Harmonized Tariff Schedule (HTS). Products eligible for GSP treatment are indicated by an "A" in the "Special" column of the HTS.

Under the GSP, an eligible product receives duty-free treatment only if 35% or more of the value of the product was added in an eligible country. There are also limitations on the volume of eligible articles that may be imported from a single country. If the volume limitation is exceeded, the product is automatically removed from the category of eligible imports from that country.

If a country is found to be sufficiently competitive, the president can remove it from the program, either entirely or with respect to individual products. This process is referred to as "graduation." In 1989, Singapore,

---

4. 19 U.S.C. §§ 2461–66 (1998).

South Korea, and Taiwan were graduated from the program entirely. Countries can also be removed from the GSP program for policy reasons, such as failure to protect intellectual property rights. A review of the program is conducted annually to determine which countries and products should be removed from or added to the program. The program is administered for the president by the U.S. Trade Representative.

The Caribbean Basin Initiative

The Caribbean Basin Initiative (CBI), like the GSP, provides duty-free treatment for products from specified developing countries—in this case, the Caribbean nations. All products are eligible except import-sensitive items such as certain textiles and sugar. The Caribbean Basin Economic Recovery Act of 1983[5] authorized the president to designate the countries that would be beneficiaries of the initiative. Eligible products are designated by an "E" in the "Special" column of the HTS.

U.S.–Israel Free Trade Agreement

Under the U.S.–Israel Free Trade Agreement,[6] all tariffs between the United States and Israel were eliminated in 1995. It is strictly a bilateral agreement, so the tariff preferences apply only to trade between the two countries and not to imports from other countries. Congress approved the agreement in the United States–Israel Free Trade Area Implementation Act of 1985.[7] Eligible articles are indicated by "IL" in the "Special" column of the HTS.

North American Free Trade Agreement

An even more significant agreement is the trilateral North American Free Trade Agreement (NAFTA).[8] The agreement provides for the elimination of all barriers to trade between the United States, Canada, and Mexico and for the free cross-border movement of goods and services between the territories of the three signatories. Designed to improve the three countries'

economies and to benefit 390 million consumers with lower-priced goods and increased investment opportunities, NAFTA established the world's largest free trade zone. Congress approved the agreement on November 17, 1993, and it went into effect on January 1, 1994.

The pact gradually phases out tariffs between the United States, Canada, and Mexico, creating a large, open regional market and providing enhanced legal protection to foreign investors. NAFTA incorporated the provisions of a bilateral agreement between Canada and the United States that went into effect in 1989 providing for the elimination of tariffs and trade barriers over a 10-year period.[9]

Under NAFTA, Mexican tariff elimination on U.S. capital goods is staged in three categories: "A," "B," and "C." Tariffs on Category A goods were eliminated in January 1994. Category A goods include automobiles. Category B goods, which include textile and apparel goods, became duty free in 1998. Category C goods, which include the majority of capital goods, will be duty free in 2003. The United States eliminated the majority of tariffs on Mexican goods on January 1, 1994.

In addition to eliminating its custom duties, each country was required to accord national treatment to the goods of the other nations in accordance with Article III of the General Agreement on Tariffs and Trade (GATT) (discussed below). The agreement also substantially reduced the barriers to government procurement and effectively results in totally open procurement by the year 2004.

The agreement prohibited new restrictions on investment and on trade in services among the three countries. It included major provisions on specific industries, such as agriculture, telecommunication, and energy. In addition, special rules of origin were established to ensure that only products originating in the United States, Canada, or Mexico enjoy duty-free treatment. Certificates of origin are required on all goods being exported between the three countries to certify that the good qualifies as an "originating" good.

The pact also provided for the adequate protection and enforcement of intellectual property rights and attempted to ensure that these rights did not become barriers to trade. Each country was required to implement several international agreements regarding intellectual

---

5. 19 U.S.C. §§ 2461–66 (1998).

6. Free Trade Agreement, Apr. 22, 1985, United States–Israel, U.S.T. __, T.I.A.S. No. __, 24 I.L.M. 653 (1985).

7. 19 U.S.C. §§ 2701–07 (1998)).

8. North American Free Trade Agreement, Dec. 17, 1992, United States–Canada–Mexico, U.S.T. __, T.I.A.S. No. __, 32 I.L.M. 605 (1993).

9. Free Trade Agreement, Jan. 2, 1988, United States–Canada, U.S.T. __, T.I.A.S. No. __, 27 I.L.M. 281 (1988).

property rights, such as the Berne Convention for the Protection of Literary and Artistic Works and the Paris Convention for the Protection of Industrial Property Rights.

NAFTA explicitly protects U.S. environmental regulations and includes a mechanism for sanctions if Mexico fails to enforce its own environmental laws. In addition, a side agreement set up a three-nation mechanism, the Commission on Environmental Cooperation, to address environmental disputes. Any country or private interest group that believes that a nation is not enforcing its environmental laws may complain. If the commission determines that a violation has occurred, it can impose a fine up to $20 million or impose trade sanctions on the offending country. Since 1992, Mexico has enacted five major environmental statutes and numerous regulations (often modeled on U.S. environmental laws) and has drastically improved its environmental enforcement regime.[10] Even so, some environmentalists have faulted the commission for not demanding more, especially in the area of transboundary cleanup and remediation.[11]

The North American Agreement on Labor Cooperation, a side agreement that established panels in the United States, Mexico, and Canada to hear complaints about worker abuse, has had little impact.[12] The panels have restricted themselves to fact-finding. They cannot levy fines or impose trade sanctions unless there is a persistent lack of enforcement of existing child labor, safety and health, or minimum employment standards.[13] Several U.S. unions have argued that violations relating to freedom of association, collective bargaining, and strikes should also give rise to fines and trade sanctions, not just the high-level ministerial consultations called for in the side agreement.[14] In the words of counsel for the International Labor Rights Fund, who litigated the five cases filed in Mexico:

> [I]n all of these cases workers are left with a piece of paper that says 'you were right.' Not a single worker was

ever reinstated, not a single employer was sanctioned, no union was ever recognized.[15]

Fruit, vegetable, and sugarcane growers in Florida were concerned that the pact would leave them open to unfair competition from Mexican growers unburdened by high labor and regulatory costs. They also feared that Mexico, which has the same growing season as Florida, could replace Florida produce in some markets. Primarily to protect the Florida growers, the treaty phases out U.S. agricultural tariffs over 15 years. In addition, during that period, any dramatic increases in Mexican fruit and vegetable imports will trigger temporary "snap-back" tariffs to protect U.S. growers.

 ## Foreign Trade Zones

Foreign trade zones are special areas within or adjacent to a U.S. port of entry, that have been designated as such by the Foreign Trade Zones Board at the U.S. Department of Commerce.[16] Merchandise may be imported into the United States directly to a foreign trade zone; import duties normally due on entry into the United States are not due until the merchandise is withdrawn from the zone.

Foreign trade zones provide several advantages. Merchandise may be imported to a foreign trade zone for demonstration purposes only; if it is reexported from the zone, no duties are owed. Merchandise may be imported into a foreign trade zone and manufactured into a new article of commerce. In that case, duties are owed on the new article of commerce when it is withdrawn from the zone for consumption in the United States. This is advantageous to the importer if the rate of duty is lower on the manufactured product than on the imported intermediate product.

 ## World Trade Organization

Besides negotiating bilateral preferential agreements, the United States participates in the World Trade Organization (WTO), the successor to the General Agreement on Tariffs and Trade (GATT) entered into in

---

10. Richard H. Steinberg, *Trade-Environment Negotiations in the EU, NAFTA, and WTO: Regional Trajectories of Rule Development*, 91 Am. J. Int'l. L. 231 (1997).

11. Joel Millman, *Nafta's Do-Gooder Side Deals Disappoint*, Wall St. J., Oct. 15, 1997, at A19.

12. *Id.*

13. *Labor, Business Say Labor Side Accord Misses the Mark; Suggest Major Changes*, 66 U.S.L.W. 2515 (May 3, 1998).

14. *Id.*

15. Joel Millman, *Nafta's Do-Gooder Side Deals Disappoint*, Wall St. J., Oct. 15, 1997, at A19.

16. Foreign Trade Zones Act of 1934, 19 U.S.C. §§ 81a–u (1998).

DENIAL OF FAST-TRACK AUTHORITY

For the first time since President Franklin Delano Roosevelt began cutting tariffs in 1934, a U.S. president lost a significant vote in Congress for trade liberalization when Congress denied President Bill Clinton fast-track negotiating authority in 1997. *Fast-track negotiating authority* allows the president to negotiate trade agreements and then submit them for an up-or-down vote by Congress with no amendments permitted.

Organized labor fought ferociously against fast track based on its belief that expanded trade undermines job security and wages in the United States. Unions have insisted that future trade agreements contain labor safeguards enforceable by trade sanctions, a demand rejected by U.S. businesses and their Republican allies in Congress. House Minority Leader and presidential hopeful Richard Gephardt (D-Missouri) blamed the North American Free Trade Agreement for a glut in the avocado and tomato markets and for various plant closings in the United States.

Denial of fast-track authority weakens the president's ability to expand NAFTA to include Chile and eventually the entire hemisphere. This has assumed new importance in light of the creation of the South American trading bloc—Mercosur—which includes Argentina, Brazil, Paraguay, and Uruguay. Members of Mercosur enjoy reduced tariffs when trading with other Mercosur countries and are in the process of negotiating a reciprocal free trade pact with the European Union.

Since 1973, the wage gap between skilled and unskilled workers in the United States has widened. In 1973, a college graduate made $1.48 for every dollar earned by a high school graduate; that increased to $1.63 per dollar by the end of 1995. Trade has played a role in

widening the wage gap, but there is no consensus as to how significant that role has been. William Cline, chief economist at the Institute of International Finance, an association of large financial service companies, estimates that 10.1% of wage inequality is due to trade, compared to 3.7% attributable to technological change, 4.4% due to the decline of unions, and 2.9% attributable to immigration.[a]

Since NAFTA took effect in January 1994, approximately 150,000 U.S. garment workers (about 16% of the garment industry's work force) have lost their jobs, largely because of import competition from Mexico and other low-wage nations.[b] However, free trade has also created jobs by increasing exports; so, on balance, it appears to have been a wash.[c] Even so, recent polls showed that a majority of Americans believe that trade agreements, such as NAFTA, destroy jobs in the United States.

In some ways, the fast-track vote became a referendum on NAFTA, which was itself negotiated using fast-track authority. Vintners and cattle ranchers in California claimed that the Clinton administration had failed to live up to its promises to open up markets in Mexico, Canada, and Europe and to reduce tariffs on U.S. goods. The California wine industry was particularly concerned that President Clinton would use his fast-track authority to expand NAFTA to include Chile, a major competitor.[d]

a. Bob Davis, *At the Heart of the Trade Debate: Inequity*, WALL ST. J., Oct. 31, 1997, at A2.

b. *Id.*

c. Helene Cooper, *Expert's View of Nafta's Economic Impact: It's a Wash*, WALL ST. J., June 17, 1997, at A20.

d. Greg Hitt, *To California Vintners, Promised a Rose Garden, Fast-Track Bill Is Wreathed in Grapes of Wrath*, WALL ST. J., Oct. 6, 1997, at A24.

1994 (GATT 1994). The WTO came into existence on January 1, 1995,[17] after the conclusion of the Uruguay Round of GATT multilateral trade negotiations.

17. Agreement Establishing the World Trade Organization, Apr. 15, 1994, 33 I.L.M. 1132 (1994).

The Uruguay Round, the eighth in the history of the GATT, was the most ambitious GATT round ever held. The 117 nations agreed to reduce their tariffs by an average of one-third over six years. In addition, agricultural tariffs were reduced by 36% in industrial nations and 24% in developing nations. For the first time, agriculture, services, textiles, and investment services were covered by international rules of fair trade. The agreement, also for the first time, protected the right of service-sector companies to operate on foreign soil free of discriminatory laws.

The WTO oversees all the agreements reached in the Uruguay Round,[18] and it is the principal multilateral mechanism devoted to the regulation of international trade. As of 1998, the WTO had 132 members with another 31 (including Russia and China) waiting to join.

The United States lost its first case before the WTO in December 1997, when the WTO rejected Eastman Kodak Company's claims that Fuji Photo Film and the Japanese government had erected internal barriers to trade in Japan. This is discussed in the "Inside Story." The United States had won outright or obtained concessions in all 14 of the other cases it had brought at the WTO. The Kodak ruling sparked criticism of the WTO. In the words of Senator John Ashcroft (R-Missouri), the ruling "raises serious questions about the credibility of this international body and of the U.S. trade representatives' capacity to secure and defend free-trade agreements."[19]

WTO Dispute-Settlement Procedures

Before the establishment of the WTO, the defendant in a GATT dispute could, in effect, block dispute-settlement procedures (including reaching an agreement on the right to retaliate) because a decision by the GATT Council to adopt a panel report had to be unanimous. Under the WTO's Understanding on Rules and Procedures Governing the Settlement of Disputes, a panel of experts is to be established at the request of the complaining party and panel reports are to be adopted virtually automatically unless they are rejected by consensus of the WTO members.

 ## The GATT

The GATT has had a profound effect on world trade since its creation in 1947.[20] It established the *most favored nation (MFN)* principle, which has been the foundation of the world trading system. Article I of the GATT states that each member country must accord to all other WTO members tariff treatment no less favorable than it provides to any other country. In other words, if the United States agrees to lower its tariff on imports of a product from a certain country, it must grant the same treatment to all other member countries of the WTO. (The GSP and other preferential agreements discussed above are exceptions to the MFN principle and are authorized by the GATT.) The theory behind the MFN principle is that world trade will be enhanced if countries avoid discriminating among themselves and creating trading blocs that expand trade within the blocs but restrict trade between them.

Under the GATT, there has been a series of multilateral trade negotiations in which the GATT members agreed to tariff reductions. Despite the complexity and length of these negotiations, they have been enormously successful. Tariffs today are a small fraction, on the average, of what they were when the GATT was formed. A second basic principle of the GATT is that of *bound tariffs*. Each time tariffs are reduced, they become bound; that is, they may not be raised again. If any country raises its bound tariffs, it must compensate, normally in the form of other tariff concessions, the other WTO members. This principle is set out in Article II of the GATT.

A third basic principle, set out in Article III of the GATT, is that of *national treatment*. WTO members may not discriminate against imported products in favor of domestically produced "like products." Thus, for example, special taxes on imported goods are illegal if not applied equally to domestic products. The determination of what is a "like product" is done on a case-by-case basis by examining such factors as (1) the product's end-uses in a given market; (2) consumers' tastes and habits, which change from country to country; and (3) the product's properties, nature, and quality.[21]

Tariffs are not the only barrier to trade. Nontariff barriers in some cases have replaced tariffs as a means of protecting domestic industries threatened by import competition. For example, the preference often given to domestic products in government procurement can

18. Final Act Embodying the Results of the Uruguay Round of Multilateral Trade Negotiations, Apr. 15, 1994, 33 I.L.M. 1140 (1994).

19. Robert S. Greenberger et al., *WTO's Kodak Ruling Heightens Trade Tensions*, WALL ST. J., Dec. 8, 1997, at A3.

20. General Agreement on Tariffs and Trade, opened for signature Oct. 30, 1947, T.I.A.S. No. 1700, 55 U.N.T.S. 187.

21. World Trade Organization: Report of the Appellate Body in Japan—Taxes on Alcoholic Beverages, WTO Docs. WT/DS8/AB/R, WT/DS10/AB/R and WT/DS11/AB/4, 1997 BDIEL AD LEXIS 27 (Oct. 4, 1996) (holding that shochu and vodka are like products, so Japan could not tax imported vodka at a higher rate than domestic shochu).

"The prince married the princess, they got most favored nation status and lived happily ever after."

reduce the volume of imports. International codes designed to reduce nontariff barriers were negotiated during the Tokyo Round of the GATT (which occurred from 1973 to 1979).

The WTO agreement requires member states to participate in the Multilateral Trade Agreements (which include updated versions of many of the Tokyo Round codes), including (1) 14 Agreements on Trade in Goods (including the GATT 1994); (2) the General Agreement on Trade in Services (GATS); (3) the Agreement on Trade-Related Aspects of Intellectual Property Rights (TRIP); (4) the Understanding on Rules and Procedures Governing the Settlement of Disputes (DSU); and (5) the Trade Policy Review Mechanism (TPRM). These agreements are binding on all members of the WTO.

The GATT encourages regional economic integration and participation in free trade areas and customs unions. A *free trade area* is created when a group of states reduce or eliminate tariffs between themselves but maintain their own individual tariffs as to other states. A *customs union* is similar but involves the establishment of a common tariff for all other states.

Once a free trade area or customs union is established, the GATT rules apply to the area or union as a whole and not to the constituent states. Members of the WTO may participate in a free trade area or customs unions only if the area or union does not establish higher duties or more restrictive commercial regulations for other WTO countries. Even so, some experts warn that regional trade pacts pose a potential threat to the GATT by (1) diverting trade from cheaper suppliers outside the region; (2) making it possible for regional groups to raise barriers against each other, thereby creating projectionist blocks; and (3) complicating the creation of new global trade rules.[22]

GATT Health and Environmental Exceptions

Article XX of the GATT gives member states the right to adopt and enforce measures "necessary to protect human, animal or plant life or health" or "relating to the conservation of exhaustible natural resources." However, such measures cannot be applied in an arbitrary or unjustifiably discriminatory manner nor may they be used as a disguised restriction on trade. To date, this exception to national treatment has been construed very narrowly.[23] A GATT dispute resolution panel declared a U.S. embargo on tuna caught by fishing methods causing high dolphin mortality to be illegal.[24] Similarly, the U.S. reformulated gasoline standards (adopted as part of the Clean Air Act Amendments in 1990), which imposed tougher baselines for foreign producers and refiners, were successfully challenged by Venezuela and Brazil.[25]

The GATT-contracting parties established a new working Committee on Trade and Environment under the auspices of the WTO to make recommendations on the need for rules to enhance the positive interaction between trade and environment measures for the promotion of sustainable development, but to date the committee has done little.

The Agreement on the Application of Sanitary and Phytosanitary Measures (SPS Agreement), adopted as part of the Uruguay Round, deals with additives, contaminants, toxins, and disease-carrying organisms in food. The SPS Agreement gives WTO member states the right to take sanitary and phytosanitary measures that are "necessary" for the protection of human, animal, or plant life and health; but the measures cannot be discriminatory, disguised restrictions on trade or more trade restrictive than required to achieve their appropriate level of protection. A measure is not more trade restrictive than required unless there is another measure reasonably available and feasible that would accomplish the same result. The European Union unsuccessfully tried to defend its nine-year ban on hormone-treated imported meat as a health-related measure in the following case.

---

22. *Fifty Years On*, ECONOMIST, May 16, 1998, at 21.

23. *See* Thomas J. Schoenbaum, *International Trade and Protection of the Environment: The Continuing Search for Reconciliation*, 91 AM. J. INT'L L. 268 (1997).

24. United States—Restrictions on Imports of Tuna, 30 I.L.M. 1598 (1992).

---

25. United States—Standards for Reformulated and Conventional Gasoline, 35 I.L.M. 274 (1996).

A CASE IN POINT	**SUMMARY**

CASE 25.2
EC MEASURE CONCERNING MEAT AND MEAT PRODUCTS (HORMONES)
World Trade Organization Appellate Body
WTO Docs. WT/DS26/AB/R, WT/DS46/ABR
(Jan. 16, 1998).

FACTS   The European Union banned the import of all meat from cattle treated with any of six growth hormones. The United States and Canada claimed that the hormone ban was not based on convincing scientific evidence and conflicted with the SPS Agreement.

ISSUE PRESENTED   Under what circumstances can a WTO member set a level of consumer protection higher than international health standards?

SUMMARY OF OPINION   The WTO Appellate Body held that WTO members have a sovereign and autonomous right to set a level of sanitary protection for their own consumers that exceeds international health standards, as long as the sanitary measures are based on a scientific risk assessment. The risk assessment for human health is not a quantitative scientific analysis, but it must cover risk in human societies as they actually exist. Responsible and representative governments may act in good

Case 25.2 continues

Case 25.2 continued

faith on the basis of a divergent scientific view coming from qualified and respected scientists. But in this case, the EU scientific report's did not support the ban because the scientific studies did not focus specifically on residues in meat from hormone-treated cattle.

RESULT   The EU ban was inconsistent with the requirements of the SPS Agreement.

COMMENTS   The EU announced that the commission would consider how to implement its international obligations and to conduct a risk assessment meeting the Appellate Body's requirements. The U.S. Trade Representative (USTR) objected to a second EU risk assessment.[26]

---

26. John R. Schmertz, Jr. & Mike Meier, *WTO Appellate Body Issues Decision in EU–U.S. Dispute Concerning Hormone-treated Beef,* INT'L L. UPDATE (Feb. 1998).

MFN Status for China

In 1998, on the eve of the first visit by a U.S. president to China since the Tiananmen Square massacre in 1989, President Clinton renewed China's MFN status for another year and proposed that it be made permanent. In 1998, the United States denied MFN status to only six nations: Afghanistan, Cuba, Laos, North Korea, and the former Yugoslavia (Serbia and Montenegro). Clinton favored a policy of constructive engagement, arguing that, "[o]n balance, the evidence is that economic prosperity and economic openness lead to greater freedom and a higher quality of life across the board."[27] He highlighted the important role of China in stabilizing South Asia and its two new nuclear powers, Pakistan and India, and the restraint it has shown in not devaluing its currency in response to the crisis in Thailand, Indonesia, and South Korea.

Critics of MFN status for China point to the Chinese government's harsh treatment of dissidents and the people of Tibet, the use of prison labor, the persecution of religious sects, the sale of nuclear technology to Pakistan, and China's barriers to access to the Chinese markets. Representative Nancy Pelosi (D-Calif.), one of the most passionate advocates for severing normal trade with the repressive Chinese government, urged Clinton

to use the threat of revoking MFN status as leverage to reduce tariffs and to open markets to more products.[28]

Cancellation of China's favorable trade status would undermine the rapid pace of China's continued economic expansion. American businesses eager to invest in China would also be hurt. Many economists argued that the key to China's uninterrupted economic expansion has been the United States. In 1997, total United States–China trade was the equivalent of 8.3% of China's economic output, as measured by gross domestic product; one-third of China's exports (approximately $60 billion) went to the United States.[29] In contrast, only 3% of U.S. exports (approximately $12 billion) went to China. This caused a U.S. trade deficit with China of almost $50 billion in 1997.

Opponents of the withdrawal of China's MFN status argued that trade status should not be linked to human rights. They stated that trade with China is so important economically to the United States and so important for encouraging political reform in China, that the effects of a cancellation would be disastrous for both American business and Chinese reform. This was based on the presumption that if trade preferences were

---

27. *Clinton: What's at Stake in China,* BUS. WK., July 6, 1998, at 32.

28. George Raine, *Despite Critics, Clinton Backs Renewal of MFN,* SAN FRANCISCO SUNDAY EXAMINER & CHRON., June 28, 1998, at B-1, B-4.

29. Karby Leggett, *China Covets U.S. Consumers, Investors,* WALL ST. J., June 26, 1998, at A12.

withdrawn, average tariffs on Chinese goods would rise from 8% to 40%, making it very difficult for China to export to the United States.

 ## Import-Relief Laws

In a series of laws, known collectively as the import-relief laws, Congress has authorized the president to raise U.S. tariffs on specified products and to provide other forms of import protection to U.S. industries. These laws vary as to the nature of the unfair practice (if any) to which they are directed, the degree of injury required in order to obtain relief, the nature of the relief authorized, the agencies authorized to provide the relief, and the amount of discretion given to the president in determining whether to grant relief.

Section 201

Section 201 of the Trade Act of 1974 (*Section 201*)[30] provides for temporary relief to domestic industries seriously injured by increasing imports, regardless of whether unfair practices are involved. It is sometimes called the *fair trade law*. The relief is designed to give

---

30. 19 U.S.C. § 2251 (1998).

ETHICAL CONSIDERATION

Your company imports electronic parts from China for use in its finished products. If MFN status were revoked, you would have to buy these parts elsewhere, at a much higher price. This would reduce your profits on your most important products by one-fourth. Some, but not all, of your competitors would be similarly affected. Your trade association is considering lobbying the president and Congress to retain China's MFN status. Should you support this effort to resist, for commercial reasons, U.S. attempts to encourage better treatment of the Chinese citizens by their government? Consider whether trade with the United States will help or hinder the development of democracy in China.

the U.S. industry a few years (normally no more than five) to adjust to import competition.

The U.S. International Trade Commission (ITC) investigates petitions filed by U.S. industries. If the ITC makes an affirmative finding of injury from imports, it recommends specific import relief, such as higher duties or quantitative limits on imports. The president must provide the recommended relief unless he or she finds that it would not be in the national economic interest as defined in the law. Because import relief always has economic costs, such as inflationary effects, the president in many cases decides not to provide relief.

The Omnibus Trade and Competitiveness Act of 1988[31] encouraged petitioning industries to submit plans illustrating how they would use Section 201 relief to adjust to import competition. It further provides that the ITC should recommend relief that not only addresses the injury caused by imports but that also will facilitate the domestic industry's adjustment to import competition. As a complement to that, the law provides that the president can grant either import relief or other appropriate relief within his or her legal authority.

Thus, the law encourages making relief conditional on the ability of the domestic industry to meet the competition or to transfer its resources elsewhere. The legislative history suggests that, with this broader authority, Congress expects that relief will be granted in almost all cases sent to the president.

An excellent example of the use of Section 201 is provided by the U.S. steel industry. In 1984, when President Reagan negotiated the new set of voluntary steel-export restraints (discussed earlier in this chapter), he did so after the steel industry had filed a Section 201 petition. The International Trade Commission recommended relief, but President Reagan decided not to impose higher tariffs or mandatory quotas under this law. Instead, he negotiated voluntary bilateral agreements with most of the major steel-producing countries.

In another case, the ITC refused to recommend relief under Section 201 for the automobile industry. A majority of the commission found that the injury being suffered by the industry was not primarily caused by imports.

In the following case, the president rejected a recommendation by the ITC for quotas on shoe imports.

---

31. 15 U.S.C. §§ 78dd-1, 78dd-2, 78ff (1998).

| A CASE IN POINT | SUMMARY |

CASE 25.3
PRESIDENTIAL
DECISION UNDER
SECTION 201:
NONRUBBER
FOOTWEAR

Statement by the President,
Aug. 28, 1985.

FACTS   Following a request from the U.S. shoe industry, the Senate Finance Committee requested an investigation of imports of nonrubber footwear under Section 201 of the Trade Act of 1974. The International Trade Commission (ITC) determined by a five-to-zero vote that imports were a substantial cause of serious injury to the domestic industry. The ITC recommended that quotas be established on imports of nonrubber footwear for five years.

ISSUE PRESENTED   Would placing quotas on shoe imports be detrimental to the national economic interest?

DECISION   President Reagan rejected the recommendation for quotas. He reasoned that, in this case, the cost of protection would be too high. Quotas would cost the American consumer almost $3 billion, and the GATT rules would require the United States to compensate its trading partners with $2 billion in trade. There was no reason to believe that quotas would help the industry become more competitive.

RESULT   The recommendation by the International Trade Commission to provide relief was rejected.

COMMENTS   Like some other U.S. industries, footwear manufacturers had made several requests for relief from imports and had been granted relief in 1977 and again in 1981. Relief under Section 201 is supposed to be temporary in nature. President Reagan in essence decided that the purpose of Section 201, which is to give temporary breathing space so that the specific industry has the chance to become competitive, had already been fulfilled.

The ITC recommended relief in approximately 50% of the investigations made under Section 201. The presidents in office granted relief in approximately half of those cases.

The Antidumping Law

The antidumping law[32] is the most frequently used import-relief law. If a U.S. industry is materially injured by imports of a product being *dumped* in the United States (that is, sold below the current selling price in the exporter's home market or below the exporter's cost of production), the law imposes an antidumping duty on such imports. The amount of the duty is equal to the amount of the dumping margin, that is, the difference between the U.S. price and the price in the exporting country. If dumping and material injury are found to exist, relief is mandatory.

The law applies a different standard to countries with nonmarket economies (such as Socialist countries) in determining what constitutes dumping of imports from those countries, on the theory that prices in such countries do not reflect market forces and are therefore not a reasonable basis for determining whether price discrimination exists.

The U.S. steel industry has generated approximately 46% of the unfair trade complaints filed with the ITC in the last two decades even though steel accounts for less than 5% of U.S. imports.[33] Even though steelmakers lost approximately 54% of the dumping and unfair subsidy cases filed in the last 10 years at the ITC, companies

---

32. 19 U.S.C. §§ 1673–77 (1998).

33. Chris Adams, *U.S. Steelmakers Win Even When They Lose an Unfair-Trade Case*, WALL ST. J., Mar. 27, 1998, at A1.

learned that the mere fact of filing a complaint can cause imports from the target companies to drop.[34]

The Countervailing Duty Law

The countervailing duty law[35] provides that, if a U.S. industry is materially injured by imports of a product benefiting from a foreign subsidy, a *countervailing duty* must be imposed on those imports, that is, an import duty that offsets the amount of the benefit conferred by the subsidy. *Countervailable subsidies* are benefits provided by a government to stimulate exports. They can take many forms, including direct grants and loans to industry at below-market interest rates. For certain countries, injury to the U.S. industry is not a prerequisite; the existence of a countervailable subsidy suffices to trigger relief. As under the antidumping law, if subsidy and (where applicable) injury are found to exist, relief is mandatory.

Section 337

Section 337 of the Tariff Act of 1930 (*Section 337*)[36] provides that if a U.S. industry is injured (or there is a restraint or monopolization of trade in the United States) by reason of unfair acts in the importation of articles into the United States, an order must be issued requiring the exporters and importers to cease the unfair acts or, if necessary, excluding imports of the offending articles from all sources. This law applies to unfair competition of all kinds not covered in other import-relief laws, but is most commonly used in cases involving patent or trademark infringement. Relief is mandatory

---

34. *Id.*
35. 19 U.S.C. §§ 1303, 1671a–h (1998).
36. 19 U.S.C. § 1337 (1998).

ETHICAL CONSIDERATION

Is it ethical to automatically file an unfair trade complaint with the ITC whenever the market for your company's product goes soft?

---

unless the president disapproves the ITC decision, which seldom happens.

The Omnibus Trade and Competitiveness Act eliminated the requirement to show economic injury in cases involving intellectual property rights (infringement of patents, trademarks, and copyrights). The act affected most Section 337 cases and made it significantly easier for U.S. companies to obtain relief under this statute. The injury requirement had caused some cases by the U.S. industry to be lost and undoubtedly caused some companies to postpone filing Section 337 complaints until imports of the offending articles reached a significant volume. The theory behind the change was that American intellectual property rights needed better protection and that infringement of those rights constituted injury in and of itself.

Section 406

Section 406 of the Trade Act of 1974 (*Section 406*)[37] is similar to Section 201. It provides for import relief if a U.S. industry is suffering material injury by reason of rapidly increasing imports from a Communist country. Relief is discretionary.

Section 232

Section 232 of the Trade Expansion Act of 1962 (*Section 232*)[38] provides for relief from imports threatening to impair U.S. national security. It has been used very rarely. Relief is discretionary.

The Buy American Act

Under the Buy American Act,[39] federal agencies, in their procurement of supplies and equipment, must give a preference to products made in the United States unless their price is a certain percentage higher than the price of the equivalent foreign product. Products are deemed to be American made, and therefore eligible for the preference, if they are manufactured in the United States and at least 50% of the components are American made.

---

37. 19 U.S.C. § 2436 (1998).
38. 19 U.S.C. § 1862 (1998).
39. 41 U.S.C. §§ 10a–d (1998).

As noted earlier in this chapter, preferences to domestic industry in procurement by governments are a common form of nontariff barrier to imports that was addressed in one of the GATT codes. Pursuant to that code (the Agreement on Government Procurement),[40] many U.S. agencies have joined foreign agencies in eliminating this preference. However, defense-related articles are not subject to the agreement and hence still receive the Buy American Act preference.

 Laws Affecting Exports

The law known as *Section 301* is intended to facilitate exports. The Export Administration Act and the Arms Export Control Act are intended to control exports.

Section 301

Section 301 of the Trade Act of 1974[41] authorizes the U.S. Trade Representative (USTR) to investigate alleged unfair practices of foreign governments that impede U.S. exports of both goods and services. Subject to the five exceptions listed below, the USTR must take action in response to foreign government practices that (1) violate trade agreements with the United States, or (2) are unjustifiable (that is, in violation of the international legal rights of the United States) and burden or restrict U.S. commerce. The USTR has discretionary authority to take action if he or she determines that an act or policy of a foreign country is unreasonable or discriminatory and burdens or restricts U.S. commerce. Section 301 has been used with growing aggressiveness by the U.S. government.

The USTR is not required to take action if (1) a GATT panel concludes there is no unfair trade practice, (2) the USTR believes the foreign government is taking steps to solve the problem, (3) the foreign government agrees to provide compensation, (4) the action could adversely affect the American economy disproportionately to the benefit to be achieved, or (5) the national security of the United States could be harmed through action.

Section 301 gives the president (acting through the USTR) the ability to take unilateral action to penalize countries with trade practices that threaten American interests without going through the GATT. More than 95 cases have been investigated since 1974. Most were settled through negotiation, but 15 resulted in sanctions. European and Asian countries have decried this unilateral approach.

The legislative history of the U.S. bill implementing the Uruguay Round and creating the WTO strongly suggests that Congress did not intend the WTO dispute resolution process to displace the unilateral power vested in the USTR by Section 301.[42] The United States was strongly criticized when it bypassed the WTO and unilaterally imposed sanctions on Japan in a dispute over automobiles in 1995.[43] Since then, the United States has indicated that it will work within the WTO.[44] Failure to abide by a WTO decision or unilateral action under Section 301 in lieu of a WTO decision would greatly weaken the WTO and subject the United States to criticism for taking a pick-and-choose approach to trade disputes.[45]

The Omnibus Trade and Competitiveness Act of 1988 created a program known as *Super 301*, which required the USTR to draw up a list of the foreign governments whose practices pose the most significant barriers to U.S. exports and immediately commence Section 301 investigations with respect to these practices.

The Export Administration Act

The Export Administration Act of 1979[46] is the primary restriction on U.S. exports. It authorizes the secretary of commerce to prohibit exports when necessary to protect national security, carry out U.S. foreign policy, enforce U.S. nuclear nonproliferation policy, and prevent the export of goods that are in short supply. Some controls are imposed unilaterally by the United States. Others are imposed jointly with U.S. allies on exports to Communist countries. These are agreed on and administered through an informal arrangement known as CoCom.

---

40. 18 I.L.M. 1052 (1979).

41. 19 U.S.C. § 2411 (1998).

42. A. Lynne Puckett & William L. Reynolds, *Current Development: Rules, Sanctions and Enforcement under Section 301: At Odds with the WTO?* 90 AM. J. INT'L L. 675, 687 (1996).

43. *See, e.g.,* Nathaniel E. Nash, *The Lonely Americans: Isolated in a Trade War,* N.Y. TIMES, May 26, 1995, at D2.

44. *Coquilles and Muscles,* ECONOMIST, Sept. 30, 1995, at 91.

45. Puckett & Reynolds, *supra* note 42, at 688–89.

46. 50 U.S.C. App. § 2401 *et seq.* (1982 & Supp. 1987).

The act's most significant restrictions are those that control high technology and its products. The explosion of high-technology industries has resulted in a radical increase in the volume of U.S. exports that are controlled under this law. This restriction has had serious adverse consequences for U.S. exporters competing for business abroad.

One particularly controversial application of the act relates to encryption software. Several U.S. companies claim that their inability to sell software with so-called strong encryption puts them at a disadvantage in applications, such as electronic commerce, that require security.

The Omnibus Trade and Competitiveness Act of 1988, reflecting the importance attached to the trade deficit and the need to promote U.S. exports, removed many controls on exports, particularly to friendly countries. The United States and its allies are further reducing controls on exports to Eastern Europe and the former Soviet Union in the light of the reduced military threat now posed by those countries.

Export Licenses The export controls are enforced by a system of export licenses. Certain categories of commodities and technical data may not be exported without an export license from the Commerce Department's Bureau of Export Administration. The bureau reviews all applications and determines whether to issue licenses. Its decision in each case is based on a number of factors, including the nature of the item to be exported, the country to which it is to be shipped, the foreign consignee, and the use to which it will be put. The restrictions vary with all of these factors.

Managers should be aware of these controls when they plan export transactions and negotiate with foreign buyers. Moreover, they must ensure that the rules are followed. The rules are complex and easily misunderstood, and the civil and criminal penalties for violations are severe.

Three points are often overlooked by exporters. First, U.S. restrictions apply not only to exports of goods but also to exports of technology (referred to as technical data). Second, U.S. restrictions apply not only to exports from the United States, but also to many reexports of U.S.-origin goods and technology to third countries by other countries. The restrictions also apply to exports from other countries of certain foreign-made articles that are direct products of U.S. technology. Third, the transfer of technical data to a foreign citizen in the United States is generally considered to be an export, which

means that an export license is required. Such transfers include verbal exchanges of technology on U.S. soil and visits by foreign nationals to U.S. plants.

The Arms Export Control Act The Arms Export Control Act[47] authorizes the secretary of state to prohibit exports of munitions and munitions technology from the United States. The act is administered by the Office of Munitions Control of the State Department, which issues the International Traffic in Arms Regulations (ITARs) and operates a licensing system similar to that of the Commerce Department, based on the United States Munitions List.[48] The Commerce and State Departments both issue advisory opinions to exporters concerning the applicability of export controls to specific transactions.

 The Foreign Corrupt Practices Act

Following the discovery that more than 400 American corporations had made bribes or questionable payments abroad, the Foreign Corrupt Practices Act (FCPA)[49] was passed in 1977 as an amendment to the Securities Exchange Act of 1934 (the 1934 Act). The bribes in question were often given to high-ranking foreign officials to secure contracts with the foreign government. Bribes were also given to low-ranking officials to expedite the granting of routine requests, such as applications for permission to import or export.

Prohibited Payments

The FCPA prohibits any payment by a company, its employees, or its agents directly or indirectly to a foreign government official or a foreign political party for the purpose of improperly influencing government decisions in order to obtain business abroad. The statute is violated even if the bribe is only offered but never paid. It is also violated if the payment is made to a private company or individual with the knowledge that it will be funneled to the government.

An exception is made for payments to low-ranking officials who merely expedite the nondiscretionary granting of a permit or license. If any of the allegedly

47. 22 U.S.C. § 2751–96 (1998).

48. 22 C.F.R. Part 121 (1990).

49. 15 U.S.C. §§ 78a–78LLL (1988).

ETHICAL CONSIDERATION

France and other European countries have typically restricted American-made programs to a maximum of 50% of the total television broadcasts and have imposed a series of taxes on movie tickets, television movies, and videocassettes. The money generated from the taxes has been used to underwrite French films.

For years, Quebec has been concerned that the U.S. media would turn Canada into a mini–United States. In April 1998, federal regulators in Ottawa adopted a requirement that at least 35% of music played on local radio stations after January 1999 be Canadian, up from 25% to 30% in 1998. Similar restrictions on Canadian ads in publications with less than 60% Canadian content were also proposed to bolster local Canadian magazines, as were restrictions on distribution of movies in Canada by U.S. movie companies. (In 1997, 95% of the movies screened in Canada were foreign films.)[a] Sheila Copps, Canadian heritage minister, claimed that this is necessary to ensure "a dynamic forum for the expression of Canadian ideas and interests."[b] Cultural policies were exempted in part from NAFTA.

An earlier attempt by Canada to impose an 80% excise tax on advertisements in split-run editions of periodicals was struck down by the WTO as a violation of Article III's requirement of national treatment.[c] (A split-run edition of a magazine is one that both (1) contains advertisements primarily directed to a market in Canada, and (2) does not appear in identical form in all editions of an issue distributed in that periodical's country of origin.)

To what extent should media companies worry about protecting local culture? Should popular tastes prevail, as in the song "I Want My MTV!"?

a. Rosanna Tamburri, *Canada Considers New Stand against American Culture*, WALL ST. J., Feb. 4, 1998, at A18.

b. Joseph Weber, *Does Canadian Culture Need This Much Protection?* BUS. WK., June 8, 1998, at 37.

c. World Trade Organization: Report of the Appellate Body in Canada—Certain Measures Concerning Periodicals, WTO Doc. WT/DS31/AB/R, 1997 BDIEL AD LEXIS 12 (June 30, 1997).

nondiscretionary tasks paid for are in fact discretionary, however, the American company will be in violation of the FCPA. A second exception is made for payments to foreign businesses, as long as they are not acting as conduits for the money to pass to the foreign government.

A troublesome clause of the FCPA prohibited payments to third persons (such as local agents) with "reason to know" that the payment would be passed on to a government official or political party. This standard was considered by many to be unacceptably vague for a criminal statute. The Omnibus Trade Act amended this clause to prohibit such payments only when they are made with actual knowledge or a willful disregard of the fact that they will be used in violation of the law.

Directors, officers, employees, or agents of the corporation who willfully violate this portion of the FCPA are subject to a $100,000 fine and up to five years in prison; the corporation can be fined up to $2,000,000 or, if greater, twice its profits from the illegal activity. The FCPA is administered by both the Department of Justice and the Securities and Exchange Commission.

Record-keeping Requirements

The record-keeping requirements of the FCPA apply to all public companies that file periodic reports with the Securities and Exchange Commission under the 1934 Act. A purely domestic public company that is not engaged in foreign trade must still comply with the FCPA record-keeping requirements.

The FCPA requires each corporation to keep records that accurately reflect the dispositions of the company's assets and to implement internal controls to ensure that the corporation's transactions are completed as authorized by management. Periodic reports must be filed.

Failure to maintain the appropriate records and procedures is a violation, whether or not there is payment of a bribe. This portion of the FCPA was designed to prevent companies from developing a slush fund and then accounting for questionable payments as legitimate business expenses. The record-keeping provisions of the FCPA do not contain any specific penalties. Violations are punished in accordance with the basic criminal and civil sanctions under the 1934 Act, discussed in Chapter 15.

Mergers

Persons working in mergers and acquisitions must pay special attention to the FCPA. All target companies must be investigated to determine whether they are in compliance with the FCPA, particularly those that conduct business abroad or have a foreign subsidiary.

Prosecution

Both the SEC and the Department of Justice have stepped up prosecutions under the prohibited payments provisions of the FCPA.[50] In one case, Young and Rubicam, a prominent New York advertising agency, was indicted under the FCPA and the Racketeer Influenced and Corrupt Organizations Act (RICO). (RICO is discussed further in Chapter 15.) The government alleged that Young and Rubicam made payments to Jamaican government officials in order to acquire the lucrative Jamaican tourist advertising campaign. Young and Rubicam pled guilty to one count of conspiracy and agreed to pay a $500,000 fine to settle charges of encouraging bribes to foreign officials. All other charges under the FCPA and RICO were dropped.

In 1995, Lockheed Corporation pled guilty to violating the FCPA by paying money to a member of the Egyptian parliament who had previously been a consultant for Lockheed. Even after becoming a member of parliament, and thereby a "foreign official" under the act, the consultant continued to help Lockheed in Egypt with the sale of aircraft to the Egyptian government. To keep the arrangement secret, Lockheed allegedly paid commissions to a company controlled by the consultant's husband.[51] Lockheed paid a $24.8 million fine, representing double its profits on a contract for transport planes. One of its executives pled guilty to corruption charges, and another—the former regional vice-president for marketing at Lockheed—fled to Syria. After being imprisoned in Syria, he returned to the United States to pay a $125,000 fine and serve an 18-month jail term.[52]

International Initiatives

American companies have complained that the FCPA puts them at a competitive disadvantage compared with foreign companies from countries that permit the payment of bribes. Relief may be in sight due to the backlash in response to the political corruption scandals in Europe, Japan, and the former Soviet Union in the early 1990s. In 1994, the Council of the Organization for Economic Cooperation and Development (OECD), which consists of 25 member states from Europe, Australia, Canada, Japan, Mexico, and the United States, adopted a recommendation that member states take "concrete and meaningful steps" to deter and combat bribery of foreign officials.[53] The OECD recommended in 1996 that bribes paid to foreign public officials not be tax deductible. In 1997, the OECD proposed a treaty to ban bribes altogether.[54] The Organization of American States (OAS) created the Inter-American Convention against Corruption, which commits member states to (1) criminalize bribery of foreign officials, (2) make bribery an extraditable offense, and (3) waive the application of bank secrecy laws in corruption cases.

---

50. *See* Dominic Bencivenga, *Anti-Bribery Campaign: SEC Cracks Down on Illegal Payments Abroad*, N.Y.L.J., Apr. 10, 1997, at 5.

ETHICAL CONSIDERATION

The FCPA creates an ethical dilemma for the corporation that seeks to engage in commerce in a country where graft is a prerequisite to getting business accomplished. Many in the business community believe it will be difficult to impose American business values in other countries. What should a manager do?

---

51. Joseph P. Griffin, *Initiatives Abroad against Foreign Bribery Raise Prospect of Putting U.S. Firms, Foreign Rivals on Level Playing Field*, BNA's CORPORATE COUNSEL WEEKLY, Aug. 10, 1994, at 8.

52. Matthew J. McGrath et al., *The Foreign Corrupt Practices Act: A Trap for the Unwary*, NAT'L CONTRACT MGMT. ASSOC. TIPS (Mar. 1997), available at <http://www.mckennacuneo.com/practice/GovContracts/GC11019970209.html>.

53. *Id.*

54. Available at <http://www.oecd.org/daf/cmis/bribery/bribery.htm>.

Export Trading Companies

Before 1982, there were complaints that efforts by U.S. companies to compete abroad by pooling their resources were hindered by the U.S. antitrust laws. The Export Trading Company Act of 1982[55] sought to address these concerns.

Under this law, the Department of Commerce may certify an export trading company formed by two or more independent companies exclusively for export purposes. If a certificate is issued (with the concurrence of the Department of Justice), the participants in the export trading company are protected from private treble damage actions and government criminal and civil suits under federal and state antitrust laws for the export activities specified in the certificate. However, the law does not protect them from private antitrust actions for actual damages. Certification is authorized for export activities that do not restrain competition in the United States and do not constitute unfair competition in the U.S. export trade.

Bank Participation

In addition to the antitrust provisions, the act encourages the formation of export trading companies by allowing banking organizations to participate in the formation of such companies. This is an exception to the general rule against the participation of banks in commercial activities. The intention is to make the banks' resources available to U.S. exporters. The act also permits the Export–Import Bank of the United States (discussed below) to guarantee loans to export trading companies and other exporters. This provision, however, applies only to short-term loans, generally with a term of 12 months or less. The intention is to make available to exporters loans that would not otherwise be available.

 ## The Export–Import Bank

The Export–Import Bank of the United States (Eximbank) was created more than 50 years ago to provide financing for the purchase of U.S. exports. Eximbank is the U.S. government's response to foreign governments' export subsidies. By offering financing at below-market interest rates, Eximbank allows U.S. exporters to compete with foreign companies.

Major Programs

The major programs of Eximbank have traditionally been direct long-term loans at fixed interest rates to foreign buyers and financial guarantees. Long-term loans or guarantees are generally reserved for exports of turnkey projects, such as manufacturing, electric power, and petrochemical plants. Short-term and medium-term bank guarantees and short-term and medium-term export credit insurance are also provided. Other programs have been introduced over the years, including the I-Match Program, which authorized Eximbank to make interest-subsidy payments to private lenders when necessary to compete with foreign subsidized financing. Another program is the Tied Aid Credit War Chest, which authorized $300 million to be used to subsidize exports and fight mixed credit financing by foreign governments. This program is part of the Treasury Department's effort to negotiate a comprehensive agreement among the industrialized countries to limit the practice of mixing foreign aid with export credit, which distorts trade.

 ## The President's Power to Restrict Trade

Over the years, Congress has authorized the president to regulate or restrict trade and other economic activity when necessary to protect the U.S. national security, foreign policy, or economy. In 1917, Congress passed the Trading with the Enemy Act, which prohibited trade with enemies during time of war. The scope of the authority granted to the president under this law was expanded gradually to include the restriction of domestic and international commercial transactions in response to declared states of emergency.

The International Emergency Economic Powers Act,[56] passed in 1977, limited the president's authority to restrict trade and other commercial transactions to instances when a national emergency had been declared

---

55. 15 U.S.C. §§ 4001–21 (1998).

56. 50 U.S.C. §§ 1701–06 (1998).

in response to an "unusual and extraordinary threat, which has its source in whole or substantial part outside the United States, to the national security, foreign policy or economy of the United States."

The economic sanctions imposed under these laws are administered by the Office of Foreign Assets Control in the Department of the Treasury, which issues appropriate regulations. To varying degrees, the regulations apply not only to transactions in the United States but also to transactions by foreign affiliates of U.S. companies and to transactions abroad involving U.S. property.

The application of the regulations to foreign operations of U.S. companies has caused considerable difficulty, particularly for companies subjected to conflicting requirements imposed by foreign governments on their foreign affiliates. U.S. firms operating internationally must be aware of the potential application of these restrictions to all of their operations anywhere in the world, as demonstrated in the following case.

A CASE IN POINT	IN THE LANGUAGE OF THE COURT

CASE 25.4
DRESSER INDUSTRIES,
INC. v. BALDRIDGE
United States District Court
for the District of Columbia
549 F. Supp. 108
(D.D.C. 1982).

FACTS   In response to the imposition of martial law in Poland in 1982, President Reagan prohibited exports of certain equipment to the Soviet Union that could be used in building a gas pipeline between the Soviet Union and Western Europe. This economic sanction was intended to pressure the Soviet Union into permitting Poland to lift martial law. The United States failed to convince its European allies to join in the economic sanction. In an attempt to prevent European companies from exporting equipment to the Soviet Union for the pipeline, President Reagan ordered that the U.S. prohibition on exports to the pipeline be extended to all persons subject to U.S. jurisdiction.

Consequently, the U.S. Department of Commerce, in its order prohibiting exports of certain equipment to the Soviet Union, applied the prohibition not only to companies in the United States but also to foreign subsidiaries of U.S. companies. In addition, it prohibited the export from any country by any company (regardless of whether U.S.-owned) of equipment manufactured from technology obtained from the United States. Subsequently, the Department of Commerce issued orders imposing sanctions against a number of European companies for violation of its order. These sanctions denied the companies all U.S. export privileges.

European governments reacted angrily, claiming that this extraterritorial application of U.S. export controls violated their sovereignty and was contrary to international law. The British government acted to prohibit British companies from complying with the U.S. order. The French government, invoking its law, ordered the French subsidiaries to meet their contractual obligations by exporting equipment to the Soviet Union for the pipeline.

Dresser (France), S.A. and its U.S. parent, Dresser Industries, Inc., sought to enjoin the sanctions imposed on Dresser (France) by the U.S. Department of Commerce.

ISSUE PRESENTED   Can a foreign subsidiary of a U.S. company obtain a court injunction against sanctions imposed for violation of U.S. export regulations?

OPINION   GREEN, J., writing for the Federal District Court:

Most acutely evident to all those involved in this case is the potential for profound harm that could injure the United States should injunctive relief issue. The

Case 25.4 continues

Case 25.4 continued

regulations that lie at the heart of this dispute, which prohibit the export of certain goods and technology to the Soviet Union, particularly those goods sought for the construction of the gas pipeline between that country and Western Europe, were promulgated as part of a major foreign policy exercise. The purpose of this foreign policy action was to effectuate the response of the United States to certain events which have transpired over the past year in Poland, creating a political situation in that country which this country's leadership has declared unacceptable and which has shown no substantial sign of reversal to previous conditions. Accordingly, the United States has a grave interest in its ability to enforce these regulations which are, in its view, essential to the accomplishment of important foreign policy objectives. As the relief plaintiff seeks would only serve to benefit them and those doing business with them, to the potentially serious detriment of the United States, it cannot be doubted that the public interest does not lie with a grant of the injunction requested by plaintiffs.

RESULT   The federal district court denied the request for an injunction. The court found that there was still a possibility of an administrative resolution of the dispute and that the plaintiffs had therefore not shown that Dresser (France) would suffer irreparable harm if an injunction were not granted. In addition, such an injunction could potentially harm U.S. foreign policy objectives and would therefore not be in the public interest.

COMMENTS   As with other U.S. government attempts to apply its export controls to foreign subsidiaries of U.S. companies, this effort was unsuccessful, even though the sanctions were upheld by the court. Companies in Great Britain and France had no choice but to follow the orders of their governments, despite the U.S. sanctions.

Similar issues arose in connection with the Iran–Libya Sanctions Act of 1996 (which required the president to impose penalties on firms that invested more than $20 million a year in the oil and gas sector of Iran and Iraq in retaliation for their sponsoring international terrorism) and the Helms–Burton Act (which required the imposition of penalties on foreign firms that invested in Cuban property seized by the state after the Communist revolution in 1959). In May 1998, the Clinton administration agreed to waive sanctions against European firms that invest in energy projects in Iran or Libya or use confiscated property in Cuba. In exchange, the EU agreed to crack down on the sale of sensitive technologies to Libya and Iraq and to try to "inhibit" future European acquisitions of property in Cuba expropriated by Fidel Castro's regime.[57] The waiver was subject to approval by the Congress.

Questions

1. What type of harm would come to the United States if Dresser (France) had honored its contractual obligations?
2. Should the United States be able to dictate the trade practices of other countries?

---

57. Helene Cooper et al., *U.S. Ends Penalties against Cuban Trade*, WALL ST. J., May 19, 1998, at A2.

The European Union

The European Union (EU), formally known and still often referred to as the European Community (EC), is an intergovernmental organization of 15 states in Europe. Founded with the intention of creating a common market, the EU has embarked on an ambitious program to achieve complete economic, monetary, and eventually political union. The member states are Austria, Belgium, Denmark, Finland, France, Germany, Greece, Ireland, Italy, Luxembourg, the Netherlands, Portugal, Spain, Sweden, and the United Kingdom.

Through a process of gradual integration, the member states have created a common market with a total population of almost 370 million people. Goods, services, people, and capital can move almost as freely within the EU as within one country. There are no tariff barriers between the states, and all states apply a single set of tariffs (called the *common customs tariff*) on goods imported from outside the EU.

The EU negotiates international trade agreements on behalf of the member states. This includes negotiations with the World Trade Organization. The EU has the exclusive power to take action against dumping in the EU by companies in nonmember countries. Agriculture is centrally coordinated through the Common Agricultural Policy, which supports prices of agricultural products and promotes the modernization of agriculture throughout the EU.

EU competition law, based on U.S. antitrust principles, has been used by the European Community to prevent companies from engaging in private restraints of trade affecting the member states. For example, the European Commission required Boeing to abandon certain exclusive contracts it had with American Airlines as a condition to obtaining European approval of its acquisition of McDonnell–Douglas. The agreements adversely affected European aircraft company Airbus Industries by locking American Airlines in to purchases of Boeing aircraft for a period of 20 years.

The EU was established through the following treaties: the European Coal and Steel Community (established in 1951), the European Atomic Energy Commission (Euratom, established in 1957), the Treaty of Rome that established the European Economic Community (EEC) in 1957,[58] the Single European Act (1987) that led to the common market in December 1992, and the Treaty on European Union,[59] also known as the Maastricht Treaty, that established the European Union in 1993.

The Treaty of Rome created the four main institutions that have responsibility for governing the EU: (1) the European Commission, (2) the Council of Ministers, (3) the European Parliament, and (4) the European Court of Justice.

The European Commission

The European Commission is the executive branch of the EU. It comprises 20 individuals appointed by the governments of the member states. Each commissioner is in charge of one or more of the commission's 26 subdivisions, called directorates-general. Commissioners are expected to act independently of their national governments. With a staff of approximately 15,000 civil servants, the commission is at the heart of the EU's policy-making process. The Council of Ministers and the European Parliament need a proposal from the commission before they can pass legislation.

The primary functions of the commission consist of initiating proposals for legislation delegated to it by the Council of Ministers and the Maastricht Treaty, ensuring that EU legislation is applied correctly by the member states, and acting as managers and executors of EU policies and of international trade relationships. To this end, the commission formulates recommendations, addresses opinions to members, and may bring member states before the European Court of Justice for failure to carry out their obligations under the Maastricht Treaty.

The Council of Ministers

The Council of Ministers, officially known as the Council of the European Union, is the legislative body of the

---

58. Treaty Establishing the European Economic Community, Mar. 25, 1957, 298 U.N.T.S. 11.

59. Treaty on European Union, Feb. 7, 1992, 1992 O.J. (C 224) 1, 31 I.L.M. 247 (1992).

EU. It enacts legislation based on proposals referred to it by the commission. Members of the council are appointed by the governments of the member states and, unlike the commission members, they represent the interests of their respective states.

At one time, the most important decisions required a unanimous vote of the council. Since the enactment of the Single European Act in 1987, however, the vast majority of cases (including agriculture, fisheries, internal market, environment, and transport policies) require a qualified majority vote (62 of 87 votes). In other cases, the qualified majority is also 62 votes, but these must be cast by at least 10 member states. Each member state has a certain number of votes, generally in rough proportion to its population.

EU legislation may be in the form of *regulations*, which are directly applicable in the member states without the need for national measures to implement them. Legislation may also take two other forms. One is the *directive*, which is a law directing member states to enact certain laws or regulations. Directives are binding with respect to the objective to be achieved but allow national authorities to choose the form and means of implementation. The third form of legislation is the *decision*, which is an order directed at a specific person or member state.

The European Parliament

The members of the European Parliament (EP) are elected directly by the citizens of the member states (it is the only community body directly elected), generally in proportion to the population of each state.

Originally, the Treaty of Rome restricted the European Parliament to a mere consultative role, not a true legislative function. Subsequent treaties have extended the EP's purview to amending and even adopting legislation so that the parliament and the council now share decision-making power in many areas. The parliament must be consulted twice on each legislative proposal: First, it considers the proposed law at the committee level, then it expresses its opinion by a vote in plenary session. The parliament can reject the proposal, in which case the law can be enacted only by a unanimous council vote. It can also amend commission proposals, whereupon, if the commission supports the amendment, it can be defeated only by a unanimous council vote. Finally, the parliament has the power to dismiss the commission and to reject the commission's annual budget.

The European Court of Justice

The European Court of Justice (ECJ) is the judicial branch of the EU. Its role is to interpret the treaties establishing the EU. The ECJ has been a major force in affirming the powers of community institutions and therefore in the development of the single market. (A subsidiary court, the Court of First Instance, was established in 1989 to improve judicial protection of individual interests and enable the ECJ to concentrate its activities on the task of ensuring uniform interpretation of community law.) In addition to hearing and deciding adversarial proceedings, the ECJ may make interlocutory (or interim) rulings on legal issues raised by national courts. It may also advise other institutions of the EU.

The ECJ is not a court of appeals from the decisions of national courts, however; it can rule only on matters of community law. Private persons and companies may bring cases in the ECJ to annul EU measures if they can demonstrate individual harm from such measures. Similarly, they may challenge the commission's or the council's failure to act. Either the commission or a member state may bring infringement proceedings against a member state for violation of its treaty obligations. Although private litigants may not bring infringement proceedings against member states, they may bring an equivalent action in a national court. The national court, in turn, may refer to the ECJ questions that involve interpretations of the Maastricht Treaty, statutes adopted by the council, or acts of EU institutions. National courts from which no appeal may be taken are required to refer such questions to the ECJ. ECJ rulings on referred questions are binding on the court from which they were received.

The following case provides an example of how the ECJ interprets the EC treaty and conforms national actions to it.

A CASE IN POINT	SUMMARY

CASE 25.5
PHYTHERON
INTERNATIONAL, SA v.
JEAN BOURDON, SA
Court of Justice of the
European Communities
Case C-352/95 (1997).

FACTS   Two French companies, Phytheron International, SA (Phytheron) and Jean Bourdon, SA (Bourdon) entered into a contract whereby Bourdon agreed to purchase from Phytheron a pesticide (Previcur N) imported from Germany that was originally from Turkey. Bourdon later canceled the order before delivery, claiming that the trademark owner had lawfully refused to allow the product to be marketed in France, making the contract unenforceable. Under French law, only the owner of a trademark registered in France or its licensee may market a product bearing the trademark in France. Phytheron sued Bourdon in France for wrongful termination of the contract, arguing that because the product was lawfully imported and marketed in Germany, it had acquired the right of free movement within the European Union by virtue of community law.

Because resolution of the dispute depended on the interpretation of the community rules concerning the principle of free movement of products bearing trademarks, the French court referred the case to the European Court of Justice for a preliminary ruling on the principle of exhaustion of trademark owner's rights under community law.

ISSUE PRESENTED   Can a product covered by a protected trademark that was lawfully acquired by an independent trader in Germany be lawfully imported into France when French law permits the owner of the trademark in France to prevent importation into France?

SUMMARY OF OPINION   The European Court of Justice began by citing Article 7 of the Trademark Directive,[60] which deals with the exhaustion of trademark rights. Article 7 provides that the "trademark shall not entitle the proprietor to prohibit its use in relation to goods which have been put on the market in the Community under that trademark by the proprietor or with his consent" unless there are "legitimate reasons for the proprietor to oppose further commercialisation of the goods, especially where the condition of the goods is changed or impaired after they have been put on the market." The court stated that it was of no importance whether the product protected by the mark had been manufactured in a nonmember country as long as it had lawfully been put into the market in the Community.

Previcur N was marketed in Germany by or with the consent of the owner of the trademark in Germany, and that trademark was owned in both Germany and France by the same company, or at least by affiliated companies. As a result, application of the principle of the exhaustion of trademark rights could not be excluded on grounds relating to separate ownership of the mark in Germany and France.

The court also noted that Previcur N was a genuine product that had not undergone any processing or any alteration in packaging, save for the addition on the label, so there was no legitimate reason for the trademark owner to oppose the importation of the product from Germany. The court concluded that neither the trademark owner nor

Case 25.5 continues

---

60. Council Directive 89/104.

Case 25.5 continued

its licensee could invoke the French trademark legislation to oppose the marketing of Previcur N in France.

RESULT   Phytheron was allowed to sue Bourdon for damages resulting from the wrongful termination of the contract. Previcur N could be sold in France without first having to obtain permission from the company owning the French trademark.

The Single European Act

The goal of the Single European Act (SEA) was to remove all barriers to trade among member states by the end of 1992. In fact, much of the implementing legislation necessary for a true single market was enacted before then. The measures included the elimination of (1) physical barriers to trade (such as immigration and customs controls); (2) technical barriers (that is, national standards and requirements on the provision of goods and services, such as product standards and professional qualifications); and (3) fiscal barriers (such as differing national tax structures). These barriers made it difficult to transfer goods, services, capital, or persons from one member state to another.

Many laws were enacted in the form of directives ordering member states to harmonize their laws so that companies and individuals could operate on the basis of a single standard or rule. Others were enacted in order to facilitate mergers and other forms of economic cooperation across member state lines.

The creation of the single EU market has had profound effects on U.S. businesses. It has facilitated the formation of bigger European companies with a larger home market and has increased large-scale research and development in Europe. At the same time, the single market has created a larger market for American goods and has made the EU a more attractive place in which to invest.

The Maastricht Treaty on European Union

The Maastricht Treaty, officially known as the Treaty on European Union, is named after the Dutch city in which it was signed. After controversial ratification, it entered into force on November 1, 1993.

The Maastricht Treaty amended and supplemented the Treaty of Rome and provided for economic and monetary union as well as political union. The treaty imposed an obligation on all member states to converge their economic and monetary policies with the goal of creating a single European currency. The convergence criteria called for the member states to harmonize their budget deficits, inflation levels, public-sector debt, and long-term interest rates at specific target levels and to achieve exchange rate stability. As explained in the "Economic Perspective," the European Monetary Union is now scheduled to begin on January 1, 1999. The European Council allowed Britain to opt out of the single-currency system for as long as it desires. Britain will not be prevented from joining at a later date.

The political component of the Maastricht Treaty expanded the Community sphere to include immigration, tourism, health, education, consumer protection, and culture. European political cooperation has also been expanded. The Maastricht Treaty's Protocol on Social Policy enables all the member states to adopt social legislation by a qualified majority vote. Britain chose to opt out of this provision as well. The Maastricht Treaty also set as a goal the creation of a common foreign and security policy for all member states.

The Maastricht Treaty represented a significant step toward political and economic integration. It adopted the concept of a European Union, which no longer consisted of a European Economic Community but rather a European Community. Integration was furthered by the new provision in the Maastricht Treaty on European citizenship, which includes the right to travel freely within the territory of the European Union.

ECONOMIC PERSPECTIVE

THE EUROPEAN MONETARY UNION

The idea of a European Monetary Union (EMU) is not new. Since the 1970s and the creation of the European Monetary System, the members have benefited from cooperation. Indeed, the true advantages of a single market cannot be realized without a single currency. The major obstacle to the EMU was the surrender of national authority over vital instruments of policy to an intergovernmental body. By giving up their national currencies, the member states relinquish control of their exchange rates and independent monetary policy to the European Central Bank and they are required to maintain tight fiscal policies.

Despite these obstacles, the major decisions on European Monetary Union culminated with the ratification of the Maastricht Treaty in 1993. Had a majority of the member states met the convergence criteria of the Maastricht Treaty in 1993, the EU would have set a date for the EMU soon after. Instead, at the Madrid Summit in December 1995, the member states agreed on an implementation strategy for the single European currency (the *euro*) and a timetable for its final stage.

The start date for the EMU is January 1, 1999. Any two or more member states that meet the convergence criteria on the basis of 1997 figures must, under the terms of the treaty, join the single currency in 1999. In May 1998, the participating member states were chosen by the council on the basis of reports by the European Commission and the European Monetary Institute. Eleven European Union members qualified for participation in the euro: Austria, Belgium, Finland, France, Germany, Ireland, Italy, Luxembourg, the Netherlands, Portugal, and Spain. Greece will not meet the convergence criteria for some time; Britain, Sweden, and Denmark were eligible but adopted a wait-and-see approach.

The European Monetary Institute is central to the EMU. Its main tasks are to strengthen coordination of the monetary policies of the member states and to make preparations for the establishment of the European System of Central Banks (ESCB), with an independent European Central Bank (ECB) at its core, in late 1998.

On January 1, 1999, all currencies of participating member states will be irrevocably locked together at a specified conversion rate, and the euro will become of-

ficial currency. National currency units will become denominations of the euro; and the European Central Bank, to be located in Frankfurt, will take control of monetary policy for the euro zone. During this transitional period, national currencies will remain legal tender in participating states, but both the euro and national banknotes will be used simultaneously with prices posted in both denominations. On June 30, 2002, the French franc, the German mark, the Dutch guilder, and other European currencies (very likely including the British pound) will cease to exist, and the euro will become the sole currency for much of Europe.

The euro will greatly impact international trade and the world's financial markets. If all the member states who wish to participate qualify, the euro zone would include nearly 300 million inhabitants accounting for 19.6% of world GDP and 18.6% of world trade. This compares with 19.6% of world GDP and 16.6% of world trade for the United States.[a] As a result, the dollar-denominated world would give way to a multipolar monetary system built around the dollar, the euro, and, to a lesser extent, the yen.

The EMU will have many potential advantages for participants. Proponents of the euro claim that it will increase European competitiveness and economic clout in the world. Companies will no longer face the added transaction costs of exchanging currency and hedging foreign currency risks. Trade among the EMU nations will increase as the elimination of exchange-rate movements reduces the risks of cross-border investments. The new transparency of the common market, due to direct comparability of prices, business, and market opportunities, will also increase efficiency of resource allocation. Investment and financing opportunities will be offered in a broader financial market strengthened by greater competition and a stable single currency.

The EMU represents a giant step towards further integration within the EU. The EMU will result not just in a single currency and common monetary policy but will require the coordination of economic policies. But the EMU also brings some major downside risks. Setting one

Economic Perspective continues

Economic Perspective continued

short-term interest rate for a group of national economies that have different GDP growth rates and unemployment levels could cause regional economic imbalances, resulting in inflation in some areas and deflation in others, higher unemployment, social turmoil, and political backlash against the European Union. These problems would be exacerbated by the considerable differences in national tax rates, welfare systems, and labor flexibility among the members of the EU. Some experts predict that the EMU will deal with this problem by allowing some fiscal policy flexibility for the member states on the 3% deficit ceiling limit once the EMU is underway and greater tax harmonization. In the long run, such regional problems should recede, but the real challenge lies in sustaining public support for the EMU in the interim.

a. *See* <http://europa.eu.int/comm/off/rep/conver/98273_en.htm>.

THE RESPONSIBLE MANAGER
Engaging in International Trade

It is important to plan in advance for import and export operations. There are many restrictions and other important rules that may affect the operation. Failure to plan can lead to inadvertent violations of law. A common mistake by exporters is providing technology to foreign persons without obtaining the prerequisite export licenses. Traveling abroad with a laptop computer loaded with strong encryption software could violate applicable law. Assigning an incorrect value to imported goods for customs purposes is another violation. Lack of planning can also cause the company to miss benefits such as duty-free treatment under the North American Free Trade Agreement and other international agreements.

Managers need to take the rapid changes occurring in world trade into account. Barriers to trade with Eastern European countries have been removed. Significant reduction of barriers to trade with other countries are being negotiated. New markets and new opportunities are arising with great speed. At the same time, these changes carry new risks for managers. They will cause increased competition not only overseas, but also in the United States. Government regulation of trade will change, but not as rapidly as the world is changing. Managers should keep abreast of regulatory changes and should also be aware of gaps between the new realities of world trade and the government's efforts to regulate.

INSIDE STORY
SNAPSHOT OF KODAK–FUJI TRADE DISPUTE

In 1997, Eastman Kodak Company (Kodak) fired its best shot in its long-standing fight against Fuji Photo Film Company (Fujifilm) and the Japanese government for access to the Japanese photographic products market. Kodak convinced the U.S. government to file a case with the World Trade Organization (WTO) alleging that Fujifilm, with the cooperation of the Japanese government, engaged in unfair trade practices that restricted Kodak's ability to compete in Japanese markets.[61]

In the 1990s, Japan had the third largest photo-finishing and photographic film and paper market in the world, after the United States and the European Union. Kodak had been in the Japanese market since before World War II, but as of 1996 had only 10% market share. Outside of Japan, Kodak was the largest manufacturer of photographic supplies, with 36% of the world market (excluding Japan), followed by Fujifilm with 33%. Kodak had spent $750 million over 10 years in Japan and still had been unable to gain market share; indeed, Kodak had seen its market share decline from its 1983 high of 18%.

Furthermore, Fujifilm was gaining market share in the United States at the expense of Kodak through aggressive pricing strategies (cutting prices by as much as 50% on some products) and exclusive supplier deals with Wal-Mart and Ritz Camera. Fujifilm's market share (based on number of rolls of film sold in the United States) increased from 12.6% in 1996 to 19.8% in 1997, while Kodak's dropped from 75.5% in 1996 to 67% in 1997.[62] Similarly, Fujifilm's share of the dollars spent in the U.S. film market increased from 11% in 1996 to 15% to 16% in 1997. (Fujifilm's share of dollars spent is less than its share based on rolls of film sold because Kodak's prices are higher.)

Fujifilm and Kodak had a history of disputes over business practices. In the early 1990s, Kodak charged Fujifilm with dumping photographic paper. Fujifilm was able to avoid the duties that were to be imposed after a U.S. Department of Commerce investigation by agreeing to raise prices. The resulting price increase caused Fujifilm to lose almost all its market share at the time, but it gained much of it back when it opened a paper plant in South Carolina to source its U.S. paper sales.

In May 1995, Kodak requested that the U.S. Trade Representative (USTR) investigate Fujifilm's business practices under Section 301, which would allow the United States to impose sanctions if the problems identified were not remedied. The USTR investigation validated many of Kodak's complaints, but the Japanese refused to negotiate under the terms of Section 301. One Japanese trade official stated, "We will not engage in consultations or negotiations with the U.S. government on issues raised in the context of Section 301 of the U.S. Trade Act because this approach, with the threat of unilateral measures, is inconsistent with international rules."

Kodak then sought relief through the Japan Fair Trade Commission (JFTC), stating that Fujifilm engaged in anticompetitive activities. The JFTC found that Fujifilm's practices did not violate Japanese antimonopoly law; but it did suggest some changes that Fujifilm might make in the way it conducted business in Japan, including reviewing its payments for sales promotions and its system of guaranteeing deposits. Other suggestions for change, such as not tying sales of photographic paper to mini–lab processing equipment, pertained to the entire industry.

In mid-1996, Kodak, injured and angry from its price war with Fujifilm and seeing further erosion in its margins due to delays in release of its digital-photography products, convinced the USTR to request consultations with the WTO regarding market access and alleged trade-agreement violations by Fujifilm and the Japanese government. The United States alleged that for three decades the Japanese government and Fujifilm had engaged in anticompetitive activities, including encouragement of integration among the retailers, wholesalers, and manufacturers (the *keiretsu* system) and specific countermeasures that limited price competition and promotions through discounts and coupons. Kodak contended that these actions prevented foreign firms from developing effective distribution systems and made it impossible to compete effectively on price.

Fujifilm, for its part, vigorously disputed all the allegations. In response to Kodak's allegation that Kodak's small market share in Japan was indicative of anticompetitive practices, Fujifilm pointed to its own similar market share in the United States (11% based on dollars spent in the U.S. market). Fujifilm argued that Kodak had perpetrated in the United States many of the activities Kodak accused Fujifilm of conducting in Japan. The biggest example of this was single-brand wholesale distribution, which Fujifilm contended is standard practice in the photographic film industry worldwide. Fujifilm also stated that if Kodak felt that these things had been problems since the 1960s, it should have brought them up with the JFTC. No private party has ever been successful in bringing a suit under Japan's antimonopoly law, however, and there are other conditions that must be met that make it unappealing for a party to file suit.

Fujifilm also contended, via documents stored on its Web site,[64] that Kodak's low market share in Japan was the result of a series of mistakes on the part of Kodak executives working in Japan. Fujifilm maintained that

Kodak could have increased market share by investing in Japanese distributors or entering into joint ventures in manufacturing, photofinishing, or distribution, even when Japanese law was restrictive on the amount of foreign investment allowed. Further, the Fujifilm documents stated that even when restrictions were relaxed to allow 100% ownership by foreign companies, Kodak did not take advantage of the opportunity.

The 1997 case before the WTO was followed with great interest. This was the first major case under the strengthened rules for dispute settlement agreed on at the Uruguay Round of the GATT that forbid members from unilaterally electing not to adopt WTO panel reports, as they had done in the past. Appeals may be made on a point of law, but rejection of the report requires unanimous approval of the WTO membership. The United States, which had not been supportive of WTO decisions in the past, had put its fate in the hands of the international body, in a case that wasn't a clear winner.

In December 1997, the WTO found that there was no evidence to support the U.S. case that Japanese protectionism was the cause of Kodak's low market share in Japan. The United States appealed the decision; but, in January 1998, the WTO confirmed its original finding, much to the dismay of Kodak and the USTR. In response to the ruling, U.S. trade officials expressed disapproval of the decision, stating that the WTO did not have the expertise or experience to adjudicate complex issues of competition. U.S. officials stated that they would monitor and test the openness of the Japanese market.

Japanese and Fujifilm officials were pleased with the results of the WTO proceeding, although unhappy with the United States call for on-going monitoring. As Fujifilm's Washington, D.C., lawyer stated, "The WTO decision was not a close call. It was a sweeping rejection of U.S. film claims about Japan. There are no private or government restrictions on Kodak's ability to sell film in Japan."[65]

Perhaps a harbinger of better times ahead, Kodak won the bid to be the official sponsor of the 1998 Winter Olympics in Nagano, Japan. This gave it exclusive rights to distribute film in and around the Nagano region during the Olympics.

---

61. For an excellent discussion of Kodak's market and nonmarket strategies for increasing its market share in Japan and competing globally with Fujifilm, *see* David P. Baron, *Integrated Strategy, Trade Policy, and Global Competition*, 39 CAL. MGMT. REV. 145 (1997), and David P. Baron, *Integrated Strategy and International Trade Disputes: The Kodak–Fujifilm Case*, 6 J. ECON. & MGMT. STRATEGY 291 (1997).

62. Robert S. Greenberger et al., *WTO's Kodak Ruling Heightens Trade Tensions*, WALL ST. J., Dec. 8, 1997, at A3, A11.

63. *Japan Official: Govt. Won't Engage In Fuji-Kodak Dispute*, DOW JONES NEWS SERVICE, Jan. 8, 1996.

64. <http://www.fujifilm.com/index2.htm>.

65. *U.S. To Monitor Japanese Photo Film Maker*, DOW JONES NEWS SERVICE, Feb. 3, 1998.

KEY WORDS AND PHRASES

QUESTIONS AND CASE PROBLEMS

1. A fast-growing U.S. beverage company wishes to import mineral water and has asked you, its vice-president for purchasing, to recommend foreign sources. You know that sources exist in France, Canada, and Australia. What U.S. trade laws should you consider in choosing among these sources?

2. Assume that you determine that the best source of mineral water for your purposes is France, but the tariff makes imports from that country noncompetitive. How could you seek a reduction in this tariff?

3. You are the vice-president for marketing at a U.S. manufacturer of electric shavers. Imports of electric shavers have been increasing rapidly in the last year, undercutting your prices and taking significant market share from your company. The shavers are coming from five countries. You know that exporters in two of these countries are selling in the United States at prices below their home market prices and that exporters in two other countries are receiving export subsidies. The single exporter in the fifth country appears to be infringing on a patent that your company holds on a particular type of electric shaver, but your lawyers have said it is not a strong patent. Which U.S. import-relief laws might be available to you to relieve the competitive pressure from these imports?

4. You are president of a U.S. engineering company. You have made a competitive bid to help design a new airport to be built by the Japanese government, but your bid has not been accepted. You believe that all significant engineering work on this project is being reserved by the government for Japanese companies. You are concerned that future projects will also be reserved for local companies. Does U.S. law provide for any relief?

5. In each of the following situations, name the U.S. government agency to which a request for assistance or petition for relief would be most appropriately addressed.

a. You believe that your company's domestic sales are being damaged by increasing imports from country X. No unfair trade practices are being employed by country X.

b. You believe that your company's export business to country Y is limited by unfair practices of that country's government.

c. Your company specializes in research and development. New technologies developed by your firm often have important military applications. The government of country Z makes your company a very attractive offer to purchase a recently developed technology. You would like to accept the offer, but you are unsure whether export of the technology is prohibited under the Arms Export Control Act.

6. Your company is U.S.-based and has a subsidiary in France. The French government is encouraging companies to do business in Shangri-la, a country with colonial ties to France but with a Marxist dictatorship. The United States has imposed an embargo on all U.S. trade with that country. Can your French subsidiary sell its products to Shangri-la? Should it?

7. You are discussing the possibility of licensing know-how to a Vietnamese company for the manufacture of personal computers. A delegation is coming to visit your company in Massachusetts to negotiate the terms of the license, to see your plant and to discuss your technology. What laws and regulations might be applicable to this meeting?

8. Glenn Levy works for Waks Enterprises, a foreign subsidiary of Curtis Holding Company, a U.S. corporation. His supervisor has in the past asked him to make payments to a low-level government employee of Aldebaran, the foreign country in which Waks Enterprises is located, to "get the paperwork moving." Levy has always made these payments. His supervisor has now asked him to make a payment to Seith Petrylak, who is known to have influence with the Aldebaron minister of finance. Levy does not know what the payment is for.

Should Levy make the payment to Petrylak? Could any of Levy's actions result in criminal penalties? Does Waks Enterprises face any criminal penalties? What about Curtis Holding Company? What is the ethical thing to do?

9. The Thailand Tobacco Acts of 1966 prohibited the importation of tobacco except by license of the director-general. No licenses for cigarettes had been issued for more than 10 years. The United States argued that this violated the GATT's prohibition on import-license restrictions on the import of products of other GATT members. Thailand argued that its ban on the importation of cigarettes came within the GATT's exception for measures necessary to protect human life or health. Result? [*Thailand—Restrictions on Importation of and Internal Taxes on Cigarettes*, GATT Doc. D510/R (Nov. 7, 1990)]

MANAGER'S DILEMMA

10. After the passage of NAFTA, several members of the Clinton administration suggested that the Super 301 program should be reinstated. Do you agree with their proposal? Why?

INTERNET SOURCES	
International Trade Law	http://itl.irv.uit.no/trade_law
U.S. Department of Commerce	http://www.doc.gov
U.S. International Trade Commission	http://www.usitc.gov
U.S. Trade Representative	http://www.ustr.gov
World Trade Organization	http://www.wto.org
A Summary of the Final Act of the Uruguay Round is available at this site.	http://www.wto.org/wto/legal/ursum_wp.htm
This site is maintained by Transparency International, a nongovenmental organization formed in 1993 to raise global awareness of corruption. It publishes an annual Corruption Index, which measures perceptions of corruption around the world.	http://www.transparency.de
This site for the International Law Section of the Academy of Legal Studies in Business provides extensive and useful links to international business law–related sites on the Internet.	http://www.wsu.edu/~legal/alsb_ils
This is the site for the *International Business Law Journal*, an on-line journal containing professional articles relating to public and private international law edited by the International Law Section of the Academy of Legal Studies in Business.	http://www.wsu.edu:8080/~legal/ijrnl/
United Nations Commission on Sustainable Development	http://www.un.org/esa/sustdev

CHAPTER 26

International Transactions

INTRODUCTION

Managing in a Global Economy

Managers in today's global economy can expect to engage in one or more types of international business transactions, including (1) sales and leasing of goods and services, (2) transfers of technology, (3) equity investments, and (4) international lending. The variety of types of transactions, potentially complex transaction structures, and diverse legal and business environments involved in international transactions create a wealth of issues and risks, but also opportunities, that may not be seen in many domestic transactions.

Chapter Overview

This chapter begins with a discussion of buying and selling goods abroad, focusing primarily on the international sales contract but also reviewing leasing, compensation trade, and processing operations. The chapter then shifts to issues involved with international transfers of technology through licensing and franchising. The threads of sales and technology transfer issues are drawn together in the context of overseas investment, which often involves multilayered cross-border relationships. The discussion of overseas investment focuses first on the planning stage, including the need to set investment goals, obtain accurate information dealing with economic and political conditions in the host country, and evaluate site options properly. The chapter then addresses operational concerns and language and cultural considerations, as well as the laws governing doing business with and litigating against foreign governments. The discussion concludes with a review of the process of managing international transactions from a U.S. perspective.

 Buying and Selling Abroad

The most common form of international business involves the buying and selling of tangible goods. Importers of foreign products to the United States must be aware of regulations governing U.S. businesses (in addition to the U.S. tariffs and trade laws discussed in Chapter 25). Exporters of U.S. products are also affected by laws (also discussed in Chapter 25) regulating export of products or information and providing benefits to certain exporters. Such U.S. regulations may apply even to transactions entirely outside the United States among non-U.S. parties.

The laws and regulations of other countries involved in a transaction may also apply, and they may impose restrictions or requirements different from or occasionally even entirely incompatible with those that exist under U.S. law. Customs and usages of international and domestic trade in other countries, as well as local industry practices, add yet another layer of complexity. Some of these are reflected in multilateral and bilateral treaties, but many other restrictions are less formal or even unwritten. By dealing through a knowledgeable agent or distributor with a presence abroad, a U.S. importer or exporter can reduce some of the risk from unforeseen foreign laws and practices. Local bankers, accountants, and lawyers can also play a valuable role. When issues have been identified, they can be addressed and risks reapportioned in the relevant agency contract, distributorship agreement, or direct international sales contract.

 The International Sales Contract

An international contract, like a domestic one, may reallocate rights, obligations, and risks in a way different from what they would be in the absence of the contract under applicable law. In an international context, however, the practices common to the parties may be fewer, their assumptions and expectations more divergent, and the risks greater. There is, in short, more ground to be covered to ensure a true meeting of the minds—and more risk and uncertainty in proceeding without one.

Applicable Law

The substantive terms of a contract are typically subject to the laws of a single jurisdiction. Those laws will clarify, modify, or even render voidable the provisions of a contract. If a contract leaves an issue open, the applicable law may fill the gap, disregarding the parties' unwritten intentions. Certain provisions may be included to address requirements of laws of other jurisdictions (for example, U.S. export controls may affect non-U.S. contracts). Even if the written contract addresses an issue, that provision may be affected by what is allowed or required under the relevant local law; it is important, therefore, to understand clearly not only what the parties wish to do but also what they are permitted to do.

On both these levels, achieving understanding can be difficult. Familiar legal terms in one jurisdiction may have a different meaning and effect in another. Only a small proportion of the business people, lawyers, accountants, and other advisors in each jurisdiction will understand the relevant differences between that jurisdiction and another sufficiently to fully address the intricacies of cross-border transactions (although an approximation is often sufficient in practice). Having advisors with this capability is important.

One technique of reducing risk is to provide that the laws of a familiar jurisdiction will govern interpretation and implementation of the contract (for example, California law might be used for an Asian–European contract). This option is available, at least in part, in most international transactions involving sales, leasing, or the licensing of goods. Explicit choice-of-law and choice-of-forum provisions are advisable in order to avoid later disputes over which law applies and which country's courts have jurisdiction. (A lawsuit brought in one country may be tried under the law of another country.) When jurisdiction and choice of law are disputed, the court in which the suit is filed will apply *conflict-of-laws* principles. Although these usually focus on the significance of each country's relationship to the contract, these principles (sometimes referred to as principles of private international law) vary in some respects from country to country and the process of litigating these issues can be extended and expensive. Consequently, addressing these issues in advance is prudent.

As explained in Chapter 8, if both parties to an international sales contract are nationals of countries that are signatories to the United Nations Convention on Contracts for the International Sale of Goods (CISG), the rules of that convention may apply, unless the parties opt out of the CISG rules. CISG rules are also applicable if the country whose law applies (as determined by the contract or by conflict-of-laws principles) is a signatory to CISG.

The way a claim is framed will sometimes determine whether the choice-of-law provision in a contract will apply and be honored, as is demonstrated in the following case.

| **A CASE IN POINT** | **SUMMARY** |

CASE 26.1
AROCHEM CORP. v.
WILOMI, INC.
United States Court of
Appeals for the Fifth Circuit
962 F.2d 496 (5th Cir. 1992).

FACTS   On September 1, 1988, Marimpex, Inc., a German oil trader, entered into a charter agreement with Wilomi, Inc., an oil company, for the transport of crude oil from Scotland to the U.S. Gulf Coast aboard Wilomi's tanker. The agreement provided that English law was to govern the agreement's construction and performance.

On September 19, 1988, while the oil was en route, Arochem Corporation, an American oil company, purchased the oil from Marimpex. The ship's destination was changed to Puerto Rico. Upon its arrival, Marimpex informed Wilomi that it was unable to pay for the delivery. Consequently, Wilomi filed lien notices with the U.S. Customs office in Puerto Rico and commenced an action in the U.S. District Court for the Eastern District of Texas. (A *lien notice* is a written notice that a claim has been placed on property for the payment of a debt.) Arochem was unaware of these actions.

A U.S. marshal *arrested* (seized) the cargo aboard the tanker in Nederland, Texas. Marimpex thereafter paid the amount owed for the freight, and the cargo was released. Arochem then brought suit for damages stemming from Wilomi's allegedly wrongful arrest. The federal district court held that U.S. law, not English law, governed the dispute.

ISSUE PRESENTED   Should U.S. law or English law govern a suit for wrongful arrest of cargo in the United States by a U.S. marshal when the cargo was originally sold under a contract providing for application of English law to which the U.S. plaintiff was not a party?

SUMMARY OF OPINION   The U.S. Court of Appeals began by noting the relationship of the United States to the cargo. The wrongful act claimed in the lawsuit was the arrest of the cargo in Nederland, Texas, after its transshipment. The transporting ship bore American registry. The legal entity claiming injury, Arochem, is a Delaware corporation with a principal place of business in Stamford, Connecticut.

Both American and English courts are equally competent and accessible. The court recognized that the charter agreement was negotiated, drafted, and executed in London and that the agreement itself provided for English law to govern its construction and performance. This factor was rendered insignificant, however, because plaintiff Arochem was not a party to the charter agreement.

Arochem's claim is for wrongful arrest by a U.S. marshal in a U.S. port. Arochem is a U.S. company, and Wilomi has a place of business and a general agent in the United States. These contacts between the transaction and the United States make it consistent and rational to apply U.S. law.

Although the contract was formed in England, the court considered it illogical to argue that England has as great an interest as the United States does in protecting an American purchaser from an unlawful arrest of cargo on an American vessel in an American port. The court upheld the district court's application of American law.

RESULT   U.S. law, not English, governed the suit for wrongful arrest of cargo.

Dispute Resolution

The choice of a forum and a procedure for resolution of contract disputes is distinct from the choice of substantive law. A contract party may be willing to accept the substantive law of the other party's country, but prefer that it be applied by a neutral body. When a neutral forum is desired, an international arbitral organization is commonly specified. Arbitration is preferable for several reasons. International arbitral bodies are often more experienced in dealing with international commercial disputes than their judicial counterparts. Many argue that arbitration is typically a more flexible, less costly, and speedier method of resolving disputes than litigation. Arbitral awards in many cases are enforceable pursuant to treaty in many countries where a foreign court's judgment would not be. Another benefit is that arbitral bodies, unlike courts, can keep the nature and the outcome of the dispute confidential, and they may provide a more level playing field than some judicial systems.

Commonly selected international arbitral forums include the International Chamber of Commerce (ICC) in Paris, the International Center for the Settlement of Investment Disputes (ICSID), the Arbitration Institute of the Stockholm Chamber of Commerce, and the Arbitration Institute of the Zurich Chamber of Commerce. Each international arbitral body has its own procedural rules. However, internationally accepted arbitration rules, such as those adopted by the United Nations Commission on International Trade Law (UNCITRAL), may also be used in conjunction with the parties' own methods of selecting an arbitral panel. This latter type of arrangement is referred to as *ad hoc* arbitration. If there is no mutually convenient venue for the arbitration, often the parties will designate a place that is comparably distant and inconvenient for both parties.

It is common for the parties to stipulate that an arbitration decision is final and binding and not subject to review by any courts. Absent such a stipulation, the dispute could be reviewed by a court without reference to the arbitration (*de novo* review), rendering the arbitration decision unenforceable. The purpose of the 1958 United Nations Convention on the Recognition and Enforcement of Foreign Arbitral Awards (often referred to as the New York Convention) is "to unify standards by which agreements to arbitrate are observed and arbitral awards are enforced in signatory countries." More than 60 countries, including the United States and most of the major trading nations, are parties to the convention. In some countries, one cannot necessarily escape the court system just by agreeing to arbitration. Arbitration abroad, or execution of the contract abroad, may be necessary to escape local courts.

Payment and Letters of Credit

Because the parties to an international sale may not be well known to each other, the buyer may be unwilling to pay for the goods before delivery and the seller may be unwilling to ship the goods without certainty of payment. As a result, the most common payment mechanism for international sales transactions is the opening (that is, the establishment) of a *documentary credit*, commonly known as a *letter of credit (L/C)*. The buyer (the *applicant*) will enter into a contract with the issuing bank, which is usually in the buyer's jurisdiction. The issuing bank issues a letter of credit in favor of the seller (the *beneficiary*). The L/C will provide for payment by the issuing bank to the beneficiary upon tender by the beneficiary (or its agent or assignee) of specified documents. The nature of these specified documents will be based on the terms of the contract between the applicant and the beneficiary.

In a transaction involving the sale of goods, the most common document to be tendered is a *bill of lading*, which the carrier (the transporter) of the goods issues to the seller. A bill of lading describes the goods received from the seller, the loading location, the name of the carrying vessel, and the destination; and it passes title to the buyer. A typical L/C requires the beneficiary to present to the issuing bank a *clean bill of lading*, that is, one with no notations indicating defects or damage to the goods when they were received for transport. When the seller presents the bill of lading (and any other documents specified by the L/C), the issuing bank makes payment. The issuing bank will then give the bill of lading to the buyer, which uses it to claim the goods from the carrier upon arrival.

Other typical documents that sales contracts often require to be tendered under the L/C include (1) an invoice, (2) a packing list, (3) a certificate of inspection issued by a designated organization confirming that the quality or condition of the goods at the time of shipment complies with the contract terms, (4) a certificate of origin (for customs purposes), (5) a certificate of

VIEW FROM CYBERSPACE

UNIFORM RULES ON DIGITAL SIGNATURES

The United Nations Commission on International Trade Law (UNCITRAL) Working Group on Electronic Commerce has drafted the UNCITRAL Model Law on Electronic Commerce to support the commercial use of international contracts in electronic commerce. It defines the characteristics of a valid electronic writing and an original document; it also provides for recognition of electronic signatures in legal documents and the admission of electronic evidence.

The Draft Uniform Rules on Electronic Signatures, issued by the UNCITRAL secretariat May 25, 1998, distinguish between the general category of electronic signatures and the narrower category of "enhanced" or "secure" electronic signatures. Authentication techniques must meet certain reliability standards. To be deemed trustworthy, an authenticity certificate must (1) be issued by a certification authority licensed by a governmental authority and accredited by a responsible accreditation body "applying commercially appropriate and internationally recognized standards," and (2) be issued in accordance with these standards. The draft rules also provide enacting states several alternatives for the endorsement by domestic certification authorities of certificates issued by foreign certification authorities and the legal recognition of foreign certificates.

On May 13, 1998, the European Commission proposed a directive governing electronic signatures.[a] To be legally recognized, an electronic signature must be (1) uniquely linked to the signatory, (2) capable of identifying the signatory, (3) created with means that the signatory can maintain under his or her control, and (4) linked to the message to which it pertains in such a way that any tampering with the message can be detected. Electronic signatures accompanied by qualified certificates issued by a qualified certification service provider will satisfy the legal requirement of a handwritten signature and be admissible as evidence in legal proceedings in the same manner as written signatures. A qualified certificate (1) identifies the signatory and the issuing certification service provider, (2) specifies the beginning and end period of the certification, (3) sets forth the value of the transactions for which the certificate is valid, and (4) specifies the service provider's liability for unauthorized transactions. The proposed directive authorizes the European Union (EU) to enter into international agreements for legal recognition of electronic signatures originating in countries outside the EU.

a. *European Commission Proposes Directive to Regulate Electronic Signature Services*, 66 U.S.L.W. 2743 (June 2, 1998).

insurance establishing that the goods are properly insured prior to shipment, and (6) a draft drawn on the issuing bank in the amount of the purchase price.

A *confirming bank* also may be involved in the transaction. This is a bank located in the seller's jurisdiction that confirms (makes a legal commitment) to the seller that it will honor the terms of the L/C issued by the issuing bank. This gives the seller greater comfort by making a more familiar local bank the paying entity. The fee for a confirmation is usually a fraction of the original L/C fee.

A seller can use the L/C as security for its own issuing bank to issue a second L/C to finance its purchase of products or materials from its supplier. This is known as a *back-to-back letter of credit*.

It is important to recognize that the purpose of documentary credits is to allow the issuing bank to pay based solely on the tender of particular documents, without requiring it to examine any extraneous facts, including the parties' compliance with their sales contract. Article 15 of the Uniform Customs and Practice for Documentary Credits (UCP), written by the International Chamber of Commerce, states:

> Banks assume no liability or responsibility for the form, sufficiency, accuracy, genuineness, falsification or legal

effect of any document(s), or for the general and/or particular conditions stipulated in the document(s) or superimposed thereon; nor do they assume any liability or responsibility for the description, quantity, weight, quality, condition, packing, delivery, value or existence of the goods represented by any document(s), or for the good faith or acts and/or omissions, solvency, performance or standing of the consignor, the carriers, the forwarders, the consignees, or the insurers of the goods, or any other person whomsoever.[1]

As a result, a sale of goods pursuant to a letter of credit involves two separate contracts. The first is the sales contract between the buyer and the seller whereby the seller agrees to deliver goods meeting the requirements of the contract of sale and the buyer agrees to pay for conforming goods. The second is an independent contract whereby the issuing bank, at the request of the buyer–applicant, promises to pay the seller–beneficiary the purchase price upon delivery of the documents specified in the letter of credit. This is shown graphically in Exhibit 26.1.

A breach of the first contract will not relieve the bank of its obligations under the second contract unless the buyer proves actual material fraud in the transaction. This fraud exception is construed very narrowly. An injunction against payment will be issued only if (1) the beneficiary has "no colorable right"[2] to draw, (2) the beneficiary's demand has "absolutely no basis in fact,"[3] or (3) the beneficiary's wrongdoing has

"vitiated the entire transaction."[4] As a result, even if the goods delivered are defective, the buyer will not have the authority to stop the issuing bank from making a payment if the seller presents the documents specified in the L/C. In other words, payment on an L/C is conditioned on tender of conforming documents, not on performance of the underlying contract. Specifying the appropriate documents is critical for both parties.

Sellers in international transactions typically require irrevocable L/Cs in dealing with unfamiliar parties. An *irrevocable letter of credit* can be amended or canceled only with the consent of the beneficiary and the issuing bank. If the buyer learns of defects in the goods that do not prevent tender of the required documents, its only recourse under an irrevocable L/C is to sue the seller for breach of the underlying sales contract.

Two sets of rules can apply to L/Cs in international sales. The first is Article 5 of the Uniform Commercial Code (UCC), which was revised in 1995 and varies slightly from state to state. The second set of rules is set forth in the International Chamber of Commerce's UCP, the most recent version of which is contained in a document often cited in bank L/C forms as *Uniform Customs and Practice for Documentary Credits*, 1993 Revision, ICC Publication No. 500. There are significant differences between UCC Article 5 and the UCP. For example, UCC Article 5, as interpreted by most U.S. courts, provides that, once established, an L/C is irrevocable unless otherwise agreed. The UCP, by its terms, establishes the opposite presumption: an L/C is revocable at the issuing bank's option and without prior

---

1. Uniform Customs and Practice for Documentary Credits, 1993 Revision, Int'l Chamber of Commerce Publication No. 500.

2. Itek Corp. v. First Nat'l Bank of Boston, 730 F.2d 19, 25 (1st Cir. 1984).

3. Dynamics Corp. of America v. Citizens & S. Nat'l Bank, 356 F. Supp. 991, 999 (N.D. Ga. 1973).

---

4. Intraworld Indus. v. Girard Trust Bank, 336 A.2d 316, 324–25 (Pa. 1925).

EXHIBIT 26.1	Letter of Credit Parallel Contracts		
Contract 1:	**Buyer–Applicant**	and	**Seller–Beneficiary**
	Payment of Purchase Price for Conforming Goods	→ ←	Delivery of Conforming Goods
Contract 2:	**Issuing Bank**	and	**Seller–Beneficiary**
	Payment of Purchase Price	→ ←	Delivery of Specified Documents

notice to or agreement of the beneficiary unless the contract and the L/C expressly state that the L/C is irrevocable. These rules, as much as the terms of the underlying sales contract, can determine the outcome of a payment dispute.

The parties can elect to have their L/C governed by UCC Article 5 or by the UCP, and they should be specific about their choice.[5] It is also prudent to expressly specify in the L/C whether it is revocable or irrevocable.

Letters of credit cost money and, in an ongoing relationship, the buyer usually presses for more favorable payment terms, including open account. In the multinational-corporation context, having a well-known parent company guarantee a local affiliate's obligations is a fairly common cost-saving alternative to L/Cs.

Overseas Offices and Subsidiaries

U.S. businesses can establish a presence in a foreign country to supervise or manage sales with little or no investment by setting up a liaison, representative, or branch office in the host country. The scope of permissible activities, capital requirements, and tax liabilities of each of these forms of representation varies with the legal scheme of the host jurisdiction.

Typically, the greater the scope of permissible activities, the more stringent the capitalization and taxation rules. In Taiwan, for example, a liaison office may not engage in any business activity other than quotation, bidding, negotiating, executing contracts, and procurement on behalf of a home office, nor may it deliver or accept any goods or cash remuneration. A liaison office has no tax obligations (because the permitted activities incur no revenue), but registration of a liaison office with the Taiwanese government is still required.

Thus, representative and liaison offices are generally limited to providing services on behalf of a home office. They cannot engage in manufacturing operations, and they are typically limited in the nature of the sales support and marketing activities they can conduct. In countries with very limited or no provision for such operations, companies may be forced to choose between use of an agent or distributor on the one hand and a branch or subsidiary on the other.

A branch office can perform certain kinds of services, such as import and export, provided it is formally capitalized, registers with local government authorities, and pays income and other required taxes. Legally, the lack of local limited liability protection is one reason not to use a branch office. Many companies have subsidiaries that are entirely separate legal entities, with their own capital structure, boards of directors, and officers. Different tax treatment is a second reason to favor a subsidiary rather than a foreign office to establish an overseas presence. Another issue that should not be overlooked is the burden of disclosing and possibly restating company financials under local regulations.

 ## International Leasing

Under a true lease, the owner of the leased goods expects to recover them at the end of the lease term. Under a *financing lease*, commonly used to finance the acquisition of expensive capital equipment and vehicles, such as airplanes, locomotives, and ships, the parties expect the lessee to purchase the leased equipment at the end of the lease term at an agreed-on residual value. Typical finance-lease transactions range from $100,000 to several million dollars.

There are several advantages of a financing lease over a direct purchase. In a financing lease, the owner retains legal title to the goods until all or most of the purchase price is paid by the lessees. In countries with an undeveloped law of secured transactions (which establishes creditors' rights to collateral for loans), this alternative offers greater comfort to the owner of the transferred goods.

For foreign banks, leasing offers a way to establish a local presence in countries that may not allow bank branches. As equipment lessors, banks operate as lenders, factoring in interest charges into the lease payments, while nominally serving a commercial function, namely, the sale of equipment. Foreign banks should consult local counsel to determine whether there are any nondisclaimable lessor obligations under local laws and whether retention of title creates any tort or other liability risks under local law.

In many countries, lessors, as owners of the leased goods, can fully depreciate those goods during the lease term, thereby gaining substantial tax benefits. Many

---

5. There are certain provisions in revised Article 5 that cannot be varied by agreement; but as a practical matter, the nonvariable rules are unlikely to conflict with any UCP rule.

countries allow the lessee to deduct all or a portion of its lease payments.

Some countries impose restrictions on the purchase of expensive imports, particularly where foreign-exchange expenditures are carefully monitored or restricted. Lease payments may escape these limitations, however, either because there is no up-front sale or because the payments can be spread out in acceptable installments. Sometimes, the installment payments can even be made from earnings generated by the leased goods.

International leasing may be subject to a wide range of other foreign laws. Local tax and accounting regulations will determine tax benefits for the owner and user of the leased goods. The creditor's rights, if any, will be determined by local laws. If creditor–debtor laws exist, there may be limitations on the lessor's rights in the event of a default by the lessee. Foreign-exchange laws may substantially affect how lease payments are calculated and made, particularly in countries in which the local currency is not freely convertible or is undergoing high rates of inflation.

Compensation Trade

Compensation trade is a variation on the simple sale or lease transaction. The foreign party transfers usage and/or eventual ownership of a good, usually equipment, to the local party, who then repays the foreign party with products produced using the foreign party's equipment. The foreign party may also supply the materials for the production process. This is known as a *processing operation*. Both types of transactions are simpler than full-scale direct investments, but may still be subject to local foreign exchange, customs, tax, and creditors' rights laws.

International Transfers of Technology

The transfer of technology across national boundaries involves many of the same legal and commercial issues as the sale of goods: the choice of applicable law, the form of payment, and the method of resolving disputes. Protecting the owner's rights in the transferred technology is a prime concern, usually accomplished by appro-

priate license terms and by taking the actions necessary to protect proprietary rights under local laws.

Licensing

Technology is protected by intellectual property laws, which vary from country to country. These laws are discussed in more detail in Chapter 11. Transfers of technology can be accomplished by sale or by operation of law as part of an acquisition. In many cases, however, technology is transferred pursuant to a licensing agreement whereby the owner of the technology (the licensor) transfers it so the user (the licensee) can manufacture specified products, normally in exchange for an ongoing royalty that is typically based on production quantity or sales of the products.

Developing countries encourage the licensing of technology to upgrade local manufacturing capabilities and expertise. This policy goal may come into conflict with the licensor's desire to restrict the use of the technology or to keep it confidential. Foreign licensors need to be especially sensitive to the nature of the host country's patent, trademark, copyright, and trade secret laws and its actual enforcement practices in dealing with foreign-owned intellectual property.

Because a technology transfer involves intangible property, its dissemination is harder to control than the sale of tangible products. This presents problems for both licensor and licensee. The licensee will be concerned with the scope of the rights it has been granted, including whether it has the exclusive right to use the licensed technology.

The licensor, which typically has invested substantial time and money in creating its technology, wants to be certain that the licensee will not disclose or use the technology without the licensor's consent. For technology that the licensor protects as a trade secret, contract provisions requiring confidentiality and restrictions on the employees who will have access to the technology are essential. In many developing countries, however, dissemination of technology is a policy objective and technology-licensing laws or administrative policies may expressly limit the terms of a license agreement and its confidentiality or enforcement provisions. These limitations may be unacceptable to a licensor.

If the licensor is also a manufacturer and exporter of products produced by the licensed technology, it will be concerned about the effect of the licensee's prospective sales on the licensor's markets. This issue can usually be resolved by imposing restrictions on the geographic markets available to the licensee. Local technology transfer laws, however, especially in developing countries, often prohibit certain types of geographic market limitations. In addition, local antitrust laws may be used to challenge such limitations. One common resolution involves a prohibition on selling efforts outside the territory but permission for unsolicited sales. These issues are all central to the transfer and use of technology, and they must be carefully negotiated in the context of local requirements.

The licensing of technology frequently involves the licensing of rights in special types of intellectual property such as copyrights, trademarks, service marks, patents, and trade secrets. The confidentiality of trade-secret technology can generally be protected, as between the contract parties, by a well-drafted, enforceable licensing contract with strong nondisclosure provisions. To protect its ownership and use rights in trademarks, service marks, copyrights, and patents against third parties in foreign countries, the licensor generally must perfect its ownership in compliance with local requirements. Obtaining protection under local patent and trademark laws can be a technical, extended process; but the protection available under those laws is essential to preserving the value of the owner's intellectual property.

International Intellectual Property Protection

Several multinational treaties seek to harmonize the application of the intellectual property laws of various jurisdictions. These treaties do not alter the differing criteria that each jurisdiction applies to determine whether an application for protection merits acceptance; instead, they seek to coordinate the registration and recognition process among signatory countries.

The scope and duration of patent and trademark protection vary from country to country. Many countries have less stringent intellectual property laws than the United States (or laws that are less rigorously enforced). A number of countries in the Middle East have been very reluctant to grant patent protection for pharmaceuticals because that would make it impossible for local companies to produce patented drugs and sell them at a fraction of the price charged by the patent

holder in other countries. As a result, the production of counterfeit goods that infringe intellectual property rights is more prevalent in such countries. U.S. trade laws (discussed in Chapter 25) may prevent the entry of such counterfeit goods into the United States, but they can only indirectly restrict the production of such goods and their sale in countries other than the United States.

For example, before enactment of updated copyright laws in Poland and the Czech Republic, copyright abuse was quite common. Computer software companies, film studios, and clothing manufacturers lost hundreds of millions of dollars from violations of international copyrights. According to some estimates, recording artists and producers lost approximately $75 million in royalties every year because of copyright piracy in Poland.[6] For example, an estimated 10,000 videocassettes of the film *Jurassic Park* were available in rental stores all over Poland long before the release of the movie by the official distributor.[7]

In most countries, if two entities file for protection of the same patented invention or trademark, protection is granted to the entity that filed first. This can be a problem for an inventor or a trademark owner who files for protection in one country and later discovers that another person has subsequently filed for protection of the same invention or trademark in another country. The International Convention for the Protection of Industrial Property Rights (popularly known as the Paris Convention) seeks to avoid this type of problem by encouraging reciprocal recognition of patents, trademarks, service marks, and similar forms of intellectual property rights among signatory nations (of which there are more than 80, including the United States). Each signatory nation agrees to grant to nationals of other signatory nations a grace period after filing in their home country within which to file corresponding patent or trademark applications in other signatory countries. These grace periods are six months for trademarks and one year for most patents; they give the filers a reasonable time to complete the filing and registration formalities in foreign countries.

The Paris Convention does not alter the substantive requirements of the laws of signatory countries, so

---

6. Matthew Brzezinski, *Polish Law Takes Aim at Copyright Piracy*, N.Y. TIMES, June 14, 1994, at D6.
7. *Id.*

patent or trademark protection in one signatory country does not necessarily translate into protection in another signatory country. Differing rules governing eligibility may mean that actions in the original jurisdiction that do not compromise protection there may forfeit protection in others (for example, disclosure or sale of inventions prior to filing for a patent). Seeking the appropriate expertise or advice in this area can help a manager avoid irreparable mistakes.

The Madrid Agreement Concerning the International Registration of Trademarks allows for centralized international registration. The owner of a trademark in its home country can file at the International Bureau of the World Intellectual Property Organization (WIPO) in Geneva for registration of its trademark in those signatory countries that it specifies.

The Pan American Convention recognizes the right of a trademark owner in one signatory country to successfully challenge the registration or use of that same trademark in another country. The issue is whether persons using or applying to register the mark had knowledge of the existence and continuous use of the mark in any of the member states on goods of the same class.

The Berne Convention for the Protection of Literary and Artistic Works and the Universal Copyright Convention extend copyright protection under the respective domestic copyright laws of signatory countries. Bilateral treaties of friendship, navigation, and commerce (FNCs), which exist between the United States and almost 50 foreign countries, and bilateral investment treaties (BITs) may afford further protection to intellectual property rights.

International Franchising

An increasingly common form of international licensing is franchising. A typical franchise agreement involves a package of licensed rights, including the right of the franchisee to use the franchisor's trademarks, service marks, patents, and confidential, unpatented know-how (including trade secrets). The franchisor may or may not also contribute equity investment, but its major contribution is usually the franchisor's goodwill—the value of the customers' recognition of a popular enterprise. If the franchisor does not properly register its trademarks and service marks locally, it can effectively lose control of its most valuable assets.

The concept of franchising as a method of doing business, and the corresponding rights and obligations between the parties, are still in a state of flux in many countries. Protection of marketing and operations methods, designs, trade dress, quality control systems, and other benchmarks of franchise businesses that are well understood domestically are often limited or unavailable internationally.

 ## Investment Abroad

Historically, the bulk of U.S. foreign investment has been concentrated in Western Europe and Canada. U.S. businesses have naturally been attracted by the political stability of these regions. Moreover, cultural affinities, similar business customs and practices, and a familiar linguistic landscape made it relatively easy for U.S. investors to set up active operations in Western Europe and Canada. In the 1970s, 1980s, and 1990s, however, the rate of growth of U.S. investment in Asia began to outpace that of investment in Europe. U.S. manufacturers scrambled for new markets and lower production costs and saw in the developing economies of Asia an opportunity to achieve both. Many of these companies have been surprised by the breadth and severity of the Asian financial and currency crisis that began in 1997 in Thailand, then spread to Indonesia, Korea, and Japan.

Investment Goals

A business plan for investing abroad must begin with an assessment of the investor's goals. The attractiveness of a prospective investment in a given host country can vary greatly, depending on these goals.

Local Market Penetration   Some markets are almost inaccessible, for legal or business reasons, to U.S. manufacturers wishing to sell their products. Developing countries may have shortages of hard currency—that is, convertible foreign exchange—and these shortages may limit their purchase of imports. Applicable laws may restrict imports of certain products, but may grant benefits to foreign investors wishing to manufacture those products locally. To penetrate these types of markets, the only practical approach may be to invest in a local manufacturing facility. Certain Asian countries permit only local companies to establish retail businesses; this is another example of restricting foreign companies from competing in certain markets.

Regional Base   U.S. businesses that wish to compete in Europe or Asia may need to establish manufacturing, marketing, and/or service centers in the relevant region to establish credibility with local customers. U.S. businesses may also need to be on-site to sustain their local sources of supplies for operations elsewhere. Regional bases can reduce transportation costs, enhance time-to-market responses, help avoid cultural difficulties, and generally help the home office monitor the business pulse of the region. They also avoid potential problems with distributors or agents not 100% committed to the products or not aligned with the foreign parent. The challenge of integrating an expatriate with the local business environment is the corollary of this issue of aligning locally hired managers with the overall corporate mission and goals.

Cheaper Production Costs   Developing countries typically offer cheaper labor and raw materials than more industrialized countries. These reduced costs are often the primary reason for U.S. business investment in foreign manufacturing operations. As discussed below, however, the assessment of true production costs is not limited to a line-item comparison of the costs of each element of production. Intangible issues such as labor efficiency, reliability of supplies, local labor law requirements, and political stability can affect the true costs of production.

Host Country Conditions

Prospective investors need to consider the economic, political, geographic, legal, and labor conditions in the host country.

Economic Conditions   The host country's economic condition is usually a high-profile issue in the investment evaluation process. Per capita income, for example, may determine whether a particular country is a realistic market for a particular product, or whether it is a likely source of inexpensive labor. Economic growth trends can suggest both a growing consumer market and increasing labor costs. The monetary system is also important. Existence of a readily convertible currency and the nature of

the currency-exchange laws will determine whether profits can be easily repatriated (that is, transferred abroad). A high inflation rate may result in local suppliers being reluctant to perform on long-term contracts, or it may make capital and working loans more expensive.

The U.S. Department of Commerce, the U.S. Foreign Commercial Service, and the U.S. Department of State regularly publish reports on the economic condition of various countries. These agencies can offer a good introduction for a prospective foreign investor. The U.S. Foreign Commercial Service has a wide-ranging network of commercial officers stationed at U.S. embassies and consulates throughout the world. They collect and analyze economic data and are available on-site to U.S. businesses to interpret how that data may be relevant to an investment project.

Political Conditions   Political instability inevitably leads to some degree of legal and economic instability. Such instability is a matter of degree. Investors are generally concerned mainly with the reliability and stability of the local legal institutions that enforce contracts and protect property rights. Changes of government in Western democracies can lead to changes in the legal and policy environment that dramatically affect the economic results of foreign investments, but without undermining the system of rule of law. Other political systems may have a stable regime but have a corrupt judicial and legislative system that does not offer effective legal recourse for investors. At the outer extreme, violent political or civil divisions can lead to a situation where the rule of law has completely collapsed. Business can still be done in such an environment, but the written contractual terms become insignificant next to practical considerations of power, possession, and protection.

A prospective foreign investor must, therefore, look beyond the reasonableness of the contract, the competence of its foreign business counterpart, and the desirability of the site to determine whether the existing government and its policies are aligned with the needs of the project and whether that government or its policies are likely to be changed in adverse ways. Managers should analyze both (1) political risks, such as expropriation, partial nationalization, and serious operational restrictions, which often stem from a change in the overall political orientation; and (2) legal risks, such as changes in tax, customs, employment, and other laws that do not represent an inherent shift against private owner-ship or against foreign investment.

One U.S. government agency, the Overseas Private Investment Corporation (OPIC), specializes in providing insurance for eligible U.S. investors against certain de-fined risks, including political risks such as expropriation. To be eligible for OPIC insurance, an investor must be (1) a U.S. citizen, (2) a U.S. partnership or corporation substantially owned by U.S. citizens, or (3) a foreign business at least 95% owned by a U.S. citizen or by a U.S. partnership or corporation. OPIC insures U.S. investor's interests only in "friendly" countries—that is, those that have investment-protection agreements (FNCs or BITs) with the United States. Coverage is also available for in-convertibility of foreign currency remittances and losses due to hostile action during civil unrest.[8]

Geographic Conditions   Climatic and geographic conditions can directly affect the production and trans-portation of products. Severe weather in certain seasons can affect delivery schedules. It is important to ascertain the breadth and reliability of the transportation system and other infrastructure available. A manager needs to keep all these conditions in mind when deciding where to locate a manufacturing site and supplier and what service and sales contract commitments for production and shipment to make.

The nature, cost, and development status of a prospective site are major considerations. In some countries, such as China, Indonesia, the Philippines, and Thailand, foreign investors are not permitted to own land but can, often with the assistance of a local partner, obtain long-term land-use rights. If the capital investment will be large relative to the parent com-pany's assets, a foreign investor may want to consider investing only in countries that offer guaranties concerning expropriation or in friendly developing countries where U.S. investors are eligible for OPIC in-surance. Sometimes, a country may seek to attract in-vestment to certain areas by offering attractive land-use terms and new infrastructure.

Common mistaken assumptions about issues such as land rights and use, flood control, power supply, fire protection, utility service, legal and informal employee

protections, and the like can present the most signifi-cant hidden operational hazard in foreign direct invest-ment. It is critical for the investor and its legal and business advisors to probe these areas aggressively in their due diligence.

Legal Conditions   Managers should ask whether local laws offer predictability, uniformity and even-handed enforcement. Also, is the judicial system speedy, effi-cient, and inexpensive? Beyond the letter of the laws, their effectiveness depends on political conditions and the nature of the legal and administrative organs that interpret and enforce them. A reliable court system or comparable dispute resolution forum (such as an estab-lished arbitration system) is a significant element, with-out which there is little leverage to enforce contracts or invoke commercial laws.

Although trade or licensing contracts may allow for choice of the law of a jurisdiction other than the host country, in foreign-investment projects the substantive laws of the host country will apply. In some instances, however, rules of interpretation and dispute resolution procedures may be governed by the rules of a third jurisdiction.

Sources of necessary supplies should be secure, and their transportation and storage not subject to rampant theft. The existence of a reasonably diligent and fair law enforcement network is a factor to be considered in this regard.

Foreign investors must obtain a working knowl-edge of the applicable host country laws and acceptable forums for dispute resolution, and they should obtain professional advice from local attorneys. These profes-sionals can also assist in providing accurate contract translations where required. It is not uncommon for a country to require that the definitive text of a contract be in the local language (for example, Mexico requires contracts to be in Spanish), but an accurate English ver-sion is critical.

Many countries offer a variety of vehicles for for-eign investment. Just as U.S. businesses can choose to operate domestically as a sole proprietorship, a general or limited partnership, or a limited liability company, or a corporation, foreign investors can select the invest-ment format most appropriate to their project in a for-eign country. Each form is subject to its own set of laws, which affect management structure, equity investment requirements, the limitation of investor liabilities, and

---

8. OPIC publishes a number of handbooks that describe its programs and ser-vices. They are available from the Information Officer, Overseas Private Invest-ment Corporation, 1129 20th Street, N.W., Washington, DC 20527.

taxation. Often, there is a less structural flexibility in foreign jurisdictions. One consideration in some countries that does not exist in the United States is the prestige attached to specific forms (for example, in some European countries, the private limited company form may be perceived as a less serious commitment than the public limited company form of entity). Country handbooks published by international accounting firms, local law firms, and the U.S. government contain a variety of useful informational items.

The licensing or contribution of technology by the U.S. business to the foreign business is often a component of an equity investment project. Some countries' investment laws or policies may limit the portion of the foreign party's equity investment that can be attributable to intellectual property (such as patents, trademarks, or know-how) as compared with cash or equipment, for example. Certain restrictions on technology use may be invalid under local technology licensing laws.

There may be bilateral tax or investment treaties that grant reciprocal rights to businesses from the host and investor countries. These treaties may offer significant benefits, such as avoidance of double taxation (that is, taxation by both the host and investor countries) and guaranties against uncompensated expropriation by the host government.

The U.S. State Department compiles records of ratified treaties and their signatories. A quick review of this information can provide a sense of the relative involvement of various nations in international conventions that affect foreign investment. Attorneys familiar with how these treaties apply locally can best advise investors in a particular jurisdiction.

Labor Conditions   A leading reason for investing abroad is to take advantage of relatively low labor costs in a foreign country. The true cost of labor, however, is more than the hourly or daily wage; it includes labor efficiency, trainability, reliability, and adherence to quality control standards. In addition, the labor and foreign-investment laws of some countries, particularly those with socialist economies, require employers to fund a wide range of employee benefits that are not expected by U.S. investors. These benefits include housing, travel, education, and food subsidies, as well as the more common retirement, health insurance, and maternity benefits. Local labor laws may limit the degree to which employees may be treated differently,

thus restricting flexibility in incentive compensation. They can also make it difficult to terminate inefficient or redundant workers, thereby reducing the employer's ability to motivate and discipline unsatisfactory employees.

Financial Issues

Several common financial concerns for an equity investor in a foreign project include currency considerations, project funding and capitalization, and taxation.

Currency Considerations   The currency in which the foreign entity does business and in which its assets and obligations are denominated can be a principal concern for a U.S. investor in many developing countries. The ideal is an open economy (1) without currency and other monetary restrictions, and (2) with a currency tied directly to the dollar or at least to another stable major currency such as the German mark or (as of January 1, 1999) the new EU common currency—the euro (which is discussed in Chapter 25). This minimizes the fluctuations in investment results due solely to currency issues relative to those inherent in the fundamental economics of the business. A second-best case is a situation in which the prices of inputs and outputs are primarily denominated in hard currency, even though the local currency is the unit of account (a common requirement). This is most typical in export and processing operations. In many cases, however, the investor will find local currency controls and financing restrictions a significant issue. Hedging contract commitments and planning capital allocation across currencies and in view of governmental restrictions is an integral part of establishing and implementing a successful financial plan.

Local financial institutions often are restricted in offering foreign currency loans. Conversely, foreign banks outside the host country may be reluctant to offer capital loans if local currency profits may not be freely convertible for loan repayment. Project proceeds, or even host country project properties, may not offer sufficient security for a loan from a foreign financial institution. The foreign investor may be required to obtain and provide security entirely outside the host jurisdiction for any loans it desires.

The availability and cost of hard currency can be a major issue when the host country currency is not freely convertible. It may be of less concern to a foreign investor who expects to earn hard currency through exports of either the project's products or other local products purchased with its local currency profits. This latter arrangement is known as *countertrade*.

Cash-flow hedging methods are increasingly common in countries in which foreign-exchange controls remain restrictive. For example, in many Eastern European countries, Western companies with both import and export activities structure import payments to match hard-currency inflows in order to reduce potential exchange-rate losses. If the local currency is rapidly depreciating, inflows of hard-currency earnings may lag behind offsetting import payments. As a currency is devalued, import costs rise. Potential exchange rate losses can be avoided by delaying the conversion of export receivables into local currency until imported goods are paid for.

Currency denomination also affects the capitalization of an investment project. For example, a foreign partner in a joint venture may agree to contribute a specified amount of U.S. dollars over time, with the host country partner making an equal contribution in local currency. If the local currency depreciates against the U.S. dollar, the foreign partner will end up making a greater than 50% contribution to the joint venture in local currency terms. Some reconciliation of paid-in capital and share pricing may be needed under local law. Unequal contributions may also arise where local law requires foreign currency capital contributions to be valued at an official exchange rate that fails to reflect the local currency's true value. These currency risks can be addressed by careful contract drafting and, where possible, through currency swaps and hedging.

Project Capitalization The foreign business to which the investor is committing an investment typically requires fixed capital (often for construction costs) and working capital for daily operations. Local laws and practices may not permit the flexibility in capital structure available in the United States. The reliability and attractiveness of a host nation in this regard may be affected by factors such as political risk, currency-convertibility laws, profit-repatriation restrictions, local banking laws and practices, and the enforceability of guaranties or security agreements.

Guaranties and Standby Letters of Credit Another important issue is the feasibility of obtaining se-

curity for those providing financing, often through a guaranty. If the political or credit risks of a country are perceived to be especially great, an entity in the host country, often an instrumentality of the host country government, may be called upon to act as the guarantor. Under a guaranty arrangement, a local financial institution guarantees, for the benefit of the project owners, that the lender will be repaid if the project principals are unable to pay, as long as the project contracts have been adhered to by the parties to the project. The choice of law for enforcement of the guaranty may be subject to negotiation. The local financial institutions authorized to issue guaranties, especially if they involve repayment in hard currencies, may be subject to a variety of local regulations that, if not adhered to, could result in the guaranty becoming unenforceable and therefore worthless.

A *standby letter of credit* is often used to secure financing for construction or similar large projects. Payment is usually conditioned upon a brief statement, in language previously agreed on by the applicant and the beneficiary, that the applicant is in default or has failed to perform an obligation to the beneficiary under the project contract and that the beneficiary is therefore entitled to payment from the issuing bank. Unlike the common form of guaranty, the creditor need only tender the specified document and need not establish that the debtor breached its obligations in the underlying contract, which could involve extended litigation or arbitration. This distinction is critical. A guarantor is liable under the guarantee only when the primary obligor is liable for the underlying obligation. The guarantor can raise any defenses that the primary obligor could raise before having to make payment to the beneficiary. In contrast, a standby letter of credit constitutes the primary obligation of the issuing bank to the beneficiary to pay upon the presentation of specified documents. As with commercial letters of credit used in connection with the sale of goods, the issuing bank cannot inquire into the underlying transaction or assert the defenses the applicant might have. It must generally pay within seven business days following presentation of the specified documents, which means that the beneficiary has the funds while the dispute between the applicant and the beneficiary is worked out or litigated.

The use of a standby letter of credit is not unusual, but it has its risks, as the following case demonstrates.

CASE 26.2
AMERICAN BELL
INTERNATIONAL, INC.
v. ISLAMIC REPUBLIC
OF IRAN
United States District Court
for the Southern District
of New York
474 F. Supp. 420 (S.D.N.Y.
1979).

FACTS   In the summer of 1978, American Bell International, a subsidiary of American Telephone and Telegraph Company, entered into a $280 million contract with Iran's Ministry of War to provide equipment and consulting services to improve Iran's international communications system. The contract provided for a down payment to Bell of more than $38 million. The Iranian government had the right to demand return of the down payment less reductions attributable to work performed by Bell and accepted by the Iranian government.

To secure the possible repayment of its down payment, Bell was required to obtain a letter of guaranty to be issued by an Iranian bank in favor of the Iranian government. The Iranian bank, in turn, required Bell to obtain a standby L/C issued by Manufacturers Hanover Trust in favor of the Iranian bank (a back-to-back credit) that provided for payment by Manufacturers to the Iranian bank upon presentation by the Iranian bank of a statement, the precise wording of which was specified in the standby L/C. The agreed-on statement would be to the effect that (1) the Iranian bank had received a payment request from the Iranian government under the letter of guaranty, (2) the Iranian bank had made such a payment, and (3) the Iranian bank was claiming payment for an amount due to it from Manufacturers. As the final element of the standby L/C transaction, Manufacturers required Bell and its parent corporation, American Telephone and Telegraph Company, to reimburse Manufacturers for all amounts paid by Manufacturers to the Iranian bank pursuant to the standby L/C.

In early 1979, the Shah's Imperial Government of Iran collapsed and was succeeded by the Islamic Republic. In anticipation of a payment claim by the Iranian government and the Iranian bank, Bell sought a preliminary injunction prohibiting Manufacturers from honoring any demand that the Iranian bank might make for payment under the standby L/C. In August 1979, Manufacturers received a demand for payment that complied with the terms of the standby L/C and proposed to make payment. Bell sought to enjoin this payment, arguing that the Iranian government had breached the consulting contract and that the demand on the letter of guaranty and the subsequent demand on the letter of credit reflected "fraud in the transaction," that is, that the Iranian government was seeking fraudulently to regain a portion of the contract deposit.

ISSUE PRESENTED   Does an issuer of a standby L/C have an absolute duty to transfer the funds if the demand for payment conforms to the terms of the letter of credit, regardless of the obligations of the parties in the underlying contractual relationship?

SUMMARY OF OPINION   The Federal District Court refused to infer a basis for fraud in the transaction and rejected Bell's request for a preliminary injunction barring Manufacturers from making payment. The court distinguished between the parties' rights under the underlying contract—including the right to claim damages for breach of that contract—and Manufacturers' absolute obligation under the standby L/C to pay the requisite amounts upon its receipt of conforming documents, regardless of whether the Iranian government breached the underlying contract.

Case 26.2 continues

Case 26.2 continued

The court was unmoved by Bell's claim that it was victimized by unforeseeable political events, saying:

> The Contract with Iran . . . was certain to bring Bell both monetary profit and prestige and good will in the global communications industry. The agreement to indemnify Manufacturers on its Letter of Credit provided the means by which these benefits could be achieved.
>
> One who reaps the rewards of commercial arrangements must also accept their burdens. One such burden in this case, voluntarily accepted by Bell, was the risk that demand might be made without cause on the funds constituting the down payment. . . . As between two innocents [i.e., Bell and Manufacturers], the party who undertakes by contract the risk of political uncertainty and governmental caprice must bear the consequences when the risk comes home to roost.

RESULT   The court refused to enjoin Manufacturers Hanover from making payment under the standby L/C.

COMMENTS   *Bell* was one of many cases resulting from the fall of the Imperial Government of Iran and the subsequent demands made by the successor Iranian government for payment under standby L/Cs obtained by foreign contractors as contract security. Almost uniformly, U.S. courts honored the L/C concept and rejected requests for injunctive relief, holding that the standby L/C mechanism should be respected independently of the question of performance in the underlying transaction.

Because U.S. law prohibits U.S. banks from issuing guaranties, the standby L/C mechanism is a useful way to provide payment or repayment comfort, especially to a party with superior bargaining power. As with letters of credit generally, however, the applicant should enter into such arrangements only with a clear understanding of how the mechanism works. Because the documentary credit transaction is independent of the underlying contract, applicants should clearly establish what the documentary conditions for payment are, in addition to establishing the terms of the underlying contract.

Taxation   Tax planning is an essential part of any foreign investor's business plan. Careful pre-planning can minimize the risk of withholding taxes and double income taxation and take advantage of local tax benefits. One simple way of addressing tax risks is a *gross-up clause* whereby the local partner or licensee is obligated to pay all taxes other than those specifically allocated to the foreign partner. In this way, the foreign party avoids the risk of tax increases or unknown taxes. However, some countries prohibit such reallocation of responsi-

bility for the payment of certain taxes and will not recognize gross-ups; and often a gross-up, though simple in concept, is not the most efficient way of addressing certain tax issues.

The United States has bilateral tax treaties with more than 50 countries. The treaties seek to avoid double taxation of U.S.-based businesses and individuals. Some treaties also impose tax ceilings on certain types of income; for example, one treaty imposes a 10% tax ceiling on passive income such as royalties from technology licenses or rental income. Bilateral tax treaties may not affect all the taxes applicable to a foreign-investment project or the taxation applicable to an individual expatriate employee's income; but when a tax treaty provision is applicable and it offers more favorable tax treatment than the comparable domestic tax rule, the treaty rule will generally apply.

Tax credits may be available to U.S. businesses engaged in foreign projects that are taxed by the host country. Such foreign-tax credits are available for the amount of foreign taxes paid up to a certain limit, which is derived by dividing the foreign-source taxable income by the total taxable income (which includes all foreign- and domestic-source income) and multiplying that fraction by the U.S. tax liability on the total taxable income. (Thus, if foreign tax rates exceed U.S. rates, no credit is available for the excess in the current year.) Foreign-tax credits for any one year cannot exceed the amount of foreign income taxes that have been paid or accrued; but taxes in excess of the limitation can be carried back two years and forward five years, subject to each year's tax-credit limit.

 ## Operational Concerns

Many noncommercial issues can affect the desirability of operating a business abroad. Some of the most common factors include language and cultural customs, ease of communication and transportation, and amenities for expatriate staff.

Language and Cultural Customs

Knowledge of the language and customs of the host country, or the use of proficient interpreters, is essential to the success of a business venture abroad. Stories abound concerning the gaffes of U.S. investors who, because of language difficulties or cultural misunderstandings, offended their foreign partners, misinterpreted contract negotiations, miscalculated the effect of their business operations, or simply could not maintain effective working relationships with their foreign counterparts. A sound fundamental business concept can be undermined by deficient communication.

Contract terms, both legal and technical, require accurate translation to ensure effective implementation. Product marketing and trademark and trade-name registration require sophisticated language skills and cultural sensitivity to ensure appropriateness for a foreign culture.

Other business customs of a host country can have a substantial impact on local business operations on very basic levels. A frank and direct management style may be welcomed in some countries; in others it may be viewed as arrogant and gauche. Gift giving may be appropriate, even expected, behavior in certain circumstances; in other situations it may be regarded as unethical and possibly illegal.

Communications

International direct-dial phones, fax machines, and electronic mail are common business tools in some regions; but in some developing countries (whose natural resources, labor skills, and markets attract foreign investors), these quick methods of communication are not available. Even postal or courier services may be unreliable. Such infrastructural deficiencies need to be reflected in contract provisions requiring timely notice or delivery of documents.

Expatriate managers without quick access to headquarters may have to be more creative and self-reliant in making decisions than their colleagues in more developed countries.

Transportation

Without reliable transportation, products and the people responsible for production cannot effectively reach their destinations. Transportation problems can affect the delivery of raw materials within a host country. Inadequate port facilities can lead to delayed shipments abroad and lost sales. Inefficient or corrupt customs officials can have similar effects in delaying business transactions and increasing their cost. These concerns must be addressed in contracts that hinge on timely delivery of equipment or products. Some of these weaknesses in the transportation infrastructure may not be readily evident; special investigation may be required.

Expatriate Amenities

In many developing countries, an expatriate manager and staff may be essential to provide needed skills. In addition, expatriate management members are also often needed to proselytize the corporate culture and goals to local staff and maintain consistency with the home office's overall strategy. To attract qualified personnel to hardship posts usually requires a compensation package that includes income premiums and benefits. The income-tax laws of the host country may disadvantage expatriate staff, and further additional compensation may have to be paid to counteract this disadvantage.

Expatriate packages often pose a problem for local personnel policy. Local managers may resent the higher compensation of their expatriate counterparts, and local laws may require that local managers receive comparable compensation. Ignoring this issue in the planning stage may prove expensive later, in terms of both cash and local management goodwill.

There can be substantial start-up costs as expatriate personnel acclimatize. In addition, some companies have found that expatriates may eventually become too acclimatized, engaging in local practices inconsistent with home office or industry practice.

Personal safety may be an issue in some countries, effectively precluding assignment of personnel with families. It may be difficult to extend comparable company health and life insurance benefits to expatriate employees.

◆ Factors to Consider When Going International

Before expanding into international markets, a firm must take into consideration not only market conditions, but also the laws and mores of the foreign country. Examples of substantive laws that may affect a foreign business are import/export regulations, employment law, tax law, securities law, and antitrust law. A company that follows the correct form of doing business but fails to recognize or understand local law may reduce its profitability. A company considering foreign investments should therefore carefully analyze the sociopolitical and economic climate of the prospective host country, in addition to obtaining a clear understanding of the legal, regulatory, and administrative regimes and the foreseeable future changes to these.

Before a company conducts business in a foreign country, it should first assess its existing and prospective competition in the region. Familiar analytical tools retain their value, but a new entrant also needs to be aware that opportunities and market positions that appear open to exploitation may be illusory for reasons that may fall within the categories of legal, cultural, and economic considerations discussed above or that may be entirely idiosyncratic. For example, apparent weaknesses in local distribution structures that appear to offer opportunities may in fact reflect deeply entrenched business practices that are resistant to change, particularly change sponsored by foreign-owned companies.

One way in which companies typically expand into the international marketplace is through direct sales to customers. Direct sales pose special problems for the company, including export regulations, international contract law, letters of credit, import regulations, and the use of local representatives.

If costs do not justify opening a local office, a firm will often retain a local representative to oversee the sale of its products. If the transaction is not correctly structured, however, the company may find that it has a dependent agent in the foreign country—that it has, under local law, opened an office in the foreign country. Transactions thought to be tax free will, in fact, be subject to corporate tax, and the local agent may have acquired additional rights and protections under local employment law.

Another manner in which a company can conduct business in a foreign country is through the acquisition of an existing company. Such transactions are governed by the laws regulating foreign investment in the country. Tax issues will play a predominant role in the determination of the form of the acquisition and the method of future operation.

A firm might also choose to create a new entity distinct from the parent corporation. This entity could be a corporation with 100% foreign ownership or a joint venture in the form of a corporation or partnership. Local law will define the regulations and restrictions to be imposed on the firm. Common restrictions include requiring majority local ownership or that a majority of the board be resident directors. Investors in many countries may have the flexibility of determining whether the entity is considered a partnership or corporation for U.S. tax purposes. Every jurisdiction seems to have some unique wrinkles in the areas of formation and administration, matters taken for granted by locals that may occasion surprise and delays for foreign investors.

Local advisors experienced in dealing with foreign investors can help smooth the process and minimize surprises on both practical issues and matters of substantive and procedural law. Special attention should be paid to coordinating tax/accounting and legal advice within the context of the investor's business goals. It must be recognized that sometimes foreign lawyers and accountants take a compartmentalized rather than interdisciplinary approach—it is not the expectation that they will go beyond their technical role and act as general business advisors. It is important for the investor's point person, the transaction manager, to actively set expectations and coordinate the advisory process.

This is perhaps nowhere more important than in the tax area. Even similar systems of tax law will differ in significant respects, and only rarely can one find a single individual who is thoroughly versed in the laws of two jurisdictions and their interrelations. It is important to coordinate carefully and start early in the planning stage to uncover potential problem areas. Obtaining tax credits is a relatively obvious issue. Other, subtle issues can appear in many contexts. An agreement, exchange of assets, or other transaction that creates no tax liability or is not deemed a tax event in one country may create income-tax liability in another. For example, stock dividends and splits are not taxable in the United States and other major economies because there is no change of economic substance. Thus, it might not occur to a U.S. manager, tax lawyer, or accountant to inquire and discover that they may be taxable in other countries.

Corporate laws also vary by jurisdiction. The U.S. system of corporate law and procedure is relatively flexible. Most other jurisdictions have less permissive rules regarding capital structure, dissolution, corporate formalities, and officers and directors, as well as different penalties for noncompliance. An investor may not be able to form, operate and close down the entity how and when it wants, and it may prove impossible or impractical to achieve the desired management structure.

If the company employs workers in the host country, it is subject to a system of employment laws, regulations, and customs that is, in most cases, more restrictive and more protective of workers than U.S. law. Employment laws are highly politicized and seek to protect local workers, particularly against foreign "exploitation." They need not make sense to U.S. managers. Restricted use of foreign personnel, required proportions of local workers, prescribed terms of employment, and difficulty in terminating unsatisfactory employees are all common issues. The foreign investor may have to compromise its employment policies in order to fit local requirements.

In some areas, such as environmental law, many developing countries are far less regulated than the United States, but the investor should expect to see these countries' legal regimes eventually catch up. Legal advantages, like business advantages, are often transitory. The investor needs to evaluate and understand both areas to develop the knowledge of and sensitivity to local conditions needed to make the right investment decision.

IN BRIEF

THINKING INTERNATIONAL

- *Market Conditions and Competition*
  - Product/Service Market Fundamentals
  - Distribution/Operational Realities
  - Personnel and Management
  - Location
  - Currency
  - Competitors
  - Achieving "Local Touch"
- *Legal Mores of Foreign Country*
  - Rule of Law
  - Corruption
  - Judicial Integrity
- *Substantive Foreign Law, including Laws regarding:*
  - Exchange Controls
  - Import/Export Costs and Controls
  - Employment Law
  - Taxes, Both Foreign and Domestic
  - Securities
  - Antitrust
  - Formation, Governance, and Dissolution of Foreign Entity
- *Sociopolitical and Economic Climate of Host Country*
  - Long-term Economic Stability
  - Stable Pro-Market Consensus
  - Attitude to Foreign Investors

◆ Extraterritorial Application of Domestic Law

Under certain circumstances, a country will seek to apply its law to conduct that occurred outside its borders. For example, as explained in Chapter 18, the United States applies its antitrust laws to activities occurring outside the United States if they cause substantial effects on U.S. exports or imports.

A related issue arises when a foreign national seeks to invoke another country's laws and use its courts to obtain relief that is not available under domestic law. Most courts will not exercise jurisdiction unless the country in which the court sits has some interest in the transaction. The following case addressed the right of an English citizen to sue an English company in the United States for securities fraud under U.S. law.

A CASE IN POINT | **SUMMARY**

CASE 26.3
ROBINSON v.
TCI/US WEST
COMMUNICATIONS,
INC.

United States Court of Appeals for the Fifth Circuit 117 F.3d 900 (5th Cir. 1998).

FACTS   Alan Robinson, an English citizen and resident, was a founder of Croydon Cable Television Limited (CCTV), one of the first cable franchises in England. Through a series of joint ventures and other investment agreements, Robinson's interest in CCTV became an interest in an English company called United Artists Communications (London South), PLC (United Artists). United Artists was controlled by Tele Communications, Inc. (TCI) and U.S. West, Inc. (U.S. West).

Robinson had sued United Artists in England after representatives of that company tried to force him to trade in his voting stock for nonvoting stock. TCI and U.S. West considered Robinson a thorn in their side and by 1993 had decided to negotiate a way to buy him out. Robinson negotiated directly with Stephen Davidson, finance director of TeleWest Communications, PLC (TeleWest), an English company formed by TCI and U.S. West. Robinson alleged that he was directed to negotiate with Davidson by Gary Bryson, a U.S. West executive in Denver, Colorado, and that Davidson was acting on Bryson's authority.

After lengthy negotiations, Robinson and Davidson reached a settlement. Robinson agreed to sell all his stock in United Artists to TCI/U.S. West (a Colorado corporation) in exchange for two payments, one to occur at the time the shares were transferred and one to occur later. Under the first payment, Robinson would receive £790,000. Robinson's second payment was to be based on a valuation of TeleWest at the time its shares were offered to the public.

Robinson's primary concern was that he be paid the full value of his stock. To that end, he said he liked this scheme because Davidson told him the valuation used to calculate his payment would be the same one used in preparation for the public offering. Thus, because it would be in TCI's and U.S. West's interests to get a high valuation, Robinson felt he was protected from an artificially low estimate.

Robinson received his £790,000 as promised. Then, in preparation for its initial public offering, TeleWest requested a valuation from an English bank. The bank valued TeleWest at $540 million. Robinson alleged that under this formula his second payment should have been worth $9 million. However, TeleWest requested that the bank prepare a second valuation for the purposes of determining the value of Robinson's payments under the settlement. This alternative valuation, when plugged into the formula, resulted in a value of zero for the second payment to Robinson.

Robinson alleged that the letter instructing the English bank to do a second valuation was actually drafted by, and faxed from the legal department of, U.S. West. Only later, he alleged, was it put on TeleWest letterhead.

In 1995, Robinson sued TCI, U.S. West, and their affiliated companies, claiming they defrauded him in violation of Section 10(b) of the Securities Exchange Act of 1934 (the1934 Act) and Rule 10b-5. The district court dismissed the case for lack of subject matter jurisdiction. Robinson appealed.

Case 26.3 continues

Case 26.3 continued

ISSUE PRESENTED Does the 1934 Act give U.S. federal courts jurisdiction over a case in which an English citizen alleged securities fraud on the part of an English company when a central act in the alleged fraud was conducted in the United States by an American affiliate of that English company?

SUMMARY OF OPINION The U.S. Court of Appeals first commented that Robinson's allegations forced it to confront the "rather nebulous issue" of the extent to which the U.S. securities laws may be applied extraterritorially. With one small exception, the 1934 Act does nothing to address the circumstances under which U.S. courts have subject matter jurisdiction to hear suits involving foreign transactions. That exception did not apply in this case. Thus, the court found itself faced with the task of "filling the void" created by a combination of congressional silence and the growth of international commerce since the 1934 Act was passed.

Courts that have previously addressed this problem created two basic tests for jurisdiction: (1) the *effects test*, which asks whether conduct outside the United States has had a substantial adverse effect on American investors or securities markets; and (2) the *conduct test*, which in essence asks whether the fraudulent conduct occurred in the United States. Courts employing the conduct test have advanced two competing strains: The restrictive conduct test states that the domestic conduct must have been of "material importance" to or have "directly caused" the fraud complained of; a more relaxed conduct test requires only that the conduct be significant to the fraud rather than a direct cause of it.

The court applied the restrictive version of the conduct test. It reasoned that because federal courts are of limited jurisdiction, "unless a contrary intent appears, [legislation] is meant only to apply within the territorial jurisdiction of the United States." Moreover, the court said, "what little guidance we can glean from the securities statutes indicates that they are designed to protect American investors and markets as opposed to the victims of any fraud that somehow touches the United States."

Applying this restrictive conduct test to the facts at hand, the court found that Robinson's complaints provided a sufficient basis for subject matter jurisdiction. It rejected the district court's rationale, which reasoned that the "lone mailing" of the instruction letter (drafted and initially faxed by U.S. West), "an event occurring months after the allegedly fraudulent inducement, cannot justify the heaving of an entire cause of action . . . across the Atlantic Ocean."

Instead, the court noted that the heart of Robinson's allegation (which the district court ignored) was that the entire scheme was directed and controlled from the United States by TCI and U.S. West. Robinson's basic claim was that the defendants duped him into selling his stock by telling him there would be only one valuation. As a result, the court said, it is self-evident that the act of requesting the second valuation (an act nominally performed by TeleWest, but allegedly directed by U.S. West) was a substantial act in furtherance of the scheme. Thus, the drafting of the instruction letter was more than just tangential to the alleged fraud; "it directly triggered the injury of which Robinson now complains."

RESULT The district court's dismissal of Robinson's claim was reversed, and the case was remanded to the district court.

The U.S. Court of Appeals for the Second Circuit reached a different result in a case involving a sale of unregistered foreign securities by an English account manager in the London branch of a French bank to a Panamanian corporation with offices in Monaco that was owned by a Canadian.[9] The account manager had proposed the investment to the Canadian owner while he was in London. The sale was consummated via a series of telephone calls and faxes to the Canadian while he was at his vacation home in Florida. When the investment soured, the Panamanian corporation sued the French bank, a Luxembourg bond fund and its Bahamian manager, and the English account manager in federal district court in New York, asserting violations of the Securities Act of 1933 (the 1933 Act) and the 1934 Act.

The Second Circuit modified the conduct-and-effects test used in extraterritorial securities fraud cases by requiring a higher level of activity to support jurisdiction over a case under the 1933 Act. The court held that the 1933 Act's registration provisions should apply only to those offers of unregistered securities that tend to have the effect of creating a market for unregistered securities in the United States.

The court acknowledged that phone calls into the United States conveying an offer to sell securities ordinarily would be sufficient to support jurisdiction for a fraud case under the 1934 Act. Nonetheless, the court held that "a series of calls to a transient foreign national in the United States is not enough to establish jurisdiction under the conduct test without some additional factor tipping the scales in favor of our jurisdiction." Although reliance on the misrepresentations may have taken place in the United States, "there is no U.S. party to protect or punish."

 Suing Foreign Governments

Sovereign immunity and the act-of-state doctrine are international legal principles that affect the rights of private commercial parties when a government becomes involved in or interferes with an international commercial transaction.

---

9. Europe and Overseas Commodity Traders, S.A. v. Banque Paribas London, Fed. Sec. L. Rep. (CCH) ¶90,223 (2d Cir. June 4, 1998).

Sovereign Immunity

The doctrine of *sovereign immunity* prevents the courts of one country from hearing suits against the governments of other countries. The rationale underlying this rule is that all sovereign states are equal, and none may subject others to their laws.

The needs of commerce have gradually tempered this rule. Because private entities often enter into commercial transactions with foreign governments, it became apparent that allowing a government to have complete immunity from all suits was not desirable. Thus, the concept of absolute immunity yielded to the restrictive theory of sovereign immunity, which allows immunity for a government's public activities but not for its commercial activities.

The Foreign Sovereign Immunities Act of 1976 (FSIA) is the U.S. codification of the restrictive theory of immunity. The FSIA was designed to eliminate the inconsistencies associated with politically initiated decisions to grant or withhold sovereign immunity in particular cases. It empowered the courts to determine when sovereign immunity applies, "by reference to the nature of the course of conduct or particular transaction or act."

The FSIA is the sole basis for obtaining jurisdiction over a foreign government in U.S. courts. The FSIA grants a blanket immunity to foreign states except in cases in which (1) the foreign state expressly or impliedly waives its immunity, (2) the foreign state engages in commercial activities, (3) the foreign state expropriates property in violation of international law (that is, seizes it without proper compensation), (4) property in the United States that is immovable or was acquired by gift or succession is at issue, (5) certain noncommercial torts are committed by the foreign state, (6) suit is brought to enforce a maritime lien under admiralty (that is, maritime) law, and (7) in a suit initiated by the foreign state, the defendant wishes to file a counterclaim. The *commercial activity exception* is probably the most important. If the nature of the foreign party to a contract or the subject matter of a contract is not clearly commercial, it may be advisable to require the foreign government to waive sovereign immunity in the contract.

In the following case, the commercial activity exception to sovereign immunity was applied to the breach of a contract by an Iraqi commercial bank and by the Iraqi government.

| A CASE IN POINT | IN THE LANGUAGE OF THE COURT |

CASE 26.4
COMMERCIAL BANK
OF KUWAIT v.
RAFIDAIN BANK
United States Court
of Appeals for
the Second Circuit
15 F.3d 238 (2d Cir. 1994).

FACTS The controversy stemmed in part from the situation in the Middle East that began with Iraq's invasion of Kuwait in August 1990 and led to the Gulf War between the United Nations and Iraq. Iraq suspended its payments under various obligations, including those at issue in this litigation.

Rafidain Bank, a commercial bank owned by the Republic of Iraq, had entered into several loan agreements and letter of credit transactions involving international banks. The Commercial Bank of Iraq (CBI), the Iraqi equivalent of the Federal Reserve in the United States, guaranteed some of Rafidain's payment obligations to assist Rafidain in obtaining loans. The Commercial Bank of Kuwait (Commercial Kuwait) participated in syndicates formed by lending banks to spread the risks of these transactions with Rafidain. Commercial Kuwait's share of the outstanding payment obligations was approximately $33 million.

Commercial Kuwait's allegations were based on CBI's guaranties of Rafidain's obligations and on a letter of credit under which Commercial Kuwait paid approximately $7.4 million. Commercial Kuwait sued Rafidain and CBI (the Iraqi Banks) for intentionally defaulting on their loan obligations. The Iraqi Banks claimed that the U.S. district court had no jurisdiction over them due to sovereign immunity.

ISSUE PRESENTED Did the Iraqi Banks enjoy sovereign immunity under the Foreign Sovereign Immunities Act (FSIA), thereby depriving the U.S. district court of jurisdiction to determine whether the Iraqi Banks willfully defaulted on their loan agreements?

OPINION FEINBERG, J., writing for the U.S. Court of Appeals:

The Iraqi Banks contend that the district court erred in applying the FSIA's "commercial activity" exception to sovereign immunity, and therefore lacked jurisdiction to consider those counts. The FSIA provides the "sole basis" for obtaining jurisdiction over a foreign sovereign in the United States. Under the FSIA, a "foreign state shall be immune from the jurisdiction of the courts of the United States and of the states" unless one of several statutory exceptions applies. . . .

The "commercial activity" exception to sovereign immunity provides, in relevant part, that a foreign sovereign or its agencies and instrumentalities: shall not be immune from the jurisdiction of the courts of the United States or of the States in any case . . . in which the action is based . . . upon an act outside the territory of the United States in connection with a commercial activity of the foreign sovereign elsewhere and that act causes a direct effect in the United States.

The Supreme Court has recently clarified the "direct effect" language of 1605(a)(2). *Weltover*[10] held that Argentina's unilateral rescheduling of bond payments had a "direct effect" within the meaning of § 1605(a)(2) because New York was the place of payment. Similarly, the agreements at issue . . . require the Iraqi Banks to make payments in U.S. dollars into accounts in New York City. The Iraqi Banks concede that these transactions constitute "commercial activity" under 1603(d). Nevertheless, they argue that the "commercial activity" exception does not

Case 26.4 continues

---

10. Argentina v. Weltover, 504 U.S. 607 (1992).

Case 26.4 continued

apply because the payments were to be made not directly to Commercial [Kuwait] but to New York bank accounts held by the lead banks of the various lending syndicates. The Iraqi Banks thus contend that, because the United States is not the place of performance of any contractual obligations owed to this plaintiff, there is no "direct effect in the United States" within the meaning of § 1605(a)(2).

We reject appellants' attempt to limit the Court's opinion in *Weltover*. The "commercial activity" exception of the FSIA withdraws immunity in cases involving essentially private commercial activities of foreign sovereigns that have an impact within the United States. This reflects the "restrictive" theory of sovereign immunity that underlies the FSIA. The focus of § 1605(a)(2) is the activity of the sovereign. If the sovereign's activity is commercial in nature and has a direct effect in the United States, then the jurisdictional nexus is met, no immunity attaches, and a district court has the authority to adjudicate disputes based on that activity.

The failure of the Iraqi Banks to remit funds in New York, as they were contractually bound to do, had a direct effect in the United States under *Weltover*. Furthermore, the requisite "material connection" between Commercial [Kuwait]'s cause of action and the "commercial activity" which is the jurisdictional basis is met despite Commercial [Kuwait]'s reliance on an agent to collect the sums due. Thus, the district court had jurisdiction to hear Commercial [Kuwait]'s claims.

RESULT   The district court had jurisdiction under the commercial activity exception to the FSIA. The Iraqi Banks did not enjoy sovereign immunity from any part of this action.

Questions

1. Do you agree with the court that the requisite material connection between Commercial Kuwait's cause of action and the commercial activity was met?
2. What type of relief should be granted to Commercial Kuwait?

The FSIA is relevant to U.S. companies that do or intend to do business with state-owned or state-managed enterprises, such as those in China and Vietnam. The exception from immunity for the commercial activities of these entities may not always be clear. In addition, if the contract is between a foreign, wholly owned subsidiary of a U.S. company and a foreign, state-owned enterprise, the fact that the U.S. parent is affected by a breach of the contract may not give rise to any remedial rights under U.S. law.

Act-of-State Doctrine

The *act-of-state doctrine* applies to the noncommercial acts of a government that affect foreign business interests within that government's territory. The doctrine was most clearly expressed by the U.S. Supreme Court in *Underhill v. Hernandez*,[11] when it stated that "the courts of one country will not sit in judgment on the acts of the government of another, done within its own territory." Pursuant to this doctrine, U.S. courts are extremely reluctant to provide a legal remedy under U.S. law for the public acts of a foreign government. As a result, U.S. businesses generally cannot look to the U.S. courts for protection from or compensation for acts such as expropriation unless there is a bilateral treaty between the United States and the

---

11. 168 U.S. 250, 252 (1897).

foreign country that specifies the procedural and substantive rights of a U.S. investor in that country. However, OPIC (the Overseas Private Investment Corporation) will insure U.S. businesses against certain host government acts, such as expropriation or restrictions on the conversion of local currency earnings.

 ## U.S. Domestic Considerations

A number of U.S. laws and business practices directly or indirectly affect U.S. investment abroad.

Trade Laws

If a U.S. investor in a foreign manufacturing facility wishes to market its foreign-manufactured products in the United States, it will face many of the same trade restrictions that are imposed on other foreign manufacturers seeking to export to the United States. In addition, if exports to the United States are a primary goal, the U.S. investor abroad should consider the advantages of preferential programs such as the North American Free Trade Agreement and the Caribbean Basin Initiative. (Trade laws are discussed in Chapter 25.)

Product Safety Standards

Exports to the United States may have to originate in facilities certified by the U.S. government or they may have to be produced according to U.S. government standards. For example, pharmaceutical products exported to the United States must be produced in facilities that adhere to the manufacturing practices established by the U.S. Food and Drug Administration (FDA). Airplanes built abroad for use in U.S. airspace must be built according to Federal Aviation Administration (FAA) standards in FAA-certified facilities. Investment contracts for such export projects need to reflect the production standards required by U.S. law.

Foreign-based U.S. manufacturers, like domestic U.S. manufacturers, need to be aware of U.S. product liability law (discussed in Chapter 10) and product standards (discussed in Chapter 19). Developing countries are increasingly enacting manufacturing safety standards and rules of manufacturer liability. Events such as the Bhopal disaster in India (discussed in Chapter 1) have shown that foreign-based U.S. investors cannot avoid liability solely by compliance with local standards. As the case that follows reveals, however, U.S. procedural law can (although it did not in this instance) insulate a U.S. company from being sued under U.S. law by foreign nationals.

A CASE IN POINT   **SUMMARY**

CASE 26.5
DOW CHEMICAL CO.
v. ALFARO
Supreme Court of Texas
786 S.W.2d 674 (Tex. 1990).

FACTS Domingo Castro Alfaro, a Costa Rican resident and employee of Standard Fruit Company, and 81 other Costa Rican employees and their wives brought suit against Dow Chemical Company and Shell Oil Company. The employees claimed that while they were working on a banana plantation in Costa Rica for Standard Fruit Company, they suffered personal injuries as a result of exposure to dibromochloropropane (DBCP). DBCP is a pesticide manufactured by Dow and Shell, which allegedly was furnished to Standard Fruit. Standard Fruit is an American subsidiary of Dole Fresh Fruit Company, headquartered in Boca Raton, Florida. The employees exposed to DBCP allegedly suffered several medical problems, including sterility.

After the U.S. Environmental Protection Agency (EPA) banned DBCP in the United States, Shell and Dow apparently shipped several hundred thousand gallons of the pesticide to Costa Rica for use by Standard Fruit. Alfaro sued Dow and Shell in Texas in April 1984, alleging that their handling of DBCP caused the employees serious personal injuries for which Shell and Dow were liable under the theories of product liability, strict liability, and breach of warranty. The defendants argued that Texas was not a convenient forum in which to litigate this case, under the doctrine of *forum non conveniens*.

Case 26.5 continues

Case 26.5 continued

ISSUE PRESENTED   Does the statutory right to enforce a personal injury or wrongful death claim in the Texas courts preclude a trial court from dismissing the claim on the ground of *forum non conveniens*?

SUMMARY OF OPINION   The Texas Supreme Court began by noting that the law of Texas allows an action to be brought in the courts of one state, even though the injury occurred in another. The court considered the defendants' claim of *forum non conveniens* in light of the U.S. Court of Appeals decision in *Atchison v. Weeks*.[12] In *Weeks*, the court discussed several of the rationales for the application of *forum non conveniens*. Among these reasons was the argument that there are many advantages to trying a case where the cause of action arises: The courts of the state in which the cause of action arose can more satisfactorily administer the laws of that state than can the courts of another state, and the expense of a trial would be less at the place of the tort than elsewhere.

In this case, judicial remedies were available in both Texas and Costa Rica. Costa Rica, however, does not allow jury trials. Because Costa Rica also does not allow for deposition of witnesses, it would have been difficult or impossible to depose Dow and Shell officials had the case been tried in Costa Rica.

The court concluded that, although there are some advantages to trying a case where the cause of action arises, the Texas court was the more suitable forum.

RESULT   The plaintiffs can bring their suit against defendants Shell and Dow in the Texas courts even though the harm occurred in Costa Rica.

COMMENTS   Both Shell and Dow argued that Texas was an inconvenient forum. It is true that there are advantages to trying a case where the cause of action arose (for example, evidence is more accessible). With improvements in technology and transportation, however, most forums today are not inconvenient nor are they cost prohibitive.

12. 254 F.513 (5th Cir. 1918).

Export Licensing

Foreign investment projects that involve U.S. technology may be subject to licensing and reexport restrictions imposed by the Export Administration Act or the Arms Export Control Act (both discussed in Chapter 25). These restrictions can extend to the reexport of products that contain specially licensed technology and to the technical training of foreign technicians in the United States. Noncompliance penalties can be severe. U.S. investors involved in foreign-investment projects with a sensitive technology component should explore these restrictions with legal counsel specializing in this area. In some cases, it may be appropriate to obtain an advisory opinion from the relevant U.S. government department.

Restrictions on Corrupt Practices

U.S. law prohibits U.S. businesses from paying or offering anything of value to foreign officials who have discretionary authority for the purpose of inducing such officials to direct business to the U.S. entity. This principle is embodied in the Foreign Corrupt Practices Act of 1977 (discussed in Chapter 25).

ETHICAL CONSIDERATION

Was the conduct of Dow Chemical and Shell Oil ethical when they shipped to Costa Rica an insecticide banned in the United States? Was Standard Fruit's use of the U.S.-banned pesticide ethical? Were the defendants arguing inconvenient forum to avoid a jury trial and Texas laws regarding personal injury and wrongful death? If so, is that ethical? If goods are not consistent with some sets of standards but are basically OK, is it ethical to sell them? If they are dangerous, how dangerous is too dangerous? Should it matter whether consumers in a developing country can afford products meeting higher but more expensive Western standards?

THE RESPONSIBLE MANAGER

Managing International Business Transactions

Managing an international business transaction, whether it be a sale, a license of intellectual property, or an equity investment, requires all the skills needed for a comparable domestic transaction and more. A broad range of foreign and domestic factors—legal, economic, social, and political—also complicate the transaction. Managers in a multinational business environment must act with these factors in mind, but cannot afford to suspend their critical objectivity and commitment to the underlying goals of the transaction. The transaction manager should be inquisitive but tactful, broad in scope of analysis but focused in attention.

A U.S. business entity is subject to the business and ethical expectations of its management, shareholders, and customers. It is also subject to both U.S. and foreign laws. All of these may constrain the extent to which the transaction manager can achieve the project goals.

Buying, selling, and investing abroad begin with identification of the project goals, which are often broader than those involved in transactions in the home market. "Penetrating new markets," "establishing a presence," and "going international" are fine-sounding goals that need to embodied in a concrete business and operational plan. Without sound and achievable goals,

transnational ventures can go wrong quickly, incurring significant costs in the process. Financial goals can be defeated by unexpected costs and efficiency problems. Profit repatriation can be frustrated by currency inconvertibility or foreign-exchange restrictions. Historically successful marketing strategies can fail under local conditions. Labor-productivity expectations can prove sadly optimistic. The objectives of local agents, management or partners can diverge from those of the U.S. company.

In many countries, a business does not have the freedom of crafting a contract within a broad field of permissible business terms that businesses in the United States enjoy. Developing countries, in particular, impose restrictions on issues that most U.S. businesses are used to treating as freely negotiable. The laws of these countries are not merely default rules that need be consulted to fine-tune a done deal or fill in gaps. They are often intended to define the principal parameters of an acceptable transaction. At the same time, they often provide incentives for certain types of transactions.

A manager will often begin with an analysis of the foreign-investment laws of the host country. Provisions of bilateral investment and tax treaties with the United States will also be relevant to crafting permissible project terms, incentives, and remedies. The manager cannot stop there, however, but must pursue the due diligence investigation of host country conditions by inquiring into the full range of potential legal and practical issues that might arise. Failure to do so can lead to embarrassment, costlier and more extended negotiations, and failure of project goals. The transaction manager is often the *only* person whose responsibility is broad enough to discover and address some of the complications that may arise.

Early use of professional services, such as those offered by legal counsel, accountants, and banking advisors with experience in the industry and the appropriate culture, can reduce negotiation costs, minimize the risk of disputes, and help prevent later surprises. Although true in the domestic context as well, it is far more critical in the international context, where physical and cultural separation, travel burdens, linguistic differences, and different sets of default expectations can more easily cause misunderstandings and disputes. Advisors can help frame the early discussion goals so as to avoid early commitments that later prove regrettable and perhaps suggest other terms that are easier to nail down favorably in the early stages of negotiation.

The choice of governing language and the selection of the party who will draft and revise the agreements to reflect the negotiations are often critical. Even if both sides negotiate the deal points thoroughly, there is a worthwhile incremental benefit in controlling the documents that is well known to every experienced lawyer. Managers should not allow the other side to assume control of the drafting as if it were a matter of little importance. Having one's lawyer involved early in the process lets a manager propose that his or her lawyer prepare the first draft, which is often a negotiating advantage.

The choice of applicable substantive law and the forum for resolving disputes are two legal issues that managers should try to resolve favorably early on rather than later, when this may be treated by the other side as a major rather than minor concession. Preparing the first draft allows a party to get its preferred terms into the contract first and not let the other side take local law and forum for granted (although one may ultimately have to concede the point under local law or for other reasons). Arbitration of disputes by a specialized forum may be more efficient and offer more confidentiality than litigation in a public court, but it may not adhere to judicial precedents and may not be easily enforceable (although arbitration awards can be more easily enforceable than court judgments in countries that are signatories to the New York Convention).

In U.S. domestic business transactions, there are various vehicles for ensuring that each party will perform the contract or will compensate the other party for failure to perform. United States laws offer a relatively sophisticated array of contractual and statutory remedies. Foreign laws may offer fewer established options. Even when effective remedies are nominally available, the legal administrative system of the foreign country may not make their use practical. The capable international manager needs to know the legal and practical remedies available in the host country if the other party fails to perform. Fortunately, third-party alternatives such as guaranties and L/Cs are also available.

Managers or their advisors should be thoroughly familiar with all applicable exchange controls and restrictions, and the transaction manager should be thoroughly familiar with the effect of exchange-rate fluctuations from both the economic and accounting perspectives. These fluctuations affect product pricing, capital contribution and distribution formulas of the respective parties, and financial results. It is also crucial to know what repatriable earnings are available from a for-

eign investment, a licensing transaction, or even the sale of products or services abroad.

Although the manager's focus will be on conditions in the host country, he or she will probably also bear responsibility for evaluating the impact of U.S. laws, ranging from tax and product liability laws to administrative regulations governing the certification of imported products. Some U.S. laws, such as the Foreign Corrupt Practices Act and the antitrust laws, affect the conduct of transactions occurring outside the United States. Having legal counsel with experience in the relevant types of international transaction available in at least a consultative capacity is indispensable.

The manager may be put in the unenviable position of having to reconcile the sometimes conflicting ethical standards of two or more cultures. For example, in some cultures, gift giving—ranging from a token company lapel pin to expensive automobiles—is an expected courtesy. In other cultures (and under the U.S. Foreign Corrupt Practices Act), gift giving, however innocently intended, may be viewed as an improper attempt to influence a business decision. United States businesses may feel hamstrung by the inability, for legal or ethical reasons, to match a competitor's gift or offer of "training"—in effect an all-expenses-paid vacation abroad—for employees of the foreign counterpart. However, the existence of relevant company policies or U.S. laws barring such actions can give a manager a face-saving, non-offensive way to decline to engage in unethical behavior.

Under pressure to make the deal happen, there can be a temptation to accept the "practical" solution rather than what is legally permissible on the argument that everyone does it. As foreign visitors, however, U.S. companies and their personnel are at particular risk of being held up as public examples of unacceptable behavior if there is a political, and perhaps business, reason for doing so. Behavior acceptable for locals is not necessarily acceptable for Americans. Nationalism, regionalism and competitive advantage are all reasons for focusing a spotlight on U.S. businesses.

Responsibly fulfilling all of these roles ultimately requires sensitivity, flexibility, and creativity. It requires familiarity with the technical needs of the project as well as practical business skill or experience. It also requires strength of character and maturity. Strength of character is needed to keep centered on the goals of the transaction rather than being swept away by deal momentum and the pressure of participants with narrower interests. Strength of character permits a manager to be receptive to foreign ways of doing things without compromising the standards of the home company or the manager's own professionalism and integrity. Maturity is needed to have the flexibility and security needed to realize one's own limitations and to accept advice and other input from a wide range of professionals and other participants.

INSIDE STORY
RESTRUCTURING THE SOCIALIST ECONOMIES OF EASTERN EUROPE

Post-socialist Eastern European societies have had no historical models for the transition from a command economy to a fully functioning market economy, although the experiences in Chile, Taiwan, and Korea provided some guidelines. As a consequence of this and local political cross-currents generated by the unsettling effect of change on existing social and economic structures, the transformation process has been one of experimentation and has proceeded at a sometimes slow and uneven pace. Nonetheless, on the whole, the transformation has proceeded with startling speed and thoroughness. The states of Eastern Europe outside the Commonwealth of Independent States (CIS) (which consists of most of the republics of the former Soviet Union) have more or less reached Western standards in terms of legal and regulatory frameworks and have achieved an economic level roughly comparable to less-affluent Western countries. Hungary, Poland, and the Czech Republic have joined NATO and are serious candidates for European Union (EU) membership early in the next decade. Estonia is now one of the freest markets in Europe and, with Slovenia, has been mentioned as a potential EU member.

These economies should be evaluated on terms similar to those used for other European countries, but with special attention to the degree of internal consensus and commitment to free markets. One must also ask how well they are coping with the negative aspects of post-socialist transition. These include widespread corruption, excessive influence of mafia-type organizations, weak environmental protections, weak and inequitable tax-collection systems, rapidly evolving laws and regulations, and loose norms of social and business behavior. State subsidization and at least indirect control of some portions of the economy remains typical. Price controls and exchange controls exist in some countries, but these have been common in other European countries as well prior to the EU taking hold in earnest after 1992. Political instability, in terms of which political party is in power and whether it tends towards capitalism or social welfarism, is also familiar elsewhere in Europe. Unemployment is another trans-European issue. Nowhere except in the CIS (and perhaps even more acutely in Belarus and the Ukraine) are there prospects of a change of power that would turn back the clock to Communism.

The former Soviet Union has encountered the most difficulty in making the transition toward a market economy. It has greater ethnic diversity, greater geographical distances with which to contend, greater diversity of political opinion, and less historical familiarity with the workings of a market economy than Eastern Europe. Often preoccupied with political issues, Russia has lagged behind in the transition, but has still made enormous progress. Substantial privatization has occurred (though not without controversy). However, the devaluation of the ruble and the Russian stock market crash in August 1998 caused a financial and political crisis that could jeopardize Russia's transition to a capitalist market economy.

Nevertheless, the material wealth of the CIS republics makes them attractive for investors hoping for bargains in undervalued assets. It is a matter of business judgment as to how much of any perceived discount represents a true bargain and how much reflects the inherent risks.

KEY WORDS AND PHRASES

act-of-state doctrine **1020**	commercial activity exception **1018**	gross-up clause **1012**
applicant **1000**	compensation trade **1004**	irrevocable letter of credit **1002**
arrested **999**	confirming bank **1001**	letter of credit (L/C) **1000**
back-to-back letter of credit **1001**	conflict of laws **998**	lien notice **999**
beneficiary **1000**	countertrade **1010**	processing operation **1004**
bill of lading **1000**	financing lease **1003**	sovereign immunity **1018**
clean bill of lading **1000**	*forum non conveniens* **1022**	standby letter of credit **1010**

QUESTIONS AND CASE PROBLEMS

1. What factors should a manager take into account when planning to expand operations outside of his or her home country?

2. Two former football players from the Chicago Winds, a defunct World Football League club, sought payment of their salaries from the club after the franchise was terminated. The original player contracts had obligated the club to secure a "domestic letter of credit" for each player in the amount of his salary. The club obtained the letters of credit, which stated that their purpose was "to guarantee payment for services rendered" by the players to the club. Each letter of credit provided that the issuing bank would pay the player upon presentation of a draft (an order for payment) and an affidavit signed by that player stating that the club had not paid him for a scheduled football game by a certain date. The players were not paid, and they presented their affidavits and draft documents to the bank. The bank refused to pay, on the grounds that the letter of credit was subject, by its terms, to the UCP. Under the UCP, the letter was unilaterally revocable by the bank. Who should prevail? [*Beathard v. Chicago Football Club*, 419 F. Supp. 1133 (N.D. Ill. 1976)]

3. The New England Petroleum Corporation (NEPCO), a U.S. corporation, obtained refined oil from its wholly owned Bahamas subsidiary refinery, PETCO. In 1968, PETCO entered into a long-term contract to purchase crude oil from Chevron Oil Trading (Chevron), a branch of a petroleum company that held 50% of an oil concession in Libya. In 1973, Libya nationalized several foreign-owned oil concessions, including Chevron's. As a result, Chevron terminated its contract with PETCO.

PETCO then entered into a new contract with the National Oil Corporation (National), which was wholly owned by the Libyan government. One month after execution of the contract, Libya imposed an oil embargo on the United States, and National canceled its contract with PETCO. Three months later, after a dramatic increase in oil prices, PETCO executed a new contract with National. National allegedly breached that contract as well.

PETCO's assignee, Carey, brought suit against National, seeking to recover damages for National's breach of the two contracts. National raised the defense of sovereign immunity. Carey claimed that there was no sovereign immunity under the Foreign Sovereign Immunities Act because the breach of contract was an act outside the territory of the United States in connection with a commercial activity that caused a direct effect in the United States. Who should prevail? [*Carey v. National Oil Corp.*, 592 F.2d 673 (2d Cir. 1979)]

4. Optomagic, Inc. is a U.S. corporation that produces optomagic gizmos. Production of optomagic gizmos involves a confidential gizmo-processing technique (which is described in printed confidential Optomagic manuals), labor-intensive processing, and inclusion of an optomagic component for which Optomagic was granted a U.S. patent six months ago. The optomagic component has widespread uses in the space, aviation, and medical industries.

Eight months ago, in the African country of Varoom, there was a relatively peaceful popular uprising that resulted in the removal of the "old guard" leaders, who had favored a strong centrally planned economy. The new provisional government called for free elections in one year, began taking immediate steps to reform the economy, and promised to liberalize foreign-investment laws to attract foreign investment.

Because the government bureaucracy is still in some disarray, it is extremely helpful, as a practical matter, to have close contacts with a government official who can speed the review and approval process for applications for foreign investment. In a recent official tour of the United States, Dr. Segun Ayantuga, the minister of health and welfare of Varoom, visited Optomagic's manufacturing facility in Boston, Massachusetts. Ayantuga is an eminent surgeon and a strong proponent of bringing advanced medical technology to his developing country so the best medical care can be made available to the public. In addition, he is interested in finding labor-intensive U.S. industries that may be able to produce products in Varoom for export to the more developed countries, to earn badly needed foreign exchange for Varoom. Optomagic is very interested in the newly emerging markets of Africa, and Varoom's in particular. Optomagic would also like to obtain gizmonium, a raw material necessary for the production of optomagic gizmos, which is found in great abundance in the mountains of Varoom, but which, under Varoomian law, is available only to Varoomian enterprises.

Two weeks after his visit to Optomagic, Ayantuga wrote to the chief executive officer of Optomagic to make the following proposal. Ayantuga and a state-owned medical clinic, Varoom Medical, are interested in establishing a joint venture in Varoom with Optomagic. Current Varoomian law limits foreign-investment interests in Varoomian enterprises to 50% of the total investment. Ayantuga states that, although under local law the Varoomian partners share equal responsibility for the management of the venture, they will in fact defer to Optomagic in all material matters related to the operation of the manufacturing facility. In addition, Ayantuga assures Optomagic that the foreign-investment law is likely to be liberalized within the year. As his investment in the venture, Ayantuga offers to contribute his lease interest in certain property in Varoom and to ensure that all the necessary government permits for the construction and licensing of the facility are obtained. Ayantuga expresses his confidence in being able to obtain all the government approvals for the proposed project because "our government has recently issued a decree emphasizing the national importance of upgrading our health-care industries."

The father of Optomagic's CEO emigrated from Varoom 60 years ago. He is excited about the developments in Varoom and finds Ayantuga to be a delightful, dynamic man. He is convinced that the time to move into Varoom is now, before Optomagic's competitors do.

Your assignment is to put together a business plan for the proposed joint venture, assuming that it's going to cost something up front but will be worth the expense in the long run. The CEO wants a preliminary report in two weeks to take to the board of directors, which will be considering establishing a wholly owned subsidiary in Cairo to operate prospective sales and manufacturing facilities in Africa. He also wants a comprehensive report to follow in another four weeks.

a. You have full access to your expert in-house legal counsel, who has experience in international projects. How can you best use him or her to assist in putting your plan together? What issues of particular importance should be addressed by counsel for inclusion in the preliminary report?

b. Given the uncertainty in the development of Varoom's foreign-investment laws (and its government), what types of terms or conditions do you think should be included in the contract for the proposed joint venture to protect against unexpected changes in the laws or government policies? What is your evaluation of the desirability of other forms of protection?

5. Assume the facts in Question 4. Are there any legal problems with including Ayantuga as an investor in the project? As a paid consultant?

6. Upon further general inquiry on behalf of Optomagic, you learn the following facts in addition to those set forth in Question 4. First, Varoom has a patent law and a trademark-registration law and is a signatory of the Paris and Madrid Conventions, but has no copyright law. Second, Varoomian law provides that licenses of foreign technology cannot (1) unreasonably restrict the geographic market for such exports, (2) impose requirements that the Varoomian party purchase components or raw materials from the foreign party, or (3) restrict use of the technology by the Varoomian licensee beyond a term of 10 years without approval from the supervising ministry (which in this case is the Ministry of Health).

What other information do you need to determine how best to protect Optomagic's intellectual property rights in the proposed venture? Based on what you do know, what steps should be taken to maximize protection of Optomagic's intellectual property rights? What U.S. laws will apply to the contribution, licensing, or other transfer of optomagic gizmo components by Optomagic to the joint venture? What license and joint venture contract terms are important to obtain?

7. Assume the facts in Question 4. Varoom Medical is prepared to invest 950 million baninis (U.S. $1 = 1,000 baninis) over the first five years of the project. Its commitment will be backed by a standby letter of credit to be issued by the National People's Bank of Varoom, a state-owned bank.

  a. What more do you need to know about the proposed capital contribution to be made by Varoom Medical and the standby letter of credit from the bank? Would you impose any additional conditions or requirements on the proposed contribution and the letter of credit?

  b. What do you propose Optomagic contribute as its share of capital to the proposed joint venture? What factors do you need to consider to make that decision?

8. Assume the facts in Question 4. You begin to consider the labor force that the joint venture will need. Ayantuga suggests that there be regular technical training visits by the venture technicians to Optomagic's facility in Boston, Massachusetts. Ayantuga also suggests that he can arrange to select the Varoomian technicians for the joint venture. Monthly salaries in Varoom for the relevant types of workers are 70% lower than in the United States. However, Varoom's labor laws require (1) payment of housing and health insurance subsidies by all enterprises to their employees, equal to 50% of their salaries; (2) mandatory arbitration with the local labor bureau prior to termination of any employee for any reason; and (3) in the case of foreign-invested enterprises, salaries and benefits to local management that are comparable with those of the expatriate management personnel of the foreign-invested enterprise.

  a. How would you assess the legal and economic advantages and disadvantages of the employees that Ayantuga proposed be hired?

  b. Is there another way to structure the workforce?

  c. What U.S. laws may apply to the training of joint venture technicians at Optomagic's U.S. facilities?

  d. Would you recommend that resident expatriate management personnel, or just visiting technicians,

be assigned to the prospective project? Why? What qualities do you think an expatriate employee in Varoom should have?

9. In addition to the facts covered in Questions 4 through 8, you learn that the banini is not freely convertible into dollars. The Varoom foreign-exchange and tax laws provide that a foreign-invested joint venture can repatriate up to 50% of its foreign-exchange earnings, subject to a repatriation tax of 15% (in addition to the tax imposed on the joint venture's income). Banini profits can be exchanged only upon prior approval by the supervising ministry (each ministry is allocated a quota of baninis for which it can approve an exchange into foreign currencies). In addition, Varoom's foreign-investment law requires that foreign-invested enterprises export a minimum of 50% of their products.

  a. What alternatives exist to repatriating foreign currency earnings in the prospective venture?

  b. What U.S. laws, if any, might apply to exports of optomagic gizmos to the United States from Varoom?

MANAGER'S DILEMMA

10. Heatwave, Inc. is a New York corporation that manufactures a highly advanced electronic instrument to measure the heat generated by electric motors operating at high speeds. The instrument has a variety of civilian and military applications. Although it can be run with different software packages available in the market, Heatwave has developed special software that it feels is superior to that of its competitors and that Heatwave claims gives a more accurate reading on the instrument. The management of Heatwave is extremely proud of its reputation as the world leader in this type of instrument and vigilantly guards against infringement of its proprietary technology and its trade name. Heatwave has a number of U.S. patents on both the instrument and the software. In addition, it uses a federally registered trademark on all its products.

  Heatwave would like to expand the production and sale of the instruments overseas. It is looking at a number of countries in both Europe and the Far East as possible markets, and it is considering using one of the following vehicles for its overseas activities: (1) licensing its technology to a foreign entity in exchange for a royalty, (2) setting up a branch in the foreign country to produce and sell the products locally, (3) establishing a wholly owned foreign subsidiary to produce and sell the products locally, or (4) establishing a joint venture with a local company to produce and sell the products locally.

Heatwave wants to protect its market in the United States and in certain foreign countries in which it is currently making direct sales. It is also concerned about maintaining the high-quality reputation of its instrument. Therefore, Heatwave would like to restrict sales

of the instrument to the local market and to require that a copy of its software be sold with each sale of the instrument. Regardless of the investment vehicle used, all rights to the software would remain with Heatwave.

a. What U.S. laws may have an impact on whether and how Heatwave expands overseas?

b. What local foreign laws may have an impact on Heatwave's decision on the type of vehicle it chooses to conduct its overseas activities and on the country into which it may expand?

INTERNET SOURCES	
The United Nations site includes the full text of the Berne Convention on Artistic and Literary Works, including the signatories.	http://www.un.or.at/uncitral
The World Intellectual Property Organization's Web site contains full text versions of the WIPO Copyright Treaty and the WIPO Performers and Phonograms Treaty.	http://www.wipo.int
The full text of the European Commission's proposed electronic signatures directive is available on the European Union's Web site.	http://europa.eu.int/comm/dg15/en/media/infso/sign.htm
This site, maintained by Professor Ray August at Washington State University, provides updates on international business law.	http://www.wsu.edu:8080/~legal/ibl
This site, maintained by C. Matthew Schulz of Baker & McKenzie, includes a "What's New?" link to information on visas and immigration.	http://www.schulzlaw.com
The International Trade Law Monitor site offers search potential and links to a comprehensive array of documents.	http://itl.irv.uit.no/trade_law
LawCrawler provides international law searching by country domains.	http://www.lawcrawler.com

Appendices

 ## Appendix A   The Constitution of the United States of America

PREAMBLE

We the People of the United States, in Order to form a more perfect Union, establish Justice, insure domestic Tranquility, provide for the common defence, promote the general Welfare, and secure the Blessings of Liberty to ourselves and our Posterity, do ordain and establish this Constitution for the United States of America.

ARTICLE I

Section 1.   All legislative Powers herein granted shall be vested in a Congress of the United States, which shall consist of a Senate and House of Representatives.

Section 2.   The House of Representatives shall be composed of Members chosen every second Year by the People of the several States, and the Electors in each State shall have the Qualifications requisite for Electors of the most numerous Branch of the State Legislature.

No Person shall be a Representative who shall not have attained to the Age of twenty five Years, and been seven Years a Citizen of the United States, and who shall not, when elected, be an Inhabitant of that State in which he shall be chosen.

Representatives and direct Taxes shall be apportioned among the several States which may be included within this Union, according to their respective Numbers, which shall be determined by adding to the whole Number of free Persons, including those bound to Service for a Term of Years, and excluding Indians not taxed, three fifths of all other Persons. The actual Enumeration shall be made within three Years after the first Meeting of the Congress of the United States, and within every subsequent Term of ten Years, in such Manner as they shall by Law direct. The Number of Representatives shall not exceed one for every thirty Thousand, but each State shall have at Least one Representative; and until such enumeration shall

be made, the State of New Hampshire shall be entitled to chuse three, Massachusetts eight, Rhode Island and Providence Plantations one, Connecticut five, New York six, New Jersey four, Pennsylvania eight, Delaware one, Maryland six, Virginia ten, North Carolina five, South Carolina five, and Georgia three.

When vacancies happen in the Representation from any State, the Executive Authority thereof shall issue Writs of Election to fill such Vacancies.

The House of Representatives shall chuse their Speaker and other Officers; and shall have the sole Power of Impeachment.

Section 3.   The Senate of the United States shall be composed of two Senators from each State, chosen by the Legislature thereof, for six Years; and each Senator shall have one Vote.

Immediately after they shall be assembled in Consequence of the first Election, they shall be divided as equally as may be into three Classes. The Seats of the Senators of the first Class shall be vacated at the Expiration of the second Year, of the second Class at the Expiration of the fourth Year, and of the third Class at the Expiration of the sixth Year, so that one third may be chosen every second Year; and if Vacancies happen by Resignation, or otherwise, during the Recess of the Legislature of any State, the Executive thereof may make temporary Appointments until the next Meeting of the Legislature, which shall then fill such Vacancies.

No Person shall be a Senator who shall not have attained to the Age of thirty Years, and been nine Years a Citizen of the United States, and who shall not, when elected, be an Inhabitant of that State for which he shall be chosen.

The Vice President of the United States shall be President of the Senate, but shall have no Vote, unless they be equally divided.

The Senate shall chuse their other Officers, and also a President pro tempore, in the Absence of the Vice President, or when he shall exercise the Office of President of the United States.

The Senate shall have the sole Power to try all Impeachments. When sitting for that Purpose, they shall be on Oath or Affirmation. When the President of the United States is tried, the Chief Justice shall preside: And no Person shall be convicted without the Concurrence of two thirds of the Members present.

Judgment in Cases of Impeachment shall not extend further than to removal from Office, and disqualification to hold and enjoy any Office of honor, Trust, or Profit under the United States: but the Party convicted shall nevertheless be liable and subject to Indictment, Trial, Judgment, and Punishment, according to Law.

Section 4.   The Times, Places and Manner of holding Elections for Senators and Representatives, shall be prescribed in each State by the Legislature thereof; but the Congress may at any time by Law make or alter such Regulations, except as to the Places of chusing Senators.

The Congress shall assemble at least once in every Year, and such Meeting shall be on the first Monday in December, unless they shall by Law appoint a different Day.

Section 5.   Each House shall be the Judge of the Elections, Returns, and Qualifications of its own Members, and a Majority of each shall constitute a Quorum to do Business; but a smaller Number may adjourn from day to day, and may be authorized to compel the Attendance of absent Members, in such Manner, and under such Penalties as each House may provide.

Each House may determine the Rules of its Proceedings, punish its Members for disorderly Behavior, and, with the Concurrence of two thirds, expel a Member.

Each House shall keep a Journal of its Proceedings, and from time to time publish the same, excepting such Parts as may in their Judgment require Secrecy; and the Yeas and Nays of the Members of either House on any question shall, at the Desire of one fifth of those Present, be entered on the Journal.

Neither House, during the Session of Congress, shall, without the Consent of the other, adjourn for more than three days, nor to any other Place than that in which the two Houses shall be sitting.

Section 6.   The Senators and Representatives shall receive a Compensation for their Services, to be ascertained by Law, and paid out of the Treasury of the United States. They shall in all Cases, except Treason, Felony and Breach of the Peace, be privileged from Arrest during their Attendance at the Session of their respective Houses, and in going to and returning from the same; and for any Speech or Debate in either House, they shall not be questioned in any other Place.

No Senator or Representative shall, during the Time for which he was elected, be appointed to any civil Office under the Authority of the United States, which shall have been created, or the Emoluments whereof shall have been increased during such time; and no Person holding any Office under the United States, shall be a Member of either House during his Continuance in Office.

Section 7.   All Bills for raising Revenue shall originate in the House of Representatives; but the Senate may propose or concur with Amendments as on other Bills.

Every Bill which shall have passed the House of Representatives and the Senate, shall, before it become a Law, be presented to the President of the United States; If he approve he shall sign it, but if not he shall return it, with his Objections to the House in which it shall have originated, who shall enter the Objections at large on their Journal, and proceed to reconsider it. If after such Reconsideration two thirds of that House shall agree to pass the Bill, it shall be sent together with the Objections, to the other House, by which it shall likewise be reconsidered, and if approved by two thirds of that House, it shall become a Law. But in all such Cases the Votes of both Houses shall be determined by Yeas and Nays, and the Names of the Persons voting for and against the Bill shall be entered on the Journal of each House respectively. If any Bill shall not be returned by the President within ten Days (Sundays excepted) after it shall have been presented to him, the Same shall be a Law, in like Manner as if he had signed it, unless the Congress by their Adjournment prevent its Return in which Case it shall not be a Law.

Every Order, Resolution, or Vote, to which the Concurrence of the Senate and House of Representatives may be necessary (except on a question of Adjournment) shall be presented to the President of the United States; and before the Same shall take Effect, shall be approved by him, or being disapproved by him, shall be repassed by two thirds of the Senate and House of Representatives, according to the Rules and Limitations prescribed in the Case of a Bill.

Section 8.   The Congress shall have Power To lay and collect Taxes, Duties, Imposts and Excises, to pay the Debts and provide for the common Defence and general Welfare of the United States; but all Duties, Imposts and Excises shall be uniform throughout the United States;

To borrow Money on the credit of the United States;

To regulate Commerce with foreign Nations, and among the several States, and with the Indian Tribes;

To establish an uniform Rule of Naturalization, and uniform Laws on the subject of Bankruptcies throughout the United States;

To coin Money, regulate the Value thereof, and of foreign Coin, and fix the Standard of Weights and Measures;

To provide for the Punishment of counterfeiting the Securities and current Coin of the United States;

To establish Post Offices and post Roads;

To promote the Progress of Science and useful Arts, by securing for limited Times to Authors and Inventors the exclusive Right to their respective Writings and Discoveries;

To constitute Tribunals inferior to the supreme Court;

To define and punish Piracies and Felonies committed on the high Seas, and Offenses against the Law of Nations;

To declare War, grant Letters of Marque and Reprisal, and make Rules concerning Captures on Land and Water;

To raise and support Armies, but no Appropriation of Money to that Use shall be for a longer Term than two Years;

To provide and maintain a Navy;

To make Rules for the Government and Regulation of the land and naval Forces;

To provide for calling forth the Militia to execute the Laws of the Union, suppress Insurrections and repel Invasions;

To provide for organizing, arming, and disciplining, the Militia, and for governing such Part of them as may be employed in the Service of the United States, reserving to the States respectively, the Appointment of the Officers, and the Authority of training the Militia according to the discipline prescribed by Congress;

To exercise exclusive Legislation in all Cases whatsoever, over such District (not exceeding ten Miles square) as may, by Cession of particular States, and the Acceptance of Congress, become the Seat of the Government of the United States, and to exercise like Authority over all Places purchased by the Consent of the Legislature of the State in which the Same shall be, for the Erection of Forts, Magazines, Arsenals, dock-Yards, and other needful Buildings;—And

To make all Laws which shall be necessary and proper for carrying into Execution the foregoing Powers, and all other Powers vested by this Constitution in the Government of the United States, or in any Department or Officer thereof.

Section 9.   The Migration or Importation of such Persons as any of the States now existing shall think proper to admit, shall not be prohibited by the Congress prior to the Year one thousand eight hundred and eight, but a Tax or duty may be imposed on such Importation, not exceeding ten dollars for each Person.

The privilege of the Writ of Habeas Corpus shall not be suspended, unless when in Cases of Rebellion or Invasion the public Safety may require it.

No Bill of Attainder or ex post facto Law shall be passed.

No Capitation, or other direct, Tax shall be laid, unless in Proportion to the Census or Enumeration herein before directed to be taken.

No Tax or Duty shall be laid on Articles exported from any State.

No Preference shall be given by any Regulation of Commerce or Revenue to the Ports of one State over those of another: nor shall Vessels bound to, or from, one State be obliged to enter, clear, or pay Duties in another.

No Money shall be drawn from the Treasury, but in Consequence of Appropriations made by Law; and a regular Statement and Account of the Receipts and Expenditures of all public Money shall be published from time to time.

No Title of Nobility shall be granted by the United States: And no Person holding any Office of Profit or Trust under them, shall, without the Consent of the Congress, accept of any present, Emolument, Office, or Title, of any kind whatever, from any King, Prince, or foreign State.

Section 10.   No State shall enter into any Treaty, Alliance, or Confederation; grant Letters of Marque and Reprisal; coin Money; emit Bills of Credit; make any Thing but gold and silver Coin a Tender in Payment of Debts; pass any Bill of Attainder, ex post facto Law, or Law impairing the Obligation of Contracts, or grant any Title of Nobility.

No State shall, without the Consent of the Congress, lay any Imposts or Duties on Imports or Exports, except what may be absolutely necessary for executing its inspection Laws: and the net Produce of all Duties and Imposts, laid by any State on Imports or Exports, shall be for the Use of the Treasury of the United States; and all such Laws shall be subject to the Revision and Controul of the Congress.

No State shall, without the Consent of Congress, lay any Duty of Tonnage, keep Troops, or Ships of War in time of Peace, enter into any Agreement or Compact with another State, or with a foreign Power, or engage in War, unless actually invaded, or in such imminent Danger as will not admit of delay.

ARTICLE II

Section 1.   The executive Power shall be vested in a President of the United States of America. He shall hold his Office during the Term of four Years, and, together with the Vice President, chosen for the same Term, be elected, as follows:

Each State shall appoint, in such Manner as the Legislature thereof may direct, a Number of Electors, equal to the whole Number of Senators and Representatives to which the State may be entitled in the Congress; but no Senator or Representative, or Person holding an Office of Trust or Profit under the United States, shall be appointed an Elector.

The Electors shall meet in their respective States, and vote by Ballot for two Persons, of whom one at least shall not be an Inhabitant of the same State with themselves. And they shall make a List of all the Persons voted for, and of the Number of Votes for each; which List they shall sign and certify, and transmit sealed to the Seat of the Government of the United States, directed to the President of the Senate. The President of the Senate shall, in the Presence of the Senate and House of Representatives, open all the Certificates, and the Votes shall then be counted. The Person having the greatest Number of Votes shall be the President, if such Number be a Majority of the whole Number of Electors appointed; and if there be more than one who have such Majority, and have an equal Number of Votes, then the House of Representatives shall immediately chuse by Ballot one of them for President; and if no Person have a Majority, then from the five highest on the List the said House shall in like Manner chuse the President. But in chusing the President, the Votes shall be taken by States, the Representation from each State having one Vote; A quorum for this Purpose shall consist of a Member or Members from two thirds of the States, and a Majority of all the States shall be necessary to a Choice. In every Case, after the Choice of the President, the Person having the greater Number of Votes of the Electors shall be the Vice President. But if there should remain two or more who have equal Votes, the Senate shall chuse from them by Ballot the Vice President.

The Congress may determine the Time of chusing the Electors, and the Day on which they shall give their Votes; which Day shall be the same throughout the United States.

No person except a natural born Citizen, or a Citizen of the United States, at the time of the Adoption of this Constitution, shall be eligible to the Office of President; neither shall any

Person be eligible to that Office who shall not have attained to the Age of thirty five Years, and been fourteen Years a Resident within the United States.

In Case of the Removal of the President from Office, or of his Death, Resignation or Inability to discharge the Powers and Duties of the said Office, the same shall devolve on the Vice President, and the Congress may by Law provide for the Case of Removal, Death, Resignation or Inability, both of the President and Vice President, declaring what Officer shall then act as President, and such Officer shall act accordingly, until the Disability be removed, or a President shall be elected.

The President shall, at stated Times, receive for his Services, a Compensation, which shall neither be increased nor diminished during the Period for which he shall have been elected, and he shall not receive within that Period any other Emolument from the United States, or any of them.

Before he enter on the Execution of his Office, he shall take the following Oath or Affirmation: "I do solemnly swear (or affirm) that I will faithfully execute the Office of President of the United States, and will to the best of my Ability, preserve, protect and defend the Constitution of the United States."

Section 2. The President shall be Commander in Chief of the Army and Navy of the United States, and of the Militia of the several States, when called into the actual Service of the United States; he may require the Opinion, in writing, of the principal Officer in each of the executive Departments, upon any Subject relating to the Duties of their respective Offices, and he shall have Power to grant Reprieves and Pardons for Offenses against the United States, except in Cases of Impeachment.

He shall have Power, by and with the Advice and Consent of the Senate to make Treaties, provided two thirds of the Senators present concur; and he shall nominate, and by and with the Advice and Consent of the Senate, shall appoint Ambassadors, other public Ministers and Consuls, Judges of the supreme Court, and all other Officers of the United States, whose Appointments are not herein otherwise provided for, and which shall be established by Law; but the Congress may by Law vest the Appointment of such inferior Officers, as they think proper, in the President alone, in the Courts of Law, or in the Heads of Departments.

The President shall have Power to fill up all Vacancies that may happen during the Recess of the Senate, by granting Commissions which shall expire at the End of their next Session.

Section 3. He shall from time to time give to the Congress Information of the State of the Union, and recommend to their Consideration such Measures as he shall judge necessary and expedient; he may, on extraordinary Occasions, convene both Houses, or either of them, and in Case of Disagreement between them, with Respect to the Time of Adjournment, he may adjourn them to such Time as he shall think proper; he shall receive Ambassadors and other public Ministers; he shall take Care that the Laws be faithfully executed, and shall Commission all the Officers of the United States.

Section 4. The President, Vice President and all civil Officers of the United States, shall be removed from Office on Impeachment for, and Conviction of, Treason, Bribery, or other high Crimes and Misdemeanors.

ARTICLE III

Section 1. The judicial Power of the United States, shall be vested in one supreme Court, and in such inferior Courts as the Congress may from time to time ordain and establish. The Judges, both of the supreme and inferior Courts, shall hold their Offices during good Behaviour, and shall, at stated Times, receive for their Services a Compensation, which shall not be diminished during their Continuance in Office.

Section 2. The judicial Power shall extend to all Cases, in Law and Equity, arising under this Constitution, the Laws of the United States, and Treaties made, or which shall be made, under their Authority;—to all Cases affecting Ambassadors, other public Ministers and Consuls;—to all Cases of admiralty and maritime Jurisdiction;—to Controversies to which the United States shall be a Party;—to Controversies between two or more States;—between a State and Citizens of another State;—between Citizens of different States;—between Citizens of the same State claiming Lands under Grants of different States, and between a State, or the Citizens thereof, and foreign States, Citizens or Subjects.

In all Cases affecting Ambassadors, other public Ministers and Consuls, and those in which a State shall be a Party, the supreme Court shall have original Jurisdiction. In all the other Cases before mentioned, the supreme Court shall have appellate Jurisdiction, both as to Law and Fact, with such Exceptions, and under such Regulations as the Congress shall make.

The Trial of all Crimes, except in Cases of Impeachment, shall be by Jury; and such Trial shall be held in the State where the said Crimes shall have been committed; but when not committed within any State, the Trial shall be at such Place or Places as the Congress may by Law have directed.

Section 3. Treason against the United States, shall consist only in levying War against them, or, in adhering to their Enemies, giving them Aid and Comfort. No Person shall be convicted of Treason unless on the Testimony of two Witnesses to the same overt Act, or on Confession in open Court.

The Congress shall have Power to declare the Punishment of Treason, but no Attainder of Treason shall work Corruption of Blood, or Forfeiture except during the Life of the Person attainted.

ARTICLE IV

Section 1. Full Faith and Credit shall be given in each State to the public Acts, Records, and judicial Proceedings of every other State. And the Congress may by general Laws prescribe the Manner in which such Acts, Records and Proceedings shall be proved, and the Effect thereof.

Section 2. The Citizens of each State shall be entitled to all Privileges and Immunities of Citizens in the several States.

A Person charged in any State with Treason, Felony, or other Crime, who shall flee from Justice, and be found in another State, shall on Demand of the executive Authority of the State from which he fled, be delivered up, to be removed to the State having Jurisdiction of the Crime.

No Person held to Service or Labour in one State, under the Laws thereof, escaping into another, shall, in Consequence of any Law or Regulation therein, be discharged from such Service or Labour, but shall be delivered up on Claim of the Party to whom such Service or Labour may be due.

Section 3.   New States may be admitted by the Congress into this Union; but no new State shall be formed or erected within the Jurisdiction of any other State; nor any State be formed by the Junction of two or more States, or Parts of States, without the Consent of the Legislatures of the States concerned as well as of the Congress.

The Congress shall have Power to dispose of and make all needful Rules and Regulations respecting the Territory or other Property belonging to the United States; and nothing in this Constitution shall be so construed as to Prejudice any Claims of the United States, or of any particular State.

Section 4.   The United States shall guarantee to every State in this Union a Republican Form of Government, and shall protect each of them against Invasion; and on Application of the Legislature, or of the Executive (when the Legislature cannot be convened) against domestic Violence.

ARTICLE V

The Congress, whenever two thirds of both Houses shall deem it necessary, shall propose Amendments to this Constitution, or, on the Application of the Legislatures of two thirds of the several States, shall call a Convention for proposing Amendments, which, in either Case, shall be valid to all Intents and Purposes, as part of this Constitution, when ratified by the Legislatures of three fourths of the several States, or by Conventions in three fourths thereof, as the one or the other Mode of Ratification may be proposed by the Congress; Provided that no Amendment which may be made prior to the Year One thousand eight hundred and eight shall in any Manner affect the first and fourth Clauses in the Ninth Section of the first Article; and that no State, without its Consent, shall be deprived of its equal Suffrage in the Senate.

ARTICLE VI

All Debts contracted and Engagements entered into, before the Adoption of this Constitution shall be as valid against the United States under this Constitution, as under the Confederation.

This Constitution, and the Laws of the United States which shall be made in Pursuance thereof; and all Treaties made, or which shall be made, under the Authority of the United States, shall be the supreme Law of the Land; and the Judges in every State shall be bound thereby, any Thing in the Constitution or Laws of any State to the Contrary notwithstanding.

The Senators and Representatives before mentioned, and the Members of the several State Legislatures, and all executive and judicial Officers, both of the United States and of the several States, shall be bound by Oath or Affirmation, to support this Constitution; but no religious Test shall ever be required as a Qualification to any Office or public Trust under the United States.

ARTICLE VII

The Ratification of the Conventions of nine States shall be sufficient for the Establishment of this Constitution between the States so ratifying the Same.

AMENDMENT I [1791]

Congress shall make no law respecting an establishment of religion, or prohibiting the free exercise thereof; or abridging the freedom of speech, or of the press; or the right of the people peaceably to assembly, and to petition the Government for a redress of grievances.

AMENDMENT II [1791]

A well regulated Militia, being necessary to the security of a free State, the right of the people to keep and bear Arms, shall not be infringed.

AMENDMENT III [1791]

No Soldier shall, in time of peace be quartered in any house, without the consent of the Owner, nor in time of war, but in a manner to be prescribed by law.

AMENDMENT IV [1791]

The right of the people to be secure in their persons, houses, papers, and effects, against unreasonable searches and seizures, shall not be violated, and no Warrants shall issue, but upon probable cause, supported by Oath or affirmation, and particularly describing the place to be searched, and the persons or things to be seized.

AMENDMENT V [1791]

No person shall be held to answer for a capital, or otherwise infamous crime, unless on a presentment or indictment of a Grand Jury, except in cases arising in the land or naval forces, or in the Militia, when in actual service in time of War or public danger; nor shall any person be subject for the same offence to be twice put in jeopardy of life or limb; nor shall be compelled in any criminal case to be a witness against himself, nor be deprived of life, liberty, or property, without due process of law; nor shall private property be taken for public use, without just compensation.

AMENDMENT VI [1791]

In all criminal prosecutions, the accused shall enjoy the right to a speedy and public trial, by an impartial jury of the State and district wherein the crime shall have been committed, which district shall have been previously ascertained by law, and to be informed of the nature and cause of the accusation; to be confronted with the witnesses against him; to have compulsory process for obtaining witnesses in his favor, and to have the Assistance of Counsel for his defence.

AMENDMENT VII [1791]

In Suits at common law, where the value in controversy shall exceed twenty dollars, the right of trial by jury shall be preserved, and no fact tried by jury, shall be otherwise re-examined in any Court of the United States, than according to the rules of the common law.

AMENDMENT VIII [1791]

Excessive bail shall not be required, nor excessive fines imposed, nor cruel and unusual punishments inflicted.

AMENDMENT IX [1791]

The enumeration in the Constitution, of certain rights, shall not be construed to deny or disparage others retained by the people.

AMENDMENT X [1791]

The powers not delegated to the United States by the Constitution, nor prohibited by it to the States, are reserved to the States respectively, or to the people.

AMENDMENT XI [1798]

The Judicial power of the United States shall not be construed to extend to any suit in law or equity, commenced or prosecuted against one of the United States by Citizens of another State, or by Citizens or Subjects of any Foreign State.

AMENDMENT XII [1804]

The Electors shall meet in their respective states, and vote by ballot for President and Vice-President, one of whom, at least, shall not be an inhabitant of the same state with themselves; they shall name in their ballots the person voted for as President, and in distinct ballots the person voted for as Vice-President, and they shall make distinct lists of all persons voted for as President, and of all persons voted for as Vice-President, and of the number of votes for each, which lists they shall sign and certify, and transmit sealed to the seat of the government of the United States, directed to the President of the Senate;—The President of the Senate shall, in the presence of the Senate and House of Representatives, open all the certificates and the votes shall then be counted;— The person having the greatest number of votes for President, shall be the President, if such number be a majority of the whole number of Electors appointed; and if no person have such majority, then from the persons hav-

ing the highest numbers not exceeding three on the list of those voted for as President, the House of Representatives shall choose immediately, by ballot, the President. But in choosing the President, the votes shall be taken by states, the representation from each state having one vote; a quorum for this purpose shall consist of a member or members from two-thirds of the states, and a majority of all states shall be necessary to a choice. And if the House of Representatives shall not choose a President whenever the right of choice shall devolve upon them, before the fourth day of March next following, then the Vice-President shall act as President, as in the case of the death or other constitutional disability of the President.—The person having the greatest number of votes as Vice-President, shall be the Vice-President, if such number be a majority of the whole number of Electors appointed, and if no person have a majority, then from the two highest numbers on the list, the Senate shall choose the Vice-President; a quorum for the purpose shall consist of two-thirds of the whole number of Senators, and a majority of the whole number shall be necessary to a choice. But no person constitutionally ineligible to the office of President shall be eligible to that of Vice-President of the United States.

AMENDMENT XIII [1865]

Section 1.   Neither slavery nor involuntary servitude, except as a punishment for crime whereof the party shall have been duly convicted, shall exist within the United States, or any place subject to their jurisdiction.

Section 2.   Congress shall have power to enforce this article by appropriate legislation.

AMENDMENT XIV [1868]

Section 1.   All persons born or naturalized in the United States, and subject to the jurisdiction thereof, are citizens of the United States and of the State wherein they reside. No State shall make or enforce any law which shall abridge the privileges or immunities of citizens of the United States; nor shall any State deprive any person of life, liberty, or property, without due process of law; nor deny to any person within its jurisdiction the equal protection of the laws.

Section 2.   Representatives shall be apportioned among the several States according to their respective numbers, counting the whole number of persons in each State, excluding Indians not taxed. But when the right to vote at any election for the choice of electors for President and Vice President of the United States, Representatives in Congress, the Executive and Judicial officers of a State, or the members of the Legislature thereof, is denied to any of the male inhabitants of such State, being twenty-one years of age, and citizens of the United States, or in any way abridged, except for participation in rebellion, or other crime, the basis of representation therein shall be reduced in the proportion which the number of such male citizens shall bear to the whole number of male citizens twenty-one years of age in such State.

Section 3.   No person shall be a Senator or Representative in Congress, or elector of President and Vice President, or hold any office, civil or military, under the United States, or under any State, who having previously taken an oath, as a member of Congress, or as an officer of the United States, or as a member of any State legislature, or as an executive or judicial officer of any State, to support the Constitution of the United States, shall have engaged in insurrection or rebellion against the same, or given aid or comfort to the enemies thereof. But Congress may by a vote of two-thirds of each House, remove such disability.

Section 4.   The validity of the public debt of the United States, authorized by law, including debts incurred for payment of pensions and bounties for services in suppressing insurrection or rebellion, shall not be questioned. But neither the United States nor any State shall assume or pay any debt or obligation incurred in aid of insurrection or rebellion against the United States, or any claim for the loss or emancipation of any slave; but all such debts, obligations and claims shall be held illegal and void.

Section 5.   The Congress shall have power to enforce, by appropriate legislation, the provisions of this article.

AMENDMENT XV [1870]

Section 1.   The right of citizens of the United States to vote shall not be denied or abridged by the United States or by any State on account of race, color, or previous condition of servitude.

Section 2.   The Congress shall have power to enforce this article by appropriate legislation.

AMENDMENT XVI [1913]

The Congress shall have power to lay and collect taxes on incomes, from whatever source derived, without apportionment among the several States, and without regard to any census or enumeration.

AMENDMENT XVII [1913]

Section 1.   The Senate of the United States shall be composed of two Senators from each State, elected by the people thereof, for six years; and each Senator shall have one vote. The electors in each State shall have the qualifications requisite for electors of the most numerous branch of the State legislatures.

Section 2.   When vacancies happen in the representation of any State in the Senate, the executive authority of such State shall issue writs of election to fill such vacancies: *Provided*, That the legislature of any State may empower the executive thereof to make temporary appointments until the people fill the vacancies by election as the legislature may direct.

Section 3.   This amendment shall not be so construed as to affect the election or term of any Senator chosen before it becomes valid as part of the Constitution.

AMENDMENT XVIII [1919]

Section 1.   After one year from the ratification of this article the manufacture, sale, or transportation of intoxicating liquors within, the importation thereof into, or the exportation thereof from the United States and all territory subject to the jurisdiction thereof for beverage purposes is hereby prohibited.

Section 2.   The Congress and the several States shall have concurrent power to enforce this article by appropriate legislation.

Section 3.   This article shall be inoperative unless it shall have been ratified as an amendment to the Constitution by the legislatures of the several States, as provided in the Constitution, within seven years from the date of the submission hereof to the States by the Congress.

AMENDMENT XIX [1920]

Section 1.   The right of citizens of the United States to vote shall not be denied or abridged by the United States or by any State on account of sex.

Section 2.   Congress shall have power to enforce this article by appropriate legislation.

AMENDMENT XX [1933]

Section 1.   The terms of the President and Vice President shall end at noon on the 20th day of January, and the terms of Senators and Representatives at noon on the 3d day of January, of the years in which such terms would have ended if this article had not been ratified; and the terms of their successors shall then begin.

Section 2.   The Congress shall assemble at least once in every year, and such meeting shall begin at noon on the 3d day of January, unless they shall by law appoint a different day.

Section 3.   If, at the time fixed for the beginning of the term of the President, the President elect shall have died, the Vice President elect shall become President. If the President shall not have been chosen before the time fixed for the beginning of his term, or if the President elect shall have failed to qualify, then the Vice President elect shall act as President until a President shall have qualified; and the Congress may by law provide for the case wherein neither a President elect nor a Vice President elect shall have qualified, declaring who shall then act as President, or the manner in which one who is to act shall be selected, and such person shall act accordingly until a President or Vice President shall have qualified.

Section 4.   The Congress may by law provide for the case of the death of any of the persons from whom the House of Representatives may choose a President whenever the right of choice shall have devolved upon them, and for the case of the death of any of the persons from whom the Senate may choose a Vice President whenever the right of choice shall have devolved upon them.

Section 5.   Sections 1 and 2 shall take effect on the 15th day of October following the ratification of this article.

Section 6.   This article shall be inoperative unless it shall have been ratified as an amendment to the Constitution by the legislatures of three-fourths of the several States within seven years from the date of its submission.

Amendment XXI [1933]

Section 1. The eighteenth article of amendment to the Constitution of the United States is hereby repealed.

Section 2. The transportation or importation into any State, Territory, or possession of the United States for delivery or use therein of intoxicating liquors, in violation of the laws thereof, is hereby prohibited.

Section 3. This article shall be inoperative unless it shall have been ratified as an amendment to the Constitution by conventions in the several States, as provided in the Constitution, within seven years from the date of the submission hereof to the States by the Congress.

Amendment XXII [1951]

Section 1. No person shall be elected to the office of the President more than twice, and no person who has held the office of President, or acted as President, for more than two years of a term to which some other person was elected President shall be elected to the office of President more than once. But this Article shall not apply to any person holding the office of President when this Article was proposed by the Congress, and shall not prevent any person who may be holding the office of President, or acting as President, during the term within which this Article becomes operative from holding the office of President or acting as President during the remainder of such term.

Section 2. This article shall be inoperative unless it shall have been ratified as an amendment to the Constitution by the legislatures of three-fourths of the several States within seven years from the date of its submission to the States by the Congress.

Amendment XXIII [1961]

Section 1. The District constituting the seat of Government of the United States shall appoint in such manner as the Congress may direct:

A number of electors of President and Vice President equal to the whole number of Senators and Representatives in Congress to which the District would be entitled if it were a State, but in no event more than the least populous state; they shall be in addition to those appointed by the states, but they shall be considered, for the purposes of the election of President and Vice President, to be electors appointed by a state; and they shall meet in the District and perform such duties as provided by the twelfth article of amendment.

Section 2. The Congress shall have power to enforce this article by appropriate legislation.

Amendment XXIV [1964]

Section 1. The right of citizens of the United States to vote in any primary or other election for President or Vice President, for electors for President or Vice President, or for Senator or Representative in Congress, shall not be denied or abridged by the United States, or any State by reason of failure to pay any poll tax or other tax.

Section 2. The Congress shall have power to enforce this article by appropriate legislation.

Amendment XXV [1967]

Section 1. In case of the removal of the President from office or of his death or resignation, the Vice President shall become President.

Section 2. Whenever there is a vacancy in the office of the Vice President, the President shall nominate a Vice President who shall take office upon confirmation by a majority vote of both Houses of Congress.

Section 3. Whenever the President transmits to the President pro tempore of the Senate and the Speaker of the House of Representatives his written declaration that he is unable to discharge the powers and duties of his office, and until he transmits to them a written declaration to the contrary, such powers and duties shall be discharged by the Vice President as Acting President.

Section 4. Whenever the Vice President and a majority of either the principal officers of the executive departments or of such other body as Congress may by law provide, transmit to the President pro tempore of the Senate and the Speaker of the House of Representatives their written declaration that the President is unable to discharge the powers and duties of his office, the Vice President shall immediately assume the powers and duties of the office as Acting President.

Thereafter, when the President transmits to the President pro tempore of the Senate and the Speaker of the House of Representatives his written declaration that no inability exists, he shall resume the powers and duties of his office unless the Vice President and a majority of either the principal officers of the executive department or of such other body as Congress may by law provide, transmit within four days to the President pro tempore of the Senate and the Speaker of the House of Representatives their written declaration and the President is unable to discharge the powers and duties of his office. Thereupon Congress shall decide the issue, assembling within forty-eight hours for that purpose if not in session. If the Congress, within twenty-one days after receipt of the latter written declaration, or, if Congress is not in session, within twenty-one days after Congress is required to assemble, determines by two-thirds vote of both Houses that the President is unable to discharge the powers and duties of his office, the Vice President shall continue to discharge the same as Acting President; otherwise, the President shall resume the powers and duties of his office.

Amendment XXVI [1971]

Section 1. The right of citizens of the United States, who are eighteen years of age or older, to vote shall not be denied or abridged by the United States or by any State on account of age.

Section 2. The Congress shall have power to enforce this article by appropriate legislation.

Amendment XXVII [1992]

No law, varying the compensation for the services of the Senators and Representatives, shall take effect, until an election of Representatives shall have intervened.

Appendix B   Article 2 of the Uniform Commercial Code: Sales [Excerpts]

Part 1 Short Title, General Construction and Subject Matter
§ 2—101. Short Title.

This Article shall be known and may be cited as Uniform Commercial Code—Sales.

§ 2—102. Scope; Certain Security and Other Transactions Excluded From This Article.

Unless the context otherwise requires, this Article applies to transactions in goods; it does not apply to any transaction which although in the form of an unconditional contract to sell or present sale is intended to operate only as a security transaction nor does this Article impair or repeal any statute regulating sales to consumers, farmers or other specified classes of buyers.

§ 2—103. Definitions and Index of Definitions.

(1) In this Article unless the context otherwise requires

(a) "Buyer" means a person who buys or contracts to buy goods.

(b) "Good faith" in the case of a merchant means honesty in fact and the observance of reasonable commercial standards of fair dealing in the trade.

(c) "Receipt" of goods means taking physical possession of them.

(d) "Seller" means a person who sells or contracts to sell goods.
. . .

§ 2—104. Definitions: "Merchant"; "Between Merchants"
. . . .

(1) "Merchant" means a person who deals in goods of the kind or otherwise by his occupation holds himself out as having knowledge or skill peculiar to the practices or goods involved in the transaction or to whom such knowledge or skill may be attributed by his employment of an agent or broker or other intermediary who by his occupation holds himself out as having such knowledge or skill. . . .

(3) "Between merchants" means in any transaction with respect to which both parties are chargeable with the knowledge or skill of merchants.

§ 2—105. Definitions: . . . "Goods"; "Future" Goods; . . . .

(1) "Goods" means all things (including specially manufactured goods) which are movable at the time of identification to the contract for sale other than the money in which the price is to be paid, investment securities (Article 8) and things in action. "Goods" also includes the unborn young of animals and growing crops and other identified things attached to realty as described in the section on goods to be severed from realty (Section 2—107).

(2) Goods must be both existing and identified before any interest in them can pass. Goods which are not both existing and identified are "future" goods. A purported present sale of future goods or of any interest therein operates as a contract to sell.

(3) There may be a sale of a part interest in existing identified goods.

(4) An undivided share in an identified bulk of fungible goods is sufficiently identified to be sold although the quantity of the bulk is not determined. Any agreed proportion of such a bulk or any quantity thereof agreed upon by number, weight or other measure may to the extent of the seller's interest in the bulk be sold to the buyer who then becomes an owner in common.
. . .

§ 2—106. Definitions: "Contract"; "Agreement"; "Contract for Sale"; "Sale"; "Present Sale"; "Conforming" to Contract; "Termination"; "Cancellation".

(1) In this Article unless the context otherwise requires "contract" and "agreement" are limited to those relating to the present or future sale of goods. "Contract for sale" includes both a present sale of goods and a contract to sell goods at a future time. A "sale" consists in the passing of title from the seller to the buyer for a price (Section 2—401). A "present sale" means a sale which is accomplished by the making of the contract.

(2) Goods or conduct including any part of a performance are "conforming" or conform to the contract when they are in accordance with the obligations under the contract.

(3) "Termination" occurs when either party pursuant to a power created by agreement or law puts an end to the contract otherwise than for its breach. On "termination" all obligations which are still executory on both sides are discharged but any right based on prior breach or performance survives.

(4) "Cancellation" occurs when either party puts an end to the contract for breach by the other and its effect is the same as that of "termination" except that the cancelling party also retains any remedy for breach of the whole contract or any unperformed balance.

. . .

Part 2 Form, Formation and Readjustment of Contract
§ 2—201. Formal Requirements; Statute of Frauds.

(1) Except as otherwise provided in this section a contract for the sale of goods for the price of $500 or more is not enforceable by way of action or defense unless there is some writing sufficient to indicate that a contract for sale has been made between the parties and signed by the party against whom enforcement is sought or by his authorized agent or broker. A writing is not insufficient because it omits or incorrectly states a term agreed upon but the contract is not enforceable under this paragraph beyond the quantity of goods shown in such writing.

(2) Between merchants if within a reasonable time a writing in confirmation of the contract and sufficient against the sender is received and the party receiving it has reason to know its contents, its satisfies the requirements of subsection (1) against such party unless written notice of objection to its contents is given within ten days after it is received.

(3) A contract which does not satisfy the requirements of subsection (1) but which is valid in other respects is enforceable

(a) if the goods are to be specially manufactured for the buyer and are not suitable for sale to others in the ordinary course of the seller's business and the seller, before notice of repudiation is received and under circumstances which reasonably indicate that the goods are for the buyer, has made either a substantial beginning of their manufacture or commitments for their procurement; or

(b) if the party against whom enforcement is sought admits in his pleading, testimony or otherwise in court that a contract for sale was made, but the contract is not enforceable under this provision beyond the quantity of goods admitted; or

(c) with respect to goods for which payment has been made and accepted or which have been received and accepted (Sec. 2—606).

§ 2—202. Final Written Expression: Parol or Extrinsic Evidence.

Terms with respect to which the confirmatory memoranda of the parties agree or which are otherwise set forth in a writing intended by the parties as a final expression of their agreement with respect to such terms as are included therein may not be contradicted by evidence of any prior agreement or of a contemporaneous oral agreement but may be explained or supplemented

(a) by course of dealing or usage of trade (Section 1—205) or by course of performance (Section 2—208); and

(b) by evidence of consistent additional terms unless the court finds the writing to have been intended also as a complete and exclusive statement of the terms of the agreement.

. . .

§ 2—204. Formation in General.

(1) A contract for sale of goods may be made in any manner sufficient to show agreement, including conduct by both parties which recognizes the existence of such a contract.

(2) An agreement sufficient to constitute a contract for sale may be found even though the moment of its making is undetermined.

(3) Even though one or more terms are left open a contract for sale does not fail for indefiniteness if the parties have intended to make a contract and there is a reasonably certain basis for giving an appropriate remedy.

§ 2—205. Firm Offers.

An offer by a merchant to buy or sell goods in a signed writing which by its terms gives assurance that it will be held open is not revocable, for lack of consideration, during the time stated or if no time is stated for a reasonable time, but in no event may such period of irrevocability exceed three months; but any such term of assurance on a form supplied by the offeree must be separately signed by the offeror.

§ 2—206. Offer and Acceptance in Formation of Contract.

(1) Unless other unambiguously indicated by the language or circumstances

(a) an offer to make a contract shall be construed as inviting acceptance in any manner and by any medium reasonable in the circumstances;

(b) an order or other offer to buy goods for prompt or current shipment shall be construed as inviting acceptance either by a prompt promise to ship or by the prompt or current shipment of conforming or nonconforming goods, but such a shipment of non-conforming goods does not constitute an acceptance if the seller seasonably notifies the buyer that the shipment is offered only as an accommodation to the buyer.

(2) Where the beginning of a requested performance is a reasonable mode of acceptance an offeror who is not notified of acceptance within a reasonable time may treat the offer as having lapsed before acceptance.

§ 2—207. Additional Terms in Acceptance or Confirmation.

(1) A definite and seasonable expression of acceptance or a written confirmation which is sent within a reasonable time operates as an acceptance even though it states terms additional to or different from those offered or agreed upon, unless acceptance is expressly made conditional on assent to the additional or different terms.

(2) The additional terms are to be construed as proposals for addition to the contract. Between merchants such terms become part of the contract unless:

(a) the offer expressly limits acceptance to the terms of the offer;

(b) they materially alter it; or

(c) notification of objection to them has already been given or is given within a reasonable time after notice of them is received.

(3) Conduct by both parties which recognizes the existence of a contract is sufficient to establish a contract for sale although the writings of the parties do not otherwise establish a contract. In such case the terms of the particular contract consist of those terms on which the writings of the parties agree, together with any supplementary terms incorporated under any other provisions of this Act.

§ 2—208. Course of Performance or Practical Construction.

(1) Where the contract for sale involves repeated occasions for performance by either party with knowledge of the nature of the performance and opportunity for objection to it by the other, any course of performance accepted or acquiesced in without objection shall be relevant to determine the meaning of the agreement.

(2) The express terms of the agreement and any such course of performance, as well as any course of dealing and usage of trade, shall be construed whenever reasonable as consistent with each other; but when such construction is unreasonable, express terms shall control course of performance and course of performance shall control both course of dealing and usage of trade (Section 1—205).

(3) Subject to the provisions of the next section on modification and waiver, such course of performance shall be relevant to show a waiver or modification of any term inconsistent with such course of performance.

§ 2—209. Modification, Rescission and Waiver.

(1) An agreement modifying a contract within this Article needs no consideration to be binding.

(2) A signed agreement which excludes modification or rescission except by a signed writing cannot be otherwise modified or rescinded, but except as between merchants such a requirement on a form supplied by the merchant must be separately signed by the other party.

(3) The requirements of the statute of frauds section of this Article (Section 2—201) must be satisfied if the contract as modified is within its provisions.

(4) Although an attempt at modification or rescission does not satisfy the requirements of subsection (2) or (3) it can operate as a waiver.

(5) A party who has made a waiver affecting an executory portion of the contract may retract the waiver by reasonable notification received by the other party that strict performance will be required of any term waived, unless the retraction would be unjust in view of a material change of position in reliance on the waiver.

Part 3 General Obligation and Construction of Contract
§ 2—301. General Obligations of Parties.

The obligation of the seller is to transfer and deliver and that of the buyer is to accept and pay in accordance with the contract.

§ 2—302. Unconscionable Contract or Clause.

(1) If the court as a matter of law finds the contract or any clause of the contract to have been unconscionable at the time it was made the court may refuse to enforce the contract, or it may enforce the remainder of the contract without the unconscionable clause, or it may so limit the application of any unconscionable clause as to avoid any unconscionable result.

(2) When it is claimed or appears to the court that the contract or any clause thereof may be unconscionable the parties shall be afforded a reasonable opportunity to present evidence as to its commercial setting, purpose and effect to aid the court in making the determination.

§ 2—305. Open Price Term.

(1) The parties if they so intend can conclude a contract for sale even though the price is not settled. In such a case the price is a reasonable price at the time for delivery if

(a) nothing is said as to price; or

(b) the price is left to be agreed by the parties and they fail to agree; or

(c) the price is to be fixed in terms of some agreed market or other standard as set or recorded by a third person or agency and it is not so set or recorded.

(2) A price to be fixed by the seller or by the buyer means a price for him to fix in good faith.

(3) When a price left to be fixed otherwise than by agreement of the parties fails to be fixed through fault of one party the other may at his option treat the contract as cancelled or himself fix a reasonable price.

(4) Where, however, the parties intend not to be bound unless the price be fixed or agreed and it is not fixed or agreed there is no contract. In such a case the buyer must return any goods already received or if unable so to do must pay their reasonable value at the time of delivery and the seller must return any portion of the price paid on account.

§ 2—306. Output, Requirements and Exclusive Dealings.

(1) A term which measures the quantity by the output of the seller or the requirements of the buyer means such actual output or requirements as may occur in good faith, except that no quantity unreasonably disproportionate to any stated estimate or in the absence of a stated estimate to any normal or otherwise comparable prior output or requirements may be tendered or demanded.

(2) A lawful agreement by either the seller or the buyer for exclusive dealing in the kind of goods concerned imposes unless otherwise agreed an obligation by the seller to use best efforts to supply the goods and by the buyer to use best efforts to promote their sale.

§ 2—308. Absence of Specified Place for Delivery.

Unless otherwise agreed

(a) the place for delivery of goods is the seller's place of business or if he has none his residence; but

(b) in a contract for sale of identified goods which to the knowledge of the parties at the time of contracting are in some other place, that place is the place for their delivery; and

(c) documents of title may be delivered through customary banking channels.

§ 2—309. Absence of Specific Time Provisions; Notice of Termination.

(1) The time for shipment or delivery or any other action under a contract if not provided in this Article or agreed upon shall be a reasonable time.

(2) Where the contract provides for successive performances but is indefinite in duration it is valid for a reasonable time but unless otherwise agreed may be terminated at any time by either party.

(3) Termination of a contract by one party except on the happening of an agreed event requires that reasonable notification be received by the other party and an agreement dispensing with notification is invalid if its operation would be unconscionable.

§ 2—310. Open Time for Payment or Running of Credit; Authority to Ship Under Reservation.

Unless otherwise agreed

(a) payment is due at the time and place at which the buyer is to receive the goods even though the place of shipment is the place of delivery; and

(b) if the seller is authorized to send the goods he may ship them under reservation, and may tender the documents of title, but the buyer may inspect the goods after their arrival before payment is due unless such inspection is inconsistent with the terms of the contract (Section 2—513); and

(c) if delivery is authorized and made by way of documents of title otherwise than by subsection (b) then payment is due at the time and place at which the buyer is to receive the documents regardless of where the goods are to be received; and

(d) where the seller is required or authorized to ship the goods on credit the credit period runs from the time of shipment but post-dating the invoice or delaying its dispatch will correspondingly delay the starting of the credit period.

§ 2—311. Options and Cooperation Respecting Performance.

(1) An agreement for sale which is otherwise sufficiently definite (subsection (3) of Section 2—204) to be a contract is not

made invalid by the fact that it leaves particulars of performance to be specified by one of the parties. Any such specification must be made in good faith and within limits set by commercial reasonableness.

(2) Unless otherwise agreed specifications relating to assortment of the goods are at the buyer's option and except as otherwise provided in subsections (1)(c) and (3) of Section 2—319 specifications or arrangements relating to shipment are at the seller's option.

(3) Where such specification would materially affect the other party's performance but is not seasonably made or where one party's cooperation is necessary to the agreed performance of the other but is not seasonably forthcoming, the other party in addition to all other remedies

(a) is excused for any resulting delay in his own performance; and

(b) may also either proceed to perform in any reasonable manner or after the time for a material part of his own performance treat the failure to specify or to cooperate as a breach by failure to deliver or accept the goods.

§ 2—312. **Warranty of Title and Against Infringement; Buyer's Obligation Against Infringement.**

(1) Subject to subsection (2) there is in a contract for sale a warranty by the seller that

(a) the title conveyed shall be good, and its transfer rightful; and

(b) the goods shall be delivered free from any security interest or other lien or encumbrance of which the buyer at the time of contracting has no knowledge.

(2) A warranty under subsection (1) will be excluded or modified only by specific language or by circumstances which give the buyer reason to know that the person selling does not claim title in himself or that he is purporting to sell only such right or title as he or a third person may have.

(3) Unless otherwise agreed a seller who is a merchant regularly dealing in goods of the kind warrants that the goods shall be delivered free of the rightful claim of any third person by way of infringement or the like but a buyer who furnishes specifications to the seller must hold the seller harmless against any such claim which arises out of compliance with the specifications.

§ 2—313. **Express Warranties by Affirmation, Promise, Description, Sample.**

(1) Express warranties by the seller are created as follows:

(a) Any affirmation of fact or promise made by the seller to the buyer which relates to the goods and becomes part of the basis of the bargain creates an express warranty that the goods shall conform to the affirmation or promise.

(b) Any description of the goods which is made part of the basis of the bargain creates an express warranty that the goods shall conform to the description.

(c) Any sample or model which is made part of the basis of the bargain creates an express warranty that the whole of the goods shall conform to the sample or model.

(2) It is not necessary to the creation of an express warranty that the seller use formal words such as "warrant" or "guarantee" or that he have a specific intention to make a warranty, but an affirmation merely of the value of the goods or a statement purporting to be merely the seller's opinion or commendation of the goods does not create a warranty.

§ 2—314. **Implied Warranty: Merchantability; Usage of Trade.**

(1) Unless excluded or modified (Section 2—316), a warranty that the goods shall be merchantable is implied in a contract for their sale if the seller is a merchant with respect to goods of that kind. Under this section the serving for value of food or drink to be consumed either on the premises or elsewhere is a sale.

(2) Goods to be merchantable must be at least such as

(a) pass without objection in the trade under the contract description; and

(b) in the case of fungible goods, are of fair average quality within the description; and

(c) are fit for the ordinary purposes for which such goods are used; and

(d) run, within the variations permitted by the agreement, of even kind, quality and quantity within each unit and among all units involved; and

(e) are adequately contained, packaged, and labeled as the agreement may require; and

(f) conform to the promises or affirmations of fact made on the container or label if any.

(3) Unless excluded or modified (Section 2—316) other implied warranties may arise from course of dealing or usage of trade.

§ 2—315. **Implied Warranty: Fitness for Particular Purpose.**

Where the seller at the time of contracting has reason to know any particular purpose for which the goods are required and that the buyer is relying on the seller's skill or judgment to select or furnish suitable goods, there is unless excluded or modified under the next section an implied warranty that the goods shall be fit for such purpose.

§ 2—316. **Exclusion or Modification of Warranties.**

(1) Words or conduct relevant to the creation of an express warranty and words or conduct tending to negate or limit warranty shall be construed wherever reasonable as consistent with each other; but subject to the provisions of this Article on parol or extrinsic evidence (Section 2—202) negation or limitation is inoperative to the extent that such construction is unreasonable.

(2) Subject to subsection (3), to exclude or modify the implied warranty of merchantability or any part of it the language must mention merchantability and in case of a writing must be conspicuous, and to exclude or modify any implied warranty of fitness the exclusion must be by a writing and conspicuous. Language to exclude all implied warranties of fitness is sufficient if it states, for example, that "There are no warranties which extend beyond the description on the face hereof."

(3) Notwithstanding subsection (2)

(a) unless the circumstances indicate otherwise, all implied warranties are excluded by expressions like "as is", "with all faults" or other language which in common understanding calls the buyer's attention to the exclusion of warranties and makes plain that there is no implied warranty; and

(b) when the buyer before entering into the contract has examined the goods or the sample or model as fully as he desired or has refused to examine the goods there is no implied warranty with regard to defects which an examination ought in the circumstances to have revealed to him; and

(c) an implied warranty can also be excluded or modified by course of dealing or course of performance or usage of trade.

(4) Remedies for breach of warranty can be limited in accordance with the provisions of this Article on liquidation or limitation of damages and on contractual modification of remedy (Sections 2—718 and 2—719).

§ 2—317. Cumulation and Conflict of Warranties Express or Implied.

Warranties whether express or implied shall be construed as consistent with each other and as cumulative, but if such construction is unreasonable the intention of the parties shall determine which warranty is dominant. In ascertaining that intention the following rules apply:

(a) Exact or technical specifications displace an inconsistent sample or model or general language of description.

(b) A sample from an existing bulk displaces inconsistent general language of description.

(c) Express warranties displace inconsistent implied warranties other than an implied warranty of fitness for a particular purpose.

§ 2—318. Third Party Beneficiaries of Warranties Express or Implied.

Note: If this Act is introduced in the Congress of the United States this section should be omitted. (States to select one alternative.)

Alternative A

A seller's warranty whether express or implied extends to any natural person who is in the family or household of his buyer or who is a guest in his home if it is reasonable to expect that such person may use, consume or be affected by the goods and who is injured in person by breach of the warranty. A seller may not exclude or limit the operation of this section.

Alternative B

A seller's warranty whether express or implied extends to any natural person who may reasonably be expected to use, consume or be affected by the goods and who is injured in person by breach of the warranty. A seller may not exclude or limit the operation of this section.

Alternative C

A seller's warranty whether express or implied extends to any person who may reasonably be expected to use, consume or be affected by the goods and who is injured by breach of the warranty. A seller may not exclude or limit the operation of this section with respect to injury to the person of an individual to whom the warranty extends. As amended 1966.

. . .

Part 4 Title, Creditors and Good Faith Purchasers

§ 2—401. Passing of Title; Reservation for Security; Limited Application of This Section.

Each provision of this Article with regard to the rights, obligations and remedies of the seller, the buyer, purchasers or other third parties applies irrespective of title to the goods except where the provision refers to such title. Insofar as situations are not covered by the other provisions of this Article and matters concerning title became material the following rules apply:

(1) Title to goods cannot pass under a contract for sale prior to their identification to the contract (Section 2—501), and unless otherwise explicitly agreed the buyer acquires by their identification a special property as limited by this Act. Any retention or reservation by the seller of the title (property) in goods shipped or delivered to the buyer is limited in effect to a reservation of a security interest. Subject to these provisions and to the provisions of the Article on Secured Transactions (Article 9), title to goods passes from the seller to the buyer in any manner and on any conditions explicitly agreed on by the parties.

(2) Unless otherwise explicitly agreed title passes to the buyer at the time and place at which the seller completes his performance with reference to the physical delivery of the goods, despite any reservation of a security interest and even though a document of title is to be delivered at a different time or place; and in particular and despite any reservation of a security interest by the bill of lading

(a) if the contract requires or authorizes the seller to send the goods to the buyer but does not require him to deliver them at destination, title passes to the buyer at the time and place of shipment; but

(b) if the contract requires delivery at destination, title passes on tender there.

(3) Unless otherwise explicitly agreed where delivery is to be made without moving the goods,

(a) if the seller is to deliver a document of title, title passes at the time when and the place where he delivers such documents; or

(b) if the goods are at the time of contracting already identified and no documents are to be delivered, title passes at the time and place of contracting.

(4) A rejection or other refusal by the buyer to receive or retain the goods, whether or not justified, or a justified revocation of acceptance revests title to the goods in the seller. Such revesting occurs by operation of law and is not a "sale".

. . .

§ 2—403. Power to Transfer; Good Faith Purchase of Goods; "Entrusting".

(1) A purchaser of goods acquires all title which his transferor had or had power to transfer except that a purchaser of a limited interest acquires rights only to the extent of the interest purchased. A person with voidable title has power to transfer a good title to a good faith purchaser for value. When goods have been delivered under a transaction of purchase the purchaser has such power even though

(a) the transferor was deceived as to the identity of the purchaser, or

(b) the delivery was in exchange for a check which is later dishonored, or

(c) it was agreed that the transaction was to be a "cash sale", or

(d) the delivery was procured through fraud punishable as larcenous under the criminal law.

. . .

Part 5 Performance

§ 2—501. Insurable Interest in Goods; Manner of Identification of Goods.

(1) The buyer obtains a special property and an insurable interest in goods by identification of existing goods as goods to which the contract refers even though the goods so identified are non-conforming and he has an option to return or reject them. Such identification can be made at any time and in any manner explicitly agreed to by the parties. In the absence of explicit agreement identification occurs

(a) when the contract is made if it is for the sale of goods already existing and identified;

(b) if the contract is for the sale of future goods other than those described in paragraph (c), when goods are shipped, marked or otherwise designated by the seller as goods to which the contract refers;

(c) when the crops are planted or otherwise become growing crops or the young are conceived if the contract is for the sale of unborn young to be born within twelve months after contracting or for the sale of crops to be harvested within twelve months or the next normal harvest season after contracting whichever is longer.

(2) The seller retains an insurable interest in goods so long as title to or any security interest in the goods remains in him and where the identification is by the seller alone he may until default or insolvency or notification to the buyer that the identification is final substitute other goods for those identified.

(3) Nothing in this section impairs any insurable interest recognized under any other statute or rule of law.

. . .

§ 2—503. Manner of Seller's Tender of Delivery.

(1) Tender of delivery requires that the seller put and hold conforming goods at the buyer's disposition and give the buyer any notification reasonably necessary to enable him to take delivery. The manner, time and place for tender are determined by the agreement and this Article, and in particular

(a) tender must be at a reasonable hour, and if it is of goods they must be kept available for the period reasonably necessary to enable the buyer to take possession; but

(b) unless otherwise agreed the buyer must furnish facilities reasonably suited to the receipt of the goods.

(2) Where the case is within the next section respecting shipment tender requires that the seller comply with its provisions.

(3) Where the seller is required to deliver at a particular destination tender requires that he comply with subsection (1) and also in any appropriate case tender documents as described in subsections (4) and (5) of this section.

(4) Where goods are in the possession of a bailee and are to be delivered without being moved

(a) tender requires that the seller either tender a negotiable document of title covering such goods or procure acknowledgment by the bailee of the buyer's right to possession of the goods; but

(b) tender to the buyer of a non-negotiable document of title or of a written direction to the bailee to deliver is sufficient tender unless the buyer seasonably objects, and receipt by the bailee of notification of the buyer's rights fixes those rights as against the bailee and all third persons; but risk of loss of the goods and of any failure by the bailee to honor the non-negotiable document of title or to obey the direction remains on the seller until the buyer has had a reasonable time to present the document or direction, and a refusal by the bailee to honor the document or to obey the direction defeats the tender.

(5) Where the contract requires the seller to deliver documents

(a) he must tender all such documents in correct form, except as provided in this Article with respect to bills of lading in a set (subsection (2) of Section 2—323); and

(b) tender through customary banking channels is sufficient and dishonor of a draft accompanying the documents constitutes non-acceptance or rejection.

§ 2—504. Shipment by Seller.

Where the seller is required or authorized to send the goods to the buyer and the contract does not require him to deliver them at a particular destination, then unless otherwise agreed he must

(a) put the goods in the possession of such a carrier and make such a contract for their transportation as may be reasonable having regard to the nature of the goods and other circumstances of the case; and

(b) obtain and promptly deliver or tender in due form any document necessary to enable the buyer to obtain possession of the goods or otherwise required by the agreement or by usage of trade; and

(c) promptly notify the buyer of the shipment.

Failure to notify the buyer under paragraph (c) or to make a proper contract under paragraph (a) is a ground for rejection only if material delay or loss ensues.

§ 2—507. Effect of Seller's Tender; Delivery on Condition.

(1) Tender of delivery is a condition to the buyer's duty to accept the goods and, unless otherwise agreed, to his duty to pay for them. Tender entitles the seller to acceptance of the goods and to payment according to the contract.

(2) Where payment is due and demanded on the delivery to the buyer of goods or documents of title, his right as against the seller to retain or dispose of them is conditional upon his making the payment due.

§ 2—508. Cure by Seller of Improper Tender or Delivery; Replacement.

(1) Where any tender or delivery by the seller is rejected because non-conforming and the time for performance has not yet expired, the seller may seasonably notify the buyer of his intention to cure and may then within the contract time make a conforming delivery.

(2) Where the buyer rejects a non-conforming tender which the seller had reasonable grounds to believe would be acceptable with or without money allowance the seller may if he seasonably notifies the buyer have a further reasonable time to substitute a conforming tender.

§ 2—509. Risk of Loss in the Absence of Breach.

(1) Where the contract requires or authorizes the seller to ship the goods by carrier

(a) if it does not require him to deliver them at a particular destination, the risk of loss passes to the buyer when the goods are duly delivered to the carrier even though the shipment is under reservation (Section 2—505); but

(b) if it does require him to deliver them at a particular destination and the goods are there duly tendered while in the possession of the carrier, the risk of loss passes to the buyer when the goods are there duly so tendered as to enable the buyer to take delivery.

(2) Where the goods are held by a bailee to be delivered without being moved, the risk of loss passes to the buyer

(a) on his receipt of a negotiable document of title covering the goods; or

(b) on acknowledgment by the bailee of the buyer's right to possession of the goods; or

(c) after his receipt of a non-negotiable document of title or other written direction to deliver, as provided in subsection (4)(b) of Section 2—503.

(3) In any case not within subsection (1) or (2), the risk of loss passes to the buyer on his receipt of the goods if the seller is a merchant; otherwise the risk passes to the buyer on tender of delivery.

(4) The provisions of this section are subject to contrary agreement of the parties and to the provisions of this Article on sale on approval (Section 2—327) and on effect of breach on risk of loss (Section 2—510).

§ 2—510. Effect of Breach on Risk of Loss.

(1) Where a tender or delivery of goods so fails to conform to the contract as to give a right of rejection the risk of their loss remains on the seller until cure or acceptance.

(2) Where the buyer rightfully revokes acceptance he may to the extent of any deficiency in his effective insurance coverage treat the risk of loss as having rested on the seller from the beginning.

(3) Where the buyer as to conforming goods already identified to the contract for sale repudiates or is otherwise in breach before risk of their loss has passed to him, the seller may to the extent of any deficiency in his effective insurance coverage treat the risk of loss as resting on the buyer for a commercially reasonable time.

§ 2—511. Tender of Payment by Buyer; Payment by Check.

(1) Unless otherwise agreed tender of payment is a condition to the seller's duty to tender and complete any delivery.

(2) Tender of payment is sufficient when made by any means or in any manner current in the ordinary course of business unless the seller demands payment in legal tender and gives any extension of time reasonably necessary to procure it.

(3) Subject to the provisions of this Act on the effect of an instrument on an obligation (Section 3—802), payment by check is conditional and is defeated as between the parties by dishonor of the check on due presentment.

§ 2—512. Payment by Buyer Before Inspection.

(1) Where the contract requires payment before inspection non-conformity of the goods does not excuse the buyer from so making payment unless

(a) the non-conformity appears without inspection; or

(b) despite tender of the required documents the circumstances would justify injunction against honor under the provisions of this Act (Section 5—114).

(2) Payment pursuant to subsection (1) does not constitute an acceptance of goods or impair the buyer's right to inspect or any of his remedies.

§ 2—513. Buyer's Right to Inspection of Goods.

(1) Unless otherwise agreed and subject to subsection (3), where goods are tendered or delivered or identified to the contract for sale, the buyer has a right before payment or acceptance to inspect them at any reasonable place and time and in any reasonable manner. When the seller is required or authorized to send the goods to the buyer, the inspection may be after their arrival.

. . .

Part 6 Breach, Repudiation and Excuse

§ 2—601. Buyer's Rights on Improper Delivery.

Subject to the provisions of this Article on breach in installment contracts (Section 2—612) and unless otherwise agreed under the sections on contractual limitations of remedy (Sections 2—718 and 2—719), if the goods or the tender of delivery fail in any respect to conform to the contract, the buyer may

(a) reject the whole; or

(b) accept the whole; or

(c) accept any commercial unit or units and reject the rest.

§ 2—602. Manner and Effect of Rightful Rejection.

(1) Rejection of goods must be within a reasonable time after their delivery or tender. It is ineffective unless the buyer seasonably notifies the seller.

(2) Subject to the provisions of the two following sections on rejected goods (Sections 2—603 and 2—604),

(a) after rejection any exercise of ownership by the buyer with respect to any commercial unit is wrongful as against the seller; and

(b) if the buyer has before rejection taken physical possession of goods in which he does not have a security interest under the provisions of this Article (subsection (3) of Section 2—711), he is under a duty after rejection to hold them with reasonable care at the seller's disposition for a time sufficient to permit the seller to remove them; but

(c) the buyer has no further obligations with regard to goods rightfully rejected.

(3) The seller's rights with respect to goods wrongfully rejected are governed by the provisions of this Article on Seller's remedies in general (Section 2—703).

. . .

§ 2—605. Waiver of Buyer's Objections by Failure to Particularize.

(1) The buyer's failure to state in connection with rejection a particular defect which is ascertainable by reasonable inspection precludes him from relying on the unstated defect to justify rejection or to establish breach

(a) where the seller could have cured it if stated seasonably; or

(b) between merchants when the seller has after rejection made a request in writing for a full and final written statement of all defects on which the buyer proposes to rely.

(2) Payment against documents made without reservation of rights precludes recovery of the payment for defects apparent on the face of the documents.

§ 2—606. What Constitutes Acceptance of Goods.

(1) Acceptance of goods occurs when the buyer

(a) after a reasonable opportunity to inspect the goods signifies to the seller that the goods are conforming or that he will take or retain them in spite of their nonconformity; or

(b) fails to make an effective rejection (subsection (1) of Section 2—602), but such acceptance does not occur until the buyer has had a reasonable opportunity to inspect them; or

(c) does any act inconsistent with the seller's ownership; but if such act is wrongful as against the seller it is an acceptance only if ratified by him.

(2) Acceptance of a part of any commercial unit is acceptance of that entire unit.

§ 2—607. Effect of Acceptance; Notice of Breach; Burden of Establishing Breach After Acceptance; Notice of Claim or Litigation to Person Answerable Over.

(1) The buyer must pay at the contract rate for any goods accepted.

(2) Acceptance of goods by the buyer precludes rejection of the goods accepted and if made with knowledge of a non-conformity cannot be revoked because of it unless the acceptance was on the reasonable assumption that the non-conformity would be seasonably cured but acceptance does not of itself impair any other remedy provided by this Article for non-conformity.

(3) Where a tender has been accepted

(a) the buyer must within a reasonable time after he discovers or should have discovered any breach notify the seller of breach or be barred from any remedy; and

(b) if the claim is one for infringement or the like (subsection (3) of Section 2—312) and the buyer is sued as a result of such a breach he must so notify the seller within a reasonable time after he receives notice of the litigation or be barred from any remedy over for liability established by the litigation.

(4) The burden is on the buyer to establish any breach with respect to the goods accepted.

§ 2—608. Revocation of Acceptance in Whole or in Part.

(1) The buyer may revoke his acceptance of a lot or commercial unit whose non-conformity substantially impairs its value to him if he has accepted it

(a) on the reasonable assumption that its nonconformity would be cured and it has not been seasonably cured; or

(b) without discovery of such non-conformity if his acceptance was reasonably induced either by the difficulty of discovery before acceptance or by the seller's assurances.

(2) Revocation of acceptance must occur within a reasonable time after the buyer discovers or should have discovered the ground for it and before any substantial change in condition of the goods which is not caused by their own defects. It is not effective until the buyer notifies the seller of it.

(3) A buyer who so revokes has the same rights and duties with regard to the goods involved as if he had rejected them.

§ 2—609. Right to Adequate Assurance of Performance.

(1) A contract for sale imposes an obligation on each party that the other's expectation of receiving due performance will not be impaired. When reasonable grounds for insecurity arise with respect to the performance of either party the other may in writing demand adequate assurance of due performance and until he receives such assurance may if commercially reasonable suspend any performance for which he has not already received the agreed return.

(2) Between merchants the reasonableness of grounds for insecurity and the adequacy of any assurance offered shall be determined according to commercial standards.

(3) Acceptance of any improper delivery or payment does not prejudice the party's right to demand adequate assurance of future performance.

(4) After receipt of a justified demand failure to provide within a reasonable time not exceeding thirty days such assurance of due performance as is adequate under the circumstances of the particular case is a repudiation of the contract.

§ 2—610. Anticipatory Repudiation.

When either party repudiates the contract with respect to a performance not yet due the loss of which will substantially impair the value of the contract to the other, the aggrieved party may

(a) for a commercially reasonable time await performance by the repudiating party; or

(b) resort to any remedy for breach (Section 2—703 or Section 2—711), even though he has notified the repudiating party that he would await the latter's performance and has urged retraction; and

(c) in either case suspend his own performance or proceed in accordance with the provisions of this Article on the seller's right to identify goods to the contract notwithstanding breach or to salvage unfinished goods (Section 2—704).

§ 2—611. Retraction of Anticipatory Repudiation.

(1) Until the repudiating party's next performance is due he can retract his repudiation unless the aggrieved party has since the repudiation cancelled or materially changed his position or otherwise indicated that he considers the repudiation final.

(2) Retraction may be by any method which clearly indicates to the aggrieved party that the repudiating party intends to perform, but must include any assurance justifiably demanded under the provisions of this Article (Section 2—609).

(3) Retraction reinstates the repudiating party's rights under the contract with due excuse and allowance to the aggrieved party for any delay occasioned by the repudiation.

. . .

§ 2—613. Casualty to Identified Goods.

Where the contract requires for its performance goods identified when the contract is made, and the goods suffer casualty without fault of either party before the risk of loss passes to the buyer, or in a proper case under a "no arrival, no sale" term (Section 2—324) then

(a) if the loss is total the contract is avoided; and

(b) if the loss is partial or the goods have so deteriorated as no longer to conform to the contract the buyer may nevertheless demand inspection and at his option either treat the contract as voided or accept the goods with due allowance from the contract price for the deterioration or the deficiency in quantity but without further right against the seller.

§ 2—614. Substituted Performance.

(1) Where without fault of either party the agreed berthing, loading, or unloading facilities fail or an agreed type of carrier becomes unavailable or the agreed manner of delivery otherwise becomes commercially impracticable but a commercially reasonable substitute is available, such substitute performance must be tendered and accepted.

(2) If the agreed means or manner of payment fails because of domestic or foreign governmental regulation, the seller may withhold or stop delivery unless the buyer provides a means or manner of payment which is commercially a substantial equivalent. If delivery has already been taken, payment by the means or in the manner provided by the regulation discharges the buyer's obligation unless the regulation is discriminatory, oppressive or predatory.

§ 2—615. Excuse by Failure of Presupposed Conditions.

Except so far as a seller may have assumed a greater obligation and subject to the preceding section on substituted performance:

(a) Delay in delivery or non-delivery in whole or in part by a seller who complies with paragraphs (b) and (c) is not a breach of his duty under a contract for sale if performance as agreed has been made impracticable by the occurrence of a contingency the nonoccurrence of which was a basic assumption on which the contract was made or by compliance in good faith with any applicable foreign or domestic governmental regulation or order whether or not it later proves to be invalid.

(b) Where the causes mentioned in paragraph (a) affect only a part of the seller's capacity to perform, he must allocate production and deliveries among his customers but may at his option include regular customers not then under contract as well as his own requirements for further manufacture. He may so allocate in any manner which is fair and reasonable.

(c) The seller must notify the buyer seasonably that there will be delay or non-delivery and, when allocation is required under paragraph (b), of the estimated quota thus made available for the buyer.

§ 2—616. Procedure on Notice Claiming Excuse.

(1) Where the buyer receives notification of a material or indefinite delay or an allocation justified under the preceding section he may by written notification to the seller as to any delivery concerned, and where the prospective deficiency substantially impairs the value of the whole contract under the provisions of this Article relating to breach of installment contracts (Section 2—612), then also as to the whole,

(a) terminate and thereby discharge any unexecuted portion of the contract; or

(b) modify the contract by agreeing to take his available quota in substitution.

(2) If after receipt of such notification from the seller the buyer fails so to modify the contract within a reasonable time not exceeding thirty days the contract lapses with respect to any deliveries affected.

(3) The provisions of this section may not be negated by agreement except in so far as the seller has assumed a greater obligation under the preceding section.

Part 7 Remedies

. . .

§ 2—703. Seller's Remedies in General.

Where the buyer wrongfully rejects or revokes acceptance of goods or fails to make a payment due on or before delivery or repudiates with respect to a part or the whole, then with respect to any goods directly affected and, if the breach is of the whole contract (Section 2—612), then also with respect to the whole undelivered balance, the aggrieved seller may

(a) withhold delivery of such goods;

(b) stop delivery by any bailee as hereafter provided (Section 2—705);

(c) proceed under the next section respecting goods still unidentified to the contract;

(d) resell and recover damages as hereafter provided (Section 2—706);

(e) recover damages for non-acceptance (Section 2—708) or in a proper case the price (Section 2—709);

(f) cancel.

. . .

§ 2—706. Seller's Resale Including Contract for Resale.

(1) Under the conditions stated in Section 2—703 on seller's remedies, the seller may resell the goods concerned or the undelivered balance thereof. Where the resale is made in good faith and in a commercially reasonable manner the seller may recover the difference between the resale price and the contract price together with any incidental damages allowed under the provisions of this Article (Section 2—710), but less expenses saved in consequence of the buyer's breach.

(2) Except as otherwise provided in subsection (3) or unless otherwise agreed resale may be at public or private sale including sale by way of one or more contracts to sell or of identification to an existing contract of the seller. Sale may be as a unit or in parcels and at any time and place and on any terms but every aspect of the sale including the method, manner, time, place and terms must be commercially reasonable. The resale must be reasonably identified as referring to the broken contract, but it is not necessary that the goods be in existence or that any or all of them have been identified to the contract before the breach.

(3) Where the resale is at private sale the seller must give the buyer reasonable notification of his intention to resell.

(4) Where the resale is at public sale

(a) only identified goods can be sold except where there is a recognized market for a public sale of futures in goods of the kind; and

(b) it must be made at a usual place or market for public sale if one is reasonably available and except in the case of goods which are perishable or threaten to decline in value speedily the seller must give the buyer reasonable notice of the time and place of the resale; and

(c) if the goods are not to be within the view of those attending the sale the notification of sale must state the place where the goods are located and provide for their reasonable inspection by prospective bidders; and

(d) the seller may buy.

(5) A purchaser who buys in good faith at a resale takes the goods free of any rights of the original buyer even though the seller fails to comply with one or more of the requirements of this section.

. . .

§ 2—708. Seller's Damages for Non-Acceptance or Repudiation.

(1) Subject to subsection (2) and to the provisions of this Article with respect to proof of market price (Section 2—723), the measure of damages for non-acceptance or repudiation by the buyer is the difference between the market price at the time and place for tender and the unpaid contract price together with any incidental damages provided in this Article (Section 2—710), but less expenses saved in consequence of the buyer's breach.

(2) If the measure of damages provided in subsection (1) is inadequate to put the seller in as good a position as performance would have done then the measure of damages is the profit (including reasonable overhead) which the seller would have made from full performance by the buyer, together with any incidental damages provided in this Article (Section 2—710), due allowance for costs reasonably incurred and due credit for payments or proceeds of resale.

§ 2—709. Action for the Price.

(1) When the buyer fails to pay the price as it becomes due the seller may recover, together with any incidental damages under the next section, the price

(a) of goods accepted or of conforming goods lost or damaged within a commercially reasonable time after risk of their loss has passed to the buyer; and

(b) of goods identified to the contract if the seller is unable after reasonable effort to resell them at a reasonable price or the circumstances reasonably indicate that such effort will be unavailing.

(2) Where the seller sues for the price he must hold for the buyer any goods which have been identified to the contract and are still in his control except that if resale becomes possible he may resell them at any time prior to the collection of the judg-

ment. The net proceeds of any such resale must be credited to the buyer and payment of the judgment entitles him to any goods not resold.

(3) After the buyer has wrongfully rejected or revoked acceptance of the goods or has failed to make a payment due or has repudiated (Section 2—610), a seller who is held not entitled to the price under this section shall nevertheless be awarded damages for non-acceptance under the preceding section.

§ 2—710. Seller's Incidental Damages.

Incidental damages to an aggrieved seller include any commercially reasonable charges, expenses or commissions incurred in stopping delivery, in the transportation, care and custody of goods after the buyer's breach, in connection with return or resale of the goods or otherwise resulting from the breach.

§ 2—711. Buyer's Remedies in General; Buyer's Security Interest in Rejected Goods.

(1) Where the seller fails to make delivery or repudiates or the buyer rightfully rejects or justifiably revokes acceptance then with respect to any goods involved, and with respect to the whole if the breach goes to the whole contract (Section 2—612), the buyer may cancel and whether or not he has done so may in addition to recovering so much of the price as has been paid

(a) "cover" and have damages under the next section as to all the goods affected whether or not they have been identified to the contract; or

(b) recover damages for non-delivery as provided in this Article (Section 2—713).

(2) Where the seller fails to deliver or repudiates the buyer may also

(a) if the goods have been identified recover them as provided in this Article (Section 2—502); or

(b) in a proper case obtain specific performance or replevy the goods as provided in this Article (Section 2—716).

(3) On rightful rejection or justifiable revocation of acceptance a buyer has a security interest in goods in his possession or control for any payments made on their price and any expenses reasonably incurred in their inspection, receipt, transportation, care and custody and may hold such goods and resell them in like manner as an aggrieved seller (Section 2—706).

§ 2—712. "Cover"; Buyer's Procurement of Substitute Goods.

(1) After a breach within the preceding section the buyer may "cover" by making in good faith and without unreasonable delay any reasonable purchase of or contract to purchase goods in substitution for those due from the seller.

(2) The buyer may recover from the seller as damages the difference between the cost of cover and the contract price together with any incidental or consequential damages as hereinafter defined (Section 2—715), but less expenses saved in consequence of the seller's breach.

(3) Failure of the buyer to effect cover within this section does not bar him from any other remedy.

§ 2—713. Buyer's Damages for Non-Delivery or Repudiation.

(1) Subject to the provisions of this Article with respect to proof of market price (Section 2—723), the measure of damages for non-delivery or repudiation by the seller is the difference between the market price at the time when the buyer learned of the breach and the contract price together with any incidental and consequential damages provided in this Article (Section 2—715), but less expenses saved in consequence of the seller's breach.

(2) Market price is to be determined as of the place for tender or, in cases of rejection after arrival or revocation of acceptance, as of the place of arrival.

§ 2—714. Buyer's Damages for Breach in Regard to Accepted Goods.

(1) Where the buyer has accepted goods and given notification (subsection (3) of Section 2—607) he may recover as damages for any non-conformity of tender the loss resulting in the ordinary course of events from the seller's breach as determined in any manner which is reasonable.

(2) The measure of damages for breach of warranty is the difference at the time and place of acceptance between the value of the goods accepted and the value they would have had if they had been as warranted, unless special circumstances show proximate damages of a different amount.

(3) In a proper case any incidental and consequential damages under the next section may also be recovered.

§ 2—715. Buyer's Incidental and Consequential Damages.

(1) Incidental damages resulting from the seller's breach include expenses reasonably incurred in inspection, receipt, transportation and care and custody of goods rightfully rejected, any commercially reasonable charges, expenses or commissions in connection with effecting cover and any other reasonable expense incident to the delay or other breach.

(2) Consequential damages resulting from the seller's breach include

(a) any loss resulting from general or particular requirements and needs of which the seller at the time of contracting had reason to know and which could not reasonably be prevented by cover or otherwise; and

(b) injury to person or property proximately resulting from any breach of warranty.

§ 2—716. Buyer's Right to Specific Performance. . . .

(1) Specific performance may be decreed where the goods are unique or in other proper circumstances.

(2) The decree for specific performance may include such terms and conditions as to payment of the price, damages, or other relief as the court may deem just.

. . .

§ 2—717. Deduction of Damages From the Price.

The buyer on notifying the seller of his intention to do so may deduct all or any part of the damages resulting from any breach of the contract from any part of the price still due under the same contract.

§ 2—718. Liquidation or Limitation of Damages. . .

(1) Damages for breach by either party may be liquidated in the agreement but only at an amount which is reasonable in the light of the anticipated or actual harm caused by the breach, the difficulties of proof of loss, and the inconvenience or nonfeasibility of otherwise obtaining an adequate remedy. A term fixing unreasonably large liquidated damages is void as a penalty.

§ 2—719. Contractual Modification or Limitation of Remedy.

(1) Subject to the provisions of subsections (2) and (3) of this section and of the preceding section on liquidation and limitation of damages,

(a) the agreement may provide for remedies in addition to or in substitution for those provided in this Article and may limit or alter the measure of damages recoverable under this Article, as by limiting the buyer's remedies to return of the goods and repayment of the price or to repair and replacement of non-conforming goods or parts; and

(b) resort to a remedy as provided is optional unless the remedy is expressly agreed to be exclusive, in which case it is the sole remedy.

(2) Where circumstances cause an exclusive or limited remedy to fail of its essential purpose, remedy may be had as provided in this Act.

(3) Consequential damages may be limited or excluded unless the limitation or exclusion is unconscionable. Limitation of consequential damages for injury to the person in the case of consumer goods is prima facie unconscionable but limitation of damages where the loss is commercial is not.

§ 2—720. Effect of "Cancellation" or "Rescission" on Claims for Antecedent Breach.

Unless the contrary intention clearly appears, expressions of "cancellation" or "rescission" of the contract or the like shall not be construed as a renunciation or discharge of any claim in damages for an antecedent breach.

§ 2—721. Remedies for Fraud.

Remedies for material misrepresentation or fraud include all remedies available under this Article for non-fraudulent breach. Neither rescission or a claim for rescission of the contract for sale nor rejection or return of the goods shall bar or be deemed inconsistent with a claim for damages or other remedy.

§ 2—725. Statute of Limitations in Contracts for Sale.

(1) An action for breach of any contract for sale must be commenced within four years after the cause of action has accrued. By the original agreement the parties may reduce the period of limitation to not less than one year but may not extend it.

(2) A cause of action accrues when the breach occurs, regardless of the aggrieved party's lack of knowledge of the breach. A breach of warranty occurs when tender of delivery is made, except that where a warranty explicitly extends to future performance of the goods and discovery of the breach must await the time of such performance the cause of action accrues when the breach is or should have been discovered.

. . .

Appendix C Title VII of the Civil Rights Act of 1964 (Excerpts)

Title VII of the Civil Rights Act of 1964—The Employment Discrimination Section

Section 703. Unlawful Employment Practices. (a) It shall be an unlawful employment practice for an employer—

(1) to fail or refuse to hire or to discharge any individual, or otherwise to discriminate against any individual with respect to his compensation, terms, conditions, or privileges of employment, because of such individual's race, color, religion, sex, or national origin; or

(2) to limit, segregate, or classify his employees or applicants for employment in any way which would deprive or tend to deprive any individual of employment opportunities or otherwise adversely affect his status as an employee, because of such individual's race, color, religion, sex, or national origin.

(b) It shall be an unlawful employment practice for an employment agency to fail or refuse to refer for employment, or otherwise to discriminate against, any individual because of his race, color, religion, sex, or national origin, or to classify or refer for employment any individual on the basis or his race, color, religion, sex, or national origin.

(c) It shall be an unlawful employment practice for a labor organization—

(1) to exclude or to expel from its membership, or otherwise to discriminate against, any individual because of his race, color, religion, sex, or national origin;

(2) to limit, segregate, or classify its membership or applicants for membership, or to classify or fail or refuse to refer for employment any individual, in any way which would deprive or tend to deprive any individual of employment opportunities, or would limit such employment opportunities or otherwise adversely affect his status as an employee or as an applicant for employment, because of such individual's race, color, religion, sex, or national origin; or

(3) to cause or attempt to cause an employer to discriminate against an individual in violation of this section.

(d) It shall be an unlawful employment practice for any employer, labor organization, or joint labor-management committee controlling apprenticeship or other training or retraining, including on-the-job training programs to discriminate against any individual because of his race, color, religion, sex, or national origin in admission to, or employment in, any program established to provide apprenticeship or other training.

(e) Notwithstanding any other provision of this subchapter—

(1) it shall not be an unlawful employment practice for an employer to hire and employ employees, for an employment agency to classify, or refer for employment any individual, for a labor organization to classify its membership or to classify or refer for employment any individual, or for an employer, labor organization, or joint labor-management committee controlling apprenticeship or other training or retraining programs to admit or employ any individual in any such program, on the basis of his religion, sex, or national origin in those certain instances where religion, sex, or national origin is a bona fide occupa-

tional qualification reasonably necessary to the normal operation of that particular business or enterprise, and

(2) it shall not be an unlawful employment practice for a school, college, university, or other educational institution or institution of learning to hire and employ employees of a particular religion if such school, college, university, or other educational institution or institution of learning is, in whole or in substantial part, owned, supported, controlled, or managed by a particular religion or by a particular religious corporation, association, or society, or if the curriculum of such school, college, university, or other educational institution or institution of learning is directed toward the propagation of a particular religion.

(f) As used in this subchapter, the phrase "unlawful employment practice" shall not be deemed to include any action or measure taken by an employer, labor organization, joint labor-management committee, or employment agency with respect to an individual who is a member of the Communist Party of the United States or of any other organization required to register as a Communist-action or Communist-front organization. . . .

(g) Notwithstanding any other provision of this subchapter, it shall not be an unlawful employment practice for an employer to fail or refuse to hire and employ any individual for any position, for an employer to discharge any individual from any position, or for an employment agency to fail or refuse to refer any individual for employment in any position, or for a labor organization to fail or refuse to refer any individual for employment in any position, if—

(1) the occupancy of such position, or access to the premises in or upon which any part of the duties of such position is performed or is to be performed, is subject to any requirement imposed in the interest of the national security of the United States. . . and

(2) such individual has not fulfilled or has ceased to fulfill that requirement.

(h) Notwithstanding any other provision of this subchapter, it shall not be an unlawful employment practice for an employer to apply different standards of compensation, or different terms, conditions, or privileges of employment pursuant to a bona fide seniority or merit system, or a system which measures earnings by quantity or quality of production or to employees who work in different locations, provided that such differences are not the result of an intention to discriminate because of race, color, religion, sex, or national origin, nor shall it be an unlawful employment practice for an employer to give and act upon the results of any professionally developed ability test provided that such test, its administration or action upon the results is not designed, intended or used to discriminate because of race, color, religion, sex, or national origin. . . .

(j) Nothing contained in this subchapter shall be interpreted to require any employer, employment agency, labor organization, or joint labor-management committee subject to this subchapter to grant preferential treatment to any individual or to any group because of the race, color, religion, sex, or national origin of such individual or group on account of an imbalance which may exist with respect to the total number or percentage of persons of any race, color, religion, sex, or national origin employed by any employer, referred or classified for employment by any employment agency or labor organization, or admitted to, or employed in, any apprenticeship or other training program, in comparison with the total number or percentage of persons of such race, color, religion, sex, or national origin in any community, State, section, or other area, or in the available work force in any community, State, section, or other area.

. . .

Section 704. Other Unlawful Employment Practices.   (a) It shall be an unlawful employment practice for an employer to discriminate against any of his employees or applicants for employment, for an employment agency, or joint labor-management committee controlling apprenticeship or other training or retraining, including on-the-job training programs, to discriminate against any individual, or for a labor organization to discriminate against any member thereof or applicant for membership, because he has opposed any practice made an unlawful employment practice by this subchapter, or because he

has made a charge, testified, assisted, or participated in any manner in an investigation, proceeding, or hearing under this subchapter.

(b) It shall be an unlawful employment practice for an employer, labor organization, employment agency, or joint labor-management committee controlling apprenticeship or other training or retraining, including on-the-job training programs, to print or publish or cause to be printed or published any notice or advertisement relating to employment by such an employer or membership or any classification or referral for employment by such a labor organization, or relating to any classification or referral for employment by such an employment agency, or relating to admission to, or employment in, any program established to provide apprenticeship or other training by such a joint-labor-management committee, indicating any preference, limitation, specification, or discrimination, based on race, color, religion, sex, or national origin, except that such a notice or advertisement may indicate a preference, limitation, specification, or discrimination based on religion, sex or national origin when religion, sex, or national origin is a bona fide occupational qualification for employment.

 # Appendix D   Americans with Disabilities Act of 1990 (Excerpts)

Title I—EMPLOYMENT
Sec. 101. Definitions.
As used in this title: . . .

(8)   **Qualified individual with a disability.**—The term "qualified individual with a disability" means an individual with a disability who, with or without reasonable accommodation, can perform the essential functions of the employment position that such individual holds or desires. For the purposes of this title, consideration shall be given to the employer's judgment as to what functions of a job are essential, and if an employer has prepared a written description before advertising or interviewing applicants for the job, this description shall be considered evidence of the essential functions of the job.

(9)   **Reasonable accommodation.**—The term "reasonable accommodation" may include—

(A) making existing facilities used by employees readily accessible to and usable by individuals with disabilities; and (B) job restructuring, part-time or modified work schedules, reassignment to a vacant position, acquisition or modification of equipment or devices, appropriate adjustment or modifications of examinations, training materials or policies, the provision of qualified readers or interpreters, and other similar accommodations for individuals with disabilities.

(10)   **Undue Hardship.**—

(A)   **In general.**—The term "undue hardship" means an action requiring significant difficulty or expense, when considered in light of the factors set forth in subparagraph(B).

(B)   **Factors to be considered.**—In determining whether an accommodation would impose an undue hardship on a covered entity, factors to be considered include—

(i) the nature and cost of accommodation needed under this Act;

(ii) the overall financial resources of the facility or facilities involved in the provision of the reasonable accommodation; the number of persons employed at such facility; the effect on expenses and resources, or the impact otherwise of such accommodation upon the operation of the facility;

(iii) the overall financial resources of the covered entity; the overall size of the business of a covered entity with respect to the number of its employees; the number, type, and location of its facilities; and

(iv) the type of operation or operations of the covered entity, including the composition, structure, and functions of the workforce of such entity; the geographic separateness, administrative, or fiscal relationship of the facility or facilities in question to the covered entity.

Sec. 102. Discrimination.

(a)   **General Rule.**—No covered entity shall discriminate against a qualified individual with a disability because of the disability of such individual in regard to job application procedures, the hiring, advancement, or discharge of employees, employee compensation, job training, and other terms, conditions, and privileges of employment.

(b)   **Construction.**—As used in subsection (a), the term "discriminate" includes—

(1) limiting, segregating, or classifying a job applicant or employee in a way that adversely affects the opportunities or status of such applicant or employee because of the disability of such applicant or employee;

(2) participating in a contractual or other arrangement or relationship that has the effect of subjecting a covered entity's qualified applicant or employee with a disability to the discrimination prohibited by this title (such relationship includes a relationship with an employment or referral agency, labor union, an organization providing fringe benefits to an employee of the covered entity, or an organization providing training and apprenticeship programs);

(3) utilizing standards, criteria, or methods of administration—

(A) that have the effect of discrimination on the basis of disability; or

(B) that perpetuate the discrimination of others who are subject to common administrative control;

(4) excluding or otherwise denying equal jobs or benefits to a qualified individual because of the known disability of an individual with whom the qualified individual is known to have a relationship or association;

(5)(A) not making reasonable accommodations to the known physical or mental limitations of an otherwise qualified individual with a disability who is an applicant or employee, unless such covered entity can demonstrate that the accommodation would impose an undue hardship on the operation of the business of such covered entity; or

(B) denying employment opportunities to a job applicant or employee who is an otherwise qualified individual with a disability, if such denial is based on the need of such covered entity to make reasonable accommodation to the physical or mental impairments of the employee or applicant;

(6) using qualification standards, employment tests or other selection criteria that screen out or tend to screen out an individual with a disability or a class of individuals with disabilities unless the standard, test or other selection criteria, as used by the covered entity, is shown to be job-related for the position in question and is consistent with business necessity; and

(7) failing to select and administer tests concerning employment in the most effective manner to ensure that, when such test is administered to a job applicant or employee who has a disability that impairs sensory, manual, or speaking skills, such test results accurately reflect the skills, aptitude, or whatever other factor of such applicant or employee that such test purports to measure, rather than reflecting the impaired sensory, manual, or speaking skills of such employee or applicant (except where such skills are the factors that the test purports to measure). . . .

Sec. 104. Illegal Use of Drugs and Alcohol.

. . .

(b) **Rules of Construction.**—Nothing in subsection (a) shall be construed to exclude as a qualified individual with a disability an individual who—

(1) has successfully completed a supervised drug rehabilitation program and is no longer engaging in the illegal use of drugs, or has otherwise been rehabilitated successfully and is no longer engaging in such use;

(2) is participating in a supervised rehabilitation program and is no longer engaging in such use; or

(3) is erroneously regarded as engaging in such use, but is not engaging in such use; except that it shall not be a violation of this Act for a covered entity to adopt or administer reasonable policies or procedures, including but not limited to drug testing, designed to ensure that an individual described in paragraph (1) or (2) is no longer engaging in the illegal use of drugs. . . .

Sec. 107. Enforcement.

(a) **Powers, Remedies, and Procedures.**—The powers, remedies, and procedures set forth in sections 705, 706, 707, 709, and 710 of the Civil Rights Act of 1964 (42 U.S.C. 2000e-4, 2000e-5, 2000e-6, 2000e-8, and 2000e-9) shall be the powers, remedies, and procedures this title provides to the Commission, to the Attorney General, or to any person alleging discrimination on the basis of disability in violation of any provision of this Act, or regulations promulgated under section 106, concerning employment.

(b) **Coordination.**—The agencies with enforcement authority for actions which allege employment discrimination under this title and under the Rehabilitation Act of 1973 shall develop procedures to ensure that administrative complaints filed under this title and under the Rehabilitation Act of 1973 are dealt with in a manner that avoids duplication of effort and prevents imposition of inconsistent or conflicting standards for the same requirements under this title and the Rehabilitation Act of 1973. The Commission, the Attorney General, and the Office of Federal Contract Compliance Programs shall establish such coordinating mechanisms (similar to provisions contained in the joint regulations promulgated by the Commission and the Attorney General at part 42 of title 28 and part 1691 of title 29, Code of Federal Regulations, and the Memorandum of Understanding between the Commission and the Office of Federal Contract Compliance Programs dated January 16, 1981 (46 Fed. Reg. 7435, January 23, 1981)) in regulations implementing this title and Rehabilitation Act of 1973 not later than 18 months after the date of enactment of this Act.

Sec. 108. Effective Date.

This title shall become effective 24 months after the date of enactment.

 ## Appendix E   National Labor Relations Act (Excerpts)

Section 3. National Labor Relations Board. (a) The National Labor Relations Board (hereinafter called the "Board") . . . as an agency of the United States, shall consist of five . . . members, appointed by the President by and with advice and consent of the Senate . . . for terms of five years each. . . . The President shall designate one member to serve as Chairman of

(6) to cause or attempt to cause an employer to pay or deliver or agree to pay or deliver any money or other thing of value, in the nature of an exaction, for services which are not performed or not to be performed; and

(7) to picket or cause to be picketed, or threaten to picket or cause to be picketed, any employer where an object thereof is forcing or requiring an employer to recognize or bargain with a labor organization as the representative of his employees, or forcing or requiring the employees of an employer to accept or select such labor organization as their collective bargaining representative, unless such labor organization is currently certified as the representative of such employees:

(A) where the employer has lawfully recognized in accordance with this Act any other labor organization and a question concerning representation may not appropriately be raised under section 9(c) of this Act,

(B) where within the preceding 12 months a valid election under section 9(c) of this Act has been conducted, or

(C) where such picketing has been conducted without a petition under section 9(c) being filed within a reasonable period of time not to exceed 30 days from the commencement of such picketing: Provided, that when such a petition has been filed the Board shall forthwith, without regard to the provisions of section 9(c) (1) or the absence of a showing of a substantial interest on the part of the labor organization, direct an election in such units as the Board finds to be appropriate and shall certify the results thereof: Provided further, that nothing in this subparagraph (C) shall be construed to prohibit any picketing or other publicity for the purpose of truthfully advising the public (including consumers) that an employer does not employ members of, or have a contract with, a labor organization, unless an effect of such picketing is to induce any individual employed by any other person in the course of his employment, not to pick up, deliver or transport any goods or not to perform any services.

Nothing in this paragraph (7) shall be construed to permit any act which would otherwise be an unfair labor practice under this section 8(b).

(c) The expressing of any views, argument, or opinion, or the dissemination thereof, whether in written, printed, graphic, or visual form, shall not constitute or be evidence of an unfair labor practice under any of the provisions of this Act, if such expression contains no threat of reprisal or force or promise of benefit.

(d) For the purposes of this section, to bargain collectively is the performance of the mutual obligation of the employer and the representative of the employees to meet at reasonable times and confer in good faith with respect to wages, hours, and other terms and conditions of employment, or the negotiation of an agreement, or any question arising thereunder, and the execution of a written contract incorporating any agreement reached if requested by either party, but such obligation does not compel either party to agree to a proposal or require the making of a concession: Provided, that where there is in effect a collective bargaining contract covering employees in an industry affecting commerce, the duty to bargain collectively shall also mean that no party to such contract shall terminate or modify such contract, unless the party desiring such termination or modification—

(1) serves a written notice upon the other party to the contract of the proposed termination or modification 60 days prior to the expiration date thereof, or in the event such contract contains no expiration date, 60 days prior to the time it is proposed to make such termination or modification;

(2) offers to meet and confer with the other party for the purpose of negotiating a new contract or a contract containing the proposed modifications;

(3) notifies the Federal Mediation and Conciliation Service within 30 days after such notice of the existence of a dispute . . .

(4) continues in full force and effect, without resorting to strike or lockout, all the terms and conditions of the existing contract for a period of 60 days after such notice is given or until the expiration date of such contract, whichever occurs later.

(e) It shall be an unfair labor practice for any labor organization and any employer to enter into any contract or agreement, express or implied, whereby such employer ceases or refrains or agrees to cease or refrain from handling, using, selling, transporting, or otherwise dealing in any of the products of any other employer, or to cease doing business with any other person, . . . Provided, that nothing in this subsection (e) shall apply to an agreement between a labor organization and an employer in the construction industry relating to the contracting or subcontracting of work to be done at the site. . . .

Section 9. Representatives and Elections.

(a) Representatives designated or selected for the purposes of collective bargaining by the majority of the employees in a unit appropriate for such purposes, shall be the exclusive representatives of all the employees in such unit for the purposes of collective bargaining in respect to rates of pay, wages, hours of employment, or other conditions of employment: Provided, that any individual employee or a group of employees shall have the right at any time to present grievances to their employer and to have such grievance adjusted, without the intervention of the bargaining representative, as long as the adjustment is not inconsistent with the terms of a collective bargaining contract or agreement then in effect: Provided further, that the bargaining representative has been given opportunity to be present at such adjustment.

(b) The Board shall decide in each case whether, in order to assure to employees the fullest freedom in exercising the rights guaranteed by this Act, the unit appropriate for the purposes of collective bargaining shall be the employer unit, craft unit, plant unit, or subdivision thereof: Provided, that the Board shall not (1) decide that any unit is appropriate for such purposes if such unit includes both professional employees and employees who are not professional employees unless a majority of such professional employees vote for inclusion in such unit; or (2) decide that any craft unit is inappropriate for such purposes on the ground that a different unit has been established by a prior Board determination, unless a majority of the employees in the proposed craft unit vote against separate representation or (3) decide that any unit is appropriate for such purposes, if it includes, together with other employees, any individual employed as a guard to enforce against employees and other persons, rules to protect property of the employer or to protect the safety of persons on the employer's premises; but no labor organization shall be certified as the representative of employees in a bargaining unit of guards if such organization admits to membership, or is affiliated directly or indirectly with an organization which admits to membership, employees other than guards.

(c) (1) Wherever a petition shall have been filed, in accordance with such regulations as may be prescribed by the Board—

(A) by an employee or group of employees or any individual or labor organization acting in their behalf alleging that a substantial number of employees (i) wish to be represented for collective bargaining and that their employer declines to recognize their representative as the representative defined in section 9(a), or (ii) assert that the individual or labor organization, which has been certified or is being currently recognized by their employer as the bargaining representative as defined in section 9(a); or

(B) by an employer, alleging that one or more individuals or labor organizations have presented to him a claim to be recognized as the representative defined in section 9(a);

the Board shall investigate such petition and if it has reasonable cause to believe that a question of representation affecting commerce exists shall provide for an appropriate hearing upon due notice. Such hearing may be conducted by an officer or employee of the regional office, who shall not make any recommendations with respect thereto. If the Board finds upon the record of such hearing that such a question of representative exists, it shall direct an election by secret ballot and shall certify the results thereof.

(2) In determining whether or not a question of representation affecting commerce exists, the same regulations and rules of decision shall apply irrespective of the identity of the persons filing the petition or the kind of relief sought and in no case shall the Board deny a labor organization a place on the ballot by reason of an order with respect to such labor organization or its predecessor not issued in conformity with section 10(c).

(3) No election shall be directed in any bargaining unit or any subdivision within which, in the preceding twelve-month period, a valid election shall have been held. Employees engaged in an economic strike who are not entitled to reinstatement shall be eligible to vote under such regulations as the Board shall find are consistent with the purposes and provisions of this Act in any election conducted within twelve months after the commencement of the strike. In any election where none of the choices on the ballot receives a majority, a run-off shall be conducted, the ballot providing for a selection between the two

choices receiving the largest and second largest number of valid votes cast in the election.

(4) Nothing in this section shall be construed to prohibit the waiving of hearings by stipulation for the purpose of a consent election in conformity with regulations and rules of decision of the Board.

(5) In determining whether a unit is appropriate for the purposes specified in subsection (b) the extent to which the employees have organized shall not be controlling.

(d) Whenever an order of the Board made pursuant to section 10(c) is based in whole or in part upon facts certified following an investigation pursuant to subsection (c) of this section and there is a petition for the enforcement or review of such order, such certification and the record of such investigation shall be included in the transcript of the entire record required to be filed under section 10(c) or 10(f), and thereupon the decree of the court enforcing modifying, or setting aside in whole or in part the order of the Board shall be made and entered upon the pleadings, testimony, and the proceedings set forth in such transcript.

(e)(1) Upon the filing with the Board, by 30 per centum or more of the employees in a bargaining unit covered by an agreement between their employer and a labor organization made pursuant to section 8(a)(3), of a petition alleging they desire that such authority be rescinded, the Board shall take a secret ballot of the employees in such unit, and shall certify the results thereof to such labor organization and to the employer.

(2) No election shall be conducted pursuant to this subsection in any bargaining unit or any subdivision within which, in the preceding twelve month period, a valid election shall have been held.

Section 19. Individuals with Religious Convictions.

Any employee who is a member of and adheres to established and traditional tenets or teachings of a bona fide religion, body, or sect which has historically held conscientious objections to joining or financially supporting labor organizations shall not be required to join or financially support any labor organization as a condition of employment; except that such employee may be required in a contract between such employee's employer and a labor organization in lieu of periodic dues and initiation fees, to pay sums equal to such dues and initiation fees to a nonreligious, nonlabor organization charitable fund exempt from taxation under section 501(c) (3) of title 26 of the Internal Revenue Code.

 # Appendix F   Sherman Antitrust Act (Excerpts)

The Sherman Antitrust Act (1890, as amended)

Section 1.   Every contract, combination in the form of trust or otherwise, or conspiracy, in restraint of trade or commerce among the several States, or with foreign nations, is hereby declared to be illegal. Every person who shall make any contract or engage in any such combination or conspiracy shall be deemed guilty of a felony, and, on conviction thereof, shall be punished by fine not exceeding $10,000,000 if a corporation, or, if any other person, $350,000 or by imprisonment not exceeding three

years, or by both said punishments in the discretion of the court.

Section 2.   Every person who shall monopolize, or attempt to monopolize, or conspire with any other person or persons, to monopolize any part of the trade or commerce among the several States, or with foreign nations, shall be deemed guilty of a felony, and, on conviction thereof, shall be punished by fine not exceeding $10,000,000 if a corporation, or, if any other person, $350,000 or by imprisonment not exceeding three years, or by both said punishments, in the discretion of the court.

Appendix G   Clayton Act of 1914 (Excerpts)

Section 3.   That it shall be unlawful for any person engaged in commerce, in the course of such commerce, to lease or make a sale or contract for sale of goods, wares, merchandise, machinery, supplies, or other commodities, whether patented or unpatented, for use, consumption, or resale within the United States or . . . other place under the jurisdiction of the United States, or fix a price charged therefor, or discount from, or rebate upon, such price, on the condition, agreement, or understanding that the lessee or purchaser thereof shall not use or deal in the goods, wares, merchandise, machinery, supplies, or other commodities of a competitor or competitors of the lessor or seller, where the effect of such lease, sale, or contract for sale or such condition, agreement, or understanding may be to substantially lessen competition to tend to create a monopoly in any line of commerce.

Section 4.   That any person who shall be injured in his business or property by reason of anything forbidden in the antitrust laws may sue therefor in any district court of the United States in the district in which the defendant resides or is found, or has an agent, without respect to the amount in controversy, and shall recover threefold the damages by him sustained, and the cost of suit, including a reasonable attorney's fee.

Section 4A.   Whenever the United States is hereafter injured in its business or property by reason of anything forbidden in the antitrust laws it may sue therefor in the United States district court for the district in which the defendant resides or is found or has an agent, without respect to the amount in controversy, and shall recover actual damages by it sustained and the cost of suit.

Section 4B.   Any action to enforce any cause of action under sections 4 or 4A shall be forever barred unless commenced within four years after the cause of action accrued. No cause of action barred under existing law on the effective date of this act shall be revived by this Act.

Section 6.   That the labor of a human being is not a commodity or article of commerce. Nothing contained in the antitrust laws shall be construed to forbid the existence and operation of labor, agricultural or horticultural organizations, instituted for the purposes of mutual help, and not having capital stock or conducted for profit, or to forbid or restrain individual members of such organizations from lawfully carrying out the legitimate objects thereof; nor shall such organizations or the members thereof, be held or construed to be illegal combinations or conspiracies in restraint of trade, under the antitrust laws.

Section 7.   That no person engaged in commerce shall acquire, directly or indirectly, the whole or any part of the stock or other share capital and no corporation subject to the jurisdiction of the Federal Trade Commission shall acquire the whole or any part of the assets of another corporation engaged also in commerce, where in any line of commerce in any section of the country, the effect of such acquisition may be substantially to lessen competition, or to tend to create a monopoly.

No person shall acquire, directly or indirectly, the whole or any part of the stock or other share capital and no corporation subject to the jurisdiction of the Federal Trade Commission shall acquire the whole or any part of the assets of one or more corporations engaged in commerce, where in any line of commerce in any section of the country, the effect of such acquisition, of such stocks or assets, or of the use of such stock by the voting or granting of proxies or otherwise, may be substantially to lessen competition, or to tend to create a monopoly.

This section shall not apply to persons purchasing such stock solely for investment and not using the same by voting or otherwise to bring about, or in attempting to bring about, the substantial lessening of competition . . .

Section 8.   . . . No person shall, at the same time, serve as a director or officer in any two or more corporations (other than banks, banking associations, and trust companies) that are—

(A) engaged in whole or in part in commerce; and

(B) by virtue of their business and location of operation, competitors, so that the elimination of competition by agreement between them would constitute a violation of any of the antitrust laws; if each of the corporations has capital, surplus, and undivided profits aggregating more than $10,000,000 as adjusted pursuant to paragraph (5) of this subsection.

 Appendix H   Federal Trade Commission Act of 1914 (Excerpts)

Unfair Methods of Competition Prohibited

Section 5.—Unfair methods of competition unlawful; prevention by Commission—declaration.   Declaration of unlawfulness; power to prohibit unfair practices.

(a) (1) Unfair methods of competition in or affecting commerce, and unfair or deceptive acts or practices in or affecting commerce, are declared unlawful.

. . .

(b) Any person, partnership, or corporation who violates an order of the Commission to cease and desist after it has become final, and while such order is in effect, shall forfeit and pay to the United States a civil penalty of not more than $10,000 for each violation, which shall accrue to the United States and may be recovered in a civil action brought by the Attorney General of the United States. Each separate violation of such an order shall be a separate offense, except that in the case of a violation through continuing failure or neglect to obey a final order of the Commission, each day of continuance of such failure or neglect shall be deemed a separate offense.

Appendix I   Robinson-Patman Act (Excerpts)

Price Discrimination; Cost Justification; Changing Conditions

Section 2—Discrimination in price, services, or facilities.

(a) Price; Selection of Customers.

It shall be unlawful for any person engaged in commerce, in the course of such commerce, either directly or indirectly, to discriminate in price between different purchases of commodities of like grade and quality, where either or any of the purchases involved in such discrimination are in commerce, where such commodities are sold for use, consumption, or resale within the United States or any Territory thereof or the District of Columbia or any insular possession or other place under the jurisdiction of the United States, and where the effect of such discrimination may be substantially to lessen competition or tend to create a monopoly in any line of commerce, or to injure, destroy, or prevent competition with any person who either grants or knowingly receives the benefit of such discrimination, or with customers of either of them; *Provided,* That nothing herein contained shall prevent differentials which make only due allowance for differences in the cost of manufacture, sale, or delivery resulting from the differing methods or quantities in which such commodities are to such purchasers sold or delivered: *Provided, however,* That the Federal Trade Commission may, after due investigation and hearing to all interested parties, fix and establish quantity limits, and revise the same as it finds necessary as to particular commodities or classes of commodities, where it finds that available purchasers in greater quantities are so few as to render differentials on account thereof unjustly discriminatory or promotive of monopoly in any line of commerce; and the foregoing shall then not be construed to permit differentials based on differences in quantities greater than those so fixed and established: *And provided further,* That nothing herein contained shall prevent persons engaged in selling goods, wares, or merchandise in commerce from selecting their own customers in bona fide transactions and not in restraint of trade: *And provided further,* That nothing herein contained shall prevent price changes from time to time where in response to changing conditions affecting the market for or the marketability of the goods concerned, such as but not limited to actual or imminent deterioration of perishable goods, obsolescence of seasonal goods, distress sales under court process, or sales in good faith in discontinuance of business in the goods concerned.

Meeting Competition

(b) Burden of rebutting prima-facie case of discrimination.

Upon proof being made, at any hearing on a complaint under this section, that there has been discrimination in price or services or facilities furnished, the burden of rebutting the prima-facie case thus made by showing justification shall be upon the person charged with a violation of this section, and unless justification shall be affirmatively shown, the Commission is authorized to issue an order terminating the discrimination: *Provided, however,* That nothing herein contained shall prevent a seller rebutting the prima-facie case thus made by showing that his lower price or the furnishing of services or facilities to any purchaser or purchasers was made in good faith to meet an equally low price of a competitor, or the services or facilities furnished by a competitor.

Brokerage Payments

(c) Payment or acceptance of commission, brokerage or other compensation.

It shall be unlawful for any person engaged in commerce, in the course of such commerce, to pay or grant, or to receive or accept, anything of value as a commission, brokerage, or other compensation, or any allowance or discount in lieu thereof, except for services rendered in connection with the sale or purchase of goods, wares, or merchandise, either to the other party to such transaction or to an agent, representative, or other intermediary therein where such intermediary is acting in fact for or in behalf, or is subject to the direct or indirect control, of any party to such transaction other than the person by whom such compensation is so granted or paid.

Promotional Allowances

(d) Payment for services or facilities for processing or sale.

It shall be unlawful for any person engaged in commerce to pay or contract for the payment of anything of value to or for the benefit of a customer of such person in the course of such commerce as compensation or in consideration for any services or facilities furnished by or through such customer in connection with the processing, handling, sale or offering for sale of any products or commodities manufactured, sold, or offered for sale by such person, unless such payment of consideration is available on proportionally equal terms to all other customers competing in the distribution of such products or commodities.

Promotional Services

(e) Furnishing services or facilities for processing, handling, etc.

It shall be unlawful for any person to discriminate in favor of one purchaser against another purchaser or purchasers of a commodity bought for resale, with or without processing, or by contracting to furnish or furnishing, or by contributing to the furnishing of, any services or facilities connected with the processing, handling, sale, or offering for sale of such commodity so purchased upon terms not accorded to all purchasers on proportionally equal terms.

Buyer Discrimination

(f) Knowingly inducing or receiving discriminatory price.

It shall be unlawful for any person engaged in commerce, in the course of such commerce, knowingly to induce or receive a discrimination in price which is prohibited by this section.

Predatory Practices

Section 3—Discrimination in rebates, discounts, or advertising service charges; underselling in particular localities; penalties.   It shall be unlawful for any person engaged in commerce, in the course of such commerce, to be a party to, or assist in, any transaction of sale, or contract to sell, which discriminates to his knowledge against competitors of the purchaser, in that, any discount, rebate, allowance, or advertising service charge is granted to the purchaser over and above any discount, rebate, allowance, or advertising service charge available at the time of such transaction to said competitors in respect of a sale of goods of like grade, quality, and quantity; to sell, or contract to sell, goods in any part of the United States at prices lower than those exacted by said person elsewhere in the United States for the purpose of destroying competition, or eliminating a competitor in such part of the United States; or, to sell, or contract to sell, goods at unreasonably lower prices for the purpose of destroying competition or eliminating a competitor.

Any person violating any of the provisions of this section shall, upon conviction thereof, be fined not more than $5,000 or imprisoned not more than one year, or both.

 # Appendix J   Securities Act of 1933 (Excerpts)

Prohibitions Relating to Interstate Commerce and the Mails

Sec. 5. (a) Unless a registration statement is in effect as to a security, it shall be unlawful for any person, directly or indirectly—

(1) to make use of any means or instruments of transportation or communication in interstate commerce or of the mails to sell such security through the use or medium of any prospectus or otherwise; or

(2) to carry or cause to be carried through the mails or in interstate commerce, by any means or instruments of transportation, any such security for the purpose of sale or for delivery after sale.

[Prospectus Requirements]

(b) It shall be unlawful for any person, directly or indirectly—

(1) to make use of any means or instruments of transportation or communication in interstate commerce or of the mails to carry or transmit any prospectus relating to any security with respect to which a registration statement has been filed under this title, unless such prospectus meets the requirements of section 10, or

(2) to carry or to cause to be carried through the mails or in interstate commerce any such security for the purpose of sale or for delivery after sale, unless accompanied or preceded by a prospectus that meets the requirements of subsection (a) of section 10.

[Prohibition Against Offers Prior to Registration]

(c) It shall be unlawful for any person, directly or indirectly, to make use of any means or instruments of transportation or communication in interstate commerce or of the mails to offer to sell or offer to buy through the use or medium of any prospectus or otherwise any security, unless a registration statement has been filed as to such security, or while the registration statement is the subject of a refusal order or stop order or (prior to the effective date of the registration statement) any public proceeding or examination under section 8.

Civil Liabilities on Account of False Registration Statement

Sec. 11. (a) In case any part of the registration statement, when such part became effective, contained an untrue statement of a material fact or omitted to state a material fact required to be stated therein or necessary to make the statements therein not misleading, any person acquiring such security (unless it is proved that at the time of such acquisition he knew of such untruth or omission) may, either at law or in equity, in any court of competent jurisdiction, sue—

[Signers of Registration Statement]

(1) every person who signed the registration statement;

[Directors and Partners]

(2) every person who was a director of (or person performing similar functions), or partner in, the issuer at the time of the filing of the part of the registration statement with respect to which his liability is asserted;

[Persons Named as Being, or About to Become, Directors or Partners]

(3) every person who, with his consent, is named in the registration statement as being or about to become a director, person performing similar functions, or partner;

[Accountants, Engineers, Appraisers, and Other Professional Persons]

(4) every accountant engineer, or appraiser, or any person whose profession gives authority to a statement made by him, who has with his consent been named as having prepared or certified any part of the registration statement, or as having prepared or certified any report or valuation which is used in connection with the registration statement, with respect to the statement in such registration statement, report, or valuation, which purports to have been prepared or certified by him;

[Underwriters]

(5) every underwriter with respect to such security.

[Purchase after Publication of Earning Statement]

If such person acquired the security after the issuer has made generally available to its security holders an earning statement covering a period of at least twelve months beginning after the effective date of the registration statement, then the right of recovery under this subsection shall be conditioned on proof that such person acquired the securities relying on such untrue statement in the registration statement or relying upon the registration statement and not knowing of such omission, but such reliance may be established without proof of the reading of the registration statement by such person.

[Defenses of Persons Other than Issuer]

(b) Notwithstanding the provisions of subsection (a) no person, other than the issuer, shall be liable as provided therein who shall sustain the burden of proof—

[Resignation before Effective Date]

(1) that before the effective date of the part of the registration statement with respect to which his liability is asserted (A) he had resigned from or had taken such steps as are permitted by law to resign from, or ceased or refused to act in, every office, capacity or relationship in which he was described in the registration statement as acting or agreeing to act, and (B) he had advised the Commission and the issuer in writing, that he had taken such action and that he would not be responsible for such part of the registration statement; or

[Statements Becoming Effective without Defendants Knowledge]

(2) that if such part of the registration statement became effective without his knowledge, upon becoming aware of such fact he forthwith acted and advised the Commission, in accordance with paragraph (1), and, in addition, gave reasonable public notice that such part of the registration statement had become effective without his knowledge; or

[Belief on Reasonable Grounds that Statements Were True]

(3) that (A) as regards any part of the registration statement not purporting to be made on the authority of an expert, and not purporting to be a copy of or extract from a report or valuation of an expert and not purporting to be made on the authority of a public official document or statement, he had, after reasonable investigation, reasonable ground to believe and did believe, at the time such part of the registration statement became effective, that the statements therein were true and that there was no omission to state a material fact required to be stated therein or necessary to make the statements therein not misleading; and

[Statement Made on Authority of Defendant as Expert]

(B) as regards any part of the registration statement purporting to be made upon his authority as an expert or purporting to be a copy of or extract from a report or valuation of himself as an expert, (i) he had, after reasonable investigation, reasonable ground to believe and did believe, at the time such part of the registration statement became effective, that the statements therein were true and that there was no omission to state a material fact required to be stated therein or necessary to make the statements therein not misleading, or (ii) such part of the registration statement did not fairly represent his statement as an expert or was not a fair copy of or extract from his report or valuation as an expert; and

[Statement Made on Authority of Expert Other than Defendant]

(C) as regards any part of the registration statement purporting to be made on the authority of an expert (other than himself) or purporting to be a copy of or extract from a report or valua-

tion of an expert (other than himself), he had no reasonable ground to believe and did not believe, at the time such part of the registration statement became effective, that the statements therein were untrue or that there was an omission to state a material fact required to be stated therein or necessary to make the statements therein not misleading, or that such part of the registration statement did not fairly represent the statement of the expert or was not a fair copy of or extract from the report or valuation of the expert; and

[Statement Made by Official Person; Copy of Public Official Document]

(D) as regards any part of the registration statement purporting to be a statement made by an official person or purporting to be a copy of or extract from a public official document, he had no reasonable ground to believe and did not believe, at the time such part of the registration statement became effective, that the statements therein were untrue, or that there was an omission to state a material fact required to be stated therein or necessary to make the statements therein not misleading, or that such part of the registration statement did not fairly represent the statement made by the official person or was not a fair copy of or extract from the public official document.

["Reasonable" Investigation and "Reasonable" Grounds for Belief]

(c) In determining, for the purpose of paragraph (3) of subsection (b) of this section, what constitutes reasonable investigation and reasonable ground for belief, the standard of reasonableness shall be that required of a prudent man in the management of his own property.

[Person Becoming Underwriter after Effectiveness of Registration Statement]

(d) If any person becomes an underwriter with respect to the security after the part of the registration statement with respect to which his liability is asserted has become effective, then for the purposes of paragraph (3) of subsection (b) of this section such part of the registration statement shall be considered as having become effective with respect to such person as of the time when he became an underwriter.

[Amount of Damages; Bond for Costs of Suit]

(e) The suit authorized under subsection (a) may be to recover such damages as shall represent the difference between the amount paid for the security (not exceeding the price at which the security was offered to the public) and (1) the value thereof as of the time such suit was brought, or (2) the price at which such security shall have been disposed of in the market before suit, or (3) the price at which such security shall have been disposed of after suit but before judgment if such damages shall be less than the damages representing the difference between the amount paid for the security (not exceeding the price at which the security was offered to the public) and the value thereof as of the time such suit was brought: Provided, That if the defendant proves that any portion or all of such damages represents other than the depreciation in value of such security resulting from such part of the registration statement, with respect to which his liability is asserted, not being true or omitting to state a material fact required to be stated therein or necessary to make the statements therein not misleading, such portion of or all such damages shall not be recoverable. In no event shall any underwriter (unless such underwriter shall have knowingly received from the issuer for acting as an underwriter some benefit, directly or indirectly in which all other underwriters similarly situated did not share in proportion to their respective interests in the underwriting) be liable in any suit or as a consequence of suits authorized under subsection (a) for damages in excess of the total price at which the securities underwritten by him and distributed to the public were offered to the public. In any suit under this or any other section of this title the court may, in its discretion, require an undertaking for the payment of the costs of such suit, including reasonable attorney's fees, and if judgment shall be rendered against a party litigant, upon the motion of the other party litigant, such costs may be assessed in favor of such party litigant (whether or not such undertaking has been required) if the court believes the suit or the defense to have been without merit, in an amount sufficient to reimburse him for the reasonable expenses incurred by him, in connection with such suit, such costs to be taxed in the manner usually provided for taxing of costs in the court in which the suit was heard.

[Joint and Several Liability]

(f) All or any one or more of the persons specified in subsection (a) shall be jointly and severally liable, and every person who becomes liable to make any payment under this section may recover contribution as in cases of contract from any person who, if sued separately, would have been liable to make the same payment, unless the person who had become liable was, and the other was not, guilty of fraudulent misrepresentation.

[Limitation on Amount of Damages]

(g) In no case shall the amount recoverable under this section exceed the price at which the security was offered to the public.

Civil Liabilities Arising in Connection with Prospectuses and Communications

Sec. 12. Any person who—

(1) offers or sells a security in violation of section 5, or

Offers or Sells by Use of Interstate Communications or Transportation

(2) offers or sells a security (whether or not exempted by the provisions of section 3, other than paragraph (2) of subsection (a) thereof), by the use of any means or instruments of transportation or communication in interstate commerce or of the mails, by means of a prospectus or oral communication, which includes an untrue statement of a material fact or omits to state a material fact necessary in order to make the statements, in the light of the circumstances under which they were made, not misleading (the purchaser not knowing of such untruth or omission), and who shall not sustain the burden of proof that he did not know, and in the exercise of reasonable care could not have known, of such untruth or omission, shall be liable to the person purchasing such security from him, who may sue either at law or in equity in any court of competent jurisdiction, to recover the consideration paid for such security with interest thereon, less the amount of any income received thereon, upon the tender of such security, or for damages if he no longer owns the security.

 # Appendix K   Securities Exchange Act of 1934 (Excerpts)

Regulation of the Use of Manipulative and Deceptive Devices

Sec. 10. It shall be unlawful for any person, directly or indirectly, by the use of any means or instrumentality of interstate commerce or of the mails, or of any facility of any national securities exchange—

. . .

[Use or Employment of Manipulative or Deceptive Devices]

(b) To use or employ, in connection with the purchase or sale of any security registered on a national securities exchange or any security not so registered, any manipulative or deceptive device or contrivance in contravention of such rules and regulations as the commission may prescribe as necessary or appropriate in the public interest or for the protection of investors.

. . .

[Directors, Officers, and Principal Stockholders]

Sec. 16. (a) Every person who is directly or indirectly the beneficial owner of more than 10 per centum of any class of any equity security (other than exempted security) which is registered pursuant to section 12 of this title, or who is a director or an officer of the issuer of such security, shall file, at the time of the registration of such security on a national securities exchange or by the effective date of a registration statement filed pursuant to section 12(g) of this title, or within ten days after he becomes such beneficial owner, director, or officer, a statement with the Commission (and, if such security is registered on a national securities exchange, also with the exchange) of the amount of all equity securities of such issuer of which he is the beneficial owner, and within ten days after the close of each calendar month thereafter, if there has been a change in such ownership during such month, shall file with the Commission (and if such security is registered on a national securities exchange, shall also file with the exchange), a statement indicating his ownership at the close of the calendar month and such changes in his ownership as have occurred during such calendar month.

[Profits Realized from Purchase and Sales within Period of Less than Six Months]

(b) For the purpose of preventing the unfair use of information which may have been obtained by such beneficial owner, director, or officer by reason of his relationship to the issuer, any profit realized by him from any purchase and sale, or any sale and purchase, of any equity security of such issuer (other than an exempted security) within any period of less than six months, unless such security was acquired in good faith in connection with a debt previously contracted, shall inure to and be recoverable by the issuer, irrespective of any intention on the part of such beneficial owner, director, or officer in entering into such transaction of holding the security purchased or of not repurchasing the security sold for a period exceeding six months. Suit to recover such profit may be instituted at law or in equity in any court of competent jurisdiction by the issuer, or by the owner of any security of the issuer in the name and in behalf of the issuer if the issuer shall fail or refuse to bring such suit within sixty days after request or shall fail diligently to prosecute the same thereafter; but no such suit shall be brought more than two years after the date such profit was realized. This subsection shall not be construed to cover any transaction where such beneficial owner was not such both at the time of the purchase and sale, or the sale and purchase, of the security involved, or any transaction or transactions which the Commission by rules and regulations may exempt as not comprehended within the purpose of this subsection.

 ## Appendix L   Rule 10b–5 from Code of Federal Regulations

§ 240.10b–5 Employment of manipulative and deceptive devices.

It shall be unlawful for any person, directly or indirectly, by the use of any means or instrumentality of interstate commerce, or of the mails or of any facility of any national securities exchange,

(a) To employ any device, scheme, or artifice to defraud,

(b) To make any untrue statement of a material fact or to omit to state a material fact necessary in order to make the statements made, in the light of the circumstances under which they were made, not misleading, or

(c) To engage in any act, practice, or course of business which operates or would operate as a fraud or deceit upon any person, in connection with the purchase or sale of any security.

[13 FR 8183, Dec. 22, 1948, as amended at 16 FR 7928, Aug. 11, 1951]

 ## Appendix M   Rule 14e–3 from Code of Federal Regulations

§ 240.14e-3 Transactions in securities on the basis of material, nonpublic information in the context of tender offers.

(a) If any person has taken a substantial step or steps to commence, or has commenced, a tender offer (the "offering person"), it shall constitute a fraudulent, deceptive or manipulative act or practice within the meaning of section 14(e) of the Act for any other person who is in possession of material information relating to such tender offer which information he knows or has reason to know is nonpublic and which he knows or has reason to know has been acquired directly or indirectly from:

(1) The offering person,

(2) The issuer of the securities sought or to be sought by such tender offer, or

(3) Any officer, director, partner or employee or any other person acting on behalf of the offering person or such issuer, to purchase or sell or cause to be purchased or sold any of such securities or any securities convertible into or exchangeable for any such securities or any option or right to obtain or dispose of any of the foregoing securities, unless within a reasonable time prior to any purchase or sale such information and its source are publicly disclosed by press release or otherwise.

(b) A person other than a natural person shall not violate paragraph (a) of this section if such person shows that:

(1) The individual(s) making the investment decision on behalf of such person to purchase or sell any security described in paragraph (a) of this section or to cause any such security to be purchased or sold by or on behalf of others did not know the material, nonpublic information; and

(2) Such person had implemented one or a combination of policies and procedures, reasonable under the circumstances, taking into consideration the nature of the person's business, to ensure that individual(s) making investment decision(s) would not violate paragraph (a) of this section, which policies and procedures may include, but are not limited to, (i) those which restrict any purchase, sale and causing any purchase and sale of any such security or (ii) those which prevent such individual(s) from knowing such information.

(c) Notwithstanding anything in paragraph (a) of this section to contrary, the following transactions shall not be violations of paragraph (a) of this section:

(1) Purchase(s) of any security described in paragraph (a) of this section by a broker or by another agent on behalf of an offering person; or

(2) Sale(s) by any person of any security described in paragraph (a) of this section to the offering person.

(d)(1) As a means reasonably designed to prevent fraudulent, deceptive or manipulative acts or practices within the meaning of section 14(e) of the Act, it shall be unlawful for any person described in paragraph (d)(2)) of this section to communicate material, nonpublic information relating to a tender offer to any other person under circumstances in which it is reasonably foreseeable that such communication is likely to result in a violation of this section *except* that this paragraph shall not apply to a communication made in good faith.

(i) To the officers, directors, partners or employees of the offering person, to its advisors or to other persons, involved in the planning, financing, preparation or execution of such tender offer;

(ii) To the issuer whose securities are sought or to be sought by such tender offer, to its officers, directors, partners, employees or advisors or to other persons, involved in the planning, financ-ing, preparation or execution of the activities of the issuer with respect to such tender offer; or

(iii) To any person pursuant to a requirement of any statute or rule or regulation promulgated thereunder.

(2) The persons referred to in paragraph (d)(1) of this section are;

(i) The offering person or its officers, directors, partners, employees or advisors;

(ii) The issuer of the securities sought or to be sought by such tender offer or its officers, directors, partners, employees or advisors;

(iii) Anyone acting on behalf of the persons in paragraph (d)(2)(i) of this section or the issuer or persons in paragraph (d)(2)(ii) of this section; and

(iv) Any person in possession of material information relating to a tender offer which information he knows or has reason to know is nonpublic and which he knows or has reason to know has been acquired directly or indirectly from any of the above.

[46 FR 60418, Sept. 12, 1980]

Glossary

A

ABANDONMENT (OF A TRADEMARK) The failure to use a mark after acquiring legal protection may result in the loss of rights, and such loss is known as abandonment.

ABSOLUTE PRIVILEGE In defamation cases, the right of the defendant to publish with impunity a statement known by the defendant to be false.

ACCEPTANCE An agreement to the amount offered for certain services or products. Acceptance may be verbal, written, or implied by action.

ACCORD AND SATISFACTION An agreement to accept performance that is different from what is called for in the contract.

ACCREDITED INVESTOR Certain investors who are so financially sophisticated that they do not need all the protections afforded by the securities laws.

ACT-OF-STATE DOCTRINE The doctrine that states that the courts of one country will not sit in judgment on the acts of the government of another done within its own territory.

ACTIONABLE Behavior that is the basis for a claim.

ACTUAL (COMPENSATORY) DAMAGES The amount required to repair or to replace an item or the decrease in market value caused by tortious conduct. Actual damages restore the injured party to the position it was in prior to the injury.

ACTUAL AUTHORITY The express or implied power of an agent to act for and bind a principal to agreements entered into by an agent.

ACTUAL CAUSE Proof that but for the defendant's negligent conduct the plaintiff would not have been harmed.

ACTUAL INTENT The subjective desire to cause the consequences of an act, or the belief that the consequences are substantially certain to result from it.

ACTUAL MALICE A statement made with the knowledge that it is false or with a reckless disregard for the truth.

ACTUAL NOTICE Concerning claims on title, actual notice refers to a claimant actually knowing of a prior interest in the real property.

ACTUS REUS **(guilty deed)** A crime; a criminal act.

AD VALOREM (according to value) TARIFF An importer must pay a percentage of the value of the imported merchandise.

ADDITIVE Anything not inherent in a food product—including pesticide residues, unintended environmental contaminants, and unavoidably added substances from packaging.

ADHESION CONTRACT An unfair type of contract by which sellers offer goods or services on a take-it-or-leave-it basis, with no chance for consumers to negotiate for goods except by agreeing to the terms of said contract.

ADMINISTRATIVE LAW JUDGE The presiding official at an administrative proceeding who has the power to issue an order resolving the legal dispute.

ADVERSE POSSESSION Ownership of property that is not occupied by its owner for a certain period of time may be transferred to those who have been unlawfully occupying it and openly exercising rights of ownership. Such a transfer is usually not reflected in the official land records. Also called squatter's rights.

AFFIDAVIT A written or printed declaration or statement of facts, made voluntarily, and confirmed by the oath or affirmation of the party making it, taken before a person having authority to administer such oath or affirmation.

AFFILIATE Any person who controls an issuer of securities, or is controlled by the issuer, or is under common control. Includes officers, directors, and major shareholders of a corporation.

AFFIRMATIVE COVENANT The borrower's promise to do certain things under the loan agreement.

AFFIRMATIVE DEFENSE The admission in an answer to a complaint that defendant has acted as plaintiff alleges, but denies that defendant's conduct was the real or legal cause of harm to plaintiff.

AFTER-ACQUIRED PROPERTY The property a debtor acquires after the execution of a security agreement.

AFTER-ACQUIRED TITLE If, at the date of execution of a grant deed, the grantor does not have title to the real property referred to in the grant deed but subsequently acquires it, such after-acquired title is deemed automatically transferred to the grantee.

AGENCY A relationship in which one person (the agent) acts for or represents another person (the principal).

AGENCY BY ESTOPPEL When the principal leads a third party to believe that a person is his or her agent, the principal is estopped (prevented) from denying that the person is his or her agent.

AGENCY BY RATIFICATION An agency formed when a principal approves or accepts the benefits of the actions of an otherwise unauthorized agent.

AGENT A person who manages a task delegated by another (the principal) and exercises whatever discretion is given to the agent by the principal.

AIDER AND ABETTOR A person with knowledge of (or recklessness as to) a primary violation who provides substantial assistance to the primary violation.

ALLOCATIVE EFFICIENCY An equilibrium in which scarce societal resources are allocated to the production of various goods and services up to the point where the cost of the resources equals the benefit society reaps from their use.

ALTER EGO THEORY When owners have so mingled their own affairs with those of a corporation that the corporation does not exist as distinct entity, it is an alter ego (second self) of its owners, permitting the piercing of the corporate veil.

AMORTIZE To pay over a period of time.

ANCHOR TENANT A key tenant of a shopping center, such as a supermarket or department store.

ANSWER The instrument by which defendant admits or denies the various allegations stated in the complaint against the defendant.

ANTICIPATORY REPUDIATION If a party indicates before performance is due that it will breach the contract, there is an anticipatory repudiation of the contract.

ANTIDEFICIENCY LAWS Statutes that restrict lenders seeking remedies against real property security from suing the borrower personally. If a lender has recourse to the borrower or to other property of the borrower, and exercises such rights, the lender may be precluded from foreclosing on real estate mortgaged by the borrower. Also called one-form-of-action laws.

ANTIDEFICIENCY STATUTE A statute that prevents the holder of a mortgage or deed of trust secured by real property from suing the borrower personally to recover whatever is still owing after a foreclosure sale.

ANTITRUST INJURY The damages sustained by a plaintiff in an antitrust suit as a result of the defendant's anticompetitive conduct.

ANTITRUST LAWS The laws that seek to identify and forbid business practices that are anticompetitive. Also called competition laws.

APPARENT AUTHORITY A principal, by words or actions, causes a third party to reasonably believe that an agent has authority to act for or bind the principal.

APPELLANT The person who is appealing a judgment or seeking a writ of certiorari. Also called a petitioner.

APPELLATE JURISDICTION The power of the Supreme Court and other courts of appeal to decide cases that have been tried in a lower court and appealed.

APPELLEE The party in a case against whom an appeal is taken; that is, the party who has an interest adverse to setting aside or reversing the judgment. Also called respondent.

APPLICANT Person (the buyer in a sales transaction) requesting an issuing bank to provide a letter of credit in favor of another party called the beneficiary (the seller in a sales transaction).

APPRAISAL RIGHTS In a merger or sale of assets, shareholders who voted against the transaction have appraisal rights, that is, the right to receive the fair cash value of the shares they were forced to give up as a result of the transaction.

APPROPRIATION OF A PERSON'S NAME OR LIKENESS Unauthorized use of a person's name or likeness for financial gain.

ARBITRARY AND CAPRICIOUS STANDARD If an agency has a choice between several courses of action, the court will presume that the chosen course is valid unless the person challenging it shows that it lacks any rational basis.

ARBITRATION The resolution of a dispute by a neutral third party.

ARBITRATION CLAUSE A clause that specifies that in the event of a dispute arising out of a contract, the parties will arbitrate specific issues in a stated manner.

ARBITRATOR The neutral third party who conducts an arbitration to resolve a dispute.

ARREST To deprive a person of his or her liberty by legal authority. Taking, under real or assumed authority, custody of another for the purpose of holding or detaining him or her to answer a criminal charge or civil demand.

ARRESTED (as to cargo) Seized.

ARTICLES OF INCORPORATION The basic document filed with the appropriate governmental agency upon the incorporation of a business. The contents are prescribed in the general incorporation statutes but generally include the name, purpose, agent for service of process, authorized number of shares, and classes of stock of a corporation. It is executed by the incorporator(s). Also called the charter or the certificate of incorporation.

ARTICLES OF ORGANIZATION The charter document for a limited liability company. Also called certificate of formation.

ASSAULT An intent to create a well-grounded apprehension of an immediate harmful or offensive contact. Generally, assault also requires some act (such as a threatening gesture) and the ability to follow through immediately with the battery.

ASSET LOCK-UP OPTION A lock-up option relating to assets of the target company.

ASSIGNMENT The transfer by a tenant of all or a portion of rented premises.

ASSUMPTION OF RISK The expressed or implied consent by plaintiff to defendant to take the chance of injury from a known and appreciated risk.

ASYMMETRIC INFORMATION Unequal information between parties.

AT-WILL CONTRACT An employment relationship of indefinite duration.

ATTACH If the three basic prerequisites of a security interest exist (agreement, value, and collateral), the security interest becomes enforceable between the parties and is said to attach. Also called attachment.

ATTORNEY-CLIENT PRIVILEGE The common law rule that a court cannot force the disclosure of confidential communications between client and client's attorney.

ATTRACTIVE NUISANCE RULE The duty imposed on landowner for liability for physical injury to child trespassers caused by artificial conditions on the land.

AUTHORITATIVE DECISION A court decision that must be followed regardless of its persuasive power, by virtue of relationship between the court that made decision and the court to which decision is cited.

AUTOMATIC CONVERSION The exchange of preferred stock for common stock that is triggered by specified events at a specified ratio.

AUTOMATIC STAY Feature of bankruptcy filing that instantly suspends most litigation and collection activities against the debtor, its property, or property of the bankruptcy estate.

AVOIDING POWERS The powers trustees can use to invalidate or reverse certain prebankruptcy transactions.

B

BACK-TO-BACK LETTER OF CREDIT A seller uses the letter of credit in its favor provided by the buyer to finance its purchase of products or materials from its supplier.

BACT (best available control technology) An emission limitation that the permitting authority determines achieves the maximum reduction of pollutants, taking into account energy, environmental, and economic considerations.

BAIT-AND-SWITCH ADVERTISING An area of deceptive pricing in which an advertiser refuses to show an advertised item, fails to have a reasonable quantity of the item in stock, fails to promise to deliver the item within a reasonable time, or discourages employees from selling the item.

BANKRUPTCY ESTATE Virtually all of a debtor's existing assets, less exempt property.

BASE RATE The lowest rate of interest publicly offered by major lending institutions to their most creditworthy customers. Also called reference rate or prime rate.

BASELINE ASSESSMENT The appraisal performed by a tenant that establishes the environmental condition of leased property at the commencement and termination of the lease.

BATTERY The intentional, non-consensual harmful or offensive contact with an individual's body or with those things in contact with or closely connected with it.

BATTLE OF THE FORMS An exchange of forms by a buyer and seller of goods in which each party claims that its own form represents the actual terms of the contract.

BENEFICIAL OWNER A person is considered to be a beneficial owner of any securities held by his or her immediate family, spouse, any minor children, and any other relative living in his or her household.

BENEFICIARY An individual who is benefited by a trust or a will.

BESPEAKS CAUTION DOCTRINE A doctrine whereby a court may determine that the inclusion of sufficient cautionary statements in a prospectus or other document renders immaterial any misrepresentations and omissions contained therein.

BEST ALTERNATIVE TO A NEGOTIATED AGREEMENT (BATNA) The outcome a person will choose if the negotiation fails.

BEST AVAILABLE CONTROL TECHNOLOGY (BACT) An emission limitation that the permitting authority determines achieves the maximum reduction of pollutants, taking into account energy, environmental, and economic considerations.

BEST AVAILABLE TECHNOLOGY ECONOMICALLY ACHIEVABLE (BAT) For toxic pollutants, BAT represents the best economically achievable performance in the category.

BEST CONVENTIONAL POLLUTANT CONTROL TECHNOLOGY (BCT) For conventional pollutants, BCT is intended to prevent unnecessarily stringent treatment that might be required under BAT.

BEST-EFFORTS UNDERWRITING An agreement among underwriters of an offering to use their best efforts to find buyers at an agreed on price.

BEST INTERESTS OF CREDITORS TEST In a Chapter 13 bankruptcy case, dissenters must be given a bundle of rights the current value of which is at least as great as the distribution they would receive through a Chapter 7 liquidation.

BEST MODE The best way the inventor knows of making an invention at the time of filing the patent application.

BEST PRACTICABLE CONTROL TECHNOLOGY CURRENTLY AVAILABLE (BPT) The average of the best existing performances by industrial plants of various sizes and ages within a point source category.

BFOQ DEFENSE Civil Rights Act of 1964 provision that states that it is not an unlawful employment practice for an employer to hire and employ an individual on the basis of his or her religion, sex, or national origin where religion, sex, or national origin is a bona fide occupational qualification reasonably necessary to the normal operation of that particular business or enterprise.

BID RIGGING An agreement between or among competitors to rig contract bids.

BIDDER The party who makes a tender offer.

BILATERAL CONTRACT A promise given in exchange for another promise.

BILL OF ATTAINDER A law enacted to punish individuals or an easily ascertainable member of a group. Prohibited by Article I, Section 9, of the U.S. Constitution.

BILL OF LADING The document carrier issues to seller that indicates what goods the carrier has received from the seller, the loading location, the names of the carrying vessel, and the destination.

BLANK CHECK COMPANY A development-stage company that has no specific business plan or whose business plan is to acquire a presently unknown business.

BLUE-SKY LAWS A popular name for the state statutes that regulate and supervise offerings and sales of securities to persons in that state.

BOILERPLATE Standardized text.

BOND Long-term corporate indebtedness.

BOUND TARIFFS The WTO principle that holds that each time tariffs are reduced, they may not be raised again.

BREAK-UP FEE An amount agreed to in a merger agreement to be paid to a friendly suitor company if the agreement with the target company is not consummated through no fault of the friendly suitor company.

BURDEN OF PROOF The requirement of a prosecutor in a criminal case to establish a defendant's guilt beyond a reasonable doubt.

BUSINESS JUDGMENT RULE In a case challenging a board decision, this rule holds that as long as directors have made an informed decision and are not interested in the transaction being considered, a court will not question whether the directors' action was wise or whether they made an error of judgment or a business mistake.

BUST-UP TAKEOVER A takeover in which the corporation, upon acquisition, is taken apart and its assets sold.

BYLAWS The internal rules governing a corporation.

C

C CORPORATION A business organization that is taxed at both the entity level and the owner level.

CALL A LOAN To terminate a loan.

CAPACITY The ability (requisite presence of mind) to enter into a binding contract.

CARTEL A group of competitors that agrees to set prices.

CAVEAT EMPTOR **(let the buyer beware)** This maxim summarizes the rule that a purchaser must examine, judge, and test for himself or herself. It does not apply where strict liability, warranty, or other consumer protection laws protect consumer-buyers.

CD Certificate of deposit.

CEASE AND DESIST ORDER An order of an administrative agency or court prohibiting a person or business firm from continuing a particular course of conduct.

CERT. DENIED Indicates that a writ of certiorari was sought but denied by the Supreme Court.

CERTIFICATE OF DEPOSIT (CD) RATE The CD rate is based on the average of the bid rates quoted to the bank by dealers in the secondary market for the purchase at face value of certificates of deposit of the bank in a given amount and for a given term.

CERTIFICATE OF FORMATION The charter document for a limited liability company. Also called articles of organization.

CERTIFICATE OF INCORPORATION The basic document filed with the appropriate governmental agency upon the incorporation of a business. The contents are prescribed in the general incorporation statutes but generally include the name, purpose, agent for service of process, authorized number of shares, and classes of stock of a corporation. It is executed by the incorporator(s). Also called the charter or the articles of incorporation.

CERTIFICATION MARK A mark placed on a product or used in connection with a service that indicates that the product or service in question has met the standards of safety or quality that have been created and advertised by the certifier.

CERTIORARI A writ of common law origin issued by a superior to an inferior court requiring the latter to produce a certified record of a particular case tried in the inferior court. The U.S. Supreme Court uses the writ as a discretionary device to choose the cases it wishes to hear.

CHECK KITING The issuing of checks from bank accounts with nonexisting funds to cover overdrafts created at other bank accounts.

CHOICE-OF-FORUM CLAUSE The clause in a contract wherein the parties agree in advance in which jurisdiction a dispute arising out of their agreement is to be litigated.

CHURNING A practice whereby insurance agents write new policies for customers and pay for the new policies with the cash value of existing policies.

CIRCUMSTANTIAL EVIDENCE The indirect (not based on personal knowledge or observation) evidence of certain facts that, taken alone, do not prove a particular conclusion but, if taken as a whole, give a trier of fact a reasonable basis for asserting a certain conclusion is true.

CLAIMS (under patent law) The description of those elements of an invention that will be protected by the patent.

CLASS ACTION SUIT A suit filed on behalf of all persons who have allegedly been harmed by a defendant's conduct.

CLASSIFIED BOARD A board on which directors serve for specified terms, usually three years, with only a fraction of them up for re-election at any one time. Also called staggered board.

CLEAN BILL OF LADING Bill of lading that has no notations indicating defects or damage to the goods when they were received for transport.

CLIFF VESTING A common vesting schedule that provides that if a person granted stock options leaves in the first year of employment, he or she forfeits all rights to any stock.

CLOSE CORPORATION A corporation owned by a limited number of shareholders, usually 30, most of whom are actively involved in the management of the corporation, that elects close corporation status in its charter.

CODE OF FEDERAL REGULATIONS (CFR) A multi-volume codification of federal regulations and rules.

CODIFY To collect and arrange items, such as statutes or regulations, systematically.

COLLATERAL The property belonging to a borrower that will become the lender's if the loan is not repaid.

COLLECTIVE ENTITY DOCTRINE Under this doctrine, the custodian of records for a collective entity (such as a corporation) may not resist a subpoena for such records on the ground that the act of production will incriminate him or her.

COMMERCIAL ACTIVITY EXCEPTION An exception to the blanket immunity from suits provided by the Foreign Sovereign Immunity Act for cases in which the foreign state was engaged in commercial activities.

COMMERCIAL IMPOSSIBILITY An excuse for nonperformance of a contract because of dramatic changes in circumstances or the relative benefits and burdens of the contract to each party.

COMMERCIAL IMPRACTICABILITY Section 2-615 of the Uniform Commercial Code states that unless the contract provides otherwise, a failure to perform is not a breach if performance is made impractical by an event unforeseen by the contract.

COMMERCIAL LEASE A contract that conveys an interest in real property from the landlord to the tenant and governs the respective rights and obligations of the parties during the lease term.

COMMERCIAL PAPER Short-term corporate indebtedness.

COMMITMENT FEE The fee payable to a lender in connection with a revolving loan as consideration for its promise to keep the commitment available, as it receives no interest on amounts not borrowed.

COMMON LAW The legal rules made by judges when they decide a case in which no constitution, statute, or regulation resolves the dispute.

COMMON MARKET The customs union in which there are no tariffs on trade among its members, and a single set of tariffs applies to goods imported from outside the union.

COMMON STOCK Stock that subjects all the shareholders to the same rights and restrictions.

COMMUNITY PROPERTY The property acquired during marriage with assets earned by either spouse during the marriage.

COMPARATIVE FAULT The liability of an injured party because of misuse or abuse of manufacturer's product.

COMPARATIVE NEGLIGENCE The doctrine by which courts decide amount of award to be given a plaintiff based on the amount (percentage) of negligence plaintiff demonstrated when injured by defendant.

COMPENSATION TRADE An international transaction in which a foreign party transfers use and/or eventual ownership of a good, usually equipment, to the local party, who then repays the foreign party with products produced using the foreign party's equipment.

COMPENSATORY (ACTUAL) DAMAGES The amount required to repair or to replace an item or the decrease in market value caused by tortious conduct. Compensatory damages restore the injured party to the position he or she was in prior to the injury.

COMPENSATORY JUSTICE Aims at compensating people for the harm done by another.

COMPLAINT The statement of plaintiff's grievance that makes allegations of the particular facts giving rise to dispute and states the legal reason why plaintiff is entitled to a remedy, the request for relief, the explanation why the court applied to has jurisdiction over the dispute, and whether plaintiff requests a jury trial.

COMPOSITION A reduction in the amount payable to creditors pursuant to a composition plan.

COMPOSITION PLAN An agreement between an insolvent debtor and his or her creditors whereby the creditors agree to accept a sooner payment of less than the whole amount in satisfaction of the whole amount.

COMPUTER FRAUD The unauthorized access of a computer used by the federal government, or by various types of financial institutions with the intent to alter, damage, or destroy information or to prevent authorized use of the such computers.

COMPUTER PIRACY The theft or misuse of computer software or hardware.

CONCERTED ACTIVITY (NLRA) The exercise by employees of their rights to band together for mutual aid and protection that is engaged in with or on the authority of other employees and not solely by and on behalf of one employee.

CONDITION PRECEDENT A condition that must be met before the lender's obligations arise under a loan agreement.

CONDITION SUBSEQUENT In contracts, a provision giving one party the right to divest itself of liability and obligation to perform further if the other party fails to meet the condition.

CONDITIONAL USE PERMIT A method of relief from the strict terms of a zoning ordinance that provides for other uses of real property that are not permitted as a matter of right, but for which a use permit must be obtained.

CONDITIONS CONCURRENT Conditions that are mutually dependent and are to be performed at the same time or simultaneously.

CONFIRMING BANK A bank located in the seller's jurisdiction that makes a legal commitment to the seller that it will honor the terms of the letter of credit issued by the issuing bank in the buyer's jurisdiction.

CONFLICT OF LAWS When choice of law is disputed, the court in which the suit is filed will apply conflict of laws principles to determine which state's or country's laws should govern the dispute. They usually focus on the significance of each country's relationship to the parties and the contract.

CONGLOMERATE MERGER A combination of firms that were not competitors at the time of the acquisition, but that may, absent the merger, have become competitors.

CONSENT DECREE A judgment entered by the consent of the parties whereby the defendant agrees to stop the alleged illegal activity without admitting guilt or wrongdoing. Also called consent order.

CONSEQUENTIAL DAMAGES Compensation for losses that occur as a foreseeable result of a breach of contract. Actual damages represent the damage, loss, or injury that flows directly and immediately from the act of the other party; in contrast, consequential damages refer to damage, loss or injury flowing from some of the consequences or results of such act.

CONSIDERATION A thing of value (money, services, an object, a promise, forbearance, or giving up the right to do something) exchanged in a contract.

CONSTRUCTION (of a statute) Interpretation.

CONSTRUCTIVE NOTICE Notice attributed by the existence of a properly recorded deed.

CONSTRUCTIVE TRUST A trust imposed on profits derived from a corporate opportunity taken by an officer, director, or controlling shareholder for personal gain when corporate opportunity was discovered during the course of business for the corporation.

CONTINUING GUARANTY A guaranty that covers all future obligations of the primary debtor to the lender.

CONTRIBUTION The doctrine that provides for the distribution of loss among several defendants by requiring each to pay its proportionate share to one who has discharged the joint liability of the group.

CONTRIBUTORY INFRINGEMENT One party knowingly sells an item that has one specific use that will result in the infringement of another's patent.

CONTRIBUTORY NEGLIGENCE Plaintiff was negligent in some manner when injured by defendant.

CONTROLLING SHAREHOLDER A shareholder who owns sufficient shares to outvote the other shareholders, and thus to control the corporation.

CONTROLLING-PERSON LIABILITY A person (or other entity), usually an officer or director of a company, responsible and liable for a securities violation.

CONVERSION The exercise of dominion and control over the personal property, rather than the real property (land), of another. Term includes any unauthorized act that deprives an owner of his or her personal property permanently or for an indefinite time.

CONVERTIBLE DEBT INSTRUMENT The document that permits conversion of debt principal into stock.

CONVERTIBLE PREFERRED STOCK Preferred stock that may be converted into common stock at a specified exchange ratio.

CONVEYANCE An instrument transferring an interest in real estate, such as a deed or lease.

COPYRIGHT The legal right to prevent others from copying the expression embodied in a protected work.

CORPORATE CHARTER The document issued by a state agency or authority granting a corporation legal existence and the right to function as a corporation.

CORPORATE DOMICILE The state under whose laws a corporation is formed.

CORPORATE OPPORTUNITY DOCTRINE The doctrine that holds that a business opportunity cannot legally be taken advantage of by an officer, director, or controlling shareholder if it is in the corporation's line of business.

CORPORATION An organization authorized by state law to act as a legal entity distinct from its owners.

CORPORATION BY ESTOPPEL When a third party, in all its transactions with an enterprise, acts as if it were doing business with a corporation, the third party is prevented or estopped from claiming that the enterprise is not a corporation.

COUNTERCLAIM A legal claim by defendant in opposition to or deduction from claim of plaintiff.

COUNTEROFFER A new offer by the initial offeree that rejects and modifies the terms originally proposed by the offeror.

COUNTERTRADE A foreign investor uses its local currency profits to purchase local products for sale abroad.

COUNTERVAILING DUTY LAW The law that provides that if a U.S. industry is materially injured by imports of a product benefiting from a foreign subsidy, an import duty that offsets the amount of the benefit must be imposed on those imports.

COUNTERVAILING SUBSIDY The benefits provided by a government to stimulate exports.

COVENANT The borrower's promise to the lender that it will or will not take specific actions as long as either a commitment or a loan is outstanding.

COVENANT NOT TO COMPETE An agreement, generally part of a contract of employment or a contract to sell a business, in which the covenantor agrees for a specific period of time and within a particular area to refrain from competition with the convenantee.

COVER In the case of a seller failing to make delivery of goods, cover refers to buyer's legal remedy of buying the goods elsewhere and recovering the cost of the substitute goods.

CRAM DOWN A bankruptcy relief plan confirmed over the objections of creditors.

CREDITOR BENEFICIARY Third party to a contract that the promisee enters into in order to discharge a duty to said third party.

CRIME An offense against the public at large; an act that violates the duties owed to the community, for which the offender must make satisfaction to the public.

CROSS-COLLATERALIZATION The collateral for one loan is used to secure obligations under another loan.

CROSS-DEFAULT Any breach by the borrower under any other loan agreement will constitute an event of default under the subject loan agreement.

CROSS-ELASTICITY OF DEMAND The extent to which consumers will change their consumption of one product in response to a price change in another.

CROWN JEWELS The most valuable assets or divisions of a target company in a takeover battle.

CUMULATIVE VOTING The process by which a shareholder can cast all its votes for one director nominee or allocate them among nominees as it sees fit.

CUSTOMER RESTRICTIONS Restrictions that prevent a dealer or distributor from selling to a certain class of customer.

CUSTOMS UNION A group of countries that reduce or eliminate tariffs between themselves, but establish a common tariff for trading with all other states.

CUSTOMS VALUATION The value assigned to an imported article by the U.S. Customs Service.

D

D'OENCH, DUHME DOCTRINE A doctrine that bars many claims and defenses against conservators and receivers that might have been valid against the failed bank or savings and loan itself. It bars enforcement of agreements unless those agreements are in writing and have been approved contemporaneously by the bank's board or loan committee and recorded in the bank's written records.

DE FACTO (in fact) CORPORATION When incorporators cannot show substantial compliance with incorporation requirements, a court may find a corporation is a de facto corporation (corporation in fact) even though it is not technically a corporation by law, if the incorporators demonstrate that they were unaware of the defect and that they made a good faith effort to incorporate correctly.

DE JURE (by law) CORPORATION When incorporators have substantially complied with incorporation requirements, the entity is a de jure corporation (a corporation by right).

DE NOVO (new) PROCEEDING An administrative agency's decision is appealed and case goes to court to be litigated from the beginning.

DEALER (1933 Act) Any person who engages either for all or part of his or her time, directly or indirectly, as agent, broker, or principal, in the business of offering, buying, selling, or otherwise dealing or trading in securities issued by another person.

DEBT SECURITIES The documents indicating that a corporation has incurred a debt by borrowing money from the holder of the document.

DEBT SUBORDINATION An agreement whereby one or more creditors of a common debtor agree to defer payment of their claims until another creditor of the same debtor is fully paid.

DEBTOR (under the UCC) The person who owes payment or other performance of the obligation secured, whether or not that person owns or has rights in the collateral.

DEBTOR IN POSSESSION Under a Chapter 11 bankruptcy, debtor may, for the benefit of all concerned, be left in possession of the bankruptcy estate.

DECISION A form of European Union legislation in which an order is directed at a specific person or member state.

DECLARATION BY THE INVENTOR Part of a patent application, the declaration by the inventor states that the inventor has reviewed the application and that he or she believes that he or she is the first inventor of the invention.

DECLARATORY JUDGMENT ACTION A lawsuit that seeks only a judicial order articulating the legal rights and responsibilities of the parties, rather than monetary damages.

DEED A written document transferring an interest in real estate that is recorded at a public office where title documents are filed.

DEED OF TRUST A loan to buy real property secured by a lien on the real property. Also called a mortgage.

DEFAMATION The intentional communication to a third party of an untrue statement of fact that injures the plaintiff's reputation or good name, by exposing the plaintiff to hatred, ridicule or contempt.

DEFAULT JUDGMENT A judgment that may be entered in favor of the plaintiff if the defendant does not file an answer within the time required.

DEFENDANT The person defending or denying; the party against whom relief or recovery is sought in an action or suit. The accused in a criminal case.

DELAWARE COURT OF CHANCERY The trial court in Delaware that hears corporate law cases.

DEMAND RIGHTS An investor's right to require an issuer to register a stated portion of the investor's shares in a public offering.

DEONTOLOGICAL THEORY An ethical theory that focuses on the motivation behind an action rather than the consequences of an action.

DEPOSITION The written or oral questioning of any person who may have helpful information about the facts of a case.

DERIVATIVE INSIDER A person, such as a tippee, upon whom the insider's duty of disclosure is imposed.

DESCRIPTIVE MARK The identifying marks that directly describe (size, color, use of) the goods sold under the mark.

DESIGN DEFECT A type of product defect that occurs when the product is manufactured according to specifications, but its inadequate design or poor choice of materials causes it to be defective.

DESIGN PATENT A patent that protects any novel, original, and ornamental design for an article of manufacture.

DETOUR A temporary turning aside from a usual or regular route, course, or procedure, or from a task or employment. To be distinguished from a frolic, which is outside of an agent's scope of employment.

DETRIMENTAL RELIANCE Occurs when an offeree has changed his or her position because of justifiable reliance on an offer.

DEVELOPMENT LOANS Loans used for the acquisition, subdivision, improvement, and sale of residential properties.

DIRECT INFRINGEMENT The making, use, or sale of any patented invention in the jurisdiction where it is patented during the term of the patent.

DIRECTED VERDICT After the presentation of evidence in a trial before jury, either party may assert that other side has not produced enough evidence to support the legal claim or defense alleged. The moving party then requests that the judge take the case away from the jury and direct that a verdict be entered in favor of the moving party.

DIRECTIVE A form of European Union legislation that is a law directing member states to enact certain laws or regulations.

DISAPPEARING CORPORATION In a merger of two corporations, the corporation that no longer maintains its separate corporate existence is the disappearing corporation.

DISCHARGE Relieve.

DISCLOSURE OF PRIOR ART A part of patent application that discusses pre-existing art that relates to a claimed invention.

DISCOVERY OF INJURY STATUTES Statutes that provide that the statute of limitations does not begin to run until the person discovers the injury.

DISCOVERY The process through which parties to a lawsuit collect evidence to support their claims.

DISCOVERY RULE The statute of limitations period does not accrue until the injured party discovers or, by using reasonable diligence, should have discovered the injury.

DISPARAGEMENT Untrue statements derogatory to the quality or ownership of a plaintiff's goods or services, that the defendant knows are false, or to the truth of which the defendant is consciously indifferent.

DISPARATE IMPACT The systematic exclusion of women, ethnic groups, or others in a protected class from employment through testing and other selection procedures.

DISPARATE TREATMENT Intentional discrimination against a person by employer by denying the person employment or a benefit or privilege of employment because of race, religion, sex, national origin, age, or disability.

DISPUTE NEGOTIATION Backward looking negotiation that addresses past events that have caused disagreement.

DISSOLUTION The designation of the point in time when partners no longer carry on their business together.

DISTRIBUTIVE JUSTICE A theory of justice that looks to how the burden and benefits of a particular situation of a system are distributed.

DISTRIBUTIVE NEGOTIATIONS Negotiations in which the only issue is the distribution of the fixed pie. Also called zero-sum negotiations.

DIVERSITY JURISDICTION The power of U.S. District Courts to decide lawsuits between citizens of two different states when amount in controversy, exclusive of interest and all costs, exceeds $50,000.

DOCTRINE OF EQUIVALENTS The doctrine that holds that a direct infringement of a patent has occurred when a patent is not literally copied, but is replicated to the extent that the infringer has created a product or process that works in substantially the same way and accomplishes substantially the same result as the patented invention.

DOCTRINE OF SELF-PUBLICATION A defamatory communication by an employer to an employee may constitute publication if the employer could foresee that the employee would be required to repeat the communication, for instance, to a prospective employer.

DOMINANT STRATEGY The strategy that is always superior to the alternatives.

DONEE BENEFICIARY Third party to a contract to whom promisee does not owe an obligation, but rather wishes to confer a gift or a right of performance.

DOUBLE JEOPARDY Fifth Amendment guarantee that protects against a second prosecution for the same offense after acquittal or conviction, and against multiple punishments for the same offense.

DRAGNET CLAUSE In a security agreement, a provision giving the secured party a security interest in all the debtor's property and in the proceeds from the sale of such property.

DRAM SHOP ACT A statute that makes a tavern liable for damage or injury caused by a drunk driver who was served drinks even though visibly intoxicated.

DRAWINGS The drawings (except in chemical cases) must show the claimed invention in graphic form.

DRUG Defined by the Food, Drug and Cosmetic Act to include (1) articles intended for use in the diagnosis, cure, mitigation, treatment, or prevention of disease; and (2) articles (other than food) intended to affect the structure or any function of the body.

DUAL AGENCY In a real estate transaction, a broker acts for both the buyer and the seller.

DUAL DISTRIBUTOR A manufacturer that sells its goods both at wholesale and at retail.

DUE DILIGENCE The identification and characterization of risks associated with property and operations involved in various business transactions. A defense available to a defendant (other than the issuer) in a securities violation case concerning a registration statement who (1) conducted a reasonable investigation, and (2) reasonably believed that (a) the statements made were true, and (b) that there were no omissions that made those statements misleading.

DUMPING Sale of imported products in the United States below the current selling price in the exporter's home market or below the exporter's cost of production.

DURESS Coercion.

DUTIABLE Import articles subject to required payment.

DUTY (1) The obligation to act as a reasonably prudent person would act under the circumstances to prevent an unreasonable risk of harm to others. (2) The required payment on imports.

DUTY OF CARE The fiduciary duty of agents, officers, and directors to act with the same care that a reasonably prudent person would exercise under similar circumstances. Sometimes expressed as the duty to use the same level of care a reasonably prudent person would use in the conduct of his or her own affairs.

DUTY OF LOYALTY The fiduciary duty of agents, officers, and directors to act in good faith and in what they believe to be the best interest of the principal or the corporation.

E

EARLY NEUTRAL EVALUATION (ENE) A dispute resolution mechanism whereby a neutral attorney familiar with the law in the area reviews the case and offers each side his or her evaluation of the strengths and weaknesses.

ECONOMIC DURESS The coercion of the borrower, threatening to do an unlawful act that might injure the borrower's business or property.

ECONOMIC STRIKE A union strikes employers when they are unable to extract acceptable terms and conditions of employment through collective bargaining.

EFFICIENT-MARKET THEORY The theory that holds that in an open and developed securities market, the price of a company's stock equals its true value.

EFFLUENT LIMITATIONS The regulations designed to impose increasingly stringent limitations on pollutant discharges based on the availability of economic treatment and recycling technologies.

EMBEZZLEMENT The acquisition by an employee of money or property by reason of some office or position, which money or property the employee takes for personal use.

EMINENT DOMAIN The power of state and federal governments to take private property for government uses for which property owners are entitled to just compensation.

EMPLOYER One who employs the services of others; one for whom employees work, and who pays their wages or salaries.

ENCUMBRANCE A claim against real property.

ENTERPRISE Any individual, partnership, corporation, association, or other legal entity, and any union or group of individuals associated in fact although not a legal entity.

ENTRENCHMENT Entrenchment occurs when a director opposes a transaction in order to maintain a place on the corporation's board.

ENVIRONMENTAL ASSESSMENT (EA) A document that identifies any significant impact of a development on the environment.

ENVIRONMENTAL IMPACT STATEMENT (EIS) A required document for any proposal for legislation or other major governmental action that may significantly affect the quality of the environment.

ENVIRONMENTAL JUSTICE The notion that decisions with environmental consequences (such as where to locate incinerators, dumps, factories, and other sources of pollution) should not discriminate against poor and minority communities.

ENVIRONMENTAL LAWS The numerous federal, state, and local laws with the common objective of protecting human health and the environment.

ENVIRONMENTAL PROTECTION AGENCY (EPA) Federal agency that administers all of the federal laws that set national goals and policies for environmental protection, except for the National Environmental Policy Act, which is administered by the Council on Environmental Quality.

EQUAL DIGNITIES RULE Under this rule if an agent acts on behalf of another (its principal) in signing an agreement of the type that must under the statute of frauds be in writing, the authority of the agent to act on behalf of the principal must also be in writing.

EQUITABLE RELIEF An injunction issued by the court to prohibit a defendant from continuing in a certain course of activity or to require a defendant to perform a certain activity.

EQUITABLE SUBORDINATION The doctrine that prevents one creditor, through fraud or other wrongful conduct, from increasing its recovery at the expense of other creditors of the same debtor.

EQUITY The value of real property that exceeds the liens against it.

EQUITY CAPITAL The cash or property contributed to an enterprise in exchange for an ownership interest.

EQUITY SECURITY (Section 16(b)) An equity security includes (1) any stock or similar security; (2) any security that is convertible, with or without consideration, into such a security; (3) any security carrying any warrant or right to purchase such a security; (4) any such warrant or right; and (5) any other security that the Securities and Exchange Commission (SEC) deems to be of a similar nature and that, for the protection of investors or in the public interest, the SEC considers appropriate to treat as an equity security.

***ERIE* DOCTRINE** In a diversity action in federal court, except as to matters governed by the U.S. Constitution and acts of Congress, the law to be applied in any case is the law of the state in which the federal court is situated.

ESCROW The system by which a neutral stakeholder (escrow agent) allows parties to a real property transaction to fulfill the various conditions of the closing of the transaction without the physical difficulties of passing instruments and funds between the parties.

ESCROW AGENT A neutral stakeholder who facilitates the transfer of real property between interested parties.

ESSENTIAL FACILITY Some resource necessary to a company's rival's survival that they cannot economically or feasibly duplicate.

ESTOPPED A defendant is legally barred from alleging or denying a certain fact when the defendant's words and/or actions have been to the contrary.

EURO The name of the currency for the European Monetary Union.

EVENT RISKS Changes in the structure of a corporation such as leveraged buyouts, mergers, or hostile takeovers that affect the credit rating or riskiness of outstanding debt.

EVENTS OF DEFAULT The events contained in a loan agreement that will trigger the lender's right to terminate the loan, accelerate the repayment obligations, and, if the loan is secured, take possession of the property securing the loan.

***EX POST FACTO* LAWS (after the fact)** The laws prohibited by the U.S. Constitution that punish actions that were not illegal when performed.

EXCLUSIONARY RULE The evidence obtained in a warrantless search cannot be introduced into evidence at trial against a defendant.

EXCLUSIVE DEALERSHIP (DISTRIBUTORSHIP) An agreement in which a manufacturer limits itself to a single dealer or distributor in a given territory.

EXCLUSIVITY CLAUSE Limits or prevents the operation of a competing store in a shopping center.

EXECUTIVE PRIVILEGE The type of immunity granted the president against the forced disclosure of presidential communications made in the exercise of executive power.

EXECUTORY CONTRACT Contracts that have not yet been performed and involve an exchange of promises.

EXEMPLARY DAMAGES Damages awarded to a plaintiff over and above what will fairly compensate it for its loss. They are intended to punish the defendant and deter others from engaging in similar conduct. Also called punitive damages.

EXEMPT PROPERTY Excluded from a bankruptcy estate, and intended to provide for the individual's future needs. Generally includes a homestead, motor vehicles, household or personal items, tools of the debtor's trade, health aids, personal injury awards, alimony or support payments, disability or retirement benefits (including IRAs), life insurance or annuities, and some special deposits of cash.

EXHAUSTION OF ADMINISTRATIVE REMEDIES A court will not entertain an appeal from the administrative process until an agency has had a chance to act and all possible avenues of relief before the agency have been fully pursued.

EXIT VEHICLE A way for investors to get their money back without liquidating a company, for example, through acquisition by a larger company or through an initial public offering of the company's securities.

EXPECTATION DAMAGES In the case of breach of contract, refers to remuneration that puts a plaintiff into the cash position the plaintiff would have been in if the contract had been fulfilled.

EXPRESS RATIFICATION Express ratification occurs when the principal, through words or behavior, manifests an intent to be bound by the agent's act.

EXPRESS WARRANTY An explicit guarantee by the seller that the goods purchased by a buyer will have certain qualities.

EXTENSION PLAN A plan by which creditors are repaid the entire indebtedness, but the period for payment is extended beyond the original due date.

EXTORTIONATE EXTENSION OF CREDIT Making a loan for which violence is understood by the parties as likely to occur in the event of nonpayment.

F

FAILURE TO WARN Failure of a product to carry adequate warnings of the risks involved in the normal use of the product.

FAIR TRADE LAW A federal law providing for temporary relief to domestic industries seriously injured by increasing imports, regardless of whether unfair practices are involved.

FAIR USE DOCTRINE The doctrine that protects from liability a defendant who has infringed a copyright owner's exclusive rights when countervailing public policies predominate. Activities such as literary criticism, social comment, news reporting, educational activities, scholarship, or research are traditional fair use domains.

FALSE IMPRISONMENT The confinement of an individual without that individual's consent and without lawful authority.

FAMILY RESEMBLANCE TEST A test for determining whether an instrument is a security by asking whether it bears a family resemblance to any nonsecurity.

FAST-TRACK AUTHORITY Legislation allowing the president to negotiate trade agreements and then submit them for an up or down vote by Congress with no amendments permitted.

FEDERAL ARBITRATION ACT (FAA) The federal law requiring courts to honor agreements to arbitrate and arbitration awards.

FEDERAL COMMON LAW The judicial interpretations of federal statutes and administrative regulations.

FEDERAL INTEREST COMPUTER A computer used by the federal government or by various types of financial institutions, or a computer that is one of two or more computers used in committing the offense, not all of which are located in the same state.

FEDERAL QUESTION When a dispute concerns federal law, namely, a legal right arising under the U.S. Constitution, a federal statute, an administrative regulation issued by a federal government agency, federal common law, or a treaty of the United States, it is said to raise a federal question.

FEDERAL RULES OF CIVIL PROCEDURE (FRCP) The procedural rules that govern civil litigation.

FEDERAL RULES OF EVIDENCE (FRE) Federal rules governing the admissibility of evidence in litigation in federal court.

FEDERALISM The doctrine that serves to allocate power between the federal government and the various state governments.

FEE SIMPLE Title to property that grants owner full right of disposition during his or her lifetime and may be passed on to owner's heirs and assigns forever.

FELONY An offense punishable by death or prison term exceeding one year.

FETAL PROTECTION POLICY A company policy that bars a woman from certain jobs unless her inability to bear children is medically documented.

FICTITIOUS BUSINESS NAME The name of a business that is other than that of the owner.

FIDUCIARY A person having a duty to act primarily for the benefit of another in matters connected with undertaking fiduciary responsibilities.

FIDUCIARY DUTY The obligation of a trustee or other fiduciary to act for the benefit of the other party.

FIDUCIARY OUT The allowance in a merger agreement for directors of target company to remain faithful to their fiduciary duties to their shareholders (for example, by recommending other unsolicited offers) even after signing an agreement with a suitor company.

FILE-WRAPPER ESTOPPEL The doctrine that prevents a patent owner involved in infringement from introducing any evidence at odds with the information contained in the owner's application on file with the U.S. Patent and Trademark Office.

FINAL-OFFER ARBITRATION A form of arbitration used most notably in baseball salary disputes; each side submits its "best and final" offer to the arbitrator, who must choose one of the two proposals.

FINANCING LEASE Under a financing lease (commonly used to finance the acquisition of expensive capital equipment and vehicles such as airplanes, locomotives, and ships), the parties expect the lessee to purchase the leased equipment at the end of the lease term at an agreed-upon residual value.

FIRM OFFER (under the UCC) An offer signed by a merchant that indicates that the offer will be kept open is not revocable, for lack of consideration, during the time stated, or for a reasonable period of time if none is stated, but in no event longer than three months.

FIRM COMMITMENT UNDERWRITING The underwriters agree to purchase the entire offering, thus effectively shifting the risk of the offering from the issuer to the underwriters.

FIRST-MOVER ADVANTAGE The competitive advantage of being the first to produce a particular product and thereby perhaps establish the standard to which all related and competing products must adhere.

FIRST SALE DOCTRINE Once the copyright or trademark owner places a copyrighted or trademarked item in the stream of commerce by selling it, the owner has exhausted its exclusive statutory right to control its distribution.

FIXTURES (under the UCC) The items of personal property that are attached to real property and that cannot be removed without substantial damage to the item.

FLOAT The difference between the amount of funds credited to a bank account and the amount of funds actually collected for that account.

FLOATING INTEREST RATE An interest rate that fluctuates throughout the life of the loan according to the interest rate that the lender would pay if it borrowed the funds in order to relend them.

FLOATING LIEN In a security interest, if the collateral is sold, exchanged, collected, or otherwise disposed of, the security interest is equally effective against cash, account, or whatever else is received from the transaction.

FOOD Defined by the Food, Drug and Cosmetic Act as (1) articles used for food or drink; (2) chewing gum; and (3) articles used for components of either.

FORECLOSE To take possession of the collateral and either sell it to pay off the debt or keep it in satisfaction of the debt.

FOREIGN CORPORATION A corporation doing business in one state though chartered or incorporated in another state is a foreign corporation as to the first state.

FOREIGN TRADE ZONE A special area within or adjacent to U.S. ports of entry, where import duties on merchandise normally due upon entry into the United States are not due until the merchandise is withdrawn from the zone.

FORGOTTEN FOUNDER A problem that can arise when several persons work together on an informal basis with a common business objective, and then one leaves. The person who left (the forgotten founder) may have ownership rights in the enterprise.

FORM S–1 The registration statement used in an initial public offering of securities.

FORM S–2 A form of registration statement that allows public companies to present certain information in a streamlined form and to incorporate previous filings by reference.

FORM S–3 A form of registration statement that is available to companies that have filed periodic reports under the Securities Exchange Act of 1934 for at least three years and have a widespread following in the marketplace.

FORM S–4 A combined securities registration statement and proxy statement.

FORM SB–1 Allows nonreporting and transitional small business issuers to register up to $10 million of securities annually.

FORM SB–2 A form for registration of any amount of securities by small business issuers.

FORUM NON CONVENIENS A doctrine whereby a suit is dismissed because an alternate, more convenient forum is available.

FORUM SHOPPING A party to a lawsuit attempts to have a case tried in a particular court or jurisdiction where party feels the most favorable judgment or verdict will be received.

FRANCHISE A business relationship in which one party (the franchisor) grants to another party (the franchisee) the right to use the franchisor's name and logo and to distribute the franchisor's products from a specified locale.

FRAUD Any intentional deception that has the purpose of inducing another in reliance upon the deception to part with some property or money. Fraud may involve false representations of fact, whether by words or conduct, false allegations, omission (especially by fiduciary), or concealment of something that should have been disclosed.

FRAUD IN THE FACTUM A type of fraud that occurs when a party is persuaded to sign one document thinking that it is another.

FRAUD IN THE INDUCEMENT A type of fraud that occurs when a party makes a false statement to persuade the other party to enter into an agreement.

FRAUD ON THE MARKET The theory that holds that if the information about a company available to the market is incorrect, then the market price will not reflect the true value of the stock.

FRAUD-CREATED-THE-MARKET THEORY A theory accepted by some courts whereby a plaintiff need not prove reliance in securities fraud cases when the alleged fraud is so pervasive that without it the issuer would not have been able to sell the securities because the information would have shown them to be worthless.

FRAUDULENT CONVEYANCE The direct or indirect transfer of assets to a third party with actual intent to defraud or have inadequate consideration in circumstances when the transferor is insolvent.

FRAUDULENT MISREPRESENTATION Deceit; intentionally misleading by making material misrepresentations of fact that the plaintiff relied on that cause injury to the plaintiff.

FREE TRADE AREA A free trade area is created when a group of countries reduce or eliminate tariffs among themselves, but maintain their own individual tariffs as to other states.

FREEZE-OUT MERGER In a merger with a controlling shareholder, some shareholders (usually the public shareholders) are required to surrender their shares in the disappearing corporation for cash.

FROLIC An activity by an employee that is entirely outside the employer's purpose. To be distinguished from a detour, which is within the scope of employment.

FRUIT OF THE POISONOUS TREE Evidence acquired directly or indirectly as a result of an illegal search or arrest.

FRUSTRATION OF PURPOSE Frustration of purpose occurs when performance is possible, but changed circumstances have made the contract useless to one or both of the parties.

FULL WARRANTY The warranty that gives the consumer the right to free repair or replacement of a defective product.

G

GAP FINANCING Financing that a developer obtains to pay off a construction loan when it becomes due before the permanent financing is available. Also called interim financing.

GARNISHMENT The legal procedure by which a creditor may collect a debt by attaching a portion of a debtor's weekly wages.

GENERAL PARTNERSHIP A form of business organization between two or more persons in which the partners share in the profits or losses of a common business enterprise.

GENERAL PLAN A long-range planning document that addresses the physical development and redevelopment of a city.

GENERAL RELEASE An agreement by person engaging in a dangerous activity to assume all risks and hold the party offering access to said dangerous activity free of all liability.

GEOGRAPHIC MARKET All firms that compete for sales in a given area at current prices, or would compete in that area if prices rose by a modest amount.

GOING EFFECTIVE Culmination of the securities registration process with the Securities and Exchange Commission. Sales can be legally consummated as of this date and time.

GOLDEN PARACHUTE A termination agreement that gives extra salary and other benefits to an executive upon a corporate change in control.

GOOD FAITH SUBSEQUENT PURCHASER A person who acquires real property for fair value without being aware of a disputed claim to the property.

GOODS (under the UCC) All things (including specially manufactured goods) that are movable at the time of identification to the contract for sale.

GOVERNMENT-CONTRACTOR DEFENSE The limited immunity available for manufacturers who produce products to the specifications of government contracts.

GRANT DEED A deed that contains implied warranties that the grantor has not previously conveyed the same property or any interest in it to another person and that the title is marketable.

GRANTEE A person to whom real property is conveyed.

GRANTOR A person conveying his or her real property.

GREENMAIL Payment by a target company to buy back shares owned by a potential acquirer at a premium over market. The acquirer in exchange agrees not to pursue its hostile takeover bid.

GROSS-UP CLAUSE The clause in foreign investment contracts by which local partner or licensee is obligated to pay all taxes other than those specifically allocated to the foreign partner.

GROUND LEASE A lease for land on which a building will be built.

GROUP BOYCOTT An agreement among competitors to refuse to deal with another competitor.

GUARANTOR The person who agrees to be liable for the obligation of another person.

GUARANTY An undertaking by one person to become liable for the obligation of another person.

GUARANTY OF COLLECTION Under a guaranty of collection, the guarantor becomes obliged to pay only after the lender has attempted unsuccessfully to collect the amount due from the primary debtor.

GUARANTY OF PAYMENT A provision that holds guarantor's obligation to pay the lender is triggered, immediately and automatically, if the primary debtor fails to make a payment when due.

GUARANTY OF PERFORMANCE A guaranty that specified nonpayment obligations will be performed.

GUARDIAN *AD LITEM* (guardian for the suit) A person authorized to bring suit for a minor.

GUN-JUMPING A violation of the securities laws that occurs when an issuer or underwriter conditions the market with a news article, press release, or speech about a company engaged in the registration of its securities.

H

HAZARD RANKING SCORE The Environmental Protection Agency ranking that represents the risks presented by certain sites to the environment and public health.

HAZARDOUS SUBSTANCE SUPERFUND Finances federal activity to investigate and take remedial action in response to a release or threatened release of hazardous substances to the environment.

HERFINDAHL-HIRSCHMAN INDEX (HHI) An aid to the interpretation of market data when determining the anticompetitive effect of a merger; the HHI of market concentration is calculated by summing the squares of the individual market shares of all the firms in the market.

HORIZONTAL AGREEMENT A conspiracy agreement between firms that compete with each other on the same level of production or distribution.

HORIZONTAL MARKET DIVISION An agreement among competitors to divide a market according to class of customer or geographic territory; it violates antitrust law.

HORIZONTAL MERGER A corporate combination of actual or prospective competitors.

HORIZONTAL PRICE FIXING An agreement between competitors at the same level of distribution to set a common price for a product. Horizontal price fixing violates antitrust law.

HOSTILE ENVIRONMENT HARASSMENT The creation of a hostile working environment, such as continually subjecting an employee to ridicule and racial slurs, or unwanted sexual advances.

HOSTILE TAKEOVER A transaction in which a third party (a raider) seeks to obtain control of a company (the target) over the objections of its management.

HUSHMAIL A repurchase of shares at a premium over market to ensure silence from a shareholder who has been critical of management.

I

IDENTIFICATION TO THE CONTRACT Setting aside or otherwise designating the particular goods for sale under a contract.

IDENTITY THEFT Taking an individual's information (such as Social Security number and mother's maiden name) and using that information to fraudulently obtain credit or commit other financial crimes.

ILLEGAL CONTRACT A contract is illegal if its formation or performance is expressly forbidden by a civil or criminal statute, or if a penalty is imposed for doing the act agreed upon.

ILLEGAL *PER SE* A practice that is illegal regardless of its impact on the market or its procompetitive justifications.

ILLUSORY PROMISE A promise that does not in fact confer any benefit on the promisor or subject the promisee to any detriment.

IMPAIRED CLAIM A claim is considered impaired if the bankruptcy relief plan does not provide for full cash payment on its effective date and it alters the creditors' legal, equitable, or contractual rights in any way (except by curing defaults and reinstating the maturity of the claim).

IMPLEMENTATION AFTER IMPASSE DOCTRINE The duty to bargain collectively in good faith prohibits an employer from unilaterally changing a term or condition of employment unless, after bargaining with the union to an impasse, the employer's unilateral changes are consistent with the union's pre-impasse proposal.

IMPLIED CONTRACT An employment agreement—implied from such facts as long-term employment; receipt of raises, bonuses and promotions; and assurance from management that the employee was doing a good job—that the employee would not be terminated except for good cause.

IMPLIED COVENANT OF GOOD FAITH AND FAIR DEALING An implied covenant in every contract that imposes on each party a duty not to do anything that will deprive the other party of the benefits of the agreement.

IMPLIED INTENT If a person does not intend a particular consequence of an act, but knew that the consequence of the act was certain, or substantially certain, and does the act anyway, intent to cause the consequence is implied.

IMPLIED RATIFICATION Implied ratification occurs when the principal, by his or her silence or failure to repudiate the agent's act, acquiesces in it.

IMPLIED WARRANTY OF FITNESS FOR A PARTICULAR PURPOSE The warranty whereby goods involving the following elements are judged satisfactory for the buyer's purpose: (1) the buyer must have a particular purpose for the goods; (2) the seller must have known or have had reason to know of that purpose; (3) the seller must have known or had reason to know that the buyer was relying on the seller's expertise; and (4) the buyer must have relied upon the seller.

IMPLIED WARRANTY OF MERCHANTABILITY The warranty by which all goods sold by merchants in the normal course of business must meet following criteria: (1) pass without objection in the trade under the contract description; (2) be fit for the ordinary purposes for which such goods are used; (3) be within the variations permitted by the agreement, of even kind, quality and quantity within each unit and among all units involved; (4) be adequately contained, packaged, and labeled as the agreement may require; and (5) conform to the promises or affirmations of fact made on the container or label, if any.

IMPOSSIBILITY An excuse for nonperformance based on the destruction of something vital to the performance of the contract or another unforeseen event that makes performance of the contract impossible.

IMPRACTICABILITY A situation in which performance is possible but is commercially impractical.

IMPROPER MEANS (UTSA) Deceitful actions through which party obtains trade secrets of another.

IMPUTED LIABILITY The imposition of civil or criminal liability on one party for the wrongful acts of another. Also called vicarious liability.

IN BANC (EN BANC) HEARING A hearing at which all the judges of a court of appeals sit together to hear and decide a particularly important or close case.

IN PERSONAM JURISDICTION Personal jurisdiction based upon the residence or activities of the person being sued. It is the power that a court has over the defendant itself, in contrast to the court's power over the defendant's interest in property (quasi in rem jurisdiction) or power over the property itself (in rem jurisdiction).

IN REM JURISDICTION Jurisdiction over property based upon the location of the property at issue in the lawsuit.

INCORPORATION The process by which a corporation is formed.

INDEMNIFICATION The doctrine that allows a defendant to recover its individual loss from a co-defendant whose relative blame is greater or who has contractually agreed to assume liability.

INDENTURE The agreement governing a bond issue.

INDEPENDENT CONTRACTOR A person is deemed to be an independent contractor only if the employer neither exercises control over the means of performing the work nor the end result of that work.

INDICTMENT Formal charges filed by a grand jury.

INDIRECT INFRINGEMENT One party's active inducement of another party to infringe a patent.

INEVITABLE DISCLOSURE DOCTRINE A doctrine that permits a former employer to prevent an employee from working for a competitor when the new position will require the employee to disclose or use the trade secrets of the former employer.

INFOMERCIAL An advertisement generally presented in the format of half-hour television talk shows or news programs.

INFORMAL DISCRETIONARY ACTION The administrative agencies' decision-making process for repetitive actions that are inappropriate to litigate in courts.

INFORMATION The formal charges filed with the court in a criminal case.

INHERENTLY DISTINCTIVE MARK Inherently distinctive marks (often called strong marks) are identifying marks that need no proof of distinctiveness.

INITIATIVE A formal petition generated by a certain percentage of the electorate to introduce legislative change.

INJUNCTION A remedy granted by the court that requires defendant to perform or cease from performing some activity.

INJURIOUS FALSEHOOD False statements knowingly made that lead to economic loss for a plaintiff.

INNOCENT LANDOWNER DEFENSE In a case under CERCLA, a potentially responsible current owner can assert this defense if the release or disposal of hazardous materials was by a third party who was not an employee and with whom the current owner had no contractual relationship. Also called the third-party defense.

INNOVATION OFFSETS Technological advantages gained by companies that met the challenge of environmental regulations and discovered lower costs and better quality products as a result.

INQUIRY NOTICE Notice attributed when reasonable inquiry would have disclosed an adverse interest, for example, if inspection of a property would have revealed that some person other than the grantor was in possession or owned the property.

INSIDE DIRECTOR A member of a board who is also an officer.

INSIDER A person with access to confidential information and an obligation of disclosure to other traders in the marketplace.

INSIDER TRADING Trading securities while in possession of material nonpublic information, in violation of a duty to the corporation or its shareholders or others.

INTEGRATION When an issuer makes successive sales of securities within a limited period of time, the Securities and Exchange Commission may integrate the successive sales; that is, it may deem them to be part of a single sale for purposes of deciding whether there was an exemption from registration.

INTEGRATED DISCLOSURE SYSTEM The system that seeks to eliminate duplicative or unnecessary disclosure requirements under the Securities Act of 1933 and the Securities Exchange Act of 1934.

the Board. Any member of the Board may be removed by the President, upon notice and hearing, for neglect of duty or malfeasance in office, but for no other cause.

Section 7. Rights of Employees.
Employees shall have the right to self-organization, to form, join, or assist labor organizations, to bargain collectively through representatives of their own choosing, and to engage in other concerted activities for the purpose of collective bargaining or other mutual aid or protection, and shall also have the right to refrain from any or all of such activities except to the extent that such right may be affected by an agreement requiring membership in a labor organization as a condition of employment as authorized in section 8(a) (3).

Section 8. Unfair Labor Practice.
(a) It shall be an unfair labor practice for an employer—

(1) to interfere with, restrain, or coerce employees in the exercise of the rights guaranteed in section 7;

(2) to dominate or interfere with the formation or administration of any labor organization or contribute financial or other support to it: Provide, that subject to rules and regulations made and published by the Board pursuant to section 6, an employer shall not be prohibited from permitting employees to confer with him during working hours without loss of time or pay;

(3) by discrimination in regard to hire or tenure of employment or any term or condition of employment to encourage or discourage membership in any labor organization: Provided, that nothing in this Act . . . shall preclude an employer from making an agreement with a labor organization . . . to require as a condition of employment membership therein . . . Provided further, that no employer shall justify any discrimination against an employee for nonmembership in a labor organization (A) if he has reasonable grounds for believing that such membership was not available to the employee on the same terms and conditions generally applicable to other members, or (B) if he has reasonable grounds for believing that membership was denied or terminated for reasons other than the failure of the employee to tender periodic dues and initiation fees uniformly required as a condition of acquiring or retaining membership;

(4) to discharge or otherwise discriminate against an employee because he has filed charges or given testimony under this Act;

(5) to refuse to bargain collectively with the representatives of his employees, subject to the provisions of section 9(a).

(b) It shall be an unfair labor practice for a labor organization or its agents—

(1) to restrain or coerce (A) employees in the exercise of the rights guaranteed in section 7: Provided, that this paragraph shall not impair the right of a labor organization to prescribe its own rules with respect to the acquisition or retention of membership therein; or (B) an employer in the selection of his representatives for the purposes of collective bargaining or the adjustment of grievances;

(2) to cause or attempt to cause an employer to discriminate against an employee in violation of subsection (a) (3) or to discriminate against an employee with respect to whom membership in such organization has been denied or terminated on some ground other than his failure to tender the periodic dues and the initiation fees uniformly required as a condition of acquiring or retaining membership.

(3) to refuse to bargain collectively with an employer, provided it is the representative of his employees subject to the provisions of section 9 (a).

(4) (i) to engage in, or to induce or encourage any individual employed by any person engaged in commerce or in an industry affecting commerce to engage in, a strike or a refusal in the course of his employment to use, manufacture, process, transport, or otherwise handle or work on any goods, articles, materials, or commodities or to perform any services; or, (ii) to threaten, coerce, or restrain any person engaged in commerce or in an industry affecting commerce, where in either case an object thereof is:

(A) forcing or requiring any employer or self-employed person to join any labor or employer organization or to enter into any agreement which is prohibited by section 8 (e);

(B) forcing or requiring any person to cease using, selling, handling, transporting, or otherwise dealing in the products of any other producer, processor, or manufacturer, or to cease doing business with any other person, or forcing or requiring any other employer to recognize or bargain with a labor organization as the representative of his employees unless such labor organization has been certified as the representative of such employees. . . Provided, that nothing contained in this clause (B) shall be construed to make unlawful, where not otherwise unlawful, any primary strike or primary picketing;

(C) forcing or requiring any employer to recognize or bargain with a particular labor organization as the representative of his employees if another labor organization has been certified as the representative of such employees. . . .

(D) forcing or requiring any employer to assign particular work to employees in a particular labor organization or in a particular trade, craft, or class. . . .

Provided, that nothing contained in this subsection (b) shall be construed to make unlawful a refusal by any person to enter upon the premises of any employer (other than his own employer), if the employees of such employer are engaged in a strike ratified or approved by a representative of such employees whom such employer is required to recognize under this Act: Provided further, that for the purposes of this paragraph (4) only, nothing contained in such paragraph shall be construed to prohibit publicity, other than picketing, for the purpose of truthfully advising the public, including consumers and members of a labor organization, that a product or products are produced by an employer with whom the labor organization has a primary dispute and are distributed by another employer, as long as such publicity does not have an effect of inducing any individual employed by any person other than the primary employer in the course of his employment to pick up, deliver, or transport any goods, or not to perform any services, at the establishment of the employer engaged in such distribution;

(5) to require of employees covered by an agreement authorized under subsection (a) (3) the payment, as a condition precedent to becoming a member of such organization, of a fee in an amount which the Board finds excessive or discriminatory. . . .

INTEGRATIVE NEGOTIATIONS Negotiations in which mutual gains are possible as parties trade lower valued resources for higher valued ones. Also called variable-sum negotiations.

INTELLECTUAL PROPERTY Any product or result of a mental process that is given legal protection against unauthorized use.

INTELLIGENT AGENTS Semi-autonomous computer programs that can be dispatched by the user to execute certain tasks.

INTENT The actual, subjective desire to cause the consequences of an act, or the belief that the consequences are substantially certain to result from it.

INTENT TO BE BOUND The oral or written statement regarding intention of parties to enter into a contract.

INTENTION TO DO WRONG Subjective intent or desire to do wrong or intent to take action substantially certain to cause a wrong to occur.

INTENTIONAL INFLICTION OF EMOTIONAL DISTRESS Outrageous conduct by the individual inflicting the distress; intention to cause, or reckless disregard of the probability of causing, emotional distress; severe emotional suffering; and actual and proximate (or legal) causation of the emotional distress.

INTERBRAND COMPETITION The price competition between a company and its competitors that sell a different brand of the same product.

INTERFERENCE WITH CONTRACTUAL RELATIONS A defendant intentionally induces another to breach a contract with a plaintiff.

INTERFERENCE WITH PROSPECTIVE BUSINESS ADVANTAGE Intentional interference by the defendant with a business relationship the plaintiff seeks to develop, which interference causes loss to the plaintiff.

INTERIM FINANCING Financing that a developer obtains to pay off a construction loan when it becomes due before the permanent financing is available. Also called gap financing.

INTERLOCUTORY Something intervening between the commencement and the end of a suit that decides some point or matter, but is not a final decision regarding the whole controversy.

INTERROGATORY Written question to a party to a lawsuit and its attorney.

INTRABRAND COMPETITION The price competition among the different dealers of the same company.

INTRUSION Objectionable prying, such as eavesdropping or unauthorized rifling through files. It includes the act of wrongfully entering upon or taking possession of property of another.

INVASION OF PRIVACY Prying or intrusion that would be objectionable or offensive to a reasonable person, including eavesdropping, rifling through files one has no authorization to see, public disclosure of private facts, or unauthorized use of an individual's picture in an advertisement or article with which that person has no connection.

INVERSE CONDEMNATION The unlawful taking of private real property by the government for a public use without just compensation. Also called regulatory taking.

INVESTIGATIVE CONSUMER REPORTING Report that contains information on character and reputation, not just credit history.

INVESTMENT CONTRACT A type of security created by an investment of money in a common enterprise with profits to come solely from the efforts of others.

INVESTORS Persons putting up cash or property in exchange for an equity interest in an enterprise.

INVITEE A business visitor who enters a premises for the purposes of the possessor's business.

INVOLUNTARY REDEMPTION RIGHTS The permission of a corporation, at its option, to redeem the shares for a specified price either after a given period of time or on the occurrence of a certain event.

IRREBUTTABLE PRESUMPTION A presumption that cannot be disputed even through the introduction of contrary evidence.

IRREVOCABLE LETTER OF CREDIT A letter of credit that cannot be amended or canceled without the consent of the seller and the issuing bank.

IRREVOCABLE OFFER Irrevocable offers arise in two circumstances: (1) when an option contract has been created, and (2) when an offeree has relied on an offer to its detriment.

ISSUER A company that offers or sells any security.

J

JOIN In cases in which more than one defendant is liable for damages, named defendant(s) may ask the court to join or add other defendants.

JOINT AND SEVERAL LIABILITY The doctrine whereby a plaintiff may collect the entire judgment from any single defendant, regardless of the degree of that defendant's fault, in a case in which the court determines that multiple defendants are at fault.

JOINT TENANCY A specialized form of co-ownership involving real property owned in equal shares by two or more persons who have a right of survivorship if one joint tenant dies.

JOINT VENTURE A one-time group of two or more persons in a single specific business enterprise or transaction.

JUDGMENT NOTWITHSTANDING THE VERDICT (JUDGMENT N.O.V.) Reverses the jury verdict on the ground that the evidence of the prevailing party was so weak that no reasonable jury could have resolved the dispute in that party's favor. Also called judgment n.o.v. (*non obstante veredicto*, notwithstanding the verdict).

JUDICIAL REVIEW The power of federal courts to review acts of the legislative and executive branches of government to determine whether they violate the Constitution.

JUNIOR DEBT Indebtedness that is subordinated under a debt subordination agreement.

JUNK BOND A form of high yield, high risk unsecured corporate indebtedness that is not investment grade.

JURISTIC PERSONALITY The characteristic of a business entity, such as a corporation, whereby the entity is treated as a legal entity separate from its owners.

K

KANTIAN THEORY An ethical theory that looks to the form of an action, rather than the intended result, in examining the ethical worth.

KICKER A percentage of gross or net income in a real estate transaction payable to lender.

KICK-OUT CLAUSE A provision in a lease that gives the tenant the right to leave if certain gross revenue goals are not met.

KNOW-HOW Detailed information on how to make or do something.

L

LAESIO ENORMIS A doctrine developed from language in the Code of Justinian that provided a remedy for those who sold land at less than half its just price.

LARCENY Theft. The taking of property without the owner's consent.

LEMON LAWS Laws designed to protect consumers from defective products that cannot be adequately fixed, such as new cars and new mobile homes.

LETTER OF CREDIT (L/C) A payment mechanism for international sales transactions involving a bank in the buyer's jurisdiction that commits to pay the seller. Also called a documentary credit.

LETTER OF INTENT An instrument entered into by the parties to a real estate transaction for the purpose of setting forth the general terms and conditions of a purchase and sale agreement until a formal legal commitment can be made through the execution of a formal acquisition agreement.

LEVERAGED BUYOUT (LBO) A takeover financed with loans secured by the acquired company's assets, in which groups of investors, often including management, use borrowed money along with some of their own money to buy back the company's stock from its current shareholders.

LIBEL A written communication to a third part by a defendant of an untrue statement of fact that injures a plaintiff's reputation.

LIBOR (London Interbank Offered Rate) An interest rate based on the cost of borrowing offshore U.S. dollars in the global interbank market, centered in several locations in addition to London.

LICENSEE Anyone who is privileged to enter upon land of another because the possessor has given expressed or implied consent.

LIEN A claim on a property that secures a debt owed by the owner of the property.

LIEN NOTICE A written notice that property is subject to a claim by someone other than its owner for the payment of a debt.

LIEN SUBORDINATION An agreement between two secured creditors whose respective security interest, liens, or mortgages attach to the same property. The subordinating party agrees that the lien of the other creditor shall have priority notwithstanding the relative priorities that the parties' liens would otherwise have under applicable law.

LIMITED GUARANTY A guaranty in which the maximum amount of the guarantor's liability is expressly stated in the guaranty instrument.

LIMITED LIABILITY COMPANY (LLC) A form of business entity authorized by state law that is taxed like a limited partnership and provides its members with limited liability, but like a corporation gives its members the right to participate in management without incurring unlimited liability.

LIMITED LIABILITY PARTNERSHIP (LLP) A form of limited partnership designed primarily for professionals who typically do business as a partnership that insulates its partners from vicarious liability for certain partnership obligations.

LIMITED PARTNERS The participants in a limited partnership whose liability for partnership business is limited to their capital contribution.

LIMITED PARTNERSHIP A form of business organization in which limited partners must refrain from actively participating in the management of the partnership but are liable for the debts of the partnership only up to the amount they personally contributed to the partnership.

LIMITED WARRANTY The warranty that limits the remedies available to the consumer for a defective product.

LINE-ITEM VETO Allowed the president to sign a bill into law and then cancel any dollar amounts that he or she believed to be fiscally irresponsible. Declared unconstitutional by the U.S. Supreme Court.

LINE-OF-BUSINESS TEST If an officer, director, or controlling shareholder learns of an opportunity in the course of business for the corporation, and if the opportunity is in the corporation's line of business, a court will not permit that person to keep the opportunity for personal gain.

LIQUIDATED DAMAGES The amount of money stipulated in a contract to be paid to non-breaching party should one of the parties breach the agreement.

LOCK-UP OPTION An option to buy assets or stock of a target company; it is exercisable only if the recipient of the option is unsuccessful in acquiring control of the target company. Depending on how it is priced, a lock-up option can have the effect of deterring other bids.

LONDON INTERBANK OFFERED RATE (LIBOR) An interest rate based on the cost of borrowing offshore U.S. dollars in the global interbank market, centered in several locations in addition to London.

LONG-ARM STATUTE A state statute that subjects an out-of-state defendant to jurisdiction when the defendant is doing business or commits a civil wrong in the state.

LOOK-AND-FEEL TEST A copyrightable work is arguably infringed by another work even if the subsequent work does not copy any individual element of the original work, if an ordinary observer would regard the subsequent work as a copy of the original work's look or feel.

LOST VOLUME SELLER A seller that can be put in as good a position as performance would have only by permitting the seller to recover the profit (including reasonable overhead) that it would have made from full performance by the buyer.

LOWEST ACHIEVABLE EMISSION RATE (LAER) The lowest achievable emission rate using best available technology.

M

MAIL FRAUD A scheme intended to defraud or to obtain money or property by fraudulent means through use of the mails.

MALICIOUS DEFENSE A tort committed when a defendant creates false material evidence and gives false testimony advancing the evidence.

MALICIOUS PROSECUTION A plaintiff can successfully sue for the tort of malicious prosecution if he or she shows that a prior proceeding was instituted against him or her maliciously and without probable cause or factual basis.

MALPRACTICE A claim of professional negligence.

MANAGERS Persons elected by the members (owners) of a limited liability company that, like a board of directors in a corporation, are responsible for managing the business, property, and affairs of the company.

MANDATORY ARBITRATION One party will not do business with the other unless it agrees to arbitrate any future claims.

MANUFACTURING DEFECT A flaw in a product that occurs during production, such as a failure to meet the design specifications.

MARKET POWER The power to control market prices or exclude competition in the relevant market. Also called monopoly power.

MARKET-SHARE LIABILITY The liability for damages caused by a manufacturer's products assessed based on a manufacturer's national market share.

MARKETABLE TITLE Title to property that is fee simple and is free of liens or encumbrances.

MARSHALING ASSETS Partnership creditors have first priority to partnership assets and, as to those assets, stand in front of creditors of individual partners themselves.

MASTER LIMITED PARTNERSHIP An entity structured as a limited partnership that has readily transferable limited partnership interests that are traded on a national securities exchange.

MATERIAL FACT A fact that a reasonable investor would most likely have considered important in deciding whether to buy or sell his or her stock.

MATURITY DATE The date a term loan becomes due and payable.

MENS REA (**guilty state of mind**) Criminal intent.

MED-ARB The parties to a dispute enter mediation with the commitment to submit the dispute to binding arbitration if mediation fails to resolve the conflict.

MEDIATION A form of dispute resolution whereby the parties agree to try to reach a solution themselves with the assistance of a neutral third party who helps them find a mutually satisfactory solution.

MEDIATOR The third party who helps the parties in mediation find a mutually satisfactory solution.

MEMBERS The owners of a limited liability company.

MERCHANT (under the UCC) A person who deals in goods of the kind or otherwise by its occupation holds itself out as having knowledge or skill peculiar to the practices or goods involved in the transaction.

MERGER The combination of two or more corporations into one.

MERGER AGREEMENT An agreement between two companies to combine those companies into one.

MERGER DOCTRINE If an idea and its expression are inseparable, the merger doctrine dictates that the expression is not copyrightable.

MERIT REVIEW A review by a state securities commissioner to determine whether the issuer's plan of business and the proposed issuance of securities are fair, just, and equitable.

MINIMUM CONTACTS As long as the person has sufficient minimum contacts with a state, such that it is fair to require him or her to appear in a court of that state, the state has personal jurisdiction over that person.

MINITRIAL A cross between arbitration and negotiation, truncated presentation of evidence conducted by lawyers, usually with business persons present.

MIRANDA **WARNINGS** Once a person is placed in custody, he or she cannot be questioned by the police unless first advised of his or her constitutional rights to remain silent and to have counsel present.

MIRROR IMAGE RULE A traditional rule of contract formation that requires the offeree's acceptance to be a mirror image of what the offeror has offered.

MISAPPROPRIATION (of a trade secret) Learning through improper means and use of the trade secret of another.

MISAPPROPRIATION THEORY (securities) The theory that holds that a securities violation occurs when a person breaches a fiduciary duty to the owner of nonpublic information by trading on that information after misappropriating it for his or her own use.

MISBRANDING False or misleading labeling; prohibited by federal and state statutes. Includes claiming unsubstantiated medicinal benefits for a food, inadequate labeling for a drug, or selling over-the-counter a drug for which a prescription is required.

MISDEMEANOR An offense lower than a felony, punishable by fine or imprisonment for less than one year (not in a penitentiary).

MISSTATEMENT (Rule 10b–5) A misrepresentation of a fact; a lie.

MISTAKE OF FACT A mistake about an underlying fact that may make a contract voidable.

MISTAKE OF JUDGMENT A mistake of judgment occurs when the parties make an erroneous assessment about the value of what is bargained for.

MITIGATE Lessen.

MITIGATION OF DAMAGES After a breach of contract, the non-breaching party has a duty to take any reasonable actions that will lessen the amount of the damages.

MONOPOLISTIC INTENT The maintenance or acquisition of monopoly power through anticompetitive acts.

MONOPOLY POWER The power to control market prices or exclude competition in the relevant market. Also called market power.

MORTGAGE A loan to buy real property secured by a lien on the real property. Also called deed of trust.

MOST FAVORED NATION (MFN) The principle that holds that each member country of the World Trade Organization (WTO) must accord to all other WTO members tariff treatment no less favorable than it provides to any other country.

MOTION FOR JUDGMENT ON THE PLEADINGS A motion filed immediately after the complaint and answer have been filed. One party, usually the defendant, argues that the pleadings alone demonstrate that the action is futile.

MOTION TO DISMISS The formal request that the court terminate lawsuit on the ground that plaintiff's claim is technically inadequate.

MULTIPLE-BRAND PRODUCT MARKET A market made up of product or service offerings by different manufacturers or sellers that are economically interchangeable and may therefore be said to compete.

MUTUALITY OF OBLIGATION Both parties in a bilateral contract are obligated to perform their side of the bargain.

N

NATIONAL AMBIENT AIR QUALITY STANDARDS The permissible levels of pollutants in the ambient or outdoor air that, with adequate margins of safety, are required to protect public health; set forth in the Clean Air Act.

NATIONAL POLLUTANT DISCHARGE ELIMINATION SYSTEM (NPDES) The principal regulatory program established by the Clean Water Act; requires permits for the discharge of pollutants from any point source to navigable waters.

NATIONAL TREATMENT The WTO principle that holds that WTO members must not discriminate against imported products in favor of domestically produced products.

NATURAL RESOURCE LAW The laws that govern wilderness protection, wildlife protection, coastal zone management, energy conservation, and national park designation.

NAVIGABLE WATERS The waters of the United States and the territorial seas, as well as lakes and streams that are not in fact usable for purposes of navigation.

NEGATIVE CONVENANT The borrower's promise of what it undertakes not to do under the loan agreement.

NEGLIGENCE A breach of the requirement that a person act with the care a reasonable person would use in the same circumstances.

NEGLIGENCE *PER SE* Violation of a statute that shifts the burden to the defendant to prove the defendant was not negligent once the plaintiff shows that the defendant violated a statute and the violation caused an injury.

NEGLIGENT-HIRING THEORY An employer is negligent if the employer hires an employee who endangers the health and safety of other employees.

NEGLIGENT INFLICTION OF EMOTIONAL DISTRESS A tort committed when the defendant negligently inflicts emotional distress that causes the plaintiff some form of physical injury.

NEGOTIATION The give and take people engage in when coming to terms with each other.

NEUTRAL GATE SYSTEM In a secondary boycott situation, the union may picket only at the gate reserved for the employees and vendors of the primary employer that is physically separated from the gate to be used by all other persons.

NEW SOURCE PERFORMANCE STANDARDS (NSPS) Require use of technology chosen as BAT for new sources of pollutants.

NEXUS The legally required relationship between a condition to a land-use approval and the impacts of the development being approved.

NOLO CONTENDERE **(I will not contest it)** A plea that means the accused does not contest the charges.

NONBINDING ARBITRATION Arbitration in which the parties are not bound by the arbitrator's decision.

NONCONFORMING USE An existing land use that was lawful but that does not comply with a later-enacted zoning ordinance.

NONINFRINGEMENT In a patent dispute, the defense of noninfringement asserts that the allegedly infringing matter does not fall within the claims of the issued patent.

NOT AN UNDERWRITER Under Rule 144, an affiliate or a person selling restricted securities is not an underwriter if certain conditions (e.g., holding period, volume limitations, manner of sale, filing of Form 144, and available public information) are met.

NOTE PURCHASE AGREEMENT The title of a loan agreement when the lender is an insurance company.

NOVATION The method of contract modification by which the original contract is canceled and a new one is written with perhaps only one change, such as substitution of a new party.

NOVEL An invention is novel if it was not anticipated; i.e., if it was not previously known or used by others in the United States and was not previously patented or described in a printed publication in any country.

NUISANCE A thing or activity that unreasonably and substantially interferes with an owner's use and enjoyment of owner's property.

O

OBVIOUS RISK If the use of a product carries an obvious risk, the manufacturer will not be held liable for injuries that result from ignoring the risk.

OFFER (contracts) A proposal to enter into a contract. Proposal may be verbal, written, or implied by action.

OFFER (securities) Every attempt or offer to dispose of, or solicitation of an offer to buy, a security or interest in a security, for value.

OFFEREE A person to whom an offer is made.

OFFEROR A person making an offer.

OFFSHORE TRANSACTION A security transaction in which no offer is made to a person in the United States and either (1) at the time the buy order is originated, the buyer is outside the United States; or (2) the transaction is one executed in, on, or through the facilities of a designated offshore securities market.

OMBUDSPERSON A person who hears complaints, engages in fact finding, and generally promotes dispute resolution through information methods such as counseling or mediation.

OMISSION (Rule 10b–5) A company or its managers fail to tell the whole truth about a fact to the investing public, and what the company does say makes it likely that reasonable investors will take away an impression contrary to the true facts.

ONE-FORM-OF-ACTION LAWS Statutes that restrict lenders seeking remedies against real property security from suing the borrower personally. If a lender has recourse to the borrower or to other property of the borrower, and exercises such rights, the lender may be precluded from foreclosing on real estate mortgaged by the borrower. Also called antideficiency laws.

OPERATING AGREEMENT A contract that sets forth the rights, obligations, and powers of the owners, managers, and officers of a limited liability company.

OPPRESSION An inequality of bargaining power that results in no real negotiation and an absence of meaningful choice for one party to the contract.

OPTION CONTRACT A contract in which the offeror promises to hold an offer open for a certain amount of time.

ORDINARY COMPARATIVE NEGLIGENCE In an ordinary comparative negligence jurisdiction, the plaintiff may recover only if it is less culpable than the defendant.

ORGANIZATIONAL STRIKE An unlawful strike whose purpose is to organize employees.

ORIGINAL JURISDICTION The power of the U.S. Supreme Court to take cognizance of a case at its inception, try it, and pass judgment upon the law and facts. Distinguished from appellate jurisdiction.

OUTPUT CONTRACT A contract under which a buyer promises to buy all the products that the seller produces.

OUTSIDE DIRECTOR A member of a board who is not also an officer.

OVER-THE-COUNTER A drug for which a prescription is not required.

P

PATENT MISUSE In a patent dispute, a defense asserting that although the defendant has infringed a valid patent, the patent holder has abused its patent rights and therefore has lost, at least temporarily, its right to enforce them.

PARENS PATRIAE **(parent of the country) ACTION** Antitrust suits brought by state attorneys general for injuries sustained by residents of their respective states.

PAROL EVIDENCE RULE If there is a written contract that the parties intended would encompass their entire agreement, oral evidence of prior or contemporaneous statements will not be permitted to vary or alter the terms of the contract.

PARTICIPATION IN A BREACH OF FIDUCIARY DUTY A tort committed when the defendant induces another party to breach its fiduciary duty to the plaintiff.

PARTICIPATION LOAN A loan in which the original lender sells shares to other parties, called participants.

PASS-THROUGH ENTITY A business organization that is not a separate taxpayer; all its income and losses are passed through and taxed to its owner. An S Corporation or limited partnership is a pass-through entity.

PASSIVE INVESTOR An investor in a business who does not materially participate in that business.

PASSIVE-LOSS LIMITATIONS The rule enacted by the Tax Reform Act of 1986 under which only owners who materially participate in a business may deduct losses against their other income.

PATENT A government-granted right to exclude others for a stated period of time (usually 20 years) from making, using, or selling within the government's jurisdiction an invention that is the subject of the patent.

PATTERN An involvement in racketeering activity demonstrated by at least two predicate acts occurring within a ten-year period.

PATTERN BARGAINING In collective bargaining, a technique of matching agreements within an industry.

PAYOFF TABLE A diagram that illustrates the results the possible outcomes of various choices in game theory.

PENUMBRA The peripheral rights that are implied by the specifically enumerated rights in the Bill of Rights.

PER SE **ANALYSIS** A form of antitrust analysis that condemns practices that are completely void of redeeming competitive rationales.

PER SE **VIOLATION** A violation without proof of anything more.

PERFECTION (under the UCC) In connection with security interests, perfection refers to making the security interest valid as against other creditors of the debtor.

PERSON (under environmental law) A party who has contributed to imminent and substantial endangerment to human health or the environment and therefore is required in a civil action to take remedial action. Person in this sense includes companies, individual employees, and officers, as well as shareholders if state law would mandate piercing the corporate veil.

PERSONAL JURISDICTION The power of state court to hear (decide) a civil case based upon residence or location of activities of the person being sued.

PERSUASIVE DECISION A well-reasoned court decision that another court, not bound by the first decision, would, when confronted with a similar dispute, probably follow.

PETITIONER The person who is appealing a judgment or seeking a writ of certiorari. Also called appellant.

PIERCING THE CORPORATE VEIL When a court denies limited liability to a corporation and hold shareholders personally responsible for claims against the corporation, the court has pierced the corporate veil.

PIGGYBACK RIGHTS An investor's right to request registration of that investor's shares in a public offering initiated by the company.

PLACEMENT AGENT A broker-dealer who distributes the private placement memorandum to suitable persons and assists in private placement of securities.

PLAINTIFF A person who brings an action; the party who complains or sues in a civil action and is so named on the record. The prosecution in a criminal case (i.e., the state or the United States in a federal case).

PLANNED UNIT DEVELOPMENT (PUD) The land use regulations for a given piece of property that reflect the proposed development plans for that property. PUD allows for mixture of uses for property not possible under traditional zoning regulations.

PLEA BARGAINING The process by which the prosecutor agrees to reduce the charges in exchange for a guilty plea from the accused.

PLEA The response by a defendant in criminal case of guilty, not guilty, or nolo contendere.

PLEADINGS The formal allegations by the parties to a lawsuit of their respective claims and defenses.

PLEDGE A type of security interest whereby the creditor or secured party takes possession of the collateral owned by the debtor.

POINTS A one-time charge to a borrower buying real property (in addition to interest) computed by a lender by multiplying the amount funded by a fixed percentage.

POISON PILL A plan that would make any takeover of a corporation prohibitively expensive.

POLICE POWER The general power granted state and city governments to protect the health, safety, welfare, or morals of its residents.

POLITICAL QUESTION A conflict that should be decided by one of the political branches of government or by the electorate. A court will refuse to decide questions of a purely political character.

POWER OF ATTORNEY A written instrument that authorizes a person, called an attorney-in-fact (who need not be a lawyer), to sign documents or perform certain specific acts on behalf of another person.

PRAYER The request for relief in a complaint.

PRE-PACKAGED BANKRUPTCY A workout plan approved by key creditors and the debtor before the debtor files bankruptcy; it becomes the plan of reorganization in a Chapter 11 bankruptcy.

PRECONTRACTUAL LIABILITY The claims by the disappointed party if contract negotiations fail before a contract has been signed.

PREDATORY PRICING The act of pricing below the producer's actual cost with the intent of driving other competitors out of the market, thus enabling the person engaging in predatory pricing to raise prices later.

PREEMPT A federal law takes precedence when state law conflicts with federal law.

PREEMPTION DEFENSE (product liability) The immunity granted manufacturers if they meet minimum standards of conduct under certain regulatory schemes.

PREFERENCES Transfers to (or for the benefit of) creditors on account of antecedent debts that are made from an insolvent debtor's property within 90 days before bankruptcy (one year if creditor is insider) and that enable the creditors to receive more than they would through a Chapter 7 liquidation.

PREFERRED RETURN The legal right to have distributions made to the person entitled to a preferred return before any distributions are made to any other equity holder.

PREFERRED STOCK Stock that has priority over common stock in the payment of dividends (and in the distribution of assets if the corporation is dissolved).

PREJUDGMENT INTEREST The interest on the amount of an award from the date of the injury to the date of judgment.

PRENUPTIAL AGREEMENT An agreement entered into before marriage that sets forth the manner in which the parties' assets will be distributed and the support to which each party will be entitled, in the event the parties get divorced.

PREPAYMENT PENALTY A clause whereby a lender imposes a penalty if the loan is paid off early.

PREPONDERANCE OF THE EVIDENCE The evidence offered in a civil trial that is more convincing than the evidence presented in opposition to it.

PRICE AMENDMENT Information concerning the price of securities and underwriting arrangement filed with the Securities and Exchange Commission once the registration statement has been informally cleared by the SEC staff, or the registrant receives notice that the registration statement will not be reviewed.

PRICE ANTIDILUTION A provision that prevents a corporation from diluting a shareholder's interests by simply issuing shares of common stock at a price below the conversion price.

PRICE DISCRIMINATION Sellers charge different prices to purchasers in interstate sales for commodities of like grade and quality.

PRICE FIXING The cooperative setting of price levels or ranges by competing firms.

PRIMA FACIE (on its face) A fact considered true until evidence is produced to the contrary.

PRIMARY DEBTOR The person with an obligation for which the guarantor becomes liable.

PRIMARY EMPLOYER (NLRA) In a secondary boycott situation, the employer with whom union has a dispute.

PRIME RATE The lowest rate of interest publicly offered by major lending institutions to their most creditworthy customers. Better practice dictates using the terms base rate or reference rate because sometimes lenders offer a loan below prime.

PRIMING LIEN A lien that is senior to a previously granted security interest.

PRINCIPAL (of a loan) The amount borrowed.

PRINCIPAL A person who delegates a portion of his or her tasks to another person who represents the principal as an agent.

PRIOR ART Developments or pre-existing art that relates to a claimed invention.

PRIOR RESTRAINTS Prohibitions barring speech before it occurs.

PRISONER'S DILEMMA A principle of game theory describing the sub-optimal outcome that results when parties do not cooperate.

PRIVATE NUISANCE Interference with a person's use and enjoyment of his or her land and water.

PRIVATE OFFERING An offering to selected individuals or entities who have the ability to evaluate and bear the risk of the investment; that is, they have the ability to fend for themselves.

PRIVATE PLACEMENT MEMORANDUM A booklet offered by entrepreneurs seeking financing from private individual investors that furnishes all information about themselves and their enterprise.

PRIVATELY HELD CORPORATION A corporation whose shares are not bought and sold among the general public.

PRIVITY OF CONTRACT The necessity for a person injured by a product to be in a contractual relationship with the seller of the product in order for the injured person to recover damages.

PROBABLE CAUSE As applied to an arrest or a search warrant, a reasonable belief that the suspect has committed a crime or is about to commit a crime. Mere suspicion or belief, unsupported by facts or circumstances, is insufficient.

PROCEDURAL DUE PROCESS The parties whose rights are to be affected are entitled to be heard and, in order that they may enjoy that right, they must be notified before adverse action is taken.

PROCEDURAL OBLIGATIONS The rules that define the manner in which rights and duties are enforced.

PROCESSING OPERATION In a compensation trade arrangement, a processing operation refers to the foreign party supplying the materials that are processed by the local party using the foreign party's equipment.

PRODUCT MARKET A product or service offering made by different manufacturers or sellers that are economically interchangeable and may therefore be said to compete.

PRODUCT LIABILITY The liability of a manufacturer or seller of a product that because of a defect, causes injury to a purchaser, user, or bystander.

PRODUCTIVE EFFICIENCY An equilibrium in which only the lowest-cost producers of goods and services survive.

PROFESSIONAL CORPORATION An organization of professionals (such as doctors, lawyers, or architects) authorized by state law to act as a legal entity distinct from its owners.

PROMISEE In contract law, the promisee is the person to whom the promise (contract) was made.

PROMISOR In contract law, the promisor is the person who made the promise.

PROMISSORY ESTOPPEL A promise that the promisor should reasonably expect to induce action or forbearance on the part of the promisee or a third person and that does induce such action or forbearance is binding if injustice can be avoided only by enforcement of the promise.

PROOF OF CLAIM A claim filed by creditors on uncontingent and undisputed debt.

PROSPECTUS (1933 Act) Any document that is designed to produce orders for a security, whether or not the document purports on its face to offer the security for sale or otherwise to dispose of it for value. The descriptive document that an issuer of securities provides to prospective purchasers.

PROTECTED EXPRESSION The part of a work that is subject to copyright protection.

PROXIMATE CAUSE A reasonably foreseeable consequence of the defendant's negligence, without which no injury would have occurred.

PROXY A written authorization by a shareholder to another person to vote on the shareholder's behalf.

PROXY CONTEST A battle for corporate control whereby someone wishing to replace the board with its own candidates seeks to acquire a sufficient number of shareholder votes to do so.

PSYCHOLOGICAL BARRIERS Barriers to negotiation that arise from the ways that negotiators see the world.

PUBLIC DISCLOSURE OF PRIVATE FACTS The publication of a private fact that is not newsworthy. The matter must be private, such that a reasonable person would find publication objectionable. Unlike in a defamation case, truth is not a defense.

PUBLIC FIGURES Individuals, who, by reason of their achievements or the vigor and success with which they seek the public's attention, are injected into the public eye.

PUBLIC NUISANCE Unreasonable and substantial interference with the public health, safety, peace, comfort, convenience, or utilization of land.

PUBLIC POLICY EXCEPTION An employer is prohibited from discharging an employee for a reason that violates public policy.

PUBLICATION Communication to a third party.

PUBLICLY HELD CORPORATION A corporation whose shares are traded on one of the national stock exchanges or the over-the-counter market.

PUBLICLY OWNED SEWAGE TREATMENT WORKS (POTWs) General and specific industry pretreatment standards are set for discharges to publicly owned sewage treatment works (POTWs).

PUFFING The expression of opinion by a seller regarding goods; not a warranty.

PUNITIVE DAMAGES Damages awarded to a plaintiff over and above what will fairly compensate it for its loss. They are intended to punish the defendant and deter others from engaging in similar conduct. Also called exemplary damages.

PURCHASE-MONEY SECURITY INTEREST A security interest created when a seller lends the buyer the money to buy the seller's goods.

PURE COMPARATIVE NEGLIGENCE A tort system in which the plaintiff may recover for the part of the injury due to the defendant's negligence, even though the plaintiff was the more negligent party.

PURE NOTICE RECORDING STATUTES Under these statutes, a person who has notice that someone else has already bought the real property cannot validate his or her deed by recording it first.

PYRAMID SELLING A scheme whereby a consumer is recruited as a product "distributor" and receives commissions based on the products he or she sells and on the recruitment of additional sellers.

Q

QUALIFIED INSTITUTIONAL BUYER Institutional investors holding and managing $100 million or more of securities.

QUALIFIED PRIVILEGE In defamation cases, the right by a defendant to make statements to (1) protect one's own personal interests; (2) protect business interests, such as statements to a prospective employer; or (3) provide information for the public interest, such as credit reports.

QUANTUM MERUIT A basis for equitable relief by a court when there was no contract between the parties, but one party has received a benefit for which it has not paid.

QUASH To declare invalid.

"QUICK LOOK" RULE OF REASON The "quick look" rule of reason is used whenever the practice has obvious anticompetitive effects but is not illegal *per se*; it allows for immediate inquiry into pro-competitive justifications.

QUID-PRO-QUO **(this for that) HARASSMENT** The specific, job-related adverse action, such as denial of a promotion, in retaliation for a worker's refusal to respond to a supervisor's sexual advances.

QUIET PERIOD (1933 Act) The time between filing of securities registration statement and the date the registration statement becomes effective.

QUITCLAIM DEED A deed that contains no warranties; the grantor conveys only any right, title, and interest held by the grantor, if any, at the time of execution.

QUORUM The holders of more than 50% of the outstanding shares of a corporation.

R

RACE NORMING OF EMPLOYMENT TESTS A device designed to ensure that a minimum number of minorities and women are in an application pool by adjusting the scores or using different cutoff scores for employment related tests on the basis of race, color, religion, sex, or national origin.

RACE-NOTICE RECORDING STATUTES These statutes protect only a good faith subsequent purchaser who recorded its deed before the prior purchaser recorded its deed.

RACE RECORDING STATUTES Under these statutes, recording is a race—the rule is "first in time is first in right." The first to record a deed has superior rights, regardless of whether he or she knew that someone else had already bought or claimed an interest in the real property.

RACKETEERING ACTIVITY The state and federal offenses involving a pattern of illegal acts, including mail and wire fraud.

RAIDER In a hostile takeover, a third party who seeks to obtain control of a corporation, called the target, over the objections of its management.

RATIFICATION A principal affirms through words or actions a prior act of an agent that did not bind the principal.

RATIONAL BASIS TEST A test under which a discriminatory classification will be held valid if there is any conceivable basis upon which the classification might relate to a legitimate governmental interest; applies to all classifications that relate to matters of economics or social welfare.

RAWLSIAN MORAL THEORY A deontological line of thought that aims to maximize the utility of the worst off person in society.

REAFFIRMATION AGREEMENT A contract with a creditor whereby an individual who has filed under Chapter 7 agrees to repay a debt even though the debt would otherwise be discharged in the debtor's bankruptcy case.

REAL ESTATE INVESTMENT TRUST (REIT) A tax-advantaged pool of real property.

RECKLESSNESS In the criminal context, conscious disregard of a substantial risk that an individual's actions would result in the harm prohibited by a statute.

RECOGNITIONAL STRIKE An unlawful strike whose purpose is to force an employer to recognize the union as the collective bargaining agent for certain of its employees.

RECOGNIZED HAZARD (OSHA) Workplace conditions that are obviously dangerous or are considered by the employer or other employers in the industry to be hazardous.

RECORD The oral and written evidence presented at an administrative hearing.

RECORDABLE FORM The requirements established by the state regarding how title to real estate is filed and recorded. Requirements generally include legibility and notarization.

RECORDING STATUTES Statutes that establish an orderly process by which claims to interests in real property can be recorded as part of the public record and resolved.

RED-HERRING PROSPECTUS Preliminary prospectus; incomplete version of the final prospectus.

REDEMPTION The buying back of shares by a corporation from a shareholder.

REFERRAL SALE The seller offers the buyer a commission, rebate, or discount for furnishing the seller with a list of additional prospective customers.

REFERENCE RATE The lowest rate of interest publicly offered by major lending institutions to their most creditworthy customers.

REGISTERED MASK WORK Highly detailed transparencies that represent the topological layout of semiconductor chips.

REGISTRATION RIGHTS An investor's right to require a company to register under applicable federal and state securities laws the shares of common stock into which the preferred stock is convertible.

REGISTRATION STATEMENT The registration statement consists of filing forms and the prospectus, the disclosure document that an issuer of securities provides to prospective purchasers.

REGULATION Z Regulations issued by the Federal Reserve Board to interpret and enforce the federal Truth-in-Lending Act.

REGULATIONS The rules of order prescribed by superior or competent authority relating to action of those under its control.

REGULATORY NEGOTIATIONS (reg-neg) A style of administrative rulemaking in which representatives of major groups convene with an administrative agency and work out a compromise through negotiation on the substance of new regulations.

REGULATORY TAKING The unlawful taking by the federal government of private real property for a public use and without just compensation.

RELIANCE DAMAGES The awards made to a plaintiff for any expenditures made in reliance on a contract that was subsequently breached.

REMAND The power of a court of appeal to send a case back to a lower court for reconsideration.

REMOTE TIPPEE Tippees of tippees other than the original tippee.

REPORTER The published volumes of case decisions by a particular court or group of courts.

REPORTING COMPANY A company registered under Section 12 of the Securities Exchange Act of 1934 that subjects issuers to various reporting requirements and to certain rules and regulations concerning proxies, tender offers, and insider trading.

REPRESENTATION ELECTION (NLRA) An election among employees to decide whether they want a union to represent them for collective bargaining.

REQUESTS FOR PRODUCTION OF DOCUMENTS Requests for documents such as medical records and personal files to be produced as part of the discovery process before a trial.

REQUIREMENTS CONTRACT A contract under which the buyer agrees to buy all of a specified commodity the buyer needs from the seller and the seller agrees to provide that amount.

RES IPSA LOQUITUR (the thing speaks for itself) The doctrine that allows a plaintiff to prove breach and causation indirectly.

RESALE PRICE MAINTENANCE (RPM) An agreement on minimum price between firms at different levels of production or distribution that violates antitrust law.

RESCIND Void or make ineffective.

RESPONDEAT SUPERIOR (let the master answer) The doctrine under which an employer may be held vicariously or secondarily liable for the negligent or intentional conduct of the employee that is committed in the scope of the employee's employment.

RESERVATION PRICE That price at which one is indifferent between the success and failure of the negotiation.

RESPONDENT The party in a case against whom an appeal is taken; the party who has an interest adverse to setting aside or reversing the judgment.

RESPONSIBLE CORPORATE OFFICER DOCTRINE A criminal law doctrine that, under certain circumstances, imposes vicarious liability on an officer responsible for compliance based on the actions of subordinates.

RESPONSIBLE PERSONS The responsible persons from whom the EPA can recover the costs of remedial work include (1) the present owner or operator of the facility; (2) the owner or operator at the time of disposal of the hazardous substance; (3) any person who arranged for treatment or disposal of hazardous substances at the facility; and (4) any person who transported hazardous substances to and selected the facility.

RESTATEMENT Former common law rules in a particular subject area (e.g., contracts, torts) integrated into formal collections that a judge or legislature is free to adopt.

RESTITUTION An award made to a plaintiff of a benefit improperly obtained by the defendant.

RESTRICTED GUARANTY A guaranty in which the guarantor's liability is enforceable only with respect to a specified transaction or series of transactions.

RESTRICTED SECURITIES Securities issued in a private placement; they cannot be resold or transferred unless they are either registered or exempt from registration. The most common exemption is pursuant to Securities and Exchange Commission Rule 144.

RETRIBUTIVE JUSTICE A theory that states that every crime demands payment in the form of punishment.

REVERSIBILITY A theory that looks to whether one would want a rule applied to one's self.

REVIVAL STATUTES State and federal statutes that allow plaintiffs to file lawsuits that have been barred by the running of the statute of limitations.

REVLON MODE A company is said to be in *Revlon* mode when a change of control or breakup of the company has become inevitable.

REVOKE To annul an offer by recission.

REVOLVING LINE OF CREDIT A line of credit that allows a borrower to borrow whatever sums it requires up to a specified maximum amount and reborrow amounts it has repaid.

REVOLVING LOAN A loan that allows a borrower to borrow whatever sums it requires up to a specified maximum amount and reborrow amounts it has repaid.

RIGHT OF FIRST NEGOTIATION Gives the holder the right to negotiate the purchase of the property before the seller enters negotiations with another party.

RIGHT OF FIRST REFUSAL A contract that provides the holder with the right to purchase property on the same terms and conditions offered by or to a third party.

RIGHT OF REDEMPTION Gives the mortgagor and certain other categories of interested persons the right to redeem or get back foreclosed property within a statutorily limited period.

RIGHT OF RESCISSION A right to cancel a contract.

RIGHT OF SETOFF Permits Party A to deduct automatically from payments due Party B amounts due from Party B to Party A.

RIPENESS A court will not hear agency cases until they are ripe for decision, that is, after a rule is adopted but before the agency seeks to apply it to a particular case.

ROADSHOW Oral presentations to large institutional investors in key cities in the United States, Europe, and Asia.

RULE OF IMPOSSIBILITY The rule under which claims of predation are rejected because the marketplace in question cannot be successfully monopolized.

RULE OF REASON The rule that takes into account a defendant's actions as well as the structure of the market to determine whether an activity promotes or restrains competition.

RULES The legislative enactments that serve as general principles and guidelines for sensitive issues not governed by law.

RUNAWAY SHOP An illegal attempt by an employer to escape its collective-bargaining obligation by shutting down a unionized operation and moving the functions of that former operation to a nearby site.

S

S CORPORATION A corporation meeting certain requirements and that is taxed only at the owner level.

S–1 REVIEW A review by the auditor of events subsequent to the date of the certified balance sheet in the registration statement to ascertain whether any material change has occurred in the company's financial position that should be disclosed to prevent the balance sheet figures from being misleading.

SALE AND LEASEBACK A simultaneous two-step transaction, whereby an institutional lender purchases real property from a company, and the property is leased back to the company for its use.

SALE (1933 Act) Every contract of sale or disposition of a security or interest in a security, for value.

SCIENTER An intent to deceive.

SEC FORMS Regulations adopted by the Securities and Exchange Commission that specify what information must be provided the public. Examples include Form S–1 for a prospectus for an initial public offering and Form 10–K for an annual report of a publicly traded company.

SECOND-STEP, BACK-END MERGER The second step in a corporate takeover whereby the shareholders who did not tender their shares receive cash or securities in a subsequent merger.

SECONDARY BOYCOTT A strike against an employer with whom a union has no quarrel in order to encourage it to stop doing business with an employer with whom it does have a dispute.

SECONDARY MEANING A descriptive trademark becomes protectable by acquiring secondary meaning, or sufficient consumer recognition through sufficient use and/or advertising of the goods under the mark.

SECONDARY OFFERING A securities offering by a person other than the issuer.

SECTION 201 Provides for temporary relief to U.S. industries seriously injured by increasing imports, regardless of whether unfair practices are involved. It is sometimes called the fair trade law.

SECTION 232 Provides for relief from imports threatening to impair U.S. national security.

SECTION 301 Authorizes the U.S. Trade Representative to investigate alleged unfair practices of foreign governments that impede U.S. exports of both goods and services.

SECTION 337 Provides that if a U.S. industry is injured (or there is a restraint or monopolization of trade in the United States) by reason of unfair acts in the importation of articles into the United States, an order must be issued requiring the exporters and importers to cease the unfair acts or, if necessary, excluding imports of the offending articles from all sources.

SECTION 4(½) EXEMPTION An exemption for a private offering of securities by an affiliate that would qualify as a private placement under Section 4(2) of the Securities Act of 1933 if made by the issuer.

SECTION 406 Provides for import relief if a U.S. industry is suffering material injury by reason of rapidly increasing imports from a Communist country.

SECURED LOAN A loan backed up by collateral.

SECURED PARTY (under the UCC) The lender, seller, or other person in whose favor there is a security interest.

SECURED TRANSACTION A loan or other transaction secured by collateral put up by the borrower.

SECURITY (1933 Act) Any note, stock, treasury stock, bond, debenture, evidence of indebtedness, certificate of interest or participation in any profit-sharing agreement, collateral trust certificate, pre-organization certificate or subscription, transferable share, investment contract, voting-trust certificate, certificate of deposit for a security, fractional undivided interest in oil, gas, or other mineral rights; any put, call, straddle, option, or privilege on any security, certificate of deposit, or group or index of securities (including any interest therein or based on the value thereof; or any put, call, straddle, option, or privilege entered into on a national securities exchange relating to foreign currency; or, in general, any interest or instrument commonly known as a "security," or any certificate of interest or participation in, temporary or interim certificate for, receipt for, guarantee, of, or warrant or right to subscribe to or purchase, any of the foregoing.

SECURITY AGREEMENT (under the UCC) An agreement that creates or provides for a security interest.

SECURITY INTEREST (under the UCC) Any interest in personal property or fixtures that is used as collateral to secure payment or the performance of an obligation.

SELF-FINANCING Generating capital by carefully managing a company's own funds.

SELF PUBLICATION A doctrine giving an employee a claim for defamation when the employer makes a false assertion in firing an employee, which the employer could reasonably expect the employee to repeat to a prospective employer.

SELF-TENDER An offer by a corporation to buy back its stock or shareholder rights for a fair price.

SELLING SHORT The sale of securities the seller does not own.

SENIOR DEBT Indebtedness that benefits from a debt subordination agreement.

SEPARATE PROPERTY Property that belongs solely to the spouse who acquired it before marriage or received it by gift or inheritance.

SEPARATION OF POWERS The distinct authority of governance granted the three branches of U.S. government (executive, legislative, and judicial) by the U.S. Constitution.

SEQUESTRATION ORDER A governmental order that requires spending levels to be reduced below the levels provided in the budget.

SERVICE MARK A legally protected identifying mark connected with services.

SETTLE When parties to a lawsuit go over claims and ascertain and agree on the balance due one another prior to taking case to trial, they have settled the lawsuit.

SHAREHOLDER A holder of equity securities of a corporation. Also called stockholder.

SHAREHOLDER DERIVATIVE SUIT A lawsuit brought against directors or officers of a corporation by a shareholder on behalf of the corporation.

SHAREHOLDER OF RECORD The persons whose names appear on a corporation's shareholder list on a specified date who are entitled to vote.

SHELF REGISTRATION The registration of a number of securities at one time for issuance later.

SHORT-SWING TRADING The purchase and sale or sale and purchase by an officer, director, or greater-than-10% shareholders of securities of a public company within a six-month period.

SHOWING OF INTEREST A sufficient number of employees who express interest in a union representation election.

SHRINKWRAP LICENSE A license that customers cannot read when they purchase software but are deemed to have accepted when they open the wrapping around the envelope containing the discs or click on the "I Accept" button on the computer screen.

SLAMMING The illegal practice of switching the long-distance telephone or electrical supplier of an individual without first getting permission.

SLANDER A spoken communication to a third party by a defendant of an untrue statement of fact that injures a plaintiff's reputation.

SLANDER PER SE Words that are slanderous in and of themselves. Only statements that a person has committed a serious crime, has a loathsome disease, is guilty of sexual misconduct, or is not fit to conduct business are slanderous *per se*.

SMALL BUSINESS ISSUERS Companies with revenues less than $25 million whose market value of publicly held securities (other than those held by affiliates) is less than $25 million.

SOLE PROPRIETORSHIP One person owns all the assets of the business, has complete control of the business, and is solely liable for all the debts of the business.

SOVEREIGN ACTS DOCTRINE The government cannot be held liable for breach of contract due to legislative or executive acts of general application.

SOVEREIGN IMMUNITY The doctrine that prevents the courts of one country from hearing a suit against the government of another country.

SPECIFIC PERFORMANCE A court order to a breaching party to complete the contract as promised.

SPECIFICATIONS The description of an invention in its best mode and the manner and process of making and using the invention so that a person skilled in the relevant field may make and use the invention.

SQUATTER'S RIGHTS Ownership of property that is not occupied by its owner for a certain period of time may be transferred to those who have been unlawfully occupying it and openly exercising rights of ownership. Such a transfer is usually not reflected in the official land records. Also called adverse possession.

STAGGERED BOARD A board on which directors serve for specified terms, usually three years, with only a fraction of them up for re-election at any one time. Also called classified board.

STANDBY LETTER OF CREDIT A method of securing a party's performance, whereby an issuing bank undertakes to pay a sum of money to the person (the beneficiary) to which performance is due on presentation of certain documents specified in the letter of credit, usually a brief statement (in language agreed on by the two parties) that

the other party is in default and the beneficiary is entitled to payment from the issuing bank.

STANDING A party to a lawsuit has standing if the person seeking relief is the proper party to advance the litigation, has a personal interest in the outcome of the suit, and will benefit from a favorable ruling.

STARE DECISIS (to abide by) The doctrine that holds that once a court resolves a particular issue, other courts addressing a similar legal problem generally follow the initial court's decision.

STATE IMPLEMENTATION PLANS (SIPs) The prescribed emission control measures for stationary sources existing prior to 1970 and on the use of motor vehicles as necessary to achieve national ambient air quality standards.

STATE-OF-THE-ART-DEFENSE A defense against claims based on a manufacturer's compliance with the best available technology (that may or may not be synonymous with the custom and practice of the industry).

STATUTE OF FRAUDS A statute that requires that certain contracts, such as contracts conveying an interest in real property, must be in a signed writing to be enforceable in a court.

STATUTE OF LIMITATIONS A time limit, defined by the statute, within which a lawsuit must be brought.

STATUTE OF REPOSE A time limit that cuts off the right to assert a cause of action after a specified period of time from the date the product is sold.

STATUTORY BAR An inventor is denied patent protection in the event that prior to one year before the inventor's filing, the invention was (1) patented; (2) publicly used or sold in the United States; or (3) described in a printed publication in the United States or a foreign country.

STOCK LOCK-UP OPTION A lock-up option relating to stock of the target company.

STOCK PARKING The temporary sale of shares to another entity or individual to avoid tax reporting requirements or the net margin requirements of the securities laws applicable to brokerage firms.

STOCKHOLDER A holder of equity securities of a corporation. Also called shareholder.

STRAIGHT BANKRUPTCY A bankruptcy in which the trustee liquidates the estate and distributes the proceeds first to secured creditors (to the extent of their collateral) and then in a prescribed order, pro rata within each level.

STRANDED COSTS The outstanding liabilities in plant and equipment that were incurred while the utilities were a regulated monopoly.

STRATEGIC ALLIANCE A source of financing by which a collaborative arrangement is entered into between an established company that has business needs or objectives complementary to another company.

STRICT LIABILITY Liability without fault. The concept that sellers are liable for all defective products. Also imposed for abnormally dangerous (or ultrahazardous) activities and toxic torts.

STRICT SCRUTINY Under this test, a discriminatory classification will be held valid only if it is necessary to promote a compelling state interest and narrowly tailored; applies to classifications based on race or religion.

STRONG ARM CLAUSE The clause that grants a debtor in possession the rights of a hypothetical creditor who extended credit to the debtor at the time of bankruptcy and who, as a result, either obtained a judicial lien on all property in which the debtor has an interest or obtained an execution against the debtor that was returned unsatisfied.

STRUCTURAL ANTIDILUTION A provision that adjusts the conversion ratio at which convertible preferred shares may be exchanged for shares of common stock, if the total number of shares of common stock is increased, for example, by a stock split.

STRUCTURAL BARRIERS Barriers to negotiation that arise from the existing frameworks and institutions within which a manager operates.

SUBDIVISION A division of land into separate parcels for development purposes.

SUBJECT MATTER JURISDICTION The specific types of cases enumerated under Article III of the U.S. Constitution to be decided by the Supreme Court and lower courts established by Congress.

SUBLEASE An act by a tenant of renting out all or a portion of property the tenant has rented from a landlord.

SUBORDINATED DEBT INSTRUMENT The document providing that a holder's right to repayment is subordinate to that of other creditors of a corporation.

SUBSTANTIAL EVIDENCE STANDARD Under this standard, the courts defer to an administrative agency's factual determinations in formal adjudications even if the record would support other factual conclusions.

SUBSTANTIAL TRANSFORMATION An article exported from its country of origin is changed into a new article of commerce in a different country.

SUBSTANTIVE DUE PROCESS The constitutional guarantee that no person shall be arbitrarily deprived of life, liberty or property; the essence of substantive due process is protection from arbitrary and unreasonable action.

SUBSTANTIVE LEGAL OBLIGATIONS The legal rules that define the rights and duties of the agency and of persons dealing with it.

SUCCESSOR LIABILITY Individuals or entities who acquire an interest in a business or in real property may be held liable for personal injury and property or environmental damage resulting from acts (including sale of products) of the predecessor entity or previous owner.

SUMMARY JUDGMENT A procedural device available for disposition of a controversy without trial. A judge will grant summary judgment only if all of the written evidence before the court clearly establishes that there are no disputed issues of material fact and the party who requested the summary judgment is entitled to prevail as a matter of law.

SUMMARY JURY TRIAL (SJT) Parties to a dispute put their cases before a real jury, which renders a nonbinding decision.

SUMMONS The official notice to a defendant that a lawsuit is pending against the defendant in a particular court.

SUPER 301 A provision of the Omnibus Trade Act of 1988 that required the U.S. Trade Representative to draw up a list of the foreign governments whose practices pose the most significant barriers to U.S. exports, and to immediately commence Section 301 investigations with respect to these practices.

SUPER DISCHARGE A type of discharge available under Chapter 13 that extinguishes otherwise nondischargeable debts such as claims for fraud, theft, willful and malicious injury, or drunk driving, but not spousal or child support.

SUPERLIEN An instrument that secures recovery of environmental cleanup response costs incurred by state agencies.

SUPERVISOR (NLRA) Anyone possessing specified personnel functions if the exercise of that authority is not of a merely routine or clerical nature, but requires the use of independent judgment.

SURPRISE The extent to which the supposedly agreed on terms of the bargain are hidden in a densely printed form drafted by the party seeking to enforce the disputed terms.

SURVIVING CORPORATION In a merger of two corporations, the corporation that maintains its corporate existence is the surviving corporation.

SUSTAINABLE DEVELOPMENT A theory that holds that future prosperity depends on preserving natural capital: air, water, and other ecological resources.

SYNDICATED LOAN In a syndicated loan, the lenders enter into concurrent direct obligations with the borrower to make a loan, typically on a pro rata basis. The loan is coordinated by a lead lender that serves as agent for all the lenders in disbursing the funds, collecting payments of interest and principal, and administering and enforcing the loan.

T

TAKE-OUT COMMITMENT An agreement by a lender to replace the construction loan with a permanent loan, usually after certain conditions, such as the timely completion of the project, have been met.

TAKEOVER A bidder acquires sufficient stock from a corporation's shareholders to obtain control of the corporation.

TARGET CORPORATION A corporation that is the subject of a tender offer.

TARIFF CLASSIFICATION The tariff on articles imported to the United States is determined by their description on the Harmonized Tariff Schedule.

TAX BASIS The amount of cash or the fair market value of property exchanged for another asset, such as a general partnership interest.

TAX-DEFERRED EXCHANGE A transfer of real property for an alternative piece of real property meeting certain requirements.

TELEOLOGICAL THEORY An ethical theory concerned with the consequences of something. The good of an action is to be judged by the effect of the action on others.

TEMPORARY INSIDERS Outside attorneys, accountants, consultants, or investment bankers who are not directly employed by a corporation, but who acquire confidential information through performance of professional services.

TENANCY BY THE ENTIRETY A special type of co-ownership of real property between husband and wife; like joint tenancy, it includes a right of survivorship.

TENANTS IN COMMON The individuals who own undivided interests in a parcel of real property.

TENDER OFFER A public offer to all the shareholders of a corporation to buy their shares at a stated price, usually higher than the market price.

TERM LOAN A loan for a specified amount funded in a lump sum or in installments to be repaid on a specified maturity date or paid off over a period of time.

TERM SHEET A letter that outlines the terms and conditions on which a lender will lend.

TERMINATION The point after the dissolution of a partnership when all the partnership affairs are wound up and partners' authority to act for the partnership is completely extinguished.

TERRITORIAL RESTRICTIONS Restrictions that prevent a dealer or distributor from selling outside a certain territory.

THIRD-PARTY BENEFICIARY One who does not give consideration for a promise yet has legal rights to enforce the contract. A person is a third-party beneficiary with legal rights when the contracting parties intended to benefit that person.

THIRD-PARTY DEFENSE In a case under CERCLA, a potentially responsible current owner can assert this defense if the release or disposal of hazardous materials was by a third party who was not an employee and with whom the current owner had no contractual relationship. Also called the innocent landowner defense.

360/360 METHOD A method for calculating interest whereby it is assumed that all months have 30 days; thus the monthly interest amounts are always the same.

365/360 METHOD A method for calculating interest whereby the nominal annual interest rate is divided by 360, and the resulting daily rate is then multiplied by the outstanding principal amount and the actual number of days in the payment period.

365/365 METHOD A method for calculating interest whereby the daily rate is determined by dividing the nominal annual interest rate by 365 (or 366, in leap years), then this daily rate is multiplied by the outstanding principal amount and the actual number of days in the payment period.

TIP Disclosure of a fact made to an individual and withheld from the general public.

TIPPEE A person who receives inside information.

TIPPER A person who gives inside information.

TOMBSTONE AD A newspaper advertisement surrounded by bold black lines identifying the existence of a public offering and indicating where a prospectus may be obtained.

TORT A civil wrong resulting in injury to a person or a person's property.

TOTAL COST Variable cost plus fixed costs, such as rent and overhead.

TOXIC TORT Any wrongful injury that is caused by exposure to a harmful, hazardous, or poisonous substance.

TRADE DRESS A manifestation of trademark law, the concept of trade dress is to protect the overall look of a product as opposed to just a particular design.

TRADE NAME A trade name or a corporate name identifies and symbolizes a business as a whole, as opposed to a trademark, that is used to identify and distinguish the various products and services sold by the business.

TRADE SECRET Information that derives independent economic value from not being generally known and that is subject to reasonable efforts to maintain its secrecy.

TRADEMARK A word or symbol used on goods or with services that indicates their origin.

TRADITIONAL SHELF OFFERINGS The registration of (1) securities offered pursuant to employee benefit plans; (2) securities offered or sold pursuant to dividend or interest reinvestment plans; (3) warrants, rights, or securities to be issued upon conversion of other outstanding securities; (4) mortgage-related securities; and (5) securities issued in connection with business combination transactions.

TRANSACTION VALUE The price of an imported article indicated on a sales invoice.

TRANSACTIONAL IMMUNITY The prohibition from prosecution granted a witness that relates to any matter discussed in that person's testimony.

TRANSACTIONAL NEGOTIATION Negotiation that is forward looking with concern for desired relationships.

TRESPASS TO CHATTELS When personal property is interfered with but not taken, destroyed, or substantially altered (i.e., not converted), there is a trespass to chattels. Also called trespass to personal property.

TRESPASS TO LAND The intentional, negligent, or ultrahazardous invasion of real property (below the surface or in the airspace above) without consent of the owner.

TRESPASS TO PERSONAL PROPERTY When personal property is interfered with but not taken, destroyed, or substantially altered (i.e., not converted), there is said to be a trespass to personal property.

TRIPLE NET LEASE A type of industrial lease that requires the tenant to pay all taxes, insurance, and maintenance expenses.

TRUST (1) A combination of competitors who act together to fix prices thereby stifling competition. (2) A manner of holding property that is controlled by a trustee for the benefit of a beneficiary.

TRUSTEE An individual who controls property held in trust for the benefit of a beneficiary.

TYING ARRANGEMENT A business arrangement whereby a seller will sell product A (the tying or desired product) to the customer only if the customer agrees to purchases product B (the tied product) from the seller.

U

UCC-1 FORM In most states, this is the form a secured creditor uses for a financing statement under the Uniform Commercial Code.

ULTRAHAZARDOUS ACTIVITY Activity that is so dangerous that no amount of care could protect others from the risk of harm.

UNAVOIDABLY UNSAFE PRODUCT A product, such as a vaccine, that is generally beneficial but is known to have harmful side effects in some cases.

UNCONSCIONABLE A contract term that is oppressive or fundamentally unfair.

UNDERCAPITALIZATION THEORY A corporation is a separate entity, but its lack of adequate capital constitutes a fraud on the public. May be a basis for piercing corporate veil.

UNDERWRITER (1933 Act) Any person who has purchased from an issuer with a view to, or offers or sells for an issuer in connection with, the distribution of any security.

UNDISCLOSED PRINCIPAL Use of an agent so that the third party to an agreement does not know or have reason to know of a principal's identity or existence.

UNDUE BURDEN Under the U.S. Constitution, a state regulation creates an undue burden when the regulatory burden on interstate commerce outweighs the state's interest in the legislation.

UNDUE INFLUENCE Sufficient influence and power over another as to make genuine assent impossible.

UNENFORCEABLE CONTRACT A contract having no legal effect or force in a court action. A contract is unenforceable if it is (1) illegal or (2) unconscionable. A contract is also unenforceable if some public policy interest dictates that the agreement should not be upheld, regardless of the desire of one or more of the parties.

UNFAIR LABOR PRACTICE STRIKE A union strikes an employer for the employer's failure to bargain in good faith.

UNFAIR LABOR PRACTICES (NLRA) Unlawful misconduct by an employer to employees.

UNILATERAL CONTRACT A promise given in exchange for an act. Offer can be accepted only by performing the act.

UNION AUTHORIZATION CARDS Generally, these cards contain a statement that the individual signing it wishes to be represented for purposes of collective bargaining by a certain union.

UNION SECURITY CLAUSE The clause in a collective bargaining contract under which employees in a particular unit are required, after a certain period of time, to become members of a union as a condition of employment.

UNIVERSALIZABILITY A theory that asks whether one would want everyone to perform in this manner.

UNJUST ENRICHMENT The unfair appropriation of the benefits of negotiation of contracts for the party's own use.

UNORTHODOX TRANSACTION The purchase or sale by an officer, director, or greater-than-10% shareholder that would otherwise result in recoverable short-swing profits but is involuntary and does not involve the payment of cash, and there is no possibility of speculative abuse of insider information.

UNREASONABLE *PER SE* Unreasonable no matter what the circumstances.

UPSTREAM GUARANTY A guaranty whereby subsidiaries guarantee the parent corporation's debt, or pledge their assets as security for the parent corporation's debt.

USE IMMUNITY The prohibition on the use of the testimony of a witness against that witness in connection with the case in which that person is testifying or another case.

USEFUL ARTICLE DOCTRINE The doctrine that holds that copyrightable pictorial, graphic, and sculptural works shall include works of artistic craftsmanship insofar as their form but not their mechanical or utilitarian aspects are concerned.

USURY Charging an amount of interest on a loan that is in excess of the maximum specified by applicable law.

USURY STATUTES State statutes that set legal caps on what interest rates lenders may charge.

UTILITARIANISM A major teleological system that stands for the proposition that the ideal is to maximize the total benefit for everyone involved.

UTILITY PATENT A patent that protects any novel, useful, and nonobvious process, machine, manufacture, or composition of matter; or any novel, useful, and nonobvious improvement of such process, machine, manufacture, or composition of matter.

V

VACATE The power of a court of appeal to nullify a previous court's ruling.

VALUE Cash, property, or compensation for past services.

VARIABLE COST The cost of producing the next incremental unit.

VARIABLE-SUM NEGOTIATIONS Negotiations in which mutual gains are possible as parties trade lower valued resources for higher valued ones. Also called integrative negotiations.

VARIANCE A method of relief from the strict terms of a zoning ordinance that allows a landowner to construct a structure or carry on an activity not otherwise permitted under zoning regulations.

V-CHIP A set of internal electronic controls in a television set that can read the TV-show ratings transmitted by television networks and block all shows with a certain rating.

VENTURE CAPITAL Money managed by professional investors for investment in new enterprises.

VENUE The particular county or geographical area in which a court with jurisdiction may hear and determine a case.

VERTICAL AGREEMENT An agreement between firms that operate at different levels of production or distribution.

VERTICAL MARKET DIVISION An agreement between a company and a dealer or distributor that prevents the dealer or the distributor from selling outside a certain territory or to a certain class of customer.

VERTICAL MERGER A combination between firms at different points along the chain of distribution.

VESTED RIGHT The right of a developer to develop property sometimes, but not always, obtained when a building permit is issued, substantial work is done, and substantial liabilities are incurred in reliance of that permit.

VICARIOUS LIABILITY The imposition of civil or criminal liability on one party (e.g., an employer) for the wrongful acts of another (e.g., an employee). Also called imputed liability.

VIEW EASEMENT An interest in property owned by another by which an easement holder is guaranteed that a landowner will not obstruct the holder's view by making changes to said property.

VOIDABLE Unenforceable at the option of one party.

VOIR DIRE Questioning of potential jurors to determine possible bias.

VOLUNTARY CONVERSION The exchange by a holder of preferred stock for common stock on the occurrence of certain events.

VOLUNTARY REDEMPTION RIGHTS The requirement of a corporation to redeem an investor's shares for cash at a specified price, provided that the corporation is not prohibited by law from buying back stock or making distributions to its shareholders.

W

WAITING PERIOD The period between the filing of the registration statement and the date the registration statement becomes effective with the SEC. Also called the quiet period.

WAIVE To refrain from exercising certain rights.

WARRANT A right, for a given period of time, to purchase a stated amount of a security (frequently, stock) at a stated price (often equal to the fair market value when the warrant is issued, permitting its holder to benefit from any increase in values of the securities).

WARRANTY DEED A warranty deed is similar to a grant deed. In addition to the implied warranties contained in a grant deed, the grantor of a warranty deed also expressly warrants the title to and the quiet possession of the property to grantee.

WHISTLE-BLOWER STATUTES Federal and state statutes that prohibit employers from discharging or retaliating against an employee who has exercised the right to complain to a supervisor or government agency.

WHITE-COLLAR CRIME Nonviolent violations of the law by companies or their managers.

WINDING UP The process of settling partnership affairs after dissolution.

WINNER'S CURSE The realization by the winner at an auction that it won because it most overvalued the item.

WIRE FRAUD A scheme intended to defraud or to obtain money or property by fraudulent means through use of telephone systems.

WORK LETTER AGREEMENT An agreement between a tenant and a landlord, often an exhibit to a lease, that covers issues regarding tenant's improvements to rented space.

WORK-PRODUCT DOCTRINE Protects information, including the private memoranda and personal thoughts of the attorney, created by the attorney while preparing a case for trial.

WORKOUT An out-of-court settlement between debtors and creditors that restructures the debtor's financial affairs in much the same way that a confirmed plan would, but it can bind only those who expressly consent.

WRAP-AROUND FINANCING The transaction in which a new lender lends the owner of mortgaged real property additional funds and agrees to take over the servicing of the first loan. In exchange, the owner executes a deed of trust or mortgage and an all-inclusive note, covering the combined amount of the first and new loans.

WRIT An order in writing issued under seal in the name of a court or judicial officer commanding the person to whom it is directed to perform or refrain from performing an act specified therein.

WRIT OF CERTIORARI An order written by the U.S. Supreme Court when it decides to hear a case, ordering the lower court to certify the record of proceedings below and send it up to the U.S. Supreme Court.

WRONGFUL DISCHARGE An employee termination without good cause that (1) violates public policy; (2) breaches an implied contract; or (3) violates the implied covenant of good faith and fair dealing.

Z

ZERO-SUM NEGOTIATIONS Negotiations in which the only issue is the distribution of the fixed pie. Also called distributive negotiations.

ZONE OF DANGER The area in which an individual is physically close enough to a victim of an accident as to also be in personal danger.

ZONING The division of a city into districts and the application of specific land use regulations in each district.

INDEX

All cases are indexed in the Table of Cases at the front of this book.